Presented To:

____

____

____

Limited Edition # 2124

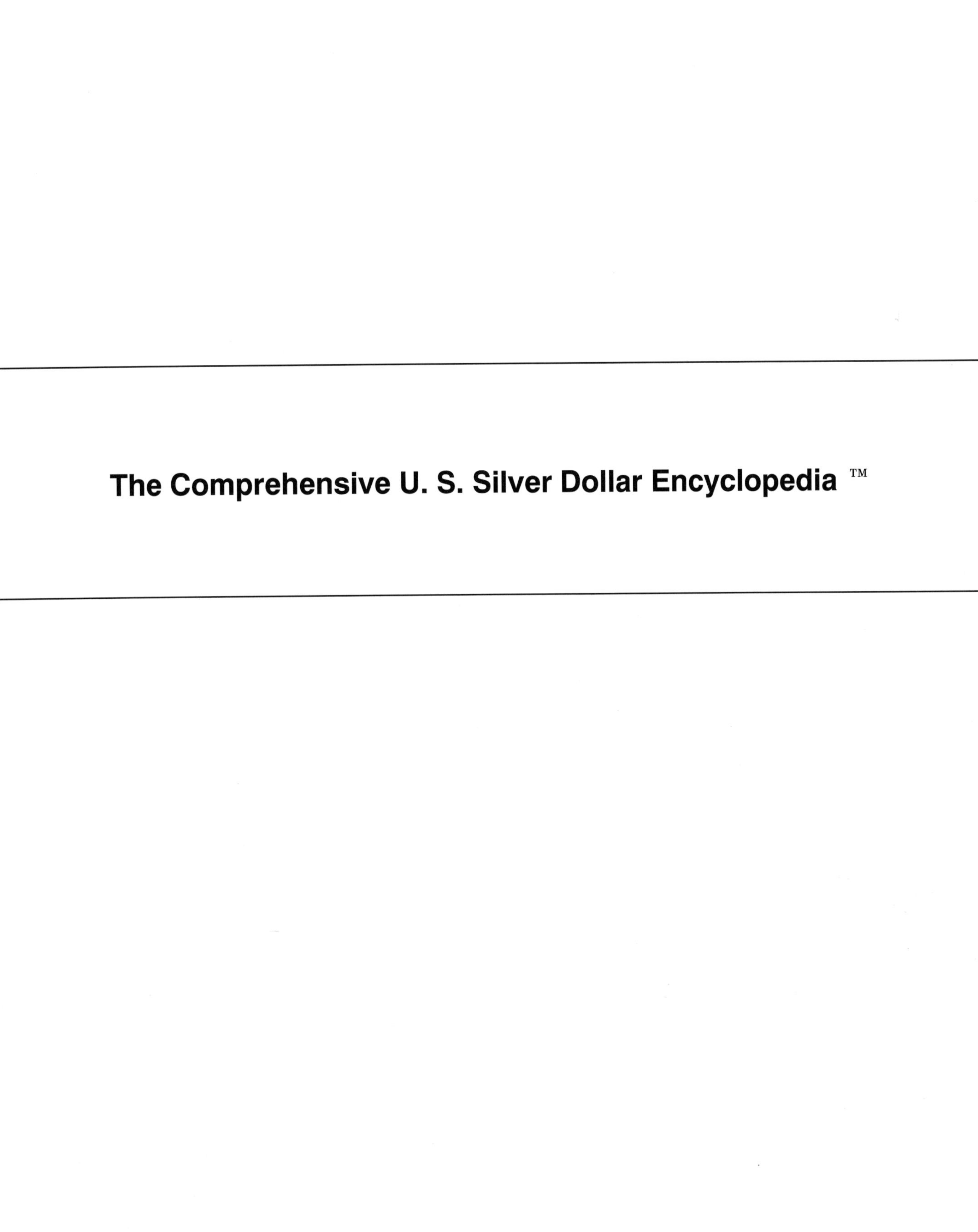

The Comprehensive U. S. Silver Dollar Encyclopedia ™

The Comprehensive U. S. Silver Dollar Encyclopedia™

John W. Highfill

Highfill Press, Incorporated
Broken Arrow, Oklahoma

Electronic Prepress by
EPIC
Digital Imaging Center
Tulsa, Oklahoma

Printing by

Tulsa Litho
Tulsa, Oklahoma

This entire book was produced electronically using

ISBN #0-9629900-0-0

Library of Congress Catalog Card Number: 91-65854

This book has been printed on *acid-free* paper to ensure long library life.

Published by
Highfill Press, Incorporated
P.O. Box 365
Broken Arrow, Oklahoma 74013

Dedicated to all my family and friends

and to the expansion of knowledge in numismatics

The Comprehensive U. S. Silver Dollar Encyclopedia™

By John W. Highfill

TABLE OF CONTENTS

FOREWORD

The transfer of knowledge from one individual to another, from teacher to student, from generation to generation through the written word is a worthy cause. In fact, it is the hope and future of the world. The hours spent by myself and each of the guest authors found within these covers were meant to serve such a goal. Looking at knowledge from another viewpoint, those following in the footsteps of the pioneers may take a valuable shortcut by the acquisition of their knowledge and experience through the written word. There may be no teacher like experience, but the words on these pages may provide the signs along the road which make the way clearer to the alert traveler.

Consider for a moment the mediums of transfer. The spoken word has been with us "forever" but the facts change with the emphasis of the storyteller in each generation. The preservation of truth and the introduction of new ideas is dependent upon the teacher. The written word is much more permanent but again the facts can change with the publication of each new work. The quality is strictly dependent upon the author. The electronic and visual transfer of knowledge is so much faster but is still restricted to the wisdom and abilities of the originator. The common thread here is continued dependency upon ourselves to provide the truth and the light for those who follow.

When I began in earnest to research material for this book, that is when I found out more and more about silver dollars. When I began to share what I knew, that is when I found that there was much more to know. Now that I have the finished work, I know that my work has just begun.

The extensive material and statistics that have been gathered in this effort are all true to the best of our knowledge. Any mistakes that have been made were not intentional and carry my sincerest apology. We have done our very best to provide you with a one-stop silver dollar reference center. Another goal is to provide a foundation upon which future references may be built. That would be very satisfying to all who have contributed in any way to this work.

IMPORTANT NOTICE: For those of you that were not able to view the PCGS "World's Finest Morgan Silver Dollars" exhibition while it was on tour, we at Highfill Press, Inc., with permission from the Professional Coin Grading Service, Inc., Newport Beach, California, are pleased to present all of the dollars from this magnificent collection as the official plate coins used in the date by date analysis. This complete in-depth date by date analysis is listed in Chapter 80 of this Encyclopedia.

The contents of this book will be news to many, interesting to others, and history to all. Some chapters reflect a nostalgic and personal touch also. There are many other authors I wished to include in this work, but regretfully, time, space, and personal reasons prevented them from becoming a part of this book.

Walter H. Breen, Editor-In-Chief indicated to me from the onset that this work was by nature an anthology. I am in complete agreement with Mr. Breen. However, it is also a full U.S. Silver Dollar Encyclopedia. Therefore the final conclusion would be that it is both an encyclopedia and an anthology combined in a massive effort to bring knowledge, wisdom and fact to everyone that enjoys coins.

Future annual supplements are anticipated which will provide an opportunity to present the work and wisdom of other authors covering a variety of topics concerning silver dollars and numismatics. We will be making sincere efforts to keep the extensive data updated on an annual basis.

James B. Osbon and Leroy Van Allen both contributed excellent books on silver dollars in 1976. These two books were completely different in style and content. Both served useful purposes. I was an avid silver dollar collector/investor at that time. I remember that both of their books regenerated my enthusiasm in all areas of silver dollar collecting and investing. Each of their works gave me the inspiration and added knowledge that I needed to achieve my goals in silver dollars to date.

If this book inspires and develops new collectors for the future of this wonderful hobby, it will be worth all of the effort required to bring it to them. Silver dollars are the backbone of all coin collecting. There has always been active market for them. I hope and believe that this book may help to "jump start" silver dollars again and place them in their proper status - that being RARE COINS.

The choreography of this book was as difficult a challenge as preparing my own material. Try reading one chapter at a time, or in any order meeting with your desires. Refer back to selected chapters as required to refresh your memory, or to supply needed facts. The "stats" area is the heart of this book and should be considered the owner's manual. Study these facts again and again as the date by date analysis contains a wealth of knowledge within its pages.

GOOD LUCK AND ENJOY!

ACKNOWLEDGEMENTS

First, I wish to express my appreciation for the efforts of the many people who made this book more than just a dream. There are too many people to list in the small space allotted in this portion of the text. However, an effort has been made to include each individual in the complete bibliography in the back of this Encyclopedia. Those listed below include family, friends, doctors and close professional business associates. A special photographic profile of additional acknowledgements and events is presented in chapter 79 of this text.

God - For everything and the inspiration to create and complete this work. Also for a second chance.

Marlene Marie Highfill - For her love, time, dedication and devotion during our seven years of marriage. Especially the four months that she spent on a roll-away hospital cot at my bedside during life's real crisis. Her determination gave me the will to come back and therefore made this book a reality.

Chelsea Marie Highfill - Her birth was the inspiration that kept me going when extremely adverse health, business and market conditions were dictating my life.

My children are listed in order of age as I love them all dearly.

Gary Wayne (Highfill) Kaplan
Michael Wade (Highfill) Kaplan
John Wayne Highfill, II
John William Highfill
Nicolette Lynn Highfill
Rebecca Ann Highfill
Jeffery James Highfill
Chelsea Marie Highfill

Bruce Amspacher - For his kindness, knowledge, insight, wisdom and vision. Most of all for just being a friend.

Yvonne "Vonnie" Berry - For all the time put in on this book above and beyond the call of duty. Vonnie and Roger spent hundreds of hours at the copier creating the prototypes and first draft manuscripts. She withstood the working conditions and pressure of deadlines. When one deadline was met, another was created. She is to be commended for meeting all of those deadlines. I personally want to thank Vonnie for her patience, kindness and understanding during this mammoth amount of work.

Walter H. Breen - His genius and vast knowledge were indispensable and have contributed greatly to a new dimension of credibility making this encyclopedia "the book" for decades to come.

John Dannreuther - For his patience, under extreme exposure and his understanding. Most of all for his friendship. He receives mine in return.

Beth Deisher - Thank you and all of the staff at Coin World for your tremendous help and many contributions.

Richard "Kenny" Duncan - One of the most dynamic and energetic new faces in the coin industry today. His market making capabilities ensure his status of becoming one of the premiere coin dealers in America for years to come. Kenny's friendship has stood the test of times and with his energy, honesty and integrity, I feel our friendship will last.

John E. English, Jr.- There would be no book without this man. I have never met anyone that could keep pace with me. John did! John has a Masters Degree and it shows throughout this work. I want to thank you a thousand pages and more. I know he uses God as inspiration, and therefore, God was again fundamental in both the transcript and completion of this book.

Vineta Mae Foreman - To my mother who I owe "everything" that I am. Your faith in me was the emphasis I needed to give me the drive and ambition to always do better. I have never met a person that didn't like my mother. She is Kindness. I love you, mom.

Bill Blue Foreman, Jr. - To my "Bro". I only got one so he's the best. He would still be even if I had a dozen. We'll have time to go fishing again soon, Promise. Love Ya' Bro!

Roger Geary - For his expertise in helping to create the color photo layout section in Chapter 78 as well as layouts for other chapters. He was put under pressure to meet many deadlines all of which he met in a timely manner. He is to be commended for his efforts on this book. I personally want to thank Roger for his patience, kindness and understanding during this time.

Dr. Rayburne "Tex" Wyndham Goen, Sr. - Cherished friend and a real life saver. To Tex and Sally, there are not enough words of kindness to describe their friendship. Tex is one of the fundamental reasons you are reading this book! The world should use this couple as a role model for human caring and sacrifice.

David Hall - His inspiration, technology, know-how and insight have proven to be the number one milestone in numismatics to date. Good luck with PCGS and its future for the numismatic community.

Leon Hendrickson - His unselfish wisdom and transfer of personal knowledge to me and others will continue to preserve numismatics for decades to come. Also to his wife Ruhama "Hamie", whose understanding completes this cycle of friendship.

John Love - For his personal friendship and taking a chance on me in my early years. To his wife Carla, whose friendship helped complete the bond we all shared. John is an institution in himself.

Dwight Manley - His unselfish friendship contributed greatly to me both personally and professionally. He has already established himself as one of the premier numismatic professionals today. He is an advocate and believer of the phrase "knowledge is king." His inspiration was a tremendous boost to making this "Encyclopedia" a reality. He is a living reason that books are the best avenue to knowledge.

J.P. Martin - Thank you and all of the staff of ANA for all of your help and contributions. I want to personally thank J.P. Martin for his continuous personal support throughout this project.

Frances Lee Maxon - To my sister. Her faith shall not go unrewarded. She is the best sister a guy could have. Don't lose faith in me, I could surprise you. God will prevail as always.

Wayne Miller - For his friendship and unselfish sharing of many of his "Textbook's" findings which appear in this book. His initial research and information has proved to be as reliable today as from his original handbook. Sometimes, no matter how much technology comes along, the "Facts" remain the same. Thanks Wayne.

Louie and Patti Moreno - Everyone should have an extra "mom and dad" like these two. They never make life dull, that's for sure. Love, patience and understanding are just a few of their qualities that stand out for all to see.

Mitchell D. O'Donnell - This man is the reason for the phrase, "I'll bet my lawyer can beat your lawyer." However, he is more than just a lawyer to me. He is a deep, loyal and compassionate friend, and this friendship will always be dear to me. Thanks for being there when it counted. I hope I am able to repay you with the same qualities.

Patricia (Trish) Pendergrass - To Trish, whose computer data entries are the number one reason the date by date analysis carry so much importance. She punched data on a daily basis for almost a year straight without interruption in order to bring you the statistical analysis that you are able to use and enjoy for years to come. She is entering data today in order to bring you "up-to-date" supplements on an annual basis. I thank her sincerely and you should too. I'll tell you how important she is to me - THERE WOULD BE NO BOOK WITHOUT HER!

Harrison Phillips - His drive, determination and influence paved the way for me to take on numismatics full time. His efforts were also pivotal to the two of us acquiring the National Silver Dollar Convention in the spring of 1982. Harrison is a true friend and believe me they are rare.

Tom Phillips - To a best friend anyone could have. Also the number one guy in hospital visits. Talk about understanding, no one understands me more than Tom. Honesty, knowledge, patience, kindness and understanding are only a few of his endless qualities. Here's back at you with friendship!

Iraj "Roger" Sayah - This genius of a businessman has entered the numismatic marketplace with a favorable and positive impact. Iraj is a genuine man that is dedicated to improving the entire numismatic community. If one man can do it, that man is Iraj. His efforts with Unitrade are unique and could prove to be the pivotal ask-based trading network that can change the way values of coins are reflected in the future. Good luck with all of your ventures. I consider your friendship a honor and mine is yours in return. Thanks for everything.

Florence Schook - Thank you for your loyal support to the National Silver Dollar Convention and to the National Silver Dollar Roundtable. Florence has been a personal and loyal friend for over a decade. It's understandable why everyone loves this lady. I love ya, too!

Joe Stephens - Thank you and all of the staff at CCE for your contributions of data for this book. Your efforts above and beyond the call of duty for the CCE statistics will bring rewards to everyone that enjoys this book.

Leroy Van Allen - For his life's work and research that made the statistical areas of this book come alive. His unselfish contributions are exhibited throughout the statistical analysis on dies and their varieties. Leroy and his beautiful wife, Marilyn, are personal friends and I only hope they see my friendship in return. Thanks again.

Mose and Kay Waldner - When times are tough you can count the friends you actually have. These are two of the best friends anyone could have. Vacations aplenty! True friends need little words to explain. Good luck in your future endeavors. Your friendship is more valuable than gold.

Bobbie Webb - There are thousands of color and black and white photos in this book which took hundreds of dedicated hours to scan their images. Bobbie spent the majority of this time along with Jim English , Trish Pendergrass, and Audrey Probert creating these quality photos. Bobbie was the catalyst of the team and without her drive, initiative, and direction, the quality of these photos would not be what they are. I personally want to thank Bobbie for her patience, kindness and understanding during the extreme pressure that the publishing of this encyclopedia put upon her.

Harlan White - To Harlan and his lovely wife Shirley whose friendship cannot be measured. I don't want to try and express with words what their friendship accomplishes. I love you both. See ya' at Tony Romas.

Bob Wilhite - Along with being a brilliant Senior Editor of Numismatic News, Bob has been a close friend of mine for the past decade. Along with all of the staff of Highfill Press, we would like to say thank you for all of your efforts to make this book what it is. Your intense and loyal support of both the National Silver Dollar Convention and the National Silver Dollar Roundtable will be appreciated forever. I can't thank you enough.

Mark S. Yaffe - For being there when I needed you (more than just once). Also his wife Christel, whose dedication and kindness progressed the relationship we all share today. Mark is a friend that is there when others seem to just disappear. Friendship has no measuring cup and if it did, Mark's cup would flow over.

Dr. Raymond A. Zekauskas - The famous surgeon, Dr. "Z" and his gay blade that saved my life on more than one occasion. Thanks can never be enough for these kind of actions. Thanks a life (or two)!

Staff of Highfill Press - Vonnie Berry, Herman Brown, John English, Roger Geary, Marlene Highfill, Trish Pendergrass, Larry Sams, and Bobbie Webb. I thank them all for their hard work, drive and determination, skills, emotional strain and just plain loyalty were all contributing factors to bringing this book to you. (Their group photo is a dozen pages forward in this book). Also, I would like to give special thanks to the part-time help, James English, Barbara Fuente, Mark Holmes, Phyllis Holmes, Edna McFarland, Michael Pendergrass, Audrey Probert, Eric Slick and Katherine "Kate" Smith. It is not necessary to individualize each and every one of them, as they all in their own way contributed to the making of this encyclopedia. **Thank you one and all!**

To all of my guest authors - Too many to list separately, but not too many to recognize. I thank you one and all for your contributions. You are all experts that are well deserved for your efforts to make this encyclopedia the mammoth work that it has become. **Congratulations! We Did It!**

JOHN W. HIGHFILL

AUTHOR, EDITOR, PUBLISHER

JOHN W. HIGHFILL, NLG

Born May 26, 1943, in San Pedro, California, John Wayne Highfill, NLG, has been a collector for over 40 years, a fulltime dealer for 15. John first started collecting in 1949. He specializes in U.S. and Canadian silver dollars, U.S. commemoratives and gold. He is President, Founder and Director of North American Coin Conventions, Inc.; President and Founder of National Silver Dollar Conventions, Inc., American Coin Conventions, Inc., Oklahoma Federated Security and Detective Corp., Oklahoma Federated Gold & Numismatics, Inc., and Oklahoma Federated Gold & Silver Exchange, Inc.; President, Founding Member and Life Member #1, Oklahoma Coin Dealers Association; President, Highfill Press, Inc. He was an original Founding Member and Life Member #1 of the National Silver Dollar Roundtable, November 12, 1982, which organization elected him to the board of governors and twice to its presidency; he was their Man of the Year for 1985. He is the Bourse Chairman for both the National Silver Dollar Convention and the National Gold Convention in Tampa, Florida.

He holds life membership in ANA, Arkansas Numismatic Society, California States Numismatic Association, Central States Numismatic Society, Florida United Numismatists, Garden State Numismatic Association, Greater Houston Coin Club, Indiana State Numismatic Association, Michigan State Numismatic Society, Numismatic Association of Southern California, Oklahoma Numismatic Association, and Tennessee State Numismatic Society. He also belongs to Alabama Numismatic Society, Canadian Numismatic Society, Clearwater Coin Club, Kansas Numismatic Association, Love Token Society, Missouri Numismatic Society, Texas Numismatic Association, Society for U.S. Commemorative Coins, PNG, RCDA, PCGS, ANE, CCE, and ANA's 1891 Club.

He has served as consultant for Compugrade™, the American Numismatic Exchange (ANE) and the Certified Coin Exchange (CCE). He is also a grading consultant for the American Numismatic Association (ANACS). He is a member of many prominent organizations and societies including the Professional Numismatists Guild, Inc., National Silver Dollar Roundtable, Numismatic Literary Guild (NLG).

For his academic achievements during his college years he was inducted into the Lambda Delta Chapter of Phi Theta Kappa Fraternity.

John is a renowned author, editor, statistician and publisher. He founded Highfill Press, Inc. which has become a leading publisher in the numismatic industry today.

John also contributes articles to many publications including, *Numismatic News*, *Red Book, Blue Book, CDN, Coin World*, *NLG Newsletter*, and the *NSDR Journal*. He also works closely with the ANA to promote education.

JOHN E. ENGLISH, JR.

SENIOR EDITOR

JOHN E. ENGLISH, JR.

John English began his lifelong "avocational" interest in numismatics a a young penny collector. Over the years, he has maintained and nurtured that interest by continuing his collections with a special emphasis towards U.S. Morgan and Peace dollars. He is a member of various numismatic organizations and enjoys continuing fellowship with collectors and investors of all numismatic items.

Mr. English has benefited from over twenty years of data processing and related business experiences which have covered many areas. Some of these include the development of document standards; preparation of system, user, and training documentation; systems analysis and project design; project development management and quality control; and management consulting.

He is currently preforming in the areas of user support, training, and system database development for a manufacturer of intelligent drafting systems based in Tulsa, Oklahoma. As a member of the development and coordination team, he recently completed development of document standards, user documentation and training manual for their major drafting system, an AutoCAD based software application for use in the sheet metal industry. He is also maintaining the database applications programs associated with the drafting system.

As President of his own consulting company, Mr. English specialized in providing data processing and related management services to companies in Northeastern Oklahoma. Projects completed include the formation of integrated system design, development, and documentation standards; and design documentation for two large integrated warehouse systems. Additional experience included the design and development of a petroleum investment management system, documentation of a collection of banking software applications, and the documentation of selected accounting systems for the energy field.

Mr. English also gained valuable experience as an Operations Officer in the operations division of a large midwestern national bank. Among his project responsibilities were the implementation of a new commercial loan system, analysis and recommendation of a new personnel / payroll system, and development and management of the system documentation program and standards. In addition, he was assigned project manager responsibilities for a number of other systems and analysis projects for the bank.

Mr. English graduated from the University of Oklahoma with a Bachelor of Business Administration degree, with a major in accounting and a minor in finance. He earned his Master of Business Administration degree from the University of Tulsa Graduate School of Business Administration. Mr. English lives with his wife Cindy and their son Jim in Broken Arrow, Oklahoma.

PATRICIA (TRISH) PENDERGRASS

MANAGING EDITOR AND CHIEF STATISTICIAN

PATRICIA "TRISH" L. PENDERGRASS

Patricia "Trish" L. Pendergrass, born February 1, 1963, in Sapulpa, Oklahoma. Trish graduated from Kellyville High School, Kellyville, Oklahoma in 1981 and furthered her education at Tulsa Junior College in Financial Accounting.

From May of 1981 to June 1986, Trish was employed by the Bank of Commerce, in Tulsa, Oklahoma. During her tenure, she held various positions ranging from Accounting to General Ledger Clerk.

In June 1986 to December 1988, Trish held the position of Lead Accounting Technician with the Federal Deposit Insurance Corporation (F.D.I.C.), in Tulsa, Oklahoma. During this time, acting as the Assistant Pro Forma (Audit) Manager, she participated in 10 bank closings, analyzing the banks' general ledger accounts and balancing them to the subsidiaries. Her additional responsibilities included supervision and training of employees on current auditing techniques and procedures.

In December 1988, Trish joined Oklahoma Federated Gold and Numismatics, Inc., Broken Arrow, Oklahoma, as the Inventory Control Manager, since that time, Mrs. Pendergrass has been promoted to the company's top position as Office Manager. She has traveled to various Coin Conventions and assisted in the conduction of both the National Silver Dollar Conventions and the National Gold Conventions, in St. Louis, Missouri and Tampa Florida.

Trish is currently associated with Highfill Press, Inc. where she is the Managing Editor and Chief Statistician. She has contributed much of her time and talents to the completion of The Comprehensive U.S. Silver Dollar Encyclopedia ™ .

Trish currently lives in Broken Arrow, Oklahoma with her husband Bob and son Michael.

MARLENE M. HIGHFILL

VICE PRESIDENT AND EDITOR

MARLENE M. HIGHFILL

Marlene M. Highfill, with over eight years as a professional numismatist, is an officer in many national and regional companies including Vice President - Oklahoma Federated Gold and Numismatics, Inc., Vice President - Oklahoma Federated Gold and Silver Exchange, Inc., Vice President - National Silver Dollar Conventions, Inc., Vice President - American Coin Conventions, Inc., and Vice President - Highfill Press, Inc.

She is the Convention Manager for the National Silver Dollar Convention and the National Gold Convention, Director for North American Coin Conventions, Inc., and Secretary of North American Coin Conventions, Inc.

Marlene Highfill is the author of several articles that appeared in Coin World, Numismatic News and the National Silver Dollar Roundtable Journal. She has edited and published the National Silver Dollar Convention and National Gold Convention Program Books for the past twelve conventions.

Marlene Highfill is a part of many national organizations and associations as listed below.

Life Member:

American Numismatic Association
National Silver Dollar Roundtable

Member:

American Numismatic Association
Central States Numismatic Society
Florida United Numismatists, Inc.
Michigan State Numismatic Society

Associate Member:

Professional Numismatists Guild, Inc.

STAFF OF HIGHFILL PRESS, INC.

Pictured L to R: Larry D. Sams, Bobbie J. Webb, Marlene M. Highfill, Roger L. Geary, Trish L. Pendergrass, W. Herman Brown, Vonnie A. Berry, John E. English, Jr., and John W. Highfill (sitting)
(Not Pictured) Barbara Fuente, Edna McFarland, Audrey Probert and Eric Slick

Welcome to the world of silver dollars and Highfill Press! We hope that your stay is pleasant, informative and profitable. Every care has been taken by each of the guest authors, and each of us, to provide you with the most current and useful information, statistics and insights within these pages. We hope that everyone benefits from the thoughts captured here, and then shares that knowledge with another person.

Thanks and good luck from all of us here at Highfill Press. It has been our pleasure!

EDITOR-IN-CHIEF
WALTER H. BREEN, NLG

Walter H. Breen entered numismatics professionally in December 1950. Wayte Raymond hired him to do research on Mint records at the National Archives, where he became a protege of Stuart Mosher (then curator of coins at the Smithsonian Institution and *Numismatist* editor), learning how to edit a magazine and to detect counterfeit coins. Breen was briefly acting Editor under the ailing Mosher. After a few weeks of work at ANS and Stack's, Breen went to Johns Hopkins University, June 1951, receiving the A.B. (Humanities Group) in June 1952, awarded Phi Beta Kappa for being the first student to graduate under the New Plan (credit for passing exams even without taking the courses). At Hopkins, Breen earned a living attributing coins for various dealers, and later also by cherrypicking rare varieties to sell to Dr. Sheldon and specialist dealers. He worked for New Netherlands Coin Co., NYC, writing much of the technical descriptions in their scholarly catalogues, 1952-1960. He also occasionally catalogued coins for other dealers, notably Stacks's (the "Anderson Dupont" collection, other than the early cents which Sheldon did). He went to night school at Columbia, completing a pre-medical course, aiming to become a diagnostician and/or work with Sheldon's constitutional psychology. He wrote poetry and music, numerous magazine articles and scholarly monographs on everything from mint history and minting methods to gold varieties and paper money; he edited little magazines. In 1958 he sold the article "Numismatics—U.S." to the *Encyclopedia Britannica*, though it was not printed until the 1965 edition. In spare time he read voluminously in hundreds of other subjects, from archaeology to zoology. He collaborated with Dr. J. Hewitt Judd on the book on U.S. Patterns, with Dr. Sheldon and Dorothy Paschal on *Penny Whimsy*, and with Eric Newman and Ken Bressett on *The Fantastic 1804 Dollar*.

In 1960, he went to Berkeley, receiving an M.A. in Sociology (1966). He wrote auction catalogues for Lester Merkin 1964-72, and articles and reviews under various names for the underground press; he became Vice President of First Coinvestors Inc. 1973-87. He continued his ongoing researches, culminating in a series of books which changed the way people thought about coins: *Encyclopedia of U.S. and Colonial Proof Coins* (1977); *Encyclopedia of U.S. Gold and Silver Commemorative Coins* (1981 with Anthony Swiatek); *California Pioneer Fractional Gold* (1983, with Ron Gillio); *Encyclopedia of U.S. Half Cents* (1984); *Complete Encyclopedia of U.S. and Colonial Coins* (1988). Several of these received NLG's "Book of the Year" award; his 1988 *Encyclopedia* also won PNG's Friedberg Memorial award. His articles have appeared in nearly every major numismatic publication, including ANS and ANA Centennial Volumes and various ANA Conference books.

He married the science-fiction and fantasy writer, Marion Zimmer Bradley (1964), best known for *Mists of Avalon*; their two children are musicians. His family founded the Society for Creative Anachronism (1966). He has received numerous awards, including the Roosevelt University Silver Medal of Honor (1966), NLG's Clemy Award (1985), and Society for International Numismatics' Silver Medal for Excellence in Numismatic Research (1991). He is listed in *Who's Who in the West*.

All of these authors were already stars. Several of them appear at times to shine brighter than others. Some seem dormant, others so deep in their own galaxy it takes a telescope to find them, while the rest are new creations in the evolutionary process. Even though they are, have been and always will be, we hope this work helps to turn:

STARS INTO STARS

John W. Highfill

"A Gathering Of Eagles"

Special Guest Authors
(In alphabetical order)

John Albanese
Numismatic Guaranty Corporation of America

Bruce Amspacher
United States Trade Dollars: 1873-1885
Prooflike Dollars

James U. Blanchard, III
Silver Dollars in the Rare Coin Market: Three Major Questions

George E. Bodway, Ph.D.
The "Bodway Set" of Morgan Dollars

Q. David Bowers
Silver Dollars, A Personal Reminiscence

Ronald A. Brandow and Joseph H. Stephens, III
The Certified Coin Exchange

Walter H. Breen
A Unique Liberty Seated Dollar: 1851-O

Walter H. Breen and John W. Highfill
The History of the Silver Dollar

Kenneth E. Bressett
The 1804 Dollar

Robert Brueggeman
Numismatic Security: Travel and Conventions

Drew R. Crowell
Common Date Uncirculated Silver Dollars

John W. Dannreuther
Liberty Seated Dollars

Ron Downing
Cartwheels & the CDN

Frank DuVall
The Lafayette Dollar Varieties

Bob H. Estremera
Computer Grading Mint State Morgan and Peace Silver Dollars "The Art Becomes Science"

Ned J. Fenton
Precious Metals, Coins and Banking

Bill Fivaz
Mint Error Dollars and the Minting Process

Rebecca Fong
A Rare Coin Experience: "The World's Finest Morgan Silver Dollars"

Michael Fuljenz
Proof Morgan Dollars

David L. Ganz
America's Bicentennial Dollar
Regulation of the Coin Industry

Lawrence S. Goldberg
How a Rare Coin Auction Works
The King of Siam Proof Set

David Hall
The Professional Coin Grading Service
Computerized Grading: The PCGS Expert™
Bear Market Bottom: The Test

James L. Halperin
Grading of U. S. Dollars

Leon E. Hendrickson and Clark A. Samuelson
The Continental-Illinois Bank Deal

Marlene M. Highfill and John W. Highfill
National Silver Dollar Convention
Conventions, Travel, Dealers and Friends: A Pictorial Bibliography

Steve Ivy
The U.S. Rare Coin Exchange

Al E. Johnbrier and John W. Highfill
National Silver Dollar Roundtable

David Lisot
The Electronic Media and its Effect on the Coin Market

John B. Love
Old Timer Stories

Andrew P. Lustig
A Price Guide To United States Pattern Dollars

Dwight N. Manley
Knowledge Is King

Wayne H. Miller
My Silver Dollar Set
Grading Circulated Dollars
Prooflike Dollars
Branch Mint Proof Morgan Dollars and Proof Peace Dollars
Counterfeit Silver Dollars

Jeff G. Oxman
Die Varieties in the Morgan Dollar Series

D. Harrison Phillips
Understanding MS60/62 Morgans

Maurice H. Rosen
Numismatic Newsletters

John H. Sack
Wall Street and Numismatics

Clark A. Samuelson and Leon E. Hendrickson
The Continental-Illinois Bank Deal

Iraj Sayah
The Unitrade Vision For The Future

John D. Schneider, Jr.
The Certified Coin, "Sight-Unseen", Electronic Trading Concept

Paul Schuyler
Network Trading Rules Revised

Philip J. Schuyler
Traits of the Certified Morgan Dollar Market
Network Trading Rules Revised

Hugh J. Sconyers and Scott A. Travers
Rare Coins As A Financial Medium

William E. Spears
The Mystique of the Carson City Silver Dollar

Joseph H. Stephens, III and Ronald A. Brandow
The Certified Coin Exchange

Anthony J. Swiatek
The Peace Dollar Series

Dean Tavenner
My Numismatic Memories

Scott A. Travers and Hugh J. Sconyers
Rare Coins As A Financial Medium

Leroy Van Allen
Total Uncirculated Silver Dollars Remaining

Chester West
Chester West Tells It As It Is - Of Federal and State Government Regulations
No Need to Change Sunday Show Schedules

Harlan White
Telling It Like It Was

Douglas Winter
Bust Dollars: The Early Years

Mark S. Yaffe
Retailing and the Marketplace

This work is designed for your wisdom and enjoyment. Search the stars for your favorites. The aura of these stars will shine in their own galaxies forever.

GOOD LUCK, STAR GAZERS!

PREFACE

This book has been prepared with the best attention, control, and diligence possible; however, the authors assume no responsibility for errors of any kind or for the accuracy or use of any information in this book.

The information contained in this book, whether in the form of comments, suggestions, or recommendations, reflects only the opinion of the writer thereof and is not to be considered a consensus of the authors of this book. The material presented herein is the sole responsibility of the respective author thereof.

A contributing author hereto may have a direct or indirect interest in various coins appearing in this book; however, no statement contained in this book shall be construed to be a solicitation of any order to buy or sell.

NOTICE
IMPORTANT INFORMATION

In addition to and in conjunction with the preceding preface, the information contained within these covers is intended for the private use of the reader, and has been prepared with the best attention, control and diligence possible. However, Highfill Press, Incorporated, its agents, and the author disclaims any responsibility for claims or any damages resulting from errors of any kind, nor for the accuracy or use of any information presented in this book.

Any recommendations, advice, or opinions given in this book by John W. Highfill or any other author are strictly the opinions of that author, and do not necessarily reflect the thinking or opinion of any other contributor to this book. In any case, no statement made by any author is a solicitation of any order to buy or sell.

Any authors involved with this book, or their affiliates, may have a direct interest in, position in, or act as a market maker for, many of the coins appearing in this book. Their actions are strictly their own and there is no connection or responsibility with respect to any information or opinions presented here.

Past price performance of coins is not necessarily an indication of the future price performance of coins. Future price levels of coins are subject to numerous variables and are not truly predictable by any scientific means. Price levels and the degree of liquidity will vary according to general market conditions and according to the particular coin involved. For some coins there may be no active market at all at certain points in time. Also, due to infrequency of auction appearance for scarce and rare date coins, price data can and may be limited.

The coin market is speculative and unregulated. Many areas of numismatics lend themselves to third party grading and authentication. Certification does not eliminate all risks associated with the grading of coins.

Highfill Press, Incorporated, recommends that all interested parties seek the counsel of qualified numismatists familiar with the numismatic marketplace before making any decisions based upon the information contained in this book.

GLOSSARY

Accumulation - A group of coins that have no specific order, or sequence.

Adjustment Marks - File marks made by the mint on a silver or gold planchet to correct its weight (from the minting process).

Annealing - The process of softening die blanks and planchets, through heat, which enables the metal to flow more freely into the cavities of the die or hub when struck. If the temperature and length of exposure to the heat are not correct in the annealing process, the design could be improperly struck up (part of the minting process).

Anvil Die - The die upon which a planchet rests prior to striking (usually the reverse die).

Arbitrage - Capitalization of inadequacies of a marketplace. Simultaneously buying something in market A and selling it in market B at a higher price.

Assay - A test undertaken to find the metallic content of a coin, ingot, or one sample.

Assay Piece - Coin selected to be assayed.

Bagmarks - Marks on a coin, caused by the coins being stored and shipped in bags. During the early years of silver dollar production, the coins were ejected from the presses and into bins or bags along with numerous other coins. The bags were frequently thrown around, creating many bagmarks on the coins. Coins with the fewest bagmarks are obviously the most desirable. One of the four criteria for the final grade of a silver dollar is the amount and degree of bagmarks on the coin.

Base Metal - A metal that is not considered a precious metal: zinc, copper, and others.

Basining - The process of polishing the surface of a die. The process consists of placing the die against a rotating zinc dish. This process was used so that the coins would strike up properly. Newly polished dies were a major factor in the production of prooflike dollars (part of the minting process).

Bit - One eighth of a Spanish dollar.

Blank - A disc of metal intended to become a coin. A blank is not a "planchet" until it goes through the upsetting mill which creates the raised rims. Blanking is done by shearing blanks from strip (same principle as a cookie cutter).

Bloom - The term used to refer to the lustrous appearance of a coin right after striking. This is caused by the reaction of the metal (steel) die striking the metal planchet.

Bogus - (Slang) False, or counterfeit. More specifically, a fake not copying a genuine prototype.

Brilliant - A mint state, uncirculated and untoned coin.

Brockage - A planchet which was struck while an unejected coin was between the planchet and the die. This produces a mirror (incused) image on the coin.

BU - Brilliant Uncirculated. Term used in classifying a condition of a coin. Choice and Gem BU are the two classes higher than BU, respectively. BU is an older method of classification than numerical grades; it may mean any MS grade from MS-60 on up.

Business Strike - A coin minted for circulation. Given only one blow from the dies, unlike proofs.

C - The mintmark used between 1838 and 1861 by the Charlotte Branch Mint for all of its coinage which consisted of gold coins.

CC - The mintmark used by the Carson City Branch Mint between 1870 and 1893 for all of its coinage.

Capped Die - A major die variety created by overpunching a small "cc" mintmark over an already existing larger "CC" mintmark on the reverse die used to produce some 1879 Carson City silver dollars.

Carbon Spot - A black discoloration on a coin which was on the planchet prior to the annealing process. The discoloration may be from burnt wood or sawdust, charcoal particles, and/or sulfides. Even the high temperature of the annealing furnaces often cannot rid the planchet of these particles (from the minting process). The term also designates black carbonate spots created by droplets of saliva.

Cartwheel - (Slang) Term used in reference to a silver dollar, or any other large size coin. Also, the (cartwheel) effect on a coin, created by the light reflecting off its fields as radii of a circle. This reflective band of light "walks" around the coin as it is turned or rotated.

Cast - Made by pouring molten metal directly into a mold. An older method used in counterfeiting coins.

Centered - Struck with all the design in the proper position in relation to the edge of the coin; borders are equally wide throughout.

Choice BU - A term used to describe a higher quality uncirculated coin.

Circulated - Showing any wear.

Clad - Describing strip, blanks, planchets or coins whose metal is a core (usually copper), bonded to two outer layers (usually copper-nickel). Clad coins were not produced by the United States until authorized by the Coinage Act of 1965.

Clashed Marks - Marks on the die caused by dies striking each other during minting, without a planchet between them ("clashing"). Each die impresses reversed portions of its design on the other.

Cleaned - Said of a coin from which toning or tarnish was visibly removed. This results in a washed out look.

Clipped Planchet - A planchet that has an area missing due to overlapping of the punches during the blanking process (part of the minting process).

Clock Position - A system of reference that is based on the dial of a clock and measured with obverse upright. For example, the bottom of the coin would be referred to as the six o-clock position.

Collar - A thick metal ring, into which the planchet is deposited, used for making the reeded or smooth cylindrical edge on a coin. The collar keeps the planchet from expanding freely when it is struck by the dies (part of the minting process).

Commemorative - Any coin whose device indicates that it was struck to commemorate a special occasion or personage.

Commercial Grade - Term used in reference to a coin graded for retail.

Common Date - A coin with a lower value due to a high mintage or number available for that date or mint.

Conservative Grade - A grade in which the buyer would be given the benefit of the doubt.

Copy - A replica of a coin, a reproduction, a modern imitation. Often made as souvenirs or novelties, not for circulation.

Cull - A coin that has a low monetary value due to the fact that it is excessively worn or damaged. These are not good for collectors and/or investors.

D - The mintmark used beginning in 1906 by the Denver Branch Mint for all of its coinage. This mintmark was also used between 1838 and 1861 at the Dahlonega, Georgia, Branch Mint where production consisted of only gold coins.

Debased - Struck to a reduced standard weight or fineness of the precious metal. This is done by increasing the alloy content or leaving the weight or both. Examples: Silver-clad Ike dollars, compared to standard silver Morgan or Peace dollars.

Defaced - Damaged, especially intentionally.

Demonetized - Declared not to be legal tender, or removed from circulation. Example: Trade Dollars.

Denomination - The face value of a coin.

Denticles - The "bumps" or "teeth" (design) around the obverse and reverse rims of a coin. Also called "dentils". Dollars had them 1794-1921, half dollars 1794-1915, etc.

Devices - The portraits and/or designs on a coin. The head of liberty, eagle, and wreath are all devices on silver dollars.

Die - An incused (depressed) design on the end of a short steel rod used to strike coins. All dies were produced at the Mint in Philadelphia.

Die Breaks - Raised, irregular areas on a coin, the result of metal from the planchet being forced through a portion of the die which has broken and fallen out. This occurs at the time of striking.

Die Cracks - Raised, irregular lines on a coin, the result of a die having cracked and metal being forced through those cracks at the time of striking.

Die Damage - Any damage occurring to the die: breakage, clashing, striking through steel fragments, etc.

Die Life - The number of coins which could be struck by a die.

Die Sinker - The person who engraves the die (part of the minting process).

Die Trial - A die trial issue consisting of a short initial die run.

Die Variety - A term used in classifying coins that were struck by the same die, distinguishable from those struck from other dies. A coin that has the same characteristics as other coins struck by the same die (from the minting process).

Die Wear - The loss of detail on a coin caused by being struck by a worn die.

Dipping - The use of a coin cleaning liquid to remove tarnish and/or dirt. Dipping should only be attempted by a person who possesses the knowledge of how to correctly dip a coin, otherwise the coin may be damaged, and/or its desirability harmed. All dips are some form of acid.

DMPL - An Abbreviation used to denote Deep Mirror Prooflike Morgan dollars. Also written as "DPL", "DM" and "DP" by some publications.

Double Strike - A coin that was struck twice by at least one die.

Electrotype - A counterfeit coin made by electroplating.

Emission - Striking of a coin, legal release, distribution.

Engraving - Term used in reference to cutting or punching a design into a die or hub (part of the minting process).

Error - A coin minted not as intended, due to some aberration in the minting process. An error may be the result of a planchet, die or striking abnormality.

Essay - A coin struck for a demonstration of the die design.

Field - Flat, open areas of a coin surrounding the raised devices.

Fineness - The amount of a precious metal in an alloy. For example the Morgan silver dollar is 900 Fine = 90% silver.

Fixed Price - Price put on a coin by a dealer (the opposite of an auction).

Flip - A special plastic holder used to store coins. Those flips containing no PVC are considered acceptable for long term storage.

Frosted Surfaces - A white texture produced on the surface of a coin during the minting process. Usually most obvious on the earliest coins off the working dies. Also see Luster.

Gem - A term used to describe a high quality coin.

Grade - A status or condition given to a coin based on the quality of the coin. Originally adjectives, now often numbers. The common system of numerical grading is known as the Sheldon Scale.

Grain - A unit equal to six hundred and forty-eight ten thousandths (.0648) of a Gram.

Gram - Metric unit of mass. A unit equal to three hundred and twenty-two ten thousandths (.0322) of a Troy Ounce. Also see Troy Weight.

Grease Marks - Aberrations on a coin's surface, caused by oil or grease dropped onto a die.

Hairlines - Scratches on a coin, usually in the fields or on the face, which are caused by rough or careless cleaning or drying of a coin. Baking soda and similar abrasive cleansers are notorious for making them.

Hammer Die - The upper die which descends to strike the planchet in the coining chamber.

High Relief - The use of a concave field on a coin for greater contrast on the raised areas of the coin. Some dollars were struck this way in order to give the illusion of a medal, notably, the 1921 Peace dollar. High relief greatly shortens die life. Coins with high relief and soft strikes sometimes are often misgraded as almost uncirculated "sliders", instead of BU. Also see Slider.

Hubbing Process - The process of producing dies from a hub. Dies have an incuse (depressed) image, while hubs have a positive (raised) image (part of the minting process).

Hubs - Working hubs are produced from the master dies. The working hubs are then used to make many working dies. Hubs are never used for minting or striking coins as they have a raised image (part of the minting process).

Ingots - Bars of metal used in the production of coins. The sizes of the bars may vary (part of the minting process).

Intrinsic Value - The value of the weight of precious metal contained in a coin.

Iridescent - Said of rainbow like interference colors, which vary with angle of view.

J - Refers to the Judd Numbers assigned to pattern coinage catalogued by J. Hewitt Judd, M.D.

Key - Short for key date. Describing a coin with a low mintage, which usually results in higher collector interest and investor demand.

Knife Rim - A piece of extruding metal on the rim of a coin caused by metal forced between die and collar (from the minting process), usually because the collar has stretched slightly.

Lamination - A layer of metal on a coin which has split away from the other layers.

Legal Tender - Whatever may legally be offered in payment of debts. If the creditor refuses it, (s)he cannot legally demand other forms of payment.

Legend - The inscription on a coin such as "UNITED STATES OF AMERICA."

Lettered Edge - Lettering around the edge (cylindrical surface) of a coin. Also seen written as "Let Edge" or "L.E." Opposed to plain edge or P.E. Also see Reeded Edge.

Lint Mark - A small, thin, irregular depression on a coin's surface, caused by a piece of lint adhering to the die or planchet during striking.

Low Relief - Said of coins struck from shallowly sunk dies, as the 1922 Peace Dollars compared to the 1921s.

Luster - The brilliance or shine of a metal. Luster is considered to be one of the four most important factors in appraising the monetary value and grade of a silver dollar. Luster will vary considerably in the Morgan dollars, but not as much in the Peace dollars. **NOTE: Alternate spelling - LUSTRE.**

Master Dies - Used for making working hubs, each of which in turn will be used to produce the working dies (part of the minting process).

Matte Proof - A coin struck by dies which were specially treated to impart a textured or granular surface and finish on a coin.

Metal Flow - A combination of heat and compression from the dies, metal and/or presses that creates a melted appearance.

Medal - A coin-like piece of metal made in honor of a person or an event. Not made to a recognized weight or fineness standard, nor intended to circulate.

Micro - Term used in reference to a very small defect. Also used to denote a much smaller than usual mintmark.

Micro D and S - Very small mintmarks appearing on the 1921-D and 1921-S Morgan silver dollar issues.

Milled - Struck on planchets cut from rolled strips. Often wrongly used to denote the reeded edge of a coin.

Minimum Bid - The smallest monetary value that will be accepted at an auction as a bid on a coin.

Mint Error - A coin that is abnormal which occurred during the minting process.

Mint Master - Old term for superintendent.

Mint Sealed or Sewn - Describing a bag of coins sealed at an official mint.

Mint Set - A set of coins that has been especially assembled and issued directly from a mint as a set. These are uncirculated coins, not proofs.

Mint State - The condition of a coin as it left the mint. Mint state coins will range from MS-60 to MS-70 and show no wear.

Mint State Rarity Indices - Estimates as to the rarity of a coin. This method is generally unscientific.

Mintmark - The mark on a coin that tells where the coin was minted. Mintmarks are: no mark for Philadelphia; "D" for Denver; "S" for San Francisco; "CC" for Carson City; and "O" for New Orleans. There is a "P" on some of the recent issues for coins struck at the Philadelphia mint. During the 1800s, gold coins were minted by the Charlotte ("C" mintmark) and Dahlonega ("D" mintmark) between 1838 and 1861. All mintmarks were placed on the dies prior to being shipped to their respective branch mints.

Mishandled Proof - Term used in reference to a proof coin which has seen numismatic abuse. Many proofs with "hairlines" are defined as mishandled.

Misstrike - An error coin which was caused by an abnormality in the striking process.

Motto - The inscription reading, "IN GOD WE TRUST."

MS - An abbreviation meaning Mint State and referring to uncirculated coins showing no trace of wear grading Mint State 60-70 on the Sheldon Grading Scale.

Mule - A coin struck from improperly matched dies (from the minting process).

Multi-Strike - A coin that has been struck more than two times.

Numismatics - The art of studying and collecting coins, medals, tokens, paper money.

Numismatist - A person who is knowledgeable in the history and collecting of coins. A dealer that has extensive knowledge of coins is considered by most as a professional numismatist.

O - The mintmark used by the New Orleans Branch Mint between 1838 and 1909 for all of its coinage.

O/CC - A major die variety caused by overpunching an "O" mintmark over an existing "CC" mintmark on extra Carson City reverse dies subsequently used by the New Orleans Branch Mint in 1900.

O/S - A major die variety caused by overpunching an "O" mintmark over an existing "S" mintmark on extra San Francisco reverse dies subsequently used by the New Orleans Branch Mint in 1882.

Obverse - The front of a coin (heads). The obverse side of a Morgan dollar, or a Peace dollar shows two different female portraits. They are described in full detail elsewhere in this book. Abbreviated as "Obv." in some references.

Off Center Strike - A coin partly out of the coining chamber at striking (resting partly atop the collar). Usually shows crescent shaped blank area opposite a region where borders or even design is incomplete.

Orange Peel Surfaces - An odd roughness on the surface of a coin, as struck, resembling the skin of an orange.

Original Roll or Bag - A roll or bag of uncirculated coins that was stored years ago, ideally in a mint sealed sack, and in its original Mint State. A bag of silver dollars consists of 1,000 coins, and a roll consists of 20 coins. Coins from an original roll or bag will often display the same luster, strike, degree of bagmarks, and die variety.

Overdate - A coin in which one or more digits of date were visibly changed in the die. Traces of the original digit must show.

Overmintmark - A coin in which a mintmark has visibly changed in the die. Traces of the original mintmark must show.

Overstrike - An error in which a set of dies strike a previously struck coin.

P - The mintmark used by the Philadelphia Mint for selected coinage. The majority of Philadelphia productions did not utilize a mintmark. The official U.S. Mint is located in Philadelphia, Pennsylvania.

Pitted - A coin whose surface(s) has depressions (damage) in it from various forms of numismatic abuse such as having been buried in the ground for many years.

PL - An Abbreviation used to denote Prooflike dollars.

Plain Edge - No lettering around the edge of a coin. Also noted as "P.E." or "Pl Edg." Also see Lettered Edge and Reeded Edge.

Planchet - The blank metal discs with upset rims, struck by dies to create a coin. The discs for dollars up until 1935 were punched from silver strips.

Planchet Striations - Lines on the surface of a coin caused by defective planchets. These can be singular or multiple (from the minting process).

POR - An abbreviation used in the coin industry meaning Price On Request.

Porous - A rough surface on a coin caused by a planchet that was in poor condition, or by burial or other prolonged contact with contaminants.

PR - An Abbreviation used to denote Proof coinage (as opposed to business strikes).

Precious Metal - Platinum, Gold, or Silver.

Presentation Piece - A term used in reference to a coin that was originally struck for presentation to a person of importance for commemoration. Very special handling is used in the making of a presentation piece.

Private Issue - Any "coin" that is issued by a private mint, and without ratification by any government. Some have special serial numbers and are limited editions. Most are for collectors and are not considered "numismatic" coins.

Promoting - The process of advertising and making the public aware of certain issues, dates, varieties, or special anniversaries of coins. Such processes are followed by a dramatic price increase as the result of increased demand.

Proof - A coin which is minted from special, carefully prepared planchets and dies. A branch mint proof is a proof coin struck at a mint other than the Philadelphia mint. Proofs are struck at least two times for more design detail.

Prooflike, Cameo - A prooflike coin whose field has a mirror finish. The fields have a mirror finish while the devices exhibit white frost, thus producing the cameo effect. Morgan dollars with these special effects are normally the first coins struck from new or polished dies. Peace dollars do not exhibit a "cameo" prooflike surface. Also see Luster and frosted surfaces.

Prooflike, Brilliant - A prooflike coin with both the field and (to a lesser degree) the devices with a mirror finish. The coin exhibits the same circumstances as Cameo, but without the contrast. The degree of mirror depends on the newly polished dies and their life cycle. Virtually all prooflikes are of the Morgan variety. Also see Prooflike, Cameo, Luster and Frosted Surface.

Prooflike, Grey Brilliant - A prooflike coin whose face has a grey luster.

Prooflike Rarity Index - The rarity of a specific date, in prooflike condition, in comparison to other dates.

Proof Set - An original set contains proof coins that have been specially packaged and sold by the mint. Assembled proof sets contain similar coins bought individually.

Raised - Said of a design in relief.

Rare - Said of a coin which only a limited number survive.

Raw - Said of any coin that has not been slabbed by a grading service.

Reeded Edge - The minting of a coin using raised parallel lines on the outside edge of the coin. Also noted as "R.E."

Reeding - The vertical indentation around the edge of a coin (part of the minting process).

Regular Issue - A business strike created for regular circulation and use. Same as Business strike.

Restrike - Any coin struck after the original striking date. Abbreviated as "Res." in some references.

Retoned - A coin which has been toned by artificial means.

Reverse - The back of a coin (tails). The reverse side of the Morgan and Peace dollars display the eagle. Abbreviated as "Rev." in some references.

Rim Dig, Rim Gouge - Terms used in describing more than minor damage to the rim of a coin.

Rim Nick - Minor damage on the rim of a coin.

Rip - (Slang) A coin purchased below the certain market price.

Rolling - Flattening metal ingots to produce a long strip of proper thickness from which the planchets will be cut (from the minting process).

Rubbing - Transferring a design by rubbing of a pencil on a piece of paper that was placed over the design.

Rusted Dies - Dies that have been damaged (pitted) by corrosion. The rusted areas on the die create raised "bumps" on the coin during the striking process, thus giving the coin a flat or dull appearance.

S - The mintmark used by the San Francisco Branch Mint beginning in 1854 for all of its coinage.

S$1 - Utilized by various organizations and publications to indicate a silver dollar.

SBA - An abbreviation used to denote the Susan B. Anthony dollar.

Scarce - Term used in reference to a coin that is not common, but not rare. Also see Rare.

Security Edge - Term used in reference to a special edge design that is placed on a coin to discourage counterfeiting.

Semi-Key - Term used in reference to a coin with a lower mintage than a common date in a series. Also see Common Date and Key.

Set - A number of coins that have been grouped together.

Sheldon (Grading) Scale - A scale created by the late Dr. William H. Sheldon for coin grading purposes.

The Sheldon Grading Scale

Descriptive	Numerical
Poor	1
Fair	2
Almost Good	3
Good	4-6
Very Good	7-10
Fine	12-15
Very Fine	20,25,30,35
Extremely Fine	40-45
Almost Uncirculated	50,55,58
Mint State	60-70

Sight-Unseen Bidding - There are multiple electronic nation-wide systems with dedicated telephone lines and/or satellite dishes that are used to post bids for "certified coins" without seeing them first. Hundreds of dealers coast to coast bid during specific trading hours daily in an attempt to buy coins at the highest bid. To date, the highest bid has resulted in 100% liquidity for certified coins.

Slab - The plastic holder used by various grading services into which graded coins are placed.

Sleeper - A coin that is underpriced at the current levels.

Slider - A coin appearing to be uncirculated, but which is slightly circulated. Commonly defined as "with a rub".

S.M.S. - Abbreviation for Special Mint Sets issued during the years 1965 through 1967.

Split Grade - A coin that has been assigned a different grade for each side of the coin. This process is unpopular even though it is more precise (purely economics).

Striking - The process of impressing an image onto a planchet (part of the minting process).

Striking Errors - Term used in reference to a mint error which occurred during the striking process.

T$1 - Utilized by various organizations and publications to indicate a Trade silver dollar.

Tarnished - Coinage displaying various colors, naturally achieved through oxidation. Also see Toning.

Technical Grading - The type of grading in which only marks caused after minting are considered. Also see Grade and Sheldon (Grading) Scale.

Thin Market - A term referring to the fact that the change in demand for BU coins of a specific date can cause changes in the wholesale value of that coin. The demand for some coins is less than others, which causes a smaller market share.

Thumbing - The process of using one's thumb in order to place a "film" on the surface of a coin to hide surface disorders.

Token Coinage - Term used in reference to a coin which has a higher face value than its intrinsic value.

Tooling - Term used in reference to the engraving of a coin, usually outside the mint, in the effort to surreptitiously increase its value.

Toning - The film, or coloring on the surface of a coin, caused by a reaction between metal and a chemical substance. The colors on a coin after toning are the result of an interesting phenomenon that is called the thin film interface. Sulfur from paper 2 X 2 envelopes was very common in creating "natural" toning. Morgan dollars are noted for being toned most often. Peace dollars that are toned are not usually very colorful.

Trans. - A transitional pattern without a legend. These pieces are not struck for circulation.

Troy Ounce - A weight used for coinage consisting of 20 pennyweights or 480 grains = 31.1 grams = 1/12 troy pound.

Troy Weight - Term used in reference to a system of weights for precious metals: see preceding.

Type Coin - A coin selected to represent a series of coins by design, not date.

Type Set - A coin set made up of one coin from each of several series.

Upsetter or Upset Mill - The machine that creates the raised rim on a coin (part of the minting process).

W - The mintmark used by the West Point Branch Mint beginning in 1984 for all of its coinage.

Want List - Term used in reference to a list of coins that an investor, collector or dealer wishes to purchase.

Whizzing - Artificial processes used on the surface of a coin to simulate mint surface. These coins exhibit a dull luster from this process. Often coins are "whizzed" and then artificially toned with various chemicals to hide the process. This practice is not popular with true numismatists, collectors, investors, and the public as a whole. Avoid these coins whenever possible.

Working Die - A die actually used to strike the coins. These dies are produced from the working hubs.

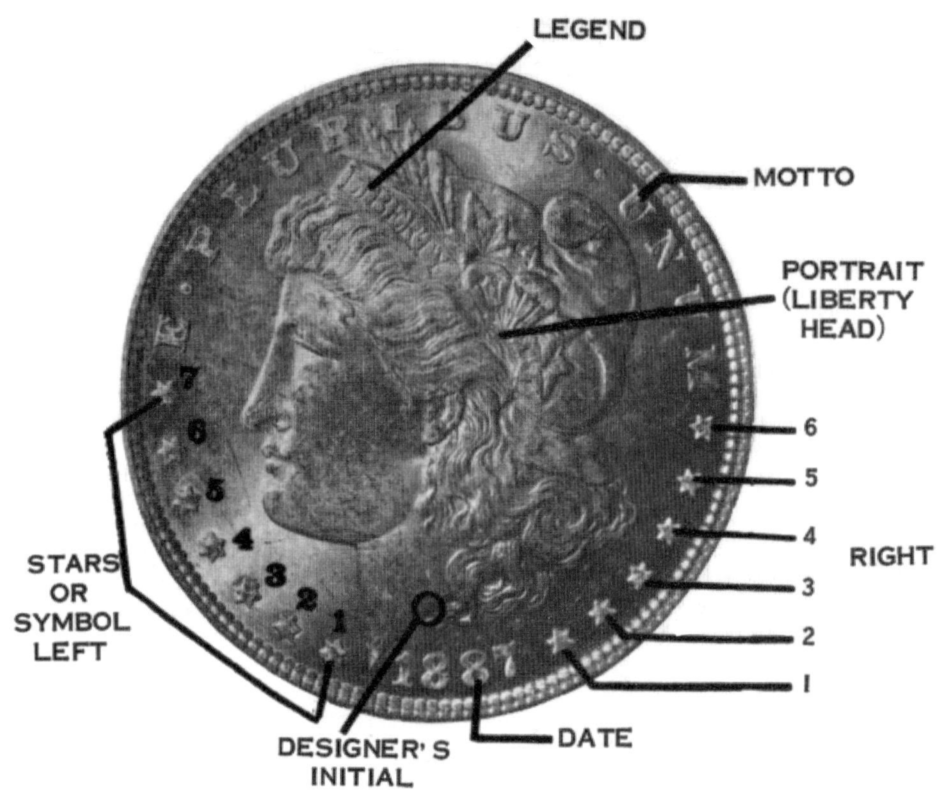

(Courtesy of Leroy Van Allen and A. George Mallis)

John W. Highfill, NLG

CHAPTER 1

The History of the Silver Dollar

by John W. Highfill, NLG and Walter H. Breen, NLG

The business world and the numismatic world both unwittingly owe much to the Habsburg Archduke Sigismund of Tyrol: he is the forefather of the "almighty dollar." In 1477 he came up with an idea whose time had come, and idea which would revolutionize world trade: *Make silver coins weighing one ounce each, recognized and accepted at par everywhere*—in every kingdom, every duchy, every principality, even the papal states. One may conjecture his motives: expand the market for Tyrolean silver mines' output; ease Tyrolean traders' task in foreign port cities; frustrate dishonest moneychangers; manifest Tyrolean honesty and Tyrolean workmanship before God and all Christian Europe. Not to mention the honor of having all Europe know who made all this happen, know by sight the Tyrolean archducal arms.

Luckily for all concerned, Archduke Sigismund had the resources to make his dream come true. He hired specialists to build and operate a mint in Hall (now Solbad Hall in Tyrol), near the silver mines of Schwaz. By 1486 (many sources say 1484), this mint's technology was advanced enough to permit quantity issue of ounce-weight silver coins, valued at one goldgulden or gold florin apiece. These soon acquired the name of *guldengroschen* 'gulden's worth of gros tournois = big little silver coin. (Until then, partly for reasons of technology, partly because silver was scarce, nobody was making large silver coins of any kind.)

As more silver mines were discovered in Tyrol and Bohemia, other rulers followed the Archduke's pioneering example and began issuing their own ounce coins to local weight standards, usually with their own portraits and coats of arms. Among the best known of these earliest issuers were Holy roman Emperor Maximiliam I before 1519, Markgraf & Elector Joachim I of Brandenburg in 1521, and Count Stephan von Schlick (locally spelled Slik) of Joachimsthal in Bohemia (now the spa town of Jachymov, Western Bohemia = NW Czechoslovakia). Schlick's coins became internationally familiar under the nicknames *Schlickthaler* from Schlick's valley and *Joachimsthaler* from St. Joachim's Valley (misrendered as *Jocondale* by French speakers, as *Jefimok* by Russians), soon shortened to *thaler* from the valley. This name became the generic term for nearly-once-weight silver coins of thousands of designs issued by hundreds of tiny German states. (Latin documents of the time called such coins *Unciales*, twelfths - {weighing} 1/12 pound = ounces.) Within a few generations, local coins of this size and nearly this weight were everywhere, often named by some mispronunciation or dialect mutation of *thaler*: Dutch *daalder* and *daldre*, polish *dalar*, Italian *tallero*, etc., eventually *dollar* itself. Other countries counterparts were variously named: dollar-size coins depicting crowns came to be called *coronae*, *kronen*, *kroner*, *kroon*, or *crowns*; those displaying prominent shields were named for them from Latin *scutum*: *scudi*, *escudos*, *ecus*. Latin American *pesos* weights, burdens, were apparently named for their weight of silver. Issues of various types of silver world crowns continued until the 1960s; they are outside the scope of this history, which must focus on the United States silver dollar.

Thalers and dollars of all kinds, unlike smaller coins, came more and more to serve public relations purposes, to propagandize the ruling families who issued them, to commemorate events the rulers believed important enough to record for coming generations, and to disperse these messages throughout the literate world. Dollars international circulation continued for centuries, thought their weight standards varied chaotically over the generations from one ruler to the next. (In practice, internationally, the coins were treated as portable silver bullion and valued by weight.) Talleros from Venice and Modena eased trade with Middle Eastern merchants, so that wealthy people could show off their carpets and spice their foods. Dutch daalders depicting a lion (a.k.a. *leeuwendaalder* lion thalers), became a common money of account in American colonies (though by then their mintage had ended); some of New York's earliest paper money (1709) valued itself in "Lyon Dollars." British rulers' policy of mercantilism aimed to keep as much gold and silver as possible in Britain, and allow as little as possible to get into American colonists' hands, lest the colonists use it to buy foreign goods. Nevertheless, the colonists came to value everything in terms of "Spanish milled dollars" —silver 8 Reales coins, primarily from Latin American mints. And the framers of the Mint Act of 1792 based the United States dollar on the Spanish in size, weight, and fineness, so that they would pass at par with the latter. Until 1857, Spanish and Latin American dollars were equally legal tender with the Philadelphia Mint's own.

The 8 Reales of 1732-71 bore one of the most famous designs in the worlds, "*Dos Mundos*" (Two Worlds'). Between the two crowned Pillars of Hercules (joining mountains and sea at Gibraltar, gate of the Atlantic from the Mediterranean) are Earth's two overlapping hemispheres (convex sides facing us) depicting Old and New Worlds. On the pillars, scrolls read PLUS VLTRA More {is} beyond {the Straits of Gibraltar}. (Contradicting the old Roman proverbial expression *ne plus ultra* 'no more beyond' = ultimate accessible point, applied since antiquity to Gibraltar as the western extremity of the classical world.) Resting on, or rather weighing down, both hemispheres is the Spanish crown; around them, the motto VTRAQUE VNUM Both [worlds are] one: as proud a royal boast as the cliche about the sun never setting on the British empire, and about as short-lived. Less than 2 centuries after the *Dos Mundos* design first appeared on the coins, no ruler in Latin America would ever again be a vassal of the King of Spain. "Look on my works, ye mighty, and despair."

(Among the side effects of all this silver: enriching rulers clerical and secular; expanding manufactures of consumer goods and of weapons; exaggerating benefactions and greed; enlarging bureaucracies and mercenary armies. Had more been available to the colonists, they would probably have defeated the redcoats faster, without so many ensuing years of financial hardship.)

Many collectors of silver dollars have become interested in coins of their Latin American ancestors. Not only were these the principal trade coins in the United States for generations, and legal tender equally with the Philadelphia Mint's, they—most of all, the Pillar Dollars—have romantic overtones: the original "Pieces of Eight", Spanish Main pirates' booty, common in treasure chests and sunken ships. Devotees collect them by county, by dates and mints, even according to which shipwrecks they came from. One of the more famous of these is the *Reygersdahl*, a Dutch East India vessel sunk in 1747 off the Cape of Good Hope; salvors in 1979 retrieved over 4,000 pillar dollars, mostly close to Uncirculated.

Dealing in any detail with world dollars would require a book; so would complete coverage of United States dollars. What we can do here, rather than merely rehash what every Red Book reader already knows, is to focus on some of the less familiar historical / economic / political / social contexts of the U.S. silver dollar.

As Robert W. Julian has pointed out, Assayer Albion Cox and Chief Coiner Henry Voigt somehow managed to convince Director David Rittenhouse that coinage at the arithmetically awkward fineness of 892.43 = 1485/1664 silver, 179/1664 copper was impractical, even to making the coins look darker than silver should, compared with coinage at 900 Fine. Dollars of 1794-95 were struck at an illegal 900 Fine standard, with about 3.5 grains extra silver per dollar, or 1% extra in the ingot. This meant that depositors got about 1% fewer silver dollars than they should for the bullion they had turned over to the Mint. One of the biggest depositors, John Vaughan, learned about this and successfully sued for the extra $2,260 due him. Dollars of 1796-1803 reverted to the 892.43 fineness; they are not noticeably darker than 1794-5's of the same grade, and some (notably of 1799 and 1802) are very brilliant. Were Cox and Voigt objecting primarily because of the awkward arithmetic? Was the alleged darkening only an excuse based on wishful thinking?

Rittenhouse was well aware of dollar coins propaganda role. After all, this underlay both the Senate's advocacy of portraying George Washington on them, and the House's insistence on a "device emblematic of liberty." All 1,758 of the 1794 dollars went to Rittenhouse, who passed them out to VIPs and others.

After about 1800, silver dollars began vanishing from domestic circulation. Latin American dollars entered the United States in quantity, being legal tender side by side with our own; the heavier ones contained about 0.5% more silver than ours, and many sooner or later went to the Philadelphia Mint for conversion into greater numbers of federal coins. Lighter ones circulated, often chopped into eights ("bits") or quarters ("two bits"), until they had lost enough weight to be refused at face. Meanwhile, federal dollars were shipped in quantity to the West Indies, where they circulated side by side with Latin American dollars, or perhaps occasionally melted for their extra value as bullion. Many others went as far away as the treaty port of Canton, China. These drains resulted in fewer federal dollars circulating in the USA, and in still fewer being minted. Those made in 1804 bore dates 1802 and 1803 (which did not prevent dollars dated 1804 from being made in later years). Mint Director Boudinot forbade further mintage after March 1804; thereafter, for over a generation, federal coinages consisted primarily of cents, half dollars, and half eagles. But circulating silver coinage was largely Latin American 1-real and 2-real pieces, cut fractions of 8 Reales, and many other foreign pieces, often counterfeit.

The backdated 1804 dollars were first made in November 1834 for diplomatic presentation purposes. One of the eight originals remains in the case in which State Department Special Agent Edmund Roberts had presented it on April 5, 1836 to King Ph'ra Nang Klao of Siam (Thailand). The case also contains a proof eagle backdated 1804, and a proof set of 1834, without the old tenor gold (with motto), and missing the half dime. The extra Class I ("original") 1804 dollars were quietly sold to collectors.

In 1858, George J. Eckfeldt, foreman of the dies, Engraving Dept., Philadelphia Mint, and his son, Theodore Eckfeldt, the Mint's night watchman (the "Midnight Minters"), made restrikes of the 1804 dollar, using a different reverse. These had plain edges (Class II), unlike the originals; collectors notified the Mint that specimens were being offered then for $75 each (or almost four oz. of gold), and in the ensuing scandal, at least four were seized, one put into the Mint Cabinet (today in the Smithsonian), the rest destroyed. Later, the Midnight Minters lettered the edges, and the seven resulting Class III 1804's were peddled in the 1870's via Capt. John W. Haseltine. Thanks to over a century of publicity, these fifteen coins are among the most famous ever minted, and among the most expensive ever sold. Several have gone well up into six figures, and the King of Siam's set has brought over $3 million.

When Mint authorities decided that the nation once again needed a silver dollar, they asked the new Second Engraver, Christian Gobrecht, to design it, from sketches by Thomas Sully and Titian Peal. Sully's Liberty Seated design was based on Britannia; Peale's flying eagle copied an actual bird, "recently killed," traditionally identified as the Mint's pet eagle Peter. Gobrecht's first working obverse (probably Nov. 1836) was signed in field above the date C.Gobrecht F. (F. = *fecit* he made it.) Some people powerful enough to make a difference objected to the signature. (almost all known impressions are restrikes made in 1858-60.) On a second working die the name appeared on the rocky base instead; this die served for 1,000 First Originals (delivered Dec. 31, 1836—600 of them to the Bank of the United States and circulation), 600 Second Originals (delivered March 31, 1837, from dies in medal alignment), and possibly over 1,000 restrikes. In 1838 the design was changed: 13 stars around Ms. Liberty, none on reverse, and no signature. The coins made in 1836 were on planchettes made to the old weight standard; those made in 1837 and later were on the new standard of 412.5 grains 900 Fine, with the same pure silver content as before.

Beginning in 1840, silver dollars were issued in quantity (larger than 1801-03, smaller than 1798-1800) from new designs (plaster models) by Robert Ball Hughes, which probably did not please Gobrecht: Liberty Seated, fattened, flattened, and blanketed; John Reich's old (1807) eagle in a refurbished version copying that on the 1839 half dollar pattern Judd 95 (the die reused on Breen 4738).

By 1849-50, so much California Gold Rush bullion had already reached the East Coast that the price of gold fell in terms of silver; U.S. silver coins became worth more than their face value in gold. Bullion dealers bought them in quantity for shipment to Europe, where many were melted. As early as 1857, silver dollars dated 1851 and 1852 were already recognized as rarities; enough so that the Midnight Minters began furnishing restrikes in silver and copper. What is thought to be the first 1851 restrike dollar used an O mint reverse in error, producing the unique 1851 O, analyzed and illustrated in a later chapter. Some restrikes dated 1851 are overstruck on other dollars dated as late as 1855.

Though the Mint had been making proof dollars since 1836, public offerings in proof sets to collectors only began in 1860, when the price of a set was raised from $2.02 (lower denominations at fact, dollar at $1.08) to $3. During and after the Civil War, proof dollars were made in more limited quantities, business strikes mostly went to the Orient. Those made from 1866 on bore the extra motto IN GOD WE TRUST, ultimately because of Rev. M.R. Watkinson's famous letter suggesting a religious motto on coins. (Dollars and smaller silver coins with this motto and dates 1863-65 were made in 1867-8 for Mint Director Henry R. Linderman.)

Western bonanzas (of which the Comstock Lode was only the most famous) created an oversupply of silver, far more than the domestic market would absorb. As if that were not enough, the Prussian state adopted the gold standard and dumped thousands of tons of silver on the market. This meant that American silver would no longer be readily salable in Europe. Silver prices began falling. Mine owners lobbied Congress and Senate for years, seeking to make the Mint into a federal subsidy market for their bullion, in a vain attempt to push up silver prices. Though they could not prevent Congress from abolishing the silver dollar in the new Mint Act of 1873, they did manage to have the new trade dollars declared legal tender (the real Crime of '73).

Trade dollars from William Barber's designs were coined to benefit traders in Chinese port cities. Acceptance of these coins by Chinese merchants meant that traders would no longer have to pay premiums for Mexican pesos, long the preferred trade coin in China. Portable bullion, in short, just as Archduke Sigismund had intended 400 years before. Or one might say that trade dollars were to Chinese merchants what talleros had been to Middle Eastern traders.

By mid 1874, trade dollars began appearing in circulation at face value in the East Coast and parts of the Midwest, while their bullion value had dropped to well under $1 apiece; by mid 1876 it was down to 85c. Congress responded by demonetizing trade dollars, but imports continued, nearly eight million in all. Factory owners bought them at bullion prices and paid them out to workers at face value. Company stores either accepted them only at bullion value or raised prices. In response to many petitions, the Treasury halted coinage in October 1877, only to resume two months later for export only. Treasury Secretary Sherman ended trade dollar coinage, Feb. 22, 1878, except for proofs. The last two dates of proofs, 1884-5, were distributed clandestinely by William Idler via Capt. John W. Haseltine. Only in 1887 did the Treasury agree to redeem unmutilated (unchopmarked) trade dollars at $1 apiece. This policy disposed of about 7,700,000. Many of these were melted down for conversion into other coins. Total silver dollar coinage, 1794-1873, came to about $8 million, compared with over $36 million in trade dollars.

Mint authorities knew that sooner or later the silver lobby would force passage of a bill mandating silver dollar coinage. They therefore hired George T. Morgan to design the new dollar. Mint Director Henry R. Linderman had chosen Morgan on recommendation from the Royal Mint's Deputy Master & Comptroller, Hon. Sir Charles Fremantle, K.C.B. Though Morgan's actual model was Anna Willess Williams, a teacher, the official cover story identified her profile as that of a Greek statue. The Bland-Allison Act of February 28, 1878 (requiring the mints to purchase $2 to $4 million in domestic silver every month) survived a presidential veto, and resulted in immense quantities of silver dollars being coined for storage in Treasury vaults, backing even more immense quantities of silver certificates for circulation: $10's up in 1878-85, lower denominations from 1886 on.

On March 11, 1878, the first Morgan dollar working dies were ready, and the first proofs (VAM 9) followed that same afternoon. The first specimen went to President Hayes, who could hardly have appreciated it; the next two went to Treasury Secretary John Sherman and Director Linderman. On March 12, 100 proofs followed; on March 13, the first 40,000 business strikes, all with 8 tail feathers. As early as March 18, Linderman demanded various changes, including that from 8 to 7 tail feathers. Fifty working reverses were reimpressed with the new 7TF hub and hardened for use, producing the "7 over 8" coins. Linderman later ordered still other changes; the version finally standardized (7TF SAF, officially "June 1878 Hub") has top arrow feather slanting and a more rounded breast.

Senator John Sherman (formerly Secretary of Treasury), to please both the silver lobby and the Populists, introduced a bill which became law as the Act of July 14, 1890, requiring the Treasury to buy at least 4.5 million oz of silver per month and (for at least the first year) to coin at least 2 million silver dollars monthly. This Act was a disaster: silver mine owners sold their bullion to the Treasury, were paid in Coin Notes (whose issue was authorized by the same Act), turned in the notes for gold, used part of the gold to buy still more silver for sale to the Treasury, etc., inexorably draining gold reserves until by 1893 they were so low as to jeopardize the government's ability to pay off bonds and other obligations in gold, and the Panic of 1893 followed. In all some 419 banks failed, and with them thousands of businesses; many were hungry and homeless. That fall, Coxey's Army of the unemployed began its months-long march to Washington to demand a federal works program (like FDR's New Deal" of forty years later), only to be dispersed by mounted police May 29, 1894. President Cleveland called Congress into special session to repeal the Sherman Act. The legislators did so only after much opposition from Rep. "Silver Dick" Bland, silver's chief congressional advocate. Bland was the front-runner presidential candidate in the 1896 campaign, until William Jennings Bryan made his "Cross of Gold" speech and won the nomination, only to lose the election to the gold bug McKinley: voters were afraid of another Sherman Act.

The Pittman Act, April 23, 1918, authorized melting 350 million silver dollars, part for conversion into smaller silver (in all 11,111,168, mostly into dimes and quarters of 1920-24), most for sale to Great Britain, though for political reasons the latter (259,121,554 at $1 per fine oz.) was diverted to India. These meltings, and others during World War II, destroyed perhaps a little under half the Morgan dollars. Pressure from the silver lobby resulted in a clause requiring that the Treasury buy enough new domestic silver to replace the entire meltage, and coin it into silver dollars. Under this mandate, the Mints struck 86,730,000 Morgan dollars in 1921, from new dies copying the old 1878 7TF PAF design.

Peace dollars, advocated by Farran Zerbe, and designed by Anthony de Francisci (winner of a design competition), were coined beginning Dec. 26-31, 1921. The first 1921's issued were satin finish proofs; a few matte proofs followed along with the 1,006,473 business strikes. Issues of 1922 and later were in lower relief to increase die life and improve striking quality. All coined through 1928 were to replace the Morgan dollars melted under the Pittman Act.

The silver lobby was still powerful enough even at the depth of the Great Depression to induce passage of the Thomas Amendment to the Agricultural Adjustment Act (May 12, 1933), authorizing the government to accept silver at 50c per oz in payment of war debt accounts, and to coin this bullion into silver dollars and lower denominations. They even persuaded President Roosevelt to issue a proclamation, Dec. 21, 1933, requiring that the Mints buy western silver for coinage into silver dollars. The silver Purchase Act of June 18, 1934 demanded that the Treasury buy silver from all sources until its market price rose to $1.2929 per oz or until the value of the Treasury's silver holdings reached 1/3 of its gold stock. Under these authorizations, the Mints coined Peace dollars in 1934-35, a little over seven million in all.

Between 1961 and 1964, the Treasury released at least 152 million silver dollars, many of them Uncs., others sliders or frankly circulated coins. These releases meant that many formerly rare dates became available. So far from killing the market in silver dollars, this event created nationwide public interest in these coins, and ultimately led to creation of this book.

The final Peace dollars were made May 15-24, 1965 but dated 1964 D. They would have benefited primarily casino owners. After 316,076 were struck, official orders came forbidding distribution. Officially, Denver Mint employees who had bought specimens of the new coins turned them all in. Unofficially, we hope that at least one was saved for the Smithsonian Institution. This effectively ended coinage at the old 900 Fine silver standard.

The mint decided to honor Neil Armstrong and "Buss" Aldrin for planting the first human footprints on the Moon, and to memorialize President Dwight D. Eisenhower, by issuing dollar coins. Some of the earliest ones were made on silver-clad planchettes; the rest were on the same nickel-clad material ("sandwich metal") as the dimes and quarters. Mintage continued through 1978, though those made in 1975 all continued to show the date 1974, and those struck in later 1975-76 bore the Bicentennial reverse by Dennis R. Williams. With the disappearance of circulating silver, we reach the boundaries of this study. Later silver dollars were made only for sale above face as commemorative coins. On these, the term DOLLAR has a meaning irrelevant to its common use in trade.

We are now further from the fulfillment of Archduke Sigismund's concept of a worldwide trade coin than our ancestors were in 1477. Perhaps it is an idea whose time is past. Dollar collectors are curators, passing into future generations mementos of an idea that had ruled world trade for five centuries.

***

RICHARD P. BLAND
(Silver and Gold,
Trumbull White)

WILLIAM B. ALLISON
(Silver and Gold,
Trumbull White)

GROVER CLEVELAND
(Silver and Gold,
Trumbull White)

JOHN SHERMAN
(Silver and Gold,
Trumbull White)

BENJAMIN HARRISON
(Silver and Gold,
Trumbull White)

WILLIAM McKINLEY
(Silver and Gold,
Trumbull White)

(Courtesy of Leroy Van Allen and A. George Mallis)

PHILADELPHIA MINT, 1901
(U.S. Treasury Dept., 1902)

PHILADELPHIA MINT, 1833-1901
(Bureau of the Mint)

NEW ORLEANS MINT, CIRCA 1890
(Illustrated History of the U.S. Mint,
George G. Evans)

(Courtesy of Leroy Van Allen and A. George Mallis)

CARSON CITY MINT, 1875
(Nevada Historical Society)

DENVER MINT, 1906 TO PRESENT
(Bureau of the Mint)

SAN FRANCISCO MINT, CIRCA 1890
(Illustrated History of the U.S. Mint,
George G. Evans)

(Courtesy of Leroy Van Allen and A. George Mallis)

CHAPTER 2

The Cycle

by John W. Highfill, NLG

Introduction

Since the beginning of time, there have been cycles. Cycles of all varieties, all lengths, for all reasons and all seasons. Cycles which occur over, and over and over again. When humans began to dwell in this world, they could not help but recognize, and fall into harmony with, all the cycles which had preceded them by eons of time. Whenever I gaze out into the ocean and watch the never ending waves beat upon the shores, I can visualize cycles. As I consider the living habits of man, cycles come into my mind. Cycles, cycles everywhere, which cause a man to think.

The coin life cycle is one of the important industry cycles which must be explored and understood by collectors and investors alike. I will elaborate on each component of the coin life cycle and its subordinate parts in the remainder of this chapter.

Pictured here is my representation of the Coin Life Cycle. I have specified categories that will present most, if not all the facets which must be seen, together with any additional elements necessary to complete the picture. There is a challenge for you however. This cycle is not unbreakable or without variation. Where there is a will, there is a way.

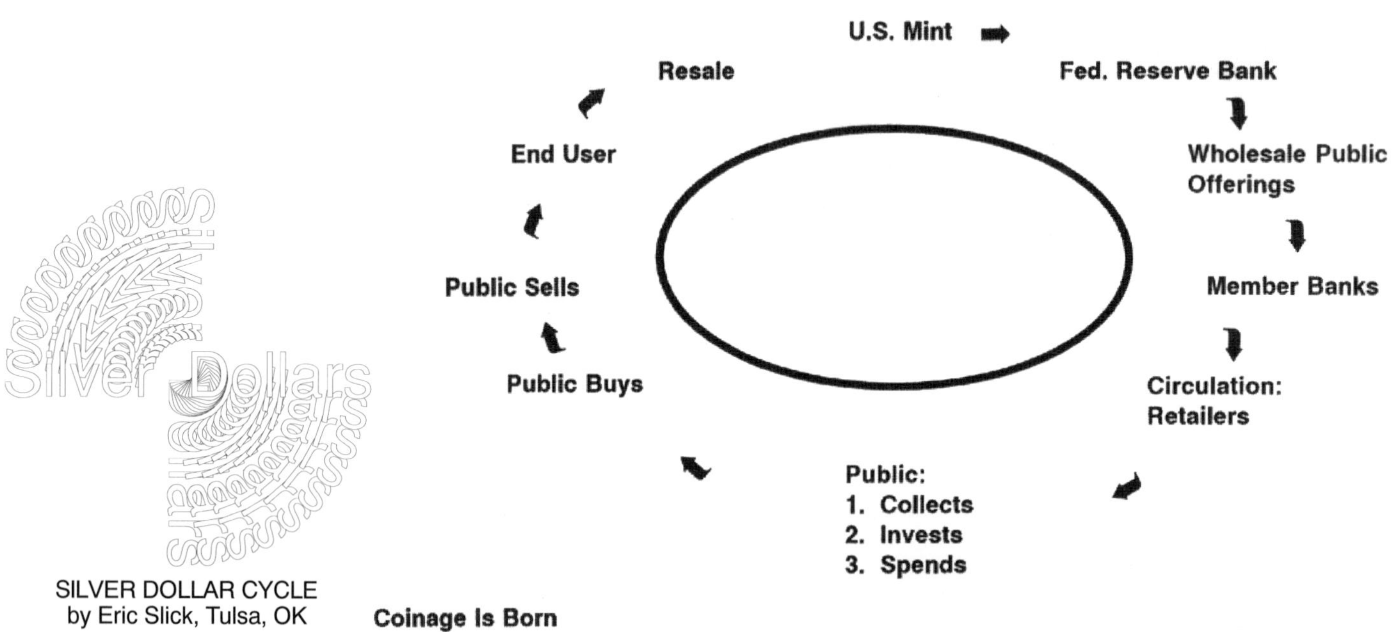

SILVER DOLLAR CYCLE
by Eric Slick, Tulsa, OK

Coinage Is Born

As an agency of the U.S. Department of the Treasury, the United States Mint has been responsible for manufacturing and initially distributing the coin of the realm since 1873. This agency also recalls those coins not desired for circulation, and acts as the custodian for the U.S. reserves of precious metals.

The current Director of the Mint is Donna Pope. As head of the agency, she is in charge of all inside functions and those of the coinage mints at Philadelphia and Denver, the Fort Knox and West Point bullion reserves, and the assay and coinage functions at San Francisco.

The minting process as it has evolved into modern times consists of several discernible steps. First, bars are made of the base metal to be used in the coinage. Then the bars are rolled into strips. These strips must conform to the required quality and specifications.

The strips are then processed and planchets (circular disks) are punched out. These planchets are carefully weighed and examined. Any that are underweight are melted and reprocessed, while those that are overweight are filed around the edge to bring them into specifications. The round edges of the planchets are then "upset": rolled to protrude beyond the surface of the coin and provide protection. The planchets are cleaned and struck by the dies to produce the finished coin. Certain coins are also reeded on their edges to aid in their handling.

The Federal Reserve System

The Federal Reserve (or central banking) system of the United States (known as the "Fed") serves as the banker for both the federal government and the banking system. Its major functions include regulating the U.S. monetary policy to achieve economic goals, issuing currency and participating in the regulation of banks. Those in charge of these activities include the Federal Reserve System Board of Governors (in Washington, D.C.) and the head officials of the twelve district Federal Reserve Banks located throughout the country.

The other main players in determining and regulating the monetary and banking policies (other than money supply decisions) are the Federal Deposit Insurance Corporation (FDIC) and the Comptroller of the Currency. The income required to keep the Federal Reserve System going is derived primarily from government securities held by the reserve banks.

All national banks are required to be members of the Federal Reserve system, but state chartered banks are members on a voluntary basis. As members, these banks must adhere to the Monetary Control Act of 1980 and meet the current reserve requirements. This act also allows the member banks to borrow reserves from the Fed at its current discount rate.

The general economy and monetary goals are accomplished through two general methods. These are changes in the required reserves and open market operations. Required reserves may be defined as the percentage of the member bank's deposits that must be kept on reserve at the Fed. If the percentage of assets (reserves) that the member banks must hold is raised, the result will be a reduction of the available money supply which may be created through the bank lending process. The reverse also holds true.

Open market operations are conducted by the Federal Open Market Committee (FOMC). These operations consist of Fed purchases and sales of U.S. government securities. Purchases, for example, would result in an expansion of the available money supply via deposits in member banks. Sales of government securities would achieve the opposite results.

By far, the most publicized method of attempting to alter the demand for money is to change the discount rate. By raising the discount rate, the Fed can discourage borrowing by member banks because of the increased cost of money. This, in turn, raises the cost of commercial and consumer loans and deters borrowing by the private sector.

In recent years, a discount rate change has affected many areas such as the stock and interest rate markets, precious metals prices, foreign currency valuation and inflation. Become aware of the current discount rate scenario and outlook. It may directly affect your current trading strategy and portfolio.

Another developing situation must be mentioned. During the 1980's, foreign money, goods and services have become increasingly important in the total economic picture for the United States. The result of these phenomena has been to lessen the economic influence of direct Fed action with respect to the money supply.

Returning more directly to our discussion of the Coin Life Cycle, our now minted coinage makes its way through the Fed to the district Federal Reserve Banks.

Wholesale Public Offerings

The demand for coinage from outside the general flow of banking activities may be described within the arena of public offerings. These numismatic oriented sales are made to the investing and collecting public. Included are such categories as proof and mint coinage, medals and medallions (items created for numismatic purposes only), and limited editions and special sets of coinage prepared for sale rather than spending.

These offerings may be subscribed to by a variety of means. These include direct sales from the Mint Bureau, mail order sales in response to special offerings, and other direct volume sales made with the intention of further distribution to the investing and collecting public.

Public offerings have certain advantages which must be mentioned. First and foremost, these sales provide the collector and investor with higher quality coinage than that obtained through normal banking channels. This includes the proof and mint state items as well as quality business strikes. Most of these are direct mail offerings by the United States Mint.

Another advantage is one of cost. Direct purchasing will reduce the number of persons (and therefore the number of markups) between you and the new coins you seek. Also, buying "early" in the life of a coin will often result in a bargain price if demand for the item picks up over a period of time.

One situation to be aware of involves heavily promoted items and special offerings. These should be purchased for the joy of their possession as collectibles rather than for investment purposes.

Member Banks

Recall that all national banks and volunteer state chartered banks are members of the Federal Reserve system. These financial intermediaries play an important and significant part in the United States economy and in the coin life cycle. It is primarily through these banks that the Fed carries out its monetary policy and economic stabilization goals. Also, it is these institutions which provide the next level of distribution as currency and coinage moves into the hands of the general public.

The member banks order their currency and coinage directly from their respective district federal reserve bank. This is the primary route for business strike coinage as it moves toward general circulation. These member banks, in turn, provide coinage on demand to their branch banks, correspondent banks and to other state chartered institutions.

For our purposes, branch banks may be defined as institutions wholly owned or controlled by federal reserve member banks. These branches look to their "mother" bank for currency destined for general circulation. Correspondent banks, for our purposes, are those non-member institutions with direct financial arrangements with member banks. These arrangements may also include obtaining currency as required to service their clientele. Other non-member institutions also meet their currency requirements through arrangements made with member banks.

Of course, coinage also moves from member banks into circulation in a direct manner through demand from depositors and retailers. This demand is the subject of the next section.

Circulation and Retailers

The demand for currency including coinage for public circulation comes from two general sources. These include the retail establishments of the country and the public. In a general sense, the currency requirement for circulation purposes reflects the general level of economic activity. Therefore, during periods of expansion, the demand for currency is greater than at other times.

A secondary purpose for coinage can be for the private collections of enterprising individuals. Coins destined for numismatists are considered withdrawn from the coinage available for general circulation.

It should be noted that small amounts of coins are lost and not recovered. Also, the federal government has been known to withdraw coinage from circulation (for instance, the silver coinage dated 1964 and earlier.) These events may influence the prices offered for certain items if there is a significant change in the number available.

Currency required to carry out the business activities of retailers is ordered based upon expected need from the commercial banks of the nation. Thus retailers may deal with their customers in an efficient manner and continue their trade (hopefully at a profit). Currency is no more than a medium of exchange used to transfer one party's goods to another.

A more specific set of retailers known as coin dealers also obtain coinage from these same sources in order to provide merchandise for their specific customers - the coin collectors. Items obtained include mint and proof sets, any special medals and offerings, BU rolls of coins, and other merchandise that they feel will appeal to their customers. Of course, they also buy coins from other dealers and from individual collectors, but that is a subject for later discussion.

Individual collectors still engage in the old practice of obtaining coinage from commercial banks in the form of rolls (pennies, nickels, etc.). This may be for purposes of perusal and selection of a small number of items for collections, or for longer term storage of a larger number of specific coins. I have already mentioned that many collectors obtain new coins directly from the mint using one of the methods previously outlined.

Private individuals also buy coins in many other ways which will be covered in the section describing public purchasing methods.

Now that we have a bit of background information under our belt, let's proceed to more exciting things and do some exploring together. And away we go!

The Public

The people of this country will generally do one or more of three things with the coinage which falls into their hands. They will spend it, invest it, or collect it. Some will even destroy it (not usually a wise action). The spending function seems to be enjoyed by most of the population. How about you? The habit of spending always seems to get into the way of the other possible objectives just mentioned. If this seems to be the case with you, I have a word of advice. Pay yourself first! Get into the habit of setting aside a percentage of your earnings before it gets away from you. You'll thank me for that one.

The three basics in life still must be food, clothing and shelter. Yes, the desire for security will always be a powerful incentive. But other very strong inducements also exist. These may include greed, the thirst for power, and a dominating ego. In any case, put money to work and it will work for you. Remember that money must be reinvested or it will be lost in time to inflation.

The business of investing in coins has provided a high return in recent years. What does the future hold? Whatever will be will be; but they are not making any more of those beautiful silver dollars of the years gone by. I believe that patient investors will be rewarded handsomely for their efforts over the longer term.

Ah - and who would forget the fascination and joy provided by collecting? Not I! It is a great pleasure to secure, view and show a fine collection of coins carefully gathered over a period of years. If this is your cup of tea, then, more power to you! Many a collection is handed down from generation to generation; or made available to museums or other organizations for public display. This is a special gift that is yours to provide if you so desire.

Most of us fall into more than one of the categories explored in the preceding paragraphs. For those with a numismatic heart, the following sources of coins can provide the thrill of victory.

Sources for the Buying Public

Following is a brief synopsis of the main sources of coins for the private individual who is in a buying mood. This is not meant to be an exhaustive list, but it does cover the areas that I have found within this industry. The ordering of the list does not have any special significance, and just reflects the sources as they came to my mind.

Private Individuals: This source of collectibles came to me first. The heart of numismatics belongs to the people. Collectors will be providing a continuing source of coins of all variety and quality. If you are buying from individuals, you must be prepared to grade and judge the coins accurately in order to obtain the desired coin for the money. If you are in doubt as to the quality of a more expensive coin, it is best to seek professional assistance in order to make a prudent purchase.

Local Coin Shop: Perhaps this is where the majority of collectors at one time or another have made their purchases. Your local dealer is in a position to get to know you and your collecting desires. When desired coins become available in the marketplace, that dealer can secure them for you and your collection. This personal service can easily justify the retail price paid for the special items you desire, but do not have the time or resources to locate. It is important to trade with a dealer you can trust, for the grading of a coin can easily make a significant difference in the final price determination.

Out-of-Town Coin Shop: Perhaps some of you are wondering why I placed this source within my list. This is in response to the "grass is greener" syndrome that lurks somewhere within all of us. But there are also other reasons. Many dealers cannot secure all the items that you desire to purchase, and an additional source can often mean the difference between owning a specific coin and not owning it. This additional dealer can also be used as a price comparison medium. This will provide you with more coin pricing knowledge, and the feeling that goes with knowing that you are paying a fair price.

Mail Order: This category may be used with success, but should be approached with a bit of caution. When buying coins "sight unseen", you are relying completely upon the integrity and business ethics of the firm you are dealing with. The grading of quality coins must be able to pass inspection without question. If you make your purchases from reputable companies with a good business record, they can make a great difference in helping you to reach your collecting and investment goals. Do not forget that most respected firms have some kind of return policy if you don't want to keep your purchase after an initial inspection (usually ten to thirty days). More and more companies are beginning to speed up the purchasing process by accepting orders transmitted by facsimile machines. Too bad they can't send your coins to you via the same medium.

Coin Conventions: Coin conventions and shows have become one of the more important entities in the buying of coins by the investing and collecting public. Conventions and shows are held throughout the United States at the local, state and national level. Generally speaking, the bigger meetings will provide a wider selection of offerings. The national conventions also provide the additional advantage of presenting some of the most prestigious names in this business as speakers or participants - an educational experience to say the least! This marketplace may be compared to visiting between 100 and 500 "mini" coin shops placed side by side. This presents a great opportunity to both buy and sell. (See Chapter 23 covering the National Silver Dollar Convention for additional information.)

Auctions: The atmosphere and thrill of a good auction is hard to beat. These auctions may be held at the local, state or national level. A national house is often the place where specialty and rare items may be purchased for collection and investment purposes. When dealing with a quality house, grading is usually not the question. It simply becomes a matter of how much you are willing to pay for what you want. However, when the coins are not professionally graded, I would be much more careful when assessing their value. I will mention that the auction process may be presented in any number of formats. Among them are the traditional outcry, mailed bids, telephone bids, and television using telephone bids. Two additional categories of auctions which may feature coins as their main bill of fare would include estate auctions and bank auctions. (See Chapter 38, "How A Rare Coin Auction Works," by Lawrence Goldberg for details.)

Telephone Retailers: Here is a category where it is important for you to know with whom you are dealing. If you are sure of the quality of the offered merchandise, and the integrity of the offering company, you may buy without impunity. In any case, you are usually buying without a visual inspection, and I would restrict this type of buying to coins that have been professionally graded by a nationally known service. You should also know that many of the better known companies offer competitive buy-backs. There are many excellent telephone retail organizations offering a wide variety of numismatic items for the collector and investor. Exercise a little caution when doing business with an unknown party. After all, you wouldn't buy your clothes, automobile, jewelry or even your home from someone without additional research.

Numismatic Publications: This category includes such things as periodicals, catalogs and books that come into possession of the buyer. A fairly good description of the offering is usually provided (often with a picture). For additional information, a telephone call is in order. This type of purchasing is closely akin to the mail order described earlier.

Limited Partnerships: A relatively new variety of numismatically oriented buying is the limited partnership. There is a growing number of large brokerage houses that are now offering this medium to their investing public. This phenomenon is undoubtedly attributable to the outstanding rate of return enjoyed by investment grade coins during the past decade. The grading of coinage purchased must be known and unquestioned (barring fraud). Limited partnerships will be a convenient way to own a portion of a large variety of high quality coins. I must also mention that the continuing growth of this method of coin ownership will have a huge impact on this industry. (For more on this subject, consult Chapter 51, Wall Street and Numismatics.)

Broker Offerings: This arena is close to limited partnerships. That is, the rate of return accruing to the holders of investment coinage. Again, only professionally graded investment coins will be offered. In fact, coins will be bought and sold much like any other stock, bond or commodity. (Refer to Chapter 51, Wall Street and Numismatics for additional insights.)

Computer Offerings: This method will probably be restricted to independent third-party graded, high quality investment coinage only. They will require computer access with the appropriate software, fees (if any) and permission to participate. I currently participate daily in the computerized marketplace and see it as the way of the future. The coin simply goes to the highest bidder according to item and grade. You should know that computer consignments are going to become a factor in the computerized coin market as this method of sales gains strength.

Public Sales: This last item on my list is simply to cover any additional selling done by organizations or individuals to the public. These are usually held on a cash and carry basis, and require some knowledge on your part as a buyer. Be sure that you know what you are doing, for there is usually no return. Sometimes these sales can be considered liquidations.

Sources for the Selling Public

What is bought is usually resold sooner or later. Coins are no different. As you begin to view my list below, it will look somewhat like the one I presented in the previous section. The difference in the lists lies in the point of view. As a seller, you very quickly become aware of the costs of doing business. The individuals and companies who were so eager to offer their merchandise to you at retail prices are only ready to buy from you at a discount. The facts of life are sometimes a little rude and that might be an understatement. Buy a car or a house and then try to sell it back to the same dealer or broker within six months. Then you'll see my point.

I will spend a moment with you now and describe my first experience as a boy with the local coin dealer in Muskogee, Oklahoma (Yes, I'm a real live "Okie from Muskogee"!), where I spent my formative years. When I was six, I realized that if I spent my allowance of fifty cents on Saturday, I would have no more until the next week. Then I found that I could obtain an additional ten cents from my mother if I would take fifty cents to the local bank, obtain a roll of pennies, and choose ten of them to save for the future. Then I would return a roll of fifty cents to the bank and enjoy the entire sum in all the ways that boys do. Notice that if all Americans would save one-sixth of their paychecks, their financial security would be assured.

As a few years passed, I found that I had a penny in my possession that was bid at one dollar. Now that was a goodly sum in those days, and I finally decided to part with that coin. But, much to my dismay, the dealer would only offer me fifty cents for it. I thought about it and finally sold it to him for the fifty cents.

The whole deal kept nagging at me the entire night through, and by morning I knew what I "had" to do. It was important for me to get that coin back. I had to have "my" coin. A quick trip to the dealer's store and I saw "my" coin under the counter glass. He had packaged it in paper and plastic with that official and special look and had placed a one dollar price tag on it! Of all the Nerve! We talked and I told him that I wanted "my" coin back for the fifty cents that I had been paid the day before. He politely explained to me that the coin would cost me one dollar now. I couldn't believe that he had marked it up 100 percent! After a lengthy discussion, he sold that coin to me for ninety cents. At least I repurchased it at ten percent back of bid! I will never forget that deal.

Now here is my list of selling sources. For ease of reference, I will put them in an order similar to the one presented earlier. Always try to provide the best information possible concerning your offering. This will enable you to receive a fair price for your holdings (and more quickly too).

Private Individuals: These persons, who are often friends or acquaintances, desire to own what you are selling. The price you receive will depend upon the degree of knowledge held by each of you and how badly you wish to sell (or the other to buy). You might be more likely to receive a higher price from a collector or investor who wants to hold the coin for a period of time, or add it to a collection.

Local Coin Dealer (Wholesale): This is the moment of truth when you find out how much your coin is really worth. Regardless of its published book value, a coin is only worth what someone will pay you for it. If you are not willing or able to advertise and market it at a retail price, you must pay someone else to do this for you. In this case, it is your local coin dealer. In order to make a living, the dealer must buy at wholesale and sell at retail prices. You are the wholesaler.

Coin Conventions: If you know someone who can market your coin for you (with or without a fee) at a convention or show, it is likely that a more competitive price can be obtained. This is due to the exposure that your coin may receive. Usually, this option is used for the disposition of investment quality coinage to be sold on a piece by piece basis. Complete sets of coins are also likely to find ready buyers at a large show.

Auctions: As the value of the coins increase, the use of auctions becomes a possibility. The fees charged are usually based upon a percentage of the price obtained, and the merchandise must be available for inspection by prospective buyers. Note that the consignment method is used by most auction houses, as opposed to a local sale under the leadership of an auctioneer. Usually you can receive an advance on your consignment subject to the appraisal by the auction company.

Certification and Resale: This is a little more sophisticated than the approaches mentioned previously. It involves submitting an investment grade coin to a third-party professional grading service expecting to receive a high grade for a coin making it more desirable and therefore more valuable. Then the graded coin is resold making the investment a profitable one. In fact, many coins used to be "cracked" from their plastic and resubmitted in order to possibly receive a higher grade. If the same grade was returned, nothing was lost. Things have changed in recent times. Now, whenever a coin is submitted for professional grading (at most services), it is graded without regard to, or knowledge of, its previous status. This could also result in downgrading and therefore provides a greater risk to the regrading process. So let the submitter beware.

Government Recall: It should be mentioned that the federal government has the right to recall certain coinage that it deems necessary to remove from circulation. In such an instance, it could become necessary to part with the specified items at the recall price. This is not the usual case and I don't expect a situation like this to arise anytime soon.

End User

This is the person at the end of the line holding the coin. After all the government handling, and after all the bank transfers, and after all the companies and dealers have dealt with the coin, it is sold to the private individual at the highest price obtainable. This individual is known as the end user.

This person may, after a period of time, choose to dispose of the coin through reselling it to another individual or dealer. But until that time, the coin is considered to be dormant and not available unless a large price change results from an increase in demand for the item. This change in circumstances may prod individuals into parting with their holdings by selling into the rising market. Special financial needs of the end user may also prompt the disposal of coins being held for the long term. From the collector viewpoint, the end user is the party that obtains the wanted coin and has no desire to part with it.

Resale

Here is where the rubber meets the road. The coin that may have been resting in your private collection for a good period of time may once again be ready for the marketplace. This can be either the easiest or toughest part of the game, depending upon your personality, needs, contacts, market conditions and geographic location.

A good rule of thumb is to begin where you left off. By this I mean to offer your coin to the dealer or contact that you purchased the coin from in the first place. This is better advice if this individual has offered a buy-back opportunity. It is like comparing apples with apples. You have only one markup to overcome - that of your original source.

Let me elaborate further on my last point. It is important that you understand. For example, if you made your purchase from a national source, your local dealer may not be able to give you the same kind of price you need when you wish to sell. This dealer may not have the same facilities and marketplace in which to buy and sell. Note that if a great deal of time has passed, this approach may not be the one to pursue.

Learn to appreciate the large national retail marketing firms that may employ dozens of people to serve you. These are the salesmen who spend the time to put the right place, right time, and the right customer all together. Also, they may provide a follow-up service on their customer's portfolios and can advise them on a continuous basis. Unfortunately, the nurturing of a customer is usually an endless and unappreciated job. Believe me, they do earn their commissions!

Another point to keep in mind is that higher overhead, facilities and research may require a sizable organization to place a larger percent markup in order to actively sell your coin for the best price. National institutions have the following costs and expenses not generated by other mediums of the industry. These being salesmen salaries, commissions, managers salaries, rent, national toll free numbers, newspaper ads, television, and other advertising. All of these add to cost of doing business which translates into the price of the coins you buy.

Let's continue our exploration of resale by reviewing a scenario that attempts to follow a transaction through several hands. Remember that the variations on this theme are endless. The prices for the various transfers are not important just now. It is important to realize the number of players that may be involved. That is why I am presenting this hypothetical example without prices for you.

The Hypothetical Scenario

In the beginning, an individual buys a BU silver dollar roll from the bank for long term storage. This person decides to give the BU roll to a nephew for a birthday present. After many years, the nephew decides to sell the BU silver dollar roll to a local coin dealer at what should be considered a wholesale price. This is transfer #1.

This dealer, in turn, wholesales it at a small profit to another dealer in same town who is known to frequent coin conventions and shows. This is transfer #2. If the roll is sold to another dealer, this scenario continues. However, if the roll sells at retail to another collector or investor, then this scenario ends.

To continue our story, let's assume that our convention bound dealer does attend the next major show and wholesales the roll (again for a small profit) to another dealer who operates in the national market. This is transfer #3.

The new owner of our traveling roll is an enterprising sort and decides to break the roll and picks it over looking for a few coins that might be graded at MS-63 to MS-65. He does find a good candidate and submits one or more coins to an independent third-party professional grading service and pays a fee for having the coin graded. This may cost from $19 to $250 depending on type and speed of grading required. Time passes and he receives the graded coin back. What luck! It is graded MS-65.

Our current owner chooses to replace the MS-65 coin in the BU roll with a substitute BU dollar, and re-markets the roll at retail to a collector. Then our fortunate dealer sells the graded coin at a profit to another dealer through one of the national certified "sight unseen" exchanges. This is transfer #4.

Our newest dealer markets the coin within his region in one of three places. The coin may be retailed at this point to an investor known to be seeking the coin thus ending this scenario. Then again, he may wholesale it again to yet another local dealer for a small premium. This is transfer #5. This local entrepreneur will retail the coin to an end user also ending the scenario. But let's choose to follow a choice to wholesale the coin at a small markup to a retail coin marketing organization. This is alternative transfer #5.

Our retail organization caters to building the portfolios of its clients and retails the coin to a client at the current retail price level. This end user may be expected to hold the coin for either the short term (which I will define as up to three to four years) or long term. A coin set aside for the long term is held from four to seven years or even more. This is especially true in cases where the collectors obtain their key coins from the retail level. In either case, this transaction ends our scenario. But what if this end user decides to give the coin to a nephew . . . ?

Summary

Now that we have been all the way around the coin life cycle, I would like to summarize. When you stop to think about it, the whole cycle is not as much of a mystery as it once was. I have presented each of the elements that I have found during my life as a numismatist. Others could choose to present a somewhat different set of titles and circumstances, but the cycle would remain the same.

Each part of this important cycle has its function in the marketplace. There are not necessarily any bad people involved with any particular aspect of it. As a collector and investor, you must be prepared to meet the market, and you will fare better as you get to know each of the market functions and objectives.

All of us must make mistakes in order to learn. This is how the business is done. But as you pay your dues, learn to understand, evaluate and appreciate the facts of numismatic life, and you will emerge a winner.

***

CHAPTER 3

The Collector: The Investor

by John W. Highfill, NLG

As a boy, I collected pennies. You just smiled, didn't you. It is one of those warm memories of youth. Did you ever stop to think about the collecting procedure? I'll bet no less than ninety-nine percent of us have pursued it. Here it is.

First, I checked each penny that I received from my parents looking for a new date. Do you remember that first dark blue tri-fold where you carefully placed each new penny as the collection grew? Did you ever get up in the middle of the night to look at your newest penny one more time? I memorized those pennies that I owned and those that I wanted so badly. Where in the world were all those 1909-S V.D.B. coins that they claimed were minted?

As the years passed, that flock that I so carefully shepherded evolved into a complete collection of Lincoln head pennies. Through this same period of time another trend began to emerge. Some of those pennies that I was so excited about when they first joined my collection just seemed to look old, rusty, scratched, cut, worn, and just plain unacceptable.

I would exchange and upgrade, upgrade and exchange, trade and trade again. Yes, I was always looking for a better coin to replace my "dogs." Then I would buy and sell, buy and sell, and buy and sell some more. It would be the best coin I could lay my hands on that would grace my collection. To summarize, the collection method of my youth was to fill, complete and upgrade.

I only wish that you and I could have embarked upon our journey at a more rapid pace. But on the other hand, I would never wish away your fond memories! In pursuit of what I will call a numismatic personality, I offer the following observations.

Categories of Numismatists

As you examine this subject further, it will become apparent that there are three general categories of numismatists served by the industry; the pure collector, the collector/investor, and the pure investor. There are many people who overlap one or more of the various categories at various times of their collecting lives.

There is also a separate category consisting of coin dealers and merchants. This group of individuals and organizations may occasionally play on turf usually belonging to the collector/investor for personal or financial reasons. Their whole reason for being is to cater to the members of the numismatic world.

These divisions aren't intended to place each numismatist into a separate and convenient box. But it does allow me to direct my remarks towards the understanding of the methods and techniques of persons affiliated with each of the four camps.

The Pure Collector

To begin, I will reflect a bit upon the pure collector. This interesting breed has only one numismatic thought, and that is to collect and hold the objects desired. Those specimens may be quite valuable, or they may be worthless to anyone else. In any case, joy of possession and value are definitely (in the eyes of the beholder) subjective.

The prices paid for the possessions are not of concern, assuming that the financial means are available. On the other side of the spectrum, it might be that collecting from existing coinage in circulation is the goal. All that really matters is that our pure collector is happily pursuing this fascinating hobby just for its own reward.

The Collector/Investor

Meet the intelligent collector/investor - John Q. Smart. This fully informed, not necessarily rich, individual has value in mind and has it all together. Mr. Smart is a talented blend of brains with a bent for assembling coins that produce a true collection that will also make a financial difference in his life. He has taken the time to become an informed collector specializing in silver dollars. Let's take a closer look at some of his techniques and premises.

Collect better, not more! He read one or more good books on the subject (too bad that he didn't have an opportunity to read this one earlier) and jumped to the front of the field in a hurry. Mr. Smart decided that if he was going to collect, it was going to be worthwhile. That meant collecting the best dates and the highest affordable grades. That combination provided not only a variety of eye appealing coins, but also an assortment with a growing net worth for the long term.

Let's delve a little deeper into this idea. When confronted with the ever-present dilemma (whether to buy common dates or rarer dates), he would always lean towards the rarer dates. This decision was made even if it meant waiting (and saving) patiently to buy the better coin. This view would also pertain to the grade of the coins that were purchased.

BUY AND SECURE! THIS IS EXTREMELY IMPORTANT. THE RARE STAY RARE.

Secure rarity before grade. Some may not be in agreement, but Mr. Smart is very conscious of rarity. You have heard the premise that the rich get richer and the poor get poorer. There is a correlation within the realm of coin collecting. Those scarce, rare and exclusive items will outperform the pack by ten to one, or 100 to one, or even 1,000 to one. And, in addition, they will furnish a great deal of satisfaction and be admired by all who view them. I must hasten to reiterate that he was also prone to purchasing the best grades that his pocketbook would allow.

He was not confused by condition rarity. This refers to the rarity associated with a high grade coin within a common issue. This type of rarity will usually not supersede true rarity for any length of time, and especially true rarity in the higher grades. True rarity may be defined as that condition reflecting lower mintage figures coupled with low surviving specimens.

Concentrate on building a set. There are as many ways to collect coins as there are people to collect them, but one of the surer routes to a successful collection is set building. The whole is worth much more than the sum of its parts, especially if that whole is a completed set. Assembling a dollar set has become a long term goal of Mr. Smart. His plans are made and in progress. I must add here that goals, once set and acted upon, can provide a zest and energy for living; and that can be very fine indeed. (See Chapter 26 covering the John W. Highfill collection.)

Buy the "key" dates first and the common dates later. Mr. Smart has always been aware that common coins are always available at some price level. Generic coins, as they are referred to, are the most common readily available value priced coins. When you want to buy the generic coins, you will be able to purchase them. It is price rather than availability that will be the important ingredient. But John Q. knows that rare coin prices will always outpace those of the generic coins. Acquiring key dates may require much more patience (and savings) than many possess. This is the part that makes the game what it is. Mr. Smart has his sights set right on the target, and he will not be deterred. His approach to the key coins has been to buy the date first, and then continually upgrade quality over a period of time.

Rotate duplicates as you upgrade your collection. Duplicates are a derivative of the upgrading process. Mr. Smart sells duplicates to generate additional cash to use in pursuit of the next coins. Some people will do this more instinctively than others. Certain collectors will find it hard to part with any coin and they will make the poorer financial decisions. After all, in a rising market, the common coins missed will be well compensated by the value of the scarcer dates already acquired.

I must add that the rotating practice carries the additional advantage of learning to contend with the process of selling coins to the numismatic community. This is the one area where I believe the collector is least proficient and the most vulnerable. "How long has it been since you have sold one or more coins?" This is the question each collector should ask himself before dismissing these comments as irrelevant.

Why do you want to collect coins? That is a question that each numismatist should consider occasionally, for the reasons will vary over the years. Our "intelligent collector" viewpoint just might not be your cup of tea. That is okay. Each of you must resolve the question in light of your personality, motivation, resources and numismatic aspirations.

I well remember the "status" given to the collecting "varieties" vogue of the 1970s. It was fun and gave us a lot to learn and reflect upon - more facts than any of us could ever remember. But many can also recollect that "pricy" bids simply faded like yesterday's flowers as many collectors turned away from varieties. I would avoid collecting fads and focus upon the proven assortment of collections involving sets, types and commemoratives. Varieties may or may not be the spice of life. (See separate chapters on "Mint Error Dollars and the Minting Process," by Bill Fivaz and Fred Weinberg; and "Die Varieties in the Morgan Dollar Series," by Jeff Oxman.)

The Investor/Collector

In the following story, the names and dates were changed for everyone's benefit. There once was an 1880-S Morgan silver dollar made by United States mint in San Francisco and released for one dollar. It grew up and decided to seek fame and fortune. The first step was to leave its original bag. It first sold for roughly $35, then $1,500, and then sold repeatedly for prices approaching $10,000 as an uncertified coin.

Finally, in the late 1980s, it went on to be certified, graded and inspected with awe. The reason for this attention was that it was awarded a status of MS-69. This coin, destined to be a star, moved to the perfect spot - just south of Hollywood at Newport Beach in the PCGS studios.

Because it was the first MS-69 silver dollar, its fame spread far and wide with predictable results - price and star status for this beautiful MS-69. What a prize! That first MS-69 dollar, so scarce and rare in that condition, began a fabulous journey that took it to a heady price level just short of $100,000 in less than one year. This was one of the biggest story lines to occur since the wild silver tales of 1980 when the price of silver bullion went from $4 to $50 and back to $10 all in one year. Unfortunately, like the rise and fall of so many stars, the coin reached its zenith and its price began to fall. The offers for this special coin fell, and fell, and fell, until it is currently trading for approximately twenty-five percent of its high. This author thinks that the bid may still be too high.

This supports the theory of condition vs. true rarity. If this coin had been an 1884-S, it would probably be trading in excess of $500,000 today and rising fast with no backsliding. It has been proven by the marketplace again and again that truly rare coins just don't backslide. Backsliding refers to a coin that sells for $1,000 and then falls to $900, continues to retreat to $800, then to $700 and below. These coins lose credibility, and then lose their liquidity and finally lose it all. Once a coin loses value and trades are made at that level, a new price floor is established. On the other hand, if no coins trade, then the price will be considered an artificial low. (See the chapters on "Market Making and Numismatics - Phase I," and "The Future of Sight-Unseen Trading - Phase II," by John Highfill.)

Without mincing words, it is rarity before grade. I do not mean condition rarity. Condition rarity refers to high grade rarity and will not usually supersede true rarity - much less rarity plus condition.

Water seeks its own level, and birds of a feather flock together. Generic coins will find their own level without any help from anyone. Rare coins are like cream that will always rise to the top. They will always be wanted, desired, coveted, and rise to higher and higher levels. I dare anyone to challenge this theory! It is simply the truth.

The intelligent investor must operate in the same manner as the collector; and that is to rotate the extras and duplicates that reside in the collection. It is wise to redistribute those multiples in exchange for various different dates in the same price range. A similar strategy would be to trade unwanted coins in order to upgrade to scarcer dates that will also enrich the investment portfolio.

Review those financial decisions and their consequences. Many an investor's dreams go unfulfilled as a result of a bad decision, or lack of any decision at all. He who hesitates is lost when he wishes for a certain date but does not take the action required to get it. And then the time for action will have passed. Another word of caution is that haste makes waste. Don't over expedite your transactions. You must make haste slowly and exercise patience in order to consummate desired transactions with the best financial results. These cliches have been used in repetition to illustrate more clearly our philosophies and viewpoints.

The Pure Investor

He is only interested in numismatics for the return it can bring for the capital invested. There is a position for this type of individual in the marketplace. Much of the big money (the kind that can spend the bucks when those extra special items come to the auction block) is investor oriented. The possession of the coins themselves is not the passion of this crowd. Their excitement results from a completed and profitable acquisition and sale. The ultimate test is the net worth of the deal. The bottom line will tell it all for these folks.

Another team is emerging on the horizon that will include the pure investor types. This is the limited partnership offered by various large brokerage houses and individual dealer organizations. People will come to consider this market as just another investment that they will never see or touch. In fact, this type of institutional investing will have a profound influence on the way coin business is done, and on the quality of inventory available for the collecting public. (See the related chapter by Hugh Sconyers entitled "Rare Coins As A Financial Medium")

Let's continue this discussion by describing the ramifications of the "bid" and "ask" quotations used in this market. If you aren't intimately involved in the coin bidding system, then you should read on. (Refer to chapters 39,40,41, and 42.)

People sometimes get confused. All bids are not absolute. The more common the coin, the lower the price. And the more there are available, the closer you can buy them to their prevailing bids. However, the higher the worth of the coin, the larger percentage you will have to pay over bid to procure it. For example, a $200 bid coin can usually be bought at $220 to $250. Likewise, a $2,000 bid item will often bring $2,500, and a coin bid at $20,000 may fetch $30,000 or more.

When you find a bid posted, it may have no relevance to the real price of the coin if you want to consummate a deal. As stated before, a mint state coin silver dollar (grade and date not important) may be bid at $200. You should be able to acquire this coin anywhere from $220 to $250. However, that special issue bid at $20,000 may not be available at ANY PRICE, or only available at a very large premium. A superb specimen bid at $200,000 is probably not available, never will be available, and most likely sold in the high six digits or low seven digits in a private and unconfirmed sale. (See Chapter 26, "Silver Dollar Price Records".)

Why does there seem to be such a discrepancy? Well, in the first place, dealers bidding for sight unseen material are taking a risk which they must be compensated for. Who is to say what that risk is in real dollar terms, and the bid prices that appear as a result? The dealers making the bids are telling you what that risk is! There is a strong sentiment towards replacing bids (bid-based system) with only quotes and numeric asks. This system will be an ask-based system and would make the markets more realistic and less volatile.

Next on the list of reasons for a "bid" and "ask" spread revolves around pure economics. That is, the cost of doing business. Dealers had better be very sure of their overhead and costs or they will not be here tomorrow to serve you. Finally, the dealer must be fairly sure that every item being bid on can be re-marketed. What good does it do to bid on items that nobody wants? That action just adds fuel to the inventory fire sale. Sometimes there are no bids at all. There is not always a market for every coin.

Finally, the result of posting bids must be considered. If the bid is "hit," the money must be produced to complete the purchase. Many dealers may not be financially prepared to purchase a $50,000 coin offered in response to your bid. There is a price to be paid for instant liquidity. Instant liquidity may become a thing of the past (unless major firms step in).

DON'T COMPLAIN ABOUT BIDS IF YOU DON'T BID! Bids are derived from many sources with the most visible being on the certified rare coin exchanges. Most of these bids are for sight unseen coins, therefore these bidders are relying upon independent third-party grading services and their ability to grade in an accurate, consistent and unbiased manner.

A bid should be viewed in reality as a **LIQUIDATION PRICE**. This concept developed in order to bring liquidity to the marketplace (liquidity in this instance being identical to liquidation). Posted prices should be considered as liquidation prices. These are not necessarily the only bid prices, but perhaps are the price of last resort. The price of last resort (as in generics) may be the real market value — sight seen or unseen.

This serves a purpose for investment-minded institutions that wish to use these networks as a foundation of security for price levels. However, as stated earlier, it is very easy to see that the higher priced the coin, the more rare the coin. This, coupled with the inability to view the coin, justifies sight unseen bids that may not reflect real market prices for the rarer issues. To be totally truthful, approximately 90% of all coins on the indexes are not available most of the time. That's why they're called "rare" coins. If every coin was available daily, we would be looking at a commodity driven market.

As a good example of this, I have been bidding in the sight unseen marketplace with thousands of bids daily since its inception. My bids have resulted in purchases of less than one percent (1%) of my daily outstanding posted prices. I must also note that of the one percent purchased, ninety percent were generic coins. This raises questions about whether this system really works. Well, for generics it does most of the time, as long as there are "asks" posted within 5-15% of the bids.

The future of the rare coin exchange lies in the "ask" prices approach of the sight unseen marketplace or, even more likely, in the nationwide independent companies that offer coins via computer on an ask basis. You may not like the price, but you can get the coin. (See the following related chapters: Chapter 51, Wall Street and Numismatics by John Sack; Chapter 36, UNITRADE, by Iraj Sayah; and Chapter 37, The U.S. Rare Coin Exchange, by Steve Ivy.)

Here is your spread - the bid and the ask. As you compare those sight unseen prices, you'll find both extremes of the price spread. You may not like either one. You may not wish to liquidate the coin at sight unseen bid, or may not wish to pay the ask price for a coin; but a transaction can still take place.

Now, let's look more closely at the selling side of coin investing. There are basically two ways to market your coin. You may either sell it for its fair market value, or liquidate the coin. Liquidation, meaning to get less than the potential for the coin, may be attributable to bankruptcy, debts or cash flow problems. Some of you may be more familiar with these ideas when they are expressed as retailing and wholesaling. Of course, we have many price levels existing between the extremes mentioned. You may choose to sell your coins at less than your asking price, but still above the liquidation price level. Many deals are made at these prices. (See the chapters on American Numismatic Exchange (ANE), by John Schneider and Certified Coin Exchange (CCE), by Ron Brandow.)

Those wishing to obtain the highest prices for their offerings must exhibit patience as they seek exposure for their coins. They must be willing to spend a little money to advertise their offerings in some way. There is a fare to be paid in order to receive top dollar. Another method is to consign your holdings to a reputable firm for sale on your behalf. The assessment is in the form of a commission. Regardless of the method you choose, highest potential value is not received without cost. (See the chapter by Lawrence Goldberg entitled "How a Rare Coin Auction Works.")

Demand Theory — A Very Short Course

Numismatically speaking, the simplest way to understand demand theory is to view one coin at one price. If two persons wish to own the same coin, it is equivalent to doubling the price. We could continue increasing the demand by adding buyers with fantastic offers being the result. Now begin to add additional coins of the same type and grade. Our offers would diminish dramatically and buyers would fade into the woodwork. The point to remember here is that the combinations are GEOMETRIC, not arithmetic progressions!

How many combinations exist? Consider these observations. Did you ever stop to realize that the basic telephone dial consists of only ten digits. With that combination of digits, it is possible to contact virtually every inhabitant of the civilized world! We're talking about "billions" of people and combinations.

Consider two basketball teams consisting of five players each. Each member is given five offensive and five defensive plays in their playbook. At half time, they switch ends of the court and play another half. Given an infinite playing time, how many different plays are possible? Do not write to me with your answer. If you guessed thousands, you are off by millions, and even I don't know the true answer. But I do know that the final score would dazzle us all.

I am demand oriented and believe in demand-side theory. Several incidents in my life have made me so. Yes, I have been conditioned by reality. Remember that the graveyards are full of economists who were fifty percent correct in their predictions. The fact that I am writing this book for you tells me that I have done as well as that. And if the "expert" economists will refrain from writing to us, I will continue (corrective criticism is welcome).

Almost everyone understands the basics of supply and demand, including their respective consequences. On the supply side, keeping the demand constant and increasing the supply will reduce prices. Likewise, if the supply diminishes given a constant demand, prices will increase. Giving equal time to demand, an increase in demand against a constant supply will increase prices, and vice versa.

The emphasis could be placed on either supply or demand, and I hypothesize that a reader poll would show that fifty percent of you would support each camp. But now I will explain why I am 100% convinced that demand is the key with the scales being tipped in its favor (especially in numismatics).

Put yourself in my shoes for a moment and suppose that you have orders (demand) for coins with stable prices. Next, you experience increased orders (more demand) coupled with the inability to expand your fixed supply which will cause prices to rise. The inevitable result is price escalation to the point where, once again, supply and demand will be in approximate equality.

"But wait," you respond, "Won't an additional supply come into the market and cause the price to decline?" In many cases, I would reply, "Okay. Make this additional supply available to me." Then you would probably answer with, "but I have no more (or an insufficient quantity) of those coins in the quality you desire." Then what other option is available to me other than to raise my price to reduce the demand for my existing supply? Generics always give a constant supply in response to demand, while rare coins operate very differently.

The whole dilemma revolves around two truths. Number one is that they simply are not making (legally) any more of those precious silver disks for the years gone by. As demand increases for the existing supply, price must become the final mediator. I will acknowledge that temporary events such as the emergence of a hoard (for instance, the Redfield Hoard, and the Continental Illinois Bank deal) or a "bear" market will cause affected prices to retreat for a short period of time. But then the demand eats up the supply and here we go again. (See the related chapters entitled "The Continental-Illinois Bank Deal," by Leon Hendrickson and Clark Samuelson; and "The Redfield Hoard," by John Highfill.)

Also, through the decades coins are lost, mishandled, melted, and taken out of the marketplace. Therefore the supply is ever diminishing. I do realize that certified coins are increasing in population, but don't get lost in the numbers game. Demand for these coins can easily be met by outside interests. (See the related chapter by John Sack entitled "Wall Street and Numismatics.")

WE HAVE ONLY JUST BEGUN TO REALIZE THE REAL VALUE OF RARE COINS (BOTH UP AND DOWN)!

Truth number two is simply a matter of risk vs. return. The price of any coin may rise to the moon, but it may also fall to the ground. To illustrate, assume that a particular item is trading at the $500 level. Your purchase of this coin will expose you to a risk of $500 or less. But the upside is unlimited and will advance to whatever the market will bear. One additional unit of demand may cause market prices to accelerate beyond reason. On the long side, the sky is the limit. With possible high inflation and a modest current price for silver bullion, I would recommend the purchase more often than not.

At the institutional level, consider that larger orders may come into being involving hundreds of coins in the $50 to $500 trading level. If many of these orders hit the market at the same time, or the same company increases its order sizes, the result would be rising prices. I have noticed an ever growing number of limited partnerships being marketed to the individual investor. For the common coins, it seems like the demand is decreasing and the supply is increasing. But the sleeping giant (i.e., institutional and limited partnership demand) will awaken and take us all by surprise.

Where do you think that coin prices will go once these funds begin to trade in earnest? And on the other hand, what will happen if a fund is forced to liquidate its holdings during a down market? We could find ourselves entering the most volatile market cycle that this industry has ever seen.

Let's spend a moment and talk about coins as a commodity. During the 1970s, there was actually a commodities contract involving bags of silver coins trading in New York on the COMEX (New York Commodity Exchange). The futures contract called for delivery of bags of silver coins worth $1,000 per bag. The volume of trading was never very high and the lack of a continuing quantity of deliverable bags was only one of the reasons for the contracts demise.

The difficulty revolves around quantities of coins which may be too large for the numismatic industry to absorb, but too small for full time Wall Street involvement. However, if the numbers become large enough, there will be full time emergence of brokerage firms selling the product. Then, with the supply fixed and the demand increasing as each new person enters the marketplace, the demand side will win over the supply side. The only way to get by the demand side of the spectrum is for price escalation to occur.

The Accidental Investor

Virtually all inventory-heavy dealers become accidental investors at some point(s) in their career. This includes all wholesale and retail businesses nationwide. The ingredients of the market causes downside corrections from time to time. If you are a pure investor, you may sell whenever you wish. However, if you are a dealer, you must sell each day to cover overhead and remain in business. Unfortunately, the overhead factor does not go away and cannot be ignored without permanent business damage. As a merchant, you must recover costs and overhead from profit, not from the liquidation of inventory. The volatility caused by the bid-driven certified exchanges has broken more than a few dealers as of the writing of this book. More will follow unless an "ask-based" system is implemented.

When unusually volatile market swings occur, you may not able to react quickly enough and market rapidly enough to reduce your inventory. By default, you are now an accidental investor. Also, you cannot hire and fire your staff every day in order to fine tune personnel costs. In periods of long range recessionary factors, you are able to trim and adjust your inventory surplus. But this is not the case in the short term volatile markets. Volatility is a direct by-product of liquidity. We should substitute "conditional liquidity" for "constant" liquidity in order to reduce volatility.

How do you become an accidental investor? By buying coins as a vendor, you will become an accidental investor. It is virtually automatic. Negative market shifts without time to sell will cause you to lose. But you may fine tune your merchandise by taking small losses. My "first loss" theory is to cut your losses and run. Yes, the first loss is the best loss. However when dramatic price swings are caused by dealer cash flow problems, hoards entering the marketplace, overextension of prices in the marketplace through promotion, or downward pressure by the larger institutions, reaction time is short to nil. The inevitable result is a real or paper loss.

Say that you have a coin with a wholesale price of $1,000 that loses thirty to fifty percent of its value in less than thirty days. Several possibilities could emerge as a result. The new price will become an artificial price level if no merchandise or little merchandise trades. Put another way, unless you buy new merchandise at the new levels and trading resumes at the new levels, this will result in an artificial price level.

Another probability looms if you sell a coin into the market at a loss and cannot replace that coin at the same condition and at the same price. You have taken a real loss. Contemplate dollar cost averaging for a moment. If you are buying new product at all price levels (i.e., $900, $800, $700, $600 and 500), but the coin is dropping due to the certified coin exchanges lack of depth, you shouldn't try to support the market by yourself. At some point in time you may have to sell these coins at a loss to cover overhead, interest charges, or other expenses of doing business. The most dangerous aspect of all this is being caught in a "bear trap" or a whip-saw effect.

One of the things that this author despises the most is a bid price that is falling without any transactions. This is akin to "limit down" trading (meaning a lack of trading) in the commodities market. In commodities trading for most markets, there is a daily limit imposed by regulations which dictate the maximum price change allowed during one trading session. If you own a contract of that commodity, you are locked into your position with no escape. If this has ever happened to you, I need say no more. In both situations, there is no immediate escape. You know what must be done, but there is nobody willing to take the other side in order to give you an exit. I BELIEVE THE NUMBER ONE PROBLEM IN THE COIN BUSINESS TODAY IS FALLING COIN PRICES WITHOUT ANY TRANSACTIONS AT ALL.

Negative market shifts will place every business (large and small) into a position of having to reduce inventory via liquidation. Cost averaging is easy to do in up and down markets, but a low price structure in the market can cause the market to back up. For example, if you buy a coin at $50, certify it for approximately $25, and sell it for $100, everything is all right. But if the current price is $40, you lose. Therefore raw coins just sit waiting for the price to go up enough to provide a profit. There's that demand side coming back once again.

Let us assume for a moment that you own inventory worth $100,000 and market moves swiftly down to $50,000. At this point, you sell, thereby losing one half of your working capital. But there is a fine line between an accidental investor and a loser. If you sell your coins for $50,000, then buy more coins for $50,000, and finally resell them for $55,000, you are still in business. What I am saying is that if you have a coin that cost you $200 and you choose to sell it for $200 less five to fifteen percent in a negative market, you can keep the business going if you can replace the inventory at prevailing market prices. You must understand, that you "still have the coin and you still have the grade." You have not really lost anything that you cannot regain. But if you liquidate that coin and cannot obtain another, then you have truly lost.

Hard assets are a storage of value. They usually keep up or outpace interest and inflation as most other investment vehicles do. Let me share a short story with you. There was a man who owned a home he purchased for $50,000. Ten years passed by. He decided to move to another neighborhood and proceeded to market and sell his current residence for $100,000. He was ecstatic! Then he began to look for a replacement home and discovered that he could not buy a dwelling equal to the previous residence for $100,000 or even $120,000. Now he was dejected and very sorry for he had lost his storage of value.

What is your storage of value worth? Your inventory is always only worth its market value. If you have 1,000 items at all kinds of prices, they are still only worth what the market will give you for them. But you must be able to sell them and replace them at five to twenty percent less. That is the money you disburse to cover overhead. If you sell coins at market on a daily basis, and then replace them on a daily basis while maintaining the 5-20 percent rule, you will stay current and on top of things.

If you complete 100 transactions within a week with 25 losers and 75 winners, you will have one of two outcomes. You will find that you have either exercised the first loss theory, or that you have made a profit. But regardless, your inventory will have retained its store of value (i.e., consistency in grade and rarity). Remember that there are always some coins that are at artificial levels and don't reflect the true value of the coins at that particular time. Therefore, it is better to trade other portions of inventory that more closely reflect their true value. You have got to maintain your inventory level while upholding your business.

The dealer may also rotate inventory by selling duplicates and replacing them with equivalently priced coins. For example, if twenty 1881-S Morgan silver dollars are on hand, most could be sold and converted into 1879-S, 1878-S and other dates. This would provide diversification and make the offerings more attractive as a variety of dates. There will be no ground lost under this strategy and, most likely, a profit can be made.

A final facet that cannot be ignored is the "thin market" syndrome. This may occur for many reasons. If there are not enough buyers for an item, then the market price can become artificial and very volatile. A special division of this condition may occur when most bids are removed at one time causing a temporary "black hole" in the market. A second contributor to this condition may be the small number of pieces available within a market. A third symptom could be a lack of interest (and therefore bids) for a certain specimen.

The Accidental Collector

Now let's look at the entire thing somewhat in reverse. We are now talking about an investor who started out buying coins strictly as an investment. In the beginning, this person had but one thought in mind, and that was to earn the best possible return for the invested funds. But over a period of time, our investor continually viewed the investment held and became entranced with the selection of coins. The next step involved beginning to desire a particular piece that would fit right in under the guise of diversification. That goal slowly transposed from one of strictly investing to one of investing in particular items.

After collecting all the colored eggs (coins) that can fit into the basket of "common dates," our individual has begun to look for eggs of a different size (price level). Yes, after buying all the dates available within price level number one, our budding numismatist moves to a different price level. Now this "investor" is all but hooked as a collector. No longer does this person wish to sell that special and growing collection. Instead, obsession can take hold. It becomes a quest to find and acquire very specific semi-key and key dates. Also, our investor/collector will begin to upgrade the collection and may perhaps become a full fledged numismatist. Some of the highest quality completed Morgan and Peace dollar sets were started with a few key coins.

The same rules already listed will apply to the accidental collector as well. The tried and true concepts of quality buying, selling duplicates to upgrade the collection, buying true rarity over condition rarity, diversification, etc., are just as valid here.

Numismatists Are Numismatists

Now that we have come full circle, so to speak, it probably has occurred to you that all these general categories of numismatists are much closer to one another than was previously thought. Most of us probably move within and around most of the categories at one time or another. This may be by design, or we may be caught up in an "accidental" manner. Dealers themselves move in their own circles. Similar to little groups or communities. Like cities are to states and states to a country. There are dollar dealers, gold dealers, type dealers, certified dealers, quantity dealers, quality dealers, bullion dealers, etc. Totally, they make up the dealer community.

New organizations entering or being formed (institutions and limited partnerships) will find themselves using the very same perceptions, but perhaps on a larger scale. I will predict that in the future of this decade, there will be a number of these "generic" players formed and available to move into the market. And when they are ready to play, nobody will be able to stem the tide.

The arena of numismatics is due for some of the most dramatic changes ever witnessed. Changes and market volatility will occur that will take our breath away. The moves will be fast and many will be caught off guard. Each of us must strive to perceive and react to those changes in order to survive. There will be no prisoners taken!

I'll close with this reminder for living. When your back is against the wall, you must do what you must do in order to survive. You will just know when that time is. All theories and advice will go out the window. You'll either make it or not. It may or may not feel right, but you will know the right thing to do. Don't ask me how, but you will know. It will be up to you and you alone.

In summary, there are collectors, investors, dealers, limited partnerships, pension plans, brokerage firms, telecommunication retailers, commodity related bullion firms, auction firms, bank loan leveraged accounts, institutional investors, Wall Street entities, etc. They all are a complex numismatic network that runs the numismatic industry of today and tomorrow. The future looks bumpy but bright. Being "in" will supersede sitting on the sidelines as the "action" goes into the 21st century with great change and positive excitement for all.

***

Q. David Bowers, NLG

I began my interest in numismatics in 1952, and entered the coin trade as a dealer in 1953, at the age of fifteen. Before long I was a major advertiser in *The Numismatic Scrapbook Magazine* and *The Numismatist*, the leading periodicals of their time. In 1958 I became associated with James F. Ruddy and formed the Empire Coin Company, Inc., which by 1961 achieved $1 million per year in sales, an unprecedented volume at the time. James F. Ruddy retired from coins in 1977, by which time our company was known as Bowers and Ruddy Galleries, Inc. In 1982 Bowers and Merena Galleries, Inc. was formed, which continues to the present day. Over the years it has been my pleasure to have catalogued and offered for sale many important collections, including the $25 million Garrett Collection sold for The John Hopkins University, the Norweb Collection, the Eliasberg Collection of Gold Coins, and many more. Along the way I have handled multiple examples of Uncirculated 1794 dollars, rare 1804 Dollars, Gobrecht dollar rarities, 1870-S dollars, and more. Silver dollars have always been one of my favorite series, and I consider them to be incredibly historical and interesting.

From 1977 through 1979 I served as president of the Professional Numismatists Guild, and from 1983 to 1985 I was president of the American Numismatic Association. I am a recipient of the Founders Award, the highest honor given by the PNG, and the Medal of Merit, given by the ANA. The author of over three dozen books, my current involvement is with *The ANA Centennial History*, commissioned by the ANA Board of Governors, a book which will be over 1,000 pages in length.

CHAPTER 4

Silver Dollars, A Personal Reminiscence

by Q. David Bowers, NLG

I first became interested in coins in 1952, and by 1953 I hung out my shingle as a rare coin dealer. Things were quieter then, electronic trading systems hadn't been invented, certified coins weren't even thought of, and prices changed on a yearly basis, whenever a new edition of the *Guide Book of United States Coins* came out.

The biggest annual convention was that held by the American Numismatic Association, the first one of which I attended in 1955. That show registered an attendance of 500 people, an all-time high. There were several other coin shows per year, perhaps a half dozen or so significant ones totally, most of which drew a couple of hundred people at best.

Most collectors centered their activities on popular series such as Lincoln cents and Indian cents, large cents, Liberty nickels, Buffalo nickels, Barber coins, Mercury dimes, Standing Liberty quarters, Liberty Walking half dollars, and commemoratives. Gold coins were mainly collected by types, rather than by date and mintmark sequence.

Silver dollars were collected by some, but were hardly in the mainstream of numismatics. If a poll were to be conducted of popularity, I doubt if Morgan dollars would have made the top ten. Still, there was enough activity in dollars that several dealers specialized in them, notably Norman Shultz, of Salt Lake City, Utah, and Bebee's, of Omaha, Nebraska. While buying from Shultz or Bebee was a nice way for the armchair collector to acquire many dates and mintmarks for a couple of dollars or so each, most who collected Morgan dollars simply went to the bank and looked through stocks there.

It must have been in 1953, certainly no later than 1954, when I decided to put together a set of Morgan silver dollars from 1878 to 1921. Equipping myself with a copy of the *Guide Book*, so as to spot the scarcer issues, I went to the Forty Fourth State Bank (Pennsylvania), located in my home town, only to find they had very few pieces.

My next stop was the Kingston State Bank, located in an adjacent community. There I was generously rewarded, for I found that as part of their cash reserves they had on hand a number of bags of dollars containing 1,000 coins each. Things were a bit more personal in those days, and the bank tellers had no problem letting me, a high school kid, post a deposit of $1,000 (representing a good part of my business capital at the time) and take a bag of 1,000 coins into a small room, where I would spend an hour or two looking through them, picking out the dates I wanted and replacing them with others. I searched through bag after bag in this manner, and was able to put together nearly a complete set.

The typical grade of a Morgan dollar was apt to be Very Fine to AU. Carson City coins, of which occasional specimens were seen, were worn the most and were usually Very Fine to Extremely Fine, typically gray-toned. The best pieces were those struck in Philadelphia, which often fit into the AU category, although a number of pieces could be called Uncirculated.

From time to time I would encounter a full bag of Uncirculated pieces, which could contain specimens of a single date, such as 1878, 1879, 1880, or 1881 — Philadelphia Mint coins which had been shipped from the nearby Federal Reserve Bank. I do not recall ever seeing an Uncirculated New Orleans Mint coin in one of these bags, nor an Uncirculated Carson City piece. A few scattered Uncirculated San Francisco pieces were encountered, but not all together in a single bag.

I never found an example of the rare 1895, and there were a half dozen others which did not come to hand. I don't recall which ones I missed, but probably the 1893-S was on the list.

Taking from my bookshelf today a copy of the 1951-1952 *Guide Book* edition, I note that in Uncirculated grade many silver dollars were priced in the $2.50 to $5.00 range. The most expensive was the 1893-S, pegged at $200, followed by 1903-O at $175. No other pieces were priced above $100. A Proof 1895 cost all of $85.

I should also mention Peace silver dollars, which I collected. All of them were priced from $2.00 up to $6.50, with the exception of the Uncirculated 1934-S which was listed for $15. A complete Uncirculated set cost considerably less than $100! In those days a coin was either Uncirculated or it wasn't. Such terms as MS-60 and MS-65 weren't unknown, but when they were used the application was strictly in the field of United States large cents, for the system had been devised just a few years earlier, in 1949, by Dr. William H. Sheldon in connection with the pricing formula he set up in his book, *Early American Cents*.

If an Uncirculated coin was particularly nice, a dealer might call it a "choice" or "gem" example, but such adjectives were not applied with any consistency, and what one person called choice, another might not give any additional description to at all. The buyer of coins could pick and choose, and those who were fussy could acquire examples with fewer bag marks, and those who didn't care would get average pieces. These was little distinction or interest in fine delineations within the Uncirculated category.

At the time the Federal Reserve possessed hundreds of millions of silver dollars. With the exception of examples sometimes used in gambling casinos in Nevada and in commerce in a few other scattered places in the West, silver dollars were not seen in everyday change. Rather, they stayed in banks, where they could be obtained for use as stocking stuffers at Christmas time, or for other gift purposes. Each year around the holiday season there was an extra call for silver dollars, and the average bank would tap the Federal Reserve system for a few bags. Sometimes these bags would contain surprises, as in the instance of a bag of 1904-S dollars released in Los Angeles in the early 1950s (when the coins catalogued less than $10 each, but still this amounted to a significant premium value) or a bag of 1889-CC dollars (value about $15 each Uncirculated) put into circulation in Montana. From time to time releases of specific dates would be reported in the pages of *The Numismatic Scrapbook Magazine* or *The Numismatist*.

In my area, in Northeastern Pennsylvania, such releases typically consisted of Philadelphia Mint coins from 1878 through the 1880s. Anyone desiring same could have bought virtually an unlimited supply of Uncirculated bags for the face value of $1,000 each.

I recall that some time in the late 1950s Abe Kosoff, one of the better known dealers at the time, had a client in California who wanted to buy a bunch of Uncirculated bags from the East, from the Philadelphia Mint, as all he could find on the West Coast were San Francisco coins. Abe sent me a check for $16,000, representing payment for 15 bags of $1,000 each, or face value, plus a $1,000 profit for me — a nice deal for me, as all I had to do was go to a local bank and place the order!

Morgan and Peace dollars continued to be of rather casual interest in the numismatic field until the early 1960s, when activity began to pick up. Philadelphia dealer Harry Forman did a lively trade in buying and selling bags of such coins as 1885-CC dollars, which were available at a price of just a few dollars per coin. Silver dollars become a popular investment medium, although not as popular as rolls of lower denominations (cents through half dollars).

The floodgates opened in autumn 1962, when it was announced that the 1903-O Morgan dollar, a great rarity at that time, listed for $1,500 in the *Guide Book*, had turned up in dealers' hands, and a few pieces were available on the market. Here indeed was a landmark rarity. Probably no more than a half dozen or so existed in collectors' hands at the time, and in 1941 when B. Max Mehl prepared his catalogue of the Dunham Collection, he specifically noted the 1903-O dollar as being one of the major rarities therein. Everyone assumed that most of the Uncirculated pieces had been melted under terms of the Pittman Act in 1918, which saw the destruction and conversion to bullion of 270,232,722 silver dollars of earlier date. No inventory was kept of the specific dates and mintmarks melted.

It soon developed that at least a bag of 1,000 1903-Os had been released, and initial coins traded hands at several hundred dollars each. A few sharpies sought to visit coin shops in remote areas and sell the coins for $1,000 each or more, figuring that they didn't know about the release. This was in the day before the teletype and electronic trading systems, and, as noted, prices did not change quickly. One enterprising individual hopped on a plane and went to London to sell Spink & Son, the well-known dealers there, a few pieces at high prices. I don't recall hearing whether or not he was successful, but an employee of Spink told me of the deception.

Harry Forman got on the telephone and alerted dealers such as me that not only had 1903-O dollars been released, and in quantities that seemed to be increasingly vast, but the 1898-O and 1904-O, also considered rarities, were available by the thousands. News of 1903-O dollars, cataloguing $1,500, but available at face value for $1 each if you were lucky enough to get one from your bank, went through the wire services. Exactly how many 1903-O dollars were eventually released, I don't know. The original mintage was 4,450,000 pieces, and undoubtedly some of these indeed were melted in 1918. I heard that over a million Uncirculated pieces were released in 1962, and know for sure that the number was at least in the hundreds of thousands. On the collector market the price never did get down to the $1 level, but I recall that it was as low as about $17.50. Dollars of 1898-O and 1904-O, valued at $300 each or more prior to the 1962 release, were much cheaper, and were available for a small premium over face value.

The rush was on, and people took wheelbarrows to banks to buy bags of dollars at face value. The rush continued through early 1963, by which time most of the treasury stocks were depleted. All sorts of early dates came to light, particularly San Francisco and New Orleans coins. Although scattered Uncirculated San Francisco pieces were not uncommon, as a class, Uncirculated New Orleans dollars were. Now all of a sudden vast quantities were available, and as nice as the day they were minted.

Just before the floodgates closed, the government decided to hold back nearly three million silver dollars of scarcer varieties, particularly Carson City Mint issues. These were subsequently marketed through a series of sales held by the General Services Administration.

Predictions were aplenty that the vast sea of Uncirculated Morgan and Peace dollars in the hands of the public would completely destroy the market, for the coins would be forever common. Prices would never be the same, and silver dollars that used to be worth $100 before the treasury release would never rise above $2 or $3.

How wrong these predictions were! While the supply of dollars in collectors' hands increased dramatically, the number of people desiring such pieces multiplied even faster, and the result was that before long nearly every Morgan and Peace dollar was priced much higher than it had been before 1962! Today, in the early 1990s, just about every variety of dollar costs substantially more than it cost in the early 1960s, the only exceptions being 1898-O, 1903-O, and 1904-O.

Silver dollars came from relative obscurity to the number one position in collectors' hearts. Today Morgan dollars are appreciated for what they are: glittering reminders of a very romantic era in American history.

***

Dwight N. Manley

Dwight N. Manley was born on February 23, 1966. As a teenager in 1981, he won an American Numismatic Association Summer Seminar scholarship which enabled him to study the history of US coinage. During 1982, he again attended the ANA Summer Seminar to learn grading and authentication of U.S. silver and gold coins. Mr. Manley attended the ANA Summer Seminar a third time in 1983 and learned about the coin minting processes. A few weeks later, at the San Diego ANA, Dwight Manley spoke on how rare coins are produced and the history of proof coinage.

Mr. Manley is a true collector. He was first inspired when he found a 1909 Lincoln Head Penny in an old coffee can. He has been collecting ever since and has become one of the largest full time numismatist in the business today. His latest acquisition was the gold and silver Panama-Pacific exposition collection that is listed in this book under the World's Finest Collections and Prices Realized chapter.

During 1983 and 1984, Mr. Manley exhibited at many state and national coin shows. He won many awards including the Junior "Best of Show" award for 1983 at the National Silver Dollar Convention in Houston, Texas. He also won designation as the "Outstanding Young Numismatist of the Year" from the Numismatic Association of Southern California.

In 1984 Dwight Manley joined the Rarities Group as a purchasing agent.

In 1985, Mr. Manley was hired by David Hall as a buyer and travelled the country looking for gem quality rare coins. Continuing to develop his expertise, he again worked for the Rarities Group buying and selling rare coins from 1986 through 1988.

Most recently, he became founder and President of Spectrum Numismatics International, Inc. The future looks bright indeed for Dwight N. Manley.

CHAPTER 5

Knowledge Is King

by Dwight N. Manley

I first went into a coin shop in the summer of 1973. A new neighborhood friend told me that his father collected coins, and there was a neat old coin shop down the road. Well having recently found a 1909 Lincoln cent in my father's coffee can, I couldn't wait to go and find out its value!

Soon, my mom took two anxious seven year olds down the road to a place that was no bigger than my bedroom. This coin shop, as small as it could be, was crammed full of old coins and "treasures." My eyes lit up at the sight of all those interesting coins. An older man came out, with a magnifying glass affixed to his glasses, and asked what he could show us. Having remembered my new friend David from previous visits, he handed David a tray of old silver dollars. The tray had a sign that said $2.50 each.

He next came to me and asked my name. He told me that coins are more than a hobby — they can be a passion. Well, having a one track mind, I pulled my very-circulated 1909 cent from my pocket, and inquired to its value. The coin dealer then put his magnifying glass to the coin, told me it was a "VG", and was worth 5 cents. Being overcome by his "instant" knowledge of value, I asked what VG meant and how did he know the value so quickly. The next thing the old man said essentially changed my life from that day on. The man handed me a 1974 black-book of U.S. coins and said, "You read this book before you ever buy a coin from me." Wow, I thought, why would someone *not* sell a coin to someone who wanted to buy one until they read a book? The man said, "The more you know about numismatics, the more you will understand. Numismatics is more than coins."

Hurriedly, we left the coin shop and went home. I immediately went to my room and began reading about the history of U.S. coinage, the first coins struck, about David Rittenhouse, first director of the U.S. Mint, and many other new stories about coins and their history. I read that book over a weekend, and by Monday, was dying to go back to the coin shop and report on my new "knowledge." I immediately asked to buy my first coin, a 1910 cent in Extra Fine condition, for 15 cents — to follow my 1909 cent. I also bought a 49 cent Whitman blue album for Lincoln head cents.

From that first purchase in 1973, coins and numismatics took a front seat in directing my life. I began subscribing to different coin magazines, attending local shows, and buying and trading coins with my neighbor, David, and other friends in my elementary school classes.

I vividly remember going to my first coin show, a NCOC show in 1975 at the Quality Inn. I had $13 saved up, and was overwhelmed by all of the different coins. I bought an 1853 arrows and rays quarter in Good condition for $4. I also bought extra souvenirs, the elongated silver dimes for around 50 cents each. Upon getting home, David and I researched our new purchases, and found out there was a variation to my arrows and rays quarter. It was an 1853 over 4 variety. The Red Book showed no price, but we soon learned it was worth $50! Armed with this new found wealth, I began actively searching for more "rarities." But I also realized I needed to study more — to know these varieties inside and out — and the only way to do this was to read. Just as I was told in 1973, and as 1950's coin dealer Aaron Feldman said, "Buy the book before the coin."

My next two book purchases were a Red Book and Photograde. The Red Book, as Walter Breen once told me, is invaluable for knowing varieties, mintages and basics. But for history and thoroughness of numismatics, it's as valuable as a wooden nickel.

As I made my rounds around the local coin stores, I came upon Fullerton Coins. Here, around 1977, I met Bill Pannier, or as I now call him, "Willy." Willy was much different from any of the coin dealers I had met before. He was fastpaced, and spit out facts and figures about coins like an out of control slot machine. I could spend hours pouring over his bidboard searching for that one bargain. The thing I remember most, though, was him pulling a 1909-S VDB cent out of his shirt pocket, and quoting me $275. Ordinarily, holding such a valuable item would make me uneasy, but with Willy, it was no big deal. He used to wear these Mexican style shirts with pockets all over the front, and as I soon found out, these "pockets" were loaded with different "rarities."

I also remember going to Bob Patchin's in 1978, and picking out beautiful Proof Franklin halves for $2.50 each. After every purchase, I would go home, package it up, and put it into a 3 ring binder for coins.

By 1980, I had a nice collection of coins and coin books. I subscribed to *Coin World* and watched as coin values rose with inflation and gold and silver prices. I remember 50 people in line just to get into local coin shops. I decided I needed to work overtime at the local banks, buying half-dollar rolls to search for silver coinage. In February 1980, at the Home Bank in Brea, I bought $100 worth of half-dollars. Upon opening them I nearly passed out. There were $70 face value of 90% silver halves. Their value was over $1,400! This almost doubled my net worth at the time. I took my profit and sent away for 10 Carson City dollars from the government on February 15. By late March I got my coins, five of which were the better 1880, 1881 and 1885 Morgans. I sold those, and now had turned $100 into over $2,500 in less than two months! Well, if I only breathed numismatics before this, now I ate, slept and breathed numismatics.

The more money I made, the more coin books I bought. My favorite was "All About Coins" by my friend Dave Bowers. As I read more, I wanted to meet more numismatists. So I called Fullerton Coins and asked where a local coin club was. He said the Orange County Coin Club meets this Wednesday. I was now 14, and eagerly awaited Wednesday so I could meet others involved in coins. I remember that December meeting very clearly. The first person to greet me was William O. Wisslead. He was very nice and introduced me to everyone including his wife Elizabeth, Peter Meyer, Herb Bergen, Bruce Davidson and many other people.

I remember the auction, where Bill Wisslead would sell some duplicate books from the CSNA library. I bought one and took it home to read. I was soon introduced to the American Numismatic Association through the Orange County Coin Club, and became an official member in March 1981 (Jr. #111353). My membership in ANA brought *The Numismatist* to my home each month.

In the April edition, there was an article about the upcoming Summer seminar in Colorado Springs, and scholarships were available. I quickly applied and on June 5, 1981, Florence Schook, then YN Chairperson for the ANA, called me to say I won the "Coin World" scholarship and was leaving on June 17. I must say that this phone call is what made another positive change in my life. Little did I know, I was about to meet one I thought was the all-time immortal numismatist — Q. David Bowers.

After arriving at the Colorado College campus, I met about 15 young numismatists like myself from around the country who loved coins. We would stay up late every night and talk about coins. We went to the ANA book sale and got old duplicates and traded them back and forth.

But the best part for me was taking the class "All About Coins" by Dave Bowers. This was right after the Garrett auctions, and Mr. Bowers had been in the press a lot. I did not think a smarter numismatist existed. I remember asking hundreds of questions, and learning about what made coins rare — that an almost uncirculated Barber half dollar was just as valuable to a collector as an MS-65; that to a collector it is the history of the coin that matters, not the value. I remember him saying, "If only a coin could talk, and tell where it had been, wouldn't a well circulated coin have more interesting stories to tell than a gem uncirculated one that just sat in a drawer for 100 years?"

Well after leaving the seminar, I began corresponding with Mr. Bowers, and asking more questions. I started going to more coin clubs; Garden Grove and Anaheim. The next year, when summer seminar #14 came, I had saved up my money for the trip. I was anxious to see my friends from the previous year.

This year, 1982, myself and three other YN's decided to attend our first ANA convention in Boston. Mrs. Schook said we could be pages to help defray the costs. Well, remembering back to the first NCOC coin show that I attended in 1975, I couldn't believe I was flying 3,000 miles for a coin show. When my friends and I arrived at the Sheraton Hotel, the first person we saw was a Santa Claus looking man in shorts, sandals, and a tie-dyed T-shirt. It was the coin genius of coin geniuses, Walter Breen!

Everywhere we looked, a famous numismatist was there. My friends, Dan, Cliff, Daniel and I checked into our room, and then quickly headed for the bourse floor. We were handed red vests and hats, and let loose to do miscellaneous errands for coin dealers. It is ironic that only eight years ago, dealer Steve Ivy of Texas was giving me a fifty cent tip to get him a hot dog and now I buy and sell millions of dollars worth of coins with his firm. I remember Kevin Lipton giving me a $5 tip to get a Bowers and Ruddy employee a coke. The last transaction I did with him was over $50,000!

But the most memorable thing at the Boston ANA was John Bergman, one of my most admired friends, loaning me $400 to buy a 1794 large cent from the John Adams collection. What was so neat about this coin was its pedigree: Ed Frossard (who illustrated it in his 1879 book), T. Harrison Garrett, John Work Garrett, Tom Morley, John Adams, and now me! This coin was the cheapest in the fixed offering, but to me, as I told Rick Bagg, the man in charge of deciding who got each coin, it had the greatest pedigree ever. I promised never to sell it if I was awarded it, and I have not. This coin became an exhibit for me that won many awards: NASC, CSNA, ANA, NCOC and others. It was buying this coin, and the experience of exhibiting it, that taught me what I know today about numismatics; that as the coin dealer told me in 1973, numismatics is more than coins, numismatics is people. It is friendships that last a lifetime; they can't be bought and sold like a coin.

Ironically, it was this exhibit that introduced me to John Highfill in 1983. John was actively pushing to expand the collector base in numismatics through his annual silver dollar shows, and he approached me about exhibiting at the 1983 National Silver Dollar Convention in Houston. I was honored and flew to Houston to show my prized coin. I was even more excited when I won Junior Best of Show. That simple encounter, brought about by sharing and learning, has blossomed into not only a very close friendship/father/son relationship, but into a very profitable business relationship as well.

Gradually, I met more people in the coin business. I began showing auction lots at Dave Bowers' auctions, attending more shows, and started thinking seriously about coins as a full time profession. I began speaking at ANA conventions, and at the 1984 NASC for Mrs. Schook.

By 1984, I was good friends with Walter Breen, and stayed with him at the NASC show in LA at the Ambassador Hotel. During all of this time, I now worked part time for Bill Pannier for $5 an hour. And I would come back from shows and seminars and tell him about the people I met and different coin transactions I witnessed. Willy would give me advice on how to behave and to always work hard. He said determination is what will get you ahead.

That year, Bowers and Ruddy moved to New Hampshire and became Bowers and Merena. Dave Bowers asked if I could help pack his office, and in exchange, I got to keep any spare coin books lying around that he did not want. This started me actively collecting old coin books, and I became even more involved with John Bergman, the world's greatest bibliophile. John is one of the most generous people I have ever met in coins, and there certainly is nobody nicer than him around. John helped me to begin a real library — something that I am convinced helped me become very successful in the rare coin business.

In 1984, I moved to Massachusetts to work for a large coin dealer. It was against my father's wishes, and was for less pay than local dealer, David Hall, offered me. My dad wanted me to go to college and become a businessman. He said that was how you become successful. But being fresh out of high school, and not having too many cares to worry about, I headed East to learn the coin business from Martin Paul, who I thought was the brightest coin dealer around.

Life back East was dramatically different from California — hot humid weather, cold winters and those bothersome toll gates. But that meant nothing when compared to working in the rare coin business. Martin was a real workaholic. Somebody that could not take a day off from coins. We worked seven days a week. And at the Detroit ANA, we worked 48 hours straight, without sleep — buying and selling coins. In the middle of the night, we would be packaging thousands of coins to submit to ANACS, the granddaddy of certified coins. After six months of this, I'd had enough. I loved coins, but I also loved to sleep too. I moved back home, took the job as David Hall's buyer, and began to take charge of the direction my career was taking.

By the age of 19, I was making six figures a year just buying and selling rare coins. My parents could not believe how successful one could become from numismatics. But as I found out from the school of hard knocks, buying overgraded coins and losing money, the coin business can be treacherous. Everybody is always trying to make money off of somebody else. For most coin dealers, they try to find someone less knowledgeable than they are to sell coins to. So to be ahead of the game, the thing I was first told came up again — Knowledge Is King.

I became partners with Sil DiGenova in Tangible Investments of America. In one year, our combined sales were over $50,000,000 wholesale, dealer to dealer. Today, the coin business side of numismatics is far different than when most of us started collecting: we have slabs, computers, million dollar coins, etc.

It appears to me that after any and all imperfections in grading services, Wall Street will come into the coin business in a very large way, with hundreds of millions of dollars, to buy high grade rare coins. Like art, coins will be treasured by different pension funds and aristocrats, and I'm sure they'll make lots of money. But no matter how much money one has, or what valuable coins they own, it can't buy the fellowship that numismatics has to offer. Always remember this. And for those of you who love coins and aspire to become "true" numismatists, read and learn; KNOWLEDGE IS KING!

***

Dean Tavenner

Dean Tavenner had a childhood hobby, collecting silver dollars, that has led to a lifetime of numismatic knowledge and memories. But before the "cartwheel" completely took over in his life, he obtained a college education and taught school in Ennis, Montana and Powell, Wyoming. This was in the early 1960s.

The "Great Silver Dollar Rush" ending in 1964 prompted Mr. Tavenner to go into the business full time, and he opened his own coin shop, "The Cartwheel," in Missoula, Montana during August 1965. Using that shop as a base, Dean Tavenner joined the band of traveling numismatists. In 1970 he closed his shop choosing to operate as a numismatic consultant and moved to Deer Lodge, Montana for a decade. California was his next home in 1980, and he has lived there ever since.

Dean Tavenner has been a "permanent fixture" on the coin show circuit from the mid-1960s until 1989, when he curtailed his annual travels to approximately five of the best known conventions.

Mr. Tavenner has contributed articles to most of the popular numismatic publications over the years. Wayne Miller dedicated the first edition of his landmark "Textbook" to both Dean Tavenner and John Love. Dean Tavenner is a member of many numismatic organizations throughout the United States. He was an initial member of the National Silver Dollar Roundtable where he served as president from 1984-1986.

CHAPTER 6

My Numismatic Memories

by Dean Tavenner

Here is a collection of my favorite "treasures." I hope that they give you as much enjoyment as they gave to me.

Telephone Book Prices

or

You Can't Collect (or invest in) What Doesn't Exist

For as long as price listings have existed (whether the "Red Book," or the trade journals,) one of the major problems in the coin hobby/business has been the attempt by people - collectors or dealers - to match a coin for every price rather than to put a price on every coin.

It becomes wishful thinking to believe that a coin exists for every price listed in the "Red Book," and yet in the silver dollar world it seems that many people wanting to collect or invest in dollars believe that because a price guide lists a price for a silver dollar, that they can tour the bourse floor of nearly any major show with their shopping carts selecting - say, for example, an 1884-S, MS-65, an 1893-CC, unc 60 with a full strike, or even a gem P/L "common date" like '89-P or '90-P. After all, most listings price these items; why not just go help yourself although you might even have to (perish the thought) pay full "bid" for what you want. After all, So-and-So last month said that one of his top recommendations for this year's investment would be full struck MS-65 1894-O dollars at bid level. Just get a few at today's prices and hold for a year - you'll make 50% or 60% or 100% - or nothin'!! You can't collect what doesn't exist! Oh, So-and-So forgot to tell you that there might have been a little wishful thinking (or self-fulfilling prophecy) written into his suggestions and recommendations.

Below I list most of those silver dollars which in my nearly 30 years experience, I believe to exist so seldom as to make a price listing superfluous. Sheldon, in "Penny Whimsy" referred to such seldom-seen items as "condition census" - coppers which were scarce enough in high grades (many times not even mint state) that each could be rated categorically as one of the best six known of that particular date or variety. A "condition census" has so far not been compiled for silver dollars; perhaps such a study is forthcoming. (It can now probably be argued that the grading service population reports have fulfilled that function.) At any rate, I believe that the following list represents those items so seldom seen as to make realistic pricing impossible.

1879-S flat breast (type of 1878) MS-65 or better.

1879-CC capped die MS66 or MS65 P/L. We know of gem '79-CC dollars, but not of the capped die variety.

1884-S MS-65+ or better. There are six or seven gem pieces now scattered in the best sets, but certainly not on the market.

1886-O MS-65 P/L. Wayne's coin has never had an equal - not even close.

1887-S MS-65 P/L. I guess they exist - I've never seen one.

1892-O MS-63+ or better. One, maybe two pieces.

1892-S MS-65 and better. A few exist in sets.

1893 MS-65 P/L. Do any exist?

1893-O MS-65+ or MS-65 P/L. Do any exist?

1893-CC MS-65 P/L. I've seen a few nice coins - never a P/L except the branch mint proofs.

1893-S MS-65 or P/L. Like the '84-S and 92-S, the few gems are in sets. Of the nice ones I've seen, none is P/L.

1894 MS-65. I know of only one.

1894-O MS-65 or P/L. All of the gems which I have been shown weren't. I've never seen a P/L (except an AU).

1895-O MS-65+. The three or four gems are really that, but I've seen pieces sell for over $40,000 which weren't even new.

1896-O MS-65+ or MS-63 P/L or better. I think this is the toughest gem to locate - I've never seen a P/L.

1896-S MS-65+ or MS-63 P/L or better. The only "wonder coin" has never been equaled - not even close.

1897-O MS-65 P/L. Some gems around; no P/L, though.

1900-O/CC MS-65 P/L. Many nice gems - no P/L

1901 MS-65 or MS-63 P/L. Do any exist?

1903-S, '04-S MS-65 are around; no P/L, however.

1921-S MS-65 P/L. No one knows what one would look like. Even the "branch mint proof" is ugly.

1923-S, 1925-S, 1928-S MS-66 or better. Existence of these correctly graded is doubtful.

I learned a long time ago that "never" is a dangerous word, much like the phrases "I'll take all you can get," or "I'll sell you as many as you can buy." Big prices can bring "wonder" coins out of hiding, but even at big bucks there seems to be some "don't exists" and "one-of-a-kinds." I know a Montana collector who is still waiting to get an '84-S which looks like the '82-S in his set. He passed the Miller piece at $210,000 when ads listed uncs at $39.50 because it wasn't nice enough (or cheap enough.) Wayne's was figured at $27,500 "raw" when he sold his set. The collector didn't even make a dime on the one he wouldn't buy.

Serendipity

A thing of beauty is a joy forever:
Its loveliness increases,
it will never pass into nothingness;
but still will keep a bower quiet for us, and a sleep
Full of sweet dreams, and health, and quiet breathing.

John Keats, "Endymion" 1818

I'm certain that John Keats had little idea that his thoughts in 1818 could be applied to the aesthetics of that fact of coin design and manufacture which yields an item which, indeed, is precisely a "thing of beauty" and a "joy forever."

I read with deep interest and amazement the notice of the sale of the 1886-O mint dollar in the recent Bowers and Merena sale for the substantial sum of $237,000.00. I had been equally as interested and amazed when the coin sold in the Superior sale of January, 1986. Why the special interest at two different times for this "thing of beauty"? These were both times when I was allowed to reflect on the past and thereby recount my personal experiences with the coin.

I attended the Utah Numismatic Society's annual coin show (as I had done for the previous eleven years) in September of 1976. I recall the year now mostly from the remembrance that shortly after the show, which was held at the old Hotel Newhouse in Salt Lake City, the hotel was blown into the next world by a dynamite crew making way for "progress." At any rate, the obliteration of the hotel brings to mind the reality of something which did really "pass into nothingness." Fortunately, my good luck at acquiring nice material at the show did not pass away.

My good friend, Jim Beem from Boise, Idaho, had set up at the show by the time I arrived, and as I walked past his table on the way to set up mine, he said (even before "Hello"), "Dean, I've got a couple of the kind of dollars which you only dream about - I'll bet a couple of CC's you haven't run across these before." If Jim gets excited enough to bet on drinks, then I had better take a look.

"Pretty nice 1886 you got there, but so what? I'm impressed with the 1892, though you got it listed as an O-mint. You know they didn't make deep proof-like '92-O dollars, particularly if they have even a little hairline or breast feathers. Get your glasses on and let's get those dudes out where we can take a look." I could already see that the 1892 was in fact an O-mint - no brain surgery degree to tell O-mints from P-mints - and certainly the 1886 was absolutely the finest Morgan I had seen in all the years I had been looking at dollars. Sometimes in life when you see the very best, you know; maybe a little bit like falling in love. Jim had it labeled 1886-O, but I still didn't believe it. See, I lost the P-mint vs O-mint identification test there and then, because I turned the coin over and there it was: O-mint; O-mint; O-mint;. . . and NOT added onto the coin.

Downplaying the excitement at seeing not one, but two things which in your life you've never seen before requires more of an acting job than I could perform and Jim sensed that he had a deal forthcoming - we hadn't even talked price yet!

$1,400.00 and $900.00 for the two pieces and it's gotta be a package deal," he bounced off of me without hesitation.

"Hell, Jim, that's ten times bid! You goin' for the get-your-buddy medal. We haven't even started drinkin' yet and you've gone crazy." Bid was about $140.00 and $90.00 at the time but in those days you just paid the price when you saw something that you'd never seen before. If you didn't, then someone else would and I knew that and Jim knew that. And I knew that Jim could go to the phone and call John (Love) or Wayne (Miller) as easily as I could, so I screamed (quietly) "I own 'em," put them in my coat pocket and went on to set up at the show.

It took no longer than five minutes before nearly every dealer at the show seem to know of the transaction. I got all the usual comments that follow a deal like this: "You're crazy! You can't pay ten times bid price and come out on the deal." "If I would've seen it first, I would've gotten it cheaper and sold it to you myself." "My best customer back home just got one which would blow this one away." You know most of the patter that issues forth; ignore it and begin to appreciate the good luck that comes every now and then.

Jim and I relaxed later at dinner that night (he bought) and he said that he had just purchased the two pieces earlier that month from a bank examiner for the Federal Reserve Bank who had picked nice dollars as he traveled in Idaho, Wyoming, and Montana. Those two pieces were the best that he had acquired and he had them since the early sixties when the dollars came out in those states.

That evening I called Wayne on the phone. He had been the strongest buyer of nice dollars and he had bought one of the more famous dollars sets put together in Montana - the Hardenburgh-Douglas set, into which, over the years when I lived in Missoula, I had sold many of the coins.

"No 1886-O ever made is worth $1,800.00," was Wayne's reply, "and if it is as nice as you say, then it has to be phony; the New Orleans mint didn't make coins that nice; I pass, but save the '92-O for me at $1,250.00. I've never seen nor heard of a proof surface '92-O and I'll just hope that it's not one of those pancake strikes. If you get real on the '86-O and if it is nice, I'll look at it later; you'll have it, no one's going to pay that much for that date, no matter what!"

The next morning a dealer-collector from Apache Junction, Arizona, stopped by the table. He had heard of the deal and since 1886-O was his personal favorite date (so he said) he figured he better take a close look at it. We settled on $1,900.00, but only with the assurance from me that I'd take it back in trade within a year if he found a better piece.

"Bring me more of those anytime; I'll stock these until I get tired of looking at them." Well, he got uncomfortable with the coin for some reason later that fall. I suppose it was too many dealers and/or friends who kept telling him that he was buried, that he had been "laid away"; you know the patter. I saw him at the winter Tucson show in January the next year, and I traded him $1900.00 worth of Saints and had my 1886-O back. This time I didn't call Wayne.

In February Wayne came from Helena to Deer Lodge to buy some classical albums and to see what new coins I had picked up at the last five or six shows I had attended.

"I'll take this and this and this 1886-P; what else you got?" "Do you think the '86 is good enough for your set? It's $2,100.00 and I think you should look closer. You passed on this one last fall."

"You're kiddin!" This is the same coin? I heard about it after you called, but I figured the piece was gone for good. How'd you wind up with it back?"

We went through the story and made the deal and the coin walked out of my life. I followed news of the coin whenever it changed hands: Miller's set to Hall-Sconyers to Superior's Sale and then to the more recent owners, then to NGC and finally to Bowers and Merena, and now to the current owner.

I ran through the old copies of CDN to January 31, 1986 to see that the news of the sale of the coin at the Superior Sale also listed the 1892-O dollar as having brought $23,100. I also see that the 1893-CC branch mint dollar in Wayne's set brought $30,800.00. I'm positive that it is the same '93-CC that I bought from Gene Henry in 1966 or 1967 for $400.00 and sold for $700.00 to Bruce Todd from Michigan from whom Wayne (directly or indirectly) acquired the coin.

The people who have owned and handled those coins since I was involved have made a lot more money than I ever did on them, but that was a different age and no one who has had anything to do with them has any fonder memories than I have from having had them for a part of my life. It's like having your cake and eating it too.

That's the World of Serendipity.

Larry

Larry was a BIG man. Larry was a HUGE man. But Larry was a big man in really many ways; physically, he scaled in at about 425 lbs when I first knew him in 1960; he was a big family man - he had six kids, three or four huge dogs and at different times an array of Montana wild animals as pets which would keep Alpo in business forever. He was a big gambler on the Cards even if they were in the cellar. He didn't acknowledge the cellar for the Cards; for him they were always on top and he'd throw in the bucks to prove it.

Larry was a beer drinker in a big way; he would always drink beer with ice cubes. I didn't understand this - but he could consume more beer than anyone I had ever met, and on the branding and fencing crews on the ranch, I had seen a few champs.

Larry was the first "big deal" man I had ever known. In my early years on the ranch I would watch as a train load of wool would go to Boston from our loading platform. I would watch as my father left to take 500 purebred rams to the annual sale in Casper, or later as we shipped 2,500 steers to Nebraska to the feed lots. But this was just regular business, these weren't "deals." It took me a long time before I realized that there wasn't much difference, but I certainly thought there was in 1960.

I had been following the release of silver dollars in Montana from about 1952 when I was old enough to realize that these wonderful pieces of silver made the world go around. I remember 1894-S dollars in cash registers in Deer Lodge in 1954; I remember 1886-S and 1888-S dollars in 1956, 1885-CC and 1878-CC in 1958. I worked in the bank in Deer Lodge when one day a bag of 1891-CC dollars came in. Until that date came in, nobody (except me) really paid any attention to coins in Deer Lodge.

One day in the summer of 1960 when I was in Bozeman at summer graduate school, I stopped at this hole-in-the-wall shop on the side street near good old Sigma Chi. Busch's Coin Shop was the sign on the window and as I looked in, I saw that maybe someone else had an eye for silver dollars because there were about six bags spread out in the window. All of them were uncirculated, all mixed together, all priced at your choice for $1.29, $119.00 per hundred pieces, or a full bag for $1,079.00. If you didn't want those in the window, Larry would get an unopened (Federal Reserve sealed) bag from the dozen or so in his huge safe. If you wanted more, he would have you come back in an hour or so and he would have gone to any of the local banks to pick up (at face value to him) any amount you needed. (Indian head pennies were about 30 cents each then, but you could have as many of those as you wanted as well.) I was impressed; these were big "deals".

We got to know one another quite well that summer and when Larry and Lavina (and all the kids had names beginning with "L") would go to coin shows, I would run the shop for him. I was like a kid in an Oreo store. There wasn't much business then but every time someone brought in a coin, it was "deal" time. What a summer!

In 1961 and 1962 I taught school at Ennis, Montana, a small town on the Madison river just north of Yellowstone Park. I was 55 miles from Bozeman and since the College was there, I had multiple reasons to go. One day in October of 1962 I got an advertising postcard from a dealer in San Francisco. He had just acquired some uncirculated '98-O and '04-O dollars and he was offering them as a Christmas deal at $59.50 each or the pair for $99.00. I didn't know of ANYONE who had an uncirculated coin of either date, and as I was just about to write and order a pair, I got a call from Larry.

"Whatever you do," he shouted in his big voice, "don't buy any late date O-mint dollars, even '03-O dollars. They are everywhere. Someone got six bags of 98-O's in Flint, Michigan. They're coming out all over and there's really going to be quantities available. But call me if you get offered any, maybe we can pick some up here in Montana."

I don't recall when I saw the first O-mint bags come into Montana, but I know a banker in Helena had '03-O's available by February of 1963. The least I ever paid for 1903-O dollars was $7.00 each. That must have been in the summer of 1963. I recall, in November of 1965, having sold five rolls of that date for a banker from Dillon, Montana, for $2,100.00, just the price of the demonstrator '65 Mustang I bought that month.

Larry had been handling some of the better date bags, and now in the fall of '62 and the spring of '63, the government really got into full swing with the dollar release program.

By June of 1963 Larry had done his homework; he had full page ads in Coin World, knew most of the dollar dealers in the country, and knew nearly every banker in Montana. During June of '63, Larry got 320 bags of dollars directly from the Helena branch of the Federal Reserve Bank. He would drive the 98 miles from Bozeman, send out what he had prepared the night before for his orders (he advertised Fed Sealed bags for $1,049.50 plus postage), drive back home to Helena and arrive by 3:45, just ahead of closing time, for another 11 bags. He would then drive back to Bozeman and after about six beers, would begin to sort dollars.

I would come from Ennis to Bozeman, arriving about 7:00 and we would sort dollars. We could tell to some extent what we had by weighing the bags. Strict BU dollars weighed 60 lbs., "two-beer" dollars (EF-AU O-mint bags, of which there were thousands) weighed 59 lbs., and circ bags were 57.5 to 58 lbs. We looked at nearly all of the circ bags because those were the bags with 93-S, 89-CC, 94-P, 95-S and the other key dates. We would guess on the 59-lb. bags, and try to find a small hole in each 60 lb. bag to see what the date was since each would be a solid date bag. We could sort seven bags a night.

One night we had all 57-pounders, so Larry said, "Let's have a beer for every 93-S we get; I've got plenty in the frig." I wasn't much of a beer drinker then, but we ran out of capacity before we ran out of beer, and we still found '93-S dollars after we ran out of capacity. Larry toasted each of the first 19 with a beer-on-ice and four more 93-S dollars went unhailed by the time we sorted all that night's bags. What a night!!

We had many nights like that and for the next year we had dollars available constantly. We had to discount bags by $25.00 to get the banks to take searched bags of dollars for deposit or exchange. At one time the Union Bank in Helena had 310 bags of searched dollars on the floor of its vault. The Fed wouldn't take them back, realizing that customers wanted only unsearched bags. Can you imagine a banker's nightmare realizing that he had $310,000 in cash that was earning nothing! Today he would be hurled out of the top floor window by Management.

It ended in April of 1964. The last dollar bags which I got at face value were from the bank in Deer Lodge during Easter vacation of 1964. I had asked the vault manager to save two for me for Friday, as I had to drive back to the ranch from teaching for the holiday. I got one bag of '88-O dollars and a bag of proof-like 1887-O dollars. They were baggy, but I'd certainly like to have another shot at them today. I sold most of the bag to Larry later on.

Larry drifted out of the coin business after dollars were no longer available for little or no premium and even though I saw him occasionally during the years I was in Missoula (1965-1970), he never was again on top of the world of silver dollars as he had been in the early sixties.

Larry was a big man in the silver dollars business and rated BIG with me, both in terms of friendship and respect.

Two-Beer Dollars

During the dollar divestiture of the late 1950's and early 1960's, the Federal Government found in its vaults thousands of bags of silver dollars which had, in fact, been placed into circulation for a very short period of time in the geographical areas near the various mints. Most of these bags were O-mint dollars and had been released for a very short period in the South. After being out there for only a brief period, they were recovered and resacked by the banks and sent in for storage at the time as bullion silver. For the past many years, and in several writings, I have referred to these as "two-beer" dollars, i.e., coins which circulated long enough to buy two beers before being returned to the vaults from circulation.

Why "two-beer" dollars? Why did they circulate such a short period of time? Which dates were involved?

It seems that most of the bags of these dollars were stored at the New Orleans mint, probably until the mint closed in 1909, and were then sent to the Federal Treasury in Washington. Here they sat in the back of the vaults until the early sixties and were among the last of the bags to be released in 1962 and 1963. We know of the uncirculated bags of 1898-O to 1904-O dollars which came out in October, 1962. Existence of bags of these dates came as a surprise to the numismatic world and collectors were able to get dates in BU condition which they had previously believed to have been consigned to the melting pots under the Pittman Act of 1918. What was nearly as much a surprise was to find high-grade 1879-O, 1880-O and 1881-O dollars (mostly not truly uncirculated) in large quantities. Before the autumn of 1962, almost the only O-mints of those dates seen were well-circulated coins, mostly VG or Fine in grade.

The reasons for the recalling of dollars during the periods of "two-beer" dollars are not clear from any reading or study I have ever done. It may have had to do with the various Reconstruction programs in the South. These changed with each administration and the influence of whichever group of carpetbaggers had its claws in the South's various legislatures. It probably had to do with a general shortage of cash in the economy of the South. It had, no doubt, to do to some extent with the fact that silver dollars were not a popular item with the general population. At any rate, millions of dollars were placed into circulation shortly after their minting and within a very brief time, withdrawn and sent to the Mint for storage. This happened primarily in 1881, and 1882, and again in 1887 and 1897.

Hundreds of bags of dollars which had been sealed in 1881 and 1882 and contained mostly coins minted in New Orleans in 1879, 1880, 1881, and 1882 were released in 1962 and 1963 in Montana through the Helena Federal branch bank. The 1879-O dollars were primarily EF-AU as were the 1880-O coins; the 1881-O dollars were AU's and sliders and the 1882-O's were nearly all high-end sliders (AU-58 coins). This explains the early belief that dollars of these dates were not struck as well as '83, '84, and '85-O dollars, but this is, in fact, not true at all. The coins that appeared had just been slightly circulated - had bought two beers, as it were - and then taken back to storage. The same scenario occurred again in 1887, the bulk of the coins in those bags being 1885-O dollars.

Again, 1886-O dollars which are really uncirculated are NOT poorly struck; the ones which are seen most of the time and passed off as weak Uncs are just "two-beer" dollars. Again, in 1897 the South cleaned the bars of dollars and sent them back to the government. This time however, most of the coins were 1896-O and 1894-O dollars, most of which were poorly struck, and a good many 1895-O dollars which were well struck. The best circulated bag of coins I ever got in those months of excitement was a bag sealed in 1897. It had about eight hundred twenty five 1896 and 1897-O dollars, about sixty five 1894-O dollars, fifty eight 1895-O dollars and the rest a mixture of various P-mints and other nondescript coins. What a person could do now with that bag!

The same policy of issuing dollars for a short period seems not to have occurred with the Philadelphia or Carson City mint dollars, and with the San Francisco mint coins only in 1885. I know of two bags - there must have been more - that came out of Montana, one in John Love's part of the state and one in Thompson Falls, a small town in the very northwestern part of the state. I got ten rolls from that bank; I think John got the entire bag from his area. We had slider 1883-S, 1884-S and 1885-S dollars for quite a while. We both ran ads offering the group of three for $39.50. Even today, the great majority of the 1884-S dollars are from these bags and others like them. Like the '86-O dollars, 1884-S dollars weren't weakly struck, they were just "two-beer" dollars.

"Two beer" bucks weighed 59 pounds a bag, so we could tell when we had one of these instead of a solid BU bag or a circulated bag. Since most of the 59-pound bags were the sliders sealed in 1882, we seldom searched these bags, because being short on time, trying to set to the next deal, we had to put our sorting time to good use. I have often wondered what we might have sent down the road to some lucky customer, or consigned to the silver furnace five or six years later in the way of some really nice high-grade dollars. If there were 1880-O, 1884-S, 1886-O, 1894-O to 1897-O (or other dates I didn't handle), they would be worth big bucks in the markets of the recent past. In the roaring markets of 1979 and 1980, most of the "BU" coins of those dates which were sold, and were in fact, good old "Two-Beer" dollars.

Holly, Dolly, Molly, and Sally

Four LOL's from DL. That's what the four great gals in the title were to me. ("Solly" would sound a bit ludicrous.) Holly was my mother's good friend; when my mother would go to town from the ranch for the day in the 1940's, she would drop off her four-year old at Holly's and Holly (who had no kids of her own) would entertain me for the afternoon. Holly's husband was a railroad engineer, one of my early heroes, because during the war anyone who had anything to do with trains - two of the transcontinental railroads paralleled each other fifty yards apart through downtown Deer Lodge - particularly an engineer, was a hero to everyone. Holly was my friend for all my life.

Molly was married to the town doctor. They arrived in Deer Lodge in 1939, became best friends of my parents, and like Holly, Molly was one of my earliest acquaintances and earliest friends. Her husband, the Doc, was a town hero as well; he delivered most of the youth of the town for thirty years.

Dolly was the rancher's wife. Con, her husband, was my Mother's cousin, and in later life the National Park Service bought his historic cattle ranch and made it the Park Service's quintessential cattle ranch of the 1870's. In spite of family relationships, she was distant; regal and intelligent, but distant and cold until I got to know her later through the coin business.

Sally was a widow at an early age, and when her husband, who owned and operated the major oil and gas bulk plant in the county, died in his thirties, he left her with several children under the age of 12. She took the challenge and ran the business herself for the rest of her life. She was a "power business" and in the days of Deer Lodge in the forties, that was a phenomenon.

So, here we are; the scenario: Four women in our small town (3,200 people, one bank which, unlike the other two, had survived the bank holiday, a state prison, two railroads, fourteen bars, and a conservative mentality that would make Orange County seem like a hotbed of radicalism), three of whom had pretty good bucks and all of whom had plenty of time to enjoy their fancies.

Enter: The government programs to liquidate the silver in the government vaults, a bank willing to work with its good customers, particularly those with money, and Larry Busch.

Sometime in the first two years of the sixties, the four ladies (and I don't know who started first) came to realize that here, with silver dollars everywhere, rolling out of the cash registers, available in any quantity at the bank for the asking, was the chance to participate in what looked to them as a pastime for middle-age which could provide entertainment, activity, sociability, and yes - profit. What a combination!

I don't know when the competition started. It was subtle and unstated, but it was one of the driving forces that completed a couple of the finest dollar sets I had ever seen, as well as some nice accumulations of dollars that were to give two of them happiness as long as they lived and two of them the retirement nest egg of which everyone dreams.

The four would independently go to the Deer Lodge Bank and pick up whatever dollars Merrill, the vault keeper, had set aside for them as the bags were delivered each day from Helena. Merrill had to be careful that he didn't give Holly a bag returned by Sally, that Dolly didn't hear what date was in the last BU bag that Molly received, or that he was "at lunch" if no bags arrived that day from Helena.

There were always plenty of bags, but each of the gals became so paranoid that she was constantly getting leftovers, that she would travel to any of the banks within a hundred miles - Phillipsburg, Boulder, Townsend, Three Forks, Anaconda - and eventually to Bozeman, Butte, and Missoula, to get bags which perhaps the other gals hadn't searched. Holly got the best bags, or at least she had the nicest coins. I guess she just had the best eye. Once, in a visit to her home, she showed me 16 rolls of '80-S's, and 9 rolls of '79-S dollars which she had cherried out of about five bags of each. There was not a coin in the group that would grade as low as MS-65. And the best of each group was the coin that she put in her set. Years later, I sold the '80-S to a major buyer; it was the first "raw" mega-buck common date so far as I know. We sold the coin for $5,000.00 and the '79-S for $2,000.00 (along with the '02-O from her set at $2,200.00). Later the '80-S slabbed MS-67 DPL, but I still think it is the finest piece located to date and so does the current owner.

Dolly had the most cash available to spend on coins and she was more willing to work through a dealer than to run to the bank herself and shuffle dollars around. She was the first, I think, to meet Larry Busch. He would come to Deer Lodge from his shop in Bozeman, at first to get dollars from the bank in Deer Lodge or from those people he could find who were regular customers of the bank and had been saving and swapping dollars. He made acquaintance of each of the "dollar-soul" sisters during this wonderful time, and he would trade with them so that they could get the dates for their sets which would not come through the banks. He could have survived handsomely on their business alone had he not needed to get onto Missoula each trip to bet on the Cards at Red's bar and play poker until the early hours. Nonetheless, his travels and contacts all over Montana gave him a chance to pick up items for his four friends.

And he worked the competition like a master diplomat. He, like Merrill, knew just which of his gals needed the extra favor at the right time, the special item to fill the space in the collection, the chance to trade in that week's extra material. He would speak to them in his deep voice (if I had a voice like his, I would just go out and attempt to repopulate the world) and they would work the trade, pay the price, and go home elated and enthusiastic as never before. He was a master working with his puppets; they loved it. But he was always fair to them. He must have sensed that retaining them as customers was better than making his fortune all at once. He easily could have.

As time crept on, the interests of the four went separate ways. Holly kept sorting and upgrading with the eventual goal of having a truly fine set. She used her many hand-picked single duplicates to trade and upgrade. She picked up a few Saints, but she stayed mostly with her first love, a wonderful set of dollars. Molly mostly finished sets of dollars (and later, other series), and was satisfied with whatever quality would fill the sets which she intended to leave eventually to the members of her family. Sally became an accumulator. Her goal was to acquire a great deal of material, as nice as possible, but not such high grades as would prohibit her from having quantities. She finally sold off the lower-grade bulk and left the better bags and rolls (yes, bags) to her lawyer and engineer sons.

Dolly put together some very nice sets and went on after the dollar run was over, to collect other series and even foreign and ancient coins. After coins, she went to stamps. Later in life, as she and Cousin Con retired and spent most of their time in La Jolla, she became the darling of several dealers around the country who save nice (they said) material for her. She should have stayed a customer of Larry Busch.

So ends chapter one of the tales of LOLs from Deer Lodge. They were wonderful friends and I'll remember them forever. We need more people like them these days. We would really have a marvelous business and hobby with the involvement and participation of people like these four gals from Montana.

The Worst 10

Recently (1984) I published a listing of my choices for the "worst 10 common date dollars" for investment. It would follow that a sequel should enumerate the "worst 10 scarce date dollars" for investment. Here goes.

Anyone can make a case for (or against) buying expensive coins versus common (now called "generic") coins on the basis of percentage return, liquidity, ego - whatever criteria one chooses. I'm omitting these criteria, however, and choosing my worst-versus-best relative to "traps" existing in these dates as investment potential, a sort of "what you see may not be what you get" red flag to warn you of problems inherent in some dates. The proper (maybe an infinite) amount of education, a like amount of exposure, and - that rare gift - a good eye, may make positives out of the negatives I give as reasons for avoiding the listed dates, but if you are on shaky ground with any of these assets (and if your ego is in place) then I suggest avoiding these scarcer dates for investment.

1. **1879-O**

2. **1880-O**. These two dates (particularly the '80-O) hardly exist BU - even real UNC 60, let alone MS-64 or MS-65. These (like '80-O and '82-O from the common list) were reasonably well-struck; they were just put immediately into circulation, most for a rather short time, withdrawn, stored, shipped around, stored longer, and then re-released in 1962 and 1963 in rather large quantities; but, there were almost no BU coins. You will never find an investment grade 1880-O at MS-65 or bid plus 25%; you couldn't get two pieces (correctly graded) at bid plus 50%, and you couldn't find five pieces at 3 times bid. You'll get offered quite a number of pieces, but they'll not make investment quality, and if your advisor tells you differently, then he's got swamp land in Florida for you, too. 1879-O's are not such a problem as '80-O's but still bad enough to warrant the "Worst 10" list.

3. **1884-S**. One of my personal favorites, but how can I invest in (or collect) something I've seen only 8 or 10 times in 24 years. The only 1884-S worth buying for investment probably is a "wonder coin," and then you probably are safe at any reasonable price. I'd be in at bid, 2 times bid, 3 times bid or whatever. (Remember this was written in 1983 or '84) But if you are uncomfortable judging a true "wonder coin," then stay out of the fire.

4. **1886-O**. The reasons for avoiding this date are the same as for '79-O and '80-O, except for two additional reasons: a. MS-65 quality in '86-O dollars (correctly graded) is more common than in '80-O; b. 1886-O dollars are priced much higher than 1880-O dollars in high grades.

As far as investment goes, don't even buy one if you need it for your collection.

5. **1887-O**. Here is a coin which has the same problems as 1888-O (in the common date worst 10.) Buy the best one you can find, pay market price, put it away for six months or six years, pull it out to reassess it, and see how the number of marks has grown while it was in storage; take it to your investment advisor (coin dealer, that is,) preferably the one who stuck you with - I mean - sold you the coin (and he'll point out all the marks which even you missed) and then sell it for 25% to 50% of what you paid for it when you (and he) thought it was nice. You now have at least a B+ in O-mint dollars 301 (advanced level) and it's one of the least expensive parts of your "college" education. See how it works?

6. **1891-P**. Like 1889-P and 1890-P, you'll never find one of the half-dozen coins the mint produced (out of millions) which is nice enough for today's STRICT MS-65/65. Besides no one wants one.

7. **1891-O**. Unlike the '91-P above, you might find the coin (at a vast sum) but you'll never find the dealer who will ever pay more than a half-vast sum for it when you want to sell it.

We skip discussion of 1892-1896 dates because of problems mostly of price and availability; besides, I'll need subject material for a whole chapter later.

8. **1897-O**. Those that look nice seldom are nice enough for resale and at the price, it's not worth taking the risk.

9. **1904-P**. Who cares? Apathy is this date's main enemy; next is the lack of knowledge which most dealers and investors have about what a gem C^4 reverse dollar looks like. It is, and always has been, scarce in investment grade, but no one wants one (and maybe never will).

10. **1921-S**. If you want to see who else besides a commodity broker can change $1200 into $50 in one transaction, just buy a 1921-S MS-65 (real 65's probably don't exist) from one dealer and sell it to any other dealer. Sometimes your own personal dealer will "lose to save face" to an extent dependent upon your client clout with him. If you are clouty enough, he might even pay you a profit (albeit small) just to prove that those dolts who write investment reports don't know what they're talking about. (Then he'll take the '21-S and sell it to the other dealer for the fifty bucks; his face is saved.) Did you ever see a buy ad for "pre-1904" Morgans only? Take my advice - apply that to investment grade Morgans as well. The off-year (1921) should be left off your investment list.

Differing opinions will be welcomed (but taken very seriously).

***

John B. Love

John Love, numismatist, has done so much for so many, it is not possible to prepare a list within this short space. John was recently presented with the National Silver Dollar Roundtable Lifetime Achievement Award. This prestigious honor was presented by this author serving as President. The honor was bestowed upon John at Ruth's Chris Steak House on November 7, 1990 in St. Louis, Missouri.

John Love is one of the largest silver dollar experts to have graced the field of numismatists through the years. His pioneer efforts paved the way for many younger numismatists. Like a silversmith passing on his trade, John has left his knowledge with a multiple of dealers and various organizations. He has secured the future of silver dollars for all of us.

CONGRATULATIONS ON YOUR MANY, MANY CONTRIBUTIONS TO THE WORLD OF NUMISMATICS!

CHAPTER 7

Old Timer Stories

John B. Love
Interviewed by David Lisot

This interview with John Love of Great Falls, Montana, was conducted by David Lisot at the 11th NSDC on November 8, 1990 in St. Louis, Missouri.

When did you get started in the coin business?

I got going in the early 60's, approximately 1961 and 62.

You are known for silver dollars and dealing in quantities. What was it about silver dollars that interested you?

First of all silver dollars were found in change in Montana, just like Nevada, and some places in Idaho. The people had them in change because gambling was legal at the time in Montana and Nevada. In Montana gambling became illegal in 1950, but the dollars were still in change. So everybody had silver dollars. All the banks had them and you could go through silver dollars any time you wanted. That's what got me started.

Were you a collector before?

Oh, yeah, I collected pennies, nickels, dimes, stamps — stuff like that — but that was years before.

Why did you collect?

It was intriguing, like history, just like a dollar, just like going through a bag of dollars. You could open up a bag of dollars and find an 1859-O sitting right on top of a bag of circulated dollars. It's kind of intriguing to open up a bag and find all kinds of numismatic treasures.

Was it the same in Idaho with silver dollars?

All three states (Idaho, Montana, and Nevada) had silver dollars that were circulating at the time. They were circulating for years, and the reason for it in Montana and Nevada were the slot machines. Of course Montana now has machines back again but they use quarters, and dollars and regular paper dollars. They have regular slot machines and keno machines just like Vegas. It's the same thing, you play five card stud and so forth.

You said that you found a lot of "P" mint bags?

Oh, yeah, usually in Montana most of the bags were Morgan bags. There weren't any Peace dollar bags at all, very, very few, because most came from Philadelphia, except for San Francisco. But Peace dollars just never got up there for some reason because the Fed (Federal Reserve Branch Bank) that sent the bags to Montana didn't have those, they had mainly Morgan dollars.

It would seem that it was mostly "S" mints or "CC"'s?

No, not at all. In fact a lot of the bags were circulated 79, 80, 81 and 82-O's that would come into the banks, and they were full bags. They'd be anywhere from XF-AU's to sliders in those bags, but you could actually tell from the weight of the bag the difference between a BU and a circulated bag. They would be two to three pounds lighter. You could walk around the vault with 50 bags on the floor and pick up the bag you wanted and know which was which. So the lightest bag was the one you wanted.

Why would you want the circ bag?

Because the circ (circulated) bag would have more rarities in it! For in most cases, they would be all circulated 93-S's, 94-P's, 03-O's, anything from the whole Morgan series. Then as the time ran out and the dollars ran short the dollars became heavier, and they were newer. You might find anything whatsoever in a mixed bag.

When did people begin to appreciate 93-S and 94-S dollars?

In the 50's, the 93-S was always scarce. The 93-P, 94-P, and of course the "O" mints were scarce in the 50's. The 98-0 through 04-0 were very scarce because all the bags were new and they had never circulated, and so very few coins had circulated which brought a lot of money at the time. A circulated 03-0 would bring $1500, until the bags broke in Alma.

Not only bags of silver dollars. You had the 3 legged buffalo nickels which broke in Wolf Point, so in Montana there were a lot of 3-legged Buffalo nickels floating around for years. I've seen a whole cigar box full of 3-legged Buffalo nickels. There were several bags of them and most of the circulation was released in Montana. Most of the coins stayed in Montana because the people found out what they had there and they kept them. I bought a least a whole cigar box at a time of different grades of Buffalo nickels.

When did collectors start to go after those pieces?

Most collectors, I would say, really started in the mid 60's and 70's as far as the avid collector goes for the price he was receiving. I think my ads ran in 1963 at $1.27 for dollars and you had your pick. Of course, each year by the date we had VG,

Fine, Very Fine, and so forth. Choice BU was used all the way up until 1978, at that point we didn't have grades like 1, 2, 3 up to 70 (referring to the mint state grades). We had BU, Choice BU, Gem, Prooflike, choice prooflike. That is what I named them. And so each denomination had a different price for their coin. Most of the people who bought anything from me in those years got really good value for their money.

You were instrumental in starting the prooflike category.

I don't know if I was instrumental or not but I thought it should be advertised because coins were so much nicer if they were nice prooflike dollars so they should be categorized in the same manner. They warranted more money. A lot of astute investors bought them — just those, and of course the ones who did in those years are quite happy with what they bought because they are worth considerably more money.

Why are some dates so common in prooflike?

I don't know for sure. From the way they struck the dies on certain coins, they either polished the dies more frequently or struck more coins and so there were more prooflike die varieties in those issues. For instance, 83-O, 84-O, 85-O — you can find a lot of those. But finding 91-O, 92-O, 93-O, in those is virtually impossible, let alone 94-O's.

One time I went to Billings and bought from an investor a bag of 96-O's that had got out somewhere down there. The man had 5 or 6 left and I bought virtually all of them. There wasn't a prooflike in the lot, let alone the strikes which were pretty weak. Usually the O-mints in the late years were pretty weakly struck, up until 98-O. You may have weak strikes normally all the way from 90-O. The 91-O's come weak, 92-O's were mainly weak, all the way up until 98-O.

How many bags would you say that you have handled?

I would say it would be in the thousands.

What was the most exciting bag deal you ever did?

I would say it was getting involved in the LaVere Redfield thing. I was buying coins from LR (LaVere Redfield) and didn't know it, through another man from Reno who was supplying me. I was buying a half a bag of 25-S's and stuff like this. At the time of his (Redfield's) death I was dealing on this bag of 93-P's, and he died and the bag kind of disappeared. A-Mark flew me all the way up from Florida to help them out, and when they finally bought the deal between Bowers and Ruddy and A-Mark. More or less to them the rarities of the coins were known and what they are worth. I was very instrumental as far as buying what I bought out of that. *At one time I had over 100 bags of 96-P, 97-P, and 98-P's in the lot*. There were a few bags of circs, 400 some bags in all.

The man (Redfield) would drop them down a coal chute into his basement. He was a very frugal man, and he left them in his basement for years. Cans of peaches would explode on them and the peach juice and acid from the juice would eat through the bag in some of the coins — kind of interesting. I never met him but the man I did business with did. The man would drive him around. He'd go to the bank and he wouldn't even put a quarter in the meter. He would go to the bank for 90% silver and the guy would either drive him around the block or put his own quarter in. The man's name was Dean Jones from Reno and he used to be a coin dealer there for years. He and LaVere were fairly close friends.

What was your main source of bags?

They came from everywhere. In the early '63 and '64 they came from banks just around town, or the Federal Reserve out of Helena, or people like that. I would buy them from Steve Rudell, whose mother was Elizabeth Rudell Smith who used to sign the dollar bills. He had access in Washington from the Fed. They would show up in banks with his mother signing the dollar bills, and he had a little better access than the guy on the street to the dollar bags. He could get more than the average guy, so if they could only get one bag, he might be able to get five.

Did you ever feel like you were paying too much for bags?

Not really, the bags started out after they went off the market at face value. They only got up to $1100 or $1200 a bag. There was a friend name Bill Holdman in Great Falls and at that time was very instrumental in a lot of dollar business. He would promote dollars way more so than I would at the time and he bought a lot of dollars. I can remember at one time he bought two bags for $1300 or $1400 that happened to be two bags of 01-S's that had just come out of Idaho and some guy brought them over.

How many people were involved in the bag business?

At the time there was Leon Hendrickson and of course Harlan White who has been in the business for a number of years. There was a fellow named Emory Redman. He was very instrumental. We used to run ads in the early 60's — full page ads, it was quite unique at the time because of the different grading that was going on at that time versus now. You had a whole different clientele because the dollars weren't very expensive. Astute collectors got involved and made a lot of money. Today you've got a topsy-turvy market and nobody knows what is going on. Nobody knows if the coin is worth $20,000 one day or $10,000 the next or $30,000 the next. It's no good.

What did you think when there got to be the huge spreads in price for a coin from its grade?

That all happened when PCGS got in the market and people started grading coins. What happens is when PCGS would grade something MS-67 it would become worth $5000 when an ordinary unc (uncirculated coin) was worth say $400.

Did you ever think the consciousness for quality would become so pronounced?

I knew it was there all the time. That's why I advertised in choice and gem BU. That was there all the time. Over 50% of the people would buy the better grade coins. They were aware of what was going on then. I also sold a lot of rolls at that time of just BU rolls of dollars that had 61, 62, and 63's in them. They would vary anywhere in price from $30 to $50 a roll.

When you bought a bag, would you cherry pick all the better coins out of it?

Normally every time I bought a bag I would go through it and obviously I would pick out the prooflikes if there were any in there. In a bag out of a thousand coins there could be 50 prooflikes, or there could be half a bagful, or there could be none. Of course your "S" mints were way better struck than your "O's", and because of this, people could not tell whether the S-mint dollars were prooflike or not. They did not understand.

People have a hard time at grading Peace dollars for the same reason. They don't know the difference between a 61 (MS-61) and a 64 or say 65. It still the same in today's market. Even coins in PCGS holders, it's the same thing. The coins are not really graded right. I'm not saying that they are graded wrong, it's just rare to find Peace dollars because of the way they were struck. They have too many scratches on them for the most part because they have too big a field.

Why is the Peace dollar not as popular as the Morgan?

That's not true. The reason is that people don't understand it. They don't know how to grade them. Anytime someone does not understand something they tend to stay away from it. So consequently some of the Peace dollars are your best buys right now and always have been. If you know what you're doing and know how to grade the Peace dollars, they are as good as any.

What has been the most exciting thing about coins for you?

I would say the most exciting thing of all is to open a fresh bag of circulated dollars and go through the bag finding little treasures here and there, like circulated 94-P's and 93-S's. Or half a bag of 1859-O's and 60-O's that are new. Things like that are just like opening a Cracker Jack box and seeing what the toy is! Some of the bags were very disappointing and some were just as exciting as could be.

Actually the most interesting thing I've ever seen at the time is a bag of 93-P's and 94-P's that broke in the early 1960's in northern California in San Francisco. That was exciting because I have never in my life seen a bag of 94-P's and never have since. That was very, very interesting.

A lot of very nice dollars got released in San Francisco, mainly "S" mints obviously. One fellow that I bought a lot of coins from had buried them in those years. It's like one guy that I know we ended up buying a lot of commems (commemoratives) from that were San Diego's 1935 and 1936. He had virtually the whole hoard. We had been buying coins from this man for years. Nobody wanted the coins at the time, nobody had any money in 1935. He ended up with virtually the whole 35 and 36 San Diego commem collection.

What is it about coins that intrigues men?

It's just like looking at a diamond or a gold slug, or a pretty piece of land or pretty whatever. It doesn't matter. They happen to like coins, and somebody else likes this. So they buy the coins, the other person buys this. It's the same thing. If a man would have bought BU bags of dollars in 1964 versus circulated bags . . . at one point in time the bags got up to where I paid as high as $250,000 for three bags of "S" mint dollars. That's over $80,000 a bag!

But the circulated bags, if he had three of those they would have been worth at that time only $75,000 or about $25,000 a bag because silver wasn't very high then. You see the difference. Or he could have bought three bags of 90% silver that would have only been worth $22,000 a bag. It's the same dollar going into each item, but each item becomes different in price at the end. It's like buying different paintings at the same price and one becomes more valuable than another because certain artists become more popular later on.

You were involved in the 79-CC capped dollar discovery.

That was just a filled die that got filled when they were striking the 79-CC. You had different dies and that was just a different die variety. The dies got clogged at the time from overuse and so they became filled. It was not any different than a 1882-O over "S", or 1887 over 86, in "O" and "P" mint marks both. A lot of time they didn't have money back then either so they would just recarve the die and use the same die again. They've done that for years.

At the time years ago there were lots of varieties that people collected as varieties and paid a little more money for them. Today people don't seem to care about the variety or which one it is. There were variety hunters in pennies, nickels, dimes, and whatever, off-struck and so forth. Today it just doesn't seem to have the pizzazz that something else might have.

You've done a lot a deals with Leon Hendrickson. How did you meet him?

Leon and I have known each other through Redman, my buddy, that I advertised with in the 1960's. Redman lived in Dayton which was near Silver Towne in Winchester, Indiana, which is probably 50 miles away. So we became good friends.

One time Leon Hendrickson, Harlan White and I bought a deal from Harvey's Wagon Wheel, the casino in Reno. We bought it through his nephew. I can remember hauling the bags to Reno, and we went up a side road. We didn't go on the main road at all. We had Harvey's guards with us and they had to open up gates all the way for us to Reno on this side road in an armored car. That was interesting. That was years ago. Harvey used the money then to build a parking garage. This was right before his casino was blown up by that kook that came out of San Francisco and blew the first 3 or 4 windows out of the Harvey's downtown casino. That's where they had the dollars stored, right on the second floor. It blew a hole right up through the first three or four floors. He was shut down for a number of years. Harvey died a few years later.

Is it true you can tell the mint mark of a Morgan dollar just by looking at its obverse?

Most people can. You can tell by looking at the rim of the coin whether it's a "P", "O", or "S" mint mark. That's because the "S" mints are usually rolled rims. The "P"'s stand up higher and the "O"'s are about in between. You can tell more or less by looking at the front of the coin pretty much tell what it is.

What was the biggest deal you ever did with Leon Hendrickson?

I imagine Harvey's deal. I've done lots with him. That deal was about 1.6 million. Back then that was a lot of money.

What about the coin market today, with the computerized trading, third party grading, and so forth?

I think it's fine. The problem is that we are trying to teach somebody by handing them a book or brochure coming through the door exactly what is going on and that will never be done. There have been books written forever on how to grade coins and how to do this or that. Everybody sees something differently by looking at a coin with their own eyes. There will never be anything that you can hand someone when they come through the door that will make them an expert. It's like looking at diamonds. How are you going to become an expert by looking at diamonds when there are so many varieties? It's the same thing with dollars or any coin, it doesn't matter. You either have it or you don't.

All these things are helpful tools. For instance, there are some coins in slabs that are listed as MS-64's that are not. They may be better than 64's or they may be worse. It just depends on who is looking at them that day. There is no cut and dried method of determining the grade of a coin. That's the reason for the ups and downs in the last year. It's been absolute turmoil.

What about some of the younger dealers with so much financial power?

There have always been younger kids in the business. Everybody has to come along at some point. I came along and I was a young kid thirty years ago, and there were a lot of people in it then. It was the same thing. It will be the same thing now or in ten years or twenty years from now. It will be the same thing again. They just get older just like I did and go on with it.

Who were your teachers and mentors when you started?

I really didn't have any, I kind of learned on my own in terms of dollars because there were so many there. You learned from experience. If you bought something you thought was this and it wasn't, you learned from getting spanked. That's the only way you learn. It's like being a doctor. You can read all the books in the world you want to read, but until you operate on people you don't know what's going on. It's the same thing, and you still don't know. The coin business is the same way. You might think it is this and it turns out to be that, or vice versa. There is no cut and dried situation. No fine line here.

John Love teaching young numismatist
Chelsea Highfill new tricks
(Courtesy of Marlene M. Highfill)

What does the future hold for the industry?

The future for coins? The biggest problem is with the government and such. Probably the dealers have lost more money than any investor ever thought of losing. They don't know what they are doing. That is the topsy-turvy part of the industry the way it is right now. It is no different than you can see a hair creme advertised on TV for $19.95 when it costs them $2. But yet they say that some guy is overcharging because he charges $5 for a coin that is worth $4, or something like that.

I don't know. The turmoil right now is awful, the situation as far as the coin dealer is concerned is that money is short and tempers are short. It's going to clean a lot of people out of the coin business, with the government's help also. The government is something that has all the time and money in the world, and most people don't. And so they will virtually eat you up from expenses on other things, which isn't ordinarily right or wrong. It could be right and it could be wrong. There are certainly people who abuse things and I think that should be corrected. But to over-abuse the other way, which they usually do . . . There is no set middle of the stream, it is always going from one extreme to the next, and that is virtually what they are doing now.

Do you think the computerized trading of coins is the answer?

We are back to the same thing again, because the coins in computerized trading, whatever is still in plastic or whatever. When you get the coin you are still going to say that I don't think the coin grades this or this looks better than that. There is no answer to any of this, there really is no definite guideline that you can print so everybody likes that, and there never will be. There has been Red Book after Red Book (*A Guide Book of United States Coins*, by R.S. Yeoman). I used to do the prices for the Red Book for Yeoman for years. It is just at the time what they were worth at that time, and tomorrow is a new day. It is just like what did gold close at today, what is it right now or then. Or what did IBM stock close at, or whatever. That is paper that stays pretty constant, so everybody can get a grasp on it because you can't change a piece of IBM stock. Tomorrow it is going to sell for something. But a coin is different, or a diamond is different — anything that is tangible.

Did you ever get politically involved?

I belong to the PNG since 1967 or 8, but as far as politics goes, I'm kind of a loner so I don't do a whole lot. I join but I just do my own thing, I don't run for President.

Will your son take over your coin business from you?

He graduated from college with a computer science degree and accounting degree both. He also went to the GIA school for diamonds. So he loves diamonds and he does work on those lines for me. He has become involved somewhat. To the extent of coins, he doesn't know that much but he is learning. He knows a lot more about diamonds, which is fine.

What kind of legacy do you want to leave?

I don't know. I'm kind of tired, right now. I mean as far as a legacy I've already left it. I mean there is nothing else I can do. I think as far as discoveries and anything else exciting it's all over with. I think it is just buying and selling now. They go up, then down, they go up and they go down. The only thing exciting is if you find a collection that has been put away for years, and somebody dies and you are able to buy it. That is exciting. And that is the only excitement left — except for eating at Ruth's Chris Steak House!

***

Harlan White

Harlan White is a true veteran of the coin business, but his experiences are wide and varied. Prior to opening his first coin shop, he moved from his long-time home in San Diego to the California/Oregon border in 1945. There he spent thirteen to fourteen years in the logging industry. While in Oregon, he also operated a grocery store and learned a great deal about retail businesses.

When he returned to San Diego in 1959, he and his wife Shirley opened the Old Coin Shop. This venture has been their business and life together for over 32 years and counting. He has seen many facets of numismatics including the influence of foreign gold coins (Japanese) in the 1960s, the varied fads of coin jewelry, and the growth and development of the most popular series of them all, Morgan silver dollars.

During the early 1980s, Mr. White was a regular on the coin circuit and visited between thirty and fifty shows and conventions per year. As the decade drew to a close, he reduced his travels to approximately twenty to twenty-five shows annually.

Harlan White is a long-time member of the Professional Numismatists Guild, a life member of the American Numismatic Association, member of the National Silver Dollar Roundtable, and other numismatic organizations. He has always believed in passing knowledge along to the next generation of numismatists and is an honored and respected representative of this industry.

CHAPTER 8

Telling It Like It Was

Two Interviews With Harlan White

Conducted by David Lisot and John English

The following interviews with Harlan White were conducted by David Lisot on February 9, 1991, in Long Beach, California, and by John English on May 1, 1991.

How long have you been dealing coins now?

Oh, for over thirty years now.

Did you start out collecting as a kid?

Well, not as a kid. I collected somewhat but not that much as a kid. I worked in the tire business, and I walked into a coin shop a couple of times and said, "Gee, this looks like fun, but I'm on the wrong side of the counter." After I got off work at night, I opened a coin shop for about four or five hours at night. Man, this was what I really liked and it was a lot of fun. It was really interesting. So I didn't collect as a kid, but I probably should have.

What were your sources of information?

You just had to loosen up and spend some money, and then when you made a mistake you remembered it more — you really did. A lot of people are so cautious and ask this and that but they really don't know until they actually spend their money on a coin, a hundred dollar coin or a thousand dollar coin, what the market is on that coin. A lot of them today just say the Greysheet says this and somebody is bidding that. They don't pay any attention to what the coin really is. They say this is the buy-sell for it, but they don't care about its history or how scarce it is. They don't know anything about the coin — Just what can I buy it and sell it for? and what does some sheet pay for it? or what does the teletype say I can get for it? So I think we really have lost a lot of the fun of coins and the real enjoyment of owning a nice coin.

Have collectors changed? Are they different since when you started?

I think so. I think there used to be more love for a coin. Now the first thing on their mind is how soon will I make a return on my money. When the kids can't find anything in circulation they just don't come around. They've got a lot of other things that they can collect like baseball cards that they can buy for a dollar or two. You can't get much of a coin for a dollar or two, and a lot of people don't want to wait on them. They say this kid has been in here for an hour and he only spent two bucks, but they can go to some of these baseball card shops, get taken care of and appreciated, and spend their two or three bucks. Then they tell their friends. It's a lot of the small hobbies that hurt us because we don't take care of them. We think that unless a guy's got $10,000 to spend, we really don't have time for him. That is absolutely the wrong attitude. We've got to back up and go to a collecting base again. And it is up to us to do it.

How have dealers related to the shows over the years?

You know there's a few successful shows like Long Beach, and a lot of the guys get into it thinking Sam is making a killing and that it looks easy. But unless you've got a following and really run the thing right, you'll get into it and then get out of it. A lot of the dealers say a show is not put on first class and they are not all that comfortable. The promoters want table fees, and maybe they don't spend much of it in advertising, and that show just doesn't last very long. I think a lot of the shows that used to be good shows, big shows, in years past have just kind of bit the dust lately. But I think that if we had half a dozen shows like Long Beach, everybody would be better off.

How have coin shows changed in the last few years?

A lot of them were hard to get into and now they are begging you to come to their shows. You've eliminated a lot of the guys, money's been tight and it is tough. It will cost me a thousand bucks to come and I can hardly afford it, but I think when things pick up we'll have all the dealers come back again.

How many coin shows do you do a year?

Probably only about twenty. I used to do a lot more. I used to do at least three a month. But along with everything else it's just awfully expensive, and with your bullion and a lot of your stuff, it's a real short margin. If you go back East it's nothing to spend three or four thousand dollars by the time you're there a week, with hotels at $100 a night (that's a bargain) and airfare at $500. If you take a couple of people, it's always four or five thousand by the time you get done. Which means you really have to make a lot of money just to cover the overhead. So I think a lot of the smaller dealers say "I can't go, I can't cut the overhead."

If people stop going to coin shows, how will the affect the way coins trade?

It would hurt us very much. You need the public. You need the public to participate. They say we had a lot of bad publicity because of the telemarketers. Maybe they got ahold of some people who had money and said "I'm too busy, I'm in business, and I'll just buy from this guy on the telephone and have him mail the coins to me." Then they get stuck once or twice and think that all coin dealers are crooked. So you've lost those guys forever and that's the people with the money. They are the ones you should take care of, but ten of those guys get hurt and tell their friends, and it really hurts a lot more than people think. A lot of people say "Well, I'm just a little dealer and it doesn't bother me." Well, he's going to need some dealer to sell his stuff to, and if that dealer who is buying his merchandise is not successful, it hurts everybody right down the line.

Do you think the recent market drop has shaken out a lot of people?

I think so. Especially a lot of the guys who came in for the fast buck. It's a lot tougher than they think. You've got to keep your nose to the grindstone. You can't just show up and go to lunch and go play golf. There's still a lot of fun and interest in it, and if you work hard at it you're going to enjoy it a lot more. The harder you work the luckier you are. I think there is still a lot of life left in collecting.

What do you think about the use of computers in homes for coins and electronic trading?

I really don't know. They've about passed me by. I guess I'm one of the old timers. I like it on a yellow sheet of paper where I can look at it and read it and figure it. The computers are here to stay but I just don't relate to them. I'm probably hurting myself by not being able to. It's like tokens or medals — that kind of thing would be a lot more fun to deal in. You've got some history and some pizzazz to them, and you can tell something about them that nobody else knows. That's real collecting.

You specialized in real rare things.

They are not as popular. I hate to say that because I have a lot of them. There is not as much demand. They're not worth as much as they were 15 years ago. You just don't have people like Amon Carter for example. Now Amon appreciated coins and could afford to buy them and was knowledgeable about them. I've been to Amon's place several times when he would pull out something. He would enjoy showing you his coins and talking about them. He collected every coin of the world by date; every country, plus paper money. Amon would get as excited about a two dollar coin as he would a ten thousand dollar coin. It wouldn't make any difference in what it was. I had a complete set of Japanese coins one time. He said "just figure out the value of the Meiji coins whatever they are, just whatever is in the ball park. I don't have that country and this looks like a good way to put the whole country together."

What impressed me was his office on the second floor of the Fort Worth Star Telegram; a great big office with two monstrous big desks, and on each end of the desk he had two 50 gallon trash barrels. That's where the trash went each day. His dad was a collector and passed the coins down. Amon would talk for a while and he would say, "Come on, let's go down and have lunch. Let's go down and have a bowl of chili." He was the most regular guy in the world. You could talk to him. He would tell his secretary "just hold my calls, I've got friends in town." I felt like somebody. One time I was at a coin show when bags were like fifteen hundred or eighteen hundred a bag and asked Amon. I said to him, "I would like to buy a bunch of bags from you." He said, "I've got a bunch. I got them out of Washington. I'll bring you a bunch of bags." So he drove down in a big Lincoln that was dragging the ground and he drove right in front of the coin show. I went out there and he must have had 15 or 20 bags! I said, "What in the world can I do with these, I can't pay you for these." He said to just go ahead and take them home. He said, "In about a month I'll need some walk around money when I go to Vegas. Just send me the money then." So I went and got a bunch of paint buckets and air freighted them home.

Do you have any other stories about Amon Carter?

Yes I do. There was a guy in San Diego with three brothers, all in their 70s whose father and grandfather had a bank in Iowa. So they all purchased the early bills that came around. One fellow came in and said they were going to get three bids for them around town and that he wanted to sell them. I looked at them and said that every third serial number was missing. "What's happened?" He said, "I have two other brothers and we just went one for you, one for me, one for you. ." They were all crisp, all early paper. So I figured what I would pay for them and he said he would check around. After a couple of weeks when I didn't hear from him, I called him. He said that he had heard that Amon Carter of Texas was a big buyer and collector and mailed him the notes. He said he had not heard back from Amon so I didn't say anything. In about two or three days I got a call from Amon saying, "I just got back in town and have all this paper money from San Diego. Do you know anything about it?" I said I looked at it and Amon said, "well it was nice stuff and I have all of it." Amon asked what I had offered and I told him. He said that I would have more fun with it than he would, so he offered less and recommended that the man sell the stuff to a dealer in San Diego. Sure enough in about a week the man came back in with it and I bought it. Amon wasn't greedy. It was worth more than that, it was all nice stuff. He looked out for the little fellow or the dealer instead of being greedy like so many other people are. You could ask other people and they would tell you the same thing.

Here's another story. At the Boston ANA Convention, Amon came in with an 1873 proof set with the gold. He tells me to figure this up. "Everybody beats my door down to buy stuff," Amon said, "but you buy stuff from me and you're fair. Just tell me what you'll pay for it." So I told him and he said it was in the ball park and sold it to me. I walked it over to Paramount when Max Humbert was there. We got together and sold it. When I got back to San Diego next week, there was a car dealer who came to me and said "look what I bought." There was the same 1873 proof set. He said, "Paramount flew a man out last week." Ray Merena came out when he was working for Paramount. He flew out and sold it. It's funny how the world works!

The old timers really weren't so greedy when you got the deal and someone else didn't. There were a lot of nice coins to go around. Today people would kill for an 1873 proof set with the gold. I just don't think that we've got many people like Amon around anymore. We really do need them. He would treat everybody right and they would treat him right.

What brings out the good and bad in a person?

I guess we are all greedy in one way or another. A lot of us think that the newcomers coming in are maybe more greedy than we think we are.

What would you say about Amon?

He was just born that way — a regular guy. He passed away and they auctioned his stuff in 1984. I bought the Kellogg piece out of Amon's collection. I paid $154,000 for it. It is right in the Red Book. We had more people who would appreciate that kind of thing in my time. Now people only think about what they can get this slabbed up to and what they can get for it. They would never think about buying it and enjoying it and putting it away for themselves. It's more of a commodity now than a collectible, which is bad.

1883 Hawaiian dollar, PCGS-64
(Courtesy of Harlan White, San Diego, CA)

What about that 1883 Hawaiian dollar in MS64?

It's awfully hard to find in 64, although I do have one graded higher by NGC. But this coin in 64 is one of the best I've ever seen. I always did like Hawaiian coins and you might say I specialize in them. They are full of history and fun to collect.

They weren't actually U.S. government issue, were they?

Not really. We made them for the Hawaiian government. They made a lot of them but this one might be the finest that I've ever held. Most of them have been used for jewelry. A lot of quarters and dimes were used in belts, and belt buckles were made using the dollars.

Wasn't that expensive for accessories?

They weren't expensive when they were made ten or twenty years ago. You could buy them all the time. But now they're more of a novelty. I used to buy them, take them apart, and sell the coins individually. You could sell Hawaiian coins for five bucks. Now they are considered a work of art and they want an arm and a leg for the stuff. There's not much of it around anymore.

There's a brand new book that just came out that has all the history in it. In fact, I was just talking to a guy in Hawaii about it just a bit ago, and he says that it's a good book. A guy by the name of Medcalf put it out. I've got a couple of them coming my way.

Any other Hawaiian coins you'd like to talk about?

I had the number one proof set at one time, but I sold it. I think it went to Japan. Back when it happened, it just seemed like another day in the coin business, you know.

You did some business in Japanese coins at one time, didn't you?

I remember the deals with the Japanese coins. Twenty to twenty-five years ago I would sell complete type sets of Japanese gold. I would take the order and guarantee delivery at $2,700 a set. Right now, just one of those pieces would bring over $20,000. In fact, a lot of those coins you could buy for just five or six hundred are worth over twenty grand now. This was about the time that Japan really got big into shipbuilding. They were ordering lots of scrap metal from this country. A lot of people made a lots of money and wanted to buy their coins back. And this is not the peak of the market. Japanese 2 yen were about $90 as a part of a roll, and so I would pick out what I wanted at 90 bucks and let the rest go. They're four to five thousand apiece today.

How about your experiences with bags of dollars?

Well now, that's another thing. A long time ago, I used to buy a few bags of "S" mint dollars at the bank. Then I'd try to sell them to my customers for $1,050 a bag, but they wouldn't pay any premium for them. They would tell me, "I can just go to the bank and get them for myself." You'd want to sell them for anything, so you could get your money back, and then go back to the bank and order some more. I'd think that if I could buy enough bags at the bank, I might get lucky and get some Carson City dollars. I got four bags of Carson City's one time and I got four dollars a coin for them. You had to sell them out, because if you turned them back in, they'd just sell them back to you next time. You had to get them off the market. Sometimes I'd sell a bag for $999 if they'd promise to keep them.

Years ago, Tom McAfee sold 1885 CC's. He'd run them in *The Numismatist* for $25 a roll. He couldn't sell enough of them, and finally he had to turn them back into the bank. In San Diego there was a lot of "S" mints like the 1888-S and 1889-S. I remember Ryan Aircraft (who made the Spirit of St. Louis) used to give these silver dollars out as Christmas presents in the 1940s.

Any other bag deals you remember?

I remember buying a lot of BU bags right here in San Diego one time about eight or nine years ago. I bought several bags of nice coins together with a gun collection right here. The man bought dollars and new pistols every time they'd come out, Smith and Wesson's and the like. He lived in a trailer at the time and put the stuff behind the walls. When he was ready to sell, I went out with a bank trust department man looking through this trailer. It had a lot of old wooden panels in it, and when we cracked one of the panels, there was a bunch of BU dollar bags. Nicest dollars in the world. The most he'd ever paid for any of them was 27 bucks a roll. John Love and Wayne Miller both bid on the lot that averaged out a $1,000 a roll. There must have been about 20 bags in the whole deal. The Bank of America handled the whole deal. I bought the dollars and the pistols too at the market highs in 1981 and 1982. The BU roll market was probably higher than at the peak of the silver market in 1980. I still got the pistols here hanging on the wall.

Over the years, I've bought bags or bag quantities from folks that must have put them into septic tanks or underground places. The bags would be moldy, deteriorated and rotten after being there for five or ten years. Some of those bags were about all eaten up and the coins wouldn't look good.

Do you think you'll ever get out of the business?

Me? No. I might slow down, but when you enjoy something, you've got to do it. What better could you do? Why would you look for something else? It would be like asking Leon Hendrickson if he was going to open a flower shop. It's ridiculous. Coins are what there is. You know, you get to meet a lot of nice people. I talked earlier about greed but basically this is an honorable business. In fact, explain to a banker how you mail a guy $30,000 — it just doesn't happen in any other business. It's just really, really enjoyable. There's just nothing else to do.

***

John W. Highfill
Young Numismatist

CHAPTER 9

Personal Stories and Numismatic Adventures

by John W. Highfill, NLG

The year was 1949 and I was in the first grade. My teacher at that time was Mrs. McNamara, and she instructed all of the class to find a hobby. Coin collecting was my decision. My first collection consisted of Lincoln cents in 1949. As a boy, between the ages of 6 and 10, growing up in Muskogee, Oklahoma, I obviously didn't have very much money. So my first collecting methods were restricted to the pennies I found in my mom's purse as change (she gave them to me). Later I made my collection grow faster by going to the bank, buying and searching penny rolls, replacing the ones I needed, returning the rolls to the bank for different ones and then going through the new rolls. Some weekends, I would go through 200 to 300 rolls of pennies. With my 60 cent allowance, I could buy a 50 cent roll and have 10 substitute pennies. After finding 10 keepers, I would then go to the Saturday morning matinee movie for 10 cents, see two hours of cartoons and stay for the regular movie free. A bag of popcorn was included in the 10 cent admission with the Rocket Man, Gangbusters, and Superman serials! A candy bar was 5 cents and a coke was 5 cents. I used the 30 cents left for the rest of the week. Wasn't life simply wonderful! I still love movies today.

There were times during my grade school years that some of my friends would go to the banks on Saturdays with me. I remember Ricky Brown, Allen Scott and Billy Stiger searching through hundreds of penny rolls during those years. At first we would mark a searched roll with an "X" in pencil. Then as time went by we began to initial the searched rolls because each of us may have been looking for different coins. Next, the bank required us to put our full name on each roll because they didn't know all of us. Finally, the banks began to discourage us by requiring us to put our name, address and telephone number on each and every roll. For a while everyone was willing to help young boys with their collections. After a period of time, my roll activity increased to the extent that I became a nuisance. By moving from bank to bank I managed to continue my activities, but I eventually became unwelcome at all local financial institutions. I remember Billy Stiger was the first one of us to find a 1909-S Lincoln cent. It's a shame those times are gone, but they aren't forgotten!

I eventually bought a cardboard box of Whitman 1 cent tubes and used a round Avery hand written label on the top of each one. They were labeled 1909-P, 1909-P V.D.B., 1909-S, 1910-P, 1910-S, etc. As I found the many different dates between 1909 and 1940, I would place them in these containers. As a learning experience, the 1930-P to 1940-S filled up quickly. I then stopped saving those years and concentrated on the 1909 thru 1933-D dates. I was very intensely involved in those years and ended up with full rolls (50 coins each) of some pretty tough dates. Some of these were 1910-S, 1911-S, 1912-S, 1913-S, 1914-S, 1915-S, 1921-S, 1923-S, 1924-S, 1926-S, 1931-D, 1932-D, 1933-P, 1933-D, etc. I had between ten to twenty rolls each of dates like 1919-D and S.

I would spend endless hours upgrading my set from AG to G to F to VF to XF to AU and finally to BU. I had to have the very best and the most complete quality set. I never bought a coin at a coin shop in those years. I found each and every date. I still collect today with the same intensity.

My youthful persistence did yield some interesting finds over the years. I used to frequently find Indian head pennies in the years I was collecting (1949 through 1952). After 1952 they became much harder to find. I didn't collect Indian head cents as I did the Lincoln head series, however, I did keep every one I had found. I sold them all in 1961. I managed to find two 1914-D Lincoln cents and three of the elusive 1909-S V.D.B. cents, but I never did find a 1922-P (at least I didn't think they were P's). The following photos show the results of my young collecting experiences. My collecting years continued through Grade School into Jr. High, but my High School years were concentrated on higher priorities. Those being girls, cars, parties and baseball!

John W. Highfill original Lincoln Cent Collection, 1909-1940; 1941-Date
(Courtesy of John W. Highfill)

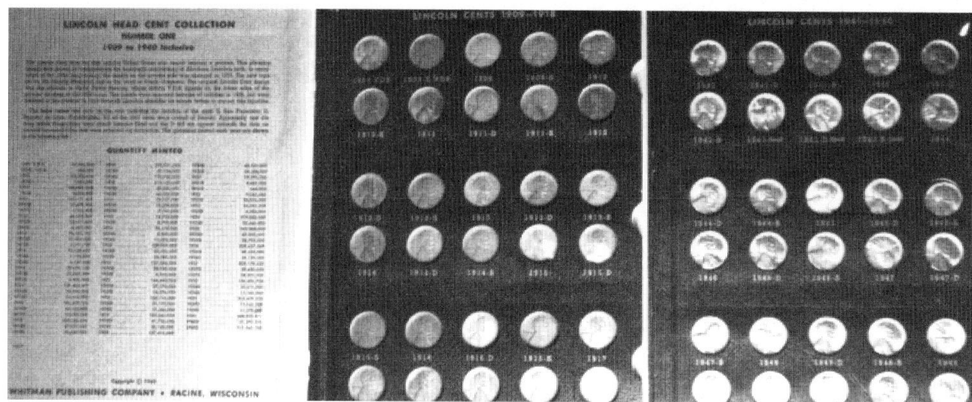

John W. Highfill original Lincoln cent collection, Circa 1949-1953 "Complete"
(Courtesy of John W. Highfill)

Charleston, South Carolina

I joined the Air Force in July of 1961 and was stationed at Charleston Air Force Base in South Carolina until July 1965. Soon after my tour of duty began, my collecting resumed. I discovered a coin shop on Reynolds Avenue. Every afternoon when my work day was finished, I visited this shop and carefully studied their entire inventory. Then on paydays (twice a month), I bought the best value I had found during the previous 2 weeks. At the time, my new and primary interest was Mercury (winged Liberty head) dimes, especially those issues with a mintage just over 1 million pieces (i.e., 1926-S, 1930-S, 1931-D, 1931-S, etc.). I lived by the Red Book mintage figures.

The owner of the coin shop and I became pretty close friends. But as time passed, the dealer noticed (after the fact) that prices changed faster than he could update them and that I was very keen and aware of prices. He thought that he had underpriced much of the merchandise I bought, and our relationship began to change. It didn't matter that he was probably still making a profit on every coin that he sold to me. He just thought that I was getting the best of him and he began to treat me as an adversary rather than a customer. Strange what money can do to a friendship, isn't it. Oh well. Perhaps it could best be described as a competitive contest. He would watch me closely to find out what I was researching at the time, and try to outguess me concerning my next purchase.

Old fashioned 25 cent slot machine that pays the winners with real silver dollars. Las Vegas, Nevada (circa 1969)

Knowledge will separate you from the crowd and in some cases, alienate you as well. As the years progressed this dealer would then "re-price" his inventory, in a somewhat paranoid manner, the day before my payday twice each month. Needless to say he overpriced everything, and lost me as a customer and virtually all of his other customers as well due to his overpriced inventory. In any case, that's the way it was in Charleston, South Carolina in the early 1960s. It was interesting, educational and fun.

Las Vegas Silver Dollars

After I was discharged from the Air Force and after my college years, I lived for a five year period in the late 1960s and early 1970s in Las Vegas, Nevada. There, I placed buys and sells in the want-ads section of the local newspaper (Las Vegas Review Journal). The ads appeared on a regular weekly basis and consisted of an offer to buy circulated silver dollars for $3.00 apiece and BUs for $4.00 each. I would, in turn, sell these coins for $3.50 (circulated) and $4.50 (uncirculated) to both Stan Zurawski, Sr. and Jr. C/O the Nevada Coin Mart on Sahara Boulevard.

People would bring their silver dollars to me and most would claim some to be uncirculated when I knew otherwise. Customer after customer would continue to try to get BU money for most if not all of their silver dollars. It was always a hassle for both them and me. After a short period of time, it dawned on me that I knew more about the grading of silver dollars than they did. Most people simply could not tell an uncirculated silver dollar from a "slider" or even a "circ."

I then changed my ad to adjust my offer to buy all silver dollars at $3.00 apiece regardless of their circulated or uncirculated status. I simply had no more questions about the condition of the coins. In addition, I had the privilege of using my knowledge to separate the uncirculated coins and sell them for $4.50, thus producing a larger margin of profit for myself.

As an aside, there was a blackjack dealer in Las Vegas, Nevada a long time ago who had me by the tail one night. I had started with $1,000 and was all the way down to ONE DOLLAR. As the last opportunity, I placed and won a $1 bet on one last hand, pushed the bet, and won again and again. I just let it ride doubling as I went. When I had recovered $512, I walked. I was positive the next bet of $512 was a loser and I didn't want to tempt fate or greed. One-half a sandwich is "always" better than none at all. I had gotten 50 percent of my money back very quickly with only a one dollar bet! I'd also rather be conservative than broke. I then bought $512 in quarters and played a twenty five cent silver dollar slot machine that paid off in "real" silver dollars. After all was said and done, I had won 301 silver dollars which I in turn sold to Stan Zurawski, Sr. on the next day for $4 each, netting me a total of $1,204. Again silver dollars seemed to be a winner for me!

The 1879-S Reverse of '78

Later in my career as a silver dollar dealer, Harrison Phillips of Memphis, Tennessee, a friend and fellow dealer, made me aware of the 1879-S flat breast variety. The flat breast (second reverse) was used on the 1879-S reverse of '78 Morgan dollar variety that grew to be one of my personal favorites. The normal reverse utilized for the 1879-S was the round breast (third reverse). Refer to the complete chapter on "The 1879-S Reverse of '78 Morgan Silver Dollar" for all of the details on this fascinating variety. This revelation led me on a multi-year search through the 1970s and the 1980s for specimens of this type. I searched many a roll of 1879-S Morgans for these examples. I would then buy the roll if I found any flat breast coins in them. Often I would go to as many as 15 coin shows in a row without finding a single flat breast.

As it turned out, I discovered the greatest concentration of them in Paramount holders from the Redfield hoard of 1879-S uncirculated silver dollars. Perhaps as much as a 20 percent concentration of the flat breast was in these holders. Before that discovery, I could search a full bag of 1879-S dollars and never find a single flat breast. Since that time most dealers have combed their inventories and recovered any available flat breast specimens. During the decade of the 1980s, this variety has gained tremendously in popularity to the point that it is considered a major Morgan dollar variety. As such, it is listed as a separate line item in all of the major coin pricing publications. The future still looks bright for this variety.

On Bags and Rolls

I had founded and incorporated Oklahoma Federated Gold and Numismatics, Inc., in 1980. As the decade of the 1980s began, we were buying and selling original bags. Most were put-together Brilliant Uncirculated (BU) bags. Original bags would have the same strike, same luster, same die variety and similar characteristics throughout the bag. A few years later, we couldn't find enough 83-O's, 79-S's, or whatever date we were looking for. So we sold mostly put-together mixed bags of "P" mints, "O" mints, S" mints and so on. Finally, we were shipping mixed BU bags of silver dollars of various dates.

During the early to mid-80s, BU singles were bought and sold for up to $50 per coin. Dealers would take their pick of dollars from $55 to $75. Bags and rolls of Morgans were a hot item and I had all the business I could handle. We dealt in thousands of silver dollars at every show and the pace was hectic to say the least. During the years spanning 1980 through 1986, I was the uncontested number one dealer for dollar rolls in America. Mark S. Yaffe, Leon Hendrickson, John Love, Wayne Miller, and a few other dealers also dealt in large numbers of dollar rolls and bags at the time. They were my only real competition.

As prices reached for the sky in the early 1980s, circulated silver dollars (bullion related) went for as much as $36 each. The BU dollar roll market was so hot at the time, we started selling half rolls (10 coins per half-sized dollar tube). Then the Hunt brothers had their problems and silver prices experienced a crash in the early 1980s. Roll prices dipped, but didn't dump, and had later recovered to $1,075 per roll (wholesale dealer to dealer) by February 1984 at the Long Beach Show. The dollar roll market promptly crashed to the $700 per roll level following a dramatic plunge in the price of silver from $12 to $8 per ounce in one single weekend! This was the worst trading plunge I had ever witnessed up to that time. By the way, just in case you missed what I just said, the silver price correction was down 33% over one weekend.

The next coin show was the mid-year ANA Convention in Colorado Springs, Colorado. I got buried in rolls at $700 per roll! It took me four or five months to get rid of the inventory dumped on me during that one show. It was truly amazing that you could sell a half million dollars of Morgans at $1075 per roll, buy them back three days later at $700 a roll, and not be able to get rid of them at the 35% lower price. The BU bag market was slowly but surely becoming a thing of the past.

I was selling dollar rolls at the time by the bagful (either government canvas bags, or rolled with 20 coins in plastic tubes with 50 tubes to a bag). We were still shipping a few original government canvas bags in the late 1970s and early 1980.

By this time most bags of dollars were shipped via packaged plastic tubes (20 coins per tube) in a custom size cardboard

Original U.S. Government canvas bag
(Courtesy of Howard W. Herz, Lake Tahoe, Nevada)

U.S. Government canvas bag tags
(Courtesy of Howard W. Herz, Lake Tahoe, Nevada)

box. The box contained 5 rolls of 5 tubes each on the bottom layer and 5 rolls of 5 each in the top layer. Postal regulations had set a limit of 60 pounds, which was very close to a fully packed box which weighed in between 58-59 pounds. Postal box size requirements were no problem due to the extreme density of the packed silver dollars. The round tubes didn't pack and ship quite as well as the tubes of today which are square on the outside but round on the inside. Next the box was wrapped and reinforced with filament tape, completely covered with the regulation post office brown tape, insured, stamped virtually all over by the post office for security purposes and then shipped registered insured.

My parent company, Oklahoma Federated Gold and Numismatics, Inc., along with many other firms used an interesting alternate method for shipping coins in the early 80s. The coins were bagged in specially labeled cloth bags, lead sealed with heavy duty wire, sealed with identifiable crimpers and shipped just like that. Slowly but surely the United States Postal Service eliminated this form of shipment and required either a pail (plastic or metal) or the kind of box described earlier.

Moving for a moment to the bullion market, we used to sell mixed 90% silver coins in bags: dimes, quarters and half dollars with a face value of $1,000. Customers could request one-half bag or one-quarter bag quantities if they so desired. We would look up that day's quotation for silver bullion and ship the desired quantity at the pre-determined calculated price. The volatility of that market pretty well dried up by the mid-1980s. Dealers still buy, sell and ship 90% bags today. However, the gross profit is in the 1-3% range per bag. Only a large volume can make this a profitable trading item.

Now back to rolls. The dollar roll market began to change dramatically in the 1980s. First there were predominantly original dollar rolls. You could tell an original roll by the similar characteristics appearing on every coin in the roll. For example, a particularly bold or weak strike, a particular die variety, special identifiable field characteristics and so on. One of my cardinal rules was then and still is "NO BAGGY BU's!" We discounted them very heavily back then if we bought them at all. Nobody wants a "baggy" silver dollar even if it was scarce. A problem coin is and will always be a problem coin! They just don't sell and have little or no eye appeal. Speaking of eye appeal, the "S" mint rolls always brought better money because the strike and luster were usually exceptional.

As long as we are on the subject of "S" mints, I remember a short story about an 1893-S. This was one I never owned. A lady came into my office one day with quite a number of

Oklahoma Federated Gold and Numismatics cloth canvas shipping bag
(Courtesy of Oklahoma Federated Gold and Numismatics, Inc.)

circulated silver dollars. She asked what I would give for the lot. I picked through her holdings and discovered a circulated 1893-S among them. Being what I thought was fair, I offered her 75% of current retail for the 1893-S and five to six dollars apiece for the rest of her dollars. You may have already guessed what happened next. She walked out the door with the 1893-S Morgan dollar, and I never saw her again. She also kept the rest of her dollars. I told you it was a short story.

During the 1980s when dollar rolls were "in", I would inspect thousands upon thousands of silver dollars. I was eventually able to differentiate the difference in strike and other characteristics associated with each and every one of the mint facilities. This enabled me to determine the mint of origin from a Morgan dollar's obverse with a ninety percent or better accuracy. Careful study of the illustrations in this book can help you learn too.

As the BU dollar rolls began to be picked over through the years, the gem dollars were consistently being removed and replaced by lower grades. They were then labeled "put-together" rolls. Sliders began to make their appearance and the dollar roll dealers had to be very careful to know what they were buying. I developed quick eye to be sure that I wasn't buying sliders instead of BU coins. It took thousands of coins with hands-on experience to be able to tell a BU silver dollar from a slider. I said back in 1982, within a decade an unpicked original roll would be news at a coin show. I was literally laughed at by some of my peers! "Deja vu." The original dollar roll market has literally dried up and died. It would be news to find an original unpicked dollar roll at a convention today, especially with PCGS, NGC ANACS and CompuGrade™ as independent third party grading enterprises. Today virtually every dollar roll is picked over before it gets to a coin convention.

During the "hey-day" of the coin show market phase, dealers would bring most of their rolls to my table. I would sort through them and buy what I needed at the appropriate price (BU money for BU coins and slider money for sliders, etc.). The roll market finally deteriorated to mostly put-together rolls with all different types of varieties! I would separate them and tube them at my table according to date and grade. People could come and buy what they wanted in any quantity. Some would bring me coins in double row boxes (300 coins of two rows each in 2x2 holders). My wife Marlene still remembers what removing thousands of coins from those types of holders did to her hands and nails. Later on I would sell bags of pre-1921 dated Morgans (1878-1904) in all grades from circulated to BU. The pre-1921 dollars always brought more money than the 1921 Morgans or any of the Peace dollar dates.

I always worked on existing orders and not on speculation. It was and is still the safest way of doing business. Your main risk (robberies aside) is nonpaying or cancelling customers. John Dannreuther told David Hall in the years of 1986-1989 that I was probably the number one volume person in America removing coins out of the wholesale marketplace. Then in 1989 I had more orders cancel on me in a month than all of the orders I had filled throughout the years. Incredible! I have obviously learned to trust customers much less since then. I could write a very interesting book on this subject alone.

Peace dollar rolls on the other hand were a very special breed. It also took a certain breed of dealers to successfully handle them. Peace dollars have always been more difficult to grade than Morgans. With Peace dollars, "sliders" are everywhere, and are much more difficult to distinguish from BU coins. You would be amazed at how many dealers that have been around for twenty years or more that never could grade them correctly! I spent a lot of time separating the wheat from the chaff in Peace dollar rolls. After some years, I became very good at grading Peace dollars which also came in handy while I was putting together my own Peace dollar set. (See the chapter, "The World's Finest Collections and Prices Realized" for a complete listing) To finalize, I had times when Morgan dollar rolls would slow down or even stop. However, there was usually somewhere to go with Peace dollar rolls. The demand was always there.

More on Original Bags

Then there is the Larry Lee story. Larry is a friend of mine and this story taught me a very good lesson. In the early 1980s, I got a call from Larry asking me if I wanted a bag of 1884-Os. I asked if the bag was original and he assured me that it was. I consented and he shipped the bag to me at $35,000. When I looked through the bag, I determined that approximately one-third of the coins were "sliders". So I called him back and he said "Just take the ones you want, write me a check and send the rest back to me." I did that and went on.

A short time later, he called me again. He said, "Do you want a bag of 1885-Os?" I asked him if the bag was original and he again assured me that it was. I decided to take a look at the bag and told him to ship it to me for $35,000. When I received the bag and opened it, about one-half of the coins were not uncirculated. I got hold of Larry and explained the situation to him. He didn't have any problems. He just told me to return the unwanted coins and send the money for the ones I took.

Some time later, he called me once again and said, "I've got an original bag of 1883-Os. Do you want it?" I was skeptical but my curiosity won out. I told him to ship 'em to me. When I opened the bag, I couldn't believe it. It was actually an original bag! I had a great time going through this bag and cherrypicking to my heart's content. THANKS, LARRY!

I could go on and on, but I think you get the picture by now. Finally, I asked him, "How do you make any money? You sell 'em to me for $35 but what do you do with the returns?" He responded, "Oh, that's no problem. There are a lot of people out there who don't know a circulated coin from an uncirculated one. I just send the bag to someone like you first. Then I take what's left and send it on to someone that's not as picky. In due time, I always rid of every coin! It's no problem." As the years passed by, I realized that "beauty is in the eye of the beholder" and he was right. I started from that day forward, letting dealers pick what they liked first and selling off the rest later to those less picky! It works fine. Thanks Larry for the inside view!

Government "CC" holders

In the late 1970s and early 80s, we sold thousands of "CC" Morgan dollars in U.S. Government holders. They were all in BU condition. These dollars were made available thanks to the G.S.A. sales of 1974-76 and 1980. Those sales were responsible for the distribution of the remaining U.S. Treasury holdings of over 3,000,000 Carson City Morgan silver dollars.

Initially, we bought and shipped "CC" dollars in both types of holders. At first, retailers wanted both of them. When they began to require only holders with "uncirculated" labeled on them. Later we had to lower our buy price for holders without the words "uncirculated." We would then pay anywhere from 10% to 20% less. We eventually had to crack out the "CC" dollars from their holders and ship them out to various retailers by the roll to get our money back. Is this where all the dealers learned to "crack out" coins? Isn't it amazing what the power of suggestion can do! We slowly but surely accumulated hundreds of black original CC government issued boxes. These boxes later sold from 50 cents to as much as a dollar apiece. Jack Beymer of Santa Rosa, California and a few other dealers were buying all he could get at that time.

Some dealers would "cringe" when they saw us cracking out "CC" dollars from their original government holders. At the time I didn't give it much thought. Later on I reflected that it would be nice to have a larger number of "CC" dollars in original government holders. However, the time for that had already passed. Note that the government's official "distribution" figures for Carson City dollars in original holders are much like those of the Red Book mintage figures. Both are accurate but both do not represent the actual numbers available today. In another perspective the "CC" Governmental figures are less proportionally reliable than either the PCGS or the NGC population reports due to their massive "crack-outs."

Next, the retailers started requiring the black original "CC" boxes with the Richard Nixon inscription inside. Then they wanted the original G.S.A. descriptive cards to be inside the boxes. Finally, it was only the serial numbered cards which matched the date of the coin inside the holder that satisfied their customers (like the one shown below). This serial number was an eight digit number preceded by the year of issue for the "CC" coin (for example, #83274303). To simplify further, the first two digits (83) indicated the year of issue and the next six digits (274303) were the serial number. We had to pay more for the serial numbered matching cards (especially for the tougher dates). At times we would buy deals where everything was intact. It was always nice to buy the serial numbered card, original black box and a government sealed plastic "CC" holder inscribed with the words "uncirculated" on them all at the same time.

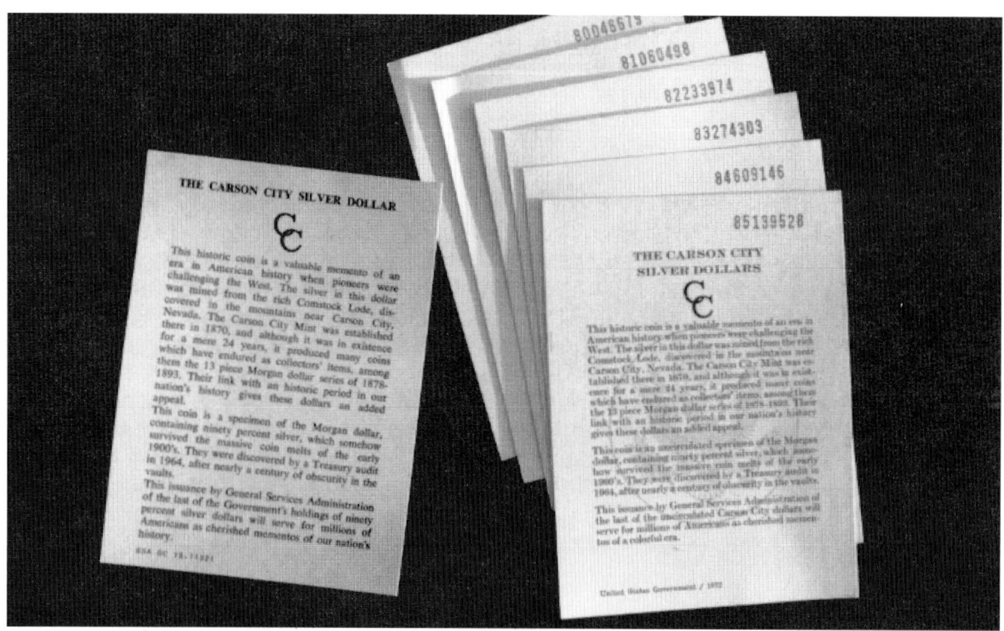

The G.S.A. Carson City Silver Dollar descriptive card
(left shows generic unnumbered card while right shows an official serial numbered card)
(Courtesy of Frank Roza, III; Sierra Nevada Coins Plus, Carson City, Nevada)

There is one special "CC" dollar story I would like to share with you. I bought a superb gem 1885-CC from Coleman Foster for $2,800 (four times bid) at the San Diego show a few years back. It was in an original G.S.A. holder. I in turn sold the coin to Louie Moreno, Jr. for $3,000. He resold it quickly to Dean Tavenner for $4,000 and Dean sold it to Ken Park for $5,000 the very next day. This was all at the *same show*! Then it was "cracked out" of its original government holder and submitted to PCGS where it was finally graded an MS-68. It was then sold to Bill Spears, who has exhibited that very coin in the PCGS "World's Finest Morgan Silver Dollars" collection. And that, my friends, is what is called a line of pedigree!

Note that I stepped out and made the initial buy at four times the posted bid. After that, the others came in realizing the quality of the coin. Sometimes one dealer's knowledge can make a whole series of transactions a reality. Now that I bragged a little bit, I should let you know that I almost passed on the coin. I also sold it for only 40% of the final price realized.

Short, Short Stories and Thoughts

I've had many long-time dealers tell me of the bags of MS 65 "Cameo" DMPL 1887-O dollars that they saw or once owned in the 1960s and 70s. But there I was submitting my best hand-picked coins to PCGS and only 1 in 25 would come back MS-65 PL or DMPL and they weren't 1887-O Morgans! By today's grading standards either the bulk of those "gems" would not make the grade, or we might have just been listening to fish stories. I've also been told of BU bags of 1884-S, 1886-O, 1889-CC, 1892-S, 1893-S, 1895-O and other very rare dates. Only time can make or break these rumors.

Looking to the future, it will be interesting to see what effect computer grading has on the ongoing grading evolution of all dates in the Morgan series. As much as change is a way of life, the tighter grading standards of today and tomorrow, will only make the coin business a better place for the future!

Back in the earlier days, I used the following methods to build my collections. Every week after the previous coin show, I would go through my new inventory, pick the very best coins, and put them away as "keepers" in the safe. Then as the weeks went by, I would review my holdings and weed out the lesser coins as upgraded specimens (rarer and better grade) became more readily available. This became a repeating cycle which I eventually refined over and over again throughout the years.

The major change of my collect, weed, upgrade, cycle process came later. After a period of time I was in a better position to determine how my inventory/portfolio was doing. It slowly became apparent that certain coins did better than others. Relatively common unpopular series did not perform nearly as well as the scarce to rare date coins in the higher grades. For example, I had a number of Buffalo nickel and Mercury dime rolls in some of the tougher dates. But when I wanted to sell them, nobody seemed to care. I did note that silver dollars, gold, commemoratives, and high grade 19th century type coins would always sell at some price level. After that, I became much more conscious of both rarity and popularity. I then concentrated on those more popular and rarer dates in the highest grades.

Another phenomenon occurred as my eye for grading got better. I would look at all of my coins with a new light and say to myself, "I remember that coin looking better than that." Sometimes it seemed as if my coins were "growing" bagmarks overnight in the safe. I kept upgrading my Morgan dollar collection until it was finally completed in MS, PL and DMPL. For a complete listing of this set, see the chapter, "The World's Finest Collections and Prices Realized," later in this book.

While I'm talking about quality coins, on May 19, 1989, myself and a partner were involved in and sold the U.S. Assayer Augustus Humbert's own personal PCGS Proof 65 1852/1 $20 gold piece in a private party transaction. The price was a record at an earth shattering $1.35 million! This was the highest price ever realized for a single United States coin. It was exciting to be part of this record making transaction to say the least. For details, again see the chapter, "The World's Finest Collections and Prices Realized" later in this book.

The Lake Tahoe John W. Highfill Collection

The weekend of April 4, 1985, at Harvey's Inn*Vitational VIP Convention, Harvey's Inn, Lake Tahoe, Nevada, was a very exciting one. The show promoters were Howard W. Herz, Bourse Chairman and Harlan White, Director. In conjunction with the show, a closed silent auction bid was held for my first personal collection. These special "keepers" were the Morgan and Peace dollars I mentioned earlier in this chapter as the "best of the best" which I had put back week after week. Each of the coins was considered "Gem BU" and was graded MS-65 or better at that time. No pedigree is available for this collection unless you are capable of tracing them through the original winning bidders.

Private invitations had been previously sent out and a number of major numismatic firms had sent representatives exclusively to bid on this collection. The sale was not publicized and the number of dealers involved was limited. The market atmosphere was very good at the time and there was a great deal of interest in the pieces I was offering. Some dealers who had not received invitations asked to be included. I regrettably had to exclude them. Those participating in the silent closed bid auction were:

Glenn Armstrong representing North American Numismatics, Phoenix, Arizona
Roger Bryan representing Bryan Ltd., Gainesville, Florida
Nick Buzolich, Jr. representing David Hall's Numismatic Investment Group, Newport Beach, California
Gary Fernandez representing Fernandez and Armstrong, Newark, California
Ronald M. Howard representing Kagin's, Inc., San Francisco, California
Wayne Hummel representing Certified Coins of America, Monroe, Louisiana
D. Harrison Phillips representing Harrison Phillips Rare Coins, Memphis, Tennessee
Dean Tavenner representing Old Coin Shop, San Diego, California

The silent closed bid auction method allowed each of the bidders in turn to view the entire selection of coins. They were only required to submit a bid on those coins which were desired. As these proceedings took place over the next couple of days, auction "fever" developed as each of the invited dealers had surveyed my collection. They placed their bids and talked very highly of the quality of the coins they had observed. Some of the coins were bid on by every dealer while others received only a few bids.

When all of the bidders had submitted their bids, a final tally was made and the winning bidder for each coin in the collection was announced. Bids were all over the board and almost every participating dealer had a high bid on at least one coin. The beauty and value as reflected by the bids was definitely in the eyes of the beholder, and nothing has changed since then. The grading was just as subjective then as it is today with the entrance of PCGS and NGC. A portion of the collection is listed here in date order with both the low bid (posted if significantly off the high bid) and the winning bid. Readers must realize that all of the participants were professional numismatists who definitely knew what they were doing.

Prices Realized

Morgan Dollars

Date	**Low Bid**	**High Bid**	**1985 Greysheet Bid**
1879-P		$1,100	$ 950
1880-CC	$ 700	1,710	1,100
1880-S		850	* 350
1881-CC	750	1,300	900
1882-S		850	* 400
1883-P		1,000*	500
1884-P		1,150*	615
1885-O Prooflike		1,200*	600
1897-O		8,000	8,700
1898-S	1,100	1,600	1,475
1900-O/CC		1,600	1,200
1902-O	650	1,500*	500
1903-S	3,925	7,500	7,000

Peace Dollars			
Date	Low Bid	High Bid	1985 Greysheet Bid
1922-D	$ 225	$1,050	$ 950
1923-P		555	400
1924-P		510	560
1925-P	350	520	495
1926-D		1,400	1,400
1934-S		7,000	7,000
1935-P	1,175	1,625	1,125
1935-S	2,150	4,010	* 2,125
Proof Morgan Dollars			
1882-P		$3,100	$1,450**
1883-P		2,900	1,450**
1892-P		2,400	1,450**

* Superb coins that sold for as much as double bid or more!
** High bid is for Proof 63 Morgans c/o the May, 1985 CDN.

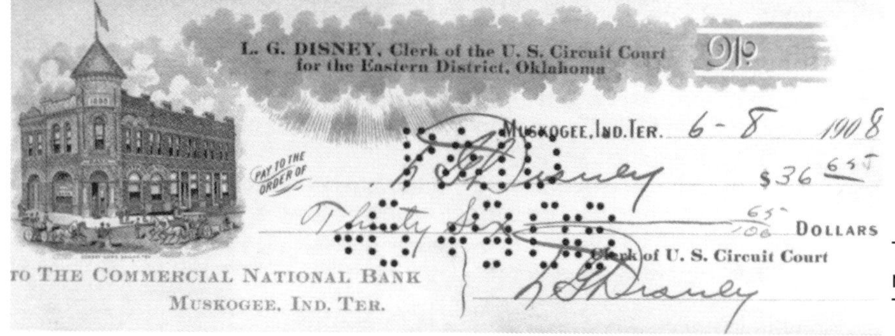
L. G. DISNEY, Clerk of the U. S. Circuit Court for the Eastern District, Oklahoma
Muskogee, Ind. Ter. 6-8 1908
Pay to the order of
$36 65/100
Thirty Six 65/100 Dollars
Clerk of U. S. Circuit Court
To The Commercial National Bank
Muskogee, Ind. Ter.

This is the bank where I first started collecting my pennies. Note then it was Muskogee, Indian Territory, now Muskogee, Oklahoma.

Showtime

Over the past fifteen years or so, I've made close to if not more than 1,000 shows and conventions (that was sometimes 2 or more shows on the same weekend!). During the late 1970s and early 1980s, the market makers were right there "in the trenches." They knew what the "greysheet" and "bluesheet" were going to publish after each week's activity before it ever came out. We were right there. This was where the "real" markets were made.

Traveling the show circuit is not for everyone. One must live out of a suitcase and a hotel room. In 1987 and 1988 I was in Tulsa, Oklahoma approximately 40 to 50 days a year. This may not sound interesting to you, but you should realize that I lived there! I've always taken the time to see the sights. Occasionally, you have to make yourself get up and do things. It's called motivation. The rewards are worth it. If you don't believe me, see some of the great photos of side trips and excursions from Cancun to Asia in Chapter 79. Some of the travel is and was what dreams are made of!

There's a very special group of people that you meet and work with on the show circuit. You see the same group week after week. It's probably a little like playing professional golf or racing cars. It is a very different lifestyle that is slowly becoming a thing of the past. Many of the larger dealers no longer attend 50 shows a year. They go to a dozen of the major conventions and that's all. The electronic trading systems and networks, shrinking profit margins, and rising travel costs have combined to make the weekly show dealer a dying breed. Too bad.

Many dealers have met at hundreds of different coin shows every year for the past decade. There are "pockets" of dealers that trade in their own circles. A good example would involve dealer to dealer sales. In that arena, the wholesale dealer sells to the same types of dealers. In a smaller perspective, the raw coin dealers deal with a certain portion of those attending the convention. The "certified" dealers mix with other "certified" dealers. There are those that deal with both. Then there are the exclusive dealers. They are sometimes, and commonly, referred to as a specialist in their own field. Some of these may be Gold, Silver Dollars, Commemoratives, Foreign, or U.S. type "specialists." The end result is that some dealers see other dealers every weekend for years and may never deal with each other. Sometimes one dealer will sell a coin to another, only to have that dealer attempt to sell the same coin back to the original owner.

A large number of dealers trade in their own circles. They all seem to have certain comfort levels with different types of dealers. Once in a while a few dealers move out of their circle of trade and make some transactions. However, they all seem to drift back to their own arena. I remember going to my 30th high school reunion at the Elks Lodge in Muskogee, Oklahoma, on July 6, 1991. I saw a lot of old friends and met some new ones. The times and the faces seem to have changed, but the people didn't. To put it simply, the same circles of people from our old high school days ventured out to meet and greet everyone, only to return to their original friends by the time the reunion was over.

I have taken the liberty of sharing some of the "good times" that these dealers and myself have enjoyed through the years in a special pictorial section in Chapter 79 of this book. I only hope that you can enjoy their memories as much as we did. There are many black and white and color collages. Hundreds of dealers are shown having a good time in this special chapter. You'll be surprised at the many memories of conventions past. You will find many people and friends that you know. You may even find yourself! HAPPY COLLECTING AND MAY YOUR TRAVELS BRING YOU GREAT REWARDS!

This following in-depth personal interview was conducted by Elsie E. Patterson, of this author's previous years in the record business and made exclusively for the PNG Report. Reproduced courtesy of the *PNG Report*, The Official Publication of the Professional Numismatists Guild, Inc., Iola, Wisconsin, Fall 1990 edition. "On the Reverse" features PNG members and others' special hobbies or interesting background stories.

On the Reverse

Former Music Man Hits the Right Note in Coin Business

By Elsie E. Patterson

Kenny Rogers. Bobby Darin. Frank Sinatra. Elvis Presley. Barbra Streisand. B.J. Thomas. Dean Martin. To most of us, these are legendary performers whose music we enjoy on records and tapes—or perhaps we've been lucky enough to see them perform in Las Vegas or Lake Tahoe. But, for coin dealer John Highfill, these luminaries were often part of his everyday work. And, he says, there were many he felt he could call his friends.

The 47-year-old Highfill says he got into the record business as a young man and started at the very lowest level: a friend hired him as a rack jobber. It was his responsibility to make the rounds of stores such as K-Mart, Sears, Woolco, and Target to fill the record racks and pick up what hadn't sold.

Highfill wasn't a rack jobber for long: he moved up the ladder at ABC Record Company and Dunhill and between 1967 and 1973 he lived in Las Vegas and Honolulu where he worked in a public relations capacity, acquired new accounts, and negotiated contracts.

Eventually, Highfill says he left his job and opened his own record store, and at one time owned three. "But," he admits, "I didn't make it. You make about 12 cents on a record and you have to sell thousands a day to break even. And we did for awhile, but it's a youth-oriented business and there's lots of theft. The cash register never balanced. That was before the days of the electronic cash register.

"I didn't file bankruptcy," says Highfill, "but I had to sell my house, car, furniture—everything—to pay my bills. I kept my credit rating, but I left the business with my tail between my legs." Highfill went to Washington, DC, as a regional sales manager for Handleman Record Co., which he says, "...was a step down from ABC Records. Plus, I was 35 years old and was working for a guy 21. It was hard on me to work for someone who was younger and didn't know as much about the business as I did. Fortunately, the company was bought out by Lieberman Enterprises Record Company and I got transferred to Memphis. And I was glad to go."

Highfill, who had collected coins since he was seven years old, says he had always done coin shows on a part-time basis. With the strong coin market in 1978 and 1979, he realized he was making more money on the side than he was with his regular job. "I moved to Oklahoma in 1979, formed Oklahoma Federated, and have never looked back," says Highfill.

Reflecting on his past experiences, Highfill says, "I'm older now and it wouldn't mean as much to me, but I was younger then. I enjoyed rubbing elbows with entertainers, it made me feel good.

John Highfill (standing) visits with Felix Caveleira of the Rascals, during the 1989 National Silver Dollar Convention.

"I learned that they were no different than anyone else. They had a job to do. Entertainers are multi-talented people, high-caliber people with super intellects. People thing they have an easy life, but they work hard for their money. 'Good' is a prerequisite for 'luck', and anyone can be a star if they get a break. There are incredible talents that never get the contract or the ads and promo behind them. Females need to be pretty, and males need to be tall and handsome. They have to act, have charisma, and the promoters want to make them bigger than life.

"The record business is fascinating," continues Highfill. "The first step is to get a contract with a record company that likes you. After you get big, they'll give songs to sing. Paul Williams was a writer, not a singer. He had a lot of talent in his head but was terrible singer. Carole King wrote for 15 years before she sang."

Highfill says he believes he had the ability to predict which songs would be hits, but he was only one voice on a board of decision makers. "Kenny Rogers," says Highfill, "said he could never predict a hit, but I could tell him what was going to be a hit and what wasn't. A song has to have mass appeal. A lot of times, it's down-home stuff like Hee Haw—no one could understand why it was number one for ten years. There are more K-Mart shoppers in the world than Nieman Marcus shoppers. You have to go for the audience, for youth-oriented songs.

"Elvis went after the kids. Actually, he was a pretty straight guy. He did his hot-doggy things in a country boy way. I met him backstage after concerts and partied with him on the 7th floor in Vegas. He wasn't overly egotistical but he didn't let intellectuals intimidate him, either. He was the star."

Today, Highfill's involvement with entertainers centers around lining up such notable groups as the Grassroots, the Association, and the Rascals to perform at the Silver Dollar Convention in St. Louis in November 1989, or Three Dog Night for the convention in 1990.

"I still like all kinds of music," says Highfill. This could well be proven by the fact that he has a collection of 28,000 albums and 20,000 45s—many of which have been personally autographed by the performers he once knew and worked with.

If you are a PNG member and would like to be featured in "On the Reverse" or know of another memer with an interesting background or hobby, please send suggestions to *PNG Report*, P.O. Box 337, Iola, WI 54945.

"On The Reverse" Interview with John Highfill by Elsie E. Patterson (Courtesy of PNG Report, Iola, Wisconsin)

***

Wayne H. Miller

Wayne Miller, 50, has been a specialist in silver dollars for 25 years. During this period he has examined over two million silver dollars, and is generally considered to be one of the leading authorities on Morgan and Peace dollars.

In January 1986, Wayne Miller's personal silver dollar collection, which is the only set ever assembled to have all of the regular issue, proof, and branch mint proof specimens, sold for over $1.2 million dollars. This was an all time highest price for a Morgan and Peace dollar collection at the time.

Wayne loves silver dollars, and is always thrilled to open an original, unsearched roll or bag (if he can still find one) of these most beautiful and exciting coins.

CHAPTER 10

My Silver Dollar Set

by Wayne H. Miller

On a hot dry August day in 1968, my wife and I were savoring the first moments of our first summer vacation together. Our two children (we subsequently added three more to our family, plus five foster children) were with my parents, and Ann and I were on the road. Our first stop was Missoula. Dean Tavenner, then one of the major forces in the silver dollar business, had told me of a fresh shipment of prooflike Morgans, and I was eager to see them. For several months an idea had been popping into my head about assembling a superb set of Morgan dollars — the finest ever. Of course, with a low paying state job and a rapidly growing family, this was sheer fantasy.

When we arrived in Missoula, our first stop was The Cartwheel, Dean's coin shop. My wife has always been tolerant of my obsession with silver dollars, even on vacations. I walked into the shop very excited at the prospect of looking through what Dean had described as a major acquisition: a roll of prooflike 1881-CC dollars.

The roll was everything Dean said it was, and I forked over $82.50 for the pick of the lot. With the acquisition of that coin, I began what I envisioned then to be a fifteen year project — to assemble a complete set of Morgan dollars in superb condition.

During the early years of the project many people laughed when they realized that the set was missing many pieces. "How can you call this a dollar set? Where's the 89-CC? Where's the 93-S?" But I determined early on that I would never put a coin in the set unless there was a reasonable assessment that this was the finest specimen that I was likely to see. It was interesting to discover through the years that the easiest coins to upgrade were those dates which were already among the finest in the set. In fact, from 1976 to 1982, during a period in which I upgraded almost 75% of the coins in the set, nearly all the upgrades were in the least expensive coins in the series.

Although I had never particularly liked the Peace dollar series, I realized that this set would also be necessary to acquire. Some of the coins in that series are among the earliest acquired in my set. The 1922-S, for example, cost me $6 in 1972; the 1935-S set me back a whopping $65 in August, 1971.

Because of my position as a silver dollar specialist and coin dealer, I was exposed to a great number of gem silver dollars. Since it was known that I would pay a "ridiculous" price for a superb gem dollar, a large number of the finest silver dollars of the period 1968 to 1983 ended up in my collection.

The 1886-O

Probably the most amazing coin in the entire collection is the 1886-O. During the negotiations for determining the value of my set, the 1886-O was figured at $60,000 to $75,000. Dean Tavenner acquired this coin for me early in 1977. Actually, he offered the coin to me initially for $1,500, (bid at the time was less than $200), sight unseen; he was at a coin show in Salt Lake. I just could not bring myself to pay that much money for an 1886-O without seeing it. Dean sold the coin at the show, and for two weeks afterward I kept hearing from various people how incredible the coin was. When Dean returned from the show he sold me an incredible 1892-O — the only cameo prooflike gem of this date I have ever seen or heard of. He told me that this coin was nothing compared to the 1886-O. Finally, I urged him to try to repurchase the coin for me. He went to a show the next week, and came over to my house. (From 1968 to 1981 I did all my coin business out of my house, and ran a good mail order business. Since I did not like going to coin shows, and since Dean loved them, we would get together after a show and I would buy whatever gems he brought back.) As I looked through his offerings no mention was made of the 1886-O. In fact, I had almost forgotten the coin. But eventually I came to what looked like the most incredible 1886-P deep mirror cameo prooflike that I had ever seen. Suddenly, I turned the coin over, and saw the "O" mintmark. The coin was mind-boggling! I would not have believed such a coin could exist. Dean was laughing by that time, and all I could say was "How much?" Dean knew that I would pay whatever he asked, but he charged me $2,075, which was about $200 more than he paid to repurchase it.

The 1878-S

At the February 1976 Long Beach coin show, while in loose partnership with John Love, I was going through his extensive inventory when I came across a group of 40 gem deep mirror cameo 1878-S dollars. Midway through the group, I came to a coin so perfect that I thought the Long Beach "light" was playing tricks with me. I soon realized that I was looking at the most perfect business strike Morgan dollar I had ever seen. The surfaces were deeply mirrored, face fully frosted, I was afraid to look at the reverse. No coin could be that perfect. It was! With as normal a voice as I could command, I asked how much? Since they were nice, $14 each for the lot. I soon resold these coins, but kept the one piece for my set. It has been the cover coin for both of my books. It realized $37,400 when the set was auctioned in 1986.

Part II

Montana has always been one of the most active areas in regard to Morgan and Peace dollars, in that it was one of only five states which utilized silver dollars as a preferred medium of exchange. Many silver dollar collections have been assembled in Montana over the past thirty years. However, very few of the dollars in my set came from individual Montana collections. There were a few exceptions however.

In December of 1970, after months of negotiations, I purchased in its entirety the silver dollar collection of John Hardenberg of Missoula, Montana. The price for the complete Morgan and Peace dollar collection (minus the 1895 Proof) was a then stratospheric $6,500. This was a peculiar collection in that the rare dates were generally of very high quality, but many of the common dates were barely uncirculated. I learned that Mr. Hardenberg was of the very sensible opinion that the rare dates should be acquired first, and the more common dates later, since they were much more readily obtainable. Three coins were pre-eminent in the Hardenberg collection: the 1884-S, the 1889-CC, and the 1895-O.

The 1884-S

Dean Tavenner had been beguiling me for several months with the information that he knew of a superb gem 1884-S, but that it was impounded in a major collection and was not likely to be offered for sale. At the time (late 1960s) the 1884-S was unknown in superb gem condition. When I inquired as to a possible price for the coin, Dean said that it would take at least $250 to buy the coin. Since the Coin Dealer Newsletter bid price at the time was $25, this was an enormous price! I gulped a few times but stated that if the coin was ever available I would like a shot at it. Being a sensible businessman, Dean did not divulge the name of the owner of the 1884-S. However, I have learned that many collectors will sell their precious collections to another collector more readily than they will to a person who is strictly a dealer. Within a few months I was contacted by a part-time dealer in Missoula, Montana and advised that a major dollar set might be available at the right price. After what I had heard of this set, I rushed over to Missoula immediately. The crafty dealer kept me waiting for nearly an hour before I got to see the set. The first plate of coins (there were five in all, in Capital Plastic holders) contained many coins of exceptional quality—the 1879-CC, the 1880-S, an 1878-7/8 VAM 41 deep mirror prooflike with all six feathers, many others lost to memory—and I was very excited. But the second plate contained the most incredible 1884-S I had ever seen. Its surfaces were nearly flawless, with a light golden tone, and the strike was very bold. Overall, it was a stupendous coin. On the reverse there was a peculiar light spot to the right of the eagle, like a water mark, but it did not detract from the coin. I was entranced by the coin, and kept tilting it and putting it under various lighting to find a flaw. There were none—the coin was magnificent.

I tried to keep my voice normal as I answered questions of the dealer who was brokering the transaction, but he could tell that the 1884-S was special. I had to own this coin!

The 1889-CC

At the bottom of the second plate was another exceptional coin. The 1889-CC was very deeply mirrored, with the usual bold strike, and the surfaces were very clean. I had handled a few gem prooflikes of this date, but this one was significantly better than any I had seen. It had a flashiness, a pizzazz that is lacking in most prooflikes of this date. I was told that Hardenberg had paid $1,000 for this coin from Dean Tavenner. I already had a gem prooflike in my set, but this was clearly superior. Another must coin!

The 1895-O

The third plate contained many exceptional specimens of rare date coins, but one coin was clearly predominant — the 1895-O. This coin was absolutely fully struck, with subdued deep mirror surfaces, and a near total absence of surface abrasions. It was not unlike the 1895-S prooflikes which are often described as branch mint proofs. (In fact, Dean still maintains that it was a branch mint proof, although I disagree). At the time I examined this set, I was not fully aware of the extreme rarity of the 1895-O in gem condition. In the succeeding 14 years, I have seen only one additional fully gem 1895-O (more on this in a later column), but I knew the coin was exceptional.

The initial asking price of the set was over $7,000. This was more than I could afford and I returned home, afraid that the set might go to someone else. But a few weeks later, I was again contacted and Hardenberg agreed to the sale price of $6,500. This set would sell today for well over $250,000.

In the past 18 years, I have been richly blessed in the coin business. I have seen and subsequently owned many of the superb gems that appeared in the market during that time. But nothing has ever compared to the thrill I felt driving home from Missoula with the Hardenberg dollar set. At that time nearly two dozen of his dates were upgrades to my collection. Even now, I rarely drive to Missoula without recalling the transaction at a certain bend in the road. Gentleman, life doesn't get much better than this!

The Proofs

By mid-1977, my silver dollar set was approaching perfection. It was becoming more difficult to upgrade. But the continuing strong demand for gem dollars meant that as a dealer I was accumulating profits which had to go somewhere. At one time I had over two double-row boxes and probably 30-50 rolls of gem single dollars, many of them just slightly inferior to coins in my set. I rarely sold these upper level coins except to special clients, to whom I was attached. Premier among these was Jack Gauya. Somehow he managed to spirit away many of the most amazing coins in my "super-cherry" box.

After a few months of frustration trying to locate upgrades for my collection, I decided to make a major expansion of my dollar set: I would assemble a complete set of proofs as well! At the time, I was quite unknowledgeable about relative rarity of proof-issue Morgan and Peace dollars, and had a bit of a problem in grading them, too. This would seem strange since I had always had a good "eye" for grading business strikes. However, most dealers will agree that it is very difficult to become expert in grading all coins — better to specialize in a few select series. This might explain why ANACS, PCGS, and NGC have been so disappointing in the consistency of their grading.

In October 1977, I bought my first proof Morgan — a superb 1890 from Julian Leidman. I paid $750, way more than the going rate. At that time, proof Morgans were not strong, and many were available. I could have bought several superb pieces in that time. But I wanted to see whether I really was committed to expanding my set to include proofs. It would be a very costly undertaking and I wanted to feel my way. During the 15 years in which I assembled my set, I tried never to buy a coin or coins if doing so would have depleted my funds and negatively impacted my business. Too many mouths to feed! But since I plowed all my profits back into coins, I could always sell off duplicates if needed.

By mid-1978 the coin boom was on, and profits were good. The sale of my first book in 1976, "Analysis of Morgan and Peace Dollars," went very well and I sold all 23,500 copies in a few years. This exposure catapulted me into the front ranks of silver dollar dealers and I had more business than I could handle. I had spent the previous year examining all the proof

Morgans I could find, trying to become more expert in differentiating the gems from the super-gems. I was not about to accumulate a group of inferior pieces which I would then have to upgrade later!

One of the most interesting hoards of proof Morgans ever assembled was made available during that period. Harlan White of San Diego had accumulated an amazing cluster of 150-175 proofs, many of them in the very upper levels of perfection. At the time, I did not realize the significance of this accumulation and so bought only a few pieces. One of the coins I passed on was a magnificent 1885. At the time I noticed it had a fairly high mintage and assumed I could always get one later, since Harlan seemed a little high. I was to learn later that some of the most difficult dates to find in gem condition are the high mintage ones and some of the dates which would seem to be rare, such as 1894 and 1895, are relatively common in superb gem condition.

Once I became committed to the proofs, they accumulated at an amazing rate. By the middle of 1980, I was lacking only 6-8 pieces for a complete set. As always, I had amazingly good luck in finding superb pieces. Some of the most amazing pieces included the 1881, acquired at the 1980 ANA sale at near the bottom of the coin market for $10,500, the only common date proof Morgan in the sale to realize more than $5,500; the 1882, traded for during the white heat of the fever market of March, 1980, for $18,000! (My trade-in was valued at $12,000); the 1888, by far the best known of that date, bought from Walt Hood while we were going through the line to the Colossus at Magic Mountain amusement park at a ridiculous price (my wife thought I was nuts negotiating for a $15,000-20,000 coin while surrounded by thousands of hungry-looking thrill-seekers); the 1895, bought in my own hometown of Helena from a major old-time collection; the 1901, an absolutely mind-boggling piece which Randy Campbell brought to my attention at the 1978 FUN Convention (I did not haggle the owner when they quoted $1,300; the 1904, a superb light-golden toned gem, the only gem of this date I have ever seen, bought from my former partner at the 1980 FUN show, Steve Contursi. Steve did not want to sell the coin, but I really did force him into it. He named a price so ridiculous no one would pay it, and I accepted without counteroffer (I knew he would pass).

There were also two coins in the set which were major rarities not because of condition, but because of the few surviving examples. One was the 1878 round breast proof, bought from David Hall for $7,500 in the depths of the dead market in 1982; David had paid around $20,000 for it in the fever market of early 1980. This was a pleasant looking coin, although it did have some noticeable hairlines. Still it is the second finest known of the 4-6 examples which survive of this date.

The other major rarity was the 1922 satin finish proof, which I acquired as a commission for arranging for the auctioning of the Henry Herrmann coin estate, in early 1979. This is the finest known of the three satin finish proofs known to exist of this date, and by far the most obviously proof of the three specimens.

By late 1979, I had acquired virtually all of the proof Morgans. For the moment, my quest was completed, but my collecting urge was unabated. Next . . .(Time will tell).

The Branch Mint Proofs

The ultimate in rarity in Morgan and Peace dollars has to be the branch mint proofs. Only four years are officially recognized: the 1879-0 (reportedly 12 struck to commemorate the re-opening of the New Orleans Mint); the 1883-0 (again 12 struck, reason uncertain); the 1893-CC (probably 12 struck, to acknowledge the closing of the Carson City Mint); and the 1921-S (24 struck, at urging of Farran Zerbe). By 1979, my silver dollar set was nearly complete, including all the Regular Issue Proofs. Therefore, I was restless to add another dimension to the set. The only area which remained was branch mint Proofs.

When I expressed my interest to other dollar enthusiasts I was told that what I was considering was a near-impossibility. At that time, there were no more than 8-10 branch mint Proof Morgan dollars of all dates known to exist. Nevertheless, I determined to add these incredible rarities to my collection. No collector had ever owned more than two specimens!

As always, just when I determined to seek out a certain type of silver dollar, within a few months the first of these elusive treasures appeared, the 1893-CC. This was the Breen discovery piece, which was the first Morgan dollar to sell for more than $10,000. I had been present at the auction in January, 1973, at the FUN coin show in Miami, when this coin was auctioned for $180,000. Imagine my excitement when I learned that this coin was included in Auction '79! I was determined to own this coin, and was the successful bidder at $39,000 — close to a record at the time for a Morgan Dollar. This is by far the finest of the four 1893-CC branch mint Proof Morgans known to exist.

The next piece I obtained was through sheer luck, since no branch mint Proof specimen of the 1883-O had appeared since 1969. At that time it was thought to be the only one in existence. Julian Leidman bought this piece in the Herbert Bergen auction late in 1979 after a fierce bidding war for $6,500. I was skeptical of Julian's claims at first, since I had been offered many coins as branch mint Proofs which turned out to be merely prooflike. But I respected Julian's expertise, so I told him to ship the coin. It was definitely a proof, although not as obviously a proof as the 1893-CC. Within six months, I had already purchased two of the four branch mint Proof issues.

In mid-1980 RARCOA, the Chicago coin firm, which was aware of my interest in branch mint Proof Morgans, called me to describe an incredible 1879-O dollar. The consignor, Leo Young, considered the coin to be merely a superb gem prooflike. However, at one glance I knew I was looking at by far and away the most magnificent branch mint proof Morgan dollar in existence. The coin was mark-free, with deep mirrored fields and a white cameo head. I purchased this coin at Auction '80 for $36,000. This became one of the four or five best coins in my entire collection, and certainly the capstone of my branch mint proofs.

The fourth and final piece of the "fearsome foursome" was the 1921-S. Although not an aesthetically appealing coin (poor strike and dull luster), it was the final piece I needed to complete my proof silver dollars. So I bought it from Leroy Lenhart for $10,000. My set was the first (and still the only) to include all regular issue Morgan Proofs, and all the four branch mint Proofs.

Reflections On My Dollar Set

Many people have asked me if I thought my silver dollar set was the finest that would ever be assembled. My answer is equivocal. In terms of completeness, no other set is likely to ever be re-assembled, since most of the great rarities were purchased by different people. Certainly many of the coins (78-CC, 86-O, 95-O, 1879-O Proof, 1893-CC Proof, 1901 Proof, 1904 Proof) are most likely the finest that ever will come to light.

However, many of the coins in my set would not have received high grades from PCGS or NGC. For example, the 1892-O in my set was by far the finest known deep-mirror prooflike of that date, and the only one with any cameo contrast. But technically speaking the coin would probably grade no higher than MS63 or MS64 because of surface abrasions.

During the time that my dollar set was being assembled (1968-1983), deep-mirror prooflike dollars were much more highly prized than they are today. Therefore, many of the coins in the set were inferior technically to a frosty specimen. For example, the 1886-S in my set was a deeply mirrored MS64-65 coin. I gave a superior piece to my good friend and partner Steve Contursi as a Christmas present: it became the first 1886-S dollar to grade MS66.

Although I have not seen the traveling PCGS silver dollar set, I am told it contains many finest-known dollars. I would urge all of you to examine this collection if it should ever come your way. I am told it contains a few coins from my collection. Maybe I will see it soon, and say hello again to some old friends.

The Wayne Miller Morgan and Peace Dollar Set

The following compilation of the Wayne Miller Morgan and Peace dollar set was presented by Bruce Amspacher in his Investment Report (BAIR), Volume 3, Number 2, July 21, 1984 [editor].

Morgan Dollars

Date	Grade	Description
1878-P 8TF	65+	Cameo PL Obv.
1878-P 7TF	65	Prooflike
1878-P 7F Round Breast	65++	Cameo PL
1878-P 7/8 TF	65+	Prooflike
1878-CC	67	Cameo PL
1878-S	69+	Cameo PL (Wonder coin)
1879-P	65++	Cameo PL
1879-CC	65	Cameo PL
1879-O	65++	Cameo PL
1879-S	68	Cameo PL (Wonder coin)
1879-S Flat Breast	64	Cameo PL
1880-P	65++	Cameo PL
1880-CC	65++	Semi PL
1880-O	67	Cameo PL
1880-S	68	Cameo PL
1881-P	65++	Cameo PL
1881-CC	65++	Cameo PL
1881-O	65	Cameo PL
1881-S	68	Cameo PL
1882-P	65+	Cameo PL
1882-CC	65+	Cameo PL
1882-O	65	Cameo PL
1882-S	65	Cameo PL
1883-P	65++	Cameo PL
1883-CC	68	Cameo PL
1883-O	65++	Cameo PL
1883-S	67	Cameo PL (not deep)
1884-P	65++	Cameo PL
1884-CC	67+	Cameo PL
1884-O	65++	Cameo PL
1884-S	65	
1885-P	67	Cameo PL
1885-CC	67	Cameo PL
1885-CC	67++	Cameo PL
1885-S	65+	Cameo PL
1886-P	67+	Semi PL
1886-O	68	Cameo PL (Wonder coin)
1886-S	65+	Prooflike
1887-P	65++	Cameo PL
1887-O	65++	Cameo PL
1887-S	65+	Semi PL
1888-P	65++	Cameo PL
1888-O	65++	Cameo PL
1888-S	65	Prooflike

Morgan Dollars

Date	Grade	Description
1889-P	65+	Prooflike
1889-CC	65+	Cameo PL
1889-O	65+	Cameo PL
1889-S	65++	Cameo PL
1890-P	65++	Light Cameo PL
1890-CC	65+	Cameo PL
1890-O	65++	Cameo PL
1890-S	65++	Cameo PL
1891-P	65+	Cameo PL
1891-CC	67	Semi PL
1891-O	67+	
1891-S	65+	Cameo PL
1892-P	65++	Cameo PL
1892-CC	65	Cameo PL
1892-O	65+	Cameo PL
1892-S	67	
1893-P	65++	
1893-CC	65+	
1893-O	65+	Semi PL
1894-P	67	Prooflike
1894-O	65	
1894-S	65+	Prooflike
1895-O	68	Semi PL
1895-S	65+	Prooflike
1896-P	67	Prooflike
1896-O	65	Semi PL
1896-S	67	
1897-P	65++	Cameo PL
1897-O	68	
1897-S	67	Cameo PL
1898-P	65+	Prooflike
1898-O	65++	Cameo PL
1898-S	65+	Cameo PL
1899-P	67	Cameo PL
1899-O	67	Cameo PL
1899-S	65++	Prooflike
1900-P	65++	Prooflike
1900-O	67	Prooflike
1900-S	65++	Prooflike
1901-P	67	Toned
1901-O	65++	Prooflike
1901-S	67	Semi PL
1902-P	67	Prooflike
1902-O	67	Prooflike

Morgan Dollars

Date	Grade	Description
1902-S	65++	Semi PL
1903-P	65++	Prooflike
1903-O	67	Prooflike
1903-S	67	
1904-P	65+	Prooflike
1904-O	67	Prooflike
1904-S	65++	
1921-P	65	Cameo PL
1921-D	67	Semi PL
1921-S	67	

Proof Dollars

Date	Grade	Description
1878 8TF	67	
1878 7TF	67	
1878 7TF Round Breast	65+	Cameo
1879	67	Cameo
1880	68	Cameo
1881	68	Cameo
1882	68	Cameo
1883	67	Cameo
1884	67	Cameo
1885	67	
1886	67	
1887	67	Cameo
1888	68	Cameo
1889	67	Cameo
1890	68	Cameo
1891	67	Cameo
1892	65++	Cameo
1893	67	Toned
1894	67	Cameo
1895	67	Cameo
1896	67	Cameo
1897	65++	Cameo
1898	67	Cameo
1899	67	Toned
1900	67	Cameo
1901	67	Some Cameo
1902	65+	
1903	67	
1904	67	
1921 Zerbe	65+	
1921 Peace	65	
1922 Peace	65	Not high relief

Peace Dollars

Date	Grade	Description
1921-P	65+	
1922-P	67	
1922-D	67	
1922-S	67+	
1923-P	67	
1923-D	65	
1923-S	63	
1924-P	65	
1924-S	65+	
1925-P	67	
1925-S	65++	
1926-P	65+	
1926-D	65+	
1926-S	67	
1927-P	68	
1927-D	65+	
1927-S	65+	
1928-P	67	
1928-S	65	
1934-P	67	
1934-D	67	
1934-S	69	
1935-P	67	
1935-S	67	

Branch Mint Proof Morgan Dollars

Date	Grade	Description
1879-O	69	Cameo
1882-CC	67	
1883-O	65++	
1893-CC	67	
1921-S	65	

References

Bruce Amspacher Investment Report (BAIR), Volume 3 Number 2, July 21, 1984

My Silver Dollar Set, three articles by Wayne Miller, *NSDR Journal*, August 1984 through February 1985, Mike Faraone, Co-Editor, Robert T. McIntire, Co-Editor and Publisher

***

CHAPTER 11

The Carson City Mint: A Branch Mint Profile

by John W. Highfill, NLG

Carson City, Nevada, is one place that speaks of the adventure and history of the old West spiced with a little old fashioned avarice. The primary reason for the existence of the Carson City branch mint was its proximity to the Comstock lode and all the other mines located in and around Virginia City, a scant 14 miles from the mint site. It was reported that more bullion was going to San Francisco than the facility there could handle. The reports also relayed the message that too much of the bullion was being exported. But I'm getting a little ahead of the story.

Once upon a time there was a deserted prairie, a range upon which the deer and the antelope played. The nearby foothills and mountains completed the scene until the arrival of settlers, prospectors and Abraham Curry.

Abraham Curry, a western traveler from New York state, wanted to buy a little real estate in the area but was having a tough time. His offers for desirable properties were rejected until he finally decided to build his own town. This led to the purchase of an old trading post located in Eagle Valley, a part of Carson County in the Western part of Utah Territory, from John Mankin, an adventurer who had bought it from a group of departing Mormons. Getting to the heart of the matter, Mr. Curry founded what was to become Carson City in 1858, accompanied by three other men (B.F. Green, Frank M. Proctor, and J.J. Musser). Meanwhile, in the foothills to the Northeast of newly founded Carson City, events were unfolding that foretold its future.

Abraham Curry, founder of Carson City (Courtesy of Nevada State Museum, Carson City, Nevada)

The Comstock Lode

The year was 1859. The man was "Old Virginny" (really James Finney of Virginia). He and a few friends made the early discoveries of gold in what was to be known as the Comstock Lode at the top of "Gold Hill." Many miners moved into the area, but no one found anything really significant. In June, Peter O'Riley and Patrick McLaughlin moved in from Johntown and discovered the Ophir bonanza of black sand containing gold and silver (although the silver content was not known until later), north of the Gold Hill discovery.

Henry Comstock heard of the Ophir find and came along to horn in on the deal. His inspection of the claim confirmed his belief, and he wormed his way into the partnership (also bringing in his own partner, Emanual Penrod, who he claimed owned the spring in the area) with a story of taking gold from the land he had previously laid out. O'Riley and McLaughlin bought the story and now there were four partners in the find. Comstock and Penrod bought out the men who had worked the area in 1858 for small amounts of money, and also bought the portion of the spring they did not already own. Comstock's brazen manner and bold actions caused the finds in the area to be called the Comstock Lode. Although he did not make either of the initial discoveries, his comments and stories resulted in the widespread belief that he was the "father of the lode."

John Winters and J.A. Osborn, who built two arrastras and provided horses, received a one-third interest in the claim on June 22, 1859. Later in June, Melville Atwood in California assayed material from the Ophir and relayed its content of one-fourth gold and *three-fourths silver*. Judge James Walsh and partner Joseph Woodworth bought into the claim (from Comstock and Penrod) as did others such as George Hearst and Francis J. Hughes. Patrick O'Riley was the last to sell and received $40,000 from J.O. Earl for his portion of the mine.

Conflicting reports reached California concerning the find, but very few investigated the activity. It seems that Californians were in the midst of a depression in 1859, after so many stories of rich mines were proved worthless. Then came the first deliveries of the rich ore from Nevada. Californians became spirited prospectors once more and led to major discoveries in the Western territories during the early 1860s. The Comstock silver discoveries were second in importance only to the fabulous gold finds in California.

Many Comstock mines were opened during the last half of 1859 and 1860. Henry De Groot researched the history of these mines during the 1870s and noted the mining companies spawned and named primarily after their founders. A few of these were the Gould & Curry (Abraham Curry), the Hale & Norcross, and the White & Murphy. The Consolidated-Virginia under the leadership of John Mackay and his partner Jack O'Brien, grew out of the old White & Murphy mine. John Mackay became a millionaire through this bonanza.

"Old Virginny," a very colorful man, was noted for all sorts of things. However, he was best honored in 1859 by those early miners who named the town near the Ophir strike Virginia City. The boom and bust syndrome invariably associated with mining activities, coupled with the seasons of the year, hit Virginia City. The population varied from 2,500 up depending upon the situation. For example, during the furor of 1863, population soared to over 15,000.

Here's something to write home about. At the height of the 1863 frenzy, stocks in the various real, bogus, and hopeful mining companies commanded a combined new worth of $40,000,000. To put this astounding figure in proper perspective, compare it with the total net worth of all companies and real estate in San Francisco at $80,000,000. In the middle of 1863, the owners of the Gould & Curry were told the truth concerning the future of their little empire. The fact was that the rich ore deposits were only present to a depth of 300-500 feet, and it would only be a matter of time before the Comstock played out. The future of the area was saved by the tremendous discoveries of Consolidated-Virginia and Crown Point in the early 1870s. By the end of 1865, the total combined net worth of all Comstock properties had dropped to $4,000,000.

President Abraham Lincoln declared Nevada a Territory of the United States on March 2, 1861, with James Nye as the first governor. The rich ore deposits of the Comstock Lode had not escaped the eyes of the U.S. Government, which was gearing up for the Civil War. Comstock production totaled less than $275,000 in 1859, $1,000,000 in 1860, $2,500,000 in 1861, $6,000,000 in 1862, an impressive $12,400,000 for 1863, and a better $16,000,000 in each of 1864 and 1865.

The Territory of Nevada politically organized itself and through a number of meetings and negotiations framed a constitution for the proposed state. Finally, the constitution was ratified, and the State of Nevada joined the Union on October 31, 1864 (the 36th state). The prominent lawyer, William M. Stewart, duly elected a Senator, was responsible for two federal mining laws, "The Law of 1866" and "The Law of 1872." The other elected Senator was James Nye, the first governor of Nevada Territory.

It was in 1864 that William Sharon came into the picture and managed to take control of the Comstock from 1867 until 1874. He made low interest loans (as bank manager) using money from the newly formed Bank of California with investors William Ralston and D.O. Mills. Hard times in Virginia City during the mid-1860s left the bank holding the majority of Comstock properties and adjoining mills. The Comstock held on until the early 1870s when the discovery at Crown Point saved the day for the bank. The Comstock Lode paved the way for the establishment of a new branch mint at Carson City, while the remaining bonanzas which were found in the surrounding areas safely secured the future of the State of Nevada and the mint.

Carson City and the Mint

"Abe" Curry did not sit idle before the days of the Comstock Lode. He had managed to sell the new Territory of Nevada land for a new prison for $80,000 (actually a conversion of his own Warm Springs Hotel). When the Comstock came in, Abe and a partner found and held a position in the Gould and Curry, but sold out too early. As time progressed, Carson City became the trade and supply center for the area. The young community was a stop along the famous Pony Express run, and was the site of a Wells Fargo office. In the later 1860s, telegraph lines, the Virginia & Truckee railroad, and several mills took their place in the Carson City landscape.

On the other side of the states in Washington, D.C., Secretary of the Treasury Salmon P. Chase was pursuing an idea — a branch mint in the Territory of Nevada. The Director of the Mint, James Pollock, was not friendly to the plan, and wished instead to expand the San Francisco facility.

Congress overlooked the mint director's recommendation and passed a bill on March 3, 1863 (presented below), to establish a branch mint in the Territory of Nevada, for two primary reasons: The cost of transporting bullion to San Francisco was high (but so was the cost of transporting finished product), and bullion was leaving San Francisco for foreign ports costing the U.S. approximately $500,000 annually. (This reason gets my vote.)

Thirty-Seventh Congress, Session III
March 3, 1863, Chapter XCVI.

An Act to establish a branch mint of the United States in the Territory of Nevada.

Be it enacted by the Senate and House of Representatives of the United States of America in Congress assembled, that a branch of the mint of the United States be located and established at Carson City, in the Territory of Nevada, for the coinage of gold and silver.

Sec. 2. *And be it further enacted*, That, for carrying on the business of said branch, the following officers shall be appointed, as soon as the public interest shall require their service, upon the nomination of the President, by and with the advice and consent of the Senate, namely: one superintendent, one assayer, one melter and refiner and one coiner; and the said superintendent shall employ as many clerks, subordinate workmen, and laborers, under the direction of the Secretary of the Treasury, as may be required. The salaries of the said officers shall be as follows: To the superintendent, the sum of two thousand dollars; to the assayer, the sum of eighteen hundred dollars; to the melter and refiner, eighteen hundred dollars; to the clerks, subordinate workmen, and laborers, such wages and allowances as are customary, according to their respective stations and occupations.

Sec. 3. *And be it further enacted*, That the officers and clerks to be appointed under this act, before entering upon the execution of their offices, shall take an oath or affirmation, before some judge of the United States or of the supreme court of said Territory, faithfully and diligently to perform the duties of their offices, and shall each become bound to the United States of America, with one or more sureties, to the satisfaction of the director of the mint, or the secretary of the Territory of Nevada, and of the Secretary of the Treasury, with the condition of the faithful performance of the duties of their offices.

Sec. 4. *And be it further enacted*, That the general direction of the business of said branch of the mint of the United States shall be under the control and regulation of the director of the mint at Philadelphia, subject to the approbation of the Secretary of the Treasury; and for that purpose it shall be the duty of said director to prescribe such regulations and require such returns periodically and occasionally, and to establish such charges for parting, assaying, refining, and coining, as shall appear to him to be necessary for the purpose of carrying into effect the intention of this act in establishing said branch; also for the purpose of preserving uniformity of weight, form, and finish in the coin stamped at said branch.

Sec. 5. *And be it further enacted*, That said branch mint shall be a place of deposit for such public moneys as the Secretary of the Treasury may direct. And the superintendent of said branch mint, who shall perform the duties of treasurer thereof, shall have the custody of the same, and also perform the duties of assistant treasurer; and for that purpose shall be subject to all the provisions contained in an act entitled "An act to provide for the better organization of the treasury, and for the collection, safe-keeping, transfer, and disbursement of the public revenue," approved August six, eighteen hundred and forty-six, which related to the treasury of the branch mint at New Orleans.

Sec. 6. *And be it further enacted*, That the superintendent of said branch mint be authorized, under the direction of the Secretary of the Treasury, and on terms to be prescribed by him, to issue payment of the gold dust and bullion deposited for assay and coinage or bars, drafts, or certificates of deposit, payable at the treasury or any sub-treasury of the Untied States, to any depositor electing to receive payment in that form.

Sec. 7. *And be it further enacted*, That all the laws and parts of laws now in force for the regulation of the mint of the Untied States, and for the government of the officers and persons employed therein, and for punishment of all offences connected with the mint or coinage of the Untied States shall be, and they are hereby, declared to be in full force in relation to the branch of the mint by this act established, as far as the same may be applicable thereto.

Sec. 8. *And be it further enacted*, That the sum of one hundred thousand dollars be, and the same is hereby, appropriated, out of any money in the treasury not otherwise appropriated, to carry into effect the provisions of this act, and to meet the expenses of the current year and for the fiscal year ending the thirtieth of June, eighteen hundred and sixty-four.

H.P. Bennett of Colorado was commissioned to select a site for the proposed branch mint, and upon arrival in Carson City, was convinced by Abraham Curry to recommend a well placed full city block. Events were delayed by Civil War efforts in the early 1860s, but were revived in 1863-64 when the Comstock was at its peak and U.S. monetary needs were great. In early 1865, the originally recommended site in Carson City, Nevada, was officially purchased by the government for its next branch mint.

Nevada's two Senators, Stewart and Nye, came forward to save plans for the branch mint in 1866 when detractors in Congress suggested that the original "branch mint" bill had lapsed. Comstock production figures came to the rescue and money was appropriated to construct the building and purchase machinery. Abraham Curry, Henry Rice and John Mills were duly commissioned to complete the construction. On July 17, 1866, Curry, also acting as general contractor, received official authorization to proceed with the work.

Carson City Mint, circa 1879
(Courtesy of the Nevada State Museum, Carson City, Nevada)

The branch mint building was built of sandstone (from the Nevada State Prison Quarry). The concrete foundation was laid seven feet below the basement floor. The structure was a two-and-a-half story building, with a frontage of 90 feet and 170 feet deep. The floors were of a double thickness; sandwiched between them was one inch of mortar. The completed cost was over $426,000 which was nearly three times the original estimate of $150,000.

The building itself was completed in late 1868, but delivery of machinery was delayed, and it was not until the middle of 1869 that all was ready. Curry was named the first superintendent of the new branch mint on April 15, 1869, and was eager to begin production as soon as personnel and dies were in place. A test run was completed during November with no problems reported. An earthquake hit Carson City on December 28, but the new building sustained only minor damage.

The Days of the Mint

Abraham Curry officially opened the branch mint for operation on January 6, 1870, but without any dies. The latest in a long series of requests for dies was dispatched to Pollock, who responded with dies dated 1870. The first delivery of 2,303 Gobrecht design "Liberty Seated" dollars went to Mr. A. Wright on February 11. The "CC" mintmark was utilized, as the single "C" designated coins struck at Charlotte, North Carolina. On February 14, 10,000 gold eagles ($10) were produced, followed in March by the coining of half-eagles ($5) and gold double-eagles ($20).

Activities at the branch mint were divided between the areas controlled by the Superintendent and Treasurer, and the assaying, melting, refining and coining operations. The Superintendent's department was responsible for bullion transfer, supplies, bookkeeping, and other administrative duties required by the mint. The assaying, melting, refining and coining areas actually converted the bullion into coinage.

1870 CC dollar
The first silver dollar issue
of the Carson City Mint
(Courtesy of the Nevada State
Museum Carson City, Nevada)

After a dedicated search for the finest men who could be secured for the available positions, the following employees were the first at the United States Mint at Carson City.

Superintendent and Treasurer: Abraham Curry
- Chief Clerk: G.G. Lyon
- Copying Clerk: Theodore R. Hofer
- Treasurer's Clerk: H.J. Peters
- Weighing Clerk: Z.S. Eldredge
- Coiner's Clerk: I. McConnell
- Calculating Clerk: H.W. Berthong
- Engineer: William Smith
- Assistant Engineer: William Mann
- Plumber: D.H. Lentz
- Deposit Melter: G.K. Laughlin
- Captain of the Watch: W.J. Cowan
- Watchmen: Edward Vore, Carl O. Appleburg, and Andrew Wright
- Messenger: Wellington Stewart
- Assay Office Laborer: Edward Wattman
- Fireman: P. McCarty
- Porter: William Lynch

Assayer and Acting Melter and Refiner: Frank D. Hetrich
- Assistant Assayer: George Atwood
- Melters: John Felix and G.W. Bryant
- Refiner: R.P. Franklin

Acting Coiner: E.W. Staley
- Annealers: Thomas Higgins and D.L. Dougherty
- Roller: H.B. Slocum

Compare the above listing of 26 employees with the 75 positions authorized for the Carson City Branch Mint by the government.

Superintendent and Treasurer:
- Chief Clerk
- Cashier
- Voucher Clerk
- Bookkeeper
- Weighing Clerk
- Computing Clerk
- Assistant Clerk
- Recording Clerk
- Seamstress
- Assistant Seamstress
- Captain of the Watch
- Watchmen (7)
- Blacksmith
- Blacksmith's Helper
- Carpenter
- Engineer
- Day Fireman
- Sweep
- Conductor
- Coalman
- Messenger

Assayer:
- Assistant Assayer
- Weigher
- Humid Assayer
- Cupeller
- Dissolver

Melter and Refiner:
- Assistant Melter and Refiner
- Weigher
- Foreman
- Melter
- Melter's Helper
- Melter of Fine Metal
- Day Foreman
- Night Foreman
- Refinery Helpers (4)

Coiner:
- Assistant Coiner
- Pressman
- Machinist
- Weigher
- Cutting Room Weigher
- Cutting Room Drawer
- Cutter
- Annealer
- Roller Helper
- Whitener
- Forewoman of Adjusters
- Adjusters (16)

As originally designed, the mint refinery was equipped to perform sulfuric and nitric acid processing, and also contained two furnaces with a refining capacity of 7,000 ounces per day. As the years passed, the mint added three coining presses, one for silver dollars and double eagles, one for half-dollars, eagles and half-eagles, and one for minor coins. The coining capacity of the mint was $500,000 in silver and $500,000 in gold coins.

The Troy pound (originating in England during the 1700s) is the unit of weight used in the United States, and therefore at the branch mints. The English original was the standard bronze weight of 5,760 grains Troy adopted by the Commission of 1758, and reaffirmed by the Commission of 1838.

Nine superintendents were appointed through the years at the Carson City. They are listed together with their initial appointment year and commentary.

1870: Abraham Curry. Curry's management team was rather unpopular with the mining community, with the result being the shipment of a great deal of bullion to San Francisco for processing. He resigned during September 1870 to run as a Republican nominee for lieutenant governor (he was defeated).

1870: H.F. Rice. The former Wells Fargo and insurance agent survived reports that the mint's charges were undermining local businesses. Coinage production doubled in 1871, processing over four tons of bullion. Germany went to a strict gold standard during 1871. This act ultimately led to the "Thirty Years War on Silver" when the price of silver went down dramatically causing big problems in "silver" country. The historic Act of February 12, 1873 was passed before Rice was forced to resign in May 1873. His ouster followed disclosure that some CC gold coins were lightweight and/or debased.

1873: Frank D. Hetrich. The first superintendent to be appointed from within the mint staff, he was the Assayer at Carson City and had been an Assayer at the Philadelphia Mint. Abraham Curry died on October 19, 1873, at the age of 58, and was mourned by all citizens of Carson City. James Pollock and Arthur Orr, who built the mint machines, came to Carson City in November 1873. After their visit, they recommended expansion of the branch facility, but funds were never appropriated. The Trade dollar made its West coast debut in Carson City on July 22, 1873, with the production of 4,500 examples. Its silver content was set at 378 grains, which made it one grain heavier than the popular Mexican dollar—a fact that far eastern merchants quickly realized.

Hetrich doubled the capacity of the branch mint with the addition of two more furnaces complete with chimneys. A second press was added in 1875 to further increase production capabilities.

OH GIVE ME A BIG SILVER DOLLAR
TO THROW ON THE BAR
WITH A CLANG

A DOLLAR ALL CREASED MAY SERVE
IN THE EAST

BUT WE LIKE OUR DOLLARS
TO CLANG !

AUTHOR UNKNOWN

(Cartoon photo of Bartender)

1875: James Crawford. A State assemblyman and mill foreman in Dayton, Nevada, he supervised the remaining production of Trade dollars which totaled 4,211,400 (about 25% of all U.S. Trade dollars). By 1876, after Congress revoked the Trade dollars' legal tender status, the value of a Trade dollar had fallen to 86 cents, causing great concern among the merchants of Carson City. Some continued to take Trade dollars at full face while others would accept them only at a discount or not at all. The last 44,148 were melted at the mint, July 19, 1878.

In June of 1875, a trial run of twenty-cent pieces began at the Carson City facility. Ten thousand of the 20 cent coins were produced in 1876, but almost all were melted on orders of the U.S. Mint. In fact, fewer than 20 examples are known to exist today.

In May of 1876, a third coining press arrived and was installed at the growing facility. However, the growth was all internal as funds for expansion of the building itself were refused time and time again. The original #1 press suffered a broken arch; the Virginia & Truckee Railroad Works constructed it and finally installed it September 21, 1878.

On February 28, 1878, the Bland/Allison act discontinued production of Trade dollars (proofs were struck at Philadelphia until 1883) and reinstated the silver dollar. The replacement was the Liberty Head (Morgan dollar) with a content of 90.8 cents worth of silver. The U.S. government decreed that these dollars were to be accepted at face value. Production of George T. Morgan's design began in April after the arrival of 10 obverse and 10 reverse dies.

There were bullion shortages during 1879 and 1880 which caused the facility to shut down for various periods. The talk of a branch mint at New Orleans did not help matters, and much political maneuvering ensued. Finally, production resumed at previous levels and all was well.

When Grover Cleveland won the presidency in 1884, Republicans at the Carson City Mint feared for their positions. Their worst fears concerning the Democratic president were later realized. Meanwhile, on March 8, 1885, Crawford suffered a heart attack and died unexpectedly, adding further uncertainty for the mint and its operations.

1885: Major William Garrard. Previously the Secretary to the Governor and a Democrat, he replaced Theodore Hofer, chief clerk at the mint, who had suspended operations as acting temporary superintendent on March 18. Garrard's first act was to close the mint and replace the department heads with Democrats. By September bullion had been emptied from the mint's vaults and shipped to Philadelphia.

On September 29, 1886, after much political hassling, Secretary of the Treasury Charles Fairchild reopened the Carson City facility as an assay office for the receipt and testing of bullion. Finally the tide turned in 1888 with the election of Republican Benjamin Harrison, a silver supporter, to the White House.

1889: Samuel C. Wright. A judge and attorney, he took his position on July 1 coinciding with the authorization to begin coinage operations immediately using the hoard of bullion accumulated during the previous years. After a short delay, production for the short year began on September 9 and resulted in high quality dollars which were widely circulated (contrasting with prior years). It is interesting to note that (in percentage terms) the 1889-CC production run contained the most prooflike examples as a proportion to total production.

Electric lighting came to Carson City during 1890, a period of time when many new inventions were becoming commercially feasible. The economy was also positive with the price of silver basking in a "bull market" beginning with Benjamin Harrison's election. Silver's value had risen to $1.20 per ounce (from 86 cents) by 1890. In a new political twist, a new law passed in 1890/91 gave the Secretary of the Treasury power over the production of silver coinage. In other political news, the Sherman Silver Purchase Act, passed on July 14, 1890, called for the purchase of 4,500,000 ounces of silver each month.

Samuel Wright died at the age of 61 of dropsy during the summer of 1892, while still holding the office of superintendent of the branch mint.

1892: Theodore R. Hofer. After Wright's death, Carson City Mint chief clerk, who was also cashier of the Bullion and Exchange Bank, became the new superintendent. The Director of the Mint was E.O. Leech. In November, Grover Cleveland, the anti-silver candidate, won the presidency for the second time. Production was running at full capacity during this period, but the end was near for the branch mint.

There was a run on the banks in early 1893 causing the gold reserves of the federal government to fall well below desired levels. Mint Director Leech resigned and was replaced by acting director Robert Preston. The Sherman Silver Purchase Act was repealed and the price of silver fell quickly to only 73 cents an ounce.

On the local scene, the Comstock and other mines were producing much less than before. Then on June 1, 1893, the Carson City Mint was ordered to cease all coining operations, but to continue with its assay and refining activities. At the time of the work stoppage, there was $1,500,000 in bullion and $8,000,000 in coins stored at the branch mint.

During 1894, the price of silver continued its decline to 60 cents an ounce. A seigniorage bill which would have authorized coining of government profits and charges stemming from the minting of coins from bullion went to the desk of the President, but Cleveland vetoed it. During May, Hofer dismissed most of the workers and was discharged as well.

1895: Jewett W. Adams. The next superintendent was a former governor of Nevada. An unfortunate situation was uncovered shortly after Adams took over. A scheme was uncovered in which gold bars were lightweight and well below the value stamped upon them. An investigation spearheaded by Andrew Mason of the New York Assay Office determined the culprits to be employees of the branch mint. Approximately $75,000 in gold was stolen and never recovered causing the mint to fall out of grace with the government. The guilty parties were eventually brought to trial and convicted.

During April 1895, the coining machinery was prepared for storage and the facility was in effect shut down. Authorization for receipt and processing of bullion was given in early 1896, vindicating the existing superintendent and staff. Appropriations for continuing operations (short of coinage) were approved for 1897.

April 1898 marked the beginning of the Spanish American War, causing the Secretary of the Treasury to call for coinage of 42,000,000 silver dollars. The Carson City branch mint's role was to provide bullion for production.

1898: Roswell K. Colcord. In September 1898, the last superintendent of the Carson City Mint was appointed. A former governor of Nevada with an engineering and mining background, he tried unsuccessfully to obtain coining responsibilities for Carson City.

On July 1, 1899, the official word was put into action. The Carson City facility was designated a United States Assay Office. In August the last coinage stored at the mint was transported from the facility. By September all machinery save the assay equipment was dismantled and shipped from Carson City, thus ending the days of the Carson City Mint.

The Legacy

The following Coinage Record shows production from the Carson City facility during its years as a United States branch mint. The branch mint produced coinage in nine denominations with a total face value of $49,274,434.30.

YEAR	DIMES	TWENTY CENT PCS.	QUARTERS	HALF DOLLARS	TRADE DOLLARS	DOLLARS	HALF EAGLES	EAGLES	DOUBLE EAGLES	NO. OF PCS.	TOTAL $
1870			8,340	54,617		12,462	7,675	5,908	3,789	92,791	$ 215,090.50
1871	20,100		10,890	139,950		1,376	20,770	7,185	14,687	214,958	545,523.50
1872	24,000		9,100	272,000		3,150	16,980	5,500	29,650	360,380	876,725.00
1873	31,191		16,462	337,060	124,500	2,300	7,416	4,543	22,410	545,882	833.274.60
1874	10,817			59,000	1,373,200		21,198	16,767	115,085	1,596,067	3,979,141.70
1875	4,645,000	133,290	140,000	1,008,000	1,573,700		11,828	7,715	111,151	7,630,684	4,963,168.00
1876	8,270,000	10,000	4,944,000	1,956,000	509,000		6,887	4,696	138,441	15,839,024	6,402,215.00
1877	7,700,000		4,192,000	1,420,000	534,000		8,680	3,332	42,565	13,900,577	3,990,020.00
1878	200,000		996,000	62,000	97,000	2,212,000	9,054	3,244	13,180	3,592,478	2,950,310.00
1879						756,000	17,281	1,762	10,708	785,751	1,074,185.00
1880						591,000	51,017	11,190		653,207	957,958.00
1881						296,000	13,886	24,015		333,901	605,508.00
1882						1,133,000	82,817	6,764	39,140	1,261,721	2,397,525.00
1883						1,204,000	12,958	12,000	59,962	1,288,920	2,588,030.00
1884						1,136,000	16,402	9,925	81,139	1,243,466	2,940,040.00
1885						228,000			9,450	237,450	417,000.00
1889						350,000			30,945	380,945	968,900.00
1890						2,309,041	53,800	17,500	91,209	2,471,550	4,577,221.00
1891						1,618,000	208,000	103,732	5,000	1,934,732	3,795,320.00
1892						1,352,000	82,968	40,000	27,265	1,502,233	2,712,140.00
1893						677,000	60,000	14,000	18,402	769,402	1,485,040.00
COINS	20,901,108	143,290	10,316,792	5,308,627	4,211,400	13,881,329	709,617	299,778	864,178	56,636,119	
TOTAL	**$ 2,090,110.80**	**28,658**	**2,579,198**	**2,654,313.50**	**4,211,400**	**13,881,329**	**3,548,085**	**2,997,780**	**17,283,560**		**49,274,434.30**

Coin Press #1
(Courtesy of the Nevada State Museum, Carson City, Nevada)

The following capsule history of the Carson City Mint original Coin Press #1 is posted on site at the Nevada State Museum, housed in the remodeled Carson City mint building, Carson City, Nevada.

Original Coin Press No. 1

This six ton coining apparatus, manufactured by Morgan & Orr of Philadelphia, arrived at the Carson City Mint in 1869. On February 11, 1870, the big press struck its first coin, an 1870 Christian Gobrecht silver dollar. The press struck coins at the Carson City Mint until the closing of coining operations in 1893.

Tremendous pressure was required to strike a sharp, clear impression on the round blanks of precious metal — up to 175 tons of pressure to strike a gold double eagle. This intense strain caused a crack to develop in the arch of the press, which had to be replaced. The foundry at the shops of Virginia & Truckee Railroad in Carson City was contracted to cast a new iron arch, at a cost of eight hundred dollars. The 6,058 pound piece was installed on the press on September 21, 1878, complete with the brass plate identifying the "Virginia & Truckee R.R. Works."

In 1899, the press was dismantled and shipped to the Philadelphia Mint. It was rebuilt in 1930 to accommodate electricity and was transferred to the San Francisco Mint in 1945 where it operated for ten years. When that mint was closed, the press was destined for destruction. Instead, it was returned to its first home as part of the exhibits of the Nevada State Museum.

But, its retirement was short-lived. The well-traveled coin press was loaned to the Denver Mint in 1964 to help alleviate a serious national coin shortage. In three years, this nearly one-hundred year old coin press stamped out 118 million quarters, dimes and pennies!

In 1967, the press was returned to the Museum. It now sees service occasionally, stamping out the commemorative bronze and silver coins available at the gift shop.

Obverse (left) and Reverse (right) of Nevada Commemorative Medallion struck using Coin Press #1
(Courtesy of the Nevada State Museum, Carson City, Nevada)

The Nevada State Museum and Virginia City

The original Carson City Mint building was reopened as the Nevada State Museum and dedicated on October 31, 1941, by the Honorable E.P. Carville, Governor, and members of the Board. The museum building was closed at least three times during the 1980s. There was a fire and life safety retrofit made during 1987, a heat and air conditioning and roofing retrofit during 1989, and a closing due to a seismic evaluation in 1990. The organizations credited with maintaining the building as a museum are the Nevada State Legislature, the Carson Nugget, and the Builders Association of Western Nevada.

The attractions within the museum include the Coin Press and mint exhibits, the Mine and Ghost Town, Weapons Gallery, USS Nevada Silver, Natural History and Anthropology Galleries, and the Hall of Regional Geology (under development).

Don Schmitz, of the Nevada City Mint in California, is shown here operating the 122-year-old Carson City coinage press, which produced the medal above.

Operating a 122 year-old coin press
(Courtesy of Numismatic News)

Dedication Bell at the Nevada State Museum
(Courtesy of Marlene Highfill)

THE MINT HAS REOPENED

AT THE NEVADA STATE MUSEUM IN CARSON CITY, NEVADA

Earliest known photograph of the U.S. Mint Building, discovered in the cornerstone of the State Capitol Building in 1870

After the fire and life safety retrofit of 1987;
After the heat and air conditioning and roofing retrofit of 1989;
After the closing due to a seismic evaluation in 1990;
And, with our gratitude and thanks to
THE NEVADA STATE LEGISLATURE
THE CARSON NUGGET
THE BUILDERS ASSOCIATION OF WESTERN NEVADA

We are once again temporarily open.

Please stop by and see your old favorites:
THE COIN PRESS
THE MINT EXHIBITS
THE MINE AND GHOST TOWN
WEAPONS GALLERY
USS NEVADA SILVER
NATURAL HISTORY AND ANTHROPOLOGY GALLERIES
together with a partial opening of our new
HALL OF REGIONAL GEOLOGY
still under delevelopment.

Museum open 8:30 am to 4:30 pm 7 days a week

HELP NEEDED!

To keep the U.S. Branch Mint open we need your support. Please write
"To All Senate and Assembly Members
c/o The Nevada State Legislature
Carson City, Nevada 89710
in support of C.I.P. Project M-32 to fund stabilization of the Mint Building."

Thank You

The Mint has reopened
(Courtesy of the Nevada State Museum,
Carson City, Nevada)

Exhibit of artifacts from the U.S. Mint at Carson City
(Courtesy of the Nevada State Museum, Carson City, Nevada)

George T. Morgan, designer of the
Liberty Head (Morgan) dollar
(Courtesy of the Nevada State Museum,
Carson City, Nevada)

Capsule history of the Comstock Lode — Sign at Virginia City
(Courtesy of Virginia City, Nevada)

The "Silver Queen"

The entrance to the Silver Queen
(Courtesy of the Silver Queen, Virginia City, Nevada)

Silver Queen Casino piece
(Courtesy of the Silver Queen,
Virginia City, Nevada)

The Story of the Silver Queen
(Courtesy of the Silver Queen, Virginia City, Nevada)

Government G.S.A. Holders and Published Statements

The following pictures show the official government holders used to hold and distribute General Services Administration "CC" silver dollars sold during the 1972-74 period, and finishing in 1980. The sales, authorized by President Richard M. Nixon, were conducted through the mail bidding system. Two categories of "CC" dollars were available; coins deemed uncirculated were placed in airtight G.S.A. holders titled "Uncirculated Silver Dollar," while coins found to be circulated or damaged were labeled "Silver Dollar." The official G.S.A. published stories and descriptions are also included together with a statement by President Richard M. Nixon:

As we approach America's Bicentennial, this historic silver dollar is one of the most valued reminders of our national heritage.

Richard Nixon

G.S.A. Government sale Uncirculated Silver Dollar holder
(Courtesy of General Services Administration)

The Carson City Silver Dollar

This historic coin is a valuable memento of an era in American history when pioneers were challenging the West. The silver in this dollar was mined from the rich Comstock Lode, discovered in the mountains near Carson City, Nevada. The Carson City Mint was established there in 1870, and although it was in existence for a mere 24 years, it produced many coins which have endured as collectors' items, among them the 13 piece Morgan dollar series of 1878-1893. Their link with an historic period in our nation's history gives these dollars an added appeal.

This coin is a specimen of the Morgan dollar, containing ninety percent silver, which somehow survived the massive coin melts of the early 1900s. They were discovered by a Treasury audit in 1964, after nearly a century of obscurity in the vaults.

This issuance by General Services Administration of the last of the Government's holdings of ninety percent silver dollars will serve for millions of Americans as cherished mementos of our nation's history.

GSA DC 73-11321

This G.S.A. description of the 1880 Carson City dollar was provided as a courtesy from the collection of Frank Roza III, Sierra Nevada Coins plus, Carson City, Nevada.

> The 1880 year group of Carson City Silver Dollars is noted for several die varieties. For example, the "80" in the figure "1880" often covers a "7" or "79", due to the fact that dies of the year 1879 were frequently used in the following year. This was accomplished by removing the "79" from the die, and putting "80" in its place. Unfortunately, the entire "79" was not always eliminated, thus leaving all or part of the "79" visible behind the "80". As such die varieties may enhance the value of the coin, we suggest that you examine the coin carefully, or perhaps have the coin inspected by a competent numismatist.
>
> GSA DC 73-13502

Not all government issues from the G.S.A. sales remained in the provided government holders. In this case, we find an 1879-P Morgan in the holder.

1879-P Morgan dollar in a G.S.A. holder
(Courtesy of John W. Highfill)

Marlene Highfill with weights and measuring equipment from the 1800's
that is located at the San Francisco Mint in California (circa 1987)

Marlene Highfill at the ANA entrance, Colorado Springs, Colorado

First Interstate Bank of Nevada "CC" Coin Collection

The First Interstate Bank of Nevada was given a complete Carson City U.S. Mint Collection by Norm Biltz, who played an important part in the financial and real estate development of Nevada. Mr. Biltz came to the Lake Tahoe and Reno area of Nevada from Bridgeport, Connecticut in 1927. He served as a member of the Nevada State Museum Board of Trustees during 1947 and 1948. The gift was made prior to his death in 1973. In honor of Mr. Biltz and in the interest of history, the First Interstate Bank has loaned the complete collection to the Nevada State Museum for display.

Appendix

The following portions of the Act of February 12, 1873, are presented to record the establishment of the United States Mint as a Bureau of the Treasury Department and naming of the Director of the Mint. Many of the sections (not shown here) of the February 12, 1873 act were made a part of the Act of June 22, 1874, pertaining to the Revised Statutes of the United States. These revised statutes are reproduced here as the most pertinent to silver dollars and the Carson City branch mint. (See other related laws in the chapter entitled "Morgan Dollars" by John W. Highfill.)

Act of February 12, 1873

An act revising and amending the laws relative to the Mint, assay offices, and coinage of the United States.

Be it enacted by the Senate and House of Representatives of the United States of America in Congress assembled, That the Mint of the United States is hereby established as a Bureau of the Treasury Department, embracing in its organization and under its control all mints for the manufacture of coin, and all assay offices for the stamping of bars, which are now, or which may be hereafter, authorized by law. The chief officer of the said Bureau shall be denominated the Director of the Mint, and shall be under the general direction of the Secretary of the Treasury. He shall be appointed by the President, by and with the advice and consent of the Senate, and shall hold his office for the term of five years, unless sooner removed by the President, upon reasons to be communicated by him to the Senate.

Sec. 2. That the Director of the Mint shall have the general supervision of all mints and assay-offices, and shall make an annual report to the Secretary of the Treasury of their operations, at the close of each fiscal year, and from time to time such additional reports, setting forth the operations and condition of each institutions, as the Secretary of the Treasury shall require, and shall lay before him the annual estimates for their support. And the Secretary of the Treasury shall appoint the number of clerks, classified according to law, necessary to discharge the duties of said Bureau. . . .

. . . Sec. 18. That upon the coins of the United States there shall be the following devices and legends: Upon one side there shall be an impression emblematic of liberty, with an inscription of the word "Liberty" and the year of the coinage, and upon the reverse shall be the figure or representation of an eagle, with the inscriptions "United States of America" and "E Pluribus Unum," and a designation of the value of the coin; but on the gold dollar and three-dollar piece, the dime, five, three, and one cent piece the figure of the eagle shall be omitted; and on the reverse of the silver trade-dollar the weight and the fineness of the coin shall be inscribed; and the Director of the Mint, with the approval of the Secretary of the Treasury, may cause the motto "In God we trust" to be inscribed upon such coins as shall admit of such motto; and any one of the foregoing inscriptions may be on the rim of the gold and silver coins. . . .

. . . Sec. 65. That this act shall take effect on the first day of April, eighteen hundred and seventy-three, when the offices of the treasurer of the mints in Philadelphia, San Francisco, and New Orleans shall be vacated, and the assistant treasurer at New York shall cease to perform the duties of treasurer of the assay-office. The other officers and employees of the mints and assay-offices now appointed shall continue to hold their respective offices, they having first given the necessary bonds, until further appointments may be required, the Director of the Mint at Philadelphia being styled and acting as superintendent thereof. . . .

. . . Sec. 66. That the different mints and assay-offices authorized by this act shall be known as "the mint of the United States at Philadelphia," "the mint of the United States at Carson," "the mint of the United States at Denver," . . .

. . . Sec. 67. That this act shall be known as the "Coinage act of eighteen hundred and seventy-three;" and all other acts and parts of acts pertaining to the mints, assay-offices, and coinage of the United States inconsistent with the provisions of this act are hereby repealed: . . .

REVISED STATUTES OF THE UNITED STATES

Act of June 22, 1874

SEC. 3495. The different mints and assay offices shall be known as:

First. The mint of the United States at Philadelphia.

Second. The mint of the United States at San Francisco.

Third. The mint of the United States at New Orleans.

Fourth. The mint of the United States at Carson.

Fifth. The mint of the United States at Denver.

Sixth. The U.S. Assay office at New York.

Seventh. The United States assay-office at Boise City, Idaho.

Eighth. The United States assay-office at Charlotte, North Carolina.

SEC. 3496. The officers of each mint shall be a superintendent, an assayer, a melter and refiner, and a coiner and, for the mint at Philadelphia, an engraver; all to be appointed by the President, by and with the advice and consent of the Senate.

SEC. 3497. The superintendents of the mints at Philadelphia, San Francisco, and New Orleans shall be, and perform the duties of, treasures of said mints respectively.

SEC. 3498. The officers of the several mints shall be entitled to the following salaries, to be paid monthly;

First. The superintendents of the mints at Philadelphia and San Francisco, to four thousand five hundred dollars a year each.

Second. The assayers, melters and refiners, and the coiners to those mints, to three thousand dollars a year each.

Third. The engraver of the mint at Philadelphia, to three thousand dollars a year.

Fourth. The superintendent of the mint at Carson City to three thousand dollars a year.

Fifth. The assayer, the melter and refiner, and the coiner of the mint at Carson City, to two thousand five hundred dollars a year each.

SEC. 3499. There shall be allowed to the assistants and clerks of the several mints such annual salaries as the Director of the Mint may, with the approbation of the Secretary of the Treasury, determine, and to the workmen employed therein such wages as may be customary and reasonable according to their respective stations and occupations, to be determined by the superintendent, and approved by the Director of the Mint. The salaries provided for in this and the preceding section, and the wages of workmen permanently engaged, shall be payable in monthly installments.

SEC. 3500. Every officer, assistant, and clerk appointed for any mint shall, before he enters upon the execution of his office, take an oath before some judge of the United States, or judge of some court of record of the State in which such mint is located, faithfully and diligently to perform the duties thereof; in addition to other official oaths prescribed by law, such oath, duly certified, shall be transmitted to the Secretary of the Treasury. The superintendent of each mint may require such oath from any of the employees of the mint.

SEC. 3501. The superintendent, the assayer, the melter and refiner, and the coiner of each mint, before entering upon the execution of their respective offices, shall become bound to the United States, with one or more sureties, approved by the Secretary of the Treasury, in the sum of not less than ten nor more than fifty thousand dollars, with condition for the faithful and diligent performance of the duties of his office. Similar bonds may be required of the assistants and clerks, in such sums as the superintendent shall determine, with the approbation of the Director of the Mint; but the same shall not be construed to relieve the superintendent or other officers from liability to the United States for acts, omissions, or negligence of their subordinates or employees; and the Secretary of the Treasury may, at his discretion, increase the bonds of the superintendents.

SEC. 3502. Whenever any officer of a mint or assay office shall be temporarily absent, on account of sickness or any other cause, it shall be lawful for the superintendent, with the consent of such officer, to appoint some person attached to the mint to act in the place of such officer during his absence; but all such appointments shall be forthwith reported to the Director of the Mint for his approval; and in all cases whatsoever the principal shall be responsible for the acts of his representative. In case of the temporary absence of the superintendent, the chief clerk shall act in his place; in case of the temporary absence of the Director of the Mint the Secretary of the Treasury may designate some one to act in his place.

SEC. 3503. The superintendent of each mint shall have the control thereof, the superintendent of the officers and persons employed therein, and the supervision of the business thereof, subject to the approval of the Director of the Mint. He shall make reports to the Director of the Mint at such times and according to such forms as the Director may prescribe; which shall exhibit in detail, and under appropriate heads, the deposits of bullion, the amount of gold, silver, and minor coinage, and the amount of unparted, standard, and refined bars issued, and such other statistics and information as may be required.

SEC. 3504. He shall keep and render, quarter-yearly, to the Director of the Mint, for the purpose of adjustment according to such forms as may be prescribed by the Secretary of the Treasury, regular and faithful accounts of his transactions with the other officers of the Mint and the depositors; and shall also render to him a monthly statement of the ordinary expenses of the mint or assay-office under his charge. He shall also appoint all assistants, clerks, one of whom shall be designated "chief clerk," and workmen employed under his superintendent; but no person shall be appointed to employment in the office of the assayer, melter and refiner, coiner, or engraver, except on the recommendation and nomination in writing of those officers, respectively. He shall forthwith report to the Director of Mint the names of all persons appointed by him, the duties to be performed, the rate of compensation, the appropriation from which compensation is to be made, and the grounds of the appointment; and if the Director of the Mint shall disapprove the same, the appointment shall be vacated. . . .

. . . SEC. 3506. The superintendent of each mint shall receive and safely keep, until legally withdrawn, all moneys or bullion which shall be for the use or the expenses of the mint. He shall receive all bullion brought to the mint for assay or coinage; shall be the keeper of all bullion or coin in the mint, except while the same is legally in the hands of other officers; and shall deliver all coins struck at the mint to the persons to whom they shall be legally payable. From the report of the assayer and the weight of the bullion, he shall compute the value of each deposit, and also the amount of the charges or deductions, if any, of all which he shall give a detailed memorandum to the depositor; and he shall also give at the same time, under his hand, a certificate of the net amount of the deposit, to be paid in coins or bars of the same species of bullion as that deposited, the correctness of which certificate shall be verified by the assayer, who shall countersign the same, and in all cases of transfer of coin or bullion, shall give and receive vouchers, stating the amount and character of such coin or bullion.

SEC. 3507. The assayer shall assay all metals and bullion, whenever such assays are required in the operations of the mint; and shall make assays of coin or samples of bullion whenever required by the superintendent.

SEC. 3508. The melter and refiner shall execute all the operations which are necessary in order to form ingots of standard silver of gold, and alloys for minor coinage, suitable for the coiner, from the metals legally delivered to him for that purpose; and shall also execute all the operations which are necessary in order to form bars conformable in all respects to the law, from the gold and silver bullion delivered to him for that purpose. He shall keep a careful record of all transactions with the superintendent, noting the weight and character of the bullion, and shall be responsible for all bullion delivered to him until the same is returned to the superintendent and the proper vouchers obtained.

SEC. 3509. The coiner shall execute all the operations which are necessary in order to form coins, conformable in all respects to the law, from the standard gold and silver ingots, and alloys for minor coinage, legally delivered to him for that purpose; and shall be responsible for all bullion delivered to him, until the same is returned to the superintendent and the proper vouchers obtained.

SEC. 3510. The engraver shall prepare from the original dies already authorized all the working dies required for use in the coinage of the several mints, and, when new coins or devices are authorized, shall, if required by the Director of the Mint, prepare the devices, models, molds, and matrices, or original dies, for the same; but the Director of the Mint shall nevertheless have power, with the approval of the Secretary of the Treasury, to engage temporarily for this purpose the services of one or more artists, distinguished in their respective departments of art, who shall be paid for such service from the contingent appropriation for the mint at Philadelphia. . . .

. . . SEC. 3513. The silver coins of the United States shall be a trade dollar, a half-dollar, or fifty-cent piece, a quarter-dollar, or twenty-five cent piece, a dime, or ten-cent piece; and the weight of the trade dollar shall be four hundred and twenty grains troy; the weight of the half-dollar shall be twelve grams and one-half of a gram; the quarter-dollar and the dime shall be, respectively, one-half and one-fifth of the weight of said half dollar.

SEC. 3514. The standard for both gold and silver coins of the United States shall be such that of one thousand parts by weight nine hundred shall be of pure metal and one hundred of alloy. The alloy of the silver coins shall be of copper. The alloy of the gold coins shall be of copper, or of copper and silver; but the silver shall in no case exceed one tenth of the whole alloy. . . .

. . . SEC. 3517. Upon the coins there shall be the following devices and legends: Upon one side there shall be an impression emblematic of liberty, with an inscription of the word "Liberty" and the year of the coinage, and upon the reverse shall be the figure or representation of an eagle, with the inscriptions "United States of America" and "E Pluribus Unum," and the designation of the value of the coin; but on the gold dollar and three-dollar piece, the dime, five, three, and one cent piece, the figure of the eagle shall be omitted; and on the reverse of the silver trade-dollar the weight and the fineness of the coin shall be inscribed.

SEC. 3518. At the option of the owner gold or silver may be cast into bars of fine metal, or a standard fineness, or unparted, as he may prefer, with a stamp upon the same designating the weight and fineness, and with such devices impressed thereon as may be deemed expedient to prevent fraudulent imitation, and no such bars shall be issued of a less weight than five ounces. . . .

. . . SEC. 3520. Any owner of silver bullion may deposit the same at any mint, to be formed into bars, or into dollars of the weight of four hundred and twenty grains troy, designated in this Title as trade-dollars, and no deposit of silver for other coinage shall be received. Silver bullion contained in gold deposits, and separated therefrom, may, however, be paid for in silver coin, at such valuations as may be, from time to time, established by the Director of the Mint. . . .

. . . SEC. 3522. From every parcel of bullion deposited for coinage or bars, the superintendent shall deliver to the assayer a sufficient portion for the purpose of being assayed. The bullion remaining from the operations of the assay shall be returned to the superintendent by the assayer.

SEC. 3523. The assayer shall report to the superintendent the quality or fineness of the bullion assayed by him, and such information as will enable him to compute the amount of the charges hereinafter provided for, to be made to the depositor.

SEC. 3524. The charge for converting standard gold bullion into coin shall be one-fifth of one per centum. The charges for converting standard silver into trade-dollars for melting and refining when bullion is below standard, for toughening when metals are contained in it which render it unfit for coinage, for copper used for alloy when the bullion is above standard, for separating the gold and silver when these metals exist together in the bullion, and for the preparation of bars, shall be fixed, from time to time, by the Director, with the concurrence of the Secretary of the Treasury, so as to equal but not exceed, in their judgment, the actual average cost to each mint and assay-office of the material, labor, wastage, and use of machinery employed in each of the cases aforementioned.

SEC. 3525. The assayer shall verify all calculations made by the superintendent of the value of deposits, and, if satisfied of the correctness thereof, shall countersign the certificate required to be given by the superintendent to the depositor.

SEC. 3526. In order to procure bullion for the silver coinage authorized by this title, the superintendents, with the approval of the Director of the Mint, as to price, terms, and quantity, shall purchase such bullion with the bullion-fund. The gain arising from the coinage of such silver bullion into coin of a nominal value exceeding the cost thereof shall be credited to a special fund denominated the silver-profit fund. This fund shall be charged with the wastage incurred in the silver coinage, and with the expense of distributing such silver coins as hereinafter provided. The balance to the credit of this fund shall be from time to time, and at least twice a year, paid into the Treasury of the United States.

SEC. 3527. Silver coins other than the trade-dollar shall be paid out at the several mints, and at the assay-office in New York City, in exchange for gold coins at par, in sums not less than one hundred dollars. It shall be lawful, also, to transmit parcels of the same, from time to time, to the assistant treasurers, depositaries, and other officers of the United States, under general regulations proposed by the Director of the Mint, and approved by the Secretary of the Treasury. Nothing herein contained shall, however, prevent the payment of silver coins, at their nominal value, for silver parted from gold, as provided in this Title, or for change less than one dollar in settlement for gold deposits. But for two years after the twelfth day of February, eighteen hundred and seventy-three, silver coins shall be paid at the mint in Philadelphia, and the assay-office in New York City, for silver bullion purchase for coinage, under such regulations as may be prescribed by the Director of the Mint and approved by the Secretary of the Treasury. . . .

. . . SEC. 3536. In adjusting the weight of the silver coins the following deviations shall not be exceeded in any single piece: In the dollar, the half and quarter dollar, and in the dime, one and one-half grains. And in weighing large number of pieces together, when delivered by the coiner to the superintendent, and by the superintendent to the depositor, the deviations from the standard weight shall not exceed two-hundredths of an ounce in one thousand dollars, half-dollars, or quarter-dollars, and one-hundredth of an ounce in one thousand dimes. . . .

. . . SEC. 3538. The coiner shall, from to time, as coins are prepared, deliver them to the superintendent, who shall receipt for the same, and who shall keep a careful record of their kind, number, and actual weight. In receiving coins it shall be the duty of the superintendent to ascertain, by the trial of a number of single pieces separately, whether the coins of that delivery are within the legal limits of the standard weight; and if his trials for this purpose shall not prove satisfactory, he shall cause all the coins of such delivery to be weighed separately, and such as are not of legal weight shall be defaced and delivered to the melter and refiner as standard bullion, to be again formed into ingots and recoined; or the whole delivery may, if more convenient, be remelted.

SEC. 3539. At every delivery of coins made by the coiner to a superintendent, it shall be the duty of such superintendent, in the presence of the assayer, to take indiscriminately a certain number of pieces of each variety for the annual trial of coins, the number for gold coins being not less than one piece for each one thousand pieces or any fractional part of one thousand pieces delivered; and for silver coins one piece for each two thousand pieces or any factional part of two thousand pieces delivered. The pieces so taken shall be carefully sealed up in an envelope, properly labeled, stating the date of the delivery, the number and denomination of the pieces inclosed, and the amount of the delivery from which they were taken. These sealed parcels containing the reserved pieces shall be deposited in a pyx, designated for the purpose at each mint, which shall be kept under the joint care of the superintendent and assayer, and be so secured that neither can have access to its contents without the presence of the other, and the reserved pieces in their sealed envelopes from the coinage of each mint shall be transmitted quarterly to the mint at Philadelphia. A record shall also be kept at the same time of the number and denomination of the pieces so taken for the annual trial of coins, and of the number and denominations of the pieces represented by them and so delivered, a copy of which record shall be transmitted quarterly to the Director of the Mint. Other pieces may, at any time, be taken for such tests as the Director of the Mint shall prescribe. . . .

. . . SEC. 3541. The superintendent shall debit the coiner with the amount in weight of standard metal of all the bullion placed in his hands, and credit him with the amount in weight of all the coins, clippings, and other bullion returned by him to the superintendent. Once at least in every year, and at such time as the Director of the Mint shall appoint, there shall be an accurate and full settlement of the accounts of the coiner, and the melter and refiner, at which time those officers shall deliver up to the superintendent all the coins, clippings, and other bullion in their possession, respectively, accompanied by statements of all the bullion delivered to them since the last annual settlement, and all the bullion returned by them during the same period, including the amount returned for the purpose of settlement.

SEC. 3542. When all the coins, clippings, and other bullion have been delivered to the superintendent, it shall be his duty to examine the accounts and statements rendered by the coiner and the melter and refiner. The difference between the amount charged and credited to each officer shall be allowed as necessary wastage, if the superintendent shall be satisfied that there has been a bona-fide waste of the precious metals, and if the amount shall not exceed, in the case of the melter and refiner, one thousandth of the whole amount of gold, and one and one-half thousandths of the whole amount of silver delivered to him since the last annual settlement, and in the case of the coiner, one-thousandth of the whole amount of silver, and one-half thousandth of the whole amount of gold that has been delivered to him by the superintendent. All copper used in the alloy of gold and silver bullion shall be separately charged to the melter and refiner, and accounted for by him.

SEC. 3543. It shall also be the duty of the superintendent to forward a correct statement of his balance-sheet, at the close of such settlement, to the Director of the Mint; who shall compare the total amount of gold and silver bullion and coin on hand with the total liabilities of the mint. At the same time a statement of the ordinary expense account, and the moneys therein, shall also be made by the superintendent.

SEC. 3544. When the coins or bars which are the equivalent to any deposit of bullion are ready for delivery, they shall be paid to the depositor, or his order, by the superintendent; and the payments shall be made, if demanded, in the order in which the bullion shall have been brought to the mint. In cases, however, where there is delay in manipulating a refractory deposit, or for any other unavoidable cause, the payment of subsequent deposits, the value of which is known, shall not be delayed thereby. In the denominations of coin delivered, the superintendent shall comply with the wishes of the depositor, except when impracticable or inconvenient to do so. . . .

. . . SEC. 3547. To secure a due conformity in the gold and silver coins to their respective standards of fineness and weight, the judge of the district court for the eastern district of Pennsylvania, the Comptroller of the Currency, the assayer of the assay-office at New York, and such other persons as the President shall, from time to time, designate, shall meet as assay-commissioners, at the mint in Philadelphia, to examine and test, in the presence of the Director of the Mint, the fineness and weight of the coins reserved by the several mints for this purpose, on the second Wednesday in February, annually, and may continue their meeting by adjournment, if necessary. If a majority of the commissioners fail to attend at any time appointed for their meeting, the Director of the Mint shall call a meeting of the commissioners at such other time as he may deem convenient. If it appears by such examination and test that these coins do not differ from the standard fineness and weight by a greater quantity than is allowed by law, the trial shall be considered and reported as satisfactory. If, however, any greater deviation from the legal standard or weight appears, this fact shall be certified to the President; and if, on a view of the circumstances of the case, he shall so decide, the officers implicated in the error shall be thenceforward disqualified from holding their respective offices.

SEC. 3548. For the purpose of securing a due conformity in weight of the coins of the United States to the provisions of this Title, the brass troy-pound weight procured by the minister of the United States at London, in the year eighteen hundred and twenty-seven, for the use of the Mint, and now in the custody of the mint in Philadelphia, shall be the standard troy pound of the Mint of the United States, conformably to which the coinage thereof shall be regulated.

SEC. 3549. It shall be the duty of the Director of the Mint to procure for each mint and assay-office, to be kept safely thereat, a series of standard weights, corresponding to the standard troy pound of the Mint of the United States, consisting of a one-pound weight and the requisite subdivisions and multiples thereof, from the hundredth part of a grain to twenty-five pounds. The troy weight ordinarily employed in the transaction of such mints and assay-offices shall be regulated according to the above standards at least once in every year, under the inspection of the superintendent and assayer; and the accuracy of those used at the mint at Philadelphia shall be tested annually, in the presence of the assay-commissioners, at the time of the annual examination and test of coins.

SEC. 3550. The obverse working dies at each mint shall, at the end of each calendar year, be defaced and destroyed by the coiner in the presence of the superintendent and assayer. . . .

. . . SEC. 3558. The business of the mint of the United States at Denver, while conducted as an assay-office, that of the United States assay-office at Boise City, and that of any other assay-offices hereafter established, shall be confined to the receipt of gold and silver bullion, for melting and assaying, to be returned to depositors of the same, in bars, with the weight and fineness stamped thereon.

SEC. 3559. The officers of the assay-offices embraced by the preceding section shall be, when their respective services are required, an assayer and a melter; each of whom shall be appointed by the President, by and with the advice and consent of the Senate. Their salaries shall not exceed two thousand five hundred dollars a year each.

SEC. 3560. The assayer at each of the assay-offices embraced by section thirty-five hundred and fifty-eight, shall have general charge of the office; and may employ, under the direction of the Director of the Mint, such clerks, workmen, and laborers as may be authorized therefor by law; and shall discharge the duties of disbursing agent for the expenses of the office under his charge. The salaries paid to clerks shall not exceed one thousand eight hundred dollars a year each. Workmen and laborers shall receive such wages as are customary according to their respective stations and occupations.

SEC. 3561. Each officer and clerk appointed at either of the assay-offices embraced by section thirty-five hundred and fifty-eight shall, before entering upon the duties of his office, take an oath pursuant to the provisions of Title XIX, "PROVISIONS APPLYING TO SEVERAL CLASSES OF OFFICERS," and shall give a bond to the United States, with one or more sureties, satisfactory to the Director of the Mint or to one of the judges of the supreme court of the State or Territory in which the office to which he is appointed is located, conditioned for the faithful performance of his duties.

SEC. 3562. All provisions of law for the regulation of mints, the government of officers and persons employed therein, and for the punishment of all offenses connected with mints or coinage, shall extend to all assay-offices as far as applicable.

SEC. 3563. The money of account of the United States shall be expressed in dollars or units, dimes or tenths, cents, or hundredths, and mills or thousandths, a dime being the tenth part of a dollar, a cent the hundredth part of a dollar, a mill the thousandth part of a dollar; and all accounts in the public offices and all proceedings in the courts shall be kept and had in conformity to this regulation.

SEC. 3564. The value of foreign coin as expressed in the money of account of the United States shall be that of the pure metal of such coin of standard value; and the values of the standard coins in circulation of the various nations of the world shall be estimated annually by the Director of the Mint, and be proclaimed on the first day of January by the Secretary of the Treasury. . . .

. . . SEC. 3586. The silver coins of the United States shall be a legal tender at their nominal value for any amount not exceeding five dollars in any one payment. . . .

Resources

Comprehensive Catalogue and Encyclopedia of U.S. Morgan and Peace Silver Dollars by Leroy C. Van Allen and A. George Mallis, FCI, New York.

Coinage Laws of the United States 1792-1894, Foreword by David L. Ganz. Wolfeboro, New Hampshire: 1991 Bowers and Merena Galleries, Inc.

Grant Smith, *The History of the Comstock Lode (1850-1920)*, Reno, Nevada: Nevada Bureau of Mines and Geology, Mackay School of Mines, University of Nevada

History of the United States Mint and Coinage, George C. Evans, Various Editions

Howard Hickson, *Mint Mark: "CC" The Story of the United States Mint at Carson City, Nevada*, Carson City, Nevada: 1990, The Nevada State Museum

Original Coin Press No. 1, history posted on site at the Nevada State Museum, Carson City, Nevada

TABLE 1
ORIGINAL GSA HOLDINGS FOR SALE

YEAR	UNC. CC	MIXED CC	MIXED UNC.	MIXED CIRC.	UNSALEABLE	UNC. COINS OUT (1975)	TOTAL
1878 CC	47,566			13,426*		1	60,993
1879 CC	3,632	490				1	4,123
1880 CC	114,941	16,587				1	131,529
1881 CC	122,708	24,776				1	147,485
1882 CC	382,912	222,116				1	605,029
1883 CC	523,852	231,665				1	755,518
1884 CC	788,627	174,008				3	962,638
1885 CC	130,822	17,462				1	148,285
1889 CC		1					1
1890 CC	3,609	339				1	3,949
1891 CC	5,176	510				1	5,687
1892 CC		1					1
1893 CC		1					1
Various			27,980				27,980
P,O,S Various				84,165	311		84,476
TOTALS	2,123,845	687,956	27,980	97,591	311	12	2,937,695

* Culled

TABLE 2
GSA CARSON CITY SILVER DOLLAR CATEGORIES

CC YEAR	UNC.	SCRATCHED/ TARNISHED	COM- BINED	REJECTS/ ERRORS	UNC. OVER- DATES	TARNISHED OVER- DATES	% MIXED CC	% MIXED CIRC.	% TOTAL MINTED
1878	47,567		13,426					14	2.7
1879	3,633		490				.07		.5
1880	114,942	12,087		4,500	(45,000)	(5,000)	2.41		22.1
1881	122,709	16,776		8,000			3.60		49.6
1882	382,913	216,116		6,000			32.29		44.6
1883	523,853	221,665		10,000			33.67		62.7
1884	788,630	159,008		15,000			25.29		84.6
1885	130,823	11,462		6,000			2.54		64.9
1890	3,610	325		14			.05		.1
1891	5,177	423		87			.08		.3

TABLE 3
GSA DOLLAR SALES

YEAR	MIN BID	OCT. 72 MAR.73	JUN.73 JUL.73	OCT. 73	FEB. 74	APR. 74 JUNE 74	TOTAL UNC & MIXED SOLD	TOTAL UNC & MIXED REMAINING	TOTAL MIXED CC 2nd&5th SALES	MIXED CC REMAIN- ING
1878 CC	15		47,564				47,564	3		
1879 CC	300				3,608		3,608	25	249	241
1880 CC	60			73,856		36,803	110,659	4,283	8,444	8,143
1881 CC	60			70,865		32,824	103,689	19,020	12,610	12,166
1882 CC	30	291,494	55,697			35,689	382,880	33	127,425	94,691
1883 CC	30	257,391	40,391			30,323	328,105	195,748	133,853	97,812
1884 CC	30	267,733	64,384			28,358	360,475	428,155	98,765	75,243
1885 CC	60			67,782		31,472	99,254	31,569	7,166	10,296
1889 CC										1
1890 CC	30		3,589				3,589	21	207	132
1891 CC	30		5,158				5,158	19	262	248
1892 CC										1
1893 CC										1
Mixed CC	15		170,299			218,682	388,981	298,975		
Mixed Unc	5		27,946				27,946	34		
Mixed Circ*	3		97,559				97,599	32		
TOTALS		816,618	512,587	212,503	3,608	414,151	1,959,467	977,905	388,981	298,975

* Includes 13,426 tarnished/scratched/error 1878CC

** Table 1, 2 and 3 charts are courtesy of Leroy Van Allen and A. George Mallis from their "*Encyclopedia of U. S. Morgan and Peace Silver Dollars*"

***

William E. Spears

William E. Spears is president of William E. Spears Investment Quality Coins, Inc., with offices in Naples, Florida and Seattle, Washington.

Bill has been a rare coin broker and numismatist since 1962. He first became fascinated with Carson City silver dollars in 1976 when he found an 1879-CC in a slot machine at Harrah's Casino in South Lake Tahoe, Nevada. After a fifteen year effort, Bill succeeded in assembling the consensus finest known Carson City Morgan silver dollar set. Each coin in the set has been the highest grades given by PCGS and in many cases is the only one assigned that grade, making this set truly unique. The set was included in its entirety in the 1990/1991 PCGS "World's Finest Morgan Silver Dollars" Tour.

Bill is a member or life member of many numismatic organizations including:

Professional Coin Grading Service — Authorized Dealer since 1986 (PCGS)
American Numismatic Association (ANA) — Life Member
American Numismatic Exchange (ANE)
Central States Numismatic Society (CSNS)
Certified Coin Exchange (CCE)
Florida United Numismatists (FUN)
Hawaii State Numismatic Association (HSNA)
National Silver Dollar Roundtable (NSDR)
Numismatic Guarantee Corp. — Associate Dealer (NGC)
Pacific Northwest Coin Dealers Association (PNCDA)
Pacific Northwest Numismatic Association (PNNA)
Society for U.S. Commemorative Coins — Life Member

Bill's hobbies include golf and collecting antique carousel animals.

CHAPTER 12

The Mystique of the Carson City Silver Dollar

by William E. Spears

Carson City (CC) Morgan silver dollars have been a favorite coin of collectors and investors for decades. The popularity can be attributed to the old west history of the CC dollar, or the unique double mint mark, or low mintages, or to the short series of 13 years. Whatever the reason, everyone agrees the CC Morgan silver dollar has a mystique that makes it special.

Carson City (the state capital of Nevada) is located only 15 miles from historic Virginia City, the site of the famous Comstock silver lode, which eventually played a major role in the production of Morgan silver dollars.

The Carson City Mint was opened July 1, 1869, and struck its first coins February 10, 1870: 3,747 silver dollars. Silver dollars with the CC mint mark were struck through 1885 and again from 1889 through 1893. The Carson City Mint struck its last coin in 1893 and was officially changed to an Assay Office on July 1, 1899 — exactly 30 years after it had opened as a branch mint. The old Carson City Mint is now the Nevada State Museum.

There was a long history of political skulduggery that led to passage of the Bland-Allison Act and the coining of Morgan silver dollars. Only those events that pertain to the Carson City Mint will be reviewed in this chapter.

The Bland-Allison Act was the result of political manipulation by western silver mine owners to combat falling silver prices by making the mint into a captive market paying inflated subsidy prices for domestic silver. This price decline was due to foreign powers dumping thousands of tons of silver on the world market, combined with the discovery of enormous quantities of silver deposits in Nevada (the famed Comstock Lode was only one of many). The Act forced the United States Treasury to buy huge amounts of new domestic silver to be used exclusively for mintage into silver dollars, and it mandated that the four U.S. mints produce a minimum of two million silver dollars per month. The Carson City, Philadelphia, and San Francisco mints started production of Morgan silver dollars in 1878, and New Orleans began in 1879.

Even though the Carson City Mint was located near the great Nevada silver lodes, it had a shortage of silver bullion during each year of production. This lack of silver accounted for the relatively low mintages of CC Morgan silver dollars, as most of the Nevada silver lode bullion used for coinage was shipped to other mints. The Carson City Mint was the smallest of the four mints. Of the two million coins (aggregate) required by law to be minted each month by all four mints, the Carson City Mint averaged only 84,000 per month. The other three mints produced the remaining 1.9 million each month. Carson City accounted for only 13.8 million of the 321.9 million coins produced by all mints for the periods 1878-1885 and 1889-1893. This amounts to only 4.3 percent of the total.

Mintages for each year the Carson City Mint produced Morgan silver dollars are as follows:

YEAR	MINTAGE	OBVERSE *	REVERSE *
1878-CC	2,212,000	30	30
1879-CC	756,000	N/A	N/A
1880-CC	591,000	N/A	N/A
1881-CC	296,000	25	25**
1882-CC	1,133,000	15	15
1883-CC	1,204,000	10	10
1884-CC	1,136,000	10	10
1885-CC	228,000	10	10**
1889-CC	350,000	10	7**
1890-CC	2,309,041	N/A	16
1891-CC	1,618,000	24	23
1892-CC	1,352,000	10	10
1893-CC	677,000	N/A	N/A
Total CC Morgan silver dollars			13,862,041

* According to Walter Breen the above numbers are the die totals for the coin date year, not for the fiscal year.

** Not all these dies were used.

Carson City Morgan dollars exhibit strong strikes for most issues. This condition is credited to the Carson City Mint having new and well-repaired Morgan and Orr presses. According to Wayne Miller in his book, *The Morgan and Peace Dollar Textbook*, the Carson City Mint struck an average of slightly more than 60,000 coins per working die pair, the San Francisco Mint approximately 120,000, New Orleans Mint over 150,000, and the Philadelphia Mint over 200,000.

Even though Morgan silver dollars were being minted in massive numbers, they were unpopular with the general public and most were subsequently shipped to the U.S. Treasury for storage. Carson City dollars were transported by horse drawn cart over 30 miles of dirt roads form the Mint to the railway station at Reno for shipment eastward to the Treasury vaults. The constant jostling in the horse drawn carts, railroad boxcars, and rough handling by Treasury employees undoubtedly account for the severe bag marks that plague most CC Morgan dollars. In the 1950s and 1960s many silver dollar bags stored in the Treasury vaults were reportedly moved about with fork lifts, sometimes with the forks penetrating the bags and thus further damaging the stored coins.

Most rarities in Morgan silver dollars are due to wholesale meltings by the government rather than low mintages. This is especially true of CC silver dollars. According to government records, over 333 million silver dollars were melted by the Treasury Department between 1883 and 1964. The Pittman Act of 1918 resulted in the melting of over 270 million silver dollars; another 52 million were melted during World War II. Additionally, when silver bullion prices climbed to over $50 an ounce in 1980, many more millions were privately melted as each silver dollar's value soared to over 36 times face value. The Treasury did not keep records of dates or mint marks which were melted. Selection of coins for melting was apparently random and was evidently dictated only by where they happened to be stored in the Treasury vaults. Subsequently, practically the entire mintage of some dates were melted. The 1895 (non-proof) Philadelphia issue is an excellent example, as Mint records indicate 12,000 coins were struck, but, to date, none have surfaced.

Morgan Silver Dollars were never popular during their years of production (1878-1904 and 1921) and were in demand only by a few sparsely populated western states. Since demand was low, thousands of mint-sealed bags of silver dollars were available to the general public at face value, but few were sold until the late 1950s. From 1960 through 1964, however, the Treasury's stock of Morgan dollars was nearly depleted in what was to be known as the **"great silver dollar rush."**

Several factors were attributed to this frantic effort to obtain silver dollars. Silver prices rose in 1960 to the point where it became profitable to melt down silver dollars for their silver content. Bags could still be bought at face value from the Treasury until March 1964. Several newspapers published articles about the diminishing supplies of silver dollars and predicted that they would soon disappear forever. These factors caused long lines of people, anxious to obtain silver dollars while they lasted, to form at the Treasury offices. According to Walter Breen in *The Complete Encyclopaedia of U.S. and Colonial Coins*, over 152 million silver dollars were dispersed by the Treasury between January 1960 and January 1964. Publicity about rare coins being obtained at face value from the Treasury prompted a government inventory. The audit revealed almost three million Carson City dollars of considerable numismatic value in the Treasury vaults. The Treasury halted public silver dollar sales in March 1964.

In 1970, President Nixon signed a bill authorizing the General Services Administration (GSA) to sell the remaining CC dollars to the public via mail bid sales. The CC dollars were segregated into two categories by GSA sorters, then sealed individually in an airtight "GSA holder." The GSA sorters were government employees, instructed by a panel of well known numismatists on what type of coin to place in each category. One category was "uncirculated", which was deemed by the sorters to be bright, uncirculated, and undamaged coins. This category of coins was placed in a holder marked "Uncirculated Silver Dollar" and sold for a premium. The second category, "Mixed CC", designated coins considered to be tarnished, circulated, or damaged. These were considered inferior and were placed in holders simply marked "Silver Dollar."

Over the years, some very interesting coins have been found among the coins originally rejected as "inferior." For example, an 1885-CC surfaced at the San Diego coin show in 1985 and immediately traded hands among dealers six times, with an eventual selling price several years later of $10,000. The coin was subsequently graded MS-67 by the Professional Coin Grading Service and is part of the consensus Finest Known Carson City Silver Dollar Set.

The GSA held a series of seven mail bid sales to liquidate the 2,937,965 CC dollars released from the Treasury. The first five sales took place from October 1972 through June 1974. Two additional sales in 1980 disposed of the rest of the Treasury hoard of CC dollars. The nearly three million coins realized over $94,000,000 in sales.

The following chart indicates the distribution of the CC dollars liquidated in the seven GSA sales:

DATE	MINTAGE	GSA HOLDINGS	GSA% of ALL MINTED
1878-CC	2,212,000	60,993	2.75%
1879-CC	756,000	4,123	.55%
1880-CC	591,000	131,529	22.25%
1881-CC	296,000	147,485	49.82%
1882-CC	1,133,000	605,029	53.40%
1883-CC	1,204,000	755,518	62.75%
1884-CC	1,136,000	962,638	84.73%
1885-CC	228,000	148,285	65.03%
1889-CC	350,000	1	.00028%
1890-CC	2,309,041	3,949	.17%
1891-CC	1,618,000	5,687	.35%
1892-CC	1,352,000	1	.00007%
1893-CC	677,000	1	.00014%
Culls and mixed circulated		84,165	
Unsalable CCs		311	
Total Mintage	13,862,041	2,909,715 *	

* The total coins sold was equal to 21% of the total CC mintage. There were 27,980 mixed non-CC dates not included in this total.

The number of coins found in the Treasury hoard affected the rarity of several dates significantly. It contained half or more of the CC coins minted from 1881 through 1885. The number of 1884-CC coins in the hoard consisted of over 84% of the total minted, and literally all of those were uncirculated. This date was considered very scarce and had carried a significant premium before the disclosure of the Treasury hoard of CC dollars. After the sale, the 1884-CC was relegated to the ranks of a semi-common date. The other dates with significant numbers in the GSA sales also had their relative rarity affected. The 1881-CC had nearly 50% of those minted in the sale, and the 1882-CC had 53% of its total mintage included. The 1883-CC and 1885-CC had almost 63% and 65%, respectively, of their total mintages offered in the sale.

Some dates that were very scarce or rare before the GSA sale remained so afterwards. The 1879-CC, and 1889-CC through 1893-CC, had minuscule percentages of their total mintage in the sale. The 1879-CC, 1890-CC and 1891-CC each had significantly less than 1% of their respective mintages offered. These dates were considered scarce before and after the GSA sale. The 1889-CC, 1892-CC and 1893-CC each had only one coin in the entire Carson City Treasury hoard. The 1892-CC remained scarce whereas the 1889-CC and 1893-CC confirmed everyone's belief that these two dates are truly rare in uncirculated condition. There is no confirmation that the single 1889-CC, 1892-CC, and 1893-CC coins delivered in the 1980 GSA sales have ever surfaced again.

Luster on CC Morgan dollars, on the average, is very good with very bright, frosty surfaces. The earlier years (1878-1885) are generally more lustrous than their later counterparts (1889-1893) which are frosty, but somewhat less brilliant in appearance. The strike on CC Morgan dollars varies significantly from date to date, even within certain dates. Most CCs have strong strikes with excellent high point detail in the hair over Liberty's ear and on the eagle's breast.

Bag marks on most CC Morgan dollars are severe and make finding a gem coin in some dates extremely difficult. The main focal point on a CC Morgan dollar — Liberty's cheek— generally has many more marks than other Morgan dollar issues. The same holds true for the reverse of most CC dollars, as the eagle's breast and surrounding fields are usually heavily abraded. The major cause is most likely due to mishandling during transportation to and storage at the U.S. Treasury.

Overall, most uncirculated CC Morgan dollars are lustrous and well struck, but very heavily bagmarked. Lower grade uncirculated pieces are plentiful in most dates, but gem specimens (MS-65 and above) are scarce. Even though huge quantities of CC dollars were released in the GSA sales, the majority have been found to be excessively bagmarked.

The following date-by-date summary is based on personal observations over the past 15 years while assembling numerous high quality Carson City Morgan dollar collections. The summary contains a brief description of each date by typical luster, characteristic strike, frequency of bag marks, and investment potential based on current price structure (early 1991). Also included is the Professional Coin Grading Service (PCGS) population of each coin in MS-65 and above. PCGS has proved to be a viable grading standard throughout the coin industry and is accepted nationwide by the majority of dealers, collectors, and investors. The PCGS Population Report, published monthly by PCGS, is considered by many dealers as an invaluable tool in determining scarcity of many coins. PCGS population references are based on the January 1991 PCGS Population Report.

1878-CC

The 1878-CC has good luster, is well struck, relatively heavy bag marks, has the flat breast reverse, and a small CC mint mark. One of the more popular CCs since it is the first year of issue. Excellent investment potential in MS-65 through MS-67 due to low PCGS populations and affordability in MS-65. The 1878-CC is one of the best CC dollar investment dates, second only to the 1890-CC in potential.

Mintage:	2,212,000
PCGS population:	MS-65 = 286
	MS-66 = 24
	MS-67 = 1

1879-CC

The 1879-CC has average luster, a fair strike, and is very heavily bag marked. The latter condition makes this a very difficult date to obtain in MS-65 or better condition. This is an excellent investment coin due to its rarity in MS-65 condition and relatively low cost in relation to its rarity. In my opinion this is one of the four best CC dollar investments.

Mintage:	756,000
PCGS population:	MS-65 = 11, none higher

1879-CC Capped Die Variety

The 1879-CC Capped Die has average to good luster, below average strike, and is very heavily bag marked. In 1879 the decision was made to enlarge the mint mark on the CC Morgan dollar. A couple of dies had already been prepared with the smaller mint mark, and, rather than discard them, the dies were reworked. This was done by attempting to remove the smaller CC with engraving tools and repunching the larger CC over them. As if that were not enough the die severely rusted before use. This unattractive reverse is known as the "Capped CC" or "Capped Die" variety. In the days before PCGS, the capped die brought 50% less than the normal CC. In early 1989, when it became apparent that the capped die variety was very rare in MS-65, the price escalated dramatically. In their first five years of grading, only one coin has been graded MS-65 by PCGS, with none higher. This variety in MS-65 now commands a premium of 300 to 500 percent over the regular CC mint mark.

This is an excellent investment coin due to its extreme rarity in MS-65.

Mintage:	Over 80,000 (estimated, included above)
PCGS population:	MS-65 = 1, none higher

1880-CC

The 1880-CC has average to good luster, poor to average strike, and few bag marks. 1880-CC Morgans can often be very pleasing coins if those with the right combination of luster and strike can be located. Many have a mellow, light golden patina that gives them a soft satiny look that is unique to this date. Some 1880-CCs can be found well struck.

The 1880-CC is another date with good investment potential in MS-66 and MS-67 due to pleasing appearance and moderately low PCGS population.

Mintage:	591,000
PCGS population:	MS-65 = 433
	MS-66 = 36
	MS-67 = 6

1880-CC Reverse of 1878 (Flat Breast) Variety

The 1880-CC Reverse of 1878 has average luster, average strike, and a few more bag marks than the normal 1880-CC. In 1880, the Carson City Mint appeared to have several defective dies (as is evidenced by the poor strikes) and decided to use some of the leftover 1878 reverse dies. The result was an 1880-CC variety with a somewhat normal appearing 1880 dated obverse, but with a reverse the same as that used in 1878 with the flat breast (concave rather than convex) eagle and a small CC mint mark. Leroy Van Allen lists up to three and Walter Breen states that two dies were used to make this variety.

Good investment potential in MS-65 and MS-66 due to moderate to low PCGS population.

Mintage:	60,000 (estimated)
PCGS population:	MS-65 = 78
	MS-66 = 6

1881-CC

The 1881-CC has exceptional luster, a very strong strike, and is often found with minimal bag marks. This date is overall the prettiest and most eye appealing Carson City issue. It is also one of the most common, despite its low mintage. Even though, at 296,000, the 1881-CC ranks as the fourth lowest mintage dollar, it is very common in uncirculated condition. This is due to the large numbers found in the Treasury vaults in early 1972. Almost half of the entire mintage was sold in the GSA sale in uncirculated condition.

This coin has average investment potential. PCGS populations are high in MS-65 and above. The beauty of this coin, however, combined with the deceptively low mintage numbers, make it a popular coin.

Mintage:	296,000
PCGS population:	MS-65 = 1,092
	MS-66 = 149
	MS-67 = 9

1882-CC

The 1882-CC has very good luster, is well struck, and has fewer than normal bagmarks. This coin is considered one of the five common date CC dollars (1881-CC through 1885-CC) in uncirculated condition. Over 53% of the total mintage was contained in the Treasury hoard. This date has only average investment potential due to relatively large PCGS population in MS-65 and MS-66.

Mintage:	1,133,000
PCGS population:	MS-65 = 1,100
	MS-66 = 127
	MS-67 = 3

1883-CC

Excellent luster, a strong strike, and fewer than normal bag marks are typical of the 1883-CC. This is the most common of the CC dollars and is easily found in MS-65 and MS-66 grades. Almost 63% of the 1883-CC total mintage was found in the Treasury hoard.

This date has only average investment potential due to its easy availability in higher grades.

Mintage:	1,204,000
PCGS population:	MS-65 = 1,971
	MS-66 = 198
	MS-67 = 3
	MS-68 = 1

1885-CC

The 1885-CC luster is excellent, the strike is very strong and the issue has a higher than average amount of bag marks. Many consider this the second nicest date, in overall appearance, behind the 1881-CC. Even though this is the lowest mintage CC dollar and the third lowest mintage Morgan silver dollar of all dates, it is relatively common in uncirculated condition. Sixty five percent of the total 1885-CC mintage was released in the GSA sale.

This coin has a slightly better than average investment potential, as PCGS populations in MS-65 and MS-66 are somewhat lower than the other "common year" CC dates. The 1885-CC is a popular year due to its low mintage.

Mintage:	228,000
PCGS population:	MS-65 = 888
	MS-66 = 127
	MS-67 = 10
	MS-68 = 1

1889-CC

After a brief hiatus of three years (1886-1888), the Carson City Mint resumed minting the CC dollar. It appears that many of the 1889-CC Morgans were released into circulation shortly after minting. The remainder that were sent to the Treasury vaults were undoubtedly lost in one of the great silver dollar melts. Only one 1889-CC was found in the Treasury hoard and offered in the GSA sales. As of 1991, it has not surfaced in private hands.

Luster on the 1889-CC is generally poor, the strike varies from weak to strong, and bag marks are very heavy. Those specimens without excessive bag marks have a washed out appearance (possibly from overdipping?), thus keeping them from gem status. This date is exceedingly rare in gem condition. As of the end of 1990, only one 1889-CC has been graded MS-65 by PCGS, with none higher. This particular coin was sold by John Love to a collector in 1962 and then repurchased in 1989. It was then sold via Dwight Manley, Jack Hertzburg, and Bruce Amspacher to Bill Spears at the 1989 ANA show in Pittsburgh, Pennsylvania. It is virtually mark-free, well struck (for an 1889-CC), and has only slightly subdued luster. Every knowledgeable dealer who has seen it has agreed that it is a true gem. It was placed in the 1990/1991 PCGS World's Finest Morgan Silver Dollar Tour.

The 1889-CC is an excellent investment due to its true rarity and low PCGS population. The only drawback is its extremely high cost which places it in a category with few potential buyers.

Mintage:	350,000
PCGS population:	MS-65 = 1, none higher

1890-CC

The 1890-CC has the highest mintage of all Carson City dollars. The 1890-CC is one of the easiest to find in circulated condition. The Treasury hoard/GSA sale only contained 3,949 1890-CC dollars in uncirculated condition which is less than two tenths of one percent of the total mintage. The luster on an 1890-CC is generally very good, the strike is usually strong, and bag marks are worse than average. The 1890-CC is a highly underrated coin in gem condition, as most uncirculated specimens are heavily bagmarked. PCGS, as of the beginning of 1991, had only graded 45 coins MS-65 with 3 higher. I consider this date to have the best investment potential of all the Carson City dollars.

Mintage:	2,309,041
PCGS population:	MS-65 = 45
	MS-66 = 3

1891-CC

The luster on an 1891-CC is excellent, the strike is usually strong, while bag marks are generally heavy. This is another CC date that was not found in large quantities in the Treasury hoard/GSA sale. Only 5,687 uncirculated pieces were found in the Treasury vaults. This amounted to slightly less than four tenths of one percent of the total mintage. This date is also one of the better investment dates in the series.

Mintage:	1,618,000
PCGS population:	MS-65 = 103
	MS-66 = 9
	MS-67 = 1

1892-CC

Luster on the 1892-CC is very good, the strike is usually strong and bag marks are heavy. This date is scarce in both circulated and uncirculated condition. There was only one 1892-CC found in the Treasury vaults. Evidently, 1892-CCs were one of the dates lost in the great silver dollar melts.

The 1892-CC rates in the top three affordable dates along with the 1890-CC and 1878-CC in investment potential.

Mintage:	1,352,000
PCGS population:	MS-65 = 66
	MS-66 = 5
	MS-67 = 1

1893-CC

The 1893-CC has average luster, most are poorly struck, and the majority are heavily bag marked. Like the 1879-CC and 1889-CC, the 1893-CC is extremely difficult to find in MS-65 or better. Only one 1893-CC was found in the Treasury hoard and was reported to be sold in the 1980 GSA sale. It has not surfaced as of this writing. Like the 1889-CC, the 1893-CC is an excellent investment due to its rarity and low PCGS population. It also carries a high price tag.

Mintage:	677,000
PCGS population:	MS-65 = 2, none higher

1900-O/CC

Although the 1900-O/CC was not minted at the Carson City Mint, it is considered by most collectors as a CC die variety and is included in many Carson City silver dollar collections. When the Carson City Mint closed in 1899, all equipment, including unused working dies, were sent to the Philadelphia Mint. In 1900, the New Orleans Mint requested more working dies. Several of the returned CC reverse dies were reworked (at the Philadelphia Mint) by imperfectly covering over the CC mint mark and repunching an O mint mark. According to Van Allen/Mallis, up to six different dies were reworked, all of which show the remains of one or both of the lower hooks of the CC mint mark. The dies were shipped to New Orleans for use in striking 1900-O series. The luster on a 1900-O/CC is generally very good, and bag marks are above average in severity. The strike is generally poor and has the typical New Orleans metal flow problems. Occasionally, a fully struck 1900-O/CC is encountered, but this is the exception. Investment potential of this date is very good, as it is popular with CC collectors and variety collectors. Gem examples of the 1900-O/CC are very scarce.

Mintage:	120,000 (estimated)
PCGS population:	MS-65 = 78
	MS-66 = 7

References:

Walter Breen, *Complete Encyclopedia of U.S. and Colonial Coins*
Wayne Miller, The *Morgan and Peace Dollar Textbook*
Leroy Van Allen and A. George Mallis, The *Comprehensive Catalogue and Encyclopedia of U.S. Morgan and Peace Silver Dollars*
Coin World Accounts of the GSA Sale, 1980
PCGS Population Report, January 1991

The Bland-Allison Act forced the production of millions of unneeded silver dollars including these Carson City silver dollars from the General Services Adminstration's sales of the 1970s and '80s.
(Courtesy of Bob Wilhite c/o Numismatic News, Iola, Wisconsin)

***

CHAPTER 13

The Redfield Hoard

by John W. Highfill, NLG

Listen my friends and you will hear
Of the Redfield hoard and the man named LaVere.
I've told it before and I'll tell it again,
For he was among the strangest of men.

He moved into Reno and purchased a farm;
No one paid attention, he did them no harm.
But he made a few friends in the banks all around,
And some tell of seeing him drive into town.

He would stop at a bank and pick up a bag,
And would toss it around like an old rotten rag.
They heard he trucked home alone with his loot,
Stashed in his basement, thrown right down the chute.

When he finally passed on in seventy-four,
The government poked around looking for more.
And what to their wondering eyes should appear
But a great hoard of dollars, from the man named LaVere!
— John English

The story of the Redfield hoard is the stuff of legend.

LaVere Redfield was a self-made man, who made his pile in oil and stocks. He lived in Los Angeles while accumulating his multimillions. When he decided to leave the world of big business in the 1930s, he moved to a large farm near Reno, Nevada. His neighbors say that Redfield enjoyed farm life, and was often seen driving his old truck around town with produce for local markets. He also invested in Nevada real estate.

His life as an inconspicuous Nevada farmer rather than a Los Angeles financier may have derived from his distrust of governments and political organizations generally; he once went to jail to avoid paying taxes. This attitude led him to hoard not paper money (government's promises to pay in silver) but silver dollars themselves: hard money with no strings attached, no paper trails. This is not the caring attitude of a collector, but the bullion-hungry attitude of a hoarder.

To feed his addiction, he befriended several people who worked for local banks. They would tell him whenever bags of silver dollars showed up. Redfield would head for the bank in his old pickup truck, buy the bags at face value, cart them home and throw them down the chute into his basement, inflicting nicks and scratches. John Love tells a story about how cans of peaches in Redfield's basement exploded, spraying corrosive acids which ate into some bags and stained the contents.

At its height, the Redfield hoard probably contained over 600 bags — over 600,000 silver dollars. About 100 bags were taken in a robbery in the early 1960s. This crime was never solved; most likely the thieves spent the dollars in the casinos of Reno and Las Vegas.

Redfield apparently sold a few bags in the early 1970s. John Love reported buying some 1925-S Redfield dollars through the Reno dealer Dean Jones, who was a friend of Redfield's and who had accompanied him on some of his bag-buying expeditions. Love was negotiating for a bag of 1893-P's when Redfield died (1974).

An IRS agent found the hoard shortly after Redfield's death, with a note addressed to relatives, admonishing them to make sure that the coins were kept out of reach of tax agents.

As part of Redfield's $200 million estate, the coins were inventoried and appraised by Stack's, who then submitted a bid for the entire lot. Most probably the inventory was only partial; there would not have been time for any coin firm to do a thorough job on over 400,000 silver dollars.

But instead of accepting Stack's or subsequent bids, authorities held a courtroom auction, January 27, 1976, without disclosing the full contents of the hoard. Knowing only that it contained 407,596 pieces, Bowers & Ruddy bid $7.2 million; Steve Markoff, who knew some more details but not all, won the hoard at $7.3 million — about $18 per coin.

Out of the 407,596 Redfield dollars, supposedly 351,259 were later graded Unc. In a brilliant marketing campaign covering three years, Markoff distributed the coins through Robert Hughes, John Love, and Paramount International Coin Corporation. The campaign generated enough public interest in silver dollars that many prices rose. Part of the collector excitement was stimulated by appearance of new gem and prooflike coins.

Though no complete list of Redfield dollars was ever published, we know most of the dates and mintmarks in the hoard: see chart below. Most of this information came from advertisements by the dealers distributing Redfield coins.

MS60 Silver Dollar from the Redfield Collection
(Courtesy Paramount International Coin Corporation)

Morgan Dollars				Peace
1878-S	1887-S	1891-CC	1897-S	1922-S
1879-S*	1888-S	1892	1898	1923-S
1879-CC	1889#	1892-CC	1898-S	1924-S
1880-S	1889-S	1893	1899-S	1925-S
1881-S	1890	1893-CC	1900-S	1926-S
1882-S	1890-S	1895-S	1902-S	1927-S
1883-S	1890-CC	1896	1903	1928-S
1885-CC	1891#	1896-S	1921-S#	1935-S
1886-S	1891-S	1897		

* Included some 7 TF PAF.
\# Very limited quantities.

The consensus of knowledgeable dealers is that no other Redfield dates are around in any quantity and that the hoard has been completely distributed.

John Love tells that after A-Mark invited him to take part in the distribution, he handled over 100 bags of 1896-98 Philadelphia Morgans. Wayne Miller bought about 50 Redfield bags from Love, and found that the quality was generally high with problems in some dates. Many were heavily bagmarked; among these, 1878-S, 1887-S, 1891-S and 1898 dollars were very dirty. Some Morgans (notably 1892 and 1897) were poorly struck and badly scratched, as were most of the Peace dollars. Many prooflike specimens of 1888-S, 1891-S and 1897-S had gray spots. Were these among the peach juice coins? Other dealers and collectors reported bad scratches on faces and wings. These are blamed on a counting machine which may have been used during initial inspection and inventory. The dates affected are 1893-CC, 1895-S, 1926-S and 1928-S.

The ten Morgan dates and four Peace dates represented in the largest quantities in the Redfield hoard are, in descending order:

Morgan	Peace
1881-S	1922-S
1880-S	1923-S
1879-S	1926-S
1878-S	1935-S
1882-S	
1896	
1898	
1891-S	
1897-S	
1890-S	

At the other end, the verified Redfield dates represented in the smallest quantities are, in ascending order:

Morgan	Peace
1879-CC	1924-S
1895-S	1925-S
1893	1927-S
1892	1928-S
1891-CC	
1885-CC	

A date-by-date analysis follows.

1878-S Fourth commonest in the hoard. Uncs., prooflike or not, took the prize for poorest quality. Most were heavily bagmarked.

1879-S Concave Breast, 7 TF PAF. Two (possibly 3) bags; these went via Paramount to Leon Hendrickson (Silver Towne). All sold out quickly, despite heavy bagmarks. To date over half are still raw.

1879-S Round Breast 7 TF SAF. Third commonest in the hoard. Most of the bags went via Paramount. These too sold out quickly.

1879-CC Scarcest in the hoard. About 400-500 found, up to MS 62; no profitless. All were of the "capped die" (large CC/small CC) variety.

1880-S Second commonest. Dozens of bags, mostly MS 61 to 64, a minority higher. Most went via Paramount.

1881-S Commonest. Dozens of bags ranging from MS 60 to 67.

1882-S Fifth commonest in the hoard. Mostly MS 60 - 64, perhaps 10-15% in higher grades.

1883-S At least several hundred Uncs., handled by Paramount, sold out quickly. They then graded MS 65; today, MS 60 - 63 by PCGS or NGC standard.

1885-CC Sixth scarcest in the hoard. About one bag (1,000), which sold out quickly.

1886-S Several bags, mostly grading MS 60 - 63. Primarily distributed by John Love, friend and legend. Most of the Uncs. known today come from the Redfield hoard.

1887-S Many bags, mostly grading MS 60 - 63, heavily bagmarked.

1888-S At least two bags, one containing PL's and DMPL's in MS 60 - 63, others ordinary MS 60's (not PL).

1889 Few bags, mostly MS 60's.

1889-S Supposedly 3 to 5 bags, some MS 63 - 64, others lower grade.

1890 Many bags, weak and heavily bagmarked, grading MS 60 - 61.

1890-S Tenth commonest. Multiple bags, MS 60 - 63.

1890-CC Possibly two bags, including several hundred fully struck DMPL's.

1891 One or more bags, mostly MS 60 - 61; no PL's.

1891-S Eighth commonest. Most were MS 60 - 63, many distributed by Paramount.

1891-CC Fifth scarcest. Possibly 3 to 5 bags. The coins were heavily bagmarked.

1892 Fourth scarcest. Possibly 1-2 bags. Most were MS 60 - 62, few in higher grades. No PL's Redfield's account for many of the surviving Uncs.

1892-CC Possibly 2 to 4 bags. Many grade only MS 60 - 63. Some were damaged by the coin counting machine.

1893 Third scarcest, variously estimated at from part of one bag to 2 or 3. These were marketed by Paramount and sold out quickly. This is aside from the bag Redfield was trying to sell to John Love via Dean Jones; nobody is sure what happened to these.

1893-CC Quality variable, but too many were damaged by the coin counting machine. Quantity unknown but not high.

1895-S Second scarcest; only a few hundred, again distributed by Paramount. Many of these were high quality but damaged by the coin counting machine.

1896 Sixth commonest; some say over 16 bags, others 20 to 40. Included in John Love's 100 bags of 1896-7-8 Philadelphia. Most raged MS 60 - 64.

1896-S Less than one full bag; mostly MS 60 - 63.

1897 Included in John Love's 100 bags of 1896-7-8 Philadelphia; some say 16-18 bags, others over 20. Mostly 60 - 64.

1897-S Ninth commonest; reportedly over 20 bags. Most graded MS 60 - 63, a minority higher.

1898 Seventh commonest. Some say 20 bags, others over 40. Included in John Love's 100 bags of 1896-7-8 Philadelphia. Most graded MS 60 - 64.

1898-S Reportedly less than one full bag, mostly MS 60 - 63, a minority higher, some PL.

1899-S Reportedly less than one full bag, mostly MS 60 - 63. Some PL's coming on the market at the same time may have been from Redfield.

1900-S Quantity unknown. Most were MS 60 - 63.

1902-S Reportedly only one bag, mostly MS 60 - 63.

1903 Small quantity (less than one bag?), mostly MS 60 - 63.

1921-S Reportedly only part of one bag, mostly MS 60 - 63.

1922-S Few bags, mostly weak MS 60 - 63; marketed by Paramount.

1923-S Few bags, mostly weak MS 60 - 63.

1924-S Limited quantities, mostly MS 60 - 63. Fewest Peace in hoard, by far.

1925-S Second fewest (3 to 4 bags), aside from the partial bag sold by Redfield via Dean Jones.

1926-S Multiple bags, MS 60 - 63. Much surface debris; many damaged by the coin counting machine.

1927-S Third fewest in hoard (3 to 5 bags?). Most seen were MS 60 - 63; many damaged by coin counting machine.

1928-S Fourth fewest in hoard.. Several bags (4 to 6?), lustrous but mostly weak, many damaged by coin counting machine.

1935-S Part of one bag; these sold out at once. Most were MS 60 - 63.

Even if more detailed information becomes available, or more hidden Redfield bags surface, the results are unlikely to affect the overall picture, and still less likely to affect the market. Whatever may be said about LaVere Redfield, his hoard of silver dollars has made available many dates long believed unobtainable Unc., and has made his name a permanent part of U.S. numismatics.

***

Leon E. Hendrickson

Silver Towne Coin officially began in 1949 out of a cigar case in the Rainbow Restaurant (in downtown Winchester, Indiana), which Leon Hendrickson owned at the time. It soon outgrew its humble beginnings and was moved to the Hendricksons' home in 1959 where it took over the entire basement and was still operated as a part-time business venture. In 1967 Leon decided the coin business was so demanding of his time and energy that it would be necessary to give up his other business ventures, which included the Rainbow Restaurant, a skating rink, a rural mail route and farming, to devote himself full time to the dream of building and managing one of the largest and most prestigious coin companies in the country.

Most people in the numismatic world will agree that he has succeeded beyond his wildest dreams. The business grew from a volume of $100,000 in 1966 to a whopping 30 million plus in 1967, thanks in a large degree to the silver certificate redemption program. The business was flourishing and growing beyond description, so in 1971 it was decided to enlarge the basement. This was thought to be all the room the shop would ever need. Not so — in 1979-80 came the big silver and gold boom. There were cars and truckloads of silver and gold waiting their turn to get in for as long as 4 and 5 hours. It was during this time the dollar volume on many days exceeded $10 million. It was soon obvious that larger and more efficient quarters were required for the more than 40 employees. A new dream emerged for Leon Hendrickson at this time. It was the new Silver Towne complex which now stands at the northeast end of Winchester, beyond the High School. This new multi-million dollar structure opened its doors to the first customers on March 15, 1982, after almost 2 years of planning and construction. The 12,200 square foot building houses a large modern sales and show room; adjacent to this is a jewelry sales area with a large selection of the latest styles in gold, silver and precious gems. There are also secluded buy areas and private offices. To the rear of the building is the laboratory and refining area which is devoted to the bullion department.

In addition to rare coins, jewelry and bullion, Silver Towne also has a large custom bar department. Specialty bars and commemorative medallions are minted for cities, states, civic organizations and businesses. Due to the immense growth in this area of the business, Hendrickson found it necessary in 1986 to enlarge the physical size of this department. Hendrickson bought a 1200 sq. ft. building at the end of Greenville Ave. and moved the manufacturing, smelting, and custom minting operations to this location.

During 1987, in keeping with Silver Towne's ever increasing expanding and growth policy, Hendrickson bought a refining factory in Jackson, Ohio, in partnership with John Engle, a former Winchester resident. This facility is capable of processing larger quantities of precious metals than the Winchester operation.

On the drawing board as we enter 1990 is a plan to enlarge the Jewelry Department and then we can only imagine what lies ahead and the dreams that Leon Hendrickson has for Silver Towne.

Clark A. Samuelson

Clark has been involved with numismatics on a full time basis since 1976 when he joined the numismatic division of Manfra, Tordella, and Brookes in New York City. Although involved with a variety of administrative as well as trading functions, his major focus was in the U.S. Gold coin market, concentrating on imports from a variety of European sources. He furthered that experience when joining the firm of Galerie des Monnaies of Geneva in their New York office.

At the invitation of Dr. George Vogt of Colonial Coins in Houston, Texas, Clark joined their staff in the fall of 1980 as a senior numismatist. It was here that he became involved in the famous Continental Illinois National Bank silver dollar hoard.

In late 1984 he started his own firm in Houston, and in 1989 joined forces with his close friend and colleague, Kenny Duncan, as a part of U.S. Coins, a company that is quickly establishing itself as one of the leading wholesalers of rare coins in the United States.

Clark is currently a member of many national and state numismatic organizations including ANA, TNA, TCDA, FUN, and CSNS, to name just a few. One of the initial members of the National Silver Dollar Roundtable, Clark now holds a seat on the Board of Governors and is a frequent speaker at their many educational forums held in conjunction with major shows across the country.

For those wishing to contact him, he can be reached at the following address: U.S. Coins, 5177 Richmond, Suite 200, Houston, TX 77056

CHAPTER 14

The Continental-Illinois Bank Deal

by Clark A. Samuelson and Leon E.Hendrickson

These separate accounts of the events and facts surrounding the Continental Illinois Bank of Chicago deal are presented by two dealers who were directly involved in the distribution of this huge silver dollar hoard. Clark A. Samuelson and Leon Hendrickson both handled multiple bags of this fascinating deal. Here are their stories.

The Continental National Bank Silver Dollar Hoard

Clark A. Samuelson

I remember that it was in the afternoon. I was sitting at my desk in the back room when the phone beeped and that slow distinctive Texas drawl began.

"Clark, come in and talk to me for a minute when you have a chance."

"Just a few minutes, George!"

I was working at Colonial Coins in Houston,Texas at the time. It was 1982. The thick, resonant Texas voice belonged to Dr. George Vogt. George was one of the pioneers of the modern coin industry in Texas. A veterinarian by trade, he had a keen interest in coins at an early age. He had founded Colonial Coins in the early 1960s. In time, he would develop it into one of the leading coin companies in the United States. George had a great deal of foresight. He was able to foresee emerging trends in our industry and capitalize on them.

I can remember him telling me the story of how he stood in line in Washington with a bunch of college kids that he had hired to buy bags of Silver Dollars that the government was selling in the early 60s. There was a limit of one bag per person. He had hired the college kids to that he could buy more. As he bought the bags he would take them over to people on the streets waiting to buy them. They were paying $1,025 each, a $25 dollar profit. He bought a lot of bags, sold them, and then brought the last ones home to sell at his shop. The price was $1.05 to pick the nicest coins. He advertised extensively but couldn't sell very many. Finally, he couldn't afford to hold them anymore so he sold them to another dealer for $1.02 each plus freight.

When he called, I really didn't expect anything out of the ordinary. Colonial Coins was a busy place. We had an active retail clientele as well as a large wholesale department to supply the trade.

When I had freed myself from the immediate things that I was doing I went in to see him.

"Do you know Ed Milas from Chicago?" he asked.

"Yes," I said. "We've met several times."

"He has some bags of Silver Dollars and I would like you to fly up there and take a look at them. They are 1880-S and 1881-S bags." he said.

"How many are there?" I asked.

"Twenty-five," and he rocked back in his chair, underneath the large paintings of the stage coach on the run from the Indians.

When George was thinking about something very important he'd rock back in that chair, cross his legs, clasp his hands together and tuck them underneath his chin. He'd get this little snicker on his face and just rock gently while his mind wandered, obviously in deep thought about the deal that was ahead. I could tell that there was more to this than met the eye.

And so marked the beginning of what many will consider to be one of the greatest numismatic events ever — the disbursement of the Continental Illinois National Bank Silver Dollar Hoard.

As many of you may remember, 1982 was not one of the greatest times in the history of our business. It had been well over a year since the "Great Boom" had ended. Both gold and silver were in a major downward trend, attempting to rally at times, but never able to sustain any positive gains. The rare coin industry wasn't much better off. The emotional prices of the 1979-1980 boom were nowhere in sight. Coins were down hard, looking for a reason to come back. The market needed a spark, something to create some excitement. It was coming.

A couple of days later I was on my way to Chicago to see Ed Milas and the Silver Dollar bags. I was glad to have an opportunity to get out of the office for a day. It was a busy place and the change of pace would do me some good. But I had already resigned myself to the fact that I had a lot of work to do. Twenty-five bags of silver dollars are a lot of coins — 25,000 to be exact. I was prepared to spend all day looking at them. I envisioned myself sitting at a desk, spot checking some of the bags, looking at every coin in others.

I landed in Chicago early and was able to get downtown to RARCOA well before lunch. RARCOA was one of the leading dealerships and auction houses in the country and Eddie's reputation as a prominent numismatist and businessman was second to none. After meeting everyone, we settled into Eddie's office and discussed the state of the world as it related to rare coins. Eddie always had the inside scoop on the business. He knew about all the big deals that were around and who was handling them. Before I'd leave him on this day, he would bring out a little box of coins and show me a few of the most amazing coins imaginable — early Large Cents, Bust Silver coinage, etc.

Besides coins, Ed Milas and George Vogt shared one other common interest — big game hunting. This was very evident sitting in Eddie's office. It was almost impossible to miss the picture of him kneeling over the great Alaskan polar bear he had taken on one of his trips. I would run into this polar bear again — hanging over the fireplace in the game room in his house. His pursuit of top quality coins was just as intense. There is little doubt that George and Eddie were a perfect team for what lay ahead.

After a few cups of coffee he asked me if I was ready to see the bags. By now I was prepared.

"Sure," I said. "Let's go see."

He took me towards the back of the office where he had a small walk-in vault. It was much longer than it was wide. Both sides were lined with shelves. As I approached the room I saw a number of buckets sitting on the floor — twenty-five, to be exact. These were the two-gallon white buckets that were commonly used to ship bags of silver coins. As I got closer I saw that each of the buckets had a canvas bag inside. The bags had been opened and the canvas was sticking up several inches over the top rim of the bucket. They were all neatly lined up along one side of the room. Eddie stayed in the doorway as I ventured in to take a closer look.

I knelt down beside the first bucket and reached in. I came up with a handful of coins (literally). Maybe fifteen pieces, all dated 1881-S. I let them spread out in my hand and I became very still as I locked into a stare. These coins were amazing. I began to select individual coins with my free hand for a closer look. Out of those fifteen coins there were two with a beautiful rainbow toning and at least three of four of the coins were solid gems.

I turned towards Eddie with what was probably a look of amazement. He responded with a short smile, that look of gleam, that sense of pride that you get when you know you have the very best. At that moment he realized that I knew what was in those bags, too.

I went down the line and did the same thing with three or four more of the bags. I found the same thing with each handful — incredible cartwheel lustre, magnificent rainbow colors, and on and on. At this point I knew that I didn't have to look anymore but I was like the kid in the candy store. This was neat. I wound up grabbing two or three more handfuls before I finally turned to Eddie and said, "Do all of the bags look like this?" Once again he said nothing. He really didn't need to. He just stood there in the doorway with that grin and nodded. I knew the answer. I also knew that it wouldn't be necessary to spend all day looking at bags of silver dollars before I could call George and tell him if I liked the bags. I asked Eddie if I could use the phone for a few minutes. I was finished and it wasn't even lunchtime yet!

Before I left the room I wanted to take a closer look at the canvas bags. As I was reaching in and out of the bags I noticed that they felt a lot thicker than I was used to. I asked Eddie if I could pull one of the canvas bags out of the bucket. When I did I could see that these bags were of double thickness and on the side of the bag, stenciled in black ink about 2 inches tall, were the letters "U.S.M." — for United States Mint. Not only were these some of the finest silver dollars that I had ever seen, but they were also in the original mint canvas bags that they were put in one hundred years ago!

After a quick sandwich I was ready to catch a flight back to Houston. Eddie would ship the bags down to Houston and they would get there in a few days.

While we awaited the arrival of the bags back in Houston, I was able to discuss the deal with George in a little more detail. I soon came to realize that this was only the beginning of the bags that would come to us from RARCOA. Although I had no idea how large the deal was, I got the impression that it might be as many as two or three hundred bags. I had no idea that it would be the largest single hoard of silver dollars ever to come to market in the United States.

The deal was originating out of the Continental Illinois National Bank in Chicago. At the time, the Bank was going through some financial difficulties. It apparently had extensive dealings with a major bank in Oklahoma that had collapsed and there were obviously other problems as well. There is no telling how long the bank had owned the bags.

Banks are required by federal law to keep a certain percentage of their "deposits" in cash at all times. This is one of their federal reserve requirements. I suspect that the silver dollar bags were kept in the bank and on their books at face value as part of this requirement. Because of the bank's financial difficulties the Board of Directors of the bank decided to sell the bags for the significant profit that they were worth over their face value to help soften the financial crisis that they faced. In time, this would not prove to be enough and the bank would wind up being taken over by the government.

The bags finally arrived in Houston and we were all anxious to take a closer look. We spent the better part of several days going through them, grading them, etc. We took some of the really superb coins and put them in 2 X 2 flips in boxes. The coins were incredible. Each bag of "S" mint dollars contained dozens and dozens of gem quality coins as well as many with magnificent rainbow toning. I recall looking at some bags that had as many as 150-200 gem coins in them, easily grading MS-65/67 by today's standards.

Before I explain the strategy used in the marketing of this great hoard, first let me set the tone of the market at that time.

Back in 1982 there were no "slabbed" coins. The Precision Grading Scale as we know it today was not fully developed. We were still using an abbreviated form of the Sheldon Grading Scale (numerical grades between 0 and 70) with the mint state grades being 60, 63, 65, and 67. If you'll go back to an old Coin Dealer Newsletter from this time, you'll find that bid levels for single coins were at the following levels:

	MS-60	MS-63	MS-65
Common "P" and "O" Mints	$26	$37	$130
Common "S" Mints	$35	$45	$100

Bid prices for common date rolls of "P" and "O" mint dollars were $550 per roll, "S" mint dollars $750 per roll. The market had rebounded ever so cautiously after experiencing an oversold condition after the big boom, but it was still somewhat lifeless and dull. It needed a boost, and it was coming.

The strategy we would use for marketing the coins was very simple. We needed to create more demand in the marketplace for the coins while at the same time being able to move sufficient quantities of the coins into the marketplace without disrupting the prices. To accomplish this, we would utilize the abilities of the entire industry — wholesalers and retailers alike. We'd start with the retailers.

We had established such a good rapport with them through the many offerings of foreign silver crowns that we were able to supply them, that this was now a perfect coin to offer. Their marketing abilities were essential to the program because we had literally hundreds of thousands of coins to sell. Through their extensive direct mail offerings they would reach literally millions of potential customers for the coins. They would offer the bulk of the coins to their clients as either singles, rolls, or bags. This would keep up from having to market the bags to the wholesale community in large quantities where they would eventually push prices down.

We'd also involve the dealer community by taking some of the nicer coins out of the bags and offering them as singles to the trade. By doing this we hoped to accomplish two things. First, we wanted to generate as much interest as possible in silver dollars. Every coin dealer in the country has at least a few retail clients and we wanted them all involved. We wanted every dealer in the country to buy some of the nicer coins and offer them to their clients. Secondly, we anticipated that, once the market for the gem quality coins (MS-65s) picked up, dealers would start offering premiums for nice original dollar rolls so that they could pick out the gems to sell to their clients. This would cause the roll market to go higher, adding a very strong price support base for the bulk coins.

We began offering coins to the retailers. Their initial success in marketing them to their clients was hugely successful. The combination of product, story, and price was a perfect fit for them. They easily sold most of the coins from the first few shipments that we received from Chicago. Because of all the publicity about dollars that the marketers were creating, word had started going around that we were handling a "neat deal of dollars" and people started to call on us to buy coins. We would sell, on occasion, a few of the nicer coins from the bags but would not allow anyone but the marketers to buy the bags. Interest was building. Dealers were starting to look to the wholesale market for coins. Dollar roll activity was picking up sharply.

Our first major venture into the wholesale market with the "hand-picked" coins came at a very opportune time — the National Silver Dollar Convention which was being held in the Astro Village Hotel in Houston in 1982. I called John Highfill, the developer of the convention, and requested two tables. He obliged by giving us the first two tables on the wall on the right hand side as you walked in the door. It was a great location.

I was really looking forward to the show for a number of reasons. First, it was a local show so we didn't have to travel very far. Second, we had by this time accumulated quite a number of the nicer dollars from the bags so I knew that we were going to have a great show. Third, John would also be giving an award for "Best Display of Silver Dollars" and I knew that we would win this award easily.

During the preceding year, Colonial Coins had been quite active in the pursuit of some of the classic silver dollars that had come to the market. In October of 1981 we had purchased, through Ed Milas, the famous Dexter-Bareford Specimen of the 1804 silver dollar from a Stack's sale in New York City. In the spring of 1982 we bought, and placed in the collection of a private client, the extremely rare 1866 No Motto Proof dollar that was being offered by New England Rare Coin Galleries. This was one of only two known examples of this coin, the other being part of the Dupont Family Collection that was stolen in 1967. This coin has never reappeared and is probably lost to the numismatic world forever. Also available at the time of the show was one of the two Lord St. Oswald examples of the 1794 silver dollar, owned at the time by Leon Hendrickson of Silver Towne, and generally considered to be one of the finest examples of the coin known.

I had gotten in touch with both our client and with Leon prior to the silver dollar show and asked if they would allow us to display the coins at the show. Both agreed and I was all set to run away with the award for the "best display." My plan was to take one of our two tables at the show and put two showcases on it. In one showcase I was going to put just three coins — the Lord St. Oswald 1794 dollar (Choice Uncirculated), the Dexter-Bareford 1804 Dollar (Choice Proof), and the 1866 No Motto dollar (Choice Proof). In the other case I was going to put out the most incredible display of rainbow toned dollars that the world had ever seen. What could go wrong?

We arrived at the show first thing Friday morning. With us we brought 24 double row boxes of handpicked dollars, each packaged in a 2 X 2 flip. Each box contained approximately 200 coins. That was a total of about 4,800 coins or almost 5 bags! As soon as I walked in the door I was besieged by people who wanted "first shot" at the dollars. One dealer even offered to pay me under the table for first pick.

I didn't want to get anyone mad so there was only one thing to do. I asked twelve different people who had expressed interest in the coins to return to our table at 11:00 am, which gave us a little over an hour to get ready. We stacked all 24 boxes on the back set-up table, got twelve chairs and put them in front of the table, and set up eight or ten lights. In between talking to people that came up to the table we were able to get everything ready except the display that would win us the award. But now it was 11:00 and time to get to work. The display could wait until later.

All twelve people came to the table exactly on time. I asked them all to have a seat, it didn't matter which one. I explained to them a little bit about the coins that they were going to be offered and then gave them the following instructions:

"These are all handpicked coins out of the dollar bags that we have been handling. All of the coins are either 1879-S, 1880-S, 1881-S, or 1882-S. Each box contains approximately 200 coins. I will make no claim that any one box of coins is any better than any other box of coins. I will give you each two boxes to start. The coins are priced at $110.00 each for the 1879-S, 1880-S, and the 1881-S. The 1882-S dollars are $150.00 each. You may buy one coin or one hundred coins, whatever you'd like. When you are done with the two boxes that I have given you, please pass them to your left. When you have all the coins that you want, please let someone else have your seat."

Over the remainder of the day and all day Saturday we had probably no fewer than 6-8 people at the table at all times. By Sunday we had sold every coin that we had brought to the show. It was absolutely incredible. I was oblivious to anything else going on at the show. We were just too busy. But that was good. Silver dollars were hot! Everyone was buying them. Some dealers bought coins, walked around the floor and sold them to other dealers, then came back and bought more. Some dealers came back four and five times over the course of two days. Everybody bought coins. It was perfect.

It was late Saturday afternoon before I finally got an opportunity to walk around the floor of the show and see what was going on. I moved over to the center aisle and started walking down the row looking into everyone's cases. As I approached

Gary Fernandez's table he stood up. We shook hands, said "Hello" and then I looked down into his case. He always had some nice dollars. I was crushed. There, in the middle of a rather impressive group of better date dollars was the award for the "Best Silver Dollar Display" that I had wanted so much to win. I glanced back at my table and saw the two cases that I was going to use for our display. I knew they were still empty. Although I showed the three rare silver dollars to several people at the show, I kept them locked in a briefcase behind the table. They were safer there. I never did get the opportunity to set the display up, but that was all right. We had done the business that we had come to do and that was the most important thing. There would always be another chance for the award.

The marketing strategy that we were using to disperse the hoard was working perfectly. Everything was falling into place. There was a great demand for gem silver dollars as well as nice rolls, a demand that at times seemed insatiable. Everyone in the wholesale arena had clients for nice dollars. The retailers that we were working with were having the same success. Dealers were entering the marketplace with higher and higher bids for nice original rolls of dollars that contained a gem coin or two. The entire silver dollar market was moving up. It was a trend that would last for another five years.

The majority of the coins that came out of the hoard were common dates — 1879-S, 1880-S, 1881-S, 1882-S, 1883-O, 1884-O, 1885-O, 1885-P, 1886-P and 1887-P. There were a dozen or so bags each of 1883-P and 1884-P and a few more single bags of some other dates. I personally know of no bags in the hoard that were dated after 1887.

To show the great success of the program and the impact that it had on the market, I have charted the price record for each of the ten dates listed above in MS-65 grade for the period 1982-1985. All prices listed represent the "bid" price as reported in the "Coin Dealer Newsletter" for the final issue of each year listed.

	1982	1983	1984	1985
1879-S	115	155	235	515
1880-S	110	150	225	500
1881-S	110	145	225	500
1882-S	150	205	275	560
1883-O	155	190	265	580
1884-O	155	190	250	540
1885-O	155	190	250	540
1885-P	150	220	265	570
1886-P	128	160	250	540
1887-P	130	165	245	545

This price chart shows the phenomenal growth rate for MS-65 silver dollars over the four year period 1982-1985. The average percentage gain for these ten coins was approximately 450%.

In 1986, with the beginning of PCGS (Professional Coin Grading Service), the industry adopted the use of the Precision Grading Scale which, for mint state coins, used all of the numbers from MS-60 through MS-70. There was a brief correction in the market as the new concept of slabbed coins was catching on and the dealers were getting used to the new grading standards, but it only took a short period of time before the silver dollar market regrouped and bid prices for these coins reached an all time high of over $800 per coin. Although not charted here, the price of MS-63 coins rose to a high of nearly $100 per coin while the MS-67 coins reached a high of over $3,000 per coin. With the adoption of the Precision Grading Scale the grades of MS-64 and MS-66 also became very important to this market. Coins of these grades reached peaks of $250 and $1,250 respectively.

The chart below gives bid prices for original silver dollar rolls from the same time period. Prices listed here also represent the "bid" price for each roll as reported in the "Coin Dealer Newsletter" for the final issue of each year listed.

	1982	1983	1984	1985
1879-S	1,000	1,175	1,300	1,250
1880-S	1,000	1,050	1,275	1,175
1881-S	925	1,025	1,250	1,175
1882-S	1,000	1,150	1,250	1,175
1883-O	650	750	825	700
1884-O	650	750	825	700
1885-O	650	750	825	700
1885-P	665	765	925	835
1886-P	660	760	825	700
1887-P	660	765	825	700

As you can see, although the initial reaction in the dollar roll was quite good, it was difficult for this market to sustain itself over the long term. As the price of MS-65 dollars continued to rise and the market for MS-64s developed, dealers would continually bid higher and higher for nice "original" rolls in order to get the few nice coins that were in them. Eventually what happened was that the dealers would replace the few nice coins that they took out of the rolls with average MS-60 quality coins and then try and recycle them back into the wholesale market. This resulted in rolls that were less than the average quality normally seen consequently pushing the prices down. With the inception of "slabbed" coins in 1986 this practice became even more widespread because even the MS-63 coins were worth pulling out of the rolls to be sent in for grading resulting in even poorer quality rolls recirculating to the market. This has continued to have a negative impact of this market and common dollar rolls are now bid at less than $300.

By the end of 1984 I decided to leave Colonial Coins and to venture out on my own. By this time, we had handled somewhere between 400 and 500 original bags of dollars out of the Continental Illinois National Bank hoard. This alone made the hoard larger than the famous LaVere Redfield hoard. But this deal was by no means finished yet. Shipments continued to come out of Chicago on a regular basis for the next year or so. As the bank's financial problems worsened, the bags came out even faster and faster. Eventually the quantity of coins coming out of the bank became so great that Eddie Milas sought the assistance of Leon Hendrickson of Silver Towne, who purchased the final lot of bags which he has also described as part of this chapter.

Besides the people at the bank itself, there may only be one person in the world who knows exactly how large the hoard really was — Eddie Milas. Eddie was never one to seek the limelight and even to this day will talk very little about the incredible deal that he handled. He was always content to sit quietly on the sidelines watching, evaluating, strategizing. He was always in control. Perhaps some day he'll tell us exactly how large the hoard was, perhaps not. I personally do not know exactly how large it was but some educated guesses are certainly possible.

Based on what we handled through Colonial Coins until the time I left in 1984 and what I was told came through Colonial Coins after I had left, combined with the figures that Leon Hendrickson cites, it is certainly possible that the hoard consisted of as many as 1,000 original bags of BU dollars as well as 500 bags of circulated coins: 1,500 bags, 1,500,000 coins. This makes it over three times the size of the famous LaVere Redfield hoard, and easily make it the largest single hoard of silver dollars ever to come to market in the United States outside of government sources. From a dollar value standpoint it is much more difficult to say. Leon ventures a guess at around $50 million. Who's to argue?

The Continental National Bank silver dollar hoard will long be remembered as one of the premier events in the history of the U.S. silver dollar market. For over two years, day in and day out, it dominated my work schedule. I would like to take this opportunity to thank both George Vogt and Eddie Milas for the confidence and trust that they placed in me. It was, without question, a once in a lifetime opportunity.

Footnote: The Marketing of Numismatic Coins

Successful marketing of any large hoard of coins, whether they be silver dollars, ancient coins, or the tons of Gold Rush coins and ingots coming from the recently discovered S.S. Central America, requires a great deal of market knowledge and planning. Certainly, as it applies to rare coins, the success is determined by being able to maintain current price levels or even increase them while still being able to move large quantities of the product into the marketplace. Most people will tell you that when supply increases sharply, demand will not keep pace and prices will fall. With proper marketing, supply can in fact help to create demand, helping to increase price levels. It is equally as important to involve the coin dealer community in the marketing of any large supply of coins.

Back in the 1970s and early 1980s, the Franklin Mint was producing and marketing large quantities of legal tender foreign gold coins and silver coins. They offered all of their material directly to the coin buying public, selling out virtually every issue. Dealers were never allowed to buy their products. At the time, the Franklin Mint officials didn't think they needed to include the dealers — but it would come back to haunt them.

In order to maintain market prices, it is necessary to have both an active and fluid secondary market. This requires participation by a broad base of dealers. To get them to participate you must allow them the opportunity to handle the product, to educate themselves and their customers. They must be allowed to sell their customers coins when the products are "fresh." It is not fair to expect them to try and maintain a legitimate secondary beginning. After all, when people want to SELL coins, where do they go? They go to coin dealers.

When the public offered their Franklin Mint coins back to the dealer community for resale they found that the coins were only worth their intrinsic, or melt value. Why? Because the dealers had never handled them before and they had no clients to buy them. Why should they be worth anything more then the intrinsic value?

If the Franklin Mint had offered 20-30% of the mintage of their product directly to the coin dealer community there would have been a much more active market for the coins when they were brought back on the market for resale. There would have been demand. There wasn't, and the Franklin Mint officials found themselves facing Harry Reasoner of "60 Minutes" one Sunday night. He was asking the same questions.

The early 1980s saw a resurgence of the same types of products that the Franklin Mint had offered. Predicated on the same marketing philosophy, they brought the same results. Obviously someone didn't pay any attention to the lessons that should have been learned.

Although the market base for any type of rarer numismatic coin is much broader than for a new issue such as the Franklin Mint produced, the principles used to market them remain the same. With proper planning and market knowledge, but most importantly with an active participation by the coin dealer community, almost any type of hoard coin can successfully be brought to market.

***

The Continental-Illinois Bank Deal

Leon E. Hendrickson

In late 1982 or early 1983, one of the great numismatic events took place. Continental Illinois Bank of Chicago began experiencing some severe financial difficulties. The Federal Deposit Insurance Corporation had to make some hard and fast decisions to try and save the bank.

It was at that time the future fate of the approximately 1,500 bags of Morgan dollars that the bank was holding in its vaults, was decided.

It was also at this time that Ed Milas of RARCOA in Chicago was contacted by the bank to purchase the bags of dollars. This was Eddie's deal from the beginning, and he must be given tremendous credit for the brilliant and quiet way he handled the disbursement of the hoard.

He contacted me and we discussed the best way to handle the sale of the dollars, so it would not adversely affect the market price.

I ultimately purchased over half of the hoard. I took all of the AU bags and at least 350 of the BU's. Of the AU's, 500 bags were 1878-1885, with most of them being 79,80,81,82 "O" mints. Dates of the BU's were 1878-1904, with most of them being 1878-88; a tremendous amount of them were "S" mints. The BU dollars, even at todays tougher grading standards, would be graded MS-63 and above for an average, with several grading in the MS-66 to 68 class.

Some of the toning on these cartwheels would make anyone's mouth water. One of the mysteries concerning the early "O" mints was the fact that some of them were mixed XF-AU-UNC all in the same bag, all with the same date and mint.

In my lifetime I have handled more than my share of dollars and I would like to go on record as stating these were among the most beautiful I have ever been privileged to see. The sheer volume and beauty of these coins was overwhelming. If you were to compare, this hoard of dollars would probably be in the $50 million range which would make it five times the Redfield Dollar Sale.

Ed and I had decided earlier that we would do our utmost to protect the market, so we took over a year to disperse of the coins. I never even took a single bag of coins to a coin show. We selected our buyers carefully to make sure they would not dump large quantities to dealers who could affect the price. A large portion went to Telemarketers, who in turn sold the coins directly to the public.

Silence and astute marketing were the key to the success of this venture. Most of my employees did not even know what was going on, as we wanted no knowledge of the true size of this transaction to leak out. As far as I was able to determine there was no visible impact on the general market at that time, which was a minor miracle given the amount of dollars that we put back into the hands of the general public and dealers.

Ed Milas and I were going so fast, and handling most of the details ourselves (so as not to involve any more people than necessary), that we never really took the time to figure out the complete financial picture. Sure, a lot of money changed hands but a final accounting was not done until near the end.

Probably late in 1984, Milas called and said he was chartering a plane to fly into Winchester, so we could sit down and finish up the financial details and close the books on the Continental dollar deal. He told me he thought I still owed him around $1 million. That sounded like a good round figure, as we really had not come to a final amount yet.

I worked on our records the rest of the day and most of the night. My final accounting showed that the reverse was true and Eddie actually owed me. Milas arrived the next day and I showed him my records — he was dumbfounded, to say the least. His words were "You mean to tell me that I chartered a plane and flew from Chicago to Winchester, Indiana to hear you tell me that!"

A couple of days later he called to tell me that I was right and he did indeed owe me. It is a testimonial to our mutual trust and friendship that a business venture of this volume could be consummated and completed on our word and a handshake.

I consider Ed Milas one of my close and personal friends, and I thank him from the bottom of my heart for including me in this once in a lifetime experience.

***

Walter H. Breen, NLG

CHAPTER 15

A Unique Liberty Seated Dollar: 1851-O

by Walter H. Breen, NLG

The Liberty Seated dollar series has long been a source of fascination — and frustration — to collectors. Not only are many dates unexpectedly hard to find in strictly mint state (1850-O, 1855, 1861-68), others are available most often in proof state (1851-2, 1858-68), and still others are elusive in any grade whatever (1870-S, 1871-CC). There are even unsolved mysteries: how many 1870-S's and why did mint records ignore them? What happened to all the 1873-S dollars? And as if all this were not enough, the Liberty Seated dollar series has just been enlarged by the discovery and authentication of a new date-mintmark combination, the first such in U.S. coins since the 1870-S half dime (1978); the only other in this century was the 1854-S half eagle (1919). Stranger still, the 1851-O is a proof; and though genuine, it was not made where or when it claims to have been.

During the 1980s, three different people told me that a new silver dollar date-mintmark combination was known; two of them said it was a new O mint, and Tom DeLorey identified it as 1851-O. Two wanted the discovery kept secret, the third (again Tom DeLorey) laid no such obligation on me. None furnished a complete description, which is why I did not list it in my *Encyclopedia* even as "Reported."

On Friday, February 2, 1990, at the Long Beach show, a California collector told me that he has the piece, that it had come from B. Max Mehl in the 1940s, and that he would show it to me at the ANA Midwinter show in San Diego. A month later to the day, he did. It not only lived up to its billing, it went well beyond; identifying its dies created more problems than it solved.

1851-O OBVERSE

1851-O REVERSE

Special thanks to the ANAAB (American Numismatic Association Authentication Bureau) for providing this photograph of the 1851-O dollar.

Obverse. Identical to that of the 1851 Philadelphia restrike, *Encyclopedia* 5446: centered date; same rust pits on r. curve of 5 and central upright of final 1 as on proof 1851 restrikes. No apparent difference in die state from the latter.

Reverse. Heavy O mintmark, from the same punch as in 1859-O and similarly placed to all three revs. of that date; higher and slightly larger than that on 1860-O revs. Inner circle at tips of dentils above UNITE. Shield does not have the same internal details as the 1858-59 proof rev. regularly used with the 1851 restrike obverse.

Both sides show evidence of double striking; obv., on dentils above stars 3-7, rev. on UNITED and claws. Outer rev. rim shows file marks, evidently to remove a pronounced knife-rim (called by Mint people a "fin"). This "fin" must have been similar to that on the 1851 and 1852 restrike dollars pictured in my *Encyclopedia*, p.439. The higher the fin, the sharper, the more risk to customers' fingers, and the more conspicuously unlike original strikings. (The other proofs showing such pronounced knife-rims — and evidence that some were filed off — are occasional restrike half cents of 1840-48, called "Group III" and "Group VI" in my half cent book.)

Mintmark appears faint; under 20x magnification it shows plain evidence of having been chiseled off, carefully so as not to disturb any more of the proof surface than necessary. (Tom DeLorey told me that ANACS had come to the identical conclusion when they authenticated the coin some years ago.)

The coin is lightweight: 400.3 grains = 25.94 grams: another feature it shares with the restrike half cents.

These confusing pieces of P-D-S evidence (Planchet, Dies, Striking) raise many questions.

1. Why would a single 1851-O dollar survive?
2. Why is it a proof?
3. Why has it a Philadelphia restrike obverse?
4. Why was it so carelessly made (double struck)?
5. Why is it lightweight?
6. Why did it have a knife-rim sharp enough to need to be filed off?
7. Why was the mintmark chiseled off?
8. When was it made?
9. Where was it made?
10. Who made it?

That chiseled mintmark is the key clue, enabling answers to all the rest.

We begin with the known history of the 1851 restrike obv. This was a second die (date central in field) stored in either the Engraver's or Coiner's vaults in the Philadelphia Mint, and either then or later polished for making proofs. Most likely it was part of the archive of old dies assembled by Adam Eckfeldt and his successor Franklin Peale, and kept in the Coiner's Vault. There is no evidence that the die ever left Philadelphia. Some time between 1858 and mid 1860, Philadelphia Mint employees used it for making restrikes in copper and silver. On July 30, 1860 it was among many dies seized by Mint Director Snowden and kept in a sealed box in the Director's vault. On May 18, 1867 a later Director, Henry R. Linderman, unsealed this box, made an inventory, and resealed it; in 1868 he reopened it, took a few impressions of some dies, and then ordered all the dies destroyed.

According to Linderman's 1867 inventory, the box contained obvs. of 1804, 1836, 1838, 1839, 1851 and 1852 dollars; of the 1827 quarter; and of half cents of almost all the proof-only dates 1836-48, 52. This circumstance links them to the 1851-O dollar and enables us to name the maker.

That this 1851 obv. was found by Mint Director Snowden and confiscated with the 1804 Dollar and half cent dies points to the Midnight Minters, George and Theodore Eckfeldt (not Snowden nor Linderman) as behind both the regular 1851 restrike dollars and the 1851-O.

Theodore W. Eckfeldt (1837-93) was the son of George J. Eckfeldt (foreman of the Engraving Dept., 1830-after 1860), who was the nephew of Adam Eckfeldt (Chief Coiner 1814-39, with the Mint in various capacities since 1792). As a teenager, Theodore Eckfeldt had worked for the Coiner's Dept., only to be fired by Franklin Peale for theft. A month later, young Eckfeldt obtained character references from both Peale and Adam Eckfeldt. A few years later, to avoid scandal, he was rehired after promising to be a good boy — and made night watchman. (Taxay says Franklin Peale did the Mint this favor, which dates the event to no later than 1854, when Peale was fired.) In 1858, apparently acting on behalf of his father George Eckfeldt, young Theodore peddled at $75 each at least three 1804 Dollars with plain edges. When the news got back to Mint Director Snowden, R. Coulton Davis (druggist and favored collector of pattern and experimental coins) gave Snowden the names of the buyers: Maj. C.P. Nichols; Edward Cogan; and another not now identified. Snowden retrieved four of the 1804's, put one into the Mint Cabinet collection, and destroyed the rest. Between then and 1860 or later, young Eckfeldt offered proof-only half cents dated in the forties, "in dozens of duplicates." Ebenezer Locke Mason, in 1882, admitted that Eckfeldt operated out of the store Mason ran, in a building owned by Dr. Montroville Wilson Dickeson, author of the best-selling *American Numismatic Manual*. This store was on the east side of North 2nd St., near Buttonwood St., Philadelphia.

The 1851-O scenario is easily reconstructed. On some night in 1858 or 1859, Theodore (with a couple of accomplices, one of whom was almost certainly his father George J. Eckfeldt) opened the Coiner's Vault and Engraver's Vault, retrieving the 1851 proof dollar obv. from the former and the nearest dollar reverse from the latter. Both dies had to be degreased, inspected, cleaned and polished; this was within George Eckfeldt's capacities as foreman of the Engraving Dept. The other accomplice (probably in the Coiner's Dept., as he would have to know how to set dies into a press) may have prepared the blanks, most likely foreign dollar-size coins polished down and with edges shaved off, rendering them lightweight. Unlike Mint Director Snowden, the Eckfeldt gang could not use regular silver planchets; like gold planchets, these were counted as money in inventories. (This circumstance explains such anomalies as Art Kagin's 1838 dollar overstruck on an 1859, and the plain edge 1804 overstruck on the Swiss shooting thaler.)

How must the Midnight Minters have felt on noticing that the very first proof specimen they struck from the 1851 dollar obverse bore an O mintmark! That would make the piece forever identifiable as not one of the rare 1851's, and possibly unsalable. There may have been no time that night to regrease and restore the proofed O mint reverse to the shelf with other dies awaiting shipment to New Orleans, find or prepare a normal proof dollar reverse, obtain or make new silver blanks, proof them and strike them, clean up all traces of their night's work, and get home quickly enough to establish an alibi if the Director or any other officers noticed anything unusual the next morning. Any others they might have struck that night were probably either melted or polished down and used for undertypes for other restrike dollars — or, at best, treated like this one. What counted was that the 1851 obverse was still intact and ready for their next get-together. By then the Eckfeldt gang would be better prepared.

Too valuable to melt down, too dangerous to sell as is: what to do with the 1851-O dollar? The obvious expedient: remove the mintmark along with the unpleasantly sharp fin, offer the coin as a regular proof 1851, and hope that buyers would not notice the traces of mintmark — or weigh the coin.

Under the circumstances, it is extremely unlikely that any others survive. The unprecedented 1851-O silver dollar is, beyond doubt, one of the most extraordinary coin rarities of the 1850s, and one of the most important coin discoveries of the century; most likely the first and most valuable of the 1851 restrikes; certainly the only coin minted in Philadelphia with an O mintmark; the only 1851-O silver dollar, unique and likely to remain so.

References:

Walter Breen, *A Coiner's Caviar: Encyclopedia of U.S. and Colonial Proof Coins 1722-1977*, NY: FCI Press 1977, rep. with additions and corrections, Wolfeboro, NH: Bowers & Merena, 1990, pp. 253-4, 262

Walter Breen's, *Encyclopedia of United States Half Cents 1793-1857*, South Gate, CA: AINR, 1984, pp. 463-65, 383-85

Walter Breen's, *Complete Encyclopedia of U.S. and Colonial Coins*, Garden City: Doubleday, 1988, pp. 173, 431-2

Eric P. Newman & Ken Bressett, *The Fantastic 1804 Dollar*, Racine: Whitman, 1962, pp. 80-86

Don Taxay, *U.S. Mint and Coinage*, NY: Arco, 1966, pp. 190-92

Appendix A: Copy for proposed ANA press release

ANACS CERTIFIES 1851-O

DOLLAR DISCOVERY COIN

The American Numismatic Association Certification Service has certified as genuine a previously unknown U.S. coin, an 1851-O Liberty Seated dollar.

The coin, described on the ANACS certificate as "1851-O Dollar-Unofficial Restrike-Proof-Mint Mark Damaged," has characteristics similar to those of the 1851 Restrike dollar in Proof, and like that issue was probably struck at the Philadelphia Mint in the late 1850's.

A comparison of the 1851-O dollar with one specimen of the 1851 Proof restrike showed that both pieces were slightly underweight, and the planchets for both pieces (in the case of the 1851-P coin a previously struck 1855 dollar) had been roughly filed around the edge prior to the striking. No sign of an undertype was seen on the 1851-O dollar.

However, a microscopic examination of the die characteristics of the two coins revealed that different collar dies were used for the two coins, as well as, of course, the mintmarked and non-mintmarked reverse dies. This makes an exact attribution of the actual date of issue impossible, but several authorities on U.S. Proof coins have agreed that the style of the die polishing or "Proofing" of the dies is typical of the 1858-1860 era.

A circumstance as mysterious as the existence of the coin itself is the fact that at some time after the coin was struck, someone tried to polish the mint mark off of the coin. Many numismatic rarities were "restruck" inside the Philadelphia Mint in the late 1850's, such as 1804 silver dollars and 1836-39 Gobrecht pattern dollars, some of the latter varieties which had not existed previously.

It is possible that the person who struck the piece, either a Mint official or a Mint employee, deliberately created it as a unique variety, but then backed off from trying to sell it as such after the scandal of the 1804 Dollars broke. Thus he tried to remove the mint mark so he could sell it as a less rare but still valuable 1851 Proof restrike.

Another possibility is that the person who bought it from the producer tried to remove the mint mark to protect himself from involvement in any scandal. The exact circumstances will probably never be known.

It is possible that other 1851-O dollars may also exist, with their mint marks either intact or else partially removed. Anyone possessing an 1851 Proof restrike dollar, or even any 1851 dollar, should check below the eagle for signs of a mint mark.

***

CHAPTER 16

The 1879-S Reverse of '78 Morgan Dollar

By John W. Highfill, NLG
with special editorial comments by Walter H. Breen

Some silver dollar rarities have been continuously recognized as rare from their discovery (e.g. 1851-2, 1870-S); some have gradually or even suddenly left the rarity class as more and more specimens have turned up (1794, 1903-O); some are mistakenly thought common at first and only later recognized as rare (1878 7/8 TF VAM 44 tripled obv., 1896-O small o.)

But how often does one encounter a rarity which was briefly famous, then forgotten for decades, only recently rediscovered as a rarity? A classic instance is the 1879-S dollar with "reverse of 1878," parallel arrow feathers, concave breast, familiarly 1879-S PAF.

For those unfamiliar with this long-neglected major type coin, a review of a few basics may be in order. Obverses first:

1879-S Morgan Dollar
Type II Obverse
Thick LIBERTY, short toe to L
Top leaf points to pellet
No lines in wheat leaves
Less details in cotton blossoms
Thick eyelash
Narrow rim

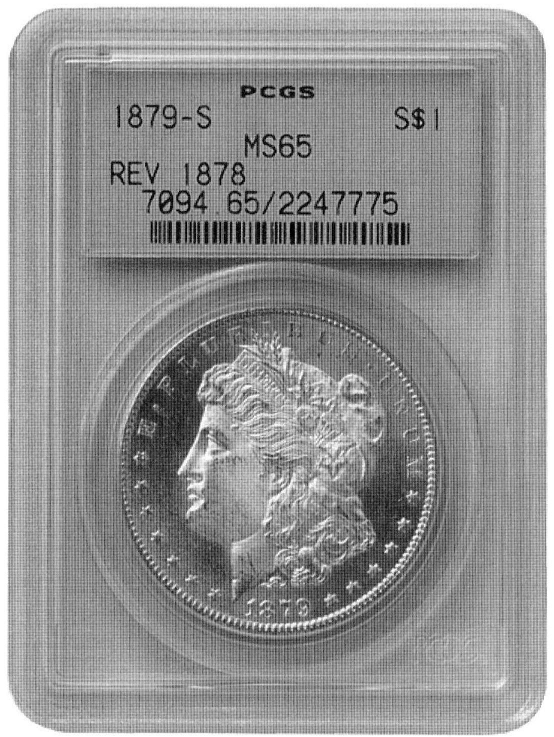

1879-S Morgan Dollar
Type III Obverse
Thin LIBERTY, longer toe to L
Top leaf points to final S
Lines in wheat leaves
More detail in cotton blossoms
Thinner eyelash
Broader rim

Morgan Dollar
Type B Reverse
PAF (Parallel arrow feathers)
"Flat" (concave) breast
A(M) touching wing
Berries 9 left, 7 right
Narrow rim
Small mintmark if any

Morgan Dollar
Type C Reverse
SAF (Top arrow feathers slants)
Convex breast
A(M) free of wing
Berries 10 left, 7 right
Broader rim
Larger mintmark if any

The Mint's official name for the Type C reverse was "June 1878 Hub." No matter how many call it "Type C", the shortest and simplest designation is SAF. Similarly, Type B is most easily remembered as PAF.

(There are a few exceptions in Type C to the larger mintmark rule: occasional dies of 1880-O (*Encyclopedia* **5539**, **5541**), 1880-CC (**5553-55**), 1896-O (**5648**), 1899-O (**5660**), 1900-O (**5669**), 1902-O (**5690**), 1903-S (**5697**). The 1880 instances were probably among the earliest Type C dies, perhaps before the larger mintmark became policy; the 1896 - 1903 examples, all rare, are thought to have been dies erroneously impressed with the quarter dollar punch. Then there is the 1879-CC "Capped Die", properly called large CC over small cc).

San Francisco coinage of Morgan dollars began April 18, 1878, from dies of type II-B (7 TF PAF). Out of the ten pairs of dollar dies shipped from Philadelphia on April 8, the San Francisco Coiner condemned three obverses and eight reverses as unusable. The other two reverses, with long nock ("center arrow feather") were used briefly, producing two varieties not in VAM (*Encyclopedia* **5517**), certainly only a very small part of the total mintage of 9,774,000. If monthly records survive for 1878-79 San Francisco dollar deliveries, it should be possible to ascertain the number minted.

The remaining 1878-S coins (7 TF PAF, short nock, **5518**) were made from 36 pairs of dies shipped in June and used until the end of the year. Some of these (used or unused) were probably held over for 1879-S coinage.

No San Francisco mint records have surfaced about numbers or dates of arrival of dies, nor of monthly coinage, let alone above the change of reverse type in 1879. The coins themselves show that apparently 6 obverses and 7 reverses were used for making 1879-S PAF's. (No one has checked to see if any of these dies had appeared on 1878-S coins.) At the then low average of 60,000 coins per die-pair at San Francisco, these dies could have made as many as 420,000 pieces, perhaps at most 0.46% of the total mintage of 9,110,000.

The discoverer of the variety, Howard Rounds Newcomb, long famous for his books on large cents, was an advanced student of varieties of United States silver — a pre-1940's counterpart of Jules Reiver. In 1913, Newcomb found an 1879-S PAF, and exhibited it at the ANA Convention as a rarity. (*Numismatist* October 1913, p. 511.) Thereafter it was ignored, then forgotten. Even after specialist collectors began distinguishing SAF from PAF in 1878 dollars, some time in the 1960's, reference works did not mention that the same types occur in 1879-S. Not even the 1971 or 1976 Scott Encyclopedias allude to them, though both editions list small and large S varieties for this date. The 1971 edition priced the small s at $4 Unc., the large at $7.50; the 1976 edition gave them separate numbers S78 and S79 respectively. What Don Taxay evidently never realized was that the small s varieties are PAF, the large S SAF; nor did most collectors. (When Taxay developed the first Scott Encyclopedia, in large part from information I (Breen) gave him in 1969, I had not yet had opportunity to examine specimens in detail).

Rediscovery can be dated to about 1963, though evidently not from any quantities in Treasury bags. The 1879 PAF's first mention in print in that period is apparently F.X. Klaes's *Die Varieties of Morgan Silver Dollars* (1963), fig. 14. A. George Mallis's *List of Die Varieties of Morgan Head Silver Dollars* (1964) lists it on p. 9 as 1879-S PAF I-1-A (K): Obv. 1: Unknown/

Rev. A : Parallel Arrow Feather Variety, indicating that he had not seen one, and that Klaes's booklet was the source. The 1965 text by Mallis and Walter Breen, *United States Silver Dollars Morgan Type*, did not mention the variety (we had not yet seen it). The 1971 Van Allen and Mallis *Guide to Morgan and Peace Dollars* listed three PAF varieties as VAM 4, 5, 6, and called each "R-3" as against the other type's R-1 and R-2 (VAM 1-3).

The earliest price list I (Breen)have found that listed it is a one-pager by Edward Nied (credited as a collaborator in the Klaes booklet), then of R.R. 1, Box 466, Northampton, Mass., undated (1963), pricing the 1879-S PAF at $3 in XF, the SAF at $1.50 XF $2 AU. For comparison, Nied priced the 1888-O Doubled Head (what today we call Hot Lips) at $12 XF, $18 AU; the 1896-O small o at $14 XF, $18 AU; the 1899-O small o at $1.50 XF, $2 AU; the Centered and Low CC varieties of 1900-O/cc Unc. at $60 and $40; the 1901-P "Shifted Eagle" (today's DDR with 14 feathers) at $12 VF; the 1902-O small o $18 Unc.; the 1903-S small s at $10 XF. Clearly neither Klaes nor Nied knew that the PAF variety was rare.

Leroy C. Van Allen's *Morgan and Peace Dollar Varieties* (1965) had apparently first called attention to the 1879-S PAF as a rarity, pp. 119-20, 150, estimating its mintage at 120,000 out of the 9,110,000 total, and valuing it in Unc. at $50 compared to the SAF's $2.50. (Taxay had probably not read the Van Allen book; his 1971 Scott Encyclopedia does not cite it as a source).

Uncirculated survivors were apparently unknown until Dean Tavenner discovered one roll in 1967. In 1975 a few more rolls turned up in Montana, but they were in EF to slider level. No larger quantities showed up until three bags were identified the Redfield hoard (1976). Leon Hendrickson (Silver Towne) bought all three, sold two to one dealer and the third to another; all three bags have been dispersed, the coins sold individually. No figures have been published about the total number of 1879-S's in the Redfield hoard (probably dozens of bags), so we do not know if the survivors in this source represent a random sample of the mintage, or if the Pittman Act meltings affected the PAF's or SAF's out of proportion to their mintages. Out of fewer than 4,000 uncs. recorded to survive, only 998 have been certified as any grade of Unc., including 59 prooflikes (less unknown numbers of resubmissions). The rest are evidently still raw.

Like other early S Mints Morgans, the 1879-S PAF comes well struck and lustrous; but those from the Redfield hoard are among the most heavily bagmarked S mints in the series. They probably were among the bags LaVere Redfield threw down the coal chute into his farmhouse basement.

During the early 1980's, I (Highfill) searched through hundreds of dealer offerings and thousands of 1879-S Morgans at coin shows and conventions, and found that the Paramount distribution coin holders contained a higher proportion of 1879-S PAF's. The thrill of the chase, and the capture!

Harrison Phillips, one of the most knowledgeable dealers in circulated Morgans, reports that occasional EF's and AU's turn up; some of these may be from the 1975 Montana rolls. In lower grades, the 1879-S PAF is evidently rarer than 1881-CC, 1885-CC or 1903-O. This consistent with the hypothesis that few were spent early, most were held in Treasury vaults and melted, probably in 1919-23 or 1942. Probably no other large hoards survive; what the market has now is unlikely to increase in supply.

Paradoxically, the Redfield hoard's impact on the variety, despite increasing supply over a hundredfold, was to increase public demand far more, so that prices have sharply risen. A major factor is determining the 1879-S PAF's future will be its separate listing as a major variety in certified population reports. Certainly if the 1882-O/S and 1900-0/CC deserve such listing, so does the 1879-S PAF, and for at least equally good reasons.

Happy hunting!

Appendix A:

In their superb book, *The Comprehensive Catalogue and Encyclopedia of U.S. Morgan and Peace Silver Dollars*, Leroy C. Van Allen and A. George Mallis describe the known "VAM" varieties for the 1879-S Reverse of '78 Morgan silver dollar. "VAM" is an acronym coined for Van Allen and Mallis who were responsible for researching the Morgan die varieties. In their "VAM Book," each die variety was given a "VAM" number which uniquely identified the variety. The number series was created in ascending order coincident with the finding of each successive variety. With permission, we are reproducing their complete listing of the known varieties from the 1981 edition (fourth printing). "I-4" means a rating of 4 on the 5-level VAM Interest Scale, where I1 refers to a normal coin for date collectors, or a variety for specialists only, and I-5 redflags a major variety of interest to all collectors.

1879-S Reverse of '78 Morgan silver dollar varieties

VAM 4: III^{2}2 * B^{2}a (PAF Reverse)
Obverse: III^{2}2 - Open 9
Reverse: B^{2}a - PAF reverse of B^2 type with small III S mint mark, R in TRUST not broken. I-3. R-4.

VAM 5 III^{2}1 * B^{2}b (Broken R)
Obverse: III^{2}1 - Closed 9
Reverse: B^{2}b - PAF reverse of B^2 type with small III S mint mark. Broken R in TRUST with upper serif partially missing. I-3. R-4.

VAM 6 III^{2}2 * B^{2}c (TIUST)
Obverse: III^{2}2
Reverse: of B^{2}c - PAF reverse of B^2 type with small III S mint mark tilted slightly to the left. Broken R in TRUST to form TIUST with upper serif completely missing. I-3. R-4.

VAM 7 III^{2}1 * B^{2}d (S/S Up)
Obverse: III^{2}1
Reverse: B^{2}d - Small III S mint mark doubled at bottom. PAF reverse of B^2 type with R in TRUST not broken. I-3. R-4.

VAM 8 $III^2 4$ * $B^2 b$ (Doubled 9)
Obverse: $III^2 4$ - 9 in date doubled at left inside and left outside of upper loop.
Reverse: $B^2 b$: I-3. R-4.

VAM 9 $III^2 5$ * $B^2 b$ (Doubled 9)
Obverse: $III^2 5$ - Closed 9 in date doubled on left outside of lower loop
Reverse: $B^2 b$: I-3. R-4.

VAM 10 $III^2 6$ * $B^2 b$ (Doubled 79)
Obverse: $III^2 6$ - 7 in date doubled at bottom of upper crossbar. Closed 9 doubled at top left outside as a short arc.
Reverse: $B^2 b$: I-3. R-4.

VAM 23 $III^2 4$ * $B^2 a$ (PAF Reverse, Doubled 9). I-3. R-4.

VAM 24 $III^2 5$ * $B^2 a$ (PAF Reverse, Doubled 9). I-3. R-4.

VAM 25 $III^2 6$ * $B^2 a$ (PAF Reverse, Doubled 7)
Obverse: $III^2 6$ - Top of 9 not broken away to form arc. I-3. R-4.

VAM 34 $III^2 5$ * $B^2 f$ (PAF, Engraved Wing Feather).
Reverse: $B^2 f$ - Feather engraved between eagle's right wing and leg. R in TRUST broken with upper serif almost completely missing. I-3. R-4.

VAM 35 $III^2 5$ * $B^2 g$ (PAF, Engraved Wing Feather)
Reverse $B^2 g$ - Feather engraved between eagle's right wing and leg. R in TRUST partially broken. I-3. R-4.

VAM 39 $III^2 1$ * $B^2 g$ (PAF, Engraved Wing Feather). I-3. R-4.

Acknowledgements:

We wish to thank the following persons for their contributions that have made this chapter possible:

Walter H. Breen
Bill Fivaz
Harry Forman
Mike Fuljenz
Leon Hendrickson
R. W. Julian
John Love
A. George Mallis
Wayne Miller
Jeff Oxman
Harrison Phillips
Tom Phillips
Paul Stoner
Dean Tavenner
Leroy C. Van Allen
Eric Vaughn
Fred Weinberg

***

Bill Fivaz, NLG

Bill Fivaz was born in Fulton, New York, in 1934. He graduated from Hamilton College in 1956, and served in the Naval Reserve until 1959. He has been employed by the Nestle Company since 1959 and is currently District Sales Manager for the Southeastern U.S. Bill married Marilyn Briggs in 1956 and has two children and two grandchildren.

Bill began collecting coins in 1950, and has shown great enthusiasm for numismatics ever since. As a consultant for ANACS, this former ANA Board member has been an educational forum speaker at the FUN convention each year since 1979, and an ANA Summer Seminar Grading Instructor each year since 1980. He has produced and made available color slide programs on a variety of subjects, and is a frequent speaker at various national, regional and local numismatic meetings.

Mr. Fivaz is the co-author of *The Cherrypicker's Guide To Rare Coin Varieties*, author of frequent articles in various numismatic publications, and a frequent contributor to the Red Book; he was co-author of the Mint Error section in the 1980 and subsequent editions. He also contributed to the VAM book, and is a frequent exhibitor at various shows with many first place and Best-of-Show awards.

He is a life member of many numismatic organizations, including: ANA (1100), FUN, Blue Ridge, Georgia Numismatic Assn., CONECA, NECA (Past President and President Emeritus). Bill is also a member of many other national and regional numismatic societies and clubs. His numismatic specialties include Buffalo nickels, Mercury dimes, Morgan and Peace dollars, Mint errors and varieties.

Bill Fivaz received the Numismatic Ambassador Award in 1982, and the ANA Medal of Merit in 1984 and 1989.

CHAPTER 17

Mint Error Dollars and the Minting Process

by Bill Fivaz, NLG
Photographs furnished by Fred Weinberg

MINT ERRORS — those intriguing, eye-catching, elusive and much-sought-after products of the mint which set them apart from the "normal" issues of the same denomination and type, and create a classically FUN collecting experience.

When do they occur? Where do they occur? *Why* do they occur?

Mint errors, regardless of the denomination and/or type, belong to one or more of three basic categories: *Planchet Errors* — those abnormalities which affect the *planchet* before the coin is struck; *Die Errors* — those usually more subtle and repetitive aberrations which occur on the *die*; and *Striking Errors* — those often spectacular and eye-popping collectibles which happen at the instant the planchet is *struck* by the dies to create a coin.

Let's take an in-depth look at each of these categories to see what kinds of errors can occur during each. We'll then review the Minting Process to determine just where, when and how they are created.

Planchet Errors:

As pointed out above, in this category, something out of the ordinary happened to the blank or planchet *before* it entered the striking chamber. Possibly the coinage strip from which the blanks are punched contained areas of improperly mixed metals, and when the blanks were produced, one or more of them exhibited copper "blotches" or discolorations which would later show up on the struck coin. Or possibly there was some occluded gas trapped in the metal as it passed through a series of rollers which reduced it down to the proper thickness. This trapped gas "bubble" could very well be represented later on the coin as a lamination — a peeled off section on the obverse or reverse, small or large, leaving "raw" metal underneath. One of the 1801 restrike proof dollars is struck on a planchet cracked from rim to B to central curl.

Another planchet error is the incomplete planchet, commonly referred to as a "clip." This occurs when the planchet strip fails to advance properly and the gang punch (several steel rods which descend and cut through the metal strip to produce blanks) overlaps an area which was previously punched. This creates incomplete planchets which appear to have a piece "clipped" out of them, much like when Mom overlapped an already cut out area with her cookie-cutter while making your favorite Toll House or molasses cookies.

A planchet error that could not have occurred prior to the advent of the clad coinage in 1965 is the "split off clad layer." This is a lamination problem where the copper-nickel outer layer is not properly bonded to the copper core of the coin and fell off. The result will be a copper colored obverse or reverse, depending on which side was improperly bonded, or, if the layer split off after striking, a very thin copper-nickel obverse or reverse with the same design on the other side, incused and quite indistinct. Other types of planchet errors include coins struck on blanks intended for other denominations (domestic or foreign), or overstruck on other coins.

Die Errors:

Often called *varieties*, these may be intentional or unintentional. In some cases, we have no way of telling for certain, but we can pretty well assume that many are *un*intentional. These latter are accurately described as *die errors*. An improperly annealed (heated) die could very well appear as a "rippled" surface on a coin, the result of improper metal flow. Die clashes were certainly unintentional. Clashmarks occur when two planchets strike or "clash" together without a planchet between them in the striking chamber. Each die transfers portions of its design to the other die and all coins struck by those dies thereafter will exhibit those clashmarks until the die is polished or retired from service.

The increasingly popular field of doubled dies comprises another die aberration which is unintentional but sometimes permitted to pass inspectors. A doubled die is created when, in the hubbing (die making) process, there is a slight shift between successive hubbings, or, as in other cases, a second entirely different hub is used. All dies require at least two strikings or impressions from a hub in order to import full design details. One hubbing will not produce the proper depth of design, so subsequent hubbings are necessary. It is extremely important to understand that between hubbings, the die must be annealed or heated in order to accept the next impression without becoming brittle. Because there is a period of time between the successive hubbings of any given die, the hub used for the initial impression may not be the one utilized on later hubbings. If the two different hubs used *are* in perfect register with each other and are lined up properly, they import a clean, sharp image to the die. If, however, one of the two hubs is distorted through prolonged use, or is not lined up properly in the hubbing press, various portions of the design on the die will appear doubled. There are many different classes of doubling, all caused by different processes, but they are too technical to get into in this chapter. Suffice to say that a doubled die will produce coins with that same doubling until it is retired from use. Some doubling may be dramatic, while other forms may be quite subtle. [For full details see Alan Herbert's new book on mint errors — Editor.]

The Engraving Department at the Mint calls the degree of doubling the "spread" and will only condemn dies where it is really conspicuous. Other die varieties which are more likely to be intentional than unintentional include Repunched Mintmarks, Over Mintmarks, Repunched Dates, and Overdates. As mentioned previously, we cannot look backward in time and know for certain on any of these areas, but we suspect that in many cases, in the effort of die economy, a date or mintmark was repunched (if it was not initially lined up properly), or one number or letter punched in over a *different* number or letter creating an overdate or overmintmark. Remember, in order to be correctly described as an *over*date or *over*mintmark, two *different* numbers or letters must be involved (8 over 7, 7 over 6, 0 over S, O over CC, for example). A *repunched* date or mintmark involves only the *same* numbers or letters. From the Mint's earlier years until at least 1900-O/CC, overdates, overmintmarks, and corrected blunders certainly represented economy. Overdates later than 1908 are die errors.

Die cracks and die breaks — occasionally, if the die is not annealed properly or if it is subjected to extended use, it may develop a crack. Upon striking, the metal from the planchet will eventually be forced into this crack, gradually or rapidly enlarging it and creating a raised, irregular line on the coin.

After repeated strikings, a piece of the die may fall out, leaving a void into which the planchet metal flows, making what appears to be a "blob" of extra metal on the coin. This in *not* extra metal, but as described above, metal from the planchet extruded into that portion of the die which was broken away. A major die break such as this is commonly referred to as a "cud."

Another die error which is relatively scarce on dollars is the rotated die, where the obverse and reverse designs are not properly lined up when the coin is flipped over. This is caused by one of the dies, usually the reverse or "hammer" die, locked in an incorrect position prior to striking, or loosening and turning from its proper position during repeated strikings. The rotation can be slight (10 degrees or so) up through 180 degrees where it appears as a "medal strike" when flipped over.

Striking Errors:

This is the most dramatic and eye-catching category of the three, all of these errors occurring *at the time of strike*. Most striking errors on dollars are quite rare, with only a few exceptions. Examples of the latter would be coins struck through grease (sometimes referred to as a "filled die"), or partial collars on the Susan B. Anthony issues.

Some of the rarer and seldom-seen striking errors, especially on Morgan and Peace dollars, are: *off centers*, occurring when the planchet fails to seat properly in the collar and is struck by the dies without the full design in the obverse and reverse; *double strikes*, which are created when a struck coin falls entirely or partially between the dies for a second strike. Most double strike errors have the first impression centered properly and the second more or less off center.

A *trial strike* or *low pressure strike* generally occurs when the press is being adjusted for proper alignment, and is exemplified by a very shallow or weak strike on *both* the obverse and reverse, with varied amounts of the design showing. A key authentication point to identify this error is to check the reeding on the edge of the coin. If the reeding is also very weak and indistinct, it is probably a low pressure (die trial) strike, as there was insufficient pressure exerted to force the metal of the planchet into the reeding of the collar, forming the raised lines or reeds on the edge of the coin. A coin *struck through grease* may exhibit many of the characteristics of a trial strike, but because it was struck with full pressure, the reeding will be sharp and full.

A *broadstruck* coin is similar to an off center strike in that the planchet fails to seat properly in the striking chamber between the dies. In most cases the reverse die is jammed in the raised position, not providing a receptacle into which the planchet can fall to be surrounded by the collar. The planchet rests, fairly well centered on top of the reverse die, and when struck, it expands outward to greater than the normal size as there is no collar present to restrain it. A broadstruck coin is called a ***centered broadstrike*** where it is spread evenly, concentrically; otherwise it is uncentered. The criterion for properly calling a misstruck coin *off center* rather than an *uncentered broadstrike* is that *a portion of the obverse or reverse design must be missing* to be an off center. Remember, on a Morgan dollar, the denticles are part of the obverse and reverse design.

Coins which are broadstruck on a Type 1 blank (without the raised rims) will be characterized by a broad, flat rim on the obverse and reverse.

A *partial collar* strike occurs when the reverse die is again jammed in an up position, but not so far up as to be flush with the top of the collar as on a broadstrike. The planchet is able to fall partially down into the striking chamber, and when struck, has reeding from the collar on only a portion of the edge. It may be a "*tilted* partial collar" or a "*full* partial collar" (commonly referred to as a "railroad rim"), depending on the angle at which the reverse die is jammed in the collar.

An *indent* striking error is another rare type on any dollar coin. This happens when a blank or a planchet falls partially or completely between the planchet in the striking chamber and the die. It is impressed into the coin, leaving a depressed, unstruck area. If the second planchet completely covers the first and there is no design at all on one side, it is called a "*uniface*" strike.

If a *struck coin* instead of a blank or planchet falls between the regular planchet and the die and is struck into the coin, that "sandwich" coin acts as a die, and its design is impressed on the newly struck coin, *incused and backward*. If this incused design doesn't cover the entire side of the coin, it is called a "partial brockage." A "full brockage" occurs when the struck coin serving as the die completely covers one side of the second coin. Early strike brockages, with sharp, undistorted incused images are much preferred over the later strikes where the "backward" design is not as distinct.

A *strike through* on a coin may involve many different substances. Struck through grease was mentioned earlier. Other items that have come between the die and the planchet prior to striking and have been impressed into the coin include cloth (usually a portion of the wipe rag the workers use to clean the machinery), wood fibers which were still on the planchet after having been stored in sawdust, stray fragments, chips, or slivers of metal from the machinery or from a broken die, and wire.

One of the rarest of all errors, in any denomination, is the coin which is struck on the *wrong planchet*. It may be a dollar struck on a planchet intended for a half or quarter dollar, or even a cent. These are extremely rare and seldom encountered, especially on Morgan and Peace dollars. With the advent of the smaller Susan B. Anthony dollar, for the first time in U.S. minting history, a *half dollar* could be struck on a *dollar* planchet. This is only possible when the smaller planchet, in this case the SBA $1, can fit into the striking chamber of the larger coin (the half). In other words, it would be impossible for a half dollar to be struck on a Morgan, Peace or even an Eisenhower planchet because the diameter of these larger dollars would preclude them from fitting into the smaller (50 cent) collar. A coin may be struck on any planchet *smaller in diameter* than its normal one, but it cannot be struck on one of *greater* diameter. Still more rarely, dollars occur overstruck on other dollars or on smaller coins.

The Minting Process

It's a generally recognized fact that in the collecting of coins, those numismatists specializing in *error* or *variety* coins have a "leg up" on other collectors. The reason for this is that in order to effectively collect in this specialty, one must study the minting process to determine if an error or variety is really that and not the result of damage or "extracurricular activity."

Once you know the various steps in the minting process and what errors *can* occur during those steps, that knowledge can very easily be applied to regular collecting and logically based determinations made in certain areas which can allow the collector to avoid some serious problems. Determinations such as: "Is this a weak strike or slight wear?"; "Is this luster original or has the coin been 'doctored'?"; "Are those lines in the field hairlines or die polishing marks?", etc.

In order to help you understand the minting process and then be able to utilize that knowledge in your collecting, I felt it would be beneficial to review it from beginning to end (without getting too technical). Also, various errors and varieties are illustrated at the appropriate point in the process where they would occur. A few are rather subtle, but many are dramatic and extremely rare, especially the striking errors on Morgan and Peace dollars.

Again, the following review will be somewhat in highlight fashion. For more information and a more in-depth study of the subject, please refer to the end of this section for the address of CONECA (Combined Organizations of Numismatic Error Collectors of America), the rapidly growing national error and variety organization. We invite you to join and add a new dimension to your collecting enjoyment.

After a particular coin design has been accepted, the actual process starts with a large plaster model of that design. This model is then coated with copper which creates what is known as a "galvano." (In recent years an *epoxy* galvano has replaced the copper version.) This galvano is then placed in a Janvier reducing machine which uses the fulcrum method to transfer and reduce the precise positive design of the galvano onto the end of a short steel rod, creating a Master Hub.

This master hub, also a positive image, is then used to produce master dies (negative images), which in turn produce working hubs (positives), and finally, working dies (negatives), which actually strike the coins.

It is during the die preparation stage that many errors or varieties can occur. Pictured here (photos #1 and #2) is the reverse of an 1883-O Morgan which has what appears to be a "wavy" surface around the letters and devices. This is the result of an *improperly annealed die*. During the die preparation, each die must be impressed by the hub at least twice in order to achieve the proper design depth. On the first hubbing the die is dramatically hardened by the enormous pressure and must be annealed or heated before it can be hubbed again. If the annealing is not done correctly, with either too much or too little heat or time in the annealing furnace, the die will be affected and all coins struck by that die will show the same problem, such as the one presented here.

#2

#1

If, after the die is made, it requires some polishing or touch-up by a mint employee, some interesting things may occur. In this photo (#3), you'll see an example of a large die gouge, extending from the far left tailfeather on this 1890-CC Morgan. This variety is affectionately known as the "Tailbar" variety and came about when a worker's tool inadvertently slipped and put a deep gouge into this particular reverse die. Remember, a die is a negative image, so any depression in that die such as a gouge, will show up raised on the coin.

#3

As mentioned above, during its preparation, a die must be heated or annealed between hubbings in order for the metal to be soft enough to accept a second impression by the hub. A certain period of time is involved between these hubbings, usually at least a few days and often weeks, so the chances are very good that an entirely different hub will be used for subsequent strikings. If this different hub is worn, spread or even *newer* than the original hub, or if it is not properly lined up in the hubbing press, some portions of the design may be doubled on all coins struck by that die. This is called a *doubled die*.

The next photos show the two most spectacular and sought after doubled dies in the Morgan series. The first (#4) is a doubled die obverse on an 1888-O which, for obvious reasons, is nicknamed "Hot Lips." The nose, lips and chin are dramatically doubled, and the variety is very rare above XF with only one mint state known, an MS-60.

#4

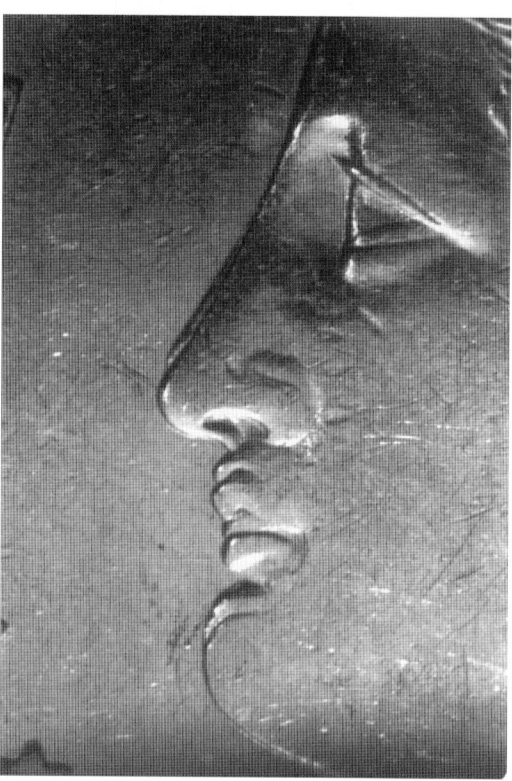

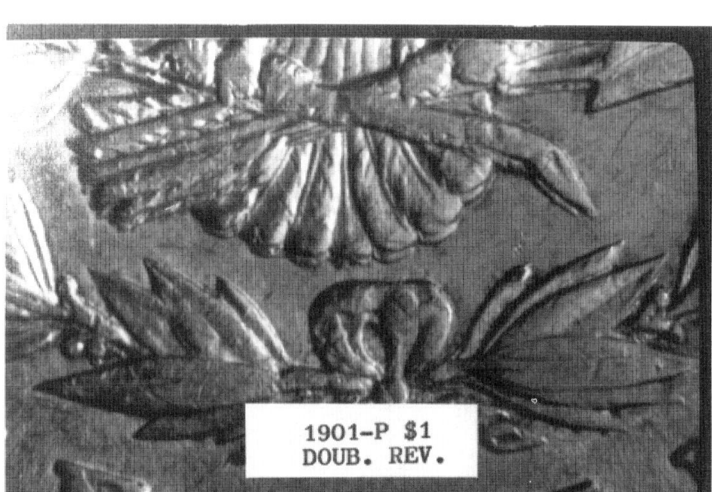

#5

The second (#5) shows a doubled die reverse on a 1901-P, with strong doubled tail-feathers, arrowfeathers, shafts, and olive branch. Again, this variety is very rare above XF with only one specimen reported in mint state.

In reviewing the minting process, it is important to understand that *all* dies are manufactured at the nation's first and largest mint in Philadelphia. Those dies to be used at the branch mints are then sent to those facilities (New Orleans, Carson City, San Francisco and Denver in the case of the Morgan dollar), where they are used for the actual striking of the coins. Prior to their shipment westward, however, the mintmark for the appropriate mint is applied by hand to each die.

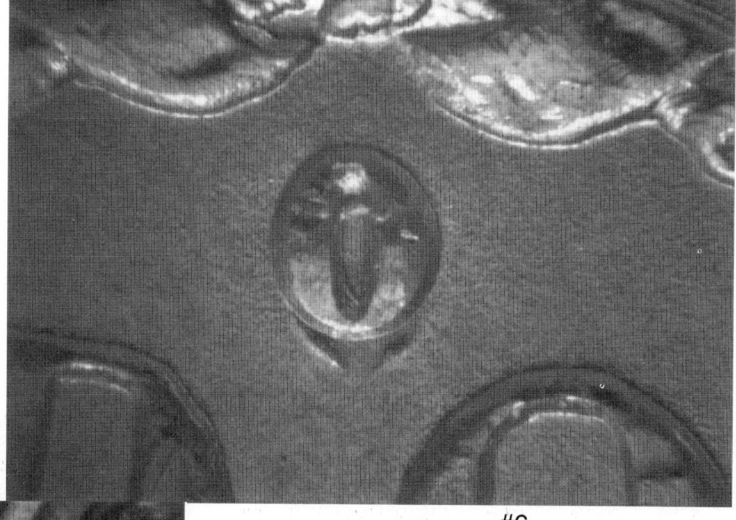

#6

Repunched mintmarks are not uncommon on Morgan dollars (but are rare on Peace). More than one impression (literally a blow with a hammer) of the mintmark punch is required to achieve the proper depth in the die. If subsequent strikings are not lined up precisely with the initial punch, a *repunched mintmark* is created and may appear as the 1882-O over Low O as shown in Photo #6.

This photo (#7) illustrated what has been described as an "O Over Horizontal O" on an 1879-O Morgan. It is identified in the VAM book as an O punched over a previous O, with the first punch in a horizontal instead of the proper vertical position. This author, along with many other variety specialists, feels it is instead an O over an O

#7

over an O, triple punched, with the first too high and the second too low. It is felt that the arcs showing inside the prime O are not in the proper configuration for the first O to have been punched in a horizontal position.

#8

Another type of mintmark variety is the "over-mintmark," where one letter is punched over a *different* letter. (A *repunched* mintmark is one letter over the *same* letter.) The 1882-O over S (#8) and 1900-O over CC (#9) over-mintmarks shown here are two examples.

#9

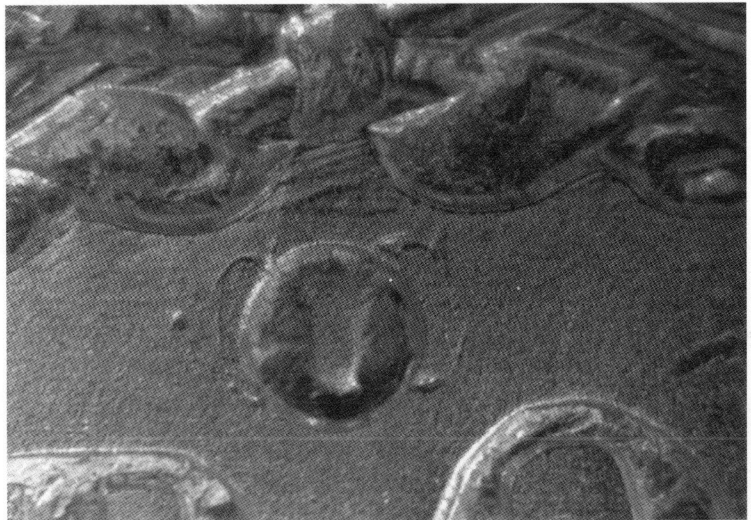

While the following are often classified as die errors because they involve something unwanted that happened to the die, they are also associated by some with the Striking category because they occur on the die after a certain number of coins have actually been struck. Examples: Photo #10 — a *die crack* on a Peace $1. Similar cracks are common on Peace dollars, especially the 1922 and 1923 issues around the date and lower bust area, and around the stars and date on the 1921 Morgan issues. They occur when a die actually cracks under the intense pressure of repeated strikings, and the metal from the planchet is forced into that fissure at each impact. On subsequent strikings the crack grows larger, more metal is forced into the opening, eventually broadening or lengthening it, or both.

#10

#11

Eventually the die breaks and a piece falls away, usually at the edge. The planchet metal forced through this cavity now is large enough to form a "blob" on the coin which is commonly referred to as a "*cud*." The large cud on the 1971-D Ike (#11) of which only two specimens are known, and the double cud on the 1979 SBA $1 (#12) are excellent examples. There is one major cud in the Morgan dollar series. The 1888-O Double Lips or "Hot Lips" variety (VAM 4) in its latest state developed cuds positioned 5:00 to 7:00, and 12:00 to 2:00 as a result of a doubled obverse die. (See EVN v2n1, page 6 (1/30/79), report by Kenneth B. Embler.)

#12

#13

Photo #13 shows an extremely strong *clashmark* on the reverse of an 1891-O Morgan which is part of "LIBERTY" on the headband from the obverse. Clashmarks occur when the obverse and reverse dies "clash" or hit together without a planchet between them and impress portions of their design on each other.

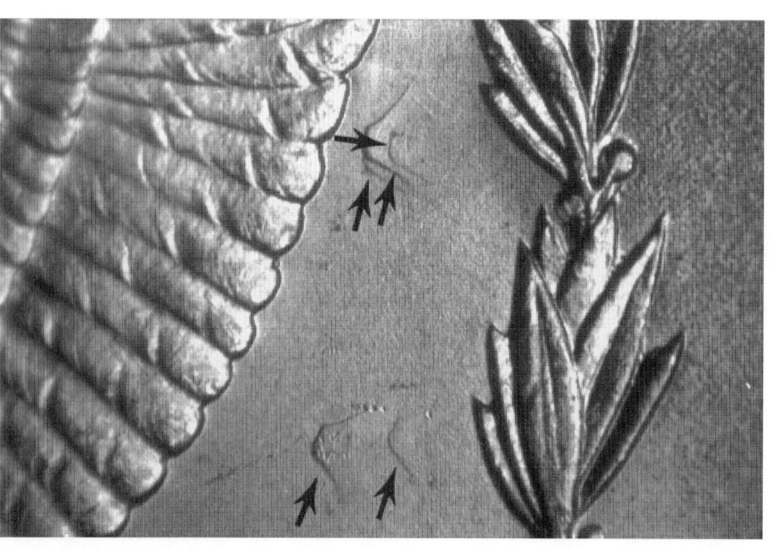

#14

Photo #14 is very interesting because it shows clearly no less than *five* clashmarks on the reverse of an 1886-P dollar. These are from the notch at the lower part of Liberty's cap on the obverse, and clearly prove that these dies clashed together at least *five times* in two widely separated positions. The two at the bottom are far out of register from the ones at the top and are the widest known in the Morgan series. Most likely the obverse die was loose for these two collisions.

#15

The final photo representing a *die* error (#15), is this *filled die* on a 1921-P Morgan. In this case grease has clogged the obverse die, precluding much of the design from being struck up. This is fairly common on some portions of Morgan and Peace dollars and even more common in certain areas of Ike and SBA's, especially around the rims.

#16

We now turn to another phase of the minting process, *planchet production*. Although in recent years some blanks are supplied by private contractors, we must assume that their production process is similar to that of the U.S. Mint.

The appropriate metals are melted in huge furnaces and combined to form large ingots which pass through a series of rollers to reduce them down to a long strip of the required planchet thickness. These long strips are then coiled and stored for future use. The strip will eventually go to the blanking room where it passes through a gang punch machine which creates the blanks from which planchets are made. (*Note*: "Blanks" are the metal discs punched out of the strip. They do not become "planchets" until they go through the upsetting mill which forms the raised edge — See Photo #29 presented later in this chapter.)

If the ingot has imperfections within it, during the rolling out process this imperfection (such as a void from trapped or occluded gas) is spread along the length of the strip. The blanks punched out of this portion of the strip will contain the imperfection and coins minted on these planchets will exhibit these abnormalities. As an example, photos #16 and #17 show occluded gas bubbles on the reverse of a Morgan dollar.

#17

Another result of improper planchet preparation has arisen in recent years since the advent of the clad coinage. Sometimes the bonding process which forms the tri-layered strip fails to adhere the three layers properly and after the blanking process one side or another of the copper-nickel outer layers may split off before striking. The two SBA dollars illustrated here (photos #18 and #19) show the obverse clad layer split off on one, exposing the center (copper) core, and the thin copper-nickel shell split off the reverse on the other.

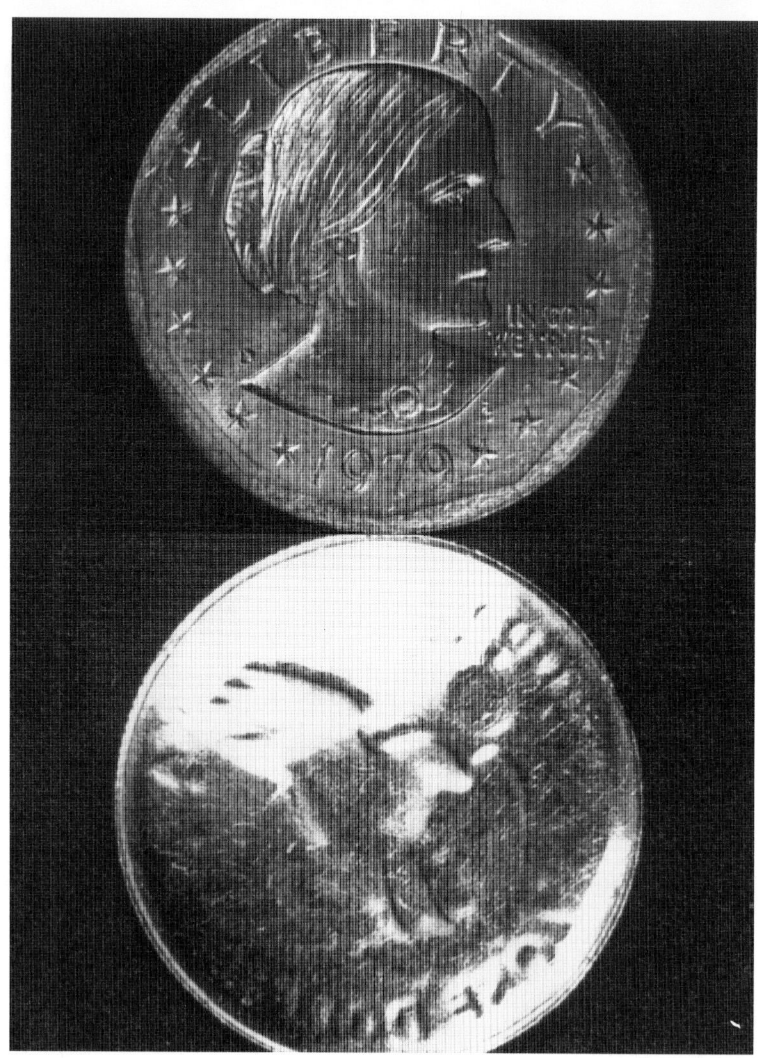

#18 ←

#19 ←

#20↑ #21↓

Specimens from which either or both clad layers have split off before striking will be weakly struck on both sides and probably edges. This is because they are thinner than normal, and the dies are set to come together to a greater distance, dictated by the normal planchet thickness. Those from which one or more clad layers have dropped after striking will have the clad side and edge normally strong.

The gang punch which produces the blanks acts essentially as a giant cookie cutter on the strip. If that strip fails to advance far enough after having a series of blanks punched out of it, the next downward stroke will overlap some of the holes, creating blanks with various size portions missing. After going through the aforementioned upsetting mill to form the raised edge, the coins minted on these incomplete planchets will show what is commonly referred to as a "clip."

#22 ←

These photos are examples of several different kinds of "clips" (incomplete planchets): Photo #20 shows a 35% curved clip on a 1979-S SBA; #21, a 40% curved clip on a 1978-P Ike; #22, a double curved clip #22 on a 1973-S Proof Ike;

#23

#23, a triple curved clip on a 1974-D Ike;

#24

#24, a straight clip (from the edge of the strip) on a 1979-S SBA

#25 An elliptical clip (one that has not cut all the way through the strip) is deep enough to break through when punched a second time after the strip has advanced. Such a planchet, when struck by the dies, is very rare.

#25

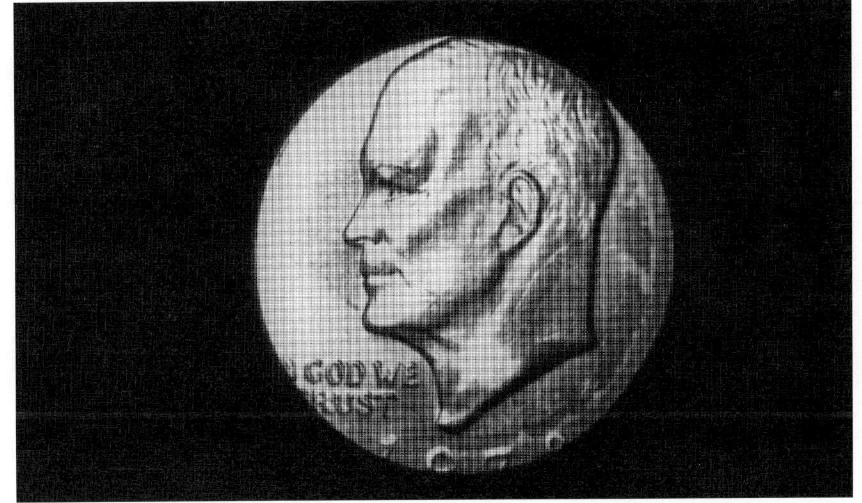

#26

Some of the more dramatic planchet errors occur when the wrong planchet, one intended for another denomination, is struck by the dies. The next photo (#26) presents a 1978 Ike struck on a 50 cent planchet.

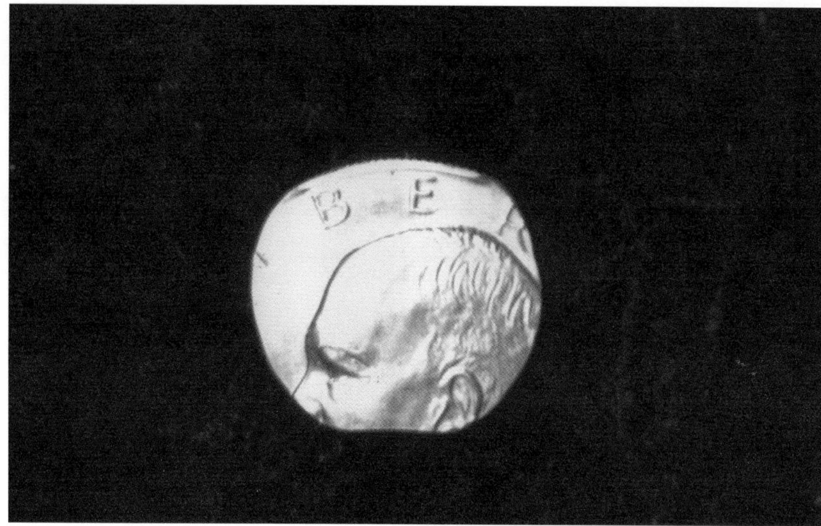

#27

Photo #27 shows an Ike struck on a (copper) 1 cent planchet!

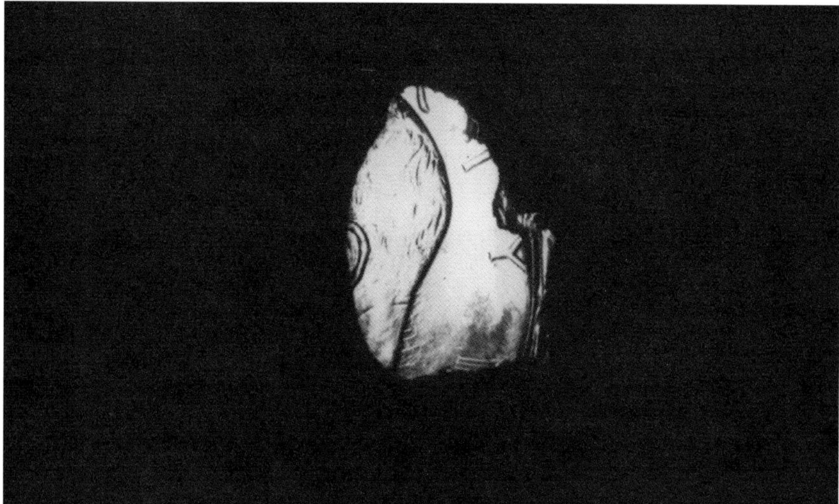

#28

The final photo of a planchet error is also quite impressive. Photo #28 illustrates an Ike dollar struck on a *fragment*, an irregular piece of scrap metal which somehow found its way under the dies. This, and the wrong planchet errors shown above, are very rare on Ike and SBA dollars and exceedingly rare in the Morgan and Peace series.

#29

Striking Errors are generally the most impressive of the three basic error categories.

After the planchets are formed and heated to soften the metal to facilitate striking (they are not still warm when they are struck, but have been well cooled beforehand), they go to the coining room where they will pass through huge, high-speed coining presses and become coins as we know them.

The planchets are fed down a chute into the coining chamber, an opening of the appropriate denomination size, surrounded by a metal collar which retains the coin's proper diameter. Occasionally a planchet fails to be struck and escapes into circulation with the normally struck coins. Photo #29 shows a planchet which has gone through the upsetting mill, forming the raised edges. This makes it easier for the design to be struck up, protects the design somewhat against wear, and facilitates stacking.

#30

When the press is just starting up or just being stopped, or if the press operator wants to ensure that the dies are lined up properly, very often a planchet is struck with far too little pressure to adequately strike up the design on both obverse and reverse. Photos #30 and #31 show a 1979-P SBA with this type of striking error.

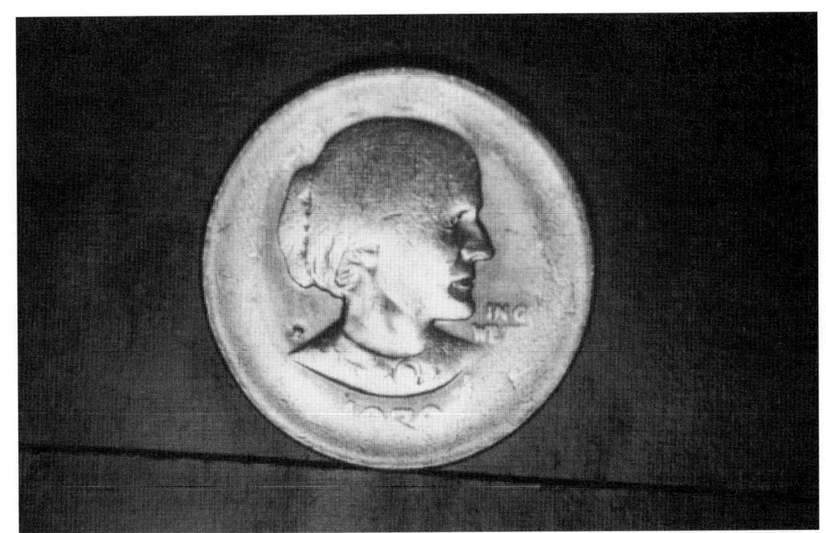

#31

(See caption beside Photo #30)

#32

Photos #32 and #33 illustrate an *extremely low pressure strike* on a Bicentennial Ike. These will have edge reeding very weak or absent.

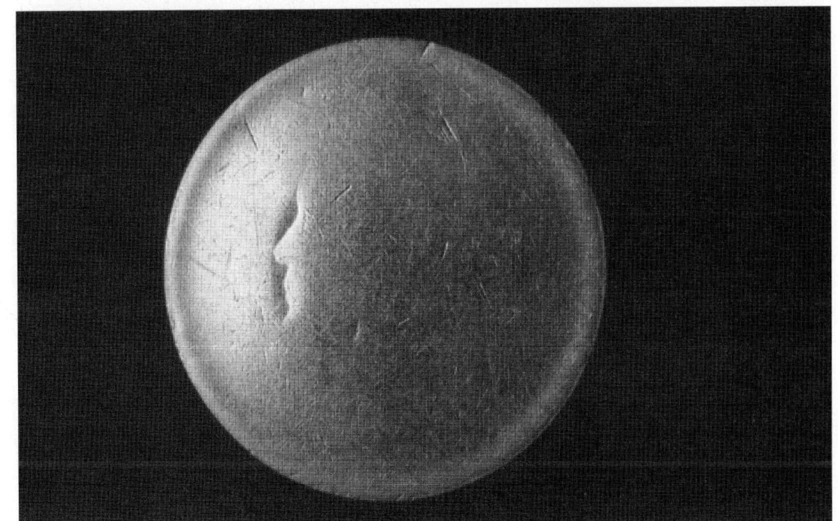

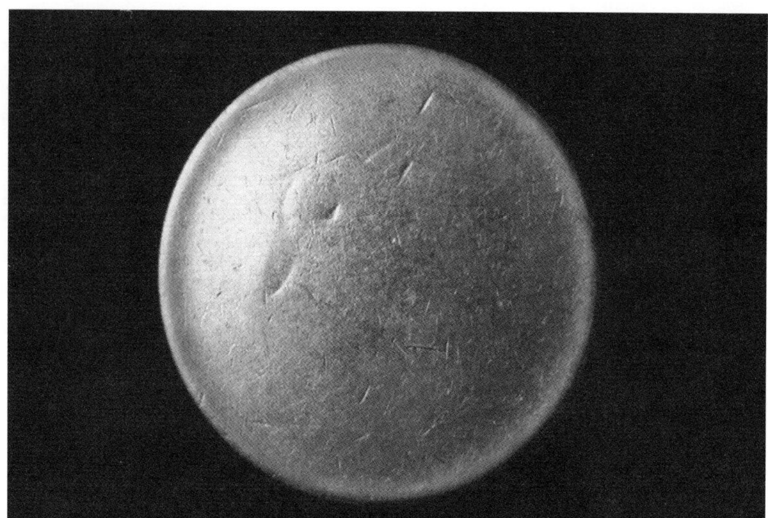

#33

(See caption beside Photo #32.)

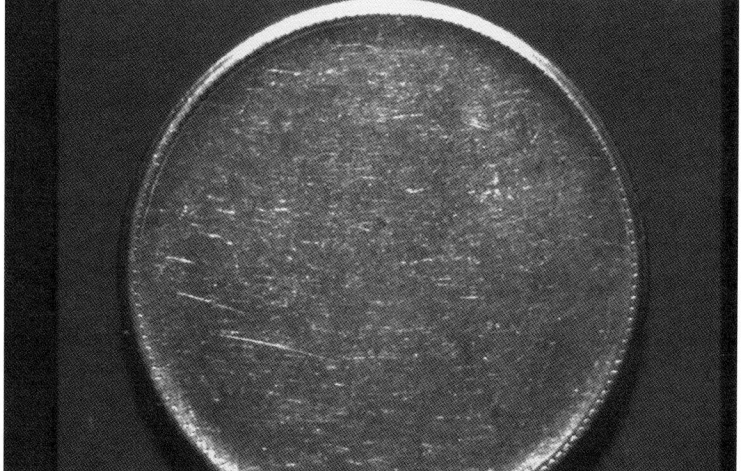

#34

Photo #34 represents an even lower pressure strike, the finest known on any denomination. If you look closely, you'll see evidence of denticles around the rim of this apparent "blank" planchet. This is proof that this planchet was struck by both dies (the weak denticles show on both sides), as they are parts of both the obverse and reverse designs. As an interesting sidelight to this error, after showing it several years ago to Tom DeLorey, former ANACS authenticator and numismatic researcher, he told me he felt quite certain that this was a *1921* Morgan struck at the *San Francisco* mint. He concluded this by the shape of the raised rim on the coin which is typical only of the Morgans struck at San Francisco in 1921. This theory was generated as Tom had seen a few off center 1921-S dollars and noticed that the raised rims on the unstruck portions were slightly different from any other date and mint.

#35

Occasionally, usually when the reverse die is jammed in the "up" position, a planchet fails to enter the striking chamber surrounded by the retaining collar and is struck *off center* or *broadstruck*. The next group of photos illustrate different percentages of off center strikes on various dollar types. Photo #35 is a 5% off center on a DMPL 1883-O, the only off center known on a DMPL.

#36

Photo #36 is a 20% off center on an 1888-O (which is also a love token!).

#39

Photo #39 is a 70% off center on a 1979-S SBA.

#40

A *broadstrike* occurs when the reverse die is also jammed in an "up" position, not allowing the planchet to fall into the striking chamber surrounded by the collar. In this case, however, the planchet lands squarely on top of the reverse die and expands outward when struck by the dies as there is no collar to retain it. Photo #40 is an example of a broadstruck 1879-P. This coin was struck on a *blank*, one not having gone through the upsetting mill, and is characterized by the broad, flat rims on both obverse and reverse.

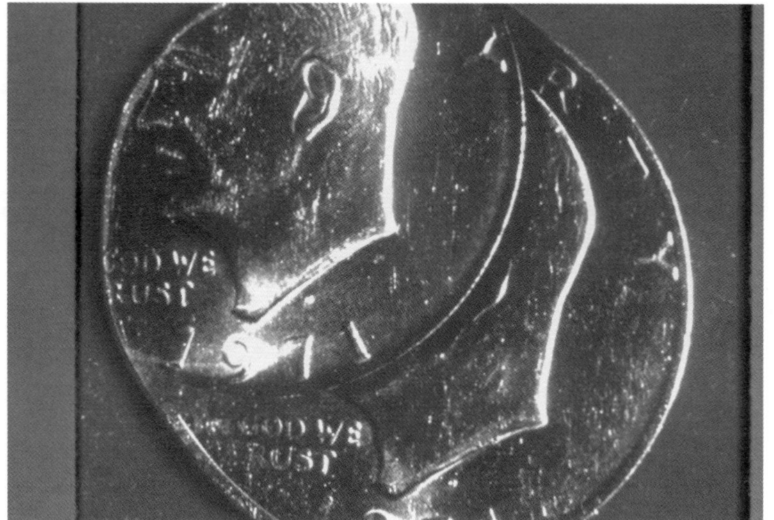

#41

Sometimes a struck coin finds its way back under the dies and is struck again (double struck). This 1971-D Ike (Photo #41) is a good example of such a striking error. Coins of this kind in which the obverse is struck over the reverse and vice versa are known as flipover double strikes.

#42

Indents are quite rare, especially when the indent is caused by another planchet of a different denomination. Somehow, a 10 cent planchet fell on the reverse die of the 1972-D Ike (#42) before the dollar planchet entered the coining chamber. Upon striking, the smaller 10 cent planchet was struck into the reverse of this coin, fell out, and undoubtedly became mixed in with the rest of the 1972-D dollars. Somewhere out there there's a 10 cent planchet with part of the Ike's reverse design on one side and blank on the other. Having both pieces of a major error such as this is an error collector's dream. Who's got it?!

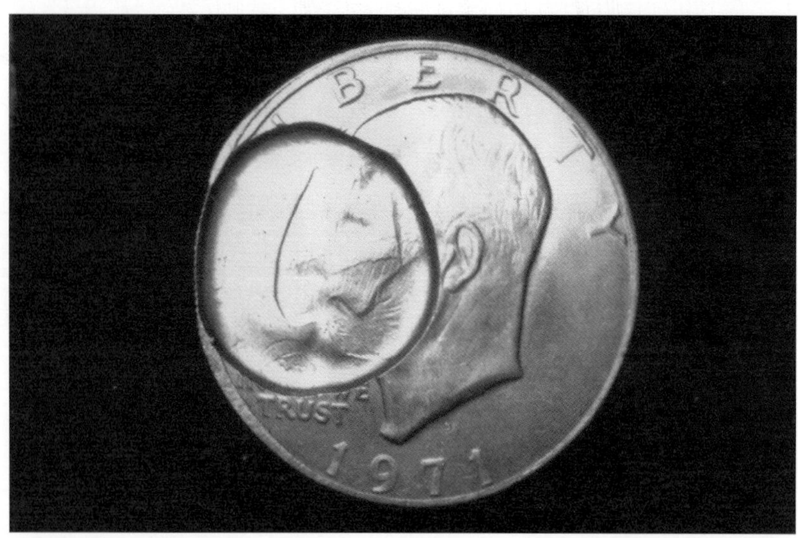

#43

Let's go one step further . . . if a 10 cent planchet *struck by the $1.00 dies* fell *on top* of an incoming $1.00 planchet and was struck into the obverse of that dollar, you would have an error such as the one in Photo #43. This creates a *brockage* strike. where a portion of the Ike obverse design (from the struck 10 cent planchet) is transferred to the obverse of the larger dollar. The 10 cent sized piece creating this very rare error would now have a portion of the obverse Ike design on one side and an expanded or somewhat distorted obverse portion on the other.

#44

Occasionally pieces of scrap, slag, cloth or a variety of foreign objects come between the planchet and either the obverse or reverse die and is struck into the coin. Not surprisingly, these are called "strike through" errors. Photo #44 shows where a long piece of metal was struck into the obverse of this 1885-O dollar and then fell out.

#45

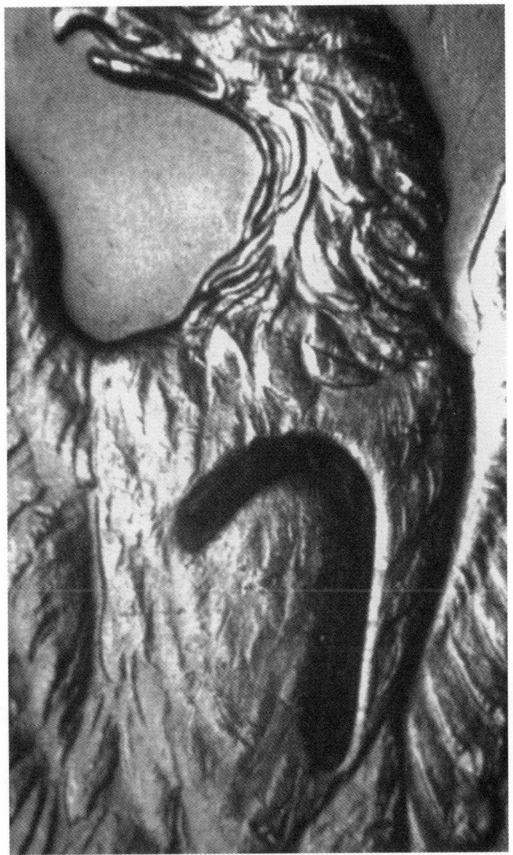

Photo #45 illustrates an even larger strikethrough, probably a piece of extraneous metal, struck into the reverse of this Morgan.

#46

Finally, Photo #46 shows a strikethrough on the reverse of an 1896-P dollar where a thick metal pin was *retained* in the coin after having been struck. Errors where the item is still imbedded in the coin are much rarer than those where the object has fallen out.

1878-CC Morgan Dollar with a 30% rotated reverse (Obverse) (Courtesy of Harrison Phillips, Memphis, Tennessee)

1878-CC Morgan Dollar with a 30% rotated reverse (Reverse) (Courtesy of Harrison Phillips, Memphis Tennessee)

This is a 1921-S Morgan Dollar. It is impossible to see the "S" mint-mark without a 20X magnifying glass. (Courtesy of Bobbie Webb, Broken Arrow, Oklahoma)

The two coins are from an original 20 roll deal in 1979. Each and every coin in those rolls had a die lamination from the middle of Miss Liberty's cheek through the date and to the rim. (Courtesy of John William Highfill, Memphis, Tennessee)

A close up view at one of the 1887-P Morgans with a major die lamination from the 1979 hoard of twenty original Bu rolls. Each and every coin had the identical die lamination! (Courtesy of John William Highfill, Memphis, Tennessee)

Morgan Dollar from the mint at Philadelphia with "unremovable" grease marks from the original minting process. (Courtesy of Yvonne "Vonnie" A. Berry, Tulsa, Oklahoma)

This concludes a brief overview of the Minting Process. It is hoped that the above will enable you to understand various aspects of the hobby a little better and that it will add to your collecting enjoyment.

For more information on errors and varieties, please write to: XAN CHAMBERLAIN, CONECA Membership Chairman, P.O. Box 915, Palo Alto, CA 94302.

I very gratefully acknowledge the assistance of Fred Weinberg who spent many hours to research, coordinate and provide the fine photographs presented in this chapter. It should also be noted that a number of the coins pictured are from Fred Weinberg's extensive personal collection.

***

Jeff G. Oxman

Jeff Oxman, whose collecting interests have spanned three decades, is, today, a respected numismatic writer, collector, researcher, and editor. For the past ten years, his primary focus has been post-1840 U.S. silver dollar die varieties, where he has devoted his energies to discovering, attributing, and cataloguing the more than 2000 known varieties. As a result of this research, Oxman is often called upon for his silver dollar expertise to attribute Liberty Seated, Morgan, Peace, and Trade dollar varieties.

A very recent turning point in his collecting career came in the fall of 1988 when a group of U.S. silver dollar specialists banded together to form the Society of Silver Dollar Collectors (SSDC). As a founding officer of the organization, Oxman has served as board member, as well as editor of its quarterly publication since its inception.

In 1989, Oxman was appointed the Assistant Editor of the *NASC Quarterly*, which, at the Summer ANA Convention in Seattle the following year, received the ANA's Top Regional Numismatic Publication award. In 1990, he assumed the editorship of the *NASC Quarterly*.

Oxman's writing talents have been featured on a number of occasions as guest columnist for the Collectors' Clearinghouse pages in *Coin World*. There, his detailed research articles have served as a resource for those interested in new silver dollar die varieties. Further, Oxman has also contributed extensively to a number of books and manuscripts which have included information about U.S. silver dollar varieties.

Oxman is currently active in a number of local and regional clubs, where he is a frequent guest speaker. In addition, Oxman has contributed articles to most of the club publications where he is a member.

What makes this specialist tick? For Jeff Oxman, it's the thrill of each new silver dollar discovery that fans the flames of numismatic interest which began over thirty years ago.

CHAPTER 18

Die Varieties in the Morgan Dollar Series

by Jeff G. Oxman

How would you like to write an analysis of each and every U.S. silver dollar variety within the space of one chapter of a book? Foolhardy, you say? Well, I agree. In the Morgan, Peace, and Trade dollar series alone, there are approximately two thousand known die varieties. Even an overview of the subject could prove to be a daunting task.

But I have been asked to boldly venture in, anyway, limiting the scope of my discussion to the ever-popular Morgan dollar series. My excuse for saying "Yes"? The late Truman Capote once wrote that "every year you live in California, you lose two points from your IQ." The sad truth is that I've been on the West Coast since 1960! Nonetheless, I view the effort as a great opportunity to convey to you some of the excitement I've personally experienced in collecting silver dollar varieties.

Mommy, Where Do Varieties Come From?

First, a basic question must be answered, "Just what is a die variety?" From a technical standpoint, a die variety consists of all coins struck from one particular pair of dies, distinguishable from all other die pairs of the same design and date by a feature or variation unique to those dies. Whew!! In a practical sense, this simply means that each unique combination of obverse and reverse dies constitutes a single die variety. Doubled dies, repunched mint marks, overdates, and repunched dates all represent die varieties.

According to Leroy Van Allen, 1,624 Morgan and 81 Peace dollar varieties had been attributed as of January 1982. And new discoveries have numbered well over a hundred since that time. But just because a certain coin is not the commonly encountered variety does not mean you'll become the next Donald Trump. Don't start negotiations for a casino on the Boardwalk just yet! The fact is that currently fewer than fifty Morgan and Peace dollar varieties could be termed premium varieties.

Knowledge Is "King"

On the other hand, it is also true that being one of those fifty silver dollar varieties *can add* significantly to the value of a given date. A prime example is the 1878-P VAM 44 with tripled die obverse. The fact that an AU example changed hands a few years ago for $2,000, at a time when the more common varieties of this date retailed for $20, is enough to get most people's attention!

Here, as in most things, "knowledge is king." The key is to recognize the premium varieties when they cross your path, and that is my purpose — to focus on the rarest, most desirable varieties in the Morgan dollar series. In the process, I hope to encourage your interest, as well as increase your knowledge, in this exciting area of numismatics.

Morgan Dollar Variety Sets

The first question on the mind of a new collector is invariably, "What should I collect?" The best answer should be "anything you like." However, a particularly satisfying approach to collecting Morgan dollar varieties involves focusing on one or more possible "sets."

The allure of "completing a set" has been instinctive to collectors down through the ages, from putting together sets of butterflies, to pressing coins into an album with spaces for specific dates and mint marks. Indeed, the "thrill of the hunt" has excited whole generations of hobbyists who hope to find that one rare specimen, which, for years, has been so elusive. Today, this dimension of numismatics is especially enjoyed by variety collectors.

In the Morgan dollar series, a number of "variety sets" could be assembled. Seven primary ones, grouped by date and mint mark, are listed in the chart below. But first a word of encouragement. The almost infinite diversity of variety collecting is what makes it so enjoyable. If your tastes run to other groupings of varieties, then so much the better!

The VAM Collector's - "MAGNIFICENT SEVEN"			
The Variety "Set"	Number in Completed Set	Rarest Variety in the Set	Notes About Rarest Varieties
1. 1878-P 7/8 TF	16 Varieties	VAM 44	15-18 Known
2. 1878-P C Rev [1]	13 Varieties	VAM 203	R-6 in VAM Book
3. 1879-S B Rev [2]	13 Varieties	Unknown	Insufficient Research
4. 1880 Overdates (P,S,O, & CC)	29 Varieties	80-P VAM 7,8	Both are Ultra-rare
5. 1882-O/S	6 Varieties	VAM 17	Less than 5 Known
6. 1887/6-P,O	2 Varieties	87-O 7/6	Tremendous Premium
7. 1990 O/CC	7 Varieties	VAM 9	Ultra-rare

[1] So called "Reverse of '79"

[2] So called "Reverse of '78"

Because die varieties are the product of a wide spectrum of causes, all with differing effects, and because the resulting varieties are scattered throughout the series, VAMs have often been considered difficult to collect in "sets." But contrary to such thinking, there *are* a number of "sets" to complete in the Morgan dollar series. Here we have seven variety "sets," which taken together, include more than 75% of the key Morgan dollar varieties.

Source: The Society of Silver Dollar Collectors.
P.O. Box 2123, Sepulveda, CA 91393. Used by permission.

The VAM Numbering System

VAM is an acronym for Leroy Van Allen and A. George Mallis, who in the early 1960's independently researched the die varieties of the Morgan dollar series. Joining forces later in the decade, their collaboration resulted in *The Guide to Morgan and Peace Dollars*, which was privately published in 1971. Five years later, the "Guide" was further refined, expanded, and then published as their magnum opus, *The Comprehensive Catalogue and Encyclopedia of U.S. Morgan and Peace Silver Dollars*. It immediately won the prestigious NLG "Book of the Year" award in 1976, and went on to become the definitive volume on Morgan and Peace dollar varieties. But its greatest accolade may simply be the fact that it is now universally accepted as the "VAM Book" by variety enthusiasts.

In the VAM book, each die variety is assigned a unique identifying number called a VAM number. The actual process is simple. As new varieties are discovered, they are assigned the next available VAM Number for that date and mint mark. There are 46 different die varieties of 1881-S Morgan dollars that have already been attributed and catalogued. So, the next 1881-S discovery will be designated VAM 47. In effect, the VAM numbers make it possible to identify and then refer to the individual silver dollar varieties in the series. Of course, it is important to know which VAM numbers represent premium varieties, because in the case of the '81-S varieties, not one currently carries a premium!

The 1878-P 7/8 TF Varieties

The 1878-P 7/8 Tail-feather varieties now enjoy an exalted position in VAM collecting, and rightly so. In the first place, many of the 7/8 TF VAMs have very dramatic variety features. VAMs 41 and 42, for example, exhibit seven underlying tail-feather tips that are so pronounced they appear to be an intentional part of Morgan's design!

Secondly, the sixteen 7/8 TF varieties are, by and large, easily detectable. 100-power microscopes are not required! I remember my first look at a VAM 31, which has incredibly doubled eagle's legs. One morning at a West Coast coin show, a dealer brought out this coveted jewel for all to see, and as people gathered around the bourse table to get a glimpse at such an oddity, amid the oohs and aahs, I knew I was hooked on VAMs!

It is a definite plus that the 7/8 TF varieties are already listed in most pricing guides, including the Red Book, the Greysheet, the Bluesheet, and the weekly numismatic publications. Although such pricing information is basically incorrect for all but the most common 7/8 TF VAMs, it does represent an important resource for new variety collectors who have no way to assign values to unpublished varieties.

Another aspect that makes 7/8 TF varieties so attractive is the range in rarity within the one set. 11 of the 16 VAMs can be obtained with only a modicum of effort, and 3 of the remaining five *do* come on the market, if rather infrequently. The last two could be considered rare, and offer a stiff challenge, but isn't that the "thrill of the hunt" I mentioned earlier! Overall, most agree that it is an exciting "set" to collect.

Featured below is a chart ranking the 16 known 1878-P 7/8 TF varieties according to their relative rarity. The rarest variety, by far, is the legendary VAM 44, of which there is only one confirmed BU example and 18 to 20 circulated specimens. At the other end of the spectrum is the VAM 33, which accounts for probably 20% of the total 7/8 TF population.

Interestingly, the rarest 7/8 TF variety, the VAM 44, and the most common, the VAM 33, share the same reverse die. It can be assumed that the VAM 44 obverse die became damaged quite early in the production run and was immediately replaced by the VAM 33 obverse. Confirming an exceedingly short die life for the VAM 44 is the fact that every known VAM 44 specimen has prooflike surfaces.

One other surprise is the total mintage of the 7/8 TF varieties. From correspondence preserved in the National Archives, Van Allen was able to pinpoint March 26, 1878 as the first day these dies were used. It appears that they were only in the presses on an exclusive basis for the next ten days, and then were replaced by the newly developed 7 TF reverse dies.

Van Allen's estimate of the total number of 7/8 TF specimens struck is a trifling 544,000. Therefore, if it were a separate date, the 7/8's would qualify, in terms of mintages, as one of the rarest dozen or so issues in the entire Morgan dollar series!

RARITY GUIDE FOR THE
MAJOR 1878-P 7/8 TAILFEATHER VARIETIES
(VAMs 30-45 Ranked in Order of Rarity)

1.	VAM 44	Exceedingly Rare	Seldom, if ever, available.
2.	VAM 32	Rare	Heavy premium when located.
3. 4. 5.	VAM 43 VAM 45 VAM 40	Very Scarce	Moderate premium to VAM collectors.
6. 7. 8. 9. 10.	VAM 34 VAM 39 VAM 42 VAM 41 VAM 31	Scarce	Not readily obtainable but nonetheless carrying only a small premium.
11. 12. 13. 14. 15. 16.	VAM 30 VAM 36 VAM 37 VAM 41A VAM 38 VAM 33	Can be elusive, but usually available	No premium over "Greysheet" listed prices.

FACT SHEET:
THE 1878-P 7/8 TF VARIETY

Nature of Variety: *Dual Hubbed Reverse Dies (New 7TF Hub over old 8TF Hub)*
Total Number of Known Varieties: *16*
Number of Different Reverse Dies: *13*
Estimated Average Die Life: *Approx. 70,000*
Rarest Variety: *VAM 44*
Most Common Variety: *VAM 33*
Estimated Total Number Struck: *544,000 (All Varieties)*
Date First Struck: March 26, 1878
7/8 TF Dies Used Exclusively: *For Approx. 10 days (Also used after April 4, 1878 with 7 TF dies)*

It surprises many collectors to learn that the first published mention of the 7/8 TF variety was as recent as 1948 — 70 years after its introduction in 1878. The seven tail-feather and eight tail-feather varieties had long been recognized, but the 7/8 TF reverse was not publicly identified in print until the January 20, 1948 issue of *Numismatic Scrapbook Magazine*. There, an inquisitive reader wrote to the editor asking if such a third variety of 1878 existed. Today's answer is a resounding "Yes!"

Source: The Society of Silver Dollar Collectors.
P.O. Box 2123, Sepulveda, CA 91393. Used by permission.

The 1878-P Varieties With "C" Reverses

First, a word about "A", "B", and "C" Reverse varieties. Confusion seems to abound about the terminology, when in fact, it is easily understood. According to the attribution system developed by Van Allen and Mallis, the "A" Reverse simply refers to the *first* reverse motif used in 1878, namely, the *eight* tail-feather reverse.

Other characteristics of the "A" Reverse include a flat eagle's breast, wide rims around the periphery of the coin, and the "I" of "In" touching the eagle's wing. First put into production at the Philadelphia Mint on March 12, 1878, this initial reverse was used in striking a minimum of 700,000 coins.

The "B" Reverse was the second major Morgan dollar reverse design used in 1878, and is easily distinguished by its flattened, low relief eagle's breast and *seven* tail-feather motif. Although a few leftover dies were employed in 1879 at the San Francisco Mint and a couple more in 1880 at the Carson City Mint, the "B" Reverse is most noted for its predominant use in 1878.

The "B" Reverse is also popularly known to collectors as the 1878 "Second Reverse," the 1878 "Flat Breast Reverse," the 1878 "Parallel Arrow Feathers (PAF) Reverse" or simply as the "Reverse of 1878."

And lastly, we come to the "C" Reverse, which is the third major motif of 1878 Morgan dollar reverse, characterized by its distinctively rounded, convex eagle's breast and seven tail-feather design with top arrow feather slanted up to left. The "C" Reverse, representing the principal reverse design identified with most of the Morgan dollar series, was introduced during June 1878, and continued in use until a new, hastily engraved hub was introduced in 1921.

More often referred to as the "Reverse of '79," the "Third Reverse of '78'", the 1878 "Round Breast" reverse, or the "Slanted Arrow Feather (SAF)" reverse, the "C" Reverse designation still remains the most technically correct.

The 13 "C" Reverse 1878-P varieties are a small, but manageable set of VAMs, once again including mostly common varieties, but also including several "stoppers." The accompanying chart represents the relative rarity of the various VAMs.

Rarity Guide For the 1878-P With "C" Reverse

VAM Number	Reverse Type	Variety Description	VAM Book Rarity #	VAM Book Int. Factor	SSDC Rel. Rarity	Rarity Ranking	Availability	Mint Mark	Breen # Cross Ref.
200	C^1	Brkn N & M	R-4	I-2	RR-7	4 th	Scarce	N/A	# 5515
201	C^1	Dbld Liberty	R-4	I-2	RR-7	5 th	Scarce	N/A	# 5515
202	C^1	Dbld "8's"	R-5	I-3	RR-4	8 th	Common	N/A	# 5516
203	C^1	Short Leaf	R-6	I-2	RR-10	1 st	Ultra-Rare	N/A	# 5516
210	C^2	Normal C^2	R-5	I-2	RR-3	9 th	Common	N/A	# 5514
210A	C^2	Line Thru R	R-5	I-2	RR-6	7 th	Scarce	N/A	# 5514
210B	C^2	Line Thru IB	R-5	I-2	RR-6	6 th	Scarce	N/A	# 5514
220	C^3	Tripled R	R-4	I-3	RR-9	2nd	Very Rare	N/A	# 5515
221	C^3	II^1 Obv.	R-2	I-1	RR-3	10th	Common	N/A	# 5514
222	C^3	II^2 Obv.	R-2	I-1	RR-2	11th	Common	N/A	# 5516
223	C^3	Polished "L"	R-4	I-2	RR-9	3rd	Very Rare	N/A	# 5514
230	C^3	Normal Rev.	R-2	I-2	RR-1	12th	Common	N/A	# 5516

Source: The Society of Silver Dollar Collectors.
P.O. Box 2123, Sepulveda, CA 91393. Used by permission.

The 1879-S Varieties With "B" Reverse

The group of 1879-S VAMs with the so-called "Reverse of '78" represents an intriguing subject for collectors interested in an unexplained "mystery." As is well documented, the reverse design of the Morgan dollar underwent numerous changes in 1878 — from the initial 8 tail-feather design; to a 7/8 TF re-impressed reverse; to a 7 TF with flat-breast eagle; to the final incarnation, a 7 TF eagle with rounded breast.

What is important here is that the Philadelphia Mint shipped an unknown number of "B" Reverse dies to the San Francisco Mint for use there in 1879, in addition to the normal "C" Reverse dies. But the plot seems to have as many twists and turns as an Agatha Christie novel.

Clearly, 1878 dies may have been used as a matter of expediency. First of all, it is quite possible that considering all the confusion of 1878, any number of obsolete Morgan dollar dies languished at the Philadelphia Mint. If, at any time, production requirements exceeded the number of dies available during 1879, it is easily imagined that a limited number of left-over dies would be used. Indeed, coinage dies were time-consuming and expensive to produce.

How many "B" reverse dies were shipped? Probably a small number, with "ten" being the most likely possibility. It is definite that the first shipments of "B" reverse dies to the San Francisco and Carson City Mints in 1878 consisted of ten reverse dies to each. The fact that seven 1879-S "B" reverses have thus far been accounted for would be consistent with that number. Finally, using such reasoning, we have some basis for the relative scarcity of the "B" reverse 1879-S Morgan dollar, which in high grades, is a major rarity of the series.

Because research into the "B" Reverse has been so sketchy, a determination of the relative rarities of the 1879-S "B" Reverse varieties has not, as yet, been possible. Indeed, until the relevant historical documents are uncovered and the individual varieties are studied further, the "Why's" and "How's" of this variety will remain something of an enigma to VAM collectors. But isn't that the fun of numismatics? (See the complete chapter on the 1879-S Reverse of '78 by John W. Highfill)

The 1880 Overdates (Philadelphia, New Orleans, San Francisco, and Carson City Mints)

For those who look at Morgan dollar varieties, and ask "Where's the beef?", the 1880 overdates may be just right for you. Look no further than the overdates of other U.S. coin series to see that they are often the key dates in the series. The 1918/7-D Buffalo nickel, the 1942/1 "Mercury" dimes, and the 1918/7-S Standing Liberty quarter represent some of the most sought after and expensive coins in their respective series.

Overdates tend to have "sex appeal" when it comes to numismatics. And 1880 was a big year for Morgan dollar overdates! 26 have already been attributed, and there are likely more to be discovered. A review of the overdate information that is presently available is summarized in the chart below.

But first, let's look at what constitutes an overdate variety. An overdate is a die variety where there is evidence that all or part of the date has been punched over the visible remains of a *different* date. Importantly, in order to be an overdate, at least one numeral in the two dates must be different. Otherwise, the coin would more correctly be termed a repunched date.

For U.S. silver dollars, overdates seem to be concentrated in the years, 1799, 1802, 1880, and 1887, and account for almost 35 different die varieties. The search for more overdates is one of today's most interesting areas of variety collecting.

1880 MORGAN DOLLAR OVERDATES
- THE PHILADELPHIA MINT-

VAM Number	Overdate Feature	Variety Description	VAM Book Rarity #	VAM Book Int. Factor	SSDC Rel. Rarity	Rarity Ranking	Availability	Mint Mark	Checkmark Feature	Breen # Cross Ref
6	8/7	Crossbar/Ears	R-5	I-5	RR-9	4th	Rare	N/A	No	# 5535
7	8/7	Crossbar	R-7	I-5	RR-10	2nd	Ultra-Rare	N/A	No	# 5535
8	8/7	Ears	R-7	I-4	RR-10	1st	Ultra-Rare	N/A	No	# 5535
9	8/7	Stem	R-5	I-3	RR-7	6th	Scarce	N/A	No	# 5535
10	8/7	Bit	R-4	I-3	RR-3	9th	Common	N/A	No	# 5535
11	8/7	Checkmark	R-3	I-2	RR-4	8th	Common	N/A	Yes	Unlisted
16	8/7	Checkmark	R-3	I-2	RR-4	7th	Common	N/A	Yes	Unlisted
23	80/79	Ear	R-5	I-4	RR-10	3rd	Ultra-Rare	N/A	No	# 5534
29	8/7	Checkmark	R-3	I-3	RR-8	5th	Rare	N/A	Yes	Unlisted

Note: 1880-P VAM 25 is listed in the 1977 VAM Book Supplement as an overdate, but such a designation is now questioned by most specialists. Breen, however, lists it as #5536

1880 MORGAN DOLLAR OVERDATES
-THE NEW ORLEANS MINT-

VAM Number	Overdate Feature	Variety Description	VAM Book Rarity #	VAM Book Int. Factor	SSDC Rel. Rarity	Rarity Ranking	Availability	Mint Mark	Checkmark Feature	Breen # Cross Ref
4	80/79	Crossbar	R-4	I-4	RR-5	7th	Scarce	Micro "O"	No	# 5538
5	8/7	Crossbar	R-5	I-4	RR-7	5th	Scarce	Oval "O"	No	# 5540
6	8/7	Ear	R-6	I-4	RR-6	6th	Scarce	Micro "O"	Yes	# 5539
6A	8/7	Ear/Spike Rev.	R-5	I-4	RR-4	8th	Common	Micro "O"	Yes	# 5539
6B	8/7	Ear/"Hangnail"	R-5	I-4	RR-10	1st	Ultra-rare	Micro "O"	Yes	# 5539
16	8/7	Checkmark	R-4	I-3	RR-7	4th	Scarce	Micro "O"	Yes	Unlisted
17	8/7	Checkmark	R-4	I-3	RR-9	2nd	Rare	Oval "O"	Yes	Unlisted
21	8/7	Checkmark	R-4	I-3	RR-8	3rd	Rare	Micro "O"	Yes	Unlisted

1880 MORGAN DOLLAR OVERDATES
- THE SAN FRANCISCO MINT-

VAM Number	Overdate Feature	Variety Description	VAM Book Rarity #	VAM Book Int. Factor	SSDC Rel. Rarity	Rarity Ranking	Availability	Mint Mark	Checkmark Feature	Breen # Cross Ref.
8	80/79	Diagonal	R-3	I-4	RR-6	4th	Scarce	Medium "S"	No	# 5544
9	80/79	Diagonal	R-4	I-4	RR-7	2nd	Scarce	Large "S"	No	# 5545
10	8/7	Crossbar	R-6	I-4	RR-10	1st	Ultra-Rare	Large "S"	No	# 5547
11	9/0	Fill	R-3	I-4	RR-5	5th	Scarce	Medium "S"	No	# 5546
12	8/7	Ear	R-3	I-4	RR-6	3rd	Scarce	Medium "S"	Yes	# 5544

1880 MORGAN DOLLAR OVERDATES
-THE CARSON CITY MINT-

VAM Number	Overdate Feature	Variety Description	VAM Book Rarity #	VAM Book Int. Factor	SSDC Rel. Rarity	Rarity Ranking	Availability	Mint Mark	Checkmark Feature	Breen # Cross Ref.
4	80/79		R-4	I-5	RR-5	3rd	Scarce	Small "CC"	No	# 5551
5	8/7	High	R-4	I-5	RR-6	2nd	Scarce	Small "CC"	Yes	# 5553
6	8/7	Low	R-4	I-5	RR-6	1st	Scarce	Small "CC"	Yes	# 5554
7	8/7	Ear	R-4	I-3	RR-4	4th	Scarce	Small "CC"	No	# 5552

The 1882-O/S Varieties

The six known 1882-O/S VAMs offer yet another case of rather exciting numismatic detective work, of which even Sherlock Holmes might have been proud. But first we must set the stage with two definitions, both central to the discussion.

1. MINTMARK: One or more letters, symbols or designs used to identify the minting facility where a coin or related item was struck. In the case of all U.S. silver dollars, an "O" represents New Orleans, an "S" represents San Francisco, a "CC" represents Carson City, and a "D" represents Denver. Silver dollars struck at the Philadelphia Mint, prior to 1983, exhibit no mintmark.[1]

2. OVER-MINTMARK: A mint mark which shows evidence of having been punched over an entirely different letter, or group of letters, that originally represented another mint. Mint marks are applied by hand at the Philadelphia Mint, using a punch to set the mint mark into the die. In the case of an over-mintmark, or "OMM" as it's more popularly called, the original mint mark has been effaced, and then replaced with a mint mark representing another mint. The key, of course, is that some of the original remains visible in and around the new mint mark.[2]

In the 1960's, the first four 1882-O/S varieties were discovered, namely VAMs 3, 4, 5, and 6. Each was identified as having the remains of an underlying "S" mint mark visible inside the "O" mint mark. Interestingly no remnants outside the various "O" mint marks could be found, but the evidence of the strong diagonal markings within the "O" on two of the varieties was compelling.

These early discoveries spurred on further searching, and in 1975, Bill Fivaz' cherry-picking efforts were rewarded with his discovery of a fifth "O/S" variety, the VAM 17. The following year yet another "O/S" variety turned up, the VAM 23, so that now the number of 1882-O MMs reached a total of six.

But the story doesn't end there. It had been observed that the surfaces of every "O/S" variety were covered with innumerable tiny, raised dots of metal, presumably from the die surfaces being rusted. This was a reasonable explanation for those who know what the humidity of New Orleans is like!

But what hadn't been noticed was the fact that the *pattern* of dots on the reverse of VAM 4 and VAM 17 was identical. After some head-scratching, it was finally agreed that both VAMs must have been produced by the same die pair. But which one came first? The VAM 17 shows only a few markings inside the "O" and VAM 4 has a complete diagonal. So the VAM 4 was first, right? Wrong!

From an examination of the varieties, it was clear that the VAM 17 was the early die state of the VAM 4, so the remains of the "S" inside the "O" on the die had actually filled in during the minting process!

Naturally at this point all the 1882-O/S varieties came under close scrutiny, and sure enough — it was discovered that VAM 3 was the late state of VAM 6. Although difficult to accept, here it was — as clear as the topmost letter "E" on your doctor's eye chart, that instead of six different 1882-O/S VAMs, there were actually only four. It then came as no surprise that VAM 23 matched up as the early die state of VAM 5, completing the story of how three different die pairs produced six different reverses.

Throwing the VAM numbering system into disarray, the final picture looked like this: VAMs 3, 4, and 5 were the late die states of VAMs 6, 17, and 25, respectively. This meant that VAM 6 became VAM 3 and VAM 3 became VAM 3A. VAM 17 became VAM 4 and VAM 4 became VAM 4A. And VAM 23 became VAM 5 and VAM 5 became VAM 5A. If you've followed me so far, you probably solve quadratic equations for enjoyment! The accompanying chart will hopefully clarify the situation for the rest of us.

I should mention for those with an eye toward investment that few Morgan dollar varieties, or varieties of any series for that matter, are as undervalued as the 1882-O MMs. Although listed in many pricing guides, the premium they usually command over their non-variety 1882-O counterparts is relatively insignificant in every grade!

The pricing confusion may originate from the fact that circulated specimens up through VF do appear with some regularity, particularly the VAM 4. But XF's and AU's are much less frequently encountered, and BU specimens, particularly those above MS62, are quite rare.

What could be more preposterous than the 1990 Red Book listing of an MS63 1882-O at $120 and the MS63 1882-O/S at $110! But therein lies the opportunity — to acquire under-appreciated varieties like the 1882-O/S for little more than their common non-variety counterparts.

As this chapter is being written, there appears to be some initial recognition as to the lack of availability of 1882-O/S varieties in MS63 or above. It could, therefore, be expected that prices for these varieties will rise in the near future to reflect their rarity.

1882-O/S Morgan Dollar Varieties

New VAM Number	Original VAM No.	Variety Description	VAM Book Rarity #	VAM Book Int. Factor	SSDC Rel. Rarity	Rarity Ranking	Availability	Mint Mark	Breen # Cross Ref.
3	6	O/S Line	R-4	I-3	RR-7	3rd	Scarce	Med. Oval	# 5567
3A	3	O/S Flush	R-3	I-5	RR-7	4th	Scarce	Med. Oval	# 5567
4	17	O/S Dot	R-5	I-3	RR-10	1st	Ultra-Rare	Med. Oval	# 5567
4A	4	O/S Depressed	R-3	I-5	RR-5	6th	Scarce	Med. Oval	# 5567
5	23	O/S Left	R-4	I-3	RR-8	2th	Rare	Med. Oval	# 5567
5A	5	O/S Broken	R-4	I-4	RR-6	5th	Scarce	Med. Oval	# 5567

Only three instances of over-mintmarks can be cited for U.S. silver dollars — the 1882-O/S and 1900-O/CC Morgan dollars and the 1875-S/CC Trade dollar. The underlying mint mark is first effaced from the die, and then, for purposes of expediency, is replaced by a mint mark representing a different Mint.

In the case of the 1882-O/S varieties, the diagonal of the underlying "S" began to fill in inside the "O" during the process of striking coins. At the point that all or part of the diagonal became visible, an "O/S" variety was created. Hence, there are distinct early and late die states for each of the three "O/S" reverse dies, resulting in six different VAMs.

Source: The Society of Silver Dollar Collectors.
P.O. Box 2123, Sepulveda, CA 91393. Used by permission.

NOTE: There is currently an 1882-O/S NGC MS64 finest known to date in the John W. Highfill personal collection — one of 11 graded to date.

The 1887 Overdates (Philadelphia and New Orleans Mints)

For those who suffer from motion sickness, forget about the 1887 Morgan dollar overdates. They're far too much of a roller-coaster ride for you! These overdates were not discovered until the early 1970's, and yet in this relatively short time span have undergone tremendous price swings, both up and down.

Looking back to 1977, the 30th edition of the Red Book listed them as follows:

DATE	VF	XF	Unc.
1887-P 7/6	150.00	250.00	350.00
1887-O 7/6	200.00	300.00	500.00
1887-P	6.50	7.50	11.00
1887-O	7.00	8.00	18.50

Ten years later, the Philadelphia and New Orleans overdates had, in a most dramatic way, fallen from grace, as the following 1987 Red Book prices would suggest:

DATE	VF	XF	MS60	MS63
1887-P 7/6	20.00	25.00	80.00	125.00
1887-O 7/6	22.00	30.00	45.00	90.00
1887-P	17.00	21.00	45.00	70.00
1887-O	17.00	21.00	60.00	110.00

What happened? Are the varieties rare or common? When Ted Clark made the first 1887-P overdate discovery in 1971, and Bob Riethe found the New Orleans counterpart in 1972, no one at that point was sure just how rare they were. So, fueled by the over-reaction to their recent discovery, the marketplace assumed they must be quite rare. After all, none had turned up before.

Soon, silver dollar enthusiasts checked their collections, and dealers inspected their inventories for these expensive overdates. Finding one was like hitting the Lottery — only you didn't have to purchase a ticket. However, on the other side of the equation, as more and more specimens were lured into the marketplace by the high prices, it became abundantly clear that such prices were not justified. The market had over-reacted.

This time, the market swung in the opposite direction, so that by the mid-1980's nearly all the premium value associated with both overdate varieties had evaporated into thin air. What is the current best assessment of their value? I would suggest that the key to understanding the interplay of prices, grade and rarity in this, as well as other cases, is a concept called "Pivotal Grade."

Any collector can tell you that some coins are common in low grades, but surprisingly rare in high grades. Other coins are nearly as common in BU condition as they are in circulated condition. Hence, in any discussion of rarity, whether considering the rarity of a particular date or a given variety, rarity is a function of grade. Without this reference point, it's like reading off all the scores of yesterday's baseball games without ever stating who was playing.

The "Pivotal Grade" is simply a point on the grade continuum, below which the date or die variety is readily obtainable, and above which its availability dramatically decreases to the point its price becomes prohibitive. The "Pivotal Grade" therefore represents the best grade that a collector can generally expect to obtain without mortgaging the house and selling the children.

From another perspective, "Pivotal Grade" is merely a visual representation of rarity. Getting back to the question of how scarce are the two 1887 overdates, using "Pivotal Grade," we can graphically depict their rarity (with the two non-variety dates for comparison purposes).

The 1887-P 7/6 Overdate

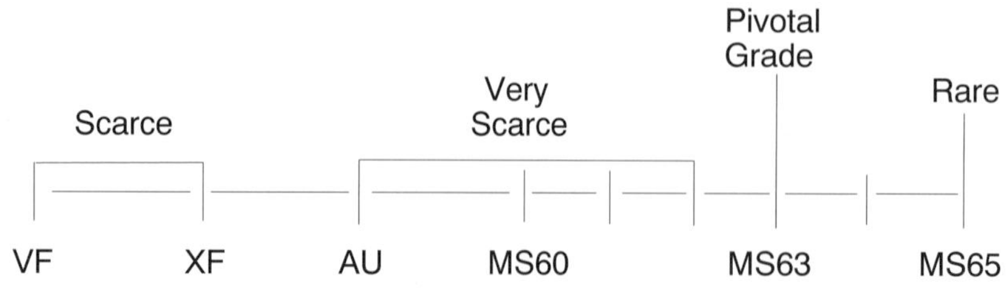

Pivotal Grade Chart

. The graphic image above portrays the variety as uncommon in any grade. Overall scarcity increases up through the MS62 level, at which time the "Pivotal Grade" is hit at MS63. Consistent with the fact that MS64 overdates are rarely offered for sale, things change markedly at the MS64 level. And MS65 represents the point at which the variety becomes a major rarity.

Source: The Society of Silver Dollar Collectors.
P.O. Box 2123, Sepulveda, CA 91393. Used by permission.

The Non-Variety 1887-P

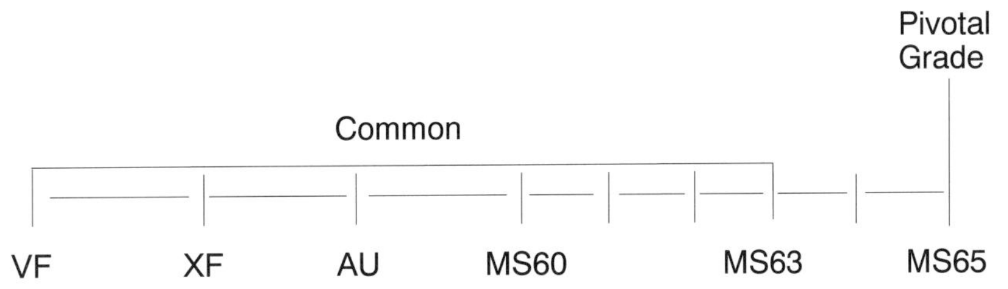

Pivotal Grade Chart

2. The situation for the non-variety 1887-P is quite different. This Pivotal Grade Chart depicts it as readily available up through all grades including MS64. MS65 is the Pivotal Grade, and it becomes more difficult to locate only in grades beginning with MS66!

Source: The Society of Silver Dollar Collectors.
P.O. Box 2123, Sepulveda, CA 91393. Used by permission.

The 1887-O 7/6 Overdate

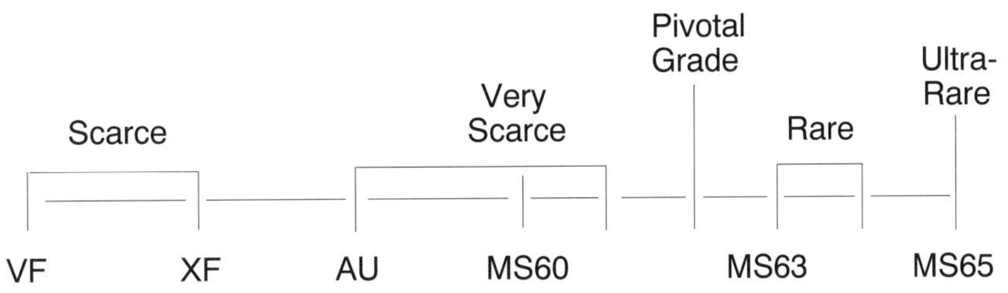

Pivotal Grade Chart

3. The 1887-O 7/6 overdate chart is rather intriguing. The overdate is pictured as not easy to obtain, even in circulated grades, and its rarity rapidly escalates to the Pivotal Grade of MS62. Market price in MS63 and MS64 becomes prohibitive, and in MS65, we have what was recently quoted as a $15,000 coin!

Source: The Society of Silver Dollar Collectors.
P.O. Box 2123, Sepulveda, CA 91393. Used by permission.

The Non-Variety 1887-O

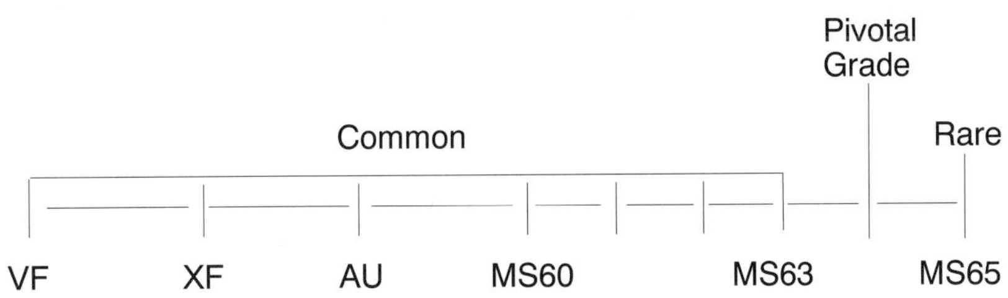

Pivotal Grade Chart

4. As can be seen, the non-variety 1887-O can be acquired without difficulty in any grade up through MS63. MS64 represents the "Pivotal Grade," and the '87-O becomes a big ticket item at the MS65 level.

Source: The Society of Silver Dollar Collectors.
P.O. Box 2123, Sepulveda, CA 91393. Used by permission.

The 1900-O/CC Varieties

When the Carson City Mint ceased its operations, one of the most interesting chapters in American coinage came to an abrupt close. It had begun with Abraham Curry buying land in 1858 with a saddlebag full of hope, $500, and some horses. It continued with the completion of a U.S. Mint in 1869 amid gala celebrations, and it ended when the last coin dropped into the hopper in 1893.

Marking its demise, the status of the Carson City Mint was officially downgraded to an Assay Office on July 1, 1899, and in September, its three coin presses, as well as related equipment and supplies used in coin manufacture, were shipped back to the Philadelphia Mint. Happily for us, among the machinery and furnishings were at least six unused Morgan dollar reverse dies!

This epilogue is well known to variety collectors. A number of Carson City reverse dies were then repunched with an "O" mint mark, and in 1900 were shipped to New Orleans for use there. The result of this re-mintmarking was one of the most popular groups of Morgan dollar VAMs, the 1900-O/CC varieties.

The Seven Known 1900-O/CC Varieties

VAM Number	Variety Description	VAM Book Rarity #	VAM Book Int. Factor	SSDC Rel. Rarity	Rarity Ranking	Availability	Mint Mark	Breen # Cross Ref.
7	O/CC Low	R-4	I-4	RR-6	7th	Scarce	Med. Round	# 5673
8	O/CC Centered	R-4	I-5	RR-7	3rd	Scarce	Med. Round	# 5673
8A	O/CC Die Chips	R-4	I-4	RR-6	6th	Scarce	Med. Round	# 5673
9	O/CC Centered Low	R-4	I-4	RR-10	1st	Ultra-Rare	Med. Round	# 5671
10	O/CC Low	R-4	I-4	RR-7	2th	Scarce	Med. Round	# 5673
11	O/CC Medium	R-4	I-4	RR-6	5th	Scarce	Med. Round	# 5671
12	O/CC High	R-4	I-5	RR-7	4th	Scarce	Med. Round	# 5673

Today, just the mention of "Carson City" conjures up images of the Comstock Lode, Cowboys, and the glory days of the Old West. And numismatists are quick to add, for a scant 24-year period, this Branch Mint seemed to produce one rarity after another. Carson City, when the final curtain closed on its minting operations, also supplied the reverse dies that were to ultimately become the 1900-O/CC varieties.

Source: The Society of Silver Dollar Collectors.
P.O. Box 2123, Sepulveda, CA 91393. Used by permission.

The Wrap-Up

For me, the collecting of silver dollars, and particularly silver dollar varieties, has been a continually rewarding adventure. Many's the time I've stared across the bourse table at a dealer who is without doubt more knowledgeable than myself about many American coin series. And yet I'm able to purchase from him a silver dollar variety that is rarer, in absolute terms, than any coin in his entire inventory! Best of all, I've paid nothing over the dealer's normal asking price. Interested in bargains? Varieties may be one of the last areas of numismatics to have them!

It is hoped that you, the reader, armed with the knowledge of what to look for, will encounter many opportunities to acquire rare silver dollar varieties. Here, we have discussed in some detail seven possible "sets" of varieties which receive much of the attention in the Morgan dollar series.

There are also other possible variety groupings. "Sets" could be organized that would include the most important VAMs grouped by variety features, such as Doubled Die Obverses, Doubled Die Reverses, Repunched Dates, Repunched Mint Marks, and a host of others.

The point is that U.S. silver dollar varieties may represent one of the few remaining frontiers in numismatics. Granted, VAMs represent only a miniscule fraction of the Morgan and Peace dollar market, but an interesting phenomenon has emerged that has turned the heads of many collectors, dealers, and investors. In the coin market tailspin of 1990, Morgan and Peace dollar prices dropped like autumn leaves. But notably, one segment of the market actually went up in terms of both demand and prices — and that area was silver dollar varieties.

Check the few VAMs already listed in the various value guides. In high grades, the variety sets such as the 1879-S with "B" Reverse, the 1887 overdates, and the 1900-O/CC OMMs were among the few bright spots in an otherwise dismal market. It may well be the case that even in the unlikely event that Morgan and Peace dollars were to fall from favor, VAMs would prove themselves in the numismatic marketplace to be swans among the ugly duckling issues.

Footnotes:

1 Source: *The Silver Dollar Dictionary*, an unreleased manuscript from the Society of Silver Dollar Collectors, compiled by Jeff G. Oxman.

2 *ibid*.

***

CHAPTER 19

Counterfeit Silver Dollars

by Wayne H. Miller

Definition

A counterfeit silver dollar is a coin made to imitate a genuine numismatic piece with intent to deceive or defraud, regardless of whether the intended deception is primarily monetary or numismatic.

Types of Counterfeit Silver Dollars

Since *Coin World Almanac* and *A Comprehensive Catalogue and Encyclopedia of U.S. Morgan and Peace Dollars* both devote several pages to a definitive exposition of the types and methods of counterfeiting, this topic will not be explored in detail. However, the author will provide specific information with regard to the counterfeiting of silver dollars, and suggestions as to methods of detection.

The following list may not be all-inclusive, but describes the most common types of counterfeited silver dollars.

A. Cast Silver Dollars

Most of the cast silver dollars in evidence today were produced from relatively crude methods many years ago, with little or no silver, in an attempt to pass for general circulation. Most cast coins have defects which are discernible upon close inspection; therefore, this method is not normally used to produce dollars with special numismatic value.

B. Die Struck Fakes

These are usually more difficult to detect than cast coins. Fake dies can be made by casting, handcutting, machine engraving, spark erosion, impact, electrochemical etching, etc. If the counterfeiter is of the patient sort, fake dies can produce an almost exact duplication of mint production methods. Comparison of a suspect coin with one known to be genuine will often reveal minor aberrations. The entire coin surface should be examined closely for defects.

Because of the large surface area which must be duplicated, fake dies are seldom used in the production of counterfeit silver dollars.

C. Altered Silver Dollars

A genuine silver dollar is sometimes altered into one of greater numismatic value. The following methods are most prevalent:

1. Mintmark Addition is probably the most common method of counterfeiting silver dollars. In this process, a relatively common date BU dollar, such as an 1896-P, can be altered to a more valuable 1896-S by adding a mintmark to the reverse. The soldering of mintmarks has been developed to a high precision. Most such altered coins cannot be detected under 45X magnification. Examine the coin carefully for disruption of metal flow around the mintmark area, or for rough edges at the base of the mintmark.

The soldering process usually results in a slight discoloration of the coin in and around the mintmark area. The entire coin is therefore dipped in a light acid bath so that the overall luster of the coin will be consistent. Such coins, although still brilliant, will lack the frosty luster of a normal silver dollar. Also, very light pitting will usually be evident under high magnification.

The enormous increase in value of rare date Morgan dollars has resulted in a corresponding increase in counterfeit specimens. The author has seen several bogus 1896-O, 1896-S, and 1897-O dollars in recent years. All of these were relatively easy to identify as being counterfeit, because the bold strike and full rims of 1896-P and 1897-P dollars makes them readily distinguishable from their branch mint counterparts, which are usually softly struck with rounded rims. However, the author has examined a few very deceptive 1886-O dollars. Since there is very little difference between genuine 1886-P and 1886-O dollars, an expert eye is needed to detect a well-executed counterfeit 1886-O. Suspect coins should be sent to ANACS for authentication.

Many counterfeiters, unfamiliar with the many design changes of the Morgan dollar, have soldered the wrong type mintmark onto a coin. The author has examined several uncirculated "1903-S" dollars onto which an inappropriate "S" mintmark has been attached. Two of the coins had been artificially toned on both sides to cover the effects of the soldering process.

The author was once offered, by a prominent type coin specialist, a BU "1889-CC" dollar, which exhibited the obviously different mintmarks of an 1878-CC dollar.

The 1884-S is another frequently counterfeited date. Many 1884-P dollars evidence a small positioning punch mark under the second "8" of the date. Since such marks are unknown among "S"-mint dollars, an 1884-S with such a mark should be considered suspect.

The most frequently counterfeited Morgan dollar is the 1893-S. However, there are several methods of detecting most such coins. Van Allen-Mallis indicate that there is only one obverse die variety of the 1893-S dollar. On all 1893-S dollars, the "3" of the date is positioned higher on the coin than the other numerals. Also, on all 1893-S dollars the "1" of the date is positioned directly above one of the denticles, which are the toothlike projections or "bumps" which form the inner half of the rim of a Morgan dollar. On all 1893-O, 1893-CC, and most 1893-P silver dollars, the "1" of the date will be positioned in between two denticles.

Assuming that no other die varieties of the 1893-S exist, then, if the "1" of a 1893-S dollar is not positioned directly above a denticle, it is not a genuine coin. If the "1" is in the appropriate position, it is either an 1893-S dollar or one of the few 1893-P dollars with this characteristic.

Another virtually fool-proof method has been discovered in recent years for detecting counterfeit 1893-S dollars. On all genuine specimens, there is a diagonal line which proceeds from lower left to upper right at the junction of the cross bars on the "T" of LIBERTY. Since LIBERTY is incuse or inset in the Morgan design, this bar is visible even on heavily circulated specimens.

Mintmarks are sometimes produced by cutting into the field of a coin with a sharp instrument to form the desired letter or letters. However, such alterations are easily detected, since the mintmark will appear to be sitting in a hole.

A September 1981 article in the Numismatist ("Embossed Mintmarks; the Newest Wrinkle in Altering Coins,") described a new method used by counterfeiters to add a mintmark onto a coin. In this process, a hole is drilled into the edge of a coin near the mintmark position with a small-bit drill. Then another tool somewhat like a needle-nosed pliers with a mintmark etched onto the inside of one jaw and either plastic or hard leather on the inside of the other jaw comes into play. The jaw with the mintmark is pushed into the hole. The handles of the pliers are then squeezed, producing pressure sufficient to raise the mintmark onto the surface of the coin. The hole is then filled and the edge filed down and smoothed to remove most of the evidence of the tampering.

Although this process has been used to alter Lincoln cents and Buffalo nickels, it is believed that it would be much more difficult to use on silver dollars because of the reeded edge, which could not be easily returned back to its original state. However, an inspection of the reeding near the mintmark area should be done when checking for counterfeits among rare date silver dollars.

John Love has a disconcerting but quite effective method of checking for mintmark additions. He inserts a very sharp knife under the mintmark and lifts up. If the mintmark has been glued or soldered on, this procedure will usually dislodge it.

Some of the processes of adding a mintmark onto a silver dollar to increase its value have become quite sophisticated. Therefore, during the past fifteen years, the author has attempted to identify certain predictable, consistent differences among dollars from different mints. If a method could be established for differentiating an "S" mint dollar from a "P" mint dollar, for example, this would greatly facilitate the detection of mintmark-added counterfeit dollars.

Silver dollar specialists can usually tell the mintmark of a silver dollar merely by examining the rims. However, despite eight years of intensive study, the author has been unable to develop a methodology which would enable an average collector or investor to make this determination.

Since all preparatory die production, including the punching in of the date and mintmark, was done at the Philadelphia mint, the central portions of all Morgan and Peace dollars will be essentially similar. However, the final preparation of the dies was performed by each mint. This included the basining of the dies. This was the process of polishing the field of the die prior to its introduction into the coining process, to obtain a radius or series of radii across the die face so that the coins would strike up properly. There definitely were differences in the basining process from one mint to the other. Variations in this process would result in subtle differences in dollars from each of the mints.

There is also some evidence that the amount of striking pressure varied from one mint to another. This could produce slight but perceptible variations among silver dollars.

The majority of mintmark-added counterfeit dollars are produced by soldering an "S" onto a Philadelphia mint dollar. Therefore, the author will present several ways in which "S"-mint dollars are **generally** different from "P"-mint dollars. The following should be considered as tendencies only, since there are many exceptions.

In general, the denticles on "S"-mint dollars are short and tend to taper into the field, toward the center of the coin. The denticles on "P"-mint dollars are longer with less tapering.

In general, "S"-mint dollars have rolled or "fade-away" rims; there is a gradual merging of the denticles with the outside rim of the coin. The rims of "P"-mint dollars are more distinctly separate from the denticles; often a ridge defines the boundary between the denticles and the outer rim. This is due to differences in die basining procedures between the two mints. At San Francisco, dies were basined in such a way as to encourage maximum flow of the metal into the central, deepest parts of the dies. This is why most "S"-mint dollars, particularly those from 1878-1882, exhibit such a bold strike. However, this bold strike resulted in less metal being available to flow out to the rims. Thus the rims are not as fully defined as those of "P"-mint dollars.

In general, "S"-mint Morgan dollars appear to be struck with slightly greater pressure than "P"-mint dollars, which causes the central details on the former to appear more prominent. However, die basining could also cause this bold center strike.

In general, the date digits of "S"-mint dollars, under magnification, evidence less taper at their edges than those of "P"-mint dollars. The digits of "S"-mint dollars appear to be sheared off like the top of a mesa, whereas "P"-mint date digits are usually more rounded. Again, this difference may be due to greater pressure utilized in the striking of "S"-mint dollars, or to differences in die basining.

In general, "S"-mint dollars evidence a luster which is slightly superior to "P"-mint dollars. Although this is an intangible phenomenon, it does provide the silver dollar specialist with another datum in his attempt to verify the authenticity of a given coin.

Some issues are so distinctly unique that they can be distinguished from all other dollars of that series. The author can usually identify an 1887-S dollar even if the date and mintmark are covered. This is also true of other issues such as 1901-P, 1903-P and 1925-P.

2. Mintmark Removal. A few Philadelphia dollars such as 1894-P, 1901-P and 1928-P are more scarce than their branch mint counterparts. Therefore, mintmarks are sometimes removed from genuine coins of these dates by any number of grinding or cutting processes. The mintmark area is subsequently polished. Sometimes the entire coin is immersed in a light acid so that the evidences of mintmark removal is blurred. These procedures can produce a coin with virtually no evidence of tampering. Therefore, one should examine the coin to see if it has the appropriate rim characteristics.

With regard to the 1894-P, this is usually distinguishable from an 1894-S by virtue of the rim differences discussed previously. Since virtually all 1894-O dollars are flat struck, the high-point detail should be examined carefully on a suspect coin. Of course, this will be possible only with specimens in the higher states of preservation.

The 1901-P is easily distinguished from an 1901-O or 1901-S dollar. On most 1901-P dollars, high-point detail is very poor. Many specimens evidence heavy metal flow; features in general are indistinct. Other less tangible differences exist.

There are observable differences between the rims of "S"-mint and "P"-mint Peace dollars; therefore, it is quite easy to distinguish a 1928-S which has been altered into a 1928-P dollar. Virtually all "S"-mint Peace dollars were struck with inadequate pressure, or from improperly basined dies, thus producing a low relief and rolled or "fade-away" rims. This is most noticeable on the left side of the coin; the "In God" part of the motto will be faint. Peace dollars from the Philadelphia mint were generally struck with greater pressure or from more correctly basined dies and evidence a higher, more distinct rim. This rim is even more pronounced on Denver mint Peace dollars. Also, "P"-mint Peace dollars will usually evidence a bolder strike than "S"-mint Peace dollars.

3. Date Alterations. Just as mintmarks are sometimes removed or added, a date digit can be changed on a genuine silver dollar. One method is to completely remove the digit and solder another into its place. Attempts are also made to alter a digit to form another one. This is sometimes done with 1898-S dollars, to produce the coveted 1893-S. Such counterfeits are usually detectable under close scrutiny.

Because of changes over the years in the size and style of the date numerals for silver dollars, date-altered dollars can sometimes be detected by examination of digit size and style. (See Van Allen-Mallis for a more detailed presentation of date and mintmark variation.)

4. Conjoining Of Two Coins. A few counterfeit dollars have been produced by merging two genuine coins of different issue to produce a key date coin. For example, the reverse of an 1890-CC dollar has been joined to the obverse of an 1889-P to produce a rare 1889-CC dollar.

The two most common processes used to join two silver dollars together are as follows: First, the surfaces of two genuine coins are machined or filed down until their combined thickness approximates that of a single coin. The two halves are then soldered together. This of course produces a seam on the rim of the coin. Such a coin will usually evidence detectable rim aberrations.

A second and more subtle method of joining two coins is to hollow out the central portions of one coin and insert a similar section from a different coin, which has been slightly shrunk by the application of dry ice or other substance. When the effects of the dry ice are gone, the insert will expand, often producing a very tight union with the coin into which it was inserted. The seam is then polished. Such coins can be difficult to detect, although the seam is usually visible under high magnification. Examine the area where the field of the coin merges with the denticles; this is the area where the connection is usually made.

Summary

The following suggestions are made with regard to the detection of counterfeit silver dollars:

1. Read anything on the topic of silver dollars or counterfeiting. Attend seminars, workshops, lectures, etc., which address themselves to counterfeiting. Ask knowledgeable dealers for tips on detecting fakes.
2. Examine as many silver dollars as possible from all the mints. After a time, the little idiosyncrasies of each mint should become familiar. Study the obverses of a number of silver dollars and attempt to guess their mintmark.
3. Become familiar with the various date and mintmark variations among Morgan and Peace dollars as described by Van Allen-Mallis.
4. Buy your silver dollars from dealers who not only are willing to uphold professional standards regarding coin authenticity, but who are knowledgeable enough about silver dollars to insure that they do not unknowingly sell a counterfeit coin to you.
5. If a coin is suspect, submit it to the American Numismatic Association Certification Service (ANACS), 818 North Cascade, Colorado Springs, Colorado 80903-3279). For a nominal fee, your coin will be examined for genuineness, and a letter of authenticity (or regret) will be provided.

Acknowledgement

The article was reprinted by permission in its entirety from Wayne Miller's *Morgan and Peace Dollar Textbook*, 1982, Adam Smith Publishing Co., Metairie, Louisiana.

***

John W. Highfill, NLG

CHAPTER 20

Counterfeit Silver Dollars: Specific Issues

by John W. Highfill, NLG

The following presentation focuses upon U.S. silver dollars up to and including the Peace dollar series. The various counterfeiting methods and characteristics known for the particular series or specific date and mintmark are presented for your information.

1794-1795 Flowing Hair Dollar

Various counterfeit coins of these years have surfaced. Most of the pieces were created using a casting process. Excessive cleaning is a characteristic of these and most other cast counterfeit coins. Most of these coins were produced in this country or in Asia. The 1795 Flowing Hair dollar is the date that has surfaced as a cast counterfeit dollar. Someone made a carb' copy of the Woody Blevins 1794.

In general, the weights and measures of counterfeit specimens often give them away. Authenticators can take specific gravity measurements to check the percentage of pure metal during the authentication process. Cast counterfeits may also be detected by porosity, bubbles, and often a greasy feel.

1799 Draped Bust Dollar

Many cast examples have surfaced over the years, with most of them cleaned to prevent detection. A characteristic of many of these pieces is an identical series of die scratches (looking like bag marks to the uninitiated) indicating counterfeit pieces. (But for this one needs to see photographs of reference coins.) Another characteristic of some castings is an imperfect "R" in LIBERTY, "D" in UNITED, and "T" in UNIT on edge.

Counterfeit: Damaged "R" in LIBERTY

Counterfeit: Damaged "D" in UNITED

Counterfeit: Damaged "T" in UNIT

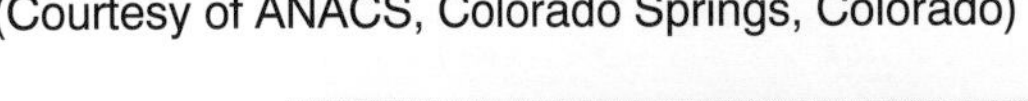

(Courtesy of ANACS, Colorado Springs, Colorado)

1799 Draped Bust Dollar: Struck counterfeit (Courtesy of ANACS)

Notice the obvious die scratch extending from the reeded edge at the bottom of the obverse to the lower right serif of the "1" in 1799.

Examine the surface area between the star and "L" of LIBERTY carefully. There is a small dig (hole or pit) on both genuine and counterfeits. The genuine pieces will have a smoother surface preservation as opposed to a more grainy surface on the counterfeits.

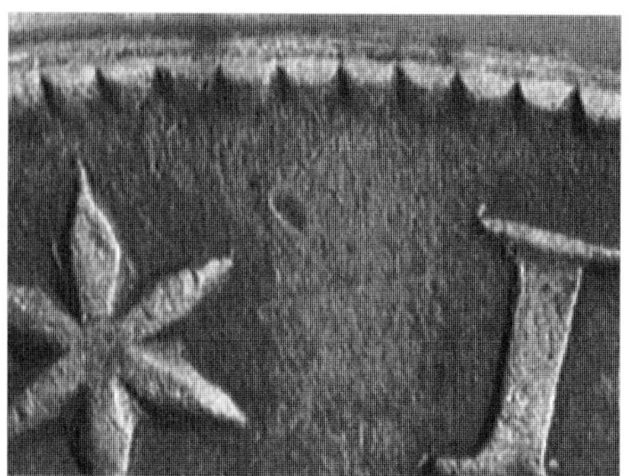

Genuine example: Star before "L" in LIBERTY
(Courtesy of ANACS)

Another example of 1799 Draped Bust dollar struck counterfeit
(Courtesy of ANACS)

Some of these cast examples have been submitted to ANACS after being sold as uncirculated coins to unsuspecting buyers. A representative of this batch of counterfeits may be uncovered by detecting non-standard weight, diameter, specific gravity and other physical improper characteristics.

Counterfeit examples have been discovered upon importation from the Far East. These pieces usually exhibit high pointed denticles, uneven reeding, porous numerals and stars and evidence of cleaning. Their weight and specific gravity tend to identify these specimens as counterfeits.

A common problem with collectors is that they do not have sufficient opportunity to inspect enough genuine dollars of this type to know a counterfeit when they see one. That is why authentication is recommended before any purchase is consummated.

Cast counterfeit 1804 Draped Bust dollar
(Courtesy of Sanford J. Durst Numismatic Publications)

1804 Dollar

Probably the most common source of 1804 counterfeit dollars is from foreign countries (notably Asia). These cast pieces were frequently sold to servicemen stationed overseas and brought back into this country. They are relatively easy to spot due to the porous texture of the field. The weight of these coins is usually less than the official weight of 416 grains. The majority of these cast counterfeit 1804 dollars were from Southeast Asia in the 1960s. Most of the cast dollars weighed between 360 and 380 grains, however, it is not unusual to encounter one that weighs the correct 416 grains or more.

Counterfeiting of the 1804 dollar via an altered date or silver electrotype process was long for commener. Electrotype copies (some made from the Mint's plain edge Class II) at least had a legitimate reason for existing: they showed what the real ones looked like back when coin photographs were rarely available. For altered dates there never was an excuse.

Gobrecht Dollars

It is said that a small number of counterfeit Gobrecht dollars have surfaced made from counterfeit dies in Europe. As the total quantity of originals number only about 3,000 pieces, it is wise to have any specimen authenticated before purchasing. The inexperienced collector/investor has probably not had the opportunity to carefully examine one of the genuine dollars, and would be easy prey for the unscrupulous seller. When in doubt, send your coins to the ANACS in Colorado Springs, Colorado for verification.

Liberty Seated dollars (1840-1873)

There have been counterfeits of this series. They have been cast. They have been molded. They have altered dates. The molded pieces can be very expertly done, and a magnifying glass in the hands of an expert may be the only line of defense against counterfeits. The molding process often leaves minute pockets of air which can cause microscopic surface cavities and give-away the true status of the coin. Again, have your coins certified for peace of mind.

Cast counterfeit 1873 Liberty Seated dollar
(Courtesy of Sanford J. Durst Numismatic Publications)

Trade Dollars

Southwest Asia for generations has produced thousands of cast Trade dollars covering a wide variety of date and mintmarks. The dull and gray surface with an almost powdery look were characteristics of these pieces. These well made counterfeits were imported and distributed by the roll as well as singly and went undetected by many for a long time. Beware of these counterfeits when purchasing Trade dollars for it is assumed that many are still "at large."

A beautiful prooflike cast counterfeit specimen of the 1873 Trade dollar was discovered in 1971. The creator was unknown and the piece itself was also lost after being used for some years as an educational specimen. Sometime around 1972, a large hoard of high quality cast counterfeits were imported from Southeast Asia and sold into the marketplace. There was a large variety of both dates and mintmarks.

1875 -1878 cast counterfeit Trade dollars
(Courtesy of Sanford J. Durst Numismatic Publications)

Morgan dollars

The casting of Morgan dollar counterfeits, although some are created in this fashion, is not nearly as prevalent as the alteration of genuine coins. The altered genuine coin is also less expensive to produce and more likely to escape detection thereby making it the preferred method used by counterfeiters. These alterations include both dates and mintmarks.

Cast counterfeit Carson City dollars have been offered for sale in official U.S. Government holders. These holders were originally opened, the genuine coins removed and replaced with counterfeit pieces.

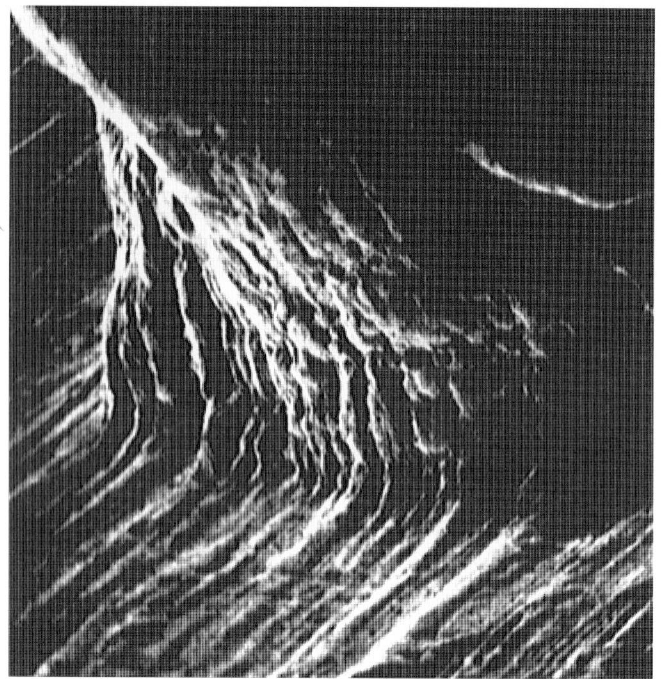

SEM 3,000-X magnification of flow-lines of genuine 1893-S mintmark area
(Courtesy of Sanford J. Durst Numismatic Publications)

In order to authenticate genuine Morgan dollars, high powered microscopes and even scanning electron microscopes are used to identify and follow the "flow lines" created during the striking process. As the coins are struck at the mint, the metal in the planchet is forced from the center toward the edge of the collar as the die is pressed onto its surface. This action produces extremely minute flow lines which add to the luster seen on the coins by numismatists. Interruptions of these flow lines (due to altered dates and mintmarks) can be detected using microscopes and counterfeits identified. In X-ray fluorescence studies, x-rays focused upon the coin's mintmark or date area. These observations are charted and surface interruptions (counterfeiter's telltale tracks) are studied.

Other microscopic studies utilized to determine genuineness include the positioning and characteristics of the date and mintmark, both of which were hand-prepared during the Morgan dollar production years. Another method of authentication requires the genuine specimens to exhibit certain die scratches and marks (when the number of dies used can be strictly identified). The following pages contain photographs showing the characteristics of specific Morgan dates.

1889-CC

There are 3 obverse and 3 reverse dies known for this date. The genuine coins produced with two of the obverse dies possess a die crack through the date area between the "8" and "9". Also on the obverse, one of the dies possesses a small die gouge on the bonnet, between the larger leaf and the smaller one to its left. None of these features will show on alterations (genuine 1889-P dollars with CC added).

Cast Counterfeit 1901-S Morgan Dollar
(Obverse and Reverse)
(Courtesy of J.P. Martin, ANACS c/o The American Numismatic Association, Colorado Springs, Colorado)

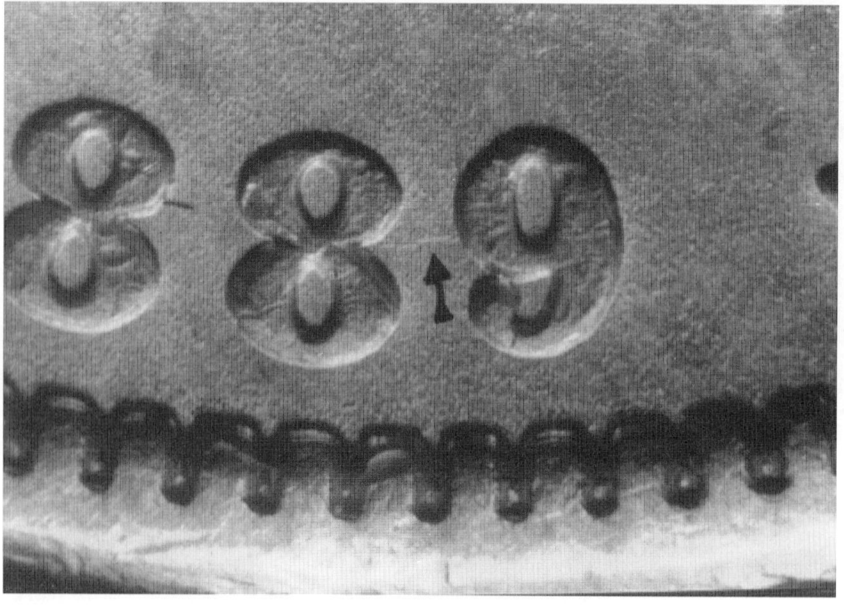

Genuine 1889-CC: Die crack between 8 and 9 of date
(Courtesy of Bill Fivaz, Atlanta, Georgia)

1884 Cast Counterfeit
Morgan Dollar
(Courtesy of J.P. Martin, ANACS c/o The American Numismatic Association, Colorado Springs, Colorado)

Genuine 1889-CC: Die gouge on bonnet between leaves
(Courtesy of Bill Fivaz, Atlanta, Georgia)

Most of the genuine pieces made with a damaged reverse die show a large number of tiny "pimples" over the eagle's body. This was primarily caused by rusted dies. Check the mintmark and surrounding area for any tampering, interruption of the metal (seam around junction of mintmark and field), and cleaning marks. Discoloration would usually confirm tampering.

Genuine 1889-CC Enlarged view of
die gouge on bonnet between leaves
(Courtesy of Bill Fivaz, Atlanta, Georgia)

1892-S

Altering genuine coins to produce a counterfeit 1892-S Morgan dollar has been tried with a number of genuine Morgans. The most successful attempts have been made utilizing 1892-P uncirculated specimens, although others have tried using the 1890-S and 1891-S dollars. Study the size of the "S" appearing on the piece and note that a small rounded "S" was used by the San Francisco Mint from 1879 to 1900. Look for the usual telltale signs of metal disturbance and cleaning around the mintmark area.

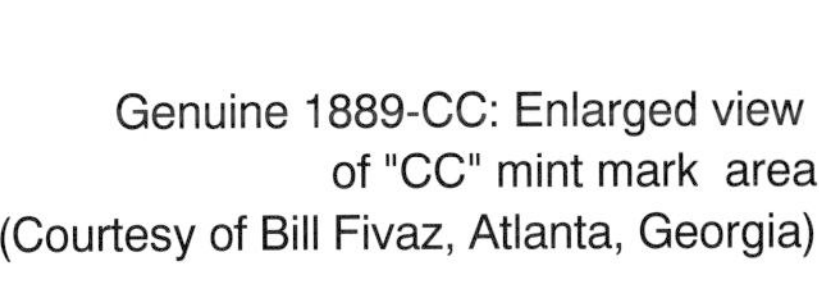

Genuine 1889-CC: Enlarged view
of "CC" mint mark area
(Courtesy of Bill Fivaz, Atlanta, Georgia)

Genuine 1893-S: With "1" centered over denticle **(see line)**
(Courtesy of Bill Fivaz, Atlanta, Georgia)

1893-S

Since this particular date and mintmark is so valuable, it is often counterfeited through altering either the date or mintmark of a genuine specimen of lesser worth. The 1898-S, 1883-S, 1892-P and 1883-P are the most commonly used Morgan dollars when alteration is attempted. Following are some characteristics of a genuine 1893-S Morgan dollar.

Study the obverse and the word "LIBERTY" looking for a raised die scratch running diagonally upward from the top of the left side of the vertical portion of the T, and two tiny die chips in the left foot of the R. It is important to remember that the letters of LIBERTY are incused into the headband. This process allows the die scratch to remain visible even on well circulated coins. The date on this obverse has the numeral "1" of 1893 placed directly over a denticle, 3 of 1893 is slightly higher than the other numerals and not doubled at the top. If the obverse does not have the die scratch on T, watch for retooling of the 93 signalling an altered piece. On the reverse, also check for possible alteration of the mintmark.

Genuine 1893-S: Diagonal die scratch on "T" (see arrow)
(Courtesy of Bill Fivaz, Atlanta, Georgia)

Genuine 1893-S: Correct "S" mintmark
(Courtesy of ANACS, Colorado Springs, Colorado)

1894-P

There is only one obverse and one reverse die known for business strikes of this date. The 1894-O dollar is most often used when alteration is attempted. The removal of the "O" is a simple task. Check the strike (lighter and weaker on the New Orleans Mint dollars) and color of the alloy (white silver in New Orleans Mint productions as compared with chrome silver). A flat strike over Miss Liberty's ear is a good indication of an altered 1894-O dollar. The obverse of 1894-P genuine coins shows two die gouges on the "R" of LIBERTY at the lower right. The point of the bust has a spike leading down from it on some pieces.

The reverse of genuine coins displays two fine die polish marks forming an "X" between the eagle's tail and the knee of the eagle's right leg. There is also a die gouge between the eagle's right leg (as you look at it) and leg feathers.

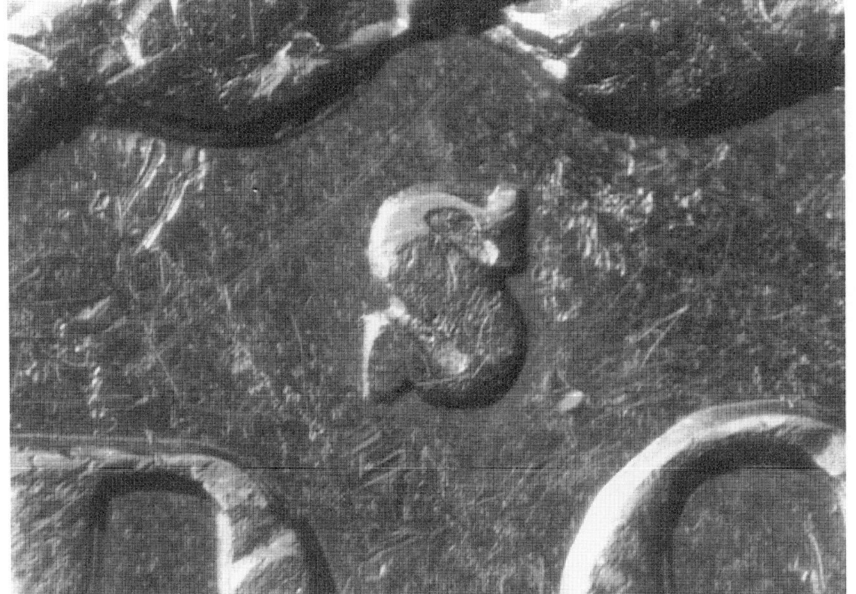

Genuine 1893-S: Correct "S" mintmark (enlarged version above) (Courtesy of Bill Fivaz, Atlanta, Georgia)

Genuine 1894-P: Two die gouges on "R" in LIBERTY(below) (Courtesy of Bill Fivaz, Atlanta, Georgia)

Genuine 1894-P: "X" shaped die polish marks next to eagle's body (above) (Courtesy of ANACS)

Genuine 1894-P: Spike below point of bust (left) (Courtesy of Bill Fivaz, Atlanta, Georgia)

Genuine 1894-P: Die gouge between eagle's right leg (as you see it) and leg feathers
(Courtesy of Bill Fivaz, Atlanta, Georgia)

Genuine 1894-P: Die gouge between eagle's right leg (as you see it) and leg feathers
(enlarged version)
(Courtesy of ANACS)

1895 Proof

The genuine specimens exhibit a number of very fine die polish marks on Liberty's eyeball and temple behind the eye. On any specimen without convincing proof surface, look carefully for uninterrupted metal surfaces around the mintmark. Other general characteristics of genuine coins include various degrees of mirror surfaces and rounded edge reeding.

Since there were only four obverse dies used in the production of 1895 Proof Morgan dollars, a microscopic study of the positioning of the hand-punched date (1895) on each was possible.

Genuine 1894-P: Enlarged date area
(Courtesy of ANACS)

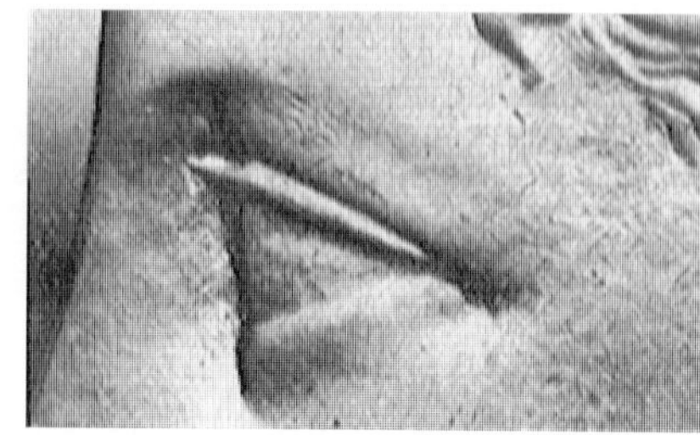

Genuine 1895 Proof: Die polish
marks on Liberty's eyeball
(Courtesy of ANACS)

Genuine 1895 Proof obverse die #1: Numeral 1 in date to the left of center over denticle. Left base of 1 over right half of denticle, right base of 1 over left edge of denticle. Lower part of serif of 1 shows repunching. Ball of 5 over right half of denticle. Date slants up slightly to the right. Photo and caption courtesy of ANACS and *The Numismatist.*

Genuine 1895 Proof obverse die #2: Numeral 1 in date centered over denticle. Left base of 1 over right edge of denticle, right base of 1 over left edge of denticle. Ball of 5 over right edge of denticle. Upper part of 5 shows repunching. The 9 on all specimens observed displays a filled lower loop. Date slants up to the right. Photo and caption courtesy of ANACS and *The Numismatist*.

Genuine 1895 Proof obverse die #3: Numeral 1 in date to right of center over denticle. Left base of 1 over right edge of denticle, right base of 1 over left half of denticle. Ball of 5 above space between denticles. Date slants up to right. Photo and caption courtesy of ANACS and *The Numismatist*.

Genuine 1895 Proof obverse die #4: Numeral 1 in date well to right of center over denticle. Left base of 1 over left edge of denticle, right base of 1 over center of denticle. Ball of 5 above space between denticles. Date is level. Photo and caption courtesy of ANACS and *The Numismatist*.

1895-S

Alterations (mostly from 1885-S) can be readily detected. Using a 20X glass or binocular microscope, check junction of 9, 5, and S with field. A seam is automatic evidence; genuine coin will show that these numerals and S are continuous with field.

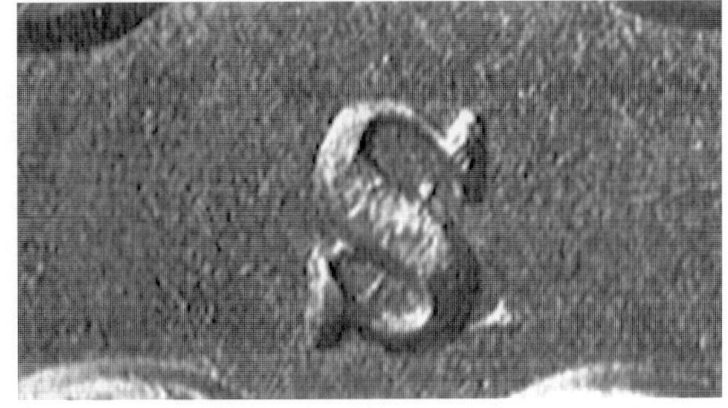

Genuine 1895-S: Horizontal "S" mintmark (Courtesy of ANACS)

1896-O

Cast counterfeits have been produced which differ from the genuine article in the following respects. The 1896 date exhibits a strong strike and good contrast as opposed to the counterfeit date which is more softly struck and displays an overall granular effect. Also check the bow on the reverse for die polish not usually present on a cast counterfeit coin.

Genuine 1896-O: Crisp die polished bow
(Courtesy of ANACS)

Counterfeit 1896-O: Grainy surface preservation
(Courtesy of ANACS)

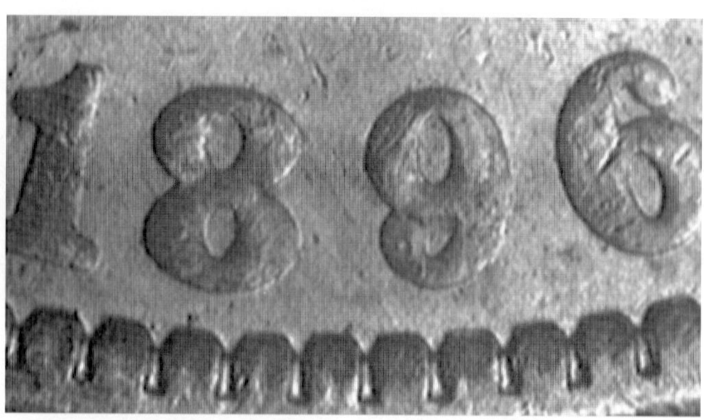

Genuine 1896-O: Exhibits strong strike and good contrast
(Courtesy of ANACS and *The Numismatist*)

Counterfeit 1896-O: Soft and displays overall granular effect
(Courtesy of ANACS and *The Numismatist*)

Counterfeit 1896-O: Raised metal between eagle's wing and olive leaves (Courtesy of ANACS)

1896-S

The 1896-P Morgan dollar is often given a transplanted "S" to make a counterfeit 1896-S dollar. Check the junction of S and field for a seam indicating that the mintmark was added later. Carefully check the rim size and characteristics: A flatted and rounded rim for San Francisco versus a wire edge rim for Philadelphia. Remember to look for signs of the placement of the "S" mintmark.

1900-O/CC

Genuine examples of this popular variety often look counterfeit in the mintmark area. The O mintmark was punched over the CC mintmark by the Philadelphia Mint on obsolete dies from the Carson City branch mint. This branch facility produced its last silver dollars in 1893, and the mint's status was officially changed to an Assay Office on July 1, 1899. The O over CC mintmark often looks glued-on, to the eyes of the uninitiated. But no counterfeit O/CC dollars are known.

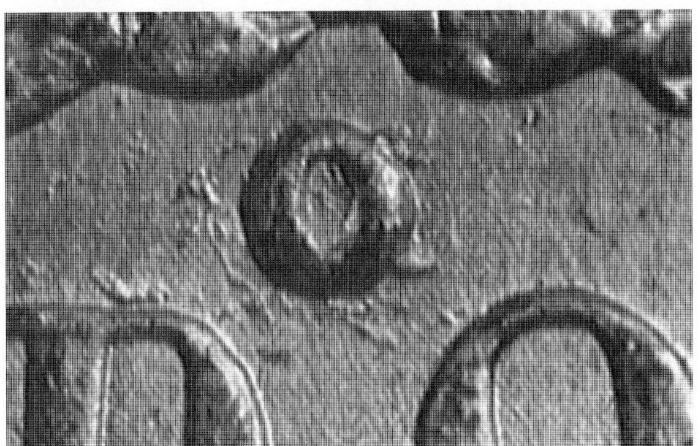

Genuine 1900-O/CC: Enlarged re-punched mintmark (Courtesy of ANACS and *The Numismatist*)

1901-P

An altered 1901-P is usually created with a 1901-O specimen. Look for any scraping or other surface abnormality in the field where mintmark might have been.

1903-S

Known counterfeits are altered from 1903-P dollar. Verify that there is no seam around the "S" mintmark. Size and shape of S are not definitive in themselves, since genuine 1903-S coins come with large and small S's.

1904-S

Beware of altered 1904-S dollars with the "S" reverse provided from a genuine reverse of an earlier period. The "S" mintmark utilized by the counterfeiter is the genuine U.S. produced mintmark but is medium-sized and rounded with pointed serifs. This type of "S" was created during the 1879-1900 period. Also, the seam created by this process is cleverly hidden in the denticles along the lower rim on the reverse of the counterfeit pieces. Altered pieces utilizing 1900-S and 1901-S Morgan dollars are also known.

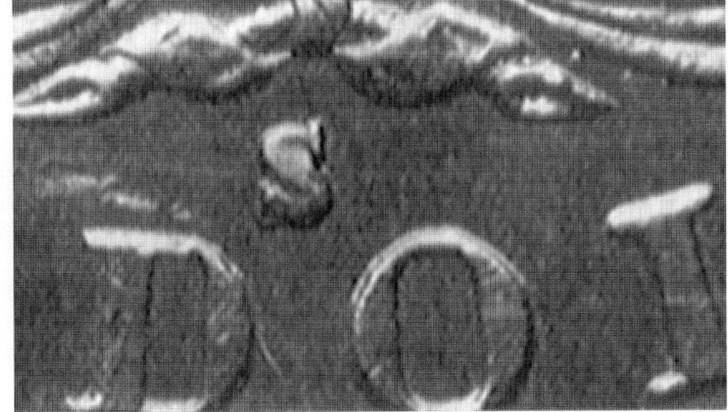

1879-1900 era "S" mintmark used to counterfeit 1903-S and 1904-S pieces (Courtesy of ANACS)

Peace Dollars

Counterfeit Peace dollars are mostly worn-looking casts, dated 1922 and 1924. The known pieces are of questionable quality and should be relatively easy to identify.

1928-P

Altered specimens have been created by removing mintmarks from 1928-S. They don't look like 1928-P's: most San Francisco Mint productions are poorly struck and may possess high wire rims. The 1923-P has also been altered by closing the left side of the "3" or by removing the "3" entirely and replacing it with an "8". Study the area around the "B" in LIBERTY. Genuine pieces exhibit fine die polish marks and a small scratch mark on the field between the first rays on the right side. There is also a small die gouge below Liberty's head under the shortest curl of hair. Some specimens display a small die scratch in the back area of Liberty's hair where it begins to flow. The rims may be sharp to faded and soft on both genuine and counterfeit specimens eliminating this factor during the authentication process. Warning: Genuine 1928 coins may exist from other dies.On the reverse, look for evidence of retooling, cleaning marks and interruptions of the metal in the area of the mintmark.

Genuine 1928-P: Obverse die #1 with horizontal die scratch mark on field between rays at right of "B"
(Courtesy of Bill Fivaz, Atlanta, Georgia)

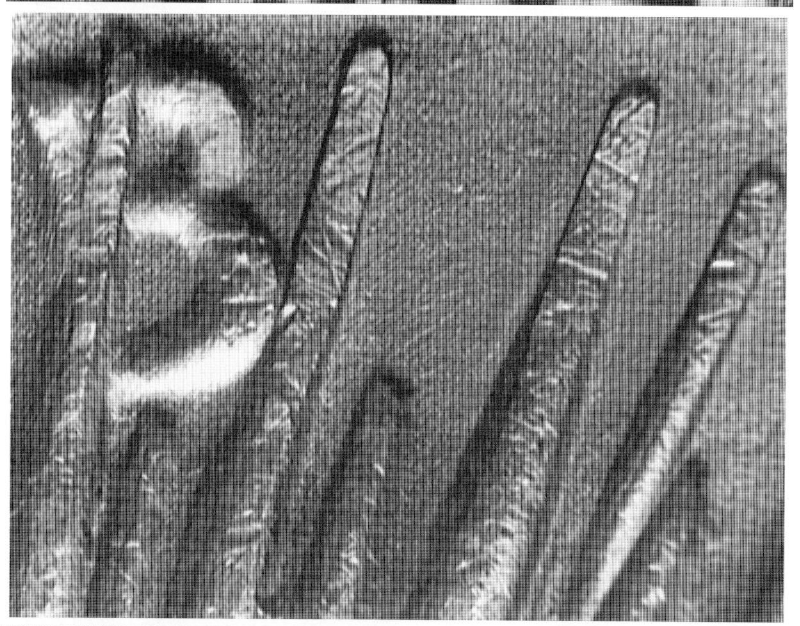

Genuine 1928-P: Obverse die #2 without die scratch
(Courtesy of Bill Fivaz, Atlanta, Georgia)

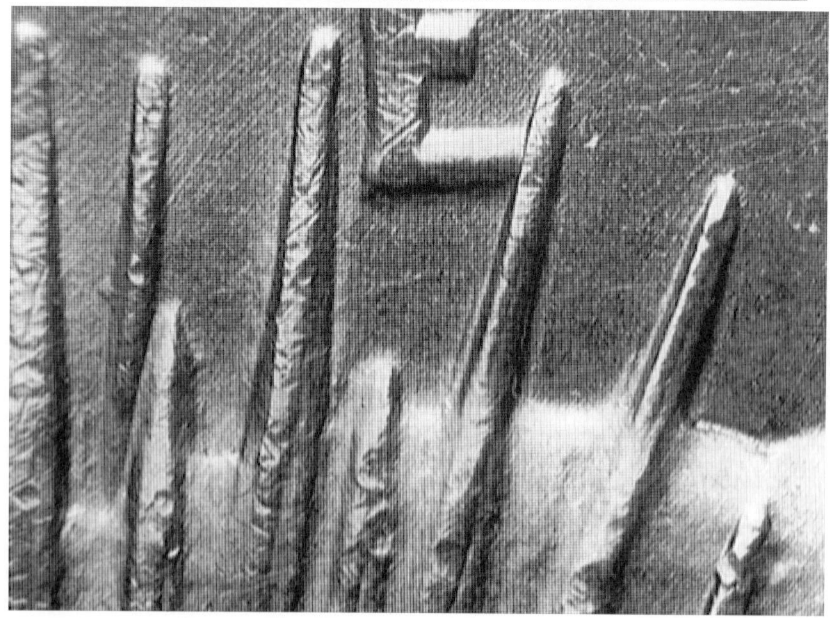

Genuine 1928-P: Obverse die #3, area of "E" in LIBERTY
(Courtesy of Bill Fivaz, Atlanta, Georgia)

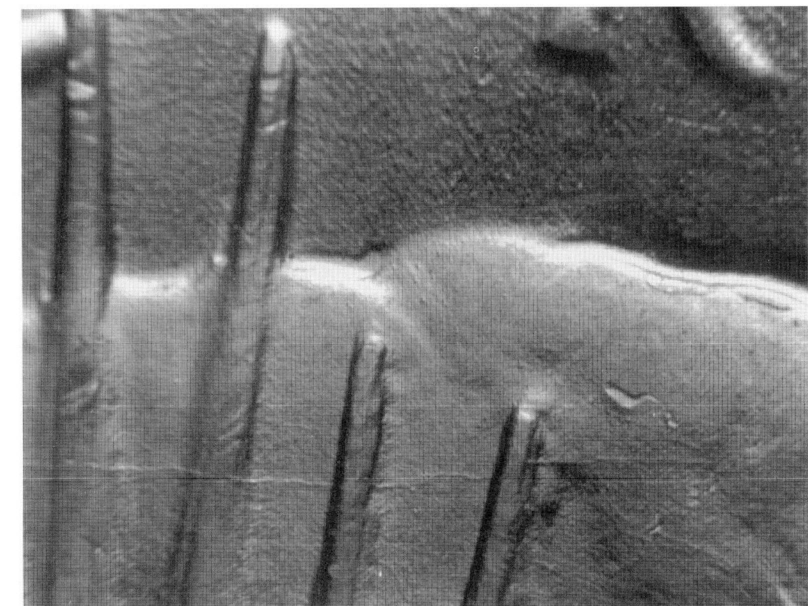

Genuine 1928-P: Obverse die #1, area of "R" in LIBERTY (Courtesy of Bill Fivaz, Atlanta, Georgia)

Genuine 1928-P: Die gouge under shortest curl of Liberty's hair (Courtesy of Bill Fivaz, Atlanta, Georgia)

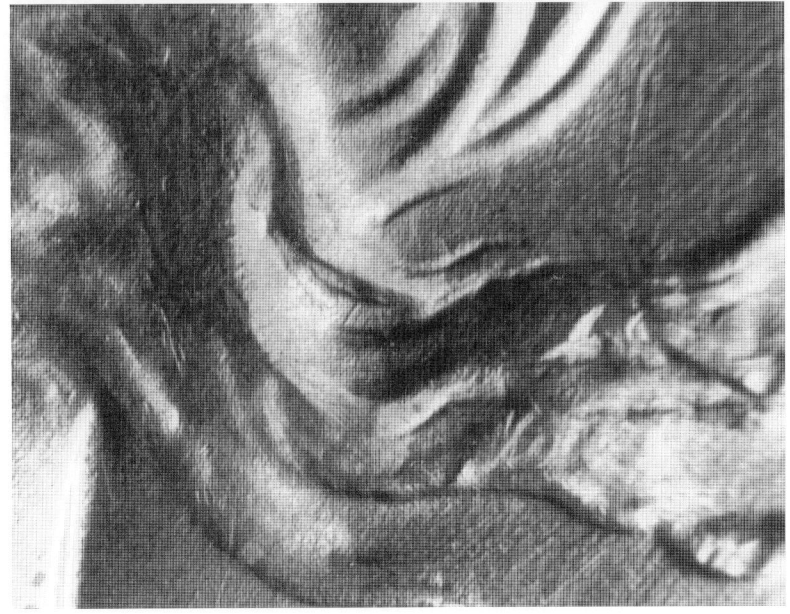

Genuine 1928-P: Obverse die #3 with die scratch in Liberty's hair (Courtesy of Bill Fivaz, Atlanta, Georgia)

1934-S

Watch for altered specimens created utilizing the 1934-P Peace dollar. Notice the strike (much sharper on Philadelphia Mint examples) of any suspect coin as well as any evidence of tampering or cleaning in the mintmark area.

Counterfeit Commemorative Dollars

The Lafayette dollar is said to be the most counterfeited commemorative piece. The methods of counterfeiting include high-pressure casting and counterfeit dies, many well made and difficult to differentiate from the originals. The cast specimens have usually been cleaned to obscure the texture. It is recommended that the Lafayette dollar and other commemorative specimens be authenticated (especially in the higher grades) before an acquisition is consummated.

The Wilson Dollar

In commemoration of the opening of a branch mint in Manila, a small number of "Wilson dollars" were produced in both silver and bronze. Production of this dollar-sized coin was limited to 2,200 silver and 3,700 bronze specimens.

Summary

The following dates are known to have been counterfeited in the past. The collector/investor should be very careful when acquiring higher priced specimens of these dates. Professional numismatic help would be advisable.

Most Counterfeited Dates

Morgan Dollars	Peace Dollars
1884-S	1928-P
1886-O	1934-S
1889-CC	
1892-S	
1893-S	
1894-P	
1895-P (Proof) *	
1896-O	
1896-S	
1897-O	
1901-P	
1903-S	

* No original business strike examples are known to exist.

The following dates are potential candidates for future counterfeiting activities. Their continuing movement towards rarity (and therefore much higher prices) coupled with the availability of an substitute "original" date and/or mint mark that could be altered puts them on our watch list.

Future Potential Counterfeit Dates

Morgan Dollars	Peace Dollars
1879-CC	1922-S
1880-O	1923-S
1883-S	1924-S
1891-O	1925-S
1892-O	1927-S
1893-O	1928-S
1904-S	

The true situation is one of "cat and mouse." Counterfeiters are utilizing the same technology available to counterfeit detectors. As a result the differences between genuine and counterfeit pieces are becoming more minute and difficult to detect. Buyers of investment grade coins should always have their prospective purchases authenticated for self-protection as well as for the protection of numismatics as a hobby and an industry.

Marlene Highfill pictured with the Morgan and Orr #C4181 press, built October 14, 1873, in Philadelphia. This Press produced #1003, the first "so-called" dollar c/o Hibler & Kappen. It was sent to the San Francisco Mint #1594 where it then struck the 1873 Trade Dollar, 703,000 were struck. The press was acquired by the ANA and placed on display in 1982.

This chapter would be incomplete without extending thanks and appreciation to those works which have contributed so much to the field of counterfeit detection and the authentication process. Very special thanks goes to Mr. J. P. Martin, ANA Numismatist/ANAAB Authenticator, who together with Florence Schook, Kenneth E. Bressett, Robert J. Leuver and Ruthann Brettell, provided numerous photos, continuous support and encouragement in the pursuit of counterfeit identification education. The following sources of information and photographs have been very valuable to the author, collectors and investors and the entire numismatic community.

John Highfill at the ANA entrance, Colorado Springs, Co.

Counterfeit Detection: A Reprint from The Numismatist, 1983, American Numismatic Association, Colorado Springs, Colorado

Counterfeit Detection: A Reprint from The Numismatist, Volume II, 1988, American Numismatic Association, Colorado Springs, Colorado

How to Detect the Genuine 1893-S Morgan Dollar, *How to Detect the Genuine 1894-P Morgan Dollar*, *How to Detect the Genuine 1928 Peace Dollar*, three articles by Bill Fivaz, NSDR Journal, Mike Faraone, Co-Editor, Robert T. McIntire, Co-Editor and Publisher

Official Guide to Detecting Altered & Counterfeit U.S. Coins & Currency, Marc Hudgeons, House of Collectibles, Inc., Orlando, Florida

Standard Catalog of United States Altered and Counterfeit Coins, Virgil Hancock and Laurence Spanbauer, 1979, Sanford J. Durst, New York

If you should require authentications you may contact both of these organizations:

ANACS
4150 Tuller Road
Suite 216
Dublin, Ohio 43017

President: Bruce Boyd
Vice President and General Manager: John McDonough
Senior Numismatist: Michael Fahey
Authenticators: Tim Hargis
Don Bonser
Randy Campbell

ANAAB
818 N. Cascade
Colorado Springs, Co. 80903-3279

Senior Numismatist and Authenticator: J.P. Martin

***

CHAPTER 21

Grading Circulated Dollars

by Wayne H. Miller

Although most collectors are able to obtain choice uncirculated specimens for common date dollars, the semi-key and key dates are usually affordable only in circulated condition. The scarcity of circulated better-date dollars has resulted in considerable hedging in grading such coins. Abuses are most prevalent among key-date dollars such as 1889-CC, 1893-S, 1895-S, 1934-S, etc.

In an effort to improve the grading of circulated silver dollars, the author will present multiple photographs with accompanying descriptive text of Morgan dollars which grade from Good to About Uncirculated. However, because of the enormous variations in strike among different dates, no photograph or text will be presented for the Peace Dollar series. After examining several dozen photographs of Peace dollars in various grades, the author has concluded that a photographic presentation is not possible. For example, the motto IN GOD WE TRUST, which is utilized as an indicator of wear, is often more pronounced on a Fine Philadelphia mint Peace dollar than on an AU San Francisco specimen. The poor strike of "S"-mint Peace dollars makes grading quite difficult. Peace dollars are best graded by their luster; but this is something which cannot be adequately presented in photographs.

Peace dollars are among the most difficult of all United States coins to grade because of the lack of design detail. However, most dates are easily obtainable in circulated condition, and pricing increments are not significant from one grade to another except for a few dates. Therefore, the grading dilemma is not as critical within this series as compared to the Morgan dollars. Again, "sliders" can be differentiated from mint state specimens by the gray appearance in the field when the coin is tilted. Unusually flat struck, dull luster or excessively abraded mint state specimens are often considered by dealers as AU pieces.

The following is a photographic and textual presentation of the various circulated grades of Morgan silver dollars:

Note: Deep gouges, cuts, planchet or striking defects, discolorations, etc. must all be considered in determining the grading of a coin. Significant imperfections will lower a coin by at least a grade, and should be fully described in any advertisements. Also, poorly struck dollars may display the luster of an AU coin, for example, but the detail of a VF coin. A realistic grade for such a coin might be EF.

G

GOOD

Obverse—Rim distinct, but some flattening of the denticles. All rim lettering intact. Only a few lines in the hair above ear still visible. LIBERTY distinct. Date clear. No detail in cotton blossoms.

Reverse—Rim distinct, with denticles flattened. All rim lettering intact. Mintmark (if any) clearly visible, although flattened. Top half of left (from observer's viewpoint) wing worn smooth.

Eight examples of Good

VG

VERY GOOD

Obverse—Rims intact, denticles quite worn, but distinct. Fine detail in hair lacking, but some line will show. Hair merges with face above ear, but hairline shows at forehead.

Reverse—Rim intact, denticles worn but distinct. Top one-third of left (from observer's viewpoint) wing worn smooth. Legs worn smooth. Rim lettering distinct.

Eight examples of Very Good

F

FINE

Obverse—Hair above forehead defined; cotton blossoms flat but distinct from the stems. Lower two cotton leaves worn at junction point but distinct from head. Curved line in Liberty's ear visible.

Reverse—Central part of upper left wing worn; little detail in Eagle's neck feathers. Eagles feet smooth; top portions of leaves in wreath are flat.

Eight examples of Fine

VF

VERY FINE

Obverse—Smooth spots on hair from forehead to ear but all lines will show except directly above the ear. Cotton blossom stems very distinct; lower two cotton leaves distinctly separate. Slight wear on grain in wheat stalks.

Reverse—All lines on Eagle's left wing (from the observer's viewpoint) will show, although some may not be clearly distinct. Few feathers show on Eagle's neck; legs show some detail on outer edges. Some leaves in wreath are worn flat. Cross point of olive branch and arrow shafts distinct.

Eight examples of Very Fine

EF

EXTREMELY FINE

Obverse—Slight wear on hair above date, ear, and forehead. Some detail in base of cotton blossoms, near the top of the stems. Cotton leaves distinct except poor edges; wheat stalks distinct. Some traces of mint luster apparent.

Reverse—All feathers in Eagle's wings clear and distinct. Neck feathers distinct; breast worn smooth, but some detail on outer edges. Legs show slight wear at center; talons worn flat. Highest raised leaves of wreath slightly worn. Traces of mint luster apparent.

Eight examples of Extremely Fine

AU

ABOUT UNCIRCULATED

Obverse—Considerable mint luster apparent, although the field will evidence a "gray" appearance when the coin is tilted. Traces of wear at highest points: Hair above ear, edges of cotton leaves, and tops of cotton blossoms. All other details clear and distinct.

Reverse—Considerable mint luster apparent, although the field will evidence a "gray" appearance when the coin is tilted. Some weakness at highest points: The center of the Eagle's breast, and the upper legs; little detail on Eagle's talons. All other details clear and distinct.

Eight examples of About Uncirculated

Acknowledgement

This article was reprinted by permission in its entirety from Wayne Miller's *Morgan and Peace Dollar Textbook*, 1982, Adam Smith Publishing Co., Metairie, Louisiana.

***

James L. Halperin, NLG

Jim Halperin has been a professional numismatist since 1969, when he opened Jim's Stamp & Coin Shop, in Cochituate, Mass. He attended Harvard College, but took a long leave of absence, halfway through his sophomore year, to become a fulltime coin dealer.

In late 1982, Jim Halperin moved to Dallas, Texas, to form a partnership with long time friend and arch-rival Steve Ivy. Jim Halperin and Steve Ivy's company, Heritage Capital Corporation, is now possibly the largest and certainly one of the most well respected coin and stamp firms in the world. Its divisions and affiliates include Heritage Rare Coin Galleries, Heritage Coin Wholesale, Heritage Numismatic Auctions, U.S. Rare Coin Exchange, U.S. Tangible Investment Corporation and the Ivy, Shreve and Mader Philatelic Auctions.

Jim is considered to be among the world's foremost experts on U.S. coins and coin grading. His other interests include late 19th and 20th century paintings and sculpture, art nouveau glass, comic art, weightlifting and racquetball.

Jim and his wife Gayle, a professor of dance who now teaches dance technique at Texas Woman's University, have set up a foundation based in Dallas to promote the teaching of daily health education courses in public schools.

Books published by Jim include the *N.C.I. Grading Guide*, his first book, and the recently published *How to Grade U.S. Coins*. Although he has written dozens of articles for numismatic publications, Jim hopes to write several other educational numismatic books, and is presently looking for ideas and suggestions of topics for his next book.

Correspondence should be addressed to: Jim Halperin 100 Heritage Plaza Highland Park Village Dallas, Texas 75205

CHAPTER 22

Grading of U. S. Dollars

by James L. Halperin, NLG

In the numismatic world, the process of determining the condition of a coin is known as grading. This fundamentally subjective process will vary from dealer to dealer and from grading service to grading service. In fact, it is not uncommon for grading services to grade a coin differently when it is submitted more than once. The truth of the matter is that grading standards are constantly changing as the nature of the coin market changes.

The standards outlined in this chapter are the approximate ones currently (as of June, 1990) employed by the Professional Coin Grading Service (P.C.G.S.) and the Numismatic Guaranty Corporation of America (N.G.C.). They represent what I believe are the most accepted standards on today's market.

I am drawing these remarks and observations exclusively from my recently published book, *How to Grade U.S. Coins* (Ivy Press, Inc. 1990). These highlights will serve to introduce the elements necessary to the grading of U.S. coins. However, experience is the final and greatest teacher.

The Sheldon Scale

This system of grading coinage was introduced by the late Dr. William H. Sheldon for the purpose of grading large cents. The system grew in popularity and eventually was adapted to all coins in the early 1970's. The Sheldon Scale, as used today, incorporates numerical grades 1 through 70 to correspond with various descriptive grades as follows:

Poor	- 1	Fine	- 12,15
Fair	- 2	Very Fine	- 20,25,30,35
Almost Good	- 3	Extremely Fine	- 40,45
Good	- 4,6	Almost Uncirculated	- 50,55,58
Very Good	- 8,10	Mint State	- 60,61,62,63,64,65,66,67,68,69,70

The Grading Process

Mint State or Almost Uncirculated? That is the question!

Perhaps the toughest part of the process of grading involves distinguishing between a mint state coin and a top grade Almost Uncirculated (A.U.) coin. Detail is not the only criterion. Sometimes an A.U. coin (or even an Extremely Fine coin) will have better detail than an uncirculated coin. This, of course, is due to the fact that some coins are struck with more detail than others.

Once you know that a coin cannot be graded solely based on detail, you can begin the process of learning how to distinguish wear. Throughout this chapter, I will use the Morgan Silver Dollar as an example of each grading technique.

Below are photographs of the obverse and reverse of a fully struck Morgan dollar. Accented in red are the high points of the design. These are the areas where the wear from circulation is most likely to appear first. Unfortunately, these are also areas which tend to lack detail if the coin is weakly struck or if it was struck from worn dies.

Obverse

Reverse

1882-S

The best way to learn to tell if a coin has wear is through actual experience. Compare a coin which you know is uncirculated to a slightly circulated (AU) coin with equal detail. Observe the coins carefully, tilting them back and forth to see how the lustre flows, especially over the high points. Look closely at the high points. You will notice a difference in the lustre. On the uncirculated coin, the full lustre will roll over the high points. On the A.U. coin, the lustre will be visibly broken, and this break will be noticeable without magnification. Thus, even to a somewhat inexperienced eye, it will convey the visual impact of slight wear (i.e., displacement of metal).

It is important to note, however, that many mint state coins will have slight "friction" on the high points or in the fields, resulting from coins rubbing against each other in rolls or bags. If the metal itself is not disturbed, and the lustre is intact (with perhaps just the slightest disturbance, usually from very tiny hairlines), the coin is probably still mint state.

This exercise is best performed, at first, using coins which have no toning. Once you have mastered untoned coins, you can try the same thing using toned coins. Just try to look "through" the toning as if it were never there. But I warn you that toned coins are many times trickier than untoned coins.

Now, here's an interesting question: If you remove the toning from a coin, all other things being equal, can that alone change the grade from almost uncirculated to fully mint state, or vice versa? The answer, surprisingly, is yes! Even though technically the removal of toning should not (and really does not) affect the presence of wear, it does affect the visual impact of wear.

Until coins are graded by computer, and possibly even after that, visual impact will be the single most important factor in grading a coin. Sometimes toning will sufficiently hide wear from even the most experienced eye. In some cases, toning will create the illusion of wear to even the most experienced eye. In these rare cases, the illusion becomes the reality, because the market will value those coins based on their visual impact.

The goal, therefore, is not to know exactly how the coin would look if the toning were removed. It is impossible to do that. Even the top experts don't always know what lurks beneath the toning of a coin. The goal is to assess the visual impact of wear on the coin, as accurately as possible.

How To Grade Mint State Coins

Like any science, language, sport, or field of study, it is best to break grading down to its basic components, and master them one at a time. I learned how to grade coins much the same way I learned how to speak English; all at once, through experience. In retrospect, however, it seems to me that both topics would be quite a bit easier to learn if one studied them one aspect at a time. This statement is especially true as a person gets older. Hence, most people learn their first language through experience. But if they learn a second language, they learn the rules first, then the vocabulary, then the sentence structures, etc. (Note, however, that by far the most effective way to learn both a second language and coin grading is by learning the rules first, and then combining that knowledge with actual experience. Either subject is nearly impossible to learn entirely from a book.)

Interestingly, it is rare that someone who learns coin grading does so in this way. Most people learn by experience far more than they do by rules, and this is especially true of those who learn to grade mint state coins. I personally have never bothered to learn any "rules" or "components" of grading. Therefore, in the course of writing this book, I have analyzed, for the first time in my life, how I grade coins. What components make up the actual process of grading uncirculated and proof coins? How important is each component in relation to the others?

After much thought, I now believe that the essence of grading a coin (once you have determined that it is definitely uncirculated or proof) can be broken down into four distinct factors:

1. Surface Preservation — This includes the presence of bagmarks, hairlines from cleaning or mishandling, and other imperfections of planchet, whether mint caused or man made. An analysis of surface preservation attempts to weigh the visual impact of these imperfections based on their degree of severity and their location on the coin.

2. Strike — Refers to the sharpness and completeness of detail, with the normal characteristics of that particular type, date and mint mark (i.e., issue) taken into account.

3. Lustre — This encompasses the brilliance, cartwheel, sheen and contrast of the coin, again taking the normal characteristics of the particular issue into account. Minor (non-hairline producing) cleaning, retoning, friction, etc., are evaluated under this category.

4. Eye-Appeal — That certain aesthetic appeal that results from the attractiveness of the toning (if any), the balance of the coin, and the effect of the combination of all of the coin's qualities.

I believe that Surface Preservation is the single most important factor in grading mint state coins. The other three factors appear to be approximately equal in value, each about half as important as surface preservation (i.e., 40% + 20% + 20% + 20% = 100%). Actually, this formula is somewhat arbitrary since it is really a function of the standards of the scales we use for each of the factors themselves. I chose this 40/20/20/20 formula mainly for its simplicity. The scales for the individual factors, outlined in the next four sections, were designed around this formula. With this in mind, I hope to teach you how to properly evaluate each factor, assign a numerical value to that factor, and then turn that information into a valid grade. You will then learn when to add to this grade other modifiers such as prooflike, full strike, rim nick, weakly struck, cleaned, etc.

Surface Preservation

As I mentioned in the previous section, an analysis of surface preservation attempts to evaluate the visual impact of the present imperfections based on their degree of severity and their location on the coin.

As you look at lots of coins, you will notice that bagmarks tend to be the most common detracting surface problem on most business strikes. Hairlines, on the other hand, are usually the most prevalent detractor of the surfaces of proof coins. This results from the physical differences between business strikes and proof coins, and the different way each type of coin tends to have been handled.

Most business strikes, at one time or another, were shipped in bags. Therefore, nearly all business strikes have some marks caused either by banging against other coins, or by some other form of mishandling after being removed from the bag.

Proof coins were handled much more carefully. Unfortunately, proof surfaces tend to magnify even the lightest mishandling into hairline scratches. Indeed, prooflike uncirculated coins generally have bagmarks and hairlines. Therefore, prooflike Morgan dollars tend to be quite a bit rarer in MS-65 grade than frosty Morgan dollars. This is one of the reasons why prooflike gems command higher prices than frosty gem Morgans.

Whenever we analyze the severity of an imperfection of a coin, we try to figure out what visual impact that imperfection will have on the eye of a trained numismatist. Obviously, the more severe the imperfection, which is measured by the amount of displaced metal, the worse the imperfection.

Of course, this statement is only true if we are comparing examples of the same type of imperfection. For example, a hairline is generally far worse than a bagmark of equal metal displacement and location, because hairlines create a lot of visual impact with very little metal displacement.

However, a mint caused planchet defect is usually not as detracting as a bagmark. This is mainly because any mint-caused imperfection is not regarded to be as detrimental as if it were man-made (i.e., post minting process). Also, very often the lustre will run unbroken through a mint caused planchet defect. This applies to planchet laminations, lint marks, die rust, die wear, or practically any other mint caused defect. (Note: Minor die scratches and clashed dies are not usually considered to be serious defects, and hardly affect the grade, if at all. In many cases, they don't even affect the value of the coin.) Of course, if a mint-caused defect is huge and ugly, it is still far worse than one that's tiny and unobtrusive — just like bagmarks and hairlines. A good rule of thumb is that a mint-caused defect will affect the grade about half as much as a bagmark or hairline of equal visual impact.

Spots, fingerprints and other discoloration, other than on copper coins, usually fall into the eye-appeal category (which will be covered later). Most spots are at least partially removable, unless the coin is copper or nickel. However, if the discoloration begins eating into the metal (i.e., corrosion), then this, too, falls under surface preservation. Any corrosion of metal must be rated on visual impact, similar to a hairline or bagmark. (Note: Major surface impairments such as harsh cleaning, blatantly artificial toning or repairs will prevent most services from issuing a grading opinion.)

Once you have determined the severity of an imperfection, this information must be measured in combination with the location of the imperfection. Refer to the photograph of a Morgan dollar, color coded as follows:

RED	- Worst (Average x 4)	GREEN	- Better (Average x 1/2)
ORANGE	- Bad (Average x 2)	BLUE	- Best (Average x 1/4)
YELLOW	- Average		

Note: These quantifications are approximate.

Obverse

Reverse

1899

For example, a mark in the red area is about eight times as serious than if the same mark were in the green area, as illustrated on the photograph. Notice that the very worst place is the middle of Miss Liberty's cheek. This area is the focal point of the coin, and the one place where experienced numismatists will invariably look first.

Also keep in mind that direction of the mark can increase or decrease its effect. For example, a vertical bagmark might be more obvious in Miss Liberty's hair than a horizontal bagmark. A horizontal bagmark would be less noticeable since it would be somewhat hidden and appear to be part of the design at first glance.

The least detrimental area to have an imperfection is on the rim. Rim imperfections tend to be less detracting and less noticeable, because the rim is the least important part of the coin's total design.

Now, the next step is to rate the surface preservation of five mint state and five proof Morgan dollars.

These examples show the worst representations of business strike surface preservation I could find, that could still merit an unqualified MS-60 grade. Anything worse, and I would have to mention the most prominent defect in my grade description of that coin. For example, a mint state coin slightly worse than the one pictured here could be described as "MS-60, scratches" or "MS-60, heavy milling marks."

Obverse

Reverse

Surface Preservation: 1

Obverse

Reverse

Surface Preservation: 2

Obverse

Reverse

Surface Preservation: 3

Obverse

Reverse

Surface Preservation: 4

Obverse

Reverse

Surface Preservation: 5

Try to compare any Morgan dollars you wish to grade to these photographs. If you think the surface preservation grades somewhere in between, feel free to use in-between grades like 2 1/2 or 4 3/4. Remember, at first your grading will involve a lot of guessing. It will take much time and practice before your grading becomes really meaningful. So try to get started practicing as soon as possible.

Strike

There are several parts of the minting process that could account for the sharpness, or lack thereof, of a coin's strike. The most important aspect is striking pressure. Striking pressure can vary tremendously from coin to coin during the minting process.

In fact, some mints (particularly New Orleans, Charlotte and Dahlonega) were usually allocated the poorer condition presses and dies. Therefore these mints tended to produce a worse than average coin in terms of strike. In addition, the sharpness of the die needs to be considered. This may vary due to wear on the die, or on the master die from which the die itself is made. Finally, the consistency and quality of the planchet can affect the quality of strike.

Here is a photograph of a fully struck mint state Morgan dollar:

Obverse

Reverse

1882-S

It is important to note that Morgan dollars dated prior to 1879 (including some varieties of 1879-S) and after 1899, simply do not have all the same die details as most Morgan dollars. This variation in no way prevents those coins from being considered fully struck, as long as they possess all the details of their particular sub-type.

Here are photographs of mint state examples of the 1879-1899 sub-type, graded by strike, 1 through 5:

Obverse

Reverse

Strike: 1

Obverse

Reverse

Strike: 2

Obverse Reverse

Strike: 3

Obverse Reverse

Strike: 4

Obverse Strike: 5 Reverse

Note that any coin struck with less detail than the coin in photo #1 must have the weakness of strike somehow noted in its final overall grade description. For example: MS-63, weakly struck, or MS-60, typical strike for this notoriously weak date.

Again, any coin having a strike grade weaker than 1 (regardless of how poorly or well struck that particular issue is normally found) must have the strike mentioned in its overall grade description. Even if this is the case, you should still use the strike grade "1" when calculating the overall grade.

Feel free to use intermediate grades (such as 3 1/2 or 2.6) when evaluating strike. Also, keep in mind that a coin might have more detail than the corresponding photograph in some areas and less detail in other areas. Occasionally, a coin may have weakness about the outer areas. A good rule of thumb is that it is only about a third as detrimental for a coin to lack peripheral detail as it is for the coin to lack the same amount of detail in the central portion.

Here is a brief synopsis of the striking characteristics of each date and mint mark of Morgan dollar (footnote 4).

Note: Any date listed as being normally softly struck, when found exceptionally well struck, may be noted as such in the overall grade description. (For example: MS-60, full strike; or MS-65, sharp strike.)

STRIKE TABLE

1878 8TF - Above average to bold
7/8 - Average7F - Above average
7FRB- Sharp and bold
CC - Sharp and bold
S - Sharp and bold

1879 P - Variable, but generally average
CC - Average
O - Average to above average
S - Sharp and bold

1880 P - Average to above average
CC - Above average to bold
O - Variable, but generally strong
S - Sharp and bold

1881 P - Above average
CC - Sharp and bold
O - Average
S - Sharp and bold

1882 P - Above average
CC - Above average
O - Average
S - Sharp and bold

1883 P - Above average
CC - Above average, to bold
O - Average to a bit soft
S - Sharp and bold

1884 P - Above average to bold
CC - Above average to bold
O - Soft to average
S - Above average

1885 P - Above average
CC - Above average to bold
O - Variable, but usually average
S - Average

1886 P - Usually sharp
O - Weak and soft
S - Usually well struck

1887 P - Usually sharp and bold
O - Variable, often weakly struck
S - Above average

1888 P - Average
O - Average, though many are weak
S - Average

1889 P - Average, though some are a bit soft
CC - Usually sharp and bold
O - Generally quite weak and soft
S - Typically sharp and bold

1890 P - Average, though some are soft
CC - Above average to sharp
O - Generally weak and soft. P-L's usually above average
S - Most sharp and bold

1891 P - Most weak
CC - Above average
O - Typically soft and weak
S - Variable, but most are sharp

1892 P - Many weak, but variable
CC - Above average
O - Almost always weak and soft
S - Sharp and well struck

1893 P - Average to above average
CC - Most are weak, especially P-L's
O - Typically weak
S - Sharp when found

1894 P - Usually well struck
O - Generally quite soft
S - Sharp and bold

1895 P - Proof only, almost always sharp
O - Weak and soft
S - Above average

1896 P - Sharp and bold
O - Weak and soft
S - Usually average

1897 P - Generally sharp
O - Average, though some weak
S - Above average

1898 P - Sharp and bold
O - Above average
S - Average to above average

1899 P - Above average to bold
O - Above average to bold
S - Above average

1900 P - Average
O - Average
S - Average

1901 P - Generally weak and soft
O - Average
S - Most weak to average

1902 P - Variable, though usually well struck
O - Average
S - Weak and soft

1903 P - Usually sharp
O - Above average
S - Sharp and bold

1904 P - Average, though some a bit soft
O - Average
S - Above average

1921 P - Average, though some a bit soft
D - Below average to average
S - Weak and soft

Lustre

During the minting process, a planchet becomes a coin once it has been struck between two dies. The striking takes place under extreme pressure. It is this pressure which is responsible for the phenomenon known as mint lustre. Mint lustre, which is a combination of cartwheel, sheen, brilliance and contrast, is defined simply as the way in which the surface of a coin reflects light.

When you grade the lustre of a coin, you basically grade the intensity, beauty and integrity of that coin's ability to reflect light, within the bounds of the lustre characteristics of that issue. For the purpose of this discussion, let us take a common date silver dollar, for example, an 1885-O. First we examine the highest points, accented in red, as illustrated here:

Obverse

Reverse

1885-O

Is the lustre as pronounced at the very highest points as it is in the fields? If not, the coin has some "friction," as discussed earlier. There is no visual impact of metal displacement (otherwise the coin would be considered AU), but there is often some disturbance of lustre. The degree of this disturbance will affect your lustre grade.

Next, examine the fields of the coin. Is the lustre absolutely booming, or is it pretty good, just so-so, or plain dull? Don't take the hairlines into account, since you've already accounted for them as part of your surface preservation grade. However, if the coin has ever been cleaned, retoned, or dipped too often, the lustre will be reduced to some degree. And, of course, some coins are made better than others.

If the coin has virtually no lustre, this must be mentioned in the description (i.e., MS-60, dull; or MS-63, but lacklustre from prolonged immersion in seawater). If any areas on the coin are polished or harshly cleaned, this too must be mentioned in the description.

Now, give the coin a grade of 1 to 5 (fractions are okay) based on its lustre. Make this evaluation with your own experience from looking at other coins of that issue (i.e., type, date and mint mark), while keeping the criteria outlined here in mind. The more experience you have had, the more meaningful your grade will be. Even if you have no idea what grade to assign, take a guess. Eventually, your guesses will become closer and closer to 100% accurate.

For additional study, here is a list of the lustre characteristics of the various issues of Morgan dollars (see footnote 1):

LUSTRE TABLE

1878 8TF - Frosty surfaces, good lustre, occasionally found with one side prooflike
7/8 TF - Frosty surfaces, good lustre, scarce in prooflike
7 TF - Full frosty surfaces, good lustre, prooflikes are available
7 TF RB - Semi-prooflike surfaces, excellent lustre, seldom found fully prooflike
S - Frosty or semi-prooflike surfaces, excellent lustre, often found fully prooflike, but heavily bag-marked
CC - Frosty surfaces, good lustre, frequently seen prooflike

1879 P - Frosty surfaces, good lustre, prooflikes not scarce
O - Frosty surfaces, excellent lustre, some prooflikes
S - Semi-prooflike surfaces, excellent lustre, fairly scarce with deeply reflective fields
CC - Variable, frosty or semi-prooflike surfaces, poor to good lustre, heavily marked

1880 P - Frosty surfaces, good lustre, prooflikes infrequent
O - Frosty surfaces, good lustre, very scarce in prooflike
S - Semi-prooflike surfaces, excellent lustre, readily available in prooflike
CC - Frosty surfaces, good lustre, scarce in P-L

1881 P - Frosty surfaces, excellent lustre, prooflikes are available, but not typically deep
O - Frosty or semi-prooflike surfaces, good lustre, heavily marked and scarce with deep mirror surfaces
S - Semi-prooflike surfaces, excellent lustre, often seen prooflike, but cameo contrast elusive
CC - Frosty or semi-P-L surfaces, good to excellent lustre, prooflikes are readily available

1882 P - Frosty surfaces, good lustre, fairly scarce in P-L
O - Frosty or Semi-P-L surfaces, good lustre, P-L's often heavily marked
S - Semi-P-L surfaces, excellent lustre, prooflikes are rare, but cameos are plentiful
CC - Frosty surfaces, good lustre, some prooflikes

1883 P - Frosty surfaces, good lustre, semi-P-L's around, though full P-L's are scarce
O - Frosty surfaces, good lustre, many prooflikes
S - Semi-prooflike surfaces, excellent lustre
CC - Frosty surfaces, good lustre, moderately scarce as P-L

1884 P - Frosty surfaces, good lustre, very scarce in true P-L
O - Frosty surfaces, good lustre, prooflikes are readily available
S - Frosty surfaces, good lustre, prooflikes are rare, as is issue in Mint State
CC - Frosty surfaces, good lustre, prooflikes available

1885 P - Frosty surfaces, good lustre, prooflikes readily available
O - Frosty surfaces, good lustre, semi-P-L's available, but true P-L's scarcer
S - Frosty surfaces, good lustre, very scarce in P-L
CC - Frosty surfaces, good lustre, not difficult in P-L

1886 P - Frosty surfaces, excellent lustre, P-L's available
O - Frosty surfaces, poor to good lustre, very rare with fully P-L surfaces, a few semi-P-L's
S - Semi-prooflike surfaces, excellent lustre, full P-L's scarce

1887 P - Frosty surfaces, excellent lustre, relatively common in P-L
O - Frosty surfaces, good lustre, P-L's appear
S - Frosty or semi-P-L surfaces, good lustre, P-L's appear, often one-sided

1888 P - Frosty surfaces, good lustre, scarce in P-L
O - Frosty surfaces, good lustre, scarce in P-L
S - Semi-P-L surfaces, good lustre, scarce in true P-L

1889 P - Frosty surfaces, good lustre, tougher issue in P-L
O - Frosty surfaces, good lustre, very scarce in P-L, especially with mark-free surfaces
S - Semi-P-L surfaces, excellent lustre, deep mirror P-L's elusive
CC - prooflike surfaces, good lustre, entire issue quite rare

1890 P - Frosty surfaces, poor lustre, very scarce in prooflike, especially with clean surfaces
O - Frosty surfaces, good lustre, P-L's more common than generally thought
S - Semi-prooflike surfaces, excellent lustre, prooflikes are available
CC - Frosty surfaces, good lustre, prooflikes seen with moderate frequency

1891 P - Frosty surfaces, poor lustre, seldom seen prooflike
O - Frosty surfaces, poor lustre, P-L's available
S - Semi-prooflike surfaces, excellent lustre, P-L's available
CC - Frosty surfaces, good lustre, prooflikes somewhat elusive

1892 P - Frosty surfaces, poor to good lustre, full P-L's fairly rare, Semi-P-L's abundant
O - Frosty surfaces, good lustre, extremely rare in prooflike
S - Semi-prooflike surfaces, excellent lustre, P-L's not rare for issue, but whole issue is rare in Mint State
CC - Frosty surfaces, excellent lustre, quite scarce in true P-L, semi-P-L's common

1893 P - Frosty surfaces, excellent lustre, extremely rare in P-L, particularly top end condition
O - Frosty surfaces, good lustre, very rare with fully P-L surfaces
S - Semi-prooflike surfaces, excellent lustre, fully P-L surfaces virtually unknown on Mint State examples
CC - Frosty surfaces, excellent lustre, P-L's quite scarce, even more so fully struck

1894 P - Frosty surfaces, poor lustre, extremely rare in P-L
O - Frosty surfaces, poor lustre, very rare in P-L, especially nice examples
S - Frosty or semi-prooflike surfaces, excellent lustre, not particularly scarce in P-L

1895 O - Frosty surfaces, good lustre, quite rare in P-L, but sharply struck when found
S - Frosty surfaces, excellent lustre, true P-L's elusive, though semi-P-L's are around

1896 P - Frosty surfaces, good lustre, relatively common in P-L
O - Frosty surfaces, poor lustre, extremely rare in full P-L
S - Frosty surfaces, good lustre, very scarce in P-L

1897 P - Frosty surfaces, good lustre, moderately scarce in P-L
O - Frosty surfaces, poor lustre, extremely rare in P-L
S - Frosty surfaces, good lustre, available as P-L

1898 P - Frosty surfaces, excellent lustre, moderately scarce in P-L
O - Frosty surfaces, excellent lustre, relatively common in P-L
S - Frosty or semi-P-L surfaces, excellent lustre, prooflikes available

1899 P - Frosty surfaces, good lustre, not difficult to locate with P-L surfaces
O - Frosty surfaces, excellent lustre, somewhat scarce as full P-L, though available
S - Frosty surfaces, good lustre, occasionally available as P-L

1900 P - Frosty surfaces, good lustre, scarce in full P-L
O - Frosty surfaces, good lustre, moderately scarce in P-L
S - Frosty surfaces, good lustre, prooflikes available from Redfield

1901 P - Frosty surfaces, poor lustre, of the highest rarity with P-L surfaces
O - Frosty surfaces, good lustre, very scarce in P-L, though well struck and pleasing when found
S - Frosty surfaces, good lustre, extremely difficult in prooflike, and when found, is weakly struck

1902 P - Frosty surfaces, good lustre, scarce, though available in P-L, seldom attractive
O - Frosty surfaces, good lustre, scarce with fully reflective fields, available as semi-P-L
S - Frosty surfaces, good lustre, very scarce in P-L, rare in fully struck P-L

1903 P - Semi-prooflike surfaces, excellent lustre, full prooflikes are very scarce
O - Semi-prooflike surfaces, excellent lustre, full prooflikes are scarce
S - Frosty surfaces, excellent lustre, rare as a prooflike

1904 P - Frosty surfaces, poor lustre, almost unknown as a full prooflike.
O - Frosty surfaces, good lustre, common as prooflike
S - Frosty surfaces, good lustre, extremely rare as a P-L

1921 P - Frosty surfaces, good lustre, moderately scarce as prooflike
D - Frosty surfaces, good lustre, very tough to locate in full P-L
S - Frosty surfaces, poor lustre, extremely rare in prooflike

Eye-Appeal

If lustre sounds subjective to you (it really isn't, it just takes a lot of experience to evaluate it), just wait until you learn about eye-appeal. Eye-appeal is, by far, the most subjective aspect of grading.

To give you an idea about the importance of eye-appeal, I will now tell you my favorite rare coin war story. In late 1979, Jerry Cohen, then a partner in the Abner Kreisberg Corporation, held a coin auction in Los Angeles. It was an especially beautiful sale with many interesting coins. One of the most interesting (and rare) coins in that sale was a 1795 Small Eagle bust dollar, described simply as Uncirculated. It was a gem coin with superb surfaces, lustre and strike. Unfortunately, the toning was positively hideous. The coin simply lacked eye-appeal.

The Coin Dealer Newsletter listed "bid" that week at $22,500 in MS-65, and most of the top dealers (myself included) were willing to bid somewhere in the $20,000 - $25,000 range for the coin. Steve Ivy, my good friend, but also at that time my arch rival (we're now business partners - how the world changes!) bought the coin for $28,000.

I expected him to "dip" the coin to remove the toning, but business was so brisk at that time that he never got around to it. The coin just sat in inventory for three or four of most explosive months in the history of the coin market. Nobody would buy the coin from him because it lacked eye-appeal. "Bid" doubled to $45,000 by February, 1980. After intensive negotiations (lasting less than a minute, I think), I managed to buy that turkey of a coin from Steve for $33,500. He had purchased the coin for 25% over bid, and resold it to me at 25% below bid. It is worth noting that grading standards throughout the industry had certainly not tightened over that time period.

I suppose I had some reservations about dipping the coin. Even for an expert, dipping a coin is a risky undertaking (and I would never recommend that a novice ever dip a coin). What if the toning hid some unpardonable flaw? Or what if the lustre became dull as a result of the dipping? Still; no guts, no glory!

A quick dip in Jewel Lustre produced the most stunning, blazing white semi-prooflike gem early U.S. silver coin I had ever seen! Really, nothing had changed except the eye-appeal factor. The coin was transformed from a "technical MS-65" with no eye-appeal, to a wonder coin, a coin that had it all. The coin that Steve couldn't sell now had suitors waiting in line. There were literally half a dozen knowledgeable buyers begging me to give them first shot at the coin. I sold it to a dealer in the Boston area for $137,000. It recently sold at auction, in a P.C.G.S. MS-65 holder, for $418,000.

Since eye-appeal can be so important, it is critical that you develop a sense for it — an art critic's eye for the aesthetically pleasing. I believe that eye-appeal can best be divided into three distinct areas: toning, balance, and that certain inexplicable aesthetic attractiveness.

First, toning. Here are photographs of five coins, all approximately equal in surface preservation, strike and lustre. They are arranged from worst to best in terms of toning.

Obverse

Reverse

Toning: 1

Obverse

Reverse

Toning: 2

Obverse

Reverse

Toning: 3

Obverse

Reverse

Toning: 4

Obverse

Reverse

Toning: 5

Note that coin #4 is approximately equal in eye-appeal grade to a coin with no toning at all. However, a flawless gem with no toning and uniform texture on both sides can still be given a 5 for eye-appeal.

The best way to grade a coin for eye-appeal is to make your own judgment as to how your coin's toning compares aesthetically to the coins photographed. Assign a grade, using fractions where appropriate. Give it a 4, if the coin has no toning at all. Then we'll make adjustments for balance and aesthetic attractiveness.

Balance can best be defined as the coin's overall consistency. Does the toning on the reverse match (or at least go nicely with) the toning on the obverse? Is the texture of the surfaces roughly equivalent on both sides, or is the obverse frosty while the reverse is prooflike (for example)? Does the coin have pleasing balance, or is it somehow lopsided?

A good general rule is to add up to a point to the toning score for perfect balance. Of course, the maximum score is always 5, so don't add anything if you already gave the toning a 5. Or, you can subtract anywhere from 0 to 50% of the toning score for lack of balance, depending on severity. In no case should the total score be less than 1.

Finally, to the number above, you can make a final adjustment for that indefinable aesthetic attractiveness. Consider the eye-appeal grade you gave your coin based on toning and balance. Now look at the coin and try to notice exactly how high or low your subconscious thinks that number is. That difference is purely aesthetic, quite subjective, and probably impossible to explain. Yet it's hard to deny its existence, as you will most likely notice it time and time again during the grading process. Just follow your heart, and adjust your final number as you see fit, just so you keep it between one and five.

Eye-appeal is the grading factor about which expert dealers will most often disagree. You know what you like, and I know what I like. Once you have looked at a few thousand coins, your opinion about the eye-appeal grade of a coin may be as valid as mine or anyone else's.

Determining Grade

Use the following formula, once you have assigned a numerical grade to the surface preservation, strike, lustre and eye-appeal of each side of a coin:

OBVERSE:

Surface Preservation (1-5) ____________ x 2	=	____________
Strike (1-5)	=	____________
Lustre (1-5)	=	____________
Eye-appeal (1-5)	=	____________
OBVERSE TOTAL:		____________

REVERSE:

Surface Preservation (1-5) ____________ x 2	=	____________
Strike (1-5)	=	____________
Lustre (1-5)	=	____________
Eye-appeal (1-5)	=	____________
REVERSE TOTAL:		____________

Next, we can relate the following totals to corresponding grades:

Total		Grade
5 to 12.99	=	MS or Proof-60
13 to 13.99	=	MS or Proof-61
14 to 17.49	=	MS or Proof-62
17.5 to 18.99	=	MS or Proof-63
19 to 20.49	=	MS or Proof-64
20.5 to 21.99	=	MS or Proof-65
22 to 22.99	=	MS or Proof-66
23 to 23.99	=	MS or Proof-67
24 to 24.49	=	MS or Proof-68
24.5 to 24.99	=	MS or Proof-69
25	=	MS or Proof-70

For example, a proof coin with an 18 obverse and a 21 reverse could be graded Proof-63/65. However, its overall grading would be Proof-63 since a coin's grade is largely determined by its worst side.

Still, usually the obverse of a coin is considered more important than the reverse. The consensus today is that the value of a coin is determined approximately 60/40 obverse to reverse. In other words, the obverse is about 1 1/2 times more important than the reverse. Practically the only exception occurs in the case of certain commemorative coins and patterns. In these cases, it is somewhat ambiguous which side is the obverse. Both sides are of approximately equal importance in these instances.

For this reason, it may sometimes be considered permissible to upgrade the reverse grade a bit if the obverse is toward the upper end of the scale of its grade. For example, a coin with a 20 obverse and an 18.9 reverse might still be graded MS-64. However, a coin with an 18.9 obverse and a 20 reverse (a far more common occurrence) must always be graded MS-63.

Is It Proof or Business Strike?

One of the most difficult parts of grading is distinguishing a "first strike" or "prooflike" uncirculated (i.e., business strike) coin from a proof. It is important to remember that "proof" is not a grade; it is a method of manufacture.

Proof coins are graded in a similar manner to business strike coins (i.e., Proof-1 through Proof-70). A coin which exists only as a proof, such as an 1895 Philadelphia mint Morgan dollar (if you believe, as I do, that all business strikes of that issue were melted) that is worn down to Very Good-8 grade, for example would still merit the grade Proof-8. Of course, some proof coins are impossible to distinguish as proofs once they are worn beyond a certain point. Therefore, circulated proofs may also be graded by their circulated grade level (i.e., VF-20 or AU-50), especially when there is some doubt as to their proof status.

When you attempt to discern between mint state and proof coins, always remember that proofs are specially made coins. They are struck under greater pressure than most business strikes, and usually they are given two or more blows of the die. In addition, they are struck on specially made, polished planchets, using polished dies (in the case of brilliant proofs).

Therefore, consider the following factors in tandem with each other, for no single factor is enough to make a conclusive decision:

1. Proof Surface — A brilliant proof should have a mirror surface. In most cases there will be little if any frost (i.e., cartwheel) in the fields. A notable exception to this rule would be the proof coins of 1860 in all denominations. For some reason, most 1860 proof coins display a lot of cartwheel, although their surfaces are still mirror-like. There will be full mirror surfaces even in the protected areas of the field, such as between the vertical lines of the shield, in the case of Seated Liberty coinage. Matte and Roman finish proofs will also lack cartwheel, and will have either dull or satiny surfaces.

Of course many business strikes have mirror or prooflike surfaces. Both prooflike business strikes and proofs will usually have some hairlines. However, business strikes are far more likely to have bagmarks as well as hairlines.

2. Strike — Proofs tend to be somewhat sharper than business strikes. In fact, most proofs are fully struck. There are a number of exceptions however. The most common exceptions in the Morgan dollar series are the proof issues of 1891, 1892 and especially 1893. These dates are often found weakly struck in the centers.

3. Edges — Most proofs will have either square edges, or wire edges in the case of some matte and Roman finish proofs. Business strikes usually do not have square or wire edges.

4. Die Variety — Proofs were usually struck from one or two pairs of dies, and these dies were often used solely for proofs. Therefore, any coin struck from proof dies is at least somewhat more likely to be a proof. Die variety, while not conclusive, can be an important factor in determining proof status.

5. Lint Marks — Proof dies and planchets were usually polished with soft cloths. Occasionally, pieces of lint would adhere to the die or planchet prior to the striking process. Therefore, lint marks are fairly common on proof coins, yet rare on business strikes.

Summary

Grading uncirculated and proof coins is a complicated subject, and many details which seem insignificant can make a substantial impact on the final grade. But in the continuing search for the "true" grade of a coin, the market itself will be the final judge.

One last bit of wisdom. As long as you're going to this much trouble, please don't forget to enjoy coins. Not only will enjoyment make the learning easier, but it also should become an end in itself. Collecting coins is interesting and fun, and I wish all of you the very best. Happy collecting!

Footnotes

1 - Striking and lustre characteristics of each date and mint mark of Morgan silver dollar are paraphrased from the following two publications: The Bruce Amspacher Investment Report, P.O. Box 9527, Newport Beach, California 92658, Subscriptions available. What Every Silver Dollar Buyer Should Know, by Steve Ivy & Ron Howard, available from the Ivy Press, Heritage Plaza, Highland Park Village, Dallas, Texas 75205.

References:

How to Grade U.S. Coins, by James L. Halperin (Ivy Press, Inc. 1990)

A Guide to the Grading of U.S. Coins, by Martin R. Bowen and John W. Dunn (Western Publishing, Inc. 1958)

Photograde, by James F. Ruddy (Bowers & Merena Galleries, Inc. 1972)

Official A.N.A. Grading Standards for United States Coins, by the American Numismatic Association (Western Publishing, Inc. 1981)

***

CHAPTER 23

National Silver Dollar Convention

by John W. Highfill, NLG and Marlene M. Highfill

Senior Editor's Note: *The Introduction was provided by Al Johnbrier — Vice President of the National Silver Dollar Roundtable.*

In the beginning, in 1980, in the old "Butler" building on the Columbus (Ohio) Fairgrounds the first coin show was held where nothing was to be displayed except "Silver Dollars."

The concept was first developed in late 1979 by Grant Smallwood, then a dealer from Tennessee, who was all but laughed out of numismatics by those who felt no show could survive with dealers displaying and selling only dollars. He showed the numismatic "Doomsday" folks that it not only could be done, but could be reasonably successful as well.

The show consisted of about 80-90 tables, where the eye could see nothing but silver dollars. For those dollar fanatics who came from around the country, I'm sure that they felt that they had discovered their Valhalla. All the "Big Name" dealers in dollars were there: names that a lot of collectors only read about through their respective ads, including Roger Bryan, Randy Campbell, Steve Contursi, Leon Hendrickson, John Highfill, Dennis Loan, John Love, George Mallis, Wayne Miller, Dean Tavenner, Leroy Van Allen, Harlan White, and many other fine dealers who dealt only in Silver Dollars. They felt that the dollars' time had finally come and this was the ultimate recognition of their loyalty, love and determination to the most popular and well recognized collectable in the world.

There were seminars throughout the show where collectors could hear first hand about the history of the dollar and meet personally the people who wrote the books and articles on their beloved series. The odd location did not dampen the enthusiasm of those attending even with the formidable presence of the Columbus, Ohio "SWAT" team as security. As I think back on how each person and dealer was scrutinized as they entered the bourse by a full uniformed "SWAT" member, no wonder there were no incidents whatsoever.

1981 Souvenir Coin Card
(Courtesy of Grant Smallwood)

Mini Silver Dollar Series
(Courtesy of Grant Smallwood)

The show was a resounding success and it was determined that a second annual convention would be held. But by the time 1981 rolled around, well, we all know what happened after the "crash" of 1980. By 1981, the market was in the "pits"; nevertheless, the 2nd Annual NSDC was held at Memphis, Tennessee, which most know is a great "Paper Money" town. It proved to be less than popular with a Silver Dollar Convention. Nevertheless, Grant Smallwood held the show but because of the negative current market factors, the show was not nearly as successful as the first. The die hard collectors who did come again got their money's worth in seminars and education.

No one knew how long the market was going to stay in the terrible condition it was in. I suppose that, along with the financial factors, is what prompted Grant to sell the convention to John Highfill of Oklahoma Federated Gold, who had some very lofty plans for the convention, which by now most had considered "Dead and Buried." Harrison Phillips of Memphis, Tennessee, was his original partner in the transfer of ownership at this time, and without him and his brother Tom, the show would have died in Memphis in 1981.

John decided to move the convention to Houston, Texas: quite a change from the fairgrounds in Ohio, or a Holiday Inn in Memphis, to the world-renowned Astro Complex in Houston, Texas. Again, the doomsayers could be heard throughout the land; but once again, the dollar's popularity won out. It had to be a labor of love on all sides, because it sure wasn't economics that drove over 100 dealers to troop to Texas in the middle of a coin depression to put on a show depicting a coin that could, at that time, be considered too plentiful to collect. But once again, the popularity of the Big Cartwheel proved overwhelming and John met his expectations not only in dealers, but attendee appearance. Texans proved that they not only knew what a Morgan and Peace dollar was, but they also proved they were willing to buy and learn all they could about the Cartwheel.

The 3rd National Silver Dollar Convention was highly advertised. Among those contributors was a Krause Publications "Special Issue" of Numismatic News entitled "National Silver Dollar Convention". We are as pleased today as we were then for the excellent coverage that Numismatic News has done.

Record set at gold sale — Page 3

numismatic news

Your Weekly Coin Collecting Guide Featuring COIN MARKET

85¢

IOLA, WISCONSIN 54990 NOVEMBER 6, 1982

SPECIAL ISSUE!!

NATIONAL SILVER DOLLAR CONVENTION

Special Issue: National Silver Dollar Convention
November 11-14, 1982
(Courtesy of Numismatic News)

Senior Editor of Numismatic News, Bob Wilhite (left)
and John W. Highfill (right)
(Courtesy of NSDC, Inc)

It was at the Astro Village Hotel in Houston that the third National Silver Dollar Convention was held. The first of many dealer invitational "Cocktail and Banquet parties" was held there. This party was hosted jointly by the NSDC and Kurt Krueger Auctions in the famous penthouse at the Astro-Village Hotel. It was called the National Silver Dollar "Indian Fire-Water Pow-Wow" — and it was just that! A REAL BARN BURNER!

It was at this show on November 12, 1982, that the National Silver Dollar Roundtable was first organized and founded by John Highfill. The initial dealer meeting was coordinated by John Highfill, Joe Buzanowski, and ANACS director Kenneth E. Bressett on an ANACS grading controversy at that time. This in turn inspired John to rally, find and enlist a large number of America's leading silver dollar specialists; and the National Silver Dollar Roundtable was born. In John's own words: "I find it exceptionally difficult to understand why a silver dollar organization has not been founded prior to this date."

Fourth National Silver Dollar Convention

November 10, 11, 12, 13, 1983
Houston, Texas

Senior Editor's Note*: The following are composite comments and statements made by John and Marlene Highfill concerning the National Silver Dollar Convention through the years.*

John: The Fourth National Silver Dollar Convention was held at the Astro Village Hotel Complex in Houston. There were 175 tables on the bourse floor. The dedication and interest of the silver dollar enthusiasts assured us that the convention was going to be with us for years to come.

Exercise is always important. Therefore, in order to promote physical activity, a basketball tournament was organized and held. The games were organized to be played 3 on 3, with each team consisting of three players. Only one of the players could be over six feet tall. The first National Invitational Basketball Tournament winners for the first year were Neil Bergelt, Brian Bauman and Bill Conroy. The basketball invitational was so well received that we expanded it to include a number of the major shows held during the years. We also had a softball tournament one year. There was really fine competition and fun for everyone.

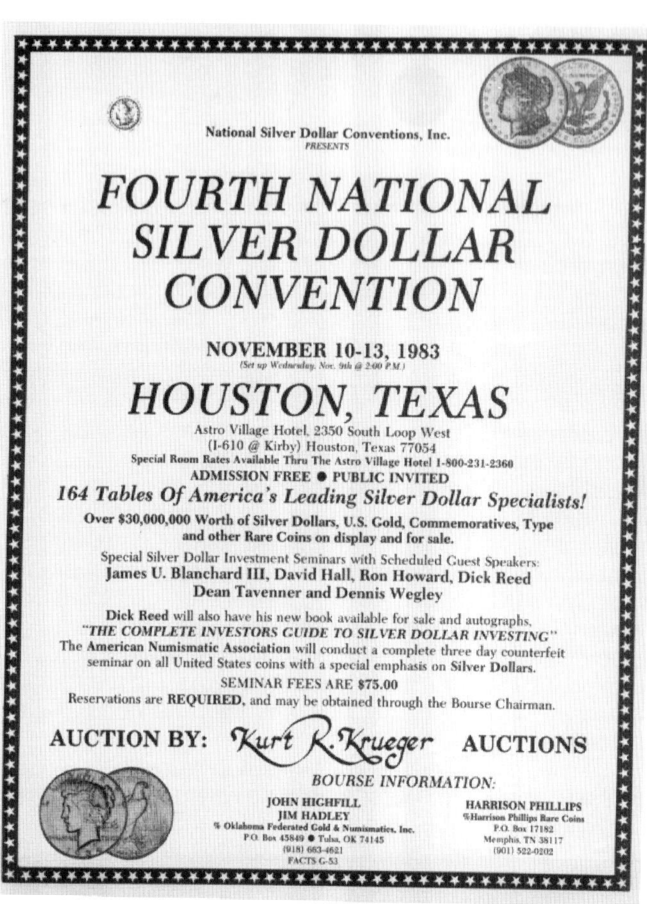

Fourth National Silver Dollar Convention Flier
(Courtesy of NSDC, Inc)

Basketball Tournament Trophy
(Courtesy of NSDC, Inc)

John W. Highfill presenting the basketball trophy to the winners of the First National Invitational Basketball Tournament
Pictured L to R: Neil Bergelt, Brian Bauman, Bill Conroy and John Highfill
(Courtesy of NSDC, Inc.)

It is always exciting to congratulate the recipients of the Special Awards. The Best of Show display award (commercial division) was presented to Dean Thornberry, Brad Johnson, and Ed Ondrick of North American Numismatics, Phoenix, Arizona. Leroy Van Allen received the award for the Best Exhibitor's Award. The Best of Show display was awarded jointly to Dick Armstrong and Gary Fernandez. The Jr. Numismatics Division award was won by Dwight Manley.

The ANACS seminars were always well planned and presented. Just prior to the actual bourse days, ANACS instructors Leonard Albrecht and Dave Jones conducted a counterfeit and grading seminar. This three day "intensive" seminar was very interesting and valuable to all who attended. The course began with the history of how coins are made and a review of the minting processes. Slide presentations were used during the grading portion and students were allowed to examine and evaluate coins. The basis of the counterfeit and altered coins portion of the seminar consisted of the way dies are made, how coins are produced and characteristics of genuine and counterfeit key coins.

The Silver Dollar Investment Forum opened with special guest speakers James U. Blanchard, III, David Hall, Ron Howard, Dick Reed, Dean Tavenner and Dennis Wegley. Numismatic information abounded and everyone left with much additional knowledge of silver dollars.

Kurt Krueger Auctions held the auction sessions for this convention. They had a good variety of offerings and everyone who attended the sessions agreed that the action was exciting.

There were a number of dealers who suggested that a central geographic location would be better for the convention. We made a search of the major midwestern cities looking for the "perfect" location.

Presentation of Awards: Pictured L to R: Dean Thornberry, Brad Johnson, Ed Ondrick, Leroy Van Allen, Dwight Manley and John W. Highfill (Courtesy of NSDC, Inc)

Presentation of award to Dwight Manley (left) by John Highfill (right) for Jr. Numismatics Division (Courtesy of NSDC, Inc)

David Jones (left) and Leonard Albrecht (right) conducting the ANACS grading seminar (Courtesy of NSDC, Inc.)

Special guest speakers
Pictured L to R: Ron Howard, David Hall, Dennis Wegley
(Courtesy of NSDC, Inc.)

After much discussion, we elected to move the convention to St. Louis, where it remained for the next seven years. (We are presenting a yearly summary of the convention during its run in St. Louis for your enjoyment.)

City of St. Louis

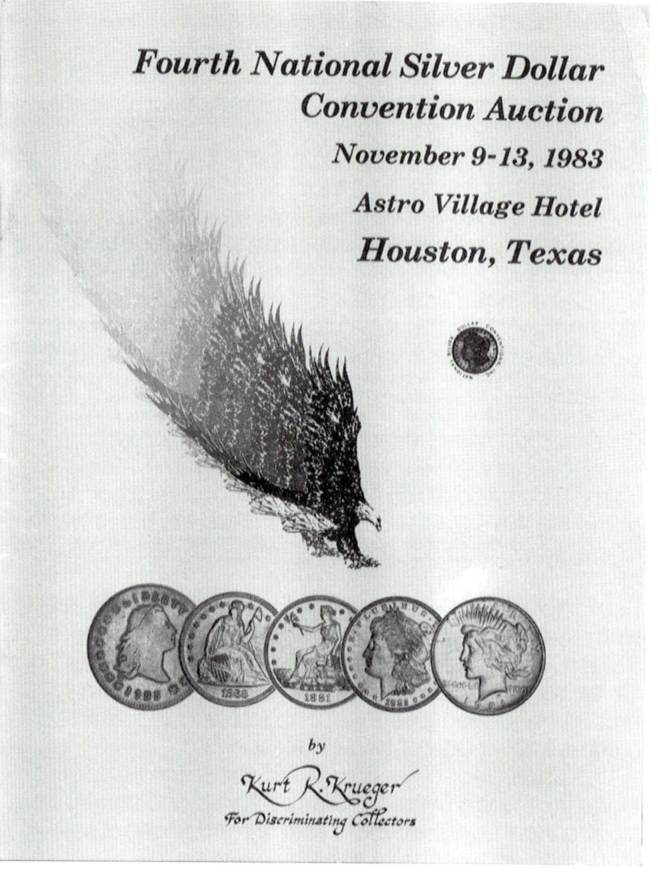

Kurt Krueger auction catalog
(Courtesy of Kurt R. Krueger)

National Silver Dollar Convention Bourse Floor prior to opening
(Courtesy of NSDC, Inc.)

Fifth National Silver Dollar Convention

November 8, 9, 10, 11, 1984
St. Louis, Missouri

John: The Cervantes Convention Center, located at 801 Convention Plaza in downtown St. Louis, was the host for this and the next six National Silver Dollar Conventions. The spacious exhibit areas together with the necessary supporting facilities made this a natural choice for the young and growing convention. It is a fine facility with ample space for the large number of convention participants and visitors.

Looking over the numismatic class collages, I don't see how Marlene ever found all the photos and put them together. It probably took the whole year to do it, but the end result brought a smile to the face of every dealer who saw it.

Putting Together the Numismatic Class of '83 Collage.
Gayle Pike, Memphis Tennessee

NUMISMATIC CLASS OF 1983

NATIONAL SILVER DOLLAR CONVENTIONS, INC.

NUMISMATIC CLASS OF 1983

NATIONAL SILVER DOLLAR CONVENTIONS, INC.

Numismatic Class of 1984
(Courtesy of Gayle Pike and Marlene Highfill)

Numismatic Class of 1985
(Courtesy of Gayle Pike and Marlene Highfill)

the COIN DEALER newsletter
Our 24th year ... a Monday morning report on the Coin Market
AUCTIONS COVER NOVEMBER CALENDAR
National Silver Dollar Convention Hits St. Louis

the COIN DEALER newsletter
Our 25th year.... ... a Monday morning report on the Coin Market
SILVER DOLLAR SHOW HITS ST. LOUIS
Auctions Continue To Pace Rare Coin Market

the COIN DEALER newsletter
Our 28th year.... ... a Monday morning report on the Coin Market
BARGAIN HUNTING DEPICTS CURRENT MARKET
National Gold Convention Headlines Week's Activity

the COIN DEALER newsletter
Our 28th year...
MARKET FIRMING IN SEVERAL AREAS
Dealers Gather At St. Louis Silver Dollar Convention

Silver Dollar Convention Headlines
via the "Greysheet"
(Courtesy of Coin Dealer Newsletter)

National Silver Dollar Convention
special issues solicitations
(Courtesy of Numismatic News)

Marlene: Personally speaking, John, I had much more fun gathering and placing the photographs for the "Class Clowns" of 1984. I still can't believe that we prepared the Numismatic Class photos for three years! I want to give Gayle Pike of Memphis, Tennessee a large share of the credit. Without her hours upon hours of labor, the project wouldn't have had the success it received. Thanks again, Gayle.

John: Special Issues had become standard policies of the numismatic trades by the time the 5th National Silver Dollar Convention rolled around. Both Coin World and Numismatic News ran special issues for the National Silver Dollar Conventions and the National Gold Conventions. There were various editorials and paid ads that ran year after year on these conventions. Below are ads, publications, editorials, auction bulletins and other various types of media. These illustrations when compiled will give you the impact of how the National Silver Dollar Convention grew tremendously in size through the years.

St. Louis Silver Dollar Show Want List

Various individual dealer's want lists listing their respective NSDC table numbers.

Editorials and ads for various National Silver Dollar Conventions.

The Colors Of Money Shine At Conventions

By William C. Lhotka
Of the Post-Dispatch Staff

Would you like to own an 1880, $4 gold piece in mint condition called "Flowing Hair"? Or do you want a five-coin commemorative collection of the opening of the Panama Canal that features two $50 gold pieces?

You can get the "Flowing Hair" collection — also known to coin collectors as "U.S. Stella" — for $95,000. The "Panama-Pacific" set goes for $67,000.

These coins are among thousands on display through Sunday at the Seventh National Silver Dollar Convention at the Cervantes Convention Center where 2,000 dealers are displaying more than $100 million in coins.

For paper money fanciers, 200 dealers are attending the World Paper Money Convention in an adjacent room. Both conventions are open to the public.

"The gleam in the collector's eye has always been gold," says Barry Faintich of Midwest Money in Clayton.

U.S. gold coins are the most popular among collectors, followed closely by silver dollars, Faintich said.

Particularly popular are the American Eagle gold coins, which were recently minted. Dealers said demand has been high for the half-ounce, $25 gold piece; the quarter-ounce, $10 coin; and the 1/10-ounce, $5 coin.

"These items have been very hot," Faintich said. "There is the feeling that the mintage in the remaining two months of 1986 could be very low." Aside from their value to coin collectors, Faintech said some people would convert the coins into jewelry.

The shortage of a coin is one of three major considerations determining the price.

The coin's condition is a second consideration — the finer its condition, the greater its value.

Lastly, the popularity of a coin determines price. The more coins collected of a certain kind, the fewer that are in circulation and the greater the price, Faintich said.

The National Silver Dollar Convention is one of the largest coin shows in the nation. It has been held here the last three years, said Marlene M. Highfill of Tulsa, Okla., vice president of the convention. "We plan to be back in 1988 and 1989," she said.

Last year, the show drew about 7,000 persons a day for the four-day event. "We had rain last year, and it's freezing cold this year," Highfill said. But the turnouts pleased the exhibitors. Dealers from every state and Britain are showing their coins this year, she said.

The convention is open to the public from 10 a.m. to 8 p.m. today, from 10 a.m. to 7 p.m. Saturday and from 10 a.m. to 4 p.m. Sunday.

Local newspaper
pre-convention coverage
(Courtesy of St. Louis Dispatch)

National Silver Dollar Convention
program books.
(Courtesy of NSDC, Inc.)

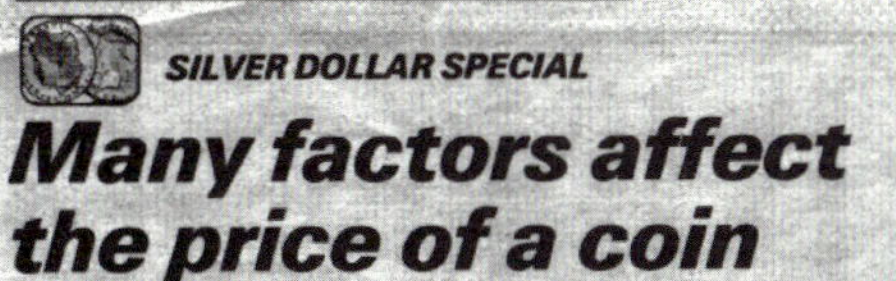

Many factors affect the price of a coin

By John Highfill
Oklahoma Federated Gold & Numismatics Inc.
Tulsa, Okla.

A lot has been noted throughout the silver-dollar industry about market conditions dictating the value of a coin.

This is probably one of the most misunderstood areas of the coin business. I'll try to explain and set some examples.

Precious metals do affect our business whether we want to admit it or not. A good example of this would be a $5,000 coin that sold easily last month when silver was, say, $13 per ounce and gold $435 per ounce.

For the convenience of illustrating a situation, let's say both gold and silver dropped to $10 and $380. The $5,000 coin is still bid at the same levels. It didn't go down in value as registered by the *Coin Dealer Newsletter* weekly report.

Gold and silver dropped almost 25 percent to 30 percent in value, but our specimen coin retained its value. Right? Wrong! Although its value has not decreased, its liquidity and salability has gone down.

There are many complex matters that go along with a dealer's business. His cash flow has suffered, and so has all his investors.

Now we take our $5,000 coin, and because we wish to sell it for whatever reasons, we can't. It's still bid $5,000, but no one wants it. Panic? No, not yet.

Sell it at a modest, reduced level that still maintains a reasonable profit — say $4,995. That isn't working either, so we are now at a K-Mart blue-light special price of $4,950. Market value seems to be $6.93.

We are getting more and more worried that we own the Edsel of numismatics.

This episode really gets thrilling with the next step. This is when your cost factor — adjusted for interest rates, inflation, air fare, hotel bill, rental car, cab fares, parking, meals, tips, etc. — has come up to $6,942.13. Meanwhile, back at the ranch, the Lone Ranger Rare Coin Co. has offered you $2,800. That's 56 percent below current CDN bid.

The masked man explains: "With the $2,800 that I offered you, I will have to sell this coin for $7,500 and only make a $557.67 profit." He says that with the initial front money of $2,800 with a cost factor — adjusted for interest rates, inflation, air fare, hotel bill, rental car, cab fares, parking, meals, tips, etc. — will come to $6,942.13. Then, if he sells it for $7,500, he will realize a profit of $557.67.

Through humor (I guess that's what we just went through), I was simply trying to illustrate how certain market conditions affect the salability of coins.

Market conditions are not just tied to precious metals. They are subject to seasonal changes, interest rates, inflation, deflation, recession, the U.S. dollar, influx of new material in the marketplace, promotions and so on.

The list can include up to 50 different varying conditions. Keep in mind that the same conditions in reverse can lead to rapid liquidation and higher prices in a hot market.

This brings about grade versus value. As it has been stated many times, "The hotter the market, the looser the grading standards. The colder the market, the tighter the grading standards."

I could write books about those two sentences, but I'll try to explain in a few paragraphs. It's very simple.

In a hot, rapidly moving market, dealers have hundreds of orders to fill. They have received funds for regular orders or advertised products and are trying to fill those orders.

Time is of the essence. They will try to find accurately graded coins. For whatever reasons, they can't find the right coins. Now they will take a lower-graded coin and ship it instead.

Now comes the slow market. The same dealer has less orders to fill. He now needs 50 coins, not 500. Obviously, he has more time, less money, and more serious customers.

Before, anyone would take anything. Now, they have been burned with their MS-63 or MS-64 coins that they paid an MS-65 price for. So they want to make darn sure it doesn't happen again. It seems that only an MS-67 coin will satisfy them now.

There is no MS-67 grade pricing anywhere. Therefore, we must bid more for our MS-65 desires.

It's now time to follow the bouncing ball: In a stable market, we trade at levels equal to MS-60, MS-63, MS-65 and sometimes MS-67 grades of uncirculated silver dollars. (Other coins tend to follow the same patterns.)

In a slow market, we must have MS-63 dollars in our rolls, we must have MS-65 dollars buying and selling at 40 percent to 50 percent of MS-65 bid, and we must have MS-67 dollars to bring MS-65 prices. (For those critics that I surely have accumulated by now, these are estimates of portions of dealers at different times, given certain circumstances during all financial conditions. In other words, "clear to partly cloudy with a chance of rain, sleet or snow.")

Next step: hot market. In case you missed it earlier, everything sells. Your AU-58 sliders sell for MS-60, the MS-60s make up nice rolls, the MS-63s sell at levels within 70 percent of MS-65 bid, the true MS-65s are selling for 20 percent above MS-65 ask, and the elusive and accurately graded MS-67 silver dollars are bringing two to four times MS-65 bid at auction.

This article in no way is intended to intimidate the collector or investor. It simply is intended to unveil some of the reasons behind the scenes as to why market conditions dictate the value of his or her coins.

(PRICE, Page 24)

Numismatic News Silver Dollar Special issue
(Courtesy of Numismatic News)

This is the fifth year for the National Silver Dollar Convention. There will be over 250 dealers in attendance with 300 of America's leading silver dollar specialists. It is sure to be one of the major coin events of the year.

The convention this year will be held in St. Louis, Missouri, November 8-11, at the Cervantes Convention Center, 801 Convention Plaza. Set up is scheduled for Wednesday, Nov. 7 at 3:00 PM.

Coin World is pleased to be able to help commemorate this 5th Anniversary with a Special Silver Dollar Convention Issue.

November 7 will be Coin World's Special Convention Issue. The deadline for this issue will be October 23.

This issue will go to our regular subscribers and an extra 500 copies will be given away at the convention.

How can you be a part of this special commemorative issue?

It's easy.
Just call us at
513-498-2111.

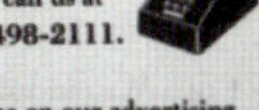

Anyone on our advertising staff will be glad to assist you.

Or you may send your ad copy to Coin World, P.O. Box 150, Sidney, Ohio 45367.

But remember, the deadline for all ads is October 23.

Setting up to film the special Silver Dollar Forum at the National Silver Dollar Convention; (L to R): David Lisot, Tony Campo and David Notowitz c/o Media Resources, Denver, Colorado (Courtesy of NSDC, Inc.)

Coin World Salutes . . .

The Fifth National Silver Dollar Convention

Be sure to stop and say "hello" at the Coin World table.

with a Special Convention Issue.

Details inside

Coin World Special Convention Issues
(Courtesy of Coin World, Sidney, Ohio)

Television News filming is a must for good convention coverage.
(Courtesy of NSDC, Inc.)

Marlene: The 300 active tables on the bourse floor for this convention presented us with a clear message, "This is the place!" The St. Louis location was also popular with the "dealer spouses" who enjoyed all that this famous city had to offer. The dealer collage contained all the photographs we could take and the resulting 11 X 14 color presentation was made available to all. The "clowns" photo is where I had as much fun as those who posed for it.

Class Clown Photo
(Courtesy of Gayle Pike and Marlene Highfill)

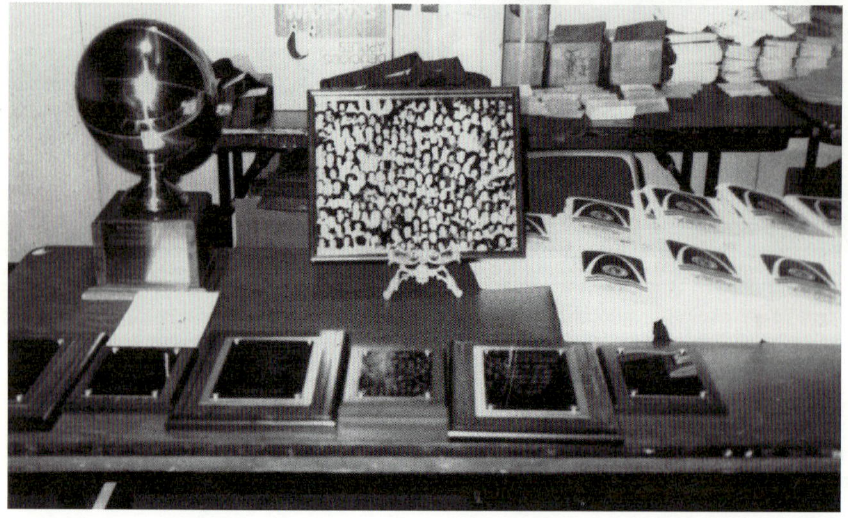

Various awards for the Annual National Silver Dollar Convention
(Courtesy of NSDC, Inc.)

John: There was something for everyone. Even the "taller" dealers were not forgotten. The NSDC Basketball Tournament was actually held at many of the bigger conventions during the year. This allowed dealers to "get physical" and work off all of their "convention tension." This year's winners were again Neil Bergelt and William Conroy along with Michael O'Higgins.

Dealers getting ready to start another basketball tournament.
(Courtesy of NSDC, Inc.)

Marlene: John presented the "Best of Show Award" to Anthony Calcagno. Leroy Van Allen won the "Best Display Award."

Presentation of the Best of Show Award to Anthony Calcagno
(Courtesy of NSDC, Inc.)

Presentation of the Best Display Award to Leroy Van Allen
(Courtesy of NSDC, Inc.)

Kenneth E. Bressett instructing a seminar for ANACS at the National Silver Dollar Convention (Courtesy of NSDC, Inc.)

Some people had more fun than others at the FireWater Pow- Wow! (Courtesy of Bill Foreman, Jr., Muskogee, Oklahoma)

Marlene: McIntire Numismatic Auctions held this year's auction with lot viewing sessions and auction sessions through the weekend. McIntire held both the NSDC and NSDR auctions and provided action and excitement for both buyers and sellers. "Auction fever" took hold as the auctioneer presided over the sale.

John: Education is always one of the highlights of each NSDC. This year's ANACS seminar covering counterfeit and grading was held prior to the convention's bourse days. Special ANACS guest speakers were Kenneth E. Bressett and Rick Montgomery. The seminar covered three days and provided good insights and information for all. The Special Silver Dollar Investment seminar was well attended and featured some of the best speakers and talent that this industry has to offer. Everyone who attended left with an addition to their knowledge of the Cartwheel. The special three hour seminar was held on Saturday featuring speakers including James U. Blanchard, III, Steve Contursi, David Hall, Steve Ivy, Wayne Miller, Dean Tavenner, and Hannes Tulving. I served as the narrator for this seminar.

Marlene: Socializing was not neglected. The Silver Dollar Firewater Pow-Wow (complimentary to all bourse table dealers) was held at the Cervantes Convention Center, featuring hors d' oeuvres, cocktails, dinner, and the best fellowship in St. Louis!

John: The National Silver Dollar Roundtable extended the invitation to all "Knights" to attend the Second Anniversary of the NSDR on Friday afternoon. Prior to that event the Board of Governors met to review the business of the NSDR. Both of these meetings were led by President Dean Tavenner and Vice President Joe Buzanowski.

1984 Silver Dollar Sale auction catalog (Courtesy of McIntire Numismatic Auctions, Inc.)

Let's Go! Dealers converging for the "Dealers Only" set up.
(Courtesy of NSDC, Inc.)

Bob Estremera and Mary Sauvain — ANACS instructors
(Courtesy of NSDC, Inc.)

Winners of the 6th National Basketball Tournament
Pictured L to R: Buddy Keller, Neil Bergelt, and Mike Bianco

Sixth National Silver Dollar Convention
November 14, 15, 16, 17, 1985
St. Louis, Missouri

John: Again, the Cervantes Convention Center, located in downtown St. Louis, was the site for this National Silver Dollar Convention. The quality of this center together with all of the support facilities came through for all who attended this convention. Over 350 dealers held the bourse floor for all attendees — and the results were excellent!.

Marlene: The ANA presented their seminar in grading and counterfeit detection, providing general information on coin production and the characteristics of genuine and counterfeit coins. This three day ANACS seminar was conducted by Bob Estremera and Mary Sauvain, expert numismatists from the ANA, with special emphasis placed on silver dollars. The Special Silver Dollar Investment Forum was presented later in the week with guest speakers Bruce Amspacher, Steve Contursi, Mike Fuljenz, David Hall, Wayne Miller, Dick Reed, Dean Tavenner, Hannes Tulving and Leroy Van Allen, and John as host. Accugrade also presented a very informative seminar featuring Alan Hager, which was well attended. Walter Perschke of Numisco rounded out the available investment seminars with a presentation on the theme, "Rare Coin Exchange." Dick Armstrong was the recipient of this year's "Best of Show Display." (Second time around for Dick!)

Bruce Amspacher "John would sometimes give the guest speakers such cute awards!"
(Courtesy of NSDC, Inc.)

John: The 6th National Silver Dollar Basketball Tournament was held at the downtown YMCA for all dealers with a desire to "let it all hang out." The rules for dealer team members were changed somewhat to allow two men per team to be over 6 feet tall. The basketball winners were Neil Bergelt, Buddy Keller and Mike Bianco. But the new event which caught the eye of some was the 1st Old Heavyweight Handicap 5K "Fun Run." How they call running 5K "fun" is beyond me, but many rose before 8:00 a.m. and participated. The winner was Jim Curtis of San Diego, CA (by the way, I did finish the race!).

1st Annual 5K Run Co-Sponsored by NSDC and Numismatic News
(Courtesy of NSDC, Inc.)

1st Annual 5K Run participants (Courtesy of NSDC, Inc.)

Winner of the 5k run was Jim Curtis (right), award presented by Joe Jones (left)
(Courtesy of NSDC, Inc.)

Marlene: The social event of the week was the Cocktails and Dinner Banquet held at the Sheraton Hotel East Ballroom. The Silver Dollar Firewater Pow-Wow was a roaring success according to all the dealers and spouses I talked to. Everyone told us to "keep it up!" No one will ever forget those Morgan and Peace Silver Dollar ice carvings — they were truly a work of art. Of course they, like most U.S. Mint holdings, eventually went for "melt" (The Highfill "Melt" Act of 1985).

A question for you from the dealers on the bourse floor, "How do you tell when a coin dealer goes on vacation? He puts a tent over his house and puts his chairs on the rooftop." (By the way, this was a joke.)

John: The National Silver Dollar Roundtable Board of Governors held their 3rd Anniversary Meeting on Friday. This was followed by the NSDR General Meeting later in the afternoon. But the NSDR event of the week was the invitation of all "Knights" to attend the National Silver Dollar Roundtable General Meeting and BREAKFAST! This was held on Friday at 8:00 a.m. — a time NOT noted for dealer activity. The exciting result was a full attendance by all "bright eyed and bushy tailed" Knights! The NSDR breakfasts are still currently held nationwide throughout the year.

Marlene: McIntire Numismatic Auctions again presented the sessions at this year's convention. The offerings provided a sale featuring high quality, desirable coins in virtually all denominations for the collector, investor and dealer. The auction sessions covered three days and were well attended with excellent prices reported at the sale.

1984 and 1985 auction catalogs
(Courtesy of McIntire Numismatic Auctions, Inc.)

Ribbon cutting ceremonies (L to R) Leo Glazer, Roger Bryan, John Foster, Florence Schook, Leon Hendrickson, John Highfill, Marlene Highfill
(Courtesy of NSDC, Inc.)

Seventh National Silver Dollar Convention
November 13, 14, 15, 16, 1986
St. Louis, Missouri

John: Let's stay with a winner! The St. Louis Cervantes Convention Center provided the facility once more for the seventh National Silver Dollar Convention. For one week of the year, this was now home to over 400 dealers as they presented a feast of cartwheels. The Professional Currency Dealers Association held their pilot annual convention in conjunction with the NSDC during the same bourse hours. They had over 100 tables filled with currency dealers from all over America. As in all of the years, Numismatic News provided complimentary National Silver Dollar Convention dealer packets (envelopes). **Thanks Always!**

Marlene: What a collection of seminars! The ANACS Counterfeit and Grading Seminar, featuring ANA special guest instructors Will Rossman and J.P. Martin, was held Monday through Wednesday. Everyone gained additional knowledge from all of these key numismatic areas. The annual Special Silver Dollar Investment Forum opened again with this year's fine slate of speakers including Roger Bryan, Mike Fuljenz, David Hall, Ron Howard, Wayne Miller, Dick Reed, Dean Tavenner, Hannes Tulving and Dennis Wegley. The investment forum was narrated by John who always seems to bring out the best in all of the guests. Numisco conducted their special investment seminar complete with complimentary cocktails and hors d'oeuvres. ICTA provided a well-received seminar covering all aspects of security. Krause Publications hosted a seminar on Friday. PCGS held a Silver Dollar Grading Seminar. Kurt Krueger conducted a seminar entitled, "Influence of the Collector returning to the market place." Completing the seminars was Martin Paul, who presented a Rarities Group Seminar entitled, "Buying Certified Morgan Dollars."

FREE
THE NATIONAL SILVER DOLLAR AND PCDA CONVENTION
November 13-16, 1986
St. Louis, Missouri
A NUMISMATIC NEWS TRADITION SINCE 1981
Pocket Bourse Guide & Convention Program
Presented by
numismatic news
Iola, Wisconsin 54990

1986 Pocket Bourse Guide and Convention Program
(Courtesy of Numismatic News)

Special Silver Dollar Seminar
Pictured L to R: Roger Bryan, Dean Tavenner, Al Johnbrier, Mike Fuljenz (speaker), Dick Reed, David Hall, Bruce Amspacher, John Highfill
(Courtesy of NSDC, Inc.)

St. Louis Dealer packets (envelopes)
(Courtesy of Bob Wilhite c/o Numismatic News)

Special Silver Dollar seminar (L to R): David Hall, Wayne Miller, Hannes Tulving, John Highfill, Dean Tavenner, Bruce Amspacher, Dick Reed, Mike Fuljenz (Courtesy of NSDC, Inc.)

Cliff Mishler (left) and Bob Wilhite (right) conducting a seminar (Courtesy of NSDC, Inc.)

John: The downtown St. Louis YMCA was the site of the 7th National Silver Dollar Basketball Tournament for all dealers to "slam dunk" their competition. This year the best numismatic athletes were Mike Abbott, Newton Mitchell, and Douglas Sharpe. Krause Publications and Numisco sponsored the 2nd annual FUN RUN (I still can't get over the naming of this event). Those who participated told me that it was fun, and I believed them.

Marlene: The social calendar included "Ladies' day out". This event combined a tour and luncheon in the St. Louis area and was a treat for everyone. The annual NSDC social event of the week was the Cocktail Party and Dinner Banquet held at the Sheraton Hotel East and Center Ballrooms. This new edition of the Silver Dollar Firewater Pow-Wow was complimentary to all bourse dealers and those dealers with their spouses loved it. The ice sculptures of Morgan and Peace dollars again provided the centerpieces at the banquet. One dealer offered "melt value" for them, but the offer was not considered. (Second time around for those of you that didn't get it before.)

John: The National Silver Dollar Roundtable Board of Governors decided to try something special this year. On Wednesday, the NSDR sponsored the first annual "**Dollar Day**" with dealers on the bourse floor displaying and selling the silver dollar. This one day affair was a tremendous success and I knew that it would be repeated in succeeding years. Again the NSDR invited all Knights to attend the National Silver Dollar Roundtable General Breakfast Meeting — Friday at 8:00 a.m. Members again responded to the call and a very good meeting was held. The 4th Anniversary NSDR Meeting was held on Friday followed by the NSDR General Meeting later in the afternoon. Finally, the schedule included an official social event — the NSDR banquet at the Sheraton Hotel West ballroom.

National Silver Dollar Roundtable Bourse Chairman for the 1st Dollar Day, Roger Bryan; also pictured (L to R): Ginger Bryan, Patti Moreno and Marlene Highfill (Courtesy of NSDC, Inc.)

Official Convention Ribbons (Courtesy of NSDC, Inc.)

This was a "must" for all Roundtable members, and a fine evening ensued for all. This was the night I took over as president of the National Silver Dollar Roundtable. It was a special moment in my life as health had been my only dictator for the previous year. In addition to the photo ID's, special ribbons were provided for auction officials, convention hosts, convention officials and for the National Silver Dollar Roundtable Honary Knights.

Marlene: McIntire Numismatic Auctions, Inc. once again were in charge of the "auction action" at this year's convention. All the excitement and thrills of the sale were felt by everyone who raised a hand to bid on the excellent and varied selection of consigned offerings.

1986 National Silver Dollar Sale
(Courtesy of McIntire Numismatic Auctions, Inc.)

Flowing Hair Liberty art by Russ VanDerLinden
Pictured L to R: Russ VanDerLinden, Robert McIntire, Florence Schook
(Courtesy of NSDC, Inc.)

Proclamation-City of St. Louis, Missouri

(Back Row L to R): John Highfill-NSDR President, Jack Keene-Mayor's Rep. City of St. Louis, Roger Bryan-President of F.U.N, Steve Taylor-President of ANA, Leon Hendrickson-PNG President
(Front Row L to R): Marlene Highfill-Convention Bourse Chairman, Florence Schook-ANA Board Member and past President
(Courtesy of NSDC, Inc.)

The following poem was submitted by Cory G. Scott and published in the Seventh NSDC program book. It is presented here with permission of National Silver Dollar Conventions Inc. for your enjoyment.

The Dollar, Silver or Not

by Cory G. Scott

Ah Liberty with flowing hair,
The years roll by with no new coin,
A real collectors must,
Until a great man came,
Then added to that great design,
Our thirty-fourth president,
Stuart draped the bust.
Eisenhower is the name.

Old Gobrecht said, "Oh Liberty,
Minted coins now bore his likeness,
A seat must be provided,
But they too didn't last,
A flying eagle on your back,
The fickle public soon ignored them,
You both must be so tired."
And so no more were cast.

The eagle's motto soon was lost,
Alas, along came Susan B.,
Changes came and went.
But for so short a time.
In God We Trust in '66
It looked more like a two-bit piece,
Was added and well meant.
And bombed before its time.

To equal all the foreign crowns,
In passing lest we not forget,
A dollar known as Trade,
Olympics had its day,
Became a standard commerce piece,
The athletes had their dollar too,
After twelve years it did fade.
For two years it held sway.

Along came mighty Morgan,
And now we have Miss Liberty,
No pirate coin was this,
Just think as speculation,
And those who hold the choice CCs
You have a choice of unc or proof,
Are smug in pleasant bliss.
But not in circulation.

The war now ended (World War One),
All fighting had to cease.
We honored all who fought the cause,
With a dollar titled Peace.

Eighth National Silver Dollar Convention

October 29, 30, 31, November 1, 1987
St. Louis, Missouri

Marlene: All were welcomed to the St. Louis Cervantes Convention Center for the eighth National Silver Dollar Convention. The addition of the second National and World Paper Money Convention folks provided a show to remember. The schedule of events included forums, seminars, banquets, special events — and of course the bourse! Ribbon cutting featured Mayor's representative Jack Keene with many honored guests.

John: For the sports minded people, the Third Annual Old Heavyweight Handicap .8 Mile & 5K Fun Run said it all. We heard that all who participated went out like a lion and came in like a lamb. The YMCA hosted the 16th National Silver Dollar Basketball tournament for dealers only. Dealers told me that this was the best exercise they had participated in for a long time. Plaques were given to Mike Bianco, Mark Chaplin and Buddy Keller.

Marlene: There were many seminars held throughout the week by organizations such as ICTA, PCGS, ANACS, Accugrade, Kurt Krueger and Krause Publications. These organizations provided top notch speakers and very educational presentations which were well attended. The NSDC/PCDA Young Numismatist Program gave all of the younger visitors a special presentation of their own.

John: One of the most informative presentations was made on Saturday. It was billed as a Special Silver Dollar Investment seminar with nationally known guest speakers. That was certainly true as the audience enjoyed comments made by Bruce Amspacher, Roger Bryan, Mike Fuljenz, David Hall, Al Johnbrier, Dick Reed, Dean Tavenner and Hannes Tulving. I served as the moderator and can say that these speakers provided a top notch and informative seminar.

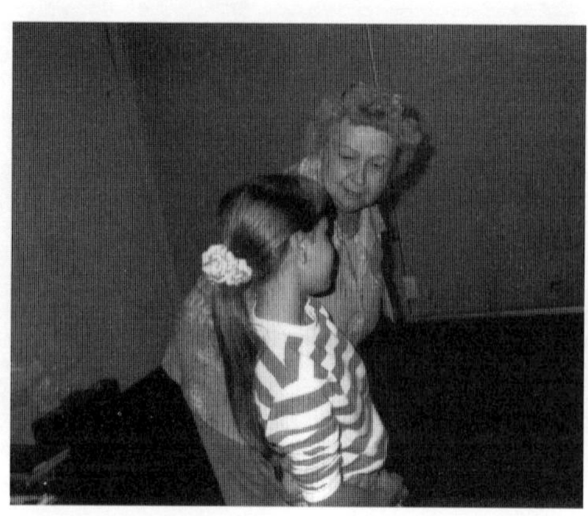

Florence Schook with Junior Numismatist
(Courtesy of NSDC, Inc.)

Marlene: One of the social highlights of the convention was the Annual Dealer Banquet with dinner. A Halloween costume party and music filled the agenda. The event was held at the Sheraton West and Center Ballrooms on Saturday night. The Silver Dollar Firewater Pow-Wow was really something! The guests, goblins, comedians, magicians, and musicians included comedians Stephen A. Sparks, J.W. Apperson, George Johnstone, and the eight piece band —Phoenix. Some of the costumes were simply "outrageous" and no one will ever forget John (as "Spuds") looking for his Bud Light. Comedy lovers were greatly entertained by a special guest appearance by comedian and juggler, Dale Jones. The "Indian chief" (Chris Verhaegh) emerged victorious in the costume contest. The event was co-sponsored by the NSDC and McIntire Numismatic Auctions.

John: The many activities of the National Silver Dollar Roundtable also took place at the convention site. These included the activities of the second annual "**Dollar Day**" and the NSDR dinner cruise on the Riverboat "Becky Thatcher." We boarded the riverboat at the foot of the Gateway Arch, and enjoyed over three hours of "Dixie-land" entertainment and a buffet style dinner. Then came the NSDR Board of Governors meeting, 5th anniversary general meeting, and the NSDR general meeting and breakfast. The "Knights" of the Roundtable were entertained in fine style. The highlight of the week was the presentation of the NSDR "Man of the Year" award. This year I was proud to present the award to two great numismatists who have contributed much to the Roundtable and the industry — Steele Eunson and Leroy Van Allen.

Marlene: It was that year on the Becky Thatcher when a few dealers had a little too much to drink. One wanted to get off the riverboat well before docking, but we all calmed him down and he went to sleep with his head on the banquet table. When the riverboat did return to the landing, we all left after putting a napkin over his head and a "rest in peace" sign and flowers all around. The captain and his men came to the rescue.

John: The U.S. Postal Service maintained a mobile unit available for all the NSDC postal needs. The Special Cancellation stamp was available for the convention free of charge. Cachet envelopes were available for purchase. The 5th anniversary of the NSDR on "**Dollar Day**" also had their own cancellation stamp for that one day.

Marlene: This year's auction sessions were again held by McIntire Numismatic Auctions. The sessions featured many interesting lots which drew considerable bids from dealers, collectors and investors alike.

Halloween costume winner!
(Courtesy of NSDC, Inc.)

5th Anniversary NSDR Cancellation Stamp
(Courtesy of St. Louis Post Office)

Third National and World Paper Money Convention Flier
(Courtesy of P.C.D.A.)

Eight National Silver Dollar Convention
Halloween Party
(Courtesy of NSDC, Inc.)

Joking on stage
Pictured L to R: Robert McIntire, Comedian George Johnstone, and Leon Hendrickson
(Courtesy of NSDC, Inc.)

Halloween costume contestants
(Courtesy of NSDC, Inc.)

Dinner & Entertainment Ticket

8th National Silver Dollar Convention

Saturday Night

October 31, 1987

7:00 p.m.

Sheraton St. Louis Hotel

(West & Center Ballroom) *$25.00*

Costumes welcome but not required.

Dinner and entertainment ticket
(Courtesy of NSDC, Inc.)

Best look alike costume — Leon Hendrickson (No costume required.)
(Courtesy of NSDC, Inc.)

"Spuds" and lady friend at NSDC Halloween party
(Courtesy of NSDC, Inc.)

Pictured L to R: Robert Hendershott, President of FUN;
Majorie Owens, Secretary of CSNS and Steve Taylor, President of the ANA
(Courtesy of NSDC, Inc.)

World's youngest and oldest numismatists
Chelsea Marie Highfill and Mr. Robert Hendershott
(Courtesy of NSDC, Inc.)

21st NSDC basketball tournament winners
Pictured L to R: Tom Paine, Mark Chaplin and John Highfill
(Courtesy of NSDC, Inc.)

Basketball tournament awards for the 20th and 21st
National Silver Dollar Conventions (Courtesy of John W. Highfill)

Ninth National Silver Dollar Convention
November 10, 11, 12, and 13, 1988
St. Louis, Missouri

Marlene: St. Louis continued to be the site for this year's National Silver Dollar Convention. Once more the Professional Currency Dealers Association held its Third National and World Paper Money Convention in conjunction with the NSDC. The ribbon cutting ceremony which opened the convention featured Jack Keene of the Mayor's Office, John and Marlene with the one who stole the show — little Chelsea Highfill! At that time Chelsea was only six months old. But none of us forgot Mr. Hendershott, who was the oldest coin dealer to come. We took the most precious photograph of the two of them. It was later entitled "the world's oldest and youngest numismatists."

John: The sports-minded dealers continued to compete in the 21st National Silver Dollar Basketball tournament at the downtown YMCA. I had one tall dealer who asked for his entry fee back. He did not like all the shorter dealers running up him to make a basket. He showed me his bruises while I tried to keep from laughing — but he didn't get a return on his fee. Now that the joking is over, the real athletes came to form this year. I WON! I had a little help from Mark Chaplin and Tom Paine (thought I'd better mention them too). Also, with the National Silver Dollar Conventions being in St. Louis, many dealers enjoyed the St. Louis Cardinals baseball games.

Coupon

Redeem for one (1) ticket to the St. Louis Cardinals Baseball Game and picnic dinner prior to game time.

St. Louis Cardinals vs. Atlanta Braves

Saturday Night, May 14, 1988

Banquet @ 6:00 p.m.
Baseball Game @ 7:05 p.m.

Must be redeemed prior to 5:00 p.m. on Thursday, May 12, 1988

St. Louis Baseball coupon

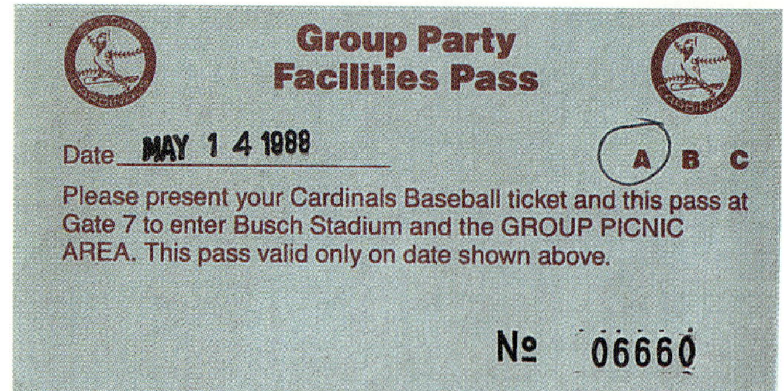

Group Party Facilities Pass

Date MAY 1 4 1988 A B C

Please present your Cardinals Baseball ticket and this pass at Gate 7 to enter Busch Stadium and the GROUP PICNIC AREA. This pass valid only on date shown above.

№ 06660

Group party facilities pass

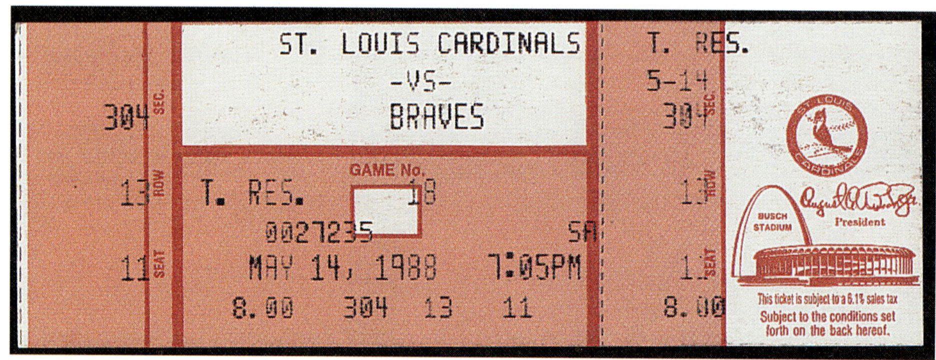

St. Louis baseball ticket

Wayne Gretzky of the Los Angeles Kings and Brett Hull of the St. Louis Blues.
Just goes to show that coin dealers and great hockey players like the same entertainment — baseball!
(Photograph taken by Jeffery James Highfill, St. Louis, Missouri)

Marlene: The seminars conducted during the week were many and all were well received. They included ANACS, PCGS, ICTA, and Anthony Swiatek.

John: All "Knights" were on hand for the National Silver Dollar Roundtable activities which included the third NSDR "**Dollar Day**," the Banquet and Cocktails gathering on the SS Becky Thatcher, NSDR breakfast, Board of Governors 6th annual meeting and 6th Anniversary general meetings. The NSDR evening aboard the SS Becky Thatcher was wonderful and afforded a beautiful view of the city from the mooring beneath the Gateway Arch. The NSDR meeting and seminar special guest speakers included myself, Roger Bryan, Steele Eunson, Leon Hendrickson, Al Johnbrier and Clark Samuelson.

Marlene: National Silver Dollar Conventions, Inc., and McIntire Numismatic Auctions teamed together to provide a top notch evening of fun and entertainment featuring dinner followed by the comedian Dale Jones and the world famous "**Grass Roots**" rock n' roll group. This event was held at the Sheraton Hotel West and Center Ballrooms. The "**Grass Roots**" were one of the hottest bands to emerge from the musical revolution of the 1960s when they charted 29 singles of which 13 went "gold." They had multiple gold albums, one of which, their greatest hits collection, went platinum and continues to be a strong seller today. Some of their more well known hits include "**Midnight Confessions**" "**Let's Live For Today**", "**The River is Wide**", "**Temptation Eyes**", "**Where Were You When I Needed You**", and many others. This was memory lane at its finest! Their show was exciting and left everyone breathless and ready for more. This first-ever numismatic "concert" was the first of many nationally known entertainers to please the dealers in the years to come.

The success of the National Silver Dollar Convention was the inspiration to launch the National Gold Convention in St. Louis, Missouri. The big name entertainment continued at the National Gold Convention on April 1, 1989 in the Sheraton East ballroom at 7:00. This time it was headlined by the **Association** from the late 60s and early 70s. They had dozens of gold records that included "**Cherish**", "**Wendy**", "**Never My Love**", "**Along Comes Mary**" and many more. Included in the excellent list of entertainers was Comedian **Jeff Sutherland** and "**Butch Wax and the Hollywoods**" dance band.

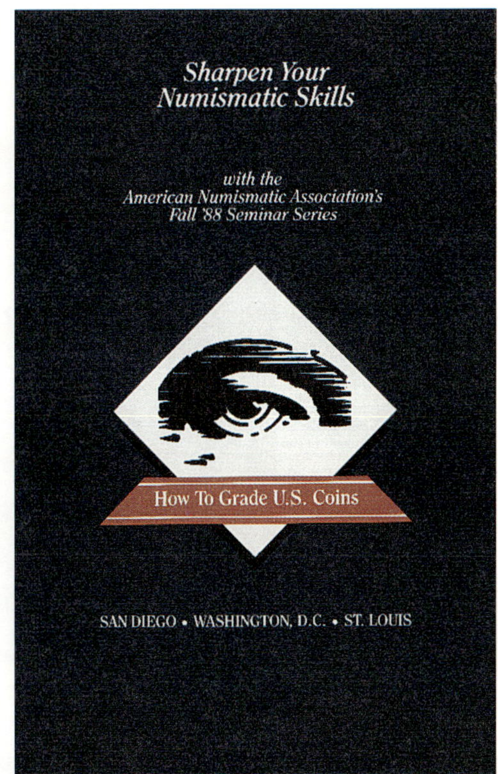

Just one of the many seminars conducted during the National Silver Dollar Convention (Courtesy of American Numismatic Association)

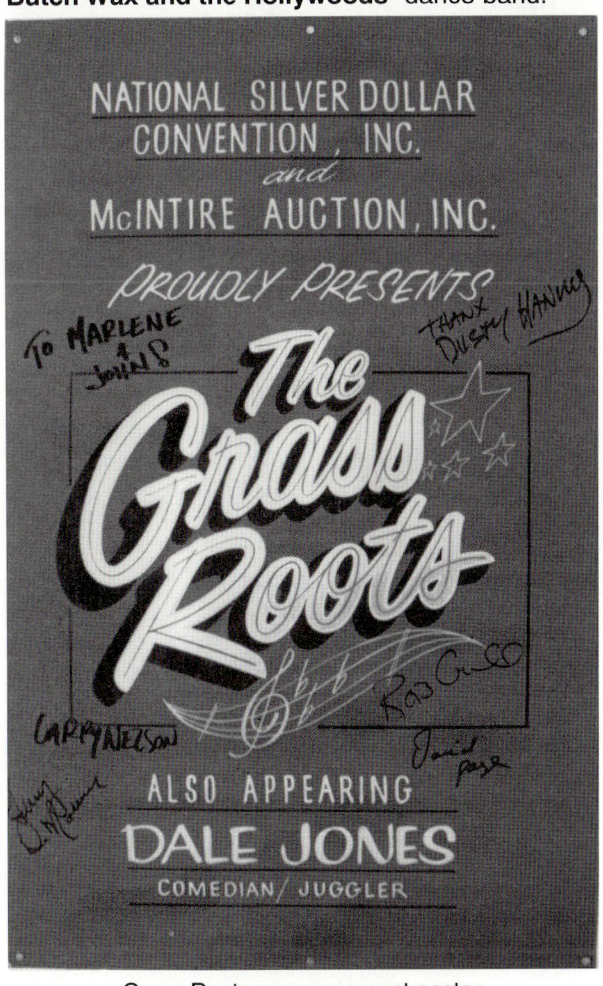

Grass Roots announcement poster
(Courtesy of NSDC, Inc.)

John and Marlene Highfill pictured with the Grass Roots
(Courtesy of NSDC, Inc.)

The Grass Roots
(Courtesy of The Grass Roots)

The Association announcement poster
(Courtesy of American Coin Conventions, Inc.)

Enjoying the entertainment at the Ninth NSDC Banquet
(Courtesy of NSDC, Inc.)

Ninth National Silver Dollar Convention souvenir cachet envelope
with cancellation stamp
(Courtesy of the U.S.P.O. and NSDC, Inc.)

John: The United States Postal Service maintained a mobile unit available for all the NSDC/NSDR postal needs. In addition, a special cancellation was again provided for the convention free of charge. Cachet envelopes were also available for purchase.

Marlene: John presented the "Best Showcase Award" to Arnie Payne (and I thought he was too old and ornery to win). It just goes to show you the cream always rises to the top!

This year's outstanding auction was held by McIntire Numismatic Auctions. The continued consignment of fine coins in a variety of series provided a great selection and interest by all who attended.

The Association
(Courtesy of The Association)

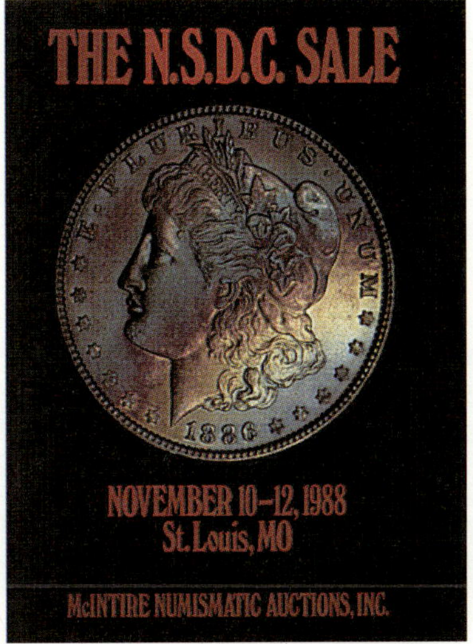

McIntire Auction Catalog
(Courtesy of McIntire Numismatic Auctions, Inc.)

Party time and dancing with The Association
(Courtesy of American Coin Conventions, Inc.)

National Silver Dollar Convention Officials
Pictured L to R: (Back Row) Harold Jagger, Melody Cunningham, Marlene Highfill, Barbara Bell, (Front Row) Patti Moreno, Vonnie Berry, Trish Pendergrass, Bobbie Webb
(Courtesy of NSDC, Inc.)

The Rascals announcement poster
(Courtesy of NSDC, Inc.)

TENTH NATIONAL SILVER DOLLAR CONVENTION

St. Louis, Missouri
November 30, 1989

7:30	Cocktails
8:00	Dinner - Banquet
8:30	Comedian *Royce Kelly*
9:00	***The Rascals'*** Featuring Felix Cavaliere Performing great hit songs such as: **Good Lovin', Beautiful Mornin', Grovin', People Gotta Be Free**, and many more.
10:30	***Butch Wax & The Hollywoods***
Midnite	Dinner and Entertainment Ends

Coat & Tie Requested
(But Not Required)

The 10th NSDC entertainment
(Courtesy of NSDC, Inc.)

Mayor's representative, Jack Keane presenting the city of St. Louis Proclamation to John and Marlene Highfill
(Courtesy of NSDC, Inc.)

The Rascals featuring Felix Cavaliere
(Courtesy of The Rascals)

Tenth National Silver Dollar Convention

November 30, December 1, 2, and 3, 1989
St. Louis, Missouri

Marlene: The Cervantes Convention Center facility continued to serve as the site of this year's National Silver Dollar Convention. The Professional Currency Dealers Association held its Fourth National and World Paper Money Convention in concert with the fourth NSDC "**Dollar Day**." The Proclamation and Ribbon Cutting was led by city representatives with myself, John, and honored guests. Those guests included ANA President Steve Taylor, FUN President Roger Bryan, ANA Past President Florence Schook, PNG President and Central States Numismatic Society President Leon Hendrickson, and others. The annual Proclamation was presented with the words, "Let the show go on!"

The seminar lineup was excellent with seminars held by ANACS, ANE, Hallmark, ICTA, NSDR, Numismatic News, PCGS and Anthony Swiatek. These organizations presented excellent educational and informative material to all who were fortunate enough to attend.

John W. Highfill (left) with Felix Cavaliere
(Courtesy of NSDC, Inc.)

John: The annual NSDC Investment Seminar held the interest of all, as many nationally known guest speakers gave of their knowledge and experience. Featured speakers were Bruce Amspacher, Roger Bryan, Mike Fuljenz, Leon Hendrickson, Hannes Tulving and David Hall. The National Silver Dollar Roundtable presented a fine state of activities which included the fourth annual "**Dollar Day**" (held prior to the official convention). The 8th NSDR general meeting and the NSDR breakfast for members was well received and had become a tradition by this time.

Marlene: The NSDR Cocktail and dinner banquet was held at the Sheraton St. Louis Hotel ballroom and featured the music of the jazz trio "**Tinted Blue.**" An exciting lineup of entertainers gathered for the NSDC cocktails and dinner banquet at the Holiday Inn Ballroom. They included **Felix Cavaliere and the Rascals** followed by **Butch Wax & The Hollywoods** and the comedian, **Royce Kelly**. **The Rascals** had a string of top 20 hits from the late 60s and early 70s. Some of them include "**Good Lovin**", "**I've Been Lonely Too Long**", "**Mustang Sally**", "**How Can I Be Sure**", "**A Beautiful Morning**" and many more!

David Lisot interviewing Elerie Arnett of Entertainment Enterprises,
Tony Campo is the cameraman
(Courtesy of NSDC, Inc.)

Winners of the 26th basketball tournament
Pictured L to R: Greg Roberts, John Highfill, Hannes Tulving
(Courtesy of NSDC, Inc.)

John: The 26th National Silver Dollar Basketball tournament at the Downtown YMCA continued to attract many dealers who put the ball through the hoop with "style and grace." You guessed it. I won again! Guess I should mention that I had a little help from Hannes Tulving and Greg Roberts.

Special cancellation stamp for the 10th NSDC
(Courtesy of St. Louis U. S. Post Office)

Heritage Numismatic auction catalog, 1989
(Courtesy of Heritage Numismatic Auctions, Inc.)

Tenth National Silver Dollar Convention cachet
(Courtesy of NSDC, Inc.)

Marlene: Those who came to St. Louis for something more than looking at those beautiful coins were not disappointed. With many historic places to visit such as the Gateway Arch and Museum, Old Cathedral, Busch Stadium, and the Sports Hall of Fame. Famous Old St. Louis, with the Anheuser-Busch Brewery, and Lacledes Landing, gave dealers and their spouses a wide variety to choose from.

John: The United States Postal Service again provided a mobile unit for all of the National Silver Dollar Convention postal requirements. The special cancellation was available for all who attended the convention. Cachet envelopes were also available for purchase.

Marlene: This was the first year for Heritage Numismatic Auctions to participate in the National Silver Dollar Convention. They were also co-sponsors for the dinner and entertainment with **Felix Cavaliere and the Rascals**. Their superior collection of numismatic merchandise in all categories was very exciting and brought many bidders into the auction sessions. Highlights of the Morgan and Peace action included the following (prices realized include the buyers premium).

Lot	Date	Category	Grade	Grading Service	Price Realized
348	1887	Morgan	MS-67	NGC	7,700
354	1890-O	Morgan	MS-65	PCGS	6,600
400	1895-S	Morgan	MS-65	NGC	18,975
420	1923-S	Peace	MS-65	ANACS	8,800
734	1890-CC	Morgan	MS-65 DMPL	PCGS	14,850

John: The entertainment has been a highlight of all the conventions through the years. The National Gold Convention for 1990 brought in The King's Manor out of Chicago. The night was full of song, food and dance with singing minstrels and a musical review.

The King's Manor announcement poster
(Courtesy of American Coin Conventions, Inc.)

The King's Manor
Chicago, Illinois

The King's Manor
"Singing Wenches"

The 11th NSDC program book
(Courtesy of NSDC, Inc.)

PCGS
AUTHORIZATION REQUEST FOR
SILVER DOLLAR CONVENTION
ST. LOUIS, MO

Dealer Name________________ Dlr. No.

Please hold the following for delivery to the Silver Dollar Convention in St. Louis, MO (check appropriate services)

______ Express Services

Gold/Type Services

______ Super Express Services

I understand that no orders will be held prior to October 31, 1990 and that specific orders cannot be designated for delivery. I further understand that no changes can be made on shipping instructions during the week of the Silver Dollar Convention (November 5th through 11th).

Authorized Signature

(Please return to Julie Uptegroff at PCGS)

PCGS Authorization Request form
(Courtesy of PCGS)

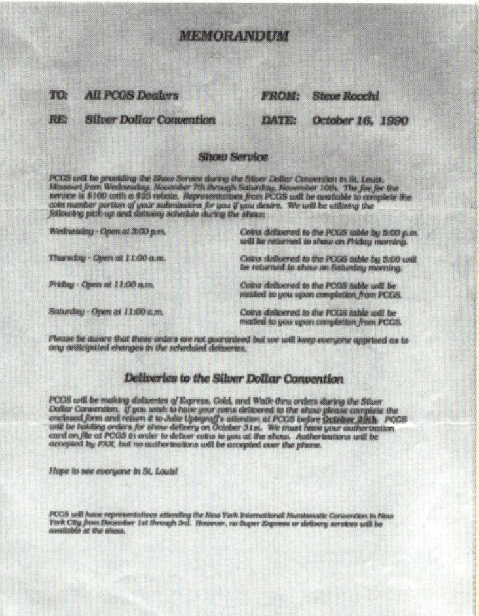

MEMORANDUM

TO: All PCGS Dealers FROM: Steve Rocchi
RE: Silver Dollar Convention DATE: October 16, 1990

Show Service

PCGS will be providing the Show Service during the Silver Dollar Convention in St. Louis, Missouri from Wednesday, November 7th through Saturday, November 10th. The fee for the service is $100 with a $25 rebate. Representatives from PCGS will be available to complete the coin number portion of your submissions for you if you desire. We will be utilizing the following pick-up and delivery schedule during the show:

Wednesday - Open at 3:00 p.m. — Coins delivered to the PCGS table by 5:00 p.m. will be returned to show on Friday morning.

Thursday - Open at 11:00 a.m. — Coins delivered to the PCGS table by 5:00 will be returned to show on Saturday morning.

Friday - Open at 11:00 a.m. — Coins delivered to the PCGS table will be mailed to you upon completion from PCGS.

Saturday - Open at 11:00 a.m. — Coins delivered to the PCGS table will be mailed to you upon completion from PCGS.

Please be aware that these orders are not guaranteed but we will keep everyone apprised as to any anticipated changes in the scheduled deliveries.

Deliveries to the Silver Dollar Convention

PCGS will be making deliveries of Express, Gold, and Walk-thru orders during the Silver Dollar Convention. If you wish to have your coins delivered to the show please complete the enclosed form and return it to Julie Uptegroff's attention at PCGS before October 29th. PCGS will be holding orders for show delivery on October 31st. We must have your authorization card on file at PCGS in order to deliver coins to you at the show. Authorizations will be accepted by FAX, but no authorizations will be accepted over the phone.

Hope to see everyone in St. Louis!

PCGS will have representatives attending the New York International Numismatic Convention in New York City from December 1st through 3rd. However, no Super Express or delivery services will be available at the show.

PCGS Memorandum
(Courtesy of PCGS)

hosted by
Professional Currency Dealers Association (PCDA)
International Bank Note Society (IBNS)
and
Society of Paper Money Collectors (SPMC)

CERVANTES CONVENTION CENTER, ST. LOUIS, MISSOURI
November 8, 9, 10 & 11, 1990

This private Souvenir Card is being issued to commemorate the International Bank Note Society (IBNS) meeting and educational program, being held in conjunction with the Fifth St. Louis Paper Money Convention. The meeting will be at 11:00 a. m. on Saturday, November 10, 1990 in Room 270 of the Cervantes Convention Center. The program will be "The Story of Currency in Kuwait." It will be presented by Mr. Armen Youssefi of Lenexa, Kansas.

Attached to this card is a Kuwait, 1/4 Dinar note, Pick 11. The note is a gift from Armen. He hopes you enjoyed his program. This offset Souvenir Card was produced by Nancy & John Wilson from Milwaukee, Wisconsin. It is number 23 in their ongoing Series. This souvenir card is limited to 60 copies. Everyone in attendance at this program will receive one free. Armen, Nancy & John thank you for attending the meeting and hope that you always support the IBNS.

Fifth National & World Paper Money Convention
(Courtesy of PCDA)

Eleventh National Silver Dollar Convention

November 8, 9, 10 and 11, 1990
St. Louis, Missouri

Marlene: The Cervantes Convention Center facility was again the site for the 11th National Silver Dollar Convention. As is now becoming a custom, the Professional Currency Dealers held their 5th annual National Paper Money Convention in conjunction with the NSDC. The NSDR held its 5th annual "**Dollar Day**" on Wednesday, November 7th. The ceremonies of ribbon cutting and issuing the Proclamation were headed by city officials with honored guests, myself and John. Would you believe that over $100,000,000 worth of silver dollars, U.S. Gold, commemoratives, type coins, jewelry, paper money and other rare coins were displayed and offered for sale at this convention! These offerings were presented by over 500 dealers with tables and 2,000 to 2,500 of America's leading gold and silver dollar specialists. They bought, sold and appraised coins among themselves and to the public.

Three Dog Night
(Courtesy of Three Dog Night)

Three Dog Night announcement poster
(Courtesy of NSDC, Inc.)

Enjoying the entertainment!
Pictured L to R: Marty Luster, Mark Yaffe, Christel Yaffe
(Courtesy of NSDC, Inc.)

Gregg Hosfeld — juggler and comedian
(Courtesy of Gregg Hosfeld)

Softball trophy and the 11th NSDC basketball trophy
(Courtesy of NSDC, Inc. and American Coin Conventions, Inc.)

This year's collection of seminars included presentations by ANACS, ANE, CCE, Hallmark, NGC and PCGS. The ANACS seminars covered the subjects of authentication, grading, and the "Sight-Seen Market for ANACS Slabs." All of the seminars were very informative and interesting for those who attended. This year's ANACS special guest instructors were Don Bonser and Randy Campbell. Both PCGS and NGC provided special show service during the Silver Dollar Conventions in St. Louis. The presence of the major independent third party grading services reaffirms creditability to our conventions.

John: The National Silver Dollar Roundtable Educational Seminar featured Leon Hendrickson, Al Johnbrier and Clark Samuelson. This year's special Silver Dollar Investment Seminar had something to offer to everyone. The speakers were Bruce Amspacher, Randy Campbell, Mike Fuljenz, Leon Hendrickson and Steve Rocchi. I was again fortunate to serve as narrator for this excellent annual event.

Marlene: The NSDR banquet was held at the Ruth's Chris Steak House. This was a steak to remember! The NSDC banquet was held at the Sheraton Hotel Ballroom. Entertainment included comedian and juggler **Greg Hosfeld**, who put everyone in good spirits. Next was the main attraction — **Three Dog Night Live in concert**! They performed hits such as "**One**", "**Easy To Be Hard**", "**Eli's Coming**", "**Mama Told Me Not To Come**", "**Joy To The World**", "**Old Fashioned Love Song**", "**Black and White**" and "**Never Been To Spain**." Everyone heard songs that brought back memories and good times. THIS WAS THE NUMISMATIC "**ENTERTAINMENT EXTRAORDINAIRE**" TO DATE! (It may never be surpassed as the top name billing for any numismatic gathering or convention.)

John: This session, the 29th National Silver Dollar Basketball tournament, was held at the downtown YMCA. This sporting event drew many dealers who have really grown to love this event. The winners were myself, along with teammates John Conner and Lee Minshull.

Marlene: Once again, the United States Postal Service opened a mobile unit for the National Silver Dollar Convention. A special cancellation was available for all, and cachet envelopes were available for purchase.

John: The National Silver Dollar Roundtable began its activities with the fifth annual "**Dollar Day**." The 9th NSDR general meeting and the NSDR breakfast continued to be well attended and provided members with meaning and fellowship.

Marlene: A rare coin "experience" occurred at the 11th NSDC. This was the exhibition of "The World's Finest Morgan Silver Dollar Collection." There were more than 100 of the "treasures" of the Morgan dollar on display. It was a fantastic collection of PCGS Morgan coins including a 1878-S MS-68PL, 1880-O MS-65PL, 1892-CC MS-67, 1887 MS-67, 1889-S MS-66. 1892-P MS-65PL, 1878 7/8 TF (Strong) MS-65 DMPL and other "gems" too numerous to mention here. Everyone who saw this collection was fascinated. (For further details see Chapter 25.) If you haven't seen this collection, do so at any one of the other conventions hosting the presentation during the nineties. This is truly an awesome display and an inspiration for all present and future silver dollar enthusiasts!

PCGS module: San Francisco and Denver Mints
(Courtesy of PCGS)

The World's Finest Morgan Silver Dollar Collection
(Courtesy of PCGS)

PCGS module: Grading rare coins
(Courtesy of PCGS)

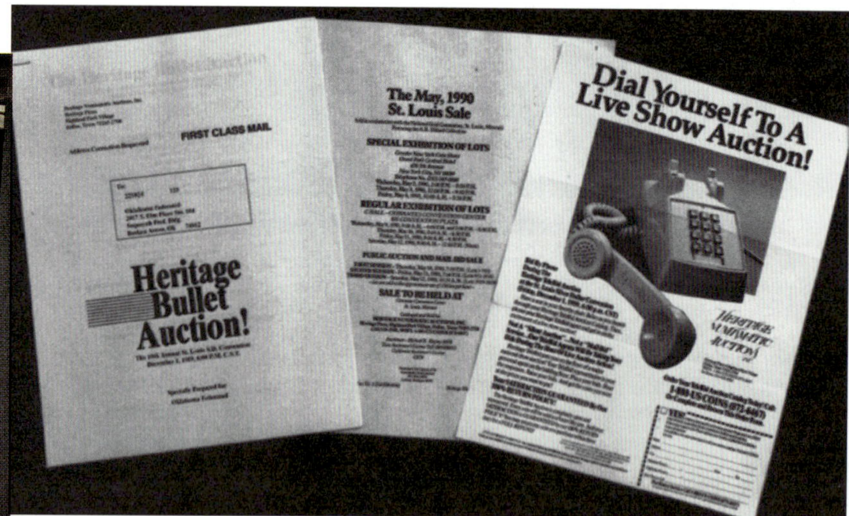

Heritage Bullet Auction
(Courtesy of Heritage Numismatic Auctions, Inc.)

Marlene: The auction was presented by Heritage Numismatic Auctions, Inc. of Dallas, Texas. Auctioneer was Michael R. Haynes, who presented in excess of 1,000 lots of rare and desirable dollars and other numismatic items on the auction block.

Twelfth National Silver Dollar Convention

October 31, November 1, 2, 3, 1991
Tampa, Florida

John: Yes, we moved to Tampa, Florida in the new and ultra-modern Tampa Convention Center. See our annual supplement for post-convention details.

Marlene: The Making of a Convention

There are a million things that must be done to put on a convention the size and complexity of the National Silver Dollar Convention. Not many of these activities are fun, but all are essential. The following remarks will give you some of the ideas brought to the convention and an idea of the rough road that the convention staff must follow in order to be there smiling when you step onto the bourse floor.

One of the first things which must be done is to schedule the facility and the dates for the convention. The NSDC is held each year in the fall. This seems easy enough, but scheduling must be done from 18 to 24 months in advance. A good start, but now we must verify that all of the supporting facilities will be present. This includes adequate bourse space, seminar rooms, security, communications, organizations to present seminars, a designated auction company, etc.

We wanted to add shows, excitement and activities to help the dealers relax, and make the show more desirable for them and their spouses. There are a lot of things to see and do in St. Louis. With the convention centrally located in St. Louis, and with the shopping malls, Gateway Arch, the top-rated St. Louis Zoo, and Grants Farm, a dealer can bring the family and make a vacation of it. This is why we picked St. Louis, and why the convention has virtually doubled in size. We also scheduled a basketball tournament and 5K run to provide exercise and release for the participating dealers. This went over so well that the NSDC has sponsored the basketball tournament in many of the major shows throughout the year. There were various softball tournaments held at both conventions in St. Louis. And for the public, numismatists and non-athletic dealers, we provided free seminars.

Other areas which are also addressed well in advance are: Notification to city officials of the event's needs and time schedule (ribbon cutting ceremonies, "National Silver Dollar Week proclamation," police and fire protection, expected visitors and money coming into the city, etc.); negotiating and contracting with the selected airlines for potential discount fares and restrictions; negotiating and securing blocks of rooms with selected hotels in the immediate area.

Bobbie Webb, "not working at all" at the Annual National Silver Dollar Convention
(Courtesy of NSDC, Inc.)

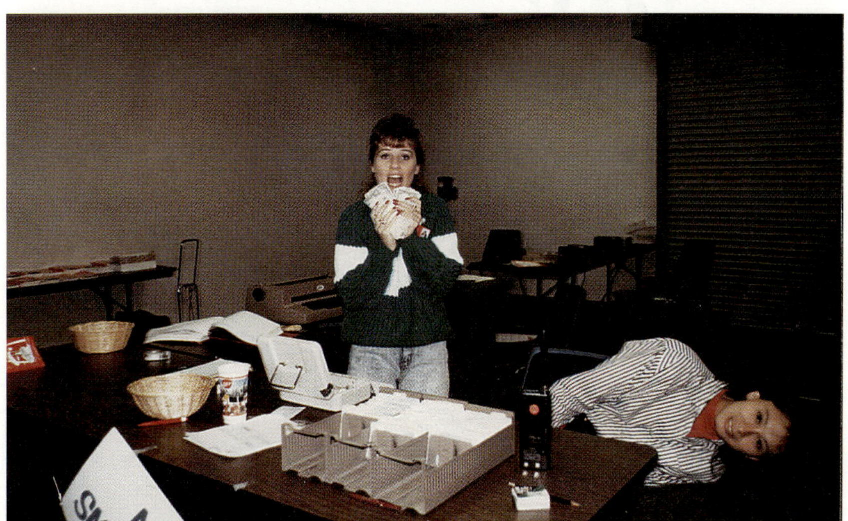

Girls pretending to be working in the Photo ID Room
Melody Cunningham (left) and Trish Pendergrass (right)
(Courtesy of NSDC, Inc.)

Tampa Convention Center
Tampa, Florida
Sight of the 1991 NSDC and the NGC

National Gold Convention dealer packet
(Courtesy of Bob Wilhite c/o Numismatic News)

ICTA DEALER DAY- A REALLY GOOD SHOW

By Diane Piret

At least that's what many of the dealers with tables told me, "My best day of the show.", "Beautiful new convention center and a great location.", and "Here's my contract for next year." were some of the comments.

First of all, let me extend my thanks to all those dealers who took the time to say nice things. Dealer Day takes a lot of time and effort, and your comments are truly appreciated.

However, ICTA Dealer Day couldn't even exist if it weren't for all the hard work and experience of Marlene Highfill, Christel Yaffe, Patti Moreno, Vonnie Berry and other support staff from Oklahoma Federated and National Gold Exchange. A special thank-you to June, Mark Yaffe's mom, who helped photo I.D. go smoothly.

Thanks to Johnson-Matthey for its donation of 10 one-oz. silver Freedom rounds for a raffle to benefit ICTA's efforts on cash reporting. Art Kagin was the winner; Ed Kuzmar "officiated" at the drawing during the cocktail party.

Marsh & McLennan sponsored the morning continental breakfast as well as the apres-Dealer Day cocktail party. Larry Waldie, VP at M & M, pointed out that, even if your inventory insurance is not with the ICTA program, you have benefited from the program's broader coverages and special rates which have caused other carriers to reduce their premiums in order to be competitive. Our thanks to M & M for its generous support of ICTA Dealer Day.

The few problems that were reported about the convention center (those air conditioning ducts were tornado force!) have been taken up with the convention center and the Mayor's office so we should have these ironed out for next year.

If any *Wire* reader would like to sponsor or co-sponsor any of the amenities of the 1992 Dealer Day, be sure to let me know. Any other suggestions or comments are welcome. And thank you to the dealers and sponsors who are at the heart of the show's success!

See you at the next Dealer Day on April 1, 1992. (April Fool's Day?!)

(Editors' Note: Many, many thanks to Diane Piret, who handles Dealer Day all by herself.)

1991 ICTA Dealer Day news release
Article on the National Gold Convention in Tampa, Florida

The 12th National Silver Dollar Convention flier
Tampa, Florida

As Spring approaches, additional projects are given the green light. These include submission of the NSDC catalog design and convention dates to the St. Louis Post Office for a special cancellation stamp; notification of local Union officials with a listing of all temporary workers required and the necessary tasks (setup, tear down, unload, serve, decorate, etc.); contacting local newspapers, radio stations, and TV stations for coverage and advertising.

During this time, all inquiries for bourse space, sign-up, bourse fees, table assignment and other dealer questions must be handled. Let me take a moment to describe the location of the 8 foot bourse tables. This is one area which must be handled very carefully and fairly. Some dealers describe the bourse floor as "Hollywood and Ventura." Everyone wants their table right up front near the entrance (Hollywood), while few want their tables near the back (Ventura). Corner tables go for more, and some dealers enjoy the exposure that can accompany a corner table even if it is located in the back section. When there is a no-show, everyone wants to move up to a better slot. This is where the fun begins.

The NSDC has assigned the tables over the years on a first come, first served basis. Careful placement of the auction lot viewing, Post Office, and other facilities and concessions has been made to encourage traffic to the left and back. The usual flow of people about the bourse floor is to enter, turn right, and move from right to left up and down the aisles. It is the NSDC standard and policy to make all tables as desirable as possible.

In 1987, I believe, we implemented a new idea. Special table space was provided to outside organizations associated with numismatics for the good of the industry and convention visitors. Organizations and agencies such as the U.S. Mint, American Bank Note Company, ANA, Numismatic News, Coin World, ICTA, Financial News Network, Professional Numismatic Guild Inc., FUN, NSDR, PNG, UNITRADE, U.S.R.C.E., PCGS, NGC, ANACS, T.I.S., Hallmark, F.N.N., CSNS, Westex Expositions, and many others displayed many items and materials for attendees. Other tables placed along the walls for public enjoyment included the British Royal Mint, U.S. Mint, Bureau of Engraving and Printing, Pobjoy Mint China Mint, and private mints such as the Hawaiian Mint. Their representatives brought literature, books, coins for display and sale.

The implementation of an official, although temporary, U.S. Post Office on the convention floor was an instant success. The Cancellation Stamp created from special artwork was fun for everyone (the Special cancellation stamp was different each year, created from art submitted 5 months prior to the convention to the St. Louis Post Office). The cachet envelope (usually 3 1/2 by 5) was another souvenir item popular with the public. The full service post office handled registered mail (100-200 per day). We also had Federal Express service twice a day.

Getting back to the pre-convention activities schedule, the Silver Dollar Convention Program book must be started three to six months before the convention date. We have handled everything including the publishing for the past nine conventions. Advertising must be sold, artwork created or received, ads completed for customers using submitted material, guest authors must be found and their work submitted, event schedules must be finalized and put into writing, entertainment must be contracted and documented, updated maps and highlights of the city must be obtained, all dealer table assignments and information must be organized, applications for numismatic related organizations must be obtained, etc.

Each year's edition provides a schedule of events, facilities description and welcome, services, bourse floor layout and participants, special event notices and seminars, entertainment, meeting announcements and advertisements. There are also dealer lists in alphabetic and table number order, as well as table telephone and fax number listings. Membership applications are provided to specific numismatic organizations. The full slate of National Silver Dollar Roundtable activities are presented with the list of "**Dollar Day**" dealers (alphabetic and by table number). Finally, "In Memoriam" remembers our numismatic friends who have passed away.

Chaos begins to enter the picture as the printing deadline approaches. When last minute changes begin to show up, it is a contest to see how many of them we can incorporate into the Program book before the printer literally rips it out of our hands! The finished program makes an excellent file for over 1,000 of the top dealers in America. Unfortunately, last minute dealer sign-ups cannot be included in the program book. As a "thank you" to all visitors to the convention the Program book is free to the public. These books over the years provide a practical and educational tool that you can use year after year.

The National Silver Dollar Convention program book is the largest to be offered by any convention in the country. The 11th NSDC edition was 124 pages filled with educational reference material, articles and advertising. There are several articles prepared by various authors in every program book, making the series collectible and providing good reading and numismatic education for years to come.

Numismatic News display at the National Silver Dollar Convention (Courtesy of NSDC, Inc.)

Coin World display at the National Silver Dollar Convention (Courtesy of NSDC, Inc.)

Johnson Matthey display at the National Silver Dollar Convention (Courtesy of NSDC, Inc.)

One special idea that I thought would add the flavor of pageantry to the convention was to hang a number of banners over the bourse floor. So I sewed and sewed and sewed! But because of these banners, I will never sew again. And when I was done, we had eight 24' by 8' banners of satin. For the following years, I only had to change the dates on the banners before they were hung above the bourse floor.

Bourse Floor Banners
(Courtesy of Marlene Highfill)

The Final Days

Approximately two weeks prior to the convention, we send the convention announcements to our pre-developed mailing list of dealers and public. This mailing will announce the show and dates to approximately 2,000 dealers and representatives, and a good number of the public who could attend. Attendance has run about 8,000 to 10,000 in recent years. Appropriate press releases are also sent to all media, both on a national and local level.

This reminds me of an interesting story. I sent a press release along with a T-shirt to Willard Scott (with the "**Today**" show). This was in 1988 and was the first time I made a neon T-shirt. Everyone said it wouldn't do, but I had done it in bright neon pink and put a silver dollar on it. This was the T-shirt I sent to Willard Scott. On the show, he said "this is what is hot!" And then he held up my T-shirt on Nationwide TV! We didn't have a single T-shirt left after that convention. This is the first year we ever sold them all. I TOLD YOU SO!

Looking back to other trinkets and goodies that have been handed out in past conventions, I remember those wooden nickels we used in 1984 through 1988 (couldn't find any wooden silver dollars). We handed out those wooden nickels to everyone who attended the show. In the beginning, they cost about 4 cents each. Over the years, the cost went up to 10 cents apiece! Talk about inflation! We decided to change to balloons and gave them away.

The United States Mint display at the National Silver Dollar Convention
St. Louis, Missouri

Thank you card from Willard Scott
(Courtesy of NBC-Today Show)

American Bank Note Company display at the National Silver Dollar Convention

But we realized that we could only hand them out outside the hall due to the lighting used inside the center. The balloons are helium filled — if they hit the lights the sound would be enough to scare the daylights out of a room full of dealers not to mention the mess left on the lights and ceiling. We had to keep them away from the bourse floor.

Now the convention is again coming up fast, and there are still many more things to do. Among them are contracting for Federal Express; finalizing seminar rooms, schedules, and speakers; providing signs for the airport to welcome dealers; hiring secretaries and others to prepare the administration of the show (ID badges, collect for bourse space, announce activities and door prizes, sign in visitors, sell T-shirts, run message center, telephones, copying machine, fax services, maintain awards and trophies, etc.). By the way, many have wondered who chooses the winners for our plaques and awards. These winners are selected by knowledgeable Non-Dealers involved with the industry. In the past, ANACS, Coin World and Numismatic News have been extremely helpful as volunteer judges.

Each year, we secure Boy Scouts and other kids to serve as pages (gophers) for all dealers. They work in pairs. They contract with dealers to clean showcases, run errands, and all sorts of related essential activities. The best pair each day get an award. These pages wear special T-shirts, special baseball "NSDC" hats, and they are very easy to spot. I don't know what we would do without them.

We spend all four days of each convention collecting table deposits for the next years convention. It would be impossible to track down dealers through the following year!

Last but not least — and just before we all crash — we send out our "Thank you for participating" letters to anybody and everybody who gave their best to the National Silver Dollar Convention!

Senior Editor: Conclusion

The concept of a convention program is not new. It is, however, an ambitious project that is not completed without the cooperation of many. After months of combined effort, NSDC along with Oklahoma Federated Gold and Numismatics, Inc. and their staff are pleased to provide convention visitors with a quality product — year after year for the last decade.

Special attention is called to the detailed list of participating dealers and the schedule of events, which is a complete listing of all the activities taking place during the National Silver Dollar Convention. The inclusion of educational articles makes the Program book a valuable tool, not only during the show, but also as a numismatic guide following the convention.

John the "crib-robber" met Marlene the "grave-robber" on May 26th 1984. Their marriage resulted in a daughter named Chelsea Marie Highfill. The second meaningful event that took place by this union was the strengthening and growth of the National Silver Dollar Convention. The third was the birth and continued growth of the National Gold Convention.

The mutual joint partnership with Alan, Mark and Christel Yaffe in 1990 was again a positive event. Their efforts combined with the Highfills' resources should make the National Silver Dollar Convention a leader in the industry for many years to come. The same process will provide a positive growth pattern for the National Gold Convention as well.

NSDC Staff pictured with comedian Gregg Hosfeld and Three Dog Night lead singer.

Very special thanks should be given to all the employees of Oklahoma Federated Gold and Numismatics, Inc., under the direction of John and Marlene Highfill, and to all the following who have combined their efforts to give you the finest numismatic conventions possible. In addition to those parties that contributed to these conventions, we have taken the pleasure to list patrons contributing to this publication.

Organizations:

AccuGrade
American Airlines
Amos Press
ANA — American Numismatic Association
ANACS. — American Numismatic Association Certification Service
ANE — American Numismatic Exchange
Asksheet — CCDN Certified Coin Dealer Newsletter Asksheet
Astro Village Hotel — Houston, Texas
ATC/FACTS — American Teleprocessing Corporation — FACTS
Blueberry Hill — Tampa, Florida
British Royal Mint
Bureau of Engraving and Printing
Busch Gardens — Tampa, Florida
CABAP — Coin and Bullion Accreditation Program
Canadian Coin Dealer Newsletter
Capital Plastics
CCDN — Certified Coin Dealer Newsletter
CCDN — Asksheet
CCE — Certified Coin Exchange (The "Certified")
CDN — Coin Dealer Newsletter
Chester West Productions
China Mint
COINage Magazine
Coin World
CompuGrade™
CSNS — Central States Numismatics Society
Embassy Suites — St. Louis, Missouri
Entertainment Enterprises
Excel Decorators, Inc. — Tampa, Florida
FNN — Financial News Network
FUN — Florida United Numismatics
Hallmark Grading Service
Harbour Island Hotel — Tampa, Florida
Hawaiian Mint
Heritage Numismatic Auctions
Highfill Press, Inc.
Holiday Inn — St. Louis, Missouri
Hyatt Regency — Tampa, Florida
ICTA — Industry Council Tangible Assets
Johnson Matthey Metals
Joe Jones Agency
Krause Publications

Organizations (cont.)

Kurt Krueger Auctions
Long Beach Expositions
M & M World Travel Service, Inc.
Marriott — St. Louis, Missouri
McIntire Numismatic Auctions
Media Resources
Missouri Numismatic Society
NGC — Numismatic Guaranty Corporation
NGE — National Gold Exchange, Inc.
NSDR — National Silver Dollar Roundtable
National Silver Dollar Conventions, Inc.
Numismatic News
OFG&N — Oklahoma Federated Gold and Numismatics, Inc.
PCGS — Professional Coin Grading Service
PCGS World's Finest Morgan Dollar Collection
Photo Certified Coin Institute
PNG — Professional Numismatic Guild
Pobjoy Mint
Positive Protection
Rarities Group
Riverside Hotel — Tampa, Florida
Riverfront "Becky Thatcher"
Ruth's Chris Steak House — St. Louis, Missouri
Sheraton St. Louis Hotel
Sho-Mor Expositions, Inc. — Tampa, Florida
St. Louis Arch
St. Louis Cardinals Baseball Organization
St. Louis Cardinals Football Organization
St. Louis Coin Club
St. Louis Police Department
Tampa Convention Center
Teletrade
T.I.S. — Tangible Information Services
T.W.A. — Trans World Airlines
U.S.R.C.E. — United States Rare Coin Exchange
U.S. Banknote Company
U.S. Bureau of Printing and Engraving
U.S. Mint
U.S. Postal Service
Unitrade
Westex Expositions
Westside Forty-Four Security
Willard Scott "Today Show"

Individuals:

Mike Abbott
John Albanese
Leonard Albrecht
Bruce Amspacher
Frank Antino
Dick Armstrong
William R. Armstrong
Elerie Arnett
Dennis Baker
Phyllis Baker
Wally Barr
Jordan Barrington
Brian Bauman
John Baumann
Jack Baxter
Barbara Bell
Lee Bellisario
Neil Bergelt

Individuals (cont.)

Van H. Berry, III
Yvonne "Vonnie" Berry
Mike Bianco
James U. Blanchard, III
Don Bonser
Ron Brandow
Kenneth E. Bressett
Earl Brown
Herman Brown
Linda Brueggeman
Robert Brueggeman
Ginger Bryan
Roger Bryan
Marcy Bush
Joe Buzanowski, Jr.
Jordan Jill Byington
Anthony Calcagno

Individuals (cont.)

Randy Campbell
Tony Campo
Linda Carlo
John Cawley
Larry Chambers
Mark Chaplin
Bob Chapman
Terry Coker
Emmett Concannon
Bill Conroy
Steve Contursi
Ron Crawley
Melody Cunningham
Jim Curtis
Connie Daigle
John Dannreuther
Beth Deisher

Individuals(cont.)

Ron Downing
Joel Edler
James Enright
Robert Enright
Bob Estremera
Steele Eunson
Becky Faber
Barry Faintich
Mike Faraone
Bryan Fazio
Gary Fernandez
Bill Fivaz
Louis Fogleman
Kevin Foley
Rebecca Fong
Bill Foreman
John Foster
Leo Frese
Mike Fuljenz
Jimmy Gaines
Roger L. Geary
Harold Greiser
Alan Hager
David Hall
Kenneth Hallenbeck
James Halperin
William E. Haugen
Michael R. Haynes
Robert Hendershott
Dave Hendrickson
Ruhama Hendrickson
Leon Hendrickson
Chelsea Marie Highfill
Jeffery James Highfill
John Wayne Highfill, II
John William Highfill
Nicolette Lynn Highfill
Rebecca Ann Highfill
Melanie Hoock
Ronald L. Horstman
Ron Howard
Steve Ivy
Sandra Jacobs
Harold N. Jagger
Mark R. Jagger
Alfred E. Johnbrier
JoAnn Johnbrier
Brad Johnson
Dale Jones
Dave Jones
Joe Jones
Art Kagin
Don Kagin
Gary Wayne Kaplan
Michael Wade Kaplan

Individuals(cont.)

Eddie Karn
Jack Keane
Buddy Keller
Kenneth Knapp
Sandy Knight
David Koble
Kurt Krueger
John Ladoto
Fred Lemons
Robert Leuver
David Lisot
Carla Love
John Love, Sr.
Marty Luster
A. George Mallis
Dwight Manley
J.P. Martin
Steve Mayer
Dennis McCormick
Matthew McCormick
Peggy McIntire
Robert McIntire
Mark Mendelson
Bob Merrill
Daren Meenahan
Wayne H. Miller
Alan Mincho
Lee Minshull
Cliff Mishler
Newton Mitchell
Paul Montgomery
Rick Montgomery
Amy Moore
Louie Moreno
Patti A. Moreno
Paul Mousseau
Melvin Neal
Michael O'Higgins
Ed Ondrick
Mike Orlando
Tom Paine
Cheryl Paul
Martin Paul
Arnie Payne
Jim Pedone
Bob Pendergrass
Trish Pendergrass
Edward M. Pereira
Dan Perloch
Harrison Phillips
Tom Phillips
Gayle Pike
Diane Augustyne Piret
Walter Perschke
Marie Portell

Individuals(cont.)

Elizabeth Rankin
Dick Reed
Steve Rocchi
Greg Roberts
Will Rossman
Russ Rulau
Clark Samuelson
Mary Sauvain
Iraj Sayah
John Schneider
Melaine Schnell
Vincent C. Schoemehl, Jr.
Florence Schook
Cory G. Scott
Willard Scott
Harold Segermark
Douglas Sharpe
Edward Shure
Grant Smallwood
Bo Smith
Katherine R. Smith
Stephen A. Sparks
Leonard Standley
Joe Stevens
Anthony Swiatek
Dean Tavenner
Steve Taylor
Randy Thern
Dean Thornberry
Elaine Todoroff
Monir Torabi
Hannes Tulving
Kevin Twellman
Leroy C. Van Allen
Marilyn Van Allen
Chris Verhaegh
Joanie Vicknair
Bobbie Webb
Dennis Wegley
Bill Wells
Chester West
Robbie Westfall
Harlan White
Shirley White
Paul Whitnah
Bob Wilhite
Ralph C. Winquist, Jr.
Jim Wolf
Linda Wood
Alan Yaffe
Christel Yaffe
Mark S. Yaffe
Curt Yemm
Brian D. Yutzy
Keith Zaner
All the "Gophers"

Entertainment:

J.W. Apperson
The Association *
Butch Wax and the Hollywoods
The Grass Roots *
Gregg Hosfeld
George Johnstone
Dale Jones

Entertainment:

Royce Kelly
The Kings Manor
Phoenix
The Rascals featuring Felix Cavaliere *
Stephen A. Sparks
Jeff Sutherland
Three Dog Night *
Tinted Blue

* These are the **original** Rock n' Roll groups from the late 60s and the early 70s.

MAY ALL OF THE CURRENT EVENTS BE POSITIVE FOR EVERYONE THAT HAS CONTRIBUTED TO MAKE THE NATIONAL SILVER DOLLAR CONVENTION THE SUCCESS IT ENJOYS TODAY.

We hope you enjoyed this chapter as much as we did in writing it. We tried to keep it from being too personal. However, we are so intimately involved conducting the conventions every year that it was impossible not to get personal.

Good Luck And Enjoy The Rest Of This Book.

***

Appendix

No Need to Change Sunday Show Schedules

by Chester West

Recently I read a letter to the editor from a collector who left his home in the northern section of a state on Sunday Morning and traveled all the way to a central city to attend a coin show. This action was taken on the outside chance that, for some unspecified hunch, all of the dealers would stick around to sever him from his dollars.

After 30 Years of national dealer desertion on Sunday morning, how could this man be so misinformed or lacking in knowledge? Gallons of printer's ink have been expended explaining and cautioning show guests that national dealers do not now — nor have they ever — waited through Sunday closing before shutting down.

Further, every coin-show regular knows that at national shows, only regional and local dealers will be on hand to greet the Sunday crowd. Let's add that anyone who would travel any great distance without consulting the show promoters by telephone is certainly fishing with a willow branch and grocer's twine.

As a conscientious show promoter, object strenuously to the implications that the dealers, show promoters, and advertising agents are some how to blame for the indiscretions of those who would blame their lack of intelligent action on someone else. It's also difficult for me to understand the call for ideas to reform a Sunday opening practice that has stood the test of general dealer and public acceptance of over three decades.

Am I being Vindictive? Absolutely not!

I have great sympathy for the unknowledgeable who don't know the industry practice and great empathy for anyone who would spend money on a fruitless trip without spending first a quarter — or a buck or two — on a phone call. But I have nothing but disgust for the idea that the entire industry practice should be changed because of the expensive disappointment experienced by an infinitesimal number of coin-show attendees.

Let me speak from great experience, Friday and Saturday will find 90 percent of all national, regional and local dealers seated and ready to buy, sell or trade. On Sunday, only local and a few regional dealers will be present.

If you have difficulty with this, re-read the last two sentences before continuing. These are the facts, from coast to coast and border to border.

Show promoters, either non-profit clubs or the "bread-and-butter" guys would rather close down on Sunday than be open. Sunday is an absolute no-profit day.

Matter of fact, it's generally a complete loss day for the promoter. Shows are kept open to accommodate local dealers and collectors and kids who can't come at any other time — plus the astute collector and investor who knows that there are great bargains to be achieved by doing their last-minute shopping after the "high rollers" have completed their transactions.

This practice, which has proven acceptable for many years, needs no reformation because a handful of dissidents would steal the small income of local dealers and great pleasures of Sunday shoppers through their voiced displeasure in national publications. It's a ridiculous premise, and I pray to God that reasonable sanity will prevail when the facts are once again explained.

Some well-meaning writers have referred to the atmosphere on Sunday at a major shows as that of a "ghost town." That's not only foolish, but completely unfounded in most cases.

Sunday morning at a coin show is a most relaxing time, and though the tables are not as well populated as they were on Friday, it's far from a deserted decor. If we are to be truthful, a well-run show looks like a small show in a large hall on Sunday morning.

Sure, over 50 percent of the dealers have shut down and headed home. But the seated dealers will provide enough merchandise to "break the bank" of the most affluent.

Sunday morning begins with dealers from the region setting up early as a few local dealers make deals with the promoter on a vacant table or two. Seated dealers bargain for additional showcases as they spread out from one table to as many as four or five. This accomplished, the dealers are ready to receive the collecting public with bargains that didn't exist at any other time during the show.

Dealers who on Friday and Saturday had a couple of cases filled with choice merchandise have now added a couple more cases with secondary coins that couldn't have been shown due to lack of space. Many times I have seen a dealer fill a complete table with minor coins and cut the prices 50 percent to please the Sunday crowd.

Let me give you a couple of examples: The Westex show have been host for many years to Richards Numismatics. Richard Malmgren and Richard Horst like to set up two adjacent corners and travel with extra double-row boxes and showcases.

On Saturday afternoon, one or both of them begin looking for vacant space that pleases their taste and make it clear to me that they desire to spread out. By Sunday morning, their operation has increased to as many as five or six tables, and the new merchandise they exhibit covers the entire realm of numismatics and exonumia.

Ken Hallenbeck and his son Tom are dyed-in-the-wool collectors whose contributions to the hobby could fill a book. Sunday you will find them spread out from their normal corner to as many as four tables covered with new and exciting offerings.

I could tell you of a dozen such moves made by regional and local dealers who spread out new merchandise to greet the Sunday crowd.

Make no mistake about it. National dealers who travel great distances will continue to leave a show when their business is accomplished, and regional and local dealers will continue to display a wealth of materials until they are chased off the floor.

In addition, the collector and investor looking for profits and good deals will populate the Sunday show until their budget is bent. And yes, the minority will continue to call for reform to the detriment of the majority. Isn't that the way it has always been?

Be happy, be healthy, get wealthy, and hold a good thought. I am Chester West.

John W. Highfill, NLG

The National Silver Dollar Roundtable was founded on November 12, 1982, at the "Third National Silver Dollar Convention," in Houston, Texas.

Mr Highfill is both Member #1 and Life Member #1. His wife, Marlene M. Highfill, is Member #223 and Life Member #61.

Mr. Highfill has served on the Board of Governors since the NSDR was founded. He has also served as a two-term President from 1986 through 1990.

Al E. Johnbrier

Al Johnbrier joined the United States Air Force in 1953, and served with distinction for 23 years. While in the Air Force, Al met and married his wife Joann. They have been married for 30 years and have three daughters. The Air Force assignment he remembers well was performing the duties of Supply Sergeant on Air Force One during the Johnson administration.

Al began collecting coins in 1961, and by 1964 his interest in numismatics led him to visit coin shows whenever possible. He helped to form the Andrews Air Force Base Coin Club in 1964 where he was secretary/treasurer. He has been associated with this club for over 25 years. The club moved to Bowie, Maryland in 1987 where he still serves as secretary/treasurer.

When he retired from active duty in 1976, he became a full time dealer. Mr. Johnbrier was one of the original founders of the National Silver Dollar Roundtable in 1982 and was appointed its first secretary/treasurer. He has been treasurer for the past eight years and was elected vice president in 1990 with his wife Joann taking over the duties of treasurer. He serves as the Roundtable representative to the Industry Council for Tangible Assets where he sits on the board as one of its founding members. Al also serves on the board of the Middle Atlantic Numismatic Association (MANA).

Al Johnbrier is a life member of the NSDR, ANA, FUN, MANA, and is a member of most of the numismatic organizations including PNG. He spends a lot of time traveling these days doing approximately 30 to 35 shows and conventions yearly.

CHAPTER 24

National Silver Dollar Roundtable

by John W. Highfill, NLG and Al E. Johnbrier

The Organization and Its People

Al: The year was 1982 and the place was Houston, Texas. The event was the Third National Silver Dollar Convention. Hosted by John Highfill, the show took place in the Astro Village Hotel. This was a big change from previous locations to the well known Houston Astro Complex. John's goals were met through dealer participation and visitor numbers. This is where the NSDC got its "second wind" which put the convention on the list of shows that many national dealers just had to attend. The show remained in Houston in 1983 and then moved to St. Louis, Missouri for a seven year stint.

Another beginning took place in Houston during the Third Annual NSDC. The idea for the NSDR came about through the efforts of John Highfill and Joe Buzanowski after a meeting with the ANACS Director, Ken Bressett, and Grader Leonard Albrecht. The purpose of that meeting was to allow dealers to air their concerns about grading standards. At that time, ANACS took the stand that strike had no influence on a coin's grade. Most silver dollar dealers believed that strike should be a major factor in the grading of a dollar, and wanted to relay that fact to Ken and Leonard. I felt at the time that they deserved credit for even appearing, if you will, in the "Lion's Den" of a bunch of very disgruntled dealers.

After the session, John asked some of us if we would be interested in forming an organization for dollar dealers and collectors, and to pass the word that there would be a meeting at 8:00 am the following morning. Now, those who know that dealers only get up that early for a hot market or a free breakfast (and then most often not even for the breakfast), would have to marvel at the turnout of nearly every table holder at the show. Approximately 65 dealers were interested enough to pledge $25 each in start-up dues.

John Highfill then quickly moved forward on the very next morning and organized a meeting of leading silver dollar dealers at the Astro Village Hotel. He was convinced that an organization of dealers for silver dollars was necessary. He was quoted at the time, "I find it hard to believe that a silver dollar organization was never founded prior to this date." After the second meeting in two days, the nucleus of the NSDR was formed, and thanks to the insight and aggressiveness of John W. Highfill the Roundtable was founded on November 12, 1982 at the 3rd National Silver Dollar Convention in Houston, Texas.

There were only 39 of the initial 65 members recruited by Mr. Highfill that joined at the time. The First National Silver Dollar Roundtable membership roster is presented below. The members are listed in alphabetical order. Each of the dealers below contributed $25 as "seed" money to found a bright new organization that was to become the NATIONAL SILVER DOLLAR ROUNDTABLE! It is a tribute to them and to the organization that the majority of these dealers are still members of the NSDR today.

Leonard Albrecht
Bruce Amspacher
Burl Armstrong
James U. Blanchard, III
Kenneth E. Bressett
Roger P. Bryan
Joe Buzanowski
Jay Cammack
Steve Contursi
Jack Copeland
John W. Dannreuther
Gary J. Fernandez
Frank Greenberg
James L. Halperin
David Hall
Leon E. Hendrickson
John W. Highfill
Ronald M. Howard
Dave Ingalls
Steve Ivy
Alfred E. Johnbrier
Kurt R. Krueger
Leroy Lenhart
Dennis Loan
John B. Love
Richard Melamed
Wayne H. Miller
Lynn Murphy
Casey Noxon
D. Harrison Phillips
Dick A. Reed
Bob C. Rose
Clark A. Samuelson
Dean Tavenner
Hannes Tulving
Leroy Van Allen
Joe Wade
Dennis E. Wegley
Harlan White

In mid January 1983, the NSDR elected Joe Buzanowski as President, Dean Tavenner as Vice President, Leroy Van Allen as Secretary, and Al E. Johnbrier as Treasurer. The Board of Governors consisted of Roger P. Bryan, Randy Campbell, John W. Highfill, Kurt R. Krueger, and Wayne H. Miller. A constitution, by-laws, ethics and logo were approved at the ANA Midwinter Convention in Tucson and the organization was off and running.

November 12, 1982 Foundation of the NSDR (left to right) J. Highfill, R. Campbell, D. Tavenner, J. Buzanowski, A. Johnbrier, (standing left to right) L. Van Allen, K. Krueger.
(Courtesy of National Silver Dollar Roundtable archives)

Membership Application and Information

NATIONAL SILVER DOLLAR ROUNDTABLE

To Join Us:

The best buy in numismatics today is a membership in the NSDR. If you fill out the attached application blank, you will be taking a big step toward more knowledge, plus more fun and prestige from your hobby of coin collecting. Detach the application, obtain the signatures of two members who will recommend you and mail it with your remittance to:

N.S.D.R.
LEROY VAN ALLEN
Secretary
Box 196, Sidney, OH 45365
(513) 492-7718

NSDR membership application
(Courtesy of Robert T. McIntire, Jacksonville, Arkansas)

The goal of the NSDR was then and still is to promote the U.S. Silver Dollar. The objective is to advance the knowledge of Numismatics, especially U.S. Silver Dollars, along educational, historic and scientific lines. NSDR assists in bringing about cooperation among all persons interested in collecting, buying, selling, grading, exhibiting and preserving U.S. Silver Dollars through educational forums, social meetings, written articles, newsletters and other publications of interest.

NSDR module with VCR Seminar Tape setup.
NSDC November 8-11, 1990, St. Louis, Missouri.
(Courtesy of National Silver Dollar Roundtable archives)

Eddie A. Karn, II receiving his membership certificate indicating that he has become an official "Knight" of the National Silver Dollar Roundtable

Al: The organization in its first year accomplished quite a bit, considering our board was spread out over eight different states from coast to coast. We developed a collector base of associate members, most of whom have been with us over the last eight years. Our regular membership has been growing steadily since our inception and we now have over 300 members, both regular, life and associate.

The NSDR was one of the founding members of the Industry Council for Tangible Assets (ICTA), and has continued to sit as a member of its board and support this important numismatic organization. ICTA is a lobbying organization and voice in Washington, D.C. and in the state legislatures. It is there to tell them our side of the story. ICTA has been funded solely by member dealer dues and membership currently stands at 650 members. All ICTA members receive the Washington Wire newsletter and a list of all ICTA members. For additional information about the Industry Council for Tangible Assets, contact Diane Piret at ICTA, 25 ST. N.W., Suite 810, Washington, D.C. 20001.

The NSDR is proud to be a member of ANA, FUN, ICTA and other major numismatic organizations and associations. It is dedicated to the continued education and advancement of numismatics.

Al: The best part of any organization is the supportive members who make it work. We have been privileged to have some of the finest names in Numismatics in our organization, and they have ceaselessly worked to make it the outstanding group it is. I would be remiss if I didn't name some of the members who have been contributing to the organization from its inception to the present and of course, first on the list is John Highfill. Without the foresight of John Highfill and also Joe Buzanowski, the group would not even have been possible. The same for our Board of Governors, and the Co-Editor of our journal, Mike Faraone, Probably a name most of you are not familiar with, Mike is a Lt. Colonel in the Air Force, stationed in Texas, who has been instrumental in putting our quarterly journal together since November of 1983 (our first issue).

First issue of the NSDR Journal, Volume 1, Number 1, first released on November 1983. (Courtesy NSDR Journal)

The NSDR Journal

A word about our NSDR journal would seem appropriate. The NSDR Journal began publication with its first issue in November 1983. This official publication of the National Silver Dollar Roundtable has been issued on a quarterly basis since that time. The months of issue include February, May, August and November of each year.

Mark Kettles of ICTA (right) presenting then President Dean Tavenner with a Certificate of Achievement for the NSDR for their efforts and contributions as a Board Member of ICTA.

Robert T. McIntire, Publisher and co-Editor of the NSDR Journal

National Silver Dollar Roundtable

JOURNAL

Vol. II No. 1 November 1984

BOARD OF GOVERNORS:

ROGER BRYAN
RANDY CAMPBELL
JOHN HIGHFILL
ROBERT MCINTIRE
WAYNE MILLER

PRESIDENT:

JOE BUZANOWSKI

VICE PRESIDENT:

DEAN TAVENNER

SECRETARY:

LEROY VANALLEN

TREASURER:

AL JOHNBRIER

NSDR JOURNAL EDITOR:

MIKE FARAONE

ADDRESS NSDR JOURNAL CORRESPONDENCE TO:
NSDR JOURNAL
BOX 395
HIGHLEY, ARIZONA 85236

ADDRESS OTHER NSDR CORRESPONDENCE TO:
NSDR
P.O. BOX 913
BOWIE, MARYLAND 20715

MY SILVER DOLLAR SET (Part II)

by Wayne Miller

Montana has always been one of the most active areas in regard to Morgan and Peace dollars, in that it was one of only five states which utilized silver dollars as a preferred medium of exchange. Many silver dollar collections have been assembled in Montana over the past thirty years. However, very few of the dollars in my set came from individual Montana collections. There were a few exceptions however.

In December of 1970, after months of negotiations, I purchased in its entirety the silver dollar collection of John Hardenberg of Missoula, Montana. The price for the complete Morgan and Peace dollar collection (minus the 1895 Proof) was a then stratospheric $6,500. This was a peculiar collection in that the rare dates were generally of very high quality, but many of the common dates were barely uncirculated. I learned that Mr. Hardenberg was of the very sensible opinion that the rare dates should be acquired first, and the more common dates later, since they were much more readily obtainable. Three coins were pre-eminent in the Hardenburg collection: the 1884-S, the 1889-CC, and the 1895-O.

The 1884-S

Dean Tavenner had been beguiling me for several months with the information that he knew of a superb gem 1884-S, but that it was impounded in a major collection and was not likely to be offered for sale. At the time (late 1960s) the 1884-S was unknown in superb gem condition. When I inquired as to a possible price for the coin, Dean said that it would take at least $250 to buy the coin. Since the Coin Dealer Newsletter bid price at the time was $25, this was an enormous price! I gulped a few time but stated that if the coin was ever available I would like a shot at it. Being a sensible businessman, Dean did not divulge the name of the owner of the 1884-S. However, I have learned that many collectors will sell their precious collections to another collector more readily than they will to a person who is strictly a dealer. Within a few months I was contacted by a part-time dealer in Missoula and advised that a major dollar set might be available at the right price. After what I had

Continued on Page 4

Copy of original 8 1/2 x 10 size NSDR Journal, November, 1984. (Courtesy of NSDR Journal)

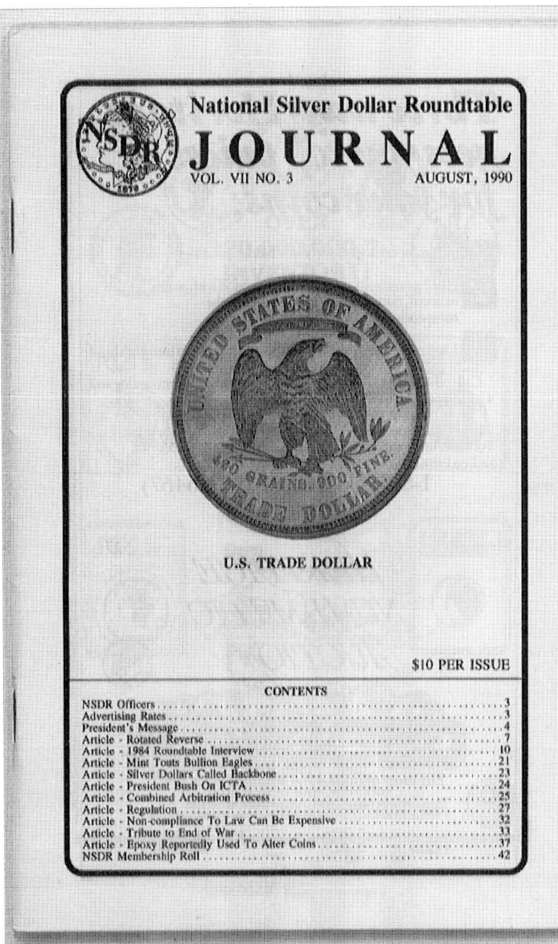

CONTENTS

NSDR Journal - Published Quarterly
(New Smaller Format)
(Courtesy of National Silver Dollar Roundtable)

Mike Faraone and Robert T. McIntire have worked with dedication to make the NSDR Journal a worthwhile publication sure to be referenced by NSDR members over the years. Both Mike and Robert are co-editors, with Mr. McIntire also serving as the NSDR publisher.

Each issue contains the presentation of the current NSDR officers and a message from the president. There are usually five to ten articles selected for publication per issue. These articles cover numismatics, silver dollars, current markets, political and tax related considerations, and special current events and situations. The variety of authors and subject material always makes interesting reading and provides a continuing source of reference material for future times. The current NSDR membership roll is also listed in each issue for use by the membership.

The February 1991 issue of the NSDR Journal contained the following articles:

NSDR Awards Presented

Four States Targeted for Exemption Drives - ICTA

Silver Dollar Educational Forum, John Highfill, Commentator - 10th NSDC, St. Louis

Peace Dollar Model Dies - *Numismatic News*

Peace Dollar Series Often Overshadowed - by Al Doyle, Courtesy of *Numismatic News*

Cash is a Four Letter Word - by Diane Piret, ICTA Director of Membership

IRS Stonewalling All Efforts - by Burnett Anderson, Washington Bureau, *Numismatic News*

ICTA Vows to Renew Legislative Battles - by Burnett Anderson, Washington Bureau, *Numismatic News*

The Market Crash of '90 - by Burton S. Blumert, Courtesy of *Numismatic News*

Pick Any Date Dollar - It's a Bargain! - by Robert R. Van Ryzin, Courtesy of *Numismatic News*

Serving in the Front Line - Courtesy of *Numismatic News*

Time to Repeal Sales Tax of Rare Coins, Bullion - by David L. Ganz

Advertising in the NSDR Journal is an excellent business decision. The NSDR Journal is read cover to cover by all of the membership. In addition, advertising rates are quite modest considering the special audience of readers.

Correspondence, advertising, copy for the Journal, and other communications may be directed to the attention of either co-editor:

Mike Faraone, 501 Rampart, Denver, Colorado 80220

Robert T. McIntire, 27 Crestview Plaza, Jacksonville, Arkansas 72076

The NSDR also runs advertisements through the year with both *Numismatic News* and *Coin World*. Robert T. McIntire is the chairman of the advertising committee of the NSDR. Listed here are two of his more creative and successful ads.

NSDR Advertisement
(Courtesy of National Silver Dollar Roundtable archives)

Goals and Objectives

That brings me to a major objective of the NSDR; that is to inform the collecting public on a timely basis of what is happening in Numismatics. We, on the board, travel as many as 45 to 50 weekends a year to shows and conventions. At these shows we present free open seminars to the public generally starting with the State of the Market and ending with a question and answer session on any numismatic subject including grading, which of course, in itself, can create quite a stimulating response. We try to show the public what coin dealers and particularly, silver dollar dealers are all about.

All of our endeavors within the organization are voluntary. We are a non-profit organization and receive no salaries or monies whatsoever. We take the time from our busy day to meet and greet the public at these seminars and inform them educationally that besides being business, numismatics and silver dollars are a labor of love. It must be to endure the constant travel, delayed planes, bad meals and even worse hotel rooms. But as soon as we get on the bourse floor, everything is all right. When we can talk to the average collector at length about our favorite subject, every bad experience is forgotten.

OF

NATIONAL SILVER DOLLAR ROUNDTABLE

UPON THE RECOMMENDATION OF ITS MEMBER

Cordially invites you to attend its

Dollar Day Bourse

on Wednesday, October 28, 1987
between the hours of 10:00 a.m. and 5:00 p.m.
(preceding the National Silver Dollar Convention)

Cervantes Convention Center
St. Louis, Missouri

Please present this card
Admission Restricted to Card Holders

NSDR "**Dollar Day**" Bourse Invitation
(Courtesy of National Silver Dollar Roundtable archives)

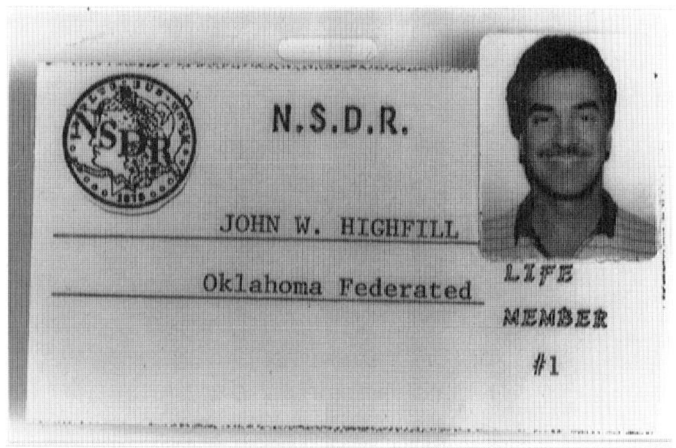

Photo ID card used for the NSDR "**Dollar Day**" at the NSDC in St. Louis, Missouri.
(Courtesy John W. Highfill)

Adhesive NSDR Invited Guest ID Badge used for "**Dollar Day**" at the NSDC show.
(Courtesy of NSDR, Al Johnbrier)

Al: When John asked me to join him in writing a chapter on the NSDR, I was going to make it fairly formal and short, but after thinking about it, that might be shortchanging some fine individuals who have been the backbone of the organization. When you're asked to write about something you've been involved with for a decade, as I have with the NSDR, many names, places and times come to mind. First is my friend and Secretary of the NSDR for those years, Leroy Van Allen. Leroy and Silver Dollars are synonymous and if you have ever read his book, *The Encyclopedia of U.S. Morgan and Peace Dollars*, that is evident. Next, the NSDR's first President, Joe Buzanowski, and its second President, Dean Tavenner and finally our third and fourth President, John Highfill. John and I have worked the closest for all those years in developing the organization into what it is today.

"Dollar Day"

The first annual "**Dollar Day**" was held at the 7th NSDC on November 12, 1986 in St. Louis, Missouri. The prevailing Board of Governors had concluded that a special NSDR sponsored dealer bourse was in the best interest of its membership body. It was a natural to launch the idea in conjunction with the annual National Silver Dollar Convention.

The concept was not necessarily a new one. The PNG (Professional Numismatists Guild, Inc., Van Nuys, California, Paul Koppenhaver, Executive Director) currently puts on a special one day bourse twice a year. One is at the CSNS (Central States Numismatic Society) in the springtime. The other is at the annual ANA (American Numismatic Association) in the late summer.

The concept of a special dealer only bourse by the NSDR was widely accepted. There were approximately 200 NSDR regular and life members at the time and the 1st annual "**Dollar Day**" resulted in 80 tables. That's a 40% attendance from the existing membership. It should be noted that 40% of any membership is an excellent turnout. The first six NSDR "**Dollar Days**" have averaged between 80 and 100 tables. Only the NSDR member and their employees are allowed to be behind the bourse table. There is a special dealer-only setup from 8-10 a.m. the day of the show. The bourse floor was open from 10 a.m. to 4 p.m. to invited guests only. Recently the open bourse has been offered to the public with no admission fee.

The first Bourse Chairman of the NSDR "**Dollar Day**" was Roger P. Bryan, Board of Governor from Gainesville, Florida. I must say that he and his lovely wife Ginger did a spectacular job. This author was appointed to the Bourse Chairman's position the next year. This was done mainly because I was also the Bourse Chairman of the National Silver Dollar Convention. To have the same identical responsibilities at the same convention was a natural. It made the job easier for everyone and has worked out great for all. There are many things that are required to do in order to make this event a success. There are a few photos below that reflect some of these responsibilities.

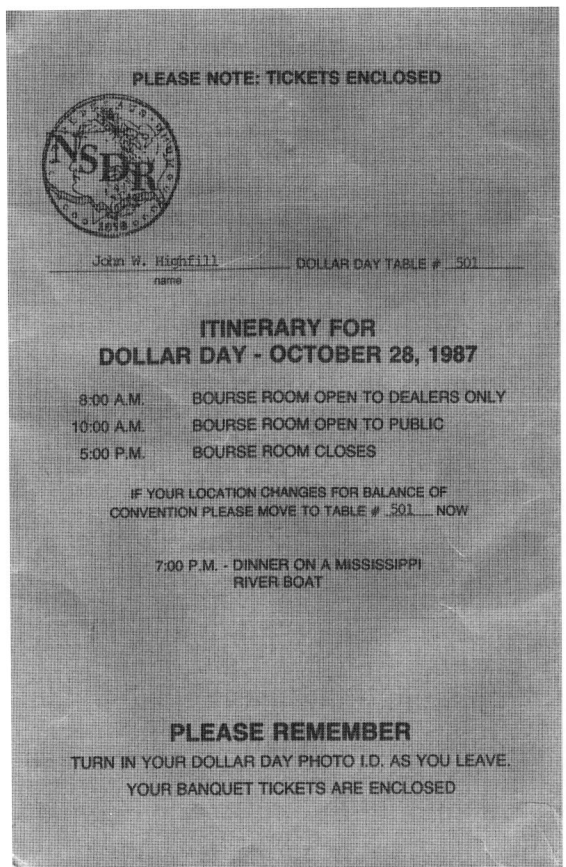

PLEASE NOTE: TICKETS ENCLOSED

NSDR

John W. Highfill DOLLAR DAY TABLE # 501
name

ITINERARY FOR
DOLLAR DAY - OCTOBER 28, 1987

8:00 A.M. BOURSE ROOM OPEN TO DEALERS ONLY
10:00 A.M. BOURSE ROOM OPEN TO PUBLIC
5:00 P.M. BOURSE ROOM CLOSES

IF YOUR LOCATION CHANGES FOR BALANCE OF CONVENTION PLEASE MOVE TO TABLE # 501 NOW

7:00 P.M. - DINNER ON A MISSISSIPPI RIVER BOAT

PLEASE REMEMBER
TURN IN YOUR DOLLAR DAY PHOTO I.D. AS YOU LEAVE.
YOUR BANQUET TICKETS ARE ENCLOSED

Dealer packet for the NSDR "**Dollar Day**", St. Louis, Missouri, October 28, 1987.
(Courtesy of Oklahoma Federated Gold & Numismatics, Inc.)

BOURSE APPLICATION
NATIONAL SILVER DOLLAR ROUNDTABLE
NSDR - 6TH ANNUAL DOLLAR DAY
OCTOBER 30, 1991
TAMPA, FLORIDA

Dear NSDR Member:

The National Silver Dollar Roundtable Board of Governors and Officers are proud to announce a one day show in conjunction with the Twelfth National Silver Dollar Convention to be held at the Tampa Convention Center, 333 South Franklin Street, Tampa, Florida for October 30 to November 3, 1991.

The Bourse fee for the NSDR-DOLLAR DAY will be $150.00. Bourse fee covers bourse table with back-up table, two show cases, and one light.

The NSDR-DOLLAR DAY will be held on Wednesday, October 30, 1991. Dealer set up begins at 8:00 A.M. and will open to the public at 10:00 A.M. The bourse will close at 4:00 P.M. Dealers with tables at the NSDR-Dollar Day can then move to their assigned table for the NSDC. If you do not have a table at the NSDC, you must vacate your table by 4:30 P.M. on October 30, 1991.

Each applicant is required to send a passport size color photo to get a dealer ID badge for this event. (If you had a badge for the 1990 show and turned it in at the close of that show, you do not need to send in a photo.) The ID badges are to be turned in at the close of the bourse at 5:00 P.M. on October 30, 1991 to the Bourse Chairman, JOHN HIGHFILL. We plan to use the ID's for the 1992 NSDR-DOLLAR DAY.

Dealer packets may be picked up at the registration area Wednesday, October 30, 1991.

Dealers are not allowed behind the annual "Dollar Day" bourse table unless they are a member of The National Silver Dollar Roundtable. They must be either an Associate, Regular or Life Member. However, only a regular or a life member is authorized to purchase a table. Employees and family members of the applicant may work behind the companys table. Any exception must be approved by the NSDR Board of Governors. Independent Dealers sharing tables must be at least an associate member of NDSR. The dues are $50.00 and must accompany the bourse application. Associate members sharing a table with a regular NSDR member will also receive a banquet ticket for the awards dinner (COAT AND TIE ARE REQUESTED) and full associate member privleges. NO CONVENIENCE HIRING WILL BE PERMITED!

If the applicant desires to cancel his table, he will be granted a full refund only if a written request for cancellation is mailed to the Bourse Chairman before October 1, 1991.

Positive Protection will provide Security for the bourse area, however, NSDR, its members or officers of the National Silver Dollar Convention will not be responsible for any loss of applicants numismatic items, materials or personal possessions, in the event of loss by fire, theft or other casualty. Dealers are expected to insure themselves against any loss which they might sustain.

A SECURITY room will be set-up by Positive Protection at 4:00 P.M. on Tuesday, October 29, 1991 in the Tampa Convetion Center, 333 South Franklin Street, Tampa, Florida, 33602.

The NSDR Banquet this year will be held at "BERNS STEAKHOUSE" here in Tampa. An event not to be missed! ONE Complimentary Dinner/Banquet Ticket will be given to each NSDR Member Tableholder. Additional tickets (space permitting) will be available for $30.00 each at the Convention Table.

6th Annual "**Dollar Day**" Bourse Application for 1991, Tampa, Florida

There is also an NSDR awards and dinner banquet every fall held in conjunction with the "**Dollar Day**" activities. There have been some great times and memories tied to these banquets. They have been held in a large variety of places. Some of the banquets were held on the riverboat "S.S. Becky Thatcher," Sheraton West Ballroom, and Ruth's Chris Steak House in St. Louis. Bern's Steak House was the host for the 6th NSDR banquet in Tampa, Florida on October 30, 1991. There is always some type of award given each year at these dinners. One example is the annual "Man of the Year" award. In addition, there is a change of officers or installation of new board members each year. This is also a time the President's Special Achievement Award is given to those individuals that have given service above and beyond the call of duty for the past year. Again, there are many photos in this chapter that illustrate banquets, good times, awards and election results from the annual NSDR banquets.

After five successful years, the 6th annual "**Dollar Day**" moved with the National Silver Dollar Convention to Tampa, Florida in 1991.

Dinner Banquets and Officer Installations

This author (Highfill) was elected as the NSDR President and took office on November 12, 1986. I was to become the first (but not the last, I hope) two term President of the Roundtable. This was a big event in my life for many reasons. I had just endured a major and considerable hospital stay at that time in my life. Therefore to take on new obligations, when I wasn't thinking of any future was in itself an exciting time. You should never take anything, especially life, for granted. It is a gift and is temporary at best.

Anyway, as I had mentioned earlier, this NSDR reception and dinner banquet was held on November 12, 1986 at 8:00-9:00 p.m. in the Sheraton West Ballroom. The room was filled to capacity. There were complimentary cocktails available and the dinner was a variety of chicken, beef, fish and vegetarian plates. There was food and drink for everyone. The photos below are reflections of the size of the dinner to individual awards. These photos are all captioned for better details of each event. The outgoing President was Dean Tavenner, and he made a memorable farewell address. Dean was always a very deliberate and articulate speaker. On the other hand my acceptance speech got by without any major embarrassment on my behalf.

However, the night was full of other officers and board members sharing the limelight. Among them were the newly elected officer seats of: Vice President - Roger P. Bryan; Secretary - Leroy Van Allen; and Al E. Johnbrier as Treasurer. The Man of the Year award for 1986 went to Al E. Johnbrier.

NSDR Dinner and Cocktails for a packed house. John W. Highfill inaugurated as NSDR President on November 12, 1986, Sheraton St. Louis Hotel, Missouri
(Courtesy of National Silver Dollar Roundtable archives)

National Silver Dollar Roundtable
cordially invites you
to attend our

Reception & Dinner

Beginning at 8:00 p.m. November 12, 1986
West Ballroom
Sheraton St. Louis Hotel

Reception 8:00 p.m.
Dinner 9:00 p.m.

Photo on left shows NSDR reception and dinner invitation, November 12, 1986, Sheraton St. Louis Hotel. (Courtesy of Al E. Johnbrier)
Photo on right taken at the NSDR banquet on November 12, 1986, at the Sheraton St. Louis Hotel. Shown left to right: Dean Tavenner, Leon E. Hendrickson and Leroy Van Allen (in right background is ANA President Stephen R. Taylor)
(Courtesy of National Silver Dollar Roundtable archives)

NSDR Dinner/Banquet, November 12, 1986 at the Sheraton St. Louis Hotel, St. Louis, Missouri. Sitting from L-R: D. Tavenner, A. Johnbrier, J. Johnbrier, S. Eunson, M. Highfill, J. Highfill,P. Moreno and L. Moreno.

The 5th Anniversary of the NSDR was held on October 28, 1987 in St. Louis, Missouri at the 8th National Silver Dollar Convention. There were many festivities for this special occasion. One of these included a special 5th Anniversary Souvenir Program that included an anthology and history of the NSDR from November 12, 1982 to date. This program book also included hundreds of photos from past events to a complete listing and individual photos of the entire membership roll. The NSDR Journal in the later years went to a smaller format with an expanded President's message such as the one illustrated below.

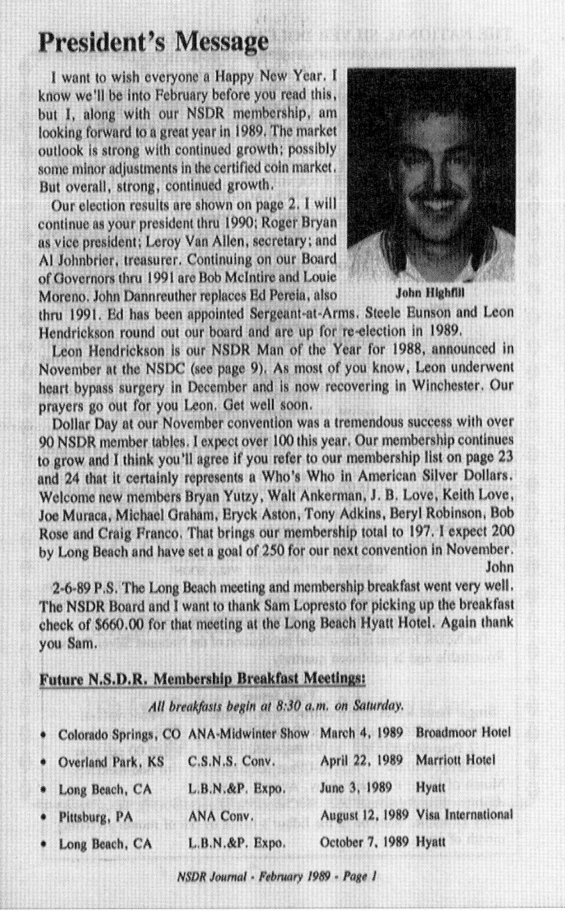

President's Message

I want to wish everyone a Happy New Year. I know we'll be into February before you read this, but I, along with our NSDR membership, am looking forward to a great year in 1989. The market outlook is strong with continued growth; possibly some minor adjustments in the certified coin market. But overall, strong, continued growth.

Our election results are shown on page 2. I will continue as your president thru 1990; Roger Bryan as vice president; Leroy Van Allen, secretary; and Al Johnbrier, treasurer. Continuing on our Board of Governors thru 1991 are Bob McIntire and Louie Moreno. John Dannreuther replaces Ed Pereia, also thru 1991. Ed has been appointed Sergeant-at-Arms. Steele Eunson and Leon Hendrickson round out our board and are up for re-election in 1989.

John Highfill

Leon Hendrickson is our NSDR Man of the Year for 1988, announced in November at the NSDC (see page 9). As most of you know, Leon underwent heart bypass surgery in December and is now recovering in Winchester. Our prayers go out for you Leon. Get well soon.

Dollar Day at our November convention was a tremendous success with over 90 NSDR member tables. I expect over 100 this year. Our membership continues to grow and I think you'll agree if you refer to our membership list on page 23 and 24 that it certainly represents a Who's Who in American Silver Dollars. Welcome new members Bryan Yutzy, Walt Ankerman, J. B. Love, Keith Love, Joe Muraca, Michael Graham, Eryck Aston, Tony Adkins, Beryl Robinson, Bob Rose and Craig Franco. That brings our membership total to 197. I expect 200 by Long Beach and have set a goal of 250 for our next convention in November.

John

2-6-89 P.S. The Long Beach meeting and membership breakfast went very well. The NSDR Board and I want to thank Sam Lopresto for picking up the breakfast check of $660.00 for that meeting at the Long Beach Hyatt Hotel. Again thank you Sam.

Future N.S.D.R. Membership Breakfast Meetings:

All breakfasts begin at 8:30 a.m. on Saturday.

- Colorado Springs, CO ANA-Midwinter Show March 4, 1989 Broadmoor Hotel
- Overland Park, KS C.S.N.S. Conv. April 22, 1989 Marriott Hotel
- Long Beach, CA L.B.N.&P. Expo. June 3, 1989 Hyatt
- Pittsburg, PA ANA Conv. August 12, 1989 Visa International
- Long Beach, CA L.B.N.&P. Expo. October 7, 1989 Hyatt

NSDR Journal - February 1989 - Page 1

Photo on left presents Special Limited Edition 5th Anniversary NSDR program, 1987 (Courtesy of Oklahoma Federated Gold & Numismatics, Inc.) Photo on right shows and example of NSDR Journal "President's Message" (Courtesy of Robert T. McIntire, Publisher and Co-Editor, NSDR Journal, Jacksonville, Arkansas)

There was also a special 5th Anniversary NSDR Cancellation Stamp that was designed by Marlene M. Highfill. The cancellation stamp itself depicts a line art drawing of the United States with a Morgan dollar centered in the map. This official U.S.P.O. Cancellation Stamp was used by the St. Louis post office station branch for the 63101 zip code area. There were special official 5th Anniversary cachet envelopes made available at the same time for the cancellation ceremonies. There was also a Second National and World Paper Money Convention Souvenir fifty cent replica note card that was made available for cancellation.

NSDR 5th Anniversary Postal Cancellation Stamp with Melanie Schnell (left) and Marlene M. Highfill (Courtesy of U.S.P.O., St. Louis, Missouri, 63101).

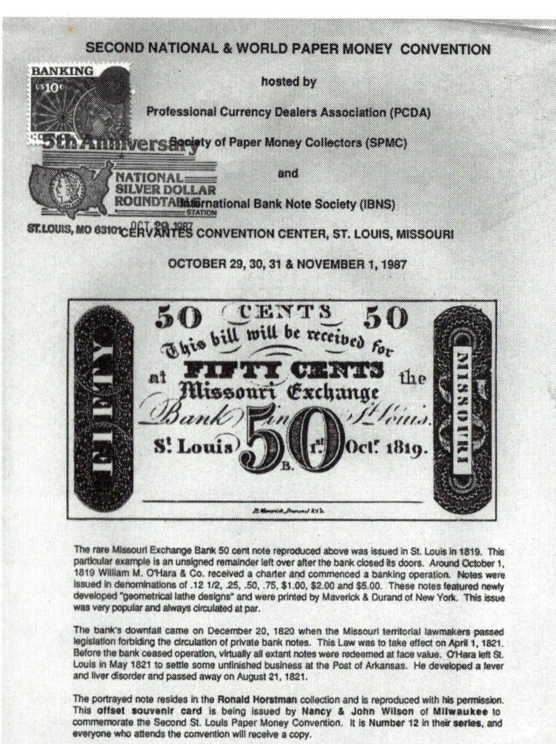

SECOND NATIONAL & WORLD PAPER MONEY CONVENTION

hosted by

Professional Currency Dealers Association (PCDA)

Society of Paper Money Collectors (SPMC)

and

International Bank Note Society (IBNS)

CERVANTES CONVENTION CENTER, ST. LOUIS, MISSOURI

OCTOBER 29, 30, 31 & NOVEMBER 1, 1987

The rare Missouri Exchange Bank 50 cent note reproduced above was issued in St. Louis in 1819. This particular example is an unsigned remainder left over after the bank closed its doors. Around October 1, 1819 William M. O'Hara & Co. received a charter and commenced a banking operation. Notes were issued in denominations of .12 1/2, .25, .50, .75, $1.00, $2.00 and $5.00. These notes featured newly developed "geometrical lathe designs" and were printed by Maverick & Durand of New York. This issue was very popular and always circulated at par.

The bank's downfall came on December 20, 1820 when the Missouri territorial lawmakers passed legislation forbiding the circulation of private bank notes. This Law was to take effect on April 1, 1821. Before the bank ceased operation, virtually all extant notes were redeemed at face value. O'Hara left St. Louis in May 1821 to settle some unfinished business at the Post of Arkansas. He developed a fever and liver disorder and passed away on August 21, 1821.

The portrayed note resides in the **Ronald Horstman** collection and is reproduced with his permission. This **offset souvenir card** is being issued by **Nancy & John Wilson** of **Milwaukee** to commemorate the Second St. Louis Paper Money Convention. It is **Number 12** in their **series**, and everyone who attends the convention will receive a copy.

5th NSDC Anniversary Cancellation Stamp of the Second National & World Paper Money Convention hosted by PCDA, SPMC and IBNS (Courtesy of Kevin Foley, Milwaukee, Wisconsin).

5th Anniversary NSDR Special Edition Cancellation First Day of Issue Cachet (Courtesy of John W. Highfill).

Different cachet envelopes used at various conventions around the world. Shown are cachet envelopes from San Francisco, St. Louis and Singapore. (Courtesy of Rudy Christians, Santa Clara, California)

Through the years, the NSDR had many memorable occasions. One of the best times that I can remember was the NSDR cocktail and dinner banquet that was held on the riverboat "S.S. Becky Thatcher". We boarded the riverboat just below the beautiful Arch on the Mississippi River in St. Louis, Missouri. There was a Dixieland band on board and we had food, fun, drink and dance for over four hours. A lot of the members and their invited guests went on top of the riverboat for a moonlit riverside view of the St. Louis city skyline. It was definitely a moment to remember. Very nice, indeed! (For more, see the related story in the 8th NSDC section of "The National Silver Dollar Convention" (Chapter 23) by John and Marlene Highfill.)

The NSDR "Belle of St. Louis" is the same company and type of riverboat as the "Becky Thatcher" used for the NSDR reception and dinner, 1987.

Moving through the memories and years are some photos of those moments to remember.

Photo on left shows incoming President John W. Highfill presenting outgoing President Dean Tavenner with a presidential solid brass gavel and presentation case in November 1986, Sheraton St. Louis Hotel, St. Louis, Missouri. Vice President Roger P. Bryan is in the background. Photo on right shows gavel presented to John W. Highfill when retiring as two-term President (1986-1990). (Courtesy of National Silver Dollar Roundtable archives)

There were also special "President's Award" plaques that were given throughout the years. This award was given to special individuals that had contributed to the National Silver Dollar Roundtable in many different ways. All of these individuals were unselfish, sharing and giving to the NSDR through the years. Those "special people" are listed below for their due credit and we plan to have many more in the future.

Yvonne "Vonnie" A. Berry
Michael Faraone
Leon E. Hendrickson
Marlene M. Highfill
Al E. Johnbrier
Joann Johnbrier
Samuel L. Lopresto
Peggy McIntire
Robert T. McIntire
Patti Moreno
Clark A. Samuelson
Florence M. Schook
Leroy Van Allen
Marilyn Van Allen
Brian D. Yutzy

National Silver Dollar Roundtable officers with ICTA award. Left to right: John Highfill, Al E. Johnbrier, Dean Tavenner, Leroy Van Allen (circa 1985)

Photo on left shows Leon E. Hendrickson receiving President's Award from NSDR President John W. Highfill at the 11th NSDC, November 7, 1990 at Ruth's Chris Steak House, St. Louis, Missouri. Photo on right shows Florence M. Schook receiving President's Award during the same evening. (Photos courtesy of Marlene M. Highfill)

There was also a very special moment that required a second President's Award to be given to Mr. Leon E. Hendrickson. This Special Achievement Award was presented to Mr. Hendrickson in conjunction with his recognition of The Numismatic News Numismatic Ambassador Award. This award is given to those individuals that are considered by Krause Publications and *Numismatic News* as: "This newspaper's method of honoring the unsung heroes at the grass roots level of collecting." From grass roots to Wall Street, Leon E. Hendrickson has been an inspiration for every coin dealer and collector in America. Congratulations are in order for the current President of the NSDR, Mr. Leon E. Hendrickson. Words fail to properly honor this man's achievements. **Thanks, Leon for all you've given us.**

Photo above shows John W. Highfill presenting the NSDR "Special Achievement Award" to NSDR President Leon E. Hendrickson, who also just received the Numismatic Ambassador Award (also pictured) on Saturday, June 8, 1991.

Photo on left presents the Numismatic Ambassador Award booklet used on June 8, 1991, in the presentation to Leon E. Hendrickson (Courtesy of Cliff Mishler c/o Krause Publications and Numismatic News)

NSDR President Leon Hendrickson presents the Presidents award for Special Achievement. Recipients were (Left to Right) Patti A. Moreno, Marlene M. Highfill, Leon Hendrickson (presenter), and Joann Johnbrier at the 12th NSDC in Tampa, Florida, October 30, 1991

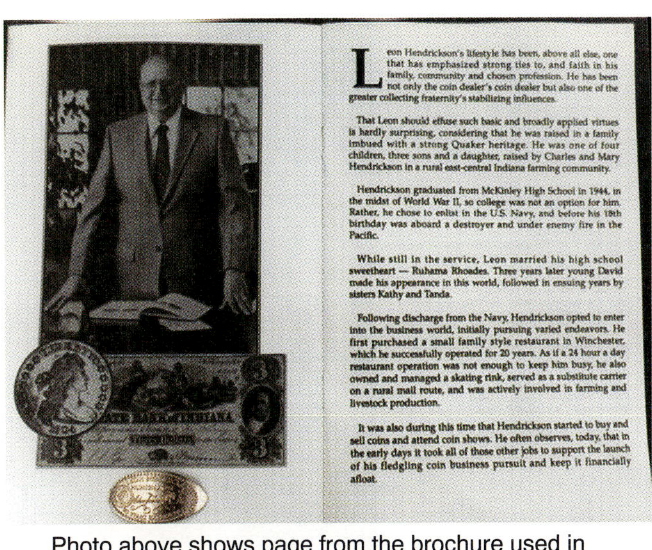

Leon Hendrickson's lifestyle has been, above all else, one that has emphasized strong ties to, and faith in his family, community and chosen profession. He has been not only the coin dealer's coin dealer but also one of the greater collecting fraternity's stabilizing influences.

That Leon should effuse such basic and broadly applied virtues is hardly surprising, considering that he was raised in a family imbued with a strong Quaker heritage. He was one of four children, three sons and a daughter, raised by Charles and Mary Hendrickson in a rural east-central Indiana farming community.

Hendrickson graduated from McKinley High School in 1944, in the midst of World War II, so college was not an option for him. Rather, he chose to enlist in the U.S. Navy, and before his 18th birthday was aboard a destroyer and under enemy fire in the Pacific.

While still in the service, Leon married his high school sweetheart — Ruhama Rhoades. Three years later young David made his appearance in this world, followed in ensuing years by sisters Kathy and Tanda.

Following discharge from the Navy, Hendrickson opted to enter into the business world, initially pursuing varied endeavors. He first purchased a small family style restaurant in Winchester, which he successfully operated for 20 years. As if a 24 hour a day restaurant operation was not enough to keep him busy, he also owned and managed a skating rink, served as a substitute carrier on a rural mail route, and was actively involved in farming and livestock production.

It was also during this time that Hendrickson started to buy and sell coins and attend coin shows. He often observes, today, that in the early days it took all of those other jobs to support the launch of his fledgling coin business pursuit and keep it financially afloat.

Photo above shows page from the brochure used in conjunction with the 33rd Anniversary Convention banquet and Krause Publications "Numismatic Ambassador Award" to Leon E. Hendrickson, June 8, 1991, Indianapolis, Indiana (Courtesy of Cliff Mishler c/o Krause Publications and *Numismatic News*).

Photo on right shows Design and Specification Sheet for the NSDR "Special Achievement Award" given in conjunction with Numismatic News and Krause Publications to Leon E. Hendrickson, June 8, 1991 (Courtesy of National Silver Dollar Roundtable archives).

Al: I've lost track of how many seminars at how many shows we've put on with such fine numismatic educators as Dean Tavenner, Wayne H. Miller, Randy Campbell, Leon E. Hendrickson, Steele Eunson, Robert "Mack" McIntire, Roger P. Bryan, Clark A. Samuelson, Louie Moreno, Jr., Joe Buzanowski and John W. Highfill. I also can't count the number of membership breakfasts we've had where we have gotten to meet some of our fine supportive associate members and who have said that our organization puts on the finest breakfast functions on the Coin Show circuit.

The NSDR breakfast meetings have become almost a ritual for the "Knights" who don't want to miss a single one. For those who may not be familiar with the breakfast "circuit," a recent annual schedule featured the following shows: **NSDC** - Tampa, **FUN** - Orlando, **NGC** - Tampa, **LBC&S Expo** (spring, summer, and fall) - Long Beach, **CSNS** - St. Louis and **ANA** - Chicago and Dallas. Now these breakfasts began at 8:00 a.m. and the members actually look forward to them in spite of the early hour. This shows the dedication of all those faithful NSDR members and associates.

All Knights are cordially invited to attend.

NATIONAL SILVER DOLLAR ROUNDTABLE GENERAL MEETING AND

Breakfast

Saturday, 8:30 a.m.
Rag Time Room

May 14, 1988
Sheraton St. Louis Hotel

NSDR Breakfast Invitation
(Courtesy of National Silver Dollar Roundtable archives)

Al: At this point (I have an occasional desire to wander), I am immediately reminded of perhaps the most neglected individuals who have been connected with the NSDR and our profession since the beginning, The Coin Wives: My wife Joann who sits alone at our table at shows and conventions while I am out doing whatever it is I do; Marlene Highfill, who is John's girl Friday (and Saturday thru Thursday too); Patti Moreno; Christel Yaffe; Peggy McIntire; Marilyn Van Allen; Ruhama "Hamie" Hendrickson; Ginger Bryan; Yvonne "Vonnie" Berry: and all the other ladies who help make the NSDR work.

From top left: Joann, Marlene, Patti, Christel, Peggy, Marilyn, Ruhama "Hamie", Ginger and Yvonne "Vonnie". (Courtesy National Silver Dollar Roundtable archives)

NSDR Pricing Guide

The NSDR Journal Pricing Guide initially appeared in the first issue of the second volume (November 1984, Volume 2, #1). The last Pricing Guide appeared in the February 1988 issue (Volume 5, #2). These quarterly Pricing Guide updates were discontinued in 1988 for several reasons. The quarterly pricing was becoming yesterday's news due to the volatility of some coin prices changing on a daily basis. Also, other trade publications were publishing weekly pricing figures. In addition, ANE and CCE daily pricing printouts were becoming available making this service a redundant (and late) one.

The NSDR Pricing Guides were published in the NSDR Journal for the sole use of the subscribers. There was never any intent to provide pricing for commercial organizations or commercial use.

The National Silver Dollar Roundtable Pricing Guide was a very innovative insert and addition to the NSDR Journal for a brief span of time. All NSDR members were polled on a quarterly basis to obtain buy-sell market prices on uncirculated Morgan and Peace dollars from MS-60 through MS-67, and prooflike grades PL-63 through PL-65. The figures submitted by all participating were averaged and the results became the NSDR Pricing Guide for that quarter. **Note that the NSDR Pricing Guide was the first publication to report MS-64 pricing within the entire numismatic industry.**

The NSDR has always considered itself very innovative and in tune with the needs of the dealers and collectors within this industry.

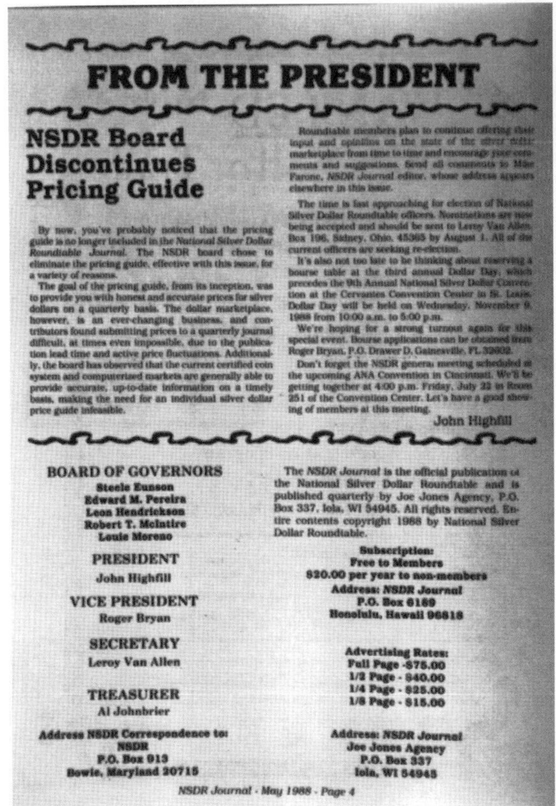

FROM THE PRESIDENT

NSDR Board Discontinues Pricing Guide

By now, you've probably noticed that the pricing guide is no longer included in the *National Silver Dollar Roundtable Journal*. The NSDR board chose to eliminate the pricing guide, effective with this issue, for a variety of reasons.

The goal of the pricing guide, from its inception, was to provide you with honest and accurate prices for silver dollars on a quarterly basis. The dollar marketplace, however, is an ever-changing business, and contributors found submitting prices to a quarterly journal difficult, at times even impossible, due to the publication lead time and active price fluctuations. Additionally, the board has observed that the current certified coin system and computerized markets are generally able to provide accurate, up-to-date information on a timely basis, making the need for an individual silver dollar price guide infeasible.

Roundtable members plan to continue offering their input and opinions on the state of the silver dollar marketplace from time to time and encourage your comments and suggestions. Send all comments to Mike Fafone, *NSDR Journal* editor, whose address appears elsewhere in this issue.

The time is fast approaching for election of National Silver Dollar Roundtable officers. Nominations are now being accepted and should be sent to Leroy Van Allen, Box 196, Sidney, Ohio, 45365 by August 1. All of the current officers are seeking re-election.

It's also not too late to be thinking about reserving a bourse table at the third annual Dollar Day, which precedes the 9th Annual National Silver Dollar Convention at the Cervantes Convention Center in St. Louis. Dollar Day will be held on Wednesday, November 9, 1988 from 10:00 a.m. to 5:00 p.m.

We're hoping for a strong turnout again for this special event. Bourse applications can be obtained from Roger Bryan, P.O. Drawer D, Gainesville, FL 32602.

Don't forget the NSDR general meeting scheduled at the upcoming ANA Convention in Cincinnati. We'll be getting together at 4:00 p.m. Friday, July 22 in Room 251 of the Convention Center. Let's have a good showing of members at this meeting.

John Highfill

BOARD OF GOVERNORS
Steele Eunson
Edward M. Pereira
Leon Hendrickson
Robert T. McIntire
Louis Moreno

PRESIDENT
John Highfill

VICE PRESIDENT
Roger Bryan

SECRETARY
Leroy Van Allen

TREASURER
Al Johnbrier

Address NSDR Correspondence to:
NSDR
P.O. Box 913
Bowie, Maryland 20715

The *NSDR Journal* is the official publication of the National Silver Dollar Roundtable and is published quarterly by Joe Jones Agency, P.O. Box 337, Iola, WI 54945. All rights reserved. Entire contents copyright 1988 by National Silver Dollar Roundtable.

Subscription:
Free to Members
$20.00 per year to non-members
Address: NSDR Journal
P.O. Box 6189
Honolulu, Hawaii 96818

Advertising Rates:
Full Page - $75.00
1/2 Page - $40.00
1/4 Page - $25.00
1/8 Page - $15.00

Address: NSDR Journal
Joe Jones Agency
P.O. Box 337
Iola, WI 54945

NSDR Journal - May 1988 - Page 4

NSDR Board discontinues pricing guide, May 1988
(Courtesy NSDR Journal)

NATIONAL SILVER DOLLAR ROUNDTABLE

PRICING GUIDE

VOL. II No. 1 PAGE I NOVEMBER 1984

NSDR PRICING GUIDE DEBUTS !

MORGAN DOLLARS

	MS 60	MS 63	MS 64	MS 65	MS 67	P-L 63	P-L 64	P-L 65
1878 8F	57	75	170	460	640	145	340	730
1878 7/8F	63	105	280	670	880	250	480	1090
1878 7F	45	65	155	410	625	125	290	680
1878 7F (Rv 79)	61	95	190	440	860	230	470	1310
1878-CC	95	130	200	400	625	150	300	650
1878-S	57	85	135	250	440	95	185	410
1879-P	42	60	200	560	830	125	375	1020
1879-CC	600	1025	2400	4900	8100	1525	3550	10300
1879-CC (C/O)	375	675	1300	2125	2460	1050	2125	5200
1879 O	44	100	320	825	1175	220	725	1875
1879 S (Rv 78)	90	135	270	390	1125	295	650	1250
1879 S	53	70	115	175	350	95	175	525
1880 P	43	60	170	350	750	125	350	950
1880 CC (Rv 78)	160	220	320	575	800	270	575	1175
1880 CC	150	195	275	550	825	190	530	1025
1880 O (8/7)	55	135	315	950	1325	250	550	1875
1880 O	50	130	330	950	1350	260	675	1925
1880/9 S	52	70	120	180	370	95	170	350
1881 P	42	65	155	430	775	125	350	900
1881 CC	155	195	270	480	875	225	440	850
1881 O	35	60	165	400	600	110	320	800
1881 S	50	70	105	170	300	90	165	350
1882 P	42	65	155	415	750	125	340	900
1882 CC	83	95	165	300	470	125	270	600
1882 O	37	60	140	375	575	100	265	700
1882 S	54	80	130	220	395	100	200	450
1883 P	42	65	150	400	650	120	330	825
1883 CC	81	95	160	285	500	125	265	575
1883 O	35	55	120	200	375	90	200	425
1883 S	330	530	1175	2550	4625	1125	2500	7950
1884 P	47	75	165	465	750	170	425	1000
1884 CC	81	95	160	285	475	125	265	575
1884 O	35	55	120	200	335	90	200	425
1884 S	975	2175	4000	11125	32500	5000	25000	40000
1885 P	35	55	130	205	355	95	200	415
1885 CC	160	200	280	490	825	185	445	880
1885 O	35	55	120	200	335	90	200	425
1885 S	83	150	375	940	1475	305	800	1925
1886 P	36	55	100	180	320	85	180	400
1886 O	250	510	1000	2725	6000	1500	3550	12250
1886 S	86	150	320	775	1150	270	575	1350
1887/6 P	60	90	140	230	575	140	285	610
1887 P	36	55	105	175	345	85	180	400
1887 O	44	75	230	690	1075	205	570	1600
1887 S	55	90	300	800	1225	275	525	1350

The NSDR PRICING GUIDE is published quarterly as an insert to the National Silver Dollar Roundtable Journal. Prices in this guide reflect the average price NSDR member dealers will pay for uncirculated coins. Member dealers are listed on Page IV of this guide. Copyright 1984. Reprint of any part of this guide without written permission is expressly forbidden by law.

First NSDR Journal Quarterly Pricing Guide
(Courtesy of National Silver Dollar Roundtable Journal)

Their leadership has been fundamental in growth and change annually in the entire numismatic community. The NSDR is an organization that takes a problem and creates a solution. We are constantly fine tuning our organization with the goal of making silver dollars and numismatics good entities through experience, knowledge and education.

For those who are curious (or wish to reminisce), here is a copy of the lead page of one of these innovative Pricing Guides.

Al: When we started the NSDR, we were not thinking in terms of "we want the biggest" etc., for we knew that there was a point when perhaps our membership would be saturated. So far that has not happened and I truly believe now it never will be. Over the last decade, some fine new Silver Dollar dealers have come upon the scene who started out as collectors and part-time dealers and developed a love and knowledge for the "Cartwheel" as I did back in 1972 when I specialized in Indian cents and Lincoln cents. It was then I met John Love who showed me that besides being "Big & Beautiful," the Morgan dollar was grossly underrated as a collector/investor coin. We talked for many hours about the Silver Dollar at a show in the Washington, DC area when the coin market was again in a slump. For many shows following, I could always be found at John Love and Wayne Miller's table. My learning process had begun.

We don't all start out as Silver Dollar dealers, but if you go to a major show, I would venture to say that over 70% of all dealers' tables will display some U.S. Silver Dollars. I, with nearly twenty years in Silver Dollars, enjoyed meeting these dealers and little by little, show after show, their dollar inventory and knowledge of the coin grew.

This is one of the reasons, I feel, that our organization will endure and still grow. As these newer dealers proliferate, so should our membership. Unfortunately, many dealers think our organization is for the elite dollar dealer and that is simply not so. I hope by writing this chapter on the NSDR, it will give the reader a better insight into the organization and from a personal view, from one who has been with the organization from its inception.

We in the NSDR like to think we are here to serve the collector and for those of you who happen to be at any of the shows or conventions that we're attending, please feel free to stop by and chat or if you want to, find out more about the NSDR. We will probably have a seminar at that particular show and we look forward to meeting with you.

I want to thank Mr. Highfill for allowing me to join him for this chapter in his book and I wish him success. I just wanted to put my thoughts on paper where I know a dollar enthusiast, be he collector or simply a novice in the field of Silver Dollars, will read and I hope enjoy and understand all of our members' love for the "King of Coins," the Silver Dollar.

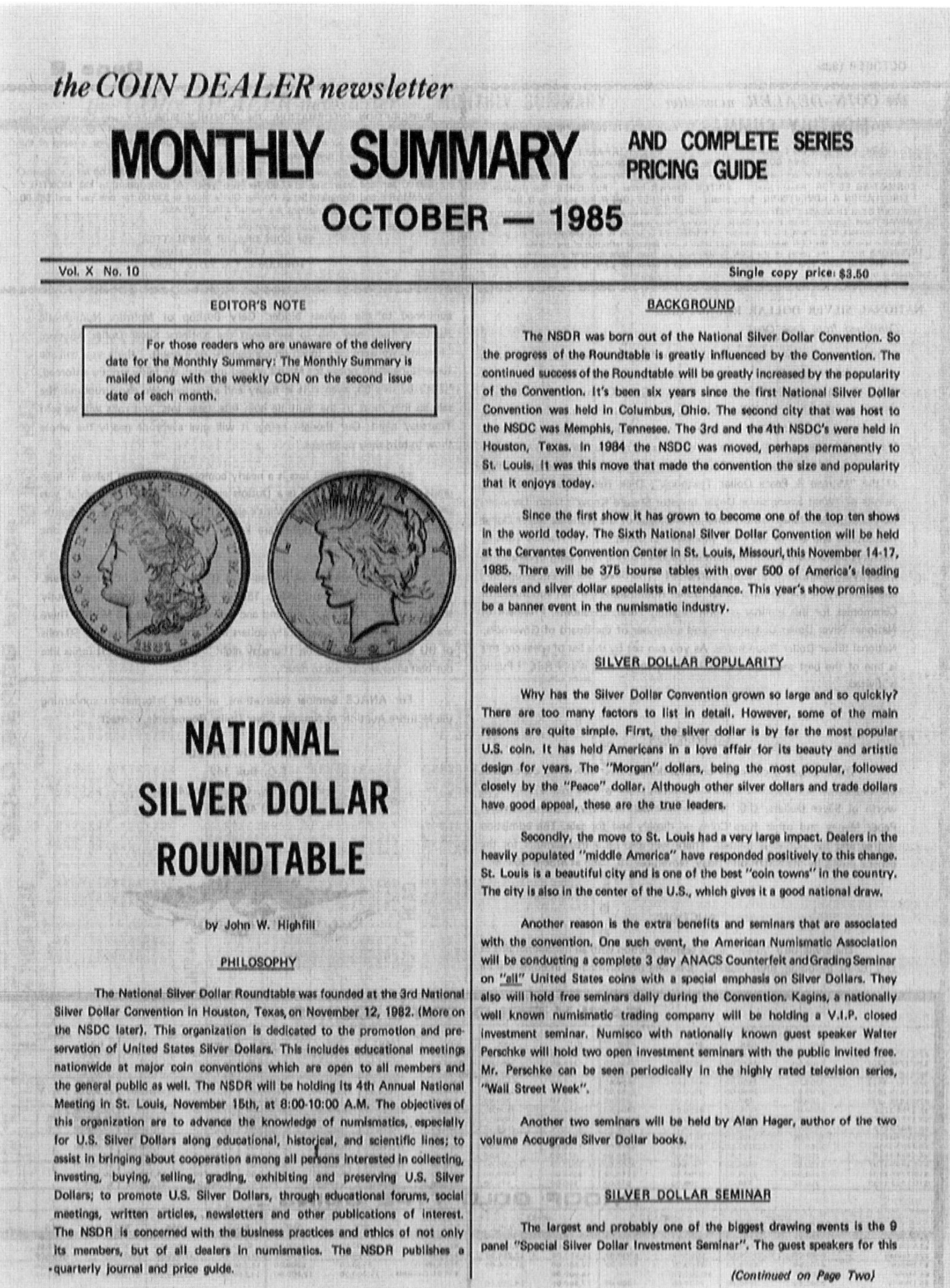

the COIN DEALER newsletter

MONTHLY SUMMARY AND COMPLETE SERIES PRICING GUIDE

OCTOBER — 1985

Vol. X No. 10 — Single copy price: $3.50

EDITOR'S NOTE

For those readers who are unaware of the delivery date for the Monthly Summary: The Monthly Summary is mailed along with the weekly CDN on the second issue date of each month.

NATIONAL SILVER DOLLAR ROUNDTABLE

by John W. Highfill

PHILOSOPHY

The National Silver Dollar Roundtable was founded at the 3rd National Silver Dollar Convention in Houston, Texas, on November 12, 1982. (More on the NSDC later). This organization is dedicated to the promotion and preservation of United States Silver Dollars. This includes educational meetings nationwide at major coin conventions which are open to all members and the general public as well. The NSDR will be holding its 4th Annual National Meeting in St. Louis, November 15th, at 8:00-10:00 A.M. The objectives of this organization are to advance the knowledge of numismatics, especially for U.S. Silver Dollars along educational, historical, and scientific lines; to assist in bringing about cooperation among all persons interested in collecting, investing, buying, selling, grading, exhibiting and preserving U.S. Silver Dollars; to promote U.S. Silver Dollars, through educational forums, social meetings, written articles, newsletters and other publications of interest. The NSDR is concerned with the business practices and ethics of not only its members, but of all dealers in numismatics. The NSDR publishes a quarterly journal and price guide.

BACKGROUND

The NSDR was born out of the National Silver Dollar Convention. So the progress of the Roundtable is greatly influenced by the Convention. The continued success of the Roundtable will be greatly increased by the popularity of the Convention. It's been six years since the first National Silver Dollar Convention was held in Columbus, Ohio. The second city that was host to the NSDC was Memphis, Tennesee. The 3rd and the 4th NSDC's were held in Houston, Texas. In 1984 the NSDC was moved, perhaps permanently to St. Louis. It was this move that made the convention the size and popularity that it enjoys today.

Since the first show it has grown to become one of the top ten shows in the world today. The Sixth National Silver Dollar Convention will be held at the Cervantes Convention Center in St. Louis, Missouri, this November 14-17, 1985. There will be 375 bourse tables with over 500 of America's leading dealers and silver dollar specialists in attendance. This year's show promises to be a banner event in the numismatic industry.

SILVER DOLLAR POPULARITY

Why has the Silver Dollar Convention grown so large and so quickly? There are too many factors to list in detail. However, some of the main reasons are quite simple. First, the silver dollar is by far the most popular U.S. coin. It has held Americans in a love affair for its beauty and artistic design for years. The "Morgan" dollars, being the most popular, followed closely by the "Peace" dollar. Although other silver dollars and trade dollars have good appeal, these are the true leaders.

Secondly, the move to St. Louis had a very large impact. Dealers in the heavily populated "middle America" have responded positively to this change. St. Louis is a beautiful city and is one of the best "coin towns" in the country. The city is also in the center of the U.S., which gives it a good national draw.

Another reason is the extra benefits and seminars that are associated with the convention. One such event, the American Numismatic Association will be conducting a complete 3 day ANACS Counterfeit and Grading Seminar on "all" United States coins with a special emphasis on Silver Dollars. They also will hold free seminars daily during the Convention. Kagins, a nationally well known numismatic trading company will be holding a V.I.P. closed investment seminar. Numisco with nationally known guest speaker Walter Perschke will hold two open investment seminars with the public invited free. Mr. Perschke can be seen periodically in the highly rated television series, "Wall Street Week".

Another two seminars will be held by Alan Hager, author of the two volume Accugrade Silver Dollar books.

SILVER DOLLAR SEMINAR

The largest and probably one of the biggest drawing events is the 9 panel "Special Silver Dollar Investment Seminar". The guest speakers for this

(Continued on Page Two)

CDN article by John W. Highfill on the National Silver Dollar Roundtable in their Monthly Summary, October 1985 (Courtesy of CDN, Torrance, California)

NSDR Officers and Awards

The National Silver Dollar Roundtable was founded in Houston, Texas, at the Third National Silver Dollar Convention on November 12, 1982. The NSDR was incorporated under the laws of the state of California in the same initial time frame.

The current slate of officers include:

President:	**Leon E. Hendrickson**
Vice-President:	**Alfred E. Johnbrier**
Secretary:	**Leroy Van Allen**
Treasurer:	**Joann M. Johnbrier**
Immediate Past President:	**John W. Highfill**
Past President:	**Dean Tavenner**
Past President:	**Joe Buzanowski**

The NSDR Board of Governors and their terms in office (each member is serving a 3 year term):

John W. Dannreuther:	1988-1991
Steele Eunson:	1989-1992
Robert T. McIntire:	1988-1991
Louie Moreno, Jr.:	1988-1991
Fred Weinberg:	1989-1990

During 1990, it was proposed, voted upon and approved by the membership of the NSDR to add 3 more members to the Board of Governors of the NSDR beginning in 1991. The amendment to the NSDR Constitution was voted in and formally approved by the current Board of Governors during their June 1, 1990 meeting at Long Beach, California. These three new Board members were duly elected to expand the scope and effectiveness of the NSDR.

Mark L. Mendelson:	1990-1993
Mark S. Yaffe:	1990-1993
Brian D. Yutzy:	1990-1993
Edward E. Fritz, Jr.:	1991-1994
Paul E. Lambert:	1991-1994
Jack R. Lee:	1991-1994
Robert T. McIntire:	1991-1994

The appointed officers of the NSDR include:

Mike Faraone:	Co-Editor of the NSDR Journal
John W. Highfill	NSDR Archives Custodian
Robert T. McIntire:	Co-Editor and Publisher of the NSDR Journal
Edward Pereira:	Sergeant-At-Arms

The coveted "Man of the Year Award" is presented as a symbol of NSDR excellence each year to the most deserving Knight. John W. Highfill was honored as the first recipient of the coveted NSDR Man of the Year Award. The past recipients of this award include:

1985: John W. Highfill - Broken Arrow, Oklahoma
1986: Alfred E. Johnbrier - Bowie, Maryland
1987: John "Steele" Eunson - Monroe, Louisiana (co-winner)
1987: Leroy Van Allen - Sidney, Ohio (co-winner)
1988: Leon E. Hendrickson - Winchester, Indiana
1989: John W. Dannreuther - Memphis, Tennessee
1990: Robert T. McIntire - Jacksonville, Arkansas
1991: Randy Campbell-Columbus, Ohio

Board of Governor Louie Moreno, Jr., with past President Dean Tavenner. (Courtesy of Oklahoma Federated Gold and Numismatics, Inc.)

Man of the Year Award, National Silver Dollar Roundtable. (Courtesy of National Silver Dollar Roundtable archives)

"Man of the Year" awards went in 1988 to two distinguished members of the NSDR. They were left to right: Leroy Van Allen and Steele Eunson. Presenting the award is John W. Highfill, the first recipient of this award in 1985 and President of NSDR at the time. (Courtesy of Marlene Highfill, NSDR Life Member #61)

COIN WORLD, Wednesday, February 26, 1986 7

World minors to appear in Chicago auction

Highfill wins NSDR award

John Highfill

Why You Should Buy Obsolete Brilliant Uncirculated World Gold Coins

Coin World editorial depicting John W. Highfill as the recipient of the NSDR Man of the Year award (Courtesy of Coin World, Sidney, Ohio)

Lifetime Achievement Award, National Silver Dollar Roundtable, Harlan White, 1991 recipient (Courtesy of Shirley White, Old Coin Shop, San Diego, California)

The NSDR Lifetime Achievement Award was first presented in 1989. This, the highest NSDR award, is presented to rare individuals who have contributed a lifetime of effort to the success of the silver dollar industry. These persons have helped the industry grow and have shown tremendous appreciation for silver dollars. The persons selected are to be considered "Landmarks" in the industry. The award winners to date are:

1989: Leon E. Hendrickson — Winchester, Indiana
1990: John B. Love, Sr., — Cut Bank, Montana
1991: Harlan White — San Diego, California

John B. Love receiving NSDR Lifetime Achievement Award from NSDR President John W. Highfill at Ruth's Chris Steak House, St. Louis, Missouri on November 7, 1990

Paul Rynearson of Dr. Paul Rynearson, Malibu, Calif.

Dean Schmidt of Dean Schmidt Rare Coin, Lawrence, Kan.

Jewelry, Cut Bank, Mont.

Ron Pettit of Ron's Coins, Cedar Rapids, Iowa.

Joel Rettew of Rare Coin Galleries,

ization, is available free of charge from Koppenhaver at P.O. Box 430, Van Nuys, Calif. 91408; telephone (818) 781-1764.

Silver dollar dealers recognized with awards

A pair of awards were presented by the National Silver Dollar Roundtable during the National Silver Dollar Convention, held Nov. 29-Dec. 3 in St. Louis.

Memphis dealer John Dannreuther was named as the organization's man of the year in voting by members of the NSDR. Primarily a wholesaler, Dannreuther specializes in high-quality U.S. certified coins.

The first Lifetime Achievement Award was presented to Leon Hendrickson of Silvertowne in Winchester, Ind.

Hendrickson was chosen for the honor by the officers and board of governors of the NSDR. The Lifetime Achievement Award was created to "honor someone who has spent a long time in the business and contributed to the industry," said Silver Dollar Convention chairman John Highfill.

"There were probably a dozen guys who could have gotten the award, but Leon really deserved it," Highfill remarked. "He got a big standing ovation when the award was presented. It was really great."

The awards were given during the NSDR dinner. More than 150 dealers are listed as members of the organzation, which is "dedicated to promoting silver dollars" and "advancing the knowledge of numismatics, especially for U.S. silver dollars, along educational, historical and scientific lines."

A second dinner was held during the convention, which has developed a reputation for featuring big-name bands of the 1960s and 1970s as post-dinner entertainment.

The Rascals appeared at the second dinner, and Highfill reported that the Turtles will be the main attraction at the National Gold Convention dinner. That show will be held May 10-13, 1990 in St. Louis.

Leon Hendrickson of SilverTowne, left, was presented with the first Lifetime Achievement Award bestowed by the National Silver Dollar Roundtable. John Highfill made the presentation at the National Silver Dollar Convention St. Louis.

TIES & CO.

The Symbol of . . . .

Numismatic News Coverage of Leon Hendrickson receiving the first Lifetime Achievement Award from President John W. Highfill on November 29, 1989 at Sheraton, St. Louis Hotel. (Courtesy of National Silver Dollar Roundtable archives)

Past NSDR Presidents:

Joe Buzanowski:	1982-1984
Dean Tavenner:	1984-1986
John W. Highfill:	1986-1988
John W. Highfill:	1988-1990*

* Two terms (maximum permitted)

Note: All past presidents are automatically entitled to become lifetime members of the Board of Governors.

National Silver Dollar Roundtable past presidents Dean Tavenner and John Highfill (Courtesy of National Silver Dollar Roundtable archives)

NSDR Committees

Accounting — In charge of acceptance and disbursement of all NSDR funds, as well as all reports and budgets. Victor Chow, Accountant, handles all of the NSDR accounting duties.

Advertising — In charge of all advertising campaigns carried out by the NSDR. Robert T. McIntire chairs this committee with the assistance of John W. Highfill and Al E. Johnbrier.

Blazers, Patches and Pins — In charge of issuing all blazers, patches and pins to the appropriate NSDR members. Al Johnbrier heads this committee assisted by Robert McIntire.

Breakfast Meetings — In charge of all preparations, dates, notifications and activities associated with the NSDR breakfast meetings. The chairman of this committee is Al Johnbrier, who is aided by members Steele Eunson, John Highfill, Robert McIntire and Louie Moreno, Jr.

Counsel — Attorney in charge of all legal matters pertaining to the NSDR. Bill Olson is the NSDR attorney.

Dollar Day Bourse — In charge of all planning, table assignments, etc., associated with **Dollar Day** held in conjunction with the NSDC. John Highfill chairs this committee with help from Steele Eunson and Louie Moreno, Jr.

Dollar Day Bourse Advisors — Advisors to the **Dollar Day** Bourse committee providing any advisory level decisions and information for **Dollar Day** activities. Marlene Highfill is the Co-chairman for this committee with the able assistance of Patti Moreno.

Eagle Distribution — In charge of distribution of the Eagle coinage to the NSDR members. Leroy Van Allen leads this activity with the assistance of Leon Hendrickson and Al Johnbrier.

Education — In charge of all educational activities including educational seminars conducted at many major conventions including ANA, Central States, FUN, Long Beach and NSDC. Steele Eunson leads the education committee with help from John Dannreuther, Leon Hendrickson, John Highfill and Al Johnbrier.

Ethics and Arbitration — In charge of all ethics related issues and arbitration of all matters brought before the committee for that purpose. Steele Eunson chairs this important committee with members John Dannreuther, Leon Hendrickson, Louie Moreno, Jr., Leroy Van Allen and Fred Weinberg. The alternate chairman is Leon Hendrickson.

Grading Standards and Listing — In charge of issuing the grading standards acceptable to the NSDR and its members, including the listing of those standards. Chairman is Robert McIntire serving with alternate chairman Steele Eunson. Members include Leon Hendrickson, John Highfill and Fred Weinberg.

ICTA Board Representative — The NSDR member(s) selected to represent the NSDR on the ICTA Board. Al Johnbrier serves the NSDR as the ICTA Board Representative with Robert McIntire as Co-Representative.

Insurance — In charge of all insurance matters involving the NSDR as the NSDR insurance company. Janet L. Horenberg of Horenberg Insurance Services, Incorporated provides insurance for the NSDR.

Journal — In charge of all activities associated with the preparation and publication of the NSDR Journal. Mike Faraone and Robert McIntire are co-editors and publishers of the NSDR Journal.

Membership Certificates and Cards — In charge of the membership rolls, dues, cards and certificates. Marlene Highfill heads this committee with help from additional members John Highfill and Leroy Van Allen.

NSDR Banner — In charge of the NSDR banner. Robert McIntire is chairman assisted by Al Johnbrier.

Public Relations — In charge of all outgoing publicity, statements of position on any question or event, and presentations geared to enhance the stature and responsibility of the NSDR. Al Johnbrier heads this committee with the assistance of John Dannreuther and John Highfill.

Budget Committee — In charge of the Annual NSDR budget and the expenditures against that budget. Al Johnbrier heads this committee with members John Dannreuther, Steele Eunson, Robert McIntire, Leon Hendrickson, Leroy Van Allen and Fred Weinberg.

Accreditation Committee — In charge of checking the application of all proposed NSDR members before the membership vote. Al Johnbrier is chairman aided by John Dannreuther, Leon Hendrickson, Leroy Van Allen, Fred Weinberg and Mark L. Mendelson.

Legal and Insurance Committee — In charge of determining the levels and types of insurance to be carried by the organization, as well as the requirement for legal assistance. John Highfill is chairman with members John Dannreuther, Al Johnbrier, Leon Hendrickson and Leroy Van Allen.

Dealer Certification and Policies — In charge of certifying member-dealers and determining the policies of the NSDR to be imposed upon its members. John Highfill is the chairman with the assistance of members Al Johnbrier, Louie Moreno, Jr., Leroy Van Allen and Fred Weinberg.

NSDR Archives Custodian — John W. Highfill

The Sergeant-At-Arms is Edward Pereira.

Membership

The National Silver Dollar Roundtable, as a non-profit educational organization, invites and welcomes to membership all worthy persons eighteen years of age and older. There are four levels of membership available within the NSDR. These include Associate Members, Life Associate Members, Regular Members and Life Members. At the present time, membership in the NSDR does not provide for club or organization memberships. All members are enrolled as individuals.

The Life Member is a special part of the NSDR. This category of membership was offered beginning in the summer of 1984. These persons are presented with a certificate showing the date and Life Member number.

The requirements of becoming a Life Member are two-fold. One is to be approved by the current Board of Governors as a candidate together with an initial annual membership fee of $250. The second is that a candidate must have been a member of the NSDR for at least one year. Then he must be approved again by the current Board of Governors, and pay a one-time fee of $1,750. After these requirements are fulfilled, the dealer will become a Lifetime Member of the NSDR. John W. Highfill was not only the first Life Member, he was awarded that status by the original officers and the Board of Governors.

A bronze and wooden plaque was presented to Mr. Highfill as Life Member number one in August 1984. This 9" by 7" wall plaque features the NSDR logo in antiqued brass placed on a solid walnut base with an engraved brass plate displaying the organization and life member information. The 2 1/2" logo itself is a work of art with a raised map of the United States and an engraved and darkened NSDR, both superimposed on a background of the 1878 Morgan dollar. This fine piece was created by Pressed Metal Products located in Vancouver, British Columbia, Canada. Bronze membership cards are provided to NSDR life members in addition to the life member plaque.

Newly elected Board of Governors for the 1991-1994 term. (L to R) Paul E. Lambert, Robert T. McIntire, Jack R. Lee, Edward E. Fritz, Jr.

THE NATIONAL SILVER DOLLAR ROUNDTABLE

WOULD LIKE TO RECOGNIZE:

John Highfill

AS A REGULAR MEMBER IN GOOD STANDING. Membership # M-1

The objectives of the N.S.D.R. are to advance the knowledge of numismatics, especially for U.S. Silver Dollars along educational, historical, and scientific lines, to assist in bringing about cooperation among all persons interested in collecting, investing, buying selling, grading, exhibiting and preserving U.S. Silver Dollars, to promote U.S. Silver Dollars through educational forums, social meetings, written articles, newsletters and other publications of interest.

NSDR

1878

Leroy Van Allen
Secretary

Joe Buczanowski
President

November 12, 1982
Date

NSDR Membership #1 presented to John W. Highfill by the original officers and elected Board of Governors, November 12, 1982

NSDR

1878

THE NATIONAL SILVER DOLLAR ROUNDTABLE

LIFE MEMBER

HAS BEEN ASSIGNED LIFE MEMBERSHIP NUMBER

BY THE BOARD OF GOVERNORS

OF THE

THE NATIONAL SILVER DOLLAR ROUNDTABLE

Date

President

Secretary

The NSDR Life Member Certificate issued to Life Members
(Courtesy of National Silver Dollar Roundtable archives)

NSDR Membership Card
(Courtesy of National Silver Dollar Roundtable Archives)

NSDR Life Member Plaque LM #1, John W. Highfill
(Courtesy of Press Metals, Vancouver, B.C., Canada)

NSDR Brass Life Member Card
(Courtesy of National Silver Dollar Roundtable Archives)

The NSDR Membership Directory (Courtesy of Robert T. McIntire, NSDR Journal Publisher)

The dealer membership directory gives everyone the opportunity to be associated with the NSDR as it is published a number of times each year. The coming membership directories will include an opening statement with the following essence.

Inclusion in the NSDR Membership Directory is not an endorsement of the dealer, but a statement of fact that the dealer, as a prerequisite for membership, has agreed to abide by the Code of Ethics. NSDR cannot assume responsibility for commercial transactions entered into with its members at any time.

Brass Board of Governors Card
(Courtesy of National Silver Dollar Roundtable Archives)

The NSDR Logo

This would be a good time to briefly relate the history of the NSDR logo. The official logo was adapted on February 25, 1983, at the American Numismatic Association Mid-Winter convention in Tucson, Arizona. There were about 35 dealers present at the NSDR meeting on that date who voted enthusiastically in favor of the logo. After their approval, the logo design was sent to the entire membership who also acknowledged their approval.

The logo previously described featured the Morgan dollar with logo and outline U.S. map in order to give the group recognition and also identify individual members to the consuming public. The logo has been used often in advertising pieces published by NSDR members.

There has been much discussion and debate on the uses and intended uses of the National Silver Dollar Roundtable Logo. The initial intent was to provide NSDR members with a distinguishing logo that would identify them as a member of the NSDR, and as such, subject to the code of ethics created by this organization. Over time, there were questions of corporate use of the NSDR logo. It has been determined by the board that a corporation can use the NSDR logo if the majority of the stock owners are NSDR members. The board is currently reviewing the question of the return of logo use to the individual members only. Individual use only will probably be the result of that review.

NSDR Logo
(Courtesy of National Silver Dollar Roundtable archives)

National Silver Dollar Roundtable Corporate Seal of gold leaf foil.
(Courtesy of National Silver Dollar Roundtable archives)

Silver dollar dealers adopt NSDR logo

Reprinted from *COIN WORLD*, Wednesday, March 16, 1983

Approximately 35 dealers attending the National Silver Dollar Roundtable's fifth meeting Feb. 25 during the American Numismatic Association MidWinter convention in Tucson, Ariz., adopted an official logo for the new national organization.

The logo, an outline map of the continental United States containing the organization's initials superimposed over a Morgan silver dollar, is intended to give the group recognition and also identify individual members to the consuming public.

"We hope our members will use this logo in their advertising," said Dean Tavenner, NSDR vice president who chaired the session.

Nearly a third of the dealers attending the Tucson meeting were prospective members.

NSDR was formed during the Third National Silver Dollar Convention in Houston in mid-November. At that time 68 dealers pledged $25 each in start-up dues.

The idea of forming such a group grew out of a session organized by Joseph Buzanowski and Ken Bressett, director of ANA's Certification Service, to allow dealers an opportunity to air their grievances about ANACS grading standards.

ANACS takes the stand that strike has no influence on a coin's grade. Many silver dollar dealers believe strike should be a factor in grading and that a weakly struck coin cannot grade Mint State 65.

Buzanowski was later elected first president of the National Silver Dollar Roundtable.

Tavenner, noting new faces among those attending the Tucson meeting, said that the organization has been busy since its formative days in Houston. He cited his meeting with ANACS staff in Colorado Springs, Colo., and a membership meeting during the Florida United Numismatists convention in Orlando in mid-January at which a board of governors was elected. The board includes elected officers Buzanowski, Tavenner, and Secretary-Treasurer Al Johnbrier as well as Roger Bryan, Randy Campbell, John Highfill, Kurt Krueger, Randall Pollock and Leroy Van Allen.

Tavenner listed a number of goals and projects he expects the organization to be involved in soon. A primary goal he said will be to resolve problems with regard to grading. Other immediate goals include promotion of silver dollars as investments, and setting membership standards.

"We want to make this a new, viable organization. We want your ideas," he told those attending the meeting.

One idea for a NSDR project which drew discussion is that of NSDR sponsoring silver dollar grading sets. As explained by Tavenner, such sets would likely include representative dates with grading of coins included agreed upon by ANACS and NSDR. A number of dealers in attendance described such sets as entry tools for new collectors and a way of promoting interest in the hobby.

Tavenner reported that the organization's constitution and bylaws, which are being prepared by Van Allen, will be presented to the membership for a vote at NSDR's next meeting which is scheduled during the Central States Numismatic Society's April convention in Dearborn, Mich.

"We're looking for everything to come together at Central States," Tavenner said.

5

Official adoption of the NSDR Logo by the membership body in March of 1983
(Courtesy of Coin World, Sidney, Ohio)

Official NSDR memorabilia patches, pins, pocket holders, name badges, lapel pins (old model and new), playing cards and brass Life Membership card.
(Courtesy of Oklahoma Federated Gold and Numismatics, Inc., Broken Arrow, Oklahoma)

Member

NSDR

National Silver
Dollar Roundtable

NSDR adhesive sticker used on the 7" x 44" Convention Dealer Bourse Table signs (Courtesy of National Silver Dollar Roundtable archives)

NSDR Logo lapel pins.
(Courtesy of Roger P. Bryan, Gainesville, Florida)

Official NSDR Patch used for officers' blazers.
(Courtesy of Al Johnbrier, Bowie, Maryland)

The logo patch appeared on the first official NSDR royal blue blazers. This combination was picked to provide a garment that would stand out but not be considered gaudy or "carnival" in style. The officers and Board members have been very pleased with the choice of color and presentation for the NSDR blazer. As the years passed, the blazer has remained the same, although a special plastic pocket insert with the gray and black logo patch on it is used by the NSDR officers and board members. This gives the officers and the board members versatility to use the mobile plastic pocket logo not only with the blue official NSDR jacket, but with any shirt or coat that they are wearing at the time.

A National Silver Dollar Roundtable banner was prepared by Robert T. McIntire for display at all major shows and conventions. The NSDR logo was placed on banner material that allowed the banner to be rolled up when not in use and displayed as needed for all NSDR purposes.

The lead original trial piece of the NSDR logo used on the Life Member plaques was auctioned on November 10-13, 1988, in St. Louis at the Ninth National Silver Dollar Convention. It was listed as Lot #2195, and was auctioned by McIntire Numismatic Auctions of Jacksonville, Arkansas. This piece was donated by Pressed Medals of Vancouver, Canada and was purchased by Mr. Highfill for his personal collection.

Plastic pocket insert used to identify officers.
(Courtesy of John W. Highfill)

NSDR LOGO

NATIONAL SILVER DOLLAR ROUNDTABLE DIE TRIAL PIECE

2195. National Silver Dollar Roundtable Die Trial Piece. A uniface impression in gray soft metal. This is the trial piece for the National Silver Dollar Roundtable Logo. An uneven size, approx. 79 mm diameter. The design is a likeness of the Morgan Dollar obverse with the United States map outline overlayed. (PHOTO)

NSDR Lead Logo Original Trial Piece — Lot #2195
(Courtesy of McIntire Numismatic Auctions, National Silver Dollar Roundtable, and the John W. Highfill Collection)

Special Programs, Offerings, NSDR Advertising and Recognition

The NSDR "donated" coinage auctions have provided an activity filled with fun and enjoyment for all. The NSDR members provided approximately 100 lots of various coins (usually silver dollars) to be auctioned off to the highest bidder in an auction held in conjunction with **Dollar Day**. This event has gathered approximately $1000 for the NSDR while providing an event filled with enjoyment for all. This contribution is added to the treasury of the NSDR.

The National Silver Dollar Roundtable commemorative medallions in one ounce silver or one ounce gold are both very attractive and desirable among NSDR members and collectors alike. The Logo is proudly displayed on the obverse with the National Silver Dollar Roundtable engraved on the reverse. These medallions were made available in 1990 by the NSDR and were very popular. The member's NSDR membership number is engraved in the edge of the one ounce gold medallions. These are limited editions of only one coin for each NSDR member.

The die trial rounds were also auctioned at the Ninth National Silver Dollar Convention. They were listed as Lot #2877, and were auctioned by McIntire Numismatic Auctions of Jacksonville, Arkansas. John W. Highfill was also successful in obtaining these heritage-rich mementos and enjoys them in his private collection today.

NSDR Medallion die trials
Lot #2877
(Courtesy of Silver Towne Mint, McIntire Numismatic Auctions, and John W. Highfill)

Original boxes and gold and silver one ounce NSDR medallions.
Also pictured is a NSDR lapel pin.
(Courtesy of John W. Highfill)

Enameled NSDR one ounce silver medallion with the map of the United States and the NSDR highlighted in black.
(Courtesy of Patti Moreno, Moreno Valley, California)

NSDR one ounce silver medallions in .999 Pure Silver
(35 MM in diameter)
Courtesy of Leon E. Hendrickson, Silver Towne, Winchester, Indiana

the
NATIONAL
SILVER
DOLLAR
ROUNDTABLE
Proudly presents....

the NSDR
COMMEMORATIVE MEDALLION
in one ounce silver or one ounce gold!

Available from

OKLAHOMA FEDERATED
GOLD NUMISMATIC, INC.
P.O. Box 25
Broken Arrow, OK 74013
(918) 451-0665

SILVER TOWNE
P.O. Box 424
Winchester, IN 47394
(317) 584-7481

NSDR brochure advertising the official one ounce gold and silver medallions.
(Courtesy of Silver Towne, Winchester, Indiana)

The NSDR is an organizing member of the American Numismatic Association's ANA 91 Club, and continues to offer its support to the numismatic industry. The ANA 91 Club was held in Chicago in conjunction with the 100th anniversary of the American Numismatic Association. The event was celebrated from August 13-18, 1991 in Chicago, Illinois.

The NSDR advertises continuously in the numismatic trades. The NSDR places full page ads throughout the year in both *Numismatic News* and *Coin World*. The full page ads run in both publications 4 times a year, and these ads usually list the NSDR membership role. Special, unusual and interesting theme advertisements appear from time to time such as the one shown here.

NATIONAL SILVER DOLLAR

Brings You Car Rental Savings Worldwide.

Now you can save money on car rentals in over 100 countries and territories around the world thanks to a special arrangement between your organization and National Car Rental. And these savings apply to both business and pleasure trips. The recap number on the identification materials below will insure that you receive your special savings. Simply attach one of the stickers to your credit card, or keep the convenient I.D. card handy, and present it when you rent from National.

We feature GM cars like this Pontiac Grand Am.

National Car Rental.
National Silver Dollar
Recap No. 5503911

National Car Rental.
National Silver Dollar
Recap No. 5503911

National Rent-A-Car Corporate Program #5503911 for NSDR members.
(Courtesy of the National Silver Dollar Roundtable archives)

NATIONAL
SILVER DOLLAR ROUND TABLE

The National Silver Dollar Roundtable, a non-profit educational organization, invites and welcomes to membership all worthy persons eighteen years of age and older.
The National Silver Dollar Roundtable is dedicated to promoting United States Silver Dollars. The objective of the organization is to advance the knowledge of numismatics, especially for U.S. Silver Dollars, along educational, historical and scientific lines. NSDR assists in bringing about cooperation among all persons interested in collecting, buying, selling, grading, exhibiting and preserving U.S. Silver Dollars, through educational forums, social meetings, written articles, newsletters and other publications of interest.

Write for a FREE N.S.D.R. Member Dealer Directory:
N.S.D.R. Secretary
P.O. Box 196
Sidney, OH 45365
(513) 492-7718

N.S.D.R. COIN SHOW
6th ANNUAL SILVER DOLLAR DAY
Oct. 30, 1991 - 10 a.m.-4 p.m.
Tampa Convention Center
333 South Franklin St., Tampa, FL
FREE ADMISSION

N.S.D.R. Quarterly Journal
1 Year Subscription: $20.00

Write:
Mike Faraone, Editor
9025 McConnell St.
Laughlin AFB, TX 78843

Proof "Theme" NSDR Ad
(Courtesy of the Robert T. McIntire, Publisher and Co-Editor NSDR Journal, Jacksonville, Arkansas)

Krause Publications, publisher of such numismatic periodicals as Numismatic News, World Coin News, Coins Magazine, Bank Note Reported and Coin Prices, presented the NSDR with a 1989 Customer Service Award. This award was presented in recognition of outstanding service to customers during the 1988 calendar year. The award further stated that the NSDR has conducted its business in conformity with the rigorous ethical standards required by the advertising policies of the family of Krause Publications.

Another benefit and service of the NSDR is membership car rental programs. The NSDR car rental program is a special part of being a member of this progressive organization. This special program was established for NSDR regular and life members. The Alamo Rent-A-Car agency was the first to offer a special deal under Alamo's Association Membership Program. This program provides a special nationwide guaranteed rate structure for members. This program is advertised in the NSDR Quarterly Journal and explains further enhancements and offerings for the program. The Alamo Association Membership program I.D. card #93232 is exclusively reserved for all of the NSDR members and their associates.

The Hertz Discount Card has been added to provide additional selection and versatility. The 4,500 nationwide locations provide V.I.P. discounts on leisure and business travel, desk toll-free number, many models, and 24 hour emergency road service. The Hertz I.D. #200927 is exclusively reserved for all NSDR members and their associates.

National Car Rental is also a part of the NSDR special rental program with locations nationwide and a wide selection of vehicles and packages. The National I.D. #5503911 is exclusively reserved for all of the NSDR members and their associates.

The NSDR Code of Ethics

The National Silver Dollar Roundtable adopted a strict and high Code of Ethics early in the life of the organization. Here is a reprint of that Code of Ethics.

I recognize my obligations as a professional dealer in silver dollars towards the numismatic collectors of the public and towards fellow coin dealers it is my desire and intention to be at all times worthy of the trust, confidence, and respect of those I deal with in the numismatic industry. I therefore make the following pledges:

In my dealings I pledge:

*To at all times use a professional conduct and approach in business dealings.

* To provide accurate and timely advice on silver dollars to my customers to the best of my ability.

*To sell coins at fair and reasonable prices.

* To buy coins at fair prices with due allowance for buyer's risks and prevailing market conditions.

* To refrain from advertising, publishing, or broadcasting in a misleading or false manner any of my goods, prices, or services or those of a competitor.

*To refrain from knowingly dealing in counterfeit, altered, or stolen coins.

In my dealings with fellow members of this organization I pledge:

* To refrain from voluntary public expression of adverse criticism or false statements of other members or their merchandise and services.

* To recognize and respect my own contracts and undertakings and those of fellow members.

* To generally cooperate towards the promotion and betterment of the silver dollar industry.

I have read and agree to abide by and support the Constitution and By-Laws of the National Silver Dollar Roundtable.

ALAMO ASSOCIATION MEMBER PROGRAM

Alamo offers you great savings on car rentals! Now enjoy **guaranteed flat rates nationwide.**

Car Category	Daily Rate* Nationwide
Chevy Chevette Economy	$28
Chevy Cavalier Compact	$30
Pontiac Grand Am Mid Size	$32
Oldsmobile Cutlass Ciera Full Size	$34
Chevy Celebrity Wagon Mid Size Wagon	$34
Buick Park Avenue Luxury	$35

Florida Daily Rates are Lower

*Four door cars add $2.00 to daily rate; $14.00 to weekly rate. Prices subject to change without notice. Similar cars may be substituted. These basic rules are subject to the terms, conditions and charges listed on the back. **Seasonal surcharges may apply.**

Alamo features fine General Motors cars such as the Buick Park Avenue and Pontiac Grand Am.

DETACH MEMBERSHIP CARD HERE

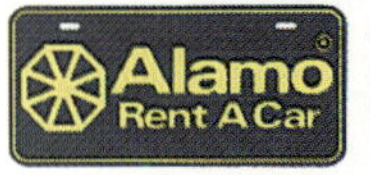

ASSOCIATION MEMBERSHIP PROGRAM I.D. CARD

Request Plan "BY" 93232
NATIONAL SILVER DOLLAR ROUNDTABLE

24 HOUR ADVANCE RESERVATION REQUIRED

Alamo Corporate Rent-A-Car program for NSDR members. Membership #93232. (Courtesy of the National Silver Dollar Roundtable archives)

Appendix

The National Silver Dollar Roundtable membership roles listed below are from the NSDR archives. The listed individuals are presented in three separate categories. These are associate, regular and life members. These roles are provided for the dual purposes of information and historic remembrance. Members listed below are both past and present.

Yvonne "Vonnie" A. Berry has diligently contributed thousands of volunteer hours by keeping the NSDR archives and membership roles up-to-date over the last 4-5 years. THANKS Vonnie, for your unselfish efforts in this massive job.

NSDR Member alphabetic list as of 10/31/91

Michael Abbott
Alan J. Ackerman
Al C. Adams, Jr.
Charles M. Adkins
Tony B. Adkins
Leonard Albrecht
Charles O. Anastasio
Walt Ankerman
Michael C. Annis
Dick Armstrong
Eryck C. Aston
Robert L. Astrich
Daniel J. Avena, Sr.
Robert M. Ball
Alex J. Barna
John Barron
Eugene Bascou
Jack M. Baxter
Brian Beardsley
Jeff Beem
Lee J. Bellisario
Jack H. Beymer
Mike Bianco
Paul Birkahn
Charles Hal Blackburn
James U. Blanchard, III
Charlie Boyd
Roger P. Bryan
John Butler
Joe Buzanowski
Nick Buzolich, Jr.
Anthony Calcagno
Randy Campbell
Jim Carr
Barry Carter
David A. Carter
John Cawley
Robert G. Chapman
John Conner
William R. Conroy
Steven L. Contursi
Jack Copeland
Jim Curtis
Steven L. Cyrkin
Jim Czachowski
William Dafcik, Jr.
John W. Dannreuther
Matthew T. De Roma
Silvano DiGenova
James DiGeorgia
William Dominick
Ronald Drzewucki, Sr.
Richard "Kenny" Duncan
Jeff Einbinder

James G. "Jim" Elrod
Steele Eunson
Warren Evans
Frank Falgiani, Jr.
Frank Falgiani, Sr.
Bryan Fazio
Gary Fernandez
Wayne Flannigan
Louis Fogelman
Bill Foreman
Coleman Foster
Craig Franco
Edward E. Fritz, Jr.
Jeff Garrett
William G. Gay
Yitzy Gedelowitz
Sal Germano
Dennis M. Gillio
Alan H. Goldsmith
Mike Golonka
Jeffrey Goodman
David Gorlin
Bob Gormillion
Michael A. Graham
Frank Greenberg
Gene C. Gress
David Griffiths
Michael S. Grodecki
Richard Gross
Paul Grosz
John Gulde
Kent Gulley
Jim Hadley
George Hallock
James L. Halperin
Larry Hanks
Leon E. Hendrickson
Jack C. Hertzberg
Robert Higgins
John W. Highfill
Marlene M. Highfill
Craig Hively
Dempsey Hodges, Jr.
Walton Hood
Donald W. Hosier
Ronald M. Howard
Wayne Hummel
Wayne Imbeogno
Rosemarie Bockhold Ingenito
Jeff Isaac
Steve Ivy
Alfred E. Johnbrier
Joann Johnbrier
Art Jorgensen
Michael Joyce
Donald H. Kagin
Edgar A. Karn, II
Jules J. Karp
Richard Kaufman
Robert F. Keller
John Keogh
Don Ketterling
Don King
Michael Kiscadden
Kurt R. Krueger
Kenneth H. Kusumoto
Paul E. Lambert
Don Lee
Jack R. Lee
Leroy Lenhart
David L. Liljestrand
Kevin Lipton
Dennis Loan
James Long
J.B. Love
John B. Love, Sr.
Keith Love
Andrew P. Lustig
John F. Maben, Jr.
Robert Magee
Dwight N. Manley
Doug Marshall
Dennis McCormick
Robert T. McIntire
Jay McNeal
Richard Melamed
Mark L. Mendelson
Mick Millard
Jay C. Miller
Wayne H. Miller
Thomas Modzelesky, Jr.
Michael C. Moline
Paul Montgomery
Louie Moreno, Jr.
Dr. W.C. Morgan
Vince Mowery
Joseph Muraca
Lynn Murphy
William J. Nagle
Thomas W. Noe
Steve Nowlin
Casey Noxon
Joseph O'Connor
Gordon O'Rourke
Ed Ondrick
Ken H. Park
Martin B. Paul
Robert M. Paul
Edward M. Pereira
Robert A. Perrine
Sanford W. Peterson
D. Harrison Phillips
Thomas B. Phillips
William Rapanotti
Dick A. Reed
Scott Reiter
Joel Rettew
Robert Rhue
Beryl P. Robinson, Jr.
Terry Rock
Ed Rockowitz
Brad Rodgers
J.R. Rol
Bob Rose
Walter S. Rubin
David A. Runfeldt
Clark A. Samuelson
Iraj Sayah-Karaji
Michael Sargent
Dean Schmidt
Sheldon Schultz
Philip J. Schuyler
Richard J. Schwary
Richard Scott
Robert M. Scott
Rick Sear
Andrew N. Seminerio
Bill Shamhart
Douglas Sharpe
Larry Shepherd
John Sladek
Craig A. Smith
Scott D. Sparks
William E. Spears
Reid Spencer
Warren "Scott" Standafer
Bryan Steger
Dennis E. Steinmetz
Barry Stuppler
Rick Sundman
Dean Tavenner
Doug Thomaston
Kim Titley
Thomas S. Tkacz
Hannes Tulving
John E. Turner
William Ulrich
Selby Ungar
Leroy Van Allen
Malcolm Varner
George Vega
Mose Waldner
Dennis E. Wegley
Fred Weinberg
George Weingart
Guy Whidden
Harlan White
Morris Wiener
Sheldon G. Wirt
J.J. Woodside
Mark S. Yaffe
Brian D. Yutzy
George Zawalonka
Stanley Zurawski, Sr.

NSDR Life Member alphabetic listing as of 10/31/91

Charles M. Adkins
Tony B. Adkins
Alex J. Barna
Eugene Bascou
Brian Beardsley
Paul Birkahn
Charlie Boyd
Roger P. Bryan
Joe Buzanowski
Nick Buzolich, Jr.
Randy Campbell
David A. Carter
Robert Chapman
Steven L. Contursi
Jack Copeland
Jim Curtis
William Dafcik, Jr.
John W. Dannreuther
Matt De Roma
Silvano DeGenova
William Dominick
Steele Eunson
Bryan Fazio
Wayne Flannigan
Louis Fogelman
Coleman Foster
Edward E. Fritz, Jr.
Alan H. Goldsmith
David Griffiths
Kent Gulley
Leon E. Hendrickson
Robert Higgins
John W. Highfill
Marlene M. Highfill
Wayne Hummel
Alfred E. Johnbrier
Michael Kiscadden
Paul E. Lambert
Dennis McCormick
Wayne H. Miller
Louie Moreno, Jr.
Martin B. Paul
D. Harrison Phillips
Thomas B. Phillips
Dick A. Reed
Joel Rettew
Ed Rockowitz
Brad Rodgers
Sheldon Schultz
Douglas Sharpe
Scott D. Sparks
Dean Tavenner
William Ulrich
Selby Ungar
Leroy Van Allen
Dennis E. Wegley
George Weingart
Morris Wiener
Mark S. Yaffe
Brian D. Yutzy
George Zawalonka

NSDR Associate Member alphabetic listing as of 10/31/91

Steven Adler
Len Albrecht
John Austin
Bobby Bagwell
Bill Barry
Michael Benyo
Steve Blum
George Bodway
Stephen Boyer
Floyd Bradford
Ronald N. Brais
Joe Bristol
Robert Brownfield
Bob Brueggeman
Gary Burhop
Lester M. Burzinski
Gerald Carsman
Barry Carter
John Caruso
John Chaney
Gary Clark
David Cohen
Dr. Robert Colby
Elsie Coriell
Steve Deeds
Jack Dempsey
Robert Destuhe
Marc Dixon
Flake Douglas
Donn Drury
Roger Dunham
Ira Einhorn
Steve Estes
Joseph Fama
Mike Faraone
James B. Fehr
Bill Fivaz
Mike Fuljenz
Don Gammel
David Ganz
Jack Gauya
Yitzchak Gedalowitz
Robert Gillespie
C.J. Haakenstad
Frank Haig
James C. Hart
Dr. Thomas Hawk
Price Headley
Brian Hendelson
Craig Hively
Joseph Jaffe
Charles Jarruit
David Jones
Joe Jones
Herbert Kaiser
Don Ketterling
Lyndon B. King
Walter Klein
Alan Kreuzer
Ronald Ladd
Robert Lecce
William Lower
Dr. Richard J. Mayer
Herbert McCann, Jr.
Randy McIntosh
Robert McNanna
Gil Michael
George Miller
William Miller
Jim O'Donnell
Jerome Parrish
Bill Patton
Bill Paul
Edward M. Pereira
John Petrecca
Diane Piret
Donald Pritchett
William Prymack
William Rapanotti
Robert Rhue
Rob Riemer
Jeffrey A. Rush
James B. Russell, III
John Paul Sarosi
Charles Schiefelbein
Florence M. Schook
Scott Sehnert
L.L. Sline
Tony Swicer
Gary Tancer
Dr. Lester Taylor
Joy Terry
Kim Titley
Gil Tribbett
Craig Watanabe
Robert Westfall
Clay Whitelaw
Bob Wilcox
Robert Wilhite
Nancy Wilson
Sheldon Wirt
Donald Withrow
Barry Wright

NSDR Member numeric listing as of 10/31/91

M-001 John W. Highfill
M-002 Joe Buzanowski
M-003 Leroy Van Allen
M-004 Dean Tavenner
M-005 Alfred.E. Johnbrier
M-006 Wayne H. Miller
M-007 Randy Campbell
M-008 Roger P. Bryan
M-009 Kurt R. Krueger
M-010 Michael Joyce
M-011 Stanley Zurawski, Sr.
M-012 Frank Greenberg
M-013 Paul Grosz
M-014 Dick Armstrong
M-015 Lynn Murphy
M-016 Robert G. Chapman
M-017 Ronald M. Howard
M-018 Steven L. Contursi
M-019 Douglas Sharpe
M-020 Jack Copeland
M-021 Dick A. Reed
M-022 Ed Ondrick
M-023 Steve Ivy
M-024 Brian Beardsley
M-025 Robert T. McIntire
M-026 Harlan White
M-027 Dennis Loan
M-028 Rick Sundman
M-029 D. Harrison Phillips
M-030 Gary Fernandez
M-031 Matthew De Roma
M-032 Guy Whidden
M-033 Joel Rettew
M-034 Nick Buzolich, Jr.
M-035 Louie Moreno, Jr.
M-036 William G. Gay
M-037 Warren Evans
M-038 Dennis E. Wegley
M-039 Dennis McCormick
M-040 Casey Noxon
M-041 John Cawley
M-042 Dr. W.C. Morgan
M-043 David A. Carter
M-044 Steel Eunson
M-045 William Ulrich
M-046 Craig Hively
M-047 Jim Czachowski
M-048 Warren "Scott" Standafer
M-049 Clark A. Samuelson
M-050 Reid Spencer
M-051 Louis Fogelman
M-052 Jack M. Baxter
M-053 Wayne Hummel
M-054 Daniel J. Avena
M-055 Jay McNeal
M-056 Leon E. Hendrickson
M-057 Ed Rockowitz
M-058 Jim Hadley
M-059 Sheldon Schultz
M-060 Silvano DiGenova
M-061 Barry Stuppler
M-062 George Weingart
M-063 Robert A. Perrine
M-064 Robert Higgins
M-065 James U. Blanchard, III
M-066 Paul E. Lambert
M-067 John Barron
M-068 Steven L. Cyrkin
M-069 George Hallock
M-070 Richard Kaufman
M-071 Thomas B. Phillips
M-072 Don King
M-073 Martin B. Paul
M-074 John Keogh
M-075 Mark S. Yaffe
M-076 Dennis E. Steinmetz
M-077 John Butler
M-078 Morris Wiener
M-079 John E. Turner
M-080 Art Jorgensen
M-081 Wayne Flannigan
M-082 Michael Abbott
M-083 Sanford W. Peterson
M-084 Walton Hood
M-085 Matthew T. De Roma
M-086 Bryan Fazio
M-087 Bill Foreman
M-088 Hannes Tulving
M-089 David Griffiths
M-090 Leonard Albrecht
M-091 Selby Ungar
M-092 Michael Sargent
M-093 Charles O. Anastasio
M-094 Yitzy Gedelowitz
M-095 James G. Elrod
M-096 Richard "Kenny" Duncan
M-097 Brad Rodgers
M-098 Gordon O'Rourke
M-099 Thomas S. Tkacz
M-100 Craig A. Smith
M-101 George Zawalonka
M-102 Richard Scott
M-103 Edward M. Pereira
M-104 David L. Liljestrand
M-105 Thomas Modzelesky, Jr.
M-106 J.J. Woodside
M-107 Robert M. Paul
M-108 Charles "Hal" Blackburn
M-109 Mick Millard
M-110 Edward E. Fritz, Jr.
M-111 Richard J. Schwary
M-112 Alex J. Barna
M-113 Gene C. Gress
M-114 Michael Kiscadden
M-115 Mose Waldner
M-116 Jack R. Lee
M-117 Mike Bianco
M-118 William Rapanotti
M-119 Kent Gulley
M-120 Jim Carr
M-121 Ken H. Park
M-122 Scott D. Sparks
M-123 Kenneth H. Kusumoto
M-124 J.R. Rol
M-125 Jeff Beem
M-126 John F. Maben, Jr.
M-127 John W. Dannreuther
M-128 Dennis M. Gillio
M-129 Coleman Foster
M-130 Ronald Drzewucki, Sr.
M-131 John Gulde
M-132 Jeff Isaac
M-133 William Dafcik, Jr.
M-134 Richard Gross
M-135 Jay C. Miller
M-136 Rosemarie Bockhold Ingenito
M-137 Don Lee
M-138 Michael C. Annis
M-139 Frank Falgiani, Jr.
M-140 Fred Weinberg
M-141 Rick Sear
M-142 Scott Reiter
M-143 Michael C. Moline
M-144 Robert F. Keller
M-145 Sheldon G. Wirt
M-146 Kevin Lipton
M-147 Doug Marshall
M-148 John Sladek
M-149 Robert M. Ball
M-150 Andrew N. Seminerio
M-151 James DiGeorgia
M-152 William R. Conroy
M-153 Alan H. Goldsmith
M-154 Larry Hanks
M-155 Jim Curtis
M-156 Paul Birkahn
M-157 Dempsey Hodges, Jr.
M-158 Eugene Bascou
M-159 William E. Spears
M-160 David Gorlin
M-161 Charlie Boyd
M-162 William Dominick
M-163 Edgar A. Karn, II
M-164 Barry Carter
M-165 Richard Melamed
M-166 James L. Halperin
M-167 Bob Gormillion
M-168 Lee J. Bellisario
M-169 Mike Golonka
M-170 William J. Nagle
M-171 Robert L. Astrich
M-172 Al C. Adams, Jr.
M-173 Don Ketterling
M-174 Sal Germano
M-175 Bryan Steger
M-176 Jeffrey Goodman
M-177 Keith Love
M-178 Walter S. Rubin
M-179 Robert Magee
M-180 Jack H. Beymer
M-181 Donald W. Hosier
M-182 Alan J. Ackerman
M-183 Mark L. Mendelson
M-184 David A. Runfeldt
M-185 Steve Nowlin
M-186 Anthony Calcagno
M-187 Philip J. Schuyler
M-188 Brian D. Yutzy
M-189 Walt Ankerman
M-190 J.B. Love, Jr.
M-191 Joseph Muraca
M-192 Michael A. Graham
M-193 Eryck C. Aston
M-194 Tony B. Adkins
M-195 Beryl P. Robinson, Jr.
M-196 Bob Rose
M-197 Craig Franco
M-198 Joann Johnbrier

M-199 Michael S. Grodecki
M-200 John B. Love, Sr.
M-201 Robert M. Scott
M-202 Leroy Lenhart
M-203 Thomas W. Noe
M-204 Frank Falgiani, Sr.
M-205 James Long
M-206 Iraj Sayah-Karaji
M-207 Doug Thomaston
M-208 Robert Rhue
M-209 Andrew P. Lustig
M-210 Donald H. Kagin
M-211 Jeff Garrett
M-212 Paul Montgomery
M-213 Dean Schmidt
M-214 Larry Shepherd
M-215 John Connor
M-216 Joseph O'Connor
M-217 Bill Sahmhart
M-218 Jack C. Hertzberg
M-219 Kim Titley
M-220 Jeff Einbinder
M-221 Wayne Imbeogno
M-222 Malcolm Varner
M-223 Marlene M. Highfill
M-224 Terry Rock
M-225 George Vega
M-226 Dwight N. Manley
M-227 Jules J. Karp
M-228 Vince Mowery

NSDR Life Member numeric listing as of 10/31/91

LM-001 John W. Highfill
LM-002 Dean Tavenner
LM-003 Alfred E. Johnbrier
LM-004 Wayne H. Miller
LM-005 Steven L. Contursi
LM-006 Roger P. Bryan
LM-007 Randy Campbell
LM-008 Leroy Van Allen
LM-009 Joe Buzanowski
LM-010 Joel Rettew
LM-011 Louie Moreno, Jr.
LM-012 D. Harrison Phillips
LM-013 Robert Chapman
LM-014 Douglas Sharpe
LM-015 Steele Eunson
LM-016 Wayne Hummel
LM-017 William Ulrich
LM-018 Selby Ungar
LM-019 David A. Carter
LM-020 Dennis McCormick
LM-021 Dick A. Reed
LM-022 Louis Fogelman
LM-023 Ed Rockowitz
LM-024 Morris Wiener
LM-025 Sheldon Schultz
LM-026 Martin B. Paul
LM-027 Thomas B. Phillips
LM-028 Wayne Flannigan
LM-029 Brian Beardsley
LM-030 Jack Copeland
LM-031 Matthew De Roma
LM-032 George Zawalonka
LM-033 Robert Higgins
LM-034 David Griffiths
LM-035 Leon E. Hendrickson
LM-036 Paul E. Lambert
LM-037 George Weingart
LM-038 Nick Buzolich, Jr.
LM-039 Mark S. Yaffe
LM-040 Coleman Foster
LM-041 Alex J. Barna
LM-042 Alan H. Goldsmith
LM-043 Michael Kiscadden
LM-044 John W. Dannreuther
LM-045 Edward E. Fritz, Jr.
LM-046 William Dominick
LM-047 Dennis E. Wegley
LM-048 Eugene Bascou
LM-049 William Dafcik, Jr.
LM-050 Jim Curtis
LM-051 Charles M. Adkins
LM-052 Bryan Fazio
LM-053 Brian D. Yutzy
LM-054 Silvano DiGenova
LM-055 Charlie Boyd
LM-056 Tony B. Adkins
LM-057 Paul Birkahn
LM-058 Brad Rodgers
LM-059 Scott D. Sparks
LM-060 Kent Gulley
LM-061 Marlene M. Highfill

NSDR Associate Member numeric listing as of 10/31/91

A-001 Mike Faraone
A-002 David Cohen
A-003 Jack Gauya
A-004 Robert Gillespie
A-005 Floyd Bradford
A-006 Michael Benyo
A-007 Bill Barry
A-008 Scott Sehnert
A-009 Craig Watanabe
A-010 Bill Fivaz
A-011 Flake Douglas
A-012 Gil Michael
A-013 Dr. Richard J. Mayer
A-014 George Miller
A-015 C.J. Haakenstad
A-016 Dr. Thomas Hawk
A-017 Donald Pritchett
A-018 Craig Hively
A-019 Yitzchak Gedalowitz
A-020 Gil Tribbett
A-021 Bill Patton
A-022 Lyndon B. King
A-023 William Rapanotti
A-024 Robert Westfall
A-025 Tony Swicer
A-026 Dr. Robert Colby
A-027 John Caruso
A-028 Jack Dempsey
A-029 John Chaney
A-030 Elsie Coriell
A-031 Price Headley
A-032 Lester M. Burzinski
A-033 Ronald Ladd
A-034 Joe Bristol
A-035 Robert Wilhite
A-036 Dr. Lester Taylor
A-037 Gerald Carsman
A-038 Joseph Fama
A-039 Herbert McCann, Jr.
A-040 Bobby Bagwell
A-041 George Bodway
A-042 Sheldon Wirt
A-043 Ira Einhorn
A-044 L.L. Sline
A-045 Walter Klein
A-046 Charles Jarruit
A-047 John Austin
A-048 Bob Wilcox
A-049 Don Ketterling
A-050 Gary Burhop
A-051 Mike Fuljenz
A-052 Gary Clark
A-053 Roger Dunham
A-054 Robert Brownfield
A-055 David Jones
A-056 Don Gammel
A-057 Donn Drury
A-058 Jerome Parrish
A-059 Steven Adler
A-060 Joy Terry
A-061 Joe Jones
A-062 Clay Whitelaw
A-063 Barry Carter
A-064 Stephen Boyer
A-065 Marc Dixon
A-066 Donald Withrow
A-067 William Lower
A-068 Steve Deeds
A-069 Randy McIntosh
A-070 John Petrecca
A-071 James B. Russell, III
A-072 Robert Destuhe
A-073 Bob Brueggeman
A-074 Len Albrecht
A-075 Robert Rhue
A-076 James C. Hart
A-077 David Ganz
A-078 Barry Wright
A-079 Robert McNanna
A-080 Jeffrey A. Rush
A-081 Frank Haig
A-082 William Rapanotti
A-083 William Prymack
A-084 Florence M. Schook
A-085 Nancy Wilson
A-086 Ronald N. Brais
A-087 John Paul Sarosi
A-088 Diane Piret
A-089 Herbert Kaiser
A-090 Ed Pereira
A-091 Kim Titley
A-092 N/A
A-093 Rob Reimer
A-094 William Miller
A-095 Charles Schiefelbein
A-096 James B. Fehr
A-097 Steve Estes
A-098 Jim O'Donnell
A-099 Robert Lecce

NSDR Associate Member numeric listing as of 10/31/91 (Continued)

A-100 Brian Hendelson
A-101 William Paul
A-102 Steve Blum
A-103 Gary Tancer
A-104 Alan Kreuzer
A-105 Joseph Jaffe
A-106 Dale DeVore
A-107 Glenn Burger
A-108 Stuart Levine
A-109 Dan Ratner
A-110 Walter Magnus
A-111 Bruce Kutcher
A-112 N/A
A-113 Kenneth Goldman
A-114 Malcolm Kurin
A-115 Walter Armitage
A-116 David Weinstein
A-117 Buddy Alleva
A-118 Doug Baliko
A-119 John Schuch
A-120 Christina Smith

Check out this license tag! NSDR A 81.
NSDR Associate #81, Frank Haig
(Courtesy of Frank Haig, Homewood, Illinois)

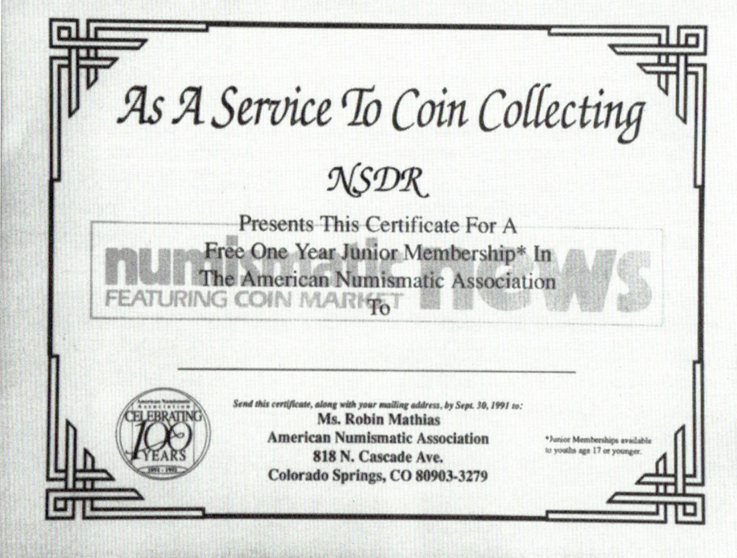

As A Service To Coin Collecting

NSDR

Presents This Certificate For A
Free One Year Junior Membership* In
The American Numismatic Association
To

Send this certificate, along with your mailing address, by Sept. 30, 1991 to:
Ms. Robin Mathias
American Numismatic Association
818 N. Cascade Ave.
Colorado Springs, CO 80903-3279

*Junior Memberships available to youths age 17 or younger.

NSDR Junior Numismatist Award Certificate in commemoration
with the 100th Anniversary of the ANA
(Courtesy of NSDR Archives)

NSDR congratulations to the ANA

I hope you have enjoyed this chapter on the
National Silver Dollar Roundtable.

John W. Highfill

***

Rebecca Fong

Rebecca Fong is the tour coordinator for Professional Coin Grading Service's World's Finest Morgan Dollar Collection. She has worked for PCGS for two years. She is currently completing her degree in Biochemistry at California State University at Fullerton.

CHAPTER 25

A Rare Coin Experience: "The World's Finest Morgan Silver Dollars"

by Rebecca Fong

On August 22, 1990, the Professional Coin Grading Service (PCGS) unveiled the World's Finest Morgan Dollar Exhibit at the 99th Annual American Numismatic Association show in Seattle, Washington. This six million dollar collection of 110 of the finest known PCGS certified Morgan dollars included coins which were produced at the main mint in Philadelphia, as well as the branch mints at San Francisco, New Orleans, and Denver. Because all of these coins were certified by PCGS, our firm played an integral role in locating the coins and coordinating such a project. Through this exhibit, PCGS hopes to acquaint people with collecting and investing in rare U.S. coins across the United States and abroad.

Those who are familiar with the history of the Morgan dollar understand why there has been such an intense effort from collectors to acquire Morgan dollars. It is believed that the Morgan dollar is the single most widely desired coin in all of numismatics. Some people contend that this coin is more beautiful and desirable than any other silver dollar minted by the U.S. Government. For its size, beauty, and variety, many people believe that there is no equivalent to the Morgan silver dollar. Consequently, a majority of the highly graded Morgans are scattered among different owners. The beauty, desire, and significance of Morgan dollars are among several reasons why PCGS decided to unify the world's finest Morgans into a spectacular exhibition to be shown for an international engagement. Other factors include education and promotion of the coin hobby, and the numismatic industry as a whole.

So far, this museum quality exhibit has toured the trade show circuit with tremendous response not only from coin collectors and numismatists, but from the general public as well. This exhibit has been scheduled to be shown in eight different cities until the end of 1991. In Japan, there is a strong interest in coin collecting Morgan dollars. Therefore, PCGS will also be considering an overseas visit to Japan.

It was important that we work with leading figures in the rare coin community in order to make the tour a reality. The silver dollar expert, Bruce Amspacher, helped us contact other noted silver dollar authorities in the industry. David Hall, William E. Spears, John Highfill, Ray Gelewski, and Joel Rettew are only a few of the rare coin industry's highly respected dealers, who also generously donated both their time and exclusive use of their coins in the exhibit. All of these people have spent many years as talented numismatists in the coin industry, often acting as consultants for such books as Scott Travers's *Investor's Guide to Coin Trading*, Travers's *Rare Coin Investment Strategy*, and James Halperin's *How to Grade U.S. Coins*, just to name a few. Due to their expertise, these people were considerably familiar with the existence of particular Morgan dollars. Through this team of experts, we were able to obtain a number of the coins currently on display. Several of these coins were loaned by the clients of these dealers.

Both PCGS' Population Report and its internal computer tracking system helped us identify the owners of these PCGS-certified coins. Although it may sound simple, tracking the owners of these coins took more time than one would expect. Several steps were necessary in order to obtain a list of possible Morgan dollar owners. The most recent issue of the PCGS Population Report furnished the number of coins which were certified at the highest and second highest grades and designations (The PCGS Population Report profiles the number of coins certified by PCGS at a given grade for each date, denomination, mint mark, and variety). We were searching for every single coin ever graded by PCGS which qualified as possessing the highest or second highest numerical designation. From this list, we consulted our computer database for more facts. The computer compiled reports detailing: 1) the dealer's number that submitted the particular coin to PCGS for grading, 2) the date it was received, and finally, 3) the PCGS invoice number. A listing of over 700 reports were drawn from this database. Even coins originally graded as far back as PCGS's first year in operation, 1986, were listed. To make our job a bit easier, we requested that the computer give us submission reports dating to coins graded within the last eighteen months.

Then, from this more simplified list, we were able to notify each dealer and ask him if he was the current owner of that particular coin or if he could assist us in contacting the present owner. While this did not always indicate a particular person still owned the coin, we were still able to track several of the coins' owners this way. After a coin has been certified, most of our PCGS dealers either sold the particular coin to a collector or another dealer. After a coin changed ownership through several different dealers, it became increasingly difficult to locate. For example, we contacted one dealer who obligingly offered to help us track the coin. He owned the coin at one time and sold it to another dealer. In turn, this dealer sold it to a collector who had his coin nostalgically attached to a private "set" of other silver dollars. No amount of persuasion would convince him to part with his coin. We amusingly compared this roundabout situation of locating tour coins as "playing tag." The certified coin was designated as "it" and the object of the game was to find "it." Fortunately, this game was not entirely hopeless for we were able to locate a few coins this way.

In some cases, coins were tied up in rare coin investment portfolios and believed impossible to obtain for the collection. Therefore, a want list, a list of coins still needed for the collection, was compiled and advertisements were placed in *Numismatic News* and *Coin World*. Our initial hope was to have a few of these seemingly "impossible to obtain" coins' owners to call about the advertisements. Actually, several individuals who owned "raw coins" (which are coins not graded or holdered) responded to our advertisements. These people believed they possessed coins which "could be the finest ever graded by PCGS." However, most of those coins could not be considered serious contenders. Further discussion revealed that these people either inherited a stockpile of silver dollars from a relative or they amassed a supply of dollars through pocket change over the years. We encouraged these individuals to submit their coins for grading, thus the condition of the coins could be

Ribbon cutting ceremony in Seattle
August 1990 — ANA Convention

Chocolate memorabilia — PCGS "The World's Finest Morgan Silver Dollar Collection" Obverse (Courtesy of PCGS)

Chocolate memorabilia — PCGS "The World's Finest Morgan Silver Dollar Collection" Reverse (Courtesy of PCGS)

determined. Unquestionably, if these coins graded the finest, we wanted to include them in the collection. So, we still did not rule out the possibility of discovering some fine specimens. Some people balked at the regular submission price of twenty-six dollars claiming it was "too expensive" to grade a silver dollar.

Despite some doubts, we were pleased when one individual did submit some surprisingly fine coins in response to our advertisements. After reading about the upcoming traveling exhibit, Colonel B.G. Cook of Virginia decided to send a dozen of his Morgan dollars for certification under our standard submission procedures. He believed several coins would be certified at a high grade, although these had never been certified before. While he is not a professional numismatist, Col. Cook has a keen eye. Both his 1878-7/8 TF weak MS65DM and 1884-O MS66DM Morgan dollars proved to be the finest known, according to both grade and designation (Only one other known; only four known). His 1903-O MS66DM Morgan dollar was certified as finest known graded in its designation, according to the July 1990 PCGS Population Report (None known at this grade). Surprisingly, of these three finest certified coins, only the 1878-7/8 TF weak MS65DM did not grade as Col. Cook expected. He was hoping for the coin to grade MS66DM. In our discussions with him, he told us that before the mention of the Morgan Dollar Traveling Exhibit, he "never dared to have coins graded before." He primarily took great joy and pride through collecting fine specimens of "raw" Morgan dollars.

In late July 1990, we encountered an interesting situation when a collector notified us that he owned several Morgan dollars for the PCGS collection. We were excited he owned so many coins initially needed on our list. But then, we informed him that a number of other collectors had already filled the vacant positions on our "want list" so there was only a need for a few of this gentleman's coins. At this, he first expressed dismay that another collector previously committed his own coins. Then he questioned the beauty and grade of the other collector's coins even though he had never seen them. Surprisingly, with one coin in particular, he offered to give us written documentation from a reputable silver dollar specialist attesting to the overall beauty of his coin. He suggested a challenge, a "grade off" whereby the two finest PCGS certified coins would compete against each other to see which was the finer of the two. Early in the project, PCGS had established a policy that the tour would accept coins on a first-come-first-serve basis.

The policy stated that the first owner of a particular issue who makes the first unqualified commitment to include it in our tour will have that coin accepted. We had not faced any difficulties in the previous months with this policy. All of the other Morgan dollar tour participants considered this an acceptable and fair rule. So, we felt that there was no need to alter the policy while we were securing coins for the tour. Fortunately, this individual believed in the value of a traveling Morgan exhibit and still decided to have us display several of his coins in the collection. We were relieved to hear this since we became quite anxious to complete the pieces for the collection in time for the upcoming August 1990 unveiling of the collection at the Seattle ANA show.

It almost seems like poetic justice with all the magnificence of this display — that the complimentary chocolate imitation silver dollars were the hit of the exhibit.

A great deal of effort was taken detailing the loan agreement which secured these certified Morgan dollars. As with all legal contracts, PCGS's lawyers were consulted in drafting this document. Even with this specifically detailed document, some collectors disagreed with key portions of the contract. One interested party argued against standard contract terms or "usual exclusions" for "(the) loss or damage due to war, invasion, acts of foreign hostilities, civil war, . . . loss by nuclear breakdown or nuclear radiation." According to our lawyers, this is a standard condition governing loans and under no circumstances could it be altered. We were glad when he finally agreed to participate in the tour, since his was the only coin known at that particular grade and designation.

Unquestionably, gathering the finest known PCGS certified Morgan dollars for the tour was not an easy task. Some collectors wanted to negotiate special conditions before lending the coins to PCGS. One person wanted PCGS to acknowledge *every* individual who owned one of the finest PCGS certified Morgan dollars. His reasoning was that he wanted others to know that at one point in time he *also* owned one of the finest known graded coins. According to the February 1991 edition of the PCGS Population Report, while a 1921-S MS65 has a population of 46, there is only one owner of the finest known 1882-O MS68 (Anonymous collector in association with Heritage Rare Coin Galleries of Dallas, Texas). Therefore, if PCGS were to recognize every owner of a particular issue with a plaque or certificate, we would need to contact and acknowledge almost 500 individual owners. This would be very difficult, since tracking down the owners of 110 Morgan dollars was challenging enough. In addition, there would certainly be more than one person that would be offended if he was not acknowledged for owning a particular coin. Therefore, we decided early in the project that participation in the tour should be unconditional. To be fair, we could not negotiate terms with different individuals in order to secure coins for the collection.

This collection of 110 of the finest known PCGS certified Morgan dollars could not have been possible if it were not for the loans of many individual collectors and PCGS authorized dealers. A serious Morgan dollar collector on the West Coast, Dr. George Bodway, owns 46 Morgan dollars traveling with the collection. Mr. William E. Spears, a collector/dealer in Seattle, Washington, owns eighteen Morgan dollar pieces: the complete Carson City collection, along with a 1895 PR67 and a 1898 MS66DM. (For details by Mr. Spears concerning Carson City dollars, please refer to the chapter entitled The Mystique of the Carson City Morgan Silver Dollar). Mr. Bodway's 1893-S MS67 ex-Norweb and Mr. Spears' 1889-CC MS-65 are the highest valued Morgans in the collection, each appraised at $750,000.

There had been extensive advertising and information programs made available to promote the tour. There were various brochures, special invitations and multiple print ads used in the promotion of this exhibit. **Senior Editor's note: This display, like the "seven wonders of the world" would be considered one of the "seven wonders of numismatics". The exhibit and tour are absolutely awesome! John W. Highfill**

Seattle start of Morgan dollars tour

What is being described as the world's finest collection of Morgan silver dollars of more than $10 million value will begin its national tour at the American Numismatic Association's 99th Anniversary Convention in Seattle, Aug. 22-26.

On consignment from various private collectors and sponsored by Professional Coin Grading Service, the touring exhibit will showcase 110 of the finest, rarest and highest graded Morgan dollars.

The PCGS traveling exhibit of Morgan dollars consists of the highest designation and grade for each date of issue. The exhibit will feature a multi-media educational display, including an interactive program that allows visitors to test their "grading" skills.

Following the ANA convention in Seattle, the Morgan dollar collection will travel to various museums and financial institutions for a year. The last stop on the tour is the ANA's 100th Anniversary Convention in Chicago in 1991.

To register for the ANA convention in Seattle, or obtain more information about accommodations, tours and other events, contact the American Numismatic Association, Convention Department, 818 N. Cascade Ave., Colorado Springs, Colo. 80903-3279, or telephone (719) 632-2646. ■

News Release — Advertisement
PCGS Dollar Tour

Professional Coin Grading Service
cordially invites you to attend
A Rare Coin Experience:
The World's Finest Morgan Dollar Collection
at the
American Numismatic Association Convention
from August 22 to August 26, 1990
Washington State Convention Center
Seattle, Washington

Exclusive VIP invitation for the premiere unveiling
of the World's Finest Morgan Silver Dollar Collection
(Courtesy of PCGS)

Cover of two-page pamphlet for
"The World's Finest Morgan Silver Dollars"
(Courtesy of PCGS)

Cover of sixteen-page deluxe brochure
(Courtesy of PCGS)

Without a doubt, this six million dollar collection is the finest known set of its kind compiled by either an individual or organization.

One of the advantages of placing a coin on display in the tour was that an owner could enjoy widespread recognition for his coin. One particular collector was primarily interested in finding a buyer for his coin. The tour would be a perfect vehicle for him to promote his coin, we explained. Many collectors knew that their coins would no longer remain locked within their bank vaults, but actually viewed by thousands of people across the U.S. Without a doubt, an exhibit of this magnitude would allow the collector to have his coins seen and appreciated by a larger audience. Unlike donations to a museum, these particular coins would still be owned by the collector while in the care of PCGS. Thus, negotiation for the release of these coins did not pose as great a problem as we originally believed.

From the start, these people shared the common desire to see this history-making collection assembled and viewed by thousands of people. There was an overall feeling of excitement that a collection of this magnitude would be included in a traveling exhibit. And with the prestige attached to this collection, many felt it would be a wonderful promotion of the coin industry, focusing the public's attention to numismatics. As the August 31, 1990 edition of the *Certified Coin Dealer Newsletter* commented,

". . . the display is almost overwhelming. No, let's be honest — it is overwhelming. It presents the very best that Morgan dollars have to offer, and in its professionalism presents the very best that numismatics has to offer. The display is sure to attract even non-numismatists."

"The World's Finest Morgan Silver Dollars" Exhibit on Tour
(Courtesy of PCGS)

Modules: The Carson City Mint and the New Orleans Mint
(Courtesy of PCGS)

Many think that this collection can somehow enjoy the prestige of the Norweb and Wayne Miller collections. The PCGS collection actually includes a few of these famous coins. We were able to secure two of the legendary Morgan dollars from the Emery May and Ambassador R. Henry Norweb collection, which are the finest PCGS certified Morgan dollars: 1893-S MS67 and 1902-S MS67. The PCGS Collection also is honored to include eight of the finest known specimens from the

Wayne Miller collection. These include the 1878-S MS68PL, 1883-S MS65, 1886-O MS67DM, 1887-O MS65DM, 1890 MS65DM, 1895-O MS66, 1901 MS65, and 1904-O MS66DM.

PCGS constantly grades an enormous number of Morgan dollars. While a coin may be known at one point in time as the finest known certified at a particular grade and designation, it can be replaced by a recently higher graded coin. PCGS pedigrees each coin which participates in the "World's Finest Morgan Dollar Collection. Even if the coin is exhibited once and becomes substituted by a higher designated and/or graded coin of the same date, it will still receive a "PCGS Tour" pedigree. Since the tour began in August 1990, seven Morgan dollars were replaced by higher PCGS graded coins. Perhaps any coin with a PCGS Tour pedigree will bring a premium for being a part of this historic event.

Although this exhibit required much planning, we began the project in early March 1990, expecting to open the exhibit at the American Numismatic Association's (ANA) Seattle show in August 1990. Within this six month time frame, we believed a museum quality exhibit could be designed that would portray both the sophistication and professionalism of the industry and PCGS. Furthermore, we wanted the exhibit to cultivate a growing interest in collecting and investing in U.S. coins. With these purposes in mind, we began our research and writing for the display. The exhibit consisted of eight free standing modules with four of them chosen to display the Morgan dollar collection. Each of these four coin modules included a central display panel describing the history behind each mint. Other intriguing components of the exhibit included an interactive computer system "**Try Your Hand at Grading a Coin**," and an audiovisual system displaying five videos.

Researching for the display panels was a wonderful opportunity for those of us involved with the project. Even those of us who had a basic knowledge of coins discovered a wealth of information surrounding the history of the Morgan dollar. We learned a variety of information which revealed an aspect of numismatic history which fascinated us all. Government agencies and authorities were contacted in order to gather research materials. The Department of the Treasury, United States Mint, in Washington D.C. was extremely helpful with information from their historical files concerning the Morgan dollar.

Extraordinary numismatic display
"The World's Finest Morgan Silver Dollars"
(Courtesy of PCGS)

Furthermore, both the Library of Congress and the National Archives generously loaned us photographs, letters, videos, and other information related to the histories of the mints, the Morgan dollar, the coin's designer George T. Morgan, and the minting process. Even though we were searching for a photograph of George T. Morgan, which would nicely illustrate one of our panels, we had a very difficult time locating one. It seems that it was not often that Mr. Morgan would sit for photographs. Fortunately, *Coin World* generously loaned us a rare photograph of the designer. This particular snapshot and an array of other information helped build a solid foundation for the development of our exhibit panels.

Besides employing historical files from government agencies and public archives, Bruce Amspacher's personal library was unparalleled as a source of information for the exhibit. To build a basic understanding of silver dollars, we referred to his many numismatic materials: newspapers, pamphlets, and books. From his exceptional knowledge of silver dollars, and particularly in the Morgan dollar, Mr. Amspacher skillfully wrote the text for the panel, "**The History of the Morgan Dollar.**" This focused on the complete story of the Morgan dollar spanning from its introduction in 1878 to its replacement by the Peace dollar in 1921.

The History of the Morgan Dollar

The silver dollar has been a significant part of American history for over 200 years. Although the first silver dollar from a United States mint was not produced until 1794, the Spanish milled dollar had circulated in the colonies since the 1730's. The Spanish coin, valued at 8 reales, was sometimes cut into pieces for use as fractional coinage: thus such terms as "pieces of eight" and "two bits" were originated.

The United States silver dollar went through several significant design changes from 1794 through 1873, including the Flowing Hair design of 1794-95, the Draped Bust Small Eagle design of 1795-1804, and the Liberty Seated design of 1840-73. The new coinage law of 1873, known at the time as the "Crime of '73," eliminated the silver dollar from the annual list of U.S. issues.

By 1878, there was severe pressure on Congress to help out the western mining interests, who were suffering from falling silver prices. The Bland-Allison Act of February 28, 1878, authorized the Secretary of the Treasury to purchase $2 million to $4 million a month in silver and to coin it into silver dollars as quickly as possible. The same day, a design submitted by George T. Morgan was officially adopted. The weight, 412 1/2 grains, and the fineness, .900, conformed to the act of January 18, 1837.

The Morgan dollar was struck from 1878 through 1904 and again in 1921. Five different mints were used for these strikings: Philadelphia (1878-1921), San Francisco (1878-1921), New Orleans (1879-1904), Carson City (1878-1893), and Denver (1921 only). The "mint mark," which designates the mint where the coin was struck, can be found below the eagle on the reverse side of the coin. The Philadelphia issues of this era have no such mark.

The Morgan dollars that were struck for circulation (actual use in commerce) are known as "circulation strikes" or "business strikes." Those terms are used to clearly designate them from proof coins, which were struck solely for collectors and never intended for general circulation (although many proof strikes did eventually reach circulation). Almost all proof coins were struck at the Philadelphia Mint. Proof coins not struck in Philadelphia were known as "branch-mint proofs," and are extremely rare.

Morgan dollars struck for circulation were stored in bags of 1,000 coins. Some of these bags, still mint sealed, exist today. Most silver dollars were eventually distributed to banks around the country. Because the supply far exceeded the demand, over 270,000,000 silver dollars were melted under the Pittman Act of 1918.

Mint records were kept on exactly how many Morgan dollars were struck in each year at each mint. Today, these mintage figures are one important factor in determining the rarity of each date of the series. Unfortunately, these figures are somewhat unreliable because no records were kept on which dates were melted in 1918.

In 1921, the minting of silver dollars was resumed using new, slightly different dies. These Morgan dollars were produced in Philadelphia, San Francisco and Denver mints. Production of the Morgans was, however, soon to be replaced by a new design.

Because World War I had reached a successful conclusion, people felt it was suitable to honor the hard won victory by designing a new dollar representing peace. Before 1921 ended, the minting of Morgan silver dollars had been replaced with the newly designed "Peace" dollar. But the Peace dollar has not diminished the Morgan dollar's appeal. The story of the dollar continues as it gains popularity with collectors and investors. Its history is still affected by politics, economics and popularity among the public.

People have hoarded Morgan dollars in attempts to avoid taxes or because they were unable to put their faith in paper currency. They traded them to foreign countries for dollars of "equal" value, but which in fact had a higher silver content. When the price of silver skyrocketed in the early 1960's, people bought bags of dollars to be melted for the bullion.

The government vaults are now nearly depleted of Morgan dollars. The fate of this beautiful and historic coin rests primarily in the hands of collectors and investors.

History of the Morgan Dollar from "The World's Finest Morgan Silver Dollars" Exhibit
(Courtesy of PCGS)

Often when historic events are described, audiences find the description dull unless they can picture these experiences. For the panel involving "**U.S. Silver Dollars and American History**" we acquired exquisite archival photographs from the California Museum of Photography of the University of California at Riverside. In May 1990, we discovered that the entire museum's collections were recently moved from the central campus into a beautiful building in the older section of Riverside. Fortunately, a few of us were invited to browse through this museum's expansive library of prints and stereoscopic slides before their opening to the public in the fall. These prints in particular, are from the museum's Keystone-Mast Collection. This panel chronicled the Congressional acts and historical events which paved the road for all silver dollars. Accompanying this time line of numismatic milestones are corresponding events in American history.

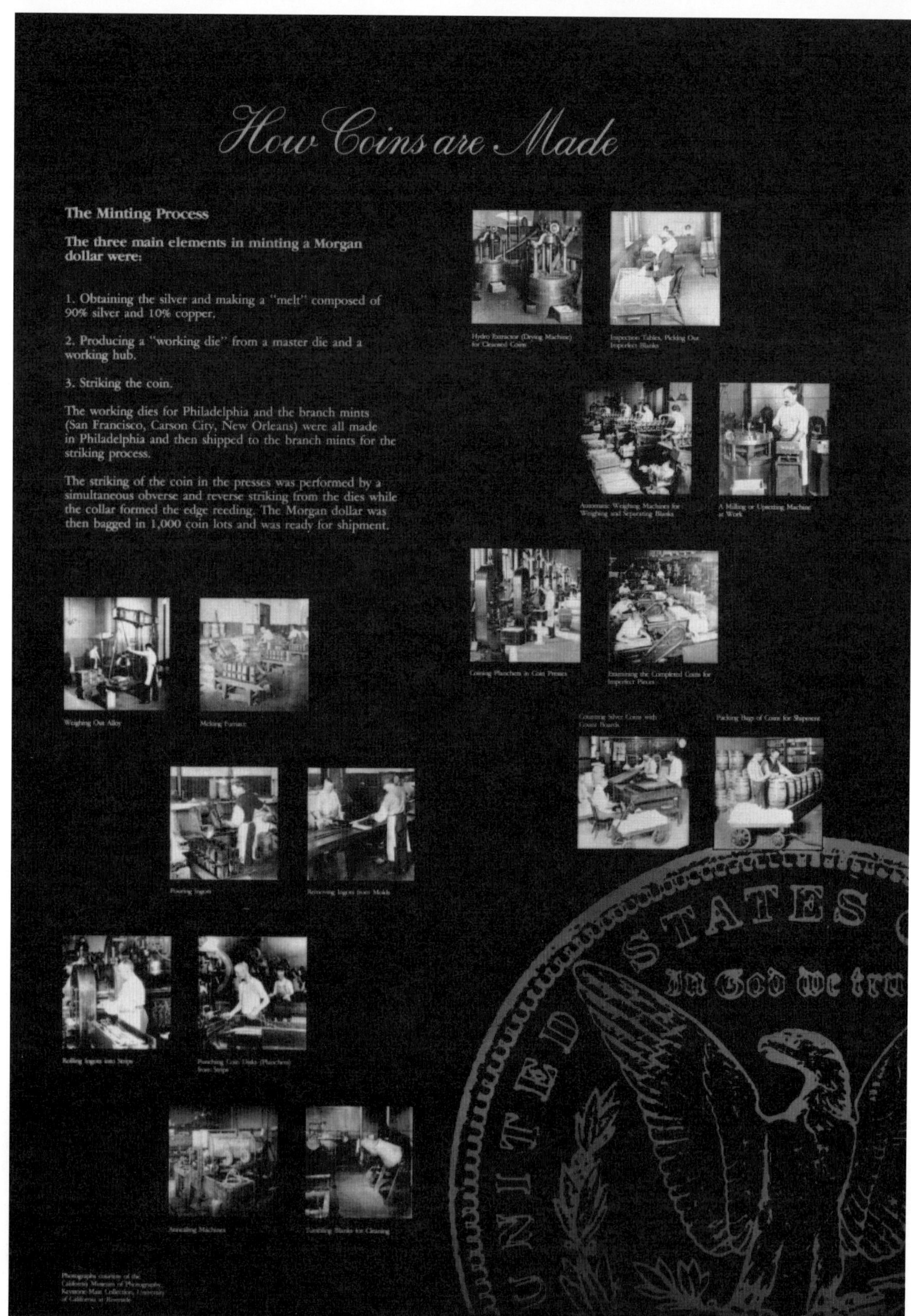

How coins are made — The minting process
(Courtesy of PCGS)

"**How Coins Are Made**," the third panel, has been one of our most popular displays because it details the steps in the minting process through sixteen archived photographs. We also obtained these invaluable photographs through the California Museum of Photography. These stereoscopic negatives from their Keystone-Mast Collection were taken from 1860 to 1960. Although only some of these 350,000 stereoscopic negatives and prints were documented with dates, the curator at the museum estimated these exquisite photographs were taken during the late 1800's. Until the early 20th century, very few changes were made in the minting process at the U.S. Mints. We were amazed that we were able to obtain such extraordinary prints for the display. From our research, we discovered only a few government agencies who had quality prints available for reproduction. Since many of our prints obtained from the California Museum of Photography were made from actual glass negatives, the quality was incomparable. They brought to life events in history for visitors to the exhibit.

Another panel, "**It Takes a Sharp Eye**", teaches the visitor how to identify various parts of a silver dollar and the specific characteristics associated with a coin's condition. A silk-screened panel shows an enlarged photograph of both the obverse and reverse of an 1878-S Morgan dollar. The mint mark, the designer's initials, the date, and other characteristics are clearly shown on both the obverse and reverse. While this display teaches the beginner or novice how to identify simple features of a coin, it also allows the advanced collector the opportunity to appreciate other aspects of a coin, such as its condition and luster.

The interactive video grading system was our most popular component of our exhibit. This system, appropriately titled "**Try Your Hand At Grading A Coin**," allows the visitor an opportunity to experience grading a Morgan silver dollar. Louis Crain, head of research and development at PCGS, was principally responsible for introducing computer grading to the numismatic industry. PCGS asked Mr. Crain to create this simple "user-friendly" software program for the Morgan Dollar Exhibit that is controlled with the push of a button.

The Video Showcase is a viewer activated audiovisual system featuring five different videos: minting, collecting, investing, grading, and trading of rare coins. Some of the unique footage used in the videos were contributed by the National Archives and Records. A great deal of time was spent researching and writing for these videos. Betsy Barta, Patricia Minassian, Bruce Amspacher, Steve Mayer and I enjoyed working closely with this aspect of the exhibit. Script after script had to be scrutinized first, by a crew of four PCGS employees, then by our lawyers. All the text was verified independently by Bruce Amspacher and Betsy Barta, then again by the rest of the team. Enormous effort was taken to authenticate all facts presented in all aspects of the display, from the information panels describing historical events to the videos illustrating the minting process.

Video Showcase — PCGS "The World's Finest Morgan Silver Dollars" Exhibit

The Exhibit

The display itself is a multi-dimensional, multi-media rare coin experience which is sure to entertain and fascinate. The coins are accompanied by a complete account of their evolution; their design by George T. Morgan; the five mints which produced them; and the events and congressional acts which directed their course through history.

The word sophistication best describes the styling of the display's monolithic modules. Classic marble and brass accents, incorporated into a traditional loden green and metallic gold motif, add warmth and elegance to this versatile design.

Security for this exhibit is essential. Security personnel are present at all times. In addition, all coins are protected by security glass cases which allow full visual access to the obverse and reverse of each coin. These specially designed cases lock into the main module and hold the coins securely. The coin cases may be separated from the larger modular structures and moved to a secure area after business hours. Each module also has an internal alarm system which is active even in the event of a power failure. The exhibit is fully insured for seven million dollars.

Module One: San Francisco & Denver

The first module in the eight module display features the 30 coins produced by the San Francisco and Denver Mints. While design and construction of the security glass coin panels allow viewing of the coins from both sides, a central graphic panel provides a brief account of the history and activities of the Mints. As an example, San Francisco was known to produce the highest quality Morgan dollars with characteristically vibrant luster and detail; while Denver's production of this silver dollar was limited to the year 1921, which marked the end of the Morgan dollar's 27-year reign.

Module Two: Philadelphia

The second coin module highlights the 33 Morgan dollars produced at the Philadelphia Mint. The first Morgan silver dollar was struck at this prolific Mint in 1878. In addition, more Morgan dollars were produced at Philadelphia than any other mint. This panel also features authentic archival photographs and an intriguing description of Philadelphia's early minting practices.

Marble Pillar Modules PCGS "The World's Finest Morgan Silver Dollars" Exhibit

Module Three: Carson City & the Grading Set

This exhibit contains 16 examples from the Carson City Mint. Established in 1870, the Mint of the Old West produced some of the rarest Morgan dollar specimens known today. Uncirculated, mint condition Carson City dollars are especially prized due to low mintages, the widespread circulation of most of these coins, and the destruction of many coins due to federal melting practices.

This module also incorporates 16 coins used for grading the condition of other collectible Morgan dollars against an established standard. These coins are only part of a comprehensive grading set assembled by the Professional Coin Grading Service in 1986. The interactive computer grading system in module eight further illustrates the significance of the grading set coins in this module.

Module Four: New Orleans & Pattern Coins

The last of the coin modules features 28 Dollars from the New Orleans Mint. Established by the congressional act of March 3, 1835, this Mint produced gold and silver coins until 1861, when it was seized by Confederate forces during the early days of the Civil War. The Mint was reopened in 1879, and continued in operation until 1909.

Module Five: Grading Rare Coins & The History of the Morgan Dollar

The second half of the exhibit contains four additional modules. The first of these discusses the evolution of coin grading as it pertains to this exhibit. The designation of grade is denoted using the widely recognized Sheldon Numerical Scale, which ranges from "one" (poor condition) to "70" (perfect condition).

The reverse of this module focuses on the complete story of the Morgan dollar — from its introduction in 1878 to its replacement by the Peace dollar in 1921.

Module Six: Investing in Rare Coins & How Coins are Made

The sixth module provides a brief study of the world of rare coin investments. Included in this panel is an overview of the roles played by independent grading firms and electronic trading networks in today's sophisticated marketplace. Such networks allow enthusiasts to trade many independently graded coins sight-unseen, via a computer network which links buyers and sellers throughout the nation.

The reverse of this module takes a detailed look at "**How Coins are Made**." This module features rare, historical photographs from the Keystone-Mast Collection, Museum of Photography, Riverside, California. The photos and accompanying text provide an interesting discussion of a typical 16-step process used in the minting of coins through the last century.

Module Seven: Video Showcase & "It Takes a Sharp Eye"

Module seven contains a viewer-activated video loop offering five, brief video selections on topics including minting, collecting, investing, grading, and trading of rare coins.

The reverse of this module asks the question: "Can you tell the difference between these two 1878 Morgan dollars?" The object here is to teach the viewer how to identify various parts of a silver dollar and specific characteristics associated with a coin's condition.

Module Eight: Interactive Computer Grading System

The last module is a particularly fascinating feature of the exhibit which allow viewers the opportunity to actually experience grading a Morgan silver dollar. This is achieved by combining the principles of coin grading with unprecedented computer technology developed specifically for the grading of coins. A simplified "user-friendly" version of this unique software program may be controlled with the push of a button. Utilizing a personal computer and a "mouse," it is the only system of its type in use today.

Completing the eighth module, and the exhibit, is a time line of events in American history which influenced the Morgan silver dollar, and shaped our nation. Archival photographs depict the era from the ratification of the Articles of the Confederation (1781) to the enactment of the First Immigration Quota Act (1921).

Physical Characteristics

The exhibit components contain eight, double sided, free-standing modules, including four con/mint modules totalling 110 Morgan dollars, six informative graphic panels, one menu-activated video monitor dedicated to a video loop on five subjects, and one interactive computerized coin grading system.

The Coin/Mint modules consist of the first four and are follows:

1 : Coins of the San Francisco and Denver Mints with graphic panels.
2 : Coins of the Philadelphia Mint with graphics.
3 : Coins of the Carson City Mint and Grading Set coins with graphic panels.
4 : Coins of the New Orleans Mint with graphics.

The Information modules complete the exhibit and are as follows:

5 a.: Grading Rare Coins.
5 b.: The History of the Morgan Dollar.
6 a.: Trading & Investing in Rare Coins.
6 b.: How Coins are Made.
7 a.: Video Showcase highlighting five subjects.
7 b.: "It Takes a Sharp Eye."
8 a.: Interactive Computer Grading System.
8 b.: Historic Time Line.

The modules and graphic panels in this exhibit were made to be interchangeable, and may be arranged or omitted to accommodate the space available.

Each module measures 5' wide by 9' high by 2' long. Each of the modules may be displayed without their decorative caps, thereby reducing the height to 7'3". The modular design gives maximum flexibility to accommodate the facilities. Space requirements range from a minimum of 10' by 25' (less than eight modules) to a maximum of 30' by 30' (using all eight modules). The average weight of each crated module is approximately 525 pounds.

The initial schedule for the exhibition is from August 1990 through October 1991. This schedule may be extended with permission of the coin owners and a described need. Several prestigious museums have made inquiries concerning the exhibition of this unique display.

This non-profit exhibit has been funded in its entirety by the Professional Coin Grading Service.

Special Recognition:

This international exhibit of 110 Morgan silver dollars has been made possible with the generous loans from the private collections of:

Bruce Amspacher
Asia Fund
George Bodway
Robert Brahms
Arnold R. Bruhn
Steve Contursi
Col. B.G. Cook
Martin Firman
Jack Gauya
Michael Gauya
Ray Gelewski
H. Grieshaber
Anonymous collector
  c/o Heritage Rare Coin Galleries
John W. Highfill
Dan Kihlstadius
K. Krivitzky
Natalie Kyle
Jim Pappas
Arnie Payne
Joel Rettew
Robert S. Riemer
Steve Ryan
Craig R. Smith
William E. Spears
Fred Weinberg

Special thanks to:

Bruce Amspacher
Betsy Barta
David Hall
Steve Mayer
Patricia Minassian
SafraBank — Encino, California
Spectrum Numismatic International, Inc.
TIA — Santa Ana, California
Valley National Bank — Tulsa, Oklahoma

Appendix

A complete listing of the coins currently "on tour" representing "The World's Finest Morgan Silver Dollars" as of this writing is presented below. As previously mentioned, the coins making up this elite group is subject to change as better specimens become available.

IMPORTANT NOTICE:

For those of you that were not able to view the PCGS "World's Finest Morgan Silver Dollars" exhibition while it was on tour, we at Highfill Press, Inc., with permission from the Professional Coin Grading Service, Inc., Newport Beach, California, are pleased to present all of the dollars from this magnificent collection as the official plate coins used in our date by date analysis. This complete in-depth date by date analysis is listed in Chapter 80 of this Encyclopedia.

Philadelphia Mint

Coin No.	Date	Grade
1	1878-8TF	MS66
2	1878-7TF Rev '78	MS65 DMPL
3	1878-7TF Rev '79	MS65 PL
4	1878-7/8TF Strong	MS65
5	1878-7/8TF Weak	MS65 DMPL
6	1879	MS66
7	1880	MS65 DMPL
8	1881	MS65
9	1882	MS65
10	1883	MS67
11	1884	MS67
12	1885	MS66 PL
13	1886	MS67
14	1887	MS67PL
15	1887/6	MS65 DMPL
16	1888	MS67
17	1889	MS67
18	1890	MS65 DMPL
19	1891	MS65
20	1892	MS65 DMPL
21	1893	MS65
22	1894	MS65
23	1895	PR67
24	1896	MS65 DMPL
25	1897	MS66
26	1898	MS66 DMPL
27	1899	MS66
28	1900	MS66
29	1901	MS65
30	1902	MS67
31	1903	MS66
32	1904	MS65
33	1921	MS67

Carson City Mint

Coin No.	Date	Grade
1	1878-CC	MS67
2	1879-CC	MS65
3	1879-CC Capped Die	MS65
4	1880-CC	MS67
5	1880-CC Rev '78	MS66
6	1881-CC	MS67
7	1882-CC	MS67
8	1883-CC	MS67 PL
9	1884-CC	MS68
10	1885-CC	MS68
11	1889-CC	MS65
12	1890-CC	MS66
13	1891-CC	MS67
14	1892-CC	MS67
15	1893-CC	MS65
16	1900-O/CC	MS66

Denver Mint

1	1921-D	MS66

New Orleans

1	1879-O	MS65 DMPL
2	1880-O	MS65 PL
3	1881-O	MS65
4	1882-O	MS68
5	1882-O/S	MS64 *
6	1883-O	MS67
7	1884-O	MS67
8	1885-O	MS67
9	1886-O	MS67 DMPL
10	1887-O	MS65 DMPL
11	1887/6-O	MS64
12	1888-O	MS66
13	1889-O	MS66
14	1890-O	MS66

New Orleans (cont.)

15	1891-O	MS65 DMPL
16	1892-O	MS65 DMPL
17	1893-O	MS65 DMPL
18	1894-O	MS64
19	1895-O	MS66
20	1896-O	MS65
21	1897-O	MS67
22	1898-O	MS67 DMPL
23	1899-O	MS67 DMPL
24	1900-O	MS67
25	1901-O	MS66
26	1902-O	MS66 PL
27	1903-O	MS67
28	1904-O	MS66 DMPL

San Francisco Mint

Coin No.	Date	Grade
1	1878-S	MS68 PL
2	1879-S	MS68
3	1879-S Rev '78	MS65
4	1880-S	MS69
5	1881-S	MS68
6	1882-S	MS68
7	1883-S	MS65
8	1884-S	MS67
9	1885-S	MS67
10	1886-S	MS66
11	1887-S	MS65 PL
12	1888-S	MS66
13	1889-S	MS66
14	1890-S	MS66
15	1891-S	MS67
16	1892-S	MS66
17	1893-S	MS67
18	1894-S	MS67
19	1895-S	MS65
20	1896-S	MS68
21	1897-S	MS67
22	1898-S	MS65 PL
23	1899-S	MS67
24	1900-S	MS66
25	1901-S	MS65
26	1902-S	MS67
27	1903-S	MS67
28	1904-S	MS65 PL
29	1921-S	MS65

PL-Indicates Prooflike
DMPL-Indicates Deep Mirror Prooflike

* The 1882-O/S MS64 was not represented on this tour.

***

Appendix

Certified Morgan display made last stop

A reprint from *Numismatic News*

A road show featuring a complete set of high-grade Morgan dollars certified by the Professional Coin Grading Service made its final appearance at the American Numismatic Association convention, held Aug. 13-18 in Rosemont, Ill.

Almost all of the coins in the exhibit were the finest-known examples graded by PCGS, and operations manager Steve Mayer was pleased with the results.

"We considered the tour to be very successful." he said. "Unfortunately, we did not get the coins into any non-numismatic venues such as museums, because they require two to three years advance notice. It would have been a logistical problem to borrow the coins for that much time."

The PCGS display appeared at such major events as the National Silver Dollar Convention and the Florida United Numismatists convention. Visitors also had an opportunity to test their grading skills.

"People had a lot of fun with the interactive grading videos," Mayer said. "They were very excited by it. Most people who viewed the coins were very impressed."

Changes were made in the traveling exhibit as coins were graded by PCGS.

"Contributors were given the opportunity to replace coins if a better one was discovered," Mayer said. "There was a lot of competition, and the contributors were very excited."

Morgan dollars that were chosen for the PCGS display were pedigreed and placed in holders noting that the coin was part of the tour.

"It's Showtime!"

CHAPTER 26

World's Finest Collections and Prices Realized

by John W. Highfill

Introduction

One of the most exciting areas of numismatics involves the review and study of the great collections amassed by both individuals and organizations. Due to the significant amounts of time, energy and money required to accumulate a truly magnificent collection, a great deal of respect should be given to those who have achieved this goal.

There are multiple collections with each claiming to be the "finest known"! The reader should review the collections in detail and rank them according to their desired criteria. This is not an exhaustive group of fantastic collections. There are many other great collections in this world that are not listed here. Other collections may surface later to lay claim to the title. Listed below are the collections contained in this chapter.

A Rare Coin Experience: "The World's Finest Morgan Silver Dollars" (PCGS World Tour)

"An Amazing Collection of United States Silver Dollars" - Superior Galleries

The Jimmy Hayes — World's Finest Specimen 1795 Dollars

Dwight N. Manley — World's Finest Known Proof Trade Dollar Set

The Wayne Miller Silver Dollar Set (1878-1935)

The William E. Spears Carson City Morgan Dollar Set (1878-1893)

The John W. Highfill Morgan Dollar Collection (1878-1921)

The John W. Highfill Peace Dollar Collection (1921-1935)

The George E. Bodway Collection of Morgan Dollars (1878-1921)

The Elliot S. Goldman Morgan Dollar Collection (1878-1921)

The Larry Shepherd Commemorative Set

The John W. Highfill Commemorative Set

The John W. Highfill Canadian Coin Collection (1935 - 1959)

The Martin B. Paul Canadian Coin Collection (1935 - 1952)

The Martin B. Paul Half Dime Collection (1792 - 1842)

The David Hall World's Finest Three Cent Nickel Collection

The David Hall World's Finest Washington Quarter Collection

Dwight N. Manley — The World's Finest Panama-Pacific Exposition Set

World Record Transactions

Prices Realized

A RARE COIN EXPERIENCE

"THE WORLD'S FINEST MORGAN SILVER DOLLARS"

This wonderful and imaginative exhibit began its tour in August 1990 at the ANA Convention in Seattle, Washington. Featuring the "World's Finest Morgan Silver Dollars," the tour schedule may be expanded beyond its October 1991 completion date to include nationally known museums. This non-profit exhibit has been funded in its entirety by the Professional Coin Grading Service.

IMPORTANT NOTICE:

For those of you that were not able to view the PCGS "World's Finest Morgan Silver Dollars" exhibition while it was on tour, we at Highfill Press, Inc. with permission from the Professional Coin Grading Service, Inc., Newport Beach, California, are pleased to present all of the dollars from this magnificent collection as the official plate coins used in the date by date analysis. This complete in-depth date by date analysis is listed in Chapter 80 of this Encyclopedia.

This international exhibit of 126 Morgan silver dollars has been made possible with the generous loans from the private collections of:

Bruce Amspacher
George Bodway
Arnold R. Bruhn
Col. B.G. Cook
Jack Gauya
Ray Gelewski
Dan Kihlstadius
K. Krivitzky
Jim Pappas
Joel Rettew
Steve Ryan
William E. Spears
Anonymous collector c/o
Heritage Rare Coin Galleries

Asia Fund
Robert Brahms
Steve Contursi
Martin Firman
Michael Gauya
H. Grieshaber
John W. Highfill
Natalie Kyle
Arnie Payne
Robert S. Riemer
Craig R. Smith
Fred Weinberg

Special thanks go to the following:

Bruce Amspacher
David Hall
Steve Mayer
Betsy Barta
Patricia Minassian

SafraBank - Encino, California
Spectrum Numismatic International, Inc., Santa Ana, California
TIA - Santa Ana, California
Valley National Bank - Tulsa, Oklahoma

A complete listing of the coins currently "on tour" representing "The World's Finest Morgan Silver Dollars" as of this writing is presented here. The coins making up this elite group is subject to change as better specimens become available. It should be noted that only one grade and specimen is selected to represent this collection. To be more specific, there is not an example of every date in all three categories of MS, PL and DMPL. There are also no NGC coins in this collection.

Date	Grade
1878-P 8TF	MS66
1878-P 7TF Rev '78	MS65 DMPL
1878-P 7TF Rev '79	MS65 PL
1878-P 7/8TF Strong	MS65
1878-P 7/8TF Weak	MS65 DMPL
1878-CC	MS67
1878-S	MS68 PL
1879-P	MS66
1879-CC	MS65
1879-CC Capped Die	MS65
1879-O	MS65 DMPL
1879-S	MS68
1879-S Rev '78	MS65
1880-P	MS65 DMPL
1880-CC	MS67
1880-CC Rev '78	MS66
1880-O	MS65 PL
1880-S	MS69
1881-P	MS65
1881-CC	MS67
1881-O	MS65
1881-S	MS68
1882-P	MS65
1882-CC	MS67
1882-O	MS68
1882-O/S	MS64
1882-S	MS68
1883-P	MS67
1883-CC	MS67 PL
1883-O	MS67
1883-S	MS65
1884-P	MS67
1884-CC	MS68
1884-O	MS67
1884-S	MS67
1885-P	MS66 PL
1885-CC	MS68
1885-O	MS67
1885-S	MS67
1886-P	MS67
1886-O	MS67 DMPL
1886-S	MS66
1887-P	MS67 PL
1887/6-P	MS65 DMPL
1887-O	MS65 DMPL
1887/6-O	MS64
1887-S	MS66
1888-P	MS67
1888-O	MS66
1888-S	MS66
1889-P	MS67
1889-CC	MS65
1889-O	MS66
1889-S	MS66
1890-P	MS65 DMPL
1890-CC	MS66
1890-O	MS66
1890-S	MS66
1891-P	MS65

Date	Grade
1891-CC	MS66
1891-O	MS65 DMPL
1891-S	MS67
1892-P	MS65 DMPL
1892-CC	MS67
1892-O	MS65 DMPL
1892-S	MS66
1893-P	MS65
1893-CC	MS65
1893-O	MS65 DMPL
1893-S	MS67
1894-P	MS65
1894-O	MS64
1894-S	MS67
1895-P	PR67
1895-O	MS66
1895-S	MS65
1896-P	MS65 DMPL
1896-O	MS65
1896-S	MS68
1897-P	MS66
1897-O	MS67
1897-S	MS67
1898-P	MS66 DMPL
1898-O	MS67 DMPL
1898-S	MS65 PL
1899-P	MS66
1899-O	MS67
1899-S	MS67
1900-P	MS66
1900-O/CC	MS66
1900-O	MS67
1900-S	MS66
1901-P	MS65
1901-O	MS66
1901-S	MS65
1902-P	MS67
1902-O	MS66 PL
1902-S	MS67
1903-P	MS66
1903-O	MS67
1903-S	MS67
1904-P	MS65
1904-O	MS66 DMPL
1904-S	MS65 PL
1921-P (M)	MS67
1921-D	MS66
1921-S	MS65

PL = Prooflike
DMPL = Deep Mirror Prooflike
PR = Proof

1732-Mo Mexico Pillar Dollar. First Year Issue. Choice Uncirculated. Finest Known.

1776 Continental Dollar. PCGS Mint State 65. Possibly the Finest Known.

1794 Flowing Hair. Neil, Carter, Wayne Miller Sale. Superb Presentation Specimen. Unique. PCGS Mint State 65.

1795 Draped Bust. Stack's "L.A. Type Set" 10/90. NGC Mint State 65.

1799 Heraldic Eagle. Superior's Heifetz Sale, 5/90. NCG Mint State 65.

1803 Heraldic Eagle. PCGS Proof 66. Auction '86. Finest Known.

1836 Gobrecht. Name below base. Norweb. NGC Proof 66. Finest Known.

1839 Gobrecht. Starless field. Norweb. PCGS Proof 65. Finest Known.

1863 No Motto. PCGS Mint State 65.

1864 No Motto. PCGS Proof 65.

1865 Judd-434. Seated Liberty Transitional coin with motto. Jimmy Hayes Collection. PCGS Proof 64.

1866 Wayte Raymond/Christies, 5/89. PCGS Mint State 66. Finest Known.

1869 Emery Nichols/Bowers & Merena, 11/84. NGC Proof 67. Finest Known.

1876 Trade Dollar PCGS Mint State 65.

1879 Trade Dollar. PCGS Proof 66.

1880 Morgan from an original Proof set. PCGS Proof 68. Finest Known for type.

1903 Morgan Dollar. PCGS Mint State 66.

1900 Lafayette Commemorative Dollar PCGS Mint State 66.

1883 Kingdom of Hawaii. PCGS Proof 65. Finest Known.

Superior Galleries Amazing Collection of United States Silver Dollars - May 26, 27, 28, 1991
(Courtesy of Superior Galleries, Beverly Hills, California)

"AN AMAZING COLLECTION OF UNITED STATES SILVER DOLLARS"

SUPERIOR GALLERIES

The following pages are reprinted courtesy of Superior Galleries, Beverly Hills, California from their May 27,28, 1991 Auction featuring "An Amazing Collection of United States Silver Dollars". The unique presentation piece is a 1794 Flowing Hair dollar. There were many other unbelievable coins available within this amazing collection. In order to better present these coins to you, the original color plates have also been printed.

A very special thanks and consideration is due to Mr. Lawrence S. Goldberg for his dedication in providing the excellent following photo analysis and descriptions. We would also like to give a special thanks and appreciation to Mr. William Conroy and Christy Boldt for their unselfish time and contributions for this section and many other portions throughout this book.

Plate 1

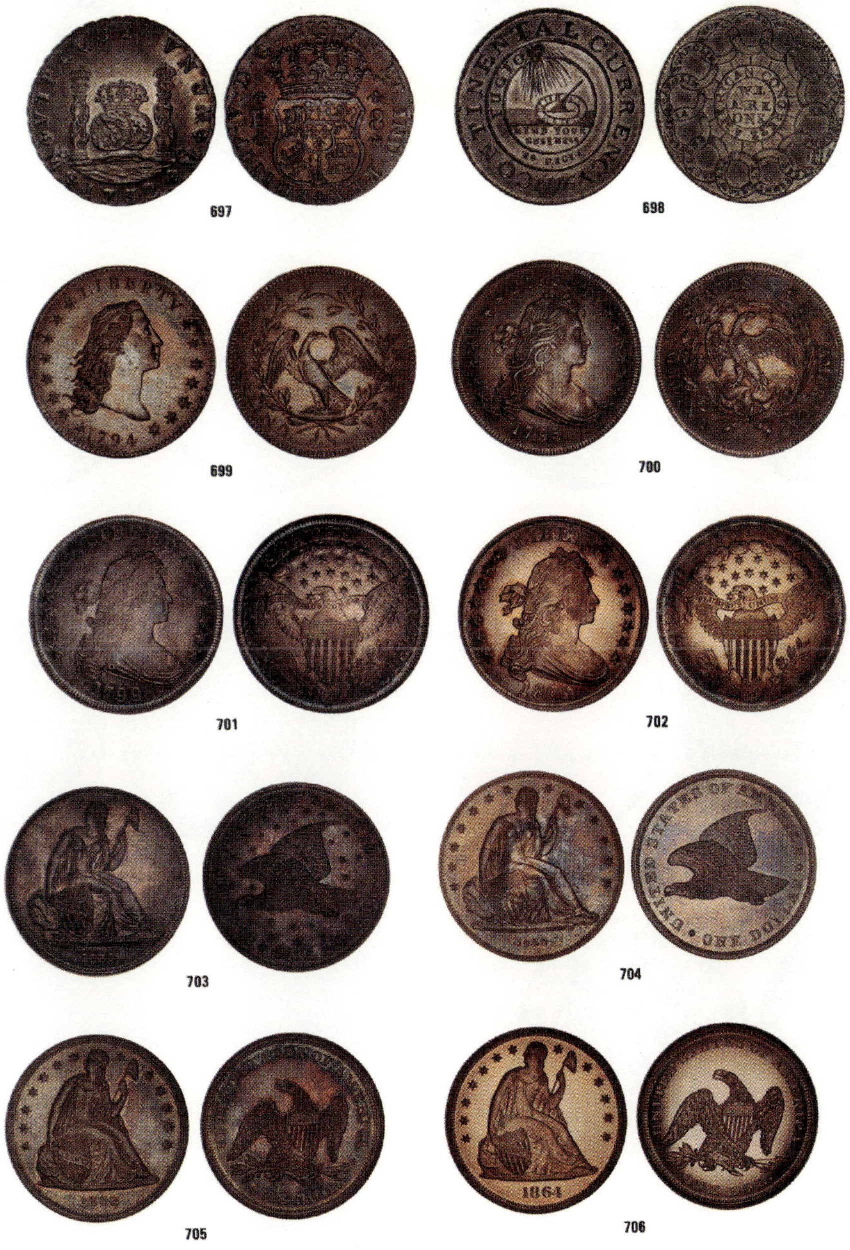

697

698

699

700

701

702

703

704

705

706

Plate 1
(Courtesy of Superior Galleries, Beverly Hills, California)

Plate 2

Plate 2
(Courtesy of Superior Galleries, Beverly Hills, California)

(Courtesy of Superior Galleries, Beverly Hills, California)

AN AMAZING COLLECTION OF UNITED STATES SILVER DOLLARS

There have been few times in numismatic auction history when such a handsome run of Silver Dollars has been offered for sale. The collector who assembled this stellar grouping aspired to expand his collecting horizon beyond the usual Federal issues. Instead, he made an effort to more completely exhibit the history of the U.S. Silver Dollar. Included along with the regular business strike pieces in the set are a "pillar dollar" struck in 1732 (the first year issue), a famous 1776 Continental Dollar struck in pewter (and in phenomenal condition, we might add), an uncompromisingly beautiful 1794 Presentation Striking Flowing Hair piece representing the first official American Dollar coin, two of Gobrecht's incomparable Seated Liberty Pattern Dollars, and a Transitional 1865 with motto IN GOD WE TRUST on the reverse.

Like all superb quality-oriented collections, this one is not, nor can it ever be, complete. Great collections generally grow and evolve. However, according to our consignor (who knew his own weakness for superb material) if his collection was not sold at this point it might end up growing out of his control as it were and cost another $20 or $30 million to complete! For this reason, these classic American rarities are being put on the auction block.

During America's colonial period, a whole slew of foreign coinage circulated here, along with odd monies like tobacco, "wampum," and various agricultural products. So when the Spanish colony in Mexico began striking 8-real "pillar dollars" in 1732, residents of North America quickly incorporated them into their commerce. With the advent of our war for independence in 1776, the Continental Congress began planning for a national coinage. That is how the Continental Dollar came into being. It's primary theme of a sundial and MIND YOUR BUSINESS motto was the brainchild of none other than Benjamin Franklin!

Finally, in 1794 actual coinage of Silver Dollars began. And the coins represented here are some of the most impressive examples you will ever get the opportunity to bid on. Before getting to the individual descriptions under each lot, readers should flip through the pages first; get a feel for the weight of high quality specimens; notice how the consignor emphasized nicely toned coins; and then marvel at the fact that so many magnificent specimens have been brought together at one time. This is, indeed, an unheard of opportunity for the perceptive buyer. In the true and proper sense of the word, this collection is amazing. First off, there is the broad scope of issues covered. Second, the consignor had an eye for quality; only the finest would do. Finally, every coin takes on added significance in the context of the entire collection. We can think of no better way for a bidder to appreciate them than to view them all together at one time. The effect is breathtaking.

SUPERB 1732 FINEST KNOWN PILLAR DOLLAR

MAGNIFICENT 1776 CONTINENTAL DOLLAR

SUPERB 1732 FINEST KNOWN PILLAR DOLLAR

697 **Mexico. 1732-Mo. 8 reales. Assayer "F" (Felipe Rivas de Angulo). So-called "Pillar Dollar." Craig-8, Choice Uncirculated**. A boldly struck example with full prooflike surfaces and in outstanding condition, to say the least! Besides being a gold toned jewel, this also happens to be not only the first year of issue for the long-running Pillars of Hercules type, but also the finest 1732 known by a long shot. To find one of these with prooflike fields is almost unheard of; to find one as fresh and original, an event.

Philip V (Filipe in Spanish) was the grandson of Maria Theresa. He reigned from 1700-1746 and it was under his rule that the New World's famed "Pillar Dollar" 8 real coinage began, 1732 being the first year of issue. The obverse features two columns representing the Pillars of Hercules — the entrance to the Atlantic ocean and once believed to mark the limits of the world. At center are two conjoined globes representing the old and new worlds, with a crown above. PLUS ULTRA ("More Beyond") on ribbons grace each pillar. The reverse depicts the Bourbon shield upon the crowned coat of arms of Castille and Leon; around this, the legend, translated into English: "By the Grace of God King of Spain and the Indies."

Pillar Dollars were struck at several Spanish colonial mints in the Americas. As collectors learn from the introduction to Yeoman's Guide Book of United States Coins, they were the forerunner of the United States Silver Dollar and saw service throughout the New World. In point of fact, they ranged throughout the eastern Pacific, as well, in effect circulating as a global trade coin. Chinese chop marks are often found on them. Here in the U.S. they remained legal tender until 1857, and were considered as an everyday coin by merchants and the public at large, along with a plethora of other worn-to-middling European coins which were also then circulating.

The shortage of small change in the U.S. was a problem in the early days since the content of the coins minted by the Philadelphia Mint was such that a profit could be had by taking worn Spanish silver in exchange for them. This caused the export of most of our new coinage as fast as it was minted. Even so late as the 1850's, the Real and Half Real continued to circulate freely, particularly in the southwest and south. Prices were often denominated in awkward sums like 6 1/4c and 12 1/2c. On February 21, 1857, Congress passed laws terminating the legal tender of foreign coins.

MAGNIFICENT 1776 CONTINENTAL DOLLAR

698 **1776. Continental Dollar. CURRENCY spelling with two R's. Struck in 95% tin. Breen-1095 with full size N in AMERICAN. PCGS graded Mint State 65.** Premium Quality. Quite possibly the finest known example. This is certainly the finest one graded by PCGS as of March 1991. And what a splendid example it is, too! Unlike most examples of America's first Continental Currency pattern coins, the fields are bright and beautiful, showing none of the usual black toning areas. They are absolutely free of flyspecks or spots as well. Moreover, as you can tell by the photographs, everything is razor-sharp on both sides. The central sun dial shows its Roman numeral digits quite as distinctly as the sun's rays which shine down gloriously upon it. Best of all, for those with an eye for quality, the surfaces are blemish-free while the rims are perfect, without nicks or bruises of any kind. And when has there been a reverse strike to compare to this one's? We doubt whether you could find another with lettering so clear, with each of the 13 interlocked rings boldly defined and having the names of each colony so plain and readable.

Turning next to the lustre, what can we add but "it's all there!" Vibrant (for tin composition), unsullied, and displaying a semblance of cartwheel effect on the obverse. Roll everything together and you have one remarkable specimen of America's most famous colonial coin. Finally, an important milestone has been reached with this specimen for the simple reason that it is the only specimen graded Mint State 65. why they didn't give it an even higher number, such as '66, is a mystery to us; for once you set your vision upon it you'll see as we do that it falls squarely in the Premium Quality class. Please consider your bids with this in mind. This is the first Continental Dollar ever slabbed by PCGS or NGC.

Listen to Breen describe this coin's historic inception and birth:

"In anticipation of Congress managing to obtain a loan of silver bullion from France, unidentified intermediaries sought out the Freehold, N.J., engraver Elisha Gallaudet with a proposal he could hardly refuse...Gallaudet was then best known for this ornamental cuts on the 1774-76 NEW-YORK WATER WORKS notes, and for the sundial and links devices on the Feb. 17, 1776 Continental Currency fractional notes...Under cover of secrecy, the agents commissioned Gallaudet to prepare dies for a mintage of coins of various denominations. These would serve a dual function: on the one hand, demonstrating to the world the United Colonies' national sovereignty the same way other nations showed theirs; on the other, propping up the paper Continental notes, showing all concerned that these were exactly what they purported to be, promissory notes redeemable in coin."

The devices chosen for Gallaudet's pieces were the same ones used on his notes. According to researchers, these were prepared from sketches done earlier by none other than Benjamin Franklin! The obverse displays a sundial with sun shining down on it, with CONTINENTAL CURRENCY around. MIND YOUR BUSINESS and the word FUGIO are also prominent on the obverse ("Fugio" meaning "I am fleeting" which refers to time or the sun arching overhead on its daily journey). Both of these mottoes were to encourage the proper use of one's time in minding one's business affairs, which Breen says was a warning aimed at farmers, merchants and patriots in their fight against the British redcoats.

For the reverse, Gallaudet chose thirteen interlocking chain links each labelled with the name of the original thirteen colonies. The symbolism is clear: America's colonies united against a common foe. At the center appears AMERICAN CONGRESS / WE ARE ONE. For added insight into this fascinating issue, see Breen's *Encyclopedia of U.S. and Colonial Coins*, pp.110-112.

Previously from Pine Tree Auction's the Altman-Haffner Sale, April 1975, Lot 677

FINEST KNOWN 1794 DOLLAR
THE WILL NEIL SPECIMEN
UNIQUE PRESENTATION PIECE

FINEST KNOWN 1794 DOLLAR—THE WILL NEIL SPECIMEN
UNIQUE PRESENTATION PIECE

699 **1794. Flowing Hair. Bolender-1. PCGS graded Mint State 65.** Premium Quality. ***Prooflike and superb***! This is "The Coin," the ***World's Finest 1794 Silver Dollar*** which has the added value of also being the only ***Presentation Specimen*** known. Although there were no 1794 Proofs officially made, there is no denying this coin received extra care when it was made. In contrast to 90% of the 100 or so 1794's remaining, here all of the stars to the left of the date are complete. Likewise, there are no signs of weakness on the corresponding part of the reverse which more often than not comes very weak.

Furthermore, the central devices — that is, Liberty's bust along with the skinny, youthful eagle on the reverse — are, quite simply, magnificent! They belong more appropriately to an issue made a century later since they are *that* strong.

Liberty's hair tresses show throughout; from top to bottom and from the lowest portion to the highest wave over her ear, every curl and strand is diamond clear. Neither are there signs of weakness elsewhere on the coin: the eagle, for this part, is incomparably bold. His every wing feather stands forth. So do the tufts on his chest, which are extraordinarily sharp for 1794; the same for his eye, his nostril, his "cheek" bone. Finally, the beak is shaped like a curving razor and comes to a spike point, ready to pierce its unwary prey; you can even make out the beak's lower segment with the naked eye. (Forgive our running on about this, but please understand how unusual these features are!) Unlike every other Mint State 1794, of which about 5 are known, there are fully developed prooflike fields behind the devices. These ***prooflike fields*** provide a wealth of beauty to the coin and give contrast to its relief details. The Mint State 65 grade also speaks volumes about its overall surface quality. In a nutshell, the fields are perfect. There are no value-impairing marks or digs or buffed-out initials to jolt your eye; and only a few barely visible adjustment marks attesting to its authenticity as an early Mint product.

When our consignor submitted it to the grading service to encapsulation, he was told in writing by Mr. David Hall "PCGS has examined and graded the Amon Carter 1794 Silver Dollar. PCGS grades the coin Mint State 65. A strong case can be made for calling the coin a Proof. It certainly is a presentation piece of some sort. "Which is why prospective bidders will want to give it extra close examination. Compare in you mind others of its kind you have seen. Compare it to the Lord St. Oswald specimen, for instance, a coin we auctioned in our Gilhousen Sale in 1973. In fairness, that specimen was a charmer in its own right. And yet it lacked many of the refinements of this piece. It was fully frosty, for one thing, lacking all signs of ever having been struck from specially prepared dies as this one does. Then, too, its eagle showed nowhere near the depth of detail this one does. (We should note here that the Ostheimer specimen brought $110,000 back in 1973, while T.V. cameras whirred recording the event.)

The question arises, is this coin Proof? When all comes to all the term "Proof" in relationship to early U.S. coinage was probably as much a matter of intent as method (method being the sole determination today). We will never know what the mintmaster who struck this coin called it. According to Breen's research, "before 1817 it is uncertain whether the coiners had figured out the trick of replacing the ejected coin (caught in a chamois or with heavy leather gloves) onto the lower die for a second impression..."What seems obvious is that presentation pieces do exist, showing evidence of unusual care in striking on carefully selected blanks, and in a few cases the recipients have been identified.

We choose to call this 1794 Dollar a presentation strike. Besides, all that really matters is that the coin is unique, far superior in manufacture to any other known 1794. That is the true ground for a coin's reputation. To use the jargon of the trade, it is a "monster." Hence, it is the ultimate United States Silver Dollar. In conclusion, we'd like to point out this coin is not merely a pattern, nor merely the finest known, nor merely a rare date. It was a special historically and important coin the day it was made, as it is today. This can be said of no 1822 Half Eagle, however rare it may be. It dwarfs the historical importance and rarity of any 1804 Dollar or 1913 Liberty Nickel. Still, this is only half the picture, for far more subtly, this coin has a quality rarely found in numismatics, a quality that grows on you: The longer you look at the coin, the more spectacular it appears. the more you become familiar with early American Silver Dollars, the more specimens you have seen, the more you will appreciate its special aura.

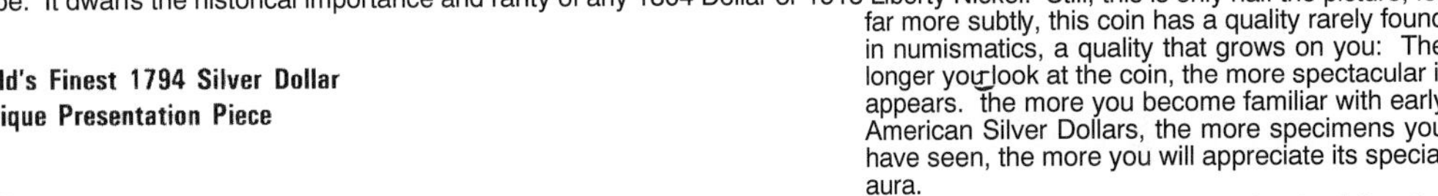

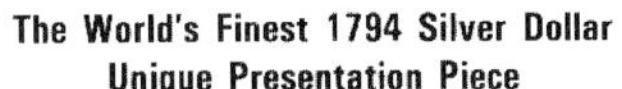

The World's Finest 1794 Silver Dollar
Unique Presentation Piece

Lot 699

Silver Dollars were authorized by the Mint Act of April 2, 1792. Those dated 1794 were from a single pair of dies prepared by Robert Scot, who had been hired by the mint in November 1793 because of his talented work on banknote plates. The head of the Silver Dollar copies the one seen on his Large Cents of 1794, except without the Liberty cap. Breen has learned that

"Because no press heavy enough for dollars had yet been built for the Mint, these coins were struck on the largest one at hand--that originally meant for cents and half dollars. Inspection of the copper proof with stars (Judd 19), which must have received two blows from the dies, suggested that this press would work satisfactorily for business strikes; actual minting proved otherwise. The new dollars were at once criticized for weakness of impression: 'the touches of the graver are too delicate, and there is a want of that boldness of execution which is necessary to durability and currency' (New Hampshire Gazette, Dec. 2, 1794). The fault, however, is less in the die than in press weakness and axial misalignment. On most survivors [but not this coin. Ed.], obv. and rev. dies were in skew (nonparallel) planes, making the l. side of the coin weaker — especially dated, stars at l., and UNITED STATES."

One explanation for why so few mint state 1794's remain (Breen thinks 5) is alluded to in *Walter Breen's Encyclopedia of United States and Colonial Proof Coins 1722-1989*; "it is known that some of the weakest 1794's were not allowed to leave the mint, but instead used as planchets for striking dollars of 1795."

As readers can see, 1794 has a wealth of history behind it. All the more reason for considering this presentation piece with its prooflike surfaces as an unusual occurrence! *Previously from Superior's Hoagy Carmichael and Wayne Miller Collection sale, January 1986, Lot 1173. Before that, from Stack's Amon G. Carter Jr. Family Sale, January 1984, Lot 207 and earlier, still, B. Max Mehl's The Will W. Neil Sale, Lot 1*

GORGEOUS 1795 DRAPED BUST SILVER DOLLAR FINEST KNOWN FOR TYPE

GORGEOUS 1795 DRAPED BUST SILVER DOLLAR
FINEST KNOWN FOR TYPE

700 **1795. Draped Bust, Small Eagle. Bolender-15. NGC graded Mint State 65. Fully Struck**. And featuring some of the loveliest gold, blue, and sunset red toning you'll ever see on an early date Silver Dollar! The colors are exquisite. As with the other specimens in this remarkable consignment of Dollars, our consignor made an extra effort to find only beautifully toned coins, coins that have color and eye appeal and that inexplicable pizzazz which says "Here I am, buy me!" Only one in a thousand get toned in this fashion. The 1795 herein offered in one of those select few.

Bolender-15 has Liberty's bust centered between the two curving rows of stars. It is also normal for this die to have a small break in the hair to the left of the ear caused by a defect in the die. The only other Small Eagle die for 1795 has Liberty pushed too far left, giving her an unbalanced appearance. This particular coin has especially strong devices and stars. It is as if it was given a double thump from the dies or, at the very least, the pressman had eaten his Wheaties that morning. For Liberty and the eagle are utterly perfect: sharp-razor-sharp, in fact-and without any of the usual contact marks on their figures to disturb them. The accompanying fields are equally fresh. More importantly, their lustre reflects back light with a warm golden red glow thanks to the toning.

As this text is being written, Los Angeles is in the midst of its Hollywood awards celebration: Emmy, Oscar, People's Choice, Golden Globes. (In fact, the husband of one of our staff members just won an Eddie award for editing from the American Cinema Editors). It is too bad Numismatics doesn't hand out an award each year for excellence in coin preservation. For if it did, we feel certain that *this* 1795 Draped Bust would win hands down for 1991! Here's how the vote tallies: as of March, 1991, NGC had graded only 1 Mint State 65 (this coin) plus 1 Specimen 65 example, while PCGS has graded 2 Mint State 65's. Neither service has graded any higher. Which makes it a gilt-edge requirement that you do not miss bidding if you are building your own top ranking Silver Dollar set.

With America's new Mint Director Henry DeSaussure at the helm, the Mint decided to upgrade Scot's Flowing Hair design. DeSaussure thought it was too unseemly for a young country and so tapped Gilbert Stuart, a famous portrait artist of the day, to rework both the obverse and reverse. Stuart came up with a conservative (and well-fed) bust of Liberty. Breen says this Draped Bust design featured a Mrs. William Bingham as Liberty. One wonders how she felt having her face appear on millions of coins.

Previously from Stack's 55th Anniversary Sale Part II, October 1990, Lot 1659.

EXTRAORDINARY MINT STATE 1799 BUST DOLLAR

EXTRAORDINARY MINT STATE 1799 BUST DOLLAR

701 **1799. Bolender-12b. Rarity-3. NGC graded Mint State 65.** And conservatively graded, we might add. This handsome coin traces back to our Heifetz Sale in the autumn of 1989. There we described it as having surfaces and strike that are original and bold: "Liberty's bust has a rich frostiness about it which literally provides a cameo look. Acting as a backdrop to her lustrous white portrait is resplendent gold, lavender, and blue toning..."From such expressions not much can be added. As we said before, we have wracked our brains in trying to recall another Heraldic Eagle 1799 as lovely as this one. Nearly two decades ago we sold the extensive Bust Dollar collection of Alfred Ostheimer, yet none of the coins from his set could compare to the present 1799. Maybe an equal exists (NGC appears to have graded 3 Mint State 65's so far), but we haven't seen it nor imagine it has the same sort of presence. Which is why we unhesitatingly recommend it for a specialized collection.

In 1799, some 11 obverse and 17 reverse dies were combined to produce 23 varieties. Bolender-12 is noted for its lack of berries in the reverse branch. Robert Scot engraved the obverse after a design by Gilbert Stuart; he engraved the reverse after the Great Seal of the United States. He seems to have accidentally transposed the arrows and olive branch when he did this, however, resulting in a heraldic boo-boo. Fortunately, so few of us understand heraldry in the late-20th Century that it matters not.

Previously from our Jascha Heifetz Sale, October 1989, Lot 3817 an prior to that ex Newcomer, Col. Green, MacAllister.

INCOMPARABLE 1803 PROOF BUST DOLLAR FINEST KNOWN FOR TYPE

INCOMPARABLE 1803 PROOF BUST DOLLAR
FINEST KNOWN FOR TYPE

702 **1803. Draped Bust, Heraldic Eagle. Bolender-7. Restrike. PCGS graded Proof 66. Premium Quality.** ***Superb! The Finest Known example***. Consider: not only is this beautifully toned Proof 66 the epitome of an 1803 Proof Dollar, it also happens to be *the finest known Proof Bust Dollar for any date, and that includes all 15 specimens of the 1804*! Even wonder why you started collecting coins in the first place? Or recommenced collecting after a layover of many years when your attention was elsewhere? Well, the present coin explains why. As Larry Goldberg, one of the principals of Superior Galleries, so aptly put it to the cataloguer the other day, although he hasn't collected coins since he was a boy (conflict of interest while running a coin business, etc), when this 1803 Proof hidden desire to possess valuable properties reawakened in him.

When you examine this coin for yourself-which you really must do, even if it is beyond your finances-you'll be awestruck by its vibrant gold and blue colors. And you'll be enraptured by its snowy cameo contrast. Taking stock of all the ones we have encountered over the years, we have never seen another Proof Bust Dollar with this much vivid white frosting on Liberty and the eagle. We do not recall having ever encountered a more delightfully deep and contrasting mirror surface. In and of itself, this would give the coin honorable mention in the halls of numismatics. But there's more! The 1803 Proof was for many, many years a mystery coin. Along with its 1801, 1802, and 1804 counterparts, coin specialist were at a loss to explain how such a coin could have come into existence. Papers were written and debates were held over their provenance. Most specialists left the debates scratching their heads. Why? Well, it turns out the Mint left no clear record. (When the story was finally pieced together, it was seen there is ample reason for the Mint having covered over its tracks). The facts were finally revealed when Ken Bressett and Eric P. Newman published "The Fantastic 1804 Silver Dollar" in 1962. Their book is required reading for collectors desiring an indepth look into Proof Bust Dollars.

Returning to the Proof 66 specimen offered here, we note that PCGS has graded only the one example in '66, with a single other specimen in Proof 65. Breen postulates that 6 to 10 specimens are known in all. Because of its majestic appearance and outstanding condition, we expect to see it bring a very strong price.

Same reverse dies as the Class I 1804 Dollar. Note distinctive die line similar to a lint mark below UM or UNUM on reverse on reverse which in seen on all 1901 and 1803 restrikes but no others. This was possible caused by a silver off foreign matter adhering to the reverse die. Edges are blundered, suggesting that-like 1804 restrikes-they were originally made with plain edges, then after the scandal of 1858, concealed until someone could find the original edge dies and jury-rig a Casting machine to impart edge lettering to the finished coins. This last supposition is from Breen. 1803 Proofs were therefore struck sometime prior to 1858 at the same time as the 1801 and 1802 Proofs as well as a portion of the 1804 Proofs.

Previously from Rarcoa's session of Auction '86, Lot 738 as "Gen Brilliant Proof"

THE EXTREMELY RARE NORWEB 1836 NAME BELOW BASE GOBRECHT DOLLAR FINEST KNOWN OF TYPE

THE EXTREMELY RARE NORWEB 1836 NAME BELOW BASE GOBRECHT DOLLAR
FINEST KNOWN OF TYPE

703 **1836. Gobrecht Dollar. C. Gobrecht F. in field between base and date. Judd-58. Breen-5410. 411.7 grains. Extremely Rare. One of perhaps a dozen known. NGC graded Proof 66.** Not only is this a spectacular example of Christian Gobrecht's monumental Silver Dollar, but it has two other noble qualities: first, it has received a hitherto unknown grade from a grading service for one of these, Proof 66; and second, it is the Norweb specimen, giving it a leg up by linking it to one of the greatest coin collections ever formed. In the Norweb sale it was described as "a glittering gem Proof, superb example of one of the most desired of all silver dollar varieties, the style with the signature of the engraver, C. GOBRECHT F. in the field between the base and date. The reverse is oriented nearly in the same direction as the obverse, medal style rather than coin style, but the eagle flying horizontally, rather than upward at a slight angle [Breen's Alignment III]. The piece was probably made in the 1850s from dies cut in 1836."

The grade speaks for itself. Where else will you find strung together a strike that is beyond reproof, surfaces that are deeply mirrored, almost "watery" in appearance, and original color? As to the coin's color, it ranges from silvery gold to pinkish gray and is the height of originality.

As we alluded to above, neither NGC or PCGS has graded another Name Below Base this high. And it seems impossible that they will ever grade another that is its equal. In fact, no other Gobrecht of any variety has yet been graded higher then Proof 65.

The story of the creation of this handsome coin is described by Bowers in the Norweb catalog: "Gobrecht, born in Hanover, York County, Pennsylvania, December 13, 1785, was apprenticed at an early age to a clockmaker. Later he moved to Baltimore where he engaged in the engraving of designs on clock bases and cases. he then prepared illustrations for various publications, for which he engraved portraits of George Washington, David Rittenhouse, Benjamin Franklin, Benjamin Rush, and others.

"In 1811 he moved to Philadelphia and set up trade as a portrait engraver, medal engraver, and die cutter. In 1825, following a design by Thomas Sully, Gobrecht engraved a medal for the Franklin Institute. Many other medals, some of which were struck by the Philadelphia Mint, were prepared by Gobrecht during the 1820s and 1830s.

"In the autumn of 1835 Gobrecht joined the Mint staff. His first task there was to prepare an obverse design of the figure of Miss Liberty, seated, from paintings and sketches by Titian Peale and Thomas Sully, following the request of Director Patterson and Engraver Kneass. The Inspiration for the subject seems to have been ultimately rooted in the neoclassicism movement of the era. Gods, goddesses, and other allegorical figures were often portrayed in long flowing robes with such accoutrements as birds, wreaths, shields, weapons, and other objects. Director Patterson's personal inspiration for the obverse motif sprang from the seated figure of Britannia, which had graced the coinage of Britain since the 17th Century.

"The reverse design portrayed a flying eagle, popularly said to have been modeled after Peter, an eagle which in the 1830s was a mascot at the mint (and who today in stuffed form is displayed in a transparent case in the lobby of the new Philadelphia Mint on Federal Square, Philadelphia). Titian Peale, it should be noted, was an ardent naturalist and painter of wildlife, and the eagle reverse might also have been taken from Peale's own sketchbook.

"In 1836 pattern silver dollars were struck. The obverse bore the newly created seated representation of Miss Liberty, the reverse a flying eagle. Director Patterson, viewing initial impressions of the die, was so delighted with the new design that he directed Gobrecht to put his name on it. Gobrecht, following the signature used on certain of his earlier medals, boldly signed it C. Gobrecht F. (The F being for *fecit*. In Latin, *made it*) in the field above the date."

Previously from Bowers and Merena's Norweb Sale Part III, November 1988, Lot 3774

THE GEM PROOF NORWEB 1839 GOBRECHT DOLLAR
FINEST KNOWN

THE GEM PROOF NORWEB 1839 GOBRECHT DOLLAR FINEST KNOWN

704 **1839. Gobrecht Dollar. J-104. Starless reverse. Silver. Plain Edge. PCGS graded Proof 65. The Norweb coin.** Another outstanding Gem Proof Gobrecht Dollar from the famed Norweb collection. This one, too, is attractively toned and has every evidence of having been handled with kid gloves down through the years. As Bowers relates, and to which we concur, "One of the nicest of the very rare 1839 Gobrecht dollars we have ever seen or handled". The weight of the present piece is 411.8 grains, and the die alignment is the same as on the preceding lot [this refers to another coin in the Norweb sale, the 1836 Name Below Base offered a moment ago]. Apparently this particular variety, with the dies aligned nearly in the same direction, but with the eagle flying horizontally, is exceedingly rare, so rare in fact that Walter Breen apparently has not confirmed the existence of an example (see notation of page 436 of his *Encyclopedia of United States Coins*, under entry 5423, line 2, where he says that this variety 'may also exist'.)

"Struck from perfect obverse and reverse dies without any breaks."

"Because documentation on existing Gobrecht Dollars has not been extensive, few examples in the past have had their die alignments studied or their weights recorded, and as additional information becomes available, prevailing thoughts on the emission sequence may change."

PCGS has graded 11 lower grade Proofs of Judd-104 as of March 1991, and only this single Proof 65. That may mean, for all intents and purposes, that this coin is the Finest Known!

Previously from Bowers and Merena's Norweb Sale Part III, November 1988, Lot 3777

SUPERB 1863 NO MOTTO SEATED DOLLAR

705 **1863. PCGS graded Mint State 65**. Beautifully toned on both sides with deep pinkish gold for the obverse and lavender and blue for the reverse. Superior in every way to the other superb 1863 we offered a year and a half ago in our Heifetz Sale. The present coin, too, has needle-sharp devices throughout combined with immaculate fields and a very handsome overall appearance. Seated Dollar enthusiasts learn the hard way that dates like 1863 are almost impossible to find in Uncirculated grade, let alone *Gem Uncirculated*. To begin with, there were only 27,200 business strikes made (along with 460 Proofs.) Of those, nearly everyone either saw circulation or went to Latin America to be melted down. This is because 1863 was a trying year for the North in America's civil war. People who had any bullion on hand kept it hidden rather than take it to the mint for coining. Uncertainty reigned. It was wiser to hoard coin and bullion.

Of the dozen or so Mint State 1863's we have auctioned, this is one of the prettiest. PCGS records 2 Mint Sate 65's as of March 1991, and 1 higher, for a grand total of 3 Gems. A jewel of such calibre may be exactly the right one for your set, so bid liberally to ensure getting it.

GEM BRILLIANT PROOF 1864 SEATED DOLLAR

706 **1864. PCGS graded Proof 65.** A second No Motto Seated Dollar, this one a Proof. and what a Proof it is! Bright, with just a hint of gold toning; deeply mirrored with the most gorgeous contrasting snow white frost imaginable; and a look of quiet elegance about it that tells you it has been revered ever since it was first sold to a collector. A spectacular Gem and would fit into any Silver Dollar set in the land. PCGS records 3 graded with none higher out of an original mintage of 470.

Because of a wide open field surrounding Liberty and the eagle on No Motto Seated Dollars, these tended to get unsightly hairlines rather easily. The present coin escaped such abuse. Which places it in a very select class.

FAMOUS "IN GOD WE TRUST" 1865 SEATED DOLLAR FINEST KNOWN

707 **1865. Pattern Dollar. Judd-434. Rarity-7. Silver. Reeded Edge. PCGS graded Proof 64. Premium Quality.** *With motto IN GOD WE TRUST on reverse.* A famous name in American numismatics, the Transitional 1865 Seated Dollar features a regular obverse of 1865 mated to the regular With Motto dies adopted in 1866. The present specimen is a razor-sharp coin and makes a wonderful adjunct to the broad-spectrum set of American Silver Dollars. In addition to its historical importance, this piece is the Finest Known, displaying attractive natural color, the sort of toning acquired only over many years.

Silver Dollar enthusiasts as well as Pattern collectors both have their tentacles out for this piece. It fits into either category quite well. And because of its unusual Transitional status, makes a great conversation piece. Of two Judd-434 specimens graded by PCGS as of March 1991, this is the finer one, the other being Proof 63. Judd considers this a Rarity-7 item, meaning only 4 to 12 are known, there may not be any sharper ones around. Please make a note of this.

Judd believes these may have actually been struck in 1865-1866. About 10 years ago an 1865 With Motto piece surfaced *struck over an 1866 regular issue coin*! We are not able to discern any undertype on the present specimen, so it may have been struck on a normal blank planchet intended from Proofs. Be that as it may a small mystery that had haunted numismatists for decades was finally laid to rest.

Previously from Stack's Jimmy Hayes Sale, October 1985, Lot 75.

UNBELIEVABLY VIBRANT 1866 SEATED DOLLAR
FINEST KNOWN BUSINESS STRIKE OF TYPE

UNBELIEVABLY VIBRANT 1866 SEATED DOLLAR FINEST KNOWN BUSINESS STRIKE OF TYPE

708 **1866. PCGS graded PCGS Mint State 66.** *Superb*! The obverse of this unbelievable Gem is summed up in four words: Bright. White. Vibrant. *Alive*! The reverse, for its part, needs a further modifier: gorgeous iridescent blue color. Now, we see by PCGS's most recent *Population Report* for March 1991 that they've graded two specimens supposedly this nice, two Mint State 66's and none higher (the other Mint State 66 was sold by Stack's as part of the Jimmy Hayes Collection). The Hayes coin does not compare to this coin's overpowering beauty, its freshness and originality of lustre and the sense of awe it inspires when you gaze upon it. Strong words, perhaps, but the coin rates nothing less. When you examine it you will see why we wax eloquent.

The Mint began introducing the motto IN GOD WE TRUST on America's silver and gold coinage in 1866. Because the nation was still on a flat money standard whereby "greenback" paper money was the primary money in circulation, most silver coinage such as this 1866 Dollar left the country as soon as it was issued. Only a relative few survived in honest-to-goodness Mint State condition; fewer, still, as unsullied as this.

Previously sold by Christie's in 1898, Formerly from Wayte Raymond.

THE EMERY NICHOLS 1869 PROOF DOLLAR
FINEST KNOWN FOR TYPE

THE EMERY NICHOLS 1869 PROOF DOLLAR — FINEST KNOWN FOR TYPE

709 **1869. NGC graded Proof 67. *Superb*!** We might as well let the kitty-cat out of the bag right up front: *this is the only Proof 67 Seated Dollar for either type graded by either service*. There are none higher. Nor will there ever be any higher if this is an example of what it takes to earn the Proof 67 label. For never will you find a more original, fresher looking specimen though you search a thousand years throughout the museums of the world and the secret master coin collections of America. Frosty white devices are here nicely offset by glowingly reflective mirror fields. And the entire coin has developed sunset gold color during its undisturbed residence in collections. Other than for some blue and lavender toning around the reverse rim, the toning is an even golden hue.

Originally, the mint struck and sold 600 Proof 1869 Seated Dollars. Collectors of the day probably cherished them as highly as we do today, but they were unfortunate to be living at a time when hard plastic holders or sulfur-free envelopes were unknown. As a consequence, most 19th Century Proof coinage got battered about. Today there are very few hairline-free Gems left for collectors to bid on at auction. That is why we consider the sale of this 1869 as a prime opportunity for the astute collector. As Bowers said when he auctioned it in 1984, "This coin appears to be totally untouched by human hands (except on the edge) in its 115 years of existence. It is truly a 'wonder coin' within this series."

Previously from Bowers and Merena's Nichols Sale, November 1984, Lot 1000.

FROSTY WHITE 1876 TRADE DOLLAR

710 **1876. PCGS graded Mint State 65**. A super example that is awash in frosty mint lustre, as white as the day it was made and a real charmer. Liberty and the eagle are boldly defined, while the lustrous fields are free from the usual bagmarks and signs of contact. It is important for us to note here that very few Trade Dollars remain in undeniable Gem Uncirculated condition. Yes, there are plenty of Mint State 60 to 63 specimens; but for the discriminating collector there are few nice, frosty white PCGS-65's of any date, not just 1876. We see where the March 1991 *Population Report* lists 6 in this category, plus 2 higher, and this out of an original mintage of over 450,000!

FROSTY WHITE 1876 TRADE DOLLAR

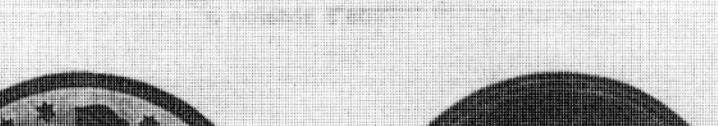

GEM TONED PROOF 1879 TRADE DOLLAR

GEM TONED PROOF 1879 TRADE DOLLAR

711 **1879. PCGS graded Proof 66.** ***A first class example with well balanced toning***. Here's a faultless example of what a Proof Trade Dollar was meant to look like. The strike is needle-sharp; the surfaces, impeccable; and the color a rich blend of blues and golden brown and smoky lavender. There were 1,541 Proofs struck in 1879. Unfortunately, most of these are no where near gem condition today, the majority having been mishandled or cleaned. As of March 1991, PCGS had seen only 8 Proof 66's and 3 Proof 67's. Because their population is so low, we recommend this specimen to all bidders looking to score big when the day comes to sell. In the meantime enjoy your new purchase as much as we enjoyed cataloguing it for you.

Provenance unknown.

FANTASTIC 1880 PROOF 68 MORGAN
FINEST KNOWN OF TYPE

FANTASTIC 1880 PROOF 68 MORGAN
FINEST KNOWN OF TYPE

712 **1880. PCGS graded Proof 68. Premium Quality.** ***Superb***! Vibrant multicolored toning circles the periphery ranging from purple to blue with dozens of shades in between giving the coin a decidedly balanced effect. We won't even attempt to restate what Rarcoa put so well when this coin last sold at Auction '90:

"**SUPERB GEM PROOF**-the ultimate condition. How do you describe a coin that comes within a hair's breadth of perfection? Basically, it is in the same state as when it left the dies at the Philadelphia Mint some 110 years ago. Perfectly struck, stored and handled for over a century, it has survived time without a mark, hairline, carbon spot or any other kind of imperfection. In fact, it centers, somewhat darker around the peripheries. A fantastic rarity in the ultimate quality. If you desire the best, then by all means bid on this lot. We fully expect it to reach a record price level. Examined by NGC and graded PF68-the one and only specimen to be so rated."

Since then it has gone sideways into a PCGS holder (probably in an attempt to see it earn a Proof 69 grade, which it deserves). Also since last summer another Proof 68 has surfaced according to PCGS's population report. Although we haven't seen that other specimen, somehow we don't think it measures up to this fantastic coin.

From an original 1880 Proof set broken up and sold separately at Auction '90.

Previously from Rarcoa's session of Auction '90, Lot 876.

THE END 1900 LAFAYETTE DOLLAR

714 **1900. Lafayette Dollar**. PCGS graded Mint State 66. Superb. And featuring superb toning with greens, golds, and blues prevailing. Here is another outstanding original toning Silver Dollar right up there among the finest known, that has been carefully stored over its lifetime. PCGS has graded 5 of these so far in Mint State 66, plus 2 higher. However, their population report fails to say whether any of the others displays similarly beautiful toning.

The occasion for this first American Silver Dollar Commemorative was the Paris Exposition of 1900. Coins were sold to the public to defray part of the cost of Paul Bartlett's equestrian statue of Lafayette at the Exposition, which the U.S. had pledged $50,000 towards. Both sides were engraved by mint engraver Charles E. Barber, the obverse layout from Peter Krider's Yorktown medal of 1881 and the reverse from an early sketch of Bartlett's statue. The inscription alludes to donations made by schoolchildren. In all, 50,000 pieces were struck, although 14,000 were melted on December 14, 1899 leaving a net mintage of 36,000.

FINEST KNOWN EXTREMELY RARE PROOF 1883 HAWAIIAN DOLLAR

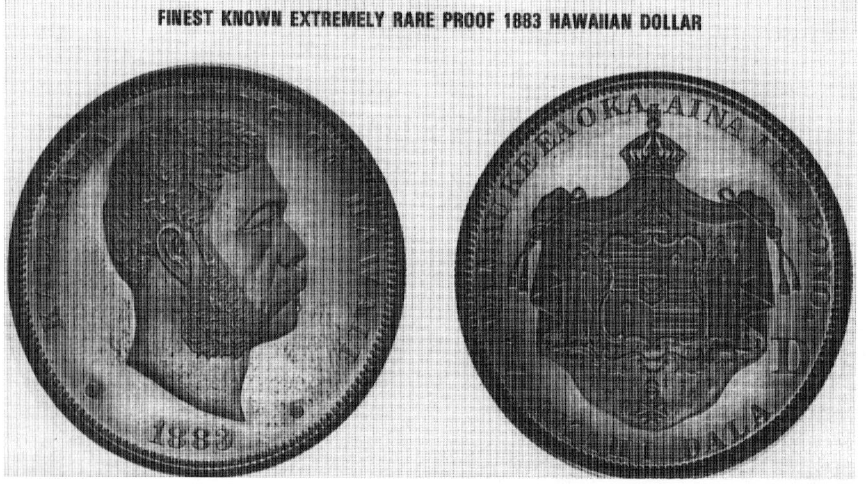

715 **1883. Kingdom of Hawaii. Kalakaua I. PCGS graded Proof 65. Beautifully toned; superb**. The obverse portrays a bust of King Kalakaua (reigned 1874-1891) with motto KALAKAUA I KING OF HAWAII. For the reverse, the Hawaiian Coat of Arms on ermine mantle with crown atop. Surrounding this, the Kingdoms (and now the State's) motto: UA MAU KE EA O KA AINA I KA PONO (loosely translated into English, "The life of the land is perpetuated in righteousness"). Proofs were struck at Philadelphia Mint from dies prepared by mint engraver Charles E. Barber. Business strikes were made at the San Francisco Mint. Only 26 Proofs struck. And this one is, without a doubt, the loveliest, freshest, most original of those surviving — by a long shot! PCGS has graded three Proofs as of March 1991. Two of these are Proof 63's, and the other, this coin, is the only Gem seen so far, a Proof 65.

Examine it if you can. Note especially its razor-sharpness; delight in its magnificent cameo contrast whereby the devices are superbly frosted; enjoy its miles-deep mirror field; and, most of all, remember that you are examining one of the classic territorial rarities in American numismatics! We expect to see bidders give this coin a good run for the money. A record breaking price realized is expected. Remember, too, that if you fail to bid high enough, you may never get another chance this century to acquire a Gem Proof Hawaiian Dollar.

A coin's story is half its charm. And the Kalakaua Silver Dollar has a dandy one. King (David) Kalakaua reigned as Hawaii's last male monarch from 1874 until his death in 1891. His sister, Liliuokalani, took over the reins of power upon his death but less than two years later was overthrown in a bloodless coup. Hawaii then went through a transition period when it became the Republic of Hawaii before being taken under America's wing in 1898 as one of our growing inventory of colonies-oops! make that "Territories."

Like all good kings before and since, Kalakaua found himself in a financial pickle in the early 1880's. Plans for a $300,000 coral block stone Palace, a navy, and internal improvements were straining the kingdom's taxpayers (mostly American businessmen). Fortunately, like all good kings, Kalakaua had close advisers. Call them idea men. Two of these were his "Minister of Everything" Walter Murray Gibson and the sugar baron, Claus Spreckels. With these two rascals on either side of him whispering into his ears, they convinced the king to borrow the money he needed ($2,000,000) via a series of bonds, with half of it coming from Spreckel's own kind generosity, terms 6%. Spreckels would be authorized to contract with the U.S. Mint for an issue of silver coinage, $1,000,000 face value in all.

This sounded fine to the king, so he gave his approval to the scheme. What he didn't realize then, but what soon came to light, was that Spreckels intended to pocket the profit (seignorage) on the coins, their bullion value being less than their face value. Jacob Adler estimates in his ***Claus Spreckels The Sugar King in Hawaii*** **that Spreckels pocketed a cool $100,000 to $200,000 on the deal. The coins were duly placed into circulation through the banks (one of which he owned, naturally).**

As was explained above in the description of the coin, the Philadelphia Mint prepared dies for each of 5 denominations, Dime, Hapawalu (12 1/2c). Quarter, Half Dollar, and Silver Dollar. Six Proofs sets were made in September 1883 without the Hapawalu, and 20 more including that denomination in September 1884, making a total of 26 Proof Silver Dollars.

Kalakaua approved the design, mintage commenced, and the coins began entering circulation in Honolulu in January 1884. Thereupon, the opposition party let out a wail, with overtones of revolution in their indictment of Kalakaua, Spreckels, and Gibson. Spreckels kept his ill-gotten seignorage. The king was able to finish his stately Palace. And the businessmen bided their time until they revolted in 1893, toppling the monarchy. Oh, yes — Claus Spreckels and Walter Murray Gibson were, after a series of other enviable scandals, unceremoniously booted out of the islands in 1887 and 1893, respectively. Collectors have this glorious 1883 Proof Hawaiian Dollar as a memento of those turbulent years!

SUPERB MINT STATE 1883 HAWAIIAN DOLLAR

SUPERB MINT STATE 1883 HAWAIIAN DOLLAR

716 **1883 Hawaiian Dollar. Portrait of Kalakaua I. Mint State 65**. A frosty Gem Uncirculated example of this one-year type having light natural toning over lovely surfaces. Kalakaua's portrait is especially bold in showing all of the curls in his beard (usually a weak area because it is high on the coin). Only a few score choice to gem Hawaiian Dollars remain out of an original mintage of 500,000. This is because of those 500,000 pieces coin in San Francisco, all but slightly over 44,000 were turned in and melted following Annexation (1898). Today, Gem Mint State 65's are highly cherished possessions.

This ends this incredible set of Silver Dollars.

CERTIFIED COIN DEALER newsletter

a weekly report on the certified market published by the Coin Dealer Newsletter (est. 1963)

Vol VI No. 22 May 31, 1991 Single copy price $3.50

1794 $1 Realizes $506K
Superior Sale Garners $7.5 Million

Teletype activity this week has been relatively subdued, as dealers crowded into Southern California for the Long Beach Show, to inspect all of the lots from the associated auctions, and to Bid on needed material for customers and inventory. The lack of plus signs can be attributed to market lethargy combined with the travelling dealers; the minus signs on the charts inside still derive from lowered sells, as dealers offered material at lower levels. We are continuing our recent policy on *Bluesheet* Bids: *We raised Bluesheet Bid on a higher posted Bid, but we didn't lower Bluesheet Bid on a lowered posted Bid; Bluesheet Bid was lowered only in response to a lower offer to Sell or Trade.*

The sale of an MS65 1893-S Morgan on the Certified Coin Exchange to the $242,000 Ask may have created a (minor) minus sign in this week's issue, but the sale of such an important coin at this level could hardly be considered negative news. A Bid that stays on the system and is never "hit" provides some valuable information: You know that the coin is worth at least the amount of the Bid, but you still don't know what the coin is really worth. A coin that sells to the ASK (as few do on CCE) provides much more exacting information on the market value of the item.

Thanks to all of the advance publicity, and a crowded audience bidding on the Amazing Collection of United States Silver Dollars at Superior Galleries' May 27, 28 Auction, we now know what some of America's finest coins are worth (see box).

ISSUE	GRADE	PRICE REALIZED
1776 Continental Dollar	PCGS65 PQ	$ 39,600
1794 Flowing Hair $1 (B-1)	PCGS65 PQ	$506,000
1795 Draped Bust $1 (B-15)	NGC65	$154,000
1803 Draped Bust, Her. $1 (B-7)	PCGS-Pr66	$264,000
1866 Seated Dollar	PCGS66	$ 60,500
1869 Seated Dollar	NGC-Pr67	$ 49,500
1880 Morgan Dollar	PCGS-Pr68	$ 39,600
1900 Lafayette Dollar	PCGS66	$ 27,500

And just to prove that the specialists also admire the finest quality in other series, an 1814 Bust Half (Overton-103) graded by NGC as MS67 realized $30,800. Total Prices realized were $7,528,564.

Heritage's Bullet Auction, to be held May 30 at the Long Beach Show, exhibits several of the changes that certification has brought to the coin auction market. In the past, we have described certified-only auctions; the concept has evolved considerably since then. The catalogue is definitely a "no-frills" affair; but no photographs and minimal lot descriptions are not a major drawback when you enjoy a clientele that is largely going to inspect the lots.

Printing the catalogues by laser means more than just being able to offer a two-week cutoff; it also means that customized catalogues can be prepared. If you are a specialist in Morgan Dollars, you can request that just the Morgan Dollar lots be included in your catalogue. Old-time numismatists who enjoy poring over old catalogues will be disappointed in this possibility, as well as those who enjoy looking at the photographs of coins outside their areas of expertise; but for an efficient system of moving coins from seller to buyer, you would be hard pressed to find technology being used more precisely.

CCDN "Bluesheet" Prices Realized - Superior's "An Amazing Collection of United States Silver Dollars"
(Courtesy of CCDN, Torrance, California)

The Congressman Jimmy Hayes Speciman (Obverse, Left; Reverse, Right) — 1795 Draped Bust Dollar
(Photo Courtesy of Jay C. Miller, Boca Raton, Florida)

Finest Known 1795 Flowing Hair ex-Garret Sale (Obverse, Left; Reverse, Right) — Jimmy Hayes Collection
(Photo Courtesy of Jay C. Miller, Boca Raton, Florida)

DWIGHT N. MANLEY

WORLD'S FINEST KNOWN PROOF TRADE DOLLAR SET

This United States Proof Trade Dollar Set was started by Dwight N. Manley in 1989 and completed during 1991. Isn't it amazing what dedication can accomplish in such a short period of time! All coins in this collection were certified by the Professional Coin Grading Service.

Date	Service	Grade
1873	PCGS	PR65
1874 *	PCGS	PR65
1875 *	PCGS	PR66
1876 *	PCGS	PR65
1877	PCGS	PR66
1878	PCGS	PR66
1879 *	PCGS	PR67
1880	PCGS	PR67
1881	PCGS	PR67
1882	PCGS	PR67
1883 *	PCGS	PR66

PR = Proof issue

* *These coins from this collection have been replaced and/or upgraded since the photograph shown with this set was taken.*

The Dwight N. Manley World's Finest Known Proof Trade Dollar Set
(Courtesy of Spectrum Numismatics, Santa Ana, California)

THE WAYNE MILLER SILVER DOLLAR SET

(1878 - 1935)

The following compilation of the Wayne Miller Morgan and Peace dollar set was presented by Bruce Amspacher in his Investment Report (BAIR), Volume 3 Number 2, July 21, 1984. This set was assembled during the years (1968 - 1983) prior to PCGS and NGC.

Morgan Dollars

Date	Grade	Description
1878-P 8TF	MS65+	Cameo PL Obv.
1878-P 7TF	MS65	Prooflike
1878-P 7F Round Breast	MS65++	Cameo PL
1878-P 7/8	MS65+	Prooflike
1878-CC	MS67	Cameo PL
1878-S	MS69+	Cameo PL wonder coin
1879-P	MS65++	Cameo PL
1879-CC	MS65	Cameo PL
1879-O	MS65++	Cameo PL
1879-S	MS68	Cameo PL wonder coin
1879-S Flat Breast	MS64	Cameo PL
1880-P	MS65++	Cameo PL
1880-CC	MS65++	Semi PL
1880-O	MS67	Cameo PL
1880-S	MS68	Cameo PL
1881-P	MS65++	Cameo PL
1881-CC	MS65++	Cameo PL
1881-O	MS65	Cameo PL
1881-S	MS68	Cameo PL
1882-P	MS65+	Cameo PL
1882-CC	MS65+	Cameo PL
1882-O	MS65	Cameo PL
1882-S	MS65	Cameo PL
1883-P	MS65++	Cameo PL
1883-CC	MS68	Cameo PL
1883-O	MS65++	Cameo PL
1883-S	MS67	Cameo PL (not deep)
1884-P	MS65++	Cameo PL
1884-CC	MS67+	Cameo PL
1884-O	MS65++	Cameo PL
1884-S	MS65	
1885-O	MS67	Cameo PL
1885-CC	MS67	Cameo PL
1885-CC	MS67++	Cameo PL
1885-S	MS65+	Cameo PL
1886-P	MS67+	Semi PL
1886-O	MS68	Cameo PL wonder coin
1886-S	MS65+	Prooflike
1887-P	MS65++	Cameo PL
1887-O	MS65++	Cameo PL
1887-S	MS65+	Semi PL
1888-P	MS65++	Cameo PL
1888-O	MS65++	Cameo PL
1888-S	MS65	Prooflike
1889-P	MS65+	Prooflike
1889-CC	MS65+	Cameo PL
1889-O	MS65+	Cameo PL
1889-S	MS65++	Cameo PL
1890-P	MS65++	Light Cameo PL

Date	Grade	Description
1890-CC	MS65+	Cameo PL
1890-O	MS65++	Cameo PL
1890-S	MS65++	Cameo PL
1891-P	MS65+	Cameo PL
1891-CC	MS67	Semi PL
1891-O	MS67+	
1891-S	MS65+	Cameo PL
1892-P	MS65++	Cameo PL
1892-CC	MS65	Cameo PL
1892-O	MS65+	Cameo PL
1892-S	MS67	
1893-P	MS65++	
1893-CC	MS65+	
1893-O	MS65+	Semi PL
1894-P	MS67	Prooflike
1894-O	MS65	
1894-S	MS65+	Prooflike
1895-O	MS68	Semi PL
1895-S	MS65+	Prooflike
1896-P	MS67	Prooflike
1896-O	MS65	Semi PL
1896-S	MS67	
1897-P	MS65++	Cameo PL
1897-O	MS68	
1897-S	MS67	Cameo PL
1898-P	MS65+	Prooflike
1898-O	MS65++	Cameo PL
1898-S	MS65+	Cameo PL
1899-P	MS67	Cameo PL
1899-O	MS67	Cameo PL
1899-S	MS65++	Prooflike
1900-P	MS65++	Prooflike
1900-O	MS67	Prooflike
1900-S	MS65++	Prooflike
1901-P	MS67	Toned
1901-O	MS65++	Prooflike
1901-S	MS67	Semi PL
1902-P	MS67	Prooflike
1902-O	MS67	Prooflike
1902-S	MS65++	Semi PL
1903-P	MS65++	Prooflike
1903-O	MS67	Prooflike
1903-S	MS67	
1904-P	MS65+	Prooflike
1904-O	MS67	Prooflike
1904-S	MS65++	
1921-P	MS65	Cameo PL
1921-D	MS67	Semi PL
1921-S	MS67	

Proof Dollars

Date	Grade	Description
1878 8TF	PR67	
1878 7TF	PR67	
1878 7TF Round Breast	PR65+	Cameo
1879	PR67	Cameo
1880	PR68	Cameo
1881	PR68	Cameo
1882	PR68	Cameo
1883	PR67	Cameo
1884	PR67	Cameo
1885	PR67	
1886	PR67	
1887	PR67	Cameo
1888	PR68	Cameo
1889	PR67	Cameo
1890	PR68	Cameo
1891	PR67	Cameo
1892	PR65++	Cameo
1893	PR67	Toned
1894	PR67	Cameo
1895	PR67	Cameo
1896	PR67	Cameo
1897	PR65++	Cameo
1898	PR67	Cameo
1899	PR67	Toned
1900	PR67	Cameo
1901	PR67	Some Cameo
1902	PR65+	
1903	PR67	
1904	PR67	
1921 Zerbe	PR65+	
1921 Peace	PR65	
1922 Peace	PR65	Not high relief

MS = Mint State
PL = Prooflike
SEMI PL = One sided Prooflike
PR = Proof

Peace Dollars

Date	Grade
1921-P	MS65+
1922-P	MS67
1922-D	MS67
1922-S	MS67+
1923-P	MS67
1923-D	MS65
1923-S	MS63
1924-P	MS65
1924-S	MS65+
1925-P	MS67
1925-S	MS65++
1926-P	MS65+
1926-D	MS65+
1926-S	MS67
1927-P	MS68
1927-D	MS65+
1927-S	MS65+
1928-P	MS67
1928-S	MS65
1934-P	MS67
1934-D	MS67
1934-S	MS69
1935-P	MS67
1935-S	MS67

Branch Mint Proof Morgan Dollars

1879-O	PR69	Cameo
1882-CC	PR67	
1883-O	PR65++	
1893-CC	PR67	
1921-S	PR65	

THE WILLIAM E. SPEARS

CARSON CITY MORGAN DOLLAR SET

The following complete set of Carson City Morgan Silver Dollars was accumulated by William E. Spears. Mr. Spears took many years to carefully assemble this astounding collection. Many of these coins were included in the PCGS sponsored Rare Coin Experience: "The World's Finest Morgan Silver Dollars." All coins in this collection were certified by the Professional Coin Grading Service.

Date	Grade	Service
1878-CC	MS67	PCGS
1879-CC	MS65	PCGS
1879-CC CD	MS65	PCGS
1880-CC	MS67	PCGS
1881-CC	MS67	PCGS
1882-CC	MS67	PCGS
1883-CC	MS67	PCGS
1884-CC	MS68	PCGS

Date	Grade	Service
1885-CC	MS68	PCGS
1889-CC	MS65	PCGS
1890-CC	MS66	PCGS
1891-CC	MS67	PCGS
1892-CC	MS67	PCGS
1893-CC	MS65	PCGS
1900-O/CC	MS66	PCGS

MS = Mint State

THE JOHN W. HIGHFILL

MORGAN DOLLAR COLLECTION

(1878 - 1921)

The John W. Highfill Morgan dollar collection was painstakingly assembled with a dedicated effort, and upgraded to its present status over a number of years. Thousands of Morgan dollars were viewed and rejected in order to find the specimens contained in this collection. Many of these coins are the "finest known" and are magnificent gems. The aura emanating from this completed set is very exciting indeed! The collection of PLs and DMPLs alone will take your breath away. Many individuals have expressed an interest in the total collection or in individual pieces. Some individual pieces have been privately placed, but the nucleus of the set is still very securely intact.

This author considers this set to be the most "totally" complete and highest quality certified Morgan dollar collection ever assembled by a private individual. This collection consists of MS, PL and DMPL categories containing many finest known examples. PCGS designates DMPL for Deep Mirror Prooflike, while NGC designates DPL for Deep Prooflike for all Morgan silver dollars. The John W. Highfill collection would rival the PCGS World's Finest Morgan Silver Dollars and other private collections. In fact, a number of these coins are a part of the PCGS tour collection (see the chapter by Rebecca Fong entitled, A Rare Coin Experience: "The World's Finest Morgan Silver Dollars"). At the time of its completion this "wonder" set contained the following coins. Abbreviations used:

Finest grade known — 133 examples
1B = One grade better known — 70 examples
2B = Two grades better known — 4 examples

Date	Grade	Service
1878-P 7TF Rev. 78	MS66	PCGS *
1878-P 7TF Rev. 78	MS65 PL	PCGS *
1878-P 7/8TF Strong	MS65	PCGS *
1878-P 7/8TF Weak	MS65	PCGS *
1878-P 7TF Rev. 79	MS65	PCGS *
1878-P 8TF	MS66	PCGS *
1878-CC	MS66	PCGS 1B
1878-CC	MS65 PL	PCGS 1B
1878-CC	MS66 DMPL	PCGS *
1878-S	MS67	PCGS *
1878-S	MS65 PL	PCGS 2B
1878-S	MS66 DMPL	PCGS 1B
1879-P	MS65	PCGS 1B
1879-P	MS65 PL	PCGS *
1879-CC	MS65	PCGS *
1879-CC	MS64 DMPL	PCGS *
1879-CC Capped Die	MS65	NGC *
1879-O	PR64**	PCGS *
1879-O	MS65	PCGS 1B
1879-S SAF	MS68	PCGS *
1879-S SAF	MS66 PL	PCGS 1B
1879-S SAF	MS66 DMPL	PCGS *
1879-S Rev. 78 PAF	MS65	PCGS 1B
1880-P	MS65	PCGS 1B
1880-P	MS65 PL	PCGS *
1880-P	MS65 DMPL	PCGS *
1880-CC SAF	MS66	PCGS 1B
1880-CC SAF	MS65 DMPL	PCGS *
1880-CC Rev. 78 PAF	MS66	PCGS *
1880-CC Rev. 78 PAF	MS65 DMPL	PCGS *
1880-O	MS65	PCGS *
1880-O	MS65 PL	PCGS *
1880-S	MS68	PCGS 1B
1880-S	MS66 DMPL	PCGS 1B
1881-P	MS66	PCGS *
1881-P	MS65 DMPL	NGC *
1881-CC	MS67	PCGS *
1881-CC	MS66 DMPL	PCGS *
1881-O	MS65	PCGS *

Date	Grade	Service
1881-S	MS68	PCGS 1B
1881-S	MS66 PL	PCGS 1B
1881-S	MS66 DMPL	PCGS 1B
1882-P	MS66	PCGS 1B
1882-P	MS65 DMPL	PCGS *
1882-CC	MS66	PCGS 1B
1882-CC	MS65 PL	PCGS 1B
1882-CC	MS66 DMPL	PCGS *
1882-O	MS66	PCGS 2B
1882-O	MS65 PL	PCGS *
1882-O/S	MS64	PCGS *
1882-S	MS67	PCGS 1B
1882-S	MS65 PL	PCGS 2B
1882-S	MS66 DMPL	PCGS *
1883-P	MS67	PCGS *
1883-P	MS65 PL	PCGS *
1883-P	MS65 DMPL	PCGS 1B
1883-CC	MS67	PCGS *
1883-CC	MS66 PL	PCGS 1B
1883-CC	MS66 DMPL	PCGS *
1883-O	MS66	PCGS 1B
1883-O	MS66 PL	PCGS *
1883-O	MS66 DMPL	PCGS *
1883-S	MS65	PCGS *
1884-P	MS67	PCGS *
1884-P	MS65 PL	PCGS 1B
1884-P	MS66 DMPL	NGC *
1884-CC	MS66	PCGS 2B
1884-CC	MS66 PL	PCGS *
1884-CC	MS66 DMPL	PCGS *
1884-O	MS66	PCGS 1B
1884-O	MS65 PL	PCGS 1B
1884-O	MS66 DMPL	PCGS *
1884-S	MS65	PCGS 1B
1885-P	MS67	PCGS 1B
1885-P	MS66 PL	PCGS *
1885-P	MS66 DMPL	PCGS *
1885-CC	MS67	PCGS 1B

Date	Grade	Service
1885-CC	MS66 DMPL	PCGS *
1885-O	MS67	PCGS *
1885-O	MS66 PL	PCGS *
1885-O	MS66 DMPL	PCGS *
1885-S	MS66	PCGS 1B
1885-S	MS65 PL	PCGS *
1886-P	MS67	PCGS *
1886-P	MS66 DMPL	PCGS *
1886-O	MS64	PCGS *
1886-O	MS64 DMPL	PCGS 1B
1886-S	MS65	PCGS 1B
1886-S	MS65 PL	PCGS *
1887-P	MS67	PCGS *
1887-P	MS66 PL	PCGS *
1887-P	MS66 DMPL	PCGS *
1887/6-P	MS65	PCGS *
1887-O	MS65	PCGS *
1887-O	MS65 PL	PCGS *
1887/6-O	MS63	PCGS 1B
1887-S	MS66	PCGS *
1888-P	MS66	PCGS 1B
1888-P	MS66 PL	PCGS *
1888-P	MS65 DMPL	PCGS 1B
1888-O	MS65	PCGS 1B
1888-O	MS65 PL	PCGS *
1888-O	MS65 DMPL	PCGS 1B
1888-S	MS65	PCGS 1B
1888-S	MS65 DMPL	NGC *
1889-P	MS66	PCGS 1B
1889-P	MS65 DMPL	PCGS *
1889-CC	MS64 DMPL	PCGS 1B
1889-O	MS66	PCGS *
1889-O	MS65 PL	PCGS *
1889-S	MS66	PCGS *
1890-P	MS65	PCGS *
1890-P	MS65 PL	PCGS *
1890-CC	MS65	PCGS 1B
1890-CC Tailbar	MS65	PCGS *
1890-CC	MS65 DMPL	PCGS *
1890-O	MS66	PCGS *
1890-S	MS66	PCGS *
1891-P	MS65	PCGS 1B
1891-CC	MS66	PCGS *
1891-CC	MS65 PL	PCGS *
1891-CC	MS65 DMPL	PCGS *
1891-O	MS65	PCGS *
1891-S	MS66	PCGS 1B
1891-S	MS65 PL	PCGS *
1892-P	MS65	PCGS *
1892-P	MS65 PL	PCGS *
1892-CC	MS66	PCGS *
1892-CC	MS65 PL	PCGS *
1892-O	MS65	PCGS *
1892-S	MS67	PCGS *
1893-P	MS65	PCGS *
1893-CC	PR64**	PCGS 1B
1893-CC	MS65	PCGS *
1893-O	MS65	PCGS *
1893-S	MS65	PCGS 1B
1894-P	MS66	PCGS *
1894-O	MS65	PCGS *
1894-S	MS66	PCGS 1B
1895-P (Proof)	PR67	PCGS *
1895-O	MS65	PCGS 1B
1895-S	MS65	PCGS 1B
1895-S	MS66 PL	PCGS *
1896-P	MS66	PCGS *
1896-P	MS66 PL	PCGS *
1896-P	MS65 DMPL	PCGS *
1896-O	MS64	PCGS 1B
1896-S	MS65	PCGS 1B
1897-P	MS67	PCGS *
1897-P	MS65 DMPL	PCGS *
1897-O	MS67	PCGS *
1897-S	MS68	PCGS *
1897-S	MS66 PL	PCGS 1B
1897-S	MS65 DMPL	PCGS 1B
1898-P	MS66	PCGS 1B
1898-P	MS65 PL	PCGS *
1898-P	MS65 DMPL	PCGS 1B
1898-O	MS67	PCGS *
1898-O	MS66 PL	PCGS *
1898-O	MS66 DMPL	PCGS 1B
1898-S	MS66	PCGS *
1898-S	MS65 DMPL	PCGS *
1899-P	MS66	PCGS *
1899-P	MS65 PL	PCGS *
1899-P	MS65 DMPL	PCGS 1B
1899-O	MS67	PCGS *
1899-O	MS66 DMPL	PCGS 1B
1899-S	MS66	PCGS 1B
1899-S	MS65 PL	PCGS 1B
1899-S	MS65 DMPL	PCGS *
1900-P	MS66	PCGS *
1900-P	MS65 PL	PCGS 1B
1900-P	MS65 DMPL	PCGS *
1900-O	MS66	PCGS 1B
1900-O	MS65 PL	PCGS 1B
1900-O	MS65 DMPL	PCGS *
1900-O/CC	MS66	PCGS *
1900-S	MS66	PCGS *
1901-P	MS64	PCGS 1B
1901-O	MS66	PCGS *
1901-O	MS66 PL	PCGS *
1901-O	MS65 DMPL	PCGS *
1901-S	MS66	PCGS *
1902-P	MS67	PCGS *
1902-P	MS65 PL	PCGS 1B
1902-O	MS66	PCGS *
1902-O	MS65 PL	PCGS 1B
1902-O	MS65 DMPL	PCGS *
1902-S	MS66	PCGS 1B
1903-P	MS67	PCGS *
1903-P	MS65 PL	PCGS 1B
1903-O	MS67	PCGS *
1903-O	MS66 PL	PCGS *
1903-O	MS65 DMPL	PCGS 1B
1903-S	MS66	PCGS 1B
1904-P	MS65	PCGS 1B
1904-O	MS67	PCGS *

Date	Grade	Service
1904-O	MS65 PL	PCGS 1B
1904-O	MS66 DMPL	PCGS *
1904-O	MS66 DPL	NGC *
1904-S	MS65	PCGS *
1904-S	MS65 PL	PCGS *
1921-P	MS66	PCGS 1B
1921-P	MS65 PL	PCGS *
1921-D	MS66	PCGS *
1921-S	MS65	PCGS *

MS = Mint State
PL = Prooflike
DPL = Deep Prooflike (NGC)
DMPL = Deep Mirror Prooflike (PCGS)

** Branch Mint Proof Issues

THE JOHN W. HIGHFILL

PEACE DOLLAR COLLECTION

(1921 - 1935)

The John W. Highfill Peace dollar collection took years of concentrated effort and searching to complete and finally upgrade. During the latter stages of my quest, I received many offers for this once in a lifetime collection. Some time after completing the set, I was persuaded to sell it separately and individually in private party sales. This beautiful and complete set brought in the mid six digit range when the final transaction had been completed! I still consider it to be a bargain. It stands as the ultimate and undisputed finest known PCGS set of Peace dollars in the world today. At the time of its completion, this fantastic set consisted of the following coins:

Date	Grade	Service	Date	Grade	Service
1921-P	MS66	PCGS *	1926-D	MS67	PCGS *
1922-P	MS66	PCGS 1B	1926-S	MS67	PCGS *
1922-D	MS66	PCGS *	1927-P	MS66	PCGS *
1922-S	MS66	PCGS *	1927-D	MS66	PCGS *
1923-P	MS67	PCGS *	1927-S	MS66	PCGS *
1923-D	MS66	PCGS *	1928-P	MS66	PCGS *
1923-S	MS67	PCGS *	1928-S	MS65	PCGS *
1924-P	MS66	PCGS *	1934-P	MS66	PCGS *
1924-S	MS65	PCGS *	1934-D	MS66	PCGS *
1925-P	MS67	PCGS *	1934-S	MS66	PCGS *
1925-S	MS65	PCGS *	1935-P	MS66	PCGS *
1926-P	MS66	PCGS *	1935-S	MS66	PCGS *

* None graded higher by any certified grading service.
1B = One better

The average grade of this entire Peace dollar set is MS-66.1 with 23 of the 24 coins in the series being finest known!

MS-65 - 3 coins
MS-66 - 16 coins
MS-67 - 5 coins

The following example of a **Certificate of Authenticity** with serialized identification has been issued on all private collections of rare coins held by John W. Highfill for pedigree purposes. A **pedigree** serves three basic and viable objectives.

(1) It serves as a historic trail of ownership.
(2) It provides a higher level of consumer confidence.
(3) It stands to the owner's advantage and adds to the coins re-marketability.

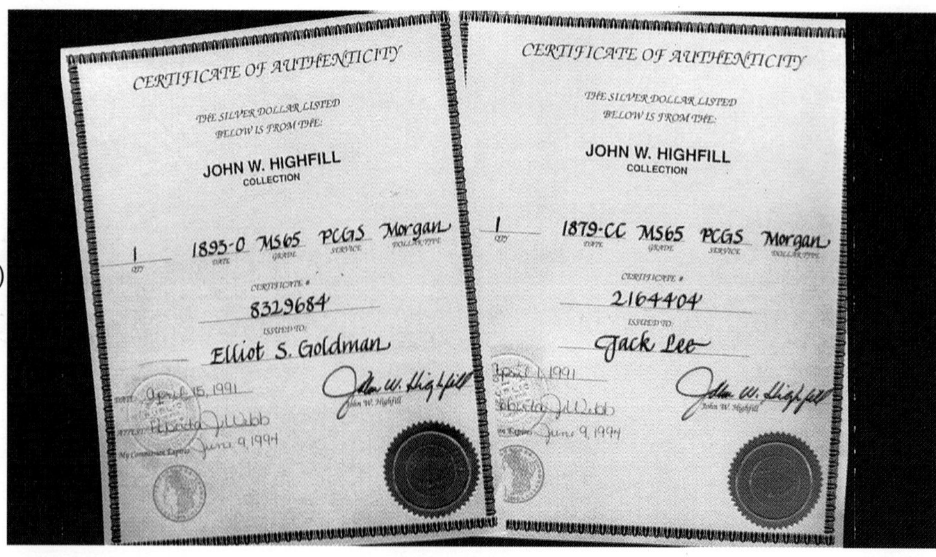

Certificate of Authenticity
(Courtesy of Elliot S. Goldman and Jack Lee)

THE GEORGE E. BODWAY COLLECTION

OF MORGAN DOLLARS

About six years ago I decided what I was going to focus my collecting efforts on uncirculated Morgan silver dollars, and to collect the highest quality complete set ever assembled.

My set is now complete and the following information will be used to describe the overall set. Of the 102 coins in the set all are certified and:

(1) The average grade of my complete set is MS 65.7 or almost an MS 66 grade. (All graded by PCGS)
(2) There are 26 coins which are graded MS 67 or MS 68 in the set.
(3) In addition there are 26 MS 66 coins.
(4) 14 are Deep Mirror Prooflike and 6 more Prooflike.
(5) 16 of the coins are unique - the only one in this grade.
(6) 35 of the coins have less than 2 other coins graded the same.
(7) 50 of them have less than 9 other coins graded the same.
(8) 71 of them have less than 29 other coins graded the same.
(9) The average grade of the 12 rarest Morgan Dollars is MS 65.4 and includes the 84-S, 86-O, 89-CC, 92-S, 93-S, 93-O, 93-CC, 94-O, 95-O, 96-O, 97-O and the 01-P.
(10) Almost half of the coins from my set are in the Morgan Dollar Set which is on a world wide tour of the finest Morgan dollars of each date (the tour is sponsored by PCGS).
(11) In addition, about two thirds of the set is or is equal to the finest known to date.
(12) 3 dates are the finest known by at least 2 grades.

Although all of the coins in my set have now been graded by third party grading services, I originally purchased the majority of them ungraded or in a raw state. The two reasons for this are one: much of my set was completed before grading services were available and two: more recently, many of the more rare coins I needed to complete my set were only available in a raw state. As a collector, you can always purchase coins which have been graded. But if you set a tough goal for yourself which consists of collecting some very rare dates, you may only be able to obtain such rare coins in an ungraded state.

Philadelphia Mint

Year-Mint	Tour	Grade	Service
1878-P 7TF Rev. 78		MS65	PCGS
1878-P 7TF Rev. 79	Yes	MS65 PL	PCGS
1878-P 7/8TF		MS65	PCGS
1878-P	Yes	MS65	PCGS
1879-P	Yes	MS66	PCGS
1880-P		MS65	PCGS
1881-P	Yes	MS65	PCGS
1882-P		MS65 PL	PCGS
1883-P	Yes	MS67	PCGS
1884-P	Yes	MS67	PCGS
1885-P		MS65 DMPL	PCGS
1886-P	Yes	MS67	PCGS
1887-P	Yes	MS67	PCGS
1887/6-P		MS65	PCGS
1888-P		MS65 DMPL	PCGS
1889-P	Yes	MS67	PCGS
1890-P	Yes	MS65 DMPL	PCGS
1891-P		MS65	PCGS
1892-P		MS65 DMPL	PCGS
1893-P		MS65	PCGS
1894-P		MS65	PCGS
1896-P		MS65	PCGS
1897-P	Yes	MS66	PCGS
1898-P		MS66	PCGS
1899-P		MS65	PCGS
1900-P	Yes	MS66	PCGS
1901-P	Yes	MS65	PCGS
1902-P	Yes	MS67	PCGS
1903-P		MS65	PCGS
1904-P		MS65	PCGS
1921-P		MS66	PCGS

Carson City Mint

Year-Mint	Tour	Grade	Service
1878-CC		MS65	PCGS
1879-CC		MS65	PCGS
1880-CC		MS67	PCGS
1881-CC		MS65 DMPL	PCGS
1882-CC		MS66	PCGS
1883-CC		MS66 PL	PCGS
1884-CC		MS67	PCGS
1885-CC		MS66	PCGS
1889-CC		MS63 DMPL	PCGS
1890-CC		MS65	PCGS
1891-CC		MS65 PL	PCGS
1892-CC		MS66	PCGS
1893-CC		MS64 DMPL	PCGS

Denver Mint

Year-Mint	Tour	Grade	Service
1921-D	Yes	MS66	PCGS

New Orleans Mint

Year-Mint	Tour	Grade	Service
1879-O		MS65	PCGS
1880-O		MS64	PCGS
1881-O		MS65	PCGS
1882-O	Yes	MS65 DMPL	PCGS
1883-O	Yes	MS67	PCGS
1884-O	Yes	MS67	PCGS
1885-O	Yes	MS67	PCGS
1886-O	Yes	MS64	PCGS
1887-O	Yes	MS65 DMPL	PCGS
1888-O		MS66	PCGS
1889-O	Yes	MS65	PCGS
1890-O		MS65	PCGS
1891-O		MS65	PCGS
1892-O		MS65	PCGS
1893-O	Yes	MS65 DMPL	PCGS
1894-O	Yes	MS64	PCGS
1895-O	Yes	MS66	PCGS
1896-O	Yes	MS65	PCGS
1897-O	Yes	MS67	PCGS
1898-O	Yes	MS67 DMPL	PCGS
1899-O	Yes	MS67	PCGS
1900-O		MS66	PCGS
1900-O/CC		MS65	PCGS
1901-O	Yes	MS66	PCGS
1902-O		MS66	PCGS
1903-O		MS66	PCGS
1904-O	Yes	MS66 DMPL	PCGS

San Francisco Mint

Year-Mint	Tour	Grade	Service
1878-S		MS66	PCGS
1879-S Rev. 78	Yes	MS65	PCGS
1879-S	Yes	MS68	PCGS
1880-S		MS66	PCGS
1881-S		MS67 DMPL	PCGS
1882-S		MS65 DMPL	PCGS
1883-S	Yes	MS65	PCGS
1884-S	Yes	MS67	PCGS
1885-S	Yes	MS67	PCGS
1886-S	Yes	MS66	PCGS
1887-S	Yes	MS65	PCGS
1888-S	Yes	MS66	PCGS
1889-S		MS65 PL	PCGS
1890-S	Yes	MS66	PCGS
1891-S	Yes	MS67	PCGS
1892-S	Yes	MS66	PCGS
1893-S	Yes	MS67	PCGS
1894-S	Yes	MS67	PCGS
1895-S	Yes	MS65	PCGS
1896-S	Yes	MS68	PCGS
1897-S	Yes	MS67	PCGS
1898-S		MS65	PCGS
1899-S	Yes	MS67	PCGS
1900-S	Yes	MS66	PCGS
1901-S		MS65	PCGS
1902-S		MS66	PCGS
1903-S	Yes	MS67	PCGS
1904-S	Yes	MS65 PL	PCGS
1921-S		MS65	PCGS

THE ELLIOT S. GOLDMAN

MORGAN DOLLAR COLLECTION

(1878 - 1921)

Starting in August 1990, Allstate Coin Co. of Tucson, Arizona, began assembling the world's finest Morgan silver dollar set. Under the instructions of Antelope Valley Newspapers Inc., Elliot S. Goldman, President of Allstate, undertook the monumental task of trying to compile the finest Morgan silver dollar of every year and mintmark graded by PCGS. Many of these dates are one or two of a kind in the highest grade. Trying to locate these coins required spending hundreds of hours on the various computer networks consulting with other dealers all over the country. Attending the largest coin shows in the country was also helpful.

There are three trustees in charge of the profit sharing trust. One of the trustees instructed Mr. Goldman to assemble the set with the idea that market conditions could not be much better for acquiring the coins at the best possible price. The trust has the goal of continually upgrading the set until the trustees decide to liquidate this numismatic treasure. This quest to acquire the finest is constantly ongoing. Every time the finest of a particular date becomes available, Goldman has been instructed to confer with the trustees about the possible purchase of the piece. At times this is extremely difficult, as many dates are one of a kind, and it is not known where the piece is located.

The owners feel that the completion of this set will enable them or its future owners to become a part of numismatic history, similar to owning an 1804 silver dollar. Being a part of the **pedigree** of this set will make any future owner proud.

Date	Grade	Service
1878-P 7TF Rev. 78	MS65	PCGS
1878-P 7/8TF	MS65	PCGS
1878-P 7TF Rev. 79	MS65	PCGS
1878-P 8TF	MS66	PCGS
1878-CC	MS66	PCGS
1878-S	MS67	PCGS
1879-P	MS66	PCGS
1879-CC	MS65	PCGS
1879-CC Capped Die	MS64	PCGS
1879-O	MS66	PCGS
1879-S	MS68	PCGS
1879-S Rev. 78	MS65	PCGS
1880-P	MS65	PCGS
1880-CC	MS67	PCGS
1880-CC Rev. 78	MS66	PCGS
1880-O	MS65	PCGS
1880-S	MS68	PCGS
1881-P	MS66	PCGS
1881-CC	MS67	PCGS
1881-O	MS65	PCGS
1881-S	MS68	PCGS
1882-P	MS66	PCGS
1882-CC	MS67	PCGS
1882-O	MS67	PCGS
1882-O/S	MS64	PCGS
1882-S	MS67	PCGS
1883-P	MS67	PCGS
1883-CC	MS67	PCGS
1883-O	MS66	PCGS
1883-S	MS65	PCGS
1884-P	MS67	PCGS
1884-CC	MS67	PCGS
1884-O	MS67	PCGS
1884-S	MS64	PCGS
1885-P	MS67	PCGS
1885-CC	MS67	PCGS
1885-O	MS67	PCGS
1885-S	MS67	PCGS
1886-P	MS67	PCGS
1886-O	MS64	PCGS

Date	Grade	Service
1886-S	MS66	PCGS
1887-P	MS67	PCGS
1887/6-P	MS65	PCGS
1887-O	MS65	PCGS
1887/6-O	MS64	PCGS
1887-S	MS65	PCGS
1888-P	MS66	PCGS
1888-O	MS66	PCGS
1888-S	MS65	PCGS
1889-P	MS67	PCGS
1889-CC	MS64	PCGS
1889-O	MS66	PCGS
1889-S	MS66	PCGS
1890-P	MS65	PCGS
1890-CC	MS66	PCGS
1890-O	MS66	PCGS
1890-S	MS66	PCGS
1891-P	MS65	PCGS
1891-CC	MS66	PCGS
1891-O	MS65	PCGS
1891-S	MS66	PCGS
1892-P	MS65	PCGS
1892-CC	MS66	PCGS
1892-O	MS65	PCGS
1892-S	MS66	PCGS
1893-P	MS65	PCGS
1893-CC	MS65	PCGS
1893-O	MS65	PCGS
1893-S	MS65	PCGS
1894-P	MS65	PCGS
1894-O	MS65	PCGS
1894-S	MS66	PCGS
1895-P (Proof)	PR67	PCGS
1895-O	MS62	PCGS
1895-S	MS65	PCGS
1896-P	MS66	PCGS
1896-O	MS64	PCGS
1896-S	MS66	PCGS
1897-P	MS67	PCGS
1897-O	MS65	PCGS

Date	Grade	Service	Date	Grade	Service
1897-S	MS67	PCGS	1901-S	MS66	PCGS
1898-P	MS65	PCGS	1902-P	MS67	PCGS
1898-O	MS67	PCGS	1902-O	MS66	PCGS
1898-S	MS66	PCGS	1902-S	MS67	PCGS
1899-P	MS66	PCGS	1903-P	MS67	PCGS
1899-O	MS67	PCGS	1903-O	MS67	PCGS
1899-S	MS66	PCGS	1903-S	MS66	PCGS
1900-P	MS66	PCGS	1904-P	MS66	PCGS
1900-O	MS67	PCGS	1904-O	MS66	PCGS
1900-O/CC	MS66	PCGS	1904-S	MS65	PCGS
1900-S	MS66	PCGS	1921-P	MS66	PCGS
1901-P	MS63	PCGS	1921-D	MS66	PCGS
1901-O	MS66	PCGS	1921-S	MS65	PCGS

MS = Mint State
PR = Proof

May 21, 1991 NUMISMATIC NEWS

High-grade $1 purchased

The only 1893-O Morgan dollar graded MS-65 by the Professional Coin Grading Service has been purchased for $157,500 by Elliot Goldman of Allstate Coin Co., Tucson, Ariz., from John Highfill of Oklahoma Federated Numismatics, Broken Arrow, Okla.

Currently the finest known specimen of that date, the 1893-O was purchased by Goldman for a client who is assembling "the finest Morgan silver set ever compiled by a private party."

The firm "has spent over $1.5 million in the past six months acquiring the finest specimens available." Other recent purchases include an 1897-O Morgan in MS-65 for $35,000 and an 1893-CC for $70,000. PCGS graded both coins MS-65.

Numismatic News release - May 21, 1991
(Courtesy of Numismatic News, Iola, Wisconsin)

THE LARRY SHEPHERD

COMMEMORATIVE SET

The World's Finest 144 piece Commemorative Set was owned by Larry Shepherd. Mr. Shepherd is president of SIMCO, Inc., Cincinnati, Ohio. Here are the facts concerning this truly fine collection carefully put together over the years by Larry Shepherd followed by Mr. Shepherd's own comments concerning this fabulous set, capped off by a complete listing of the set itself.

- Fully 102 of the 144 pieces are the highest known grade.
- Ninety-two pieces have a certified population of less than 15.
- All 50 piece "type" coins are graded MS-66 or higher.
- 75 of the 144 pieces (52%) are graded MS-67 and MS-68!
- All PCGS Coins have been pedigreed with "Shepherd" on the inset label.
-

The following table presents the grade breakdown of the Set.

Certified Grade	Number of Pieces
MS65	14
MS66	55
MS67	60
MS68	15

Over the last ten years I have spent thousands of hours attending hundreds of coin shows and auctions, to assemble what is now widely recognized as the finest 144 piece commemorative collection ever assembled. Over this period I viewed several hundred thousand commemoratives and actually bought and sold around 5,000 pieces to arrive at the current set. Each coin was selected for the highest combination of surface quality and spectacular eye appeal. I never bought a coin just for the grade on the label. Instead, I have always bought the finest coins available, regardless of the label. Each of the 144 pieces is the finest I have ever seen during my experience.

All 144 pieces have been graded MS-65 or higher by PCGS or NGC. Over one-half the set (75 of 144 pieces) have a grade of MS-67 and MS-68! All 50 types are represented in MS-66 and higher. Of the 144 pieces, 102 are the highest graded by their service. Many coins have populations of 1,2, or 3, and each displays the most spectacular, colorful toning and eye appeal you will ever see.

Larry Goldberg of Superior Galleries has stated that, in all his years of experience and considering the many record setting collections they have handled, this is the most amazing and beautiful collection they have every seen. Obviously PCGS was equally impressed, since they recently reholdered all the pieces in the main set graded by them with my name on the insert label. By pedigreeing the set they have not only paid me a marvelous tribute, but have also added a distinct identity to each of the coins that will add to their overall appeal, as long as they remain in the PCGS holder.

On Sunday, August 11, 1991, Superior Galleries auctioned my entire collection. This sale, which was held at the Embassy Suites Hotel in Rosemont, Illinois just two days prior to the 100th anniversary meeting of the ANA, included every individual lot in my 144 piece set, as well as over 200 extra high quality duplicates. Many of these duplicates would themselves rank as the second or third finest known pieces.

This exciting event was a "happening" for the commemorative market and for my collection in particular. I feel very positive about the outlook for the commemorative market in the future, particularly the most exquisite pieces. If anyone thinks I sold my set because I lost faith in the market, they are wrong. I sold it because my set was complete, and I could no longer improve it in a meaningful way. Putting it on the market regenerated interest in dozens of collectors about completing their sets, and generated several new collectors who will start building sets. Hopefully this was a very positive boost to my business in the future and to every other dealer who specializes in the commemorative market.

Highlights of the Sale

- Isabella Quarter PCGS MS-68: Exquisite Toning
- Lafayette Dollar PCGS MS-67: Beautifully Toned
- Alabama 2x2 PCGS MS-66: Beautifully Toned
- All Arkansas dates with beautiful toning and eye appeal, including 3 graded MS-67 and matched PDS sets.
- 1935/34 PDS Boone set and 1938 PDS Boone set, both graded MS-67, 68, and 67.
- 1936 PDS Columbia set from Statehouse time capsule.
- 1892 Columbian PCGS MS-67, the only MS-67 of either date by either service (it graded MS-67 at both NGC and PCGS).
- The two Columbian half dollars pictured on the cover of the Swiatek-Breen book, including the proof Columbian said to be the first commemorative coin ever struck.
- Grant with star PCGS MS-66, the only one graded by PCGS and one of only a handful known to exist without the die clash at the collar.
- Hawaiian NGC MS-66

- Hudson PCGS MS-67: Population 2
- Missouri PCGS MS-66: Population 3
- Monroe PCGS MS-66: Beautifully Toned
- An amazing set of Oregon Trails, including 4 MS-68's plus the highest graded matched 1938 and 1939 sets in existence, both graded PCGS MS-67, 68, 67.
- Pan-Pac PCGS MS-67: From the Garrett Collection
- Sesqui PCGS MS-66, with beautiful toning (and in my opinion, the toughest and most valuable commemorative coin in this condition).
- Several spectacular Texas, including 3 MS-68's and an MS-67 1938 set.
- Vancouver and Vermont, both graded MS-67.
- The only complete set of Booker T. Washington's in existence, with all 18 coins graded MS-66 and MS-67.
- Several beautiful, rare multicolored Washington Carvers.
- Numerous MS-68 type coins, such as Antietam, Iowa, Norfolk, and York (17 MS-68's in total).
- One of only three known San Diego satin finish proofs.
- Roanoke proof.
- Two Rhode Island proofs.
- A special collection of ultra scarce commemoratives graded prooflike (PL). Many are one of a kind or finest known.
- Plus over 200 duplicate silver commemoratives grading MS-64 through MS-68 — each put away over the years for their extra desirability.
- A superb collection of commemorative gold.

Variety	Date	PCGS NGC	MS Grade	Prices Realized
Isabella	1893	PCGS	68 *	$63,250
Lafayette $1	1900	PCGS	67 *	115,500
Alabama	1921	PCGS	65 *	N/A
Alabama 2x2	1921	PCGS	66	13,750
Albany	1936	PCGS	67 *	N/A
Antietam	1937	PCGS	68 *	14,850
Arkansas	1935	PCGS	66	2,200
	1935-D	PCGS	67 *	6,875
	1935-S	PCGS	66 *	2,035
	1936	PCGS	66 *	2,750
	1936-D	PCGS	67 *	8,250
	1936-S	PCGS	66	2,530
	1937	PCGS	66 *	2,035
	1937-D	PCGS	66	2,310
	1937-S	PCGS	65	N/A
	1938	PCGS	66 *	N/A
	1938-D	PCGS	67 *	7,425
	1938-S	PCGS	65	1,210
	1939	PCGS	66 *	N/A
	1939-D	PCGS	66 *	N/A
	1939-S	PCGS	66 *	N/A
Bay Bridge	1936-S	PCGS	67 *	5,280
Boone	1934	PCGS	67 *	2,640
	1935/34	PCGS	67 *	N/A
	1935/34-D	PCGS	68 *	N/A
	1935/34-S	PCGS	67 *	N/A
	1935	PCGS	67 *	1,980
	1935-D	PCGS	66	N/A
	1935-S	PCGS	66	770
	1936	PCGS	67 *	1,870
	1936-D	NGC	66	770
	1936-S	NGC	68 *	N/A
	1937	PCGS	67 *	2,530
	1937-D	PCGS	67 *	N/A
	1937-S	PCGS	67 *	N/A
	1938	PCGS	67 *	3,520
	1938-D	NGC	68 *	3,520

Variety	Date	PCGS NGC	MS Grade	Prices Realized
Boone (cont.)	1938-S	PCGS	67 *	2,310
Bridge Port	1936	PCGS	66	2,970
California	1925-S	PCGS	67 *	5,060
Cincinnati	1936	PCGS	66 *	3,740
	1936-D	NGC	67 *	14,850
	1936-S	PCGS	66 *	4,400
Cleveland	1936	NGC	67 *	N/A
Columbia, S.C.	1936	PCGS	66 (SET)	4,180
	1936-D	NGC	67 *	
	1936-S	PCGS	66	
Columbian	1892	PCGS	67 *	41,800
	1893	PCGS	65	5,500
Connecticut	1935	PCGS	67 *	9,350
Delaware	1936	PCGS	67 *	9,350
Elgin, Illinois	1936	PCGS	67 *	N/A
Gettysburg	1936	PCGS	67	6,875
Grant Memorial	1922	PCGS	66	4,180
Grant w/ Star	1922	PCGS	66 *	31,900
Hawaiian	1928	NGC	66 *	13,750
Huguenot Walloon	1924	PCGS	66	3,520
Hudson, New York	1935	PCGS	67 *	26,400
Illinois Centennial	1918	PCGS	67 *	12,100
Iowa	1946	PCGS	68 *	3,740
Lexington Concord	1925	PCGS	66 *	8,525
Long Island	1936	NGC	67 *	7,975
Lynchburg	1936	PCGS	67 *	N/A
Maine	1920	PCGS	66	2,530
Maryland	1934	PCGS	66	2,777
Missouri	1921	PCGS	66 *	15,950
Missouri 2x4	1921	PCGS	65	N/A
Monroe	1923-S	PCGS	66	12,100
New Rochelle, N.Y.	1938	PCGS	67 *	N/A
Norfolk, Virginia	1936	PCGS	68 *	N/A

Variety	Date	PCGS NGC	MS Grade	Prices Realized
Oregon	1926	PCGS	67 *	3,190
	1926-S	PCGS	68 *	7,700
	1928	PCGS	67 *	4,400
	1933-D	PCGS	66	2,750
	1934-D	PCGS	66	2,420
	1936	PCGS	67 *	6,600
	1936-S	PCGS	66	2,530
	1937-D	PCGS	68 *	2,860
	1938	PCGS	67 *(SET)	16,500
	1938-D	PCGS	68 *	
	1938-S	PCGS	67	
	1939	PCGS	67 *(SET)	14,850
	1939-D	PCGS	68 *	
	1939-S	PCGS	67	
Panama-Pacific	1915-S	PCGS	67 *	18,150
Pilgrim	1920	PCGS	65	1,650
	1921	PCGS	66 *	3,080
Rhode Island	1936	PCGS	66	N/A
	1936-D	PCGS	66	1,540
	1936-S	PCGS	65	N/A
Roanoke	1937	PCGS	67 *	3,960
Robinson-Arkansas	1936	PCGS	67 *	9,350
San Diego	1935-S	PCGS	67 *	3,300
	1936-D	PCGS	66	1,925
Sesquicentennial	1926	PCGS	66 *	33,000
Spanish Trail	1935	PCGS	67 *	9,350
Stone Mountain	1925	PCGS	67	3,520
Texas	1934	PCGS	68 *	5,060
	1935	PCGS	66	1,210
	1935-D	PCGS	67 *	1,595
	1935-S	PCGS	67 *	1,320
	1936	PCGS	68 *	3,740
	1936-D	PCGS	68 *	3,190
	1936-S	PCGS	67	2,035
	1937	PCGS	67 *	1,870
	1937-D	PCGS	67 *	1,375
	1937-S	PCGS	66	935
	1938	PCGS	67 *	3,190
	1938-D	PCGS	67 *	2,970
	1938-S	PCGS	67	2,750
Vancouver	1925	NGC	67	3,960

Variety	Date	PCGS NGC	MS Grade	Prices Realized
Vermont	1927	PCGS	67 *	14,850
Booker T. Washington	1946	PCGS	66 *	N/A
	1946-D	PCGS	66 *	N/A
	1946-S	PCGS	67 *	N/A
	1947	PCGS	66 * (SET)	4,840
	1947-D	PCGS	66 *	
	1947-S	PCGS	66 *	
	1948	PCGS	66 * (SET)	3,685
	1948-D	PCGS	66 *	
	1948-S	PCGS	65	
	1949	PCGS	66 (SET)	1,705
	1949-D	PCGS	66 *	
	1949-S	PCGS	66 *	
	1950	PCGS	66 *	1,320
	1950-D	PCGS	66 *	990
	1950-S	PCGS	67 *	2,310
	1951	PCGS	67 *	2,310
	1951-D	PCGS	66 *	770
	1951-S	PCGS	66	330
Washington Carver	1951	PCGS	65	577
	1951-D	PCGS	65 *	605
	1951-S	PCGS	65	330
	1952	PCGS	66 *	1045
	1952-D	NGC	65	605
	1952-S	NGC	66	1100
	1953	PCGS	66 *	1265
	1953-D	PCGS	65 *	742
	1953-S	NGC	66	1320
	1954	PCGS	65	770
	1954-D	PCGS	65 *	990
	1954-S	PCGS	66 *	1815
Wisconsin	1936	PCGS	67	2310
York County, Maine	1936	PCGS	68 *	N/A

* Highest grade known

Prices Realized courtesy of William Conroy c/o Superior Galleries, Beverly Hills, California

The Larry Shepherd Collection of U.S. Silver Commemorative Coins - Plate 1
(Courtesy of Superior Galleries, Beverly Hills, California)

The Larry Shepherd Collection of U.S. Silver Commemorative Coins - Plate 2
(Courtesy of Superior Galleries, Beverly Hills, California)

THE JOHN W. HIGHFILL

COMMEMORATIVE SET

This complete 144 piece Commemorative Set was acquired over a period of time and owned by John Highfill. May 1989 this magnificent set in its entirety was sold in the three-quarter million dollar range to a private party and has since been put away for the long term.

Variety	Date	PCGS	MS Grade
Isabella	1893	PCGS	66
Lafayette $1	1900	PCGS	65
Alabama	1921	PCGS	65 *
Alabama 2x2	1921	PCGS	65
Albany	1936	PCGS	66
Antietam	1937	PCGS	66
Arkansas	1935	PCGS	66
	1935-D	PCGS	66
	1935-S	PCGS	66 *
	1936	PCGS	65
	1936-D	PCGS	65
	1936-S	PCGS	65
	1937	PCGS	65
	1937-D	PCGS	65
	1937-S	PCGS	65
	1938	PCGS	65
	1938-D	PCGS	65
	1938-S	PCGS	65
	1939	PCGS	65
	1939-D	PCGS	66 *
	1939-S	PCGS	65
Bay Bridge	1936-S	PCGS	66
Boone	1934	PCGS	66
	1935/34	PCGS	66
	1935/34-D	PCGS	66
	1935/34-S	PCGS	66
	1935	PCGS	66
	1935-D	PCGS	66
	1935-S	PCGS	66
	1936	PCGS	66
	1936-D	PCGS	66
	1936-S	PCGS	66
	1937	PCGS	66
	1937-D	PCGS	66
	1937-S	PCGS	66
	1938	PCGS	65
	1938-D	PCGS	65
	1938-S	PCGS	66
Bridgeport	1936	PCGS	66
California	1925-S	PCGS	67 *
Cincinnati	1936	PCGS	66 *
	1936-D	PCGS	66
	1936-S	PCGS	66 *
Cleveland	1936	PCGS	66
Columbia, S.C.	1936	PCGS	67
	1936-D	PCGS	67 *
	1936-S	PCGS	67
Columbian	1892	PCGS	66
	1893	PCGS	65
Connecticut	1935	PCGS	67 *
Delaware	1936	PCGS	66
Elgin, Illinois	1936	PCGS	66

Variety	Date	PCGS	MS Grade
Gettysburg	1936	PCGS	67
Grant Memorial	1922	PCGS	66
Grant w/ Star	1922	PCGS	65
Hawaiian	1928	PCGS	66 *
Huguenot-Walloon	1924	PCGS	66
Hudson, New York	1935	PCGS	67 *
Illinois Centennial	1918	PCGS	66
Iowa	1946	PCGS	67
Lexington-Concord	1925	PCGS	66 *
Long Island	1936	PCGS	66
Lynchburg	1936	PCGS	67 *
Maine	1920	PCGS	66
Maryland	1934	PCGS	66
Missouri	1921	PCGS	65
Missouri 2x4	1921	PCGS	65
Monroe	1923-S	PCGS	65
New Rochelle, N.Y.	1938	PCGS	67 *
Norfolk, Virginia	1936	PCGS	67
Oregon	1926	PCGS	66
	1926-S	PCGS	67
	1928	PCGS	66
	1933-D	PCGS	66
	1934-D	PCGS	66
	1936	PCGS	67 *
	1936-S	PCGS	66
	1937-D	PCGS	67
	1938	PCGS	66
	1938-D	PCGS	66
	1938-S	PCGS	67 *
	1939	PCGS	67 *
	1939-D	PCGS	67
	1939-S	PCGS	67
Panama-Pacific	1915-S	PCGS	67 *
Pilgrim	1920	PCGS	66
	1921	PCGS	66 *
Rhode Island	1936	PCGS	66
	1936-D	PCGS	66
	1936-S	PCGS	65
Roanoke	1937	PCGS	67 *
Robinson-Arkansas	1936	PCGS	67 *
San Diego	1935-S	PCGS	67 *
	1936-S	PCGS	66
Sesquicentennial	1926	PCGS	65
Spanish Trail	1935	PCGS	66
Stone Mountain	1925	PCGS	67
Texas	1934	PCGS	66
	1935	PCGS	66
	1935-D	PCGS	66
	1935-S	PCGS	66
	1936	PCGS	66
	1936-D	PCGS	67
	1936-S	PCGS	67

Variety	Date	PCGS	MS Grade
Texas	1937	PCGS	66
	1937-D	PCGS	66
	1937-S	PCGS	66
	1938	PCGS	66
	1938-D	PCGS	66
	1938-S	PCGS	66
Vancouver	1925	PCGS	66
Vermont	1927	PCGS	66
Booker T. Washington	1946	PCGS	66 *
	1946-D	PCGS	66 *
	1946-S	PCGS	66
	1947	PCGS	66 *
	1947-D	PCGS	66 *
	1947-S	PCGS	66 *
	1948	PCGS	66 *
	1948-D	PCGS	66 *
	1948-S	PCGS	66 *
	1949	PCGS	66
	1949-D	PCGS	66 *
	1949-S	PCGS	66 *

* Highest Grade Known

Variety	Date	PCGS	MS Grade
Washington	1950	PCGS	65
	1950-D	PCGS	65
	1950-S	PCGS	66
	1951	PCGS	65
	1951-D	PCGS	66 *
	1951-S	PCGS	66
Washington Carver	1951	PCGS	65
	1951-D	PCGS	65 *
	1951-S	PCGS	66 *
	1952	PCGS	66 *
	1952-D	PCGS	65 *
	1952-S	PCGS	66
	1953	PCGS	65
	1953-D	PCGS	65 *
	1953-S	PCGS	66 *
	1954	PCGS	65
	1954-D	PCGS	65 *
	1954-S	PCGS	66 *
Wisconsin	1936	PCGS	67
York County-Maine	1936	PCGS	67

THE JOHN W. HIGHFILL

CANADIAN COIN COLLECTION

(1935 to 1959)

The John W. Highfill Canadian coin collection was one of his first to be assembled. The listed sets were acquired after a diligent search through thousands of coins from the "friendly lands to the north." The popularity of Canadian coinage has developed over many years, during which this outstanding group of specimens were obtained. This market should stand the test of time and become an excellent opportunity for the future.

Date	Grade/Service	Date	Grade/Service
1937 Canadian Set-Matte	PCGS	1945 Canadian Set	NGC
1 Cent Canadian	SP65RD	1 Cent Canadian	SP63BN
5 Cent Canadian	SP66	5 Cent Canadian	SP66
10 Cent Canadian	SP66	10 Cent Canadian	SP66
25 Cent Canadian	SP66	25 Cent Canadian	SP66
50 Cent Canadian	SP66	50 Cent Canadian	SP66
Canadian Silver $	SP66	Canadian Silver $	SP66
1937 Canadian Set-Mirror	PCGS	1948 Canadian Set	NGC
1 Cent Canadian	SP66RD	1 Cent Canadian	SP65RB
5 Cent Canadian	SP67	5 Cent Canadian	SP65
10 Cent Canadian	SP65	10 Cent Canadian	SP65
25 Cent Canadian	SP66	25 Cent Canadian	SP66
50 Cent Canadian	SP66	50 Cent Canadian	SP65
Canadian Silver $	SP66	Canadian Silver $	SP65

Canadian Dollar Set

Year	Grade	Service	Year	Grade	Service
1935	MS66	PCGS	1949	PL66	PCGS
1936	MS65	PCGS	1950	MS66	PCGS
1937	MS65	PCGS	1950	PL65	PCGS
1937 Mirror	SP65	NGC	1950 Arnprior	MS65	PCGS
1937 Matte	SP66	PCGS	1951	MS65	PCGS
1938	MS65	PCGS	1952	MS66	PCGS
1939	MS65	PCGS	1952 N W/L	MS65	PCGS
1945	MS64	PCGS	1953	MS65	PCGS
1945	MS66	NGC	1953 No Strap	MS65	PCGS
1945	SP66	NGC	1954	PL65	NGC
1946	MS65	PCGS	1955	PL65	PCGS
1947 Pt. 7	MS65	PCGS	1955	PL67	PCGS
1947 Blunt 7	MS65	PCGS	1955 Arnprior	PL67	PCGS
1947 Maple Leaf	MS65	NGC	1956	PL66	NGC
1948	MS63	PCGS	1957	PL66	PCGS
1948	SP65	NGC	1958	PL67	PCGS
1949	MS66	PCGS	1959	PL66	PCGS

MS = Mint State
PL = Prooflike
SP = Specimen
RD = Red
RB = Red Brown
BN = Brown

THE MARTIN B. PAUL

CANADIAN COIN COLLECTION

Martin Paul's interest in Canadian dollars resulted in the Specimen Canadian collection presented here. Specimen coins are among the most sought after Canadian coins as they were unusually well struck. The finish used on the coins varied over the years with the 1937 coinage of George VI available in both a bright mirror finish and an overall satin (or matte) finish. During the years from 1938 to the mid-1940s, a polished appearance was attributed to the specimen coins. All of these coins are Specimen Canadian dollars in gem condition graded by PCGS.

Description	Year	Grade *	Service
Canadian Dollar	1935	SP68	PCGS
	1936	SP67	PCGS
(Mirror)	1937	SP66	PCGS
	1937(Matte)	SP66	PCGS
	1938	SP64	PCGS
	1939	SP67	PCGS
	1945	SP66	PCGS
	1946	SP66	PCGS
(Pointed 7)	1947	SP65	PCGS
(Blunt 7)	1947	SP67	PCGS
(Maple Leaf)	1947	SP66	PCGS
	1948	SP67	PCGS
	1949	SP65	PCGS
	1950	SP66	PCGS
	1951	SP66	PCGS
(Waterlines)	1952	SP66	PCGS

* **SP** = Specimen

THE MARTIN B. PAUL

HALF DIME COLLECTION

(1792 - 1842)

"In execution of the authority given by the legislature, measures have been taken for engaging some artists from abroad to aid in the establishment of our Mint. Others have been employed at home. Provisions have been made for the requisite buildings, and these are now putting into proper condition for the purposes of the establishment. There has been a small beginning in the coinage of half dismes, the want of small coins in circulation calling the first attention to them."

— President Washington's Fourth Annual Address, November 6, 1792

1792 Half Disme, Breen 1360, Judd-7, R.3, PKG MS66

According to Walter Breen's Encyclopedia (p. 153) the name *disme*, 'tenth,' later (about 1836) anglicized to *dime*, is a neologism of the polymath Simon Stevin van Brugghe, alias Simon Stevinus (1548-1620). Stevin invented the decimal system as a convenient alternative to fractions, and published it in a pamphlet, *De Thiende* {1585} [editor].

From Washington's quotation above one might conclude that the 1792 half dime was struck as circulating coin of the realm, rather than as a pattern as has so often been assumed. Further verification for this belief comes from the widely accepted story that George and Martha Washington donated silverware worth about $100 for the nation's first coinage. This was enough silver to strike approximately 1,500 half dimes — a very large mintage for a pattern coin.

Presumably, Robert Scot copied the obverse design from the Birch cent patterns struck in the same year. Legend has it that Liberty was modeled after Martha Washington, but that is doubtful. Around the edge of the obverse is the Franklinesque legend: LIB. PAR. OF SCIENCE & INDUSTRY. The reverse features a scrawny eagle in flight with UNITED STATES OF AMERICA around the edge and HALF DISME below.

The vast majority of half dimes that survive today (perhaps 100 to 200 pieces) show evidence of extensive wear. Most pieces grade Good to Fine with only half a dozen or so known in mint condition. Most survivors also show planchet laminations — evidence of the difficulty early mint employees had in preparing planchets for striking. Many also show adjustment marks from filing in the mint, it being strongly believed that if coins of the new republic were to find acceptance alongside the commonly encountered coins of the world, then they must weigh very close to established standards — no more, no less.

The coin currently offered is one of only two MS66 half dismes to have been graded by PCGS or NGC. As one can infer from the grade, the surfaces are uncommonly free from impairments - both those that could have been produced in the mint and the myriad possibilities outside the mint. There is no planchet flaking on either side. In the center of the reverse are a series of light, diagonal adjustment marks, but these have little effect upon the visual appeal of the coin. The strike appears fully brought up in all areas. Frankly, we have never seen such a finely struck coin, and have found detail on this coin that we were unaware existed. Over the expanse of 200 years this piece has been spared cleaning and the surfaces have been left to tone naturally, leaving a warm golden patina in the center of each side that is surrounded by thin bands of bright iridescence around the edges.

One has to wonder how much longer a coin such as this can remain in private hands. Over the past fifty years more and more important coins and collections have been given to museums. Each time this coin is offered for sale increases the chance that eventually a civic-minded collector will acquire the coin and later donate it to an institution. One can certainly make a case that this coin should be available to the largest number of people in this country. Perhaps some day we will look back and remember when truly great and historic U.S. coinage was available for private ownership. Whether one considers the 1792 half dimes as patterns or as coins struck for circulation, they nevertheless remain among the most historic, intriguing, and desirable of all U.S. coins.

1794 PCGS MS63. Breen 1-A and 2965, V-1, R.7, Widest Date.

The V-1 variety is the rarest by far of the four varieties struck bearing the 1794 date. Most likely all four varieties were included in the delivery of 7,756 half dimes of March 30, 1795.

A single presentation piece is known of this variety — from the Leian Rogers collection. It was struck on a burnished planchet with exceptional detailing. This piece seems to have also been struck on a polished planchet, but apparently not as much care was given to the quality of the striking as with the Rogers presentation piece. This coin does show very sharp detailing on the hair and stars, the wings of the eagle are also very strong, but the breast feathers are characteristically soft. All mint state 1794 half dimes come from a single source of about 15 pieces, saved as first of their kind.

In addition to the surfaces having a brightness not seen on other early mint state half dimes, both sides are toned a lovely deep blue, olive, and red. The coin also has very few surface blemishes, the few there are only being visible with a magnifier. Undoubtedly the finest known specimen of this rare variety and one of three pieces of this date that have been graded MS-63.

1794 PCGS MS64. Breen 2-A, V-2, R.4, Two Specimens.

One outstanding feature of the Martin Paul collection of half dimes is that not only is the collection the most complete set ever assembled, but there are duplicates of many rare dates and duplicate varieties of some rare dates. "Obsession" is a word that comes to mind when viewing this collection. Obsession with not only the series and each member of that series, but also with the finest quality coin available of each date.

The collection contains two 1794 V-2 coins. The surfaces of both have a similar fabric: slightly reflective and showing very minor planchet irregularities. Yet they differ in important ways from each other also. The one coin (let's call it the blue coin) has distinctive underlying blue toning with reddish-golden accents scattered around the edges. The strike shows a bit of softness on the hair curls when compared to the other coin, but we doubt that this would be noticeable as a weakness unless one had another high grade 1794 to compare it to. The blue coin has one thin cut along the lower cheek and there are a couple of light diagonal grease stains in the lower reverse field. These so-called defects are of little or no consequence to the overall eye appeal of the coin and are mentioned for the sake of accuracy and to aid catalogers in the future who may wish to trace the pedigree of the coin.

The second, "green" coin does indeed have a deep olive-green patina with an underlying reddish tint. The strike is fully brought up with clearly defined hair detail, in the lower portions having an almost etched appearance. The surfaces are exceptionally clean and seem to be virtually unaffected by abrasions caused by coin to coin contact. In the field below and to the left of the eagle's left leg are a series of very faint planchet rifts that at first appear to be streaks of a darker color. An extraordinary pair of 1794 half dimes. PCGS has graded ten coins MS64 of this first official year of issue, but none finer, making these two pieces tied with the other eight as finest known for this date.

1794 PCGS MS62. Breen 2-B, V-3, R.5

Half dimes were not struck again until 1795. All 1794 half dimes were struck either during or after February 1795.

This piece is well struck with good details on both Liberty and the eagle. There is a slight loss of definition in the center of the eagle's breast and a few small marks noted on each side, but these minor defects are more than made up for by the originality of surfaces and attractive reddish-russet color in the centers that deepens to a royal blue at the edges. According to the current Population Report from PCGS only three other coins of this date have been similarly graded.

1795 PCGS MS65. Breen 8-E, V-4, R.4

In the late 1870's or early 1880's the Wadsworth-Rea hoard of some hundred high grade 1795 half dimes was dispersed by coin dealer William Elliot Woodward. Most of the coins from this hoard are of the V-4, 5, and 6 varieties. The existence of this hoard however, should not diminish the true rarity and importance of this date, which is nevertheless a rare one and of the utmost importance to the type collector (with 1794 coins not usually available in high grade).

This coin has an extraordinarily clean obverse with no marks visible even with a magnifier. The reverse has a couple of small marks on the eagle's wing and in the field, but these are of little consequence when one considers the overall beauty of the coin. The strike is certainly adequate but shows the slight central weakness common to this variety and many of the coins from the hoard. The centers are toned a deep reddish-violet with the edges having taken on a bright blue tone. One of only four coins to have been so graded by PCGS.

1795 PCGS MS65. Breen 7-D, V-6, R.5

There were a few V-6 coins in the Wadsworth-Rea hoard of some hundred high grade 1795 half dimes was dispersed by coin dealer William Elliot Woodward. Most of the coins from this hoard are of the V-4 and 5 varieties. The existence of this hoard, however, should not diminish the true rarity and importance of this date, which is nevertheless a rare one and of the utmost importance to the type collector (with 1794 coins not usually available in high grade).

This coin has an extraordinarily clean obverse with no marks visible even with a magnifier. The reverse has a couple of small marks on the eagle's wing and in the field, but these are of little consequence when one considers the overall beauty of the coin. The strike is certainly adequate but shows the slight central weakness common to this variety and many of the coins from the hoard. The centers are toned a deep reddish-violet with the edges having taken on a bright blue tone. One of only four coins to have been so graded by PCGS.

1795 PCGS MS65. V-6, R.5

Probably also from the Wadsworth-Rea hoard. An extraordinarily lustrous coin that exudes originality with its red-violet centers and blue-green edges. There are no contact marks to speak of, the coin obviously having been taken care of by knowledgeable and caring owners since dispersal of the hoard. There are however, numerous die cracks on each side and in the center of the obverse there are several light, parallel adjustment marks. Sharply struck except in the centers which show slight striking weakness as usual for the variety. Again, one of only four gem coins to have been so graded by PCGS.

1795 NGC MS65. Breen 6-C, V-8, R.7

A very rare variety and one not included in the Wadsworth hoard. Breen estimates that perhaps only five pieces are known, the finest being the Eliasberg presentation piece. Similar to the Eliasberg coin (that is a superb prooflike piece), this coin also has a glimmer of PL surface in the fields. This is not immediately apparent as the surfaces have taken on a muted gray and blue patina. There are also several darker spots of color on each side. The strike is very sharp with almost all details complete, lacking only the breast feathers as usual — but these are partially in evidence, being obscured only by the adjustment marks in the center of the reverse. Although graded the same as the V-4 and V-6 above, this coin is much rarer and should have a value far greater than the others because it is not a hoard coin, thus being subject to another 85 years of possible mishandling between 1795 and 1880.

1796 PCGS MS67. V-1, R.4

The Martin Paul collection of half dimes represents the finest collection ever assembled of this denomination. All major rarities and patterns are included. But of all the coins in the collection, this 1796 represents one of the most extraordinary examples of rarity in both date and grade.

Conditions in the mint during this period were difficult. In a few short months two mint directors were appointed. The personnel hired had little artistic inclination and even less ability to transfer an artistic notion onto a working idea. Additionally, yellow fever took an annual toll on both employees and production.

Even though there was a major design change in 1796, few people seem to have taken notice of it. Few coins were saved of this or the next year in mint condition. But this one extraordinary coin was preserved. This 1796 half dime is head and shoulders above the other known coins of this year. While we realized that the condition census for a given issue may be far removed from what is indicated by the PCGS and NGC Population reports, these publications can still serve as a useful guide. According to the reports the coin that most closely approaches this one is three grades away, an NGC MS64. Beyond that there have been two other coins graded in mint state with MS60.

The coin is extraordinary in all respects. Struck from heavily clashed dies, these clash marks are the only superficial disturbances in the otherwise pristine fields. The strike is unparalleled in our experience with the Draped Bust/Small Eagle type. Not only are the hair curls fully defined, but the eye and beak of the eagle are complete, as well as showing full details on the breast feathers. Weak central detailing is almost diagnostic for this type, leading us to wonder if perhaps this coin has been struck twice in order to achieve such completeness. The center of each side is light, almost brilliant, gradually shading to a warm and ever deeper golden-brown hue with deep blue at the edges. One of the finest early type coins in existence, regardless of denomination.

1801 PCGS MS65. V-1, R.4

Of the five different dates represented in the Heraldic Eagle half dime series, certainly the 1801 is the poorest struck. Usually the center of the obverse is weak and various portions of the clouds and wings on the reverse show incomplete or missing details. Valentine considered the 1801 "probably the most difficult date in the series, and certainly the most underrated". He also believed the mintage of 1801 dated coins to be considerably less than the officially recorded figure of 33,910 pieces.

Both varieties of 1801 half dimes are found in well worn condition. In his Encyclopedia, Breen has recorded the finest known specimen as being the Allenburger piece that reappeared in Auction '82. This coin is definitely not that piece, and comparing this coin to the plates in the Auction '82 catalog the present specimen appears noticeably finer than the Allenburger coin. Both were struck from an advanced state of the V-1 dies, but the Allenburger coin was obviously struck later and shows considerably less peripheral detail than this piece.

This coin has an extraordinarily strong strike. The only areas to show weakness are the two uppermost clouds and the feathers at the juncture of the shield and eagle's right wing. The hair curls show just a touch of softness behind the forehead. Otherwise the design was very well brought up, even the stars around the edge of the obverse are sharp in spits of the advanced beak in the dies. The surfaces are highly lustrous with smooth, unbroken mint frost. Each side has blue and gray color in the centers with a bright iridescence at the edges. This is the finest 1801 half dime that either service has graded. The closest coin to rival it is an MS62, graded by PCGS. We do not know if this MS62 is the Allenburger coin but we do not hesitate to state that this piece is finer, thus making this coin the finest known.

1838-O No Stars NGC 63. V-1

Struck from uncracked dies that appear to have been polished. Apparently this coin was struck in the earliest state of the dies before cracks developed.

There were approximately 70,000 pieces struck, but very few survive in mint condition as these coins were used extensively in the channels of commerce in Louisiana alongside the Mexican medio (valued at 6 1/4 cents). Naturally, any coin that passes for more than its face value will see extensive use, and so it is not surprising that most of the surviving 1838-O half dimes are in the Good to Very Good range. Valentine considered the 1838-O to be extremely rare in mint state. In his Encyclopedia, Breen called it "prohibitively rare unc." There are however, four coins that have been graded in various conditions of mint state by both the major grading services. PCGS has graded one MS60 and one MS61. NGC has only graded this piece and one other, undoubtedly the finest known, an MS65. This coin is neither the Garrett, Robison, nor the Gilhousen specimen. Its pedigree is unknown to us. To those wishing to trace its provenance it may be identified by a series of four small milling marks in the left obverse field and a scratch from Liberty's left arm extending down to the upper thigh. While mostly brilliant, both sides show scattered bits of light iridescent tone.

Aside from the above mentioned surface flaws there are very few abrasions noted on either side. A feature we find most curious on this coin is its completeness of strike. Both varieties of this issue are known for their weak strikes. On this coin the fullness of strike coupled with the reflectively in the fields lead us to conclude that this must have been one of the first coins struck from the V-1 dies, and possibly for some special purpose. An extraordinary example of this very rare issue that was believed to be the second finest known.

1838 No Drapery PCGS MS66

First year of the three year No Drapery type. While not an especially rare date relative to other early half dimes, the 1838 is nonetheless very scarce in such superior condition. PCGS has only graded three other coins of this date MS66, and none are finer.

This piece is fully struck in all areas including all the stars and the head area. Semi-prooflike, the coin shows evidence of having been struck from polished dies as both sides have light die striations in the fields. The coin has great visual interest with both sides being covered by blue-gray and red toning with scattered spots of original brilliance seen in the fields. The luster is frosted and swirls around the coin as it is angled beneath a light. A superb example of this first year of the With Stars and No Drapery type.

1840 No Drapery MS68

Final year of issue for the No Drapery type. Not only is this one of the finest half dimes we have ever seen regardless of date, but it is also one of the finest coins we have ever seen - regardless of denomination. Struck from lightly striated dies, the fields have a semi-prooflikeness that brightens the surfaces and makes the natural patina glow and shimmer beneath a light. Fully struck, every detail engraved into the die was completely brought up on this coin.

Obviously struck from the terminal state of the obverse die, there is a pronounced die crack that traverses the entire obverse vertically from rim to rim. Otherwise the surfaces are absolutely immaculate and free from any post-striking impairments or defects. Although one might expect technical perfection from a coin that grades MS68, mere freedom from abrasions cannot account for the grade. Doubtless were type coin brilliant or covered with a drab or indifferent toning, it would not grade as highly as it does. But in addition to clean surfaces, the grade is derived from the tremendous eye appeal this coin possesses due in no small part to the sea-green, violet, and golden-rose toning on each side and the thick, frosted mint luster that rolls around the surfaces as the coin is slowly tilted beneath a light.

This is the finest known example of this date, only one NGC graded MS67 approaches it. It is also the highest graded coin of the type. In fact, only one other coin has been given such a lofty grade by PCGS in the entire series of half dimes up to 1873. A historic offering.

1841-O NGC MS65

Although not recognized as a great rarity in its own right as is the 1849-O, the 1841-O is rare enough that most serious collectors and dealers have never seen a choice uncirculated one, and perhaps never even seen one in mint state at all.

This piece has lovely muted blue, red, and gray toning, evenly matched on both sides, and adding considerable visual interest to the coin. The bright lustrous fields glimmer and further enliven the toning. This piece possesses a complete strike in all areas, including the head. Full head detail on some dates in this series is almost impossible to find, and not made any easier by the loose and easy attitude toward production assumed by some employees of this mint. Struck from lightly rusted dies, the reverse shows three die cracks that travel from the rim inward to the wreath or just beyond.

This is one of only two coins of this elusive issue to have been so graded by NGC, and none are finer. The highest grade given by PCGS is MS64.

1842 PCGS PR64

Mint records do not exist documenting how many proofs were struck of this date. It is believed that eight proofs are known of this date. In his 1977 Proofs book, Walter Breen lists seven proofs known at that time. The #3 coin is the Valentine plate coin exhibited at the ANS at their legendary 1914 Exhibition. This coin however, is struck from the V-1 dies, as Breen indicates all seven listed coins are. But Valentine loaned two proof 1842 half dimes to the ANS for their exhibit. One is listed in the catalog as having the date near base, this would be from the V-1 dies. A second proof is listed as having the date away from the base. The second coin is not among those in Breen's pedigree list and this piece may very well be the second proof shown at the 1914 Exhibit. It is obviously a proof and just as obviously not struck from the V-1 dies, the date being well away from the base.

The coin has very deeply mirrored fields with a significant amount of mint frost on the devices. It is lightly toned and there are a few stray lint marks in the fields apparently caused by polishing the dies. This coin may be distinguished from the other seven known proofs by the presence of a long, hook-shaped lint mark just below star nine on the obverse. A historically significant proof that may well be the only one of its kind.

THE DAVID HALL

WORLD'S FINEST THREE CENT NICKELS

Over the years, I decided to put together the world's greatest collection of Proof Three Cent Nickels. I picked Three Cent Nickels because they were historically important, reasonably priced, and because the complete set was challenging but not impossible to complete.

For two years I've searched for coins at all the major coin shows and auctions. I bought coins for the set any time I found one. After I had acquired all the dates I continued to search for upgrades. Now, after two years of work, I'm ready to present a real showpiece set. I am convinced that no finer set could exist. And I am absolutely convinced that this set could not be duplicated at double the price.

There are 26 coins in the set. All of the coins have been graded by PCGS. Fourteen grade PR65, four grade PR66, six grade PR67 and two grade PR68. The two Proof 68's are the only Three Cent Nickels graded PR68 by PCGS! Here's a complete breakdown of this fabulous set;

Year	Grade	Population	Graded Higher
1865	PR65	32	4
1866	PR66	2	0
1867	PR65	24	2
1868	PR65	23	0
1869	PR65	35	3
1870	PR65	23	3
1871	PR65	41	1
1872	PR65	31	1
1873	PR65	30	1
1874	PR65	34	1
1875	PR65	17	0
1876	PR65	40	2
1877	PR65	116	18
1878	PR66	31	3
1870	PR67	8	0
1880	PR66	51	0
1881	PR68	1	0
1882	PR67	34	0
1883	PR68	1	0
1884	PR67	8	0
1885	PR67	8	0
1886	PR67	11	0
1887	PR65	71	5
1887/6	PR65	108	10
1888	PR66	38	1
1889	PR67	6	0

The 1865 is the lowest mintage of the entire series. It has always sold for a big premium. All of the 1865 to 1876 issues are difficult to find in grades above PR64. The 1877 and 1878 are classic Proof only issues. The later dates are unsurpassed in quality. And the 1881 and 1883 are the finest Three Cent Nickels ever graded by PCGS.

THE DAVID HALL

WORLD'S FINEST WASHINGTON QUARTER SET

For years, I have been working on putting together the world's finest set of Washington Quarters. Here's some of the highlights of this showpiece set;

Year	Grade	Population	Graded Higher
1932	MS66	7	0
1932-D	MS65	11	0
1932-S	MS65	17	0
1934-D	MS65	33	3
1935-D	MS66	9	0
1935-S	MS66	18	0
1936	MS67	4	0
1936-D	MS66	11	1
1936-S	MS66	17	1
1937-D	MS66	26	0
1937-S	MS66	25	0
1938	MS66	33	3
1938-S	MS66	46	3
1939-S	MS66	23	0
1940-D	MS67	3	0
1940-S	MS66	44	0
1942-S	MS67	2	0
1943-D	MS67	1	0
1943-S	MS67	6	0
1944	MS67	1	0
1944-S	MS67	2	0
1945	MS67	2	0
1946-S	MS67	2	0
1951-S	MS67	7	0
1953	MS67	2	0
1957-D	MS67	6	0

The complete set features 83 coins. All of the coins have been graded by PCGS. There are 24 coins that grade MS65. There are 37 coins that graded MS66. And there are an unbelievable 13 coins that grade MS67. There are 9 of the later dates (all very inexpensive coins) that grade MS64. Note that Washington Quarters are really tough to find in MS67. They are much rarer in that grade than Walking Liberty Halves or Mercury Dimes, for example.

This set was an incredibly difficult project to complete. I have helped build some truly great collections in my time. I must say that I found the Washington Quarter set to be one of the most difficult sets I've ever worked on. They are truly underrated rarities in top condition.

THE WORLD'S FINEST PANAMA-PACIFIC EXPOSITION SET

DWIGHT N. MANLEY

The Dwight N. Manley Panama - Pacific Exposition Set is simply wonderful to behold. All coins in this collection were certified by the Professional Coin Grading Service.

Charles E. Barber designed the Pan-Pac 50 cent piece issued in 1915 by the San Francisco Mint to celebrate the opening of the Panama Canal. The gold dollar Panama-Pacific Exposition piece was designed by Charles Keck, while the quarter-eagle bears the design fashioned by Charles E. Barber and George T. Morgan. The fifty-dollar gold piece completed this series and was designed by Robert Aitken. This coin was issued in both round and octagonal shapes. These coins were the first commemorative coins to display the motto, "IN GOD WE TRUST."

Description	Date	Service	Grade
Pan-Pac 50c	1915-S	PCGS	MS67
Pan-Pac Gold Dollar	1915-S	PCGS	MS67
Pan-Pac Gold $2.50	1915-S	PCGS	MS67
Pan-Pac $50 Round	1915-S	PCGS	MS65
Pan-Pac $50 Octagonal	1915-S	PCGS	MS65

1915-S Panama-Pacific Exposition Half Dollar

PCGS graded Mint State 67. Superb! When have you ever beheld a more amazing Pan-Pacific Half Dollar than this. Not only is it close to perfection, but its toning is something only the angels could duplicate. The coin remained in an original copper frame along with its gold companions, apparently until just before being submitted for grading. In that time it developed an incredibly beautiful halo of colors around the obverse periphery. With the centers offering the lightest hues, the color marches outward toward the rim in an overlapping blend from gold to red to magenta to turquoise blue! They are almost beyond belief. It is as if a summer rainbow had visited the coin and left its shadow thereon.

Equally beyond belief is the grade, since this is one of the few Mint State 67's graded by PCGS (19) from an original mintage of 27,134. We have seen a number of high grade specimens sold over the years. And we can say without fear of contradiction, this is the most beautiful rendition of a Panama-Pacific Half we have ever been privileged to sell. We hope that its new owner will not simply lock it away in a vault somewhere, but instead will let others admire its remarkable beauty from time to time. Truly, it belongs in an exhibit case sitting on a velvet rise beneath a golden spotlight.

1915-S Panama-Pacific Exposition Gold Dollar

PCGS graded mint State 67. Superb! From an original set in copper frame, of which the other pieces are also offered in this special section along with the frame. Collectors have long known that Panama-Pacific Dollars generally come nice, but never this nice! That is, until this one was submitted to PCGS for grading. Then, upon emerging from their test of fire (which in many ways is more rugged than the Twelve Labors of Hercules was) the numismatic community learned that there is, indeed, a Mint State 67 example. It ran their gauntlet and came out shining. Both figuratively and literally, this one outshines all others of its kind. And in the set it is a glowing centerpiece.

1915-S Panama-Pacific Exposition Quarter Eagle

PCGS graded Mint State 67. Superb! Here is one to match the spectacular Pan-Pacific gold Dollar in the preceding lot. Everywhere you examine this Quarter Eagle you will find virtual man-made perfection. Throughout its entire fabric it is a precious rendition of coin artistry and workmanship wrought in gold. Not only is the strike incomparably bold, but the surfaces, the luster, are smooth, satiny, and free from the usual scuffs and nicks. Unlike 99% of all Pan-Pacific Quarter Eagles we are offered, this one has escaped the harsh realities of numismatic "circulation". It is bright, never having been cleaned; it is beautiful, with delicate natural color, and it belongs in the finest set in America.

Upon examining a recent PCGS Population Report, we found this is the only Mint State 67 example graded, with none higher. Moreover, because so few original pieces remain intact uncleaned and fresh, we fail to see how another Mint State 67 could ever surface. Take it, then, that this is the quintessential 1915-S Pan-Pacific $2.50 gold piece, the Finest Known.

The 1915-S Panama-Pacific Exposition was held at a time in our history when the art world was throwing off the constraints of its staid, Victorian ways. Many new techniques were being tested on our coinage: matte proofing, rims lacking denticles, fancy lettering, textured fields. As can be seen , the coins struck for the exposition, such as this handsome Quarter Eagle, capture the flavor of these changes. Instead of a traditional design, the artist proposed an unusual motif featuring Columbia seated on a mythological hippocampus, a half-horse and half-sea serpent creature! The reverse eagle, too, was rendered in a way never before seen on an American production coin, having been modeled upon a similar eagle seen on one of our rare Pattern issues. These devices are obviously a far cry from our usual "traditional" coinage art.

1915-S Panama-Pacific Exposition $50 Round

PCGS graded Mint State 65. This and the $50 Octagonal should be examined by anyone who has any sense of aesthetic appreciation. For without a doubt, the present $50 Round is unmatched by any other example we have ever heard of. Its surfaces are sublime original, satiny, the picture of perfection. And its stern-looking owl stares out at his ogling viewers in a proud, stately fashion, knowing full well he graces the finest $50 Round Pan-Pacific gold piece of them all. As we said, everything here is the picture of perfection. Whether you judge a coin by its strike or is surfaces or its overall impression on your visual sense, the coin offered here outdistances any contender for Finest Known. In spite of there having been 483 Rounds sold, the average grade for one of these seems to be Mint State 62 to 63. They must have been so heavy that they received more than the usual number of bumps and scratches from mishandling. How did this one escape? How did it survive unscathed? We can only place it to the fact that it resided in an original copper frame until our consignor had it encapsulated by PCGS. Should you examine the frame you will see how it, also, is clean and unblemished.

America's fairs and expos are usually centered around a chosen theme. For 1915, the fair organizers honored the discovery of the Pacific Ocean (1513) and the completion of the Panama Canal (1914) as two anchor points for their theme. A series of 5 coins was struck for the occasion, including complete sets mounted in metal frames or leather cases sold for $200. Many sales were made to banks and other novices; for this reason, high grade examples are especially hard to find; the larger the denomination, the harder to locate. Some were carried as souvenir pieces, in fact. When all was said and done, only 483 Round and 645 Octagonal $50 gold pieces were sold. And though no specific records were kept in this regard, one can assume that numerous pieces in the hands of the public were melted after the federal government sized America's gold coins in 1933. We estimated there are perhaps 200 of the round pieces left today, along with 300 to 350 in the octagonal format.

1915-S Panama-Pacific Exposition $50 Octagonal

PCGS graded Mint State 65. A superb spectacular, utterly amazing $50 gold piece! Its surfaces are alive with dancing golden color, a deep yellow-gold hue suggesting long residence in its purple velvet-lined copper frame of issue (offered in another Lot). There are no defects to mention on this Gem Uncirculated specimen, nothing but overwhelming beauty and originality, nothing but the sharpest, brightest, most dazzling perfection we have ever seen in an Octagonal Pan-Pacific $50. From an original mintage of 645 can be deducted 75% for those which have been cleaned or lost or banged about. Then of the remaining 25% only 1 or 2 approach this one's delightful color and glow. Finally — and this is of prime importance to value minded buyers — this is the only Mint State 65 example graded by either grading service! It, along with the $50 Round is one of only two Mint State 65's awarded to such a mammoth coin. Were this a smaller coin like a Gold Dollar it would probably have gotten a Mint State 68 or 69 grade. However, the grading services are uncommonly strict when grading big gold coins; especially are they strict on these satin finish jewels from the 'teens.

Imagine the advances in technology which had to occur before these massive gold coins could be struck. The Philadelphia Mint's fourteen-ton medal press was shipped by train and set up at the San Francisco facility for the striking ceremonies for the Panama-Pacific fifty-dollar gold pieces. It is claimed this press could strike a coin with a pressure of 450 tons per square inch! By comparison, Morgan Silver Dollars required only 150 tons of force. This steel behemoth struck 1,500 of each $50 gold piece, for a total of 3,000 coins or nearly 7,500 ounces of gold (value today with gold at $370 an ounce = $2,775,000.00) Unfortunately, there were few takers at the $100-per-coin asking price and so only 645 Octagonal 'fifties were sold. The remainder were melted.

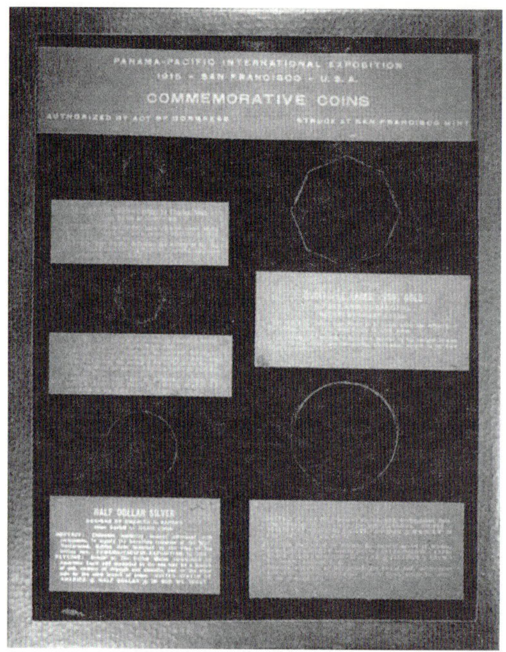

Original copper frame for a Panama-Pacific Set
(Courtesy of Superior Galleries, Beverly Hills, California)

Panama-Pacific Collection
(Courtesy of Christy Boldt c/o Superior Galleries, Beverly Hills, California)

Augustus Humbert 1852/1 $20 Pioneer gold coin (PCGS PR-65) sold May 19, 1989, by John W. Highfill (Oklahoma Federated Gold & Numismatics, Inc., Broken Arrow, Oklahoma) and Mark S. Yaffe (National Gold Exchange, Inc., Tampa, Florida) for $1,350,00 in a private transaction! The current owner wishes to remain anonymous.

U.S. Assayer Augustus Humbert personally owned this fabulous coin for many years. Then ownership passed to noted collectors Andrew Zabriskie and James Ellsworth. Next, it was acquired by James Work Garrett in 1923. The coin remained in the Garrett Collection until being sold at auction by Bowers & Ruddy in 1980 for $325,000.

Volume 30 Issue 1536
Sept. 20, 1989

Entire Contents Copyright 1989 by Amos Press Inc., Sidney, Ohio 45365 (USPS No. 120700) (ISSN 0010-0447)
Single Copy U.S. $1.25

Coin World®

• THE WEEKLY NEWSPAPER OF THE ENTIRE NUMISMATIC FIELD •

Gold coin breaks $1 million barrier

By Robert M. Lacewell
COIN WORLD Staff Writer

A single United States coin, an 1852/1 Augustus Humbert $20 pioneer gold coin,

(Courtesy of *Coin World,* Sidney, Ohio, Sep 20, 1989)

numismatic news
FEATURING COIN MARKET

VOL. 38 NO. 37 September 12, 1989 • IOLA, WISCONSIN 54990

©1988 Krause Publications, Inc. ISSN 0029-604X $1.25

Record shattered!
Territorial gold sells for $1.35 million

By David C. Harper

It's official. The million-dollar price barrier for an individual U.S. numismatic item has been broken. An Augustus Humbert 1852/1 $20 Territorial gold piece was sold May 19 for $1.35 million. The private-treaty transaction was consummated between a partnership of a

(Courtesy of *Numismatic News,* Iola, Wisconsin, Sep 12, 1989)

COIN MARKET CELEBRATES FIRST MILLION-DOLLAR COIN

September marked a major milestone for the rare coin market: the announcement of a U.S. coin selling for more than $1 million.

The coin, an 1852/1 Humbert $50 gold piece graded PCGS PR65, was sold by two prominent ANE dealers to a private investor for $1.35 million. The sale, which took place in May, was disclosed in September to stop "exaggerated rumors" of its existence, according to the dealers.

We announced in August the $990,000 sale of the Dexter specimen 1804 silver dollar – at that time the highest known price ever paid for a U.S. coin. That purchase, which took place at Auction '89 sale in July, postdates the Humbert transaction by two months.

The 1852/1 Humbert overdate is among the rarest and most famous of U.S. coins. The coin was struck by Augustus Humbert, the U.S. assayer of gold during the California gold rush. Unlike most pioneer gold coins, the Humbert coin was an authorized issue of the U.S. mint. The specimen sold is the finest of three examples known of this variety.

For many years, this coin remained the property of Augustus Humbert. It subsequently was handled by noted collectors Andrew Zabriskie and James Ellsworth before being purchased by James Work Garrett in 1923. The coin remained in the Garrett Collection until being sold at a 1980 Bowers & Ruddy auction for $325,000.

The Exchange Report
Published Monthly By:
American Numismatic Exchange, Inc. (ANE)
9040 Roswell Road, Suite 400
Atlanta, GA 30350
Telephone: (404) 587-1454
Fax: (404) 587-2365

Article from The Exchange Report regarding the sale of the 1852/1 Humbert $20 gold piece
(Courtesy of American Numismatic Exchange, Atlanta, Georgia)

STOCK MARKET JITTERS

Continued from page 1
according to a study by major Wall Street brokerage firm, rare coins have appreciated at an average annual rate of 17%; stocks, by comparison, returned an average of 13% and T-bills 9% during this same period.

If the financial markets continue to look vulnerable — and judging by recent news, it looks as if they will — it's fair to speculate that the *Big Money* will be eager to exploit other investment opportunities... Rare coins should be big winners.

This is why rare coins should attract strong attention if higher inflation returns. Just as *big money* investors remember the impact of inflation in the late 1970's on financial assets, they also remember the upward spiral of rare coin prices during the same period.

If the financial markets continue to look vulnerable — and judging by recent news, it looks as if they will — it's fair to speculate that the *Big Money* will be eager to exploit other investment opportunities. It may be reasonable to assume that with inflation widely perceived as a threat, these investors will consider placing 5-10% of their funds into what are considered "inflation hedges" — precious metals, stamps, art, diamonds and rare coins.

Rare coins should be big winners. The *money power* that institutional investors represent is mind-boggling. In aggregate, these individuals and firms control over $5 trillion in assets. With such a large bankroll, even a 1% shift in funds to tangible assets would amount to a $50 billion commitment. Although precious metals and stocks tied to precious metals recovery and refining will be major beneficiaries of the reshuffled priorities, the rare coin market would receive its multi-billion dollar share.

The sight-unseen trading of rare coins is a fresh product with a compelling future. Also, rare coins have "pizzazz". One element previously highlighted in any due diligence review of rare coins was the matter of liquitidy; prior to 1986, rare coins had not been known for their ease of liquidation. But in the past 3 years with the formation of American Numismatic Exchange (ANE) and the advent of its computerized, sight-unseen electronic trading network for certified coins, a liquid two-way market for rare coins is growing.

So is Wall Street's acceptance of rare coins. The heightened confidence level of *big money* in rare coins has been reflected recently by the several exciting numismatic ventures announced by various Wall Street brokerages. In 1988, Merrill-Lynch introduced a $40 million limited partnership of ancient coins and artifacts.

In March, 1989, Kidder, Peabody & Co. announced the American Rare Coin fund, a $40 million partnership to be comprised of U.S. coins; most of these coins were to be certified by Professional Coin Grading Service or Numismatic Guaranty Corp.. The news of a $40 million influx of funds into the rare coin market sent it, according to one prominent dealer, "into interstellar overdrive." Prices rose across-the-board, as much as 20 percent to 30 percent a month for several months. Higher-quality and rarer issues doubled, and in many cases tripled.

The sight-unseen trading of rare coins is a fresh product with a compelling future. Also, rare coins have "pizzazz".

Until the American Rare Coin Fund was announced, the largest limited partnership of certified U.S. rare coins had been approximately $5 million. This partnership therefore represented a quantum leap in the acceptance level by *big money* of rare coin products certified by third-party grading services.

The fund has provided an enormous boost in the demand for the rare coin "classics"; the ultra-rare and often extremely expensive coins that are the highlight of any collection or auction. In July, 1989, the Dexter specimen of the 1804 silver dollar sold for $990,000. Less than two months ago, in September, the $1 million barrier for a U.S. coin was broken when the 1852/1 Augustus Humbert $50 gold piece sold to an investment consortium for $1.35 million.

If a $40 million influx of cash produces "interstellar overdrive" in the market, what will a billion dollars do to it? This amount of money inserted into what traditionally has been considered a "thin" market could make the price gains experienced in early 1989 seem trivial by comparison.

The first glimmer of this new interest in rare coins from the *Big Money* is now on the horizon. Reports of other major brokerage firms offering their own rare coin limited partnerships abound. If they prove true, the rare coin market could be in for a quick awakening from its five month slumber.

But even if the reports prove premature, the October 13 stock market "correction" has set the stage for a fundamental evaluation of financial assets by *Big Money* investors. Tangible assets will be under intense scrutiny by institutional investment managers in the weeks and months ahead. Any tangible asset that can provide the *Big Money* with reasonable returns on investment and liquidity will be in for a profound expansion on the demand side.

In this environment, how should investors react? For starters, the opinion is that we've reached the bottom of the current rare coin Bear Market. Even investors who are not convinced that rare coins are headed for significant price increases should make some adjustments to their portfolio to adjust to higher inflationary expectations.

The first glimmer of this new interest in rare coins from the *Big Money* is now on the horizon. Reports of other major brokerage firms offering their own rare coin limited partnerships abound. If they prove true, the rare coin market could be in for a quick awakening from its five month slumber.

It is obvious that the *Big Money* is already making such preparations. It is only prudent that smaller investors do the same. ☐

Dexter Specimen 1804 Sold!
(Courtesy of American Numismatic Exchange, Atlanta, Georgia)

Dexter Specimen 1804 acquired by Hugh Sconyers, American Rare Coin Fund, Beverly Hills, California, $990,000, July 1989!

The Legendary King of Siam Set
(Courtesy of Superior Galleries, Beverly Hills, California)

The 1804 King of Siam Set was consigned to Superior Galleries "The Father Flanagan's Boy's Town Collection" sale held May-June 1990 where it sold for $3,200,000 to Iraj "Roger" Sayah!

Many other spectacular sales have taken place making rare coins more visible within the entire spectrum of collectibles while attracting the attention of investors at the highest level. Here is a sampling of prices realized for several extraordinary specimens.

1776 Continental Penny, EG FECIT, tin, Breen No. 1095, PCGS 65, $39,600 (see Lot #698 - Superior Galleries "An Amazing Collection of United States Silver Dollars" Catalog, May 27, 28, 1991 Auction).

1794 Dollar, Superior, presentation strike with prooflike surfaces, ex W.W. Neil, Amon Carter, Jr., $506,000 (see Lot #699 — Superior Galleries "An Amazing Collection of United States Silver Dollars" Catalog, May 27, 28, 1991 Auction).

1795 MS65 NGC Draped Bust small eagle, $154,000 (see Lot #700 - Superior Galleries "An Amazing Collection of United States Silver Dollars" Catalog, May 27, 28, 1991 Auction).

1795 MS65 PCGS Draped Bust dollar realized $250,000 in a private sale - no photograph available

1803 Draped Bust dollar, Bolender 7, PCGS Proof 66, $264,000 (see Lot #702 - Superior Galleries "An Amazing Collection of United States Silver Dollars" Catalog, May 27, 28, 1991 Auction).

1866 Seated Liberty dollar, PCGS 66, $60,500 (see Lot #708 - Superior Galleries "An Amazing Collection of United States Silver Dollars" Catalog, May 27, 28, 1991 Auction).

PRICES REALIZED

The sight-unseen certified bid reporting mechanism does not work especially in the case of scarce and/or rare date silver dollars. The numismatic trades over the past few years have chosen to use only the electronic Coin Exchange posted bid prices to reflect the "values" of certified third-party graded silver dollars. This can only be described as inadequate reporting and does not reflect the true "market value" of all the affected coins. The discovery of true values in the case of scarce to rare silver dollars is one involving actual transactions and the asking prices of those who actually hold the coins. The same case rests for all esoteric rare coins.

The following transactions representing prices realized are within a 0-5 percent range of accuracy. These prices may actually shock some people, but can also help others understand the reasons as to why they are never able to buy these rarer date issues on any sight-unseen system. Note that these coins were dealer to dealer transactions, and remember that these are prime examples of coins for those who want only the very best.

The prices realized versus sight-unseen bid levels ranged from 100% to 1000%. Bids have not been printed because they are irrelevant to true market value (i.e., 1893-O bid at $10,000 sold at $157,500 which is 15.75 times bid).

For a complete listing of the first year's activity (**May 22, 1990 through May 22, 1991**) for the Morgan and Peace silver dollars on the Certified Coin Exchange, see the chapter entitled "The Certified Coin Exchange," by Ronald A. Brandow and Joseph H. Stephens, III. A complete annual chart for Morgan and Peace silver dollars that traded sight-unseen on the CCE for their first fiscal year is listed in complete detail. Very interesting!

Record sale price data for the majority of the Carson City Silver Dollars were accumulated by William E. Spears. The chart figures are for the highest price paid for "CC" silver dollars from each of the Carson City production years. For some years, the listing may include two coins with different mint state grades. (Note: PCGS designates DMPL for Deep Mirror Prooflike, while NGC designates DPL for Deep Prooflike for all Morgan silver dollars.)

There is a group of dealers that deal with the finest known coins. Those that have contributed to these private sale transactions are that group and here are their reports for both the finest known examples and their prices realized at the time. The dollars listed below are all in PCGS or NGC holders unless otherwise noted. These are exceptional coins with high market values. **MANY ARE ONE OF A KIND. THEY ARE ONLY AN ELITE SAMPLING AND DO NOT REFLECT THE ENTIRE MARKET**. There are multiples of other dates and grades that trade daily within a 5% range of the posted CDN bid levels.

Bruce Amspacher
Robert L. Astrich
Barry Bellefontaine
Michael Blodgett, Ph.D.
George E. Bodway, Ph.D.
Kent Brennan
John Connor
John W. Dannreuther
Silvano DiGenova
Richard "Kenny" Duncan
Jack A. Ehrmantraut, Jr.
Steele Eunson
Michael Fuljenz
Roger L. Geary
Elliot S. Goldman
David Hall
Jack C. Hertzberg
Robert Higgins
John W. Highfill
Wayne Hummel
Steve Ivy
Donald H. Kagin
Dan Kihlstadius
Jack R. Lee
Dwight N. Manley
Jay C. Miller
Wayne H. Miller
Paul Montgomery
Jay Parrino
Martin B. Paul
Arnold "Arnie" Payne
D. Harrison Phillips
Thomas B. Phillips
Steve Ryan
Clark A. Samuelson
Iraj "Roger" Sayah
Larry Shepherd
William E. Spears
Dean Tavenner
Mark S. Yaffe
Brian D. Yutzy

You wanna pay WHAT?

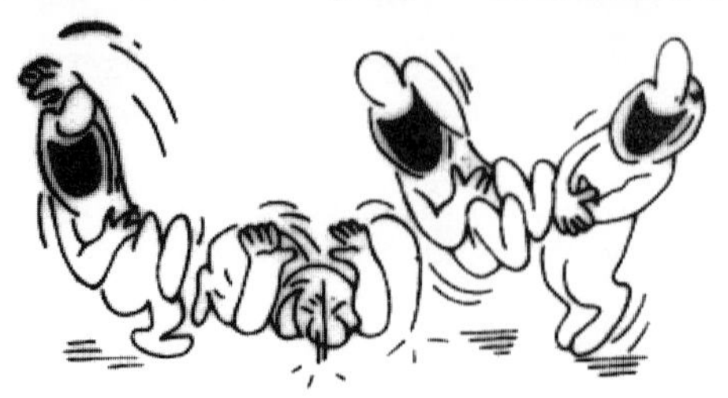

Morgan Dollars:

Date	Grade	Price Realized In Past 2 Years
1878-P 8TF	MS66	25,000
1878-P 8TF	MS66	14,700
1878-P 7TF	MS66	25,000
1878-P 7TF	MS65 PL	9,500
1878-P 7TF	MS65 DMPL	15,000
1878-P 7/8TF	MS65 (Weak)	7,500
1878-P 7/8TF	MS66 (NGC)	19,500
1878-CC	MS66	20,000
1878-CC	MS66 DMPL	11,000
1878-CC	MS67	30,000
1878-CC	MS65 DMPL	16,000
1878-S	MS67	15,000
1878-S	MS67	17,500
1878-S	MS67	12,250
1878-S	MS67	12,500
1878-S	MS67 (NGC)	17,500
1878-S	MS65 DMPL	9,000
1878-S	MS66 DMPL	15,500
1879-P	MS66	20,000
1879-CC	MS65	28,500
1879-CC	MS64 DMPL	9,500
1879-CC CD	MS65	60,000
1879-CC CD	MS65	100,000
1879-CC CD	MS65 (NGC)	37,500
1879-O	MS65	6,600
1879-O	MS66	17,500
1879-O	MS66	14,580
1879-S	MS68	11,000
1879-S Rev.78	MS65	32,000
1879-S Rev.78	MS65	20,000
1879-S Rev.78	MS65	17,500
1879-S Rev.78	MS65	15,000
1879-S Rev.78	MS65	14,000
1879-S Rev.78	MS65	9,500
1880-P	MS65	4,950
1880-P	MS65	7,250
1880-P	MS65 DMPL	17,500
1880 Proof	PR68	39,600
1880-CC	MS67	25,000
1880-CC	MS65 DMPL	15,000
1880-CC	MS65 DMPL	15,500
1880-CC Rev.78	MS66	28,500
1880-CC Rev.78	MS65 DMPL	30,000
1880-O	MS65	135,000
1880-O	MS65	90,000
1880-O	MS65	95,000
1880-O	MS65	60,000
1880-O	MS64 DMPL	7,500
1881-P	MS65 DPL (NGC)	12,500
1881-P	MS65 DMPL	12,500
1881-CC	MS66	5,600
1881-CC	MS67	20,000
1881-CC	MS66 DMPL	14,000
1881-CC	MS66 DMPL	14,500
1881-O	MS65	4,190
1881-S	MS68	12,500
1881-S	MS68	9,250
1881-S	MS68	11,500
1881-S	MS69	65,000
1882-P	MS67	19,400
1882-P	MS65 DMPL	12,000
1882-P	MS65 DMPL	11,000
1882 Proof	PR65	15,950
1882-CC	MS67	25,000
1882-CC	MS67	50,000
1882-CC	MS66 DMPL	19,000
1882-CC	MS66 DMPL	15,000
1882-O	MS67	19,400
1882-O	MS66	15,000
1882-O	MS65 PL	11,000
1882-O/S	MS64	5,500
1882-S	MS68	21,500
1882-S	MS68	25,000
1882-S	MS66 DMPL	12,500
1883-P	MS65 DMPL	8,500
1883-P	MS66 DMPL	25,000
1883 Proof	PR65	18,700
1883-CC	MS67	12,500
1883-CC	MS67 PL	25,000
1883-CC	MS66 DMPL	12,750
1883-O	MS67	12,500
1883-O	MS66 PL	11,750
1883-O	MS65 DMPL	8,500
1883-O	MS66 DMPL	10,000
1883-S	MS64	5,250
1883-S	MS65	35,700
1883-S	MS65	65,000
1884-P	MS65 DPL (NGC)	8,750
1884-P	MS66 DMPL	14,500
1884-CC	MS67	25,000
1884-CC	MS67	17,850
1884-CC	MS68	40,000
1884-CC	MS66 DMPL	11,750
1884-O	MS67	11,880
1884-O	MS67	11,000
1884-O	MS66 DMPL	9,650
1884-O **Proof (Br.)***	PR64	20,900
1884-S	MS64	106,000
1884-S	MS64	75,000
1884-S	MS65	390,000
1884-S	MS65	400,000
1884-S	MS65	425,000
1885-P	MS66	1,850
1885-CC	MS67	25,000
1885-CC	MS68	75,000
1885-CC	MS68	90,000
1885-CC	MS66 DMPL	13,500
1885-O	MS66 PL	8,500
1885-O	MS66 DMPL	11,000
1885-S	MS65 PL	9,500
1885-S	MS65 DMPL	25,000
1886-P	MS66 DMPL	11,500
1886-O	MS64	9,000
1886-O	MS64 DMPL	35,000
1886-O	MS67 DMPL	231,000
1886-S	MS65	5,250

Morgan Dollars:

Date	Grade	Price Realized In Past 2 Years
1886-S	MS65 PL	9,750
1887-P	MS67	15,000
1887-P	MS67	17,500
1887-P	MS67	15,500
1887-P	MS67	9,000
1887-P	MS66 DMPL	10,500
1887/6-P	MS65 DMPL	30,000
1887-O	MS65 PL	14,000
1887-O	MS65 DMPL	18,000
1887-S	MS65	7,500
1887-S	MS65	5,900
1887-S	MS66	18,500
1887/6-O	MS64	8,900
1888-P	MS65 DMPL	10,000
1888-P	MS66 PL	9,750
1888-O	MS65 PL	4,750
1888-O	MS65 DMPL	8,750
1888-S	MS65	6,150
1888-S	MS65 DMPL	23,700
1888-S	MS65 DPL (NGC)	21,000
1889-P	MS65 DMPL	14,500
1889-CC	MS64	36,700
1889-CC	MS65	450,000
1889-CC	MS65	310,000
1889-CC	MS64 DMPL	100,000
1889-CC	MS64 DPL (NGC)	115,000
1889-O	MS65	7,400
1889-O	MS66	25,000
1889-O	MS66	11,880
1889-O	MS65 PL	15,000
1889-S	MS66	14,500
1890-P	MS65 PL	11,500
1890-CC	MS65	8,000
1890-CC	MS65	11,500
1890-CC	MS66	27,500
1890-CC	MS66	25,000
1890-CC	MS66	25,200
1890-CC	MS65 DMPL	16,000
1890-CC	MS65 DMPL	12,000
1890-CC (Tailbar)	MS65	15,000
1890-O	MS65	12,500
1890-O	MS65	8,500
1890-O	MS66	15,000
1890-O	MS66	13,500
1890-S	MS65 DMPL	16,000
1891-P	MS65	15,000
1891-P	MS66	26,000
1891-CC	MS66	16,000
1891-CC	MS67	40,000
1891-CC	MS65 DMPL	25,000
1891-O	MS65	14,500
1891-O	MS65	14,750
1891-O	MS65	14,000
1891-O	MS65	12,500
1891-S	MS65	14,300
1891-S	MS65 PL	10,000
1891-S	MS65 DPL (NGC)	13,000
1892-P	MS65 DMPL	30,000

Date	Grade	Price Realized In Past 2 Years
1892-CC	MS66	33,000
1892-CC	MS66	16,800
1892-CC	MS67	55,000
1892-CC	MS65 PL	15,000
1892-O	MS65 DMPL	45,000
1892-O	MS65 DMPL	25,000
1892-S	MS66	118,000
1892-S	MS66	115,000
1892-S	MS66	94,000
1892-S	MS67	275,000
1892-S	MS67 (NGC)	157,500
1893-CC **Proof (Br.)***	PR64	90,000
1893-CC	MS65	110,000
1893-CC	MS65	85,000
1893-CC	MS65	150,000
1893-O	MS65	157,500
1893-O	MS64	15,000
1893-S	MS65 (RAW) **	*** 357,500
1893-S	MS65	242,000
1893-S	MS65	375,000
1893-S	MS65	450,000
1893-S	MS65	250,000
1893-S	MS65 (NGC)	150,000
1894-P	MS65	25,000
1894-P	MS66	82,000
1894-O	MS64	4,700
1894-O	MS65	28,875
1894-O	MS65	55,000
1894-S	MS67	75,000
1895 Proof	PR67	125,000
1895 Proof	PR67	75,000
1895 Proof	PR67	115,000
1895 Proof	PR67	89,000
1895 Proof	PR67	102,500
1895-O	MS65	135,000
1895-O **Proof (Br.)** *	PR65 (RAW) **	60,250
1895-S	MS65	22,260
1895-S	MS65	14,850
1895-S	MS66 PL	75,000
1896-P	MS65 DMPL	6,500
1896-P	MS65 DPL (NGC)	6,500
1896-P	MS66 PL	12,500
1896-Proof	PR65	16,500
1896-O	MS64	17,500
1896-O	MS64	24,200
1896-S	MS65	24,200
1896-S	MS65	35,000
1896-S	MS66	60,000
1896-S	MS66	57,500
1897-P	MS65 DMPL	9,000
1897-O	MS64	18,000
1897-O	MS65	32,000
1897-O	MS65	34,125
1897-O	MS65	37,500
1897-O	MS65	52,800
1897-O	MS66	80,000
1897-O	MS67	250,000
1897-S	MS65	13,750

Morgan Dollars

Date	Grade	Price Realized In Past 2 Years
1897-S	MS68	25,000
1897-S	MS65 DMPL	9,000
1897-S	MS65 DPL (NGC)	7,500
1898-P	MS65 DMPL	7,250
1898-O	MS67	6,200
1898-O	MS66 DMPL	9,750
1898-O	MS67 DMPL	27,000
1898-S	MS65 DMPL	15,000
1899-P	MS65 DMPL	12,500
1899-P	MS65 DPL (NGC)	7,500
1899-P	MS66 DMPL	15,000
1899-O	MS66 DMPL	8,750
1899-S	MS65 DMPL	12,500
1900-O	MS66	2,200
1900-O	MS67	14,500
1900-O	MS67	15,660
1900-O	MS67	17,500
1900-O	MS65 DMPL	12,750
1900-O	MS65 DPL (NGC)	11,000
1900-O/CC	MS66	12,000
1900-S	MS65	18,700
1900-S	MS66	10,750
1900-S	MS66	7,500
1900-S	MS65 DMPL	15,000
1901-P	MS64	55,000
1901-P	MS64	60,000
1901-P	MS64	35,000
1901-P	MS64	50,000
1901-O	MS66 PL	12,500
1901-O	MS65 DMPL	12,500
1901-S	MS66	51,000
1901-S	MS66	21,500
1902-P	MS67	17,500
1902-P	MS65 PL	7,000
1902-O	MS66	2,470
1902-O	MS65 PL	5,000
1902-O	MS65 DMPL	12,750
1902-O	MS65 DMPL	7,500
1902-O	MS65 DMPL	14,500
1902-S	MS67	19,800
1902-S	MS66	11,000
1902-S	MS66	9,000
1903-P	MS67	12,500
1903-P	MS67	21,750
1903-P	MS67	11,250
1903-O	MS65	7,480
1903-O	MS65 PL	4,900
1903-O	MS66 PL	10,500
1903-O	MS65 DMPL	12,500
1903-O	MS65 DPL (NGC)	12,500
1903-S	MS65	10,000
1903-S	MS65	14,500
1903-S	MS65	14,000
1903-S	MS66	18,500
1903-S	MS67	30,000
1904-O	MS67	15,000
1904-O	MS65 DMPL	4,250
1904-O	MS65 DPL (NGC)	4,500
1904-O	MS66 DMPL	10,500
1904-S	MS65	14,500
1904-S	MS65	10,450
1904-S	MS67 (NGC)	91,000
1904-S	MS65 PL	35,000
1921-P	MS66	2,090
1921-P	MS65 PL	5,750
1921-D	MS65 DPL (NGC)	18,000
1921-D	MS66	2,090
1921-S	MS64 DMPL	15,000
1921-S	MS65 PL (NGC)	25,000
1921-S	MS64 DPL (NGC)	15,000

MS = Mint State
PL = Prooflike
DPL = Deep Prooflike
DMPL = Deep Mirror Prooflike
PR = Proof

* Branch mint proof. The 1895-O branch mint proof is undocumented. The only reported 1895-O branch mint proof, H.R. Lee, American Numismatic Society, one reported, Stack's sale 1947, Louis Eliasberg collection [Walter H. Breen, Berkely, California].

** Uncertified grades

*** This coin was later certified and graded MS67 by PCGS

Note: Many coins with the identical date, mintmark and grade may have sold at different prices depending upon the time sold and prevailing market conditions. To put it in more simple terms, an identical coin may have been listed multiple times having been sold at different price levels at various times. A very small percentage of the coins were sold prior to the past two years and the prices realized reflect that fact.

Peace Dollars:

Date	Grade	Price Realized In Past 2 Years	Date	Grade	Price Realized In Past 2 Years
1922-P	MS67	22,500	1926-D	MS67	33,500
1922 MP High Relief	PR65	46,200	1926-D	MS67	33,000
1922 MP Reg. Relief	PR65	35,200	1926-D	MS67	25,000
1922-D	MS65	1,750	1926-S	MS67	33,500
1923-P	MS67	28,500	1927-D	MS66	50,000
1923-S	MS65	9,900	1928-S	MS65	38,000
1923-S	MS67	75,000	1928-S	MS65	28,000
1923-S	MS67	80,000	1928-S	MS65	25,300
1925-P	MS67	28,500	1934-S	MS65	11,500
1925-S	MS65	16,000	1934-S	MS65	15,000
1926-D	MS67	28,500	1934-S	MS66	34,600
1926-D	MS67	31,500	1934-S	MS66	37,000

MS = Mint State
PL = Prooflike
DPL = Deep Prooflike
DMPL = Deep Mirror Prooflike
PR = Proof

Commemoratives:

1900 Lafayette	MS66	27,500
1900 Lafayette	MS67	125,000

Gobrecht Dollars — 1836-1839

1836	MS64 (NGC)	35,000
1838	MS65 (NGC)	150,000
1839	MS65 (NGC)	150,000

There are many other excellent collections, individual coins and prices realized which are not represented in this chapter. As other fantastic collections are accumulated and price records broken, they will be captured in the limelight for all to see. The world of numismatics is growing more exciting with each passing decade, and as you will see, "The Best is yet to come!"

***

George E. Bodway, Ph.D.

Dr. George E. Bodway is manager of corporate planning for Hewlett-Packard. Prior to this assignment in 1989 he was Director of Hewlett-Packard's System Program Planning Organization, a position which he assumed in late 1986.

Dr. Bodway joined Hewlett-Packard in 1965 as an engineer in Palo Alto, California. He became general manager of the division's Technology Center in 1970 and supervised its move to Santa Rosa, California during the period of 1972 to 1975. While in Santa Rosa Bodway served on the Board of Directors of the Santa Rosa Chamber of Commerce during which time he was elected Vice President and subsequently President of the Santa Rosa Chamber of Commerce in 1981. While in Santa Rosa he directed the company's acquisition of a new site in Rohnert Park, California until he was named general manager the Computer Integrated Circuits Division in Cupertino, California. As a result of his work with the city of Rohnert Park one of the city streets near the plant was named after Dr. Bodway. In 1984, he became general manager of HP's Information Technology Group, directing the activities of one operation which produced integrated circuits for HP's use and three other operations concerned with the development and manufacturing of advanced computer systems technologies. He held that position until being named to his current planning assignments in 1986.

Dr. Bodway was born in Oakland, California in 1935. He has three degrees in engineering physics from the University of California at Berkeley, his bachelor's, masters and doctoral degrees having been awarded in 1960, 1964 and 1966 respectively. He is the author of a number of patents in the field of solid-state integrated circuits and has published several articles on solid-state devices and microwave design techniques. He is a member of the American Physical Society and on the Board of Directors of the Semiconductor Industry Association (SIA). He was one of the original founders of the Semiconductor Research Corporation (SRC) and a member of its original Board of Directors. He is also currently on the Board of Directors of SEMATECH, a semiconductor manufacturing consortium.

Dr. Bodway is involved in numerous hobbies such as trout fishing, hunting, downhill skiing, tennis, golf, gun collecting, wood working, as well as numerous investment activities including rare coin collecting. He has been a serious collector of U.S. coins for more than 20 years and has become friends with many people in the industry.

Dr. Bodway is married to a beautiful young lady named Joan, and has 5 children and 10 grandchildren.

CHAPTER 27

The "Bodway Set" of Morgan Dollars

by George E. Bodway, Ph.D.

Preface

The following story about the "Bodway Set" of Morgan dollars consists of three parts. The first part is an introduction which describes the set from an overall perspective, talks about the rewards I received from putting the set together, and ends with a list of suggestions I offer for other new collectors based on my experiences.

The second part of the story consists of a detailed listing of the "Bodway Set" sorted in a number of interesting ways.

The final part includes a short description, pedigree information and a little history for twelve coins from the "Bodway Set." These twelve dollars are among the rarest and most difficult to obtain in this high level of condition in the entire Morgan dollar series.

Part One: Introduction
Part Two: "Bodway Set" Listing
Part Three: Description, Pedigree and History

Introduction

I have been collecting coins for more than 20 years. For me the potential financial returns from an investment point of view are secondary to many of the other rewards, although this potential financial return certainly encourages me to invest more of my assets in the hobby than otherwise would be the case.

I started out by collecting many different kinds of U.S. coins, but as time went on it became apparent that it would be better to focus on a few areas and be really knowledgeable in these areas. As a result of this gradual transition from a broad based collector to a specialist I ended up focusing on uncirculated Morgan dollars. In fact I eventually sold off all my other coins such as type, Peace dollars and U.S. gold coins and put all of my energy into this one area.

About six years ago I decided on a specific goal for my Morgan dollar collection and became even more focused. The goal was to complete a Morgan dollar set in as high a quality as possible. Shortly after I made this decision the introduction of reliable third party grading services such as PCGS occurred. These services provided an increased confidence in the quality of coins in one's set, and even more important to me is that a coin in your set is now recognized and respected for what it is to a far greater degree than before third party grading. For example, prior to PCGS, if you said you had a coin you believed to be of a certain quality people would discount the information and say to themselves "No way." Half a dozen or more people could and did believe they had the finest coin for a particular date and mintage. Prior to PCGS, the only way that a coin received credibility was for a so called "Industry Expert" to make a statement in a public article proclaiming its relative condition. This did make for a lot of very interesting reading on the subject. Unfortunately this public hype about particular coins by the experts is almost non-existent now and this I believe is unfortunate for the hobby.

Another big advantage of the third party grading services has been the publication of population statistics. There have been enough Morgan dollars graded now to be able to extrapolate the most likely number of coins available in each grade. There have probably been more than 10% of the available uncirculated Morgan dollars graded by now and probably a much higher percentage of the rarer and high grade samples. In early 1987 after about a year of grading by PCGS I was able to use advanced statistical analysis to predict the ultimate availability of Morgan dollars in each grade. This allowed me to identify early some coins that would always be extremely rare. This also contributed or reinforced my decision to focus on completing a high quality Morgan dollar set. A more detailed analysis of the statistical work appeared in the National Silver Dollar Roundtable publications of August 1987 and February 1988.

What I would like to do now is discuss the Morgan dollar set that I have put together in general terms that describe the overall set rather than any one particular coin. Hopefully you will then have some idea of what I have been up to. With that as a background, I will point out from my vantage point what some of the rewards are in collecting coins and some of my recommendations for other collectors.

Bodway Morgan Dollar Set:

About six years ago I decided what I was going to focus on and what the goal was going to be.

Focus: Uncirculated Morgan silver dollars
Goal: Highest quality complete set ever assembled

My set is now complete. Of the 102 coins in the set all are certified and:

1) The average grade of my complete set is MS 65.7 or almost an MS 66 grade. (All graded by PCGS)
2) There are 25 coins which are graded MS 67 or MS 68 in the set.
3) In addition there are 25 MS 66 coins.
4) 14 are Deep Mirror Prooflike and 6 more Prooflike.
5) 16 of the coins are unique — the only one in this grade.
6) 35 of the coins have less than 2 other coins graded the same.
7) 50 of them have less than 9 other coins graded the same.

8) 71 of them have less than 29 other coins graded the same.
9) The average grade of the 12 rarest Morgan Dollars is MS 65.4 and includes the 84-S, 86-O, 89-CC, 92-S, 93-S, 93-O, 93-CC, 94-O, 95-O, 96-O, 97-O and the 01-P.
10) Almost half of the coins from my set are in the Morgan Dollar Set which is on a world wide tour of the finest Morgan dollars of each date (the tour is sponsored by PCGS).
11) In addition, about two thirds of the set is, or equals the finest known to date.
12) 3 dates are the finest known by at least 2 grades.

Although all of the coins in my set have now been graded by third party grading services, I originally purchased the majority of them ungraded raw. Much of my set was completed before grading services were available; more recently, many of the more rare coins I needed to complete my set were only available raw. As a collector, you can always purchase coins which have been graded. But if you set a tough goal for yourself which consists of collecting some very rare dates, you may only be able to obtain such rare coins in an ungraded state.

Rewards

These are some of the rewards I have found in putting together this set of Morgan dollars.

1) The incredible challenge of trying to find and complete a particularly difficult set and the resulting thrill of finding many of the specimens I had been seeking for many years.
2) Getting to know on a personal basis, and making lasting friendships with, many people in the business, both dealers and collectors.
3) The sense of accomplishment that comes with reading and absorbing the information and history about the particular area one is working on.
4) A sense of pride that is reinforced by the experts in the field as they are aware of your goals and progress as you get closer to achieving that goal.
5) The opportunity to be the expert in social situations when the subject of coin collecting is the topic being discussed (usually brought up by yourself).
6) The fun and excitement of attending coin shows. The local shows are important in getting new collectors and introducing local collectors to each other and local dealers. The regional shows are important because they draw from a broader population base, offer seminars, classes, exposure to the larger coin collecting community and have access to a greater availability of material.
7) The excitement of seeing particular coins in your set discussed in books, monthly or weekly publications and newsletters.
8) The satisfaction of seeing the value of your coins go up. Unfortunately they also go down at times which is not nearly as much fun.

Suggestions:

These are some of the suggestions I would have for my fellow collectors.

1) Focus so that you can become an expert in your area of interest. It will pay off big dividends in your sense of accomplishment.
2) Set a goal so that there is a direction to your efforts, and you will end up using better judgment on individual decisions.
3) Don't give up; follow through and be patient in pursuing your goal. You will feel a better sense of accomplishment in achieving the goal and you will be more successful financially than if you keep changing your mind along the way and sell one series to start another. The buying and selling costs are high.
4) Set a goal that is both a challenge and is achievable within your expected means. Set a tough goal so that you will really be challenged and stick to it, but within your means so that you can eventually reach your goal.
5) Understand your goal. Know how difficult it is going to be, how long to complete, what it will cost versus time (prices trend up over the long haul); and if it involves a comparative goal such as mine, then know in detail what has been done in the past, and what the competition is currently doing and where they are going.
6) Work on the most difficult part of the goal first because it will take the longest to achieve and you can't afford missing any opportunities if it is a difficult goal.
7) Strive for the highest grades on the rarest coins in your set if you want to also achieve a good financial return. This is in opposition to many others' recommendations.
8) Sell some coins along the way so that you develop a real grasp of value and the liquidity of your collection.
9) Read everything that you can get your hands on about the area of collecting that you are focusing on. Become as knowledgeable as the professionals in a narrow area so that you can make your own judgments and decisions. It will pay off in your confidence level, accomplishments, and long term financial results.
10) Attend coin shows and auctions. In particular, attend some major shows and auctions so that you have a perspective on the market place and can accumulate vital information that is not available in any other way.
11) Use many dealers or at least as many as you can manage the relationships with. No single dealer will have access to all of the coins that you will want. In addition most dealers love the field and will go out of their way to help you learn, and of course each dealer has something new to teach you.
12) Bargain. Most prices are set with the expectation that there will be some bargaining so you may pay more than necessary if you don't negotiate.

"Bodway Set" Listings

This section shows the detailed listing of my set and is sorted in several different ways.

By Mint and Grade:

Here is where the entire set is listed by mint in order of "S" (San Francisco), "P" (Philadelphia), "O" (New Orleans), "D" (Denver), and "CC" (Carson City) mints. The other information (in all of the listings) includes the year of mintage, a "yes" for those dollars that are included on the PCGS World Wide Tour of the finest Morgan Dollars, the grade, Prooflike condition (if applicable), the date I obtained the coin, the dealer who helped me obtain it; and a description of the variety if it applies. You may notice that three of the sets (the S, P and D sets) are all MS 65 or better. The S and P sets are in themselves unequaled in quality. The whole set is also unequaled in quality and has only 5 coins less than MS 65, but even these 5 are extraordinary coins with much history. You may also observe by the "yes" that almost half of the set is involved in the PCGS World Wide tour.

By Dealer:

This listing sorts the coins by dealer. All of the dealers on the list were very helpful, fun to work with and to learn from. Even though everyone was very important to the completion of the set the following 5 individuals made a special contribution and were enormously helpful.

1) Dave Carter 15 coins
   Specialty: Impossible dates, many other contributions and the 93-S
2) Bill Spears 16 coins
   Specialty: High grade tough dates. 13 MS 67 and MS 68 coins
3) David Hall 10 coins
   Specialty: Impossible dates in extraordinary condition.
4) Kent Brennan 8 coins
   Specialty: Great friend and teacher.
5) Jack Hertzberg 9 coins
   Specialty: Tough dates in high quality and the 83-S.

By Prooflike and Deep Mirror Prooflike:

This listing separates the coins by prooflike condition. In sum there are 6 Prooflikes and 14 deep mirror Prooflikes. The wonder coins in deep mirror prooflike include the 98-O and 81-S in 67 DMPL and the 04-O in 66 DMPL. In addition the following unique or very low population coins are included in deep mirror; 93-O, 87-O, 92-P, 90-P, 82-O, 93-CC, 89-CC and 82-S.

By On Tour:

This lists the 51 dates that have been participating in the PCGS World Wide tour of the finest Morgan dollars.

By Year:

This lists all the coins in the set by ascending date. Of interest is the unique MS 67 year set for 1884.

Description, Pedigree and History:

Most of the coins in my dollar set have a very interesting history, pedigree and are of spectacular quality. For example I have been very discriminating with regard to strike as well as all of the other quality aspects such as color, originality, lack of marks and just the "look." For a coin to be in my set it has to have a full strike; for example, all breast feathers, full hair detail over the ear, stars, numbers and rim detail. Being this insistent on quality in general and strike in particular means that the population of available coins for my set is much smaller than the PCGS population statistics suggest and therefore most of the coins in my set are at the extreme upper end of the grade. In addition very few of these coins have been graded more than once even though most people say when they look at some of the coins that they would probably move up a grade if they were regraded. Since I have to limit myself in this section, I will provide some descriptive, pedigree and historical information on just twelve of my coins. The twelve coins I will select are some of the most difficult dates to find in the Morgan dollar series, let alone in the kind of quality we have been discussing. I will leave a more lengthy dissertation for these twelve and similar information on the rest of the "Bodway Set" for another time.

The list of 12 dates follows:

1) 1883-S	MS 65	7) 1895-O	MS 66
2) 1884-S	MS 67	8) 1895-S	MS 65
3) 1892-S	MS 66	9) 1896-S	MS 68
4) 1893-S	MS 67	10) 1896-O	MS 65
5) 1893-0	MS 65 DMPL	11) 1897-O	MS 67
6) 1893-CC	MS 64 DMPL	12) 1901-P	MS 65

Note that the average grade of this list of the rarest Morgan dollars is 65.8 or slightly higher than the average grade of my whole set.

#1 1883-S

Description: An incredible specimen of the Morgan dollar series. Absolutely fully struck in all detail. Pristine mark-free surfaces with beautiful light toning increasing in intensity toward the rim on the obverse. Very reflective semi prooflike surfaces.

Purchased from: Jack Hertzberg

Previous Owners: Wayne Miller

Wayne purchased this coin as part of a high quality collection put together in Montana between 1940 and 1968 by an unidentified collector.

Quotes: "This is the finest 83-S I have ever seen by a mile." Kent Brennan

"The finest 1883-S specimen known." Larry Goldberg

"If there was ever an MS 66 dollar, this is it." Bill Spears

#2 1884-S

Description: PCGS 67 Wonder coin. Extraordinary color and vibrancy, full strike and virtually mark free.
Purchased from: David Hall
Previous Owners: Chuck Walanka
Quotes:"This is a super Gem nearly perfect Morgan Dollar." David Hall's Book
"This coin has been referred to publicly over the last 10 years as one of the most incredible dollars in existence along with the 96-S." Numismatic Publications

#3 1892-S

Description: A gorgeous white almost fully prooflike silver dollar. Completely and fully struck with blemish free surfaces.
Purchased from: David Carter
Previous Owners: Ed Milas of RARCOA purchased this coin along with a 97-O and 96-O from an undisclosed midwest collector in 1987. They had been in this collection for decades. Dave and I purchased these three coins raw from Ed between Auction 87 and the 1987 ANA Convention. The only time they have been seen by the public was at the 1987 ANA prior to the PCGS tour. The 92-S subsequently graded MS 66 as did the 97-O while the 96-O was graded MS 65, all by PCGS.
Quotes:"This is the finest 92-S I have ever seen." David Hall (1987 ANA) (David saw the 92-S graded MS 67 in the raw state 2 weeks before seeing this coin)
"An amazing coin." ANA Attendants

#4 1893-S

Description: Incredibly clean and mark free. It looks as if it was minted yesterday. Superb color, strike and luster with no toning. It is very similar in appearance to the 96-S in MS 68. It looks like it was caught with a gloved hand directly from the press.
Purchased From: David Carter
David Carter and I purchased this coin raw with Ed Milas' help at the Norweb Auction.
Previous Owners: Mrs. R. Henry Norweb
Quotes: "Several graders gave this coin an MS 68 grade". David Hall
Numismatic Publications Have referenced this specimen dozens of times in the last 4 years as being the single most important Morgan Dollar.
"This 1893-S was probably obtained directly by the mint as a specimen strike". Q. David Bowers

#5 1893-O

Description: Deep mirror cameo prooflike Morgan Dollar. Brilliant color, exceptional contrast and flash with absolutely no hairlines and virtually mark free. An absolutely incredible Morgan Dollar for any date.
Purchased From: David Carter
Previous Owners: Leo Young, Barbara Goldfried
Quotes:"Barbara's 1893-O is unequaled." Dean Tavenner
"The best 1893-O is Barbara Goldfried's coin." Bruce Amspacher
"By far the finest known 1893-O is Barbara's coin." Wayne Miller
"This is the finest known 1893-O." Auction 80 and 87

#6 1893-CC

Description: PCGS 64 DMPL Authenticated by PCGS as a business strike. This was confirmed at the 1987 Long Beach October Show as being correct by Walter Breen. Walter states that this is a presentation strike and was single struck by the proof dies but after the dies had been polished. As such, this is the only known fully struck deep mirror prooflike 1893-CC. In addition it is probably the finest known 1893-CC business strike.
Purchased from: Tony Calcagno
Previous Owners: Garrett (lot #719), Barbara Goldfried
Quotes:"This 1893-CC is a full gem." Bruce Amspacher
"This is the finest 1893-CC business strike prooflike." Auction '87
"This coin must be an MS 65." Bill Spears

#7 1895-O

Description: PCGS 66 A captivating nearly perfect semi prooflike wonder coin.
Purchased from: David Hall
Previous Owners: Wayne Miller
Quotes:"The MS 66 coin that was in Wayne Miller's set is one of the all time Morgan Dollar turn-ons." David Hall
"A virtually flawless semi prooflike Morgan Dollar." Bruce Amspacher
"The finest known 1895-O Morgan Dollar I have seen." Wayne Miller
"The neatest coin to appear in the market in 1986." Anastasio
"The neatest coin to appear in the market in 1986." LaBlanc

#8 1895-S

Description: PCGS 65 This coin is absolutely mark free and an exceptionally strong strike. It has captivating color and luster and looks like it was minted yesterday.
Purchased from: Dean Tavenner
Previous Owners: Unknown collector, New England, Bruce Amspacher.

Quote:"The finest Morgan Dollar I've seen of any date." Ron Howard
"A virtually perfect coin, superb MS 69." Bruce Amspacher
Most people who see this coin say "This has to be at least an MS 67 graded Morgan Dollar."

#9 1896-S

Description: PCGS 68 Probably the finest known Morgan Dollar of any date or mint mark.
Purchased from: David Hall
Previous Owners: Chuck Walanka
Quotes:"Chuck's 'wonder coin' has not been matched — not even close." Dean Tavenner
"The 1896-S in PCGS 68 was the neatest coin to appear in the market in 1986." Buzolich
"The 1896-S in PCGS 68 was the neatest coin to appear in the market in 1986." Spears

#10 1896-O

Description: A superb flawless gem. A wonder coin that is virtually perfect and absolutely fully struck. The original owner purchased this dollar directly from the mint in 1896 and it has been in the same family and unknown until it appeared at the ANA show in 1987. The coin was viewed there with absolute awe, but was already sold.
Purchased from: David Carter (See 1892-S)
Previous Owners: Private collector family.
Quotes:"I will give you $100,000 + for that 1896-O." Major California Dealer (This was in 1987 and for a raw coin.)
"This is the finest known." Auction '87 Catalog
"The 1896-O is the rarest Morgan dollar in gem condition." David Hall

#11 1897-0

Description: PCGS 67 Probably the most perfectly struck Morgan Dollar of any date or mint mark and it's a 97-O. When you start looking at it you can't take your eyes away from it. It is so captivating, superb luster and color, virtually mark free.
Purchased from: Steve Ivy
Previous Owners: Steve Ivy, David Hall, David Hall Customer
Quotes:"This 1897-O approaches MS 70. The impeccable surfaces show no significant marks. The strike is nothing short of incredible." Steve Ivy / Ron Howard's book.

#12 1901-P

Description: PCGS 65 Probably the only 1901-P gem business strike in existence. Superb strike, mark free and gorgeous multicolored toning.
Purchased from: David Hall
Previous Owners: Wayne Miller, Steve Ivy, Hannes Tulving
Quotes:"Owned by a virtual who's who in silver dollars. A guaranteed gem 1901-P Morgan Dollar." Bruce Amspacher
"The toned 1901-P is the neatest coin I ever owned." Hannes Tulving
"This 1901-P is the only fully gem dollar I have ever seen." Wayne Miller
"Prohibitively rare." David Hall

SORTED BY YEAR

YEAR	MINT	TOUR	GRADE	OBTAINED	DEALER
1878	P	YES	MS65	08-01-88	BRENNAN
1878 7TF REV 78	P		MS65	08-01-88	BRENNAN
1878 7TF REV 79	P	YES	MS65 PL	01-01-89	KIHLSTADIUS
1878 7/8 TF	P		MS65	03-01-88	HERTZBERG
1878	CC		MS65	04-01-88	MODERN COINS
1878	S		MS65	05-01-88	HERTZBERG
1879	P	YES	MS66	01-01-91	CARTER
1879	CC		MS65	04-01-88	MODERN COINS
1879	O		MS65	05-01-88	BRENNAN
1879 REV 78	S	YES	MS65	09-01-88	SCHUYLER
1879	S	YES	MS68	04-01-87	SPEARS
1880	P		MS65	04-01-88	HERTZBERG
1880	CC		MS67	02-01-88	SPEARS
1880	O		MS64	06-01-90	HERTZBERG
1880	S		MS66	03-01-79	HALL
1881	P	YES	MS65	10-01-88	SPEARS
1881	CC		MS65 DMPL	04-01-85	MILLARD
1881	O		MS65	06-01-88	ELLESMERE
1881	S		MS67 DMPL	05-01-88	SPEARS
1882	P		MS65 PL	06-01-85	ARMSTRONG
1882	CC		MS66	10-01-89	CAPPER
1882	O	YES	MS65 DMPL	11-01-85	CARTER
1882	S		MS65 DMPL	11-01-85	CARTER

YEAR	MINT	TOUR	GRADE	OBTAINED	DEALER
1883	P	YES	MS67	01-01-88	CALCAGNO
1883	CC		MS66 PL	03-01-86	ARMSTRONG
1883	O	YES	MS67	07-01-89	SUPERIOR
1883	S	YES	MS65	08-01-88	HERTZBERG
1884	P	YES	MS67	06-01-88	SPEARS
1884	CC		MS67	07-01-88	SPEARS
1884	O	YES	MS67	08-01-90	SPEARS
1884	S	YES	MS67	01-01-87	HALL
1885	P		MS65 DMPL	03-01-85	ARMSTRONG
1885	CC		MS66	03-01-88	ELLESMERE
1885	O	YES	MS67	03-01-88	HALL
1885	S	YES	MS67	07-01-88	SPEARS
1886	P	YES	MS67	03-01-88	HALL
1886	O	YES	MS64	05-01-90	HUANG
1886	S	YES	MS66	08-01-88	HALL
1887	P	YES	MS67	08-01-90	ELLESMERE
1887	O	YES	MS65 DMPL	02-01-86	MILLER
1887	S	YES	MS65	08-01-89	MARLING
1887/6	P		MS65	02-01-90	MARLING
1888	P		MS65 DMPL	02-01-87	SUPERIOR
1888	O		MS66	11-01-90	PETERS
1888	S	YES	MS66	10-01-89	MANLEY
1889	P	YES	MS67	06-01-88	SPEARS
1889	CC		MS63 DMPL	01-01-91	CARTER
1889	O	YES	MS65	04-01-88	HERTZBERG
1889	S		MS65 PL	01-01-86	BRENNAN
1890	P	YES	MS65 DMPL	01-01-86	SUPERIOR
1890	CC		MS65	10-01-88	SPEARS
1890	O		MS65	10-01-80	HUGHES
1890	S	YES	MS66	03-01-88	MANLEY
1891	P		MS65	01-01-88	BRENNAN
1891	CC		MS65 PL	03-01-88	ELLESMERE
1891	O		MS65	07-01-88	KIHLSTADIUS
1891	S	YES	MS67	02-01-88	SPEARS
1892	P		MS65 DMPL	10-01-85	CARTER
1892	CC		MS66	09-01-88	KIHLSTADIUS
1892	O		MS65	11-01-88	HERTZBERG
1892	S	YES	MS66	10-01-89	CARTER
1893	P		MS65	10-01-85	CARTER
1893	CC		MS64 DMPL	10-01-88	CALCAGNO
1893	O	YES	MS65 DMPL	09-01-87	CARTER
1893	S	YES	MS67	08-01-90	CARTER
1894	P		MS65	07-01-87	CARTER
1894	O	YES	MS64	01-01-91	BRENNAN
1894	S	YES	MS67	07-01-88	AMSPACHER
1895	O	YES	MS66	06-01-86	HALL
1895	S	YES	MS65	04-01-87	TAVENNER
1896	P		MS65	10-01-90	CARTER
1896	O	YES	MS65	01-01-88	CARTER
1896	S	YES	MS68	09-01-86	HALL
1897	P	YES	MS66	05-01-89	KIHLSTADIUS
1897	O	YES	MS67	07-01-87	IVY
1897	S	YES	MS67	05-01-87	SPEARS
1898	P		MS66	05-01-89	COMMEM TOWNE
1898	O	YES	MS67 DMPL	06-01-88	SPEARS
1898	S		MS65	05-01-87	SWEENEY
1899	P		MS65	07-01-87	HALL
1899	O	YES	MS67	01-01-88	CALCAGNO
1899	S	YES	MS67	05-01-87	SPEARS
1900	P	YES	MS66	05-01-89	KIHLSTADIUS
1900	O/CC		MS65	04-18-88	SPEARS
1900	O		MS66	05-01-89	IVY
1900	S	YES	MS66	09-01-88	CALCAGNO
1901	P	YES	MS65	02-01-87	HALL
1901	O	YES	MS66	08-01-88	HERTZBERG
1901	S		MS65	04-01-88	PARKS

YEAR	MINT	TOUR	GRADE	OBTAINED	DEALER
1902	P	YES	MS67	08-01-90	JAY MILLER
1902	O		MS66	08-01-90	ELLESMERE
1902	S		MS66	01-01-88	HERTZBERG
1903	P		MS65	01-01-88	BRENNAN
1903	O		MS66	06-01-88	CARTER
1903	S	YES	MS67	06-01-88	SPEARS
1904	P		MS65	06-01-88	HALL
1904	O	YES	MS66 DMPL	01-01-86	MILLER
1904	S	YES	MS65 PL	07-01-87	CARTER
1921	P		MS66	06-01-86	AMSPACHER
1921	D	YES	MS66	01-01-85	BRENNAN
1921	S		MS65	03-01-88	SCHUYLER

SORTED BY MINT AND GRADE

1879	S	YES	MS68
1896	S	YES	MS68
1893	S	YES	MS67
1903	S	YES	MS67
1881	S		MS67 DMPL
1894	S	YES	MS67
1899	S	YES	MS67
1884	S	YES	MS67
1885	S	YES	MS67
1891	S	YES	MS67
1897	S	YES	MS67
1890	S	YES	MS66
1888	S	YES	MS66
1886	S	YES	MS66
1878	S		MS66
1892	S	YES	MS66
1902	S		MS66
1880	S		MS66
1900	S	YES	MS66
1879 REV 78	S	YES	MS65
1895	S	YES	MS65
1889	S		MS65 PL
1883	S	YES	MS65
1882	S		MS65 DMPL
1901	S		MS65
1898	S		MS65
1887	S	YES	MS65
1904	S	YES	MS65 PL
1921	S		MS65
1884	P	YES	MS67
1889	P	YES	MS67
1886	P	YES	MS67
1883	P	YES	MS67
1902	P	YES	MS67
1887	P	YES	MS67
1900	P	YES	MS66
1897	P	YES	MS66
1898	P		MS66
1921	P		MS66
1879	P	YES	MS66
1880	P		MS65
1888	P		MS65 DMPL
1885	P		MS65 DMPL
1890	P	YES	MS65 DMPL
1887/6	P		MS65
1896	P		MS65
1892	P		MS65 DMPL

SORTED BY MINT AND GRADE

1893	P		M S65
1899	P		MS65
1891	P		MS65
1901	P	YES	MS65
1878 7/8 TF	P		MS65
1903	P		MS65
1904	P		MS65
1881	P	YES	MS65
1878 7TF REV 78	P		MS65
1878	P	YES	MS65
1878 7TF REV 79	P	YES	MS65
1894	P		MS65
1882	P		MS65 PL
1897	O	YES	MS67
1883	O	YES	MS67
1884	O	YES	MS67
1885	O	YES	MS67
1898	O	YES	MS67 DMPL
1899	O	YES	MS67
1888	O		MS66
1901	O	YES	MS66
1902	O		MS66
1895	O	YES	MS66
1904	O	YES	MS66 DMPL
1903	O		MS66
1900	O		MS66
1889	O	YES	MS65
1890	O		MS65
1881	O		MS65
1900	O/CC		MS65
1879	O		MS65
1896	O	YES	MS65
1893	O	YES	MS65 DMPL
1882	O	YES	MS65 DMPL
1891	O		MS65
1892	O		MS65
1887	O	YES	MS65 DMPL
1894	O	YES	MS64
1880	O		MS64
1886	O	YES	MS64
1921	D	YES	MS66
1880	CC		MS67
1884	CC		MS67
1892	CC		MS66
1882	CC		MS66
1883	CC		MS66 PL
1885	CC		MS66

SORTED BY MINT AND GRADE

1878	CC		MS65
1891	CC		MS65 PL
1879	CC		MS65
1881	CC		MS65 DMPL
1890	CC		MS65
1893	CC		MS64 DMPL
1889	CC		MS63 DMPL

SORTED BY PL AND DMPL

1883	CC		MS66 PL
1891	CC		MS65 PL
1878 7TF REV 79	P	YES	MS65 PL
1904	S	YES	MS65 PL
1889	S		MS65 PL
1882	P		MS65 PL
1898	O	YES	MS67 DMPL
1881	S		MS67 DMPL
1904	O	YES	MS66 DMPL
1882	S		MS65 DMPL
1887	O	YES	MS65 DMPL
1893	O	YES	MS65 DMPL
1885	P		MS65 DMPL
1888	P		MS65 DMPL
1892	P		MS65 DMPL
1890	P	YES	MS65 DMPL
1882	O	YES	MS65 DMPL
1881	CC		MS65 DMPL
1893	CC		MS64 DMPL
1889	CC		MS63 DMPL

SORTED BY TOUR

1878	P	YES	MS65
1878 7TF REV 79	P	YES	MS65 PL
1879	P	YES	MS66
1879	S	YES	MS68
1879 REV 78	S	YES	MS65
1881	P	YES	MS65
1882	O	YES	MS65 DMPL
1883	P	YES	MS67
1883	O	YES	MS67
1883	S	YES	MS65
1884	P	YES	MS67
1884	O	YES	MS67
1884	S	YES	MS67
1885	O	YES	MS67
1885	S	YES	MS67
1886	P	YES	MS67
1886	O	YES	MS64
1886	S	YES	MS66
1887	P	YES	MS67
1887	O	YES	MS65 DMPL
1887	S	YES	MS65
1888	S	YES	MS66
1889	P	YES	MS67
1889	O	YES	MS65
1890	P	YES	MS65 DMPL
1890	S	YES	MS66

SORTED BY TOUR

1891	S	YES	MS67
1892	S	YES	MS66
1893	O	YES	MS65 DMPL
1893	S	YES	MS67
1894	O	YES	MS64
1894	S	YES	MS67
1895	O	YES	MS66
1895	S	YES	MS65
1896	O	YES	MS65
1896	S	YES	MS68
1897	P	YES	MS66
1897	O	YES	MS67
1897	S	YES	MS67
1898	O	YES	MS67 DMPL
1899	O	YES	MS67
1899	S	YES	MS67
1900	P	YES	MS66
1900	S	YES	MS66
1901	P	YES	MS65
1901	O	YES	MS66
1902	P	YES	MS67
1903	S	YES	MS67
1904	O	YES	MS66 DMPL
1904	S	YES	MS65 PL
1921	D	YES	MS66

David Hall

David Hall is chief executive officer, chairman of the board and one of the principal owners of the Professional Coin Grading Service (PCGS). He has been directly involved with the PCGS Expert project from its inception, and has provided much background grading information for the actual programming of the system.

David has been actively involved in numismatics since 1961 and has been a major force in the rare coin industry since 1972. Today he is considered one of the true pioneers in the rare coin investment field. Many of the major developments in the rare coin market within the past decade — including the marketplace's obsession with quality, guaranteed grading programs, daily cash bid/ask prices, the Professional Coin Grading Service (PCGS), and the American Numismatic Exchange (ANE) — originated with David Hall.

David Hall has been a life member of the American Numismatic Association since 1973 and is a charter member of the California Professional Numismatists' Association. He was a founding member of the Industry Council for Tangible Assets (ICTA), and he's also on the Board of Governors of the Institute of Numismatic and Philatelic Studies at Adelphi University.

David Hall has handled virtually every United States coin, including numerous six-figure rarities. He has also been involved in several milestone numismatic transactions and was the underbidder (at 7.2 million dollars) in the 1976 sale of the LaVere Redfield Estate, at that time the largest numismatic transaction in history. In 1984, David Hall set another price record when he purchased the famous Wayne Miller Silver Dollar Collection for over one million dollars.

David Hall is one of the industry's most respected and astute grading experts and was a major contributor to the official American Numismatic Association grading guide, for which he personally wrote standards for several series, including Morgan and Peace dollars.

In addition to his duties at PCGS, David Hall publishes the monthly *Inside View*, the coin industry's most influential and largest circulation investment advisory newsletter. He is a contributing editor to *Gary North's Investment Coin Review*. In 1986, his book, *A Mercenary's Guide to the Rare Coin Market*, was published by the American Bureau of Economic Research. David Hall is also chairman of the board of David Hall's Numismatic Investment Group, which is one of the industry leaders in the sale of high quality rare coins.

CHAPTER 28

The Professional Coin Grading Service

by David Hall

It's hard to believe that only six years ago the world had never heard of PCGS. But in 1985, there weren't any electronic coin exchanges. There was no ANE, CCE, TIS, etc. There was no Certified Coin Dealer Newsletter. There was no sight-unseen bidding on rare coins. There was no Merrill Lynch, Shearson or Kidder Peabody. There was no computer grading. There were no regrades, crossovers, crack-outs, or walk-thru's. There were no slabs. There was no PCGS.

In just over five years the rare coin market has been totally revolutionized. The entire structure of the market place has changed. PCGS was the catalyst for the coin market revolution. Before PCGS, product misrepresentation was rampant in the rare coin industry. Unless the buyer was a grading expert, he was totally at the mercy of the coin seller when it came to the grades of the coins he bought. The inherent conflict of interest present when the seller of the product determined the price of the product based on his own interpretation of the product's quality was a limiting factor standing in the way of significant market growth. The grading problem had to be solved. The solution was the Professional Coin Grading Service. Here's how it all began.

In the 1960's, very few people paid attention to the grades of coins. Grade was a component of price, but it took a very distant back seat to rarity. "Mintage" was the most frequently used term in coin advertisements.

In the 1970's, this country experienced inflation like nothing since before the Constitution was adopted. Correspondingly, in the 1970's, the rare coin market experienced price increases that it had never seen. In a ten year period many prices increased ten to twenty fold! With huge price increases, minute differences in quality became increasingly important. People began to pay attention to quality. Grading descriptions became more refined. A numerical grading scale (the Sheldon 1 to 70 scale) began to see widespread use.

In the early 1980's a new problem emerged for the first time. This was the problem of changing grading standards. A coin's grade could fluctuate according to market conditions. When the market was down, buyers tended to be especially picky about the coins they purchased. If money was tight, they were inclined to demand higher quality coins for bargain prices. This led more buyers to become more critical when grading. Whether they realized it or not, their grading standards changed to reflect the changes in the market. If the market was "hot", grading between buyers and sellers tended to be inflated rather than adhering to a standard grading scale. If the market was "cold," grading become ultra conservative.

Since all dealers had personal grading standards which did not necessarily match the standards used by others, grading was subjective and varied significantly from dealer to dealer. While books were written on the subject of grading, there was no single widely recognized standard used to measure the condition of coins. When grading was limited to only the participants in a transaction, grading fluctuated because each person had a vested interest in either buying or selling the coin in question. Since the grade of a coin is a major component of its value, an individual could be tempted to claim a lower grade when buying a coin and a higher grade when selling the coin.

Unscrupulous telemarketers also arrived on the scene in the early 1980's. These companies would mislead consumers into believing there were fortunes to be made, if only consumers would buy their coins. The telemarketers used the lack of a grading standard to blatantly rip off the coin buying public. They sold horribly overgraded coins at prices that were sometimes as much as 10 times their wholesale value. These practices of product misrepresentation cast a shadow over the industry and aroused the attention of Federal regulators. The reputable dealers were worried about the state of their industry. The grading problem had to be solved. The rip-offs had to stop.

The challenge for the coin industry was to come up with a viable grading standard that would be accepted by the entire marketplace. A plan to implement the grading standard was also needed. At the time (1985), I was involved in a massive book writing project with three friends of mine; Bruce Amspacher, John Dannreuther and Gordon Wrubel. We were going to set the rare coin record straight with an eleven volume rare coin encyclopedia. But we kept getting stuck on the same conceptual problem, namely that there was no grading standard in the rare coin industry . . . no standard on which to determine price . . . no standard on which rarity and price research could be based. But in addition to presenting an obstacle for our writing project, the lack of a grading standard was ruining our industry. As long time coin dealers, all four of us were worried about this problem. We decided to focus our energies on the grading problem.

After much discussion and analysis we reached the opinion that six things were needed to solve the grading problem:

1) *A grading service*. One that used professional graders, the world's best if possible, to grade coins with the highest humanly possible degree of accuracy and consistency.

2) *A grading standard*. One that would be accepted by virtually the entire numismatic community.

3) *A tamper proof holder*. So that once a coin was graded, it could trade based on an unchanging grade.

4) *A grading guarantee*. To solidify the concept, it had to be backed by money on the table.

5) *A dealer network*. Reputable dealers that would go along with the concept and promote it with the public.

6) *An electronic trading exchange*. So that coins could trade on the basis of the new grading standard.

The first step was to form a grading service. All four of us wanted to be involved and we needed help. We asked two world class grading experts, Steve Cyrkin and Silvano DiGenova, to join our company and we incorporated as the Professional Coin Grading Service. One of the new things that PCGS did was to use world class coin graders, i.e., full-time, veteran coin dealers, to grade coins. All six owners of PCGS were recognized by the coin industry for their grading expertise. This instilled confidence in the grading on both the public and dealer level.

The second step was to create a grading standard that would be acceptable to the coin community. We sought the input of major market-makers. Our dealer friends helped us build a grading set — a group of coins that would serve as permanent examples of the PCGS grading standards. PCGS was the first grading service to have a permanent grading set. Today, the PCGS grading set contains 591 coins with a value of $462,155.

The PCGS grading system took numerical grading a set farther and utilized the full 11-point grading scale from MS-60 to MS-70. Prior to PCGS, the increments of MS-60, MS-63, MS-65, MS-67, and MS-70, were utilized by the American Numismatic Association and others. The grade MS-64 was used in the silver dollar market. Frankly, many people called us crazy for using all eleven grades between MS-60 and MS-70, but the eleven point Mint State Scale is now accepted by the entire industry and used by all grading services. The use of the full 11-point scale was an improvement over the MS-60, MS-63, MS-65, MS-67 and MS-70 scale because more precise grading and pricing were possible.

A third step was the PCGS coin holder or "slab." PCGS encapsulates coins in a clear plastic, tamper-resistant holder which protects both the coin and a certification tag, which lists the grade, an identification number, and information about the coin itself. Not only does this holder allow the coin to be easily examined by the viewer, but it also prevents the coin from being damaged or "switched" after it has been graded by PCGS.

As long as the coin remains intact in the PCGS holder, PCGS will stand behind the grade of the coin with the "PCGS Guarantee of Grade and Authenticity". . . the fourth step in our plan. This was the first time in history that a grading service actually backed its product with a cash buy-back guarantee. To date, PCGS has repurchased 463 coins for $693,720 under the terms of its grading guarantee.

The fifth step of the PCGS plan was to create a dealer network to support and promote grading standards. Initially, 32 well-known dealers agreed to participate in the PCGS program. PCGS dealers agreed to accept the grades assigned by PCGS and initially they agreed to make sight-unseen bids for PCGS coins. For the first time in history a coin buyer could buy a coin from dealer A and sell it over the phone to dealer B — without dealer B needing to see the coin. This greatly improved the liquidity of the rare coin market.

Prior to the advent of PCGS, the concept of sight-unseen trading was unheard of in the rare coin industry. Back then, it was essential that a buyer have the coin in his hand and actually see it before he agree to purchase it. To trust that another party graded it correctly was wishful thinking, rather than a reality. However, today sight-unseen transaction are used daily by market makers in the rare coin industry. Hundreds of thousands of dollars worth of coins now trade between dealers sight-unseen every day.

The sixth step in the PCGS plan was the creation of the electronic coin exchanges. The owners of PCGS along with most of the original PCGS dealers got together and formed the American Numismatic Exchange (ANE). Today, there are several other electronic exchanges, including the Certified Coin Exchange (CCE) and Tangible Information Systems (TIS). All of the electronic exchanges have one thing in common: they feature sight-unseen trading of certified coins.

The response to the PCGS plan was phenomenal. Since February 1986, PCGS has graded 2,420,375 coins with a declared value of $2,809,646,071. These coins have been through a growing network of authorized coin dealers in the United States and abroad. There are now 618 PCGS dealers including dealers in Japan, Switzerland, England and Canada.

That brings us to 1991. The revolutionary changes in the rare coin market have been extremely beneficial to the coin buying public. If you buy certified coins you no longer have to worry about receiving a MS-63 coin represented as MS-65. You can buy and sell coins sight-unseen. The market is much more liquid, efficient and safe.

Has PCGS solved the grading problem? Well, if we define the problem as the lack of an industry-wide grading standard, then the answer is a resounding yes! There is now a grading standard that is used by virtually everyone in the coin industry.

Has PCGS stopped rip-offs? Unfortunately, the answer is no. Certified grading has made it more difficult to rip-off the public. There are fewer boiler rooms, but they do still exist. The coin industry is a lot cleaner than it was five years ago, but it's up to all of the industry leaders, including PCGS, to do everything possible to make it totally clean.

What does the future hold for PCGS? First, PCGS will continue to do its job of grading independent grading for the rare coin industry. Grading will get even better — more confident and more efficient. Second, PCGS will get involved with other collectible fields. The PCGS concept should work for other markets. PCGS will soon be grading baseball cards and authenticating autographs.

The coin industry has changed dramatically in the last five years. Because of the efforts of PCGS and many others, the coin market is a lot better place for the coin buying public. It's an exciting time to be involved with rare coins. The decade of the 1990's should see even more beneficial changes as the rare coin market revolution continues.

Staff of PCGS — Newport Beach, California
(Courtesy of PCGS)

CURRENT PCGS GRADER ROSTER

Graders : Gordon Wrubel, Ron Howard, Nick Buzolich, Miles Standish, Thad Olson, Keith Kelman, Rich Montgomery, Walt Armitage, Mike Sargent and Randy Pollock.
Type and Gold Graders : Walt Armitage, Ron Howard, Miles Standish, Thad Olson, Rick Montgomery, Keith Kelman and Mike Sargent.
World Coin Graders : Walt Armitage, Ron Howard and Gordon Wrubel.
Coin Verifiers : Rick Montgomery and Mike Sargent.
World Coin Technical Verifier: Walt Armitage.
Double Verifiers : Rick Montgomery is head of the double verification team.
Director of Grading : Gordon Wrubel.
Canadian Coin Consultants : Charles Moore and Sandy Campbell.
English Coin Consultants : Steve Fenton and Bruce Lorich.
Japanese Coin Consultants : Al Tom and Ron Gillio.
Swiss Coin Consultant : Marcel Haberling.

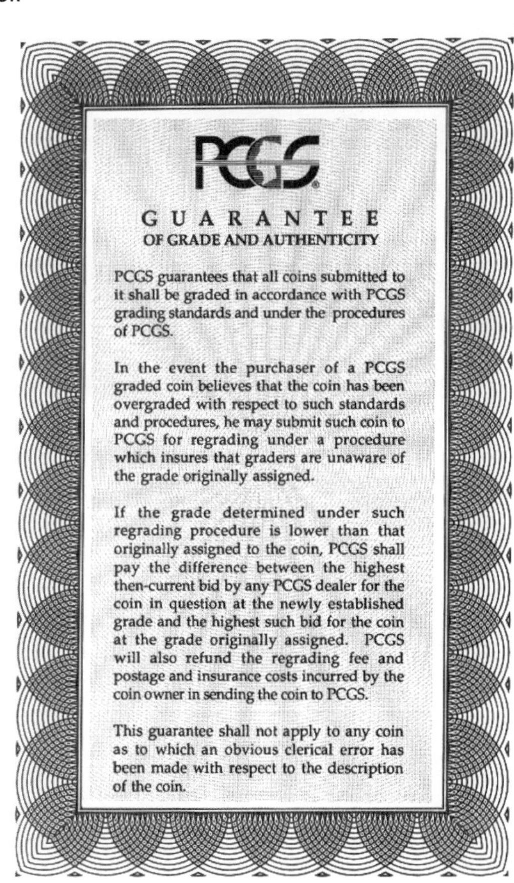

PCGS

GUARANTEE
OF GRADE AND AUTHENTICITY

PCGS guarantees that all coins submitted to it shall be graded in accordance with PCGS grading standards and under the procedures of PCGS.

In the event the purchaser of a PCGS graded coin believes that the coin has been overgraded with respect to such standards and procedures, he may submit such coin to PCGS for regrading under a procedure which insures that graders are unaware of the grade originally assigned.

If the grade determined under such regrading procedure is lower than that originally assigned to the coin, PCGS shall pay the difference between the highest then-current bid by any PCGS dealer for the coin in question at the newly established grade and the highest such bid for the coin at the grade originally assigned. PCGS will also refund the regrading fee and postage and insurance costs incurred by the coin owner in sending the coin to PCGS.

This guarantee shall not apply to any coin as to which an obvious clerical error has been made with respect to the description of the coin.

PCGS Guarantee of Grade and
Authenticity Certificate
(Courtesy of PCGS)

***

John Albanese

John Albanese is the founder and chairman of the Numismatic Guaranty Corporation of America (NGC), based in Parsippany, New Jersey. Mr. Albanese spent many years in numismatics as a very successful coin dealer before deciding to embark on this new venture in 1987. The change in activities was just as dramatic. The order of the day is providing a high level of service and strictly graded certified coins.

His talented and enterprising management team includes president Mark Salzberg (whose activities as the grading finalizer are nationally known), executive vice president Kenneth Krah who is the NGC foreign coin expert, vice president Mark Feld, and operations manager Peter Carrigan who painstakingly oversees the grading process and NGC operations.

Mr. Albanese is now launching the New Jersey Coin Exchange. This dealer cooperative offers an accessible central location for participating dealers to carry on their business. Shared services and a convenient bourse add to this unique concept.

CHAPTER 29

Numismatic Guaranty Corporation of America

by John Albanese

The Company

The Numismatic Guaranty Corporation of America was founded to fill the recognized need for an independent, unbiased, highly credible coin grading service.

Previously, grading services had been involved in buying and selling the product they graded or been an ancillary part of an organization whose primary task was not grading coins. NGC, in addition to representing the highest professional standards, expressly prohibits its management from buying, selling or trading coins for commercial profit.

We have also restricted our organization's activity to a coin grading service only. We believe that this oneness of purpose is unique, and will allow us to provide you with the finest service available.

Now, for the first time, a consumer can purchase a coin that is independently evaluated by experts whose sole purpose is to determine the exact quality of that coin. This "arms-length" evaluation will give the consumer assurance that he is purchasing precisely what is stated, analogous to the services performed by stock and bond rating companies, that have long been a fixture in the financial marketplace.

As the coin marketplace has shifted from a loose, unrestricted hobby/collecting activity to a more organized, investment-oriented one, the need for independent and objective evaluation has been long overdue. The industry and the coin-buying public has needed such independent analysis to give numismatics its much needed credibility as a true investment option and an equal partner in an investment portfolio.

The Service

As you know, a coin's value is determined by two factors: *rarity and condition*. Rarity is simply determined by low mintage figures, or in some cases by small amounts of known examples. For higher mintages, condition is the determining factor of value. In accordance with industry practice, NGC has adopted the Sheldon Numerical Grading System (from 0 to 70) in assigning a grade to a coin. Over the years this Numerical Grading System has proved to be more accurate than the previous used adjective grades (gem, choice, etc.).

Without a specific *numerical* grade, his coin must be *seen* by a purchaser for him to be quoted a price. Numerical grading allows sight-unseen price quoting.

NGC incorporates the latest in modern technology to all phases of our operations. Understanding the importance of security, NGC designed a system that guarantees a protected environment for your coin.

The grading facilities are the most modern and well-equipped in the industry. Special lighting has been scientifically installed to give true readings of the coin's color and luster.

NGC has developed a hard plastic, sonically sealed, tamper-proof holder that encapsulates the coin and grading information label in a permanent, safe package.

This holder is the culmination of almost a year of extensive design, engineering, and rigorous testing. It provides an attractive display setting, and a safe, chemically inert, environment for the coin and its grading information.

The clear, colorless plastic exterior allows an unobstructed view of both the front and back of the coin as well as its true natural color. This, along with the hologram, gives you added security. The rim of the front is raised to protect the main surface from scratching. The back contains a ridge that can interlock with the front rim of another holder, allowing them to be stacked for more compact storage. The edge or rim of the holder is also reeded to detect any tampering.

The interior section of the holder grips the coin by its entire rim. It applies pressure evenly (not at pressure points), and will not damage the coin in any way. The chemically inert paper grading label has the coin information (i.e., type, denomination, mint mark if any, and grade) clearly shown.

NGC's hologram (a 3-D image of the company's scales-of-justice logo) was produced by the American Bank Note Company's holographics division in Elmsford, New York. A hologram is a three dimensional picture created by lasers. The hologram logo is reproduced and firmly embedded into NGC's holder. This insures that the holder and the coin contained within it are genuine.

$20 Saint Gauden in NGC holder
(Courtesy of Numismatic Guaranty Corporation of America)

From the moment a coin is received at NGC to the moment it leaves our premises, it is given the most rigorous, personalized care in the industry.

A custom designed computer inventory and tracking system is set in motion. The coin is tagged, logged, and checked within minutes of entering our secure offices. An expert checks to see that information supplied by the dealer is accurate.

Next, the coin is scheduled for grading according to a rigorous timetable. Then, it is stored in our vaults until it is scheduled to be taken to the grading room.

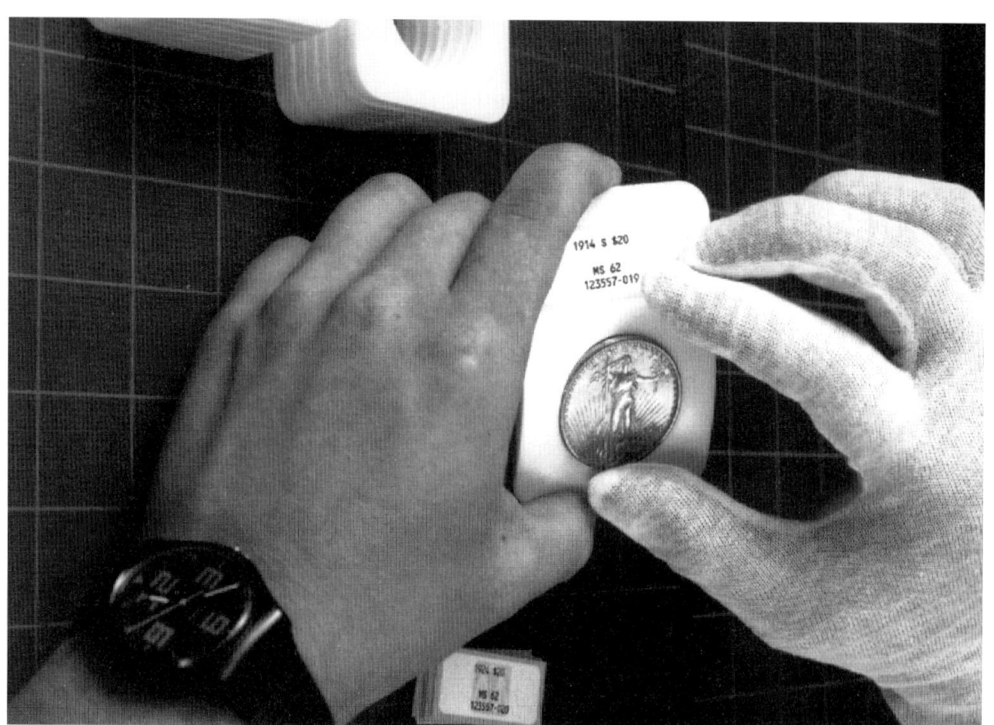

Example of placing a coin in a NGC holder
(Courtesy of Numismatic Guaranty Corporation of America)

Grader verifying coin (Courtesy of Numismatic Guaranty Corporation of America)

Even in a high tech world, NGC continues to rely solely on experience, expertise and judgment of our graders. Each grader possesses a lifetime of skill and knowledge that cannot be computerized or automated.

A team of 3 to 5 graders independently evaluates each coin. A senior grader, or "finalizer," is then responsible for making the judgment that will determine the coin's published grade. If his grade does not concur with the team, further evaluation follows.

From there the coin goes to the encapsulation room where, in a dust-free atmosphere, the coin and its label are sonically sealed in our custom holder. The coin is then packed in our protective foam package and promptly shipped back to the dealer.

During each step of the process the coin is handled by experts and protected by a multi-tiered security environment. Internal checks and balances have been created to reaffirm the integrity of all employees.

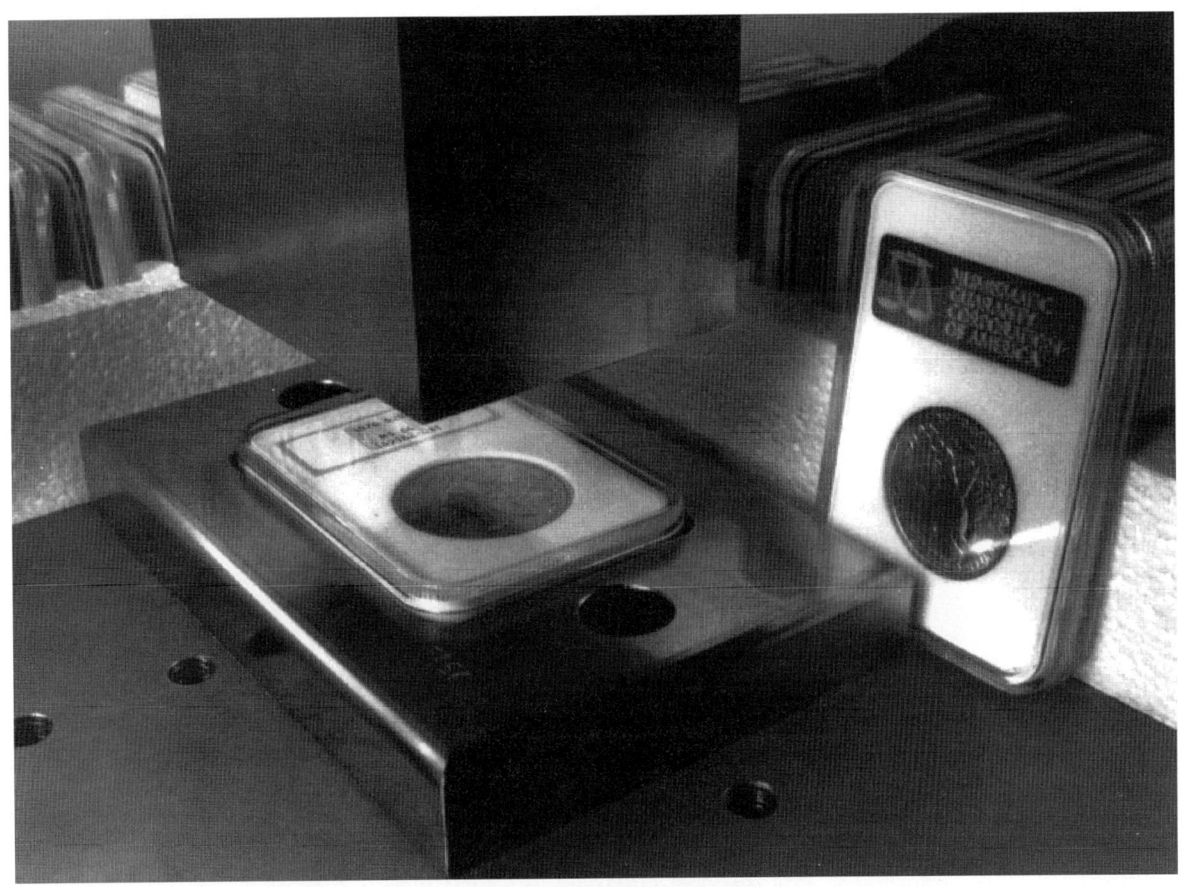

Process of coin encapsulation
(Courtesy of Numismatic Guaranty Corporation of America)

The NGC Network and Services

One of the features of a NGC certified coin is its liquidity. Coin investors can easily verify the liquidity of their NGC certified coin by referring to trade and other highly respected national business publications. (There may not be a market for every coin at all times.)

Whatever brings the consumer to coins, whether its the joy of collecting rare and beautiful objects or the search for a viable investment option for a balanced portfolio, we at NGC want the consumer to be secure in the knowledge that his hard-earned dollars will be safer and more liquid with NGC graded coins. We believe that a NGC graded coin is readily accepted as the best numismatic product available.

General services available at NGC are extensive and present a variety designed to fit the needs of submitting dealers and their clients. Here is a current listing of the services provided by NGC.

* WALK THROUGH: By appointment only. Same day service if received before 3 p.m. Pan Pac Octagonals must be submitted through this service.

* Dispatch: 24 to 48 hours. Coins valued over $10,000 must be submitted through this service or WALK THROUGH.

* Express: 5 to 10 working days. Coins valued over $3,000 must be submitted through this service or Dispatch or WALK THROUGH.

* Early Bird: 4 weeks approximate. Coins less than $3,000 may be submitted through this service.

* Generic: This new tier service as of July 1990 was developed to help expedite certain common date coins. Allow 3 to 4 weeks approximate time. Only coins of generic type and valued at less than $3,000 may be submitted through this service.

Additional services include Certified Pre-grade, Resubmission, PVC, Reholder, Deep Prooflike and Hologram. Allow 3 to 4 working days for these Processes.

Consumers Cannot Submit Coins Directly to NGC for Grading.

We have, by way of distancing ourselves from commercial transactions, created a dealer/member network of some of the most respected dealers in numismatics today. And it is only these dealers who can submit coins to us.

Months of careful examination and screening preceded the assembling of the NGC dealer network. These efforts were expended in an effort to identify dealers who agreed to honor the NGC commitment to integrity and service.

Guarantee

NGC guarantees that all coins submitted to it shall be graded by a minimum of three (3) NGC grading experts in accordance with NGC grading standards and procedures. In the event the purchaser of an NGC coin believes that the coin has been overgraded or undergraded with respect to such standards and procedures, the purchaser may submit any such coin to NGC for regrading under a procedure which assures that graders are unaware of the grade originally assigned. The fee for such regrading shall be $20.

If the grade determined under such regrading procedure is lower than that originally assigned to the coin, NGC shall pay the difference between the fair market value of the coin, as determined by arm's-length current bids of NGC dealers, at the newly established grade and the grade originally assigned to such coin.

Warning: Exception to NGC guarantee. Copper coins can oxidize after sealing. In such an event, the coin grade may diminish. Therefore, the NGC guarantee shall not be applicable to copper coins.

Clerical error with respect to the description or grade of the coin which would be readily noticed on inspection shall not be subject to the NGC guarantee herein stated.

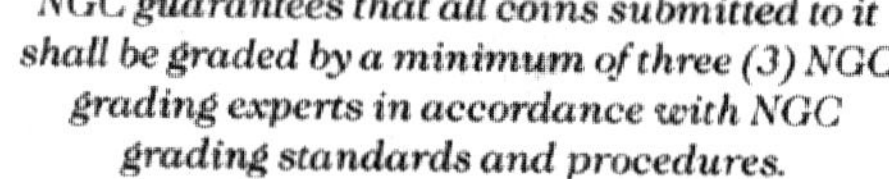

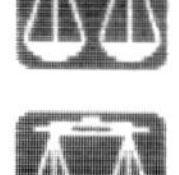
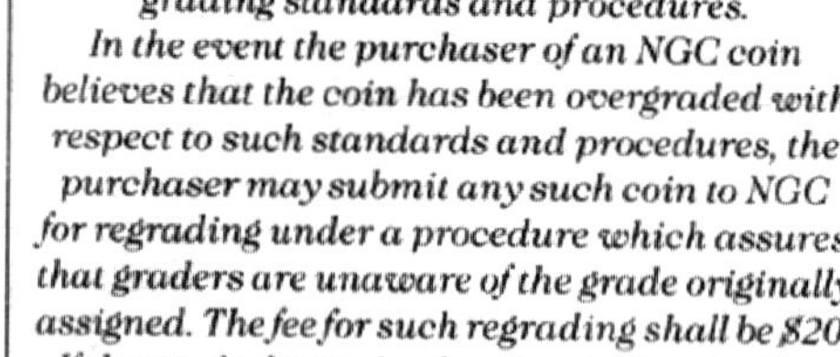

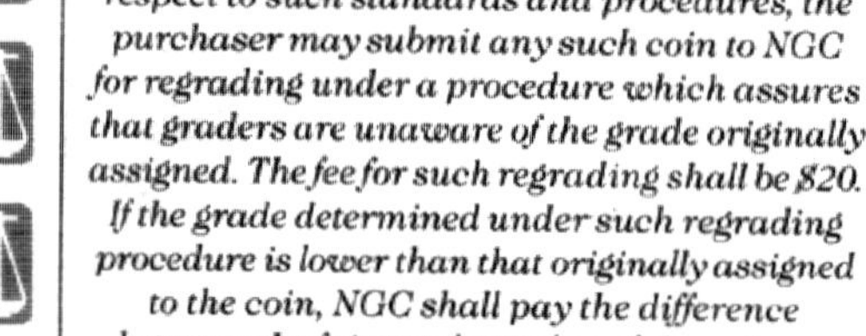

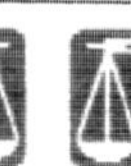

Guarantee

NGC guarantees that all coins submitted to it shall be graded by a minimum of three (3) NGC grading experts in accordance with NGC grading standards and procedures.

In the event the purchaser of an NGC coin believes that the coin has been overgraded with respect to such standards and procedures, the purchaser may submit any such coin to NGC for regrading under a procedure which assures that graders are unaware of the grade originally assigned. The fee for such regrading shall be $20.

If the grade determined under such regrading procedure is lower than that originally assigned to the coin, NGC shall pay the difference between the fair market value of the coin, as determined by arm's-length current bids of NGC dealers, at the newly established grade and the grade originally assigned to such coin.

WARNING: EXCEPTION TO NGC GUARANTEE COPPER COINS CAN OXIDIZE AFTER SEALING. IN SUCH AN EVENT, THE COIN GRADE MAY DIMINISH. THEREFORE, THE NGC GUARANTEE SHALL NOT BE APPLICABLE TO COPPER COINS.

Clerical error with respect to the description or grade of the coin which would be readily noticed on inspection shall not be subject to the NGC guarantee herein stated.

Numismatic Guaranty Corporation of America
Certificate of Guarantee
(Courtesy of NGC)

Grading of Foreign Coins

The many demands of collectors and investors have prompted NGC to open the grading services of the corporation to grading coins from many foreign countries beginning in 1989. Since its inception, the certification of international coins has been expanded to include additional countries with more planned for the future. The same diligence and care that NGC is known for is used to grade coins from the following countries and years.

Canada (including Maritimes)	1858 thru 1958
Cuba	1897 thru 1953
France (post reform)	1794 thru 1945
Germany / German States	1800 thru 1940
German East Africa	1890 thru 1916
German New Guinea	1894 thru 1895
Great Britain	1797 thru 1947
Hong Kong	1863 thru 1950
Japan	1870 thru 1941
Netherlands	1816 thru 1945
Philippines	1903 thru 1947
Puerto Rico	1895 thru 1896
Sarawak	1863 thru 1941
Straits Settlements	1845 thru 1935
Switzerland	1795 thru 1968

Coins and Types that Cannot be Submitted for Grading

NGC has always been concerned for the coin-buying public, and has conscientiously graded all mint state coins up to 1964 as well as Proof Franklin half dollars. It is the responsibility of grading services to police the market and educate the unsuspecting public. The major concern is the marketing of late-date coins and late-date proof coins at prices far exceeding their true market value. Therefore, it is NGC's policy not to accept the following coins and types for grading.

Coins minted after 1964
Colonial coins
Bullion coins (i.e., Krugerrands, Maple Leafs or U.S. Gold or Silver Eagles)
Ike dollars
Proof Jefferson 5-cent pieces dated 1956 thru 1964
Proof Roosevelt dimes dated 1956 thru 1964
Proof Washington quarters dated 1956 thru 1964
Proof Kennedy half dollars dated 1964

Numismatic Guaranty Corporation of America Census Report

NGC incorporates the latest in modern technology to all phases of its operations. Totals for coins certified by NGC are compiled and stored in our highly advanced computer database. At the end of each month, information is pulled for publication. NGC's Census Reports, now a monthly 8 1/2" x 11" paperback, have been well received. The different sections of the monthly Census Report include:

* Population Type Coin Totals: Total coins graded to date for type coins listed.

* Coin Population by Date: Total population of coins graded for all grade categories using the Sheldon Grading Scale. Major die varieties are listed as well as prooflikes (PL), deep mirror prooflikes (DPL's) and proofs (PF). Commemoratives, Territorial issues and Patterns are also included. Totals for each grade are published for each coin type (i.e., Morgan dollar, etc.).

The NGC Census Report is an invaluable tool if consulted correctly. However, persons using the NGC Census Report are cautioned that the report is not a reliable guide for determining a coin's rarity, and that buyers should seek the advice of a qualified numismatist before buying coins based upon the NGC Census Report. Additionally, rarity is only one of the factors that determines the value of a coin. This warning is issued to educate consumers and combat "boiler room" operations which tout common coins with low populations on the report as rarities.

The factors contributing to inaccuracy in reported populations include lack of submittals of non-investment grade (low price) coins, and resubmittals of already certified coins removed from their holders in hopes of getting a higher grade. Resubmittals will incorrectly add to population totals.

In order to properly inform the public, the following disclaimer appears at the front of each published Census Report.

CAUTION

The utilization of this Report as a tool for assessing the population and value of certified numismatic coins in any character or grade is unreliable.

The following characteristics inherent in the marketplace undermine the accuracy of this Report.

1. Inexpensive coins which are not submitted for certification appear scarce but are not.
2. Numismatic coin certification services are predominantly utilized for investment grade coins.
3. Often certified coins are cracked out of holders without notice to the grading service, therefore, computer tallies utilized to publish grading reports may be misleading.
4. Rarity is only one factor which must be weighed in determining economic value of a numismatic coin.

Numismatic Guaranty Corporation of America encourages all numismatic coin collectors and investors to seek the counsel of qualified numismatists familiar with the certified coin marketplace before making any purchase based upon this Report.

Conclusion

NGC is proud to have over 500 charter and associate members. A corporate video was designed to assist our members in their current marketing strategies and promotions. Many have found it to be an effective marketing tool for introducing clients to NGC. In February 1990, NGC offered readers a sample of a NGC certified coin. The response was incredible. The initial ad drew thousands of requests for information about NGC and its dealer/member network.

The NGC educational and advertising program includes weekly and monthly ad placements in well respected trade journals including: *The Wall Street Journal,* the *New York Times, U.S. News and World Report, Business Week, and Barron's.*

For too long numismatics has been an industry whose growth has lagged far short of its true potential. Major obstacles to this growth have been the lack of critically needed support from the individual investor and the investment community. The Numismatic Guaranty Corporation of America has answered this challenge and will continue to honor its commitment to provide the industry with an independent, credible and superior coin grading service.

And NGC is planning a great deal more. Educational programs are on the drawing boards. In the coming months announcements will be made concerning a series of new plans and projects designed to foster the industry's pride, and promote professionalism and growth.

Appendix

The following excerpts are from a press release dated January 16, 1991, concerning the Coin Exchange planned in New Jersey.

COIN EXCHANGE PLANNED IN NEW JERSEY

Dozens of coin dealers — possibly 50 or more, in all — will do business at one location under an innovative plan devised by John Albanese, founder and president of the Numismatic Guaranty Corporation of America (NGC).

The plan calls for participating dealers to join forces and purchase a large office building in northern New Jersey, a major hub of activity in the numismatic field. Each will then receive office space in the building — to be known as the *New Jersey Coin Exchange* — and use it as a base of operations.

The dealers will continue to operate independently, but will reap substantial savings and enjoy expanded services through cooperative activities with all the other participants in the venture. . . .

. . . Albanese said, "For a total outlay of not much more than $1,000 a month, each dealer would have a comfortable office in a conveniently located building with armed guards on the premises, a secretarial pool and other services not available to them — or prohibitively expensive — at their present place of business."

"Little retail business will be carried out at the Exchange," Albanese said. "It is intended as a place where member dealers will conduct transactions by telephone, teletype and computer with other dealers or face to face with dealers in the building. A place where they will receive and ship coins. Retail clients will be permitted to visit, but special arrangements must be made and security precautions must be observed."

Details have not been finalized, but Albanese anticipates that each member dealer will have at least 400 square feet of office space. In addition, there will be a large bourse area where the dealers can assemble to do business with each other or with visiting non-member dealers. Tentative plans call for periodic dealer-to-dealer shows in the bourse, possibly on a regular monthly basis. . . .

. . . Albanese is seeking a site for the Exchange in northern New Jersey. He chose this general area partly because he knows it well from living and working in the vicinity; NGC is based in Parsippany, New Jersey, some 35 miles northwest of midtown Manhattan. "The most important reason however," he said, "is that North Jersey is already the home base for many potential participants and is readily accessible to many others." . . .

. . . "I envision this becoming the Northeast's mecca for coin trading," he declared. "And it this works out, there is no reason why similar exchanges can not be established in other parts of the country as well, such as Florida, Chicago or California. This would all be very positive for the whole industry." . . .

. . . "In today's market, with the real estate recession in the Northeast and the high vacancy rates, we should have no problem buying the kind of building we need for roughly $2.5 million," he related. . . .

. . . "Essentially," Albanese said, "we are talking about an initial outlay of $12,000 per dealer and a monthly payment of possibly $1,100. To get something comparable elsewhere, a dealer would have to pay five or six thousand dollars a month, and he would not have nearly the same services or do as much business."

Albanese notes that the project's cooperative nature will result in a great many benefits.

One of the most obvious is the enhanced security. Plans call for several armed guards on the premises, as well as an elaborate system of electronic safeguards. These would be far too expensive for the typical individual dealership.

A secretarial pool will serve the entire building. . . .

. . . A shipping room will also be available. . . .

. . . Arrangements will also be made to have a bank send representatives to the Exchange on a daily basis to pick up dealers' deposits. . . .

. . . "Doing more business is really the whole point of the New Jersey Coin Exchange," Albanese stressed.

. . . Beyond the day-in, day-out advantages provided by such services as security and secretarial support, Albanese also sees numerous other ways in which the Exchange's dealers can reap important benefits and pocket significant savings.

For one thing, he said, "The members' collective clout will enable them to purchase a special computer and set up an in-house travel agency to handle all arrangements when they journey to coin shows and other engagements." . . .

. . . In addition, he suggested, members of the Exchange could enjoy further savings — as well as greater convenience and heightened security — by chartering special buses with armed guards aboard to transport them in a group while traveling to and from airports. . . .

. . . Savings should also be possible on insurance, he suggested. . . .

. . . *NGC is sending information about the Exchange to all its member dealers and inviting them to participate. However, Albanese emphasized that the venture is not limited to NGC dealers and associates*. . . .

. . . "NGC will certainly assist; we will help set it up and promote it. But we do not look at this as a moneymaking scheme; there will not be any money in it for NGC. This is for the coin dealers."

Among other things, NGC will assist in setting up the physical facilities. . . .

. . . Albanese is so confident the Coin Exchange will succeed that he intends to relinquish his duties at NGC in order to devote himself more intensively to the new enterprise. . . .

. . . Albanese made it clear that NGC is in good health and also in good hands. . . .

. . . Albanese disclosed that during the coming months, NGC will unveil yet another new initiative; an educational program . . .

. . . Albanese intends to implement the plan [New Jersey Coin Exchange] as soon as enough dealers have committed themselves to the venture. He said the Exchange could be operational before the end of the year. . . .

. . . Dealers interested in further details regarding the New Jersey Coin Exchange should write to NGC at P.O. Box 1776, Parsippany, NJ 07054.

NGC Logo

Mark Salzberg — President
Numismatic Guaranty Corporation of America

Kenneth Krah — Vice President
Numismatic Guaranty Corporation of America

***

CHAPTER 30

Computerized Grading: The PCGS Expert™

by David Hall

Professional Coin Grading Service — Background

On May 16, 1990, the Professional Coin Grading Service announced a major breakthrough for the rare coin industry with the successful development and implementation of a highly sophisticated computer system which actually graded coins.

The firm named its computer grading system the "PCGS Expert™." The Expert™ was developed as part of PCGS's ongoing efforts to better serve the needs of the rapidly expanding numismatic investment marketplace. The unprecedented computer system simulates human processes to provide highly accurate, efficient and consistent grading.

PCGS was the first to incorporate computerized grading into its on-line operations in what PCGS billed as "the next giant step for the rare coin industry." The Expert™ began grading Morgan dollars in tandem with its human counterparts on May 17, 1991.

"This technological breakthrough is the result of more than two years of intensive research and development. We enlisted the expertise of specialists in computer software and hardware and combined their knowledge with that of the PCGS graders in order to develop the Expert™ system," states Louis M. Crain, PCGS Director of Research and Development.

PCGS has made its mark in the rare coin industry by providing a consistent coin grading standard for collectors and investors since Feb. 1986. In addition, PCGS pioneered the concept of coin encapsulation as a means of reinforcing its grading guarantee. Today, PCGS's overwhelming success may be evidenced by the fact that it has graded 2,614,378 coins with a total declared market value of $3,151,078,882.

"The rare coin industry is evolving at a break-neck pace, with guaranteed third party grading, sight-unseen computer trading networks, Wall Street rare coin funds and now, a machine that grades coins", says PCGS Chief executive Officer, David Hall. "All of these major events have occurred in less than five years. It's amazing!"

The Expert™ is an integrated computer system which combines advanced functions such as robotics, expert systems, real time video, image enhancement, image processing and an on line image database. These components come together for a simulation of the human grading process and enable each Expert™ system to perform the following functions: Automated computer grading of rare coins; computer aided grading; image archiving; and digital fingerprinting.

* Automated computer grading is the process by which the Expert™ captures many images of a coin. It then processes those images using the sophisticated software program developed by the PCGS team, resulting in a final grade for the coin using the Sheldon Numerical Scale.
* Computer aided grading is an expanded version of automated grading used in special circumstances. After automated grading is complete, the detail of the processes and decisions made by the computer are available to human graders. This enables them to utilize and interpret this data and reach a decision as to the final grade of the coin.
* Image archiving is the process by which one or more images of every coin graded by the Expert™ are saved for future reference. The images are transferred to an optical laser compact disk for storage. This allows for easy access for possible verification at a later date.
* Digital fingerprinting is an expansion of the image archiving process. It stores a set of key metrics, calculated during grading, to laser compact disk. It is believed that this set of numbers is a unique numerical representation of each coin much the same as a fingerprint is unique to a human. This information can be reviewed to provide additional support for issues such as authenticity and tampering.

The computer hardware consists of the Macintosh IIX, using a 50-megahertz Motorola 68030 with a floating point co-processer, high speed cache, eight-megabyte memory, erasable optical laser compact disk, video capture hardware, high precision robotics, and an attached special purpose processor.

The Morgan dollar, due to its vast popularity among collectors and investors, is the first and currently the only, issue graded by the Expert™. Current plans call for the expansion of the PCGS Expert's programming to include other frequently traded coins, such as $20 St. Gaudens, Walking Liberty half dollars, Peace dollars, Mercury dimes and Franklin half dollars.

"The fact that grading coins by a machine is a reality should create tremendous excitement among everyone interested in rare coins," said David Hall. "Grading has now progressed to a point where accuracy, consistency and efficiency is at its highest level ever." All of this translates to even more confidence in rare coins for consumers.

PCGS Expert™ — Introductory Questions

1. What is the PCGS Expert™?

The PCGS Expert™ is a powerful and unique computer system which is programmed to grade rare coins. The Expert™ combines state-of-the-art computer technology with leading edge software and peripheral hardware. The system employs robotics, expert systems, real time video, image enhancement, image processing and an on line image database. All of these components come together to simulate the human process of grading coins.

2. How did PCGS develop the Expert™?

PCGS has maintained its leadership position in the grading industry by constantly striving to meet the needs of the marketplace. PCGS is always focused on future trends, as well as ways to improve our products and services. In our continuing effort to incorporate new technology and methods into our operations, PCGS began researching the feasibility of the Expert™ in 1987.

PCGS concluded that a system could be designed to grade coins emulating human methods. Various specialists in software development and hardware capabilities joined forces with members of the PCGS grading staff to create the working prototype.

After defining the hardware requirements, software was developed based upon input from PCGS graders and owners. Morgan silver dollar examples from the permanent PCGS grading set were used as the grading reference for the Expert. The PCGS standard is based upon these and hundreds of other coins in the grading set.

3. Why computer graded coins?

Computer grading by the PCGS Expert™ enables PCGS to continue to address many fundamental obligations to the numismatic community. These obligations include providing the most accurate, efficient and consistent grading methods with the highest volume capabilities. These enhanced operations translate directly to a better product because all refinements to the system are done using human methods based upon our established standards. In addition, the repeatability of the service coupled with increased volume capabilities should draw more and more participants into the numismatic marketplace.

4. How does the Expert™ work in tandem with PCGS's team of world-class grading specialists?

PCGS feels that the human element is important in grading and this has been programmed into the Expert™ system. Because the PCGS Expert™ has been created with human defined methods, simulating the human visual system, the PCGS Expert™ can stand alone as a grader. Currently the PCGS Expert™ is programmed to grade Morgan dollars, but even as other series are added to its capabilities, PCGS plans to utilize a human verifier on all coins graded by the Expert™.

Certification by PCGS does not guarantee protection against the normal risks associated with potentially volatile markets.

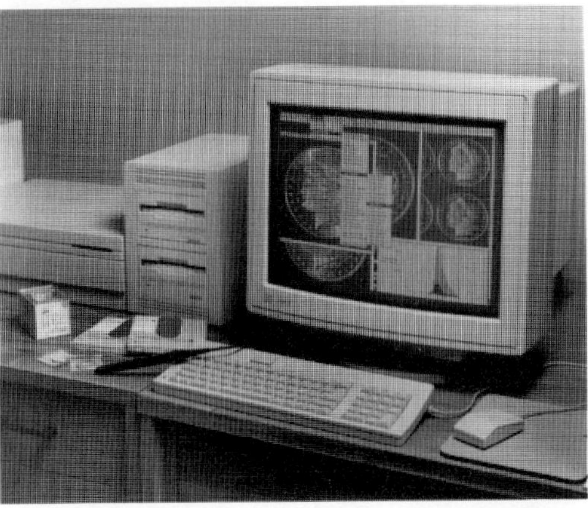

The PCGS *ExpΣrt*™ incorporates accelerated standard computer hard-ware, state-of-the-art software, and a specially designed parallel computer to provide optimum efficiency.

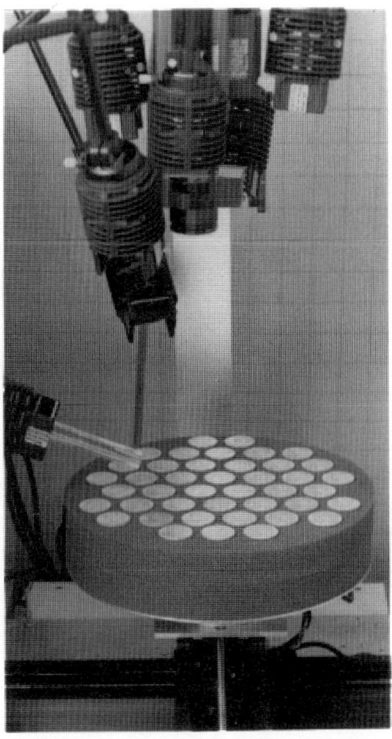

The PCGS *ExpΣrt*™ utilizes real time computer imaging and precision robotics in an expert system uniquely designed for the grading of rare coins.

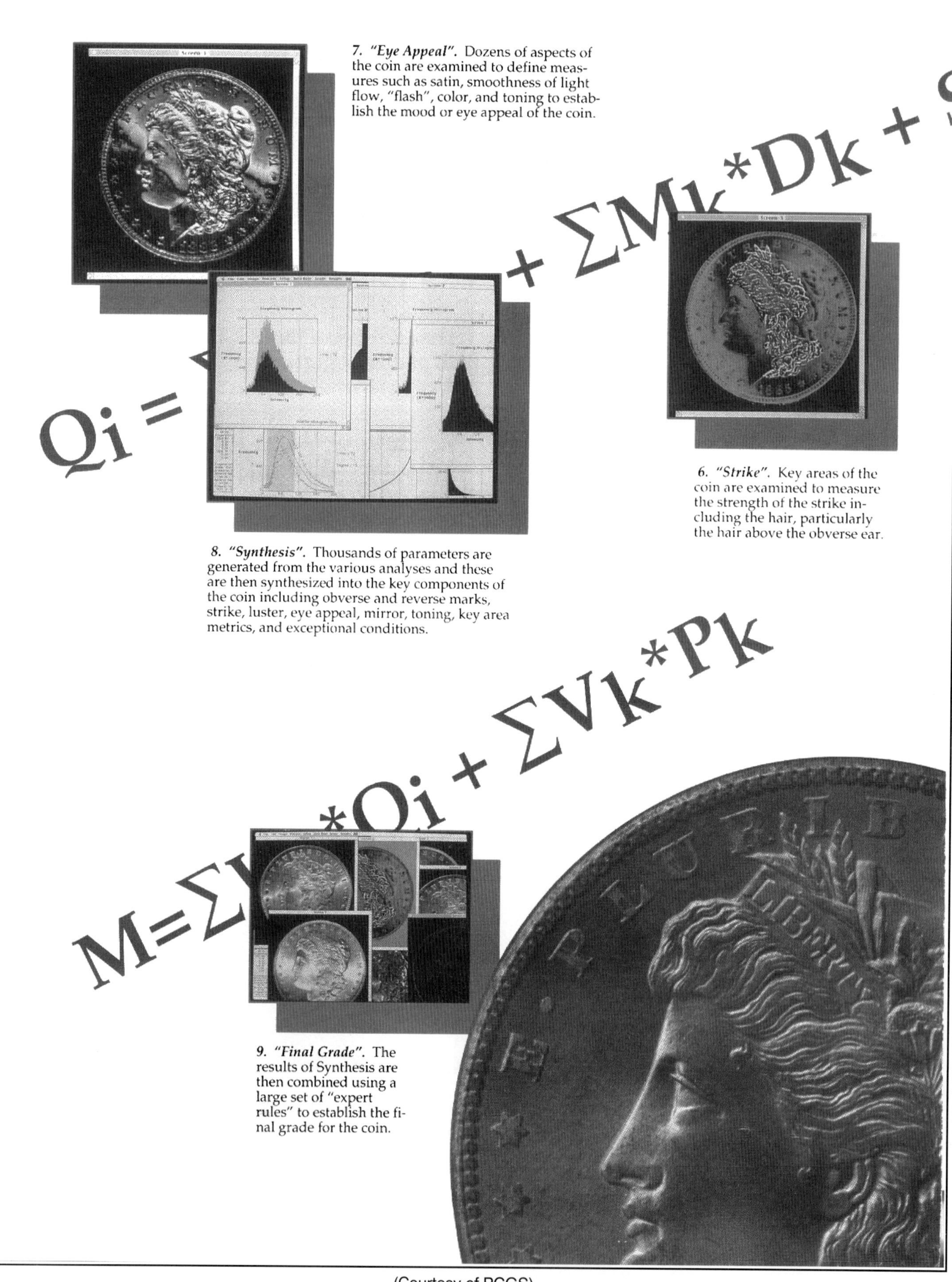

7. "Eye Appeal". Dozens of aspects of the coin are examined to define measures such as satin, smoothness of light flow, "flash", color, and toning to establish the mood or eye appeal of the coin.

6. "Strike". Key areas of the coin are examined to measure the strength of the strike including the hair, particularly the hair above the obverse ear.

8. "Synthesis". Thousands of parameters are generated from the various analyses and these are then synthesized into the key components of the coin including obverse and reverse marks, strike, luster, eye appeal, mirror, toning, key area metrics, and exceptional conditions.

9. "Final Grade". The results of Synthesis are then combined using a large set of "expert rules" to establish the final grade for the coin.

(Courtesy of PCGS)

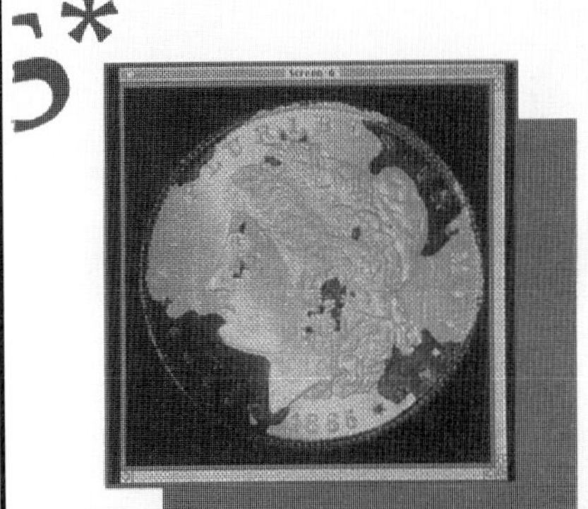

4. *"High Frequency Marks Analysis".* Secondary regions of the coin are examined to identify flaws that exist in busy background regions such as the hair, letters and rim. These flaws are then classified, measured and scored.

5. *"Mirror and Luster".* A light flow and reflectance analysis is used to precisely measure the mirror as well as the inherent luster of the coin.

3. *"Low Frequency Marks Analysis".* The key regions of the coin are examined in great detail to identify, classify, measure, and score all flaws.

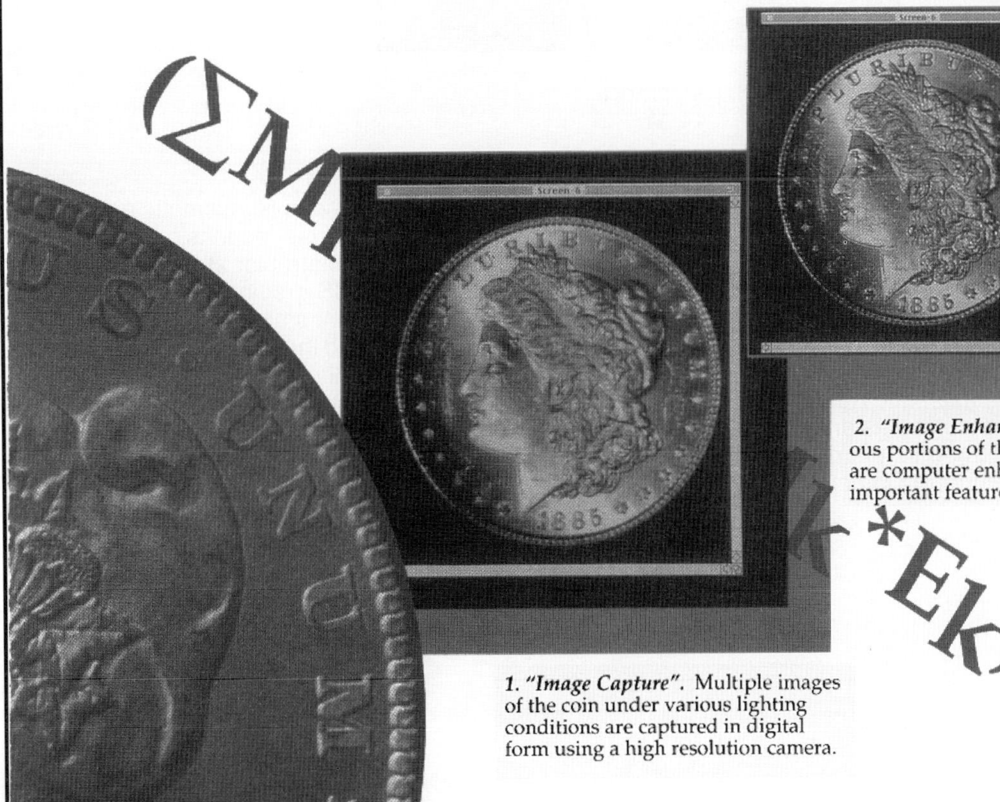

2. *"Image Enhancement".* All or various portions of the captured images are computer enhanced to bring out important features of the coin.

1. *"Image Capture".* Multiple images of the coin under various lighting conditions are captured in digital form using a high resolution camera.

(Courtesy of PCGS)

Bob H. Estremera

Bob Estremera began his numismatic career in the photographic department of the American Numismatic Association in 1981. He was promoted to the ANA certification service (ANACS) in 1984. While in ANACS his responsibilities included being a final grader, and he was particularly well known as an effective and energetic grading instructor at the ANA summer seminars and traveling seminars. In 1985, Bob drafted the initial proposal to create the ANACS grading "reference sets" to help stabilize production grading standards and facilitate the implementation of the 11 point mint state scale by the ANA.

While in the employ of the ANA, Bob has provided expert witness testimony for the F.B.I. and the New York State Attorney General's office. He has also been a consultant in private civil litigation involving grading fraud. His grading articles have been published in *The Numismatist* and *Numismatic News*.

Since leaving the ANA, Bob has worked as an account representative at Heritage Rare Coin Galleries in Dallas, Texas, and as the manager of a retail coin shop in Miami, Florida. He is currently the numismatic grading specialist for the New Orleans based computer grading company, CompuGrade™ .

CHAPTER 31

Computer Grading Mint State Morgan and Peace Silver Dollars

"The Art Becomes Science"

by Bob H. Estremera — Numismatic Grading Specialist for "CompuGrade" ™

Many independent grading services have been created since the American Numismatic Association began its foray into third-party grading of U.S. coins in 1979. Despite their best intentions, these various grading services have been plagued with a nagging and serious problem.

Accurate and consistent results are elusive in the production grading environment for several reasons. One of the principle reasons is that human grading is a subjective exercise in the first place. Each professional grader, however expert, has his or her own personal grading biases. Other human factors including temperament, fatigue, and the need to keep up with production requirements all contribute to an observable lack of accuracy and consistency in the final product.

It has long been felt that if a computer grading system could be developed, it would be able to eliminate most of the problems associated with modern commercial grading. We now have the technological capabilities that allow us to bridge the gap between numismatics and computer science. Just as ANACS and PCGS utilize grading reference sets to establish grading standards that they try to adhere to, a computer grading system could have a tremendous reference set as part of a huge data base that it would constantly refer to. The application of these technologies has transformed the "art" of coin grading into the "science" of coin grading by the ability of programmers and numismatists to "quantify" the subjective factors of grading.

Silver dollars have long been the favored "first series" of grading instruction, for people or computers. The coin is large and shows the degree of original mint lustre easily. Bag marks and surface abrasions are easily seen, while a few year and mint mark combinations display weak strikes that must be factored into the "final grade". These factors led numismatists and computer experts to the obvious conclusion that Morgan and Peace dollars should be the first step for computer grading.

The Benefit — Predictable Performance

The principle benefit of the computer grading process is that of predictable performance. All criteria of the mint state grading process can be accurately and consistently measured and combined into the final grade. The grading process is now demonstrably predictable in its outcome. A well designed computer grading system has the ability to document its required criteria for any grade and issue in terms of lustre, contact marks, strike and eye appeal and to uniformly apply those criteria in the same manner all the time. The educational possibilities are enormous. It is now possible for the astute numismatist to learn a precise, scientifically derived methodology of grading Morgan and Peace silver dollars that is both accurate and repeatable.

The First Step — Letting Go of Grading Fallacies

One of the most significant obstacles to the acceptance of computer grading is the firmly entrenched idea that only the human element has the ability to consistently evaluate the appropriate lustre and "look" of any particular silver dollar in any particular grade. As the designers of computer grading systems will tell you, most of what we graders do to arrive at the proper grade for a coin is quite an interesting blend of human data retrieval and a little "voodoo." We tend to greatly exaggerate our abilities to recognize what is normal lustre, what is impaired lustre, how a coin of a specific date and mint mark usually comes and how all of these considerations should effect the final grade. As we investigate the methods and results of computer grading it will become apparent that computer imaging and data retrieval systems allow for more accuracy and precision when properly programmed. Modern numismatic grading is at the cross-road of replacing the old system of human imprecision with the new accuracy of high-tech computer grading. If we take out time to move slowly and carefully with an open mind into this new age, we will reap the considerable rewards of a true numismatic science and more educational material than we ever dreamed of.

The Process — Duplicating the Human Sequence

In the computer grading scenario, two essential processes occur. The first is the image acquisition phase and the second is the data processing phase. Any necessary attributions concerning specific varieties will be done by the numismatic quality control personnel, leaving the computer system free to perform its primary task.

The image acquisition phase is the process that records all of the surface characteristics of the coin. Measurements are carefully made of the degree of original mint lustre, the presence and severity of contact marks and other surface abrasions, and the fullness of the strike. Image acquisition can be accomplished by the application of laser scanning devices or a simple high resolution optical video camera. The laser technology, although extremely thorough in its ability to resolve the most minute details of a coins surface, is too slow to be effective for production grading. It is important to render the image to the computer in much the same way that it would look to a human grader. Therefore, a video lens used in conjunction with a sophisticated lighting system is the most effective combination. This approach allows the computer grading system to "duplicate the human sequence" of grading. The duplication by the computer system of what humans do is essential because it facilitates the ability of the numismatists and the science personnel to interact with each other and the system during the early development phase. It also serves to ensure quality control later on. After the images have been recorded they are digitized and the second phase of the computer grading system begins.

The data processing phase is the most complex part of the entire computer system. In this phase, all of the previously digitized data must be "crunched" to become a single mint state grade. This is no small task considering that tens of millions of calculations are made to arrive at that final grade. The reason the data processing phase is so difficult is because the relationship between the number of contact marks and their effect on the final grade is, as scientists say, totally non-linear. In other words, you don't just add up the bag marks.

It takes many man-hours of research by image technologists, computer programmers and numismatists to arrive at the proper relationships between: the amount of surface imperfections, the location of the imperfections relative to prime focal areas, the severity of the marks and the effect of available mint lustre. All of these factors must be painstakingly documented, calculated and re-calculated in order to arrive at a suitable grading algorithm (equation) that will work predictably for a large population of silver dollars.

Identifying a Consensus Standard

Despite the differing grading standards that are evident when inspecting certified coins from the various grading services, there is a more narrow range of consensus among top quality professional graders than their final products would indicate. When given the time to properly evaluate a coin's condition and assign an accurate grade, most professionals are surprisingly close to each other.

The following steps are necessary to ensure that the computer grading system will be "trained" with accurate and repeatable grades that are accepted by the numismatic community.

First, a test population of randomly selected certified coins from different mints and in various grades is located and catalogued. Care must be taken to include "problem" coins and that the top certification services are used.

Second, a panel of proven numismatic grading experts must be assembled to grade the test population. The certified grades must be covered so that the graders are not influenced. Each grader assigns the lowest reasonable grade, the highest reasonable grade and his or her "preferred grade" for each coin. The grades used to train the computer are the averaged "preferred grade" for each coin as they are considered the most accurate. The average low and the average highest reasonable grades are computed to ensure that the computer system does not deviate above or below a range of acceptability. Using this approach, the computer grading system can now "lock in" a scientifically derived accurate grading standard.

Grading Basics

Grading Morgan and Peace dollars, as with other coins, is a matter of prioritizing certain aesthetic properties and assigning a numerical grade to the final analysis. The essential properties are lustre, surface preservation, strike, and eye appeal. We will explore the ways that the state-of-the-art computer grading system accomplishes its task of duplicating the human analysis of each of the aesthetic properties involved in grading silver dollars and then to distill this analysis into a final grade.

Lustre

Like a gem, the brightness of a coin's surface changes as the direction of the illuminating light changes. This property is called lustre and is most easily seen as a cartwheel of light that moves when the coin is manipulated under a directional light source. By comparing multiple images to each other, the computer system can measure the strength and sharpness of the lustre at each point on a coin's surface. Lustre "maps" of each coin are then generated and printed by the system. The lustre maps are so accurate they appear like a photograph of the coin and are used by the design team to be sure the computer system is "seeing" the coin's lustre as a human grader would. Because the computer "remembers" every coin it has ever graded it can compare the lustre measurements with other coins of the same mint and date. This allows the modern computer grading system to "know" that the lustre of an 1903-P does not have the same levels of brilliance as the 1885-P mint and will factor these and other lustre differences into the final grade.

In practice, lustre can be effectively used to "bracket" appropriate grade ranges. Another important benefit the computer grading system provides is coins that have been "processed" by the application of surface contaminants will display abnormal lustre data and will be "flagged" for a down-grade or a no-grade, depending on the nature and severity of the contamination. Also, the application of some type of lustre "index" on the certification label itself would allow the interested buyer or seller of a coin to know whether it exhibits below average, average or exceptional lustre.

Another aspect of lustre determination that the computer system is better suited for is the recognition of the different lustres that can be observed from coins of the same year and mint. For instance, an original 1924 Peace dollar can display a rough, uneven surface with its characteristically soft lustre or it can be seen with a smooth surface and a more dramatic and lively "cartwheel." These and other similar anomalies can be input as data to the computer system and will be effectively "remembered" with far more consistency and accuracy than is currently possible using human graders.

Surface Preservation

Bagmarks, hairlines, and wear interrupt the lustre on a coin and lower its grade. The computer grading system detects these defects and measures their location, severity, and size. Defects in key areas are weighted more heavily than those in peripheral areas. Keep in mind that measuring a flaw on a coin means more than locating it. The measurement must reflect how a coin and the marks on it *look* to a human grader. That is one of the reasons why the high resolution camera is superior to a laser light approach. As with lustre measurements, defect "maps" are generated and printed by the computer system and are used by the programmers, image technologists and numismatists to ensure that surface imperfections are being sensed by the system as they appear to human graders.

Strike

The amount of high point detail is measured to determine the strength of strike. The computer measures the relief at these high points and compares it to other coins of the same issue. Certain degrees of strike (depending on year and mint mark) can be programmed to exist before upper mint state grades will be assigned. For example, the practical application of strike data makes it possible for the computer to "know" that an 1892-CC Morgan, or a 1921 Peace dollar can display less high point detail, grade for grade, than coins that are normally fully struck.

Planchet defects, whether in the form of planchet striations, struck-throughs (grease, fragments, etc.) or pitted dies are all recorded by the imaging system. Since the planchet defects have lustre, the system will downgrade for them but not as severely as it does for actual contact marks that are more "specular" (bright and reflective) in nature. This is an important duplication of the human sequence in the way that humans approach the planchet defect problem and is an excellent example of why the optical video camera is superior to the laser scanning system.

Color

Color can easily be included into the grading process by recognizing factors such as the presence of primary colors and the symmetry of the pattern. In this way, the desirability of original "rainbow" toning can be factored into the final grade. Similarly, the presence of dull, gray, mottled or otherwise unattractive toning can be recognized and factored into the grading algorithm. All considerations of toning are of an extremely subjective nature and should be used sparingly.

Eye Appeal

Eye appeal has long been considered the single most unattainable quality for a cold, impersonal computer to determine.In practice, it is actually one of the easiest factors of grading for a state-of-the-art computer grading system. In many people's opinions, if human production graders were so good at factoring eye appeal into a final grade, the rampant practice of "crack-outs" and re-submissions would not be so wide spread and the erosion of confidence in sight-unseen bidding would not be taking place.

Positive eye appeal is simply the determination that a particular coin possesses extraordinary lustre and strike for its year and mint mark. Conversely, negative eye appeal is the observing of less than normal lustre and strike. Also, the distribution of bagmarks affects eye appeal as does the strength, symmetry and color of the coin. These determinations are most effectively made by the imaging system rather than by human graders because the computer has the ability to immediately access its huge data base, make a scientific comparison against known values and then factor the eye appeal information into the final grade.

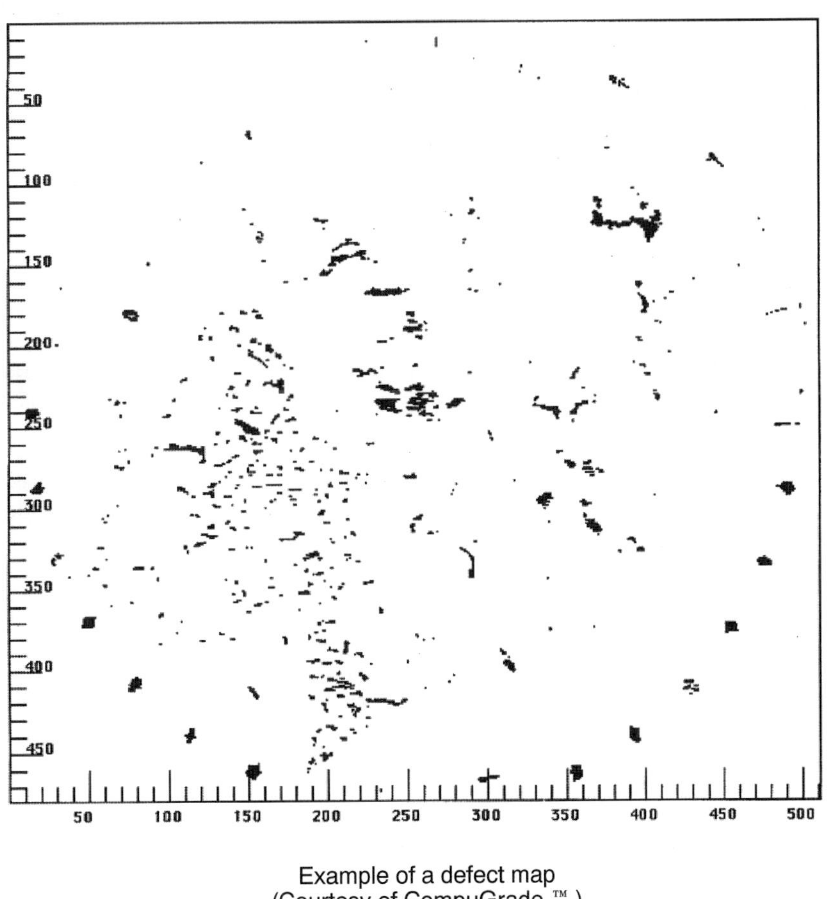

Example of a defect map
(Courtesy of CompuGrade ™)

Final Grade

The final grade is now ready to be computed from all the measured properties of the coin. The luster, marks, strike, and eye appeal are all factored into the final grade which should be expressed to the tenth of a grade. Fractions of a grade are essential to computer grading for several reasons. A principal reason is that the repeatability of a real computer grading system is within one tenth of a grade and that repeatability could not be verified without one tenth grade increments. Also, if the final grade is rounded down to the nearest whole grade as some firms would do, a whole grade difference will result if the coin was graded MS64.9 the first time and MS65.0 the second time, even though the difference is only one-tenth of a grade.

Repeatability would be lost. Lastly, the upper increments would consistently and impartially denote PQ (premium quality) coins.

ProofLike Coins

As with the other grading criteria, designations of prooflike or deep mirror prooflike are best made by the imaging system. The amount of prooflike properties is a simple measurement of the degree of reflectivity from the field areas of the coin's surface and can accurately be expressed on a 100 point scale. A great advantage of the computer system is that the amount of "cameo" can also be expressed on a 100 point scale as it is simply the amount of contrast between the devices and the field. With the application of both the P/L scale and the cameo scale, prooflike Morgan dollars can be effectively described sight-unseen with absolute accuracy and consistency.

Low Population Coins

Low population issues do not present a problem for the computer grading system. In fact, grading low population coins accurately and consistently has been much more of a problem for human graders and the services at which they work than for a state-of-the-art computer grading system. Let's be realistic. The human graders at any of the major grading services haven't seen that many low-population silver dollars themselves. The idea that the computer won't know how to grade its first MS65, 1896-O or 1928-S silver dollar falls into the "grading fallacy" department. The most pertinent question when confronting the grading of low-population silver dollars is whether to grade them on a different standard. CompuGrade ™ , the New Orleans based computer grading service polled a number of silver dollar specialists including members of the Silver Dollar Roundtable to find out whether they thought rare, low population silver dollars should be graded differently than the more common issues. All of these experts agreed that all other factors being equal, there should not be any difference in the grading standard between common dollars and their more rare counterparts. They felt strongly that the grading should be uniform across the board and the market should set the price for low-population coins. So then, for the computer system, the first high grade 1889-CC or 1934-S silver dollar it encounters will be graded with all the accuracy and consistency the system affords.

In Closing

Computers have been making life and work easier for us for a number of years now. Every form of analyzing and "figuring" has been streamlined and simplified by the appropriate applications of computer technology. There is no reason to think that grading U.S. coins is any different. Although we professional human graders hate to admit it, once properly programmed, the computer grading system has the ability to effectively "see" a coin, measure every aspect of its condition and give it an accurate grade, every time! We can even program it to remember if it has seen the coin before and what grade it gave it! The human element is inefficient for production grading because its data base is limited, it lacks an accurate retrieval system and is greatly influenced by external forces.

As the marriage between numismatics and computer science evolves and becomes more widely accepted, we will be able to look back and see how the great "cartwheels" of George T. Morgan and Anthony De Francisci were the first bold step in this exciting numismatic advancement.

Appendix A:

Following are excerpts from an article entitled, "CompuGrade ™ Quantifies Morgan Mint Lustres," by Bob Estremera, including "histograms" which graphically illustrate the lustre characteristics of selected Morgan silver dollars as compiled by CompuGrade ™ , the New Orleans based numismatic research and development company.

Original mint lustre, a key consideration when grading mint state coins, has been a primary focus of preliminary CompuGrade ™ research. Human graders rely on their years of experience to determine whether a given coin has retained its original "mint bloom." This determination is essential to properly assigning a mint state grade, especially in the upper ranges. The patented CompuGrade ™ system is creating a useful and extensive data base in order to store the acceptable ranges of original Morgan dollar lustre by date and mint mark.

When comparing the lustre of common "O" mint dollars to their "S" mint counterparts, Morgan dollar enthusiasts learn that the San Francisco products exhibit a more "flashy" brilliance often characterized by dark fields and brighter "frosty" devices. The New Orleans mint, on the other hand, produced a whiter more even lustre. These and other lustre characteristics have been measured and quantified by CompuGrade's RESEARCH AND DEVELOPMENT staff.

The diagrams shown are graphic representations of the numerical distribution of lustre as measured by CompuGrade's proprietary computer system. These diagrams are commonly known as histograms.

The following histograms illustrate the measured differences of lustre characteristics between an 1884-O and an 1880-S dollar. Figures 1a and 1b are lustre measurements of the field area, figures 2a and 2b are measurements of the face lustre. Although the data used to generate these histograms is complex, CompuGrade ™ can compress the information to a simple representation.

Figures 1a and 1b graphically illustrate the differences in field lustre between the two coins. The 1884-O has a peak contrast index of 2500, whereas the 1880-S peaks at 16000! This represents a difference of approximately 6 to 1. These histograms also show that the 1884-O reflects more middle tone values than the 1880-S at equivalent contrast levels.

Referring to figures 2a and 2b you will note that both coins have a more even distribution of lustre in the face. The ratio between them there is now only 2 to 1. However, the steeper transitions of the 1881-S histogram tell us that its face lustre has more contrast.

The practical application of these types of histograms will be significant. It affords CompuGrade ™ an effective tool to consistently determine lustre parameters for any given mint state grade by year and mint mark. Histograms can also be invaluable as an in-line authentication backup for altered Morgan dollars.

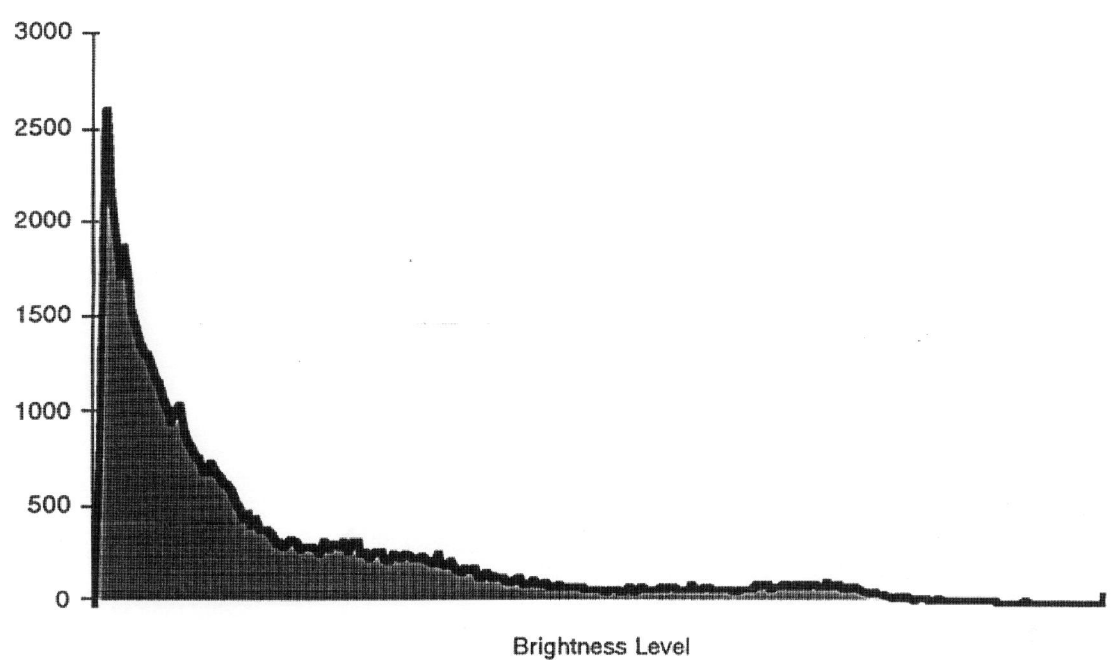

Figure 1a: 1884-O Field Lustre Histogram
(Courtesy of CompuGrade ™)

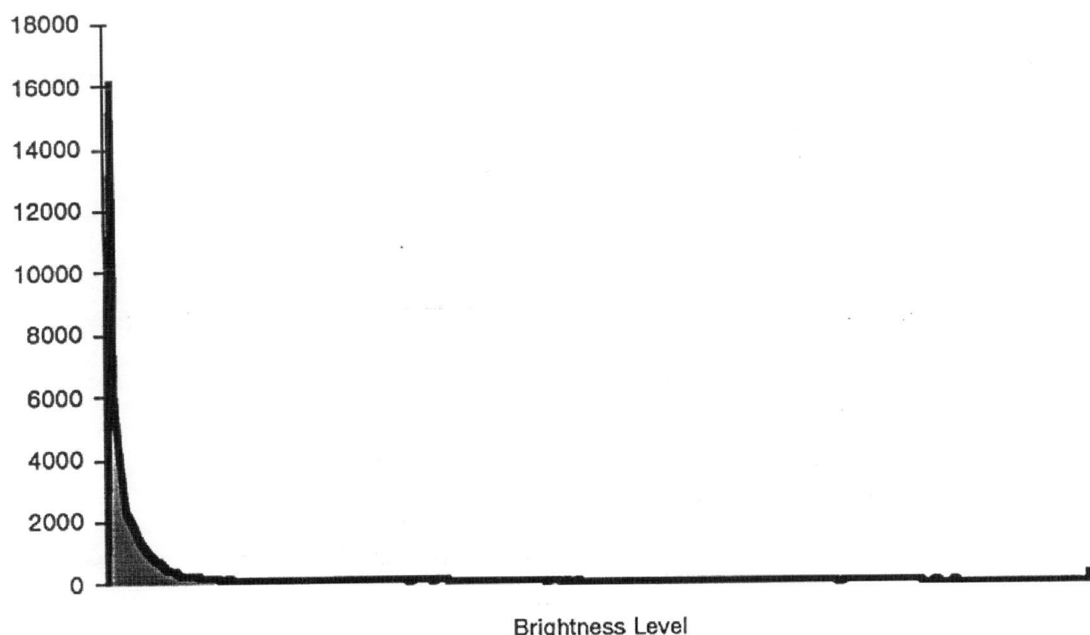

Figure 1b: 1880-S Field Lustre Histogram
(Courtesy of CompuGrade ™)

Figure 2a: 1884-O Face Lustre Histogram

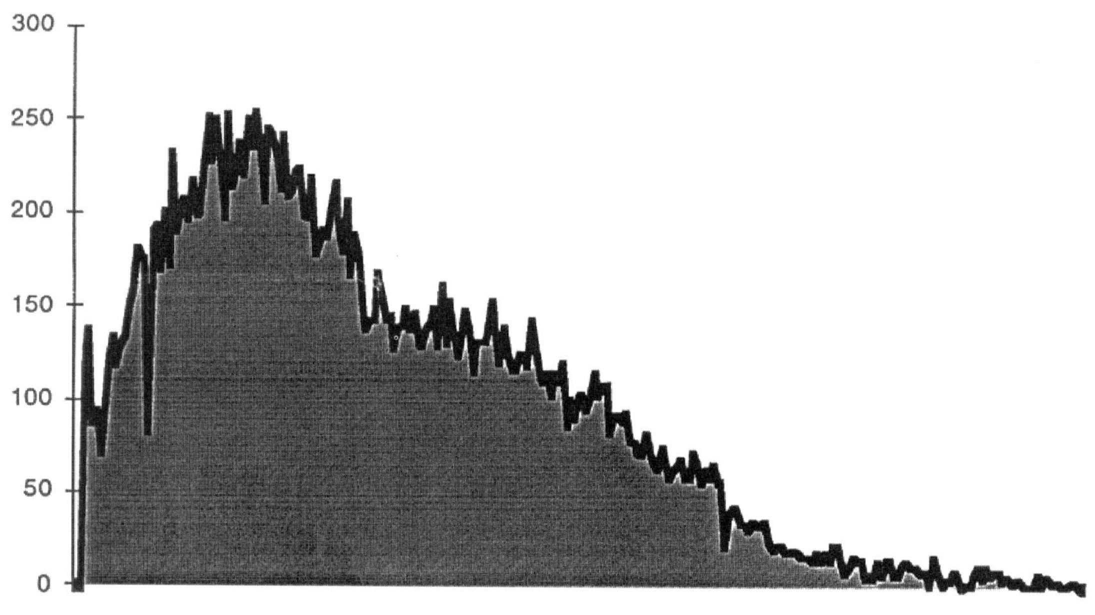

Brightness Level

Figure 2a: 1884-O Face Lustre Histogram
(Courtesy of CompuGrade ™)

Figure 2b: 1880-S Face Luster

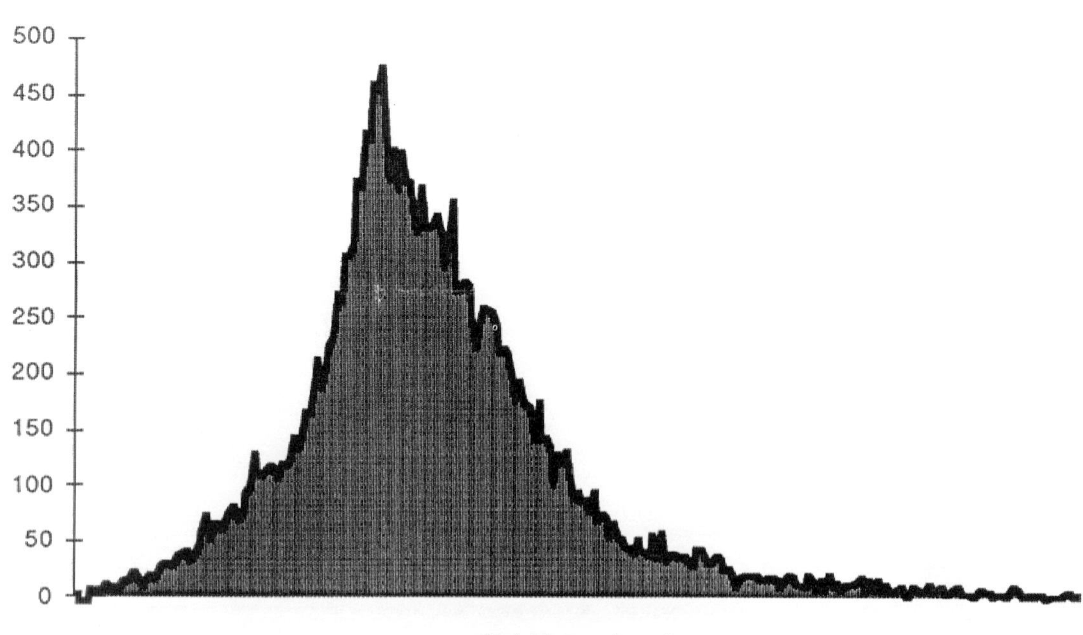

Brightness Level

Figure 2b: 1880-S Face Lustre Histogram
(Courtesy of CompuGrade ™)

Appendix B:

Additional "grading tools" were developed to assist in the testing of the computer grading system concept. One of these was a grade comparison model developed to allow CompuGrade ™ to measure its computer grading system with expert human graders. Refer to the comparative graph showing CompuGrade's computed grades versus human "actual" grades during the following discussion.

To perform this test, several human grading experts (Morgan dollar specialists) were brought to the CompuGrade ™ New Orleans site. The invited numismatists included Bill Fivaz, Mike Fuljenz, John Highfill, Wayne Hummel, Bill Panitch and myself. The job of these advisors was to grade each of the Morgan dollars provided in order to "teach" the computer. Additional input was provided by CompuGrade's own specialist. The other factor used was the existing PCGS certified grade of the coin.

The procedure required each expert to give each coin the highest and lowest reasonable grade, as well as the "preferred" grade. Next, the CompuGrade ™ representatives performed their statistical work and used the grading information to "train" the computer. This procedure allowed CompuGrade ™ to develop a grading "standard" for the test population using accepted expert grading opinions.

Turning attention to the graphic presentation of the results of this exercise, the number of coins utilized in the tested population is presented on the horizontal axis. The test population in this case consisted of 100 coins. The mint state grades from MS-60 to MS-66 are arranged up the vertical axis.

The results were very interesting. Ninety-six of the hundred coins were within three tenths of the calculated average "preferred" grade. All 100 coins were well within the spread between the average high grade and average low grade. Only four coins varied by as much as one-half of a grade. As other tests were conducted and the results calculated and compared, the CompuGrade ™ computer grading system continued to provide similar accuracy.

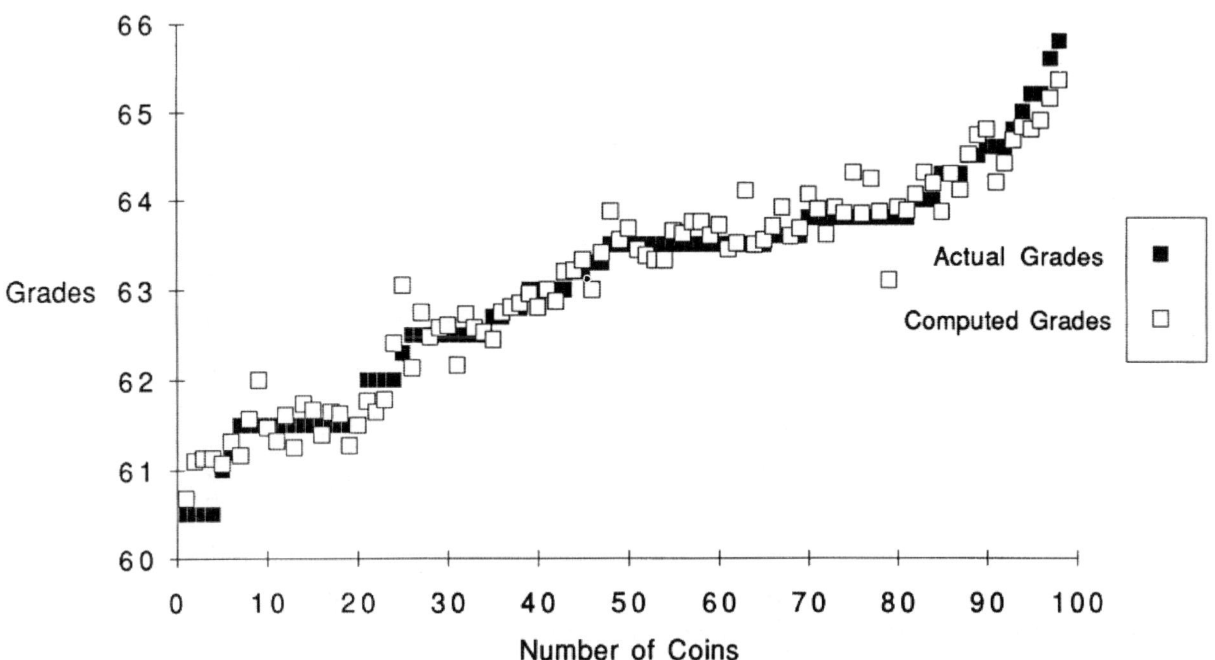

Grades given by expert graders and grades computed by the computer
(Courtesy of CompuGrade ™)

***

John D. Schneider, Jr.

John D. Schneider, Jr., born on December 2, 1949, was educated at the University of Southwestern Louisiana, where he graduated as the Outstanding Senior in 1972.

Mr. Schneider was elected a County Commissioner and City Councilman during the 1972-76 period. He continued his education and obtained a J.D. degree from the Louisiana State University Law School. This led to his founding his own legal firm where he was the sole practitioner during the years 1976 through 1984 in Lafayette, Louisiana.

Also during this same time period John Schneider founded JSE, Inc., a sports marketing and management firm. As president, he negotiated player, licensing and endorsement contracts for athletes. He was the co-founder and chairman of Graham, Schneider Associates, Inc., an advertising, marketing and public relations firm.

In March 1984, Mr. Schneider became the president and chief executive officer of the American Numismatic Exchange, Inc., a national firm that serves the rare coin industry. During his tenure, John Schneider established a national telecommunications network utilizing computers and satellites for the "real-time" trading of rare coins similar to stocks on NYSE, as well as drafted and enforced rules and regulations to govern the daily trading. Over 200 firms in 40 states traded $250 million annually on the network.

CHAPTER 32

The Certified Coin, "Sight-Unseen", Electronic Trading Concept

by John D. Schneider, Jr.

In January 1986 two firms — American Numismatic Exchange (ANE) and Professional Coin Grading Service (PCGS) — banded together to develop a concept where certified coins could be traded sight-unseen for specific bid and ask prices, just like stocks.

The move was revolutionary because of its parallel to Wall Street activities and the companies' attempt to address irregularities of grading and liquidity and restore credibility to rare coin trading. The certification of coins (even by an independent third party, i.e., PCGS) as to their condition or "grade" was not a new concept. What was innovative was the placement of coins in sonically sealed holders and then having these coins electronically traded, "sight-unseen" on a trading exchange based on the grade stamped on the holder.

Prior To "Sight-Unseen", Electronic Trading

Before 1986, coin dealers communicated price information the "old fashioned way." i.e., via printed price lists transmitted through the mail. The prices, however, were not binding and invariably callers were informed that the price in question was the "old price" or "last week's price."

The ability of dealers to be "flexible" in trading coins based on printed price lists had an interesting impact on the market. When the coin market went down, liquidity was the first casualty, not value. If a coin had traded at $750 when the market was hot, dealers might still bid $700 for it when the market declined. But the same dealers would tighten their grading standards.

A very large percentage of coins "weren't quite there" in a down market. Dealers simply chose not to accept most coins and they lost their liquidity, except at much lower price levels. As a result, printed price lists never showed the true magnitude of any market decline because on paper the bids remained strong. The introduction of electronic coin trading exchanges introduced a new era with new rules.

OKLAHOMA FEDERATED GOLD & NUMISMATICS, INC.

3778 South Elm Place • Broken Arrow, Oklahoma 74011

VOLUME 1 NOVEMBER, 1986

Buying PCGS Coins
Call for Quotes or Confirmation
(918) 451-0665

P.C.G.S. U.S. GOLD

DATE/MM	AU-58	MS-60	MS-61	MS-62	MS-63	MS-64	MS-65	MS-66	MS-67
$1 TYPE I	360	725	775	1175	1750	3300	6700	QUOTE	QUOTE
$1 TYPE II	2200	4400	5200	6400	10350			QUOTE	QUOTE
$1 TYPE III	340	700	750	1050	1700	2900	5175	QUOTE	QUOTE
$2 1/2 LIBERTY	385	825	875	1000	1700	2850	4250	QUOTE	QUOTE
$2 1/2 INDIAN	235	360	400	525	1150	2400	4350	QUOTE	QUOTE
$3 PRINCESS	1650	3000	3200	3850	5750			QUOTE	QUOTE
$5 LIBERTY	230	360	385	525	1125	3150	5700	QUOTE	QUOTE
$5 INDIAN	425	800	875	1125	2500	4200	7450	QUOTE	QUOTE
$10 LIBERTY	300	375	450	725	1875	3800	6400	QUOTE	QUOTE
$10 INDIAN	540	750	800	1050	1825	3750	6400	QUOTE	QUOTE
$20 LIBERTY	490	590	615	775	1450	2950	6300	QUOTE	QUOTE
$20 SAINT	590	690	720	815	1215	2200	3750	QUOTE	QUOTE
$20 SAINT-1908	560	650	710	810	1150	2150	3750	QUOTE	QUOTE

P.C.G.S. WALKING LIBERTY HALVES

1941-P	40	42	60	115	200	375	550	750
1941-D	45	50	70	150	285	485	600	800
1941-S	150	160	225	450	725	1000	1275	1600
1942-P	40	42	60	100	200	375	550	750
1942-D	50	55	70	185	250	475	600	800
1942-S	85	95	105	250	300	550	725	925
1943-P	40	42	60	90	200	375	550	750
1943-D	50	55	70	165	275	550	700	925
1943-S	80	90	105	260	350	640	800	1025
1944-P	40	42	60	90	200	375	550	750
1944-D	45	50	70	160	285	475	625	825
1944-S	50	55	70	160	415	825	1050	1350
1945-P	40	42	60	90	200	375	550	750
1945-D	45	50	70	115	250	440	600	800
1945-S	50	55	70	115	225	525	650	825
1946-P	40	42	60	110	220	425	600	825
1946-D	45	50	60	90	200	390	550	800
1946-S	50	55	70	110	210	500	650	850
1947-P	50	55	60	120	210	450	600	800
1947-D	50	55	70	100	215	450	600	800

FOR A FREE COPY OF OUR NEXT PCGS BUYING LIST . . .

NAME: __________

ADDRESS: __________

CITY/STATE/ZIP: __________

PHONE: __________

P.C.G.S. MORGAN SILVER DOLLARS

DATE/MM	AU-58	MS-60	MS-61	MS-62	MS-63	MS-64	MS-65	MS-66	MS-67
1903-P		40	45	55	80	400		QUOTE	QUOTE
1903-O	150	200	210	225	325	575	950	QUOTE	QUOTE
1903-S	400	1350	1650	1850	2600	4000	7500	QUOTE	QUOTE
1904-P	25	70	75	110	235	700		QUOTE	QUOTE
1904-O	16	25	29	38	70	240		QUOTE	QUOTE
1904-S	300	650	700	900	1650	2200		QUOTE	QUOTE
1921-P		18	20	25	55	225		QUOTE	QUOTE
1921-D		25	30	35	70	300		QUOTE	QUOTE
1921-S		20	25	38	80	450		QUOTE	QUOTE

P.C.G.S. PEACE SILVER DOLLARS

DATE/MM	AU-58	MS-60	MS-61	MS-62	MS-63	MS-64	MS-65	MS-66	MS-67
1921-P		155	175	215	350	1150		QUOTE	QUOTE
1922-P		20	22	25	50	210	600	QUOTE	QUOTE
1922-D		25	30	40	75	350		QUOTE	QUOTE
1922-S		25	30	40	85	425		QUOTE	QUOTE
1923-P		20	22	25	50	210	600	QUOTE	QUOTE
1923-D		25	30	40	100	410		QUOTE	QUOTE
1923-S		25	30	40	110	425		QUOTE	QUOTE
1924-P		25	30	35	55	250	625	QUOTE	QUOTE
1924-S		110	140	175	325	1150		QUOTE	QUOTE
1925-P		25	30	35	55	210	625	QUOTE	QUOTE
1925-S		95	105	150	250	850		QUOTE	QUOTE
1926-P		40	50	70	150	450		QUOTE	QUOTE
1926-D		50	55	75	150	460		QUOTE	QUOTE
1926-S		40	55	70	110	450		QUOTE	QUOTE
1927-P		80	85	110	185	675		QUOTE	QUOTE
1927-D		170	225	275	500	1150		QUOTE	QUOTE
1927-S		120	130	170	265	700		QUOTE	QUOTE
1928-P		180	195	205	340	750		QUOTE	QUOTE
1928-S		90	110	125	280	700		QUOTE	QUOTE
1934-P		70	75	110	180	675		QUOTE	QUOTE
1934-D		75	100	125	265	725		QUOTE	QUOTE
1934-S	325	1100	1150	1300	2200	3500	7000	QUOTE	QUOTE
1935-P		45	50	65	110	415		QUOTE	QUOTE
1935-S		110	150	175	325	800		QUOTE	QUOTE

TERMS: PRICES ARE "INDICATIONS ONLY" AND ARE SUBJECT TO CHANGE. CALL FOR CURRENT QUOTES & CONFIRMATION. ALL ORDERS C.O.C. (IF KNOWN PARTY). TRADING HOURS ARE MONDAY-FRIDAY 10:00 - 4:00 P.M. (CENTRAL TIME). CLOSED HOLIDAYS.

************* SHIPMENTS MUST BE POSTMARKED WITHIN 48 HOURS *************
COINS MUST BE IN P.C.G.S. HOLDERS.

OKLAHOMA FEDERATED GOLD & NUMISMATICS, INC.
3778 S. ELM PLACE • BROKEN ARROW, OKLAHOMA 74011
(918) 451-0665

Sight-unseen bid sheets - Nov. 1986
(prior to electronic trading)
(Courtesy of Oklahoma Federated Gold and Numismatics, Inc.)

The Basic Structure of an Electronic Coin Trading Exchange

An electronic coin trading exchange such as American Numismatic Exchange is a member firm organization. These members are permitted to post bid (the price for which a dealer will buy a coin) and ask (the price for which a dealer will sell a coin) quotations directly on the electronic trading network operated by the exchange.

Each dealer posting a bid price on the exchange for an "approved certified coin" — a coin graded by an independent, third party grading service recognized by the exchange — is *required* to purchase a minimum dollar value or quantity of that coin, i.e., $1500 or 10 coins (whichever comes first) — from any other member firm wishing to sell the coin.

As to any ask price for an approved certified coin posted on the exchange, the member firm is required to sell at least one such coin at the quoted price when contacted by another member firm.

All bid and ask quotations pertain to approved certified coins and are effective on a "sight-unseen" basis. That is, any bid price quoted for a particular coin is good for any approved certified coin of the designated grade, without inspection by the bidding party. Likewise, if a member firm wishes to post an ask price for an approved certified coin, another member firm purchasing from him at that price agrees to buy it *without inspection*.

The prices quoted on the exchange from time to time are subject to change without notice. The rights and obligations of member firms with respect to quotations posted on the exchange are subject to additional rules and regulations which, in some cases, limit their obligations.

Bid and ask prices posted on the exchange are, in effect, *wholesale* prices offered between and among member firms of the exchange. Thus, interested parties who are not member firms of the exchange may or may not be able to obtain and/or sell approved certified coins at the quoted figures. In most cases, member firms will offer to buy approved certified coins from non-member firms or individuals at their own bid prices for such coins less a commission or transaction charge and will agree to sell such coins at their ask prices plus a commission or transaction charge.

Exchange rules require that all bid and ask prices posted on the exchange by member firms are determined and quoted by each dealer independently. The member firms individually make markets in different areas of actively traded issues of approved certified coins. Not all member firms make markets in all U.S. coins. Also, there may not exist a market through the exchange for every approved certified coins.

An approved certified coin for which an active market exists at one point in time later may not have an actively traded market. Like many other items which are actively bought and sold, the prices quoted for approved certified coins are subject to a high degree of volatility. Factors such as supply and demand, interest rates, commodity prices and general economic conditions, all of which are changeable and unpredictable, have a strong influence on the prices of numismatic coins.

Since the Establishment of "Sight-Unseen", Electronic Trading

Since the establishment of "sight-unseen" electronic trading of certified coins, the concern of liquidity has been reduced in both up and down markets for most actively traded coins graded by approved certification services such as PCGS and NGC (Numismatic Guaranty Corporation) coins.

Electronic trading performed the role of facilitating the sight-unseen trading of certified coins in various market climates. Hundreds of major coin dealers are linked up via various computer networks and given the ability to post bid and ask prices daily on thousands of certified coins.

Real-time prices are communicated nationwide to all parties in less than 3 minutes. Importantly, these are prices at which the dealers are not only willing but required to trade coins. The era of printed price lists with "flexibility of adherence" is nearing an end.

Although electronic trading has achieved a primary goal of facilitating the sight-unseen trading of certified coins in various market climates, prices on electronic trading networks are not always the exclusive indicator of the levels at which coins trade.

During *rising* markets, certified coins trade at a premium over bid prices on electronic exchanges. The reason is that the coin industry is not a closed market. Interested parties are not legally restricted to transact trades only through member firms of these exchanges; parallel this scenario with the way stock trades are handled only by licensed brokers.

Nevertheless, in a rising market, price information on electronic exchanges is extremely valuable to all parties in a coin transaction because such data is the basis from which sellers determine the asking prices for their coins; invariably demanding (and receiving) offers for their coins in the wholesale market that are 10-30% over the bid prices on the electronic exchanges.

One may ask, "Why don't bidders on the exchanges merely raise their prices 10-30% to reflect sellers' ask prices?" The reason is that, "Sellers would then demand (and receive) 10-30% over the new bid prices." The origin of a bull market in certified coins can partially be traced to exchange bidders trying to keep pace with sellers' ask prices.

Even though coins trade at exchange price levels during a *falling* price market, it is important that interested sellers during this period be aware of certain characteristics *presently* inherent in any electronic coin exchange.

First, such an exchange is a bid-oriented market. Exchange founders were so determined to enhance the liquidity for certified coins — the ability to sell coins easily whenever one so desires — that the focus of the electronic network was placed on encouraging member firms to post bid prices.

Also, this focus continued a decade-long pattern in the coin industry — reflected in most printed price lists — of reporting only bid prices (not ask prices) for coins. Dealers have long felt that it was more important to know what price someone was willing to pay for a coin rather than what price someone was willing to sell a coin.

However, such an orientation, when coupled with the exchange rules that bidders are *required* to buy a minimum number of coins at their posted prices, has had a profound impact on coin market volatility. Remember, prior to the "sight-unseen", certified coin market, price guides never showed the true magnitude of a market decline because on paper the bids remained strong; dealers simply chose not to accept most coins and they lost their liquidity.

Now, bid prices on electronic exchanges may drop dramatically in a down market because earnest bidders are obligated to back up their prices with real dollars. The notice, however, that all sellers in falling markets must be aware of and remember, is that electronic exchanges may sometimes overstate the severity of any drop in the market.

Why? Although the number of member firms on various electronic coin exchanges has grown from a small core of 45 major dealers to an expanded network of several hundred firms, cumulative cash reserve of all the players are not yet large enough to provide an orderly decline in exchange market prices in the midst of a major selling frenzy. Exchange bid prices may drop dramatically in a down market more as a reflection of the lack of cash reserves of member firms as opposed to a decline in coins' true values.

This temporary cash shortage, however, is not the only problem. The union of a cash shortage factor and a bid-oriented factor (and the absence of ask prices) creates a situation where lower exchange bid prices (rather than ask prices) quickly become the actual trading levels in the market.

Consider this analogy frequently used by several dealers in analyzing this particular situation in the coin market. You paid $150,000 for your home three years ago. The real estate market in your area is now weak; Realtors appraise your home at $145,000. Imagine if real estate brochures listed a "bid" price rather than your "ask" price for the home. An interested buyer knows the market is weak and makes a lowball offer of $100,000 that appears in next week's real estate price sheet; it quickly becomes the market value basis on which all offers are made. Do you sell at that price or focus your sale presentation on the appraisal report? Hopefully, you do the latter.

Coin sellers in falling markets must recognize that exchange prices during these periods may be more a reflection of the market factors stated above rather than true value of the coins. Unless it is imperative that one sell coins during falling markets, it may be best to hold on to the coins until the market corrects itself. Also, it may be an excellent time to acquire coins at the lower *perceived* levels.

The Future of the "Sight-Unseen" Marketplace for Certified Coins

Rare coin liquidity is not a great deal better than it was prior to the establishment of electronic exchanges. And as more traders with more money continue to come onto the exchanges, liquidity will continue to improve.

The "sight-unseen" market will broaden, and more importantly, deepen. The coin market will continue to experience periods of price volatility, but the industry will continue to head in the right direction.

Industry leaders are developing plans to establish in the near future a coin exchange "clearinghouse" to process daily trades. Besides providing guaranteed cash settlements of trades, the clearinghouse will help ensure that exchange prices reflect the daily price levels at which coins trade; especially in rising markets.

Also, exchange price levels will be based on actual transaction prices reported to the clearinghouse and, thereby, the bid-oriented focus of the exchanges that has exacerbated the decline in prices during a falling market will be lessened.

An exciting coin market has arrived, and a great deal of credit must be given to the development of "sight-unseen" electronic trading exchanges.

***

Ronald A. Brandow

Ronald A. Brandow is the founder, president, and principal shareholder. For the past 25 years he has been a leader in the telecommunications industry. He pioneered the growth of intelligent networks with the growth of ATC in the terminal and switching business. Most recently Mr. Brandow has led ATC in network development. He has a B.S. in Electrical Engineering from the University of Illinois and an M.S. in Computer Science from Southern Methodist University.

Joseph H. Stephens, III

Joseph H. Stephens, III is Vice President of Finance. In addition to day-to-day financial responsibilities, he has been directly involved in the company's acquisitions. Mr. Stephens has several degrees, including a B. Mus. and an M.A. from Sam Houston State University and an MBA in finance and accounting from the University of Houston. Mr. Stephens is a CPA and came to ATC from Ernst and Whinney, where he specialized in tax matters with emphasis in real estate partnerships and construction.

CHAPTER 33

The Certified Coin Exchange

by Ronald A. Brandow and Joseph H. Stephens III

The Certified Coin Exchange (CCE) was formed in March, 1990 as a result of American Teleprocessing Corporation's strategy to provide tiered trading network services to various trading markets, in this case, the numismatic market.

ATC had acquired the FACTS Numismatic Trading Network from AutEx (a division of Xerox) in March of 1984. FACTS was a very valuable franchise that we acquired while we were seeking to acquire the Computer Dealer's Network, which used the same software and communications platform. FACTS had been in existence since 1962, and had gone through various technical metamorphoses and owners.

"FACTS" is an acronym meaning, to the best that we can determine, "Fox and Crabbe Teletype Service."

ATC invested over 1.5 million dollars in converting the communications platform from AT&T leased lines to the hybrid satellite/phone lines that are now in place. The investment was well worth it however, and by 1986, ATC operated a very economic and reliable communications network. We continued our technical enhancement by putting spot metal prices on the screen, and this became a key feature of our service.

We began providing network services to the individual members of the American Numismatic Exchange (ANE) in 1987, many of whom were already subscribers of FACTS, and we continued to do so until late June, 1990.

Contract difficulties began to occur with the ANE in the summer of 1989, and they continued to worsen until June, 1990, when we agreed to go our separate ways.

The early part of 1990 was an era of extremely high risk for ATC, where strategy and execution were critical to the profitability and market share we had enjoyed.

We had on our side the FACTS network, which included over 600 dealers of which about 150 were not concerned with certified sight unseen trading. Also, we had signed up about 120 of the ANE dealers to Charter membership in the CCE. Another strong point of ATC was out technical experience in communications and the existing communications platform that currently existed.

We began writing the trading rules on 3/12/90, starting with a blank page. After several pages were written, we consulted with dealers. We wrote more, we consulted more. Mike Byers, Bruce Amspacher, Paul Birkahn, Mark Yaffe, Ron Downing, Sil DiGenova, John Highfill, and many, many others contributed.

Principle contributors to the CCE's trading rules were Ron Downing, Sil DeGenova, Mark Yaffe, and Tom Noe, the founders of NUTREX. The concepts that they envisioned that all bids are firm, and that exchange data is recorded and verifiable, are the basis of the CCE trading rules.

The CCE realized that these were the members' rules, not our rules. The CCE would not be trading with these rules, but the members would. So, we built governing power into a committee system that would be turned over to the dealers in the form of a dealer-elected Board of Governors.

We had a meeting in the Central States Show in Milwaukee in early April, 1990 to unveil our concept and announce the beginning of live trading on April 16, 1990.

We wanted control over trading. It was not enough for us to take someone's word that a phone call deal had been made. We needed objective proof of the agreement. Also, we wanted to record all trades that occurred on the exchange, not just the ones that had a problem associated with them. We understood that using a trading system as a pricing system was just fine, but the pricing had to come out of trading, and all posted bids had to be firm: no exceptions.

We saw a bid as a contingent liability, not as a pricing mechanism. The software was designed to allow bidders to specify lot-size bid for, so the bidder has an actual known maximum liability.

We began by using a form, which contained the data that would form the basis for a trading summary. This would then be used to give the dealer statements of his activity. We would summarize the dealer's activity and put it on his printer at night, and publish a Last Trade Report, which was essentially the equivalent of an auction prices realized report.

We wanted to perform a true exchange service, but we stopped short of a true clearing service, and a true depository service, because we feel that at this time, that is not demanded by dealers or the retail public. When the demand from the dealers for this service is there, we will be there to fill it.

The reception to our presentation at the ANA show was skeptical at best, and we went back to Houston with a lot of work to do. We came up with excellent software, opened the exchange for live trading with the form software, and did trading testing during late April and early May. We knew that the solution to a major ANE problem, which we referred to as the "waiting period after transaction execution," was for the dealer to be able to post lot size bid or asked for, which would be decreased after transaction execution. The ATC programming staff developed excellent and thoroughly tested trading software which was implemented in the field on 5/22/90.

All that was required for the dealer to execute a trade was to go to the market page, press a sequence of function keys, and the trade would be executed by matching the trade parameters between the terminal and the mainframe. Each dealer was responsible for keeping his bids updated.

The first day of trading with the automated trading software, there were about 50 trades, and the next week, our volume held. Everyone who participated was very pleased with the results.

After the May 90 Long Beach, trading picked up considerably. We are able to disassociate ourselves from the ANE in mid June, and were able to devote our technical resources to our own network. We implemented the Last Trade Report in June, and it has become a much referred to tool by our dealers. Volume has been as high as 367 trades with dollar volume of $440,000 per day. Typical volume for the Fall of 90 period is 100 — 150 trades with dollar volume in excess of $100,000 per day.

As of this writing, there are over 140 Member firms posting over 20,000 bids and over 3,000 asks. Whenever a decision or a problem confronts us as operators of the exchange, we ask ourselves what the theory of fair markets would dictate.

We at ATC are very concerned with the current marketing tactics that some coin firms use to promote the sale of certified rare coins. To the extent that major investment firms choose to purchase certified coins, liquidity will be injected into the market, but to the extent that they choose to sell certified coins, liquidity will be removed from the market. It's a two way street. Just look at what the American Rare Coin Funds LP has done to the market. They are a source of supply, not a source of demand. They can remove liquidity as well as add it.

The talk of "Wall Street" was supposed to bring respectability to the rare coin market, but rare coins, properly graded and sold in a fair market need only the rarity and the beauty of the asset, and the checks and balances inherent in a fair market to convince knowledgeable buyers of the intrinsic value.

One recent book on investing in rare coins said that "Wall Street" has "leapt into the rare coin market." Wall Street firms are strictly interested in making money through fees, and a rare coin market that is in a steep decline is not a very saleable investment vehicle at this time.

ATC serves our customers, our dealers. To the extent that we can be a help to our dealers by helping the end user we will do so, and it we can publish our wholesale prices to end users on which the dealers can charge a markup, we will do so. We want to be able to encourage the buying public that coin information is available, and that they don't need to fear being triple charged for an MS-65RB Indian Cent. We are not the only source of numismatic pricing information. You all know the *Coin Dealer's Newsletter*, *Numismatic News*, *Coin World*, and of course the omnipresent Red Book, to mention a few.

But our pricing information is for dealers, and our trading service is for dealers. We have delivered to our dealers an efficient market for certified rare coins; the Certified Coin Exchange.

Appendix A

April 25, 1991

For Immediate Release

Certified Coin Exchange Completes First Year of Trading

April 24, 1991 marks the end of the first year of trading on the Certified Coin Exchange, a sight-unseen exchange for PCGS, NGC, and ANACS certified rare coins operated by American Teleprocessing Corporation, and carried by the FACTS Numismatic Trading System's communications network.

Despite its short history, the CCE has provided a consistent and reliable sight unseen trading opportunity for the CCE member firms and their customers Monday through Friday, from 12:00 ET to 5:00 throughout the year.

Trading volume began to increase on 5/22/90 (see graph) with the introduction of software that made it possible for bids and asks to be deleted upon a trade's execution. This gave real meaning to the term "all bids and asks are live" because the dealer's liability was limited to the bid/ask for quantity only.

Trading increased steadily throughout the summer, and heated up considerably after the Seattle ANA convention when a great deal of better material was sold to bidders. After another near panic sell-off during and after the October Long Beach show, the market began to recover and selling to bidders at their posted levels slowed, with activity moving to the ask side. Some days in November exhibited a greater number of trades on the ask side than the bid side. As the prices firmed, volume on the CCE slowed during the holiday season.

Beginning in late January, however, volume increased with selling mainly to bidders. This caused a decrease in the prevailing bid levels. Very high volume continued through March and April, with a record number of transactions being executed on 4/1/91.

The CCE is planning several changes for the coming year. The number of coins that can be traded will be expanded to include all U.S. coinage. The CCE Clearing Corporation will also be introduced shortly to increase dealer's posting of asks on high priced material. Also, CCE is considering moving to an ask based system for rare coins, to reduce the reliance on the bid in coin price negotiations.

We at the CCE are proud of the acceptance that the dealer community has extended to our concept of a live electronic trading system in its first year and we hope to be serving the dealer community and their customer base with trading services and pricing information for years to come.

For more information on the CCE and ATC numismatic trading services, or a referral to a CCE Member Firm in your area, please write the CCE at P.O. Box 19337, Houston, Texas 77224.

Joseph H. Stephens III
Executive Director

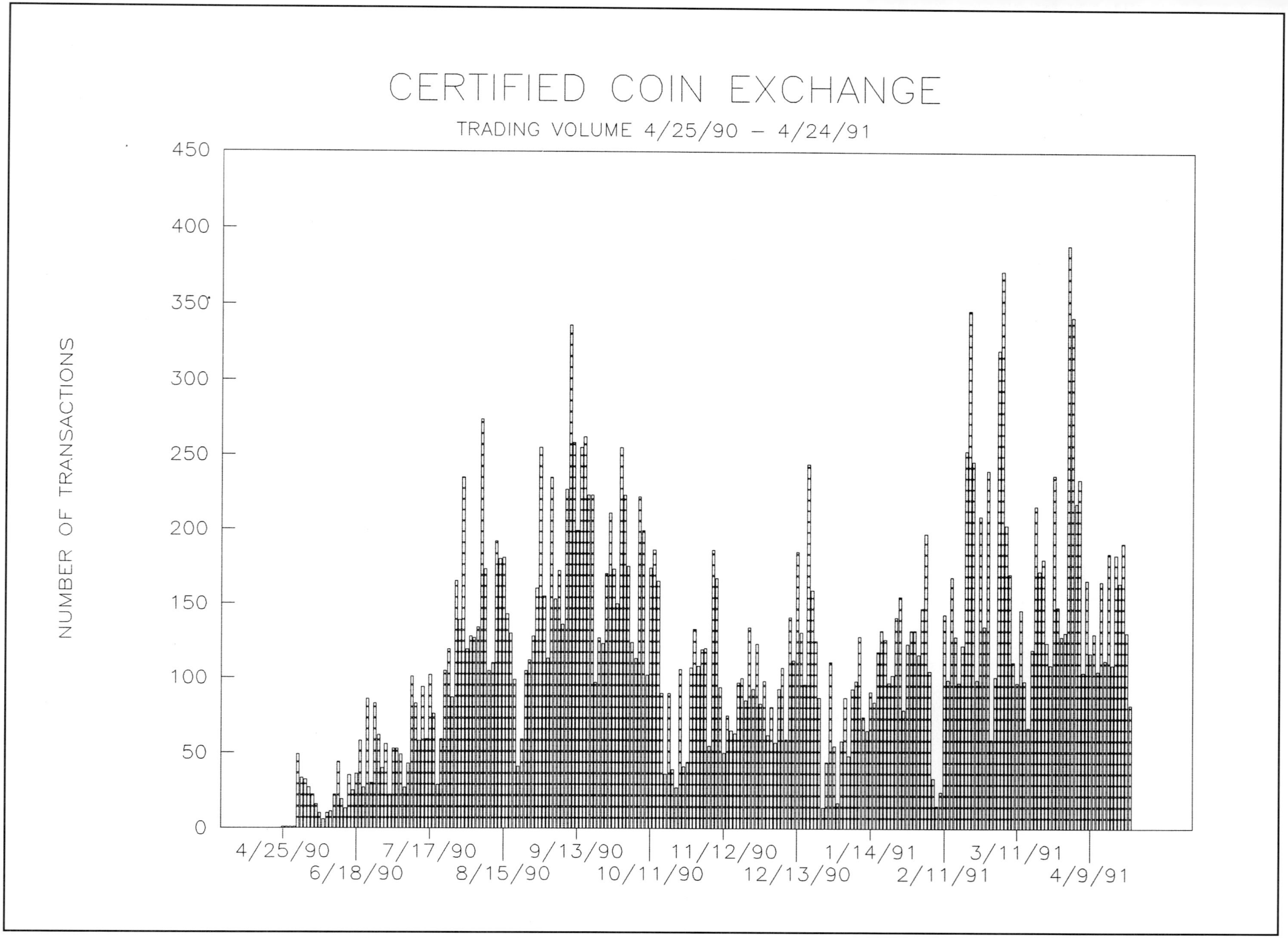

CERTIFIED COIN EXCHANGE

TRADING VOLUME 4/25/90 – 4/24/91

NUMBER OF TRANSACTIONS

Certified Coin Exchange Trading Volume (courtesy of the Certified Coin Exchange)

SIGHT-SEEN MARKET

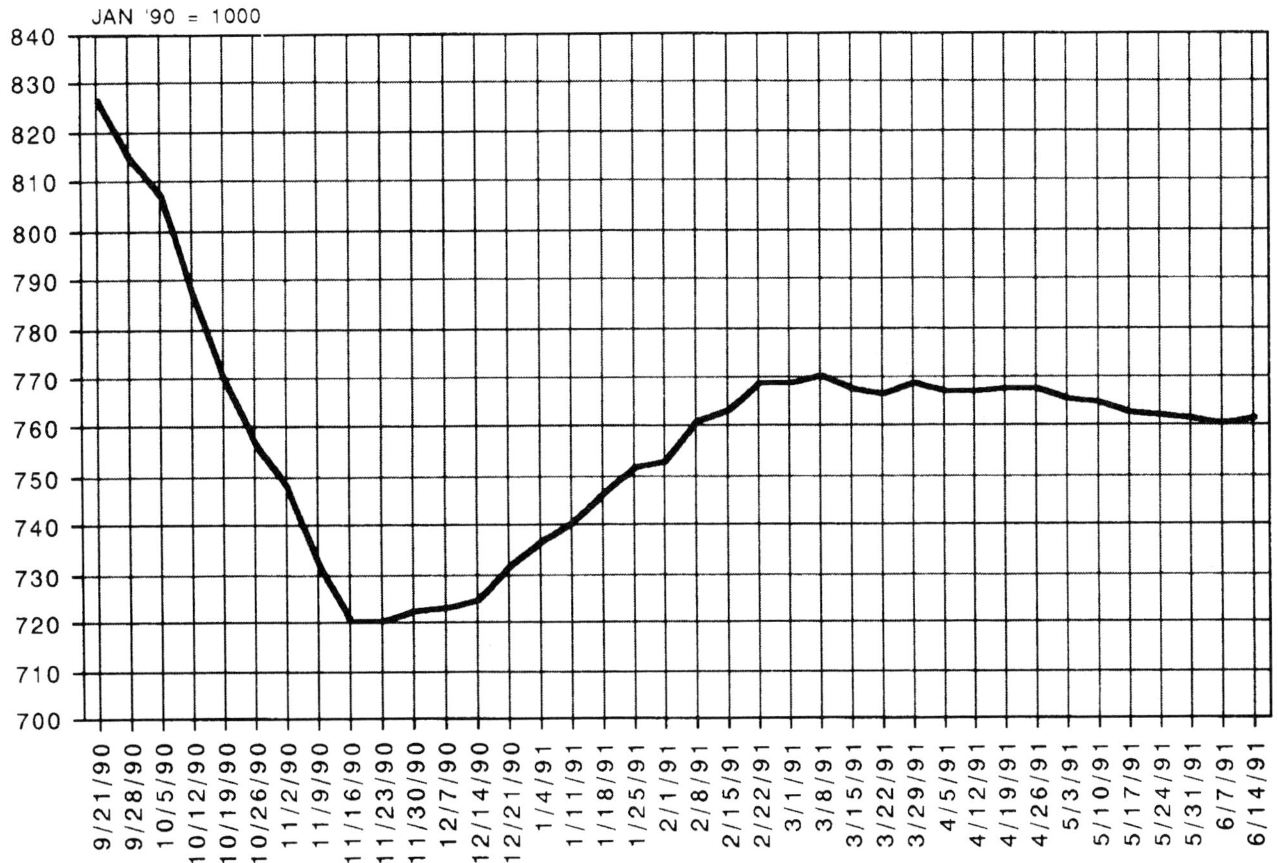

Graph courtesy of the Certified Coin Dealer Newsletter, Box 11099, Torrance, CA 90510

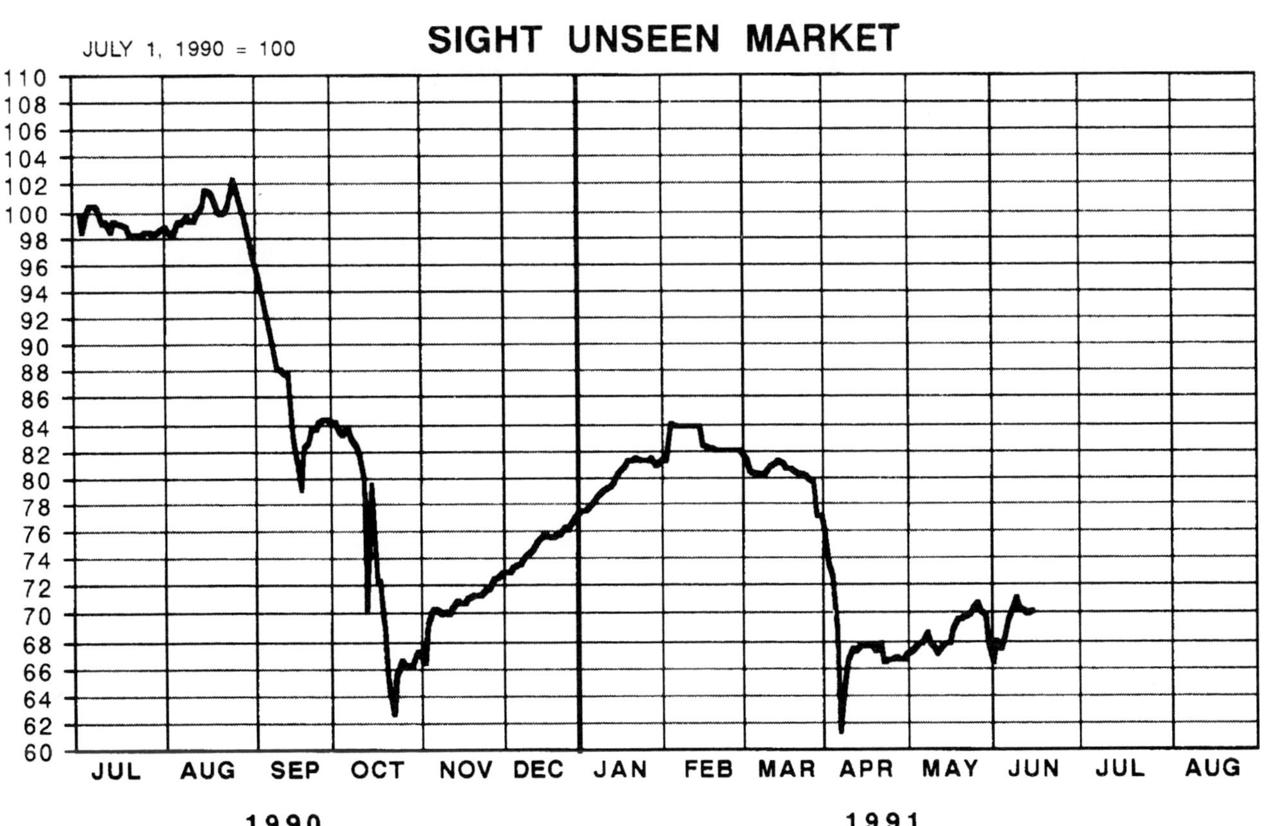

P.O. BOX 19337, Houston, Texas 77224-9337
(713) 465-9618, FAX (713) 973-8321
FACTS STATION I.D. Z11

Last Trade Report between 05/22/90 and 05/21/91

Last Prices for coins traded on CCE between 05/22/90 and 05/21/91

TRADING ACTIVITY ANALYSIS

GRADING SERVICE ASKS/BIDS/TOTALS		# OF TRADES	# OF COINS	$ VALUE	AVERAGE $/TRADE
PCGS	ASKS	2308	7034	3,835,809	1,662
PCGS	BIDS	24475	57334	25,770,368	1,053
TOTALS FOR PCGS		26783	64368	29,606,177	1,105
ANAC	ASKS	3	6	1,842	614
ANAC	BIDS	74	234	44,433	600
TOTALS FOR ANAC		77	240	46,275	601
NGC	ASKS	223	385	233,956	1,049
NGC	BIDS	3286	6171	3,123,907	951
TOTALS FOR NGC		3509	6556	3,357,863	957
TOTAL	ASKS	2534	7425	4,071,607	1,607
TOTAL	BIDS	27835	63739	28,938,708	1,040
TOTALS FOR CCE		30369	71164	33,010,315	1,087

CERTIFIED
COIN
EXCHANGE

P.O. BOX 19337, Houston, Texas 77224-9337
(713) 465-9618, FAX (713) 973-8321
FACTS STATION I.D. Z11

Last Trade Report between 05/22/90 and 05/21/91

Last Prices for coins traded on CCE between 05/22/90 and 05/21/91

COIN.GR	COIN DESCRIPTION		GRADING SERVICE	DATE OF TRADE	LAST PRICE $	LAST QTY	TOT QTY	B/A
07072.60	1878 - 8TF MORGAN		PCGS	11/21/90	30	1	1	B
07072.62	1878 - 8TF MORGAN		PCGS	05/20/91	44	1	4	B
07072.63	1878 - 8TF MORGAN		NGC	02/11/91	54	1	1	B
07072.63	1878 - 8TF MORGAN		PCGS	04/03/91	62	1	10	B
07072.64	1878 - 8TF MORGAN		NGC	08/07/90	275	1	1	B
07072.64	1878 - 8TF MORGAN		PCGS	02/19/91	246	1	23	B
07072.65	1878 - 8TF MORGAN		PCGS	02/11/91	1,620	1	2	B
07073.63	1878-8TF Morgan	PL	PCGS	03/06/91	140	1	1	B
07074.62	1878-7TF MORGAN Reverse of 1878		PCGS	04/30/91	26	1	2	B
07074.63	1878-7TF MORGAN Reverse of 1878		PCGS	05/15/91	70	2	81	B
07074.64	1878-7TF MORGAN Reverse of 1878		NGC	05/13/91	150	1	4	B
07074.64	1878-7TF MORGAN Reverse of 1878		PCGS	04/30/91	252	1	31	B
07074.65	1878-7TF MORGAN Reverse of 1878		PCGS	02/27/91	1,700	1	12	B
07075.64	1878-7TF Morgan Rev of 1878	PL	NGC	09/14/90	450	1	3	B
07076.63	1878-7TF MORGAN Reverse of 1879		PCGS	04/02/91	102	1	9	B
07076.64	1878-7TF MORGAN Reverse of 1879		PCGS	04/23/91	400	1	11	B
07076.65	1878-7TF MORGAN Reverse of 1879		PCGS	01/21/91	2,620	1	3	B
07078.60	1878-7/8TF MORGAN Strong Variety		PCGS	05/30/90	41	1	1	B
07078.61	1878-7/8TF MORGAN Strong Variety		PCGS	06/11/90	46	2	5	B
07078.62	1878-7/8TF MORGAN Strong Variety		PCGS	01/09/91	50	1	2	B
07078.63	1878-7/8TF MORGAN Strong Variety		NGC	03/12/91	80	1	1	B
07078.63	1878-7/8TF MORGAN Strong Variety		PCGS	09/26/90	85	3	7	B
07078.64	1878-7/8TF MORGAN Strong Variety		PCGS	03/08/91	356	1	11	A
07080.62	1878-CC MORGAN		PCGS	04/30/91	59	1	8	B
07080.63	1878-CC MORGAN		NGC	02/12/91	88	1	2	B
07080.63	1878-CC MORGAN		PCGS	05/08/91	87	4	35	B
07080.64	1878-CC MORGAN		NGC	02/20/91	260	1	6	B
07080.64	1878-CC MORGAN		PCGS	05/06/91	226	1	34	B
07080.65	1878-CC MORGAN		NGC	04/24/91	1,350	1	1	B
07080.65	1878-CC MORGAN		PCGS	05/02/91	1,510	1	12	B
07080.66	1878-CC MORGAN		PCGS	02/19/91	4,800	1	2	A
07081.64	1878-CC Morgan	PL	PCGS	08/14/90	440	1	1	B
07082.61	1878-S MORGAN		PCGS	04/30/91	21	1	2	B
07082.62	1878-S MORGAN		PCGS	05/06/91	24	5	31	B
07082.63	1878-S MORGAN		PCGS	05/07/91	25	1	178	B
07082.64	1878-S MORGAN		NGC	04/02/91	55	3	6	B
07082.64	1878-S MORGAN		PCGS	05/13/91	56	2	117	B
07082.65	1878-S MORGAN		NGC	04/02/91	230	4	12	B
07082.65	1878-S MORGAN		PCGS	05/06/91	190	1	42	B
07082.66	1878-S MORGAN		PCGS	04/04/91	1,010	1	8	B
07082.67	1878-S MORGAN		PCGS	01/17/91	8,500	1	1	A
07083.63	1878-S Morgan	PL	NGC	03/12/91	55	1	1	B
07083.64	1878-S Morgan	PL	NGC	09/12/90	120	1	1	B
07083.64	1878-S Morgan	PL	PCGS	01/24/91	100	1	2	B

07083.65	1878-S	Morgan	PL	PCGS	09/12/90	800	1	3	B
07084.62	1879	MORGAN		PCGS	04/12/91	21	2	3	B
07084.63	1879	MORGAN		NGC	03/07/91	28	1	1	B
07084.63	1879	MORGAN		PCGS	05/08/91	36	1	40	B
07084.64	1879	MORGAN		NGC	02/20/91	170	1	5	B
07084.64	1879	MORGAN		PCGS	05/17/91	132	1	69	B
07084.65	1879	MORGAN		NGC	06/19/90	1,975	1	1	B
07084.65	1879	MORGAN		PCGS	04/19/91	1,060	1	8	B
07085.63	1879	Morgan	PL	PCGS	08/16/90	86	1	1	B
07086.61	1879-CC	MORGAN		PCGS	08/22/90	1,120	1	1	B
07086.62	1879-CC	MORGAN		PCGS	05/06/91	1,270	1	6	B
07086.63	1879-CC	MORGAN		PCGS	04/22/91	1,910	1	6	B
07086.64	1879-CC	MORGAN		PCGS	02/22/91	3,000	1	2	B
07088.60	1879-CC	MORGAN Cap Die		PCGS	04/08/91	805	1	1	B
07088.61	1879-CC	MORGAN Cap Die		PCGS	01/18/91	890	1	1	B
07088.63	1879-CC	MORGAN Cap Die		PCGS	04/26/91	1,580	1	5	A
07088.64	1879-CC	MORGAN Cap Die		PCGS	02/08/91	3,900	1	1	B
07090.60	1879-O	MORGAN		PCGS	04/19/91	25	3	3	B
07090.61	1879-O	MORGAN		PCGS	04/19/91	36	4	9	B
07090.62	1879-O	MORGAN		PCGS	04/19/91	85	1	12	B
07090.63	1879-O	MORGAN		PCGS	05/08/91	208	1	12	B
07090.64	1879-O	MORGAN		PCGS	04/26/91	615	1	10	B
07090.65	1879-O	MORGAN		PCGS	09/28/90	3,325	1	4	B
07090.66	1879-O	MORGAN		PCGS	01/17/91	13,500	1	1	A
07092.63	1879-S	MORGAN		PCGS	04/30/91	24	1	4	B
07092.64	1879-S	MORGAN		PCGS	04/12/91	44	3	19	B
07092.65	1879-S	MORGAN		PCGS	02/21/91	130	2	3	B
07092.66	1879-S	MORGAN		PCGS	04/17/91	334	1	3	B
07093.63	1879-S	Morgan	PL	PCGS	02/14/91	78	1	1	B
07093.64	1879-S	Morgan	PL	PCGS	01/25/91	77	1	2	B
07093.65	1879-S	Morgan	PL	PCGS	07/11/90	450	1	1	B
07093.66	1879-S	Morgan	PL	NGC	10/12/90	600	1	1	B
07093.66	1879-S	Morgan	PL	PCGS	09/05/90	700	1	2	B
07093.67	1879-S	Morgan	PL	PCGS	09/25/90	1,650	1	2	A
07094.60	1879-S	MORGAN Reverse of 1878		PCGS	05/02/91	75	1	4	B
07094.61	1879-S	MORGAN Reverse of 1878		PCGS	05/02/91	85	1	10	B
07094.62	1879-S	MORGAN Reverse of 1878		NGC	12/06/90	47	1	1	B
07094.62	1879-S	MORGAN Reverse of 1878		PCGS	03/08/91	130	1	3	A
07094.63	1879-S	MORGAN Reverse of 1878		PCGS	03/04/91	262	1	4	B
07094.64	1879-S	MORGAN Reverse of 1878		PCGS	09/14/90	910	1	1	B
07094.65	1879-S	MORGAN Reverse of 1878		PCGS	10/11/90	7,000	1	3	B
07095.63	1879-S	Morgan Rev of 1878	PL	PCGS	02/01/91	550	1	1	B
07096.63	1880	MORGAN		PCGS	04/22/91	32	1	60	B
07096.64	1880	MORGAN		NGC	04/29/91	110	1	4	B
07096.64	1880	MORGAN		PCGS	05/14/91	110	1	30	B
07096.65	1880	MORGAN		NGC	06/11/90	2,075	1	1	B
07096.65	1880	MORGAN		PCGS	03/04/91	1,750	1	16	B
07100.61	1880-CC	MORGAN		PCGS	10/09/90	106	1	1	B
07100.62	1880-CC	MORGAN		PCGS	05/09/91	106	2	21	B
07100.63	1880-CC	MORGAN		NGC	04/04/91	72	1	1	B
07100.63	1880-CC	MORGAN		PCGS	05/06/91	120	1	23	B
07100.64	1880-CC	MORGAN		NGC	03/19/91	250	1	4	A
07100.64	1880-CC	MORGAN		PCGS	05/14/91	182	1	21	B
07100.65	1880-CC	MORGAN		PCGS	05/03/91	760	1	35	B

07100.66	1880-CC	MORGAN			NGC	09/05/90	5,500	1	1	B
07100.66	1880-CC	MORGAN			PCGS	05/03/91	3,160	1	6	B
07100.67	1880-CC	MORGAN			PCGS	03/15/91	11,900	1	1	A
07101.63	1880-CC	Morgan		PL	PCGS	04/25/91	210	2	3	B
07101.65	1880-CC	Morgan		PL	NGC	05/13/91	1,000	1	1	B
07101.65	1880-CC	Morgan		PL	PCGS	09/19/90	1,650	1	2	B
07108.63	1880-CC	MORGAN	Reverse of 1878		PCGS	02/21/91	180	1	3	B
07108.64	1880-CC	MORGAN	Reverse of 1878		NGC	09/05/90	335	1	1	B
07108.64	1880-CC	MORGAN	Reverse of 1878		PCGS	05/03/91	450	1	6	B
07108.65	1880-CC	MORGAN	Reverse of 1878		PCGS	05/08/91	1,420	1	6	B
07108.66	1880-CC	MORGAN	Reverse of 1878		PCGS	11/30/90	4,760	1	1	A
07114.58	1880-O	MORGAN			PCGS	09/17/90	15	1	1	B
07114.60	1880-O	MORGAN			PCGS	11/26/90	28	3	3	B
07114.63	1880-O	MORGAN			ANAC	03/13/91	276	1	1	B
07114.63	1880-O	MORGAN			NGC	09/04/90	200	2	2	B
07114.63	1880-O	MORGAN			PCGS	02/25/91	330	1	11	B
07114.64	1880-O	MORGAN			PCGS	04/02/91	1,050	1	7	B
07115.62	1880-O	Morgan		PL	PCGS	07/26/90	125	1	1	B
07118.64	1880-S	MORGAN			PCGS	04/24/91	44	1	5	B
07118.65	1880-S	MORGAN			NGC	04/29/91	120	3	3	B
07118.66	1880-S	MORGAN			NGC	05/08/91	350	1	3	B
07118.66	1880-S	MORGAN			PCGS	04/17/91	330	1	3	B
07118.67	1880-S	MORGAN			PCGS	05/14/91	1,130	1	1	B
07119.64	1880-S	Morgan		PL	PCGS	11/21/90	70	2	8	B
07124.62	1881	MORGAN			PCGS	07/11/90	24	1	1	B
07124.63	1881	MORGAN			PCGS	05/17/91	29	1	26	B
07124.64	1881	MORGAN			NGC	04/29/91	126	1	3	B
07124.64	1881	MORGAN			PCGS	05/20/91	124	1	21	B
07124.65	1881	MORGAN			PCGS	05/07/91	1,650	1	6	B
07126.62	1881-CC	MORGAN			PCGS	04/30/91	116	1	2	B
07126.63	1881-CC	MORGAN			PCGS	05/20/91	128	1	13	B
07126.64	1881-CC	MORGAN			PCGS	05/14/91	206	1	45	B
07126.65	1881-CC	MORGAN			PCGS	05/08/91	478	1	64	B
07126.66	1881-CC	MORGAN			NGC	03/13/91	1,300	1	2	B
07126.66	1881-CC	MORGAN			PCGS	05/16/91	1,050	1	27	B
07126.67	1881-CC	MORGAN			PCGS	05/07/91	7,000	1	3	A
07127.63	1881-CC	Morgan		PL	PCGS	09/12/90	200	1	1	B
07127.64	1881-CC	Morgan		PL	NGC	08/07/90	420	1	1	B
07127.65	1881-CC	Morgan		PL	PCGS	09/14/90	1,000	1	3	B
07127.66	1881-CC	Morgan		PL	PCGS	09/26/90	2,600	1	1	A
07128.63	1881-O	MORGAN			NGC	02/11/91	37	1	1	B
07128.63	1881-O	MORGAN			PCGS	03/13/91	55	1	29	B
07128.64	1881-O	MORGAN			NGC	01/23/91	180	1	1	A
07128.64	1881-O	MORGAN			PCGS	05/20/91	140	1	20	B
07128.65	1881-O	MORGAN			NGC	04/15/91	1,500	1	2	B
07128.65	1881-O	MORGAN			PCGS	05/17/91	2,080	1	12	B
07130.64	1881-S	MORGAN			PCGS	03/25/91	44	4	8	B
07130.65	1881-S	MORGAN			NGC	04/29/91	120	3	3	B
07130.65	1881-S	MORGAN			PCGS	02/22/91	126	1	1	B
07130.66	1881-S	MORGAN			NGC	04/29/91	346	1	1	B
07130.66	1881-S	MORGAN			PCGS	02/14/91	426	1	2	A
07130.67	1881-S	MORGAN			PCGS	07/25/90	2,000	1	1	B
07132.61	1882	MORGAN			PCGS	08/08/90	22	1	1	B
07132.62	1882	MORGAN			NGC	09/11/90	18	1	1	B

07132.63	1882	MORGAN		NGC	09/11/90	25	1	1	B
07132.63	1882	MORGAN		PCGS	05/02/91	27	3	27	B
07132.64	1882	MORGAN		NGC	03/22/91	92	1	4	B
07132.64	1882	MORGAN		PCGS	05/13/91	76	1	62	B
07132.65	1882	MORGAN		NGC	03/05/91	500	1	3	B
07132.65	1882	MORGAN		PCGS	05/15/91	500	1	24	B
07134.61	1882-CC	MORGAN		PCGS	05/09/91	45	1	1	B
07134.62	1882-CC	MORGAN		PCGS	05/09/91	48	4	6	B
07134.63	1882-CC	MORGAN		NGC	11/27/90	57	1	2	B
07134.63	1882-CC	MORGAN		PCGS	05/17/91	63	1	42	B
07134.64	1882-CC	MORGAN		NGC	03/01/91	112	2	5	B
07134.64	1882-CC	MORGAN		PCGS	05/13/91	96	1	82	B
07134.65	1882-CC	MORGAN		NGC	02/15/91	410	1	3	B
07134.65	1882-CC	MORGAN		PCGS	05/20/91	300	1	99	B
07134.66	1882-CC	MORGAN		NGC	02/19/91	1,500	1	3	B
07134.66	1882-CC	MORGAN		PCGS	05/16/91	1,400	1	17	B
07134.67	1882-CC	MORGAN		PCGS	03/15/91	9,000	1	1	A
07135.63	1882-CC	Morgan	PL	NGC	01/24/91	65	1	1	B
07135.64	1882-CC	Morgan	PL	PCGS	05/14/91	134	1	2	B
07135.65	1882-CC	Morgan	PL	PCGS	09/12/90	625	2	3	B
07136.62	1882-O	MORGAN		PCGS	04/30/91	19	1	21	B
07136.63	1882-O	MORGAN		PCGS	04/30/91	24	3	47	B
07136.64	1882-O	MORGAN		PCGS	05/21/91	110	7	49	A
07136.65	1882-O	MORGAN		PCGS	04/01/91	1,780	1	15	B
07136.66	1882-O	MORGAN		PCGS	03/14/91	8,300	1	2	B
07140.63	1882-S	MORGAN		PCGS	04/30/91	24	6	6	B
07140.64	1882-S	MORGAN		PCGS	04/05/91	45	3	8	B
07140.65	1882-S	MORGAN		PCGS	05/06/91	112	1	3	B
07140.66	1882-S	MORGAN		PCGS	04/03/91	354	1	8	B
07140.67	1882-S	MORGAN		PCGS	10/31/90	1,110	1	2	B
07141.64	1882-S	Morgan	PL	NGC	03/12/91	85	1	1	B
07141.64	1882-S	Morgan	PL	PCGS	05/16/91	71	1	2	B
07141.65	1882-S	Morgan	PL	NGC	09/05/90	425	1	2	B
07141.65	1882-S	Morgan	PL	PCGS	03/05/91	250	1	7	B
07141.66	1882-S	Morgan	PL	NGC	07/10/90	1,200	1	1	B
07141.66	1882-S	Morgan	PL	PCGS	01/28/91	685	1	2	A
07142.64	1883	MORGAN		ANAC	03/19/91	34	1	1	B
07142.64	1883	MORGAN		PCGS	04/02/91	45	2	22	B
07142.65	1883	MORGAN		NGC	04/02/91	166	2	5	B
07142.65	1883	MORGAN		PCGS	05/21/91	130	1	137	B
07142.66	1883	MORGAN		PCGS	05/20/91	560	1	27	B
07142.67	1883	MORGAN		PCGS	04/01/91	4,100	1	1	A
07143.64	1883	Morgan	PL	NGC	09/12/90	150	1	1	B
07143.64	1883	Morgan	PL	PCGS	02/20/91	164	1	1	B
07144.61	1883-CC	MORGAN		PCGS	05/09/91	44	1	1	B
07144.62	1883-CC	MORGAN		PCGS	05/09/91	46	4	9	B
07144.63	1883-CC	MORGAN		NGC	04/22/91	67	3	4	B
07144.63	1883-CC	MORGAN		PCGS	05/09/91	66	3	91	B
07144.64	1883-CC	MORGAN		NGC	04/22/91	95	2	8	B
07144.64	1883-CC	MORGAN		PCGS	05/21/91	94	1	139	B
07144.65	1883-CC	MORGAN		NGC	05/03/91	250	1	10	B
07144.65	1883-CC	MORGAN		PCGS	05/20/91	202	1	131	B
07144.66	1883-CC	MORGAN		NGC	04/16/91	1,100	1	2	B
07144.66	1883-CC	MORGAN		PCGS	05/10/91	960	1	35	B

07145.62	1883-CC	Morgan	PL	PCGS	08/07/90	60	1	1	B
07145.63	1883-CC	Morgan	PL	PCGS	03/18/91	70	1	2	B
07145.64	1883-CC	Morgan	PL	PCGS	04/01/91	130	1	2	B
07145.65	1883-CC	Morgan	PL	NGC	11/12/90	450	1	1	B
07145.65	1883-CC	Morgan	PL	PCGS	04/04/91	432	1	13	A
07145.66	1883-CC	Morgan	PL	PCGS	02/19/91	2,150	1	3	A
07146.64	1883-O	MORGAN		PCGS	04/02/91	44	1	2	B
07146.65	1883-O	MORGAN		NGC	05/14/91	126	1	6	B
07146.65	1883-O	MORGAN		PCGS	05/06/91	126	1	44	B
07146.66	1883-O	MORGAN		NGC	04/16/91	850	1	1	B
07146.66	1883-O	MORGAN		PCGS	05/13/91	910	1	9	B
07147.65	1883-O	Morgan	PL	PCGS	11/09/90	450	1	2	B
07147.66	1883-O	Morgan	PL	PCGS	09/26/90	2,000	1	1	A
07148.60	1883-S	MORGAN		PCGS	08/16/90	250	1	1	B
07148.62	1883-S	MORGAN		PCGS	05/08/91	420	1	2	B
07148.63	1883-S	MORGAN		PCGS	11/09/90	625	1	2	B
07148.64	1883-S	MORGAN		PCGS	05/06/91	3,300	1	6	B
07150.63	1884	MORGAN		PCGS	02/21/91	30	1	6	B
07150.64	1884	MORGAN		NGC	03/11/91	45	1	4	B
07150.64	1884	MORGAN		PCGS	05/13/91	42	1	37	B
07150.65	1884	MORGAN		NGC	03/15/91	294	1	2	B
07150.65	1884	MORGAN		PCGS	05/13/91	286	1	61	B
07150.66	1884	MORGAN		PCGS	02/27/91	1,450	1	4	B
07151.65	1884	Morgan	PL	PCGS	09/19/90	1,400	1	1	B
07152.60	1884-CC	MORGAN		PCGS	05/09/91	43	1	1	B
07152.61	1884-CC	MORGAN		PCGS	05/09/91	44	1	3	B
07152.62	1884-CC	MORGAN		PCGS	05/09/91	46	6	14	B
07152.63	1884-CC	MORGAN		NGC	05/09/91	58	2	6	B
07152.63	1884-CC	MORGAN		PCGS	05/17/91	63	1	65	B
07152.64	1884-CC	MORGAN		NGC	04/22/91	106	3	7	B
07152.64	1884-CC	MORGAN		PCGS	05/21/91	94	2	135	B
07152.65	1884-CC	MORGAN		NGC	05/17/91	270	1	5	B
07152.65	1884-CC	MORGAN		PCGS	05/17/91	210	2	120	B
07152.66	1884-CC	MORGAN		PCGS	04/25/91	1,130	1	26	B
07152.67	1884-CC	MORGAN		PCGS	04/03/91	17,000	1	1	A
07153.63	1884-CC	Morgan	PL	PCGS	04/04/91	68	1	1	B
07153.64	1884-CC	Morgan	PL	PCGS	05/08/91	134	1	6	B
07153.65	1884-CC	Morgan	PL	PCGS	03/18/91	400	1	10	B
07154.64	1884-O	MORGAN		NGC	03/26/91	42	1	1	B
07154.65	1884-O	MORGAN		NGC	05/20/91	126	1	6	B
07154.65	1884-O	MORGAN		PCGS	02/14/91	138	1	4	A
07154.66	1884-O	MORGAN		PCGS	04/01/91	710	1	34	B
07155.65	1884-O	Morgan	PL	PCGS	11/09/90	390	1	2	B
07156.58	1884-S	MORGAN		PCGS	08/17/90	675	1	1	B
07156.63	1884-S	MORGAN		PCGS	09/26/90	15,250	1	1	B
07158.65	1885	MORGAN		NGC	04/29/91	126	3	3	B
07158.65	1885	MORGAN		PCGS	04/17/91	120	1	29	B
07158.66	1885	MORGAN		NGC	02/19/91	575	1	2	B
07158.66	1885	MORGAN		PCGS	05/14/91	460	3	26	B
07159.64	1885	Morgan	PL	PCGS	09/12/90	75	1	1	B
07159.65	1885	Morgan	PL	PCGS	04/02/91	402	1	2	B
07160.61	1885-CC	MORGAN		PCGS	03/15/91	160	1	1	B
07160.62	1885-CC	MORGAN		PCGS	05/17/91	180	1	15	B
07160.63	1885-CC	MORGAN		NGC	06/21/90	211	1	1	B

07160.63	1885-CC	MORGAN		PCGS	05/10/91	190	3	53	B
07160.64	1885-CC	MORGAN		NGC	01/23/91	230	1	2	A
07160.64	1885-CC	MORGAN		PCGS	05/20/91	234	1	49	B
07160.65	1885-CC	MORGAN		NGC	04/02/91	665	1	5	B
07160.65	1885-CC	MORGAN		PCGS	05/06/91	635	1	59	B
07160.66	1885-CC	MORGAN		PCGS	05/13/91	1,550	1	20	B
07160.67	1885-CC	MORGAN		PCGS	03/15/91	7,500	1	1	A
07161.63	1885-CC	Morgan	PL	ANAC	04/26/91	186	1	1	B
07161.64	1885-CC	Morgan	PL	PCGS	08/16/90	390	1	1	B
07161.65	1885-CC	Morgan	PL	PCGS	05/08/91	950	1	6	B
07161.66	1885-CC	Morgan	PL	PCGS	07/30/90	7,500	1	1	B
07162.65	1885-O	MORGAN		PCGS	12/17/90	156	1	1	A
07162.66	1885-O	MORGAN		NGC	04/25/91	440	1	1	B
07162.66	1885-O	MORGAN		PCGS	05/20/91	352	1	61	B
07162.67	1885-O	MORGAN		PCGS	02/22/91	3,460	1	4	B
07163.64	1885-O	Morgan	PL	PCGS	08/08/90	100	1	2	B
07163.65	1885-O	Morgan	PL	PCGS	11/08/90	390	1	3	B
07164.61	1885-S	MORGAN		PCGS	03/18/91	52	1	1	B
07164.62	1885-S	MORGAN		PCGS	09/27/90	60	1	6	B
07164.63	1885-S	MORGAN		PCGS	05/17/91	190	1	24	A
07164.64	1885-S	MORGAN		NGC	03/26/91	310	1	1	B
07164.64	1885-S	MORGAN		PCGS	05/03/91	396	1	7	B
07164.65	1885-S	MORGAN		NGC	04/10/91	1,300	1	3	B
07164.65	1885-S	MORGAN		PCGS	02/14/91	2,300	1	5	A
07164.66	1885-S	MORGAN		PCGS	03/27/91	6,450	1	1	B
07165.63	1885-S	Morgan	PL	PCGS	04/02/91	190	1	1	B
07165.64	1885-S	Morgan	PL	NGC	08/06/90	850	1	1	B
07166.64	1886	MORGAN		PCGS	04/24/91	43	1	1	B
07166.65	1886	MORGAN		NGC	04/29/91	120	2	3	B
07166.66	1886	MORGAN		NGC	03/26/91	466	1	4	B
07166.66	1886	MORGAN		PCGS	05/14/91	380	1	43	B
07166.67	1886	MORGAN		PCGS	10/12/90	1,850	1	1	B
07167.64	1886	Morgan	PL	PCGS	10/02/90	80	1	1	B
07167.65	1886	Morgan	PL	NGC	04/11/91	400	1	1	B
07167.65	1886	Morgan	PL	PCGS	08/31/90	700	1	2	B
07168.60	1886-O	MORGAN		PCGS	05/17/91	198	1	12	B
07168.61	1886-O	MORGAN		PCGS	05/16/91	252	1	14	B
07168.62	1886-O	MORGAN		PCGS	05/08/91	446	1	6	B
07168.63	1886-O	MORGAN		PCGS	05/06/91	1,190	1	6	B
07168.64	1886-O	MORGAN		PCGS	11/26/90	4,760	1	1	A
07170.62	1886-S	MORGAN		PCGS	01/29/91	106	1	1	B
07170.63	1886-S	MORGAN		NGC	03/25/91	190	1	1	B
07170.63	1886-S	MORGAN		PCGS	04/22/91	240	1	5	A
07170.64	1886-S	MORGAN		NGC	02/13/91	575	1	1	B
07170.64	1886-S	MORGAN		PCGS	05/03/91	580	1	10	B
07170.65	1886-S	MORGAN		NGC	02/26/91	2,100	1	1	B
07170.65	1886-S	MORGAN		PCGS	04/11/91	2,150	1	4	A
07171.64	1886-S	Morgan	PL	NGC	08/03/90	950	1	1	B
07171.64	1886-S	Morgan	PL	PCGS	06/20/90	850	1	1	B
07172.64	1887	MORGAN		PCGS	04/30/91	43	1	1	B
07172.65	1887	MORGAN		NGC	02/25/91	130	1	1	B
07172.65	1887	MORGAN		PCGS	12/21/90	132	1	2	B
07172.66	1887	MORGAN		NGC	05/13/91	500	1	3	B
07172.66	1887	MORGAN		PCGS	05/16/91	580	1	12	B

07172.67	1887	MORGAN		PCGS	11/28/90	6,000	1	1	B
07173.64	1887	Morgan	PL	PCGS	08/06/90	110	1	2	B
07173.65	1887	Morgan	PL	PCGS	05/13/91	270	1	11	B
07173.66	1887	Morgan	PL	PCGS	04/11/91	2,450	1	4	B
07174.62	1887/6	MORGAN		PCGS	05/15/91	500	1	15	B
07174.63	1887/6	MORGAN		PCGS	05/17/91	1,200	1	10	B
07174.64	1887/6	MORGAN		PCGS	05/21/91	1,350	1	7	B
07176.61	1887-0	MORGAN		PCGS	04/10/91	22	5	6	B
07176.62	1887-0	MORGAN		PCGS	04/11/91	37	7	11	B
07176.63	1887-0	MORGAN		NGC	11/19/90	48	1	1	B
07176.63	1887-0	MORGAN		PCGS	05/21/91	130	1	21	B
07176.64	1887-0	MORGAN		NGC	02/21/91	675	1	7	B
07176.64	1887-0	MORGAN		PCGS	03/07/91	700	1	19	B
07176.65	1887-0	MORGAN		PCGS	08/20/90	8,650	1	1	B
07178.62	1887/6-0	MORGAN		PCGS	03/05/91	400	1	1	B
07178.63	1887/6-0	MORGAN		PCGS	10/29/90	1,030	1	3	B
07180.63	1887-S	MORGAN		PCGS	05/06/91	196	1	13	B
07180.64	1887-S	MORGAN		PCGS	04/22/91	605	1	7	B
07180.65	1887-S	MORGAN		PCGS	04/19/91	3,700	1	11	B
07182.63	1888	MORGAN		PCGS	10/29/90	26	1	1	B
07182.64	1888	MORGAN		NGC	04/04/91	42	1	2	B
07182.64	1888	MORGAN		PCGS	04/12/91	45	1	36	B
07182.65	1888	MORGAN		PCGS	05/14/91	200	2	88	B
07182.66	1888	MORGAN		PCGS	05/08/91	1,510	1	6	B
07183.65	1888	Morgan	PL	PCGS	08/15/90	1,925	1	1	B
07184.63	1888-0	MORGAN		PCGS	05/08/91	33	1	34	B
07184.64	1888-0	MORGAN		NGC	03/01/91	100	1	2	B
07184.64	1888-0	MORGAN		PCGS	05/13/91	75	1	95	B
07184.65	1888-0	MORGAN		NGC	02/19/91	850	1	6	B
07184.65	1888-0	MORGAN		PCGS	05/16/91	850	1	22	A
07185.63	1888-0	Morgan	PL	PCGS	08/01/90	61	1	1	B
07185.65	1888-0	Morgan	PL	PCGS	09/17/90	1,425	1	1	B
07186.60	1888-S	MORGAN		PCGS	11/29/90	65	2	2	B
07186.62	1888-S	MORGAN		PCGS	03/05/91	96	1	2	B
07186.63	1888-S	MORGAN		PCGS	05/16/91	226	1	3	A
07186.64	1888-S	MORGAN		PCGS	04/22/91	585	1	9	B
07186.65	1888-S	MORGAN		PCGS	04/26/91	3,520	1	5	B
07187.63	1888-S	Morgan	PL	ANAC	03/15/91	300	1	1	B
07188.62	1889	MORGAN		PCGS	08/14/90	19	1	1	B
07188.63	1889	MORGAN		PCGS	03/05/91	25	1	2	B
07188.64	1889	MORGAN		NGC	02/20/91	45	1	3	B
07188.64	1889	MORGAN		PCGS	05/02/91	50	1	19	B
07188.65	1889	MORGAN		NGC	04/09/91	500	1	2	B
07188.65	1889	MORGAN		PCGS	05/15/91	630	2	29	B
07188.66	1889	MORGAN		NGC	05/07/91	2,600	1	1	B
07188.66	1889	MORGAN		PCGS	03/01/91	3,500	1	4	B
07190.58	1889-CC	MORGAN		PCGS	02/01/91	2,500	1	1	A
07192.62	1889-0	MORGAN		PCGS	08/30/90	60	4	4	B
07192.63	1889-0	MORGAN		NGC	02/05/91	126	1	2	B
07192.63	1889-0	MORGAN		PCGS	04/26/91	186	1	8	B
07192.64	1889-0	MORGAN		PCGS	01/16/91	550	1	9	A
07192.65	1889-0	MORGAN		PCGS	12/19/90	4,000	1	4	A
07192.66	1889-0	MORGAN		PCGS	12/03/90	11,000	1	1	A
07194.63	1889-S	MORGAN		PCGS	05/21/91	176	1	6	A

07194.64	1889-S	MORGAN		NGC	05/14/91	326	1	1	B
07194.64	1889-S	MORGAN		PCGS	05/03/91	386	1	8	B
07194.65	1889-S	MORGAN		PCGS	05/17/91	1,630	1	12	B
07194.66	1889-S	MORGAN		PCGS	09/12/90	8,250	1	1	B
07196.62	1890	MORGAN		PCGS	04/29/91	21	1	3	B
07196.63	1890	MORGAN		PCGS	04/29/91	40	5	63	B
07196.64	1890	MORGAN		NGC	05/16/91	216	1	4	B
07196.64	1890	MORGAN		PCGS	05/03/91	242	1	19	B
07196.65	1890	MORGAN		PCGS	04/19/91	3,860	1	7	B
07198.62	1890-CC	MORGAN		PCGS	05/20/91	176	1	5	B
07198.63	1890-CC	MORGAN		PCGS	09/06/90	300	1	2	B
07198.64	1890-CC	MORGAN		PCGS	05/14/91	860	1	4	B
07198.65	1890-CC	MORGAN		NGC	02/28/91	3,960	1	1	B
07198.65	1890-CC	MORGAN		PCGS	07/23/90	5,250	1	2	B
07198.66	1890-CC	MORGAN		PCGS	04/03/91	24,000	1	1	A
07199.62	1890-CC	Morgan	PL	PCGS	12/12/90	218	1	2	B
07199.64	1890-CC	Morgan	PL	NGC	09/12/90	1,300	1	1	B
07200.62	1890-O	MORGAN		PCGS	03/18/91	40	1	2	B
07200.63	1890-O	MORGAN		NGC	01/28/91	95	1	2	B
07200.63	1890-O	MORGAN		PCGS	04/24/91	85	1	16	B
07200.64	1890-O	MORGAN		NGC	05/13/91	160	1	3	B
07200.64	1890-O	MORGAN		PCGS	05/14/91	110	1	12	B
07200.65	1890-O	MORGAN		PCGS	09/11/90	3,200	1	3	B
07200.66	1890-O	MORGAN		PCGS	03/19/91	15,000	1	1	A
07201.63	1890-O	Morgan	PL	PCGS	09/27/90	45	1	1	B
07202.60	1890-S	MORGAN		PCGS	03/12/91	24	3	3	B
07202.61	1890-S	MORGAN		PCGS	03/12/91	26	4	5	B
07202.62	1890-S	MORGAN		PCGS	03/12/91	28	1	5	B
07202.63	1890-S	MORGAN		PCGS	05/08/91	48	1	20	B
07202.64	1890-S	MORGAN		PCGS	04/26/91	180	1	15	B
07202.65	1890-S	MORGAN		NGC	05/17/91	710	1	2	B
07202.65	1890-S	MORGAN		PCGS	04/04/91	830	1	20	B
07202.66	1890-S	MORGAN		PCGS	11/01/90	2,000	1	5	B
07204.60	1891	MORGAN		PCGS	03/21/91	24	1	1	B
07204.63	1891	MORGAN		NGC	05/03/91	102	1	1	B
07204.63	1891	MORGAN		PCGS	05/16/91	112	1	8	B
07204.64	1891	MORGAN		NGC	02/13/91	800	1	3	B
07204.64	1891	MORGAN		PCGS	04/29/91	565	1	12	B
07204.65	1891	MORGAN		PCGS	08/01/90	7,700	1	1	B
07206.60	1891-CC	MORGAN		PCGS	03/21/91	85	1	2	B
07206.61	1891-CC	MORGAN		ANAC	03/19/91	85	1	1	B
07206.61	1891-CC	MORGAN		PCGS	04/03/91	102	3	5	B
07206.62	1891-CC	MORGAN		PCGS	05/08/91	112	2	8	B
07206.63	1891-CC	MORGAN		PCGS	05/20/91	200	3	36	B
07206.64	1891-CC	MORGAN		NGC	05/13/91	550	1	4	B
07206.64	1891-CC	MORGAN		PCGS	05/01/91	625	1	6	B
07206.65	1891-CC	MORGAN		PCGS	08/22/90	3,700	1	2	B
07206.66	1891-CC	MORGAN		PCGS	09/11/90	8,000	1	1	B
07207.64	1891-CC	Morgan	PL	NGC	10/09/90	1,000	1	1	B
07208.62	1891-O	MORGAN		PCGS	05/14/91	58	1	6	B
07208.63	1891-O	MORGAN		PCGS	04/03/91	210	1	2	B
07208.64	1891-O	MORGAN		NGC	02/20/91	720	1	2	B
07208.64	1891-O	MORGAN		PCGS	05/08/91	780	1	18	B
07208.65	1891-O	MORGAN		PCGS	07/23/90	11,000	1	2	B

07210.62	1891-S	MORGAN		PCGS	12/06/90	30	3	3	B
07210.63	1891-S	MORGAN		PCGS	04/19/91	92	4	14	B
07210.64	1891-S	MORGAN		PCGS	05/14/91	240	1	21	B
07210.65	1891-S	MORGAN		NGC	09/17/90	675	1	2	B
07210.65	1891-S	MORGAN		PCGS	03/11/91	1,500	1	6	B
07210.66	1891-S	MORGAN		PCGS	03/06/91	4,300	1	3	B
07212.62	1892	MORGAN		PCGS	05/03/91	99	1	3	B
07212.63	1892	MORGAN		NGC	02/15/91	160	1	1	B
07212.63	1892	MORGAN		PCGS	04/25/91	202	1	8	B
07212.64	1892	MORGAN		PCGS	02/06/91	560	1	9	B
07212.65	1892	MORGAN		PCGS	01/28/91	3,500	1	2	B
07214.61	1892-CC	MORGAN		PCGS	10/12/90	220	1	1	B
07214.62	1892-CC	MORGAN		PCGS	08/29/90	370	1	1	B
07214.63	1892-CC	MORGAN		PCGS	04/08/91	670	1	8	B
07214.64	1892-CC	MORGAN		PCGS	01/16/91	1,150	1	2	A
07214.65	1892-CC	MORGAN		NGC	02/27/91	4,060	1	1	B
07214.65	1892-CC	MORGAN		PCGS	05/14/91	3,900	1	7	B
07214.66	1892-CC	MORGAN		PCGS	04/03/91	16,000	1	1	A
07215.63	1892-CC	Morgan	PL	PCGS	09/17/90	635	1	1	B
07216.63	1892-O	MORGAN		NGC	04/22/91	136	1	1	A
07216.63	1892-O	MORGAN		PCGS	04/26/91	150	1	48	B
07216.64	1892-O	MORGAN		PCGS	05/06/91	500	1	10	B
07216.65	1892-O	MORGAN		PCGS	03/19/91	5,500	1	3	A
07218.66	1892-S	MORGAN		PCGS	11/06/90	125,000	1	1	A
07220.63	1893	MORGAN		PCGS	01/21/91	470	1	1	A
07220.64	1893	MORGAN		NGC	05/02/91	825	1	3	B
07220.64	1893	MORGAN		PCGS	05/16/91	1,050	2	10	B
07220.65	1893	MORGAN		PCGS	08/15/90	6,750	1	1	B
07222.60	1893-CC	MORGAN		PCGS	09/27/90	665	1	2	B
07222.61	1893-CC	MORGAN		PCGS	04/11/91	820	1	5	B
07222.62	1893-CC	MORGAN		PCGS	12/21/90	1,100	1	7	A
07222.63	1893-CC	MORGAN		PCGS	10/09/90	1,830	1	8	B
07222.64	1893-CC	MORGAN		PCGS	08/14/90	6,100	1	1	B
07222.65	1893-CC	MORGAN		PCGS	04/03/91	65,000	1	1	A
07224.63	1893-O	MORGAN		PCGS	03/19/91	3,360	1	4	A
07224.64	1893-O	MORGAN		PCGS	03/19/91	15,000	1	1	A
07224.65	1893-O	MORGAN		PCGS	04/02/91	158,000	1	1	A
07226.63	1893-S	MORGAN		PCGS	10/24/90	44,000	1	1	A
07228.61	1894	MORGAN		PCGS	12/31/90	780	1	1	A
07228.63	1894	MORGAN		NGC	10/30/90	1,280	1	1	B
07228.63	1894	MORGAN		PCGS	10/18/90	1,450	1	2	B
07228.64	1894	MORGAN		PCGS	09/28/90	2,650	1	1	B
07228.65	1894	MORGAN		PCGS	01/15/91	13,500	1	1	A
07230.63	1894-O	MORGAN		PCGS	10/10/90	855	1	1	B
07230.64	1894-O	MORGAN		PCGS	10/02/90	3,750	1	2	B
07230.65	1894-O	MORGAN		PCGS	11/21/90	35,000	1	1	A
07232.63	1894-S	MORGAN		PCGS	04/19/91	460	1	3	A
07232.64	1894-S	MORGAN		PCGS	05/20/91	1,320	1	9	B
07232.65	1894-S	MORGAN		PCGS	05/15/91	4,100	1	5	B
07236.55	1895-O	MORGAN		PCGS	03/26/91	620	1	1	B
07236.64	1895-O	MORGAN		PCGS	10/25/90	17,500	1	1	A
07238.60	1895-S	MORGAN		PCGS	08/06/90	705	1	1	B
07238.61	1895-S	MORGAN		PCGS	08/02/90	855	1	1	B
07238.63	1895-S	MORGAN		PCGS	12/26/90	1,600	1	3	B

07238.64	1895-S	MORGAN		PCGS	08/17/90	3,900	1	2	B
07238.65	1895-S	MORGAN		PCGS	04/09/91	21,200	1	2	A
07239.62	1895-S	Morgan	PL	PCGS	02/18/91	1,230	1	1	B
07240.64	1896	MORGAN		NGC	02/20/91	43	1	1	B
07240.64	1896	MORGAN		PCGS	04/10/91	45	9	26	B
07240.65	1896	MORGAN		NGC	04/16/91	210	1	1	A
07240.65	1896	MORGAN		PCGS	05/15/91	180	1	39	B
07240.66	1896	MORGAN		PCGS	05/13/91	1,380	1	6	B
07241.64	1896	Morgan	PL	NGC	02/05/91	58	1	1	B
07241.64	1896	Morgan	PL	PCGS	03/06/91	100	1	2	B
07242.61	1896-O	MORGAN		PCGS	04/11/91	725	1	3	A
07242.62	1896-O	MORGAN		PCGS	05/17/91	1,400	1	1	A
07242.64	1896-O	MORGAN		PCGS	03/19/91	17,500	1	1	A
07244.61	1896-S	MORGAN		PCGS	04/11/91	585	1	2	A
07244.62	1896-S	MORGAN		PCGS	05/20/91	650	1	5	B
07244.63	1896-S	MORGAN		PCGS	04/02/91	920	1	7	B
07244.64	1896-S	MORGAN		PCGS	12/06/90	1,300	1	4	A
07244.65	1896-S	MORGAN		PCGS	04/08/91	12,500	1	1	A
07246.63	1897	MORGAN		NGC	04/04/91	26	3	3	B
07246.63	1897	MORGAN		PCGS	04/22/91	26	1	4	B
07246.64	1897	MORGAN		NGC	03/01/91	42	3	4	B
07246.64	1897	MORGAN		PCGS	04/09/91	53	1	27	B
07246.65	1897	MORGAN		PCGS	04/01/91	364	1	19	B
07246.66	1897	MORGAN		PCGS	05/20/91	1,900	1	6	B
07246.67	1897	MORGAN		PCGS	05/13/91	12,000	1	1	A
07247.64	1897	Morgan	PL	PCGS	09/11/90	200	1	2	B
07248.60	1897-O	MORGAN		PCGS	04/10/91	310	1	2	B
07248.61	1897-O	MORGAN		PCGS	06/21/90	465	1	1	B
07248.62	1897-O	MORGAN		PCGS	04/11/91	1,150	1	9	A
07248.63	1897-O	MORGAN		PCGS	01/10/91	2,400	1	2	A
07248.64	1897-O	MORGAN		PCGS	04/16/91	15,000	1	1	A
07248.65	1897-O	MORGAN		PCGS	04/02/91	32,000	1	1	A
07250.62	1897-S	MORGAN		PCGS	04/12/91	27	1	6	B
07250.63	1897-S	MORGAN		PCGS	05/16/91	59	2	85	B
07250.64	1897-S	MORGAN		NGC	02/20/91	150	1	3	B
07250.64	1897-S	MORGAN		PCGS	05/08/91	146	1	14	B
07250.65	1897-S	MORGAN		NGC	09/12/90	570	1	2	B
07250.65	1897-S	MORGAN		PCGS	04/01/91	625	1	9	B
07250.66	1897-S	MORGAN		PCGS	05/16/91	1,900	1	6	B
07251.63	1897-S	Morgan	PL	PCGS	07/30/90	75	1	1	B
07251.65	1897-S	Morgan	PL	PCGS	03/01/91	1,150	1	3	B
07252.63	1898	MORGAN		PCGS	06/15/90	30	1	2	B
07252.64	1898	MORGAN		NGC	12/26/90	41	1	1	B
07252.64	1898	MORGAN		PCGS	05/13/91	41	3	26	B
07252.65	1898	MORGAN		NGC	03/25/91	276	1	5	B
07252.65	1898	MORGAN		PCGS	05/13/91	270	1	25	B
07252.66	1898	MORGAN		PCGS	12/18/90	2,100	1	3	A
07253.63	1898	Morgan	PL	PCGS	08/01/90	51	1	1	B
07253.64	1898	Morgan	PL	PCGS	09/11/90	170	1	1	B
07253.65	1898	Morgan	PL	NGC	12/20/90	226	1	1	A
07254.64	1898-O	MORGAN		PCGS	03/19/91	45	1	6	B
07254.65	1898-O	MORGAN		PCGS	05/06/91	124	1	25	B
07254.66	1898-O	MORGAN		PCGS	05/21/91	520	1	25	B
07255.64	1898-O	Morgan	PL	PCGS	02/28/91	110	1	1	B

07255.65	1898-O	Morgan	PL	PCGS	09/17/90	540	2	2	B
07256.62	1898-S	MORGAN		PCGS	05/08/91	114	1	4	B
07256.63	1898-S	MORGAN		NGC	08/15/90	100	1	2	B
07256.63	1898-S	MORGAN		PCGS	04/08/91	150	1	3	B
07256.64	1898-S	MORGAN		NGC	03/26/91	392	1	2	B
07256.64	1898-S	MORGAN		PCGS	04/17/91	426	1	7	A
07256.65	1898-S	MORGAN		PCGS	03/28/91	1,650	1	7	B
07256.66	1898-S	MORGAN		PCGS	04/22/91	8,250	1	2	A
07258.62	1899	MORGAN		ANAC	05/09/91	60	2	2	B
07258.62	1899	MORGAN		PCGS	05/15/91	58	1	10	B
07258.63	1899	MORGAN		ANAC	05/08/91	65	1	1	B
07258.63	1899	MORGAN		PCGS	04/24/91	95	1	10	A
07258.64	1899	MORGAN		NGC	03/26/91	200	1	2	B
07258.64	1899	MORGAN		PCGS	05/16/91	152	1	28	B
07258.65	1899	MORGAN		PCGS	05/13/91	950	1	13	B
07258.66	1899	MORGAN		PCGS	11/14/90	2,700	1	3	B
07260.63	1899-O	MORGAN		NGC	11/20/90	26	1	1	B
07260.64	1899-O	MORGAN		PCGS	04/30/91	43	1	1	B
07260.65	1899-O	MORGAN		PCGS	04/29/91	120	2	51	B
07260.66	1899-O	MORGAN		NGC	09/13/90	750	1	1	B
07260.66	1899-O	MORGAN		PCGS	04/08/91	650	1	10	B
07260.67	1899-O	MORGAN		PCGS	02/11/91	4,000	1	2	B
07261.64	1899-O	Morgan	PL	PCGS	08/20/90	240	1	1	B
07261.65	1899-O	Morgan	PL	PCGS	05/06/91	550	1	1	B
07262.62	1899-S	MORGAN		PCGS	05/02/91	110	1	1	B
07262.63	1899-S	MORGAN		NGC	01/24/91	156	1	1	A
07262.63	1899-S	MORGAN		PCGS	05/08/91	202	1	6	B
07262.64	1899-S	MORGAN		PCGS	04/19/91	426	1	13	A
07262.65	1899-S	MORGAN		PCGS	04/22/91	1,910	1	8	B
07262.66	1899-S	MORGAN		PCGS	04/04/91	4,100	1	3	B
07264.63	1900	MORGAN		PCGS	05/13/91	25	5	5	B
07264.64	1900	MORGAN		PCGS	05/13/91	41	2	36	B
07264.65	1900	MORGAN		NGC	03/26/91	230	1	3	B
07264.65	1900	MORGAN		PCGS	05/13/91	210	1	63	B
07264.66	1900	MORGAN		PCGS	05/08/91	1,450	1	7	B
07265.64	1900	Morgan	PL	NGC	04/18/91	260	1	2	B
07265.65	1900	Morgan	PL	PCGS	04/11/91	1,100	1	1	B
07266.64	1900-O	MORGAN		PCGS	04/10/91	45	1	14	B
07266.65	1900-O	MORGAN		NGC	03/26/91	164	1	6	B
07266.65	1900-O	MORGAN		PCGS	05/13/91	140	1	51	B
07266.66	1900-O	MORGAN		PCGS	05/20/91	980	1	10	B
07267.64	1900-O	Morgan	PL	NGC	08/22/90	165	1	2	B
07267.64	1900-O	Morgan	PL	PCGS	07/16/90	165	1	1	B
07268.63	1900-O/CC	MORGAN		PCGS	08/16/90	219	1	1	B
07268.64	1900-O/CC	MORGAN		PCGS	11/01/90	500	1	4	A
07268.65	1900-O/CC	MORGAN		PCGS	09/17/90	2,200	1	1	B
07268.66	1900-O/CC	MORGAN		PCGS	03/19/91	11,000	1	1	A
07270.62	1900-S	MORGAN		PCGS	05/06/91	104	1	4	B
07270.63	1900-S	MORGAN		NGC	01/24/91	156	1	1	B
07270.63	1900-S	MORGAN		PCGS	05/08/91	170	1	9	B
07270.64	1900-S	MORGAN		PCGS	04/19/91	340	1	6	A
07270.65	1900-S	MORGAN		NGC	02/26/91	1,020	1	1	B
07270.65	1900-S	MORGAN		PCGS	05/16/91	1,600	1	4	B
07270.66	1900-S	MORGAN		PCGS	08/20/90	6,750	1	1	B

07272.58	1901	MORGAN		NGC	04/15/91	276	1	1	B
07272.60	1901	MORGAN		PCGS	06/20/90	600	1	1	B
07272.62	1901	MORGAN		PCGS	04/19/91	2,760	1	6	B
07272.63	1901	MORGAN		PCGS	04/02/91	7,500	1	1	A
07274.64	1901-O	MORGAN		NGC	04/04/91	42	1	4	B
07274.64	1901-O	MORGAN		PCGS	05/17/91	43	1	25	B
07274.65	1901-O	MORGAN		NGC	12/03/90	180	1	3	B
07274.65	1901-O	MORGAN		PCGS	05/07/91	272	1	33	B
07274.66	1901-O	MORGAN		PCGS	07/06/90	2,400	1	1	B
07275.64	1901-O	Morgan	PL	NGC	08/24/90	190	2	2	B
07275.65	1901-O	Morgan	PL	PCGS	05/13/91	850	1	2	B
07276.61	1901-S	MORGAN		PCGS	04/22/91	186	1	1	B
07276.62	1901-S	MORGAN		PCGS	08/08/90	180	1	1	B
07276.63	1901-S	MORGAN		NGC	03/05/91	228	1	1	B
07276.63	1901-S	MORGAN		PCGS	07/23/90	195	1	1	B
07276.64	1901-S	MORGAN		PCGS	05/08/91	720	1	13	B
07276.65	1901-S	MORGAN		PCGS	03/19/91	3,250	1	4	B
07278.62	1902	MORGAN		PCGS	04/15/91	32	2	3	B
07278.63	1902	MORGAN		NGC	04/04/91	34	1	1	B
07278.63	1902	MORGAN		PCGS	04/15/91	42	3	19	B
07278.64	1902	MORGAN		NGC	01/24/91	106	1	1	A
07278.64	1902	MORGAN		PCGS	04/22/91	126	1	29	B
07278.65	1902	MORGAN		NGC	03/19/91	410	1	4	B
07278.65	1902	MORGAN		PCGS	05/14/91	490	1	28	B
07278.66	1902	MORGAN		PCGS	04/15/91	1,550	1	6	B
07280.62	1902-O	MORGAN		PCGS	06/28/90	24	1	1	B
07280.64	1902-O	MORGAN		PCGS	05/13/91	41	1	8	B
07280.65	1902-O	MORGAN		PCGS	05/06/91	180	1	48	B
07280.66	1902-O	MORGAN		PCGS	05/07/91	1,580	1	18	B
07281.64	1902-O	Morgan	PL	PCGS	10/03/90	80	1	2	B
07281.65	1902-O	Morgan	PL	PCGS	08/15/90	1,750	1	2	B
07282.62	1902-S	MORGAN		PCGS	04/22/91	144	1	1	B
07282.63	1902-S	MORGAN		PCGS	05/21/91	268	1	5	B
07282.64	1902-S	MORGAN		PCGS	05/14/91	640	1	14	B
07282.65	1902-S	MORGAN		PCGS	01/22/91	3,000	1	4	B
07282.66	1902-S	MORGAN		PCGS	03/19/91	11,000	1	2	A
07284.61	1903	MORGAN		PCGS	08/07/90	19	1	1	B
07284.62	1903	MORGAN		PCGS	04/29/91	29	2	3	B
07284.63	1903	MORGAN		PCGS	05/06/91	37	1	24	B
07284.64	1903	MORGAN		NGC	02/20/91	70	1	4	B
07284.64	1903	MORGAN		PCGS	05/20/91	62	1	47	B
07284.65	1903	MORGAN		PCGS	05/06/91	210	1	47	B
07284.66	1903	MORGAN		PCGS	05/15/91	940	1	20	B
07284.67	1903	MORGAN		PCGS	04/22/91	2,100	1	1	B
07285.64	1903	Morgan	PL	PCGS	01/16/91	252	1	1	B
07286.62	1903-O	MORGAN		PCGS	05/03/91	136	2	5	A
07286.63	1903-O	MORGAN		ANAC	05/08/91	130	1	1	B
07286.63	1903-O	MORGAN		PCGS	04/29/91	140	1	10	B
07286.64	1903-O	MORGAN		NGC	02/12/91	150	1	1	B
07286.64	1903-O	MORGAN		PCGS	05/13/91	164	1	34	B
07286.65	1903-O	MORGAN		NGC	03/07/91	386	1	2	B
07286.65	1903-O	MORGAN		PCGS	05/06/91	480	1	48	B
07286.66	1903-O	MORGAN		PCGS	05/20/91	1,400	1	9	B
07288.63	1903-S	MORGAN		PCGS	08/15/90	2,950	1	1	B

07288.64	1903-S	MORGAN		PCGS	10/02/90	2,800	1	5	B
07288.65	1903-S	MORGAN		PCGS	08/23/90	5,700	1	1	B
07290.60	1904	MORGAN		PCGS	11/29/90	35	1	1	B
07290.61	1904	MORGAN		PCGS	01/09/91	38	1	1	B
07290.63	1904	MORGAN		NGC	03/19/91	130	1	2	B
07290.63	1904	MORGAN		PCGS	03/21/91	140	2	7	B
07290.64	1904	MORGAN		NGC	11/29/90	376	1	1	A
07290.64	1904	MORGAN		PCGS	04/01/91	525	1	23	B
07290.65	1904	MORGAN		PCGS	02/27/91	3,700	1	3	B
07292.62	1904-O	MORGAN		PCGS	09/11/90	24	1	1	B
07292.65	1904-O	MORGAN		PCGS	05/08/91	112	1	39	B
07292.66	1904-O	MORGAN		PCGS	04/15/91	815	1	9	B
07293.63	1904-O	Morgan	PL	PCGS	05/14/91	50	1	1	B
07293.64	1904-O	Morgan	PL	PCGS	05/14/91	75	1	3	B
07293.65	1904-O	Morgan	PL	NGC	06/14/90	550	1	1	B
07293.65	1904-O	Morgan	PL	PCGS	04/29/91	240	1	3	B
07294.62	1904-S	MORGAN		PCGS	09/14/90	805	1	2	B
07294.63	1904-S	MORGAN		PCGS	10/31/90	875	1	3	B
07294.64	1904-S	MORGAN		PCGS	05/02/91	2,050	1	5	A
07294.65	1904-S	MORGAN		PCGS	04/17/91	9,500	1	2	A
07296.61	1921	MORGAN		PCGS	08/07/90	11	1	1	B
07296.62	1921	MORGAN		PCGS	08/07/90	13	1	1	B
07296.63	1921	MORGAN		PCGS	05/17/91	16	1	83	B
07296.64	1921	MORGAN		NGC	01/14/91	31	10	10	A
07296.64	1921	MORGAN		PCGS	05/03/91	30	5	197	B
07296.65	1921	MORGAN		NGC	04/05/91	120	1	4	B
07296.65	1921	MORGAN		PCGS	05/16/91	170	1	46	B
07296.66	1921	MORGAN		PCGS	05/20/91	1,250	1	5	B
07297.63	1921	Morgan	PL	NGC	04/02/91	55	1	1	B
07297.63	1921	Morgan	PL	PCGS	12/13/90	45	1	1	A
07297.64	1921	Morgan	PL	PCGS	12/24/90	48	40	40	A
07298.62	1921-D	MORGAN		PCGS	08/08/90	17	2	2	B
07298.63	1921-D	MORGAN		PCGS	04/16/91	33	1	29	B
07298.64	1921-D	MORGAN		NGC	02/19/91	128	1	8	B
07298.64	1921-D	MORGAN		PCGS	05/21/91	126	1	46	B
07298.65	1921-D	MORGAN		NGC	02/20/91	570	1	13	B
07298.65	1921-D	MORGAN		PCGS	05/13/91	414	1	26	B
07298.66	1921-D	MORGAN		PCGS	04/01/91	2,700	1	2	B
07299.64	1921-D	Morgan	PL	NGC	09/05/90	850	1	1	B
07300.63	1921-S	MORGAN		ANAC	03/22/91	39	20	20	B
07300.63	1921-S	MORGAN		NGC	02/19/91	30	1	1	B
07300.63	1921-S	MORGAN		PCGS	04/12/91	43	2	14	B
07300.64	1921-S	MORGAN		NGC	02/04/91	200	1	6	B
07300.64	1921-S	MORGAN		PCGS	05/08/91	180	1	16	B
07300.65	1921-S	MORGAN		PCGS	03/18/91	3,000	1	6	B
07310.61	Morgan Dollar		PR	PCGS	05/13/91	740	1	13	B
07310.62	Morgan Dollar		PR	PCGS	04/04/91	1,020	2	10	B
07310.63	Morgan Dollar		PR	NGC	04/01/91	1,410	1	2	B
07310.63	Morgan Dollar		PR	PCGS	05/02/91	1,520	1	18	B
07310.64	Morgan Dollar		PR	NGC	05/15/91	1,930	1	5	B
07310.64	Morgan Dollar		PR	PCGS	05/13/91	2,200	1	15	B
07310.65	Morgan Dollar		PR	NGC	02/20/91	4,700	1	3	B
07310.65	Morgan Dollar		PR	PCGS	05/07/91	4,100	1	9	B
07310.66	Morgan Dollar		PR	NGC	04/01/91	8,050	1	4	B

07310.66	Morgan Dollar	PR	PCGS	03/28/91	7,500	1	3	B
07310.67	Morgan Dollar	PR	NGC	03/28/91	13,000	1	1	B
07310.67	Morgan Dollar	PR	PCGS	03/06/91	15,800	1	1	B
07311.63	1878-8TF MORGAN	PR	PCGS	08/29/90	2,600	1	2	B
07329.62	1894 MORGAN	PR	PCGS	08/30/90	1,400	1	1	B
07329.63	1894 MORGAN	PR	PCGS	07/31/90	2,500	1	1	B
07330.62	1895 MORGAN	PR	PCGS	10/10/90	11,500	1	1	B
07330.63	1895 MORGAN	PR	PCGS	09/27/90	13,600	1	1	B
07330.67	1895 MORGAN	PR	PCGS	04/10/91	115,000	1	1	A
07355.58	Peace Dollar		PCGS	10/16/90	9	1	1	B
07355.60	Peace Dollar		PCGS	04/08/91	12	1	1	B
07355.61	Peace Dollar		PCGS	04/02/91	14	2	5	B
07355.62	Peace Dollar		NGC	04/24/91	12	4	10	B
07355.62	Peace Dollar		PCGS	04/29/91	15	1	253	B
07355.63	Peace Dollar		ANAC	03/14/91	14	3	3	B
07355.63	Peace Dollar		NGC	04/26/91	16	10	86	B
07355.63	Peace Dollar		PCGS	05/15/91	17	50	1470	A
07355.64	Peace Dollar		NGC	05/21/91	34	1	327	B
07355.64	Peace Dollar		PCGS	05/13/91	34	7	2284	B
07355.65	Peace Dollar		ANAC	04/18/91	140	1	2	B
07355.65	Peace Dollar		NGC	05/15/91	150	1	102	B
07355.65	Peace Dollar		PCGS	05/20/91	160	16	659	B
07355.66	Peace Dollar		NGC	02/20/91	1,600	1	2	B
07355.66	Peace Dollar		PCGS	05/13/91	1,220	1	39	B
07356.60	1921 PEACE		PCGS	01/28/91	90	1	1	B
07356.61	1921 PEACE		PCGS	05/08/91	100	1	1	B
07356.62	1921 PEACE		NGC	01/11/91	110	1	1	B
07356.62	1921 PEACE		PCGS	05/15/91	110	1	14	B
07356.63	1921 PEACE		NGC	04/25/91	180	1	3	B
07356.63	1921 PEACE		PCGS	05/09/91	190	2	34	B
07356.64	1921 PEACE		NGC	05/15/91	376	1	3	B
07356.64	1921 PEACE		PCGS	04/29/91	350	1	21	B
07356.65	1921 PEACE		NGC	05/14/91	1,650	1	5	B
07356.65	1921 PEACE		PCGS	04/02/91	1,730	1	15	B
07357.62	1922 PEACE		NGC	02/27/91	20	3	3	B
07357.63	1922 PEACE		NGC	02/27/91	21	3	3	B
07357.63	1922 PEACE		PCGS	04/11/91	17	1	1	B
07357.64	1922 PEACE		NGC	04/23/91	37	1	6	B
07357.64	1922 PEACE		PCGS	05/13/91	35	2	10	B
07357.65	1922 PEACE		NGC	04/29/91	166	2	3	B
07357.65	1922 PEACE		PCGS	05/08/91	160	1	14	B
07357.66	1922 PEACE		PCGS	03/19/91	3,100	1	1	B
07358.62	1922-D PEACE		PCGS	11/13/90	18	1	1	B
07358.63	1922-D PEACE		PCGS	03/15/91	46	1	19	B
07358.64	1922-D PEACE		NGC	01/29/91	106	2	2	A
07358.64	1922-D PEACE		PCGS	05/21/91	128	1	36	B
07358.65	1922-D PEACE		NGC	05/14/91	980	1	2	B
07358.65	1922-D PEACE		PCGS	05/20/91	1,040	1	18	B
07358.66	1922-D PEACE		NGC	04/12/91	3,600	1	2	B
07359.62	1922-S PEACE		PCGS	03/04/91	23	1	5	B
07359.63	1922-S PEACE		NGC	03/07/91	45	1	3	B
07359.63	1922-S PEACE		PCGS	03/26/91	62	1	26	B
07359.64	1922-S PEACE		NGC	02/20/91	260	1	1	B
07359.64	1922-S PEACE		PCGS	02/04/91	288	1	13	B

07359.65	1922-S	PEACE	PCGS	01/14/91	3,000	1	1	A
07360.62	1923	PEACE	NGC	02/27/91	19	2	2	B
07360.62	1923	PEACE	PCGS	04/05/91	19	1	1	B
07360.63	1923	PEACE	NGC	02/27/91	19	2	2	B
07360.63	1923	PEACE	PCGS	02/26/91	20	10	10	A
07360.64	1923	PEACE	NGC	04/23/91	35	3	3	B
07360.64	1923	PEACE	PCGS	05/13/91	34	6	19	B
07360.65	1923	PEACE	NGC	05/01/91	160	1	3	B
07360.65	1923	PEACE	PCGS	11/07/90	162	1	5	B
07360.66	1923	PEACE	PCGS	02/20/91	1,710	1	2	B
07361.63	1923-D	PEACE	PCGS	05/03/91	78	1	17	B
07361.64	1923-D	PEACE	NGC	03/15/91	226	1	1	B
07361.64	1923-D	PEACE	PCGS	05/10/91	260	2	29	B
07361.65	1923-D	PEACE	PCGS	05/20/91	2,300	1	9	B
07362.62	1923-S	PEACE	NGC	02/27/91	34	1	1	B
07362.62	1923-S	PEACE	PCGS	05/13/91	27	1	4	B
07362.63	1923-S	PEACE	ANAC	03/14/91	55	1	1	B
07362.63	1923-S	PEACE	NGC	03/18/91	60	1	2	B
07362.63	1923-S	PEACE	PCGS	04/19/91	64	1	24	B
07362.64	1923-S	PEACE	NGC	02/20/91	310	1	2	B
07362.64	1923-S	PEACE	PCGS	04/23/91	372	1	8	B
07362.65	1923-S	PEACE	NGC	03/05/91	3,400	1	1	B
07362.65	1923-S	PEACE	PCGS	10/10/90	3,000	1	4	B
07363.62	1924	PEACE	PCGS	04/12/91	19	1	1	B
07363.63	1924	PEACE	NGC	04/05/91	18	4	4	B
07363.63	1924	PEACE	PCGS	04/26/91	23	4	42	B
07363.64	1924	PEACE	NGC	04/23/91	47	1	3	B
07363.64	1924	PEACE	PCGS	05/13/91	42	1	55	B
07363.65	1924	PEACE	NGC	03/07/91	210	1	1	B
07363.65	1924	PEACE	PCGS	05/15/91	194	1	55	B
07363.66	1924	PEACE	PCGS	03/15/91	2,260	1	3	B
07364.62	1924-S	PEACE	PCGS	10/24/90	75	1	1	B
07364.63	1924-S	PEACE	PCGS	04/24/91	372	1	21	B
07364.64	1924-S	PEACE	PCGS	04/03/91	1,350	1	12	B
07364.65	1924-S	PEACE	PCGS	01/16/91	1	1	2	A
07365.62	1925	PEACE	PCGS	03/04/91	19	1	1	B
07365.63	1925	PEACE	NGC	03/07/91	17	2	2	B
07365.63	1925	PEACE	PCGS	05/14/91	20	1	10	B
07365.64	1925	PEACE	NGC	05/06/91	37	1	4	B
07365.64	1925	PEACE	PCGS	05/08/91	35	3	39	B
07365.65	1925	PEACE	NGC	05/01/91	176	2	5	B
07365.65	1925	PEACE	PCGS	04/04/91	166	1	16	B
07366.62	1925-S	PEACE	NGC	02/27/91	68	1	1	B
07366.62	1925-S	PEACE	PCGS	05/15/91	55	1	6	B
07366.63	1925-S	PEACE	NGC	01/30/91	150	1	2	B
07366.63	1925-S	PEACE	PCGS	05/09/91	136	1	41	B
07366.64	1925-S	PEACE	PCGS	04/03/91	840	1	14	B
07366.65	1925-S	PEACE	NGC	10/12/90	9,000	1	1	B
07367.61	1926	PEACE	PCGS	08/07/90	18	1	1	B
07367.62	1926	PEACE	PCGS	03/07/91	22	1	9	B
07367.63	1926	PEACE	NGC	04/24/91	40	1	4	B
07367.63	1926	PEACE	PCGS	05/08/91	45	1	27	B
07367.64	1926	PEACE	NGC	05/02/91	95	2	6	B
07367.64	1926	PEACE	PCGS	05/03/91	84	1	30	B

07367.65	1926	PEACE	NGC	05/06/91	480	1	4	B
07367.65	1926	PEACE	PCGS	04/29/91	500	1	17	B
07367.66	1926	PEACE	PCGS	08/14/90	4,700	1	2	B
07368.62	1926-D	PEACE	PCGS	01/09/91	37	2	2	B
07368.63	1926-D	PEACE	PCGS	04/03/91	76	1	10	B
07368.64	1926-D	PEACE	NGC	05/06/91	190	1	9	B
07368.64	1926-D	PEACE	PCGS	04/26/91	186	1	13	B
07368.65	1926-D	PEACE	NGC	04/29/91	935	1	3	B
07368.65	1926-D	PEACE	PCGS	01/22/91	895	1	7	A
07368.66	1926-D	PEACE	PCGS	04/24/91	3,520	1	7	B
07368.67	1926-D	PEACE	NGC	08/31/90	24,000	1	1	B
07368.67	1926-D	PEACE	PCGS	08/07/90	24,000	1	1	B
07369.62	1926-S	PEACE	PCGS	05/06/91	32	2	2	B
07369.63	1926-S	PEACE	PCGS	05/13/91	63	1	20	B
07369.64	1926-S	PEACE	NGC	11/01/90	70	1	1	B
07369.64	1926-S	PEACE	PCGS	04/02/91	216	1	21	B
07369.65	1926-S	PEACE	NGC	08/27/90	1,500	1	1	B
07369.65	1926-S	PEACE	PCGS	05/06/91	1,700	1	11	B
07370.60	1927	PEACE	PCGS	08/03/90	43	1	1	B
07370.61	1927	PEACE	PCGS	09/24/90	48	1	1	B
07370.62	1927	PEACE	PCGS	04/26/91	60	1	12	B
07370.63	1927	PEACE	NGC	03/11/91	100	1	1	B
07370.63	1927	PEACE	PCGS	05/03/91	116	1	32	B
07370.64	1927	PEACE	PCGS	05/21/91	430	1	20	B
07370.65	1927	PEACE	NGC	04/02/91	3,400	1	1	B
07370.65	1927	PEACE	PCGS	02/04/91	5,500	1	5	A
07371.62	1927-D	PEACE	PCGS	05/06/91	210	1	10	B
07371.63	1927-D	PEACE	PCGS	04/30/91	462	1	10	B
07371.64	1927-D	PEACE	PCGS	11/21/90	800	1	5	A
07371.65	1927-D	PEACE	NGC	05/10/91	4,020	1	1	B
07371.65	1927-D	PEACE	PCGS	01/15/91	7,500	1	1	A
07372.62	1927-S	PEACE	PCGS	05/06/91	71	1	37	B
07372.63	1927-S	PEACE	NGC	02/18/91	220	1	4	B
07372.63	1927-S	PEACE	PCGS	05/06/91	170	1	98	B
07372.64	1927-S	PEACE	PCGS	03/08/91	995	1	9	A
07372.65	1927-S	PEACE	PCGS	10/01/90	12,000	1	1	B
07373.62	1928	PEACE	PCGS	04/26/91	186	1	10	B
07373.63	1928	PEACE	NGC	06/19/90	175	1	1	B
07373.63	1928	PEACE	PCGS	05/13/91	254	1	34	B
07373.64	1928	PEACE	NGC	01/23/91	450	1	1	A
07373.64	1928	PEACE	PCGS	05/03/91	600	1	18	B
07373.65	1928	PEACE	NGC	04/30/91	3,100	1	1	B
07373.65	1928	PEACE	PCGS	01/15/91	5,500	1	4	A
07374.60	1928-S	PEACE	PCGS	04/26/91	50	1	3	B
07374.61	1928-S	PEACE	PCGS	04/02/91	62	3	4	B
07374.62	1928-S	PEACE	PCGS	04/02/91	90	9	22	B
07374.63	1928-S	PEACE	NGC	03/26/91	276	1	2	B
07374.63	1928-S	PEACE	PCGS	03/18/91	320	1	21	B
07374.64	1928-S	PEACE	NGC	04/10/91	1,350	1	1	B
07374.64	1928-S	PEACE	PCGS	05/06/91	1,460	1	10	B
07375.61	1934	PEACE	PCGS	05/03/91	53	1	1	B
07375.62	1934	PEACE	PCGS	04/23/91	65	1	10	B
07375.63	1934	PEACE	NGC	02/04/91	112	1	2	B
07375.63	1934	PEACE	PCGS	03/07/91	120	1	13	A

07375.64	1934	PEACE	NGC	02/19/91	260	1	4	B
07375.64	1934	PEACE	PCGS	05/13/91	202	1	16	B
07375.65	1934	PEACE	NGC	02/26/91	900	1	1	B
07375.65	1934	PEACE	PCGS	04/22/91	1,760	1	9	B
07376.61	1934-D	PEACE	PCGS	09/26/90	62	1	1	B
07376.62	1934-D	PEACE	PCGS	05/20/91	81	1	5	B
07376.63	1934-D	PEACE	NGC	01/15/91	200	1	2	B
07376.63	1934-D	PEACE	PCGS	05/21/91	164	1	24	B
07376.64	1934-D	PEACE	NGC	01/15/91	550	2	2	B
07376.64	1934-D	PEACE	PCGS	05/13/91	625	1	11	B
07376.65	1934-D	PEACE	PCGS	05/03/91	1,980	1	5	B
07376.66	1934-D	PEACE	PCGS	02/20/91	5,300	1	3	B
07377.61	1934-S	PEACE	PCGS	11/21/90	860	1	1	B
07377.62	1934-S	PEACE	PCGS	02/19/91	1,500	1	7	B
07377.63	1934-S	PEACE	PCGS	03/15/91	2,310	1	8	B
07377.64	1934-S	PEACE	PCGS	04/22/91	3,960	1	9	B
07377.65	1934-S	PEACE	PCGS	01/15/91	10,500	1	2	A
07377.66	1934-S	PEACE	PCGS	04/11/91	34,600	1	1	A
07378.61	1935	PEACE	PCGS	01/09/91	32	3	4	B
07378.62	1935	PEACE	PCGS	04/25/91	46	1	4	B
07378.63	1935	PEACE	NGC	02/04/91	69	1	1	B
07378.63	1935	PEACE	PCGS	05/13/91	60	1	46	B
07378.64	1935	PEACE	NGC	02/14/91	172	1	4	B
07378.64	1935	PEACE	PCGS	05/21/91	166	1	22	B
07378.65	1935	PEACE	PCGS	05/03/91	965	1	5	B
07379.62	1935-S	PEACE	NGC	02/27/91	100	1	1	B
07379.62	1935-S	PEACE	PCGS	04/26/91	120	1	3	B
07379.63	1935-S	PEACE	PCGS	12/27/90	204	1	12	B
07379.64	1935-S	PEACE	NGC	05/20/91	346	1	2	B
07379.64	1935-S	PEACE	PCGS	11/09/90	240	1	8	B
07379.65	1935-S	PEACE	NGC	03/26/91	1,180	1	2	B
07379.65	1935-S	PEACE	PCGS	03/26/91	1,250	1	9	B
07379.66	1935-S	PEACE	PCGS	01/10/91	4,760	1	1	A

***

Ron Downing
Publisher of the Coin Dealer Newsletter

Ron Downing started his career in numismatics as a teenage coin collector. He spent more than two decades as a professional numismatist with his mother, Pauline Miladin, at Coin-A-Rama in Hawthorne, CA. Ron was the principal buyer and wholesaler for the firm, and was a well-known figure in numismatic circles. Their partnership purchased the Coin Dealer Newsletter in June of 1984.

Ron is a collector at heart, and the purchase of the **Greysheet** required a major change in his collecting habits. Denied the joys of collecting coins (to absolutely avoid a conflict of interest), Ron refocused his attention on antiques. Ron not only savors the *purchasing* of fine pieces, he also enjoys living with antiques. One of his areas of specialization is coin glass, naturally, and he takes special pride in his museum-quality collection. Ron is still looking for a few more important pieces, and then hopes to send his collection on tour. Ron is also an avid sportsman, and has most recently enjoyed buffalo hunting in Colorado and salmon fishing in Alaska.

CHAPTER 34

Cartwheels & the CDN

by Ron Downing

American silver dollars were there (almost) at the beginning — the beginning of the Greysheet, that is! The Coin Dealer Newsletter (also known as the CDN or the Greysheet) was a unique idea that arose from most unusual circumstances. In 1962, eight separate coin dealers were operating out of a single shop in Hawthorne, California, known as Coin-A-Rama City. At that time, there were four separate teletype systems linking American dealers; only real old-timers in the coin business would remember that even the PNG had its own teletype system! In an age of personal computers with the power of the mainframes of twenty years ago, and silent laser printers with 150 type faces, the massive (and deafening!) teletype machines of the early 60s seem almost prehistoric.

Housed in large olive cabinets, the term "Green Monster" was not always used affectionately, especially not when all four were printing at the same time. While these were then the latest in technology, there was always something basically contradictory about their use as communication devices. They allowed you to talk to dealers across America, but prevented you from having a conversation in your office. And if I sound like I lack the proper nostalgia for the "good old days", I will point out one of the disadvantages of growing up in a family of coin dealers — we had one of the teletype machines at home whose very loud incoming-message bell served as my morning alarm clock!

Orvil L. Payne, one of the Coin-A-Rama associates, believed that there would be great benefit to a printed consolidation of prices from the various teletypes, as well as a listing of other dealer-to-dealer transactions. In June of 1963, in the back room of Coin-A-Rama, the first issue of the National Coin Broker's Bulletin was created. By the second issue the name had changed to the Coin Dealer Newsletter, and an uninterrupted string of 27+ years of weekly issues began. James and Pauline Miladin (my parents), together were one of the eight Coin-A-Rama companies, and were intimately involved in the CDN from its founding. James was the first writer for "The Market in Depth" column, and Pauline was the statistical editor, consolidating the pricing information gathered each week from many sources.

While thinking about this article, and the way the Silver Dollar market and the CDN have grown up together, I went back to the very first issue of the "the National Coin Brokers Bulletin". I was very surprised to discover that among all the Roll prices listed, Dollars weren't even mentioned! I could have lost BIG money betting on that particular point. Within months Morgan and Peace Silver Dollars had assumed a major role in the Coin Dealer Newsletter, even if the prices now seem strangely low. It seems hard to believe that, at a time when satellites were already whizzing through space, BU Morgan Rolls could still be purchased for $25!

My mom, Pauline Miladin, was one of the first female coin dealers in America to achieve recognition. Her work with the CDN ended when her husband became gravely ill. Allen Harriman, who had been learning the business under their guidance, assumed responsibility for much of the writing and pricing research. Allen was joined in his efforts by Edward Judd, who was to become his future partner.

Upon my dad's passing in October 1965, my mom asked me to join her at Coin-A-Rama City. This ended our association with the CDN (at least, for the time being!). I took the opportunity to learn the coin trade from her, beginning a close relationship that has continued to this day. Pauline, recognizing the growing potential of the coin market, began buying out the remaining Coin-A-Rama dealers; by the late 1960's, she was the sole owner.

At the same time, Allen Harriman and Edward Judd assumed complete responsibility for the CDN, and ultimately became its owners. During these years we were in nearly daily contact with Allen and Edward. As the coin market grew, so did the importance of the CDN to dealers across America (and throughout the world). As collectors attended coin shows and conventions, they couldn't help but notice that virtually every dealer in U.S. coins was using the now-familiar Greysheet in determining buying and selling prices. In time, even the professional's "Greysheet" nickname passed into public usage.

Mint State Morgans & More

As coin prices began to rise during the 1960s, we began to see the development of additional grades. Jim Ruddy, the numismatist whose Photograde grading reference book (now in its 18th printing!) revolutionized the coin business, recently reminisced about Mint State grades:

"In the old days, it just didn't matter. We didn't care because most of our customers didn't care. And the price differences weren't that great between the top coins — primarily because the top grades 'didn't exist', at least not in our minds. The market was driven by rarity more than quality."

The initial Photograde reference dealt with circulated coins, and was based on the principle that the best way to "describe" what any particular EF looked like was simply to photograph it. Jim spent many hours looking through the junk boxes and "circ" trays at Coin-A-Rama buying what Mom and I thought were the most unusual coins. Since the book project was kept an absolute secret (and Jim knew how to keep a secret!), none of the dealers could figure out what he was up to. We all knew the quality of coins he normally bought and sold, but then he would sit for two hours, look at 2,000 coins and buy a VG shield nickel. More than one dealer tried to anticipate a major market swing and ended up with an inventory of low grade circs!

All this attention focused on looking at your coins soon had major ramifications for the uncirculated material as well. As the collectors (and consequently their dealers) began to look more closely at the condition of all of the coins that they were buying, an entirely new awareness of quality emerged — followed by an acceptance of the concept of premium pricing for premium quality. As the spreads in prices between grades began to grow, the need for intermediate grades also began to grow.

The CDN began to differentiate Bids for "MS-60" and "MS-65" silver dollars in 1975. Three years earlier the spreads in gold had brought the new BU and Gem BU designations to gold (where wider spreads had first developed). The rest of the series would follow suit, as the industry began the long journey towards quality consciousness. In 1975, the premiums for Gem coins (which seemed huge at the time) seem almost quaint today. The 1882-CC Morgan was Bid at $19 and $23; the 1894-S at $130 and $220.

PAGE 6 **THE COIN DEALER Newsletter** December 6, 1963

BU SILVER DOLLARS MARKET CLOSING PRICES

MORGAN DOLLARS

YEAR	SINGLES BID	SINGLES ASK	ROLLS BID	ROLLS ASK
1878 8tf	------	------	265.00	295.00
1878 7tf	------	------	------	------
1878 7/8tf	4.25	------	80.00	155.00
1878-CC	------	------	165.00	165.00
1878-S	------	1.50	25.00	29.00
1879-P	------	2.00	------	25.00
1879-CC	90.00	95.00	-----	------
1879-O	4.00	------	------	------
1879-S	------	------	26.00	30.00
1880-P	------	------	------	27.00
1880-CC	26.50	------	450.00	450.00
1880-O	3.00	------	------	55.00
1880-S	------	------	------	24.00*
1881-P	------	2.00	------	------
1881-CC	42.50	------	------	885.00
1881-O	------	------	32.50	------
1881-S	------	1.85	-----	24.00*
1882-P	------	------	------	26.00
1882-CC	15.00	16.50	300.00	360.00
1882-O	------	------	32.00	60.00
1882-S	2.50	------	29.00	35.00
1883-P	1.35	---- -	26.00	27.00
1883-CC	14.00	16.50	------	290.00
1883-O	------	------	------	30.00
1883-S	5.00	9.50	150.00	------
1884-P	1.40	------	------	26.00
1884-CC	22.50	-----	------	400.00
1884-O	-----	-----	------	28.50
1884-S	5.00	10.00	350.00	------
1885-P	1.35	1.65	24.50	24.50
1885-CC	42.50	------	700.00	850.00*
1885-O	------	------	------	28.00
1885-S	4.00	------	85.00	---- -
1886-P	---- -	1.60	26.00	27.50
1886-O	12.00	------	------	------
1886-S	14.00	------	300.00	360.00
1887-P	------	1.50	25.00	25.75
1887-O	------	------	------	90.00
1887-S	5.00	------	150.00	------
1888-P	------	------	------	27.00
1888-O	------	4.00	-----	------
1888-S	17.50	------	300.00	500.00
1889-P	------	------	------	25.00
1889-CC	------	------	-----	------
1889-O	------	------	------	70.00
1889-S	22.50	------	400.00	------
1890-P	-----	------	------	------
1890-CC	7.00	------	175.00	200.00
1890-O	4.50	------	------	60.00
1890-S	2.50	------	60.00	------
1891-P	------	------	------	------
1891-CC	7.00	------	175.00	200.00
1891-O	------	------	------	------
1891-S	4.00	------	80.00	-----
1892-P	4.00	------	130.00	------
1892-CC	25.00	------	450.00	------
1892-O	4.45	------	70.00	95.00
1892-S	125.00	------	------	------
1893-P	21.00	25.00	500.00	550.00

MORGAN DOLLARS Continued

YEAR	SINGLES BID	SINGLES ASK	ROLLS BID	ROLLS ASK
1893-CC	65.00	-----	------	------
1893-O	55.00	------	------	------
1893-S	850.00	------	------	------
1894-P	70.00	80.00	1800.00	------
1894-O	7.50	10.00	-----	------
1894-S	15.00	------	240.00	------
1895-P	------	------	-------	------
1895-O	55.00	------	------	------
1895-S	150.00	------	------	------
1896-P	------	------	------	27.50
1896-O	6.00	------	------	------
1896-S	60.00	------	800.00	------
1897-P	------	------	28.00	29.00
1897-O	6.00	-----	------	------
1897-S	2.75	------	80.00	------
1898-P	------	------	------	25.00
1898-O	1.40	-· 1.50*	35.00	36.00
1898-S	------	------	300(00	------
1899-P	20.00	23.00	415.00	41.50
1899-O	------	------	------	25.00
1899-S	30.00	------	300.00	------
1900-P	------	------	------	25.50
1900-O	------	------	------	25.00
1900-S	10.00	------	175.00	------
1901-P	15.00	------	------	------
1901-O	-----•	------	------	26.50*
1901-S	-----	------	200.00	250.00
1902-P	------	------	------	------
1902-O	20.00	------	------	26.00
1902-S	------	------	------	------
1903-P	1.40	------	36.00	------
1903-O	35.00*	------	610.00	610.00
1903-S	65.00	------	600.00	------
1904-P	------	------	39.00	60.00
1904-O	1.50	------	30.00	31.50
1904-S	55.00	------	600.00	------
1921-P	------	------	------	------
1921-D	2.50	------	------	------
1921-S	2.50	------	50.00	------

PEACE DOLLARS

YEAR	SINGLES BID	SINGLES ASK	ROLLS BID	ROLLS ASK
1921-P	15.00	19.50	------	95.00
1923-D	4.00	-----	------	95.00
1924-S	17.50	-----	------	------
1925-S	9.00	9.50	------	------
1926-P	5.50	------	111.00	------
1926-D	------	------	------	115.00
1926-S	------	4.50	------	------
1927-P	------	16.50	------	400.00
1927-D	10.00	------	------	190.00
1927-S	14.00	-----	------	------
1928-P	40.00	40.00	------	------
1928-S	10.00	------	------	------
1934-P	12.50	18.00	-----	-----
1934-D	7.50	12.50	------	------
1934-S	80.00	80.00	------	------
1935-P	7.50	10.50	------	------
1935-S	16.00	18.00	------	------

PROOF SETS

	BID	ASK		BID	ASK		BID	ASK
1936 (3,837)	510.00	540.00	1950 (51,386)	118.00	118.50	1958 (875,652)	9.55	------
1937 (5,542)	215.00	230.00	1951 (57,500)	64.00	65.00	1959 (1,149,291)	---- -	4.80
1938 (8,045)	120.00	140.00	1952 (81,980)	36.00	36.00	1960 (1,691,602)	------	4.70
1939 (8,795)	100.00	110.00	1953 (128,800)	23.00	24.00	1960sm(	44.00	45.00
1940 (11,246)	75.00	85.00	1954 (233,300)	17.00	17.50	1961 (3,028,244)	2.60	2.65
1941 (15,287)	65.00	65.00	1955 (378,200)	18.00	18.75	1962 (3,218,019)	2.45	2.60
1942 (21,120)	46.50	52.50	1956 (669,384)	9.25	9.75	1963	3.30*	3.40*
1942 t2	70.00	70.00	1957 (1,247,952)	5.60	5.65			

Page 6 of the CDN, December 6, 1963
(Courtesy of CDN)

MARKET CLOSING PRICES BU SILVER DOLLARS

Gem (MS-65/70) specimens bring more than the prices listed below.

MORGAN DOLLARS

	MS-60 SINGLES BID	MS-60 SINGLES ASK	MS-65 SINGLES BID	MS-65 SINGLES ASK	ROLLS (MS-65) BID	ROLLS (MS-65) ASK
1878 8tf	17.00	19.00	22.00	– 24.00	425.00	– 465.00
1878 7tf	9.00	10.00	12.00	13.50	225.00	245.00
1878 7/8tf	24.00	26.00	36.00	+ 39.00	675.00	+ 725.00
1878-CC	22.00	24.00	27.50	29.50	525.00	570.00
1878-S	7.00	7.75	10.00	+ 11.25	190.00	+ 202.50
1879-P	8.00	9.00	11.00	12.50	200.00	212.50
1879-CC	340.00	375.00	575.00	+ 625.00	—	—
1879-O	9.00	10.00	12.50	14.00	230.00	255.00
1879-S	6.25	7.00	7.75	8.50	150.00	160.00
1880-P	7.00	7.75	10.00	11.25	185.00	197.50
1880-CC	53.00	56.50	64.00	68.00	1200.00	—
1880-O	11.50	13.00	24.00	26.50	450.00	495.00
1880-S	5.50	6.00	7.15	+ 7.75	137.50	+ 145.00
1881-P	7.00	7.75	10.00	11.25	185.00	197.50
1881-CC	55.00	58.50	66.00	70.00	1250.00	—
1881-O	5.75	6.25	7.75	8.50	145.00	155.00
1881-S	5.50	6.00	7.15	+ 7.75	137.50	+ 145.00
1882-P	6.75	7.50	9.50	10.75	175.00	185.00
1882-CC	19.00	21.00	23.00	– 25.00	450.00	– 485.00
1882-O	5.75	6.25	7.25	8.00	137.50	+ 145.00
1882-S	5.75	6.25	7.50	8.25	145.00	155.00
1883-P	6.25	7.00	8.75	9.50	165.00	+ 175.00
1883-CC	19.00	21.00	23.00	– 25.00	450.00	– 485.00
1883-O	5.50	6.00	6.50	7.00	125.00	131.50
1883-S	125.00	140.00	300.00	+ 340.00	—	—
1884-P	6.00	6.75	8.50	9.25	160.00	170.00
1884-CC	19.00	21.00	23.00	– 25.00	450.00	– 485.00
1884-O	5.50	6.00	6.50	7.00	125.00	131.50
1884-S	270.00	300.00	700.00	+ 775.00	—	—
1885-P	5.50	6.00	6.50	7.00	125.00	+ 131.50
1885-CC	54.00	57.50	61.00	65.00	1150.00	—
1885-O	5.50	6.00	6.50	7.00	125.00	131.50
1885-S	27.50	29.50	37.00	+ 40.00	700.00	760.00
1886-P	5.50	6.00	6.50	7.00	125.00	131.50
1886-O	60.00	64.00	105.00	+ 112.00	1900.00	—
1886-S	60.00	64.00	105.00	+ 112.00	1900.00	—
1887-P	5.50	6.00	6.50	7.00	125.00	131.50
1887-O	9.75	11.00	13.00	+ 14.50	230.00	+ 255.00
1887-S	22.00	24.00	35.00	+ 37.50	650.00	710.00
1888-P	5.50	6.00	6.75	7.25	130.00	137.50
1888-O	6.00	6.50	7.50	+ 8.25	145.00	+ 155.00
1888-S	57.50	61.00	100.00	107.00	1850.00	—
1889-P	5.50	6.00	6.75	7.25	130.00	137.50
1889-CC	1600.00	1900.00	2575.00	+ 2800.00	—	—
1889-O	21.00	23.00	32.00	+ 35.00	575.00	+ 630.00
1889-S	46.00	50.00	70.00	74.50	1300.00	—
1890-P	6.75	7.50	9.00	10.00	170.00	180.00
1890-CC	50.00	53.50	60.00	64.00	1150.00	1275.00
1890-O	17.00	19.00	26.00	+ 28.50	460.00	+ 510.00
1890-S	12.50	14.00	21.50	23.50	400.00	440.00
1891-P	13.00	14.50	24.00	26.00	440.00	485.00
1891-CC	40.00	43.00	46.00	– 49.00	875.00	– 950.00
1891-O	21.00	23.00	32.00	+ 35.00	575.00	+ 630.00
1891-S	16.00	17.50	25.00	27.00	460.00	500.00
1892-P	35.00	38.00	60.00	+ 65.00	1100.00	+ 1225.00
1892-CC	130.00	145.00	185.00	+ 200.00	—	—
1892-O	34.00	37.00	80.00	86.00	1500.00	—
1892-S	3700.00	4000.00	9500.00	—	—	—
1893-P	125.00	137.50	170.00	180.00	—	—
1893-CC	400.00	445.00	660.00	+ 720.00	—	—
1893-O	375.00	410.00	625.00	+ 675.00	—	—
1893-S	15,000.00	17,500.00	27,500.00	+ —	—	—
1894-P	340.00	375.00	525.00	+ 575.00	—	—
1894-O	125.00	150.00	300.00	+ 330.00	—	—
1894-S	130.00	155.00	220.00	+ 245.00	—	—
1895-P	5500.00	5950.00	7750.00	+ 8250.00	—	—
1895-O	900.00	1000.00	1600.00	+ 1800.00	—	—
1895-S	950.00	1050.00	1500.00	+ 1700.00	—	—
1896-P	5.75	6.50	8.00	8.75	150.00	160.00
1896-O	115.00	125.00	200.00	+ 220.00	—	—
1896-S	265.00	295.00	425.00	+ 470.00	—	—
1897-P	8.50	9.50	11.00	12.50	200.00	215.00
1897-O	115.00	125.00	200.00	+ 220.00	—	—
1897-S	18.00	20.00	30.00	+ 33.00	550.00	+ 600.00
1898-P	6.00	6.75	8.50	9.50	160.00	170.00
1898-O	6.25	7.00	7.50	8.25	141.50	+ 149.00
1898-S	76.00	80.00	112.50	120.00	—	—
1899-P	35.00	37.50	41.00	44.00	780.00	– 825.00
1899-O	5.75	6.50	6.75	7.25	130.00	137.50
1899-S	115.00	122.50	175.00	190.00	—	—
1900-P	6.00	6.75	7.50	8.10	140.00	150.00
1900-O	5.75	6.50	6.75	7.25	130.00	137.50
1900-S	72.00	76.00	105.00	112.50	—	—
1901-P	300.00	340.00	850.00	+ 950.00	—	—
1901-O	6.75	7.50	9.50	10.50	180.00	192.50
1901-S	83.00	87.50	115.00	+ 122.50	—	—
1902-P	14.50	16.00	24.00	26.00	450.00	495.00
1902-O	5.75	6.50	6.75	7.25	130.00	137.50
1902-S	110.00	117.50	215.00	+ 230.00	—	—
1903-P	10.00	11.50	15.00	17.00	280.00	305.00
1903-O	48.00	51.00	55.00	58.50	1075.00	1175.00
1903-S	700.00	775.00	1250.00	+ 1375.00	—	—
1904-P	23.00	25.00	40.00	43.00	760.00	+ 825.00
1904-O	6.00	6.75	6.85	+ 7.35	132.50	+ 140.00
1904-S	310.00	340.00	450.00	495.00	—	—
1921-P	4.75	5.25	5.50	6.00	105.00	111.00
1921-D	7.00	8.00	16.00	18.00	285.00	+ 310.00
1921-S	7.00	8.00	12.00	13.50	215.00	+ 235.00

PEACE DOLLARS

	MS-60 SINGLES BID	MS-60 SINGLES ASK	MS-65 SINGLES BID	MS-65 SINGLES ASK	ROLLS (MS-65) BID	ROLLS (MS-65) ASK
1921-P	65.00	69.50	105.00	115.00	1950.00	—
1922-P	4.50	5.00	5.25	5.75	103.00	108.00
1922-D	7.75	8.75	15.00	+ 16.50	260.00	285.00
1922-S	7.75	8.75	15.00	+ 16.50	260.00	285.00
1923-P	4.50	5.00	5.25	5.75	103.00	108.00
1923-D	8.50	9.50	15.00	+ 16.50	260.00	285.00
1923-S	8.00	9.00	15.00	+ 16.50	260.00	285.00
1924-P	5.00	5.50	6.25	6.85	122.50	130.00
1924-S	47.00	50.00	80.00	+ 85.00	1500.00	—
1925-P	5.00	5.50	6.25	6.85	122.50	130.00
1925-S	39.00	42.00	56.00	+ 59.50	1000.00	1100.00
1926-P	11.50	13.00	15.50	17.00	280.00	310.00
1926-D	13.50	15.00	24.00	+ 26.50	440.00	+ 480.00
1926-S	12.50	14.00	20.00	22.00	380.00	415.00
1927-P	30.00	32.50	45.00	48.00	850.00	925.00
1927-D	47.00	50.00	80.00	+ 85.00	1500.00	—
1972-S	80.00	85.00	130.00	+ 140.00	—	—
1928-P	127.50	135.00	150.00	162.50	—	—
1928-S	46.00	49.00	85.00	+ 90.00	1550.00	—
1934-P	32.50	35.00	44.00	47.00	850.00	925.00
1934-D	43.00	45.00	65.00	69.50	1200.00	—
1934-S	425.00	475.00	725.00	+ 795.00	—	—
1935-P	24.00	26.00	38.00	41.00	740.00	800.00
1935-S	60.00	64.00	100.00	107.00	1900.00	—

EISENHOWER DOLLARS

		SINGLES BID	SINGLES ASK	ROLLS BID	ROLLS ASK
1971-P	47.799	—	—	27.00	29.00
1971-D	68.587	—	—	25.00	27.00
1971-S	6.869	2.75	3.00	—	—
1971-S Proof	4.265	4.85	5.20	—	—
1972-P	75.890	—	—	23.00	+ 25.00
1972-D	92.549	—	—	23.50	+ 25.50
1972-S	2.193	2.90	3.15	—	—
1972-S Proof	1.182	5.75	6.10	—	—
1973-P	2.000	5.65	6.15	110.00	120.00
1973-D	2.000	5.65	6.15	110.00	120.00
1973-S	1.883	3.90	4.20	—	—
1973-S Proof	1.006	19.50	21.00	—	—
1973-S Cl. Pr.	2.770	3.10	3.35	60.00	65.00
1974-P	27.366	—	—	21.50	23.00
1974-D	35.466	—	—	21.50	23.00
1974-S	.585	2.80	3.05	—	—
1974-S Proof	1.315	6.05	6.45	—	—
1974-S Cl. Pr.	2.617	2.40	2.65	44.00	47.00
1976-P					
1976-D					
1976-S Cl. Pr.		4.50	5.00	85.00	95.00

PROOF SETS

		BID	ASK
1936	(3,837)	1200.00	1300.00
1937	(5,542)	550.00	– 600.00
1938	(8,045)	270.00	295.00
1939	(8,795)	260.00	282.50
1940	(11,246)	185.00	195.00
1941	(15,287)	180.00	190.00
1942	(21,120)	180.00	190.00
1942t2		225.00	245.00
1950	(51,386)	165.00	172.50
1951	(57,500)	105.00	112.00

		BID	ASK
1952	(81,980)	69.50	73.00
1953	(128,800)	37.00	39.50
1954	(233,300)	22.50	23.75
1955(box)	(378,200)	22.00	23.25
1955(f.p.)		23.00	24.25
1956	(699,384)	9.75	10.35
1957	(1,247,952)	6.00	6.35
1958	(875,652)	9.25	9.75
1959	(1,149,291)	6.00	6.35
1960	(1,691,602)	5.40	5.70

		BID	ASK
1960sm		16.00	17.00
1961	(3,028,244)	4.15	4.40
1962	(3,218,019)	4.15	4.40
1963	(3,075,645)	4.15	4.40
1964	(3,950,762)	4.25	– 4.55
1968-S	(3,041,509)	3.80	+ 4.05
1968-S"P"10c		5000.00	—
1969-S	(2,934,631)	3.75	+ 4.00
1970-S	(2,632,810)	8.45	+ 8.95
1970-S sm		36.00	39.00

	BID	ASK
1970-S"P" 10c (2,200)	360.00	+ 390.00
1971-S (3,224,138)	3.90	+ 4.15
1971-S"P" 5c (1,655)	470.00	+ 510.00
1972-S (3,267,667)	4.00	+ 4.25
1973-S (2,769,624)	10.50	+ 11.25
1974-S (2,617,350)	8.00	8.50
1975-S	19.50	+ 21.00
1976-S (3 pc 40%)	14.00	+ 15.50

MINT SETS

1946-58 are Treasury issued double sets (2 of each coin as issued); 1959 to date are single sets of government issue.

	BID	ASK		BID	ASK		BID	ASK		BID	ASK
1946	127.50	135.00	1954	23.00	25.00	1962	5.25	5.75	1970	14.50	15.50
1947	85.00	90.00	1955	22.00	– 24.00	1963	5.25	5.75	1971	2.00	2.20
1948	46.00	49.50	1956	10.50	11.50	1964	5.25	5.75	1972	2.05	2.25
1949	210.00	227.50	1957	15.50	16.75	1965 sms	1.95	2.10	1973	12.50	13.50
1950	97.50	104.00	1958	14.75	16.00	1966 sms	2.15	2.35	1974	3.85	4.10
1951	115.00	121.50	1959	6.75	7.25	1967 sms	2.85	3.10	1976-S (3 pc. 40%)	10.50	+ 12.00
1952	66.00	70.00	1960	5.75	6.25	1968	1.90	2.10			
1953	48.00	51.50	1961	5.50	6.00	1969	1.90	2.10			

Page 6 of the CDN, August 15, 1975
First 1975 Gem listing page (Courtesy of CDN)

As “BU” evolved to “BU and GEM BU” and ultimately to “BU, Choice BU, and Gem BU”, the numismatic industry also began to “experiment” with applying Dr. William Sheldon’s 70-point grading scale for Large Cents to all coins. MS-60, MS-63, and MS-65 terminology became the rage. According to Jim Ruddy, the numerical system became popular because “the numbers made it all seem very scientific. A ’Choice BU’ label is vague; an ’MS-63’ label is precise.”

As dealer usage of the “new” intermediate grades (MS-63, MS-64, MS-67, etc.) became accepted in the marketplace, they were added to the Greysheet. In 1980 the Greysheet added an MS-63 column, and in 1985 MS-64 became a standard feature.

the COIN DEALER newsletter

. . . a Monday morning report on the Coin Market

Vol. XVIII No. 39 | September 26, 1980 | Single copy price: $2.50

"MS-63" COLUMN ADDED TO DOLLAR CHARTS!

Minimum Bid Of $775 Recorded For BU Pre-1921 Morgan Rolls; Singles Strong

The Market in Depth

ALLEN HARRIMAN

Readers will note that, with this issue, we have added a MS-63 bid-ask column to both the Morgan and Peace dollar charts! This new category of prices is in line with

uncirculated coins---not the brown "sliders" so often offered as unc.) Prices have also advanced for the later XF and AU specimens of both denominations---with the needed quantities not being located thus far.

NICKELS: All three of the early half-dimes are again bid at higher levels in all grades from Good thru AU. These little devils are particularly difficult to find without defects of one sort or another; pieces with problems, of course, bring lower prices. There is

CDN Headline, September 26, 1980
(Courtesy of CDN)

the COIN DEALER newsletter

. . . a Monday morning report on the Coin Market

Vol. XXII No. 10 | March 8, 1985 | Single copy price: $3.50

U.S. GOLD WITH EYE APPEAL WANTED IN ALL DENOMINATIONS

"MS-64" Column Added To Dollar Charts!

The Market in Depth

YEAR: 1985

QUESTION: What does it take for a coin to command today's MS-65 "bid"?

Before this question can be answered, some background information is required. The

quarters look very nice with the naked eye. But, upon close examination with a magnifying glass, little pin marks may show up on many of the coins. The obverse does not display much detail; it has a smooth (not weak) surface. There are not many locations where bag marks can hide.

HALVES: Walking Liberty halves seem to be the second most popular silver coin behind silver dollars. It is large and enjoys extravagant detail in which minute bagmarks can hide. Nevertheless, if those marks show up in the field to the right of Liberty, or on the sun to the left, or on the reverse feathers, the many buyers of this coin will

CDN Headline, March 8, 1985
(Courtesy of CDN)

We believe that the CDN played a major part in the growth of the Morgan and Peace Dollar Market through its unique role as an independent source of pricing information. People unsure of the true value of a coin are not likely to be willing to "stretch" to purchase it. The Greysheet acted as a reliable source of information on pricing and the market, and that allowed the buyers to feel more comfortable in the sometimes intimidating numismatic marketplace. And that information wasn't just confined to the Morgan and Peace dollars; in 1971, the CDN began to list Type prices for other dollars. We now include Bids & Asks for Flowing Hair Dollars, Draped Bust Dollars (small and large eagles), Seated Liberty Dollars (no motto and motto), Trade Dollars, and Gobrecht Dollars.

Along with all the changes in the marketplace during the 1980s, there was one other major change at CDN — ownership passed to the partnership of my mom and myself. This was certainly a major change in my life, as one of the requirements was that I leave the coin business. The CDN was too important to the coin market to be confronted by possible charges of conflict of interest; we could not allow our reputation for independence and accuracy to be challenged by anyone claiming self-dealing. So I stopped being a coin dealer and became a publisher.

Certified Coins

From its creation in 1986, the Certified Coin Dealer newsletter (the "Bluesheet") reflected the new realities of the coin market. That is not to say that there haven't been additional changes in that market; there have, and they have been important changes. But all of the recent refinements have been predicated upon the market's interest in individual, quality-grade coins, and the relative consistency of third-party grading.

August 22, 1986 — ***CERTIFIED COIN DEALER newsletter*** — **Page 3**

MORGAN DOLLARS

Soft struck coins will not command bid levels where full strikes normally exist.
NB - Represents no bid at this time.

	ANACS				NCI		PCGS					
	MS62/63 MS62/62	MS63/64 MS63/63	MS64/64 MS64/65 MS65/64 MS65/63	MS65/65	MS64	MS65	MS61	MS62	MS63	MS64	MS65	MS66
1878 8TF	75	110	320	NB	150	NB	65	75	120	400	1,750	NB
1878 7/8TF	85	135	390	NB	184	NB	70	85	145	525	2,000	NB
1878 7TF	65	85	300	1,450	140	525	55	65	90	350	1,400	2,000
1878 7TF (Rev. 79)	80	100	325	1,800	150	NB	70	80	100	375	1,750	NB
1878 CC	125	185	425	1,400	200	545	105	125	200	550	1,450	1,950
1878 S	65	100	330	900	150	330	55	65	110	375	950	1,300
1879	55	80	300	1,400	145	490	45	55	90	450	1,400	NB
1879 CC	NB	1,950	NB	NB	NB	NB	1,200	1,400	1,950	3,500	8,600	NB
1879 CC Capped Die	NB	1,050	NB	NB	700	NB	700	750	1,100	1,750	2,350	NB
1879 O	75	145	595	NB	280	NB	60	75	175	700	NB	NB
1879 S (Rev. 78)	110	140	445	NB	210	NB	100	110	135	450	2,200	NB
1879 S	60	110	175	500	85	180	50	60	100	210	510	1,050
1880	50	82	275	950	130	385	40	50	90	300	1,000	1,500
1880 CC	195	275	595	NB	280	700	160	195	300	775	1,800	2,600
1880 O	110	170	660	NB	310	NB	70	110	190	850	NB	NB
1880 S	60	90	175	500	85	175	45	60	100	210	500	1,000
1881	50	80	250	900	115	335	35	50	90	285	900	1,225
1881 CC	250	340	595	1,350	130	525	215	250	360	725	1,500	2,050
1881 O	40	80	320	1,180	150	420	40	50	100	475	1,250	1,450
1881 S	60	110	160	450	75	165	45	60	100	200	475	1,000
1882	50	80	275	900	130	340	35	50	90	325	900	1,250
1882 CC	125	175	460	900	185	375	100	125	200	450	925	1,250
1882 O	40	74	280	900	130	335	40	50	100	400	900	1,250
1882 S	60	95	180	525	85	195	45	60	100	210	525	1,100
1883	45	80	240	775	115	300	35	45	90	280	800	1,100
1883 CC	125	175	365	810	170	315	100	125	200	450	925	1,250
1883 O	40	65	180	550	85	220	30	40	85	210	550	1,100
1883-S	NB	790	1,150	NB	540	NB	400	515	850	1,250	4,250	6,000
1884	55	90	280	900	125	350	35	55	100	300	900	1,300
1884 CC	125	175	390	900	185	350	100	125	200	450	925	1,225
1884 O	40	70	180	550	85	210	30	40	85	210	550	1,100
1884 S	NB	3,200	NB	NB	NB	NB	1,450	2,000	3,200	7,500	22,500	NB
1885	40	70	185	575	85	210	30	40	85	210	575	1,100
1885 CC	265	340	600	1,600	280	580	235	265	360	700	1,650	2,125
1885 O	40	70	180	550	85	210	30	40	85	210	550	1,100
1885 S	145	220	510	1,600	240	630	115	145	235	650	1,600	2,000
1886	40	75	180	525	85	195	30	40	85	210	525	1,100
1886 O	410	650	1,400	NB	660	NB	325	410	700	1,750	4,950	NB
1886 S	185	265	635	NB	300	750	150	185	285	750	2,150	2,500
1887	40	70	190	550	90	235	30	40	85	210	550	1,100
1887/6	75	92	320	720	150	280	65	75	93	380	800	1,100
1887 O	60	87	190	NB	150	580	55	60	100	550	1,500	NB
1887/6 O	90	110	385	NB	180	665	80	90	210	600	1,900	NB
1887 S	120	210	620	NB	290	665	85	120	230	725	1,725	2,325
1888	40	75	195	650	90	225	30	40	85	225	650	1,100
1888 O	40	80	235	875	110	310	30	40	90	340	825	1,100
1888 S	200	275	615	NB	270	NB	180	200	300	725	2,000	3,000
1889	40	80	255	900	120	350	30	40	85	300	1,000	NB
1889 CC	NB	7,250	NB	NB	NB	NB	5,100	5,750	7,300	10,000	21,250	NB
1889 O	115	215	595	NB	280	NB	80	115	230	700	3,100	NB
1889 S	170	250	595	NB	280	630	135	170	250	700	1,700	2,250
1890	40	85	300	1,100	140	420	30	40	95	350	1,200	NB
1890 CC	255	360	575	NB	270	700	210	255	385	675	1,800	2,400
1890 O	70	95	400	NB	200	550	60	70	105	525	1,575	NB
1890 S	85	125	330	1,000	155	385	75	85	135	375	950	1,375
1891	90	135	550	NB	260	NB	70	90	150	650	2,150	NB
1891 CC	250	355	575	NB	270	665	210	250	375	675	1,700	2,500
1891 O	100	175	700	NB	330	NB	70	110	190	825	4,250	NB
1891 S	90	130	320	975	150	340	75	90	140	375	975	1,375
1892	185	310	765	NB	360	NB	130	185	325	900	2,925	NB
1892 CC	390	520	785	NB	370	NB	340	390	525	925	2,200	3,175
1892 O	170	350	675	NB	330	NB	115	170	375	825	3,825	NB
1892 S	NB	7,250	NB	NB	NB	NB	4,000	5,000	7,250	11,000	32,250	NB
1893	350	540	975	NB	460	NB	280	350	575	1,150	3,375	NB
1893 CC	975	1,600	NB	NB	NB	NB	690	975	1,700	2,800	8,500	NB
1893 O	NB	1,900	NB	NB	NB	NB	875	1,175	1,900	5,500	NB	NB
1893 S	NB	24,500	NB	NB	NB	NB	NB	NB	NB	NB	NB	NB
1894	NB	1,300	NB	NB	NB	NB	825	975	1,350	2,950	9,000	NB
1894 O	NB	950	NB	NB	NB	NB	385	550	950	NB	NB	NB
1894 S	NB	600	925	NB	440	NB	295	475	650	1,100	2,925	NB
1895 Proof	NB	16,500	NB	NB	NB	NB	NB	NB	16,500	18,000	31,500	40,000
1895 O	NB	4,800	NB	NB	NB	NB	1,800	2,750	4,000	NB	NB	NB
1895 S	NB	1,400	NB	NB	NB	NB	850	1,000	1,300	3,250	7,800	NB
1896	40	75	200	700	95	245	30	40	85	225	670	1,100
1896 O	NB	1,300	NB	NB	NB	NB	650	850	1,200	5,300	27,500	NB
1896 S	NB	800	1,500	NB	720	NB	485	580	850	1,800	5,200	NB
1897	40	80	270	750	120	270	30	40	85	300	775	1,100
1897 O	NB	825	NB	NB	NB	NB	325	495	900	2,200	9,000	NB
1897 S	105	175	360	1,050	160	350	75	105	185	400	1,000	1,425
1898	40	75	225	725	100	270	30	40	85	225	725	1,100
1898 O	40	75	200	640	90	230	30	40	85	225	650	1,100
1898 S	190	325	800	NB	340	NB	165	200	350	850	2,000	2,600
1899	115	180	375	1,450	175	550	90	115	185	450	1,400	1,850
1899 O	40	80	220	650	105	235	30	40	90	225	675	1,100
1899 S	150	310	750	NB	320	NB	125	150	325	800	2,150	2,550
1900	40	65	225	800	100	290	30	40	85	225	775	1,100
1900 O	40	75	200	600	90	220	30	40	85	225	600	1,100
1900 O/CC	130	190	425	NB	200	630	110	130	200	500	1,600	NB
1900 S	150	280	675	NB	280	560	115	165	300	700	1,450	NB
1901	NB	2,100	NB	NB	NB	NB	825	1,200	2,300	7,500	25,200	NB
1901 O	40	80	225	950	100	360	30	40	85	250	1,000	NB
1901 S	290	550	1,000	NB	480	NB	235	300	600	1,250	3,450	NB
1902	65	105	375	1,325	175	510	55	65	110	440	1,500	NB
1902 O	40	80	200	700	90	265	30	40	85	225	700	1,100
1902 S	250	400	650	NB	305	NB	200	260	400	750	2,250	NB
1903	65	105	315	925	150	350	50	65	100	350	1,100	1,250
1903 O	255	310	500	1,100	235	420	240	255	310	550	1,150	1,500
1903 S	1,900	2,800	NB	NB	NB	NB	1,550	1,950	2,700	4,000	8,000	NB
1904	140	260	460	NB	220	NB	85	140	275	550	2,400	NB
1904 O	40	60	200	575	90	210	30	40	85	225	550	1,100
1904 S	975	1,775	2,000	NB	NB	NB	775	1,050	1,700	2,250	4,500	NB
1921	30	50	155	525	70	195	25	30	55	175	550	1,100
1921 D	40	85	295	1,025	140	395	35	40	85	345	1,125	NB
1921 S	40	95	320	1,300	160	510	30	40	95	400	1,450	NB

PEACE DOLLARS

	ANACS				NCI		PCGS					
	MS62/63 MS62/62	MS63/64 MS63/63	MS64/64 MS64/65 MS65/64 MS65/63	MS65/65	MS64	MS65	MS61	MS62	MS63	MS64	MS65	MS66
1921	220	340	800	NB	380	NB	190	240	375	900	4,275	NB
1922	30	50	175	625	80	210	22	30	55	200	625	1,000
1922 D	50	80	300	1,080	140	420	40	50	90	325	1,000	1,450
1922 S	45	93	340	NB	160	560	45	55	100	400	1,350	1,925
1923	30	50	175	625	80	210	22	30	55	200	625	1,000
1923 D	60	105	310	1,800	145	700	45	60	95	365	2,000	NB
1923 S	55	115	350	NB	170	NB	43	65	120	425	2,400	NB
1924	45	65	220	650	100	235	35	45	70	250	650	1,100
1924 S	175	335	850	NB	440	NB	140	200	350	1,050	3,200	NB
1925	45	65	200	650	95	230	35	45	70	250	650	1,100
1925 S	160	275	625	NB	290	NB	120	170	300	700	2,600	NB
1926	65	100	340	1,125	160	440	50	65	100	400	1,100	1,600
1926 D	85	145	375	1,530	175	595	65	85	150	425	1,700	NB
1926 S	60	105	300	1,300	160	510	50	65	105	400	1,200	1,725
1927	130	210	425	1,800	200	700	95	130	210	500	2,000	NB
1927 D	300	520	900	NB	420	NB	200	300	500	1,050	3,825	NB
1927 S	170	290	450	NB	230	NB	140	185	265	575	2,200	NB
1928	260	370	610	NB	285	NB	210	260	350	700	2,850	3,650
1928 S	150	295	425	NB	240	NB	110	170	265	600	2,600	NB
1934	125	205	480	1,900	220	NB	85	125	200	550	1,850	2,575
1934 D	155	285	510	2,400	240	NB	95	155	260	600	2,600	NB
1934 S	NB	2,250	NB	NB	NB	NB	1,250	1,500	2,200	3,500	8,150	NB
1935	80	130	375	1,300	175	510	60	80	125	440	1,250	1,825
1935 S	190	360	550	NB	290	NB	150	210	350	700	2,250	2,950

Page 3 of the CDN, August 22, 1986 (Courtesy of CDN)

"One of the grand traditions of the CDN," my mom is fond of saying, "has been our ability to make changes and improvements over the years to reflect changes in the market. When certified coins began growing in popularity, we were able to gather information quickly, utilizing old contacts and gaining some new ones. We started The Certified Coin Dealer newsletter because there was a market need for that reliable information. Gathering it made both us and the market stronger."

With PCGS's introduction of the additional mint state grading numbers (MS-61 through 70), the market began to look at uncirculated coins even more closely. The Bluesheet started listing grades from MS-61 through MS-66, as that was where most of the action was (and consequently where reliable information could be obtained).

CERTIFIED COIN DEALER newsletter

a weekly report on the certified market
published by the Coin Dealer Newsletter (est. 1963)

Vol. V No. 37 September 14, 1990 Single copy price $3.50

Plus Signs Signal Increased Demand As Buyers Step to the Plate

After the incessant "bad" news of the last several weeks, it is a pleasure to report that we are starting to see increased bidding activity – **and at higher levels**. Since autumn nearly always inspires us to baseball metaphors, it is good to see the solid hitters taking charge at the plate. This is not to deny that minus signs still dominate some charts, and still represent some very serious declines. But overall, the lowered levels have brought out some equally serious buyers who are willing to push Bids in the "plus" direction. As a leading dealer recently pointed out, lowered levels not only made many coins more 'affordable', they also meant that the coins would carry less risk. This becomes more apparent as the market starts to turn around.

While we are heartened by the week's Bids, we must also report that there remain many dealers who are predicting that some coin prices may still have a way to fall. They point to two leading factors: 1) the liquidation that has been occurring in the coin market for several years now, marked by consistent declines in prices for the *bulk* of the material in the marketplace, and 2) general economic uncertainty that has many other investments also declining in value. While they too cheer the recent plus signs, they see such activity as an interlude, as a calm time between the waves of liquidation.

Also significant in this ever-changing market is the fact that it has become more difficult to "find" the highest Bidder. In the 'good old days', someone who needed a coin would advertise that 'demand" in as many places as possible. Now, the message may appear only once on only one service; miss the message and you miss the opportunity. Anyone selling coins could easily miss the highest Bid. If you are liquidating coins for another party, your **fiduciary duty** to find that highest Bid has become more difficult in this market – and not utilizing every source of information available could easily result in dereliction of duty to your customer. This could become a serious problem; we have seen instances where one group of messages has resulted in turning more than 100 minus signs into **plus** signs. One thing is sure – more messages like that and the market may turn around a lot quicker!

This week also marks the introduction of improved versions of our graphs. Heretofore, we offered "Composite" graphs which tracked the total **dollar** amount of all of the Bids appearing on the underlying chart; this technique had a stabilizing effect, as it equally weighted all **dollars** (which naturally made the higher grade and value coins have a greater influence). We have listened to many dealers voice their opinion that it would be more suitable to have each **coin** weighted equally, instead of each **dollar** bid.

We have been convinced, although it took one very good Bid for one MS-67 Peace Dollar to clinch their argument. Accordingly, we have now adopted an entirely new approach to the graphs, and one that we think will fulfill your requests for an accurate depiction of the current market. For each coin listed in each grade, we are comparing its current Bid to its Bid level on January 5, 1990. For Peace Dollars, that means we are calculating percentages for 24 issues times seven grades (MS-61 through MS-67) times 2 grading services (PCGS & NGC). This produces 336 weekly percentage changes (increases or declines), and we take the average of those results for a final depiction of that series. If half of the coins went down 20% and half went down 10%, we would show the market average down 15%; this method makes it irrelevant whether that 15% decrease equals $10 or $1000.

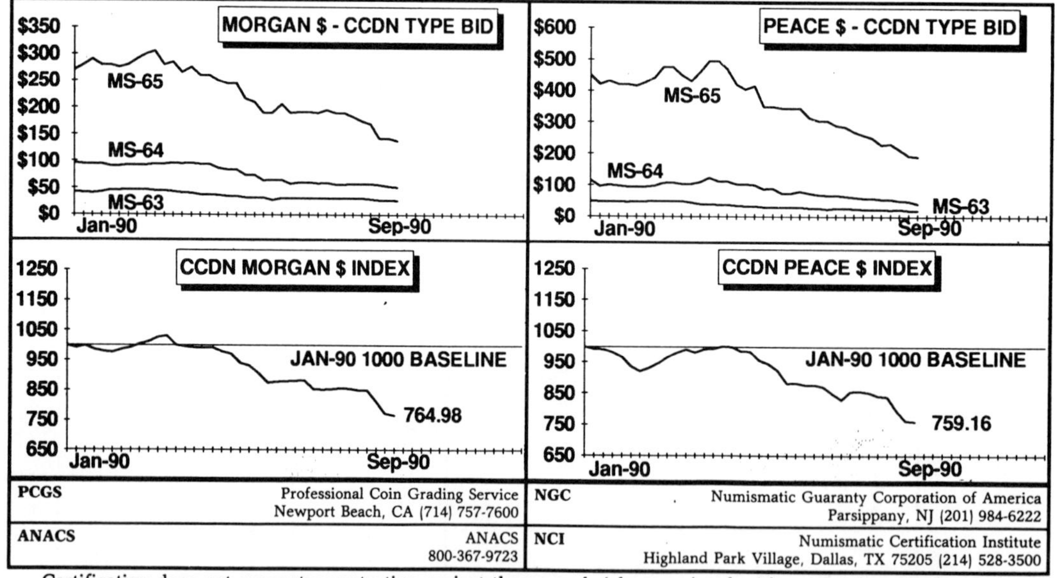

PCGS	Professional Coin Grading Service Newport Beach, CA (714) 757-7600	**NGC**	Numismatic Guaranty Corporation of America Parsippany, NJ (201) 984-6222
ANACS	ANACS 800-367-9723	**NCI**	Numismatic Certification Institute Highland Park Village, Dallas, TX 75205 (214) 528-3500

Certification does not guarantee protection against the normal risks associated with potentially volatile markets. Client or sight-seen sales may command a substantial premium above *Bluesheet* Dealer-to-Dealer Bids.

CDN Headline, September 14, 1990 (Courtesy of CDN)

Later, as MS-67 specimens began to appear with more regularity, that column was added. Most of the changes in the Bluesheet over the last five years have involved the extension of our charts as increasing numbers of coins (and coin types) were certified.

Of course, there have also been some changes as the relative importance of certification firms changed in the marketplace. When the Bluesheet began publishing, PCGS was the dominant factor in slabbed dollars; ANACS was a major presence in the third-party grading, and NCI was also a strong contender. ANACS' late adoption of encapsulation (or "slabbing"), after Numismatic Guaranty Corp. had captured second place with its own slab, relegated them to a relatively minor role in the certified market.

September 14, 1990 — CERTIFIED COIN DEALER newsletter — Page 3

MORGAN DOLLARS

PCGS DMPL and NGC DPL Bids are for fully Deep Mirror Prooflike coins. Bids for PCGS PL and NGC PL dollars (semi-prooflike or one-sided PL) will be listed monthly in a supplemental insert. CDN *(Greysheet)* Bids have always represented fully, deep mirror prooflike specimens.

	PCGS										NGC									
	MS61	MS62	MS63	MS63 DMPL	MS64	MS64 DMPL	MS65	MS65 DMPL	MS66	MS67	MS61	MS62	MS63	MS63 DPL	MS64	MS64 DPL	MS65	MS65 DPL	MS66	MS67
1878 8TF	+ 36	+ 40	+ 61	+ 320	220	+ 1,100	+ 1,900	+ 6,160	12,000	17,500	31	35	57	270	- 180	+ 1,150	1,650	5,200	11,000	14,000
1878 7/8TF	50	53	+ 77	500	- 225	- 1,450	2,900	- 5,500	5,000	9,000	45	48	70	450	- 210	- 1,300	2,750	- 5,350	- 5,000	- 9,500
1878 7TF	22	+ 27	+ 39	- 340	105	+ 1,070	2,000	+ 6,450	- 8,500	16,000	22	25	37	- 325	100	+ 1,100	1,900	6,000	- 8,250	14,000
1878 7TF (Rev. 79)	22	+ 28	+ 65	- 485	250	- 1,075	+ 2,750	6,500	5,000	9,000	24	26	55	425	240	- 1,050	2,600	6,500	- 5,150	- 10,000
1878 CC	+ 71	+ 76	78	- 360	170	- 525	+ 1,350	4,000	+ 4,100	15,000	62	67	77	- 350	160	- 500	1,350	3,850	- 5,500	- 14,500
1878 S	19	+ 23	+ 35	465	63	800	+ 227	4,000	+ 1,300	5,750	16	21	33	400	60	- 625	215	3,850	- 1,500	- 5,500
1879	18	+ 21	+ 31	290	120	1,120	- 1,175	6,700	- 4,000	- 7,000	16	21	30	275	110	1,000	- 1,150	6,000	- 4,250	- 7,000
1879 CC	1,035	1,600	2,000	3,800	3,500	6,000	10,500	18,000	19,000	32,000	1,000	1,500	2,350	3,750	3,450	6,000	- 10,000	- 17,500	- 18,500	- 30,000
1879 CC Capped Die	910	1,150	+ 1,400	+ 4,720	3,500	6,000	20,500	29,000	32,000	47,500	875	1,075	1,350	4,400	3,450	6,000	18,550	27,500	31,000	45,000
1879 O	26	+ 50	+ 110	+ 585	+ 355	1,750	4,100	+ 13,000	10,750	19,000	27	44	90	525	340	+ 1,800	3,600	9,250	10,500	18,500
1879 S (Rev. 78)	+ 72	85	- 115	+ 1,870	+ 925	+ 4,790	6,800	- 15,000	12,500	23,000	70	80	- 120	1,600	900	4,000	6,750	- 14,000	12,000	22,500
1879 S	18	- 19	- 27	+ 87	- 50	- 195	- 138	1,050	- 385	- 1,400	16	18	- 23	80	- 43	- 180	125	1,000	380	1,475
1880	- 18	+ 21	+ 33	- 270	125	- 525	+ 1,825	4,750	+ 8,100	12,500	20	22	27	- 250	120	- 500	1,500	4,250	7,500	12,000
1880 CC	110	115	130	280	- 175	- 700	- 875	5,650	3,500	10,500	105	110	130	275	- 165	- 675	850	5,250	5,500	10,000
1880 O	33	+ 62	+ 300	735	1,425	- 3,300	19,500	+ 55,000	36,000	60,000	30	+ 47	225	700	1,250	- 3,250	15,500	+ 45,000	35,000	55,000
1880 S	18	- 19	- 27	85	+ 55	- 195	- 138	860	- 385	- 1,400	16	18	- 23	80	- 43	- 180	125	850	380	1,475
1881	18	+ 21	+ 32	375	- 117	+ 1,045	1,250	+ 6,885	- 4,000	- 7,500	20	22	30	350	110	+ 900	- 1,200	6,500	- 4,500	- 8,000
1881 CC	120	+ 129	155	- 360	204	- 650	+ 425	3,000	+ 1,540	8,100	120	125	150	- 350	200	- 625	425	3,000	+ 1,900	8,000
1881 O	18	+ 21	+ 35	+ 320	+ 150	1,800	+ 2,250	- 4,750	3,600	7,000	16	20	30	260	125	1,500	2,150	- 5,000	- 3,500	- 7,000
1881 S	18	- 19	- 27	85	- 52	- 195	- 138	860	- 385	- 1,400	16	18	- 23	80	- 43	- 180	125	850	380	1,475
1882	- 18	+ 21	31	230	- 60	+ 710	600	4,700	+ 2,200	- 6,500	+ 17	20	30	225	- 60	+ 700	575	4,250	2,150	- 7,000
1882 CC	- 51	57	75	100	115	- 200	300	1,825	+ 1,510	- 9,100	55	58	75	95	105	- 190	320	1,925	- 1,650	- 9,000
1882 O	20	22	+ 32	+ 172	100	900	+ 1,750	6,000	7,000	25,000	20	22	28	160	100	875	1,400	5,000	- 6,850	12,000
1882 S	18	+ 21	28	170	- 50	- 525	- 140	2,000	- 385	+ 1,650	16	18	- 23	160	- 43	- 500	125	- 1,900	400	1,950
1883	18	+ 21	29	+ 87	- 50	- 290	180	3,800	+ 900	3,150	16	20	25	90	46	300	- 150	3,150	800	3,000
1883 CC	50	+ 54	72	100	+ 108	- 195	260	1,625	1,200	7,500	52	55	70	90	99	- 190	+ 260	2,000	1,575	- 7,250
1883 O	18	- 19	- 27	85	- 50	- 195	- 150	2,250	+ 1,200	- 4,500	16	18	- 23	80	- 43	+ 290	150	2,100	1,050	- 5,000
1883 S	+ 290	+ 335	+ 1,050	+ 2,710	+ 2,900	3,750	+ 24,500	34,000	36,000	42,500	270	310	950	2,500	2,600	- 3,500	19,000	26,000	30,000	40,000
1884	18	+ 21	32	170	64	+ 710	330	3,800	+ 1,425	12,000	16	20	30	150	- 43	+ 625	280	- 3,500	1,500	10,000
1884 CC	52	57	72	+ 90	115	- 195	260	1,625	+ 1,500	8,500	52	56	70	90	105	- 190	+ 270	1,975	2,000	7,000
1884 O	18	- 19	- 27	85	- 50	- 195	- 138	1,500	+ 810	+ 2,800	16	18	- 23	80	- 43	+ 300	125	1,600	- 800	2,100
1884 S	5,250	7,000	- 16,000	20,000	35,000	55,000	150K	+ 180K	180K	290K	4,500	6,350	14,000	20,000	33,500	52,000	130K	155K	140K	240K
1885	18	+ 21	28	85	- 50	- 195	- 138	1,460	520	- 2,500	16	18	- 23	80	- 43	+ 300	125	1,800	- 650	- 2,450
1885 CC	170	180	+ 200	245	240	- 475	685	2,625	+ 1,875	+ 7,500	170	175	190	- 230	230	+ 550	650	2,425	2,000	7,000
1885 O	18	- 19	- 27	+ 87	- 50	- 195	- 138	1,375	600	- 1,700	16	18	- 23	80	- 43	- 180	125	1,675	650	- 2,000
1885 S	60	+ 72	120	+ 1,685	310	+ 3,185	+ 2,700	8,750	6,000	- 11,500	55	70	110	1,525	300	2,950	2,400	8,000	- 6,000	- 11,000
1886	18	- 19	- 27	85	- 50	+ 300	- 138	1,750	+ 525	+ 1,650	16	18	- 23	80	46	+ 225	125	1,800	675	1,750
1886 O	355	535	1,450	+ 4,000	- 6,000	13,500	- 12,000	- 40,000	- 22,500	- 42,500	320	460	1,400	3,600	6,000	13,000	- 12,500	- 38,500	- 24,000	- 45,000
1886 S	+ 67	+ 87	+ 170	+ 1,385	+ 435	+ 3,050	2,800	8,850	- 7,000	13,000	65	85	120	1,150	400	2,600	2,750	6,750	7,250	12,500
1887	18	20	- 27	+ 87	- 50	- 195	- 138	1,800	+ 770	- 5,500	16	18	- 23	80	46	+ 290	125	+ 1,775	700	- 6,000
1887/6	+ 60	- 100	- 500	+ 1,380	875	+ 4,050	+ 4,500	+ 9,160	7,000	12,500	40	95	400	1,200	800	3,650	4,000	8,000	- 6,750	- 12,000
1887 O	+ 24	+ 35	+ 55	285	525	+ 1,800	6,000	12,000	11,000	20,000	25	34	50	275	425	900	- 5,500	11,500	11,000	20,000
1887/6 O	- 105	+ 305	1,400	+ 3,880	2,650	+ 6,350	- 4,000	- 11,500	- 7,200	15,000	- 100	250	1,200	- 3,250	2,500	5,850	- 4,000	- 12,000	- 7,500	- 14,500
1887 S	46	+ 62	+ 140	- 925	+ 440	+ 2,700	3,850	+ 7,000	+ 15,000	22,000	40	55	95	- 900	400	- 2,250	3,650	5,500	12,000	20,000
1888	18	+ 21	- 27	225	- 50	- 525	240	3,950	+ 1,875	12,250	16	20	- 26	200	48	- 500	200	3,750	1,750	10,000
1888 O	18	+ 21	+ 33	100	70	- 350	+ 725	4,200	- 4,000	7,000	16	20	30	100	70	- 325	650	3,500	- 3,850	- 7,000
1888 S	72	+ 92	+ 155	435	+ 440	- 1,350	3,000	10,250	20,500	28,000	70	90	135	425	375	- 1,300	3,100	9,500	16,500	22,000
1889	18	20	- 27	235	60	+ 830	+ 600	6,800	+ 3,100	- 5,600	16	20	- 26	220	52	750	525	6,000	3,150	- 6,000
1889 CC	5,500	6,750	- 10,500	15,500	- 24,000	51,000	+ 130K	185K	150K	180K	4,850	6,350	- 10,000	15,000	23,000	42,000	90,000	175K	140K	175K
1889 O	- 47	+ 63	+ 116	- 785	+ 455	- 1,900	+ 4,650	16,500	- 12,000	22,000	- 45	55	+ 86	- 700	410	- 1,850	4,650	12,500	- 11,500	20,000
1889 S	56	+ 72	+ 114	- 925	225	1,750	+ 1,700	- 4,500	- 8,250	16,000	55	65	100	- 900	220	1,600	1,600	- 4,350	- 8,000	16,000
1890	18	+ 21	32	+ 270	+ 220	- 1,350	+ 5,150	8,500	8,100	14,000	- 18	22	30	230	200	1,450	4,150	8,250	7,850	13,500
1890 CC	160	+ 185	+ 300	425	+ 860	1,800	4,500	7,950	+ 9,050	16,000	150	165	240	400	750	1,800	4,250	7,250	8,750	- 15,500
1890 O	+ 26	+ 29	57	+ 232	- 200	800	+ 3,350	8,100	10,000	18,000	24	28	50	200	190	750	3,000	6,500	9,500	17,500
1890 S	+ 25	+ 28	+ 52	460	125	+ 1,435	+ 750	- 5,750	+ 2,420	4,100	22	26	40	- 375	110	1,350	650	5,250	2,250	4,000
1891	22	+ 35	+ 103	+ 1,040	+ 640	4,900	+ 6,250	- 11,000	- 13,000	27,500	22	30	+ 80	- 900	500	4,400	6,000	- 10,500	- 12,500	25,000
1891 CC	90	+ 112	185	+ 485	- 535	- 1,600	2,800	- 12,500	+ 8,100	13,000	90	110	150	460	450	- 1,550	- 2,750	12,000	7,000	12,500
1891 O	38	+ 42	124	+ 1,775	+ 740	+ 3,850	7,500	+ 27,500	13,000	22,000	37	40	95	1,700	500	3,650	7,000	18,000	12,750	21,000
1891 S	25	+ 29	+ 56	580	- 160	1,470	+ 1,170	- 5,750	3,600	+ 6,100	24	26	50	- 450	- 150	1,400	1,050	- 6,000	3,500	6,000
1892	66	75	+ 146	975	+ 500	2,300	+ 3,600	9,350	6,000	11,000	60	70	110	- 825	- 475	2,250	3,350	7,600	5,850	10,500
1892 CC	+ 230	400	595	+ 1,160	925	- 2,500	3,500	- 9,000	10,250	- 20,000	210	285	475	- 1,100	725	- 2,350	- 3,250	- 9,000	10,000	21,000
1892 O	57	+ 68	+ 140	+ 1,805	+ 380	+ 3,010	4,800	17,000	8,750	16,000	51	65	130	1,175	325	2,900	3,500	13,500	8,500	16,000
1892 S	10,000	14,000	16,600	22,000	22,500	30,000	55,000	90,000	110K	- 130K	9,000	12,500	14,000	21,000	19,000	30,000	50,000	90,000	95,000	- 120K
1893	232	+ 265	+ 405	+ 1,585	- 810	+ 5,540	+ 4,700	- 11,000	+ 8,100	16,000	220	240	400	1,430	- 775	5,200	4,250	- 10,500	- 8,000	16,000
1893 CC	+ 810	1,170	- 2,000	+ 5,420	+ 4,250	+ 8,625	+ 45,000	67,500	62,000	75,000	850	1,100	- 1,900	5,250	4,000	8,000	37,500	65,000	52,500	70,000
1893 O	1,170	+ 1,375	3,950	+ 6,600	+ 8,400	15,000	- 13,500	87,500	- 27,000	- 52,500	1,110	1,200	3,750	6,500	8,000	15,000	- 13,000	66,000	- 25,000	- 50,000
1893 S	15,000	17,000	36,000	55,000	49,000	75,000	185K	210K	220K	340K	13,000	16,500	30,000	54,000	50,000	72,500	160K	205K	210K	270K
1894	725	+ 935	+ 1,535	- 6,100	3,150	- 10,000	+ 11,500	- 20,000	28,000	40,000	750	900	1,300	- 5,500	2,400	- 10,000	- 11,000	21,000	23,500	40,000
1894 O	300	+ 445	+ 830	+ 4,000	+ 4,200	8,000	- 20,000	36,000	- 38,000	55,000	270	355	775	3,700	4,000	- 7,850	- 22,500	- 35,000	- 36,500	50,000
1894 S	225	+ 295	330	+ 1,575	+ 1,050	+ 3,320	+ 4,050	7,750	+ 8,800	15,500	255	300	325	1,400	750	3,000	3,750	- 7,500	8,500	15,000
1895 Proof	11,500	12,100	+ 13,600	--	17,000	--	25,000	--	37,500	60,000	10,750	11,200	13,000	--	17,000	--	24,500	--	33,500	55,000
1895 O	3,200	5,400	+ 8,800	11,500	+ 14,200	22,500	+ 54,000	87,500	- 75,000	- 105K	2,700	5,000	7,750	10,000	12,500	21,000	40,000	65,000	- 70,000	- 100K
1895 S	+ 730	985	+ 1,850	+ 3,440	3,400	6,000	+ 12,750	20,000	33,000	40,000	800	970	1,750	3,100	3,000	6,000	12,000	20,000	25,000	37,500
1896	18	- 19	- 27	100	- 52	- 245	- 240	3,500	+ 1,800	3,000	16	20	28	90	46	- 225	- 200	3,250	1,550	3,000
1896 O	760	- 1,375	+ 3,050	+ 7,790	+ 6,500	+ 12,200	+ 62,000	+ 71,000	70,000	75,000	760	1,175	3,000	7,550	5,500	11,500	40,000	47,500	50,000	60,000
1896 S	+ 460	550	925	+ 3,020	2,200	+ 7,150	7,100	- 15,000	13,000	23,000	450	- 525	900	2,600	2,150	7,000	- 6,750	- 15,500	- 12,500	22,500
1897	18	+ 21	28	200	- 54	575	400	3,400	+ 2,550	4,500	16	20	28	- 165	- 52	500	400	3,350	2,200	- 4,250
1897 O	475	1,000	2,150	+ 10,000	+ 6,300	13,000	+ 24,000	35,000	38,000	66,000	450	1,000	2,000	- 6,000	- 6,000	- 11,000	21,000	32,500	37,500	55,000
1897 S	26	+ 29	40	+ 182	100	455	+ 650	2,550	+ 2,300	4,500	23	26	- 38	160	100	425	+ 570	2,500	2,250	4,250
1898	18	+ 21	28	- 165	- 52	- 375	- 265	3,500	- 1,700	- 4,250	16	20	27	- 140	46	400	- 225	3,450	- 1,650	- 5,000
1898 O	18	+ 21	28	- 85	- 52	- 235	145	1,800	+ 635	+ 2,200	16	18	25	- 80	46	+ 325	125	1,950	700	1,850
1898 S	100	125	+ 142	+ 595	+ 380	+ 1,600	2,100	+ 6,790	+ 6,100	11,000	- 100	120	130	550	310	1,450	1,900	6,000	- 6,000	10,000
1899	55	57	85	275	+ 125	- 600	+ 930	+ 3,000	- 2,850	- 5,750	50	55	70	275	100	- 575	- 900	+ 3,150	- 3,000	- 6,000
1899 O	18	+ 21	- 29	- 170	- 52	+ 350	145	+ 1,450	- 660	+ 2,450	16	18	- 30	- 140	46	300	125	2,000	850	- 2,350
1899 S	64	+ 81	+ 137	+ 870	+ 355	+ 1,100	- 1,400	+ 5,770	+ 5,100	- 12,000	65	70	85	- 800	+ 300	- 950	- 1,750	4,750	- 5,000	- 11,500
1900	18	+ 21	28	+ 570	- 52	+ 2,230	- 175	+ 5,270	+ 1,900	3,200	16	18	25	475	46	1,950	- 160	5,000	1,900	- 3,500
1900 O	18	+ 21	28	+ 835	- 52	+ 1,150	- 175	4,025	+ 1,225	- 4,500	16	18	25	675	46	1,100	- 140	3,750	1,200	- 5,000
1900 O/CC	+ 97	+ 110	+ 210	+ 1,360	+ 450	+ 3,600	2,500	- 9,000	+ 4,500	7,500	85	95	170	1,150	410	3,350	2,400	- 9,500	4,100	7,500
1900 S	60	+ 72	+ 105	+ 1,610	+ 202	+ 3,310	+ 1,650	6,300	+ 5,500	10,000	55	65	80	1,400	170	3,000	1,650	6,000	5,150	9,000
1901	915	- 2,500	4,600	- 8,400	19,000	35,000	+ 58,000	75,000	77,500	110K	835	- 2,400	4,250	- 7,750	18,500	32,500	50,000	65,000	70,000	95,000
1901 O	18	+ 21	28	650	- 52	1,525	- 275	4,250	+ 2,550	4,250	18	20	25	- 500	46	- 1,250	275	4,000	2,400	- 4,000
1901 S	+ 162	+ 182	+ 225	+ 1,570	+ 565	+ 3,360	+ 3,500	10,000	- 14,250	- 21,000	150	175	185	1,375	420	3,000	3,350	8,450	- 13,500	- 20,000
1902	22	+ 29	+ 44	+ 775	+ 130	+ 1,830	+ 460	+ 6,550	+ 1,850	+ 3,700	22	26	32	680	105	1,575	400	6,250	- 1,750	- 3,650
1902 O	18	+ 21	28	655	- 52	1,510	- 180	+ 6,220	+ 1,975	3,200	16	20	25	- 550	46	1,300	- 165	- 5,250	1,800	- 3,000
1902 S	18	+ 102	+ 145	+ 1,540	- 325	+ 3,340	+ 2,650	6,300	9,500	- 20,000	75	90	110	1,300	- 300	3,050	2,500	- 6,000	9,500	- 22,500
1903	+ 20	+ 27	+ 38	+ 835	- 61	+ 2,140	320	+ 6,250	+ 1,575	- 6,200	22	26	34	725	60	1,850	280	6,000	1,200	- 6,000
1903 O	145	148	155	760	170	1,275	480	5,000	1,300	3,300	145	150	155	725	170	- 1,200	450	4,750	1,250	- 3,500
1903 S	+ 1,425	1,700	2,600	+ 4,840	3,000	5,400	+ 5,250	- 11,000	15,000	18,250	1,375	1,650	2,500	4,500	2,850	- 5,250	5,000	- 10,500	13,000	18,000
1904	37	+ 46	+ 90	+ 1,335	+ 480	+ 3,550	+ 4,200	6,750	- 10,000	20,000	36	42	70	1,100	450	3,310	4,000	6,500	9,000	16,500
1904 O	18	24	27	110	- 50	285	+ 160	2,275	+ 960	- 5,500	16	18	25	100	46	+ 335	125	2,250	900	- 6,000
1904 S	595	825	1,150	+ 3,100	1,900	+ 5,010	+ 6,600	- 13,000	13,000	- 30,000	575	700	1,100	- 2,600	1,750	- 4,250	6,000	- 12,500	10,000	- 30,000
1921	16	17	19	+ 1,740	- 40	+ 2,640	- 190	+ 4,350	+ 1,700	- 7,850	16	17	18	1,300	40	2,550	- 170	4,000	1,500	- 7,500
1921 D	- 16	- 18	+ 33	+ 1,840	115	+ 3,190	- 390	+ 6,860	+ 2,850	3,300	- 16	- 18	28	1,750	110	2,800	- 400	6,000	2,150	- 3,000
1921 S	- 16	- 18	+ 30	+ 1,950	+ 167	+ 3,420	- 2,500	+ 18,000	4,250	8,000	- 16	- 18	28	1,800	110	3,000	- 2,250	+ 25,000	4,000	- 7,750

PEACE DOLLARS

	PCGS							NGC						
	MS61	MS62	MS63	MS64	MS65	MS66	MS67	MS61	MS62	MS63	MS64	MS65	MS66	MS67
1921	120	130	170	- 380	1,800	6,500	+ 17,250	110	125	165	- 375	1,700	6,000	12,500
1922	14	- 15	- 21	- 43	200	4,600	+ 17,250	11	14	20	- 40	185	3,750	9,000
1922 D	- 18	24	- 48	+ 135	+ 1,200	+ 4,350	+ 17,250	- 18	- 23	- 45	100	900	3,750	10,250
1922 S	- 18	24	41	320	+ 3,050	9,500	+ 17,250	- 18	23	40	300	2,900	9,000	15,000
1923	14	15	21	- 43	192	1,900	17,250	11	14	20	- 40	- 175	- 1,500	9,000
1923 D	- 18	- 20	- 60	+ 200	+ 1,460	- 7,250	+ 17,250	- 18	- 22	- 55	180	1,100	- 7,000	11,500
1923 S	- 18	22	+ 44	+ 425	+ 7,500	12,500	+ 32,500	- 18	22	40	360	7,000	10,500	20,000
1924	14	- 15	- 21	- 43	+ 215	+ 2,500	+ 17,250	11	14	- 20	- 40	185	2,250	9,000
1924 S	75	+ 88	350	+ 1,075	+ 9,450	16,750	22,000	70	85	320	975	8,500	13,500	20,000
1925	14	15	- 21	- 43	195	- 1,875	17,250	11	14	20	- 40	185	- 1,500	9,000
1925 S	55	60	120	+ 810	+ 12,750	19,000	24,000	- 45	55	- 100	750	- 11,000	16,000	22,000
1926	20	+ 24	- 30	+ 74	375	4,000	+ 17,250	16	20	- 30	68	350	3,750	9,000
1926 D	35	+ 42	71	+ 160	+ 930	+ 4,500	20,000	32	40	65	125	700	3,750	- 19,000
1926 S	27	+ 31	60	+ 180	+ 1,630	4,650	17,500	26	- 30	- 55	140	1,500	4,250	- 16,000
1927	48	55	105	+ 420	+ 4,100	+ 14,000	23,000	40	50	- 90	380	4,000	10,000	21,000
1927 D	+ 125	175	+ 435	+ 1,500	+ 7,425	20,500	32,000	115	160	410	1,425	6,750	17,500	25,000
1927 S	68	+ 85	+ 325	+ 875	+ 12,250	27,500	40,000	55	70	190	725	11,000	25,000	37,500
1928	+ 160	+ 180	+ 255	600	4,800	9,000	+ 17,250	150	160	230	- 575	- 4,650	7,750	14,000
1928 S	65	74	200	+ 1,150	+ 17,000	20,000	27,000	60	70	165	875	14,500	- 17,500	22,500
1934	47	+ 60	105	220	+ 1,650	6,000	+ 17,250	41	55	90	190	1,350	4,000	10,500
1934 D	60	75	+ 205	750	- 2,000	- 5,750	+ 17,250	60	+ 150	180	725	- 2,150	5,350	12,500
1934 S	- 1,325	- 1,700	- 2,600	+ 5,500	+ 10,500	27,500	31,500	- 1,400	- 1,750	3,200	4,500	9,500	19,500	26,000
1935	32	+ 37	60	+ 140	+ 830	+ 4,000	+ 17,250	- 30	36	55	125	750	3,650	9,500
1935 S	71	85	+ 175	+ 240	1,400	+ 5,450	+ 17,250	70	80	160	225	1,350	4,500	11,000

Page 3 of the CDN, September 14, 1990 (Courtesy of CDN)

According to dealers' Bidding acceptance, NCI's continued use of its own grading standards appears to have hurt their efforts to maintain their earlier prominence. As the marketplace voted with their Bids and their checkbooks, the CCDN changed its format. Our Weekly issues feature Bids for PCGS and NGC now, with a special monthly supplement for ANACS and NCI Bids.

One of the nicest aspects of the certified market is that the collector can put together a relatively inexpensive "grading set" for his own use. Even if collectors don't particularly care whether the rest of their collection is in or out of plastic, having a standard of grading gives them that much more accurate information about the rest of their coins.

Dollar Rolls

Looking at that very first issue of the Greysheet also reminded me of another major piece of historic trivia. Those early issues were marketed as a "resume of all BU Roll Bid and Ask Prices". Imagine, or even worse, remember when the coin market was a roll market, and many dollar rolls were barely rare enough to be included. Life is change! A Greysheet survey of the market in 1965 (covering the previous twelve months) revealed that 79 BU Rolls had increased an average 79%, while 118 BU singles had shown growth of only 21%. One only had to look at the investment success of Rolls like the 50-D nickel to know how to best invest. No question where the smart money was in that market.

BU Dollar Roll prices weakened through the late 60s, but grew stronger during 1970. While Dollar Roll prices were lower, there was at least active trading. Interest in Rolls of the lesser denominations was also waning, and waning fast. During 1971, BU Dollars continued to be the most active part of the market, but even then the demand was seen as shifting to better quality individual pieces. In a 1971 editorial, the CDN reported:

"This very active Bidding has also continued to extend into the better date rolls. Of particular interest this week were such rolls as 1878 (7TF), 80-O, 85-S, 86-O, 87-O — and choice BU single Peace Dollars . . . Assembling a BU Peace Dollar set is a reasonably easy task — and so many collectors are obviously trying to put together superb sets while they are at it. This, obviously, is part of the fun in collecting — searching for just the right coin. Those investors who are also particular when buying find that it definitely pays off when they decide to sell." Not bad advice for 1971. Or 1991!

Following the CDN listings of BU dollar rolls over the years is to trace the disappearance of the better material from the market. In 1971, the CDN still listed such rolls as the 1883-S, 1888-S, 1892-P, 1892-O, and 1901-S. The emergence of the Redfield hoard in the mid-70s prolonged the availability of some of the better dates, but not for long. In fact, in the later 70s, rolls were purchased not as investments, but to provide the opportunity to search them for just the best singles that would command a premium.

Over time, as the rolls were increasingly searched and the better quality coins removed, the average grade of the roll naturally began to drop. This phenomenon was partly both cause and effect of the market's growing interest in quality single coins. Roll Bids dropped as roll quality dropped, and the phrase "Original Roll" was greeted with great suspicion. By the early 'eighties, the dollar roll boom was pretty much over. Dollar rolls are still offered, but now they are generally purchased only after careful examination of the individual coins, and at a price based on their individual quality.

Prooflike Dollars

One of the more intriguing ways that both the CDN and CCDN have evolved along with the Morgan marketplace involved the market's usage of the terms "Prooflike" and "Deep Mirror Prooflike". Among the most confusing actions in the coin market (with an obvious parallel to the many changes that have occurred in grading standards), has been the affixing of new definitions onto old words. Just as many of today's MS-65s are very different from most of the MS-65s of the 1970's, today's "prooflike" is also very different.

The confusion resulted from PCGS's usage of the old term "prooflike" to describe some non-fully reflective coins that had been previously known as "semi-PL". At first, PCGS did not differentiate between coins that were nearly deep mirror and those that were fully deep mirror. As a market developed within the PL ranks, Bids were confused as to whether they applied to the (old) full or (old) semi-prooflikes. The new extended definition was therefore viewed as unsatisfactory, so in late 1988 PCGS and NGC slabs began to appear bearing the term "DMPL" or "DPL" (Deep Mirror ProofLike) for the fully reflective coins, and "PL" for anything less. NGC used the term "DPL" for the deep mirror prooflikes, while PCGS preferred "DMPL".

The new definitions created a small problem for the Coin Dealer Newsletter, since our policy has always been to reflect the prevailing standards in the marketplace. After all, the CDN is only a useful tool to look up the value of that MS-65 if you know what an MS-65 is; if you know the grade, we give you the price. When the grading services redefined the old grading terms, the Greysheet reflected those new definitions as soon as they dominated market activity. However, the Morgan Dollar "Prooflike" Bids in the weekly Greysheet had always been for fully reflective coins (on both sides), since MS65 Prooflike Singles were first included in January 1979.

While the marketplace was trying to figure out which definitions would be used when and where, and before the new definitions began to be widely used and accepted, we were put in the uncomfortable position of listing DMPL Bids in a chart titled "Prooflike". Our decision to change our caption was made much easier when we received reports that a few unscrupulous telemarketers (we refuse to call them "coin dealers") were selling new PL slabs (the old semi-PL coins) at Greysheet PL Bid (the new DMPL Bids). In November of 1989, the Greysheet began to caption those Bids as "Deep Mirror ProofLike".

This part of the PL/DMPL imbroglio was relatively easily settled, but there was another difficulty in presenting accurate Bid information on the Bluesheet side: how to report sight-unseen Bids on the PL slabs, which might have been either old high-end prooflike (AKA the still older semi-PL) or the old DMPL (AKA the still older "prooflike"); or the new "PL" average prooflike (AKA the still older semi-PL). Ten minutes of explaining this dilemma to an old (dealer) friend generated the following response: "Huh?". Life in numismatics is never dull!

Type Dollars

While full date and grade charts for Morgan and Peace Dollars have long been a constant feature of both the Greysheet and the Bluesheet, we have also long recognized the need for information about Type dollars as well. During the 1970s, type collecting became increasingly popular as rising prices meant that it simply wasn't possible to complete most sets of rare coins. Type collecting had the advantage of giving the collector more diversity in designs and denominations. The benefit of a diversified portfolio is easily understandable to anyone who has tried to explain to a glazed-eyed neighbor why that tiny S-mintmark on the reverse of a Morgan means all that much — and the lover of Morgans cannot help but be a little deflated when that same neighbor replies that "they all look alike to me!"

The Coin Dealer Newsletter included its first Type chart in the February 19, 1971 issue. Bid and Ask prices for Liberty Seated Dollars and Trade Dollars in Choice BU, and Liberty Seated Dollars, Morgan Dollars, and Trades Dollars in Choice

Proof were all the neophyte would have found to guide him. Bids for circulated dollars (in one grade! — Good or Better) were added in early 1973. Less than twenty years ago, and that was the limit of market interest in type coins!

Over the years, our listings grew as market interest grew, of course. Today's Coin Dealer Newsletter covers a much wider range of dollars. Our uncirculated type charts include prices for both Draped Bust Dollars, both types of Liberty Seated Dollars, and the Trade Dollar, in MS-60, MS-63, MS-64, and MS-65. The Proof Type charts include the five basic types, in Pr-60, Pr-63, Pr-64, and Pr-65. The Circ Type chart lists six grades, from Flowing Hair to Trade Dollars. Today's Bluesheet covers Mint Type Dollars from Flowing Hair to Trade in seven grades (MS-61 through MS-67), and the six Proof Types in seven grades as well.

the COIN DEALER newsletter

. . . a Monday morning report on the Coin Market

Vol. XVII No. 1 January 5, 1979 Single copy price: $2.00

EXPANDED MARKET COVERAGE ADDS MS-65 PROOFLIKE MORGANS

"Year Of The BU Rolls"—Part One Of A Review

The Market in Depth

ALLEN HARRIMAN

With this first issue of 1979, the CDN is very pleased to announce a major ex-nsion of our silver dollar market coverage. The page six charts now include a D RANGE for MS-65 PROOFLIKE Morgan Dollars---an addition that we el will be of invaluable help to those many dealers, investors and collectors o are involved in this area of numismatics! It must be stressed that the bid nges listed are for fully prooflike and strictly MS-65 specimens. To qualify r this category, the coin must be sharply struck and relatively free of major g marks. Softly struck or heavily bag marked pieces are worth considerably s than the listed prices. Conversely, superb specimens (MS-65+) usually sell r considerably more. Also, to be considered true prooflikes, both sides of e coin must have highly reflective (almost like a mirror) fields. Beware of mi-reflective or one-sided prooflikes offered at full prooflike prices!

"The year of the BU rolls" is certainly an appropriate term for 1978! After veral year's of taking a definite "back seat" to numerous other areas of the rket, BU roll exploded into action during '78---with the various series "taking f" at differing intervals during the year. All of the series from Buffalo nickels ru Franklin halves participated in the often frantic activity---leaving only the ncoln cents basically unaffected. In this and next week's issue we will examine e frequently extroardinary advances registered by the BU roll market during e past twelve months.

The Buffalo nickels were rather late entrants into the action but, nonetheless, ins made during the last months of '78 were very impressive indeed. Beginning th this 1934-38 group, we will also take a look this week at the Mercury dimes d Walking Liberty halves; next week's issue will examine the remaing series. rst, the Buffalos:

	Bid Jan. 6 '78	Bid Jan. 5 '79	% Gain		Bid Jan. 6 '78	Bid Jan. 5 '79	% Gain
34-P	$ 825	$1350	64%	1936-D	$ 375	$ 700	87%
34-D	1480	1900	28%	1936-S	390	710	82%
35-P	350	725	107%	1937-P	255	665	161%

	Bid Jan. 6 '78	Bid Jan.5 '79	% Gain		Bid Jan. 6 '78	Bid Jan. 5 '79	% Gain
1943-P	$ 140	$ 290	104%	1944-S	$ 180	$ 625	247%
1943-D	170	420	147%	1945-P	125	290	132%
1943-S	375	1250	233%	1945-D	160	565	253%
1944-P	142	290	104%	1945-S	160	575	259%
1944-D	165	460	179%				

The 1934-47 Walking Liberties, for the most part, also fared extremely well during 1978! Bidders placed particular emphasis upon the twenty issues in the 1941-47 "sh set"--but all of the previously overlooked pre-1941 P-mints (along with 1938-D and 1939-D & S) did enjoy a substantial measure of the activity. It is interesting to note that 1934-37 mintmarked singles continue to lag behind the remainder of the Walkin Liberties. It will be equally interesting to see if these eight dates begin to "catch up" during 1979. The chart below covers the year's gains for all issues in this group; numerous important comparisons can be made from these figures:

	Bid Jan. 6 '78	Bid Jan. 5 '79	% Gain		Bid Jan. 6 '78	Bid Jan. 5 '79	% Gain
1934-P(sgl)	$ 35	$ 100	186%	1941-D	$ 480	$1325	176%
1934-D(sgl)	185	200	8%	1941-S	1400	2150	54%
1934-S(sgl)	425	460	8%	1942-P	275	665	142%
1935-P	540	770	43%	1942-D	410	905	121%
1935-D(sgl)	195	220	13%	1942-S	760	1695	123%
1935-S(sgl)	260	285	10%	1943-P	275	660	140%
1936-P	460	760	65%	1943-D	510	1010	98%
1936-D(sgl)	95	110	16%	1943-S	425	850	100%
1936-S(sgl)	120	127	6%	1944-P	280	660	136%
1937-P	540	780	44%	1944-D	380	715	88%
1937-D(sgl)	190	225	18%	1944-S	360	825	129%

CDN Headline, January 5, 1979
(Courtesy of CDN)

The Future?

One of the interesting (and at times difficult) challenges in writing the editorials for our publications is to avoid making predictions. It's easy enough to avoid the typical predictions of some dealers' publications ("MS-63 McKinleys are going to go up — so buy now and I happen to have a good deal on them on page 3.") It is harder to avoid an editorial slant that might result from our assumption that the market is going to continue to go up (or down), or that its direction is going to reverse soon. If we hear enough dealers making the same predictions, we might repeat them, and maybe even offer a contrary opinion, but we do try not to inject our own predictions. We follow a "simple" rule when deciding what to print — it's our job to print the news, not to make it.

All that said, I will make a few observations. For several years, I have been watching a general liquidation in the coin market, especially in the generic material. As the population reports of the certification services have revealed, there really are a large number of high quality Morgan Dollars out there. Unless we see new demand emerge from some unexpected source, I don't expect to see any major upward swings in generic dollars. And I don't see Wall Street as a major source of demand for generics.

January 5, 1973 **THE COIN DEALER NEWSLETTER** **Page 5**

MARKET CLOSING PRICES **CIRCULATED ROLLS**

CENTS

	BID	ASK
1934-D	2.75	3.00
1935-D	1.25	1.50
1935-S	1.50	1.75
1936-D	1.25	1.50
1936-S	2.00	2.25
1937-D	1.25	1.50
1937-S	1.50	1.75
1938-D	5.00	5.50
1938-S	6.50	7.00
1939-D	8.00	9.00
1939-S	1.15	1.30
1940-D	1.10	1.25
1940-S	.90	1.00
1941-D	1.25 +	1.50
1941-S	1.25 +	1.50
1942-S	1.25	1.50
1943-P	1.15	1.30
1943-D	4.00	4.50
1943-S	3.25	3.60
1947-S	1.00	1.15
1948-S	1.10	1.25
1949-S	1.50	1.75
1954-P	1.75	2.00
1954-S	.90	1.00
1955-S	5.50	6.00
1960-Dsm	.80	.95

NICKELS

	BID	ASK
1938-P	3.00	3.25
1938-D	30.00	32.00
1938-S	60.00	63.50
1939-P	2.75	3.00
1939-D	95.00	100.00
1939-S	11.00	12.00
1940-D	2.75	3.00
1940-S	2.75	3.00
1941-D	2.75	3.00
1941-S	2.75	3.00
1942-D	3.00	3.25
1942-P(2)	3.85	4.10
1942-S	4.00	4.25
1943-P	3.60	3.85
1943-D	18.50	20.00
1943-S	3.60	3.85
1944-P	3.60	3.85
1944-D	4.00	4.25
1944-S	3.75	4.00
1945-P	3.60	3.85
1945-D	4.00	4.25
1945-S	3.60	3.85
1946-D	3.00	3.25
1946-S	3.00	3.25
1947-D	3.25	3.75
1947-S	2.75	3.00
1948-D	3.00	3.25
1948-S	3.25	3.50
1949-D	2.75	3.00
1949-S	3.50	3.75
1950-P	6.25	6.75
1950-D	250.00	265.00
1951-D	2.85	3.10
1951-S	7.00	7.75
1952-D	2.75	3.00
1952-S	3.00	3.25
1953-S	2.75	3.00
1954-S	2.75	3.00
1955-P	7.25	8.00

DIMES

	BID	ASK
1934-D	14.00	15.50
1935-D	8.25	8.75
1935-S	7.75	8.25
1936-D	8.25	8.75
1936-S	7.75	8.25
1937-D	8.00	8.50
1937-S	7.75	8.25
1938-D	22.50	25.00
1938-S	10.00	11.00
1939-D	7.50	8.00
1939-S	8.50	9.25
1940-D	7.50	8.00
1940-S	7.50	8.00
1946-P	7.00	7.50
1946-D	7.00	7.50
1946-S	7.50	8.00
1947-P	7.10	7.60
1947-D	7.50	8.00
1947-S	7.25	7.75
1948-P	7.10	7.60
1948-D	7.25	7.75
1948-S	7.25	7.75
1949-P	7.50	8.00
1949-D	7.50	8.00
1949-S	9.25	10.00
1950-P	7.25	7.75
1950-D	7.25	7.75
1950-S	7.25	7.75
1951-P	7.25	7.75
1951-D	7.25	7.75
1951-S	7.25	7.75
1952-P	7.10	7.60
1952-D	7.10	7.60
1952-S	7.25	7.75
1953-P	7.50	8.00
1953-D	7.10	7.60
1953-S	7.25	7.75
1954-P	7.10	7.60
1954-D	7.10	7.60
1954-S	7.50	8.00
1955-P	17.00	18.00
1955-D	7.50	8.00
1955-S	7.50	8.00
1958-P	7.25	7.75

QUARTERS

	BID	ASK
1932-P	17.50	19.00
1934-P	14.50	15.00
1934-D	24.00	26.00
1935-P	14.50	15.00
1935-D	15.00	15.50
1935-S	15.00	15.50
1936-P	14.50	15.00
1936-D	15.00	15.50
1936-S	15.25	15.75
1937-P	14.50	15.00
1937-D	14.75	15.25
1937-S	115.00	120.00
1938-P	14.75	15.25
1938-S	23.00	25.00
1939-P	14.50	15.00
1939-D	14.75	15.25
1939-S	26.50	29.00
1940-P	14.50	15.00
1940-D	25.00	27.00
1940-S	14.50	15.00
1941-D	14.50	15.00
1941-S	14.50	15.00
1942-D	14.50	15.00
1942-S	14.50	15.00
1943-D	14.50	15.00
1943-S	14.50	15.00
1944-D	14.50	15.00
1944-S	14.50	15.00
1945-D	14.50	15.00
1945-S	14.50	15.00
1946-D	14.75	15.25
1946-S	17.00	18.50
1947-D	14.75	15.25
1947-S	15.00	15.50
1948-D	14.50	15.00
1948-S	14.50	15.00
1949-P	14.75	15.25
1949-D	14.50	15.00
1950-D	14.25	14.75
1950-S	14.25	14.75
1951-D	14.25	14.75
1951-S	14.75	15.25
1952-D	14.25	14.75
1952-S	14.50	15.00
1953-D	14.25	14.75
1953-S	14.50	15.00
1954-D	14.25	14.75
1954-S	14.50	15.00
1955-P	14.50	15.00
1955-D	50.00	52.50
1958-P	14.75	14.25

HALVES

	BID	ASK
1934-D	15.50	16.00
1935-D	14.50	15.00
1935-S	14.50	15.00
1936-D	14.50	15.00
1936-S	14.50	15.00
1937-D	26.50	29.00
1937-S	16.00	17.50
1938-P	15.00	15.50
1939-D	14.50	15.00
1939-S	15.00	15.75
1940-S	14.50	15.00
1946-D	20.00	21.50
1946-S	14.50	15.00
1947-P	14.50	15.00
1947-D	14.50	15.00
1948-P	43.00	46.00
1948-D	16.00 +	16.75
1949-P	14.50	15.00
1949-D	15.50 +	16.25
1949-S	16.00 +	16.75
1950-P	14.50	15.00
1950-D	14.50	15.00
1951-P	14.25	14.75
1951-D	14.50	15.00
1951-S	14.25	14.75
1952-P	14.25	14.75
1952-D	14.25	14.75
1952-S	14.75	15.25
1953-P	42.00	45.00
1953-D	14.25	14.75
1953-S	14.75	15.25
1954-P	14.25	14.75
1954-D	14.25	14.75
1954-S	14.75	15.25
1955-P	84.00	87.50
1956-P	16.00 +	16.75
1957-P	14.75	15.25
1957-D	14.25	14.75
1958-P	15.25 +	16.00
1958-D	14.25	14.75
1959-P	14.50	15.00
1959-D	14.50	15.00
1960-P	14.50	15.00
1960-D	14.25	14.75
1961-P	14.50	15.00
1961-D	14.25	14.75
1962-P	14.25	14.75
1962-D	14.25	14.75
1963-P	14.25	14.75
1963-D	14.25	14.75

MISCELLANEOUS COMMON DATE CIRCULATED ROLLS

	BID	ASK
INDIAN HEAD CENTS	15.75	16.75
LIBERTY HEAD NICKELS	8.50	9.50
BUFFALO NICKELS	3.60	3.90
BARBER DIMES (average circ)	19.50	21.00
BARBER DIMES (Good/better)	22.50	24.50
MERCURY DIMES	7.50	8.25
BARBER QUARTERS (average circ)	25.00	27.00
BARBER QUARTERS (Good/better)	27.50	29.50
STANDING LIBERTY QUARTERS (average circ)	24.00	26.00
STANDING LIBERTY QUARTERS (VG/better)	28.00	30.00
BARBER HALVES (average circ)	37.50	40.00
BARBER HALVES (Good/better)	42.00	44.50
WALKING LIBERTY HALVES	15.00 +	15.75
MORGAN/PEACE DOLLARS (VG/better)	54.50	56.00

CIRCULATED TYPE COINS

(Good or Better)

	BID	ASK
HALF CENTS	7.50	8.25
LARGE CENTS	2.50	3.00
FLYING EAGLE CENTS	3.50	4.00
COPPER-NICKEL CENTS	1.25	1.50
TWO-CENT PIECES	2.00	2.50
THREE-CENT PIECES (Nickel)	2.00	2.50
THREE-CENT PIECES (Silver)	3.50	4.00
SHIELD NICKELS	2.75	3.25
BUST HALF DIMES	5.75	6.50
SEATED LIBERTY HALF DIMES	2.00	2.50
BUST DIMES	5.25	6.00
SEATED LIBERTY DIMES	1.80	2.25
TWENTY-CENT PIECES	16.50	18.00
BUST QUARTERS	9.00	10.00
SEATED LIBERTY QUARTERS	3.50	4.00
BUST HALF DOLLARS	8.00	9.00
SEATED LIBERTY HALF DOLLARS	4.00	4.65
BUST DOLLARS	80.00	90.00
SEATED LIBERTY DOLLARS	25.00	27.50
TRADE DOLLARS	23.00	25.00

MISCELLANEOUS CHOICE BU TYPE COINS

(Superb specimens bring proportionately more than the prices listed below)

	BID	ASK
Common Date HALF CENTS (Brown Unc)	40.00	45.00
Common Date HALF CENTS (BU)	135.00	150.00
Common Date LARGE CENTS (Brown Unc)	47.50	52.50
Common Date LARGE CENTS (BU)	145.00	162.50
FLYING EAGLE CENTS	160.00 +	175.00
COPPER-NICKEL CENTS (1859)	125.00	135.00
COPPER-NICKEL CENTS (1860-64)	28.00	31.50
INDIAN HEAD CENTS	13.50	15.00
TWO-CENT PIECES	55.00	60.00
THREE-CENT PIECES (Nickel)	25.00	28.00
THREE-CENT PIECES (Silver) Type I	72.50 +	80.00
THREE-CENT PIECES (Silver) Type II	265.00	—
THREE-CENT PIECES (Silver) Type III	72.50 +	80.00
SHIELD NICKELS (with rays)	105.00 +	112.50
SHIELD NICKELS	39.00 +	42.50
LIBERTY HEAD NICKELS (no cents)	12.50	14.00
LIBERTY HEAD NICKELS	24.00	27.00
BUFFALO NICKELS (Type I)	11.00	12.50
BUST HALF DIMES	135.00	150.00
SEATED LIBERTY HALF DIMES (no stars)	245.00	265.00
SEATED LIBERTY HALF DIMES (no drapery)	120.00	130.00
SEATED LIBERTY HALF DIMES (stars obv.)	65.00	70.00
SEATED LIBERTY HALF DIMES (arrows)	110.00	120.00
SEATED LIBERTY HALF DIMES (legend obv.)	60.00	65.00
BUST DIMES (large size)	750.00	—
BUST DIMES (reduced size)	400.00	430.00
SEATED LIBERTY DIMES (no stars)	575.00	625.00
SEATED LIBERTY DIMES (no drapery)	150.00	165.00
SEATED LIBERTY DIMES (stars obv.	65.00	70.00
SEATED LIBERTY DIMES (with arrows) 1853-55	180.00	197.50
SEATED LIBERTY DIMES (legend obv.)	60.00	65.00
SEATED LIBERTY DIMES (arrows) 1873-74	215.00	230.00
BARBER DIMES	40.00	43.00
TWENTY-CENT PIECES	250.00 +	275.00
BUST QUARTERS (large size)	1000.00	—
BUST QUARTERS (reduced size)	750.00	825.00
SEATED LIBERTY QUARTERS (no drapery)	500.00	—
SEATED LIBERTY QUARTERS (no motto)	150.00	165.00
SEATED LIBERTY QUARTERS (arrows & rays)	435.00	—
SEATED LIBERTY QUARTERS (with arrows) 1854-55	240.00	260.00
SEATED LIBERTY QUARTERS (with motto)	140.00	155.00
SEATED LIBERTY QUARTERS (with arrows) 1873-74	240.00	260.00
BARBER QUARTERS	115.00 +	122.50
STANDING LIBERTY QUARTERS (Type I) Full Head	80.00	86.50
STANDING LIBERTY QUARTERS (Type II)	30.00	33.00
STANDING LIBERTY QUARTERS (Type II) Full Head	50.00	55.00
BUST HALF DOLLARS	150.00	165.00
BUST HALF DOLLARS (reeded edge)	275.00	300.00
SEATED LIBERTY HALF DOLLARS (no drapery)	1000.00	—
SEATED LIBERTY HALF DOLLARS (no motto)	185.00	200.00
SEATED LIBERTY HALF DOLLARS (arrows & rays)	875.00	—
SEATED LIBERTY HALF DOLLARS (with arrows) 1854-55	275.00	300.00
SEATED LIBERTY HALF DOLLARS (with motto)	170.00	185.00
SEATED LIBERTY HALF DOLLARS (with arrows) 1873-74	335.00	365.00
BARBER HALF DOLLARS	225.00 +	245.00
SEATED LIBERTY DOLLARS (no motto)	250.00	270.00
SEATED LIBERTY DOLLARS (with motto)	240.00	260.00
TRADE DOLLARS	180.00 +	195.00

MISCELLANEOUS CHOICE PROOF TYPE COINS

(Superb specimens bring proportionately more than the prices listed below)

	BID	ASK
INDIAN HEAD CENTS	38.00	41.50
TWO-CENT PIECES	95.00	105.00
THREE-CENT PIECES (Nickel)	39.00	42.50
THREE-CENT PIECES (Silver) Type III	130.00 +	145.00
SHIELD NICKELS	52.50	57.50
LIBERTY NICKELS (no cents)	46.00	49.50
LIBERTY NICKELS	44.00 +	47.50
BUFFALO NICKELS	125.00	135.00
SEATED LIBERTY HALF DIMES	80.00 +	86.50
SEATED LIBERTY DIMES	80.00 +	86.50
SEATED LIBERTY DIMES (with arrows) 1873-74	275.00	300.00
BARBER DIMES	100.00 +	107.50
MERCURY DIMES	20.00	22.50
TWENTY-CENT PIECES	310.00 +	335.00
SEATED LIBERTY QUARTERS	150.00 +	165.00
SEATED LIBERTY QUARTERS (with arrows) 1873-74	300.00	325.00
BARBER QUARTERS	155.00 +	170.00
SEATED LIBERTY HALVES	175.00	190.00
SEATED LIBERTY HALVES (with arrows) 1873-74	410.00	440.00
BARBER HALVES	245.00 +	267.50
WALKING LIBERTY HALVES	60.00	65.00
SEATED LIBERTY DOLLARS	340.00	370.00
MORGAN DOLLARS	210.00	225.00
TRADE DOLLARS	325.00	360.00

Page 5 of the CDN, January 5, 1973
(Courtesy of CDN)

However, I have watched Morgans over many decades perform the role of "soul" of the American market. Few collectors can avoid being attracted to the coins. They are large, silver, historical, and pretty. There is a lot to be said for eye appeal in developing increased demand. From the perspective of a current soft market, I see the coin market five to ten years out as very healthy, and I see Morgan and Peace Dollars playing a major role in that market.

I also recognize that it is a fact of life that few collectors will attempt to complete a Morgan Dollar or Peace set, especially if they are collecting in high grade. To that extent, I expect type coins to continue their popularity. I see the average collector working on his type set, but holding a couple of dozen Morgan and Peace dollars picked up along the way because they were just too pretty to pass up. Hopefully, there will always be room in numismatics for the buyer who acts just because the coin is attractive.

I know that coin prices will go up or down, or both, and some series will move in and out of favor. Certainly we can expect more government intervention in the coin business, but it seems safe enough to say that we can expect more government intervention in every other aspect of life as well. Coins may be in or out of plastic, and may trade sight-seen or sight-unseen. As long as there is a supply of coins and some demand for them, the marketplace will determine the proper trading levels.

Summary

The CDN family of publications fill two distinct needs in the community of coin dealers and advanced collectors, who can find price levels in the charts, and commentary on activity in the editorials. Dealers need both to add to their knowledge about current market conditions. This was the role of the CDN in 1963, and it still is.

The coin market is still largely governed by the forces of supply and demand, and demand can only grow if more buyers chase a constant number of rare coins. A large component of the demand, especially in these times of super-high prices for many rare coins, is the level of comfort the purchaser has with the price that he must pay to add that one particular item to his collection, portfolio, or inventory. And the same holds true for dealers who may be buying outside of their particular sphere of expertise. To make informed buying and selling decisions, numismatists need an independent source for prices and market information. A source that has demonstrated that it is independent, reliable, accurate, and timely. For 28 years, the CDN has been that source, and we intend to remain the market leader. Silver Dollar prices may rise or fall, but you can be sure that you will get the straight story in our publications.

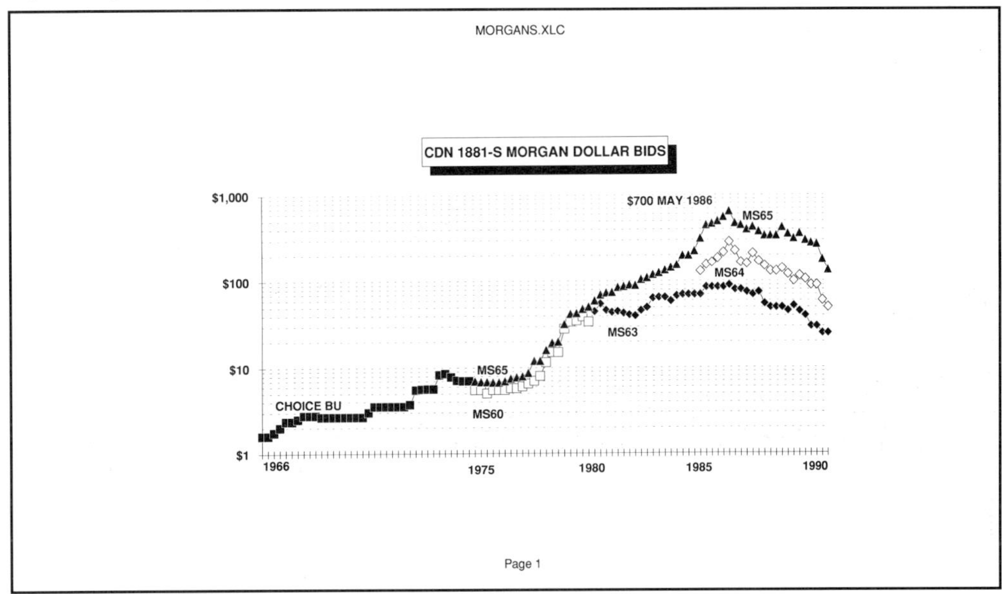

CDN 1881-S Morgan Dollar Bids (Courtesy of CDN)

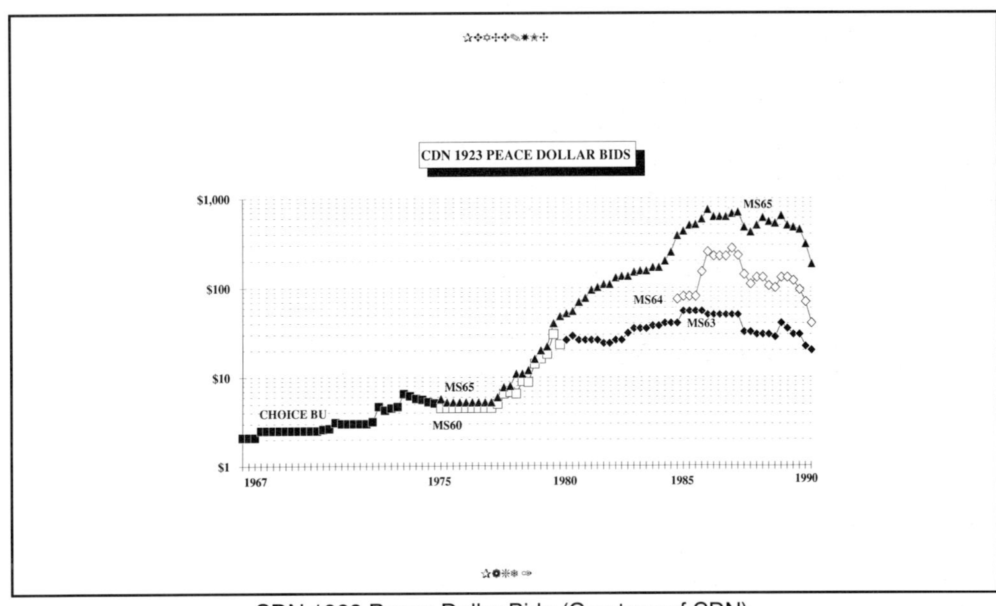

CDN 1923 Peace Dollar Bids (Courtesy of CDN)

the COIN DEALER newsletter

MONTHLY SUMMARY

AND COMPLETE SERIES PRICING GUIDE

JUNE — 1984

Vol. IX No. 6 Single copy price: $2.00

MS GRADING SYSTEM: TYPE COINS AND SILVER DOLLARS

by John W. Highfill
of Oklahoma Federated Gold & Numismatics, Inc.

This article has a primary purpose of trying to educate, philosophize, and or define the complex nature of the mint state (MS) grading system. To somewhat limit the complexity of this discussion, I will speak toward silver dollars only.

The majority of the difficulties in today's grading of coins comes from the MS coins. Practically all collectors, either novice or advanced, have some degree of knowledge in grading circulated coins. There are very explicit books with photographs that are available to help determine the grades of G-4 thru AU-55. Two such books are, photograde, by Brown and Dunn and the ANA's (American Numismatic Association) Official Grading Guide. There are many other commercial books which have been written with chapters included on grading. Most of these have been written within the past five to ten years; this being the time frame that inflation has paved the way for investors to enter the marketplace in a very serious manner. Many of these investors were collectors at one time; therefore they have minute problems in the area of grading. However, those prudent investors that are very serious-minded are careful to protect themselves with expert and knowledgeable dealers or ANACS papers. The numismatic industry has shifted from the collector oriented base to those more investment minded. Therefore, when the money is on the line, the grading had better be accurate ! ! !

Now that we have the basics behind us, we will proceed to mint state grading. There are extreme price differences between the MS-60, MS-63, and MS-65. Especially between the MS-63 and the MS-65 grades in the Morgan and Peace silver dollar series. There are a few auction companies that have recently begun to install and implement the MS-64 grade in their respective auctions. One author has gone to print advising the price projections for MS-60, MS-63, MS-65 and the MS-64 grade.

We hear the argument, that if you start grading a coin MS-60, MS-63, MS-64, MS-65 and MS-67, then what about MS-61, 62, 66, 68 and 69? At some point, we have to get serious about the value versus the grade of a coin. I believe that most knowledgeable and professional dealers agree that there are different grades of uncirculated coins. Thus, we have a base for MS-60, MS-65, and MS-67.

When the MS-63 was first introduced in a 1982 C.D.N. there was a lot of controversy at that time. We all agreed that there was a lot of silver dollars that are better than MS-60 and not good enough for MS-65. Thus, the birth and installation of the MS-63 grade. We are at the same crossroads once again. Enter the argument for the MS-64 grade. There are many silver dollars that are better than MS-63 and not good enough to be classified as MS-65's. With this philosophy in mind, an MS-64 grade would likely be "a good candidate for grading, and defining a value for investment grade silver dollars that are not as good as an MS-65 and better than roll quality MS-63 silver dollars" Currently they are referred to as MS-63+ dollars.

Now we will enter into another argument. Currently, we have low inflationary times and moderately stable market conditions. A silver dollar under those conditions will have to be almost perfect to bring the historical high MS-65 prices. Those coins "not quite there" will not bring the MS-65 grade. Now comes the main idea of this entire series of events. Are we paying MS-65 prices for MS-67 coins? Many dollar experts believe that to be the case. If so, are the "not quite there" coins really MS-65's and the so called near perfect coins MS-67's? It seems to this writer that MS-60, MS-63, MS-65 and MS-67 are the categories that we should work within.

Instead of MS-64 being worth less than MS-65 and more than MS-63, we are really in essence saying that MS-64's are actually MS-65's and MS-65's are truly MS-67's. After all, if a coin is near perfect, it should be classified as an MS-69 or even MS-70. (God forbid). It would be nice to be able to read columns that have price guides that are realistic in direct proportion to their value. An example is: 1884-O Morgan Dollar MS-60 - $42, MS-63 - $55, MS-65 - $150 and MS-67 - $275. The MS-60 being the most common and sold frequently in roll form is valued at $42. The MS-63 would most likely be a nice BU coin with a minimum amount of bagmarks and a good to above average strike. All mint

(Continued on Page Two)

by Dennis E. Steinmetz
of Steinmetz Coins and Currency, Inc;

In this article I would like to discuss the silver Unc and Proof type coin that just miss making the full MS-65 grade. I will also be listing the gold Unc type coins that grade as such.

In my opinion this area offers some of the best potential for profit in the rare coin field. As most dealers will readily admit, many of today's strict MS-64 type coins sold easily as MS-65 and MS-65+ in the Bull Market of 1979-80. With another major Bull Market there is a good likelihood that this would reoccur.

Below is some commentary on individual type coins and bid ranges for the material in strict MS-64 grade;

THREE CENT SILVER

In Choice MS-64 the Type one and Type three are available in the current bid ranges. On some occasions small hoards have surfaced. The Type two in both Unc and Proof are very scarce and excellent values. The Type three is one of the easier Proof-64 type coins to obtain.

BUST HALF DIME

Truly scarce in MS-64 grade. One of the best examples of today's MS-64 trading as MS-65 in 1979-80. Excellent value at up to $2000.

SEATED HALF DIME

Common date stars and legend half dimes are also available in today's market place in current bid ranges. The no stars and no drapery varieties do surface from time to time with bids at approximately $1500-$2000. The arrows variety is a good value at $900-$1300. Proof-64's are available in current bid ranges.

BUST DIME

A true rarity when strictly graded and highly recommended. Be prepared to pay premium prices for slightly better dates or exceptionally attractive pieces.

SEATED DIME

The stars variation seated dime has excellent growth potential in strict MS-64. The legend variety is fairly common in relation to all other types. The no stars and no drapery varieties are seldom seen in strict MS-64. Legend seated dimes in PR-64 offer superior value with a relatively small investment per coin.

BARBER DIME

Available in PR-64 and MS-64 without too much difficulty.

TWENTY CENT PIECE

Excellent value and highly recommended in PR-64 and MS-64. One of the high flyers of 1979-80. Full strike necessary on MS-64 pieces.

BUST QUARTER

Very rare and seldom seen. Strict uncleaned pieces a must. Almost always overgraded.

SEATED QUARTER

No motto type in MS-64 available due to several hoards. (Especially 1858 in frosty MS-64). With motto type also available in both PR-64 and MS-64. Arrows and rays type and both arrow varieties truly scarce in MS-64.

BARBER QUARTER

Very popular and also obtainable at current bid levels in both PR-64 and MS-64.

BUST HALF

Exceptional value in MS-64. I sometimes wonder what it takes for a bust half to be worth MS-65 bid!

SEATED HALF

Difficult to locate no motto or motto type in strict MS-64. PR-64's are often quoted at near PR-65 prices. Arrow varieties are seldom seen and somewhat unappreciated as to rarity.

BARBER HALF

Available and popular in both MS-64 and PR-64 in current bid ranges.

(Continued on Page Two)

Monthly Summary, June 1984
"MS Grading System: Type Coins and Silver Dollars" by John W. Highfill
(Courtesy of CDN)

***

David Lisot, NLG

David Lisot has long been involved in the world of collectibles. He started as a child saving marbles and comic books; his interests grew to include most major categories of interest to the collector. Coins, watches, postcards, stamps, old stocks and bonds, books, guns, and glass are but a few of his many areas of expertise.

Mr. Lisot worked as the business reporter for the Financial News Network in cable television from 1986 to 1990, covering the numismatic market. His program, The Coin Report, won the Numismatic Literary Guild award for best television reporting in both 1989 and 1990. His educational program Rare Coin Magazine has been shown for several years in schools and universities on The Learning Channel, a national cable television station. He conducted several interviews in this volume.

Creation of educational programming focusing on collecting has been a source of primary activity for Lisot. He feels that the use of technology is integral to the expansion of the collector base for any hobby. He continues to help promote interest in collecting as a form of enjoyment and a way to appreciate the world in general.

Lisot is a graduate of the University of Colorado and a lifetime member of the American Numismatic Association since 1973.

CHAPTER 35

The Electronic Media and its Effect on the Coin Market

by David Lisot, NLG

Introduction

During the last 50 years, dramatic technological changes have occurred in our society. Television has been created, satellites have been launched, computers are now in most homes and businesses, and information about an incredible variety of things is readily available to more people than ever before. These changes have affected every walk of life, including the hobby of coin collecting.

The pastime many people consider to be nothing more than "saving pennies out of their pockets" now functions at a very "high tech" level. Advancements in technology have been applied to the trading of coins in ways that have gone beyond the scope of ordinary imagination. Coins are now evaluated by experts, or even computers, to determine their state of preservation and are sonically sealed in plastic holders. These encapsulated coins are then listed for sale on electronic trading exchanges whose information is delivered by satellite to hundreds of downlink locations across the country. Transactions can then take place without the coins ever having been seen by the parties buying or selling until the coin is finally delivered to the end consumer.

Prices for numismatic rarities have reached levels where many coins now sell for hundreds of thousands of dollars. A sale for a single coin has been reported for over one million dollars. Estimates of the total dollar volume for coin sales reach into the billions. Advances in technology have contributed to the increasing popularity of owning coins. There is a reason why so much technology has been applied to an area as esoteric as numismatics. We will explore the various facets of the coin industry, how they have developed and the ways in which this new technology in the electronic media is part of that development.

Historical Background

The hobby of coin collecting encompasses many levels of interest and appreciation. They are small articles of value that may be transported by individuals to allow the procurement of goods and services. They are timeless windows into the past with each small metallic disk containing a story of important men, great events, or revered symbols of a past country and culture. Coins are items of intrigue. They represent wealth in several ways; their face value as denoted by a government, as a measured amount of a precious metal, and as an item of value to a collector for their historical importance. To many it is the precious metal aspect that is the most important. Even the Bible shows how early man's appreciation of gold was established. The second chapter of the Book of Genesis refers to the Garden of Eden being near the land of gold and the onyx stone, indicating that it was a valuable piece of property.

Collecting coins was a hobby comprised of collectors and historians interested in the romance of coins, joined by their mutual love of coins. These hobbyists usually belonged to coin clubs where they traded coins, swapped stories and exchanged information. They bought and sold coins for their collections, upgrading when they could or adding a rare variety when one came along. Knowledge was the key to successful collecting and the person who knew the most about coins, their strikes and wear characteristics, actual mintages and availability, had the advantage over the other coin collectors and dealers. The hobby was dominated by the people with the most knowledge and money.

Current Market

Today there are more people buying and selling coins than ever before. The hobby has grown to become an industry in which coins are considered to be an area of investment as well as items for enjoyment and the pastime of collecting. This new attitude towards a hobby turned industry has caused the application of the new technology in the electronic media to numismatics.

No collectible has as sophisticated a trading market as the coin market. Why has there been such growth in the application of technology to numismatics that goes beyond what has been applied to other areas of collecting? What is needed is an understanding of the different forces that comprise the coin market and how they function together to constitute today's modern coin industry.

Forces Affecting the Current Market

The United States government is a major force behind the renewed popularity for collecting coins. In 1982 a new series of commemorative coins was started to honor great Americans and special events. These coins have been advertised and promoted throughout the world. In 1986 the U.S. Mint began striking the American gold and silver Eagle coin for both bullion investors and coin collectors. Each year millions of new people are exposed to numismatics through the promotional efforts of the U.S. Mint.

These collectors enjoy sharing with others of similar interest and often belong to one of the many organizations that promote coins and collecting. One of the oldest organizations is the American Numismatic Society located in New York City that was founded in 1858. The largest organization devoted exclusively to the study of coins and paper money is the American Numismatic Association of Colorado Springs, Colorado, founded in 1891. There are also numerous state and local clubs devoted to the fraternity of coin collecting. Each of these organizations helps promote the hobby to the local community as well as often being organized into larger statewide and nationwide infrastructures.

Many of these organizations and clubs hold coin conventions where the public is invited to view displays of coin collections and stroll through bourse rooms full of coin dealers offering coins and paper money for sale. There may also be lectures and seminars presented where specialists in a particular field of collecting share their knowledge and research. These groups are funded by membership dues, donations, revenue from coin conventions, and even the sale of books and videotapes about collecting. Their goals are usually to bring collectors together and to share information.

There are also hundreds of commercial coin conventions that take place where collectors and dealers go to buy, sell and trade as well as keep touch with the other collectors and dealers. These conventions are organized by entrepreneurs involved in promoting coins.

For the person who becomes a professional coin trader there are coin dealer organizations. The Professional Numismatists Guild is the most widely known of the national dealer organizations and has been in existence since 1955. There are also state groups that deal with more local issues. These groups create ethical guidelines and offer services to help their members in business. As with other professional organizations, these groups add a degree of stability and accountability to the industry. Many of these organizations function as watchdog agencies to help maintain a high standard for trading and advertising in the hobby as a whole.

There is a national lobbying organization in Washington, D.C. called the Industry Council for Tangible Assets. ICTA represents the legislative interests of the coin and precious metals industry at a national level and works to keep coin dealers aware of current legislation and reporting requirements that affect their businesses. This group provides a needed service for an industry that is becoming more scrutinized by the federal and state government. The degree of technological sophistication and the dollar volume of coins sold has made the numismatic market a new area of focus for the various regulatory agencies.

There are even national print publications that focus on news, activities, and pricing information for the numismatic marketplace. These are published on a regular basis to help keep participants informed about what takes place both nationally and internationally. These different journals allow dealers to advertise their wares and services and as a forum for collectors to express their opinions.

There are now several companies who provide the service of grading a coin. This process, called third party grading, allows a coin to be examined by several numismatic experts and a grade assigned that has been arrived at by a consensus of opinions, rather than the judgement of one individual. These graded coins are then sonically sealed in plastic holders to prevent damage and tampering. The condition of a coin is a major factor in determining its value and the creation and relative acceptance of third party grading has contributed enormously to the popularity and expansion of coin collecting.

The final force to be factored into this equation of the forces of the market is the coin dealer. There are basically two categories of these traders of coins. The first are the institutions that have large pools of capital representing major financial commitments used to make markets, post buy and sell prices, and maintain a daily business of trading coins. They often have inventories of rare coins representing millions of dollars. The creation of limited partnerships by various Wall Street firms and the participation of banks that loan money against coins as collateral represents a profound difference in the coin market compared to other collectible areas.

There are thousands of smaller dealers and companies who buy and sell coins. These entities range from substantial corporations down to what are called “vest pocket dealers,” traders who buy and sell literally out of their briefcases or vest pockets. Each of these participants represents part of the conduit that funnels the supply of coins through the various channels of numismatics.

These forces comprise the modern numismatic industry. It is the existence of each of these entities that are part of the hobby that has now developed into a billion dollar industry.

Satellite Communications in the Coin Market

Satellite communications is an area of technology that has changed the coin marketplace and hobby forever. When coin trading began to grow in popularity after the turn of this century the only way to transmit information about coins and their prices was by fixed price lists, print publications, the telephone, or by sitting down with the person who owned the coins and asking how much they cost.

Now national numismatic trading exchanges exist that use celestial orbital technology as a way to transmit information about coin prices. Communication satellites circle the earth at fixed positions over 22,000 miles above the planet's surface. Mainframe computers store coin price information gathered from the marketmakers who belong to the trading exchange. This pricing information is beamed up by an uplink transmitter to a satellite whose sensors capture the information and aim it back down to earth to be intercepted by member firms of the trading exchange. Members of the trading exchange access this electronic information directly with a receiving dish through their personal computer or by phone line direct to their personal computer from the mainframe computer. This process creates up-to-the-minute pricing information to be available simultaneously to the entire country and world. It allows additional information about the number of coins that exist in a particular grade to be known, their availability, last trade pricing information and number of trades over a given time period.

Electronics and Advertising

Coin dealers have advertised for years, but the usual method to reach the public was to place a print ad in one of the major numismatic trade publications. This was done in an attempt to sell specific coins in the traditional numismatic marketplace where coin collectors looked to find their wanted items. Marketing by this method worked well to sell individual coins but it did not do much to bring new collectors into the industry. Its primary market was an audience already interested in coins.

The electronic media has begun to contribute to the expansion of the numismatic industry in new ways. The message and benefit of coin ownership has begun to be shared with the public by the use of advertising and information through the electronic media. Electronics has benefited the coin industry by taking the message of coin collecting to a massive new audience.

One of the most effective ways to reach a large new audience has been through the use of television. There are over 92 million households in America with a TV set and virtually every family spends a part of their day in front of this most persuasive visual medium.

Although TV has long been considered the most efficient means to gain access to a large number of potential consumers, for years it was too expensive for most businesses to benefit from its broad reach. The cost of commercial air time coupled with high cost of production made TV advertising prohibitive to most businesses until technology advanced to a new level.

One difficulty with advertising on television was understanding how the medium worked. Reaching people through television was a numbers game. Advertisers paid so much to reach so many people. The more people reached on a particular station or network, the more expensive the advertising time. The major television networks charged tens of thousands of dollars for their advertising time because they reached so many viewers that the expense justified the price. When a car manufacturer advertised a new automobile they wanted the huge numbers of viewers that national network television offered. Since the possible consumer for the new automobile was virtually every person in driving age, it was worthwhile to reach as many people as it could in that category.

In the 1970's cable television was introduced on a national scale. Networks were created that were delivered by satellite that had programming in specialty areas like movies, sports, news, financial news, ethnic programming, religion, and other called "narrowcast" concepts. This proliferation of television networks created smaller , more competitively priced advertising markets. An advertiser could now buy commercial time on a network at a much cheaper price whose audience would be more likely to have an interest in their product. With so many networks to choose from, TV advertising reached price levels that many businesses could afford. The opportunity to place a message on TV had come within the reach of the numismatic industry. The industry began to benefit by having the message of numismatics advertised on television as a few intrepid numismatic advertising pioneers ventured forth into the world of TV commercials.

Cable television offered the specialized audience that would be interested in the products that coin dealers had to sell. Rather than having to buy expensive ad time on network television, the growing numismatic industry could take advantage of the more affordable advertising rates on cable television and benefit from the more targeted audience. It was obvious that a business audience that watched networks like the Financial News Network or the Consumer News and Business Channel would be potential buyers of coins if they were told the investment angle. Cultural channels like Arts & Entertainment or The Discovery Channel could show people the historical aspects of coin collecting and the enjoyment of the hobby. Television programming was created devoted exclusively to coins. A daily news segment on the Financial News Network called the *Coin Report* aired from 1986 to 1991 and a half hour program called *Rare Coin Magazine* currently aired for several years during that same time on The Learning Channel, a national cable television channel.

Conclusion

Coin collecting has grown from a hobby of collectors and historians into an industry of investors and professional traders. This growth has been based upon the infrastructure of the collectors, the organizations, the publications, and the application of the technological advances in the electronic media.

Many factors are present that will continue to contribute to the growing interest in coins. The United States Mint is spending millions of dollars each year to promote the American gold and silver Eagle coins and its commemorative coin program. A change in the circulating coins in our pockets may occur that will help awaken people to coins and collecting. The possible discontinuation of the one cent coin adds interest. If a new dollar coin is introduced and the dollar bill withdrawn, this will also help to create interest in coin collecting. Plus there are an increasing number of modern circulating coins with doubled dies and rotated reverses that have true collector value, causing people to look at their coins again in the hopes of finding a valuable treasure.

Of the many forces that contribute to the strength and vitality of coin collecting, it is the use of electronics that has had the most dramatic effect on the market overall. The sophistication of the market and the interest of so many people has encouraged the introduction and utilization of the latest technology available to enhance and facilitate trading in coins. Satellites and computers have helped make numismatics a vital and growing industry. For the industry to grow in size and strength, the number of coin collectors must increase. If dealers and traders just buy and sell coins back and forth to one another, the market will remain at its current level. If the coin industry is to grow and prosper, more participants are needed to enter the market.

Those who have the vision of contributing to the strength of numismatics as a whole realize that people must be reached who are not active in coins but would become so if they had the opportunity to see what coin collecting was all about. There are several means to reach this new audience and the one that holds the most promise is the technology of the electronic media. As more coin dealers and collector organizations take their numismatic messages to the airwaves of radio and television, satellites and computers, the more people will learn about the pleasures of the pieces of metal in their pockets.

Coin collecting has been around as long as there have been coins. The enchantment with the flattened metallic orbs has affected people from many walks of life, each enjoying some aspect of the myriad of things that numismatics represents. Although the coin industry is subject to cycles of price highs and lows and trading volume, the overall future of the numismatic industry is bright. The spirit of the entrepreneur pervades the coin market and each major advance in technology finds its way into what some consider to be just "saving the pennies out of their pockets." But in truth coin collecting has been and will continue to be known as the hobby of kings!

***

Iraj Sayah

Iraj Sayah is an international businessman who has 30 years experience as a trader in different industries.

In 1980 Mr. Sayah moved to the United States where he became fascinated by the history and romance of American coins. Since then he founded UNIGOLD, a multimillion dollar rare coin holding company. He plans to develop the world's most sophisticated retail computer trading network, UNITRADE.

Iraj deeply believes that coins represent one of the most exciting and interesting markets in which he has ever been involved. He feels that the trading of rare coins has the potential to grow to dynamic new levels, depending on the ability of the industry and its people to work together. He is sincerely devoted to achieving this ideal.

CHAPTER 36

The Unitrade Vision For The Future

by Iraj Sayah

Today's coin market offers extreme promise either for the person seeking the enjoyment of a pleasurable collecting hobby or the pursuit of a new investment and business opportunity. Coins have long had a tremendous fascination for many people as pieces of history and as art objects. But it is not only this historical attraction that is stimulating the development of a new business area and investment market.

Compare the coin industry to other areas of business that are at a higher level of development. Although the coin business has come a long way in recent years, its practices are still primitive from many business points of view. It has been called a hobby even though coins have been traded for thousands of years. It has not been considered by many as a true business area.

Now, a new environment created by the advent of third party grading services, sight-unseen buying and selling, telecommunications and trading networks has resulted in the ability of coins to be traded in bigger volume and in a more efficient manner, which has made coins an attractive business market.

We have seen the coin business grow very fast over the last few years. More and more players have come into the industry attracted by the sight-unseen trading. In the last two years, large Wall Street firms have joined the market. They too, see a strong future for coins.

As a planted seed becomes a fruitful tree, so shall the coin market progress into an even larger and more powerful industry. People will still love coins as objects of history and art, but they will also view coins as traded items of value like other financial assets, because of the potential of coins to increase in value as do other tangible assets. If your money loses buying power, you lose assets, while coins have the potential to be a storehouse of value.

The coin industry, like other businesses, could not ignore the fact that technology had improved, and that's why computerization started taking place in the industry. Currently several computer trading exchanges exist, but they are not meeting the overall need of the market. When the first computer exchange, American Numismatic Exchange (ANE), was established in January 1986, the initial concept was to provide a center where certified coins could be traded sight-unseen for specific bid and ask prices, just like stocks.

Before 1986, coin dealers exchanged price information the "old-fashioned way," i.e., via printed price lists transmitted through the mail. ANE and other computer exchanges that followed have been effective in introducing the concept of computer trading to the coin market; however, most of these exchanges are primarily oriented towards the "bid" price, which is not the same as a system based on the "ask" price. Exchange founders were so determined to enhance the liquidity for certified coins (the ability to sell coins easily whenever one so desires), that the focus of the electronic network was placed on encouraging member firms to post bid prices. This determination also reflected a long-standing industry practice of dealers being more concerned with knowing what price someone was willing to pay for a coin rather than at what price someone was willing to sell a coin. Exchange rules have fostered this bid price orientation.

Each dealer posting a bid price on the exchange for an "approved certified coin" — a coin graded by an independent, third party grading service, recognized by the exchange — is *required* to purchase a minimum dollar value or quantity of that coin, i.e., $1500 or 10 coins (whichever comes first) — from any other member firm wishing to sell the coin.

Very soon dealers realized that the bid system has many problems; the system allows bids for coins that do not even exist; some coins exist but are not available since a collector or investor may have them and not want to sell them, and the critical factor that dictates most bids for coins is the cash reserves of the participating dealers. Therefore, many bids are not a true reflection of the value for the coins, because they do not always reflect the true price level of the market. Bids for some coins have been listed on exchanges for a year and no trades have taken place.

Bids may show the power or willingness of people to buy coins but bids alone do not show the real value of the coin at the level where it is actually trading. During *rising* markets, coins trade at a premium over bid prices on electronic exchanges. During *falling* markets, bid prices frequently overstate the severity of the drop in the market because earnest bidders are obligated to backup their prices with real dollars. Again, if cash reserves are tight, bid prices may be intentionally lowered beneath true market levels to curtail selling. Although vast strides have been made in expanding the number of participants in the coin market, cumulative cash reserves supporting a bid-oriented system have yet to reach the level necessary to prevent severe price volatility.

This brief commentary on the weaknesses of the bid system is not intended as an advocacy of its abolition. The bid system fulfills a purpose in any financial market and this is true of the coin market but a bid system alone is not enough. There must be an "ask-based" system that shows the last trade price; the last price at which the coin was actually traded; and more information about each single coin available for trade; and centralization of all trades. Ask prices provide a counter-balance to the bid prices, and allow buyers and sellers (be they dealers, investors or collectors) to properly determine what is the true market level for a coin.

Unitrade responds to the need for a more complete computer trading system and intends to play an influential role in the future growth of the coin industry. The basis of the Unitrade concept is to use the latest technology and have the largest source of coins available for sale centralized in a massive database where potential buyers can easily have access to this inventory through Associate members in the Unitrade system. The stated weaknesses of the bid system will be counter-balanced; ask prices will be there for coins that actually exist and are available; price levels will be determined as much by what someone wants to sell a coin for, as by what someone wants to buy a coin for.

There are many other added benefits of Unitrade. Dealers and brokers will no longer be concerned if they do not have a large inventory of coins on hand in the office for potential customers. Simply by looking at the Unitrade computer, they will have ready access to a multi-million dollar inventory. They will be able to serve their collector and investor customers with reduced exposure to market volatility. Unlike a bid-based system where sellers control the transaction and buyers are required to acquire coins "sight-unseen" based on their posted buy prices, the Unitrade Associate will allow the buyer to control the transaction.

There is no obligation to purchase. An interested buyer may even be able to request that a coin, which is offered for sale on a "sight-seen" basis, be sent to him for evaluation before a trade is finalized. Buyers can study the market before making a purchase and only need to do so when they have a customer.

Unitrade will incorporate the better elements of the "bid-oriented" systems in its "want" list feature. Dealers will be able to list specific coins not only by type but even by each date and special remark that they are interested in purchasing and respective prices either "sight-seen" or "sight-unseen" that they are willing to pay for the coins. Dealers will be able to indicate whether the price is "firm," meaning a computer automatic trade can be initiated by the selling dealer from his office with notification being forwarded electronically to Unitrade and to the buying dealer, or "confirmation required," meaning that a telephone call need to be placed by Unitrade to the buying dealer prior to executing a trade via computer to confirm that the buyer is still in the market for the coin. Again, Unitrade's "want list" feature will be a refined version of the "bid-oriented" system and more, however, it will be a secondary feature to the huge coin inventory offered for sale through the Unitrade "ask-based" system.

How a dealer interacts with the system is very easy. Once having joined as an Associate, the new member will be provided a computer for the listing and accessing of coins.

Associate members of the Unitrade network will be able to list extensive information on individual coins that they have for sale; sale price, strength of strike, toning, marks, population by type and grade, pedigree, auction record, historical price performance graph and other data will be available. Coins will be listed at the price that the Associate independently elects. If the member has a coin that he feels should bring a "premium," he may describe it as such and ask a higher price. The Associate also may think that the coin is so nice that he selects to list it as a coin available on a sight-seen basis and ask even more.

Once the information is entered at the Associate's office, the data will be transmitted by telephone line to Unitrade's main computer and integrated into the master inventory with all the other coins listed. Then, the new coin information will be transmitted by satellite to the individual computers of all other Associate members. In 3 years, Unitrade intends to have more than one thousand Associates on line, all having access to the largest single source of coins in the world.

Another avenue available to Associates will lead to secured inventories of coins held by listing banks. The associate may choose to authorize the listing bank to list certain coins on Unitrade's main computer and master inventory. Once these coins have been registered, other Associate members may elect to purchase these coins electronically. The funds will be transferred to the listing bank on behalf of the selling Associate, and the coins released and delivered to the buyer.

System activities available to Associates will include being able to buy from the system, sell on the system, delete coins, put coins on "hold" for a prescribed period of time for a pending customer and participate in a weekly computerized auction to buy or sell coins. Coins by individual dates — the entire available coin population — and not just by generic type, will be listed. Once the coin is sold, the price at which the coin sold will be retained in the computer and shown as the last trade price.

Detailed population data, i.e., how many coins of a particular type and grade have been graded by each independent third party grading service, will be available on each coin. Coins of all recognized grading services will be available on Unitrade, as will coins that have not been placed in holders, i.e., "raw" or "unslabbed" coins.

Unitrade's software program has been custom designed and developed to permit use by even the most novice computer user. Simple key strokes supported by on-screen instructions will "walk" the Associate through the program to produce the desired results. Various "parameter" screens have been inserted in the program to allow the Associate to "focus" his search or selection process. For example, if the associate only wants to view a coin of a particular date, mintmark, population size, and price range, he will be able to specify his request on each of these areas and the computer will automatically search the massive database and exhibit only those coins that meet the pre-determined criteria.

Typed reports of selected coins or detail reports showing complete categories of coins will be easily printed. Again, the "parameter" screens will allow an Associate to "focus" his range of coins to be printed as narrow as he desires. The printed reports can even be "customized" for distribution to customers. The Associate will be able to indicate his wish to have the customer's price list reflect a percentage or dollar markup above the wholesale price, as well as the customer's name printed on the report.

The Unitrade weekly computer auction to buy or sell coins will be the first known instance of auctions being conducted by computers. The process will be simple. Associates will be able to consign coins to Unitrade for inclusion in one of its weekly auctions. Each coin will be listed separately in the auction with any detailed description that the consignor wants to submit. The consignor may set a pre-determined "reserve" on the coin; a minimum price that he is willing to accept for the coin.

Other Associates will be able to review an auction "lot" and the current high bids on the coins simply by calling up the auction page on his computer in his office. If he is interested in bidding on one or more of the coins, all he has to do is enter his bid in the appropriate box on the computer screen, press a function key, and the new bid is automatically forwarded to the Unitrade's central computer and simultaneously broadcasted to all other Associates' computers across the country. This process will allow all Associates to have the latest, "real-time" high bids on each of the coins in an auction. They will be able to monitor the auction throughout the week, raising their bids as they desire, and, on the last day, the weekly auction will be closed and the high bidder will own the coin. Beginning with the close of one auction, the next auction will immediately commence with Associates being able to see a detailed description on each coin in the new auction and to input any bids that they may have. A new era for the coin industry and, ultimately, the entire collectible market will be unveiled with Unitrade's auction feature. On the other hand Unitrade auction will be the world's first "real-time, computerized auction" using computers and satellites. The Unitrade auction will be patterned after actual, current coin auctions, utilizing the Unitrade computer in his office, an Associate on his own behalf or for a client, will be able to bid on any coin, or item, as if he is present in person on the auction floor. Unitrade's main computer will perform the role of an auctioneer and thereby reduce the chance of human mistakes.

This enhancement will not be the last. Unitrade will earmark thousands of dollars in an on-going software research and development program to keep pace with rapid technological changes. Historical price graphs will soon be available both for screen viewing and color printing. Vivid "images" of the type of coins for sale displayed on the computer screen also will soon be part of Unitrade.

Equally important, Unitrade's involvement in the coin industry is not the limit of its business purpose. Ultimately, the Unitrade concept will be expanded to the entire collectibles industry, i.e., baseball cards, stamps, diamonds and gemstones, etc. Over 25 collectible areas have been targeted for inclusion in Unitrade.

There is no requirement to the amount of business that an Associate must or should do. Some associates may have 20 coins listed worth $100,000, some may have just 2 coins worth $2,000, while others may have $1,000,000 inventories listed. Some Associates may be just buyers, while some might just be sellers, and there will be a group which will do both. It does not matter. However, if a member does not transact a minimum dollar amount of trades monthly, he will be charged a reasonable fee for accessing the information.

Unitrade will automatically work to make the prices competitive. If twenty people offer the same coin for sale — for example, a 1923 St. Gaudens — all offers can be listed on the system. The various prices will be integrated into one master inventory database. When a person using the Unitrade computer searches for a coin of this particular type and date, all of the 20 coins will be listed accompanied by each respective sale price. Although the lowest priced coin of a particular type and grade should sell first, the additional data on each coin will allow buyers to be selective. Importantly, these ask prices combined with the last trade prices will show a true current market for a coin.

The coins will be listed in the order of price; the lowest price will be listed first. If coins are priced the same, the earliest entry on the system will be listed first. If there are coins on the Unitrade "want" list, the highest bid will be posted first.

It is important to emphasize the competitive nature of the Unitrade system. With so many people listing coins for sale, the price will be the lowest possible, because people are competing with one another to sell to this large subscription base. No one person can manipulate the market.

Confidentiality will be an important feature of the Unitrade system. The buyer or seller's identification will not be disclosed. This feature will be offered because most dealers do not want others to know that they are selling or buying certain coins. Unitrade will function as a clearing house for trades. Unitrade will create a committee to oversee the trades on the system and create a Code of Ethics to govern trading. Committee members will be drawn from the American Numismatic Association, the National Silver Dollar Roundtable, the Professional Numismatists Guild, the Industry Council for Tangible Assets, and other regulatory groups.

The amount of time required to process a transaction will vary based on different factors. Associate members will be able to execute "automatic trades" against posted prices (except if the listing firm requests prior confirmation). If the coins are in the possession of Unitrade, the trade will be confirmed immediately. If the coins are not in Unitrade's possession, the transaction may take a little longer. In either case, the computer will indicate how long it will take for the delivery of the coin.

Coins of all grading services will be listed, as well as coins priced from $10 to millions of dollars such as the "King of Siam" proof set. Even raw coins will be listed, although these coins will normally be traded sight-seen. New issue, certified, and world coins also will be listed. There will be a return privilege for coins offered for sale sight seen.

The central focus of Unitrade is to help the dealer better serve the collector and investor by making coin trading more efficient. Unitrade will not directly deal with the public, all trades are conducted through Associate members. Unitrade information is based solely upon rare coin prices and inventory data supplied by Associates. Unitrade is not responsible for Associate transactions with any customer at anytime. Unitrade needs the individual dealers to help personally educate the consumer, take him by the hand to explain the subject of coin buying and selling. The dealer is the major force in Unitrade. Unitrade will help dealers provide better service to consumers.

Unitrade has unique services available for its Associate members. First you have read how the ask-based computer trading system works. Second, if an Associate needs a cash advance on coins in his inventory, the coin or coins may be shipped to Unitrade and a cash advance will be given at a fair interest rate. After the sale of the coin(s) the remaining balance will be sent to the Associate. Associates may obtain a credit line to purchase coins or they may deal on a cash and carry basis.

Furthermore, Unitrade will also work to expand the number of participants in the coin market. Whenever a trade takes place on the system, Unitrade will take one percent of the gross dollar amount and spend it on advertising. This one percent could amount to more than a million dollars a year. These funds will be used to promote and advertise the whole concept of coins, provide greater consumer awareness of coins and encourage greater coin trading. No one person can afford to promote the concept of the whole industry, but a system of this collective size and volume can, through the one-percent advertising expenditure, help in doing what is necessary.

Fortunately, the American Numismatic Association is working with the young people to help create new collectors. Many Americans have not yet seen gold and silver coins. Unitrade can introduce the concept to a new audience. If coin education programs can be conducted outside of the existing coin market, it will be good for everyone.

Within 5 years, Unitrade hopes to see all coin dealers linked to this state of the art computerized trading network, with one giant inventory database of all the coins on the market. The most important factor and goal is to serve the customer with fair pricing, better service, and more information. If this goal can be achieved, the coin industry will have overcome many of its weaknesses. We will have a mutual understanding between coin customers and dealers. Right now, customers do not know where to go to find all of the coins they want and dealers do not have sufficient inventories to be able to satisfy the varying needs. Unitrade is poised to address these concerns.

Unitrade wants to minimize expenses for the dealers in order to provide the best price possible for the customer. The achievement of this goal can give the coin industry a stronger business capability, a better business environment, a larger source of inventory and a more efficient vehicle for buying and selling.

Therefore, Wall Street firms will continue to be attracted to the coin industry. Although Wall Street participation is not essential, such participation could offer tremendous growth for the industry. The foundation of the coin industry will continue to be collectors but the influence of Wall Street will add to the growth of the industry by introducing coins to a greater audience.

Previously, one of Wall Street's concerns has been the question of enough coins of value to warrant involvement. Another concern has been the issue of coin pricing. Unitrade intends to address both of these concerns. Unitrade will bring to a single source the largest inventory of coins for sale and at competitive market prices with the same technology used in Wall Street.

There is room in the coin industry for Wall Street firms, as well as "mom and pop" operations. The Unitrade concept works for both parties because it addresses the issues of, "where can I find the coin? What is a fair price for the coin? How can I acquire it easily and efficiently?"

Unitrade will help insure competitive prices and no market manipulation with a large inventory of coins available to everyone. The coin market is the initial collectible area that Unitrade will target. Soon, the Unitrade concept will be expanded to other collectible markets. The world of collectibles will be open to everyone through Unitrade!

***

Steve Ivy, NLG

In 1970, Company founder Steve Ivy first opened the doors of Steve Ivy Rare Coin Company in Dallas, Texas. After thirteen years of successful operation, the name was changed in 1983 to Heritage Rare Coin Galleries.

At that time, renowned numismatist and coin dealer James L. Halperin joined with Ivy as partner and co-owner. That merger made Heritage the world's largest dealer of rare coins with annual sales in excess of $100 million. In 1987, Heritage was featured as the 7th largest company of the "INC. Magazine 500" list of the fastest growing companies in America.

Today, Heritage Rare Coin Galleries is one of eight independent companies affiliated under the parent name Heritage Capital Corp.

Steve Ivy is founder of Heritage Capital Corporation. A recognized leader in the coin world, he is a consultant to the American Numismatic Association, a member of the Numismatic Literary Guild, and co-author of the book *What Every Silver Dollar Buyer Should Know*. Steve is also a member of most leading national and regional coin organizations, including the prestigious Professional Numismatists Guild (PNG).

CHAPTER 37

The U.S. Rare Coin Exchange

by Steve Ivy, NLG

The introduction of inexpensive personal computers into the numismatic world, combined with the development of third-party grading as a credible foundation for sight-unseen coin buying and selling, has led to the establishment of computerized coin trading networks. While the first networks of this type were originally established for wholesale trading among dealers, the inevitable was soon to follow: an electronic trading network accessible by both dealers and retail buyers.

On October 1, 1990, the U.S. Rare Coin Exchange (USRCE) was introduced by Numismatic Technologies, Inc., a subsidiary of Heritage Capital Corporation, the world's largest rare coin dealer. Unlike its predecessors, the USRCE is available to anyone who wants to buy or sell certified coins. It is a necessity for any serious coin buyer. In short, the USRCE provides a computerized listing of the inventories of nearly 100 different dealers, continually updated.

Technically speaking, USRCE is not a trading network but an electronic listing service. Sellers who want to sell coins through the USRCE list them for a fee in much the same way that an advertiser publishes lists of coins for sale in numismatic journals like *COIN WORLD* or *NUMISMATIC NEWS*.

For a nominal six-month or annual subscription fee, buyers gain access to these listings. When a buyer sees a coin he wants to purchase, he is given information on how to contact the seller, and the deal is concluded directly between seller and buyer. USRCE is not involved in the transaction and charges no fees for it.

What is the U.S. Rare Coin Exchange?

To conclude that the USRCE is simply a vast electronic bulletin board for coins is to overlook the power of the computer to influence significantly the coin marketplace.

Sellers' listings on the USRCE, for example, provide the following information on each coin: type, date, grade, population, mint mark, and price. For an additional charge, sellers may also include a description of a coin and/or a statement of terms and conditions of sale (see figures 1 and 2). The real advantages of the computer are seen in the selection and "browsing" functions. Buyers are able to sort coins according to any of the above criteria, and view only those coins which meet their particular specifications. For example, a buyer may wish to examine Morgan Dollars, graded above MS-65, with populations under 25 pieces and priced at less than $2,000. Within seconds, his computer screen would fill with all the listed coins with those attributes.

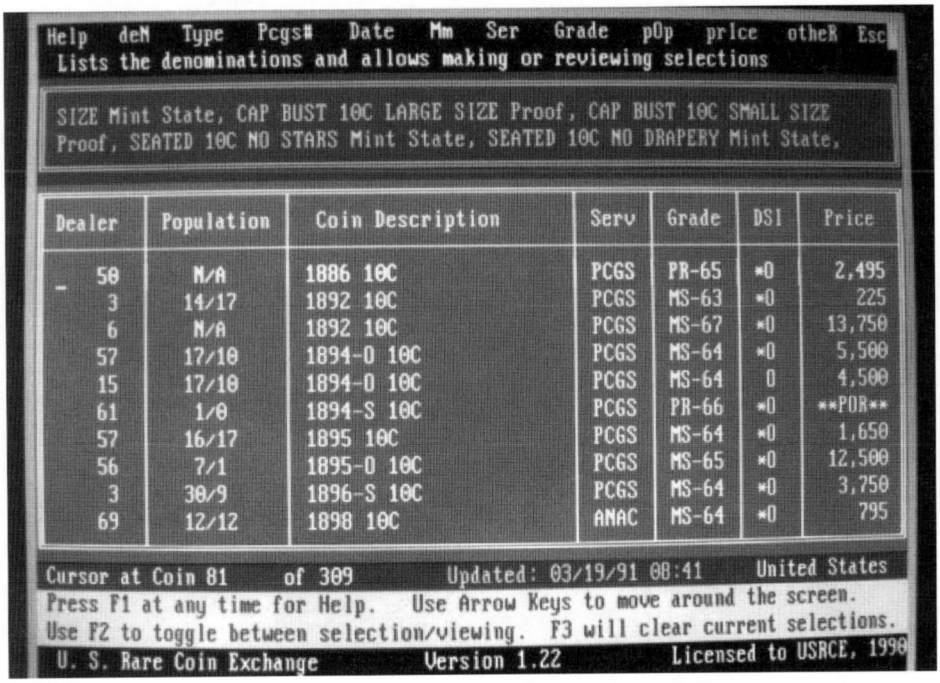

Help deN Type Pcgs# Date Mm Ser Grade pOp price otheR Esc
Lists the denominations and allows making or reviewing selections

SIZE Mint State, CAP BUST 10C LARGE SIZE Proof, CAP BUST 10C SMALL SIZE Proof, SEATED 10C NO STARS Mint State, SEATED 10C NO DRAPERY Mint State,

Dealer	Population	Coin Description	Serv	Grade	DSI	Price
58	N/A	1886 10C	PCGS	PR-65	*0	2,495
3	14/17	1892 10C	PCGS	MS-63	*0	225
6	N/A	1892 10C	PCGS	MS-67	*0	13,750
57	17/10	1894-O 10C	PCGS	MS-64	*0	5,500
15	17/10	1894-O 10C	PCGS	MS-64	0	4,500
61	1/0	1894-S 10C	PCGS	PR-66	*0	**POR**
57	16/17	1895 10C	PCGS	MS-64	*0	1,650
56	7/1	1895-O 10C	PCGS	MS-65	*0	12,500
3	30/9	1896-S 10C	PCGS	MS-64	*0	3,750
69	12/12	1898 10C	ANAC	MS-64	*0	795

Cursor at Coin 81 of 309 Updated: 03/19/91 08:41 United States
Press F1 at any time for Help. Use Arrow Keys to move around the screen.
Use F2 to toggle between selection/viewing. F3 will clear current selections.
U. S. Rare Coin Exchange Version 1.22 Licensed to USRCE, 1990

Figure 1: Example of dimes listed on the USRCE
(Courtesy of USRCE)

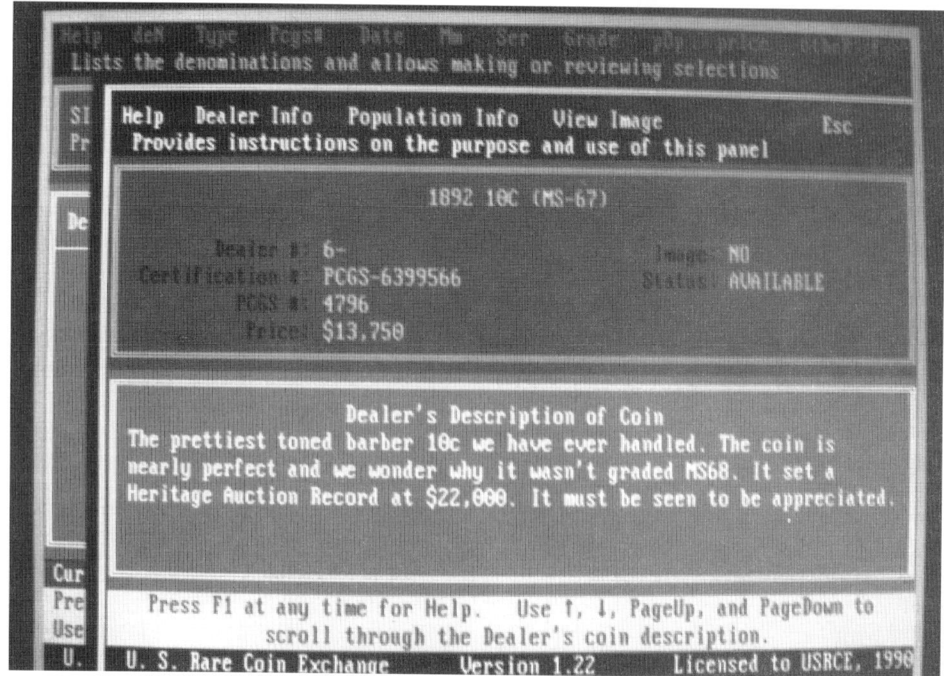

Figure 2: Listing of a specific coin with a description
(Courtesy of USRCE)

For coins of particularly outstanding eye-appeal or unusual value, a full-color, high-resolution image of the coin can also be featured (see figure 3). For users of the Exchange with high-resolution monitors, the quality of these enlarged coin images is so remarkably detailed that a sharp numismatic eye can actually grade from them with reasonable accuracy.

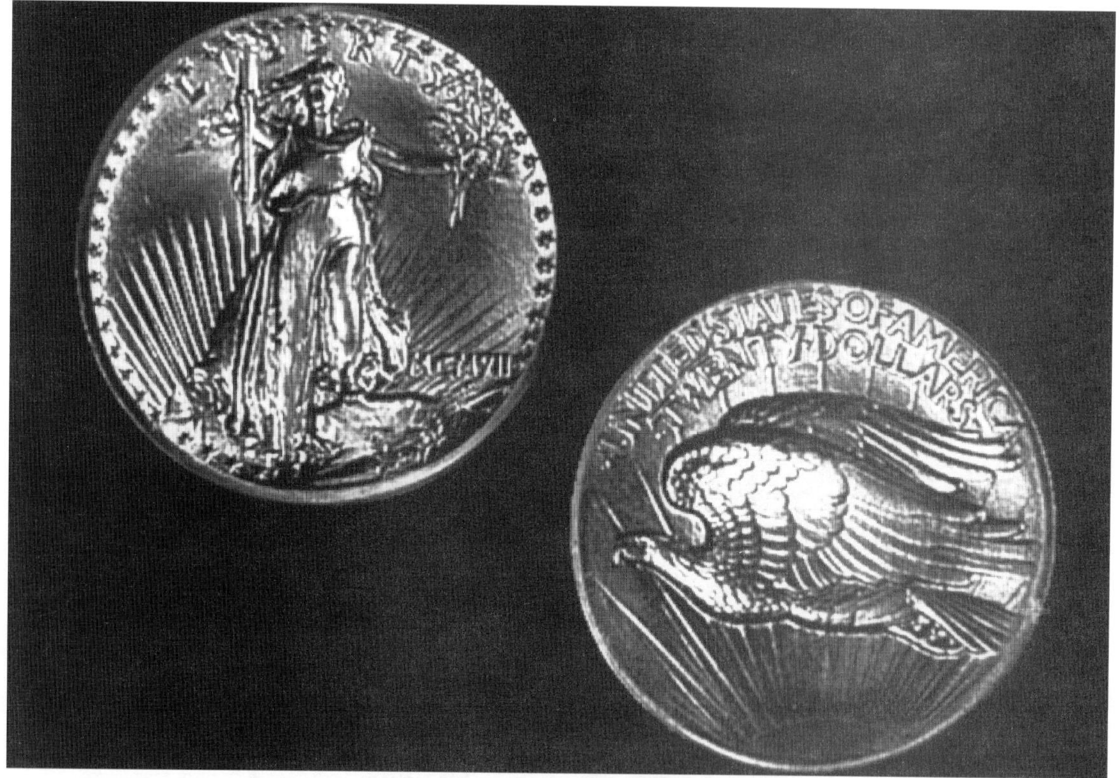

Figure 3: Computer image of a MS68 High Relief
(Courtesy of USRCE)

How to Receive the "National Database"

Buyers can access this information using their home computers and a telephone modem. To accommodate the traditionally conservative numismatic world (which is hardly known for its cutting-edge approach to high technology), the USRCE is also accessible through a printed catalog version of the Exchange, the RARE COIN MARKET EXPRESS. Using the latest laser printer technology, new editions of the RCME are printed daily, and mailed once a week to thousands of dealer and collector subscribers.

The IBM-compatible micro computer is by far the most efficient medium for using the USRCE. In fact, the Exchange provides a floppy disk of proprietary software exclusively designed for manipulating USRCE information.

Upon accessing the USRCE via telephone lines with a phone modem, users may specify the particular kinds of coins they are interested in, according to type, date, grade, population, mint mark, price range, and/or any combination of these parameters. The Exchange then provides listings on only those coins that meet their criteria.

After downloading this information into their IBM-compatible home computers, they can then terminate their communication, which saves long-distance telephone charges for many users. Using the software provided, they are able to manipulate the listings they have requested at their leisure, in order to make their coin-buying decisions.

Subscribers to the Exchange whose computers are not IBM-compatible can perform most of the same functions by maintaining their phoneline communication with the Exchange.

The Rare Coin Market Express

The RARE COIN MARKET EXPRESS is a laser-printed version of the Exchange sent to subscribers monthly, twice monthly, or weekly. Like the electronic Exchange, it gives basic coin listings plus whatever descriptions sellers have included on particular coins. Also like the electronic service, users can request that the RARE COIN MARKET EXPRESS be tailored to their particular coin interests. By indicating on a Survey Form their specific coin interests, subscribers receive a RARE COIN MARKET EXPRESS catalog featuring only those coins. For example, a collector of circulated gold coins could restrict his copy of the RCME to only those coins. Many copies of the EXPRESS are unique, custom made catalogs. The advantage over wading through endless dealer listings is obvious.

Listing Your Coins on the Exchange

Listings can be communicated to the Exchange in a variety of ways. Sellers can provide the information by mail or FAX, which is then keyed by hand into the system. Floppy disks (IBM Compatible) may also be sent to the USRCE for electronic transfer of listing information. But by far the most efficient method is direct transfer from the seller's personal computer to the Exchange mainframe via telephone lines. To facilitate this process, USRCE provides exclusive software to sellers whose volume of listings requires frequent contact with the USRCE.

Because the Exchange is electronic, additions and deletions on the system are on-going, thus keeping the information provided to buyers fresh and up-to-date.

A proprietary program called PriceMark allows prices to be adjusted continuously according to current market conditions. Sellers may direct the USRCE to maintain a consistent mark-up on their listings based on a percent of CCE bid price on a respective type and grade of coin. As the CCE bid prices fluctuate, prices shown on their USRCE listings are adjusted automatically. As a result, unlike printed listings and catalogs, prices on the Exchange are far more likely to be accurate, and sellers who still have the option of quoting a price change to a prospective buyer are far less likely to do so.

Another significant factor regarding the prices of coins listed on the USRCE is the price-competitive nature of this selling environment. Coins are sorted according to the parameters specified by the user and displayed in ascending order by date (if more than one date is requested). If more than one listing of a particular coin of the same type, date, grade, etc., is shown, the order is determined by the length of time the listing has been on the system from the oldest to the most recent. The effect then is instant side-by-side comparison of coins by price. As you can imagine, this makes for extremely competitive prices, usually a true wholesale or very close to it.

Buying Coins on the Exchange

While descriptions, imaging, and terms of sale are certainly factors in a buyer's decision to choose one coin over another, the opportunity to view several listings of the same kind of coin invites the buyer to choose the coin with the lowest price. Budget-minded buyers who may have shopped coin shows and dealer inventories for weeks to find the lowest price on a coin can make their price comparisons in seconds.

Primarily to serve investors and bulk purchasers of the most commonly traded coins, a special section of the Exchange is devoted to "generics." Generic listings are grouped into 18 of the most commonly traded coin types and dates. The listings display the coins by type, grade, and grading service only with prices listed in quantities of 1, 10, and 100, emphasizing discount volume buying for buyers who are solely interested in coins by type, grade, and grading service.

This price-competitive environment might seem at first to weigh the USRCE in favor of the buyer, but in fact, coin dealers — the most frequent sellers of coins — are the heaviest users of the Exchange. Why? There are two primary reasons.

First, for the low daily listing fee of $1 or less per coin, they can expand their customer base from their local region of buyers to a nationwide market. Many dealers attend coin shows to accomplish this very same purpose, and view the Exchange like a nationwide coin show where the costs of travel and bourse fees are eliminated.

Likewise, dealers often attend coin shows to buy. They want to find those coins that will fill their customers' want lists or to replenish their inventories. These same needs are served by the USRCE. The Exchange serves dealers as an extension of their own inventories where they can search for coins specifically requested by their customers without the costs of maintaining them in stock. Theoretically, a dealer could operate with no inventory at all simply by buying coins through the Exchange to fill his local customers' requests.

Using the Want List

USRCE offers a "Want List" software package to facilitate this very process. Using the software, collectors and dealers alike can fill their own or their customers' want lists instantly by inputting information on the coins desired and receiving a comprehensive sort of all listings on the Exchange in the various categories requested.

The computer that manages this nationwide Exchange is a $2 million IBM mainframe Model 3081, the largest computer in the numismatic world. With a storage capacity of more than 10 trillion bytes, it can maintain listings on a virtually unlimited number of coins. It could, for example list the entire population of PCGS coins, some 2 million entries, ten times over.

Its ability to access and process this database rapidly is equally impressive. Handling over 14,000,000 instructions per second, it can serve up to 500 users simultaneously with no slow-down in response. When an individual subscriber requests specific parameters by type, date, grade, etc., the USRCE can sort and respond with the appropriate data usually in about three seconds, regardless of how many other users are on the system at a given time. And the USRCE computer is in operation 24 hours a day, seven days a week.

USRCE Software

Designers of the U.S. Rare Coin Exchange emphasize that its computer capabilities are still not nearly realized. New services and software programs are in preparation to serve the numismatic community. For example, new software for dealers will soon be offered that integrates the Exchange with a dealer's management of inventory, invoicing, cash flow, accounting, grading service submissions, and client files.

For collectors and investors, similar programs will assist with record maintenance such as pricing and pedigree, budget management, and tracking the market value of a collection or portfolio.

Add-on services of the Exchange will soon include:

— a U.S. Coin Auction Catalog, an electronic listing of lots for all current coin auctions;
— a U.S. Coin Bulletin Board, an electronic listing of events and shows around the country;
— a U.S. Coin Archive, featuring every coin ever listed on the Exchange and its pricing history.

The U.S. Rare Coin Exchange is a prime example of the influence of the computer on the numismatic marketplace. The power and capability of electronic information processing itself is changing the way coins are being bought and sold. What appears at first as simply an electronic version of the printed catalogs and coin listings that have been around for years, in fact becomes a national coin inventory accessible by anyone interested in buying and selling coins. The numismatic marketplace has for decades relied on the provinciality and diversity of its character as the foundation for its traditional structure of wholesale and retail dealers and collector/investors who buy at the store-front and bourse-table level. By offering a buying/selling resource accessible to everyone, the USRCE is transforming that structure fundamentally.

With wholesale dealers, retail dealers, collectors, investors, even estate executors and other coin "outsiders," buying and selling off the same Exchange, the whole notion of wholesale pricing, for example, loses its meaning altogether. Side-by-side price competition produces a leveling effect where margins are increasingly narrowed.

On the other hand, the ease with which buyers can find and acquire the coins they want using the USRCE increases the volume of sales, which in market terms translates into increased demand. While dealers may fondly long for the "good old days" of 50 and 100% mark-ups, they will also welcome a lively market where heated buying activity keeps the market strong and sales brisk.

***

Lawrence S. Goldberg

I was born in Los Angeles, California on April 26, 1942. When I was just 10 years old, my father Harold Goldberg, started me on a career in the stamp and coin business. I began by dusting and cleaning our store located on 4th Street in downtown Los Angeles and began to learn a tremendous amount about coins. After a few years, I was very much involved in the numismatic aspect of the business and developed my own "department" in the company. At 18, after gaining much experience, I cultivated a client who wanted to collect every U.S. coin ever made in all metals. He also wanted to collect gem quality worldwide coins.

For 12 years, I worked on his collection and in the process acquired an excellent knowledge of U.S. gold coins. Finally, my client decided to auction the entire collection. I personally cataloged and photographed his coins for three important sales we conducted in 1973. Known as the Gilhousen Auction, these sales were to become the largest auction sale ever held at that time.

Also in 1972, my cousin, Ira Goldberg, and I purchased the Dr. Ruby collection on behalf of Superior Stamp & Coin Co., Inc. This $1 million purchase was, at that time, the largest single purchase ever made by a coin dealer. In 1974, we began selling off the Dr. Ruby collection by auction and private treaty. It took over five years to sell this incredible hoard of coins. In 1975, Superior Stamp & Coin Co., Inc. was awarded the American Numismatist Association's Auction Sale in Los Angeles. We decided we wanted to showcase this event. The sale grossed over $3.3 million and was included in the Guinness Book of World Records as the largest grossing auction sale ever.

In the early 1980's, we decided it was time to expand and in 1983, I begin promoting and advertising to create a more successful auction business. The gross prices realized rose from $3,743,565 in 1983 to $62,000,000 in 1990. The year by year gross prices realized at Superior auction sales are presented at the end of this chapter.

In 1985, we conducted the Dr. Jerry Buss Auction Sale, which featured two very famous coins — the 1913 nickel and the 1804 silver dollar. That one sale put Superior Stamp & Coin on the top and set a record price for two great coins. We conducted the Buddy Epsen Auction Sale in 1987, which realized nearly $8 million. The coins were unbelievable and brought record prices. This was the largest grossing auction sale ever. In 1990, we sold the King of Siam United States Proof Set, including the great 1804 silver dollar, for $3,190,000 — an all time auction record for a set of coins.

I married Marilyn Morris in 1981, and have four children: Laurie is 26, Jason is 20, Ashley is 6 and our newborn son, Sean, was born November 8, 1990. My hobbies include golf, swimming, snorkeling, collecting art and glass.

Information concerning the many organizations to which I belong, my specialties, and my contributions to books are also listed at the end of this chapter.

CHAPTER 38

How a Rare Coin Auction Works

by Lawrence S. Goldberg

Selling your coins through auction can be one of the most rewarding experiences in your collecting career. If you choose your auction house well, and if you learn the ins and outs of how auctions work, you will come away from the sale knowing you have sold your coins for their peak value. You will also have — through the auction catalog itself — a memorable document of your collection; a remembrance in years to come of those endearing treasures you once called your own.

Buying coins through auction can be an equally advantageous, equally rewarding experience. Again, if you have done your homework well, you'll be able to capture rare and desirable pieces for your collection that might otherwise pass you by. Collectors who have never bought a coin from an auction are missing 50% of the pleasure of numismatics. For they have never experienced the rush of the action and the joy of being the successful bidder at their price, not someone else's.

Rare coin auctions have been an integral part of American numismatics since the 1860s. From the very beginning, famous collections put together by well-known collectors or prominent men of the day elicited excitement and large crowds when they were sold. Such big name sales as J.J. Mickley, Stickney, Adams — and in the modern era, Dunham, Dupont, Farouk, Miles, and Heifetz — provided numismatic scholars a wealth of information to study, to discuss, to write about.

Why did these collectors, among so many thousands of others, choose to sell their coins through auctions in the first place? A prime factor, no doubt, was that they could reach a broader market of buyers than otherwise. They could scarcely afford to run costly, repetitive ads in the local press or coin publications of their day; nor did they want to wait while their coins sold piecemeal if consigned to a dealer. Another crucial drawback to selling coins yourself instead of all at once in an auction is obvious if you think about it for a moment. Which coins sell first? Which pieces do knowledgeable buyers snap up if once given a chance to "cherry pick" such a consigned collection? Naturally, the best ones would go first; or those which were underpriced because neither the consignor nor the dealer representing him knew they were undervalued.

Problems like these are swept aside when one sells his holdings at auction. For instead of one seller with limited knowledge of the market (either the collector himself or his agent, the dealer), the seller can tap the combined knowledge of hundreds — if not thousands — of specialists. Each buyer in this broadly based auction market has his or her specialty. So each buyer knows exactly what to pay. And if there are many competitors for the same series of coins, as is usually the case in an auction, these veterans will tend to bid aggressively against one another; bid aggressively and be willing to pay top dollar for pieces they need. Rarely will the seller's collection of coins be cherry picked in an auction. Adam Smith's "invisible hand" of the marketplace sees to this. Or, put another way, the very process of bringing numerous bidders together for one sale precludes it.

Yes, you can sell your coins direct to a dealer or to another collector. However, what happens if the dealer or collector can afford only a portion of your coins? Will he make a lower offer than he might otherwise if funds were more available? What happens if you cannot be paid "until this time next year", as so often happens when you sell direct. By selling your coins through auction on the other hand you can wave this problem aside like you wave aside a bothersome insect with a flick of the hand.

Another point to consider is, what if you have a large estate or a specialized collection for sale, say of Large Cent die varieties or a collection of U.S. Proof sets, 1858 to 1916 or a multi-million dollar holding? What if you have a complete run of rare U.S. pattern coinage which your corner coin shop is entirely unfamiliar with? Here the answer is crystal clear: auction is the only intelligent way to go. For how else will your coins attract the diverse buyers who are scattered across the country from one end to the other; a major auction will bring them together, whereas no other method seems adequate to do so.

Therefore, there are clear-cut advantages to selling one's coins through an auction. What are some of the buyers' advantages? How can collectors profit from bidding for coins in an auction sale? Again, there are many advantages. We will touch upon only a few of them here as it would take a considerable volume to describe them fully. First, virtually every advanced collector sooner or later finds he needs certain issues or rare mintmarks which are not easily found. Even major dealers may not be able to supply his needs for particular pieces. What is he to do? This is where auctions come in. It is an axiom as old as the hills that just as surely as there are thousands of new collections being formed as you read this, there are also dozens of old collections coming up for sale each year. And it is from major old-time collections that buyers are able to find those elusive pieces they have been searching for.

Like with any precious commodity, rare coins are by their very nature hard to come by. It is only when a collector assembles his set of rarities over many years — one coin at a time — that he is able to accumulate a large number of hard to find issues. He builds his collection one piece at a time, but sells it all at once. In other words, buyers who attend auction sales, especially major sales, have many rare pieces offered to them in one location at one time. It's clear, then, why buyers find that going to auctions can be extremely rewarding. Since others have done much of the work for them, they need only inspect the coins, attend the sale, and bid for those pieces which are on their want lists.

Another "plus" for buyers or bidders in an auction sale is that each can set a personal limit on how much he will pay. Bidders set prices themselves in line with how they value each item, although the competition keeps everyone in line so that bargains are usually very limited. A third advantage for bidders (as well as sellers, for that matter) is that one can remain anonymous if he chooses to do so. Many famous personages like movie actors, wealthy businessmen and art connoisseurs, sports figures, etc., collected coins in the past or do so today. It is easy to see why they would tend to want to remain anonymous. If need be, anonymity can be achieved by designating an agent to bid in your name. This has been done all along by big bidders. Ask your auction house for recommendations.

Pick an auction house that will work with both buyer and seller; a firm who will educate buyers on grading and how to price coins, and instruct sellers on whether their coins should be sent in for third-party grading or "slabbing" (more on slabbing later). It is very important that you choose a firm where you can always talk to the owners or principals. No one likes to get a run-around; nor should you be passed from department to department while waiting on hold for someone to come on the line who can make a decision.

What about guarantees of authenticity? After all, every collector wants to be assured he is buying genuine coins. Here, too, the auction house provides greater expertise than a general coin dealer who handles fewer rare coins. For auction houses by their nature see untold thousands of coins each year; coins which rarely come on the market; coins which, through experience, the auction specialist knows to be genuine. Therefore, their directors are familiar with nearly every issue and can spot a counterfeit coin usually at arms length. Bogus pieces rarely make it into auctions because of this. It goes without saying any auction house of repute will honor its commitment to back every questionable coin that passes through their sales with a money-back guarantee. They usually spell this out in both their consignment agreement form as well as their rules for bidding (Terms of Sale). Make certain you see a house's guarantee of authenticity in its publications. If they do not have one — and 99% of them do — steer clear. Which brings up another important area for prospective auction sellers and buyers to consider:

How to Choose an Auction House

Whether you are contemplating selling your coins or are looking for an auction house which is capable of supplying your needs, here are several key points to consider when making your selection:

- Reputation — how many years in the business?
- Financial strength
- Insurance
- Clear and concise written consignment agreement
- Size of mailing list
- Catalog quality
- Professional auctioneer
- Past performance
- Are they experts?

The key here is reputation. Is the auction house you are thinking about employing run by experts? Are they pros. Have they been in business for many years through thick and through thin, during recessionary times as well as business up-cycles? If so, they have learned the necessary lessons for selling your coins in a professional manner. They are prepared to give you skillful service.

A major segment of a firm's qualification, and one on a par with their reputation and years in the business, is financial strength. Do they have the financial resources to attract large consignments, to prepare first class catalogs, to give consignor advances, to cover any contingency which may arise? In other words, is this a healthy, well run company? If it is your chances of success are multiplied manyfold. Your chances of getting premium prices for your coin consignment are enhanced. And your confidence will be assured from the day you mail in your coins until the day you cash your proceeds check. If you have a valuable consignment, it might be advisable to ask their bank what sort of line of credit they have. It never hurts to find out early whether you are dealing with a well funded company or one that is operating on a shoe-string budget.

It goes without saying your coins should be insured while they are in the hands of the auction house. Be sure to inform yourself whether or not the company carries insurance. If you have a large collection to consign, insist on getting an insurance endorsement. Surprisingly, smaller auction firms, and those which are euphemistically called "fly-by-night operations" tend to cut corners when it comes to insurance. By doing your homework ahead of time, by insuring that your coins will be fully covered while out of your hands, you'll minimize any possible future difficulties.

All reputable auction firms will have you read and sign an auction consignment agreement form. This stipulates the terms of consignment; everything from commission rate to date of sale, and from insurance coverage — whether you are covered or not — to details on how the firm will handle the cataloging of your collection. Make sure you read the consignment agreement and understand it; if you have any questions call the firm for clarification. They will be happy to explain any points you are uncertain about.

If possible, find out what the size of their mailing list is. How many clients will they be sending the catalog to; which means, how many potential buyers will there be for your coins? And are they important buyers? Do they include the big hitters in the world of numismatics? For if you have significant holdings you will want to be assured that there will be big buyers at the sale bidding.

Turning from mailing list size to catalog preparation, it is important to find out what the auction house's catalog looks like. There is nothing more enticing to buyers than a clean layout, plenty of black and white photographs (even of moderately priced coins), color coverage for outstanding pieces, upbeat descriptions that are clear and readable, detailed Terms of Sale, and, hopefully, historic tidbits to give background to the coins being sold. Remember, too, this will be your sale; your coins will be described and photographed and will go down in the record books. Will you want some collector 100 years from now to find the catalog interesting and informative? If so, select a firm that is known for its professional cataloging, its professional air.

Something not to be overlooked either is whether the auction sale itself will be presided over by a talented auctioneer. For there is nothing more frustrating to bidders than to have an inept auctioneer. Or worse, an auctioneer who immobilizes his audience by his abrupt, argumentative manner. You do not want someone who harasses your pool of potential bidders. Instead, you are looking for an auctioneer who first of all knows who the buyers are in a sale; by keeping tabs on who is buying, he will rarely miss a bid. Then, too, the auctioneer should be fast and move along at a good rate and keep the audience's attention. Nothing is more tiring to bidders than a plodding slow sale. Put yourself in their place. If people grow bored with the pace they'll either leave early or let their attention wander. And your consignment will suffer accordingly. Neither of these is profitable to consignors.

Finally, prospective consignors and bidders should examine the past performance of an auction firm's sales. If their sales sparked active bidding, if they brought healthy prices realized, and if they were afterwards written up in the numismatic press and talked about on the convention bourse floor, then you know you've picked a winner. Attend a few sales. Talk to those who are auction regulars. Judge for yourself before deciding.

In the end, it all boils down to whether or not the owners or directors of the firm are experts. If they know what they are doing, and if they have a 24 carat reputation, then chances are excellent you will enjoy your business dealings with them. Both you and they will profit.

Buying at Auction

Bidders have several responsibilities they must attend to when buying coins in an auction. Oddly enough, many fail to read the Terms of Sale. These are always published in the front of every auction catalog and spell out the various aspects of what is to take place. Such items as guarantees of authenticity, warranties, bidder commission, lot viewing, grading, floor bidding, mail bids, sales tax, when payment is due, lot pickup, and the like are listed under the heading Terms of Sale. Some of this may seem tedious, but it is always best to take the time to read the Terms of Sale carefully. Just as a basketball team learns its signals and practices its plays before the big game, so also must bidders prepare themselves prior to the big event — the auction sale.

Bidding in Person

American auctions, like their European counterparts, charge a buying commission rate, usually 10%. Be sure to factor this 10% in when estimating your bids and remember it while bidding, since the price at which you are awarded the coin when the auctioneer says "Sold!" has that 10% buyer's fee added in when your account is settled after the sale.

View the lots if it is at all convenient for you to do so. Lot viewing times are published in the front of the catalog. If you cannot view the lots in person, you may want to appoint an agent to do this for you. (Numerous reputable dealers who attend sales regularly act as agents for bidders. They usually charge a nominal commission fee. And if asked, they will examine the lots and bid for you, while your participation remains completely anonymous.)

When estimating values for coins which are of interest, see if the auction firm will work with you. Most leading houses are happy to oblige. Their years of expertise — and the fact that they are up-to-date on the market — often proves invaluable. Ask them for current wholesale of dealer bid prices. See if they have sold similar coins recently through one of their sales.

As the big day nears it is important for you to establish credit with your auction firm. Phone them several weeks in advance for details, especially if you contemplate buying a large dollar amount at the sale. And when the big day arrives, sign in at the table set up near the entrance to the auction room. You will be given a bidder card at this time with your number on it. Do not lose it. The employee at the table can help you with any last minute questions you may have about the workings of the sale (although he or she may be unable to help with numismatic questions like how much such-and-such a lot will bring).

Floor bidding begins at an opening bid. This is set by the auction house at either (1) a slight discount from the highest mail bid they've received, or (2) what the house deems is a reasonable starting price when no mail bids for the particular lot have been received. In some cases where a high ticket item is to be sold, the auctioneer will either publish a "Bidding Will Commence At" price or announce it to the audience. This happens when a consignor places a Reserve on his lot. Reserves are more often encountered in art sales than rare coin auctions, though, so there are usually few reserved lots.

Bids rise in increments set by the auctioneer but controlled by tradition. At pre-established junctures, the dollar amounts jump from, say $25 per advance to $100 per advance, etc. Although you may call out a lesser bid than the auctioneer has asked for, do so sparingly. How would you feel if you were an underbidder who is outbid by only a tiny increment? Higher priced coins, wherein the bids jump in large increments, sometimes justify an intermediate bid called from the floor. Never be afraid to stop the sale if you have a pertinent question.

When the auction is underway, what happens if you raise your hand accidently and are awarded a coin you didn't intend bidding on? Immediately raise your hand and tell the auctioneer you made a mistake. Do not wait until 10 or 20 lots have passed before doing so, do it immediately. Auctioneers are people just like you; they make mistakes, too. He will simply reopen the lot for bidding. Or, what happens if you had your hand up but were skipped over? Be sure to call out or stop the action. It is in the interest of all parties to have lots sell to the highest bidder. Again, do not wait until 10 or 20 lots have passed. In cases where you failed to bid on a lot that you wanted, if you wait the auctioneer will not allow the lot to be reopened. Therefore, keep on your toes, keep your attention focused on the sale, and you will rarely make a mistake.

If you intend picking up your lots after the sale, talk to one of the firm's employees who are set up at the entrance to the auction room. They will give you necessary directions where to go to obtain your lots. Do not forget — there are no return privileges for bidders bidding from the floor, except where a coin might prove to have been counterfeit. Minimize your uncertainties beforehand so you won't have to live with your mistakes afterwards.

Bidding by Mail or Phone

Those who wish to bid by phone should make arrangements well in advance. Call the company for requirements several weeks before the sale. By all means, talk to the person who will be executing your bids on the auction floor.

If you are bidding by mail, read the Terms of Sale carefully, decide which coins you'd like, and fill in the bid sheet. Then check it. Then check it again — to make absolutely sure you are bidding the correct amounts on the correct lots. Reread the part about mail bidders' return privileges in the front of the catalog. Do not forget that sales tax will be charged where applicable unless you are a dealer with a resale permit; also, there is a 10% buyers fee, and postage. Like when bidding in person, it is always advisable to establish credit well before the sale so there will be no surprises. Call the firm if you have any questions, including questions about grading.

Consigning Coins for Auction

You have selected an auction company to consign your coins to. Now there are several things you must do in order to get the ball rolling. First and foremost, after having discussed your collection with the company, package your coins securely for shipment. Sign and include a copy of the auction consignment agreement form, and — this is quite important — make a detailed inventory. Do you understand the payment schedule? The commission rate? How your coins will be listed and described? If not, phone for details.

Auction houses establish their commission schedules differently, although there are similarities in all of them. For example collectors who have significant consignments, those ranging from $100,000 on up, can often get reduced rates. This is only natural, since much of the cost to the company in processing a consignment is in the paperwork and employee time required. Larger consignments take little extra staff time and so, on a coin-per-coin basis, have a lower unit cost. Smaller collections ($2,000 to $10,000) — but especially unusual ones like tokens or books or numismatic oriented collectibles — require more work for the value received; hence, they are charged a higher fee. Fees range, on average, from 2% for larger collections and estates up to 10% or 15% for smaller consignments which take more time to prepare and catalog. Many firms will negotiate commissions individually on very expensive coins. If you have such properties for sale, you should learn what their policy is. Discuss this with an owner or principal.

We said above that you should find out if your coins are insured while out of your hands. You will sleep better at night if you know they are from the moment they are received and signed for. Is an extra charge required for photography? If so, you might want to stick to those companies who cover all expense of photography and advertising as part of the overall commission rate. No one likes surprises after their coins are consigned.

Ask if you can work with the cataloger or if you can provide him or her with background information on your more important pieces. This way you will receive an error-free description that gives added weight to the coin (as well as added dollars to your pocketbook). And along these lines, find out who will be working on your coins — removing PVC film from them, grading them, photographing them, preparing them for cataloging, etc. Only qualified people who know how to handle coins properly should be working on them, not novices. After all, these are your prize coins.

In addition to getting qualified people to prepare and catalog your coins, you may want to have your higher grade pieces sent in to one of the third-party grading services for "slabbing." Ask who pays for this service, you or the house. Have the owner or principal select which grading service is best for your coins (NGC and PCGS are the two we recommend). And if, by chance, your coin comes back with a grade on the conservative side, be sure to instruct the right people to put a Premium Quality label on the slab and give its population report in the catalog description. Each one of these points about slabbing increases the likelihood your coins will receive high bids — which is what you are seeking.

During the 1980s, third-party grading (or slabbing as it is known in the trade) became an integral part of the business. Top condition coins that have received consensus grading by either NGC or PCGS often bring double or triple the prices realized of their unslabbed counterparts. Some collectors may be uncertain whether putting collector coins in plastic slabs is advisable. Being collectors, they prefer to handle and store their coins in albums, etc. Regardless, that is the direction the market has taken. And since the market is nothing more nor less than the market participants themselves, this means that you get the most for your coins when you follow the lead of the marketplace. If you try to go your own way you may not receive full value for your consignment. That is why many of the larger auction houses encourage their consignors to have their coins graded by one of the third-party services. As always, the choice is yours.

One of the advantages to having your coins slabbed is that they then go into a large database stored at the grading service. Every month they publish updated population reports or census figures on what has been graded. This provides the market with valuable information on rarity. It is also a good indication of the relative rarities within a series. For example, a Mint State 65, 1913 Barber Quarter might turn out to be many times rarer than a similarly graded 1912-S. Whereas for years the 1912-S might have been priced higher than the 1913, now it is seen that 1913 is many times rarer grade for grade. The market comes into line with these new figures and those who were fortunate enough (or wise enough) to buy 1913 when it was considered less rare, reap the benefits.

Ask the firm when your coins will be offered. Are there any events scheduled around the sale which may generate more bidders such as a local coin convention. We have found over the years that auctions which are held just prior to a major convention bring the best prices. Not during the convention, but prior to it. During a coin show dealers and collectors are too busy walking around the bourse room floor to have time to view lots. Also, if they've purchased coins at the show they will undoubtedly have less money available for bidding in an auction; better to have your coins sell before a convention, while everyone still has a bulging wallet.

Since you are hoping to sell your coins to the widest possible audience, check to make certain the sale will be extensively advertised. Ask the auction house how many ads will be placed in the numismatic press. Check through past editions to see how comprehensive their advertising was.

Many consignors prefer to take an advance on the auction prices realized. When you did your checking earlier to see if the firm was well grounded and financially secure, you most likely learned whether they also give auction advances. If you wish to avail yourself of this service, talk to either the auction department head or one of the firm's principals to discuss terms. Most charge interest at two, three, or four percentage points over prime. And most advance between 50% and 70% of expected prices realized. Because auction advances are important to many consignors, and because some firms are rather stingy with their checkbook, it behooves you to look into this early on, before you commit your coins.

Typically, consignors are paid 45 days after the sale — exactly 45 days. Consignor checks go in the mail on the 45th day. This is standard practice throughout the United States since buyers normally have 30 days in which to pay. If your check does not arrive soon thereafter, notify the company immediately.

Lastly, if you are consigning particularly rare coins or coins that belonged to notable collectors of the past, be sure to provide pedigree information if you have it. This way your coins will be described fully. They will also receive loftier bids if they have an extended pedigree behind them, since a pedigree is like a scorecard or track record for future bidders and owners.

This wraps up the general overview of how auctions work, both for consignors wishing to sell their collections as well as for prospective buyers interested in bidding in sales. We close with some often-asked questions and answers:

1. Can I submit my coins for auction pregraded with the grades I would like to see them sell for?

Yes, by all means include grades when you consign your coins. If the auction house feels they are accurately portrayed, they will use them as is. If, on the other hand, they feel they are on the high side you will be notified before cataloging begins. In our firm, we often advise that they be sent in to PCGS or NGC. This can be especially profitable to you if you have very high quality pieces that have the "old time" natural toning today's buyers demand. If your coins have high value many firms will pay the grading fee for you.

2. Can I review your auction descriptions before the catalog goes to press?

It is always wise to get some indication from the auction house how they will describe your better pieces. Coins with unusually low populations or mintages, those with beautiful toning, or high value pieces with pedigrees should get detailed descriptions. You might even wish to include suggestions at the time you consign your material. If these suggestions are well written and readable, they will often be used verbatim, either in part or in whole.

3. Can a consignor (owner) bid on his own coin? And if so, what will be the cost of buy backs?

Nearly all firms allow consignors to bid on their own coins. Some charge a set buy-back commission fee; others have a sliding scale depending upon the individual coin involved. Buy-backs range up to 5% commission charge, on average. Be sure to alert the auctioneer ahead of time if you are submitting bids on your own material. This will help alleviate any possible misunderstanding later on. You can also have an agent bid for you if you prefer to remain anonymous.

4. When is the best time to sell a coin or collection?

There are no fast and hard rules here, but if past history is any guide, from mid-January through February is a good time, since buyers seem to come out of the woodwork, as it were, near the beginning of the year. Tax time is out, of course. So, too, the holiday season, particularly around Christmas and New Years. Any potential bidders have their minds (and their bank accounts) on other things then. The fall is an excellent time to have your coins sold. With everybody back from summer vacations people have more time to devote to their hobbies. Another outstanding time to sell is prior to a large coin show. Since shows draw in thousands of collectors and dealers from around the country, you'll have a much larger potential audience for your coins. However, as we said earlier, sales that take place at the same time as a show — on the same days and in competition with the coin convention — tend to be overshadowed by all the other activities going on; activities like seminars, exhibits, tours, and the bourse floor hustle-bustle itself.

5. What about advertising and publicity for the sale. Will my coins get good coverage?

They will if you place your coins with a firm that is known for its large advertising budget. If you regularly see full-page spreads in the numismatic press advertising upcoming sales, you are on the right track. Also, well established firms bring in the local media, from television crews to town papers, to publicize the event. All advertising should be paid for by the auction house. As consignor, you should not have to be assessed a fee for this.

6. How can I know there will be a large number of mail bidders for my coins?

Be sure to question your auction house about the size of the mailing list and how many catalogs they prepare; also find out it they mail out a pre-auction announcement brochure, as many do for big name sales. Learn, too, if your coins will be seen by collectors nationwide or if their listing is exclusive to only a small region of the country.

7. How many of my coins will get photographs?

Your best bet here is to examine sample auction catalogs from all of the major firms. See which coins are pictured. Do they photograph only $10,000 and above giants, or are the less expensive pieces given regular coverage as well. Although photographs take up valuable space in a catalog (printing costs are steep nowadays), nevertheless, your coins do draw in more bidders and realize higher prices when they are pictured. Although you cannot expect to have every coin you consign photographed, you should expect anything that is choice or out of the ordinary done.

8. How do I know my coins will be in good company with other nice pieces in a sale?

Ask the auction house. Find out when their next big sale is. For example, if you have a specialized collection of Large Cents or Bust Dollars by die variety, you'll want to have it placed in the front of the catalog if it warrants this. Or, of you know that a major variety collection will be sold in six months or a year, you can piggyback your set along with others who will be doing the same. There are hundreds of famous "big name" collections that have brought extra strong prices for those who have similar material to what has been consigned by the estate or prominent collector. Keep a close eye on *Coin World* and *Numismatic News* accounts of future sales.

Here's an example: when we at Superior sold the Jack Robinson collection of Large Cents by die variety, price records were broken time and time again. Because many of Mr. Robinson's coins had been off the market for years, and because many new collectors had come into coins in the intervening time, they were hungry to buy his coins; and they showed their eagerness by topping each other's bids as we said, time and time again; it was one of our best attended — and certainly one of our most hectic — auction sales ever. It never hurts to place your coins in excellent company where they will be in the spotlight.

In Summary

I guess if I had to sum up in a paragraph everything you'll need to be a successful auction participant, I would recommend to all prospective sellers and to all prospective buyers, to do your homework first so as to be one-up on the competition: know your coins; know your competition; know the market; know the rules of the game; know 10% more than everyone else. If you follow these rules, success will be yours.

Additional information concerning Lawrence Goldberg:

Organizations

— Life member of the American Numismatic Association, #845, since 1971
— Member of the Professional Numismatists Guild, #154, since February 1969
— Member of the American Numismatic Society since 1969
— Life member of the Society of International Numismatics
— Member of the John Reich Society
— Member of the International Association of Professional Numismatists

Specialties

Mr. Goldberg is a recognized expert in the following fields:

— United States coinage from 1793 to 1950. This includes all coins in gold, silver, nickel and copper.

— Mexican coinage. Starting with our first auction sale which specialized in Mexican coins, we became the top auction firm in the world in selling Mexican and Spanish colonial coinage. We have even written a book on Mexican Revolutionary coinage.

— World gold and silver coinage. I have contributed to many foreign catalogs. Many years ago when the American Numismatic Association decided to put out a standard catalog for grading coins, I was one of the experts who helped perform this important task and today it is one of the standards used by numismatists throughout the United States.

— Appraising United States and foreign coins. I have been hired by almost every leading bank in California and have even done some work for the FBI and the Secret Service.

— I have written numerous articles. Some of the publications in which articles of mine have been published include: The *Numismatist*, *Coin World*, *COINage* Magazine, *Numismatic News*, the Los Angeles Times, the Herald Examiner newspaper and various other leading publications throughout the world.

— I have formed some of the largest collections for clients. Many of these collections have appeared in our auction sales and become quite famous. These auction sales include: The Gilhousen Collection, The Wolfson Collection, The Bernard Turkus Collection, The Federico Claveria Collection of Mexican Coinage, The Miguel Munoz Collection of Mexican Coins, The Merrill Bothamley Collection, etc.

— Moneytalks. In the early 1980's, I hosted a live television program which aired on a local financial news network once a week for 15 minutes. This program lasted over two years and dealt with investing in coins.

— Contributor on prize-winning catalog. Superior Galleries won the 1987 Numismatic Literary Guild Award for the Robinson Brown Catalog, September 1986.

Gross Prices Realized At Superior Auction Sales

1983	$ 3,743,565
1984	4,848,028
1985	10,340,354
1986	14,370,695
1987	25,079,573
1988	24,480,674
1989	44,712,673
1990	62,000,000

Contributions to Books

— A Guide Book of United States Coins (the "Red Book"), by R.S. Yeoman. It is the sixth all-time best selling nonfiction book. I have been a contributor since 1970.
— United States Pattern, Experimental and Trial Pieces.
— The Standard Catalogue of World Coins, by Chester L. Krause and Clifford Mishlin.
— A Guidebook of Modern United States Currency, by Neil Shafer.
— Current Coins of the World, by R.S. Yeoman.
— A Catalog of Modern World Coins, by R.S. Yeoman.
— Handbook of United States Coins ("Blue Book"), by R.S. Yeoman.
— Mexican Revolutionary Coinage, by Guthrie.
— A Guidebook of Mexican Coins, 1822 to Date, by Buttrey.
— Eight Reales and Pesos of the New World, by Elizondo.
— Coins of Mexico, by Grove.
— Official ANA Grading Standards for United States Coins.

Other interests

In 1979, my partners Ira and Mark Goldberg and I purchased an interest in the National Basketball Association's Indiana Pacers and sold our shares a few years later.

***

Market Making and Numismatics — Phase I

by John W. Highfill

Senior Editor's comment:

During the fall of 1990, and I do mean the FALL of 1990, the precipitous crash of rare coin values was felt by all. Everyone experienced some degree of loss as the market plunged taking many dealers out of the industry forever, and placing many more in jeopardy.

As a response to these events, John Highfill prepared a series of four separate articles addressing the probable causes and possible cures for the ailing coin market. He widely distributed these essays in order to inform the industry leaders of his findings and encourage them to act in positive ways to stem the tide, turn the market around and create a marketplace that would be more immune to the events of the past.

Many positive responses were received but the required actions were not forthcoming quickly enough nor in the necessary degree. Therefore, in the continuing effort to educate and stimulate those who are in a position to take appropriate action, these articles are reported in their entirety within this book.

We would like to use these essays as a historical viewpoint to a problem unsolved at the time. However, if the problem still exists as you read these pages, you may be able to solve or at least understand the problems of a bid-oriented electronic sight-unseen trading system.

CHAPTER 39

Market Making and Numismatics — Phase I

(Release date: October 5, 1990)

CHAPTER 40

The Future of Sight-Unseen Trading — Phase II

(Originally Released October 15, 1990)

CHAPTER 41

In Search of Electronic Trading Excellence — Phase III

(Preliminary Release date: October 29, 1990)

CHAPTER 42

The Aftermath — Phase IV

(Preliminary Release date: April 8, 1991)

CHAPTER 39

Market Making and Numismatics — Phase I

(Release date: October 5, 1990)

by John W. Highfill, NLG

Art is not appreciated or understood by everyone. Only the artist is acutely aware of the creation, the emotion, the obstacles, and the sweat! There are many critics — consisting mostly of those who are not participants. They can't paint but they know what the picture should look like (or what they want it to be).

Market making is most certainly an art — with a distinctive flavor and color all its own. I consider this activity to be the core of the numismatic industry while the collectors and investors are the lifeblood. The dealers form the indispensable network through which the coins move continually from hand to hand.

To get to the future, we must begin with the past. Many people have said "you don't know where you're going if you don't know where you've been." With that in mind, let's pause for a quick review.

Prior to the conception of independent third-party grading in the mid 1980s, dealers had to agree on both grade and price to complete a transaction. This usually required the dealers to meet in order to inspect the coin, and agreeing upon a grade was one of the biggest problems within the industry. Price was determined only after the grading question was resolved. This method of doing business tended to restrict the size and growth potential of the numismatic marketplace.

Third-party grading gave birth to a new concept — the sight-unseen marketplace. This method of trade allowed the market to expand to include more numismatists and non-professional players. With the grade of certified coins previously established, all could buy with confidence. Of course, this led to the growth of collectors and investors in the market.

The idea and concept of sight-unseen trading is excellent. It has utilized the variables of grade and price, and then set grade constant through independent third-party grading. Grading in this manner has served the industry very well from its inception to this time. As of today, except for individualists who still believe that they can do a better job of grading, the industry and general public have learned to accept independent third-party grading.

In the future, computer grading may supersede the current concept — but that remains to be seen. Grading is a subjective process with each individual possessing varying skills and personal habits. Computerized grading, when implemented, could overcome all of the "people" problems and provide extremely consistent grading. The keys to computer grading lie in a large accessible base of data and an accurate "picture" of the coin. Possibilities at the present time remain very high and positive. This appears to be the biggest potential change as far as the grading process is concerned.

Turning to the variable of price, I submit that all bids are guesses at best. Some of them are better guesses than others. If the answers are wrong, they will go through the evolutionary process to arrive at an acceptable market value. This results in a viable and healthy market (if there are asking prices in place to keep bids within a competitive spread or margin).

The variable (price) is more unscientific — and will most likely remain so into the future. This is where the free market enters the equation. If you apply the basic economics of supply and demand (supply being equal to third-party graded coins), supply can be documented to within 10%, by using PCGS and NGC population reports. The level of accuracy is lessened due to loss, crackouts (resubmissions), etc.

Looking back, we were all taught that supply is limited, but now the supply of certified independent third-party graded coins is growing. The government may not be making any more, but the services are certifying more! In the long run, the "certified" supply will give this industry a tremendous boost. In the near term we are running short on the demand side.

The shortage of demand involves a lack of capitalization in the certified coin market. Without adequate participation from the collecting and investing public, dealers are forced to use their limited resources to support both prices and market activity. More and more dealers are choosing to leverage their inventories to acquire additional capital.

This strategy is based on the premise that coins will either continue to increase in value or additional funds will enter the market to reduce inventories. If the bid prices for coins continues to advance, dealers have no problem maintaining their position and selling into a rising market. Looking at the entry of additional capital, this also gives the dealer no problems because new funds are available to purchase dealer inventories.

On the other hand, if the coin market suffers a decline in values, the leveraged position of dealer inventories is now in jeopardy. The dealer must either reduce inventory or infuse additional cash to hold the position. Dealers who cannot maintain or sell their inventory at a profit or break-even level suffer real losses when forced to liquidate to raise cash. If liquidation is done during an extreme low in market prices, this may also literally put the dealer out of business. These circumstances must not be allowed to happen as they threaten the very existence of many small and mid-sized dealers. Low-ball bids without transactions can create an illusionary "artificial" low. This initial domino could cause extreme hardships for everyone if allowed to go "unregulated."

The additional supply of coins coming into the market was expected to be absorbed by Wall Street in the late 1980s. This just hasn't happened, and I don't know when (or if) it will happen, but I do know that we can all go broke just sitting and waiting around for Wall Street (or any other source of demand).

Every month the population of certified coins increases. The marketplace must have the mechanisms in place to move these coins off the market. Looking down the road, the "creation" of certified coins will finally begin to decline steadily. This event will spur the market onward and upward as well as reinforce our traditional position with regard to the supply of coins.

A Look at Computerized Trading Systems

The potential for sight-unseen trading allowed computerized systems to make an entrance and provide an "organized" marketplace for the market maker. The emergence of several computer "bid" and "ask" oriented systems has attracted a number of dealers and significantly expanded the scope of their acquisitions and offerings.

Systems such as the American Numismatic Exchange (ANE) and Certified Coin Exchange (CCE or "Certified") have provided a view of the "bid" side of the market for better date and rare date coins. It is an unfortunate side effect that multiple quote systems lead to reduced participation and contribute to an already thin market, especially for higher priced material.

My pet peeve and the number one problem with sight-unseen trading via computer is that prices can fall with little or no actual transactions taking place. Generic coins can pull down the bids for rare coins without those rare coins trading at all. Why should the bid on a coin drop when no coin was, is or will be available? The idea that any tangible asset can go down in value without supply coming into the marketplace defies the basics of economic supply and demand. How can this be? If the supply is not there, how can demand diminish? Even if demand and supply go to zero, the price should theoretically remain the same. However, the thrust is that these declines should not occur for any reason other than asking prices (supply) responding to the bids. To quote a comment: "The bid-based systems have created a market with inadequate price discovery mechanisms." THEY HAVE THEM, THEY JUST HAVEN'T USED THEM.

NOT ONLY HAVE WE ESSENTIALLY TURNED COMMON "GENERIC" COINS INTO A COMMODITY, BUT WE ARE ALSO TRYING (THROUGH THE "BID-BASED" SYSTEM) TO DO THE SAME WITH RARE COINS. Last week an 1884-CC PCGS-65 traded on the CCE for $146! By the "rules" we play by now, all the PCGS-65 1884-CC's in the U.S.A. are worth only $146 each. I don't know about you, but if I have any, my asking price will be far more than that! I guess I would have to sell one of my "rare" 1881-S PCGS-65 Morgan dollars and give up an extra twenty bucks to pay for this deal.

Looking a little deeper, a number of factors which contribute to a fall in prices must be mentioned. First, the negative psychology that accompanies a fall in generic prices will cause market makers and dealers to lower their bids for higher priced items. Verbal abuse and negative thinking will drive coins down without trading. This is undesirable, does no one any good and it must be stopped. A dealer who removes his bid for whatever reason will make the second bidder the high bid. If the second bid is substantially lower, the "perceived" price goes down without any transaction. This has been happening for the last 18 months and is virtually the number one problem (domino) in the destruction of the entire numismatic community! Setting generics aside, the (approximate) 10% of the coins traded set the pricing "tune" for the entire market (90% of these haven't traded).

Another factor that affects the bidders quotations is the availability of cash which may be used to cover acquisitions. If the dealer is expecting to cover purchases with past or present sales receipts, anything which interrupts the flow of cash can lead to an emergency liquidation. These "fire" sales intended only to satisfy a need for immediate cash are very damaging to most dealers, and to the entire numismatic industry as well. Dealers are facing an unstable customer base and are currently concerned with every new purchase. They have no conceivable idea of the "perceived" value of any coin, much less every coin.

Fear of the unknown will motivate bidders to remove or reduce their bids. If "ask" quotations are not readily visible, nobody knows when and if their bids might be hit. The fear of ownership can be a great deterrent to sight-unseen bidding, especially when the financial exposure cannot be readily determined. Therefore, bidders have less incentive to bid. We are losing bidders every day, and some will never bid again on the system! Dealers — your attention please. Currently, there are billions of dollars of PCGS and NGC coins alone in the marketplace.

Finally, outright panic will cause bidding action to cease entirely, or lead to liquidation on a large and very damaging scale. This is a market phenomenon which we must diligently guard against.

The lack of participating bidders in the computerized marketplace has been a problem from the inception of sight-unseen trading. No bidder can hold up the entire market! There are now billions of dollars in the marketplace. The identification and management of potential liability is paramount to the survival of all market makers. A larger base of market makers and bidding dealers is required to insure fiscal responsibility with a more orderly and less volatile market. This could be achieved by a Wall Street type of exchange and a "governing board of trade" (still a possibility).

In 1989 ANE initiated an exclusive market maker bid/ask system for MS-63 Morgan and Peace dollars. This was initiated to increase the liquidity of these coins and to narrow spreads. On the current bidding systems (ANE and CCE) dealers may post a bid and/or an asking price for a coin. The posted asking price may be at any level without regard to the prevailing bids. There were times when bids for coins dropped substantially to artificially low levels. Trading ceased until either bids were raised or asking prices dropped to a level that would promote trading once again. This process occasionally left the affected coins with no market until normal spreads were restored. But all in all, the generics have maintained a market meeting most of its objectives.

If the "ask" side of the picture were to be posted in the better date and rare date market, we would obtain a clearer indication of the prevailing bid-ask spread. The "Ask" side of the market should offer no more advantage than "bid" side. Asking prices can put a lid on bids and, in downward cycles, can cause bids to fall. This condition is acceptable and understandable — anything different would not make economic sense.

The "bid" system as it exists at the time of this writing, with asking prices unknown, leaves the bidders as a distinct disadvantage. The holders of the coins are well ahead of the game. They can just sit back and watch the bids rise or fall and simply hit the bids whenever they wish. They don't actively have to work to maintain the system.

By the way, when you currently buy a coin, your bid is dropped from the system. At that time your coin suffers an automatic decline in market value as the next lower bid becomes the high bid. This would not be the case if the last transaction prices were posted by the system. It is not right to suffer an immediate paper loss (according to the system) whenever your bid is hit. Posted transaction price data would be quite valuable in assessing the "real" market value for better and rare date items. The "perceived" value (bid) is currently being published as the real value and is the number one "journalistic injustice" to everyone involved in coins. (This includes dealers, collectors, investors, banking institutions, pension plans, limited partnerships, etc. — EVERYONE!)

The "Bidders" in the Computerized Marketplace

The market makers providing the bids entered into the computerized market are of three general groups. These include large market makers supporting a large portion of the market, small market makers supporting their special interests, and other dealers who do not support the market but occasionally bid as their needs dictate. Let's take a closer look at each of these three categories of bidders.

The large market makers who bid "across the board" and provide support for the market are the backbone of computerized bidding. Without these bidders, liquidity "at any price" for a number of items would simply not be available. Computerized systems would probably disappear altogether without the support of the large market makers and hundreds of separate market makers. Current dealer capitalization is simply not even close to being adequate. If the hundreds of market makers we need to make daily spreads were available, those specialists would become just that — specialists!

I have been bidding in the sight-unseen marketplace on a daily basis from the beginning. These bids for each day have numbered in the thousands, but have resulted in purchases of less than one percent of my daily outstanding bid prices. Another interesting fact is that purchases of generic coins made up about ninety percent of that total. These are very interesting figures and seem to be consistently accurate in both bull and bear markets. (Most will buy close to the top and very little after the fall.)

Special interest market makers are small and medium sized dealers who use the computer trading systems to make a market in only those coins in which they have an interest. This does not necessarily mean that they currently own inventory in these issues, but rather that they are willing to support and acquire the coins they are bidding for.

Occasional dealers bidding for coins in order to satisfy immediate needs or to take advantage of what they perceive to be low market prices make up the third group. This is a small assembly making up less than ten percent of all bidders on the computerized trading systems.

We all have been lectured by critics of those who have supported bids across the board. They have said things like "Don't bid a coin that you don't wish to buy," and "We must stop the bidders that bid on their own coins." If you eliminate all these market makers or dealers who bid on their own coins, the result is simply a blank screen.

If you don't like the bids, either HIT THE BID, BID MORE or POST AN ASK. Don't criticize a high ask if it is the only ask. If you don't like an ask , HIT THE ASK, POST A LOWER ASK, or GO HIGH BID.

The market will take care of those who bid on their own coins. These dealers may be protecting their inventory, bidding for more coins, acquiring special positions, or looking for buy-sell spreads on their own inventory. A few may be trying to inflate their inventory through artificial market manipulations, but the market will take care of itself in all of these cases.

What we need is more bidders — but more bidders has been only one answer from day one. It's time to re-invent the wheel! We must develop a system that encourages them to bid without fear of being loaded up (ask-based). There are many dealers that don't think five seconds before unloading inventory bought just a week ago to raise cash. This produces unnecessary volatility and an unstable market. Solutions are available to deter this kind of trading.

Market Psychology and Market Making

Positive thinking breeds positive thinking. Negative thinking breeds negative thinking. Nothing profound here — but these concepts are still the largest psychological contributors to numismatic market cycles. Consider the great silver boom of early 1980s. During that short period of time, there was talk of phenomenal prices and a never-ending upward spiral making millionaires of us all. What did everyone say in 1982 when the market was in the midst of a large correction? It was only talk of gloom and doom with no end in sight. As of this writing, the industry is suffering a severe downturn and lack of demand sufficient to meet the growing supply of certified coins. Negative thinkers abound and their pronouncements just serve to drive the market down even further.

All this talk has contributed to the negative psychology and low-ball offers by both big and small money men for your inventory — just when you need cash and they don't necessarily need the coins. Incidentally, there has been a constant flight of high quality coins moving into strong investor hands. Their funds are growing through a combination of capital infusion and the selling of lower quality merchandise to finance their rare coin purchases.

What does it take to turn the market around? It simply takes money and support. The money comes from the largest industrial players who desire the inventory for future gain, and possess the amounts of capital required to buy and hold large amounts of certified coins. The support comes from all those in the industry who will climb aboard when they realize that the money (demand) has returned to the marketplace. Positive markets lead to positive thinking! If we induce confidence within ourselves, we will be able to re-induce that same confidence into the end-users.

I would like to make a comment concerning "contrarian" trading. A definition would be taking a position in the market when everyone is thinking in the opposite direction. Some of you have heard me say, "You can't go north when everyone else is going south!" This is essentially true — unless you are the captain of the ship! Think about it.

At some point in time during every bear market cycle, the big money men will step in and reverse the trend. They will accomplish this by absorbing everything in sight and bidding for even more. To the outsider, this phenomenon will seem to be akin to "contrarian" trading, but in fact, it is simply the decision of those in charge that they cannot buy the coins for any less. Their pockets are deep and can stand much adversity if their purchases turn out to be premature. Most of the time, their actions generate enough activity and confidence among the industry followers that the entire market picks up and moves to the upside with little ongoing effort other than the steady increasing of their bids. This can be put into checkmate by asking prices. The ask can slow down a rapid escalation of prices, but will not stop all issues or a "real" bull market. By the way, speaking of market psychology, has anyone even considered that we may be looking at a bear trap?

I never thought I'd be saying this, but it may be time to put rhetoric and discussion aside and let the computers do the talking for us. It is better for computers to show the bids and asking prices instead of using the mentality of the coin dealer (i.e., negative psychology). Nobody likes change, but sometimes change, if given enough time, can put things back into the proper perspective.

Bottom Lines

Here is a collection of thoughts, ideas and facts that you may be able to identify with and relate to. These statements come as a result of many years of experience and hard knocks. This is the bottom line.

Set generics aside for a moment as they have only become a by-product of the "bid-ask" quandary. It has been documented by the CCE starting on May 22, 1990, that an excess of 90% of the listed coins have not traded at any price. Yet 100% of the index has gone down 50-75% in the last 120 days. There are no reasons other than fear, panic, negative psychology, etc., for this decline. We are dying from friendly fire. If this was self-orchestrated, they could not have done a better job. Even the large dealers who wish to buy at lower levels did not expect this. We haven't shot ourselves in the foot, we have shot everyone within bullet range. "Take no prisoners" has been the order of the market.

Until large retail merchandising enters the market, generics will continue to draw the life blood out of the business. It is utterly asinine and deplorable that common generic coins can make rare coins go down in value without actually even being available for sale.

With the two divided systems, there are not enough bidders to bid on every coin sight-unseen that has been graded by PCGS (let alone NGC). A split system cuts the action and bids from 100% to 10%. (This is not a math error. Proportionate performance prevails here.) Extreme thinness of the market is the result of this division. Referring to the previous "critics" paragraphs — if you had a blank system before, you have absolutely nothing now. Couple that with the multiple commercial "ask-based" systems in the marketplace, and the dealer-oriented system may suffer terminal damage.

Currently everyone is a loser if the market stays in its current cycle. Coin dealers inventories have gone down approximately 50% in 90 days, and bank portfolios are on margin. Investors and collectors have lost one-half of their investment portfolios. Large inventories including limited partnerships and other institutional money stand to lose half of their invested value if liquidation were to be completed at this time. Staying power will hold through these temporary paper losses.

We are losing small dealers forever, and losing small to medium sized dealers daily. Collectors are staying on the sidelines and investors are leaving the marketplace never to return. Credibility in the industry is at a historic low, and unless we stop the degradation of numismatic values, we will lose it all.

We must address regulation rather than be afraid of it. Self regulation is ideal and can be attained only through unselfish contributions for the good of the industry. Recently, a steering committee has been elected for a self-regulating organization chaired by Hugh Sconyers. I wish them the best in their quest for making the coin business a "good business."

Moving on, consider fully implementing one of ANE's first concepts — to put a willing buyer together with a willing seller. Be careful of software updates that simply band-aid the symptoms. This will only prolong the agony while not eliminating the problems. Don't take aspirin for a brain tumor!

Put both bids and asking prices on the same screen. Spreads for generics are already there. The esoterics won't fall unduly and the move will encourage bids. The asking prices will move the bids into proper alignment. The investors will not suffer additional paper losses on their inventory due to unknowledgeable and low-ball bids. We must stop the downward price spiral. The vast majority of coins are going down with virtually no trading. The "ask" side has a distinct sight-unseen advantage (due to asks not being posted). In the future the sellers would have to update their asking prices. They will have to go to work for the first time in over five years! We have tried the bid-based system for the last five years. Let's give equal time for the ask-based system!

All the coins in the U.S. are being held hostage by the bidders, and the publications are reporting the blood bath. Remember the "golden rule" — he who owns the gold makes the rules. In a bid-based system he who doesn't own the gold makes up the price (rules). Consider a coin with a population of 1,000. If one low-ball bid is posted and reported in a market with no trading, that bid is picked (and published) over the unposted asking price of each of the 1,000 people who hold the coin. If this is right, I'm in the wrong business. The bottom line of this entire essay is: There must be an ask prior to a bid being posted. If a bid is even allowed at that time it would have to be within 15-25% of the ask. No longer should a bid be able to determine the price of a coin.

This move will also reduce or eliminate "fair weather bidders" — bidders who bid only when bids are low hoping to pick off a coin or two. It will also dispose of the need for policing a lateral rule if dealers must post an ask before "hitting" the bid.

Couple 24 hour posted asking prices with the last transaction price on the same screen, and this industry would stabilize in a hurry. In addition, these moves will serve to increase the amount of negotiated trades and private dealings.

PRICE KNOWLEDGE IS VITAL TO THE SURVIVAL OF THIS INDUSTRY! Let's get out of this fear-ridden tumbling price syndrome which can only lead to panic liquidation and the demise of many dealers. We must make computers work for us. Blank screens can and will become the order of the day. The only thing worse than an "organized" boycott is an "unorganized" boycott of the system!

Better yet, take out fear and put buyers and sellers together on the same screen with 24 hour lag time. We must alleviate the pressure. This is not an overreaction, but a viable solution to an ongoing problem existing since the inception of the sight-unseen marketplace. Let the software take care of monitoring the required time lag while we take care of business.

Laziness usually is not overcome. But the benefits are there if people can bid with knowledge. By posting an ask first, you will stop a lateral market and eliminate the lateral rule. There will be no more "hit and run" because dealers will be required to post an asking price 24 hours prior to hitting your bid.

If sellers were on a thirty day pay schedule, watch what would happen. The sellers would disappear for the most part. This would alleviate much of the pressure on both dealers and prices. The result would be a more orderly market and a reduction of hitting the bids, hit and runs and laterals. Dealers wouldn't be able to sell purchased inventory immediately to pay their bills. (Critics: please refer to blank screen paragraph.) If an ask-based system were in place of the bid-based system, there would be no need for credit extension. This credit policy is only a band-aid idea at best.

Bids will stabilize and asking prices will back off the bids. More bidders will come into the marketplace. Increased consumer confidence will emerge with dealer time to purchase a coin, inventory the coin, market the coin, wholesale the coin, advertise the coin, retail the coin, etc. The payment for the coin will be received to pay for the coin in an orderly manner instead of the haste-makes-waste cash crunch which has existed for five years. In the future fewer coins will be shipped via Federal Express. Instead, we will be making vault to vault transfers.

Dealers who buy too many coins may go bankrupt. With a business oriented payment policy, these dealers will have the opportunity to stay in the business of buying and selling coins.

We would like to commend the numismatic oriented lending institutions covering bank loan financing and leveraged portfolios. Even when required by this market turmoil to ask for additional margin, they haven't gone overboard in a panic and tried to unload collateralized inventory at liquidation prices. Their dumping would only add to the current demise, and would also be unfair to the thousands of collectors and investors who are holding coin portfolios. They realize that the bid-based systems reflected values are not the true values of these portfolios. They are also very concerned that our marketplace has shown that it is not able to control itself. Looking forward, the movement toward self-regulation, together with the emergence of an ask-based system, will help these lending institutions to maintain this approach. This is similar to the President's remarks made with respect to the savings and loan institution liquidators not to dump real estate in depressed areas for instant cash at the sacrifice of the market.

This market volatility we are experiencing is completely unjustified, unwarranted, unwanted and will completely turn everyone away. This includes the collector, investor, dealer and Wall Street. Volatility must be harnessed and placed under control.

HOW LONG CAN YOU TREAD WATER?

Answers

It's quite easy to criticize but very hard to correct. If the answers were easy, I would simply type a couple of paragraphs and give them to you. But the strategies are complex and require a real effort from each and every one of us. There is one easy answer to the dilemma which is facing each of us today.

WE MUST HAVE INCREASED DEMAND THROUGH CAPITAL INFUSION COUPLED WITH AN INCREASED DEMAND FROM THE COLLECTORS AND INVESTORS.

That is not really a revelation to any of us. But the tough ingredients of the answer must now be explored. There are two general strategies that we may employ to achieve the desired end. We may either:

1. Do nothing and wait for the inevitable bottom and eventual turn-around of the coin market cycle.

or

2. Perform a radical reformation within the industry by putting aside our differences, addressing our problems and becoming the master of our own destiny. Don't be disturbed by the word "radical." This is not Bart Simpson speaking here, but changes in the wind.

The results of the "do nothing" approach (number 1) are generally predictable, but not lasting. It is true that, if we literally do nothing to alleviate the demise of the market, the coin cycle will eventually complete this bear market and move into another bull market phase. History may repeat itself but it comes back differently each time. In the past, an infusion of capital has come from the natural turn of the cycle with the investors and collectors coming in. But three very big negatives lurk before us: (a) the cost in bankrupt dealers, lost customers, personal pressure, and stress will be very high, (b) we will have learned and gained nothing from the experience that will serve us in the future, and (c) the future will be no different than the past when the next bear market comes upon us. Whether the bear is real or artificial is unimportant, especially if it is not recognized by the numismatic price publications. The reporting of fully researched prices is a duty and not just a job. IT IS ESSENTIAL!

On the other hand, the outcome of successfully implementing the strategies associated with approach number 2 will produce a different list. The results include: (a) the ability and organization within this industry required to meet and achieve price stabilization (and any other worthwhile goal), (b) the ability to attract collectors, investors, institutions and other financial entities who will enter the coin industry with confidence, and (c) the ability to stabilize prices in order to minimize the drastic negative effects of a bear market (especially and "artificial" bear trap).

You already know which of these two strategies I am recommending to you now. We cannot sit down and wish for something to happen. WE MUST MAKE SOMETHING HAPPEN! I have always believed in action, but no one can do it alone. We all need to concentrate our talents, thoughts, and desires to do whatever it takes to alter our path. We are obviously on the wrong track at this time.

WE MUST PURSUE A COURSE OF RADICAL REFORMATION RIGHT NOW!

The next step is to organize a committee to represent the industry and address its existing problems. A formal group must be arranged for the following reasons: (a) this group must have decision-making power to carry out the required actions for the good of this industry, (b) this group must contain high-level representatives covering each of the industry functions vital to the achievement of the objective, (c) this group must provide the leadership necessary to turn the current negative market psychology into a positive and driving force, and finally (d) this group must be able to plan efficiently, develop and assimilate ideas, and work diligently at a pace necessary to stabilize the market in the near term. The PNG currently serves the majority of these needs.

For your consideration and review, we will open with the following suggestions for the computerized market making arena.

1. The last transaction price must be posted on the computer trading system and come to a ATP-A (average trading price — annual), ATP-SA (semi-annual), and ATP-Q (quarterly). We need either all or a combination of the above averages. The last transaction price alone is helpful, but coupling that with the current bid, ask and averages will make for a more realistic price analysis. Price information, not market swings, should be the information of top priority. We seem to be getting reports on market interpretation rather than price dissemination.

2. An asking price must be posted 24 hours prior to hitting the bid and must also be within 15-20% of the current high bid. This will stop bids from running to artificial highs and stop cash liquidations against an unsuspecting bidder. The better solution would be no bids. However, the possibilities include:

(a) The bid will be removed. In case of multiple bidders one or more of those bidders may disappear — however, this will simply reinforce that the bid was too high in the first place. This may seem negative for the person who posts an asking price, but it is good for the policing action of the sight-unseen marketplace and the numismatic industry as a whole. The seller will therefore chase the bids down to a valid level until the requirements for a trade are met. Bids and asking prices will be closer together for generics, while the better and rare dates will most likely carry a larger spread (this can be verified by prices realized in auctions and sales).

(b) The high bidder will sit tight and wait for the seller to hit the bid. If the bidder actually wants the coin, this is the action that will prevail in a stabilized market.

(c) Another bidder wanting the coin will raise the bid and become the high bidder. In a rising market, the bidders will not use this opportunity to chase the market to unrealistic highs as long as the sellers are there to check the advance.

(d) The asking price will be hit and bids may rise.

If we move to post an asking price 24 hours prior to hitting a bid (after a start-up period) "ask" should become more commonplace and therefore bids will react to asks and asks will react to bids. This will lead to a more concrete marketplace than the bid "guess" system that we currently operate under. After all is said and done, bids in a one-sided trading system are a guess at best (and usually low — even in rising markets). The unchecked and "unregulated" lowering of bids without transactions is the number one reason for the market collapse. Coupled secondly by the mass influx of generics with diminished demand, together they have destroyed a business we all have grown to love. The real answer is to post asks only.

Call To Arms

Now is the time for all of us to set aside our internal bickering, petty jealousies, self interest, innuendos, uncorrected criticism, etc. We must unify for our own survival.

What the coin business needs today is unbiased leadership looking for a positive and healthy industry as the highest reward. Those who wish to enter and make suggestions that only benefit their companies are not recognizing the gravity of the situation. We must be prepared to sacrifice here to benefit our industry in the long term by addressing the real problems.

This type of a plan may not please everyone, but before the Monday morning quarterbacks kick in, please hear us out and make constructive statements, objective comments and positive suggestions. We know where we have been, and where we are, but we must move together now to insure a brighter future.

Several steps must be taken, and the first of these is the installation of the ask-based system. Action on our part today will in itself begin to alleviate the negative psychology and encourage those on the sidelines to reenter the marketplace. We are at the crossroads. If we do not act now, we will be destined to meltdown after meltdown until it is over. STEP FORWARD AND BE COUNTED. NOW IS THE TIME FOR ACTION!

LET ME HEAR FROM YOU!

OPEN LETTER TO ALL COIN DEALERS FROM THE AMERICAN RARE COIN FUND L.P.

Dear Coin Dealers:

In the past eighteen months there have been many changes in our industry. The Bid-Based systems, which are now prevalent in the rare coin industry, have created a market with inadequate price discovery mechanisms. Bid prices at times tend to be elusive, unstable and unrealistic. As a result, coins are traded from dealer to dealer with insufficient public participation. The coin industry needs to serve investors and collectors by providing them with a way to accurately value their coins. Otherwise, they will be driven out of the industry.

The effects of our Bid-Based systems have been devastating and have raised serious concerns about the state of our industry. The dealer community is undercapitalized for Bid-Based systems. The coin market is a billion dollar market. Due to dealer undercapitalization and reliance on only Bid-Based systems, the market has experienced harmful volatility.

The American Rare Coin Fund L.P. (ARCF) is one of the largest buyers and sellers of rare coins in the country. Since April, 1989, we have spent more than $64 million on rare coin purchases. Every day we must make many complex purchasing decisions. Although ARCF seeks to have an ongoing relationship with as many dealers as possible, it is impossible to speak to every dealer on an individual basis about the coins he has available that day. We believe, however, we have found a way to achieve an equivalent benefit, and also contribute to the stability needed in our industry while attracting investors and collectors who are so vital to the market.

A decade ago, a dealer would show his inventories to another dealer who would select what he wanted to purchase. The seller would quote his ask price. The buyer purchased coins he believed had profit potential, and which were within his financial means. This system worked. The old fashioned Ask-Based system can work again, and even more efficiently, because dealers no longer need to thumb through boxes of coins. Thanks to third-party grading, dealers can buy coins sight unseen from computer generated listings.

Effective October 1, 1990, ARCF began making most of it's purchases on an Ask-Based system, sight unseen, from those dealers who have listed their inventories with a firm ask price on Tangible Information Systems, Inc. (TIS). This allows us to study and make actual purchase decisions with respect to a list of coins organized by individual date, mint mark, grade, and grading service. We cannot do this by studying other listings that carry bid and ask prices on a generic coin basis. Although ARCF will gladly consider deals that are not appropriate to list on TIS, and will continue to be an active participant in the major auctions, TIS will likely be the major source for ARCF purchases. ARCF will, of course, consider purchasing on the basis of any other firm Ask-Based system; and it may from time to time use Bid-Based systems as well when it is deemed appropriate.

We understand that TIS will, on a daily basis, provide ARCF and all subscribers with a listing of all transactions from the previous day. This information will not only list coins purchased by ARCF the day before, but all other subscriber's purchases as well. This information...the last transaction...is the information which we feel is most relevant in determining the price of a coin.

We believe that the current Bid-Based systems will benefit from our move to an Ask-Based system. This will allow dealers to post bids based on actual coin selling prices. As prices are actually realized on TIS, dealers will be able to place competitive bids on ANE and CCE, hoping to buy coins which they will feel more confident about selling on an Ask-Based system like TIS. We will continue our efforts to make our current Bid-Based systems better and to support them.

ARCF is taking the steps outlined in this letter in an attempt to achieve a more stable and realistic market. We hope others of you will do the same. We believe unless these steps are taken, we will be doomed to repeat the coin melt downs which have been recurring in our industry.

We would appreciate hearing your views on this approach and suggestions on how we can make the steps we are taking even more effective. We look forward to an ongoing relationship with each and every one of you.

Sincerely,

Hugh Sconyers for
Sconyers Rare Coins, Inc. Manager

The above editorial was released on October 12, 1990 as an open letter advertisement from
Mr. Hugh Sconyers of Sconyers Rare Coins, Inc.
(Courtesy of CDN)

***

CHAPTER 40

The Future of Sight-Unseen Trading — Phase II

(Originally Released October 15, 1990)

by John W. Highfill, NLG

I wish to thank all those who have provided comments, ideas, and suggestions in response to my last paper on Market Making and Numismatics. This paper expands on those ideas and discusses the future of this industry. It is not only my thoughts, but a consensus of thoughts from many persons that will help to determine our future. These ideas are intended for the salvation of us all, and not just for any splinter groups such as bidders, producers, investors, collectors, institutions, etc.

State of the Markets

The comments I made in my previous paper (phase I) still hold with respect to the current state of the coin market. Coin prices are continuously making new lows. Bids continue to deteriorate and more and more dealers are simply withdrawing from computerized sight-unseen trading. A blank screen is the order of the day on CCE, while ANE has enforced a short moratorium on trading altogether. Morale is still declining and negative thinking is the only bill of fare.

As the coin market suffers a decline in values, the leveraged position of dealer inventories is in jeopardy. The dealer must either reduce inventory or infuse additional cash to hold the position. Dealers who cannot maintain their inventory, or sell their inventory at a profit or break-even level, suffer real losses when forced to liquidate to raise cash. If liquidation is done during an extreme low in market prices, this may literally put the dealer out of business. These circumstances must not be allowed to happen as they threaten the very existence of many small and mid-sized dealers. It's not a joke — a brilliant numismatic mind is a terrible thing to waste. Talent lost forever. Some professional numismatists are going into other business ventures and leaving us permanently. What a terrible blow to the numismatic field.

Salomon Brothers presents the rare coin market as #1 for a 30 year period. What do they say now? Can we go from number one to the cellar in less than ninety days? This could only result from news reporting without adequate interpretation as to values. We've been compared to the Elliott wave, etc. I just don't believe it.

Reviewing other facts, the United States government is wrestling with the budget, and looking for the best political way to present bad news to the people. It is simply a matter of transferring additional wealth from the people to the government. In any case, the discretionary funds available for investing will be affected. One point that must be understood is that an extreme decrease in spending by the government will, in itself, cause or contribute to a recession. This effect would be moderated by any increase in spending by the public sector. The reality is that double-digit inflation is looking down our throats for the next six months and possibly longer. Only a favorable Mid-East solution could turn economic events around.

The stock market continues to hover around the 2400 range while everyone places their bets on the depth and longevity of a recession. I know that they have not begun to place their bets on the side of recovery — that is when the stock market will move to the upside. There is a mountain of available cash in the hands of institutions and money managers. They do have the power to support the stock market, but are not willing to do so at the present time. An interesting fact is that much of this reserve cash is being placed into debt instruments — most of which are losing base value while interest rates are creeping higher. We find this scenario uncomfortably similar to the numismatic marketplace.

The precious and industrial metals markets continue to decline in value at a rapid pace. New 14 year lows are being registered by silver bullion prices on a daily basis. The market is in a free fall — and nobody is pulling the cord to activate the parachute. The price of gold has been a bit more stable, but gold is very vulnerable to selling by the U.S.S.R. and South Africa in order to raise cash to finance their own economies. Even Saudi Arabia is selling gold to obtain British Pounds for transaction purposes. Platinum is reeling from a double blow: the lack of investment demand from the Japanese (who favor platinum as the preferred precious metal), and the current state of automobile sales (or lack thereof).

A flight to cash ties and binds — but there are billions of dollars out there! While real estate is off 20-30%, silver has lost its reputation as a precious metal and is also down 20-30%. Autos are in the dungeon, while luxury spending is going fast and the stock market is off 20%. Why are coins off 50-60% — when everybody wants them? The demand for generics may be off, however, the esoterics are in demand. The influx of certified rare coins into the marketplace continues, but the demand is not there to meet the growing supply. This in itself is not altogether bad, but when coupled with an extreme lack of buying, it has led to a complete collapse of the market.

The domino effect: After 90% of coins have retreated 50% in one month, then fear shifts into high gear and panic ensues. The end result should be tons of coins dumping into the marketplace right now. Instead we have a minimum amount of coins trading with no coins available at current levels — just the opposite. WHY? If you're looking for signals, this is one that indicates we're at a bottom. If you think bids can go down more, perhaps you are correct. The problem is that there won't be a mass dumping of inventory (outside of cash flow liquidations). For example, the recent Long Beach show proved to be a very slow show. Purchases were virtually impossible, and when we came back to work on Monday, bids still went down substantially. Actually, everyone gave up on the bid side of the marketplace. Some bidders will probably never bid again. If they would place asks, the requirement to bid across the board would be greatly diminished.

The move from a bid-based system to an ask-based system is analogous to self-adjusting brakes. In other words whenever bids need adjusting they will automatically do so by the natural balance of supply and demand. To further relate, dumping in an ask-based system will be more orderly and only the coins (categories) concerned would suppress their own portion of the marketplace. As it is with the bid-based system, bidders lower their bids across the board in anticipation or apprehension. Therefore the entire coin industry (index) suffers unjustly because of this unbelievable and ludicrous system as it stands today. The bid based system is comparable to someone with a terminal illness. You know it's going to die, but not when.

If this was a true market correction, coins would be offered at lower and lower prices (some are, but mostly just "stuff"). But note that majority of ask prices have declined only 5-10% (generics aside) in the last six months. Even with the extreme cash crunch suffered by dealers nationwide, we have yet to see mass dumping and free falling asking prices! Let the coins actually for sale determine their own destiny and value. THE LAST THING A BID REFLECTS IS THE TRUE VALUE OF A COIN! A bid is no more than one person's buying price for a coin, not his selling price.

In fact, let's play dominos using silver dollars because it is pertinent to all of us. Let's use the 1881-S Morgan. This coin in MS-65 is beautiful, artistic, historic and a great acquisition for almost any American — collector and investor alike. It has traded for as much as $850 and is now bid as low as $108. Some say that it may go lower. What happened? The government wasn't minting any more and grading is not subjective any more. The coin still has great numismatic value. Why doesn't anybody want it? The PCGS population in MS-65 as of October 1990 population report is 19,278. This amounts to $2,082,024 at today's bid. If you could buy 100 coins at $120 each, and if you purchased 100 coins a week quietly in an undisturbed market, within two months you would accumulate a bag. However, any twitch or capital infusion of any size, and it wouldn't be 30 days before the price would be $200! If you sold your position into this market, you would be very lucky to even get back in! And then you would enter stage 3 — after fear and panic, you have greed. To put it bluntly, I wouldn't short 100 of these coins to anybody right now. I would sell them, but not short them.

Some say we have already crashed and burned and everyone is already lined up for the funeral. But I notice a lot of smart, savvy, and cash available groups including the institutional investors standing on the sidelines during this ceremony. If they step forward, the coffin will be empty.

Let me close this section with a list some of the telltale signals of both market tops and market bottoms. See how many of these you can find in today's scenario.

Signals of a market top include the following:

a. That sounds cheap — I'll buy it (no other reason!)
b. Foreign coins are cheap vs. U.S. coins — I'll buy some with my extra cash.
c. I'll buy it! How much? (pre-bought conclusion — They don't even know the price and are ready to buy)
d. Net buyers become sellers at the wholesale level all of a sudden
e. Volatile escalation of prices in limited time frame (bid run-up)
f. Record auction prices (for other than ultra-rare coins)
g. Certified bids start getting hit on a regular daily basis
h. When end users say, "We have plenty this week but keep buying! We'll need more next week." (slowdown coming)
i. We have no time for meetings or seminars, just making deals
j. When the whole country is trying to get you to short coins

Signals of a market bottom include the following:

a. That sounds expensive
b. I don't need U.S. coins — why should I buy foreign coins?
c. How cheap is it?
d. No interest in coins at any level!
e. No buyers at any price
f. Only extremely rare coins sell occasionally for respectable prices
g. Isolated non-generic bids hit — and stir panic
h. New organizations are formed such as the Retail Coin Dealer's Association, PNG, NSDR, ICTA, SRO (as humorous as this may seem, it is only in times of extreme stress, anger, demise, and chaos that these organizations come out and meet and solve the crises). COUNT THE ORGANIZATIONS AND YOU CAN COUNT THE CRISES. The SRO will probably fade as dealers will be financially unable to support such a venture. It will be re-addressed later in the decade as the "hobby" expands and requires greater scrutiny.

Market Psychology

Positive thinking breeds positive thinking. Negative thinking breeds negative thinking. Nothing profound here — but these concepts are still the largest psychological contributors to numismatic market cycles. Consider the great silver boom of early 1980. During that short period of time, there was talk of phenomenal prices and a never-ending upward spiral making millionaires of us all. What did everyone say in 1982 when the market was in the midst of a large correction? It was only talk of gloom and doom with no end in sight. As of this writing, the industry is suffering a severe downturn and lack of demand sufficient to meet the growing supply of certified coins. Negative thinkers abound and their pronouncements just serve to drive the market down even further.

Extreme thinking and mass action often signal the top or bottom of the market. From my point of view, it seems almost inconceivable that there is practically no confidence in the market now. We've passed the fear stage and are possibly entering the panic stage. In just a short period of time many have stopped trading coins and are sitting on the sidelines with their hands in their pockets. Others have started liquidating coins instead of marketing coins. Still others have removed all bids from the computerized marketplace — unwilling buyers at any price.

As of October 15, 1990, I want to share some facts with you (although I realize that this is an extreme example) to show what fear can do. PCGS graded MS-65 generic Peace dollars were bid at $110, but the ask was listed as "QUOTE." You have an "ask" ashamed of "bid" at this moment. What is wrong with this picture? What more can fear do than to produce a holder of a $100 — $200 coin ashamed to put up an ask? By the way, NGC Peace dollars were bid $157 at the same time. If you wish to thrive on misinterpretation of information, the headlines would read MS-65 quality Peace dollars currently trading on NGC at 50% premium over PCGS MS-65 Peace dollars. This is how misinformation (on purpose or otherwise) can make for a nonsense market — a market that is out of context and completely out of control.

On October 22, 1990, the high bid was $350 for a quantity up to 5 of 1922-S Peace dollars in PCGS-65. The ask was $4,000 on the same date. The last trade recorded was $3,750. Next day, the bid was $600 and two days later the bid was $2,200. The ask remained at $4,000 during this time. What can we say about these numbers? One report might read, "MS-65, 1922-S Peace dollar falls to extreme low of $350, down almost 92%!" Another might say, "Volatility of the Peace dollar series — down 92% and then up 600% within two days. Boom! Market explodes." Notice that the ask of $4,000 did not change during this entire period — zero volatility on the ask side of the equation!

Additional Examples: Refer to the CCE trading history report dated October 5, 1990. On August 31, an 1881-CC MS-67 Morgan dollar traded at $8,000, but the current bid is $3,600 only 30 days later. This is extreme, but these extremes are not unusual. For a more practical example, an 1882-CC PCGS MS-66 Morgan traded for $3,000 on June 20, traded for $1,475 on September 13, with no trades since that time. Again we are faced with someone who doesn't own a coin unilaterally telling someone who does what it is worth. Aren't we just a little backward here? I know I'm confused. How about you? To peace meal information and conversation in a "out of context" manner is considered dis-information and is usually harmful to most parties.

If these examples seem outlandish, go back and read the last 90 days of numismatic journals interpretations of our market. The word "market" is used and definitely abused. Reporting of prices has gone from information to forecasting. They say the best forecasting economists are only 50% correct. If that is true, the numismatic "economists" are at the bottom of the class. REPORT IT, DON'T FORECAST IT!

All this talk and action has contributed to negative psychology and low offers for your inventory — just when you need cash and they don't really need the coins. Incidentally, there has been a flight of high quality coins moving into strong investor hands. Their funds are growing through a combination of capital infusion and the selling of lower quality merchandise to finance their rare coin purchases. Why do you think generics are off as much as 70% in the last six months? Did you really believe the markets were that overpriced?

What does it take to turn the market around? It simply takes money and support. The money comes from the largest industry players who desire inventory for future gain, and possess the amounts of capital required to buy and hold large amounts of certified coins. The support comes from all those in the industry who will climb aboard when they realize that the money (demand) has returned to the marketplace.

I would like to make a comment concerning "contrary-opinion trading." A definition would be taking a position in the market when everyone is thinking in the opposite direction. Some of you have heard me say, "You can't go north when everyone else is going south!" This is essentially true — unless you are the captain of the ship! Think about it.

At some point in time during every bear market cycle, the big money will step in and reverse the trend. They will accomplish this by absorbing everything in sight and bidding for more. To the outsider, this phenomenon will seem to be akin to "contrary-opinion trading," but in fact, it is simply the decision of those "in charge" that they cannot buy the coins for any less. Their pockets are deep and can stand much adversity if their purchases turn out to be premature. Most of the time, their actions generate enough activity and confidence among the industry followers to pick up the entire market and move it to the upside with little ongoing effort other than the steady increasing of their bids.

Certified Coin Exchange: Interesting Figures and Viewpoints

The following figures are estimates only, but are based upon verbal statistics obtained from the management of the Certified Coin Exchange. There have been approximately $70 million in bids posted on daily basis (includes multiples), with the average trading dollar volume at $250,000 per day. this amounts to .0035 of one percent per day — LESS THAN FOUR ONE-THOUSANDTH'S OF ONE PERCENT PER DAY. The daily average trade is $1800. There have been a total of 200 trades in an average day. From May 22 through September 30, there have been a total of 9,705 trades involving 26,233 coins with a dollar volume of $13,080,792.

Trading on CCE since Long Beach (October 1990) has averaged less than $40,000 per day. They call this dumping with huge volumes? One report states, "There is no certainty that any buyers currently exist at these levels." I'm sorry but my interpretation is 180 degrees out of phase. I would have said, "There is no certainty that any sellers currently exist at these levels." Here is a classic philosophical case of the glass half full versus the glass half empty. Aren't you inspired by this "positive" piece of journalistic forecasting? If we haven't already run off all of our customers, a few more of these "jewels" will certainly finish off the rest of them. Sometimes I feel that words of caution said too often create a definite false sense of negative security. Think about it for awhile. Who do we think we are trying to protect?

It is interesting to note that there are dozens of coin companies that do more volume than reported above on a daily basis. If CCE was the only place you could buy coins, then the trading volume would increase 100 times or more. The only way this would be possible is to increase bids on the current bid-based system. A move that is potentially dangerous in itself. The bid based system is like an engine with a vapor lock. It works some of the time but it always breaks down. I'll go one step further and say it never worked. It just fooled everyone.

From May 22 through October 5, the total amount of trades on CCE for MS-65 or better Morgan dollars amounted to a total of only $1,054,479. This was a period of four and one-half months with figures good to within 1-2 percent.

Take a hypothetical company that must be completely dependent upon CCE for the following comments. Notice that if this company bought every coin (Morgan MS-65 or better) during the 100 business days since May 22nd, the volume would equal ten thousand dollars a day. Assuming a profit range of 5-10 percent, this company would be making only $500 to $1000 per day. That company would have to have a minuscule overhead or be going broke!

My figures may be a fraction off, but they are continually in the ball park. If you wish to do your own research, contact the CCE, get the data since May 22 and do some investigating. Draw your own conclusions and share them with us all. The efforts that I have spent in these studies coupled with other findings would be very useful when going to bat. I am very interested in obtaining details for each category and grade specification covering the entire coin index from CCE to date. CCE prints its trades out daily. They also make available all of the past trades by category. Contact them for your own research. (Author's note: Since this initial writing a complete one year report from CCE is listed for silver dollars as an appendix to the CCE chapter by Ron Brandow and Joe Stephens.)

If you take the total quantity of coins available and compare it with the total amount of dollars traded per category, I would not be surprised to learn that 4/1000 of each category traded (i.e., use every coin — because approximately 94% of the entire coin index have never traded at any price since May 22, 1990).

Another interesting fact would emerge if all coins had a potential for trading at the current low. Using the most common coin (the 1881-S) as an example, it would take in excess of $10 million in available funds to support the market if all were traded in one day. As of this writing, the 1881-S Morgan in MS-64 is bid at approximately $40 with a population in excess of 30,000. If you equate the total sales of 1881-S coins sold since May 22 (i.e., documented sales), I'll guess that probably less than 4/1000 of one percent have traded on this system. With these numbers growing through certification, it is impossible for a bid system to support itself. There are simply not enough dealers with enough money and desire to support the market. (Large institutions with commodity minded traders could do it.)

Using 4/1000 as a trading percent, if 25 times as many bids were hit, we still only have one percent of the bids trading! The dealers could not handle that increase in volume with their present funds. This could result in 99% of listed coins going down because dealers would pull their bids to escape the financial exposure. The bottom line would become "Don't bid on a coin unless you really want it." Then there would be virtually no bids! Dealers in support of the bid-based system have certainly witnessed a meltdown during a five month trading cycle with volume consisting of 4/1000 of one percent from the posted bids. What is the future if the major market makers quit and volume increased? The question of the day follows. What comes next after a real meltdown? I definitely don't want to see this scenario.

Food for thought: Using the 4/1000 percent of coins trading daily for the last five months ($250,000 per day), 90 percent of these trades were in generic or common coins. With the entire coin business revolving around the current bid with bids in a free fall, it is no wonder that generics (the only real items being traded) are in an over-reactionary phase. Not a forecast of things to come — but an observation of things done.

Signal as of October 17: MS-63 Saints are bid at $460, ask $560 (a $100 spread) a signal of no buyers, low bids and cautious sellers. Remember, this is one of the if not the most generic coin available on a daily basis and a $100 buy-sell spread is ludicrous!

Problems, Problems, Problems

The entire system doesn't work right now. It is very difficult to sell rare coins today. For example, assume for a moment that you as a dealer pick up the phone and call Dr. ZZZ who is an inactive investor. He has been sleeping on a goodly sum that you believe can be profitably invested in rare coins at this time. You introduce yourself as a professional numismatist with multiple numismatic credentials. You present your product (certified rare coins) and explain the value of independent third-party grading. You have prepared a proposed investment portfolio which suits his budget, and now he is posing some questions. "Why should I buy now when each week the pricing references are reporting lower and lower bids for the coins I already own?" "Why are your asking prices two, three, four or more times as much as the reported bids?" "Why can't I buy the coins I want at or near the bid prices I see each week?"

In response, you carefully close the door as you leave the room. What can you say to these legitimate questions being asked by investors all over the country? Don't you see that the current bid oriented trading system and the publicly reported bid-only information is killing us?

The idea that dealers can occasionally bid on a coin at their leisure, or bid on a coin for a customer, and call that a "market" is absurd! ONE COIN PURCHASE DOES NOT MAKE A MARKET. We have a sight-unseen reporting deficiency: incomplete pricing information is being sold directly to the public. It's a tough business when over 90 percent of the coins that we are not able to buy on an inadequate system are being sought after nationwide by thousands of collectors and investors at 5 percent less than the pricing guides! Why is the public, desiring to buy coins, misled into believing that they can take a pricing guide, find a coin and price, and expect a dealer to get it for them at that price (or at ANY price)? The only consolation is the disclaimer at the bottom of the pricing guide stating, "Client or sight-seen sales may command a substantial premium above dealer to dealer bids." Really! Fooled me. One governmental agency has told an independent third-party grading service that they could not back up their advertisements. That agency would have a field day with this mis-interpretation of public/private information.

I want to commend those retailers and many other members of the industry who are actively trying to market coins! I am holding one dealer's September 1990 offers to sell coins. He is making a supreme effort to market his coins. What a fight! His prices are 2 to 4 times the current bid levels on CCE. "Your mission, if you should choose to accept it, is to market coins at super premiums over PUBLISHED bids." I admire them all for their efforts! This is not a cheap shot by any means, for they are trying to sell coins in an "unbearable" scenario. The crash of 1990 makes the 1982 market seem like kindergarten! At least back then you could buy and sell at levels back of bid. Today you can't buy under bid or sell above bid. A terrible scenario and it is real.

Speaking of selling coins, I went to an ANA coin convention in the summer of 1988 and had close to a $4 million dollar show, Dealers were buying and selling and business was brisk. At the last show I just attended, I had less than 2 percent of that figure. Business was lethargic at best and action was slow to nil. What happened to all of the dealers who used to buy and sell? Is the coin business doomed or are we just getting a bad rap?

On another front, Tangible Information Systems, Inc. (T.I.S.), UNITRADE, U.S. Rare Coin Exchange and other "ask" based systems are entering the marketplace. These systems do offer real coins for available prices, and that might cause the sight-unseen bid system marketplace to disappear — literally become "unseen." These large firms with their own independent ask-based systems are moving forward rapidly, and if we don't act to solidify our own independent ask-based network, we will have no future say in the asking prices of coins. Another point to remember is that their listings are sent directly to the end user as well as to dealers. The Unitrade system, if successfully launched, will provide a tremendous boost to the marketing technique of the rare coin industry and other tangible assets.

Looking at the bid side once more, generic coins are continuing to negatively affect the bids for rare coins even when those coins are not trading at all. This is not right. How can a bid on a coin drop when there is none trading? How can a bid on a coin drop when NOBODY WANTS TO SELL? This is utterly ridiculous! If bids and asks are both dropping with trading taking place in an orderly manner, then we have no quarrel with the market. But the blood bath that we have recently witnessed is not the result of "normal" market actions or conditions.

If the numismatic press would only analyze the bid figures, the answer would quickly surface. The public reporting of unrealistic and unobtainable bid prices in the weekly and monthly numismatic pricing guides serves absolutely no one. The owners and editors must carefully consider the consequences of their actions and determine if this is their conscious choice and their business desire. To undervalue coins artificially is as serious as to overvalue them. Think about this.

Collectors and investors all want to buy coins — at today's prices. Do you realize that they are being discouraged by dealers unwilling to take a 25-50% loss in a 30 day time frame? They feel immobilized and are not taking positive action. I can sympathize with the position of the dealers, but this isn't moving coins out of the marketplace. Dealers — if you can replace the sold inventory at today's prices, then you have not lost anything. It is the turnover in inventory at a businessman's profit that will revive the business and your business as well. GET THE COINS OUT OF THE WHOLESALE ARENA and develop a retail customer base, not a wholesale dumping ground. If a stable price is established for a coin, whether it be $500 or $1,000, it will sell and demand will increase. Another point to remember is that with the calendar year ending, tax planning should be considered. Is it to your advantage to market a portion of your replaceable inventory prior to December 31 of each year?

Those without large inventories today are approaching the market in an intelligent manner. However, they shouldn't try to destroy the customers who have bought their inventories. If they didn't have the customer base, then these wholesalers are hurting their dealer's own customer base. There is no need for a battle when we are truly on the same side and for the same objectives. If all would attempt to really understand the advantages of the ask-based system, then this market could turn around in a hurry! Even I, when trying to be objective in this, find it hard to believe it when I see low-ball bids (i.e., Arkansas types at $200). Is a 1922-S PCGS MS-65 Peace dollar really worth only $350? When I see bids like this going on while the whole community is trying to revamp and restructure because of the demise of the bid-based system, I get very upset (and this is what I call friendly fire). And just enough coins are liquidated at these unreasonable low prices to keep the fire coming. It just gives those few buyers a reason to say they are buying all they want at the new levels. You can buy all you want in any market, but getting what you want is not always possible (i.e., I believe you heard what I said, however, I don't believe what you heard is what I said).

Liquidity on our system as it stands today is impossible without the support and bids of hundreds of dealers — not the handful of participants we have now. The promise of sight-unseen trading liquidity has been met on a limited basis only. At low volumes in the generics, liquidity is a reality. But as volumes escalate, liquidity goes out the window. In the better and rare dates, liquidity at very low volumes is available only with an unbelievable price concession. The number of financially able dealers is much too low, and I don't see a plan that will increase their numbers.

A bid based system in constant degradation with a volatility factor of 10 to 30 percent in one day is completely insane! Bids are UNREGULATED and out of control. There have never been enough bidders and probably never will be enough. How do you bid against a huge unknown supply. The industry cannot afford to ignore this problem any more. Each day, more and more dealers are throwing up their hands and giving up.

It is not necessary or desirable for dealers to quietly sit on the sidelines doing nothing, entering no bids, and not participating — to the detriment of all. Our own lack of supporting bids and lack of bidding has partially contributed to the state of emergency existing today. I'm not sure who will post bids in the future. Those that own the coins, I guess. If this answer is correct, then we need to address the obvious — THE ASK-BASED SYSTEM. If you own the coin, don't post a bid to protect it, simply post an ask and let someone compete with you on that side of the equation. It's actually very simple. Only 10 to 20 percent of the coins will be posted — that's because only 10 to 20 percent of all coins are available today, yesterday and tomorrow. If 100% were available, you would just go to the local "non-rare coin store" and get what you wanted. Then again, it wouldn't be called the rare coin business anymore.

Objectives

I'M A BULL, NOT A BEAR! But reality is here. Procrastination of even one more day or week could result in a total industry meltdown. I believe coins can and will move upwards after a short "period of adjustment," but we have to have all the information in order to play the game. Today's game plan will not work in tomorrow's field of numismatics. We must progress and move on.

In order to reach any objective, it is necessary to establish a sound plan consisting of practical and ordered steps leading to the desired results. This plan must allow for update and change as no industry is static for any length of time. The group or "committee" that I recently proposed would be an ideal organization to lead us toward a revitalized and dynamic industry once more.

The following general objectives must be accomplished without delay in order to save our industry:

1. We must move to stabilize the market place into one of two general categories: an upward trend (obviously preferred), or a flat non-trending market.
2. We must work with the officials of CCE and ANE To change sight-unseen computerized trading to an ask-based system for the betterment of the industry. One trading exchange would be the more ideal situation.
3. We must refine and expand the dealer information and reporting sector of the numismatic marketplace to include: Bid, Ask, Last transaction, and Monthly, Quarterly, Semi-Annual and Annual price averages. Another important ingredient is the percentage volume of trades versus their respective populations. Get all of the information, not just today's liquidating price.

Let's take a closer look at each of these objectives.

Objective 1: Stabilize Market

We must diffuse what I currently consider a compete meltdown of the coin industry, and understand why we are at these crossroads. Some were disturbed at my use of the word "radical" in my last paper. Use any word you like but the need is still the same. How would you describe the market in the last 3 months? Would you describe it as "radical" or "extreme?" It takes a like reaction to neutralize an action. We must take "radical" or "extreme" (or whatever you wish to call it) action to overcome the current market demise and bring us out of this chaos! This action must be extreme today because we have procrastinated for the last 2 to 3 years. The producers have had a free ride for five years — going to the Bahamas while we nursed our bids day in and day out. Those times may be gone forever!

Up and down cycles in the coin market are becoming more rapid and getting bigger. The spread is growing very wide in the sight-unseen marketplace. Setting generics aside, just enough coins are trading to fuel the downward market spiral together with the pulled and/or lowered bids. It seems that regardless of the position within the cycle, one percent of traded coins is enough to create a "chicken little" down market, or develop feverish bids chasing coins up (refer to the June 1989 peak).

Another signal that we are unstable and in trouble is when a rare coin can trade for $100,000 and then trade very soon for either $95,000 or $105,000, depending upon the need or the greed of the owner, whichever comes first. Like a commodity, these isolated instances are just enough to make people think that all coins are tradable at, or very near, the prevailing bids.

Many investors and Wall Street institutions would like to see rare coins trade like any other "normal" investment. This may be asking too much of a market consisting of a truly limited original supply and a real scarcity of rare coins (either by date or condition). Generics would be their only answer.

We must act to move coins out of the wholesale marketplace and into the retail arena. This will require an infusion of money and capital provided by institutions, collectors and investors returning or entering the market. THE STABILIZATION OF THE MARKET WILL BE THE FIRST STEP THAT WILL BEGIN TO ATTRACT THE ATTENTION OF THESE GROUPS. Every building must start with the first brick. This will not occur overnight, but over a period of time as we address and overcome each obstacle standing in our way.

The methods by which this objective can be met are, (1) changing the current psychology (via publications and statements by numismatists) from negative to positive— or at least neutral, (2) changing the sight-unseen trading system from a bid-based system to an ask-based system, and (3) changing the current price reporting methodology from bid-based reporting to ask-based reporting including the last transaction and four price averages as well. The multiple price averages could be presented in monthly publications or by the individual trading exchanges on a monthly basis similar to the current population reports.

Objective 2: Ask-Based System

We have all learned the "hard way" with the bid-based system and were told to shush! Don't say it doesn't work. Well I'm saying it now — and the market is saying it now — and the collectors and investors are saying it now — IT DOESN'T WORK! With an ask-driven market the better date and rare coins will dominate and stabilize the market. If a market should rise from an ask-driven market, it will be real coins driving the market.

Looking back to the beginning of sight-unseen trading, the goal of the American Numismatic Exchange Inc. (ANE) was stated as, "... provide timely, real-market price information of actively traded certified coins that facilitates sight-unseen trading between a willing buyer and a willing seller at a mutually agreeable price." Some of these original goals have actually been met. These include consummation of sight-unseen trades without grading discrepancies, knowledge of the price and terms at the time of the trade, and liquidity within the market (at least for the generics). Since one of the main purposes for the ANE system was to put a WILLING buyer with a WILLING seller, the best deal is when both parties are satisfied. The objective is still there but we took a wrong turn at the fork in the road — we took the bid direction instead of the ask direction.

This reminds me of a true story that happened quite a while ago. It was getting late in the day and I was leaving Tupelo, Mississippi heading for Memphis, Tennessee to celebrate my son's birthday. I was driving along thinking of a million things when all of a sudden, my mind snapped back to the highway. I was watching the sun set in my rear-view mirror, together with the welcome sign to the state of Alabama! I was going the wrong way on the right highway. I had been driving for 1.5 hours to the east. Double indemnity struck then and there. I quickly turned around and made my way west to Memphis — late, but not too late, for my son's birthday. This is one of those times for this industry. We are on the right road, but we are going in the wrong direction. IT IS NOT TOO LATE FOR US TO TURN AROUND AND MOVE QUICKLY IN THE PROPER DIRECTION!

As the recent market decline has unfolded, it is painfully obvious that the bid-based system as originally designed does not do the job. It is time to redefine the reason for the existence of sight-unseen systems. It is time to consider replacing the current bid-based system with an ask-based system. This will stabilize markets and eliminate the unbelievable fluctuations we have been experiencing.

Nobody likes change, even if the change is for the better, and most tend to fight it at first. But I am convinced that the change to an ask-based system is a must for the long term survival of the certified rare coin marketplace. Even if it contains flaws, I'll give you a 100% guarantee that it cannot be any worse than it is right now (I'm currently looking at a blank screen). With a few isolated and low-ball bids, coins are showing 100 to 200 percent bid spreads, coupled with virtually no transactions. We are facing a short-term fix trying to rejuvenate the bid-based system that will last 90 days to 6 months at best before the next crisis. One of the two exchanges is exercising a 2 WEEK TRADING HALT TO STOP THE HEMORRHAGING. I always wondered if coins could be moved to a position worth less than zero — is it through a trading halt?

Don't expect to buy an ultra-rare coin from either the bid or ask on the ask-based system. You will grow old and go broke (or both) waiting to make a living on the RARE coins. This point holds just as well for the bid-based system existing today. You can't look for "home run" trades to the detriment of your bread and butter business.

Critics think that any one should be able to place a bid at any time, however, to bid for coins or search for coins on any system should not reflect the VALUE OF A COIN. The acquisition of a coin through a bid or ask will at that time reflect the last transaction price which can be the transaction price of a coin (and not the entire series for that moment). Markets are made and will be made by the generic coins and their spreads. Non-generic coins will drive a market through an ask-based system with generics following rather than leading. In simple terms, with an ask-based system, the rare coins will stabilize and lead the market. This is as it should be.

A new development in the reporting of prices by major auction houses needs comment. In the past, auction prices were listed for every lot in the auction regardless of whether the coins changed hands (except lots withdrawn prior to the sale). Prices bid below the minimum price set by the consignor were listed, as well as coins repurchased by the consignor. Realizing the possible confusion, several firms have announced a new policy — unsold lots will no longer be listed in the firm's prices realized. These companies include Heritage Numismatic Auctions, Inc., Dallas, Texas, Superior Galleries, Beverly Hills, California, and Mid-American Rare Coin Auctions, Lexington, Kentucky. We applaud the efforts of these leading houses and others expected to quickly follow suit. This action will provide a better picture of market and a more accurate auction report of prices realized.

A BID SHOULD NEVER REFLECT THE VALUE A COIN — IT SHOULD BE A COMBINATION OF THE ASK AND/OR LAST TRANSACTION PRICE. Average price data should be used if the last transaction hit a low-ball bid. ONE COIN DOES NOT A MARKET MAKE. One coin transaction may reflect the value of that coin at the time, but not all coins at that time! (See the 1884-CC story in my previous paper.)

Consider the following:

a. An ASK must be posted before any bids appear (i.e., the coin must be available on the system before any bidding can take place). After all, isn't this a RARE coin market? Requiring an ask to be posted first, the bids will follow automatically. Rather than bidding for unknown material, the bidder will be posting a bid with knowledge of the coins available. In addition, the ask should be free to move either higher or lower. I will repeat, the obvious answer would be to have no bids. If bids are allowed, they should be on a generic bid-ask spread basis only, with a central control exchange.

b. You can't bid without an ask showing, and the bid must be posted within 20% of the asking price. If a bid is not desirable within the 20% rule, then put up a "QUOTE." A function key could be defined to produce the highest "QUOTE" bid price, or the lowest "QUOTE" asking price. Any "QUOTE" should be considered an active attempt to purchase a coin by a respective dealer at the indicated buy price. We don't wish to stop the progress of the smaller dealer with a collector/investor base and a genuine need to bid on individual coins. By denying him the ability to bid on individual coins that are infrequently traded may seem unfair, however to publish these want lists, bulletin board requests, and bids as accurate and true value (guesses) of coins has become the cardinal sin of the business. THE NUMBER ONE SIN IS LOW BIDS CAUSING PRICES TO FALL WITH NO TRADING. The number two sin is reporting sin number one. The combination of these two sins is the biggest problem of the industry and has contributed tremendously to its current demise. Yes, virtually all of the market swings are attributed to these two "sins."

c. No one may hit the bid without posting an ask first. This is really for the betterment of both the buyer and the seller. Who knows — some dealer may have been looking for that coin and is willing to hit the ask where it stands rather than risk losing the trade. On the other hand, the bidders know that their bid may be hit, and they can take the desired action. This rule will also eliminate "lateral" trades. This step would be eliminated if step "a" is used.

d. No ask prices should be posted for coins priced over $50,000. These should be entered as "QUOTE." This will help to prevent one undesirable side effect, price manipulation, and maintain a more orderly market. We must prevent and discourage a seller from using the system to post a unrealistic high ask in order to market a coin to the public, or to anyone for that matter. This requires a two tier system as the higher prices have both a much thinner market and the possibility of violations without proper constraints. **REMEMBER ASKS ARE ASKS AND MOST ARE VARIABLE IN A TANGIBLE FREE MARKET NUMISMATIC MARKETPLACE. IT IS NOT UNUSUAL FOR A COIN TO TRADE AT 10-30% BELOW AN ORIGINAL ASKING PRICE!**

e. If a buyer and seller wish to make a trade "off the exchange," they may do so on their own. This trade should not be considered or reported as a trade made on the exchange. Manipulation of the market will be reduced through non-reporting of off system trades.

f. If no bids were posted, meaning only quotes on the bid side and asking prices on the other, this would be the best solution and would eliminate the need for bids as discussed in "a" through "e" above. By the way, this is the answer to the entire "equation." (Remember over 90% of the available type coins will still have bids in this scenario.)

NO BID SHOULD GO UNCHECKED OR UNREGULATED. This would be an open invitation for any regulating government agency to investigate, halt trading, levy fines, etc. We must self-regulate the market with the ask-based system. This must include all bids regardless of the possible price range of the material. If not, we leave room for low-ball bids on non-generic items, manipulation of the market, and all of the things that we are endeavoring to correct. Enter a "QUOTE" if no market is showing, and realize that a market cannot really exist without a tangible item (ask).

Regarding a trial period, there are some who say we should try the ask-based system for 30 days. Why not try this for 5 years as we did the bid-based system? We have to make a commitment — this is the bottom line. Then possibly after 10 years we can determine which one is best. I realize that 5 years is an exaggeration, but we must give it an honest try, not just a 30 day stand in a marketplace that is currently confused and unorganized.

People need to understand that adoption of the ask-based system can stabilize the market and induce consumer confidence. This, in turn, will cause the market to rise in a natural manner. Would you rather sell 1 coin at $100 or 10 coins at $100? And what if instead of selling 10 at $100, you could sell 10 at $300 (earning the higher margin of profit)?

Another area to consider is the time of payment which would accompany an ask-based system. There will be real product for real prices on an ask-based system. While on a bid-based system we had asked for a 30 day pay period; now with an ask-based system the theory is reversed and 7 day pay would be the proper maximum. The 7 day pay period would prevail for bid as well as ask. It is not right to give the ask side a 2 to 7 payment ratio advantage. This would only serve to maintain a constant unwarranted lid on the bids. Bid is real and must pay in 7 days. The ask should pay in the same time frame. If bid equals demand and ask equals supply, equal payment terms will provide an economic balance. After all, the basis of all economics is supply versus demand. A well organized exchange would make these objectives and serve to "police" the transactions.

Objective 3: Reporting Dealer Information

Since its inception in 1963, *The Coin Dealer Newsletter*, published by CDN Inc., has provided weekly reports on rare coin bid and ask levels. The "greysheet" has covered many markets including gold, dollars, commemoratives, mint and proof sets, type coins and rolls. For many years, information was obtained from teletyped dealer reports. As the Sheldon Grading Scale gained popularity, additional columns of information were added (both grades and prices).

In 1986, with the advent of the certified coin market, the "bluesheet" was born. *The Certified Coin Dealer Newsletter* reports weekly the highest national sight-unseen bids for the most actively traded coins certified by PCGS and NGC. A special monthly supplement provides prices for ANACS and NCI graded coins. Changes in the format of the bluesheet involved the extension of the charts shown and the coverage of additional certified coins and coin types.

Since its inception, the bluesheet has been dedicated to reporting the bids. They didn't have complete electronic breakdown information prior to May 22, 1990. They utilized dealer figures found on the ANE and CCE. They continue to only print the last high bid available before press time. I must state again that a bid is just that: A bid, not necessarily the value of the coin.

A "Ghost" Story: Once there was a coin dealer known as "The Dealer." He was sitting at his convention table on a slow day and dozed off. It seemed as if a man walked up to the table and introduced himself as "Gunther." Gunther told the dealer, "I know about every coin in your case." He also said, "I know the bid on each and every coin and I want to make sure that everything goes right." With these comments, Gunther sat down with his back to The Dealer. The Dealer asked Gunther if he would like to see some coins and Gunther replied, "No. Like I said, I already know about all the coins that you have here." It seemed as if "Tommy Trader" stepped up to the table and Gunther rose to meet him. Gunther asked what he wanted and Tommy replied, "I wish to buy coin #1 over there, coin #4 and coin #12." Gunther replied that he knew exactly what those coins were worth and that Tommy should pay $1,000 for coin #1, $1,500 for coin #4 and $800 for coin #12 — for a total of $3,300. Gunther also told Tommy that the dealer would try to get more for the coins. Tommy said, "Thank you," and went to retrieve his checkbook.

Gunther just seemed to disappear and "The Dealer" was aroused by Tommy, who was knocking on the table. The Dealer asked Tommy if he could be of service and Tommy replied, "Yes. I wish to buy these three coins from you and have prepared a check for $3,300 to cover my purchase." The Dealer looked at coin #1 and said, "I have to have $1,550 for that coin which is just a bit over what I have in it." Tommy countered, "He told me that you would say that." The same kind of conversation took place over coin #4 and coin #12. Finally, Tommy pulled out the current pricing guide and remarked while pointing at each of the coins. "Look! See what these coins are worth. How come you are asking so much? I don't want to hear any more. Goodbye!" With those comments, Tommy rushed off. The Dealer was left without a word. For you see, Gunther was the ghost of the pricing guides coming to haunt him. The numismatic press has posted bids and asks for decades. This wasn't a problem prior to sight-unseen trading. Now it is a major problem. The CDN and the other numismatic pricing guides are not the fault. They are reporting what we the dealers give them as transactions. This will change as more and more electronic price reporting data becomes available.

The following reportable information is available today on the CCE. This includes the last transaction price, average prices for the last monthly period, quarterly period, semi-annual period, and annual period (when a full year of data is available). We need on-line information similar to the population reports on a daily basis via a separate function key, and on a monthly basis for public or commercial use. Publications such as the "bluesheet," *Coin World*, *Numismatic News*, etc., need this information desperately. We need separate indexes for the entire coin business (by series), not just MS-64 1881-S or MS-63 $20 Saints. I believe in the generic index, but without all of the information we will still play the game of not knowing what's sold or available at what price level. We need reliable indexes on type, nickels, dimes, quarters, half-dollars, Morgan and Peace dollars, gold, commemoratives, etc. All of them!

Another observation concerns the reporting of an isolated low-ball trade. This does not make a market or indicate the direction of the market as a whole. But its reporting gives credence to the trade as a "market maker" and serves to fuel the downward spiral of the remainder of the coin market (with no averages available to counteract the report). This, in turn, continues to hammer at the psychology of all who read the report. The message published is loud and clear — NEGATIVE, DOWN, and LOWER! WE MUST REVERSE THIS PSYCHOLOGICAL SPIRAL NOW!

My objective is that correct price information be made available to everyone on a timely basis, and reported accurately by the reporting agencies. I have two recommendations:

a. When (and if) the ask-based sight-unseen trading system is established, publish the Certified Coin Dealer Newsletter (bluesheet) to reflect the latest bid and ask prices, when available, on the CCE. I realize that if both prices are published, that would in effect double the size of the newsletter and increase the cost to produce it. I also realize that if only the bid prices were published according to the rules of the proposed ask-based system, there would be many items listed only as "QUOTE." This would reflect REALITY because there would not be any (or extremely few) trades consummated at unrealistically low bids anyway.

b. Publish a monthly document produced by the exchanges or by CDN with the following contents: Last bid, last transaction price, last ask (if available), monthly average, quarterly average, semi-annual average and annual average prices. With all of these numbers available, each individual could draw his own conclusions. Also, this would present a much more realistic view of the rare coin market as it really exists, with greater opportunity for trading at the reported price levels. *Coin World*, *Numismatic News*, and other numismatic publications could get more detailed information for analysis on a monthly basis. This could be MORE valuable than a Population Report which shows populations consistently growing with no knowledge of their current price status. Price information is more important than populations, and price information can be virtually exact!

An interesting combination of trading volume and population could be presented in a "Population Percentage Index." This index would indicate the percentage of the volume of trade for the reporting period versus the available population. The index could be compiled and reported by one or more of the numismatic newsletters and periodicals on a monthly basis. For example, take the 1897-O, PCGS-63 Morgan dollar in which less than one coin traded on both the exchanges in a year. With a current total population of 43 coins, the percent of trades to annual volume would be 1/100 of one percent to just under 1 percent. We would therefore conclude that, "One coin does not a market make."

As a final concern in this area, a deplorable situation exists with respect to the negative letters sent to the editors of numismatic publications. These are published every week or month without contradiction or rebuttal. I have no desire to restrain freedom of speech, but I do feel that each story has two sides, both of which deserve to be presented. Let a knowledgeable numismatist answer or provide additional insight to such letters. Fear is Public Enemy Number One. If fear and anxiety are removed from the marketplace, confidence and positive thinking that we so desperately need will rise to take their place. We would have no need to "shoot the messengers" if their research and homework was completed prior to printing their reports.

The End Result

This is the time for us to realize and re-evaluate our situation and understand why we are here. I'm putting this in print and therefore will create adversaries, critics and perhaps enemies (composed of self-interest groups). I will need you — even if you don't agree — to at least advise and provide corrective criticism and support. We need all the support we can muster! If we are wrong on the issues or the solutions, time will determine that. Please (yes, I said please) send me constructive criticism rather than "hate" mail. Your opinions count. If I'm totally off base, don't send me a one page rebuttal. Send me your own typed 12 page report. Research and think first before you reply.

I want to commend the numismatic banking community for using restraint in these times of obvious misrepresentation of pricing. Bank liquidation of coin inventories would only compound the situation and send the wrong signal, questioning the governmental role of liquidation in an unregulated market. After all, the U.S. government through savings and loans, is not in the business of making markets, just as the numismatic banking community is not in the business of making or disrupting markets.

Change in anything is never easy, but standing up to our obvious problems is the best thing to do. To liquidate your inventory in a panic driven market can and will probably produce a whip-saw effect that will put dozens (if not hundreds) of both small and large dealers into bankruptcy. You fix the system and you will fix the market! It's not a radical change, it is an obvious change. You keep the sight-unseen certified system and change it from bid driven to an ask driven system. Change it from reverse to obverse. Retreating bids without transactions will be stopped cold.

If all of the "producers" from individuals to institutions were to place their own product upon arrival from the third-party grading services, there would be no dumping into the system. This would serve as a system "pressure valve." Also, the wealth and debt of the industry participants would remain in balance. Such a plan of distribution would place a "just" burden on the producer instead of today's plan which places an unjust burden on the bidders within the system.

Self-regulation can work, but somebody has to take a leadership role. What can we do to stop the demise of the coin business? Ask-based systems are one answer to the need for self-regulation. Only asks can check a bid up or down. We put lid on the bid on the upside. but how about downside? Simple — there cannot be a bid placed unless it is within 20% of the ask. HOWEVER, NO BIDS AND QUOTES ONLY ARE THE REAL ANSWER. You must bid against a tangible object — a coin. If you don't want to do that then don't bid. By using the ask-based system, we will automatically become somewhat self-regulated. After all, ask is equivalent to a real coin, and bids are nothing more than daily want lists for dealers at "their" price. In times of weakness, they tend to place the lowest possible bids for coins. Understandable but sad. I never said we weren't in a bear market. But let's at least see what the correct prices are in "all" markets. Remember that "ask" are not the value of a coin either! Only multiple combinations of price transactions calculated in a accurate proportionate matter may determine the range of a coin's value.

This is the time for us to utilize the concept of self-regulation and put it to work for us. The ask-based system and related reports will begin to work for us immediately upon implementation. This is self-regulation at its best. The ask prices will "regulate" the bids in the marketplace. Bidders will stand up and take notice. All who have been waiting on the sidelines will realize that the period of low-ball bids and unrealistic prices is over and done. They will begin to grow concerned about their ability to acquire the pieces they desire (as well they should). If only .0035% of the index has traded in the last five months, it will be interesting to see some of the first "asks" that appear on the exchanges. In short, THE MARKET WILL BEGIN TO TURN AROUND!

We are currently the "Revolutionary" forces in this world of numismatics. We are not enemies. I and others are just trying to help the industry including all of the dealers, collectors and investors. Give us support and constructive criticism. Together, we can create a system that works for all of us.

LET ME HEAR FROM YOU NOW!

***

CHAPTER 41

In Search of Electronic Trading Excellence — Phase III

(Preliminary Release date: October 29, 1990)

by John W. Highfill, NLG

I appreciate the many supportive responses received after the release of my last article on The *Future of Sight-Unseen Trading — Phase II*. As a composite essay presenting the thinking of many in this industry, the *Phase II* paper, among other issues, presented the case for an ask-based system and called for accurate reporting of prices. The intent of this paper is threefold: (1) to review the current situation and potential problems, (2) to clarify, expand and further explore the validity and necessity of the ask-based system as recommended for electronic sight-unseen trading, and (3) to continue the discussion concerning the misrepresentation of prices being reported to the numismatic community.

The need for positive and fully implemented action is reinforced daily by those unfortunate dealers who have been driven out of this business (perhaps forever) by the recent market volatility and meltdown. These essays have come too late for them and I am truly sorry. We are losing tremendous talent and numismatic knowledge on a daily basis. We must take immediate action to deter other dealers from making the decision to quit. I realize there is some repetition in these articles, however considering their strategic placement, they become necessary. Your understanding is certainly appreciated.

Current Market Conditions

Coin prices seem to be stabilizing at current levels (although bid price reporting practices are still the same). This is the first positive sign that I've seen since September. The syndrome of the "blank screen" that I have witnessed on CCE still persists, but I am beginning to see some activity. This carries a very dangerous side effect. That side effect is the tendency to let matters slide and to put the problems on the back burner. We cannot let that happen for the cost to dealers and others in the numismatic community is much too high to ignore. We will "re-melt." It's just a matter of time. Dealers will ignore this and pass it off as "just another cycle." It's more than that.

There are still far too many dealers who are in a leveraged position and severe cash bind that a stable market by itself will not relieve. Many dealers are still in the position of forced liquidation of inventory in order to raise much needed cash. This translates to "real" losses with no chance to recoup. This whip-saw effect will take out quite a few smaller dealers. The answer for them requires a rising market, proper price reports and interpretations from numismatic publications, and increased buying activity from collectors and investors. In fact, collector buying activity has been up. I will elaborate on this later.

We overshot the bottom by over 50% in certified coins (with low-balling, electronic blank screens and the reporting of these bids). With the market stabilizing recently, some are wondering if we are still in a bear market. Have we reached bottom? Is the bull around the corner, or is this just a rebound — a "bear" market rally? MANY PRICES ARE SO LOW ON THE ELECTRONIC EXCHANGES THAT RAW DEALERS ARE BUYING THE COINS FROM UNSUSPECTING SLAB DEALERS, "CRACKING" OUT THE COINS AND SELLING THEM RAW AND DOUBLING THEIR MONEY.

On the national front, the threat of war still hovers over us as more and more of our forces are being positioned in the Middle East. Do any of you old timers remember World War I? How about World War II and Korea? Most of us remember Vietnam and its victims. Are we now going to commit the same errors in the Middle East? When will we ever learn? War will come and go, but it will only temporarily solve the issues.

The budget issue has basically been resolved, but at a great cost to the taxpayer — and at no loss to the government in terms of power or revenue. The real hidden spending factor for us to contend with is the "insurance policy" that the American taxpayer is paying on for the savings and loan institutions. We are being asked to take all of the risk associated with insuring the banking industry but we get none of the rewards. Not only that, but we must continue to blindly insure the nation's banks to the full extent of our wealth regardless of the consequences! Like it or not, we are all going to go down with this ship someday. Probably our children or their children will pay the necessary price.

Election time is here, but no one seems to be unduly concerned with the current budget or potential war situations. Other domestic issues are more evident in the campaigns that I have been following. Higher income and energy taxes, when put into place, will translate into a modest decrease in funds for investment purposes. Inflation looks higher with the price of energy leading the way. In short, the hard asset investors may begin to emerge from the woodwork in full force once more!

The Dow Jones Industrial Average has not made a significant move in either direction after its 20% fall from the 3000 level. I don't expect to see much action either way unless the Middle East situation deteriorates or improves. More of a decline has been registered by the broader market averages and the smaller companies. There may be some "bargain hunting" but most of the available institutional cash remains on the sidelines. Small stocks will lead the next bull market.

I must note that the percentage loss registered by the DOW is small when compared to the losses of 50-70% sustained by rare coins during the same period of time. Am I the only one who believes this to be way out of proportion? I know of many who would give much for the privilege of owning some of the rarities that I've seen recently. These losses are "artificial" due to the biased and harmful reporting of "bid prices" as representing the "true value" of rare coins. The "gospel according to the pricing guides" needs to be reworked entirely and immediately to honestly reflect the real value of these coins.

Let's take a closer look at percentages. If a coin worth $1,000 goes down to $200, it is down 80%. This can happen (and has happened) with the inadequate bid system we have now. Then suppose the price of the coin rises 80%. Some believe that all is now well. One dealer says to me, "The market is stable. It has gone down 80% and come back 80%." BUT THE VALUE OF THIS COIN IS ONLY $360! The market is still down over 60% from the original price. What? If you think he's confused, what do you think other people are saying? People not intimately familiar with the issues are often LOST IN PERCENTAGES.

Taking a different approach to percentages, consider the following. When a coin trades at a number (low or high), it is just exactly that — one coin trading. If a population (available supply) of that coin is 50, 100, or even 1,000, all we have determined at this point is a price for a coin. A minute percentage of the available supply. Does the market possess the right to price the rest of the coins on the basis of one listed trade? PERHAPS WITH THE GENERICS, BUT CERTAINLY NOT WITH THE SCARCE AND RARE COINS!

Moving to the precious metals, gold bullion prices have been stable during the last couple of weeks. There is a good deal of support evident at the recent lows. Silver prices dropped to below $4.00 per ounce in the latest fall. This is certainly extreme, and accentuates the fact that silver has been downgraded to a role as an industrial metal. The silver/gold ratio has been rising to unbelievable heights, and spread traders are watching the action very closely. If (or rather when) silver bullion regains its status as both a precious and industrial metal, this ratio should move quickly to more reasonable levels. The entry of additional hard asset investors would accelerate this transition to a more traditional relationship. I'm sorry to say, but silver still has some short term downside potential.

The supply of certified rare coins is continuing to grow, which is one negative factor in a market which is showing mixed demand. The collector, who has been purchasing "raw" coins all along, is beginning to perk up and realize that the certified prices are just not right. The material being purchased is generic and available but not at the quoted bid price levels. The rarer items (either condition or date oriented) are not close to available at the published prices. The numismatists are finally going to realize that they have been completely misled by the bid price quote method of reporting coin values. This is when corrective action we must have will gain the additional support of the American collector. WE HAVE USED THE BID FOR SO LONG, IT WILL SEEM ODD TO ASK SOMEONE WHAT HE WANTS FOR A COIN.

The investor on the other hand is still sitting on his hands and doesn't yet realize that the time to buy is at hand. But those investors will rise up, when the optimum time has passed, and jump into the arena once more. This is when they will be exposed to the truth that we already know. THE RARER COINS ARE NOT AVAILABLE, OR ARE NOT AVAILABLE AT (OR EVEN NEAR) THE PUBLISHED PRICES. If this situation has not been corrected by this time, there will be many questions asked by many people.

There is another thing I want to talk about. Many dealers are beginning to pick up the standard and shout "It is time to buy!" But when the collector answers the call, two things are occurring with more frequency: (1) The collector is offered existing inventory at inflated price levels prevailing in the summertime before the collapse in prices occurred, and (2) The collector is being advised to purchase other available coins when the wanted coins are not possessed by the dealer (is this akin to "bait and switch"?). Both of these activities are natural responses by dealers with burdensome high-priced inventories and cash flow problems. Dealers must guard against this potential conflict of interest with respect to their most valuable asset — the collector!

We need to review the status of several market bottom signals presented in Phase II. Several of these statements and observations are occurring (or have already occurred). Many (especially collectors) are beginning to feel that prices are not expensive any more. The question, "How cheap is it?" is being replaced by "Why can't I buy it at this price?" The collector is beginning to show an interest in coins at these levels. The buyers are beginning to realize that there are a minimum number of coins available near these price levels. On the other hand, there are still situations which have not been overcome. These include: (1) only extremely rare coins sell for respectable prices, (2) isolated non-generic bids are hit — and stir panic, and (3) forced liquidations and bankruptcies occur on the part of dealers.

Where are the institutional and investor groups right now? Most are standing on the sidelines watching to see if (1) the bottom of the market is at hand, and (2) any really good material is to be liquidated to generate cash for an unfortunate player. Let's take a look at the current market from the psychological viewpoint.

Current Market Psychology

The complete negative psychology that I have been witnessing has been supplanted in several cases with "bargain basement" headlines. Let me explain. Look at the latest copy of your favorite numismatic publications. Are they telling you to look for bargains now? Are they explaining how ridiculously low prices are? Are their articles (not advertisements) shouting at you to "BUY NOW" without any hesitation? These are early indications that the currently prevailing conditions of fear and panic are about to be replaced by GREED.

Could it be that there are excellent buys in certified coins which should be made today? Are they going to get away from you? Comments like these can contribute to the reorientation of the thinking process. Negative thinking is no longer breeding only negative thinking. In fact, I can make a case for the existence of a two-tiered market. On one hand, the collector has been willing to buy "raw" coins throughout this entire ordeal at a slower but acceptable pace. On the other hand, those dealing mainly in certified coins have experienced extreme volatility in pricing coupled with weak demand for their product.

An analogy can be made using the consumer and the concepts of an economic slowdown and recession. The actions of the collector may be compared with an economic slowdown — purchases of "raw" coins are made at a reduced pace, but on a continuing basis. The actions of the investor compare more readily with an economic recession. The investor is sitting on the sidelines making few purchases — watching the certified bid price erosion and wondering when to begin buying again.

There are still quite a number of negative thinkers (and those who want to take advantage of negative thinkers) in the marketplace. They talk in terms of low-ball bids and in the biased and irresponsible reporting of bid prices as reflecting the true value of rare coins. Their victims are those who listen to the gloom and doom and decide to sell their coins for whatever they will bring. The other victims are those dealers who are forced to liquidate inventory to meet their cash requirements. These actions on the part of the victims only serve to continue the decline.

Some of the biggest misconceptions and generalizations that I have heard recently are: (1) the market was overpriced anyway, (2) I remember when silver dollars could be bought at the bank for $1 each, (3) volatility is something we are going to have to learn to live with, (4) if it weren't for bank-loan financing, we wouldn't be in this trouble, (5) it's all "plastics" fault, (6) get rid of the electronic system and all of our problems will go away, and (7) the markets are all manipulated anyway. If you believe any or all of the above, you don't understand the issues, and you need to talk to someone who does (and one who is not motivated solely by their own interests). There are those of us out there who still believe that we can make a difference.

Imagine that a car dealer had the following vehicles in stock. One Chevrolet (priced at $10,000), one Oldsmobile (priced at $20,000) and one Cadillac (priced at $30,000). Someone offered the dealer $10,000 for the *Caddie* hoping to pick it off. The dealer offered the Chevrolet, but was not interested in letting the Cadillac go (notice that the VALUE OF THE CADILLAC HAS NOT CHANGED). Other bidders offered the dealer $20,000 for the Cadillac — but still no sale (and no value change). Finally, one bidder came in with the $30,000 and bought the premium Cadillac. Doesn't this sound familiar? Many of the low-ball bidders in today's electronic coin market are involved in a similar scenario. The difference is that today's biased price reporting system is telling the world that the rarer coins (that have not traded) are only worth what the low-ball bidder would like to pay for them. This goes beyond the asinine! I can't believe that I have to even address this issue!

Look at the lack of trading experienced by 90% of the market in recent months, and then consider the possible psychology behind the lack of offerings. Maybe the owners are investors with longer term holding periods in mind. These people are not ready to part company with their previous plans. Perhaps the owners are collectors who do not wish to part with their collections at any price. These numismatists have carefully built their collections and simply have no desire to sell. It could be that, at current prices, owners are contrary thinkers and believe that prices are incorrect. These owners are correct, and probably will not dump their portfolios into this marketplace. Some owners will not part with material at a price below their original purchase price. People who possess this mind-set will just hold on until they can at least make a profit (if they have the staying power). Dealers tend to have less staying power than their customers because the must trade daily instead of investing. (See related chapter entitled "The Collector/Investor".)

To summarize, their lack of trading may be summarized as follows. THE PRODUCT WAS NOT FOR SALE AT THE CURRENT BID, OR EVEN AT TEN TIMES THE CURRENT BID. THE PRODUCT WAS NOT EVEN OFFERED IN THE MARKETPLACE. AND IF THIS IS THE CASE, HOW CAN SOMEONE'S BID MAKE IT WORTH LESS? This gives the private owners no say in the value of their portfolios, while dealers are selling their inventory and lowering their bids just to sell their new inventory again, and then to replay the game at the next lower level.

Why is there so little support and respect for the "certified" market at these levels? We must begin to trade coins once more. That is what we are in business for — isn't it? Numerous dealers are cautious because they are not confident that their purchases can be sold at a profit. They feel that they are at the mercy of a bid-based reporting system with no concept of reality. The bid-based market is in complete disarray with no rationale for pricing or stability. For these dealers, the answer is twofold: (1) fully implement the ask-based electronic trading system to develop price confidence, and (2) report actual transactions and asking prices with developed averages (including monthly, quarterly, semi-annual and annual) and type indexes covering specific market segments. Other dealers are simply short of funds or are overstocked with inventory. In many cases, the answer for them is the same: DEVELOP OR REVITALIZE YOUR CUSTOMER BASE AND BRING NEW CAPITAL INTO THE BUSINESS NOW!

Just a few comments concerning market exposure. Remember when we used to go to the convention, buy the coins we wanted at a fair price and sell them for a 5 to 10% profit all day long? Now there is no price consistency. We cannot buy coins at $150 for we do not know what their price will be tomorrow. In our business, we do not have the luxury of hedging inventory. Therefore, dozens of dealers are out the business, either temporarily or permanently. Inventory values can be changed by a whim, and rampant volatility is the order of the day. Financial considerations are uppermost in the minds of us all. Our customers have been shown the door. We cannot go on this way! I may start playing dominoes.

Dominoes

When I was young, I learned one of the basic principles I have lived by my entire life. One of my Jr. High teachers asked me what I had learned one day. I replied, "Nothing." He said, "Yes you did. You just don't know it." Then he asked, "Do you pray every night?" I said, "I try to." He responded, "Every night when you pray, thank God for the things you have learned today and then name them. All this will come back to you."

I know that I'm going to learn something every day. The secret to learning is to identify it. Everyone learns something every day. Take time to determine what it is and then apply it. KNOWING WHAT TO DO AND DOING NOTHING IS EQUAL TO DOING NOTHING AT ALL.

Just like chemistry, science, and other constantly changing fields, our marketplace is ever changing. The evolution which originated in my previous *Phase I* and *Phase II* articles is continuing in the development of *Phase III*. I am sure that as long as there are issues and I continue to write, there can be infinite phases. The later thoughts may even seem to contradict earlier thoughts as the progression unfolds. After all, we do tend to learn from our mistakes. I make mistakes daily, how about you?

One of the main thrusts of these essays is to pass on what we have learned to those who are following. For people who, at this time, think coins are too cheap, coins will rise again to the pinnacle (and fall again to the depths with a bid-based system). Are we destined to relive history with no change? There is a danger in this, not that we haven't learned, but that inexperienced new players enter the marketplace and learn the hard way (what we are already supposed to know).

Is it possible to relate the numismatic blank trading screen I see before me now to the stock market crash of 1987? On "Black Monday" (after a 500 point one-day debacle) the specialists on the floor of the stock exchange turned to the banking community for support in the face of huge losses. The banks refused until the Federal government decided to back up the banks and specialists. Now is the time for the leaders of the numismatic industry to step in and stop the current demise.

Speaking of Wall Street, brokers have been dropping us hints for the last 3 years, but their statements are never exact, carry no liability, and have not resulted in much trading activity. As we fail to meet their expectations (and so far we have), they just stand aside. We are the big losers by their suggestive, but not explicit, instructions. None of us are brokers, but many are traders with experience. We learned through OJT (on the job training) and become "street-wise" in order to survive. Maybe Wall Street is trying to make brokers of us all — and I for one am balking.

There are quite a few of the old "market makers" who have indicated to me that they will never bid again. However, there are new bidders coming in every day who will have to learn the hard way. Some of these bidders unknowingly start as "low-ballers" who are not yet buying anything. Soon they will raise their bids until they are buying. Then they will chase each others bids all the way to the next high. It does not have to be this way. If we will develop responsible numismatic electronic trading standards and reporting policies, things will change. The new players would be able to enter an ask-based environment with an appreciation for rare coins, a more stable marketplace, and the knowledge that they can build a business for the future.

Sometimes examples, parallel thinking, philosophy, and comparisons, are all required before plain common sense can take over and come to a rational decision. Some of these issues are involved. I'm not trying to justify them — I'm just laying them out for you.

We have been trying to bid correctly for the last five years, — and we never found out how. The reason is quite simple. BIDS ARE JUST BIDS — THEY HAVE NO OTHER MEANING. It is what someone is willing to pay at any given time for any given product without regard for its numismatic value. I could put up thousands of bids for the rest of my life and rarely buy a coin (and possibly be the high bidder for 50% of the those coins). If anyone thinks this is the best way to do business, they need to rethink their decision. None of us were traders with schooling, or even knew what we were doing when we started bidding, and we became the casualties of the numismatic wars. All of us (yes — all of us). It just took until now for all the rest of the pack to catch up.

More on this question of bidding. The bidders have tried everything for the past five years. Posting bids across the board, posting selective bids, being the high bidder, being second bidder, being third bidder, or just being on the screen (for identity). Very few asks were posted because they were considered stoppers. Everyone likes a rising market — the DOW retreating to under 2400 from 3000 did not make very many people happy. Therefore, they bid in quantum leaps and continual incremental bidding. They tried and tried to become professional numismatic electronic traders.

If I were the principal of the numismatic electronic trading school, AFTER FIVE YEARS OF COLLEGE, I WOULD GIVE NONE OF THE STUDENTS A DIPLOMA. NO ONE WOULD GET A PASSING GRADE, BECAUSE NOTHING WORKED. We saw the market go to an all time high in June 1989, with less than 1-5% of coins trading on the exchange (relatively accurate figures) and we didn't learn on the rise. Bids fell to an all time low, and some still haven't learned. There was absolutely no difference from the rise of '89 and the crash of '90. There was the same percentage volume of trade in both markets.

The group CHICAGO recorded the song, "Does Anybody Really Know What Time It Is?" My line reads, "Does Anybody Really Know What Bid Is?" I have mentioned before that bids are guesses at best. Numismatic market (esoteric) values are anything above intrinsic melt value. It doesn't take a *ROCKET SCIENTIST* to figure that the bid system doesn't work, never has worked, and never will work. The only possibility of a bid-based area would be within the generic index, using a required percentage point bid-ask range (similar to that devised by ANE in their market maker program in the MS-63 Morgan and Peace dollars). If enough financially sound institutional players were to be developed, and an exchange born with a governing board, this concept would have a chance. Wall Street has been in existence for over a century and they're still trying to get their thing down.

Let me address one of the most common questions, "Why can't I bid for a coin if I want one?" Due to the complexity of the indexes, thinness and rarity factors, and the knowledge of the market required, this is a complex question. For your concept to work, there would have to be 12,000 people like you in order to support the 12,000 coins currently on the CCE index. My next question would be, "What are you going to do if you get hit with 10 coins?" The next question is, "Will you continue to bid on that coin?"

Putting the same question within a larger scale, if you were one of 100 bidders, how would you finance your portion of the marketplace (the 120 coins you would have to carry). With your honesty, ability to price each of your coins correctly, and integrity, you still must be financially sound. Also, how would you respond to the adversity that is sure to come sooner or later (i.e., now)?

There actually have been no more than one dozen major electronic bidders at any one time in the last five years. This will probably not change. We find that it is impossible to find enough good players. If they give up, where will the next group of soldiers be coming from? I say one dozen, because those who are "in the know" have all come to this decision. There are hundreds of subscribers available to bid daily, but only a dozen or so dealers consistently dominate the boards.

Ask-driven or Not Ask-driven — That is the Question

Since the release of *Phase II*, the proposed CCE Board of Governors has agreed to develop the software required to implement an "ask-driven bid/ask system." The essence of the electronic trading rules includes the following:

(1) Where asks exist, bids that are less than 70% of the ask will appear as "QUOTE" except where the high bid is under $1,500.
(2) Where no asks exist, bids are shown as "QUOTE" except where the high bid is under $1,500.
(3) Where the high bid is under $1,500, the bids and asks are shown with no restrictions as to spread.
(4) The last trade and date will be posted on the screen.
(5) Asks will be added to the high-bid list (i.e., to eliminate the high bid only printout).

This is a step in the right direction but, as the detailed analysis that follows will show, does not solve the current problems with respect to the market. We have taken "one small step for man," but no giant step for this industry. A compromising solution, such as the one presented by CCE, is not the answer. Why compromise when there is so much more to be gained by going all the way? This is like sending in the Little League cellar-dwellers to play the world champions.

Let's go to work! IT HAS BEEN CONCLUSIVELY SHOWN THAT A BID-ORIENTED SYSTEM ISN'T WORKING, WON'T WORK AND CANNOT WORK! The evidence has been presented in the *Phase I* and *Phase II* essays. Now we have a proposal for a bid-system *DISGUISED* as an "ask-driven" system. We have not solved a thing. This is a SELLOUT of the ask-based system requirement and a SMOKE SCREEN. This is NOT an ask-based system! THIS IS A BID-DRIVEN SYSTEM CAMOUFLAGED AS AN ASK-DRIVEN SYSTEM.

This concept leads to one of the subjects I wish to address. We are working under the assumption that the ask-based system will provide the best solution to rebuilding the future of numismatics. I currently find it inconceivable that, even prior to electronic trading and reporting, we have used bids as a guideline for numismatic pricing. Now we are getting ready to make the mistake of implementing a system as an ask-based system that does not even qualify. This is not a forecast, this is an observation. I realize that changes take time, but because we are 5 years behind the complete change needs to be made rapidly. NOW! Not next week, next month, or especially next year.

We have bid electronically for 5 years. To turn on a dime and expect an ask-driven system to be perfect is asking too much. It will have to be fine-tuned for a period of time before it really begins to work. But to explore the potentials of an ask-based market by implementing a revised bid-based system (labeled as ask-driven) is not going to get the job done.

Don't argue with me, or with a friend, in favor of the bid-based system. Stop, look, listen and think carefully of the ask-based formula. For example, if there were no electronic systems, how would you sell your coins? You could either sell them at retail, wholesale, or liquidate them for whatever you would receive. You would contact potential buyers and tell them how much you wanted for your material. If interested, they would either buy at your price or present a counter offer, and a deal would finally be consummated at the negotiated price.

The only way for the rest of the coin community to function electronically is to post asking prices offering REAL PRODUCT at desired levels to stimulate transactions. There need be NO BIDS for these coins. Rare coins, after all, should not be subjected to commodity-like transactions. Unless we do this, even the rarest of rare will have the volatility and instability of the most common coins. If you believe that this is the way to do the coin business, then you've got it right now! If you think that right now means 30 to 90 days, then you have made a mistake in the interpretation of this article. Right now means RIGHT NOW!

The negative incentive to post asks on the systems will consistently go away when the bids disappear. After all, no one is embarrassed to post a low ask. If the ask is too low, the coin will be sold. Not many people are embarrassed to post a high ask, but if the price is not competitive, their coins will not be sold. After the implementation of the ask-based system, there should and will be rules committed to keeping asking prices from being manipulated on the high side. If your asking price is too high, then either go lower to compete, or stay put until the other coin is sold and you are the low ask.

There needs to be asks and no bids except on generic coins. Due to the nature of this segment of the business, generics require bids and asks, and can operate in this environment (controlled bid and ask with two way markets only). No one should be able to put a bid or ask between the market maker (market makers would operate within an approximate spread range of 5-15%).

The proposal is to allow bids within 30% of the asking prices to be posted prices. This is much too large! Even if we go one step at a time to get to asking prices only, then 15-20% should be the maximum spread. The reported CDN spreads on the entire coin business prior to electronic trading averaged 8-10% for the past 25 years.

Turning to the $1,500 portion of the proposal. This is just a Band-Aid compromise for small traders. Unfortunately, manipulation is very possible within even these constraints. For example: With asking prices of $5,000 to $15,000, the posted bids can be $1,490 but not over $1,500 and still be viable according to the rules. The possibility exists for a multiplicity of manipulation with low-ball bids just under the $1,500 wire (for coins with no asking prices). Remember that this price range represents 90% of all coins available. NINETY PERCENT OF COINS TRADE IN THIS RANGE AND, THEREFORE, 90% CAN STILL BE MANIPULATED! We have accomplished nothing as of today! We got sold out to the bid-based supporters. This is not an observation, but a fact.

The $1,500 limit for bidding without an asking price being posted is ludicrous. I understand the concerns of some people. Don't use $1,500 as a stepping stone or a quick-fix to the generic index. This is just a stop-gap measure and will not do the real job. We must go to the ask-based system. There are just enough old-timers and people that don't want to implement the ask-based system to cause this $1,500 rule to be implemented. I'll tell you why it doesn't work: Pick your dates they are easy to find. There are hundreds if not thousands of bid and ask spreads of $400-$500. Then there are bids of $300 and asks of $1,500. How about bids of $1,400 and asks of $4,000? These situations will destroy the numismatic marketplace if they are allowed to exist! Our credibility is and will be zero!

The producers who are so worried that their dumping ground will disappear shall quickly understand that the low ask will be the first coin sold (i.e., don't hit the bid, just put up a low ask). This may not produce instant liquidity, but liquidity at a POSSIBLE BETTER PRICE. An additional blessing resides in all of this. When the dumping ground is not there, producers may actually use coin conventions and more traditional methods to meet coin dealers and collectors to conduct their business. Self-sufficient producers will greatly contribute to a more stable marketplace.

By the way, the proposed CCE elected board of governors need to hear from the people. They don't have the power they think they have. The job of providing a stable and viable electronic trading network is a great challenge. They must have your input and support to use their power wisely.

We've had a great number of replies that tell me that we're on the right track but the train is moving much too slowly. Put more coal into the boiler, and let's move on down the line!

Future Price Reporting

We foresee that if immediate steps aren't taken by the current numismatic price reporting agencies, new competition will enter the marketplace. With viable and reliable ask-based pricing information available from networks such as UNITRADE, T.I.S., and USRCE, a new breed of price reporting mechanisms is very likely to emerge. Publications of this nature with the accumulation of the combined asking prices would be superior to anything we currently have. (It can't come too soon.)

Let's review the state of numismatic reporting to the industry and to the numismatic public (and the result of this reporting). Since the entry of the current publishers, the numismatic pricing publications have come under frequent, if not at times constant, fire and criticism. We understand that whenever something is put into print, the publisher is open to criticism.

Rephrasing from *The Future of Sight-Unseen Trading — Phase II*, ". . . Denying the dealer the ability to bid (on the electronic exchanges) for individual coins that are infrequently traded may seem unfair. But publishing these want lists, bulletin board postings, requests, and bids as accurate and true values (guesses) of coins has become the cardinal sin of the business.

THE NUMBER ONE SIN IS LOW BIDS CAUSING PRICES TO FALL WITH NO TRADING. THE NUMBER TWO SIN IS REPORTING SIN NUMBER ONE. The combination of these two sins is the biggest problem of the industry and has contributed tremendously to its current demise."

WHAT WE NEED IS FOR THE PUBLISHERS TO CONCENTRATE ON CORRECTING SIN NUMBER TWO, WHILE THE ELECTRONIC EXCHANGES CONCENTRATE ON CORRECTING SIN NUMBER ONE!

Let me present some comments, ideas, and suggestions for consideration. Publishers are in constant contact with PCGS, NGC and various higher level Wall Street firms and lending institutions. They have informed me and others that the majority of the numismatic community seems to feel that there is a negative perspective projected by numismatic publications on a weekly basis. Everyone is trying to change the world. I object to personal criticism, but I always consider *corrective* criticism.

We already have the FTC telling PCGS what they can and can't say. Don't believe that this can't happen to you. The power of suggestion has already been implanted in the minds of government agencies prior to these writings. Negative influence can and will be considered equally damaging in the decision making and timing of all investors liquidating their portfolios.

Inadequate price information, and inadequate reporting of certified price information is hurting our industry and all of its members. The public comes in wanting to buy at these prices — and cannot do so (for all of the reasons that I have previously covered). The dealers may try to sell the public alternate items that are available and priced within their price range. The public is going to become very disillusioned with reported certified prices in general, and with dealers in particular.

Publications are often negligent in their research. They print a bid, or a last transaction, but they have no concept of price reality (or if they do realize what they are doing, they have another kind of problem).

Let's pause for a quick look at the headline of the November 2, 1990 issue of the Coin Dealer Newsletter, "MARKET RIPE FOR 'PICKING'." What does the word market mean? Where is the recipe for the market being down or up? What total composite numbers have been analyzed about the state of the market to arrive at this conclusion? I'm sorry, but I don't find this amusing, objective or positive, and the timing is tasteless to say the least.

Turning to price reporting: it is very obvious to me that if a coin is bid at $500 and offered at $4,000, at least one (if not both) of these two parties is incorrect in their perception of market value. I don't suggest that either is right — but all of the numismatic publications apparently do — by printing the bid only! Now I will tell you what I think — I believe that this is incorrect. Notice that I still didn't say that the ask was correct, but it may be. Remember that the ask prices have not moved more than 5-10% during the last 90 days or even in the last year. If the holders needed or wanted to sell, the asking prices would have fallen much more dramatically. These publications can correct the entire issue by printing the entire picture, not just part of this story.

For example, the various numismatic pricing guides can (and should) print bid (if available) or quote, last transaction price and the ask. We understand that this would result in an additional publishing expense. I believe that this additional expense is essential to the survival of the indexes as a viable entity. Competition will arise.

Some reporting by publications is full of disclaimers within the text of their "market based" articles. These publications would be much better off by simply writing a full disclaimer and putting it at the bottom of the first page of each issue or newsletter as the FTC would put it: **IN TEN POINT BOLDFACE HELVETICA TYPE.**

Looking at in depth analysis, with almost 6 months of trading data available, we are getting close to being able to present some "true" facts with respect to pricing, volume, and trading history. We have been stuck in a damaging mode for the last 5 years since the advent of electronic trading, It is not that there is or is not a MARKET, but the word has been used by everyone for their own benefit.

Consider printing on a weekly basis only those coins with transactions (this is consistent with the financial reporting of other industries). On a monthly basis, the value guides could present a summary of all coins consisting of a bid, quote, ask and last transaction. Consider asking prices on coins of $500, $600 and $950. If they stay in that order without adjusting to each other, a quasi composite asking price of approximately $683 can be calculated. This is still not a composite price — only an average. However this is a reflective average that can be used as a viable price gauge.

Reporting agencies need to have a standard disclaimer explaining how they derived the bid, ask, last transaction, averages, composite asks, and trends (average transaction prices for monthly, quarterly, semi-annual and annual periods). With this information readily available, it would be a wealth of information which could be published on a monthly basis that every concerned numismatic entity would be vitally interested in. The CDN, *Coin World*, *Numismatic News* and all other journalist price reporting agencies should take heed. CDN would be ideal for my suggested changes because they have been and are the top viable (reliable) price reference vehicle for the past 25 years. Western Union used to be involved in only telegraphs. Read the writing on the wall. Regroup and prosper.

A little food for thought. This information is available currently from the CCE, and either they or others (with permission) could make this information available with a revenue generating income for someone to publish monthly price indexes. This new product has a lot of financial potential — AND I MEAN A LOT OF POTENTIAL.

Getting back to our thoughts, bids do not determine the price of a coin. CCE TRADING VOLUME OF LESS THAN 1% DOES NOT INDICATE A MARKET, OR MAKE A MARKET. It may suggest a direction, but false interpretation can cause positive or negative dominoes that affect everybody's lives. As I have presented earlier, the majority of asking prices prevailing during this bid-driven downward spiral have moved down in response to the bids. However they have only demonstrated a 5-10% volatility. Because of documentation reporting that 94% of all coins are not traded on the exchange, then the 100% bids reported as real numbers should be considered "ghost bids."

As I have said previously, "ONE COIN DOES NOT A MARKET MAKE." This can be restated and developed to read, "ONE COIN TYPE DOES NOT A MARKET MAKE." For example, silver dollars can be up, gold can be down and commemoratives can be flat. This total picture would indicate that the overall market is mixed. To refine this even further, one could find silver dollars in different price ranges in different grades going down at the same time that other coins in other price ranges can be going up. This is the concept of markets within markets which needs to be explored fully by the numismatic publications.

By the way, the word "market" is used and abused more than any other word (for at least as long as I have been in the business). I get so tired of hearing that the market is this, or the market is that, when all they really want to do is INFLUENCE you so they can buy or sell coins. A classic example follows: A coin was purchased at auction for approximately $125,000. Due to multiple factors, a majority of them being traced to negative market reporting (which slows sales, discourages new purchases and backs up everyone's cash flow), someone offered to buy the coin for $75,000 before the auction bill was even paid. This becomes the "chicken and egg" syndrome, After all, it took 100 years for this coin to come to the marketplace in encapsulated form — worth $125,000 at auction. How could it be that the same coin is worth $75,000 in less than 30 days? Is it actually possible that a dealer's cash flow problem can make an ultra-rare coin worth 33% less in one month? There are dominoes that can make this coin worth $50,000 to another cash-hungry seller or even $200,000 to an end consumer. But this kind of volatility is unwarranted. This coin sold a couple of weeks later for $150,000.00. **Congratulations for not submitting to negative market pressures**. Rare coins are just that — rare coins — and should not be exposed to the problems of the business and treated as liquid as a common generic MS-63 Saint. If you want me to write 500 pages, I will show you other coins in detail — situations where ultra-rare coins have been traded with no mercy only to meet auction bills or other short term cash flow problems.

To summarize, we must develop unbiased electronic standards of reporting price information. It is no transaction when only a bid exists for a coin. It is a transaction when one coin trades at a price, but that price is only good for that coin and grade. That transaction will be forgotten (except by the averages) when the next transaction takes place. The collective averages present a much more complete picture of the total market, as opposed to the isolated single trade. The averages can be properly interpreted to indicate trends. We should focus on these rather than on the extreme high and low prices paid for a specific coin.

In Closing

Generic two-way indexes need to be made. The $1,500 bid rule must be done away with and replaced with "QUOTE" on the bid side of the equation (except for the generic indexes). Currently, we have been sold out to the bid-based supporters with the $1,500 dollar bid limit. Abolish this and we can begin to rebuild. There are billions of dollars looking for an alternate investment at this time. Cash is king, but on the other hand, few investments are attractive. GOLD AND COINS ARE ATTRACTIVE NOW!

LET ME HEAR FROM YOU!

***

CHAPTER 42

The Aftermath — Phase IV

(Preliminary Release date: April 8, 1991)

by John W. Highfill, NLG

Highfill's Sight Unseen Coin Law:

You can't win,
You can't lose,
You can't tie,
You can't even quit the game!

Coin Values

We have just begun to find the true value of coins (both up and down). Independent third-party grading services opened a new arena for numismatics and ushered in a new era with opportunities for large limited partnerships. These groups with a large capital base are positioned to take advantage of the sight unseen market possible with certified coins. Bank loan financing is available for larger dealers and others willing to leverage their inventory for an opportunity to make additional profits, although leverage carried to an extreme can be devastating if the market crashes and additional margins must be posted.

The value of a coin is crucial for many reasons, but that value is very elusive and not easily determined. THE VALUE OF A COIN IS NOT A BID! It **IS** what the market will bear. It is **NOT** a sight unseen bid on an electronic exchange. It **IS** a trend of various buy/sell spreads. It is **NOT** an isolated trade of an esoteric coin. It **IS** in the spread of an actively traded coin. It is **NOT** a bid, or an ask, or a last transaction. It **IS** closer to a combination of a bid, ask and last transaction. It is **NOT** what a potential buyer wishes he or she could pick up at "fire sale" prices. It **IS** what the owners of the coins are willing to sell them for in a competitive market.

The sight-unseen concept was an excellent first step. However, the "ask" side of the equation is the next step in the evolution. The bid-based system is not working and the posted bids (as reported and used by financial institutions and others) are putting many dealers out of the business forever. Only a change to an ask-based system will place prices in line with actual inventories for sale and result in realistic price levels for all concerned. Coin warehousing has become a losing proposition just as cash flow is at its lowest level in years. Dealers, collectors and investors have watched the value of their holdings decline before their eyes with very little trading or no trading. The bids simply submarined the entire marketplace. Inactivity reduces profits, and existing overhead provides another nail in the coffin for dealers.

Turning to volatility in the marketplace, a specific situation will present the picture best. For example, a 1922-S Peace dollar with a last transaction price of $4,250 was bid, during the crash of 1990, in a two week period at $350, $600, $800, $1,700, $800, $440, $1,200, $2,200, and then $800. That is down 80%, then up 700%, and back down 65%. Inexcusable and unreal volatility within a short time frame; a problem that an ask-based system would not have created.

Let me create a scenario for you. On April 27, 1991, a 1926-P Peace dollar in MS-65 (a semi-generic coin) showed bids ranging from $216 to $505, and asks ranging from $575 (for 3 coins) to $2,100 (for 1 coin) to "quote" for "x" coins. Now this is a test!

1. What is bid on this coin?
2. What will be the bid on this coin in the morning?
3. What is the ask on this coin?
4. What would you have to pay to get 4 of these coins?
5. What would you have to pay for a fifth coin?
6. Can you buy or locate six or more coins?
7. How many coins are available for sale on this exchange?
8. Is the first coin white, toned, tarnished, PQ, overgraded, undergraded . . . ? Now, how about the others?
9. What will be the reported value of this coin by the numismatic trends?
10. What is the market value of this coin?
11. What is the "Perceived Value" of this coin?

The bigger players in this industry are way ahead of the other dealers. They know the bid based systems are not the way to go, and can never last. That's why the smart dealers have implemented their own ask based systems. Examples include the U.S. Rare Coin Exchange (U.S.R.C.E.), Tangible Information Systems, Inc. (T.I.S.), and Unitrade. All of these systems feature real coins available at real prices. Comparative "shopping" is encouraged, however, read any descriptive material as PQ coins are usually sold at a premium. Better quality coins offered at realistic prices will move quickly, while others will become "stale" listings.

The ask based systems require looking at the market from a different point of view, but the basics are still the same. The collector determines the coins to be acquired and finds acceptable examples within the bounds of available funds. The technician searches for emerging longer term trends and purchases coins producing those trends. The contrarian buys when others are selling, perhaps specific coins or currently unpopular series (hopefully holding quality better date coins for appreciation). The hidden key to achieving a profitable strategy lies in selling holdings at the top of a coin cycle, except in the case of a collector who may find the "profit" in owning the coins themselves.

The opportunity that exists today is one that limited partnerships and other well capitalized entities may take advantage of at their leisure. This won't always be the case. Telecommunications and electronic ask-based systems will provide a more competitive market with current offerings and information readily available to all. But always remember, YOU CAN'T BUY OR INVEST IN WHAT YOU CAN'T GET!

Private transactions are a very important factor, but sometimes go unreported, and are not an ingredient in the determination of current market prices. If these transactions are kept private, there is no way for the numismatic marketplace to utilize this valuable information for price determination. Most private transactions involve coins which are considered scarce to rare, and deals are consummated at prices well above prevailing bid levels. *Coin World* and other publications state that they are willing to utilize documented private transactions when developing their value indexes. There would be many additional entries for the "prices realized" charts if all private transactions were known. (Some of these are listed in the chapter entitled "World's Finest Collections and Prices Realized" by John W. Highfill.)

"Yuppie" coin dealers emerged in the 1980s as the new generation of coin dealers interested primarily in the value of a slabbed coin, rather than the history, story, and numismatic characteristics of the coins they hold. Quality in grade is the thing, but only as it relates to price. The evolution of grading standards and the importance given to various aspects of the grading process have combined to undermine the previous values given to coins. In other words, the emergence of grading services such as PCGS and NGC with perhaps "stricter" grading standards has resulted in yesterday's MS-65 specimens emerging in slabbed form as today's MS-64 or MS-63 coins.

Don't underestimate the influence that PCGS had on this industry beginning on February 3, 1986. The advent of certified third party grading instilled confidence in many who purchased U.S. rare coins for the first time in the later 1980s. Grading was ever-changing prior to that time depending on who was buying, who was selling, and the status of the market (up or down). With the grading issue resolved, the issues of price and quality captured first place in the minds of some, while others began to trade sight-unseen creating a commodity-like comparison. Spreads between bid and ask prices on generic issues began to narrow, creating the potential for a "squeeze" on dealer profits with any decrease in volume. At the time of this writing, volume is down and dealers are feeling the pinch in profits and cash flow. Numismatics issued the invitation but Wall Street forgot to come to the party. What else can I say?

Price is becoming "number one", but the popularity of the series or the coin still ranks high in the minds of collectors and investors alike. With price as the number one variable, market volatility is becoming more important. This does not lead to a stable marketplace, and those who do not own their coins outright may find themselves in a precarious position. There were promises made of Founders, pioneers, heroes and even a Purple Heart. No such things emerged. Only producers, cash flow requirements and market corrections resulting from lower bids with less volume of trading.

Someone said, "That which does not kill you makes you stronger." I wish I had an answer (and a dollar) for all the people who have asked me where the market and the coin business is going from here. But after every crash, from out of nowhere, bidders (bottom scrapers) always seem to show up with their new low "high" bid, and be willing to take up to 100 coins each! They quickly disappear when the bids increase like a flash in the pan. They didn't buy anything at the bottom or on the initial rise either. Before we look further ahead, let's fall back and regroup.

Monitoring the Crash in the Fall of 1990

(September 7)

Following the early waves of selling as the market slide continued in early September 1990, the sight-unseen demand and therefore the bids rested at lower levels. There were quite a number of bidders at the lower levels with "the tail wagging the dog" syndrome beginning to show. In other words there was little to no trading in the more scare and rare issues, but their bids were dropping along with the more active generic issues. The fact still remained that the coins usually could not be purchased at the new lower levels.

The coin market cycle was definitely in a downward spiral with negative psychology prevailing. This translated into a lack of demand and withdrawal from the marketplace by many dealers and investors.

Dealers, experiencing a decline in demand from their customers, were beginning to reduce their inventory as much as possible. There were dealers who had "bailed out" near the top increasing the supply of coins and reducing demand at the same time. Another developing situation revolved around reduced cash flow on the part of dealers. For those dealers with leveraged holdings, an additional problem will occur if lending institutions call for additional margins to cover their positions.

Increasing customer demand during market declines is usually difficult, and revolves around the opportunity to pick up desired coins at more favorable market prices. Unfortunately, most collectors and investors are not "contrarian thinkers" at heart, and the result in the short term is decreasing demand. Moving coins into the hands of consumers will create cash flow, as well as allowing dealers to replenish their inventory at comparable prices. Another point to recognize is that reducing inventory by selling to other dealers only increases the available supply while depressing market prices even further.

(Mid-September)

There was a rally in prices of many coins coupled with greater bidding activity. Both of these are favorable circumstances and everyone was holding their breath (and turning purple) watching to see if the market would hold its rally. Not all issues were up but the market as a whole was in a positive mode and encouraging. Perhaps calm before the next storm.

There was actually more competitive bidding on the electronic exchanges as dealers realized that prices were quite a bit lower when compared with summer levels, and that the risk associated with holding inventory at these levels was lower. In cases where a "spike" bottom occurs, the market makes a definite and marked rebound, and never looks back. This does not feel like that kind of rally, and therefore we must look for either new lows or a test of the bottom before a lasting rally can get going.

Liquidity is still not present in the marketplace, and cash flow problems abound among dealers. This is another question mark in the face of the market's rally. Yet another area of concern revolves around possible military conflict in Iraq. Uncertainty seems to cause many to stand aside watching, and this time is no exception. Margin calls are being issued to dealers with leveraged inventories. This is causing available cash for affected dealers to be taken from the marketplace, and in extreme cases, resulting in liquidation of inventory at unfavorable prices.

(October)

History repeats itself. Yes, history does repeat itself, but manages a disguise which fools many. The speed of today's market causes many to miss the signs on the road which mark the way. New players who have not gained from the experiences of the past also contribute to the masses doomed to repeat yesterday's mistakes.

The relatively short respite was only that. The market has dropped in another downward spiral, again due to the continual drop in sight unseen bids. Cash is even more precious than in September, and many are receiving daily calls for additional money to protect or pay for their holdings. More dealers are throwing in the towel and giving up for good. Mass psychology is terribly negative and there is no white knight riding in with a capital infusion.

Worse still, commitments by dealers to auction houses are coming due, and some are not able to meet their obligations. Market values have eroded to the point where forced liquidation or worse is being experienced by some specialists.

How long can this go on?

(November — December)

It takes more than dealers trading coins to dealers trading coins to dealers to create a healthy market. Producers are slabbing coins, and not finding a ready retail buyer, dumping them to the highest bidder on the sight-unseen market. Thus that bid is removed from the screen and replaced with the next highest (lower) bid. This spiral of self-destruction must stop. Dealers must be responsible for marketing their inventories to retail customers.

The American Numismatic Exchange (ANE) has halted trading operations for the time being. This event transfers focus of electronic trading more directly to the Certified Coin Exchange (CCE). It is unknown at this time whether ANE will again emerge as a trading network.

Transaction data and trading volume from May 22, 1990 through the end of the preceding month is electronically available. Through May 21, 1991, a total of 30,369 trades occurred involving 71,164 coins with a total market value exceeding $33 million. This information is in addition to the daily report already accessible.

The market is stabilizing now. It appears that the worst is behind us. Prevailing price levels are again attracting serious buyers who are stepping in. Also, collectors and investors who have been watching the proceedings are purchasing certified coins in greater numbers. Particular areas within the Morgan series receiving increased demand include Carson City dollars, MS-65 specimens, DMPL Morgans, and key dates in both uncirculated and circulated condition. It should be mentioned that raw coins in popular collector series have not suffered the tremendous fall in prices shown at the certified level. They have been "immune" to the bids posted on the electronic exchange.

The words PRICE CHANGE, CASH CRISIS, and LIQUIDATION best express the market during the past year. Today, a collector can buy an MS-64 at yesterday's MS-63 prices plus a little from a liquidating dealer. Likewise an MS-65 can be bought for a bit more than an MS-64 of a few years back, if the money is available. But unlike the early 1980s, a certified MS-65 is still a certified MS-65 regardless of the market level. Earlier, a weaker market would usually result in stricter grading of raw coins by dealers, and therefore lower bid prices. The bid-based system has taken the place of the "stricter grading" methods of the past. Thus dealers simply lower their bids now in times of market corrections. In other words, if grade remains constant, prices must fluctuate.

On another tier, portfolio owners of the better material are simply holding on. They are not interested in selling at these depressed levels (barring a forced sale). They worked too hard to find their gems, and will not part with them at these prices.

Inventory-heavy dealers have other problems. It will take over one full year for those dealers to downcost and balance their inventories. Virtually all large inventory dealers rarely have extra cash. They always sell coins to raise needed cash. Large inventory dealers that sold their inventories to pay their obligations are unable to repurchase new coins at these (or any) levels. Therefore their market-making capabilities and their influence in the marketplace are greatly diminished for the near term.

Submissions of coins to third-party grading services are down from last year, and the only other change in the wind revolves around computer grading. Will computer grading result in stricter grading and yet another round of coin revaluation? It's too early to tell, but keep your eyes open on this one.

Economically speaking, the appearance of higher inflation (4-5 percent range) coupled with public payment of bills without additional investments could be a dangerous combination. A substantial amount of big money has been parked in hard assets (mostly gold), and will not be available for investment at this time. Ironically, public investment in numismatics itself was done partly to combat inflation, but if today's coin index is that future, there goals have not been met.

The following 1990 market review is reprinted from *The Winning Edge*, Issue 155, January 10, 1991, written and edited by Paul Schuyler and Philip Schuyler.

The Five Biggest Coin Market Events of 1990

To those of us who buy and sell coins for a living, the severe decline in rare coin values that took place from August through November was by far the most significant market event of 1990. It was the steepest drop in the history of the certified coin market. Even truly scarce issues lost over 40% of their value; more common coins fell 60% to 90% from their peak values. As anyone that has been following the market is aware, historically, certified rare coins are now cheaper than cheap.

To buyers who choose to look beyond their current net worth as a function of inventory market value (non-dealers), the numismatic events of 1990 were not at all negative. Rather, they highlighted rare coin market improvements and expansion. Here are, in my opinion, the five most significant coin market events of 1990 listed in chronological order.

1. February 8. Merrill Lynch underwrites $50 million rare coin fund limited pa**rtnership.**

The NFA World Coin Fund L.P. managed by Numismatic Fine Arts, Inc. and Superior Stamp and Coin, Inc. was the second major limited partnership underwritten by a Wall Street firm, lending credence to the idea that Wall Street is taking rare coins seriously as an investment vehicle. Not coincidentally, the two months following the announcement of the Merrill Lynch fund were the two strongest of the 1990 market.

2. May 16. PCGS unveils computer grading.

Inconsistencies inherent in rare coin grading have been a shortcoming of our industry since grading began. On May 16, PCGS started grading Morgan silver dollars with a machine. Being an evolutionary process, it will take years before all coins can be computer-graded, but the ultimate in rare coin grading consistency is now within reach. It's a huge achievement, with far-reaching positive ramifications for the industry. The impreciseness of human grading had always been a hump to get over for mainstream and institutional buyers of rare coins.

3. May 28. The sale of the King of Siam set.

The King of Siam set is the centerpiece of American numismatics. The nine-coin set was one of four produced by the mint for the U.S. State Department in 1834, earmarked as gifts for use in trade negotiations. Of those, only two were delivered, one to King Ph'ra Nang Klao of Siam, the other to the Imaum of Muscat. Since no silver dollars or gold eagles were issued in 1834, the mint struck one of each of the documented last year of issue, 1804, for the sets, creating four of the eight known "original" 1804 dollars. (The other four originals were extras; these seven known restrikes were struck in 1858-9).

On May 28, 1990, the King of Siam set was purchased for $3.19 million from Superior's Father Flanagan's Boys Home Sale by Iraj Sayah and a partner, setting a new record price for a set of U.S. coins. Representatives of the major brokerage firms in attendance were appropriately impressed.

4. October. Improvements in electronic trading rules and technology encourage the posting of ask and last transaction prices in addition to bids.

The rare coin market lacks the efficiency, the volume, the continuity, and the capitalization for standing offers to be the basis of rare coin values. Stock market trading rules didn't work in coins for the same reasons they don't work in real estate. Without market "thickness," without sufficient bidding competition, bids tend to be well under actual trading levels. The amount that a bidder would like to pay for a coin can be less than half of what the coin actually brings in the marketplace. Bids therefore have little meaning unless reported in the context of ask prices and actual trading levels.

Before the rule changes, a lone buyer with a bunch of take-a-shot bids could do more to depress reported market levels (which in turn depress true market levels) than millions of dollars worth of coins coming onto the market. Prominent dealers and officials of the Certified Coin Exchange are now aware that in an inefficient market, a bid price alone can be a misleading indication and a depressant of market value.

5. August — November. The meltdown.

Rare coins lost half of their value in four months. The decline affected virtually every U.S. coin. From their high, MS66FB mercury dimes were down 74% (from $340 to $90), MS66 walkers were off 73% (from $1,450 to $395), MS64 Morgans were down an incredible 90% (from $450 to $45), MS65 Morgans were down 81% (from $850 to $165), MS64 Saints were off 68% (from $2,650 to $850).

Today, prices have begun to increase from the November low. Most rare coins offer surprisingly good value at today's levels. With prices so low and starting to climb again, the second half of 1991 could blossom into a full blown market comeback.

Coin market flips to tail end of price index

By Joyce Harris
USA TODAY

Investors trying to make heads or tails of the coin market are finding that tailspin is more like it.

After hitting a peak two years ago, the numismatic coin market — or collectors' coin market — has fallen sharply:

▶ An index based on prices of 17 types of coins has fallen 38% from 9,402 to 5,860 since May 1990, according to *Numismatic News*, which compiles the index.

▶ The price of a Morgan silver dollar, considered a bellwether coin, has been falling, too. The rare 1896 Morgan minted in New Orleans and in near-mint condition has fallen 49% to $30,000 today from $59,000 in 1990. A more common 1883 Morgan minted in Carson City, Nev., has fallen 64% to $270 from $760 in 1990. And an 1880 San Francisco-minted Morgan sells for about $19 vs. $22 in 1990 — down 14%.

Prices on some coins are as low as they were in 1979, says Ira Friedberg, vice president of the Coin & Currency Institute in Clifton, N.J.

The key reason for the fall is that like the art market, the coin market overheated in the late 1980s. The same 1896 Morgan selling for $59,000 last year had risen from $17,650 in 1985 — a 234% rise. Telemarketing firms began pushing coins as hot investments. Even Wall Street's interest rose. Brokerages Kidder, Peabody & Co. and Merrill Lynch & Co. set up coin limited partnerships.

"People in the trade were enthused about Wall Street money coming in," says Bob Wilhite, senior editor of *Numismatic News* in Iola, Wis. "All these things were coming together about the same time and the market went up. It was a euphoria thing."

In 1989, speculators sensed the peak was was near and rushed for the door causing a glut. Then last year, the Federal Trade Commission charged several coin telemarketers with deceptive practices. Meanwhile, the economy began to sour. Investors tend to avoid speculative investments during recessions.

"Business is very bad in the coin business right now," says Friedberg.

In the past month, however, the market has leveled off as some serious collectors seem to be taking advantage of today's lower prices. "The intelligent collector is re-entering at the prices he understands," says Harvey Stack, partner in Stack's, a New York coin dealer.

Still, today's buyers might not see big profits soon. "I don't expect the market to take off unless some new money comes into the market," says Wilhite of *Numismatic News*.

(Reprint courtesy of USA Today, May 30, 1991)

Personal Reflections

I know that you may find this hard to believe, but I tried to maintain bids and find appropriate levels in a semi-scientific manner for practically 365 days a year, 12-14 hours a day, for almost 5 years. It was to no avail. To say that I lived and breathed price levels and populations of silver dollars would be a gross understatement. The sight-unseen bidding war made every participant into a casualty. This includes many who never placed a bid. As it turned out no one knows what the correct value is and each coin will seek what the market will bear.

Take a moment to consider "prehistoric bid hitting." The selling dealer would call the buying dealer between 10 am and 4 pm and learn why the buying dealer was not going to honor his bid. Then came the electronic age featuring R2D2, C3PO and the F4 button (the automatic "hit the bid" key). No more excuses! Guess which dealers' bids vanished or went south? You're right!

When bids are pulled, and the next lower bids are reported, everyone loses. This includes bidders, buyers, sellers, collectors, and investors. Some may ask why a buyer is affected by this circumstance. How many times have you stepped to a table at a show, asked the price of a coin, and mentally or verbally compared it with a known bid (completely non-reflective of the true value of the coin)? Need I say more?

I found that bidders came and went on sometimes a daily basis. There were all kinds of bidders. There were market makers, market supporters, fair weather bidders, lowballers, and those who bid just on their own inventory. To compete with all of these various types on a daily basis proved to be the number one reason that rare coins became as volatile as common commodities. Prices on some coins would go up and down on the same day making market volatility completely unacceptable for any financial investment.

OKLAHOMA FEDERATED GOLD & NUMISMATICS, INC.

3778 South Elm Place • Broken Arrow, Oklahoma 74011

VOLUME 1 NOVEMBER, 1986

Buying PCGS Coins
Call for Quotes or Confirmation
(918) 451-0665

P.C.G.S. U.S. GOLD

DATE/MM	AU-58	MS-60	MS-61	MS-62	MS-63	MS-64	MS-65	MS-66	MS-67
$1 TYPE I	360	725	775	1175	1750	3300	6700	QUOTE	QUOTE
$1 TYPE II	2200	4400	5200	6400	10350			QUOTE	QUOTE
$1 TYPE III	340	700	750	1050	1700	2900	5175	QUOTE	QUOTE
$2 1/2 LIBERTY	385	825	875	1000	1700	2850	4250	QUOTE	QUOTE
$2 1/2 INDIAN	235	360	400	525	1150	2400	4350	QUOTE	QUOTE
$3 PRINCESS	1650	3000	3200	3850	5750			QUOTE	QUOTE
$5 LIBERTY	230	360	385	525	1125	3150	5700	QUOTE	QUOTE
$5 INDIAN	425	800	875	1125	2500	4200	7450	QUOTE	QUOTE
$10 LIBERTY	300	375	450	725	1875	3800	6400	QUOTE	QUOTE
$10 INDIAN	540	750	800	1050	1825	3750	6400	QUOTE	QUOTE
$20 LIBERTY	490	590	615	775	1450	2950	6300	QUOTE	QUOTE
$20 SAINT	590	690	720	815	1215	2200	3750	QUOTE	QUOTE
$20 SAINT-1908	560	650	710	810	1150	2150	3750	QUOTE	QUOTE

P.C.G.S. WALKING LIBERTY HALVES

1941-P	40	42	60	115	200	375	550	750
1941-D	45	50	70	150	285	485	600	800
1941-S	150	160	225	450	725	1000	1275	1600
1942-P	40	42	60	100	200	375	550	750
1942-D	50	55	70	185	250	475	600	800
1942-S	85	95	105	250	300	550	725	925
1943-P	40	42	60	90	200	375	550	750
1943-D	50	55	70	165	275	550	700	925
1943-S	80	90	105	260	350	640	800	1025
1944-P	40	42	60	90	200	375	550	750
1944-D	45	50	70	160	285	475	625	825
1944-S	50	55	70	160	415	825	1050	1350
1945-P	40	42	60	90	200	375	550	750
1945-D	45	50	70	115	250	440	600	800
1945-S	50	55	70	115	225	525	650	825
1946-P	40	42	60	110	220	425	600	825
1946-D	45	50	60	90	200	390	550	800
1946-S	50	55	70	110	210	500	650	850
1947-P	50	55	60	120	210	450	600	800
1947-D	50	55	70	100	215	450	600	800

FOR A FREE COPY OF OUR NEXT PCGS BUYING LIST . . .

NAME: ______

ADDRESS: ______

CITY/STATE/ZIP: ______

PHONE: ______

P.C.G.S. MORGAN SILVER DOLLARS

DATE/MM	AU-58	MS-60	MS-61	MS-62	MS-63	MS-64	MS-65	MS-66	MS-67
1903-P		40	45	55	80	400		QUOTE	QUOTE
1903-O	150	200	210	225	325	575	950	QUOTE	QUOTE
1903-S	400	1350	1650	1850	2600	4000	7500	QUOTE	QUOTE
1904-P	25	70	75	110	235	700		QUOTE	QUOTE
1904-O	16	25	29	38	70	240		QUOTE	QUOTE
1904-S	300	650	700	900	1650	2200		QUOTE	QUOTE
1921-P		18	20	25	55	225		QUOTE	QUOTE
1921-D		25	30	35	70	300		QUOTE	QUOTE
1921-S		20	25	38	80	450		QUOTE	QUOTE

P.C.G.S. PEACE SILVER DOLLARS

DATE/MM	AU-58	MS-60	MS-61	MS-62	MS-63	MS-64	MS-65	MS-66	MS-67
1921-P		155	175	215	350	1150		QUOTE	QUOTE
1922-P		20	22	25	50	210	600	QUOTE	QUOTE
1922-D		25	30	40	75	350		QUOTE	QUOTE
1922-S		25	30	40	85	425		QUOTE	QUOTE
1923-P		20	22	25	50	210	600	QUOTE	QUOTE
1923-D		25	30	40	100	410		QUOTE	QUOTE
1923-S		25	30	40	110	425		QUOTE	QUOTE
1924-P		25	30	35	55	250	625	QUOTE	QUOTE
1924-S		110	140	175	325	1150		QUOTE	QUOTE
1925-P		25	30	35	55	210	625	QUOTE	QUOTE
1925-S		95	105	150	250	850		QUOTE	QUOTE
1926-P		40	50	70	150	450		QUOTE	QUOTE
1926-D		50	55	75	150	460		QUOTE	QUOTE
1926-S		40	55	70	110	450		QUOTE	QUOTE
1927-P		80	85	110	185	675		QUOTE	QUOTE
1927-D		170	225	275	500	1150		QUOTE	QUOTE
1927-S		120	130	170	265	700		QUOTE	QUOTE
1928-P		180	195	205	340	750		QUOTE	QUOTE
1928-S		90	110	125	280	700		QUOTE	QUOTE
1934-P		70	75	110	180	675		QUOTE	QUOTE
1934-D		75	100	125	265	725		QUOTE	QUOTE
1934-S	325	1100	1150	1300	2200	3500	7000	QUOTE	QUOTE
1935-P		45	50	65	110	415		QUOTE	QUOTE
1935-S		110	150	175	325	800		QUOTE	QUOTE

TERMS: PRICES ARE "INDICATIONS ONLY" AND ARE SUBJECT TO CHANGE. CALL FOR CURRENT QUOTES & CONFIRMATION. ALL ORDERS C.O.C. (IF KNOWN PARTY). TRADING HOURS ARE MONDAY-FRIDAY 10:00 - 4:00 P.M. (CENTRAL TIME). CLOSED HOLIDAYS.

************* SHIPMENTS MUST BE POSTMARKED WITHIN 48 HOURS *************
COINS MUST BE IN P.C.G.S. HOLDERS.

OKLAHOMA FEDERATED GOLD & NUMISMATICS, INC.
3778 S. ELM PLACE • BROKEN ARROW, OKLAHOMA 74011
(918) 451-0665

Prehistoric bid sheet

The ability of bidders to come and go at will slowly but surely created instability in the marketplace. All it took was for a few major dealers to pull their bids and the market would seemingly crash. This crash, when published and read by others, created a false sense of security for the market at that time. This in turn created a negative atmosphere for all of numismatics. The negative domino effect of this scenario even caused raw coins to go down in their "perceived" value.

The electronic trading exchange may be compared to a pawn shop with no return privilege. "I'll buy it back later" is the comment made by many dealers who are dumping material in favor of cash flow. Trouble is, the better material will not be there later. In fact, with the "no return privilege" aspect in mind, those coins are not even available on the very next day, except perhaps at a substantial premium.

There is no way to document the volume of trades of raw coins, but the end result was close to the same. Very few coins traded at the new lower levels and business stalled. And as more and more investors turned away from our business, the more real the prices became. I had discussions with various dealers on their concepts of the market, and I remember saying at the time that if a price stays down there long enough, "it will become the new price level." I also forecast in the BAIR newsletter in early 1988 that generics could go down in value while the more rare coins may go up (both in the same market time frame). This not only held true prior to its actual occurrence, it will hold true in the future as well. The rarer the coin, the less volatility it has. Bid is a deplorable excuse for value for truly rare coins.

Take a break for a milestone. On April 24, 1991, the *Coin Market*, published by *Numismatic News*, celebrated its 15th anniversary. Congratulations! Bob Wilhite reminisced on the fact that Morgans were listed in the beginning as either uncirculated (MS-60) or choice uncirculated (MS-65). The price for an 1881-S back in those days was $7 in MS-60 and $8.75 in MS-65. He also made a classic understatement when he said, "It would be safe to bet that most coins that traded as MS-65 on that April date in 1976 would not make that grade today under the certified standards." How's that for insight!

Generics will be the first indicator in any bull market, for the simple fact is that they are the most available coins. When money enters the marketplace, it is usually not in search of any specific rarity. In other words, money is usually in a hurry and does not have time to wait on specific coins. If money had its preference over time, it would choose specific coins. However, in most (if not all) bull markets, he who hesitates is lost. As in both bear and bull markets, haste makes waste. (You should mark this paragraph and study it later.)

Bids and asks are simply the wants and desires of individuals attempting to buy as low as possible and sell as high as possible. This is the same in all marketplaces. Jeff Isaac put it very well when he said, "In reality bids represent levels at which coins are not trading, essentially representing a price level under market levels. Occasionally these bids rise to or over the changing market levels and transactions take place until the bid falls below the market again."

We have witnessed PCGS MS-64 "generic" Morgan dollar type bid/ask spreads of $40/$41 for 100 coin lots. On the other extreme, this author sold a PCGS MS-65 1893-O in a dealer to dealer wholesale transaction for $158,000 while the sight-unseen bid was a mere $10,000. I had just paid over $125,000 for this coin with no specific customer in mind! I paid over 12 times bid myself! Are we crazy, or do we seem to have a feel for the higher grade rarer date issue of Morgan and Peace dollars? (See related chapter on World's Finest Collections and Prices Realized by John W. Highfill.)

TALK ABOUT "THIN" MARKETS! Try to make broad based markets in early date buffalo nickels, Winged Cap dimes or especially foreign coins. I liked what Bob Wilhite had to say; "There is a difference in bidding for generic coins and rare coins. Generic coins are readily available and trade on a supply and demand basis. Rare coins are exactly that: RARE." Great quote, Bob!

Here's another interesting truth for you. Every time I get hit with a decent coin on the electronic exchange, guess what happens? Many of those would-be (but not really) bidders call me up and say they want to buy the coin from me. I know they saw the report showing I was hit with the coin, and I ask them why they didn't bid on the coin if they wanted it. All of the excuses in the world are what I hear in reply. As Leon Russell once sang, "It's a strange world that we're living in." Eighty to ninety percent of the member dealers don't bid anymore. The dealer base is entirely too thin for the sight-unseen marketplace to reflect true coin values in the case of non-generic coins.

Before PCGS, I used to make markets at over 50 coin conventions a year. Every weekend, I would buy and sell coins. The one thing that always bugged me then was for someone to "base" me. That is the term I used when someone would get my buy price and use it as a base level from which to try and sell to others. I never minded bidding or giving out my buy price to others. It's just when they took my "bids" (buys) and tried to sell to everyone in the convention for a little bit more, and when unsuccessful came back to me and tried to sell it to me at my original offer.

I would repeatedly ask them what they were buying the same coins at. Their reply would always be the same. "I'll get back to you later on that." The same scenario has happened to the market makers on the electronic exchanges from day one. You currently have almost 300 CCE members, but only one or two dozen dealers produce 75%-85% of the bids. They used us for years to "BASE" from. We always showed our hole card. We placed the bid and took the exposure of market shifts, while the other dealers simply bought and sold around our "bids" at their leisure. Oh well, all good things must come to an end. With the inevitable demise of the bid-based system, he who knows the most will win! From here on, no one can sell you out for the extra buck and they will have to go to their own school, not yours, for their bids. There will be no more follow the leader, especially when no one knows who the leaders are.

The strength of the numismatic marketplace is NOT measured by the high bid, or by a single bid. The underpinnings of the market lie within the depth of the market. For example, when the high bid is hit or removed, what underlying bids are present to maintain the market? Depth of this nature requires large capitalization and bigger players. If these bidders stand aside, the market will fall due to lack of stabilization, lower volume, and psychological factors. The 12,000 bids which constitute the electronic marketplace do not have 12,000 market makers with the capital necessary to support the market.

Back in the 1960s, many bags and rolls changed hands with large volume the order of the day. During the 1970s, collectors began recognizing, and much numismatic research followed. Bids remained approximately the same with coins selling at 10-30% back of bid in slower times with less volume. Quality coins increasingly entered the marketplace with the advent of third-party certified grading services. Today, if bids aren't increasing at a progressive pace and begin to stall, they start to fall automatically with or without trading. Bids can fall 20-50% as a mass result of the fear factor alone. Just because bids are stalling is not the reason for coin index values to fall. It is natural that the coin market should have periods of slower trading and lower activity, like any other market. But undercapitalization of the bid-based dealer system causes extenuating circumstances with extreme volatility and undue price fluctuations with no trading in the majority of issues.

One of the differences between the coin markets of 1981 and 1991 is the way dealers handled their bids and their business. In 1981 bids drifted lower over a period of time as opposed to a one day and/or week "perceived" crash. Back then, a dealer could buy merchandise at 25% to 30% back of bid and sell it from 20% to 30% back and still make a profit. But using the sight-unseen system today a dealer can't buy coins for more than 1-2% back of bid and can't sell them for more than 1-2% above. The problem is compounded during periods of extreme volatility when a dealer may be holding inventory that has not yet been resold. The risk of holding merchandise when dealing with a small profit margin is often much greater than the profit to be gained from the transactions.

Looking ahead, the continuing evolution of electronic trading continues to create a more competitive marketplace coupled with an immediate inventory of available coins. This fact, coupled with high travel expenses, has caused more and more dealers to frequent fewer and fewer coin shows and conventions. In the future only the large competitive conventions will survive. Also, the spreads available to dealers in lower priced merchandise have narrowed, with volume trading providing only a meager living. The net result of all these factors will be the disappearance from the market of many coin dealers who can't compete. A whole generation of dealers with numismatics as their reason and mode of living is in jeopardy. Think about it.

The Ask-Based System Environment

The first attempt at a sight-unseen ask-driven trading environment was only that — a first attempt. The first level demanding ask-driven trading was coins valued at over $1,500 by masking the bids at this level. The second criterion for masking bids was for coins where the highest bid was less than 70 percent of an existing ask. That level was soon raised to $3,000 which, for practical purposes, returned the electronic exchange to the bid-based system. After they moved to unmask all bids up to $5,000, the cat was out of the bag. We were 100% back to the old bid system.

These first rules provided for asks for coins of higher value that did not constitute more than 10 percent of all trading on the electronic exchange. The dealers were thus able to sidestep this attempt and continue to operate in the bid-based manner of the past five years. The result was not a solution and did not even placate those who were looking for a change.

With a broader ask-based electronic trading system on the horizon, it would be well to look at that environment in more detail. These considerations are presented with that goal in mind.

An "ask" is the value one places in an attempt to produce a transaction. A seller that sells at or below a posted ask in negotiation with a buyer constitutes a most reliable pricing transaction index. Inherent within the ask-based system is the obligation to accept a "hit" ask and deliver the sold coin. Under normal circumstances this is expected and acceptable, but becomes a problem when the buyer is deemed to be a financial risk. In that case a guarantee of payment would provide the incentive to deliver the coin as promised. This would best be accomplished through the exchange itself with a mechanism to insure payment and fund provided by the participating dealers. The Certified Coin Exchange has recently announced the formation of a Clearing Corporation to provide secured clearing of trades posted on the ask side exceeding $3,000. Such an organization could instill confidence and provide security for the asking dealer. For a fee, the Clearing Corporation will receive the coin and the funds in collected form, and forward each to the other dealer when both are received. Business, at least on the electronic sight-unseen exchange, could be successfully conducted on an ask basis at all price levels.

The CCDN Asksheet and other publications reporting last trade or ask prices appearing on the sight-unseen electronic market would be closer to presenting real coins at real prices. There would no longer be imaginary (wishful) bid prices reported as the value of coins in the dealer to dealer wholesale marketplace. Financial institutions with outstanding loans would be better able to assess their exposure to the market, and become more responsible in their approach to dealers with leveraged inventory positions.

Transaction prices are a good indication of value if they are taken as a group or series, and not on an isolated or individual basis. Rare coins are traded at conventions, auctions, on all ask based systems, and from other from dealer to dealer transactions. Value might better be determined if all of these factors were brought together in a larger database for the numismatic community to view.

The current bid-ask system that exists for generic issues is working well and could easily remain in place. The volume of trading together with the narrow spread existing for these coins provides a ready market. Electronic trading in generic coins has not been a problem in the past, and is not seen as a problem for the future. However, an exchange must be set up somewhat similar to the Chicago Board of Trade to handle the transactions.

The liquidity aspect of the market would change. Instant liquidity (albeit at "fire sale" prices) would be exchanged for a short period of time while a lower posted ask attracted a buyer for the interested seller. That's how it appears on paper. In reality, the scarce to rarer issues involved would not usually be traded at bid prices to begin with, the exception being a very occasional fire sale. In fact, it could be that a buyer would be uncovered and a sale consummated more rapidly if a real coin were exposed for sale at a lower ask. For those who consider limited liquidity a problem, WE MUST COMPROMISE LIQUIDITY FOR MARKET VALUE STABILIZATION AND RETENTION OF THE STORAGE OF VALUE (HARD ASSETS).

The matter of competition would require some exploration on the part of dealers and market makers. In order to compete in an ask-based environment, a lower ask would be required. Asks may drive asks down through competitive selling of a real tangible product. If no desire existed to move the coin, the dealer(s) would simply sit tight and wait for the lower ask to be "hit" exposing their ask as next in line. When the market is in an uptrend, dealers would be likely to raise their asking prices accordingly, although "high-balling" and lack of value knowledge for low population issues can confuse buyers. If they got ahead of the market, the asks would be adjusted independently by dealers to generate sales as required. Very limited (if any) manipulatory situations would be present due to the existence of other ask-based systems including Unitrade, U.S.R.C.E., and T.I.S. Asks, unlike bids, reflect real product available in the marketplace for sale at a price. A question for you to ponder: "Why do these ask-based systems not allow bids?" We've been saying "What's bid?" for years, but this will change. In fact, this group of ask-based exchanges could lead to the preparation and publication of an "average coin values" index. Who will be the first to take advantage of this opportunity? After all, we have always asked what someone wants for his coins at conventions for the past thirty years or so. Why change now?

The ask-based electronic trading system should not be expected to take the place of good old fashioned retail marketing and sales. If that were to be the case, the exchange would have to expand their membership and membership requirements; something that they are not prepared for at the present time.

There was a meeting held during April of 1991 at New Orleans between the Certified Coin Exchange, Certified Coin Dealer Newsletter, and a large number of major member dealers. The purpose of the meeting was to explore the computerized bid/ask system and make decisions concerning its future. After that meeting, many numismatic articles were printed stating that the results called for the elimination of the bid driven system for rare and esoteric coins in favor of an ask-based system. The bid system would not be abolished entirely under this plan, and would remain in place for the generic issues and type coins. As of this writing, these changes have not been implemented, but they are of great interest to the numismatic community. We will report on this ongoing saga in future supplements. If these agreements turn political in nature and stone-walling persists, the dealers will probably create their own ask based system. They will simply remove all of their bids and post ask only. This would be considered a voluntary move, not a boycott. A boycott would be to quit the entire system, and this still remains a possibility. **AS LONG AS THERE IS A BID-BASED SYSTEM THAT IS RECOGNIZED IN THE NUMISMATIC COMMUNITY, ALL RARE COINS WILL BE VOLATILE AND TREATED AS A COMMODITY AND THEIR VALUES UNCERTAIN.**

Appendix

Network Trading Rules Revised

by Paul and Philip Schuyler

The following is reprinted in its entirety with permission from *The Winning Edge*, Ellesmere Numismatics, Issue 161, May 1, 1991, edited by Paul and Philip Schuyler.

Certified Coin Exchange to eliminate bidding on scarce issues

Hello, all. Hope things are well on your end.

Lots to cover this month — so much that the article is a page longer than usual. In early June, the Certified Coin Exchange, the major trading network for PCGS and NGC coins, will ban bidding on all non-generic issues. What follows is a discussion of the reasons for the decision and possible ramifications of the change.

A Rare Coin Exchange

Rewind to 1985. Coins were strong, but buyers were getting fed up with grading discrepancies. They were tired of watching their coins appreciate on paper only to find that their MS65 purchases could not be sold at any grade level above MS64. Floating grading standards made it virtually impossible for a non-professional buyer to profit.

In February 1986, PCGS began to certify coins. Unlike its predecessors, PCGS reinforced the validity of its grading assessments with a money back guarantee. The guarantee generated a new level of confidence in certified coins — such confidence that dealers started to accept PCGS graded coins at the PCGS grade level sight unseen.

There was debate over the sight-unseen concept. On one hand, coins had always drawn a portion of their market value from their appearance. Trading them sight unseen, as commodities, blurred their individuality and reduced premium value derived from the aesthetic appeal of any one piece. On the other hand, it was important that our industry oil the wheel that squeaked loudest first: grading discrepancies. In this regard sight-unseen trading was a resounding success. Gradeflation abruptly ended. Coins bought as MS65 could always be sold as MS65. Collectors and investors could sell their coins for an immediate sight unseen offer over the telephone. No coins would be rejected.

Next would come a sight unseen trading network. It would be the New York Stock Exchange for certified rare coins. Hundreds of dealers buying for inventory and trying to fill customer orders would participate. The best coins would draw the strongest bids and the most bidders. Unpopular or infrequently traded coins would draw weaker offers. The free market — buyers and sellers — would determine rare coin trading levels. Sellers of certified coins could post ask prices, or if they chose, they could sell to the high bidder.

The American Numismatic Exchange (ANE), and later the Certified Coin Exchange (CCE), would function not only as a trading forum for dealers, but also as a comprehensive provider of market levels for the industry. Rare coin values would be determined by standing offers. Every regularly traded certified coin would have a bid price and therefore a floor value.

The liquidity created by competitive bidding would benefit every segment of the market. Instant liquidity would entice new collectors and investors and even Wall Street. It would stimulate demand like never before. The scenario was mouth-watering. Small and finite supply of investment quality rare coins; escalating mainstream demand. How could coins go anywhere but up?

In Practice

Fast forward five years to the present. Generic coins have lost 70% to 85% of their 1989 peak value. Even truly scarce issues are down 40% to 70%. Virtually nothing is up from 1989. Trading has slowed to a crawl. Rare coin firms that formerly employed fifteen people now employ five. Dealers are heavily in debt; so is the industry. It's a time of bankruptcies, mergers, consolidation, and austerity budgets.

Ask ten dealers and you'll get ten different reasons why coins are at giveaway prices today. Most acknowledge that the competitive bid structure, the attempt to provide a standing offer for all regularly traded certified coins, has been a factor in the erosion of market values. The question is, how big a factor? There are two camps: those who feel that a bid network has done more harm than good and should be scrapped, and those who acknowledge its flaws but feel it should be retained.

Biggest problem: Bidding doesn't fill in sufficiently to accurately reflect rare coin values as determined by other yardsticks of value because rare coin demand is not and never has been order-based. Orders activate less than 10% of all rare coin sales. Most sales are made by dealers marketing their existing inventory. A coin dealer has only two legitimate reasons to bid for coins — to fill an order, or to "rip" underpriced coins for inventory. Without standing orders, dealers have no incentive to bid competitively. They bid primarily to rip coins, which means that their bids are well below existing market levels. But since their bids are the only *printed* market levels, their bids tend to become the new market. Dealers want to pay under market, so when the market retreats to their bid levels, they lower their bids, again lowering the market. And the cycle repeats itself.

Because rare coin demand is not order-based, most bids are the product of dealer speculation. And unlike bids to fill orders, speculative bids are optional. More than one hundred major dealers choose not to bid at all. Of the few dozen who do bid, many will either lower or delete all of their bids during a show, or while on vacation, or when their cash flow is poor, or when they feel that the market is weakening, or for any reason. Market values for an industry with more than 100,000 participants are based on the actions of a few dozen dealers with no incentive to pay market value for coins.

Even when a dealer does have orders to fill, he has little incentive to bid on the Certified Coin Exchange. If he enters a bid higher than the existing bid, his bid rarely results in a purchase. It simply creates a new higher market level. The last thing the dealer wants to do is raise the market value of a coin he is trying to buy. Better to not bid and try to buy the coin over the telephone or at a show at a price relative to the existing high bid.

Over the past five years, at least fifty major dealers, including Ellesmere, have maintained bids, then discontinued it. They found it to be a waste of time and an unnecessary liability (bids do produce purchases when prices are falling). A Catch 22 determines coin prices. Our industry bases market values on a competitive bidding structure that discourages competitive bidding.

The degenerative nature of the bid structure tends to feed on itself. Wholesalers find that it's not worth the search to get an extra percent or two over the high CCE bid for their coin — it's easier to sell to the bidder and take the weak price. It costs retailers at least 15% extra to move coins, which means that they need at least 20% extra to earn a 5% net profit for their efforts. Many have found it easier to discontinue retail, save the expenses, and sell their coins cheap to the high CCE bidders.

Think of the overall effect. Both wholesalers and retailers are selling coins *into* the market. Few sellers still market coins to end buyers and fewer try to entice mainstream investors anymore. The costs are too high. So coins travel from one bidder to the next, staying on the market, sopping up capital. The competitive bid structure that was to provide liquidity and create demand instead draws coins into itself. It stifles rather than stimulates the flow of coins to end buyers, and perpetuates a market glut.

Bid System Economics

Our industry tried to create liquidity where liquidity did not exist as a natural extension of demand. Can't be done. When there is demand, there is liquidity. Without demand, there isn't. Liquidity cannot be installed by middlemen or sellers; only buyers can make an investment liquid. Trying to provide liquidity for coins irrespective of real demand is like trying to provide job security for employees when there isn't any work. In either case, where do the necessary funds come from?

Our industry tried to create liquidity in an attempt to increase demand. That's inverted logic. Liquidity doesn't create demand. Demand creates liquidity.

Because the liquidity provided by the Certified Coin Exchange is rooted in dealer speculation and not in collector and investor demand, it is superficial, one-directional, and extremely costly to maintain. True liquidity comes free with true demand. CCE liquidity is merely cash borrowed from dealers against future sales. As more dealer capital is tied up in this manner, less is available to provide bids and therefore market value. Ultimately, the cost of maintaining standing offers is incurred by all of us in the form of reduced equity in our holdings. The price in market value of attempting to provide standing offers for all rare coins at all times is impossible to calculate, but it appears enormous.

Dealers who feel that CCE bidding is the correct basis of market values make the point that if demand is weak, then coin prices *should* be this cheap. The system isn't doing anything to lower market values beyond their true levels. If coins were truly underpriced, bidders would jump in and levels would increase. Adam Smith was right. The free market works. Dealers are a bunch of moaners that want to tamper with the system because they don't like the true levels.

Adam Smith was right. But Smith's understanding of market mechanics was deeper than that of his modern adherents, who tend to believe that markets work automatically if just left alone. Smith alluded to "market failures," cases in which *imperfect competition* destroys the natural self-regulatory ability of the free market to maintain order and appropriate prices. "Imperfect competition" is a technical economic term that refers to a market in which one firm or consumer can have a considerable effect on market price. A monopoly is one example of imperfect competition. A collusive oligopoly like OPEC is another.

A third type of market failure is caused by a form of imperfect competition called *monopolistic competition*. This refers to a market in which there is a large number of similar products, but not so similar that they are perceived as being interchangeable with one another. When a market contains a high number of slightly different products, competition in any one segment is too sparse to result in efficient pricing. Competition is fragmented by the narrowness of each market segment.

Monopolistic competition is prevalent in the airline industry. There are many airlines, but there is such a large number of routes that only a small number of airlines compete for each route. It you're looking for a nonstop from Tampa to Tucson, your choice of carrier will be very limited. A limited number of participants in any one market lessens price competition.

In coins, on the Certified Coin Exchange, observers can witness this any day. Say I own an 1879-CC dollar graded MS65 by PCGS. After polling five dealers I find that the market is evaluating the coin at $18,000. But I don't want to sell the coin for $18,000. I think it's worth a lot more and there are no other sellers of the coin on the system so I post an ask price of $36,000. It's double what everyone want to pay, but what the heck. There aren't any other ones around at the time. The lack of competitors results in a monopolistic ask price.

No one has any trouble ignoring my ask price. A few dealers ask me if I'm a lunatic pricing the coin that high, but other than that, nothing happens. The ask price is not reprinted on the CCDN or anywhere else. It is considered meaningless.

Now, lets move to the bid side. Same issue — 1879-CC dollar MS65 — but this time say I want to make an offer on one. I don't have an order to fill; I just think they're cheap. No one else is bidding on the coin so I put up a bid of $9,000 — half of what the market says the coin is worth. Why not? No reason to bid more: The lack of competitors results in a monopolistic bid price — precisely the same situation as before, but now on the bid side.

Here's the difference: my monopolistic bid price is *not* ignored. Dealers around the country use it as a basis of worth. "What's bid? Nine thousand." "What's bid? Nine thousand." "What's CCE on it? Nine thousand." The question is asked and answered day after day in dealer shops and offices all over the country. "$9,000" is reprinted by the CCDN. At first, everyone thinks $9,000 seems too cheap but over time it becomes self-fulfilling. After seeing $9,000 as the high bid day after day, dealers no longer want to pay $18,000 for the coin. They only want to pay $14,000, then $12,000.

Because a sight unseen bid price on the CCE is backed up by a cash offer, it has credibility. Once my $9,000 bid becomes entrenched as representative of market value, then the former worth of the coin, the $18,000 worth as determined by professional numismatists, is forgotten. Regardless of its accuracy, the printed number triumphs in the same way that an unsound argument can win through lack of opposition.

There is an interesting inconsistency here. If insufficient competition among sellers leads to market failure in the form of unrealistically high ask prices, then insufficient competition among bidders leads to market failure in the form of unrealistically low bid prices. Yet, post an ask price that's too high, it is meaningless; post a bid that's too low, it is Gospel.

Why doesn't anyone bid more for the 1879-CC dollar? If there truly is demand for rare coins, why doesn't the bidding fill in better? Why isn't there more competition on each issue? Because rare coins are the quintessential monopolistic competition products. Large number of individual markets? On CCE there are 17,810 different coins to bid on (1,370 issues times 13 grades for each issue). That's about 15 times as many listings as on the New York Stock Exchange.

One hundred dealers with $1 million each to spend could not sustain a bid structure under these circumstances for more than a few months. As the new capital filtered through the market, it would quickly be dissipated over the huge quantity of issues. A few dozen dealers in debt certainly can not sustain a market structure of such breadth. It doesn't work. Fundamental economics and five years of hands on experience say it can't work.

The good news is, it doesn't have to work. Think about how real estate is evaluated. Approximate value is determined by location, square footage, zoning, condition of the property, sale prices of nearby properties, etc. A seller and a buyer determine a specific transaction level. (Note that the seller's ask price is the starting point, not the bid price.) The actual sale price then becomes public record and the information is used by other buyers to interpolate values of other properties. Standing offers for all properties are not required to provide market value.

What would your house be worth if its value were determined solely by a lone bidder? What would all real estate in the U.S. be worth if values were determined by the standing offers of Realtors? What is today a $200,000 house might have a high offer (and therefore a market value) of $12,500.

For 150 years, until 1986, rare U.S. coins traded like real estate. Ballpark prices were determined by rarity, grade, popularity, historical worth, etc., then transaction levels were determined by the interaction of a buyer and a seller. It worked. As in real estate, the industry did not find it necessary to provide a standing offer to imbue a coin with value. Proponents of the current system feel that dealers in favor of eliminating it are meddling in the free market. What they don't realize is, the coin market that existed prior to competitive bidding was the coin market that evolved naturally. The initiation of electronic bid systems was the meddling in the free market.

And none of us knows how much the attempt to provide a standing offer for every PCGS and NGC certified coin has cost.

The Change

Perhaps we'll start to have some idea late this year. In June 1991, CCE will end competitive bidding on all non-generic coins. Plentiful coins will still be bought and sold in quantity on CCE. Bid systems tend to work for generic coins because trading volume is sufficient for perfect competition to evolve.

In all other areas, CCE will permit only ask prices. By eliminating monopolistic bidding, there will no longer be a forum for self-fulfilling depressants of market value. Also, there will no longer be a forum for dealer promotion of already-owned coins.

The group affected most adversely by the change will likely be the "producers" — dealers that crack out coins to ship to PCGS or NGC attempting upgrades. They will no longer be able to dump their coins on CCE. With fewer bids, producers will be forced to spend less time looking for crackouts and more time selling their coins off the market. It will be the beginning of the end of a system that draws coins into itself. There will be renewed incentive for dealers to expand their customer bases, thereby expanding the rare coin market.

Capital currently being used wastefully — being dissipated over 17,810 issues to provide standing offers — will be consolidated. Less will be required. By curtailing the number of bids, CCE will not only create incentive for dealers to move coins off the market and expand our industry; it will also free up the capital required to do so.

Collectors and investors lose no advantages, unless you consider a $2,000 offer on a coin you bought at $6,000 an advantage. Remember, it is not the sight unseen concept that is under fire; it is the competitive bid structure. All grading guarantees remain intact. PCGS and NGC coins will still trade sight-unseen. Ellesmere and other dealers will continue to make offers over the telephone for your certified coins. Little will change, except that over time the elimination of bidding may bring about a significant increase in market values.

The key words in that last sentence are "over time." During June and July you will likely see substantial price increases on virtually all non-generic coins. Know, however, that this will *not* be true appreciation. The elimination of bids means that price information will start to come from ask and transaction levels, both of which are well above the bids. The increases you will be seeing on price guides in June and July will be the result of a one-time shift in the basis of market values.

Over the next month or two, the hype level will also be up a couple of notches. Aggressive marketers in favor of the change are prone to explain it as the latest reason coin prices are poised to skyrocket. Some will use the June and July increases as validation. The change could trigger a boom, but given the state of the industry, confusion followed by a 2-3 month period of confidence building as dealer re-learn to evaluate coins on their own, seems more likely. True appreciation may very well follow, but don't get excited too quickly. The damage done by monopolistic bidding is great. The industry is not healthy.

Dealers against the change may publish a few caustic statements and articles about illiquidity, collapse, ruin, pestilence, etc. Relax, the outlook just improved — a lot. The elimination of a system that has had a deleterious effect on rare coin values for five years *must* be considered positive for market values over time and for the industry as a whole.

Regular *Winning Edge* readers will note that since 1986, our position regarding ANE/CCE has been constant: the systems do more harm than good. Over the past five years, the problems of relying on a bidding structure for evaluation and liquidity have been addressed in fifteen different issues of The Winning Edge and three special reports. The CCE decision to discontinue bidding on all non-generic certified coins is an intelligent one.

In the future, rare coin values will likely be higher but less well-defined than in the past, and that's an issue we'll get into next month. No changes will take place between now and mid June.

EDITOR'S NOTE: In a September 23, 1991 memo from Joe Stephens of CCE, the "sight-seen" trading software was scheduled to be implemented on October 12-13, 1991. From a direct quote; "A sight-seen status will apply to both the bid and the ask side...". From another quote in the same memo; "On high-bid/low-ask sheets, the high bid, whether sight-seen or sight-unseen will be shown...".

The final result of this change should be higher bids whether coins increase and/or decrease in actual trading activity. This is probably a positive move, however it complicates the process more for the consumers. Again this is another concept of trying to achieve a "perceived value" for coins.

Summary

The electronic sight-unseen system is very complex and presents a great challenge. In order to overcome the problems currently facing the bid-based system contained in this electronic marketplace, those involved must successfully understand and address the issues, implement important changes in a timely manner, and continue to monitor this vital component of the numismatic marketplace. Inaction will guarantee a future no better than the past (and probably worse). Phase IV does not mark the end of the presentation of critical issues and their possible solutions. Continuing efforts to educate and inform the numismatic community will be forthcoming in ensuing publications.

***

CHAPTER 43

Bear Market Bottom: The Test

by David Hall

Editor's note: The following pages present the contents of David Hall's Inside View (Issue 119), An Inside Report on the Rare Coin Market. This issue was published after the crash in the fall of 1990.

The Test

Every five or six years the rare coin market gives everybody a test. The name of the test is market bottom.

For the coin buying public, their performance on the test determines whether they remain in the coin market. For coin dealers, the test is more serious. Their performance on the test determines whether they remain in business.

The coin buying public suffers from a very strong urge to sell at the bottom. Many throw in the towel at the very worst time. A few have a longer term view and buy at the bottom. For those few, the rewards are enormous.

The coin dealers suffer from the cash flow problems that plague independent entrepreneurs throughout the business world. And at a market bottom, many are forced to liquidate their inventory at the very worst time. Some dealers go out of business during market bottoms. The strong survive. Right now, all the dealers I know are losing their butts.

Top or Bottom?

At a market top, dealer inventories and cash positions are very high. They have lots of coins and lots of cash. At a market bottom, dealer inventories are low and cash positions are miserable. What do we have today? Dealer inventories are very low. There have been massive liquidations at recent coin shows and auctions. Dealer cash positions are nearly non-existent. Several big dealers are teetering on the edge of bankruptcy and several have already gone out of business. Dealer inventories and cash positions are telling us that rare coins are at a market bottom.

At a market top, the coin market receives very favorable publicity. We're in the news and everybody loves us. At a market bottom, the coin market receives bad publicity. What do we have today? This year, the coin industry has received terrible publicity. Numerous major multi-part articles in the L.A. Times, Wall Street Journal and other important papers and magazines. Publicity indicates that the coin market is at a bottom.

At a market top, dealer sentiment is extremely high. If you would have walked around the February 1980 Long Beach show and asked dealers whether prices would be higher or lower in six months, you would have received a 95% plus response on the side of much higher prices. That's even though coin prices had risen spectacularly for four years in a row. Of course what happened was that within two months, the market peaked sharply and prices declined for nearly two years.

At a market bottom, dealer sentiment is extremely low. Here's a few examples:

> "The crash came last March. 'Suddenly there were all sellers and no buyers', says Jack Friedberg, president of Capital Coins. Rare-coin specialist Benjamin Stack, of Stack's Coins, who predicted the great coin crash, has little sympathy for any fellow dealers who are in trouble. 'They cut their own throats and now they're wallowing in their own blood', he says. 'Some 15% of all coin dealers have gone out of business and I predict we'll lose another 15%. . . .'"

- Forbes Magazine, October 1, 1965

> "You don't understand, David We sold Seated quarters for ten grand. That will never happen again."

- Ron Downing, 1982, when Seated quarters were selling for $2,000. In 1989, MS-67 Seated quarters reached over $20,000.

And what do we have today? Here's an example:

> "When I get home, I'm looking for another business to buy."

- A coin dealer friend who's been a major force in the rare coin industry for over 30 years, at the October 1990 Long Beach Show.

Coin dealers are depressed, startled, confused, and for the most part feel that the coin business is permanently dead. Coin dealer sentiment is telling us that the coin market is at a major bottom.

Finally, at a market top, buyer sentiment is extremely positive. That's what makes a market top. Everyone is so positive about coins that all of the buyers have bought all the coins they possibly can. There's no one left to buy so prices start to go down. At a market bottom, buyer sentiment is extremely negative. Everyone is so negative about coins that all of the sellers have sold every coin they possibly can. That's what makes a market bottom. There are no more sellers, so prices start to go up.

This buyer psychology works in all markets. If you've ever bought stocks, you know what I mean. When the Dow is at 2900, you love stocks, think the stock market is great and think you are a genius for buying stocks. When the Dow drops 600 points you hate stocks, think the stock market consists of nothing but crooks and con men and you wonder how you were ever stupid enough to buy stocks.

And what do we have today? Long time subscribers are familiar with the David Hall definition of a coin market top:

"When you have the irresistible urge to buy coins, when you want to mortgage your house, your children's houses and your neighbor's houses to buy coins, then the market is at or near a top."

Is that how you feel today? I doubt it. Everyone I talk to hates coins. And I'd bet a lot of money that I'm going to get a lot less Christmas cards this year. I don't mean to speak for you, but if you're like most of the coin buyers I talk to, you don't want to buy coins, you want to get rid of the coins you have (if you haven't already). We all suffer from the very human urge to buy at the top and sell at the bottom. And today, buyer sentiment is telling us that the market is at a major bottom.

There are no guarantees. Prices could go lower. However, with prices at a fraction of their old highs, with cash bidders on permanent vacation, with dealers looking to change jobs, and with the electronic exchanges in total disarray, it looks like a market bottom to me. ALL INDICATIONS POINT TO A MAJOR MARKET BOTTOM!

Meltdown!

Let's take a look at exactly how far prices have come down. I'll go through a couple of the most important areas of the market and we'll look at the recent high price watermark of the past few years and compare them with today's current prices. For most of the more frequently traded issues the highs will be in mid-1986. For most of the gold issues, the highs were in mid-1989.

First, let's take a look at generic coin issues. These are the bread and butter issues of the entire rare coin marketplace. Since mid-1986 they have slowly but surely collapsed in price. The chart below shows exactly how cheap these coins have become:

Coin	All Time High Bid	Current Market	Percentage of High Bid
Morgan dollars			
MS-63	$ 85	$ 32	37.6
MS-64	405	45	11.1
MS-65	825	135	16.4
Peace dollars			
MS-63	120	25	20.8
MS-64	440	50	11.4
MS-65	900	195	21.7
$20 Liberties			
MS-64	4,650	1,475	31.7
MS-65	13,300	4,650	35.0
$20 St. Gaudens			
MS-63	1,450	535	36.9
MS-64	2,550	700	27.5
MS-65	4,200	1,525	36.3
Walking 50C			
MS-64	205	57	27.8
MS-65	550	126	22.9

The chart above shows that mainstays of the rare coin market have dropped between 62% and 89% in price in the past few years. They are selling for twenty to thirty cents on the dollar of their all-time highs. MS-64 Morgan Dollars are selling for eleven cents on the dollar!!

As you can see, the blue chips of the rare coin market have been slaughtered in price in the past few years. Now let's look at the major gold issues and compare their highs to recent price levels and note that the "High Bid" represents dealer buy prices, while the "Current Market" is what *you* can buy the coins for today.

The blood bath has been just as severe in nearly every other market area:

Silver Commemoratives-Slashed in half.
Better Date Dollars-Totally hammered.
20th Century-Way down.
Type Coins-Had actually gone up in price between 1986 and early 1990 but then had a free fall.
Rarities-Most aren't worth 50% of their highs.
The bottom line is that nearly all rare coin prices are a lot cheaper than they used to be.

IF COINS ARE SO GREAT... WHY HAVE PRICES COME DOWN SO MUCH?

I could talk about how the major electronic trading exchange split into several factions and put too much financial pressure on a thinly capitalized, entrepreneurial financial support base. I could talk about the bad publicity the industry has received this year. I could talk about Wall Street being a whimper and not a bang (so far, anyway). I could talk about the contraction of the economy of this country. But this is not the real point.

The real point is that price corrections and Bear markets are a natural part of the coin market cycle. Since I've been involved in coins, we've had Bear markets in 1965, 1969 & 1970, 1975 & 1976, 1981 & 1982 and now in 1989 & 1990. Bear markets are a natural part of any free market. Bear markets are healthy. They show that the coin market is real.

The facts are that rare coins are one of the premier long term performers. Even after the past price collapse, top quality rare coins have a superb long term record.

Here's a chart which shows the long term price history for many major issues. We have some Type coins, Dollars, Gold, 20th Century and Silver Commems. I've focused on the MS-65 grade because that's the grade for which we have the most accurate price information. The coins are randomly picked. You will find similar results for nearly every coin the these five major market areas.

I've used the last three market cycles. This includes the major market bottoms of 1976, 1982 and 1990 and the major market tops of 1974, 1980 and the double top (May, 1986 for generics and May 1989 for rarities) of the last cycle.

TYPE	1983-1990	1977-1982	1970-1976
Bust 10C MS-65			
High	$ 20,300	$ 5,850	$ 1,000
Low	7,900	3,500	850
Trade $1 PR-65			
High	17,300	10,000	1,200
Low	9,850	2,500	1,100
Twenty Cents MS-65			
High	14,500	8,800	850
Low	9,850	5,450	1,400
Barber 25C MS-65			
High	5,000	2,500	220
Low	3,330	1,000	155
Barber 50C PR-65			
High	7,425	5,500	500
Low	4,750	2,150	485
$2 1/2 Libs MS-65			
High	8,260	2,650	170
Low	2,970	1,375	160
$2 1/2 Inds MS-65			
High	11,600	2,850	160
Low	6,450	1,500	150
$5 Indians MS-65			
High	31,850	4,800	265
Low	16,500	2,700	250
$10 Libs MS-65			
High	15,100	4,000	250
Low	7,500	2,300	195
$20 Libs MS-65			
High	13,300	1,900	320
Low	4,650	1,700	205
$20 St. Gaudens MS-65			
High	4,200	1,400	295
Low	1,525	1,200	215
Morgan $1 MS-65			
High	825	110	8
Low	135	88	7
Peace $1 MS-65			
High	900	135	6
Low	195	102	5
Buffalo 5C MS-65			
High	150	48	7
Low	38	18	6

TYPE	1983-1990	1977-1982	1970-1976
Walking 50C MS-65			
High	550	200	14
Low	126	50	11
Lafayette $1 MS-65			
High	18,600	7,500	600
Low	9,750	4,250	500
Delaware 50C MS-65			
High	1,900	535	87
Low	975	350	80
Hawaiian 50C MS-65			
High	15,700	4,000	1,000
Low	6,875	2,000	800
Missouri 50C MS-65			
High	18,600	2,100	480
Low	8,900	1,700	465
Texas 50C MS-65			
High	655	185	36
Low	275	160	34

The chart clearly shows that rare coins have been a great long term appreciating asset. Each high is higher than the previous high. Each low is higher than the previous low. That's a long term appreciating asset.

Now if you bought rarities in May, 1989 or the generic mainstays in the first part of 1986, you probably don't think much of rare coins. But the facts are that if you bought properly graded coins anytime between 1970 and 1983, you have probably seen spectacular gains. Since 1984, the results have been mixed. But that's mostly because our current price reference is today's cheap levels and they very possibly represent a major market bottom.

What To Do

I have some very specific suggestions as to what to do today! Here's a three step plan.

STEP ONE - MENTAL ATTITUDE. If you want to be a successful participant in the rare coin market you have to have the right attitude. I've seen lots of big winners in rare coins and they all have the following things in common. All of the big winners I've seen have a long term perspective. They buy the very best and they hold their coins long term. When prices get real high they always sell at least a few coins. When prices get cheap they scoop up the bargains. They are long term players.

You need to ask yourself if you have the long term attitude. If you want to be a long term player then you should proceed to step two and three. If you don't want to be a long term player then you should probably sell your coins and do something else.

STEP TWO - GET YOUR HOUSE IN ORDER. It's always appropriate to do the right thing to-maintain the right position-to hold the right coins. But at a market bottom it's critical that you get your house in order.

First of all, you should have all of your coins graded by PCGS. If you own un-certified coins you are taking an unnecessary risk on the grades of your coins. If you have coins that haven't been graded, get them graded by PCGS today.

Second, if you have lower quality coins you should trade them for higher quality coins at today's cheap price levels. Beware of the lessor quality proponents who seem to come out of the woodwork during every market bottom and say, "See, I told you so. Look how much these so-called MS-65 coins have come down in value". Of course, what the "semi-numismatic" coin proponents fail to tell you is that the coins they recommend have also come way down in value (or never went up in the first place) and that semi-numismatic coins have a far inferior long term performance record. It's never appropriate to hold less than the best in your rare coin portfolio.

Finally, if you're a long term player in the rare coin market, you shouldn't sell any MS-64 or better quality coins. Now is one of the worst possible times to be selling coins.

STEP THREE - BUY A BARGAIN TODAY. If you're a long term player in the rare coin market, you must be a buyer today. Now is the time when you can buy the very best coins for bargain prices. It's a buyer's market. There's not much competition around. You can pick your coins and pick your price. If you understand coins you should have a smile on your face and you should buy a bargain today!

I have some specific suggestions. Here's my opinion of the best deals - in order:

1. The All-Time Classics. Close your eyes and imagine your secret fantasy coin... that true rarity that you always wanted to buy but never could afford. Well, guess what? Today you can buy that fantasy coin. If you've ever wanted a Proof Trade dollar, Twenty Cent Piece, Proof gold coin, Lafayette dollar, etc., your time has come.
2. Extremely High Quality Coins. Now is the time to buy MS-67 Type coins, MS-66 and MS-67 Gold coins, MS-67 and MS-68 Dollars, 20th Century and Silver Commemoratives. Only at market bottoms can you buy the caviar of the coin market at cheap prices.
3. Major Gold Issues. Look at the gold coin charts on page two. Today you can buy the world's most important rare coins - Gem quality U.S. gold coins - at ridiculously cheap prices.

4. Better Date Silver Dollars. More people collect silver dollars than any other U.S. coin series. The better dates are selling at 25% to 50% of their high water marks of eighteen months ago. This is a great long term play.
5. Generic Coins. Check out the coins on page two and three of this chapter. On a few of these coins, all they'd have to do is get back to 25% of their all-time high and you'd double your money. This seems like a very low risk play.

Generic Issues - A New Inside View Position

The mainstays of the rare coin market ($20 St. Gaudens, Morgan and Peace Dollars, Buffalo Nickels and Mercury Dimes) have had their prices annihilated in the past four years. Early this year (when prices were 50% to 100% higher) I advised all clients and subscribers to throw in the towel and either liquidate or trade out of their generic coin positions. I'm now going to change that recommendation.

With prices at absurdly cheap levels, I don't believe it's right to sell the generic issues of the coin market. I'm not prepared to issue an all out buy recommendation, but I definitely think generics deserve a close look.

Consider the following. You can buy a PCGS graded, 100 year old Gem quality, MS-64 Morgan dollar - one of the world's most beautiful coins - for only $45. And in 1986 dealers were paying over $400! That's eleven cents on the dollar. That means you can buy ten coins for $450 - about the same price as one coin used to be. Doesn't it seem like it's time to take a flyer on generics?

The New Frontier

There is one area of the market where prices haven't gone down. That's because prices have been the same for the last ten years. In the last *Inside View*, I discussed the great opportunities in the world coin market. Let's talk about what's been going on with world coins.

Even though the general market conditions are horrible, world coins are still hot. They're still easy to sell. In short, all of my comments in the last *Inside View* still apply. I recommend that 2% to 10% of your rare coin portfolio consist of PCGS graded, superb quality world coins.

***

CHAPTER 44

Traits of the Certified Morgan Dollar Market

How degree of rarity influences value, price movements, cost, and liquidity

by Philip J. Schuyler

The rare coin market before 1986

It was August 1977 at the Bay State Show in Boston when I first witnessed the nature of rare coin trading as it existed before guaranteed third party grading. I was looking through a box of raw Morgan dollars at the table of a well-known dealer whose conversation consisted of, "*That* one's a beauty," with regard to each coin I set aside for him to price.

Another dealer, a knowledgeable fellow named Steve, was also looking through boxes of dollars at the same table. I watched as he pulled out an 1892-O Morgan and asked for a price. The selling dealer quoted $2,500. Steve offered $2,000 and showed a complete lack of interest at a nickel more. Following some obligatory complaining about the weakness of the offer, the dealer accepted $2,000 and in the end seemed quite satisfied with it.

Fifteen minutes later I happened to be looking at coins at a table on the other side of the room when Steve walked up and offered the 1892-O dollar he had just purchased to the dealer seated behind the table. "How much?" asked the dealer. "Three thousand," replied Steve. "Twenty-five hundred," countered the dealer after inspecting the coin. "Twenty-eight is the absolute best," said Steve. After a pause the dealer said, "I own it."

What a rip, I thought. Steve just paid $2,000 for the coin and sold it for $2,800. An eight-hundred dollar, forty percent profit in fifteen minutes — for walking the coin across the room?

But then I began to realize that the dealer Steve bought the coin from was pleased to get $2,000 for it and the dealer he sold it to was happy to pay $2,800. Both were experienced, successful dealers. They knew what they were doing. So how could they be so far apart in their assessment of the coin's worth? Was rare coin grading *that* ambiguous?

I got my answer the next day when the same 1892-O dollar was in another dealer's case. He told me he had just purchased it that morning. He quoted me $4,000 on it, exactly double what I had seen Steve pay for the coin not twenty-four hours earlier. Grading — or more specifically, evaluation — was that ambiguous.

In fact, transactions like the previous one were common before 1986. The value of a rare coin was based on a combination of the technical grade of the coin, the grade it would pass for, the aggressiveness and numismatic knowledge of the buyer, and the salesmanship of the seller. Given these circumstances, it was difficult for anyone but professional coin traders to profit.

Before 1986, grading was a matter of individual preference. Since one grading point can translate to thousands of dollars in value, traders tended to have a subtle double standard. When buying they were strict, even harsh, in their assessment of grade. When selling, they graded more liberally.

A common saying before 1986 was, ownership is worth half a point. The owner of a coin was on average a half point optimistic in his grading, the non-owner a half point conservative. That put buyers and sellers a grading point apart. Differences of opinion were routine even among experts and far more trades fell through than were consummated.

Grading discrepancies severely hampered rare coin liquidity on an industry-wide scale. And the fewer coins a dealer could sell, the more profit he needed to earn on each piece. Vague evaluation methods and poor liquidity created a high-markup, low-volume rare coin market.

Due to grading haziness, buyers frequently found that they were unable to sell their coins at the same grade level at which they had been purchased. Even in bull markets, few realized more than paper profits. Grading discrepancies and liquidity problems excluded rare coins from serious consideration by most mainstream investors.

Guaranteed third-party grading

Rare coin investment changed profoundly in February 1986 when the Professional Coin Grading Service (PCGS) was founded in Newport Beach, California. There were other grading services before PCGS, but PCGS was the first to back up their grading assessments with a money back guarantee. If a PCGS coin is found to be graded too high, PCGS will correct the grade free of charge and pay to the owner the difference between the value of the coin at the initially certified grade and the value at the newly assessed grade. Or, at the owner's option, PCGS will purchase the coin from the owner at the higher of the two grades.

That guarantee changed the industry permanently. Individual grading standards quickly came into line with those of PCGS. For the first time, grading was uniform. Since the buyer of a PCGS coin knew that the grade was guaranteed, PCGS coins began to trade sight-unseen, like commodities, unheard of in the rare coin business. A seller could simply call his dealer, tell him the coin and PCGS grade, and the dealer would make a binding offer to purchase. If the seller chose to accept the offer, he shipped the coin, the dealer sent him a check, and the deal was done.

PCGS gave the market what it needed most: an answer to grading inconsistencies. For the first time, most certified rare coins were instantly salable. Soon hundreds of dealers were trading PCGS coins over the telephone, without seeing them. No grading discrepancies. No coins rejected.

Since bids for PCGS coins were real, binding offers to purchase, bid levels published in price guides began to reflect true market values — what you could actually get for a coin — rather than prices a dealer might pay if he happened to agree with the grade. Sight-unseen trading solved the ancient problem of price definition by tying each actively traded PCGS coin to a specific bid level, like a commodity.

The concepts of guaranteed third party grading and sight-unseen liquidity caught on fast. Eighteen months after PCGS, the Numismatic Guaranty Corporation (NGC) located in Parsippany, New Jersey, started to certify and encapsulate coins. Since NGC's standards and guarantees were nearly identical to those of PCGS, NGC further eliminated grading discrepancies, enhanced liquidity, and solidified long term consistency in grading standards.

During the first few years of PCGS and NGC, it became apparent that guaranteed, third-party grading had brought a new level of consumer protection to rare coins. Better liquidity and improved price definition cut dealer buy/sell spreads in half. Much was written about the improved climate in rare coins and the impending entrance of Wall Street into the market. But another aspect of the metamorphosis, perhaps the most important one of all in the end, received little attention at the beginning.

The first empirical definition of rarity

Before PCGS and NGC, no one knew how many of each coin in each grade were really out there. But every coin certified by PCGS and NGC has been documented. The totals are published monthly in the PCGS and NGC population reports. The reports were initially considered little more than PCGS and NGC marketing devices, but they marked a permanent change in how rarity — and consequently, value — would be determined in the rare coin market.

Scarcity, coin by coin, was no longer an educated guess agreed upon by numismatists. Scarcity, for the first time, was being determined by empirical data. *Supply* in the supply/demand equation was actually being measured.

The new data redefined Morgan dollar rarity. Over time the population reports made it apparent that some dates were more abundant than anyone guessed; others were scarcer than had been realized. From nearly five years of PCGS population data, what follows is a ranking of Morgan dollars based on total population in all uncirculated grades, MS-60 through MS-69. (A possible source of error is resubmissions, which would make some date-mintmark combinations appear commoner than they actually are; this might affect some dates much more than others.) Dates are listed in order of rarest to most common. The first number is population rank. The number following the date of the coin is the percentage of the entire Morgan series made up by that date. The number on the right is the rank of rarity in February 1985, one year before PCGS began grading.

RANK	DATE	% of SERIES	1985 RANK
1.	1893-S	0.002	1
2.	1892-S	0.003	3
3.	1895-O	0.004	2
4.	1884-S	0.01	6
5.	1889-CC	0.02	12
6.	1901-P	0.02	4
7.	1887/6-O	0.02	38
8.	1893-O	0.03	7
9.	1903-S	0.03	10
10.	1894-O	0.03	8
11.	1896-O	0.04	5
12.	1879-CC C/D	0.04	27
13.	1895-S	0.04	13
14.	1894-P	0.04	9
15.	1897-O	0.04	11
16.	1887/6-P	0.06	89
17.	1904-S	0.06	17
18.	1896-S	0.06	16
19.	1886-O	0.08	19
20.	1880-CC R'78	0.08	52
21.	1879-CC	0.09	15
22.	1883-S	0.10	18
23.	1893-CC	0.10	14
24.	1894-S	0.10	24
25.	1901-S	0.12	21
26.	1900-O/CC	0.13	49
27.	1893-P	0.13	23
28.	1899-S	0.14	37
29.	1879-S R'78	0.14	55
30.	1892-P	0.14	26
31.	1898-S	0.15	39
32.	1878-P R'79	0.15	56
33.	1902-S	0.16	31
34.	1886-S	0.16	43
35.	1891-O	0.18	20
36.	1889-O	0.19	25
37.	1904-P	0.19	28
38.	1888-S	0.19	42
39.	1900-S	0.20	57

RANK	DATE	% of SERIES	'85 RANK
40.	1892-CC	0.20	30
41.	1880-O	0.21	33
42.	1891-P	0.21	29
43.	1887-S	0.21	46
44.	1890-CC	0.23	40
45.	1892-O	0.26	22
46.	1889-S	0.26	48
47.	1891-S	0.28	68
48.	1887-O	0.28	47
49.	1902-P	0.29	36
50.	1879-O	0.30	34
51.	1885-S	0.30	35
52.	1921-S	0.31	50
53.	1878-P 7TF	0.33	62
54.	1878-P 8TF	0.35	44
55.	1878-P 7/8TF	0.36	45
56.	1899-P	0.38	55
57.	1890-S	0.38	69
58.	1897-S	0.40	65
59.	1881-P	0.41	73
60.	1891-CC	0.43	41
61.	1879-P	0.44	58
62.	1890-O	0.44	32
63.	1890-P	0.45	61
64.	1880-P	0.49	71
65.	1880-CC	0.50	53
66.	1881-O	0.52	72
67.	1921-D	0.55	63
68.	1903-O	0.56	51
69.	1882-P	0.60	74
70.	1897-P	0.61	82
71.	1882-O	0.65	77
72.	1888-O	0.69	80
73.	1884-P	0.70	70
74.	1878-CC	0.70	64
75.	1903-P	0.72	67
76.	1898-P	0.75	88
77.	1885-CC	0.77	59
78.	1881-CC	0.81	60

RANK	DATE	% of SERIES	1985 RANK
79.	1889-P	0.92	60
80.	1901-O	0.94	75
81.	1883-P	1.15	76
82.	1900-P	1.22	78
83.	1882-CC	1.22	79
84.	1888-P	1.25	83
85.	1896-P	1.27	86
86.	1878-S	1.45	81
87.	1900-O	1.61	92
88.	1902-O	1.61	90
89.	1921-P	1.65	94
90.	1884-CC	1.80	85
91.	1883-CC	1.81	84

RANK	DATE	% of SERIES	1985 RANK
92.	1899-O	2.04	87
93.	1885-P	2.33	96
94.	1898-O	2.64	91
95.	1883-O	3.47	97
96.	1882-S	3.71	95
97.	1904-O	3.96	93
98.	1886-P	4.04	99
99.	1887-P	4.65	100
100.	1879-S	4.69	102
101.	1884-O	5.24	101
102.	1885-O	5.54	98
103.	1880-S	6.83	104
104.	1881-S	12.09	103

Naturally, the numerical rank would be different if only higher grades were used in the survey. If just MS-65 through MS-69 pieces were used, for example, dates with very low populations in just the top grades like 1886-O, 1893-CC, 1896-O, and 1901-P would appear scarcer. Other dates tend to be more evenly distributed among the range of grades. Dates that are generally scarce in all uncirculated grades like 1895-S, 1896-S, and 1903-S would rank lower than shown if only MS-65 and higher pieces were considered.

But an MS-65 through MS-69 ranking would assume that a Morgan dollar has to grade MS-65 or higher to be considered rare, which is not the case. Also, it is statistically most accurate to use the largest number of uncirculated grades possible because a larger sample yields a more reliable and enduring assessment of rarity. If only the highest grades were chosen, rank of rarity would be determined by single-digit populations in many cases, which could be rendered inaccurate by the certification of a few additional high-grade coins.

The differences in rarity between one date and another can be immense. The twenty most common Morgan dollars make up almost three quarters of the total uncirculated Morgan dollar population. The twenty rarest dates make up about three quarters of one percent. For every uncirculated 1893-S dollar seen by PCGS, there are nearly five bags of uncirculated 1881-S dollars certified.

On the whole, it is surprising how accurately the free market had established rarity before PCGS began certifying coins. More than half of the coins — 56 out of 104 — were ranked correctly within five positions of their empirical rarity as later ascertained by PCGS. Only six dates differed by more than twenty positions from their 1985 ranking and all six are special-case, variety issues: 1878-P reverse of '79, 1879-S reverse of '78, 1880-CC reverse of '78, 1887/6-P, 1887/6-O and 1900-O/CC.

These six issues need a category of their own because they are really subsets of regular issues. Demand for subset issues is thinner. The market tends to value varieties at prices less than commensurate to their populations.

Excluding these six variety issues, a ranking of Morgan dollars by value would look very similar to the ranking of the 104 dates by population as shown. This is to be expected since population is a measurement of scarcity and scarcity is the chief determinant of rare coin value.

How the two "pops" determine Morgan dollar value

The other key component in the value of a rare coin is demand, as measured by *popularity* with collectors and investors. No matter how rare a coin is, if it isn't sought after, it isn't going to be worth much. Some dates of Morgan dollars have always been more popular than others. Value is determined by the combination of the two "pops," population and popularity. Each has a broad and a specific dimension, creating a total of four factors that determine the value of a Morgan dollar.

1. Population in the grade in question

The obvious one. The lower the population, the higher the value. An MS-65 1889-O Morgan is worth 6-7 times as much as an 1888-O because 1889-O is several times more scarce. 1892-O is a scarce date, but 1893-O will always bring more because fewer exist. Note, however, that ratios of population to value are not directly proportional. If Morgan dollar A has a population one eighth as large as Morgan dollar B, A will bring more, but not necessarily eight times as much. Population in the grade in question is the single largest determinant of the value of a Morgan dollar, but it should be used as a ballpark guide only because the following three factors also apply.

2. Population in other uncirculated grades

Historically, MS-65 1887-O Morgans have traded for about 60% of what 1904-S Morgans have brought in the same grade. Yet the two have similar populations. Has 1887-O been undervalued by the market or has 1904-S been overvalued? Or both? The answer is neither. The 1904-S is worth almost twice as much because, although 1904-S has about the same rarity as 1887-O in MS-65 condition, 1904-S is five times as rare when all uncirculated grades are considered.

Population one grade up or one grade down influences value too. An MS-64 Morgan with an MS-64 population of 200 and an MS-65 population of 15 will have a greater value than an MS-64 Morgan with an MS-64 population of 200 and an MS-65 population of 60. Both MS-64s have populations of 200, but a greater number of buyers will seek the coin with the smaller MS-65 population. Unable to locate an MS-65 sample, many will settle for an MS-64, increasing demand for the MS-64.

1880-O and 1891-P have similar populations in MS-64 condition, but 1880-O is worth about twice as much as 1891-P because 1880-O is very rare graded MS-65, which increases MS-64 demand for 1880-O.

3. Popularity of the date in general

Popularity is a tough one to quantify. Why were cars with fins popular from 1957 to 1961? Why was shag carpeting popular in the seventies, but not any more? Psychologists can come up with reasons for a trend, but rationalizations after the fact don't help much in trying to determine present and future value. Wall Street newscasters can back up any occurrence in the stock market with reasoning, but they are unable to make accurate forecasts.

Some aspects of Morgan dollar demand have been around for decades. Carson City Morgans tend to bring premiums to their population rarity. Flatly struck dates or those that come dull like 1891-P or 1921-D tend to bring less than their rarity would suggest. CCs are more popular than S mints; both are more popular than O mints; P mints are the least popular of all. But these are generalizations. The most prudent way to estimate demand is as a function of supply because scarce coins are more popular than common coins. A very rare Morgan dollar stimulates its own demand. An MS-65 1893-S dollar — the series key in the highest achievable grade — is as popular as any six-figure coin. Low-population Morgans enjoy widespread popularity.

Common dates are not popular. They have become thought of as generic, replaceable. Collectors are not interested in coins extant in quantities of tens of thousands. Investors don't buy them because they aren't scarce. The least popular Morgans are common dates in common grades. Buyers have a shoulder-shrug attitude toward MS-63 1881-S dollars because they feel they can acquire any quantity of them at any time, so why buy now?

4. Popularity in the grade in question

When a Morgan has a big spread in value between one grade and the next, it is usually popular in the less expensive grade. Buyers figure, why pay ten or fifteen times as much for an MS-65? Better to buy a nice MS-64 sample and save 90%. The funds in one's checking account can make a persuasive case for buying for value.

Low grade uncirculated coins are not popular. Even MS-60 and MS-61 better dates can be difficult to sell at a strong price. The rare coin market is more commodity-oriented than ever before, but most buyers still try to avoid buying heavily bagmarked pieces.

The most popular grade for most Morgan dollars is the lowest grade at which buyers perceive them to be scarce. For the common dates, MS-66 and MS-67 are the most popular grades; for most dates, MS-65 and MS-66 are the most popular grades. The rarest dates, like 1884-S, 1889-CC, 1892-S, 1893-S and 1895-O are the most sought after in MS-63 and MS-64 condition.

How rarity affects price movements of certified Morgan dollars

The rarity of a Morgan dollar influences its short and long term price movements. For ease of reference, the Morgan dollar series is broken into three categories below: common dates, better dates, and rare dates. Designations are based on total uncirculated populations. Any date with an uncirculated population of more than seven-tenths of one percent of the entire series is considered common. Dates with total uncirculated populations that make up between one tenth and seven tenths of one percent of the total are considered better dates. Rare dates are those with populations of less than one tenth of one percent of the total population of all uncirculated Morgan dollars certified by PCGS.

Common dates	Better dates	Better dates (cont.)	Rare dates
1878-S	1878-P 7TF	1890-CC	1879-CC
1879-S	1878-P 8TF	1890-O	1879-CC C/D
1880-S	1878-P R'79	1890-S	1880-CC R'78
1881-CC	1878-P 7/8	1891-P	1883-S
1881-S	1878-CC	1891-CC	1884-S
1882-CC	1879-O	1891-O	1886-O
1882-S	1879-P	1891-S	1887/6-P
1883-P	1879-S R'78	1892-O	1887/6-O
1883-CC	1880-CC	1892-P	1889-CC
1883-O	1880-O	1892-CC	1892-S
1884-CC	1880-P	1893-P	1893-CC
1884-O	1881-P	1897-P	1893-O
1885-P	1881-O	1897-S	1893-S
1885-CC	1882-P	1898-S	1894-P
1885-O	1882-O	1899-P	1894-O
1886-P	1884-P	1899-S	1894-S
1887-P	1885-S	1900-O/CC	1895-O
1888-P	1886-S	1900-S	1895-S
1889-P	1887-O	1901-S	1896-O
1896-P	1887-S	1902-P	1896-S
1898-P	1888-O	1902-S	1897-O
1898-O	1888-S	1903-O	1901-P
1899-O	1889-O	1904-P	1903-S
1900-P	1889-S	1921-D	1904-S
1900-O	1890-P	1921-S	
1901-O			
1902-O			
1903-P			
1904-O			
1921-P			

Long-term trends

Over time, the effect of rarity on the performance of certified Morgan dollars is well-documented. Past performance is never a guarantee of future results, but the track record of PCGS certified Morgan dollars to date suggests that the rarest dates appreciate most. Over the past five years, the coins in the third group have more than doubled in value on average. Graded MS-65, the group has risen 410% on average. 1883-S, 1884-S and 1887/6-P have increased more than ten times in value over the past five years!

The dates not scarce enough to be labelled rare, those in the middle group, have also registered outstanding results over the most recent five years. Of the 50 dates in this category, 39 have more than doubled in value. In MS-65 condition, the better dates have increased an average of 362%, almost as much as the rare dates. The big winners were 1878-P 7tf, 1878-P r79, 1879-S r78, 1880-O, 1881-O, 1887-O, 1887-S, 1890-P and 1891-P. Each of these dates increased in value more than five times over the past five years. Only 1884-P, 1902-P and 1903-O have fallen in value. Not surprisingly, these are three of the most plentiful dates in the category.

As of this writing, common date Morgans have been depreciating since the inception of PCGS. The ten most common dates have lost 60% to 80% of their initial value. As more have been certified and come onto the market, supply has continued to grow, but demand has not. This slide in value will likely continue until prices for common date Morgans become cheap enough that buyers are once again enticed. At that level (no one can say what it is for sure) demand will pick up. As demand increases, common date Morgans will disappear from the market and prices will turn around.

Since common date Morgans may be insufficiently scarce to provide a fundamental reason to rise in value faster than the inflation rate, an investment in that area is essentially a matter of good timing. In a market that does not register a favorable performance over time, it is necessary to buy at or near cyclical lows and sell at highs to profit.

The better date Morgans and especially the rare dates have a built-in advantage for investors: they *are* coins that have a fundamental reason to rise in value because they are truly scarce. They have low populations and are sought after by both collectors and investors. In addition, as more coin buyers become aware of the advantages of scarcer Morgans as opposed to common dates, a gravitation toward the rarer coins is likely. Demand for the scarce Morgans will likely increase from both outside and within the coin market.

Short-term price movements

While long-term performance is primarily a function of scarcity, daily, weekly, and monthly price movements of Morgan dollars are determined by competitive teletype bidding.

For common date Morgan dollars, the sight-unseen bids are an accurate, reliable way to determine market value. Common dates are bellwether coins, they tend to characterize the direction of the rare coin market as a whole. What's good for common date Morgan dollars is good for the rare coin market. With dozens of buyers and sellers ready to participate, common date Morgans make up one of the most efficient markets in rare coins. Prices tend to move fast, then correct quickly. Because the market is efficient, buy/sell spreads are tight.

One misconception about common date Morgan dollars is that they are among the most volatile of rare coin investments. On the contrary, since huge quantities exist, the market is broad and relatively deep. There are plenty of sellers with plenty of coins to offset a steep rise. Market depth provided by dozens of bidders cushions steep drops in value. Short-term price movements of common date Morgans are less severe than those of almost any other rare coins. While bid levels for many U.S. coins have changed 20% to 40% before in a single day (that's rare, of course), 10% is considered a major change in value for common date Morgan dollars, and they have never moved 20% in a day.

Better date Morgans trade in what can be called a semi-efficient market. There are usually a number of buyers for any date, but in the slowest markets, there may be only one or two bidders. Better dates trade at bid levels occasionally, but since there are fewer of them on the market, better dates often bring 5% to 20% over posted bid levels at wholesale, depending on market conditions.

Teletype bidding is an understated but reasonably accurate way of determining true wholesale worth for better date Morgans. Understated, because asks are ignored. By publishing bids alone, price guides report like-to-buy-it-at-prices. Asks are like-to-get-for-it-prices. Neither constitute the actual market, which is somewhere in between the two. Most price guides depict only the lower half of the market, which is why it is difficult, if not impossible, for collectors and investors to buy better date Morgans at published bid levels. In most cases, even dealers can not acquire coins at the bids.

Because the market for better date Morgans is less efficient than the market for common dates, short term price movements are more extreme. The top two teletype bidders for a coin might be tied at $6,000 each, with a third bid at $4,800. If one of the two high bidders fills his need and deletes his bid, the other bidder no longer has any reason to bid $6,000 with the next highest bidder at $4,800 and may lower his bid to $4,800 as well. Look what happens if he does. Because one bidder has filled a need for one coin, printed price levels drop 20%, from $6,000 to $4,800. The market for better date Morgans can be that thin.

Upward movements can be sudden as well. In the previous example, another buyer may know that $4,800 is an unrealistically low bid price for the coin and enter a new bid of $5,500, which would result in a 15% increase in value for the coin.

If you feel that something is wrong with a market in which one bidder with one need routinely causes a 10% or 20% change in value on a coin, you're not alone. Thin-market economics dictate that coins not in need at the moment will not receive realistic bids and their values will be understated. Coins needed for orders will tend to be overbid and therefore overvalued. Unfortunately, the only solution appears to be the eventual growth of the industry. If more bidders, each with more orders, compete for coins in the future, bids for better date Morgans will gradually become more representative of actual worth.

Whereas bids for better date dollars can be spotty and understate value, bids for the rare dates are almost meaningless. At wholesale, rare date Morgans can and do bring 50% to 100% premiums above published bid levels; high-grade pieces can bring multiples of bid. For example, bid on the American Numismatic Exchange for an 1893-S Morgan graded MS-67 was $100,000 when one brought $357,000 at the Norweb sale in November, 1988.

If there is no realistic bid for a rare date Morgan, which is often the case, using whatever bid is highest as an indicator of value is a mistake, because, once again, the ask price is ignored. If your house is worth $300,000 and a buyer offers you $75,000, the offer would be ignored. If real estate were evaluated like rare coins, however, home buying guides in your area the following week would show a picture of your house with the caption "$75,000" underneath it. The real worth of a coin is what it trades at; not what someone would like to pay for it, what they *have* to pay for it.

Why are the teletype bids so low relative to the actual trading worth of very scarce Morgans? The lack of bids is a natural extension of the lack of standing orders for six-figure coins. In addition, most teletype dealers do not bother to maintain bids for very rare coins. Bidders know that they are very unlikely to buy such coins over the teletype and they don't want to spend time maintaining bids that don't produce. Bidding is therefore ultra-thin. One bidder might be at $60,000 on a coin, the next might be at $22,000. The coin may be worth $100,000 or more. The value of a truly rare coin is determined to a great extent by the needs and whims of the *seller*, rendering bid levels irrelevant.

Teletype bids for rare Morgan dollars can be misleading in the other direction too. The owner of a very rare coin can bid on the issue, creating a market level that might otherwise be lower. As buyers can be unrealistically low in their assessment of the value of a very rare coin, owners can be unrealistically high.

Truly rare Morgan dollars, like great works of art, are too few in number and their values are dependent on too few people to trade efficiently like commodities. When real value is most open to individual interpretation, buyers and sellers are farthest apart. That's why the industry's use of bids as the basis for the published value of very rare coins is misleading. Worth cannot be determined by efficient bidding in a market that precludes efficient bidding.

As for price levels and movements of rare Morgan dollars, the best advice is to ignore teletype quotes and weekly price guides entirely. Use auction prices realized and a wide range of professional opinions to estimate the worth of a rare Morgan dollar. As in the earlier days of the business, you'll have to do some interpolating.

The industry's embrace of sight-unseen trading has ushered in a new era in rare coin liquidity and price definition; and on balance, sight-unseen trading has been a positive. But sight-unseen bids constitute a lowest-common-denominator interpretation of value and are a poor indication of actual worth for truly rare coins.

Like famous homes or renown works of art, great coins don't lend themselves to commodity-oriented liquidity. When a special piece of property or an old master comes onto the market, the price it brings is a result of marketing, time allotted for inspection and appraisal, negotiation, amassing of capital, arrangement of financing, and other factors. If the potential buyer were required instead to make an immediate sight-unseen offer, that was indefinitely binding, under fixed terms, without financing, the offer would be much lower. Instant liquidity isn't free and it doesn't work for truly rare coins. Our industry pays a high price in market value to try to make it work.

How rarity influences acquisition and liquidity

Strictly speaking, a liquid asset is one that is readily convertible to cash. On that basis, all rare U.S. coins are liquid. But for practical purposes, a better definition of liquidity is convertibility to an *appropriate amount* of cash. Under this definition, a coin that can only be sold by offering it at 30% of its published market value is not considered liquid. To be liquid, a coin must be easily saleable at or very near its full market value.

Rule of thumb: Rare coin liquidity is inversely proportional to rarity.

Since common date Morgan dollars are plentiful, they are among the most liquid of all PCGS certified U.S. coins. High availability and tight buy/sell spreads make common date Morgan dollars easy to acquire. Printed price guides reflect the wholesale market for them accurately and depending on terms, quantity, general market conditions, and so forth, they can be purchased from any of hundreds of dealers for a few percent to twenty percent over bid levels. What common date Morgan dollars lack in scarcity, they make up for in ease of acquisition and liquidation.

To sell common date Morgans, an owner can call several dealers, compare their offers, all of which will be very close, and commit his coins over the telephone to the high buyer. This is not only the easiest way to liquidate common date Morgans, it's the smartest. Odds are, you wouldn't get any more and you might get less at a show, shop, or auction. Common date Morgans have a very narrow trading range, so you won't get significantly more money for them regardless of how you choose to sell them. You might as well commit them sight-unseen — that's the cheapest, easiest way to liquidate certified coins.

The better dates are a bit more elusive. If you're looking for a specific date or two, it can take weeks or even months to find the right coin — but they are out there. Expect to pay about 10% more relative to a price guide for better dates than for common dates. In other words, 15% to 30% over published bid levels. Remember, bids depict what dealers want to pay, not what they have to pay. Better date Morgans often cost dealers more than published levels, so they'll cost end buyers a premium too.

Better date Morgans are also highly liquid. Timing plays a major role in the acquisition or liquidation of better date Morgans. The best time to liquidate is when three or more bidders are competing for a date, and when the coin seems fully priced relative to its population, its price history, and current market parameters.

The best method of liquidation depends on the coin itself. If the coin is unattractive in any way, a telephone call to a few sight-unseen buyers will work best. If the coin is very high in grade or has unusual attributes — gorgeous rainbow color, pristine surfaces, etc. — it might be worthwhile to use one of the sight-*seen* methods of liquidation. You can consign the coin to an auction, walk it around at a show, or ship it to a dealer that specializes in premium quality coins for an offer upon inspection. Better date Morgans that bring the best prices are those that are so close to the next highest grade that a buyer thinks the coin has a possibility of being upgraded in a resubmission.

Rare date Morgans are hard to locate. Since very scarce dates are bid at unrealistically low prices on the trading systems, they are difficult to evaluate accurately. When they surface at major shows or auctions, they routinely bring giant premiums or multiples of their published values. It's difficult to know how much is too much to pay. Dealers hold out for top dollar on coins that they know will be irreplaceable so, assuming you can make a good estimation of value, your best chance to purchase at a favorable price is to make an offer. A firm offer will sometimes buy the coin. If not, at least it shows the dealer that you are serious about purchasing and the offer will make him more open to price negotiation.

Acquiring a rare date Morgan is a process that involves locating the coin, inspecting and evaluating it, feeling out the seller, negotiating a price and other terms, and possibly financing. The process can be cumbersome. Investing in the common of better dates is much easier. Regardless, if you are able to acquire a truly rare Morgan dollar at a fair price in a weak or normal market, the trouble is worth it because rare date Morgans have performed exceptionally well over time.

The best way to liquidate a rare Morgan is through a major auction. Since you likely had to outbid others to buy the coin, it will be advantageous for you to create similar competitive interest to sell the coin at a favorable price. You could offer the coin to a number of dealers, but unless you know a dealer that specializes in rare date Morgans, you're likely to get offers that are based in part on the prevailing sight-unseen bids. Unless the market is high, do not accept teletype-related offers for rare date Morgans. They are almost always worth more. After all, you couldn't acquire the coin at a teletype-related price; don't settle for it when you sell. Sight-unseen liquidation over the telephone is a convenient, efficient way to sell common dates and sometimes better dates, but rare date Morgans trade more like works of art than commodities.

Strange things can happen at a major auction. At worst, your rare Morgan won't bring your minimum and you'll pay a fee or percentage to buy it back. More often than not, it will sell. Occasionally, a great coin will bring an outrageous price. Buyers may think that the coin has a chance to upgrade, or two or more bidders might want it desperately for a collection. The right coin at the right time can realize literally two to ten times printed bid levels at a major sale.

Risks and rewards

Any investment has a risk/reward ratio. The risks and rewards of an investment in Morgan dollars are directly related to the scarcity of the pieces you choose to acquire.

Since common dates are plentiful, they may be insufficiently scarce to register the kind of appreciation possible in rarer issues. That is the rub against the common dates and it's a serious one. It may be the only one, however.

Common date Morgans are easy to acquire. Trading levels are well-defined; a few telephone calls to check dealer prices is all you need. They can not be easily promoted, so there is little risk of paying an inflated price for them. Since they enjoy broad demand, common date Morgans are easy to liquidate at full market value.

In addition, there is something to be said for investing in the least expensive samples of the most popular coin in numismatics — like buying the cheapest piece of real estate in a great location. Common date Morgan silver dollars are the right coins for investors that want basic, conservative holdings, don't plan to spend a lot of time delving deeper into numismatics, and don't mind forgoing some profit potential in exchange for commodity-style ease of liquidation. A buyer of silver or gold bullion coins making a foray into numismatic issues, for example, might start with MS-65 common date Morgan dollars.

For a novice, an investment in better date Morgans incurs more risk and more profit potential. For a buyer with a little background knowledge, however, the risks inherent in better date Morgans are no greater than those associated with common dates and the potential rewards are higher.

There are two chief risks in an investment in better date Morgans: volatility and population explosion. The better dates tend to rise more in up markets, and fall more in down markets, which means that an investor has to keep his eye on weekly and monthly price movements as well as long-term performance. "Volatility" has a negative connotation, but volatility creates both risk and opportunity. Risk because prices can fall quickly, opportunity because they can rise as fast. A buyer that is able to develop a perspective over time of what constitutes "cheap" and "expensive" for most of the middle-rare dates of the Morgan series can make volatility work for him.

The other risk is that a hoard of a one date is discovered. This happens rarely, but once in a while a number of gem rolls of a certain date are certified, thereby increasing its population and putting downward pressure on prices. Unless the supply of new coins is huge, however, the drop is usually temporary.

In addition to potent short-term opportunities in better date Morgans, there is the bigger, better reason to buy them: long term appreciation potential. As buyers of common date Morgans gravitate towards the better dates, demand will increase. The supply is limited, especially for Morgans graded MS-65 and higher. The total number of better date Morgan dollars graded MS-65 and higher — all dates combined — makes up only one percent of all uncirculated Morgan dollars.

For the same reasons, the rare dates have even greater potential to appreciate. There are literally millions of coin collectors, tens of thousands that concentrate on Morgan silver dollars. The ten rarest dates combined, in all uncirculated grades combined, make up less than two one-thousandths of all uncirculated Morgan dollars. Virtually every collector needs them. Investors want them because of the lopsided supply/demand ratio.

The risks of investing in rare date Morgans are like those associated with the better dates. Since rare dates have the lowest populations of all, transactions are few and teletype levels are unreliable, leaving values poorly defined. A deeper knowledge of numismatics, including price and population histories for individual dates, is required to invest in rare dates safely. Also, it will take perseverance to find and acquire key date Morgans.

But buyers who do the necessary background work, put in the time and effort required to locate the best dates, and who are willing to step out and pay the price, will ultimately reap the greatest rewards — not least of which is the pride of owning the rarest dates in the most popular series of them all, Morgan silver dollars.

Philip Schuyler graduated from Morrisville College in 1976. After his graduation, he founded Ellesmere Numismatics with his brother Paul Schuyler in 1978. The company they founded has prospered over the years and is now specializing in high quality PCGS and NGC certified coins. Mr. Schuyler is a member of many numismatic organizations and a contributor to numerous numismatic publications including Coin World, Numismatic News, COINage, and Coin Dealer Newsletter. He is the publisher of the well known tri-weekly numismatic newsletter, The Winning Edge.

***

James U. Blanchard, III

James U. Blanchard, III is the gold bug with the golden touch. In 1971, he invested $50 into a kitchen-table business. Fifteen years later, he sold the business — grown to a $100 million-a-year rare coin firm — to the third largest corporation in America.

In 1974, he organized the first National Committee for Monetary Reform conference. Now known as the Annual Blanchard Investment Conference, it ranks as the largest gathering of private investors on earth.

In the early 1970s, Jim successfully fought for the right of Americans to own gold, buzzing President Nixon's 1973 inauguration with a "Legalize Gold" banner towed behind a biplane, and publicly defying the U.S. Treasury to throw him into jail for possessing a two-ounce gold bar.

Through the years, he has managed to fly in a Soviet helicopter to the North Pole, cheat death on four continents, airlift tons of freedom literature behind the Iron and Bamboo curtains, help found the Industry Council for Tangible Assets, help reverse several U.S. laws on behalf of American investors, and write several books, including his autobiography, *Confessions of a Gold Bug*. He is also co-founder of the Blanchard Group of Funds, operated by Sheffield Management, Inc., with over $475 million under management.

Jim is now in private enterprise once again. His new company, Jefferson Financial, Inc., is diversified into many areas, including investment information publishing and the sale of high quality antique manuscripts and newspapers.

CHAPTER 45

Silver Dollars in the Rare Coin Market: Three Major Questions

by James U. Blanchard, III

Introduction

I'll end any suspense in the first sentence of this chapter: I THINK SILVER DOLLARS WILL BE ONE OF THE GREATEST INVESTMENTS OF THE 1990s. To illustrate why, I've organized the chapter into three major questions.

1. Hard Money Investors and Rare Coins: What's the Connection?
2. Will There Be Sufficient Growth in the Silver Dollar Retail Business to Cause an Increase in Silver Dollar Prices?
3. How Rare are U.S. Silver Dollars?

Question 1:

HARD MONEY INVESTORS AND RARE COINS: WHAT'S THE CONNECTION?

I'm often asked it there is a connection between gold and rare coins. Or the question is sometimes raised in another way: Are U.S. rare coin buyers hard money investors, or are they simply investors who understand the investment advantages in coins? Back in the 1950s and 1960s most U.S. rare coin buyers were collectors. There may have been a few maverick investors who bought U.S. rare coins solely because they were good investments, but for the most part the coin market was dominated by the local corner coin shop and a few large auction houses.

All that began to change dramatically in the late 1960s, when Lyndon Johnson took the silver out of United States coinage and savvy American investors suddenly began to save their silver coinage, creating hundreds of thousands of coin "investors."

I began to save my silver coinage in the mid-1960s. There was a local hangout where my college buddies and I enjoyed going for a few beers. Beer was only a quarter, but even when I had the proper change I always gave the bartender a dollar so I could receive three quarters in change.

In fact, it was partly this appetite for saving my silver change that led to my first investments in uncirculated U.S. silver dollars. I began reading *Coin World* and other coin publications, and eventually began buying common-date Morgan dollars and then better-date type coins, U.S. double eagles, etc.

As I continued to buy rare coins, I was going through a self-education process which led me to an understanding of the inherent disadvantages of government managed fiat currency systems versus a currency system based on gold.

It was during those days of research that I read one of the most memorable quotes concerning paper money by my favorite economist, Ludwig Von Mises: "Government is the only agency that can take a useful commodity like paper, slap some ink on it and make it totally worthless."

The Hard Money Movement Gains Momentum

Apparently, there were a lot of other investors who agreed with Von Mises, because in 1968 both gold and silver entered their first modern bull markets. The price of gold increased form $35 to $42, and the price of silver rose from $1.29 to $2.54. As the metals gained momentum, so, too, did the modern hard money movement in the United States. The movement was started by several thousand loosely organized individuals who correctly predicted that the major trend of the 20th century would be a depreciating dollar and increasing precious metals and hard assets prices.

Because gold bullion was illegal, most of these investors limited their hard money investing to precious metals mining shares. But a small number of the early hard money investors who wanted the real metal bought U.S. gold Double Eagles. (At that time, double eagles were selling for about $45, and the price of gold was set at $35.)

The next gold bull market began in the early 1970s and peaked at just under $200 an ounce when gold was legalized on December 31, 1974. Even though gold bullion entered a bear market until September 1976, hard money investors were encouraged by the increased availability of legal bullion, and hard money investors, who previously had invested solely in gold mining shares, were now investing heavily in gold bullion coins, such as the Krugerrand and the Maple Leaf.

The most popular gold bullion investment coin was the Krugerrand. Although the first Krugerrand was minted in 1967 with a relatively small mintage of only 50,000, by the time production of the Krugerrand was discontinued in 1988, a total of 40 million one-ounce Krugerrands had been produced.

But a funny thing was beginning to happen to many of these hard money investors: Slowly, a small percentage began to experiment in buying non-bullion coins, or what I have always referred to as semi-numismatic coins, such as common-date Morgan silver dollars and common-date U.S. gold double eagles.

The far-sighted investors who bought such coins in the mid-1970s enjoyed enormous profits. Many of these coins increased twenty times in value by the time the bullion and rare coin markets peaked on January 21, and April 16, 1980, respectively.

Coin Market Changes for the Better

Another dramatic metamorphosis occurred in the rare coin market during the 1970s. The U.S. rare coin had previously been dominated by collectors who frequented local coin shops and a few large auction firms (such as Stack's in New York). But as the hard money coin buyers entered the market, several national coin companies were founded entirely to serve this new breed of coin investor. Companies like Investment Rarities and James U. Blanchard and Company began to introduce innovative marketing strategies that helped bring tens of thousands of new rare coin investors into the market. These companies began mass-marketing rare coins via direct response and direct mail advertising to hard money mailing lists.

Clients were educated about the benefits of investing in rare coins through well researched educational and polished promotional materials, and by coin brokers via toll-free telephone. In many ways, these large national coin companies were the rare coin market's equivalent of a stock brokerage firm.

The market had indeed changed for the better. In the past, local coin shops serviced perhaps several thousand clients, of which only several hundred were active buyers. But these new national direct mail and telemarketing coin firms communicated to millions of potential clients every year, generating increased demand never before witnessed in the rare coin market. By the 1980s, these firms had sold rare coins to several hundred thousand investors who had not even heard of rare coins as an investment ten years earlier.

But has this influx of new coin buyers really changed the focus of the rare coin market? In other words, is the rare coin market dominated by the collector or by the investor? In my opinion the answer is clear: The rare coin market is now dominated by the investor (of course, some investors become collectors as well), and this will increasingly be the case.

After twenty years in the business, I am convinced that the vast majority of investors in rare coins today are hard money investors. That is to say, these investors have more faith in assets such as gold and rare coins than in the traditional equity markets comprised of stocks and bonds.

Profile of the Hard Money Population

One should not underestimate the staggering numbers and monetary muscle of the so-called hard money investment community. There are several resources available for estimating the number of so-called hard money investors.

One of the best ways is to add up the number of subscribers to hard money oriented newsletters. Doing so provides a figure of approximately 500,000 unique names. Of course, even this figure doesn't tell the whole truth because it represents only the wealthiest investors — those who choose to subscribe to the generally high priced, hard money newsletters (some of which sell for several hundred dollars per year).

It is estimated that the average net worth of hard money newsletter subscribers is $500,000, meaning the total investment potential of hard money investors is approximately $250 billion. And this is probably understating the case because there are a lot of extremely wealthy, multi-millionaire hard money investors.

Another figure comes from the World Gold Council which estimates that as many as 12.5 million Americans have purchased gold coins (primarily gold bullion coins).

One can also get a broad picture of the growing interest in hard money investments by counting the number of new gold mutual funds. It is interesting to note that in the early 1970s only two gold mutual funds existed. Today, over 30 gold mutual funds exist, with a combined equity of over $14 billion. Further, it is estimated that the combined equity of individually owned (non-institutional, non-mutual fund) gold mining shares in North America is almost $100 billion.

Almost by definition, the owners of these equities are hard money investors. It is my contention that it is these investors who offer the most fertile ground for being the newest source of U.S. rare coin buying in the years ahead. After all, it is estimated that private Americans already own approximately 250 million ounces of gold, mostly in the form of gold bullion coins, but also in the form of ingots, bars, etc. At $370 an ounce, that's $92.5 billion in value!

So in all, the two most popular investment holdings of hard money investors — gold mining shares, gold bullion and bullion coins — have at least $200 billion in equity.

Ironically, even considering the huge amounts of capital dedicated to gold and gold shares, most hard money investors have a much larger proportion of their total investment assets in cash instruments (money market funds, T-bills, etc.) than in gold mining shares or bullion. The consensus among hard money financial analysts is that hard money investors are waiting on the sidelines to see which way the economy goes — inflation or deflation. Once gold breaks out of the $450 level, these analysts expect huge amounts of new money to enter the gold equity and gold bullion markets.

These circumstances look very promising for the future of rare coin prices. If hard money investors were to invest only 10% of their current equity in bullion, bullion coins and mining shares, approximately $20 billion would be infused into the relatively thin rare coin market.

In such a market, it would not be unreasonable for a $20 Saint Gaudens double eagle in MS-61 condition to sell for $2,500, or for a Morgan silver dollar in MS-64 condition to sell for $600, or higher.

After twenty years in the coin business, I've come to know many other coin dealers, and I can tell you this: I've rarely met a coin dealer who wasn't basically a hard money man. If you read the newsletters and promotional materials produced by the prominent coin dealers, with few exceptions, they are extremely hard money oriented.

Obviously, all of this argues well for my proposition that today's coin market is dominated by the investor, and more precisely the hard money investor. In the future, I think this will be even more the case.

Assuming my premise is correct, what events have brought about the metamorphosis?

First and foremost, I think it is obvious that rare coins are hard assets. They are the opposite of paper investments. Hard money investors apparently understand that stocks depend on the economy, which looks shaky as we enter the 1990s, and even government T-bills and bonds depend on the value of the dollar, which, of course, depends on the integrity of the money managers.

As we enter the shaky 1990s, it is likely that we will experience a prolonged bear market in the dollar, and that the huge bull market in the U.S. stock market of the 1980s will likely turn into a bear market. Hard assets of all types should benefit from this change in market climate.

Also, inflation is now triple what it was just three years ago, and even though official government figures claim 1989 inflation was only 5%, real inflation is probably more like 7%. If you have your money in a money market fund earning 8%, after paying taxes and accounting for loss through inflation, you are really not making any money.

The hard money investors are also concerned about (1) the possibility of our major economic problems eventually causing a depression and (2) how rare coins would perform in a depression. As Paul M. Green pointed out in "Coin Market Performance During Hard Times," (Blanchard's American Rarities, Winter 1990) coins actually increased in value during the Great Depression, while most other assets lost approximately 80% of their worth between 1929 and 1936.

For example, during the 1920s and 1930s, one of the largest coin dealers was B. Max Mehl. A recent study shows that 30 coins he auctioned in 1929 had increased 48% in value by 1936, while most Americans lost an average of 80% in other assets. Because hard money investors fear not only inflation, but also the possibility of a depression, coins provide the perfect double play insurance against either economic calamity.

There are other contributing reasons to explain hard asset investors' love for rare coins. Even though the precious metal content of a $5,000 rare coin has little to do with its market price, who can argue that the precious metal in a rare coin is not at least psychologically attractive to hard money investors.

Also, there are some gold-oriented hard money investors who fear that the U.S. government may once again confiscate privately owned gold, as Roosevelt did in 1934. To protect themselves, many hard money investors have taken advantage of a provision in the law: The 1934 Gold Reserve Act, which authorizes the president to confiscate gold at any time, specifically excludes rare numismatic coins from confiscation powers.

In conclusion, while it may not initially appear logical, there is definitely a close connection between gold and rare U.S. coins. In fact, it appears that gold and rare coins move together, especially during a bull market.

In fact, during a future gold bull market, rare coins are likely to outperform gold as they did in the 1976-1980 gold market. If I am correct in predicting a massive new bull market for gold during the 1990s, all indications suggest rare coins should do even better.

Question 2:

WILL THERE BE SUFFICIENT GROWTH IN THE SILVER DOLLAR RETAIL BUSINESS TO CAUSE AN INCREASE IN SILVER DOLLAR PRICES?

If you are looking for a healthy U.S. silver dollar market (and of course this applies to any other U.S. rare coins as well) and if the market is dominated 90% by wholesalers making a few dollars on trading between each other and a few retail clients, and 10% organized retail coin companies and brokerage firms, then the answer is we are not going to have consistently increasing silver dollar prices in the 1990s.

The bottom line is there is an absolute need for the retailer, whether it's a nationally respected telemarketing firm specializing in rare coins and silver dollars, and acting much like a traditional stock and bond broker, or whether it is the new entry of Wall Street and regional brokerage firms.

Obviously it is essential to have both a healthy wholesale and retail market. The wholesaler provides several valuable functions including accumulating and storing inventory for the retailer, market making, etc. But, it is the retailer who provides the critical function of selling coins to the retail coin customers who may be collectors or investors, or who may be both. Unless we have a growing number of retail customers, both collectors and investors, we are obviously not looking at healthy growth in the coin industry. It will be a continual boom and bust cycle dominated by the wholesalers.

Am I optimistic in the growth of the American retail coin business? The answer is ultimately yes. In the short term, there may be problems. For example, with Murphy's Law, everyone in 1989/1990 expected that the major Wall Street brokerage firms would cause almost an immediate huge boom in the coin market: it simply didn't happen. There's another important point to keep in mind about the large Wall Street brokerage firms. The existence of several large coin funds is not going to create a healthy long term environment for silver dollars and other rare coins. Ultimately, and I believe this will happen, the major Wall Street brokerage firms as well as dozens of regional brokerage firms will actually have their thousands of brokers selling individual coins. . .and this is great news for silver dollars. Many coin dealers have become negative on generic U.S. silver dollars and generic U.S. gold. But, it is just these coins that are available in fairly large quantity, that the major Wall Street and regional brokerage firms are going to first get their clients into. Also, this is where they can create the most liquid market. Ask yourself this question: Is it easier for a relatively numismatically uneducated stock and bond broker to sell 10 different MS-65 Morgan Dollars or to sell a $25,000 Barber Quarter?

The Importance of the Large Specialist Retail Coin Dealers

Some coin commentators have suggested that as the large Wall Street firms and regional securities firms enter the coin market, small and large U.S. coin retailers will become obsolete. This is absolutely not the case!

There is a vital role to play for the specialist in U.S. coin retailing (as opposed to the traditional equity brokers). It is these retailers, both large and small, who must provide the ongoing in-depth education about U.S. silver dollars and other rare coins, in order to develop an underlying base of hundreds of thousands of serious collector-investors or investor-collectors. It is these retailers who will have the most knowledgeable specialist coin brokers and the marketing departments to produce highly specialized silver dollar and other rare coin educational and sales literature. And finally it is extremely important for the major coin wholesalers to realize that it is to the wholesaler's benefit to support extremely expensive retailing operations because developing new clients means growth in the industry. This undoubtedly will involve help in marketing dollars for the retailer as well as providing other informational and trading services.

Question 3:

HOW RARE ARE U.S. SILVER DOLLARS?

In the period 1988 to 1989, I was astonished at how fickle many coin dealers became on the issue of whether generic U.S. silver dollars and generic U.S. gold are good investments. At one time, almost everyone unanimously agreed that generic U.S. silver dollars and generic U.S. gold were super investments for many reasons. Big money would be entering the gold market, the coin market would be growing, major Wall Street money would be entering the market, regional brokerage firms would be entering the market, coin funds would cause further public interest, etc. All this meant higher generic prices. Then when the generic markets for various reasons had a major cyclical correction, these same dealers dropped the generic market, or any favorable mention of the generic market, like a hot potato. It is my contention that generic silver dollars and other generic coins such as double eagles will be superb investments for the 1990s, and it is not because the major brokerage firms will have little to choose from except U.S. generic silver dollars and U.S. generic gold. The fact is that both of these categories are much rarer than most dealers, collectors and investors realize. For example, as of mid-September of 1990, there were approximately 100,000 third-party certified MS-65 Morgan dollars. At that time, the bid on these coins was approximately $140 per coin (by the way, a price which I think is an incredible bargain). The bottom line is the total value at $140 bid for the 100,000 MS-65 Morgans as of mid-September, 1990 was a pitifully small $14 million. Compare this to the hundreds of billions of dollars that trade daily on world equity markets and the trillions of dollars that are traded on the foreign exchange markets. With the growth of the American retail coin business, I believe generic U.S. silver dollars, both Morgan and Peace, will be the major means of introducing new investors to rare coins.

Upon superficial analysis, it seems that United States silver dollars, typically of the Peace and Morgan type, are anything but rare. Over nine hundred million Morgan and Peace dollars were minted between the years 1878 and 1935, yet as the records clearly show, the government officially melted approximately half of the total mintage of all Morgan and Peace silver dollars, and in subsequent years many more millions of silver dollars were melted.

Most other silver dollars remain today in circulated (non-investment) condition.

According to the National Silver Dollar Roundtable Journal (Volume 2, Number 1, November, 1984) in the article entitled "Total Uncirculated Silver Dollars Remaining," by Leroy Van Allen, the quantity of remaining uncirculated condition silver dollars is dramatically lower than most people believe. Van Allen estimated that 40-50 million pre-1921 Morgans and 30-40 million Peace dollars exist today in uncirculated condition. And, of course, the vast majority of these silver dollars exist in common date lower grade MS-60/MS-61 condition. The higher quality MS-63, MS-64, MS-65, MS-66 and MS-67 coins are only a tiny minority of this total. Of course, the easiest way to estimate the exact number of the higher grade MS-63 and over Morgan and Peace silver dollars that exist is to check the population reports. Yes, the population of these coins will grow as the prices rise in the future and more coins are submitted for third-party grading, but even if the number of MS-65's approached several hundred thousand, that would still be small in comparison to the total amount of investment capital available for this type of material.

What About Liberty Seated and Trade Dollars?

I am convinced that the uncirculated Morgan silver dollars down even to the lowest uncirculated grade of MS-60, will be the mainstay of a rejuvenation of the investor and collector market in U.S. silver dollars. Young collectors can start Morgan date sets in MS-60, MS-61, and MS-62 grades and investors can concentrate on the higher grade and better date MS-63, MS-64, MS-65, and MS-66 and higher grades, and those investors with even deeper pockets can go for the early silver dollars minted from 1794-1804 and Liberty Seated dollars minted from 1840-1873, as well as Trade dollars minted from 1873-1885. Liberty Seated and Trade dollars are incredibly rare compared to Morgan and Peace dollars by any comparison. For example, there were only 42.2 million Liberty Seated dollars minted while a total of only 35.9 million Trade Dollars were minted. This compares to over nine hundred million Peace and Morgan silver dollars. Of course, the vast majority of Liberty Seated dollars and Trade Dollars were melted. This is especially true of Trade Dollars where, of the total minted of 35.9 million, 27 million were exported, most ending up in the melting pot.

By the way, my favorite U.S. silver dollar is the Liberty Seated dollar. They are incredibly scarce in uncirculated condition. Of the original mintage of 42.2 million Liberty Seated dollars, in mid-August 1990 PCGS reported that only 599 no motto mint-state Liberty Seated dollars existed in uncirculated condition, and only 188 motto mint-state Liberty Seated dollars. What this means is that in Liberty Seated material, even MS-60 coins are super rare! (See the related chapter on the Liberty Seated Dollars by John Dannreuther.)

The bottom line is as we enter the 1990s and hundreds of thousands of new investors and collectors enter the market, the first coins they will be able to afford is U.S. silver dollars from generics to early U.S. silver dollars: Price gains should be extraordinary!

***

The Fabulous Norweb-Farouk 1885 Trade Dollar

One of Five Known Specimens

1848 **1885 Proof-60 to 63.** An attractive sharply struck example with nearly all details strongly defined. The fully lustrous devices beautifully complement the reflective fields. The obverse is brilliant with splashes of amber and gray toning. The reverse has a suggestion of golden brown around the letters and the central device. This example would deserve the Proof-65 classification if not for the presence of light hairlines.

Truly a great rarity, the 1885 trade dollar is one of the most highly prized issues in American numismatics. It terms of rarity, it is about three times rarer than the 1804 silver dollar and is even rarer than the 1787 Brasher doubloon.

Below is an list of examples of the 1885 trade dollar updating Walter Breen's census. The presently offered specimen is enumerated first.

1) The Norweb coin. From Sotheby's sale of the King Farouk Collection, February 1954, Lot 1680. Said by Breen to have been in the Atwater Collection.

2) The Menjou-Baldenhofer-NERCG coin.

3) The Green-Johnson-Roe-Amon Carter coin. Recently in Stack's sale of the Amon Carter Jr. Collection, January 1984, Lot 441, to Kevin Lipton, and subsequently in Superior's section of Auction '84, Lot 192.

4) The Clapp-Eliasberg coin.

5) The Olsen-Ewalt-Young coin. In RARCOA's section of the Auction '80 sale, Lot 1626, and subsequently in the same firm's section of Auction '84, Lot 1810.

This great rarity stands as one of the most important American coins to cross the auction block in recent times, and as one of the foremost highlights of the Norweb Collection. It has been off the market since 1954, 34 years ago. Once sold, it may be another generation until it once again appears.

1885 Proof trade dollar, Lot 1848, Proof, sold by Auctions by Bowers and Merena, Inc. as part of the Ambassador and Mrs. R. Henry Norweb Collection, March 1988. $121,000.

Auctions by Bowers and Merena, Inc., "America's Leading Rare Coin Auctioneer," Box 1224, Wolfeboro, NH 03894. Toll-free 800-222-5993.

Maurice H. Rosen, NLG

Maurice Rosen is President of Numismatic Counseling, Inc., a Plainview, New York rare coin firm specializing in the assembling of investment portfolios for clients. Since 1976, he has been the editor of The ROSEN NUMISMATIC ADVISORY, which provides in-depth analysis and commentary. The RNA is a multiple winner of the "Best Newsletter of the Year Award" from the prestigious Numismatic Literary Guild. Mr. Rosen is frequently quoted in numismatic and investment periodicals and a popular speaker at investment conferences, trade shows and seminars.

Mr. Rosen's strong pro-consumer advocacy stance has earned him considerable respect. Some of his controversial writings include: An article in the September, 1981 Monthly Summary of the CDN titled, "The 1980/81 Grading Renaissance;" his 1982 RNA report exposing the weaknesses of ANACS grading; and his widely reprinted 1984 RNA report on the Fallacy of Rare Coin Historical Price Performance Data. Such reports have firmly established him as an outspoken analyst/critic who pulls no punches.

From 1987 through 1990, Mr. Rosen had been a regular, part-time grader at Numismatic Guaranty Corporation of America (NGC). His grading abilities and market expertise have been sought by various financial institutions and courts. He was a contributor to the ANA Grading Standards of U.S. Coins, was a founding officer in the Liberty Seated Collectors Club, and holds memberships in several collector organizations. His firm is an authorized PCGS dealer and is a Charter Member of NGC.

Mr. Rosen completed credits leading to a M.B.A. degree in Finance and Investments (1970) at The Baruch School of The City College of C.U.N.Y., and worked as a securities analyst before becoming a full-time numismatic professional in 1968.

CHAPTER 46

Numismatic Newsletters

by Maurice H.Rosen, NLG
President of Numismatic Counseling, Inc.,
Editor of *The Rosen Numismatic Advisory*

Our fascination with the future is as old as mankind itself. We've always looked to the stars and the gods, to prophets, seers and soothsayers, to help explain to us the mysteries of the past and to enthrall us with the marvels and wonders of the future.

We have, figuratively, crouched in awe at the feet of people who, due to some special supernatural talents (perhaps the blessings of "touching" of the gods), seemingly hold the key to unlocking secrets of the future, such that if only but a few drops of those persons' overflowing rivers of wisdom could fall on us we'd be blessed with untold riches beyond our dreams.

Such claimed (and imagined) abilities to see in the future were adopted by many people for different purposes: power, privilege, prestige, amusement, counsel and gain, to name a few motivations. For the most part, however, such predictors were often clever practitioners of being obscure, such that they could fudge their errors without losing much of their mystical auras. Still, despite their frequent predictive lapses, we always came back for more. After all, someone for sure must "know" the future!

As the modern world took shape, and people strove to better their lot by means of financial endeavor, such sages assumed various cloaks. One of them has been the publishing of investment newsletters (or advisory letters), in our case those concerned with the reporting of developments and opportunities in the numismatic marketplace.

I will attempt here to present you with virtually "all you ever wanted to know" about numismatic newsletters. I aim not to merely give you some helpful do's and don'ts, advantages and disadvantages, and so on, but to probe beneath the surface to isolate and discuss the essence behind what motivates people to write - and people to read - newsletters. In the end, I hope you will view newsletters in a different light as the best and worst of what they have to offer is illuminated here for you.

I must admit to you that I am a "newsletter junkie." That's probably due to a combination of things: (1) my financial and investment training; (2) my fondness to collect and save things; (3) my love to analyze and research; and, (4) since 1968, my own career as a newsletter writer (*FCI Advisory Letter*, 1968-75; *The Rosen Numismatic Advisory*, 1976-current; *Maurice Rosen's Rare Coin Confidential*, 1987-88). To give you some idea as to the length of time I have been affected by this passion, I have several file cabinets filled with financial and numismatic newsletters, some dating back to the 1950s. Yellowing with antiquity, these chronicles of the past offer me a ready source of research and fond memories.

If I need to check on what *The Forecaster* said about BU Morgan $1 rolls in 1974, no problem. You want to know what Dave Bowers predicted in 1963 in his *Empire Investors Report* for the 1950 proof set? I've got it! Have an urge to know what Les Fox in 1984 wrote about ANACS in his *The Fortune-Teller*? Be back to you in a couple of minutes. Want to check up on the recommendations of David Hall, Mike De Falco, Bruce Amspacher, James Blanchard or Ray Mercer? I'm your one-man research center!

If you have the impression that I am about to deride and ridicule my newsletter fraternity for promising far more than it has delivered - you're partially right! I'll do that because they deserve to be knocked down a peg or two, and you need to know their weaknesses and failures so you can make informed and reasoned decisions. But, I will also here praise and honor some of them for standing tall among their peers, for providing their readers with far more value than the subscription fees they paid, that value being the wisdom, insight and confidence allowing readers to take positive financial steps.

Types of Numismatic Newsletters

In my files I have over 50 titles of numismatic newsletters. They can be broadly placed into one of three categories: Objective, Promotional and In-Betweeners. These categories signify the *raison d'etre* (reason for being) of any particular newsletter. It doesn't necessarily pertain to the competency or sincerity of their advice; rather, it cubbyholes them according to their purpose.

Objective (or nearly so) - Typically written by a person or firm trying their best to present an accurate analysis of the market and to make worthy recommendations. There is very little or no self-promotion, few if any accompanied "inserts" of coin offerings, few pleas for your business or advertisements of any kind. Their purpose is to largely sell you advice, to provide you with knowledge and insight that you could not otherwise obtain via more rudimentary means. *Objective* newsletters comprise about 25% of the newsletter universe.

Promotional - The overriding purpose of these newsletters is to sell coins to you. Some of the more clever ones do it by dressing their copy in a cloak of sophistication and authority. Others are more circus-like; they sound the drums and the trumpets to razzle-dazzle you with hard-sell and colorful copy. Few subscribers actually pay for these newsletters; they get them free as clients or prospects of the firm. They are more kindly referred to as house organs.

As you would expect, they are almost always bullish, full of great "Buying Opportunities," exude a highly-charged exuberant outlook for the market and their recommendations. Coverage of the market is usually light and sophomoric, with little analytical depth, perhaps for fear of educating their readers. Sometimes it is written by an outside source. Often there is a distinct, formularized style of hype and exaggeration. It is almost always accompanied by a parcel of "insert" offerings. *Promotional* newsletters comprise about 25% of the universe.

In-Betweeners - These are simply, all the rest - with varied weights of objectivity and promotion. They are typically written by a person or firm wearing two hats: publisher and dealer who must come to terms with their own level of bias and conscience.

Since the business of selling subscriptions to coin investment advisories has not proven to be very profitable, it is the actual coin business which results as an extension that provides the bulk of income to the publisher. The *In-Betweeners* have been about 50% of the newsletter universe.

Why Do People Write - and Other People Read - Newsletters?

Basically, coin advisories are written as an adjunct to a dealer's business of buying and selling coins. Dealers either do the writing themselves or hire someone. I've found that the better, more responsible dealers publish the more credible newsletters, that is; light on hype and heavy on useful advice.

Over the years, newsletters have generally gained a heightened stature of respect and appreciation. Whether that's because people have become used to reading newsletters in other fields (stocks, economic, health-related, etc.) or because some people attach great weight to the printed word - I don't know for sure. So, this "ego fulfillment" may account for some newsletters to be written. Too, the launching of a newsletter is often a good way for a budding dealer to acquire a following and a list of clients.

What about the readers, why do they subscribe to coin newsletters? For sure, there's the "search for the Grail" urging I suggested earlier. But, there's also the natural curiosity and need for intelligent people to expand their understanding, to become privy to so-called restricted or confidential information made available only via the relatively expensive means of a two to twelve page newsletter.

Such readers realize that one good idea is worth the few dollars per issue cost, especially when they have thousands at stake in their investments. It's been the growth of this type of reader in the 1980s that has prompted newsletters to mature and respond to the call for improved analytical substance and responsible research. The occasional slipshod days of the past are over. You readers won't tolerate it. It can be instructive to read of the evolution of the species. Accompany me now as I take you down newsletter memory lane.

Evolution of Numismatic Newsletters

Era I: The Rollicking BU Roll Years

In general, financial newsletters did not make much of an appearance until the 1950s, about the same time that coin market advisories debuted. Since the trading of BU rolls and proof sets of modern coinage (cents through halves, dated 1934-up) was where the action was during those years, a number of publications came forth promoting and romanticizing the riches made and to be made by investing in such coins.

To be sure, such boisterous exploitation of our long-thought pastoral hobby was looked down upon by the more traditional rare coin dealers of the time. For these dealers, age and rarity dated to the 18th and 17th centuries and earlier, not to the 1930s and 1940s! Even wet-behind-the-ears Maurice Rosen at the time saw more merit chasing down a few BU rolls of 1950-P Jefferson Nickels at $80 each, rather than buying a few Gem Proof Trade Dollars for the same $80.

The wisdom of the purists - and the foolishness of the naive - proved out as the BU roll madness crashed after mid-1964, never to come back with nearly as much fervor or respect. That the 1950-P 5-cent rolls are now $26 and Gem Proof Trade Dollars are $4,000 and up (allowing them to conservatively qualify as today's Proof-64), clearly dramatizes the error of my old ways and the evolving, volatile nature of our marketplace.

Perhaps the granddaddy of the genre is George W. Haylings who, as early as 1947 in his book, *Hidden Dollars*, and later in his 1964 "Waterloo" book, *The Profit March of Your Coin Investment, 1935-1971*, probably did as much to publicize coin investing early on as anyone else. Later in 1968 he would return with the publication of *Coin Investing Communique*.

Other notable, long-running newsletters include: *The International Coin Investor*, by Frank S. Arko, from 1954 to the 1970s; and *The Forecaster*, since 1962, of which I'll have more to say soon. Recognition must also go to Harry J. Forman for his 1971 book, *How You Can Make Big Profits Investing In Coins*, followed in 1974 by *How You Can Keep On Making Big Profits Investing In Coins*, for being one of the industry's distinguished prophet of profits.

Curiously, at the same time the BU roll fad was at its strongest, a rare coin/modern coin combination newsletter was born in 1963, *The Empire Investors Report*. Published by Empire Coin Co., Inc. (later Windsor Research Publications, Inc.), the writer should be known by most readers of this book, Q. David Bowers. The last issue I have is December, 1965. I lost interest as their coverage of the BU roll market disappeared and they devoted much space to foreign coins. Thus, one of the most prolific numismatic writers of all time includes among his many credits one of the first numismatic investment newsletters!

The Forecaster: After a quarter century of writing *The Forecaster*, editor John V. Kamin is still going strong. First published by Bill "Mr. I. Predict" Willoughby Coin Exchange until November, 1967, and thereafter by Kamin, we might ask "What accounts for its amazing durability?" Apparently, it has been Kamin's ability to identify a niche in the marketplace and successfully provide it with a "Strategy for Profit," as its masthead states.

In these old days of coin advisories (1960s and 1970s), *The Forecaster* was a force, clearly among the leaders in the field providing advice to its swelling legion of mostly hard-money principled investors. In fact, for me it was required reading such was its immediacy and impact. Early on it was published 48 times a year, then 44, now 40. Over its near three decade history, that's an amazing 1,200 issues (exceeded only by *The Coin Dealer Newsletter*).

What distinguished *The Forecaster* from most others was its continuous accent on economic advice and philosophy. For many budding numismatic enthusiasts, I suspect *The Forecaster* was their first introduction to economic theory and principles and how they applied to the marketplace. I was a high school student when it began and looked forward to Kamin's articles on contrary opinion, real estate investment strategies, negotiation tactics, consumer tips and tax tips and monetary theories. Such advice is still offered by Kamin, augmenting his coverage of the bullion and numismatic markets. The advice tends to be of the meat-and-potatoes variety, with a distinct, pro-entrepreneurial flair.

During, and somewhat after, these hectic years for the BU roll and proof set markets, items recommended in *The Forecaster* were almost certain to be demanded by many subscribers, thus driving up the price. For sure, such impact wore thin as over the years those markets lost interest and money for their owners. Still, *The Forecaster* has continued to follow them, as well as MS60-63 grade Morgan and Peace dollars, commemoratives and type coins.

Perhaps it has been *The Forecaster's* general avoidance of recommending higher quality coins that has earned it a loyal following. Kamin has been skeptical of paying big premiums for high quality coins, preferring to accentuate low-mintage, key-date issues. In fact, to this day whenever my attention is focused on certain coins I recall *The Forecaster's* fondness for them (1955-P 10 cent, 1955-D 25 cent, 1881-CC / 85-CC / 88-O / 01-O and 03-O Morgan dollars, among others).

Perhaps the Theory of Contrary Opinion which Kamin extols will one day turn the long sleeping BU roll market into a roaring bull again. Should that happen, I'll be ready with my files of old *Forecasters*!

How a Trashcan Gave Birth to the Coin Dealer Newsletter!

Yet another member of the Quarter Century Club is none other than *The Coin Dealer Newsletter* itself. As unusual as it seems, you can say the CDN was born in a trashcan! First published on June 12, 1963, the CDN was a "natural," yet early controversial outgrowth of the first teletype coin exchange, the American Numismatic Exchange (ANE - do these initials sound familiar?) out of Houston, Texas. The following information comes from the *1965 Coin Investors Manual*, by Payne Publishing Co., Inc.

Before the days of the teletype, and later on for those dealers who did not have access to it, the flow of pricing information was slow, relating more to the publication schedules of the coin papers and magazines. Within a matter of months, the two faces of the coin market became readily apparent. Dealers without teletype facilities grew aware of their handicap and some made arrangements with those who did to monitor trading. Others couldn't make those arrangements and were at a competitive disadvantage.

The need for up-to-date pricing information was filled on June 12, 1963 with the initial issue of the CDN. However, not everyone was pleased. By balancing the inequity which existed between informed and uninformed dealers, the CDN had eliminated a portion of the profit edge which informed dealers had been enjoying. Some teletype dealers argued that the CDN was infringing in their business, was publishing confidential information, and that it must cease publication. Pressure was applied to the Exchange to cut off the information sources of the CDN, and they did.

The CDN negotiated secretly with three teletype dealers to secure tapes and continued to publish. Necessary steps were taken to preserve these information sources. A trashcan served as one drop point, a bowling alley locker as another. Towards the end of 1963, this pressure dwindled and finally ceased.

Mention must be made of Allen Harriman, initially the Associate Editor of the CDN under Orvil L. Payne, later Editor from October 1964 to June 1984, when Dennis R. Baker became Editor and Harriman became Consulting Editor until he passed away on May 1, 1985. It was Harriman's devotion to the CDN and his integrity to its responsibilities which contributed so strongly to make it first and foremost in the field. It would not be an over-statement to say that the very existence of the CDN was a major cause of the coin market's growth.

From October 1966 to August 1969, the CDN included within its pages frequent excellent research reports on various coinage series and additional market commentary. From some reason, these well-written and timely analyses ceased to be part of the CDN. However, seven years later, one of the finest of all newsletters was launched.

In August 1976, the CDN Monthly Summary was born. The "Summary" reported more in-depth coverage than the weekly CDN, providing quotes for all dates in various 20th and 19th century series. Importantly, the first two pages were often devoted to highly specialized market commentary or coin analysis by an array of guest contributors. What sets apart the Summary in this regard has been its ability to attract always pertinent and important articles that otherwise likely would not have been published. They included some excellent research and date-by-date studies for many series, including:

Morgan Dollars (David Hall, Bruce Amspacher);
Gold Coins (William Mitkoff, Les Fox, John Dannreuther, Gordon Wrubel and Q. David Bowers);
Barber Coins (Gene Edwards);
MS Grading Systems: Type Coins & Silver Dollars (John Highfill).

The Summary would also occasionally serve as a sounding board of important and sometimes controversial subjects, including: Grading Changes, Coin Preservation, "Wonder" Coins and Third-Party Grading.

Were it not for the immense distribution of the Summary, it is doubtful if the broad investing public would otherwise ever be so highly and stimulatingly informed by what these contributors had to say.

The Man Who Called the BU Roll Bust

Ever dream of making a one and only magical appearance at bat during your baseball team's desperate ninth inning attempt to overcome the awesome pressure of being down three runs and win the ball game? "Who was that masked man," is what some in the crowd would euphorically cry as you modestly mount your stallion and ride into oblivion leaving the perfect record: one time at bat, grand-slam home run!

No newsletter I ever read can claim that record, but one special report which comes close was "Coin Market Crash Coming, An Interpretive Analysis" by Alexander Hamil. It was released during early 1964 - until then the dawning of the hobby's most frantic and hectic bull market of its history.

For sure there were doubters and scoffers at the time, some who wrote passionately to the coin periodicals with diatribes attacking the "BU roll boys for taking over and ruining the hobby." But no one else I know of took to their typewriter and banged out a newsletter (one-shot or otherwise), which in a stark, uncharacteristically analytical and persuasive manner for the times pulverized the rollmeisters with a giant bat of logic and reality. I have yet to see anyone so wield a literary bat. Here is an excerpt, typical of the Report:

"Let us listen for a moment to the voice of the optimist and try to discover his philosophy. The Articulate voice is that of the coin dealer . . . and investment advisor. He bears little resemblance to the bespectacled numismatic clerk of yesterday. While his business future depends upon a continuing active market, we will not question his motive but accept his advice as sincere. He promises. He entices by painting a picture of an ever-expanding market. This he justifies by pointing to recent growth in interest and recent past history of value increases. He happily tells you of the huge fortunes missed by yesterday's overcautious. He insists that while large sum investments are best there is still room for the little man who can surely afford one roll of 1958-P nickels BU for only $36, which having already come from $2 to $36 in just five years must inevitably continue to rise despite its mintage of almost 18 million pieces. This reveals an economic outlook strikingly akin to that of the John Jay unlimited expansion days of American capital. Drawing on a seemingly unlimited public domain of new, interested purchasers the market is in its infancy."

Who, indeed, is — or was — Alexander Hamil? And, where was he when we needed him after 1964?! I've not been able to find a trace of him. Such was his swift and unpretentious departure from the pre-crash days of early 1964. So, in belated tribute to this true sage, seer and soothsayer of the past, for posterity's sake this writer's one and only issue is now deservedly memorialized. May he serve as an inspiration to us all to one day issue another correct "out of the park" sell signal!

Era II: Rolls Recede, Rarity Reigns

The decade of the '70s took on a new character, thus ushering in new advisory letters and resigning others to the shadows. Rolls were out, single rare coins were in. The grip of inflation provided the impetus for marketing-savvy rare coin dealers to position their "product" as life rafts amid a sea of sinking dollar-denominated paper assets.

Many newcomers to the rare coin marketplace came from the related bullion area. There they were weaned on the likes of $20 gold pieces, Mexican 50 Pesos, British Gold Sovereigns, 90% junk silver coins and BU silver $1 rolls. Since they were making a giant leap from the hefty and bulky world of bullion to the often-confusing and minute world of high-priced single coins, rare coin advisory letters needed to fill the void by upping their level of sophistication to appeal to this new, well-monied audience. Four such come to mind: *The FCI Advisory*, the *Numisco Letter*, *The Fortune-Teller*, and my own, *The Rosen Numismatic Advisory* (1976-current).

The FCI Advisory was published by First Coinvestors, Inc., one of the first rare coin telemarketing firms. Founded in 1967 (under the name First Mutual Coin Investors Corp., later First Coin Collectors Co., then FCI), the company went public by the selling of shares in November 1969. The firm struggled throughout the '80s, going out of business in 1989.

Limited as FCI was in certain ways, its vision of selling coins through the printed word was broad. It's now hardly-known, though revolutionary for the time, Summer of 1970 issue of its Advisory was titled "A New Direction." That heralded in the era of U.S. Type Coins as an investment sector, supplanting the former status of BU rolls. With thousands of Advisories going out to prospective buyers — mostly novices — the opportunities of investing in single rare coins was exposed to a vast, new marketplace.

Moreover, FCI showed brilliant foresight by hiring some of the hobby's most revered writer/researchers: Walter Breen, Don Taxay and Sylvia Haffner, to name a few. The Advisory also contained articles on such diverse areas as Colonial Coins and Currency, Large Cent varieties, Fractional Currency and Bust Half-Dollar varieties. No bread and butter advisory here.

Nonetheless, because it was biased towards the marketing of material it was selling (mostly to novice coin buyers), it tended to support the firm's selling strategies and relatively high markup requirements.

The *Numisco Letter* introduced a new twist to the field. Written by Walter Perschke beginning in 1973, an expert commodities trader and analyst as well as a coin dealer, the NL often included competent articles pertaining to precious metals, currencies and related economic matters. Considering the times, this was a timely and authoritative-looking marriage. At times the NL recommended BU rolls and proof sets, but mostly stressed rare coins and interesting market commentary. Perschke's attention to quality analysis produced a fine study of the Harold Bareford Auctions of 1979 and 1981.

Les Fox, a coin dealer from 1969 until the later 1980s, was a writer who always sparked controversy. Some people called him abrasive, brash and cocky ("ABC"). Others, myself included, eagerly awaited his writings which often provoked and aroused a theretofore rarely incited industry which, to be honest, from time to time needed its nose tweaked and its participants stirred up. Few since fulfilled this role as well as Fox.

In 1969 he started *The Profit Prophet*, a private circulating letter to some 50-100 subscribers. During 1975-76, as an employee at Deak-Perera in New York City, Fox wrote the "Coin Report," in which his "ABC" writing style took shape, though was necessarily guarded because his employer was a very conservative "old world" type of company frowning on high-profile publicity and controversy. But, from 1979 to 1986, when *The Fortune-Teller* was published, Fox (a boxing fan) took the gloves off and supplied the "oomph," as he put it, lacking in his earlier writings.

While Fox's recommendations often proved quite successful, for me it was his direct writing style and frequent, heated chafing of dealers, organizations and industry developments for which he deserves kudos and a special place in the Honor Roll of Numismatic Advisory Letters. Some may say it was my good fortune to have avoided his admonishments (to the contrary, having earned his accolades), that causes me to see him as a crusading, consumer advocate, not as an "ABC" dealer out to feather his own nest by pulling apart others'. But I'll put on the gloves to defend Fox, if not so energetically to continue tweaking the noses of the deserving.

Fox's ardent consumer advocacy is also shown by the brief, but provocative, publishing history of *Review of Numismatics and the Law*, later titled *The Counsellor*. Only four issues were published, 1981-82, in conjunction with The Numismatic Legal Referral Service, a non-profit service available to subscribers of *The Fortune-Teller*. It contained excellent articles pertaining to the legal aspects of numismatics, taxes, estate planning and reports on dealers of questionable reputation. It was a bold undertaking, stepping on some important toes in the industry.

Fox is also to be remembered for his promotional abilities - ever resourceful to recognize an opportunity and make hay. This was best shown by his series of "Silver Dollar Fortune-Telling" books (well over 150,000 sold in 6 editions from 1977 to 1985), co-authored by his wife, Sue. These books were an instant and continuing success. In an easy-to-read format, they convincingly put forth a very bullish argument for investing in silver dollars. The main section of each edition presented a detailed, date-by-date analysis with price projections and estimates of surviving specimens broken into four or more grade categories. It was a brilliant presentation, a powerful sales tool for many dealers - including, of course, the authors.

Those various editions also included pertinent and highly informative chapters on a variety of subjects relating to silver dollars, including the Redfield hoard, grading, pricing, proof-likes, interviews with noted dealers, and the pains of "fessing up" to the change in grading standards over the years.

Perhaps Les Fox left the field when the getting out was good. Perhaps, the tremendous buildup and subsequent heart-breaking disappointment of his Amazing Gold Rarities investment program was the trigger. Suffice it to say while *The Fortune-Teller* was published, the industry was at the very least more "on guard" of its own shortcomings, foibles and vulnerabilities. For sure it was bolstered by increased sales as a result of Fox's promotions.

Although Les and Sue Fox wrote that their 1985 edition of Silver Dollar Fortune-Telling was to be the final one, and the last issue of *The Fortune-Teller* was in 1986, I, for one, hope there remains a degree of passion still burning in them to again tweak the industry's noses, while making pungent and pointed commentary on the coin market.

Era III: The 1980s - The Good, The Bad and the Ugly

The decade of the '80s began with enormous tension and is ending the same way. It was those first few, glorious, heart-pounding and crazy months of 1980 ("If it was new, round and had a date on it, it was MS-65!") which gave way to a series of mini eras, as follows:

(1) The Great Market TOP and Subsequent Bust: 1980-82;

(2) Recovery Amid Inflations Revival: 1982-83;

(3) The Telemarketing Frenzy: 1983-86;

(4) The PCGS "Revolution": 1986-current.

Whereas the mission of newsletters during the 60s and 70s was, in retrospect, an easy one, namely to keep you in the market by buying rare coins at reasonable prices, their duty in the 80s was to provide coin buyers with helpful advice. This new mission was fraught with great challenge, complexity and difficulty. Some of the older newsletters folded while new ones were born. The changes in newsletters' mission are worth exploring.

For one, the bloody bear market of 1980-82 had to be dealt with editorially, including recognition of the tightened grading standards which hurt portfolios' values and prior recommendations' credibility.

Secondly, those newsletters which stressed BU rolls and proof sets were to be increasingly seen as adhering to an antiquated strategy. They found themselves out of step with the demanding and sophisticated market of the 80s brought about by better educated coin buyers seeking rare coins, not bulk.

Thirdly, the waves of new investors who entered the field during the 70s to act out a hard-money philosophy - and so were laden with heavy losses in both bulky, bullion material and essentially overgraded rare coins - required a convincingly heightened approach to the merits of staying in coins. This became an opportunity for some medium-sized, savvy dealers to start a newsletter as a marketing tool. The investors wanted reassurance that the coin field still offered financial reward to them and the writer-dealers saw that as an opportunity to present themselves as expert numismatic advisors. To be sure, not all fulfilled their promises.

Fourth, as the decade progressed and the industry became increasingly competitive, so that dealers needed to work on slimmer profit margins while expenses were mounting, and often fewer new customers were converted per marketing dollar expended, newsletters were in a less than thriving environment. This was made especially worrisome as the PCGS "revolution" served, among other things, to cause a leveling of numismatic knowledge needed to play in the market. The "opening up" of the true marketplace to professional and novice alike removed some of the mystery and ambiguity that seemed to always exist when the dealers held all the cards and the buyers all the money. These barriers removed, investors felt more confident to act on their own behalf.

Telemarketing Turmoil

Curiously, as the industry was internally experiencing the beginning of a trend to increased consumer sophistication, externally some dealers were displaying a different face. The age of rare coin telemarketing was to kick into high gear during mid-decade. This came about for a few reasons, including:

(1) The prosperous 80s created a new wealthy class, largely at ease with the concept of buying merchandise over the telephone;

(2) The sales pitch of soaring inflation, runaway government spending, and coin investing privacy was still a convincing one, especially with the formidable respect of the Salomon Brothers Investment Study showing rare coins as a #1 performer;

(3) The huge profit margin which the telemarketers needed and received enabled them to spend lavishly on gifted salespeople and on flashy, expensively printed brochures, often formula-written to pack a powerful selling punch;

(4) Until well into the 80s, the regulatory climate was relatively easy, encouraging these rip-off merchants to thrive.

What did the newsletters of these spreaders of deceit recommend? Mostly silver and gold coins that were easy to buy in quantity. Silver $1 singles and rolls; BU rolls of late-date Roosevelt dimes, Washington quarters and Franklin halves; $20 gold pieces and BU foreign gold coins were constantly touted — all at markups up to 200-700%, or more. One of the larger and more dramatic of the bunch took every opportunity to steer customers to their "Premium BU" coins and rolls, professed to be MS63-65 and, unsurprisingly, priced at two to four times the prices of their regular BU quality rolls. Whether there was any difference between premium and regular is open to question, but the practice reinforced their "ours is better than theirs" arguments. One might say it sold a lot of gas.

Except for a still lingering few, these rats have deserted their ships, sunk by any of three torpedoes: The Federal Trade Commission's investigations; the broadened public awareness of PCGS and NGC; or the over-exploitation of a shrinking, gullible marketplace. Good riddance.

Kudos to the Good

Some of the best numismatic newsletters ever produced started in the 1980s, during or just after the 1982-83 market recovery. It's my pleasure to describe them to you.

Bruce Amspacher Investment Report (April 1982 - July, 1990): Known to regular readers of the CDN Monthly Summary from his several articles on Morgan and Peace dollars, Kansas City coin dealer Bruce Amspacher launched his own newsletter in April, 1982. Nicknamed the BAIR, Amspacher's newsletter displayed a unique blend of expertise, humor and wit to fashion one of the best "from the trenches" coin market advisories.

Those trenches were over 20 years spent attending hundreds of coin shows, servicing many customers at various firms, befriending dozens of active dealers, and developing a forceful and highly readable writing style to educate people on the finer points of rarity, condition, and value.

Still, as lavishly as I compliment Bruce, our crossed paths have not always been harmonious ones. Perhaps this is the risk when two iconoclasts are publishing advisory letters. Sometimes toes are stepped on or faces muddied. Whereas on most coin matters we agreed, on one point friction resulted. This stemmed from my occasionally expressed reservations for the prospect of the Morgan and Peace $1 market. These clashed with Bruce's more enthusiastic outlook. I never viewed such feuding as being personal, but rather as two strong critics with opposing views (a la Siskel & Ebert on movies). Such conflict caused lively copy, all in the interest of advising our subscribers to the best of our abilities.

Bruce's humor was multi-faceted and enlivened his perceptive articles. To me, the ones concerning Phineas Q. Whiplash a fictional stereotyped coin investor — were the best. PQW was often portrayed as a somewhat myopic player who thought he knew everything about the business, but who really knew little despite Bruce's calm and reasoned attempts at educating him. For the many dealers who read the BAIR, PQW was typical of at least one person they each had known. I suspect creating PQW was Bruce's satirical way of exposing some people to their own foibles.

Bruce ceased publishing the BAIR after the July 1990 issue, citing health and other reasons as demanding too much of his time. Although Bruce still writes occasionally, I hope he'll be able to republish the BAIR in the future. In any case, those eight volumes are a prized treasury of numismatic commentary and wit.

Numismatic Investment Advisory, Jack Ehrmantraut, 1984-current: Another superb "from the trenches" writer/dealer continues to produce an excellent and timely newsletter on investment opportunities in the high quality sector of the rare coin market.

Perhaps it's the breed, but like mine, Jack's iconoclastic and sometimes rough-hewn past articles have ruffled some feathers in the industry. He too has poked at Morgan and Peace dollars, excoriated market manipulators and vilified abusive telemarketers. Yet Jack's commanding knowledge of various series and the intricacies of the market and the timing of his recommendations (buy and sell) have been an integral part of each issue of the NIA. Some of his more notable issues have analyzed nickel and Barber coinage. Importantly, Jack's love for the business and concern for his subscribers comes through in each issue. These are hard-to-find qualities in a numismatic newsletter.

The Numismatic Investment Journal, by James S. Iocova and Raymond G. Mercer, October 1982 to June 1987: If the NIJ is to be labeled a "from the trenches" newsletter, don't expect the writers to necessarily be chumming about with their other so-called trenchmates. Rather, it's likely you'll find them in the corner drafting a biting, penetrating expose on the myopic and foolish involvement of some dealers who hype coin investing and craft various clever ways of reaching into their clients' wallets. Editors Iocova and Mercer never sought to wrap themselves in the "making money in coins" rat race pursued by so many other dealers and writers. Oh, sure they frequently made recommendations about what to buy (definitely on what to sell!), but the action stressed was to buy coins the reader enjoyed to collect, not to necessarily monetarily profit from.

Lest you think the NIJ was the equivalent of a numismatic religious school text about proper behavior and attitudes, let me correct that vision. For the NIJ was arguably the best numismatic advisory letter ever published. It was highly readable, skillfully produced, often humorously cynical and brutally realistic about the manipulative aspects of the marketplace. Yet, it was refreshingly optimistic about the fun and satisfaction to be derived from the sensible pursuit of buying coins as a collector/investor.

Iocova and Mercer didn't need a PQW to represent the mentally-limited coin investor; they took on the industry's collector organizations, grading services, major coin investment firms, telemarketers, you name it. They poked, they prodded, they hammered away at the false hopes, duplicity and hype they saw as misdirecting the gullible public's money and attention.

If Ehrmantraut and I (among others) were labelled as guarded on the outlook for the prices of Morgan and Peace dollars, by comparison Iocova and Mercer should be called mudslingers. Every tick increase above $200 bid for common-date MS-65 Morgans since 1984 they viewed as another sign that the silver dollar market would explode as if it were a helicopter to be blasted from the skies in a James Bond movie!

They continued to argue persuasively against the 11-point numerical mint state grading system, stating that only three clear gradations existed.

They pulled open the curtains of the "guaranteed buy-back" dealers who claimed to be working on 20% spreads (i.e., buy $500, sell $600), by asserting that their profits needed to be closer to 100% (buy $300, sell $600). In fact, the NIJ boldly and candidly alleged that a fair dealer retail spread required to be in the area of 50% (buy $400, sell $600) to enable the dealer to operate a successful business and provide the client with accurately graded coins and competent service. Much less of a spread meant the dealer was cutting corners, they avowed.

Beyond all this consumer advocacy, Iocova and Mercer were widely acknowledged experts on U.S. Commemoratives. In 1979, Iocova wrote *A Comprehensive Guide to U.S. Commemorative Coins*. And throughout the life of the NIJ, several studies were published examining each commemorative issue in detail. In fact, their dedication and commitment to educating their subscribers about commems (among other series) and the market for coins in general have been hallmarks of the NIJ from the start.

Among their many superb feature reports were "The Invisible Empire" (December, 1985) and "The Invisible Empire Strikes Back" (May and June 1986). These were two tremendously fascinating and eye-opening interviews with "Jack," a professed rip-off coin telemarketer. They were hilarious, but at the same time pathetic indictments of a gullible public and a too compliant industry.

Yet another was their "skull & crossbones" issue of April 1986. There they tore into the dangerous world, as they saw it, of chasing after the overpromoted coins of "guaranteed buy-back" dealers (and others). For many people, their helicopter was shot to pieces as, for example, MS-65 Morgans tumbled from the $800-1,000 area after May of 1986. Yet those who heeded the warnings in the NIJ and cashed in such coins in time safely averted the crashing debris.

The May/June 1987 issue of the NIJ was the last. "We didn't have enough time to continue writing it as we wanted to," admitted Mercer to me, "besides, after telling people for over two years to sell their overvalued coins, how much longer could we beat them over the head with the same message?"

Here, perhaps, is a major reason why highly principled, consumer advocate newsletters have not been very successful. People tend to flock more to those who promise or imply that they offer "inside" secrets to making money - that is tips - than to advisors, who some may feel are lecturing to them. Consequently, hard-to-swallow educating in a fast-food-newsletter-world for some folks is the wrong menu.

Special Mention

Here is a listing of several other fine advisories worthy of note.

Analysis & Outlook, by R.W. Bradford (1971-current)
As I See It, by Donald Kagin (1988-current)
Gary North's Investment Coin Report, (1984-current)
Inside View, by David Hall (1979-current)
The Jeffcoat Report, by Arnold Jeffcoat (1983-86)
Marketwise, by Michael G. De Falco (1982-86?)
"*On Guard*", by Philip Kominos (1985-86?)
The Reader's Edge, by Larry Hanks (1989-current)
The Swiatek Report, by Anthony Swiatek (1982-current)
The Winning Edge, by Paul & Philip Schuyler (1986-current)

How to Tell the Good From the Bad

Uppermost is your mind should be to identify the raison d'etre of the particular newsletter you are reading. In general, is it of the Objective type, the Promotional type, or an In-Betweener? Those in either of the first two categories will not be too difficult to identify. There will be some overlapping and fuzziness with the In-Betweeners, making it difficult for you to always identify this third group.

Clearly the most harmful to your wallet are the Promotional newsletters, though every once in a while they give me a hearty chuckle. I'm still amazed at their occasional brashness, inane analysis and utter disregard for providing truthful, responsible advice.

> As brash and as boastful as some people regarded *The Fortune-Teller*, it never featured a 4-color layout recommending with panting enthusiasm rolls of proof Franklins at $395 each.

> As down-to-earth and practical as has been the *Numismatic Investment Journal*, they've never announced such ridiculous hype as "The Ticking Time Bomb of Debt & Inflation;" "The Coming Credit Collapse;" "Discovered Hoard Offers Amazing Profit Potential;" or, "Silver Dollar Prices Poised to Orbit;" and, "Buy Before the Funds Dry Up the Entire Supply."

> As proud and flattering of his own firm as Dave Bowers has written, he's avoided saying: "Our buyers combed the vaults of Europe to locate this fabulous hoard;" or, "Our clients are sitting on tens of millions in profits and we plead with them to ruthlessly expect more, much more!" Or, "How a $10,000 investment today can send your child through the best college."

> As expert as Bruce Amspacher is on rarities and identifying good deals in the marketplace, he never made pronouncements such as: "These Australian Gold Sovereigns are as rare as MS-63 Liberties, but only 1/5th the price!" Or, "With MS-63 Morgan dollars going for $60 each, these Mexican Onzas are a steal at $11." Or, "At $325, the 1961-P Washington 25 cent roll in Premium BU grade has 550-700% profit potential in 3-5 years!"

The message here? When a newsletter oozes forth with unfounded hoopla and hyperbole as it extols the merits of its "recommendations," you can be sure your wallet and not your loyalty is what the publisher wants to get its hands on.

Some of these "uglies" are crafty and cunning enough to masquerade their true intentions beneath the cloak of credible numismatic affiliations, accompanied impressive economic and market analysis, interviews with top-notch authorities and other business enterprises which tend to present the publisher as being a stalwart of honesty and competence. They are the most insidious; for, their outward trappings play a dangerously seductive role to entrap their prey. Still, their hidden agenda (raison d'etre) should be detectable if they display a few of these traits:

(1) The newsletter is too slick, too professionally edited, its copy too formulated. Such production costs are expensive, difficult to justify if all they are doing is selling advice. Some of the best advisory letters ever published were/are done as modest, unassuming efforts. Whereas, some of the biggest rip-off promotional newsletters would win design and production awards. Go by the Smell Test: If it smells fishy . . .

(2) The Promotional newsletters often - if not always and abundantly - stuff their mailing envelopes with various offerings. Whether it's a passionate plea for coins, insurance products, other investment services or seminars, you can tell by such excess tonnage that you're merely viewed as a guppy with money.

(3) "Super-Duper" renewal offers can be a tip-off. I've yet to see any of the better advisories offer their renewals at bargain-basement prices. Nor do they promise you loads of "Special Reports" for renewing or other grandstanding and razzle-dazzle offers. Typically, renewal notices are a simple slip announcing that your subscription is up at a certain date. Sure these good guys want you to renew, but they are not going to resort to flamboyant histrionics to entice you to send a check.

(4) A suspicious giveaway is a newsletter's failure to write about wholesale trading levels and other actual, in-the-field activities. Let's face it. If I want to sell you "Choice BU" rolls of 1883-O Morgan dollars at $1,195 a pop, I'm not going to tell you that CDN bid for typical BU rolls is $270 . . . but, MY rolls are original and handpicked! You'll probably see fancy, but fallacious charts, read mumbo-jumbo about rarity and profit potential, maybe how only 10 rolls of these babies can put your child through college. But, will they tell you what you can sell the coins for in the wholesale market?

(5) Their writings on the coin market are generalities. Their paper is too valuable to be wasted on non-marketing features. A date-by-date analysis of Liberty Seated Dollars? No way, they can't get any to sell, plus they don't have any one on staff who knows enough to write about the coins. A discussion of the population rarity of mint state Trade Dollars? Whom are you kidding? Ah, but an article on Ike dollars, followed by a recommendation for the 4-piece silver proof set at a mere $99, with a picture of the 5-Star General poring over a map while planning D-Day . . . *that* you may read!

Sensible Selection Advice on Subscribing to Newsletters

(1) **Word of Mouth**: Chances are if a coin dealer or two you know and respect has complimentary things to say about a coin advisory letter, it is worthy of your attention. Knowledgeable dealers can see through a less than top-notch newsletter in a flash.

(2) **Knowledgeably Written and Well Reasoned**: The writer should convince you of his numismatic expertise, not his hyped-up, formulated optimism. Moreover, the quality of the presentation, the arguments and the analyses used should be such that they do not insult nor ridicule basic statistics. The field has matured considerably since the "old days." Slipshod research, careless analysis and hasty arguments won't do for today's more demanding and sophisticated audience.

(3) **Unbiased Advice**: This takes several forms. You know the old saying, "Never ask a shoemaker if you need new shoes." Extended to coins, never ask a silver dollar specialist if he would recommend silver dollars! Of course he does, so his advice may be biased. Such specialized newsletters could be a means of conveying an impression that the writer is an expert - thus the dealer from whom you should be buying your silver dollars (or your gold coins, or your commems, etc.).

I'm not knocking specialization, for there are many fine dealers who have stellar reputations in their chosen niches, some being writers. But you are seeking financial advice, counseling and direction. Someone who is too close to his "tree" may not be able to see the "forest," not be able to provide you with the broad, diversified wisdom you need.

If you are using that advisor's newsletter on a select, narrow basis, okay. But, be cautious when he travels too far from his specialty. I wouldn't ask a silver $1 expert for his opinion on early copper coins, or a commem specialist for advice on gold rarities.

Another thing to look out for is a writer constantly "I'ing" you. One who brags about himself is someone you should probably avoid. Look for authoritative humility - confident opinions, yes, but not someone who can't seem to get enough of himself.

Perhaps the most obvious bias is when the newsletter is a house organ. A large coin firm which puts out a newsletter as a means of establishing a reputation for itself can have cross purposes. If they acquired a large hoard of "CC" Morgans, might they not be pressured to feature an enthusiastic recommendation of these coins? In contrast, a commendable situation is when a newsletter recommends the purchase of a coin - but has none in stock and refers you elsewhere!

(4) **Winning Advice**: Last, but not least, is this newsletter helping you to make profitable investment decisions? Such advice can come on different levels and you should recognize the value of each level:

(A) **Recommendations**: How is its track record? Can it make winning recommendations? Are they reasonably available picks? I remember a well-known newsletter which some 18 years ago issued a major recommendation for the uncirculated 1836 Reeded Edge Bust 50 cent piece. It had a $350 Red Book valuation at the time - but it was impossible to find one even remotely close to that price. Later on when the coin's valuation rose spectacularly, the same newsletter bragged about its great pick!

(B) **Market Outlook**: The newsletter should give you a well-reasoned case for either a bullish (positive) or a bearish (negative) outlook for the market as a whole. It should serve as a guide to most of your investment decisions, taking not only a short-term view, but a long-term one as well. However, because many newsletters are written by dealers, there is that natural bias to stress a bullish posture and underplay a bearish one.

Nonetheless, the responsible newsletter will face up to market reality and inform you of the scope of current conditions and likely future ones. No newsletter has ever been perfect, or even close (Alex Hamil excepted), so it is commendable if one is humble and sincere by admitting to mistakes and bad advice, as well as keeping you out of the market when the risks are too great.

(C) **Consumerism**: As insiders of the coin business, some newsletter writers are privy to certain situations which are potentially gaping pitfalls. A newsletter that dares to publicize some of these traps is performing a great service. Remember: Successful investing is not only making profitable decisions, it is to avoid making unprofitable ones, too.

Unfortunately, by exposing some of the seedier aspects of the industry, a writer can be tagged as a troublemaker, thus alienating himself to some degree. But done fairly and professionally, such active consumer advocacy is to be applauded.

(D) **Supporting Economic Analysis**: You need to be at least acquainted with economic and monetary developments which influence the coin market. At times, coin prices can act as if in a world of their own, but their price activity is soon impacted by outside forces - and that's where economic analysis comes in.

While it's unfair and unrealistic to expect a rare coin advisory letter to also provide you with competent economic commentary, you should expect the better ones to at least pay heed to non-numismatic forces. Moreover, they should be able to support their positions if at great variance with the conventional wisdom.

Review

Separating the good newsletters from the not so good ones is fairly easy. Usually the bad ones are mere promotional sheets for the firm and are devoid of analytical substance, are anything but impartial, and avoid the least bit of controversy, lest they dwell from their formulated purpose. That they are not worth the paper they are printed on is usually shown by them being given away free to those people merely inquiring about the firm.

On the other hand, the good ones perform a commendable service providing you with pertinent information and stimulate your interest in market awareness. As such, they can be a valuable learning experience and a source of renewed study over the years long after they are published.

One last tip. As a subscriber to a newsletter service, there is one significant perk which is often available to you, though not widely advertised. You can pick up the telephone and speak personally to the editor-writer. Inquisitive and perceptive subscribers may be able to glean much valuable information about the newsletter's merits when conversing with the editor. I can attest to this and have not been shy in the past to call various editors (coins, economics, stocks, commodities, etc.) to get a more intricate understanding of a subject discussed in the newsletter.

Quite often you'll find the editor not only available to you, but a willing party to the conversation. I'm always pleased to speak to a subscriber, especially one who is not only urging me to clarify or expand upon a certain point but who is responding in such a manner as to make the conversation pleasant and stimulating for me.

In fact, at times I've come away from such encounters with ideas for future articles and helpful feedback on how to improve my newsletter. Consequently, writers are most willing to speak with a subscriber - a win-win situation. You will benefit by getting to know your newsletter writer better and by having a no-fee private consultation - an important perk if you use it wisely.

Yet another tip. Want to take a peek at a newsletter without subscribing to it or even paying for a single issue? Write a nice original note (not photocopied) to the publisher requesting their current issue. Write that you have heard fine things about them and want to see if it can be useful to you. Enclose a self-addressed-double-stamped envelope, a courtesy practiced by few, but distinguishing yourself as a "mensch."

Advantages and Disadvantages of Newsletters

Calling upon my 30+ year history of reading newsletters (including 23 years writing 3 of them), I have my own ideas as to their overall usefulness. Clearly, most of you are not "junkies" as I am, but I assume you are serious collector/investors. As such, it may be worthwhile to take measure of the group's pluses and minuses.

Advantages:

(1) The good ones provide you with independent, knowledgeable insights of market developments and opportunities that otherwise might not be made available to you.

(2) They will also at times contain research and analytical approaches that you may not find elsewhere. These can serve as examples for you to apply them to other situations. Thus, you can learn of new tools to aid your collecting and investing decisions.

(3) As a subscriber, you might have telephone access to the editor-writer. As described earlier, this can be a valuable benefit. Also, a few newsletters offer telephone "hotline" services. These are usually weekly updated reports of up-to-the-minute developments and recommendations. Since most advisories are monthlies, such a service can be of great help.

Disadvantages:

(1) They are costly. Instead of paying 50 cents or so for an issue of Coin World or for Numismatic News, the good newsletters will set you back about $5-15 per issue on a subscription basis. For that price, they should deliver pertinent, valuable information. Still, you should not hold them to an unrealistically high level of expectation month in and month out. Occasionally an issue or two won't be helpful to you, but another may hit home causing you to make a winning decision that pays for many years of renewals.

(2) You risk being given advice (sincere as it may be) that is underlaid with bias or is bad. Such frequent failings prompt people to often ask, "If you're so smart, how come you're not rich?" There is a ring of truth to that question. Furthermore, because most newsletters are written by dealers, there could be a tendency to hesitate divulging negative news and bearish opinions or to withhold market commentary that might shake your confidence in the market or, for that matter, the idea itself of buying coins as an investment. Such slanted tendencies are found elsewhere (stocks, insurance, real estate, etc.). Nonetheless, such bias is a distinct disadvantage. For instance, while newsletters frequently write of "buying opportunities," they will rarely warn you of "selling opportunities."

(3) Furthermore, as my walk down memory lane has shown you, even the first-rate advisories are not perennial. They can fold with the first hint of winter's frost, leaving you without a continuation of the advice upon which you acted. To some, we are "sunshine advisors," there to write newsletters when it pays, folding our tents when it doesn't. Message: Don't be overly dependent upon any one newsletter, especially if it has not been publishing for a long time.

Summary

Were numismatic newsletters priced at 50 cents an issue, they'd probably enjoy no more respect or allegiance than they do now when they cost much more. Nor would their quality be much enhanced if present subscription fees were doubled. But if the cost is not the issue, what is? Their ability to enable you to make reasoned, objective and winning decisions is their main selling point - indeed, probably the sole purpose for you to be reading them. I know I've been repetitive on that point, but I don't want you to overlook it.

The Future of Numismatic Advisory Letters

Whither the numismatic newsletter? Considering the rise and fall of several excellent ones during the 1980s, I occasionally wonder what's in it for others to enter the marketplace: Ego? A means to boost coin sales? Attract a following? Surely it's not to solely profit from its publication, for with only minor exceptions, most have been a losing proposition for their publishers.

I wonder. Is this because coin collectors and investors have always been used to getting free advice? After all, we are an industry selling a product. Or have they been at the most paying little for such advice via articles in the traditional periodicals? Is it because some coin buyers are, at times, given to arrogance, overconfidence or distrust (a la Phineas Q. Whiplash)? Or, dare I say, is it because the genre has failed to deliver on its promises . . . its predictions . . . its principles?

Then again, is it fair to denounce us because we have been urged to deliver the undeliverable? For sure, a bull market makes geniuses of us all, but the inevitable bear markets often devour even the most principled and skilful of coin newsletter publishers. Is there a future for us in an uncertain world? Do you really care?

You should. I hope my article has given you a new appreciation for the value of newsletters. Yes, many are bad. Some are sophomorically written or offer incompetent advice. Others are overly self-promotive. Still others have been dangerously misleading or outright wrong in their recommendations. And then there are the brilliant, relatively awesome exceptions which have delivered valuable guidance to their subscribers — all I hope here duly praised.

You see, dear reader, you are, for the most part, on your own, LIMITED TO YOUR OWN WITS AND SENSIBILITIES IN THIS OR ANY OTHER FIELD OF FINANCIAL DECISION MAKING. Indeed, there are the good, the bad and the ugly in any field of human endeavor. I hope that ample motivation and drive exists for competent and sincere numismatists to be encouraged to find a ready and receptive market to offer their counsel and advice as future newsletter publishers. The good ones, indeed, more than make up for the bad. I hope I have illuminated the way for you to find them.

> "We futurists know only one thing for certain about the future: It cannot be predicted. Therefore, we leave predictions to fortune-tellers, horserace touts, fools, and economists!"
>
> James O'Toole

THE EXCHANGE REPORT

Vol. I, Number 6 © 1988 ANE December 1988

THE RARE COIN MARKET IN 1989

OVERVIEW

The revolution that has taken place in the rare coin market in the past three years since the establishment of PCGS will increase in intensity and impact in the next twelve months.

1989 will see the continued replacement of old concepts, obsolete products and stagnant approaches with new concepts, fresh products and innovative approaches.

Coin dealers will find it much more difficult to do business "the old fashion way." But fortunately, it will be much easier to be a member of the coin-buying public.

A LOOK BACK

The numismatic revolution of the past three years has been so total in its scope because the number one beneficiary of this revolution is you, the coin consumer.

This revolution has brought us major changes in four aspects of the coin industry - volume, margins, liquidity and volatility. Let's take a look at each of these areas.

First, in terms of volume, the rare coin marketplace has moved to a total undreamed of level. Here's a significant example. Five years ago, a major wholesaler could do several hundred thousand dollars worth of volume at a major show and perhaps as much as $500,000 to $1,000,000 worth of business at the annual American Numismatic Association (A.N.A.) convention.

Today, million dollar coin shows are becoming fairly commonplace for more and more dealers. And at the most recent A.N.A. show this past July, there were five different major dealers who each transacted between $4,000,000 and $5,000,000 in business at that one show.

The impact of this tremendous surge in volume is just beginning to be realized throughout the industry. But as big as the increase in volume has been, it may just be scratching the surface.

Soon, maybe in 1989, but in the immediate future, a major wholesaler is going to have a coin show where he does $10,000,000 in sales. Continued on page 2

AMERICAN NUMISMATIC EXCHANGE • 1117 Perimeter Center West • Suite 500 E • Atlanta, GA 30338 (404) 392-3318

The Exchange Report
By: American Numismatic Exchange, Inc. (ANE)
(Courtesy of ANE)

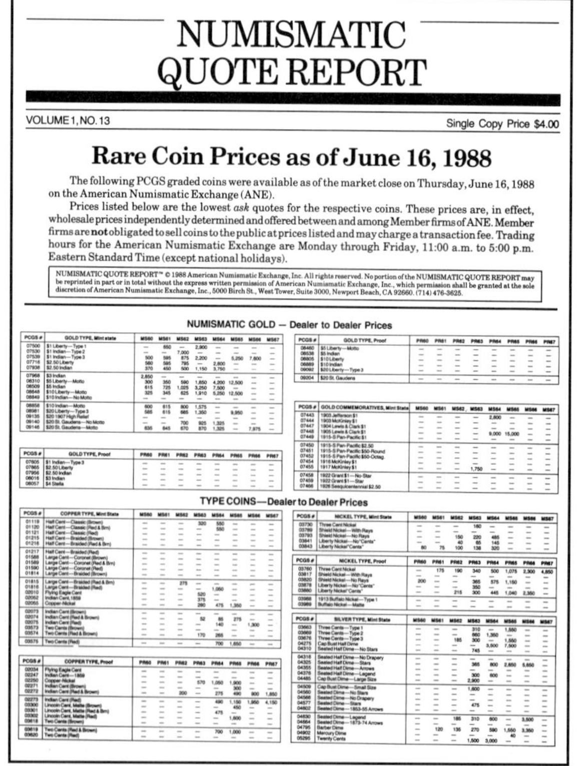

NUMISMATIC QUOTE REPORT

VOLUME 1, NO. 13 Single Copy Price $4.00

Rare Coin Prices as of June 16, 1988

The following PCGS graded coins were available as of the market close on Thursday, June 16, 1988 on the American Numismatic Exchange (ANE).

Prices listed below are the lowest *ask* quotes for the respective coins. These prices are, in effect, wholesale prices independently determined and offered between and among Member firms of ANE. Member firms are **not** obligated to sell coins to the public at prices listed and may charge a transaction fee. Trading hours for the American Numismatic Exchange are Monday through Friday, 11:00 a.m. to 5:00 p.m. Eastern Standard Time (except national holidays).

NUMISMATIC GOLD — Dealer to Dealer Prices

TYPE COINS—Dealer to Dealer Prices

The Numismatic Quote Report
By: American Numismatic Exchange, Inc. (ANE)
(Courtesy of ANE)

BRUCE AMSPACHER

INVESTMENT REPORT

P. O. BOX 9527 NEWPORT BEACH, CA 92658 (800) 821-3985 / (714) 250-3187

Volume 6, Number 6 & 7 December 15, 1988

Chestnuts roasting on an open fire, Jack Frost nipping at my nose......

It's that time of year once again, with yuletide prognostications ready for release, filled with optimism of the great future we're all going to share. The fresh start of 1989 is eagerly anticipated, especially after 1988 left almost everyone, and certainly both of me, a little schizo. First the good news, then the **really** good news.

The annual Silver Dollar Convention in St. Louis was the first major test of the question: "Is the market ready to roll again?" The happy answer is "Yes." Going into November 1988, the coin market was still suffering the post-ANA blues, with market prices down in most areas 20% or more in only three months. The show was well attended, active, upbeat, much better than expected (ask **anyone**), and something unusual happened. After the show, prices continued **up**. Recently, the action following a major show has been soft, as overspent dealers decided to get into stronger cash positions. **This time**, there was more money around than coins, and the ANE/NQS system has been a plethora of plus signs for weeks. A complete set of Morgan and Peace dollars, all PCGS graded and mostly MS65 or better, traded **three** times at the show, starting out at $750,000 and then trading again at $800,000 and $850,000. Common MS65 dollars traded at just over the $300 level at the show, but have since been testing the $350 barrier as the market heats up again. Silver dollars? Looking **strong!**

Speaking of strong, immediately following the Silver Dollar Convention came the Norweb III auction, conducted by Bowers and Merena and featuring some of the neatest coins to come along since the Garrett sales nearly a decade ago. The highlights could take pages to list, but here are a few Morgan and Peace dollar prices that will be memorable for generations to come. The star attraction was an 1893-S Morgan, a "whopper" by all accounts, that sold for.....

$357,500. That's "Three and a quarter plus the juice" in coin dealer parlance. That's a world record in **any** language. **Mais oui!** The coin was purchased for a major California collection that is quickly becoming the number one set of Morgan Dollars in the world. Some other prices of the "Wow, can you believe that?" category include:
1882 Proof 65---$15,950***1883 Proof 65---$18,700***1884-O "Proof" 64---$20,900***1891-S MS65---$14,300***1896 Proof 65---$16,500***1896-S MS65---$24,200***1897-O **MS65---$52,800***1897-S MS65---$13,750***1900-S MS65---$18,700***1902-S MS65---$27,500***1903-O MS65---$7480***1922 Matte Proof 65 (High relief) $46,200***1922 Matte Proof 65 (Regular relief) $35,200***1928-S MS65---$25,300 (can that be **right?**) and......on and on.

If there was a "real bargain" from the Norweb III sale it was the sale of the 1861 Paquet Reverse $20 gold coin. The price was hardly weak at $660,000 (!), yet it was hoped by many that this would be first U.S. coin to realize $1,000,000 or

BAIR Investment Report
By: Bruce Amspacher (BAIR)
(Courtesy of Bruce Amspacher)

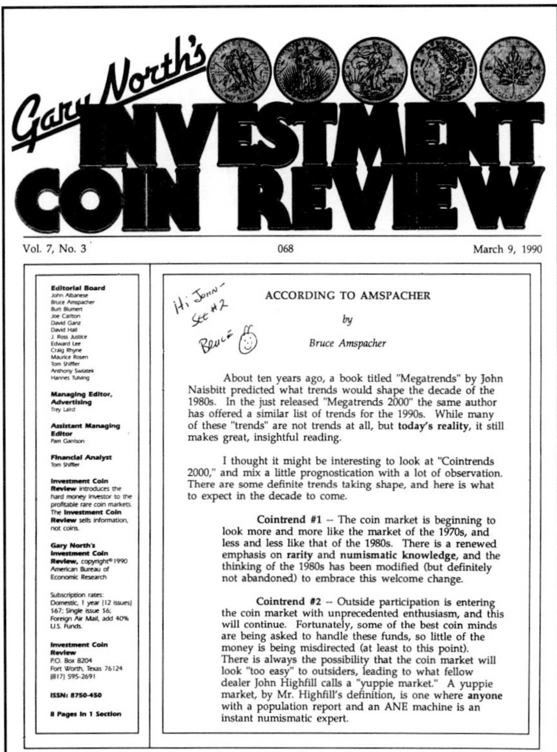

Gary North's INVESTMENT COIN REVIEW

Vol. 7, No. 3 068 March 9, 1990

Editorial Board John Albanese, Bruce Amspacher, Burt Blumert, Joe Carlton, David Ganz, David Hall, J. Ross Justice, Edward Lee, Craig Rhyne, Maurice Rosen, Tom Shiffer, Anthony Swiatek, Hannes Tulving

Managing Editor, Advertising Trey Laird

Assistant Managing Editor Pam Garrison

Financial Analyst Tom Shiffer

Investment Coin Review introduces the hard money investor to the profitable rare coin markets. The **Investment Coin Review** sells information, not coins.

Gary North's Investment Coin Review, copyright© 1990 American Bureau of Economic Research

Subscription rates: Domestic, 1 year (12 issues) $67; Single issue $6; Foreign Air Mail, add 40% U.S. Funds.

Investment Coin Review P.O. Box 8204 Fort Worth, Texas 76124 (817) 595-2691

ISSN: 8750-450

8 Pages In 1 Section

Hi John – See #2 Bruce

ACCORDING TO AMSPACHER

by

Bruce Amspacher

About ten years ago, a book titled "Megatrends" by John Naisbitt predicted what trends would shape the decade of the 1980s. In the just released "Megatrends 2000" the same author has offered a similar list of trends for the 1990s. While many of these "trends" are not trends at all, but **today's reality**, it still makes great, insightful reading.

I thought it might be interesting to look at "Cointrends 2000," and mix a little prognostication with a lot of observation. There are some definite trends taking shape, and here is what to expect in the decade to come.

Cointrend #1 -- The coin market is beginning to look more and more like the market of the 1970s, and less and less like that of the 1980s. There is a renewed emphasis on **rarity** and **numismatic knowledge**, and the thinking of the 1980s has been modified (but definitely not abandoned) to embrace this welcome change.

Cointrend #2 -- Outside participation is entering the coin market with unprecedented enthusiasm, and this will continue. Fortunately, some of the best coin minds are being asked to handle these funds, so little of the money is being misdirected (at least to this point). There is always the possibility that the coin market will look "too easy" to outsiders, leading to what fellow dealer John Highfill calls a "yuppie market." A yuppie market, by Mr. Highfill's definition, is one where **anyone** with a population report and an ANE machine is an instant numismatic expert.

Investment Coin Review
By: Gary North
(Courtesy of Investment Coin Review)

the COIN DEALER *newsletter*

Our 27th year... *...a Monday morning report on the Coin Market*

Vol. XXVII No. 14 April 7, 1989 Single copy price: $3.50

ACTIVE BIDDING FORCES MARKET HIGHER

BU Silver Rolls Only Area Not Participating At Higher Levels

The Market in Depth

This Week's Market

Coin Dealer Newsletter: Certified Coin Market Indicator™

Greysheet
The Coin Dealer Newsletter
(Courtesy of CDN)

the COIN DEALER newsletter

MONTHLY SUMMARY AND COMPLETE SERIES PRICING GUIDE

FEBRUARY— 1990

Vol. XV No. 2 Single copy price: $3.50

1989 RECAP

WHAT GOES UP, MUST COME DOWN, MUST GO UP...

WHAT GOES AROUND, COMES AROUND...

COINS ARE FOREVER; COIN CYCLES ARE FOREVER...

1881-S MORGAN, PCGS MS-65
Volatility Even Struck Generics!

(Continued on Page Two)

Greysheet - Monthly Summary
(Courtesy of CDN)

CERTIFIED COIN DEALER newsletter

a weekly report on the certified market
published by the Coin Dealer Newsletter (est. 1963)

Vol. III No. 47 | November 18, 1988 | Single copy price $3.50

Sight—Seen Auction Action Accentuates Slabbed Sales

The certified coin market exhibits many facets that are not as well publicized as some of its more commonly discussed characteristics. The topics of liquidity, market coverage, and grading consistency have been thoroughly examined. One of the *least* discussed issues has to do with the **regrading** of certified coins. Regrading usually occurs when the dealer submitting the coin or coins is not happy with the grade assigned; it can be taken for granted that regrading will occur only when he thinks the grade should be higher.

The regrading is usually accomplished in one of two ways. First, the dealer can physically break the coins out of the plastic slabs, and resubmit them (as though they had never been graded in the first place). This second submission is performed with the hopes of the coin reaching a different (and *more lenient*) second group of graders. The result? Hopefully, a higher grade and a *substantial* increase in value. When such coins are recycled through the system without notification, it naturally has the effect of making the population reports slightly skewed - some of the count in a particular category may belong to the same resubmitted coin. We have heard of one example where it took a dealer six tries to finally achieve the grade he wanted - in this case, the population count for MS-65 is at least **five** too high.

Second, a dealer can resubmit coins whose grading he challenges with the coins left in their slabs. The coins can then be reviewed to determine if the grade should be changed. Again, there may be a different set of graders viewing the coins differently. If their consensus is that the grade should be raised, the coin can be reslabbed with the population report amended. Naturally, this method is not as popular with the dealers since the very existence of the slab tends to limit independent observation of the coin.

All this is brought to mind because of the recent sale of a complete set of Peace Dollars in McIntire Numismatic Auctions' N.S.D.C. Sale last week. The matched set, graded PCGS-64, realized $27,500. *Bluesheet* Bid at that time was $16,605 for PCGS-64, and $87,254 for PCGS-65. For many weeks, we have been mentioning that selling coins **sight-seen**, as at an auction, will vastly improve the price realized over selling them **sight-unseen**; likewise, that sight-unseen Bids have been particularly low as dealers wished to avoid adding unwanted coins to inventory. Are those the reasons for paying such a substantial premium over *Bluesheet*? Or, are many of these coins destined for resubmission? If just a couple of the rarer dates "make it", the whole process will be well worth it.

One of the really big events of the just completed Silver Dollar Show was the sale of a complete set of PCGS graded Morgan and Peace Dollars, including varieties. Consisting of mostly high grade, 65 and better, the set sold for $750,000, dealer-to-dealer. This was approximately $50,000 over Bid at the time.

PCGS Professional Coin Grading Service: Established in 1986 to grade and authenticate U.S. coins. Located in Newport Beach, CA. You must submit coins through authorized PCGS dealers. Contact PCGS at (714) 250-1211 for a list of authorized dealers (currently over 250 throughout the U.S. and Canada). PCGS has more than 15 graders on their staff and a minimum of three must agree on the grade of a coin before the final PCGS grade is determined. The service costs $22 per coin, plus postage and insurance, no matter how valuable the coin is. When graded the coin is sonically sealed in an inert, hard plastic container and returned to the customer.

Many PCGS dealers make sight unseen bids for PCGS coins. PCGS identifies color on copper (red, red and brown, or brown), full bands on Mercury Dimes, full head on Standing Liberty Quarters, and Prooflike and Deep Mirror Prooflike on Morgan Dollars. PCGS has a comprehensive grading set which includes most major series. PCGS publishes monthly population reports. PCGS has a cash-backed grading guarantee.

NGC Numismatic Guaranty Corporation of America: Established in 1987, to grade and authenticate U.S. coins. Located in Parsippany, New Jersey. You must submit coins to NGC through authorized NGC dealers. Phone: (201) 984-6222. NGC has more than 15 graders on its staff and every coin is viewed by a grading team of 3-5 members. A finalizer assembles the grades and verifies the final grade. The finalizer must not be in the buying or selling end of the coin business. The service costs a minimum of $23, plus postage and insurance, no matter what the value of the coin. After it is graded, it is then placed in a "lab-tested" (inert), hard plastic holder and sonically sealed, then returned to the customer.

There are over 250 authorized NGC dealers who will send coins in for grading. Many of these dealers will make sight unseen bids for NGC graded coins. NGC will not grade coins dated after 1964. Their grading philosophy is designed to be strict no matter what condition the coin market is in. The principals of NGC do not buy or sell coins for commercial profit: "Arm's length". NGC has a grading set for the popular series and is currently working on sets for other series.

ANACS American Numismatic Association Certification Service: First authentication service, established by the American Numismatic Association in 1972 (to which grading was added in 1978). The ANA is a nonprofit, educational organization chartered by Congress. ANACS proceeds are channeled into ANA membership services. ANACS renders independent, third-party opinions that are free of market influences. The Service employs a team of authenticators/graders, three of whom must agree to determine a final grade. ANACS utilizes nearly 100 expert numismatic consultants to reaffirm authentication and grading opinions.

The ANA Certification Service issues certificates displaying color photographs of the obverse and reverse. Luster, surfaces, eye appeal and strike are described on the back of the certificate. They do not identify color (red, brown) on copper, full split bands on Mercury dimes, full head for Standing Liberty quarters, or prooflike on dollars.

CCDn Bids reflect 1986 and newer certified coins. Certificates may not have any negative comments to command bid prices. ANACS is currently working on the establishment of grading sets for every series possible. Costs range from $10 to $20, depending on the type of service rendered. On request, ANACS will certify coins in sealed holders. Contact ANACS at 818 N. Cascade Ave., Colorado Springs, CO 80903-3279, phone 719-632-2646. Due to current trading volume, ANACS coins will only be listed once a month.

NCI Numismatic Certification Institute: Organized in June, 1984, to grade and authenticate U.S. coins. NCI guarantees the authenticity of every coin it certifies. They are located at 311 Market St., Dallas, TX 75202. Phone: (214) 742-2200. NCI uses three graders in a determination of a final grade, and thirty professional dealers act as consultants. Many of these dealers also market NCI coins.

Grading is based on the philosophy of James Halperin ("N.C.I. Grading Guide") which may be considered somewhat liberal (commercial) when compared to the other three services listed. Minimum cost is $24 per coin and turnaround time is approximately twelve business days or less. You may request a specific grade and if NCI can certify at that grade or higher, a certificate will be issued; if not, the coin will be returned ungraded for a $7.50 charge. They will certify coins already in holders without removal, if requested.

NCI has established grading sets for silver dollars, $20 St. Gaudens, and Walking Liberty halves. They also have reference sets for silver dollars pertaining to "eye appeal", "luster", "surface preservation", and "strike". Due to current trading volume, NCI coins will only be listed once a month. *CCDn* Bids reflect 1987 and newer certified coins.

The *Bluesheet* reports the national certified coin market on a weekly basis.

Bluesheet
(Courtesy of CDN)

the CURRENCY DEALER newsletter

OCTOBER 1987

a monthly report on the Currency Market
published by the Coin Dealer Newsletter

Vol. 8 No. 10 | Single copy price: $3.50

DEMAND STRENGTHENS FOR LARGE SIZE NOTES

MPC—UPDATE

ACTIVITY ...across the market

By Frank A. Nowak

This year's ANA continued a trend which has been evident for the past few years, that is, paper money was not in abundance at the ANA nor were the paper money collectors. The big event for paper is now the Memphis Show in June, with the fall show in St. Louis, running second. Most major dealers were present at the Atlanta ANA, but those looking to buy found pickings slim. Most dealers reported decent sales, but with the inability to replenish inventories the result can only be an upward pressure on current prices.

LARGE SIZE NOTES

The large size type note market, and this includes "type" nationals, continues to gather steam. Quality items at the ANA were in short supply. Lightly circulated notes (XF or better) are snapped up almost instantly when offered. A number of dealers at the ANA were seeking the lower grade large size types (affectionately known as "swill"), but met with only limited success. Even the various pre-ANA shows proved a bit frustrating for dealers seeking paper money.

SMALL SIZE NOTES

This area of the market is rapidly expanding. Notes which many dealers wouldn't even stock a couple of years ago are now being sought and dealers are also stocking circulated grades of notes previously wanted only in top condition. Again, dealers seeking specific issues are finding it tough going. Five $100 1966A legals surfaced at the ANA and were resold to dealers at prices up to $550 each. Coin dealers have rarely brought their small size notes to conventions, it simply not being worth the effort or the case space to display it. However, with the current activity in small size, they should reconsider their decision, at least as far as uncirculated notes are concerned. Red seal $5's and $1 silvers in CU are currently being strongly sought, whether for telemarketing or promotional purposes we do not know.

FRACTIONAL CURRENCY

There always has to be at least one dark cloud around and currently it's fractional. It just isn't moving. Truly choice notes should be bought if they can be found (at current price levels). A couple of knowledgeable dealers are buying the cream at current levels, but they are not really interested in selling at current levels. Lower grade fractional, preferably in lots, is about the only activity in fractional currency.

NATIONAL BANK NOTES

Nationals can best be described as a modestly burning fire with a couple of intense hot spots. The hot spots are "type" nationals, and most of all, notes from banks for which there are immediate "homes". The rest of the nationals are somewhat of a wasteland. The current increased interest by collectors in small size types (and hence, soon if not already, the large size types) may soon spill over to the nationals and at least partially rectify this situation.

MISCELLANEOUS

Obsoletes remain one of the strongest segments of the market. Dealers are having the usual problem, they can't find enough of the "right" notes to buy. Confederate also is doing quite well. Telemarketing has swept considerable low-end confederate material off the market. Foreign banknotes remain healthy with collectors, and hence dealers, seeking condition pieces. Stock and bond material remains quite popular.

MILITARY PAYMENT CERTIFICATES ... an update

Reverse of Series 692 $10

by Tom Knebl

In 1981, Fred Schwan published a much needed reference on the subject of military payment certificates. It was a very comprehensive book which covered virtually all aspects of the subject as well as could be expected with the limited information available at the time. It was the MPC bible.

Six years have passed and much new information has become available, which should be made known to the MPC collector. In view of this, a second edition of this reference is about to be released, and in fact, will be by the time of this publication.

Some of the features of this new edition are an essay on the fascinating and ever mysterious series 651 fractional notes; an up to date listing of MPC coupons with more of these coupons illustrated than ever before, plus, detailed information on replacement certificates. The survey of MPC replacement notes now includes more than 1500 serial number reports along with additional information and illustrations. Never before published information and illustrations of the yet to be released series 691 and 701 are also included. The catalog section is also updated as to values and an essay on the investment aspects of MPC is also included. There are also many other new features and revisions.

This new edition will be available in three versions. The first is the regular softbound edition, the second will be a hardbound edition which will hold up to heavy use much better, and the third will be a special collectors' edition which will be especially prepared on an individual basis for each person who orders one. This last version will have a special binding and other features not found in the first two versions. It will also be limited to no more than the first fifty persons who order it.

The book may be ordered from the publisher;

BNR Press
132 East Second Street
Port Clinton, OH. 43452

Softbound $20.00
Hardbound $30.00
Collectors' Special Edition $65.00
(Add $2 for postage)

The book may also be ordered directly from the author: Fred Schwan, Drawer 409, Leavenworth, KS. 66048; (913) 651-2878.

Greensheet
(Courtesy of CDN)

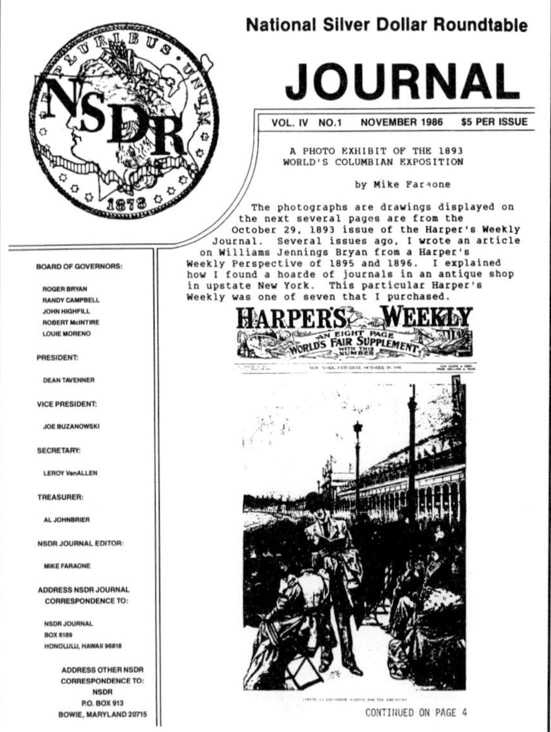

National Silver Dollar Roundtable

JOURNAL

VOL. IV NO.1 | NOVEMBER 1986 | $5 PER ISSUE

BOARD OF GOVERNORS:
ROGER BRYAN
RANDY CAMPBELL
JOHN HIGHFILL
ROBERT McINTIRE
LOUIE MORENO

PRESIDENT:
DEAN TAVENNER

VICE PRESIDENT:
JOE BUZANOWSKI

SECRETARY:
LEROY VanALLEN

TREASURER:
AL JOHNBRIER

NSDR JOURNAL EDITOR:
MIKE FARAONE

ADDRESS NSDR JOURNAL CORRESPONDENCE TO:
NSDR JOURNAL
BOX 6189
HONOLULU, HAWAII 96818

ADDRESS OTHER NSDR CORRESPONDENCE TO:
NSDR
P.O. BOX 913
BOWIE, MARYLAND 20715

A PHOTO EXHIBIT OF THE 1893 WORLD'S COLUMBIAN EXPOSITION

by Mike Faraone

The photographs are drawings displayed on the next several pages are from the October 29, 1893 issue of the Harper's Weekly Journal. Several issues ago, I wrote an article on Williams Jennings Bryan from a Harper's Weekly Perspective of 1895 and 1896. I explained how I found a hoarde of journals in an antique shop in upstate New York. This particular Harper's Weekly was one of seven that I purchased.

CONTINUED ON PAGE 4

The NSDR Journal (Quarterly)
(Courtesy of National Silver Dollar Roundtable Journal)

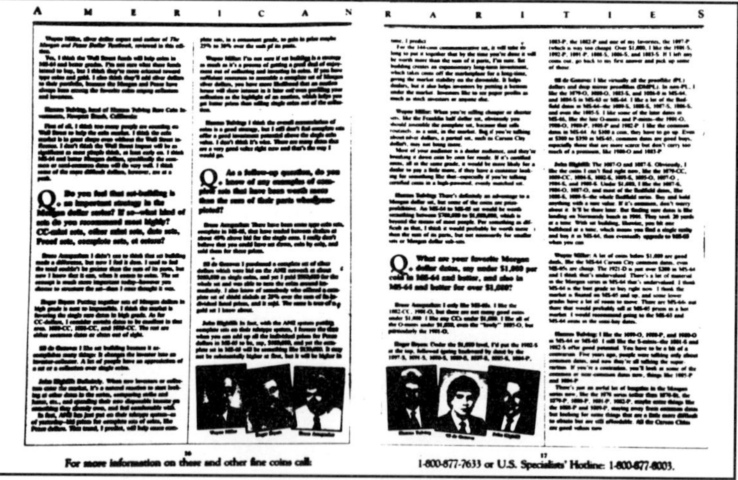

A M E R I C A N R A R I T I E S

For more information on these and other fine coins call: 1-800-877-7633 or U.S. Specialists' Hotline: 1-800-877-8003.

American Rarities Newsletter
(Courtesy of James U. Blanchard and Company)

PNG revises ethics code

Collector's needs to take priority

By David L. Ganz

Please see PNG Page 16

Support strong for Columbus coins in House Banking hearing

By Richard Feeney

KENNETH E. HALLENBECK, above, testifies during May 14 hearing on H.R. 600 and H.R. 1107. Below, Lt. Gen. Donald W. Jones, left, testifies, as Eugene Essner, Deputy Director of the U.S. Mint, right, looks on.

Please see HEARING Page 7

Gulf update:

Influx of fake gold coins may increase

By Maj. Greg Dubay

Please see UPDATE Page 24

Coin World
(Courtesy of Coin World)

100th ANA Anniversary Special Issue
Numismatic News
(Courtesy of Krause Publications)

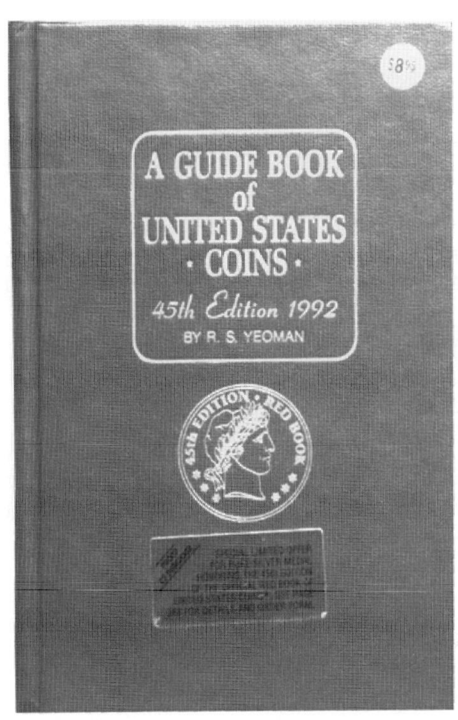

A Guide Book of United States Coins
(Red Book)
(Courtesy of Ken Bressett)

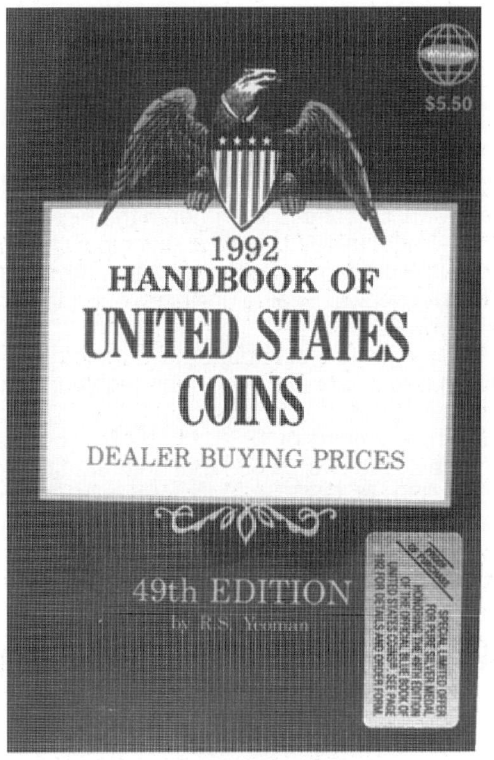

Handbook of United States Coins
(Blue Book)
(Courtesy of Ken Bressett)

***

Mark S. Yaffe

Today, Mark S. Yaffe is a partner in the highly successful National Gold Exchange. In the beginning, coin dealing was a hobby for Mr. Yaffe. In 1976, while a junior in high school, he and his brother Alan opened a small retail coin store in Medford, Massachusetts and named it Markal Coins. From 1977 to 1980, Mark attended Boston College full time as well as traveling to all major coin shows. Seeing unlimited opportunity in coins, Mr. Yaffe left Boston College in his senior year to pursue coins on a full time basis.

In 1981, Mr. Yaffe first imported U.S. gold coins from Europe to the United States. By 1985, as the business had grown to $50 million size, Mark and Alan changed their firms name to National Gold Exchange to more accurately reflect the coins they were trading.

During the Summer of 1988, Mr. Yaffe moved his operation from Massachusetts to Tampa, Florida. In late 1989, Mr. Yaffe was one of the two parties that sold the first coin to trade for over $1 million (U.S. Assayer Augustus Humbert's own Proof 1852/1 $20, PCGS Pr-65). In June of 1990, Mr. Yaffe again made numismatic history. He purchased a complete type set of coins. The purchase price for the 130-coin set was in excess of $8 million. This purchase was even greater than the Redfield dollar deal.

Although he has handled many great rarities and finest known coins like the 1796 quarter PCGS MS67, 1799 dollar PCGS MS66, 1798 $2½ gold PCGS MS65 and the 1796 half dollar NGC MS64, his daily business involves coins valued between $50 and $10,000.

Mr. Yaffe is a life member of the ANA, NSDR, PNG, and many other numismatic organizations. He is also an annual contributor to the "Red Book". Mr. Yaffe is currently a member of the Board of Governors of the National Silver Dollar Roundtable.

CHAPTER 47

Retailing and the Marketplace

Two Interviews With Mark S. Yaffe
Conducted by David Lisot and John W. Highfill

The following interview with Mark S. Yaffe was conducted by David Lisot on November 10, 1990 in St. Louis, Missouri. This interview focused upon Mark's interest in the gold coin market.

How did you get started in coins?

It was a hobby. As a kid in school when I got good grades, my parents would give me a dollar for every 'A'. I could go into Boston and take the subway and go to coin stores on Bromfield Street and buy coins with the money that I had. I used to buy old Indian head pennies for 20 cents apiece, or 6 for a dollar.

Did you have one person who inspired and helped you get started in collecting?

When I first started being involved with coins as a business, I did a lot of coin buying from Eddy Leventhal at J. J. Teaparty. The person who probably introduced me the most to coins and got me involved and took me around was Eddy Aleo in Boston. He runs the Boston coin show now.

Did you ever think you would get involved to the level you have?

Definitely not. I never thought coins would be what they are. It was a hobby when I was a kid, something I fooled around with in high school. I never thought in my wildest dreams I would be doing what I'm doing today.

You have a lot of experience in dealing with the European coin market.

We buy gold in Europe and have been importing gold U.S. coins into America since 1980. Now we import them and slab them. In the old days we would bring them in and sell them as raw coins in the different grades, MS-61, 62, 63 and so forth, whatever it may be.

Why are there so many U.S. gold coins in Europe?

Europeans in the 1920's and 30's did not deal in paper money or believe in paper money, so when the U.S. government or businesses had to pay their bills, they shipped over gold. Then when gold became illegal in 1933, the Europeans would pay $21 for a $20 gold coin. So it made sense to take the coins from America and sell them in Europe, except the Europeans were smarter because now we're paying $400 and $500 for the same $20 gold coins.

How do the coins surface, what is a typical transaction like?

Different ways. The basis is the coins start from private people. They either have coins on deposit in a bank or in their safe deposit boxes or the basement of their houses. They usually take it to a store and the store either calls us or other coin dealers that they know, usually Americans. Sometimes they take it to a bank or a bigger dealer and then it gets sold and it eventually ends up back in America.

How do you solicit business while your in Europe?

Like here, we have a regular clientele of different banks in Switzerland. We deal with different coin places in France, or Belgium or Germany. We call them up and say "What do you have" or go visit their stores and offices. They show us coins and we make offers and if the prices are accepted they sell us the coins.

How did you break into the European market?

It wasn't easy. When I first started in 1981 I went over with my father because at the time I was 21 years old and a Swiss banker wasn't going to talk to a young kid. So I had my father come, who knew nothing about coins, and act as the boss of the business and he would talk to them. I would tell him what to say and they would show him coins that he would show to me. We would make the prices and we started that way. It took a lot of door pounding. There was one bank we went to, Bank Leu in Zurich, we probably went to for one year before they would even show me a coin. It took a lot of persistence.

What is the most important thing to the Europeans in terms of doing business?

They value correct business. They don't want someone who is going to play games. This is the price. If you offer them $400 they don't expect you to buy a coin that is worth $600. If they find out that you have taken advantage of them they just won't do business with you. When you pay it is cash and carry, unlike in America where you pay by check or you ask for two weeks or four weeks, or you buy coins at retail and you put them on lay away. Theirs is a cash only business: "This is the price, wire me the money, I send you the coins."

What was the most interesting deal to come out of Europe?

In 1985 we bought a deal in Switzerland where we had 2,000 1904 $20 Liberty gold coins. They were in mint sealed bags of 250 coins per bag. We bought the coins. We had no idea what we bought, we had to buy the coins without looking at them. When we got back to the States, they ranged anywhere from MS-60, not because they were worn but because they were beat up in the bag, to coins that would grade MS-64 and 65. The whole spectrum of coins. It was pretty amazing. We got the coins into the States and took them up to our office and opened the bags and just stacked them up and looked at them. It was pretty neat.

How difficult is it to deal with customs for transporting the coins, both in this country and overseas?

In the U.S. it's no problem to bring them into the States. Coins are duty free. There is no tax on it. All you need is a broker and to declare the coins with a value, proof of purchase, country of origin and invoices. When you export coins, the laws vary from country to country. Each country has different export laws. In Switzerland you don't need any papers. In Belgium they serve papers. In France it's legal now if you're a licensed business, but if you're a private person and try to take coins out of the country they will confiscate the coins at the border. Every country has its own set of rules and laws. If somebody thinks about buying coins outside the country, like anything else, just know what you're doing before you start to do it.

Of all the European countries, which is the best to do business with, which is the worst?

The easiest in the western European countries is Switzerland because you go to a bank, they have the coins, they tell you this is what they want or you can make them an offer and it's yes or no. That's the end of the discussion.

The worst would probably be business in France because nothing is cut or dry. A lot of people are afraid they may sell a coin too cheap and they may even want to solicit your offer and wait to get five more offers before they feel they have maximized the price of the coin. So I'd say that France is the worst with Switzerland being the easiest.

Is there much reciprocal business that goes on, where you can take coins over there to be sold?

They are interested in European coins. They don't like American coins so much. When the dollar goes down and the premiums in America go down, they buy lower grade gold, we ship it from the States back to Europe, but this only happens maybe two or three times a year. In general they are net sellers of gold.

Why are they selling U.S. gold coins back to us right now?

The premiums are high. There are a lot of European coins you can buy in nice condition, compared to $20's which are not rare but relatively common coins. You can buy Swiss 20 francs, you can buy French Roosters or British sovereigns or Belgian Alberts, coins in the 1800's and early 1900's in nice uncirculated condition, the equivalent of the $20 gold piece sell for a few percent over melt. So why buy a U.S. gold coin that you may pay 20 or 30% more [for]? They would rather sell the U.S. and buy the European coins, and still keep more ounces of gold for the same dollar value invested.

How aware are the Europeans of the American infatuation with grading?

They never used to be, but they are very, very in tune now. We are slabbing coins for Europeans and they pay us 2 or 3 percent to sell the coins for them. They come to all the major coin shows. The Swiss banks and private dealers set up at ANA conventions. Eight or ten years ago they were not that attuned to the market in the U.S., but now they are as good or smarter than any American dealer.

Will we ever see third party grading in Europe?

Someday I think you will and I don't think it's too far off. That was a radical concept in the U.S., and it was fought, and people tried not to do it. But once it was done and accepted everyone loved it. It makes sense that the Europeans should do the same.

Do you ever get rare dates and good coins out of Europe, or is it just bullion?

You definitely do, but you don't get them for free. Everybody has Red Books or Greysheets or Bluesheets and they have a good idea of the values. If they don't, they call up the States and they may call an auction company and find out what the approximate value of a coin may be. We do have a customer over there who sells us U.S. gold coins who has a 1927-D $20 St. Gaudens, but they don't want to sell it. They have had it for years. We've offered them many hundreds of thousands of dollars and they still want to keep the coin. The people who have the neat stuff don't need to sell it, they would just as soon keep the coins.

After you get the coins out of Europe and back to the States, what do you do with them?

It depends. On the low grade coins we sell them raw to different dealers or over the counter in our store retail. We recommend low grade U.S. gold instead of the modern day Eagle because for the same price people can buy a hundred year gold coin with a little romance and history versus a modern day coin that is freshly minted. The higher grade coins we encapsulate with either PCGS or NGC, and then we sell them in the slabs.

Is there a formula type of deal that happens out of your European trading?

Not really. There is no rhyme or reason to anything. One day or week you could be buying Very Fine $20 Liberty gold coins and the next buying original rolls of BU $20 Saints that are all MS-64's, 65's, and some 66's. You could see all kinds of deals crop up. I've seen dealers buy original government bags of "O" and "S" mint silver dollars in 1985. I don't know how they got there but they were there. In 1986 I saw a dealer buy a U.S. large cent that they sold for $37,000, a rare variety, that they bought in a flea market in the south of France. You never know what will come up. [This is probably the VF+ 1793 Liberty Cap, S-16, which sold at $25,000.00, and resold at $35,000.00 spring 1987. Compare *Coin World* 7/1/87, p.38; 8/5/87, p.23.]

Is there a lot of competition to do business with the Europeans?

There are not a lot of people. It's not like there are 50 or a hundred or hundreds of people going around. It is more like there are five or eight of us. We are all very, very competitive. We all know the same people and we are all trying to get to the deal first before the other one gets the coins. A lot of the smarter dealers that get the bigger deals, have their offices set us up in different booths and take bids from us. They show us a lot of coins, get us to write down our price, then show it to the next dealer and the next dealer. Then they break up the deals and whoever offers the most for each individual lot gets to buy the coins. It's more like a silent auction.

Will this source of coins dry up and the game be over?

At some point it will dry up; like anything the supply will stop, but I don't foresee it anytime in the next couple of years. I think in maybe 10 or 15 years it will stop. It's kind of like oil. You never know when it will run out but they'll keep finding new supplies and eventually it will run out, maybe in 50 or 100 years. But coins are more limited than oil.

Let's talk about telemarketing. What is the difference between a telemarketer and a regular coin dealer?

A regular coin dealer's main emphasis is selling coins wholesale; calling up another coin dealer and saying this is the price, do you want it, yes or no. A telemarketer is a retailer of a coin that will usually solicit business on the phone, seeking individual people. They will call them up and ask if they are interested in coins, and send them more information. A brochure will explain to them about coins, about past performance, price history, etc. A good telemarker is like a teacher. They teach people about coins, versus the dealer who just takes a coin and offers it with a price and that's it.

Why have telemarketers gotten a bad name?

There are some companies over the years that have taken advantage of people. People don't think about or remember the companies that have been honest or give fair value. People only like to talk about negatives. Negatives being the companies that have gone broke, the companies that have misrepresented coins or overpriced them, overcharged the people. It is just human nature. People like to gossip and you can't gossip about this one who gave me a good deal, and how I made a lot of money on this coin. They only want to talk about the negative and bad. So naturally when you say telemarketing, people think of all the companies that have taken advantage of the people. They just don't want to talk about the companies that have done good.

How does a telemarketer decide what to price his coins?

It depends, some of them mark up coins double, or a hundred or two hundred percent. But they're not the ones you should be doing business with. They are the fly-by-nights. They are not the ones who have been in business ten years or twenty years. They are not the ones that have clean records, no complaints with the Better Business Bureau or the FTC. The ones with good clean track records usually mark coins up 20%, and 20% is not an unreasonable markup for the product. When coins go up in value, 20% can be made in the span of a few weeks, versus the 100% or 200% markups that could take forever for the person to make a profit. A person needs to look for the dealer with a fair markup.

Are there other countries where coin hoards exist?

Coins are everywhere. A deal was bought out of El Salvador in, I believe, 1985 that is rumored to have been as high as $30 million. It had 20,000 U.S. double eagle gold coins in it, and that came from the national treasury. The King of Siam set wasn't in America. The one that recently sold in the Superior Boys Town Auction Sale, came from the Far East. King Farouk of Egypt had one of the finest coin collections ever assembled in the 1950's. Lord St. Oswald of British royalty, had one of the finest sets of silver dollars. A lot of American coins come up in the strangest places, you don't know where. Who knows what will turn up with free trade in Eastern Europe. We don't know what will turn up there. There could be nothing or there could be some of the great numismatic rarities that have been lost for hundreds of years. I mean, you could find a 1793 Chain Cent in MS-67 red, it could come up. It's unlikely, but it could happen.

Of all your dealings, which do you enjoy the most?

I guess I like dealing in the really neat rare coins. Coins that are a lot of money, that I can't afford to keep. I'd like to keep them and regret when I sell them. We sold a 1796 quarter in MS-67 at the 1990 Seattle ANA Convention for over a million dollars, and we had the proof Humbert in PCGS MS-65 the year before that. Coins that are truly unique and rare. Once in a lifetime coins. The only bad thing is they are a lot of money, and you can only have one at a time. But they are so much fun when you have them and when you sell them.

Why do U.S. gold coins command such a significant premium over their gold bullion value compared to other world gold coins?

Americans like American coins and Americans have more money and disposable income per capita than Europeans. The average European (my wife is from Belgium) lives in a small apartment or house, assuming they are fortunate enough to have a house. They are really just getting by. Gas is three or four dollars a gallon. Taxes are high, unlike the U.S. where the top rate is around 33%. In Belgium the top rate is 80%! So people just get by and make a living.

Do you see the industry changing from when you started to where it is now?

The industry is always changing. In the late 50's and early 60's, people were buying BU rolls of nickels and dimes. Things that are really common, they considered rare. In the 70's it was BU rolls of silver dimes, quarters, halves, and Walkers. In the early 80's it was commems, in 1985 it was small U.S. gold $1's, $2's, 1/2's, $5's. In 1987 and 1988 it was Pandas, Dragons and foreign coins.

I think the market has come into its own in the last two or three years. People are now buying high grade U.S. coins, type coins, proof gold, commemoratives, things like that. So the market is evolving. It was seeking direction over the last 30 years and now it is being more fine tuned. Coins that go up in value are the better type coins, better high grade coins. The coins that are becoming, I won't say worthless, but have no real significant value, are the generic coins. The MS-63 silver or 63 Saints, coins that there are truckloads of, and truckloads will be made.

***

The second interview with Mark S. Yaffe was conducted by John W. Highfill in February 1991. This interview focused on Mark's experiences in the silver dollar market.

When did you first get interested in silver dollars?

As a kid I thought they were really neat, they were one hundred years old and at the time they were probably worth two to three dollars. It just seemed that something so old that was worth so little had to be rare.

When did you first start buying and selling silver dollars to make a profit with them?

When I was in high school, I started trading silver dollars. That was in 1975 and 76. I used to go to local mall shows, flea markets and things like that. I used to find nice BU rolls of "S" mints for $140 and sell them for $145. At the time it just seemed amazing that coins that were almost 100 years old and only worth six or seven dollars apiece. Never could understand it. I still think silver dollars are too cheap.

You used to buy a lot of silver dollars "raw" — before PCGS. What was the roll market at the time, and how did you fit into that marketplace?

Well in the 1980's when we started doing all of the major shows, we did lots of rolls of silver dollars. Telemarketers used to recommend them as a hedge against inflation and as a silver medium, and they were really popular. They still are popular. Only now the rolls have dropped tremendously in price from the high of about $1,000 for a common date dollar roll in 1982 to today when they are around $275. The big difference being all the MS-63, MS-64 and MS-65's have been pulled out of the rolls and now the rolls are strictly MS-60 quality.

There were a lot of retail marketing firms that sold quantities of silver dollars by the roll and even in bag quantities. How fundamental were you in the wholesaling to those retailers in large quantities in the 1980's?

In the late 70s and all through the 80's, we used to buy rolls, bags and singles of dollars and ship them up to different telemarketing companies like Investment Rarities in Minneapolis. They would take the coins, pick what they liked, and sell them to their customers. We'd go to every major show and buy as much as we could, because we were selling all we could buy. We shipped bags and bags from shows. There was a very big business at the time.

Were most of the rolls original, or put-together? Were there original bags? How did the whole process evolve?

It varied. We would buy single coins, put them into make up rolls, or we would buy individual original rolls if they were available. Of course when bags and bag deals came about, we'd buy those also. We'd just sell whatever we could find. Rolls, singles, bags — just anything that was a silver dollar and was uncirculated.

What did you sell the most of at the time — Morgan or Peace dollars?

Morgans because Morgans are much more common than Peace dollars. Peace dollars are really a much tougher coin than people give it credit for. So to answer the question, Morgan dollars.

Do you believe that the silver dollars are the backbone of the coin business?

They always have and they always will be, because they are affordable to everyone, are popular, and they're attractive.

There have been times when they have said that the 1881-S is the most pivotal coin in the coin business. Do you believe that the coin business follows in the way of the 81-S. In other words, if the 81-S is down and sells for a very low price, does it seem to be a market indicator?

The 81-S's may show that the cheaper coins are down in value, but has absolutely no bearing on rare coins. The 1893-S dollar in MS-65 has no correlation to an 81-S dollar in 65.

Do you believe that investors, if they are buying coins, should buy the 1881-S, of if they could buy a coin that's got a lower population for about the same money, they should go with it?

Anyone that can afford a little better coin with a lower population should go for lower population coins. But if all you can afford is an 81-S, then that's what you should buy.

You visit a lot of conventions. If there was a surge in the marketplace, would you be able to go to most of the conventions, and pick up the coins you need for the upward swing?

As soon as there is any pent up demand for coins, we'll see prices escalate 20 to 30 percent overnight, because there is a definite lack of material. The only reason prices are down is if there is a shortage of money. Once people realize there aren't a lot of coins around, and they get orders from their retail customers, which is now starting to happen, you will see prices escalate very rapidly.

Would you explain the price difference in a situation where you had a bag of MS-65 dollars for sale versus a situation where you wanted to buy a bag of 65 dollars.

From any good market maker, you may have a spread of $5 or $10, which turns into a percentage in this market of around 2 percent. That's virtually nothing when you think about it. You get one or two good size orders, the market can move up ten or twenty dollars, and you can recoup the dealer buy-sell spread without batting an eye.

Do you think if there was a large demand for 5,000 MS-64 Morgans at one time, that the spreads would widen?

Of course. Because there wouldn't be a lot of coins around and the sellers (as soon as they got wind of a big order) would raise their ask prices and then the bidders (realizing a shortage of coins) would raise their bid prices, so you would see an immediate rise in the marketplace with the spread widening. Sellers would be more reluctant to sell, and bidders would be paying more to try to buy the coins.

After this order is filled, would it quiet back down to a narrow spread trading range again, or would there be a void in the marketplace?

The market always corrects itself, so there would be a big void momentarily, but in due process the spreads would narrow, and we would go back to a tight trading spread with business as usual.

This doesn't necessarily mean that prices would go down. It just means that the margin would tighten up. Is that correct?

Right. Because with a lot of coins taken off the market, and the market would trade at a narrower spread, but at a new higher level. The only reason the market would go down is when a big order is dumped on the market.

What do you see in the future for silver dollars — raw coins or certified? Do you think that bag lot quantities are a better deal, or do you think that certified bags would be the way to go?

Well if people don't want to pay the big premiums for high quality coins, they're better off buying nice BU rolls of Morgans which today are worth around $275. Because the coins at around $14 a coin would be a good value. They are relatively close to bullion, and you still get an uncirculated coin that could be 100 years old. On the other hand, if you want to put your money into something that could appreciate tremendously, then high grade Morgans in MS-65, 66, 67, or rarer dates in MS-63 or 64 are the way to go.

Do you think if someone bought bag quantities of slabbed coins in MS-63, 64, or 65, that they would make a good investment?

With the ridiculously low prices of today, I don't see how people can help but make money. I mean that the coins are just so cheap, anyone can make money in today's market.

What do you think the outlook for the future for silver dollars and for coins in general would be?

I think the market looks very "up" and very positive. Coins, as everyone knows, made a major correction in the Fall of 1990, and today, in the Spring of 91, they are at ridiculously low levels, and the only way they can go is up. I think that wise money will be buying now. A few years from now we'll look back at today's levels and laugh at how cheap coins were, and how stupid we were for not buying more than what we could at the time.

What is life all about?
It's not doing coins 24 hours a day.

***

CHAPTER 48

Merchandising, Advertising, Publications and Silver Dollars

by John W. Highfill, NLG

Brass Souvenir U.S. Mint Name Plate, c/o San Francisco (Not a Regular Mint Issue) (Courtesy of Vineta Mae Foreman, Muskogee, Oklahoma)

Destroyed Original U.S. Mint Dies (4 Different Denominations) (Courtesy of Oklahoma Federated Gold and Numismatics, Inc., Broken Arrow, Oklahoma)

The Morgan dollar is a coin with class! During its 43 year "lifetime" it has been associated with one of the richest historical periods in America. The design is considered to be one the best ever presented on a United States coin, and won its designer, George T. Morgan, a permanent place in the "numismatic hall of fame." The Morgan dollar was very popular (although not as a circulating piece) at the time. It was collected, jeweled and bedecked to the hilt. Jewelers and craftsmen made pendants, watch fobs, belt buckles and all matter of jewelry and even "love tokens." Personalized love tokens were made by smoothing off the reverse and then engraving images such as flowers and hearts capped off with a romantic saying and perhaps initials or a name. These tokens would be holed and worn on a chain or mounted in a setting.

Advertisers of all kinds quickly realized the potential "circulating" medium offered by the popular Morgan dollars. They would smooth the reverse and replace it with their own individual advertising messages. Realize that these altered coins were still acceptable as legal tender and, as such, these advertising pieces would circulate (usually in the local area) and the ad would be noticed.

Others could place copper "collars" or covers around the coins and display their advertising message on those collars. Another large segment of advertising associated with Morgan dollars involved the manufacture of rounds and medallions utilizing the Morgan dollar design (especially the obverse). There were many advertisers looking for engravers who could successfully imitate the Morgan dollar design.

The United States Mint and Silver Dollars

The history and merchandising of coinage within the United States has been told in many ways. One of these is to observe and study a few of the thousands of available pictures relating to the subject. Under this title, the following categories are represented: photos of selected souvenirs, medallions, elements used during the minting process, and items used for storage, transportation and distribution.

Obverse

Reverse

One Ounce Brass Souvenir Medallion - Old San Francisco Mint, San Francisco, California

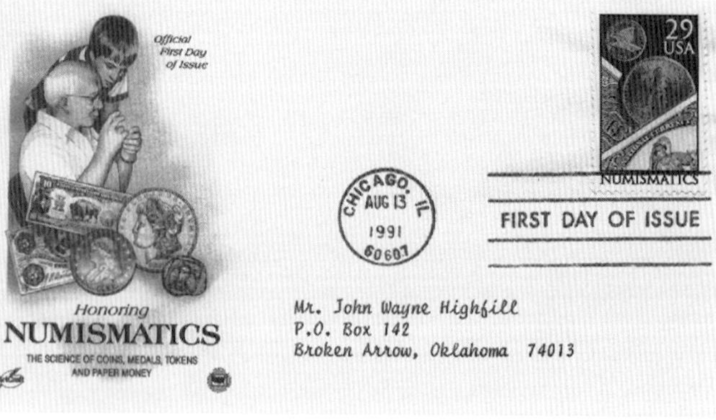

First Day of Issue Cancellation Numismatics Stamp

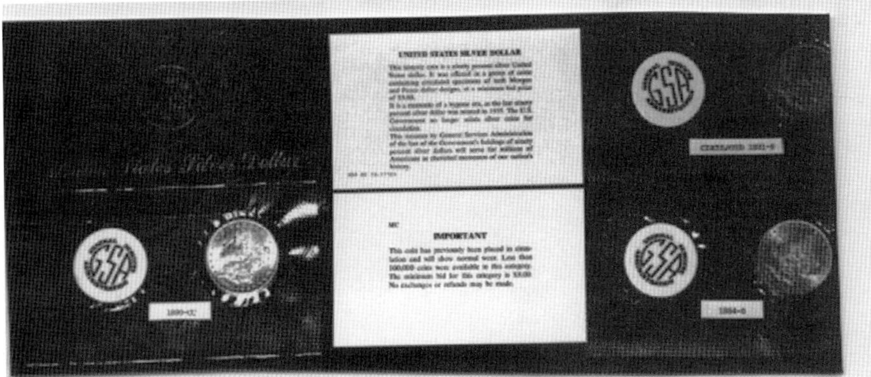

Government Packaged G.S.A. U.S. Silver Dollars "CC", BU and circulated examples (Courtesy of Oklahoma Federated Gold and Numismatics, Inc.)

THE CARSON CITY SILVER DOLLAR

This historic coin is a valuable memento of an era in American history when pioneers were challenging the West. The silver in this dollar was mined from the rich Comstock Lode, discovered in the mountains near Carson City, Nevada. The Carson City Mint was established there in 1870, and although it was in existence for a mere 24 years, it produced many coins which have endured as collectors' items, among them the 13 piece Morgan dollar series of 1878-1893. Their link with an historic period in our nation's history gives these dollars an added appeal.

This coin is a specimen of the Morgan dollar, containing ninety percent silver, which somehow survived the massive coin melts of the early 1900's. They were discovered by a Treasury audit in 1964, after nearly a century of obscurity in the vaults.

This issuance by General Services Administration of the last of the Government's holdings of ninety percent silver dollars will serve for millions of Americans as cherished mementos of our nation's history.

GSA DC 73-11321

G.S.A. Information card that was enclosed with "CC" Dollars. (Courtesy of Oklahoma Federated Gold and Numismatics, Inc.)

The first CC "Slabbed" BU dollars (circa 1960s) California Club, Reno Nevada (Courtesy of Oklahoma Federated Gold and Numismatics, Inc.)

IMPORTANT

This coin has never been placed in circulation by the U.S. Government. However, due to its heavy scratches or tarnish it was culled out of the "Uncirculated" category and was offered in a special category ("Mixed Carson City") at a $15.00 minimum bid price. Your coin was selected from this category which includes Carson City dates 1879, 1880, 1881, 1882, 1883, 1884, 1885, 1890, and 1891. Exchanges for different years may not be made.

GSA DC 73-11321

Mixed lot "CC" card (Courtesy of Oklahoma Federated Gold and Numismatics, Inc.)

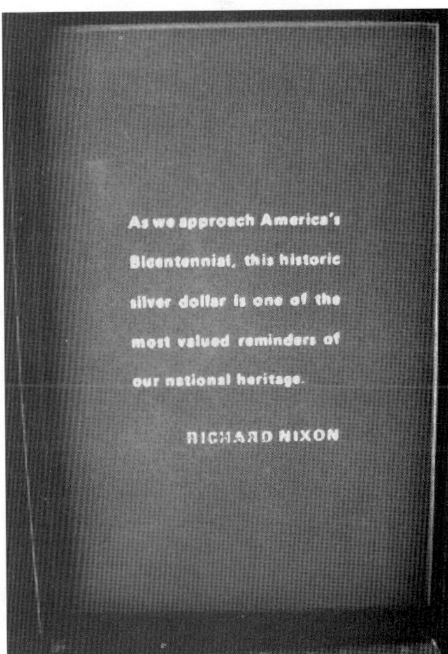

Inside of G.S.A. box holder with inscription from then president Richard M. Nixon (Courtesy of Oklahoma Federated Gold and Numismatics, Inc.)

Original Mint Canvas Bag - Treasury $1000.00 Washington (Courtesy of Howard W. Herz, Lake Tahoe, Nevada)

Silver Dollar Hotel, Virginia City, Nevada (Courtesy of D. Harrison Phillips, Memphis, Tennessee)

Front

Back

"Bag Tags" Philadelphia, Pennsylvania - U.S. Treasury

Silver Dollar Replicas

The extreme popularity of the Morgan dollar and, to a lesser extent, the Peace dollar has resulted in a great many replicas. Companies of all kinds used replicas of these silver dollars to market and distribute a wide variety of bullion related products. Some of these coins were produced in bronze and other materials. Here is a group of replicas that may bring this concept to life.

One Pound "Cameo" Morgan Dollar Replica (.999 Fine Pure Silver) (Courtesy of Rebecca and Nicholette Highfill)

Various U.S. mint tags and seals for original canvas mint-sewn bags. (Courtesy of Howard W. Herz, Lake Tahoe, Nevada)

The Morgan and Peace Dollar used in Multiple Ideas and Designs. (Courtesy of John William Highfill, Memphis, Tennessee)

One, Five and Ten Ounce Silver Bars and Medallions. The One Ounce "Morgan" Replica Medallion is an Obverse and the "Peace" is a Reverse Example. (Courtesy of Oklahoma Federated Gold and Numismatics, Inc.)

Obverses (left) Reverses (right) Replicas of Morgan Dollar, one troy ounce, .999 fine silver, 39MM (Courtesy of Oklahoma Federated Gold and Numismatics, Inc., Broken Arrow, Oklahoma)

Various .999 Fine Silver Dollar Replicas. (All are One Ounce, 39mm) (Courtesy of Oklahoma Federated Gold and Numismatics, Inc.)

Obverse Reverse

Clipped Planchet One Ounce "Peace" Dollar Replica Medallion.
(Courtesy of Oklahoma Federated Gold and Numismatics, Inc.)

Original Dies used in First Run Production of "Peace" Dollar Replica. One Troy Ounce Medallions (circa 1981). Obverse is on Left in Photo. (Courtesy of Oklahoma Federated Gold and Numismatics, Inc.)

Bronze Medallions From Hong Kong, Shanghai, Singapore, and the Great Wall of China in Presentation Cases. (Courtesy of Brad Rodgers, c/o Numismatic Emporium, Inc., Sherman Oaks, California)

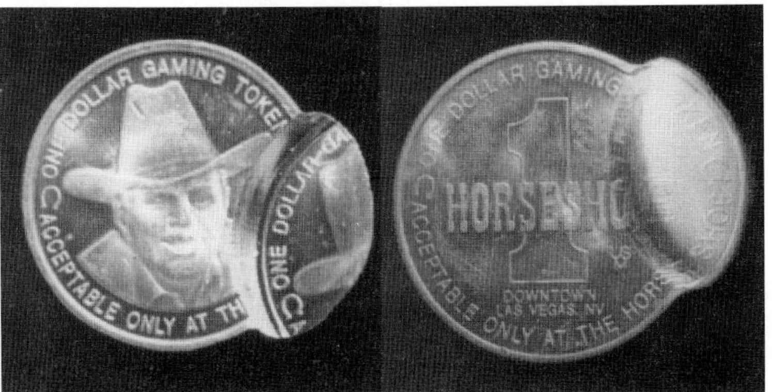

Obverse Reverse

Error (rare) gambling token - Horseshoe Casino, Las Vegas, Nevada

One Ounce Silver Dollar Medallions: Promotional Sales Brochure
(Courtesy of Oklahoma Federated Gold and Numismatics, Inc.)

Obverse Reverse

This Morgan Dollar was used in a belt buckle. The obverse was recessed and remained BU, while the reverse was worn down to XF on the inside of the belt
(Courtesy of John Michael Ford, Denver, Colorado)

Retailers "Packaging"

One important aspect of merchandising silver dollars (or any product for that matter) involves packaging. The aesthetic look and eye appeal of the package, holder, album, or other decorative material and information often makes the difference in a successful campaign. A number of packaging concepts are presented here. Perhaps you may remember seeing some of these through the years.

Coin Album for U.S. Dollars
(Courtesy of Roger Geary, Broken Arrow, Oklahoma)

Various dollar merchandising and presentation methods including white labeled "Okie" from Muskogee, Western Motel souvenir dollar
(Courtesy of Tidy House Products, Co.)

Plastic holders by Capital Plastics, Inc.
Three different variations of 3" x 3" presentations
(Courtesy of Capital Plastics, Inc., Massilon, Ohio)

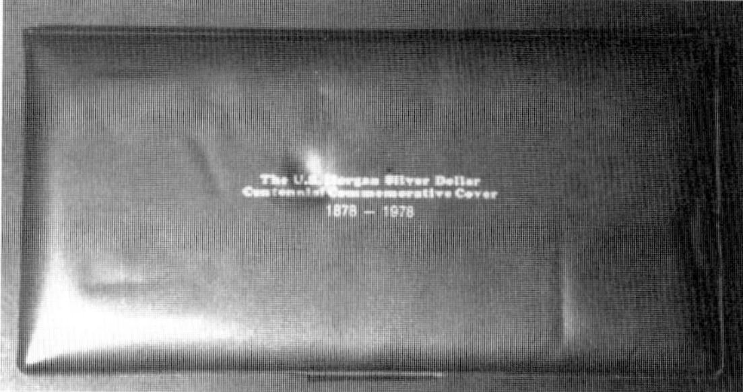

Coin Leather/Vinyl Wallet
"Centennial Commemorative Cover"
(Courtesy of First Coinvestors, Albertson, New York)

Susan B. Anthony first day of issue cancellation cachet stamped envelope.
(Courtesy of Frances Lee Maxon, Independence, Missouri)

Silver dollar package 1945, c/o United Pacific Insurance Company
(Courtesy of Fred Lemons, Tulsa, Oklahoma)

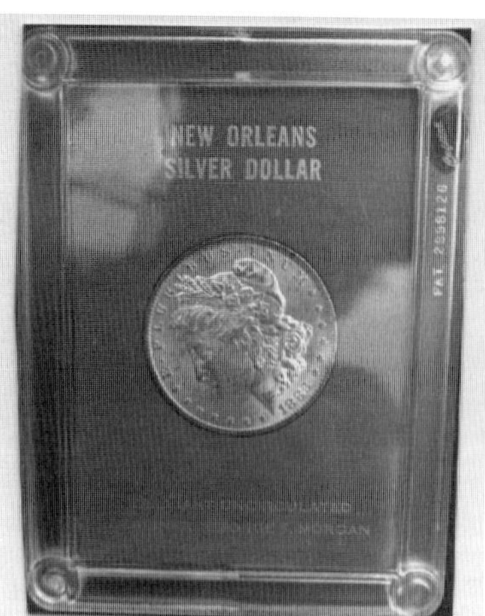

CERTIFICATE OF AUTHENTICITY

The New Orleans Silver Dollar

O

This is to certify that the accompanying New Orleans Silver Dollar is an authentic U.S. Government Brilliant Uncirculated Morgan Silver Dollar, minted at the long closed New Orleans Mint. Although in existence for a very brief period, this historic U.S. Mint produced many coins which have endured as collectors' items. Foremost among them is the Morgan Dollar Series. Their link with an historic period in our nation's history gives these dollars an added appeal.

Surviving the massive coin melts of the early 1900's, this historic 90% Silver Dollar, designed by George T. Morgan, is one of the most valued reminders of our national heritage.

This sale of New Orleans Silver Dollars by the National Minting Distribution Center will serve for many Americans as cherished mementos of a colorful era.

Obverse Holder

New Orleans Mint promotional packaging.
(Courtesy of Thomas B. Phillips, Memphis, Tennessee)

Depictions and Assorted Presentations

There are as many ways to present a theme built around the silver dollar as there are people to create them. They run the gamut from record album covers to jewelry. They have been used as an attractive decoration in almost every setting. Conversation pieces are as varied as their designers, and have been used for economic, romantic, and devious purposes. Here is just a sampling.

The Art of Coins

There are many talented artists who have been intrigued and inspired by the designs appearing on United States silver dollars. Only a few of them appear here, but a legion of pictorial presentations have been seen over the years. They have been prepared for collectors of coin art in its many variations as well as for those desiring themed decorative pieces.

Retail packaging by Tulsa Coin Company in conjunction with ad placed thru *Coins Magazine* and *Numismatic News*. (Courtesy of Don Brown, Tulsa, Oklahoma)

Trade Dollar Locket that was used to smuggle cocaine into the U.S. from the Orient in the 19th century (Courtesy of D. Harrison Phillips, Memphis, Tennessee)

This U. S. Morgan silver dollar receives a lot of wear. This one is concrete and is one of the stepping stones in my yard.

Inside of "The Silver Dollar Country" LP depicting an 1887-P BU Morgan Dollar scotch taped to a map on the state of Montana. (Courtesy of The John W. Highfill Personal Record Collection)

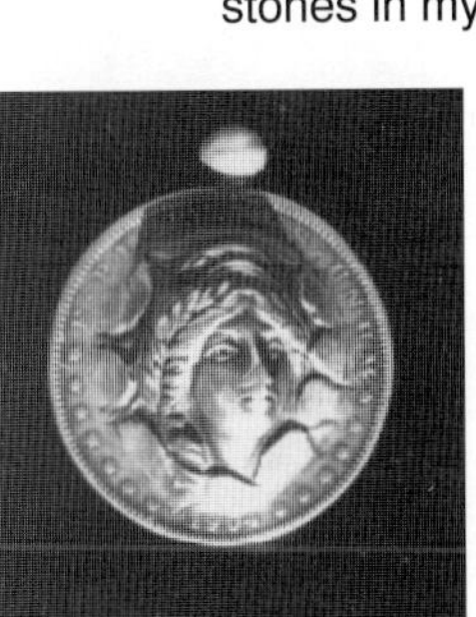

"Punched-Out" Morgan Jewelry (Courtesy of John Wayne Highfill II, Las Vegas, Nevada)

Peace Dollar issued as salary to National Guard Soldiers (Courtesy of Mark R. Jagger, Baltimore, Maryland)

"The Silver Dollar Country" silver dollar record album by Lanny Ross (Courtesy of The John W. Highfill Personal Record Collection)

Inspiration for American Coinage - The Bald Eagle (Courtesy of Nevada State Museum, Carson City, Nevada)

Obverse Reverse

Aluminum Sleeve with Morgan Dollar Insert - 1963 (Courtesy of Oklahoma Federated Gold and Numismatics, Inc.)

Obverse

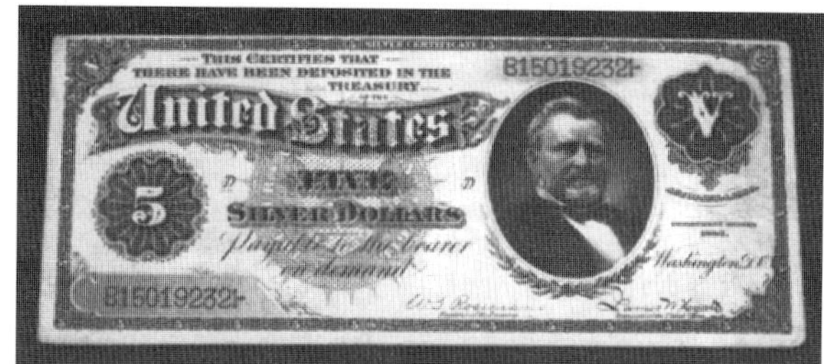

Reverse

Silver Certificate - $5.00
(Courtesy of Thomas B. Phillips, Memphis Tennessee)

Metal Replica of "Morgan" Dollar Silver Certificate
(Courtesy of Oklahoma Federated
Gold and Numismatics, Inc.)

The CoinArt collector's series piece was designed, sculpted and framed by artist and sculptor John Morgan of Tulsa, Oklahoma. The framed work measures two foot square and presents an excellent replica of the elusive 1895-P business strike Morgan dollar. The background decor of dark blue and silver enhances the beauty of the "coin" and makes it a perfect selection for the office or home.

"Morgan Dollar" Framed Sculpture
by John Morgan - Artist, Tulsa, Oklahoma.
(Very Exclusive Limited Edition)
(Courtesy of CoinArt c/o Highfill Press, Inc.,
Broken Arrow, Oklahoma)

Collectors Edition: 1991 Special Issue
(Courtesy of Gabriele Armstrong,
Los Angeles, California)

David Andrade "The Illustrator for the Numismatic Industry"
(Courtesy of Gabriele Armstrong, c/o The Collector's Edition,
Los Angeles, California)

Memorabilia

There are many ways to hold a coin or its picture in your hands. How about a deck of playing cards or decorated glass in its many forms? Collector items from historical occasions and places abound with the silver dollar theme. The 100th ANA Convention in August 13 -18, 1991 at Chicago, Illinois brought a great many memorable collector items into existence by both organizations and individuals. Here is a small representative group.

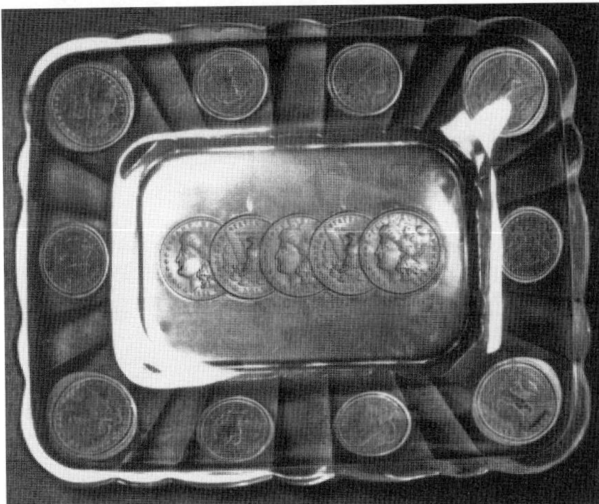

Silver Dollar glass serving plate (replica)
(Courtesy of Gayle Pike, Memphis, Tennessee)

"Coin Cards" Different Promotional Playing Cards Depicting Various Coins and Promoters.
(Courtesy of Oklahoma Federated Gold and Numismatics, Inc., and Thomas B. Phillips, Memphis, Tennessee)

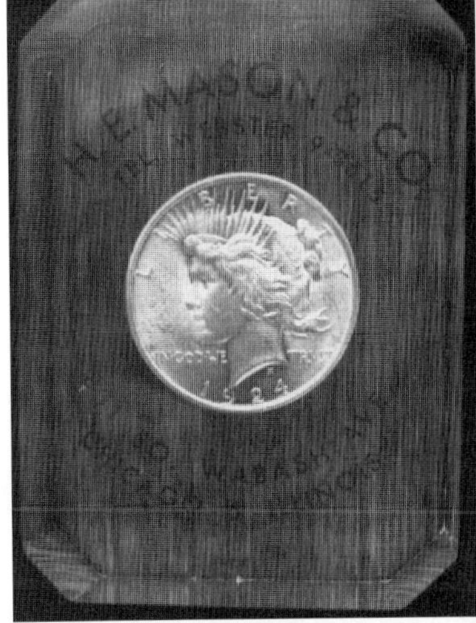

Plastic "Paper Weight" with BU 1924 Peace Dollar enclosed (circa 1982) (Courtesy of Bob Chapman c/o Kansas Federated Gold & Numismatics, Inc. Wichita, Kansas)

1879 Tumbler, hand blown — Circa: 1879 (also see lower left) (Courtesy of John W. Highfill Broken Arrow, Oklahoma)

Various NSDC and NSDR Merchandising Techniques. Wooden Nickels, Playing Cards and Mini Dollar Series Cards.
(Courtesy of Grant Smallwood, Las Vegas, Nevada and Al E. Johnbrier, Bowie, Maryland)

1879 Tumbler, hand blown - Circa: 1879 (Courtesy of John W. Highfill, Broken Arrow, Oklahoma)

Obverse

Reverse

Morgan Dollar Decanter c/o Avon Products (Courtesy of Julie Maxon, Independence, Missouri)

Silver Dollar Pure Rye Whiskey - Circa: 1920
(Courtesy of Thomas B. Phillips)

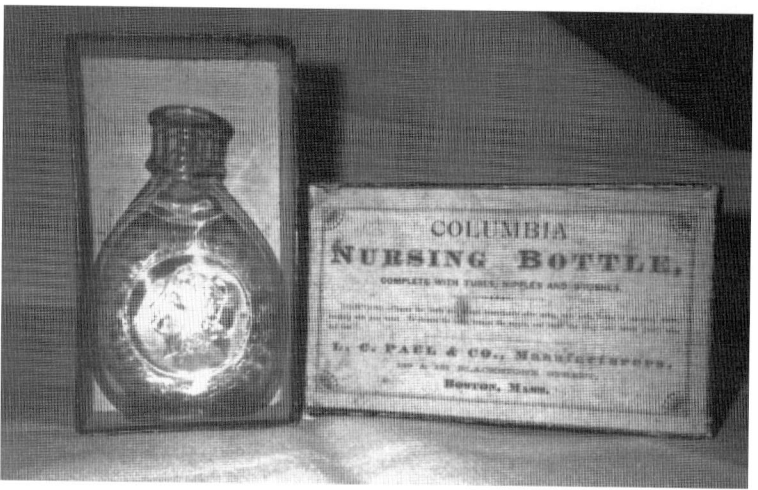

Columbia Baby Nurser, hand blown (1880s)
(Courtesy of Thomas B. Phillips)

Obverse Reverse
Chicago Worlds Fair Medal
(Courtesy of Thomas B. Phillips)

Obverse (Heads) Reverse (Eagle)
1896 Political Whiskey Nip, hand blown, William Jennings Bryan.
(Courtesy of Thomas B. Phillips)

Advertising Items 100th Anniversary ANA Convention, Chicago, Illinois, August 13-18, 1991
(Courtesy of American Numismatic Association, Colorado Springs, Colorado)

Whiskey Nip depicting an 1885 Morgan Silver Dollar
(only one known)
(Courtesy of Thomas B. Phillips)

Obverse Reverse
1892 Toothpick Holder, pattern molded pressed glass, Chicago Worlds Fair - Circa: 1892
(Courtesy of Thomas B. Phillips)

Expanded Collapsed
Collapsible Aluminum Shot Glass
(Courtesy of Thomas B. Phillips)

Numismatic Lapel Pins
(Left to Right, Top to Bottom)
PNG, ICTA, ANA 1891 Club, Original NSDR, Current NSDR and Enameled Black Highlighted NSDR Pins.

(Courtesy of John W. Highfill)

Souvenir glass mug commemorating the "Dealer Fest" at the Mid-Winter ANA convention — Little Rock, Arkansas, March 10, 1988

Certificate of Authenticity
John W. Highfill Collection 1893-O, 1895-Proof, and 1897-O
(Courtesy of Elliot S. Goldman, c/o Allstate Coins, Tucson, Arizona)

Special Guest Speaker award given at the 11th NSDC on November 8, 1990 — St. Louis, Missouri — (award was to represent that the business was in the toilet at the time)

ANA/PNG balloon "Money Bag" (advertisement)
(Courtesy of Glenda Koppenhaver — PNG, Van Nuys, California)

100th Anniversary ANA glass mug
(Courtesy of Roger L. Geary, Broken Arrow, Oklahoma)

100th Anniversary ANA Ribbons
(Courtesy of Oklahoma Federated Gold and Numismatics, Inc.)

96th ANA anniversary commemorative Coca-Cola bottle Atlanta, Georgia, August 26-30, 1987

Numismatic Lapel Pins PNG and PNG Associate
(Courtesy of Paul Koppenhaver, c/o PNG, Van Nuys, California)

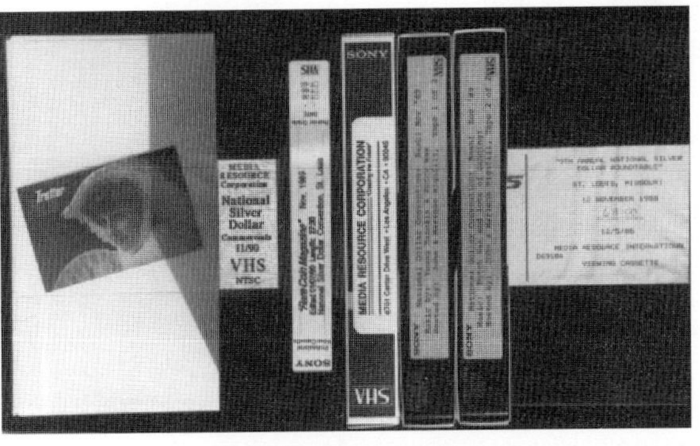

Various VHS Video Tapes and Ad Spots and Seminars
(Courtesy of David Lisot, c/o Media Resource Corporation, Denver, Colorado)

100th Anniversary ANA ceramic mug
(Courtesy of Marlene M. Highfill, Broken Arrow, Oklahoma)

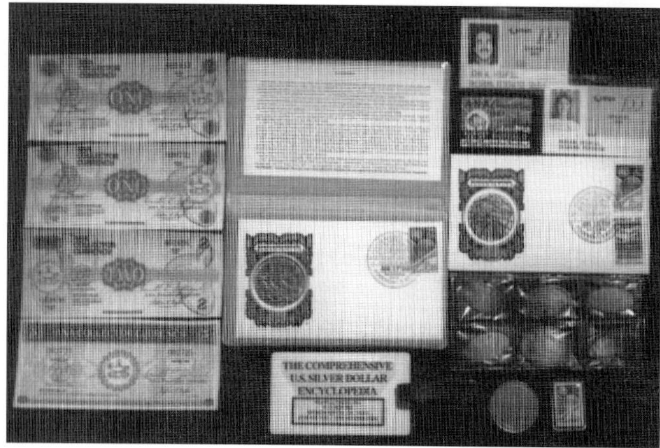

100th ANA anniversary memorabilia — photo includes luggage tag, coin world token, ANA stamp pin, photo ID, U.S.P.O. special metal and cachet cancellation, ANA currency, 1947 ANA (Buffalo) stickers. (Courtesy of John W. Highfill)

Special 100th ANA anniversary medallion stamp (Courtesy of John William Highfill, Memphis, Tennessee)

Books and Publications

More has been written about silver dollars and numismatics than any one person could read. Millions of words describing the history, availability and future value of coins. Analysts abound in books, periodicals, newsletters and other types of publications. It seems that there will always be something for another person to say about the "cartwheel." This text alone offers close to if not in excess of a million words! This is a very small pictorial listing. Refer to the Bibliography for a more extensive listing.

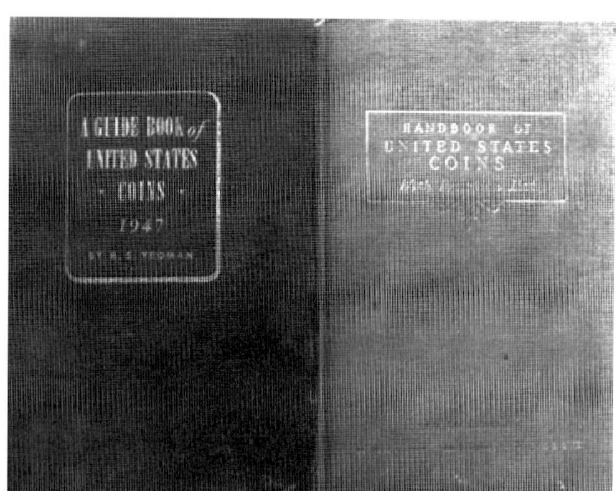

The Early Years: 1947 Red Book and 1943 Blue Book (Courtesy of John W. Highfill)

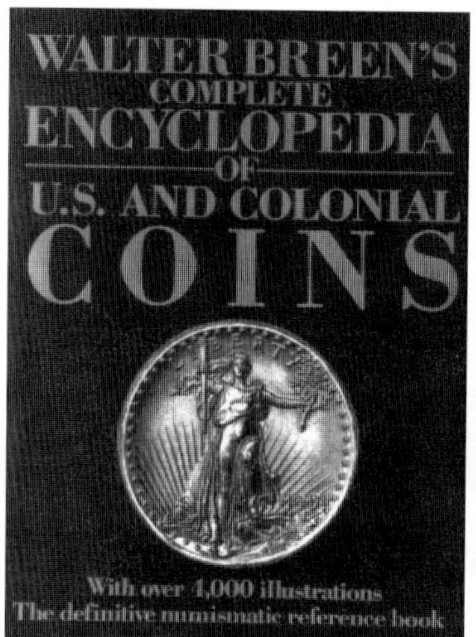

Walter Breen's Encyclopedia of U.S. and Colonial Coins
(Courtesy of Walter Breen, Berkeley, California)

The Comprehensive U. S. Silver Dollar Encyclopedia TM
(Courtesy of Highfill Press, Inc., Broken Arrow, Oklahoma)

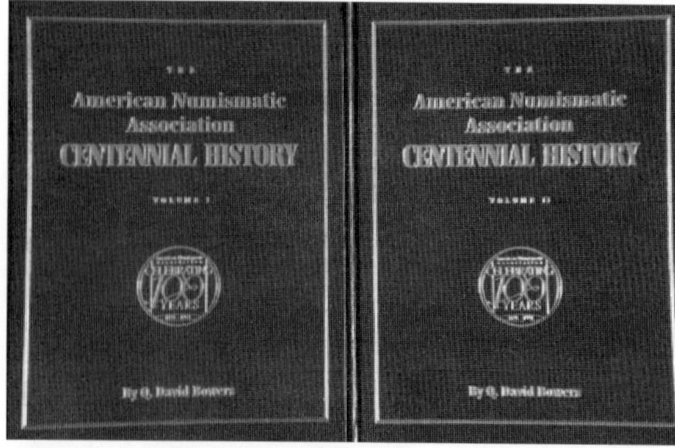

American Numismatic Association Centennial History, Volumes I and II
(Courtesy of Q. David Bowers, Wolfeboro, New Hampshire)

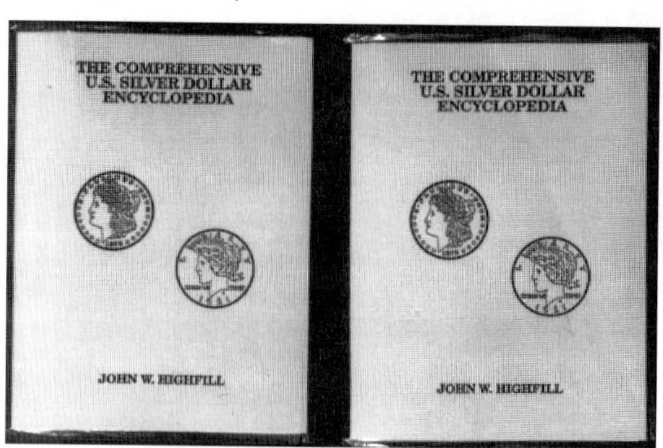

The prototype of The Comprehensive U.S. Silver Dollar Encyclopedia (Courtesy of Highfill Press, Inc.)

COINage Magazine commemorating the 100th Anniversary of the ANA (Courtesy of COINage, Iola, WI)

The Commemorative Trail Newsletter (Courtesy of Society for U.S Commemorative Coins, Don and Helen O'Carmody, c/o Huntington Beach, California)

the COIN DEALER newsletter

Our 29th year...

SELECTED ISSUES STILL RISING

It Takes Visible Demand To Move Market

The Market in Depth

This Week's Market

Coin Dealer Newsletter Certified Coin Market Indicator

BULLION, FOREIGN GOLD, & PLATINUM COINS

SILVER BULLION PRICES

FOREIGN GOLD

U.S. GOLD

"Old Reliable" The *Coin Dealers Newsletter Price Guide* (Courtesy of Ron Downing c/o CDN, Torrence, California)

The Encyclopedia of U.S. Morgan and Peace Dollars, by Leroy Van Allen (Courtesy of Leroy Van Allen, F.C.I. Press, Inc. New York, New York)

ANA Official Grading Guide (Courtesy of J.P. Martin, ANAAB, Colorado Springs, Colorado)

Silver Dollar Encyclopedia, by Jim Osbon 2nd Edition — A Landmark Publication (Courtesy of James B. Osbon, Richmond, Virginia)

Informational brochure (Courtesy of Professional Numismatists Guild, Inc.)

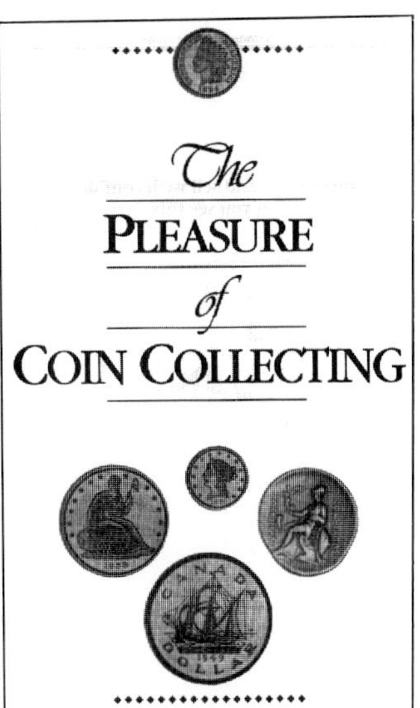

The Pleasure of Coin Collecting (Courtesy of Professional Numismatists Guild, Inc.)

Summary

Limited space has permitted only a small overview of the many methods of presenting, advertising, merchandising, publicizing and describing silver dollars. It is clearly a subject that could occupy a complete book if treated in its entirety.

***

Drew R. Crowell

Drew Crowell started his numismatic career at the age of 15 working at the Plaza Coin Shop in Tampa, Florida. Later, after graduating from Furman University with a degree in Economics and Business Administration, he worked for the Citizens and Southern National Bank of South Carolina.

In 1982 he joined Don McAlvany's investment firm, International Collectors Associates, in Denver, Colorado. He is the head numismatist and coin buyer for the company and serves on their executive advisory board. Drew resides in Denver with his wife and two children.

CHAPTER 49

Common Date Uncirculated Silver Dollars

by Drew R. Crowell

One of the oldest axioms in the numismatic market is, "always buy the rarest and highest quality that you can afford." Time and price performance have proven this to be sound investment advice. We are constantly reminded by Salomon Brothers and others that rare coins continually find themselves at the top of the list of investment vehicles. Even though these studies don't account for the dramatic grading changes over the years, nor indicate the very significant mark-ups and spreads on rare coins, they still offer compelling evidence that the true rarities have done well.

If rarity and quality are key ingredients to successful rare coins investing, why would anyone seriously consider common date, lower-grade (MS60-MS63) silver dollars as an investment? Since they are by definition not a rare coin, but rather a semi-numismatic, they fail to meet the most basic investment criteria.

Consider the following facts:

1. According to R. S. Yeoman there were a staggering 571 million Morgan silver dollars minted from 1878-1904;
2. There were an additional 277 million silver dollars minted from 1921-1935 (including the 44 million 1921 Morgans);
3. In total there were about 850 million silver dollars minted from 1878-1935.

These figures clearly indicate that common date silver dollars are not rare coins. But are they as common as they first appear? Taking the Morgan dollars minted from 1878-1904, the casual observer might think there are still 571 million coins at large. However, several things happened to greatly reduce the population of these coins. In 1918, under the provisions of the Pittman Act, over 270 million silver dollars were melted down. This left a population of only 300 million coins. It is estimated that of this figure only 10% survived in uncirculated condition, or about 30 million coins. With all the fervor lately about how many Morgans the PCGS has certified, it should be remembered that they have only graded a little over 2% of the surviving uncirculated coins. That figure represents only 1/10 of 1% of the original mintage of the Morgan silver dollars! These numbers will either scare off every future potential silver dollar investor or cause them to realize that there is still only one coin available for every ten people in the United States!

Simply on its merits as a rare coin, a common date MS60 silver dollar doesn't appear to have much of an investment future. Are there, however, other factors that might affect the price performance of silver dollars? This chapter will address factors that might have a dramatic effect on the future price of common date silver dollars.

Unlike most other numismatic coins, silver dollars derive part of their value from their bullion content. Although they contain only .77 ounce of silver, this is more significant than it may at first appear. The U.S. public has long held a fascination for the U.S. Silver Dollar. The size and silver content have always given the bearer a sense of genuine value, even back in its day of regular circulation. The mystique of the coin has grown over the years. Silver dollars were the standard fare at Las Vegas casinos for decades, until visitors finally took most of them home. They were regularly given to children as gifts for almost every occasion, and it was very common for grandparents to pass them on to their grandchildren.

Silver dollars are a symbol of an earlier America. An America without many of its social, political and economic problems that it faces today; a time of economic stability and certainty based on a currency backed by gold and silver. It's partly due to these traditional values that the silver dollar remains the most widely held collectible in the world today. It also explains why the public gladly accepted the opportunity to buy and absorb the government's many bags of Carson City dollars, as well as the Redfield hoard. More importantly it indicates that the U.S. Silver Dollar is the most marketable coin in the industry. It has the broadest appeal and is viewed as a genuine value, largely because of its size, age and bullion content.

The price of silver dollars is certainly affected by the price of bullion silver, but to a great degree the price of silver dollars is dependent on the public's perception of future silver prices. The expectation of the future price of silver has an even greater effect on silver dollar prices than the current spot price of silver. The investor tries to anticipate the direction of the market, and bases his investment decision on that anticipation. After the collapse of the gold and silver bullion prices in 1980, silver dollars fared remarkably well. As a matter of fact, they continued to rise and didn't reach their peak until the mid 1980's. Several factors were at work in the marketplace. There was a strong belief in the hard-money camp that gold and silver were preparing to take off again. Helping to nurture this expectation, several large and successful marketing firms arose who specialized in selling U.S. gold coins and uncirculated U.S. silver dollars. It was in this environment that silver dollars reached their peak, while silver was actually hovering at only $5 to $6. Some have blamed the subsequent fall in the price of these dollars on more and more new hoards being discovered and sold into the market place. Although this explanation is partially correct, it is also fairly misleading. The real answer lies more on the demand side of the equation; demand simply dried up. After years of dashed hopes, it finally became apparent that silver wasn't on the verge of another explosion upward. As public interest waned, and investor patience ran out, the silver dollar market responded accordingly — it crashed.

The thoughtful reader will ask himself at this point what possible hope does anyone have who has invested in silver dollars. Not only is there a huge supply, but there is currently little to no demand for them. The answer is relatively simple: market conditions and investors' expectations must return to something similar to what they were between 1979 and 1986. Are the conditions that existed then likely to repeat themselves? Will the U.S. public once again be lured into the silver market, or has it finally had enough? Will precious metals live up to their name and once again become precious, or will they continue to erode in value and merely become relics of times gone by?

It is appropriate at this point to review some of the issues that could have a bearing on the future price of silver. Keep in mind that since Biblical times gold and silver have been regarded as valuable and used for money. Virtually every major civilization incorporated precious metals into their monetary system. In fact, it has only been since 1964 that silver was removed from our coinage and since 1971 that the U.S. dollar was no longer redeemable by foreign governments for gold. Money in the United States was backed by some combination of gold and silver for nearly 200 years, but now is backed by nothing. It is also important to remember that no fiat currency (what the U.S. dollar is now) has ever withstood the test of time. The U.S. dollar is backed by the full faith and credit of the U. S. Government, but its ability to live up to that promise is eroding every day.

Because the economic discipline which was once imposed on our politicians has now been removed (they could not create more money than there was gold and silver to back it), we have entered the most dangerous economic period in U.S. history. In the 1980's alone, the United States went from being the largest creditor nation on earth to the largest debtor nation on earth. We have accumulated more debt in the last eight years than in the previous 200 years put together. We have enjoyed a prolonged period of expansion, but it has been financed by debt — not productivity. And the cracks in the system have begun to show up. The country is currently experiencing the greatest number of personal and corporate bankruptcies since the great depression. 1700 S&L's have gone out of business in the past 10 years, with 500 more projected for the next two years. 1400 banks are currently on the FDIC problem list, and the insurance companies are overloaded with junk bonds and rapidly depreciating real estate. Combine all of this with the fact that our Federal Budget Deficit continues to grow at an out of control pace, and you have the makings of a real financial disaster.

Because our currency is no longer backed by the stability of precious metals, continued erosion of the U.S. dollar is inevitable. Since 1939, the U.S. dollar has lost an astounding 97% of its purchasing power. Whether we continue to suffer gradual long-term inflation or a more direct devaluation of our dollar, the result will be the same — people will seek investments that will preserve their capital. The answer certainly won't be found in the stock market. The outlook for the stock market is not at all healthy. Corporate profits are suffering from heavier debt burdens, new taxes, smaller profit margins, and slowing consumer spending. This has pushed stock prices lower in recent months, but not nearly as low as they are expected to go.

Nor does the answer lie in the real estate market. Not only is real estate extremely non-liquid, but its long-term prospects are dismal. The changes in the 1986 tax laws touched off a domino effect in the real estate market that will continue for a number of years to come. As investors turned away from real estate developing as a tax shelter, developers found themselves saddled with too much real estate. As they sold their holdings, real estate prices began to drop, which caused serious problems for both the real estate developers and their creditors. The first creditors to get hit financially were the S&L's, but there are serious consequences still unfolding for both the banking industry and the insurance industry. As these two enormous financial industries continue to slip into trouble, a great deal of money is going to seek out a safe investment vehicle. Gold and silver have always been sought out as havens from economic uncertainty, and as investment money begins to seek a refuge, gold and silver prices will rise dramatically.

But how will this affect the U.S. silver dollar market? As money begins to flow into precious metals, the stage will be set for a repeat of the early 1980's scenario. Marketing firms will again arise that will cater to the public's insatiable appetite for gold and silver coins. The mystique and fascination of the U.S. silver dollar will be rekindled, and will be enhanced by the rising silver market. It is estimated that less than 1% of the American public participated in the first bull market in precious metals from 1971 — 1974, when gold rose from $35 to $197.50. Probably only 3% of the public participated from 1976 — 1980, when gold rose from $102 to $850, and silver spiked to $50. However, it is estimated that 10-15% of the public will participate in the next bull market in precious metals. This means there will potentially be five times as many investors participating in the next bull market. In this scenario the balance between supply and demand will be reversed. Instead of demand for silver dollars drying up, supply will dry up. With a fixed supply and a possible five-fold increase in demand, prices will have no place to go but straight up.

Common date, uncirculated silver dollars remain a very valid investment vehicle. Considering their age, beauty, history and bullion content they could very well be the most undervalued coin on the market today. Virtually everyone can afford this coin, which increases its potential market place dramatically over other rare coins. The U.S. silver dollar represents American history, and owning them always gives the investor a sense of pride. Their popularity with the public insures an ongoing two-way market, as well as future involvement by marketing firms in promoting them. It is important to remember, however, that the price of the U.S. silver dollar will continue to be directly affected by the bullion price of silver. Therefore, the wary investor should enter the silver dollar market when expectations for silver are unusually low (an environment like today), and plan to exit the market when everyone is projecting new highs.

Appendix

UNDERSTANDING MS 60/62 MORGANS

By D. Harrison Phillips

MS 63 to MS 65 (and higher) dollars are the most popular with the investor and investor oriented dealers, but the vast majority of mint state dollars fall into the MS 60/62 grade. In the 1960's, when dollar collecting became popular, and through out the 1970's people basically made one of 3 types of morgan sets.

1. **Circulated set** (although these sets almost always included a few uncirculated on the dates that are much rarer in circulation than uncirculated - ie: 1884-CC, 1885-CC, 1898-O, 1903-O.)

2. **Mixed set** with as many uncirculated as possible and the highest grade circulated affordable or obtainable for the rest.

3. **Uncirculated set** (with or without the proof, only 1895). Many times these sets also contained a proof 1901 due to the rarity and lack of quality of uncirculated 1901-P's. The 1960's and 1970's was a time before the application of the MS grading system to dollars. During this time most people just wanted a full uncirculated dollar (in today's terms MS 60 or better). Although there were some exceptions, large premiums for better quality uncirculated dollars were unusual.

D. Harrison Phillips

In 1991, with the strengthening of the collector market verses the investor market, there seems to be a new interest in building uncirculated (MS 60 or better) dollar sets. We see much demand for the key dates in just full uncirculated (MS 60/62) for set building, i.e. 1879-CC, 1884-S, 1889-CC, 1892-S, 1893-O, 1893-S, 1894-P, 1894-O, 1895-O, 1895-S, 1897-O, 1901-P, 1903-S, 1904-S.

Some rare date morgans are almost unobtainable above MS 62 (ie: 1884-S, 1895-O, 1901-P). Some of the other rare dates are actually scarcer in MS 60/62 than MS 63 and above (1892-S, 1893-S, 1903-S). Some of the best values in the Morgans dollar series exist in the key dates in MS 60/62 in comparison to many of the more common dates in MS 64 to MS 66.

In general "CC" dollars in MS 60/62 are priced higher than others in MS 60/62 dollars of similar scarcity due to the popularity of CC dollars and "CC Dollar sets". Some dollars are overpriced in MS 60 due to popularity, scarcity in Circulated, and former scarcity. Although it is priced at well over $100 in MS 60, the 1903-O is more common in MS 60 than some of the other "O" mints that sell for less in MS 60 (ie 1889-O, 1890-O, 1891-O, 1892-O). Before the bags of 1903-O's were released, it was one of the keys to the morgan set in circulated or BU, now it is relatively common in uncirculated with one or more sizeable hoards probably remaining.

The relative scarcity of MS 60/62 dollars cannot be analyzed properly by the use of grading service population reports due to four main factors.

1. It does not pay to submit inexpensive dollars for grading, which makes the populations of the lower grades not comparable with the higher grades.

2. Except for rare dates most *investors* want MS 63 or better. Most submissions to grading services are for ultimate sale to investors.

3. Many MS 60/62 dollars are full uncirculated but are "no-graded" due to cleaning, nicks, discoloration, questionable toning, or damage.

4. Many rare date dollars MS 60/62 are broken out of holders and resubmitted to try for a higher grade. Unless the submitter returns the grading insert to the grading service the same coin may appear two or more times in the population report.

RELATIVE SCARCITY OF MS 60/62 MORGANS

The Most Common

1921-P singles, rolls and common bags still available.

Common Dates

1878-S, 1879-S,1880-S,1881-S,1882-S,1883-O,1884-O,1885-P,1885-O,1886-P,1887-P,1888-P,1889-P,1896-P,1897-P, 1898-P,1898-O,1899-O,1900-P,1900-O,1901-O,1902-O,1904-O,1921-D. Singles and rolls common bags about two thirds of above dates came up for sale on a regular basis. Bags of the other third occasionally.

Relatively Common

1878-P 7TF, 1878-P 8TF, 1879-P, 1880-P, 1881-P, 1881-O, 1882-P, 1882-O, 1883-P, 1884-P, 1888-O, 1890-P, 1890-S, 1891-S, 1897-S, 1903-P, 1903-O (See previous comments), **1921-S**.

"CC" - 1878-CC, 1882-CC, 1883-CC, 1884-CC (Singles relatively common due to GSA sales). Rolls frequently encountered. Bags occasionally.

Less Common

1878-P 7/8F, 1879-O, 1880-O, 1887-O, 1887-S, 1890-O, 1891-P, 1891-CC, 1899-P, 1902-P.

Singles available, rolls of all dates above still seen from time to time. Bags almost unheard of today, although they used to occasionally surface.

Tougher Dates

1880-CC, 1881-CC, 1885-CC, 1886-S, 1888-S, 1889-O, 1889-S, 1891-O, 1890-CC, 1892-P, 1892-O, 1898-S, 1899-S, 1900-S, 1900-O/CC

Singles available although not as common as previous group. Rolls occasionally seen of most dates. Bags almost unheard of today. "CC" 1880-1885 were in bag quantities in Government GSA Hoard (sold as singles). "S" mints in bags or part bags in Redfield Hoard. Most of the other dates probably stored in bags at least at some time in history after minting.

Scarce Dates

1885-S, 1892-CC, 1893-P, 1901-S, 1902-S, 1904-P.

Scarcer than previous group but singles available. Rolls rarely seen today. Bags - probably at one time.

Semi-key Dates

1894-S, 1896-S, 1895-S, 1893-CC.

Singles only available now. Rolls available in the 70's. Bags or part bags Redfield 1895-S + 1896-S. Reportedly, a bag of 1894-S was sold in Montana in the 60's which supposedly contained a roll of BU 1893-S.

1879-CC - An available but scarce and very popular coin. Many of today's MS 60/62 specimens are in or have been removed from GSA holders.

1879-CC Cap Die - Scarcer than the regular variety but priced less due to the unattractive "Capped Die" mint mark.

1883-S, 1886-O,1894-O, 1896-O, 1897-O. Scarce Coins in True BU, but available in AU and sliders which keeps prices down and makes them seem more common.

THE TOP TEN (In Order)

1. **1893-S** - RARE COIN IN ANY UNCIRCULATED (MS 60 or Better) grade. When true uncirculated specimens are found they are more likely to be MS 63 or above. Scarcer than 1892-S in the over all spectrum of uncirculated grades, but a close call in MS 60/62. As mentioned previously, reportedly a BU roll of 1893-S contained in a 1894-S bag sold in Montana in the 60's.
2. **1892-S** - RARE COIN IN UNCIRCULATED (MS 60 or Better) grade. When true uncirculated are found they are more likely to be MS 63 or above than MS 60/62. Some super sliders trade as uncirculated. Close call with 1893-S for #1 in MS 60/62 survey. Underpriced in MS 60/62 in comparison with 1893-S.
3. **1895-O** - RARE COIN IN TRUE UNCIRCULATED (MS 60/62) again AU's and sliders keep price and perception down.
4. **1884-S** - RARE COIN IN TRUE UNCIRCULATED (MS 60/62) AU and sliders keep the price and perceived scarcity down.
5. **1903-S** - When found usually MS 63 or better, therefore a higher rank in this survey. As far as total BU's go, several places higher (more common). In MS 65 would rank many places higher (more common) expensive but available in mint state. A very scarce coin in MS 60/62.
6. **1889-CC** - Very scarce and very popular. Rumors of a bag dumped on the gambling tables in Las Vegas years ago could be true.
7. **1894-P** - Very Scarce
8. **1893-O** - Very Scarce
9. **1904-S** - When found BU frequently 63 or higher therefore it receives a higher ranking than in a higher grade or total BU survey.
10. **1901-P** - Very scarce on the BU (MS 60/62). Price and perceived scarcity kept down due to AU's and sliders.

Note: 1895-P unknown in mint state — proofs only (therefore not included).

***

Ned J. Fenton

Ned Fenton, Executive Director of the Collateral Loan Division of SafraBank (California), founded the division in March 1979. During these last 11 years, the Collateral Loan Division has helped over 100,000 borrowers by extending over $6 billion in loans secured by both numismatic coins and precious metals.

Mr. Fenton serves on the Board of Directors of ICTA and the Federal Regulatory Affairs Committee, and is currently Chairman of the California Regulatory Sub-committee.

SafraBank (California) is a full service commercial bank, part of the Safra family of banks, affiliated with Republic National Bank of New York, which is recognized as one of the largest and best capitalized banks in the United States. Republic National Bank of New York enjoys an international reputation as a specialist in precious metals.

CHAPTER 50

Precious Metals, Coins and Banking

by Ned J. Fenton

Historical Overview

Gold, silver, platinum and the other precious metals in various forms of bullion, coin and jewelry have proven lasting and trustworthy as wealth, money and collateral throughout the ages.

Because they are rare, durable and divisible, precious metals have been regarded as a storehouse of value and have been used as a practical medium of exchange in the day-to-day trade of goods and services. Coinage accelerated economic growth by facilitating exchange between individuals, organizations and countries.

Even the origin of today's convenient paper currency can be traced to precious metals. Deposits of precious metals were placed in the vaults of goldsmiths for safekeeping. Written demand receipts were issued by the goldsmiths to the depositors. Soon merchants and traders were exchanging these demand receipts rather than the metal that was on deposit.

In time, the goldsmiths would become what we today know as banks; and the redeemable paper receipts that were written for deposits of gold and silver, we now call cash or currency.

Eventually, the issuance of currency was assumed by governments. Most world currencies were backed principally by the gold reserves of the issuing nation. Certainly much of the world's economic growth in recent centuries can be attributed to the confidence and convenience of currencies backed by the gold standard.

Perhaps renowned historian Will Durant stated it best with the profoundly accurate observation that "Gold and civilization wax and wane together."

Today's Perspective

Since precious metals have been used as money for centuries, why would one want to borrow currency or bank credits against *real* money — gold, silver and platinum? *The answer is simple. By borrowing against bullion, coin or numismatics, working funds are gained and ownership or control of the metal is not lost.*

The flexibility and versatility afforded by a bank that lends to owners of precious metals and numismatics is considerable. It provides new opportunities, dimensions and dynamics to owners of gold, silver, platinum and many numismatic items.

The bank will lend an individual or company a percentage of the current market value of the precious metals or numismatic coin pledged to the bank as collateral. The bank holds the precious metals as collateral until the loan and interest have been re-paid.

There are three situations in which bank financing might be used:

1. When an individual or company wishes to generate cash flow from precious metal or numismatic coin it owns without selling it. The owner pledges the metal or coin to the bank as collateral for a loan. The loan proceeds can be used by the owner for any purpose.
2. Individuals or companies may wish to use presently owned metal or coin as collateral to generate a cash down payment on the purchase of additional holdings. In this way, the individual or company can increase the size of their holdings, with no additional cash outlay.
3. An individual or business may wish to purchase precious metals, or has an opportunity to buy a collection of numismatic coins. By using the bank to finance the purchase, the buyer can expand the power of his purchasing funds.

Between fifty and eighty percent of the value of bullion and numismatic coins can be used as the basis for a bank loan advance which is generally short term (six months to one year). These loans are often renewable and there is usually no penalty for early repayment.

Interest charged on a bank collateral loan made against precious metals or numismatics is typically at or near the prime rate with a single loan fee to cover storage, insurance, collateral verification and documentation. The fee can be added to the loan balance in most cases.

Risks faced by the individual or company in taking a collateral bank loan are primarily in the volatility of market prices for the specific collateral pledge. Multiple pressures affect the price of metals and numismatic coins as traded on international markets. While prices for these items can remain relatively stable for extended periods, they can also experience long term price increases or declines. Prices can also fluctuate greatly, day to day, hour to hour and even minute to minute, resulting in losses or profits in the value of the collateral.

When the difference between the value of the collateral and principal loan balance (equity) declines to an unacceptable level as determined by the bank, the bank may call for additional equity which typically can be met by the payment of additional money paid on the principal balance of the loan, or by adding additional collateral.

In addition to price volatility, one must understand that a bank will charge interest and loan fees for making a collateral loan and these costs must be considered in addition to the purchase price of precious metals and numismatics when calculating the extent of the price increase necessary to be financially beneficial.

As we enter the 21st Century, precious metals and numismatic coin will continue to play a vital role as they have through centuries past.

Now, with bank financing available for the ownership and management of metals and coin, the opportunities in the 21st Century are and will be more flexible and versatile than ever.

***

John H. Sack

John H. Sack is a First Vice President in the Futures Division of Lehman Brothers, in New York City. He has participated in commodity markets for over ten years and manages Lehman's Retail Metals Department.

John has taken an active role in the numismatic community since 1987 and is considered an expert in the bullion coin and bar business. After recognizing the parallels between the bullion coin business and the certified numismatic coin business John brought his expertise to Numismatics and has been influential in the development of the current numismatic marketplace.

CHAPTER 51

Wall Street and Numismatics

by John H. Sack

Since the inception of third-party grading the rare coin marketplace has made major strides towards becoming a mainstream investment. In order for the marketplace to continue its progress, it needs a more solid foundation to build on. In this chapter, I will briefly address how the marketplace has arrived to where it is today, the major problems confronting it now, and most importantly, solutions for moving forward in order to insure the continued success for the certified sight-unseen rare coin revolution.

The Past

Before the advent of acceptable third party grading, the rare coin marketplace was destined to be limited in size. Dealers had to meet in order to agree on the three main aspects of a transaction, grade, price, and terms of the sale. The most important of these being grade. Once the grade issue was clarified, price and terms could be settled by phone.

The first of the independent third party grading services to enter the scene was sponsored by the American Numismatic Association. This program began in 1979 and continues today under the acronym ANACS (ANA Certification Service). The ANA realized that their leadership was required in order to move the industry forward into a new decade. One of the biggest problems to be overcome was the fact that the process of grading is subjective. The problem was addressed with grading reference sets and standards geared to overcome the human factor. Consistency of grading was vastly improved, but not fully realized.

In the mid 1980's, a group of numismatic professionals again set out to conquer the grading of U.S. coins. This led to the organization of the PCGS (Professional Coin Grading Service) which began operations in February 1986. The "team grading" approach taken by PCGS, together with encapsulation of the graded coins, moved the industry even closer to the desired goal. The Numismatic Guaranty Corporation (NGC) and others followed with their own third party grading services.

In 1987, the American Numismatic Exchange (ANE) added yet another block to the numismatic building. They sponsored the first sight-unseen trading network for U.S. coins. This was made possible by the growing population of "certified" coins. The liquidity provided by those bidding on the "Annie" system raised the level of investor confidence and involvement in trading of certified coins. Third party grading and sight-unseen trading had combined to open the market to part-time and non-professional players by making the market more efficient.

With the grading issue well in hand, it was only natural that the demand for certified coins grew tremendously and the number of participants in the market would escalate.

The Present

By early 1989 coin prices were increasing and both PCGS and NGC were turning out record numbers of certified coins. Dealers and buyers alike began to use the PCGS population reports to help determine, and in some cases realign, the true value of rare coins. With over two million coins graded, research and statistics were not only possible, but also relevant.

Dealers were delighted by talk that "Wall Street was coming" and envisioned endless profits by providing less coins than there would be an appetite for. Many dealers were trying to position themselves for increased activity by computerizing inventories, creating new company brochures, offering bid-ask spreads to other dealers, even wearing suits and ties.

While dealers were busy sprucing up their own companies, they were neglecting the marketplace in general. The market was clearly not ready for the influx of business that was anticipated. As business increased, several deficiencies began to appear.

The most important of these deficiencies was the lack of capitalization in the certified coin market and a coherent plan to attract it. Without a broader based participation from the general public, dealers were forced to use their limited capital to support both prices and market activity. As business increased, dealers found it necessary to leverage their inventories in search of additional capital. This strategy was based on the premise that coins would either continue to increase in value or additional funds would enter the market to take inventories off dealers hands. If at any time these circumstances were not taking place the market would be vulnerable to a price collapse which in turn would bring the dealers down.

Every month the population of certified coins continues to increase. Dealers and investors alike are beginning to view the certified coin marketplace in terms of an increasing supply and varying demand. Instead of the historical view of a "fixed supply," the independent third party grading services are "creating" additional certified supplies every day. Therefore, the marketplace must have the mechanisms in place to remove coins from the market. Producers are unable to move their growing supply of certified coins into the retail marketplace. Their answer is to "sell" to the wholesalers at a volume level inconsistent with the available capital. Several ideas were toyed with in 1989 and 1990, yet none were implemented in time to prevent the substantial decline in prices that has occurred in 1990.

In the next section I will discuss ideas to increase the base level of participation in order to support increased activity in the coin market.

The Future

One of the first and most important steps required of the industry is the dissemination of price information. This one step would either directly or indirectly address many of the major problems facing the market today. Let me first explain what I mean by price information dissemination. There are two principal ways of achieving this goal. The first is a nationally recognized coin index. Many dealers today send their own index to their clients monthly. Both dealers and clients are aware of the advantages of following a market via an index. But each dealer's index lacks one major ingredient — it is not nationally recognized. I believe the industry needs to appoint a committee to form an index that is representative of the rare coin market. Although this will not be an easy task it can be accomplished by consensus from leaders within the industry. Next, a track record of this index needs to be assembled, most probably from the Coin Dealer Newsletter prices. Then comes the hard part. The entire industry must refer to this national index. No longer should dealers send their own index to their clients. Each dealer should send out the National Index. Only then will the National Index begin to achieve its goals. Once the industry has a National Index to refer to, it can then be published as other financial information is.

The second principal way to disseminate price information would be the actual publishing of selected rare coin prices. These prices could be selected either daily or weekly from one of the two current pricing systems (Certified Coin Exchange or American Numismatic Exchange). But there are problems with publishing prices based upon the sight-unseen marketplace: (1) one intent of the sight-unseen marketplace is to provide a liquid wholesale trading arena, not a retail market; (2) given the continually increasing certified volume of coins, the bid prices posted on ANE and CCE carry a tremendous financial exposure out of scope with the capital available to the current bidding participants; (3) bid prices posted can greatly distort market "values" when there are no competitive asking prices or transaction prices to provide a balance (a thin market prevails for other than generic coins); (4) the reported bid prices are unrealistic and the vast majority of listed coins are either not attainable or unavailable at these prices (rare coins carry a very substantial premium over posted bid prices).

Mentioning another approach, there are a number of emerging systems based upon asking prices. Systems such as Tangible Information Systems, Inc. (T.I.S.), UNITRADE, and U.S. Rare Coin Exchange (USRCE) are now in operation with others coming soon. The combined offerings by these systems total millions of dollars of coins available at prevailing asking prices. It could be that these prices should be gathered and reported. Eventually the industry should be trying to achieve its own section of the business page of America's newspapers.

As I see it, one of the main problems of the coin market today is the way coins are sold. They are sold by telemarketers, dealers who call their clients, newsletters and hype about past performance such as the famed Salomon Brothers Index. Not very often are coins bought on an unsolicited basis. The reason for this is that collectors and investors, until recently, have not had easy access to the information they need in order to enter and exit the market on their own.

With the recent advent of the computerized asking price systems mentioned above, this could all change. For modest fees, individuals may access listings of available coins in a variety of formats suited to their goals and pocketbooks. Transactions may be consummated in accordance with the rules set down by the system being accessed. The dissemination of this price information would be the catalyst to both bring in thousands of new clients, and create extra transactions from existing clients. With the volatility coins have experienced in the last three years, clients more than ever need unbiased information in order to buy coins. If the coin client could follow prices on his own then that investor would more likely act when he saw prices enter (or test?) new trading levels. It happens in almost all other financial products. Why not coins?

Reliable price information is the key to expanding the number of retail coin clients. Once coin prices are listed in daily newspapers the task of educating new clients would become easier. The problem is still one of determining which prices to report, and the consolidation of prices, grades and indexes for reporting purposes has not been fully developed by the industry. It takes leadership and a period of time for a major index and pricing methodology to be developed, disseminated and accepted on a national basis.

Instead of dealers pushing coins in general they could be talking about the benefits of collecting type sets, silver commemorative, proof gold, etc. The consumer would be comfortable with coins in general and would be looking for specific advice of what to buy. By listing prices, consumers would be able to check to see if coins being offered were at a reasonable price. This alone would raise comfort levels of clients to new heights.

The dissemination of price information would immediately raise demand for rare coins. Once demand increases, numerous opportunities would arise on the supply side. More investment brokers would be willing to provide coins to their clients, a new round of limited partnerships would appear, coins would be touted by investment analysts, just to name a few. I cannot overemphasize the importance of price dissemination. Once this happens, the future of the coin market will begin to take shape.

Another answer to a few of today's problems in the coin market is that of the addition of market-making specialists for many of the coins with higher populations. The American Numismatic Exchange began to organize this concept with two coins in 1989. They were MS-63 Morgan dollars and MS-63 Peace dollars. The theory behind this attempt was to increase liquidity of these coins and to narrow spreads. On the current bidding systems (ANE and CCE) dealers may post either a bid or an asking price for a coin, or both. Dealers may post any price they wish regardless of whether they make economic sense or not. The bid may be miles away from the ask in percentage terms. This method brought about many days when bids for coins dropped considerably to levels many dealers felt were not where the "real" market was. In effect trading dried up until either bids were raised or asking prices dropped to a level that would facilitate a two-way market. Unfortunately sometimes several days would pass before the situation rectified itself leaving the coin market in limbo. To put it mildly, this type of system doesn't work very well and can often lead to no liquidity at all.

A market making system should be organized along the following lines. Depending upon the population and price of a coin, a number of market-makers would be selected to post both a bid and an ask price for a coin. The bid-ask spread would have to be within a certain percentage of each other and the market-maker would be obliged to honor his price for a minimum number of coins. Several dealers feel there is insufficient capital in the market for this type of system to work. One way to begin this would be to bring in as many market-makers as possible regardless of their capital. With hundreds of dealers throughout the country. These dealers would select whatever they feel comfortable with. For instance, a very small dealer might be willing to post a two-way market for MS-65 Stone Mountain commemoratives. Perhaps the dealer would only make his spreads good for three coins. How much capital would he have to commit for the good of the marketplace? With hundreds of dealers to contribute and many of the better capitalized ones willing to make a market for more than one coin, then the beginning of a real market would materialize. The purpose of this would be two-fold.

First, a dealer would have no reason to lower his bid if he is not buying any coins. For if he lowered his bid, he would have to lower his ask for the same coin. Why sell for less if there is no need to? Second, liquidity for all coins would increase.

Certainly coins would still not be "liquid" in a Wall Street sense (and rarer coins will never be truly liquid), but it would be a major improvement over today's market.

The next step would be to open the market-making function to anyone who agrees to play by a basic set of rules. Those rules would consist of posting "live" spreads for six hours a day, five days a week, and honoring those spreads by sending either cash or coins within two business days. The purpose of opening to more market-makers would be to achieve an acceptable level of capitalization and liquidity desired to enhance a broader based market. With increased trading, more players would want to become market-makers, for when dealers are hitting your bid and taking your ask, the market-maker earns the spread. The marketplace would find people willing to do this from outside today's coin market. More players, more trading; more trading, more liquidity; more liquidity, more profits; more profit, more players.

The final area I will touch upon would be a well financed public relations campaign touting both the benefits of certified coins and the developments in the marketplace. After both price dissemination and market-makers are established the industry needs to let the public know about the improvements that have taken place. There are thousands of people who wish to participate in the ownership of rare coins but are reluctant because of either past negative experiences or simply that they don't know how easy it is to play. As liquidity improves and customers are able to follow prices, investors and collectors will flock to the market.

Once the marketplace begins to attract a new and higher level of retail participation, only then can it grow in new directions. These solutions will spark a chain of events that will make the certified rare coin market the market of the 90's.

***

Hugh J. Sconyers

Hugh J. Sconyers is president of Sconyers Rare Coins Inc. of Beverly Hills, California. He also is manager of the American Rare Coin Fund, a private-placement limited partnership established by KP Futures Management Corp.

Mr. Sconyers has been a professional numismatist since 1972, when he joined World-Wide Coin Investments in Atlanta. He entered the field shortly after graduation from the University of Florida, where he received a master's degree in mathematics in 1971. He also holds a Bachelor of Science degree in mathematics from the University of South Florida. His interest in coins dates back to his boyhood; he started a collection at the tender age of 8.

Mr. Sconyers' knowledge of higher mathematics has come in handy during his career in numismatics. In 1976, for example, while serving as president of A-Mark Coin Company in Los Angeles, he helped negotiate the purchase of the famous LaVere Redfield Hoard of 407,596 silver dollars, for which A-Mark paid an eye-popping $7.3 million. That same year, he also acquired on A-Mark's behalf the Wilkison Collection including the unique 1907 Indian Head $20 gold piece, considered by many experts the most beautiful U.S. coin ever minted.

In 1977, Mr. Sconyers left A-Mark to start his own investment business, which, among other things, specialized in the trading of rare coins. In the mid-1980s, he played an important role in conceptualizing the Professional Coin Grading Service. He became affiliated with the American Rare Coin Fund in 1989.

Mr. Sconyers is a contributor to *A Guide Book of United States Coins*, the best-selling reference work popularly known as the "Red Book.." Hugh J. Sconyers, Sconyers Rare Coins Inc. 8601 Wilshire Blvd., 8th Floor, Beverly Hills, California, 90211.

Scott A. Travers, NLG

Scott A. Travers is president of Scott Travers Rare Coin Galleries Inc. in New York City. He also is co-director of the Numismatic Guaranty Education Foundation, a non-profit organization dedicated to the promulgation of knowledge about rare coins.

Mr. Travers established a mail-order coin business in 1976, at the age of 14, and soon impressed a growing list of customers with his knowledge, integrity and service. He became a full-time professional numismatist in 1983, following graduation from Brandeis University in Waltham, Massachusetts, with a Bachelor of Arts degree in politics.

In 1977, the American Numismatic Association honored Mr. Travers as Outstanding Young Numismatist in the nation. Seven years later, the ANA cited him as Adult Advisor of the Year for his work in developing a new generation of young collectors.

Mr. Travers now ranks as one of the most influential coin dealers in the world. He serves as numismatic advisor to a number of major investment funds and has supervised the liquidation of numerous important coin collections. He specializes in supergrade certified coins.

His name is familiar to readers around the world as author of three best-selling books on coin investment: *The Coin Collector's Survival Manual*, *Travers' Rare Coin Investment Strategy* and *The Investor's Guide to Coin Trading*. All three have won book-of-the-year awards from the prestigious Numismatic Literary Guild. A new book by Mr. Travers, *One-Minute Coin Expert*, is scheduled for release by Dell Publishing in September 1991 as a mass-market paperback.

Mr. Travers is a contributing editor of *COINage* magazine and a regular contributor to other numismatic periodicals. He also is a frequent guest on radio and television programs and public forums, where he has gained an impressive reputation not only as a coin expert but also as a forceful consumer advocate for the coin-buying public. His work has earned him the nickname of "the numismatic Nader." He may be reached at Scott Travers Rare Coin Galleries Inc. , P.O. Box 1711, F.D.R. Station, New York, N.Y. 10150.

CHAPTER 52

Rare Coins As A Financial Medium

by Hugh J. Sconyers and Scott A. Travers, NLG

The story made national headlines. A single United States coin — a high-grade example of the rare 1804 silver dollar — brought just under $1 million at Auction '89 in Chicago.

Million-dollar collectibles are always news, of course. But this one was particularly special. First, it set a record as the highest-priced U.S. coin ever to change hands at public auction. Second, it provided dramatic new evidence of the financial service industry's involvement in the rare coin market, for the buyer — the American Rare Coin Fund L.P. — was a private-placement limited partnership established by KP Futures Management Corp., an affiliate of Kidder, Peabody & Co., Inc.

Just in case anyone had any doubts, this transaction made it clear that rare coins have become a big business, a business big enough to appeal to what coin enthusiasts have come to refer to as "Wall Street."

Around the same time, in a private transaction, two coin dealers paid a reported $2.2 million for a set of 11 coins produced in the 1830s as a gift for the King of Siam from President Andrew Jackson. Less than a year later, this "King of Siam Set" was resold at auction for more than $3 million.

Many rare coins are uncommonly valuable today. And coin collecting has grown into more than just a pastime or diversion: It now forms the basis of a high-stakes, high-powered market where millions of dollars change hands routinely.

The Wall Street Connection

Wall Street investment firms have taken due note of this transformation, and are moving with characteristic caution to carve a niche for themselves in this fascinating marketplace. They haven't entered the market as fully or as quickly as some coin analysts expected or might have wished, but the fact that they are doing so at all demonstrates how far rare coins have come. And it holds out the prospect of greatly expanded horizons in the not-too-distant future when the coin market's acceptance as a major investment medium is complete.

- During 1989, KP Futures Management Corp. spent $42 million on rare coins through the American Rare Coin Fund L.P.
- Merrill Lynch Pierce Fenner & Smith has set up two different limited partnerships with multimillion-dollar investments in ancient coins, and has taken steps to establish a similar fund with investments in rare U.S. and world coins.
- Shearson Lehman Hutton has been purchasing coins on a sight-unseen basis at the wholesale level through electronic trading.

The impact of this activity hasn't yet been as dramatic as some had hoped, but this is a case of great expectations getting ahead of reality. The fact is, rare coins have made an impressive start toward winning acceptance on Wall Street, and what we have been witnessing is not a retreat or reconsideration by the investment firms, but rather an understandable exercise of prudence on their part.

The financial service industry remains the single greatest source of potential new growth for the rare coin market, and there's good reason to look for fulfillment of this promise during the 1990s. The result could easily be the greatest market boom in rare coins' history. A steady, ongoing influx of big new Wall Street money would override other factors that normally play key roles in determining price levels — factors such as the presence or absence of inflation and ebbs and flows in bullion prices. Simply stated, rare coins could soar to unprecedented heights in such a market.

Historical Perspective

Not so many years ago, the notion of buying coins specifically as an investment would have been considered quite unusual. People did make money from coins in those days: they simply didn't view themselves as investors. As recently as the late 1960s, the coin market was populated almost exclusively by dealers and collectors. "Investors" from outside the confines of the hobby were all but unknown.

A combination of factors led non-collectors to start buying coins in the early and mid-1970s. One of these was the sale of surplus silver dollars from the U.S. Treasury's vaults. Another was the lifting of the federal government's ban on ownership of gold in bullion form, a ban that had been in place for more than four decades.

Attracted by the publicity surrounding silver dollars and gold bullion, thousands of investors developed an awareness of rare coins in general, and many began to buy them. This expanded the coin market's base and helped propel prices to unprecedented heights within a few short years.

In 1972, shortly before the influx of investors began in earnest, headlines proclaimed the sale of two rare coins — a 1913 Liberty Head nickel and an 1804 silver dollar — for a combined total of $180,000. That kind of money was unheard of in the coin market at the time.

Within two years, several coins had topped the $200,000 mark. And by the end of the decade, the stakes had increased considerably: In 1979, a Brasher doubloon was hammered down for $725,000 at the Garrett Sale in New York, setting a record that stood for nearly 10 years. As this is written, the king of the hill remains the Dexter specimen of the 1804 silver dollar, which changed hands at Auction '89 for $990,000.

Old-Time Collections

Although they weren't assembled with profit and investment as primary objectives, many of the coin collections formed by old-time hobbyists turned out to be remarkable investments indeed. The coins that were collected with such tender loving care have played a pivotal role in luring wealthy investors into the coin market and driving up prices across the board.

A well-known case in point is that of Harold Bareford, a New York City lawyer who began acquiring coins about 1940. Bareford hardly ever paid more than a few hundred dollars for any coin, but he bought with discrimination unusual for that time: Unlike most collectors, who were satisfied with less, he insisted upon the very highest quality. In all, Bareford spent $40,000 putting together sets of U.S. coins — but following his death in 1978, these coins were sold at auction for a total of more than $3 million. In other words, the coins were sold for 77.5 times as much as Bareford paid for them. That's a nice return on any kind of investment, and it isn't diminished at all by the fact that Harold Bareford probably didn't view his collection of coins as an investment.

Numerous other examples can be cited of old-time collections that earned phenomenal profits for their owners or their heirs.

- The Garrett Collection, begun in the late 19th century by railroad magnate T. Harrison Garrett, realized a total of more than $25 million when sold at a series of four public auctions from 1979 to 1981. Yet it contained a great many coins acquired for face value during the late 1800s and early 1900s — coins for which investors paid thousands of dollars apiece at the four auctions.
- The Norweb Collection, painstakingly assembled by Cleveland philanthropist Emery May Norweb and her husband, Ambassador R. Henry Norweb, over a period of more than half a century, electrified the coin market when offered for sale at a series of three auctions in 1987 and 1988. It realized a total of nearly $20 million — even without some of its greatest prizes, which the Norwebs had already donated to museums.
- The Eliasberg Collection won fame for its owner, Baltimore numismatist Louis Eliasberg, when Life Magazine spotlighted it in 1951. As the magazine reported, his was the only collection ever put together which included every date in every metal in every denomination ever struck by any United States mint. In 1982, six years after Eliasberg's death, the gold coins from this collection were sold at a single record-breaking auction for $12.4 million. Remarkably, the sale coincided with one of the coin market's deepest depressions.

The Redfield Hoard

LaVere Redfield wasn't a coin collector, but few people have had as much influence in shaping today's coin market.

Redfield was regarded as a wealthy, eccentric miser in his hometown of Reno, Nevada, and seems to have lived up to this reputation. But after his death in 1974, coin collectors learned that this shy, reclusive man had left an enduring legacy to their hobby: 12 tons of U.S. silver dollars — some 407,000 coins, in all. The hoard was purchased by a Los Angeles coin company for $7.3 million and subsequently dispersed to dealers, collectors and investors in a process that lasted for years.

The emergence of these coins, soon dubbed "the Redfield Hoard," sent shock waves through the silver dollar market. As is was, the market was already in the process of digesting millions of coins from the U.S. government's "Great Silver Sale" of Carson City cartwheels. Understandably, there were fears that the Redfield coins would create an enormous glut and depress prices seriously.

Looking back, it's apparent that the Redfield Hoard had exactly the opposite effect. Instead of precipitating a collapse in market values, it led to a dramatic increase in prices. It did this by attracting many new customers to the market. The media exposure surrounding the discovery and sale of the Redfield coins more than compensated for the extra supply of coins. In other words, these coins created new demand along with the new supply. This, in turn, did much to keep silver dollars in the forefront of the coin market during the years that followed.

The Redfield case demonstrates the importance of marketing and media exposure in promoting the sale of coins. Clearly, the publicity surrounding this mammoth hoard drew thousands of new enthusiasts into the collecting of rare coins in general and silver dollars in particular.

One can only speculate how much the hoard would have realized if Wall Street financing had been available. Undoubtedly, there would have been more competitors for the coins in that event; and competition, of course, would have driven up the price, already quite impressive for that period.

The Redfield hoard was almost entirely composed of coins that were brilliant uncirculated. And many scarcer dates were discovered in the hoard. No inventory was ever released detailing the contents, probably out of fear that this might depress the prices of dates that were represented in larger numbers. It's now known, however, that the hoard contained a high proportion of better-date Morgan dollars from the San Francisco Mint — including many examples of the 1887-S, 1888-S and 1889-S. Not only was the overall quality quite high, but many better-date prooflike examples were discovered.

The Grading Revolution

The arrival of investors in the rare coin market was accompanied by demand for exceptional quality — what one hobby periodical characterized as "the search for the perfect coin." Traditionally, collectors had tended to place more emphasis on rarity, but investors proved to be preoccupied instead with quality: They wanted their coins to be in pristine levels of preservation.

This emphasis on condition soon came to be reflected in market values. Premiums rose dramatically for coins in mint condition, and buyers and sellers began to recognize several distinct grades within the mint-state range. This, in turn, made it more vital than ever that coins be graded accurately — particularly coins in mint condition.

By the mid-1980s, the market had developed a grading system involving no fewer than 11 different mint-state grades, ranging from Mint State-60 (for a coin barely qualifying as uncirculated) to Mint State-70 (for a coin in perfect condition).

Even slight deviations in grade — the difference between Mint State-64 and Mint State-65, for example — could lead to great disparities in price. As a consequence, accurate grading was imperative. But many buyers and sellers felt existing grading standards had changed over the years, calling into question the accuracy of the grading for any given coin.

By 1986, the market was in turmoil. Then, in February of that year, West Coast coin dealer David Hall announced the establishment of the Professional Coin Grading Service (PCGS). The new company offered a novel service: For a fixed fee, it would certify and grade coins that were submitted for review and encapsulate them in sonically sealed, tamper-resistant hard plastic holders.

Almost overnight, PCGS revolutionized the marketplace. Its expert graders provided investors with unprecedented reassurance regarding the grade of each coin they were buying — and since grade determines price, the investors could now purchase coins with much greater confidence that they were receiving good value.

PCGS also established a viable resale market, since each of its dealer members agreed to purchase any and all coins graded by the service, and pay their current price for the grade that had been assigned to each coin.

Before long, rare coins housed in PCGS "slabs" were being traded routinely from coast to coast. Many dealers even started trading them "sight unseen," accepting the grade assigned by the service without first examining each coin.

This grading revolution put rare coins back on the track as vehicles for investment. The uncertainty engendered by the perceived change in previous grading standards, and accompanying abuses perpetrated by unscrupulous sellers, had threatened to derail the market — but PCGS's emergence saved the day. PCGS served as the medium which transformed coins into a commodity, making it possible for casual investors to get involved with coins as never before.

In 1987, PCGS was joined by a second grading service with impeccable credentials. Veteran coin dealer John Albanese, one of the founders of PCGS, broke away and formed the new service, the Numismatic Guaranty Corporation of America (NGC). At NGC, final graders (including Albanese) have always been barred from buying and selling coins commercially, a policy now observed by PCGS, as well. NGC's service is similar to that of its competitor: It encapsulates each coin in a distinctive plastic holder — likewise sonically sealed and tamper-resistant — along with a paper tab stating the grade. NGC's holders have a white insert, while PCGS's are clear.

NGC and PCGS are the two most reliable and most widely respected coin grading services today, but other services also play important roles. Among these is ANACS, owned by Amos Press of Sidney, Ohio.

Generic Coins

High-grade examples of common-date coins are known as "generic coins" and enjoy enhanced liquidity when graded and encapsulated by one of the leading certification services. These coins are said to be "fungible," which means they can be interchanged readily with other common-date coins of the same kind and grade. A number of investors like these coins because they are very much like the stocks, bonds and other investment vehicles with which they have long been familiar; in short, they are like commodities. Within each series, all of them trade within the same price range, and buying them doesn't require specialized numismatic knowledge.

Common-date Morgan dollars are the single most widely traded generic coins. These include such dates as the 1880-S, 1882-S, and, most common of all, the 1881-S. All these coins exist in large numbers in desirable mint-state grades, and this is reflected in the population and census reports from PCGS and NGC, which show that these services have certified many thousands of these coins in grades of Mint State-63, 64 and 65.

Other routinely traded generic coins include common-date Saint-Gaudens double eagles (or $20 gold pieces), Walking Liberty half dollars and commemorative coins. Again, these coins exist in substantial numbers in the mint-state grades that investors prefer.

Generic coins are much more likely to trade sight-unseen than coins of less common types or less common dates. By their very nature, scarcer coins require more specialized knowledge, and often they possess some distinctive characteristic that diminishes their interchangeability with other coins of the same series.

As this is written, generic coins are suffering from a loss of buyer confidence because of downward adjustments in market values. However, they have considerable potential and could go up in price in the months and years to come — especially if a major brokerage firm were to offer them for sale with a view to long-term holding. That would help remove the surplus from the market, firm up price levels and create new confidence.

Coin-Price Cycles

The first edition of *Rare Coin Investment Strategy* by Scott A. Travers, published in 1986 by Prentice-Hall Press, stated that the typical coin-price cycle was a four-year, four-phase process. There are still four phases in the cycle, but subsequent developments have compressed the typical cycle into a much smaller time frame: Today, it's likely to take less than a year for all four phases to unfold. And if current trends continue, the process could be compressed even further — perhaps to as little as two or three months.

Phase One is the acquisition stage. During this phase, the buyer's objective should be to purchase high-quality coins at the lowest possible prices. It's wise to focus on coins that seem depressed the most, following the contrarian philosophy of buying when everyone else is selling and vice versa.

Phase Two is the momentum stage — a period when prices rise dramatically and coins go up in value on an almost continual basis. It's perfectly all right to continue buying coins during this period, but greater care should be exercised: Peripheral areas and off-quality coins should be avoided and purchases should be limited to high-quality coins of proven rarity.

Phase Three is the full-throttle stage — a time when even skeptics have been transformed into believers and everyone's convinced that the boom will go on forever. It won't of course, and this phase is actually the time to sell, while prices are at their peak.

Phase Four is the burnout stage, when the overheated market runs out of gas and prices plunge. This is definitely *not* the time to sell; rather, it's a time to capitalize on other people's panic by purchasing coins of proven rarity and quality at bargain prices.

Every coin gets a turn in the market-cycle process — though some get turns more frequently than others. No coin is ever a totally lost cause; even the least active or least popular coin will decrease in value only so far before turning around and going up. That, after all, is what market cycles are all about. The marketplace might be likened to a pillow: No matter how much you punch it, it always bounces back — but some pillows bounce back faster than others.

Those who are impatient, or can't afford to bide their time, may decide a given item isn't worth the wait. In that case, they might sell it, take a loss, and move on to something else. Chances are, however, that if they could hold out a little longer, they'd catch the rising tide of a new market cycle.

Market Volatility

Rare coins enjoy considerable liquidity today. Their liquidity isn't continuous; at time, interruptions occur. But it's greater today than it was in the past, due in large part to certification and sight-unseen trading.

For the very same reasons, rare coins are also subject to much greater market volatility today than in years gone by. Now that many coins can be traded like commodities, they also react to marketplace influences much more quickly and dramatically than in the past — just as commodities do.

It's important to remember that the rare coin industry is made up, for the most part, of thinly capitalized entrepreneurs. They're sensitive to news and even rumors, good and bad, and tend to respond in a somewhat exaggerated manner. Thus, if they detect slight buyer resistance to certain coins, they're often prone to magnify this softness — and that, in turn, can drive prices sharply lower, certainly much lower than circumstances warrant. Conversely, if they see a modest rise in prices on one of the sight-unseen trading networks, they may raise their own bids to an even higher level, giving those prices further upward impetus that really isn't justified by objective market factors.

The coin market's long-term outlook is highly positive, and prices should rise substantially over time. But the increased volatility will lead to zigs and zags along the way — some of which could be quite pronounced. This won't be an ideal place for the faint of heart, but for those with a taste for adventure it could be both exciting and rewarding.

A New Breed of Buyer

The rare coin market has become a favorite stomping ground for a new breed of buyer. This healthy, vibrant breed is part collector, part investor — motivated by both the pure collector's love of the hobby and the strict investor's quest for financial gain. The collector/investor seeks — and obtains — the best of both worlds.

Many collector/investors are members of the baby-boom generation who cut their teeth on coin collecting during their youth, then drifted away from the hobby to pursue other interests such as college, courtship and careers. Now that they're settled down, they've returned to coins again — this time with the benefit of greatly expanded financial resources and much sharper business acumen. Instead of seeking scarce Lincoln cents in pocket change, they're now buying certified coins with price tags in the tens of thousands of dollars. But they're bringing the same enthusiasm to this new pursuit as they did to the hobby of their youth.

This new breed of buyer shares the old-time collector's deep appreciation for coins' intangible values. Like the old-timer, he admires rare coins for their history, artistry and cultural significance. But he also brings great savvy and sound business judgment to the marketplace. Profit and profit potential always have a bearing on his buy-and-sell decisions, and he balances these factors against the intangibles.

Collector/investors' presence has given new strength to the marketplace. At the same time, it has added to the market's volatility — for unlike pure collectors, these new-breed participants are willing to take a profit when coins go up in value. This results in a much more frequent turnover of valuable coins — and when the supply rises to meet the demand, prices drop.

Collector/investors are plunging into the coin market with the same kind of zest they brought years ago to the pure collecting pursuits of their younger days. They're attending shows, reading books and periodicals and buying coins certified by the leading services. They're familiar with marketing tools; they know about the population and census reports issued by PCGS and NGC, for example. And they use these tools shrewdly to enhance the profit potential of their purchases.

In years to come, collector/investors may play a pivotal role in determining rare coins' market values. They know what they're doing, so few can take advantage of them. Thus, to keep them as customers, dealers will have to hold their profit margins to much slimmer levels than might otherwise be the case.

"Supergrade" Coins

Collector/investors and other knowledgeable buyers have shown a decided preference in recent years for "supergrade" coins. These are coins in the highest available levels of preservation — generally those graded Mint State-66 (or Proof-66) and above by PCGS or NGC.

Coins in these levels have tremendous appeal to today's coin buyers. They've gone up in value more rapidly and dramatically than many others. There's good reason for this: These coins are not only the best-preserved and therefore the most beautiful, but they're also the scarcest within each series, since precious few were saved in such flawless condition. This is apparent from the population and census reports of the two leading certification services, which consistently show extremely low numbers for coins in upper-end mint-state grades.

The combination of quality, rarity and beauty is irresistible — not only to investors, but also to pure collectors. Thus, supergrade coins hold great allure for buyers across the spectrum. No wonder they're in such demand — and given the great demand and small supply, no wonder they hold such potential!

Supergrade Glamour Coins

The most desirable of all rare coins are those which combine supergrade quality with extreme rarity. Among the coins which fall under this heading are early silver dollars — those of the Flowing Hair, Bust and Seated Liberty types. These coins were minted in very small quantities, for the most part, and few were preserved in mint condition. Thus, *any* mint-state example commands a handsome premium. In supergrade levels the premiums can be staggering.

Collector/investors from the baby-boom generation find supergrade glamour coins irresistible, and are willing to pay big prices to obtain them. At that, these coins could be among today's biggest bargains. Many astute observers believe that in the not-too-distant future, these coins — now selling for $70,000 and $80,000, in many cases — could be worth upwards of half a million dollars.

Rare Coins' Potential

Over the last two decades, rare coins' price performance has been impressive. Surveys show that they've outperformed much more entrenched investment vehicles, including stocks, bonds and real estate. But many believe that, in the words of famed entertainer Al Jolson, "You ain't seen nothing yet!"

Those who have been associated with the coin market for many years marveled when the Dexter specimen of the 1804 silver dollar flirted with the million-dollar mark at Auction '89. But those with a broader perspective point out that in comparison to other collectibles, coins such as this are relative bargains.

Famous paintings sell for tens of millions of dollars. Prized collector cars, such as Bugattis, sell for upwards of $10 million apiece. Even antique chairs sell for millions of dollars each. Rare coins haven't yet come close to such levels — but many believe their rarity and popularity justify comparable prices.

This is a major reason why institutional investors feel confident today in purchasing rare coins for prices in the 25 and 50 thousand-dollar range. They see these prices not in terms of the much lower values of coins in years gone by, but rather in terms of the much higher values of certain other collectibles today. In a word, they see *potential*.

One leading investment banker who is himself a heavy investor in coins predicts that today's $25,000 and $50,000 coins will be selling before long for six to eight times those amounts. This, of course, is strictly a personal opinion — but given this man's experience and expertise, it certainly carries a great deal of weight. It also reveals the kind of excitement brought to today's coin market by the new generation of baby-boomer buyers — for this man is a member of that group. Unlike old-time hobbyists, these people are comfortable with today's price levels and have their sights set firmly on where the market is headed, not where it may have been 20 years ago.

If Inflation Strikes

Today's investment market is much more mature than the one that existed back in the 1970s, when rampant inflation first kindled widespread interest in rare coins' possibilities as a hedge. If the same kind of inflation were to strike again today, investors would be far better prepared to cope with it and respond to it.

During the late 1970s and early 1980s, we saw a great deal of trial and error. Not being certain how to proceed, many investors resorted to techniques that lacked sophistication. Today, they know the ropes and would use them to good advantage. We'd almost surely see large-scale purchases of gold and silver bullion and very heavy investments in rare coins. That, in turn, would drive prices higher right across the board for investment-quality coins.

Silver Dollars' Role

Silver dollars have played a central role in rare coins' emergence as a major investment vehicle. They appeal to investors strongly; their heft, their silver content, their age and their generally high condition all are very attractive to many investors. Their ample supply has been big a plus, as well — and this, of course, was reinforced by the Redfield Hoard and the federal government's sale of "CC" dollars. Silver dollars were not only the single biggest beneficiary of the rare coin boom of the late 1970s and early 1980s, but also quite arguable one of the biggest causes.

Many believe that silver dollars will continue to occupy center stage as the coin market moves to the next stage of its development in the wider investment arena.

***

David L. Ganz, NLG

David L. Ganz is a lawyer admitted to practice law in the Courts of the States of New York, New Jersey and the District of Columbia. He is managing partner in the firm of Ganz, Hollinger & Towe of New York City, and Ganz & Sivin P.A., of Fair Lawn, N.J. A graduate of Georgetown University's School of Foreign Service (BSFS 1973), he was awarded his law degree form St. John's University Law School (JD 1976). He is admitted to practice in the highest state court in each state in which he is licensed, and all federal courts including the U.S. Tax Court and the Supreme Court of the United States.

Appointed legislative counsel to the American Numismatic Association in 1978, a post he continues to hold today, he is an elected member of the American Numismatic Association Board of Governors and vice president-elect for the 1991-3 term. He is also a member of the Board of Directors of the Industry Council for Tangible Assets. He has served as general counsel to the Professional Numismatists Guild, Inc., since 1981, and formerly served as general counsel to the National Association of Coin & Precious Metals Dealers before it merged into ICTA.

The author of a number of articles published in legal periodicals since 1977, as well as thousands of articles in various numismatic publications since 1965, he is a Fellow of the American Numismatic Society, an Affiliated Member of the PNG, an ANA Life Member since 1972, and was appointed by President Nixon to the 1974 Annual Assay Commission.

The assistance and comments of Jerrietta R. Hollinger, Esq., (JD Univ. of Maryland, LL.M. (Tax) N.Y. University Law School) is specifically acknowledged and appreciated. The views expressed in this article are the author's alone.

CHAPTER 53

Regulation of the Coin Industry

by David L. Ganz, NLG

As coin collecting moved from a hobby to a growth industry, government agencies (federal, state, and municipal) have grown geometrically and their regulations have grown exponentially. The numismatic market is drowning in an alphabet soup of governmental agencies.

Where once the Federal Trade Commission handled anti-trust claims, it is now intimately acquainted with the coin field and seeking redress against perceived wrongs against consumers. Where the Internal Revenue Service once confined itself to quiet revenue rulings that permitted or prohibited like-kind exchanges of certain coins and numismatic properties on a tax-free basis, it now has a role of attempting to regulate the reporting of income — if some versions are to be believed — from sales as low as a single silver Roosevelt dime produced (to a tune of over 2.2 billion pieces) in 1964.Where once the Post Office did little but assist collectors in receiving payment for lost registry parcels, it now has sought convictions for mail fraud, has brought claims against false advertising of numismatic products against mass-marketers, and has actually sent coin dealers to jail for selling over-graded rare coins. Where the Securities and Exchange Commission, in the back waters of time, permitted rare coins to be described as a good "investment", now there has been a crackdown by the Securities and Exchange Commission on rare coins. Just a few years ago SEC won a case — and a conviction for violation of the nation's Securities laws — from someone who was selling nothing but rare coins and some ancillary services.

The long march from hobby to a security predated Wall Street's real entry into the rare coin market by more than a dozen years. For many years it was impossible to own gold bullion in any form — it was declared illegal during the Roosevelt administration — the Treasury Department (Bureau of the Mint) now produces gold and silver bullion coins and markets them through a wholesale network to investors. Like other bullion, yet another governmental agency is involved in its regulation: the Commodity Futures Trading Commission (CFTC). And, while years earlier, the Office of Domestic Gold and Silver Operations (ODGSO) of the Treasury Department regulated the foreign gold coins that could and could not be sold within the United States, the office is now long-since abolished; more than 30 countries marketed their gold coinage in the United States this year, and after a hiatus of a half century, the U.S. Mint is again producing gold coins of a commemorative nature. On a state level, the so-called "Blue Sky" laws have been utilized by attorneys in more than a dozen states to halt sale of rare coins upon the grounds that "securities" were being marketed; in some cases penalties were imposed, and in others, the sometimes unsuspecting merchant was frequently left liable for substantial civil damages in a barrage of lawsuits. These same state governments, in large measure because of the rapid rise of the price of gold and silver in 1980 — also enacted a series of repressive "holding laws", which, to summarize, frequently require the purchaser of a coin to hold it for a lengthy period of time prior to reselling.

The aim is to prevent fencing of stolen property and to protect the community at large; the result, however, places many of the purchasers of such items at substantial risk of market fluctuations which have grown violent. The result: to make the purchase, because of the added risk factor, the price paid the consumer is invariably minimized. Also on a state (and sometimes on a municipal) level, the auction laws have been changed substantially. The aim is to eliminate the fly-by-night sellers who prey on the unsuspecting public; often, however, the result has been the creation of a [substantially difficult to manage] business operation that is unwieldy to manage. Moreover, some of the rules and regulations seem more honored in the breach than in compliance, in large measure because they run contrary to the way the numismatic auctions have been held for hundreds of years.

Regulation of the coin industry has also resulted (taken place) from a number of sources other than those traditionally thought of. Sometimes, it can come as the result of private litigation which results in a decision that has adverse consequences which are perceived by many; for example, several years ago, a claim was brought in Minnesota in which a collector/investor was sold rare coins by a dealer who guaranteed to buy them back "in the same grade sold" and at the then-current price for that grade. As grading standards changed, the dealer's argument was that the MS-65 was now a different grade. A court ruled, however, that promise was a contract, was legally binding, and that while pricing may be different, the critical issue of grade had already been discussed by the parties, and resolved by contract. Other court cases through the years have had similar results based upon widely disparate issues. Insofar as regulatory agencies go, each is equal — but some are more equal than others. Depending upon the circumstances, it is important — indeed, vital — for the collector, the investor, and the dealer to keep up with what the currents status is for each agency, and how it affects various numismatic matters.

Federal Trade Commission

Federal Trade Commission activity with numismatics actually stretches back across three decades to the 1970's when the Hobby Protection Act became law. Primarily designed to prevent the unauthorized reproduction of numismatic items (without labelling them as a "copy") the Federal Trade Commission did have a considerable amount of activity in the early 1970's and brought several enforcement proceedings to require those making reproductions of numismatic items to utilize the word "copy" on each specimen. Actions were brought against jewelry firms, dealers, and manufacturers. The full force and effect of the law resulted from the enactment of rules placed in the Code of Federal Regulations, which are enforceable by the Federal Trade Commission, and by private action brought by any person claiming to have been damaged. The statute is unusual because it is one of just about 20 enacted by Congress that authorize a prevailing party to receive reasonable attorney fees.In the mid-1980's, rare coins had already moved from a hobby to a quasi-investor status. One of the results of this was that the Federal Trade Commission began to look at some of the advertising claims that were being made — some of the promotional aspects — and concluded that the claims were deceptive practices in interstate commerce. Squarely, this put the actions under the Federal Trade Commission Act, which is designed to prevent or prohibit such practices in interstate commerce. In particular, the initial examinations of the Federal Trade Commission focused on disparities that could be characterized as overgrading: a dealer systematically purchasing coins as MS-60 or MS-63 then selling them as MS-65's. Still later, complaints were brought to include over-pricing aspects. No claim has ever been made by the Federal Trade Commission that a coin dealer cannot sell a coin at whatever price it wants to; although the Uniform Commercial Code may impose its own restraints based on "unconscionability". If a coin dealer wants to sell a 1990 proof set, without the "S" mint mark on the one cent coin for its $11 cost — or for $3,000 or more — it is permissible. The Federal Trade Commission, instead, focused on the linking of price to the selling of an "investment." Specifically, rulings were sought — and obtained — that where a seller represented that a numismatic item was a good investment, it could not be a good investment if the seller's markup was 100% or higher, for the investor would have to double the dealer's acquisition cost in order to simply "break even".

The first leading case brought by the Federal Trade Commission was the claim against *Security Rare Coins*, 1989 US Dist Lexis 15958, 1989 WL 134002 (U.S. Dist. Ct. Minn. 1989). In edited form, portions of the Court's 38 page findings of fact, conclusions of law, and order for judgment appear below:

> Defendant Security is a corporation organized and existing under the laws of the State of Minnesota. Security no longer does business. During 1985 and 1986, Security actively promoted the sale of coins through advertisements in Capital Gains $, Financial Security Alert, and Investment Forum and via flyers that were mailed to subscribers of these publications. In addition, Security occasionally placed advertisements in publications such as USA Today. Security normally routed a response by an individual who receive an advertisement to a sales representative employed by Security and called a "monetary specialist." Generally, the same monetary specialist would handle all of an individual customer's transactions with Security. Security's advertisements and other sales efforts resulted in coin sales. * * * Defendant CCE is a corporation organized and existing under the laws of the State of Minnesota. CCE no longer does business. During 1985 and 1986, CCE purchased all of the coins that Security later sold to individuals. CCE also purchased coins which it sold to other coin dealers and coins which Security had repurchased from its customers. CCE employed "graders" to separate and grade the American silver and the foreign gold coins which Security offered for sale. When Security sold the coins that it obtained from CCE it sold them at the grades that CCE placed on them, and it remitted a portion of its retail price to CCE as payment to CCE for those coins and services. The portion remitted of Security's retail price varied based upon the coin sold, and changed over time. Much of the consolidated profit realized by Security and CCE on the sales of coins to consumers was reported as that of CCE.
>
> The defendants acknowledge that the prices CCE charged Security for coins and the prices Security paid for coins were not the result of arms-length transactions and were the result of an internal allocation of profits and expenses. * * *
>
> [Note: An arms-length transaction is the price agreed to by a willing buyer and willing seller. CCE charged high prices to Security — higher than Security would have paid from other buyers — so it could legitimately claim it sold goods at little more than "cost." Profits were made at the other end.]
>
> The FTC's case against defendants involves four categories of coins: American silver dollars; modern-date American dimes, quarters, and half dollars; foreign gold coins; and American gold coins. The dates, mint marks, and grades of the coins involved in the promotion and sale by defendants in 1985 and 1986 which the FTC contends violated Section 5(a) of the FTC Act are as follows:
>
> * * * [American Silver Dollars, MS-63 and MS-65, Total Net Sales: $18,921,370; Modern-Date American Dimes, Quarters, and Half Dollars Total Net Sales: $ 7,655,128; Foreign Gold Coins Total Net Sales: $ 7,606,016] * * * Various U.S. gold coins, MS-63, Total Net Sales: $ 15,232,975 * * *
>
> The FTC claims that defendants defrauded consumers by representing that their products were valuable, low-risk investments when, in fact, the markup over the coins' real value was so high that defendants' customers faced a substantial probability of losing a significant portion of their investments. The FTC also claims that defendants defrauded consumers by misrepresenting the grades of certain of the coins. As to American gold coins, the FTC seeks redress only for those persons whose coins were appraised during the course of these proceedings and whose appraisals were introduced into evidence. In addition, the FTC is not challenging the grading of either the modern-date American dimes, quarters, and half dollars, or of the foreign gold coins, with the exception of the 1931 Italian 50 Lire; FTC's case with respect to these types of coins was based entirely on the alleged misrepresentations of their value as investments. * * *
>
> CCE employed approximately 35 to 40 graders. CCE's graders took the coins given them by their supervisors and separated the coins into individual categories. Each grader had a desk work station with a coin grading board, which had the various coin grades between MS-60 and MS-70 broken down into individual numbers, and, in some instances, into half numbers. CCE's grading supervisors checked the graders' work. [The company President] supervised the grading supervisors and sometimes checked grading himself, by checking on the coin graders at their desks and by checking rolls of coins from the inventory drawers. When Ulrich or a supervisor noticed a mistake, the coins were regraded. Graders would be required to regrade a roll three or four times if necessary.
>
> Graders were instructed to grade coins according to CCE's standards. Initially, sample coins were available in flipettes, to enable the graders to compare coins. By the end of 1985 or by early 1986, CCE had developed sample grading boards. The grading boards showed five obverse and two reverse sides for each grade. Grading boards were developed for dimes, quarters, half dollars, Franklin half dollars, Walking Liberty half dollars, Mercury dimes, Washington quarters, Roosevelt dimes, Kennedy half dollars, Morgan silver dollars, Peace silver dollars,

Eisenhower silver dollars and foreign gold coins. [The company president] testified that Security established its prices by taking into account CDN prices, competitors' prices, acquisition costs and overhead, and forecasts of future activity in the market. He did not, however, demonstrate how these factors were considered in setting prices for any of the particular coins at issue in these proceedings. * * *

Numismatists classify coins into two general categories: "circulated," i.e., coins showing wear, and "uncirculated," i.e., coins without wear. Among uncirculated coins, there are two types: (1) coins intended for circulation, or "mint state" and (2) coins intended for collectors, or "proof state."

The value of a rare coin depends on its condition. In evaluating a coin's condition or "grade," a number of factors are considered, including: (1) the coin's overall appearance and eye appeal; (2) the number of marks and scratches it has; (3) its toning, color, and tarnish; and (4) its "strike" or the clarity of the impression made in the minting process. Different grading systems and individual graders may weight these factors differently in grading coins. Thus, for example, some graders may be more strict about overall eye appeal, while others give more emphasis to the amount of rubbing and bagmarks. * * *

However, most coin dealers in the United States measure the condition of American coins on a numerical scale — known as the Sheldon scale — of 1 to 70. Circulated coins are graded 1-59, with coins ranging from 50 to 59 classified as "about uncirculated" or "AU." Uncirculated coins occupy the upper range of 60 to 70, with mint state uncirculated coins denoted "MS" and proof state coins denoted "PF." * * *Grades MS-61, MS-62 and MS-64 were officially recognized by the American Numismatic Association (ANA) in 1986. The adjectival descriptions that would correspond with today's grades of MS-60, MS-63 and MS-65 would be "brilliant uncirculated," or "BU," "choice BU," and "gem BU," respectively. * * *The Coin Dealer Newsletter (CDN or "the GreySheet") reports the bid and ask prices among dealers for a particular type of coin at grades MS-60, MS-63, MS-64, and MS-65. It also lists quotes for BU rolls of U.S. silver coins. The bid price is a guide to the prices that dealers are offering for an average coin in that grade, while the ask price is a guide to the prices that dealers are asking for an average coin in that grade. * * *

There are a number of grading services. Today, the most accepted grading service is the Professional Coin Grading Service (PCGS), an independent grading service established in early 1986 and based in California. Before PCGS gained acceptance, the American Numismatic Association Certification Service (ANACS) was the most widely used service and was widely recognized during 1985 and 1986, even though some dealers raised questions about its reliability. * * *

The grading of coins is an art, not a science, and always involves a certain amount of subjectivity. In addition, grading standards have changed over the years. * * *

The Official ANA Grading Standards for United States Coins (3d ed. 1987) ("ANA Book") is published and endorsed by the American Numismatic Association. It states:

Interpretations of grades within the uncirculated category MS-60 to MS-70 are apt to vary from person to person. Further, such interpretations could change over a period of time, as it has not been possible to define these grades photographically or verbally on a precise, consistent basis. * * *

The ANA Board of Governors has recognized that grading differences of less than four points on the 1-70 scale is reasonable. Thus, an MS-65 graded coin could reasonably be interpreted to be an MS-63 by some or an MS-63 uncirculated coin might reasonably be called MS-65. An MS-60 coin would be overgraded if it were termed MS-67 * * *.

That experts can differ in assigning grades was illustrated by two FTC experts, * * * who graded the same 31 U.S. gold and silver coins and disagreed as to 19 of them, in five cases by more than two points. One coin, a $20 gold piece (Def. Exh. 91-3), was assigned four different grades by five FTC experts, ranging from AU-58 to a "very nice" MS-63. Another gold piece (Def. Exh. 91-5) was graded MS-63 by one expert and MS-60 by another * * *

It is not possible to define precisely when changes in grading standards occurred, since the changes were gradual, and were recognized by different dealers at different times. The weight of the evidence indicates that the tightening of grading standards, while largely complete in 1985, continued into 1986. The Court also finds that the changes in grading standards primarily affected the higher grades (grade MS-64 and higher) but also affected grade MS-63. The ANA Book indicates that: [I]n 1985 and 1986 commercial interpretations of such grades as MS-63, MS-65, and MS-67 tightened considerably . . . . Interpretations of the grading standards can and have changed over the years and may continue to do so in the future. * * * The ANA Statement indicates that: The marketplace—composed of collectors and dealers — has tightened its interpretation in recent years and ANACS has reflected those changes. Accordingly, the ANA Grading Service, endeavoring to keep in step with current market interpretations (rather than create interpretations of its own), has in recent times graded coins more conservatively than in the past, in many instances. Hence, it may be the situation that a coin which was graded MS-65 by the Grading Service in 1981 and 1982, for example, may, if regraded in 1985 or 1986, merit the current interpretation of MS-63 or less. Similarly, dealers and others in the commercial sector have found that coins that were graded MS-65 several years ago may merit MS-63 or lower interpretations today. . . . Because of its imprecise nature, which admits a great deal of subjectivity and opinion, it may be the case that the interpretation of grading standards will continue to change in the future, as indeed has accrued over a long period of past years. * * *

Defendants represented to consumers that the coins they were selling were excellent, low-risk investments sold at or near market value with superior liquidity and profit potential. They did so by making frequent claims that rare coins as a whole were a very profitable, low-risk investment, thus clearly implying that their coins possessed the same qualities. They also made similar claims about particular coins that they were promoting. Defendants projected that coins sold in grade MS-63 or higher during 1985 and 1986 would yield a profit between 200% and 850% in three to five years. * * *

Defendants also represented to customers that the coins they were purchasing were accurately graded. * * *

In order to allay concerns about investing in rare coins, defendants represented to consumers that they maintained a buy-back policy, whereby Security would buy coins back from its customers at a discount off the company's prevailing sales prices. The amount of the discount varied over time. During 1985 and 1986, it ranged between approximately 15% and 22%. After the FTC filed its suits, the figure increased to approximately 35%. Later in 1987, Security discontinued the buy-back program altogether.* * *

[Security] did not maintain a reserve of funds to satisfy buy-back requests. If only 10% of defendants' customers had sought to take advantage of the buy-back, defendants would have had insufficient funds to satisfy their requests. Given that so many of defendants' coins were consistently overpriced, it could have been anticipated that many customers ultimately would seek to take advantage of the buy-back program. * * *

The Court finds that defendants' grades and prices for its MS 63-65 silver dollar rolls were consistently and significantly higher than those prevailing in the marketplace during the applicable period. The Court does not, however, find that the grades and prices were fraudulent, since grading standards in the applicable range were undergoing change during the time period in question.

The FTC's experts testified that subjectivity in grading and changes in grading standards did not account for the disparities in grading they observed. Several experts testified that the tightening of grading standards that occurred during 1985 and 1986 affected mostly coins in the higher grades (grades MS-64 and greater). The Court concludes, however, that grades in the MS 63-65 range were not sufficiently established during this period to warrant a finding that defendants' grading of silver dollars was fraudulent. * * *

The standard industry retail markup for modern-date rolls of dimes, quarters and half dollars is 20% to 40%. Defendants consistently marked up these coins by 100% to 200%. * * *

The Court [also] finds that defendants misrepresented the value of the products as investments in two ways. First, defendants promoted foreign gold coins as low-risk, highly profitable investments, even though these coins had little numismatic value and were being sold at two to eight times their real worth. Second, defendant charged substantial premiums between their MS-63+ and MS-64+ foreign gold coins, and between the MS-64+ and MS-65+ coins, when the market did not then recognize, nor does it currently recognize, any significant differences in value among the three grades for coins of this type. * * *

[P]rices did not bear a reasonable relationship to the then-prevailing market values of these coins. Further, from 1985 through 1987, the market did not recognize the differences in value among grades that defendants maintained. * * *

The FTC contends that defendants misrepresented some of their American gold coins as good investments when the coins lacked investment value because they were overgraded. The FTC does not contend that the evidence shows a general pattern of overgrading for the American gold coins. It does contend that the evidence supports a finding that certain of the American gold coins were regularly overgraded by defendants. FTC seeks relief with respect to those coins for which appraisals are part of this record.

The Court does not believe that overgrading has been sufficiently established as to the American gold coins. The extent of any overgrading is not so great that it can be said that subjectivity in grading does not account for the differences. Further, a significant number of the coins at issue were sold at grades that were affected by changes in grading standards during the applicable period. The Court recognizes that the FTC seeks relief only with respect to coins for which appraisals are part of the record. Nevertheless, the Court declines to grant that relief, in view of its concerns about subjectivity in grading standards as to these coins, and about changes in the grading standards during the applicable period for many of the American gold coins at issue.

Conclusions of Law

Defendants have engaged in certain "unfair or deceptive acts or practices in or affecting commerce" which are unlawful under Section 5(a) of the FTC Act, 15 U.S.C. 45(a). Specifically, the Court concludes that the following constituted unfair or deceptive acts or practices: misrepresenting, via a form letter sent to customers who had placed orders, that the price charged reflected the market at the time the transaction was executed; misrepresenting that defendants would maintain their buy-back policy; misrepresenting the investment value of the modern-date dimes, quarters and half dollars sold; and misrepresenting the investment value of the foreign gold coins sold. * * * This is a proper case for an award of consumer redress against defendants * * * The proper measure of redress is the monetary equivalent of rescission, which, in this case, is equal to the difference between the sale price of the defendants' coins and their market value * * *Although rumors existed that there was a formula used by the Federal Trade Commission — 20% over "greysheet" or something similar — in fact, nothing of the sort ever existed. The extracts above do show, however, a clear position by the government as to some of the elements that it will not tolerate, and of the judiciary as to how it will react to perceived facts, even if they are inaccurate. As 1990 drew to a close, the case was on appeal to the Court of Appeals for the 8th Circuit where the Federal Trade Commission was challenging some of the judgment.

What seemed clear enough to the Federal Trade Commission, however, and to the judges interpreting the Federal Statutes, was that the word "investment" by itself connotes that the purchaser has an expectation of making a profit. The profit expectation may be over a short term, or a long term — it is largely irrelevant.

However, if an item is selling everywhere else at $100, is purchased by a dealer for resale at $90, and sold to a customer for $200, it is not a good investment for that customer. The reason:

An instant guaranteed substantial loss in the event of liquidation, and (perhaps more importantly) a substantial likelihood that it would be a long time before a person was able to cash themselves out of the alleged investment vehicle.

With each new case brought by the Federal Trade Commission, those with a bent for challenging regulatory activity thought up a better widget: some sought low-population coins for which there was no ready market price (allowing for extensive mark up); some sought to do price comparisons with gains of coins listed in the Salomon Brothers Studies which bore no relevance whatsoever to the coins they were actually selling. (For example, someone comparing a 1961 quarter with the rarities of the Salomon Study is not comparing even apples and oranges; it is more likely not comparable at all.)

Yet, through it all, the Federal Trade Commission itself never defined any precise set of standards — indeed, it was prone to simply define prohibitive conduct. In particular, the Federal Trade Commission has made claims that various sellers made false fraudulent representations to consumers that the coins sold were valuable and low risk investments.

The mark ups on the real value of the coin was claimed by the FTC to be so high that the customers faced a substantial probability of losing a significant portion of their investment. In one example, the Federal Trade Commission charged that one seller "routinely priced 10-20 times higher than dealer-to-dealer prices" and claimed that "losses would equal as much as 90% or more of their original investment" if a purchaser sought immediate liquidation.

The Federal Trade Commission also brought claims that various sellers of rare coins fraudulently represented that their coins were worth prices quoted in industry pricing publications such as the "greysheet." The claim is the sellers knew or had reason to know that the coins that they were selling were of a different quality.

Moreover, sellers were alleged by the FTC to have misrepresented that the grades of all grading services were equal, when it was well known that ANACS-graded coins from the 1980 period of time differed from ANACS-graded coins of 1985, and that ANACS-graded coins of 1990 were in fact different from either of those two periods of time; the same held true for other grading services.

In the same vein, one of the early claims by the Federal Trade Commission in the 1986 case was that certificates bearing an inflated grade were utilized; a parallel case that came subsequently was that the actual supplier of the coin (not the seller) also had liability for substantially overstating the condition or quality of the coins.

There have also been complaints filed by the Federal Trade Commission alleging that the supplier of coin directed and encouraged the public to believe that the coins were of a high grade and investment quality when they were not. As a corollary, a claim was made that the suppliers assisted retailers in preparing portfolios utilizing certificates that filled the customers order but in fact consisted of little more than blatantly overpriced and overgraded coins.

There were even claims of coins that rare coin sellers acquired them from captive companies at a cost that was less than arms length and then resold them to consumers to show that there were only making a "small profit" when in fact the profit made was a substantial one.

One of the major complaints of the Federal Trade Commission was that sellers of rare coins made false representations as to the market value of coins or other investments, and that they falsely or fraudulently told customers that the coins purchased would substantially increase in value within several months of acquisition, or within a period of time of up to five years.

Parallel to this was the complaint that the Federal Trade Commission found that some sellers falsely told customers that they would repurchase or buy back the coins from them at a profit or the fair market value, when they either did not do so or would not do so, or could not.

Misrepresentation of the liquidity of rare coins was another major FTC complaint — and one which has had a significant impact in the coin market place as a whole. Sometimes, Federal Trade Commission lawyers complained, representations were made that coins could easily be bought and sold — just like a stock.

In other instances the FTC charged, there was an implication that a coin that was encapsulated by one grading service or another was "more liquid" than that of other grading services.

Liquidity notions aside, what the FTC ultimately said — or at least implied — was that rare coins were not like stock, are not a bond, and are not a certificate of deposit, but rather are goods which requires a willing buyer and a willing seller in order to obtain a price. Because the market place is not homogeneous, that price will and can vary even among seller to seller at the same time and place. (Any person who has ever attended a convention of the American Numismatic Association — where hundreds of dealers gather — knows that this is true; it is not uncommon for someone to purchase a coin from one dealer and sell it to another and keep as a profit the difference.)

In their claim against the Professional Coin Grading Service, the Consent Decree of August 16, 1990, requires as an affirmative disclosure that the rare coin market is "a highly speculative, unregulated market" which constitutes heady words from a government regulatory agency.

In the same vein, the FTC has argued strenuously that it is important for sellers of rare coins to disclose to purchasers the importance of securing third party opinions about the grade and quality of items purchased, as well as using proper descriptions of the grades of coins — whether they are adjectives, numbers, or some other means of description.

State Attorneys General

Implementation of various blue-sky claims by the various Attorneys General is not a new phenomenon. The number of cases has in fact grown substantially.

Blue-sky laws are so-named because the only security that an investor has is the depth of the blue sky, which is to say that in some instances (as alleged by various states) to enforce them, the blue-sky laws (when not complied with) offer the investor no protection at all. Worse, it is outright illegal to not comply with the various blue-sky laws, and both civil (and, in some cases, criminal) penalties may ensue.

As early as 1974, the Attorney General in New York brought a claim under its blue-sky laws involving a claim that at least peripherally touched on numismatic matters. Since then, numismatic sales have been the focus of "blue sky" actions brought by Idaho, Minnesota, California, Missouri, Wisconsin, Georgia, and other states claiming that sellers were offering investors a lot of blue sky — and not much numismatic material.

Some states, in fact, have had multiple actions for alleged blue-sky law violations against a variety of corporate and individual entities. In almost every instance, the focus is substantially identical: is an "investment contract" being offered to a resident of the state in a manner calculated to flout registration requirements?

In some instances, an application to the State Securities Office is made prior to the commencement of business; in nearly every instance, particularly when the methodology of doing business is disclosed, it has resulted in an opinion from the Attorney General's Office which strongly suggests that sales may not take place in the absence of compliance with the blue-sky laws and registration with the local Securities Bureau.

In most cases, the State Attorneys General has but a single interest: protection of the citizens of the state. Their aim, and their goal, is to assure that if rare coins or other investment vehicles are being sold within their state, that they are only done so if the person offering them is registered within the meaning of the local Securities Law.

That, of course, is no guarantee that the Federal Securities and Exchange Commission will exempt the transaction, and their requirements can be even more stringent.

Securities and Exchange Commission

The Securities and Exchange Commission draws its power and its theory that rare coins can be involved in a security from a 1946 Supreme Court case entitled *SEC v W.J. Howey & Co.* 328 U.S.293 (1946). *Howey* set forth a three-pronged test for determining whether a transaction involves an investment contract which itself is subject to the Federal Securities Laws.

The Supreme Court defined an investment contract in *Howey* as 1) an investment, 2) a common venture premised upon the reasonable expectation of profits which are 3) derived from the entrepreneurial or managerial efforts of others.

Where the fortunes of an investor are interwoven with and dependent upon the efforts and success of those either seeking the investment, or third parties, many courts have held that this constitutes a common enterprise. Where there is a link between the fortunes of the investor and the efforts of the promoter, there is also a view in many courts that the *Howey* test has been met.

The leading case in recent times in which the SEC argued that coins were security is *SEC v. Brigadoon Scotch*, a 1975 case brought in U.S. District Court for the Southern District of New York. There, an entity known as the "Federal Coin Reserve," a private company, chose coins for prospective purchasers. They also provided a number of incidental services such as insurance, accounting, and tax advice. A reasonable reading of the facts of the case by an objective, dispassionate observer would conclude seller committed egregious actions that caused many consumers to lose quite a bit of money; not surprisingly, the seller was held to be marketing a security.

A more recent case, involving Rare Coin Galleries of America (against which firm the Federal Trade Commission also brought action) had a different result — but one whose precedent might well cause a different finding in parts of the country that adhere to the notion that "commonality" in a venture can be implied based on the management efforts of the promoter.

The Court in that case was specific in its findings, and they bear some repetition (though they have been edited to omit some citations and footnotes included in the original opinion):

> The plaintiffs, desiring to invest some money, were advised by the defendants to purchase some rare coins. The defendants informed the plaintiffs that Rare Coin Galleries of America (RCGA) was a reputable rare coin dealer, and provided the plaintiffs with promotional literature on RCGA. According to this literature, the purchasers would buy rare coins from RCGA. The coins would, however, be selected by RCGA based on their professed expertise in the rare coin market. The gallery would also advise the purchasers when to sell the coins, and would help place the coins in auction houses, where the coins would be auctioned. The gallery would also negotiate with the auction houses in order to obtain the lowest auctioneer's commission possible. There is no indication that RCGA was to receive any compensation other than the profit received on the initial sale of the coins to the plaintiffs. The gallery also guaranteed that the coins sold were authentic and were accurately graded. Much of the literature extolled the virtues of rare coins as an investment, and emphasized the relative advantages of investing in coins over investing in stocks or bonds. The plaintiffs decided to invest in rare coins through RCGA, and paid the gallery $20,000. They never received their coins, and RCGA eventually filed for bankruptcy. The defendants first argued that the counts alleging violations of federal securities laws should be dismissed for failure to state a claim upon which relief can be granted. The defendants contend that the contract for sale of rare coins is not a security within the meaning of the federal securities laws. Both parties agree that in order for the sale contract to come within the purview of the securities exchange laws, it must fall within the definition of an investment contract under 15 U.S.C. 77b(1).

Citing first to the *Howey* case, the Court in *Rare Coin Galleries* stated succinctly "The principal issue in this case is whether the sale of rare coins involved a common venture, thus satisfying the second prong of *Howey*.""Some courts have adopted a "horizontal commonality" approach, some have adopted a "vertical commonality" approach, while others use both," the Court began, noting that a "horizontal commonality" approach requires a pooling of the interests of a number of investors in order to establish a common enterprise with the added requirement that the fortunes of each investor must be intertwined with the success of the pool.

Among courts that have adopted the vertical commonality approach, there is disagreement over whether to apply the strict approach or the broader approach. Under the strict vertical commonality definition of a common enterprise, the "fortunes of the investor are interwoven with and dependent on the efforts and success of those seeking the investment or third parties." The person seeking the investment, or the third party who is providing the entrepreneurial skill, must share in both profits and losses with the investor. If the person seeking the investment profits from the investment without sharing in the potential losses, there is no common enterprise under this view. Under this approach, there must be a link between the fortunes of the investor and the efforts of the promoter, rather than between the fortunes of both as required under the stricter approach. This view, however, has been expressly rejected by several courts; as one court noted, the broad vertical commonality merges the second element of the Howey test with the third element, thus eliminating one prong.

On the close question of whether RCGA's fortunes were tied directly to the plaintiffs' success in the rare coin market, the plaintiffs argue that commonality exists because RCGA guaranteed the coins' authenticity and the accuracy of the grading. Thus, RCGA stood to lose money if they selected coins that were not authentic, or if they improperly graded and valued the coins.

The Court found that in such a scenario, however, the plaintiffs would not lose anything, since RCGA would be obligated to refund the full purchase price plus 20% interest. The plaintiffs would not share in the losses incurred in that situation. On that basis, the Court claimed it would not establish a common enterprise.

"More importantly, the gallery would not gain or lose anything if the coins had appreciated or depreciated in market value. The transaction entered into by the plaintiffs was more akin to a contract for the sale of goods and incidental services than to a common investment enterprise. The primary risks and rewards — appreciation or depreciation in market value — rested on the plaintiffs."

Accordingly, the Court found that there was no common enterprise — hence no security. But it takes only a little variation of the facts to see how a security could easily be found, even in a circuit that had adopted a different approach.

While it by no means portends how other courts would look at securities issues — for indeed, a number of courts have said that coins are not securities — it would appear that in the coming decade, the "securities" issue involving rare coins is more likely to be determined, and made into law by private actions, against firms and individuals based upon the principles of *Howey*, *Brigadoon Scotch*, and their progeny.

Internal Revenue Service

The Internal Revenue Service activity with rare coins, or numismatic items in general, has increased to some extent in recent years. A review of the Internal Revenue *Bulletin* will find Revenue Rulings, however, which make it abundantly clear that IRS has been interested in the rare coin field for some time.

Most recently, however, controversy has revolved around Section 6045 of the Internal Revenue Code which was initiated by the 1982 Tax Equity and Fiscal Responsibility Act ("TEFRA"), Public Law 97-248.

Origins of the controversy concerning Regulation Section 6045 date back to early 1983 when the IRS promulgated regulations that went into effect in July of that year. Specifically, Section 6045 of the Internal Revenue Code was amended by TEFRA, to require the IRS to issue regulations dealing with broker reporting.

Basically, the Regulations provide that a report must be filed with the Internal Revenue Service for certain specified transactions covered under the terms of the regulations. Easy enough, as far as it goes.

The initial proposed regulations published in the Federal Register of November 15, 1982, defined broker to mean a person willing to transfer property, redeem securities, retrieve indebtedness or engage in a closing transaction "in securities, commodities for forward contracts for others."

None of that sounded particularly threatening to coin dealers, coin buyers, or collectors. In fact, the original Proposed Regulation Section 1.6045-1(a)(6)(i) only included property regulated by the Commodity Futures Trading Commission plus sales of certain other designated items.

But, in the Alice-in-Wonderland world of tax law, that arcane science of legalistic interpretation, even the word effecting "sales" has a different meaning than the ordinary English language. Regulation Section 1.6045-1(a)(9) defines sales to mean "any disposition of securities, commodities and regulated futures contracts . . ." Reg. Section 1.6045-1(a)(9).

Sounds rational enough; however "securities" doesn't have its conventional meaning, and neither does "commodity". For example, securities means stocks in a corporate entity as well as an interest in other entities according to one subparagraph found in Regulation Section 1.6045-1(a)(3)(i)-(vi).

For their part, commodities were defined as any type of personal property "the trading of regulated futures contracts in which has been approved by the Commodity Futures Trading Commission" in Regulation Section 1.6045-1(a)(5)(i), and also included other specific properties.

Given this mishmash of definitions within definitions, it is instructive to review the final operative paragraphs and "plug" definitions into them.

The actual reporting requirements are set forth in Reg. Section 1.6045-1(c) which provide in pertinent part:

> (c) Reporting by brokers.
>
> 1. Requirement of reporting. Any broker shall, except as otherwise provided, report in the manner prescribed in this section.
>
> 2. Sales required to be reported. Except as provided in paragraphs (c)(3), (c)(5), (g) and (p)(1), a broker shall make a return of information with respect to each sale by a customer of the broker effected by the broker in the ordinary course of a trade or business in which the broker stands ready to effect sales to be made by others.
>
> 3. Exceptions. (i) Sales for exempt recipients. No return of information is required with respect to a sale by a customer that is an exempt recipient described by Section 3452(c)(2)(A) through (E) or (G) through (I) * * *

Within the law, and the regulations, there are numerous sub-definitions that have shaded meaning that is not necessarily English, and is more like a translation from a foreign tongue (the Legal language to English). For example, the simple word "sales" does not mean the act of selling or exchanging property (Webster's New Universal Unabridged, 2d ed. 1979, p. 1598) but instead the word sales is deigned to mean "any disposition of securities, commodities and regulated futures contracts . . ." Reg. 1.6045-1(a)(9).

Commodities, which is defined in the dictionary to mean "any article which is bought or sold" (Webster's New Universal Unabridged, 2d ed. p. 365) is specifically held in the Regulations to include items "the trading of regulated futures contracts which has been approved by the Commodity Futures Trading Commission", Reg. 1.6045-1(a)(5)(i) plus other specific properties *plus* those subsequently determined, Reg. 1.6045-1(a)(5)(ii)-(iii) — a contradiction in terms.

Restating this as the definitions themselves would, this would mean in form modified for clarification as follows: (a [bracket] indicates the statutory word; bold faced words are from the definitional section; other words are per existing regulation. Some syntax and modifications have been made to avoid having the gobbledygook being totally incomprehensible — but it still has an Alice-in-Wonderland quality that reminds you why Will Rogers is reported to have quipped that most law-writers wanted to be Congressmen badly . . .

Here's what the text says, in translation — substitution each separately defined word with its definition:

> (c) Reporting by Brokers.1.
>
> Requirement of reporting.
>
> Any [broker] **person that, in the ordinary cause of a trade or business stands ready to [effect] act as an agent for a party, or as principal in order to carry out [sales] any disposition of securities [commodities] any type of personal property or an interest (other than securities) the trading of regulated futures contracts in which have been approved by the Commodity Futures Commission**, shall except as otherwise provided, report in the manner prescribed in this section.
>
> 2. Sales required to be reported. Except as provided *** [below], Any [broker] **person that, in the ordinary course of a trade or business stands ready to** [effect] **act as an agent for a party, or as principal in order to carry out** [sales] **any disposition of securities** [commodities] **any type of personal property or an interest (other than securities) the trading of regulated futures contracts in which have been approved by the Commodity Futures Commission**, shall make on return of information with respect to each [sale.] **disposition of securities** [commodities] **any type of personal property or an interest (other than securities) the trading of regulated futures contracts which have been approved by the Commodity Futures Commission**, by a customer of the [broker] **a person that, in the ordinary course of a trade or business stands ready to** [effect] **act as an agent for a party, or as principal in order to carry out** [sales] **any disposition of securities** [commodities] **any type of personal property or an interest (other than securities) the trading of regulated futures contracts which have been approved by the Commodity Futures Commission**, shall except as otherwise provided, report in the manner prescribed in this section *** in the ordinary course with a trade or business in which the [broker] **person that, in the ordinary course of a trade or business stands ready to** [effect] **act as an agent for a party, or as principal in order to carry out** [sales] **any disposition of securities** [commodities] **any type of personal property or an interest (other than securities) the trading of regulated futures contracts which have been approved by the Commodity Futures Commission**, stands ready to effect [sales] **any disposition of securities,** [commodities] **any type of personal property or interest (other than securities) the trading or regulated futures, contracts in which have been approved by the Commodity Futures Trading Commission**, to be made by other.

Small wonder no one understands what it means. Ordinary words have their meaning changed; verbs become nouns. If Regulation writers were paid like Dickens — by the word — the arcane would be explainable (though not understandable). Lamentably, this is neither.

These regulations would require reporting of purchases of any commodity where the CFTC had authorized a contract to be traded; that would include bags of silver coins (which are no longer traded, but which were authorized at the time that the regulations went into effect).

As of June, 1983, the Commodity Futures Trading Commission had approved trading for the following relevant units: 100 ounce gold bars, Comex, New York; MidAmerica Commodity Exchange, and Chicago Board of Trade, 33.2 troy ounces [1 kilo]; 1,000 ounce silver bars, Chicago Board of Trade; 5,000 ounce silver bars, Comex. These are the items that trade daily. Palladium is approved in 100 ounce bar form, and platinum in 50 ounce bars.

U.S. silver coins in bags of $1,000 face (without mixing denominations therein) were also approved. Krugerrands were approved in December 1983 with other bullion coins on the Comex and Chicago Mercantile Exchange. As of December 27, 1984, Krugerrands and silver coins had not traded in more than six months, and under the rules of the exchanges, and CFTC rules, could not be traded without re-applying to the CFTC for approvals, 17 CFR sec 5.2.

Although a number of futures contracts have been authorized in a variety of markets, H. Rep. No. 97-395, 97 Cong. 1st Sess. at 62 (1981) [17th Report by the House Committee on Government Operations] that not every quantity authorized in fact is sold. Still, high volume is regulated. In a given day, the Comex recorded trades of 35,000 contracts of 100 troy ounce gold (3.5 million ounces, valued at $1.4 billion), and 24,000 contracts for 5,000 ounce silver (120 million ounces valued at $1.3 billion); MidAmerica reports 2,100 trades of its 33.2 ounce contract of gold, and the Chicago Board of Trade for kilo gold reports 1,100 trades.

The trading bars sold by federally registered dealers or brokers — which are actually traded on massive levels, appears to be within the scope of what Congress intended to cover, and what the Regulations themselves contemplate. *See* e.g.,

Reg. Section 1.6045-1(c)(4) (examples 103); Proposed Reg. Sec. 1.6045-1 (Special analysis states "the Secretary of the Treasury certifies that the regulations proposed . . . will not have a significant impact on a substantial number of small entities.")

The problem with the IRS interpretation that even dormant contracts are covered is that the history of the legislation makes clear that any fractional part of such a contract is also reportable. Taken to its most absurd position, this means that a 1964 silver dime, or quarter — a fractional part of a tradeable bag of 90% silver — is a reportable transaction.

Cost of the paperwork, alone, on such a transaction removes the possibility of profit from the dealer making a purchase and would constitute an onerous reporting requirement that would be ill-served. Clearly, it would appear that was not what Congress intended.

Indeed, the Senate Report 97-494, 97th Cong. 2d. Sess. at 245 (1982) explains that the law itself "clarifies the definition of broker to explicitly include persons . . . who (for consideration) regularly act as *middlemen* with respect to property of services," which is not what a coin dealer typically is. In fact, *middleman* is defined as someone who is not at risk, and stands indifferent between two or more people brought together by him (Black's Law Dictionary, p. 1143 (4th ed. 1968), where a coin dealer buys for his own account and is at risk.

The underlying definitions in the Regulations proved to be so confusing that the IRS then proposed new regulations that would alter the relationship and clarify what had to be reported.

It is useful to review the revised proposed regulations to Section 6045, which offer several specific examples which may also be of assistance in at least presenting the IRS viewpoint:

> Example 16. W, a coin dealer, regularly advertises that it will purchase gold items for their bullion value. Since W stands ready to effect sales to be made by others, W is a broker. [The transaction is reportable.]
>
> Example 17 X, a coin dealer, regularly buys gold items when they are offered for sale and this is known to sellers of such items. Since X stands ready to effect sales to be made by others, X is a broker whether or not it advertises.

There is also some confusion that has arisen as to whether or not "rare" or "numismatic" coins are exempt from reporting which has to do with the lack of specifics in the regulations, and a series of Treasury Department Revenue Rulings and policies which appear to contradict each other.

For example, Revenue Ruling 82-96, *Int. Rev. Bull. 1982-20*, 8, holds that "because the value of gold content in each Canadian Maple Leaf gold coin greatly exceeds its face value, it is not a circulating medium of exchange." This reasoning concludes that this somehow transforms the coin into property and not money, but offers no authority for the proposition. If the underlying premise is correct, it would suggest that at any time the bullion value of a coin "greatly exceeds" its face value, it ceases to be a medium of exchange, loses numismatic properties and becomes bullion alone.

This position seems to be inconsistent. It would appear that a 1964 half dollar, with .36 troy ounces of silver (worth about $1.40 with silver at $4 an ounce) is no longer a medium of exchange. This is, of course erroneous, as the "Circulation Finds" column that has appeared from time to time in *Numismatic News* indicates so clearly, and as any serious numismatist knows.

Worse, it also would tend to mean that there is no predictability as to when a coin or other piece or type of money is in fact a medium of exchange. In fact, it seems reasonable to conclude that a coin always remains a medium of exchange, whether its value rises or falls below a par value. For that reason, the U.S. Post Office (or the Treasury Department) itself, would accept a $20 gold piece at its nominal value.

For example, in 1919, the selling price of silver rose above the nominal value of American currency when the price of silver topped $1.38 an ounce. A silver dollar, struck in 1904 (the last year of issue to that time) or earlier contained .7734 troy ounces of silver.

With silver valued at $1.06 in the coin, it was "worth" more than face value. But there is no hint that the coins were no longer used as legal tender, or lost status as a currency even though the government itself (utilizing the provisions of the Pittman Act) did melt down millions of dollar coins.

The same holds true with gold coinage. The break-even point for bullion into coinage was $20.67 for most of the 19th century; the Coinage Act of January 18, 1837, set this value. Yet, by 1862, gold rose to $23.42, making a $20 gold piece worth $22.65 in bullion, and by 1864, gold's price rose to $41.96, giving rise in the value of a $20 gold piece to $40.59. (The history of this is conveniently found in volume 1 of *Rep't to the Cong. of the Comm. on the Role of Gold in the Domestic & Int'l Monetary Systems* at page 220, table SC-16 (1982)).

Yet, in 1862, the Mint at San Francisco produced 854,173 double eagle gold pieces, and in 1864, when gold was even higher, 793,660 double eagles were produced at San Francisco, alone. The distinction drawn about coins and valuation therefore, flies in the face of history and logic.

As the price of a precious metal rises and falls, the basal value of the denomination remains constant. For example, gold was officially pegged at $35 an ounce in 1934. Yet, on January 16, 1970, the official price of gold fell below that, to $34.95 on the "free Market".

It must be noted that the existing IRS regulations are "unclear" whether "certain forms of personal property are commodities" within the meaning of Section 6045. 49 Fed. Reg. at 646 (Jan. 5, 1984). As a result, proposed regulations change this interpretation by specifically re-writing the definitional section to provide that any form or quality deliverable as a CFTC contract (even if not in full quantity), provided it has been approved by the CFTC (irrespective of whether or not it may be currently traded) is included in the scope of intended coverage. Prop. Reg. Sec. 1.6045-1(a)(5)(i)(A).

The proposed regulations, which would modify the existing regulations, make clear that all gold and silver coins are intended to be covered unless they were *numismatic* items — which are then defined to mean having a price of more than fifteen (15%) percent above bullion content. Proposed Reg. Sec. 1.6045-1(a)(5)(ii)(D).

The Treasury does not appear to aim at numismatic coins, since such coins are not regulated by the CFTC. Still, defining numismatic coins is difficult. There still remains no precise definition of what is or is not a numismatic coin. It may be defined, alternatively, as coins being purchased for an investment in the coin itself, rather than primarily for its metallic content, which is alluded to in a 1982 Revenue Ruling by the IRS.

Or, it might be viewed as being gold coins which are sold at a premium of ten percent (10%) or more above the spot price of gold on any given day. (This reasoning is by analogy, per the Treasury Department's apparent standard two decades ago in a funnily entitled case, *United States v. One Solid Gold Object in Form of a Rooster*, 208 F. Supp. 99, 101-102 (D. Nev. 1962.)

The Treasury's currently proposed regulations use a 15% test, *See*, 49 Fed. Reg. 645, 647 (Jan. 5, 1984). Prop. Reg. Sec. 1.6045-1(a)(5)(ii)(D), which seems reasonable enough on paper, but will be difficult in practice.

The reason: it will slip and slide all year long — in fact, all *day* long, depending on different gold fixes that are utilized and the marketplace's response to it with larger-denominated gold coins such as double eagles, which contain nearly an ounce of gold.

The IRS viewpoint, as evidenced in the proposed regulations issued in January 1984, was that purchases of Krugerrands, as well individual silver coins, were covered under the law. (Krugerrands may still be acquired, though they are no longer favored in the marketplace because they cannot be imported into the United States, thanks to a 1985 Congressional law).

IRS amplified its view in a press release dated June 8, 1984, (#84-57), which stated in pertinent part (relying on the proposed regulation): "The IRS today stressed that since January 1, 1984, information reporting is required on certain sales of South African Krugerrand, Canadian Maple Leaf, and Mexican one-ounce gold coins. Broker reporting regulation. . . require information reporting on sales or property that could be delivered to satisfy a contract approved for trading by the CFTC. This is so whether or not contracts are actively traded."

The same release notes that "reporting is not required for sales of coins in which the coins do not meet CFTC contract requirements as to form or metal quality until the publication of amended regulations under section 6045." It emphasizes that where few or more than the CFTC contract number are acquired — and that is the only ground for distinction — a report must be filed.

In partial response to this, the Senate Committee on Appropriations issued a report, S. Rept. No. 98-562, 98th Cong., 2d, Sess. at 33 (July 17, 1984) which stated that the regulation "incorrectly interpreted the scope of the law." Thereafter, on July 25, the chairman of the Senate Finance Committee disagreed with that interpretation calling it "both reasonable and clearly consistent with congressional intent in enacting the provision." Cong. Record p. S9136 (daily ed. July 25, 1984).

Summing up broker reporting, one can only conclude that it is an area of confusion. Penalties for noncompliance are stiff and unyielding, principally because a goof-up is treated as if it were withholding tax not withheld or paid.

To illustrate: assume someone tenders a single Maple Leaf that they bought for $600 several years ago and is paid $400 for it by a dealer (or "broker" under the Act), a reasonable market price. (The dealer would probably be willing to re-sell the item for $420, a profit of about $20).

If no taxpayer identification number is received, and no 1099-B report filed, the IRS could impose a penalty equal to 20 percent of the amount *received* — the "backup" withholding penalty, or $80.

Then, there is a penalty assessment of 5 per cent per month for five months (25 percent total), or another $20. Then interest at the rate of 16 percent annually is added for, say, three years (total $48). Plus a $50 penalty for not filing the form.

Grand total: $198 penalty *per transaction* on a potential profit of no more than $20.

Based on this inconsistency, it appears that the following are the solid points that may be relied upon: (1) the Internal Revenue Service has issued regulations which it claims requires the reporting of virtually all bullion coin sales/purchases; (2) that by press release, IRS has indicated that if, by reason of fineness (metal quality) or type (form) it is considered a non-trading unit by CFTC, no reporting is required at this time; and (3) the legislative history, and construction suggest a substantial amount of confusion as to what the intent of Congress was, and what Congress in fact authorized the IRS to do.

Reporting is clearly required for a trading size bar, that is, a silver or gold bar which is accepted for settlement by the CFTC. For regular U.S. gold coins, even $20 gold pieces bought and sold primarily for their bullion content, and even devoid of numismatic value, there is currently no reporting requirement under either the original regulation or the proposed regulation (the press release exempts the one possibility — that there is less than fifteen (15%) percent difference between bullion and the price, unlikely except for a "cull" double Eagle).

For regular mixed silver coins acquired or packaged bulk (i.e., in $1,000 units, or more, or less), since this is not tradeable — commodity exchange regulations require all of the same denomination to settle — this is not reportable.

For Krugerrands, and other "bullionlike" coins, there is no current CFTC contract, the coins cannot be utilized to settle any other precious metal CFTC-approved contract, and thus it appears that this is not reportable, though it would be under the regulations currently still proposed.

In coming months and years, ICTA may assist in the resolution of this matter.

Of some interest, as well, are some of the prior Revenue Rulings of the IRS relative to like-kind exchanges. For example, you can exchange (without tax consequences) a Canadian Maple Leaf for a U.S. Eagle bullion coin. (The actual revenue ruling uses a Krugerrand with a Maple Leaf, but the principle is the same.)

What if you want to exchange a Canadian Maple Leaf (gold) for a Canadian Maple Leaf (silver) coin? Revenue Ruling 82-166 addresses the issue with these facts:

> An individual taxpayer, who is not a dealer in gold or silver bullion, purchased gold bullion in the cash market and held it as an investment. In 1980, after the gold bullion had appreciated in value, the taxpayer exchanged the gold bullion for silver bullion of equal total fair market value. A gain was realized by the taxpayer as a result of the exchange. The taxpayer holds the silver bullion as an investment.

The IRS analysis begins with the definition of "like kind". Though not defined in *Black's Law Dictionary*, it means goods that are essentially the same. You can exchange one home for another, one auto for another, a $100 bottle of Lafitte for two $50 bottles of Margaux. The IRS then cobbles it up. Treas. Reg. Sec. 1.1031(a)-1(b) states: As used in section 1031(a) of the Internal Revenue Code, the words "like kind" have reference to the nature or character of the property and not to its grade or quality. One kind or class of property may not, under that section, be exchanged for property of a different kind or class. The fact that any real estate involved is improved or unimproved is not material, for that fact relates only to the grade or quality of the property and not to its kind or class.

The balance of the Revenue Ruling is useful because it discusses other rulings in which numismatic items are found to be like-kind, because it shows the type of analysis that the IRS utilizes, and because of the areas that it affects:

> The fact that both the gold and silver are in bullion form is significant only in establishing that the value of each comes essentially from the metal itself and not from the form the metal is in, such as numismatic-type coins or rare jewelry. See Rev. Rul. 79-143, which states that bullion-type gold coins, unlike numismatic-type gold coins, represent an investment in gold on world markets rather than in the coins themselves.
>
> Thus the question here is whether the metals gold and silver are of like kind. The metals are defined in *Webster's Third New International Dictionary* pp. 974 and 2119 (unabridged 1961) as follows:
>
> [G]old: a very malleable, ductile, yellow trivalent and univalent metallic element that . . . is hardened or changed in color for commercial use (as in coins, jewelry, dentures) by alloying with copper, silver, zinc, cadmium, and other metals.
>
> [S]ilver: a white metallic element that is sonorous, ductile, very malleable, capable of a high degree of polish, and chiefly univalent in compounds, that has the highest thermal and electric conductivity of any substance, that is . . . one of the noble metals in view of its resistance to oxidation or corrosion except tarnishing by combination with sulfur, that is usually alloyed with copper to increase its hardness, and that is used for coinage, tableware, jewelry, plate, and a great variety of articles in photography, in electrical contacts, and as a catalyst.
>
> We believe these definitions make clear that, although gold and silver have some similar qualities and uses, they are essentially different metals that do not have the same nature or character.
>
> A test that is applied for determining if gain or loss is recognized when properties are exchanged is whether the taxpayer's economic situation after the exchange is fundamentally the same as it was before the transaction occurred. * * * The test is based on Congress' reason for allowing non-recognition when like kind properties are exchanged which was that the taxpayer's economic situation before and after the exchange is fundamentally the same. * * *
>
> Congressional intent for section 1031(a) was reinforced by the addition of section 1031(e), which provides that the exchange of livestock of one sex for livestock of the other sex is not an exchange of property of like kind for purposes of the nonrecognition provision of section 1031(a). The Senate Finance Committee Report states that the different sexes of livestock are not of like kind because they represent investments of different types, in one case an investment for breeding purposes and in the other an investment in livestock raised for slaughter. * * *
>
> The Service applied the test in Rev. Rul. 79-143, supra, with respect to the exchange of numismatic-type gold coins for bullion-type gold coins. The revenue ruling states:
>
> > [A]lthough the coins appear to be similar because they both contain gold, they actually represent totally different types of underlying investment, The bullion-type coins, unlike the numismatic-type coins, represent an investment in gold on world markets rather than in the coins themselves. Therefore, the bullion-type coins and the numismatic-type coins are not property of like kind.
>
> Applying this test to the situation here, the question is whether the taxpayer who exchanges gold bullion for silver bullion is in essentially the same economic situation after the exchange as he or she was in before the exchange. The argument might be made that investments in gold and silver are alike because they are both considered by some investors to be hedges against inflation. Of course, many other kinds of property, such as art, diamonds, and real estate, are also considered by some to be hedges against inflation, and certainly they are not all like kind properties. Gold and silver are commodities and are traded as such on commodity exchanges along with other metals such as copper, palladium, platinum, and zinc. Their prices are determined by the same forces that determine the prices of other commodities — supply and demand. These market forces vary greatly between gold and silver. For example, if a large new supply of gold or silver is discovered, it will tend to drive down the price of the metal discovered but it will not ordinarily affect the price of the other metal. If, on the other hand, a new use is discovered for gold or silver and the demand for the metal increases, the price of the metal will also tend to increase. Although some events, such as a decline in the value of the dollar, may tend to affect similarly the prices of gold and silver, most factors that are involved in determining their respective prices are not related. We believe that gold bullion and silver bullion, like the numismatic-type and bullion-type gold coins considered in Rev. Rul. 79-143, represent totally different types of underlying investment.
>
> We believe, therefore, that a taxpayer who exchanges gold bullion for silver bullion is not in essentially the same economic situation after the exchange as he or she was in before the exchange. We do not agree with the proposed revenue ruling because, in our view, gold bullion and silver bullion are not like kind properties for purposes of section 1031(a) and there is recognition of gain when the properties are exchanged.

There are many other tax issues that the IRS deals with from time to time; it is best, typically to consult with your accountant or your lawyer before undertaking a significant monetary transaction that could have tax consequences. Merely calling the IRS to obtain an informal opinion is just not sufficient; the telephone advice is *not binding* on the IRS (they can, in fact, take a contrary position). This includes cash reporting of $10,000 or more under Regulation 6050-I and a host of other issues.

U.S. Postal Service

Most people don't think of the Postal Service as a regulatory entity of any kind, yet through its enforcement mechanism the Postal Service brought a case against a coin dealer that resulted in a substantial prison sentence, *U.S. v. Kail* 804 F.2d 441 (8th Circuit, 1986).

The *Kail* case, never widely reported within the coin industry, ought to send shock waves to anyone involved with rare coins who, initially, claims that grading is entirely subjective and that reasonable differences may be tolerated. The facts of the case, as stated by the United States Court of Appeals for the 8th Circuit (slightly edited for the convenience of readers) is enlightening:

> From April 1983 to March 1984 Kail was president of Coin & Stamp Gallery, Inc., a Minnesota corporation dealing in the sale of investment quality coins. Kail was responsible for hiring personnel, and in this capacity recruited several brokers and other employees from his former employer * * * The brokers contacted their former customers * * * usually by mail, and informed them that they now worked at Coin & Stamp Gallery. One letter, drafted by Kail, described him as "one of the most knowledgeable numismatic experts in the country." The brokers informed customers that Coin & Stamp Gallery dealt in the finest investment quality coins which would provide a much better investment than the lower-grade coins and bullion offered by [the former company]. Throughout all of their dealings with their customers, Coin & Stamp Gallery brokers emphasized the investment potential of rare silver and gold coins, although Kail did caution them that they were not to sell the coins as securities or represent that profit was guaranteed. Customers purchased coins from Coin & Stamp Gallery brokers based upon the representations that this would be an excellent investment in that the coins were sold at their fair market value. The fair market value of coins sold to customers was often confirmed by letter. In addition, Coin & Stamp Gallery assured its clients that it would repurchase coins at current market value if the client wanted to sell them. Subsequent appraisals of the coins purchased by Coin & Stamp Gallery clients, however, established that many of the coins had been purchased at a price far in excess of the fair market value, making them almost worthless as an investment vehicle. In most instances the price listed on the broker's inventory sheets was two to three times higher than the price at which Kail originally purchased the coins, therefore misleading the sales personnel as to the true value of the coins they were selling. After individual customers had brought numerous complaints about the fraudulent transactions, the government conducted additional appraisals of the coins. To determine the market value of a particular coin and its condition ("mint state"), the appraisers routinely consulted The Coin Dealer Newsletter, ommonly referred to as "the gray sheet." The gray sheet reports on a weekly basis the wholesale and retail price of coins traded nationwide by hundreds of coin dealers. Dealers commonly mark up the retail price of coins 20 to 30 ercent above cost. Not only were the coins being sold at prices far above their market value, they were also being sold at prices significantly higher than those recommended by Kail's chief supplier * * * [D]oubts among Coin & Stamp Gallery brokers increased in early 1984 after several customers complained and requested refunds of their purchases. In several instances, Kail refused to repurchase coins at the request of customers. On March 6, 1984 postal inspectors, investigating complaints of mail fraud, executed a search warrant at the Coin & Stamp Gallery offices. Among the business records seized was the Coin & Stamp Gallery commission ledger in which Kail's wife, Maggi, had recorded the actual purchase price of the coins.
>
> *** The search warrant authorized inspectors to seize: (1) evidence of mailings of coins in bullion shipments; (2) books, records, papers and documents relating to the sale and purchase of coins and bullion; (3) accounting ledgers or records, checkbooks, monthly statements, cancelled hecks, and deposit slips; (4) inventory records, records of safety deposit boxes, safety deposit keys and coins; and (5) customer files, client lists, letters and mailings from clients, checks, cash, coins or bullion shipments sent as payment for purchases and advertising materials. * * * Kail asserts that there was insufficient evidence to support the jury's verdict in light of the fact that there were honest differences of opinion and judgment as to the grade and value of the coins, therefore furnishing no basis for a finding that the defendant had committed fraud. He maintains that because the valuation of coins is inherently subjective, it cannot be fraud to sell coins at high prices. [Kail], however, mischaracterizes the nature of the charges against him. He was not charged with marking up the prices of the coins, but with misrepresenting the coins as valuable investments. In the record before us, the evidence demonstrates that Kail's representations with regard to the market value of the coins were false, and that these representations were made with an intent to defraud. The evidence established the existence of official grading standards promulgated by the American Numismatic Association which, while not having the force of law, were recognized by the government's experts as having wide acceptance in the industry. Moreover, The Coin Dealer Newsletter ("the greysheet") is almost universally relied upon by dealers to determine current market value of coins. Therefore, Kail's assertion that there is an absence of standards in the industry must be in doubt from this record. In addition, in spite of the fact that the coin grading process is inherently subjective, the experts' appraisals of coins sold by Kail's firm were consistent in demonstrating a pattern of over valuation. In some instances, the markups exceeded the cost tenfold. As a result, the jury could reasonably infer that the pricing practices of Coin & Stamp Gallery were so far beyond the limits of custom and practice in the industry as to constitute mail fraud. Finally, even if there were reason to believe that the subjective nature of the coin valuation process would make it difficult to prove criminal fraud, we nonetheless conclude there was abundant evidence presented that Kail operated his business dishonestly. He misled his brokers as to the cost basis of the coins that they were selling. His records reveal the actual cost of the coins had been concealed. Kail

even deceived his chief supplier by marking up grades and prices of consigned coins without apparent justification. And when customers, alerted to the fraud, demanded refunds, Kail refused on several occasions to honor his buy-back guarantee. We would therefore conclude the jury could reasonably find that Kail's pricing and sale of the coins was not conducted in good faith and amounted to mail fraud.

Postal Service Decision

Kail asserts that the trial court erred in excluding a 1977 Postal Service administrative decision in which the administrative law judge found that there were no industry-wide standards for the grading and valuation of coins. *Security National Rare Coin Corp. and Riverside Coin Co.*, Postal Service No. 5/130 (May 10, 1977). Kail offered the administrative decision in order to establish that the Postal Service acknowledged the absence of uniform coin grading standards and that in this prosecution the Postal Service was violating its own policy. The district court sustained the government's objection on hearsay and relevance grounds. On appeal, Kail argues that it was error to exclude the evidence since the administrative decision was admissible as a public record under Rule 803(8) of the Federal Rules of Evidence, and was relevant in that it supported his claim of good faith. To be admissible under F.R.E. 401, the Security National decision must be probative of a fact of consequence in this case. The trial court noted that the opinion proffered by Kail was dated 1977 and the testimony in this case indicated that there had been standards developed since that date by the American Numismatic Society ([sic] should read American Numismatic Association) which have been widely accepted by experts in the field. In addition, the district court noted that the finding of an administrative law judge in 1977 in a totally unrelated proceeding did not bear any relevance to the issues or was a proper way to decide issues involved in this case. The record before us demonstrates that Coin & Stamp Gallery was not incorporated until 1983. In addition, Kail himself utilized the standards promulgated in 1977 by the ANA in his grading of coins. Moreover, there is no evidence presented that Kail was in any way aware of the administrative law judge's decision until the time of his own trial. The administrative decision, therefore, was not relevant to any issue of consequence in this trial. In addition to the administrative decision's marginal relevance, we believe that the district court properly excluded it because its probative value was substantially outweighed by the danger of misleading or confusing the jury. F.R.E. 403. We believe that it is implicit in a situation in which an administrative decision is submitted as an exhibit to the jury that the jury would be forced to decide legal rather than factual questions. Moreover, it is apparent that allowing Kail to introduce the opinion into evidence might well have distracted the jury from the real issue in this case — Kail's intent to defraud. We believe that Kail had ample opportunity to present his good faith defense through his extensive cross-examination of experts, who were able to describe the prevailing practices among coin dealers during the relevant time period. We would therefore conclude that there was no prejudice to his case by the exclusion of this evidence and would affirm the decision of the district court.

The sentence that the Court of Appeals affirmed: "Kail was sentenced on May 30, 1985, to serve a total of seven years imprisonment and ordered to pay restitution in the amount of $501,738."

The Postal Service has also brought a number of different cases involving a variety of other abuses that they perceive. For example, they have brought action seeking relief against firms who used the word "mint" in their title, have brought suit going back to 1977 on coin grades that were allegedly abused, and have even gone so far as to bring a proceeding against those who believe that their numismatic products come from "guarded vaults" or a hoard.

All of this authority derives from the Postal Service Statute which specifically authorizes them to protect consumers and others from inherent abuses of the mail.

Summing Up

There ought to be no doubt, as the 90's begins, that government activity has basically affected virtually every area of the rare coin field. No longer can a seller (whether dealer or collector) claim ignorance as an excuse for shoddy practices. In fact, some have gone so far as to argue that coins are like a stock certificate — requiring disclosure and presumptions running against the seller. In the process, some believe that the rare coin field has now turned around to bite the hand that once fed it.

What is also abundantly clear is that with regulation, the buying and selling of coins — indeed, their collecting — will never again be the same.

For further reading on industry self-regulation:

Regulation of the coin industry is not new, nor has it lacked for coverage in the numismatic press. Below is a selected bibliography of articles written by the author that have been published in *COINage* Magazine, *Coin World*, and *Numismatic News* from 1974 until the present. They form a good bibliographic study of the field, and the view about government regulation within it.

"Ganz Believes Disclosure Vital to Industry," *Coin World*, September 3, 1986, p. 36.
Ed., "Numismatics and the Law," in *Coin World Almanac*, 3rd ed. (1978), pp. 47-110; 4th ed. (1984), pp. 53-129; 5th ed. (1987), pp. 43-144; 6th ed. (1990), pp. 47-164.
"'Bogeyman Woes Haunt Collectors for 13 Years: Grading Changes Prompt Fears," *Coin World*, September 19, 1990, p. 94.
"12 Guidelines for Coin Buyers and Sellers," *COINage*, March, 1988, p. 78-80.
"35 Hidden Truths of Coin Buying: Guidelines for Every New Collector-Investor," *COINage*, Dec. 1986, p. 74, 82.
"Certification [of dealer] process exciting move," *Coin World (Backgrounder)*, April 8, 1987, p. 4, 62.
"Certification [of dealers] may be essential," *Coin World (Backgrounder)*, April 15, 1987, p. 71, 78.
"Coin Grading Controversy Is Not Unsolvable Puzzle," *Numismatic News Weekly*, September 27, 1975, 12, 40.
"Coin Industry Under Fire: Forbes Attacks Broadside," *Numismatic News Weekly*, Feb. 1, 1975, p. 38.
"Coin market remains classic frontier," *Coin World (Backgrounder)*, June 10, 1987, p. 85.
"Educating the Buyer: Using Common Sense Will End Many Market Abuses," *COINage*, April, 1988, pp. 76, 78.
"Education important for consumers," *Coin World (Backgrounder)*, June 4, 1986, p. 54.
"FTC, postal officials investigate firms," *Coin World (Backgrounder)*, June 3, 1987, p. 42, 46.
"Ganz offers revised draft of FTC Brochure," *Coin World*, Feb. 10, 1986, p. 60.
"Grading Board Proposal Now Hotly Debated Issue," *Numismatic News Weekly*, September 20, 1975, 28, 29.
"Ike, CC Dollar Promotions Dampen Hobby Enthusiasm," *Numismatic News Weekly*, May 29, 1973, p. 27.
"Noncollecting Consumer of Coins Also Needs Protection With Law," *Numismatic News Weekly*, ("Under the Glass") July 31, 1973, p. 22.
"Numismatic industry at crossroads," *Coin World (Backgrounder)*, July 23, 1986, p. 96.
"Professional membership right step," *Coin World (Backgrounder)*, April 1, 1987, p. 76, 81-2.
"Regulation of the Coin Industry: An Overview," 1 *Review of Numismatics and the Law* 12-16 (1981).
"The Coin 'Professionals': Programs to Certify Those Who Sell Coins," *COINage*, Nov. 1987, p. 41, 42.
"The Government Regulators Look at the Coin Field," *COINage*, (May, 1986), pp. 49-52.
"The time has come [for self-regulation]," *Coin World (Backgrounder)*, July 15, 1987, p. 58, 60.
"Toward a Revision of the Minting and Coinage Laws of the United States," 26 *Cleveland State Law Review*, 175-257 (1977).
"USPS enforcing postal regulations," *Coin World (Backgrounder)*, May 6, 1987, p. 92, 99.
"Valuation of Coin Collection," 5 *Proof of Facts* 3rd 577-655 (1989).
"When Coins Trade Hands: What Should be Disclosed in a Coin Transaction?", *COINage*, June 1987, p. 57, 58.
"Winds of Change: Government Regulation of Coin Collectors," Bowers & Merena *Rare Coin Review*, Summer, 1985, pp. 47-49.
14 Bits: A legal and legislative history of 31 U.S.C. sec. 324d-324i (1976).

Selected Relevant Cases

Arizona v Reed, (March 1, 1989)*Corp. Comm'r v Schoolhouse Coins*, Cal. Ct. App. April 8, 1987)*FTC v Liberty Financial of North America, Inc.*, (US DCt. Ariz. June 27, 1990)*FTC v Vilkin, Civ.* 89-5674R (US DCt. CD Cal. 1989)*FTC v Rare Coin Galleries of America, Inc.*, Slip Opin. Sept. 16, 1986 (DCt. Mass.)*FTC v Numismatic Certification Institute*, (US DCt. SD Fla)*FTC v Rare Coin Galleries of America, Inc.*, (US DCt. Mass. Oct. 23, 1986)*FTC v Security Rare Coin & Bullion Corp.*, (DCt. Minn. 1988)*FTC v Standard Financial*, (US DCt. D. Mass 1987) *FTC v Numismatic Funding Corp.*, (US DCt. EDNY)*FTC v Schoolhouse Coins*, (US DCt. C.D. Cal. 1987).*FTC v Rare Coins of Georgia*, (US DCt. N.D. Ga. 1987)*FTC v Certified Rare Coin Galleries*, (US DCt. SD Fla. Aug. 30, 1990)*FTC v Certified Rare Coin Galleries*, (US DCt. SD Fla)*FTC v Professional Coin Grading Service*, (DCt. D.C. 1990) *Investment Rarities, Inc.*, (SEC 1975)*Longines Symphonette Soc.*, (SEC 1972)*Matter of Wilbert*, Opin. Georgia Comm'r of Securities, 1988 *Matter of Schoolhouse Coins, Inc.*, Wisc. Securities Comm., 1986*Matter of Numismatic Rarities, Inc.*, Wisc. Securities Comm'n, 1988*Matter of Numismatic Rarities, Inc.*, Wisc. Securities Comm'n, 1988*Matter of Numismatic Funding*, Missouri Securities Comm'n, 1987*Matter of Domaine Numismatics*, Missouri Securities Comm'n, 1986*Matter of Atlantic Numismatics*, Missouri Securities Comm'n, 1987*Matter of Omega Precious Metals & Coins*, Wisc. Securities Comm. 1986*Matter of A.G. Rothchild & Assoc.*, Washington Securities Div., 1988*People v Monex*, 380 NYS2d 504 (1974)*SEC v Brigadoon Scotch*, 388 F.Supp. 1288 (SDNY 1975)*SEC v Western Pacific Gold & Silver Exchange*, D.C. Nev. 1975)*SEC v Suter*, (ND Ill. Civ. 1983)*SEC v Comstock Coin*, (D.C. Nev. June 16, 1964)*State of NY v First Meridian Planning Corp.*, (Sup. Ct. 1987)*State of Minnesota v Coin Wholesalers Inc.*, (Sup Ct. Minn. 1976)*State of Idaho v A-Mark*, (US DCt. Idaho 1988)

IRS & Regulation 6045

Ganz (ed.) Numismatics and the Law in Coin World Almanac (6th ed. 1990). Covers Section 6045; a number of other regulations referred to in the materials are also reprinted in whole or in part in the chapter (pp. 47-164).

Logan [D. Ganz], "A Hobby Victory: An Intelligent Coin Lobby and New IRS Regulations," *COINage*, April 1984, p. 46, 48.
"IRS To Issue Final Regulations on Coin Dealer Reporting," *Coin World*, November 27, 1985, p. 1, 3.
"IRS Proposal Confusing," *Coin World*, Feb. 1, 1984.
"IRS Rules on Tax Status in Gold Coin Exchange," *Coin World*, Aug. 11, 1976.
"Reporting need tied to definitions," *Numismatic News*, January 16, 1990, p. 4, 18.

***

Chester West

CHAPTER 54

Chester West Tells It As It Is

Of Federal and State Government Regulations

The morning was an unusually peaceful one, and I was grateful, inasmuch as I had been in front of the tube most of the night. My very nature causes me to be a "Cspan-a-holic" and last night the senate hearings kept my attentive glands in an angry mood as I watched the guardians of freedom exercise their lack of knowledge in the Senate chambers.

On an adjacent channel, the bags under my eyes grew as the House of Representatives performed other important functions that test credulity in the mind of any reasonable person.

Why did I find the sessions upsetting? Well, let me relate a couple of the actions taken without naming the persons or perpetrators.

There was an elected official who molested someone. He had his hands slapped. You would have gone to jail. There was one who had "absentmindedly" forgot to pay scores of parking tickets, probably due to the fact that his home was being used for a brothel (without his knowledge — he said). He got his hands slapped. You would have gone to jail. Then, another who had used his position to swindle the taxpayers with unauthorized vouchers. He too had his hands slapped. You would have done time. Yes, I was angry and further surprised that you weren't.

It was in this atmosphere that I received the call from John Highfill asking me if I would write a chapter for this book on the subject of federal and state government regulations. After I informed him that I would, he added that he would desire that I be factual but to make it interesting reading. You know, a little on the light side.

Over the years my reading, research, and experience has loaded my memory with volumes of information on the subject, and my eagerness to perform the task was apparent to anyone who saw the "goose bumps" rise. But, how do you do this in a comical or even interesting manner?

Government Harassment Long Forgotten

There was a young man in the northwest who purchased for sale a few replicas of a dollar bill enlarged to an enormous size and inscribed with a bit of clever comedy. The Secret Service invaded the shop and unceremoniously, physically confiscated the bills against the protest of the merchant. A scuffle ensued — the "SS" won and the merchant was outraged. The teletypes hummed with enraged conversation on the subject for days. Can you find anything funny about this government regulated action?

In 1973, in Illinois, a couple was aroused as their bedroom door was demolished and armed men appearing as bums rushed in hollering and cussing. They brandished their guns, ransacked the house, destroyed much personal property and threatened the lives of the couple. These men were from the United States Justice Department, but they never identified themselves or produced a search warrant. As a matter of fact, it turned out that they were even in the wrong house. Charges were filed by the couple to be compensated for their frightening, life threatening, and costly experience, but nothing ever came of it. What's so funny about this kind of government interference allowed by your elected officials?

Shortly before I moved to California in 1964, Los Angeles County condemned a piece of property in order that an entertainment museum could be constructed on the site. The guy that owned the residence just didn't want to move out of his home. He barricaded himself with a shotgun and held off the deputies for weeks. Finally he was evicted and received jail time as a trouble maker and for resisting arrest. The museum was never built and the property when last I heard was making money for someone else as a parking lot. Can you find something amusing about this action endorsed and condoned by your elected representatives?

I was sorely tempted to call John and tell him that the exercise couldn't be completed if it must be done in a lighter vein. My mind pondered the political actions over the years that have been adverse to those whose only interest is collecting or servicing the collector. It would appear that such a small segment of the population would attract virtually no attention from such an austere group as the elected representatives in every governmental agency. It seems that operating funds could be spent more judiciously than trying to force unreasonable regulation on such a small industry. And isn't it true that the Federal Government profits handsomely from the numismatic and collecting activities of the citizens?

Whenever I am faced with incongruous actions, it has been my practice to "find the money bag." Who makes or loses money? Whose bull is being gored — so to speak?

A Time of Unrestricted Activity

Let's take a little trip back to 1963. At that time, collectors collected for fun and pleasure and the word "investor" was seldom used. There were in fact investors, but the part they played in the scheme of numismatics was very limited. It worked this way and still does to some extent. If a dealer purchased more stock than his immediate needs required or his pocketbook could handle and he wished to hold on to some popular items, he would sell them to a friend or customer in bulk at a reasonable price with the right to buy them back at a future time. This "investor" became a warehouse for collectibles. This situation was very limited in scope and made no impact on the market or price of coins.

In those days the collector filled his needs from coin clubs, mail order, bid boards, and the ever present local dealer. Every one had fun and enjoyed the educational hobnobbing and excitement of coin shows and conventions.

There was virtually no governmental interference or unreasonable regulations. Oh yes, every now and then an agent or enforcement arm of the law would flex his muscles and show his importance at a coin show by picking up some holed coins, love tokens or coins that were used as jewelry — but not often. I don't believe I ever saw an arrest. They just confiscated the "offending" material and left the dealer or collector to hide his embarrassment and contemplate his losses.

Silver Dollars and Government Decree Against the Public Will

In recent years, the first instance of serious governmental interference in the business or hobby of Numismatics was the release of bags upon bags of silver dollars in Washington, D.C. from the Treasury Department. Some dollars that were considered scarce and rare were suddenly plentiful, and the sudden release played havoc with some dealers stocks. Overnight some dealers lost thousands in inventory value. Generally, the collector didn't care about value enough to consider the loss. He had bought his coin to fit the set he was putting together and the fluctuations really don't mean anything until it's time to sell.

We can't be too harsh on the officials for this act, in as much as the government and the people had been trying to eliminate this huge stock of silver dollars since the second year of production.

1878 ranks high on the list of just plain preposterous bureaucratic regulation. Millions of taxpayers' dollars have been wasted in purchasing the silver, minting the coins, building and rebuilding vaults to store them, melting them down and then recoining them, and spending tens of thousands of hours arguing about them on the floor of both chambers. You see, the public didn't want them and refused to use them, and the government wasn't to be dictated to by the public's wishes.

President Hayes in 1880 said, "We have minted 72 million silver dollars and we have spent a lot of dough trying to keep them in circulation, but they keep coming back. The people don't want them. I think we should melt 700 of them and make an Aztec Calendar for General John W. Foster."

In 1881 President Arthur said, "The minting of silver dollars is unnecessary. We have coined 102 million of these dollars and only 34 million are in circulation."

In 1882 he said, "We now have 128 million of these "jingers" and only 35 million are being used. We don't have room in the vaults for them. The public doesn't want them. Why do we make them?"

In 1884, "Well, we got a mess of these things now. We made 185 million and only 40 million are out."

President Grover Cleveland took up the chant in 1885, "We've coined 215 million silver dollars and no one uses them. We have spent great sums building new vaults to house 165 million of them."

In 1886 President Cleveland lamented the horrendous loss caused by elected officials who were adamant that their regulations prevail regardless of the cost or the desires of the people, "Last year we spent 23 million dollars plus labor and storage for silver dollars that no one wants. Now we have 247 million of them. This gamble on a silver price increase is a bust. In the beginning, when we bought the silver, the dollar content was 94.5 cents. On the 31st day of July, 1886, silver dropped to its lowest price. Now these things are only worth 78 cents."

In 1888, "This silver gamble is a bad deal. Now we have made 312 million and only 60 million are being used."

President Benjamin Harrison in 1889 said, "In the beginning, when we started this exercise, silver was $1.20 an ounce and the cost of the silver dollar plus storage and labor was 93 cents. Now we have accumulated 343 million of these dollars and the public just doesn't want to pay a dollar for something worth only 70 cents."

This could go on and on, but my purpose is to show that regulations, which assault the reason of thinking men, flowing from the pens of our elected officials is nothing new. Even then the will and the desire of the people took a back seat to the preferential treatment of a few at the expense of the many.

History shows that eventually a great portion were ordered to be melted only to be restruck again at the expense of the people beginning in 1921.

Discriminating Action Moves Silver Dollar Hoard

In 1960 the mint reported 485,000 bags of silver dollars in reserve. This accumulation of silver dollars which began the very first year of minting has always caused much speculation of the part of Numismatists. There had been so much confusion in the striking, storing, melting and restriking process that the serious collector or historian had no knowledge concerning exactly what was in the treasury's closet. We know that in about 1893 the branch mints of Denver, Carson City, and San Francisco suspended silver dollar operations and sent the dollars back to the treasury vaults. Therefore, it was safe to assume that the 1963 sell off of silver dollar bags, in the beginning, was made up largely of these branch mint returns.

It reasons that in the exercise of 1963, the bottom of the stack was the Carson City dollars — then the New Orleans dollars. Toward the top of the stack the bags become a mixture of Philadelphia, Denver, and San Francisco, which came from their regular production runs.

Rumors ran rampant. Speculation and rumor concerning the 1903-O dollar was that the entire stock of 4,450,000 was on top of the heap and consequently comprised in its entirety a portion of the 90 million dollars melted for India. This theory was also held in part for the 1904-O dollar.

In 1963 collectors found that bags of 1903-O dollars were being shipped to the FED for Christmas business. The price of the 1903-O dollar dropped from around $1,500 to $15.00.

Now if the 1903-O and 1904-O dollars weren't a large part of the India melt — what else is in the huge stock of dollar bags which are considered rare and are not at all?

The treasury maintained a window where anyone could pick up all the silver dollars they wanted for cash. Collectors and dealers and those interested in silver dollars headed for Washington and purchased unopened bags of silver dollars for face value. They quickly opened the bags — removed what they wanted and headed for the closest bank to exchange them for paper money. Then back to the treasury window for another bag or bags. This became a melee when others discovered what was going on and stood in the same line — sometimes as long as ten hours.

Every day silver dollars which were previously traded at a premium were discovered causing the hobby market to tumble; but, of a more ominous nature, in the background were the industrialists, waiting to buy silver dollars for the melting pots.

Plainly in evidence were also the representatives from the Nevada gaming houses, waiting their turns to buy hundreds of bags for use in the casinos. Although it is certain that they were successful in obtaining their share, the acquisition was merely a shot in the arm for the gambling industry. It was a losing struggle for the casinos to hang on to their supply of silver dollars — they disappeared as fast as they were placed into play. The casino customers, caught up in the frenzy and maintaining a belief that somehow these dollars were rare, just pocketed them and took them home. Frustrated casino operators even tried grinding off the dates. It didn't work.

Dealers set up shop in Washington and began advertising and shipping full bags across the country in thousands and thousands of bags for up to $1,350 per bag.

As the stockpile became smaller and smaller the Denver dollars disappeared and then San Francisco and New Orleans and Philadelphia.

Sometime in early 1964 the rarest of them all, the Carson City dollar, appeared. Here was a low mintage series which commanded and would always command a premium as long as there were collectors. A bag of CC dollars could easily be sold for a profit of ten to twenty thousand dollars. The ensuing scene was worse than a rock festival. Crowds of people stood in line for blocks, sometimes as many as five abreast, for hours. Runners were hired by some to do their buying for them. The whole thing got out of control and the treasury suspended the sale of the dollars.

It was the Friday before Easter 1964 and the treasury had moved and the public had absorbed the entire stock save an estimated 3,000 bags of dollars known or almost surely thought to be Carson City dollars.

It was this lot that ultimately received the kind of treatment any business man would have afforded something he know nothing about. Eventually they hired a committee of experts — as I recall Fred Weinberg was one of them — who were called to Washington to inspect the bags. This action preceded the release of the "Nixon Silver Dollars."

As is usually the case, the decision to move the dollars at face value was made without any concern about the thousands of dollars in time and energy that would have to be paid. Many dollars could have been saved by both the government and industry if the bags had been randomly distributed to the banks across the country through everyday channels. Distribution to the citizenry would have been much more equitable. But, the government was rid of its dollars — at a fantastic cost to the taxpayers.

Restrictive Distribution of Proof Sets

In 1964 the mighty arm of the government pointed a digit again at the collecting fraternity. Up until that time, the general public paid little or no attention to proof sets or ordering procedures. Some collectors ordered a set or two and dealers were known to order in the hundreds for distribution to their customers. Someone in Washington decided to do a bit of regulating and limited the number available to any one customer to five sets.

It should have been clear to any one that such a regulation would not prevent the dealer from servicing his customers. He just placed more orders under the names of his friends who had no desire to own them. The collector didn't give a hoot either because he was going to complete his series with or without government intervention. It was of little consequence that this action caused higher handling and mailing costs, which of course was charged to the taxpayer.

What did happen was a gigantic display of the chaos caused when people in government, who have a great propensity for error, have the power to make far reaching decrees without first obtaining a practical knowledge of the consequences of its actions.

Before the end of the year the price of the 1964 proof set had soared to as high as $25. Because there were fewer made? Not true. The 1964 issue was 3.9 million and the three prior years were right at 3 million.

If the government had in mind saving silver, it failed; thirty percent more proof sets were sold. If they had in mind curbing speculation, it failed miserably. This regulation fired one of the biggest "ding dong" speculation sprees I have ever seen. Everyone became a coin collector or hoarder. Prices soared and anyone who left the house with an extra twenty dollars in the morning bought something with it before he came home. He knew that tomorrow he would make a profit.

Government Debases Coins and Creates Panic Atmosphere

A short time later the government debased the coinage and the public started going through their change and scooping out all of the silver coin they could afford to keep. I was in California at the time and my banker asked me if I could get him a couple of bags of dimes, quarters, or halves. I was quite puzzled at the request and asked why. He informed me that the change that came into the bank was usually rolled by the FED and returned. In recent weeks they had been sending it in to the FED but not getting it back. Every indication was that the government was melting silver coin, though no one knew for sure. In any event the shortage of change was placed squarely on the shoulders of the collecting public.

In those days, it was possible to go through change and find collectibles, and I jumped at the chance to be of service to the bank and find a stock in trade in exchange for labor. I told him that I would take his bags of loose coin and roll them for him at no charge over the week end — explaining of course my reason.

During the remainder of the week I pressed every one I knew for a loan until Monday morning in order that I could pay for the bags of loose change. I managed to raise $3,000 which I believed was probably sufficient. When I arrived at the bank, I was directed to the business manager who had readied ten bags for my weekend activity. To say I was speechless is an understatement. I began to apologetically explain that I didn't have the funds when he interrupted to explain his terms. I was to give him a check on Friday night for ten thousand and on Monday he would return it to me and get a good check for the amount of coin I had kept. This went on for the better part of four months.

The government with another disastrous decision had nearly depleted the coin flow necessary to conduct business. Who got the blame? You can rest assured that the government didn't take it. They blamed the coin collector and dealer.

Government Melts Coins — John Q. is Arrested

During this period, the commodity markets in silver began to make waking up noises. The government was taking in the silver coin and melting it and replacing it with debased coinage.

To my knowledge the treasury didn't admit melting the silver coin until 1967 when they reported that they had retrieved 1,673,735 ounces from the melt. It was clear at that time that an inflationary trend was well established and that the government was short of silver. The stocks had dropped to 270 million ounces, and the melt continued.

Private citizens saw a chance to profit from coin melt and began melting silver coin the same as the government was doing. Enforcement agents were quickly on the scene to prevent this outrageous destruction of (government) property.

Citizens were harassed and charged for doing the same thing the government was doing. Citizens were even arrested and charged for taking silver coin out of the country.

In May 1969 the double standard which prohibited private citizens from doing what the government openly did was ended. The ban on melting and exporting silver coinage was lifted.

It would appear to anyone watching these events that somewhere along the line those who dream up regulations would take a breather. Such is not the case.

Promises Redeemed in Granules

The backing was removed from the silver certificate with a regulation that said you had a time period during which the government would honor its promise to pay the long-established one ounce of silver for one dollar, and after that period it would have no intrinsic value. The redemption method must have been dreamed up after an all night poker game somewhere. Let's look at it.

If a customer wishes to purchase silver bars from a dealer, he gets a good looking well struck certified bar or round — most of the time with an interesting design, which is tradeable without question. The government delivered nondescript bars with the weight affixed with a marking pen. This opened up the back door for crooks to alter the weight and in some cases even drill them out and fill them with other than silver. Those who didn't qualify for large bars were given the final insult — a packet of granules that looked like silver. The silver certificate was rendered worthless — without intrinsic value. If that wasn't bad enough, it was regulated that you must accept this worthless paper as money in any negotiation — under threat of penalty.

Silver Granules issued by the U.S. Treasury
(Courtesy of John W. Highfill)

U. S. Silver Certificate
(Courtesy of Fred Lemons, Tulsa, Oklahoma)

Justice is the Corner Stone of a Free Society

The long and short of it is just this. One of the functions of the government in a "free society" is to protect its citizens from force and fraud rendered by others. This should not imply that the agencies of government are excluded from the "Others." The use of force, devious schemes, intimidation and harassment toward the citizenry was not the intention of the Founding Fathers and is not the desire of the people in a "Free Society."

The subject of duty, law, regulation, necessity, and injustice is a most complex one. Somewhere along the line each is dependent on the other, but it becomes almost an impossible task to assign each its position in the scheme of things to the satisfaction of all men. It is easy to lay down general ideas of our own definitions of what is right and just, but care must be taken when applying these broad definitions to the masses.

Justice is the most important and the most elusive attribute to be observed when measuring the worth or value of any law or regulation. Justice is the cement that binds all lasting relationships between men. It binds successful negotiations between nations, between man and his family, and between government and citizen.

Any discussion of justice, duty, and law must be based on the platform that "man is free" and this freedom in a free society such as ours must never be infringed upon by fraud or force. If any action by any person or body of persons imposes restrictions on the moral free actions of others against their will under the guise of necessity or desire, the action is unjust. It's as simple as that.

Therefore, in the matter of legislation, which is the topic of this chapter, the injurious action to be avoided is the legislation of unfair and unequal rules against the will of free men under the banner of necessity to fulfill the desires of another.

Throughout the history of man, all governments who have robbed Peter to pay Paul have fallen out of favor with the governed and have ultimately failed when Peter found out he was being robbed. You can take only so many bites out of one cherry. The historical demonstrations and uprisings of John Q. Public have emerged in every instance because he felt the sword of injustice slashing his rights.

Unconscionable government interference in private industry and the lives of the citizens is nothing new. It has been permitted by the citizen and practiced by bureaucracies for centuries. The premise for this meddling is that mankind is not able to think for himself in an orderly manner without guidelines set forth by a governing body. I hasten to add that "**it might be true**." Interestingly, those who are charged with the responsibility — under oath — of setting these guidelines are for the most part the least equipped to understand the problem or the remedy.

We are told that our representatives come from all walks of life, and judging from recent newsprint, it occurs to me that we would all be a bit better off it they didn't. Youngsters have been lied to for years. They've been told that if they study and learn and live a good life without lying, cheating, or stealing, they could grow up to be a Senator or Representative or even Governor or President. This being said, they are further told that if they lie, cheat, or steal — "God will getcha."

Nothing could be further from the truth. To be elected you need only the desire to be elected, an organization with money and pull behind you, and votes.

The Greatest Form of Government — But Who Will Serve?

I am blessed with a firm conviction (which my investigations into the governments of the world will bear out) that this is the greatest land and the greatest form of government in the world. My point is that most of our representatives are not schooled in the leadership requirements needed to properly understand and administer our rights as set down by our Constitution and Bill of Rights; most are somewhat less than suited for the task of governing according to the will of the people. And maybe I'm right. Let me ask you: "Would you run for office? Choose the best of all the intelligent management people you know. Do you know one who would run or serve?" Of course you don't. If that's so, you're left with those who find being elected some kind of advancement or ego serving vehicle.

The ballots are filled with the names of housewives whose claim to knowledge is based on a diploma and whose management skills were acquired by successfully managing a shopping list. And men whose management skills were acquired by managing the family hearth and offspring. In many cases found in the reports, the managing of the offspring was a "flop." In recent years notably, the governing of this great nation has been accomplished with the aid of an astrologer — a seer. Another group that populates the ballot are those who are adept at compromise, the ability and skill needed to trade beliefs for votes.

And who elects them? Voters who can tell wheat from chaff? Absolutely not. They're elected by puppeteers who have something to gain: gun lobbies; money lobbies; labor lobbies; minority lobbies; and special interests hoping for special treatment. Are the officials crooks? Not necessarily. Will they stay honest? Not necessarily.

There is a reluctance of people with ability to run for any public office. It is very seldom that we elect one of our top management people to the office of president or any other office for that matter. Look over the list for the last 70 or so years and you'll be shocked at the very few who had any leadership or management ability at all. When something goes wrong or a devious action is found out in the headlines, there is sure to be a consensus in the "bull pen" that, "Aw, they're all crooked." Is it any wonder that intelligent men are happy to "let George do it"?

There's a story among aircraft pilots that if you sit in the cockpit long enough, you'll feel and know that you could get the plane off the ground — and it's true. Anyone can. But, landing that sucker is another story.

Of Potholes and Highways

These people aren't crooks. They just become experts on everything overnight by public acclaim. When a new face shows up in the political arena (and that isn't often, because it's populated by incumbents), he might have the greatest of morals and honesty, but before long he will be found trading his vote to "fix the potholes" in your state for your vote to "run a highway" through his. You and I know that this is certainly devious, if not indeed just plain crooked. He gets the highway and his "colleague" gets his potholes fixed at the expense of the taxpayers in other states. He doesn't look at it that way at all because he can wave a banner of accomplishment before his lobby, and that's good for votes at a future date and an authorized free meal or two (deductible of course at the taxpayers expense).

Watch the proceedings at any session and you will hear the chairman's gavel constantly rapping in an attempt to maintain order. You will notice members moving from desk to desk with papers in their hands. Believe me, they are not discussing the baseball scores. They're making deals for "potholes."

Rights in the Market Place Violated

I find no action in the bills which have adversely effected the Numismatic Fraternity, that is contrary to rights or freedoms, if you will. Then we must ask, what's wrong with the regulations — holding laws — tax requirements — reporting requirements — government competition in private industry? None of these things attack or hinder any of these named rights.

But there is another right which has been tampered with — violated — regulated and restricted which, in my opinion, is the greatest of all freedoms. We have the right to conduct our affairs in the market place without "mind boggling" controls and regulations that decrease our effectiveness in pursuing our legal and productive goals.

The government does indeed have a legal and moral charge to assure that no citizen be hampered through coercion — fraud- or force by anyone and that includes governments. However, as a citizenry, we have allowed the government to do just that and in most instances the contrary actions of government were initiated by the very people who under oath declared their allegiance to the Constitutional rights of the people.

This whole fiasco is not present only in hobby related items. It pervades virtually every financial activity engaged in by the public. The list of forced economic compliance is much to long for this chapter, but let's look at a few. There are Unemployment Compensation, Social Security, Minimum Wage Acts, Sales Taxes paid over and over on the same piece of merchandise, and Hidden Taxes of every kind and nature. These and many other hindrances and interferences into the private lives of individuals and companies force the citizen to act without choice on matters of hiring, firing, producing, giving, or contracting as he wishes (without force or fraud) in the interest of his own fulfillment and accomplishments.

If all legislation hampering or forcefully controlling legitimate action in the market place were removed, most of the activity in both the Senate and the House would be eliminated.

It is no secret that strong lobbies looking for preferential treatment in the arena of business have been largely responsible for curtailing or hampering the freedoms of smaller businesses to gain a competitive edge. It happens every year.

Even the government deliberately and unjustly markets it's production to your customers and many times in a most biased manner. Case in point would be the marketing of collector coins through outside channels — and only those with megabucks may be considered. That's certainly discriminatory. Or selling the same coins that you make a market in without assessing the customary required sales tax. That's blatantly unfair competition. A thinking person must ask himself, "What justification does any branch of government have to compete in any private business at any time for any reason?" I suggest they have none.

Money Plus Numbers Equals Not Enough to Accomplish the Task

Coin Dealers and collectors have had no organization like the NRA to make a call to arms and produce sufficient numbers or dollars to champion their cause — and never will. Oh yes, I know we have ICTA who in recent years have attempted to bring our cause to the attention of the law makers but, in the process they almost went broke and I suspect that the scenario will be repeated in the future. It takes a lot of money to keep a lobby on the Washington scene and if you had the entire membership of ANA backing the action — it would still not be enough.

To give the reader an idea of the dollars involved, consider if you will that over $150,000 was expended by ICTA in the most recent attempt to have the Senatorial eyes consider the unfairness of the reporting law as outlined in S.1349. The reported results of this expenditure of effort and money was a favorable report from 13 Senators. It must be considered that at least four of these Senators were already on our team. This then being the case, where will the funds come from to gain a favorable reaction from over 500 more law makers? Simple mathematics will indicate that our numbers and our dollars do not measure up to the task.

The question naturally arises, "So what? What's so bad about the status quo? Why the objection to making reports to the IRS on purchases and sales? What's wrong with holding laws? What's wrong with Sales Taxes on coins purchased as investment vehicles? What's wrong with Estate Taxes on coin collections as well as other personal property?"

That's a bunch of "What's Wrongs."The global answer to all of these questions is that they are uniquely unfair and in every case (except Estate Taxes) discriminatory.

There is No Status Quo

The negative involved in the status quo is that there is none. No one knows precisely what is required of them concerning many of the regulations. Those who have had access to the written regulations (and that's not everyone) are unable to read them and have no legal counsel on retainer to even attempt an understanding. Neither the agencies nor the government forwards the regulations they enact until a citizen is confronted by an enforcement team. It is interesting to note here that the enforcers generally are not able to interpret the context of the entire documents or the intended meaning. When inquiry is made to the governing body for clarification, they either do not respond or make a partial and ambiguous interpretation which may or may not govern the enforcer. These laws, rules, and interpretations for the most part have never been known to the alleged offender and those which are known are difficult or impossible for the average person to comprehend. Laws which are unknown can not reasonably be obligatory and laws written in high and mighty words sprinkled with "where as — if — and — but — and refer to Baxter 749-6669-1a" that none can read or interpret cannot be reasonably obligatory.

These facts do not deter the enforcement arm of the government from levying tremendous fines and penalties and unreasonable interest charges. Worse yet is that you must pay them regardless of your thought. They have all the money — the power — and the guns. You will pay!!

There is no "status quo."

1099B — A Death Knell to an Industry

Why the objection to making reports to the IRS on 1099B or Magnetic Media? The answer here again is that there is no objection to making reasonable reports that are required by an intelligent law deemed proper by the citizens and clearly directed to the industry intended by the law makers in the first place. None of these criteria exist in the case of the ruling requiring a 1099B. Let me add that this answer should in no way indicate that the writer believes that such reports are valid in a supposed free society — they are not. However, one of the great objections is that such reporting as outlined in the requirement and as explained by regional enforcement agents are not only unreasonable — they are unfathomable and smack of rank intimidation from a position of strength. I have read reports where a dealer was charged and fined for not reporting the purchase and/or sale of an Indian Head Cent. The closest independent interpretation of the ruling which not only defies understanding but is cloaked in every violation of grammatical structure known to mankind — is that the purchase of a 1960 Roosevelt Dime would of necessity under threat of penalty require the paperwork involved in filing a 1099B. To say the whole concept is ridiculous would be far too charitable. The whole thing smacks of "Hitlerism." If the transaction was a fair transaction, the dealer would profit less than five cents, and this is or should be known to those who profess to possess a sufficient quantity of knowledge to act as public servants.

Further on this subject is that the government agency has arbitrarily placed a "Broker" status on coin dealers and collectors that does not exist in most instances and no attempt has been made to segregate the few where the term "broker" might exist from the many where no applicable connection can possibly be made. The coin dealer is a coin dealer and the precious metals dealer may or may not be a broker. A broker by the most accurate definition is an intermediary who makes deals between parties or acts as an agent between or for parties. A coin dealer on the other hand buys his stock in much the same way that the hobby store buys theirs. He places it in his counters and waits for someone to come by who wishes to purchase one of those jingers. To place all in one class is not just plain unjust — it's criminal in this case and violates the very freedom from harassment promised to every citizen.

In addition to that, if the government insists on forcing these regulations on any industry, they should at least have some idea of what they are doing before it's done by consulting with the industry at length to make sure that they don't violate the rights of others not involved. It seems ridiculous to mention that after the dastardly deed is accomplished by the elected representatives, it would seem logical to any honest entity that notification of the regulation and its requirements would properly be disseminated to all who were affected by the act long before the enforcement crowd arrived on the scene claiming "non-compliance." It would also seem fair and just that the enforcement people should be clear about the contents and what constituted a violation and — that should apply to all citizens falling in the same category regardless if the habitat was Minneapolis or Mobile or Havre or Timbuctoo. We have had instances where individual Regional Offices have proffered their independent interpretations after being asked to do so, and even these interpretations defied interpretation by counsel. This is not a healthy intelligent state of affairs when the regulation itself requires compliance or extreme penalty.

Make no mistake about it. The "intent" of the law maker, must be read into the letter of the law. The "purpose" of the law placed into the body of the law illuminates the text. Statutes on the same subject matter should be logically construed together, and no part of the obvious legislative intent should be allowed to perish through construction. Such is not the case with the law governing the implementation of 1099B.

Then we must investigate the depth in absurdity the regulation requires, as read by counsel. On the face of the regulation, it would require extensive paperwork between the buyer and the seller, then further paper work between the buyer and the seller and the IRS, on a transaction that historically involves less then fifty cents that produces a gross profit of less than ten cents. Additionally, it would require reports on Magnetic Media — we assume that's computer floppy disk — if the transactions in one year exceeded a certain figure (believed to be 250 at this writing). This assumes that the shop on the corner has a computer and the software and knows how to use it. Did I say absurd? You bet it is!!

Is there anything else? Yes, many things, but the ultimate result is that the lack of interest shown for the taxpayers interest and welfare in allowing these enforcement actions sounds a "death knell" to an industry effecting hundreds of thousands of people.

This is No Way to Do Business

Senator David Pryor said very clearly, "There seems to be confusion within the IRS as to the proper enforcement of these regulations. Some IRS agents require taxpayers to file 1099B reports on all transactions. Some agents ignore the regulations altogether. While other agents have suggested an arbitrary de minimis limit, such as one ounce of gold or one silver coin. All the while, these business people around the country do not know when the other shoe will fall, and the IRS will come in and decide retroactively whether or not their businesses are in compliance with the regulations."

"Mr. President, this is no way to do business. If the Federal Government is going to require taxpayers to comply with costly and time consuming reporting requirements, the least we can do is clarify the law so that people know whether or not they are in compliance with those laws."

That sounds pretty clear to me — how about you? I presented this paragraph to my ten year old grandson and asked him to tell me what it said. He had a small problem with "de minimis" and "retroactively," but his interpretation of these words was "right on."

The IRS Has Overstepped Its Limits

Senator Steve Symms is clear, "This restrictive interpretation (by the IRS) has caused untold frustration for thousands of small dealers and collectors who have to file and report transactions as small as forty cents. The IRS has overstepped its limits in making every mom-and-pop coin dealer report these transactions."

Representative Mathew Martinez of California said, "When ordering to pay, IRS auditors are policemen."

William Hawkins, Tax Commissioner of Virginia came across heavy handedly when he said, "Fear causes compliance in Virginia. We have a right to padlock and sell businesses."

IRS Commissioner Fred Goldberg said, "Complex rules and forms cost 35 billion dollars (I assume per year) and bury IRS and taxpayers alike in needless forms and correspondence. Our employees need training and tools and we need to reduce the paperwork burden on taxpayers."

I have other quotes along the same line, but in most instances the replies to my inquiries have been side stepped by the elected representative I queried with some kind of "canned gobbledygook" and a thank you for calling this to my attention. Then again, I don't have anything to trade to get my "potholes" fixed.

If what I say is true, what reason has been given for directing such a regulation at the hundreds of coin dealers and tens of thousands of collectors in the nation?

That's a good question and I usually avoid it because the reason given would insult the sensibilities of anyone with just a smattering of knowledge of logic and math. First of all, you must understand that the Bill approved by the government legislative bodies had absolutely nothing to do with coin collecting, coin collectors or coin dealers whose dealings are monetarily modest by any standards. The bill was intended to be aimed at Stock and Commodity Brokers who deal in hundreds of thousands of dollars and on occasion sell a contract involving silver and gold coins. These actions by any stretch of the imagination cannot and were not intended to include the citizen or his dealer who were engaged in a transaction to collect a set of Roosevelt dimes.

As cases of arbitrary interpretation and intimidating action came to light, members of the Numismatic Fraternity turned to the law makers and their personal elected representatives for relief. At this writing, no relief is in sight. I have personally spoken to dozens of elected representatives and in almost every case they have informed me that the story is so absurd that it can't be true. None the less, it is true — every word.

Capital Gains for a Coin Collector?

Politicians have informed me that one of the reasons for this legislative action was to force the citizen to more honesty in the matter of reporting "capital gains." It seems the IRS reported that they were only able to get reports on sixty percent of capital gains.

You have to admit that the collection of only sixty percent of the moneys due is far from an efficient operation and should certainly be looked into. Let's see how legislating and enforcing the reporting requirement on those who collect coins will aid in swelling the purse of the Federal Government. If a collector starts to put together a set of circulated Roosevelt Dimes one at a time, over a period of time he will have made 48 separate purchases and spent well under thirty dollars. It's silly to even discuss this because, if he ever sold them, (and most don't) — he couldn't buy a steak dinner for him and his wife with the entire proceeds and probably couldn't pay the tab at McDonald's with the profits. Capital gains — indeed.

Converting a Quarter Mil in Drug Money at the corner Coin Store

The reason given by some of those in power is that they wish to put some kind of curb on the laundering of drug money.

Unless you have been "hermitting" in a cave for the last couple of decades, you know that drug dealers operate in six figures and up. Can you possibly conjure a picture of anyone — even someone playing with a short deck — trading in coins 500 — 1,000 or even 5,000 dollars at a clip to move $250,000 in ill gotten drug money? The idea is ludicrous and becomes more contrary to possible reality when you consider that over three quarters of all the coin dealers in the land have less than $50,000 worth of inventory and thousands of shops operate on less then $20,000. Laundering drug money — it sounds like the incoherent mumbling of a kid trying to explain why the lawn didn't get mowed. If the law makers made a mistake of omission, or the IRS was over zealous in it's interpretation, shouldn't the "keepers of the light" be big enough to correct the error and get on with it? Is it really necessary to require an industry to spend hundreds of thousands of dollars in lobby fees and promotional activity to have the wrong righted? Is it necessary to continue to intimidate an industry with the threat of complete ruin and elimination by a ruling which is ill conceived at best and economically impossible to comply with?

It must be clear to anyone that "laundering drug money" is a pretty lame reason resting on a flimsy foundation. If the truth were known, the IRS probably has too many people on the payroll and in order to keep them busy the directors look for tasks that are apparently easy. You will note here that finding coin dealers is an easy thing to do. They are family raising, church going, property owning, tax paying citizens who have generally been in the same location for years.

Let me tell you right now that the shop on the corner whose average sale is less than fifty dollars does not engage in nefarious schemes to launder "drug money." You really don't have to be intelligent to perceive this and you have to be pretty badly advised to think otherwise. In any case, wasting hundreds of thousands in man hours and labor of the nation's income investigating and harassing these people is a travesty reflecting the actions of Diocletian.

Hundreds of Thousands of Reports — No Convictions

What's wrong with holding laws? My direct answer will tend to make me "persona non grata" by many of my readers. There is probably nothing wrong with holding laws, in my opinion, but I reserve the right to define the meaning of "holding laws." There is little doubt that obtaining merchandise in an illegal manner by some members of society is a problem that has always been with us and will always be with us. It is also clear that the law enforcement agencies are ill equipped in both man power and knowledge to successfully hunt down — arrest — and convict these persons without intruding on the privacy of others.

Punishing the innocent to excuse the lack of ability to intelligently and efficiently track down the guilty is nothing new. It has been a method resorted to by every failed government and dictatorship since the beginning of time — though it is not something to be associated with freedom. Be that as it may, the elected representatives goaded on by law enforcement have resorted to "holding laws" as a method for tracking down criminals and giving no thought whatsoever to an intelligent method that would produce the least inconvenience to the honest businessmen who were forced to comply. Here again, it's easier to find and intrude on the routines of an honest businessman than it is to wear out a little shoe leather finding the crook. The dealer has been on the corner for years and if you miss him there you can find his home close by. He'll be in the back yard playing with the kids.

If some investigative inquiry was directed before the writing of these acts, they would include only those items which can be positively identified. It's no secret that most cases never come to trial and when they do, they are lost for lack of evidence or the inability of the case to prove other than presumption or circumstantial evidence.

What then should be included in the holding laws? I've already answered that. Only those items that can be positively identified at a future date would qualify as an item that should be made a part of this very costly "witch hunt." Certainly, coins for the most part are absolutely unidentifiable to the extent that such identification would hold up in court.

I have on my desk at this writing a teletype notice that reads, ". . .the guy who did the robbing and killing took lots of bullion gold and a bunch of high grade raw Morgans — the only thing identifiable was a Pan Pac 2 1/2 gold. . ." This information was from a veteran coin dealer to other coin dealers across the nation. With this in mind — that a large robbery took place and a great quantity of coins were stolen and even dealers couldn't identify them at a later date — how could a law enforcer, attorney, judge, or jury have any use for them at all? And let me further state that the author of the teletype notice was in error. You know and I know that the Pan Pac could not be "positively" identified under any circumstance.

(Since the above paragraph was written, the culprit was apprehended and charged in Alaska. The positively identifiable item was the watch that was removed from his victim. The writer of this news added the footnote that some sharp shyster will get him off on some "mickey mouse" technicality.)

That's what's wrong with the holding laws. If they applied to identifiable items only, there would be some semblance of reason found other than the pure harassment that exists as a result of them. Let my reader understand positively that these instances in no way should suggest that the writer compromises his belief that all of these uses of forceful compliance are contrary to the promises of freedom in a free society.

We can't logically leave the question of holding laws without considering the damage done to a free market by the enforcement that currently exists. It must be clear to anyone that merchandise which is traded on the basis of a market is traded historically at very small spreads. Such items when they must be held for a period of time cannot be purchased by any dealer at a fair price. Therefore, the citizen loses and in many cases even the dealer loses when the market declines after the buy was made. This action decimates a free market and renders it inoperative. This restrictive action by government has produced nothing but higher costs, higher taxes, and a frustrated environment with virtually no results. Out of the hundreds of thousands of reports that have been made and the hundreds of thousands of items that have been held as required, a very, very, small percentage has produced the expected results. None the less, the enforcement continues.

The Greatest Discrimination of All

What's wrong with sales tax on coins? I suppose any experienced writer could write a book on this subject, but I will limit my comments to a couple of paragraphs. Actually, the whole thing could be tied up in one sentence, "They're ill conceived, poorly written laws and I can say without fear of contradiction that they are discriminatory." It should be noted here that "Discrimination in and of itself is not illegal, but discrimination between or against like qualifications — might be."

A large amount of Numismatic activity is across state lines and city to city within state borders. This provides a most unreasonable atmosphere for the dedicated businessman doing business with frugal people. If a collector is spending $50 for a coin that has a fair market traded price of $50 and the sales tax is 7% in location "A", he must cough up an additional $3.50 to conclude the purchase. If the coin is traded a mile or so away in city "B", and the tax is 4%, he adds only $2.00 to his cost. This certainly discriminates against the dealer at point "A", and causes him to lose business because of a government forced regulation. The end of the story is even worse. If the same buyer wishes to wait a few days for delivery, he can purchase the same coin without tax from out of state point "C". You don't have to be a genius to see the incongruity of these government restrictions.

That fairly well demonstrates discrimination and it's a serious matter, but let me relate a story of the actions in Colorado. Over the years tens of thousands have been spent by Colorado dealers in money (not counting thousands of hours of lost time) in an effort to bring some semblance of justice and equality to the Sales Tax Regulations. In recent months, the ruling body revised the rules to reasonable standards to place the industry in a competitive atmosphere with others. You would think that the air was clear and the wrong had been righted. Nothing could be further from the truth. Before the ink had dried on the Act, another greater bureaucratic problem was discovered which presented a worse discrimination than the one which existed. In Colorado, the city sales tax varies from town to town and now each town council must be approached to achieve the results hoped for over the years and already achieved in the state legislature. The sales tax laws that still exist in the cities and towns in Colorado have worsened the problem. All dealers in Colorado collect a different sales tax from their customers — except one. His village has "no sales tax". Representatives who vote without knowledge on matters that clearly dictate inequality through law and enforcement will never know the devastation their vote caused.

The Nation's Largest Coin Dealer Escapes All Regulations

The "broth thickens" when you consider that the largest coin dealer in the nation, the very entity responsible for unreasonable meddling — the United States Government — sells coins throughout the nation without assessing one dime of sales tax. They are not subject to the reporting requirements when some drug dealer wants to launder "$200 in drug money" or some citizen wants to invest a grand or two in "Government issued" coin sets. Banks throughout the nation sell coins without sales tax or reporting requirements. Commodity brokers sell coins without sales tax. The citizen is assessed sales tax only when he purchases from a licensed coin dealer and then the amount is variable depending on the location. The situation covers more than just coins also. It is not unusual for the U.S. Government to be on hand at coin shows and conventions selling currency and novelty items or commemorative sets to the public without the assessment of any tax or reporting records.

The question must now be answered.

"What can we do about it?"

The following are probably the toughest paragraphs I have to write on the subject. There is little history to draw on to discover a plan that is economically feasible. That leaves us with drawing up our own course of action.

Let's first investigate the facts. The hobby of collecting at this time is everything but booming. The collector has less time to devote to his hobby and less money to use. The coin dealer, as he was known in previous years, has undergone a change and offers many items and collectibles other than coins in an attempt to survive this slow business cycle. Overhead in even the smallest of operations has escalated. Wage and hour laws and sundry labor taxes have prohibited him from hiring the people needed to expand his operation. Established membership organizations refuse to contribute either effort, personnel, or funds to accomplish the job. Elected Representatives have turned a deaf ear to the requests made by their constituents. All government entities are up to their ears in debt and going further and further in that direction every day. Our activities in regard to the hobby are markedly different than the activities performed in most other businesses. We have no established lobby such as the one established by sportsmen and gun collectors. Our business caters to all walks of life — the poor and the wealthy alike. A large section of our customers are youngsters. Coin dealers are not wealthy individuals. Many in our ranks are retired people enjoying their retirement and not inclined to actively participate. Some of the buying — selling — and trading is done between collectors in the pursuit of their hobby.

There are hundreds of other factors that you are fully aware of; but, they all indicate the fact that we are not large enough or equipped enough financially or otherwise to engage successfully, in a short period of time, the people in government charged with the responsibility of dispensing equitable and fair treatment.

The recent events vigorously engaged in by ICTA and a very small number of coin dealers and interested public over the last few months have shown that a small degree of success is unattainable even though a couple of hundred thousand dollars have been expended. There is no cohesiveness apparent in the ranks of dealers and collectors.

Even the ANA with a membership of 33,000 and a recent "windfall" of a million and a half dollars found only $1,000 available for a cause that was initiated to bring equity into the dealings of their membership. Another thing to be considered here is that the disagreements about the accuracy of grading services are largely responsible for the eyes of the Federal Government looking our way in the first place.

If the ANA with their huge membership, whose future in the hobby of collecting may be at stake, can find only $1,000 and have expended virtually no space in *the Numismatist* concerning the problem or rallying the membership — what chance do you really believe we have in following the present course of action? We have no chance.

There Will be No Relief Unless. . .

On the other hand, if all (I repeat all) of those affected will put forth an effort, the task can be accomplished because the regulations are unfair. A plan that will insure success would include these four steps.

ESTABLISH CONTACT WITH YOUR REPRESENTATIVES

* Every coin dealer and collector, collector organization, and numismatic publication, will establish a communication link with their elected representatives. Letters and phone calls must be made monthly and preferably more frequently.

ESTABLISH CONTACT WITH ALL REPRESENTATIVES

* Each of the above mentioned persons will write and phone the representatives from other states. Letters and phone calls must be made at least once a month.

ENLIST THE AID OF YOUR FRIENDS

* Every person who belongs to an organization (VFW — American Legion — etc.) must enlist the aid and support of their organizations to alleviate this situation.

CIRCULATE AND RETRIEVE PETITIONS

* Everyone must be responsible to get hundreds of petitions. Coin show promoters must be actively engaged in getting petitions signed by those who attend the show.

There will always be collectors and there is little that legislatures can do about that; but, dealers as we know them cannot possibly survive in the oppressive atmosphere generated by senseless reports on small sales or random regulations on small businesses. Further, if the dealers and collectors do not establish some kind of favorable rapport with their elected officials, they deserve everything they get.

Be Happy, Be Healthy, Get Wealthy, and Hold a Good Thought.

I am Chester West.

***

Robert Brueggeman

Robert Brueggeman is president of Positive Protection, Inc., a company which provides maximum safety and security to individuals and organizations planning a convention, auction, or transfer. With his superior understanding of the specialized needs of rare coin, stamp and jewelry dealers, he has provided consulting services as well as polished security teams and equipment for many events and conventions.

Since the inception of Positive Protection, Inc., Mr. Brueggeman has developed security and protection services in many areas. These include executive protection, electronic alarm systems, loss prevention, security guards, and special services including management consulting, convention planning and special event coordination.

Mr. Brueggeman is dedicated to the education of the numismatic community as well as its protection and security. He is well known and respected as an expert in this vital arena of numismatic activity.

CHAPTER 55

Numismatic Security: Travel and Conventions

by Robert Brueggeman

Security Tips

When you're away from home on an extended trip, some of the things that you can accomplish for safety and security are as follows:

1. Have someone pick up the mail for you or arrange for the post office to hold your mail until you return.
2. Have the newspaper delivery service stopped so that there isn't a stack of papers out front. Of course, lock all your doors and windows.
3. If you have a dog, a good suggestion is to tape the dog barking under normal situations such as the ringing of the doorbell, and attach your tape recorder to a timer. Turn on the tape recorder so that neighbors and others can hear the dog barking as if you were at home. Use the same strategy with your lights. Set your lights in the same type of sequence as you would if you were at home, to give the appearance that you are there. Set your timers so that lights are lit in the bathroom and the bedroom in the morning, and in the evening lights are lit in the living room. You may also attach the TV to a timer to turn on at your normal viewing hours.
4. Telephone answering machines can signal your absence from home. Set your response so that when someone calls, the message states you will be back shortly. For example, "Sorry, not available at the moment, stepped out to go the grocery store," or "Went shopping at the mall, be back in an hour or two." Be sure when you set up your message, that you check in for messages everyday so that you can call back just in case someone is trying to time your response interval.
5. If you have an alarm system always set your alarms. Your alarm system should be a central station alarm system, in case the alarm goes off during your absence.

Also make sure that your entire home is well lit around the exterior. If you don't want to keep your home lit at all times, there are units available with microwave or motion detectors attached to the lights so that when a human moves into the unlit area, the light automatically turns on. When you're not at home it appears that you are turning on the lights when someone approaches the home. Always be sure that there are no dark areas on the outside of your home. I suggest an external alarm as well as an internal alarm. If someone has broken a window or penetrated the roof area the external alarm would be a first line of defense. The second line of defense would be an internal alarm set off by someone walking into your living room or bedroom. I also suggest a small safe, not a closet safe that can be easily moved, but something that is attached or cemented to the floor to prevent moving the safe out.

Another important security protection device is a panic button. Place them at three or four locations where you feel you would need one in case of a break-in or emergency situation. Make sure your panic system is always on, even when your external alarm is on.

Alarm systems now do far more than make noise. We now have systems that can be armed or disarmed through a telephone call that can be attached to telephone systems and even appliances. For example, before you board the plane, you call your home and turn on the air conditioner so that your home will be cool when you arrive. You can also turn a certain door penetration alarm on and off. For instance if your housekeeper always comes on Wednesday, you tell the housekeeper to come in a special door, then you call your home telephone number, punch in a few codes, and disarm that door so that she can enter to clean and rearm when she leaves.

Vehicle Security

When transporting articles, always keep the passenger doors locked and the windows up. If you're riding in a cab always make sure that the doors are locked and the windows are up. Keep your valuables in your area When traveling to and from shows. Always travel in twos. Find a partner who is going to the show and have him drive the point car or the backup car and vary the load. Sometimes place the load in the point car and other times place the load in the backup car. Or divide the load between both vehicles using walkie-talkie communication if possible. Citizen band communication would be preferable so that if one car stops for any reason and you lose sight of it, assistance can be immediately called. If you can afford it, a cellular phone is a definite must to summon the police in an emergency situation.

When traveling in a vehicle to and from a show, eat in fast food restaurants. Without leaving your car, use the drive-up window, order your food, pay for your food in your car and continue your drive. It's not suggested to stop anywhere and have your dinner and set yourself up as a target. You want to make sure that you're always on the move, making it difficult for anyone to attack you or mark you.

When you arrive at the convention site and unload, it's a good idea to let the valet park the car. Never use the car again during your trip. Let's just assume for a moment that a "perpetrator" has marked you: he's gone to your table in the convention, he sees that you're the man he wants to hit, he's going to watch you, he's going to trail you, he's going to see where you go at night, what hotel you are staying in, and what car you're driving. If he discovers that you're driving your own personal car, with a personal state license plate on it, he's going to make the assumption that you are going to use that same car to return home. If he makes that assumption and he finds where that car is parked, he can then puncture your tires, set your tires on a slow leak, or put a distributor cap disengage on your engine. He will watch your car, follow it and make his hit. When driving an automobile, always keep the big picture in mind. What do I mean by big picture? That means know who is in front of you, at the side of you, and behind you at all times. Before you get into your car always check your tires, check your spare tire, and check your oil. Know that everything is a go prior to loading the car and unloading the car. Always load and unload in the front of the hotel in the open in full view. Always have a second person there with you so that you can watch the material while they do the loading. Of course, when feasible and economical, always have a security guard with you on the load or unload. At some conventions, a security guard is available during loading and unloading, and at times even with you to the nearest thoroughfare.

When traveling to and from shows via air, whenever possible have an escort pick you up at the office. Have him escort you from the passenger's side of the metal detector to your transportation then on to the convention. When economics do not allow for armed security guards, I suggest that coins and valuables being carried with you never leave your side. A suggestion that I've made in the past is to place a little cat gut around the handle of your attache case. Take the cat gut and attach it to your belt. It's a noticeable method of keeping control of your case and, if you are distracted for any reason, you'll know when the case is being grabbed, because the thief will be pulling your pants off! If you're using a cart, remember not to just place the cases on the cart, but lock them with the plastic hooks that come with the cart. Use either a metal cable with a plastic coating or chain to wrap them to the cart. Remember if you use the elastic that comes with the cart, the plastic can be easily cut or sliced with a knife, and cases grabbed while you're pulling it. Which brings me to another point. Never drag the cart behind you. Always push the cart in front of you so that you are aware at all times of who is surrounding and who is near your cart. Again, always travel in pairs.

Convention Security

When at conventions, be sure to conform to all rules and regulations. If an I.D. is required, don't get upset. Photo I.D. is extremely beneficial to the security of a show. The guards check whether dealers and assistants are behind the proper table. Other dealers may wander behind your table because they're disoriented, especially on the first day of the show. When you're working tables at any convention, especially the larger ones, always travel, if possible, with more than one person. With a minimum of two persons at the table, then you can follow the rules of never leaving the table alone at anytime. Take shifts for lunch, restroom breaks, coffee breaks, etc.

While at the table, always keep the front cases locked, unless showing coins to potential clients.

Always know your customer. Know whether he is an old customer and can be trusted or whether he's a new customer and should be watched. Never take anything for granted. When you are alone at the table while showing coins, if you turn to the rear for any reason, make sure you lock that case before you turn. Coins can be lifted from the case ever so quickly. When using Brinks cases or the like on the backup table, it's a good ideal to place the Brinks cases on top of the table with chains through the handles attached to the tables. In this way, if you are distracted for any reason your case can not disappear, and secondly when that case is not in use the cover can be slid down, a lock can be placed through the clasp while you're facing front.

At closing time, many dealers place a cover over their showcases and some chairs. This of course, prevents any obvious tampering. A new system that many dealers are using is a large canvas type closure which goes over the top of the table. All of their goods are placed on the top of that front table and the entire bag is zipped up and locked, which makes it very difficult for anyone to tamper with the coins during the evening. Otherwise some tampering may occur because of the need for service by the clean up crew, electricians, and air-conditioning personnel.

Be sure that the security for the convention you're attending is satisfactory to you. Just because a promoter is putting together a convention doesn't mean that he has hired the proper security needed. Many times security is based on budget, and therefore, the security may not be the caliber you expect for the show. Always find out in advance what type of security is being provided and by whom.

Remember, at all major shows, security does not allow the clean up crew to come in unless there is one security guard per crew member walking the hall and preventing anyone from wandering behind the booths or exhibits.

For vest pocket dealers: If there's a security room at the convention, use it. Don't take coins out of the show area. Coins are not secure in a hotel room. Pass keys can be used by engineering and staff to enter the room.

Ninety-nine percent of the time security room operations at large conventions are the safest locations that you can find there. Also look for closed circuit television, tape recorders, and claim checks. Make sure that the claim checks are three parted, one part for the files, one part for the system and one part for you. Before placing coins into a security room, be sure materials are always placed in a locked bag or attache case. Run tape around the cases and the locks. Sign your name across the overlap to prevent any tampering during the period of time that it is in the security room.

Contrary to popular opinion, it is best to keep the cases as light as possible. This eases checking into the security room, and facilitates appropriate filing and handling. The lighter the cases the better. When cases are attached to dollies, or to pullcarts, please leave both pieces with the men in the security room. If cases are chained together, as I suggested before, check them in as one unit for one claim check. This will facilitate the speed in which materials are checked in and out of security rooms.

Don't ever give your hotel number, room, or key to anyone. Keep that as secret as possible. Never bring any of your valuables to your hotel room. Always do your trading on the bourse floor.

See that the hotel is very stringent in the manner in which they hand out keys. In some hotels you can step up to the counter and say, "I'm Bob Brueggeman and I'm in Room 212 and I lost my key. May I have another one?" If they don't ask you for I.D., then you may be staying at the wrong hotel. Complain to your promoter about insufficient hotel security.

I think, in general, it's important to realize that 99.9 percent of coin show robberies take place when you lose control of your valuables. If for one moment you are distracted or you set down your cases to help someone, you are at risk. Always be aware of your valuables. This is your livelihood. This is your life. This is the way you earn a living. Please be sure to keep yourself alert and keep the big picture in mind.

Air Travel Security

The following portion of this chapter appeared in Numismatic News on February 26, 1991, and is reprinted here.

Air transportation systems in the United States are a necessity to the coin dealer traveling the show and convention circuit. The threat of terrorist attacks, as well as personal theft, calls for special procedures in airports and during air travel.

You can further lessen the risk by taking some reasonable precautions and by making a very conscious effort to avoid placing yourself in hazardous situations as you travel to coin shows.

Before heading to the airport, call an hour before to determine if your flight is on schedule. This will help avoid prolonged waits if the flight is known to be delayed and therefore decrease your risk of exposure. Always know your scheduled time of departure and plan your arrival at the airport so that you have just sufficient time for processing, taking into consideration baggage check-in, seat selection, and the security checkpoint.

Upon your arrival at the airport, say goodbye to your friends at the vehicle, and unless you have been accompanied on the trip, proceed alone to accomplish all the necessary pre-flight procedures.

Many terminals are not allowing your checking of luggage at the curbside at this time, but check at curbside whenever possible. This will allow you to avoid long lines at the counter and speed up the check-in process.

Always bear in mind the "Big Picture." While waiting at the gate area, always be aware of your belongings. Be on the lookout for persons who may be attempting to switch your bag for another, or seeking to distract your attention from your bags.

Always seat yourself in an area that can afford a clear view and avoid a large expanse of glass. Sit as close to a structural support column as possible and make sure there is no unattended luggage anywhere near. While waiting, always anticipate that a problem may occur, and what your reaction to it would be. Pick a shelter area such as behind a cigarette machine, a soda machine of a support column, and be prepared to seek that shelter immediately in the event of an incident.

Look around and always identify any emergency exits in the waiting area and if possible, check to see where they lead. If at any time airport officials order an evacuation of the area, take a position at the center of the group with as many people around you as possible. Do not take a lead or straggling position.

When it comes to selecting a seat on the aircraft, always request one next to a wing emergency exit. While in that seat read the instructions posted there regarding the operation of that exit window. It is a Federal Aviation Administration regulation that the person in that seat operate the exit in case of an emergency. Sitting here allows you to be the first passenger out of the plane.

If it is impossible to obtain a seat near the preferred exit, select a position that will bring you as close as possible to an alternate exit. Always select a window seat whenever possible, as this will keep you a seat or two from anyone who may be causing a disturbance in the isles.

Always be aware. Do not ignore any of your feelings; if something feels wrong it may indeed be wrong. What sounds like a gunshot or explosion may well be a gunshot or explosion. Be aware that any disturbance could be a deliberate diversion.

Below are some important points to remember as you travel concerning possible terrorist action.

In the event of a high-jacking, those who do the actual high-jacking usually take any documents that you have on your person or in any carry-on luggage. Therefore, it is important that you have no provocative or incriminating information on your person or in your carry-on baggage. Specifically:

- Do not carry a passport which shows any extensive overseas travel. Many visits to the same country or travel to countries of controversy such as Israel or Jordan might be dangerous. Your U.S. passport can be taken to any U.S. Post Office, Passport Office, or Department of State field office, to be exchanged for a new, clean passport. The cost is approximately $35. Any optional information such as your home address and addresses and telephone numbers of your next of kin should not be included in the passport.
- Avoid identification cards for the military reserve, police reserve organization, political party, political action group, veterans organization or any group that can be considered controversial.
- Don't carry any business cards of associates that may be in the armament defense industry, as that may also be a point of issue by terrorists.
- Don't carry personal letters. Personal data could be used to pressure you into talking or taking actions or making statements against your will. Some business data can do the same, so try to leave home any financial information. Documents like these could provide information regarding your wealth to the high-jacker and will tend to agitate radicals.
- Leave your checkbook and the savings account register at home. This may indicate wealth and make you an important target. Also, very expensive jewelry, large diamond rings, gold chains, gold watches and so on should be left at home. Don't wear clothing that may set you apart from the rest of the passengers.
- Don't bring any magazines, books or papers that may be considered offensive to other cultures (i.e., books by noted anti-communists or Israelis or any religious texts).

A very important subject is what to do in the event of an actual high-jacking. In case of a high-jacking, the airline crew will be doing everything in its power to keep the passengers safe, but they will be limited and their concerns must encompass all the passengers as a group. Therefore, you as the traveler are obliged to look out for your own preservation. One of the major steps in avoiding unpleasantness as a result of a high-jacking is to try to remain as invisible as possible so as not to be singled out for any reason.

Here are some of the guidelines:

- Follow the instructions of the high-jacker. Do not argue or ask questions. Don't volunteer anything and don't volunteer to do anything, such as function as spokesman for the passengers. If you are accused of being in charge, don't display any authority, disdain or arrogance, and be as neutral as you can in all situations.

In the beginning, during the first 20-30 minutes of the incident, avoid making any eye contact with any of the perpetrators. Experience has shown that in the initial stages of a high-jacking those responsible are especially nervous and agitated, therefore they are the most dangerous during this period. If and when the high-jackers set out to confiscate valuable documents or personal items, don't attempt to hide anything. Do not ask for special permission to do anything such as smoke or go to the lavatory unless absolutely necessary.

- Don't offer any position whatsoever to the high-jackers. Don't make comments either for or against them or their cause. If you are asked for an opinion say that you are not knowledgeable enough to comment either way. If the high-jacker wants to talk about his cause, listen but without any agreement or disagreement. Always remain as calm as you can throughout the incident and conserve any strength you have for any future need.
- Again, just like sitting at the airport while waiting for the plane to leave, you should rehearse your actions in case the situation deteriorates to violence and you must move quickly. Keep the area between you and the seat in front of you clear of clutter. You may have to crouch down to protect yourself in case of gunshots. Try to have a coat or blanket handy in order to protect you head. At the sound of any gunshots or any other disturbance you should crouch down as low as possible between the seats and remain in that position until you either determine that it's safe to sit up or that you must take further action for your safety.

Protecting Yourself

This group of very pertinent and important subjects is reprinted from Bob Brueggeman's security newsletter, *Protecting Yourself*. This newsletter is dedicated to those people who need protection and security, and is published quarterly by Positive Protection, Inc., 3950 Concordia Lane, Fallbrook, Ca. 92028.

KEEP RIGHT! This One Could Have Been Prevented!

One dealer using a safety deposit box at the hotel, placed his coins in a little red box carrying case on the floor, When he stood up to replace the safety deposit box, he lost sight of coins for a split second and they were instantly whisked away. In as much time as it has taken you to read this far, his coins were gone and all he saw was a shadow running through the restaurant and out of the door with his valuables. It is obvious the dealer lost contact with his coins, that is a Cardinal Sin, but what happened behind the scene is more important. This dealer walked through the streets with an auction catalog in his hand without wrapping, identifying him as a dealer. In addition he was walking through the streets with the same little red box, empty. What an advertisement! He would not have alerted as many if he had an ad in *Coin World*. Certainly if I were looking for a target, this victim would be most obvious.

Keep all your valuables in a closed case and carry that case on your person at all times. Never let a closed case leave your side. While attending functions and walking the streets with your valuables, try using cases other than easily identifiable attache cases. Sport cases and shoulder cases are very difficult to grab and run with even if both your hands are busy. This helps you have the case under control. It is best if the shoulder bag is a well-constructed type such as Samsonite brand.

Remember the incident we all read about in *Coin World*, of the loss at one of our shows, where they used three(3) people at a table to accomplish the theft. This was accomplished by one talking to the dealer, one opening the case, and one grabbing the box of Saint Gaudens to carry out the theft. They were caught and apprehended which is commendable to the show security and the dealers surrounding the victim, but again, the only reason the loss was sustained was that there was an open show case. If it were not open, the dealer would have been better protected and the loss not sustained.

Food for thought — these people were picked up and arrested. They are now out on bail. This dealer has learned from his mistakes. HAVE YOU?

NO PASSING: On Safes and Storage

A safe provides physical security in a permanent location, protecting against fire, humidity and theft.

For storage of valuables away from home or office, a safe deposit box or private security vault would be more practical.

Safes come in a wide variety of sizes, types, grades and prices. Your specific needs will determine which one you select. Look for the following features when choosing a unit.

GRADING — All safes should be graded by at least one of the following: UL (Underwriters Laboratories), ISO (Insurance Service Office), JIS (Japanese standards), or DIN (German standards).

FIRE RESISTANCE — Safes are rated for their ability to maintain an interior temperature that protects particular kinds of records for a specific period. Temperature categories are 350 degrees F for paper, 150 degrees F for magnetic tapes, and 125 degrees F for flexible computer disks. Time period include 1, 2, 3 and 4 hours of safety. A typical good-quality, fire-resistant model is the Mosler Model K-2.

HUMIDITY CONTROL — Tapes and disks must be protected from moisture during fire exposure and cooling period. Make sure specific relative humidity levels are assured in your model.

BURGLAR RESISTANCE — ISO and UL grade safes for burglar resistance. ISO grades run from B up to the top level G. UL grades use a combination of letters to indicate what implements or materials have been used to force entry during controlled tests and numbers to indicate the length of time the unit will resist such attach. A TXTL60 safe, for examples, will withstand entry attempts with tools, cutting torches, and explosives for 60 minutes. One popular model in this category is the Mosler ER201612.

INSTALLATION — Home safes are installed in the walls or buried in concrete basement floors. Typical wall units include the Diebold model 1436 and the WVD model. Examples of popular floor models are the Diebold 18804 and Pacific Securities VC 25 and VC 40. All free-standing safes should be bolted and cemented to the floor.

When traveling out of town, valuables can be stored in a safe deposit box at a bank or placed in a rented space at a private security vault. Both provide excellent protection. Both have pros and cons:

SAFE DEPOSIT BOX

+ Less expensive
+ Available nationwide
— Liability may be limited
— Relatively small storage space

SECURITY VAULT

+ Better humidity and temperature control
+ Permits anonymity
+ Carry higher liability insurance
— Available only in larger metropolitan areas
— More expensive

Always check a firm's reputation and available liability limits before entrusting valuables. For extra protection, talk to an insurance agent about policies specifically written to cover contents of safe deposit boxes and vaults outside the home.

SIGNAL AHEAD! The Truth — The Whole Truth — Nothing But The Truth

How to know if someone is lying:

NOTE THE MANNER OF RESPONSE, the body language. Is the person's posture open and unthreatened? Is their tone hostile or challenging?

DISTINGUISH HOW BELIEVABLE someone appears from what he is saying. Sift through the actual information being supplied.

LISTEN for what someone is NOT SAYING. A guilty person will avoid the subject, leading the conversation elsewhere.

AVOID INTERRUPTING when someone is telling his version of something. Listen closely. Take notes for future reference.

ASK QUESTIONS in a way which will elicit the most information. Use specific questions that are short and simple.

EXHAUST POSSIBILITIES. Don't assume that you have the complete answer after only one question.

USE A JOB APPLICANT AS HIS OR HER OWN REFERENCE. Ask about short-term jobs no on the application. Why were they omitted? Fired? Laid off?

DISTINGUISH SUGGESTIONS OR OPINIONS FROM FACTS. Listen for verbs like "seemed," "think," "thought," and qualifiers like "pretty sure."

DON'T LET PRECONCEPTIONS close your mind. If you have already decided what is the truth, you may not ask questions which could clarify the situation.

WITH DIFFERENT STORIES from two people, look for both areas of agreement, and dispute. If there is a significant disagreement, isolate it and concentrate on trying to resolve it through additional questioning.

OFFER A "FACE SAVING" WAY OUT.

BE ALERT FOR SELF-VALIDATING STATEMENTS. A guilty person often offers unsolicited statements trying to prove innocence.

USE ROLE-REVERSAL QUESTIONS. A true culprit, when asked what punishment fits the crime, will usually shy away from an answer or suggest a minor penalty.

CONSIDER WHAT THE "AVERAGE MAN" WOULD HAVE DONE, compared to what your suspect describes. Watch for statements such as "I know this sounds crazy, but. . ."

ACCEPT THE SIMPLEST SOLUTION.

SOME CIRCUMSTANCES CREATE QUESTIONABLE EYEWITNESSES. Moments of stress and tension may cause an eyewitness to be unreliable.

WATCH FOR THE MOMENT OF SURRENDER in a deceitful person. When a deceitful person is convinced that further lying may worsen his circumstances, the most common response is withdrawal.

DON'T TRY FOR THE "WHOLE ENCHILADA." Offer a guilty person a chance to preserve a little dignity with gradual admissions.

Finally, remember that most people are honest and will tell the truth if you have the courage to seek it.

(Taken from an article written by James R. Wygant.)

WARNING! Avoid The Credit Card Sting

You can prevent unauthorized credit card purchases by observing these warning signals offered by Elan Financial Services of Milwaukee.

- The signature on the card does not match the signature on the sales slip.
- The signature panel on the card has been altered or the word "VOID" appears on the panel.
- The cardholder appears to be underage.
- The cardholder is making random purchases without concern for price.
- Effective immediately all MasterCards must have a hologram. All Visa Cards have had a hologram since December, 1986.
- The card has expired.
- The account number and/or names and expiration dates are not clearly embossed.
- The surface of the card is uneven or "wavy" or taped together.
- The colors on the card appear to be faded.

REMEMBER: When a valid card is used to complete a credit purchase, the risk is the responsibility of the card-issuing institution. However, in the case of telephone or mail order purchases where the card is not presented, the retailer assumes the risk.

CAUTION! Avoid Check Frauds — Save $$$$

Follow these simple precautions to avoid accepting forged, bogus and insufficient-funds checks.

- Identify the endorser. Ask for identification which includes signature and photograph. In addition to a driver's license, obtain and record numbers from credit card, social security card, etc.

- Inform each check presenter that his identity is being verified. Fraudulent check passers may be reluctant to provide requested information.
- Call the bank on which the check is drawn for verification.
- Instruct employees on check cashing procedures. Allow only trusted employes to handle checks. Have them initial any they receive for future reference.
- No postdated checks.
- Beware of checks with more than one endorsement.
- Establish a card identification system. Require each person presenting a check to have a card on file.
- Call the police immediately if a bad check is passed.
- Always prosecute. Earn the reputation that YOU WILL NOT accept worthless checks.
- If in doubt, don't accept the check.

By establishing a rigid check-cashing policy, you won't be cheated out of thousands of dollars by the passers of worthless paper.

Summary

Among the groups of people who are most conscious of the need for security are those persons active in the numismatic industry. There is no better time than right now for these dealers, auction houses and convention owners to formulate and implement a security business plan. This critical aspect of numismatics cannot be left to chance or addressed after the fact. It is hoped that the ideas and suggestions presented here will educate and inform all those who require the protection and security discussed herein.

Positive Protection, Inc., Staff

***

Andrew P. Lustig

Andrew P. Lustig, president of Vanguard Rare Coin Corporation, is a professional numismatist based in Hackensack, New Jersey. He began his career "sometime between the lessons of toilet training and the memorization of the multiplication tables, " and is considered a cradle-to-grave numismatist by all but the world's greatest optimists.

Mr. Lustig is a life member of the American Numismatic Association, and was elected to the Professional Numismatists Guild, Inc. in 1988. He also holds a B.S. in economics from Fairleigh Dickinson University.

CHAPTER 56

A Price Guide To United States Pattern Dollars

by Andrew P. Lustig

"United States patterns are among the most beautiful, rare and historically important numismatic treasures known to mankind." Ask any collector of patterns why he buys patterns, and that's one of many similar answers you may get. But then, almost invariably, the greedy little demon of competitive materialism pokes his head from behind the collector's facade. The seemingly pure numismatist pauses, but then unabashedly exclaims, "I don't know why the darned things are so cheap, but one day the world will wake up and I'll be rich, I tell you, rich!"

The pattern collector need not be ashamed of his commercial instincts. It is wonderful to recognize unappreciated things of greatness, to boldly go where few have gone before, and to be later showered with riches for ones courage and foresight.

When one compares the rarity and numismatic importance of patterns to their regular issue counterparts, the pattern collector's enthusiasm is easy to understand. It is obvious that patterns are ridiculously underpriced. Yet, few collectors and only a handful of dealers seriously pursue the field. Ask the typical big-time dealer why he has no patterns in stock, and you'll see his super-confidence melt before your eyes. "Well, uh, sure they're rare, um, but, well you know, how do you know what they're worth?"

It's true. There are no reliable price guides for patterns. The Judd book is unusable as a pricing tool, only as a guide to rarity. Auction prices realized give clues as to values, but the data is spotty and erratic. The only way to price patterns has been to rely on knowledge and instinct, rare commodities on the bourse floor.

Until now. On the pages that follow, you will find a price guide to United States pattern dollars, in all grades from 60 to 65. Please remember, however, that these prices are often purely theoretical. The coin may not even exist in the specified grade. Furthermore, prices vary from day to day, dealer to dealer, and auction to auction. Patterns do fluctuate with the rest of the coin market, albeit not with as much volatility. Also, given the rarity of both the coins and the collectors, competition for any given piece may cause its price to far exceed the listed price.

Still, the guide should provide a useful framework for pricing most pattern dollars. Even as the market changes, most relative price relationships should hold steady.

It is my hope that at least a few collectors who had previously found the pattern field unapproachable will find this guide helpful in entering the pattern collecting fraternity. I trust you will enjoy the field immensely. And may you be showered with riches!

Editor-In-Chief note: *The prices listed below are estimates of values for United States Pattern dollars. They are not to be mistaken for exact or current market values. Some prices however do reflect actual transactions and confirmed auction sales. They are not identified separately from the rest of the coins. These estimates are to be used as a price guide only and not to be misinterpreted as prices realized or bid/ask levels.*

SILVER DOLLAR PATTERNS

Year Judd No.	60	61	62	63	64	65
The Patterns of 1794:						
J-18	Unique — Porous EF, 40,000					
J-19	Unique — Smithsonian — choice PL Unc. — 500,000					
The Patterns of 1836:						
J-58	13500	15000	18000	30000	55000	150000
J-59 R	12000	13500	15000	20000	30000	50000
J-59 RB	11000	12500	13500	16500	22500	38500
J-59 B	10000	11500	12500	15000	20000	35000
J-60	5500	6000	7000	11500	25000	75000
J-61	25000	30000	35000	45000	100000	200000
J-62 R	12000	13500	15000	20000	30000	50000
J-62 RB	11000	12500	13500	16500	22500	38500
J-62 B	10000	11500	12500	15000	20000	35000
J-63	27500	32500	40000	60000	100000	200000
J-64 R	12000	13500	15000	20000	30000	50000
J-64 RB	11000	12500	13500	16500	22500	38500
J-64 B	10000	11500	12500	15500	20000	35000
J-65	22500	27500	32500	42500	100000	200000
J-66 R	12000	13500	15000	20000	30000	50000
J-66 B	11000	12500	13500	16500	22500	38500
J-66 RB	10000	11500	12500	15500	20000	35000

The Patterns of 1838:

J-84	11000	12500	13500	20000	40000	100000
J-85	13500	15000	18000	30000	55000	150000
J-86 R	12000	13500	15000	20000	30000	50000
J-86 RB	11000	12500	13500	16500	22500	38500
J-86 B	10000	11500	12500	15000	20000	35000
J-87 R	12000	13500	15000	20000	30000	50000
J-87 RB	11000	12500	13500	16500	22500	38500
J-87 B	10000	11500	12500	15000	20000	35000
J-88	20000	25000	30000	40000	80000	175000
J-89 R	12000	13500	15000	20000	30000	50000
J-89 RB	11000	12500	13500	16500	22500	38500
J-89 B	10000	11500	12500	15000	20000	35000
J-90 R	12000	13500	15000	20000	30000	50000
J-90 RB	11000	12500	13500	16500	22500	38500
J-90 B	10000	11500	12500	15000	20000	35000

The Patterns of 1839:

J-104	7500	8500	10000	16500	30000	90000
J-105	17500	22500	27500	37500	60000	150000
J-106 R	12000	13500	15000	20000	30000	50000
J-106 RB	11000	12500	13500	16500	22500	38500
J-106 B	10000	11500	12500	15000	20000	35000
J-107 R	12000	13500	15000	20000	30000	50000
J-107 RB	11000	12500	13500	16500	22500	38500
J-107 B	10000	11500	12500	15000	20000	35000
J-108	22500	27500	32500	42500	100000	200000
J-109 R	15000	16500	18000	25000	37500	75000
J-109 RB	13500	15000	16500	20000	30000	50000
J-109 B	12500	13500	15000	18500	27500	45000

The Patterns of 1851:

J-132 R	2750	3000	3750	6000	10500	18000
J-132 RB	2500	2750	3000	4500	8000	12000
J-132 B	2250	2500	2750	4000	6500	10000
J-133	5000	5500	6000	9000	16000	32000

The Patterns of 1852:

J-134 R	2750	3000	3750	6000	10500	18000
J-134 RB	2500	2750	3000	4500	8000	12000
J-134 B	2250	2500	2750	4000	6500	10000

The Patterns of 1853:

J-154 R	2750	3000	3750	6000	10500	18000
J-154 RB	2500	2750	3000	4500	8000	12000
J-154 B	2250	2500	2750	4000	6500	10000

The Patterns of 1863:

J-345	6000	6750	7500	10000	18000	30000
J-346 R	2500	2750	3500	5500	10500	16500
J-346 RB	2250	2500	3000	4500	8000	12500
J-346 B	2000	2250	2750	4000	6750	10500
J-347	2500	2750	3500	4250	6250	12500
J-348 R	2250	2500	2750	3500	6250	15000
J-348 RB	2000	2250	2500	3000	5000	10000
J-348 B	1750	2000	2250	2750	4250	7500

The Patterns of 1864:

J-396	6000	6750	7500	10000	18000	30000
J-397 R	2500	2750	3500	5500	10500	16500
J-397 RB	2250	2500	3000	4500	8000	12500
J-397 B	2000	2250	2750	4000	6750	10500
J-398	3000	3250	3750	5000	7500	15000
J-399	3500	3750	4250	6500	10000	20000

The Patterns of 1865:						
J-434	9000	10000	12000	15000	25000	45000
J-435 R	3000	3250	4000	6000	12500	20000
J-435 RB	2750	3000	3500	4500	8500	13500
J-435 B	2500	2750	3250	4250	7250	11500
J-436	3000	3250	4000	6000	10000	17500
J-437 R	2250	2500	2750	3500	6250	15000
J-437 RB	2000	2250	2500	3000	5000	10000
J-437 B	1750	2000	2250	2750	4250	7500
The Patterns of 1866:						
J-540	50000	60000	75000	100000	150000	250000
J-541 R	1800	2000	2200	2900	5000	10000
J-541 RB	1650	1800	2000	2400	3800	8000
J-541 B	1500	1650	1800	2200	3500	7000
The Patterns of 1867:						
J-592 R	2250	2500	2750	3500	6250	15000
J-592 RB	2000	2250	2500	3000	5000	10000
J-592 B	1750	2000	2250	2750	4250	7500
J-593	2000	2400	2750	4000	6500	12500
The Patterns of 1868:						
J-652	2000	2250	2500	3000	5000	10000
The Patterns of 1869:						
J-763 R	2250	2500	2750	3500	6250	15000
J-763 RB	2000	2250	2500	3000	5000	10000
J-763 B	1750	2000	2250	2750	4250	7500
J-764	2000	2250	2500	3000	5000	10000
J-765	2500	3000	3250	4500	8750	17500
The Patterns of 1870:						
J-996	2000	2400	3000	4500	9500	17500
J-997	2000	2400	3000	4500	9500	17500
J-998 R	1500	1650	2000	2750	5000	12500
J-998 RB	1350	1500	1750	2250	4000	7500
J-998 B	1250	1350	1500	2000	3600	6000
J-999 R	1500	1650	2000	2750	5000	12500
J-999 RB	1350	1500	1750	2250	4000	7500
J-999 B	1250	1350	1500	2000	3600	6000
J-1000	1350	1500	1750	2250	4000	7500
J-1001	1350	1500	1750	2250	4000	7500
J-1002	2000	2400	3000	4500	9500	17500
J-1003	2000	2400	3000	4500	9500	17500
J-1004 R	1500	1650	2000	2750	5000	12500
J-1004 RB	1350	1500	1750	2250	4000	7500
J-1004 B	1250	1350	1500	2000	3600	6000
J-1005 R	1500	1650	2000	2750	5000	12500
J-1005 RB	1350	1500	1750	2250	4000	7500
J-1005 B	1250	1350	1500	2000	3600	6000
J-1006	1350	1500	1750	2250	4000	7500
J-1007	1350	1500	1750	2250	4000	7500
J-1008	2000	2400	3000	4500	9500	17500
J-1009	2000	2400	3000	4500	9500	17500
J-1010 R	2000	2250	2500	3500	6250	15000
J-1010 RB	1750	2000	2250	3000	5000	10000
J-1010 B	1500	1750	2000	2750	4250	7500
J-1011 R	2000	2250	2500	3500	6250	15000
J-1011 RB	1750	2000	2250	3000	5000	10000
J-1011 B	1500	1750	2000	2750	4250	7500
J-1012	1750	2000	2250	3000	5000	10000
J-1013	1750	2000	2250	3000	5000	10000
J-1014	2000	2400	3000	4500	9500	17500
J-1015	2000	2400	3000	4500	9500	17500
J-1016 R	2000	2250	2500	3500	6250	15000
J-1016 RB	1750	2000	2250	3000	5000	10000
J-1016 B	1500	1750	2000	2750	4250	7500

The Patterns of 1870: (Continued)

J-1017 R	2000	2250	2500	3500	6250	15000
J-1017 RB	1750	2000	2250	3000	5000	10000
J-1017 B	1500	1750	2000	2750	4250	7500
J-1018	1750	2000	2250	3000	5000	10000
J-1019	1750	2000	2250	3000	5000	10000
J-1020 R	2250	2500	2750	3500	6250	15000
J-1020 RB	2000	2250	2500	3000	5000	10000
J-1020 B	1750	2000	2250	2750	4250	7500
J-1021	2000	2250	2500	3000	5000	10000
J-1022	2250	2500	2750	3500	5500	12500

The Patterns of 1871:

J-1120	2000	2400	3000	4500	7500	17500
J-1121	2000	2400	3000	4500	7500	17500
J-1122 R	2000	2250	2500	3750	7000	17500
J-1122 RB	1750	2000	2250	3250	5000	11000
J-1122 B	1650	1800	2000	3000	4250	8000
J-1123 R	2000	2250	2500	3750	7000	17500
J-1123 RB	1750	2000	2250	3250	5000	11000
J-1123 B	1650	1800	2000	3000	4250	8000
J-1124	2500	3000	3500	4500	5000	15000
J-1125	2500	3000	3500	4500	5000	15000
J-1126	2000	2400	3000	4500	9500	17500
J-1127	2000	2400	3000	4500	9500	17500
J-1128 R	2000	2250	2500	3750	7000	17500
J-1128 RB	1750	2000	2250	3250	5000	11000
J-1128 B	1650	1800	2000	3000	4250	8000
J-1129 R	2000	2250	2500	3750	9500	17500
J-1129 RB	1750	2000	2250	3250	9500	11000
J-1129 B	1650	1800	2000	3000	6750	8000
J-1130	1750	2000	2250	3250	5500	11000
J-1131	1750	2000	2250	3250	4500	11000
J-1132 R	2250	2700	3300	5750	6750	22500
J-1132 RB	2000	2400	3000	4500	5500	15000
J-1132 B	1850	2200	2700	4000	4500	13500
J-1132aR	2250	2700	3300	5750	7500	22500
J-1132aRB	2000	2400	3000	4500	7500	15000
J-1132aB	1850	2200	2700	4000	9500	13500
J-1133	2000	2400	3000	4500	9500	17500
J-1134	2000	2400	3000	4500	6750	17500
J-1135 R	1750	1850	2250	3500	5500	15000
J-1135 RB	1600	1750	2000	2750	4500	10000
J-1135 B	1500	1650	1750	2500	6750	8500
J-1136 R	1750	1850	2250	3500	5500	15000
J-1136 RB	1600	1750	2000	2750	4500	10000
J-1136 B	1500	1650	1750	2500	5500	8500
J-1137	1600	1750	2000	2750	5500	10000
J-1138	1600	1750	2000	2750	11500	10000
J-1138a	2500	3000	3750	6000	7500	20000
J-1138b	2000	2500	3000	4500	6750	15000
J-1139	2000	2500	3000	4500	11500	15000
J-1140	2000	2500	3000	4500	7500	15000
J-1141 R	1750	1850	2250	3500	6750	15000
J-1141 RB	1600	1750	2000	2750	9500	10000
J-1141 B	1500	1650	1750	2500	9500	8500
J-1142 R	1750	1850	2250	3500	7000	15000
J-1142 RB	1600	1750	2000	2750	5000	10000
J-1142 B	1500	1650	1750	2500	4250	8500
J-1143	1600	1750	2000	2750	7000	10000
J-1144	1600	1750	2000	2750	5000	10000
J-1145	2000	2400	3000	4500	4250	17500
J-1146	2000	2400	3000	4500	5000	17500
J-1147 R	1750	1850	2250	3500	5000	15000
J-1147 RB	1600	1750	2000	2750	10000	10000
J-1147 B	1500	1650	1750	2500	7500	8500

The Patterns of 1871: (Continued)

J-1148 R	1750	1850	2250	3500	7000	15000
J-1148 RB	1600	1750	2000	2750	5000	10000
J-1148 B	1500	1650	1750	2500	4250	8500
J-1149	1600	1750	2000	2750	5000	10000
J-1150	1600	1750	2000	2750	5000	10000
J-1151 R	2250	2500	2750	3500	6250	15000
J-1151 RB	2000	2250	2500	3000	5000	10000
J-1151 B	1750	2000	2250	2750	4250	7500
J-1152	2000	2250	2500	3000	5000	10000
J-1153	2500	3000	3250	4500	8750	17500
J-1154	3000	3500	4000	6000	15000	30000
J-1155	3000	3500	4000	6000	15000	30000
J-1156 R	2250	2700	3300	5750	11500	22500
J-1156 RB	2000	2400	3000	4500	7500	15000
J-1156 B	1850	2200	2700	4000	6750	13500
J-1157 R	2250	2700	3300	5750	11500	22500
J-1157 RB	2000	2400	3000	4500	7500	15000
J-1157 B	1850	2200	2700	4000	6750	13500
J-1158	2500	3000	3500	5000	11000	22500
J-1159 R	2000	2250	2500	3750	6750	17500
J-1159 RB	1750	2000	2250	3250	5500	11000
J-1159 B	1650	1800	2000	3000	4500	8000
J-1160	3250	3750	4250	6500	15000	30000

The Patterns of 1872:

J-1205	20000	23000	27000	40000	60000	110000
J-1206 R	11000	12500	15000	24000	36000	65000
J-1206 RB	10000	11500	13500	20000	30000	45000
J-1206 B	9000	10500	12500	18000	25000	37500
J-1207	15000	17500	20000	25000	35000	60000
J-1208	2000	2400	3000	4500	9500	17500
J-1209	2000	2400	3000	4500	9500	17500
J-1210 R	2250	2500	2750	3500	6250	15000
J-1210 RB	2000	2250	2500	3000	5000	10000
J-1210 B	1750	2000	2250	2750	4250	7500
J-1211	2000	2250	2500	3000	5000	10000
J-1212	2000	2400	3000	4500	9500	17500
J-1213	2000	2400	3000	4500	9500	17500
J-1214	2000	2400	3000	4500	9500	17500
J-1215	2000	2400	3000	4500	9500	17500
J-1216 R	2000	2250	2500	3750	6750	17500
J-1216 RB	1750	2000	2250	3250	5500	11000
J-1216 B	1650	1800	2000	3000	4500	8000
J-1217 R	2000	2250	2500	3750	6750	17500
J-1217 RB	1750	2000	2250	3250	5500	11000
J-1217 B	1650	1800	2000	3000	4500	8000
J-1218	1750	2000	2250	3250	5500	11000
J-1219	1850	2000	2500	4000	7500	15000
J-1219aR	2750	3250	3750	6500	13500	30000
J-1219aRB	2500	3000	3500	5000	10000	20000
J-1219aB	2250	2750	3250	4500	9000	16500
J-1220	2000	2400	3000	4500	9500	17500
J-1221 R	2000	2250	2500	3750	6750	17500
J-1221 RB	1750	2000	2250	3250	5500	11000
J-1221 B	1650	1800	2000	3000	4500	8000
J-1222	2000	2250	2500	4000	7500	15000
J-1223	3000	3600	4500	6500	12500	30000

The Patterns of 1873:

J-1274 R	3000	3250	3500	5500	9000	20000
J-1274 RB	2750	3000	3250	4500	6000	12000
J-1274 B	2500	2750	3000	4000	5500	10000
J-1275	2750	3000	3250	4500	6000	12000
J-1276	1750	2000	2250	3000	5000	12500
J-1277	2250	2500	2750	3750	6500	15000
J-1278 R	2000	2250	2500	3500	6000	15000
J-1278 RB	1750	2000	2250	3000	4500	10000
J-1278 B	1650	1850	2000	2750	4000	8000
J-1279	2250	2500	2750	3500	5000	12500
J-1280	2000	2250	2500	3500	5000	12500
J-1281	2000	2250	2500	3250	5500	13500
J-1282	2500	2750	3000	4000	7000	17500
J-1283 R	1800	2000	2250	3500	5500	13500
J-1283 RB	1650	1850	2000	2750	4000	9000
J-1283 B	1500	1650	1800	2500	3500	7500
J-1284	2250	2500	2750	3500	5000	12500
J-1285 R	1800	2000	2250	3500	5500	13500
J-1285 RB	1650	1850	2000	2750	4000	9000
J-1285 B	1500	1650	1800	2500	3500	7500
J-1286	3000	3250	3500	5000	7500	17500
J-1287	3000	3250	3500	5500	8500	20000
J-1288 R	3500	3750	4500	9000	15000	27500
J-1288 RB	3250	3500	4250	7500	11500	20000
J-1288 B	3000	3250	4000	6750	10000	17500
J-1289 R	3500	3750	4500	9000	15000	27500
J-1289 RB	3250	3500	4250	7500	11500	20000
J-1289 B	3000	3250	4000	6750	10000	17500
J-1290	3000	3250	3750	5000	8500	15000
J-1291	3000	3250	3750	5000	8500	15000
J-1292	2000	2250	2500	3000	5000	10000
J-1293	1750	2000	2250	3000	5000	12500
J-1294	2250	2500	2750	3750	6500	15000
J-1295 R	1800	2000	2250	3500	5500	13500
J-1295 RB	1650	1850	2000	2750	4000	9000
J-1295 B	1500	1650	1800	2500	3500	7500
J-1296 R	1800	2000	2250	3500	5500	13500
J-1296 RB	1650	1850	2000	2750	4000	9000
J-1296 B	1500	1650	1800	2500	3500	7500
J-1297	2500	2750	3000	4000	7500	15000
J-1298	2500	2750	3000	4000	7500	15000
J-1299	2500	2750	3000	4000	7500	15000
J-1300	3000	3250	3750	5000	8500	15000
J-1301 R	2750	3000	3500	5000	9000	20000
J-1301 RB	2500	2750	3000	4000	7500	15000
J-1301 B	2250	2500	2750	3750	7000	13500
J-1302 R	2750	3000	3500	5000	9000	20000
J-1302 RB	2500	2750	3000	4000	7500	15000
J-1302 B	2250	2500	2750	3750	7000	13500
J-1303	2500	2750	3000	4000	7500	15000
J-1304	2500	2750	3000	4000	7500	15000
J-1304a	3500	3750	4250	5750	10000	20000
J-1305 R	1800	2000	2250	3500	5500	13500
J-1305 RB	1650	1850	2000	2750	4000	9000
J-1305 B	1500	1650	1800	2500	3500	7500
J-1306	1650	1850	2000	2750	4000	9000
J-1307	2500	2750	3000	4000	7500	15000
J-1308	3250	3500	4000	6000	10000	20000
J-1309	1750	2000	2250	3000	4500	10000
J-1310	2000	2250	2500	3250	5500	13500
J-1311	2500	2750	3000	3750	7500	17500
J-1312 R	1800	2000	2250	3500	5500	13500
J-1312 RB	1650	1850	2000	2750	4000	9000
J-1312 B	1500	1650	1800	2500	3500	7500
J-1313	1750	2000	2250	3000	4500	10000
J-1314	1750	2000	2250	3000	4500	10000
J-1315	2000	2250	2500	3250	5500	13500

The Patterns of 1873: (Continued)

J-1316	2500	2750	3000	3750	7500	17500
J-1317 R	2250	2500	2750	3500	5500	13500
J-1317 RB	2000	2250	2500	3000	4500	9000
J-1317 B	1850	2000	2250	2750	4000	8000
J-1318	2500	2750	3000	3750	7500	15000
J-1319	2500	2750	3000	3750	7500	15000
J-1320	2750	3000	3250	4000	8000	17500
J-1321 R	2250	2500	2750	3500	5500	13500
J-1321 RB	2000	2250	2500	3000	4500	9000
J-1321 B	1850	2000	2250	2750	4000	8000
J-1322	2000	2250	2500	3250	5500	13500
J-1323	2500	2750	3000	3750	7500	17500
J-1324 R	2000	2250	2500	3500	5250	12500
J-1324 RB	1850	2000	2250	2750	4250	8500
J-1324 B	1750	1850	2000	2500	3750	7500
J-1325	2000	2250	2500	3250	4500	10000
J-1326	1750	2000	2250	3000	4500	10000
J-1326 a	2500	3000	3500	5000	8500	16500
J-1326 b	2000	2250	2500	3500	6000	12500
J-1327 R	1800	2000	2250	3500	5500	13500
J-1327 RB	1650	1850	2000	2750	4000	9000
J-1327 B	1500	1650	1800	2500	3500	7500
J-1328	1800	2000	2250	2750	4500	10000
J-1329	2000	2250	2500	3500	6750	13500
J-1330	2000	2250	2500	3500	6750	13500

The Patterns of 1874:

J-1363 R	1800	2000	2250	3500	5500	13500
J-1363 RB	1650	1850	2000	2750	4000	9000
J-1363 B	1500	1650	1800	2500	3500	7500
J-1364	1800	2000	2250	2750	4500	10000

The Patterns of 1875:

J-1420	3500	4000	4500	7500	15000	30000
J-1421 R	2250	2500	2750	4500	10000	20000
J-1421 RB	2000	2250	2500	3750	7500	15000
J-1421 B	1850	2000	2250	3500	6750	13500
J-1422	3500	4000	4500	6000	10000	20000
J-1423	3500	4000	4500	7500	15000	30000
J-1424 R	2250	2500	2750	4500	10000	20000
J-1424 RB	2000	2250	2500	3750	7500	15000
J-1424 B	1850	2000	2250	3500	6750	13500
J-1425	3250	3500	4000	5500	9000	17500
J-1426	3500	4000	4500	7500	15000	30000
J-1427 R	2250	2500	2750	4500	10000	20000
J-1427 RB	2000	2250	2500	3750	7500	15000
J-1427 B	1850	2000	2250	3500	6750	13500
J-1428	2000	2250	2500	3750	7500	15000
J-1429	3250	3500	4000	5500	9000	17500
J-1430 R	1800	2000	2250	3500	5500	13500
J-1430 RB	1650	1850	2000	2750	4000	9000
J-1430 B	1500	1650	1800	2500	3500	7500
J-1431	1650	1850	2000	2750	4500	10000

The Patterns of 1876:

J-1457	12500	13500	17500	25000	40000	75000
J-1458 R	3500	4000	4500	7500	12500	25000
J-1458 RB	3250	3500	4000	6000	10000	17500
J-1458 B	3000	3250	3500	5000	8500	15000
J-1458aR	3500	4000	4500	7500	12500	25000
J-1458aRB	3250	3500	4000	6000	10000	17500
J-1458aB	3000	3250	3500	5000	8500	15000
J-1459	12500	13500	17500	25000	40000	75000
J-1460 R	3500	4000	4500	7500	12500	25000
J-1460 RB	3250	3500	4000	6000	10000	17500
J-1460 B	3000	3250	3500	5000	8500	15000

The Patterns of 1876: (Continued)

J-1461 R	4250	4500	5000	8500	15000	30000
J-1461 RB	4000	4250	4500	7000	12000	20000
J-1461 B	3750	4000	4250	6000	10000	17500
J-1462	12500	13500	17500	25000	40000	75000
J-1463 R	3500	4000	4500	7500	12500	25000
J-1463 RB	3250	3500	4000	6000	10000	17500
J-1463 B	3000	3250	3500	5000	8500	15000
J-1463aR	5500	5750	6000	10000	17500	30000
J-1463aRB	5000	5250	5500	8500	13500	25000
J-1463aB	4500	4750	5000	7500	12500	20000
J-1464	12500	13500	17500	25000	40000	75000
J-1465 R	3500	4000	4500	7500	12500	25000
J-1465 RB	3250	3500	4000	6000	10000	17500
J-1465 B	3000	3250	3500	5000	8500	15000
J-1466 R	4250	4500	5000	8500	15000	30000
J-1466 RB	4000	4250	4500	7000	12000	20000
J-1466 B	3750	4000	4250	6000	10000	17500
J-1467	7500	8500	10000	17500	30000	50000
J-1468 R	3500	3750	4250	6000	13500	25000
J-1468 RB	3000	3250	3750	4500	8500	17500
J-1468 B	2500	2750	3250	4000	7000	15000
J-1469 R	3500	3750	4250	6000	13500	25000
J-1469 RB	3000	3250	3750	4500	8500	17500
J-1469 B	2500	2750	3250	4000	7000	15000
J-1470	12500	13500	17500	25000	40000	75000
J-1471 R	3750	4000	4500	7000	15000	30000
J-1471 RB	3250	3500	4000	5000	10000	20000
J-1471 B	2750	3000	3500	4500	8000	16500
J-1472	12500	13500	17500	25000	40000	75000
J-1473 R	2500	2750	3250	5500	10000	20000
J-1473 RB	2250	2500	2750	4000	6250	12500
J-1473 B	2000	2250	2500	3500	5000	10000
J-1474	12500	13500	17500	25000	40000	75000
J-1475 R	3500	3750	4250	6500	13500	30000
J-1475 RB	3000	3250	3750	5000	9000	20000
J-1475 B	2500	2750	3250	4500	7000	16500
J-1476 R	2500	2750	3250	4000	7500	15000
J-1476 RB	2250	2500	2750	3500	5000	10000
J-1476 B	2000	2250	2500	3250	4250	8500
J-1477	2250	2500	2750	3500	5000	10000

The Patterns of 1877:

J-1542 R	3500	4000	4500	7500	12500	25000
J-1542 RB	3250	3500	4000	6000	10000	17500
J-1542 B	3000	3250	3500	5000	8500	15000
J-1543 R	4500	5000	5500	8000	15000	30000
J-1543 RB	4000	4500	5000	6500	12000	20000
J-1543 B	3500	4000	4500	5500	10000	17500
J-1544 R	3500	4000	4500	7500	12500	25000
J-1544 RB	3250	3500	4000	6000	10000	17500
J-1544 B	3000	3250	3500	5000	8500	15000

The Patterns of 1878:

J-1550	2000	2250	2500	3500	5500	12500
J-1550 a	2000	2250	2500	3500	5500	12500
J-1551 R	2000	2250	2500	3500	6000	15000
J-1551 RB	1800	2000	2250	3000	4500	10000
J-1551 B	1650	1850	2000	2750	4000	8500
J-1552	3000	3250	3500	4500	8500	17500
J-1553 R	2750	3250	3500	4500	8500	17500
J-1553 RB	2500	2750	3250	4000	7000	12500
J-1553 B	2250	2500	3000	3600	6000	11500
J-1554	2250	2500	2750	3750	6500	15000
J-1555 R	2000	2250	2500	3500	6000	15000
J-1555 RB	1800	2000	2250	3000	4500	10000
J-1555 B	1650	1850	2000	2750	4000	8500

The Patterns of 1878: (Continued)

J-1556	2500	2750	3000	4000	7500	15000
J-1556 a	2250	2500	2750	3500	7000	13500
J-1557	1500	1750	2000	2500	3500	7500
J-1558	1150	1350	1600	2000	3000	6000
J-1559 R	1350	1650	1850	2400	3500	7500
J-1559 RB	1250	1500	1750	2000	3000	5500
J-1559 B	1150	1350	1600	1850	2750	4500
J-1560	1750	2000	2250	3000	4250	10000
J-1561	1350	1500	1750	2250	3500	7500
J-1562 R	1350	1650	1850	2400	3500	7500
J-1562 RB	1250	1500	1750	2000	3000	5500
J-1562 B	1150	1350	1600	1850	2750	4500
J-1563	1650	1800	2000	2750	3750	8500
J-1564	1350	1500	1750	2250	3500	7500
J-1565 R	2750	3000	3500	5500	10000	20000
J-1565 RB	2500	2750	3000	4250	7500	15000
J-1565 B	2250	2500	2750	3750	7000	13500

The Patterns of 1879:

J-1603	5000	6000	7500	12500	20000	40000
J-1604 R	3500	4000	4750	9000	16000	25000
J-1604 RB	3250	3750	4250	7000	12000	18000
J-1604 B	3000	3500	4000	5500	10000	15000
J-1605	4000	5000	6000	9000	15000	35000
J-1606 R	2750	3250	4000	7000	12500	30000
J-1606 RB	2500	2750	3000	4000	7500	15000
J-1606 B	2250	2500	2750	3500	6000	12000
J-1607	3000	3250	3500	5000	10000	20000
J-1608	25000	30000	37500	50000	75000	150000
J-1609 R	20000	22500	25000	35000	45000	90000
J-1609 RB	17500	20000	22500	27500	32500	60000
J-1609 B	15000	17500	20000	25000	30000	50000
J-1610	5000	6000	7500	10000	15000	25000
J-1611	2500	2750	3000	4000	7500	15000
J-1612 R	2000	2250	2500	3500	4500	10000
J-1612 RB	1800	2000	2250	2750	3850	7500
J-1612 B	1650	1850	2000	2500	3500	6500
J-1613	2500	2750	3000	4000	7500	15000
J-1614 R	2000	2250	2500	3000	4500	10000
J-1614 RB	1800	2000	2250	2750	3850	7500
J-1614 B	1650	1850	2000	2500	3500	6500
J-1615	3000	3250	3500	4500	9000	16500
J-1616 R	2250	2400	2700	3750	5500	12000
J-1616 RB	2000	2100	2400	3250	4500	9000
J-1616 B	1750	1850	2200	3000	4000	7500
J-1617	1250	1500	1750	2250	3000	6000
J-1618	1000	1200	1500	2000	2700	5000
J-1619 R	1200	1400	1600	2000	3500	7500
J-1619 RB	1100	1300	1500	1850	2500	4000
J-1619 B	1000	1200	1400	1650	2250	3500
J-1620	1250	1500	1750	2500	4000	7500
J-1621	2000	2250	2500	3000	4000	6000
J-1622	1500	1650	1850	2750	4250	8500
J-1623 R	1350	1650	1850	2500	4000	8000
J-1623 RB	1200	1350	1500	2000	3250	5750
J-1623 B	1100	1250	1350	1850	2750	5000
J-1624	1500	1650	1850	2500	4000	7500
J-1625	2000	2250	2500	3750	6500	12500
J-1626	1250	1500	1750	2000	3250	6750
J-1627	1000	1200	1500	1800	2700	5000
J-1628 R	1350	1650	1850	2400	3500	7500
J-1628 RB	1250	1500	1750	2000	3000	5000
J-1628 B	1150	1350	1600	1850	2750	4250
J-1629	1250	1650	1850	2350	3500	7500
J-1630	2000	2250	2500	3000	4000	6000
J-1631	1500	1750	2000	3000	5000	10000

The Patterns of 1879: (Continued)

J-1632 R	1400	1600	1850	2700	4250	10000
J-1632 RB	1250	1400	1600	2250	3400	7500
J-1632 B	1150	1300	1450	2000	3000	5750
J-1633	1500	1750	2000	2750	4000	8500
J-1634	2000	2250	2750	4000	7500	15000

The Patterns of 1880:

J-1645	1500	1800	2100	2500	3750	7500
J-1646 R	1200	1400	1600	2000	3500	7500
J-1646 RB	1100	1300	1500	1800	2500	4000
J-1646 B	1000	1200	1400	1650	2250	3500
J-1647	2000	2250	2500	3000	5000	10000
J-1648	1350	1650	1850	2750	4250	8500
J-1649 R	1350	1650	1850	2500	4000	8000
J-1649 RB	1200	1350	1500	2000	3250	5750
J-1649 B	1100	1250	1350	1850	2750	5000
J-1650	2000	2250	2500	3000	5000	10000
J-1651	1350	1650	2000	2500	3750	7500
J-1652 R	1350	1650	1850	2400	3500	7500
J-1652 RB	1250	1500	1750	2000	3000	5000
J-1652 B	1150	1350	1600	1850	2750	4250
J-1653	1250	1650	1850	2350	3500	7500
J-1654	1500	1750	2000	3000	5000	10000
J-1655 R	1400	1600	1850	2700	4250	10000
J-1655 RB	1250	1400	1600	2250	3400	7500
J-1655 B	1150	1300	1450	2000	3000	5750
J-1656	1500	1750	2000	2750	4000	8500

The Patterns of 1882:

J-1702	12000	15000	20000	27000	40000	75000
J-1703 R	9000	11000	13500	20000	32000	50000
J-1703 RB	8500	10000	12500	17500	25000	37500
J-1703 B	8000	9000	11000	15000	21000	30000
J-1703aR	2500	2750	3250	5000	9000	20000
J-1703aRB	2250	2500	2750	4000	6500	13500
J-1703aB	2000	2250	2500	3500	5500	11500
J-1703bR	2500	2750	3250	5000	9000	20000
J-1703bRB	2250	2500	2750	4000	6500	13500
J-1703bB	2000	2250	2500	3500	5500	11500

The Patterns of 1883:

J-1720aR	2500	2750	3250	5000	9000	20000
J-1720aRB	2250	2500	2750	4000	6500	13500
J-1720aB	2000	2250	2500	3500	5500	11500

The Patterns of 1884:

J-1731 R	2500	2750	3250	5000	9000	20000
J-1731 RB	2250	2500	2750	4000	6500	13500
J-1731 B	2000	2250	2500	3500	5500	11500
J-1732 R	2500	2750	3250	5000	9000	20000
J-1732 RB	2250	2500	2750	4000	6500	13500
J-1732 B	2000	2250	2500	3500	5500	11500

The Patterns of 1885:

J-1747	3000	3250	3750	5000	7500	15000
J-1748 R	2250	2500	2750	4000	6250	12500
J-1748 RB	2000	2250	2500	3000	4250	8500
J-1748 B	1800	2000	2200	2700	3750	7500
J-1749	2500	2750	3000	4250	6500	13500
J-1750	2250	2500	2750	4000	6000	12000
J-1750aR	2500	2750	3250	5000	9000	20000
J-1750aRB	2250	2500	2750	4000	6500	13500
J-1750aB	2000	2250	2500	3500	5500	11500

* **R** = RED **RB** = RED BROWN **B** = BROWN

Douglas Winter, NLG

Douglas Winter graduated with an honors degree in English from the University of North Carolina (Chapel Hill) in 1982. After working for a large rare coin firm in Texas for three years, he formed his own firm in 1985.

Douglas Winter Consulting specializes in high quality rare date 19th century United States gold coinage, 18th and early 19th century United States silver coinage, Territorial gold, California Fractional gold and pattern coinage. In addition to being a strong wholesale and retail presence, the firm also does consultation work for many leading rare coin auction firms, limited partnerships and funds, banks, estates and financial institutions.

Winter is a member of all leading numismatic organizations including the Professional Numismatists Guild, in which he holds membership #399. He has written three books and is having a fourth published in conjunction with Unitrade in the spring of 1991. He has also written dozens of articles for leading numismatic publications as well as many of the most significant rare coin auction catalogs from the past decade.

Winter lives with his wife Kerrin, a well-known photographer, in University Park, Texas.

CHAPTER 57

Bust Dollars: The Early Years

by Douglas Winter, NLG

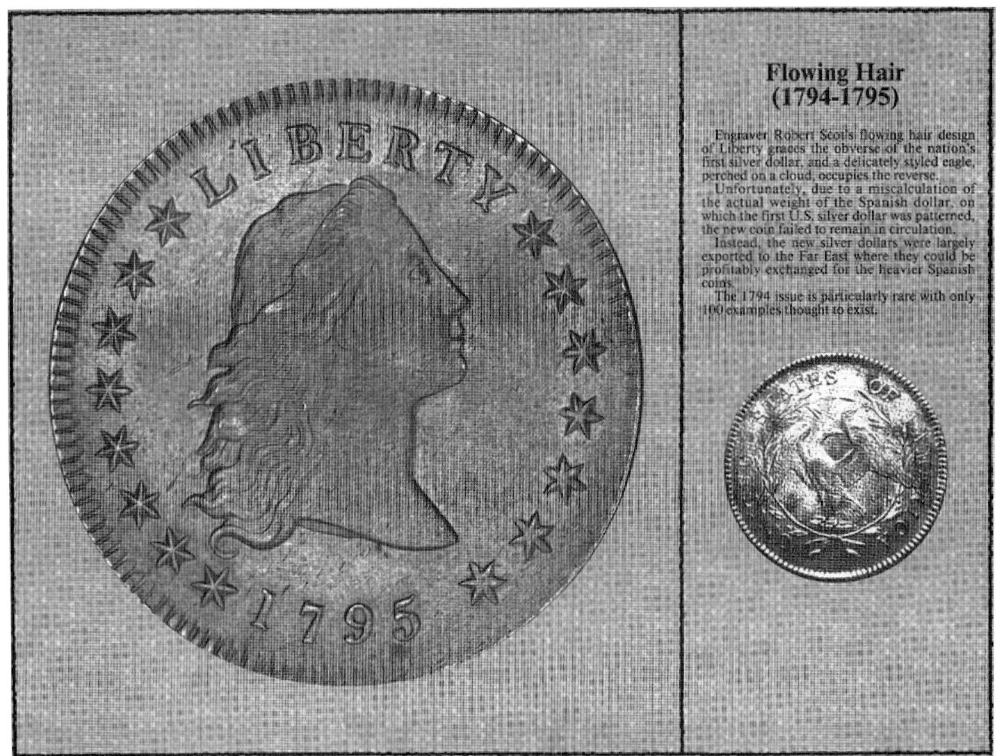

Bust Dollars: The Early Years Flowing Hair (1794 — 1795)
(Courtesy of Krause Publications)

Bust Dollars: The Early Years Draped Bust, Small Eagle (1795 — 1798)
(Coin courtesy of Milton O. Lynn)
(Photo provided by Krause Publications)

For a variety of reasons (most of which will be discussed in detail by experts elsewhere in this book), Bust dollars are the unloved step-child of all American silver dollars. Most investors do not even know these coins exist and only a handful of dealers and collectors can rightfully be called experts in this field.

However, Bust dollars have a number of factors which make them an extremely interesting collecting field. They are very scarce in comparison to Morgan and Peace dollars yet are very reasonably priced. They have a very attractive design and are far less standardized than these later types. They include a number of rare and important varieties which can often be purchased for the price of a common "type" example. And they are not subject to dramatic ups and downs in their price levels, as are certain heavily promoted common issues within the Morgan and Peace dollar series.

The Mint Act of April 2, 1792, authorized, among other things, the coinage of silver dollars. These new dollars were to pass at par with Mexican and Spanish dollars. They were, as well, to weigh 416 grains and contain the unwieldy ratio of 179 parts copper to 1664 parts silver.

Albion Cox, the Assayer of the Mint, and David Rittenhouse, the Mint's Director, both complained that this fineness ratio was impossible to work with. They recommended a reduction of the copper to 10% and a revised weight standard of 412.5 grains. Congress, for some unknown reason, vehemently opposed this suggestion. Rittenhouse compromised by proposing that the silver content be increased from 371.25 to 374.75 grains. This, in turn, would create a 900/1000 fineness. Thomas Jefferson and Alexander Hamilton both found this proposal to be practical. Rittenhouse firmly believed that Congress would approve his plan and he then set about coining the 1794 dollars.

Technically, the 1794 dollar is an illegal coin in that it was struck in a non-standard ratio. By coining the 1794 (and 1795 Flowing Hair) dollars at an unauthorized standard, Rittenhouse unknowingly created a situation whereby depositors of silver bullion met substantial losses. 2.5 grains of extra silver had to be put into each dollar they received; this represented a net loss of 1% from what they would have received had the dollars been coined at legal fineness.

On October 15, 1794, a total of 1758 pieces were struck from a single pair of dies cut by the Engraver Robert Scot. The coins were put into circulation immediately; contemporary records indicate that they were sent to the New England region of the United States. Further contemporary accounts criticized these coins for their weak strikes. The December 2, 1794 issue of the *New Hampshire Gazette* wrote: "The touches of the graver are too delicate and there is a want of boldness of execution which is necessary to the durability of the currency."

However, the fault lies in the manufacturing process and not in the design. After only a few pieces were struck, the dies became misaligned vertically (i.e., they were no longer in parallel planes). Therefore, the left side of 1794 dollars is almost always weak and it is common to see heavy clashmarks at the centers. Recent research has shown that the dollars were struck in a press which was intended for Eagles and Half Dollars; given this fact, the unevenness of strike seems inevitable.

As with most first-year-of-issue coins, an abnormally high percentage of 1794 dollars were saved as souvenirs. However, this is still a genuinely rare coin with an estimated 100-125 pieces known to exist. The majority of these grade from Fair to Very Good. In the middle circulated grades, this issue becomes quite rare. Mint State examples are, as one might imagine, extremely rare and in great demand. It is estimated that between five and seven strictly Uncirculated examples exist.

Among the Mint State 1794 dollars are two pieces which were acquired at their time of issue by Sir Rowland Wynn, later Major the Lord St. Oswald, a British nobleman and coin collector who had the foresight to obtain a number of United States coins on a visit to America in 1795. These coins were forgotten until St. Oswald's estate was auctioned by Christie's in 1964. One of the coins was subsequently sold to Mrs. Henry Norweb. It remained in her collection until 1988 when it was auctioned and sold to a West Coast Limited Partnership. This coin has been graded MS-63 by PCGS. In my opinion, the finest known 1794 is the prooflike Amon Carter coin which has been graded MS-65. This piece has superb color and is remarkably well struck. It is currently owned by a New Jersey dealer who values it at over $1 million!

Obverse

Reverse

1794 Dollar

The 1794 dollars are very difficult to properly grade. In addition to the striking problems described above, many pieces show serious adjustment marks. Normally, adjustment marks do not adversely affect a coin's grade. But how does one value a coin with, say, "Very Fine" sharpness but which has heavy clusters of adjustment marks?

Another problem with 1794 (and most Bust dollar issues as well) is that a number of pieces have been cleverly repaired. As an example, there are probably as many as twenty 1794 dollars floating around which have either been plugged or which show evidence of removal of names or initial. While such coins will not be graded by the services, they certainly still have some value. The new collector needs to learn how to check for damage on Bust dollars (some tips will be offered later) and should, as a rule, avoid such pieces.

Other forms of repair which are often seen on Bust dollars include tooling, burnishing, strengthening of the hair details and removing edge bumps. The first two repair techniques are relatively easy to detect although they can be masked, somewhat, by subsequent application of artificial color. It is advisable to carefully study the fields of any Bust dollar and look for any areas which appear irregular. On coins with strengthened hair detail, the quality of the work can range from excellent to ridiculously bad. If a coin with what appears to be a considerable amount of wear has surprisingly strong hair detail, check it carefully with a strong magnifying glass or show it to an expert. Coins with repaired edges can best be detected by inspecting the edges and looking for unnatural, smooth areas.

As mentioned above, the grading services will not intentionally grade repaired Bust dollars. But they will grade certain coins which have scratches or which show signs of cleaning. In recent years, such coins have been "net graded." As an example, a 1794 dollar which has the sharpness of Very Fine-25 but which has some severe scrapes on its obverse might trade at a price level equivalent to a Very Good-8. Thus, the grading services will take this into consideration and may choose to award the coin a Very Good-8 grade. While the grading services generally do an admirable job at grading early dollars, it is advisable for the collector to learn how to grade these coins. And it is never advisable to buy such coins on a strictly sight-unseen basis.

The Flowing Hair type continued into 1795. A total of 160,295 1795 Flowing Hair dollars were struck. Approximately 5,000-6,000 of these have survived with the great majority of these grading Poor to Fine. Pieces which grade Extremely Fine are fairly scarce and popular; About Uncirculated examples are sometimes available but are very scarce. Fully Mint State pieces are sometimes offered for sale but many of these are overgraded; choice examples are very rare and in great demand as type coins.

It is very difficult to locate a well struck 1795 Flowing Hair dollar. Most coins are weakly struck at their centers and are apt to lack fine details on the eagle's breast and the uppermost portion of the wings. Coins with adjustment marks are commonly seen as well.

The dies for the 1795 Flowing Hair dollars were prepared by both Robert Scot and his assistant John Smith Gardner. It is possible to distinguish which dies were cut by which engraver as each man's work contained a number of unique characteristics. Scot's obverse dies are readily identifiable by their lack of a truncation line below the bust on the obverse. Gardner's obverses show a truncation line. Scot's reverse dies show two inside leaves below the eagle's wings and drooping leaves above the head of the eagle. On Gardner's reverses, there are three leaves below the eagle's wings and all of the leaves have a larger overall size. Altogether, Scot was responsible for three obverse dies and eight reverse dies. Gardner created seven obverse dies and two reverse dies.

There are a total of 18 die varieties known to exist for 1795 Flowing Hair dollars. About 90% of the surviving coins are from one of three pairs of dies. One of these shows the 7 in the date cut over an erroneous 1. The other two show die defects in the left obverse field which appear like a raised "bar" to the naked eye. While there is not a great amount of interest in the other, rarer, die varieties, it is sometimes possible to acquire a 1795 Flowing Hair dollar which is from a very rare die pair for the price of a common variety.

In October 1795, the new Draped Bust design was introduced to the dollar denomination. This design was the result of plans by the Mint's new director Henry William DeSaussure to improve the appearance of all United States coinage. The famous artist Gilbert Stuart was hired to depict Liberty, and his image was, in turn, adapted to coinage form by John Eckstein and Robert Scot.

Two pairs of dies were used in October 1795 to coin 42,738 Draped Bust dollars. On one, the obverse portrait is well-centered while the other shows the portrait with better centering. Approximately 2,000-2,500, 1795 Draped Bust dollars have survived. Low grade examples are easy to find although most have been cleaned or show a blatant lack of eye appeal. This type really does not become rare below the Mint State level but Uncirculated coins have survived on a higher proportionate basis than for the 1795 Flowing Hair dollars. Most examples are better defined on the obverse than on the reverse. Even Uncirculated coins are apt to show considerable weakness on the eagle's breasts and feathers.

A few really spectacular 1795 Draped Bust dollars have survived. The finest which I can ever recall seeing is the piece which was sold as Lot #3816 in Superior's Heifetz Sale of October 1989. A PCGS graded MS-65 example which was sold as Lot #3876 in Superior's May 1990 Boys Town Sale, realized $418,000 which is unquestionably a record for any 1795 dollar. In addition to these two gems, there are three or four other pieces known which qualify at or near today's Mint State-65 interpretation.

Some 1795 Draped Bust dollars are known which exhibit an appearance somewhat similar to a Proof coin; these include the memorable Garrett II: 680 piece and others. While these pieces are not Proofs in the truest sense of the word, it is highly possible that they are some sort of presentation pieces made specially for DeSaussure to demonstrate the new design and to pass out to dignitaries.

Coinage of the Draped Bust Small Eagle reverse type dollars continued into 1796. Production was made very difficult by a lack of good steel for the making of dies, the scarcity of bullion and a general lack of public support and governmental backing for the Mint.

The 1796 Dollars can be conveniently sorted into three distinct types: Small Date/Small Letters, Small Date/Large Letters and Large Date/Large Letters. The rarest of these three types is the Small Date/Small Letters type, followed by the Large Date/Small Letters and the Small Date/Large Letters respectively. In terms of numbers known, the 1796 dollar is about as rare as the 1795 Draped Bust. However, this date is significantly rarer in the high grades.

Any type of 1796 dollar is genuinely scarce in Extremely Fine and full About Uncirculated coins are quite rare. Mint State 1796 Dollars are extremely rare; dozens of times more so than the more well-known Dimes and Quarters of this date. I have only viewed two examples which qualified as Uncirculated. These are a piece owned by Heritage in August 1986 and the MS-60+ which was sold as Lot #358 in the 1989 ANA Sale. I also recall seeing an exceptional example in the 1796 "Proof Set" which is owned by a famous Mid-Western dealer and which was exhibited a few years back at an ANA Convention.

The quality of strike for this date is almost always very poor. The typical example will appear to be almost a full grade weaker on the reverse than on the obverse. Many pieces are poorly centered and show weak milling as a result. The quality of the average planchet used to strike 1796 dollars is inferior to that found on 1795's and, thus, some coins will show Mint-made roughness. Another problem is locating coins with a good degree of eye appeal. After examining a good number of 1796 dollars, I sometimes wonder if there are any left which haven't been cleaned or which do not show nasty marks and/or scratches. In 1988, I was putting together a type set of Bust dollars for a client. It took me close to a year to find an acceptable Extremely Fine example and even that piece was hardly what I would call "choice for the grade."

The internal problems which plagued the Mint in 1796 became even worse in 1797. As a result, the production of silver dollars was severely limited. Production runs, such as they were, occurred in February, late May to late June and in August. During each striking period, different die pairings were employed. Thus, three distinct types exist, each from a single pair of dies.

The 16 Stars (9x7)/Small Letters coins were struck first. The sixteenth star was added to signify the admission of Tennessee to the Union. The reverse die had already been employed once in 1795 and twice in 1796. By 1797, it was well worn and this accounts for the weakness which is diagnostic to this variety. Its resurrection is a poignant reminder of just how badly off the Mint was in 1797.

The next group of 1797 dollars to be struck shared the same obverse with those struck earlier in the year. A new Large Letters reverse die was paired with the obverse, creating yet another type. Both dies cracked early; the obverse enough so that the last coins struck show this die all but obliterated. As a result, the quality of strike for the 16 Stars (9x7)/Large Letters reverse is always very poor.

Sixteen Stars (10x6)/Large Letters coins were the final 1797 dollars to be struck. The reverse is slightly different from the preceding type as it shows the lowest berry near the ribbon on the outside of the wreath.

The year 1797 marks the rarest individual date of any Bust dollar struck from 1795 until 1803. Approximately 600-800 pieces survive with somewhere in the area of 50-60% of these being of the 16 Stars (9x7)/Small Letters reverse type. However, most of the choice examples known of this date are of the 16 Stars (10x6)/Large Letters type.

The typical 1797 dollar grades from Poor to Very Good. This date becomes scarce in choice Very Fine and is very rare in About Uncirculated. Fully Mint State examples are extremely rare although not quite as much so as the 1796. The finest example which has been sold in many years is the piece offered as Lot #3715 in Superior's October 1990 Sale and graded MS-64 by NGC. The Eliasberg Collection is said to include a gem example but I have never had the pleasure of viewing this coin.

The 16 Stars (9x7)/Small Letters reverse type is one of the most underrated of all United States silver coins. Only 342 pieces were originally struck. Remarkable, the "Red Book" only assigns this type a value which is double that of a more "common" 1797 dollar type. When available (which is not very often), examples of this rarity tend to come in very low grade and are wretchedly struck. There is just one piece known which even approaches Mint State (the Amon Carter: 218 coin) and just a few pieces exist in Extremely Fine. The reverse is always very weak due to this die having been re-used for the fifth time since 1796 and most pieces are poorly centered as well.

Because of their poor manufacture, it is hard to grade 1797 dollars. The most accurate way is to judge the detail visible on the hair of Liberty and to note if there is any remaining luster. The obverse should play a much greater role in determining the grade than on most coins due to the quality of the reverse dies which were employed.

This is another date which will prove extremely frustrating to the finicky buyer. Any 1797 dollar which grades Very Fine-30 or better and which is clean and free of problems is worth well in excess of current published valuations.

The 1798 silver dollars form the most challenging and misunderstood issue within the Bust dollar series. There are a total of 33 different die varieties including a number of significant and rare issues.

The first two issues of this year employed the Small Eagle reverse which is also found on dollars dated 1795-1797. The first type has 13 stars on the obverse while the second has 15 obverse stars. The rest of the coins struck in this year employ the new Heraldic Eagle reverse created by Robert Scot.

The total mintage figure for all types of 1798 dollars is 327,536. Of these it is estimated that around 7,000-8,000 coins survive. Both Small Eagle reverse varieties are scarce, although lower grade examples are not as hard to locate as was once felt. In higher grades, the 1798 Small Eagle reverse dollar is very rare and I have never seen a coin which graded higher than AU-55.

A number of important types are known which use the Heraldic Eagle reverse. There are three different date sizes and varieties are known with both a Plain 9 and a Knobbed 9. These can be broken down further into sub-varieties by the star configurations on the reverse.

Two patterns of stars can be found on the Heraldic Eagle reverse 1798 dollars. These are classified as "arc" and "cross." The cross configuration is found on the earliest reverses. This pattern has stars above the eagle's head in intersecting straight lines. The stars are arranged in two groups of six which are, in turn, shaped in triangular formations. The thirteenth star is isolated above the head of the eagle and the straight lines formed by the triangles intersect through this star.

The arc star pattern is found on those reverses completed later in 1798 and on all dollars dated 1799 to 1803. (There is one exception; a very scarce 1799 variety which employs a leftover 1798 reverse.) This pattern has stars arranged with the top row paralleling the clouds and the middle row forming an arc of a smaller concentric circle.

It is impossible to state exactly why there are two distinct star patterns. As mentioned above, the "cross" pattern was designed before the "arc" pattern. It is possible that it was cut by an assistant to Robert Scot and the design was later modified by Scot. Or, perhaps, Scot himself cut the abnormal pattern but decided to (or was forced to) standardize the reverse.

The 1798 Heraldic Eagle (or Large Eagle) dollars are much easier to obtain than their Small Eagle counterparts. Nice Extremely Fine and About Uncirculated examples can be located with patience. Mint State coins are rare. The finest single coin I can recall having ever seen was the piece sold as Lot #3877 in Superior's Boys Town Sale of May, 1990. This coin sold for $52,250 and was later being offered for $72,500 in an East Coast firm's fixed price list.

The quality of strike for 1798 dollars varies greatly. The Small Eagle varieties are usually sharper on the obverse than on the reverse. Nearly all pieces lack full definition on the head and the breast of the eagle and it is hard to locate a piece with full milling on both the obverse and the reverse. Certain die varieties are always weak on the stars above and behind the head of the eagle due to die failure. Other varieties will show sporadic areas of weakness due to die breakage.

Grading coins which show diagnostic Mint-made weakness of strike due to poor conditions of the die(s) requires expertise. For example, a certain die variety may show the detail of an Extremely Fine-40 coin in most places but may be extremely weak on Liberty's hair due to strike. Since the grading services are generally not familiar with the striking characteristics of each and every variety of Bust dollar, they may unfairly downgrade such a coin to, say, a Very Fine-25. By becoming familiar with the striking characteristics for specific dates and varieties, the knowledgeable collector may be able to purchase some severely undergraded pieces for this collection.

As with all of the issues in the Heraldic Eagle reverse type, the collector should be on the lookout for coins which have been plugged, repaired or retoned. I have seen some coins which were so expertly plugged that they were nearly impossible to detect with the naked eye. During the 1970's, many Bust dollars were whizzed. Some have acquired attractive natural coloration since that time and appear "original" to the naked eye. To detect such a piece, it is advisable to look at the flow of the metal near the lettering on the obverse and the reverse. Whizzed coins will show a "build up" of metal near these raised areas. Most experts have a pre-determined conception of just how a whizzed coin should appear and if a coin does not have a bright, unnatural "whizzed" appearance, a coin which has retoned or been recolored since the whizzing can be missed on quick examination.

The 1799 Bust dollars are among the most common issues, on an individual basis, within the entire type. 423,515 pieces were struck and it is probable that as many as 8,500-9,000 have survived.

There are a few very interesting varieties which can be found on 1799 dollars. There are two 1799/8 varieties. One shows thirteen stars on the reverse while the other shows fifteen stars. The latter variety is the result of a blunder by the engraver who subsequently tried to efface his mistake by enlarging the clouds. His attempted camouflage was not entirely successful as the bottom points of the extra stars can be seen at the far left and the far right clouds.

Both 1799/8 varieties are fairly easy to obtain in grades up to and including Extremely Fine. About Uncirculated pieces are scarce while fully Mint State pieces are rare. While the thirteen star reverse variety is a bit more common overall than the fifteen star, it is much rarer in Mint State. The finest known examples include the 1989 ANA: 369 and Amon Carter: 224 coins. Approximately six or seven Uncirculated 1799/8 fifteen star reverse dollars are known. The finest of these is the piece which was last sold as Lot #3878 in Superior's May 1990 Sale and which had earlier been offered in three of the "Apostrophe Sales" between 1983 and 1986.

All normal date 1799 dollars have thirteen obverse stars arranged seven by six with the exception of one which has its arranged eight by five. It is possible that this variety is a blundered die. The engraver may have thought he was cutting the dies for an Eagle and began by placing eight stars at the left. This variety is overrated in lower grades but it is extremely rare in Mint State.

In higher grades, this date is one of the easier of all Bust dollars to locate. It is probable that around 40-50 Uncirculated examples are known with most of these grading Mint State-60 to Mint State-62. A few really spectacular 1799 dollars are known including a piece which has been graded MS-66(!) by PCGS.

The quality of strike for 1799 dollars is fairly similar to that described above for 1798's. When selecting a type coin, the collector should seek a piece with nice original color, good centering and a good overall balance between the obverse and the reverse.

Some fairly deceptive counterfeit 1799 dollars are known. These pieces first surfaced about a decade ago. One of the tell-tale signs which all of these counterfeits show is a small raised dot on the left side of the R in LIBERTY which appears to break this letter. Edges are sharp, with a narrow blank area outside the dentils. Most of these coins, apparently better than EF, have dull, lifeless surfaces which make them appear as if they have been heavily cleaned at one time.

In all, there are twenty-two die varieties known to exist for 1799 dollars. None of these are extremely rare but, then again, very few people seem to care.

The 1800 is another fairly common date by the standards of Bust dollars. Of the 220,920 pieces originally struck, it is estimated that 4,500-5,000 survive today.

Most 1800 dollars are found in low grades. The typical piece will grade about Good-Fine. Extremely Fine pieces can be located with some amount of patience. In About Uncirculated, this date becomes scarce. Fully Mint State pieces are very rare with probably no more than 15-20 currently known to exist.

The quality of strike for this date tends to be fairly good although it is hard to locate pieces which are very sharp at their centers. For some reason, many 1800 dollars are found on slightly oversized planchets and, as a result, they will show full milling on both the obverse and on the reverse.

Unlike the 1798 and the 1799, this date does not include many interesting and/or spectacular varieties. The best known variety is the so-called "AMERICAI." A raised die flaw which looks like an "I" can be seen after the second A in America. This issue is quite common in lower grades and becomes rare only in Mint State. Nearly all known examples are very weakly impressed at the centers.

Beginning in 1801, mintage figures for silver dollars dropped considerably from previous years. Because of this fact, fewer dies were used and fewer varieties exist.

While the reported mintage for 1801 was 54,454, it is believed that this figure includes a number of pieces dated 1800. It is difficult to estimate the number of surviving pieces but when examining the availability of this date, one fact immediately arises: it is much scarcer than generally believed.

Most 1801 dollars grade from About Good to Fine. This date becomes fairly scarce in Very Fine and is legitimately tough in Extremely Fine. Full About Uncirculated examples are rare and Mint state pieces are extremely rare. In Uncirculated, this date rivals the 1796 and the 1797 and is easily the rarest date bearing the Heraldic Eagle reverse. The only Mint State piece I have seen was the Amon Carter: 232 coin which was Prooflike and very choice.

The 1801 dollars tend to come weakly struck at the center of the obverse. Even high grade coins will lack strong hair detail, especially on the strands near Liberty's forehead. The reverse is usually better impressed although certain coins will show die rust and subsequent weakness on the feathers nearest the shield.

For some reason, this date tends to show heavy marks on the planchet and many pieces show post-striking damage. Rim bumps are also common. A general rule of thumb for this issue is that if you are offered a truly choice example, you should be prepared to pay a strong price for it.

In 1802, the reported mintage for silver dollars was 41,650 coins. This date is not as scarce as its low mintage would indicate, because (by die state evidence) some pieces dated 1802 were struck in 1803 and 1804.

Varieties are known with a normal date and a 1802/1 overdate. The normal date variety with broken foot of T in LIBERTY is the more common of the two, especially in higher grades. In fact, the normal date is one of the easier Heraldic Eagle dollars to obtain in higher grades. The overdate is not hard to locate in grades up to and including Very Fine but it becomes rare in About Uncirculated and very rare in Mint State.

Many 1802/1 dollars show significant weakness of strike at the centers; particularly so on the obverse. The normal date coins, on the other hand, tend to come with a better overall quality of strike. The luster on many normal date 1802 dollars is excellent and this makes these coins very popular with type collectors.

The exact mintage figure for 1803 silver dollars is unclear, as of the 85,364 pieces which were reportedly struck, at least 19,570 were delivered in 1804 and some of them were dated 1802. Varieties exist with a small 3 and a large 3 in the date, the former scarcer.

While not as rare in high grades as the 1801, this date is another significantly overlooked issue. Low grade pieces are common but at the choice Extremely Fine level, this issue becomes scarce. About Uncirculated pieces are rare and fully Mint State pieces are very rare. The finest example of this date which I can recall seeing is the NGC MS-63 which was sold as Lot 3879 in Superior's May, 1990 Sale. This coin sold for $35,200 which proves that its rarity in Mint State is not totally unrecognized.

The 1803 dollars invariably are found with soft strikes and, as a result, they can be difficult to grade. Many are quite flat at the center of the obverse while others show an overall "mush" impression on the reverse. The reason for this is that the reverse die used to strike the most common variety had been used in 1801 and again in 1802. By 1803, it was showing noticeable wear and this can usually be seen by strong metal flow near the edges.

Production of silver dollars came to a halt in 1804 and this denomination would not be resurrected until 1836. Demand for silver dollars had become very limited and the production of such coins had become increasingly expensive. Simply put, while the silver dollar has always been regarded as the most prestigious of all silver denominations, it has never been a practical one.

However, 1803 was not the last date which would appear on a silver dollar bearing the Draped Bust Heraldic Eagle reverse design. The 1804 dollar, one of the most famous of all American coins, would be struck in 1834 (and again in the late 1850's). A more complete history of this issue can be found in the chapters entitled "The 1804 Dollar," by Kenneth E. Bressett; and "The King of Siam Proof Set," by Lawrence Goldberg.

Collecting Bust Dollars

On page 428 of his *Encyclopedia of United States Coins*, Walter Breen makes the following comment: "Only in recent years have early silver dollars begun to attract collector attention as intense as the smaller denominations despite the shortcomings of available reference books. Were some future researcher to produce a book on the series in a class with Sheldon ("Penny Whimsy") on 1793-1814 cents, doubtless early dollars would eventually rival the cents' popularity."

The first published reference on early dollars was John Haseltine's *Type Table Catalogue*. Haseltine was a coin dealer from Philadelphia who held a number of important auction sales during the 1870s and the 1880s. His sale of November 28, 1881 featured in-depth variety collections of Bust quarters, Bust halves and Bust dollars. The collections themselves (and probably the actual cataloging) were the work of J. Colvin Randall, a leading numismatist of the era. The Haseltine work contained some important errors and omissions but it served as an important reference work well into the 20th century.

In 1950, Haseltine's work was replaced by Milfer H. Bolender's *United States Early Silver Dollars From 1794 to 1803*. Bolender, a resident of Illinois, was a coin dealer active in the 1920-1950 era. He was best known for his auctions and conducted 197 sales. During his long career, he became on expert on early dollars and in 1950 he published the culmination of four decades of research.

Bolender's work was a huge improvement over the Haseltine "Type Table." Bolender formulated levels of rarity for each variety, recorded (or deleted from Haseltine's work) important diagnostic criteria, created identification charts for the varieties of 1795, 1798, 1799 and 1800 and generally made attribution easier.

However, there were some inherent flaws in the Bolender work. His arrangement of die varieties was designed to correspond with the long-outdated Haseltine work. A more logical system would have listed each year's varieties in an emission sequence, as Sheldon later did for the early cents. A number of dubious varieties were retained and included in the new numbering system. The attribution criteria for certain dates (especially 1798 and 1799) were ambiguous and often proved frustrating to the new collector.

While the Bolender book has been reprinted (and slightly revised) a number of times since 1950, Breen is correct in his assertion that it needs to be replaced. A number of new varieties have been discovered since 1950 and many of Bolender's rarity levels are highly inaccurate. This situation could change soon, however, as it is rumored that a totally new book on early dollars is in the works.

There are many ways to collect Bust dollars. All of these methods can provide the newcomer to this area with considerable pleasure and will prove to be challenging as well.

1. By Date: The date collector seeks to purchase an example of each dollar struck between 1794 and 1803. The typical set will grade from Very Fine to About Uncirculated with the 1794 usually in a lower grade. A date set does not differentiate between major varieties. In a set like this, the collector will seek to obtain a single 1795 as opposed to both the Flowing Hair and the Draped Bust types.

2. By Red Book Variety: The current edition of *A Guide Book of United States Coins* lists a total of 37 major varieties of Bust dollars. While some of these varieties are admittedly esoteric, others are very significant. None of these are impossible to locate (at least in lower grades) and a set such as this could be completed, with patience, over the course of a year or two. It should be stressed that the collector should be patient and not buy problem coins merely to fill a gap. It makes sense to buy evenly matched, problem-free and original coins in a grade range in which the collector feels comfortable. A famous quote is "A problem coin will always be a problem coin."

3. By Grade: The collector who subscribes to the "gem or nothing" theory can forget Bust dollars. Most dates are all but nonexistent in Mint State-60; let alone Mint State-64 or 65. After some preliminary research, the collector should be able

to devise a “grade tolerance” level for each date. By this, I mean he should be able to determine in which grades each date becomes unobtainable. For example, the grade tolerance level for an 1801 dollar is About Uncirculated-50. In this grade, or below it, the 1801 dollar is an obtainable coin. Above this grade, it is essentially impossible to locate. Thus, do not set unrealistic goals for yourself in creating a high-grade set of early dollars.

4. By Die Variety: There are 115 different die varieties of Bust dollars. To the best of my knowledge, no one has ever completed this set, although I know of at least two collectors who are only lacking three or four varieties. In my opinion, Bust dollars should be much more actively collected by die variety. Whether or not the lack of a good reference to blame is a subjective point. The real reason is more likely the cost. Excluding the 1794, a nice Bust dollar should cost in the area of $1000-$2000. Assuming that every rare variety could be purchased at little or no premium, a die variety set of low to middle grade coins would still represent an investment in the area of $115,000 to $230,000. Therefore, the best solution is to focus on a specific year. I feel that the 1795, 1798 and 1799 issues are the most interesting to collect by die variety. The 1795’s are the hardest to obtain and the most expensive; the 1798’s and the 1799’s contain more coins but no great rarities. Die variety collecting is not for everyone but, at least in the case of Bust dollars, I feel that it offers fertile ground for the collector.

Some Buying Tips

For the collector or investor who is purchasing Bust dollars, there are a few pointers which I can offer.

1. If you have absolutely no clue how to grade Bust dollars, start out with PCGS or NGC graded examples. But learn how to grade these coins yourself. I don’t think it is essential to buy lower grade examples which have been slabbed. I wouldn’t tell an investor to purchase a “raw” Mint State-66 Morgan Dollar, but I don’t think rampant overgrading of raw coins is as much a problem with Bust dollars as it is with super-grade investment pieces.

2. Learn to spot problem coins. As I mentioned above, a good number of Bust dollars have been plugged, tooled, burnished, etc. You should avoid these coins at any cost. You should be able to avoid this problem if you buy an independent third-party graded coin. These services don’t intentionally grade coins that have been plugged, tooled, burnished, etc.

3. Avoid coins which have been harshly cleaned, over-dipped or artificially toned. A coin with a natural gun metal grey appearance is far preferable to a bright, unnatural piece. Whenever possible, try to purchase pieces with pleasing toning. The majority of artificially toned Bust dollars look terrible. But before you buy coins, again look at PCGS and NGC graded examples. Learn what real color looks like and keep a picture of it in your mind when you look at other coins.

4. Find a dealer who either specializes in Bust dollars or who understands the series. While there are no “Bust Dollars-R-Us” firms, there are a number of dealers who do handle enough nice pieces to (a) have a selection of pieces available and (b) know how to price and grade the series.

5. Follow auction prices for Bust dollars as this is probably the best way to figure out what these coins are worth; especially rare varieties. I would particularly recommend subscribing to Superior, Stack’s, and Bowers and Merena’s Sales. These firms handle a number of coins, they know how to grade them and they know how to properly attribute them.

6. Join the John Reich Collector’s Society. This is a club which is dedicated to the study of Bust coinage of all denominations. The club publishes an excellent journal a few times a year. You can meet other collectors of Bust dollars though the JRCS, read interesting articles and attend their annual meeting which is held at the American Numismatic Association.

AVAILABILITY OF BUST DOLLARS

DATE/TYPE	GRADE G-VF	XF	AU	UNC
1794	R	RR	RR/RRR	RRR
1795 Flowing Hair	C	S	VSA	R/VR
1795 Draped Bust	C	C	S	R
1796 (all kinds)	C	S	RR	RRR
1797 (all kinds)	S	R	RR	RRR
1798 Sm. Eagle	S	R	R/RR	RRR
1798 Lg. Eagle	C	C	S	RR
1799/8	S	S/R	R	RR
1799	C	C	S	R
1800	C	C	S	RR
1801	C	S	R	RRR
1802/1	C	S/R	R	RR
1802	C	C	S	R
1803	C	C	S	RR

Key:

C = Common	R = Rare
S = Scarce	RR = Very Rare
VS =Very Scarce	RRR = Extremely Rare

Conclusion

I could go on and on about why I think Bust dollars are better than other types of dollars. I don’t think this is the appropriate place to do so. But, I hope, I have been able to share my enthusiasm for these beautiful, historic and fascinating coins.

Obverse

Reverse

1795 Flowing Hair

Obverse

Reverse

1795 Draped Bust

Obverse

Reverse

1797, 9 Stars Left, 7 Stars Right — Small Letters

Obverse

Reverse

1797, 10 Stars Left, 6 Stars Right

Obverse

Reverse

1798 Small Eagle

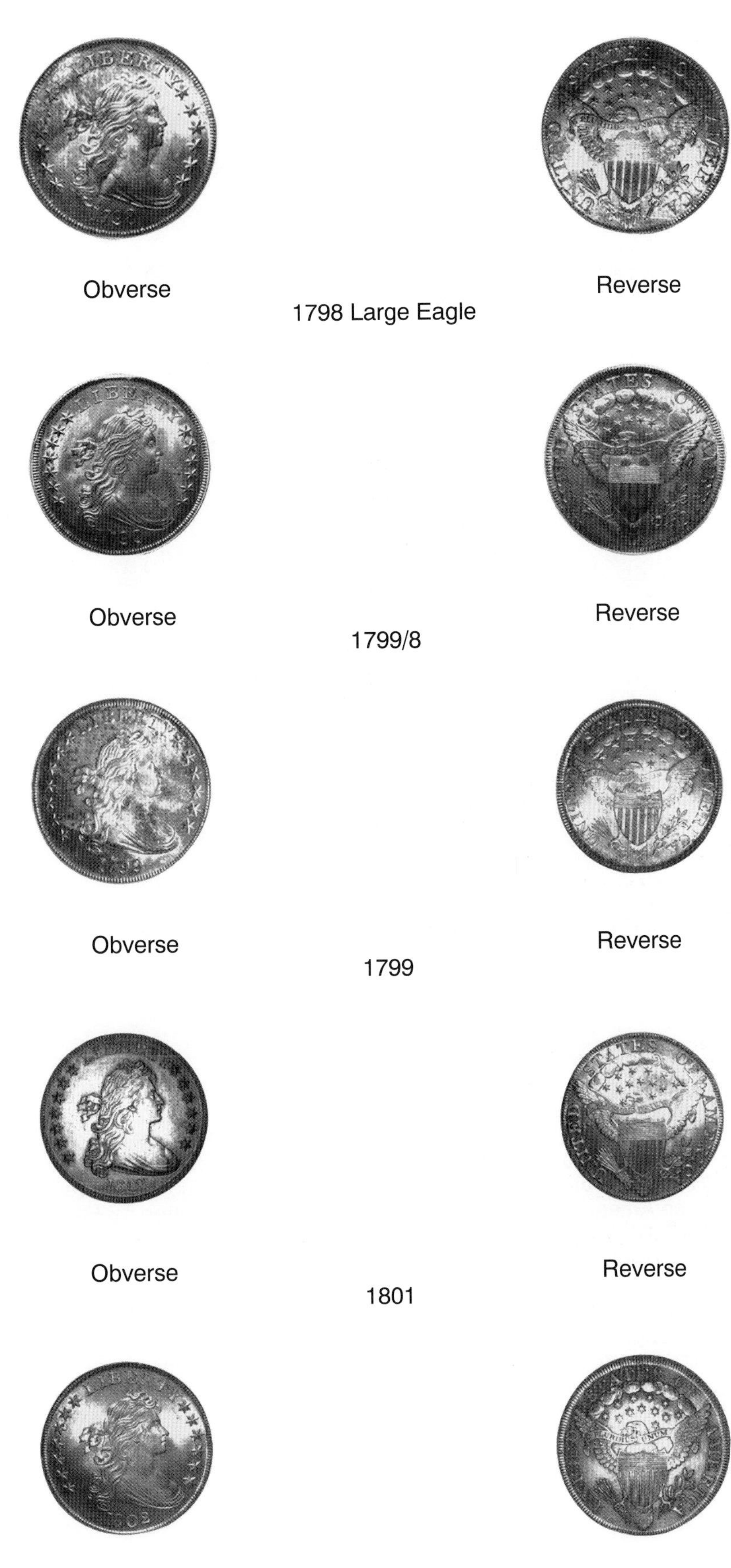

Obverse

Reverse

1798 Large Eagle

Obverse

Reverse

1799/8

Obverse

Reverse

1799

Obverse

Reverse

1801

Obverse

Reverse

1802

The author greatly acknowledges the assistance of Superior Galleries in assembling the photographs in this chapter. Special thanks go to Su-Z Kono for her patience and help.

***

Kenneth E. Bressett, NLG

Ken Bressett's numismatic experience is extensive. For over 25 years he has served as coordinating editor of *A Guide Book of United States Coins*, and has authored numerous coin collectors' reference books, among them *Let's Collect Coins*, *Buying and Selling United States Coins*, *The Guide Book of English Coins*, and *Basics of Coin Grading For U.S. Coins*.

In addition, Mr. Bressett has written many articles for the coin collecting hobby, and served as Managing Editor of the monthly "*Whitman Numismatic Journal*" from 1964 through 1968. He has also done extensive research and writing on Early American coins, and serves on the American Numismatic Society standing committee for Far Eastern Coinage.

In 1977 Ken coordinated the editing and publishing of the American Numismatic Association's Grading Standards book, and is a consultant and instructor for the ANA grading and certification service, after serving as Director of ANACS for two years.

He is a life member of the American Numismatic Association, and a Fellow of the American Numismatic Society, and the Royal Numismatic Society of England. In 1966 he was appointed to serve on the United States Assay Commission by President Lyndon Johnson. While Director of Education for the ANA, Ken was responsible for implementing various seminars and programs including the publication of numismatic information in all forms from books to TV and video programs. One such project took him to the bottom of the ocean in search of the sunken treasure ship Atocha.

Ken Bressett currently serves on the Board of Governors of the American Numismatic Association.

CHAPTER 58

The 1804 Dollar

by Kenneth E. Bressett, NLG

The 1804 Dollar
(Coin courtesy of Leon Hendrickson and George Weingart)
(Photo provided by Krause Publications)

Everyone seems to agree that the 1804 Dollar is one of the most famous and valuable coins of the world. What they do not agree upon is just why it is so valuable, or how this piece came to be held in such high regard that it has been called "The King of Coins." Its history has been so shrouded in mystery and so questionable, that it is a wonder why any collector would ever seriously want to own one. Still, even with its bastard birth it is today one of the most desirable and highest priced of all United States coins.

The origin of the United States 1804 silver dollar has all the makings of an exciting mystery novel. Official Mint records show that 19,570 dollars were struck in the year 1804. To date, however only a handful have survived. Why? Many stories have been propagated over the years as to its fate: Barbary coast pirates, ransoms, even sunken ships. But the real story behind this rarity is even more colorful than the myths.

Were any of the known 1804 Dollars actually made that year? Absolutely not. They could not have been because the Mint machinery used to make these coins was not installed in the Mint until nearly 30 years later. All of the dollars made in 1804 must have been dated 1803 or earlier, a practice that was not unusual at that time to save on the expenses of making new dies. The dollars dated 1804 that are now considered so rare and valuable were made much later as we shall see, and in at least two batches at different times.

My fascination with the 1804 Dollar started over 50 years ago when I chanced upon a copy of a promotional piece sent out by Texas coin dealer B. Max Mehl to stimulate sales of his *Star Rare Coin Encyclopedia*. He was selling the 200 page book for $1.00, and it was advertised heavily throughout the country. The book was actually a good bargain at a time when there was little other available information about the value of rare coins. It was essentially a buying list for Mehl, and his prices seemed ridiculous by today's standards, but there was little else for a kid to read. He made every coin seem like something glamorous, and the 1804 Dollar, together with his pet, the 1913 Liberty Head nickel, were jewels in the numismatic crown.

I clearly remember that he offered to pay $1,250 for any specimen of the 1804 Dollar. That was an incredible amount of money in 1940, and seemingly more than any coin could be worth. He mentioned stories of how one of these dollars had recently been found in circulation by a ticket seller at a theater, and how even I could possibly do the same. Wow! Those were exciting times. I wanted to learn more about this incredible coin, and just why it was so valuable. Several years were to pass before I took up the pursuit, but I had vowed to find out more about what did indeed seem to be the king of coins, as Mehl had named it.

In 1946 the first edition of R.S. Yeoman's *Guide Book of United States Coins* was published, and I managed to get a copy the following year. It contained a full page and a half of pictures and information about the 1804 Dollar, and renewed my interest in the subject. Here for the first time in my limited experience was a logical study of the rarity and origin of this strange coin. The story presented a brief overview of both sides of the controversy surrounding the possible origin of the coin, and ended with this challenge: "Unless some new evidence is uncovered, the mystery of its existence or disappearance will always be a matter of speculation for the numismatic fraternity."

In the early 1950's Walter Breen had begun researching and writing on many topics. In his monograph *Proof Coins Struck by the United States Mint 1817-1921*, he mentioned the 1804 proof pieces and shed new light on the subject by describing the specimens known to him. This information was further expanded in his later works, and inspired me to compile a file of every scrap of data that I could locate. About that time I started reading the back issues of *The Numismatist* and found a great many both real and imaginary accounts of the origin and existence of the 1804 Dollars.

During that same time I was doing research in Boston at the Massachusetts Historical Society and one of the first coins that I asked to see was their specimen of the 1804 Dollar. This coin had been given to them in 1905 by William Sumner Appleton, and held in storage for many years. Few people even knew that they still had it, and they were somewhat reluctant to get the coin out for me to examine. When they found that my interest was more than mere curiosity, one of the curators did manage to find the piece and set up an appointment so that I could see and photograph it.

That trip to Boston was an exciting one for me, for it was the first time that I had ever examined an actual specimen of the legendary coin. I sat in the curator's office almost in a sweat waiting for him to get the coin from wherever it was stored. At length he returned to the desk where he had stationed me to set up my photographic equipment. He sat on the opposite side of the desk and slid the coin out of an old letter envelope. Then he said "Here it is — catch." At that he placed the coin on his forefinger and with his thumb flipped the coin through the air in my direction. I was dumbfounded, and how I ever caught it I will never know, but somehow I did so with the best numismatic care; and then turned white.

"Do you know how valuable this is?" I asked. At that time it had an estimated worth of around $10,000, or about two years salary for most people. The curator responded with something that seemed to indicate that it was just another coin as far as he was concerned, and a real bother to locate every time someone wanted to see it. A record with the coin indicated that the last time anyone had looked at it was about twenty years earlier. Years later, in 1970, this coin was offered for sale in a Stack's auction where it was sold to a Chicago collector for $77,500. In January 1974 it was sold by private treaty through Stacks for $150,000 to Reed Hawn who presently owns the piece.

Prior to 1960 I also had a chance to see both of the pieces in the Smithsonian Institution. The "original" specimen had been a part of the collection since shortly after it was made in November 1834. The unique Type II piece with plain edge had been added to the collection after it was confiscated from the employee who made it in 1858 or 1859. It was a pleasure to examine these coins because of their pristine condition. I was not allowed to photograph either of the pieces at that time, but was supplied with glossy black and white prints at a later date.

By 1960 I was convinced that a solution to the mystery of the origin of the 1804 Dollars could be found by studying the coins. My research had progressed far enough to lead me to collaborate with Walter Breen and Eric P. Newman who by then were both involved in the quest. We agreed to work together on the age old problem and to share each other's information in an attempt to determine the origin of these dollars, and to set to rest the rumors of them possibly having been made in 1804. The result of this study was published in 1962 in our book entitled *The Fantastic 1804 Dollar*.

During the period of research for the book, I found the opportunity to locate and examine most of the other known specimens of the legendary coin. One was rumored to be in Chicago. The piece had been sold by dealer R. Green in 1945. I was fortunate to have known Ruth Green for many years, and asked her one day if she would introduce me to the owner so that I could see the coin. Within a few months arrangements were made for me to visit the current owner who was the son of the man who had originally purchased the coin. The meeting was one of the most enjoyable and fortunate ever for me, and the beginning of a lasting friendship with years of sharing information and knowledge between the two of us.

In researching this coin, which at that time had been known as the Brand specimen, I discovered that it could be traced back to an early Chapman sale where it was reported to have come from the Walters collection in England before 1917. A thorough search of all catalogs of that period failed to locate any such collection, but did turn up the sale of the C. A. Watters collection. He did indeed have a specimen of the 1804 Dollar that he supposedly bought from a pawn broker in Liverpool. In looking through this auction catalog I was struck by the fact that it contained nearly a full proof set of 1834 silver coins. That would be unusual in any context, but in conjunction with a specimen of the 1804 Dollar was enough to convince me that these coins could have come from one of the original proof sets that were given to foreign diplomats in 1835-6. I subsequently concluded that it was most likely from the set given to the Imaum of Muscat.

The last time that I saw this incredible coin, which I think is the finest condition piece of all known specimens, was in the owner's home. He had it there for me to see as a special treat during my visit. When we left for dinner he put it on top of a china cabinet for "safe keeping." Weeks later he asked if I remembered where he had hidden it as he wanted to put it back in the bank. Only he knows where it is today!

I had a chance to see the Stickney specimen sometime in the early 1960's at two of the several displays of the Louis Eliasberg collection. The coins were under glass, and a bit difficult to see, but they were available for close inspection thanks to the lovely display panels that he had constructed. On my second viewing I attempted to get photographs of the key coins in the display. That of course was a real challenge because the collection consisted of one of each date and mint of every coin in the entire United States series! My challenge here was to build a camera system small enough to be carried into the display area and shoot the pieces quickly with available light. Nothing like that had ever been done before, and although I was one of the very few early coin photographers using any kind of portable equipment, I was not sure that it could be done.

Through a piece of luck I had earlier found a used German 35mm camera that had been liberated from the Luftwaffe during the war. It took 55 small-sized frames on a standard roll of 35mm film, and it had a very fast lens for those times. I had rigged it up with a special supplemental magnifying lens, and a focusing device in the form of a post that kept the camera a fixed distance from the subject. Using this set-up, I only had to place a coin in front of the camera and shoot with available light. I felt sure that I could get some kind of pictures of the Eliasberg coins if they would just let me try.

After examining and recording everything that was on display I started to photograph the most special coins. Then in came Doris Eberding, Eliasberg's secretary who pretty much cared for the entire collection. She asked what I was doing, and I explained. Then with a laugh she said that it was impossible but she certainly did not care if I tried. She then helped me to arrange some of the material for better viewing and work. I shot many pictures that day, and most of them came out very well considering the conditions. I was particularly pleased with the quality of the 1804 Dollar and 1894-S dime shots. The silver portion of the Eliasberg collection, along with the 1804 Dollar, is still intact and in the possession of the family since the death of Louis in 1976.

I never did get to see the Cohen specimen of the Type I 1804 Dollar. This is the piece that is in worn condition and owned by the Lammot duPont family. I suspect that the wear on this coin is artificial and put there to make it look like it came from circulation. At any rate it was stolen in a home robbery in 1967 and has never been recovered. Since that time I have examined countless pieces that were reported to be this missing specimen, but the truth is that it has never turned up and perhaps has even been destroyed by now. The duPont collection had a second specimen of the dollar, one of the Class III pieces. I'll tell more about that coin when I get to the "restrike" pieces.

The Parmelee specimen of the first striking of these coins, has been on display off and on in Omaha for many years. It was bequeathed by Byron Reed to the city in 1891, but placed in a bank vault for safekeeping in 1966 after several burglary attempts. It is now in the Omaha History Museum.

I first saw the original Dexter specimen of the '04 dollar at a meeting of the New York Numismatic Club when it was owned by Harold Bareford. He was very proud of his coin and always happy to share it with interested numismatists. As work on the book progressed, and everyone became convinced that none of the 1804 Dollars were ever minted in that year, I started to share some of the information with Harold. He never did accept that fact that his piece was anything but a genuine coin made at the Mint in 1804, and at one point vowed to sue me for damages if I published such a heresy about his coin.

The piece was sold by Stacks in 1981 for $280,000 to Rarcoa, and in 1985 was purchased in partnership by Leon Hendrickson and George Weingart for a reported $500,000. It was only after that time that the small letter D was discovered punched on the second cloud from the right on the reverse. I had never noticed it before, although photos show that it was there. I have never figured out what the letter stands for, but it seems safe to assume that it was probably Dexter's secret mark of identification. [Others have conjectured that it was Dunham's D.]

When I was employed by Premier Investments of Minneapolis in 1988 we had a client who wanted to purchase a specimen of the 1804 Dollar. The Dexter specimen was quietly being shown for sale, and we arranged to borrow it for presentation to the customer. The client was slow in making up his mind about the coin. He had his eye on two or three other pieces and did not know if he wanted one super rare coin, or the other items. While he vacillated, we were scheduled to attend a couple of major investment shows, and decided to bring the dollar with us as a showcase attention getter. To insure the safety of the piece, and get additional attention, an armed guard accompanied the coin at all times. The excitement that it generated was phenomenal, and I ended up "baby sitting" the coin on several occasions. We offered the piece for sale at $750,000, but with no takers, and the client eventually decided on the other coins. When this specimen finally did sell in 1989 it went at auction for $990,000.

The eighth specimen of the 1804 Dollar did not turn up until 1962. Our book was actually on press when David Spink of London made his historic announcement at the ANA Convention, and the world first learned of the King of Siam set. It was the final piece in the puzzle. Without it our book would have been outdated the moment it hit the market. I rushed to the nearest telephone and called the publisher with my first and only request for anyone to "Stop the Press!"

Over the next few weeks Newman and I worked feverishly on chapters VIII and IX, "The Diplomatic Gift Background" and "The Origin of 1804 'Originals'." The Siam set was a wonderful addition to our book, and proved for once and for all when and why these coins had originally been minted. The most recent sale of the King of Siam set was in 1990 when it was auctioned for $2.9 million (plus the 10% buyers fee). I have examined the set both before and after it was plastic slabbed, and must say that it was far more exciting and attractive in its original plush case. Regardless of its origin, this is probably the most desirable and interesting of all United States coin sets, and will probably remain the most valuable.

1804 Silver Dollar — PCGS graded Pr-65
(Courtesy of Superior Galleries)

We now know that the Class III pieces were made in the Mint somewhere around 1858. They were made at a time when there was a surge of interest in coin collecting and rare coins like the 1804 Dollar were bringing record prices. The temptation for Mint officials to restrike a few additional specimens was just too great for them to resist. The original obverse die was still around at that time, but apparently the reverse could not be located. A second die was prepared and the restrikes made on whatever available planchets could be found. At least one was even struck over a foreign crown size coin.

Some, if not all of these pieces, had a plain edge. This was an oversight that led to their quick detection by potential buyers, and forced the perpetrators to take them off the market. They were all supposedly returned to the Mint, with only one being preserved in the National Collection. Most likely what really happened was that they were taken back to the Mint to see what could be done about applying a lettered edge to the pieces. In time the problem was solved, and the edges decorated with crude lettering. The pieces were then held until about 1869 when they were offered to collectors one at a time through a few dealers and auction houses.

The first of the "restrike" coins that I had a chance to examine was the Rosenthal specimen that had been owned at one time by Farran Zerbe. This was yet another one of the dollars that has been artificially worn to make it appear to be an authentic coin. It was supposedly received in change by a freed slave who gave it to his son who held it for over 40 years. The entire story of course was a fabrication, but offered some excuse for its existence when it surfaced in 1893.

This specimen was sold to the Chase National Bank along with the rest of the Zerbe collection in 1929, and was on public display there for many years. When the Chase Manhattan Museum of Moneys of the World was disbanded in 1978, a 10-year loan gift arrangement was made for transferring the Rosenthal dollar from the Chase to the collection of the American Numismatic Society in New York City. I last saw this piece in the 1986 ANS exhibit at the "America's Silver Coinage" conference, where I had a chance to examine it a little closer and determine that it is in Extremely Fine condition rather than only Very Fine, as I previously believed.

The Class III (restrikes) owned by Edwin Hydeman, Samuel Wolfson, and Amon Carter were rarely displayed during the time that they owned them. I think that I saw each of them on one or more occasions at coin shows of the period, but they were never readily available for examination. Amon, Jr. was always happy to share his treasures with students, and at one time allowed Eric P. Newman and me to borrow his Proof dollars of 1801, 1802 and 1803 for study in connection with the 1804 story, but I do not recall seeing all four pieces together at the same time. The entire group is now owned by an unidentified West Texas collector.

T. H. Garrett acquired the Berg specimen in 1883, and this piece eventually went into the collection of the Johns Hopkins University in Baltimore, Maryland. The story that it had originally come from auction in 1875 through Messrs. Koch & Co. of Vienna was only partially true. It is doubtful that the piece ever traveled to Europe for the sale, but in fact probably remained in Philadelphia with dealer John W. Haseltine who both consigned, and purchased the piece, to create a legitimate sounding origin for the coin.

Many collectors, including myself, had a chance to see this specimen while it was on display at the University. It is a lovely coin and created great excitement when it was offered for sale in the 1980 Bowers' auction of the great Garrett collection. The piece had changed hands several times since then, and in the last sale of record it went to Martin Paul of the Rarities Group, Inc. Subsequently it was reportedly sold to a person identified only as Mrs. Sommer.

The Davis specimen of the 1804 Dollar that was owned by Samual Wolfson has been one of the most troublesome coins to pedigree. Past owners have been rather secretive, and the piece has not been publicized since its last sale in 1971. It originally entered the market around 1877 through dealer J. W. Haseltine who was responsible for the first appearance of most of the restrike pieces. At one time it was owned by Ben Koenig (a New York collector who had investments in Alaska) and known simply as the "Fairbanks Collection" coin. In the 1971 Stack's auction it was reportedly sold to James McConnell who still owns the piece.

Willis H. duPont acquired his two 1804 Dollars from the old family collection. The Linderman Class II 1804 specimen was stolen along with his Cohen Class I dollar when a major portion of the duPont numismatic collection was taken at gunpoint by five masked men during the 1967 robbery of his Coconut Grove, Florida residence. The total loss was somewhere around $1,500,000, principally in rare coins including the two 1804 Dollars. During the period up to 1974, approximately 34 of the coins were recovered through aggressive action by investigators and payment of ransom and rewards. One of the recovered pieces was a 1787 Brasher gold doubloon.

In 1980 and 1981, rumors of the existence of a mysterious specimen of the 1804 Dollar began to surface, and at least some of the fragmentary evidence seemed to point to the possibility of it being one of the missing duPont coins. On at least two occasions I was asked to supply information about the Linderman specimen, and thus became aware that something was in the wind. Checking out "new" or stolen 1804 Dollars was nothing new for me. I had worked with the FBI and others on several occasions, and learned to expect that the suspected coins would turn out to be modern cast fakes. In the late 1960's and 1970's there were thousands of cast dollars of 1803 and 1804, as well as Trade Dollars, that servicemen picked up in the Orient for prices ranging from $12 to $50. By the time they got to this country many were attempted to be passed off as genuine and someone was always trying to find out what their new treasure was worth.

On one such occasion, I was called by a "businessman" in Chicago who was sure that he had a genuine coin and wanted it valued and authenticated. I said that I would be happy to take a look at the piece if he would get it to me, and we set up a date for him to bring the coin to Racine. The day came for our appointment and he arrived right on time. With him were two of the biggest bruisers that I had ever seen outside of a wrestling ring. He introduced them simply as his lawyers, but I remained a bit suspicious of their size and pin-striped suits. I was sure that I could see bulges that looked strangely like guns in their jackets.

In preparing for the meeting I had dug out photographs of a genuine 1804 Dollar, and similar enlargements of one of the common cast pieces that has a die flaw after the final A in AMERICA. I had a hunch that this piece would be such a fake, and wanted to be able to show graphically what a genuine coin should look like. The visitor stood in front of my desk flanked by his "lawyers", took the 1804 out of his vest pocket, and placed it on the velvet pad I had provided. I did not even have to turn the piece over to know what it was, but I felt obliged to scrutinize the thing so that they would think that I was giving it full consideration.

When I finished my "examination" I told them with a very serious voice that this was a modern reproduction and worth nothing. I also pointed to the photographs and showed them the obvious differences. The businessman then said, "are you sure that it is not worth $50,000 or more?" I assured him that it was not. That was the full extent of his visit and conversation. He threw a $100 bill on my desk, turned and hurried out of the room. I never saw or heard from any of them again, but I watched the Chicago papers for several weeks after that to see if anyone found in the river might have put up a rare coin for collateral on some kind of a loan.

Something quite different than this happened with the Class III Linderman specimen that had been stolen from duPont. In that case the coin really did pass through the underworld of crooks and thieves, and by 1981 someone wanted to sell it and cash in on its value. When it was found that all rare coins of that caliber had to be authenticated and "papered", they brought it to Colorado Springs for examination by ANACS. The piece was immediately recognized as the missing Linderman specimen by authenticator Tom DeLorey who convinced the agent that he would have to retain the coin for a short time for review and study. When the man returned to pick up the piece, the FBI was waiting to arrest him and recover the coin.

I was called in to testify at the grand jury investigation of the matter and got to see the coin on several occasions. I had little trouble convincing the attorneys that it was highly improbable that this man's father had received this coin in change. It was his only defense, but still there was no way to prove that he actually stole the coin. The jury, after 16 hours of deliberation, found the man not guilty of stealing the coin, but the rightful ownership of the piece was established and it was returned to duPont. During the hearings I spent several hours visiting with Mr. duPont and getting to know him. He did not have any interest in getting the coin back after all of the trouble that it had cost him, and later he agreed that it would be lent to the American Numismatic Association for safekeeping, study and display. I have had a chance to examine the piece on several occasions, and although it is not always on public display, it is still there for everyone to study.

The Idler specimen, once owned by Edwin Hydeman, is best known as the Jerry Buss coin. He purchased it in 1979 after it had passed through the hands of several dealers. When his collection was sold at auction by Superior Galleries in 1985, the coin realized $308,000, and was purchased by Aubrey Bebee of Omaha. I never had a chance to examine this coin carefully before it was owned by Buss and Bebee. It had been kept as a private investment most of the time before that, and rarely shown. The illustration of the coin that I used in *The Fantastic 1804 Dollar* book was actually that of the Adams specimen from Mehl's 1950 Golden Jubilee Sale, rather than the Idler coin. The correct photograph did appear in the Atwater and Neil sales as well as all subsequent sales, but in this case it is the only one in the *1804* book that was not of the actual coin under discussion.

Before the Idler dollar was owned by H. O. Granberg of Oshkosh, Wisconsin from 1908 until about 1940, he had bought another specimen which he thought was genuine. In this case it was nothing more than an altered 1800 dollar with the date changed to 1804, but Granberg believed that it was original in every way. It had supposedly been found on the body of a sailor who was found washed up on the beach in Chesapeake Bay. It was tested by the Mint in 1906 and they could not find anything wrong with it (but they also said that many other 1804 Dollars were genuine). Granberg later purchased the Idler piece for his collection, but he went to his grave believing that someone, someday would find that his first piece was genuine. Unfortunately, this altered piece remained in the family, and the heirs believed it genuine ever since. I attempted to dispel the misconception in 1989, but old beliefs die hard. The coin is actually a Bolender-1 1800 dollar with final 0 altered to 4.

The genuine Idler coin purchased by Aubrey Bebee in 1985 was loaned for display at the American Numismatic Association in 1989, and is now a special part of the ANA's outstanding exhibit which is the only one to feature two specimens of the Class III 1804 restrike.

The saga of the 1804 Dollar seems never ending. We now know that all of the so-called "original" pieces were made at the Mint in the period 1834-35, for presentation proof sets. The first specimen known to collectors was obtained from a Mint officer by Matthew Stickney on May 9, 1843. Since that time a total of eight of the Class I pieces have surfaced. The latest appearance being in the King of Siam proof set which was brought to light in 1962.

When the Mint ran out of their original supply of 1804 Dollars someone found the obverse die and proceeded to make an additional batch of at least seven more pieces to satisfy the collector market. These were produced somewhere around 1858 or 1859, and released to the trade over the next 20 years mostly through dealer John W. Haseltine. There remains no more mystery or question about when or why these coins were made. We probably will never know exactly who made them, or if there are more of these rare pieces still hidden away for future generations to discover.

Regardless of their origin, the 1804 Dollars have remained among the most desirable and valuable of all United States coins probably because of all of the legends and tales that have persisted in conjunction with them. Even now when the truth is finally known, they continue to bring higher prices than ever before. The King of Coins, was originally made for a king, and has held its royal place ever since. The King is not dead. Long Live the King!

***

CHAPTER 59

The King of Siam Proof Set

by Lawrence S. Goldberg

The world famous King of Siam Proof set was specially ordered in 1834 by President Andrew Jackson for delivery to the King of Siam (modern day Thailand). It consists of an 1804 silver dollar, 1804 gold eagle ($10), and 1834-date Proof examples of the half cent, large cent, dime, quarter, half dollar, gold quarter eagle ($2.50) and gold half eagle ($5). All were mounted at the time of issue in a tawny yellow box with purple recesses for the coins. As individual coins, each piece averages Rarity-7, meaning that between 4 and 12 examples have been traced. The illustrious 1804 silver dollar is one of 15 known. All were struck twice from highly polished dies giving them genuine Proof mirror fields. Because the recesses in the dies were *frosted* when they were prepared, the resulting coins become impressive *cameos*, their Liberty heads and raised reverse designs stand out boldly against the mirror background like jewels.

By all accounts, the King of Siam Proof set is unique. There is nothing else quite like it in numismatics. Not only does it contain *Proof* samples of America's coinage from the period, but because of the unusual background of the set, and the mystery surrounding its major coin, the 1804 dollar, it has an aura of majesty about it, of nobility. Its history — its *story* — is unrivaled from a standpoint of origin, numismatic research value, and pedigree. Collectors began unraveling its secret nearly a century ago. But their efforts seemed merely to lift back a corner of the veil which hid its past from our eyes. Finally, in the 1960s, the tale you are about to read was completed. Like a Beethoven symphony with its various movements and climax, the King of Siam's clouded history was ultimately revealed with a flourish, a climax, by the 1962 publication of Eric P. Newman's and Ken Bressett's *Fantastic 1804 Dollar*.

One can not ask for a more intriguing story than the one behind this splendid Proof Set; for as often as not, life's river of history takes the curious twists and turns which, when these turns appear, seems inconsequential to its players at the time but are of major concern to future generations. Researchers who came on the scene years after the set was struck, years after these now almost forgotten events unfolded, were met by a string of loose ends, an array of disjointed facts.

Until 30 years ago, when *The Fantastic 1804 Dollar* was published, the story's outline was sketchy. True, scholars knew long ago that the U.S. government had prepared several complete sets of coins which were used for diplomatic purposes. A November 11, 1834, letter to Samuel Moore, Director of the Mint, from John Forsyth of the State Department, authorized their striking:

Dept. of State

Washington Nov. 11, 1834

Sir:

The President has directed that a complete set of the coins of the United States be sent to the King of Siam, and another to the Sultan of Muscat. You are requested, therefore, to forward to the Department for that purpose, duplicate specimens of each kind now in use, whether of gold, silver, or copper. As boxes, in which they are to be contained, may be more neatly and appropriately made at Philadelphia, under your direction, than they could be here, you are desired to procure them, if it will not be too much trouble, and have the coins suitably arranged in them before they are sent on. They should be of a small a size as is consistent with the purpose in which they are intended; and should be of wood, covered with plain morocco. The color of one should be yellow, and the other crimson.

You are authorized to draw upon the Department for the value of the coins, and the expense of the boxes.

I have the honor to be, Sir,

Very respectfully

Your obed. serv

John Forsyth

To Dr. Samuel Moore

Director of Mint

Here is where a glaring hole appears in our story. For nowhere in Mr. Forsyth's letter was it explained what "a complete set of coins of the United States" meant. Mr. Moore, being Director of the Mint and fully aware of diplomatic protocol, took it as a given that presentation sets were just that, coins of presentation quality; that is, Proofs. This posed no problem for mint personnel since all denominations save the silver dollar and ten dollar gold Eagle were then in production.

Most likely a search was made at the Mint in an effort to find original dies used to strike 1804 silver dollars and 1804 $10 pieces (the last years these two were believed to have been officially struck). Actually, there were *never* any 1804 silver dollars minted in 1804; pieces reported for that year were from earlier-dated dies, and were probably dated 1802 or 1803. And although 1804 $10 pieces had been struck, evidently no original dies could be located either.

So, with all good intent the Mint did the logical thing; they ordered William Kneass to engrave new dies bearing the date 1804 for the dollar and $10 pieces. Thus the set could contain examples of these two important denominations.

Both sets were duly made. The one in a yellow box was given to the King of Siam as part of a diplomatic exchange, a trade treaty being the purpose of the exchange. Yellow was chosen because this was the regal color of the kingdom. The other set, that in red morocco, was handed to Said Said bin Sultan (1804-1856), Imaum of Muscat. (Muscat is on the Arabian peninsula in the middle of today's OPEC oil cartel states.)

As the years sped by, collectors forgot all about these two Kingly treasures; forgot about them, or rather, came to believe they no longer existed. Individual pieces from the Muscat set evidently surfaced in a 1917 auction in England. All but the gold coins were distributed at the time; no one today knows the fate of the Muscat gold pieces.

The King of Siam set has come down to us with two mystery empty spaces in it, two unfilled spaces, one of which was clearly intended for the 1834 half dime. The other slot poses a problem. In point of fact, scholars may never know what it contained. There are, however, two candidates which could have met the requirements. One, it may have contained a With Motto variety 1834 quarter eagle, since its opening is the right size. But some numismatists today counter this with a compelling argument; there should also have been space provided as well for the other With Motto coin made that year, the *half* eagle. Which there isn't. The other possibility is a specimen of the 1833 medalet struck by the U.S. Mint for President Andrew Jackson's second inauguration; this medalet, struck in gold, would fit the space provided. According to Stack's — New York City coin firm — who favors this second option: "It would also occupy a nearly central position within the top row of the pieces in the case, would present a portrait of our country's elected leader at the time the set was made, and would do so in the 'royal' metal without claiming royalty (since it was of a size comparable to the smallest circulating gold denomination of the period)."

Be that as it may, it wasn't until 1962 that the King of Siam Proof set reappeared in its present form, and in England of all places. Mr. David Spink, owner of Spinks, the English rare coin dealership, bought the set from an undisclosed source. How it could have travelled half way around the world from its royal home in Thailand remains veiled in fog. Perchance, during Great Britain's heyday when the sun never set on her vast Empire, an English statesman or diplomat may have come into possession of the set.

Whatever its source, this legendary set was discreetly sold to Mr. Spink in 1962. It was kept by him until 1979 when he consigned it to Lester Merkin, a long time dealer, who sold it to a prominent Eastern family now residing on the West Coast. While they owned it the set was loaned to the Smithsonian Institution (1983-1984) where it was placed on public display. Next, a few years later, it was consigned to Bowers and Merena's auction (October 1987) and, when it did not meet the reserve, it was reconsigned to Stack's of New York City in May 1989.

On October 18, 1989, Martin Paul of The Rarities Group finalized purchase negotiations for the King of Siam Proof set with Stack's for $2.25 million. Shortly thereafter it was consigned to Superior Galleries "The Father Flanagan's Boy's Town Collection" sale held May-June 1990 where it sold for $3.19 million.

How does one analyze the rarity and significance of such a set? Against what does one compare it? For such a set is unique. There are no others. There is nothing like it outside of museums, either here in America, or in Europe. In the true and proper sense it is a treasure, comparable, say, to Thomas Gainsborough's "Blue Boy" painting or an original of our Declaration of Independence. Now that its mystery shroud has been partially removed, one can see the set in a clearer light, a light of history and romance that is the very reason for the science of numismatics.

I would especially like to thank the following for their past and present contributions to this chapter.

Ken Bressett
Martin Paul
Iraj Sayah

The King of Siam Proof Set

(Courtesy of Superior Galleries, Beverly Hills, Ca.)

Finest Known 1804 Silver Dollar PCGS graded Proof 65 - Obverse
(Courtesy of Superior Galleries)

Finest Known 1804 Silver Dollar PCGS graded Proof 65 - Reverse
(Courtesy of Superior Galleries)

***

CHAPTER 60

Gobrecht Dollars

by John W. Highfill, NLG

(Coin courtesy of Gordon E. Krohn)
(Photo provided by Krause Publications)

Christian Gobrecht, one of this country's best known engravers, was born in 1785 in Hanover, Pennsylvania. During most of his adult years, he performed as a medal engraver and die cutter. He was not asked to join the staff of the United States Mint until he was fifty years old, although the quality of his work was known to mint officials. He was hired by Dr. Robert M. Patterson for the position of associate engraver (not assistant) with William Kneass, who was suffering from a stroke. In this capacity, Gobrecht further established his reputation by preparing the Gobrecht dollar from a design based on paintings and sketches by Thomas Sully and Titian Peale.

These artists were commissioned by Patterson in the summer of 1835 just after he assumed the director's position. The suspension of Silver dollar coinage was lifted in 1831. The Sully design was a seated Liberty inspired by the British coinage of the day. Titian Peale's eagle design was of an eagle in flight, perhaps modeled after Peter, the storied Philadelphia U.S. Mint pet eagle.

The design and engraving of the dollar was only part of a larger plan to produce new devices for the entire spectrum of United States coinage. The resulting seated Liberty design was utilized for decades on U.S. coinage. One of his disappointments associated with the design of the Gobrecht dollar was that his engraved reverse "onward and upward" eagle was not retained after 1839. Gobrecht became Chief Engraver of the Mint in 1840 and retained that position until 1844, the year of his death.

Stepping back in time for a moment, it had been over thirty years since the last regular issue silver dollar had been struck. The first U.S. silver dollars were produced during the period beginning in 1794 and ending in 1803. Depositors created the demand for these early dollars, but few were actually circulated and many were exported to foreign countries. Elias Boudinot was Director of the Mint in 1804 when production of silver dollars was halted. The next two mint directors, Robert Patterson (1805 - 1824) and Samuel Moore (1824 - 1835), were not able to reinstate the silver dollar as a regular issue during their terms. The famous 1804 dollars were actually struck in late 1834 to become a part of diplomatic presentation sets.

The silver dollars struck in the year 1804 were actually dated 1803; not an unusual practice in those days. Robert Patterson became the Mint Director in 1835, and continued to work towards the reinstatement of the silver dollar as a regular issue coin. (See related chapter entitled "The 1804 Dollar" by Kenneth E. Bressett and "The King of Siam Set" by Lawrence S. Goldberg).

Under Patterson in 1836, about eighteen Golbrecht dollar proof specimens were struck. Under Patterson's direction, Golbrecht's name prominently displayed in the field above the date. The name was engraved as "C.GOBRECHT F." The initial "F" stood for "fecit," meaning, in literal translation, "Christian Gobrecht made it." The word "fecit" (abbreviated "F"), was used by Italian violin makers of the 1600s and 1700s, and then later adopted by other craftsmen and artists. The public outcry against the bold signature caused it to be moved into position on the rock base underneath Liberty on the obverse. The signature was omitted entirely in the 1838 obverse design and thereafter.

Additional criticism resulted from the stars placed in the field on the reverse around the flying eagle. The 26 stars were representing the existing states (with Michigan included expecting it to be admitted to the Union). The 13 original states were represented by the 13 larger stars, while the smaller stars were for the additional states.

The original Gobrecht dollar design as engraved featured the traditional plain edge, which allowed for imprinting. As edge lettering was being phased out of most world coinage during this time, the plain edge was eventually abandoned in favor of the reeded edge which was adopted for the Liberty Seated coinage. A reeded edge may be described as very closely spaced vertical lines engraved all around the edge of a coin causing ribs or valleys between the lines. Plain edge Gobrecht dollars were produced from various dies in 1836 and 1837 with the name in the rock base under Liberty and stars on the reverse. The pieces struck in 1839 were produced with a reeded edge, no name and no stars on the reverse.

The 1836 Gobrecht obverse design as modified was accepted and its use was expanded into the design of the 1837 half dime and dime. Thirteen stars were added to the Gobrecht obverse in 1838. The quarter and half dollar with stars already added to the design changed from capped bust to the seated motif in 1838 and 1839 respectively. The reverse eagle which replaced the flying eagle was taken from the John Reich and William Kneass design. This design featured the shield chested eagle perched with head left and wings extended. The eagle's claws contain arrows and olive branches. This design was used on the quarter dollar beginning in 1815, and the half dollar beginning in 1807. The Liberty Seated dollar coinage utilizing the shield chested eagle was produced from 1840 until 1873. The flying eagle design did make somewhat of a comeback, however, and was incorporated into the Flying Eagle cent produced from 1856 through 1858 as designed by James Longacre.

During the late 1850s and 1860s, a number of Gobrecht dollar restrikes (believed to exceed the total original production of 1,900) were produced unofficially by mint personnel to meet the demand of influential persons and collectors. Walter H. Breen discovered and recorded a precise test for originals versus restrikes in his Encyclopedia (p. 434). Here is the test in his own words.

> "The quickest way to test if Gobrecht dollar of any date is an original or a restrike is die alignment. Four alignments are distinguishable, and no specimen is ambiguous as to which was used. To test for die alignments I and III, hold the coin (obv. up) by the edges at 9:00 and 3:00 between thumb and finger, rotate along this *horizontal* axis, and notice position of eagle. If eagle is still belly up, test for die alignments II and IV by holding the coin (obv. up) at 12:00 and 6:00 edges between thumb and forefinger, rotate along this *vertical* axis, and notice position of eagle. These procedures will yield one of the four alignments below."
>
> "Alignment I: Eagle flies "onward and upward," two pellets flanking ONE DOLLAR are level after rotation along *horizontal* axis. Originals only, 1836-39; same as most U.S. coins since 1792."
>
> "Alignment II: The exact opposite. Eagle flies "onward and upward," two pellets flanking ONE DOLLAR level after rotation along *vertical* axis. Second original issue,, March 1837."
>
> "Alignment III: Eagle flies horizontally, two pellets flanking ONE DOLLAR not level (l. one low) after rotation along *horizontal* axis. Restrikes only. This alignment copies the 1856-58 Flying Eagle cents, on which eagle is intentionally horizontal."
>
> "Alignment IV: Eagle flies horizontally, two pellets flanking ONE DOLLAR not level (l. one low) after rotation along *vertical* axis. Restrikes only."

Production totaled 1,900 pieces over the years 1836-39 not including patterns and restrikes. In 1836, 1,000 pieces were struck, on the standard of 1792, weighing 416 grains. In 1837, 600 pieces dated 1836 were struck on planchets weighing 412 1/2 grains under the new standard authorized by the Act of January 18, 1837. In 1839, 300 pieces, all proofs, were struck under the new 412 1/2 grain standard.

There has been a long discussion over the decades concerning the status of the Gobrecht dollar issues. Were they patterns or regular issues? Walter Breen reported the following in his *Encyclopedia* (p. 434) as the answer to this question.

> "The 1,600 dated 1836 with name on base, delivered pursuant to Director's Warrants with other regular issue coins, including those sent to the Bank of the United States for release into circulation, were beyond doubt regular issues. The 300 delivered in 1839 at legal standards, and mentioned in the Director's Annual Report with other coins of regular issue, likewise qualify as regular issues, though minted as proofs. About the similar 1838's there is doubt primarily because the tiny mintage was omitted from the Director's Report; however, that negative argument loses its force when we consider that the half cents of 1836-48, quarter eagles of 1841, and other proof-only issues of regular design were also ignored in Director Patterson's reports, though clearly belonging to

the regular series because included in proof sets as issued from the Mint. Other varieties, with die alignments III and IV, in silver and copper, have all proved to be restrikes."

Walter Breen has carefully and completely outlined the Gobrecht Flying Eagle design in his *Complete Encyclopedia of U.S. and Colonial Coins*. The succinct outline covers specifications, grading and varieties. This superb presentation and analysis is given below in its entirety (p. 434-436).

Gobrecht's Flying Eagle Design

Designers, obv., Thomas Sully; rev., Titan Peale. Engraver, Christian Gobrecht. Mint, Philadelphia. Diameter, 25.5/16" = 39 mm. Edges, 1836 plain, 1838-39 reeded; exceptions (restrikes) as noted. Weight standards, originals of 1836 only, 416 grs. = 26.96 gms.; all others, 412.5 grs. = 26.73 gms. Composition, silver: originals of 1836 only, 892.43 + Fine; all others, 900 Fine. Authorizing Acts, originals of Dec. 31, 1836, Act of April 2, 1792; other originals, Act of Jan. 18, 1837.

Grade range, POOR to ABOUT UNC.; unworn specimens are proofs. GOOD: Date and all letters except LIBERTY legible. VERY GOOD: Traces of gown details, few feather details. At least three letters of LIBERTY legible. FINE: All letters of LIBERTY legible (some will be weak); partial details of hair, cap, upper drapery; at least half wing-feather details. VERY FINE: Over half gown and feather details; LIBERTY fully clear, scroll edges visible. EXTREMELY FINE: Isolated tiny rubbed spots only, mostly at knees, breasts, tops of wings, and eagle's breast. At least some traces of proof surface should remain. NOTE: Most surviving proofs have been cleaned; pristine (uncleaned) proofs bring a high premium over others. Beware of abrasion marks from baking soda paste or similar mechanical cleaners.

5409: 1836 Name below base; starry rev. Original. [18?] Ex. rare. Judd 58; Julian 1.416 grs. = 26.96 gms. Die alignment I: See introductory text. Not to be confused with next. None authenticated in many years.

5410: 1836 Name below base; starry rev. Restrike. Very rare. Judd 58; Julian 6, 7, respectively die alignments III and IV: See introductory text. 1979 ANA:1037, $20,000. Possibly 25-30 survivors. Later impressions sometimes show knife-rims; some show cracks through OLLA and tops of NITED STATES O. See Breen {1977}, p. 258. It is not yet known which die alignment is rarer. The copper restrikes (Ex. rare) have die alignment III.

5411: 1836 Name below base; starless rev. Restrike. Ex. rare. Judd 63; Julian 9. Die alignment III or IV. 1) Anthon, T. H. Garrett, John Work Garrett (1976):252, $19,000. 2) Woodin, Newcomer, Boyd, Farouk, Kaplan, Baldenhofer, Ostheimer, Merkin 9/68:329. 3) Maj. Lenox R. Lohr.

5412: 1836 Name on base; starry rev. First Original. [1,000] Rare. Judd 60; Julian 3. Weight, fineness as 5409. Die alignment I: See introductory text. Issue of Dec. 31, 1836. Not to be confused with either of next 2. Usually worn, from the 600 paid out by the Bank of the United States. Pristine proofs are very rare.

5413: 1836 Name on base; starry rev. Second Original. [600] Very rare. Judd 60; Julian 4. 412.5 grs. = 26.73 gms., 900 fine. Die alignment II: See introductory text. Usually worn; pristine proofs are Ex. rare.

5414: 1836 Name on base; starry rev. Restrike. Plain edge. Scarce. Judd 60; Julian 11, 12. Early impressions have die alignment III or more often IV; line in die slants up pointing between AT. Later impressions form repolished rev. have die alignment III; partial knife-rims, line in die slants up pointing to O(F); repunching on 83 faded out; cracks developing through OLLA and NITED STATES O. Over 2/3 of the Gobrechts offered at auction or fixed prices in the last 30 years belong to this number, including many circulated pieces (pocket pieces? spent during one of the later financial panics?).

5415: 1836 Name on base; starry rev. Restrike. Reeded edge. Ex rare. Judd 61; Julian 14. Die alignment III or IV, unchecked. 1) DeWitt Smith, Granberg, Woodin, Newcomer, Baldenhofer:993, discovery coin, NUM 5/11. p. 179. 2) Farouk:1713.

5416: 1836 Name on base; starless rev. Restrike. Plain edge. Ex rare. Judd 65; Julian 15. Die alignment III or IV, unchecked. 1) William J. Jenks, J.W. Garrett II:700. 2) Ralph J. Lathrop, Jay:173. 3) Farouk:1715.

5417: 1838 Starless rev. Original. Reeded edge. [25P] Ex. rare. Judd 84; Julian 2. Die alignment I: See introductory text. None seen in many years. Not to be confused with next 3.

5418: 1838 Starless rev. Restrike. Reeded edge. Very scarce. Judd 84; Julian 17, 18, respectively die alignments III, IV: See introductory text. Possibly 60-80 survive. Carter:244, $22,000. Later die states show knife-rims, obv. occasionally with field rust marks, rev. cracked through NITE and AMERI. Compare next. A single specimen is known overstruck on an 1859 dollar (clear date): Louis Werner (ca. 1958), A.M. Kagin. Others may exist. Kagin {1961}.

5419: 1838 Starless rev. Restrike. Plain edge. 6-8 known? Judd 85; Julian 19. Die alignment III or IV. Auction 80:801, $23,000. See partial roster in Breen {1977}, p. 259. Quality of ills. in many auction catalogs renders pedigree tracing doubtful especially after coins have been repeatedly cleaned.

5420: 1838 Starry rev. Restrike. Plain edge. Ex. rare. Judd 88; Julian 22. Die alignment III or IV. Late cracked rev. as in 5414. 1) Maris, Parmelee, Woodin, Newcomer, Boyd, Col. Curtis, Farouk, Randall, Baldenhofer, Ostheimer, Merkin 9/68:332 (ill. in Adams-Woodin {1913}). 2) Lohr, Miles, "Autumn":310, $12,000. The similar reeded-edge coin reported by Adams-Woodin (their no. 62 = Julian 25) is unverified.

5421: 1839 Starless rev. Original. Reeded edge. [300P] Rare. Judd 104; Julian 5. Die alignment I: See introductory text. Comprises under 1/3 of proof 1839's offered, but the majority of worn ones.

5422: 1839 Starless rev. Restrike. Reeded edge. Scarce. Judd 104; Julian 26. Die alignment III; may also exist with alignment IV (Julian 27): See introductory text. Later strikings show knife-rims and various states of cracks through NITED S and MERI. Over 2/3 of the proof 1839's offered belong to this number, with a smaller number of worn ones.

5423: 1839 Starless rev. Restrike. Plain edge. Ex. rare. Judd 105; Julian 28. Die alignment III; may exist with alignment IV. 1) Granberg, Woodin, Newcomer, Boyd, Menjou I:2083, Col. Curtis, Farouk, Baldenhofer, Ostheimer, Merkin 9/68:334. Lint mark below O(NE); many file marks at rounded rims (inflicted at the Mint to remove irregular sharp knife-rims: Breen {1984}, pp. 379, 398, 421, 424). 2) Jay, Miles, "Autumn":312, $12,00. Border weak below E DOLLA. 3) Allenburger, Donlon, 1975 ANA, Treglia, Pine Tree Auctions, 1978. Lint mark above space between 39. One other may survive.

5424: 1839 Starry rev. Restrike. Plain edge. Ex. rare. Judd 108; Julian 31. Die alignment III; heavily cracked rev. 1) Parmelee, DeWitt Smith, Granberg, Woodin, Brand, Boyd, Farouk, pvt. coll. 2) W. W. C. Wilson, Lenox Lohr, Miles, "Autumn":313, $15,000. NUM 5/11, p. 185. Rumored to exist also with reeded edge: Julian 32.

In order to present the story of the Gobrecht dollar from another perspective, we turn to R.W. Julian, who has spent a great deal of time understanding and writing about this interesting series. A background study and summary of the "The Gobrecht Dollars of 1836-1839" was prepared by R.W. Julian for *Legacy* Magazine, and appeared in their November-December 1988 issue. This article in its entirety is being reprinted with permission of the publisher, Mark Van Winkle, *Legacy* Magazine, Dallas, Texas..

The Gobrecht Dollars of 1836-1839, R.W. Julian, NLG

In the 19th century one of the most popular series of coins among collectors was the silver dollars struck from 1836 to 1839. Although numismatists considered them patterns, Gobrecht Dollars were strongly sought after, and most believed that a good collection was not complete without at least one of these rare coins.

The Gobrecht design was more than just something found on silver dollars. In 1837 the Seated Liberty was put on the dime and half dime, with other denominations following closely behind. Until 1891, the American public saw little else on its silver coinage; and today these coins are making a comeback among serious collectors.

The Philadelphia Mint began to strike silver dollars in 1794, but they never really entered active use in the marketplace. Many were used as backing for paper currency issues by banks, but others were exported to foreign lands, never to return.

By 1803 the government realized that the minting of silver dollars was a losing proposition, even though the depositors wanted these in return for their bullion. In 1804, Mint Director Elias Boudinot ordered a halt to dollar coinage and forced depositors to accept half dollars instead. This suspension came reluctantly, as there were many who felt that the dollar was a flagship coin and represented the country abroad.

Robert Patterson, who succeeded Boudinot as director in 1805, considered dollar coinage, but it was rejected because most of the coins would have gone abroad within a short time. Patterson's successor (and son-in-law), Samuel Moore, was also interested in dollar coinage and nearly succeeded in achieving this during his tenure of office, 1824-1835.

Moore checked the origins of silver being deposited at the mint very closely. In late 1830 and early 1831, he noted that silver bullion had been received from Canton, something that had never happened before. In the past, American exporters had normally sent silver to the Orient to pay for luxury items, but the reverse deposit meant something special. When other deposits of a similar nature occurred, Moore decided that it was time to act.

In April 1831 Moore wrote Treasury Secretary Samuel Ingham, asking that the prohibition against dollar coinage be lifted and that he be permitted to coin silver dollars. Ingham discussed the matter with President Andrew Jackson and, as a result, a letter was sent on April 18 with the president's permission.

Mint Director Robert M. Patterson, responsible for the production of the Gobrecht dollars.

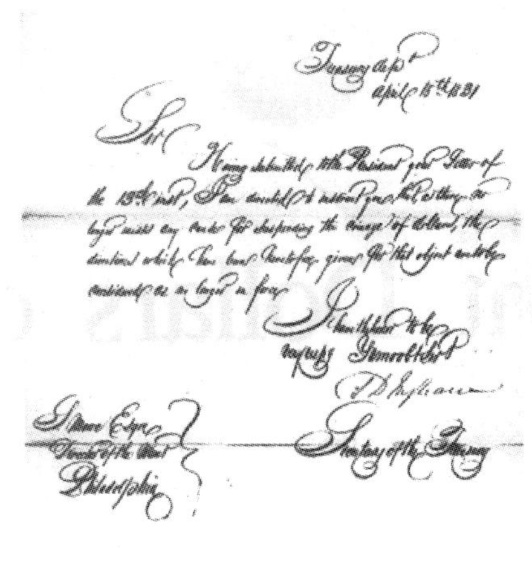

Letter of April 1831 authorizing dollar coinage; at the same time it removed the prohibition of 1806.

Mint Director Samuel Moore, responsible for many technical improvements in U.S. coinage beginning in 1828.

(Courtesy of *Legacy* Magazine)

Moore had the necessary dies cut (using the old hubs of 1798-1803), but they were not dated or hardened. The director wished to make certain that the new silver dollars would not be exported, as had been the case prior to 1805. Unfortunately, Moore discovered that the imports from Canton had indeed been a fluke, and the reverse window was once more closed. The dies were laid aside.

Due to an unexpected turn of events, Moore used the special dies that had been prepared in 1831. In late 1834, the State Department ordered the mint to make up special sets of U.S. coins as presents for potentates in the Middle and Far East. Diplomat Edmund Roberts was preparing to negotiate commercial treaties and thought that sets of coins should be given as gifts.

The State Department orders were ambiguous, and Moore interpreted them to mean that he should strike the dollar and eagle, last made in 1804. As a result, and obverse die was given the old date, and the famous 1804 silver dollars were the result.

For Moore, the incident again whetted his desire for a regular coinage of dollars, but the export problem remained and he was forced to bide his time. However, he decided to return to private life in 1835 and resigned on June 30.

In June, Moore asked President Jackson to hire Christian Gobrecht (1785-1844) for the mint engraving department. The director had two things in mind; the first was related to the March 1835 law that added three mints to the system. More dies would be needed, and Moore felt that adding an additional engraver was a good idea.

The other reason was more complex. Beginning in 1828, Chief Engraver William Kneass had executed revised dies for the coinage, but with the same basic design. Coins were now being struck in a collar and the diameters were reduced. By mid-1835 all U.S. coins except the cent and half dollar had been accorded the revised Kneass dies.

Moore knew that his successor (and brother-in-law), Dr. Robert Maskell Patterson, was very much interested in continuing the progress made to date. The two men had discussed the possibility of silver dollar coinage, and Moore realized that one engraver would be hard put to furnish both the extra dies for the new branch mints and revised (or new) designs for the coinage.

Dr. Patterson arrived at the mint in early July 1835 to take up his post, but found that nothing had been done about hiring Gobrecht. Within a matter of weeks, however, the new director had decided to go ahead with plans for a silver dollar coinage, with or without an additional engraver.

In early August 1835, Patterson asked famed portrait painter Thomas Sully to design a Liberty seated figure for a new dollar coinage. At about the same time, naturalist (and artist) Titian Peale accepted a commission to draw an eagle flying "onward and upward." The director wanted a coin that would be admired the world over.

Just after Patterson had commenced this historic project, Engraver William Kneass suffered a paralytic stroke. Now the employment of Gobrecht was a necessity, not just a luxury. The president soon approved his joining the mint as "second" engraver, not as an assistant to Kneass. (In time, Kneass recovered to a certain extent and did limited engraving work until his death in 1840).

Top Row: Drawings for the Seated Liberty coinage as done by William Kneass, Titian Peale and Thomas Sully. Botton Row: Early drawings for the reverse of the Seated Liberty coinage as done by Titian Peale.
Library Company of Philadelphia and American Philosophical Society Library.

(Courtesy of *Legacy* magazine)

Patterson derived his idea for the seated Liberty figure directly from the contemporary British coinage, but the origin of this concept goes back to ancient Greece. It was adopted by the Romans and used as a personification of Britannia on the coinage. In the 1670s King Charles II ordered London Mint engravers to re-create this famous symbol. One of his mistresses is said to have posed for the likeness of Britannia. (At present she graces the fifty-pence coin.)

Toward the end of September, Sully finished some rough sketches of a seated Liberty and sent them to Patterson. The director was pleased and instructed Gobrecht to execute a copperplate etching of the best drawing, which was finished and ready for use by mid-October 1835. A few prints were soon made and distributed.

One of these prints was sent to Treasury Secretary Levi Woodbury for transmission to the White House. President Jackson showed it to his cabinet on the 16th and on the following day Woodbury wrote Patterson of the result of the discussions. There was general satisfaction, but a few minor suggestions for improvement as well. In particular, Jackson asked that the Liberty pole be made a bit longer, so that there would be no question of its significance and importance.

The print was shown to others in the Philadelphia area, especially artists and the well educated. Patterson knew that the final design would have to please many people, and he solicited criticism from all quarters.

When all of the critical remarks had been received, Gobrecht set to work on a brass die for the obverse. Gobrecht was so far advanced with his task by the end of 1835 that Patterson proudly noted in his annual report that "one of the engravers of the mint is engaged in preparing a die of the dollar size..."

Tetradrachm of Alexander III with seated figure of Zeus on the reverse.

Sestertius of Hadrian with Britannia reverse.

1799 British one-penny with Britannia reverse.

(Courtesy of Legacy Magazine)

On January 8, 1836, this first die was completed and a few pieces in fusible metal (probably pewter) were struck. One of these was sent to the president for his examination. Jackson repeated his criticism of the pole being too short, but otherwise felt that the effort was a strong step in the right direction.

Patterson and Gobrecht discussed the first pattern very carefully, with an eye toward meeting the president's suggestions. Gobrecht made the corrections directly into the original brass die. Revised patterns were then made and sent to Washington. These were quickly approved by the proper officials, and work on a steel obverse die commenced.

Gobrecht had barely begun the steel die (in late January) when the Treasury interrupted with something more urgent, at least in their view. Secretary Woodbury had long been interested in introducing a gold dollar, although both Moore and Patterson were opposed; Gobrecht was instructed to prepare suitable dies. (Woodbury was also considering a $1.50 gold piece!)

The gold dollar dies occupied Gobrecht during February and a portion of March. On March 14, patterns were struck and forwarded to the Treasury, but Patterson's strong opposition was to bury the idea for some years; it would be 1849 before Congress would approve the denomination.

Gobrecht was now able to proceed with the dollar obverse die in steel. (He was partially freed from the more mundane engraving work because the chief coiner, Adam Eckfeldt, oversaw the preparation of many of the working dies). It was a slow process, however, and the die was not completed and hardened for use for nearly a month.

Although the first steel die for the obverse was finished in April 1836, the reverse die, with the eagle flying "onward and upward," had not even been started by the engraver. The reason for the lack of progress was quite simple: Patterson had yet to approve a single one of Titian Peale's drawings as suitable for the design he had in mind. Peale had already submitted more than thirty sketches without success, but just as the obverse steel die was completed, he produced one that caught Patterson's fancy.

In early April, a trial strike from the steel obverse die and Peale's approved drawing for the reverse were sent to the Treasury for a decision. On April 11, the Treasury notified Director Patterson that the obverse had been approved as well as the Peale drawing. All who saw the sketch praised it with just a few exceptions.

The President thought the eagle ought to have its mouth closed instead of open. The director was able to persuade him that his (Patterson's) concept was the correct one by noting that drawings had been prepared with the mouth closed and had been found unsuitable. (In all of the correspondence there is no mention of Peter, the mint's pet eagle, despite popular legend that Titian Peale used him for a model).

There were several interruptions in the spring of 1836, and Gobrecht was delayed in beginning work on a second steel obverse die until June. Changes were now made to the design, including lengthening Liberty's neck.

With the new obverse finished in June, Gobrecht was able to commence work on the reverse eagle designed by Titian Peale. The engraving went slowly, primarily because Gobrecht was a careful artist, but also because of the difficulty of the design. Patterson wanted the finest possible work, and that took time. However, toward the end of August 1836 all was in readiness to strike patterns.

On August 27, the Treasury formally approved both designs and gave permission for Patterson to proceed with regular coinage. Authority had been also granted in April 1831 but that would have been with the old dies and not the design of 1836.

Chief Coiner Adam Eckfeldt, who had served the mint in varying capacities since its inception in 1792, was directed on September 22 by Patterson to prepare for a coinage of silver dollars. The mint originally intended to coin the new dollars by steam power, but this proved impractical, and Eckfeldt was ordered to use the old screw press.

Andrew Jackson, taken from an 1845 daguerrotype.

Mint Director James Ross Snowden, ordered the restriking of the Gobrecht dollars in the late 1850s.

(Courtesy of *Legacy* Magazine)

Eckfeldt was also directed to prepare the actual working dies, added proof that the engraver's department did not prepare all of the dies used for coinage. At Patterson's express command, Gobrecht added his name in the field above the date: C. Gobrecht F. (Christian Gobrecht Fecit, Latin for Christian Gobrecht made it). It was a bold act for the time for a U.S. coinage die had never been signed.

When word got out, the "conceited German" came under attack for his supposed arrogance. Patterson ordered the offensive signature placed on the base of the figure, inconspicuous, but still there for those who wanted to see it. No United States coin since that time has carried the full name of the artist, although initials are common.

It is sometimes said that eighteen pattern dollars of 1836, with name below base, were struck, but the figure is purely a traditional one without a shred of archival backing. It is the only true pattern coin of 1836, although this status is sometimes claimed for some of the restrikes produced in the 1850s.

Perhaps the dispute over the name delayed coinage, but whatever the reason, Eckfeldt did not begin striking the new dollars until mid-December 1836. Patterson ordered that all of them be struck in proof so that the public could see the high quality of the new design. Proof coinage is, however, slow, and it took time to strike the 1,000 specimens delivered in December.

Of the first 1,000 pieces, 600 were sent to the Bank of the United States for public distribution, while the mint kept 400. All of these coins were made on the 416-grain standard of 1792, not the standard of 1837 (412.5 grains), as was reported in the past when researchers believed all of these to be patterns instead of coins for circulation. The low mintages misled numismatists into thinking this as early as the 1850s.

The issue of 1836, with name on base is a legal coinage, and type sets are not complete without it. In the past this was generally made a part of such sets for mere tradition, but now there is concrete reason for doing so.

On January 18, 1837, President Jackson signed a mint bill that made many changes in the monetary system. The most important of these, for our purposes, was the official alteration of the old silver fineness (0.8924+) to 0.900. The weights of coins were adjusted so that there was no real change in the amount of silver contained.

The Bank of the United States had paid out the 600 dollars on hand, and the mint now proceeded, in March 1836, to make another small coinage just for the bank. Six hundred were struck from the dies of 1836. To distinguish the coins of December from those of March, the dies were reversed; the December dies had normal alignment (180 degrees), while those of March were inverted (0 degrees).

The easiest way to visualize this special change is to examine your pocket change. Note that current U.S. coins are aligned in "coin" fashion, as has always been the case. The 1837 dollars are aligned in "medal" style, as on coins of Canada and Britain.

There were soon discussions about putting the Seated Liberty design on minor silver coins. This was done to the half dimes and dime in 1837 and on the silver dollar of 1836, with the stars were left off the obverse. However, at the beginning of 1838, it was noticed that this left the coin somewhat unbalanced.

For a variety of reasons the half dime and dime obverses were changed at the beginning of 1836 by adding thirteen stars around the figure (Outdated dies of the 1837 style were sent to New Orleans in 1838.) This led to Patterson considering changes on the dollar to correspond with the minor coins. The quarter dollar was introduced in 1838 with the new design on the obverse (including stars) but the old reverse.

In July 1838 the treasury asked Patterson for fifty silver dollars. These were duly sent, but the director noted that all were of the December 1836 coinage, none of the 1837s being on hand. The Treasury asked for an additional twenty-five on July 7. This request apparently triggered the execution of dies dated 1838 with the stars now switched from reverse to obverse. There is no record of the twenty-five dollars being sent to Washington, but presumably this was done.

The 1838 dollar is a true pattern coin, just as the 1836 with name below base is. Both are of the highest rarity, and originals are virtually never seen in the numismatic marketplace. It is quite possible that less than ten pieces exist for each date.

In December of 1839, the new chief coiner, Franklin Peale (brother of Titian Peale), executed 300 silver dollars, the last coinage with the flying eagle reverse. An original 1839 dollar is extremely difficult to locate. There may be as few as seventy-five originals in existence, and these show up at auction very rarely.

The coinage of silver dollars resumed on a larger scale in 1840, but the magnificent flying eagle reverse was not used. Instead the director opted (perhaps at Treasury insistence) to use the old eagle from 1807. The reverse was thereby the same as the quarter and half dollar.

During the 1840s there was little interest in the Gobrecht dollars because available specimens outnumbered collectors. Putting a silver dollar into a collection in those days was also an expensive proposition because of wage levels. It was not until the mid-1850s that there was a numismatic awakening in this country.

When the first Gobrecht restrikes were made is a fact lost to history, but it probably did not come before 1854 or 1855 under Mint Director James Ross Snowden. He was interested in building up the national collection of coins and medals, especially those relating to George Washington, and spared no effort in doing this.

By late 1857, restriking of old and rare coins at the mint had become a fact of life, though it was done on a small scale at first. Snowden was more interested in trading his restrikes for specimens not in the mint collection. From this it gradually turned into a situation where Snowden sold the newly made coins and used the funds obtained to buy rare coins.

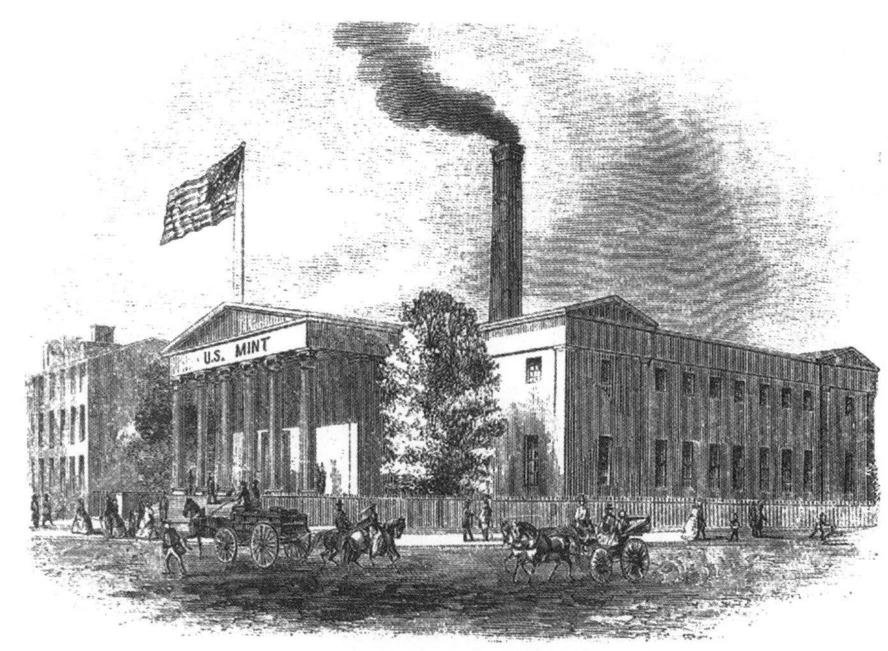

U.S. Mint circa 1859

(Courtesy of *Legacy* Magazine)

Although no written records survive to confirm the supposition, it is almost certain that Snowden ordered the Gobrecht restrikes to be made in such a way that he could determine if the piece were original or not. If one rotates an original coin (whether medal or coin turn) the eagle will be flying upward, but on a restrike the eagle will be flying level (flat). It is as simple as that. (Walter Breen rediscovered this in the 1970s).

There are many today who believe that only original Gobrechts of 1836-1839 are proper for their collections. It is true that the December 1836 striking (name on base, coin turn) is available for a price, but the others are not, and the astute collector will obtain one of the restrikes for his type set. The demand for Gobrechts intended for type sets can only grow in the next few years to a point where even the restrikes will be virtually unobtainable except at very high prices.

The various mules (struck with mismatched obverse and reverse dies) will continue to bring high prices — all are restrikes — but it is more likely that interest in such pieces will become subordinated to the regular designs, whether original or restrike.

This series of coins is one of the most fascinating in our entire numismatic history, and the last word on the subject will probably never be written. As long as there are collectors, the Gobrecht dollars will be topic of conversation.

Profile of Christian Gobrecht
Token and Medal Society

(Courtesy of Legacy Magazine)

Gobrecht Dollar Collecting

In May 1989, Mark S. Yaffe, National Gold Exchange, Tampa, Florida, acquired the world's finest Gobrecht dollar set of regular issue coins. Each of the coins in the set has been certified by the Numismatic Guaranty Corporation (NGC) to be an original and, as such, comprise the finest known examples of this series. Since that time, these particular specimens have changed hands and are currently held in a private collection. The prices realized for the coins in this collection are also noted.

Date	Grade	Service	Prices Realized
1836	MS-64	NGC	$ 35,000
1838	MS-65	NGC	150,000
1839	MS-65	NGC	150,000
Total:			$ 335,000

In addition to the "real thing" there have been thousands of artistic pictures, replicas and designed pieces prepared utilizing the Gobrecht dollar devices. These have been sought and collected by numismatists and others for decades. One such piece is the special five-ounce commemorative silver medallion pictured below.

Obverse

Reverse

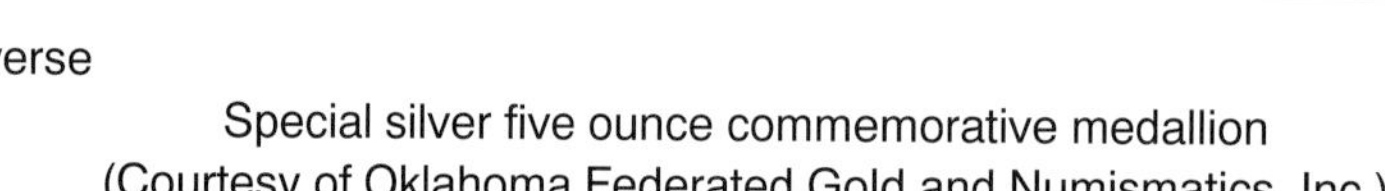
Special silver five ounce commemorative medallion
(Courtesy of Oklahoma Federated Gold and Numismatics, Inc.)

The Gobrecht dollars will always hold a high place in the minds of collectors and investors alike. Type coin collectors create a special demand for the extremely limited supply of these specimens. A very select group of series collectors have taken up the challenge of acquiring pieces from either the original series and/or the various restrikes. Pattern collectors, as usual with early U.S. series, are always looking and waiting for one of the few rare specimens to be offered for sale. Investors will find top quality specimens extremely difficult to locate, and then perhaps more difficult to acquire as holders of the finest pieces are not usually in the market to sell. When found, competition for the best Gobrecht dollars should be keen among the many collectors and investors looking to acquire these coins. Historically and otherwise, this fascinating series, born just after the belated appearance of the 1804 dollars, will retain its high rank in the eyes of all, and the interest of numismatists for decades to come.

Acknowledgements

Walter Breen's Complete Encyclopedia of U.S. and Colonial Coins, Walter H. Breen, Garden City: Doubleday, 1988

"The Gobrecht Dollars of 1836-1839", R.W. Julian, *Legacy*, for the contemporary numismatist, November-December 1988, Volume 1, Number 5, Steve Ivy and James L. Halperin, Dallas, Texas. Exclusive rights held and permission granted by the publisher, Mark Van Winkle, to reprint from *Legacy* Magazine.

Dollar Gobrecht (1836-1839)

An American classic, the Gobrecht Liberty Seated design, modeled after drawings by Thomas Sully and Titian Peale, was first introduced on the pattern and circulation silver dollars of 1836.

At the suggestion of Mint Director Robert M. Patterson, Gobrecht's name and the Latin "F" for "he made it" were prominently displayed below the base of the Liberty design.

Criticism arose in the local press over the display of the engraver's name. Gobrecht offered to remove it, but Patterson preferred its retention.

In the end, Patterson compromised by having the engraver's name appear in a reduced size, located inconspicuously in small letters on the base of Liberty.

The reverse of the first Liberty Seated dollars displayed a flying eagle modeled after "Peter the Mint Eagle," the Mint's mascot during the 1830's. When regular coinage began again in 1840, this attractive design had been replaced by a more conservative heraldic eagle.

(Courtesy of Krause Publications)

***

John W. Dannreuther

John West Dannreuther was born May 5, 1948, in Canton, Mississippi. As a youngster, John was a collector of both coins and stamps. He continued to collect during his younger years, mainly collecting coins — dollars, Lincoln cents, and Indian cents were early favorites.

After attending the University of Mississippi, Mr. Dannreuther graduated with a B.A. in English and Chemistry in 1970. For the next three years, he was mainly involved in music, moving to Memphis, Tennessee in 1972 with a band that had signed a record contract. In early 1973, his father consigned much of his collection to John and his second era of numismatics had begun.

After several years of owning his own business, John was hired in 1976 to head New England Rare Coin Galleries Wholesale Division. In 1977, he moved to Miami as a buyer for Numismatic Investments of Florida and partial owner of a wholesale company, Commercial Coin Exchange of Florida. In January of 1979, John restarted JDRC, and in December moved back to Memphis. JDRC, Inc. has been located there since.

Mr. Dannreuther has written articles for the Coin Dealer Newsletter, contributed to David Hall's book, *A Mercenary's Guide to the Rare Coin Market*, and was voted "Man of the Year" in 1989 by the National Silver Dollar Roundtable. He is a member of the ANA, PNG, ANS, FUN, TNA, MNA, CSNS, and NSDR.

CHAPTER 61

Liberty Seated Dollars

by John W. Dannreuther

(Coin courtesy of Gordon E. Krohn)
(Photo provided by Krause Publications)

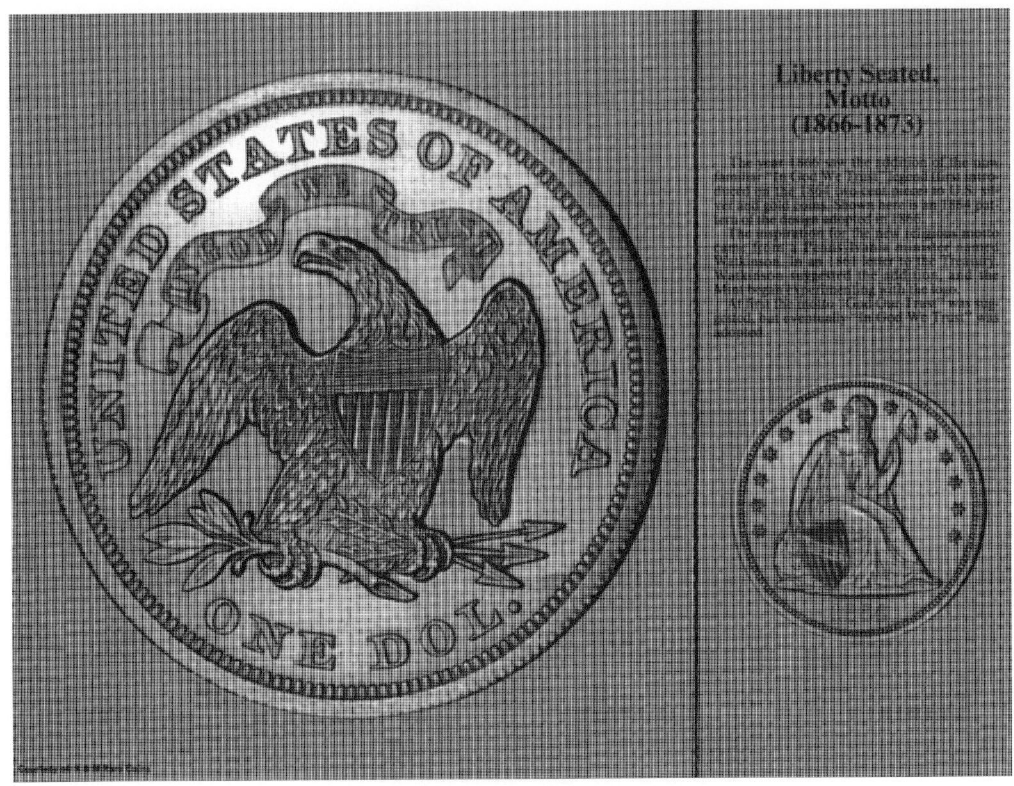

(Coin courtesy of K & M Rare Coins)
(Photo provided by Krause Publications)

Although we usually think of the Liberty Seated series as starting with the 1837 coinage, and Liberty Seated Dollars with the 1840, the first Liberty Seated coinage was the 1836 Gobrecht Dollar. When William Kneass become incapacitated in 1835, Christian Gobrecht began revamping virtually all our coinage. In 1836 he designed the obverse of the Liberty Seated coinage which (with modifications by Robert Ball Hughes) would be used on all the silver issues until 1891. The beautiful "Flying Eagle" reverse, unfortunately, was only used from 1836 to 1839, and only on the dollar.

The debate as to whether the 1836-39 Gobrechts were patterns or regular issues has been going on for quite some time. The fact that they were all proofs (no other regular issues for circulation save the 1856 Flying Eagle Cent, which also comes in mint state, were issued as proofs) makes a case for them as patterns, but they were released into circulation, pursuant to the Director's Annual Report: Those of 1836 and 1839 must be called regular issues, even though they were proofs. The other Gobrechts, the various restrikes and varieties, can rightfully be called patterns, so I guess both arguments "hold water."

With Robert Ball Hughes's reworking of the Gobrecht obverse for the Quarter and Dollar came another curiosity. The Gobrecht reverse was abandoned in favor of a modification of the old John Reich eagle reverse. Hughes's modifications of the obverse also included the adding of 13 stars around the edge (copied from 1838). So in 1840, we now had the Liberty Seated Dollar, minus the "onward and upward" Flying Eagle reverse: the Liberty Seated No Motto design with which we are all familiar.

No matter how one feels about the changes, the Liberty Seated series is still very beautiful. This dollar series is one of the most interesting of all United States coinages. It contains some of the greatest rarities and a few mysteries. When I was queried for a wonderful Bruce Amspacher article in the Greysheet Monthly Summary a few years back, I was asked to comment on the various dates and mint marks in Liberty Seated Dollars and Bruce had included the 1873-S. My comment was very simple, in fact it was only two words — Good date! This comment is appropriate for many coins in this series, but the 1873-S is basically unknown. I say basically because the rumors of this coin have been around for quite some time, sometimes attributed to reliable sources and since the 1870-S Half Dime was unknown for over 100 years, (I know, we knew since there was the 1870-S Three Dollar Gold there should be a Half-Dime, what with it being the year of the famous cornerstone) a 1873-S Dollar in P-L MS-66 is bound to show up. Dreaming, just dreaming. The excitement that an 1873-S would generate at an auction is . . . oh well, you see how I feel about this wonderful series.

As I said earlier, this series contains some of the rarest of United States coinage to the extent that all grades and almost every date is a condition rarity. There really is no "commonest" date MS-65 Seated Dollar. Even the most common Seated Dollar (1860-O) is very tough in MS-65, and MS-64 for that matter. I have always thought of this series as an "impossible" to do, though I guess with enough money, anything is possible, but there is another stopper in the set, especially in condition, because the best 1870-S known is AU. Maybe there is a proof or prooflike 1870-S out in coinland, but there I go dreaming again.

I think the easiest way to think about Liberty Seated Dollars is to group them as the "Forties," "Fifties," and the "Sixties-Seventies". The "Forties" dates are all scarce in all grades, with the 1840 being the most "common" proof and the 1842 and 1847 the easiest dates to obtain in uncirculated. Although there are more proof 1840's than other dates in the "Forties," it is obviously a very rare coin, as are most proof coins before 1856. In fact the most common "Liberty Seated Dollar" in proof prior to 1859 is the 1836. A trick question.

The Forties

1840. Since this is the first year of mint state circulation issues, one would think this date would be relatively, at least for the 1840's, common. But no, it is as tough in mint state as any other of the 1840's dates. In proof, as I mentioned before, it (with the 1846) is seen, though none of the 1840's proofs are really "available." They show up in auctions sometimes when "name" collections are sold. In all grades of mint state I doubt that over 25-30 1840's still exist, mostly in 63 and less. The best proofs I have ever seen are the Garrett coin and the one I purchased from Julian Leidman in 1980, which was with a beautiful 1850 proof. Talk about value — I paid a little over ten grand . . . for the pair! Would whomever I sold these coins to, please call? My phone number is . . .

1841. This date is slightly more common than the 1840 in mint state grades. Still it is quite rare in mint state, especially so in MS-63 and above, although PCGS has graded one coin MS-65. Proofs are excessively rare with PCGS having graded none.

1842. This is slightly more common than the 1841 in mint state with a few MS-64 and MS-65's known. The Bernard Turkus specimen was a very nice coin as was the gem I handled with another dealer in the late 1970's, which we sold for the "high" price of $4,000. As a proof it is like the 1841 — almost never seen, though PCGS has graded a PR-64. Many of the mint state coins exhibit obverse, and occasionally reverse, die striations. These mint caused lines tend to make these semi-prooflike and after wearing out or polishing off the die, fully prooflike.

1843. Similar to 1841 in mint state rarity. Seldom seen in MS-64 and better. Rarer than 1840 and 1846 in proof, thought all of these dates are so rare it is hard to call a coin with a PCGS population of two rarer than a coin with a population of one. They are all of extreme rarity.

1844. This date has the famous doubled obverse die variety (just a bit of humor there, folks). There are very few die varieties in the Seated Dollar Series, mainly because of the minuscule issuance of virtually every date. 1844 is on a par in rarity with 1841 and 1843 in mint states. As usual, excessively rare in proof with PCGS having graded exactly . . . none. This is also the second lowest mintage of the Forties with a paltry 20,000 coins struck.

1845. This might be the rarest of the Forties in mint state, and it is also one of the rarest of all mint state Seated Liberty Dollars, PCGS never having graded one higher than AU-58. It is also the third lowest mintage of the 1840-49 era with only 24,500 struck. In mint state this coin is rare and above MS-63 it is excessively so — just not available. PCGS has graded a PR-64 specimen which could easily be the finest known.

1846. Although it is still more available than prior years in mint state, it still is of a rarity level equal to the 1842. In MS-64 and better it is certainly as rare as the earlier dates. Perhaps it is more common in proof than the other dates of the Forties, since Breen enumerates a few more specimens then the other dates, including the 1840. PCGS has even graded a PR-65 which is probably the finest known proof.

1846-O. At one point, I considered this date the key of the Forties. In MS-64 or better it is probably nonexistent. There has, however, been a persistent rumor for quite a few years of a bag of uncirculated 1846-O's. This fantasy emanates, I'm sure, from the Treasury's early 1960's release of 1859-O and 1860-O bags, along with a few other Seated Dollar dates. The rumor of a roll or partial roll is believable, as I once purchased 18 uncirculated 1854-O dimes at a coin show in the early 1980's, a date which probably had less than a dozen true mint state coins known at that time. No matter, whether there are 15 or 35 uncirculated 1846-O's known, it is still a mint state rarity.

1847. The most "common" date of the Forties in mint state is the distinction of the high mintage (140,750) 1847. This date is available occasionally in MS-64 and higher, but still only occasionally. Trying to rank Seated Dollars as to availability in mint state is a futile effort, since a "hoard" of five pieces can swing the rarity rating. A proof rears it's head once or twice a decade, so don't expect to see it in your local coin shop next week. Wouldn't a complete set of Gobrechts and Seated Liberty Dollars in proof make a nice display! OK, whoever is holding all those PR-65 Gobrechts and 1840's Seated Dollars, bring'em to the next show, . . . please!

1848. This year has a wonder coin — a coin I tried to buy in the 1977 Fairfield sale but fell a few bucks short to William Mitkoff's $4,750 bid. I did get to handle it at the 1985 Central States show, though, and I believe it still resides in that coin dealer's collection. PCGS later graded it MS-65! That coin, along with an amazing non-PL 1857, are probably my favorite Seated Dollars that I have personally handled. By the way, the same dealer has the 1857 in his collection also. A single proof has been graded by PCGS, and it's a PR-65!

1849. Now this date has a wonder, wonder coin. PCGS graded it MS-66 and it easily made that grade. It is also an ex-Fairfield collection coin that I was a tad short of buying; Bill Mitkoff got that coin too. Even with that coin, 1849 is a very rare coin in MS-64 and higher. (There are some coins, and this 1849 is one of them, that simply boggle the mind that they could exist in such superb condition.) PCGS has also graded a single proof of this date and wouldn't you know it, it's a PR-65! That would make a nice pair of cufflinks for Mark Eaton, wouldn't it? Nah, put the proof in the 1836-1849 proof display and use the MS-66 for a reverse display!

The Fifties

1850. The Fifties Seated Dollars, especially the early fifties, represent some of the series' most celebrated rarities. 1850 is one of them. An extreme rarity in mint state above MS-63; I have never seen a gem of the 7,500 issued. The single proof seen by PCGS is graded PR-64 and might be the coin I handled with the 1840 proof that I mentioned earlier. Certainly as rare as any of the Forties dates in proof. Beginning with this date there are restrike proofs known, but they too are very rare and command prices at or near originals.

1850-O. Earlier I said that the 1848 and 1857 in mint state that I handled were personal favorites of mine. Well, the 1850-O from Auction 79 certainly is another one I can add to the list of personal favorites. This is surely the MS-64 that PCGS graded, which, by the way, is one of the only two mint state 1850-O's they have graded! The other is a MS-62. Enough said, this is certainly one of the rarest Seated Dollars in mint state.

1851. This date comes in mint state and proof as originals and, as I mentioned earlier, there are proof restrikes. The originals have the third lowest circulation mintage of the Seated Dollars series (excluding the 1873-S), though PCGS has graded a MS-65. There is controversy as to whether any of the originals are really proofs, as the striking qualities as not up to norm, and the fact that 1851 coinage in proof is probably the rarest overall in the post 1840's era, lending doubt to the few pieces even claiming to be proof strikings. The restrikes leave no doubt, though, and are easily distinguished from originals as they have a different obverse with the date centered. (On the originals the date is placed high.) Certainly one of the rarest in the series. A new discovery is a Proof 1851 dollar with a reverse with a mostly effaced "O", probably from a die that was intended to be shipped to New Orleans!

1852. This date has the lowest circulation mintage of any Seated Dollar (again excluding 1873-S, which I will explain later why I keep excluding), and the population data bears this fact out. PCGS has just two mint state specimens: a MS-64, and believe it or not, a MS-65! There is also a PR-65! What a pair. As a matter of fact, these coins traded as a pair in 1989 for six figures each! What more can you say? The rarest of the rare. Again there are a few restrike proofs out there in coinland and one that is probably a restrike with the reverse of 1840-49, though Walter Breen and others who have examined this specimen (in the ANS museum) are uncertain. The restrikes that are certainly restrikes have the reverse of 1858-59, which leaves no doubt as to when they were struck-after 1858! The 1850 and 1851 restrikes have this reverse die also.

1853. Starting with 1853, the circulation strikings increased. This "high mintage" Fifties date had over 46,000 coins struck for commerce. How many uncirculated ones survived? A few, including one PCGS graded as MS-66! This might be the Auction '79 coin which brought a whopping $17,000! Sounds pretty reasonable today, though. There don't appear to be any original proofs, though one could show up someday. The restrikes again are obvious, since they have a different obverse and the reverse of 1862! Supposedly only 12 silver ones were struck, so this date is as rare as prior years.

1854. Now this is a hoard date. Why I once saw 5 (!) uncs at one time at Lanham, Maryland show (boy, does that bring back memories — of the coins and of the poor facilities for that show). Please, no cards or letters, as I mean no disrespect for that show or Maryland. Of course, one of those uncs had a scratch on the reverse. This is the first date in this series for which there have been several gems available. The Harmer-Rooke Spring 1985 sale specimen and the Numismatic Investments of Florida late 1970's specimen are certainly two of the finest I have ever seen. Proofs, again, are very rare though not quite as rare as prior years, so in PR-62 and below they can be had for a price. I have never seen a gem proof, though I'm sure somebody out there will stick one under my nose someday. Please! There are no restrikes of this date reported.

1855. This date really is a hard-date! Fifty scruffy uncs showed up in a 1975 Superior sale. Where these are now no one knows, I guess, for PCGS has graded only three mint state coins, with the highest graded only a MS-62! A very rare coin in high condition. This is the first date that there are quite a few proofs known (Breen estimates 50-60 survive), though you wouldn't guess it from PCGS population numbers as they have graded only three coins, with the finest a PR-64. They still are quite rare in PR-64 and better. I personally think that the number of proofs extant is under 40.

1856. This has a "very high" mintage of 63,500. Whoa, Nelly! You still won't find these with the modern proofs sets at K-Mart. Like most Seated Dollars, the population above MS-64 is "Mohave-like" — sparse, dry, thin, mirage, etc. Proofs were made in similar quantity to 1855, though still nothing like the later years. In fact, 1856 marks the year that all United State proof coinage becomes more available. As with the business strikes, you will probably have to settle for a PR-64 or below, as in gem they are super rare.

1857. The gem 1857 that I mentioned earlier is the exceptional 1857: not only for condition, but because it is not prooflike as many of the uncirculated coins of this date, nor are the stars weak. MS-63 and 64 specimens are available of the 94,000 issued, though they are, as mentioned, weakly struck with the stars and the head of Liberty and the eagle's neck and wing sometimes so weak that it is mistaken for wear. Some of the proofs of this year are also weak, probably carelessly made since the mint was now striking quantities of proof coinage and obviously the care taken in prior years was not employed. Proofs are more often seen than previously, though by no means are they common.

1858. Now here's a date that is really rare in mint state! Whoops, it should be, since it is a proof-only issue. This is by far the most common proof of the 1840-1858 era, but is still quite scarce in PR-64 and better. The mint also began promoting proof coins and sets in this year, thus the estimate of 80 struck seems to be about right. They come with the reverse of 1857 and 1859, so there is speculation that this date was restruck, which is consistent with the mint "happenings" of 1858-60. The best one I remember handling was the 1980 Metro New York show specimen that I paid $27,000 for at the peak of the market. Now that brings back memories!

1859. With a mintage of 256,500 one would think this would be an easy date, but as I said before, there are no easy dates, in fact PCGS has graded none higher than MS-64. They just weren't saved by many collectors in 1859. They could buy proofs for $1.08 so who would want an MS-68 business strike? Although from here on the proofs are relatively common (PCGS has graded more 1859's than all the dates combined from 1840-1857!), they are No Motto's and as such are very scarce in PR-65 or better.

1859-O. Now we've come upon a truly "common" Seated Dollar. At least in MS-62 and below, you will find this date. A bag or two of uncs came out in the early 1960's when the Treasury discovered the mother lode in her vaults (obviously most of what was held were Morgan and Peace dollars). It's still a common misconception that 1859-O's are available in gem condition. Those bags were bagged around quite a bit and all Seated Dollars, as I am sure you have figured out by now, are rare in MS-65 and above!

1859-S. See what I mean? Bring me all three mint state 1859-S's that PCGS has graded. Might be those three MS-62's could be one and the same coin! Only the submitter knows for sure! As rare as rare can be! In the same mint state rarity class as 1850-O, 1851 and 1852. The last of the Fifties Seated Dollars is one of the rarest of the rare!

The Sixties — Seventies

Obverse

Reverse

1873 Liberty Seated Dollar
(Courtesy of Heritage Numismatic Auction)

1860. Again, this is a date that is available in MS-64 and below, but it's just an ordinary Seated dollar in MS-65 and above-rare! Proofs are like the 1859 and are available in PR-64 and below and killers in anything above that, though there is one PR-66 graded.

1860-O. What can you say? A common coin, easily obtained in MS-60 to 62. Baggy uncs from the 1960's hoard are around of this third highest mintage date (515,000). What is forgotten is that 1860-O is a rare coin in MS-65 and above, with only one MS-65 graded by PCGS. I must tell you one story here as a footnote to the Treasury hoard. It's a wonderful little ditty about one of the 1860-O bags that was related to me in the early 1970's. I presume it is true. A bank in a small town in Arkansas wanted to give away a silver dollar as a promotion (opening a new account), so they ordered a bag of silver dollars from the New Orleans Federal Reserve. (My Mother worked in our local bank in the 1960's and we ordered a bag a week, all they would allow, for numerous weeks, but only got one date — 1904-O.) Anyway, one of the Arkansas bank's officers happened to walk by one of the tellers and glanced in the cashier's drawer and said, "What are these?" The tellers response was, "Those are the dollars we are giving out in our promotion!" The officer quickly stopped that promo, but supposedly over half the bag had already been dispersed. A local customer of mine started buying them from the bank and eventually ended up with about a hundred or so of them. As I said, it's a great story and it's probably true.

1861. This is one of the common "P" mint 1869-65 era, though PCGS has graded only one MS-65. The low mintage (11,540) of business strikes is due to the Civil War, but the higher than normal survival ratio is due to the same circumstances. People hoarded coins (both silver and gold) during the war, thus the "nifty" specimens that show up occasionally are due to this. Quite a few of this year and the following war years were exported. The proofs can be had for a price.

1862. This date is rare in all grades and very rare in uncirculated. There was one obverse and two reverses for business strikes. Of the 550 proofs coined, 430 were sold in sets. Most of the others were melted in 1863 as unsold.

1863. One of these guys is an MS-66! Again, available mainly in MS-64 and below. There are two minor proof varieties. Available up through PR-65, though quite rare above that.

1864. No MS-66, but PCGS has graded one MS-65. It is probably the most common PR-65 No Motto dollar, but common is a pretty relative word in this case.

1865. For some reason this seems to be slightly rarer than the 1860-64 coins in mint state, especially in gem. In proof it is about the same rarity as the 1864, with a few less PR-65's but with two PR-66's! This is the last of the No Motto Seated Dollars struck for circulation (the two 1866 No Motto's are proofs).

1866. The start of the Seated Dollar With Motto variety (In God We Trust added above the eagle on the reverse). It is more common than the 1860-65's in mint state, especially in high grade, though not much different in overall mint state rarity. Examples include 1) Jimmy Hayes, $31,900; 2) Auction '86:747. "gem", $15,950; 3) Auction '87:249. The two No Motto proofs (one is missing now having been stolen from the Willis duPont collection in 1967) are controversial. Breen calls them "pieces de caprice", reportedly struck as a favor for Robert Coulton Davis, though they have been listed in catalogues as "transitional" items for so long that they are generally accepted as such. The With Motto proofs are available in grades PR-65 and below, though there is one PR-66 from an original proof set which came from Auction '79.

1867. This date is rarer than 1866 in mint state, obviously so in MS-65 and better. With a "medium" high mintage (for Seated Dollars anyway) of 47,525, one would expect it to be available in mint state, but with all Seated Dollars, this is not the case and it is very rare in high grade. The proofs are seen with about the same frequency as 1866's, although in PR-65 and above the 1867 is probably a bit tougher.

1868. This date is tougher in high grade than either the 1866 or 1867, although the B & M New York Public Library specimen was amazing. This is possibly the NGC MS-65 . That coin traded hands three times (!) at a Southern California show in the mid-1980's. Proofs seem to be slightly more common in higher grades than 1866 or 1867. PCGS has even graded two PR-66's!

1869. This date is rumored to exist in hoards, though I have no personal knowledge of such and doubt that they exist. There is one MS-66 graded by PCGS, but this date is rare in higher grades also, with this coin the exception. Proofs seem to be about available as 1868's, with one PR-66 graded by PCGS.

1870. The first Philadelphia Seated Dollar of the Seventies has a wonder coin also. The "Mint Set" MS-66 is probably the finest known business strike. This set (half-dime, quarter, half dollar, and dollar) is probably a "put together" set, but who cares, as the dollar — like the other coins — is spectacular. One would think that with a mintage of 416,000 that this date would be relatively easy to obtain in mint state, but it is actually as rare as many other dates in MS-65 and above and only slightly more common in lesser grades. The proofs are on the same rarity plane as 1866-1869, though NGC has graded one PR-66 specimen.

1870-CC. This is the "commonest" CC Seated Dollar in mint state. Certainly the Liberty Seated Dollar series is filled with as many rarities as any U.S. series. This date, though a few mint state coins are known, is very rare in mint state and many of the uncs that have been offered would not be called mint state by the grading services. An extremely rare coin above MS-63 and really, an overall rarity rating near the 1850-O, 1851, 1852, and 1859-S, etc.

1870-S. The king of mint state Liberty Seated Dollars, the 1870-S! It has to be king because the best known and the best likely to be known is AU. What more can be said? A moot point. The AU Norweb coin may forever be the finest known of this coin that has no record of mintage. If the San Francisco Mint Building cornerstone is ever unearthed and the coin is still there and if there is no damage from the elements and . . . I can always hope and dream! PR-67!

1871-CC. This ranks with the 1850-O, 1851, 1852, 1859-S, and a few others as a monster mint state rarity. PCGS has graded none in mint state and NGC has seen a couple. Usually seen in XF or AU at best and prohibitively rare above MS-63. Norweb: 3828.

1872. There still is doubt but a least one bag of a thousand coins was dispersed in the Treasury disgorging of the early 1960's. I say doubt, for when one looks at the population data, you would say this highest mintage Seated Dollar (1,106,450) is just as rare as many other dates. The highest graded is MS-65 by PCGS and there aren't many more graded in all mint state grades, but they can be found. Proofs are available in PR-64 and PR-65, though no PR-66's are yet graded.

1872-CC. Another of the "virtually impossible to find in mint state" CC's. The Bareford coin was uncirculated and there have been a few others, but this date ranks with the other "super" dates of Seated Dollars. These dates are so close in overall rarity and a hoard, which I would guess for Seated Dollars would be five or more coins, might show up and skew the rarity relationship. Norweb: 3830.

1872-S. Another mystery date. 9,000 supposedly struck, but quite rare in mint state. PCGS has graded an MS-63 coin which may be the coin Ken Goldman had (Fairfield coin I think) or possibly the Robison specimen or the B. Max Mehl-Garrett coin. There aren't many possibilities, you see, so put it with the rarest of the rare.

1873. Not as often seen in mint state as 1871 and 1872, though still available up to MS-64. The mintage of 293,600 explains those coins. A very tough date in MS-65 or higher. Better buy a proof, since this is one of the easiest ones to get in PR-65 or 66.

1873-CC. A few AU's of this date are available and there were 3 uncs that were taken from a Carson City cornerstone. Neither PCGS or NGC has seen one that they will call mint state. Possibly the second rarest mint state Seated Dollar trailing only the 1870-S, though a piece or two of this date in unc is imaginable, especially if one of the cornerstone pieces surfaces. Norweb: 3833.

1873-S. We come to the most controversial date of them all. 700 (?) minted? All melted? All dated 1872-S? Rumor of a coin persists. I would pay a fancy sum just to gaze upon it. What a fitting way to end this treatise on my favorite series of United States coinage. This series has been underappreciated in the dollar series for too long. Perhaps if there weren't so many "stoppers," promoters would have hyped them as they have with their better known cousins — Mr. Morgan and Mr. Peace. Alas, not so. But that doesn't detract from this fabulous series. What more can be said? Oh, that's an easy one, I'll come close with a statement that I mentioned earlier that was my comment about this date in the past. This remark is valid for almost all the dates in the Liberty Seated Dollar series. When asked to comment on this date, all I could come up with was the lame answer: "Good Date!"

That's it. What a fabulous series!

***

Senior Editor's note: The Liberty Seated Collectors Club is an organization dedicated to Liberty Seated dollar collectors and enthusiasts. Membership information for the club may be obtained by writing to John Kroon, P.O. Box 1062, Midland, Michigan, 48641. Dues are $11 per year.

Mr. Christian Gobrecht, ChristianGobrecht
Designer of The Liberty Seated Dollars
(Courtesy of Nevada State Museum)

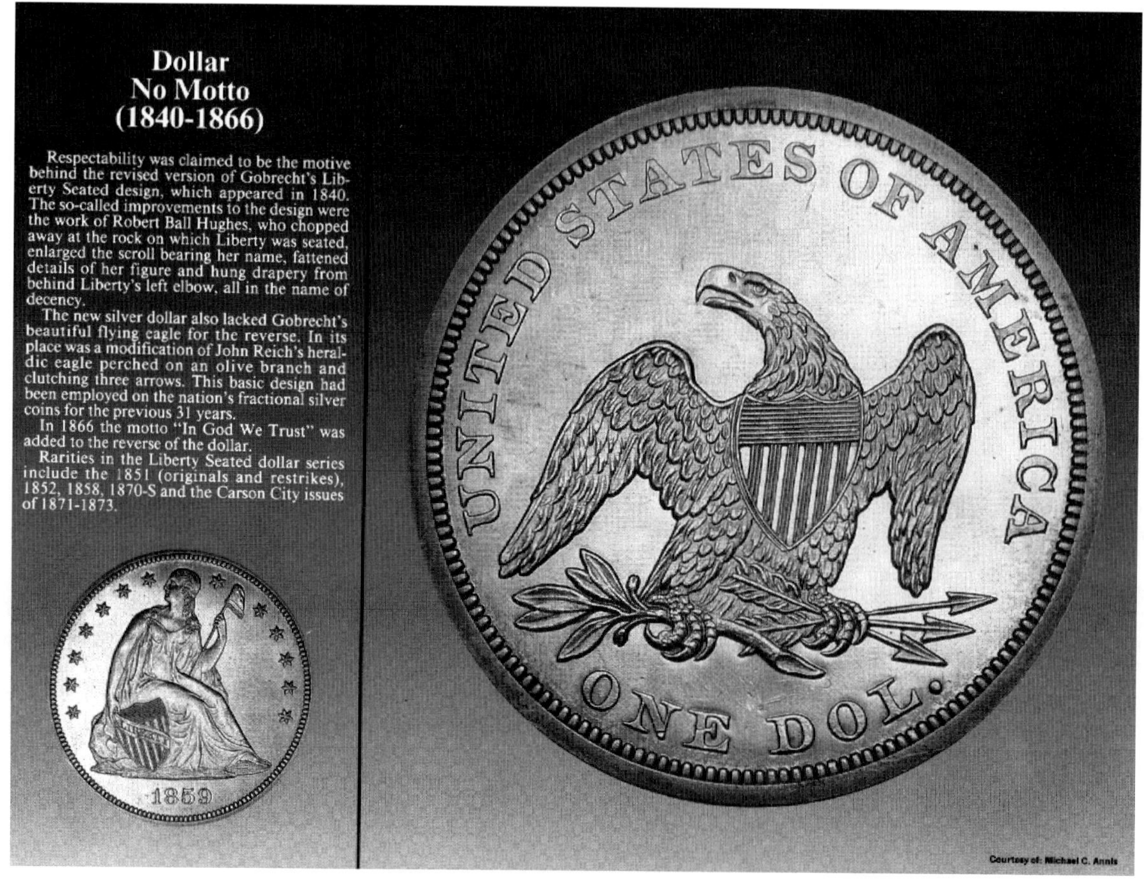

(Coin courtesy of Michael C. Annis)
(Photo provided by Krause Publications)

Gem Uncirculated 1886-O Dollar

MS-67 DPL (NGC)

"The Most Spectacular Morgan Dollar Now Known"

400 **Gem Uncirculated 1886-O Morgan Dollar. MS-67 DPL (NGC).** The identical specimen described by Wayne Miller in *The Morgan and Peace Dollar Textbook* (n.d.) as **"The incredible deep mirror cameo** [this coin] **is universally considered to be the most spectacular Morgan dollar now known, considering the extreme rarity of this date in gem prooflike condition." THE ULTIMATE MORGAN DOLLAR!** This is the **Wayne Miller Plate Coin** pictured on p. 113 of the above referenced text. In his description, Wayne notes that "The typical 1886-O is heavily bag marked, with indifferent lustre." He goes on to say that ". . . Mint State specimens are very scarce. Because of heavy surface abrasions present on most specimens, gems are rare." This example is absolutely, incredibly, pristine, with deep prooflike surfaces which one could get lost in! In fact, even at full arm's length, the surfaces perfectly and clearly reflect anything presented to them, exactly like a mirror. The obverse and reverse central devices, Miss Liberty's bust to the left and the displayed eagle, are perfectly, completely, and beautifully frosted, without a mark, abrasion, or sign of handling on them. It would appear that this piece was struck from a very early state of the dies, before many, if any, had been coined, and carefully preserved at the New Orleans Mint from the moment of its striking. Its quality must have been acknowledged even as early as the day it was struck, for it has been carefully handed down from owner to owner in its original pristine condition for more than 100 years! Who was the original owner? Was he the New Orleans Mint superintendent at the time, the mint's coiner, an important person from New Orleans society, we may never know. What we can say, with absolute certainty is that no matter how far one looks today, no matter how much effort and time and money is expended, no finer Morgan dollar is presently known or available to collectors.

No other 1886-O Morgan dollar has been graded higher than this example. The July 31, 1990 NGC *Population Census* shows the following: No examples graded by this service in MS-60, one graded MS-61, none graded MS-62, one graded MS-63, **none graded higher!** The PCGS mid August 1990 *Population Report* shows a similar grading trend: two graded MS-60, one graded MS-61, one graded MS-62, one graded MS-63, one graded MS-64, **none graded higher.**

The opportunity presented by the auction appearance of this phenomenal specimen cannot be overemphasized. No other 1886-O Morgan dollar has been graded higher than this one, and in fact, it outranks all other known examples of this date by a full three grading points. When the chance to acquire this example has passed, when will another present itself? Clearly, many, many years may pass before a collector might obtain a second chance at acquiring this outstandingly beautiful, memorably breathtaking dollar, which has been justifiably called **the most spectacular Morgan dollar now known.**

1886-O Gem Prooflike dollar, Lot 400, sold by Auctions by Bowers and Merena, Inc. as part of the Chris Schenkel Collection Sale, November 1990. $231,000.

Bruce Amspacher

Bruce Amspacher has been a full time rare coin dealer and numismatic writer since 1968. His articles have appeared in dozens of publications, including *The Coin Dealer Newsletter*, *Gary North's Rare Coin Investment Review*, *Numismatic News*, *Coin World*, *Legacy*, and his own *Bruce Amspacher Investment Report (BAIR)*.

Mr. Amspacher is one of the founders of the Professional Coin Grading Service (PCGS), and has done many radio and television programs, seminars, and open forums promoting the numismatic industry.

CHAPTER 62

United States Trade Dollars: 1873-1885

by Bruce Amspacher

U.S. Trade Dollar (1873 - 1885)
(Courtesy of Krause Publications)

This article is dedicated to the memory of Michael Gauya

The opening interview with Bruce Amspacher was conducted by David Lisot on November 8, 1990 in St. Louis, Missouri.

How are you working with John Highfill for the Silver Dollar book?

I've written a chapter on trade dollars, a date by date analysis, a little about die varieties, condition rarity, and history of the Trade dollar, all those things went into that article. Throughout the book there will be other articles by dealers in their respective areas of expertise. My understanding is John W. Dannreuther is doing Seated dollars, William E. Spears is doing Carson City dollars, and there will be other dealers in the book in their areas of specialty.

Why did you pick Trade dollars?

Actually, Trade dollars were picked for me. John called and asked if I would do Trade dollars. The word in the coin business was that I know a lot about Trade dollars. I had written a couple of articles about trade dollars for the Coin Dealer Newsletter Summary a few years ago. I have always dealt in them. I like the big coins, silver dollars, Liberty Seated dollars, and Trade dollars. I was the designated expert in that area.

What is it about the Trade dollar that intrigued you?

For one thing, I'm very much into condition on coins. I'm a big believer in MS-65 and better coins and Trade dollars is one of the rarest series for a short lived series to find in gem condition. There are a great number of coins in the series that are extremely rare in MS-65 or better. Meaning that there are two, one, or none known in MS-65 or better. That is a very significant rarity. It's hard to get rarer than none known! There are some coins, for example the 1876-CC is unknown better than MS-63. The 1877-P is unknown in MS-65, there are no 74-CC known in MS-65, no 77-CC known in MS-65, there is only one 74-P known in MS-65, and only three proofs of 1874 known in MS-65. It is something that would really surprise you, a lot of the coins that people relegate to the common date status are in fact extremely rare. You can add 1874-S also, a coin with a mintage of over 4 million with no MS-65 coins known.

To what would you attribute the scarcity of the high grade coins?

The coin was originally designed and adopted to use for trade in China. The accepted currency in China was the Mexican peso, the old style Mexican peso, and the U.S. silver dollar was underweight in relationship to that. So the American traders had to go buy Mexican pesos in order to do trade with China and had to frequently pay premiums of 15 or 20% over their value in order to get them in order to do their trading. So the U.S. needed a heavier coin and they designed the Trade dollar. Almost the entire mintage of 1873 went to China and the coins ended up being mishandled, they had no numismatic value to them, they were just coins. Many of them were heavily cleaned and chopmarked and impaired in some other way. So very few coins actually survived.

In 1876 it was declared that they were no longer legal tender in the United States, so for that reason they weren't saved. People actually wanted to get rid of them because they were worth only about 80 cents in melt after the silver crash of 1876 and since they weren't legal tender, it was just a problem coin. Sort of a Susan B. Anthony type situation, where there was a coin that nobody wanted, so the coin was not saved. Now that the collectors have come along and want it they find there are no condition coins for them to buy. It's an extremely rare coin in top condition.

Why was the series discontinued?

The series was discontinued because of the questionable legal tender status. The coin was worth about 80 cents in melt value after the silver crash. The merchants would not accept the coin at a dollar face, but people were getting them in their pay envelopes. For instance, if someone who owned a mine would buy them for 83 cents and put them in people's pay envelopes at a dollar, and then the people would go to spend them, the merchants either would not take them or would only take them at a value of about 80 cents. For this reason they took the legal tender status away from them completely in 1876 so that people would not be paid with them. But they did continue to strike them in 1877 and 1878. They also struck some proof coins up through 1883. Later on, 1884 and 1885 Trade dollars were also made. They did not appear until 1908.

Were the coins accepted by the Chinese?

Very much so, they were very happy with them, the coins were a tremendous success abroad. They were very happy with them because of their weight. They weighed the same as the old style Mexican peso, the full 420 grains and that was what they were interested in. The value came in the amount of silver, so they were a tremendous success abroad.

What about the stories about bags of Trade dollars still in China?

There may very well be, and if there are, they are probably cleaned and chopmarked. I've been to Hong Kong three times in the last five years and we always go around and go to the coin shop buildings and run up and down the stairs and see all the different people. All the Trade dollars that I've run across are cleaned and/or chopmarked. I have a feeling that even if they come to the door uncleaned and unchopmarked, that the dealers will clean them before they offer them. It seems to be the way of the Orient, that everything has to be shiny before it can be offered. So most of the coins are ruined, even if they do show up in original condition. I really cannot imagine that there are any significant number of Trade dollars in collector condition. I hope it is true, but I can't imagine it.

With so many mints striking Trade dollars, where did all the coins go and why were none saved by collectors then?

A lot of the mintage was melted, most of the mintage went to China. It was not popular in the U.S. and a lot of the coins received heavy wear. Unlike the Morgan dollar, where there seems to be a roll or two or five now and then of almost anything, there are very few Trade dollars. There was a very nice group of 1878-S coins that came out some time in the last year with some MS-65 and MS-66 coins in it, but basically almost with that exception there has never been a significant hoard of quality Trade dollars. There was a hoard that Worldwide Coin Investments found in the early 70s and a lot of dates were in it but they were mostly MS-60+ quality or lower and many chopmarked coins and many cleaned coins. There were a lot of Carson City coins in that deal also.

To collectors, how does the Trade dollar compare in interest to the Seated dollar compared to the Morgan and Peace series?

The Trade dollars actually seem to have more interest than the Seated dollars do because they are not quite so esoteric. The Seated dollars have so many rarities in them that it is really staggering. The Trade dollar is a much shorter series. The Seated dollar ran from 1840 to 1873, or some might say 1836 to 1873, if they count the Gobrecht patterns. Whereas the Trade dollars were actually only from 1873 to 1878, was all the years that they made coins for circulation. There were some proof only issues, from 78-83 and 84 and 85. Trade dollars seem to be of more interest to collectors because the set is shorter and more completible, even though they have to ignore the 1884 and 1885. Even in relatively poor condition an 1884 Trade dollar is worth $30-40,000 and the 1885 is worth much more.

Introduction to the Trade Dollar

Obverse Reverse

1878-S Trade Dollar PCGS 66 "A Pristine Example!"
(Courtesy of Heritage Numismatic Auctions)

The Trade Dollar may be America's most unusual coin. At the time of its issue it was controversial: loved abroad and despised in its land of origin. It was heavier than the just-repealed silver dollar; in fact, its weight was the reason for its existence, since it was to be used in foreign commerce. The design by William Barber was considered uninspired (at least at the time), and all too soon the coin became an economic nightmare.

The Trade Dollar, as a collector series, is equally unusual, filled with minuscule mintages, condition problems, odd die varieties, a few highly touted "wonder" coins, and two of the most famous rarities in all of numismatics.

Trade Dollars were issued for circulation from 1873 through 1878. Proofs (known as "proof-only" issues **after** 1877) were struck from 1873 through 1883. In addition, 1884 and 1885 Trade Dollars were struck sometime prior to 1908, though almost certainly not in 1884-85.

To begin at the beginning, the Trade Dollar had its origins out of necessity. Americans trading with the Orient found the silver dollars of 1840-73 unacceptable because they were underweight relative to the Mexican pesos so liked by the Chinese. In order to do business, Americans were forced to purchase pesos, frequently at highly inflated prices. The Act of February 12, 1873 authorized the new, heavier coin, and by October of that year the first American Trade Dollars had reached China.

While the Trade Dollar was a success overseas, it was a disaster at home. When silver prices crashed in 1876, the Trade Dollar (of legal tender status to the limit of $5 per transaction) flooded the American economy. It had a "real" value of about 80 cents, but a face value of one dollar. While such a problem is almost inconceivable today, when coins have virtually no intrinsic value, it was a serious setback for the already jittery economy of 1876. On July 22, 1876, Congress withdrew the Trade Dollar from legal tender status.

The rarity of quality Trade Dollars for collectors is due to three significant factors. One, the **mintage** for many issues is small; incredibly so when compared to the issues of today. For instance, eight different issues have a mintage of less than 2,000 coins. Two, **melting** of some Trade Dollars took place, and it is believed that nearly one-half of the 1878-CC mintage was lost due to melting. Three, many Trade Dollars that reached the Orient were damaged due to **chopmarks** (counterstamped ideograms, often firm names). In addition, enormous numbers of Trade Dollars have suffered mishandling and abusive cleaning.

From this awkward history the collecting of Trade Dollars was born, and many of the collectors have been as legendary as the coins they owned. Looking at only one issue, **1884** Trade Dollars have been owned by Adolphe Menjou, King Farouk, Colonel Green, Jerome Kern, Dunham, Baldenhofer, Wolfson, Clapp, Eliasberg, Atwater, and Neil - a literal "roll call" of American numismatics from the first half of the 20th century. What about Idler, Haseltine, Adams, Brand, Norweb, Granberg, Woodin, and Johnson? They owned **1885** Trade Dollars. Of course, many of the aforementioned persons owned both.

Charles E. Barber, Designer
The Trade Dollars

A Brief Date-by-date Analysis Of The Top Survivors Known Of Each Issue.
First, The Proof Trade Dollars Of 1873-85.

1873 - Mintage of 865 coins. Usually seen with a low degree of reflectivity characteristic of proofs of 1873-76. **Rare** in "gem" (Proof 65 or better) condition. Most specimens known today have been cleaned to some degree. A minor softness of strike is characteristic of this issue.

1874 - Mintage of 700 coins. The **rarest** of the non-clandestine issues in "gem" condition. Most known specimens are heavily impaired; unusual, considering that all 700 coins are believed to have been issued with the original proof sets of that year.

1875 - Mintage of 700 coins. Struck from two distinct reverse dies. Type I (Berry under claw, as in 1873-4) is much rarer than Type II (No berry under claw). A somewhat controversial issue, as many low quality proofs are offered as "prooflike" uncirculated coins. Many proofs of 1875 are weakly struck, especially in the area of Miss Liberty's head. **Rare** in "gem" condition.

1876 - Mintage of 1150 coins. Almost all known specimens have the "Type II" reverse (No berry under eagle's claw on viewer's right). Notorious for poor quality, both from mediocre mint work and post-minting mishandling. **Rare** in "gem" condition.

1877 - Mintage of 510 coins. The minting quality of the proof Trade Dollars improved dramatically from 1877 through 1883, probably due, at least in part, to the new obverse hub introduced in 1877. **Rare** in "gem" condition, and popular due to the extreme rarity of the 1877 business strikes in top condition.

1878 - Mintage of 900 coins. The first of the "proof-only" issue Trade Dollars from the Philadelphia mint. San Francisco and Carson City continued producing coins for circulation through 1878. **Rare** in "gem" condition, although the majority of the finest pieces extant are not only "gem," but **superb**. To put it another way, the coin is seen in Proof 66 grade more often than it is seen in Proof 65 condition. [Only 683 sold; 217 were "released into circulation" in 1879, according to Robert W. Julian.]

1879 - Mintage of 1541 coins. **Scarce** in "gem" condition (actually quite rare, but we are speaking in relative terms). Proof-only issue, as are all that follow. Some known specimens have heavily frosted devices and deeply mirrored fields.

1880 - Mintage of 1987 coins. The most commonly seen date in Proof 65 or better, but still considered **scarce** in "gem" condition. A beautifully made coin (at its best), with the look of a modern issue medal.

1881 - Mintage of 960 coins. **Scarce** in "gem" condition and about twice as rare as the 1879 and 1880 dates, both in mintage and survival rates. Several so-called "wonder" coins are known of this date. Many have a flat head and strike.

1882 - Mintage of 1097 coins. Almost exactly equal in rarity to the 1881; **scarce**. Some flatness is characteristic of strike, especially on the obverse. Breen attributes this to a deteriorating hub, which is unquestionably a correct assessment, as each year the strike quality is slightly inferior to the preceding year.

1883 - Mintage of 979 coins. **Scarce** in "gem" condition; about equal in rarity to 1881 and 1882. Popular as last year of "collectible" type. Slightly sub-par in overall quality (strike, depth of mirror, eye appeal) compared to issues of 1879-82.

1884 - Mintage of 10 coins. **Unknown** in "gem" condition. Invariably seen in moderately impaired condition (Proof 60-63). Unknown until 1908. Most examples, and possibly all, have been traced to Idler/Haseltine. Breen reports that one coin has "allegedly" been in a Chicago estate since the 1890s. One of the most famous of all U.S. coins, yet almost undoubtedly a "fantasy coin."

1885 - Mintage of 5 coins. **Unknown** in "gem" condition, and, as is true with the 1884 issue, always seen in Proof 60-63 condition. Even more famous than the 1884 Trade Dollar, and of the same provenance. All five known 1885 Trade Dollars are thoroughly pedigreed, and mintage figures are probably correct as no sixth coin is known or rumored. All known examples are traced to Idler/Haseltine. Breen notes that no records account for the bullion used to make the coins, there is no record of making the dies, and no striking or delivery dates exist. Undoubtedly a "fantasy coin."

The "circulation strike" or "business strike" Trade Dollars are dated from 1873 through 1878, and were struck in Philadelphia (no mint-mark), San Francisco ("**S**" mint-mark), and Carson City, Nevada ("**CC**" mint-mark). There are seventeen different date/mint-mark combinations, one overmintmark (1875-S/CC), and countless varieties. Below is a brief date-by-date analysis of the **business strike** Trade Dollars. **Note**: There are references to Type I and Type II **obverses** and **reverses**. On the Type I *obverse*, the ribbon (or scroll) with "LIBERTY" written on it points to the observer's left at the base; RT, ST about touch. The Type II obverse details a ribbon that points downward; RT and ST apart. The *reverse* Type I variety, as mentioned earlier, shows a berry below the eagle's claw on the viewer's right. On the Type II reverse, this berry is missing.

1873 - (Philadelphia mint issue) - Mintage of 397,000 coins. Scarce in all mint-state grades, **rare** in "gem" condition. Almost the entire mintage was shipped to China. Frequently seen with strike weakness, especially on Miss Liberty's head and eagle's leg on viewer's right. Several high quality pieces have been seen with a heavy, nearly "muddy," patina. In great demand as a first year of issue.

1873-S - Mintage of 703,000 coins. Scarce in all mint-state grades, **rare** in "gem" condition. Nearly all shipped to China. Long regarded as a rarity in mint state (i.e., this date has always carried a heavy price/date premium).

1873-CC - Mintage of 124,500 coins. Rare in all mint-state grades, **extremely rare** in "gem" condition (in fact, I have never seen a coin that graded above MS-63). Once again, nearly the entire mintage was shipped to China. At least half of the mint-state examples known came from a hoard dispersed by World Wide Coin Investments in the early 1970s.

1874 - (Philadelphia mint issue) - Mintage of 987,100 coins. Scarce in all mint-state grades, **extremely rare** in "gem" condition. This date has only recently become appreciated for its rarity in top grades; in the early '70s it was relegated to the "common" status (a mistake based on mintage rather than actual observation, as recognizing "condition rarities" was a little-known form of numismatic research at that time).

1874-S - Mintage of 2,549,000 coins. Scarce in mint state, **extremely rare** in "gem" condition. See comments on 1874-Philadelphia issue. Almost mystifyingly rare considering the mintage. Most mint-state examples known have softly struck areas, especially around the head of Miss Liberty.

1874-CC - Mintage of 1,373,000 coins (Possibly 1,373,200 coins). Scarce in all mint-state grades, **extremely rare** in "gem" condition. Notorious for weakly struck and oddly struck examples. Usually has subdued luster similar to the New Orleans mint Morgan dollars of 1895-97.

1875 - (Philadelphia mint issue) - Mintage of 218,200 coins. Scarce in mint state, **extremely rare** in "gem" condition. One famous "wonder" coin is known of this date: ex-Pine Tree, "Fairfield" auctions (graded MS-68 by PCGS). First year of the "type two" reverse, even though this date and others of 1875-76 are found with both reverses. Because of the rarity of top quality business strikes of this date, some proofs (usually impaired) are offered at times as "gem uncirculated, prooflike."

1875-S - Mintage of 4,487,000 coins. Relatively common in mint state, **scarce** in "gem" condition. Frequently seen with a "blob" mint-mark characteristic of the San Francisco issues of 1875 (also seen on the 1875-S dime and twenty cent piece). Many strike problems, but, because of high mintage and survival rates, an inordinately high number of quality pieces exist today.

1875-S/CC - Mintage unknown; part of 1875-S mintage. Rare in mint-state, **extremely rare** in "gem" condition. The most significant and popular of the Trade Dollar die varieties. Two distinct reverse die varieties exist; one (extremely rare) with "CC" far to the right of the "S." Almost all examples known today have one "C" partially obscured by the over-mint-mark "S."

1875-CC - Mintage of 1,573,700 coins. Scarce in mint state, **extremely rare** in "gem" condition. Some mint-state examples have a heavily striated obverse die. Highly lustrous for a "CC" issue, and popular because of the "look" of the coin. A small hoard dispersed in the 1970s is probably responsible for most mint-state examples known today.

1876 - (Philadelphia mint issue) - Mintage of 455,000 coins (According to Breen, 145,000 of these are the Type I obverse/reverse variety). Relatively common in mint-state, **scarce** in "gem" condition. Relatively high survival rate for a low mintage coin. Unusually well struck for a Trade Dollar, except for the eagle's claw on the observer's left.

1876-S - Mintage of 5,227,000 coins - Relatively common in mint state, **rare** in "gem" condition. This date is sometimes collected by die variety due to the pairing of Type I and Type II obverse dies with the Type I and Type II reverse dies in all but one of the possible combinations (I haven't seen or heard of a pairing of the Type II obverse with the Type I reverse). The finest specimens of this date have an extremely intense luster; most examples have a minor striking problem.

1876-CC - Mintage of 509,000 coins - Rare in mint state, **unknown** in "gem" condition. One of the true rarities of the series, along with the 1873-CC, 1877-CC, and 1878-CC. I have asked many veteran dealers about this date, and almost without exception they state that they have "never seen a nice one." I have not seen enough mint-state examples to report on any characteristics.

1877 - (Philadelphia mint issue) - Mintage of 3,039,710 coins. Relatively common in mint state, **extremely rare** in "gem" condition. An unusual situation, similar to the 1874-S, where many mint-state survivors still produce **no** "gem" specimens, at least to date. Noted with usual problems of strike and excess marks from bag storage or improper handling.

1877-S - Mintage of 9,519,000 coins. Relatively common in mint state, **rare** in "gem" condition. This is the most frequently seen date in mint condition, as the mintage would suggest. At its best, one of the prettiest dates of the series, with outstanding luster.

1877-CC - Mintage of 534,000 coins. Scarce in mint state, possibly **unknown** in "gem" condition. "Average" in overall appearance, with good (but not great) luster, a good (but not great) strike, etc. Usually seen heavily marked or with some cleaning.

1878-S - Mintage of 4,162,000 coins. Relatively common in mint state, **relatively common** in "gem" condition. This is the "common date" of the series in "gem" condition, as about three dozen pieces are known in MS-65 or better. This shows the true rarity of "gem" quality Trade Dollars, in my opinion, when the "common date" is one where **one coin** out of every 115,000 (!) survived in top condition.

1878-CC - Mintage of 97,000 coins. Scarce in mint state, **extremely rare** in "gem" condition. This date has been considered the number-one rarity, or "key," of the series for decades. Recent research into condition rarity shows that the 1878-CC is actually fourth or fifth in overall mint-state rarity, despite the low mintage. A famous and popular coin.

I am deeply indebted to two books that were used extensively in researching this article. Rather than burden my text with dozens of footnotes, I have decided to save the accolades for last. The books I am talking about are Walter Breen's *Complete Encyclopedia of U.S. and Colonial Coins* and Walter Breen's *Encyclopedia of United States and Colonial Proof Coins*. Without these two works, the research on this article would have taken dozens of hours longer. Each book is a fountain of reliable and accurate information, filled with scholarship and wit.

Well, tell me the truth, aren't Trade Dollars absolutely fascinating?

Trade dollar (1873-1885)

Designed by William Barber, the Trade Dollar was introduced in 1873 in response to demand for a bullion piece for use in trade with the Far East.

Several factors — including nonacceptance by Oriental merchants and its limited legal-tender status of $5 in the U.S. — caused the Trade Dollar to quickly become a drug in domestic markets.

Ironically, though it contained more silver than any previous or subsequent U.S. silver dollar, the Trade Dollar found only limited acceptance in the U.S., where it was heavily discounted and rejected.

In 1876 the Trade Dollar's legal-tender status was revoked by Congress, but it continued to be coined for circulation until 1878 and for collectors until 1885.

The retirement of this handsome, but unloved coin became a major point in President Chester A. Arthur's annual message on Dec. 3, 1883. In 1887 the government redeemed an estimated 8 million of the over 36 million Trade Dollar coins minted — most of which were by then in the hands of speculators.

Trade Dollar (1873-1885)
(Courtesy of Krause Publications)

***

John W. Highfill, NLG

CHAPTER 63

Morgan Dollars

by John W. Highfill, NLG

(Coin courtesy of Leroy Van Allen)
(Photo provided by Krause Publications)

The Liberty Head (popularly known as the Morgan) dollar was the heart of the mightiest hoard of silver dollars ever assembled. When the presses finally ceased production of Morgans in 1921, a total of 657,013,609 dollars had been minted during the 43 year life of the Morgan series that began in 1878. Millions and millions of silver dollars! How could this have happened? Why were they produced? Where did they all go?

In order to understand the Morgan dollar and the reasons for its existence, one must look to events which took place prior to the striking of the first of the "new standard dollars" in 1878. The prime motivators and champions of silver and the silver dollar were the owners of the vast silver mines discovered in the West during the 1860s and 1870s. They had suffered a severe blow when Germany dumped silver in the world market, and another when the Act of February 12, 1873, established the one dollar gold piece as the standard. (See "The Carson City Mint: A Branch Mint Profile" for additional information on this Act.)

The Liberty Seated design by Christian Gobrecht, the existing silver dollar, was replaced by William Barber's Trade dollar, a heavier dollar designed to compete with Mexican dollars for acceptance by Chinese merchants via treaty. Congress mistakenly made these legal tender — as a favor to the silver lobby.

Germany led the countries of the world to the gold standard when it took that step in 1871 and dumped several thousand tons of silver into the market. This fact coupled with the overwhelming quantities of U.S. silver which became available during the 1870s (via the Comstock Lode and other discoveries) brought the price of silver down significantly. Western U.S. silver was overproduced. The United States was able to purchase all the foreign silver it wanted at discount prices. Consumers had no need for the enormous amounts of available domestic silver bullion — and still they kept producing, while prices kept falling. The Western silver lobbyists intensified their efforts and won the support of Congressmen such as Senator William B. Allison (R-Iowa) and, Representatives Richard P. Bland (D-Mo.), John A. Kasson (R-Iowa) and William D. Kelley (R-Pa).

The next Congressional action of the "Silver Dick" Bland campaign even partly in favor of the silver interests was the Act of July 22, 1876, which consisted of a joint resolution for the issue of silver coins. The Act abolished the Trade dollar as domestic legal tender, limited its production to existing export demands, and authorized silver bullion purchases for certain uses.

Act of July 22, 1876

Resolved by the Senate and House of Representatives of the United States of America in Congress assembled, That the Secretary of the Treasury, under such limits and regulations as will best secure a just and fair distribution of the same through the country, may issue the silver coin at any time in the Treasury to an amount not exceeding ten million dollars, in exchange for an equal amount of legal-tender notes; and the notes so received in exchange shall be kept as a special fund separate and apart from all other money in the Treasury, and be reissued only upon the retirement and destruction of a like sum of fractional currency received at the Treasury in payment of dues to the United States; and said fractional currency, when so substituted, shall be destroyed and held as part of the sinking-fund, as provided in the act approved April seventeen, eighteen hundred and seventy-six.

SEC. 2. That the trade dollar shall not hereafter be a legal tender, and the Secretary of the Treasury is hereby authorized to limit from time to time the coinage thereof to such an amount as he may deem sufficient to meet the export demand for the same.

SEC. 3. That in addition to the amount of subsidiary silver coin authorized by law to be issued in redemption of the fractional currency it shall be lawful to manufacture at the several mints, and issue through the Treasury and its several offices, such coin, to an amount, that, including the amount of subsidiary silver coin and of fractional currency outstanding, shall, in the aggregate, not exceed, at any time fifty million dollars.

SEC. 4. That the silver bullion required for the purposes of this resolution shall be purchased, from time to time, at market rate, by the Secretary of the Treasury, with any money in the Treasury not otherwise appropriated; but no purchase of bullion shall be made under this resolution when the market-rate for the same shall be such as will not admit of the coinage and issue, as herein provided, without loss to the Treasury; and any gain or seigniorage arising from this coinage shall be accounted for and paid into the Treasury, as provided under existing laws relative to the subsidiary coinage: *Provided*, That the amount of money at any one time invested in such silver bullion exclusive of such resulting coin shall not exceed two hundred thousand dollars.

That was a start, but the silver mine owners wanted much more. Their goal was legislation requiring large purchases of domestic silver for minting into silver dollars. On the economic front, the price of silver and gold was coming together at a propitious moment for Bland, Allison and their supporters. During 1877, the thrust of their efforts was twofold: (1) to authorize production of silver dollars as legal tender once more, and (2) to compel the U.S. Treasury to purchase tremendous quantities of domestic silver for coinage into silver dollars. Mint authorities realized that passage of such a bill would be only a matter of time; the question was not *if* but *when* they would have to make unprecedented quantities of silver dollars.

The eventual designer of the "new standard dollar," George T. Morgan, was born during 1845 in Birmingham, England. After receiving his education, he became associated with the Royal Mint in London under the tutelage of Leonard C. Wyon, noted designer and modeler of British Empire coinage. When Mint Director Linderman asked the Royal Mint's Deputy Master C.W. Fremantle, to recommend a designer for the new dollar, Fremantle nominated Morgan. Linderman at once hired the 32 year old Morgan as assistant engraver. One of Morgan's initial assignments was to create a design for a new silver dollar. This assignment amounted to a competition between Morgan and then chief engraver William Barber for the new design. William Barber, designer of the Trade dollar, wanted no part of this newcomer or his designs.

Meanwhile, on Capitol Hill, Richard Bland and William Allison seemed to be in sight of the finish line with a bill which met all of the silver interest's wildest dreams. Only a few hurdles remained. Critical Congressional votes were won through a compromise in which the silver interests agreed to support an unwanted tariff bill. The final obstacle was the vote to override President Rutherford B. Hayes's veto of the proposed bill. When the dust had settled, the victorious Bland and Allison had secured passage of the Act of February 28, 1878 (commonly known as the "Bland-Allison Act"). The major sections of the Act re-established the silver dollar as legal tender and authorized its production from dictated bullion purchases of between two and four million dollars per month. The notification of each branch of Congress overriding the President's veto is also presented.

George T. Morgan (1845 - 1925) was the designer of the Liberty Head (Morgan) Dollar and later chief engraver of the U.S. Mint.

(Bland-Allison Act)Act of February 28, 1878 (Bland-Allison Act)

Be it enacted by the Senate and House of Representatives of the United States of America in Congress assembled, That there shall be coined, at the several mints of the United States, silver dollars of the weight of four hundred and twelve and a half grains troy of standard silver, as provided in the act of January eighteenth, eighteen hundred thirty-seven, on which shall be the devices and superscriptions provided by said act; which coins together with all silver dollars heretofore coined by the United States, of like weight and fineness, shall be a legal tender at their nominal value, for all debts and dues public and private, except where otherwise expressly stipulated in the contract. And the Secretary of the Treasury is authorized and directed to purchase, from time to time, silver bullion, at the market price thereof, not less than two million dollars worth per month, nor more than four million dollars worth per month, and cause the same to coined monthly, as fast as so purchased, into such dollars; and a sum sufficient to carry out the foregoing provision of this act is hereby appropriated out of any money in the Treasury not otherwise appropriated. And any gain or seigniorage arising from this coinage shall be accounted for and paid into the Treasury, as provided under existing laws relative to the subsidiary coinage: *Provided*, That the amount of money at any one time invested in such silver bullion, exclusive of such resulting coin, shall not exceed five million dollars: *And provided further*, That nothing in this act, shall be construed to authorize the payment in silver of certificates of deposit issued under the provisions of section two hundred and fifty-four of the Revised Statues.

SEC. 2. That immediately after the passage of this act, the President shall invite the Governments of the countries composing the Latin Union, so-called, and of such other European nations as he may deem advisable, to join the United States in a conference to adopt a common ratio between gold and silver, for the purpose of establishing, internationally, the use of bi-metallic money, and securing fixity of relative value between those metals; such conference to be held at such place, in Europe or in the United States, at such time within six months, as may be mutually agreed upon by the Executives of the Governments joining in the same, whenever the Governments so invited, or any three of them, shall have signified their willingness to unite in the same.

The President shall, by and with the advice and consent of the Senate, appoint three commissioners, who shall attend such conference on behalf of the United States, and shall report the doings thereof to the President, who shall transmit the same to Congress.

Said commissioners shall each receive the sum of two thousand five hundred dollars and their reasonable expenses, to be approved by the Secretary of State; and the amount necessary to pay such compensation and expenses is hereby appropriated out of any money in the Treasury not otherwise appropriated.

SEC. 3. That any holder of the coin authorized by this act may deposit the same with the Treasurer or any assistant treasurer of the United States, in sums not less than ten dollars, and receive therefor certificates of not less than ten dollars each, corresponding with the denominations of the United States notes. The coin deposited for or representing the certificates shall be retained in the Treasury for the payment of the same on demand. Said certificates shall be receivable for customs, taxes, and all public dues, and, when so received, may be reissued.

SEC. 4. All acts and parts of acts inconsistent with the provisions of this act are hereby repealed.

Sam J. Randall,
Speaker of the House of Representatives.
W. A. Wheeler,
Vice-President of the United States and President of the Senate.

IN THE HOUSE OF REPRESENTATIVES U.S.
February 28, 1878

The President of the United States having returned to the House of Representatives, in which it originated, the bill, entitled "An act to authorize the coinage of the standard silver dollar, and to restore its legal-tender character," with his objections thereto; the House of Representatives proceeded in pursuance of the Constitution to reconsider the same; and

Resolved, That the said bill pass, two-thirds of the House of Representatives agreeing to pass the same.

Attest: GEO. M. ADAMS,
Clerk.
By GREEN ADAMS,
Chief Clerk.

IN THE SENATE OF THE UNITED STATES
February 28, 1878

The Senate having proceeded, in pursuance of the Constitution, to reconsider the bill entitled "An act to authorize the coinage of the standard silver dollar, and to restore its legal-tender character," returned to the House of Representatives by the President of the United States, with his objections, and sent by the House of Representatives to the Senate with the message of the President returning the bill;

Resolved, That the bill do pass, two-thirds of the Senate agreeing to pass the same.

Attest: GEO. C. GORHAM,
Secretary of the Senate.

Returning to the discussion of the design of the new silver dollar, Morgan persuaded Anna W. Williams to model for his design of Miss Liberty. Miss Williams, a schoolteacher concerned for her position, consented to model only after assurances that she would not be identified. His design was along traditional lines with a Liberty head obverse and heraldic type eagle reverse. Both George T. Morgan and William Barber submitted designs for consideration, but Linderman selected Morgan's design after noting striking problems associated with Barber's work.

The obverse design features the traditional Liberty head facing left, adorned with a Phrygian cap marked "LIBERTY" together with two heads of wheat and two cotton blossoms. The words "E PLURIBUS UNUM" appear along the top rim of the coin with the date at the bottom. The remainder of the perimeter of the piece contains seven stars on the left edge and six stars on the right. The initial "M" of the designer is placed at the bottom of the neck above the lowest curl of hair.

The main device on the reverse is the eagle with wings outstretched. The eagle is holding an olive branch in its right talon and three arrows in its left talon. Two laurel branches tied with a bow surround the lower body of the eagle. Words all around the rim of the coin includes "UNITED STATES OF AMERICA" at the top and "ONE DOLLAR" at the bottom. The motto, "IN GOD WE TRUST" appears just above the head of the eagle completing the reverse design.

Critical specifications of the new dollar included a net weight of .77344 ounces of silver in a composition of .900 fine silver and .100 copper. The diameter of the coin was set at 38.1 millimeters with a total weight of 26.73 grams.

After minor alterations were made, Morgan's design became official on February 28, 1878. First production of the new silver dollar was at Philadelphia. The first three proofs were delivered on March 11, 1878, to President Hayes, Secretary of the Treasury John Sherman (the future author of the Sherman Silver Purchase Act), and Mint Director Linderman. On the next day, 100 more proofs were struck at the Philadelphia Mint. The initial popularity of the Morgan dollar among the public was due to the new design; among the silver interests, to rejuvenation of their dreams of a captive subsidy market. Under provisions of the Bland-Allison Act, 378,166,793 Morgan silver dollars were produced.

The Act of March 3, 1887 and Act of March 3, 1891 authorized silver dollars to be produced using bullion obtained from Trade dollars as well as from Trade dollars existing in the U.S. Treasury. The conversion of Trade dollars led to the minting of 5,078,472 Morgan dollars.

Three additional laws were directly responsible for the amount of Morgan dollar production during the years 1891 through 1904. These were the Act of July 14, 1890 (known as the Sherman Silver Purchase Act); the Act of November 1, 1893 (repealing the Sherman Silver Purchase Act); and the Act of June 13, 1898. The first of these, the Sherman Silver purchase Act authored by Senator John Sherman, contained three sections of interest. Section 3 directed mintage of silver dollars after July 1, 1891, to be limited to the amount required for possible redemption of Treasury notes, while Section 5 repealed the portion of the Bland-Allison Act requiring monthly bullion purchases of not less than two million dollars and coinage of same (In place of the repealed requirement, up to four million five hundred thousand ounces of silver was to be purchased each month). The bonanza for the silver interests was that the newly purchased silver was to be paid by Treasury Notes of 1890 (redeemable in gold) and coined only into silver dollars. These Treasury Notes (alias Coin Notes) were recycled again and again by the silver mine owners who hoarded all of the gold received for their silver bullion.

Act of July 14, 1890 (Sherman Silver Purchase Act)

Be it enacted by the Senate and House of Representatives of the United States of America in Congress assembled, That the Secretary of the Treasury is hereby directed to purchase, from time to time, silver bullion to the aggregate amount of four million five hundred thousand ounces, or so much thereof as may be offered in each month, at the market price thereof, not exceeding one dollar for three hundred and seventy-one and twenty-five hundredths grains of pure silver, and to issue in payment of such purchases of silver bullion Treasury notes of the United States to be prepared by the Secretary of the Treasury, in such form and of such denominations, not less than one dollar nor more than one thousand dollars, as he may prescribe, and a sum sufficient to carry into effect the provisions of this act is hereby appropriated out of any money in the Treasury not otherwise appropriated. . . .

SEC. 3. That the Secretary of the Treasury shall each month coin two million ounces of the silver bullion purchased under the provisions of this act into standard silver dollars until the first day of July eighteen hundred and ninety-one, and after that time he shall coin of the silver bullion purchased under the provisions of this act as much as may be necessary to provide for the redemption of the Treasury notes herein provided for, and any gain or seigniorage arising from such coinage shall be accounted for and paid into the Treasury.

SEC. 4. That the silver bullion purchased under the provisions of this act shall be subject to the requirements of existing law and the regulations of the mint service governing the methods of determining the amount of pure silver contained, and the amount of charges or deductions, if any, to be made.

SEC. 5. That so much of the act of February twenty-eighth, eighteen hundred and seventy-eight, entitled "An act to authorize the coinage of the standard silver dollar and to restore its legal-tender character," as requires the monthly purchase and coinage of the same into silver dollars of not less than two million dollars, nor more than four million dollars' worth of silver bullion, is hereby repealed. . . .

The Sherman Act enabled 168,674,682.53 fine ounces to be purchased at a cost of $155,931,002.25 for which Treasury Notes were issued.

By 1893, serious consequences had developed as a result of the Sherman Silver Purchase Act of 1890, under which production of Morgan dollars amounted to 36,087,285 pieces prior to the repeal of the silver purchase authority on November 1, 1893; 42,139,872 were coined between November 1, 1893 and June 12, 1898; and 108,800,188 were coined as directed by the act of June 13, 1898. This came to a final total of 187,027,345 silver dollars responsible to the Sherman Silver Purchase Act. Under the Acts of March 3, 1887 and March 3, 1891, authorized coinage from Trade Dollar Bullion and Trade Dollars then in the Treasury, 5,078,472 standard silver dollars were minted. U.S. international obligations were payable only in gold (of which the U.S. Treasury had only an inadequate supply) while the Treasury vaults bulged with silver dollars useless for international debt. The panic of 1893 ensued with 419 bank failures. President Grover Cleveland called a special session of Congress to repeal the Sherman Silver Purchase Act. The repealing Act of November 1, 1893, resulted in no further purchases of silver bullion.

Act of November 1, 1893

Be it enacted by the Senate and House of Representatives of the United States of America in Congress assembled, That so much of the act approved July fourteenth, eighteen hundred and ninety, entitled "An act directing the purchase of silver bullion and issue of Treasury notes thereon, and for other purposes," as directs the Secretary of the Treasury to purchase from time to time silver bullion to the aggregate amount of four million five hundred thousand ounces, or so much thereof as may be offered in each month at the market price thereof, not exceeding one dollar for three hundred and seventy-one and twenty-five one hundredths grains of pure silver, and to issue in payment for such purchases Treasury notes of the United States, be, and the same is hereby repealed. And it is hereby declared to be the policy of the United States to continue the use of both gold and silver as standard money, and to coin both gold and silver into money of equal intrinsic and exchangeable value, such equality to be secured through international agreement, or by such safeguards of legislation as will insure the maintenance of the parity in value of the coins of the two metals, and the equal power of every dollar at all times in the markets and in the payment of debts. And it is hereby further declared that the efforts of the Government should be steadily directed to the establishment of such a safe system of bimetallism as will maintain at all times the equal power of every dollar coined or issued by the United States, in the markets and in the payment of debts.

The Act of June 13, 1898, mandated that all silver bullion previously purchased under the Sherman Silver Purchase Act be coined into silver dollars. Production of Morgan dollars under the provisions of this Act amounted to 108,800,188. During the years 1878 through 1904, a total of 570,283,609 Morgan dollars were struck. Once that supply was exhausted in 1904, production of silver dollars stopped, and the mammoth U.S. Treasury hoard including 27 years of silver dollars was at its highest level.

One of the most well known pieces of legislation to affect the quantity of surviving Morgan dollar specimens was the Act of April 23, 1918. In what is known as the Pittman Act, the main purposes of Congress were to protect the gold supply of the United States, permit trade balance settlement in silver and provide silver for subsidiary coinage, stabilize the price of silver and encourage its production. Here is the text of this important Act that led to the melting of 270,232,722 (the maximum authorized was 350,000,000) Morgan silver dollars.

Act of April 23, 1918 (Pittman Act)

Be it enacted by the Senate and House of Representatives of the United States of America in Congress assembled, That the Secretary of the Treasury is hereby authorized from time to time to melt or break up and to sell as bullion not in excess of three hundred and fifty million standard silver dollars now or hereafter held in the Treasury of the United States. Any silver certificates which may be outstanding against such standard silver dollars so melted or broken up shall be retired at the rate of $1 face amount of such certificates for each standard silver dollar so melted or broken up. Sales of such bullion shall be made at such prices not less than $1 per ounce of silver one thousand fine and upon such terms as shall be established from time to time by the Secretary of the Treasury. [Notes 1 & 2]

SEC. 2. That upon every such sale of bullion from time to time the Secretary of the Treasury shall immediately direct the director of the Mint to purchase in the United States, of the product of mines situated in the United States and of reduction works so located, an amount of silver equal to three hundred and seventy-one and twenty-five hundredths grains of pure silver in respect of every standard silver dollar so melted or broken up and sold as bullion. Such purchases shall be made in accordance with the then existing regulations of the Mint and at the fixed price of $1 per ounce of silver one thousand fine, delivered at the option of the Director of the Mint at New York, Philadelphia, Denver, or San Francisco. Such silver so purchased may be resold for any of the purposes hereinafter specified in section three of this Act, under rules and regulations to be established by the Secretary of the Treasury, and any excess of such silver so purchased over and above the requirements for such purposes, shall be coined into standard silver dollars or held for the purpose of such coinage, and silver certificates shall be issued to the amount of such coinage. The net amount of silver so purchased, after making allowance for all resales, shall not exceed at any one time the amount needed to coin an aggregate number of standard silver dollars equal to the aggregate number of standard silver dollars theretofore melted or broken up and sold as bullion under the provisions of the Act, but such purchases of silver shall continue until the net amount of silver so purchased, after making allowance for all resales, shall be sufficient to coin therefrom an aggregate number of standard silver dollars equal to the aggregate number of standard silver dollars theretofore so melted or broken up and sold as bullion. [Note 3]

SEC. 3. That sales of silver bullion under authority of this Act may be made for the purpose of conserving the existing stock of gold in the United States, of facilitating the settlement in silver of trade balances adverse to the United States, providing silver for subsidiary coinage and for commercial use, and of assisting foreign governments at war with the enemies of the United States. The allocation of any silver to the Director of the Mint for subsidiary coinage shall, for the purposes of this Act, be regarded as a sale or resale.

SEC. 4. That the Secretary of the Treasury is authorized, from any moneys in the Treasury not otherwise appropriated, to reimburse the Treasurer of the United States for the difference between the nominal or face value of all standard silver dollars so melted or broken up and the value of the silver bullion, at $1 per ounce of silver one thousand fine, resulting from the melting or breaking up of such standard silver dollars.

SEC. 5. That in order to prevent contraction of the currency, the Federal Reserve banks may be either permitted or required by the Federal Reserve Board, at the request of the Secretary of the Treasury, to issue Federal reserve bank notes, in any denominations (including denominations of $1 and $2) authorized by the Federal Reserve Board, in an aggregate amount not exceeding the amount of standard silver dollars melted or broken up and sold as bullion under authority of this Act, upon deposit as provided by law with the Treasurer of the United States as security therefor, of United States certificates of indebtedness, or of United States one-year gold notes. The Secretary of the Treasury may, at his option, extend the time of payment of any maturing United States certificates of indebtedness deposited as security for such Federal reserve bank notes for any period not exceeding one year at any one extension and may, at his option, pay such certificates of indebtedness prior to maturity, whether or not so extended. The deposit of United States certificates of indebtedness by Federal reserve banks as security for Federal reserve bank notes under authority of this Act shall be deemed to constitute an agreement on the part of the Federal reserve bank making such deposit that the Secretary of the Treasury may so extend the time of payment of such certificates of indebtedness beyond the original maturity date or beyond any maturity date to which such certificates of indebtedness may have been extended, and that the Secretary of the Treasury may pay such certificates in advance of maturity, whether or not so extended. [Note 4]

SEC. 6. That as and when standard silver dollars shall be coined out of bullion purchased under authority of this Act, the Federal reserve banks shall be required by the Federal Reserve Board to retire Federal reserve bank notes issued under authority of section five of this Act, if then outstanding, in an amount equal to the amount of standard silver dollars so coined, and the Secretary of the Treasury shall pay off and cancel any United States certificates of indebtedness deposited as security for Federal Reserve bank notes so retired.

SEC. 7. That the tax on any Federal reserve bank notes issued under authority of this Act, secured by the deposit of United States certificates of indebtedness or United States one-year gold notes, shall be so adjusted that the net return on such certificates of indebtedness or such one-year gold notes, calculated on the face value thereof, shall be equal to the net return on United States two per cent bonds, used to secure Federal reserve bank notes, after deducting the amount of the tax upon such Federal reserve bank notes so secured.

SEC. 8. That except as herein provided, Federal reserve banknotes issued under authority of this Act, shall be subject to all existing provisions of law relating to Federal reserve banknotes.

SEC. 9. That the provisions of Title VII of an Act approved June fifteenth, nineteen hundred and seventeen, entitled "An Act to punish acts of interference with the foreign relations, the neutrality, and the foreign commerce of the United States, to punish espionage, and better to enforce the criminal laws of the United States, and for other purposes," and the powers conferred upon the President by subsection (b) of section five of an Act approved October sixth, nineteen hundred and seventeen, known as the "Trading with the Enemy Act," shall in so far as applicable to the exportation from or shipment from or taking out of the United States of silver coin and silver bullion, continue until the net amount of silver required by section two of this Act shall have been purchased as therein provided.

Note 1: Under Section 1, only 270,232,722 silver dollars were melted, out of the 350,000,000 authorized. Some 259,121,554 (about 96% of the total number melted) were earmarked for sale as bullion to Great Britain. To avert protest from silver lobby and silver speculators, this shipment was diverted to India — about 209 million ounces of fine silver. Did this bullion become part of the large 1919 mintages of Bombay and Calcutta rupees and Bombay half rupees?

Note 2: The other 4% (11,111,168 silver dollars) went to the melting pots to be converted into dimes, quarters, and half dollars. Because each silver dollar weighs 6.92% more than two halves or four quarters or ten dimes, in theory this amount would have made $11,880,136 in small change, primarily dimes and quarters. We have not seen the actual amounts going to each mint for any of these denominations. But the melted dollars may well have contributed to the large mintages of 1920 Philadelphia quarters and dimes and possibly 1923 dimes, with smaller amounts to other mints and denominations.

Note 3: Sections 2 and 3 perverted the Act's purpose into yet another subsidy for politically powerful western silver mine owners. The 270,232,722 melted Morgan dollars were replaced (at taxpayer expense: $1 per oz plus expenses) with 86,730,000 1921 Morgan and 183,502,722 Peace dollars through 1928. *VAM*, pp. 11-13.

Note 4: All knew that silver dollars could not be forced to circulate so long as paper dollars continued. All knew that a "contraction of the currency" (major lowering of the amount of paper currency in circulation) would be disastrous — though obviously they forgot by 1929. To avert this, the Act's framers authorized issue of $1 and $2 Federal Reserve Bank Notes, Series of 1918, along with more of the higher denominations already in use; these would be withdrawn after enough paper dollars were coined. The $1 and $2 notes actually issued far exceeded the face value of the 1921 Morgan and Peace dollars struck: $478,892,000 in $1's and $135,192,000 in $2's from the twelve districts, total $614,084,000. As not all Series of 1918 quantities issued have been publicized, they are printed here; all figures are in millions of pieces:

Branch	**$1**	**$2**	**$5**	**$10**	**$ 20**
Boston	39.600	12.468	0.440		
New York City	106.724	15.216	6.400	0.200	
Philadelphia	51.056	8.004	1.600		
Cleveland	46.240	4.320	2.600		
Richmond	23.384	3.736			
Atlanta	35.760	2.300	1.200	0.184	0.096
Chicago	64.432	9.528	3.000	0.200	
St. Louis	27.908	3.300	1.524	0.100	0.024
Minneapolis	17.320	1.672	0.828		
Kansas City	24.820	2.652	4.000		
Dallas	17.864	1.252	0.300		
San Francisco	23.784	3.188	0.500		
	478.892	67.636	22.392	0.684	0.120

Plus 4,000 $50's from St. Louis. Over 99% of all these have been recalled.

In 1921, a final year of Morgan dollar production brought 86,730,000 pieces of the amount required by law to replace coins melted under the Pittman Act. This brought the total number of Morgan dollars minted to 657,013,600.

Morgan Dollar Mintage: Annual Summary

Turning to the production sites, Morgan dollars were coined at five United States facilities. They were the mints at Philadelphia, Carson City, Denver, New Orleans and San Francisco. The following table shows the years of production at each facility.

Philadelphia	1878 through 1904, 1921
Carson City	1878 through 1885, 1889 through 1893
Denver	1921
New Orleans	1879 through 1904
San Francisco	1878 through 1904, 1921

(From *Annual Report of the Director of the Mint*, 1885)

	1884	1885
Philadelphia	$.0130	$.0189
New Orleans	.0155	.0149
San Francisco	.0437	.0580
Carson City	.0728	.0913

(The cost of coinage was principally the cost of striking)

The regular Morgan dollar series consists of 96 different date and mintmarks. Production exceeded one million pieces in 82% of those issues (79 of the 96). The award for the largest production year and mintmark of the entire series goes to the 1921-P, of which 44,690,000 were struck.

Morgan Dollar Mintage By Year (Including Proofs)

Year	Total Mintage	Year	Total Mintage
1878	22,495,550	1892	6,333,245
1879	27,560,100	1893	1,455,792
1880	27,397,355	1894	3,093,972
1881	27,927,975	1895	862,880
1882	27,574,100	1896	19,876,762
1883	28,470,039	1897	12,651,731
1884	28,136,875	1898	14,426,735
1885	28,697,766	1899	15,182,846
1886	31,423,886	1900	24,960,912
1887	33,611,710	1901	22,566,813
1888	31,990,833	1902	18,160,777
1889	34,651,811	1903	10,343,755
1890	38,043,004	1904	8,812,650
1891	23,562,735	1921	86,730,000

The individual dies for the Morgan dollar series were created at the Philadelphia Mint. The desired mintmark was then punched directly onto the dies before they were shipped to the proper branch mint for their use. Each branch mint would do the final work on the dies before placing them into production at their facility.

Wayne Miller reported in his *Morgan and Peace Dollar Textbook* that the Carson City Mint struck an average of 60,000 coins per working die pair, San Francisco averaged 120,000, New Orleans averaged 150,000 and Philadelphia Mint averaged over 200,000 per working die pair.

Carson City Morgan Dollars

This special word about Carson City acknowledges the many Carson City silver dollar collectors. These avid collectors find the historic and romance of the old West coupled with the relatively small number of coins required (only thirteen production years) irresistible. Carson City is located 14 miles from historic Virginia City, the site of the famous Comstock Lode and many other Nevada silver mines. The Carson City Mint was opened July 1, 1869, and struck its first coins in 1870.

The last coin was struck in 1893 and the Mint was officially converted to an Assay Office on July 1, 1899, 30 years after its opening. The total number of Morgan silver dollars produced at Carson City was 13,862,041. (Note to collectors: Many 1889-CC Morgans were released into circulation shortly after minting, which contributes to the scarcity of uncirculated specimens.)

Carson City dollars not released were shipped to the U.S. Treasury for storage. This long and arduous trip covered over 30 miles of dirt roads from the Carson City Mint to the railway station at Reno, Nevada. Then railroad boxcars and rough handling continued to damage the coins and inflict severe bag marks. Finally, mint employees tossed the canvas bags of coins as they were moved to a more or less permanent storage location. Abusive bagmarks were an unavoidable result of this rough treatment.

In 1970, President Nixon signed a bill authorizing the General Services Administration to sell the remaining Carson City dollars via mail bids. All of these coins were delivered in airtight G.S.A. holders. G.S.A. held seven mail bid sales to liquidate 2,937,965 Carson City dollars. Five sales took place from October 1972 through June 1974. Two others were held in 1980. Nearly 3 million coins realized over $94 million in sales. These sales relieved the U.S. Treasury of its remaining silver dollar hoard.

Designs and Varieties

There were basically four different obverse and reverse designs used in the Morgan dollar series. Wayne Miller described them so well and succinctly in his *The Morgan and Peace Dollar Textbook* that I would like for you to read his descriptions.

"The first obverse design type depicts Liberty with an evenly divided ear lobe; on the reverse, the breast of the eagle is flat and concave. The eagle has eight tail feathers. This design was utilized only in 1878, for the striking of a few hundred thousand dollars at the Philadelphia mint."

"The Second obverse design evidences an unevenly divided ear lobe, with the fuller part toward the face. On the reverse, the breast of the eagle is flat and concave, but the eagle exhibits seven tail feathers. There are two varieties of this design, with long and short center arrow feathers. This design was used in the striking of the majority of other 1878 silver dollars, and for some 1879-S and 1880-CC dollars."

"The third obverse design involved only slight modifications of the second design. However, the reverse of the third design exhibits two major changes: The breast of the eagle is rounded and full, and the top arrow feather in the bundle is not longer parallel to the others but slants upward. This design was utilized for most 1879-S and 1880-CC dollars, and for all other dollars from 1879-1904."

"The fourth obverse design was utilized for the striking of all 1921 Morgan dollars. Although many changes were made, these are the most noticeable: The hairlines are more deeply etched; the eye lash is missing; there is no crease above the chin; and the latter is "tucked up" more than on earlier designs. On the modified reverse design the eagle's breast is flat and concave, the arrow feathers are parallel, and the stars are larger."

The Type IV and C4 dies

The Type IV obverse and reverse dies were used only in the 1921-P,D and S Morgans. They are crude copies of 1878 7TF. The hairlines are more distinct, deeper and somewhat different above Miss Liberty's ear on the obverse. Her cheek is flatter also. The reverse shows an almost concave (flat) breast instead of the usual more rounded breast. The stars on the reverse are larger and all of the arrow feathers are parallel. The "S" is a "micro-S" and is very hard to see on the 1921-S. The "D" is a "micro-D" and is also very hard to see on the 1921-D. Sometimes you have to tilt the coin at just the right angle and light to see both of these tiny mint marks.

The C4 reverse was from a new master die and was used during the years 1900 through 1904. The reverse eagle breast feathers will not be as deep and may appear to many as a weak strike. The C4 reverse also has a "wet" look that would make one believe it was "metal flow" instead.

The C4 reverse displays a number of identifying characteristics. The eagle's breast feathers are not sharply defined, and may give the appearance of being softly struck. There is a greater distance on the right side of the eagle's wing from where the wing joins the eagle's neck. The junction is U-shaped, not V-shaped. The reverse stars are larger. These are the most significant differences which must be taken into account when grading these coins.

In the year 1901, the Philadelphia Mint started to use gas furnaces for the annealing process instead of the older wood burning furnaces. The problem is there was not enough oxidation. There was also too much heat for the annealing of the silver strips prior to the punching of the planchets. This total process created problems with the "metal flow" and strike in all the years thereafter (1901-P through 1904-P).

The C4 reverse was first used in 1900 thus creating a new major variety. The dates using the C4 reverse die for all or a portion of the mintage were:

The following Morgan dollar dates were totally and exclusively minted using the C4 reverse die.

First Reverse Design
Type A — 8 Tail Feathers

Total C4 Mintage	Partial C4 Mintage
1902-P	1900-P
1902-S	1900-S
1903-P	1901-P
1903-O	1901-O
1903-S	1901-S
1904-P	1902-O
1904-O	
1904-S	

Die Varieties

Leroy Van Allen and A. George Mallis have made an extensive search into all known die varieties associated with the Morgan dollar series are responsible for the following facts concerning the mintmarks and variations used in production of the series. There was a total of seventeen mintmark variations used for the Morgan silver dollars by the branch mint facilities. The Carson City Mint utilized five variations of their distinctive "CC" mintmark. Denver presented the "D" and micro-D, while New Orleans supplied four mintmarks. San Francisco presented the most mintmark variations with a total of six. In the "A Comprehensive Catalog and Encyclopedia of U.S. Morgan and Peace Dollars" by Leroy Van Allen and A. George Mallis, there are descriptions and photographs of more than one thousand die varieties. Since that book was released the author's have discovered over one thousand more die varieties.

Concerning die varieties and their collectibility, Wayne Miller has given this subject a great deal of thought. It is with thanks and appreciation that we reproduce the following personal list of significant Morgan dollar die varieties as contained in Wayne Miller's *Morgan and Peace Dollar Textbook* with minute updated editing. Each of these major varieties is visible without magnification.

1. **1878-P 8TF** (8 tail feather). Actually there are over twenty different die varieties of the 1878 8-tail feather dollar. VAM 23 is the most spectacular, with obverse and reverse doubling.

2. **1878-P 7TF** SAF (Third Reverse, Round Breast). Again, there are many slight die variations among this issue.

3. **1878-P 7/8** VAM 30 Doubled Talons. Both of the Eagle's legs have an extra talon shifted to the left.

4. **1878-P 7/8** VAM 31, with doubled legs and talons, shifted to the right.

5. **1878-P 7/8** VAM 33. The Eagle's legs are 1 1/2 times normal width with a double set of claws.

6. **1878-P 7/8** VAM 38, doubled LIBERTY with shift to the left — the largest shift of this kind known among the entire Morgan silver dollar series.

7. **1878-P 7/8** VAM 41, seven tail feather ends showing. Strongest tail feather overstrike known.

Type IV Obverse
(Courtesy of Leroy Van Allen and A. George Mallis)

C^4 Reverse
(Courtesy of Leroy Van Allen and A. George Mallis)

D Reverse
(Courtesy of Leroy Van Allen and A. George Mallis)

8. **1878-P 7/8** VAM 43, doubled legs and talons shifted to the left.

9. **1879-S** PAF (Second Reverse, Flat Breast). Several slight die variations exist. Very popular variety (See entire chapter on this special variety, co-authored by both John W. Highfill and Walter H. Breen, entitled the 1879-S rev 78.

10. **1880-P, 8/7** Variety, VAM 6. The top of the 7 is clearly visible above the second 8. There are several 1880-P overdates; this is the most pronounced.

11. **1880/79-CC**, PAF VAM 4. The 80 is clearly repunched over the 79 in the date. Second reverse with the flat breast design.

12. **1880-CC 8/7** low, VAM 6. The 8 is repunched over the 7 in the date with the original 7 punched low. Third reverse, round breast. The scarcest of the major 1880-CC overdate die varieties.

13. **1880-O**, VAM 4. The 80 is repunched over the 79 in the date. Such specimens are often prooflike.

14. **1880-S**, VAM 8 and 9. The 80 is repunched over the 79 in the date.

15. **1882-O/S**, VAM 3, 4, 5 and 6. What appears to be the center shaft of an "S" mintmark is clearly visible within the "O" mintmark. These varieties exhibit very small dots of metal, particularly upon the raised surfaces, due to rusted dies.

16. **1887-P, 7/6** overdate. VAM 2. The remains of the base of the 6 are clearly visible under the 7 of the date.

17. **1887-O** VAM 2, Doubled 2 and tripled 7 in date. One of the largest date doubling shifts known. Most specimens are heavily bagmarked.

18. **1887-O 7/6** overdate VAM 2. The bottom loop of the 6 is visible at the bottom of the stem of the 7, curving upward. All specimens known to the author are flat struck.

19. **1888-O** VAM 4, doubled head variety with two complete sets of lips, chin and nose clearly visible. Also known as "Hot Lips." Very rare in grades above EF.

20. **1888-O** VAM 1A. Clashed die marks on the reverse reveal the "E" of LIBERTY below the Eagle's tail feathers on the left side. This phenomenon also occurs among 1886-O and 1891-O dollars but the 1889-O "E" clash is by far the rarest, with fewer than five specimens known in any grade. A partial "E" clash has been found on 1878-P, 1880-P, 1883-O, 1884-P and 1887-P dollars.

21. **1890-CC** VAM 4, the tail bar variety. Extra metal caused by a gouge in the die extends from the junction of the Eagle's tail feathers and arrow feathers down to the wreath.

22. **1900-O/CC** VAM 7 through 12. The remains of the "CC" mintmark are visible under the "O". VAM 7 and VAM 10 are the most common, and evidence the least amount of anomaly.

23. **1901-P** VAM 3, the shifted Eagle variety. Much of the Eagle is strongly doubled, particularly the tail feathers.

24. **1903-S** VAM 2, with very small mintmark. This phenomenon is also observable among specimens of the 1896-O, 1899-O, 1900-O and 1902-O. With the exception of the 1899-O, these "micro" mintmarked dollars are very rare in grades above VF; even the 1899-O is very scarce in uncirculated condition.

25. **1921-P** VAM 2, infrequent reading. On this variety the edge has about 15 percent fewer reeds per lineal inch than normal.

Note: VAM is derived from Van Allen-Mallis.

The following list comprises the consensus top 12 major die varieties (in Brilliant Uncirculated condition). There are three basic reasons.

1. Each of the listed varieties appear weekly in the *Coin Dealer Newsletter*, *Certified Coin Dealer Newsletter*, *Coin World* and *Numismatic News*.
2. All are recognized by both PCGS and NGC grading services and appear in their respective population reports.
3. They are listed and traded by Unitrade and the Certified Coin Exchange electronic trading exchanges.

The VAM numbers associated with each of these die varieties has been provided courtesy of Leroy Van Allen and A. George Mallis. These reference numbers are shown after each date.

Die Varieties	Date	VAM Numbers
3	1882-O/S	3,4,5,6,17,23 *
1	1887/6-O	3
1	1879-CC Capped Die	3
1	1887/6-P	2
3	1880-CC Rev. 78	2,4,7
16+	1878-P 7/8 TF (Weak)	32,33,34,36,37
13	1879-S Rev. 78	4-10,23,24,25,34,35,39
12	1878-P 7TF Rev. 79	200-203,210,215,220-223,230
16+	1878-P 7/8 TF (Strong)	38,39,40,41,42
33	1878-P 8TF	1-14,14-1 to 14-9,15-23
54	1878-P 7TF Rev. 78	70,79-84,100,110-122,130-133,140-146,160-171,185-188,190,195-199
7	1900-O/CC	7,8,9,10,11,12

*VAM numbers 6,17 and 23 are sub-varieties of VAM numbers 3,4 and 5.

The 1879-CC "Capped Die" Variety

The 1879-CC "Capped Die" silver dollar is one of the most interesting Morgan dollar varieties. An original Carson City reverse die (third reverse with seven tail feathers and rounded breast) for 1879 was punched with a small CC mint mark continuing the 1878 style. Before the die was used, a decision was made by the U.S. Mint to change the look of the mint marks on the Morgan dollars to mirror the Trade dollar (which was all but discontinued). As a result the die was repunched with the larger CC punch.

John Love is among my dearest of friends and without his help and inspiration throughout the years, this book would not be a possibility. One of his in-famous quotes on the 1879-CC Capped Die: "Back then dies got clogged at the time from overuse and so they became filled." Interesting selection of words but otherwise sounds okay to me!

The larger mint mark was applied too low on the die and the tops of the small CC remained visible above the larger ones. This gave the mint mark a capped look and led to the "capped die" nickname. Leroy Van Allen assigned VAM number 3 to this variety.

After the die had been altered, the mint engraver tried to hide the original CC by tapping around the mint mark with a blank punch. When the die had been used for a period of time, a press operator at the Carson City Mint caused additional damage to the mint mark area while trying to eliminate the extra CC. This made the mint mark look as if it had been glued on and has led many people to doubt its authenticity. In any case, it would be wise to certify any 1879-CC capped die specimen before purchasing it in a high mint state grade.

Total Silver Dollars Melted (1883-1964)

The following table is provided by Leroy Van Allen and A. George Mallis from their classic text, *A Comprehensive Catalogue and Encyclopedia of U.S. Morgan and Peace Dollars*. The figures cover total silver dollars melted between the years 1883 and 1964. The vast majority of all silver dollars melted were Morgans with Peace dollars in second place. The figures are presented by U.S. fiscal year ending each June 30.

Fiscal Year	Total Melted	Fiscal Year	Total Melted	Fiscal Year	Total Melted	Fiscal Year	Total Melted	Fiscal Year	Total Melted
1883	621	1902	1,893	1921	113,064	1940	366	1959	332,669
1884	--	1903	1,777	1922	2,447	1941	407	1960	191,585
1885	1,850	1904	1,304	1923	2,635	1942	562	1961	196,520
1886	--	1905	2,298	1924	1,918	1943	8,080,983	1962	333,175
1887	8,929	1906	909	1925	1,773	1944	44,658,876	1963	1,080,724
1888	14,055	1907	1,548	1926	2,594	1945	394,317	1964	1,293,378
1889	1,342	1908	1,170	1927	3,638	1946	97,072		
1890	11,977	1909	1,293	1928	1,394	1947	688,946	**Total: 333,022,048**	
1891	10,800	1910	961	1929	852	1948	362,240		
1892	42,881	1911	1,320	1930	1,329	1949	242,666		
1893	10,500	1912	1,024	1931	1,193	1950	274,623		
1894	15,055	1913	4,757	1932	442	1951	334,439		
1895	18,580	1914	785	1933	513	1952	351,642		
1896	2,034	1915	823	1934	504	1953	378,993		
1897	1,898	1916	1,092	1935	649	1954	498,034		
1898	1,365	1917	961	1936	638	1955	669,317		
1899	1,734	1918	68,753,583	1937	339	1956	1,700,211		
1900	1,341	1919	91,370,031	1938	607	1957	216,481		
1901	1,786	1920	10,001,164	1939	629	1958	190,531		

The two most important pieces of legislation authorizing the melting of silver dollars were the Pittman Act of April 23, 1918 and the World War II Silver Act of December 18, 1942. Both of these Acts caused millions of silver dollars to be melted from the gigantic hoard stored in the U.S. Treasury. The Pittman Act led 270,232,722 Morgan dollars to the melting pot, while the World War II Act caused 52,738,933 Morgan and Peace dollars to be melted. The silver bullion resulting from the World War II Act was used in the war effort.

Moving from the general discussion of the Morgan dollar, it's time to review the status of individual date and mintmarks. In order to better understand the position of the individual Morgan dollar dates and their relationships, the following comments are provided.

Categories of Morgan Dollars

Consider the following selected dates from the Morgan dollar series as presented in four somewhat overlapping categories. These are the Common date, Semi-common date, Semi-key date and the Key date Morgans.

Common dates: The most common dates often find their way into beginning collections. They are upgraded over time, or perhaps sold in order to acquire semi-key or key date coins. Investors who purchase common date Morgan dollars will do so for a profit motive, and will sell them if the price is right. As a result of these activities, these coins will recycle in the marketplace over time.

Semi-common dates: Semi-common dates are often collected for the intermediate term as these coins are better than common dates, but not good enough to quality as semi-key dates. They will usually be sold and replaced with a better coin if one comes along. Investors who purchase these coins will offer them at a profit providing a return of these pieces into the marketplace.

Semi-key dates: These specimens are continually sought by collectors, and are acquired and put into collections for the long term. These coins are usually sold only when upgrading a collection or in special situations where cash is needed. Investors acquiring these pieces usually do so for the longer term, and are willing to part with them at the right price.

Key dates: These dates and mint marks are always actively sought by collectors and investors alike. Once found and secured by a collector, they are rarely if ever sold. Investors will part with these rarities only when their objectives are completely met. The highest graded specimens will usually be sold at auction or through a private transaction. Key date coins in higher mint state condition are commonly referred to as "keepers". Most people don't let them go after they finally acquire them.

In order to better understand the details associated with each date and mintmark, refer to the date by date analysis of the Morgan dollar series presented in chapter 80. This date by date analysis is authored by one of the most knowledgeable men in U.S. Silver Dollars in the world today — John W. Highfill. The chapter is also fully color illustrated with every silver dollar from the PCGS "World's Finest Morgan Silver Dollars" tour being used as the official plate coins for this encyclopedia.

Common Dates

The 25 most common dates (in Brilliant Uncirculated condition) as determined from information contained in the certified population reports issued by the two largest grading services, PCGS and NGC include:

Rank	Date	
1.	1881-S	[Commonest]
2.	1880-S	[Not including overdates]
3.	1885-O	
4.	1884-O	
5.	1879-S	[SAF]
6.	1887-P	[Not including 1887/6]
7.	1886-P	
8.	1904-O	
9.	1882-S	
10.	1883-O	
11.	1898-O	
12.	1885-P	
13.	1883-CC	

Rank	Date	
14.	1884-CC	
15.	1899-O	[Large O]
16.	1902-O	[Large O]
17.	1921-P	(M)
18.	1900-O	[Not including O/CC]
19.	1878-S	
20.	1882-CC	
21.	1896-P	
22.	1888-P	
23.	1883-P	
24.	1900-P	
25.	1889-P	[25th commonest]

Remember that the vast number of Morgan silver dollars as well as their size and beauty has served to make this series the most popular in all of numismatics. Some have been too quick to criticize the large numbers of available Morgans without realizing that the very availability of these dollars has generated great interest by the mass of collectors as well as allowing a tremendous number of dealers to make a living specializing in the "cartwheel."

Morgans are favored over all other series by numismatic collectors who study the coins and their many varieties. Collectors favor Morgan dollars for the wide available price ranges found in the various dates, mintmarks, varieties, and condition. Bullion dealers have long used the lowest grade Morgans as an investment medium for their purposes. During the magical silver boom of 1980, the silver in a Morgan dollar was worth over $36! Roll collectors used to have a field day with Morgan dollar rolls (this author handled thousands and thousands of BU Rolls in the 1970/80s), but this form of collecting is declining as the quality and quantity of Morgan dollar rolls diminishes. The series is favored by collectors for the large quantities of semi-prooflike, prooflike, and proof coins available. (The die polishing methods used for the Morgan dollars created the great quantities of semi-prooflike and prooflike coins.) All favor the Morgan dollar issues because they are the most available, price aside.

The area of the country where the "cartwheel" ruled was definitely the old West. Morgan dollars were used in saloons and gambling halls of all territories, and "The Silver Dollar" sign was visible in establishments all over the place. Marksmen used the dollars for practice and contests on a continual basis. Showmen developed all sorts of tricks and presentations revolving around the popular silver dollars. The Morgan dollars were trusted in banking transactions as well, and were much more readily received in the West where paper money was still a bit suspicious. Morgans also became associated with wealth, position and power. Capitalists always seemed to have a large number of them at their disposal. Politicians had been involved in many long disputes concerning silver and its status, and many political campaigns were won or lost on the position of the candidate concerning silver, gold and their relationship. Nevada, Idaho and Montana had vast hoards of silver dollars mainly due to legalized gambling in those states during the middle of this century.

Over the years, the Morgan dollar series has been analyzed in every conceivable manner (but somehow, we still come up with an additional way to view this spectacular market). The advertising and merchandising efforts of Morgan dollar dealers have been reviewed within these covers under the chapter entitled "Merchandising, Publications and Silver Dollars by this author. The number of books, publications, articles, presentations and seminars covering this glorious series have been legion. The number of collectors with interests in Morgan dollars is unparalleled in all of numismatics. Morgan dollars are almost an industry in their own right. Think about all of these points and realize that if the great volume of Morgans was not available, there would be only average interest in the series and little additional dealer activity.

Dealers were especially active in the silver dollar market during the late 1970s and early 1980s. During the bullion boom of 1980, they were willing to buy silver dollars in any condition as they worked to satisfy the public demand.

The 1881-S (most common of all Morgan dollars) has a story to tell. When the Continental Illinois Bank hoard came into the market in the early to mid-1980s, thousands and thousands of gem uncirculated pieces were marketed to hungry collectors. Prices were quoted in several financial publications, drawing a great response. These Morgans were successfully distributed with little trouble in an organized marketing effort. (See the chapter entitled "The Continental-Illinois Bank Deal" by Clark A. Samuelson and Leon E. Hendrickson.)

Another area that should be discussed in buying Morgan dollars by the roll (i.e., in plastic tubes containing 20 specimens of the same date and mintmark). During the early 1980s, rolls were traded by the thousands, their quality was generally good, and a good number of them were still "original" rolls (i.e., not cherrypicked). Over the years, the quality and number of rolls has decreased dramatically. The common problems with buying rolls today are: (1) The rolls have been picked over more than once leaving the vast majority as "put-together" rolls; (2) The rolls are more and more apt to contain some "sliders" rather than uncirculated specimens; and (3) buying and holding a large number of one particular date and mintmark makes the owner more susceptible to changes in value of that particular issue (inadequate diversification).

Semi-common Dates

The 20 leading Semi-common dates (in Brilliant Uncirculated condition) as determined from information contained in the certified population reports issued by the two largest grading services, PCGS and NGC are as follows:

Rank	Date	
1.	1891-CC	[26th commonest]
2.	1897-S	
3.	1890-O	
4.	1880-P	
5.	1890-P	
6.	1880-CC	
7.	1903-O	
8.	1921-D	
9.	1881-O	
10.	1897-P	
11.	1882-P	
12.	1882-O	
13.	1903-P	
14.	1884-P	
15.	1888-O	
16.	1878-CC	
17.	1898-P	
18.	1885-CC	
19.	1881-CC	
20.	1901-O	[45th commonest]

As far as condition rarity is concerned, the relatively strict grading standards of today (as compared to the past) have continued to push many coins into lower grades. This effectively reduces the supply of Morgan dollars salable as gems. Couple this with the fact that there are more coin collectors today than ever before, and realize in which direction the supply/demand ratio is heading.

A corollary of this fact comes to light when some of the long-time dealers reminisce about those bags of "gem" dollars from the past. It could be that their memory has enhanced the quality of the bulk of those coins over the years, and the true fact may be that the large numbers of gem coins are simply not out there.

Intermediate mint state grades such as MS-61, MS-62 and MS-64 are especially prevalent when grading Morgan dollars. For example, pieces submitted to the grading services which do not warrant the MS-63 grade will come back MS-62. Likewise, many MS-64 examples are coins which were submitted in hopes of receiving an MS-65 grade. Some of these coins are submitted a number of times seeking the MS-65 rating creating "padded" numbers on the PCGS and NGC certified population reports. Collectors and investors can purchase intermediate grade coins when upgrading from a lower grade, or when their pocketbooks do not allow the expense of acquiring a higher grade.

Another factor affecting values of Morgan dollars is the existence of a number of prooflike and deep mirror prooflike specimens in the series. The method of die preparation used in those days allowed early strikes from a well-prepared die to be of prooflike quality. Buyers seeking quality coins are willing to pay premiums in order to acquire these coins. Third party grading services recognize and record prooflike and deep mirror prooflike characteristics when grading Morgan dollars. The premium given to prooflikes has shown a tendency to vacillate rather widely creating an additional risk in buying and selling these coins. Another consideration is that prooflikes in the lower mint state grades show scratches and bagmarks quite vividly due to their mirrored surfaces. For that reason, many buyers will only purchase prooflikes in the higher mint state grades (i.e., MS-65 and higher).

Yet another area which should be addressed involves toned Morgan dollars. The oxidation process involving various chemicals upon the surface of the dollars over time (due to reaction with the 10% copper content) has created a rainbow of surface colors on a large number of specimens. Colors vary and may include yellow, gold, blue, purple, gray, green — virtually all colors of the rainbow. This surface toning is appealing on some coins and detrimental to the looks of others. See the "Color Photo Section" chapter later in this volume for superb color pictures of a selected variety of toned pieces. Sellers often ask premium prices for toned specimens, and those who want them are willing buyers. Unfortunately for some, those sellers may use toning as a negative factor when purchasing toned coins. In any case, the subjectivity involving toned Morgan dollars and their value can create a large divergence between their buying and selling prices. One final warning — beware of artificially toned coins, especially when used to cover other deficiencies. These "doctored" coins are often difficult to detect making it imperative for buyers of expensive toned coins to have their prospective purchases certified.

Semi-key dates

The top 25 Semi-key dates (in Brilliant Uncirculated condition) as determined from information contained in the certified population reports issued by the two largest grading services, PCGS and NGC are:

Rank	Date	
1.	1898-S	[26th Rarest]
2.	1902-S	
3.	1891-O	
4.	1886-S	
5.	1904-P	
6.	1889-O	
7.	1900-S	
8.	1888-S	
9.	1891-P	
10.	1887-S	
11.	1892-CC	
12.	1892-O	
13.	1880-O	
14.	1889-S	
15.	1890-CC	
16.	1891-S	
17.	1902-P	
18.	1887-O	
19.	1921-S	
20.	1885-S	
21.	1879-O	
22.	1890-S	
23.	1899-P	
24.	1881-P	
25.	1879-P	[50th rarest]

Surprisingly enough to some, several of the semi-key dates listed above are among those issues with over one million coins originally struck. The reason for their semi-key date status lies in the *surviving* mint state mintage figures in the certified population reports issued by PCGS and NGC. The large number of Morgans destroyed as a result of the Pittman Act and the World War II Act meltings have caused analysts to recognize that the original mintage figure is only one factor in determining the surviving population of an issue.

Other components include the certified population (which after five years has become statistically significant), the numbers released by the U.S. Treasury during the "great silver dollar rush" of the early 1960s, and the quantities of a particular issue which may surface through private hoards such as the Redfield hoard and the Continental Illinois Bank hoard. Morgan dollars of nearly all dates and grades have been made into jewelry and other pieces, forever removing them from the BU coin supply.

As time goes forward and the certified population reports begin to reach the point of diminishing returns (i.e., as fewer raw coins are submitted for certification), more and more accurate "guesstimates" will be made concerning the surviving specimens of each date and mintmark. These estimates will enable the marketplace to place a more reliable rarity estimates on each specific issue. There will always be the possibility of additional hoards coming into the market on occasion, but these should be few and far between.

The reason for the inaccuracy of current surviving numbers is due to the many unknowns associated with the Morgan dollar series. From the known mintages we plunge into the unknown numbers of each date which were melted in response to the Pittman Act. Then we ponder the numbers used in jewelry, lost, damaged or destroyed. Next, the number of mint state specimens must be calculated based upon the best available information (certified population reports). Finally, the possible additional sources of Morgans yet to surface (hoards released in the future) must be kept in mind. This is an inexact science to say the least!

Looking for a moment at the current status of the San Francisco issues, the order of rarity for the later dates is interesting to note. The rarity order for the dates 1897-S through 1904-S is presented below. You might refer to this chart when researching the other "S" mint dates involved. The 1903-S is the most rare and the 1897-S is the most common.

1. 1903-S
2. 1904-S
3. 1901-S
4. 1899-S
5. 1898-S
6. 1902-S
7. 1900-S
8. 1897-S

Among the Carson City issues, there was a realignment of prices and values after the Government Services Administration sales. The 1881-CC was one of the coins which moved to Semi-common status after these sales. Other Carson City dates were given lower rarity ratings after the sales, but collector interest ballooned and easily absorbed the increased supply. On the other hand, the 1879-CC, 1889-CC and 1893-CC Morgans retained their rarity ratings after the GSA sales, for they were virtually non-existent in the distributions.

Key Dates

The Key dates to the Morgan series are shown here. The top 25 (in Brilliant Uncirculated condition) as determined from information contained in the certified population reports issued by the two largest grading services, PCGS and NGC include:

Rank	Date
1.	1893-S [Rarest]
2.	1892-S *
3.	1895-O
4.	1884-S
5.	1901-P
6.	1895-P (Proof) **
7.	1889-CC
8.	1903-S
9.	1893-O
10.	1894-O
11.	1896-O
12.	1894-P
13.	1895-S
14.	1897-O
15.	1896-S
16.	1904-S
17.	1886-O
18.	1883-S
19.	1879-CC
20.	1894-S
21.	1901-S
22.	1893-CC
23.	1893-P
24.	1892-P
25.	1899-S [25th rarest]

* Currently tied in all BU grades for first with the 1893-S. Each of these coins has a total of 24 BU pieces graded by PCGS and NGC as of this writing.

** The 1895-P is a Proof only issue.

Take some time to study the impact on rarity caused by the distribution of Morgan dollars from the major hoards. These include the all-important U.S. Treasury distributions, the Redfield hoard and the Continental Illinois Bank hoard. Early indications of the U.S. Treasury's intent to disperse its holdings came in 1956 when uncirculated bags showed up in banks located in Nevada, Montana and Idaho. These particular areas with their concentration of gambling activities created a natural outlet for silver dollars. The marketing of multiples of uncirculated bags of Morgans from the three major hoards has redefined the rarity of some issues while reinforcing the rarity of others. Some dates considered scarce to rare surfaced in bag quantities from the hoards, while other dates were not represented at all. The lack of government records concerning the great "melts" resulted in many surprises as new supplies came to market from concentrated sources.

As an example, the 1903-O Morgan dollar lists an original mintage of 4,450,000. As late as September 1962, collectors assumed that most coins of this issue were melted under the provisions of the Pittman Act. Uncirculated pieces were extremely difficult to locate and the premium rose accordingly. However, in October 1962, a group of uncirculated 1903-O specimens began to surface. It soon became apparent that many bags of uncirculated 1903-O Morgans had been distributed by the U.S. Treasury in the early stages of the "great silver dollar rush."

The rush accelerated as the general public realized that these and other rarities might be available from the government's holdings. Some watched helplessly as prices for their "rare" 1903-O dollars dropped drastically. Others saw an opportunity to acquire this once rare issue at very modest prices. Those who had actually received the bags of 1903-O Morgans from the Treasury experienced windfall profits as they unloaded their holdings at whatever price the market would bear. Other formerly rare dates lost their premium as quantities were released by the U.S. government. Some dates were released as early as 1958. Two previously rare dates surfacing during the early 1960s include the 1898-O and 1904-O. In fact the 1898-O was among the top five rarest Morgans in mint state condition prior to 1962.

The importance of surviving mintages with respect to both rarity and value have led analysts and numismatists to pour over the mountainous compilations of data associated with the Morgan dollar series for decades. Collectors, investors, dealers and authors have either performed research or studied the research prepared by others looking for any facts shedding light on the situation. Due to melts, hoards, and other outside factors, determining surviving numbers of Morgan dollar issues is inexact at best and a pure guess at worst. Predictions based upon the existing PCGS and NGC population reports have been given additional credence as the statistical significance of the numbers increases over time. Barring the surfacing of large additional hoards (perhaps from Las Vegas or elsewhere in Nevada), population reports will continue to heavily influence valuation of this series. One thing is certain, the last word on Morgan dollars has not been written.

Summary

The Morgan dollar is a coin with class! During its 43 year lifetime it was associated with one of the richest historical periods in America. The design is considered to be one of the best ever presented on a United States coin, and won its designer, George T. Morgan, a permanent place in the numismatic hall of fame. The coin was very popular (although not as a circulating piece) at the time and was collected, jeweled and bedecked to the hilt. Jewelers and craftsmen made pendants, watch fobs, belt buckles and all matter of jewelry and even "love tokens." (Personalized love tokens were made by smoothing off the reverse and then engraving images such as flowers and hearts capped off with a romantic saying and perhaps initials or a name. These tokens would be holed and worn on a chain or mounted in a setting.)

The silver dollar has played a significant role in American history for almost 200 years. The Morgan (Liberty Head) dollar is firmly intrenched in this long history. The Morgan silver dollar holds the prestigious position of being the most popular with American coin collectors. In fact, the Morgan silver dollar is believed to be the single most sought after coin in all of numismatics!

References

Walter Breen's Complete Encyclopedia of U.S. and Colonial Coins, Walter H. Breen, Garden City: Doubleday, 1988

Coinage Laws of the United States 1792-1894, Foreword by David L. Ganz, Wolfeboro, New Hampshire: Bowers and Merena Galleries, Inc., 1991

A Comprehensive Catalogue and Encyclopedia of U.S. Morgan and Peace Dollars, Leroy Van Allen and A. George Mallis, NY: FCI/Arco, 1976

Wayne Miller, *The Morgan and Peace Dollar Textbook*, Metairie, Louisiana: Adam Smith Publishing Co., 1982

***

Superb Gem 1893-S Dollar

3887 **1893-S MS-65** or finer. A superb gem coin, a piece with delicate, lustrous, satiny fields. Quite possibly one of the pieces reserved for examination by the Assay Commission at the time of issue.

The surfaces maintain nearly full original mint brilliance, overlaid with delicate light brownish gold toning. The striking is excellent, the aesthetic appeal is superb, and in every other respect here is one of the very finest known examples of the greatest of all Morgan dollar rarities.

In 1893 at the San Francisco Mint, 100,000 silver dollars were produced. As examples in lower grades are rare today, it is evident that only a small percentage of the mintage actually reached circulation, possibly only a few thousand. Most were later melted, undoubtedly under the provisions of the Pittman Act, 1918, which saw the destruction of 270,232,722 dollars of earlier dates.

In 1893, interest in collecting by mintmark varieties was at its nascent stage, and in that year the landmark publication *Mint Marks*, by Augustus G. Heaton, reached print. However, it was not until 1909, about 15 years later, that mintmark collecting caught on in a big way. In 1893 there was very little interest in collecting Morgan dollars by mintmark varieties, and it is probably safe to say that no more than a half dozen numismatists aspired to acquire current issues when they were released, and even this number may be on the high side.

In 1962-1963, when the Treasury Department released its vast hoard of silver dollars of earlier dates, large numbers of issues considered earlier to be rare, such as the Carson City pieces of the early 1880s, came to light in quantity. However, no 1893-S dollars were among this treasure trove.

Contrary to the laws of supply and demand, or perhaps as a corollary to it, the sudden availability of several hundred million silver dollars of different dates depressed the prices of a few issues for a short time, but before long virtually all Morgan dollars—with just a handful of exceptions—were selling for significantly *more* than they were before the Treasury release!

Earlier, and this goes back to the days when the Norweb and Holden families were collecting, Morgan dollars were much scarcer, and dealers had very low stocks of them. There were not enough around to create much interest, so when Abe Kosoff took a survey of the most popular series with collectors around the year 1960, heading the list was the category of Buffalo nickels, and Morgan dollars didn't finish even close. After 1963 the situation changed dramatically, dozens of dealers specialized only in silver dollars, new markets were created, and the demand increased far greater than the supply of coins increased. Indeed, today in 1988, Morgan dollars are the most popular single series in American numismatics, each year a special convention is given over to the subject of silver dollars, and any professional firm counts the area of silver dollars as a foundation for revenue. A few years ago (we haven't checked since then) the American Numismatic Association Certification Service reported that over 80% of the coins it graded were silver dollars!

Although an 1893-S dollar in Uncirculated grade was a rarity years ago, in proportion to the vastly larger quantities of other dates in collectors' hands since 1962-1963, it is a much greater rarity today. Literally thousands, if not tens of thousands of numismatists have an Uncirculated 1893-S dollar on their want list, and yet so far as true MS-65 or finer pieces are concerned, they are so rare that in the past 35 years we have handled just three or four examples (including the Wayne Miller coin which we placed in a leading private collection in 1987).

1893-S Uncirculated silver dollar, lot 3887, sold by Auctions by Bowers and Merena, Inc. as part of the Ambassador and Mrs. R. Henry Norweb Collection, November 1988. $357,500, a price which stands today as the highest ever realized for ANY Morgan silver dollar of any kind. (First page of multiple-page catalog description shown above.)

Auctions by Bowers and Merena, Inc., "America's Leading Rare Coin Auctioneer," Box 1224, Wolfeboro, NH 03894. Toll-free 800-222-5993.

CHAPTER 64

Prooflike Dollars

by Bruce Amspacher and Wayne H. Miller

Editor's Note: ***John W. Highfill***

Prooflike Dollars presents a wonderful blend of the combined talents of Wayne H. Miller and Bruce Amspacher. With their combined years of experience and wisdom, each of them presents an aspect of prooflike Morgan dollars that complements the other. Wayne Miller opens with a discussion of prooflike characteristics and types. He also explores the minting processes which led to prooflike Morgan dollars. This portion of the chapter was reprinted by permission in its entirety from Wayne Miller's *Morgan and Peace Dollar Textbook*.

The remainder of this chapter features a superb date-by-date analysis of prooflike Morgan dollars prepared by Bruce Amspacher. He presented this in-depth study during the "pre-PCGS" years (between June 1982 and May 1986) in his well known newsletter, the *Bruce Amspacher Investment Report* (BAIR). The PCGS population reports subsequently verified Bruce Amspacher's analysis as *right on target*. **The prices listed at various times in the study reflect those prevailing at the time of writing and are not meant to represent current values**. As a final note, Bruce Amspacher adds to the credits of Oklahoma numismatic products as a graduate of the University of Oklahoma, (Yeah, Bruce!)

Sincere gratitude and thanks go to both of these well known and respected numismatists. Wayne Miller's "Textbook" has withstood the sands of time, and we just turned the sand clock over for him again. Bruce Amspacher's BAIR has been given high praise by all numismatic organizations, as well as by respected newsletter publishers such as Maurice Rosen. The information they present will be reviewed and studied many times by any and all who desire to know more about Prooflike Dollars. This trip down memory lane makes a person stop and think about the extreme price differences over the last decade for prooflike Morgan dollars.

Opening Analysis by **Wayne H. Miller**

Definition

A prooflike silver dollar is a coin struck from a highly polished die which produces a mirror-like, reflective surface upon the field and sometimes the devices of a coin. Since prooflike coins are business strikes, intended for circulation, they will evidence abrasions from being jostled in mint sealed bags. Prooflike dollars will sometimes evidence a flat strike. However, with the exception of some 1884-O, 1885-O, 1887-P, 1887-O, 1890-O, 1892-P, 1892-O, 1893-CC, 1902-O, and 1904-O dollars, and a few others, most prooflike dollars are boldly struck.

Although fully prooflike dollars are readily distinguishable from the more common frosty-luster specimens, this difference was not articulated until the early 1960's. Dean Tavenner, then proprietor of The Cartwheel in Missoula, Montana, is believed to have been the first major dealer to publish a separate price listing for prooflike silver dollars.

Due to the enormous increases in the price of rare date uncirculated silver dollars, many collectors have given up the idea of acquiring a complete mint state set, and are instead collecting individual pieces of exceptional quality. Because of their generally superior characteristics, prooflike dollars have become one of the most popular items in all of numismatics.

Very little useful information has ever been provided regarding prooflike dollars, despite their enormous popularity. This author has been fascinated with prooflike silver dollars for the past twenty years, and has endeavored to learn as much as possible about the different types of prooflike Morgan dollars and the factors which produced them.

Some original bags of silver dollars not opened since the year of issue will contain two or three hundred prooflike pieces. Many persons have wondered why the entire bag would not be prooflike. This is explained by the fact that a bag of silver dollars (1,000 pieces) usually contains the products of several dies. Silver dollars were weighed after the striking process. Underweight dollars were mixed with correct weight and overweight dollars in order to achieve a correct weight for the bag. Therefore, the products of several dies were often merged into one bag. Prooflike dollars, the product of one die, would thus be merged with frosty specimens struck from other dies.

Prooflikeness is a matter of degree. Some dollars evidence very deep reflective surfaces, and are unmistakably prooflike. Other dollars, while brilliant and somewhat reflective, are more appropriately termed semi-prooflike. Most of the early "S" mint dollars evidence superior luster, and brilliant specimens are often incorrectly described as prooflike.

The percentage of prooflike dollars in relation to frosty uncirculated specimens also varies widely from one date to another. Some dates such as 1884-P and 1921-S are relatively common in mint state condition, but fully prooflike specimens are rare. Relatively speaking, prooflikes of these dates are much more rare than those of dates such as 1889-CC and 1892-S, which are very rare in mint state but which have a relatively high percentage of prooflikes. The 1921-S is by far the rarest Morgan dollar in prooflike condition in relation to the number of available mint state specimens. Although a very common coin in mint state, there are fewer than a dozen known fully prooflike 1921-S dollars.

The degree of prooflikeness also varies from date to date. Among some dates such as 1879-S, 1880-S, 1884-CC, 1885-P, 1885-CC, 1888-O, 1889-O, 1890-CC, 1891-P, etc., prooflike specimens will usually evidence deep mirror fields and frosty devices. However, other dates such as 1881-S, 1882-S, 1887-P, 1897-P, 1900-P, 1904-O, etc. will not usually evidence this contrast, even though the coins may be deeply mirrored. A few dates, such as 1902-P, 1903-P, and 1904-P, will display gun-metal or gray brilliant mirror surfaces. In order to appreciate a prooflike specimen of a given date, one must be aware of the general characteristics of prooflikes of that date.

Types of Prooflike Dollars

The degree of prooflikeness which a gem dollar exhibits is dependent primarily upon three factors: First, the depth or reflectivity of the mirror surface; second, the degree of contrast, if any, between the field of the coin and the raised devices; third, surface imperfections such as bagmarks which disrupt the reflective surfaces, and factors such as exposure to salt water or other corrosives or to temperature and humidity extremes which can dull the luster of the dollar. Prooflike silver dollars can thus be divided into the following categories:

A. Cameo Prooflike

A cameo prooflike is a coin on which the reflective mirror finish is confined to the fields of the coin. The devices will evidence the natural frost of silver, thus producing a very striking contrast. Cameos are the most desirable of all prooflike dollars. They are also the most easily identifiable as being prooflike because of the contrast between the field and the devices.

Cameo prooflikes are produced from highly polished dies. During the basining process, which was performed on all Morgan dollar dies, the field of the die was polished by holding the die face against a slowly revolving dish-shaped zinc lap. The first several hundred coins struck from such a polished die would be cameo prooflikes. The depth of the mirror surface in the field of the coin would be determined by the amount of polishing which the field of the die received, and the fineness of the grit used in the polishing process. There is considerable evidence that polishing of the dies occurred intermittently throughout the life of the die, and not just prior to its introduction into the coining process.

Since the devices are recessed on a die it would not have been difficult to confine the polishing operation to the field of the die. The frosty white surface of the devices (the head of Liberty on the obverse, and the Eagle on the reverse) is due to a surface roughness in the die cavity. This roughness diffuses the natural reflectivity of silver, the most reflective of all metals. The incredible deep-mirror cameo proof coins issued by the mint in recent years are due to a process wherein the central portion of the dies are sandblasted with abrasive grit and glass beads prior to chrome plating of the die field.

Although all cameo prooflike dollars will exhibit a contrast between the field and the devices, this contrast may vary considerably from one coin to another due to factors such as duration and extent of the polishing process, deterioration of the reflective field due to repeated striking, variations in planchet luster, fineness of the grit in the die polishing process, surface imperfections, etc. Therefore, deeply mirrored cameo prooflike dollars are usually advertised at significant premiums.

Morgan dollars which are most frequently available in cameo prooflike condition include 1878 8-tail feather (obverse only), 1879-S, 1880-S, 1882-CC, 1883-CC, 1884-CC, 1885-CC, 1885-P, 1888-O, 1890-CC, 1898-O, 1899-O, etc.

Artificial Cameo Prooflikes

Through the years the demand for deep-mirror cameo prooflike dollars has been incredible. Dealers find it impossible to keep them in stock, regardless of the prices placed on them. It is perhaps inevitable that a few unscrupulous individuals would experiment with methods in which to artificially impart a cameo prooflike surface upon a Morgan dollar. Some of these efforts have been laughable, although even clumsy attempts can dupe the unwary collector.

Several years ago an elderly gentleman proudly exhibited a year set of Morgan dollars at a Long Beach coin convention. Each coin appeared at first glance to be a deep-mirror cameo prooflike dollar. All the coins were identical in appearance and were obviously artificially processed. The fields were indeed deeply mirrored, and the devices frosty. However, the mirror surfaces were the result of the application of a buffing wheel, and the frosty devices had been painted on. Although these coins were instantly recognizable to a trained eye as counterfeit (altered) cameos, the owner was convinced they were genuine.

At the 1980 ANA Convention this author was asked to resolve a dispute regarding a group of cameo prooflike dollars. Although not advised that any of the coins were processed, the author picked out about fifteen very skillfully processed coins out of a group of twenty pieces. The parties exclaimed that I had picked out the exact coins which had just been purchased by a dealer at the convention from one individual. A major West Coast auction in the late 1970's contained a grouping of a 1921-P, D, and S dollar which had all been processed to appear as cameo prooflikes.

After diligent effort the author managed to track down the person responsible for the processing of these coins, and warned him that if any others were discovered and traced back to him that he would be exposed. While he never overtly admitted his guilt, the production of these spurious coins did cease.

Most artificial cameos can be detected by a close examination of the point at which the field intersects with the devices of the coin. Usually the "frost" which has been painted on will either extend into the field, or the devices will be devoid of frost in various places. Also, under magnification the field of the coin will exhibit hairline swirls from the buffing wheel used to impart a mirror surface to that area. However, sometimes these swirls can be confused with inadequate die polishing by the mint. For this reason, the latter coins usually command a lesser price because of the suspicion that their surface may be artificial.

The best of the artificial cameo prooflikes can be detected only by the most highly skilled silver dollar specialist. For these, the swindler selects a coin which is already very choice and which may even possess some degree of mirror surface. A dental tool is then utilized to paint a white surface onto the devices, which exaggerates the contrast between the field and the devices of a coin. It is not always necessary to process the field, although this is usually done to some degree. An expert who is aware of the types of prooflikes which exist for a given coin can often spot a fake cameo by comparing it mentally to other prooflikes that he has seen for that date. Also, fake cameos often exhibit a dark shadow on the frosty devices when the coin is tilted way from direct light. As a final test, much of the artificially applied frosting will come off if the coin is dipped in a coin cleaning solvent.

The beginning collector of prooflikes should not be frightened into abandoning the search for deep-mirror cameos, however, since the processing of artificial pieces is not widespread and they can be detected by an expert at no charge at a coin show. However, the author feels that the collecting public should be aware that such coins exist.

B. Brilliant Prooflike

A brilliant prooflike is a coin in which the reflective mirror finish is evident in both the field and the devices. Only the most deeply recessed parts of the die, such as the date, lettering, and mintmark, will not exhibit reflective surfaces. Although the fields are often as reflective as those of a cameo prooflike, brilliant prooflike dollars will not usually appear to be as deeply mirrored, because of the lack of contrast between fields and devices.

The factors which produced brilliant prooflike dollars are detailed in the next section. Dates which usually occur in brilliant prooflike condition include 1878-S, 1881-S, 1882-S, 1887-P, 1888-P, 1895-S, 1897-P and 1904-O.

C. Gray Brilliant Prooflike

A gray brilliant prooflike is distinguished by a subdued luster. Although reflective, such coins will not evidence the full brilliance of a cameo or brilliant prooflike dollar. There will be no contrast between fields and devices. Gray brilliant prooflikes are not to be confused with impaired or dull prooflike pieces, since the subdued luster of the former is the result of mint processes, and not to mistreatment after the coins had left the mint.

Because of their subdued luster, gray brilliant prooflikes are not as desirable as cameo or brilliant prooflikes. Also, many specimens, particularly 1900-P and 1903-P, evidence die polishing hairlines in the field. Such pieces are sometimes difficult to differentiate from a whizzed or buffed coin. Gray brilliant prooflikes are largely confined to later date Morgan issues. All known 1902-P, 1903-P, 1903-S, and 1904-P prooflikes are gray brilliant, as are the majority of 1900-P and 1902-O dollars. Prooflikes of the 1878-P, 1878-7/8, 1889-P, 1890-P, 1896-P, 1898-P, 1901-O, 1903-S, 1901-S and 1902-S are also frequently of the gray brilliant variety.

D. Impaired Prooflike

Although not a category in itself, it should be noted that impaired specimens of either cameo, brilliant, or gray brilliant prooflike dollars must be considered differently from undamaged specimens. The very delicate, fragile surfaces of prooflike dollars are easily marred. Bagmarks or other abrasions tend to be very noticeable. Even the slightest wear will be readily distinguishable on a prooflike dollar.

In addition to a sensitivity to abrasions, the mirror surfaces of prooflike dollars are easily dulled. Cleaning substances which are harmless to frosty specimens can sometimes dull the surfaces of a prooflike dollar. It also appears that extreme temperature and humidity changes over several years' duration can affect prooflike surfaces; the coin alternately "sweats" and dries, sometimes producing a clouded mirror surface which may or may not be removable. Salt water also has a deleterious effect producing gray or white spots upon coin surfaces.

Some of the prooflike dollars in the Redfield hoard exhibit distracting hairline swirls caused by the failure to complete the die polishing process. This is particularly noticeable on the majority of the prooflike-obverse 1887-S dollars. All three of the fully prooflike 1896-S dollars from this hoard also are hairlined from incomplete die polishing. Many of the deep-mirror 1888-S Redfield dollars exhibit gorgeous, unimpaired, deep-mirror obverses, with dull gray, heavily hairlined reverses. Although the hairlines on these coins are the result of mint processes, their unattractiveness decreases their value significantly.

Many of the extremely rare prooflike dollars such as 1886-O, 1892-O, 1893-O, 1896-O, 1896-S, 1897-O, 1903-S, etc., are impaired prooflikes. The eager buyer should not pay an excessive premium for such a coin merely because of the presence of mirror surfaces.

Some dates which are rare in prooflike condition are not fully appreciated by collectors because prooflikes of these dates are usually inferior in appearance to their frosty-luster counterparts. Examples: 1893-P, 1900-S, 1902-P, 1902-S, 1903-P, 1903-S.

Prooflike Dollars: Causality

Many people are puzzled as to the tremendous variation in the depth and extent of mirror surfaces among silver dollars. This is explained by the fact that there are several different causes for the presence of a mirror surface upon a silver dollar. The following list is not all-inclusive but is the author's best perception as of this writing.

A. The Master Die was a Cameo

The master die for the Morgan dollar had cameo surfaces. This cameo effect was transferred to the working hubs and hence to the working dies actually used to strike coins. Van Allen estimates that this cameo effect would be transferred to the first 500-2,000 coins from a given working die before it weakened and eventually disappeared.

Cameo prooflike dollars are most common during the earlier years of the Morgan series, and virtually unknown after 1900. This is probably due to the fact that the cameo effect eventually disappeared from the working hubs as they prepared the working dies. The latter, of course, then produced progressively fewer cameo prooflikes.

B. Basining of the Dies

This was the process of polishing the field of the die prior to its introduction into the coining process by holding the die face against a slowly revolving dish-shaped zinc lap. A fine lens-grinding compound and water on the lap did the actual polishing of the field of the die. The first several hundred coins struck from such a polished die would be cameo prooflikes. (This process is still used to polish the mirrors of optical instruments.) Obviously, the designers of the Morgan dollar were aware of the aesthetic value of contrasting fields and devices.

Because of basining of the dies and because undetailed surfaces are greater reflectors of light, silver dollars will usually evidence more brilliance in the field than in the devices; this is true even among non-prooflike dollars. This phenomenon has confused many novice collectors, especially when examining early "S" mint specimens, nearly all which evidence brilliant fields.

Although authorities are agreed that most cameo and brilliant prooflike dollars were produced from polished dies, the latter has sometimes been incorrectly interpreted to mean that a substance rather than a process was applied to the dies. In other words, many have thought that a polishing substance was actually rubbed onto the field and sometimes the devices of a coin just prior to striking to create the desired mirror or prooflike surface.

This process would have been relatively inconvenient, and its effect would not be of long duration. Therefore, another process or processes must have been applied to dies or planchets to produce prooflike dollars.

This author (Miller) feels that most cameo prooflike dollars can be attributed to basining of the dies. The lens grinding compound and the water, when applied to the die field by the revolving zinc lap for a sufficient period of time, would produce a highly reflective surface. This surface, being very smooth and relatively free from imperfections, would be transferred to the field of a coin. This theory is substantiated by the fact that most cameo prooflike dollars are well struck, and are obviously the product of new dies.

The continued striking of coins would result in a gradual deterioration of the reflective mirror surface of these dies. Successive coins would evidence less deeply mirrored fields; soon they would be termed semi-prooflike. If the basining of the dies was not repeated, the polishing effect would deteriorate, and succeeding dollars would evidence little or no mirror surface.

Each mint was responsible for basining its own dies. This explains why, for example, the 1879-S is easily available in cameo prooflike condition, while the 1879-P and 1879-O are relatively scarce. It also explains the existence of flat-struck prooflikes such as 1881-P, 1884-O, 1885-O, 1887-O, 1892-P, 1893-CC, etc., apparently worn dies were occasionally subjected to the basining process.

C. Polishing out Clash Marks

Occasionally during the striking process a planchet failed to feed into the press, and the obverse and reverse dies came into contact with one another. This resulted in clash marks, which are impressions of the obverse die upon the reverse of a coin, and vice versa. If the clash marks were heavily impressed into the die, the die setters would usually attempt to polish them out. This would result in a mirror surface upon the die. Since the clash marks would be in evidence both in the field and the devices of the die, this polishing was probably extended to the entire die face. Therefore, coins struck from such dies would produce brilliant rather than cameo prooflikes, since the dies would likely have struck sufficient coins to have worn away the cameo effect upon the devices.

Polishing of the devices to remove clash marks would tend to erode some of the fine design detail on the die. This explains why many brilliant prooflike dollars do not exhibit the bold design of cameo prooflikes.

D. Polishing of the Dies by the Planchets

The process of producing silver dollars from silver planchets involved the application of tremendous pressure: As much as 150 tons per square inch. All those factors which impinged upon the planchet prior to striking would be relatively insignificant compared to the effects of this pressure. Therefore, it is believed that the great majority of prooflike Morgan dollars were the result of polished dies rather than polished planchets. (Possible exceptions are enumerated in succeeding sections.)

After the basining effect had disappeared from the dies, subsequent silver dollars would evidence frosty rather than mirror surfaces. The dies, because of different composition and treatment, were much more durable and resistant than the planchets. However, repeated strikings, with the attendant pressure and friction of planchet metal against die surfaces, would tend to produce a polishing action upon the dies. This may explain the occurrence of brilliant prooflike dollars, wherein the entire coin except for the most deeply recessed areas (date, lettering, mintmark), evidences reflective surfaces. It would also explain why the majority of brilliant prooflike dollars do not evidence the bold strike of cameo prooflike dollars, which are usually struck from new dies.

E. Polishing of the Planchets

After the planchets had been punched from the long, flat ingot strips, they were immersed in a potent solution of soap, borax, and water. After being rinsed in water, they were steam-dried, run through the upsetting mill for the formation of the raised edge, and annealed. They were then dipped into a weak sulfuric acid and water solution, rinsed in boiling water, and tumbled in a revolving drum filled with saw dust. Variations in this cleaning and polishing process from one batch to another could have produced variations in luster.

It is also possible that the planchet strip, or the planchets themselves, were polished prior to striking. However, this would have been a rather difficult, time-consuming chore. It would have been especially difficult to polish the underside of the planchet strip. Therefore, polishing of the planchets was probably done only for proof coins.

F. New Rollers in the Rolling Mill

The condition of the rollers in the rolling mill which converted the large, bulky ingot into a thin planchet strip through several successive runs could also affect the luster of the planchet. New rollers with relatively few surface imperfections would produce a more perfect planchet strip, which would be more reflective because of the smoothness of its surface.

G. Condition of the Drawing Bench

For Morgan dollars a drawing bench was used to obtain a consistent final thickness for the silver planchet strip after it had been run through the rolling mill. The planchet strip was pulled through the jaws of the drawing bench, which compressed it to the desired thickness. If these jaws were new, with smooth gripping edges, the final planchet strip would tend to be more reflective because of the smoothness of its surface.

H. Leftover Proof Planchets

Gray brilliant prooflikes are scarce in comparison to cameo or brilliant prooflike dollars. It is possible that some prooflikes were actually produced from leftover proof planchets. This conjecture is supported by the fact that all later date proof Morgan dollars (from 1902-1904), exhibit the same subdued gun-metal toning as the gray brilliant prooflike dollars of these years. This would also explain the relative rarity of gray brilliant prooflike dollars, as well as the fact that most occur among Philadelphia specimens.

I. Leftover Proof Dies

The total number of proof Morgan dollars struck in any given year seldom exceeded 1,000 pieces. Consequently, dies utilized in the striking of proof Morgan dollars would have had considerable die life remaining after their primary function had been effected. It is therefore possible (Mallis concurs; Breen does not) that proof dies were occasionally utilized for striking regular issue dollars. Such pieces would tend to be brilliant or gray brilliant rather than cameo prooflikes, and would evidence a very bold strike. It is possible that more than a few prooflike Philadelphia Morgan dollars from 1896-1904 were the products of proof dies. There is considerable evidence that a few hairlined proof dies were used in striking 1921-P Morgan dollars. These are often confused with proofs of this issue, since the latter were also struck from hairlined dies.

Prooflike Peace Dollars?

One topic which has been debated for years among silver dollar specialists is why the Peace dollar is not available in fully prooflike condition. Although this author has seen a few 1922-D, 1927-S, 1934-D, and 1934-S dollars which might be termed semi-prooflike, even these are very rare. The 1925-P and 1934-D silver dollars pictured below and on the following page are the closest to being fully prooflike of any Peace dollars this author has seen.

1925 Obverse

1925 Reverse

1934-D Obverse

1934-D Reverse

The most logical explanation for the non-existence of cameo prooflike Peace dollars is that the dies utilized in the striking of Peace dollars were not basined. The curvature of the Peace dollar master die at the Philadelphia mint eliminated the need for basining each working die. This was not possible during the Morgan dollar era, since presses were not standardized then and each working die had to be basined differently. Also, the design of the Peace dollar curves gently into the field as opposed to the sharply defined design of the Morgan dollar. Therefore, basining a Peace dollar die would have caused erosion of design detail.

Since the basining process is believed responsible for virtually all cameo prooflike Morgan dollars, discarding the basining and attendant polishing process would result in a coin with no contrast between field and devices. This is precisely the case with Peace dollars, which evidence an even, homogeneous luster upon their entire surface.

The unavailability of brilliant and gray brilliant prooflike Peace dollars is more difficult to explain, since these types of prooflikes are produced by several different factors. Many brilliant prooflike dollars are the result of polishing out clash marks. The author knows of very few examples of die clashing among Peace dollars. The mint must have corrected this problem and therefore had no further need to polish out clash marks, a process which could have produced brilliant prooflike Peace dollars.

The lower relief of the Peace dollar meant that less pressure was necessary to bring up the details of the coin. Less pressure meant less friction of planchet metal against die surfaces, thus decreasing the polishing action upon the dies.

It has also been suggested that a change might have been made in the cleaning and polishing process to which the planchets were subjected just after being annealed and prior to being run through the upsetting mill for the formation of the raised edge or rim. If the concentration of sulfuric acid in the cleaning and polishing process were to be increased, the planchets would evidence a frostier luster. (The lovely frosted proof dollars of recent vintage are due to acid treatment of the dies.) This is supported by the fact that Peace dollars generally exhibit a frosty, coruscating luster.

This author welcomes any other suggestions as to possible reasons for the non-existence of prooflike Peace dollars.

Prooflike Morgan Dollars: An In-Depth Study

by Bruce Amspacher

When a coin is referred to herein as "rare," this degree of rarity being discussed is for MS-65 or better Prooflike coins only. Not only do I not recommend that you buy MS-63 (or worse) Prooflike dollars, I also do not consider them to be of significance. For example, the 1893-CC Dollar is not rare in Prooflike condition. However, a fully struck Prooflike 1893-CC in true MS-65 is one of the rarest of all Morgan Dollars.

Secondly, a coin may not be rare in MS-65 Prooflike condition but may be extremely rare in MS-67 or in Deep Mirror Cameo Prooflike. This is true of the common 1904-O, for instance.

Thirdly, this is one area of the market where Coin Dealer Newsletter bid ranges frequently have no bearing on what the coin is actually worth. If an 1891-P Prooflike sells for $6,000 and bid is only $2,200, it might appear that the buyer would lose $3,800 if he wanted to sell it. Not necessarily so! Even with a cost of $6,000 the buyer might make an instant profit — it depends on *many factors* besides CDN bid.

All of the following factors can (and do) influence the value of a Prooflike dollar.

1) Bagmarks
   a) number of bagmarks
   b) size of bagmarks
   c) location of bagmarks
2) Mirror surfaces
   a) depth of mirror
   b) contract to devices
   c) bagmarks
3) Contrast
   a) amount of contrast — none to slight to solid "white" cameo
   b) eye appeal of contrast
   c) Rarity of given amount of contrast in given date
4) Strike
   NOTE: Prooflike dollars are not always fully struck or even sharply struck.
5) Rarity
   NOTE: A cameo Prooflike "wonder coin" 1884-CC might bring "only" three times bid while an 1890-P in the same condition would easily bring eight times bid.

Other factors include desirability, popularity of the date, affordability, past price records, demand, and even the situation in which the coin is sold. On Prooflike dollars, "bid" doesn't come close to telling the whole story — and it doesn't pretend to. As this study continues keep all these factors in mind.

NOTE: All prices reflected in this chapter are from the years of 6/82 through 5/86.

1878-P 8-Tail Feather Variety = 8TF

The first Morgan struck for circulation, it has the appearance of a higher relief than later dates. This appearance is both reality and illusion, the latter heightened by the flat breast on the eagle, giving the coin a concave reverse/convex obverse look. The strike is usually exceptional.

Because so many die pairs were used for this type, Prooflikes often come with prooflike obverse/frosty reverse or vice versa; and there are assorted degrees of semi-prooflikes. Most Prooflikes have good or better contract, especially on the obverse.

The obverse-is-prooflike/reverse-isn't prooflike phenomenon is frequently called a "one-sided Prooflike." One sided Prooflikes are not as desirable as two-sided Prooflikes, but they definitely are worth buying.

Despite the relatively short life of the dies, a large percentage of this date exhibits no prooflike surface at all.

The great demand for the 1878 8TF as a first year of type coin and a one year variety has put a lot of pressure on the small supply of MS-65/better Prooflikes.

Formerly considered "somewhat scarce," this variety can be considered (at least) very scarce by today's more exacting standards.

Price record known to me is $1,800 although the actual record is probably much higher. Current bid: $625.

1878-P 7/8 Tail Feather Variety

This variety was created by re-impressing the 7-tail feather hub onto 50 8-tail feather reverse dies.

This variety is rare in Prooflike condition, and, like the 8TF, it is difficult to match the obverse and reverse. This issue is worth buying even if the obverse is Prooflike and the reverse isn't. Do *not* buy this variety unless at least four of the eight tail feathers show under the seven on top. (But check first for the tripled obverse die, VAM 44; look at cotton blossoms and leaves. All known specimens of this extreme rarity have some Prooflike surface.)

Wonder coin Prooflikes are hardly ever encountered, and judging from how long (years sometimes) this date stays on want lists, this is obviously an underrated coin. When you do find the two-sided Prooflike, contrast is usually poor.

Price record known to me is $2,500, although the right coin (1878 8TF) would easily bring twice that amount. Current bid: $910.

1878-P 7-Tail Feather Variety (flat breast) = 7TF PAF

The Philadelphia Mint found that the new Morgan Dollar design needed much debugging. This is the third of four types produced in 1878.

Once again, many Prooflikes are one-sided. The obverse is usually a "frosty" Prooflike, fully mirrored but somewhat lacking in depth. Gem Prooflike pieces are scarce; cameo examples are rare.

The depth of field is almost never equal to the best specimens from the branch mints. This is ironic, considering the following letter quoted by Van Allen-Mallis in their book *The Comprehensive Catalogue and Encyclopedia of U.S. Morgan and Peace Dollars*. The letter, quoted in part, is from William Barber to Mint Superintendent James Pollock:

"The new silver dollar dies from the new hubs will not basin on any specific basin but require three different grades . . . a matter of some pains and skill to us of long practice. I hesitate to put the task on the western mints which have not had the experience."

The western mints may have lacked experience, but they were fast learners! The early branch mint Morgan Dollars are far superior in quality to the work done in Philadelphia.

NOTE: The term "die basining" refers to the process of polishing the fields of a working die prior to the striking of the coin, imparting a slight but varying curvature. This was supposed to improve the appearance of the coin. Sometimes the results were spectacular, frequently the results were mixed or even disastrous.

Price record known to me is insignificant; reported sales of $1,500+. Current bid: $520.

1878-P 7-Tail Feather Variety (round breast) = 7TF SAF

This is the first Morgan to exhibit what can be considered the standard reverse; the basic design survived until 1900 or so. This date proves that not only did the "experienced" Philadelphia Mint experts know little about die basining, they knew practically nothing about striking pressure. Most examples are softly struck with dreary luster.

Prooflikes are scarce, Cameo Prooflikes are rare, and wonder coins are nearly non-existent. I have seen only one wonder coin, and sold it in 1976 for the then crazy price of $250 (or maybe less, I'm not certain).

I owned a bag of this date (1,000 coins) in 1974. At the time of purchase, I didn't know they were the round breast variety. Only six pieces graded MS-65 (even by the looser standards of eight years ago) and none was a true Prooflike. Price record known to me is insignificant; the 1976 coin would easily bring $5,000 today — probably more. Current bid: $650.

1878-CC PAF

This exceptionally well struck issue is relatively easy to find in Cameo Prooflike, although wonder coins are quite scarce and the reverse seldom exhibits either the depth of mirror or contrast of the obverse.

All '78-CC dollars have the flat breast reverse. This date is highly popular as a first year of type, a "one year" variety (although some 1880-CC Dollars have the flat breast reverse, also), and in demand because of the romance of the Carson City Mint.

The above factors sometimes push prices above the norm for a date of this rarity. Still, it is a coin held in high regard by some, and MS-65 examples get tougher to locate each year. Price record known to me is $1,600. Current bid: $420.

1878-S PAF

Years ago, the black and white cameo 1878-S wonder coin was easily located. If you paid $30 for one, you were considered by many to be unknowledgeable ("they're all over the place") or to have more money than you had sense.

Chalk up another victory for the foresight of buying wonder coins. They've vanished. There are still some great looking '78-S Dollars around, but they're not quite the equal of the old days and prices have zoomed.

The current bid of $300 is considered high by some, but that is the result of misinterpretation of what kind of coin is wanted for the price. Price record known to me is insignificant; reported sales of at least $750.

1879-P

Usually sharply struck, frequently highly lustrous, this date still proves elusive in Gem Prooflike condition. The problem is bagmarks. When clean PLs are located, they usually have the same look as the Philadelphia Dollars of 1878 — a frosty, semi-PL appearance. Deep mirror cameos are known, of course, but are rare. Price record known to me is $1,500.

1879-O

This is one of the most difficult of all the medium priced Prooflikes to locate. The typical PL is well struck, average to deeply mirrored, has better than average to excellent contrast, and (there's always a catch) looks like it was peppered with ten rounds of buckshot at 20 paces. As this study continues, this description of a "typical PL" will pop up again and again. How many times in my writings on dollars have you read these words: "The problem is bagmarks"?

Judging from the confusion that swirls around this series, it still hasn't been written nearly enough that the problem usually is bagmarks. There are people (dealers included) who will tell you that the 1879-O Dollar is not rare in Prooflike. A *Gem* Prooflike *is* rare, however, I have them on want lists literally from A to Z. Some of those want list cards have yellowed edges. This coin is *rare*.

The price record known to me is insignificant. The last Gem PL I owned (it ended up in Wayne Miller's personal set) sold for $500. It's worth more today, of course, by a factor of seven or so.

Twelve Branch Mint Proofs were struck, four are known today, and the price record is an impressive $36,000.

1879-S PAF

The 1879-S variety with the reverse of 1878 (flat breast) is an unappreciated rarity. Although some bags of this variety surfaced from the Redfield hoard, almost no Gem PLs were uncovered.

If a flat breast 79-S PL Gem is ever offered to you at anything close to current bid level ($450) jump on it (figuratively speaking, of course). Maybe I've led a sheltered life, but I've seen less than five Gem PLs of this variety ever.

No significant price record.

1879-S SAF

This is one of the most common of all Prooflike Dollars, because a large percentage of mint state survivors are Prooflike and a relatively high percentage of the Prooflikes are Gems. Outstanding strike, contrast, and surfaces typify this issue.

Price record known to me for a round breast 1879-S is $1,000.

1879-CC

Did you know that the 1884-P Dollar is rarer than the 1879-CC in Gem Prooflike condition? Did you know the 1879-CC is "overpriced" and actually only a "so-called" rarity? I didn't "known" these "fact" either, until I recently read them in *Coin World*. I'm certainly glad I got straightened out on this matter, however. Just in time, too! Otherwise, I would have told you that the 1879-CC is among the rarest of all Morgans in Gem Prooflike, exceeded only by the "impossible" dates like 1893-CC, 1894-O, 1901-P, and a few others. I would also have mentioned that Wayne H. Miller finally put a '79-CC Prooflike in his personal collection that had a planchet flaw on the face because he could never find a better one. I would have told you that David Hall wrote in the "Coin Dealer Newsletter" that the 1879-CC with capped "CCs" was *unknown* in Gem PL. a piece of information I considered accurate because I'd never seen or heard of one, either.

I would have told you that there is no significant price record on this date because no coin of "price record quality" has appeared on the market in over a decade.

I would have told you these things, but I won't now. Thanks to the recent *Coin World* ad, we are all saved from such ignorance. I'll keep you posted on further developments as Silver Dollar "research" is updated to new heights of excellence.

1880-P

All the "P" mints from 1879 to 1883 have multiple similarities in prooflike condition. They range from frost PL to deep mirror, with good contrast and above average strikes. I haves seen rolls of all the dates.

Why, then, do these dates have price records well into four figures? You guessed it . . . bagmarks. The *clean* cameo prooflikes are rare.

1880-O

1880-O dollars are usually well struck. Now, for the bad news. Gem prooflikes are virtually non-existent. Of the few I've seen over the years, over 50% were overdates.

"I read in the BAIR a few months ago," said the caller today, "that a Gem Prooflike 1880-0 was worth $5,000. Would you like to buy one?" "Sure, if it's a Gem," I answered. "Well, It's Gem on the back. The front is scratchy, though." "A Gem has to be a Gem on both sides. Lots of Prooflike dollars have Gem reverses. Find one with a Gem obverse and reverse and we'll talk." "Okay," said the caller, and hung up. I thought I'd made it clear. One more time, this series is about Gem Prooflike dollars. Gem Prooflike dollars are Gem on the front and Gem on the back. Both at the same time. I don't want to sound patronizing, condescending, impatient, or self-important. I just want it to be clear. But the caller was an intelligent person. He buys coins from me. He subscribes to the BAIR. That's two signs of extraordinary intelligence right there. If he doesn't understand this series, others may not as well.

Numerous cameo PL "sliders" exist, as do PL MS-60 and MS-63 coins. The current "bid" of $1,775 is meaningless; a true gem would easily bring $5,000 wholesale.

1880-S

At the just completed Boston ANA (1982), Memphis dealer John W. Dannreuther turned down an offer of $500 per coin for seven pieces of superb PL 1880-S dollars. Although this is one of the easiest (probably the easiest) dates to locate in gem prooflike condition, the demand for the near-perfect Morgan dollar is so great that prices have continue upwards through bullish, bearish, and flat markets. At this rate, we'll see "common date" superb prooflikes at $2,500+ by 1986.

Can it happen? It not only *can* happen, it *has* to happen. Semi-common dates have already shuttered the $2,500 "barrier", with such prices as $7,000 for an 1881-O, $3,000 for an 1897-S, $3,000 for an 1881-P, and others.

This date features a great strike, super contrast, excellent depth of mirror and an outstanding overall appearance.

1880-CC

Although this date is frequently grouped with the 1881-CC (Same "bid" in both MS-65 and MS-65 prooflike), the 1880-CC is much scarcer in *both* conditions.

Fair contrast, good depth of mirror, and an above average strike characterize this date in Gem PL. Most 1880-CC dollars are overdates of one kind or another. The 1880-CC variety with the reverse of 1878 (flat breast) is rare in Gem prooflike.

No meaningful price records are known to me for this date.

1881-P

With sales records to $3,000, this date commands some respect, as do the other "P" mints from 1879 to 1883. Expect good depth of mirror, excellent contrast, above average strike. Demand clean surfaces, as on all prooflikes you buy.

1881-O

In 1982, a prooflike 1881-O Dollar sold for $7,000 to a dealer. There's a message there, and I'm certain you can read it.

An Ms-65PL will usually have good to excellent contrast, good depth of mirror with a degree of frost in the fields (sort of semi-PL plus plus), a sharp strike with slightly fuzzy breast definition, and overall eye appeal.

This description has nothing to do with the average BU 1881-O Dollar, which is mushy, baggy, and dull.

1881-S

This common date "S" mint does not look like its older brothers , the 1879-S and 1880-S.

The 1881-S is much more difficult to find with Cameo devices, as most PL's of this date are without noticeable contrast and exhibit brilliant fields. Rare? I'd get in trouble with any rating above "slightly scarce", yet I have seen a few pieces that would easily bring a four figure price today.

1881-CC

This date comes with a "wonder strike", shimmering white frost, and exceptionally clean surfaces. Even some of the non-prooflikes have Cameo devices.

With all this going for it, the MS-65/better Prooflike would seem to be an easily located coin. It's easier than some, of course, but hardly easy.

The Prooflikes are generally not deep mirror and not nearly as clean as their frosty counterparts.

Price record known to me is $1,800.

1882-P

I'll be glad to get out of the "P" mint dollars of 1879-1883; they are so similar in strike and rarity characteristics that the descriptions become a little repetitious. While prooflikes of this date are sometimes seen by the roll, 99% are so scruffy they have little or no premium value. Superb deep mirror cameos are occasionally found, however. Expect good depth of mirror, sharp contrast, and a nice strike.

The price record known to me is $1,000, although I am certain several pieces have sold for more.

1882-0

The strike on this issue ranges from terrible to great; depth of mirror ranges from "semi-PL" to "black and white" cameo. Although scarce, it is one of the easier "O" mints to locate. The O/S variety, however, is extremely rare in prooflike.

Price record known to me is $1,500.

1882-S

This is another "common" date that is frequently grouped (incorrectly) with the 1879-S and 1880-S.

Cameo prooflike 1882-S dollars are much tougher than the 1881-S, which, as noted earlier, is tougher than the 1880-S. Expect an excellent strike, little or no contrast (usually), and a deeper mirror on the obverse than the reverse.

No significant price record is known to me.

1882-CC

Since well over 50% of the total mintage of this date is extant today in mint state, it would seem logical that a prooflike would be easily located (it is) and a Gem would be relatively easily located (it isn't). As the premiums increase, the Gem PLs get scarcer (true collector's market). This date is not rare, but compared to the equally priced 1884-CC, the '82-CC is unquestionably underrated. The 1882-CC has good depth of mirror, good contrast, and an above average strike.

I once sold an 1882-CC dollar to another dealer for a price well into five figures. If that isn't the record, I'll eat a copy of *Coin World*. That coin was, of course, a previously unknown branch mint proof. There are two other price records for a "regular" Gem PL in the $1,500 range.

1883-P

If you don't mind the bagmarks, a Cameo PL 1883 dollar is easy. At $125 a coin, dealers can cover you up in them. There is also a Gem Cameo PL on the market at $2,150. At a little less, I'd buy it. Current bid is $675 for an MS-65 Prooflike. So it goes.

1883-0

A common PL, except that:

1) They're too baggy.
2) They're frequently PL only on the front.
3) The reverse is usually flat or too weak.
4) Nobody has any nice ones for sale.

Current bid is $310 for an MS-65 Prooflike. As Montana dealer Don Harris says: "Stack 'em up until I can't see over them."

1883-S

The 1883-S, like the 1892-S and 1903-S, occasionally turns up in near perfect condition. The near perfect *Prooflike*, however, doesn't turn up. One famous coin, graded MS-70 Prooflike in an auction years ago, turned up again in 1983. As usual, it took a little "imagination" to locate the "Prooflikeness", but it still realized a nice price. A deep Cameo PL with nice surfaces would easily bring a five-figure price.

1883-CC

You can frequently tell an '83-CC from other "CC" dollars just by looking at the breast feathers; the definition is so fuzzy the reverse has a C^4 look to it. Cameo Gems are available at times, but the prices can be right up there with the "tough dates."

Kent Brennan sold what he called a "shallow PL" for $1,500 recently and says he would pay that to buy it back. At the Houston Silver Dollar Show, a deep, clean Cameo PL sold for $2,400. This is the record price known to me. Current bid is $420.

1884-P

Remember Gary Patch? He once wrote in *Coin World* that a Gem Prooflike 1884-P dollar was rarer than an 1879-CC in the same condition. You can "learn" a lot about coins by numismatic publications. Unfortunately, a lot of it is pathetic misinformation such as the above. It's still a tough coin in Gem PL. The 1884-P usually has average to excellent depth of mirror, zero to good contrast, and a nice strike.

The price record known to me is only $1,250, a meaningless record since much more common coins have sold for more.

1884-0

I have concluded that this is the easiest "O" mint Morgan to locate in Gem PL. I also paid over $1,700 for one recently. Expect excellent contrast, very good to excellent depth of mirror, and an outstanding strike from this issue.

The price record is $2,250.

1884-S

A Gem Prooflike? How do you write about the characteristics of a coin that is virtually nonexistent? The prices for *non*-Prooflikes can be staggering: $75,000 was turned down for a Superb 1884-S in 1980. The best I've seen was a clean Cameo PL with minor obverse hairlines. Many Prooflike *sliders* exist. If a Gem PL does, it is a tremendous rarity.

1884-CC

This is the easiest of the CC Prooflikes, which must be interpreted as the relative statement that it is. Expect excellent depth of mirror, very good to outstanding contrast, and a great strike. Watch for the ones with clean faces and pleasing surfaces. Some PL 1884-CCs have a halo cameo effect, where the frost on the devices "bleeds" over onto the mirrored fields.

The price record known to me is $2,200.

1885-P

This is one of the most frequently encountered dates in prooflike condition. Depth of mirror ranges from semi-PL to deep mirror cameo. Expect an excellent strike.

The price record known to me is $1,450.

1885-0

Another common date, although it is increasingly difficult to locate in superb prooflike. Can be found in *deep* mirror cameo, although usually too baggy to command a premium. To digress a moment, I would like to illustrate how difficult it can be to locate even the common date prooflikes in *Gem* condition. I have a client who has worked for years on building one of the best dollar sets ever assembled. According to Wayne H. Miller's *Morgan and Peace Dollar Textbook*, the "finest known" examples of the following dates are all in this one client's collection: 1892-S, 1893-S, 1894-0, 1895-S, and 1921 Peace. There are other "finest known" pieces in his collection that Wayne has not seen. As you will see by reading the book, I obtained many of the coins in this collection for him. The point? I also found the 1885-0 dollar for his collection about two months ago.

The price record known to me is only $950, which is probably *not* the actual record.

Some people say there are "too many" books on silver dollars. Others say you could publish books on dollars *forever* and not get it all said. Obviously, I agree with the latter opinion. It is not only the characteristics of each date that can be written about again and again, but the values and the interpretations of quality. The first time I paid $5 for an 1885-0 dollar, I heard snickering in the background. The first time I paid $100 for an 1885-0, it was a record. The $1,000 1885-0? Show me one that is nice enough, and I'm in. As prices increase, the interpretation of quality becomes more exacting. The search for the near perfect dollar is both frustrating and rewarding. "Standards are getting so tough", said dealer John Albanese at the recent Miami Show, "that people are starting to grade Morgan Dollars like Barber Halves. This will drive prices up 400% if it continues." It will continue. Keep that in mind. Prooflike dollar prices are not on the ground floor any longer. They're on the 20th floor. But it's the 20th floor of a 500-story building.

1885-S

This toughie is extremely scarce. The 1977 "hoard" (a few superb pieces) was swallowed up in short order; no nice pieces have appeared in several years, at least that I've seen. Many "prooflikes" are mirrored only on the obverse; others, only on the reverse. Some PLs show little or no contrast and a few have fully frosted devices.

No significant price record is known to me.

1885-CC

Quality ranges from semi-PL to deep mirror cameo. Several pseudo branch mint proofs have appeared over the years. The price record is $3,600.

Currently bid in the $600/700 range, this date always brings more, frequently much more. At the 1982 Silver Dollar show I sold a superb prooflike for $2,500. At a recent show in the east, I saw the man that bought the coin. He complained that the price had been too high and that the coin was worth only "$800 or so." Since he had the coin with him, I looked at it again and offered him a substantial profit. "Oh, I don't want to sell it," he said, "but I did pay too much." Will someone explain that logic to me?

1886-P

While priced with the 1885-P and 1887-P, the 1886 is much tougher, especially a deep mirror cameo. Expect an excellent strike, good lustre, and medium depth of mirror. This issue covers the spectrum from grey-brilliant to deep cameo, although the latter is quite scarce.

The price record I have listed is $475. Obviously, an *old* record.

1886-0

Many "slider" prooflikes exist, and it is from those that we learn the characteristics of this date: deep mirror, good contrast, good strike.

No matter how you define "rare", this coin is rare in Gem prooflike condition. The coin in Wayne H. Miller's set is in another world; he reportedly turned down $50,000 for it! It's *better* than the picture in the book shows it to be. Another Gem prooflike appeared in 1976, sold for $1,500 (megabucks at the time), and would easily realize a five figure price today.

1886-S

The prooflikes of this date that were in the Redfield hoard had little effect on the supply of *Gem* pieces; few true Gems are seen and practically none has appeared recently. When located, they are usually very nice, with excellent contrast and mirror. Strike is good.

The price record known to me is $1,400, but I have sold non-prooflikes for more.

1887-P

Not nearly as rare as the 1886, although the two dates are priced about the same. This coin is available, or used to be before the entire series "magically" became rare. Expect a good strike, excellent depth of mirror, and average to excellent contrast.

The price record known to me is $1,500.

1887-0

The problems with this date are many:

1) Poor strike on feathers and area over the ear.
2) Lustre. Many prooflikes are "dead".
3) Need I say it? Bagmarks.
4) Contrast. (sounds like a lot of dates).

A true gem prooflike is *tough*, and of course, getting tougher. A few wonder coins are known, such as one handled several years ago by Jay C. Miller of NPI that sold into an eastern collection and another in a Texas collection that is called by some a branch mint proof. In frosty gem BU and prooflike gem BU, this date has great potential.

The price record known to me is $4,250.

1887-S

This date is frequently found with a prooflike reverse/frosty obverse and vice versa. Very few of either combination are gems. The PL obverse/reverse pieces that I have seen usually had poor contrast despite excellent depth of mirror.

The price record known to me is $1,800, which is cheap.

1888-P

When a clean cameo prooflike 1888-P dollar traded at the recent Long Beach Show for $1,300, I was pressed to recall the last time a Gem PL had been on the market. In spite of the prooflike bag that Wayne Miller reported was in Reno in 1976, practically no Gem pieces have appeared on the market in recent years. When seen, there is usually some contrast but seldom enough to call "cameo". Depth of mirror is usually fair, at best.

Price record? $1,300.

1888-0

Although this date is notorious for soft strikes, most prooflikes are sharply struck and flashy. The depth of mirror, on a scale of one to 100, touches *every number* on the scale. Some are deep mirror cameos of outstanding quality, other barely touch the boundaries of reflective. With today's demands for mirror and clean surfaces, the 1888-0 has become, like most other dates, difficult to locate.

The price record is $3,500.

1888-S

I purchased several clean prooflike 1888-S dollars from the Redfield hoard; each coin had incredible depth of mirror but absolutely zero contrast. It seems as the contrast improves, the facial marks increase. A superb cameo PL would be a great coin, indeed.

It has been proved time and time again in the coin market that supply creates demand. It has also been proved that no matter how high the demand, no one can create supply on truly rare coins. Increased bids have produced zip in recent years; this coin is rare in true Gem prooflike.

The price record known to me is $2,500.

Since I've been on my soapbox this issue, there is one more misconception about the market that I'd like to talk about. *The prooflike dollar craze!* That's the label attached to one area of the market by another faction that doesn't understand what's going on. There is no prooflike dollar craze. In fact, prooflike dollars, per se, are about as weak an area of the market as there is.

The *Gem* prooflike dollar market is a different subject altogether. As has been true for years, there are millions of dollars (the kind you spend) out there begging to be spent on Gem prooflike dollars. For the most part, the money is going unspent.

1889-P

Of the few Gems known, most have excellent depth, a good strike, and very good contrast.

A Gem cameo prooflike of this date surfaced at the Silver Dollar Show. It was the first one I'd seen in four years. The dealer who owned it had paid $2,600 for it, but he refused to price the coin to anyone. This is a common occurrence when oddball dates show up; there are buyers but no sellers!

1889-CC

Where did these go? Once considered an overrated coin in Gem PL, but the surplus has dried up. I have seen fewer than five pieces in the last ten years, after seeing six at one time in 1971. There are *lots* of sliders, including some with cameo devices and deeply mirrored fields. The clean surfaced Gem is rare.

The price record known to me is $27,000 — for a coin that was too baggy for me (or for you, I hope).

1889-0

Although this date is tough, too, it seems to be fully appreciated. By that I mean there are many other dates that are equally rare, or rarer, that are bid at a lot less money. This date comes flat, soft, sharp, or full in the strike department. The same is true of depth of mirror: semi, full, deep, deep cameo. Some *true Gems* are known.

The price record known to me is $4,800.

1889-S

Another rarity, although (here we go again) many baggy cameo PLs are seen around the shows. A '90-S is like most other S-mint dollars from this era — the problem is marks.

The price record known to me is a weak $1,250; the right coin will bring much more.

1890-P

This date is seldom encountered in Gem Prooflike. At least two deep mirror cameo Gems are in one eastern collection. Aside from those, the usual PL has moderate or little contrast with a somewhat washed out appearance. The 1890-P is a rare coin.

The price record known to me is $3,000.

1890-0

Expect some cameo, a good strike, and overall nice eye appeal, as less desirable pieces are washed out and somewhat flat.

I once bought forty Gem PL 1890-0 dollars for $42 per coin. I picked them out of a 200 piece lot. As late as 1975, I purchased a wonder coin for $135. That coin was significantly better than the Amon Carter coin (which realized $8,800 in January 1984), yet was returned by a Michigan collector as a "rip-off" at $165. Today's lesson: Thomas W. Noe and I figured in 1983 that the $10,000 worth of coins that the Michigan collector returned in 1975-76 has a conservative value of $250,000 today. The 1890-0, like everything else, is quite scarce today.

1890-S

Another "easy" date that *vanished*. Prooflikes of this date used to command a small premium at best. The coin became more appreciated after the Redfield hoard broke, because that hoard produced an odd assortment of striated planchets, one-sided PLs, PLs with no contrast, shallow PLs with good contrast and even a few of the regular kind. Expect good contrast, excellent depth, and a long wait.

The price record is a meaningless $1,000.

1890-CC

A hoard of 1890-CC Prooflikes broke in 1978 — a *bag* or so — and many of the lesser pieces are still around. The Gems were swallowed up quickly, of course, and this is another of those dates you don't see anymore in the desired grade. When you find clean surfaced Prooflike, many will have a foggy look in the fields. Deep cameo PLs exist, though, so don't give up.

The price record known to me is $1,500 which means it's time to update a few prices.

1891-P

If the words "a real rarity" do not apply to this date, then the words have no meaning. I have not seen a Gem PL since May of 1980, and few before that time. Scruffy shallow PLs with a weak reverse are relatively common, but the "deep and clean" 1891-P is a true numismatic prize. Expect a good cameo, a medium strike, good to excellent depth of mirror, and a big price.

The price record known to me is $3,600.

1891-0

"No matter how nice you think the coin is going to be, it's nicer." That was how I described the "Auction '80" 1891-0 dollar to the customer who eventually bought it. Aside from that wonder coin, there have been few other Gems to appear on the market over the years. Notable coins include one that came from a Maine dealer in 1979 at around $9,000, the Carter coin which most dealers didn't like but brought big bucks anyway, and a couple of others. MS-63 PLs are seen more frequently, and usually have a very weak obverse periphery.

The price record is $18,400.

1891-S

On the day that everyone finally learned that "clean PLs" were 100 times rarer than "deep PLs", the Gem PL 1891-S became a very scarce coin. The Redfield hoard (you've heard this story before) had little influence on the supply of Gem pieces. Expect a great strike, good to excellent depth of mirror, and moderate cameo effect.

The price record is $1,100 (that I know of).

1891-CC

Wayne H. Miller calls the problems of the PL 1891-CC "aesthetic deficiencies". I couldn't have said it better. The coin usually has no eye appeal, as most PLs are washed out, shallow, and little contrast. A few deep, clean PLs are known.

The price record known to me is $2,000.

1892-P

Of the "P" mints of 1878 to 1892, this date ranks third behind the 1891 and 1889. I have seen prooflike 1892's that were flat, had average detail, or were fully struck, and had medium depth, great depth (of mirror), some contrast, good contrast, or even, super contrast. Usually, the contrast is better on the reverse than on the obverse.

Two great coins have surfaced in recent years, each selling in the $9,500 range. The price record known to me is $10,000.

1892-0

Want to fix those "boiler room" callers trying to sell you coins you don't want? Tell them: "Why, yes, there is one coin I need to complete my collection. I need a fully struck gem cameo PL 1892-0 dollar. Let me know the minute you find it. Thanks so much. What's that? No, nothing else." The coin is R*A*R*E. The only gem known to me is in Wayne H. Miller's ex-set. Open the book to page 134 and drool.

1892-S

Wayne H. Miller says "prooflike specimens of the 1892-S seem to be no rarer than frosty specimens." Well, that's sort of true. It all depends on how you define "prooflike".

What I have seen offered or sold as prooflike in this date would be considered "semi-PL" in, say, an 1882-S; i.e., brilliant, slightly reflective fields, low contrast, minor striations, moderate eye appeal. Prooflike, but not worth as much as a flashy non-PL (at least to me). Did I mention that this date is also R*A*R*E?

I know of no meaningful price record, although one was quoted to me at $90,000 in 1981.

1892-CC

This is by far the easiest mintmark of the four 1892 issues. Even so, I haven't seen a gem PL since 1980, except for that rag Kent Brennan has that he won't sell to me. Despite a nice strike, good depth, and excellent contrast, the problem is (surprise!) bagmarks. This is one of the choppiest dates of the series.

I have no meaningful price record for this date.

1893

One might summarize all four mints' PLs:

1893-P - Rare
1893-O - Rarer
1893-CC - Even Rarer
1893-S - Rarest

I'm tempted to leave it at that, but I won't. If you took all the Gem PL 1893 dollars (all four mints) that have appeared in the last ten years and put them in your hand, you'd still have enough room left in you hand for a Big Mac and fries. First of all, these four dates seldom appear in MS-65 with or without PL surfaces. Wayne H. Miller didn't have any of these dates in prooflike. I have seen and handled two Gem PL 1893-P dollars, one in 1976 (sold to Wayne H. Miller, oddly enough, who sold it to a Connecticut collector) and one in 1980. That's all I know of.

1893-O

Many, many prooflike 1893-O dollars are known. Pennsylvania dealer Art Leister once had a roll of them. "There wasn't a breast feather on any of 'em," Art said. That, of course, is the problem.

The best is Barbara Goldfreed's coin from Auction '81 at $57,000. The coin is Gem, Cameo, and Prooflike. It is 90% or so fully struck. The Amon Carter coin was not as deep but it was a steal at under $15,000.

1893-CC

The Garrett coin at $33,000 was a Gem, but many argued it was a branch mint proof — and that doesn't count. One Gem PL is known that is absolutely superb. It originally sold in 1974 as a proof for $11,000. Then, Walter H. Breen said it definitely was not a proof. The coin was returned, then sold to John B. Love at the 1974 ANA for a song. John sold it to Harlan White, then it ended up with Robert L. Hughes (when David Hall was working for him). I had a chance to buy it for $5,000 — too much, David and I agreed — and then it vanished. I see the owner now and then when I'm in Florida. He just smiles.

1893-S?

None known.

1894-P

The room was alive with tension. Morgan dollar freaks from around the country had gathered in New York to buy the 1894-P, a gem prooflike being auctioned by Paramount. "Let's play 'high bid,'" another dealer suggested, "since we both know that either you or I are going to buy it." He wrote down his bid and showed it to me, confidently. He bid was $6,750. I showed him my bid. It was $30,000. "You're a goose," he said. "Thank you," I answered. If I was a goose, then the room was a gaggle. At $30,000, there were four other hands in the air. Wayne H. Miller outlasted us all, claiming the coin to a spattering of applause. The new record was $36,000. Wayne now owned the finest known PL 1894-P and the second finest known, too. He sold me his "reject" (the one that had been in his set). My customer was happy. Wayne was happy. I was happy. Don't you just love a happy ending?

1894-O

"What'll you pay for a gem PL 1894-O dollar?" asked the eager beaver at my table. "Let's see it," I said. "It's a deep mirror fully struck gem. A cameo." "Let's see it," I said. "What'll you pay?" he asked again. "$20,000 if I like it," I said. "Hah," he said, "There's no way I'd sell it for less than $30,000." "$30,000 if I like it," I said. He raced to his table. He was back in an instant. "Ever seen one before?" he asked. "I've seen flat ones, but no full strikes," I said. He handed me the coin. "I still haven't seen one," I said. "But it's clean and deep and fully struck," he whined. "Yes, but it's not Unc. They have to be Unc. to be worth 30 grand." "That's what someone else said, too," he said, crestfallen. Not all stories have a happy ending.

No coin = no price record.

1894-S

"Did you see the 1894-S dollar in the TNA sale?" Doug Sharpe asked me. "Yes," I said. "What did you think?" he asked. "I think I own it," I answered. "Let's split it," Doug suggested. We did, but first we had to get by that same dealer who had the $6,750 bid on the '94-P. This time he had a bid he was executing for a Tennessee collector. A serious bid. After Doug and I bought the coin, I paid him a profit for his half.

I ran the coin in *Coin World*. The Tennessee collector called. "I'd like to make an offer on that coin," he said. "Okay," I said. His offer was less than my cost. I told him so. "Didn't you buy it out of the TNA sale?" he asked. "Yes," I said, "but I had a partner on the coin. After I bought his share at a profit to him, my cost is more than your offer." "Harrumph," he said, and hung up.

Meanwhile, an eastern collector decided to buy the coin. Later, the Tennessee collector decided he wanted it, too. "Sorry, I sold it," I said. The eastern collector was happy. I was happy. Doug was happy. The Tennessee collector hasn't spoken to me in three years. Some stories have mixed endings. Happy and sad.

The price record is $10,500.

1895-O

It was back in the winter of '75 — January 3, 1975 to be exact — and I was at a show in Beverly Hills. Wayne H. Miller came bopping by. "What do you think of this?" Wayne asked. I looked at the coin. A virtually flawless, semi-PL Morgan. Absolutely gorgeous. "It's amazing," I said, "even for an '85-O." "It's a '95-O," Wayne said, "I just offered the guy $5,000 for it." *$5,000!* Let's put that in perspective. I had just bought a gem BU 1859 Indian cent for $80 from Bob Emmer. Marc Emory had a run of gem BU Seated half dimes for sale at $120 per coin. The market was the pits. "You mean he didn't take the offer?" I asked, incredulous. "Not yet," Wayne said, "but he's weakening." *I should hope so*. "I've been trying to get the coin from him for a long time," Wayne continued, "I think if I take some other stuff he'll let me have it." He's letting you have it, all right, I thought. Still, it was such a sensational coin, maybe it was worth it . . . A little over nine years later, that coin sold for $100,000 (estimate) as part of the sale of Wayne's set. O ye of little faith.

Since that coin was semi-PL, or shallow PL at "best", perhaps it doesn't belong in the PL price records. A deep PL sold for $65,000 a few years back. A dealer friend of mine in the northeast, -er, northwest, turned down $75,000 for his sensational '95-O that is frosty white with no trace of prooflike surface.

What's the record? Sometimes a story has no ending.

1895-S

It was the first annual National Silver Dollar Convention. We were actually holding a coin show in a pig barn in Columbus, Ohio. Soooey! A well known silver dollar collector came running over with his latest find. "How does this '95-S compare to the one you sold for over $30,000 a few years ago? I just picked this baby up for 15 grand!" he said. I looked at the coin and answered: "Well, the one I sold was better struck, it was deeper, it was cleaner, it had more contrast, and it had more eye appeal. Aside from that, they're identical." The collector turned and yelled to his buddy across the room. "Bruce says they're identical!" And that says it all in the world of prooflike dollars. If you like it the best, it's the best. And that's the best ending of all.

The record is $33,000.

1896-P

Although this date is scarce, there was a hoard of gem prooflikes on the market in the early '70's that were so deep and clean that many of them were sold as proofs. The average '96-P PL is brilliant with moderate contrast and a good strike. Very few gems have appeared in the past few years. Almost all of the Redfield coins were ugly — grey and baggy.

The price record known to me is $2,250.

1896-O

Since this coin is almost unknown in MS-65, it follows that an MS-65 prooflike is an ultra-rarity. The only coin known to me that is even arguably MS-65 PL is the Auction '80 coin from the Leo Young/Paramount offering. That coin sold for $29,000 to Kent Brennan. Other "gem PLs" haven't stood the test of time. A gem *non*-prooflike sold for $17,500 at the 1979 ANA; another gem non-PL turned up at the same show that eventually sold for $22,000.

As I wrote in a *Coin Dealer Newsletter* article in 1979, "If you are looking for a superb example of this date, remember this: You have a better chance of being hit by a meteorite."

1896-S

I purchased a gem PL 1896-S dollar out of a set at an L.A. show in 1975. That's the last one I've seen. There were some "whirly" prooflikes in the Redfield hoard; coins that appeared to the untrained eye to be buffed or abrasively cleaned.

So little can be written about prooflikes that non-PLs have the most notable price records. A frosty "wonder coin" sold for $15,000 or so at the 1983 Silver Dollar Show. This date is as rare as almost any other. I wish I could tell you more.

1897-P

A "brilliant" Prooflike is usually referred to as such because the coin has little or no contrast, despite brilliancy in the fields. A "grey brilliant" usually has poor contrast and lacks flash in the fields as well. An example? 1902-P. The typical 1897-P Prooflike is a "brilliant" PL. Even when the coin is Gem, it's not very inspiring.

The Redfield Hoard produced some of the best examples, and Wayne H. Miller notes a small hoard of cameo PLs exist.

The price record known to me is $1,000 — a relatively weak price reflecting the unavailability of this coin in Gem PL in recent years.

1897-O

Here's another classic rarity. I know of only two Gem Prooflikes; one in a Rhode Island collection, the other in a New Jersey holding. Both coins turned up about the same time — 1979 and 1980. While working for Fred Sweeney in 1980, I bought and sold one of the 97-Os. It was clean cameo Prooflike, believe it or not.

The coin traded hands four times in a matter of days — Steve Ivy, Joe Flynn, Fred Sweeney, New Jersey collector — and eventually sold for a record $23,000.

1897-S

In recent months, 1897-S dollars have been setting records right and left. At the mid-winter ANA in 1984, one traded hands at $3,000. At the 1984 National Silver Dollar Convention in Houston, Texas, another coin traded at $5,200. Now the shocking news — *neither coin was Prooflike.*

It's becoming more and more common for the non-PL price record to be greater than the P-L price record. The coin that brings the most money today is the coin that's the nicest regardless of Prooflike surfaces.

The Prooflike price record known to me is $3,000.

Since I've talked about other dealers here (David Hall, Les Fox), it's only appropriate that I now talk about Wayne H. Miller. Wayne's two silver dollar books have had as much to do with the current success of the silver dollar market as any other one — or two — things. When I asked Wayne if a third volume was forthcoming, he said, "I'd rather walk out on the highway and get hit by a truck."

I know what he means. I love to write, don't get me wrong, but this "technical analysis" stuff isn't my cup of oolong. I'm not going to abandon it, though, especially since it's one of the most popular sections of the BAIR. So, with gritted teeth, here goes...

1898-P

Although deep cameo prooflikes are rare, this date is sometimes seen with deep fields and little contrast or with heavy contrast against "shallow-PL" fields. The "grey-brilliant PLs" from the Redfield hoard were not pretty coins, but at least they looked better than most of the '97-P's.

Years ago (I was a mere child), a small hoard of deep cameo PLs surfaced in — of all places — Oklahoma. Dallas dealer Donald Willis socked 'em away at about $6 a coin. Over the years I bailed him out at about $900 a coin.

Let's see now, at 25% a year. . . . The price record known to me is $2,500.

1898-O

One of the best dollars I've ever seen was a '98-O. At the February 1978 Long Beach show, a dealer had a superb cameo PL. A killer. $200 would have been a big price, but I decided if the coin was $600 or less, I was going to buy it. I wanted that coin. I asked the price. "$2,500," the dealer said. *$2,500!* I envisioned Fred (I worked for Fred Sweeney at the time) locking me in the office for six months if I bought the coin. I looked at the coin again. Wonder coin. "I own it," I said. I swear my voice cracked. "You gotta take the rest of 'em," the dealer said. "The rest of *what*?" I asked. "The rest of the coins in the case. They're $2,500 each as a lot." The "rest" included a 1921 Morgan in XF and other choice material. I figured if I bought the rest of the case at what it was worth, I'd be in the '98-O at $87,999. I'd already agreed to pay 77 times bid, but that was enough. I got out of the area in a hurry.

That evening, I told the story to another dealer. "He's been teasing people with that coin for years," the dealer said, "but he's got something else that's even more bizarre." I declined to even speculate what it might be. "He's got a BU roll of 1916-D dimes or at least he says he has. He won't show 'em to anyone, but he says that if you'll bet him $10,000 that he doesn't have the roll, then he'll show 'em to you." Just another day in the coin business, folks.

Wonder coins notwithstanding, this date comes in deep cameo PL, shallow cameo PL, with moderate contrast, and, occasionally, with virtually no contrast. Most have heavy abrasions.

The price record known to me is $2,000.

1898-S

Since this is a study of *gem* prooflikes, then this date deserves its rightful place in the "nearly impossible" category. The problem? Bagmarks! Like the 1888-S and 1896-S, it appears that every coin was dropped right on its face. As with the other mints in 1898, the "S" is found with cameo contrast, almost no contrast, and (most often) with a brilliant shallow PL. Strike can be a problem. No stories with this date.

The price record known to me is $3,000.

1899-P

The shallow PL '99-P is more common, but, like most dates, the clean faced gem (deep, frosty, or in-between) is getting scarcer and scarcer.

There have been some deep cameo prooflike wonder coins of this date appearing over the years. A hoard (hoardlet?) of seven pieces turned up in 1970. "I thought they were proofs at first," said Montana dealer John Diekhans. They sold for as much as $125 a coin — a staggering price at the time. At least one showed up every year until 1982, then the "flow" stopped. The best one (maybe) appeared in a Robert L. Hughes Auction in 1978. It brought $1,200.

The price record is $5,250.

1899-O

At the Houston ANA in 1978, Florida dealer Walt Hood had the 1899-O dollar. He says the price was $475; I remember it being $875. Whatever it was, it was too much for me at the time. It sold, though, and I spent too much time years later trying to track that coin down for a customer.

In 1984, an even better coin turned up in a Bowers and Merena Sale. Kansas City dealer Lyn F. Knight said, "I hadn't even looked at the lots in the sale, but I knew the '99-0 had to be the wonder coin of the decade. The first six people I saw said, 'Did you see the 1899-O dollar?'" In the next two days the coin had five different owners, eventually selling for a record $5,500.

1899-S

They're not pretty. If all Morgan prooflikes looked like '99-S prooflikes, few people would collect PL Morgan dollars. No contrast. Lots of pecks on the cheek. Very little *oomph*! The "creamy satin surfaces" noted by Miller on the Redfield coins are semi-PL in my opinion; the true prooflike gem is rare.

The price record is $6,000.

1900-P

Long a recognized rarity, this date has less eye appeal than perhaps any other date. Many "prooflike" 1900-P dollars are prooflike on the obverse only. The reverse is usually frosty, similar to the 1878-8TF. If you do locate a true PL, expect very little if any contrast, minimum depth of mirror, and excessive die polishing marks." This coin is rare in gem PL.

The price record known to me is $1,500.

1900-O

This is another tough "common" date, but it's not nearly as scarce as the 1900-P. I have handled several gem PLs in recent years, including one with good cameo contrast. Die polishing marks are a characteristic of this date. That "swirly stuff" bothers a lot of collectors, and they frequently think the coin has been whizzed.

One variety of this date, the 1900-O/CC, is unknown in PL condition.

The price record known to me is $2,000, although a non-P-L recently realized $2,200 in a private sale.

1900-S

They're flat, they're baggy, they're dull, and they're rare in gem prooflike. The Redfield hoard only added to the population of undesirable prooflikes. Most have the C^4 reverse, too, just to add to the problems.

Mike DeFalco recently handled a gem PL with excellent contrast and far above average mirrored field. That coin sold for a record $3,500.

1901-P

There's no denying it. The Bruce Todd 1901-P dollar has a bagmark, a heavy one, over the ear. Regardless, it is one of the most famous of all Morgan dollars, with deep mirror surfaces, flash, oomph, and rarity. It is also worth MS-65 money, which arguably I admit, makes it MS-65. The coin, originally purchased by Dean Tavenner from a Montana banker who found it in a bag of dollars in his vault, has graced the collections of Bruce Todd, Wayne H. Miller (who sold it to me), Earl Green, and the current owner, a New Jersey collector.

Several well-known dealers have also owned the coin, each of whom remembers the acquisition as "special". Why such a high regard for a coin with a gash over the ear? Because the coin has an ineffable aura; it's the right coin.

The price record is $9,000. That's because the coin hasn't traded for six years.

1901-O

It's not in a class with the 1901-P, but not many coins are. Regardless, this is a *tough* coin in MS-65 PL. Very few Morgan dollars minted after 1900 are "prooflike" in the sense that 1880-S dollars are prooflike. But even that oversimplifies the matter. The 1901-O cannot be compared with other post 1900 dates, let alone with an '80-S or even an 1898-O. Let me explain what I mean.

Wayne H. Miller notes: "Like the 1898-O and 1899-O, the 1901-O evidences a wide range in quality from one coin to another." That statement, of course, is true. What it *doesn't* say is that within that wide range the '98-O and '99-O are found in fully struck gem, both frosty and PL, while the 1901-O really isn't found in top grade.

This coin, frankly, doesn't trade. Attribute it to a "grading change" or increased knowledge or an aberration of unavailability; whatever the reason, the Gem PL 1901-O needs to be re-evaluated from scarce to rare.
The price record known to me is $1,000.

1901-S

Same song, second verse. Can a coin be flat and still be MS-65? Well, it can be flat and still be worth MS-65 money. When a flat prooflike 1901-S sold for $4,200 at auction in 1979, no objective opinion or grading certificate, or die analysis, meant doodley compared to the opinion of the buyer. And, since the buyer had an underbidder, there were at least two people in one room who felt the coin was worth $4,000 or more and were willing to back that opinion with their money.

Why did I get off on this tangent? Because it is the most frequently misunderstood aspect of coins, especially dollars. The strike can excuse some things about the surfaces, but the surfaces can excuse a lot more about the strike. If a "problem" coin brings big money, then the problem is usually strike, not surfaces. The 1901-P mentioned earlier is an exception, and one of the *few* exceptions.
The price record known to me is $4,250.

1902-P

In your hand is a Susan B. Anthony dollar. It is XF, with spots. There is a big cut on the face. Not a pretty picture, right? Well, the average prooflike 1902-P is even less pretty (if you can imagine). Put all this into one coin — subdued lustre, cloudy surfaces. baggy face and field, C^4 reverse and you have the hardest coin to sell since the market collapsed on "atheist" cents. The market does reflect the problem: MS-63 PL bid $260/290; MS-65 PL bid $2,900/3,300. Yes, some prooflikes have even bigger spreads between MS-63 and MS-65, but few coins have a greater disparity in real value; it's closer to $150 vs. $7,500.
The price record known to me is $950.

1902-O

As George Carlin says, "*This* one doesn't even belong on the *list*." Why not? Because you can actually find them occasionally. Maybe three or four every *decade* or so. Humph! Hardly worth mentioning. Because this date lacks contrast, it takes a deep mirror to give the coin a prooflike appearance. Add to this the usually mushy strike and baggy face . . . need I say more?
The price record known to me is $1,900.

1902-S

This issue of the BAIR will be complete as soon as I finish writing about the 'O2-S. I stared at the paper for 20 minutes. I took a peek in Miller's book to see if I could "borrow" an idea from him. Nothing. This date is extremely rare (yawn) and seldom encountered (yawn) and has many problems (yawn) including striated planchets, weak strike, poor contrast, and bagmarks (snore).
The price record is $6,600.

1903-P

In non-prooflike, the '03-P is considered to be an "easy" coin, as many gem and near gem pieces exist. In gem prooflike, however, the story changes. As is true with other post-1900 dates, most "prooflikes" aren't prooflike in the classic sense. Instead, there is a grey-brilliant look to the coins, with little depth of mirror and not much flash. Many prooflike 1903-P dollars are so heavily striated that they have a "whizzed" appearance. The deep mirror gem 1903-P is rare.

Regardless, the prices this date brings when available are surprisingly reasonable because of the unpopularity of the date.
The price record known to me is $2,500.

1903-O

Once the ultimate rarity of the Morgan series, then a $25 coin in the late 1960's, today the 1903-O dollar is a "solid" coin with renewed popularity and high demand. The prooflike '03-O is, like the '03-P, usually subdued or, at best, lacking in contrast. Some deep mirror cameo pieces exist. Most deep mirror examples are weakly struck about the periphery of the coin. Gems are rare.
The price record is $6,000.

1903-S

Like the 1892-S, the 1903-S is difficult to locate in high grades. Also like the 1892-S, when true mint state 1903-S dollars are located an amazingly high percentage are gem. Prooflikes are (you guessed it) extremely rare, and exhibit that same grey brilliant look typical of this era.

All of the known gem prooflikes could be pedigreed in the space of a quarter page or less. The most recent one to appear on the market recently sold for nearly $20,000 at auction.
The price record known to me is $27,000.

1904-P

This highly unpopular date is a great rarity in gem prooflike. The average specimen is dull, baggy, and usually "semi-PL" when any reflectivity is evident. Most of the "big money" 1904-P prooflikes have been, in my opinion proofs. A proof 1904 dollar is so shallow and "rounded" that it gives the appearance of being a business strike to the untrained eye.
The price record known to me is $10,000.

1904-O

Although the '04-O is common in prooflike condition, a gem PL is extremely scarce, due to facial abrasions. Almost every '04-O has heavy marks in quantity due to 60 years of poor handling in Treasury vaults. Depth of mirror is usually minimal, and, when depth is good, the planchet is usually hairlined from die polishing marks.

The price record known to me is $2,500.

1904-S

Long a recognized rarity, this date is extremely rare in gem PL although the coin is available in MS-63 PL and MS-64 PL. The problems are characteristic of most C^4 issues; marks, poor lustre, less than great strike, and minimal depth of mirror.

The price record is a meaningless $9,000.

1921-P

In 1921, the Philadelphia mint struck 44,690,000 silver dollar-sized pieces of junk. The moderate change of design was uninspired, the lustre was drab, and the overall coin still leaves collectors wondering what happened. The few gem prooflikes that exist are grey-brilliant almost without exception, lacking in flash and depth of mirror.

Two unquestioned proof coins exist; one purchased by Gary Sturtridge from ARCOA in 1974, the other a sensational cameo proof offered by Stack's for $30,000 at the 1983 San Diego ANA. Many other probable proofs exist, called "Zerbe" and "Chapman" proofs. Other business strikes are seen that came from the same die pair as the Zerbes.

The price record known to me is $1,500.

1921-D

This is a true rarity in gem prooflike, yet the unpopular modified design keeps the price down when such coins are offered. The deepest '21-D might be considered "semi-PL" if it were an '81-S. Some exist with cameo devices, but even then the fields are shallow.

The price record known to me is $4,250.

1921-S

Very few exist. Even with that, the case is overstated because the prooflikes that do exist exhibit heavy die polish and strike problems. The best known are technically non-prooflikes with blazing lustre and a hint of mirror. 1921 was the last year of the Morgan dollar, but the mint definitely didn't save the best for last.

The price record known to me is $5,250. This concludes the in-depth study of the prooflike series.

NOTE: All prices reflected in Mr. Amspacher's analysis are from the time frame between June 1982 and May 1986.

BRUCE AMSPACHER

INVESTMENT REPORT

P. O. BOX 9527 NEWPORT BEACH, CA 92658 (800) 821-3985 / (714) 250-3187

Volume 6, Number 6 & 7

December 15, 1988

Chestnuts roasting on an open fire, Jack Frost nipping at my nose......

It's that time of year once again, with yuletide prognostications ready for release, filled with optimism of the great future we're all going to share. The fresh start of 1989 is eagerly anticipated, especially after 1988 left almost everyone, and certainly both of me, a little schizo. First the good news, then the **really** good news.

The annual Silver Dollar Convention in St. Louis was the first major test of the question: "Is the market ready to roll again?" The happy answer is "Yes." Going into November 1988, the coin market was still suffering the post-ANA blues, with market prices down in most areas 20% or more in only three months. The show was well attended, active, upbeat, much better than expected (ask **anyone**), and something unusual happened. After the show, prices continued **up.** Recently, the action following a major show has been soft, as overspent dealers decided to get into stronger cash positions. **This time,** there was more money around than coins, and the ANE/NQS system has been a plethora of plus signs for weeks. A complete set of Morgan and Peace dollars, all PCGS graded and mostly MS65 or better, traded **three** times at the show, starting out at $750,000 and then trading again at $800,000 and $850,000. Common MS65 dollars traded at just over the $300 level at the show, but have since been testing the $350 barrier as the market heats up again. Silver dollars? Looking **strong!**

Speaking of strong, immediately following the Silver Dollar Convention came the Norweb III auction, conducted by Bowers and Merena and featuring some of the neatest coins to come along since the Garrett sales nearly a decade ago. The highlights could take pages to list, but here are a few Morgan and Peace dollar prices that will be memorable for generations to come. The star attraction was an 1893-S Morgan, a "whopper" by all accounts, that sold for.....

$357,500. That's "Three and a quarter plus the juice" in coin dealer parlance. That's a world record in **any** language. **Mais oui!** The coin was purchased for a major California collection that is quickly becoming the number one set of Morgan Dollars in the world. Some other prices of the "Wow, can you believe that?" category include:
1882 Proof 65---$15,950***1883 Proof 65---$18,700***1884-O "Proof" 64---$20,900***1891-S MS65---$14,300***1896 Proof 65---$16,500***1896-S MS65---$24,200*****1897-O MS65---$52,800*****1897-S MS65---$13,750***1900-S MS65---$18,700***1902-S MS65---$27,500***1903-O MS65---$7480***1922 Matte Proof 65 (High relief) $46,200***1922 Matte Proof 65 (Regular relief) $35,200***1928-S MS65---$25,300 (can that be **right?**) and......on and on.

If there was a "real bargain" from the Norweb III sale it was the sale of the 1861 Pacquet Reverse $20 gold coin. The price was hardly weak at $660,000 (!), yet it was hoped by many that this would be first U.S. coin to realize $1,000,000 or

The Bruce Amspacher Investment Report (BAIR)
(Courtesy of Bruce Amspacher, Newport Beach, California)

The Dimple Sheet

Continuing Bruce Amspacher's interest in prooflikes and deep mirror prooflikes, "The Dimple Sheet" was born. It presented wholesale market prices (bids) for prooflike and deep mirror prooflike dollars (PCGS coins only). These sheets were published monthly for a two to three year period ending in 1989. The prices listed were not offers to buy or sell, but represented the current bid prices at the time through a national survey of PCGS marketmakers. Some bids were for coins that did not exist in PCGS holders at that time (and may not exist today), but willing buyers existed if the coins were to appear.

PCGS began listing Prooflikes (PL) in their population reports beginning in April 1987. PCGS Deep Mirror Prooflikes (DMPL) made their PCGS debut in January 1988. NGC began reporting PLs in October 1988, while DPL (Deep Prooflike equivalent of PCGS DMPL) reporting started in January 1989. When the Bluesheet (October 1988) and Greysheet (November 1989) initiated DMPL price reporting, the need for "The Dimple Sheet" was diminished and eventually it was discontinued.

"The Dimple Sheet," fully copyrighted, was published monthly by the Bruce Amspacher Investment Report. All rights reserved. This information was prepared by Bruce Amspacher, William E. Spears, David Hall, Leroy Van Allen, Ronald M. Howard, Nick Buzolich, Jr., Wayne Hummel, Tom Culhane, Dwight N. Manley, Joel Rettew, Dan Kihlstadius, and John W. Highfill.

MARCH 1989

****The Dimple Sheet****

Wholesale market prices (bids) for deep mirror prooflike dollars--PCGS coins only. Prices current through March 15, 1989. The prices listed below are not an offer to buy or sell, but represent the current sight unseen bid prices through a national survey of PCGS marketmakers. Some bids are for coins that do not exist in PCGS holders at this time, but willing buyers exist if the coins were to appear.

"The Dimple Sheet" is fully copyrighted, and is published monthly by the Bruce Amspacher Investment Report. All rights reserved. This information was prepared by Bruce Amspacher, William Spears, David Hall, Leroy Lenhart, Leroy VanAllen, Ron Howard, Nick Buzolich, Wayne Hummel, Tom Culhane, Dwight Manley, Joel Rettew, Dan Kihlstadius, and John Highfill.

"DMPL" = Deep Mirror Prooflike. "PL" = Prooflike.

	MS64DMPL	MS65DMPL	MS66DMPL	MS64PL	MS65PL	MS66PL
1878-8TF	1,150	8,500	13,500	960	3,650	9,050
1878-7/8TF	**1,400**	**10,000**	**16,500**	**900**	**5,250**	**11,225**
1878-7/8TF(weak)	1,200	5,000	8,500	-	-	-
1878-7TF	**750**	**6,250**	**9,500**	**385**	**3,000**	**8,850**
1878-7TF(rev79)	1,500	11,000	16,000	700	4,875	11,500
1878-CC	**800**	**6,000**	**10,000**	**500**	**3,375**	**6,550**
1878-S	300	3,250	8,500	180	995	4,350
1879	**700**	**7,000**	**15,000**	**460**	**3,875**	**7,700**
1879-CC	8,000	25,000	42,000	5,500	19,500	37,000
1879-CC(capped)	**7,500**	**15,000**	**26,000**	**7,500**	**17,750**	**24,750**
1879-O	1,800	15,000	24,000	700	7,225	11,200
1879-S	**260**	**1,350**	**3,250**	**146**	**540**	**1,200**
1879-S(rev78)	6,000	27,000	39,000	2,550	17,100	20,000
1880	**700**	**10,000**	**16,000**	**360**	**4,000**	**7,700**
1880-CC	850	4,500	13,500	435	2,325	6,425
1880-CC(rev78)	**1,000**	**5,250**	**12,000**	**700**	**3,600**	**8,000**
1880-O	4,500	50,000	85,000	3,600	23,100	41,000
1880-S	**260**	**1,350**	**3,000**	**146**	**540**	**1,150**
1881	800	7,000	10,000	450	3,800	6,450

The Dimple Sheet issue of March 1989, BAIR
(Courtesy of Bruce Amspacher, Newport Beach, California)

Acknowledgements

Wayne H. Miller's portion of this chapter was updated, re-edited and reprinted by permission in its entirety from *The Morgan and Peace Dollar Textbook*, Wayne Miller, 1982, Adam Smith Publishing Co., Metairie, Louisiana.

Bruce Amspacher's in-depth study of prooflikes appeared over a period of years (June 1982 - May 1986) in his nationally known newsletter, the *Bruce Amspacher Investment Report*, (BAIR), Newport Beach, California.

***

Michael Fuljenz, NLG

Mike Fuljenz, most importantly, is married and the father of two wonderful children, Jake and Katie. He enjoys basketball and spending time with his family. He is a former teacher, principal and camp leader and loves working with kids.

Mike Fuljenz is the Chief Numismatist for Blanchard and Company, Inc. the largest retail dealer in rare coins and precious metals in the United States.

Mike has written the award winning Market Forum column in the American Numismatic Association magazine, *The Numismatist*, for the past eight years. In this column he analyzes the coin market monthly for its members. This column was voted the Numismatic Literary Guild's Magazine column of the year in 1986. He has also contributed to leading price guides like the *Red Book*, *Blue Book* and *Coin Dealer Newsletter Monthly Summary*.

Mike Fuljenz has spoken at numerous numismatic and financial conferences of state and national scope and welcomes the opportunity to participate in such events. These have included American Numismatic Association and Florida United Numismatists Conventions, Howard Ruff and James Blanchard conferences. He also has routinely been among the featured speakers at the National Silver Dollar Convention.

Mr. Fuljenz was president of the Southwest Louisiana Coin Club four times in the early 1970's; he was a Vice President for the Society for U.S. Commemorative Coins and head of the American Numismatic Association Certification Service Committee from 1987 to 1989.

Mike Fuljenz has contributed to leading books on Walking Liberty and Franklin halves, proof coinage, and U.S. Commemoratives over the past decade. He also contributed to *Walter Breen's Complete Encyclopedia of U.S. and Colonial Coins*, and to leading works on consumer protection by Scott Travers and the postal service. He is a major contributor to *A Consumers Guide To Coin Investment*, prepared with the United States Postal Service and the Consumer Information Center by Blanchard and Company, Inc.

Mr. Fuljenz has been featured locally and nationally on television having routinely appeared on CNBC's production "Smart Money" hosted by Ken and Daria Dolan. Since 1982, Mike also has enjoyed teaching summer seminars for the American Numismatic Association, on topics ranging from gold coins and commemoratives to silver dollars.

Mike Fuljenz can be reached by writing c/o Blanchard & Co., Inc., 2400 Jefferson Highway, Jefferson, LA 70121.

CHAPTER 65

Proof Morgan Dollars

by Michael Fuljenz, NLG

For the last eight summers, I've taught a regular week-long seminar in Colorado Springs for the American Numismatic Association (ANA). In this course (called the "Supercourse" by the ANA) over $1 million worth of gold coins, commemorative coins and silver dollars are examined and discussed in depth. While it is important to remember the old numismatic adage, "Buy the book before the coin," the first thing I tell my seminar students is "the lab is more important than the lecture." As a former chemistry teacher, I find that this statement hits home. All the book knowledge in the world is not as important as practical hands-on skills with coins. One of the fundamental mistakes neophytes make is overestimating their skills after reading a few of the leading texts or newsletters in a particular field. Practical skills only come through examining numerous coins, and are enhanced and expedited if done with the assistance of a real expert in the field. Those whom *MANY* would consider the experts can be found among the contributors to this book, who lecture at major coin conventions, and contribute also to leading publications and price guides. If someone is truly respected for character and ability in the numismatic field, (s)he will usually fit into one or more of the above categories.

In this chapter, I hope to impart lessons I and others have learned about Proof Morgan Dollars "the hard way" as well as provide a guide to the series for the collector, investor and dealer.

Remember #1: No book, not even this one, is a substitute for time spent personally studying coins. The book augments and guides but never supplants hands-on time and skills gained with a true expert and thousands of coins.

Definition: A proof coin is a "Sunday go to meeting" coin. By that I mean it is intended to be the best a particular coin can look. It is the pride of everyone involved in its design and production.

To produce a proof Morgan dollar, metal blanks (planchets) are carefully selected. Heavy digs or other flaws in a planchet may still remain after striking if this is not done. These premium planchets are then highly polished. The dies are also specially prepared and polished. Finer grit than that used on business strikes is used to create mirrored surfaces. The coin's devices, where the finer grit is not used, appear frosty giving a cameo contrast. The presses at the mint used for the production of proof coinage are run at a slower rate and exert far more pressure than with business strikes. The blanks are carefully fed by hand and retrieved likewise to minimize damage. The end result is the ultimate Morgan Dollar in terms of detail, luster, lack of imperfections and overall eye appeal.

Remember #2 : A proof Morgan Dollar is intended to be the best product that a coin can be.

Criteria for Proof Morgan Dollars

A. *Superb Detail*. The details of the coin are exceptionally sharp including the high points of the coins and those tough-to-fill recesses in the dies (like the hair over the ear and eagle's breast feathers). Be aware that proof Morgans from the late 1880's early 1890's and 20th century can exhibit a lack of high point detail. While proofs exhibiting full detail from these years are available and are preferred, most dealers and grading services tend to give this deficiency little weight in their appraisals.

B. *Squared Off Rims*. Extra pressure and multiple striking on proof coinage results in a rim that appears square compared to business strikes, which appear rounded under 10 power magnification. This characteristic is especially helpful in determining proof status on coinage where proof dies were used to produce business strikes or where mirrored surfaces were lacking on proof coinage.

C. *Lack of Bag Marks*. Proof Morgans have different problems from business strikes. Proofs should have few if any nicks from other coins as they weren't dropped into bags with other dollars. What usually is the nemesis to these coins are hairline scratches from improper cleaning.

D. *Mirror-like Fields*. A proof Morgan dollar should always have mirrors so deep "you could shave in them." Unlike some proof silver and nickel coinage of the 19th century that have frosty surfaces, proof Morgan Dollars are usually deeply mirrored. The dates 1902 to 1904 have more cupronickel proof appearance than silver. Next time you are at an auction or coin convention, look for this.

Intention: For many numismatists and grading services to acknowledge a coin's proof status, it not only must have proof characteristics beyond reproach but also must have been intended to be a proof by the U.S. Treasury. Thus some coins that appear to be proofs, like certain branch mint proof Morgans, may not be designated as such by a grading service due to lack of historical backup. There is an inherent risk, and lack of liquidity, in buying proof Morgan dollars that are not considered such by leading grading services.

Remember #3: If you are not an expert, to be safe, buy only proofs that would be certified as such by leading grading services. Proof Morgans, intended to be proofs by the Mint, should have superb detail, squared off rims, a lack of bag marks, and mirror-like fields.

Proof Morgan Dollar Characteristics

I. Toning

Toning, tarnish to the masses, is the result of oxidation of metallic surface with sulfur or oxygen that a coin has been exposed to during storage. Toning can either enhance or detract from a coin's desirability and grade. It can be of varying depths, patterns and colors. The following list contains generalizations regarding toned proof Morgans, and exceptions do exist to these observations.

A. Toning on 1878 coinage is usually the darkest and drabbest of any of the 19th century issues.

B. Proof Morgans from 1902, 1903 and 1904 often have brown unattractive toning. An explanation is included in the date by date analysis.

C. Vibrant toning in rainbow shades can often bump a coin's grade up a whole point. In fact the only way a coin gets to proof 67 or better is with vibrant toning or (black, white) cameo contrast.

D. Bull's-eye toning is typically exhibited by coins stored in albums; the periphery, especially the rims, are dark and the toning gradually lightens toward the center of the coin.

E. Coins stacked on one another often exhibit bright round areas where a smaller coin rested on the larger piece.

F. Dark lines across a coin's surface could be from a rubber band used to hold numerous "flips" together. They do not often dip away completely and are often best seen when a coin is viewed under fluorescent light in an otherwise dark room.

G. Artificial toning is most often used to hide imperfections on a proof Morgan. Be especially careful when inspecting proofs with heavy toning over small areas where a scratch or nick may reside. Poor artificial toning jobs often show abrupt delineation between toned and untoned areas. Key areas such as the face and field in front of the face are prime targets for artificial toning. Use a professional numismatist and a top flight grading service to minimize this risk. Brown and fluorescent blues and golds are the artificial colors most often seen. Don't let this deter you from buying attractively toned pieces.

H. Proofs stored in envelopes usually exhibit even overall toning on both sides, while a coin lying flat in a cabinet will only show significant toning on one side.

I. Proof Morgans stored in PVC (Polyvinyl Chloride) flips for a prolonged time can be damaged with resulting cloudy splotching of the mirrored surfaces.

J. Moderate toning on proof Morgans usually dips off, resulting in a beautiful mirrored example. It is remarkable how many glorious cameos are hidden by toning. Darkly toned proofs do not dip well as they often take on a washed-out, slightly "off" look. Also toning can hide or subdue virtually unnoticed imperfections like light hairline patches which will leap out upon dipping off the toning. Carefully examine any toned proof for hidden traps before dipping. Only dip a coin if you've practiced on similar cheaper coins and preferably with the assistance of an expert. The best bet is to not dip in most cases.

K. Toning can form a protective barrier of oxidation to atmospheric contaminants and thus can serve to protect a coin's state of preservation.

Remember #4: Toning is most often a positive attribute on Morgan Proofs due to its verification of a coin's originality, protection of surfaces, and attractiveness. Thus it usually enhances rather than detracts from the grade of a particular coin.

II. Imperfections

A. *Hairlines*. The primary problem in proof Morgans is hairlines. I define a hairline as a scratch so fine you have to tilt a coin at just the right angle to an incandescent light, in an otherwise dark room, to view it. They are practically invisible to the naked eye under fluorescent light or sunlight. Be careful when examining proofs under unfamiliar lighting like in bank vaults or at coin shows. A 7-10 power loop may aid you in seeing them but is not necessary despite other text statements to the contrary.

Hairlines are caused by wiping a coin's mirrored surfaces with an abrasive material. Even a dirty rag can do this. Scrubbing coins with baking soda and water was a prime culprit of the 1970's, especially when used to neutralize dipped coins. Sloppy mint workers have been known to hairline coins when wiping them against their clothing.

Almost every proof, even a proof 67, has hairlines. Proof 65's can have a small patch. Often graders are overcritical and undergrade as often as they overgrade hairlined proof coins. A minor hairline patch on an overall perfect coin is the prime target of those who artificially tone coins.

B. *Slidemarks*. These are moderate scratches caused by the edges of old album slides and more recently by the edges of hard plastic flips. A slidemark is not that noticeable at certain angles to an incandescent light. Depending on the quantity, location and severity of slidemarks on a particular proof, its grade can be dramatically lowered. Typically, slidemarks occur at focal high points which make them especially unattractive. A Morgan proof with even one slidemark rarely grades above proof 64.

C. *Scratches*. Scratches on coins are most often the result of improper removal of a coin from a coin holder. I can't stress enough how important it is to take a little extra time and remove every staple from a 2x2 holder. Recently screwdrivers or pliers have been ruining coins in the "crack out" process for slabbed coins. Sometimes scratches are due to attempts to clean spots or other isolated areas of a coin with a metal object. No other imperfection on a coin results in such varied grading opinions by experts except maybe high point friction. A coin with a scratch rarely grades above proof 65, and depending on the depth, length and location, it may be deemed ungradeable by a grading service. A scratch, unlike hairlines or slidemarks, is excruciatingly obvious upon initial inspection of a proof Morgan at any angle to the light.

D. *Struck-Throughs*. A piece of hair, sawdust or small thread or lint are the most common foreign objects struck into a proof coin's surface. These are considered by most to be part of the minting process and not as detrimental as post-manufacture damage. Since the strike-through does not contrast with the rest of the coin as sharply as damage that exposes fresh metal, its effect on a coin's grade is also minimal. In fact one of the most amazing cameo proof Morgans I've ever seen was an 1893 $1 graded proof 68 by PCGS that had a minor strike through on the reverse above the eagle's head.

E. *Abrasions or Nicks*. Proof Morgan dollars were not put in bags, thus any nicks or abrasions found are due to mishandling and unusual contact with other coins. A proof Morgan dollar with nicks or abrasions in focal points like the cheek or field in front of the face rarely grades above proof 64. But I have seen proof 67's with pin point nicks on the periphery at 5 o'clock in the field. So don't automatically "kill" the grade of an otherwise incredible proof Morgan if this category of imperfection is minute and not readily apparent.

F. *Altered Surfaces*. Cameo proof Morgans are sometimes the target of "coin doctors" who try to artificially frost the devices, especially the cheek, of proof Morgans. Substances most commonly used are bondo and dental wax. Look for scratches that would normally form a shiny contrast with frosted devices but are unusually subdued. Don't confuse incused damage with raised die polish lines that are quite common and contribute to mint made frosty devices. Again, buy certified coins graded by leading grading services to protect against this, and have a prominent numismatist verify your purchases' originality. Grading services are going after the "coin doctors", so look for a decrease in this activity in the future. Coins suspected of being "done" are not graded by grading services and are often designated altered surfaces on their holders when returned.

G. *Weak Strikes*. Despite extra blows from special presses, some proof Morgan dollars have poor high point detail. The hair above the ear and the corresponding reverse breast feathers can be poorly defined. These are the deepest recesses of the dies that metal is squeezed into. Problem years include 1888 to 1893 and to a lesser extent coins listed to 1901 - 1904 with 1892 and 1893 specially a problem. One can speculate about faulty dies or wrong pressure settings, but it all boils down to poor craftsmanship during this era as excellent strikes are found just as often as those lacking in detail. When given the choice, always opt for the better detailed piece over all other factors being comparable, but a little loss of high point detail is preferable to noticeable hairlines or other significant imperfections.

Remember #5: All coins have different combinations and severities of imperfections. Numismatists balance these with a proof Morgan's attributes in determining its grade.

III. Die Polish Marks

These are fine raised lines on the surface of a coin from polishing the surfaces of a die with a coarser material than was used to previously polish the die. It is most prominent on the cheek of cameo proof Morgan dollars of the late 1890's and especially 1899. Die polish marks are rarely detrimental to the grade of a coin, and in some series they are why cameos of certain dates exist. Be careful in identifying raised die polish marks as without a "loupe" (10 x magnification); they can be confused by beginners with hairlines, which are incused damage to the surface of the coin.

IV. Cameos

The term refers to the contrast shown between deeply mirrored fields and frosted devices. This is a highly coveted effect, and when combined with a whisper of peripheral rainbow toning and immaculate surfaces, it is the "stuff" proof 68 and 69's are made of. Cameos are most prevalent from 1880 to 1885 and 1890 to 1901. Smooth powdery to silvery white devices are the rule up until the late 1890's when more die polish is interspersed among the frost. Cameos from 1902 to 1904 do not occur. Many toned coins from the cameo years if dipped reveal nice cameos. This should only be attempted by an expert on a lightly toned coin with great care.

V. Mintages vs Populations

Known mintages for proof Morgans range from a low of 50 (1878 7TF SAF) to a high of 1355 (1880). The surviving population is generally in line percentage-wise with the mintages, although in some years the percentage seen by the grading services in high grade is abysmal. Check the numbers provided in the date by date analysis if you desire to compare mintage to survival rates in greater detail. Remember that populations are still increasing at about 10-20% a year in this series and that about 20% of all certified coins have been cracked out for resubmission or other reasons. With grading services revising numbers when old tags are returned, this percentage should decrease relative to the number of coins certified.

VI. Date Pressure

Certain dates of proof Morgans are especially sought after due to the rarity of their mint state business strike counterparts. Those almost often needed are the 1895, 1894 and 1901 in that order. Lately, most all dates except the 1895 have started to be priced more by their populations than by conventional date pressure thinking. Thus the premium on the 1894 over other dates has decreased significantly. Certain dates like the 1878, 1892, 1899, 1900 and 1904 are in demand due to beginning or ending a particular series or era.

Remember #6: The more intersecting demand factors on a particular date, the more valuable that proof Morgan will be.

VII. Pricing

Up until the early 1970's many dealers and collectors considered all proof Morgans to be of about the same value unless obviously mishandled. It was possible to pick out what would today be considered a gem coin for little if any premium over other average quality pieces. In the late 1970's as the bull market began it was not unusual at major conventions to see gem specimens trading numerous times from dealer to dealer at multiples of then current price guide indications.

Today price guides are as accurate as they've ever been, yet they are still just a guide. Some are more timely than others. Some represent only sight unseen coins, and others can't keep up with infrequently traded issues. While price guides are a good beginning, a professional can help provide additional insights such as auction records, private transactions, and ask prices on currently available comparable pieces to better approximate the value of a particular coin. It is not unheard of for nice cameo examples of proof 65 and better Morgans to bring 50% over current sight unseen levels at auctions in 1991.

Remember #7: Pricing coins involves many factors, and any guide sheet or guide book will be only one piece of the puzzle. A specialist can help put all the pieces in place.

In studying the price history of proof Morgans over the last 40 years a few comments are in order about the 3 excellent publications used.

1. *The Guidebook of U.S. Coins*. Often called the Red Book, was the best guide for pricing proof Morgans from 1952 to 1970. It is the best annual of its kind and its contributors relish being listed as such. Since it is only issued yearly, it can become out of line with a moving market. It is a retail price guide indicating prices a dealer would sell coins at. From 1952 to 1970 it had only 1 designation for proof Morgans and that category represented a coin that today would be considered anywhere from a Proof-63 to Proof-65. Remember gem examples often traded at relatively small premiums over average, but not mishandled, quality pieces.

2. *The Coin Dealer Newsletter*. Began publishing weekly wholesale bid indications for proof Morgans in 1971 under the designation "Choice Proof". That category would correspond to today's proof 63 to proof 65 category also with little price differentiation for coins of the better quality. To translate wholesale bids to retail, Red Book, prices would require an increase of 20 to 50% at this time.

In 1976 the *Coin Dealer Newsletter*, nicknamed the greysheet due to its grey paper stock, provided 2 proof designations, Proof-60 and Proof-65. The Proof-60 was more like today's Proof-62, and the Proof-65 ranged from Proof-64 to Proof-66 by today's standards.

In 1979 and 1980 the greysheet couldn't keep up with rapidly increasing bids. The market premium factor for proof 65 and better Morgans ranged from 150% to 8 times bid depending on the "Oh my God", "It's a Moose", or "Godzilla Gem" impression the coin had on 2 or more competent and sober professionals at a major show.

In 1981 the greysheet further divided proof Morgans into 3 categories and changed the "choice" designation for Proof-65 to "gem" shortly thereafter. In 1979 and 1980, a Proof-63 or better specimen could bring proof 65 bid as the market was that hot. In 1982 it took a solid to better than Proof-65 Morgan to bring bid as the market was very soft.

In 1986, the greysheet began a sister publication, *The Certified Coin Dealer Newsletter* to list sight unseen bids monitored on electronic exchanges — the first was ANE — in grades Proof-61 to Proof-66. In 1988, the grade Proof-67 was included. Four grading services' products are monitored with PCGS and NGC the most relevant to date. Currently the leading wholesale electronic exchange monitored is the Certified Coin Exchange.

Remember #8: In trying to determine what a coin was worth at a particular time period, (wholesale or retail) it is best to consult with someone who actually dealt those coins at that time, or track a particular coin that traded in the past and is now slabbed and properly valued. A price guide such as that which follows is only a guide.

Forty year (1952 to 1991) Proof Morgan Dollar Price History

Red Book Pricing (Retail)

DATE	PROOF
1952	$ 11.00
1954	12.00
1956	14.00
1959	50.00
1965	75.00
1967	180.00
1970	220.00

Coin Dealer Newsletter Pricing (Wholesale)

	DATE	CHOICE PROOF
December	1971	$ 175.00
December	1972	210.00
December	1973	320.00
December	1974	485.00
December	1975	550.00

	DATE	PROOF 60	PROOF 65
December	1976	$ 350.00	$ 625.00
December	1977	300.00	575.00
December	1978	365.00	925.00
December	1979	1,200.00	4,000.00
December	1980	1,350.00	5,000.00

	DATE	PROOF 60	PROOF 63	PROOF 65
December	1981	$ 675.00	$1,700.00	$4,000.00
December	1982	400.00	925.00	2,600.00
December	1983	675.00	1,450.00	5,600.00
December	1984	675.00	1,450.00	5,600.00
December	1985	675.00	1,800.00	7,500.00

PCGS CCDN Pricing (Wholesale)

DATE	PROOF 64	PROOF 65	PROOF 66	PROOF 67
8-22-86	$4,100.00	$7,250.00	$8,700.00	0
9-12-86	3,900.00	8,500.00	8,700.00	0
10-10-86	3,750.00	8,000.00	8,700.00	0

DATE	PROOF 64	PROOF 65	PROOF 66	PROOF 67
11-14-86	3,750.00	8,100.00	8,740.00	0
12-12-86	4,000.00	8,100.00	8,740.00	0
1-09-87	3,700.00	7,800.00	8,750.00	0
2-13-87	3,500.00	7,500.00	9,000.00	0
3-13-87	2,600.00	5,800.00	9,000.00	0
4-10-87	3,000.00	5,800.00	8,000.00	0
5-08-87	2,500.00	5,250.00	7,300.00	0
6-12-87	2,550.00	5,800.00	7,500.00	0
7-10-87	2,550.00	5,800.00	8,400.00	0
8-14-87	2,700.00	6,750.00	9,000.00	0
9-11-87	2,850.00	6,750.00	9,000.00	0
10-09-87	2,700.00	6,750.00	9,000.00	0
11-13-87	2,700.00	6,300.00	8,400.00	0
12-11-87	2,600.00	5,900.00	8,000.00	0
1-01-88	2,600.00	5,150.00	8,000.00	0
2-12-88	2,500.00	5,000.00	8,200.00	13,500.00
3-11-88	2,500.00	5,000.00	8,250.00	13,000.00
4-08-88	2,500.00	5,000.00	8,250.00	11,200.00
5-13-88	2,600.00	5,100.00	8,250.00	13,000.00
6-03-88	2,750.00	5,500.00	8,425.00	13,500.00
7-08-88	3,000.00	5,950.00	8,700.00	13,900.00
8-05-88	3,150.00	6,525.00	9,525.00	15,800.00
9-02-88	3,175.00	6,750.00	11,200.00	18,000.00
10-07-88	3,275.00	6,500.00	11,625.00	18,750.00
11-04-88	3,275.00	6,300.00	11,100.00	18,300.00
12-02-88	3,275.00	6,300.00	11,250.00	19,000.00
1-06-89	3,275.00	6,575.00	12,350.00	26,700.00
2-03-89	3,275.00	6,575.00	12,000.00	23,000.00
3-03-89	3,275.00	6,575.00	12,000.00	24,000.00
4-07-89	3,275.00	7,000.00	12,200.00	26,000.00
5-05-89	4,300.00	9,000.00	16,200.00	32,000.00
6-02-89	5,000.00	10,000.00	22,000.00	41,000.00
7-21-89	4,400.00	8,000.00	15,600.00	30,500.00
8-11-89	3,900.00	7,400.00	15,750.00	31,000.00
9-01-89	3,750.00	7,150.00	13,500.00	29,500.00
10-06-89	3,800.00	7,150.00	13,250.00	26,000.00
11-08-89	3,925.00	7,650.00	14,000.00	28,500.00
12-01-89	3,650.00	7,500.00	13,000.00	27,000.00
1-05-90	3,650.00	7,600.00	13,000.00	26,000.00
2-02-90	3,650.00	7,900.00	13,750.00	26,000.00
3-02-90	4,000.00	8,100.00	14,500.00	29,000.00
4-06-90	3,850.00	8,100.00	13,000.00	28,250.00
5-04-90	3,600.00	7,900.00	14,000.00	29,000.00
6-01-90	3,500.00	7,600.00	12,000.00	27,500.00
7-06-90	3,400.00	7,250.00	12,200.00	27,000.00
8-03-90	3,700.00	7,300.00	12,750.00	27,500.00
9-14-90	3,300.00	6,600.00	11,500.00	25,000.00
9-21-90	3,300.00	6,600.00	9,600.00	23,000.00
12-21-90	2,500.00	4,500.00	8,000.00	15,500.00
3-15-91	2,400.00	4,100.00	7,200.00	14,500.00
4-12-91	2,200.00	4,000.00	7,000.00	14,000.00
5-10-91	2,310.00	4,100.00	7,000.00	11,500.00
6-14-91	2,200.00	4,100.00	7,000.00	11,500.00

VIII. Capitalization

The populations for most issues increase monthly. The amount of money available to buy newly certified coins and previously certified pieces offered for sale, in part, determines current bid levels. By studying populations, bids and capitalizations (population times bid) over the past couple of years a few conclusions can be drawn.

First, the amount of money entering the market has not been sufficient to support the bid levels of 1989 for proof Morgans or most other series for that matter. Even capitalizations are down.

Second, it is easy to see that a minimal, when compared to other financial markets, increase in capitalization in this area could result in significant bid increases even if the increase just approached prior capitalization.

Third, population increases are slowing down. Fourth, Many proof Morgans bought at higher levels will not come on the market until those levels are approached again and most dealers personal holdings have been liquidated to survive the almost soft market. Thus, there is little resistance to achieving price levels of 1989 in the next bull market.

Remember #9 : By studying population reports for proof Morgans, and noting the capitalization of dates in certain grades and the series as a whole, it becomes obvious that opportunities exist to cherrypick certain dates in high grade at virtually no premium over higher population and capitalization dates. When this series gets listed by date on electronic exchanges, look for premiums like those associated with proof walkers to develop.

POPULATION INCREASE VS PRICE

PCGS POPULATION THROUGH JUNE 1989		BID JUNE CCDN		CAPITALIZATION
PROOF 64	699	X	$ 5,000.00	$ 3,495,000.00
PROOF 65	300	X	10,000.00	3,000,000.00
PROOF 66	106	X	22,000.00	2,332,000.00
PROOF 67	10	X	41,000.00	410,000.00

PCGS POPULATION THROUGH JUNE 1990		BID JUNE CCDN		CAPITALIZATION
PROOF 64	937	X	$ 3,500.00	$ 3,279,500.00
PROOF 65	404	X	7,600.00	3,070,400.00
PROOF 66	148	X	12,000.00	1,776,000.00
PROOF 67	34	X	27,500.00	935,000.00

PCGS POPULATION THROUGH MAY 1991		BID MAY CCDN		CAPITALIZATION
PROOF 64	975	X	2,200.00	2,145,000.00
PROOF 65	444	X	4,100.00	1,820,400.00
PROOF 66	217	X	7,000.00	1,519,000.00
PROOF 67	69	X	11,500.00	793,500.00

IX. Uncertified Proof Morgans

While there are still numerous uncertified proof Morgans in old time collections, A sizable minority of Morgan proofs have probably been certified. Dealers are the ultimate collectors and their coins were certified. There are some proof set runs with proof Morgans but most of those sets will remain intact when certified, thus not causing as much downward pressure on bid in a slow market or conversely quenching demand in a bull market. Look for population increases to decrease yearly. Unlike mint state issues where bags exist uncertified, hoards of these low mintage dates are unheard of and are not likely to exist.

Remember #10 : Hoards of proof Morgans by date are unheard of and limited by miniscule mintages in comparison to their mint state counterparts.

X. Books with information on Proof Morgans

Remember #11: Buy only books by Q. David Bowers, Walter H. Breen, John W. Highfill, Wayne H. Miller, Scott A. Travers, and the Van Allen-Mallis encyclopedia. Beware, as there are many vanity books filled with misinformation in the field. Auction catalogues can also be a good source of information.

The Morgan dollar proof population report figures listed here are based on the June 1991 PCGS and May 1991 NGC Population Reports.

Date by Date Analysis

1878 8TF

	PR60	PR61	PR62	PR63	PR64	PR65	PR66	PR67	PR68	PR69	PR70	TOTALS
PCGS	3	8	10	26	17	8	4	0	0	0	0	76
NGC	0	1	2	3	11	4	3	1	0	0	0	25
												101

MINTAGE 500 % OF MINTAGE **20%** % OF MINTAGE 65 OR BETTER **4%**

This was the first year of issue and the first of 3 types struck in that year. Most proof examples seen are medium to deeply toned with the occasional brilliant example exhibiting minimal cameo contrast. Toning tends to not be extremely attractive on average, but I did recently see a nice light cameo specimen with gorgeous rainbow peripheral toning in a complete 1878 proof set.

This is the fifth rarest proof Morgan in proof 65 or better condition. Since the two rarest are the other types of this year, it is often the issue of choice for many needing an example from 1878. This extra demand factor along with demand from those needing first year of issue coins makes this specimen trade at a significant premium over dates of similar population like the 1902, often in the range of 50 to 100% more.

Other demand factors found on this date as well as other dates come from those building denomination sets, complete sets or sets of all reverse types. All of these demand factors, more than on most dates, make this a coin that is seldom offered outside of some set as an individual example.

1878 7TF PAF Seven Tail Feathers (Flat breast or breast of 1878)

	PR60	PR61	PR62	PR63	PR64	PR65	PR66	PR67	PR68	PR69	PR70	TOTALS
PCGS	2	3	4	12	10	5	0	1	0	0	0	37
NGC	0	0	0	8	6	5	1	0	0	0	0	20
												57

MINTAGE 250 % OF MINTAGE **12%** % OF MINTAGE 65 OR BETTER **2.6%**

This is the second rarest proof Morgan dollar by certified population and mintage and is also the second rarest in proof 65 or better. Most examples are medium to deeply toned and not that attractive. Maybe because of the way coins of 1878 and to a lesser degree 1879 were packaged and subsequently stored, they tended to tone darker than any other years and are less attractive on average. Maybe Wayne Miller's excellent explanation of their film interference also plays a part in explaining how our eyes perceive the coloration on these issues and those of 1902-1904 that most regularly come unattractively toned compared to all other dates.

While cameos are virtually unheard of, the magnificent NGC proof 66 that came out of an East coast proof set run in 1990 was a remarkably brilliant specimen with moderate cameo contrast and gorgeous peripheral rainbow toning.

Some weakness in strike may be evident on specimens of this date, but unless horrible, should not inhibit a buyer from obtaining one of this series' great rarities. Dipping issues of this year often leaves undesirable "washed out" luster and is not advised. Specimens in gem condition have commanded prices of 2-4 times common dates recently.

1878 7TF SAF Seven Tail Feathers (Round Breast or Breast of 1879)

	PR60	PR61	PR62	PR63	PR64	PR65	PR66	PR67	PR68	PR69	PR70	TOTALS
PCGS	0	0	1	2	0	0	0	0	0	0	0	3
NGC	0	1	0	2	0	0	0	0	0	0	0	3
												6

MINTAGE APPROX. 25 % OF MINTAGE **24%** % OF MINTAGE 65 OR BETTER **0%**

This is the rarest Philadelphia mint proof Morgan by a mile. As of June 1991, PCGS and NGC have only noted 6 examples seen in grades proof 60 and better. (Unsurprising with a mintage of only 50 of which 15 were spent!) the best specimen extant to date is only proof 63.

The quality of production was better than that of the flat breasts and known specimens do exhibit much more cameo contrast on brilliant examples.

This issue, as with the other two types of this date commands premiums over more common dates of extreme significance even in lower grades.

1879

	PR60	PR61	PR62	PR63	PR64	PR65	PR66	PR67	PR68	PR69	PR70	TOTALS
PCGS	7	10	24	42	47	21	9	5	1	0	0	166
NGC	0	2	6	15	18	8	4	1	0	0	0	54
												220

MINTAGE 1100 % OF MINTAGE **20%** % OF MINTAGE 65 OR BETTER **4.5%**

The 1879 proof Morgan is one of the most common for the series in all grades according to population reports but just seems to show up less than comparable population dates. It also has less cameo contrast than the dates that immediately follow when they are found relatively untoned. The luster is typically a little less vibrant than proofs of 1880 to 1882 and toned coins typically lean toward being rather dark.

1880

	PR60	PR61	PR62	PR63	PR64	PR65	PR66	PR67	PR68	PR69	PR70	TOTALS
PCGS	4	18	31	48	58	29	16	16	3	0	0	223
NGC	1	0	5	16	27	21	11	7	1	0	0	89
												312

MINTAGE 1355 % OF MINTAGE **23%** % OF MINTAGE 65 OR BETTER **6.9%**

This date is by far the most common date of the series in all grades, even in proof 65 and better condition, a fact which corresponds with it having the highest mintage. Cameo examples abound and have powdery white devices of moderate strength. Gorgeous toned examples also are seen more often than with most dates. The mirrors in the fields of this year often have an extra sparkly look that enhances eye appeal. Depth and eye appeal of the mirrored surfaces on the dates from 1880 to 1885 are some of the best in this entire series along with issues from 1892 to 1898. Even though this is the most common date in the series, exceptional cameos can command up to 50% over common date prices at auction. Incredible cameos should never be sold at sight unseen bid levels. In fact, typical cameos of any date fall into that guideline.

1881

	PR60	PR61	PR62	PR63	PR64	PR65	PR66	PR67	PR68	PR69	PR70	TOTALS
PCGS	12	11	19	37	44	15	9	2	2	0	0	151
NGC	2	0	2	7	16	13	3	3	0	0	0	46
												197

MINTAGE 975 % OF MINTAGE **20%** % OF MINTAGE 65 OR BETTER **4.8%**

This was a great year for the craftsmen at the Philadelphia Mint. Attractive mirrors, good cameo contrast and eye-appealing toning are as prevalent as with any issue in the series. But, curiously enough, there aren't as many proof 65 and better examples noted by population reports as your guesswork might indicate. Maybe more sets of coinage from 1880 and 1881 are broken up making more single dollars available than with years that have more set building demand. Anyway, if you are looking for a great type coin, this is a great year to consider.

1882

	PR60	PR61	PR62	PR63	PR64	PR65	PR66	PR67	PR68	PR69	PR70	TOTALS
PCGS	4	8	21	42	45	17	7	3	0	0	0	147
NGC	0	1	4	15	29	20	8	5	1	0	0	83
												230

MINTAGE 1100 % OF MINTAGE **21%** % OF MINTAGE 65 OR BETTER **5.5%**

This year is a little more common overall in proof 60 and proof 65 and better conditions than the 1881, in line with a slightly higher mintage. Examples of this year are as attractive as the 1880 and 1881 issues, which exhibit some of the most beautiful specimens in the series. In fact, all of the proof 68 specimens seen by PCGS and NGC in the 1880's are found among the issues dated 1880 to 1882.

1883

	PR60	PR61	PR62	PR63	PR64	PR65	PR66	PR67	PR68	PR69	PR70	TOTALS
PCGS	6	7	23	25	42	22	6	2	0	0	0	133
NGC	1	0	6	17	25	23	4	0	0	0	0	76
												209

MINTAGE 1039 % OF MINTAGE **20%** % OF MINTAGE 65 OR BETTER **5.4%**

This issue has surviving specimens in line with its relatively high mintage, and proof 65 and better examples are relatively common. But more issues are deeply toned in average, forgettable, shades than the previous dates of the 1880's. Brilliant examples do exhibit cameo contrast, yet it is not as strong as earlier dates. This date is popular for set building due to three different types of proof nickel coinage being struck this year as well as a modest business strike mintage on the 3 cent piece.

1884

	PR60	PR61	PR62	PR63	PR64	PR65	PR66	PR67	PR68	PR69	PR70	TOTALS
PCGS	3	9	23	28	36	19	7	1	0	0	0	126
NGC	0	1	2	13	16	17	4	0	0	0	0	53
												179

MINTAGE 875 % OF MINTAGE **20%** % OF MINTAGE 65 OR BETTER **5.0%**

The proof Morgans of this year appear in total and in gem condition as often as their mintage would indicate. Powdery white devices along with nicely mirrored fields are common on brilliant examples. Specimens in proof 66 and better are little tougher than one might first think.

1885

	PR60	PR61	PR62	PR63	PR64	PR65	PR66	PR67	PR68	PR69	PR70	TOTALS
PCGS	8	10	22	32	30	13	14	2	0	0	0	131
NGC	0	1	1	8	25	16	1	0	0	0	0	52
												183

MINTAGE 930 % OF MINTAGE **19%** % OF MINTAGE 65 OR BETTER **4.9%**

This year exhibits moderate cameo contrast when untoned, but many examples are toned especially in medium amber hues. Overall, gems and other certified grades are seen as often as the mintage would indicate. There is no extra demand factors for coins of this year, and since many other denominations have high populations it is not a favorite of those building denomination sets. Dates like this trade at common type prices.

1886

	PR60	PR61	PR62	PR63	PR64	PR65	PR66	PR67	PR68	PR69	PR70	TOTALS
PCGS	2	10	23	26	23	16	10	0	0	0	0	110
NGC	0	0	4	5	18	16	1	0	0	0	0	44
												154

MINTAGE 886 % OF MINTAGE **17%** % OF MINTAGE 65 OR BETTER **4.0%**

From 1886 to 1891 the overall eye appeal of proof Morgans diminished. The mirrored surfaces were not as "sparkly", although still deep, and cameo contrast was lessened. Dipping toned examples often resulted in a "washed out" appearance. The result is fewer proof 65 to proof 68 examples from many of these issues.

The 1886 has not had a proof 67 noted by the grading services, and along with the 1888 is the only date lacking in such high quality examples being recorded. No extra demand factors come to mind about this date.

1887

	PR60	PR61	PR62	PR63	PR64	PR65	PR66	PR67	PR68	PR69	PR70	TOTALS
PCGS	8	13	23	18	40	22	6	2	0	0	0	132
NGC	0	1	1	4	19	11	8	0	0	0	0	44
												176

MINTAGE 710 % OF MINTAGE **24%** % OF MINTAGE 65 OR BETTER **6.9%**

A few more proofs of this date have been noted than the mintage would suggest. Gems are also more abundant relative to the low mintage figures. The fact that even pristine examples aren't usually as "flashy" as same grade examples from the early 1880's makes finding that "just right" piece tough at times. Toned specimens are usually not pretty, but again often drab brown. Cameos are usually only light silvery ones when located. No extra demand factors for this date are present thus it usually trades at common type price levels for the grade of specimen offered, unless exceptionally eye appealing.

1888

	PR60	PR61	PR62	PR63	PR64	PR65	PR66	PR67	PR68	PR69	PR70	TOTALS
PCGS	6	6	23	23	21	11	1	0	0	0	0	91
NGC	0	2	3	10	15	3	0	0	0	0	0	33
												124

MINTAGE 832 % OF MINTAGE **14.9%** % OF MINTAGE 65 OR BETTER **1.8%**

This year and 1889 boast some of the lowest percentages of survivors in all grades and in gem condition. In fact, this is the third rarest proof Morgan when all grades are considered, despite having a typical mintage of 832. The 1888 $1 has one of the lowest proof 65 and above populations with only 1 proof 66 or better example recorded by PCGS and NGC combined as of June, 1991. The year 1888 marks the beginning of the poorly detailed Morgan proofs discussed earlier, and this factor along with relative lack of cameo contrast, unexciting mirrored fields and drab toning resulted in few gem examples seen to date.

This year also has other denominations with unusually low populations as do the years 1889 to 1891 that follow. While this may be perplexing, it is a demand factor as set builders seem to focus on dates where low population proof coinage can sometimes be located at common date prices. This lack of premium for coins up to five times rarer in popular grades will probably change when Morgans are someday listed complete by date on electronic exchanges and popular price guides.

1889

	PR60	PR61	PR62	PR63	PR64	PR65	PR66	PR67	PR68	PR69	PR70	TOTALS
PCGS	5	14	16	26	20	8	7	0	0	0	0	96
NGC	1	2	2	8	20	6	4	1	0	0	0	44
												140

MINTAGE 811 % OF MINTAGE **17%** % OF MINTAGE 65 OR BETTER **3.2%**

Like the 1888, this date isn't that pretty and isn't found in high grade in virtually every denomination of this year in proof. Cameo contrast is often slight although strike is not as big a detraction as on the previous year. Pretty 1889 proof Morgans in gem are really a tough find, and this year has a lower than average survival rate of all proof Morgans. An attractive gem of this year should command a premium as those constructing low population sets of particular years should be attracted to this date.

1890

	PR60	PR61	PR62	PR63	PR64	PR65	PR66	PR67	PR68	PR69	PR70	TOTALS
PCGS	2	7	15	16	32	18	14	8	0	0	0	112
NGC	0	0	3	12	13	11	7	1	0	0	0	47
												159

MINTAGE 590 % OF MINTAGE **26.9%** % OF MINTAGE 65 OR BETTER **10%**

This year has the lowest mintage outside of the 1878 issues for the regular issue proof Morgans. But its populations in proof and in gem condition are significantly higher than those of the preceding two years. Moderate cameos do exist; By and large striking problems took a one year hiatus, and toned examples are more pleasing than in the past couple of years, thus its percentage of high grade examples is greater than average, for its mintage, compared to most other dates. Most denominations of this date have a lower than typical population in gem proof condition resulting in extra demand being found in this year as well.

1891

	PR60	PR61	PR62	PR63	PR64	PR65	PR66	PR67	PR68	PR69	PR70	TOTALS
PCGS	2	7	9	24	31	18	5	1	0	0	0	97
NGC	0	0	3	7	20	8	7	0	0	0	0	45
												142

MINTAGE 650 % OF MINTAGE **21%** % OF MINTAGE 65 OR BETTER **6%**

This low mintage issue had some striking problems although not as often nor as pronounced as the following two years. This issue is often found medium to deeply toned, thus dipped examples often take on a washed out appearance. Many untoned examples have cameo contrast but not as striking as the rest of the dates in the 1890's. The mirrored surfaces are not as sparkling as the rest of this decade's issues, and toned coins are little less attractive on average too. The fact that only one proof 67 has been seen to date is a reflection of this date's slight deficiencies in eye appeal.

This date is additionally tough as it is locked away in sets of 1891 proof coinage as this was the final year for the minor silver coins to be of the seated liberty design.

1892

	PR60	PR61	PR62	PR63	PR64	PR65	PR66	PR67	PR68	PR69	PR70	TOTALS
PCGS	7	13	26	46	51	22	8	5	1	0	0	179
NGC	3	1	2	12	29	11	6	1	0	0	0	65
												244

MINTAGE 1245 % OF MINTAGE **19%** % OF MINTAGE 65 OR BETTER **4.3%**

From 1892 to 1898 the U.S. Mint produced proof coinage with the best cameo contrast and prettiest mirrored surfaces of any years to date. Unfortunately in 1892 and 1893 central high point detail wasn't the best on about 50% of examples I've examined. This weakness is not nearly as dramatic as on pancake "O" mint dollars where breast feathers are completely flat and up to half the hair strands from Miss Liberty's ear to the top of her head are nonexistent. On these proofs, the weakness usually only encompasses the first three or four hair strands above the ear and is a minor detraction when factored into grading such a specimen. The reverse breast feathers are just not as sharp as they should be but still present.

This year has extra demand as it marked the beginning of Barber coinage for the minor silver issues.

Toned examples are usually as attractive as any in the series. The devices on this date tend to be silvery white as opposed to the frosty white on some of the years that followed.

1893

	PR60	PR61	PR62	PR63	PR64	PR65	PR66	PR67	PR68	PR69	PR70	TOTALS
PCGS	8	8	18	18	26	16	6	0	2	0	0	102
NGC	0	1	4	8	9	11	4	2	2	0	0	41
												143

MINTAGE 792 % OF MINTAGE **18%** % OF MINTAGE 65 OR BETTER **5%**

For the date 1893, weakness of strike is often overcome by a glorious cameo effect. In fact, this is one of the best dates for finding amazing cameos in every denomination of proof coinage. This balance is demonstrated by the fact that the percentage of proof 65 or better examples is a healthy 5% of mintage and the 4 proof 68's seen is the most for any date. Although many pieces may have medium to dark toning of average beauty, other examples have lovely toning. With patience, an eye appealing example of this date can be found, but, if you want absolute full hairstrand detail, your task will be more formidable as over half of them are lacking in this trait.

1894

	PR60	PR61	PR62	PR63	PR64	PR65	PR66	PR67	PR68	PR69	PR70	TOTALS
PCGS	13	9	29	28	48	19	6	1	0	0	0	153
NGC	0	1	6	9	30	17	3	1	2	0	0	69
												222

MINTAGE 972 % OF MINTAGE **22%** % OF MINTAGE 65 OR BETTER **5%**

Date pressure used to be always mentioned whenever this issue was offered in the past, but it is not the factor it used to be. Premiums over common prices have slipped over the past couple of years in proof 64 or better, as this date has a relatively high number of such specimens, at least enough to handle what little demand that may present itself from mint state collectors who "just can't wait."

This date has a good strike and comes, when found untoned, with nice cameo contrast. But many examples have medium depth toning that is not particularly pleasing. Gorgeous examples should always command some premium for this date.

1895

	PR60	PR61	PR62	PR63	PR64	PR65	PR66	PR67	PR68	PR69	PR70	TOTALS
PCGS	15	10	29	25	38	16	12	4	0	0	0	149
NGC	1	0	6	13	24	13	4	0	0	0	0	61
												210

MINTAGE 880 % OF MINTAGE **24%** % OF MINTAGE 65 OR BETTER **5.5%**

This date has long been considered magical and the "King of Morgan Dollars." Even though it is no longer the most expensive date in high grade, the fact that no unquestionable business strike examples have been recorded provides the ultimate date pressure.

Proof Morgans of this year, when untoned, and not harshly dipped, show beautiful cameo contrast between watery deep mirrored surfaces and white frosted devices.

The number of examples certified is a healthy 24% of mintage but is probably high owing to the extra value involved over common dates, thus providing an extra incentive for submitting this date to grading services for owners.

The percentage of proof 65 and better examples is also a healthy 5.5% of mintage. The supply of these currently is such that a few examples are always available if someone is willing to pay the price. It is kind of like gem High Relief double eagles in that respect in an average to weak market. But, in hot markets, the supply of both is quickly gobbled up by the intense demand for these key issues.

Mark Yaffe sold a gorgeous proof 67 in the worst time of the 1991 market at $67,500 wholesale. It was one of only four proof 67's seen by PCGS and NGC had not graded one at that time.

1896

	PR60	PR61	PR62	PR63	PR64	PR65	PR66	PR67	PR68	PR69	PR70	TOTALS
PCGS	4	8	13	25	52	28	12	2	2	0	0	146
NGC	0	2	6	17	33	11	5	1	0	0	0	75
												221

MINTAGE 762 % OF MINTAGE **29%** % OF MINTAGE 65 OR BETTER **8%**

When comparing original mintages to survival rates overall and in proof 65 and better, this date is the second highest in both categories. Why this is so would be a good topic for club meetings. In fact, almost 50% more examples by percentage have been noted by grading services for this date than what is typically seen (29% to 19%).

Proofs of all denominations of this year come with amazing cameo contrast and sparkling mirrored surfaces. From 1896 to 1898 the Mint did a superb job of maximizing cameo contrast on its coinage. Toning is usually as attractive as that seen on any date in the series.

1897

	PR60	PR61	PR62	PR63	PR64	PR65	PR66	PR67	PR68	PR69	PR70	TOTALS
PCGS	8	9	15	15	28	10	8	0	2	0	0	95
NGC	2	6	5	8	5	9	9	1	0	0	0	45
												140

MINTAGE 731 % OF MINTAGE **19%** % OF MINTAGE 65 OR BETTER **5.3%**

The typical untoned example of this date has striking cameo contrast with watery deep sparkling mirrored surfaces. The fact that over 5% of its mintage has been noted in proof 65 or better condition attests to the high quality product produced this year compared to most other years. In fact the same could be said about most of the 1890's when one compares the average to the issues of the 1880's or 1900's. The other proof coinage of 1897 also comes with excellent cameo contrast, so proof sets of this year can be really stunning when seen intact. Toning for this year tends to be as attractive as any year in the series.

1898

	PR60	PR61	PR62	PR63	PR64	PR65	PR66	PR67	PR68	PR69	PR70	TOTALS
PCGS	7	5	18	25	31	18	14	6	0	0	0	124
NGC	0	0	2	6	22	12	8	4	2	0	0	56
												180

MINTAGE 735 % OF MINTAGE **24%** % OF MINTAGE 65 OR BETTER **8.7%**

This date was probably the best made date of the entire series. This is confirmed by the fact that, (with the exception of the high mintage 1880), this year has far and away more proof 65 and better specimens noted by PCGS and NGC than any other year. This is even more amazing when one notes the surviving specimens overall are not that remarkable in number. Note the percentages of surviving specimens and surviving specimens in gem condition that accompany the date by date analysis section of this chapter if you desire to make interesting date comparisons.

The typical example of this year in any proof denomination has excellent cameo contrast and vibrant toning. If you are looking for the ultimate type coin, this may be the year you end up with. Also, if you have to buy a coin sight unseen or ship a coin to a first time buyer, this date has a good chance to stick.

1899

	PR60	PR61	PR62	PR63	PR64	PR65	PR66	PR67	PR68	PR69	PR70	TOTALS
PCGS	6	6	17	32	28	10	4	3	0	0	0	106
NGC	1	1	4	7	18	6	2	0	1	0	0	40
												146

MINTAGE 846 % OF MINTAGE **17%** % OF MINTAGE 65 OR BETTER **3%**

This is the sixth rarest issue in proof 65 or better condition, and the fourth rarest date as the three 1878 types break up that year's population. With only 146 examples in proof 60 or better noted by both grading services, this is the least seen date after 1898.

Die polish is often very noticeable on the face of cameos, and, although nicely frosted devices are fairly common on untoned specimens, the mirrored fields often lack the sparkle characteristic of the issues of the 1890's. The toned 1899 issue pictured in this book, while deeply toned, is one of the most attractive deeply toned proof Morgans I've ever seen. This is an exception as toned specimens begin to be found predominantly in forgettable medium to dark shades. This year is under strong demand as it is the last year of the century and most denominations have low populations in gem proof. Appreciating examples of this issue may take some getting used to, as even the most glorious cameos are due in part to heavy die polish which is a "turn off" to some. If die polish is not your cup of tea, you may be after "the impossible dream."

1900

	PR60	PR61	PR62	PR63	PR64	PR65	PR66	PR67	PR68	PR69	PR70	TOTALS
PCGS	5	7	16	33	30	12	13	0	0	0	0	116
NGC	0	3	0	8	14	8	4	3	0	0	0	40
												156

MINTAGE 912 % OF MINTAGE **17%** % OF MINTAGE 65 OR BETTER **4%**

This date and the 1903 are the two most common dates of the 20th Century, but, when it comes to the 1900, that is misleading information. The 1900 issue has strong demand from collectors who want an example from the turn of the century. Also, because of it being a popular year, intact sets are less frequently broken up and new 1 cent through dollar sets are popular to complete. Thus want lists for proof Morgans of this year in any grade often go unfilled for longer times than populations would suggest. Also when populations are examined note that in all grades this date is twice as rare as the most common date, the 1880, at 312 to 156. Also it is rarer in proof 65 and better than three-fourths of the issues. This date is a prime candidate to develop a premium over more common dates in the future.

While nice cameo examples do exist of this date, this is the beginning of a reduction in cameos seen in the series.

1901

	PR60	PR61	PR62	PR63	PR64	PR65	PR66	PR67	PR68	PR69	PR70	TOTALS
PCGS	6	9	16	28	38	10	4	0	0	0	0	111
NGC	2	3	2	10	25	9	3	1	1	0	0	56
												167

MINTAGE 813 % OF MINTAGE **20%** % OF MINTAGE 65 OR BETTER **3%**

This is the last year that proof Morgans sometimes come with significant cameo contrast. Most cameos lean toward having silvery, rather than white devices. It also is the last year for mirrored surfaces that have a "silvery" sparkle to them. The 1902 to 1904 issues have chrome looking mirrors much like on our non-silver late date proof coinage. This date has routinely traded at a premium to common dates due to its low overall population in proof 65 or better (7th rarest), and the demand created by the rarity of mint state examples. While "date pressure" is a factor, it is a bit overrated in most cases including this one. Most collectors of mint state coins do not substitute a proof but will wait until a mint state example becomes available.

This date is popular, and, when found in a particularly attractive state for a grade, should always be worth a premium.

1902

	PR60	PR61	PR62	PR63	PR64	PR65	PR66	PR67	PR68	PR69	PR70	TOTALS
PCGS	0	12	21	24	39	4	3	0	0	0	0	103
NGC	3	0	7	8	20	7	5	0	0	0	0	50
												153

MINTAGE 777 % OF MINTAGE **19%** % OF MINTAGE 65 OR BETTER **2.4%**

This year begins the era of the deep "chrome look" mirrored surfaces and a virtual lack of cameo contrast on proof Morgans. It also ushered in an era of light to moderate drab brown toning. Whether this toning resulted from Mint packaging or the phenomenon of thin film interference is a topic to debate. The resulting look of 1902 proof Morgans is not what one has grown accustomed to. While this issue has a fairly low survival number overall, the lack of eye appeal on stone original pieces results in it being the fourth rarest issue in proof 65 or better condition. In fact, this year and the 1904 have no proof 67's noted to date.

It does have a demand factor in that the other proof denominations of this year tend to have low populations. If you find an eye appealing example of the grade for a 1902 proof Morgan you should buy it, as finding another may take a long time.

1903	PR60	PR61	PR62	PR63	PR64	PR65	PR66	PR67	PR68	PR69	PR70	TOTALS
PCGS	6	9	16	35	22	15	7	5	0	0	0	115
NGC	0	2	3	10	12	6	1	5	0	0	0	39
												154

MINTAGE 755 % OF MINTAGE **20%** % OF MINTAGE 65 OR BETTER **4.9%**

This year does come nicer than the 1902 and 1904 in regards to toning, although the lack of cameo contrast and "sparkling" mirrors keeps appeal below that of the issues of the 1890's. Without cameo contrast to dip for, more of this issue is found in its original undipped state. Toning found ranges from drab brown to rich reds, blues and violets. The population reports support the position that more high grade examples exist of this date. Ten proof 67's have been seen compared to none for the 1902 and 1904, despite the 1903 having a much lower population total in all grades than the 1904 and virtually the same as the 1902.

1904	PR60	PR61	PR62	PR63	PR64	PR65	PR66	PR67	PR68	PR69	PR70	TOTALS
PCGS	12	12	23	32	37	16	5	0	0	0	0	137
NGC	0	4	4	10	26	13	3	0	0	0	0	60
												197

MINTAGE 650 % OF MINTAGE **30%** % OF MINTAGE 65 OR BETTER **5.6%**

As this is the last regular issue and tied for second lowest mintage of proof Morgans it is more popular than most dates in the series. Also contributing to its demand is a bit of date pressure as the mint state counterpart is relatively scarce. While survival rate is high for its mintage in all grades and in proof 65 or better, finding attractive gems is a challenge. This becomes readily evident when one notes no proof 67's have been seen by PCGS or NGC as of June 1991. This lack is due to "chrome like" mirrors, no cameo contrast and drab toning being the rule. It makes one long for those deep, silvery mirrors of years gone by with cameo contrast and light to medium rainbow coloration that allows the luster to burst through. Even strike was a minor problem for these years (1902-1904).

Conclusions and Recommendations

1. Proof Morgan dollars will continue to be one of the blue chip areas of the entire coin market due to exceptional artistic beauty, collector investor demand and an excellent long term track record of price appreciation.
2. When our country's recession ends watch out for this series which is full of underpriced sight-seen issues.
3. Read all the (remembers) in this chapter for a quick (Cliffnotes) synopsis of my key points for proof Morgans.
4. This important book should do great things for the dollar market and the rare coin market in general.

Pictorial Presentation of Morgan Proofs

The following pages depict a number of proof Morgan dollars for study. All of these examples have been PCGS or NGC graded Proof-65 or higher.

Obverse

Reverse

1882 Proof 66 Morgan dollar
(Courtesy of Michael Fuljenz, Blanchard and Company, Inc., Jefferson, Louisiana)

Obverse

Reverse

1884 Proof-66 Morgan dollar
(Courtesy of Michael Fuljenz, Blanchard and Company, Inc., Jefferson, Louisiana)

Obverse

Reverse

1885 Proof-66 Morgan dollar
(Courtesy of Michael Fuljenz, Blanchard and Company, Inc., Jefferson, Louisiana)

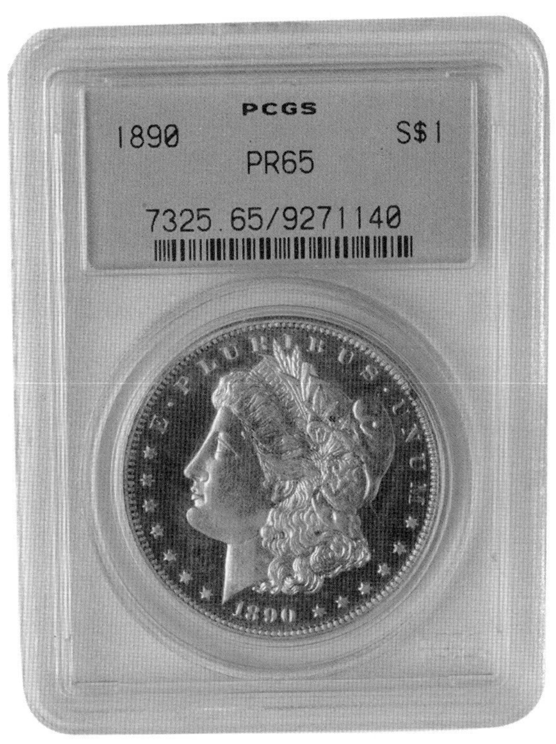

Obverse

Reverse

1890 Proof-65 Morgan dollar
(Courtesy of Michael Fuljenz, Blanchard and Company, Inc., Jefferson, Louisiana)

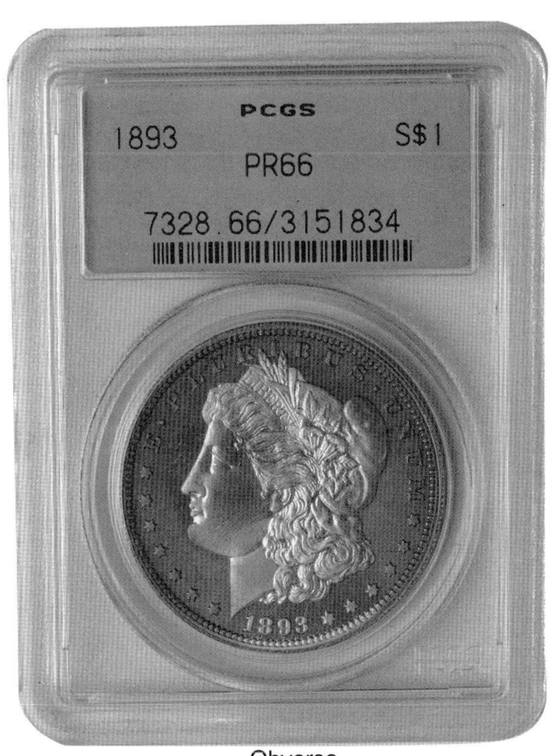

Obverse

Reverse

1893 Proof-66 Morgan dollar
(Courtesy of Michael Fuljenz, Blanchard and Company, Inc., Jefferson, Louisiana)

Obverse

Reverse

1894 Proof-66 Morgan dollar
(Courtesy of Michael Fuljenz, Blanchard and Company, Inc., Jefferson, Louisiana)

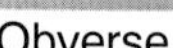

Obverse

Reverse

1897 Proof-66 Morgan dollar
(Courtesy of Michael Fuljenz, Blanchard and Company, Inc., Jefferson, Louisiana)

Obverse

Reverse

1898 Proof-66 Morgan dollar
(Courtesy of Michael Fuljenz, Blanchard and Company, Inc., Jefferson, Louisiana)

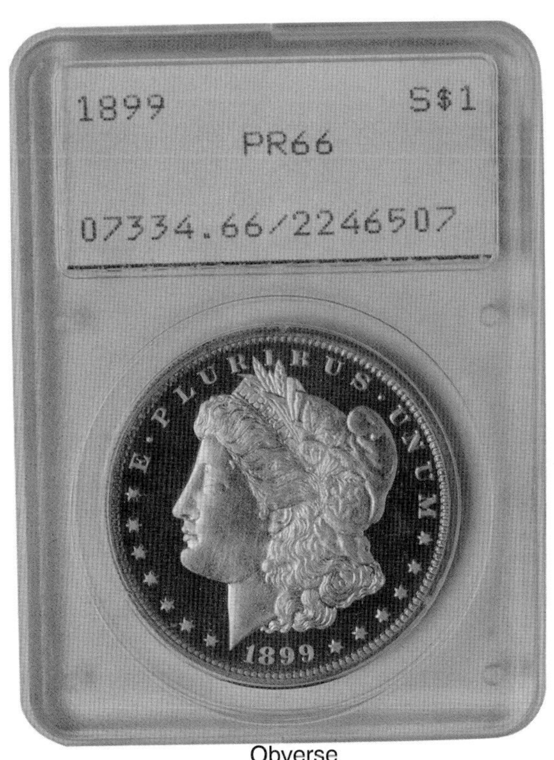

Obverse

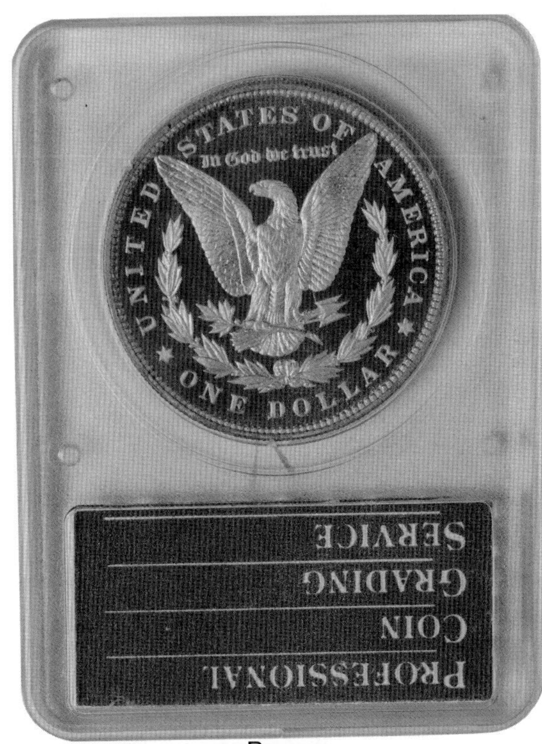

Reverse

1899 Proof-66 Morgan dollar
(Courtesy of Michael Fuljenz, Blanchard and Company, Inc., Jefferson, Louisiana)

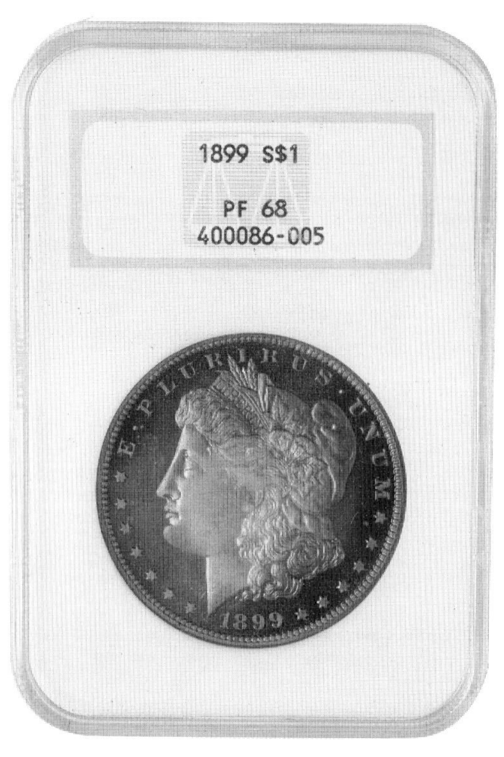

Obverse

Reverse

1899 Proof-68 Morgan dollar
(Courtesy of Michael Fuljenz, Blanchard and Company, Inc., Jefferson, Louisiana)

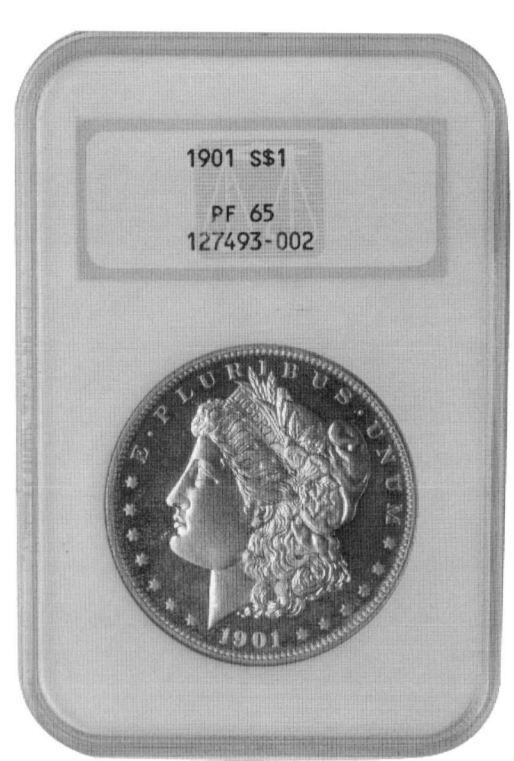

Obverse

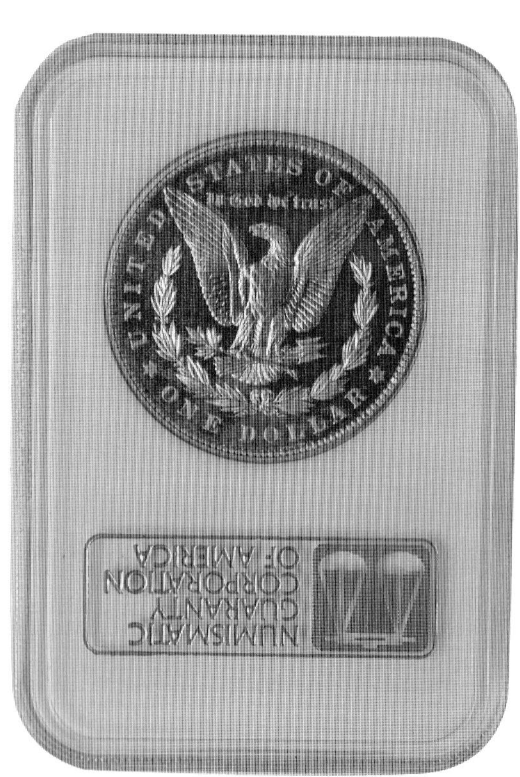

Reverse

1901 Proof-65 Morgan dollar
(Courtesy of Michael Fuljenz, Blanchard and Company, Inc., Jefferson, Louisiana)

***

CHAPTER 66

Branch Mint Proof Morgan Dollars and Proof Peace Dollars

by Wayne H. Miller

Definition and Method of Manufacture

A branch mint proof silver dollar is a coin struck at one of the branch mints (San Francisco, Carson City, or New Orleans) from carefully selected, highly polished planchets. The dies were also highly polished, and buffed frequently during use. After being ejected from the die the coins were individually handled and not allowed to touch each other.

The dies for all Morgan and Peace dollars, whether business strikes or proofs, were produced in Philadelphia. However, because of the lack of standardization of the coin presses during the 19th Century, considerable work had to be performed on each die so that it would conform to the press for which it was intended. Therefore, the final steps of basining and polishing the dies were performed at each of the mints. Because of the lack of hydraulic presses at the branch mints, proofs were struck on the same presses as were business strikes. However, the pressure was usually adjusted to the maximum in order to produce the strongest strike possible, and each planchet was struck twice.

It is not known whether the Philadelphia mint shipped a special die to the branch mints, or whether a business strike die was modified for striking of proof coins. The extremely low mintages of branch mint proof Morgan dollars, and their infrequent issuance, would not appear to justify the creation of a die just for this purpose. It is significant that the 1921-S branch mint proof exhibits the same exceedingly weak strike as the majority of business strikes of that year.

Reference Material

Of all the specialized areas of numismatics none is more rife with misinformation, speculation, hyperbole, controversy, etc. than branch mint proof Morgan dollars.

Much of this is due to absence of accurate information. Virtually nothing has ever been written regarding branch mint proof Morgan dollars. This is not surprising since they are excessively rare (The largest estimated mintage of any issue is twenty-four!) and since the first reliably reported specimen of any date was the 1893-CC in the 1973 FUN auction.

Branch mint proof dollars are mentioned very briefly in the Scott Catalogue [Don Taxay's *Comprehensive Catalogue and Encyclopedia of United States Coins*, Scott Publishing Company, New York] with no comments except for estimated mintages. The *Guide Book of United States Coins*, which supposedly includes a listing of every coin ever minted in this country, has no listings for branch mint proofs, even for the four which are well-documented.

The most extensive discussion thus far regarding branch mint proof Morgan dollars is contained in Walter Breen's book on proof coinage. Breen discusses the possibility of no fewer than twelve different dates of branch mint proof Morgans. He also provides detailed information regarding the events which occasioned their striking; estimates of total mintages; locations of known specimens; etc. However, much of Breen's information is based on conjecture. For example, he lists several possible branch mint proofs in the massive Amon Carter collection, but has not had occasion to examine them. Of the specimens which he himself has examined, none are described in detail.

Authentication

The determination as to whether a given coin is a branch mint proof can be difficult. This is due to the following factors:

First, the branch mints did not have the huge hydraulic presses used by the Philadelphia mint in the manufacture of proof coins. Therefore, since less pressure was utilized in their production, branch mint proofs usually do not exhibit the square rims of their Philadelphia counterparts. Also, the design details of the coin are not quite as bold.

Second, the personnel at the branch mints had very little experience in the production of proof coins. Therefore, many of the fine touches which were second nature to Philadelphia coiners were not performed. On some dates such as 1883-O, the dies and/or planchets seem to have received insufficient polishing. On the very mediocre 1921-S, it appears that a die utilized for business strikes, which was very lacking in high-point detail, was pressed into service for the hasty production of twelve to twenty-four "proof" dollars for the influential Farran Zerbe. Actually, considering the limitations of the branch mints, most of the proofs they produced are of amazingly high quality.

Third, many branch mint proof Morgan dollars show evidence of careless handling. This disturbs the perfection of the fragile mirror surface and makes the determination as to whether a coin is a proof or merely a business strike prooflike very difficult. The reason for this careless treatment is that most collectors were not aware of the existence of branch mint proof Morgan dollars. They therefore assumed that their coin was merely an exceptional business strike. Hence they did not give these coins the special handling required of a proof. Many of the branch mint proof Morgans which have surfaced in recent years were not known to be proofs by their owners. This includes the magnificent 1879-O from the Leo Young collection, and the 1883-O from the Herbert Bergen collection.

Fourth, there is some evidence that occasionally one of the branch mints would take special pains in the production of a business strike coin, with brand new polished dies, and special handling after striking. Such a coin can be very difficult to differentiate from a branch mint proof coin, because of some of the limitations of the latter.

Who Performs Authentications

An authenticator of branch mint proof issues of any denomination must meet two qualifications: First, he must possess the requisite experience to perform such a difficult task. Second, he must command sufficient respect in the numismatic field so that his authentications convey the weight of authority.

There are more than a few individuals who meet the first requirement. But during the past thirty years there has been but one individual whose letters of authentication are accepted universally. For three decades one man has been the final arbiter as to whether a given coin is or is not a branch mint proof. Even an obvious specimen is less saleable without his letter of authenticity. This man is, of course, Walter Breen.

Walter Breen is possibly the greatest scholar in the history of numismatics. He is an eccentric genius with an incredible store of knowledge, and an eidetic memory which enables him to recall, with great clarity, the pertinent details of coins seen as far back as forty years ago. He has examined many major collections both public and private, including significant portions of the Smithsonian Institution holdings. He has served as an advisor to many of the major collectors and dealers in this country. He is the author of several of the most important numismatics reference works. His tremendous learning, and his willingness to share this learning, has enriched us all.

Walter Breen issued the first letter of authenticity for a branch proof Morgan dollar, in 1963. This was for the 1883-O owned by Harry Forman. Breen subsequently authenticated the first branch mint proof 1893-CC in 1972, the first 1879-O in 1973, and the first 1921-S in 1976. More than any other person, Walter Breen has been responsible for developing an awareness of branch mint proof Morgan dollars.

Since Walter Breen is universally regarded as the ultimate authority in the authentication of branch mint proof coins of all denominations, it may seem sacrilegious for anyone to question any of his attributions. However, in analyzing the data regarding branch mint proof Morgan dollar, this author disagrees with some of Breen's authentications. The following section will be devoted to an analysis of the twelve different Morgan dollars which Breen lists as possible branch mint proofs, with comments by the author.

1879-O: Mint records confirm the production of this coin. It is described in detail elsewhere in this chapter. The author has examined three of the four known specimens, and concurs with Breen's branch mint proof attribution.

1883-O: The existence of this coin is well documented. It is described in detail elsewhere in this chapter. The author has not seen the Harry Forman piece authenticated by Breen. The Amon Carter, Jr. specimen, not verified by Breen but examined by the author, appears to be a deep-mirror, bagmarked business strike prooflike rather than a branch mint proof.

The reason for confusion regarding this and several other coins in the Amon Carter, Jr. collection can be traced to ambiguities in a 1955 Max Mehl auction catalogue, which listed several Morgan dollars subsequently purchased by Carter. Mehl described certain silver dollars as "brilliant semi-proof, almost brilliant proof." The term "semi-proof" is meaningless. However, a coin can be described as semi-prooflike. This is obviously what Mehl meant. Therefore, those dollars which were listed in the catalogue as being "semi-proof" were actually meant to be described as semi-prooflike.

1883-CC, 1891-O, 1892-O, 1895-S: These four dates are listed by Breen as possible branch mint proofs in the Amon Carter, Sr. Estate, but were never examined by him. In 1979, this author visited Amon Carter, Jr., who inherited his father's vast coin collection and has added to it considerably over the past thirty years. Amon Carter is a wonderful man who enjoys sharing his collection with others. Several hours were spent in a detailed examination of Mr. Carter's magnificent Morgan dollar collection. Although the 1883-CC, 1891-O, 1892-O, and 1895-S dollars were indeed gorgeous coins they were not branch mint proofs. The 1891-O and 1892-O, in particular, were among the most beautiful business strikes of these dates the author has seen. Since gem prooflikes of these two dates are virtually unknown, it is not surprising that they might be considered to be branch mint proofs.

In a 1980 Kagin auction, an 1895-S with Breen's branch mint proof authentication papers realized $19,000 to a mail bidder. The author examined this coin extensively and concluded without doubt that the coin was not a branch mint proof. This judgement was shared by all knowledgeable dollar dealers in attendance at the auction. The coin was a deeply toned prooflike which exhibited little or no square rim, was not boldly struck, and was bagmarked. It was, in sum, a relatively unattractive business strike prooflike coin. Since neither the Carter or the Kagin coins are proofs, this casts much doubt upon the legitimacy of a third 1895-S "proof" attributed by Breen, the Dupont specimen.

1884-CC: Breen authenticated this piece for Arthur Kagin several years ago. This author examined this coin around 1973, while it was in the possession of John Troyan, a Florida dealer. Although I was not sufficiently knowledgeable at the time to make a definite determination, it was my opinion, and that of several other who examined the coin, that it was a superb gem prooflike rather than a proof.

1890-O, 1893-O: Breen lists these as being part of the huge Dupont collection, with the implication that he has verified both of these pieces as branch mint proofs. In addition, Breen also lists a 1891-O in the Dupont collection. The author has not examined any of these specimens.

As mentioned previously, New Orleans dollars from this period are very rare in gem prooflike condition. The few that the author has seen have been deep mirror cameos which are significantly above the quality normally associated with business strike dollars of these dates. The natural tendency is thus to elevate the status of such remarkable specimens to that of a presentation piece, or even a proof. Therefore, it is probable that these three coins are superb prooflike business strikes, rather than branch mint proofs.

1892-CC: Breen lists one piece and indicates that he has not verified its status. Superb, deep mirror cameo prooflikes of this date do exist, and could easily be confused with a branch mint proof.

1893-CC, 1921-S: The existence of these coins is well documented. They are described in detail later in this chapter. The author has seen all of the specimens listed by Breen except for the impaired MTB 1893-CC and concurs in the branch proof designation.

Other Possible Branch Mint Proofs

When I began the study of branch mint proof Morgan dollars six years ago, I was skeptical of the possibility of any additional dates other than the well-documented 1879-O, 1883-O, 1893-CC, and 1921-S. However, during the past six years a few intriguing coins surfaced which have forced me to modify my thinking. These will be discussed in the order of their appearance.

1887-O: At the 1976 ANA convention in New York, Amon Carter Jr. showed me several superb gem dollars, including a steel-toned, full strike, deep mirror prooflike 1886-O, and a superb prooflike 1891-O and 1893-O. These coins were among the finest I had ever seen of these dates.

The final coin which Mr. Carter handed to me was, at first glance, an obvious proof 1887 Morgan dollar. Upon examining the reverse of the coin, I was amazed to see an "O" mintmark.

This coin exhibited a light blue peripheral coloration yielding to a beautiful yellow at the center. It was very boldly struck. This was significant, since virtually all prooflike business strike 1887-O dollars are somewhat lacking in high-point definition. There were a few obverse rim nicks, but otherwise no contact marks at all. The rim was square around much of the circumference of the coin. In summary, it was a gorgeous coin, an obvious branch mint proof, and the sensation of the convention. Mr. Carter refused several offers up to $7,000 for the coin.

1884-O: This coin appeared at the 1980 ANA convention in Cincinnati, as part of a West Coast silver dollar collection. The author, who was actively seeking out branch mint proof Morgan dollars at the time, refused the coin at $1,500. This piece exhibited a strong strike, and was very deeply mirrored. However, it had been badly mishandled and was quite unattractive. Because of its condition the author was unable to determine whether the mirror surface was that of a mishandled proof or whether it had been augmented by artificial means. Julian Leidman and John Ford, among others, also felt that the coin could not be authenticated as a proof.

The coin was later sold at the convention for $500 to a prominent New England coin company, which obtained a quick bourse-floor authentication from Walter Breen and resold the coin to a collector for a reported $22,500.

1882-CC: In November of 1980 Bruce Amspacher called to offer me a proof 1882-CC silver dollar. Since Bruce is one of the few people capable of distinguishing a proof from a deep-mirror prooflike business strike, I was intrigued. The price was outrageous, and there was nothing to suggest the possibility of the existence of a proof of this date. But after expressing considerable skepticism I told Bruce to ship the coin.

1882-CC Branch Mint Proof
(Photo courtesy of Wayne Miller)

1881-O, possible Branch Mint Proof
(Photo courtesy of Wayne Miller)

This coin, pictured above left, is an obvious branch mint proof. Its chocolate brown toning does not obscure the deep-mirror proof surfaces, which are evident both in the field and the devices. The photograph brings out these mirror surfaces and emphasizes the bold strike typical of a proof. There is a full, square rim around much of the circumference of the coin, both obverse and reverse. The coin has no bagmarks, but does exhibit a few hairlines which are largely hidden by the dark toning. In summary, this 1882-CC essentially fulfills the requirements for a branch mint proof Morgan dollar.

1881-O: In April of 1982 Kevin Lipton sent me the coin pictured above right, having just purchased it in an auction the week previously for $3,500. The coin has a partial square rim on both obverse and reverse, and very deep mirror surfaces. The periphery of the coin is toned a light brown. There are several contact marks in the fields and on Liberty's face. The latter shows no sign of being struck from a polished planchet. The strike is not full over Liberty's ear. The reverse is slightly dull, but the strike is very strong. The coin shows some evidence of handling. This makes the attribution of such a piece very difficult.

In the end, the author declined to authenticate the coin as a proof, in part because of the lack of proof surfaces on Liberty's face, but largely because the coin did not present the overall appearance of a proof coin. In comparing the coin with known branch mint proofs, there were dissimilarities. However, it was a very difficult determination, and others might rightly call it a proof. It is therefore considered by the author to be a possible but doubtful proof.

1885-CC: Bruce Amspacher recently advised me that a major Midwestern dealer sold an 1885-CC as a branch mint proof about ten years ago to a California collector. In Bruce's opinion, the coin was a superb, deep-mirror business strike prooflike rather than a branch mint proof. Since prooflikes of this date often exhibit very deep-mirror fields and frosty devices it is understandable that such a coin could be mistaken for a proof. However, the author has not had the opportunity to examine this coin to render an opinion.

Summary

The branch mints lacked the huge hydraulic presses used by the Philadelphia mint, and their personnel had very little experience in the production of proof coins. Also, many branch mint proof Morgan dollars show evidence of careless handling. Consequently, the determination of a branch mint proof can be difficult. Legitimate differences of opinion may exist among knowledgeable people as to whether a given coin is or is not a branch mint proof.

Because of the excessive rarity of branch mint proof Morgan dollars (of the estimated fifty to seventy-five pieces which were produced, fewer than fifteen fully authenticated branch mint proof Morgan dollars are known to exist), they of course command very high prices. There is thus a tendency to describe a coin as a branch mint proof if it shows **any** of the characteristics of a proof such as an extremely bold strike, extraordinarily deep mirror surfaces, square rims, etc. However, because of the extreme rarity of branch mint proof dollars, the likelihood that such a coin is merely a "peculiar" or unusual business strike is much greater. The burden of proof must always rest with the person who is trying to verify branch mint proof status.

The following is a listing of all definite, possible, and doubtful branch mint proofs of which the author is aware, in descending order of certainty. The author has tried to be conservative in these determinations.

I. 1879-O, 1883-O, 1893-CC, 1921-S, are **authorized, definite** branch mint proofs. These are four dates for which proofs were authorized and subsequently issued.

II. 1882-CC and **1887-O** are **unauthorized** but **definite** branch mint proofs. These are two coins for which authorization does not exist but which must be considered as proofs because they meet the necessary criteria.

III. 1881-O, 1884-O, and **1884-CC** are considered to be **possible** but **doubtful** branch mint proofs. These are three coins which might be proofs, specimens of which the author has seen but which do not meet his conservative criteria.

IV. The **1890-O, 1891-O, 1892-O**, and **1895-S** from the Dupont collection; the Colonel Green 1892-CC listed by Breen; and the 1885-CC sold by the Midwestern dealer, are considered as **doubtful** branch mint proofs. These are coins which the author has not seen but which are of doubtful proof status.

V. The **1883-CC, 1891-O**, and **1895-S** from the Amon Carter, Jr. collection; and 1895-S from the Kagin auction, are coins rumored to be branch mint proofs which the author has seen and which are definitely not proofs.

Date-by-Date Analysis

The following pages will be given to a date-by-date analysis of the four authorized, definite branch mint proof Morgan dollars, the Zerbe and Chapman Morgan proof dollars, and the proof Peace dollars.

Morgan Branch Mint Proofs

1879-O Proof (Mintage: 12)

There is considerable documentation for the existence of the 1879-O Proof Morgan dollar. According to the best sources, twelve pieces were struck on February 20, 1879 to commemorate the reopening of the New Orleans mint, and the first Morgan dollar struck there.

1879-O Branch Mint Proof
(Photo courtesy of Wayne Miller)

At this time there are four known specimens. The author has owned all but the piece in the Smithsonian Institution. They are described as follows, in ascending order of condition:

1. This piece first came to light in the 1973 Central States Numismatic Society auction conducted by Rarcoa, where it realized $7,500. It later surfaced in Auction '79, and was purchased by the author for $14,500. The coin was subsequently resold to Fred Sweeney, Inc. through Bruce Amspacher for $20,000. Walter Breen attributed the coin and raved about the "extreme sharpness of the eagle's breast feathers, claws, legs, inner details of the leaves. . ." However, aesthetically speaking the coin is rather unattractive, with toning so dark and heavy that it inhibits the reflectivity of the fields. Additionally, although the coin does not evidence actual wear, it presents a rather "tired" appearance with some hairlines in evidence. Nonetheless, the coin is an obvious proof, and as such is an extreme rarity.

2. The Smithsonian Institution piece. The author has not seen this coin but it is reported that the coin is attractive but not superb.

3. I first saw this piece while it was owned by Alan Brotman in early 1973. Previous provenance was McDermott, another collector (Bass perhaps?), and Brownlee. Brotman apparently consigned the coin to the Kagin Sale of the 70's held on November 2 and 3, 1973. The coin was bought by Robert W. Barker for $8,250. Julian Leidman obtained the coin for the author in 1980.

This coin is much superior to the Rarcoa coin, with light golden-brown toning and very few hairlines. There are two tiny rim nicks behind the mouth of Liberty. The strike is extremely bold; every feather on the eagle is fully articulated. The coin has a partial wire rim on the obverse, and a virtually full rim on the reverse. The proof surfaces are very evident under the toning and the coin is identifiable as a proof at first glance.

4. The pictured piece is by far the finest known branch mint proof Morgan dollar of any date. It was purchased by the author at Auction '80. The piece was consigned by Leo Young, who thought of the coin as merely a superb gem prooflike. The coin is absolutely fantastic - one of the most beautiful proofs known of any date. It evidences virtually no wire rim, but the strike is very bold. It exhibits amazing cameo contrast; the fields are very deep and the devices are snow white. There are some very light lines on the cheek of Liberty from a plastic insert visible only under magnification, a light thin stain over the "8" in the date, and a tiny cut above Liberty's cap. Otherwise the coin is flawless.

1883-O Branch Mint Proof
(Photo courtesy of Wayne Miller)

1883-O Proof (Estimated mintage: 12)

Very little is known of the background of the 1883-O proof Morgan dollar. According to Walter Breen twelve coins were made for presentation to officials in New Orleans, probably relating to some event in the cotton industry or with the establishment of Tulane University as the State University of Louisiana. They were first mentioned in the *American Journal of Numismatics* in 1884 by the superintendent of the New Orleans mint. Harry Forman of Philadelphia reported the first specimen in 1963; it reappeared in a Harmer-Rooks auction in 1969, realizing $1,600. As has been the case with all branch mint proof Morgans, most people were not aware of this coin until Breen's excellent work.

The only other 1883-O proof to appear on the market is the piece pictured, which was auctioned by Superior Coin and Stamp in 1979, as a part of the Herbert Bergen collection. Although described as a gem prooflike instead of a gem proof, the coin was bid up to $6,500 by Julian Leidman, and subsequently resold for $15,000.

The coin is described as follows: Light brown toning around the periphery. Fields are deeply mirrored but gray brilliant. There are a very few light hairline cuts on Liberty's chin and cheek, and a deeper cut above the eagle's head, which may be a rim nick. Otherwise there are no discernible bagmarks. The strike is very bold, with partial square rims on the reverse. The coin presents an overall proof appearance. Obviously Julian Leidman and Jim Halperin (the underbidder) were convinced that this coin was a proof. Walter Breen, who has recently become very cautious in attributing proofs, states, "I think it is, but I have to see the other one (Harry Forman had it) to be sure." The author has examined the coin extensively and has concluded that this coin is one of the twelve 1883-O branch mint proof dollars.

The 1883-O dollar in Amon Carter's vast collection has long been rumored to be a proof, but the author has examined this and all other Carter Morgan dollar holdings, and is reasonably certain that the coin is a business strike. The coin is deeply mirrored, but fairly heavily bagmarked. The strike is strong but not as bold as on a proof dollar. (See the introduction for more data on this and other dollars in Carter's collection.)

1893-CC Branch Mint Proof
(Photo courtesy of Wayne Miller)

1893-CC Proof (Mintage: 12)

Considerable documentation exists for the 1893-CC proof Morgan dollar. According to Wayte Raymond a total of twelve pieces were struck to commemorate the closing of the Carson City Mint in 1893. The existence of these pieces was largely unknown until 1973, at which time Rarcoa introduced the finest, and at the time, the only known piece in its January FUN Auction. Since then three other specimens have been identified.

Of all the dates of which branch mint proofs are known or suspected, the 1893-CC is with the 1879-O, the easiest to identify.

The author has examined three of the four known 1893-CC proof dollars. They are described in ascending order of quality.

1. The firm of Manfred-Tordella-Brookes owns a specimen which by all accounts is polished and heavily abraded. The author has not seen this piece but due to its very poor state of preservation attribution would be difficult. It is therefore listed here as a possible rather than as a definite proof specimen.

2. The Amon Carter specimen, an obvious proof, but with extensive hairlines in the obverse field. This coin is a very deeply mirrored cameo and still quite attractive despite the hairlines.

3. Lot #719 of the Garrett Sale, 1980. This coin was not listed as a branch mint proof by the cataloguers (although the chief authenticator of the firm which conducted the auction, Bowers and Ruddy Galleries, concurs with the proof designation). Nevertheless, the coin still realized $30,000. The author examined the coin extensively and concludes that the coin is a proof, for the following reasons: It would otherwise be the only business-strike Morgan dollar from 1880-1904 listed in the Garrett Collection; the coin was fully struck on the reverse - only one other fully prooflike 1893-CC dollar has had full feathers; the coin evidenced square rims. In summary, it presented an overall proof rather than prooflike appearance. It is possible the coin referred to by Wayte Raymond back in the 1940's; he would have been cognizant of the Garrett collection at that time.

4. By far the finest known is the discovery piece, attributed in great detail by Walter Breen in August 1972, and sold in the January 1973 Rarcoa Auction of the Bruce Todd silver dollar collection. It realized $18,000 at that time, the first Morgan dollar to break the $10,000 barrier. It surfaced again in Auction '79 where it was bid up to $39,000.

The description of this coin is as follows: Although some cameo contrast is evident especially on the reverse, this coin is more brilliant than cameo proof. The fields are deeply mirrored, and the strike is very bold. The piece is an obvious proof at first glance. There are some very light abrasions in the obverse field. Liberty's cheek is pristine. There is a small rim dent at the lower left of the coin.

1921-S Proof (Estimated mintage: 24)

In a 1951 conversation with Wayte Raymond, his mentor and a legend in the coin profession, Walter Breen was told that two dozen 1921-S proof Morgan dollars had been struck for Farran Zerbe, probably to complement the Philadelphia proofs which Zerbe had also caused to be produced.

Only four or five specimens of the 1921-S proof Morgan dollar are known. Breen indicates that the American Numismatic Society and the Chase Bank in Manhattan each have one. The author has also heard of two pieces in Eastern collections, but has not been able to confirm this.

1921-S Branch Mint Proof
(Photo courtesy of Wayne Miller)

The fifth piece, and the only one the author has seen, is pictured right. It was first attributed as a proof by Breen, and repurchased by the consignor for $1,900 in a 1975 GENA sale by Pine Tree Auctions. In 1981 it was sold by Leroy Lenhart of American Coin Company to the current owner for $10,000.

This coin is by far the least attractive of all the known branch mint proof Morgan dollars. It is very flat struck, which is unique for a branch mint proof dollar. A considerable percentage of business strike 1921-S dollars also exhibit a similar lack of high-point detail. Therefore, it is possible that a die which has been used for business strike coins was commandeered for the production of the two dozen proofs. The fact that these proofs appear to have been made as an afterthought, toward the close of the year 1921, under pressure from one person (Zerbe), tends to support this hypothesis.

The coin is toned an unattractive light brown. The surfaces are mirrored, but are those of a dull gray brilliant proof. Further, the coin exhibits minor contact marks, mostly on the obverse.

The author has been unable to examine any of the other specimens of the 1921-S proof Morgan dollar. However, it may be assumed that the other specimens exhibit the same poor strike and dull gray brilliant surfaces.

With five or fewer specimens known, the 1921-S proof Morgan dollar must be considered a major rarity. However, the mediocre condition of such pieces will probably prevent them from realizing a price which is commensurate with their true rarity.

Zerbe and Chapman proof Morgan dollars

**1921-P "Proof" Morgan (Zerbe)
(Estimated mintage: 20-200)**

1921-P "Proof" Morgan (Zerbe)
(Photo courtesy of Wayne Miller)

In 1920 the American Numismatic Association, through the considerable energies of Farran Zerbe, one of its most active and influential members, was clamoring for the release of a new Peace dollar. The first release was delayed until the end of 1921. So to appease Zerbe and his numismatic colleagues, a number of presentation-quality 1921 Morgan dollars were produced. The exact mintage is unknown, with estimates of 20-200 most commonly cited.

The quality of these "Zerbe proofs," as they were later termed, is much inferior to any of the Morgan proofs minted from 1878-1904. Although the strike is quite bold, the fields are not deeply mirrored, and exhibit little or no cameo contrast. The devices show very little polishing. Surface abrasions are often heavy; many appear to have been in physical contact with other coins. "Zerbe proofs" are very difficult to differentiate from prooflike business strikes. However, Zerbe specimens all have a light die scratch from the second "U" in "UNUM" to the denticles at the rim.

In the author's opinion, these Zerbe dollars do not meet the criteria for a proof coin; their fields are not sufficiently mirrored and the strike is not unusually bold. Also, there is some evidence that business strike dollars with prooflike surfaces were struck from these same dies. The "Zerbe proof" Morgan appears to be something in between a business strike and a proof, much like the Special Mint Set coins of 1965-1967.

Obverse Reverse

1921-P PCGS PR-61 Zerbe Proof Morgan Dollar
(Photo courtesy of George Alexander Frudakis)

1921-P ANACS graded MS-64 Morgan dollar struck from Zerbe proof dies

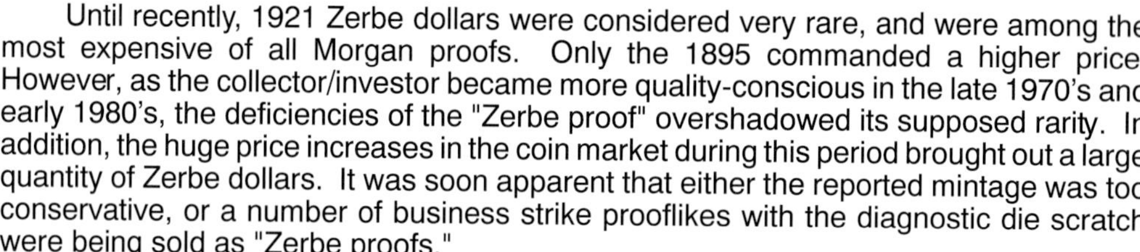

Until recently, 1921 Zerbe dollars were considered very rare, and were among the most expensive of all Morgan proofs. Only the 1895 commanded a higher price. However, as the collector/investor became more quality-conscious in the late 1970's and early 1980's, the deficiencies of the "Zerbe proof" overshadowed its supposed rarity. In addition, the huge price increases in the coin market during this period brought out a large quantity of Zerbe dollars. It was soon apparent that either the reported mintage was too conservative, or a number of business strike prooflikes with the diagnostic die scratch were being sold as "Zerbe proofs."

Currently, 1921 Zerbe dollars bring much less than proof Morgans of the 1878-1904 era.

1921-P "Proof" Morgan (Chapman)
(Estimated mintage: 12)

Late in 1921 Henry Chapman of Philadelphia, who had for over forty years been one of the most influential coin dealers in America (he conducted his first numismatic auction in 1879 with his brother Samuel) decided that if Farran Zerbe could persuade the Philadelphia mint to issue a 1921 proof-quality Morgan dollar, that he should be able to do the same. At his urging twelve silver dollars, now known as Chapman proofs, were struck.

The author has examined four of the twelve Chapman proofs. They are vastly superior to "Zerbe proofs," primarily in the depth of their fields. Contrary to the Zerbe dollars, they are readily discernible as a proof at first glance. All are gray-brilliant proofs, similar to the 1902-1904 issues, but with a slight amount of cameo contrast. Luster is somewhat subdued and mellow. The fields exhibit a "polished" look, as though the dies had been hastily pressed into service before the basining/polishing process had been fully completed. None of the four show any evidence of contact with other coins, as is so often the case with "Zerbe proofs."

1921-P "Proof" Morgan (Chapman)
(Photo courtesy of Wayne Miller)

In 1977 the author purchased a Chapman proof from Harlan White and sold it to a prominent Connecticut collector for $4,500. The pictured piece, now in the R.J. Sheppard collection, brought near $20,000 in Auction '80, as a part of the Leo Young collection. These two were fully gem proofs, with mellow, glowing mirror surfaces and a slightly soft strike. Another piece, listed as a Proof-63, was sold in a 1980-81 auction by Bowers and Ruddy. A fourth piece is quite hairlined and somewhat dull, yet still an obvious proof.

Possible because of the negative attitudes which have developed in recent years toward the inferior "Zerbe proof," the prices realized for 1921 Chapman proofs have not been commensurate with their true rarity. This coin was minted in far smaller quantities than any other Philadelphia Morgan dollar, with the possible exception of the 1878 Round Breast proof. As this coin becomes more well known, its price should increase dramatically.

Peace Dollar Proofs

1921 Proof Peace Dollar (Mintage: Unknown with estimate 20-50)

There are two distinctly different types of 1921 proof Peace dollars; each will be discussed separately.

1921 Peace Dollar: Matte Proof. The existence of this variety has been well documented. Walter Breen lists five specimens in his book. The author has seen three, one at the 1976 ANA Convention and another at the 1979 ANA mid-winter convention. The details of the third piece are lost to memory.

1921 Satin Finish Proof Peace Dollar
(Photo courtesy of Wayne Miller)

All three specimens exhibit a very bold strike, with high-point details plainly visible - something which does not occur on business strikes of this date. Luster is very subdued, as is typical of matte proofs. All three coins have a rather unappealing blue-gray coloration and are, to many collectors, aesthetically inferior to a gem business strike, except for the incredible high-point detail and the absence of surface abrasions. However, due to the overall extreme rarity of proof Peace dollars, and as the first year of the Peace dollar design, 1921 matte proof Peace dollars have always commanded substantial prices. During the "fever" market of 1979-1980, one specimen reportedly sold for more than $100,000.

1921 Peace Dollar: Satin Finish Proof. This variety was unknown until 1975, when Walter Breen made the first attribution at the ANA convention. Initially this variety was thought to be even more rare than the matte proof type. However, the market of 1979-1980 brought out several examples, most of which were immediately sent to Breen for his all-important attribution papers. However, like the 1921 Zerbe, a number of deceptive business strikes appear to have been produced from the same dies which produced the satin finish proof. Breen eventually refused to authenticate any further specimens as proofs. It is possible that some of the proofs which were authenticated were business strikes.

The author observed nearly a dozen of these coins, and in his judgement only two or three qualified as proofs. The pictured specimen purchased from Steve Ivy in 1979 for $10,000, is the finest known satin finish proof Peace dollar. Charles Adkins of New York also owns a superb 1921 Peace dollar, with Breen's attribution as a proof.

Although the satin finish 1921 proof Peace dollar is possibly as rare as the matte proof variety, the former have always brought a much lower price for the following reasons: First, the matte proof variety has been known and documented for a much longer period of time. Second, the satin finish proofs are not mentioned in any mint report. Thus, they lack the all important official legitimacy of the matte proof variety. Third, matte proofs are readily distinguishable from business strikes, whereas it is sometimes difficult to differentiate a satin finish proof from a business strike produced from the same dies.

1922 Proof Peace Dollar (Mintage: Unknown with estimate 20-30)

There are two distinctly different types of 1922 proof Peace dollars; each will be discussed separately.

1922 Peace Dollar: Matte Proof

The existence of the variety is well documented. Apparently high relief Peace dollars were contemplated for mintage in 1922, and a few matte proof pieces were coined. However, the problems of the high relief design resulted in its discontinuance. Walter Breen states that five are known, and provides attribution for three. The author has seen two, which are additional to the three attributed by Breen.

The Bruce Todd collection of prooflike Morgan dollars, auctioned at the 1973 FUN convention in Miami, contained a 1922 matte proof Peace dollar which exhibited the startlingly bold relief of a 1921 Peace dollar. The coin was a rather dull gray and like most matte proofs did not display deeply reflective fields. The coin was marred by a few very heavy gouges, one right behind Liberty's mouth. Nevertheless, it realized approximately $8,500 - a higher price than a choice BU 1893-S dollar would have brought.

Another specimen consigned to Manfred-Tordella-Brookes of New York was offered at the $75,000 level. The author examined this coin at the 1978 mid-winter ANA convention. The coin was again a rather unappealing dull gray matte proof.

Bowers and Ruddy Galleries offered a 1922 high relief matte proof Peace dollar in May, 1980, near the height of the "fever" market. This piece was subsequently sold for approximately $100,000. According to their research, six specimens of this variety were known at that time.

1922 Peace Dollar: Satin Finish Proof

This variety was unknown until the first specimen was attributed by Walter Breen at the February, 1977 Long Beach convention. Its owner, Robert J. Riethe, had purchased it shortly before in the auction of the old-time John Beck estate as a business strike. After reading of the coin in Breen's book, the author agreed to purchase this coin from Riethe for $14,000, subsequent upon the author's acceptance of the coin as a proof.

This coin exhibited very dark toning on much of the reverse and part of the obverse. It was very sharply struck, although not nearly as bold as the high relief variety. Some slight mirror surface was evident. The coin definitely was unusual. However, the author was not persuaded that the coin was a proof and declined to purchase it. Riethe subsequently sold this coin late in 1981 for an undisclosed figure.

Early in 1979 the author was commissioned to disperse the massive coin collection of the late Henry F. Herrman of Hays, Kansas. Included in this accumulation was a 1922 satin finish proof Peace dollar, pictured at left. The strike is very bold, with very deep brilliant proof mirror surfaces. It is an obvious proof at first glance, much more so than the Riethe piece. The coin has numerous hairline scratches on Liberty's cheek, probably from the plastic inserts in a coin album. Otherwise it is a superb gem proof.

This coin was purchased as a proof by Mr. Herrman from Paul B. Volk and Sons of Boston in May of 1945 for the sum of $4.50 - the same price he paid for an 1895 proof Morgan three years later.

A harshly cleaned Proof-60 1922 Satin Finish Peace dollar was offered by New England Rare Coin Galleries in an August, 1982 auction. It was accompanied by a letter of authentication from Walter Breen. In the letter Breen indicated that the only other specimens he was aware of were the two pieces described above.

Although satin finish 1922 proof Peace dollars are much more rare than the matte proof variety, the latter will probably always bring a higher price for the following reasons: First, the matte proof variety has been known and documented for a much longer period of time. Second, the high relief to matte proofs makes them more desirable. Third, the satin finish proofs are not mentioned in official mint reports. They thus lack official sanction. Fourth, since there are only three satin finish proofs known, they lack the exposure necessary to command a price commensurate with their extreme rarity.

1922 Satin Finish Proof Peace Dollar
(Photo courtesy of Wayne Miller)

Acknowledgement

The article was reprinted by permission in its entirety from Wayne Miller's *Morgan and Peace Dollar Textbook*, 1982, Adam Smith Publishing Co., Metairie, Louisiana.

CHAPTER 67

Peace Dollars

by John W. Highfill, NLG

Peace Dollars (1921-1935)

"The war to end all wars" was over, and in 1920 Farran Zerbe, a past president of the American Numismatic Association and editor of its journal, *The Numismatist,* proposed that a new design be produced representing the theme of peace.

The result was the Peace Dollar designed by Anthony De Francisci.

De Francisci used his wife Teresa — an immigrant, who fondly remembered as a child posing like Liberty upon first arriving in America — as the model for his Liberty design. She would later describe her modeling for the coinage design as the "realization of my fondest childhood dream."

The Peace dollar was coined from 1921-1935, with the exception of the years 1929-1933.

On August 3, 1964, an act was passed providing for 45 million Peace Dollars to be produced. Records indicate that 316,076 1964-dated Peace Dollars were struck at the mint in Denver. Plans were altered, and the official word is that all examples were melted.

Peace dollar Liberty Obverse and Eagle Reverse
(Coin courtesy of Robert T. McIntire)
(Photo provided by Krause Publications)

Numismatists often begin any discussion of the Peace dollar with references to Farran Zerbe, the influential historian for the American Numismatic Association, who first proposed the Peace dollar at the ANA convention on August 25, 1920.

Some historically oriented collectors begin with the surrender of Germany to the allies and the Treaty of Versailles ending World War I. This official act prompted calls for a peace-oriented commemorative coin.

Those interested in sculpture and engraving of coinage tend to study the coin through the artist himself, Anthony de Francisci, and trace the development and acceptance of the design through the competition sponsored by the federal Commission of Fine Arts.

Social interests have developed the story of the Peace dollar through the eyes of Teresa de Francisci, who modeled for her husband and was designated the "Lady of Peace."

Others have concentrated on the Act of September 26, 1890, which amended the Revised Statutes of the United States and provided for new designs of United States coins. They also recall the Pittman Act of April 23, 1918, which provided bullion for Peace dollars — and congressional opposition to the project. They may even mention the silver lobby's role in both the 1921-28 and 1934-5 coinages.

Still others, focusing on the collecting and investing aspects of the Peace dollar, extol the virtues of this 20th century series. They explore the production and rarity of the various dates together with their certified populations and profit potential.

Still other numismatists focus their attention on the errors made during the minting process. These include defective planchets, rotated and damaged dies, striking errors, and other mint errors.

The Creation of the Peace Dollar

Numismatists agree that Farran Zerbe was the prime motivator in the spirited move for the Peace dollar. Zerbe was very well known and respected in numismatic circles during the early 1900s. He founded the Chase Manhattan Bank Money \Museum with his own superb collection, and was at the core of the ANA in 1920 when he presented his historic paper, "Commemorate the Peace with a Coin for Circulation." The following statement was made within the paper. "Our Peace coin should be of good size for art effects, and if it be one for popular use by all the people, the half dollar . . . would be a common choice. But, should we resume the coinage of the silver dollar, that coin should be a consideration." Zerbe was aiming at a new design for the half-dollar, but wanted silver dollar coinage if that option presented itself. He knew that a silver dollar was possible as a result of the Pittman Act of 1918.

Originally, Zerbe and the ANA were considering commemorative coinage, but were asking for a circulating coin. Precedents from the past allowed for commemoratives as fund raisers and collector coins not intended for circulation. As official language developed later, the commemorative aspects of the proposed coin were downplayed in favor of a "Peace" silver dollar for general circulation.

His paper inspired the ANA to the extent that a committee was formed headed by Judson Brenner with Zerbe and the following additional members: Congressman William A. Ashbrook of Jamestown, Ohio; Dr. J.M. Henderson of Columbus, Ohio; and Howland Wood of New York City. The Chairman of the House Committee of Coinage, Weights and Measures at the time was Albert H. Vestal (R-Ind.). Vestal was convinced by the ANA committee of the need for the "Peace" coinage and prepared a joint resolution to Congress on May 9, 1921, to obtain their approval. Here is the verbiage of that Joint Resolution:

> "RESOLVED by the Senate and House of Representatives of the United States of America in Congress assembled, that as soon as practicable after the passage of this resolution, all standard silver dollars coined under the provisions of Section 2 of the Act entitled 'An Act to conserve the gold supply of the United States; to provide silver for subsidiary coinages and for commercial use; to assist foreign Governments at war with the enemies of the United States; and for the above purposes to stabilize the price and encourage the production of silver,' approved April 23, 1918, shall be of an appropriate design commemorative of the termination of the war between the Imperial German Government and the people of the United States."
>
> "Such design shall be selected by the Director of the Mint with the approval of the Secretary of the Treasury. Each standard silver dollar of such design shall be known as the 'Peace Dollar'."

An attempt by Vestal to place the joint resolution on the unanimous consent calendar failed, and the subsequent debate on the issue did not bring it to a vote. Resistance to a silver dollar coin was high, given all that had taken place since 1878, and Congress was reluctant to pass a resolution authorizing a silver dollar coin.

While this was going on, Zerbe and others were disturbed to find the San Francisco Mint producing Morgan dollars beginning on May 9, the same day as Representative Vestal's resolution. These coins were made possible via a section of the Pittman Act which forced the purchase of enough bullion to match all of the melted dollars. In all, the Philadelphia, Denver and San Francisco mints coined 86,730,000 Morgan dollars that year, commemorating not peace, but silver lobby greed.

As it turned out, ingenuity saved the day. The Act of September 26, 1890, which amended the Revised Statutes of the United States, Section 3510, provided the vehicle which Zerbe and others required. The approval of Congress was not necessary as the Morgan design was over 25 years old, (actually 43), and could be replaced under the Act of 1890. The text of that Act follows:

Act of September 26, 1890.

"Be it enacted by the Senate and House of Representatives of the United States of America in Congress assembled, That section thirty-five hundred and ten of the Revised Statutes of the United States be, and the same is hereby, amended so as to read as follows:"

> "SEC. 3510. The engraver shall prepare from the original dies already authorized all the working dies required for use in the coinage of the several mints, and, when new coins, emblems, devices, legends, or designs are authorized, shall, if required by the Director of the Mint, prepare the devices, models, hubs, or original dies for the same. The Director of the Mint shall have power, with the approval of the Secretary of the Treasury, to cause new designs or models of authorized emblems or devices to be prepared and adopted in the same manner as when new coins or devices are authorized. But no change in the design or die of any coin shall be made oftener than once in twenty-five years from and including the year of the first adoption of the design, model, die, or hub for the same coin: *Provided*, That no change be made in the diameter of any coin: *And provided further*, That nothing in this section shall prevent the adoption of new designs or models for devices or emblems already authorized for the standard silver dollar and the five-cent nickel piece as soon as practicable after the passage of this act. But the Director of the Mint shall nevertheless have power, with the approval of the Secretary of the Treasury, to engage temporarily for this purpose the services of one or more artists, distinguished in their respective departments of art, who shall be paid for such service from the contingent appropriation for the mint at Philadelphia."

It is sometimes amazing how fast the wheels of government can turn. The Pittman Act of April 23, 1918, provided for melting of up to 350,000,000 silver dollars (270,232,722 Morgans were actually melted), and for purchase of enough bullion to replace the melted dollars. The Secretary of the Treasury agreed with the ANA that a Peace coin should be issued, and took matters into his own hands. President Warren G. Harding signed an Executive Order on July 28, 1921, putting all material aspects of the new coin among the responsibilities of the head of the Federal Commission of Fine Arts.

That Commission announced a design competition for the new dollar on November 23, 1921. Entries all had to be submitted in one month. Nine first rate sculptors were invited to compete with eight accepting. Each was asked to prepare a model for the new proposed coinage. The one month time period was very short for the creation of coin design, and the participants were working at a feverish pace with little time for research.

One of the entrants was an Italian immigrant named Anthony de Francisci. He was responsible for designing the Maine Centennial commemorative half dollar issued in 1920. This sculptor modeled his obverse design after his wife, Teresa, then 23 years old. She related later that he sat her beside an open window to create a windblown hair effect. His design of a youthful and alert Liberty with parted lips was also inspired by the crown of the Statue of Liberty. He wished to acknowledge the vitality and spirit of America's new generation.

Francisci's original design sketches submitted on December 13, 1921, caught the eye of the Fine Arts Commission which declared his model the winner on December 19. Not all aspects of the design went unchallenged. The reverse showed the eagle breaking a sword to symbolize peace, but detractors insisted that it symbolized defeat. Without consulting Francisci, the Mint Bureau ordered Morgan to get rid of the sword. Morgan remodeled the eagle to stand with an olive branch atop a mountain peak inscribed PEACE. These changes were approved and the Peace dollar was almost a reality.

Teresa, the "Lady of Peace," was the last model to pose for a representation of Liberty for a U.S. coin. A plaque was given to her in 1970 to honor the 50th anniversary of the first striking of the Peace dollar. She was celebrated by many numismatic organizations throughout the years and passed away at the age of ninety-two on October 20, 1990.

Peace dollar model Teresa Cafarelli de Francisci (Courtesy of Krause Publications, Numismatic News, Iola, Wisconsin)

1922-P: Contender for the "World's Flattest non-1921 Peace Dollar" award

The Peace Dollar

The Peace dollar, like its predecessors, contains .77344 ounces of pure silver in a composition of .900 silver and .100 copper. The diameter is 38.1 millimeters with reeded edges and weighs 26.73 grams.

The obverse features a youthful Liberty with the crown of rays and windblown hair in a strong yet simplistic design within a plain field. LIBERTY appears across the top of the coin at the rim, with the motto, IN GOD WE TRVST split between the neck of Ms. Liberty. The designer's monogram appear under the neckline. The date completes the design at the bottom of the obverse. The reverse presents the redesigned eagle with olive branch perched atop a mountain peak with the rays of sunlight in the background. Verbiage includes UNITED STATES OF AMERICA above *E PLURIBUS UNUM* at the top, the denomination ONE DOLLAR split by the eagle, and PEACE at the bottom completing the reverse design. The mintmark appears on the reverse under the ONE at the left of the eagle's tail feathers.

The high relief design provided by Francisci was not fully tested before the striking of coinage. This provided problems. Still intent on producing Peace dollars during 1921, the dies were quickly prepared by the Philadelphia Mint. The first production date was December 26, 1921, and there were 1,006,473 Peace dollars struck during the last week of December. On January 3, 1922, the first strikes were delivered to President Harding, the Secretary of the Treasury, and the Director of the Mint. Soon, the new Peace dollar was released into circulation. The high relief design served to shorten die life, and when striking pressure was reduced, the result was a Peace dollar of diminished central detail, as on most 1921's.

In response to the high relief die problems, George Morgan made further modifications in January of 1922. Obverse changes included intensifying the details of the hair and adding two additional short rays on Liberty's tiara. The eagle's feathers and mountain peak were re-engraved on the reverse completing the modified design. Only three high relief proofs with a matte surface were struck using the modified design before additional modifications were made, thereby creating a rarity in the series.

With the situation still unresolved, Anthony de Francisci himself was called to Philadelphia to assist in creating usable working dies, but all he was permitted to do was watch helplessly. Morgan made additional major changes, lowering the relief and flattening the concave fields. The consequence was a flat coin which lost much of the beauty intended by the designer. The Peace dollars struck after this action were bland and belied the boldness of Ms. Liberty.

Cameo prooflike Peace dollars are virtually nonexistent; semi-prooflikes are few and far between. The major reason usually advanced for this void was the lack of die basining of the Peace dollar dies coupled with the uniform presses available at the time. The master die curvature precluded the need for basining of the working dies, which almost guaranteed no contrast between the devices and the fields. Another factor is the design of the Peace dollar flows smoothly into the fields eliminating the need for basining. In fact, basining would have led to a deterioration of the device details — an event a Peace dollar struck in low relief could ill afford.

Brilliant prooflikes, usually produced by polishing of the dies, are also unavailable, leading to the conclusion that polishing of the dies was unnecessary. Clash marks were seldom noticeable during production of Peace dollars, which gave no reason for additional die polishing that could have led to brilliant prooflikes. The low relief and long life of working dies contributed to lackluster examples of Peace dollars.

Walter Breen reported the following four types of proof Peace dollar issues in his celebrated *Complete Encyclopedia of U.S. and Colonial Coins*. All were created in 1921 and 1922 with no further proofs struck for the Peace dollar series.

1. 1921 Matte Proof, high relief with possibly six to eight known examples. Features a fine-grain matte surface with sharp hair and feathers.
2. 1921 Satin Finish Proof, high relief, discovered at the 1975 ANA Convention. No trace of mint frost; sharp hair and feathers. These were the first Peace dollars struck December 26, 1921; in Auction '87: 1885 was the documented #20 specimen. Business strikes are known from the same dies, but display only ordinary striking quality (flat in central hair and on many feathers, notably leg and forward parts of wing).
3. 1922 Type of 1921 High Relief Proof with concave fields and a matte surface. Six to eight pieces exist of this type, the only high relief 1922 Peace dollars known. High relief design differs with 1921 in ways described earlier in this chapter. Norweb: 3931
4. 1922 Regular design Proof, low relief, flat fields, thinner letters and numerals with only three examples known to exist. At least ten were made, two with sandblast finish, sold by George T. Morgan to Ambrose Swasey, March 1, 1922: the story is at Norweb: 3932-3. No business strikes are known from this die although the new 1922 low relief design was utilized throughout the remainder of the Peace dollar series.

The *Annual Report of the Director of the Mint* for the fiscal year ended June 30, 1922, gave the following accounts as listed under the Operations of the Mint Service.

New Coin Designs

"The 'Peace dollar' takes the place of the old design of the standard silver dollar, which was first issued in 1878. This coin commemorates the declaration of peace between the United States, Germany, and Austria, exchanges of peace treaty ratifications having been made in Berlin of November 11, 1921, and in Vienna on November 8, 1921, and peace having been proclaimed by the President of the United States on November 14 and 17, 1921, respectively. No special congressional authority was required for the change in design of the silver dollar, since the law permits changing the design of any of our coins not more frequently than once in 25 years. The design of the 'Peace dollar' was selected by the Fine Arts Commission from models submitted by a number of prominent sculptors, and is the work of Anthony de Francisci. On the obverse is a female head emblematic of Liberty, wearing a tiara of light rays, and the word 'Liberty'; on the reverse is an eagle perched on a mountain top, holding in its talons an olive branch, witnessing the dawn of a new day; the word 'Peace' also appears. Other mottoes and inscriptions are as required by the coinage laws. The design for the silver 'Peace dollar' was approved in December, 1921, and 1,006,473 pieces were executed by the close of the calendar year. Subsequent coins of this design will bear the year in which made. At the close of the fiscal year on June 30, 1922, a total of 24,701,473 of the new design coins had been struck. . . ."

Engraving Department

". . . The dies for the peace dollar were made from models approved by the same commission [Fine Arts Commission], and over 1,000,000 pieces were struck in 1921. Before the dies for the 1922 issue were finally ready considerable experimenting to reduce the relief was necessary because of the extreme difficulty in coinage. . . ."

Dies Manufactured

Regular silver coinage:	
Unused	280
Issued to mint at Philadelphia	835
Issued to mint at San Francisco	280
Issued to mint at Denver	270
Total prepared	1,665

Mintage

The legal goal of the Peace dollar was to replace the 270,232,722 dollars melted under the Pittman Act. This objective was completed with the striking of the 1928 Peace dollars; production halted.

Thomas Amendment

The Thomas Amendment was attached to the Agricultural Adjustment Act that was approved on May 12, 1933. President Roosevelt was authorized within a five month time frame to receive silver in lieu of payment on war debt account at a maximum of 50 cents per ounce of .900 fine silver. The cap or total amount to be collected was not to exceed $200,000,000.

Silver certificates were authorized to be issued for the silver received to the total value at which the silver was accepted. The total silver received was to be used to mint standard silver dollars and subsidiary silver coins as required at the option of the Secretary of Treasury.

The Western U.S. silver interests regrouped and managed to induce passage of a December 21, 1933 proclamation, signed by President Franklin D. Roosevelt. The essence of the document was a requirement to coin silver dollars with newly purchased domestic bullion. This resulted in over 7,021,528 Peace dollars struck in 1934 and 1935, which completed the series. The Silver Act passed in 1934 provided for backing of silver certificate paper money with both bullion and coinage, which in turn eliminated the requirement for coinage of silver dollars for that purpose. The depression was another factor reducing the need for silver dollar coinage at this time.

By the end of 1935, a total of 190,577,279 Peace dollars had been coined. The actual mintage figures for each year and mintmark follow:

Peace Dollar Mintage (1921-1935)

Date:	Mintage:	Proof Mintage:	Date:	Mintage:
1921-P	1,006,473	20+ *	1926-D	2,348,700
1922-P	1,737,000	10+ *	1926-S	6,980,000
1922-D	15,063,000		1927-P	848,000
1922-S	17,475,000		1927-D	1,268,900
1923-P	30,800,000		1927-S	866,000
1923-D	6,811,000		1928-P	360,649
1923-S	19,020,000		1928-S	1,632,000
1924-P	11,811,000		1934-P	954,057
1924-S	1,728,000		1934-D	1,569,500
1925-P	10,198,000		1934-S	1,011,000
1925-S	1,610,000		1935-P	1,576,000
1926-P	1,939,000		1935-S	1,964,000

* Estimated Mintage

There is one final episode in the saga of the Peace dollar series. The Act of August 3, 1964 authorized production of 45 million silver dollars of the Peace design. Trial pieces were struck in Philadelphia, where all but two were destroyed. The working dies for the 1964-D dollars were sent to Denver for actual production, and 316,076 Peace dollars were coined during the period, May 15 through May 24, 1965. For uncertain reasons, President Lyndon B. Johnson rescinded the order for the Peace dollar coinage, requiring that all struck pieces were to be reclaimed and melted.

In the final analysis, the last of the .900 fine Peace dollars were named "trial strikes" and not legally issued. All were presumably destroyed (by weight rather than by count). According to Denver coin dealer Dan Brown, Fern Miller of the Denver Mint suggested that mint employees were allowed (by custom) to purchase two of each newly produced coin, but supposedly all were returned.

Any 1964-D Peace dollars found today would be subject to seizure by the Treasury Department as they were not legally released. Other coins of the past in this category include the 1933 double eagles. Numismatists are hoping that one of these coins will be donated to the Smithsonian Institution for all to see.

1964 Peace dollar design
(Courtesy of Bob Wilhite c/o Numismatic News)

Peace Dollar Characteristics and Varieties

Generally speaking, the Peace dollar series was a lackluster affair with relief and detail problems. The series has not been in vogue with collectors since the extreme run-up ending in 1980. Artistically, the inherent beauty of the high relief coupled with the bold design was lost early in the life of the Peace dollar and never recovered. Problems with the high relief dies of 1921 revolved around die breakage; accordingly, most 1921s were made with reduced pressure and were flat and weak, with central device details blurred. Later dates in lower relief, are often too weak on letters.

Generally, the "barren" fields of the Peace dollars tend to exaggerate bagmarks, scratches and other surface abrasions, distracting to the observing eye. The low relief strike of thin and rounded numbers and letters certainly did not help the aesthetic quality.

The Philadelphia Mint was singled out as presenting colored spots (of an off-white shade) on a number of coins made during the years, 1922, 1923, 1924 and 1925. This discoloration must have occurred during the minting process, and is a permanent characteristic of the affected coins.

Die cracks occur on the Denver issues of 1922 and 1923, less often on other dates. In an effort to produce a higher quality dollar, striking pressure was briefly increased to the extent of damaging the dies. The 1922-D and 1924-P have been singled out as the "orange peels" of the series, referring to the rough surface caused by excessive die wear.

Contrary to the reputation earned during production of the Morgan series, the San Francisco facility was known for its poor, light strikes of Peace dollars. The low relief die pairs were good for an unprecedented 500,000 coins: another sacrifice of art to economics.

Few significant varieties occur in the Peace dollar series. The most prominent of these is the high relief and low relief which occurred in 1921 and 1922. Other noteworthy varieties are not as obvious and require further explanation.

The 1921 is known with an unusual reeding pattern on the edge of the coin. This variety was the result of a collar which did not contain the usual number of grooves, and commands a modest premium.

The 1928-S was produced with a very small "S" mintmark as well as a larger "S". The larger "S" variety is very rare and commands a substantial premium.

The 1934-D is found with a "micro D" mintmark as well as a larger "D". Both of these varieties are known with a doubled obverse die and these are rare. The doubled obverse die varieties bring a large premium.

The 1935-S has two varieties of the reverse, one with three rays below the "ONE", and a new reverse die with four rays. Both of these varieties are equal in rarity.

Turning attention to grading for a moment, uncirculated specimens must show no wear and will be graded based upon strike, bag marks, luster and eye appeal. About Uncirculated specimens will show only slight signs of obverse wear on the hair above the eye and ear of Liberty. On the reverse slight wear will be visible on the top and outside edge of the eagle's right wing. Other circulated grades will show increasing amounts of wear concentrated in the areas listed for About Uncirculated pieces.

Peace Dollar Statistics

The following chart presents the Peace dollar dates broken down into four categories. These include Common Dates, Semi-Common Dates, Semi-key Dates and Key Dates, in ascending or descending order as noted. Mintages are also repeated for reference purposes.

Peace Dollar Categories and Mintage

Common Dates		**Semi-Common Dates**		**Semi-Key Dates**		**Key Dates**	
Year	**Mintage**	**Year**	**Mintage**	**Date**	**Mintage**	**Date**	**Mintage**
1922-P	51,737,000	1922-D	15,063,000	1922-S	17,475,000	1921-P	1,006,473
1923-P	30,800,000	1923-D	6,811,000	1923-S	19,020,000	1924-S	1,728,000
1924-P	11,811,000	1926-P	1,939,000	1927-P	848,000	1925-S	1,610,000
1925-P	10,198,000	1926-D	2,348,700	1934-P	954,057	1927-D	1,268,900
		1926-S	6,980,000	1934-D	1,569,500	1927-S	866,000
				1935-P	1,576,000	1928-P	360,649
				1935-S	1,964,000	1928-S	1,632,000
						1934-S	1,011,000

The next chart displays the Peace dollar series arranged in certified population order. There are two columns of data. The first column shows independent third-party graded PCGS and NGC MS-65 coins in population order as of this writing (reflecting condition rarity). The second column shows the series arranged in certified population order for all mint state grades as of this writing.

Peace Dollar Series: Certified Population

Certified MS-65 Only			**Certified All Mint State Grades**		
Rank	**Date**	**Population**	**Rank**	**Date**	**Population**
1.	1928-S	16	1.	1934-S	673
2.	1925-S	21	2.	1927-D	1,070
3.	1927-S	22	3.	1924-S	1,118
4.	1924-S	28	4.	1934-D	1,154
5.	1927-D	29	5.	1935-S	1,262
6.	1923-S	38	6.	1928-S	1,276
7.	1928-P	50	7.	1923-D	1,555
8.	1927-P	51	8.	1934-P	1,689
9.	1934-S	53	9.	1927-P	1,896
10.	1922-S	90	10.	1926-D	1,940
11.	1934-D	96	11.	1927-S	1,982
12.	1934-P	112	12.	1923-S	2,003
13.	1923-D	113	13.	1928-P	2,086
14.	1926-S	149	14.	1925-S	2,088
15.	1935-S	155	15.	1926-S	2,141
16.	1921-P	202	16.	1922-S	2,196
17.	1935-P	208	17.	1935-P	2,566
18.	1926-D	263	18.	1922-D	2,670
19.	1922-D	296	19.	1921-P	3,530
20.	1926-P	529	20.	1926-P	3,980
21.	1924-P	1,016	21.	1924-P	9,177
22.	1922-P	1,313	22.	1925-P	13,537
23.	1925-P	2,352	23.	1922-P	20,977
24.	1923-P	4,227	24.	1923-P	43,828

The quantity of Peace dollars, being produced after the days of the Pittman Act of 1918, have not been reduced by melting to the extent of the Morgan series. There were unknown numbers of Peace dollars melted during World War II, after the silver dollar rush of 1964, and again during the crazy days of 1979-80. These dollars were melted for bullion purposes and probably consisted of the more common dates and lower grades. That leaves a large portion of the original Peace dollar production in public hands today, consisting primarily of lower quality pieces. The James M. West Hoard (1957) contained over 271,000 dollars, mostly Peace type; unfortunately nobody has furnished an inventory.

The Peace dollar series consists of only 24 coins, but a quality collection is more difficult to obtain than is realized at first glance. A gem set of Peace dollars will take a number of years to put together. Collectors would do well to concentrate on the key dates first. The 1921-P, being a high relief issue, is of special interest and should be acquired early on. The quality strike of a gem specimen shows the Peace design as it was initially intended. The difficulty in finding quality pieces representing the 1934-S, 1925-S, 1927-S and 1928-S makes these dates a challenge. San Francisco was not noted for high quality Peace dollar strikes, 1922-28. The 1934-S, on the other hand, has presented a large number of quality coins in hoards discovered on the West coast as reported by Wayne Miller and others.

The semi-key dates are more difficult to find in gem condition than one would expect, given their production figures. The reason lies in the general low quality exhibited by the vast majority of the issues. Similar comments apply to the semi-common and common dates as well.

The legacy of the Peace dollar series has many perspectives. Readers viewing these early 20th century silver dollars and the events surrounding their existence, will find a wealth of information and enjoyment. The world of numismatics has been greatly enhanced and enriched by the presence and vitality of the Peace dollar series.

Appendix

Errors created during the minting process have always provided a special interest to numismatists. The following assortment of Peace dollar errors includes pieces from a special group put together by this author for informational and educational purposes.

Obverse

Reverse

1922 Peace dollar featuring rotated dies

Obverse

Reverse

1928 Peace dollar showing the results of a planchet flaw at nine o'clock

Obverse of 1922 Peace dollar showing lamination flaw from Miss Liberty's hairline through her ear and into her neck.

Obverse of 1922 Peace dollar showing a double clipped planchet, one at four o'clock and the other (less noticeable) at eleven o'clock.

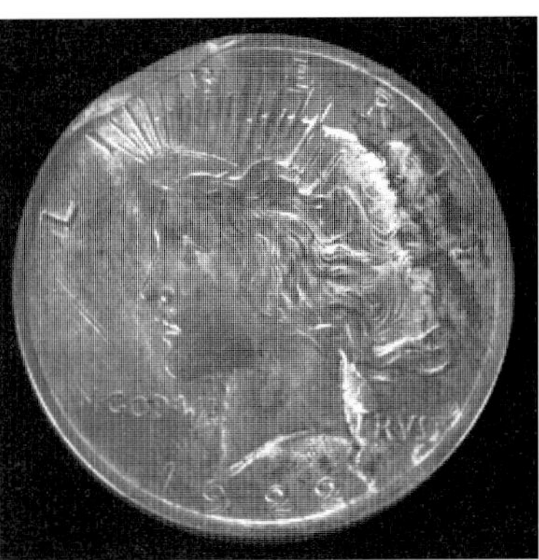

Obverse of 1922 Peace dollar showing a large curved clip at eleven o'clock.

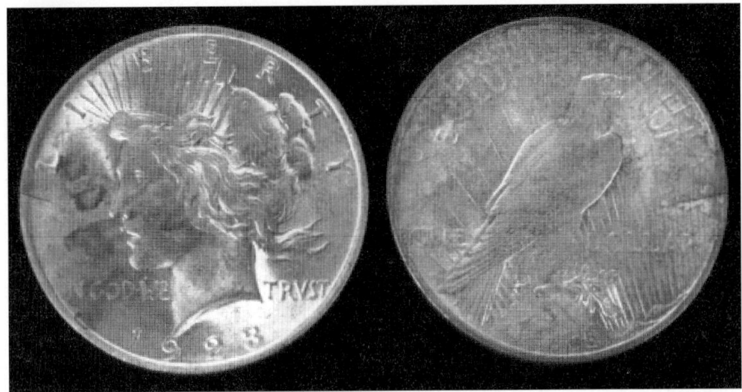

Obverse and Reverse of 1923 Peace dollar showing cracked planchet

Reverse of Peace dollar showing grease marks on die

Obverse of 1921 Peace dollar showing clipped planchet at nine o'clock

Obverse pair of 1922 Peace dollars showing clipped planchets (coin on left at eleven o'clock, coin on right at noon)

Perspective is interesting. A room full of people discussing Peace dollars may well bring up any or all of these points of view and agree or disagree on certain aspects of the subject. In fact, a room full of people will not contain two of them with identical viewpoints.

For an instant study in perspective, consider the following two photographs. They were both taken (by coincidence) at precisely the same moment as each picture recorded the flash of the other camera. This author was present and sitting at the table where the action occurred. It was sheer accident that the two pictures were discovered and matched. Wouldn't it be interesting to know what each person witnessing this action was thinking? It would also be enlightening to know what each of you "observers after the fact" have to say about these two unusual pictures. Here are the photographs courtesy of Mr. X and Mr. Y. (This perspective is similar to the examples of the "Bridge of San Luis Rey" and "Rashomon".)

Imagine 100 or even 1,000 photographs (flashes) at the same moment in time. It would be a kaleidoscope of perspectives. The man in the photo is Randy Crews of Tulsa, Oklahoma (his wife Vicki is sitting at the table).

Getting back to the subject of the Peace dollar, let's explore each of the above "perspectives." In reality, they are interwoven into the fabric of the Peace dollar story, and looking at only one aspect, or even one aspect at a time, will not do justice to the facts.

The Peace dollar series provides a wealth of interest and information for all numismatists. Their perspective may be one of history and the laws, design and creation of a coin, collecting of the series, or even mint errors. Regardless of the point of view, the rich heritage and story provided by the Peace dollar series will be told again and again to each numismatic generation.

Acknowledgements

Annual Report of the Director of the Mint, Fiscal year ended June 30, 1922, Office of the Director of the Mint, Government Printing Office, Washington, D.C.

Walter Breen's Complete Encyclopedia of U.S. and Colonial Coins, Walter H. Breen, Garden City: Doubleday, 1988

Coinage Laws of the United States 1792-1894, Foreword by David L. Ganz, Wolfeboro, New Hampshire: Bowers and Merena Galleries, Inc., 1991

A Comprehensive Catalogue and Encyclopedia of U.S. Morgan and Peace Dollars, Leroy Van Allen and A. George Mallis, NY: FCI/Arco, 1976

Wayne Miller, *The Morgan and Peace Dollar Textbook*, Metairie, Louisiana: Adam Smith Publishing Co., 1982

***

Anthony J. Swiatek, NLG

Anthony Swiatek is a recognized contemporary authority on silver and gold commemoratives. Swiatek is co-author of *The Encyclopedia of United States Silver and Gold Commemorative Coins 1892-1954,* which received the Numismatic Literary Guild's Book of the Year Award in 1981. He testified before the House Banking, Finance and Urban Affairs Subcommittee on Consumer Affairs and Coinage regarding U.S. commemorative coinage, and his opinions and work are cited in the new Library of Congress study "*Issuing Commemorative Coins; An Historical Overview*." He again testified before the same Subcommittee, to help support its Chairman, Frank Annunzio, in his quest to attain better Olympic Coinage designs for the collector and hobbyist.

Mr. Swiatek was invited by Donna Pope, Director of the Mint, to strike the fifth George Washington ceremonial commemorative half dollar, as well as the thirteenth striking of our Olympic commemorative dollar. He was also honored by being asked to strike other ceremonial issues including the 1986 Statue of Liberty five dollar gold proof, the 1 oz. 1986 American Eagle bullion specimen and the 1987 Constitution uncirculated dollar. He was later an invited guest at the White House presentation of Olympic coins to the Olympic Museum by President Reagan.

He is a Consultant to ANACS. He has written the ANA's Home Study Course dealing with Commemorative Coinage. He has lectured in many education forums at major coin shows and coin clubs throughout the United States. He conducts numismatic awareness classes, during the spring and fall semesters for the Continuing Education Programs in Manhasset, N.Y. This successful program's write-up has appeared on several occasions in the New York Times. He is also publisher of the popular Swiatek Numismatic Report (SNR), voted Best Numismatic Investment Newsletter of the Year 1983-84; 1984-85; and 1987-1988 (first place tie). He also received the N.L.G.'s literary awards for Best Magazine Article and Best Book on U.S. Coins, *The Walking Liberty Half Dollar*, in 1984.

He has written for *COINage* Magazine, *Coins* Magazine; Gary North's Investment Coin Review, The B.A.I.R., the Red Book, and contributed to the Official ANA Grading Standards for Coins, developing today's grading standards for the commemorative coinage of the United States of America, and is a contributor to Scott A. Travers's *The Coin Collectors Survival Manual*.

Mr. Swiatek received his Master's Degree from The City College of New York (CCNY). With many years of experience in numismatics, Swiatek, 46, is a life member (#1099) of the ANA, AINA, CSNA, FUN, GENA, GSNA, MSNA, and many other numismatic organizations.

He received the American Numismatic Association's Adult Advisor Award and was elected President of the Society for U.S. Commemorative Coins at the 1983 San Diego Convention for the years 1983-1985. He was elected Vice President for the 1985-1986 term and served as editor (1987-1988) of the Society's newsletter, the famous *Commemorative Trail*. He is a recipient of a 1990 ANA Medal of Merit and the Wayte and Olga Raymond Memorial Award for Distinguished Numismatic Achievement In The Field of United States Numismatics.

CHAPTER 68

The Peace Dollar Series

by Anthony J. Swiatek, NLG

Introduction

Aside from my well-known love for U.S. commemorative coinage, there exists additional U.S. Mint creations which occupy special places within my numismatic heart. A deep passion for the Saint-Gaudens and Coronet double eagle coinage has dwelled there, for as long as my interest in the commemorative series. It simply was a greater challenge to first explore the virgin territory of the latter. Thus, new and more meaningful undiscovered information could be shared with the entire numismatic world.

Within other locations are some of America's most beautiful coinage designs: The Indian Head 5-cent series, the seated Liberty and Barber coinage, the Walking Liberty half dollars, plus the Morgan and Peace dollars. At this time, I would like to submit my own personal analysis of the Peace dollar series.

A little more than 67 years ago, on May 9, 1921, Congress was presented with a joint resolution to authorize a coin to commemorate the end of World War I. The catalytic agent of responsibility, for the most part, was the American Numismatic Association. Fortunately, due to the provision of the Pittman Act of April 23, 1918, authorization took place without congressional action. Finally, in November 1921, nine artists were given just three weeks to present their drawings and four additional days to create models. (Let's ask Elizabeth Jones and John Mercanti if this sounds familiar.)

Anthony de Francisci, an Italian sculptor living in New York and pupil of James Earle Fraser, was chosen. His obverse is based on the model by Saint-Gaudens for the 1907 Indian Head $10 eagle. He deviated from the latter because he wanted to reflect the intellectual speed, vigor and vitality of America. Using his wife, Teresa Cafarelli de Francisci, as a model, the designer created an alert Liberty with windblown hair, hair bun, small eyes and parted lips. His reverse eagle, resting on a mountain oak, is based on the birds of Saint-Gaudens and Bela Lyon Pratt for the redesigned 1907 Indian Head eagle, 1908 Indian Head eagle and the 1908 Indian Head quarter eagle.

Originally the Peace dollar design was to be struck in high relief. The initial idea sounds wonderful for the current Mint-produced collector coinage. Unfortunately, great striking pressure was required to strike the coins. Die life was shortened and coin stacking posed a problem. Thus, less pressure was used, bringing an end to high point detail on the hair above Liberty's ear and the wing feathers of the eagle.

The following year, Chief Mint Engraver George T. Morgan had the relief lowered and fields flattened. Die life was increased to an average of 500,000 creations and the true beauty of the coin was sacrificed.

I believe the goal of many collectors and investors is to obtain a coin which will offer pride of ownership, as well as future growth potential. Needless to say, numismatic investigation into the area will be required. Readers will discover that most discussed dates will not be recommended in circulated grades, or in grades Mint State 60 through MS-63, due to poor strike or other numismatic negatives, haunting the latter's collection or investment potential.

It should also be understood that there is nothing wrong with purchasing or owning individual pieces or rolls of common-date Peace dollars grading from Good to MS-60+. Just know that they are available and will most likely offer only insignificant future price increases. However, should inflation make its presence felt, or you be fortunate to sell into a promotional upswing, money can be made. Nevertheless, should you, the collector or investor, like it or simply desire it, by all means buy it. This is what the joy of collecting is all about.

Date: 1921 **Mintage: 1,006,473**

Analysis:

The 1921 Peace dollar was the only one issued for circulation featuring the extremely high relief design. Luster can vary from an awful-looking grey to a brilliant frosty to an eye appealing satin to prooflike surfaces. Strike can range from weak to full. Weak or soft strikes will be the norm, and are not recommended for purchase, unless Liberty speaks to you. Strongly or well-struck specimens grading MS-64+ or low end MS-65 coins are almost always in demand. The fully struck specimen grading MS-65+ is a rare bird and extremely difficult to obtain. Highly recommended is the MS-64+ (low end MS-65) specimen, possessing full original luster, strong strike, a clean face on Liberty, a virtually clean eagle and no detracting field marks.

The issue is quite popular among collectors in grades AU-55, MS-60 and MS-63. However, abide by the aforementioned guidance. Matte Proof (eight pieces?) and Satin Finish Proof (three to five pieces?) specimens do exist for this date. I examined examples of both several years ago in New York City. The Matte Proof specimen sold for more than $100,000 in 1980. Beware of the Satin Finish Proof offering, even with attribution papers. A specimen recently graded by Anthony Swiatek's Grading Service Inc. was a rare prooflike business creation. The coin lacked the needed strike to achieve Proof status. However, I would purchase the Satin Finish Proof, which is rarer than the Matte Proof dollar, from a reputable dealership or auction house. At a New York auction in October 1987, a cleaned specimen brought $9,900. Why? There are vast amounts or future potential that exists for this super rarity, which may be considered rarer than the Proof 1895 Morgan dollar.

Date: 1922 **Mintage: 51,737,000**

Analysis:

Now we encounter George Morgan's die changes. The 1922 Peace dollar usually presents the beholder with good frosty luster and strike, but possesses many contact marks and surface marks. Lack of lower relief and light tan to dull white unremovable stains (caused by improper washing, then drying after the planchet's acid bath) make this issue too often — undesirable.

I highly recommend the elusive MS-65+ or high-end specimen for purchase, if funds allow. Yes, high end really means MS-66. The MS-65 prices as currently seen in the price guides reflect (in my opinion) the MS-64+ or low end MS-65 coin. Beware. Coins now graded MS-66 can be the MS-65 pieces of 1985-1986, when standards were quite strict. That's all right, since what was then sold as a strictly graded "MS-65" is a slab-graded MS-66. Grading of "Raw" coinage was very questionable. Problems arose when there were few coins to market as MS-65. Thus, we again experienced the lowering of standards to satisfy the nagging demand.

I have seen too many optimistically graded slabbed promotable coins which rise in value and fall flat on their faces. The buyer usually gets hurt, because the sellers know how much hype and air make up the inflated worth. Remember what happened with the 1881-S dollar and other promotable dates?

About Uncirculated-55 sliders abound for this date. Beware of those put together "original rolls" or so-called original rolls harboring such pieces. Pass on heavily marked coins contained in roll form. Purchase only if the price is very right. Pass on this promotable date in "so called MS-65," as well as other promotable dates to be mentioned, even if slabbed.

If you can't resist and are astute to the market happenings, purchase, but take an early exit. Knowledgeable buyers will be quite reluctant to secure at higher levels. Were it not for greed, one might believe they are living proof man can exist without brains. The trick is not to be greedy. Try to understand that this material must exist in quantity. Otherwise, it would not have been promoted. After all, no one can merchandise or sell a coin if few or none exist. Who do you deem will purchase this material which is scheduled to be pushed to highly inflated new levels? The promoter(s)? History just seems to repeat itself, doesn't it? Remember the 1881-S dollar, which rapidly dropped from $850+ to $140.

I would suggest acquisition of coins grading MS-60 through MS-63 only for the joy of collecting, which is what our hobby is all about. However, if the price is fair and the coins are properly graded, they are a pleasure to own and be a storehouse of value. Matte Proof (five?) and Satin finish Proof (five?) coins do exist.

Date: 1922-D **Mintage: 15,063,000**

Analysis:

Exceptionally eye appealing MS-64+ and better specimens accompanied by a strong strike are great additions to your collection with wonderful future potential. Sounds good. The problem is that the Denver Mint specimens are usually heavily contact marked. Luster for the most part is just acceptable to semi-prooflike. Due to excessive use of the dies, a rough surface can be revealed to the beholder, known as the orange peel effect.

Liberty's hair detail is struck rather well, but a distinctive weakness is encountered on the eagle's wing feathers. Unfortunately, the latter is characteristic throughout the series and keeps many specimens out of the higher grade (MS-64+ and MS-65+) categories. Die crack lovers will enjoy what they encounter on the obverse of this issue. Unless it appeals to you, pass this date by. MS-65+ specimen can bring high premiums. All is dependent on how much of a coin you are examining.

Beware of the AU-55 coins. Needless to say, should the desire to acquire from grades Good to MS-63+ be so intense for the joy of collecting, satisfy the need.

Date: 1922-S **Mintage: 17,475,000**

Analysis:

Horrid strikes plague the 1922-S issue. The motto is often difficult to read. Luster is for the birds. Surface marks are abundant. Low-end MS-65 (MS-64+ specimens) labeled or slabbed as MS-65 can be valued across the board.

Leave this date for the knowledgeable. The kind of silver disk desired by 99 44/100 percent of our earthly seekers, for the most part, resides in the collection of the deity. Legitimate MS-63+ rolls, put together from original bags, should be held by their owners. Definite MS-60 or MS-60+ roll offerings should be passed, unless desired for the joy of ownership. Hold if the item now resides in your collection.

Date: 1923 **Mintage: 30,800,000**

Analysis:

Strike and luster present the prospective buyer with few problems on the 1923 coin. Contact marks, abrasions and those degreasing solution stains (which cannot be removed by tarnish removing liquids) do create difficulties. MS-63+ through MS-64+ or low-end MS-65 specimens should not be difficult to locate. What might be thought of, or promoted as a good deal, would be a MS-63+ and MS-64+ (low-end MS-65) offerings. That means knowing how weak or how strong of a "64" or "65" you have.

Beware of those plentiful AU-55 coins. Do not refer to them as sliders because that would indicate a coin which has all the requirements of a MS-65 silver dollar, except for a trace of wear on its high points. The translates into the needed luster, strike and clean surfaces. Such is designated as AU-55. Pass on MS-60 and MS-63 low-end offerings, unless price is very right or you want to acquire it for the joy of collecting. Should you possess true MS-63+ rolls, hold; for the time may not be right to sell lesser grade material.

Date: 1923-D **Mintage: 6,811,000**

Analysis:

The plus side of the 1923-D coin is a good frosty luster and a strong strike barring the habitual weakness on the eagle wing feathers. The negative side is plagued by heavy contact marks, abrasions, and obverse die cracks. True MS-65+ specimens are very difficult to obtain. Apply the same price-grading logic here as presented for the 1922-S issue. Beware of those lightly circulated specimens which are plentiful. Pass this date. Hold, should you currently possess original rolls ranging from MS-60 to MS-63.

Date: 1923-S **Mintage: 19,020,000**

Analysis:

The 1923-S coin simply lacks charisma. Its characteristic makeup: Average luster, heavy surface abrasions, dreadful strike, especially on the reverse. MS-65 specimens are nearly impossible to locate. Pass on the About Uncirculated, MS-60 and MS-62+ offerings. Consider rejecting this date. Hold on to those original MS-60/63 rolls, until silver climbs drastically in value or some promoter offers you this date claiming that his coin, when purchased, will bring you luck and increase your chances of hitting the lottery.

Date: 1924 **Mintage: 11,811,000**

Analysis:

Specimens of the 1924 coin can be located in MS-64+ and better conditions. Luster can vary from the dull to a lovely white frosted surface. Strike can deviate from satisfactory to strong, on both sides of the coin. What we desire is a MS-64+ (Low-end MS-65) specimen or a MS-65+ specimen blessed with full original eye appealing luster, clean devices and a minimum of minute surface mars or contact marks (as only seen with the aid of low magnification). Deep cuts, scratches, gouges and detracting surface abrasions are not acceptable. No, I did not forget strike — it must be strong.

However, the MS-67+ asking price for this issue can be too high. Same for the MS-65+ specimen when it can be obtained. Pass on this date in all grades, unless the price is very right. Think about this. The 1924 issue is not close in rarity to the dates we have discussed, or not yet covered. But, if priced in the same range as the 1922-P or the 1923-P in a stable market, buy!

About Uncirculated coins are in abundance. I suggest passing on this date in higher grades, unless you are knowledgeable and the price is right. However, original BU rolls, grading MS-63+, should be held at this time. Reject anything lower, unless desired for the joy of collecting or the price on the properly graded coins resides between right and very right.

Date: 1924-S **Mintage: 1,728,000**

Analysis:

The 1924-S coins bear unattractive to just average luster, combined with heavily contact-marked surfaces and strike problems, especially on the reverse eagle, which make this coin a candidate for "not receiving the second look." Once in a blue moon, examples which can be labeled finer than the norm will make their appearance. Their asking price is usually too steep for a coin flaunting full luster, only a better than average obverse strike and fewer than the typical number of contact marks present on the masses.

A dangerous item, recommended only for those who are totally familiar with the series. True MS-64+ (low-end MS-65) coins are very difficult to locate. Mint State 65+ specimens are virtually impossible to obtain. I have seen slabbed specimens graded MS-64 which were worth low-end MS-64 (MS-63+) money. Beware of those abundant AU-55 specimens.

How do we grade and value — the key word — an amazing coin which is seldom encountered in such condition, but has a small dig or contact mark, say on the reverse eagle? Let us "assume" that a MS-64 and MS-65+ are within their given price guide values. If the coin was available or not that difficult to obtain (as seen or examined), it would be graded MS-64+. However, when it is so difficult to locate, as originally described, a higher price is not realistic. A high MS-65 value might also be viewed or looked upon as one with no real substance. This is because if one is even located, in a MS-64+ or low-end MS-65 grade, the knowledgeable might have to pay an extremely high premium. Why? It could be the finest piece encountered.

Should one hold or have the knowledge of where such a coin resides, be informed that ownership is something special. Place with a person trustworthy to market your coin or place the coin in a quality auction. Its true value will be attained. I have done the aforesaid for many clients and will be happy to do the same for you.

Date: 1925 **Mintage: 10,198,000**

Analysis:

The 1925 date is not that difficult to locate in MS-64+ and MS-65+ condition. Nevertheless, it does mean that they are easy to acquire, as the 1881-S Morgan dollar. It broadcasts a strong strike, lovely luster and surfaces with less than average contact marks. Should an amazing Peace dollar be desired, your wish will materialize. Just believe that current price levels offer no buys. A lower figure is desirable, since this Philadelphia creation is the easiest of the Peace dollars to attain in top condition. However, our current asking price might seem cheap by the year 2000.

The problem which always exists is that we are programmed by "long term" promoters, via their advertisements, newsletters and so on, about buying a coin that will be worth more in the years to come. It usually takes the **LONG TERM** for most of us to profit. After a market correction, we can expect these market makers to come right back and offer those items which caused great losses to others, to the new customers.

This popular date is a promotable date which will quickly rise in value when the market warms up. Recall what was mentioned about such material. If you own original MS-63+ rolls, hold. Lower grade roll specimens should be sold, but only if funds are needed. About Uncirculated 55 specimens exist in large numbers.

Date: 1925-S **Mintage: 1,610,000**

Analysis:

Luster on the 1925-S Peace dollar can range from average to full frosty. Most surfaces will exhibit a plethora of deep contact marks, plus surface mars. Characteristic strike must be labeled weak, usually caused by prolonged die usage. Full hairlines on Liberty and fully defined feathers on the reverse eagle, for all practical purposes, do not exist.

Due to the last-mentioned situation, specimens which reflect a better than characteristic flat strike, possess original frosty luster and the least possible amount of contact marks have been sold as MS-65 and MS-66 coins. Why? They are not abundant and are above the norm. Their true value must be determined only by the knowledgeable prospective buyer. Purchase the lower grades simply for the joy of collecting.

Date: 1926 **Mintage: 1,939,000**

Analysis:

Collectors hear the date 1926, recall its low mintage and tend to give it special significance in grades AU through MS-62. This is due to the more abundant and available common date 1922 through 1925 Philadelphia specimens making their presence known. Luster can vary from dull frosty to bright frosty. Strike will range from weak to strong with normal given the passing grade. Surface abrasions will deviate from excessive irritations to the very minimum, making the beholder smile.

Highly recommended are specimens grading MS-64+ and MS-65+. Price range depends on how much "coin" you are examining. It must flaunt full original frosty luster, strong strike for the issue and surfaces with a minimum of irritations. Clean devices and insignificant field abrasions are a must. The date is certainly available in AU, MS-60 and MS-62+ condition. Original MS-63+ rolls, depending upon their condition, are good to hold in your collection. Beware of the slider specimens offered at higher grades. Examine your high points for friction or loss of metal.

Date: 1926-D **Mintage: 2,348,700**

Analysis:

Luster will range from an appealing satiny to frosty on the 1926-D Peace dollar. Strike will be strong, thanks to the use of more striking pressure. It could be that someone at the Denver Mint cared and took pride in the finished product. Many Peace dollars flaunted all of, if not most of, the eagle's feather definition. Due to this extra pressure, you can observe some weakness of strike at the coin's 5 to 7 o'clock position in some specimens. Surface abrasions will range from minimum to heavy.

Highly recommended are specimens grading MS-64+ and MS-65+. Realize that the price range is dependent or contingent upon a coin's flash, eye appeal, color, toning or location of numismatic negatives. Add to the latter the possible lack of knowledge of the seller. These specimens possess excellent future potential (eight — ten years).

In this date, we possibly look at the easiest Denver creation to obtain in MS-65+ condition. It should be priced lower based on a rarity scale. Higher value is caused by availability and demand. Good roll to own in original MS-62+ or low-end MS-63 condition. Note: This item is **NOT COMMON** in AU condition.

Date: 1926-S **Mintage: 6,980,000**

Analysis:

Luster ranges from passable to very eye appealing frosty for this date. Strike is stronger than most San Francisco creations, especially on the eagle. However, it's those surface irritations which will appear in abundance. The coins which bear the minimum defects are difficult to cross paths with. Mint State 64 prices can reflect a MS-63+ or low-end coin.

Real MS-65+ pieces can be expensive depending on the offered specimen's praiseworthy qualities. Price must be based on eye appealing luster, strong strike for the date and those illusive surface characteristics (bearing clean devices and fields with a minimum of surface abrasion).

A coin can have just a bit too many irritations, but possess the required luster and strike. On the other hand, it may have amazing strike and surface, but display average or below average luster, or it may flaunt tempting surfaces and eye appealing luster, but may have a strike which is not strong enough. Thus, strike, luster and surface abrasions must be weighed to establish a price for the coin in question, no matter what its raw or slabbed grade reflects.

This issue is a good roll date to own in original MS-62+ and MS-63+ condition. If you possess original MS-60+ rolls, hold them.

Date: 1927 **Mintage: 848,000**

Analysis:

Contact marks and surface mars cast the mass of the 1927 issue into the MS-60+ and MS-63 low-end category. Frosty luster can be described as average to better than average. Strike can be labeled from average to well struck. Due to its low mintage, past collectors put this issue away, allowing us to take pleasure in today's offerings. It is highly recommended in MS-64+ condition, but only for the astute. Remember, that means low end MS-65.

We are wanting a specimen with full original, eye appealing luster, a very strong strike and a minimum of abrasions. Price determination must be based on "how much coin do you have" or the weighing of its total constituents. Review what was noted in the 1926-S analysis.

The 1927 is another common date in AU condition, and a good date to own in original MS-60+ condition by the single or roll.

Date: 1927-D **Mintage: 1,268,900**

Analysis:

Fate permitted most of the 1927-D issue to possess a good strike, frosty or satiny luster and surface mars that can be labeled as not excessive. Sounds great, doesn't it? Unfortunately, the latter existing negatives are deep and therefore, distracting to their beholders. Too many coins were not blessed, in this respect.

It is highly recommended in MS-64+ condition and MS-65+ condition, but only for the astute. This is due to the neophyte's difficulties in determining how much coin he has for the money. Naturally, if purchased from a dealer you know, you should be a future long-term winner.

It appears that most of this date was placed into circulation. It is a great roll date in strict AU-55 through MS-62+ condition. However, should your specimen or the offered coin possess no wear, but is a candidate for the "ugly duckling" award because of excessive cuts, hits and so on, its value will diminish.

Date: 1927-S **Mintage: 866,000**

Analysis:

The 1927-S issue is blessed with luster which varies from bright, to satiny, to semi-prooflike; accompanied by a minimum of surface mars. Unfortunately, when we examine the typical weak strike on the eagle's wing feathers, the smiling face turns into a frown. Price range for an MS-64+ specimen once more depends on "how much coin" is possessed. Remember, this grade means low-end MS-65. Your slab or "raw" card insert will indicate that a MS-65 card is enclosed. Just know the total makeup of your coin.

Apply same for a MS-64 coin. Coins can be labeled such because of eye appealing luster, a minimum of marks and so on. The strike can be somewhat better than normal. I personally would recommend this date only to the very knowledgeable.

It also appears that much of this issue was placed into circulation. Great roll date in strict AU-55 through MS-62+ condition.

Date: 1928 **Mintage: 360,649**

Analysis:

The 1928 Peace dollar is a very popular date possessing brilliant frosty luster, a minimum of surface irritants and a strike that ranges from acceptable to strong. However, the latter is not the norm. This lowest mintage Peace dollar is highly recommended in low-end MS-65 or MS-64+ condition.

The price spread can be based upon the total makeup or "how many positives does the coin possess?" In other words: How minimum are those surface abrasions? How strong is the strike? How flashy is the luster? Does appealing natural toning grace the issue? Don't expect Santa Claus to pay you a visit in the middle of July. Beware of flashy AU-58 slider coins sold as Brilliant Uncirculated MS-60 and higher. BU should not mean "been used." Recommend roll purchase in strict AU-55, MS-60+ and MS-62+ condition.

Guard against the following two possibilities:

Since the digit 3 is a closed looking 3, it can resemble the digit 8. I have seen collections over the years which housed a 1923 coin in the 1928 slot. Also I have encountered 1923 individual specimens in paper envelopes and flips marked 1928 BU, MS-63. Most owners were surprised about their misfortune.

The Mint mark at times is removed from the 1928-S issue, creating the rarer Philadelphia issue. Fortunately, the branch unit creation's rims will not be bold and the motto "IN GOD WE TRUST" will be weakly struck.

Date: 1928-S **Mintage: 1,632,000**

Analysis:

The 1928-S Peace dollar usually possesses good luster, but is virtually haunted by poor strike, abrasions and contact marks. Quality specimens must possess a strong strike, eye appealing luster and a minimum of abrasions. These grading low-end MS-65 or MS-64+ or MS-65+ are, needless to say, quite difficult to encounter along the path, as are so many dates within the series.

Please apply what was noted relating to prerequisites concerning make up and price for other issues. I suggest passing on this date in the higher grades. However, nothing is wrong in possessing MS-60+ through low-end MS-63 original dollar rolls.

Date: 1934 **Mintage: 954,057**

Analysis:

Luster, strike and abrasion present the 1934 issue with its problems. So what else is new? I have encountered a number of offerings possessing a strong strike, combined with clean surfaces. However, they were not flashy enough, lacking the needed full original Mint luster.

We have here an issue that I find difficult to recommend. It can be ticklish to grade, causing the potential buyer much difficulty.

For whatever reason, collectors seem to believe that the coin is rare and a good investment in MS-60 condition. Actually, there exists an ample supply of AU-55 coinage. Mint State 60 coinage is not the greatest item to retain and should be sold during the next silver dollar boom. Hold at present. I wouldn't mind owning MS-62+ or MS-63+ original rolls. I believe this is the best place to be with this date, unless your collection houses a legitimate high grade specimen.

Date: 1934-D **Mintage: 1,569,500**

Analysis:

The last of the Denver Mint's business strike production is the 1934-D. It's blessed with a strong strike and eye appealing frosty luster. It is hurt by the presence of deep and distracting contact marks. Thus much of this date resides in the MS-60 through 63 state. I recommend this issue in grades MS-63+, MS-64 and MS-65+. Nothing is wrong in owning original rolls grading strict MS-63. Individual coins may also be held with a bid reflecting a constant value. Good future long range potential resides in this issue.

Date: 1934-S **Mintage: 1,011,000**

Analysis:

The 1934-S, an extremely popular date, blessed with a strong strike and eye appealing frosty luster. Thanks to angelic protection, a large number of coins display a minimum of surface mars. I like the coin in circulated grades of EF-45 and AU-55. Pass on pieces that display heavy contact marks, cuts, dings or which have been whizzed, polished or treated in some fashion. Excellent long-term potential (eight to ten years) in MS-60+, MS-63+, MS-64+ and MS-65+ condition.

Date: 1935 **Mintage: 1,576,000**

Analysis:

The strike on the 1935 Peace dollar can vary from good to well struck. Luster will range from blah to beautiful, frosty bright. Surface mars will run from light to excessive. Highly recommended are specimens grading MS-64+ and MS-65. Please review what we have discussed in the analysis of other dates (1924-S, 1926-S, 1927-S and so on), concerning grade and price determination. This issue is quite available in AU-55 condition. The MS-62+ or low-end MS-63 and MS-63+ or low-end MS-64 original or put together rolls, will possess excellent future investment potential.

Date: 1935-S **Mintage: 1,964,000**

Analysis:

The chances of locating the 1935-S issue in MS-64+ and better condition will be greater than all of the aforementioned dates. Luster, strike and abrasion problems do not haunt this date to the degree it does the others. Collector, investor and promoter desirability are created. However, that's not to say pieces won't be seen weakly struck or void of numismatic negatives. By the way, a reverse variety was created for some of this issue. A fourth ray was added below the reverse word ONE, as well as a seventh ray below the eagle's tail. Is it rare? Should you run out and buy it? Not really. It is equal in rarity with the original design.

Recommended purchase is in MS-64+ condition. Remember, we are speaking of a low-end MS-65 specimen. It might be slabbed as MS-65 because standards for a number of pieces encountered were lowered. A coin can be slabbed or raw and be listed as MS-64 or MS-65. But is it a low-end or a high-end specimen? In my opinion, the MS-64 coin is not the exceptional coin. It's a flashy low end or middle-of-the-road coin. In other words, how much "64" do you have?

The price tag reflects the strict MS-65 coin of post-January 1985 grading standards and the dollar amount needed to acquire such a lovely piece. At that time, a MS-66 coin or better for the most part became the new MS-65 coin. That "old 65" was not an MS-64 or MS-64+ coin. An MS-65+ coin is an MS-66 specimen. An honestly graded, fairly priced specimen should reflect how much "65+" is possessed.

Although easier to acquire than almost every other date in top condition, there are not enough high-grade MS-65+ 1935-S specimens to meet the demand. Also, recall most of the other Peace dollar dates are extremely rare in MS-65+ condition. Some might not even exist. The exception being the 1925 Philadelphia creation. Remind yourself that it is the coin that counts. We are looking for a clean face on Liberty and a virtually mark-free eagle. Those primary focal areas are so important. It's critical for my purchase and other dealer purchases. It should be the same for you.

BU vs. AU (Brilliant Uncirculated vs. About Uncirculated)

Also beware of those AU-55 or lightly circulated specimens. If the coin has MS-65 qualities, but possesses definite slight wear on the high points, grade it AU-58 or super slider. These coins can bring MS-63 money, depending on the date. Look for wear on the cheek and hair in the area which covers Liberty's ear, as well as the eagle's feathers on the right wing and left leg. Full mint luster in these areas is a must. However, don't confuse the common weak strike (caused by insufficient striking pressure or improper die spacing) in the aforesaid areas with wear. These areas can be covered with frost but will exhibit that difference in metal texture that we call wear, which it will have a dull grayish-white appearance.

What about strike?

Strike will vary from weak to strong, to full. Weak or soft strikes and average strikes for their respective issues are the norm. When we speak of a strong strike, we refer to strong definition on Liberty's hair with slight weakness present only on the highest strands. The reverse should display a bold outline combined with discernible wing feather definition. If two pieces were identical twins, their worth would be the same. If one flaunted stronger feather detail, this coin would attain a greater value. However, those leg feathers can display weakness and be labeled strong.

Full strike means that all details must be bold with no weakness seen on Liberty's hair strands. On the reverse, the eagle must be boldly struck and all of his wing feathers strongly defined. Some weakness on his legs can be acceptable. Needless to say, fully struck pieces are rare birds. Obtaining a common date, fully struck specimen grading MS-60 or MS-63 is great for the joy of collecting. Collectors will usually pay more for it. More emphasis and worth was placed on strike in 1979 and early 1980. Today, the strike can be labeled strong. Still, if other requirements are not present, sorry, Charlie. Nonetheless, if the date is seldom seen, much more may be paid for the coin. All is dependent upon the buyer and seller.

What about grading?

Here is a creation which was accepted as MS-65 or even MS-65+ earlier than January, 1985, before standards become so strict and were unofficially changed by market makers. Such a coin must possess original full luster, strong strike and a minimum of abrasions.

Minimum translates into no deep scratches, cuts, nicks, reed marks, contact marks or large surface abrasions or mars on the primary focal areas. That's Liberty's face, neck and fields (in front of her face and below her head), as well as the eagle's body, his neck and neighboring fields. Her face can show a very minor hit or abrasion, but must possess the overall clean look. Same for the eagle, two reed marks on the cheek might be a bit too deep, thus the MS-64+ changes to an MS-64 low end coin.

A slabbed coin or "raw" coin's insert might indicate and MS-64 grade, but is it high or low end? The low-end MS-64 creation can have a lovely eye appeal and rather clean surfaces. However, it may possess a strict defect which leaves more to be desired on one or both sides of the coin. It can also display a hit or deep cut which is simply too distracting on Liberty's face or on the reverse eagle. It can have an amazing obverse, but its reverse will reveal just too many abrasions on the eagle and so on. Thus, these coins are better than average, but may lack what it takes to attain the higher grade and/or price.

Here, we do not have a case of strict grading on my part. Other dealers grade the same way when buying coins or when they must spend big dollars. My grading is derived from years of experience and market realities.

When grading standards were unofficially changed just before January 1985, market makers were suddenly grading or calling previously graded MS-66 and MS-67 coinage gem MS-65 or MS-65. Thus, much could be rejected when offered. Coins which previously graded MS-65 and MS-65+ were now called MS-64. Many of these were to be purchased at lower levels. How much pressure existed to fill orders? What percentage of these were later offered at MS-65 gem prices? You tell me. These are the coins which can drive coin prices downward upon entering a bear market.

Hot market action was then reflected in the price guide MS-65 columns because no influential MS-66 and MS-67 columns existed. The columns could be created after overgraded MS-65 specimens were pushed to their overpriced limits. Prices could be drastically lowered, and coins then bought back, as MS-65. Within the last few years, look at what happened to the 1881-S dollar, the MS-64 Saint-Gaudens double eagle, and the MS-65 Saint-Gaudens double eagle. Prices moved substantially lower.

Requirements for an MS-65+

Mint State 65+ means high-end MS-65 or MS-66. Such a coin should possess the following: full original eye appealing luster, strong strike, a few barely noticeable abrasions or marks in critical areas, which are seen only with the aid of a magnifying glass. I did say barely! The obverse portrait should possess a clean face. More grading weight and value is given to the obverse. In other words, it would be better to have the minute mark on the reverse eagle than on Miss Liberty's face.

Requirements for MS-67 are full, original, eye appealing luster; full strike; and virtually flawless surfaces with minuscule contact marks, which are only seen with the aid of a magnifying glass. Any Peace dollar which resides in this category must be considered rare. Its acquisition will require many dollars. However, in the future, it may be considered a bargain. This holds true for all the recommended issues. In fact, the next time we encounter a bull market, most of the given values will be left in the dust.

Please don't use a magnifying power higher than 3X or 4X on an MS-67 coin. When observing people using 16X, or 10X or 8X, I wonder if they are giving Liberty a retinal exam or attempting to locate fleas on the reverse eagle. Such high power distorts surface negatives. Use lower power first. Then, use higher power to examine the high points for wear. Thus, you will arrive at a much better evaluation.

Summary

The primary objective of this encyclopedic analysis is to help enlighten the reader about the "numismatic facts of life," relating to one of my numismatic loves, the Peace dollar series. I hope you enjoyed consuming its contents as much as I had writing this opus for the Comprehensive U.S. Silver Dollar Encyclopedia.

Senior Editor's Note:

Mr. Swiatek's original article was published as a three-part series in the March 8, 1989, March 15, 1989 and March 29, 1989 issues of Coin World. Anthony Swiatek has updated this material and prices to reflect the market conditions and knowledge as of this writing. We gratefully acknowledge permission from Coin World to "reprint" this article as updated.

***

CHAPTER 69

The Lafayette Silver Dollar

by John W. Highfill, NLG

Lafayette Commemorative (1900)
(Coin courtesy of Harford Coins)
(Photo provided by Krause Publications)

The History

One of the areas often neglected when writing or studying in the field of numismatics is the history behind the coin. In this case, I am referring to the life of the man who is commemorated by the coin — Marquis de Lafayette. We all know of course that George Washington, our first president, and Lafayette are both featured on the obverse of the Lafayette dollar. Most of us know something about Washington, but few know much about Lafayette. Therefore, I am presenting a career in capsule form for your enlightenment.

Marie-Joseph-Paul-Yves-Roch-Gilbert du Motier, marquis de Lafayette, was born on September 6, 1757 to a noble family in what is now Chavaniac-Lafayette in France. He received his education at the College Louis-le-Grand in Paris and then joined the French army. He served from 1771 to 1776 and rose to the rank of captain. The American Revolution won his heart and he traveled to America to offer his services. In 1777, the young Congress commissioned Lafayette as a major general in the Continental army. He soon developed a close relationship with General George Washington and was assigned to his staff. During the Battle of the Brandywine, Lafayette was wounded. He recovered and was given the title of division commander.

Soon thereafter, France and America entered into an agreement and alliance against the powerful British. This action officially brought France into the war. Lafayette returned to France for a short time in early 1779 and gathered military aid for the Americans. In April 1780, he came to America again and fought in Virginia. This offensive eventually led to his trapping Lord Charles Cornwallis at Yorktown and to the British surrender, October 19, 1781.

Back in France, Lafayette was a liberal leader in the French Revolution and became a member of the National Assembly. He participated in French politics and military efforts, but became disenchanted with the regime of Napoleon Bonaparte. This caused Lafayette to reduce his involvement with French affairs until the fall of Bonaparte. Beginning in 1815, he once again served in the forefront of French politics. He made a triumphant visit to the United States in 1824-25. He died in Paris on May 20, 1834 after a distinguished career.

The Background

Looking forward from the late 1890s, the coming 1900 Paris Exposition was to be a monumental event to say the least. It was to be properly celebrated by all of France, and the United States wished to be a part of the formal presentations. The United States offerings were to consist of an equestrian statue prepared by Paul Wayland Bartlett and a commemorative silver dollar prepared by the United States Mint.

This coin was not only being created as a part of the U.S. government's presence in the 1900 Paris Exposition, but also in commemoration of the 1899 centennial of George Washington's death. The other reason for its existence was to help finance Bartlett's statue.

Lafayette Monument Committee first requested 100,000 half dollars, to be sold at a premium. This would result in profits that would be used to finance the cost of the monument. But this proposal was later changed by the committee which then supported a silver dollar commemorative souvenir.

March 3, 1899 was the important day for U.S. silver commemorative coinage enthusiasts. This was the official Congressional "authorization" day for the Lafayette dollar, a project which Charles Barber took upon himself to deliver. By early April, he had prepared the preliminary design of the coin. There was considerable interaction with the Lafayette Memorial Commission, and especially with Robert J. Thompson, secretary. These discussions revolved around the design and size of the proposed commemorative piece.

There were sketches prepared which featured the dual heads of Washington and Lafayette, a prayer presentation for the reverse as well as a single figure (or equestrian) reverse. Charles Barber copied Peter L. Krider's 1881 Yorktown medal conjoined heads design for the obverse, and used an early sketch of Bartlett's equestrian statue for the equestrian reverse. The design decision was actually made by Mint Director George Roberts, without the Commission's initial consent. This decision became a matter of public knowledge through a premature announcement made in the April 1899 issue of the *American Journal of Numismatics*.

The issue involving the size of the coin was resolved without much difficulty. Mr. Thompson initially favored a "medallic" size somewhat larger than the existing silver dollar. Charles Barber won the decision using the coin's legal tender status and the requirement for a single strike to produce the coin. Additionally, the "two heads" design for the obverse necessarily demanded a higher relief that would suffer under an increase in size without multiple strikes from the dies.

The youth of America also played a part by contributing towards the Lafayette monument. During 1899 there was a national campaign under which school children contributed their pennies to help meet the United States pledge of $50,000. Their efforts were honored in an unusual manner by an inscription on the reverse of the Lafayette dollar, "ERECTED BY THE YOUTH OF THE UNITED STATES IN HONOR OF GEN. LAFAYETTE." The monument was officially unveiled in Paris and presented to France on July 4, 1900.

The Coin

The Lafayette dollar was the first United States coin to present the portrait of an American President. For anyone who has ever been associated with presentations, the term "upstaging" never had a more applicable meaning. The obverse was shared with Lafayette with their heads presented "cheek to cheek," but the dollar's namesake got full billing on the reverse.

Obverse

Reverse

1900 Lafayette Dollar

Charles E. Barber utilized two sources for the head of Washington. One was the familiar Jean Antoine Houdon bust of Washington, and the other was the "Washington before Boston" medal by Du Vivier. Although their relationship and joint role in the Revolutionary War occurred when Lafayette was young, the sculpted design used for Lafayette on the commemorative piece were taken from a later time. The Lafayette likeness was fashioned from the 1824 "Defender of American and French Liberty" medal by F. Augustin Caunois, and the Centennial of Yorktown medal by Peter L. Krider.

Lafayette's equestrian pose on the monument, as designed on the coin's reverse, presents him in parade surrounded by the honorary words, "ERECTED BY THE YOUTH OF THE UNITED STATES IN HONOR OF GEN. LAFAYETTE," with "PARIS 1900" at the bottom. Unfortunately, the design of the coin was completed and engraved before the monument was completed. As a result, the actual statue differs from Charles Barber's version, specifically in the sword held aloft and the horse's tail shorter and bound up. The coin copies a plaster model exhibited at the Louvre.

The Distribution

George Washington died on December 14, 1799. Honoring that date, the Philadelphia mint struck 50,000 coins (plus an additional 26 for assay purposes). Because the coins were struck in 1899, the date 1900 could not be officially expressed as the year of mintage (which would have violated the Mint Act of 1873). Instead, 1900 was considered the year of the Paris Exposition and of the monument. The Mint Act of 1873 required that all United States coinage display the year of mintage as the date. Therefore, the Lafayette dollar was not in complete compliance with the law.

On December 14, 1899 (the centennial day of Washington's death), at 11:15 AM, Miss Gleary started up the old Merrick press (the same one the Philadelphia Mint had used at expositions). At 80 coins per minute = 4,800 per hour, the 50,000 coins (plus 26 for assay) took somewhat over 10 hours, including interruptions to change dies. At least four obverses and five reverses were used in six combinations.

There was an offer of $5,000 made for the first coin off the press. But President McKinley had already promised the first piece to be taken in an elaborate presentation case by Mr. Thompson as Special Commissioner of the United States to the President of the French Republic, Mr. Thompson presented the coin to President Loubet of France on February 22, 1900.

To officially establish the procedure for subscription, the Lafayette Memorial Commission prepared the following letter to be sent to potential subscribers of this commemorative silver dollar.

OFFICE OF THE LAFAYETTE MEMORIAL COMMISSION

CHICAGO, December 8, 1899.

TO THE PUBLIC:

Within the next few days there will be struck at the United States Mint in Philadelphia the most unique and significant coin issued in modern times. It is the Lafayette Dollar authorized by Congress in aid of the Lafayette Monument.

This coin, which is a legal tender dollar, bears upon its face in bas-relief a double medallion of the heads of Washington and Lafayette and upon its reverse a miniature reproduction of the equestrian statue of Lafayette used for the Monument. The inscription on the dollar explains its purpose (struck in commemoration of Monument erected by school youth of United States to General Lafayette, Paris, France, 1900).

The Lafayette Dollar thus serves not only to aid the Memorial work but forms a new and beautiful tie between the two great republics of Europe and America, and therefore the coin must be regarded as an international emblem. It constitutes a most desirable souvenir and memento of the Children's Monument to the "Knight of Liberty," the Universal Exposition of 1900 at Paris, and the opening of the twentieth century. The limited number issued will make these coins extremely rare and in very great demand.

The first coin to be struck of the 50,000 will be presented to the President of the French Republic.

Popular subscriptions for these coins will now be entered, and honored in the order received. The price fixed on them by the Commission is two dollars. All orders for coins must be accompanied by payment in full and be in the hands of the Commissions on or before December 20, 1899, on which date the popular subscription closes. Drafts, currency or Money Orders will be accepted in payment. Drafts and Money Orders must be made payable to Edwin A. Potter, Treasurer of the Commission.

The Commission reserves the right to limit the number of coins (above fifty) allotted to each subscriber. ORDERS FOR ONE COIN SHOULD BE COMBINED AND SENT IN ONE SUBSCRIPTION, ENABLING THE COMMISSION TO DELIVER TO ONE ADDRESS. IF POSSIBLE, SEND THROUGH LOCAL BANK OR EXPRESS OFFICE.

Inquiries and subscriptions for coins to be addressed to Robert J. Thompson, Secretary, in care of American Trust & Savings Bank, Chicago.

THE LAFAYETTE MEMORIAL COMMISSION.

WM. R. DAY
WM. B. ALLISON
EDWARD EVERETT HALE
W. T. HARRIS

ARCHBISHOP IRELAND
JOHN W. MACKAY
MELVILLE E. STONE
CHAS. A. COLLIER

ROBERT J. THOMPSON
ALEX. H. REVELL
EDWIN A. POTTER
CHAS. G. DAWES
FERDINAND W. PECK

In fact, the Commission actually offered the coins to the public at a price of two dollars each for a number of months beginning in December 1899. The coins were distributed by the American Trust and Savings Bank of Chicago. A relative small number were sold to coin collectors, and after the Exposition closed its doors, the bank held large quantities unsold.

Over the years, about 36,000 were distributed with the remaining 14,000 remaining in the vaults of the Treasury. In 1945 Aubrey Bebee of Omaha, Nebraska, believing that the remaining Lafayette dollars were being hoarded by the government, tried to buy the lot, but was informed that they had been previously melted.

Therefore, the surviving count is limited to a maximum of 36,026 pieces. As it turns out, most of the known Lafayette dollars are found in circulated condition (Fine to AU). Mint state examples are few and far between with gem specimens (with no evidence of cleaning) are very scarce. "Sliders" are abundant and must be avoided by those desiring true mint state examples. There have been counterfeits identified (including prooflikes) which makes authentication of gem specimens a wise choice. Anthony Swiatek has reported one authentic brilliant proof Lafayette dollar.

Several die varieties have been discovered throughout the years. Research by George H. Clapp (then Alcoa president) and Howland Wood (the counterfeit expert) presented the following four die varieties from three obverse and four reverse dies. A fifth combination was reported by Anthony Swiatek. Frank Duvall described the sixth.

Obverse 1. The AT in STATES high; point of Lafayette's bust above top of L; small point on bust of Washington. With Reverses A, B, and C.

Obverse 2. The A in STATES high; final A of AMERICA double punched at left foot. With Reverse C.

Obverse 3. The final S in STATES low, AT repunched; both F's defective; AMERICA poorly spaced, RI close; pellet between OF A is closer to A than to F; point of Lafayette's bust is beyond right top of L. With Reverse D.

Obverse 4. CA spaced far apart. E of STATES and first E of LAFAYETTE repunched. ATE successively lower, L of LAFEYETTE high. With Reverse E.

Reverse A. Branch with 14 long leaves and long stem; point of lowest leaf above 1 in 1900; B below Y in BY. With Obverse 1.

Reverse B. Branch with 14 shorter leaves and short stem; point of lowest leaf over space between 1 9. Later, cracked through legend. With Obverse 1.

Reverse C. Branch with 14 medium leaves and short stem bent down; point of lowest leaf above center of 9. With Obverse 2.

Reverse D. Branch with 15 thin leaves and short stem, bent up;point of lowest leaf above center of 9. With Obverse 3.

Reverse E. Branch with 13 thin leaves; lowest leaf point to left of 1 in date; first 0 in 1900 low; H in THE high (both times); A in STATES high. With Obverse 4.

The following combinations are known to exist:

From Clapp and Wood:

1. Obv. 1, rev. A. Scarce
2. Obv. 1, rev. B. Not as scarce as the others. Copied by counterfeiters.
3. Obv. 2, rev. C. Rare
4. Obv. 3, rev. D. Very rare

From Swiatek:

5. Obv. 1, rev. C. Very rare

From Duvall:

6. Obv. 4, rev. E. Very rare

The typical mint state specimen is often poorly struck, with a dull luster and heavy bag marks. The government issued holders (cardboard) did not promote good preservation, and many pieces were cleaned over the years.

The obverse areas showing early wear are George Washington's cheekbone and Lafayette's lower curls on the obverse. The reverse targets include the boot, thigh, rear leg and blinder. The strike in many cases is weak in these areas. Beware of "full boot" phobia defining the full boot as a separation of the top of Lafayette's boot and leg. Some coins have even been altered in order to present a false full boot.

There have been 814 Lafayette mint state examples certified by PCGS as of this writing, with 61 specimens grading MS-65 and higher. NGC reports 355 certified mint state examples with 39 grading MS-65 and above. As it turns out, the 1900 Lafayette dollar is one of the rarest commemorative coins in gem MS-65 condition. Most mint state Lafayette dollars will grade only MS-60 due to the factors mentioned above. Sliders and AUs are plentiful.

When purchasing an MS-65 or better specimen, pay particular attention to the coin's luster. If the piece is toned, the toning should be natural. The cheeks of Washington and Lafayette should be free of slide marks and abrasion. Finally, the piece should be well struck and be relatively free of bag marks.

Collectors of silver dollars need one of these coins to complete their sets. So do collectors of U.S. commemoratives. The Lafayette dollar is a great acquisition and recommended in all BU grades. Good luck in your search for the gem Lafayette dollar!

Obverse

Reverse

Special Two Troy Ounce .999 Fine
Silver Commemorative Reproduction

the COIN DEALER newsletter

Our 29th year...

Single copy price $3.50 Vol. XXIX No. 33 August 16, 1991 *. . . a Friday morning report on the Coin Market*

100 YEARS, 100,000 MEMORIES
100,000+ = ONE LAFAYETTE

The Market in Depth

Well, it took 100 years to arrive, but it's finally here - the *100th Anniversary* of the **American Numismatic Association.** The major dealers from across the country are in Chicago this week, hoping that business will steadily increase through the final weekend. Even with the many celebratory events planned, dealers and collectors are making time for some 'good old' coin trading.

The celebration started off with a real "bang" with the pre-convention 'piggy-back' auction of the **Larry Shepherd Collection of U.S. Commemorative Coinage**. Only someone who has devoted countless hours to assembling a world class collection could understand the mixed emotions of seeing it auctioned, but Shepherd expressed himself as extremely pleased with the results. Prices were very strong, and the 150 + floor bidders simply stole the battle from the book. The 144-piece set yielded more than **$850,000**, but, according to Shepherd, perhaps most pleasing was the knowledge that most of the coins were being sold to collectors who were working on their own great collections. The strength of the action was sometimes formidable. The Isabella, in MS68, opened at $22,500 before being hammered at **$63,250**. The Lafayette in MS67 opened at $37,500 before soaring to **$115,500!** The Antietam in MS68, which just may have been Shepherd's favorite coin, realized $14,850.

Despite the relative quiet in the recent market, the strong showing of the Shepherd coins is helping create an upbeat mood for the ANA. Initial Convention reports are in line with recent predictions: Trading is somewhat active, although not a barn-burner; prices are somewhat sporadic; there are some discounted bargains available from 'hungry' sellers. Dealers are interested in viewing the abundant high-quality coins available and negotiating before making any decisions; the strength of the negotiations seems to be largely determined by the "look" of the coin, its rarity, and the strength of the Want List [the certainty of the customer]. Dealers who arrived well-armed with Want Lists may have the time of their lives, and a few are quietly buying material for their own accounts, especially when available at a discount. Demand seems especially strong for high-quality circulated specimens, as collectors are taking advantage of depressed prices to pick up splendid coins whose only drawback is some evidence of honest circulation. It just may be that the tone of this anniversary celebration, the whole idea of *remembering* when the coin "business" involved dealers inspecting and haggling, may remind them how their livelihood prospered.

This Week's Market

CENTS THRU HALVES: Weeks with major conventions are normally very slow on the teletype systems, especially so in the BU roll market. This week is following that pattern as trading is quite slow. However, there are a few dealers willing to pay current Bids for specific items in limited quantities.

DOLLARS: Although common (MS63, 64 & 65) Dollars remain mostly steady in today's market, it appears that some of the 'not so common' Dollars are inching their way up slightly. If these can hold firm, it could be a stage which precedes advances for other issues. While this sounds good for the market, it is not without some despair. Several minus signs still cover the MS65 column.

PROOF SETS AND MINT SETS: Most Proof and Mint Sets are stable at today's levels; many issues are on want lists at current Bids. There are even a few plus signs in the Mint Set chart.

COMMEMORATIVES: The number of Bid changes in the Commem chart is commensurate with the last several weeks. A few plus signs and a few minuses keep this series moving, although, most of the activity is still to the downside.

TYPE: Type coins should be one of the most active areas at the ANA this week in Chicago. The Type charts are spotted with changes, about evenly divided between increases and decreases. Many dealers have recently reported that they have active want lists for properly graded Type coins.

GOLD: Mint State U.S. Gold continues to trade in a positive vein. Bids may not be moving up much, but they are active at somewhat higher levels. We have even noticed a few transactions which have taken place at about 20% over current bids for single items on want lists. These are usually less-frequently traded issues.

EAGLES: American Proof Gold Eagles are trading at: 1986 1oz-$371.50/$380, 1987 1oz-$373/$383, 1/2oz-$184/$200, 1988 1oz-$380/$440, 1/2oz-$185/$205, 1989 1oz-$395/$455, 1/2oz-$190/$235, 1990 1oz-$510/$565, 1/2oz-$325/$375. Proof Silver Eagles are trading at: 1986-$15.25/$16.50, 1987-$14.50/$15.75, 1988-$77/$85, 1989-$14.50/$15.75, 1990-$23.50/$27. BU 1986 Silver Eagles wholesale at $11.75/$12.50.

Coin Dealer Newsletter Certified Coin Market Indicator™

SERVICE	LOW	HIGH	AVERAGE
PCGS	93.36%	104.75%	100.26%
NGC	87.73%	107.58%	98.73%
ANACS	68.75%	91.14%	83.10%
NCI	13.90%	83.27%	42.21%

BULLION, FOREIGN GOLD, & PLATINUM COINS

SILVER BULLION PRICES Silver bullion items based on spot price of $3.95 per oz.

FOREIGN GOLD

U.S. GOLD (Prices are for the most common date of each type.)

August 16, 1991 CDN
(Courtesy of Coin Dealer Newsletter)

Acknowledgements:

I wish to thank the following persons for contributions that have made this chapter possible:

Walter H. Breen
George H. Clapp
Tom Culhane
Anthony Swiatek
Howland Wood
Frank Duvall

Appendix

The Lafayette Dollar Varieties

by Frank DuVall

Frank DuVall is a renown collector and has written many numismatic editorials for CDN, Coin World, Numismatist, NSDR Journal, Commemorative Trial and many others

Many references have documented the varieties of the Lafayette dollar with descriptive methods of attributing the different varieties. Indeed there are a number of differences between the varieties, but only a few of these are needed to determine diagnostically which variety is being examined. The photographs accompanying this article provide a ready reference for the simplified narrative which follows:

To attribute the obverses quickly use these diagnostic characteristics:

1. Note if the second "S" in the word STATES is doubled — if so, this "Obverse 2."
2. Note if the dot between the words OF and AMERICA is close to the letter "A" (rather than being centered)—if so, this is "Obverse 3."
3. Note if the letter "C" in the word America is recut at the top (in the "C")—if so, this is "Obverse 4."
4. If none of these characteristics (1-3 above) are observed, then this is "Obverse 1."

The reverse attribution is slightly more complicated, but diagnostic tools exist as follows:

1. Starting from the right end of the limb below the statue base, move left along the stem to the first leaf below the stem.
   Note the position of the tip of this first lower leaf relative to the date 1900. If the tip of the first lower leaf is above the 1 of 1900, then this is a "Reverse A."
2. If the tip of the first lower leaf is above the space between the 1 and the 9 of 1900, then this is "Reverse B."
3. If the tip of the first lower leaf is above the 9 of 1900, the leaves should be counted. If there are 14 leaves, then this is "Reverse C."
4. If the tip of the first lower leaf is above the 9 of 1900 and there are 15 leaves, then this is "Reverse D."
5. If the tip of the first lower leaf is above the space to the left of the 1 of 1900, then this is "Reverse E."

Observed marriages of the obverses and reverses are as follows: 1-A, 1-B, 2-C, 3-D, 4-E.

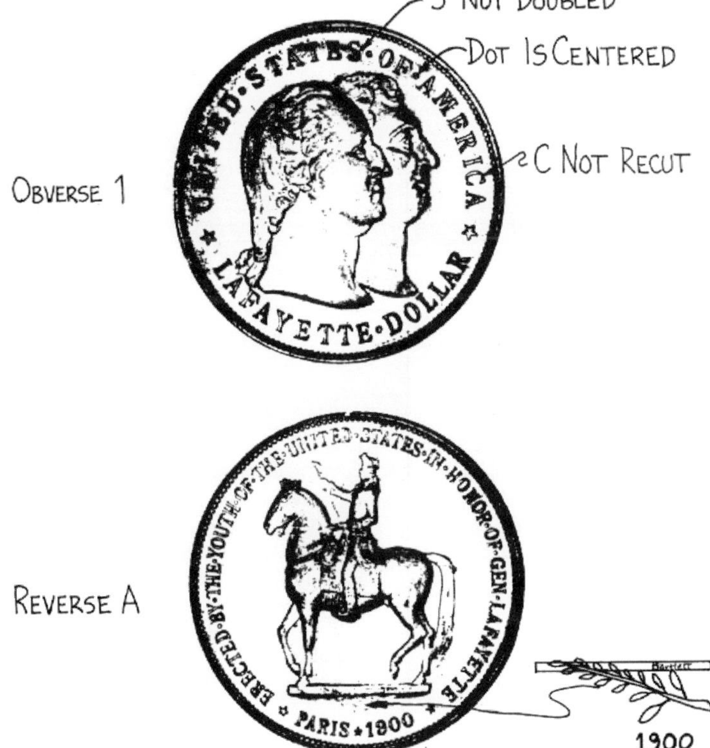

Lafayette Dollar 1-A
(Courtesy of Frank DuVall, Huntsville, Alabama)

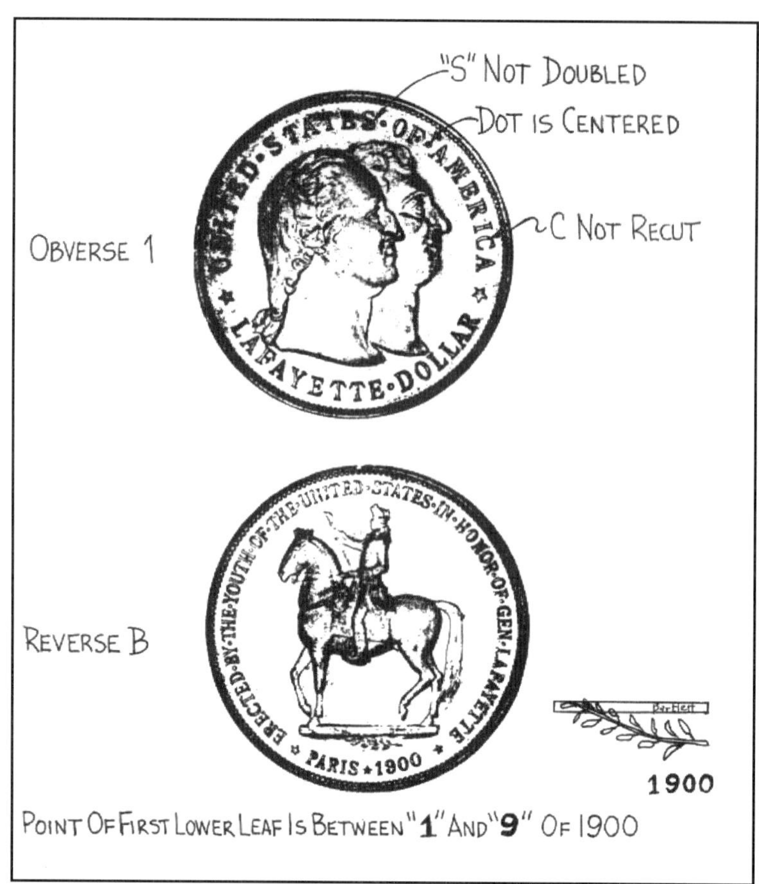

Lafayette Dollar 1-B
(Courtesy of Frank DuVall, Huntsville, Alabama)

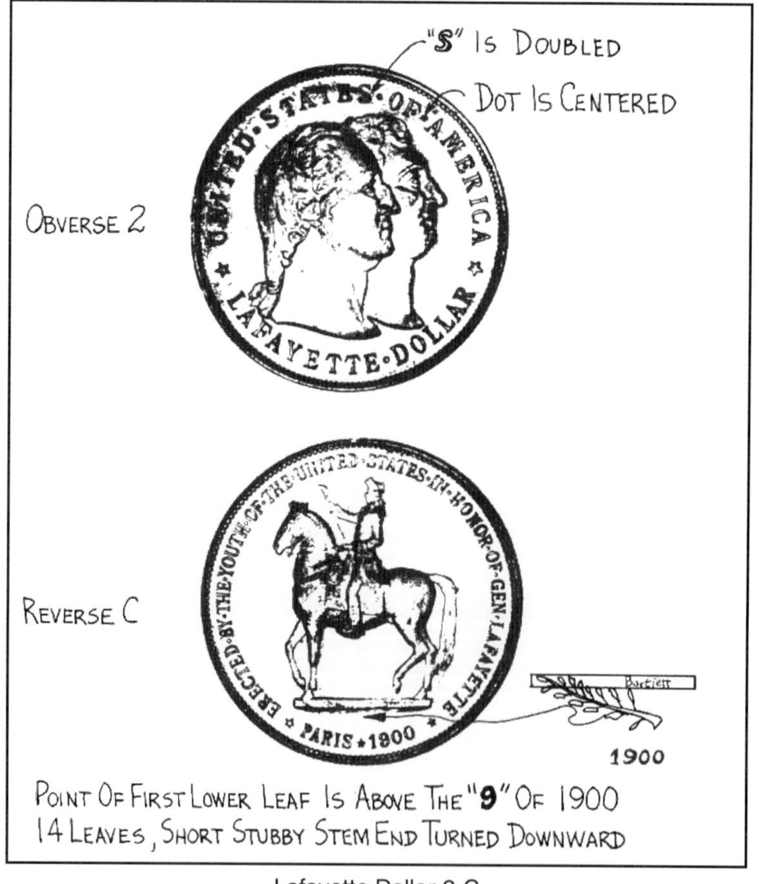

Lafayette Dollar 2-C
(Courtesy of Frank DuVall, Huntsville, Alabama)

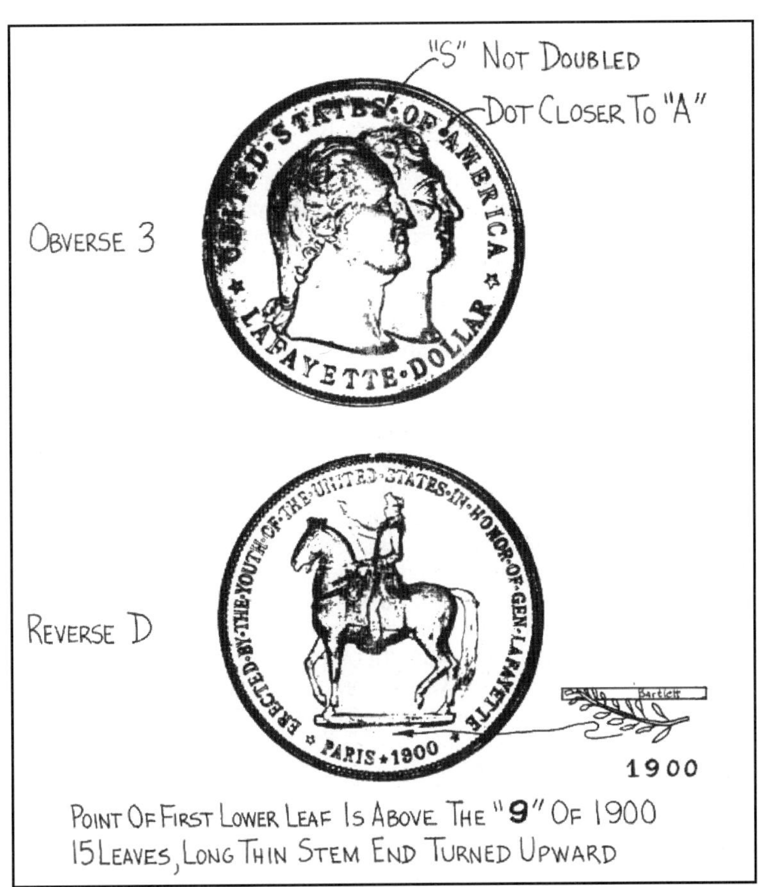

Lafayette Dollar 3-D
(Courtesy of Frank DuVall, Huntsville, Alabama)

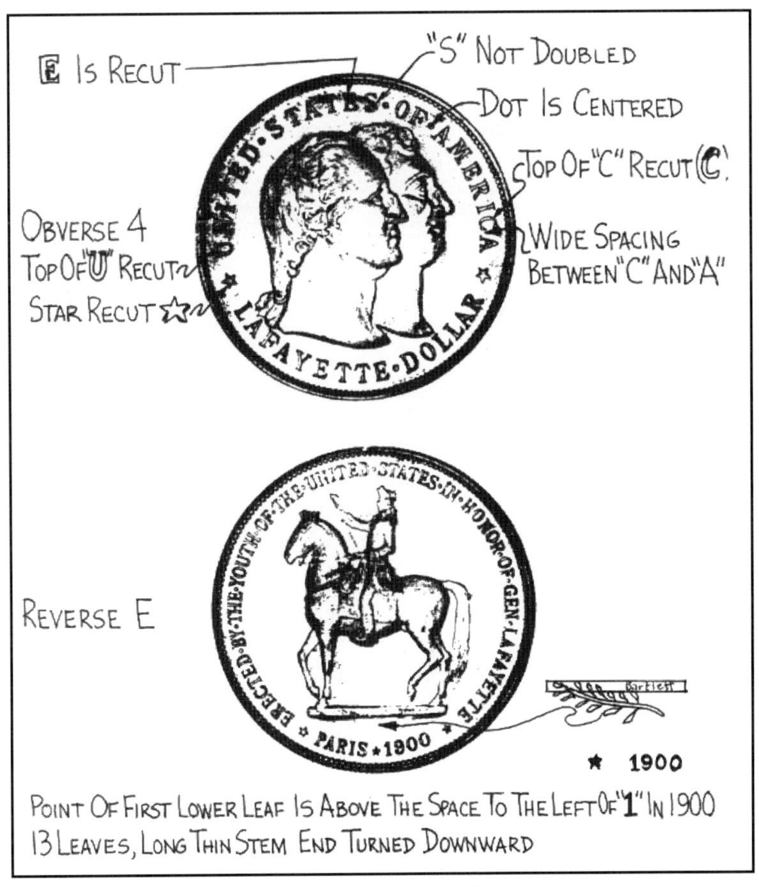

Lafayette Dollar 4-E
(Courtesy of Frank DuVall, Huntsville, Alabama)

I read with great interest — and great appreciation — the excellent article "The Lafayette Dollar" by Tom Culhane, R-1103, NJ in the Fall '88 issue of TCT. Tom is to be congratulated on such a marvelous find, and for his historical research, and for sharing the good news with society members. I own a somewhat proof-like Lafayette Dollar and look forward to the time that I might view the coin that Tom writes about. It is finds such as Tom's that add immense pleasure to Commemorative coin collecting.

For some time, I have speculated on the events that actually took place during the Lafayette Dollar striking on December 14, 1899. To set the stage for what follows, reference is made to the following excerpts from Tom Culhane's article:

The Chicago Record of June 20, 1899 reported the following: "Engravers will soon commence the preparation of ** a ** die for the Lafayette souvenir coin..." and "As soon as it is known that they have given it, the engravers at the mint will undertake the preparation of ** a ** die and have it ready within 2 months. The coins can then be struck in a day..." and "The 100th anniversary of the death of Washington, Friday, December 14, 1899 was chosen as the appropriate date to strike the 50,000 Lafayette Dollars and the first was struck at exactly 11:15 AM..." and "The coin press was an old one in the mint..." and "The press, turning out 80 coins a minute completed the entire issue on Friday....." and finally "Anthony Swiatek, who was not entirely convinced that it is the number two coin did verify that the die combination is correct so that is could possibly be the second piece. If it had been one of the other die combinations, right away the story would not hold up." End of quotes.

The fact that the newspaper accounts consider only ** one ** die and ** one ** press is somewhat incompatible with the fact that at least 3 obverse dies and 4 reverse dies were used. [By way of digression, and to explain why 50,000 coins were struck and only 36,026 are noted in the literature, we have the interesting story that 14 bags (14,000 coins) of unsold Lafayette Dollars were discovered at the mint in 1945. Before a "Purchase-type" telegram from Aubrey Beebe could trickle down channels at the mint, the 14,000 coins were melted. What is so exciting about the "melt" is speculation of how many of each variety were actually melted, and — could there have been other die varieties, none of which survived?].

Several questions now arise: "Why was not a master die - hub - die process used?" and "Why were so many dies hand cut?". Since all the coins were to be struck in one day, did mint officials want to be certain that enough dies would be on hand in case early dies would break? If only one press was to be used and could only produce 80 coins per minute, it is mathematically sound to assume that the 50,000 coins would take over 10 hours (at 4800 per hour), assuming there were no problems. Since the first coin was not struck until 11:15 AM, this means that the single press striking would ensue to at least 9:15 PM. It is not too logical to me that mint officials would wish to gamble on achieving a perfect schedule (much less working into the night on a single issue).

My speculation (and it is only speculation) has been that several dies were cut in anticipation that several presses would be used in parallel to insure that all of the coins could be struck in a single day. The fact that I have not seen any "broken die" coins (they could have been destroyed) could support the parallel striking theory. Further, since only 50,000 coins were to be struck, it appears logical that only one, or two, and certainly not more than three dies would have been adequate for a sequential (broken die) striking.

One could further speculate about whether the "ceremonial" coins were struck during the public ceremony, and others were struck in another area either simultaneously or later. This, too, could have a bearing on which of the die combinations were "right" for the Tom Culhane coin to be the second coin struck. As it stands, the benefit of the doubt leans in Tom Culhane's favor.

In summary, despite the newspaper accounts, there is enough evidence to speculate that the mint may have operated differently from the news articles. Hopefully, new evidence will appear to clarify the questions raised above.

This is another quest!

***

CHAPTER 70

The Eisenhower Dollar and the Coinage Act of 1965

by John W. Highfill, NLG

Eisenhower, Apollo II (1971 — 1978)
(Courtesy of Krause Publications)

Dwight David Eisenhower! How that name inspired men to serve and to achieve. And the United States citizens were destined to commemorate him in coinage very soon after his life had ended.

He was born on October 14, 1890, to a poor Mennonite family in Denison, Texas, moved to Abilene with his family, and graduated from high school in 1910. He was brought up with a strong sense of self-reliance and was taught to pay for everything in cash, owing nothing to any man. The beginnings of his outstanding leadership abilities were cultivated at the United States Military Academy at West Point, where he played football and graduated in 1915.

After his graduation, the eager Eisenhower was assigned to the 19th U.S. Infantry at Fort Sam Houston, Texas. It was there that he met and married Mamie Geneva Doud in 1916. They had two sons. Dwight David was a victim of scarlet fever while yet an infant. John Sheldon Doud was born in 1922 and enjoyed a successful military career.

Eisenhower was promoted to Captain while stationed at the Tank Training Center at Camp Colt. He did not see overseas duty at any time during World War I, but was awarded the Distinguished Service Medal for his capabilities. Between World Wars I and II, Eisenhower attended the Army General School at Leavenworth, Kansas, and graduated at the top of his class. Next, he attended the War College located in Washington, D.C., and mastered the strategies employed during World War I.

General Douglas McArthur received "Ike" as an aide in 1932 and joined him in the Philippines in 1934. Eisenhower assisted in the development of the Philippine Army and rose to the rank of Lieutenant Colonel.

As a Colonel, Eisenhower was assigned to the 15th Infantry and was soon designated Chief of Staff of the Third Army. He earned the rank of Brigadier General through his excellent record with the Third Army.

World War II began and Eisenhower found himself in the War Plans Division of the U.S. Army. In 1942, he commanded the Allied Landing Forces in North Africa and ended the war in this area within six months. This victory earned him the rank of General. Further victories during the invasion of Sicily caused President Roosevelt to appoint him the Supreme Commander of all Allied Forces. As Commander, General Eisenhower organized and led the successful invasion at Normandy, France, remembered by all as D-Day. This eventually led to the surrender of the Germans at Rheims, France, on May 8, 1945.

Eisenhower was pressured by President Truman to run for the presidency, but instead chose to become President of Columbia University in 1948. Nevertheless, both political parties pursued "Ike", and the Republicans elected him president of the United States in 1952 and again in 1956. His ability to achieve results in the political arena was well known, and he used all of his skill to lead this country into a great expansionary era. After a long and successful career, he died on March 28, 1969, in Washington, D.C.

Background

In order to better understand the politics surrounding the decision to commemorate General Eisenhower on a clad metal dollar denominated coin (with silver issues made especially for collector interests), the situation surrounding and leading to the Coinage Act of 1965 should be reviewed.

Public Law 88 - 36 of 1963

This was in essence a repeal of the Silver Purchase Act of 1934 and later legislation regarding silver and authorized the issuance of #1 and #2 Federal Reserve Notes to eliminate the requirement of Silver as a backing of those denominations. Therefore silver dollars were not needed to back the silver certificates, since silver bullion could be used for that purpose. With the new law the Federal Reserve Notes became the new currency and the silver certificates went out of circulation in the late 1960's as they were redeemed for silver dollars, silver bullion and silver granules. Public law 88-36, June 4, 1963 states: "Silver Certificates shall be exchangeable on demand at the Treasury of the United States for silver dollars or, at the option of the Secretary of the Treasury, at such places as he may designate, for silver bullion at a monetary value to the face amount of the certificates."

Remember the great silver dollar rush of the early 1960s? During the period beginning in 1958 and ending in 1964, the United States government distributed 217,013,000 silver dollars from its tremendous hoard. Public purchases of silver dollars from government holdings increased dramatically in early 1964 with the rising price of silver, forcing the U.S. Treasury to close the silver dollar window on March 26, 1964.

The developing situation involving the rising price of silver during the early 1960s led to a government sponsored study by the U.S. Treasury's Office of Financial Analysis with cooperation from the Bureau of the Mint, Office of Domestic Gold and Silver Operations, the Treasurer's Office, and the Office of the General Counsel.

Portions of the final conclusions are reprinted from the *Digest of the Treasury Staff Study of Silver and Coinage*, U.S. Government Printing Office, Washington, D.C.

Digest of the Treasury Staff Study of Silver and Coinage

I. Summary of Conclusions and Recommendations

1. The fundamental finding of this study is that the world and the U.S. silver supply and production situation and outlook do not warrant continuation of the large-scale use of silver in the U.S. coinage.

2. Cupronickel is the best permanent material for a new subsidiary coinage, ignoring the vending machine problem. However, cupronickel coins would require "factory" adjustment of the coin rejectors in some 6 million coin-operated vending machines, entailing significant costs and public inconvenience.

3. Since extensive experiments confirm that cupronickel clad on a copper core operates successfully in unaltered vending machine rejectors, preferable options are available. Cupronickel-clad coins can be used during a transition period, or permanently. An overriding requirement with cupronickel-clad coins is the production feasibility of the strip and the assurance of an adequate supply for processing in the Mint.

6. Subsidiary silver coinage of reduced content, such as silver-copper alloys clad on a low-content silver-copper core, suffers both from difficult transitional problems and incomplete assurance that the subsidiary coinage would not be imperiled again within a fairly short period of time, due to the shortage of silver. If any silver is to be retained in the subsidiary coinage system, it should be limited to a clad silver 50-cent piece of 400 fineness. There is no suggestion that the silver content of the silver dollar be changed.

7. During the installation of any new coinage system, it will be obligatory to hold the market price of silver at its current level of $1.29+ in order to protect the existing coinage. Since this will remove the incentive to melt the existing coinage, controls over melting would probably not serve any useful purpose. Effective controls on the hoarding of coin appear impractical. Controls on the export of coin may serve a useful purpose during the transition period. There is something to be said for having standby authority to invoke controls. A prompt transition to base alloy coinage would make the actual use of controls unnecessary.

8. New coins should be placed in circulation through normal channels. Every effort should be made as soon as possible to prepare for extremely high rates of production of the new coins.

II. Criteria by Which a New Coinage Can Be Judged

Summary of Criteria

The criteria are listed in the order in which they are discussed rather than in descending importance. However, it is felt that *the single most essential objective must be the facilitation of the orderly flow of financial and commercial transactions*.

A new coinage should meet the following principal criteria:

1. No interruption of essential medium of exchange function.
2. Promise of requiring minimum changes for a long period of time.
3. Assured access to raw materials.
4. Public acceptability in terms of-
   a. Need for the charge
   b. Technical characteristics of the coins
   c. Degree of inconvenience the new coinage imposes.
   d. Absence of extreme hardship to any group or region.
5. Minting characteristics and coinage costs:
   a. Assurance of high levels of production.
   b. Minimization of dollar cost.
   c. Minimization of any adverse impact upon balance of payments and international financial position.
6. Compatibility with present coinage:
   a. Probable need for side-by-side circulation.
   b. Vending machines usage

III. Silver Market Trends

The discussion of silver market trends is divided into two parts. First, the dimensions of the growing imbalance in world silver markets are established and the implications for Treasury policy are discussed briefly. Second, the extent to which production and consumption of silver would adjust to higher prices is examined in order to reach a preliminary judgement as to the feasibility of reduced content silver coinage. [*To avoid misunderstanding, it should be stressed that while this preliminary examination of silver markets does not definitely rule out the possibility of a low-content silver coinage system, that possibility is ruled out by a later examination (Section V) of the specific difficulties of achieving a safe transition*.]

1. Recent years have seen the development of an enormous gap between Free World production and consumption of silver. The overall deficit, inclusive of coinage demands, was 200 million ounces in 1963 and almost 340 million ounces in 1964. Even if all coinage demands, United States and foreign, are subtracted, a deficit remains.

2. U.S. Treasury stocks of silver declined to 1,218 million ounces by the end of 1964 and may be down to 1,000 million ounces or less by mid-1965. Legislative action by 1965 on a new coinage system is essential while Treasury stocks of silver are still large.

3. On the basis of past experience, higher silver prices and increases in base-metal production promise to increase world silver production. The independent influence of higher silver prices cannot be estimated with any precision, but there is no reason to doubt that substantially higher prices would lead to some expansion in silver output. However, the current production deficit is so large that it cannot be closed from the production side.

4. During the last 15 years, most of the growth in the industrial consumption of silver has occurred in foreign countries; U.S. consumption has grown more slowly. There were some signs that the recent increases in silver prices had checked the overall growth in world industrial use of silver, but only temporarily, and in 1964 there was a sharp advance in silver consumption, here and abroad.

5. A simple extension of the postwar trend of silver prices suggests that $2 an ounce might easily be reached by 1980 or 1985. Analysis of supply-and-demand factors does not yield any precise estimate of the level that silver prices might reach in a free market. The analysis does suggest that there is a very appreciable risk that the price could reach $2 and ounce then, or even much sooner. Battelle's detailed quantitative projections of the rate of exhaustion of Treasury stocks lead to an even more pessimistic appraisal since with coinage of 50 percent silver content they can foresee the complete exhaustion of Treasury silver as early as 1969.

6. In view of these considerations, it does not appear that reduction of silver content to 800, 700, or 600 fineness would constitute a long run (20 to 25 year) solution to the coinage problem. On the basis of longrun supply-and-demand factors, *there is an unmistakable risk that a rising market price of silver would soon imperil coinage of 500 fineness. That risk would be overwhelming even for lower silver contents if future U.S. coinage demand could not be met exclusively from Treasury silver holdings. . . .*

. . . V. Problems With a Changeover to Reduced Content Silver Coinage

The present section examines the feasibility of achieving a successful transition to a new coinage system using low-content silver alloys. An appendix considers the possibility of a silver 50 cent piece of 400 fineness. Major conclusions can be summarized as follows:

1. The transition to silver coinage of reduced content would be an extremely risky undertaking, and Treasury silver stocks would probably be depleted within a relatively short period of time. If there is a partial and limited exception to this overall conclusion, it arises with 400 fineness where a high proportion of the existing coinage is recovered at a rapid rate.

2. Even there the risks would have to be judged intolerably great unless there were clear evidence, at the time a decision was reached, that the coin shortage had ended and subsidiary coinage was temporarily redundant. (This is clearly not the case at the present time.) No one could be sure in any case that the price of silver would not be driven again to the melting point of subsidiary coinage; this might not occur within the immediate future. *In general, analysis of the special problem of the transition to reduced content silver coinage suggests that attention can appropriately be concentrated from this point in the study upon the base alloy alternatives*.

VI. The Relative Merits of the Base Metal Alloys

This section first considers the respective merits of the four remaining alloys: cupronickel, nickel silver, 95 percent nickel (Inco coin), and cupronickel clad on a copper core. The nature of the production effort required for a smooth transition is described and the possible use of controls is examined, and largely rejected. Major conclusions are summarized below.

1. Assuming that vending machine rejectors were to be modified, the choice of permanent coinage material lies primarily between cupronickel and nickel silver. The difference between these homogeneous alloys is not great, although in most respects cupronickel is slightly superior. The preference would be for cupronickel subsidiary coinage with the present 5-cent piece unchanged.

2. The cupronickel (or nickel silver) clad on a copper core has the great advantage of avoiding the need for modification of vending machines. The Inco coin does not work acceptably, and, even if it did, it would be superior to the clads only on the basis of appearance. The clad coin is to be preferred since it would lead logically and easily to a permanent coinage of cupronickel, or nickel silver, or, as seems equally desirable, could be retained as the permanent coinage material.

3. Full replacement of the existing subsidiary coinage with straight cupronickel could be achieved in less than 3 years with existing and planned Mint capacity, even more rapidly if capacity were expanded further. The Mint is conducting an exhaustive investigation of the supply situation in the case of cupronickel clad on copper.

4. Standby authority to impose controls on the melting and export of coin might be a useful backstop. A prompt transition to base alloy coinage would make the use of controls unnecessary.

This study served as background information in support of the submittal of the proposed Coinage Act of 1965, presented at the following hearings. 1) Hearing before the Committee on Banking and Currency House of Representatives, Eighty-Ninth Congress, First Session on H.R. 8746, a bill to provide for the coinage of the United States, June 4, 7, and 8, 1965; 2) Hearing before the Committee on Banking and Currency United States Senate, Eighty-Ninth Congress, First Session on S.2080, A bill to provide for the coinage of the United States, June 9, 1965.

Turning our attention to the Senate, Mr. A. Willis Robertson, Virginia (for himself and Mr. Wallace F. Bennett, Utah) introduced the following bill (S.2080) on June 3, 1965, during the 89th Congress, 1st Session, which was read twice and referred to the committee on Banking and Currency.

The Senate Committee on Banking and Currency was chaired by A. Willis Robertson of Virginia. The members of the committee consisted of many familiar names as you can see from the following roster.

John Sparkman, Alabama
Paul H. Douglas, Illinois
William Proxmire, Wisconsin
Harrison A. Williams, Jr., New Jersey
Edmund S. Muskie, Maine
Edward V. Long, Missouri
Maurine B. Neuberger, Oregon
Thomas J. McIntyre, New Hampshire
Walter F. Mondale, Minnesota
Wallace F. Bennett, Utah
John G. Tower, Texas
Strom Thurmond, South Carolina
Bourke B. Hickenlooper, Iowa

Matthew Hale, Chief of Staff
Woodlief Thomas, Chief Economist
John R. Evans, Minority Clerk

President Lyndon B. Johnson
Henry H. Fowler, Secretary of the Treasury
Eva Adams, Director of the Mint

The Committee on Banking and Currency met in Washington, D.C. on Wednesday, June 9, 1965, to discuss the proposed Coinage Act of 1965. Excerpts from the proposed bill are presented here for your review.

A Bill
To provide for the coinage of the United States

Be it enacted by the Senate and House of Representatives of the United States of America in Congress assembled, That this Act may be cited as "The Coinage Act of 1965."

Title I

Section 1. (a) The Secretary of the Treasury is authorized to cause to be minted and issued the following coins:

(1) A half dollar or fifty-cent piece which shall be composed of an alloy of eight hundred parts of silver and two hundred parts of copper per each one thousand parts by weight clad on a core of a silver-copper alloy of such fineness that the composition of each coin shall be four hundred parts of silver and six hundred parts of copper out of each one thousand parts by weight.

(2) A quarter dollar or twenty-five-cent piece and a dime or ten-cent piece each of which shall be composed of an alloy of 75 per centum of copper and 25 per centum of nickel clad on a core of pure copper.

(b) The cladding alloy used for the outside layers of such coins shall comprise not less than 30 per centum of the weight of each coin. Such coins shall be of the same diameter, respectively, as the coins of the United States of corresponding denominations current at the time of the enactment of this Act.

(c) The weight of the half dollar provided for herein shall be eleven and fifty one-hundredths grams, of the quarter dollar five and sixty-seven one-hundredths grams, and of the dime two and two hundred and sixty-eight one-thousandths grams.

SEC. 2. Subject to the requirements of section 1, the methods of manufacture of the coins therein provided, the wastage allowances, and the allowable deviations in the metallic percentages and weights, shall be as determined by the Secretary of the Treasury. Such coins shall be subject to the laws pertaining to the designs and inscriptions on coins of the United States. . . .

SEC. 3. All coins minted pursuant to the provisions of this Act shall be legal tender for all debts, public and private, public charges, taxes, duties, and dues.

SEC. 4. Nothing herein contained shall be deemed to prohibit the continued minting of coins of the United States authorized by law at the time of enactment of this Act.

SEC. 5. Whenever in the judgment of the Secretary of the Treasury such action is necessary to protect the coinage of the United States, he is authorized under such rules and regulations as he may prescribe to prohibit the exportation, melting or treating of coins of the United States.

SEC. 6. The Secretary of the Treasury is authorized to sell on such terms and conditions as he may deem appropriate, at not less than the monetary value thereof, any silver of the United States in excess of that required to be held as reserves against silver certificates.

SEC. 7. The Secretary of the Treasury is authorized and directed to purchase at the price of $1.25 per fine troy ounce silver mined after the date of enactment of this Act from natural deposits in the United States or any place subject to the jurisdiction thereof and tendered to a United States mint or assay office within one year after the month in which the ore from which it is derived was mined. The bullion fund provided by section 3526 of the Revised Statutes, as amended (31 U.S.C. 335), may be used for such purchases. . . .

. . . SEC. 10. The first sentence of section 3558 of the Revised Statutes, as amended (31 U.S.C. 283), is amended to read as follows: "The business of the United States assay office in San Francisco shall be in all respects similar to that of the assay office of New York except that until such time as the Secretary of the Treasury determines that the mints of the United States are adequate for the production of ample supplies of coins, its facilities may be used for the production of any coins of the United States authorized by law." . . .

. . . SEC. 14. Section 485 of the Act of June 25, 1948 (18 U.S.C. 485), is amended by striking out "the gold or silver coins" and inserting in lieu thereof "gold, silver, silver-clad, or cupronickel-clad coins".

SEC. 15. The Secretary of the Treasury is authorized to issue such regulations as he may deem necessary to carry out the provisions of this Act.

SEC . 16. Whoever knowingly violates any of the provisions of section 5 hereof or of any order, rule, regulation, or license issued pursuant thereto shall, upon conviction, be fined not more than $10,000 or imprisoned not more than five years, or both. In addition, there shall be forfeited to the United States any coins exported, melted, or treated in violation of this Act or any order, rule, regulation, or license issued hereunder, or any metal resulting from such melting or treating of coins. Such coins or metal may be seized and condemned by like proceedings as those provided by law for the forfeiture, seizure, or condemnation of property imported into the United States contrary to law. . . .

The following excerpts are reprinted from the June 1965 "Message From the President of the United States Relative to Silver Coinage" to the Congress of the United States.

From the early days of our independence the United States has used a system of coinage fully equal in quantity and quality to all the tasks imposed upon it by the Nation's commerce.

We are today using one of the few existing silver coinages in the world. Our coins, in fact, are little changed from those first established by the Mint Act of 1792. For 173 years, we have maintained a system of abundant coins that with the exception of pennies and nickels is nearly pure silver.

The long tradition of our silver coinage is one of the many marks of the extraordinary stability of our political and economic system.

Continuity, however, is not the only characteristic of a great nation's coinage. *We should not hesitate to change our coinage to meet new and growing needs. I am, therefore, proposing certain changes in our coinage system — changes dictated by need — which will help Americans to carry out their daily transactions in the most efficient way possible.*

There has been for some years a worldwide shortage of silver. The United States is not exempt from that shortage — and we will not be exempt as it worsens. Silver is becoming too scarce for continued large-scale use in coins. . . .

. . . We expect to use more than 300 million troy ounces — over 10,000 tons — of silver for our coinage this year. That is far more than total new production of silver expected in the entire free world this year. Although we have a large stock of silver on hand we cannot continue indefinitely to make coins of a high silver content . . .

. . . The legislation I am sending to the Congress with this message will insure a stable and dignified coinage, fully adequate in quantity and in its specially designed technical characteristics to the needs of our 20th century life. It can be maintained indefinitely, however much the demand for coin may grow. . . .

THE NEW COINAGE

. . . I propose no change in either the penny or the nickel. The new dime and the quarter — while remaining the same size and design as the present dime and quarter — will be composite coins. They will have faces of the same copper-nickel alloy used in our present 5-cent piece, bonded to a core of pure copper. The new dime and quarter will, therefore, outwardly resemble the nickel, except in size and design, but with the further distinction that their copper core will give them a copper edge.

This type of coin was selected because, alone among practical alternatives, it can be used together with our existing silver coins in the millions of coin-operated devices . . .

THE HALF DOLLAR

. . . Our new half dollar will be nearly indistinguishable in appearance from the present half dollar.

It will continue to be made of silver and copper, but the silver content will be reduced from 90 to 40 percent. It will be faced with an alloy of 80 percent silver and 20 percent copper, bonded to a core of 21 percent silver and 79 percent copper. The new half dollar will continue to minted with the image of President Kennedy. Its size will be unchanged.

THE SILVER DOLLAR

No change in this famous old coin, or plans for additional production, are proposed at this time. It is possible that implementation of the new coinage legislation that I am proposing, greatly reducing the requirement for silver in our subsidiary coinage, will actually make feasible the minting of additional silver dollars in the future. Certainly, without this change in the silver content of the subsidiary coinage, further minting of the silver dollar would be forever foreclosed.

It is our intention that the new coinage circulate side by side with our existing coinage. . . .

. . . I want to make it absolutely clear that these changes in our coinage will have no effect on the purchasing power of our coins. The new ones will be exchanged at full face value for the paper currency of the United States. . . .

OTHER AUTHORITY REQUESTED

First. — As a useful precautionary measure, I request standby authority to institute controls over the melting and export of coins to assist the protection of our existing and our new silver coinage.

Second. — I request authority to purchase domestically mined silver at not less than $1.25 per ounce.

Third. — I am asking for authority to reactivate minting operations temporarily at the San Francisco Assay Office.

Fourth. — As a safeguard for assured availability of the new coinage, I am asking for new contracting authority for the procurement of materials and facilities related to it.

Fifth. — I propose the establishment of a Joint Commission on the Coinage composed of certain Members of the Congress, the public, and the executive branch of the Government, to report to me later the progress made in the installation of the new coinage and to review any new technological developments and to suggest further modifications which may be needed.

WHY THE SILVER CONTENT OF THE COINAGE MUST BE REDUCED AT THIS SESSION

These recommendations for revision of our silver coinage rest upon extensive study of the silver situation, and of alternatives to our present coinage, by both governmental and private specialists. The Treasury Department's comprehensive report, known as the Treasury Staff Silver and Coinage Study, is being released today as background to my recommendations. Its principal finding *was that the supply of silver in the free world has become progressively incompatible with the maintenance of silver in all our subsidiary coins. . . .*

. . . There is no dependable or likely prospect that new, economically workable sources of silver may be found that could appreciably narrow the gap between silver supply and demand. The optimistic outlook is for an increase in production of about 20 percent over the next 4 years. This would be of little help. . . .

. . . Short of controls that are undesirable in a peacetime free society there is no way to diminish the bounding growth of private demand for silver for use in jewelry, silverware, photographic film, and industrial processes. The one part of the demand for silver that can be reduced is governmental demand for use in coinage.

Most free world countries no longer use silver in their coins. A few — as we now propose — continue to make limited use of it. It is true that U.S. coinage does not currently depend upon new silver production, because for many years we have supplied silver for our coinage out of large Treasury stocks, which still amount to 1 billion troy ounces.

But — and this is the crux of the matter — at the present pace, this stock cannot last even as much as 3 years. We would then be shorn of our ability to maintain the coinage, and , if there were no alternative to our present silver coinage, the Nation would be faced with a chronic shortage. That is why definitive action is necessary at this session of the Congress.

PROTECTION OF THE COINAGE

It is necessary for the U.S. Government to have large stocks of silver in addition to the quantity needed for coinage.

We need these stocks because our silver coins in circulation must be protected from hoarding or destruction. Protection of the silver coinage will continue to be a necessity. . . . Our silver coins are protected by the fact that the Government stands ready to sell silver bullion from its stocks at $1.29 a troy ounce. This keeps the price of silver, as a commodity, from rising above the face value of our coins. This, in turn, makes hoarding or melting of the silver coinage unprofitable.

It is as additional protection for the existing coinage that I am requesting standby authority to institute controls over the melting, treating, or export of U.S. coins. . . .

. . . We believe our present stocks of silver to be adequate, once the large present drains from coinage are greatly reduced, to meet any foreseeable requirements for an indefinite period. *However, prompt action on a new coinage will help us protect the silver coinage by freeing our silver reserves for redemption of silver certificates at $1.29 per ounce. Thus, we can assure that no incentive will be created for hoarding our present coins in anticipation of a higher price for their silver content. . . .*

. . . It is for the purpose of protecting the silver producer from a precipitate drop in the price of silver resulting from the action of the Government that I am requesting authority for the Secretary of the Treasury to purchase any newly mined domestic silver offered to him, at the price of $1.25 per troy ounce.

THE SAN FRANCISCO ASSAY OFFICE

Coinage operations at the San Francisco Mint were ended in 1955. Legislation converting the mint to the San Francisco Assay Office was passed in 1962. As part of our efforts to overcome the coin shortage of the past year, coin blanks have been cut and annealed at the San Francisco Assay Office. Present law forbids full minting there. However, we will temporarily need the facilities of this plant to move into large quantity production of the new coinage and to continue production of existing coins until enough new small money is made to make certain we have adequate supplies. *Consequently, I am asking for authority to reactivate minting operations at San Francisco on a temporary basis. . . .*

WHY COMPOSITE COINS ARE RECOMMENDED

We have no choice but to eliminate silver, for the most part, from our subsidiary coinage. The question was: What would be the best alternative? After very thorough consideration of all aspects of this highly complex problem, we have settled upon the two types of composite, or clad, coins I have already described. . . .

. . . This type of coin was found to be necessary if the new coinage is to be compatible with the existing silver coinage in all the 12 million coin-operated devices in use in the United States. . . .

. . . Six million of our coin-operated devices, including nearly all vending machines, have selectors set to reject coins or imitations of coins that do not have the electrical properties of our existing silver money. . . .

. . . To be compatible in cooperation with our existing coinage, therefore, our new coins must duplicate the electric properties of a coin that is 90-percent silver. No single acceptable metal or alloy does so. The composite coins, made of layers of differing metals and alloys, that I am asking the Congress to approve, are coins made to order to duplicate the electrical properties of coins with a high silver content. . . .

. . . *The coins that I am recommending to you do this, and do it well, because they were specifically designed for the task.*

The new half dollar was designed with the strong desire in mind of many Americans to retain some silver in our everyday coinage. We believe that by eliminating silver from use in the dime and the quarter, we will have enough silver to carry out market operations in protection of our existing silver coinage — and to make a half dollar of 40 percent silver content. . . .

THE COINAGE — CURRENT AND PROSPECTIVE

I am pleased to report to the Congress substantial progress toward overcoming the coin shortage the Nation has been experiencing. Greatly increased minting has eliminated the shortage of pennies and of nickels. We are still somewhat on the short side of the demand for dimes and quarters, but this deficit is rapidly being overtaken. A severe shortage of the half dollar continues, due to the popularity of the new 50-cent pieces bearing the image of President Kennedy. . . .

. . . *There is no reason for hoarding the silver coinage we now use, because there is no reason for it to disappear*. . . .

I am satisfied that, taking into account all of the various factors involved in this complex problem, the recommendations that I am making to you are sound and right. Your early and favorable action upon the proposed legislation will make it possible to produce and issue to the public a coinage that will be acceptable, provide the maximum convenience, and serve all the purposes — financial and technical — of modern commerce. In considering this problem the needs of the economy and the convenience of the public have been placed ahead of all other considerations. They are the factors that have resulted in my recommendations to the Congress. I urge their approval at the earliest possible date.

Lyndon B. Johnson.

The White House, June 3, 1965.

The Congressional hearings were brought to a successful conclusion with the approval of the Coinage Act of 1965 by President Lyndon B. Johnson on July 23, 1965.

The last business strike 90 percent silver coins with 40 percent silver content were struck in 1964, these being the Kennedy half dollars dated 1964. The last of the coins produced for circulation containing silver were the Kennedy 40 percent silver half dollars which were struck at Denver until 1969. (Coins dated 1970-D were issued only in mint sets.)

An interesting sidelight to these governmental activities took place in Denver, Colorado, where historical records state that 316,076 dollars bearing the Peace design were struck during mechanical testing operations in 1965. All of these coins were destroyed under strict supervisory and accounting procedures, required by Mint regulations, after a supplemental appropriation request for $675,000 to produce 50 million silver dollars was not approved. There is no additional historical information on record.

Procedures used by the Mint were considered a part of normal operations within the federal government. Any records created as a result of these procedures may have been subsequently destroyed in accordance with records management regulations established by the National Archives and Records Administration.

Congressional Actions and Reactions along the Way

The Joint Commission on the Coinage, having been originated by Lyndon Johnson, set the wheels in motion to honor the late Dwight D. Eisenhower on the coinage of the United States. The leadership of the committee consisted of the four officers of the executive branch most directly concerned with matters affected by the coinage: the Secretary of the Treasury, the Secretary of Commerce, the Director of the Budget Bureau and the Director of the Mint. Their proposal included a dollar denomination coin, but with no silver for the commemoration.

Highlights: 1969 — 1970

* Senator Peter H. Dominick (R-Colo), pressed for a coin containing silver.

* The price of silver exceeded $3.00 per ounce.

* James A. McClure (R-Idaho), working with Mary Brooks of the Mint, drafted a bill in the House supporting a 40 percent—*1990 Eisenhower silver dollar.*

* In July, Senator Dominick introduced a bill in the Senate calling for an amendment to the Coinage Act of 1965. This bill would authorize 100 million dollar coins be struck each year for three years with silver content.

* James McClure introduced a second House bill to amend the Coinage Act of 1965. The essence of the bill was identical to the Senate bill.

* Gerald R. Ford (R-Mich) introduced a bill asking for a commemorative coin honoring the flight of Apollo 11 and man's first walk on the moon. The denomination of this commemorative was to be a half dollar.

* H.R.13252: This House bill honoring Eisenhower was delayed, debated, amended, but not discarded.

* An amendment by Rep. Bob Casey (D-Texas) and Rep. Leonor Sullivan (D-Mo.) was approved by the House. This legislative draft championed an Eisenhower dollar with a reverse commemorative the moon flight of Apollo 11.

* S.J.Res. 158 was drafted for the purpose of authorizing the use of silver in the proposed Eisenhower coinage.

* The House Banking and Currency Committee, chaired by Wright Patman (D-Texas), wanted no silver in the proposed coin.

* Amendment to H.R. 6778 was drafted authorizing the striking of 150 million Eisenhower dollar coins utilizing 40 percent silver. H.R. 6778, important to Wright Patman, dealt with bank holding companies.

* In December 1970, the Senate and House both passed H.R. 6778, with amendments.

* December 31, 1970, President Nixon signed Public Law 91-607 which approved the production of the Eisenhower dollar.
The Eisenhower dollar was to be struck in copper-nickel sandwich metal for circulation. The legislation also specifically approved 150 million Eisenhower dollars to be struck with 40 percent silver for the collector market. (Specific instructions were required due to the provisions of the Coinage Act of 1965.)

The Eisenhower Coin

Frank Gasparro, Chief Sculptor and Engraver for the United States Mint created the design of the Eisenhower dollar. His obverse portrayed General Eisenhower facing left, using available photographs and personal material. The words LIBERTY run along the rim at the top, IN GOD WE TRUST appears under Eisenhower's chin, and the date is at the bottom: a layout echoing that on the Washington quarter.

The reverse of the coin was adapted from Michael Collins' and James Cooper's NASA insignia for the Apollo space flights to the moon. The eagle dropping his olive branch onto the Plain of Tranquility alluded to the lunar module and its historic message, "The Eagle Has Landed." The earth as seen from the moon is seen in the background. There are 13 stars placed in an arc around the central design. The words UNITED STATES OF AMERICA run along the upper rim with E PLURIBUS UNUM placed above the eagle. ONE DOLLAR representing the denomination appears at the bottom of the reverse design. Mint Director Mary Brooks presented the galvanos for the new coin to Mamie Eisenhower on January 1, 1971.

The Eisenhower Dollar

The following is a listing of the mintage for each date and mint mark in the Eisenhower dollar series which ran from 1971 through 1978. The issues were copper-nickel clad unless noted as silver clad.

Date:	Mintage:	Proof Mintage:
1971-P	47,799,000	
1971-D	68,587,424	
1971-S (silver)	6,868,530	4,265,234
1972-P	75,890,000	
1972-D	92,548,511	
1972-S (silver)	2,193,056	1,811,631
1973-P	2,000,056 *	
1973-D	2,000,000 *	
1973-S		2,760,339
1973-S (silver)	1,883,140	1,013,646
1974-P	27,366,000	
1974-D	45,517,000	
1974-S		2,612,568
1974-S (silver)	1,900,156	1,306,579
1977-P	12,596,000	
1977-D	32,983,006	3,251,152
1977-S		
1978-P	25,702,000	
1978-D	33,012,890	3,127,781
1978-S		

* A total of 1,769,258 pieces each of the 1973-P and 1973-D were sold in mint sets and not released into circulation. The unsold coins (439,899) were destroyed in 1974 at the mint.

The Bicentennial dollar featuring Eisenhower on the obverse and the Liberty-Moon reverse was dated 1776-1976. For details, see the next chapter entitled "America's Bicentennial Dollar" by David L. Ganz.

Trial strikes were made beginning on January 25, 1971, at the Philadelphia Mint. Later first-strike festivities were held at the San Francisco facility on March 31.

The Mint personnel in all three facilities were relatively unfamiliar with the striking of dollar-sized coins, as the Denver Peace dollars in 1965 were the last ones made at any branch since Peace dollar production ended in 1935. As problems arose, the obverse and reverse designs were changed to improve the coins' striking quality. The only Eisenhower dollars scheduled to possess any silver were the San Francisco branch mint proof strikes and special uncirculated coins. Proof production was moved to San Francisco in 1968 when the U.S. Mint once again produced proof sets. None of the business strikes produced at the Philadelphia or Denver facilities contain any silver. The pieces produced for circulation were made of a copper nickel alloy which served as an outside clad layer over a pure copper core. The silver clad coins produced in San Francisco contained two outside layers of .800 silver with the rest copper bonded to an inner core of .210 silver with the remainder being copper. This combination contained a total of 40 percent silver composition by weight.

Of the silver coins produced in San Francisco during the first year, 6,868,530 uncirculated pieces were struck in low relief, while the 4,265,234 proof silver dollars were struck in higher relief. The 1971-S proof sets did not contain a silver Eisenhower dollar, and collectors were advised to place separate orders for the Eisenhower proof dollars. The proof sets were expanded in 1973 and later years to include the Eisenhower dollar. The copper-nickel circulation strikes for 1973 were not released for general circulation, but were offered only through purchases of mint sets.

While we are on the subject of relief, there is more. The 1972-S 40% uncirculated coins were made in high relief (all of the proofs were produced in high relief). The total 1971 issue of copper-nickel coins were produced in low relief. In 1972, the Philadelphia issues came in both low relief and high relief. The Denver branch mint production in 1972 was entirely of the low relief variety.

The special uncirculated 40% silver specimens struck at San Francisco were packaged in blue government holders while the 40% silver proofs were packaged in brown holders. Unfortunately, some unscrupulous individuals have been known to change coins in the holders, therefore, don't buy on the basis of the holder color alone. The 40% silver coins are white or faintly pink on the edge, while the copper-nickel clad coins display a visible clear-cut red copper core.

There is one "key" coin in the regular Eisenhower series, and that is the 1973-S proof silver. Counterfeits are known silverplated on, or cast from the similar copper-nickel Ike dollars. The semi-key for the series would be the 1974-S proof silver. The mintage figures for all of the proofs was in excess of one million. This coupled with the relatively low quality makes these coins an easy acquisition.

Varieties

The low and high relief varieties of the 1971 Eisenhower dollar have already been presented. Another variety of the 1971-S Ike dollar possesses an "R" without serifs on the left foot in "LIBERTY" on the obverse (the "peg leg"). This variety was reportedly seen again in 1972.

The U.S. Mint made reverse die changes in 1972 which led to three distinct relief varieties: Type I produced in low relief, Type II produced in higher relief on the obverse and reverse, and Type III described by Walter Breen in his *Complete Encyclopedia of U.S. and Colonial Coins* as follows. Modified high relief as in 1973-74. No incuse outline behind lower r. crater; three distinct Caribbean islands l. of Florida. The Eisenhower issues for 1973 were in high relief due to the enhanced dies.

It has been reported that varieties of the 1974-S silver proof and special uncirculated issues exist with repunched mintmarks.

The rarest variety in the entire Eisenhower series is the 1974-D dollar in 40 percent silver rather than copper-nickel. These coins were struck on rejected silver-clad proof blanks shipped from San Francisco to Denver. About 30 pieces are known to exist according to Walter Breen. This variety was discovered by a Las Vegas blackjack dealer, and exhibited at the ANA convention in 1974.

Dwight D. Eisenhower First Day of Issue
Special Cancellation Cachet Envelope

Conclusion

The Eisenhower dollar was born in compromise, and its production largely went to meet the requirements of casinos' dollar slot machines. As a general circulating coin, it failed; the public as a whole ignored it or saved an Ike or two as a memento or souvenir. The longer range plans of the U.S. Treasury, which began to come to light with the Susan B. Anthony dollar, revolved around the elimination of the paper one dollar bill. The public showed its dislike for that alternative by shunning the SBA dollar completely. On the commemorative aspect of the situation, the Eisenhower dollar was successful in meeting its objective; that of commemorating the life and accomplishments of Dwight David Eisenhower.

Resources

Digest of the Treasury Staff Study of Silver and Coinage. Washington, D.C.: U.S. Government Printing Office

Hearing before the Committee on Banking and Currency House of Representatives, Eighty-Ninth Congress, First session on H.R. 8746, a bill to provide for the coinage of the United States, June 4, 7, and 8, 1965. Washington, D.C.: 1964/5, U.S. Government Printing Office

Hearing before the Committee on Banking and Currency United States Senate, Eighty-Ninth Congress, First session on S.2080, A bill to provide for the coinage of the United States, June 9, 1965. Washington, D.C.: 1965, U.S. Government Printing Office

Walter Breen's Complete Encyclopedia of U.S. and Colonial Coins. Garden City: Doubleday, 1988

***

David L. Ganz

David L. Ganz of New York City has been a collector for more than 30 years. Starting in 1965, he began a column in *The Coin Shopper*; in 1967, his column *Under the Glass* began to appear monthly in *The Coin Collector*. The column moved to *The Coin Collector & Shopper*, when Krause Publications acquired it in 1968.

Starting college at Georgetown University in Washington, D.C. in the fall of 1969, he began writing spot news stories for *Numismatic News Weekly* that fall, and in January, 1970, his *Under the Glass* column made its debut in *Numismatic News Weekly* where it ran weekly for more than six years. From 1969 until 1974, he was Washington Correspondent for Krause Publications, and in such capacity was admitted as a member to the Periodical Press Gallery of the United States Senate, which he covered together with the House of Representatives and the various federal agencies that then were involved with regulating, or affecting, the rare coin field. He was appointed by President Nixon as a member of the 1974 Assay Commission.

As a free-lance writer, his articles have appeared in virtually every major numismatic publication, including *Coin World* and *COINage* Magazine (both since 1971), *The Numismatist*, *Numismatic Circular*, *Numismatic Scrapbook*. *The Forecaster*, *TAMS Journal*, *Coins Magazine* and others. His column "Coin Market Perspective" ran monthly in *Coins* Magazine for a decade and covered the economic side of the numismatic market. "Backgrounder" is the column that he has written for *Coin World* since 1974, where it presently appears biweekly. "Coin Market Insider's Report" has run for the past 16 years each month in *COINage* Magazine.

Joining the American Numismatic Association as a junior member in 1967 (J-59168) and later becoming Life Member 1072 in October, 1972, Ganz became legislative counsel to the ANA in 1978, two years after graduating form St. John's University Law School in New York. In 1985, he was elected to the ANA Board of Governors.

As managing partner in the New York City law firm of Ganz Hollinger & Towe, he has continued to write his numismatic columns, but has also taken the opportunity to focus his research on numismatic-legal issues.

Books written by him include *14 Bits: A legal and legislative history of 31 U.S.C. 324d-324i* (1976); *The World of Coins and Coin Collecting* (Scribner's, 1980; rev. 2d ed. 1985); *A Critical Guide to Anthologies of African Literature*, African Studies Ass'n, 1973 [In Library of Congress reference collection].

Married since 1981 to the former Sharon R. Lewis, he has three children well-known to the readers of his "Coin Market Insider's Report" column that runs monthly in *COINage* and *The Numismatist*: Scott (age 8), Elyse (6) and Pamela (3-1/2). All are life members of the ANA.

Ganz has been general counsel to the Professional Numismatists Guild, Inc. since 1981, and is a founding member of the Board of Directors of the Industry Council for Tangible Assets (ICTA). The views presented in this chapter are his own.

CHAPTER 71

America's Bicentennial Dollar

by David L. Ganz, NLG

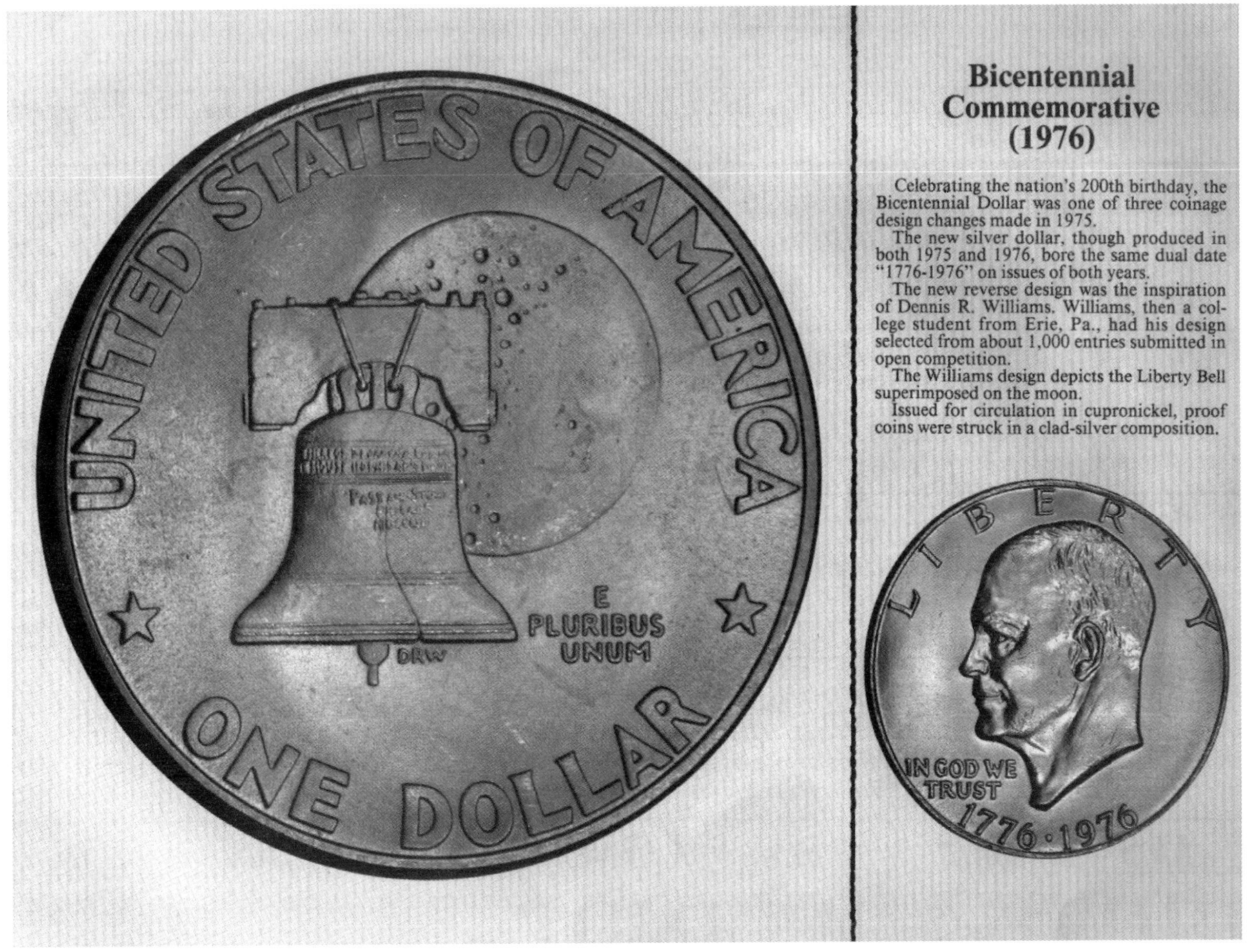

(Courtesy of Krause Publications)

Genesis for America's bicentennial dollar and a legal tender commemoration of the 200th anniversary of American independence, owes itself to the foresight of a medalist, and the tenacity of a mint director, with a strong push from several members of Congress acting on behalf of their constituents.

William Trees Louth, then president of the Medallic Art Company, whose hydraulic coin presses were first used to test the St. Gaudens designs at the turn of the century, deserves credit for first proposing legal tender commemorative coinage for America's bicentennial, then a decade in the future. From his little noticed proposal, the distinctive circulating legal tender commemorative of the bicentennial emerged, struck in copper-nickel cladding, and also specially produced for collectors in a non-circulating legal tender silver-clad version.

About three years after the American Revolution Bicentennial Commission (ARBC) was created by Act of Congress, Rep. Leonor K. Sullivan (D-Mo), Chairman of the Subcommittee on Consumer Affairs of the House Committee on Banking and Currency, made an electrifying speech before the American Numismatic Association's annual convention, held that year at the Chase Park Plaza Hotel in her home town of St. Louis.

Entitled "Numismatic Views From the Hill," and largely written by her key aide, Charles B. ("Chuck") Holstein, the speech gave an important hint of the view of one member of Congress of the possibility of changing coin designs, of the use of commemoratives, and of the possibility that the bicentennial of American independence would be treated differently than commemorative coins had been over the preceding four decades.

Starting in the mid-1930's, the Treasury Department had opposed the issuance of commemorative coins, largely on spurious grounds. First, they argued that commemoratives were confusing to the public at large. Next, they claimed that commemorative coinage gave rise to the possibility of increased counterfeiting. Third, they called issuance of non-circulating commemorative coinage incompatible with the monetary system. Finally, they argued with increasing success that commemorative coinage was the subject of a pattern of abuse that allowed for private profiteering.

In 1939, the abuses had become so notorious that the treasury urged the abolition of commemoratives in their entirety, or, at a minimum, placing serious limitations upon them in terms of the number of pieces produced, the circumstances under which they could be struck, and most importantly, the distribution system under which they could be sold. They induced Congress to pass the Act of August 5, 1939, revoking all remaining authority to strike commemorative coinage.

Dating back to at least the 1929-33 term of Herbert Hoover, the Treasury Department, on its own, had successfully argued for the veto of several commemorative coinage bills, using identical grounds that ultimately were repeated nearly verbatim by Presidents Roosevelt, Truman, and Eisenhower.

By the time that consideration was being initially given to bicentennial coinage, the objections of the Treasury Department had become codified in Treasury Department practice, and, hence, there was strong opposition to the issuance of non-circulating commemorative coinage, even as to any change in coin design.

That changing coin designs should be opposed by the Treasury Department from the late 1920's, until today, should not be a real surprise. Even in the 1990's, as consideration is given to legislative proposals designed to change the features on each circulating U.S. coin, Treasury Department opposition has been adamant. In particular, although the U.S. Senate had passed such a proposal no less than six times since 1988, and even though more than half the House of Representatives has approved the measure, Treasury opposition has stultified design change. So it too with America's bicentennial dollar — at least initially.

In early 1939, a young Washington, D.C., numismatist named Harry X Boosel in large measure wrote a typescript of abuses then existing in the commemorative coinage distribution schemes permitted by the mint based on deficiencies written into law by Congress that expressly permitted them. Boosel, who two years earlier had served as General Chairman for the ANA convention held in Washington, later went on to become the 1966 Chair of the Diamond Jubilee Convention of the ANA in Chicago and election to the ANA Board of Governors.

His views were adopted wholeheartedly by Chairman Cochran, Chairman of the House Committee on Banking and Currency, where a then obscure Representative from Texas named Wright Patman (D-TX) was still serving as an apprentice after 15 years in Congress. Cochran issued H.R. Rept. 101, 76th Congress, 1st Session (1939) which detailed the abuses and suggested a solution.

By the 1960's, Patman had become Chair of the powerful Banking and Currency Committee, and was nearing the close of a career that spanned nearly 50 years of service to his country in the House of Representatives. One of his key aides, Baron Shacklett, was a coin collector — a circumstance which proved propitious, and ultimately would bode well for the tale of the bicentennial dollar.

Up until 1963, the House Banking Committee had subcommittees which were simply denominated numerically, though they were assigned different functions. In that year, subcommittee number three had its name changed to reflect its subject matter: Consumer Affairs, a function that it maintains to this very day. Congresswoman Leonor Sullivan (D-Mo) was the Chair of the Subcommittee; she was also Chair of the Subcommittee of Merchant Marine and Fisheries, and was a political power in her own right, both in St. Louis and on Capitol Hill.

Mrs. John B. Sullivan was elected to Congress after her husband died in 1951, succeeding him — as many women have their spouses — in a time honored manner. She quickly put her own imprimatur on the job and the seat, and for the next quarter century represented her district and her country with distinction.

Initially, however, her principal identification with her late — and she used the socially acceptable "Mrs. John B. Sullivan," rather than her first name Leonor. In fact, when Charles B. ("Chuck") Holstein, then a newspaperman from Pittsburgh, first met her in an interview, she declined to give her first name, saying only that she was "Mrs. John B. Sullivan," which is also how her name appeared on the November ballot.

Chuck Holstein was also an amateur coin collector, though in a very casual way, and it was simply by chance that an orphan issue such as numismatics was given to the Consumer Affairs Subcommittee. As Mrs. Sullivan herself related years afterwards, "no one wanted it."

It is ironic that the dominant political issue of the 19th century — which was paramount in every presidential election form 1876 until the turn of the century — was all but relegated to backdrop by the 1960's. Yet, in short order it was to move to the forefront as America faced a shortage of coins and ultimately found that it could no longer retain precious metal coinage as the price of silver became too dear to support such an endeavor.

As the nation slipped into a coin shortage it was as if the Mint had sneezed and the nation's cash registers caught pneumonia. Suddenly there were no one cent coins, silver dimes, or quarters, and half dollars were but a faded memory. Even silver dollars, once ubiquitous at the nation's banks (where they could be obtained by exchanging a silver certificate or for that matter a Federal Reserve note), began an incremental march in value.

President Lyndon B. Johnson perhaps recalled the silver dollars of his youth when he directed the Mint to begin production in 1965 of the first silver dollars struck in some 30 years. The old Peace dollar design was utilized, the date for that of the previous year, 1964, because of the date freeze in effect as a result of Congressional action.

Congress slammed the door down on more than 300,000 Peace dollars bearing the 1964 date, and specifically prohibited the further minting of dollar coins for a five year period of time. The expiration of that time frame neatly coincided with the creation of the — 1990 Eisenhower silver dollar.

The politics of the era could be characterized readily as a battle anew over the silver interests. With Richard Nixon inaugurated as President, the Treasury Department made a serious miscue with Patman, ostensibly backing a proposal for a copper-nickel coin while simultaneously allowing the legislative pursuit of a silver dollar.

Patman was furious at the perceived double-cross — really a misunderstanding based on conflicting political interests on a regional and local level — and stymied efforts to bring forth a coin. From the October 1969 hearings, it was clear that there would be a long wait before Patman was willing to approve of any silver dollar, even if it were to honor the late President Eisenhower.

With this as a backdrop, in January 1970, the Advisory Panel on Coins and Medals of the American Revolution Bicentennial Commission (ARBC) met in Washington for the first time, and held extensive hearings on precisely what ought to be done to commemorate America's bicentennial.

Chairing the panel was restaurateur George Lang, while Eric P. Newman, of St. Louis, provided the historic backdrop and numismatic expertise. Others who were active at the time were Co-Chairman Margo Russell, then editor of *Coin World*;

Clifford Mishler, editor of *Numismatic News Weekly*; Ralph J. Menconi, the celebrated medallic sculptor; with cameo appearances by writer Don Taxay; Herbert M. Bergen, ANA President; Henry Grunthal, a curator at the American Numismatic Society; and the ubiquitous John Jay Pittman. Federal agencies were represented by Dr. Vladimir Clain-Stefanelli and Mrs. Elvira Clain-Stefanelli of the Smithsonian; Rep. Fred Schwengel (R-Iowa); and others.

Full and complete details of what the Advisory Panel on Coins and Medals debated and, indeed, not until an inquiry was made under the Freedom of Information Act (FOIA) were transcripts of the proceedings furnished. Significant extracts have appeared together with the substance of what transpired. [1]

Treasury Department opposition to a bicentennial coinage was severe; all of the tired arguments of the Thirties were drawn out, and at least initially, succeeded, though the Coins and Medals Advisory Panel actually wanted to change the designs on all coins, cent to dollar, for the monumental event honoring America's bicentennial. Initially, Treasury was enthusiastic only about a medals program, which no doubt was exactly what William Trees Louth did not want, though he recognized the appropriateness of creating some official medals. Joseph Segal, president of the Franklin Mint, vigorously opposed a medallic program — arguing that it would cut into private enterprise and could not be properly marketed.

What emerged, however, was a proposal that (at least initially) seemed as if it might become the sole numismatic commemoration for the bicentennial: a national medals proposal starting in 1971 that would ultimately culminate with multiple issues in 1976. Imaginatively, it included philatelic-numismatic combinations, though none were in fact imaginative in design. Restrikes of America's first medals were also proposed.

But, alas, initially, there continued to be substantial opposition within the Treasury Department to a bicentennial coin — even a single dollar — and for a time, it appeared that it would end that way: a bicentennial celebration with no legal tender dollar coin, nor indeed any other true coin of a commemorative nature.

The Treasury Department was adamant that no commemorative coin be utilized. In delivering the official administration position, Mary T. Brooks, Director of the Mint, said that "the Treasury Department opposes the minting of special-event, non-circulating commemorative coins" utilizing the same arguments stated by President Hoover in his 1929 veto of commemorative legislation: coins "do not serve as a medium of exchange, are not readily available and recognizable to the public, invade the production capacities of the Mint, and have been the subject (in the past) to hoarding and profiteering." [2]

Summarizing the arguments of Presidents Hoover, Roosevelt, Truman, and Eisenhower, Mrs. Brooks concluded that — in the words of the Treasury Department, but perhaps not in her own views — "commemorative coins tend to defeat the purpose of the coinage system." [3]

Clifford Mishler, an astute observer of numismatic matters for more than 30 years, summed up the Treasury viewpoint by stating that if the Advisory Panel on Coins and Medals had any thought of recommending a commemorative coinage for the bicentennial, it had "better secure an Act of Congress ordering it." [4]

William L. Dickey, Deputy Assistant Secretary of the Treasury, followed Mrs. Brooks to the witness stand, and also opposed any change in coin of the realm. He acknowledged Congress and its "expertise . . . in the sentiment of the American people," and noted that Congress could make the judgment that Treasury was simply not "in a position to." [5]

Numismatic researcher, Don Taxay, a panel member, recalled the great design changes of 1892, but Dickey, speaking for the Mint, noted that "a general conversion of the coinage . . . taxes the capacity of the Mint" (*ibid*., page 72).

Debate on the coin portion of the panel was extraordinary. Initially, there was the definitional question as to whether or not any coin honoring a person or event was a commemorative. Eric P. Newman suggested that definition (Executive Session of September 31, 1970, page 50), and the deal was accepted. A suggestion was made early on of using a double date, "1776-1976," in the context principally of no design change at all but that alteration. Eric P. Newman called the suggestion "meaningless" (Executive Session, page 28), however, Clifford Mishler then suggested that the reverse only be changed (Executive Session, page 33). Dr. Vladimir Clain-Stefanelli, Curator of the Smithsonian's Numismatic Collection, also made a similar suggestion (*ibid*., page 31).

The first mention of the Eisenhower dollar as a bicentennial vehicle came from the then President of the American Numismatic Association, and panel member Herbert Bergen. (Executive Session, September 30, 1970, page 60.)

The problem with the dollar was expressed by Margo Russell best when she said that "I am afraid that the man on the street will not receive the coin" (*ibid*., page 60).

George Lang, as Chairman, finally suggested the Panel vote on whether a "single dignified commemorative coin should be recommended in conjunction with the bicentennial" (Executive Session, page 71), and after a miscounted ballot, ten members voted in favor, Mint Director Brooks voted against (in accordance with Treasury instructions) and two members abstained (Executive Session transcript, page 72). Strangely, having voted for a single commemorative, the Panel then voted 12-1 (Mint Director Brooks, again opposing) in favor of changing all coinage designs (transcript of Executive Session, page 93).

Treasury Department opposition all but killed the Coins and Medals Advisory opinion. The vote was similar to one taken in President Lincoln's Cabinet where he voted in favor, the entire Cabinet against. "The ayes have it," he is reported to have said.

Enter Wright Patman, Chairman of the House Banking Committee, who wrote to David J. Mahoney, Chairman of the ARBC, on October 1, 1970, and changed, in a single letter, more than 30 years of Treasury opposition, and a similar period of Congressional disapproval. "While it has been the policy of (House Banking and Currency Committee) for many years not to authorize the striking of special coins of the design different from those of the regular circulating coins . . . We would certainly be willing to give careful consideration to any proposals from the Bicentennial Commission for legislation authorizing either a new series of circulating coins or of special commemorative coins minted in limited quantities . . . It is my firm opinion that numismatic materials created by the Bicentennial Commission as part of this great national observance should be approved by Congress and should be made in the Mint as U.S. coins . . . " [6] **Congress had bought into the deal.**

If there was one man behind Patman's letter, it is without question Clifford Mishler, who knew Baron Shacklett, Patman's key aide, for many years. Shacklett was a subscriber to *Numismatic News*, and Mishler had visited him many times on Capitol Hill. Little wonder then that he was able to write to Lang on October 5 that he had been "requested by Congressman Patman's aid(e)s to provide his office with the guidelines of a drafting of required legislation."

The Advisory Panel on Coins and Medals continued to meet, as did the American Revolution Bicentennial Commission. Exactly 1,776 days before the bicentennial, the American Revolution Bicentennial Commission formally endorsed a comprehensive coinage change — across the board.

The Mint Bureau, so soon after a coin shortage in the previous decade, was practically apoplectic. The reason was clear: a fear, whether ill-founded or not, that new designs would mean the withdrawal of older coins from circulation — and a nearly impossible task of supplying the nation's coinage needs.

Quietly, Mint Director Mary T. Brooks began to search for alternatives to the Department's hard position that supported limited-issue medallions, and opposed coins of any kind whatsoever. Gradually, she was able to soften the views of Treasury Secretary George Schultz, who had succeeded John Connally. (Connally's contribution to silver dollar history is perhaps best remembered by his remark terming the profits on silver Eisenhower dollar sales to collectors "unconscionable.")

June 12, 1972 marked the departure of John Connally as Secretary of the Treasury, and George P. Schultz' oath of office as successor. Mint Director Mary T. Brooks utilized the opportunity to lobby hard in favor of bicentennial coinage — and in particular, a bicentennial dollar and half dollar. So, too, did the members of the Advisory Panel on Coins and Medals — who, having unanimously (with a single reservation) approved an across- the- board change in coinage designs, intensively lobbied individual members of Congress in favor of the proposal.

Margo Russell, then editor of *Coin World* and vice chairman of the Panel, wrote in November 1972 to Dr. Lynn Carroll, Deputy Executive Director of the ARBC, hoping for the possibility of a coinage change. It was she who, in that same letter, suggested an "open (wide open to the public) or semi-open (to professional sculptors)" coin design competition in 1976.

As Wright Patman gave bicentennial coinage a nudge on January 4, noting that his committee would "consider legislation for a new coin to be placed in circulation with appropriate design symbolizing the origin and history of our great nation," the Advisory Panel of Coins and Medals readied for its January 12, 1973, meeting. Eric P. Newman, as chairman of the panel, asked for a report from the Director of the Mint at that meeting "as to the possibilities with respect to the striking of United States coins."

Newman, himself an accomplished numismatist, and renowned author and attorney, stated to the panel members that they would "recall that our committee recommended a design change for all denominations. It was a rather elaborate request and . . . the Treasury Department was in opposition to that" (Transcript of 1973 Advisory Panel meeting, page 134).

Mint Director Brooks responded with humor, noting that she was "about as popular as Typhoid Mary by the time I got through reading my paper" during the 1970 Bicentennial Advisory Panel hearings. (1973 Transcript, page 135, referring to the 1970 Advisory Panel transcript at pages 25 through 30.)

Mint Director Brooks then swore the Advisory Panel on Coins and Medals "all to secrecy, or it may blow up in our faces, but there is some progress. Further than that, I am sorry I cannot tell you at this point, today. Two weeks from now, it may be that we can talk about it. But, I have made some progress." (1973 Advisory Transcript, page 135.)

What Mint Director Brooks declined to tell the Advisory Panel on Coins and Medals is that she had persuaded the Secretary of the Treasury, George Schultz, to sponsor a bicentennial coinage proposal — one that would include the dollar coin and the half dollar coin.

Documents on file with the American Revolution Bicentennial Commission, signed by the legislative reference staff of the Office of Management and Budget in a "legislative referral memorandum," sought OMB approval to "provide a new coinage design and date emblematic of the bicentennial of the American Revolution for dollars and half dollars," and requested a response within 30 days.

On March 5, 1973, Treasury's legal counsel had a draft bill signed by Secretary Schultz and sent to Capitol Hill. In particular, it mandated that the "reverse side of all dollars and half dollars minted for issuance on or after July 4, 1975, and until such time as the Secretary of the Treasury may determine, shall bear a design determined by the Secretary to be emblematic of the bicentennial of the American Revolution."

The bill was introduced by Representative Wright Patman, Representative Leonor Sullivan, and Representative William Widnall (representing the leadership of the House Banking Committee relative to coinage matters) as H.R. 5244 on March 4, 1973; in the Senate, Senators John Sparkman and John Tower, the ranking and minority members of the Banking Committee, introduced it jointly as S. 1141 on March 8, 1973.

Representative Wright Patman, nearing the end of a long career, explained in his typical fashion why he supported the legislation. The explanation came in his 1848th weekly newsletter to his constituency: "1976 should be a year when all Americans close ranks in recognition of their heritage. Appropriate designs on our coinage are a small reminder of the courage and beliefs that made these States a Nation United." (Wright Patman's 1848th *Weekly Newsletter*, March 22, 1973, page 1.)

March 5, 1973, marked the day that Treasury Secretary Schultz sent the administration's bicentennial coinage bill to Capitol Hill; it also was the moment Mrs. Brooks won the battle for bureaucratic turf, and the Mint (under the Secretary of the Treasury's formal proposal) would produce circulating half dollars and dollars (in limited quantity) that would be struck in copper-nickel, and a special silver-clad version for collectors.

The event was historic, because for the first time, the Treasury Department had acknowledged the feasiblity of a circulating commemorative coin that would be issued for a limited duration — the half year preceding the bicentennial, and the bicentennial period itself.

As events worked out, Representative Leonor Sullivan would listen to the fervent plea of John Jay Pittman, by then President of the American Numismatic Association, that a truly circulating copper-nickel coin also be included: the quarter. But that was months away, and in the interim, coinage once again moved to the forefront as special interest groups sought to influence the legislation in one manner or another.

The resulting Public Law 93-127, approved October 18, 1973, is deceptively simple verbiage. As laws go, it was quite short. Yet, from Treasury Secretary Schultz' proposal to enactment involved two sets of hearings, a report by the House and the Senate, a conference report, much compromise, and considerable political drama.

Initially, returning precious metal coinage became an attractive goal to a number of members of Congress and some thought it might be the opportunity to start a new tradition of gold coinage — even though its ownership had been illegal, except under certain circumstances, since 1933.

Before the tussling could begin, hearings were necessary — and in May 1973, the House Banking Subcommittee on Consumer Affairs slated hearings in which the administration proposal was placed alongside that of the ARBC, and Mint Director Brooks pilloried (unfairly, as history bears out) for her publicly espousing the party line while privately arguing for an expanded program.

Historically, the Senate Banking Committee handled coinage matters within the full committee, rather than in a smaller subcommittee unit; however, a junior member was itching for a subcommittee chair, and one was created especially for the situation: the ad hoc subcommittee on minting and coinage to which William Hathaway, Democrat of Maine, was named the chair. June hearings were set by the Hathaway subcommittee, and again, the issue was extensively studied.

Just how the coins would be designed and what display they would show was the subject of considerable discussion. Ralph Menconi had always declared that "every Congressman is an artist," and argued that for this reason, American coinage design was destined to mediocrity. What evolved — in the form of a design competition — was an attempt to solve that problem, though some would argue it was an unsuccessful effort.

Just two short months after the bill was introduced, the first hearings were held, May 2-3, 1973: a remarkable series of days on Capitol Hill. Mint Director Mary Brooks testified before the Subcommittee on Consumer Affairs of the House Banking and Currency Committee; she announced that the Mint endorsed a two-coin proposal (dollar and half dollar) and was closely followed by Hugh A. Hall, Acting Director of the ARBC, who claimed that "we have been impressed by . . . concern for the severe strain which a wholesale change in the design of U.S. coinage would place on the production capacity of the U.S. Mint." [7]

Hall went on to endorse the two-coin proposal that itself resulted solely from salesmanship of Mary Brooks. Both Margo Russell and Chester Krause were outraged at the sellout. Krause offered a devastating attack: "I feel the birthday party is being seriously short changed by the Mint's proposal." [8]

Bringing up the vanguard, John Jay Pittman, President of the American Numismatic Association, suggested the addition — at a minimum — of a Washington quarter with a bicentennial theme.

June 6, 1973 marked the start of the Hathaway subcommittee hearings on the bicentennial coinage legislation. Mint Director Brooks capitulated readily and incorporated the quarter — what ultimately became the three-coin bicentennial proposal. The capitulation was that of the Treasury Department, not Mrs. Brooks. In an interview she disclosed, "when I read that approved paper (before the Bicentennial Panel in 1970) I thought I was wrong. I felt that (the bicentennial) was an important enough occasion to allow for more change. So I proceeded to go through channels to try and change it . . . When it was agreed we could use West Point (as a mint) that added flexibility gave us a way that worked." [9]

A week after the hearing, the ad hoc Subcommittee on Minting and Coinage met and approved the Treasury proposal with the addition of the quarter dollar; it also favorably voted on a gold coin bill added by Mark Hatfield, Republican of Oregon, a longtime collector. The following day, June 14, the Subcommittee on Consumer Affairs so voted in favor of the new Treasury proposal, but excluded a gold coin proposal by Representative Philip M. Crane, Republican of Illinois.

June 20, 1973, was a gold letter day. It was also one of politics, as Senator Edward Brooke/(R-MA) moved to amend the bicentennial legislation to require the mandatory production of 60 million bicentennial coins of a silver clad material.

Sen. Brooke, a legislator of extraordinary accomplishment, was actually acting on behalf of a constituent in Massachusetts who produced silver cladding; nonetheless, Mint Director Brooks became apoplectic, particularly because the possibility of silver coinage might have an effect on Representative Patman. "Any controversial amendment causing the delay and the passage of this bill would seriously endanger the changes of having any bicentennial coinage," she declared. [10]

As this simmered overnight, on June 21, 1973, the Senate Banking Committee made a proposal to require 60 million silver clad bicentennial coins to be struck by the Mint prior to July 4, 1980, and authorized the possibility (but not the requirement) that a gold coin likewise be issued.

It was but two short weeks later on July 11, 1973, that Senator Hatfield — while the Senate was considering S. 1141 — took to the floor and with only six other colleagues present, required Treasury Secretary to mint gold coins. [11]

The following week, on July 19, the House Banking and Currency Committee met and reached an opposite conclusion. Although Leonor Sullivan did not oppose silver commemorative coinage, she thought a bargaining chip was appropriate to deal with an obstinate Senate. Five days after that on July 24, 1973, the Banking Committee issued the "Report on New Coinage Design and Date Emblematic of the Bicentennial of the American Revolution," (House Report 93-391) which argued, strenuously, in favor of the administration proposal. The Honorable Chalmers P. Wiley, Republican of Ohio, ranking member of the Subcommittee, stated "the object of this bill is to provide a coin for use by every man, woman, and child, to symbolize a rededication to the great American ideal and values." (House Report, page 11.)

How the coins, once approved, would be designed had also been determined: "an open [design competition] rather than one restricted only to members of [the National Sculpture Society]. All citizens would be eligible to compete." (H.R. Rep. 93-391, page 7.)

What finally emerged was an agreement that did not produce 60 million of the clad coins, but rather required 45 million silver clad pieces to be produced — with an option to increase it to 60 million pieces should the demand arise. The conference report, H.R. Rep. 93-521 (September 24, 1973), reprinted in the *Congressional Record* of the same day (page H. 8223-24) details the specific compromise.

On October 4, 1973, both the Senate and House elected to act on a conference report to S. 1141 which was the bicentennial bill that emerged from both Houses. Also on October 4, 1973, the matter was debated on the House floor. Representative H. R. Gross (R-Ia), a perennial gadfly, criticized the proposal: "I thought we would fittingly celebrate our 200th anniversary with the same scrap metal coins that we have been using and probably will continue to use" (Congressional Record, October 2, 1973, daily ed., page H-8660), making an obvious reference to the clad coinage.

The measures were finally approved, and on October 18, 1973, President Nixon signed Public Law 93-127, authorizing the creation of bicentennial coinage.

Mere passage of the law, of course, did not create the coins. The Treasury Department opened a $5,000 bicentennial coin design competition and about 15,000 inquiries were received by both the Mint and the National Sculpture Society.

Eligibility, as indicated, was open to "all sculptors who are citizens of the United States and who are capable of executing a plaster model compatible with the coining process." (Rules of the Competition, page 1.)

There were some limitations. Design had to be "emblematic of the bicentennial of the American Revolution — 1776-1976"; the statutory legends "E PLURIBUS UNUM" and "UNITED STATES OF AMERICA," had to appear.

A total of 900 entries reached the West Point Bullion Depository, the location chosen for preliminary judging. Many came from school children, though there was some from professional sculptors, artists and amateurs who had heard about the competition. One was submitted by a young college student majoring in art named Dennis R. Williams; his design of (a project assigned by one of his professors) was a well-thought-out sketch of the Liberty Bell superimposed over the lunar surface. It was to become the model for the $1 coin.

Ultimately, a mere dozen designs would be chosen: and at that point denomination was largely irrelevant. On March 1, 1974, six finalists were selected: Jack Ahr, Ogden Dalrymple, Seth Huntington, Dean McMullen, Brydon Stewart, and Dennis R. Williams.

Precisely a year and a day after Secretary Schultz sent his letter to the Senate and the House asking for consideration, the winners were announced in Washington. At the age of 22, Dennis R. Williams had become the youngest coin designer in American history.

Once the designs had been selected, it was necessary to assure that they could properly be immortalized in metal. Frank Gasparro, Chief Engraver and Sculptor of the United States, and long-time employee of the Mint, revised parts of the design in order to make them historically accurate. He retained, however, the initial design as created by Williams — which had a certain crudity in the lettering that almost seemed as if it was part of a Colonial die engraving. Williams, as did the other sculptors, agreed with the changes and assisted in the process. [12]

Even as Watergate swirled, President Nixon issued a proclamation for National Coin Week noting the new designs that "will appear on the backs of the dollar, half dollar, and quarter" and the double dating on the front of the coins. "When in circulation, these bicentennial coins will reach every citizen and serve as reminders of our rich national heritage and continuing dedication to freedom and self government . . ." (Presidential Proclamation 4286, April 1974).

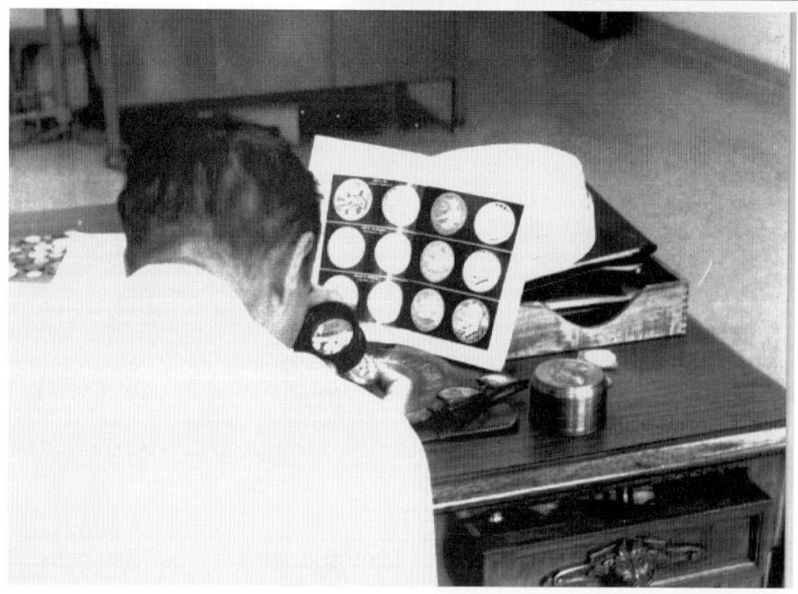

Frank Gasparro looks at his die for the Eisenhower Bicentennial Dollar

Galvanos were ready during National Coin Week, and Williams, Huntington, and Ahr travelled to Washington to pick up their prizes in a presentation ceremony attended by then Treasury Secretary-designate William E. Simon (after signing in the private dining room of outgoing Secretary of the Treasury Schultz). They also met with Presidential counselor Ann L. Armstrong, and the administrator of the American Revolution Bicentennial Administration John Warner (now Senator from Virginia) at the White House. Extensive photographs were taken of this well documented meeting.

In the meantime, the Williams design — originally drawn as a quarter dollar — had been transformed to a dollar, and the bell line of the Liberty Bell softened from a round to a flat surface. The craters on the moon were similarly strengthened to give a more accurate impression of the lunar surface.

(Pictured L to R) William E. Simon, Seth Hunnington, Dennis R. Williams

Counsellor Anne Armstrong, on behalf of the President, congratulates Dennis R. Williams of Columbus, Ohio. (left) on his winning design for the reverse of the dollar. Center is Mr. John W. Warner, Administrator of the American Revolution Bicentennial Administration. Mr. Williams is one of the three winners of the National Bicentennial Coin Design Competition for reverse designs for the dollar, half dollar and quarter.

Dennis Williams indicated that he had produced his sketch as part of a college project. Born October 26, 1952, at the time of the award, he was a junior at Columbus College of Art and Design in Columbus, Ohio, majoring in sculpting. His sculptor instructor assigned him the National Bicentennial Coin Design competition as a design problem. In an interview, he disclosed that "I worked 15 hours on it after studying the design for a long time. Once I started, I just couldn't stop." He revealed that to obtain the right sense of the Liberty Bell, he purchased a 1963 uncirculated Franklin half dollar for $2.50.[13]

August 12, 1974, marked the first strike ceremony at the Philadelphia Mint. Dennis Williams, in attendance, remarked, "the coin is a lot better than my original design."[14] The coins that were produced at the first strike ceremony — based on Williams' design and Gasparro's galvano — were immediately placed on board a jet with Mint Director Brooks and they were unveiled before crowds assembled at the 83rd Anniversary Convention of the American Numismatic Association.

(Pictured L to R) Leonor K. Sullivan, Dennis R. Williams, Mint Director Mary T. Brooks.

The coins were unique in a number of respects, and these proof or specimen pieces are distinctive for an entirely different reason. Walter Breen notes in his authoritative *Complete Encyclopedia of U.S. and Colonial Coins* that these initial proofs were produced without a mint mark. He notes that they are "probably silver clad" — though it may be confirmed that they were in fact struck in silver-clad materials. Breen further notes that three specimens were known; the first of which he claims went to President Ford, the second to his Appointment Secretary, and the third to the Bureau of the Mint.

If there is some confusion as to who has these specimens (if indeed they survive at all) it can easily be forgiven: just five days earlier, Richard Nixon was the first President of the United States to ever resign from office, given the choice between that and impeachment.

There is a subsequent history to the bicentennial coins, and one that is interesting insofar as the pieces were formally presented to the President. On November 18, 1974, Mint Director Brooks met at the White House with President Ford, John W. Warner, and an assembled crowd to formally announce to the public — as opposed to the numismatists — bicentennial coins. Mrs. Brooks said, "The dollar is made by a student, and he had the Liberty Bell on the moon. He was a student in an art school in Columbus, Ohio." (Presidential Documents, Gerald Ford, 1974, page 1439.)

The note accompanying the remarks shows that "Mrs. Brooks and Mr. Warner presented the President with first strikes of the newly designed bicentennial coins," thus giving some indication that these pieces — without the mint mark — were not melted as Breen perhaps suspects.

Almost as soon as the first of the bicentennial dollars was struck, mint production officials in the Office of Technology recognized that the design was fine for proof coinage production, all doubly struck, but did not lend itself well to high-speed mass production. Minor changes were made on the obverse though the majority of them were permitted on the reverse to facilitate that type of production. Two varieties of these dollars resulted.

The first variety has the thick, block style letters created by Dennis R. Williams. It has a nearly closed E with a straight tail on the R; the second variety has a thinner and much more contoured lettering which is more typical of the lettering used on the obverse, but distinctively different from a colonial type design created by Williams.

As a historical post script, the debate over the silver coins proved problematical. Indeed 60 million silver-clad coins proved wildly optimistic — there was simply no market for 20 million dollars, or, for that matter, the other denominations. In fact, even at the rolled-back level of 45 million — 15 million apiece — the market place was not prepared to absorb them given the then price of silver and interest in the coins.

Although 15 million were produced, many were melted, and the actual number that remains was further reduced by the price of silver in 1980 when it topped out a $48 an ounce — making the bicentennial silver coins an attractive melting target.

Of additional historical interest is that the type two variety, also produced in silver-clad, has at least one known example without a mint mark — the same style of rarity as was created in the first strike ceremonies in 1974.

Mintage figures for the bicentennial dollars are:

1776-1976 Copper-nickel clad, variety I	4,019,000
1776-1976 Copper-nickel clad, variety II	113,318,000
1776-1976D Copper-nickel clad, variety I	21,048,710
1776-1976D Copper-nickel clad, variety II	82,179,564
1776-1976S Copper-nickel clad, variety I Proof	2,845,450
1776-1976S Copper-nickel clad, variety II Proof	4,149,730
1776-1976S Silver clad, variety I	4,294,081
1776-1976S Silver clad, variety II Proof	3,262,970 [15]

1776-1976 Bicentennial Proof Eisenhower Dollar

Quietly, as the bicentennial year ended, the design receded into the American consciousness.

It forms a fascinating sidelight to collecting of dollars, and without question forms a bridge between early non-circulating legal tender commemorative pieces from 1892 to 1954, and those of the present era whose only basis came based upon the success of the Mint's bicentennial program.

Footnotes:

1. Ganz, "200 Years of Freedom: the Story of How the United States Got Its Bicentennial Coinage," 88 *The Numismatist* 499 (1975), revised and updated in *14 Bits: A Legal and Legislative History of America's Bicentennial Coinage*, page 3,4, 1976.

2. American Revolution Bicentennial Commission Advisory Panel on Coins and Medals, plenary session, September 29, 1970, transcript of proceedings at page 25.

3. *Ibid*, pages 25, 26.

4. *Ibid*., page 43.

5. *Ibid*., page 69.

6. Letter of October 1, 1970, reprinted in Hearings before the Subcommittee on Consumer Affairs and Coinage of the House Committee on Banking and Currency, 92nd Congress, First Session, on H. R. 7987 (June 29, 1971) page 52.

7. House Bicentennial Coinage hearings, page 29.

8. House Bicentennial Hearings, page 60.

9. Interview of the Honorable Mary T. Brooks, Washington, D.C., January 16, 1974; quoted in Ganz, *14 Bits, A Legal and Legislative History of America's Bicentennial Coinage*, page 41, at footnote 367.

10. Ganz, "Senate Unit OK's Plan for Silver Bicentennial Coins," *Numismatic News Weekly*, June 3, 1973, page 1-6.

11. *Congressional Record*, July 11, 1973 and Ganz, "Ownership of Gold, Bicentennial Coin Approved by Senate", *Numismatic News Weekly*, July 24, 1973, pages 1 and 30.

12. Ganz, "Three New Coins are Born," *COINage* Magazine, July 1974, pages 32 through 42 (interviews with three designers).

13. Ganz, "Three Coins are Born," *COINage* Magazine, July 1974, page 36 (interview at the White House).

14. "First Bicentennial Coinage Struck," *Coin World*, August 28, 1974, page 1.

15. Yeoman, *A Guidebook of United States Coins*, 44th edition 1991, P. 182; Breen, *Encyclopedia of U.S. and Colonial Coins* (1988). p. 464, 465.

Selected Bibliography and Listing of Selected Primary Source Documents

Feb. 15, 1972, Pub. L. 92-228, 86 Stat. 37.
Bicentennial medallic commemoration authorized.

Oct. 18, 1973, Pub. L. 93-127, 87 Stat. 456, 31 U.S.C.
Bicentennial coinage legislation (creates new reverse for quarter, half dollar and dollar, authorizes dual-date obverse, and silver-clad collector coins)

Pub. L. 93-179, Dec. 11, 1973, 87 Stat. 697
American Revolution Bicentennial Administration created as successor to Bicentennial Commission.

Dec. 11, 1973, Pub. L. 93-179, 87 Stat. 704.
Bicentennial medal program curtailed.

Pub. L. 93-441, Oct. 11, 1974, 88 Stat. 1262
Authorizes transfer of 10 percent of Ike dollar sales to Eisenhower college; authorizes date changes for Bicentennial coins; allows compositional change in cent to zinc-copper until 1977.

Dec. 26, 1974, Pub. L. 93-541.
Amends Bicentennial legislation to permit simultaneous production of Bicentennial coinage and other dates during calendar year 1975 and gives Mint additional time to produce the whole 45 million silver-clad commemorative collector issues.

Bicentennial medals. Hearing on H.R. 7987, 6/29/71 (House Banking Subcommittee on Consumer Affairs).

Bicentennial coinage, Hearing on H.R. 5244, 5/2-3/73, House of Representatives, Subcomm. on Consumer Affairs, House Banking Committee.

Hearing on S. 422 and others, 6/6/73, Ad Hoc Subcommittee on Minting & Coinage of the Senate Banking Committee

H. Rept. 93-391) 9/12/73; 10/4/73;
S. Rept. 93-144) 7/11/73; 10/4/73;
Conference Rept. H. Rept. 93-521

"Numismatics and the Law," *The Coin World Almanac*, 3d edition (1978); 4th edition (1984); 5th ed., 1987 (pp 43-144); 6th ed. (1990).

"Toward a Revision of the Minting and Coinage Laws of the United States," 26 *Cleveland State Law Review*, 175-257 (1977).

14 Bits: A legal and legislative history of 31 U.S.C. 324d-324i (1976)

"Proposing the Authorization of a Gold Coin: Writing a Final Chapter to the Bicentennial," *Congressional Record*, June 11, 1975 p. S-10330-1 (daily ed.).

"Treasury & Federal Officials Scramble to Explain Inadvisability of Bi' Gold Coin," *Congressional Record*, June 11, 1975 p. S-10331-2 (daily ed.).

"200 Years of Freedom: The Story of America's Bicentennial Coinage" vol. 88, *The Numismatist*, p.499 *ff.* (June-Dec., 1975).

David L. Ganz — Summary of Legal Writings

Among his writings in the numismatic area of the law are: "Valuation of Coin Collection," 5 *Proof of Facts* 3rd 577-655 (1989); "Toward a Revision of the Minting and Coinage Laws of the United States," 26 *Cleveland State Law Review*, 175,257 (1977); "Probative Value of 'Currency Dating' for Income in Respect of a Decedent," 51 *N.Y. State Bar J.* 487-495 (1978); "Regulation of the Coin Industry: An Overview," 1 *Review of Numismatics and the Law* 12-16 (1981); "Numismatics and the Law," in *Coin World Almanac*, 3d ed. (1978), pp. 47-110; 4th ed. (1984), pp. 53-129; 5th ed. (1987), pp. 43-144, 6th ed. (1990), pp. 47-164; "Dollar Coin Controversy Brewing on Front Burner — Decade of Discussion at End?" 136 *Cong. Record* E1634-04 (May 21, 1990); "A New Silver Coin from the U.S. Mint" *Congressional Record*, August 8, 1984, p. 10064 (daily ed.); "A 1984 Morgan Dollar? — Congress Considers Some Exciting New Ideas," August 2, 1983, pp. 11367-8 (daily ed.); "Drop dollar bills; we need $1 coins," *USA Today* May 23, 1990, p. 10A (Guest Columnist, "Face-Off").

He is also the author of a number of other legal publications, including "Legal Ethics: When A Lawyer's Obligation begins (and Ends)," 125 *N.J. Law J.* 1742 (June 28, 1990); "A Mingles Agreement," in Irwin, *Mingles: A Home Buying Guide for Unmarried Couples* (McGraw-Hill, 1984); "Rent Control," in R. Irwin, ed., *Handbook of Property Management*, (N.Y.: McGraw-Hill, 1986) pp. 333-350; "The United Nations and the Law of the Sea," 26 *Int'l & Comparative Law Quarterly* 1-53 (1977), and others.

***

CHAPTER 72

Susan B. Anthony Dollar

by John W. Highfill, NLG

Susan Brownell Anthony was born on February 15, 1820. Her early life was spent in the Battensville, New York, where she was educated as a Quaker. Her father encouraged her to teach and she began her 15-year education career in Rochester, New York, when she was 15.

Her career as a teacher gradually ended when she became active in the temperance movement from 1848 to 1853, helping form the Women's State Temperence Society of New York. It was in 1851 that she met Elizabeth Cady Stanton, who was already working for women's rights. Elizabeth Stanton wrote speeches while raising her young children, and Susan B. Anthony delivered them throughout the New York area. They worked together during the years 1854 to 1860 to reform the New York State laws which discriminated against women. In conjunction with these activities she became an agent of the American Anti-Slavery Society which she supported until 1861. During the Civil War she founded the Women's Loyal League to promote freedom for all slaves.

After the war, she became convinced that the road to women's rights must start with the right to vote. In 1869 she helped organize the National Woman Suffrage Association. The organization's primary purpose and goal was to bring about a constitutional amendment which would allow women to vote.

Their newspaper, *Revolution*, addressed the injustices and discriminations suffered by women as well as their desired rights. This publication coupled with intensified public speeches and protests brought much attention and interest to the fight. The dictum under which the newspaper existed was, "The true 'republicmen', their rights and nothing more; women, their rights and nothing less."

She traveled outside the country and while in Europe, she helped local activists form the International Council of Women in late 1880's. Back in the United States, she worked persistently toward her goals until the age of 80, when she cut back to a partial schedule of speeches and lectures for the National American Woman Suffrage Association. In 1904 she organized the International Woman Suffrage Alliance.

She spent the majority of her adult life in the long struggle to win, for women, the right to vote. It was somewhat sad that she did not live long enough to see the Nineteenth Amendment adopted (on August 26, 1920). When Susan B. Anthony died in Rochester, New York, on March 13, 1906, Women's Suffrage was a reality in four states, as well as in New Zealand and Australia.

The "Birth" of the Anthony Dollar

After the Eisenhower dollar had been in production for approximately five years, various political comments began to surface which indicated a new coin on the horizon. Frank MacDonald, temporary mint director, responded to public rumors with the announcement that the mint was studying the potential for a smaller size dollar coin (possibly with 11 sides) through the Research Triangle Institute. Another mint official was reported to have said, "Eisenhower dollars are too big and bulky." The size being considered was between that of a half dollar and a quarter.

The Research Triangle Institute's September 15, 1976 recommendation consisted of three parts. One was to reduce the diameter of the one dollar coin; the second was to eliminate the half dollar; and the third was to eliminate the one cent coin by 1980. These recommendations were not the only ones taken into consideration by Mary Brooks, who was the new director of the mint.

The vending industry was also looking into the situation and seemed to favor a dollar sized token, although it would consider a reduced size round dollar token. In any case the cost of upgrading vending machines would be substantial, and would have to be carefully planned and coordinated with the U.S. Treasury if "official" coinage was going to be used.

Nevada casinos were also very interested in the future and fate of the Eisenhower dollar and any possible replacement. Their tables were equipped to handle the Eisenhower dollar or private token of 38.1 millimeters. A significantly smaller dollar would require great expense to upgrade their equipment, and generated much concern as to the long-term implications of these decisions.

Analysis by the U.S. mint was focusing on a smaller dollar coin with ten or eleven sides and a weight that would make it easy to differentiate from a quarter. The estimated cost per dollar was about three cents, with an estimated life of 15 years. This was compared to the Bureau of Engraving's reported cost of less than three cents for a Federal Reserve Note with an estimated life of less than 18 months. The future intent was very clear. The U.S. Treasury was intending to introduce a smaller dollar as a new circulating coin that would eventually replace the one dollar bill in this country.

Finally, the Treasury published a paper entitled *A New Smaller Dollar Coin — Technical Considerations*. This paper focused upon a smaller dollar coin, and seemed to attribute the lack of circulation of the Eisenhower dollar to its traditional dollar size. The big users of these dollars were members of the casino industry, and those who were looking for a souvenir. It was later learned (in 1980 when the big silver boom occurred) that many people were holding Ike dollars on the belief that they contained silver. As these dollars came out of hiding and were offered for their silver content, thousands of disappointed people found out the truth — no silver in the Ikes.

The legislative branch began to take a more prominent interest in the proceedings in 1977. Michael Blumenthal, Secretary of the Treasury, in early 1977 told the House Committee on Banking, Finance and Urban Affairs that the U.S. Treasury was willing to support a smaller dollar coin. The House Banking Subcommittee on Historic Preservation and Coinage also became interested in the situation, noting that the Office of Management and Budget was not taking any action.

Focus on size began to give way to a new concern: the design of the new dollar coin. The current proposal presented by Blumenthal was a Gasparro design of a modernized Flowing Hair type Liberty such as the one appearing on the 1794 dollar. This design proposal was criticized by Senator William Proxmire (D-Wis), who was much more favorably impressed with a commemorative design. There were many supporters in the House of Representatives who advocated a picture of Susan B. Anthony; a position that gathered strength throughout early 1978.

Blumenthal continued his "crusade" with a draft bill to the Senate. The purpose of this bill was to reduce the size of the dollar coin. Interestingly enough, the bill also advocated the continuance of the Eisenhower dollar with silver content. Protests immediately came from the ABA (American Bankers Association) in the House of Representatives during May of 1978. But the bottom line is that the U.S. Treasury had gathered enough legislative support to present a winning case for the smaller dollar coin.

The final version of the necessary bill (H.12904) was submitted by House member Mary Rose Oakar (D-Ohio) in late July 1978. The House Banking, Finance and Urban Affairs Committee accepted a recommendation for a smaller dollar measuring 26.5 millimeters in diameter, portraying Susan B. Anthony. The commemoration of Anthony was approved by the Senate Banking Committee in early August. Senator Proxmire then presented the bill that paved the way for the design of the smaller Anthony dollar in late August 1978.

The design of the Susan B. Anthony dollar was made by Frank Gasparro, chief engraver of the U.S. Mint. His initials appear below the portrait on the obverse and below the eagle on the reverse. Susan B. Anthony was the first woman explicitly portrayed on a United States circulated coin.

His obverse presented the portrait of Susan B. Anthony in profile. Her hair was in the familiar bun with firm and focused features in the portrait. The word "LIBERTY" appeared at the top of the obverse with the words, "IN GOD WE TRUST" to the right of the coin. The date of issue was at the bottom below the bust in the center, with the mint mark (either P, D or S) located above her right shoulder. The thirteen stars were presented in a circular array with six stars on the right hand and seven stars on the left.

The American eagle was the feature of the reverse. This is the same eagle that appears on the Eisenhower dollar, with the same inscription, adapted from the Apollo IX insignia designed by Michael Collins and James Cooper from NASA.

This design and smaller size was advanced in the legislation which President Jimmy Carter signed into law on October 10, 1978. The three mints at Philadelphia, Denver and San Francisco made their preparations for the 1979 debut of the Susan B. Anthony dollar.

The initial composition of the coin consisted of a copper core with a clad sandwich layer of copper and nickel. The diameter of the Anthony dollar was 26.5 millimeters which is somewhat larger than a quarter, but smaller than a half dollar. The edge of the issue was reeded, and the interior edge of the coin presented an 11-sided rim. The purpose of the polygonal rim was to distinguish the dollar coin from the quarter which was only slightly smaller.

Production and Circulation of the Anthony Dollar

In the first year of production, 761,490,919 Anthony dollars were produced at the three mints including 3,677,175 San Francisco mint Proofs. After the initial interest by the public and collectors in the coins, nobody seemed to want them on a circulating basis. Thus the U.S. Treasury was once again left with a hoard of hundreds of millions of unwanted dollar coins.

It seemed as if some people were just waiting in the wings for an opportunity to express their negative opinions over the coin. The press went to work publishing reports featuring their "concerns" over the size of the coin. It was easily mistaken for a quarter in change. Changemaking machines and vending machines either rejected "Susies" as counterfeits or ate them as quarters. Some women's rights advocates were concerned that the coin picturing a female was partially responsible for its unpopularity. Some thought the portrait was too prettified, others too ugly.

The legislature was not silent either. The Dollar Coin Enhancement Act was introduced as a bill by Jerry Lewis (R-Calif) to cease production of the Anthony dollar and recall all pieces. This bill did not gain the required support but the point was made.

The U.S. Treasury responded to this bombardment of protest with a $655,000 publicity campaign designed to educate the public and promote the Anthony dollar. U.S. Post Offices presented the coins (unless they were refused) in change at their facilities. Approximately 15 million Anthony dollars reached circulation in this manner. But the merchants were returning them to the banks as fast as they were received in business transactions.

In late fall 1980, the Treasury experimented on military personnel overseas, by paying them only in $2 bills and "Susies", while PXs rounded up prices to multiples of 5 cents to phase out the cent. After the Deutsche Bank valued "Susies" at 1 Deutschmark apiece, while paper dollars traded at 1.75 DM, protests followed, and the Treasury dropped the policy in January 1981.

The size of the coin and the way it was forced upon the American public probably were the main contributions to its short life as a minted issue. There was never a great demand for purposes of circulation and public usage.

Nevertheless, the Mint proceeded to produce Anthony dollars in 1980 at a reduced pace. Then, in 1981, only coins destined for the 1981 Proof and Mint sets were struck, none for circulation. The U.S. Mint proposed some changes intended to give the Anthony dollar new life. The proposal for a change in the composition of the coin to give it a brown or brass hue involved adding silicon. There was also a suggestion to place a large number "1" on the reverse in place of the eagle. Both of these were designed to make the coin more easily distinguishable while circulating.

Then the action that virtually everyone was expecting took place. The funds to continue the Anthony dollar were not placed into the 1982 budget. The Susan B. Anthony dollar was officially dropped and the paper dollar has not been challenged since. This made 1979, 1980 and 1981 the years of record for the Susan B. Anthony dollar. The mintage figures for the Anthony dollar are presented here.

Year	Mintage
1979-P	360,222,000
1979-D	288,015,744
1979-S Proof	3,677,175
1979-S	109,576,000
1980-P	27,610,000
1980-D	41,628,708
1980-S Proof	3,554,806
1980-S	20,422,000
1981-P	3,000,000 *
1981-D	3,250,000 *
1981-S Proof	4,063,083 *
1981-S	3,492,000 *

* No coins were struck for circulation in 1981. Coins were produced for Proof and Uncirculated Mint sets only.

The grading of the Susan B. Anthony dollar utilizes all the usual categories of surface preservation, strike, luster, and eye appeal. Particular attention should be focused on the cheekbone of Susan B. Anthony, and to the hair above her ear. These areas of the obverse will usually be the first to show wear. On the reverse, pay attention to the eagle's left wing and chest (the same locations that would first show wear on the Eisenhower dollar). Uncs. of 1979 from all three mints are often weak at mouth and nose.

Susan B. Anthony Varieties

Although there were only three years of coinage, varieties have emerged to pique the interest of numismatists. One of these occurred in the proof issue of 1979. The "Filled S" (Type I) and "Clear S" (Type II) proofs exist, with the "Clear S" trading at a substantial premium in Proof-65 or better condition.

The "Filled S" (Type I) coin when observed gives the impression that the "S" mint mark was filled in. This was due to the extended use of the old San Francisco Mint punch which, as used, gave an unattractive and rather undefined mint mark. There were unsuccessful attempts made to encourage the creation of a new punch prior to the striking of the Anthony dollar proofs of 1979. During 1979, this offensive mint mark punch finally became unusable, and a new one was ordered. The Official mintage for the "Clear S" variety was about 500,000, with the mint sets delivered in late 1979 containing approximately 350,000 examples. The fate of the remaining 150,000 is unknown. By the way, die variety collectors should know that extensive die polishing for the proof issues eventually resulted in the "third star" variety (with the third star markedly smaller than the other two).

The new "S" mint punch was quite clearer and provided the "Clear S" (Type II) proof examples later in 1979. There are definite indentations in both the upper and lower loops of the "S" mint mark. Thus the key points for identification of Types I and II proofs are the rather undefined "Filled S" with straight edges on the right and left edges of the letter on Type I, versus the well-defined "Clear S" with openings on both the upper and lower loops on Type II..

Fate struck again in 1981 for the San Francisco proof Anthony issues. In this year the "S" die punch broke, and another mint mark punch was made. Therefore, we have the Type I and Type II "S" proofs for the 1981-S coins as well. Additional similarities include the less defined "S" for Type I specimens, and a much smaller mintage for Type II (making the Type II more valuable). The "third star" variety for the 1981-S proof Type II also exists due to overpolishing of the die.

Another of the Anthony varieties originated in Philadelphia in late 1979. A modification in the design of the coin was made in order to widen the rim on the obverse. The widening of the border rim came about as a result of public reaction to the size of the dollar and its confusion with the existing quarter coinage. This new design featuring the wide rim with the date nearly touching was first struck with the "P" mint mark very late in the year. The original "far date" design carried a date with thick numbers away from the obverse rim (a "thin" numbers variety also exists for the "far date" design). The modified "near date" design continued for all Susan B. Anthony dollars issued for the years 1980 and 1981. All numismatists agree that the 1979-P "near date" struck with the wide border rim is a scarce item with a substantial premium paid for ownership.

To summarize, there are 16 coins currently required to "complete" a set of Anthony dollars as of this writing. First there are the business strikes and proofs for the years 1979 through 1981. Then add the 1979-P "wide border" or "near date" variety to the more common "far date" variety. Next, the 1979-D with a broken lower serif on the "D". Finally the Proof mint mark varieties (Type I and II "S" mint marks) for both 1979 and 1981.

This ends the story of the U.S. dollar produced for circulation, which began in 1794 with the Flowing Hair design, and ended in 1981 with the Anthony commemorative design. However, this was not the end for the U.S. dollar coin, since the modern commemorative and bullion silver dollars have emerged to take their place. The U.S. silver dollar is still very much alive and thriving!

***

CHAPTER 73

Commemorative and Modern Silver Dollars

by John W. Highfill, NLG

The commemorative era of silver dollars produced in the United States presents a fine collection of attractive coins issued for several different events and reasons. The first of these is the popular Lafayette silver dollar issued in 1900. Quality specimens are hard to come by and command a price tag commensurate with its scarcity. On the other hand, collectors of contemporary commemorative coinage possess well struck and attractively packaged issues ready for display. Also, the cost of acquisition for most contemporary items is modest and within the reach of most collectors. Yet another reason for many Americans to purchase these offerings is to support the cause the coins promote.

The designs are not nearly as stereotyped as those required for circulation. In addition, the size of the silver dollar piece is excellent for the imaginative designs built around the theme of the piece or set. Finally, it provides an opportunity for the numismatic community to admire and own coins designed by a number of sculptors whose work might not otherwise be represented on any United States coinage.

This chapter explores the modern commemorative silver dollars as well as the Silver Eagle bullion silver dollar.

The Lafayette Silver Dollar

Although a more complete discussion of the Lafayette dollar is presented earlier in this book, a brief entry is made here in order to properly include this dollar among the United States dollar commemorative issues. One purpose of the piece was to commemorate Lafayette. Another was to aid the United States participation in the 1900 Paris Exposition in France through financing of Paul Bartlett's equestrian statue of Lafayette. A final objective was to commemorate the centennial of George Washington's death.

Charles E. Barber's design presents the heads of Washington and Lafayette on the obverse with the words UNITED STATES OF AMERICA and LAFAYETTE DOLLAR appearing on the perimeter of the coin. The reverse features an equestrian statue of Lafayette based upon Bartlett's piece which was not yet finished at the time, accounting for the differences between the two. The words ERECTED BY THE YOUTH OF THE UNITED STATES IN HONOR OF GEN. LAFAYETTE, surround the statue with PARIS 1900 at the bottom.

The coinage by each mint for the 1900 Lafayette dollar follows.

Date	Mintage	Proof Mintage
1900	36,026	None

Modern Commemorative Silver Dollars

The first set of contemporary silver dollar commemorative coins was issued in connection with the twenty third Olympiad held in Los Angeles in the summer of 1984. The coins were prepared to help defray the cost of the Games as well as to provide a collectible momento of the event.

This set consisted of two coins, one design issued in 1983 and the other in 1984. Each of the active mints, Philadelphia, Denver and San Francisco, participated in each of the two years. Thus a complete set of the Olympic silver dollars amounted to six coins. There was also a set of gold commemorative coins produced for the Olympiad.

The first of the Olympiad coins was designed by the chief engraver of the mint, Elizabeth Jones. She prepared a design featuring a Greek discus thrower on the obverse with the body of an American eagle on the reverse. Her obverse of the traditional Olympian was inspired by the ancient sculptor Myron. The five Olympic rings and the Olympiad identification are also present on the obverse together with the inscription LIBERTY, IN GOD WE TRUST and the date and mint mark. The reverse eagle is surrounded by the words, UNITED STATES OF AMERICA above and ONE DOLLAR below. The final touch is the traditional E PLURIBUS UNUM placed to the left of the eagle.

The coinage by each mint of the 1983 Discus Thrower commemorative silver dollar follows.

Date	Mintage	Proof Mintage:
1983-P	294,543	
1983-D	174,014	
1983-S	174,014	1,577,025

The second Olympic silver dollar commemorative was produced in 1984 based upon a design by Robert Graham which complemented the 1983 design. His design replicated the "Gateway" sculpture he created and set in front of the Los Angeles Memorial Coliseum. The obverse of two ceremonial Olympians has the Memorial Coliseum in the background. The obverse also announces the Olympiad with the words LIBERTY, IN GOD WE TRUST and the date and mint mark. The reverse depicts a perched eagle with the inscription, UNITED STATES OF AMERICA above and ONE DOLLAR to the right. E PLURIBUS UNUM is set below the eagle.

The coinage by each mint of the 1984 Olympic Coliseum commemorative silver dollar was approximately the same as for the 1983 offering.

Date	Mintage	Proof Mintage:
1984-P	217,954	
1984-D	116,675	
1984-S	116,675	1,801,210

The Statue of Liberty silver dollar commemorative piece was issued in 1986 to memorialize Ellis Island and its role as the "Gateway to America." The issue consisted of two silver coins bearing the Statue of Liberty design. The Philadelphia and San Francisco mints participated in producing the regular and proof commemorative set. The total Statue of Liberty offering also included a commemorative clad half dollar and five dollar commemorative gold piece.

The design for this commemorative was by John Mercanti, a U. S. Mint artist. He was assisted by Matthew Peloso in modeling the reverse. His design was inspired by the Statue of Liberty and features it on the obverse of the coin. The background consists of the Ellis Island Immigration Center with the words, ELLIS ISLAND and GATEWAY TO AMERICA presented to the left of the statue. LIBERTY, IN GOD WE TRUST and the date and mint mark complete the obverse definition. The reverse presents the torch of Liberty centered on the coin together with the famous Emma Lazarus lines, GIVE ME YOUR TIRED, YOUR POOR, YOUR HUDDLED MASSES YEARNING TO BREATHE FREE. The reverse is completed with UNITED STATES OF AMERICA above the torch, ONE DOLLAR and E PLURIBUS UNUM below.

The coinage by each mint of the 1986 Statue of Liberty silver dollar follows.

Date	Mintage	Proof Mintage
1986-P	723,635	
1986-S		6,414,638

The next commemorative silver dollar to be produced was the Constitution Bicentennial. This innovative piece was designed by Patricia Lewis Verani to commemorate the 200th anniversary of the United States Constitution. It was issued in conjunction with a smaller five-dollar gold commemorative piece.

The coin's obverse features a page of parchment with the calligraphic inscription *We The People* and a quill pen. The words, THE U.S. CONSTITUTION 200TH ANNIVERSARY, and 1787 LIBERTY 1987 together with the motto IN GOD WE TRUST complete the obverse design. The reverse displays a unique assembly of Americans from many lifestyles and periods of U.S. history. The wording includes E PLURIBUS UNUM at the top, DOLLAR 1 in the lower middle above UNITED STATES OF AMERICA located at the bottom.

The coinage by each mint of the 1987 Constitution Bicentennial commemorative silver dollar follows.

Date	Mintage	Proof Mintage
1987-P	451,629	
1987-S		2,747,116

The twenty-fourth Olympiad in Seoul, South Korea, was the inspiration for the 1988 Olympic commemorative silver dollar. A five dollar gold commemorative piece was also issued in honor of U.S. participation in this event.

Patricia Lewis Verani was again called upon to design the obverse of this coin. She created an obverse featuring the lighting of the ceremonial Olympic torch. Wording included OLYMPIAD at the top, LIBERTY at the bottom and IN GOD WE TRUST with the date on other side.

The reverse was designed by Sherl J. Winter, a mint sculptor and engraver. Her reverse centered the five Olympic interlocking rings between two branches. The inscription UNITED STATES OF AMERICA surrounds the coin. The 1 DOLLAR denomination is shown at the top, with U S A just above the Olympic rings. E PLURIBUS UNUM appears at the bottom of the reverse to complete the design.

Each mint's output of 1988 Olympiad commemorative silver dollar follows. The Denver mint participated in commemorative silver dollar production for the first time since 1984.

Date	Mintage	Proof Mintage
1988-D	191,368	
1988-S		1,354,366

The Congressional Bicentennial commemorative silver dollar was issued in 1989 to celebrate the 200th anniversary of the Congress of the United States. The coin was issued in conjunction with the Congress Bicentennial half dollar and five dollar gold piece.

The coin was designed by artist William Woodward and features the Statue of Freedom on the obverse. This statue is found at the peak of the dome on the Capitol building in Washington, D.C. LIBERTY appears around the top of the obverse with the dual dates 1789 and 1989 on the left and right sides respectively, and IN GOD WE TRUST around the bottom. The reverse presents the Mace of the House of Representatives. This staff is always on the House floor when the House is in session. An eagle sits on the world globe on top of the Mace. Wording includes UNITED STATES OF AMERICA around the top, E PLURIBUS UNUM to the left of the Mace, BICENTENNIAL OF THE CONGRESS to the right, and ONE DOLLAR denomination at the bottom of the reverse.

Production figures for each mint mark of the 1989 Congress Bicentennial commemorative silver dollar follow.

Date	Mintage	Proof Mintage
1989-D (Clad)	163,753	
1989-D (Silver)	135,203	
1989-S (Clad)		767,897
1989-S (Silver)		762,198

The next in the series of modern commemoratives is the Eisenhower Centennial silver dollar. This coin was issued to commemorate the 100th anniversary of the birth of Dwight David Eisenhower, who was the 34th president of the United States.

The obverse design was created by Mint engraver John Mercanti. It features two profiles of Eisenhower, one facing right superimposed over the left profile of Eisenhower as a five-star general. Wording includes EISENHOWER CENTENNIAL around the top, LIBERTY to the left of the two profiles, IN GOD WE TRUST to the right and the dual dates 1890-1990 at the bottom.

The reverse design by Marcel Jovine depicts the home of Eisenhower at Gettysburg. This home is now a National Historical Site. UNITED STATES OF AMERICA appears around the top with E PLURIBUS UNUM under the Eisenhower home and ONE DOLLAR denomination at the bottom.

Production figures for each mint mark of the 1990 Eisenhower commemorative silver dollar follow. Notice that the commemorative strikes were made at the West Point mint facility.

Date	Mintage	Proof Mintage
1990-W	240,677	
1990-P	5,840,110	1,139,134

Date	Mintage	Proof Mintage
1991-W	240,720	
1991-P	1,139,887	635,843

The first commemorative to be issued in 1991 as authorized by the Mount Rushmore National Memorial Coin Act was the Mount Rushmore commemorative set. Its ceremonial debut took place on February 15, at Ford's Theater in Washington, D.C. This commemorative issue honoring the 50th anniversary of the Mount Rushmore National Memorial contains a silver dollar, gold half eagle and copper-nickel half dollar.

The obverse of the silver dollar was designed by Marika Somogyi, Berkeley, California, while the engraving was by Chester Y. Martin, sculptor/engraver of the U.S. Mint. The obverse design features Mount Rushmore itself with the busts of the four presidents: George Washington, Thomas Jefferson, Theodore Roosevelt and Abraham Lincoln. Mount Rushmore itself exists in Black Hills, South Dakota, where the busts were carved into granite on site by Gutzon Borglum and his staff during a 14 year period of time. The words displayed on the obverse includes LIBERTY above the monument, 1991 just below the busts, GOLDEN ANNIVERSARY MOUNT RUSHMORE NATIONAL MEMORIAL surrounding the lower half of the monument, and the motto IN GOD WE TRUST presented on the center portion of the wreath at the bottom of the piece.

The reverse was both designed and engraved by Frank Gasparro, a name well known to all as he was the former chief sculptor/engraver at the U.S. Mint. This design presents the Seal of the United States superimposed upon a map of the Union and embellished by rays emanating from the seal. The legend, UNITED STATES OF AMERICA is around the rim at the top, E PLURIBUS UNUM is under the map, and ONE DOLLAR is seen at the bottom of the coin.

Production figures for the Mount Rushmore are not available as of this writing, but the uncirculated coins were struck by the Philadelphia Mint while the proof examples were produced by the San Francisco Mint. A limit of 2.5 million silver dollars was imposed by the Coin Act.

Date	Mintage	Proof Mintage
1991-P	125,591 *	
1991-S		673,287 *

*** Figures as of September 27,1991**

The second commemorative issued in 1991 was the Korean War silver dollar commemorating the thirty eighth anniversary of the end of the Korean War in 1953. Production began on May 6, 1991, with an elaborate ceremony held at the Philadelphia Mint. First strike at Philadelphia Mint: the Korean War Veterans Memorial coin ... Attending for the ANA, President Ken Hallenbeck, who struck coin the 22nd coin during the ceremony.

The obverse was designed by Mint sculptor/engraver John Mercanti, and features a U.S. soldier advancing up a hill with a background of naval ships complete with F-86 aircraft flying overhead. There are eight stars to the upper right along the rim. The wording includes THIRTY EIGHTH ANNIVERSARY COMMEMORATIVE KOREA together with the motto IN GOD WE TRUST. The double dates of 1953 and 1991 appear at the solder's left foot and LIBERTY is at the bottom.

The reverse was designed (and later redesigned) by James Ferrell, sculptor/engraver of the U.S. Mint. The final design presents a map of Korea divided by the line known as the 38th Parallel. The Yin Yang symbol is placed in South Korea and an eagle's head appears to the right. The denomination ONE DOLLAR is at the top, E PLURIBUS UNUM at the left of the Korean map, and UNITED STATES OF AMERICA appears along the lower rim of the coin.

Uncirculated specimens were produced by the Denver branch mint facility while proof specimens were created by the Philadelphia Mint. Production figures for this commemorative were unavailable as of this writing.

Date	Mintage	Proof Mintage
1991-D	186,189 *	
1991-P		505,741 *

*** Figures as of July 19,1991**

The future of modern commemorative silver dollars looks bright with a wide range of historical events available for commemoration during the coming years. Many designers are hoping for an opportunity to present their work on commemorative coinage. In fact, as of this writing, the U.S. Mint has initiated an open competition for the Olympic commemorative coinage of 1992. The specifications of the proposed one-dollar silver coin include a composition of 90% silver and 10% copper, a diameter of 1.5 inches, a weight of 26.73 grams, and an estimated thickness of 0.116 inches. Collectors are also eager for these issues representing fine workmanship and historical significance.

The United States Silver Eagle

The United States Silver Eagle is often referred to as a "bullion-related" coin together with the Gold American Eagle. The Silver Eagle may be spent as legal tender in this country and is valued at one dollar for this purpose. The Gold American Eagle is also legal tender and comes in a variety of values ($5, $10, $25 and $50).

The design of the Silver Eagle contains something old, something new, something borrowed, but nothing blue. The "something old" is the beautiful Liberty Walking half-dollar obverse designed by Adolph A. Weinman. The "something new" on the reverse was actually developed from "something borrowed." The heraldic eagle design by John Mercanti presents a modern view of the traditional eagle so prominent on the early United States coinage.

The Liberty Walking half dollar which first featured this obverse design (commonly called "Walkers") was produced from 1916 through 1947. On the original coin, the initials of Mr. Weinman were placed under the tip of the wing feathers on the reverse eagle. As there were two designers involved in the case of the Silver Eagle, Mr. Weinman's initials were placed on the obverse on the hem of Miss Liberty's gown.

The Silver Eagle contains one ounce of fine silver. The coin is composed of 99.93 percent silver and .07 percent copper. The coin presents a reeded edge with a diameter of 40.6 millimeters, and it "weighs in" at 31.101 grams. Following is the mintage for each date and mint mark of the United States Silver Eagle.

Date	Mintage	Proof Mintage	Date	Mintage	Proof Mintage
1986-P	5,393,005		1988-S		557,370
1986-S		1,446,778	1989-P	5,203,327	
1987-P	11,442,335		1989-S		617,694
1987-S		904,732	1990-P	5,840,110	
1988-P	5,004,646		1990-S		700,000

There has been an organized and coordinated production and marketing effort by the U.S. Treasury, aimed at matching the number of coins produced with the public orders received. The coins have been rather well received as collectibles, which was the probable intent of the U.S. Treasury in the first place.

Beginning in 1990, there was a significant change in the marketing aspect of the Silver Eagle proof coinage. The "limited edition" concept was used with an established fixed mintage for proof coins. The established ceiling for 1990 proof coinage was set at 700,000. The proof coins were delivered in an encapsulated protective plastic case ready for display together with a certificate of authenticity.

The United States silver dollar is alive and well, albeit in a collectible form rather than as a circulating coin. The current design is very attractive while at the same time preserving tradition. As far as the modern collector is concerned, things are going "just fine."

The Hawaii 1883 Silver Dollar

No procession of silver dollars produced by the United States Mint would be complete without an example of the Hawaiian silver dollar. This coin was one in a group of silver coins in various denominations produced in 1883 by the United States for King Kalakaua I. Minted under authority of the Act of 1874, which allowed the United States Mint to produce coins for other countries, the silver dollar was issued to provide circulating coinage for the islands, on the recommendation of sugar tycoon Claus Spreckels..

The coin's design was approved by then Mint Director Horatio C. Burchard and prepared by Charles E. Barber. The obverse features the bust of King Kalakaua I facing right surrounded by the inscription, KALAKAUA I KING OF HAWAII. The date (1883) is at the bottom. The reverse presents the mantled Hawaiian coat of arms with the denomination AKAHI DALA at the bottom.

Today's numismatists are split in their interpretation as to whether the Philadelphia Mint's Hawaiian dollar is an official U.S. silver dollar. Many collectors do add this dollar to their sets. You should draw your own conclusions.

Production began with six proof sets made at Philadelphia, September 1883; 20 more followed in 1884 for presentation to Hawaiian dignitaries. The San Francisco Mint struck the uncirculated coins between November 17, 1883 and June 1884, from five pairs of dies.

Date	Mintage	Proof Mintage (Sets)
1883	46,348	26

Actually, 500,000 were struck, but 453,622 were recalled and melted (1904 -). After Hawaii became a Territory of the United States, the Treasury decided to replace all Hawaiian coins with regular U.S. coins. [Other Reference — Chapter 26 World's Finest Collections — Lot # 715 Entitled "Finest Known 1885 Hawaiian Dollar and Lot # 716 "Superb Mint State 1883 Dollar"]

***

Leroy Van Allen, NLG

Leroy Van Allen was born in Seattle, Washington, and received bachelor's and master's degrees in electrical engineering from the University of California at Berkeley. During 25 years as an electrical engineer he prepared many studies, technical reports, and analyses of advanced electronic and ship systems and co-authored a book entitled "Arctic Environment and Resources" published by the Arctic Institute of North America.

Since the early 1960s he has been a researcher and writer on U.S. Morgan, Peace and Eisenhower dollars. He is the author of the book "Morgan and Peace Dollar Varieties" privately published in 1965. In 1971, after several years of collaboration, he co-authored with A. George Mallis the book "Guide to Morgan and Peace Dollars" which became the standard reference for these two U.S. coin series. This book was revised in 1976 as "Comprehensive Catalogue and Encyclopedia of U.S. Morgan and Peace Silver Dollars" which received the 1977 "Book of the Year" award by the Numismatic Literary Guild. In 1979 he compiled for the Numismatic Error Collectors of America Club a book entitled "Dollar Varieties and Errors Scrapbook." He has been a regular contributor to numismatic journals treating such subjects as the cause of the Morgan dollar seven over eight tailfeathers variety, the die varieties in the General Services Administration sale of Carson City Morgan dollars, the high value of Eisenhower dollar errors, how Morgan dollar overdates were made, and the causes of prooflike Morgan dollars, die wear and machine strike doubling. He received the 1975 Numismatic Literary Guild Best Writer award from *Coins* magazine. Since 1980 he has been a full time coin dealer specializing in silver dollars.

He is a member and served several terms as president of the Maryland Numismatic Society, served as president of the Numismatic Error Collectors of America, is secretary of the National Silver Dollar Roundtable, and is a member of the American Numismatic Association and Numismatic Literary Guild.

CHAPTER 74

Total Uncirculated Silver Dollars Remaining

by Leroy Van Allen, NLG

Introduction by John W. Highfill

I wish to give credit to Leroy Van Allen for his indispensable research into the die varieties displayed by the Morgan silver dollar series. His unending labor of love and persistence has provided much more reliable and organized data concerning the dies produced and also to the facts behind the annual reports of the Director of the Mint.

Leroy Van Allen has spent a lifetime of numismatics researching these die varieties. For him to give us his "bottom-line" figures on every Morgan and Peace dollar is unheralded. Leroy Van Allen is a close friend of mine. For his recognition, we wish you to take the time to appreciate the magnitude of his work in providing these die variety totals for every date. (It seems inappropriate to put such an important factor in only a little box in the date by date Morgan and Peace analyst.)

The same honor and credits are due to A. George Mallis. THANK YOU VERY MUCH!

Leroy Van Allen reports that the VAM Collector Society is not currently active. This society was founded just after the release of the "VAM" book and met for several years on an annual basis during the ANA convention. The organization was led by First Coin Investors.

The following article appeared in the National Silver Dollar Roundtable Journal — Vol. II, No. 1, November 1984. Leroy Van Allen has updated this article for your knowledge and benefit.

Total Uncirculated Silver Dollars Remaining

As collectors, investors and coin dealers know, there is a tremendous number of uncirculated Morgan and Peace silver dollars around. Several hundred thousand bags of these silver dollars were released by the Treasury Department in the early 1960s. The stock of silver dollars held by the Treasury was cleaned out by 1964 by speculators and investors as the price of silver steadily advanced to $1.29 per ounce when their bullion value equaled their face value. Even twenty-five years later in the late 1980s, bags of silver dollars were still being dumped on the market. Rumors persisted of private hoards of 20 to 200 bags of dollars still in existence. The question is, how many uncirculated Morgan and Peace dollars remain in the hands of collectors, investors and dealers today?

To answer this question, the Treasury Department records on production quantities and amounts in circulation have to be examined. Some 570 million Morgan dollars were minted between 1878 and 1904. About 270 million of these were melted in 1918 and 1919 under the Pittman Act. Another 86 million Morgan dollars were minted in 1921, and 190 million Peace dollars were minted from 1921 to 1935. Over 52 million silver dollars were melted in 1943 and 1944 for wartime uses. About 10 million mutilated and damaged silver dollars were melted by the Treasury Department from 1945 to 1964. Many more millions of circulated and some 1921 Morgan and common date Peace uncirculated silver dollars were also melted commercially during late 1979 and early 1980 when the price of silver soared for a short time to $50 per ounce. In all, over 340 million Morgan and Peace silver dollars were melted.

The total stock of silver dollars was 484,722,100 in 1964 which was later reduced by probably about 10 to 30 million during the 1979 and 1980 silver melts. Thus, something like 250 million dollars still exist, about 60 to 70 million 1921 Morgan dollars exist and about 150 to 160 million Peace dollars exist.

The accompanying charts show the total stock of silver dollars and amounts held by the Treasury Department and in circulation. During the coinage of the Morgan dollar from 1878 through 1904, only about one-fourth to one-eighth of the coins were actually in circulation at any given time. Most silver dollars were held by the Treasury as backing for silver certificate paper, which the public preferred. The vast quantities of silver dollars coined just sat unused in the Treasury vaults to back the silver certificate paper money. This was also true for the Peace silver dollar which never saw much circulation either. Many of the silver dollars released into circulation didn't remain there very long and were returned to the Treasury after just light circulation.

Silver Dollar Distribution *

Date	Total Coinage	In Treasury Backing Silver Certificates	In Treasury In Excess	In Circulation
1885	210,759,431	93,656,716	71,827,005	45,275,710
1895	423,289,309	342,409,504	22,525,713	58,354,092
1905	568,228,865	454,864,708	39,779,821	73,584,336

* From the annual reports of the Director of the Mint.

By the late 1950s only half of the silver dollars were in circulation by Treasury Department figures. Most of these however, were not actually in circulation but were in various commercial bank vaults and private hoards such as the Redfield estate and gambling casinos. Few silver dollars were actually used regularly by the public in the eastern states. They only saw appreciable circulation in the western states where some of the public preferred hard currency.

Silver Dollar Distribution *

Date	Total Stock	In Treasury	In Reserve Banks	In Circulation
1957	488,435,800	229,200,021	6,628,920	252,606,859
1964	484,722,100	2,943,295	57,866	481,720,939

* From the annual reports of the Director of the Mint.

Based on the relatively low quantities of silver dollars that were in circulation until the 1950s, it is estimated that about one-sixth to one-fifth of the pre-1921 Morgan dollars never reached circulation. It is also estimated that one-fifth to one-quarter of the 1921 Morgan and Peace dollars never circulated. This would mean that about 40 to 50 million pre-1921 Morgans, 10 to 50 million 1921 Morgans and 30 to 40 million Peace dollars exist today in uncirculated condition. Total uncirculated Morgan and Peace dollars are estimated at 80 to 100 million out of a total of about 450 to 470 million surviving silver dollars.

This may seem like an excessively large estimate of the quantity of uncirculated silver dollars to some people. But it must be remembered that almost 3 million uncirculated Carson City dollars were held back by the Treasury in 1964 because they were scarce compared to other Morgan dollars. Vastly greater quantities of uncirculated common date S, O, and P mints of pre-1921 Morgans were released and available at that time as well as large quantities of uncirculated 1921-P Morgan and common date Peace dollars of 1922-P and 1923-P.

No other contemporary U.S. coin is available in such quantities in uncirculated condition. Compared to the Barber quarters and halves and the coins of the 1920s, this is a tremendous quantity of surviving uncirculated coins. Gold coins of the comparable time period were too expensive for many people to hoard. Subsidiary coins circulated extensively for commerce with few being held by the Treasury from year to year in uncirculated condition. Not many subsidiary coins were hoarded by rolls and bags throughout the silver dollars production time period. Only the U.S. Government could afford to store millions and millions of silver dollars unused for many decades to back the silver certificates. Whereas silver dollars are available by the rolls and bags, most other contemporary uncirculated coins are traded only by individual pieces.

It is this very availability of the uncirculated silver dollar that such a large coin market has developed with them. At $30 to $50 average price per coin, the value of the uncirculated silver dollars is something like 2 to 3 billion dollars. The 350 to 390 million circulated silver dollars at $10 to $15 per coin represents 3.5 to 6 billion dollars in value. And that makes silver dollars one of the largest segments in the current U.S. coin market.

Appendix

The following chart lists the dies produced for each fiscal year (July 1 - June 30) and mint for the Morgan silver dollar series. Since the fiscal year extends from July 1 of one year to June 30 of the next, the numbers only approximate the quantities of dies used to strike the coins in any given calendar year.

Morgan Dollar Dies Produced *

Year	Philadelphia	New Orleans	San Francisco	Carson City
1878	92	0	192	100
1879	157	40	192	30
1880	199	80	110	25
1881	148	119	200	50
1882	92	50	80	30
1883	127	92	105	20
1884	128	60	80	20
1885	131	124	40	20
1886	161	80	0	0
1887	107	108	8	0
1888	116	136	80	0
1889	104	150	20	10
1890	95	60	80	50
1891	81	100	73	40
1892	15	30	33	30
1893	16	20	30	20
1894	0	20	20	
1895	4	10	38	
1896	40	40	40	
1897	70	50	98	
1898	40	34	58	
1899	37	140	40	
1900	45	230	40	
1901	114	210	80	
1902	136	300	40	
1903	142	180	20	

* The above figures include proof dies.

Morgan Dollar Average Pieces Struck Per Die Pair

The following calculation presents the average pieces struck per die pair produced. This calculation uses totals for the entire Morgan dollar series without production for 1921 (86,730,000).

Total Pieces	Die Pairs	Average No. Strikes Per Die Pair	
260,779,667-P	1,198-P	217,679-P	
186,137,529-O	1,231-O	151,208-O	
109,493,373-S	898-S	121,930-S	
13,862,041-CC	222-CC	62,441-CC	
570,272,610	3,549	160,411	**Sub Totals**
86,730,000			
657,002,610			**Total**

Morgan Dollar Die Varieties

The Morgan dollar die varieties for each year and mint are presented in the following chart.

Year	Die Varieties
1878-P 8TF	33
1878-P 7/8TF	16
1878-P 7TF	54
1878-P 7TF (Rev. 79)	12
1878-CC	26
1878-S	53
1879-P	36
1879-CC	3
1879-CC (C/D)	1
1879-O	28
1879-S	31
1879-S (Rev. 78)	13
1880-P	40
1880-CC	7
1880-CC (Rev. 78)	3
1880-O	39
1880-O (8/7)	9
1880-S	69
1880-S (0/9)	1
1881-P	17
1881-CC	6
1881-O	29
1881-S	53
1882-P	23
1882-CC	6
1882-O	37
1882-S	27
1883-P	15
1883-CC	4
1883-O	39
1883-S	8
1884-P	12
1884-CC	12
1884-O	36
1884-S	8
1885-P	21
1885-CC	4
1885-O	15
1885-S	8
1886-P	20
1886-O	16
1886-S	4
1887-P	17
1887-P (7/6)	1
1887-O	21
1887-O (7/6)	1
1887-S	8
1888-P	19
1888-O	18
1888-S	10
1889-P	22
1889-CC	3
1889-O	18
1889-S	11
1890-P	14
1890-CC	13
1890-O	20
1890-S	25
1891-P	9
1891-CC	4
1891-O	12
1891-S	13
1892-P	7
1892-CC	9
1892-O	11
1892-S	7
1893-P	5
1893-CC	5
1893-O	5
1893-S	1
1894-P	2
1894-O	8
1894-S	7
1895-P	N/A
1895-P (Proof)	3
1895-O	4
1895-S	4
1896-P	21
1896-O	19
1896-S	8
1897-P	10
1897-O	7
1897-S	11
1898-P	10
1898-O	19
1898-S	13
1899-P	6
1899-O	30
1899-S	13
1900-P	23
1900-O	33
1900-O/CC	7
1900-S	12
1901-P	11
1901-O	32
1901-S	9
1902-P	11
1902-O	38
1902-S	11
1903-P	9
1903-O	5
1903-S	31
1904-P	8
1904-O	8
1904-S	5
1921-P (M)	25
1921-D	7
1921-S	7

Peace Dollar Die Varieties

The Peace dollar die varieties for each year and mint are presented in the following chart.

Year	Die Varieties	Year	Die Varieties
1921-P	2	1926-D	2
1922-P	11	1926-S	3
1922-D	3	1927-P	1
1922-S	2	1927-D	1
1923-P	8	1927-S	2
1923-D	1	1928-P	1
1923-S	2	1928-S	3
1924-P	5	1934-P	1
1924-S	1	1934-D	5
1925-P	1	1934-S	2
1925-S	1	1935-P	1
1926-P	1	1935-S	3

Morgan Dollar Top 12 Die Varieties (BU)

The next chart lists the top 12 die varieties (BU). These have been selected because they are (1) listed weekly by the Coin Dealer Newsletter, Certified Coin Dealer Newsletter, Coin World and Numismatic News, (2) recognized by both PCGS and NGC grading services, and (3) listed by the Unitrade (ANE) and CCE electronic trading exchanges.

The VAM numbers associated with each of these die varieties has been provided courtesy of Leroy Van Allen and A. George Mallis. These reference numbers are shown after each date.

Die Varieties	Date	VAM Numbers
3	1882-O/S	3,4,5,6,17,23 **
1	1887/6-O	3
1	1879-CC Capped Die	3
1	1887/6-P	2
3	1880-CC Rev. 78	2,4,7
16 *	1878-P 7/8 TF (Weak)	32,33,34,36,37
13	1879-S Rev. 78	4-10,23,24,25,34,35,39
12	1878-P 7TF Rev. 79	200-203,210,215,220-223,230
16 *	1878-P 7/8 TF (Strong)	38,39,40,41,42
33	1878-P 8TF	1-14,14-1 to 14-9,15-23
54	1878-P 7TF Rev. 78	70,79-84,100,110-122,130-133,140-146,160-171,185-188,190,195-199
7	1900-O/CC	7,8,9,10,11,12

* There are 16 die varieties for both types (weak and strong) of the 1878-P 7/8 TF (NOT 32 COMBINED!).

** VAM numbers 6,17 and 23 are sub-varieties of VAM numbers 3,4 and 5.

Major Die Varieties

Editor's note: Wayne Miller has given a great deal to numismatics over the years. It is with thanks that the following personal list of significant Morgan dollar die varieties are presented with permission as contained in Wayne Miller's *Morgan and Peace Dollar Textbook*.

In their monumental work, *A Comprehensive Catalogue and Encyclopedia of U.S. Morgan and Peace Dollars*, Leroy Van Allen and A. George Mallis included descriptions and photographs of more than one thousand die varieties. Since that time an additional seven or eight hundred varieties have been discovered. Most, however, are of interest only to the most avid die variety specialist. The following is a list of die varieties, all visible without magnification, which Wayne Miller feels are of major significance:

1. **1878 8-Tail Feather**. Actually there are over twenty different die varieties of the 1878 8-tail feather dollar. VAM 23 is the most spectacular, with obverse and reverse doubling.
2. **1878-P Third Reverse** (Round Breast). Again, there are many slight die variations among this issue.
3. **1878-7/8** VAM 30 Doubled Talons. Each of the eagle's legs has an extra talon shifted to the left.
4. **1878-7/8** VAM 31, with doubled legs and talons, shifted to the right.
5. **1878-7/8** VAM 33. The eagle's legs are 1 1/2 times normal width with a double set of claws. Rarer still (R-7) is VAM 44, same reverse, triple obverse, plainest in cotton blossoms and leaves.
6. **1878-7/8** VAM 38, doubled LIBERTY with shift to the left — the largest shift of this kind known among Morgan dollars.
7. **1878-7/8** VAM 41, seven tail feather ends showing. Strongest tail feather overstrike known.
8. **1878-7/8** VAM 43, doubled legs and talons shifted to the left.
9. **1879-S** Second Reverse (Flat Breast). Several slight die variations exist.
10. **1880-P 8/7** VAM 6 Variety. The top of the 7 is clearly visible above the second 8. There are several 1880-P overdates; this is the most pronounced.
11. **1880/79-CC**, VAM 4. The 80 is clearly repunched over the 79 in the date. Second reverse with the flat breast design.
12. **1880-CC (8/7 low)**, VAM 6. The 8 is repunched over the 7 in the date with the original 7 punched low. Third reverse, round breast. The scarcest of the major 1880-CC overdate die varieties.
13. **1880-O**, VAM 4. The 80 is repunched over the 79 in the date. Such specimens are often prooflike.
14. **1880-S**, VAM 8 and 9. The 80 is repunched over the 79 in the date.
15. **1882-O/S**, VAM 3, 4, 5 and 6. What appears to be the center shaft of an "S" mintmark is clearly visible within the "O" mintmark. These varieties exhibit very small dots of metal, particularly upon the raised surfaces, due to rusted dies.
16. **1887-P (7/6 overdate)** VAM 2. The remains of the base of the 6 are clearly visible under the 7 of the date.
17. **1887-O** VAM 2, doubled 2 and tripled 7 in date. One of the largest date doubling shifts known. Most specimens are heavily bagmarked.
18. **1887-O (7/6 overdate)** VAM 2. The bottom loop of the 6 is visible at the bottom of the stem of the 7, curving upward All specimens known to the author are flat struck.
19. **1888-O** VAM 4, doubled head variety with two complete sets of lips, chin and nose clearly visible. Very rare in grades above EF.
20. **1889-O** VAM 1A. Clashed die marks on the reverse reveal the "E" of LIBERTY below the eagle's tail feathers on the left side. This phenomenon also occurs among 1886-O and 1891-O dollars but the 1889-O "E" clash is by far the rarest, with fewer than five specimens known in any grade. A partial "E" clash has been found on 1878-P, 1880-P, 1883-O, 1884-P and 1887-P dollars.
21. **1890-CC** VAM 4, the tail bar variety. Extra metal caused by a gouge in the die extends from the junction of the eagle's tail feathers and arrow feathers down to the wreath.
22. **1900-O/CC** VAM's 7 through 12. The remains of the "CC" mintmark are visible under the "O". VAM 7 and VAM 10 are the most common, and evidence the least amount of anomaly.
23. **1901-P** VAM 3, the shifted eagle variety. Much of the eagle is strongly doubled, particularly the tail feathers.
24. **1903-S** VAM 2, with very small mintmark. This phenomenon is also observable among specimens of the 1896-O, 1899-O, 1900-O and 1902-O. With the exception of the 1899-O, these "micro" mintmarked dollars are very rare in grades above VF; even the 1899-O is very scarce in uncirculated condition.
25. **1921-P** VAM 2, infrequent reading. On this variety the edge has about 15 percent fewer reeds per linear inch than normal.

***

CHAPTER 75

United States Dollar Mintage Figures

by John W. Highfill, NLG

This chapter is presented as a reference guide to the mintage figures for each date and mintmark of all dollars produced by the United States Mint. This handy directory includes production information on each U.S. dollar date, type, mintmark, and major die variety, presented in date order.

Continental Currency (1776)

Obverse

Reverse

Date:	Mintage:
1776 "Curency" — Pewter	Unknown
1776 "Curency" — Brass	Unknown
1776 "Curency" — Silver	Unknown
1776 "Currency" — Pewter	Unknown
1776 "Currency" — Pewter, EG FECIT	Unknown
1776 "Currency" — Silver, EG FECIT	Unknown
1776 "Currencey" — Pewter	Unknown

Flowing Hair Type (1794-1795)

Obverse

1794

Reverse

Obverse

1795

Reverse

Date:	Mintage:
1794	1,758
1795	160,295

Draped Bust Type, Small Eagle Reverse (1795-1798)

Obverse

Reverse

Date:	Mintage:
1795	42,738
1796	72,920
1797	7,776
1798	327,536

Draped Bust Type, Heraldic Eagle Reverse — Initially used in 1798

Reverse

Draped Bust Type, 1799 over 98, Stars 7 and 6

Obverse

Draped Bust Type, Stars 8 and 5

Obverse

Date:	Mintage:	Date:	Mintage:
1798	N/A	1801	54,454 *
1799	423,515	1802	41,650 *
1800	220,920	1803	85,634 *

* There was an unknown number of proof restrikes for each of these three years.

The 1804 Dollar

Obverse

Second Reverse

19,570 silver dollars were produced in 1804. Believed that these dollars were minted with 1802 and 1803 obverse dies.

Date:	Known:	Date:	Known:
1804 1st Rev.	8	1804 2nd Rev.	7

Gobrecht Dollar (1836)

Obverse

Reverse

Gobrecht Dollars (1838-1839)

Obverse

Reverse

The following is a listing of the mintage for each date of the Gobrecht silver dollar. This includes both "pattern" and "circulation" issues. Unauthorized restrikes were produced in the late 1850s.

Date:	**Mintage:**
1836 (pattern)	N/A
1836	1,000
1836	600 *
1838 (pattern)	25+
1839	300

* Mintage for 1836 pieces struck in 1837. These have dies aligned medalwise, unlike most U.S. coins.

Liberty Seated Dollar — No Motto (1840-1865)

Obverse

Reverse

Liberty Seated Dollar — Motto (1866-1873)

Obverse

Reverse

Following is a listing of the mintage for each date of the Liberty Seated silver dollar. Proof quantities struck for the early years are unknown.

Date:	Total Mintage: *	Proof Mintage:
1840-P	61,005	
1841-P	173,000	
1842-P	184,618	
1843-P	165,100	
1844-P	20,000	
1845-P	24,500	
1846-P	110,600	
1846-O	59,000	
1847-P	140,750	
1848-P	15,000	
1849-P	62,600	
1850-P	7,500	
1850-O	40,000	
1851-P	1,300	
1851-O	-	1 (known) **
1852-P	1,100	
1853-P	46,110	
1854-P	33,140	
1855-P	26,000	
1856-P	63,500	
1857-P	94,000	
1858-P		80 Estimated
1859-P	256,500	800
1859-O	360,000	
1859-S	20,000	
1860-P	218,930	1,330
1860-O	515,000	
1861-P	78,500	1,000
1862-P	12,090	550
1863-P	27,660	460
1864-P	31,170	470
1865-P	47,000	500
1866-P (no motto)	2 (known)	
1866-P (with motto)	49,625	725
1867-P	47,525	625
1868-P	162,700	600
1869-P	424,300	600
1870-P	416,000	1,000
1870-CC	12,462	
1870-S	N/A	
1871-P	1,074,760	960
1871-CC	1,376	
1872-P	1,106,450	950
1872-CC	3,150	
1872-S	9,000	
1873-P	293,600	600
1873-CC	2,300	
1873-S	700***	

* The total mintage includes the Proof mintage also. (Example: The "official" mintage for the 1873-P business strike is 293,000. The Proof mintage is 600. Therefore the total mintage is 293,600.)

** Walter H. Breen reports one known specimen which is fully covered in Chapter 15 entitled "A Unique Liberty Seated Dollar: 1851-O."

*** None known to have survived

Trade Dollars (1873-1885)

Obverse

Reverse

Following is a listing of the mintage for each date of the Trade dollar. Only Proof quantities were struck after 1878.

Date:	Total Mintage: *	Proof Mintage:
1873-P	397,500	865
1873-CC	124,500	
1873-S	703,000	
1874-P	987,800	700
1874-CC	1,373,200	
1874-S	2,549,000	
1875-P	218,900	700
1875-CC	1,573,700	
1875-S	4,487,000	
1875-S/CC	N/A	
1876-P	456,150	1,150
1876-CC	509,000	
1876-S	5,227,000	
1877-P	3,039,710	510
1877-CC	534,000	
1877-S	9,519,000	
1878-P	900	900
1878-CC	97,000	
1878-S	4,162,000	
1879-P	1,541	1,541
1880-P	1,987	1,987
1881-P	960	960
1882-P	1,097	1,097
1883-P	979	979
1884-P	10	10
1885-P	5	5

* The total mintage includes the Proof mintage also. (Example: The "official" mintage for the 1876-P business strike is 455,000. The Proof mintage is 1,150. Therefore the total mintage is 456,150.)

Morgan (Liberty Head) Dollar (1878-1921)

Obverse

Reverse

Date	Unc. Mintage:	Proof Mintage:
1878-P 8TF	699,300	500
1878-P 7TF Rev. 78	4,900,000*	
1878-P 7TF Rev. 79	4,300,000*	
1878-P 7/8TF (Strong)	544,000**	200
1878-P 7/8TF (Weak)	544,000**	
1878-CC	2,212,000	
1878-S	9,774,000	
1879-P	14,806,000	1,100
1879-CC	756,000	
1879-CC Capped Die	250,000*	
1879-O	2,887,000	12
1879-S	9,110,000	
1879-S Rev. 78	4,000-5,000*	
1880-P	12,600,000	1,355
1880-P 8/7	N/A	
1880-CC	591,000	
1880-CC 80/79	N/A	
1880-CC 8/7	N/A	
1880-O	5,305,000	
1880-O 8/7	N/A	
1880-S	8,900,000	
1880-S 80/79	N/A	
1880-S 8/7	N/A	
1881-P	9,163,000	975
1881-CC	296,000	
1881-O	5,708,000	
1881-S	12,760,000	
1882-P	11,100,000	1,100
1882-CC	1,133,000	
1882-O	6,090,000	
1882-O O/S	N/A	
1882-S	9,250,000	
1883-P	12,290,000	1,039
1883-CC	1,204,000	
1883-O	8,725,000	
1883-S	6,250,000	12
1884-P	14,070,000	875
1884-CC	1,136,000	
1884-O	9,730,000	
1884-S	3,200,000	
1885-P	17,786,837	930

Date:	Unc. Mintage:	Proof Mintage:
1885-CC	228,000	
1885-O	9,185,000	
1885-S	1,497,000	
1886-P	19,963,000	886
1886-O	10,710,000	
1886-S	750,000	
1887-P	20,290,000	710
1887-P 7/6	N/A	
1887-O	11,550,000	
1887-O 7/6	N/A	
1887-S	1,771,000	
1888-P	19,183,000	832
1888-O	12,150,000	
1888-S	657,000	
1889-P	21,726,000	811
1889-CC	350,000	
1889-O	11,875,000	
1889-S	700,000	
1890-P	16,802,000	590
1890-CC	2,309,041	
1890-O	10,701,000	
1890-S	8,230,373	
1891-P	8,693,556	650
1891-CC	1,618,000	
1891-O	7,954,529	
1891-S	5,296,000	
1892-P	1,036,000	1,245
1892-CC	1,352,000	
1892-O	2,744,000	
1892-S	1,200,000	
1893-P	389,000	792
1893-CC	677,000	12
1893-O	300,000	
1893-S	100,000	
1894-P	110,000	972
1894-O	1,723,000	
1894-S	1,260,000	
1895-P	12,000	880
1895-O	450,000	
1895-S	400,000	

Morgan Dollars (Continued)

Date:	Unc. Mintage:	Proof Mintage:	Date:	Unc. Mintage:	Proof Mintage:
1896-P	9,976,000	762	1901-P	6,962,000	813
1896-O	4,900,000		1901-O	13,320,000	
1896-S	5,000,000		1901-S	2,284,000	
1897-P	2,822,000	731	1902-P	7,994,000	777
1897-O	4,004,000		1902-O	8,636,000	
1897-S	5,825,000		1902-S	1,530,000	
1898-P	5,884,000	735	1903-P	4,652,000	755
1898-O	4,440,000		1903-O	4,450,000	
1898-S	4,102,000		1903-S	1,241,000	
1899-P	330,000	846	1904-P	2,788,000	650
1899-O	12,290,000		1904-O	3,720,000	
1899-S	2,562,000		1904-S	2,304,000	
1900-P	8,830,000	912	1921-P	44,690,000	
1900-O	12,590,000		1921-D	20,345,000	
1900-O/CC	N/A		1921-S	21,695,000	
1900-S	3,540,000				

* Estimated mintage
** Estimated mintage (includes both strong and weak varieties).

Peace Dollars (1921-1935)

Obverse

Reverse

Date:	Mintage:	Proof Mintage:	Date:	Mintage:	Proof Mintage:
1921-P	1,006,473	13-18 *	1926-P	1,939,000	
1922-P	51,737,000	9-11 *	1926-D	2,348,700	
1922-D	15,063,000		1926-S	6,980,000	
1922-S	17,475,000		1927-P	848,000	
1923-P	30,800,000		1927-D	1,268,900	
1923-D	6,811,000		1927-S	866,000	
1923-S	19,020,000		1928-P	360,649	
1924-P	11,811,000		1928-S	1,632,000	
1924-S	1,728,000		1934-P	954,057	
1925-P	10,198,000		1934-D	1,569,500	
1925-S	1,610,000		1934-S	1,011,000	
			1935-P	1,576,000	
			1935-S	1,964,000	

* Estimated

Eisenhower Dollars (1971-1978)

Obverse

Reverse

Eisenhower dollars were copper-nickel clad unless noted as silver clad.

Date:	Mintage:	Proof Mintage:
1971-P	47,799,000	
1971-D	68,587,424	
1971-S (silver)	6,868,530	4,265,234
1972-P	75,890,000	
1972-D	92,548,511	
1972-S (silver)	2,193,056	1,811,631
1973-P	2,000,056 *	
1973-D	2,000,000 *	
1973-S		2,760,339
1973-S (silver)	1,883,140	1,013,646
1974-P	27,366,000	
1974-D	45,517,000	
1974-S		2,612,568
1974-S (silver)	1,900,156	1,306,579
1977-P	12,596,000	
1977-D	32,983,000	
1977-S		3,251,152
1978-P	25,702,000	
1978-D	33,012,890	
1978-S		3,127,781

* A total of 1,769,258 pieces each of the 1973-P and 1973-D were sold in sets and not released into circulation. The unsold coins were destroyed at the mint.

Bicentennial Dollar Dated 1776-1976

Obverse

Reverse

The Bicentennial dollar featuring Eisenhower on the obverse and the Liberty-Moon reverse was dated 1776-1976. The issues were copper-nickel clad unless noted as silver clad. Var.I coins were made in 1975; Var II in 1976.

Date:	Mintage:	Proof Mintage:
1776-1976 Var. I	4,019,000	
1776-1976 Var. II	113,318,000	
1776-1976-D Var. I	21,048,710	
1776-1976-D Var. II	82,179,564	
1776-1976-S Var. I		2,845,450
1776-1976-S Var. II		4,194,730
1776-1976-S Var. I (silver)	4,294,081	3,262,970 *

* Approximate mintage

Susan B. Anthony Dollar (1979-1981)

Obverse

Reverse

The following is a listing of the mintage for each date and mint mark in the Susan B. Anthony dollar series.

Date:	Mintage:	Proof Mintage:	Date:	Mintage:	Proof Mintage:
1979-P	360,222,000		1980-P	27,610,000	
1979-D	288,015,744		1980-D	41,628,708	
1979-S	109,576,000		1980-S	20,422,000	3,554,806
1979-S		3,677,175 *	1981-P	3,000,000	
			1981-D	3,250,000	
			1981-S	3,492,000	4,063,083

Lafayette Dollar 1900

Obverse

Reverse

Date:	Mintage:
1900	36,026

United States Silver Eagle (1986 to Date)

Obverse

Reverse

Date:	Mintage:	Proof Mintage:
1986-P	5,393,005	
1986-S		1,446,778
1987-P	11,442,335	
1987-S		904,732
1988-P	5,004,646	
1988-S		557,370
1989-P	5,203,327	
1989-S		617,694
1990-P	5,840,110	
1990-S		700,000

Los Angeles XXIII Olympiad — 1983

Obverse

Reverse

Date:	Mintage:	Proof Mintage:
1983-P	294,543	
1983-D	174,014	
1983-S	174,014	1,577,025

Los Angeles XXIII Olympiad — 1984

Obverse

Reverse

Date:	Mintage:	Proof Mintage:
1984-P	217,954	
1984-D	116,675	
1984-S	116,675	1,801,210

Statue of Liberty — 1986

Obverse　　Reverse

Date:	Mintage:	Proof Mintage:	Date:	Mintage:	Proof Mintage:
1986-P	723,635	N/A	1986-S	N/A	6,414,638

U.S. Constitution Silver Dollar — 1987

Obverse　　Reverse

Date:	Mintage:	Proof Mintage:	Date:	Mintage:	Proof Mintage:
1987-P	N/A	451,629	1987-S	N/A	2,747,116

Olympic Silver Dollar — 1988

Obverse　　Reverse

Date:	Mintage:	Proof Mintage:	Date:	Mintage:	Proof Mintage:
1988-D	191,368	N/A	1988-S	1,354,366	N/A

Congress Silver Dollar — 1989

Obverse Reverse

Date:	Mintage:	Proof Mintage:
1989-D (Clad)	163,753	N/A
1989-D (Silver)	135,203	N/A
1989-S (Clad)		767,897
1989-S (Silver)		762,198

Eisenhower Silver Dollar — 1990

Obverse Reverse

Date:	Mintage:	Proof Mintage:
1990-W	240,677	N/A
1990-P	N/A	1,139,890*

* Figures as of August 23, 1991

Mount Rushmore Silver Dollar — 1991

Obverse

Reverse

Date:	Mintage:	Proof Mintage:
1991-P	121,701*	
1991-S		593,487*

* Figures as of July 1991

Korean Silver Dollar — 1991

Obverse

Reverse

Date:	Mintage:	Proof Mintage:
1991-D	186,189	
1991-P		505,741

* Figures as of July 1991

***

CHAPTER 76

Statistics and Comparative Analysis

By John W. Highfill, NLG

Introduction

THIS IS YOUR OWNER'S MANUAL! Read it over and over again! Refer to it repeatedly. The descriptive analysis in the date-by-date section of this book is concise and to the point. Pages and pages could be written on each date using many adjectives, but the data published here is focusing on the bottom line. Only the main and important issues and facts are presented for your reference. The charts, figures and graphs tell their own story.

A brief summary of the United States dollar goes like this. The origin of the dollar is found in Europe with dollar-sized silver coins derived from the word "thaler." The forerunner of the U.S. dollar was the Spanish 8 Reales. The Mint Act of 1792 defined the silver dollar to contain 416 grains of silver with a fineness of 892.43. The Coinage Act of 1965 officially all but removed silver from the coinage of the United States and "fiat" money has prevailed ever since.

Morgan, Peace and all other dollars were struck at the active United States mints during the time of their production. The mintmarks used together with the mint of origin and the years of operation are presented in the following tables.

Philadelphia, Pennsylvania (1792-Present), P mintmark or none *
San Francisco, California (1854-Present), S mintmark
New Orleans, Louisiana (1838-1909), O mintmark
Carson City, Nevada (1870-1893), CC mintmark
Denver, Colorado (1906-Present), D mintmark
West Point, New York (1984-Present), W mintmark

* The P mintmark was used for the Jefferson "war year" nickels of 1942-54, the entire Susan B. Anthony dollar series, and on other modern issues beginning in 1979.

Business Strike Coins are divided into two categories; circulated and uncirculated. Using the Sheldon grading scale, circulated coins are graded from AG-3 through AU-58. Uncirculated coins are graded Mint State-60 through MS-70. Proof strike coins are listed using grades PR-50 through PR-70. A summary in chart form is listed below.

Circulated	**Uncirculated**	**Proof**
AG-3 . . . AU-58	MS-60 . . . MS-70	PR-50 . . . PR-70

TO PROJECT PRICE INCREASES IS NOT THE PURPOSE OF THIS BOOK! In the past when dollars projections were estimates and guesses at best. Projecting $10 coins rising to $100, or even $1,000 specimens rising to $10,000. That was easy to do. But to project a piece selling today for $25,000 to rise to $100,000 within a few short years is not a very good or practical idea. It is much more realistic and smarter to LET THE MARKET FORECAST ITS OWN FUTURE. Supply and demand will take care of the basic economics of numismatics as well.

On economic forecasting: Never make forecasts. Those that come true usually only temporarily remain so. As economic situations change, so do the forecasts. They become just like yesterday's newspapers - HISTORY!

Isn't it interesting to note that the United States Mint and its branch mints over all the years minted nearly ONE BILLION Morgan and Peace silver dollars (847,590,888 to be exact). It gets even more interesting when, in light of this fact, you take a closer look at the surviving "guesstimates" and certified services population figures that have been gathered during the last five years. Look at the numbers.

Total Morgan dollars minted (1878-1904) - 570,283,609
Morgan dollars minted in 1921 - 86,730,000
Total Morgan dollars minted - 657,013,600
Total Peace dollars minted - 190,577,279
Total Morgan and Peace dollars minted - 847,590,888
Melted as a result of the Pittman Act of 1918 - 270,232,722
Meltage of 1918 designated for export to India via England - 259,121,554
Morgan and Peace dollars melted as a result of the World War II Act of 1942 - 52,738,933 *
Morgan and Peace dollars melted between 1883 and 1964 - 333,022,048 *
"Great Silver Dollar Rush" government distribution from 1958 through March 26, 1964 - 217,013,000
Total G.S.A. sales - 2,825,849 (mainly "CC" Morgans) ***
Total surviving Morgan and Peace dollars - approximately 514 million (not allowing for losses) **
Meltage - 1964 silver dollar rush **
Meltage - 1980 silver explosion **

* Accurate estimates
** There were unknown quantities of silver dollars "melted" by unauthorized persons as a direct result of the dramatic rise of the price of silver during the "Great Silver Dollar Rush" and later in the 1960s. In addition, there were millions of all dates and grades of silver dollars melted in 1979-1980 when the price of silver sky-rocketed to $50 an ounce.
*** There were 27,980 non-CC mixed dates listed in the G.S.A. inventory for sale at the time.

There were millions upon millions of Morgan and Peace silver dollars minted for circulation. But there were many minting problems, large melting of coins, lost and hoarded quantities. Now only extremely minute percentages of pieces are known to exist today in MS-65 or better condition. Consider the following PCGS population figures for a few selected pieces in MS-65 or better condition. TAKE YOUR TIME AND LET THESE FIGURES SINK IN YOUR MIND!

Most Rare:

Date	PCGS Certified MS-65	Official Mintage
1893-O	1	300,000
1896-O	1	4,900,000
1889-CC	1	350,000
1884-S	1	3,200,000
1901-P	1	6,962,813
1892-S	2	1,200,000
1895-O	2	450,000
1893-S	3	100,000

Common to Semi-Common:

Date	PCGS Certified MS-65	Official Mintage
1888-P	approx. 1,050	19,183,832
1889-P	approx. 290	21,726,811
1885-P	approx. 3,000	17,787,767
1881-S	approx. 20,000	12,760,000
1921-P (M)	approx. 825	44,690,000

The majority of dates were held by government directives and decisions as silver bullion governmental reserves and were not released into circulation. A number of reasons have been suggested for this action. They include requirements placed upon government officials as a result of the Bland-Allison Act and other U.S. legislation concerning the maintenance of war reserves. The Pittman Act of 1918 caused 270,232,722 Morgans to be melted. Of this amount, 259,121,554 were ear-marked to be shipped to India as stated earlier. Possible reasoning:

1. The legal requirement for the United States government to maintain a silver stockpile for internal and foreign bullion needs.
2. There is better than a 50-50 chance that there was a strategically related requirement for the government to maintain a "war reserve" of silver.
3. Another reason that did not directly involve legislation was the lack of acceptance of the silver dollar as a circulating coin by the public.

As the federal reserve banks did their periodic vault inventories, they abruptly moved the bags of silver dollars from one location to another through the century. This one action by itself has probably contributed to over half of the bagmarks displayed by the "surviving" original mint state coinage today.

Looking at an overview of the mintage of silver dollars, we find that the Morgan series in all of its years presented the United States with 657,013,609 coins. Talk about a hoard! After 1904 the U.S. discontinued the production of the Morgan dollar, primarily due to the short supply of government owned silver. The Morgan dollar was again struck in 1921 as a one year issue. The Pittman Act of 1918 melted 270,232,722 prior to this striking. But the Peace dollar series took up the slack and produced 190,577,279 coins during its 1921-1935 run. The demands of the World War II war effort took 52,738,933 of the gigantuate government holdings. Remember, the majority of the coins melted in 1942 were Peace dollars!

It took government distributions, sales and time to finally dispose of and/or distribute all of those millions and millions of dollars. These distributions were the U.S. Treasury's release from 1958 through 1964 that is commonly referred to as the "Great Silver Dollar Rush." The other were the two General Services Administration (G.S.A.) sales of the "CC" Morgans at premium prices in 1972-74 and later in 1980.

Acts, Hoards and Government Sales

The following Acts, hoard and sales should be reviewed in order to arrive at a better understanding of the concept of "surviving original mintage." In many cases, the exact dates and quantity of coins involved are not known. In these instances, the best that can be done is to provide the results of the available research and perform statistical calculations to arrive at the "guesstimated" surviving examples for each date and mint mark. Let's look at each of these very significant factors.

1. **Pittman Act of 1918.** There was one significant portion of this piece of legislation as passed by Congress. This Act authorized the melting of 270,232,722 Morgan dollars from the governments huge hoard. The bullion obtained from this great "melt" was to be used for two general purposes. One was to provide 259,121,554 to be shipped to England (bound for India), and to maintain a strategic silver stockpile (perhaps for war as well as for other uses). The other was to obtain bullion for the future minting of additional silver coinage. Of course, no Peace dollars were included. The Peace dollar coinage was first produced in 1921.
2. **World War II Act of 1942**. This was another piece of legislation that required a great melting of Morgan and Peace dollars held by the government. There were much more Peace dollars melted at this time than Morgans, although no one knows the exact figures. The melt has been listed at 52,738,933. The government used the bullion created by the meltage for the war effort which was moving into high gear at that time.

There were unreported amounts of silver dollars melted outside of the United States over the years. No records were kept of foreign melting of U.S. coins. This has contributed to the difficulty in calculating the potential surviving population data. There were millions upon millions of circulated and BU Morgan and Peace dollars melted by independent refineries during the silver run-up in 1980. Leon Hendrickson of Silver Towne alone was reported to have sent 30,000 1923-P Peace dollars to one refinery along with a large hoard of 1883-O Morgans.

Of the Morgans melted as a result of the Pittman Act, 259,121,554 were sold to England and shipped to India and the remaining 11,111,168 were to be used in the production of smaller silver denomination coinage in the next fiscal year.

3. **Coinage Act of 1965** signed into law by President Lyndon B. Johnson on July 23, 1965. This Act was the culmination of the millions of Morgan dollars that were distributed by the government during the years 1958 through 1964. By this time, the U.S. Treasury holdings had been reduced dramatically, the price of gold and silver was on the rise, and there was in fact a "run" of sorts for silver bags at the federal branch banks. This "run" caused the U.S. Treasury to close its windows during March of 1964. The higher price of silver was reflected in the cost to the government to produce coinage. The government realized that is must reduce or eliminate the silver content of its coinage immediately.

The Act authorized the government to take steps to reclaim circulating silver coinage as well as to eliminate silver from all coinage except the half-dollar. The last business strike coins containing 90 percent silver were struck in 1964, these being the Kennedy half dollars dated 1964. The Kennedy 40 percent silver half dollars were struck until 1969. Some 1974-D (Breen reports "about 30 known") and 1977-D (Breen reports "about 15 known") Eisenhower dollars were made using a silver-clad composition, but these were made in error. This is the real key to completing a set of the Eisenhower dollars. Walter Breen reports in his Encyclopedia (p. 463):

"The rarest coins of this design are the 1974-D's struck on heavy silver-clad blanks. On Oct. 10, 1974, a Las Vegas blackjack dealer brought the first one to *Coin World*. The Mint Bureau confirmed that an unknown number of silver-clad blanks were accidentally included among nickel-clad blanks rejected as unfit for proof coinage and shipped from San Francisco to the Denver Mint. *CWA*, p. 181."

The price of silver started to rise dramatically in the early 1960s, and the "Great Silver Dollar Rush" really caught on. This was apparent beginning in 1962, although the U.S. Treasury had been distributing silver dollars by the millions beginning in 1958. This "rush" for dollars was due to the rising price of silver which made the dollars more valuable. The 35,584,000 dollars distributed in 1962 making this year the largest of the "rush" years up to that time.

The majority of the dates from the "Great Silver Dollar Rush" were first observed to be released around October 1962. Those dates with the most notoriety and rarity at the time were the 1898-O, 1903-O and 1904-O. Many of the 1879-O through 1882-O U.S. mint sewn original bags from the New Orleans Mint had circulated coins in them. Some solid date bags had one, two, three or all four New Orleans dates in them (1879, 1880, 1881 and 1882). It appears that the bags were all recalled in late 1882.

The reasoning for this thesis revolves around the number of coins found in the bags for each of the dates. That is, most of the circulated coins found were dated 1879-O. The next largest number were dated 1880-O, followed by the 1881-O pieces and finally the 1882-O circulated coins. The date presenting the most sliders was 1882. If the coins were recalled earlier than 1882, other sliders would have been found representing the earlier dates. There would also have not been any 1882-O Morgans in them.

Another reason supporting the 1882 recall date is that some bags of 1879-Os contained 5-10% circulated 1880-O, 1881-O and 1882-O dollars. The same situation was discovered in selected bags of the 1880-O and 1881-O Morgans. In addition, some "BU" coins in these bags were of lower quality, grading XF to AU to slider.

The majority of the New Orleans circulated coins found were in 1882-O bags (approximately 40%). Next came 1881-O with 30%, 1880-O with 20% and 1879-O with 10%. This coordinated in theory to the time in circulation and the respective grades uncovered in the original mint sewn bags.

Larry Busch, a big silver dollar dealer from Montana, handled quite a number of these dollars in the early 1960s. John Love, also from Montana, handled a bag of "slider" Morgans dated 1883-S, 1884-S and 1885-S. All three of the dates were in one "original" U.S. mint sewn bag. This was similar to the way the New Orleans Mint did it in the same era of time (i.e., New Orleans 1879-1882-O; San Francisco 1883-1885-S).

However, this is the only known and/or reported San Francisco bag to date. New Orleans had 350 bags in the Continental Illinois National Bank of Chicago hoard above. Leon Hendrickson of Silver Towne handled these bags.

There were also "original" U.S. mint sewn canvas bags of 1887-O Morgans that were partly or all lightly circulated sliders. They also had some circulated 1886-Os in them! The same situation occurred at the New Orleans Mint in 1897. A few 1897-O "original" bags contained circulated 1897-O and 1896-O Morgans. If you will notice, there were no reports of bags containing circulated coins with a date succeeding the "breakoff" years in them! The "breakoff" or ending years include 1882, 1887 and 1897 for the New Orleans Mint and 1885 for the San Francisco Mint. Put another way, there were no dates later than 1882 in the "original" New Orleans bags of 1879 through 1882.

THERE SEEMS TO BE SOME INDICATION OF GOVERNMENT DIRECTION IN THESE RE-CALLS OF MORGANS (1879-1882-O, 1883-1885-S, 1887-O, AND 1897-O).

Dean Tavenner refers to all of these re-called Morgans as "two-beer" dollars. His explanation and interpretation was that they were in circulation just long enough to buy a couple of beers before the U.S. government mints re-called them. John Love and Dean Tavenner suggest that circulated bags tended to weigh 57 pounds, while "slider" or "two-beer" bags weighed 59 pounds. Full original BU bags weighed 60 pounds. Guess which ones these dealers went for, and why? They wanted the circulated bags for the possible rarer dates. The emphasis was not on quality at that time. They were looking for pieces like the 1884-S and 1893-S Morgans, or 1859-O and 1860-O Liberty Seated dollars.

Then in 1963 the public really got excited and took 66,883,000 silver dollars out of the hands of the U.S. Treasury. As 1964 began to unfold, the excitement was building to a new high. January saw 1,299,000 leave the Treasury. In February 2,987,000 were taken. Then came March when 21,429,000 were taken in a wild frenzy before the government closed the doors on March 26, 1964. Thereafter, silver certificates were redeemable only in silver granules. (See photo and related story in Chapter 54 entitled "Chester West Tells It As It Is".)

As far as the "silver certificate" was concerned, June 1968 was the last date they could be redeemed for silver. The redemptions were available at all of the active mints - Philadelphia, Denver and San Francisco. In the mid 1960s when the price of silver was slowly rising, many dealers began offering a premium for the public's supply of silver certificates. The dealers, in turn, redeemed the certificates by the millions and marketed the silver bars they received in exchange.

Here is an approximate listing of the silver dollars released by the U.S. Treasury during the "Great Silver Dollar Rush" between 1958 and March 26, 1964. The frenzy grew as the media jumped on the band wagon. Stories of "rare" coins being acquired at face value added fuel to the fire, and the rush for silver dollars intensified.

Date	**Troy Oz. (millions)**	**Mintage**
1958	12.7	16,493,000
1959	15.7	20,390,000
1960	16.2	21,039,000
1961	23.8	30,909,000
1962	27.4	35,584,000
1963	51.5	66,883,000
1964 (Jan)	1.0	1,299,000
1964 (Feb)	2.3	2,987,000
1964 (Mar)	16.5	21,429,000
Totals:	167.1	217,013,000

The following list presents the dates released by the U.S. Treasury during the "Great Silver Dollar Rush" between 1958 and 1964.

Dates Known

1881-CC *	1900-O
1884-CC *	1901-O
1885-CC *	1902-O
1889-O *	1903-P
1893-O *	1903-O
1898-O	1904-O
1899-P	1925-P **
1899-O	

* Very limited quantities.

** It was very interesting that the 1925-P was the only Peace dollar date known to be held through the years in the vaults of the U.S. Treasury!

4. **Redfield dates**. The hoard of LaVere Redfield consisting of some 407+ bags of silver dollars (407,596) were distributed by A-Mark and Paramount International among others. This hoard was distributed starting in the year 1976. The net result of this distribution was a great rejuvenation of interest in silver dollars and a large influx of new collectors. The known dates contained in the hoard are listed in this chapter for your review and study. (For more details, see Chapter 13 entitled "The Redfield Hoard" by John W. Highfill.)

The number of bags involved in the Redfield hoard for each of the represented dates provides "Redfield rarity" information. This data is valuable when making a before and after price comparison of the Redfield dates, or when calculating the mint state surviving mintage of the Redfield dates.

The top ten most common Redfield dates are all from the Morgan series. In ranking order, they are presented with the four most common Peace dollar Redfield dates.

Rank	**Morgan Dates**	**Rank**	**Peace Dates**
1.	1881-S	1.	1922-S
2.	1880-S	2.	1923-S
3.	1879-S	3.	1926-S
4.	1878-S	4.	1935-S
5.	1882-S		
6.	1896-P		
7.	1898-P		
8.	1891-S		
9.	1897-S		
10.	1890-S		

The top nine most rare uncirculated dates recorded in the Redfield hoard do not include those dates which are questionable and not verified by actual dealer activity during the distribution of the hoard. These dates for the Morgan and Peace dollar series are ranked as follows:

Rank	Morgan Dates	Rank	Peace Dates
1.	1895-S	1.	1924-S
2.	1879-CC	2.	1925-S
3.	1889-P	3.	1927-S
4.	1891-P	4.	1928-S
5.	1893-P		
6.	1892-P		
7.	1891-CC		
8.	1885-CC		
9.	1921-S		

Contrary to myth, previous beliefs and other statements, there is less than two percent of any date Morgan or Peace silver dollar available by the bag in MS-65. The possibility of those available dates would include the 1879-S, 1880-S, 1881-S, 1882-S Morgans and the 1923-P Peace dollar. Other dates would be hard pressed to yield one bag in MS-65 condition. This type of bag just isn't available today. This is the main reason Wall Street traders haven't successfully handled our product. There aren't enough coins to actively trade on a daily basis. Perhaps through future demand, lower grades in large quantities will be traded. If this were successfully done, silver dollars would explode in price and lead the way for all numismatics. If Wall Street seriously entered the market using certified coins as a daily trading product, they would probably trade computer-graded bag lots on MS-60, 61 and 62 Morgan and Peace dollars. It may not sound right to you now, but the possibility exists.

5. **The U.S. Treasury** distributed many millions of silver dollars during the "Great Silver Dollar Rush." Some dates were released as early as 1958. They continued to be released annually until the "window" was closed on March 26, 1964. Only the Carson City minted dollars were held back for later disposal and sale in the G.S.A. programs of 1972-74 and 1980.

6. **G.S.A. Sales of 1972 through 1980**. These sales relieved the government of all of its remaining silver dollars. These sales were held on a bid basis and there were both minimum bids and strict limits imposed upon the bidders in an effort to minimize the advantage to any group of potential buyers. The dates involved in the sales are listed here.

G.S.A. inventory as of October 1972.

Date	Inventory	
1878-CC	60,993	
1879-CC	4,123	
1879-CC Capped Die Variety	600	*
1880-CC	131,529	
1881-CC	147,485	
1882-CC	605,029	
1883-CC	755,518	
1884-CC	962,638	
1885-CC	148,285	
1889-CC **	1	
1890-CC	3,949	
1891-CC	5,687	
1892-CC **	1	
1893-CC **	1	
Total:	2,909,715	***

* Included in the 4,123 1879-CC totals.

** These dates were sold in the "mixed lot" category. There were 977,600 pieces left over from the 1972-74 G.S.A. sales. They were offered again and sold through G.S.A. sales in 1980.

*** There was a total of 27,980 mixed non-CC dates not included in this total. When added, the grand total is 2,937,695.

G.S.A. inventory as of February 1979 according to their own records.

Date	Inventory
1880-CC	4,300
1881-CC	19,000
1883-CC	195,700
1884-CC	428,100
1885-CC	31,500
Mixed *	299,000
Total	977,600 **

* The mixed group of the Carson City dates consisted of specimens with bad rim nicks, very heavy bagmarks and scratches, bad toning or other severe damage. There were also 27,980 non-CC mixed dates included in this total.

** The total inventory also included 84,165 "culls" & mixed circulated CC dollars (other unsalable CC dollars totaled 311).

7. **The Continental Illinois National Bank of Chicago hoard**. This tremendous hoard of approximately 1500 bags of Morgan silver dollars is the largest private hoard known to date. These coins were distributed by Colonial Coins of Houston, Texas, and Leon Hendrickson of Silver Towne, during the early to mid 1980s. The well organized and planned efforts of those in charge of the distribution resulted in an orderly market with no adverse effects. (See the chapter entitled, "The Continental Illinois Bank Deal," by Leon Hendrickson and Clark A. Samuelson.) There were approximately 1,000 original U.S. mint sewn canvas bags and 500 circulated bags in the entire hoard. The known dates involved are listed here.

BU Bags (1000)	XF/AU Circ. Bags (500)
1879-S	1879-O *
1880-S	1880-O *
1881-S	1881-O *
1882-S	1882-O *
1883-P	Various Mixed Dates
1883-O	
1884-P	
1884-O	
1885-O	
1885-P	
1886-P	
1887-P	

* The 1879-O through 1882-O run of dates consisted of 350 of the 500 "circulated" bags.

No dates after 1887 were known to be included in this hoard. The 1887-P bags represented the last year involved.

Original Mintage Versus Surviving Mintage

THE PERCENT OF CERTIFIED BU MORGAN DOLLARS AND PEACE DOLLARS IN COMPARISON TO TOTAL "OFFICIAL" MINTAGE RECORDS IS THE NUMBER ONE STATISTIC FOR THE ENTIRE BOOK!

The one number that you must grasp, realize and utilize in all you do within the world of silver dollars. The one number that will change the way you think about silver dollars. The bottom line!

It is the Percent of Certified BU Morgan dollars and Peace dollars in comparison to TOTAL "OFFICIAL" MINTAGE RECORDS. (i.e., before the melts, after PCGS, etc., hoards, G.S.A., Redfield, etc.). There were 847,590,888 million Morgan and Peace dollars minted according to the official records. The breakdown consisted of 657,013,609 million Morgans and 190,577,279 million Peace dollars. ALMOST A FULL BILLION DOLLARS! THINK ABOUT IT!

Sometimes we lose perspective of things. Isolated and individual collectors fear populations of one, ten, one hundred or even 1,000 coins. They don't realize there are billions of dollars in numismatic items traded annually in the U.S. rare coin marketplace. And that number is increasing every day! THINK ABOUT IT AGAIN! Every decade encounters price-shock! There are more to come.

Before we go any farther, let's discuss a grave misunderstanding held by many collectors. This is what I will call the "Mintage Syndrome." It is the mis-use of the original mintage information presented in publications such as the "Red Book." This mintage information presented therein is the most authoritative of which I am aware, and the publishers and contributors have done a superb job. But there is a great tendency among many collectors to consider the mintage figures to be the one and only indicator as to the availability of a date and mint mark within a series. This is exactly where this "Encyclopedia" will give you the wealth of information required to make prudent buying decisions.

For example, take a look at the 1892-S and 1893-S Morgan silver dollar. The original mintage figures are as follows.

Date	Original Mintage
1892-S	1,200,000
1893-S	100,000

At first glance, it would appear that the 1892-S would be 12 times more available than the 1893-S. But consider these facts. Nearly the entire available mintage of 1892-S and 1893-S coins were melted! The best indications are that neither of these dates were included in the Redfield hoard, so that is not a mitigating factor.

Next, we need to look at the certified third party graded mint state examples. The statistics published by PCGS and NGC are not conclusive evidence, but they are becoming more and more statistically significant as time goes on. As of this writing, the numbers below are exact.

1892-S	PCGS	NGC	1893-S	PCGS	NGC
MS-60	0	0	MS-60	1	0
MS-61	3	0	MS-61	2	1
MS-62	6	0	MS-62	3	3
MS-63	1	1	MS-63	5	3
MS-64	4	0	MS-64	1	0
MS-65	2	1	MS-65	3	1
MS-66	3	1	MS-66	0	0
MS-67	1	1	MS-67	1	0
TOTALS	20	4	TOTALS	16	8

The unavoidable conclusion is that the 1892-S is giving the 1893-S a run for its money! We can argue about how many MS-65's and above there are of each and so forth, but the facts still remain. How many months and years of certified population reports must you see to be convinced? The 1892-S is RARE! The original mintage is only the starting point for determining the surviving and available mint state examples of any given date.

For those who are still not convinced, consider the 1886-0. The original mintage is listed at 10,710,000. Do you realize that as of this writing there have been no MS-65 examples graded by PCGS or NGC. NONE! Did you consider this issue available in MS-65 before reading this? Do you believe multiples of MS-65's will be certified soon? Later? At all?

Turning attention for a minute to the Peace dollar series, the original mintage for the 1922-P is 51,737,000, while the 1923-P is listed as 30,800,000. This is okay as far as that goes, but do you realize that due to the various losses sustained, the 1922-P is actually two times more scarce in mint state condition than its teammate despite a 40% higher official mintage?

Look at the 1928-S (mintage of 1,632,000) and the 1928-P (mintage of 360,649). The 1928-S is a Redfield date, has been widely distributed, and is considered a semi-key date. The 1928-P is a key date to the series and has always maintained that status. Now the fact. THE 1928-S IS 2 TO 4 TIMES AS RARE IN VARIOUS MINT STATE CONDITIONS. PCGS certified totals to date showed the following.

Date	PCGS BU	PCGS MS-65 and above
1928-P	1761	43
1928-S	1116	9

Individual opinions vary, and that is very healthy for numismatics, but we've taken an unbiased statistical approach to arrive at undeniable conclusions.

In the past, many dates were unpopular for various reasons. The inception of independent third party grading, computer grading, limited partnerships, leveraged borrowing, long term pension plans, institutional investing, population reports, electronic sight-unseen trading, new collectors and dealers have changed that. This trend will continue as scarce and rare will be just that, "SCARCE AND RARE." The numbers and the computers will do all the talking in the future. The human psychological factors will be greatly diminished. There will be less coin conventions and the ones that survive will be stronger than before.

Yes, thanks to PCGS and NGC, more accurate and conservative "guesstimates" are now available to enhance the perception of what's out there. Another important statistic derived from the population data is the "proportionate ratios of grade" information.

We are in the process of redefining the status of coins. This book has taken the liberty of working to change the status from common to semi-common, and from semi-common to semi-key, etc. This is due to the availability of more precise statistical information by the way of certified population reports which are pointing out so many times that CONDITION RARITY IS A FACT! These statistics are slowly unveiling this truth and showing us what is really available. (See both PCGS and NGC population report disclaimer listed in this chapter.)

Mint Conditions Affecting Strike

There are a number of conditions which can affect the strike associated with a given mint or with a given year or series of years. This can greatly affect the quality of the surviving pieces and their perceived value in the marketplace.

Beginning in 1888, the Philadelphia Mint began to let the dies self-destruct. They had many poor strikes, sub-par luster and overall lower quality compared to the earlier years (1878-1887). This process continued through 1894. The return to quality wasn't made until 1896.

For example, let's take a look at the strikes produced by the Philadelphia Mint from the years 1888 through 1894. During these years, various factors contributed to striking problems. For instance, overuse and abuse of the dies. The high ratio of dies used to coins minted left no other alternative to soft and/or flat strikes for the majority of the issues. Two particular problem areas are above Miss Liberty's ear and on the reverse eagle's breast feathers. In fact, some dies were used to the point of rusting, cracking or breaking. Improper basining of the dies often led to "metal-flow" problems. This caused a lack of definition of the device details. There were also many strike problems and varieties caused by the positioning, punching and repunching of the dates. (See Bill Fivaz's chapter #17 cited above.)

Turning our attention to New Orleans, we generally find a weaker strike in almost all of the issues. During many years and especially the later years, 1886 through 1897, the strike has been labeled "flat." Even the earlier years did not produce a strike which could be labeled as "full." Lack of quality control and perhaps outright negligence led to these conditions. Lack of attention to the basining of the dies was at the heart of many of the striking problems (i.e., thick rims and metal flow). It could also be that the equipment available at New Orleans was not in the best of condition. This could help to explain the generally insufficient striking pressure associated with New Orleans coinage. This mint was also guilty of die overuse, and reflected the tremendous government mintage requirement coupled with inadequate funds to do the job. (See the related chapter #17 entitled, "Mint Error Dollars and the Minting Process", by Bill Fivaz.)

During the coining process, it is relatively common for a combination of oil, grease, and dirt to cause an incomplete strike of the planchet. Many examples are available with small areas which were not completely struck due to the presence of die grease and dirt. Do not be surprised to find a specimen with part of the date missing, or with a small portion of the design barely struck. This is a much more common phenomenon than is popularly believed, and does not add numismatic value to the coin in the vast majority of cases.

Do you know...

1. That silver dollars are not nearly as common as believed.
2. Why some dates sell for 5000% of published bids and are still a great deal.
3. Why some dates sell for 1% spreads between bid and ask.
4. Why some dates have a volatility of 50% a month.
5. That certain silver dollars can be worth as much as a million dollars apiece.
6. That over 10 different dates have traded in excess of $100,000 in MS-65 and higher during the 1980s and were not publicly reported.
7. Why there are not bags and bags of gem dollars still out there.
8. That estimated coin survival figures of the past that were considered liberal were actually ultra-conservative. Many were off by factors of 10!

Here are some insights into each of the items mentioned in the previous list.

1. Silver dollars are not nearly as common as many believe due to a number of reasons. One of the largest contributing factors was the great "melts" of the twentieth century. These were a result of the Pittman Act of 1918 and the World War II Act requiring precious metal resources for the war effort. Another element was simply the disappearance of coins into collections, hoards, melting pots, or wherever lost coins go. There were 270,232,722 Morgan dollars exclusively melted under the provisions of the Pittman Act. There were both Morgan and Peace dollars melted under the World War II Act of 1942. The majority of these were believed to be Peace dollars.

Another piece of the puzzle depends upon the quality of coinage under discussion. If MS-65 is the governing requirement, then silver dollars may not be that common, they may be considered scarce to rare! If we are including the entire mint state grades, then silver dollars are certainly more available. But they are not making any more Morgan and Peace dollars, and the number of collectors and investors is steadily growing. There were 847,590,888 Morgan and Peace dollars minted by the U.S. Treasury. Many MS-60/62 grade dollars have not been certified for obvious financial reasons. However, as of June 1, 1991, PCGS has graded 758,992 Morgan dollars and 118,715 Peace dollars. NGC has graded 135,588 Morgan dollars and 23,312 Peace dollars. This is a total of 1,036,607 silver dollars certified by both services. STOP AND THINK ABOUT THIS FOR A MINUTE. THERE IS LESS THAN .01 OF ONE PERCENT OF THE ENTIRE MORGAN AND PEACE DOLLAR MINTAGE THAT HAS BEEN CERTIFIED IN ALL BU GRADES (.07 OF 1% PEACE, AND .0128 OF 1% MORGAN). Currently one in every 250 Americans could own a PCGS or NGC graded silver dollar.

2. There are silver dollars that sell for many, many times their published bids, and their buyers are "tickled pink" to make their purchase. The bids reported for the truly rare silver dollars are not in any way reflecting the worth or market value of these pieces. These bids are simply "lowball" numbers thrown out without any thought, or in a vain attempt to draw the desired coins out of their hiding places. When the "rare" coins change hands, both parties know that they are worth far in excess of any published bids. These coins may be sold privately or at auction, but you can be sure that the buyer is willing to pay a very high premium for the privilege of holding just one of those fabulously rare coins! You tell me. What is the value of the highest certified graded silver dollar within each date and series. What are these unique coins really worth?

3. Some dates present spreads between bid and ask of 1 percent or even less, while others command much higher spreads. Also spreads of the same date will vary according to market conditions. The common date Morgan silver dollars ("generics") will show spreads of 1 percent in a down market as the bid and ask prices move very close to each other in a relatively liquid market. But as the market rises, these spreads tend to widen and the bid and ask prices move farther apart.

If we examine the scarce and rare dates of the series, the bid and ask prices, when presented at all, will tend to reflect thin market conditions and lack of liquidity. The coins trade much less often with a resulting market spread reflecting the conditions of the market and the reason for the sale.

4. Why do some dates have a volatility of up to 50% in a single month? The answer revolves around the bid-based electronic trading system. When the bids are allowed to be posted at any price, at any time, there is no control. This is only one-half of the equation, and the wrong half at that. First, there is often no trading in certain coins while their "value" is being batted around like a racquetball as a result of irresponsible bidding. Second, one bid used in this fashion can bring the perceived value of hundreds of coins of that date down at the same time - without a single trade taking place! Believe it! You witnessed it in the "*MELTDOWN*" during the crash in the fall of 1990.

This action was aided and abetted by negative psychology and the presence of leveraged positions challenged by unparalleled margin calls which in turn created a lack of ready cash in the entire market. This caused cash poor market-makers to pull back (or off) their bids and the market went into free fall. As markets fell further, pressure on existing margins and new margin calls by auction houses, banks and other collateral based lending institutions ultimately created the ultimate electronic trading meltdown. The market crashed 50-80% without coins actually selling on the way down. The only coins traded on the way down were from auction bills and involuntary forced margin calls for settlement by various lending institutions. The dominoes kept falling. Some lending institutions showed little restraint in trying to cover the exposure. Because of these institutions squeezing the life blood (cash) out of the major market makers, it caused undue harm for the entire industry. This was the largest meltdown in numismatic history and it happened in less than 90 days! INCREDIBLE!

There were quite of number of reasons for the Incredible Meltdown of 1990. The fact that these actions occurred so rapidly and in concert added to the demise. Here is a listing to consider.

a. The bank loans that had been made to finance coin inventories and further leveraged business activities came under "attack" as the market faded during the fall. These banks, in turn, required additional margin from the leveraged dealers just when cash flow was most needed. This led to a severe cash crunch and some dealers were forced into liquidation of their holdings. The war and recession turned bank examiners into "credit crunch criminals." Some lending institutions put a moratorium on new loans irrespective of the credit worthiness of the borrower or collateral.

b. An additional result of reason a was the ever-growing reluctance of lending institutions to finance new inventory which also contributed to the already serious cash shortage.

c. The numismatic press added fuel to the fire with their extensive and continual negative reporting of the lowest possible prices they could find. It was the "I can beat your story" syndrome at its worst, with the pace accelerating with every new issue. Extreme negative psychological impact was the only possible result from this action.

d. The split of the major electronic sight-unseen trading exchanges was ill-timed at best. The separate ANE and CCE networks were doomed to add fuel to the fire. This action contributed to ranks of ever-thinning market makers who were continuing to withdraw bids altogether, or post lower and lower bids ("lowballing") for items that would normally never sell at those levels.

e. As the fall progressed, a new threat entered the picture. This was the threat of war in the Middle East. The first response of this type of threat was a withdrawal from activity. This can be due to personal priorities taking over, or just standing aside to assess the situation and probabilities.

f. Recession was also in the wind. This added to the negative thinking prevailing in the marketplace. The length and depth of this economic downturn was unknown and led to an overly cautious attitude. Consumer spending hit a brick wall. It stopped!

g. Fear and panic seemed to gain ground with each new week. Market reports, personal comments, and financial worries all combined to drive psychology into negative territory. Fear breeds fear. Panic begets panic! This is the kind of environment that can lead to blowoffs of significant proportions. The market responded by overshooting a more normal correction and bottom by a huge margin.

h. The auction dealers were hit with their auction bills when available cash was shrinking fast, and new sources were drying up or non-existent. They found themselves inventory rich, cash poor and overextended. The result was inevitable. Many dealers were forced into "fire-sales" or even full liquidation in order to meet their obligations. Auction houses that had been in business for decades didn't recognize the magnitude of the unique situation. They just wanted to be paid. Most showed little or no sympathy.

i. Additional auction related cash flow problems resulted from future auction consignment margin calls. These loans were called for additional margin as the market continued its unbelievable and unparalleled collapse.

j. In times of market downturns, there seems to be a inclination to grade using tighter standards. This tendency is due to a number of factors including the character of the market (going from a sellers market to a buyer's market), a reduction of ready cash to make desired purchases, a need to hedge bets concerning tomorrows prices for todays purchases, and a little greed when dealers perceive a seller in trouble.

k. "Crackouts" is a term that is used when a independently certified third party graded coin is broken out of its holder and resubmitted for grading. The major reason behind "crackouts" is the hope of receiving a higher grade. Other considerations include resubmission to another grading service for marketing "pricing and popularity" reasons. Some coins have been resubmitted as many as 10 to 20 times. This affects the accuracy of the graded population reports issued by third party grading services. The point of diminishing returns for many coins has been reached drastically reducing the flow of "crackouts" to the various grading services. "Crackouts" receiving a lower grade only compounded the cash flow problems at the time and led to further liquidations.

l. The so-called "generic" coins were a much too significant part of the total market spectrum. They not only led the way down, but they took the rarer coins with them (with virtually no trading in the higher grades of the scarce and rare dates). The tail was wagging the dog and the entire dog-house!

m. A real concern during the market crash was that the whole story and true facts were not reported. Information was either misunderstood, withheld, or distorted by the numismatic press and other information reporting centers. Most dealers did not really know all of the leading causes for the demise. This author prepared three important releases during this period of time in order to present the true facts, and offer solutions to preserve an orderly market. (See the chapters covering this very critical situation in Phases I, II, III and IV.)

n. The crux of the market's problems were imbedded in the bid based system practices used by ANE and CCE in the dealer to dealer sight-unseen electronic trading arena. This was given undue importance through the reporting of the "lowball" bids as representing the true value of the coins. The fact that trading was virtually non-existent in over 95% of the items was totally ignored.

o. As of today, nobody seems to have learned anything from the past 1990 crash. ANE has suspended trading indefinitely and CCE has returned to the "dark ages" and reinstated the bid-based system.

5. Certain silver dollars can be worth as much as a million dollars apiece. This is not so astounding when you consider the entire field of collectibles, and the prices brought at auction for those famous and valuable pieces of art, sculpture, etc. The most recent famous example of such an item was the 1804 Dollar sold in 1990 as a part of the King of Siam set by Superior Galleries in the "Boy's Town" auction for $3.19 million. How do you value a real treasure? One that cannot be replaced at any price. The first official million dollar coin in a single transaction involved the sale of the PCGS Proof-65 Augustus Humbert 1852/1 $20 territorial gold piece. This author concluded that sale at a record price of $1.35 million in May of 1989. A "Guinness" record at that time in history.

A PCGS MS-65 1794 dollar recently was sold to Jay Parrino for a silver dollar auction record price of $506,000. Also a PCGS MS-65 1893-S Morgan dollar in a private transaction for $475,000 and the one PCGS graded MS-65 1884-S sold for $425,000 in a private sale.

The price record for a U.S. coin belongs to the Augustus Humbert 1852/1 $20 Pioneer gold coin (PCGS PR-65). This piece was sold May 19, 1989, by John W. Highfill (Oklahoma Federated Gold & Numismatics, Inc., Broken Arrow, Oklahoma) and Mark S. Yaffe (National Gold Exchange, Inc., Tampa, Florida) for $1,350,000 in a private transaction.

6. Over one dozen different dates have traded in excess of $100,000 in MS-65 and higher during the 1980s, and were not publicly reported. Why were they not reported? In many cases, these were private dealer to dealer transactions. Others were private sales to collectors or investors who wished to remain unknown in the numismatic world. A good trivia question for you would be to find out these dates and their respective grades! All were MS-65 or better except one. Your first correct answer would be an 1884-S in MS-64.

7. There are always some dealers who remember large numbers of great coins, bags and rolls. Could it be that their memories have faded over the years and left them with an exaggerated impression of what was really there? Now as the grading standards (and their "fish story syndrome" memory) have changed, so have the end results. They only think they're still out there. There may be hoards still available but the majority of the bags they saw that had been dispersed are "not as remembered." Sorry!

8. Estimated coin survival figures of the past that were considered liberal were actually ultra-conservative. Many were off by millions of coins, especially in the higher mint state grades! If we look carefully at the statistics presented by PCGS and NGC since their inception, it becomes very clear that the actual number of coins available for collectors and investors is dramatically below previous estimates. As we see the certified point of diminishing returns being reached by one date after another, the "guesstimates" of the surviving mintage in mint state condition become more and more believable. The truth is that the coins are not really out there in quantity and/or quality, as believed by many numismatists. If they really aren't out there, they need to be looked at in a new light. See the multiple charts listed in this chapter. YOU MAY BE SHOCKED!

The point of diminishing returns may also be described as the "point of diminishing submissions." It is that point in time when the continuing submission volume of coins for certification begins to decline. For each date, this will be a different time. Some coins have already begun their submission decline, while others have not yet peaked. As the point of diminishing submissions is reached for each date, it will be easier to "guesstimate" the number of examples actually available. Another hint of the coming point of diminishing submissions is the diversification of the various grading services into baseball cards and other collectibles. There were 2.5 million U.S. coins graded in the first 5 years of PCGS. There will not be that quantity in the next 5 years (we're talking U.S. coinage here). PCGS has researched and looked into taking steps to grade the coins of many other countries including ancient coins, as well as different type collectibles such as baseball cards, stamps and possibly autographs.

ANACS Grading Standards

The grading and certification environment before 1985 was the domain of The American Numismatic Association Certification Service (ANACS), which began formally grading coins in 1978. From then until 1985, this service was the "only game in town" and performed a much needed benefit to the coin industry in the United States.

Among other things, the adopted grading standards called for a stated grade on the obverse and reverse of the coin being evaluated. For example, if a coin was graded MS-65/63, this split grade meant that the obverse was rated an MS-65 while the reverse only graded MS-63. An MS-63/63 rating meant that the coin was graded MS-63 on both sides. The consensus grade was often an average between the split grade given the coin, and could be open to negotiation by both buyer and seller depending on the appeal of the specimen, current market conditions and other factors.

As concerns about the grading standards utilized by ANACS began to surface, ANACS director, Ken Bressett and grader Leonard Albrecht participated in a meeting with a number of dealers in Houston, Texas during the third National Silver Dollar Convention. The heart of the dispute revolved around the significance of the strike with respect to the grade given a coin. ANACS held that strike had little or no influence on the grade while many dealers felt that strike should be considered as a major factor. The ramifications of this continuing struggle with grading factors and their relative significance gave birth to the Professional Coin Grading Service.

The Professional Coin Grading Service (PCGS)

February 3, 1986 was the day the Professional Coin Grading Service (PCGS) first opened its doors. They used a grading reporting method which differed from the existing procedure used by ANACS. Each coin was given only one reported grade instead of a grade for the obverse and another for the reverse (examples: MS-65 versus MS-65/65; MS-65 versus MS-65/64;

MS-63 versus MS-63/64; etc.). The other major change in the grade reporting involved the grades of the Sheldon scale used. Previously, the accepted mint state grades were MS-60, MS-63, MS-64, MS-65 and MS-67. PCGS elected to report grades using the entire mint state scale from MS-60 through MS-70 inclusive. This decision added MS-61, MS-62, MS-66, MS-68, MS-69 and MS-70 to the previously utilized set. It is interesting to note that the only mint state grades used in the early 1970s were MS-60, and later, MS-65.

The first coin to be independently graded as MS-70 was by PCGS. It was a 1986 Silver American Eagle, serial number 1172618. It was reported by the Wall Street Journal as well as the various numismatic publications at the time.

There are several areas worthy of mention that have been affected by PCGS over the last five years.

a. **Credibility**: Independently graded coins, once encapsulated and guaranteed by PCGS to be authentic, became eligible for lending activities. This paved the way for lending institutions to loan against existing inventories of certified coins.

b. **Authentication**: PCGS graded coins were given a guarantee of authenticity. This made the encapsulated certified coins more acceptable for trading by less knowledgeable collectors and investors.

c. **Sight-Unseen**: The sight-unseen marketplace for certified coins developed as a direct result of the grading service. Dealers promised to accept certified coins using an electronic trading network (ANE). In fact, it was one of the stated goals of PCGS.

d. **Grading Consistency**: The PCGS methodology used a team of professional graders to provide an unbiased third party grade to coins submitted for certification. As time has proven, there has been a consistency of grading standards used by PCGS in its grading process.

e. **Improved liquidity**: PCGS has directly affected the liquidity of its certified coins in the marketplace. These specimens are readily accepted both by the network of dealers and market makers, as well as by collectors and investors. Transactions may take place quickly as the question of grade has already been decided.

f. **Population Reports**: The next most visible result of PCGS activities, after the certified coin itself, is the population reports that have been published. These reports have provided a wealth of information leading to more "modern" guesstimates of surviving mintages in mint state condition. One older dealer has even suggested that there was too much information available today!

g. **ANE Electronic Trading Network**: PCGS was able to support this successful sight-unseen electronic trading network for subscribing market makers and dealers. This has added to the liquidity of certified coins, but has also contributed to greater volatility as a bid-based system. ANE's pioneering efforts paved the way for updated systems such as Unitrade, CCE, T.I.S., and U.S. Rare Coin Exchange.

h. **Bar Coding**: PCGS used bar coding to enhance the electronic reading of the encapsulated coin's information. This has promoted electronic handling of certified coinage. The identification number of the coin and the grade as well as the serial number could be entered into a computer without hand typing all those numbers.

i. **Hand Held Scanners**: These scanners are used to read the bar codes provided by PCGS during the encapsulation process.

j. **Accepted Numerical Coin Identification Numbers**: Each coin listed has been assigned a unique identification number. This enables computer systems to quickly identify, sort, and process certified coin information after scanning.

k. **Computer Grading**: This newly developed capability is a natural extension of the grading process in the electronic age. Computer grading will serve to remove most, if not all, of the problems associated with "human" grading. These grading systems, however, will only be as good as the databases and programmers used in the process. Refer to David Hall's "Computerized Grading: The PCGS Expert™" for additional information.

l. **Foreign Coin Grading**: PCGS has expanded into the grading of foreign coins. This is consistent with the growing interest of collectors and investors for these issues in countries around the world.

m. **Authorized Dealer Network (International)**: This expanded dealer network is a natural extension of foreign coin grading. This also provides an expanded market for U.S. coins as well as potential additional capital and liquidity for electronic trading. The European community, along with the Japanese have a strong interest in the future of all PCGS/NGC coins, domestic and/or foreign.

n. **Inventory Control**: The combination of coin identification numbers, coin serial numbers, bar coding, hand-held scanners and computer inventory processing has led to the potential of computerized inventory control. The addition of computer grading and electronic trading networks to this group of electronic processes leads us to the door of complete computer processing from start to finish.

o. **Certified Coin Exchange (CCE)**: The CCE expanded on the original ideas used by the ANE electronic exchange by offering a sight-unseen market with on-screen editing, a collection of management and market reports, a message service, and a subscriber elected Board of Governors. The trading summary reports covering the period since May 1990 provide excellent analytical material for sight-unseen trading frequency and content analysis. This network has been fundamental in the trading of PCGS coins on a sight unseen basis.

p. **Counterfeit Deterrent**: The independent third party grading services have worked diligently to grade authentic coins only. The PCGS/NGC guarantee of authenticity concerning its graded coins are examples. The growing ability (especially with the help of computers) to distinguish counterfeit specimens from the real thing is very beneficial to the numismatic marketplace. NGC has taken similar steps in their grading procedures.

Population reports should accomplish the following:

1. Provide information that may be used for statistical analysis and reference purposes.
2. Give you approximate relationships and proportions to other dates and allow estimates of surviving mintages.
3. The population reports should not be misinterpreted. The majority of the better dates were submitted from collectors and investors whose only intent was to get them certified. They were never for sale!
4. Provide information used to monitor "generic" coin populations.
5. Many lower value coins are not submitted for obvious reasons. The price of submission sometimes exceeds the value of the coin. This is referred to in Oklahoma as "**country boy philosophy**." In the rest of the world, it's called COMMON SENSE!

Most dealers really do know what they're doing. For example, using original dealer submissions, the MS-60 PCGS certified population for the 1881-S is 123, while the MS-60 population for the 1886-P is 66. The better date 1885-S has an MS-60 population of 52. Now the dealer can make money certifying and marketing the 1885-S in MS-60, but how can you make any money on a certified 1881-S or 1886-P? There are multiples of Morgan and Peace dollars out there, but they are usually MS-60/63 and not worth submitting for certification at this time.

There is a story being circulated which goes like this. The boiler rooms are touting and selling low population, low mint state grade coins as "rare" coins. They are talking about the 1961-D Washington quarter in MS-60, and similar coins. Of course, nobody is submitting them for certification. Therefore, the population reports show few or none of this type of coin. DON'T GET LOST! Realize what is takes for a dealer to submit coins for certification. A recent certified population report lists the 1881-S in MS-60 at 123, and in MS-65 at over 10,000 pieces. None of us would say that the 1881-S in MS-60 was more rare than the same date in MS-65.

The population figures published by PCGS and NGC are more of a "reality" in both scope and vision than the older publications that relied on original mintage figures. As these independent third party grading services certify a greater number of coins, their population reports will continue to grow as the reliable source for statistical data concerning surviving specimens in mint state condition. Remember that the lower mint state grades of common dates will not reflect the true number of coins out there due to the economics of submission for certification. However, MS-64 and higher grades can be used with greater reliability as a tool for calculating surviving mintages.

This book has chosen to rely heavily upon the published population reports of independent grading concerns in order to predict surviving pieces with a greater degree of certainty. This is revolutionary but, as time goes on, the "certified population" approach will gain more and more validity. Statistically speaking, its time has come. This author was on the American Numismatic Exchange (ANE) Board of Governors when the PCGS population report was initially discussed and approved. This was a milestone as far as numismatic availability for historical data research is concerned.

It is always interesting to note the truth about the truth. What I am referring to is the collector's perception of the truth versus the real truth. It has been said that it does not really matter what truth is; what does matter is what people perceive to be true. This situation exists today in the perception of surviving quantities of mint state Morgan and Peace silver dollars. The real truth is that these surviving quantities are much smaller than most collectors realize. In fact, it would be better stated that the Morgan and Peace dollars in MS-66 and higher are RARE!

Following are a number of reasons to explain why there are so few MS-60 through MS-62 and circulated certified coins graded and listed in the population reports issued by PCGS and NGC. This is not an issue of philosophy, but simply of doing business.

1. Only a few circulated rarer date coins are submitted to be graded due to the relatively low value of other coins compared to the actual submission costs.

2. The mint state grades MS-60/62 are also often valued at a price that does not make submitting those coins to be graded economically feasible.

3. The rarer dates such as 1892-S, 1893-S, 1894-P and 1895-O have higher prices than their circulated and MS-60/62 "cousins." But the small number of coins available in the marketplace has restricted the number submitted for grading. The coins for sale could economically be submitted for certification. Those coins held by collectors who are not planning to sell their holdings are usually not submitted.

4. One special situation has been responsible for a number of the certified coins in the MS-62 population figures. This is partly due to submissions by dealers and collectors looking for a certified grade of MS-63. The MS-63 grade for most investment grade coins is THE PIVOTAL GRADE AND PRICE POINT! Mint state-63 and higher is considered the investment starting point (not to be confused with each date's actual Pivotal Grade Point).

The following Professional Coin Grading Service (PCGS) Important Notice and format is reprinted for your attention with permission from the Professional Coin Grading Service, P.O. Box 9458, Newport Beach, California, 92658.

IMPORTANT NOTICE - Please Read Carefully

The PCGS POPULATION REPORT profiles the number of coins certified by PCGS at a given grade for each date, denomination, mint mark and variety. BECAUSE THE POPULATION REPORT CONTAINS INFORMATION ONLY WITH RESPECT TO THOSE COINS WHICH HAVE BEEN SUBMITTED TO AND CERTIFIED BY PCGS, IT SHOULD NOT BE RELIED UPON TO DETERMINE ACTUAL OR RELATIVE VALUES OF PARTICULAR COINS IN THE MARKETPLACE. The values of many issues, such as most proof coins minted after 1954, do not justify submission to PCGS for grading. The populations reported herein for such coins are therefore significantly lower than the actual numbers available in the marketplace.

The information contained herein is compiled from the computer data base maintained by PCGS for this purpose. Information is posted to this data base on a daily basis, and population figures for any given coin can change substantially over a short period of time. These population figures represent the number of coins processed from PCGS and may not reflect any reduction for coins that have been lost, destroyed, or removed from PCGS holders. Note that dealers often remove coins from PCGS holders and re-submit them in hopes of receiving a higher grade. Sometimes the dealers return the old inserts to PCGS so that coins can be removed from the Population Report, but sometimes they do not. PCGS makes reasonable efforts to maintain and publish accurate information, however, it disclaims any responsibility of liability for the accuracy or completeness of the information contained herein.

SPECIAL NOTICE: PCGS has been grading world coins (Canada, Switzerland, Germany, England, Japan, etc.) for an extremely brief period of time. Population Report information for world coins is very preliminary. At this early stage you should not make any assumptions on the rarity of any world coins based on PCGS population information.

Certification of PCGS does not guarantee protection against the normal risks associated with potentially volatile markets.

The degree of liquidity of PCGS certified coins will vary according to general market conditions and according to the particular coin involved. For some coins there may be no active market at all at certain points in time.

The following Numismatic Grading Corporation (NGC) words of caution and format is reprinted for your attention with permission from the Numismatic Grading Corporation, P.O. Box 1776, Parsippany, New Jersey, 07054.

CAUTION

The utilization of this Report as a tool for assessing the population and value of certified numismatic coins in any character or grade is unreliable.

The following characteristics inherent in the marketplace undermine the accuracy of this Report.

1. Inexpensive coins which are not submitted for certification appear scarce but are not.
2. Numismatic coin certification services are predominantly utilized for investment grade coins.
3. Often certified coins are cracked out of holders without notice to the grading service, therefore, computer tallies utilized to publish grading reports may be misleading.
4. Rarity is only one factor which must be weighed in determining economic value of a numismatic coin.

Numismatic Guaranty Corporation of America encourages all numismatic coin collectors and investors to seek the counsel of qualified numismatists familiar with the certified coin marketplace before making any purchase based upon this Report.

IMPORTANCE NOTICE:

The coin market is speculative and unregulated. Many areas of numismatics lend themselves to third party grading and authentication. Certification does not eliminate all risk associated with the grading of coins.

PCGS celebrates milestone

A gem quality 1894-S Morgan silver dollar was designated Mint State 66 by the Professional Coin Grading Service on December 21, 1988, as the industry leader certified its one millionth coin.

This numismatic rarity was certified by PCGS graders Gordon Wrubel, Charles Browne, Ronald Howard and finalized by Steven Cyrkin, and represents a major milestone in PCGS history as the firm approached its third anniversary.

The one millionth coin carried an insured value of $17,000, bringing the cumulative declared market value of all PCGS-graded coins to $883,264,859 at the time. This author bought and sold this coin shortly after it came into the marketplace.

1894-S MS66
(Courtesy of Professional Coin Grading Service)

Prooflikes are not all alike

There is a possibility for confusion over the different prooflike categories as reported by the various services and numismatic publications. Let's take a look.

Definitions:

PL	=	Prooflike (both NGC and PCGS)
DPL	=	Deep Prooflike (NGC)
DMPL	=	Deep Mirror Prooflike (PCGS)

Description:	**Service**	**Starting Date:**
PL	PCGS	April 1987
DMPL	PCGS	January 1988
PL	NGC	October 1988
DPL	NGC	January 1989 *
PL	Greysheet	December 1979 **
DMPL	Greysheet	November 17, 1989
PL	Bluesheet	January 2, 1987
DMPL	Bluesheet	October 1988

* NGC designates DPL to be virtually identical in grade standards to DMPL as described by PCGS.

** Note that CDN has indicated that the PL title used since 1979 should have been DMPL from the beginning. The DMPL category replaced the PL category on November 17, 1989. There are currently no price records available for PLs by the CDN or CCDN. There also was no great price change in the transformation from PL to DMPL. The DMPLs did not actually go up in value, however, the PLs were destroyed by a simple reporting policy change. The same thing happened to MS-63 coins with the introduction of the MS-64 grade without prior notice. MS-63 coins crashed and/or became MS-64 due to the less strict grading standards in use at that time.

Coin Holders

The progress of coin holders is one that is not usually presented in a historical fashion, but there is always a first time for everything. The first coin holders were really the coin drawer cabinets that held the coins (and created sliders via the opening and closing of the drawers). The other best known carrier (and therefore holder) of coins were the mint sewn canvas bags used by the U.S. Treasury. Looking at individual coin holders, envelopes and other cloth protection was placed around the coins in the 18th and 19th centuries. This allowed the chemicals associated with the holding materials as well as elements in the atmosphere and foreign substances to tone, tarnish and otherwise alter the surface appearance of the coins.

When the early "coin flips" were designed, they were still of paper origin and therefore still subject to earlier sulphur problems. By the 1960s, coin flips had advanced to forms of plastic and another method was also gaining popularity. This was the stapled 2 by 2 coin holders. Information concerning the coin was written on the outside of the coin holder. Heavier plastic holders were also being designed to provide further protection to the coins inside. Plastic holders developed further to include 3 by 3 holders which were screwed or snapped together to protect the coin inside.

The custom plastic snap holders (3 by 3) developed from their earlier "relatives." By the middle of the 1980s when PCGS was formed, holders were developed to fully seal and protect the coin inside. Further development of holders continued the technology of fully sealed holders to those which we see today. The future of coin holders will be determined by technological advances as well as the economics of high volume grading services.

The older problems of PVC (Poly Vinyl Chloride) damaging coins is no longer an issue. PVC was especially prevalent in the "soft" plastic coin flips. These flips were welcomed at the time as a favorable alternative to the "hard" plastic flips that would damage the skin around the fingernails as the coins were placed inside. "Kointains"® were used as protection against PVC materials. This method involved two separate hard plastic cases that would fit very close together with the coin inside. The smaller of the two portions of the case would be inserted (with the coin) into the slightly larger receiving portion.

Electronic Sight-Unseen Trading Volume Considerations

The advent of third party certification led to an electronic marketplace which has been used, abused and probably misunderstood by those who have tried to make bid-based electronic trading work. For a complete discussion electronic trading including its effect on the numismatic marketplace, refer to this author's coverage of the subject in chapter 39, 40, 41 and 42 (Phase I, II, III and IV) of this volume.

There are not enough dealers to support the electronic marketplace as it exists today. The potential dollar volume far exceeds their combined capital available for market activities.

However, on the other side of the equation, there are not enough coins to support Wall Street institutions, and their commission structure, volume requirements, liquidity needs and other considerations.

It is impossible to make a "complete" two-way market for every date in MS-65 Morgan dollars. Here is a summary of "categories" and associated comments.

1. Some dates have not yet been graded in any or all grades by any certified grading service. There have not been any coins submitted, and there may never be.

2. Some dates have 1-5 examples and are gone forever. Those that have these "once in a lifetime coins" are not going to let them go. They are "**Keepers**."

3. Those issues with 10-25 examples are sold and don't re-enter the marketplace. These prized specimens are the cornerstones of most important collections and will be held for the long term.

4. Those dates with 25-100 examples trade infrequently and the mint state coins in an current inventory status would be 5-10% available. The bid would be (100%) consistent with little or no ask. They can be obtained with a diligent effort, but the price would surprise you!

5. Those dates with over 100-500 examples would have only 10-20% availability at any given time in the marketplace. They will trade infrequently, and could not be expected to be in the market much at all. The spreads would be large and could approach 200 -300% or more.

6. Those dates possessing 250-500 pieces would have 20-30% availability, and be a little more accessible. Collectors would still be motivated to hold these coins, and be rather reluctant to sell them. The spreads here would still be large, but beginning to come down a bit.

7. Those dates with 500-1000 coins *may* have 30-40% availability. These would definitely be traded, but not at the whim of a potential buyer. Spreads would still be rather large (50-150%) depending upon market conditions.

8. Those dates with over 1,000 will trade 40-50% of the time with spreads from a low of 10-20% up to and including as much as 100%. These coins should be obtainable within a short period of time. The price and spread would vary depending upon the demand for the purchase and sale (current market conditions).

9. The most common and "generic" dates will be available daily. Depending upon market conditions, quote spreads will vary from a low of 1-2% to a high of 10-15%. Collectors and investors could expect to obtain these coins at will, with condition and demand being the major factors. These are and will remain volatile during price fluctuations.

THEREFORE YOU WILL NEVER, AND I SAID NEVER, HAVE A COMPETITIVE (NARROW) SPREAD ON THE MAJORITY OF ALL MORGAN AND/OR PEACE DOLLAR DATES. You will have a better chance of competitive (10-20%) spreads on the common date MS-65 and/or PR-64/65 type coins in the 19th century. There are numismatic "traders" that will buy and sell every date and/or grade with a small percentage spread. You should buy your coins from these dealers if they should encounter the rarer issues. Go back and read this entire paragraph again. COMPREHEND IT CAREFULLY. It is one of the best pieces of advice you will get from this entire book!

The Wall Street type of brokerage trading may dictate the way the common "generic" dates trade in the U.S. and foreign markets. Independent third party graded MS-60 Morgan dollars may trade in 1000 coins lots from one country to another in the future. The price could be from $50 to $500 per coin. This is not a forecast, but an observation of things that are entirely possible.

Take a moment to consider that silver dollars are completely different from any other *type* of coin on the CCE. The bids can move up constantly on a daily basis as dealers attempt to locate the scarce and rare dates. The dates are listed individually as well as by type.

Certain coins are in constant demand from collectors. This group of coins make good investment vehicles. It is a little like a dividend which shores up the value of a good stock during slack market periods. Demand for these coins creates the backbone of the entire numismatic marketplace. For example, coins like the 1938-D Buffalo in MS-65, and the MS-63 Barber dimes can virtually remain at the same bid/ask spread for an entire year.

It is interesting to compare pricing and marketing operations existing at the coin shows with those of the electronic trading systems. Many dealers lower their bids on the electronic sight-unseen market system, and try to buy the desired coins for less at the coin shows. SURPRISE! There have no good coins (or very few) available for the dealers to buy, and those that are for sale command a higher price than the dealers expected to pay.

In fact, coins today sell anywhere and everywhere if the price is right. Coins do not have to be brought to coin shows anymore to be sold. Here is a commonly heard sentence. "I can't believe how few good coins are here (at the show)." This remark is heard so often at all the shows these days. It's like a bad joke. It seems as if they never learn. The majority of all rare coins are in private collections, various museums, limited partnerships, pension plans, various financial funds, leveraged borrowing accounts (regular or "accidental" investor), and savvy dealer's private inventory that's "NOT FOR SALE!" It takes a major effort to obtain anything other than common or lower grade collectible coins. DON'T LOOK FOR THIS TREND TO CHANGE!

Doom and gloomers and other forecasters/writers say some MS-65 better date dollars are not worth between five and ten thousand dollars. But note the guesstimate totals of MS-65's were off 90-95% in the past (so were the BU totals!). Grading then changed and so did condition rarity in direct proportion to prices. All silver dollars are now the MOST collected and have the largest demand (this is "reclassifying" what is RARE). Many non-dollar dealers consider all silver dollars as common, but they will soon have to re-evaluate their positions. In Prooflikes, the percentage of PL in proportion to the original mintage will also lead to a redefinition of the term "rare." There are 129 dates and mint marks (excluding varieties) available in the Morgan and Peace series. The demand for these silver dollars assures them of a high place in the world of numismatics.

If you think that silver dollars are common, take a minute to study this chart and let the truth slowly sink in. The chart presents a picture of the entire population of certified Morgan and Peace dollar coins. Look at all of the available MS-66's and higher. Do they look common to you?

	Morgan Dollars		Peace Dollars	
	PCGS	NGC	PCGS	NGC
MS-60	4,684	573	806	110
MS-61	12,889	1,899	2,173	460
MS-62	63,877	8,543	12,457	1,636
MS-63	225,183	34,175	45,976	6,200
MS-64	239,272	50,495	42,838	9,194
MS-65	101,745	21,612	8,896	2,932
MS-66	13,764	1,943	301	94
MS-67	11,183	136	9	3
MS-68	63	5	0	0
MS-69	5	0		
Totals	672,665	119,381	113,456	20,629

These figures are based upon the January 1, 1991 population totals.

The "Red Book" has proven over the years of its existence to be the most valuable tool in its service to the numismatic community. However, the most common misinterpretation of the Red Book by many collectors is the original mintage figures for the Morgan and Peace silver dollar series. The mintage figures ARE correct. It's their interpretation that needs changing. For example, take a look at some of the examples and the spread between some of the Morgan and Peace dollars.

BU Chart Population

	Morgan Dollars			Peace Dollars	
Date	**Mintage**	**Certified ***	**Date**	**Mintage**	**Certified ***
1881-CC	296,000	7,127	**1922-D**	15,063,000	2,670
1885-CC	228,000	6,919	**1922-S**	17,475,000	2,196
1889-CC	350,000	220	**1923-S**	19,020,000	2,003
1887-O	11,550,000	2,423	**1928-P**	360,649	2,086
1889-O	11,875,000	1,587	**1928-S**	1,632,000	1,403
1896-O	4,900,000	326	**1934-S**	1,011,000	673

* The Certified figures are a combination of both PCGS and NGC as of this writing.

Are you looking for the "Lost Dutchman" mine in "Numismatic-Land?" Where are those silver dollars that you see all over the place in those original mintage figures? Where did they go? Isn't it time for a "reality" check? If those silver dollars were really available, they would be sending them in by the droves to be certified and then sold to waiting collectors and investors. But the want lists remain unfulfilled for the most part. And that's the simple truth!

For the Date Only Collector

The date-only collector is interested in collecting one example from each date, and does not require one specimen of each mint mark for a given date of issue. The usual procedure is to buy the date first. Then the upgrading process takes place over a period of time. Often, date only collectors will expand their horizons and begin to acquire the different mint marks available for each date. This action will lead them toward the accumulation of a complete set and another "full set" collector will be born. Of course, investors may often move down the same path of buy and secure, upgrade and finally expand (a collector in the making). With this in mind, the following charts present the most common and the rarest date Morgans by year and mintmark for the benefit of date only collectors. This chart is for MS-60 specimens.

Most Common BU By Year	Rarest BU By Year	Most Common BU By Year	Rarest BU By Year
1878-S	1878-P 7/8TF	1892-O	1892-S
1879-S	1879-CC	1893-P	1893-S
1880-S	1880-O	1894-S	1894-P
1881-S	1881-P	1895-S	1895-O
1882-S	1882-O	1896-P	1896-O
1883-O	1883-S	1897-P	1897-O
1884-O	1884-S	1898-O	1898-S
1885-O	1885-S	1899-O	1899-S
1886-P	1886-O	1900-O	1900-S
1887-P	1887-S	1901-O	1901-P
1888-P	1888-S	1902-O	1902-S
1889-P	1889-CC	1903-P	1903-S
1890-P	1890-CC	1904-O	1904-S
1891-CC	1891-O	1921-P Morgan	1921-S

All Peace dollars are scarce in grades above MS-64. For example, counting common date issues, less than 1% of the "surviving" original mintage is in MS-65 condition or above. It is also estimated that less than 5% of the original mintage is available in any BU mint state grade. The following chart lists the PCGS graded Peace dollar figures for MS-65, MS-66 and MS-67 courtesy of the PCGS Population Report, June 1, 1991, Newport Beach, California.

PCGS Graded Peace Dollars in MS-65, MS-66 and MS-67

Date	MS-65	MS-66	MS-67
1921-P	176	12	1
1922-P	1,064	17	0
1922-D	276	11	0
1922-S	53	2	0
1923-P	3,506	8	1
1923-D	105	2	0
1923-S	24	0	1
1924-P	778	26	0
1924-S	23	0	0
1925-P	2,123	108	2
1925-S	13	0	0
1926-P	485	12	0
1926-D	213	16	4
1926-S	97	9	1
1927-P	42	1	0
1927-D	26	2	0
1927-S	18	1	0
1928-P	43	1	0
1928-S	9	0	0
1934-P	86	8	0
1934-D	91	10	0
1934-S	41	3	0
1935-P	189	15	0
1935-S	138	11	0

Condition Rarity

CONDITION RARITY IS REAL AND ALWAYS WILL BE! John Love of Cut Bank, Montana, was probably the originator of the prooflike designation for silver dollars. He found that many of his discriminating customers were willing to pay a higher premium for the best quality pieces. He advertised the higher quality and experienced great success and many happy customers.

The wealthy want the best of everything at any price. This special distinction given to the highest quality has always been sought by those with the money and taste for only the very best. It may be egomania or it may be the driving force of a collector who will not rest until he has those few magnificent pieces. This can be compared to art, antiques, automobiles and/or even wine. Refer to John Highfill's chapter entitled "World's Finest Collections and Prices Realized" for a large listing of Morgan and Peace dollar price records.

Collectors of all means seem to gravitate towards a similar goal. That is to buy and secure the very best with the resources at hand. This is usually a process of upgrading over a long period of time. The collector who has a coin in MS-60 will upgrade to an MS-63 if given the opportunity. The MS-63 will later be exchanged for an MS-64 if possible. Likewise an MS-64 will be converted into an MS-65 and so forth. It is a cycle that is destined to repeat itself. UPGRADING CAN BE VERY REWARDING FOR BOTH THE COLLECTOR AND INVESTOR ALIKE.

Did you know . . .

1. The 1880-S is the most common date in DMPL followed closely by the 1884-CC. The 1881-S is seventh!
2. The BU 1892-S and 1893-S are in a 24 to 24 tie according to the certified population figures published independently by PCGS and NGC. This includes all BU graded coins to date.
3. Forty-one dates and mint marks do not have a single MS-65 DMPL representing them.
4. The 1889-CC boasts that 47.7% of its existing BU certified population is prooflike (in either PL and DMPL condition).
5. There are 129 different dates and mint marked Morgan dollars. This excludes the different die varieties.

Notes for Investors

It is always interesting to look for variations of the familiar 80-20 rule. For instance, it is reported that approximately 80% of gross sales taken in by retail department stores is attributed to only 20% of the merchandise offered in their stores. It is also true that only 20% or so of those in an organization are active to any degree. The coin industry has something to say along these lines — but is a little more extreme. The published record of sales on the sight-unseen electronic marketplace shows an incredible 95% of total sales involving only 5% of the available offerings! That means that there is only a recorded market in only 1 out of every 20 listings. The other nineteen have no recorded trades at all.

It is important to develop a properly diversified portfolio based upon that portion of the total funds available for numismatic investment or collection purposes.

Collector "A" has $25,000 to commit to a numismatic portfolio. He decides to buy one coin for the entire amount of $25,000. This collector is quite vulnerable to a number of considerations including volatile market movements, the "popularity" of that particular date, an unexpected increase in the independent third party graded population of that date and condition, and a possible future emergency cash need which would call for selling the coin at a "liquidation" price. The same situations could arise for any portfolio of this magnitude containing under five different coins.

Collector "B" is also willing to put $25,000 into U.S. coinage on a long term basis. This collector elects to acquire 25 coins at a price of $500 to $2000 each. The coins selected represent diversified dates and series which have shown relative stability in the past. Collector "B" has a much better and more diversified portfolio which would provide more protection against adverse market conditions, continuing popularity for the majority of the dates held, a cushion against unforeseen increases in the population of the coins in the portfolio, and the ability to sell only a portion of the portfolio if special cash needs arise. These are some of the advantages of developing a diversified numismatic portfolio.

The same considerations apply when the numismatic funds available are over one million dollars. The dollar amounts may be different but the percentages are still the same. Don't put 100% of the available funds into only one coin. Forty to fifty coins with a market value of $10,000 to $40,000 would be more appropriate. In any case the cardinal "rules" of acquisition are still the same (i.e., buy the rarer dates first and upgrade; buy the highest grade possible within the budgeted price parameters; and buy a high quality coin within the selected grade).

A large amount of available money does not eliminate the need or the responsibility to create a broad-based portfolio. Sadly enough, the availability of larger sums often leads to mismanagement of those funds coupled with a less caring attitude. If you buy coins with little downside, you will usually buy a coin with little upside also. Speculation: No Pain — No Gain; No Risk — No Reward.

Everyone talks about the "fluff" built into markets when they are on the high side. Well, the price lows reached in the crash of 1990 by the full range of issues on the electronic sight-unseen trading network took any and all "fluff" away (along with the cash reserves of many of the dealers). The price tags for material in the Spring of 1991 were "bare bones" and represented an excellent entry point for both collectors and investors. One up and coming potentially famous dealer marked his calendar with March 15, 1991, as the bottom of the market and start of a new bull market. These comments will stand the test of time over any number of coin market cycles, so tuck these away for use again and again.

The theory of "*cointrary*" opinion should be understood by collectors and investors alike. One side effect of the information offered in the population reports published by PCGS is a decrease in the mystery, mystique, and romance of coins in the eye of the reader. The presence of this body of knowledge leaves much less to the imagination. IT'S TIME TO RETHINK THIS!

Do you realize that, of coins graded by PCGS in the Morgan series, there is only ONE MS-65 for the 1884-S, 1889-CC, 1893-O, 1901-P, etc? (Look for yourself and be convinced.) There have been only 10 1882-O/S pieces PCGS graded MS-64, and only 11 1896-O specimens graded MS-64. If these examples don't excite you, GO OUT AND FIND ONE! Then see what you have to give to own one (assuming that it is even for sale). Use your imagination to visualize what continued and growing demand from an increasing number of collectors and investors must do to the asking prices for these coins. You will soon develop your own "*cointrary*" opinion!

Most decisions in life are 50/50. Nothing is clear cut. That can include religion, culture, science, coins and even mathematics. Try to compare life to a final basketball score of 101 to 100, a baseball game of 4 to 3, or even a Congressional vote of 273 to 272. Even war is never clear cut. Nobody really wins and sometimes everyone loses. Look at grading today: MS-60, 61, 62, 63, etc. Look at computer grading for tomorrow: MS-60, MS-60.1, MS-60.2, MS-60.3, etc. As you can see by these examples, most decisions are subjective and marginal at best.

Bottom Lines

The coin business is like all other businesses in this way. IT IS AS STRONG AS ITS WEAKEST LINK. THAT LINK IN SILVER DOLLARS IS THE 1881-S IN MS-63/65 RANGE. Many dealers keep one eye on this particular coin in the marketplace looking for indications of strength or weakness. Any large order coming into the market could very easily spark a rally which could affect the entire silver dollar series.

On the other side of the spectrum, lower populations indicate several things. One thing that immediately comes to mind is that LOWER POPULATION COINS ALREADY HAVE HOMES! That goes for all rare issues, and even applies to some degree to conditionally rare issues. Another indicator applying to low population issues is the tendency for these coins to trade at many times bid. The interest for high quality, low population specimens has always been present and always will be.

"Turnover" and its relationship to the surviving mint state population of U.S. rare coins is not very well understood. For example, assume there is a declared value of $3 billion in PCGS certified coins as of this writing. Some of these coins may, upon grading, prove to be undervalued, while others may be overvalued. The number of coins graded by PCGS from its inception to date is approximately 2.5 million.

Next, assume $2 billion of that amount resides in the hands of collectors and investors for the intermediate and/or long term, and that $1 billion is "circulating" within the marketplace on a continual basis. The coins in private hands may only trade on a decade by decade basis, with the most valuable pieces surfacing less often than that. Of the circulating coins, approximately 90 percent are "generic" and/or lower grade with the remainder considered scarce to rare.

What coins make up this "circulating" volume of business? Before jumping to the conclusion that the 90+ versus 10- is the proper relationship, one additional factor must be explored. The velocity of turnover is a major (and often ignored factor). For example, generic coins may experience an annual turnover rate of between 5 and 10, but scarce to rare items could appear only once or twice per year. This additional factor could change the makeup of the "circulating" volume substantially. It could be argued that 97 to 99 percent of the "circulating" volume of annual business is in "generic" and/or lower grade coins.

BUY-SELL SPREADS ON GENERIC COINS WILL ALWAYS BE SMALL. BUY-SELL PRICING ON ESOTERIC COINS WILL ALWAYS BE LARGER OR EVEN EXTREME AND TOTALLY SUBJECTIVE TO WHAT THE MARKET WILL BEAR.

Coin dealers should always take the time necessary to assess their operating margin (buy-sell) and measure that percentage against the volatility percentage factor for that same market. These percentage comparisons must be made using the same time frame to properly allow for inventory turnover. In other words, the dealer must be able to determine in advance the approximate selling price for coins that are inventoried. And likewise, the approximate price of replacing sold inventory items must be ascertained ahead of time. Just like any other business in the world, the lower the turnover ratio, the higher the profit margin must be. In slower markets, even generics need higher profit spreads to substitute for the lack of volume in trading.

For example, assume an operating margin of 5 percent for a monthly turnover in generic Morgan dollars. Next, assume that the market volatility on a monthly basis for the same market is 15 to 20 percent. Given these facts, the dealer cannot operate profitably on a consistent basis without a great deal of luck. The dealer's buy-sell spread must be consistently within the market volatility for the time period required to turn the inventory. Buying and selling during periods of higher market volatility is just a gamble and nothing more.

AS THE VOLATILITY INCREASES, THE VOLUME DECREASES. AS THE VOLUME DECREASES, THE PERCENTAGE OF PROFIT MUST INCREASE. THE OVERHEAD WILL OTHERWISE BE THE DICTATOR.

Inventory based dealers will give way to large firms and/or financial institutions that are able to maintain profitable spreads on their inventory. The days of independent dealers with large in-house inventories are numbered.

Do you remember when there were thousands of small farmers? They lost their livelihood, merged with other farmers to survive, or sold out to larger farms. The same trend has been happening to dealers over the last decade and will continue to do so. It will be close to impossible for a single entrepreneur to compete with larger firms in the future.

BROKER! Yes, brokering coins will be the only way to financially survive in the future. The auction companies have been profitable for decades using this formula. You can too. I don't mean open your own auction firm. You will have to find the customer and his needs, then find the coin(s) and sell them.

The population figures reported by the various independent third party grading services represent those submitted for certification (including resubmissions). Coins with higher values will be submitted, while those with low values will not due to the cost of certification versus the economic worth of the coins. This practice has led to population figures which do not properly represent the numbers of lower quality coins. Therefore a low population figure for a more common coin, or for a lower grade, may not actually reflect the rarity of that coin. On the other hand, resubmissions may cause the population of rare coins or conditionally rare coins to be overstated. As a result, the population figures should be studied considering all of the possibilities before being used to "guesstimate" the number of surviving examples of any particular coin and condition.

There are multiple ways to approach a collection of Morgan silver dollars based upon the pocketbook of the collector and the time available for this fascinating venture. Here is a list of some of the favorite set combinations.

1. A complete set of Morgan dollars consists of one coin for each date and mintmark making a collection of 96 coins. The two rarest dates are the 1893-S and the 1895 Proof. The total rises to 129 if the major recognized die varieties are to be included.

2. A Morgan date Set consists of one coin representing each date for a total of 28 coins. A representative piece for the year 1895 is the most expensive to acquire (i.e., the 1895-S).

3. A Morgan dollar first year of issue set contains one of each example for the year 1878 making a total of 7 coins. The collection includes the 1878 8TF, 1878 7TF, 1878 7TF (Rev. 79), 1878 7/8TF (Strong), 1878 7/8TF (Weak), 1878-CC, and 1878-S. The 1878-8TF is the lowest mintage dollar among these.

4. A Morgan dollar last year of issue consists of three coins including the 1921-P, 1921-D and 1921-S. The most difficult coin is the 1921-S.

5. A complete set of Morgans by each mint consists of five coins. These include one example each from Carson City, Denver, New Orleans, Philadelphia, and San Francisco. A coin representing the Carson City mint would be the most expensive.

6. A Morgan set of Carson City dollars would contain one example of each date for a total of 13 coins. The most expensive coin in the series is the 1889-CC.

Here is a word to the collector and investor concerning funding and the acquisition of coins. First, never place funds required for necessary items into coins, but rather use discretionary cash for this purpose. Second, consider a varied collection and portfolio with no more than 20% of the available capital tied up in any one piece. On the other hand, don't purchase coins that require less than 2% of the anticipated cash to be used for acquisitions.

The latest available PCGS figures going into press time reveal that PCGS has certified 758,992 Morgan dollars in uncirculated grades. This is hardly an overwhelming number considering the collector base and continued investor interest in this series. Next, realize that common date Morgan dollars are selling for the lowest prices since the bottom of the last coin cycle in 1982. Now this is an opportunity. But how do we reconcile the fact that the pricing of common date Morgans has managed to drag the value of rarer pieces down with them? Now this is unbelievable! Putting it another way, the twenty most common dates in the Morgan series comprise over 530,000 of the certified population. These coins are regulating the price of all the other dates including the twenty rarest dates which include approximately 5,300 certified Morgans. The tail is certainly wagging the entire dog at this time.

Population reports should accomplish the following:

1. Provide information that may be used for statistical analysis and reference purposes.
2. Give you approximate relationships and proportions to other dates and allow estimates of surviving mintages.
3. The population reports should not be misinterpreted. The majority of the better dates were submitted from collectors and investors whose only intent was to get them certified. They were never for sale!
4. Provide information used to monitor "generic" coin populations.

Date by Date Analysis Terminology

The commentary in the date by date analysis (chapter 80 and 81 of this volume) will utilize the following general categories when mentioning BU rolls and/or bags in MS-60/63.

1. **May be assembled "put-together" rolls**
2. **May be original rolls**
3. **May be original bags**
4. **May be original mint sewn bags**
5. **May be unsearched original bags or rolls**

This author has (at multiple coin shows and conventions) bought and sold from 3 to 5 bags per week, 52 weeks per year, from 1979 through 1987. This quantity of rolls and bags approximates between 2 to 3 million silver dollars. Let's take a closer look at each of these 5 categories.

1. **May be assembled or "put-together" rolls**. These are not original rolls. Dealers have bought the silver dollars as single coins and put them together in 20 coin lots of the same date and mint mark. Some of these coins may have even been "super sliders," but that is often a matter of opinion by various dealers. One dealer's BU may be another dealer's "super-slider." There is a very fine line between these two grades. These rolls will grade MS-60 to MS-63 with the majority being MS-60/61. The die varieties will be mixed in the rolls. The dates and the mint marks will be the same.

2. **May be original rolls**. These rolls will begin as original rolls. The dealers who have handled these coins have probably "cherrypicked" the rolls, and replaced the coins with lower quality BU coins. There will usually be a few lower-end MS-63 dollars left in for "spice." Original rolls will all have the same characteristics and usually be of the same die variety. If original rolls are picked over and the replacement coins are of different varieties, the roll will then become a "put-together" roll (see example #1 above).

3. **May be original bags**. The original bags will have been handled like the originals rolls discussed in the previous paragraph. They are probably cherrypicked with few lower-end MS-63 coins left in. Again, the coins will all be of the same die variety. After original bags are picked over, they are no longer complete bags. They have become MS-60/62 original rolls (see example #2 above).

4. **May be mint sewn bags**. Here we have unsearched bags of uncirculated coins. The quality will vary according to the date and mint mark, strike, luster and bagmarks. One special situation which should be mentioned concerns the New Orleans Mint. In some years (1879-1882, 1887 and 1897), this mint has released coins into circulation, recalled those coins, and placed them into mint sewn bags as uncirculated pieces. They were later released as "original" mint sewn bags. Leon Hendrickson handled approximately 350 U.S. mint sewn original bags of 1879-O through 1882-O. These were from the Continental Illinois National Bank of Chicago. They were all XF to AU with multiples of sliders. The identical situation occurred with this author in the early 1980s. John Love and Dean Tavenner handled the same type "O" mint bags from the early 1960s. The San Francisco mint did the same thing in the years 1883-1885.

5. **There is still a quantity of rolls and bags that are not mint sewn and are still unsearched**. The expected breakdown for a search of the majority of "virgin" rolls or bags is as follows. (This example would be for average dates and mint marks.) The San Francisco and Carson City mints would have higher quality bags in comparison to Philadelphia, Denver and New Orleans.

Grade		Precentage
MS-60/62	-	30 to 40%
MS-63	-	20 to 30%
MS-64	-	10 to 20%
MS-65 and above	-	5 to 10%

Pivotal Point (Grade)

It is very important for you to grasp the concept and significance surrounding the pivotal point presented in the date by date analysis section. The "pivotal point" is a significant mint state grade where two main conditions are present.

First, when reviewing the certified third party grading service population reports and the population number graded shows a decline of at least 50% or more between two mint state grades. That is a factor. For example, the recent certified population of the 1901-S Morgan is as follows:

Grade	Price
MS-63	322
MS-64	210
MS-65	47
MS-66	2

Looking at these numbers, we would be inclined to select a "pivotal" grade of both MS-65 and MS-66. Since the MS-66 population is so very small in comparison, and since the MS-65 population certainly falls within the "50% rule," it would lean toward the MS-65 at this "point." REMEMBER THIS! EVERY DATE THAT HAS A COIN GRADED HIGHER THAN ITS INITIAL PIVOTAL GRADE, WILL HAVE A SECOND AND MORE DRAMATIC PIVOTAL GRADE. THE REASON BEING, THE HIGHER THE GRADE THE MORE PIVOTAL IT BECOMES!

Now let's look at the second criteria. The pricing indexes are required to exhibit at least a 100% price jump between the mint state grade to be considered the pivotal point. Once again, let's use the 1901-S and review a recent price report.

(Non-current estimated price only)

Grade	Price	
MS-63	260	
MS-64	500	
MS-65	3,000	Initial (primary) pivotal grade #1
MS-66	7,500	Secondary (sometimes more dramatic) pivotal grade #2

The price really takes two jumps. Once between MS-64 and MS-65, and once again between MS-65 and MS-66. For the simplicity of interpreting the charts, the "initial" pivotal grade only is designated.

In cases where the pivotal point could fall to either one of two grades, the judgment of the analyst must enter into the final decision. Knowing that the consensus pivotal point over a majority of the Morgan series, and virtually all of the Peace series, the MS-65 would probably become the end result. It is the combination of these two factors, POPULATION AND PRICE, that must both be taken into consideration in order to properly arrive at the initial "pivotal point."

The difference in price between "EVERY POINT" in the mint state grades (MS-60 through MS-70) of the Sheldon scale can be thousands of dollars. Make absolutely sure you don't pay BU money for a "slider" (AU-55/58).

One important word that is used often when referring to Almost Uncirculated coinage is "slider." This word has a story to tell. In the early days of the Morgan series, it was a common practice to store minted coins in cabinets filled with drawers. This occurred at the mints as well as in BU coin shops and other dealer locations. These drawers were rather narrow from top to bottom (rather like a jewelry box drawer) and were fitted with a specially prepared and "holed-out" section of wood. After the BU coins were placed in the "counting board" (a partitioned flat wooden surface with parallel slots running the entire length - somewhat like an old washing board) and counted, they were simply transferred to the drawers by sliding them into the prepared slots (holes) in the wood.

As these drawers were opened and closed, the newly minted coins would tend to slide within their somewhat loose wooden holders. This action would sometimes produce a trace of wear on the most pronounced areas of the coins. The repeated opening and closing of the drawers caused the enclosed coins to "slide" back and forth. Thus, coins displaying this type of condition became known as "sliders."

The "Slider dates" list is provided for the benefit of those who may be considering BU quality coins. Beware of "sliders" being offered as BU examples. PRICE DIFFERENCE CAN BE AND USUALLY IS SUBSTANTIAL.

1878-CC	1886-S	1892-CC	1895-O	1897-O
1883-S	1889-CC	1892-S	1895-S	1899-S
1884-S	1890-CC	1893-S	1896-O	1902-S
1886-O	1891-CC	1894-O	1896-S	1903-S
				1904-S

Every Peace dollar date! (1921-1935 P,D, and S)

Vocabulary

To the uninitiated, here are a few descriptive words that need to be mentioned concerning cleaned and artificially colored or resurfaced coins.

1. California prooflikes: These are coins that have been especially cleaned with the aid of items such as a dentist drill and fine polisher. Now some of the "artists" were very good, and their products were blazing to behold, their cameo prooflikes too good to be true! A number of the more prominent perpetrators of these coins hailed from California, and these coins were so named.

2. Whizzed coins: Yet another name for coins that have been given the "dentist drill and polish" treatment. These super-cleaned coins were dubbed "whizzed" coins by those in the know.

3. Cloroxing: Using specially prepared solutions, coins would be cleaned and polished to give them a shiny new look and glow. Most examples were later "artificially toned." Very nice to view — but that's all.

The independent third party grading services have contributed much to the grading of coins. One of their excellent "contributions" has been a refusal to grade coins that have been altered in surfaces using techniques such as those just described. This has prevented an uninitiated collector or investor from being sold a piece that would only cause problems later. The financial loss also could be tremendous.

Slider Versus Bagmarked Coins

A "slider" coin is best described as a nice AU-58 example with only the slightest rub and no other marks of circulation. Bagmarks are different and are present on uncirculated coins as a result of their "travels" in U.S. mint sewn canvas bags. The AU coins are usually lustrous and fully struck. The first presence of circulation is found on the breast of the eagle on the reverse and over the ear of Miss Liberty on the obverse.

A "baggy" mint state 60 (or other mint state graded) specimen is not a "slider." Bagmarks may often be confused with circulation by the new collector. In fact there are "slider" MS-63 and even MS-65 examples.

Collectors have developed the "eye appeal" approach to the coins they acquire for their collections. Most of them will opt for a nice looking AU-58 piece versus a baggy "technical BU" specimen. Toned coins are also collected by some and shunned by others. It just depends upon the individual collector.

Silver Dollar Categories

The general categories of silver dollars used in this chapter and the date-by-date analysis need to be explained. There are four groups to be addressed including Key dates, Semi-key dates, Semi-common dates, and Common dates.

Key dates - These are the dates and mint marks that collectors are always actively seeking. Once found and secured, they are rarely if ever sold.

Semi-key dates - Collectors continually and actively seek the semi-key date coins. These examples are acquired and put into collections for the long term. These coins are usually sold only in emergency situations or in order to upgrade their collection.

Semi-common dates - Since these coins are better than common dates, but not good enough to qualify as semi-key dates, collectors will obtain them for collections for the intermediate term. They will usually be sold if the price is right, or if a better coin comes along. Investors will also participate in this arena expecting to recycle the coins at a profit.

Common dates - Collectors often seek and find these coins as they begin their collections. They will sell these coins to upgrade their collection, or to acquire a semi-key or key date example. They will usually be sold if the market presents the holder with a profit too good to pass up. Investors will enter the market and buy these coins with a profit motive only. As a result, these coins will recycle in the marketplace over time.

***

CHAPTER 77

Morgan and Peace Dollar Quick Reference Charts

by John W. Highfill, NLG

This collection of quick reference charts represents the results of research compiled into an easily used chart format. The purpose of these charts is to provide a ready source of informational knowledge to collector and investors alike. For your convenience, the charts are numbered and presented in the following order.

(1) Morgan Dollars: Dies Produced
(2) Morgan Dollars: Average Pieces Struck Per Die Pair
(3) Morgan Dollars: Die Varieties
(4) Peace Dollars: Die Varieties
(5) Morgan Dollars: Top 25 MS-65 Certified Rare Dates
(6) Morgan Dollars: Top 25 MS-65 Certified Common, Semi-Common, and Semi-Key Dates
(7) Morgan Dollars: Top Certified BU Dates
(8) Peace Dollars: Certified MS-65 and BU in Population Order
(9) Morgan Dollars: Rarity Chart in Rarity Factor Order
(10) Peace Dollars: Rarity Chart in Rarity Factor Order
(11) Morgan Dollars: Top Certified "Rarest" MS-65 PL and DMPL
(12) Morgan Dollars: Top 25 Certified BU and DMPL Common Dates
(13) Morgan Dollars: Top Common Prooflikes (Percent of Total BU Graded)
(14) Morgan Dollars: *NO* MS-65 Certified DMPL or DPL Specimens
(15) Morgan Dollars: Hardest and Easiest PL (Date Order)
(16) Morgan and Peace Dollars: Branch Mint Proofs, Certain Morgan Proofs, and Peace Proofs
(17) Morgan and Peace Dollars: MS-60 Coins With Potential
(18) Morgan Dollars: Top 25 Circulated (Scarcest and Rarest)
(19) Peace Dollars: Circulated (Scarcest and Rarest)
(20) Morgan Dollars: Philadelphia Mint Dollars in Rarity Order
(21) Morgan Dollars: Carson City Mint Dollars in Rarity Order
(22) Morgan Dollars: Denver Mint Dollars in Rarity Order
(23) Morgan Dollars: New Orleans Mint Dollars in Rarity Order
(24) Morgan Dollars: San Francisco Mint Dollars in Rarity Order
(25) Morgan Dollars: Pivotal Grades
(26) Morgan Dollars: Characteristics
(27) Peace Dollars: Characteristics
(28) All Issues: PCGS Grading Summary Totals by Grade and Type
(29) Original GSA Holdings For Sale
(30) GSA Carson City Silver Dollar Categories
(31) GSA Dollar Sales

(1) MORGAN DOLLARS: DIES PRODUCED

The following chart lists the dies produced for each year and mint for the Morgan silver dollar series. The number of dies listed are for each fiscal year (July 1 — June 30). Very special thanks and appreciation go to Leroy Van Allen for the information and research contained in the first four die and variety charts. The dies and die varieties information is also presented in the date by date analysis section (within the statistical blocks).

Year	Philadelphia.	New Orleans	San Francisco	Carson City
1878	92	0	192	100
1879	157	40	192	30
1880	199	80	110	25
1881	148	119	200	50
1882	92	50	80	30
1883	127	92	105	20
1884	128	60	80	20
1885	131	124	40	20
1886	161	80	0	0
1887	107	108	8	0
1888	116	136	80	0
1889	104	150	20	10
1890	95	60	80	50
1891	81	100	73	40
1892	15	30	33	30
1893	16	20	30	20
1894	0	20	20	
1895	4	10	38	
1896	40	40	40	
1897	70	50	98	
1898	40	34	58	
1899	37	140	40	
1900	45	230	40	
1901	114	210	80	
1902	136	300	40	
1903	142	180	20	

(2) MORGAN DOLLARS: AVERAGE PIECES STRUCK PER DIE PAIR

The following calculation presents the average pieces struck per die pair produced. This calculation uses totals for the entire Morgan dollar series without production for 1921 (86,730,000).

Total Pieces	Die Pairs	Average No. Strikes Per Die Pair
260,779,667-P	1,198-P	217,679-P
186,137,529-O	1,231-O	151,208-O
109,493,373-S	898-S	121,930-S
13,862,041-CC	222-CC	62,441-CC
570,272,610	3,549	160,411
86,730,000		
657,002,610		

(3) MORGAN DOLLARS: DIE VARIETIES

The numbers of known Morgan dollar die varieties for each year and mint are presented in the following chart.

Year	Die Varieties	Year	Die Varieties
1878-P 7TF	54	1890-P	14
1878-P 7TF (Rev. 79)	12	1890-CC	13
1878-P 7/8TF	16	1890-O	20
1878-P 8TF	33	1890-S	25
1878-CC	26	1891-P	9
1878-S	53	1891-CC	4
1879-P	36	1891-O	12
1879-CC	3	1891-S	13
1879-CC (C/D)	1	1892-P	7
1879-O	28	1892-CC	9
1879-S	31	1892-O	11
1879-S (Rev. 78)	13	1892-S	7
1880-P	40	1893-P	5
1880-CC	7	1893-CC	5
1880-CC (Rev. 78)	3	1893-O	5
1880-O	39	1893-S	1
1880-O (8/7)	9	1894-P	2
1880-S	69	1894-O	8
1880-S (0/9)	1	1894-S	7
1881-P	17	1895-P	N/A
1881-CC	6	1895-P (Proof)	3
1881-O	29	1895-O	4
1881-S	53	1895-S	4
1882-P	23	1896-P	21
1882-CC	6	1896-O	19
1882-O	37	1896-S	8
1882-S	27	1897-P	10
1883-P	15	1897-O	7
1883-CC	4	1897-S	11
1883-O	39	1898-P	10
1883-S	8	1898-O	19
1884-P	12	1898-S	13
1884-CC	12	1899-P	6
1884-O	36	1899-O	30
1884-S	8	1899-S	13
1885-P	21	1900-P	23
1885-CC	4	1900-O	33
1885-O	15	1900-O/CC	7
1885-S	8	1900-S	12
1886-P	20	1901-P	11
1886-O	16	1901-O	32
1886-S	4	1901-S	9
1887-P	17	1902-P	11
1887-P (7/6)	1	1902-O	38
1887-O	21	1902-S	11
1887-O (7/6)	1	1903-P	9
1887-S	8	1903-O	5
1888-P	19	1903-S	31
1888-O	18	1904-P	8
1888-S	10	1904-O	8
1889-P	22	1904-S	5
1889-CC	3	1921-P (M)	25
1889-O	18	1921-D	7
1889-S	11	1921-S	7

(4) PEACE DOLLARS: DIE VARIETIES

The numbers of known Peace dollar die varieties for each year and mint are presented in the following chart.

Year	Die Varieties	Year	Die Varieties	Year	Die Varieties
1921-P	2	1924-S	2	1927-S	1
1922-P	11	1925-P	3	1928-P	1
1922-D	3	1925-S	1	1928-S	1
1922-S	2	1926-P	1	1934-P	1
1923-P	8	1926-D	2	1934-D	5
1923-D	1	1926-S	1	1934-S	2
1923-S	2	1927-P	3	1935-P	1
1924-P	5	1927-D	1	1935-S	3

(5) MORGAN DOLLARS: TOP 25 MS-65 CERTIFIED RARE DATES

The following chart ranks the top 25 MS-65 Certified Morgan dollar rare dates (PCGS and NGC combined) as of this writing (Sept. 1991).

Rank	Date	Population	Rank	Date	Population
1.	1886-O	0	14.	1892-S	6
2.	1884-S	1	15.	1880-O	8
3.	1901-P	1	16.	1895-S	8
4.	1893-O	1	17.	1879-CC	13
5.	1896-O	1	18.	1894-P	14
6.	1889-CC	2	19.	1879-S Rev. 78 *	16
7.	1895-O	2	20.	1891-O	20
8.	1879-CC C/D *	2	21.	1896-S	21
9.	1893-CC	3	22.	1891-P	26
10.	1894-O	3	23.	1887-O	27
11.	1893-S	4	24.	1904-S	27
12.	1883-S	4	25.	1892-O	28
13.	1897-O	5			

* Major die varieties

(6) MORGAN DOLLARS: TOP 25 MS-65 CERTIFIED COMMON, SEMI-COMMON, AND SEMI-KEY DATES

The following chart ranks the top 25 MS-65 Certified Morgan dollar common dates, semi-common dates, and semi-key dates (PCGS and NGC combined) as of this writing (Sept. 1991).

Rank	Common	Rank	Semi-Common	Rank	Semi-Key
1.	1881-S	1.	1921-P (M)	1.	1878-P 7TF Rev. 78
2.	1880-S	2.	1903-P	2.	1885-S
3.	1879-S	3.	1884-P	3.	1898-S
4.	1882-S	4.	1898-P	4.	1890-O
5.	1885-O	5.	1903-O	5.	1900-O/CC
6.	1886-P	6.	1901-O	6.	1881-O
7.	1887-P	7.	1880-CC	7.	1892-CC
8.	1884-O	8.	1897-P	8.	1886-S
9.	1898-O	9.	1897-S	9.	1880-CC Rev. 78
10.	1885-P	10.	1921-D	10.	1902-S
11.	1904-O	11.	1888-O	11.	1887-S
12.	1883-CC	12.	1902-P	12.	1879-O
13.	1883-O	13.	1878-CC	13.	1892-P
14.	1899-O	14.	1882-P	14.	1921-S
15.	1884-CC	15.	1889-P	15.	1901-S
16.	1883-P	16.	1899-P	16.	1890-CC
17.	1900-P	17.	1890-S	17.	1888-S
18.	1882-CC	18.	1879-P	18.	1878-P 7TF Rev. 79
19.	1878-S	19.	1881-P	19.	1878-P 7/8TF STRONG
20.	1881-CC	20.	1880-P	20.	1904-P
21.	1888-P	21.	1889-S	21.	1890-P
22.	1902-O	22.	1900-S	22.	1903-S
23.	1896-P	23.	1878-P 8TF	23.	1894-S
24.	1900-P	24.	1899-S	24.	1889-O
25.	1885-CC	25.	1891-S	25.	1893-P
		26.	1891-CC		

(7) MORGAN DOLLARS: TOP CERTIFIED BU DATES

The following chart ranks the top 25 Certified BU Morgan dollar Common, top 20 Semi-Common, top 25 Semi-Key, and top 25 Key dates (PCGS and NGC combined) as of this writing (Sept. 1991).

Rank	Common	Rank	Semi-Common	Rank	Semi-Key	Rank	Key
1.	1881-S	1.	1901-O	1.	1879-P	1.	1899-S
2.	1880-S	2.	1881-CC	2.	1881-P	2.	1892-P
3.	1885-O	3.	1885-CC	3.	1899-P	3.	1893-P
4.	1884-O	4.	1898-P	4.	1890-S	4.	1893-CC
5.	1879-S	5.	1878-CC	5.	1879-O	5.	1901-S
6.	1887-P	6.	1888-O	6.	1885-S	6.	1894-S
7.	1886-P	7.	1884-P	7.	1921-S	7.	1879-CC
8.	1904-O	8.	1903-P	8.	1887-O	8.	1883-S
9.	1882-S	9.	1882-O	9.	1902-P	9.	1886-O
10.	1883-O	10.	1882-P	10.	1891-S	10.	1904-S
11.	1898-O	11.	1897-P	11.	1890-CC	11.	1896-S
12.	1885-P	12.	1881-O	12.	1889-S	12.	1897-O
13.	1883-CC	13.	1921-D	13.	1880-O	13.	1895-S
14.	1884-CC	14.	1903-O	14.	1892-O	14.	1894-P
15.	1899-O	15.	1880-CC	15.	1892-CC	15.	1896-O
16.	1902-O	16.	1890-P	16.	1887-S	16.	1894-O
17.	1921-P (M)	17.	1880-P	17.	1891-P	17.	1893-O
18.	1900-O	18.	1890-O	18.	1888-S	18.	1903-S
19.	1878-S	19.	1897-S	19.	1900-S	19.	1889-CC
20.	1882-CC	20.	1891-CC	20.	1889-O	20.	1895-P (Proof) **
21.	1896-P			21.	1904-P	21.	1901-P
22.	1888-P			22.	1886-S	22.	1884-S
23.	1883-P			23.	1891-O	23.	1895-O
24.	1900-P			24.	1902-S	24.	1892-S *
25.	1889-P			25.	1898-S	25.	1893-S

* Currently tied in all BU grades for first with the 1893-S. Both coins have 24 BU pieces each totally graded by PCGS and NGC as of this writing (Sept. 1991).

** The 1895-P is a Proof only issue.

Note: The major die varieties are not included here.

(8) PEACE DOLLARS: CERTIFIED MS-65 AND BU IN POPULATION ORDER

The following chart ranks the Independent Third-Party Graded PCGS and NGC MS-65 Coins and BU Coins in Population order (condition rarity) as of this writing (Sept. 1991).

Rank	Date	MS-65 Population	Rank	Date	All BU Grades Population
1.	1928-S	16	1.	1934-S	673
2.	1925-S	21	2.	1927-D	1,070
3.	1927-S	22	3.	1928-P	1,086
4.	1924-S	28	4.	1924-S	1,118
5.	1927-D	29	5.	1934-D	1,154
6.	1923-S	38	6.	1935-S	1,262
7.	1928-P	50	7.	1928-S	1,276
8.	1927-P	51	8.	1923-D	1,555
9.	1934-S	53	9.	1934-P	1,689
10.	1922-S	90	10.	1927-P	1,896
11.	1934-D	96	11.	1926-D	1,940
12.	1934-P	112	12.	1927-S	1,982
13.	1923-D	113	13.	1923-S	2,003
14.	1926-S	149	14.	1925-S	2,088
15.	1935-S	155	15.	1926-S	2,141
16.	1921-P	202	16.	1922-S	2,196
17.	1935-P	208	17.	1935-P	2,566
18.	1926-D	263	18.	1922-D	2,670
19.	1922-D	296	19.	1921-P	3,530
20.	1926-P	529	20.	1926-P	3,980
21.	1924-P	1,016	21.	1924-P	9,177
22.	1922-P	1,313	22.	1925-P	13,537
23.	1925-P	2,352	23.	1922-P	20,977
24.	1923-P	4,227	24.	1923-P	43,828

NOTE: The only proof Peace dollars are 1921-P and 1922-P. These issues are in matte and satin Proof and are rare. Proof strikes for both of these years were of the high relief design, except for the March 1922 Morgan-Swasey

(9) MORGAN DOLLARS: RARITY CHART IN RARITY FACTOR ORDER

The following chart presents the Morgan dollar series arranged according to this author's rarity factor by date. The rarest dates are listed under the heading R-1, while the most common are listed under the R-5 heading.

R-1	R-2	R-3	R-4	R-5
1879-CC	1878 7/8 TF Weak	1878 8TF	1878-CC	1879-S SAF
1879-CC Capped Die	1878 7TF SAF	1878 7TF PAF	1878-S	1880-S
1882-O/S	1878 7/8 TF Strong	1879-O	1879-P	1881-S
1883-S	1879-S PAF	1882-P	1880-P	1882-S
1884-S	1880-CC PAF	1885-S	1880-CC	1883-CC
1886-O	1880-O	1887-O	1881-P	1883-O
1887/6-P	1886-S	1889-S	1881-CC	1884-CC
1887/6-O	1887-S	1890-P	1881-O	1884-O
1889-CC	1888-S	1890-CC	1882-CC	1885-P
1892-S	1889-O	1890-O	1882-O	1885-O
1893-P	1891-P	1890-S	1883-P	1886-P
1893-CC	1891-O	1891-CC	1884-P	1887-P
1893-O	1892-P	1891-S	1885-CC	1898-O
1893-S	1892-CC	1899-P	1888-P	1899-O
1894-P	1892-O	1902-P	1888-O	1902-O
1894-O	1898-S	1921-S	1889-P	1904-O
1894-S	1899-S		1896-P	1921-P (M)
1895-P (Proof)	1900-O/CC		1897-P	
1895-O	1900-S		1897-S	
1895-S	1902-S		1898-P	
1896-O	1904-P		1900-P	
1896-S			1900-O	
1897-O			1901-O	
1901-P			1903-P	
1901-S			1903-O	
1903-S			1921-D	
1904-S				

(10) PEACE DOLLARS: RARITY CHART IN RARITY FACTOR ORDER

The following chart presents the Peace dollar series arranged according to this author's rarity factor by date. The rarest dates are listed under the heading R-1, while the most common are listed under the R-5 heading.

R-1	R-2	R-3	R-4	R-5
1924-S	1921-P	1922-D	1926-P	1922-P
1925-S	1922-S	1923-D		1923-P
1927-P	1923-S	1926-D		1924-P
1927-D	1935-S	1926-S		1925-P
1927-S		1934-P		
1928-P		1935-P		
1928-S				
1934-D				
1934-S				

(11) MORGAN DOLLARS: TOP CERTIFIED RAREST MS-65 PL AND DMPL

The following chart presents the top 30 Certified MS-65 rarest PL, top 25 Certified MS-65 rarest DMPL, and top 30 rarest PL and DMPL combined Morgan silver dollars (PCGS and NGC combined) as of this writing (Sept. 1991).

Rank	PL Date	Rank	DMPL Date	Rank	PL and DMPL Combined Date
1.	1893-S	1.	1893-S	1.	1886-O
2.	1892-S	2.	1892-S	2.	1884-S
3.	1895-O	3.	1895-O	3.	1901-P
4.	1884-S	4.	1884-S	4.	1896-O
5.	1901-P	5.	1901-P	5.	1895-O
6.	1889-CC	6.	1889-CC	6.	1889-CC
7.	1903-S	7.	1903-S	7.	1879-CC Capped Die *
8.	1893-O	8.	1893-O	8.	1893-O
9.	1894-O	9.	1880-O	9.	1894-O
10.	1896-O	10.	1894-O	10.	1893-CC
11.	1894-P	11.	1896-O	11.	1893-S
12.	1895-S	12.	1894-P	12.	1883-S
13.	1897-O	13.	1895-S	13.	1897-O
14.	1886-O	14.	1897-O	14.	1892-S
15.	1883-S	15.	1896-S	15.	1880-O
16.	1879-CC	16.	1904-S	16.	1895-S
17.	1894-S	17.	1886-O	17.	1894-P
18.	1901-S	18.	1883-O	18.	1879-S Rev. 78 *
19.	1893-CC	19.	1879-CC	19.	1879-CC
20.	1893-P	20.	1894-S	20.	1891-O
21.	1902-S	21.	1901-S	21.	1896-S
22.	1891-O	22.	1893-CC	22.	1891-P
23.	1886-S	23.	1893-P	23.	1887-O
24.	1904-P	24.	1902-S	24.	1904-S
25.	1896-S	25.	1891-P	25.	1892-O
26.	1880-O			26.	1893-P
27.	1904-P			27.	1889-O
28.	1879-O			28.	1903-S
29.	1898-S			29.	1890-P
30.	1921-S			30.	1894-S

* Major die varieties.

(12) MORGAN DOLLARS: TOP 25 CERTIFIED BU AND DMPL COMMON DATES

The following chart presents the top 25 Certified BU most common date, and top 25 Certified DMPL common Morgan dollar issues (grades MS-60 through MS-65) as of this writing (Sept. 1991). The most common date is presented first in this chart.

Rank	BU DMPL Date	Rank	BU DMPL Date	Rank	BU Date	Rank	BU Date
1.	1880-S	14.	1886-P	1.	1881-S	14.	1884-CC
2.	1884-CC	15.	1898-O	2.	1880-S	15.	1899-O
3.	1883-CC	16.	1904-O	3.	1885-O	16.	1902-O
4.	1884-O	17.	1890-CC	4.	1884-O	17.	1921-P (M)
5.	1885-O	18.	1896-P	5.	1879-S	18.	1900-O
6.	1881-S	19.	1883-P	6.	1887-P	19.	1878-S
7.	1885-P	20.	1888-O	7.	1886-P	20.	1882-CC
8.	1883-O	21.	1898-P	8.	1904-O	21.	1896-P
9.	1882-CC	22.	1882-S	9.	1882-S	22.	1888-P
10.	1887-P	23.	1882-O	10.	1883-O	23.	1883-P
11.	1885-CC	24.	1880-CC	11.	1898-O	24.	1900-P
12.	1879-S	25.	1881-O	12.	1885-P	25.	1889-P
13.	1881-CC			13.	1883-CC		

(13) MORGAN DOLLARS: TOP COMMON PROOFLIKES (PERCENT OF TOTAL BU GRADED)

The following chart presents the top 20 most common Prooflikes (Percent of total BU surviving population).

Rank	Date	Rank	Date	Rank	Date	Rank	Date
1.	1890-S	6.	1895-O *	11.	1880-CC	16.	1884-CC
2.	1889-CC *	7.	1879-CC *	12.	1882-CC	17.	1879-S
3.	1892-S *	8.	1886-S	13.	1878-CC	18.	1891-S
4.	1897-S	9.	1883-CC	14.	1892-CC	19.	1899-S
5.	1880-S	10.	1893-CC *	15.	1900-S	20.	1885-CC

* You will note that quite a few rare dates are on this list. The percentage of prooflikes in their total mint state population is higher than the other dates. You will also notice the 1881-S IS NOT ON THIS LIST. You should study this chart carefully. Seventy five percent of these dates are key and/or scarce dates!

Only 5 of the top 20 most common BU Morgans made this percentage of prooflike chart. They were the 1879-S, 1880-S, 1882-CC, 1883-CC, and 1884-CC.

Note: Die varieties are not included in this analysis.

(14) MORGAN DOLLARS: NO MS-65 CERTIFIED DMPL OR DPL SPECIMENS

The following chart lists Morgan Dollar dates in MS-65 or Better where no examples have been certified Deep Mirror Prooflike (DMPL). Also listed are the dates that NGC has not graded DPL (equivalent to DMPL) as of this writing (Sept. 1991). The dates are not listed in rarity order, but in chronological order. NO MS-65 CERTIFIED DMPL OR DPL SPECIMENS!

PCGS	PCGS	PCGS	NGC	NGC	NGC
1878-P 7/8 Strong	1889-S	1895-S	1878 7TF Rev. 79	1886-S	1892-O
1879-CC	1891-P	1896-O	1878 7/8 TF	1887-S	1893-CC
1879-CC Capped Die	1891-O	1896-S	1879-P	1888-O	1894-S
1879-S Rev. 78	1892-CC	1897-O	1879-CC	1889-CC	1895-O
1880-O	1892-O	1900-CC	1879-S Rev. 78	1889-O	1895-S
1881-O	1892-S	1901-P	1880-CC Rev. 78	1889-S	1896-O
1882-O/S	1893-P	1901-S	1880-O	1890-P	1897-O
1883-S	1893-CC	1902-P	1881-O	1890-CC	1898-S
1884-S	1893-S	1902-S	1882-P	1890-S	1899-S
1886-O	1894-P	1903-S	1882-O	1891-P	1902-P
1887/6-P	1894-O	1904-P	1883-S	1891-CC	1921-D
1887/6-O	1894-S	1904-S	1885-S	1892-CC	
1887-S	1895-P *	1921-D			
1889-CC	1895-O	1921-S			

* The entire nonproof mintage apparently melted.

(15) MORGAN DOLLARS: PL — HARDEST AND EASIEST TO FIND (Date Order)

This is a presentation in date order of the hardest and easiest to find Prooflike coins in the Morgan dollar series. These charts do not have their respective dates in rarity order.

Hardest to Find Dates			Easiest to Find Dates	
1879-CC Capped Die *	1892-S	1900-O/CC *	1878-P 7TF PAF*	1885-CC
1879-S PAF*	1893-P	1901-P	1878-S	1885-O
1880-O	1893-O	1901-S	1879-S	1886-P
1882-O/S *	1893-S	1902-P	1880-S	1887-P
1883-S	1894-P	1902-S	1881-CC	1897-S
1884-S	1894-O	1903-P	1881-S	1898-P
1886-O	1894-S	1903-S	1882-CC	1898-O
1887/6-O *	1895-P **	1904-P	1882-S	1901-O
1889-O	1895-O	1904-S	1882-CC	1902-O
1891-P	1895-S	1921-P (M)	1883-O	1904-O
1891-O	1896-O	1921-D	1884-CC	
1892-P	1896-S	1921-S	1884-O	
1892-O	1897-O		1885-P	

* Major die varieties.
** Unknown in nonproof.

(16) MORGAN AND PEACE DOLLARS:

BRANCH MINT PROOFS, CERTAIN MORGAN PROOFS, AND PEACE PROOFS

Accurate information is difficult to obtain concerning branch mint proofs issued for the Morgan dollar series, Zerbe and Chapman Proofs, and Proofs for the Peace dollar series. There has been an extensive search with the following information reported to the numismatic community.

Date	Estimated Mintage	Known
1879-O *	12	4
1883-O *	12	2
1893-CC *	12	2
1921-P (M) (Chapman)	20 - 30	14
1921-P (M) (Zerbe)	100 - 200	43
1921-S **	24	5
1921-P High Relief	6 - 8	6 - 8 Matte Surface
1921-P High Relief	20+	7 - 10 Satin Surface
1922-P High Relief	6 - 8	6 - 8 Matte Surface
1922-P Regular Design	10+	3 Satin Surface
		2 Sandblast Surface***

* Authorized branch mint proofs.
** Authorized branch mint proofs supposedly created for Farran Zerbe.
***Made by order of Morgan for Ambrose Swasey.

(17) MORGAN AND PEACE DOLLARS: MS-60 COINS WITH POTENTIAL

The following chart presents the Morgan dollar MS-60 coins with potential. Order is date, not degree of potential. This is not a recommendation to invest.

Morgan Dollars	Morgan Dollars	Peace Dollars
1878-P Rev. 79 *	1892-O	1921-P
1879-CC	1892-S	1924-S
1879-CC Capped Die *	1893-P	1925-S
1879-S Rev. 78 *	1893-CC	1927-P
1880-CC Rev. 78 *	1893-O	1927-D
1880-O	1893-S	1927-S
1882-O/S *	1894-O	1928-P
1883-S	1894-S	1928-S
1884-S	1895-O	1934-D
1885-CC	1895-S	1934-S
1885-S	1896-O	1935-S
1886-O	1896-S	
1886-S	1897-O	
1887/6-P *	1900-O/CC *	
1887-O	1901-S	
1887/6-O *	1902-S	
1887-S	1903-O	
1888-S	1903-S	
1889-CC	1904-P	
1889-S	1904-S	
1890-O		
1891-O		

* Major die varieties

(18) MORGAN DOLLARS: TOP 25 CIRCULATED (SCARCEST AND RAREST)

The following two lists are comprised of the scarcest circulated Morgan dollars. The first list is composed of the top 25 dates most difficult to locate (Number one is the scarcest). The second list indicates the top 25 most valuable circulated dates. The comparative value of the dates on the second list was determined using: 1) mintage, 2) scarcity, 3) popularity, 4) their value in uncirculated grades, and 5) current market conditions. Note that five of the coins on the first list do not appear on the second list.

NOTES: 1895 circulated proofs do exist and are the most difficult to obtain. This coin was not included in the scarcity rating since it was not a business strike. The 1895-P business strike Morgan would be the rarest circulated date, however, none are known to exist.

The 1880-O 8/7, 1880/9-S, 1882-O/S, 1887/6-P and 1887/6-O were not included due to their infrequency of being traded and sought after **in circulated grades**.

Research was provided by Tom Phillips of Memphis, Tennessee and friends. Notice that the dates in this ranking do not directly correspond with the ranking of certified BU Morgan dates.

List 1:

Rank	Hardest to Find
1.	1885-CC
2.	1903-O
3.	1898-O
4.	1893-S
5.	1881-CC
6.	1895-S
7.	1884-CC
8.	1904-O
9.	1894-P
10.	1883-CC
11.	1889-CC
12.	1882-CC
13.	1893-CC
14.	1878-P 7/8 TF (both weak & strong) *
15.	1900-O/CC *
16.	1880-CC PAF *
17.	1880-CC
18.	1878-P 8TF *
19.	1885-S
20.	1893-O
21.	1902-O
22.	1895-O
23.	1879-CC
24.	1899-P
25.	1893-P

List 2:

Rank	Highest in value
1.	1893-S
2.	1885-CC
3.	1894-P
4.	1893-O
5.	1889-CC
6.	1895-S
7.	1881-CC
8.	1884-CC
9.	1893-O
10.	1893-CC
11.	1893-P
12.	1880-CC
13.	1880-CC PAF *
14.	1879-CC
15.	1892-S
16.	1882-CC
17.	1883-CC
18.	1879-CC Capped Die *
19.	1892-CC
20.	1899-P
21.	1891-CC
22.	1890-CC
23.	1878-CC
24.	1900-O/CC *
25.	1884-S

* Major die varieties included in this analysis.

The list of dealers that completed this analysis are the same as for the circulated Peace dollar rarity charts. They are Bill Dafcik, Jay King, David McHenry, Harrison Phillips, Tom Phillips and Leonard Standley.

(19) PEACE DOLLARS: CIRCULATED (SCARCEST AND RAREST)

The following two lists of Peace dollars have been determined on the same basis as the Morgan lists. Credit and organization for this analysis goes to Tom Phillips of Memphis, Tennessee. Tom is a true friend of mine and one of the premier "behind the scenes" dealers in America today.

List 1

Rank	Hardest to Find
1.	1928-P
2.	1934-P
3.	1934-S
4.	1921-P
5.	1927-P
6.	1927-D
7.	1924-S
8.	1935-P
9.	1927-S
10.	1935-S
11.	1934-D
12.	1928-S
13.	1926-D
14.	1925-S
15.	1926-P
16.	1926-S
17.	1923-D
18.	1925-P
19.	1924-P
20.	1922-D
21.	1923-S
22.	1922-S
23.	1922-P
24.	1923-P

List 2

Rank	Rarest in Value
1.	1928-P
2.	1921-P
3.	1934-S
4.	1927-P
5.	1927-D
6.	1934-P
7.	1928-S
8.	1934-D
9.	1927-S
10.	1935-P
11.	1924-S
12.	1926-P
13.	1926-D
14.	1926-S
15.	1935-S
16.	1925-P
17.	1925-S
18.	1924-P
19.	1923-S
20.	1923-D
21.	1923-P
22.	1922-S
23.	1922-D
24.	1922-P

Again, the list of dealers who combined their expertise to furnish this data includes Bill Dafcik, Jay King, David McHenry, Harrison Phillips, Tom Phillips and Leonard Standley.

Thomas B. Phillips — Professional Numismatist
Memphis, Tennessee

(20) MORGAN DOLLARS: PHILADELPHIA MINT DOLLARS IN RARITY ORDER

The following chart presents the Philadelphia Mint Morgan dollars in rarity order (most rare first). The first column presents BU rarity while the second column presents MS-65 certified rarity.

BU Rarity

1.	1895-P *	15.	1897-P
2.	1901-P	16.	1884-P
3.	1894-P	17.	1903-P
4.	1893-P	18.	1898-P
5.	1892-P	19.	1889-P
6.	1904-P	20.	1900-P
7.	1891-P	21.	1883-P
8.	1902-P	22.	1888-P
9.	1899-P	23.	1878-P **
10.	1881-P	24.	1896-P
11.	1879-P	25.	1921-P (M)
12.	1880-P	26.	1885-P
13.	1890-P	27.	1886-P
14.	1882-P	28.	1887-P

MS-65 Certified Rarity

1.	1901-P	15.	1882-P
2.	1894-P	16.	1902-P
3.	1891-P	17.	1897-P
4.	1893-P	18.	1898-P
5.	1895-P (Proof)	19.	1884-P
6.	1890-P	20.	1921-P (M)
7.	1904-P	21.	1903-P
8.	1892-P	22.	1900-P
9.	1880-P	23.	1896-P
10.	1881-P	24.	1888-P
11.	1879-P	25.	1883-P
12.	1899-P	26.	1885-P
13.	1878-P **	27.	1887-P
14.	1889-P	28.	1886-P

* No 1895-P business strikes are known to exist. The entire original mintage of 12,880 is believed to have been melted.

** Includes all die varieties. All 1878 die varieties would "individually" rank higher on each list.

(21) MORGAN DOLLARS: CARSON CITY MINT DOLLARS IN RARITY ORDER

The following chart presents the Carson City Mint Morgan dollars in rarity order (most rare first). The first column presents BU rarity while the second column presents MS-65 certified rarity.

	BU Rarity		MS-65 Certified Rarity
1.	1889-CC	1.	1889-CC
2.	1879-CC	2.	1893-CC
3.	1893-CC	3.	1879-CC
4.	1892-CC	4.	1890-CC
5.	1890-CC	5.	1892-CC
6.	1891-CC	6.	1891-CC
7.	1880-CC	7.	1878-CC
8.	1878-CC	8.	1880-CC
9.	1885-CC	9.	1885-CC
10.	1881-CC	10.	1881-CC
11.	1882-CC	11.	1882-CC
12.	1884-CC	12.	1884-CC
13.	1883-CC	13.	1883-CC

NOTE: Die varieties are not included in this chart.

(22) MORGAN DOLLARS: DENVER MINT DOLLARS IN RARITY ORDER

The following chart presents the Denver Mint Morgan dollars in rarity order (most rare first). The first column presents BU rarity while the second column presents MS-65 certified rarity. This was not a difficult chart to research and prepare for the 1921-D was the only Denver Mint Morgan dollar issue.

BU Rarity	MS-65 Certified Rarity
1. 1921-D	1. 1921-D

(23) MORGAN DOLLARS: NEW ORLEANS MINT DOLLARS IN RARITY ORDER

The following chart presents the New Orleans Mint Morgan dollars in rarity order (most rare first). The first column presents BU rarity while the second column presents MS-65 certified rarity.

BU Rarity

1.	1895-O	14.	1903-O
2.	1893-O	15.	1881-O
3.	1894-O	16.	1882-O
4.	1896-O	17.	1888-O
5.	1897-O	18.	1901-O
6.	1886-O	19.	1900-O
7.	1891-O	20.	1902-O
8.	1889-O	21.	1899-O
9.	1880-O	22.	1898-O
10.	1892-O	23.	1883-O
11.	1887-O	24.	1904-O
12.	1879-O	25.	1884-O
13.	1890-O	26.	1885-O

MS-65 Certified Rarity

1.	1886-O	14.	1890-O
2.	1896-O	15.	1882-O
3.	1895-O	16.	1888-O
4.	1894-O	17.	1901-O
5.	1893-O	18.	1903-O
6.	1897-O	19.	1902-O
7.	1880-O	20.	1900-O
8.	1891-O	21.	1899-O
9.	1887-O	22.	1883-O
10.	1892-O	23.	1904-O
11.	1889-O	24.	1898-O
12.	1879-O	25.	1884-O
13.	1881-O	26.	1885-O

This presentation does not include major die varieties.

(24) MORGAN DOLLARS: SAN FRANCISCO MINT DOLLARS IN RARITY ORDER

The following chart presents the San Francisco Mint Morgan dollars in rarity order (most rare first). The first column presents BU rarity while the second column presents MS-65 certified rarity.

BU Rarity		MS-65 Certified Rarity	
1.	1893-S	1.	1884-S
2.	1892-S	2.	1892-S
3.	1884-S	3.	1893-S
4.	1903-S	4.	1883-S
5.	1895-S	5.	1895-S
6.	1896-S	6.	1896-S
7.	1904-S	7.	1904-S
8.	1883-S	8.	1903-S
9.	1894-S	9.	1894-S
10.	1901-S	10.	1888-S
11.	1899-S	11.	1901-S
12.	1898-S	12.	1921-S
13.	1902-S	13.	1887-S
14.	1886-S	14.	1902-S
15.	1900-S	15.	1886-S
16.	1888-S	16.	1898-S
17.	1887-S	17.	1885-S
18.	1889-S	18.	1891-S
19.	1891-S	19.	1899-S
20.	1921-S	20.	1900-S
21.	1885-S	21.	1889-S
22.	1890-S	22.	1890-S
23.	1897-S	23.	1897-S
24.	1878-S	24.	1878-S
25.	1882-S	25.	1882-S
26.	1879-S	26.	1879-S
27.	1880-S	27.	1880-S
28.	1881-S	28.	1881-S

(25) MORGAN DOLLARS: PIVOTAL GRADES

The following chart presents the Pivotal Grades for each date and noted variety in the Morgan series.

Date	Pivotal Grade	Date	Pivotal Grade
1878 7/8 TF Weak	MS-65	1888-O	MS-65
1878 8 TF	MS-65	1888-S	MS-65
1878 7TF PAF	MS-65	1889-P	MS-65
1878 7TF SAF	MS-65	1889-CC	MS-63
1878 7/8 TF Strong	MS-65	1889-O	MS-65
1878-CC	MS-65	1889-S	MS-65
1878-S	MS-65	1890-P	MS-64
1879-P	MS-65	1890-CC	MS-64
1879-CC	MS-64	1890-O	MS-65
1879-CC Capped Die	MS-64	1890-S	MS-65
1879-O	MS-64	1891-P	MS-64
1879-S	MS-66	1891-CC	MS-64
1879-S PAF	MS-64	1891-O	MS-64
1880-P	MS-65	1891-S	MS-65
1880-CC	MS-65	1892-P	MS-65
1880-CC PAF	MS-65	1892-CC	MS-65
1880-O	MS-64	1892-O	MS-64
1880-S	MS-66	1892-S	MS-60 *
1881-P	MS-65	1893-P	MS-65
1881-CC	MS-66	1893-CC	MS-64
1881-O	MS-64	1893-O	MS-64
1881-S	MS-66	1893-S	MS-60 *
1882-P	MS-65	1894-P	MS-65
1882-CC	MS-65	1894-O	MS-64
1882-O	MS-64	1894-S	MS-65
1882-O/S	MS-60	1895-P (Proof)	PR-65 **
1882-S	MS-65	1895-O	MS-60 *
1883-P	MS-65	1895-S	MS-65
1883-CC	MS-65	1896-P	MS-65
1883-O	MS-65	1896-O	MS-63
1883-S	MS-64	1896-S	MS-64
1884-P	MS-65	1897-P	MS-65
1884-CC	MS-65	1897-O	MS-64
1884-O	MS-65	1897-S	MS-65
1884-S	MS-63	1898-P	MS-65
1885-P	MS-65	1898-O	MS-65
1885-CC	MS-65	1898-S	MS-65
1885-O	MS-65	1899-P	MS-65
1885-S	MS-65	1899-O	MS-65
1886-P	MS-65	1899-S	MS-65
1886-O	MS-64	1900-P	MS-65
1886-S	MS-65	1900-O	MS-65
1887-P	MS-65	1900-O/CC	MS-65
1887/6-P	MS-65	1900-S	MS-65
1887-O	MS-64	1901-P	MS-63
1887/6-O	MS-64	1901-O	MS-65
1887-S	MS-64	1901-S	MS-65
1888-P	MS-65	1904-P	MS-65
1902-P	MS-65	1904-O	MS-65
1902-O	MS-65	1904-S	MS-65
1902-S	MS-65	1921-P (M)	MS-65
1903-P	MS-65	1921-D	MS-65
1903-O	MS-65	1921-S	MS-65
1903-S	MS-65		

* The Pivotal Grades are much lower for these rarer issues.

** Proof only.

(26) MORGAN DOLLARS: CHARACTERISTICS

The following categories may be used to study the physical characteristics of the Morgan silver dollar. The categories presented are Strike, Bagmarks, and Luster. This author has organized the information in date order under each category.

Strike Characteristics — Chart #1

Soft/Weak	Soft/Weak	Average	Average To Bold	Sharp/Bold	Sharp/Bold
1879-CC Capped Die	1893-CC	1878 7/8TF Weak	1879-P	1878 8TF	1886-S
1882-O	1893-O	1878 7TF PAF	1880-CC	1878-CC	1889-CC
1882-O/S	1894-P	1878 7TF SAF	1880-O	1878-S	1889-S
1883-O	1894-O	1878 7/8TF Strong	1881-P	1879-S	1890-CC
1884-S	1895-O	1879-CC	1883-P	1880-S	1890-S
1885-S	1896-O	1879-O	1883-CC	1881-CC	1891-S
1886-O	1896-S	1879-S PAF	1884-O	1881-S	1892-S
1887-O	1897-O	1880-P	1887-P	1882-CC	1893-S
1887/6-O	1900-O/CC	1880-CC PAF	1891-CC	1882-S	1894-S
1888-P	1901-P	1881-O	1892-CC	1883-S	1895-P (Proof)
1888-O	1901-O	1882-P	1893-P	1884-P	1896-P
1889-P	1901-S	1885-O	1895-S	1884-CC	1897-P
1889-O	1902-O	1887/6-P	1897-S	1885-P	1898-P
1890-P	1902-S	1887-S	1899-P	1885-CC	1903-P
1890-O	1904-P	1888-S	1899-O	1886-P	1903-S
1891-P	1921-P (M)	1892-P	1899-S		
1891-O	1921-D	1898-O	1902-P		
1892-O	1921-S	1898-S			
		1900-P			
		1900-O			
		1900-S			
		1903-O			
		1904-O			
		1904-S			

Bagmark Characteristics — Chart #2

Light	Moderate	Moderate (cont.)	Moderate To Heavy	Heavy
1879-S	1878 7/8TF Weak	1887/6-O	1878-CC	1879-S PAF
1880-S	1878 8TF	1889-CC	1879-CC Capped Die	1882-O/S
1881-CC	1878 7TF PAF	1889-S	1880-CC	1890-P
1881-S	1878 7TF SAF	1890-O	1882-CC	1900-O/CC
1882-S	1878 7/8 TF Strong	1890-S	1883-S	
1892-S	1878-S	1891-O	1884-P	
1893-P	1879-P	1891-S	1885-S	
1893-S	1879-CC	1892-P	1886-O	
1894-S	1879-O	1892-CC	1887-O	
1898-P	1880-P	1892-O	1887-S	
1899-O	1880-CC PAF	1894-P	1888-P	
1899-S	1880-O	1894-O	1888-O	
1902-P	1881-P	1895-O	1888-S	
1903-P	1881-O	1895-S	1889-P	
1903-O	1882-P	1896-P	1889-O	
1903-S	1882-O	1897-P	1890-CC	
	1883-P	1897-O	1891-P	
	1883-CC	1897-S	1891-CC	
	1883-O	1898-O	1893-CC	
	1884-CC	1898-S	1893-O	
	1884-O	1899-P	1896-O	
	1884-S	1900-P	1896-S	
	1885-P	1900-O	1901-P	
	1885-CC	1900-S	1901-O	
	1885-O	1901-S	1904-P	
	1886-P	1902-O	1904-O	
	1886-S	1902-S	1921-P (M)	
	1887-P	1904-S	1921-D	
	1887/6-P		1921-S	

Luster Characteristics — Chart #3

Poor	Average	Good	Very Good	Excellent
1890-P	1878 7/8TF Weak	1878 7TF PAF	1883-S	1878-S
1891-P	1878 8TF	1878 7TF SAF	1885-P	1879-S SAF
1891-O	1878 7/8TF Strong	1878-CC	1891-CC	1880-S
1895-O	1879-P	1879-CC Capped Die	1892-S	1881-CC
1896-O	1879-CC	1879-O	1893-P	1881-S
1897-O	1881-O	1879-S PAF	1893-CC	1882-S
1901-P	1882-O	1880-P	1898-O	1885-CC
1904-P	1883-P	1880-CC	1898-S	1886-P
1921-S	1886-O	1880-CC PAF	1900-O	1889-S
	1887/6-P	1880-O	1903-P	1890-S
	1887/6-O	1881-P	1904-O	1891-S
	1887-O	1882-P		1892-CC
	1888-P	1882-CC		1893-S
	1888-O	1882-O/S		1894-S
	1889-P	1883-CC		1895-P (Proof)
	1889-O	1883-O		1895-S
	1892-P	1884-P		1899-O
	1892-O	1884-CC		1903-O
	1893-O	1884-O		1903-S
	1894-P	1884-S		
	1894-O	1885-O		
	1896-P	1885-S		
	1896-S	1886-S		
	1901-O	1887-P		
	1901-S	1887-S		
	1902-P	1888-S		
	1902-O	1889-CC		
	1902-S	1890-CC		
	1904-S	1890-O		
	1921-P (M)	1897-P		
	1921-D	1897-S		
		1898-P		
		1899-P		
		1899-S		
		1900-P		
		1900-O/CC		
		1900-S		

(27) Peace Dollars: Characteristics

Focusing on the visual characteristics of the Peace dollar, the listings below present this author's view of the following categories: Strike, Bagmarks, and Luster. I'll bet you didn't realize the 1934-S and the 1935-S were among the best strikes in the Peace dollar series.

Strike Characteristics — Chart #1

Soft/Weak	Average	Average To Bold	Sharp/Bold
1921-P	1922-P	1926-S	1923-P
1922-S	1922-D	1928-P	1924-P
1923-S	1923-D	1934-D	1925-P
1924-S	1927-D	1934-S	1926-P
1925-S		1935-S	1926-D
1927-S			1927-P
1928-S			1934-P
			1935-P

Bagmark Characteristics — Chart#2

Light	Moderate	Moderate To Heavy
1925-P	1921-P	1922-D
1927-P	1922-P	1922-S
1928-P	1923-P	1923-S
1934-P	1923-D	1924-S
1934-S	1924-P	1925-S
1935-P	1926-P	1926-S
	1926-D	1928-S
	1927-D	
	1927-S	
	1934-D	
	1935-S	

Luster Characteristics — Chart #3

Average	Good	Excellent
1921-P	1923-P	1922-S
1922-P	1923-D	1925-P
1922-D	1923-S	1926-D
1925-S	1924-P	1926-S
1934-P	1924-S	1927-S
	1926-P	1934-S
	1927-P	1935-P
	1927-D	1935-S
	1928-P	
	1928-S	
	1934-D	

(28) All Issues: PCGS Grading Summary Totals by Grade and Type

The following chart is a summary presented by permission from the Professional Coin Grading Service (PCGS). The report is dated May 1991 and lists the entire number of coins in all denominations graded by type and grade including totals.

U.S. Grading Summary Coin Totals by Type

Grade	Copper	Nickel	Silver	Gold	Total
1-15	454	88	1,451	375	2,368
20-35	524	85	2,367	3,267	6,343
40-45	408	134	2,902	6,995	10,439
50-58	1,583	2,211	25,276	42,860	71,930
MS60	320	363	9,598	29,833	40,114
MS61	287	377	23,373	55,980	80,017
MS62	1,742	2,925	116,235	104,082	224,984
MS63	7,869	10,098	386,352	96,419	500,738
MS64	18,401	20,936	494,777	48,520	582,634
MS65	14,010	28,812	277,867	13,722	334,411
MS66	2,874	8,045	55,016	1,672	67,607
MS67	201	104	5,994	240	6,539
MS68	3	3	251	22	279
MS69	0	0	5	6	11
MS70	0	0	0	0	0
PR60	36	91	1,228	100	1,455
PR61	56	173	2,089	165	2,483
PR62	323	875	5,409	342	6,949
PR63	2,185	4,190	11,297	658	18,330
PR64	6,456	11,422	25,962	1,180	45,020
PR65	3,503	8,251	32,021	609	44,384
PR66	505	2,166	18,800	185	21,656
PR67	63	273	6,370	29	6,735
PR68	1	15	937	0	954
PR69	0	2	66	0	68
PR70	0	0	0	0	0
Other (Pattern and Modern Issues)					33,373
Totals	**61,804**	**101,639**	**1,505,644**	**407,361**	**2,109,821**

* Courtesy of PCGS, Newport Beach, California

(29) ORIGINAL GSA HOLDINGS FOR SALE

Year	Unc. CC	Mixed CC	Mixed Unc.	Mixed Circ.	Unsaleable	Uncirculated Coins Out (1975)	Total
1878 CC	47,566			13,426*		1	60,993
1879 CC	3,632	490				1	4,123
1880 CC	114,941	16,587				1	131,529
1881 CC	122,708	24,776				1	147,485
1882 CC	382,912	222,116				1	605,029
1883 CC	523,852	231,665				1	755,518
1884 CC	788,627	174,008				3	962,638
1885 CC	130,822	17,462				1	148,285
1889 CC		1					1
1890 CC	3,609	339				1	3,949
1891 CC	5,176	510				1	5,687
1892 CC		1					1
1893 CC		1					1
Various P, O, S			27,980				27,980
Various				84,165	311		84,476
TOTALS	**2,123,845**	**687,956**	**27,980**	**97,591**	**311**	**12**	**2,937,695**

* Culled

(30) GSA CARSON CITY SILVER DOLLAR CATEGORIES

CC Year	Unc.	Scratched/ Tarnished	Combined	Rejects/ Errors	Unc. Over-Dates	Tarnished Over-Dates	% Mixed CC	% Mixed Circ.	% Total Minted
1878	47,567		13,426					14	2.7
1879	3,633		490				.07		.5
1880	114,942	12,087		4,500	(45,000)	(5,000)	2.41		22.1
1881	122,709	16,776		8,000			3.60		49.6
1882	382,913	216,116		6,000			32.29		44.6
1883	523,853	221,665		10,000			33.67		62.7
1884	788,630	159,008		15,000			25.29		84.6
1885	130,823	11,462		6,000			2.54		64.9
1890	3,610	325		14			.05		.1
1891	5,177	423		87			.08		.3
TOTALS	**2,123,857**	**637,862**	**13,916**	**49,601**	**(45,000)**	**(5 ,000)**	–	**14**	–

(31) GSA DOLLAR SALES

Year	Min Bid	Oct. 72 Mar. 73	Jun.73 Jul. 73	Oct. 73	Feb. 74	Apr. 74 June 74	Unc & Mixed Sold	Unc & Mixed Remaining	Mixed CC 2nd&5th Sales	Mixed CC Remaining
1878 CC	15		47,564				47,564	3		
1879 CC	300				3,608		3,608	25	249	241
1880 CC	60			73,856		36,803	110,659	4,283	8,444	8,143
1881 CC	60			70,865		32,824	103,689	19,020	12,610	12,166
1882 CC	30	291,494	55,697			35,689	382,880	33	127,425	94,691
1883 CC	30	257,391	40,391			30,323	328,105	195,748	133,853	97,812
1884 CC	30	267,733	64,384			28,358	360,475	428,155	98,765	75,243
1885 CC	60			67,782		31,472	99,254	31,569	7,166	10,296
1889 CC										1
1890 CC	30		3,589				3,589	21	207	132
1891 CC	30		5,158				5,158	19	262	248
1892 CC										1
1893 CC										1
Mixed CC	15		170,299			218,682	388,981	298,975		
Mixed Unc	5		27,946				27,946	34		
Mixed Circ*	3		97,559				97,599	32		
TOTALS		**816,618**	**512,587**	**212,503**	**3,608**	**414,151**	**1,959,467**	**977,905**	**388,981**	**298,975**

* Includes 13,426 tarnished/scratched/error 1878CC

** Table 1, 2 and 3 charts are courtesy of Leroy Van Allen and A. George Mallis from their "*Encyclopedia of U. S. Morgan and Peace Silver Dollars*"

***

CHAPTER 78

Color Photo Section

by John W. Highfill, NLG

Toned Morgan dollars are among the most beautiful coins in the world. Many Numismatists have specialized in toned coins and enjoy viewing and collecting these magnificent specimens. This chapter contains many specially selected beautiful photographs of toned coins. I sincerely wish to thank the following individuals and companies who have generously contributed photos for this presentation.

EDITOR'S NOTE: There are many breath-taking color photographs in the chapter entitled "World's Finest Collections and Prices Realized" by John W. Highfill.

American Numismatic Association, Colorado Springs, Colorado

Coin World, Sidney, Ohio

Roger L. Geary, Broken Arrow, Oklahoma

Julie Uptegraff, c/o PCGS, Newport Beach, California

Kenny Duncan of U.S. Coins, Houston, Texas

McIntire Numismatic Auctions, Jacksonville, Arkansas

Mid-American Rare Coin Auctions, Inc.

National Silver Dollar Conventions, Inc., Broken Arrow, Oklahoma

Numismatic News, c/o Krause Publications, Iola, Wisconsin

Oklahoma Federated Gold & Numismatics, Inc., Broken Arrow, Oklahoma

Patti Moreno, Moreno Valley, California

Superior Galleries, Beverly Hills, California

Wayne H. Miller, Helena, Montana

Special Acknowledgements

I am especially appreciative of the layout and editing by **Roger L. Geary**, Broken Arrow, Oklahoma to prepare and display the many toned photographs appearing in this chapter. Very Special thanks are also due to **Wayne H. Miller** who contributed the photos appearing in his discussion of toning. Thank You!

Editor's Note: Wayne Miller's commentary is reprinted in its entirety with his permission from The Morgan and Peace Dollar Textbook, Adam Smith Publishing Co., Metairie, Louisiana.

Toning

As used here, toning or patina refers to a very thin film, coloring, or mellowed appearance upon the surface of a silver dollar as a result of the chemical combination of the metal in the coin with another element such as sulfur or oxygen, over a long period of time.

Although the creation of this thin film is due to a chemical reaction, the colors which are perceived by the eye or other optical instrument are the result of a phenomenon known as thin film interference. There are thus two factors which must be present in order to produce toning.

The first factor in creating the phenomenon of toning involves the chemical process wherein the silver in the coin unites with another element, usually sulfur, over a long period of time, with the resultant formation of a very thin layer or layers of film upon the surface of the coin. These layers are so thin that they are usually transparent to light in varying degrees. For this reason, it is often possible to detect mirror or prooflike surfaces through the toning of a dollar.

Soon after striking, most silver dollars were sealed into sturdy cloth sacks and stored away for long periods of time. Toning often occurred through long-term contact or certain coins in the bag with the sulfur-impregnated cloth from which the bag was made. Only those coins which were actually touching the bag were so affected. This explains why most silver dollars are toned on one side only. It also explains why some dollars exhibit only a "crescent" of toning: One coin overlapped part of another, thus permitting only part of the coin to interact chemically with the sulfur in the bag.

Toning can also occur through contact with sulfur-impregnated paper dollar wrappers. Most such "original rolls," as they are often termed, remain unopened for several years, during which time the sulfur interacts chemically with the silver dollar on each end of the roll. Often the folded-over parts of the wrapper have left a darker, richer toning near the center of these coins.

Toned Peace dollars are much more scarce than toned Morgan dollars, and very seldom show bright, vivid colorations. This is due to the following factors: First, the toning of silver dollars is usually a long-term process. Being minted much more recently, Peace dollars did not have as much time to interact with the sulfur in the bags in which they were stored. Second, there is some evidence that the acid bath into which planchets were plunged after annealing to remove discoloring oxidation was more highly concentrated for Peace dollars, in order to maximize the frosty whiteness of the planchets. This could serve as a detriment to subsequent interaction of the silver planchet metal with sulfur or oxygen, thus retarding the toning process.

The silver dollars pictured here all exhibit the "crescent" of toning discussed earlier. Parts of these coins were covered bu other coins and therefore did not react chemically with the sulfur in the mint bag.

The gorgeous toned dollars shown above are all patterns. These were designs which were considered at one time by the Mint but were passed over in favor of other designs. All these patterns exhibit the Morgan obverse, matched with reverses which were rejected during the selection process. The oversized copper pattern is Judd 1565. There are two or three known specimens. The pictured coin is from the Garett collection.

The top coin is Judd 1550, and very similar to the design which was eventually accepted. This coin is from the R.J. Sheppard collection.

The middle and bottom coins are Judd 1613 and 1615 and are by far the finest known specimens of these two beautiful patterns.

Unless the toning is very deep (as on the cobalt blue 1888-O at top left), prooflike surfaces are usually visible under the colorations. The oversized 1884-CC was purchased by Henry F. Herrman in 1947 as a proof. It is now known to be a superb business strike toned prooflike.

Some toned dollars are monochromatic; their surfaces evidence only one coloration. This is the result of several years' contact with a sulfur-impregnated source, wherein the surface of the dollar is exposed evenly to the sulfer.

The dollars pictured at the top are toned black, which is the natural color of silver sulfide. On these the sulfide film is so thick that thin film interference does not occur. Most monochromatic dollars are either blue or yellow-gold.

Oxygen sometimes interacts with silver dollar surfaces to produce toning. However, since silver dollars which have been exposed to the air under uniform temperature and humidity conditions for several years seldom become toned, it is felt that oxygen is not the usual source of toning.

A silver dollar can also be toned by impurities in the air. Hydrogen sulfide, for example, will effect a black patina over a relatively short period of time, if present in sufficient concentrations. One puff of cigarette smoke, exhaled at close proximity to a silver dollar will produce a light brown coloration, which deepens with each succeeding puff.

Toning or patina is sometimes artificially applied to silver dollars and other coins in order to cover a flat strike, wear, abrasions, counterfeiting, carbon spots, etc. Such artificial toning is prevalent among 1892-S dollars, where the difference between an AU coin and a mint state specimen is several thousand dollars; and among 1921 Peace dollars, in an effort to cover up a very flat strike.

Because of the manner in which toning occurs it is usually (but not always) present only upon one side of a coin. Therefore, scarce date dollars which are toned on both sides should be examined carefully. Artificially toned dollars often evidence bright, almost fluorescent colorations, with a predominance of blues and violets. Some specimens exhibit such colors about their periphery, while the center of the coin evidences a light golden toning. Although the experienced collector can readily identify such a specimen as being artificially toned, such pieces are quite striking and therefore appealing to novice collectors.

Another reason that coins are toned artificially is that some collectors incorrectly assume that a toned coin is always an uncirculated coin. Toning is not de facto proof of a mint state coin. A toned coin may obscure details such as a flat strike, poor luster, abrasions, or just plain wear.

Because the film which produces the effect of toning is very thin, it is easily removed by the introduction of a chemical (usually in liquid form) which will disrupt the bond of the silver compound. The most popular toning remover contains thiourea, itself a compound of a uric acid and sodium thiosulfate. In most cases the application of a cleaning substance will not diminish the frosty, reflective luster of a silver dollar. However, if the toning is very dark (dark green, blue, purple, black) the surface of a coin thus cleaned will often be lacking in luster. It appears that some of the silver compounds are etched deeply enough so as to destroy the coin's mint luster. The author knows of no substance which will clean a darkly toned coin and restore its natural mint luster.

The second factor in creating the phenomenon of toning involves the perception of the thin silver compound film by the eye or other optical instrument. Many people have long been puzzled by the abundance of different colorations upon a single toned dollar. Since under normal conditions silver is not an especially active element, this variegation of color cannot be explained in chemical terms. In other words, the colors cannot be attributed to variations in the silver compounds which comprise the film on the surface of a toned dollar.

These colorations can be explained by an optical phenomenon known as thin film interference. Color is perceived as a difference in the length of light waves which radiate or are reflected from an object. Short length waves are perceived by the eye as blue; medium length waves as green, and long waves as red. The length of these waves is extremely short; the range of light waves which the eye can perceive varies in length from one to two 100-thousandths of an inch.

It is known that sufficiently thin films of all transparent bodies, although themselves colorless, can exhibit brilliant colors. These can be observed in thin films of oil upon water, or in soap bubbles.

With regard to the thin film upon the surface of a toned silver dollar, a beam of light which penetrates the film to reflect from the surface of the dollar will confront another beam of light which is reflected from the surface of the film. If the film is of the right thickness (between one to two 100-thousandths of an inch), the reflected wave will meet the entering wave in opposition to it, and interference will occur. The colors on a toned silver dollar, then, represent the light from the source (light bulb, sun, etc.) minus the thickness of the film as expressed in wave lengths. If, for example, the dollar exhibits a yellowish toning at some point, the thickness of the film there is such as to cause interference of blue light. If at another point the film looks blue-green, the film is slightly thicker, so as to cause interference of the longer red waves and to cancel them. The varying colors upon a toned silver dollar, then, are caused by varying thicknesses of the film upon its surfaces.

The phenomenon of thin film interference explains why that portion of a coin which is most closely touching the sulfur-impregnated bag will usually appear to be toned a black, blue-green, green, or purple color the long red, yellow and orange waves are absorbed by the thicker toning and the eye perceives the toning to be black, blue-green, or purple. On the other hand, dollars toned by only a few years' exposure to the sulfur in paper wrappings are almost always yellow, orange, or light red. Since the toning layer on these coins is thinner, the shorter wave lengths (blue-green, green, purple) are absorbed, and the eye perceives the longer wave lengths of red, yellow and orange.

When the thickness of the film increases to the point that thin film interference cannot occur, a black toning, which is the natural color of most silver compounds, will appear.

Many people love toning on a silver dollar. To some, toning makes the coin more beautiful, and enhances its nostalgic and reminiscent value, since toning, or patina is equated with the past which for them is rich in memories. Others feel that toning makes a coin look "genuine," and that it is de facto proof of the mint state condition of a coin. Still others feel that since toning is different on every coin, that it adds to the uniqueness of a particular coin. Some individuals like toning because it hides or masks abrasions, carbon spots, or other surface imperfections.

Perhaps an equal number of individuals do not like toning. Some toned coins are returned to dealers with statements such as "This coin has been in a fire," or "What are you trying to hide?" Many people prefer to perceive the surfaces of a coin without the subtle masking effects of toning, which can often hide deep scratches, carbon spots, poor strike, etc. Such individuals feel that silver dollars should exhibit the frosty, reflective surfaces of a silver coin.

The blotchy, uneven toning of these dollars was produced by the paper wrappings which enclose a roll of silver dollars. These coins were all end coins in the rolls. The overlapping ends of the wrapper were folded and creased several times, thereby producing an uneven exposure of the dollar to the sulfer in the wrappings.

On this page and the next are pictured some of the most beautiful toned dollars in existence. The 1882-S obverse and 1883-O reverse, are depicted as oversized photos on this page. These coins were all toned from exposure to the sulfer in a mint-sealed bag for many, many years.

Until recently, silver dollars with attractive multicolored toning usually commanded a price above the MS-65 Bid levels of the Coin Dealer Newsletter, whether or not they were of gem quality. However, recent huge increases in these levels have made buyers much more quality-conscious. Toned dollars with heavy abrasions or flat strikes are no longer saleable at big premiums, regardless of their beauty. In fact, many buyers categorically refuse all toned dollars, because of the difficulty of ascertaining the grade of such coins. This is unfortunate, since gem toned dollars can be very beautiful.

Sometime, unless a silver dollar is of relatively common issue or exhibits exceptionally lovely toning, a few dealers may dip toned dollars in cleaning liquid to remove toning. However, the consensus opinion would be that unless the toning definitely detracts from the overall appearance of the coin, it should not be removed. The reasons for this are two-fold: First, many deeply toned dollars, after being cleaned, will often reveal a loss of mint luster. Second, the cleaning process usually renders the coin more vulnerable to corrosion than before, since the thin silver compound film which is dissolved by the cleaning agent is no longer present to protect the coin.

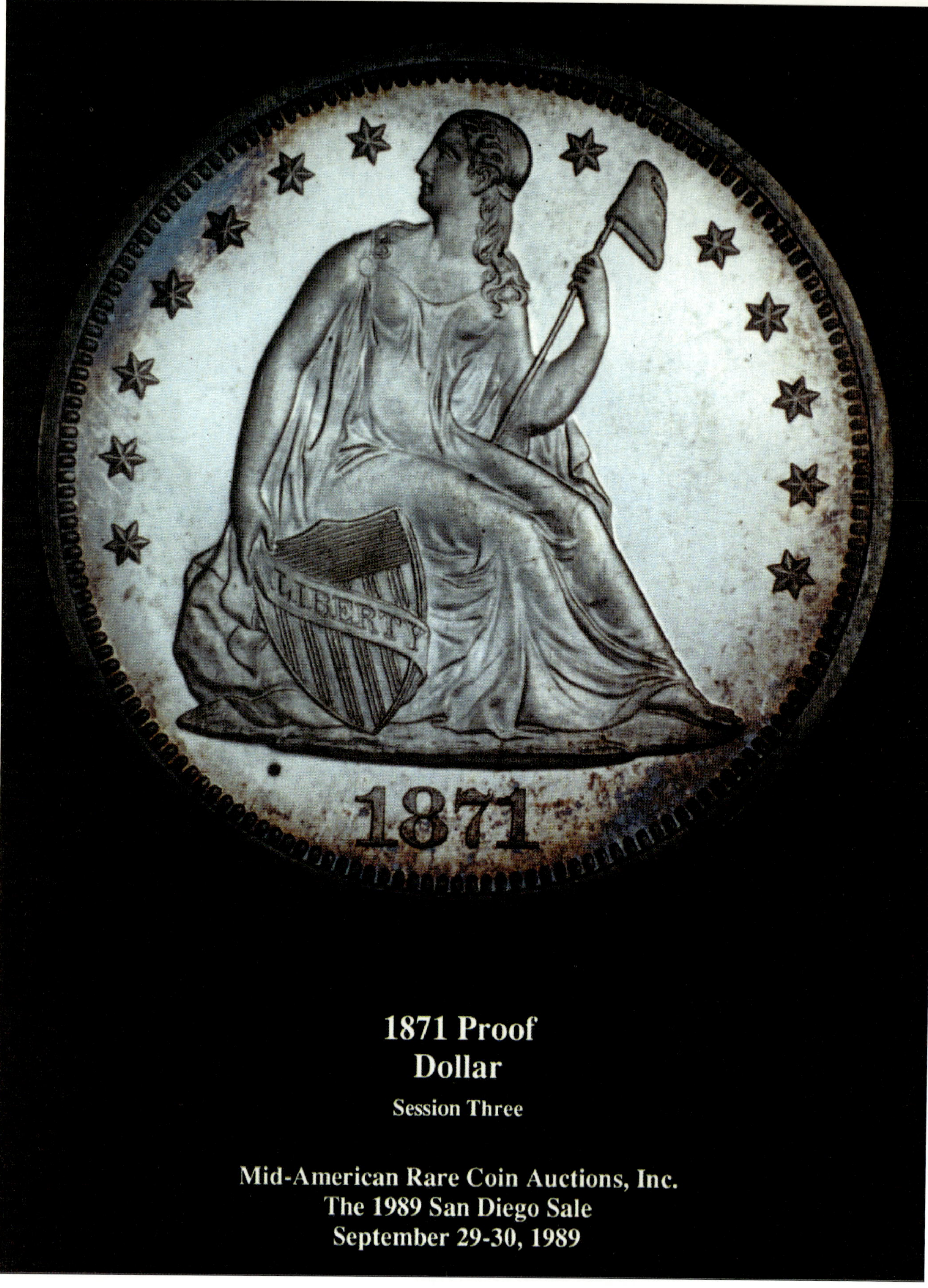

1871 Proof Dollar
(Courtesy of Mid-American Rare Coin Auctions, Inc., Lexington, Kentucky)

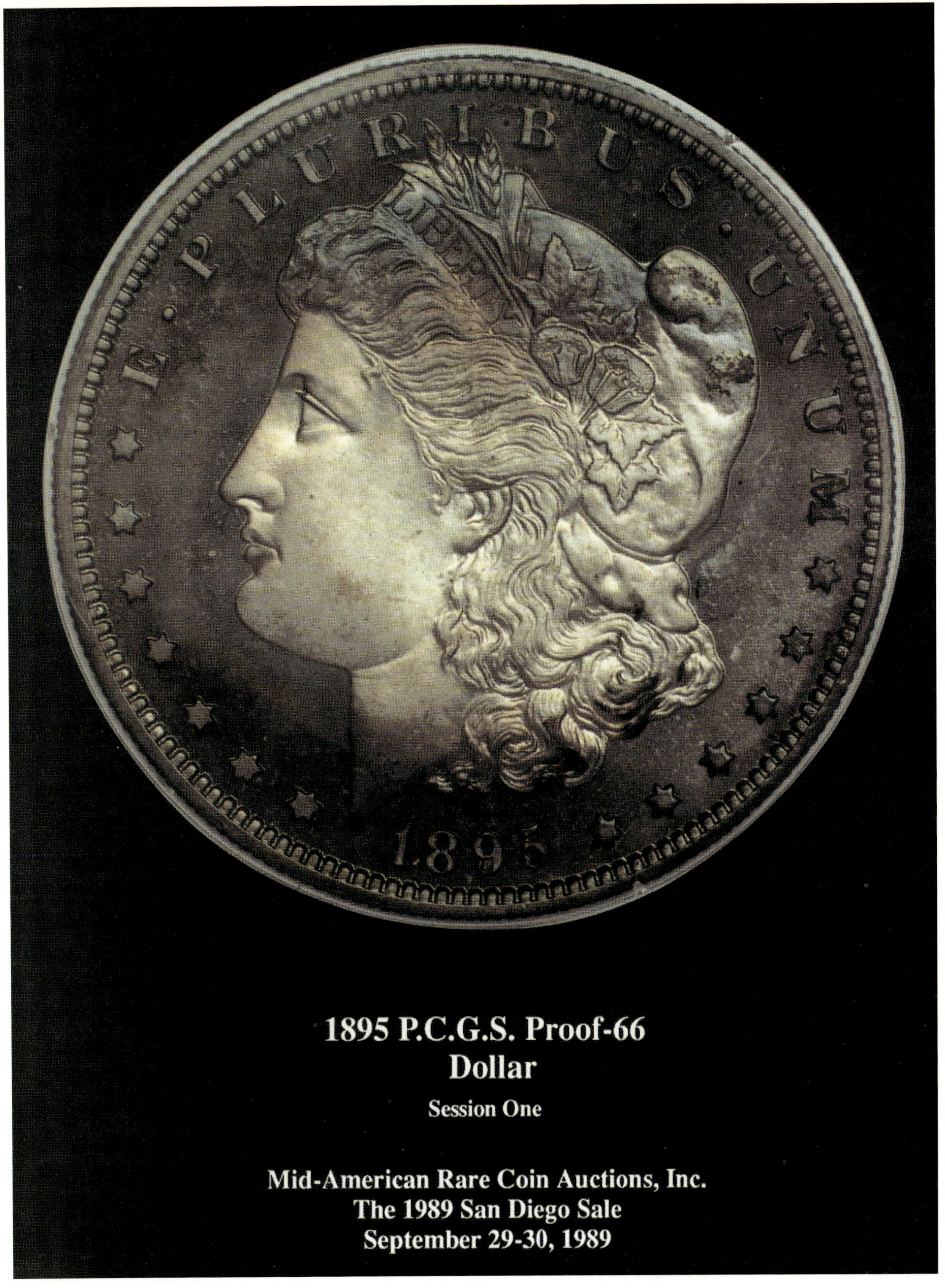

1895 PCGS Proof 66
(Courtesy of Mid-American Rare Coin Auctions, Inc., Lexington, Kentucky)

1888-O Morgan Dollar
(Courtesy of Mid-American Rare Coin Auctions, Inc.)

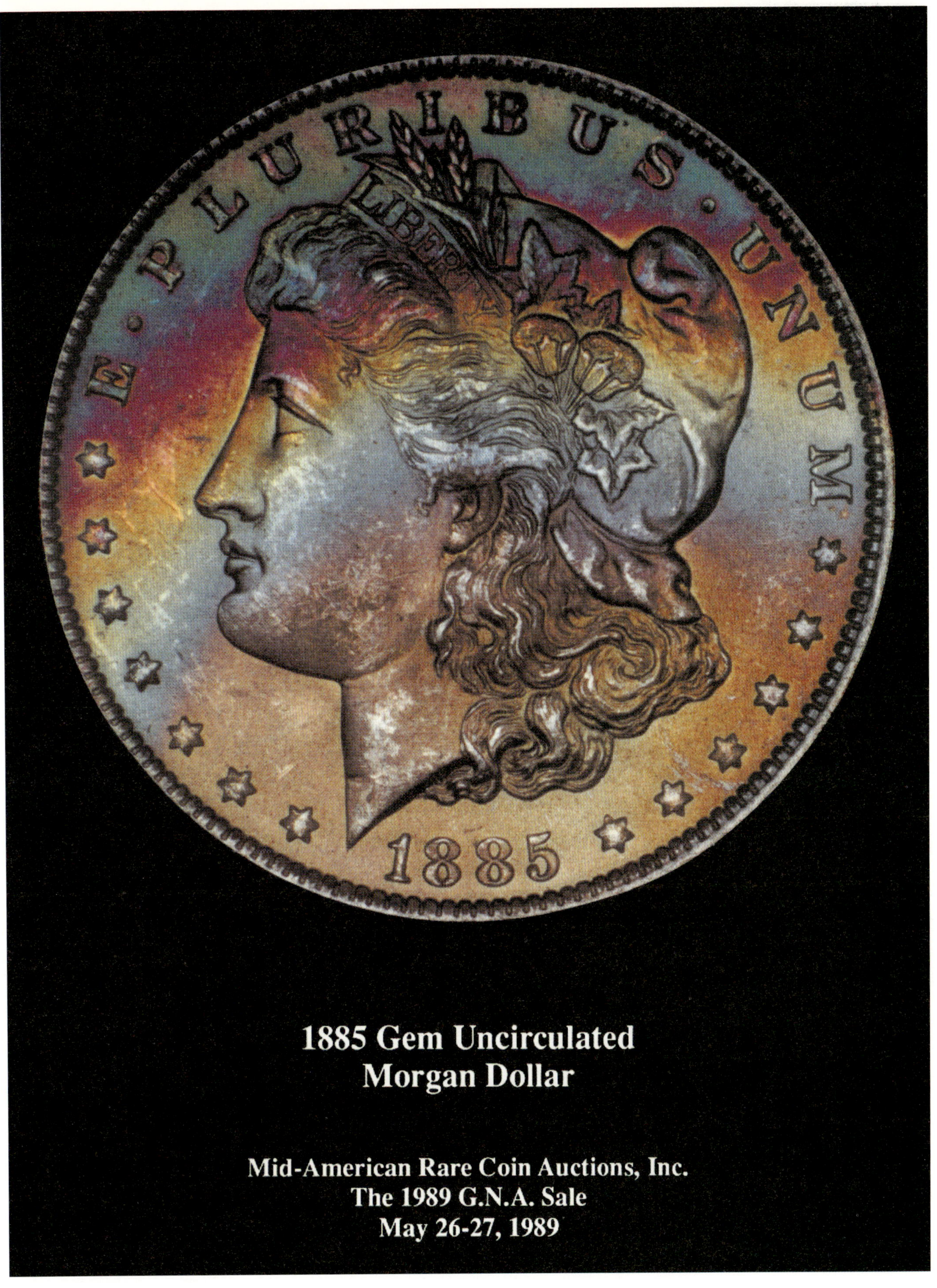

1885 Morgan Dollar
(Courtesy of Mid-American Rare Coin Auctions, Inc.)

1921 Proof Dollar
(Courtesy of Mid-American Rare Coin Auctions, Inc.)

THE N.S.D.C. SALE

NOVEMBER 10–12, 1988
St. Louis, MO

McINTIRE NUMISMATIC AUCTIONS, INC.

(Courtesy of National Silver Dollar Conventions, Inc., Broken Arrow, Oklahoma and McIntire Numismatic Auctions, Inc., Jacksonville, Arkansas)

(Courtesy of Julie Uptegraff, c/o PCGS, Newport Beach, California)

1895 proof 65 PCGS Encapsulated Morgan dollar "King of the Morgans" sold in a private sale in June 1991 for $20,000. (Courtesy of Oklahoma Federated Gold and Numismatics, Inc., Broken Arrow, Oklahoma)

12th dollar released from 1st 100 ever coined at Denver mint Thomas Annear — Superintendent. 1921-D: Presentation Piece. (Courtesy of John W. Highfill)

1923-S plate coin used in *The Morgan & Peace Dollar Textbook* by Wayne Miller (Courtesy of Kenny Duncan c/o U.S. Coins, Houston, Texas)

Brightly colored enameled one, five and ten troy ounce .999 fine silver "Morgan" and "Peace" replicas. (Courtesy of Patti Moreno, Moreno Valley, California)

TONED DOLLARS

FLOWING HAIR | GOBRECHT | LIBERTY SEATED | MORGAN (PROOF)

LIBERTY SEATED - OBVERSE/REVERSE

LIBERTY SEATED - OBVERSE/REVERSE

MORGAN DOLLAR - OBVERSE/REVERSE

PATTERN DOLLAR - OBVERSE/REVERSE

PEACE DOLLAR - OBVERSE/REVERSE

(Courtesy of Roger L. Geary, c/o Highfill Press, Inc., Broken Arrow, Oklahoma)

SEATED DOLLARS

Light Brown

Light Brown

Dark Brown/Brown

Brown/Lt Brown/Blue

TRADE DOLLARS

Brown/Gold

Lt Brown/Champagne

Brown/Burnt Orange

Superb color! Brown Blue/Purple/Pink Gold

Dark Brown/Brown

Brown/Lt Blue/Blue

P.L. Cameo

Champagne

Brown/Gold Brown

Brown/Golden Brown

Brown/Lt Purple

Brown/Violet Golden Brown

Champagne

Brown/Lt Brown

Lt Brown/Gold

Brown/Lt Brown Lt Blue/Rust

(Courtesy of Roger L. Geary, c/o Highfill Press, Inc.)

LIBERTY SEATED DOLLARS/TRADE DOLLARS/MORGAN DOLLARS

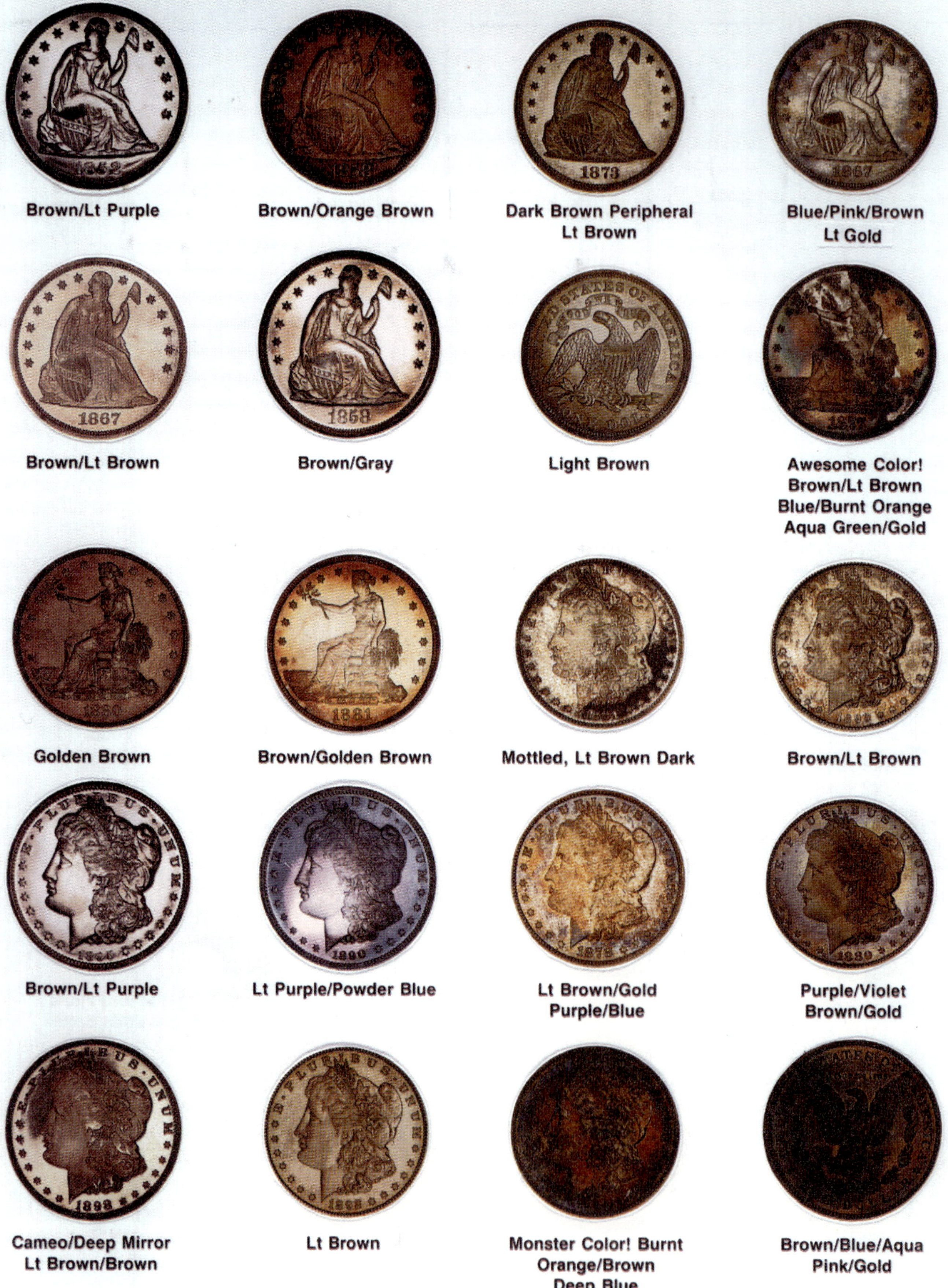

Brown/Lt Purple

Brown/Orange Brown

Dark Brown Peripheral Lt Brown

Blue/Pink/Brown Lt Gold

Brown/Lt Brown

Brown/Gray

Light Brown

Awesome Color! Brown/Lt Brown Blue/Burnt Orange Aqua Green/Gold

Golden Brown

Brown/Golden Brown

Mottled, Lt Brown Dark

Brown/Lt Brown

Brown/Lt Purple

Lt Purple/Powder Blue

Lt Brown/Gold Purple/Blue

Purple/Violet Brown/Gold

Cameo/Deep Mirror Lt Brown/Brown

Lt Brown

Monster Color! Burnt Orange/Brown Deep Blue

Brown/Blue/Aqua Pink/Gold

(Courtesy of Roger L. Geary, c/o Highfill Press, Inc.)

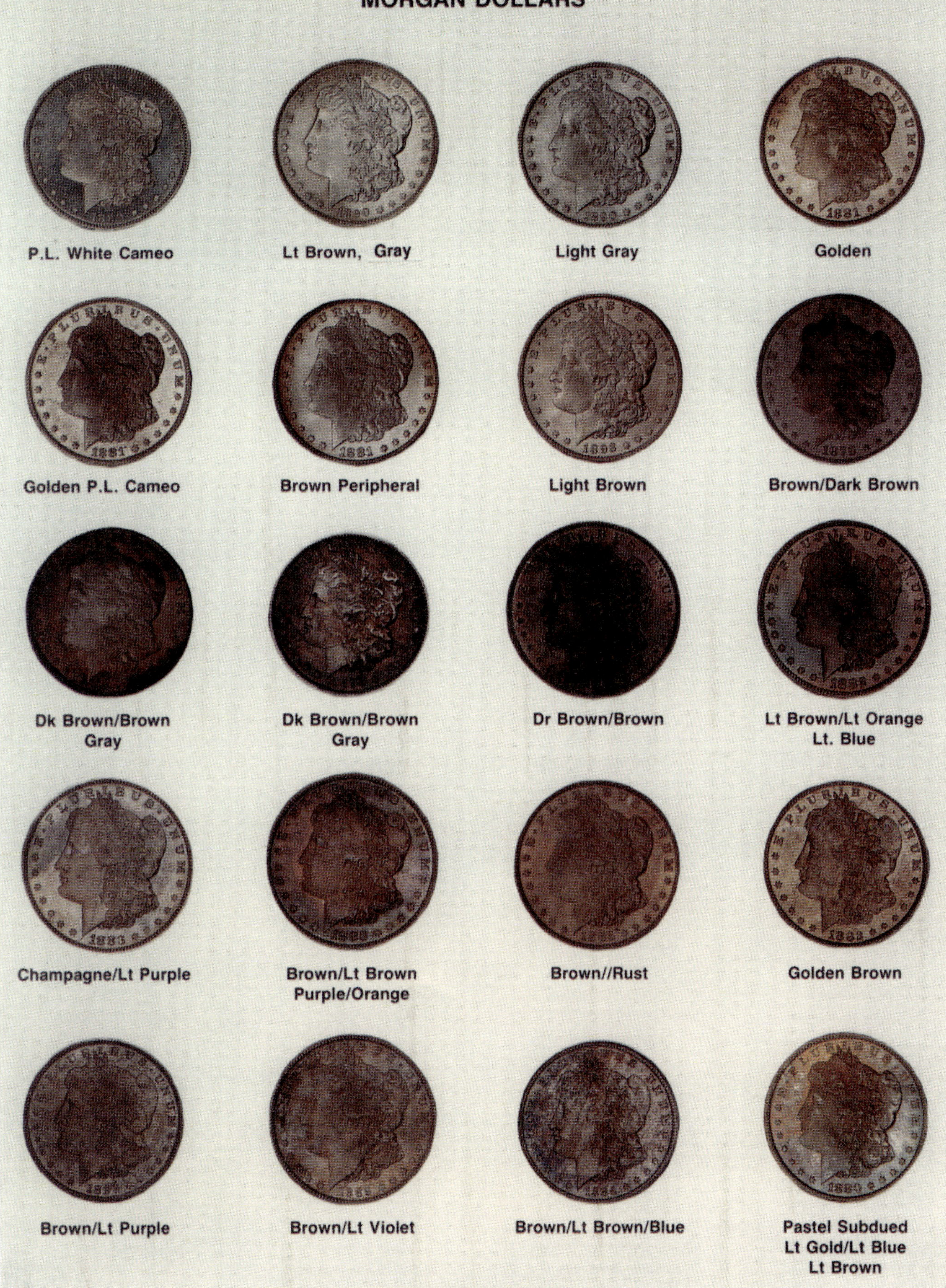

(Courtesy of Roger L. Geary, c/o Highfill Press, Inc.)

MORGAN DOLLARS

Olive	Dark Brown/Rust	Blue/Orange/Brown	Turquoise
Lt Brown/Rose	Dk Brown/Brown Purple	Cameo/Proof Like	Brown/Deep Blue Burnt Orange
Dk Brown Rims Brown Field/Cameo	Brown Rims P.L. Surfaces/Cameo	Mottled Brown Lt Blue/Rainbow Edge	Outward Peripheral Lt Brown/Brown/Blue
Partial Gold Lt Brown/Lt Blue	Partial Rainbow Red/Gold/Blue/Yellow	Blue/Purple, Aqua/Brown	Vivid Bold Aqua/Dk Brown
Flashy Vivid Gold Orange/Blue/Brown	End of Roll/Lt Gold Lt Blue/Lt Brown	Bold/Brown Violet/Blue/Purple	Brown/Rust/Blue White Cameo

(Courtesy of Roger L. Geary, c/o Highfill Press, Inc.)

There are tens of thousands of color photo examples available. An entire book could be done on the toning of coins. We have only tried to briefly illustrate the beauty of toned dollars through a selective sampling. Much attention was given to the selection of the group of coins in order to provide a wide and interesting assortment of toned coins. Although space was limited, selected specimens will provide viewing pleasure again and again. Thanks again to all photograph contributors, and we hope that everyone is inspired by their contributions.

"Awesome Color Toning" 1882-S Morgan dollar
(Courtesy of *Coin World*, Sidney, Ohio)

***

John and Marlene Highfill

A Decade of Memories: "Yours and Ours"

This is the time we would like to show you photographs of conventions, travel, dealers and friends. During our travels, we've had many wonderful memories with hundreds of friends and dealers. We would like to share these personal moments with all of you, and to those of you who were fortunate (or unfortunate) enough to be with us when we had a camera nearby. THANKS! Only a small portion of these memories have been recorded in photographs, and these photos are dedicated to **EVERYONE**.

Hundreds of coin dealers gather every weekend somewhere in America at a coin show or convention. Sometimes they bring their families. The following chapter illustrates with hundreds of photos in a collage format the multiple faces of many traveling dealers.

I love all of my children. Chelsea Marie Highfill appears in many photos because she was present during the time frame when most of these photos were taken. She was the youngest member of the ANA (Junior Associate Member JA-146705). She would also like to show you her many personal friends in a special pictorial collage of her own.

We sincerely, and do mean sincerely, hope that you enjoy this chapter as much as we did putting it together for you. **LIFE IS ENTIRELY TOO SHORT. TIME IS PASSING US BY SO QUICKLY. TAKE SOME TIME AND SMELL THE ROSES!**

CHAPTER 79

Conventions, Travel, Dealers and Friends: A Pictorial Bibliography

by John and Marlene Highfill

John Highfill and friend, Bali, Indonesia (September, 1988)

Many authors in other chapters have coordinated their business related stories and have tied silver dollars and the coin business together. These photos both personal and business are a vivid reflection of the adventure and travel (necessary and pleasure) that is as much of the coin business as anything else in this book. John, Marlene, Iraj and Monir are in many pictures for the simple reason that they took the majority of the photographs themselves.

There are hundreds of individual portraits and other various photos in the following pages. Some of the more humorous pictures have been captioned separately for your pleasure. The majority of dealer photos are in a "special collage" presentation. Each individual photo collage has its on theme and merit. Some of these are strictly portraits of dealers from old convention photo ID badges. There are many collages of dealers and their wives at various cocktail/dinner parties throughout the coin circuit. I want to personally thank Iraj "Roger" Sayah and Monir Torabi of Unitrade for the great photos that they have contributed to this chapter. Coin conventions are held annually all over the world also. You'll find fascinating photos from New York to the Great Wall of China! It's a small world after all, especially when it comes to the travels and adventures of a coin dealer. REMEMBER, "COIN DEALERS ARE PEOPLE, TOO!"

Travel can be no fun unless you make the most of it. Here are some of our memories and possibly yours. If you weren't fortunate enough to have been there, we hope you may still enjoy these moments. There are hundreds of dealers that were not caught by the camera's eye, however, no one has been excluded if a photo was available. Some dealers are in more than one collage and not for any special reason. "IF A PICTURE HAS A THOUSAND WORDS, THEN A THOUSAND PICTURES MUST HAVE A MILLION WORDS."

The following "Headline" appeared in the Silver Dollar City News after much encouragement and hoopla proffered by John English. Silver Dollar City, located just outside of Branson, Missouri, features an excellent assortment of artisans practicing their trade, entertainment of all sorts, and lots of activities and rides for people of all ages. It just seemed natural for Silver Dollar City to be the site of the first public announcement of John's new book.

Many of the photos of this chapter are the courtesy of Oklahoma Federated Gold & Numismatics, Inc., Broken Arrow, Oklahoma

FROM THE CRAFT & ENTERTAINMENT CAPITAL OF THE OZARKS

SILVER DOLLAR CITY NEWS

Vol. 1, No. 1 — Silver Dollar City, Missouri — Founded 1960

John Highfill To Publish Limited Edition: Silver Dollar Book!!

Adventure and Vision Form City's Past

HOLDUP! Bolen Gang Assaults Train (again)

CITY POST OFFICE Established — Serves all 28 citizens

(Photo courtesy of John English, Senior Editor, Highfill Press, Inc.)

CONVENTIONS, BADGES, RIBBONS, PHOTO ID'S, MEDALS, AND OTHER MEMORABILIA

CONVENTIONS, BADGES, RIBBONS, PHOTO ID'S, MEDALS, AND OTHER MEMORABILIA

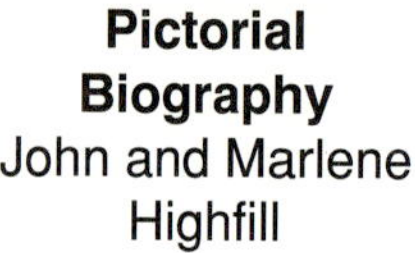

Pictorial Biography
John and Marlene Highfill

Marlene with villagers in Indonesia, Summer 1987

This is a test...Can you detect something out of the ordinary in this photo? Marlene M. Highfill
Bali, Indonesia, September 1988

OK, Already! Let's eat or start the show!!

John and Marlene on Top Of The Incline above Hong Kong. Hong Kong Coin Convention, September, 1987
(Courtesy of Brad Rodgers, Sherman Oaks, CA)

I'm thinking of buying this place and settling down!

The women in my life

Can I sell you something?

"Typical day at the office"

JOHN AND MARLENE HIGHFILL — A PICTORIAL BIOGRAPHY

An evening and a sunset to go in Hawaii. What a combination! Marlene M. Highfill, October, 1986

Marlene at Lake Tahoe in June 1984

Marlene as Miss Bloomington in the Miss California Beauty Pageant Venus USA. Los Angeles, CA, 1983 (Second Runner Up)

One of my favorites of my wife, Marlene

Marlene Highfill with "Little Anthony", Arizona Coin Convention, Scottsdale, Arizona, 1988. (Courtesy of Gordon Wrubel, Newport Beach, California)

Marlene Marie Highfill with Willie Nelson's buses — "The Red Headed Stranger" and "Me and Paul." Willie sings the "unofficial" coin dealer national anthem, "On The Road Again", Lake Tahoe, Nevada, 1990

John & Marlene in Beijing, China. Side trip from Hong Kong International Coin Convention, September, 1988 (Courtesy of Mose and Kay Waldner, Las Vegas, Nevada)

John in Hong Kong, Sept. 1987

Beijing, China, September 1988

Marlene...

Another of my favorites of Marlene...John

MARLENE M. HIGHFILL — A PICTORIAL BIOGRAPHY

A PERSONAL FAMILY PICTORIAL ACKNOWLEDGEMENT AND DEDICATION TO MY CHILDREN: GARY, MICHAEL, JOHN II, JOHN WILLIAM, JEFFERY, NICOLETTE, REBECCA, AND CHELSEA HIGHFILL

CELEBRITIES, DEALERS, AND FRIENDS OF CHELSEA MARIE HIGHFILL

AFTER HOURS AT THE OLE' BALL GAME WITH JEFFERY AND FRIENDS, CENTER PHOTO (right to left) BRETT HULL AND WAYNE GRETZKY — MAY 1990
(Courtesy of American Coin Conventions, Inc., Broken Arrow, Oklahoma)

MARLENE'S FAMILY PHOTO COLLAGE

HOME, CARS, TRAVEL, FAMILY AND FRIENDS

A GATHERING OF EAGLES! Guest authors (from left to right - top to bottom) include: J. Oxman, A. Johnbrier, G. Bodway, W. Spears, J. Schneider, J. Love, J. Sack, L. Hendrickson, R. Brandow, Iraj Sayah, A. Swaitek, R. Downing, L. Goldberg, W. Breen, Marlene and John, W. Miller, S. Travers, B. Fivaz, K. Bressett, J. Albanese, M. Rosen, D. Hall, L. and M. Van Allen, J. Dannreuther, M. Yaffe, A. Lustig, C. West, D. Lisot, H. White, B. Amspacher, Q.D. Bowers, D. Ganz, R. Brueggeman & Co., J. Halperin, C. Samuelson, H. Sconyers, D. Crowell, S. Ivy, D. Manley, M. Fuljenz, D. Winter, N. Fenton, R. Fong and D. Tavenner. Authors whose photos were not available at the time of this picture include: J. Blanchard, III, B. Estremera, J. Stephens, III and P. Schuyler.

Jennifer and James Fairfield, Jr., Lake Tahoe Queen at Sunset (August 1989), Lake Tahoe, Nevada

Edward E. Fritz, Jr. and Mary Sauvain, Lake Tahoe, Nevada, 1989

(Left to right) Eric Aston, Robert and Linda Brueggeman, Louis Moreno, Jr., Karen and Bryan Fazio, Lake Tahoe, Nevada, August, 1989

"Trish", Bob and Michael Pendergrass "Hanging Out",

Al and Joann Johnbrier, "Good Friends," 1991

The guy wins a NSDR lifetime achievement award and now he thinks he's Frank Sinatra! John Love at Ruth's Chris Steak House, NSDR Awards Banquet, St. Louis, Missouri, November 8, 1990

Randy and Vickie Crews and Family Tulsa, Oklahoma, 1991

There's "Iraj" and then there's "Rog". Both are wonderful human beings. This one is Roger Geary of Tulsa, Oklahoma at the Dallas Mid-winter ANA, March 1, 1991

Charles and Lisa Anastasio "What A Great Couple!"

GREAT PHOTOS OF GREAT FOLKS, HAVING GREAT TIMES.

John B. Hamrick, Jr. and family at Christmas, 1990, Atlanta, Georgia

Can you name all of these dealers and their family members?
Tahoe Queen Riverboat ride, Lake Tahoe, September 1988

Dr. Rayburne "Tex" Wyndham Goen, Sr.
The Best Doctor in the whole wide world!

David Hall and Staff

Barry Bellefontaine and staff, Honolulu, Hawaii, 1991

(Left to right) Shirley and Harlan White, Jim Beem, Lake Tahoe Queen, August 1989, Lake Tahoe Coin Show, Lake Tahoe, Nevada

FIND YOURSELF OR A FRIEND...

The "biggest" little coin dealer in America celebrating his first birthday party ever! Dan Kihlstadius, San Diego ANA, 1990

Who is this "mystery man" from Memphis? Photo taken at Reno Coin Show, Reno, Nevada, April 19, 1991

"Yow!" BBFJ, Muskogee, Oklahoma

"We're just friends, **Really!**"
Gordon Wrubel and Nick Buzolich, Jr.

Can you name them all?
(Courtesy of NSDC, Inc., Broken Arrow, Oklahoma)

NSDC staff "acting" like they are working! (left to right) "Trish", Marlene, Phyllis, Patti, Bobbie, Melody NSDC, St. Louis, Missouri

Halloween office party, October 1990

Halloween 1991, (L to R) Marlene Highfill, Chelsea Highfill, Kate "Grandma" Smith

"You know what I mean, Vern?"

"Silver Dollar Cycle"
by Eric Slick, Tulsa, OK

FIND YOURSELF OR A FRIEND...

Mose parting the waters at the Black Sand Beach, Kalapana outside of Hilo, Hawaii, October, 1985 (Courtesy of Mose and Kay Waldner, Las Vegas, Nevada)

John & Marlene on Kauai island in Hawaii, October, 1985 (Courtesy of Bill and Janie Foreman, Muskogee, Oklahoma)

Diamond Head Sunset Dinner & Cruise — Hawaii State Coin Convention, November, 1990 (Courtesy of Barry Bellefontaine, Honolulu, Hawaii)

Frankie & Johnny (Courtesy of Frank Antino, Toms River, New Jersey)

"I came into this world with nothing and I still have most of it." Jack M. Baxter, Universal City, Texas

"I'm ready. Let's party!" (Louie Moreno, Jr.)

What can I say? It's absolutely beautiful in Cancun, Mexico everyday!

My home away from home, Cancun, Quintan Roo, Mexico

Dan Kihlstadius making an "extra buck" from Dave Hendrickson during the crash of '90 (Courtesy of David Hendrickson, Silver Towne, Winchester, Indiana)

FIND YOURSELF OR A FRIEND...

I can't stop this guy from kissing me! John Highfill and Tom Phillips on the Lake Tahoe Queen, Lake Tahoe, Nevada in August, 1987 (Courtesy of Thomas B. Phillips, Memphis, Tennessee)

"It's **MY** birthday party and **THIS** is the size of the cake I get? **Some party!**"
Louie Moreno, Jr., October, 1985
(Courtesy of Patti Moreno, Moreno Valley, CA)

The Sherilles backstage after performing at the Arizona Coin Convention Cocktail and Dinner Party in Scottsdale. (circa 1988)
(Courtesy of George Weingart c/o The Coin and Stamp Gallery, Phoenix, Arizona)

Ghiradelli Square Chocolate Factory, Fisherman's Wharf, San Francisco, California

"Home Sweet Home" . . . John Highfill

Underwater at Cancun, Mexico, with Harold, Melody, Marlene and John

Michael Wade (Highfill) Kaplan "singing" at Blueberry Hill, Tampa, Florida, National Gold Convention, March 29, 1991

Millions of words of reference text were researched and reviewed over a period of years in order to complete this encyclopedia.
(Courtesy of Highfill Press, Inc., Broken Arrow, OK)

Writing a book is no small task, writing a multi-authored encyclopedia is an absolute nightmare! Photo depicts 3 file cabinets, a 16 bin file cabinet, and a floor full of paperwork and research materials.
(Courtesy of Highfill Press, Inc., Broken Arrow, OK)

FIND YOURSELF OR A FRIEND...

Dean Tavenner posing as Charlton Heston aboard the Tahoe Queen Riverboat

Making all of the collages was hard work, but a lot of fun!

Dealers night at the ole ball game in Milwaukee, Wisconsin. Scott, Elizabeth, Louie and Marlene (Courtesy of Elizabeth Rankin, San Diego, California)

John English, "Class of '43", Senior Editor for Highfill Press on his 48th birthday, January 30, 1991, Broken Arrow, OK

"Hi!"

This is where I'm going to play when this book is finished!

John Highfill, Lisa Anastasio, Jack & Sondra Beymer on the Tahoe Queen, during the Annual Lake Tahoe Invitational Coin Convention, October, 1989 (Courtesy of Jack & Sondra Beymer, Santa Rosa, CA)

You don't know me. I'm here because I'm beautiful! (Photo taken by BBFJ in Cancun, Mexico, December 1989)

Elba Shepard and Dean Tavenner on the Tahoe Queen during the Lake Tahoe VIP Invitational Coin Convention, October, 1988 (Courtesy of Elba Shepard, Los Angeles, CA)

FIND YOURSELF OR A FRIEND...

Dealers playing volleyball every 4th of July at the Clearwater Coin Club Show, Clearwater, Florida. (1990) (Courtesy of Oklahoma Federated Gold & Numismatics, Inc.)

This view of Waikiki Beach and Diamond Head is one of the reasons dealers flock to the Hawaii State Coin Convention every year. (Courtesy of Barry Bellefontaine, Honolulu, Hawaii)

The Association autographing The National Gold Convention's Headliner Poster. The lady in background is Miss Elerie Arnett of Entertainment Enterprises, National Gold Convention — April 1, 1989, St. Louis, Missouri

A "motley crue" in Hawaii — a night to remember! October, 1985 (Courtesy of Oklahoma Federated Gold & Numismatics, Inc.)

John and Marlene at the 10th NSDC December, 1989, St. louis, Missouri

Mom, John and Frances (Courtesy of Vineta Mae Foreman, Muskogee, OK)

FIND YOURSELF OR A FRIEND...

FIND YOURSELF OR A FRIEND...

FIND YOURSELF OR A FRIEND...

FIND YOURSELF OR A FRIEND...

CHELSEA MARIE HIGHFILL — MODELING FOR "THE CHILDREN'S HOUR" BY JAN BRIGGS, SPRING 1991

THE COIN GIRL CALENDAR: "HOW ABOUT THESE GUYS AND DOLLS?"
(Courtesy of Gabriele Armstrong, Los Angeles, California)

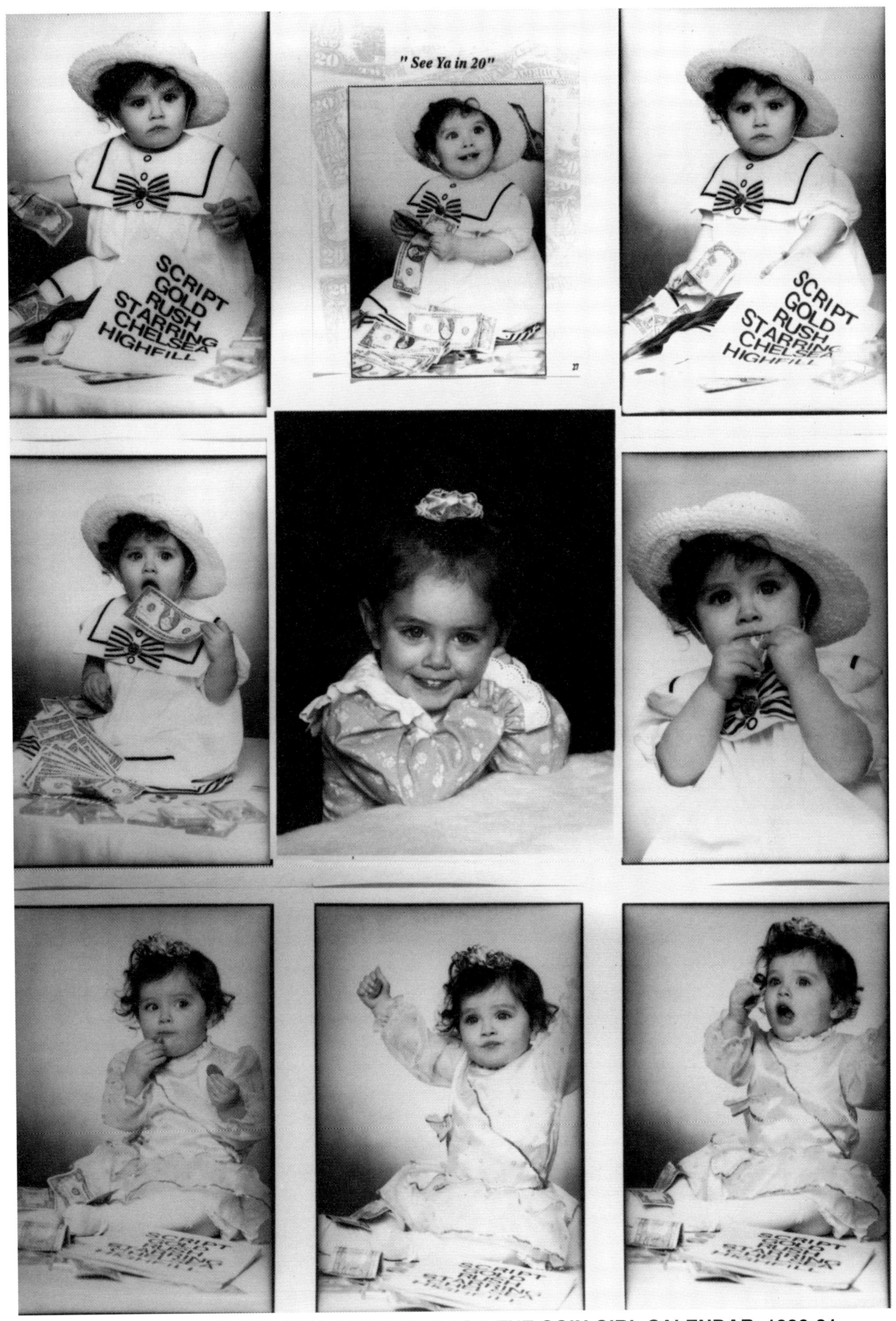

CHELSEA MARIE HIGHFILL MODELING FOR THE COIN GIRL CALENDAR, 1990-91

NUMISMATIC "COIN MAP" OF THE UNITED STATES
(Courtesy of Gabriele Armstrong, Los Angeles, California)

FIERCE BASKETBALL COMPETITION AT THE NSDC AND OTHER NATION-WIDE CONVENTIONS
(Courtesy of National Silver Dollar Conventions, Inc., Broken Arrow, Oklahoma)

SUNSET ON THE TAHOE QUEEN WITH DEALERS AND FRIENDS. LAKE TAHOE, NEVADA
(Courtesy of Oklahoma Federated Gold & Numismatics, Inc., Broken Arrow, Oklahoma)

HOME AWAY FROM HOME IN CANCUN, MEXICO...
OUR FAVORITE PHOTOS OF PLACES, FRIENDS, & THE SEA

ASIA & FOREIGN ADVENTURES...

HONG KONG, SHANGHAI, BEIJING, SINGAPORE & BALI WITH FRIENDS AND DEALERS

HONG KONG, SHANGHAI, BEIJING, SINGAPORE & BALI WITH FRIENDS AND DEALERS

RICHARD SCOTT SAYS, "LET'S PARTY!"

HALLOWEEN PARTY AT THE 8TH NSDC IN ST. LOUIS, MISSOURI
"GREAT COSTUMES, GREAT FRIENDS, GREAT FUN!" OCTOBER 29, 1987
(Courtesy of National Silver Dollar Conventions, Inc., Broken Arrow, Oklahoma)

DEALERS DANCING THE NIGHT AWAY...
PHOTOS FROM A COMBINATION OF VARIOUS COCKTAIL AND DINNER PARTIES

GRAND BALLROOM — HOLIDAY INN DOWNTOWN ST. LOUIS, MISSOURI
FIND YOURSELF OR A FRIEND....
(Courtesy of American Coin Conventions, Inc., Broken Arrow, Oklahoma)

THE KINGS MANOR: "WHAT A PARTY THIS WAS!" WE SPENT A MONTH THERE THAT NIGHT!
(Courtesy of The National Gold Convention, St. Louis, Missouri)

"First Rate Entertainers" NSDC, St. Louis. Missouri

The Association, The Grassroots, The Rascals, Three Dog Night, and Charley Daniels

(Courtesy of National Silver Dollar Conventions, Inc., Broken Arrow, Oklahoma)

Autographed Albums by some of the greatest entertainers of all time including **Elvis Presley, Richard and Karen Carpenter, Glen Campbell, Fats Domino, Bobby Darin, Tom Jones, Englebert Humberdinck, The Osmonds, Barbara Mandrell, Kenny Rogers, Roy Orbison,** and many others. (Courtesy of the John W. Highfill personal record collection)

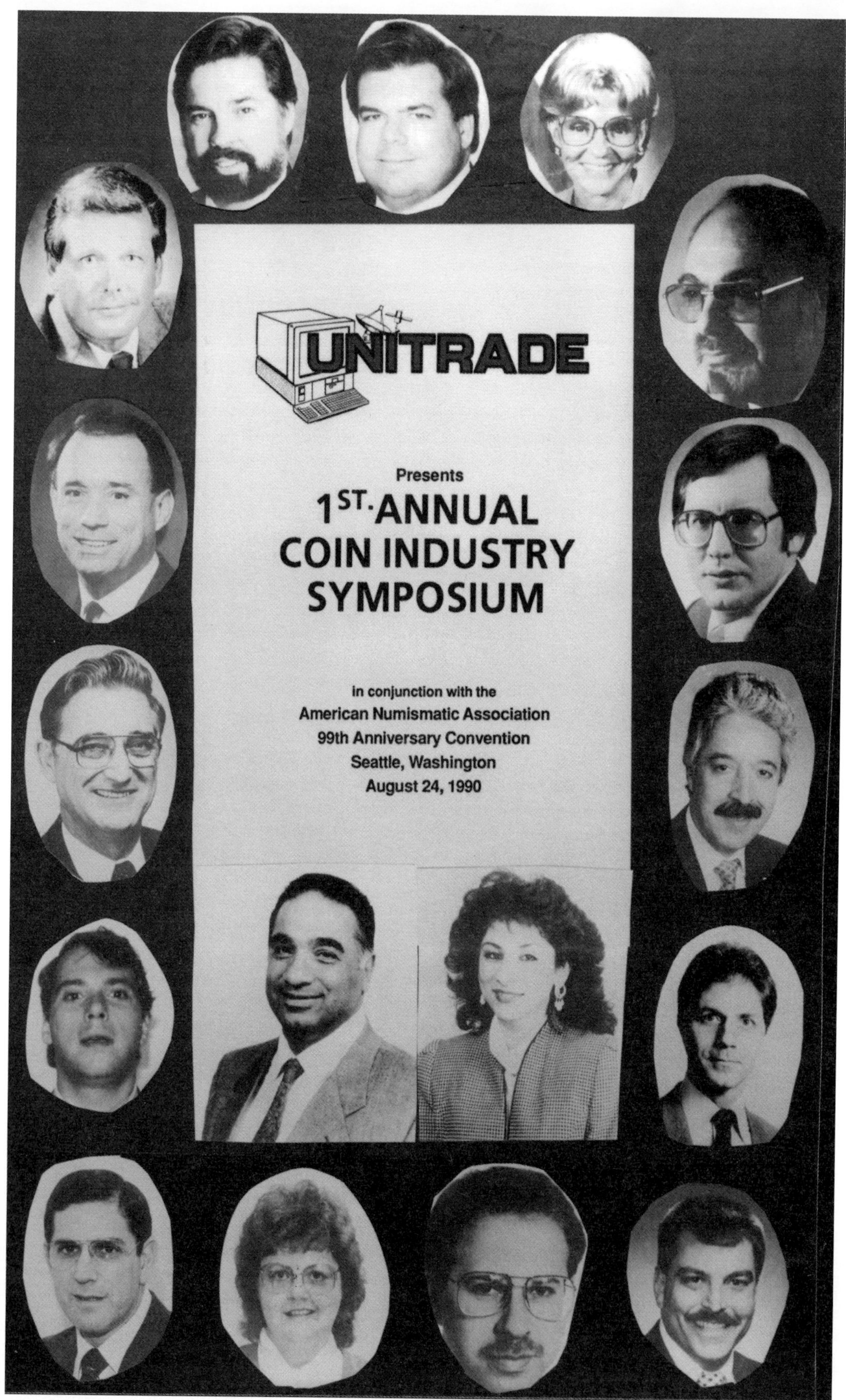

Unitrade 1st Annual Coin Industry Symposium Guests (from left to right - top to bottom) include: David Hall, Bruce P. McNall, Donna Pope, James U. Blanchard, III, Luis Vigdor, John D. Schneider, Jr., Robert B. Korver, Robert J. Leuver, Richard Schwary, John H. Sack, Iraj Sayah, Monir Torabi, David Lisot, Barry J. Cutler, Beth Deisher, Mark Salzberg, Thomas W. Noe, (Photo of Ned Fenton unavailable.)
(Courtesy of Unitrade, Inc., Encino, California)

Top left photo (L to R) John Highfill, Monir Torabi, Iraj Sayah, and Marlene Highfill
(Courtesy of Unitrade, Inc., Encino, California)

Hundreds of photos were made available in order to present this portion of dealers and their travels. It was a massive effort and I believe Iraj "Roger" Sayah and Monir Torabi of Unitrade need to be highly commended for their outstanding contributions. As usual, they were unselfish and giving. I wish to very sincerely thank you.

John W. Highfill.

"THE PARTY" - DO YOU REMEMBER? IT WAS ANOTHER GREAT PARTY HOSTED BY UNITRADE AT THE HYATT, LONG BEACH, CALIFORNIA

(Courtesy of Iraj "Roger" Sayah and Monir Torabi c/o Unitrade Inc., Encino, California)

1ST ANNUAL INTERNATIONAL NUMISMATIC FRIENDSHIP PARTY
(Courtesy of Iraj "Roger" Sayah and Monir Torabi c/o Unitrade, Encino, California)

1ST ANNUAL INTERNATIONAL NUMISMATIC FRIENDSHIP PARTY
(Courtesy of Iraj "Roger" Sayah and Monir Torabi c/o Unitrade, Encino, California)

1ST ANNUAL INTERNATIONAL NUMISMATIC FRIENDSHIP PARTY
(Courtesy of Iraj "Roger" Sayah and Monir Torabi c/o Unitrade, Encino, California)

2ND ANNUAL INTERNATIONAL NUMISMATIC FRIENDSHIP PARTY
"DEALERS" ALL DRESSED UP WITH "*SOMEWHERE*" TO GO FEBRUARY, 1991"
(Courtesy of Iraj "Roger" Sayah and Monir Torabi c/o Unitrade, Inc., Encino, California)

"WONDERFUL PEOPLE" — 2ND ANNUAL INTERNATIONAL NUMISMATIC FRIENDSHIP PARTY
LONG BEACH, CALIFORNIA — FEBRUARY, 1991
(Courtesy of Iraj "Roger" Sayah and Monir Torabi c/o Unitrade, Inc., Encino, California)

"MORE WONDERFUL PEOPLE" — 2ND ANNUAL INTERNATIONAL NUMISMATIC FRIENDSHIP PART
LONG BEACH, CALIFORNIA — FEBRUARY, 1991
(Courtesy of Iraj "Roger" Sayah and Monir Torabi c/o Unitrade, Inc., Encino, California)

MORE WONDERFUL PEOPLE...
(Courtesy of Iraj "Roger" Sayah and Monir Torabi c/o Unitrade, Inc., Encino, California)

2ND ANNUAL INTERNATIONAL NUMISMATIC FRIENDSHIP PARTY, LONG BEACH, CALIFORNIA
(Courtesy of Iraj "Roger" Sayah and Monir Torabi c/o Unitrade, Inc., Encino, California)

2ND ANNUAL INTERNATIONAL NUMISMATIC FRIENDSHIP PARTY, LONG BEACH, CALIFORNIA
(Courtesy of Iraj "Roger" Sayah and Monir Torabi c/o Unitrade, Inc., Encino, California)

2ND ANNUAL INTERNATIONAL NUMISMATIC FRIENDSHIP PARTY, LONG BEACH, CALIFORNIA
(Courtesy of Iraj "Roger" Sayah and Monir Torabi c/o Unitrade, Inc., Encino, California)

NUMISMATIC CLASS OF 1983

NATIONAL SILVER DOLLAR CONVENTIONS, INC.

NUMISMATIC CLASS OF 1983

NUMISMATIC CLASS OF 1984

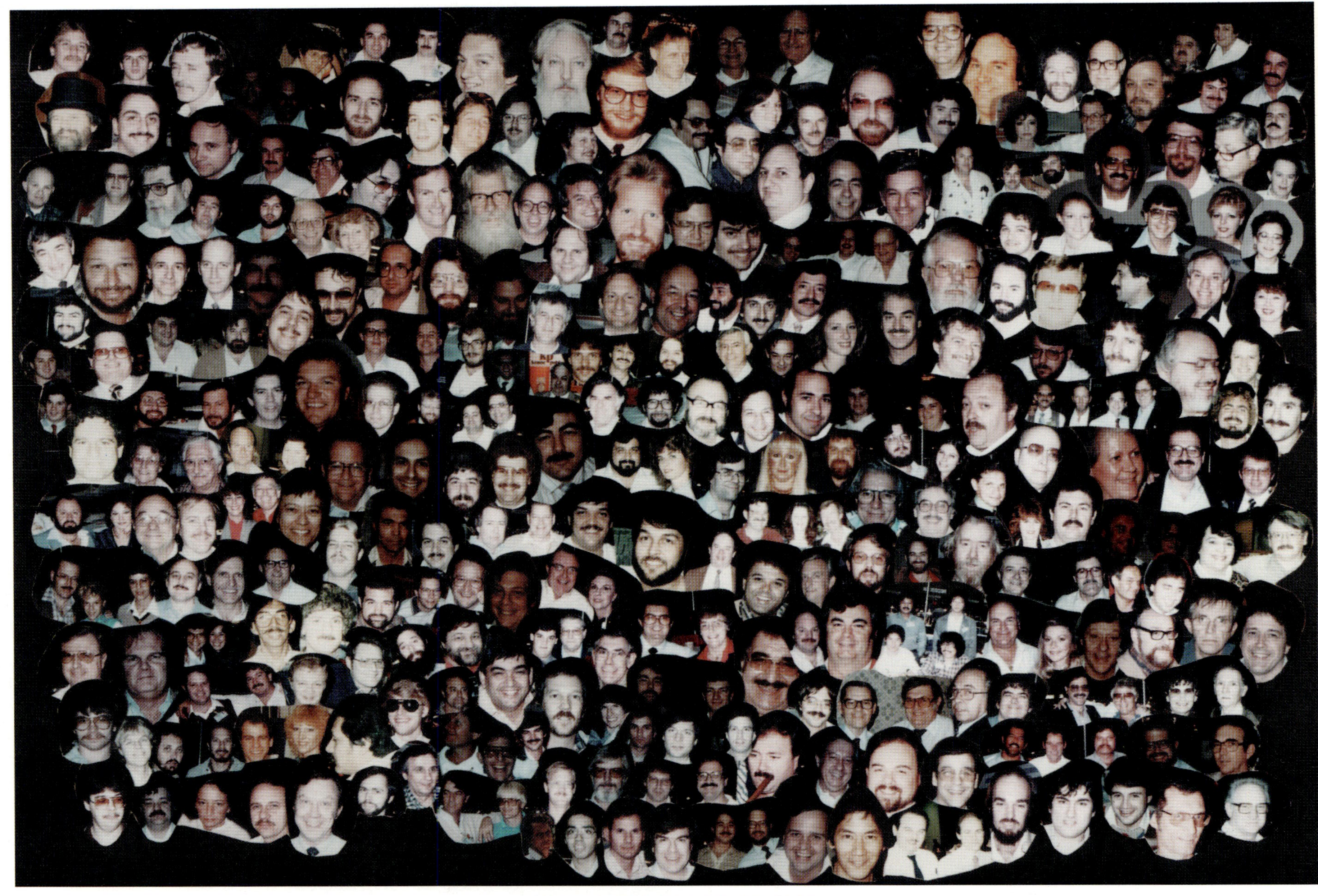

NUMISMATIC CLASS OF 1985

NUMISMATIC CLASS OF 1991

NUMISMATIC CLASS OF 1991

NUMISMATIC CLASS OF 1991

NUMISMATIC CLASS OF 1991

★★★

John W. Highfill, NLG

CHAPTER 80

Morgan Dollars — Date By Date Analysis

by John W. Highfill, NLG

THE MORGAN DOLLAR

(1878 - 1921)

IMPORTANT NOTICE:

For those of you that were not able to view the PCGS "World's Finest Morgan Silver Dollars" exhibition while it was on tour, we at Highfill Press, Inc., with permission from the Professional Coin Grading Service, Inc., Newport Beach, California, are pleased to present all of the dollars from this magnificent collection as the official plate coins used in this Morgan dollar date by date analysis.

PROPOSAL:

The U.S. silver miners persuaded noted politicians Senator William Allison (R-Iowa) and House members Richard Bland (D-Mo.), John Kasson (R-Iowa) and William Kelley (R-Penn.) to support a proposal for a new silver dollar in the late 1870s. After continued lobbying and negotiation Richard Bland (who earned the name, "silver dick,") introduced a bill with Senator William Allison to resurrect the silver dollar.

LEGISLATION:

The proposed coinage act would require the Treasury to purchase a minimum of $2 million per month in domestic silver bullion to be coined into only silver dollars. The Bland-Allison Act was approved by Congress in spite of the veto of President Rutherford Hayes on February 28, 1878.

INSPIRATION:

The vast hoards of silver discovered in the United States (such as the Comstock Lode near Virginia City, Nevada) coupled with the political and economic maneuvers of the mining industry.

AUTHORIZATION:

The Bland-Allison Act gave legal tender status to the silver dollar. Production was halted in 1904 when the government supply of silver bullion was depleted. The Pittman Act of April 23, 1918 created the return of the Morgan silver dollar in 1921 for one final year.

COMPETITION:

George T. Morgan, who had been hired as assistant engraver by mint director Henry R. Linderman, faced a determined chief engraver, William Barber. After many design changes reflecting the constant rivalry, Morgan's design was accepted by the mint director on February 28, 1878 (the same day Congress gave its approval).

DESIGNER:

George T. Morgan, formerly of the London Royal Mint, designed the Morgan dollar using a traditional Liberty and reverse eagle. The model was Miss Anna Willess Williams.

DESIGN:

Obverse: Liberty head facing left with obverse legend (E PLURIBUS UNUM) and stars surrounding Miss Liberty. The date is at the bottom with the artist's initial "M" placed just below the neckline.

Reverse: American Bald eagle with wings spread holding an olive branch and arrows in its talons. The words, UNITED STATES OF AMERICA are circled around the top with IN GOD WE TRUST centered below. ONE DOLLAR is at the bottom. A wreath of branches surrounds the lower half of the eagle.

SPECIFICATIONS:

Weight is 26.73 grams composed of .900 silver and .100 copper, giving a net weight of .77344 ounces of pure silver. Diameter is 38.1 millimeters with a reeded edge. These specifications were made to conform with the Act of January 18, 1837.

CONTRIBUTING MINTS:

Philadelphia, Carson City, Denver, New Orleans and San Francisco. The Denver facility was only used for production in 1921. Mint marks are on the reverse below the wreath.

FIRST YEAR PRODUCTION:

Production of the Morgan dollar began in 1878 when 22,495,550 coins were made at the Philadelphia, Carson City and San Francisco facilities.

PROOFS:

Proof Morgan dollars were made at Philadelphia in all production years. The 1921 issues consisted of the scarce "Zerbe" and "Chapman" proofs which were issued for special commemorative reasons. There were branch mint proofs by the respective branches in selective years.

For accuracy of the following statistics, the rarity factor is illustrated as the degree of rarity of a certified population. The formula for statistics in a rarity class will be based upon the total certified population. The rarity factors may change in time as the population totals change.

The price data shown in the statistical graphs for each date and mint mark begins in 1979. This is due to the volatility and price changes that began since the price boom in the 1979-1980 period. Price data begins in 1979 only for uncertified (raw) pricing data.

Imagine a complete and detailed essay on each of the dates presented in the Morgan and Peace dollar series. Now, assume that you have been given an assignment. You must cover the total analysis in the space of one-half page per date and mint mark. That will give you an idea of what this author went though to provide the bottom line summary as we cut each individual date analysis down to the bone of necessity. Instead of pages of text we have summarized in graph form what would have taken thousands of words to explain.

How to Interpret and Use the Date By Date Analysis

The statistical date by date analysis pages presented in chapter 80 and 81 of this *Encyclopedia* have been prepared to provide a synopsis of information concerning the Morgan and Peace dollar series. These comments and observations are provided to enable the reader to make the best use of the information contained in these pages.

The first part of each date by date analysis page consists of a verbal summary describing the characteristics, history, and availability of that particular issue. This is followed by the summary of facts in chart form showing the following.

MINTAGE	PROOF	STRIKE	LUSTER	BAG MARKS	REDFIELD
3,720,000	0	Weak To Average	Very Good	Moderate to Heavy	No
DIES	**DIE VARIETIES**	**% OF PL**	**% OF DMPL**	**PIVOTAL GRADE**	**RARITY FACTOR**
180*	31	4.9	1.1	MS 65	R-5

* Fiscal Year 1903 data

Morgan Dollar Information:

Mintage: Official U.S. Government mintage.

Proof Mintage: Official U.S. Government proof mintage.

Strike: The average strike for the date and mintmark.

Luster: The average luster for the date and mintmark.

Bagmarks: The average amount of bagmarks for the date and mintmark.

Redfield Status: "YES" if any examples of the issue were found in the Redfield hoard; "NO" otherwise.

Dies Produced: Number of dies produced for the issue. (Fiscal Year Figures)

Die Varieties: Number of die varieties known for the issue.

Percentage of PL: Using total number of PL's certified by PCGS and NGC combined for each issue, divide that total by the total of all certified coins of that same issue.

Percentage of DMPL: Using total number of DMPL's certified by PCGS and DPL's by NGC combined for each issue, divide that total by the total of all certified coins of that same issue.

Pivotal Grade: (1) point where decline of 50% or more exists between two mint state grades (using PCGS and NGC population reports); and (2) price makes at least a 100% jump between the mint state grades found in number (1).

Rarity Factor: The comparative rarity of the certified total (PCGS plus NGC). Rarity factors range from R-1 (most rare) to R-5 (most common).

For accuracy of these statistics, the rarity factor is illustrated as the degree of rarity of a certified population. The formula for statistics in a rarity class will be based upon the total certified population. The rarity factors may change in time as the population totals change.

Peace Dollar Information:

Mintage: Official U.S. Government mintage.

Proof Mintage: Official U.S. Government proof mintage.

Strike: The average strike for the date and mintmark.

Luster: The average luster for the date and mintmark.

Bagmarks: The average amount of bagmarks for the date and mintmark.

Redfield Status: "YES" if any examples of the issue were found in the Redfield hoard; "NO" otherwise.

Category: Common, Semi-Common, Semi-Key or Key.

Die Varieties: Number of die varieties known for the issue.

Pivotal Grade: (1) point where decline of 50% or more exists between two mint state grades (using PCGS and NGC population reports); and (2) price makes at least a 100% jump between the mint state grades found in number (1).

Rarity Factor: The comparative rarity of the certified total (PCGS plus NGC). Rarity factors range from R-1 (most rare) to R-5 (most common).

The statistical summary is followed by a series of graphs representing volume and pricing information for differing periods of time. This allows for more detailed study of populations, trends, pricing comparisons, and coin price history. A more detailed description of each available graph follows.

PCGS Population Chart

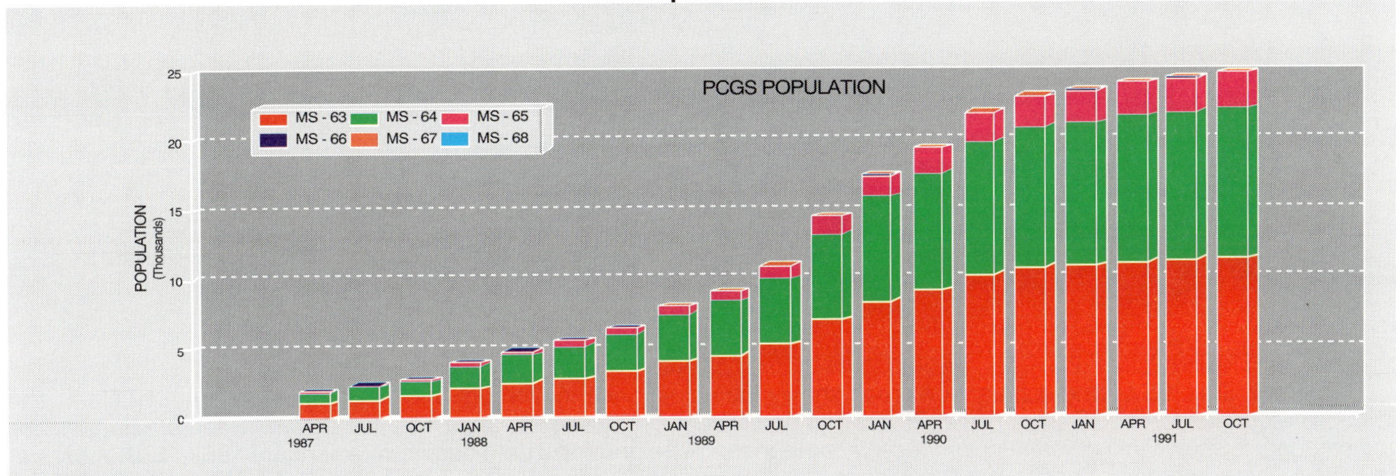

The PCGS population graph shows the **TOTAL** PCGS certified population data presented in graph form using the following grades: MS-63, MS-64, MS-65, MS-66, MS-67 and MS-68. The **TOTAL** for each grade is shown in a different color according to the legend in the upper left corner. The **TOTAL** for all grades is shown as a multi-colored bar for each quarterly time period beginning in April 1987. We began with April 1987, as it was the first year PCGS began publishing their population reports.

NGC Population Chart

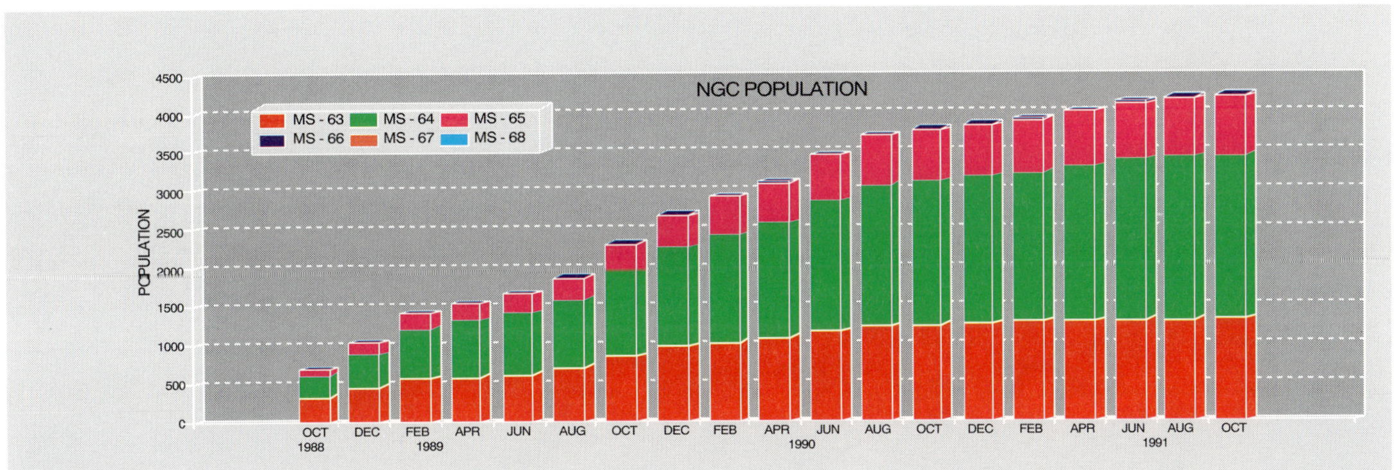

The NGC population graph shows the **TOTAL** NGC certified population data presented in graph form using the following grades: MS-63, MS-64, MS-65, MS-66, MS-67 and MS-68. The **TOTAL** for each grade is shown in a different color according to the legend in the upper left corner. The **TOTAL** for all grades is shown as a multi-colored bar for each bi-monthly time period beginning in October 1988.

Totals began with October 1988, which was the date NGC first started publishing their population reports. We have used PCGS and NGC data only since these are the current two dominant grading services. However, other grading services are becoming more available.

Mint State 65 Pricing Comparison

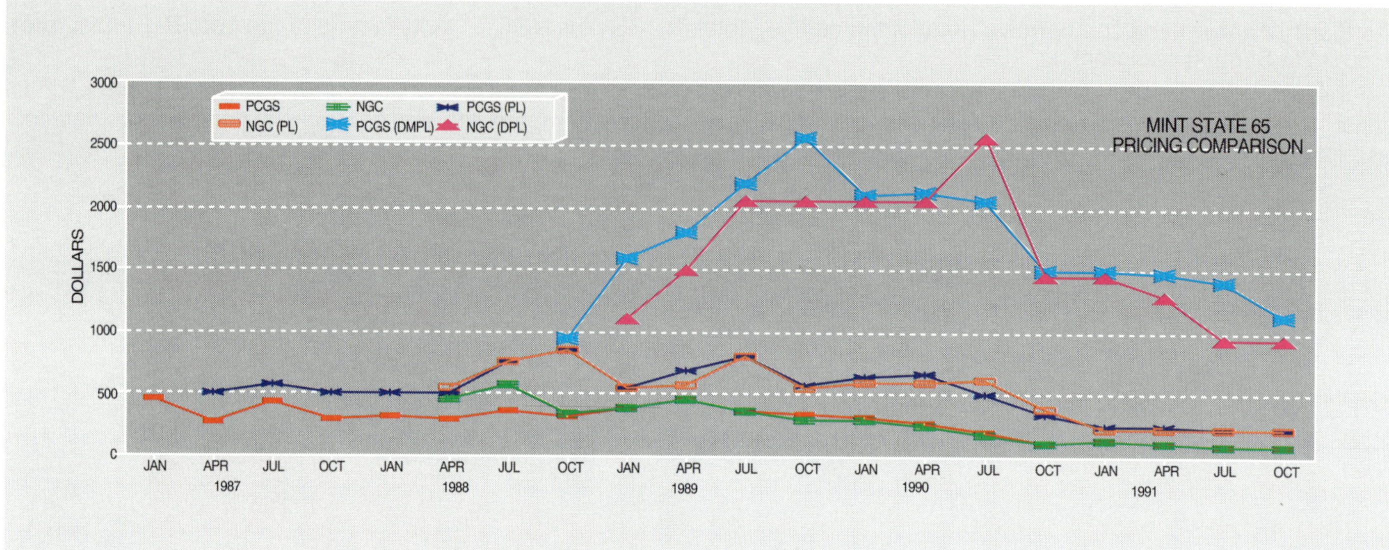

The Mint State 65 pricing comparison graph shows the actual price movement of Mint State 65 dollars over time. The certified categories for PCGS (Mint State, PL, DMPL) and NGC (Mint State, PL, and DPL) are shown. Each grading service and category is shown in a different color for easy comparison. The graphical data begins with January 1987. **Editors Note:** All lines in the graph do not begin with the January 1987 data. NGC coins, Prooflike and DPL had different starting points depending on their charted dates. These charts are based on prices published in the Certified Coin Dealer Newsletter (CCDN — *Bluesheet*)

Mint State Pricing Comparison And Market Trends

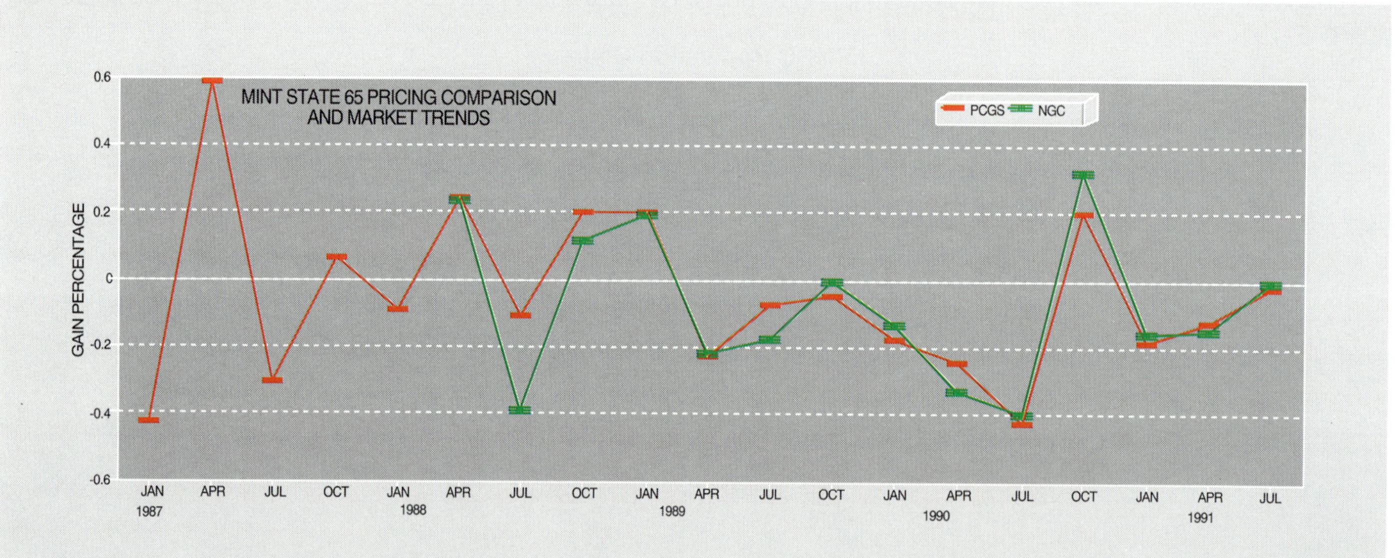

The Mint State 65 pricing comparison and market trends graph shows the percentage of price change over time for PCGS and NGC certified coins for Mint State 65 dollars. Each service is shown in a different color for easy comparison. The percentage change from period to period is shown as opposed to actual price levels. The graphical data begins with January 1987. The graph also shows the market trends and swings of mint state 65 silver dollars from January 1987 through April 1991. The percentage gains and/or losses from the above chart have been determined also from the Certified Coin Dealer Newsletter (CCDN — *Bluesheet*). For example: The April 1987 graph mark shows approximately a .6 or 60% gain. This is based on price comparisons from April to July.

Coin Price History By Grade

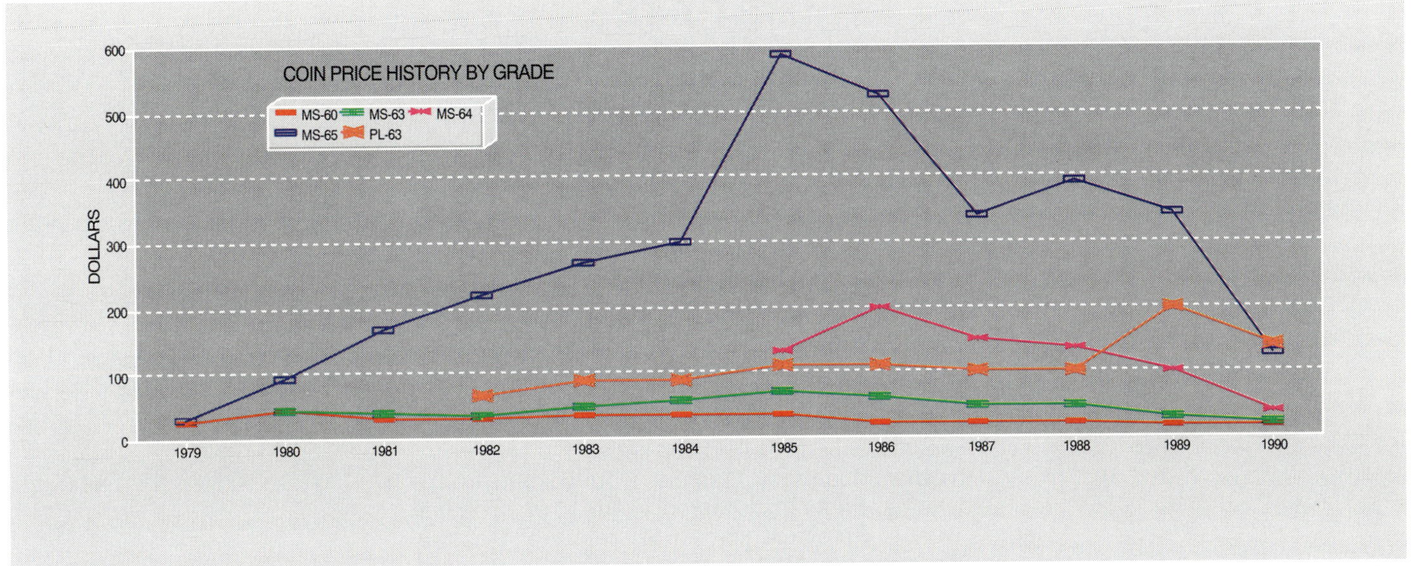

The final graph presents uncertified coin pricing over time for both Mint State and Prooflike examples of the issue. The Mint State and Prooflike categories are color coded for easy identification. The uncertified price data shown begins in 1979. **Editors Note:** This chart is based on prices published in the Coin Dealer Newsletter (CCDN — *Greysheet*).

Graphical Research

The cumulated PCGS and NGC certified population data may be studied for overall volume or rate of increase over time. For example, the rate of increase of the certified populations in many of these graphs focuses attention on the fact that the issues they represent are being submitted for certification at a reducing rate, leading to the "point of diminishing return" for that issue. Notice that for the 1904-O (and all of the Morgan and Peace dollar Population charts) the MS-63 and MS-64 graded certified populations are the largest by far.

The Pricing Comparison graphs (dollars and Percentage Gain) for the various categories and the two grading services over time can reveal trends not previously recognized. The Pricing Comparison Percentage Gain graph focuses on percentage change relationships on a period to period basis rather than on actual price levels. Study the comparative price relationship over time to reveal relational percentage and directional price movements.

The Coin Price History data presents over a decade of information and allows trend analysis for each of these two categories as well as comparisons between them.

The data presented in the five graphs for each date and mintmark of the Morgan and Peace dollar series may be used for research, trend analysis, determining the "point of diminishing returns" and other valuable insights.

Additional Historical Research

There are many references to Walter Breen's Complete Encyclopedia of U.S. and Colonial Coins in both the Morgan and Peace dollar date by date analyses.

Walter H. Breen not only served as the Editor-in-Chief for this encyclopedia, but was also supplemental in the text portion of the individual Morgan and Peace dollar dates.

Editor's Note: The PCGS labels on the reverse of the illustrated Morgan Dollars were inverted for better cosmetic appearance and eye appeal.

***

1878-P 8 TF

PCGS
1878 8TF
S$1
MS66
7072.66/7258711

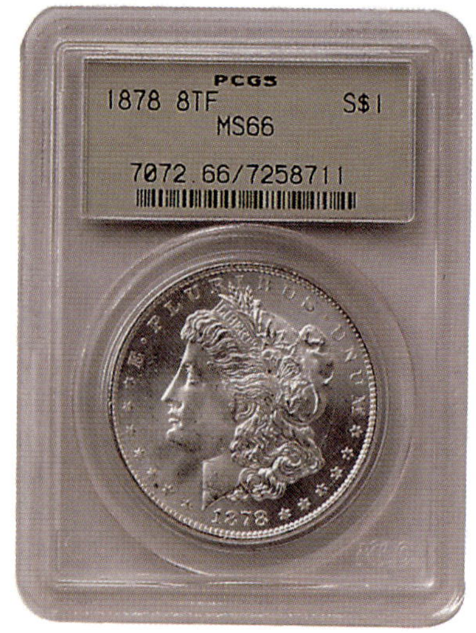

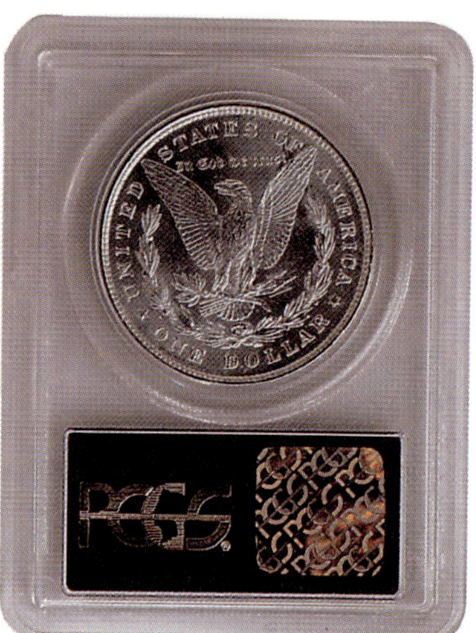

The first adopted design of Morgan dollar. Common partly because saved as first of their kind, partly because many turned up in Treasury bags.

At least 749,500 struck, March 12-26, 1878.

The earliest have Type I rev., with blunt beak; about 33 varieties. *Encyclopedia* 5500. A small minority show doubled obv. die, *Ency*. 5501, VAM 15-17.

Controversy regarding the number of tail feathers on the American eagle, the dies were later changed to seven tail feathers. Later coins have Type II rev., pointed beak over blunt beak (doubled die rev., from two hubs). Normal obv., *Ency* 5502; doubled obv. die, *Ency* 5503.

Recommended in MS 64 or better.

Proofs: Much rarer than one would expect from a 500 mintage. First struck March 11 (VAM 9). The first three went to President Hayes, Secretary of Treasury John Sherman and Mint Director Henry R. Linderman. Most later 8TF proofs are the earliest state of VAM 14-3 (spine from eyeball), including probably most of the 100 of March 12, and all the 100 March 15 and the 300 of March 18.

Prooflikes: Often one-sided (obverse only): mirror fields around cameo head, but frosty reverse fields. Especially above grade 64, two-sided PL's are much scarcer, DMPL's rarer still and seldom in gem state.

MINTAGE	PROOF	STRIKE	LUSTER	BAG MARKS	REDFIELD
749,500	500	Sharp & Bold	Average	Moderate	No
DIES	**DIE VARIETIES**	**% OF PL**	**% OF DMPL**	**PIVOTAL GRADE**	**RARITY FACTOR**
92*	33	10.6	3.6	MS 65	R-3

*Includes all dies used at the Philadelphia Mint - FY 1878

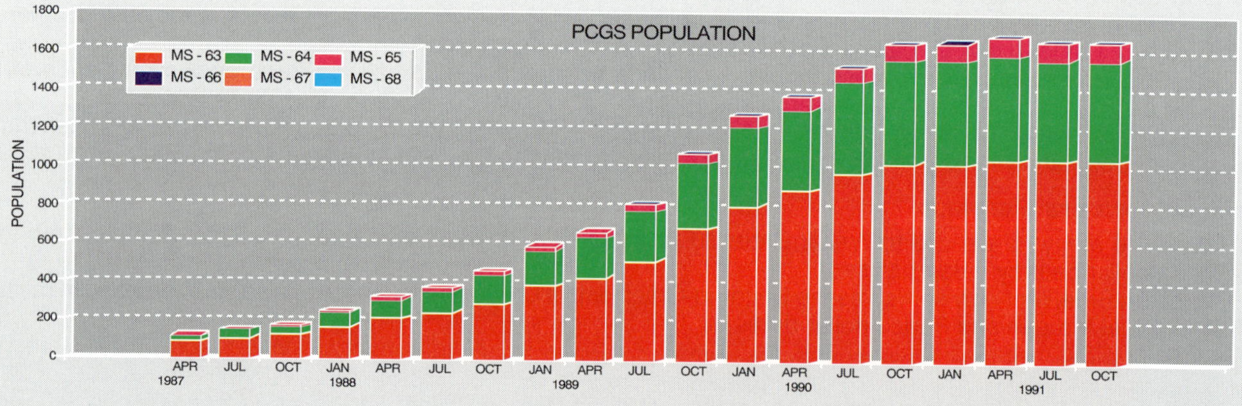
PCGS POPULATION
MS - 63
MS - 64
MS - 65
MS - 66
MS - 67
MS - 68
POPULATION
1800
1600
1400
1200
1000
800
600
400
200
0
APR 1987
JUL
OCT
JAN 1988
APR
JUL
OCT
JAN 1989
APR
JUL
OCT
JAN
APR 1990
JUL
OCT
JAN
APR
JUL 1991
OCT

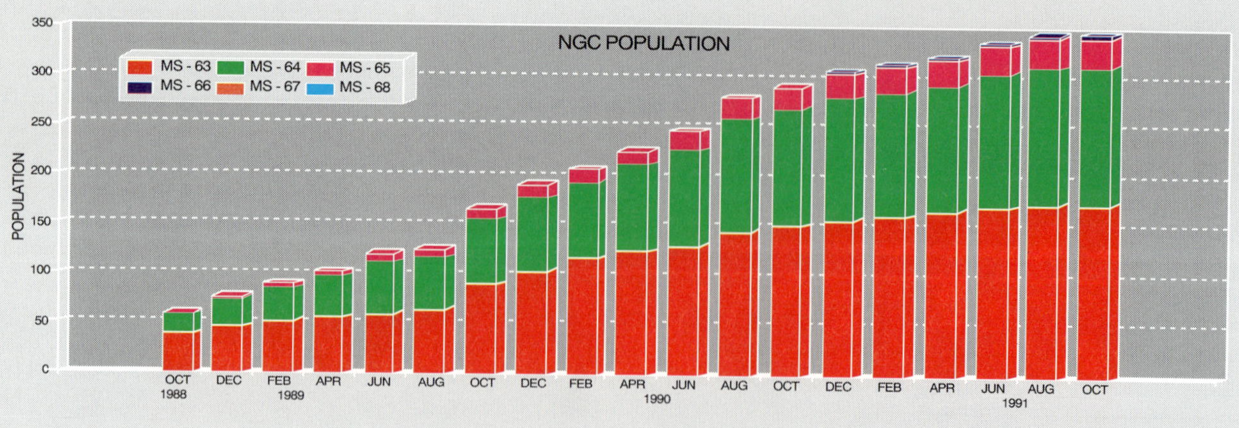
NGC POPULATION
MS - 63
MS - 64
MS - 65
MS - 66
MS - 67
MS - 68
POPULATION
350
300
250
200
150
100
50
0
OCT 1988
DEC
FEB 1989
APR
JUN
AUG
OCT
DEC
FEB
APR 1990
JUN
AUG
OCT
DEC
FEB
APR
JUN 1991
AUG
OCT

1878-P 8 TF

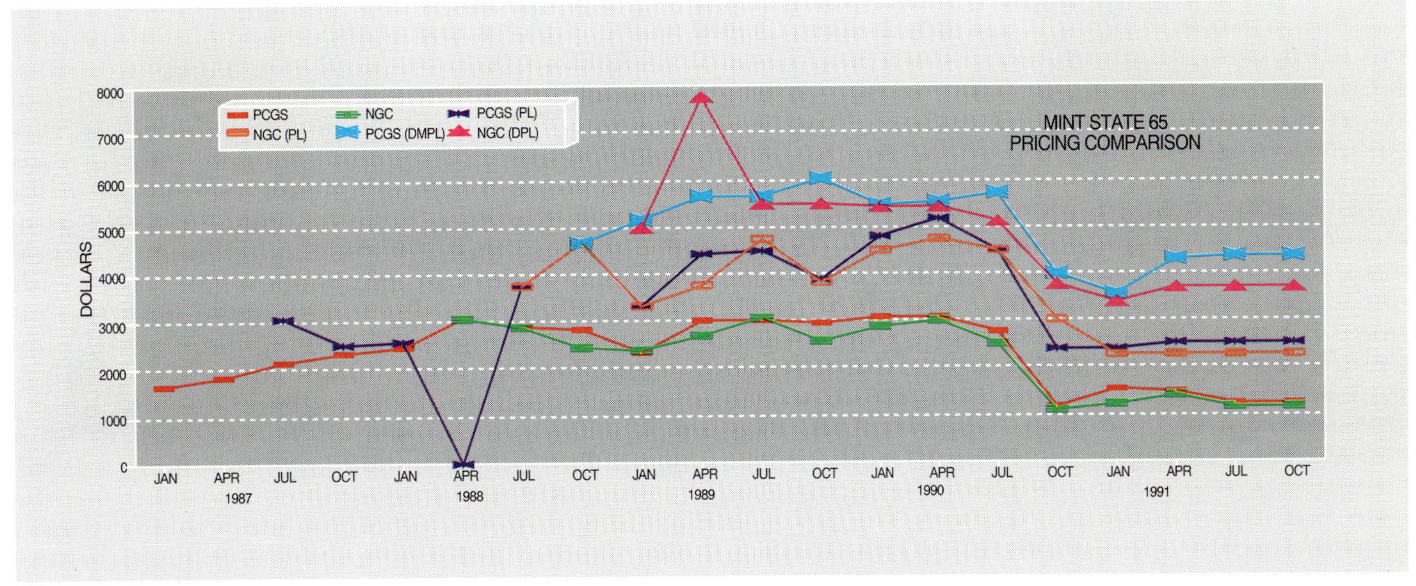

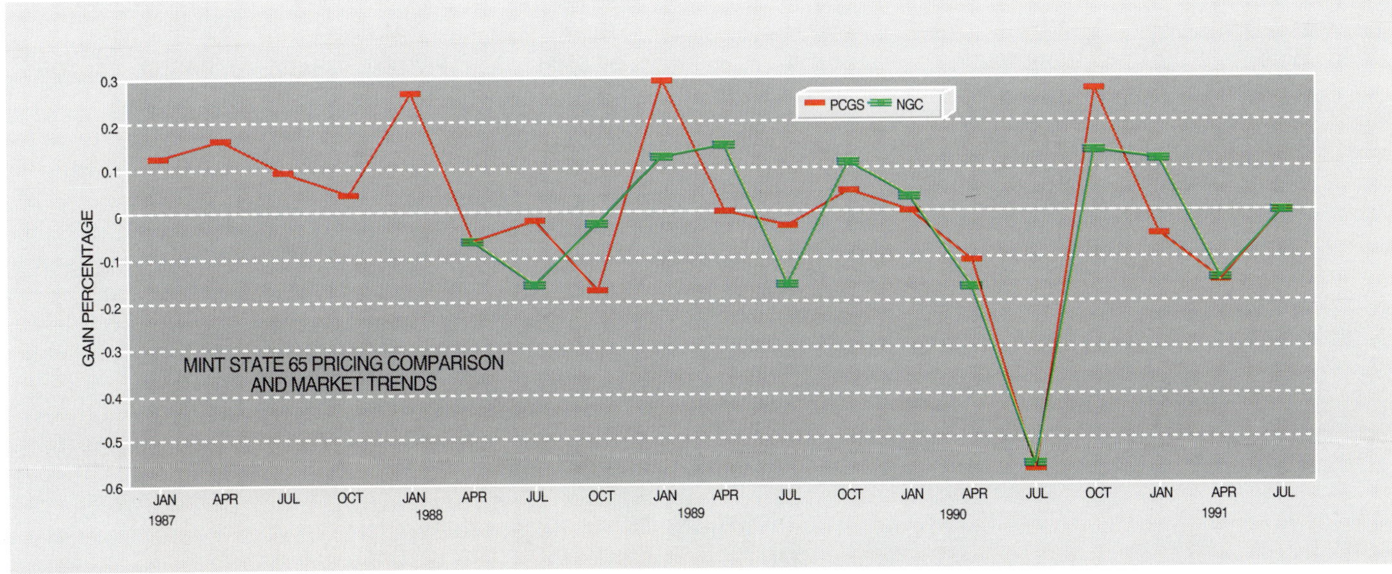

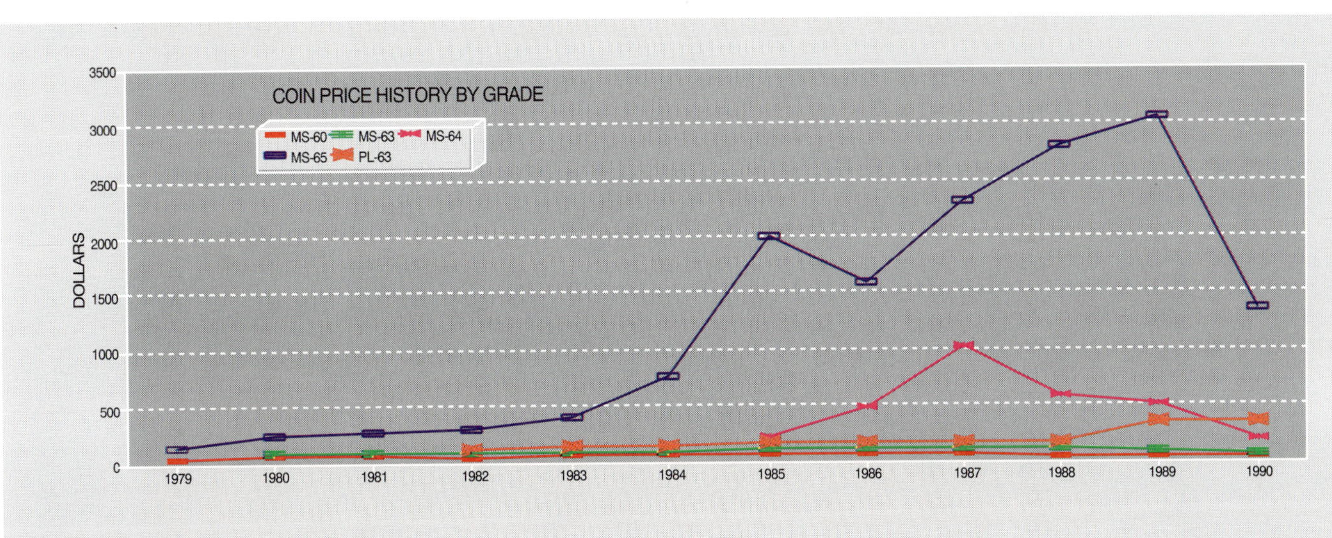

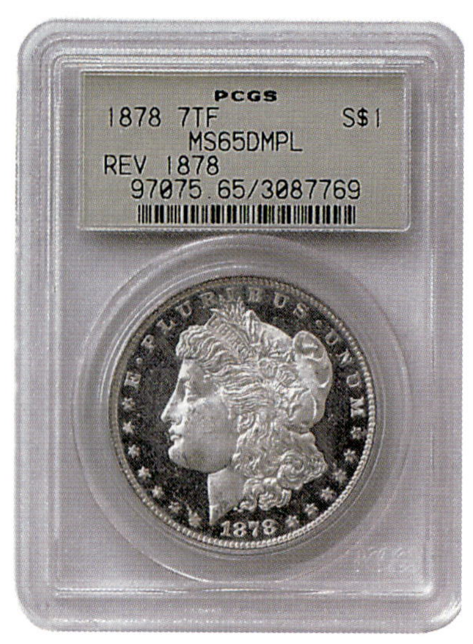

1878-P 7 TF (Reverse of '78)

Concave Breast, Type II obverse, Type B reverse.

Struck April 4 - June 28 (4,900,000), in response to media criticism of the 8TF design; eagles have odd numbers of tail feathers, not even. Common in all grades at least through MS 64. The 115 die varieties include the 8TF, 7/8 Weak and Strong, Rev '78 and Rev '79.

Proofs: Many of the 200 VAM 131's struck March 26 were spent. Next to this, the 1895 is common.

Prooflikes: Scarce, more so above MS 64; DMPL's are still more so. Cameos are very scarce, especially in higher mint state grades.

MINTAGE	PROOF	STRIKE	LUSTER	BAG MARKS	REDFIELD
4,900,000 *	200	Average	Good	Moderate	No
DIES	**DIE VARIETIES**	**% OF PL**	**% OF DMPL**	**PIVOTAL GRADE**	**RARITY FACTOR**
92**	54	12.1	6.0	MS 65	R-3

* Estimated by these authors ** Includes all dies used at the Philadelphia Mint - FY 1878

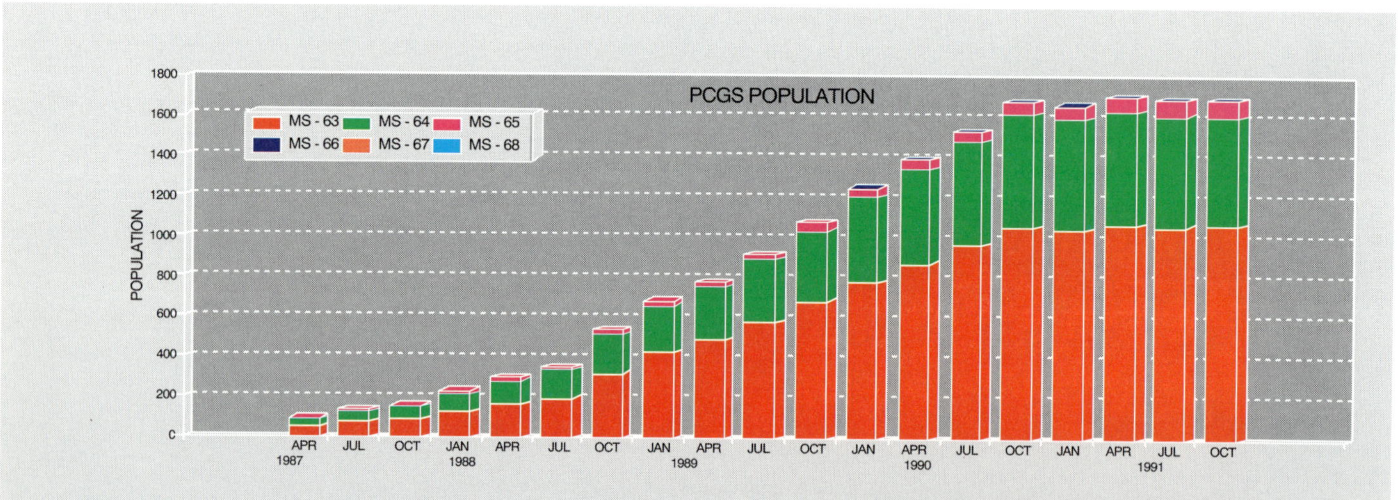

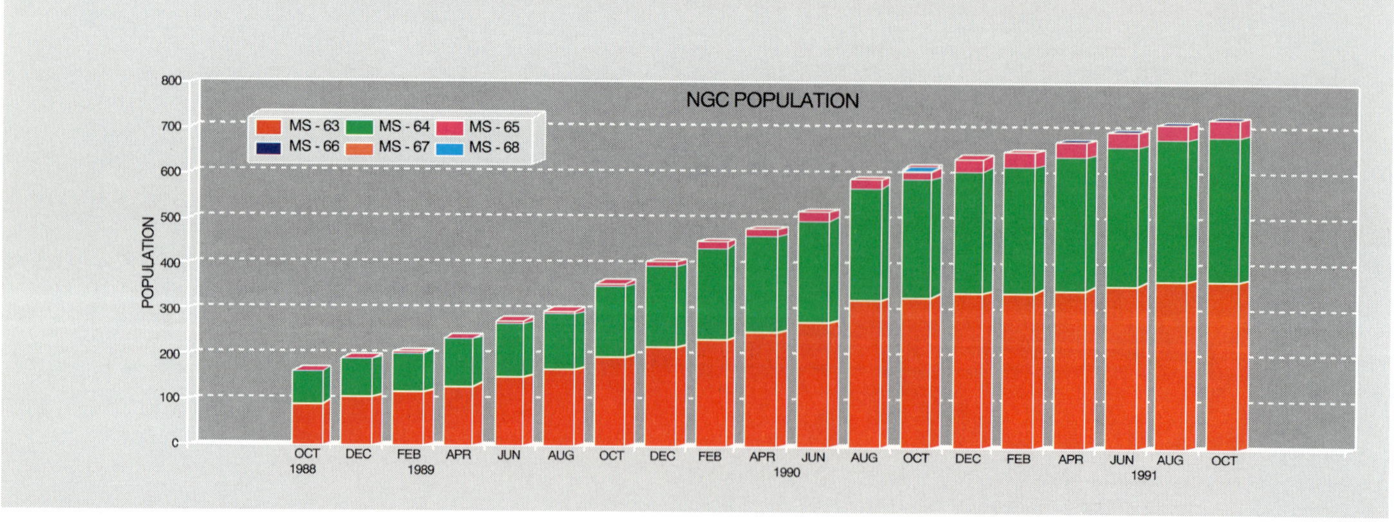

1878-P 7 TF (Reverse of '78)

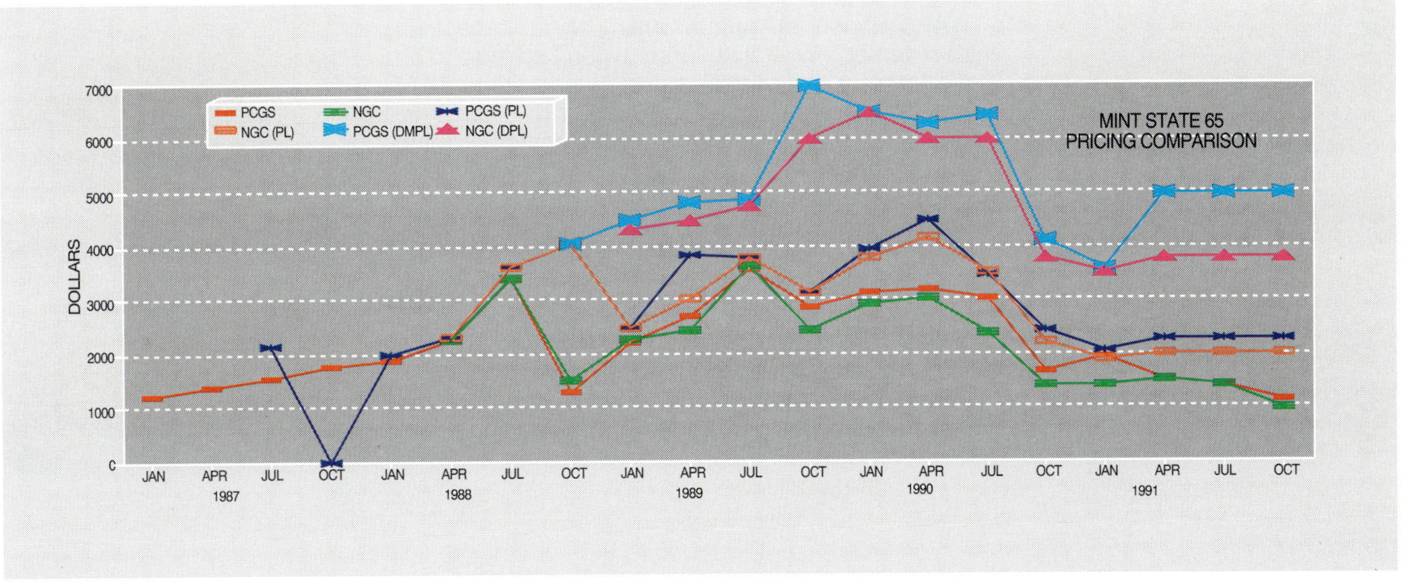

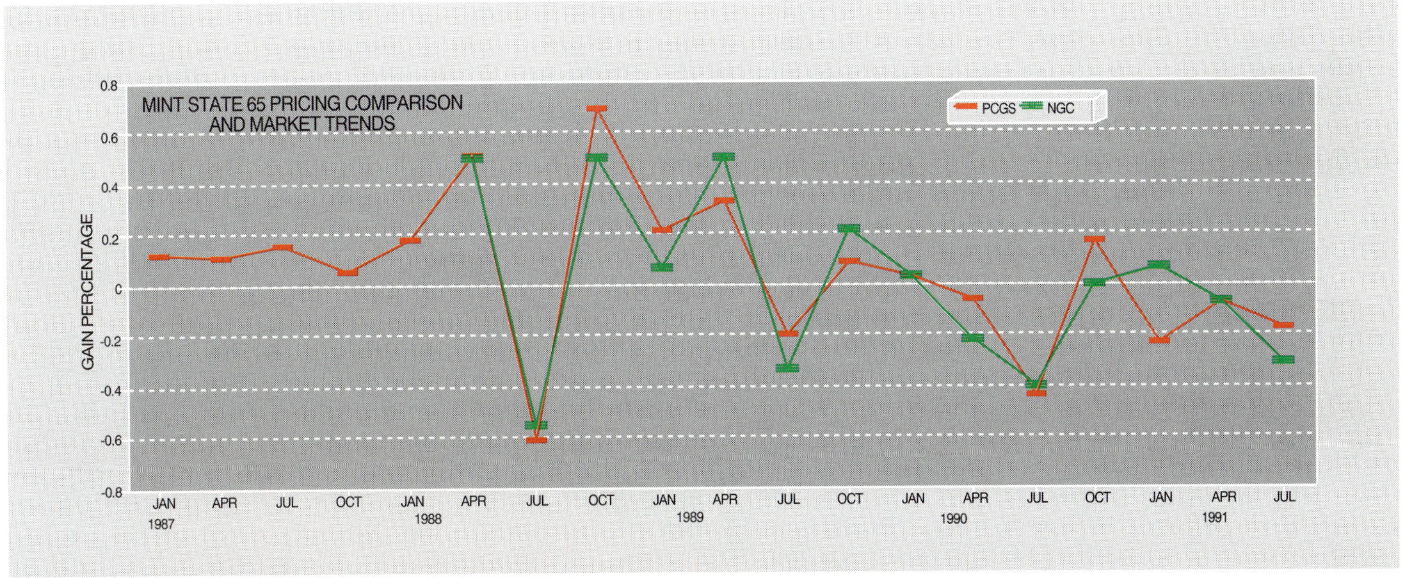

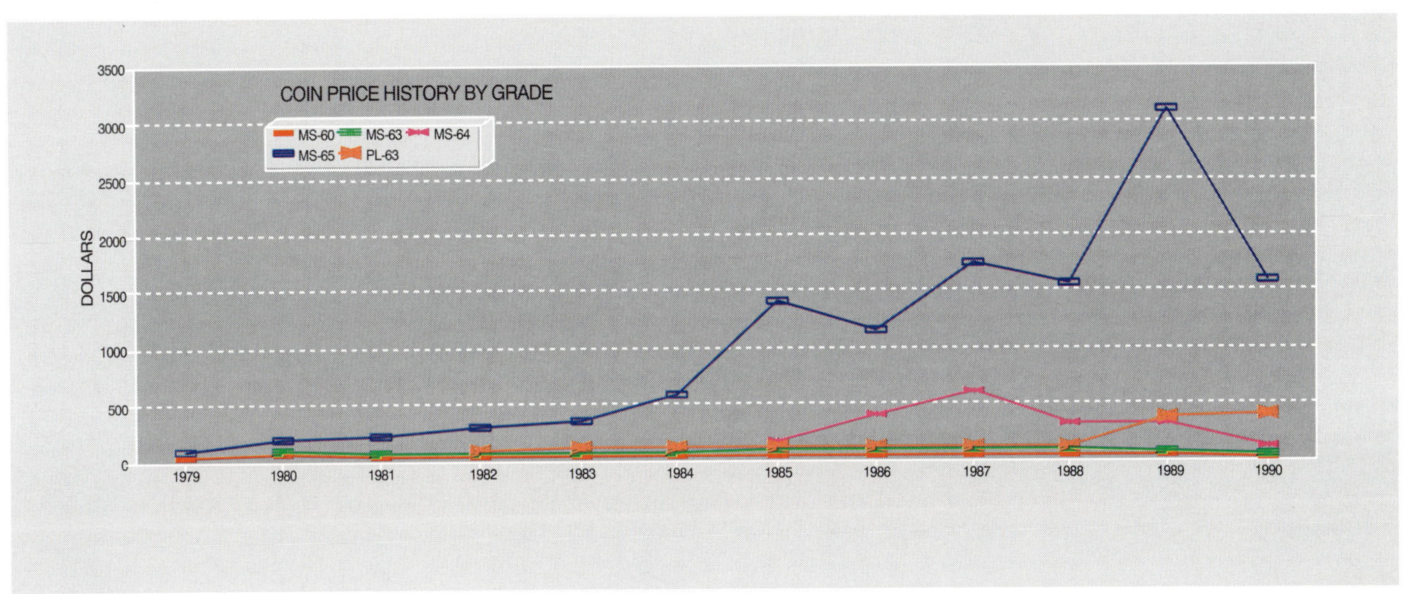

1878-P 7TF (Reverse of '79)

Also known as "round breast" or "full breast" or "third reverse." Type II obverse, type C reverse. The Mint's term for this modified design was "June 1878 Hub." Production began on June 28, 1878; total 4,300,000 plus 50 proofs. (SAF designates Slanted Arrow Feather variety.)

Proofs: Out of the 50 VAM 215's delivered November 8, 34 were sold, the rest spent January 1879. The rarest Morgan proof before 1921. As long ago as February 1974, one was sold to the dealer Harlan White (a longtime friend) at Bowers & Ruddy's Stanislaw Herstal sale, for $4,600. Not over 10 seen to date, including impaired ones.

Prooflikes: Often one-sided. Very scarce, two-sided more so; rare above grade 64, especially DMPL.

MINTAGE	PROOF	STRIKE	LUSTER	BAG MARKS	REDFIELD
4,300,000*	50	Average	Good	Moderate	No
DIES	**DIE VARIETIES**	**% OF PL**	**% OF DMPL**	**PIVOTAL GRADE**	**RARITY FACTOR**
92**	12	6.6	3.2	MS 65	R-2

*Estimated by the authors **Includes all dies used at the Philadelphia Mint - FY 1878

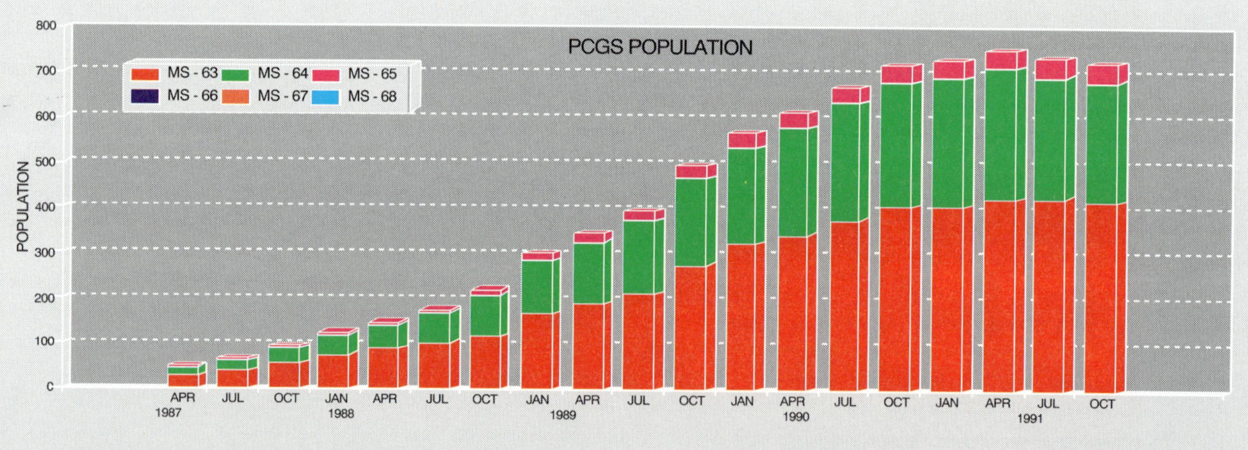

PCGS POPULATION

MS - 63 MS - 64 MS - 65 MS - 66 MS - 67 MS - 68

POPULATION

0 100 200 300 400 500 600 700 800

APR 1987 JUL OCT JAN 1988 APR JUL OCT JAN 1989 APR JUL OCT JAN APR 1990 JUL OCT JAN APR JUL 1991 OCT

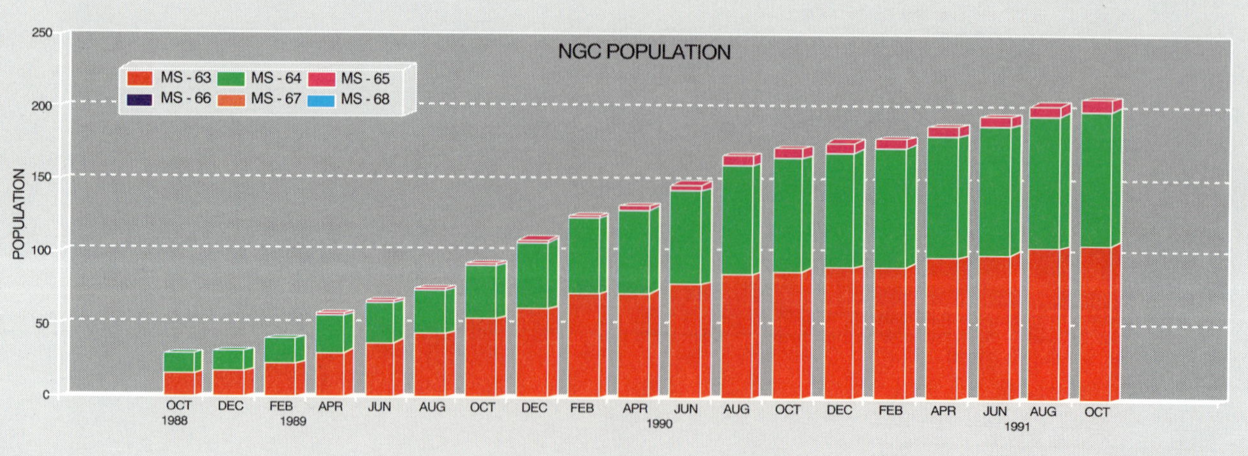

NGC POPULATION

MS - 63 MS - 64 MS - 65 MS - 66 MS - 67 MS - 68

POPULATION

0 50 100 150 200 250

OCT 1988 DEC FEB 1989 APR JUN AUG OCT DEC FEB APR JUN 1990 AUG OCT DEC FEB APR JUN 1991 AUG OCT

1878-P 7TF (Reverse of '79)

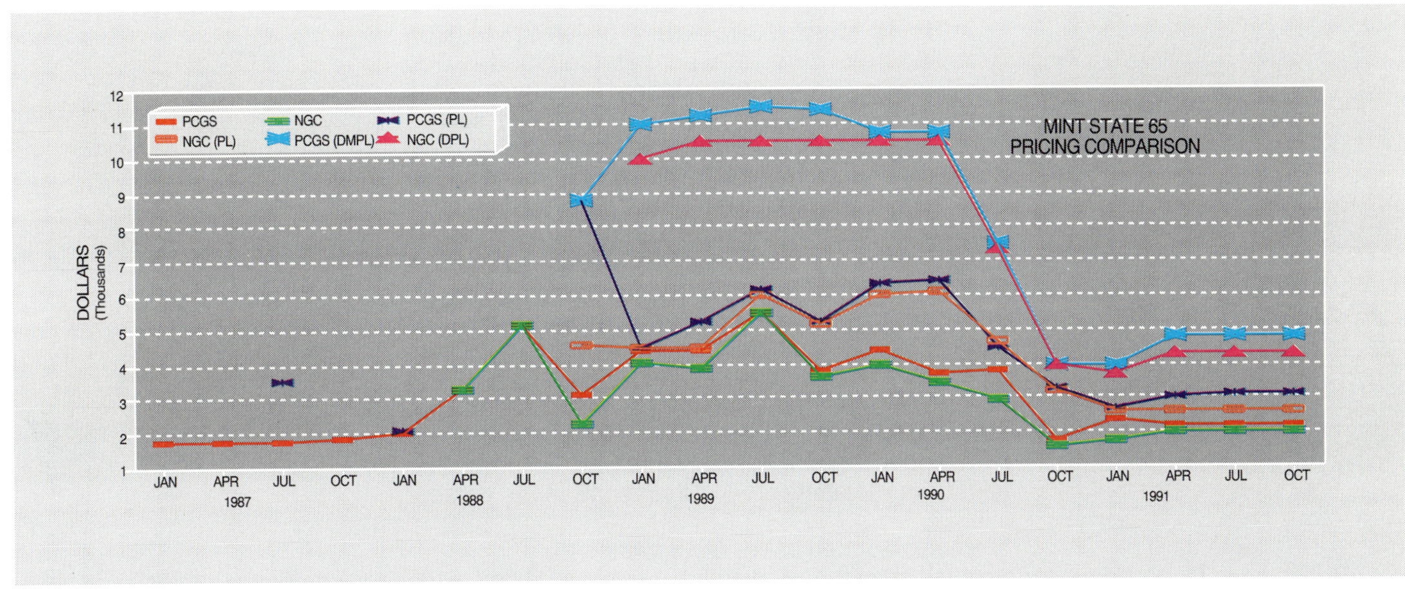

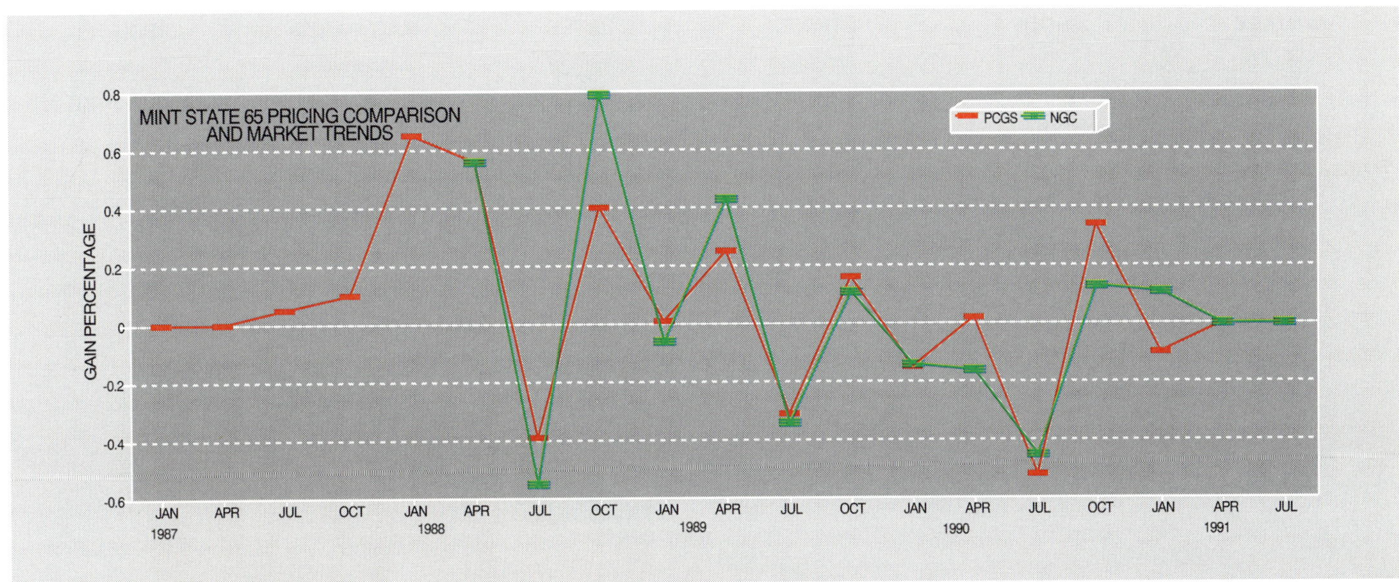

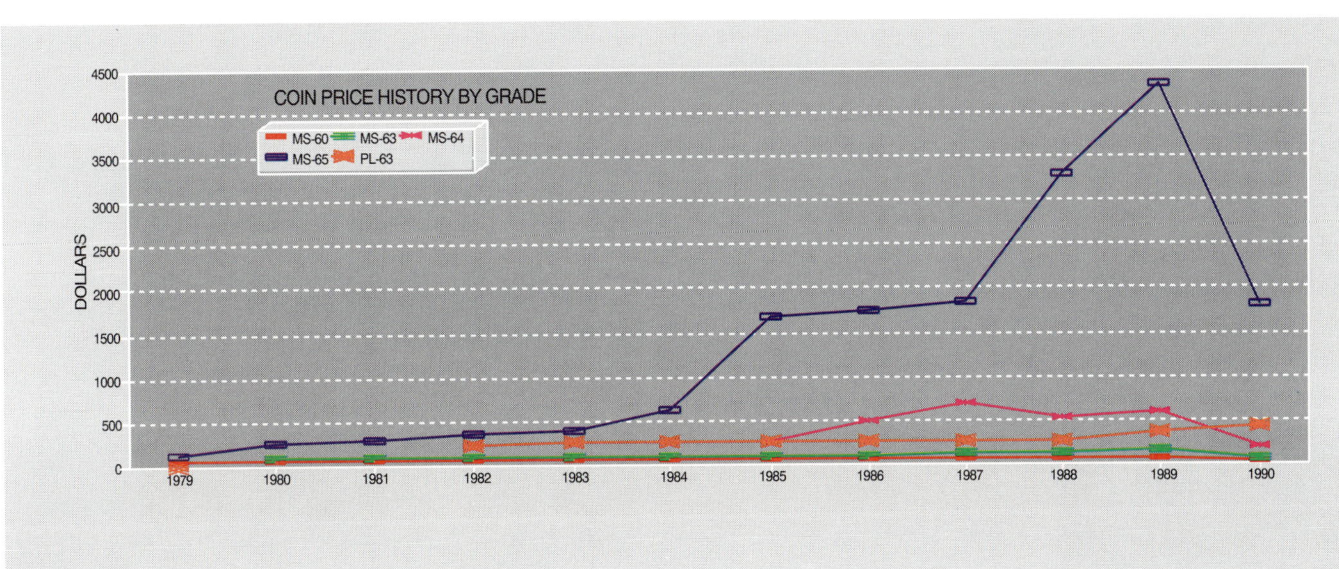

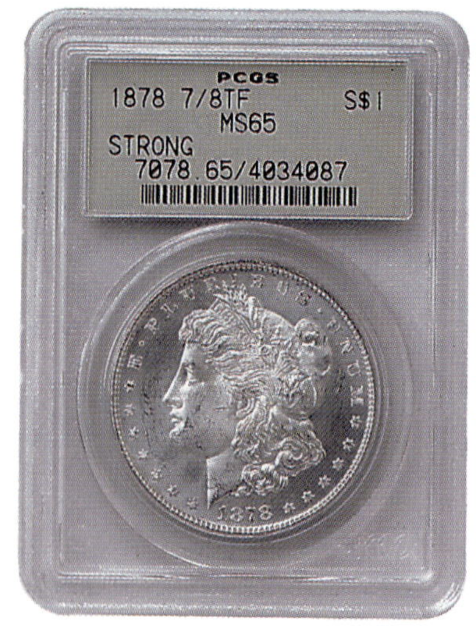

1878-P 7/8 TF (Strong)

PCGS
1878 7/8TF S$1
MS65
STRONG
7078.65/4034087

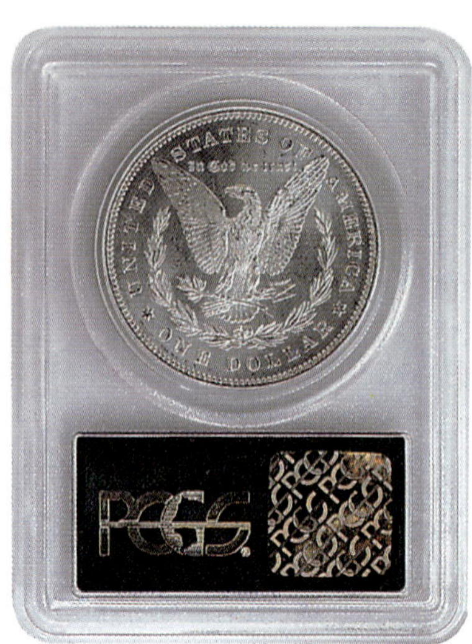

Struck March 26 to April 4 or later (544,000), from 50 rev. dies, not all yet identified. See *Encyclopedia* 5504-5508. Many collectors divide these into "weak" (3 or 4 extra tail feathers) and "strong" (5 to 7 extra feathers). Both "weak" and "strong" have rare and common varieties. The "strong" has been so much sought after that the "weak" 7/8's have become sleepers.

Perhaps the most remarkable varieties have doubled talons (VAM 30, 45), doubled legs (VAM 31, 43), or tripled obv. die (VAM 44). None of these is common; the VAM 44 is extremely rare. Cherrypickers hunting this one should look on lower edges of cotton leaves and blossoms. About 20 survivors are traced, all with some prooflike surfaces; and AU sold a few years ago at $2,000, and only one Unc. is know. See Jeff Oxman's variety study, Chapter 18 in the present volume.

Recommended in MS 64 or better.

Prooflikes: One-sided are more often seen than two-sided. Very hard to find, especially cameos. Both PL and DMPL are rare above grade 64. The finest VAM 41 (all 7 extra feathers show) is the John Hardenberg, Wayne Miller DMPL.

MINTAGE	PROOF	STRIKE	LUSTER	BAG MARKS	REDFIELD
544,000*	0	Average	Average	Moderate	No
DIES	**DIE VARIETIES**	**% OF PL**	**% OF DMPL**	**PIVOTAL GRADE**	**RARITY FACTOR**
92**	16	9.3	3.9	MS 65	R-2

*Estimate includes both weak and strong varieties ** Includes all dies used at the Philadelphia Mint - FY 1878

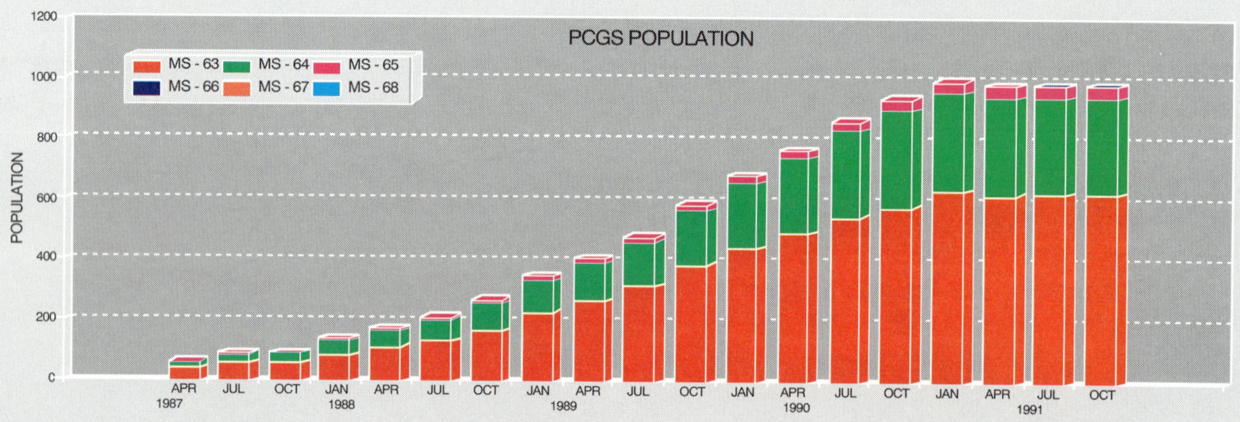
PCGS POPULATION
MS - 63
MS - 64
MS - 65
MS - 66
MS - 67
MS - 68
POPULATION
1200
1000
800
600
400
200
0
APR 1987
JUL
OCT
JAN 1988
APR
JUL
OCT
JAN 1989
APR
JUL
OCT
JAN
APR 1990
JUL
OCT
JAN
APR
JUL 1991
OCT

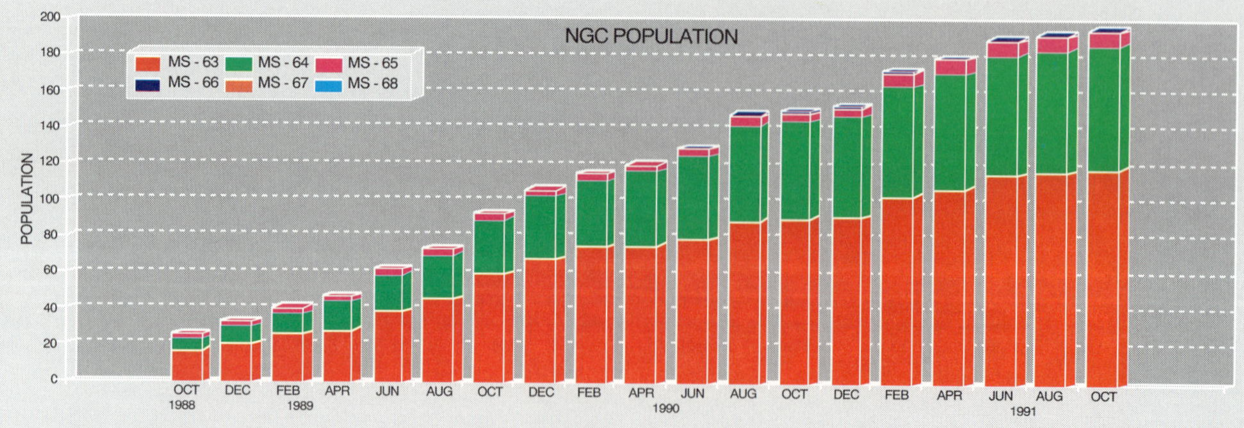
NGC POPULATION
MS - 63
MS - 64
MS - 65
MS - 66
MS - 67
MS - 68
POPULATION
200
180
160
140
120
100
80
60
40
20
0
OCT 1988
DEC
FEB 1989
APR
JUN
AUG
OCT
DEC
FEB
APR 1990
JUN
AUG
OCT
DEC
FEB
APR
JUN 1991
AUG
OCT

1878-P 7/8 TF (Strong)

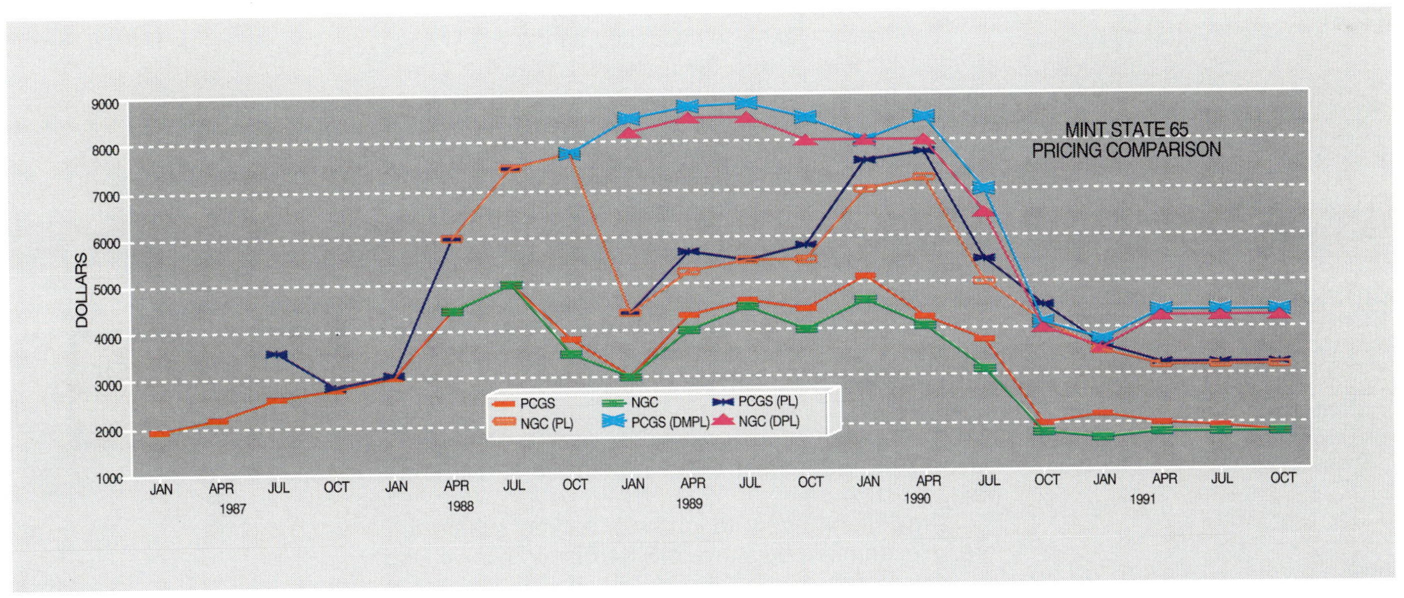

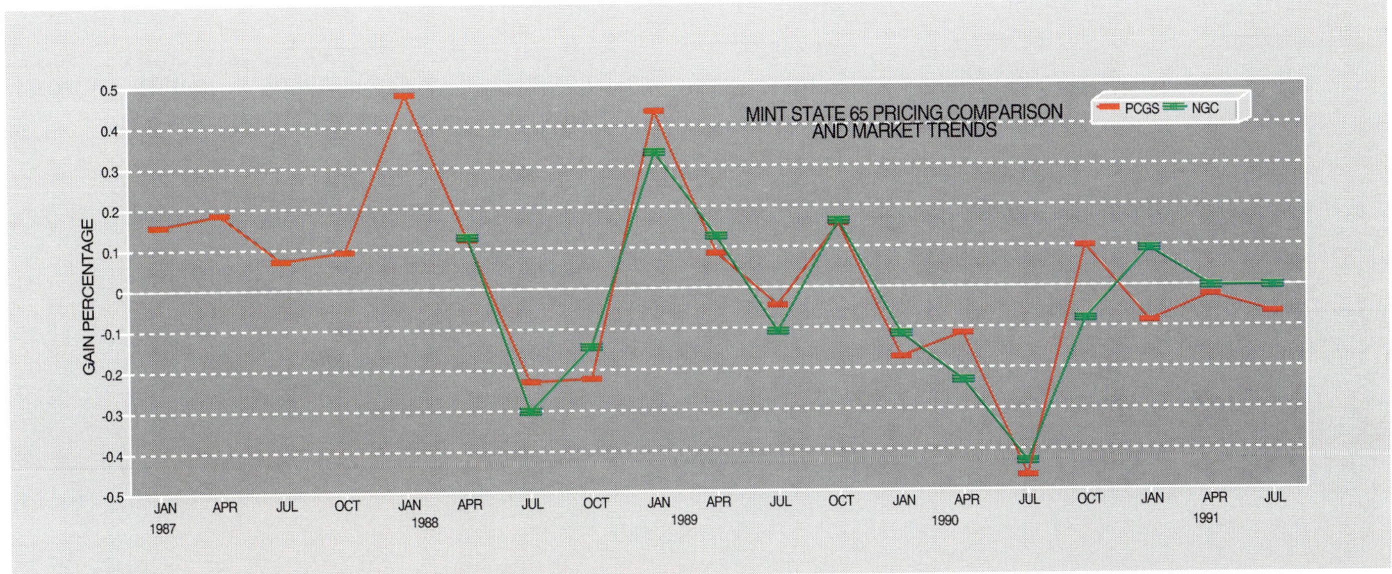

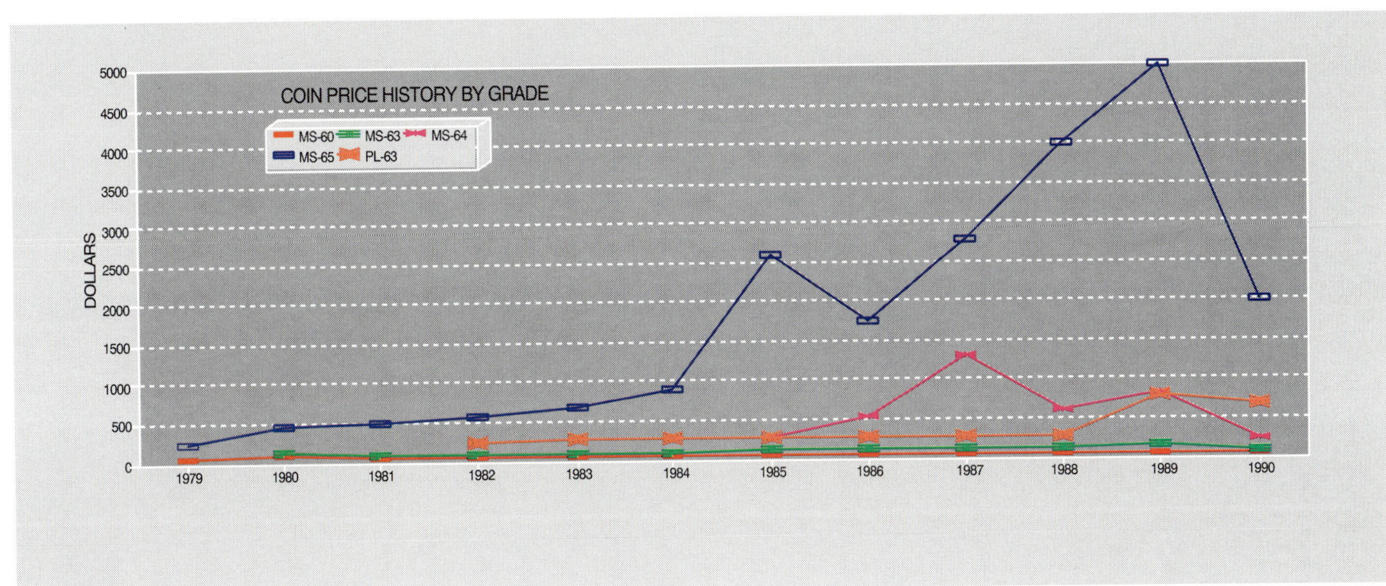

1878-P 7/8 TF (Weak)

The "weak" variety is described as the 7/8 TF die variety with less than 5 tail feathers below the 7 tail feathers on top. In the past, the strong variety has always been the most desirable; and well it should be from a "pure numismatic viewpoint." However, because of the strong demand for "complete" collections, this largely ignored variety is not as common in BU as the "strong" variety. Giving way to the pure economic (supply and demand) viewpoint, the "weak" variety at this time is a real "sleeper."

One should obtain the "weak" first from the supply side theory. Very tough to get in grades above MS 64. This author's (Highfill) estimate is approximately 50,000 pieces.

There were approximately 50 reverse dies used for the 7/8 TF(the same used in both the strong and weak varieties).

Prooflikes: Very tough, with cameo scarce to rare. Recommended above MS 64 PL and MS 64 DMPL.

MINTAGE	PROOF	STRIKE	LUSTER	BAG MARKS	REDFIELD
544,000*	0	Average	Average	Moderate	No
DIES	**DIE VARIETIES**	**% OF PL**	**% OF DMPL**	**PIVOTAL GRADE**	**RARITY FACTOR**
92**	33	10.6	3.6	MS 65	R-3

*Estimate includes both weak and strong varieties ** Includes all dies used at the Philadelphia Mint - FY 1878

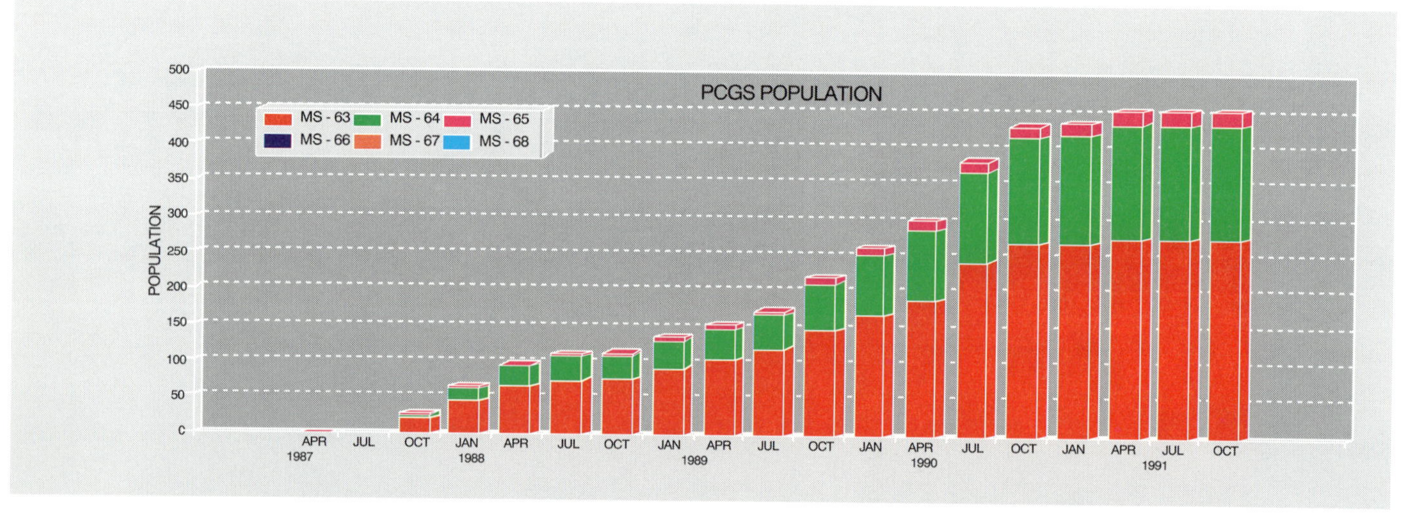

NGC does not recognize the difference between "weak" and "strong" in the 1878-P 7/8 TF series. Please refer to the NGC Population chart on page 931 for information on the 1878-P 7/8 TF series.

1878-P 7/8 TF (Weak)

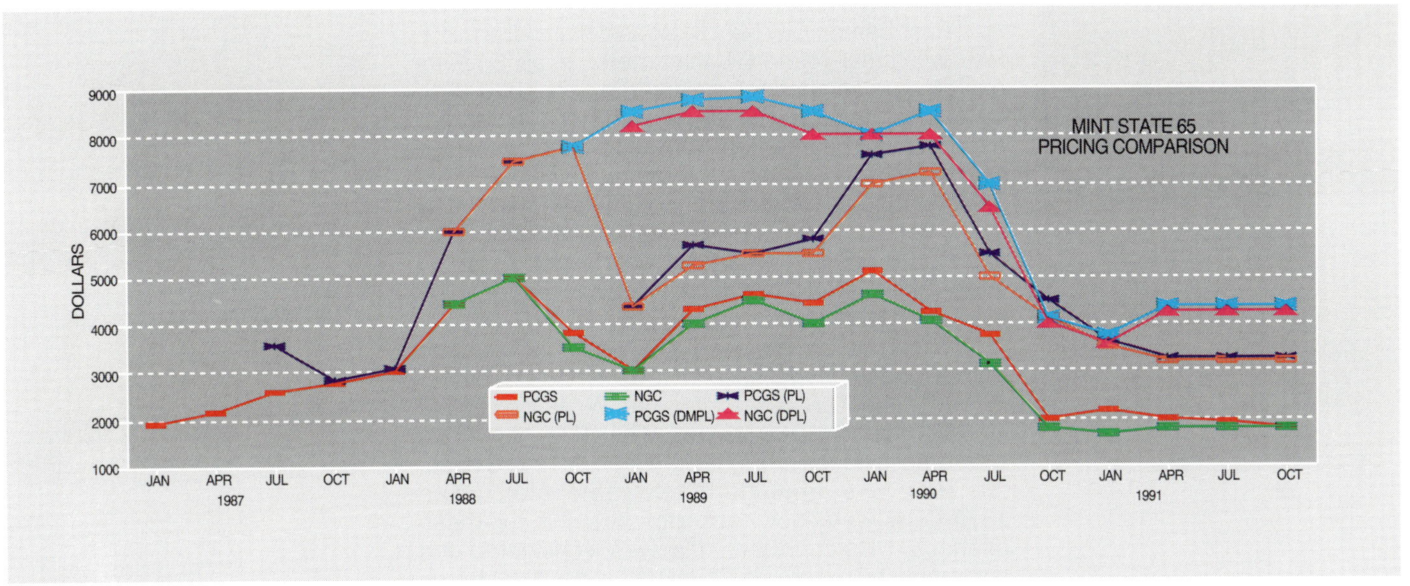

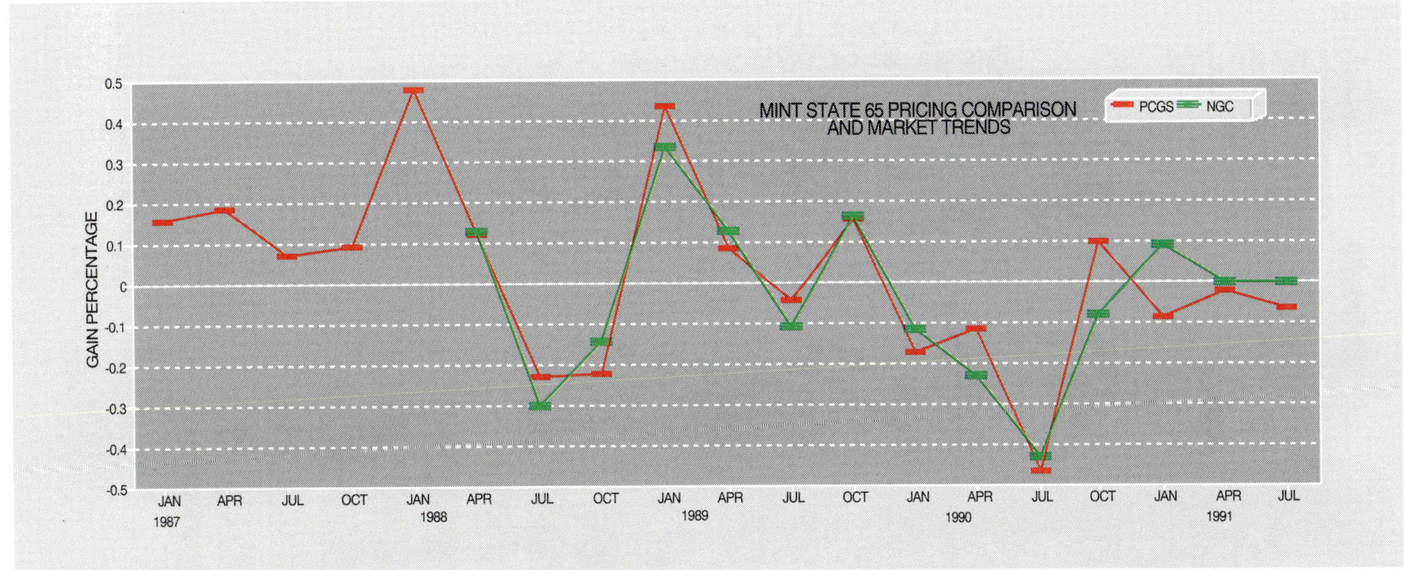

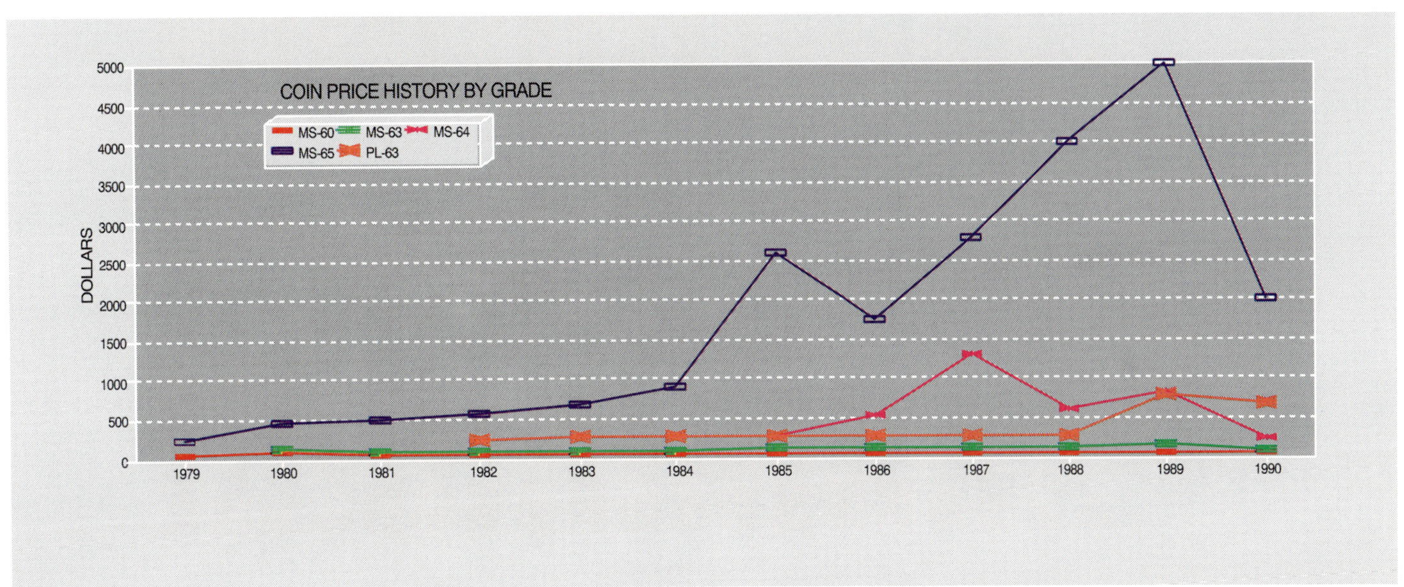

1878-CC

First Carson City Mint Morgan dollar. All are 7TF PAF, with small round CC mint mark. In all, 30 pairs of dies were shipped for making the 2,212,000.

Uncs., though well struck with good luster, are often heavily bagmarked from shipments via stage coach and railroad through the mountains, and from being carried or shoved around in the same canvas sacks from one part of a bank vault to another. Only one PCGS MS 67 has been graded in their first 2.5 million coins; as of this writing, NGC has graded none 67. Low quality Unc. rolls still survive.

The Treasury released a few bags in Montana (1958), and nearly 70 bags in 1963-4. On December 6, 1971, the U.S. Depository at West Point sold 47,566 Uncs. of the 60,993 in GSA's 1972-74 mail bid sales, most pieces brought winning bids of $16 each; the rest, $15 (minimum allowable bid). The 1878-CC's were sold out after the fifth of these offerings. Before then, this was considered the commonest CC date and the least expensive; this is no longer the case.

Recommended in MS 64 or by the roll in MS 63.

Prooflikes: Many are one-sided. Two-sided PL's are scarce, DMPL's more so. A few of these have high cameo contrast.

MINTAGE	PROOF	STRIKE	LUSTER	BAG MARKS	REDFIELD
2,212,000	0	Sharp & Bold	Good	Moderate To Heavy	No
DIES	**DIE VARIETIES**	**% OF PL**	**% OF DMPL**	**PIVOTAL GRADE**	**RARITY FACTOR**
100	26	9.7	4.4	MS 65	R-4

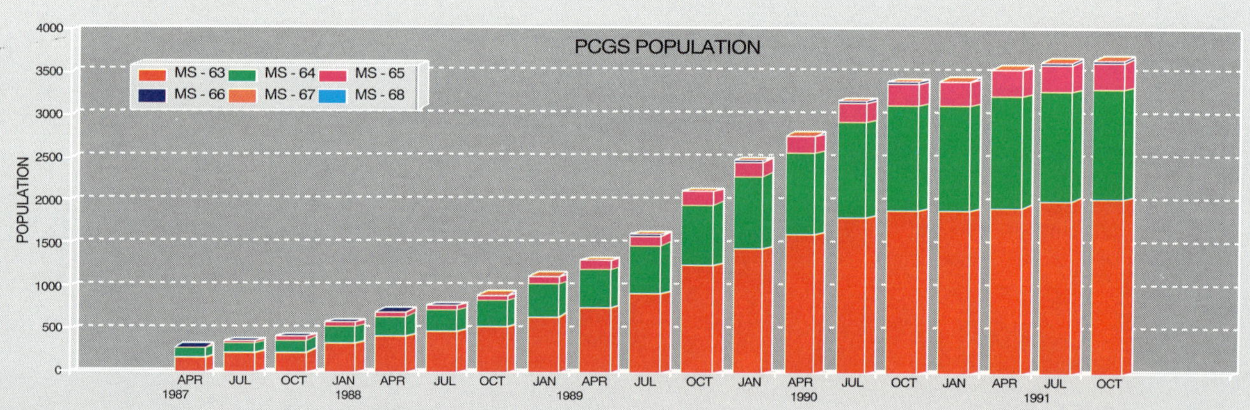

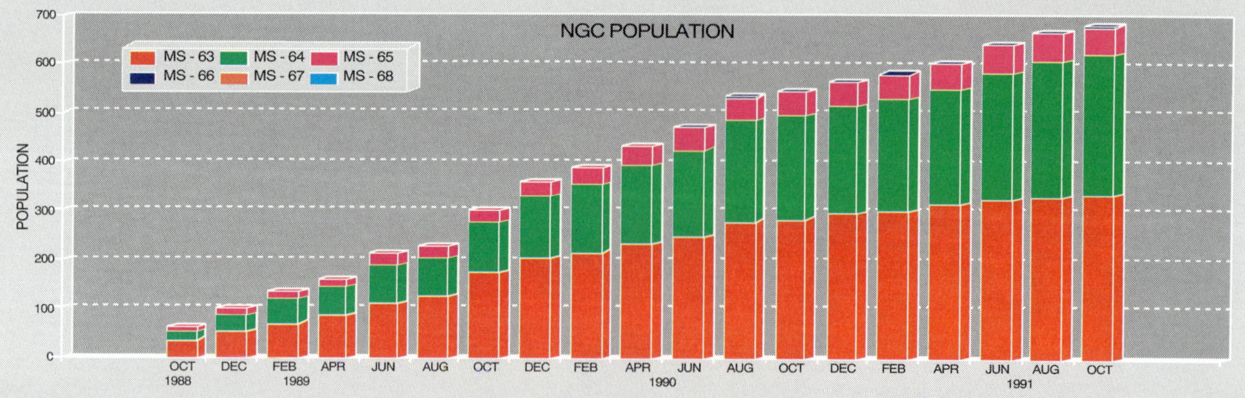

1878-CC

MINT STATE 65
PRICING COMPARISON
PCGS
NGC
PCGS (PL)
NGC (PL)
PCGS (DMPL)
NGC (DPL)
DOLLARS
7000
6000
5000
4000
3000
2000
1000
C
JAN
APR
JUL
OCT
1987
1988
1989
1990
1991

MINT STATE 65 PRICING COMPARISON
AND MARKET TRENDS
PCGS
NGC
GAIN PERCENTAGE
0.8
0.6
0.4
0.2
0
-0.2
-0.4
-0.6
JAN
APR
JUL
OCT
1987
1988
1989
1990
1991

COIN PRICE HISTORY BY GRADE
MS-60
MS-63
MS-64
MS-65
PL-63
DOLLARS
3000
2500
2000
1500
1000
500
C
1979
1980
1981
1982
1983
1984
1985
1986
1987
1988
1989
1990

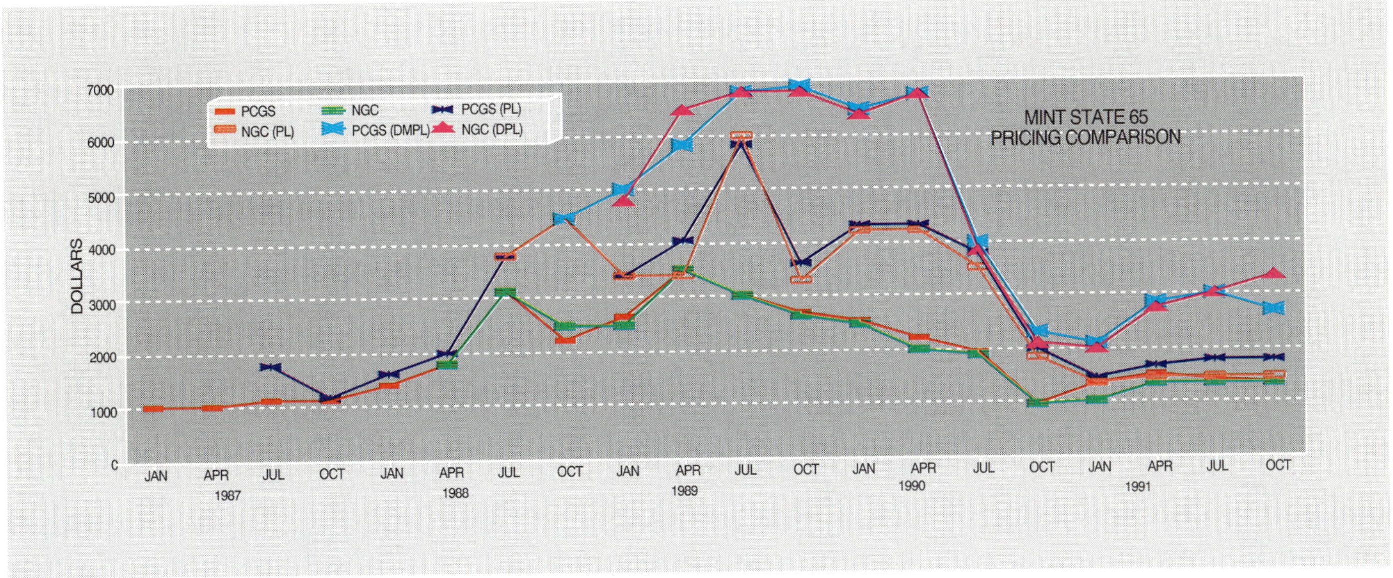

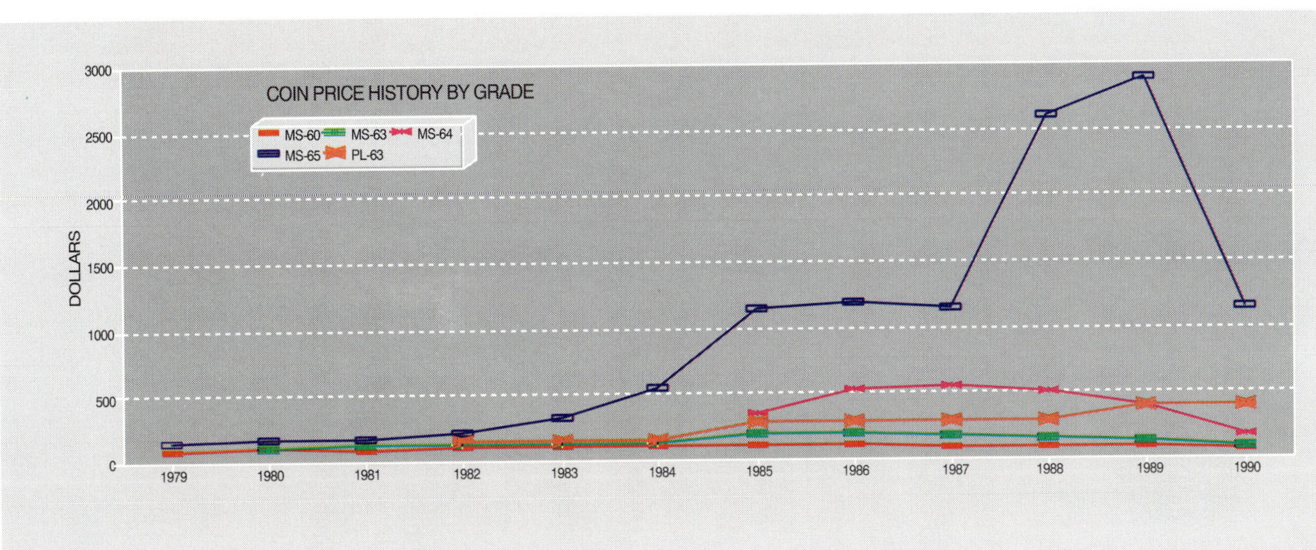

PCGS
1878-S S$1
MS68PL
7083.68/4015424

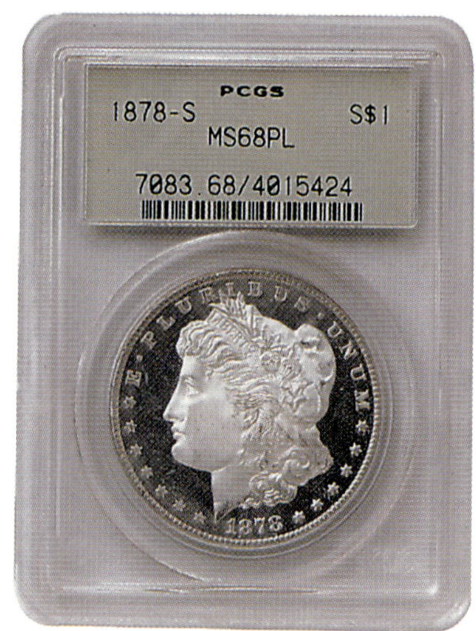

1878-S

First San Francisco Mint Morgan dollar, saved as first of its kind; fifth commonest of its mintmark. The 9,774,000 made came from 36 pairs of dies.

Always 7 TF PAF. (Parallel Arrow Feather) One of the rarest varieties has long nock or "center arrow feather" (*Encyclopedia* 5517, not in VAM, discovered December 1979); see illustration at *Ency* 5509, compare with the short nock at *Ency* 5510. Long nock coins were made beginning April 18 from only two usable reverses; survivors are all in low grades.

Uncs. are often brilliantly lustrous and well struck. Many lower quality Uncs. in Redfield hoard (possibly 5 bags).

Prooflikes: PL's are perhaps 8 to 10 times more often seen than DMPL's, but 20 times scarcer than regular Uncs. Many are one-sided.

PCGS

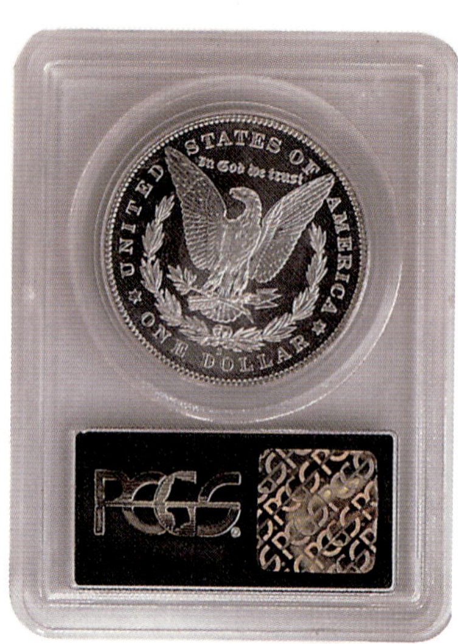

MINTAGE	PROOF	STRIKE	LUSTER	BAG MARKS	REDFIELD
9,774,000	0	Sharp & Bold	Excellent	Moderate	Yes
DIES	**DIE VARIETIES**	**% OF PL**	**% OF DMPL**	**PIVOTAL GRADE**	**RARITY FACTOR**
192	53	6.8	1.2	MS 65	R-4

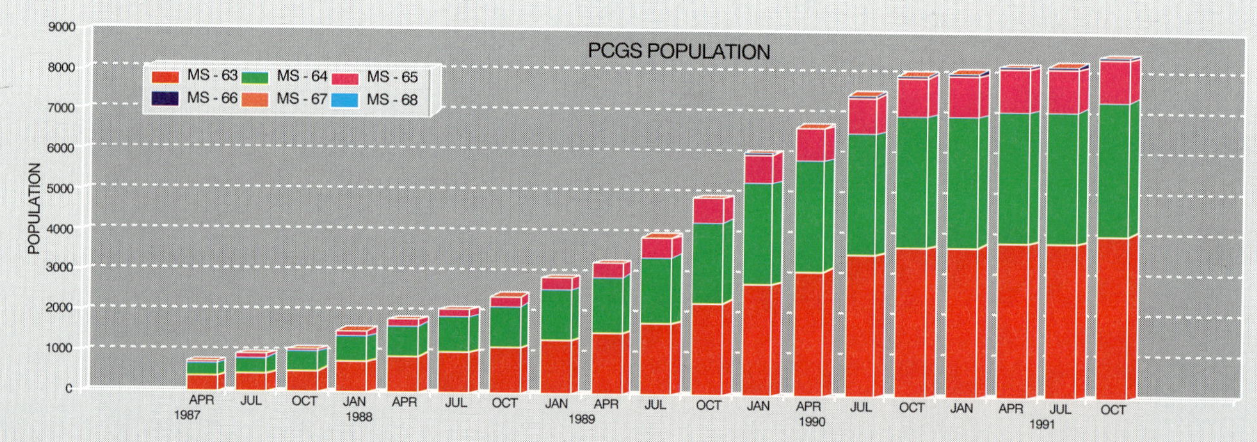
PCGS POPULATION
MS - 63 MS - 64 MS - 65
MS - 66 MS - 67 MS - 68
POPULATION
9000
8000
7000
6000
5000
4000
3000
2000
1000
0
APR 1987
JUL
OCT
JAN 1988
APR
JUL
OCT
JAN 1989
APR
JUL
OCT
JAN
APR 1990
JUL
OCT
JAN
APR
JUL 1991
OCT

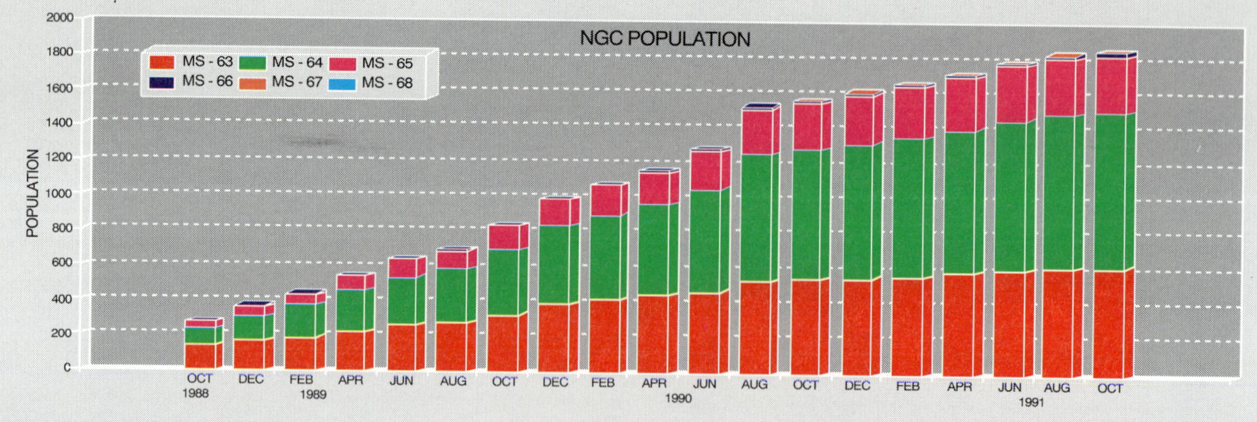
NGC POPULATION
MS - 63 MS - 64 MS - 65
MS - 66 MS - 67 MS - 68
POPULATION
2000
1800
1600
1400
1200
1000
800
600
400
200
0
OCT 1988
DEC
FEB 1989
APR
JUN
AUG
OCT
DEC
FEB
APR 1990
JUN
AUG
OCT
DEC
FEB
APR
JUN 1991
AUG
OCT

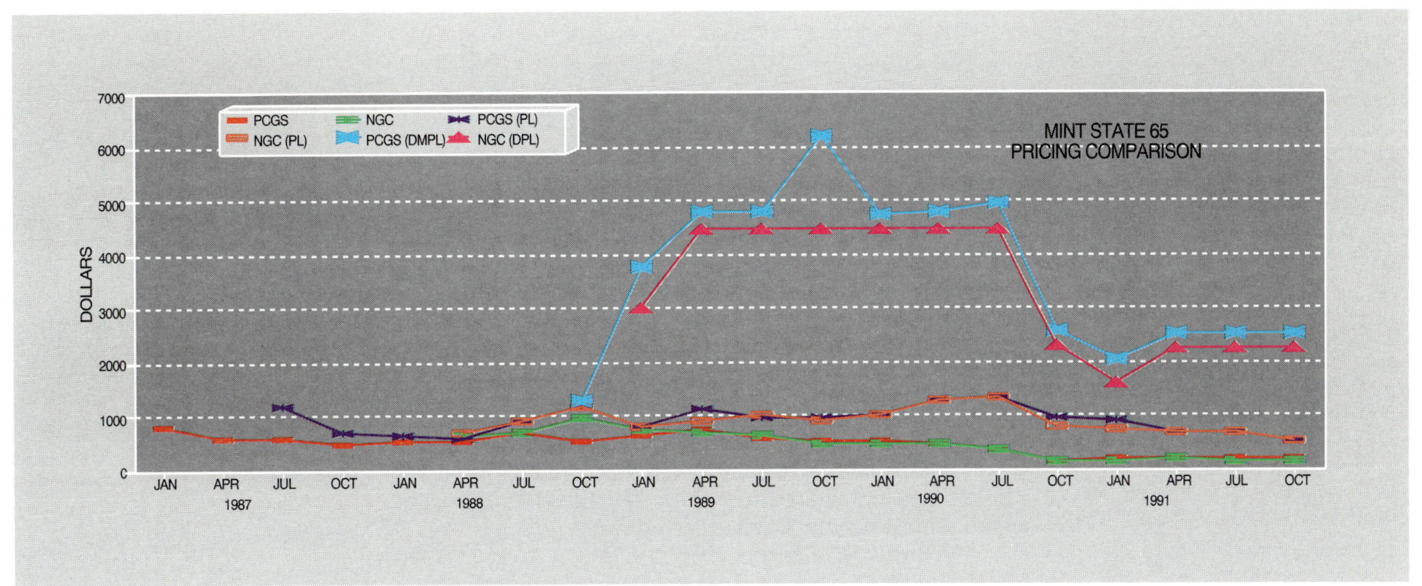
MINT STATE 65
PRICING COMPARISON
PCGS
NGC
PCGS (PL)
NGC (PL)
PCGS (DMPL)
NGC (DPL)
DOLLARS
7000
6000
5000
4000
3000
2000
1000
0
JAN APR JUL OCT JAN APR JUL OCT JAN APR JUL OCT JAN APR JUL OCT JAN APR JUL OCT
1987
1988
1989
1990
1991

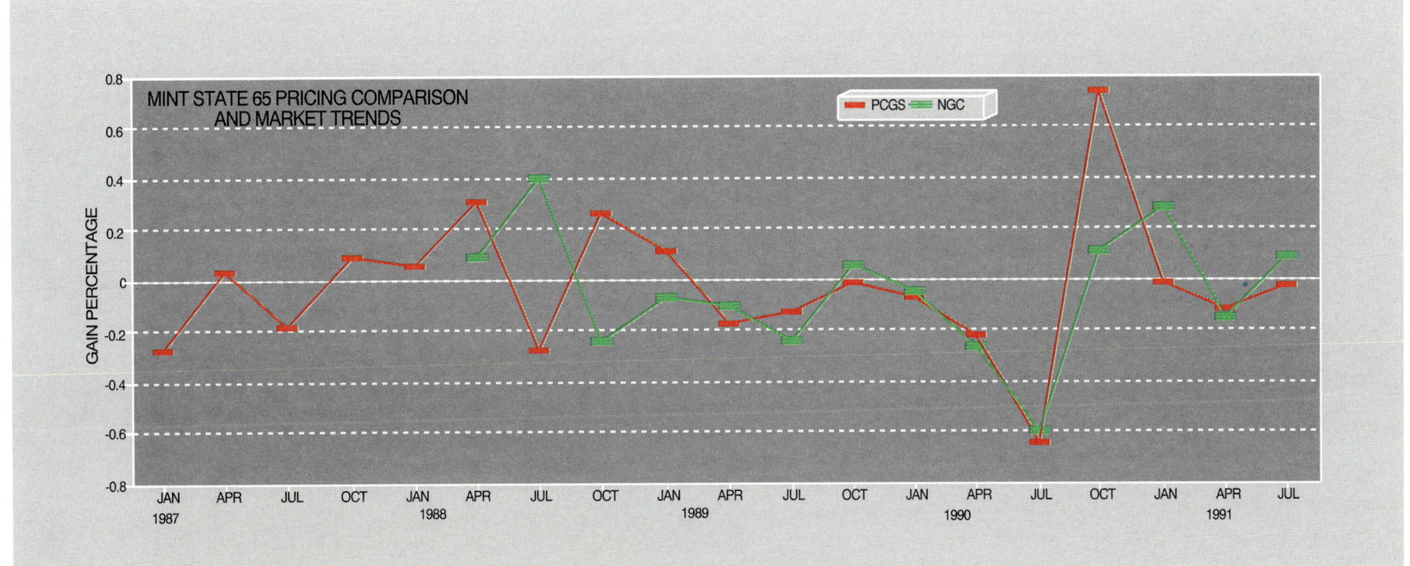
MINT STATE 65 PRICING COMPARISON
AND MARKET TRENDS
PCGS
NGC
GAIN PERCENTAGE
0.8
0.6
0.4
0.2
0
-0.2
-0.4
-0.6
-0.8
JAN APR JUL OCT JAN APR JUL OCT JAN APR JUL OCT JAN APR JUL OCT JAN APR JUL
1987
1988
1989
1990
1991

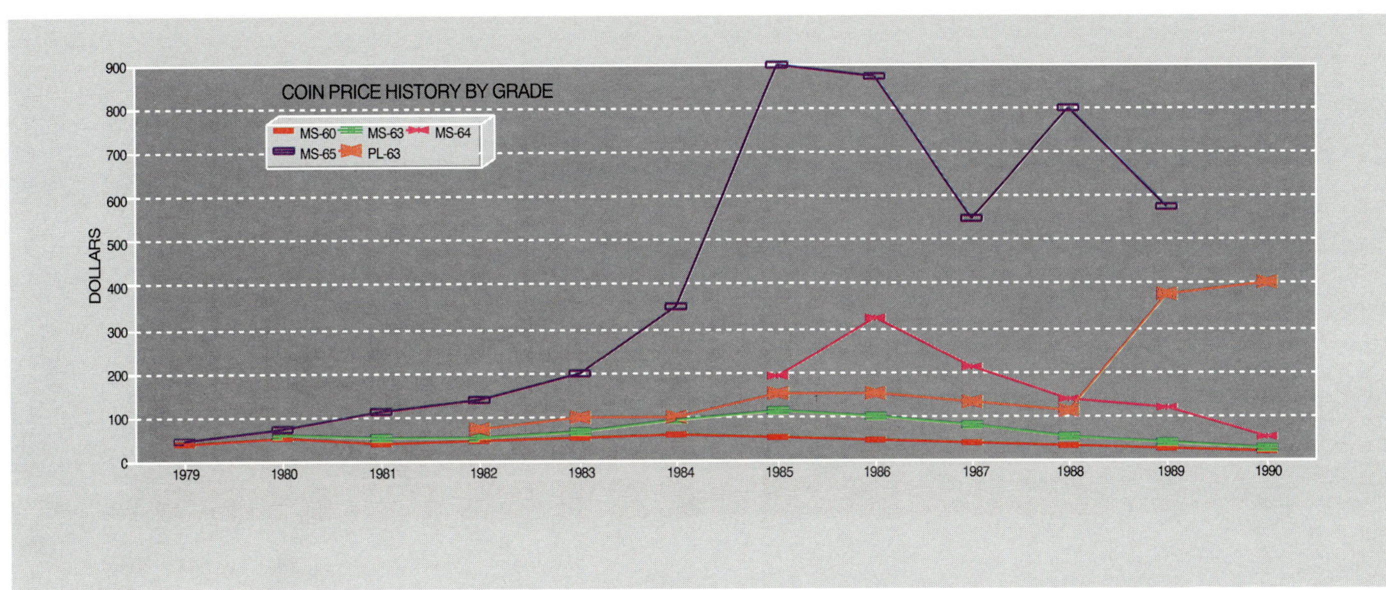
COIN PRICE HISTORY BY GRADE
MS-60
MS-63
MS-64
MS-65
PL-63
DOLLARS
900
800
700
600
500
400
300
200
100
0
1979 1980 1981 1982 1983 1984 1985 1986 1987 1988 1989 1990

1879-P

The 7 TF SAF (Slanted Arrow Feather) reverse continues without noticeable change until 1899. The 129 obvs., 86 revs. were probably all used along with leftover 1878 reverses, for making the 14,806,000.

Many working dies were used past the point of no return — the same way some people use their cars today.

Despite enormous mintage and large quantities of survivors, this date is hard to locate in MS 65; by PCGS or NGC, fewer that 1 per 100,000 qualify at that level. Most survivors are low grade Uncs. or sliders, often struck with flat breast feathers.

Proofs: Controversy over the number minted (650 or 1100?) has resulted in the 1879 carrying a premium over some later proofs. They answer the description of VAM 1, but with die polish leaving a small blank area in hair around Morgan's initial M, and die file marks between back of neck and wing.

Prooflikes: Very scarce above MS 64 in PL OR DMPL, despite a hoard of several hundred found in San Francisco in 1977. Few are cameos; many are one-sided.

MINTAGE	PROOF	STRIKE	LUSTER	BAG MARKS	REDFIELD
14,806,000	1,100	Average To Bold	Average	Moderate	No
DIES	**DIE VARIETIES**	**% OF PL**	**% OF DMPL**	**PIVOTAL GRADE**	**RARITY FACTOR**
157	36	3.9	3.2	MS 65	R-4

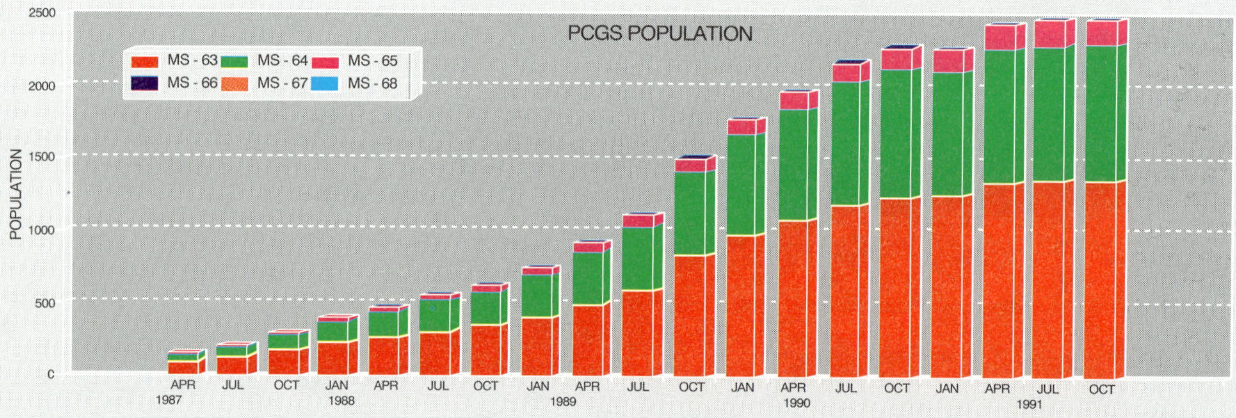

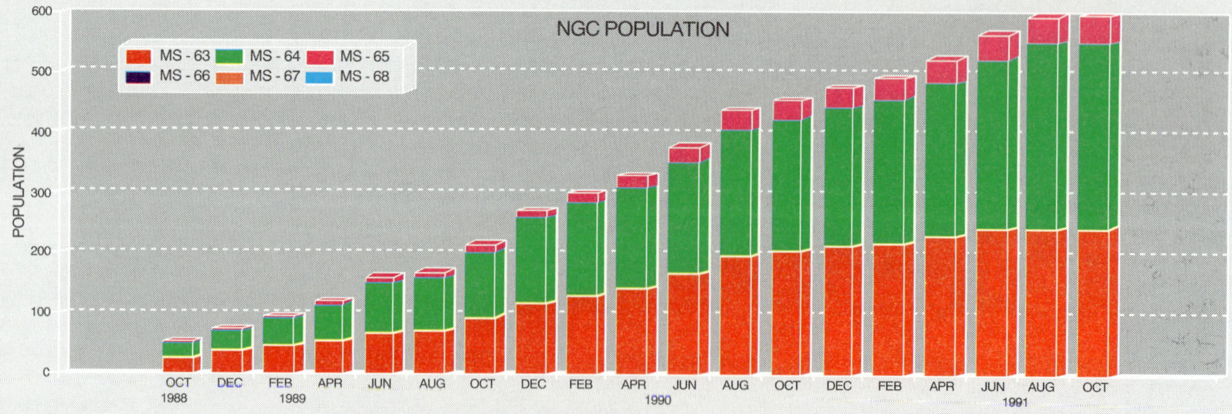

PCGS POPULATION

MS - 63 MS - 64 MS - 65 MS - 66 MS - 67 MS - 68

POPULATION

2500 2000 1500 1000 500 0

APR 1987 JUL OCT JAN 1988 APR JUL OCT JAN 1989 APR JUL OCT JAN APR 1990 JUL OCT JAN APR 1991 JUL OCT

NGC POPULATION

MS - 63 MS - 64 MS - 65 MS - 66 MS - 67 MS - 68

POPULATION

600 500 400 300 200 100 0

OCT 1988 DEC FEB 1989 APR JUN AUG OCT DEC FEB APR 1990 JUN AUG OCT DEC FEB APR JUN 1991 AUG OCT

1879-P

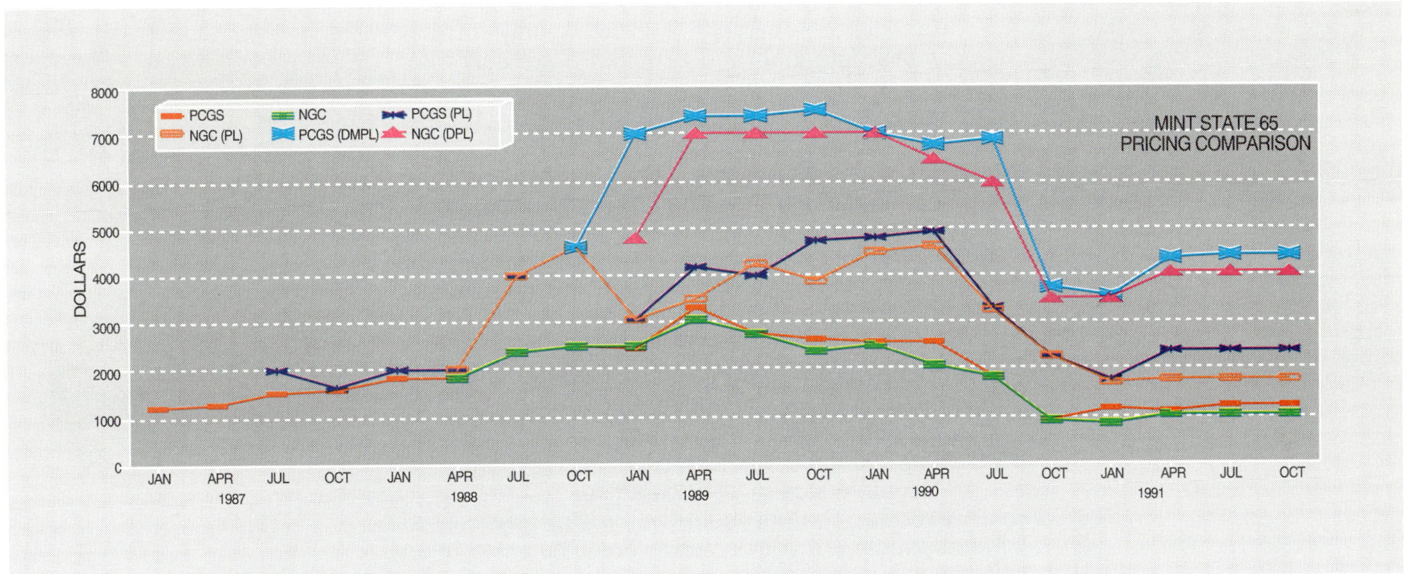

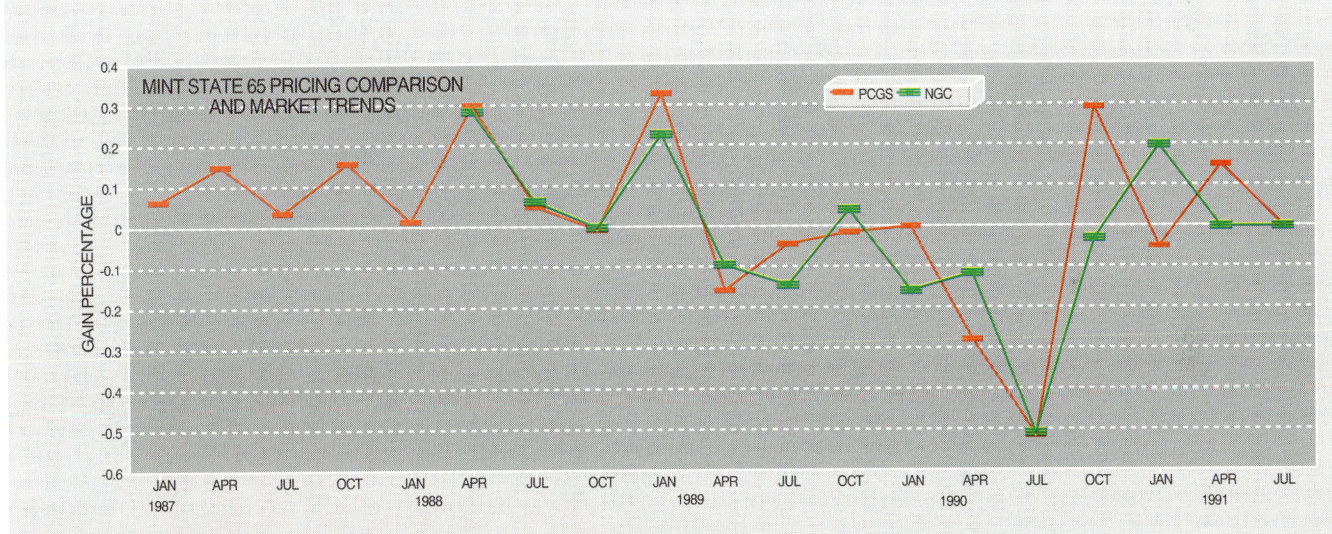

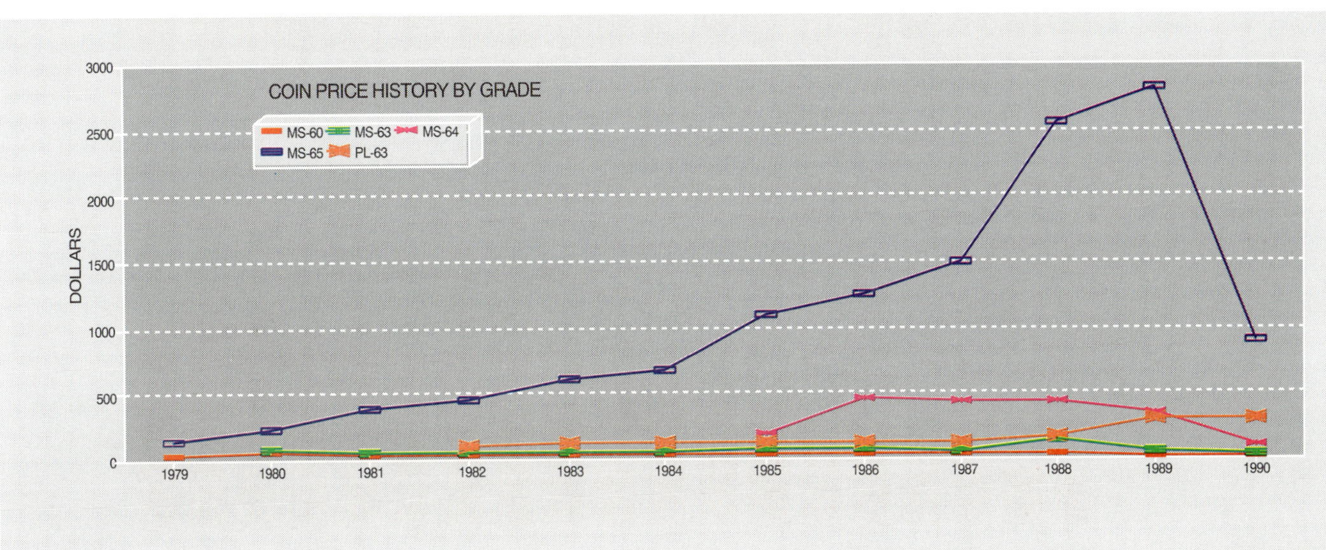

PCGS
1879-CC
S$1
MS65
7086.65/6271755

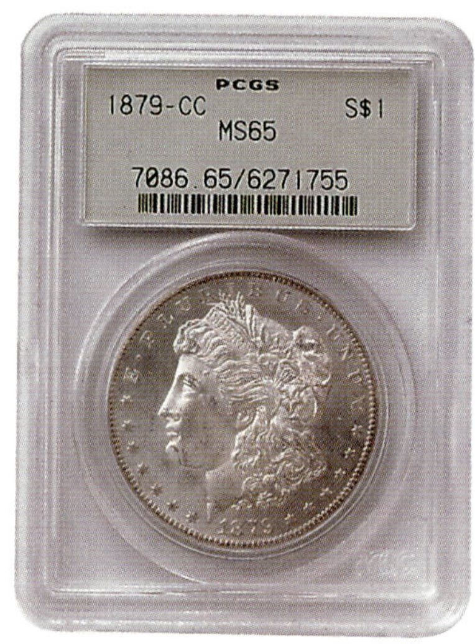

1879-CC

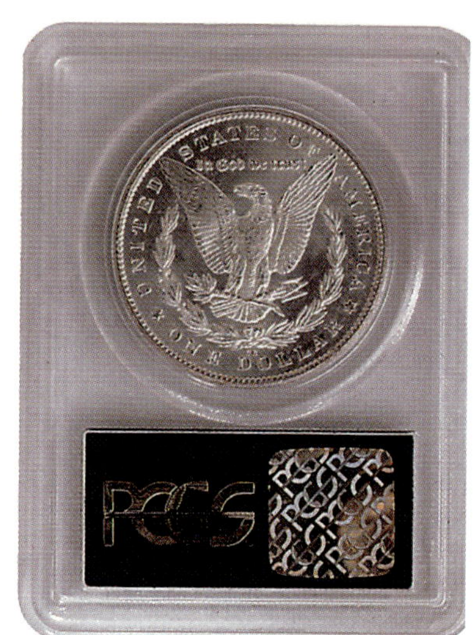

Partly from low mintage (756,000), partly from low supply, this date long ago acquired a reputation for rarity. (It is very scarce even in circulated condition.) It retained most of its reputation even after 4,123 BU examples were auctioned by GSA (1972-74). The winning bid was $300 each. About 600 of these were the "capped die" variety. The LaVere Redfield hoard was alleged to have 400 to 500 pieces. As in all Redfield issues, the exact quantities are unknown. As in 1878-CC and for similar reasons, this date comes very "baggy".

The "capped die" (VAM 3) shows tall CC over small round CC and extreme die rust around mintmark. Tops of small CC show above tops of large CC. To date, only one coin of this variety has been certified MS 65 by both PCGS AND NGC.

Recommended in all BU grades.

Proofs: The one from the Brock, University of Pennsylvania, Rovensky collections has not been verified.

Prooflikes: Often one-sided. Very scarce to rare MS 64 up PL, rarer in DMPL.

PCGS

MINTAGE	PROOF	STRIKE	LUSTER	BAG MARKS	REDFIELD
756,000*	0	Average	Poor To Average	Moderate	Yes
DIES	**DIE VARIETIES**	**% OF PL**	**% OF DMPL**	**PIVOTAL GRADE**	**RARITY FACTOR**
30**	3	12.5	4.1	MS 65	R-1

* Includes estimated 500,000 1879-CC and estimated 250,000 1879-CC/CD **Includes capped die varieties

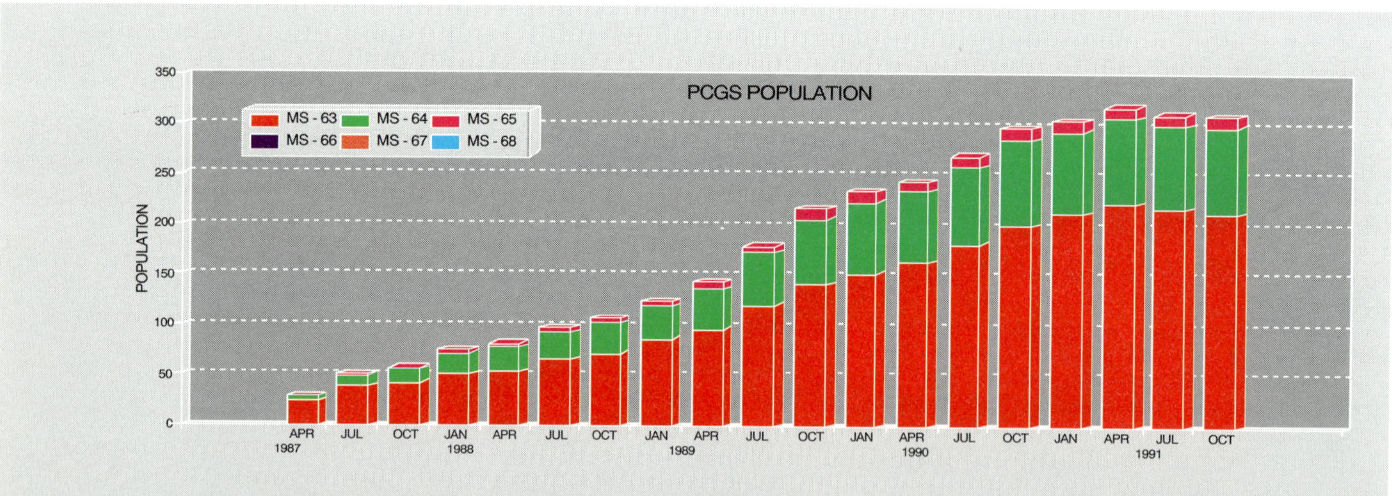
PCGS POPULATION
MS - 63
MS - 64
MS - 65
MS - 66
MS - 67
MS - 68
POPULATION
350
300
250
200
150
100
50
0
APR 1987
JUL
OCT
JAN 1988
APR
JUL
OCT
JAN 1989
APR
JUL
OCT
JAN
APR 1990
JUL
OCT
JAN
APR
JUL 1991
OCT

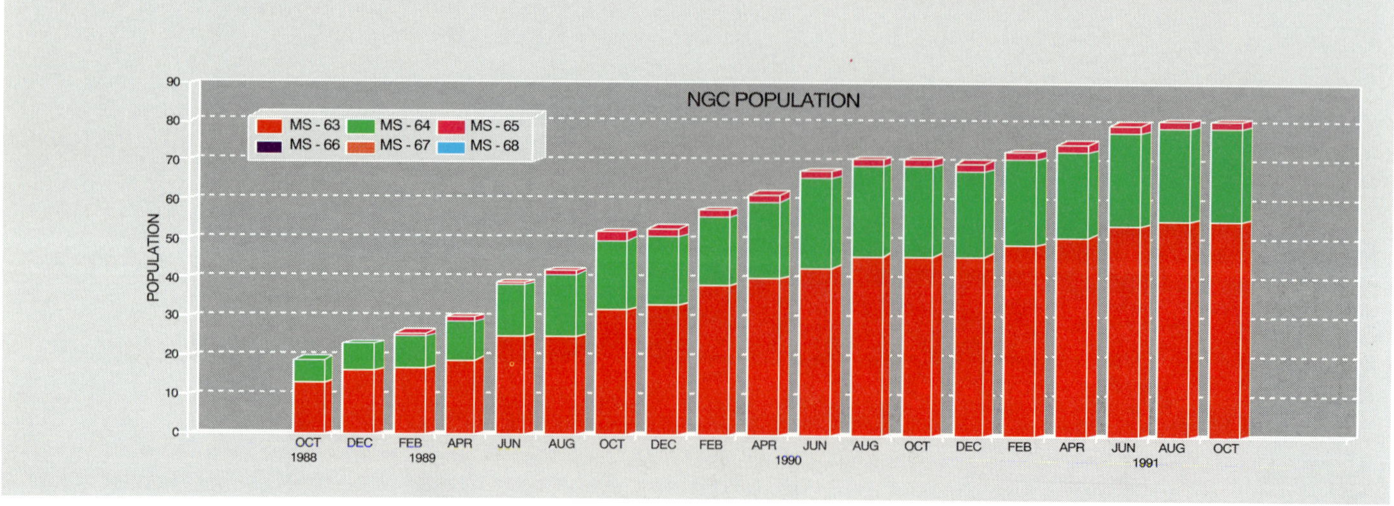
NGC POPULATION
MS - 63
MS - 64
MS - 65
MS - 66
MS - 67
MS - 68
POPULATION
90
80
70
60
50
40
30
20
10
0
OCT 1988
DEC
FEB 1989
APR
JUN
AUG
OCT
DEC
FEB
APR 1990
JUN
AUG
OCT
DEC
FEB
APR
JUN 1991
AUG
OCT

1879-CC

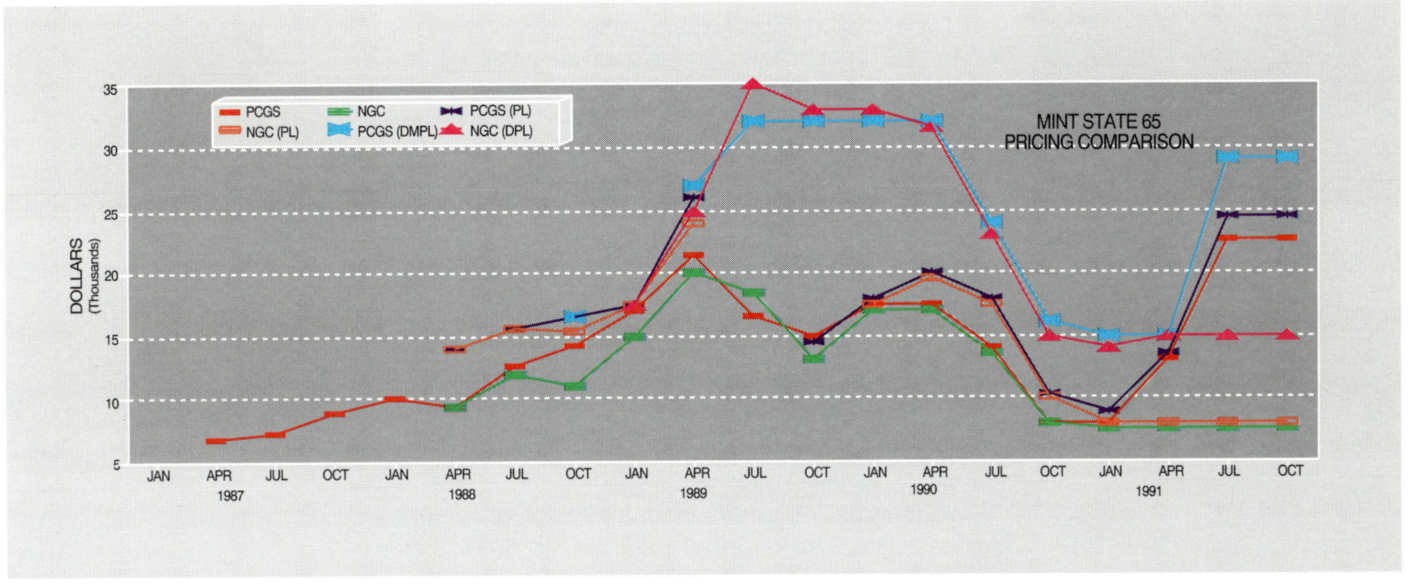

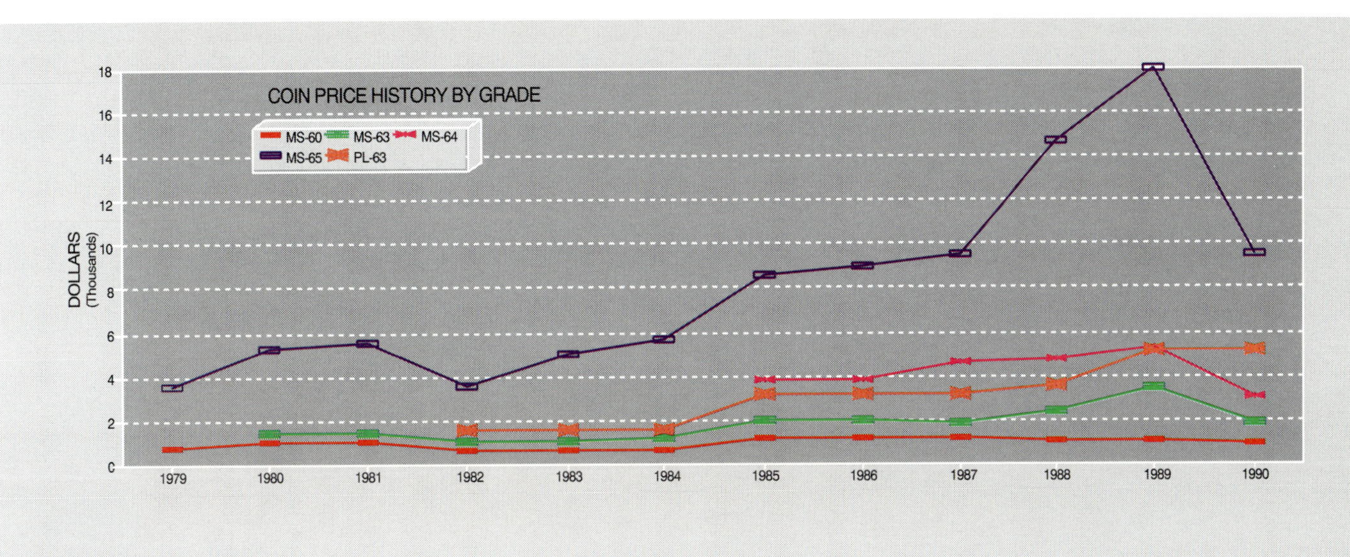

1879-CC (Capped Die)

The 1879-CC comes in two varieties - the "perfect die" and the "capped die." The capped die (VAM 3) had a small CC mint mark on the Morgan dollar. The original die was repunched with a larger CC directly on top of the smaller CC. The punch was applied too low and the tops of the small CC were visible above the larger CC. A larger CC of the capped die variety looks much like an altered mint mark!

This coin comes "baggy". It is estimated that approximately 600 pieces were sold in the 1972/74 GSA Auction.

The capped die is twice as scarce in all BU grades and is currently ten times as rare in MS 65. Only one capped die has been graded MS 65 by both PCGS and NGC as of this writing. This coin is also very scarce in circulated condition.

Recommended in all BU grades.

Prooflikes: Prooflikes are often only one-sided. This issue is scarce to rare all grades in MS-64 PL and DMPL categories. This coin when encountered comes "cameo".

MINTAGE	PROOF	STRIKE	LUSTER	BAG MARKS	REDFIELD
250,000	0	Weak	Good	Moderate To Heavy	Yes
DIES	**DIE VARIETIES**	**% OF PL**	**% OF DMPL**	**PIVOTAL GRADE**	**RARITY FACTOR**
30**	1	7.6	2.5	MS 64	R-1

*Includes estimated 500,000 1879-CC and estimated 250,000 1879-CC/CD **Includes regular die varities

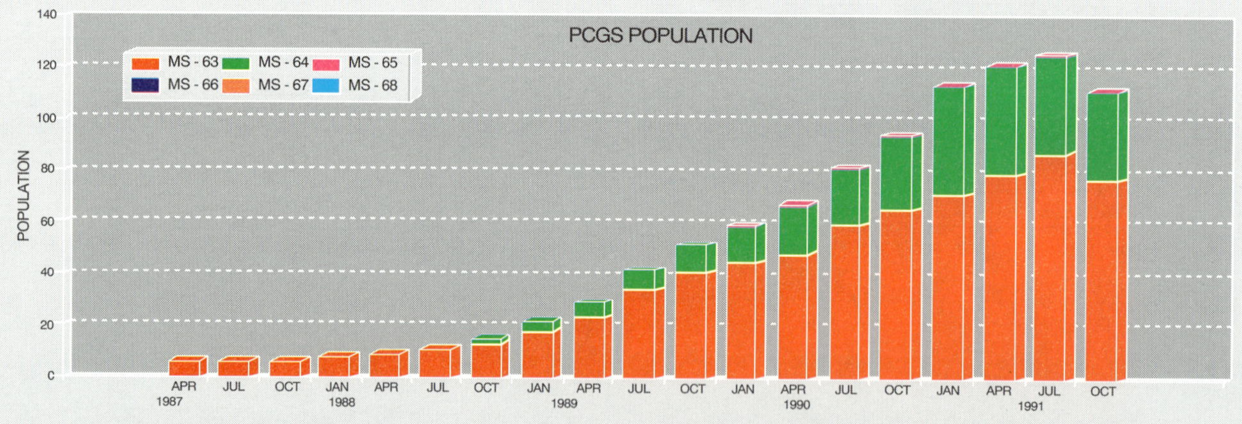

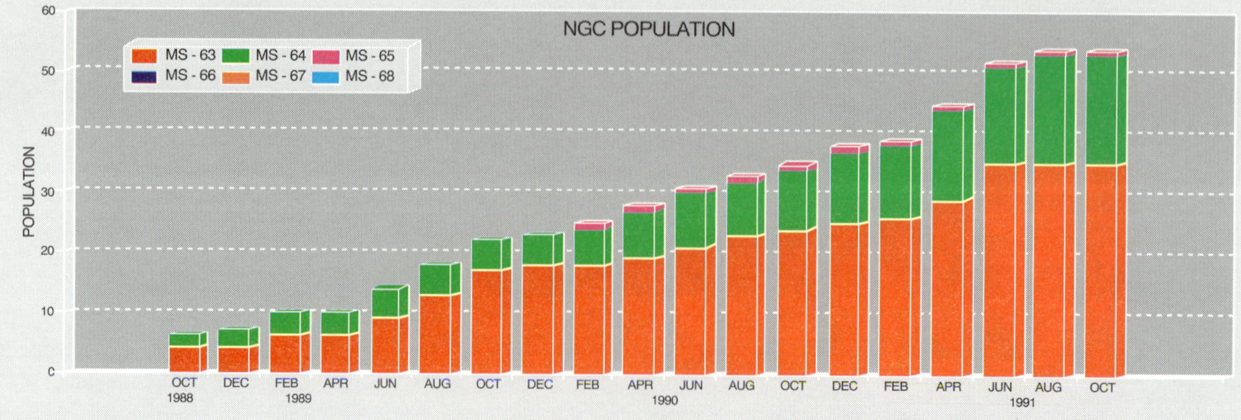

PCGS POPULATION

NGC POPULATION

1879-CC (Capped Die)

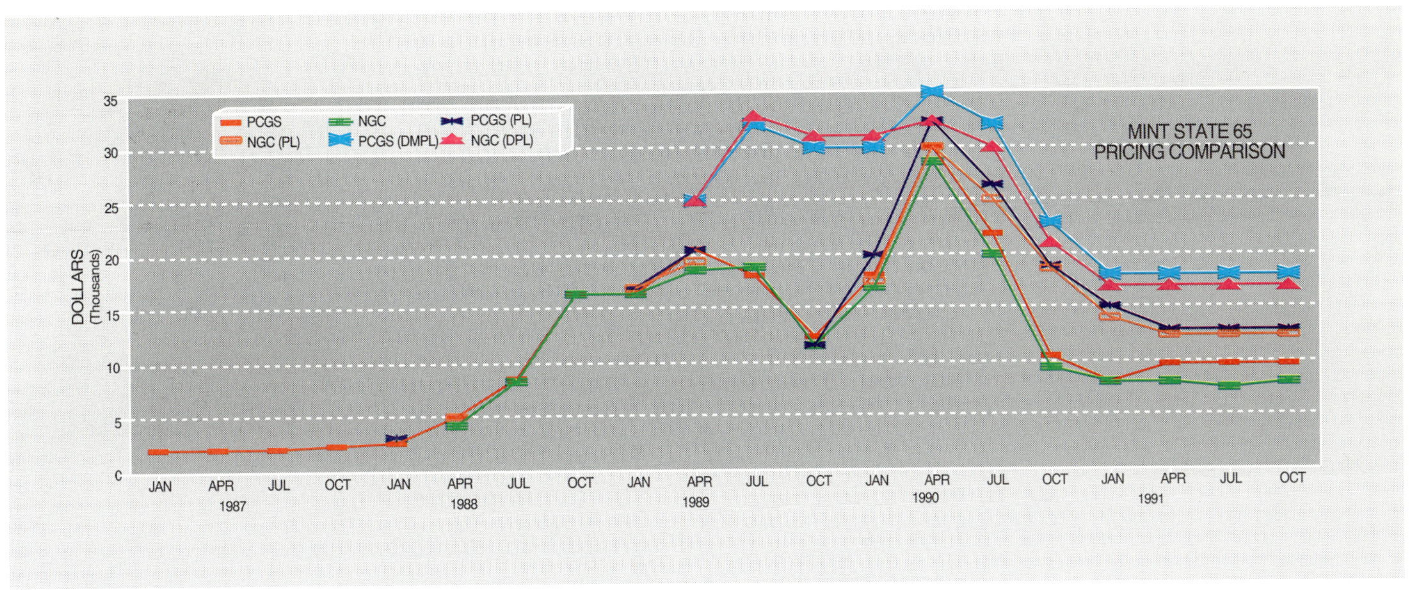

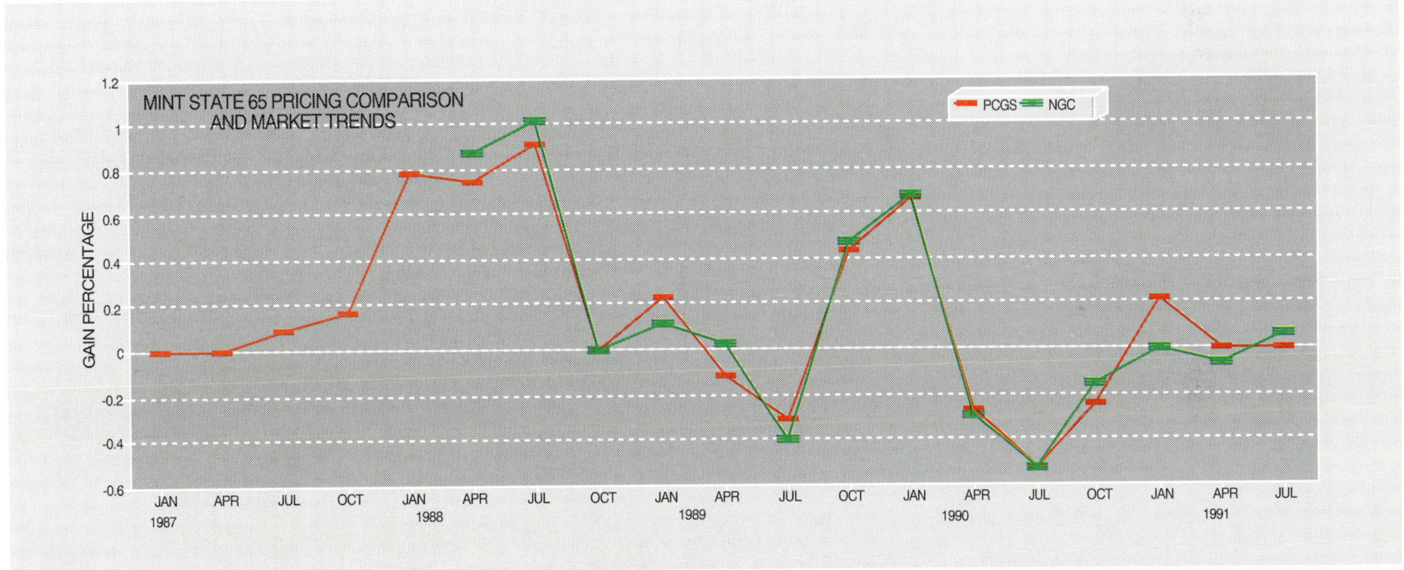

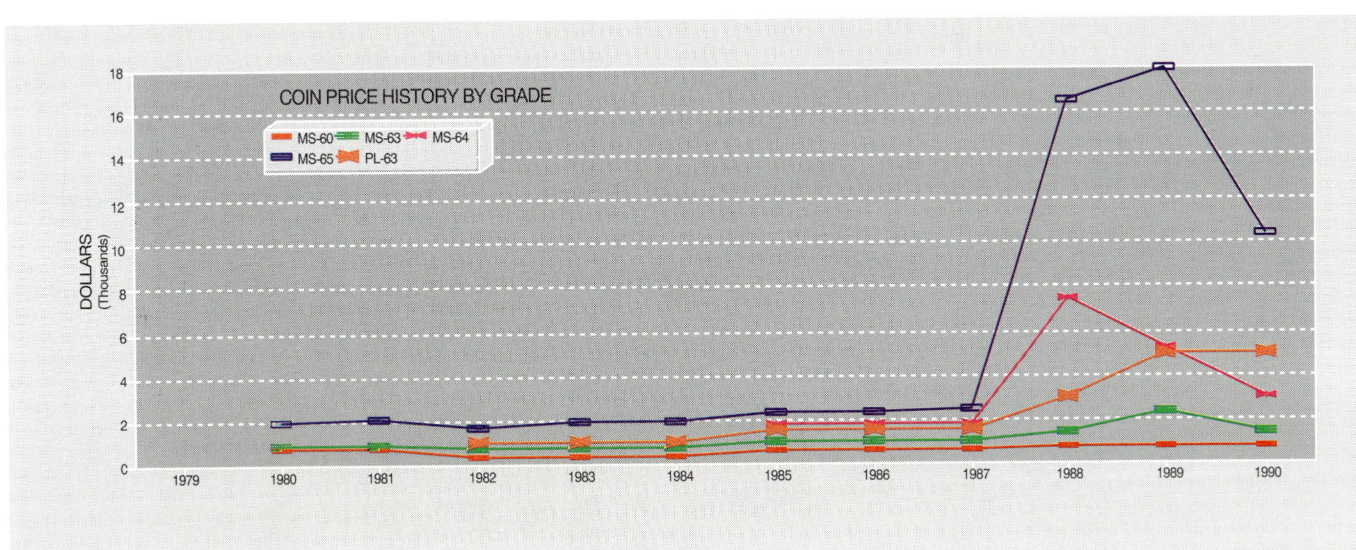

1879-O

PCGS
1879-O S$1
MS65DMPL
97091.65/8145801

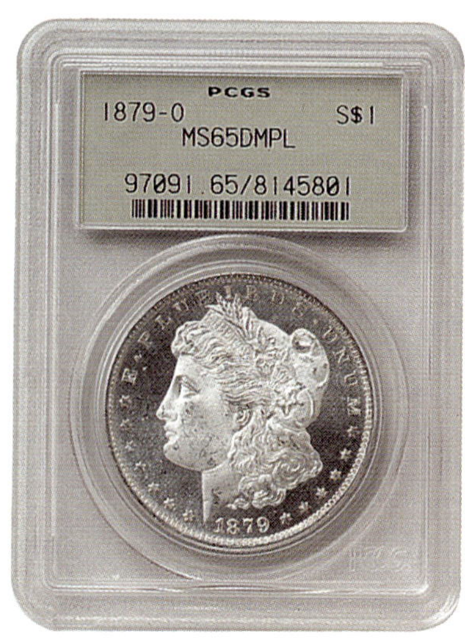

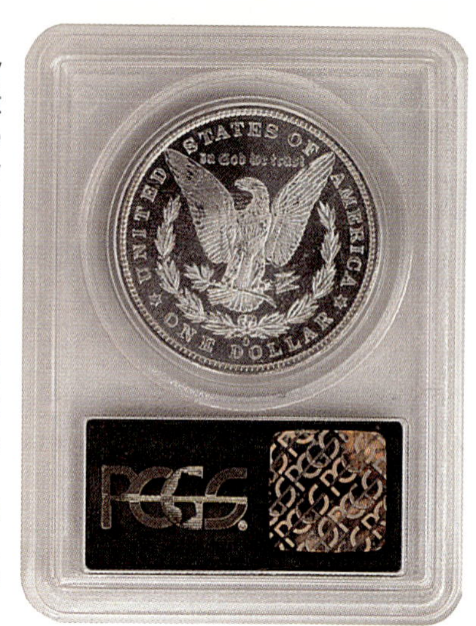

First New Orleans Morgan dollar. Reasonably well struck, which is more than can be said for most later O Mints. Many of the 2,887,000 made were released briefly into circulation, then found their way back to banks where they were resewn into mint sacks (about 1882); Dean Tavenner calls these "two-beer" dollars (see his article, Chapter 6). Many of these turned up in and after the 1960's, others in the Continental Bank hoard (see under 1879-S), proving to contain 80-90% sliders with small numbers of P, S and CC coins. Typically, the 1879-80 O's were VF to AU, the 1881-O's AU and sliders, the 1882-O's sliders with a few BU's.

Not much difference in rarity between the round O and tall O mintmarks. VAM 4, *Encyclopedia* 5528, the triple O, sometimes called O over horizontal O, is very scarce and usually found in EF - AU.

Proofs: On February 20, 1879, 12 were made to celebrate the reopening of the Mint (closed since 1861). Of these at least four are traced, one in the Smithsonian Institution. They are among the most carefully made New Orleans proofs.

Prooflikes: Rare above MS 64, especially DMPL's. Cameos are few.

MINTAGE	PROOF	STRIKE	LUSTER	BAG MARKS	REDFIELD
2,886,988	12	Average	Good	Moderate	No
DIES	**DIE VARIETIES**	**% OF PL**	**% OF DMPL**	**PIVOTAL GRADE**	**RARITY FACTOR**
40	28	5.4	2.4	MS 64	R-3

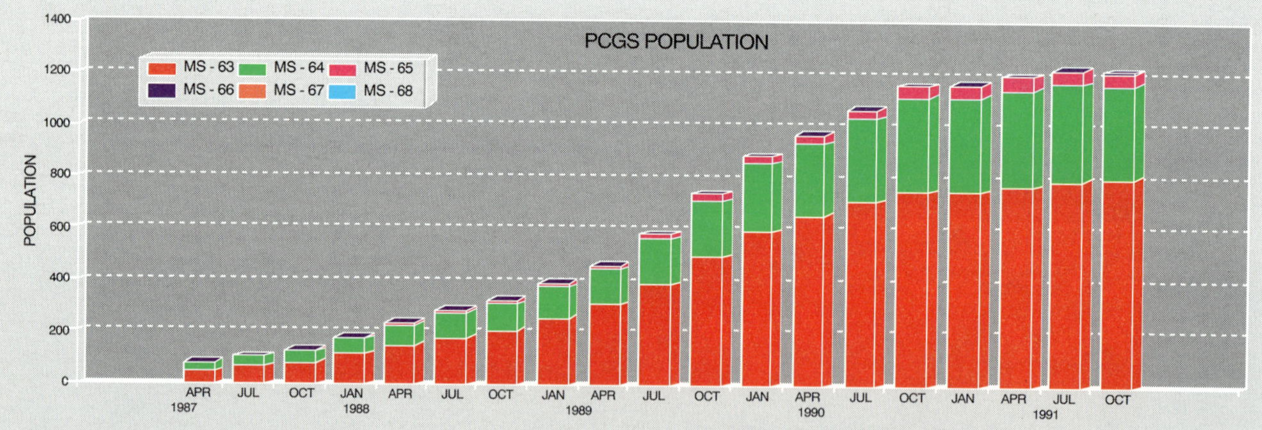
PCGS POPULATION
MS - 63
MS - 64
MS - 65
MS - 66
MS - 67
MS - 68
POPULATION
1400
1200
1000
800
600
400
200
0
APR 1987
JUL
OCT
JAN 1988
APR
JUL
OCT
JAN 1989
APR
JUL
OCT
JAN
APR 1990
JUL
OCT
JAN
APR
JUL 1991
OCT

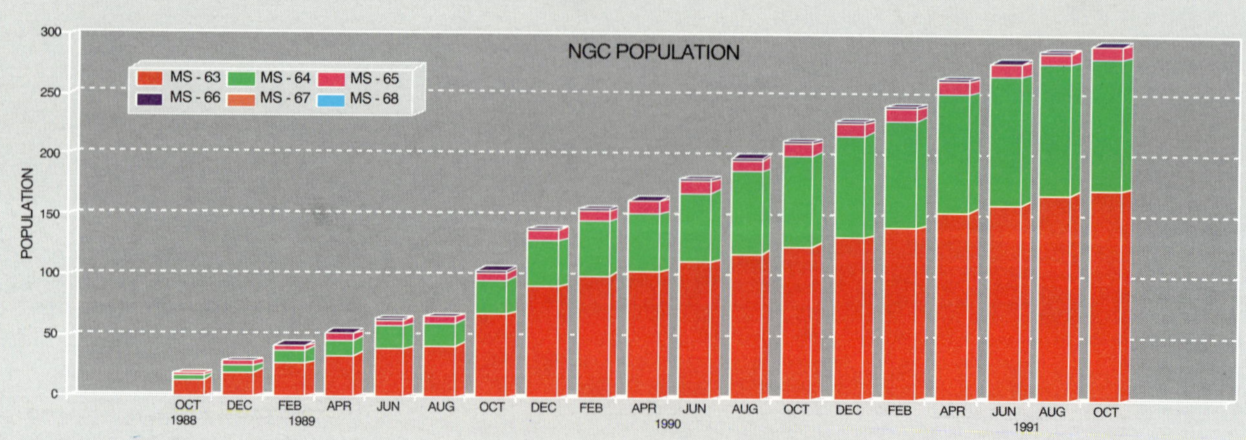
NGC POPULATION
MS - 63
MS - 64
MS - 65
MS - 66
MS - 67
MS - 68
POPULATION
300
250
200
150
100
50
0
OCT 1988
DEC
FEB 1989
APR
JUN
AUG
OCT
DEC
FEB
APR 1990
JUN
AUG
OCT
DEC
FEB
APR
JUN 1991
AUG
OCT

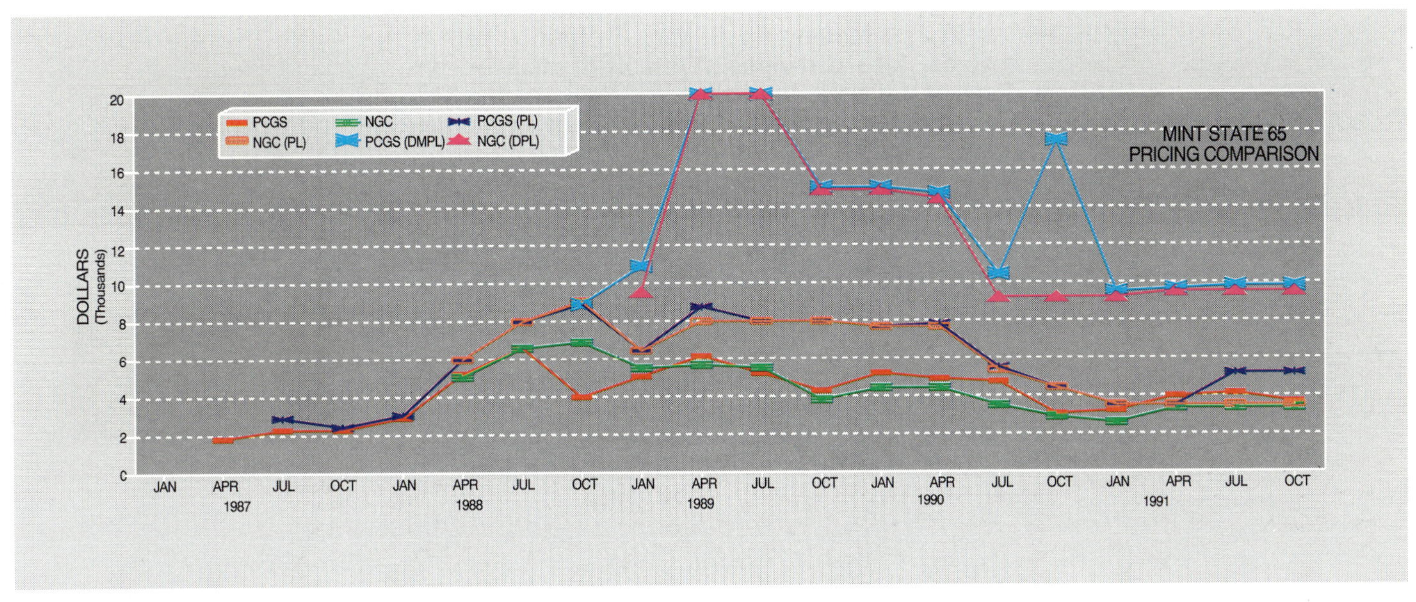
PCGS
NGC
PCGS (PL)
NGC (PL)
PCGS (DMPL)
NGC (DPL)
MINT STATE 65
PRICING COMPARISON
DOLLARS
(Thousands)
20
18
16
14
12
10
8
6
4
2
0
JAN
APR
JUL
OCT
JAN
APR
JUL
OCT
JAN
APR
JUL
OCT
JAN
APR
JUL
OCT
JAN
APR
JUL
OCT
1987
1988
1989
1990
1991

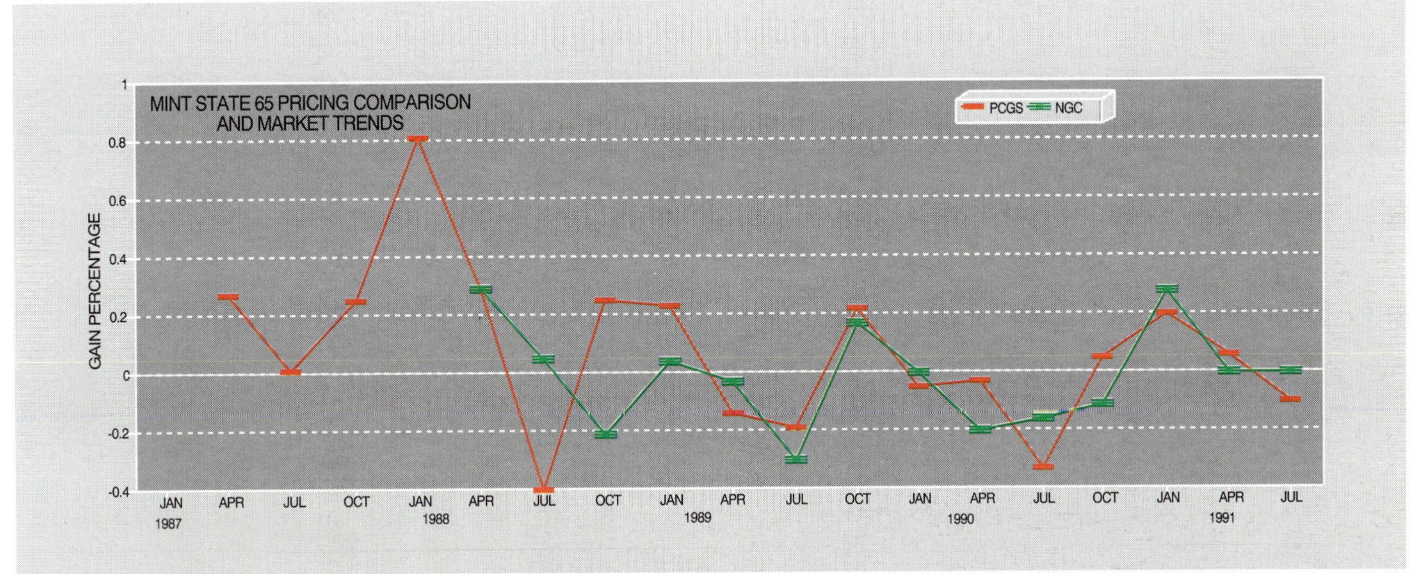
MINT STATE 65 PRICING COMPARISON
AND MARKET TRENDS
PCGS
NGC
GAIN PERCENTAGE
1
0.8
0.6
0.4
0.2
0
-0.2
-0.4
JAN
APR
JUL
OCT
JAN
APR
JUL
OCT
JAN
APR
JUL
OCT
JAN
APR
JUL
OCT
JAN
APR
JUL
1987
1988
1989
1990
1991

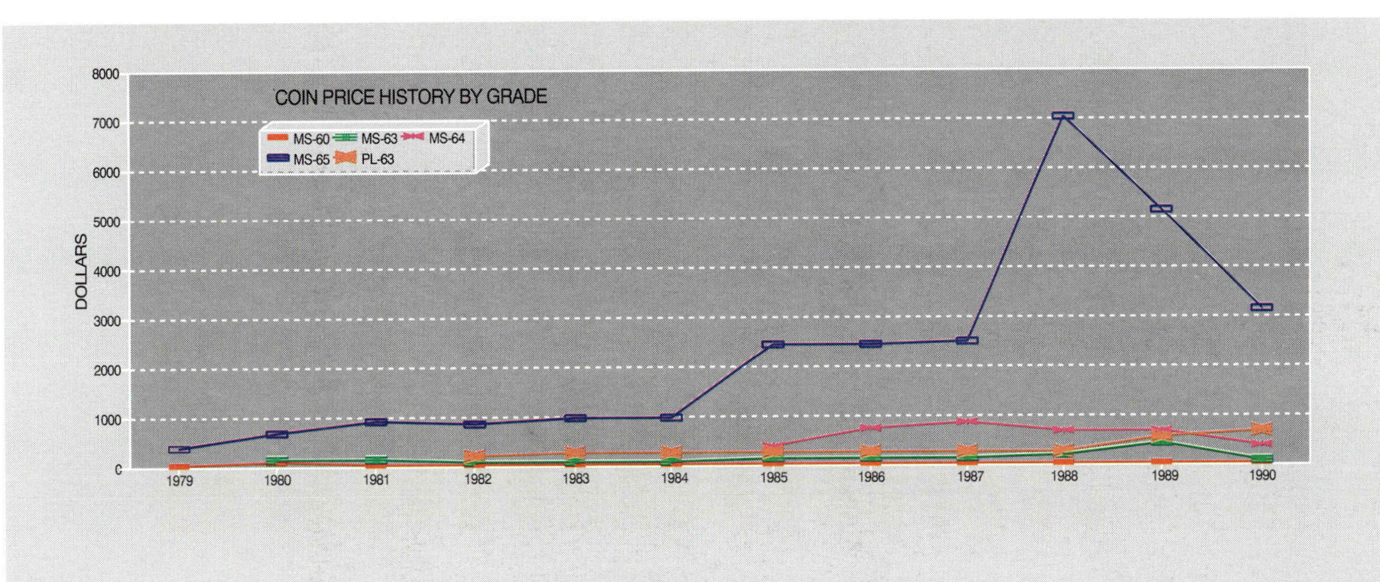
COIN PRICE HISTORY BY GRADE
MS-60
MS-63
MS-64
MS-65
PL-63
DOLLARS
8000
7000
6000
5000
4000
3000
2000
1000
0
1979
1980
1981
1982
1983
1984
1985
1986
1987
1988
1989
1990

1879-S

Third commonest S Mint Morgan. Type III obverse, Type C reverse. Available in quantity from Treasury, Redfield, and Continental Bank hoards. This list comprised approximately 1,500 bags of Morgan dollars in the vaults of the troubled Continental Illinois National Bank of Chicago (1983-4). These included about 850 Unc. bags of common dates and approximately 750 bags in lower grades to sliders. According to Leon Hendrickson, about 500 bags each of 1879-82-O were EF and AU. So far no accurate figures are available for each date. The 1879-S had the third highest numbers in the Redfield hoard.

Proofs: The one reportedly in the Jerome Kern sale has not been available for checking.

Prooflikes: Many brilliant PL's; about 1/10 as many DMPL's. Scarce in DMPL MS 66 or higher.

MINTAGE	PROOF	STRIKE	LUSTER	BAG MARKS	REDFIELD
9,110,000*	0	Sharp & Bold	Excellent	Light	Yes
DIES	**DIE VARIETIES**	**% OF PL**	**% OF DMPL**	**PIVOTAL GRADE**	**RARITY FACTOR**
192**	32	8.7	1.2	MS 66	R-5

*Includes estimated 9,106,000 1879-S and estimated 4000 1879-S Rev 78 **Includes all dies used at the San Francisco Mint - FY 1879

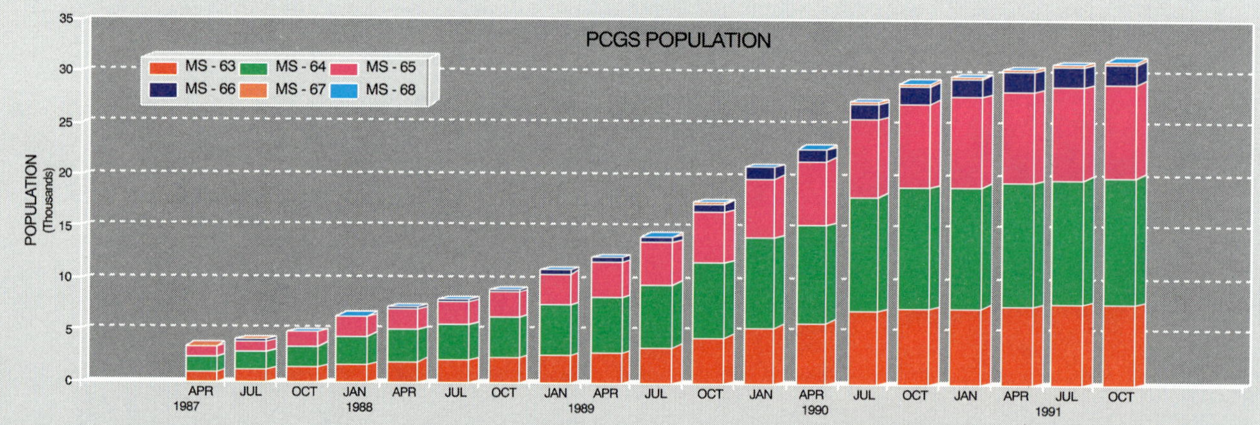

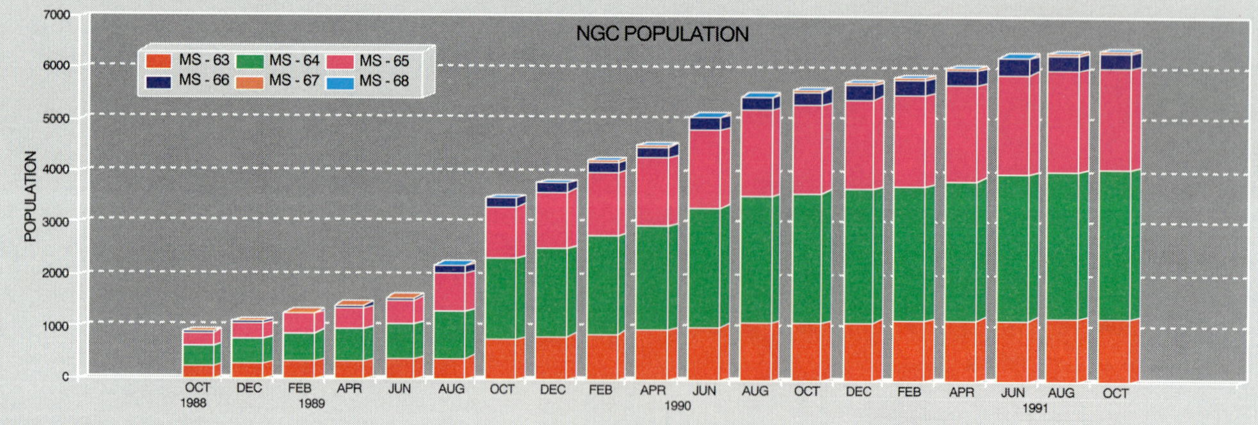

PCGS POPULATION

MS - 63 MS - 64 MS - 65
MS - 66 MS - 67 MS - 68

POPULATION (Thousands)

35 30 25 20 15 10 5 0

APR 1987 JUL OCT JAN 1988 APR JUL OCT JAN 1989 APR JUL OCT JAN 1990 APR JUL OCT JAN 1991 APR JUL OCT

NGC POPULATION

MS - 63 MS - 64 MS - 65
MS - 66 MS - 67 MS - 68

POPULATION

7000 6000 5000 4000 3000 2000 1000 0

OCT 1988 DEC FEB 1989 APR JUN AUG OCT DEC FEB APR 1990 JUN AUG OCT DEC FEB APR JUN 1991 AUG OCT

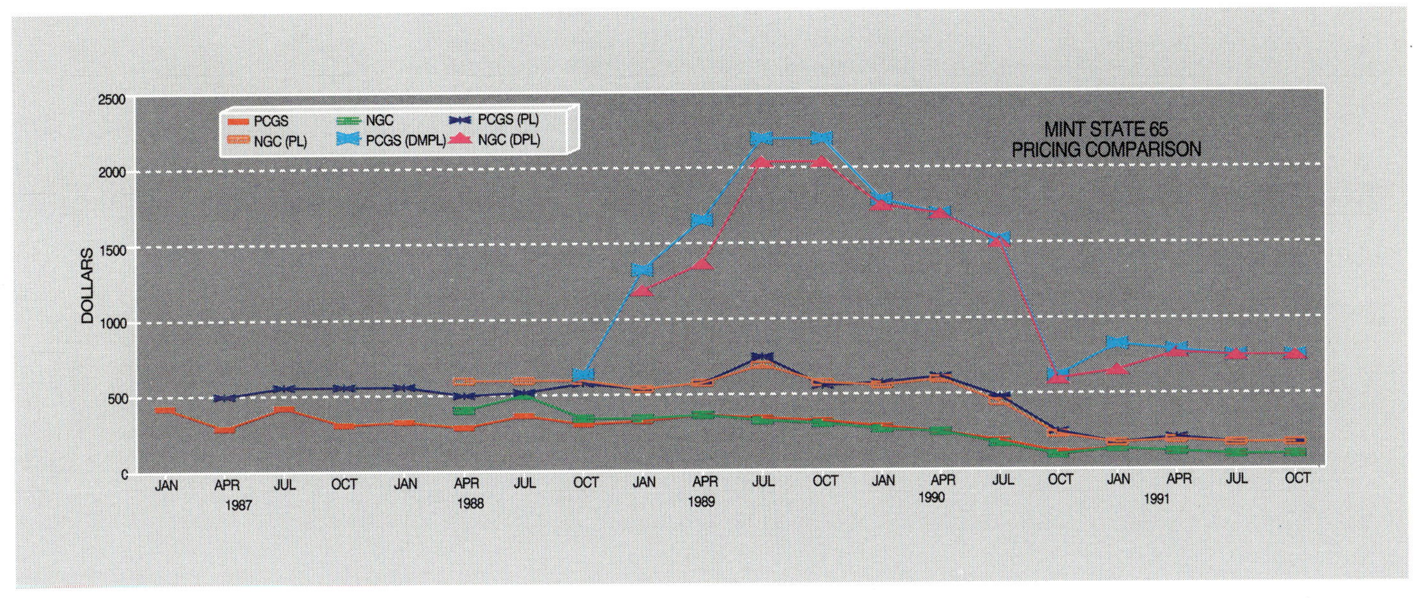
MINT STATE 65
PRICING COMPARISON
PCGS
NGC
PCGS (PL)
NGC (PL)
PCGS (DMPL)
NGC (DPL)
DOLLARS
2500
2000
1500
1000
500
0
JAN
APR
JUL
OCT
1987
1988
1989
1990
1991

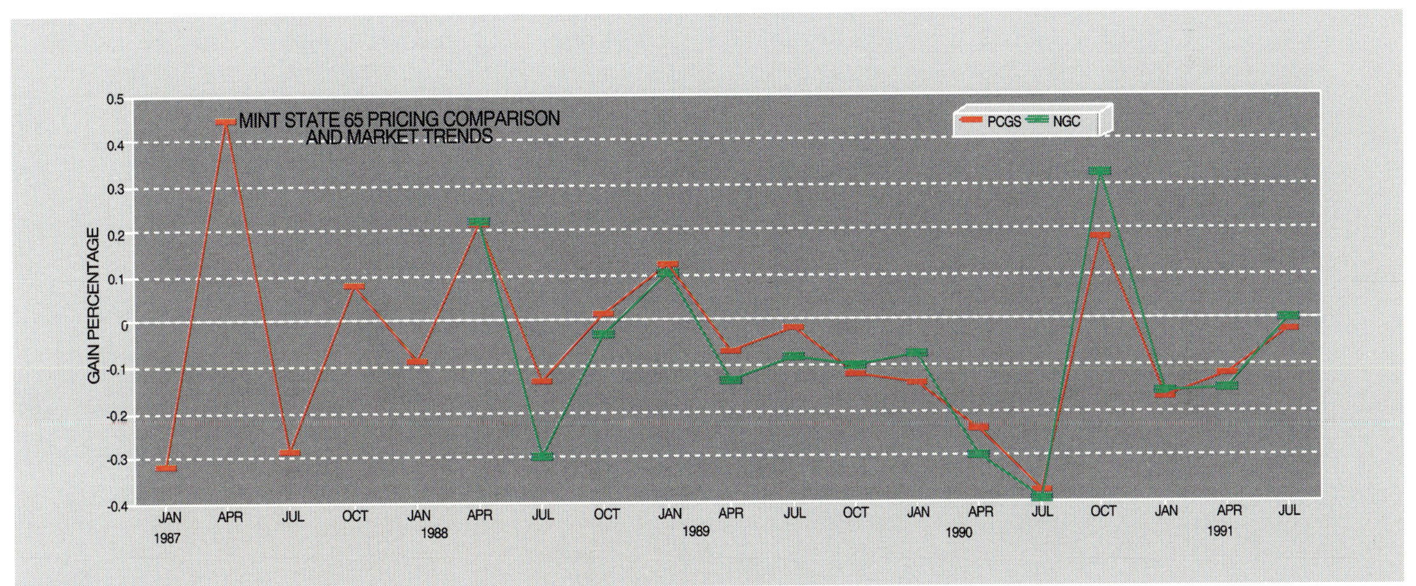
MINT STATE 65 PRICING COMPARISON
AND MARKET TRENDS
PCGS
NGC
GAIN PERCENTAGE
JAN
APR
JUL
OCT
1987
1988
1989
1990
1991

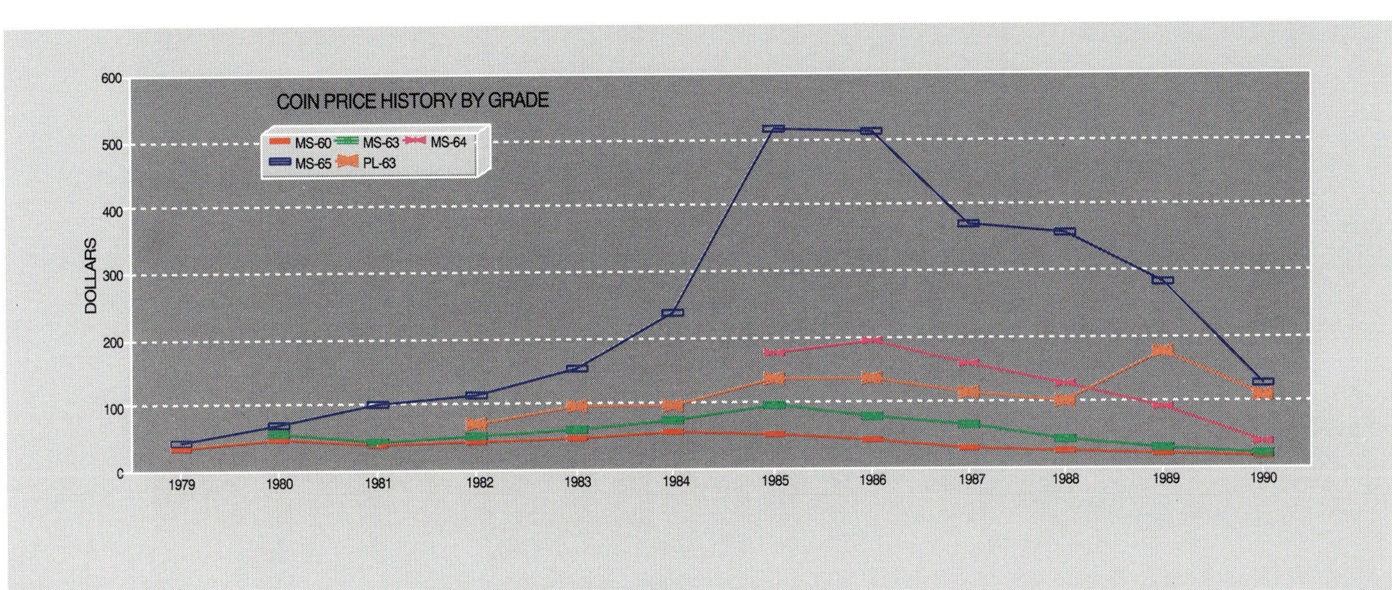
COIN PRICE HISTORY BY GRADE
MS-60
MS-63
MS-64
MS-65
PL-63
DOLLARS
1979
1980
1981
1982
1983
1984
1985
1986
1987
1988
1989
1990

PCGS
1879-S S$1
MS65
REV 1878
7094.65/2247775

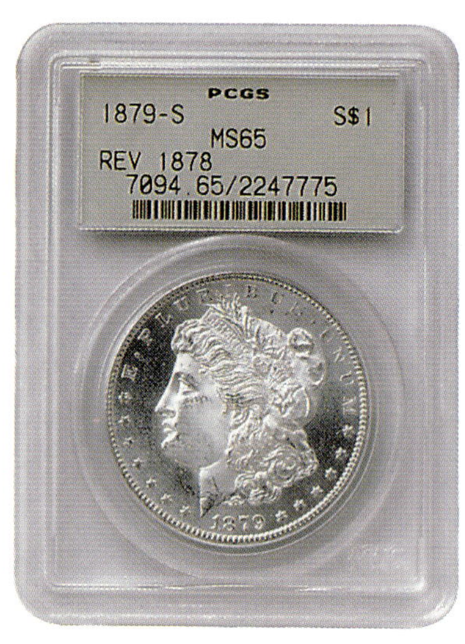

1879-S (Reverse of '78)

Though discovered by Howard Newcomb in 1913, it was forgotten until 2 or 3 bags turned up in the Redfield hoard, 1976. These were sold by A-Mark through Paramount and NSDR President Leon Hendrickson (Silver Towne) of Winchester, IN; the entire supply sold out. Fewer than half have been slabbed. These must have comprised only a few percent of the 9,110,000 struck. Concave Breast, Type III obverse, Type B reverse.

The two bags contained 13 varieties from seven reverses (VAM 4-10, 23-25, 34, 35, 39), mostly heavily bagmarked. For the full story see Chapter 16.

Prooflikes: To date only 35 PL's have been certified — and no DMPL's are traced.

PCGS

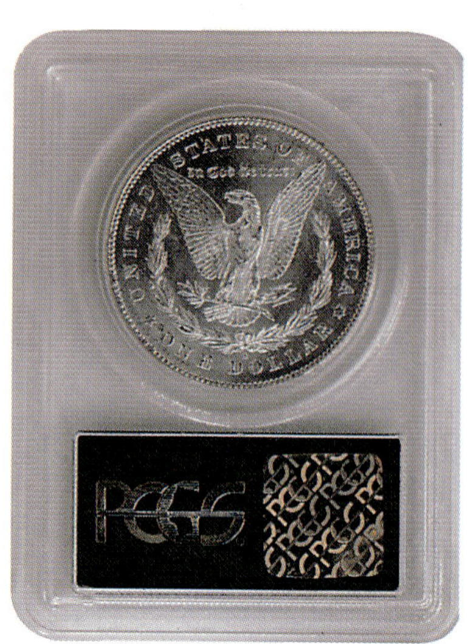

MINTAGE	PROOF	STRIKE	LUSTER	BAG MARKS	REDFIELD
4,000*	0	Average	Good	Heavy	Yes
DIES	**DIE VARIETIES**	**% OF PL**	**% OF DMPL**	**PIVOTAL GRADE**	**RARITY FACTOR**
192**	13	4.6	0.6	MS 64	R-2

* Estimated 4000 known **Includes all dies used at the San Francisco Mint - FY 1879

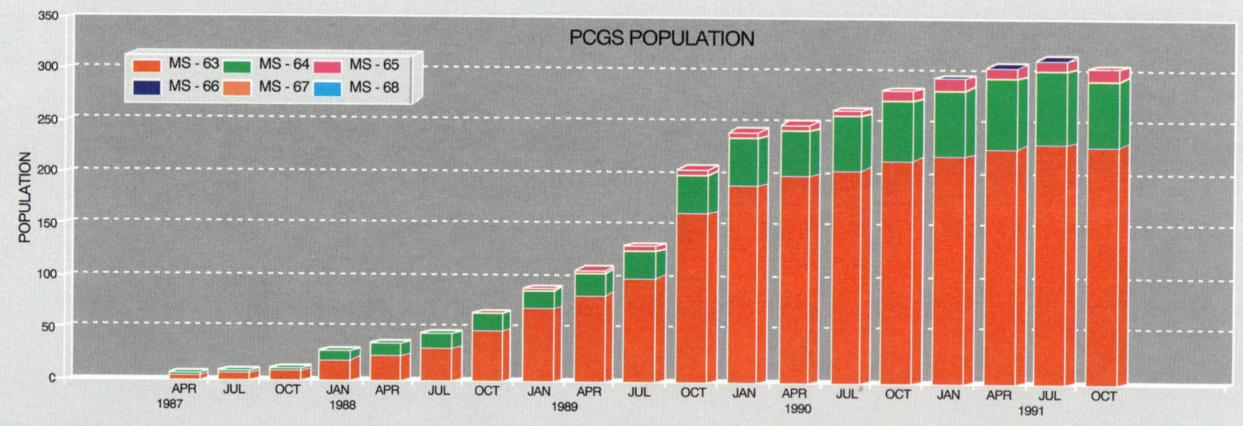
PCGS POPULATION
MS - 63
MS - 64
MS - 65
MS - 66
MS - 67
MS - 68
POPULATION
350
300
250
200
150
100
50
C
APR 1987
JUL
OCT
JAN 1988
APR
JUL
OCT
JAN 1989
APR
JUL
OCT
JAN
APR 1990
JUL
OCT
JAN
APR
JUL 1991
OCT

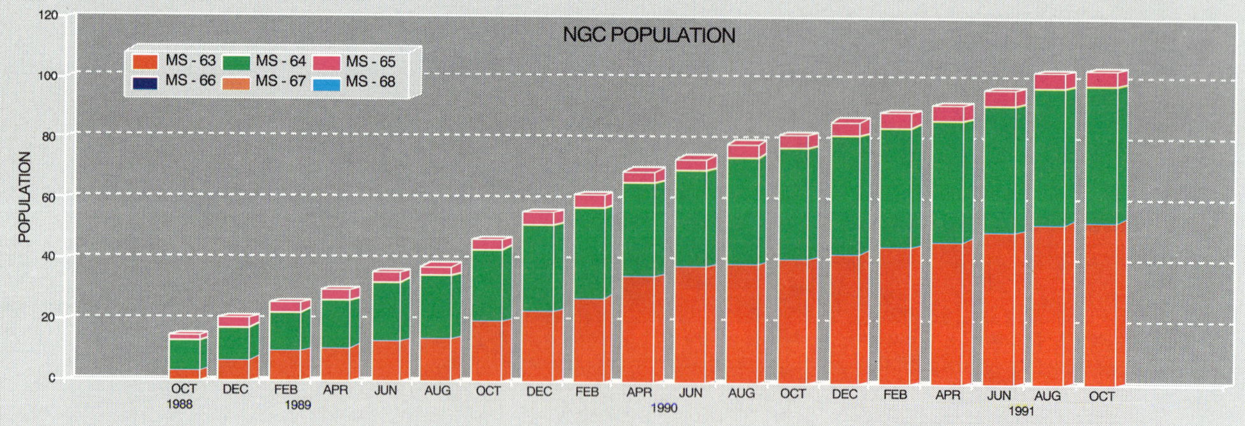
NGC POPULATION
MS - 63
MS - 64
MS - 65
MS - 66
MS - 67
MS - 68
POPULATION
120
100
80
60
40
20
C
OCT 1988
DEC
FEB 1989
APR
JUN
AUG
OCT
DEC
FEB
APR 1990
JUN
AUG
OCT
DEC
FEB
APR
JUN 1991
AUG
OCT

1879-S (Reverse of '78)

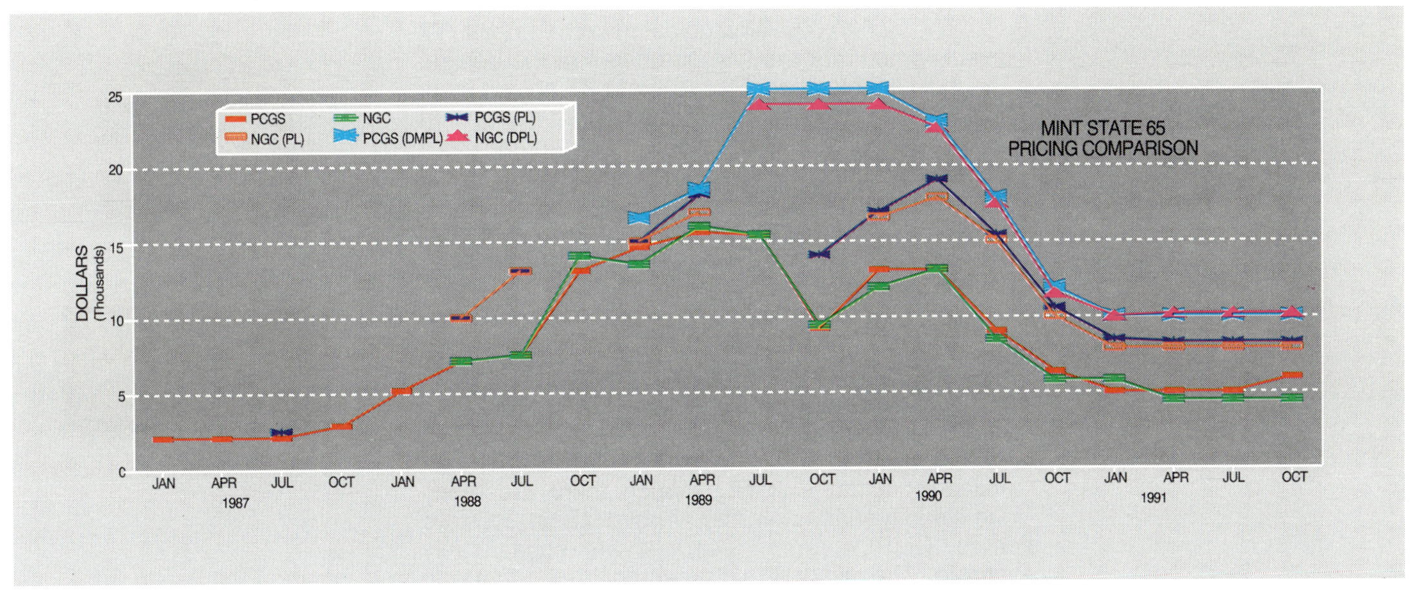

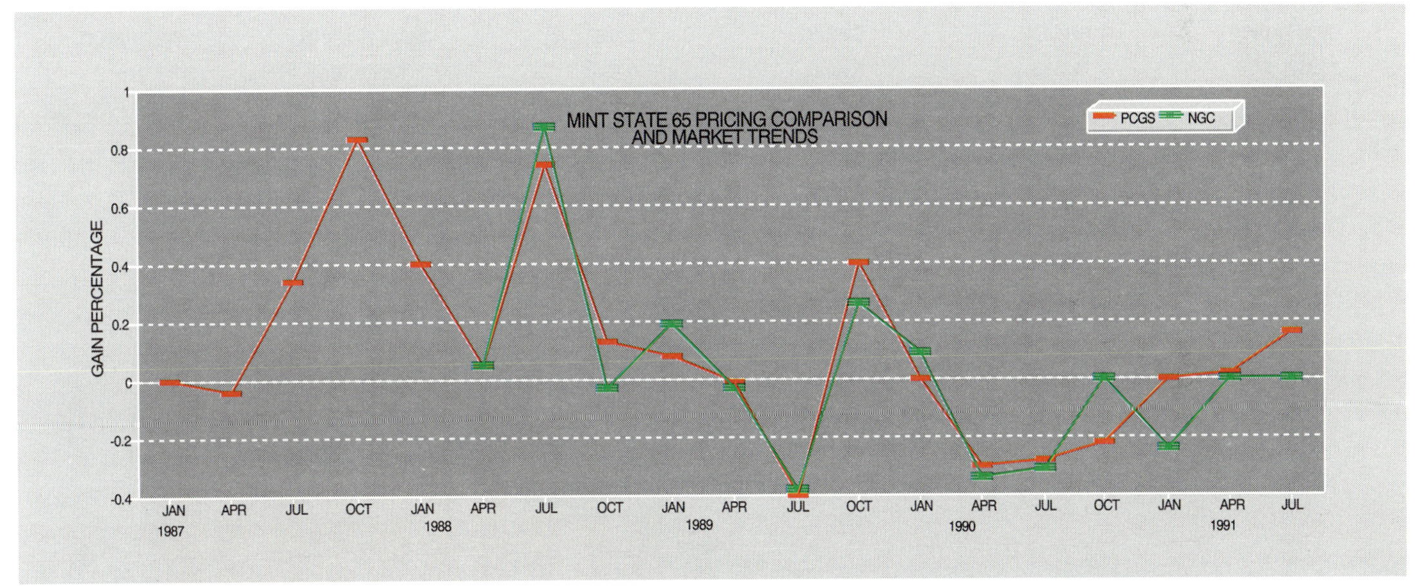

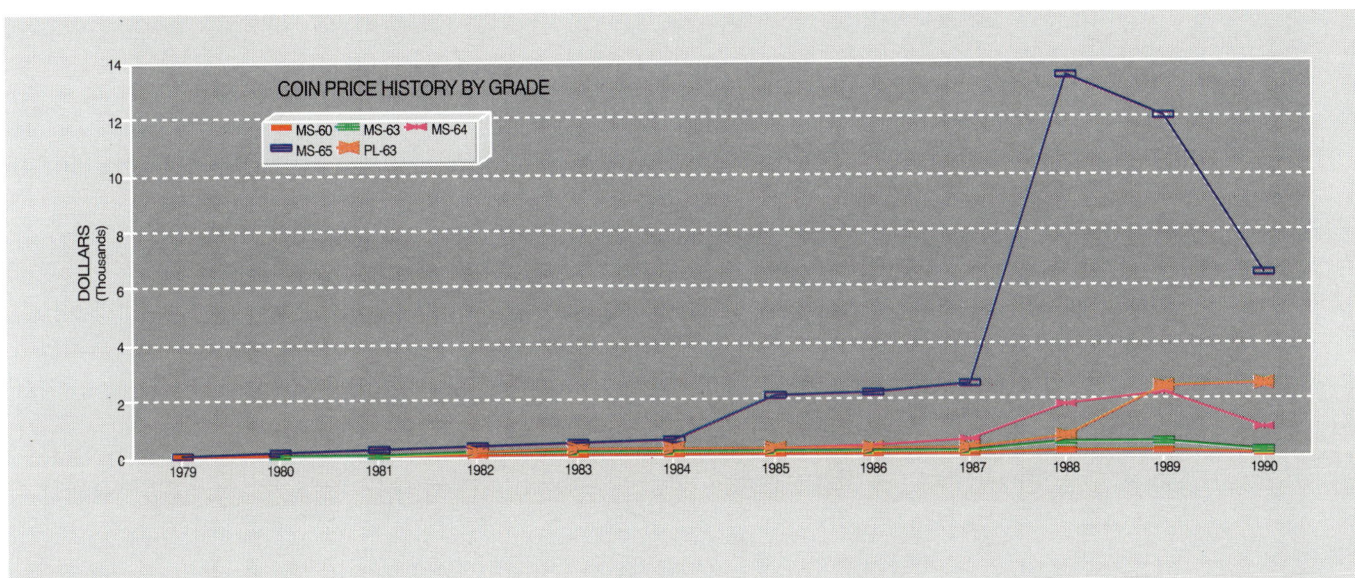

1880-P

The 12,600,000 mintage came from 91 obvs., 77 revs. Famous for the first overdates of the design. The most spectacular of these, VAM 23, shows parts of 79 in thick raised parts of 80, with corner of 7 at upper right curve of 8. Discovered by Anthony and Dazelle Morano in 1964. The "Red Book" price reflects this overdate.

Normal dates are semi-common, though scarcer above MS 64. Roll and bag quantities of MS 60/62 are still available.

Recommended in MS 65 or by the roll in MS 64.

Proofs: VAM 13, minute repunching on base of 1; rev. of 1879 with the same die file marks. The 1,355 coined should have required a second pair of dies, but none is yet identified.

Prooflikes: Among the more difficult Philadelphia dates in PL, though there are many one-sided (usually obverse). Above MS 64, PL's are scarce, DMPL's rarer. Cameos are occasionally available. The bag of PL's discovered in 1971 has long been dispersed.

MINTAGE	PROOF	STRIKE	LUSTER	BAG MARKS	REDFIELD
12,600,000	1,355	Average	Good	Moderate	No
DIES	**DIE VARIETIES**	**% OF PL**	**% OF DMPL**	**PIVOTAL GRADE**	**RARITY FACTOR**
199	40	3.4	2.9	MS 65	R-4

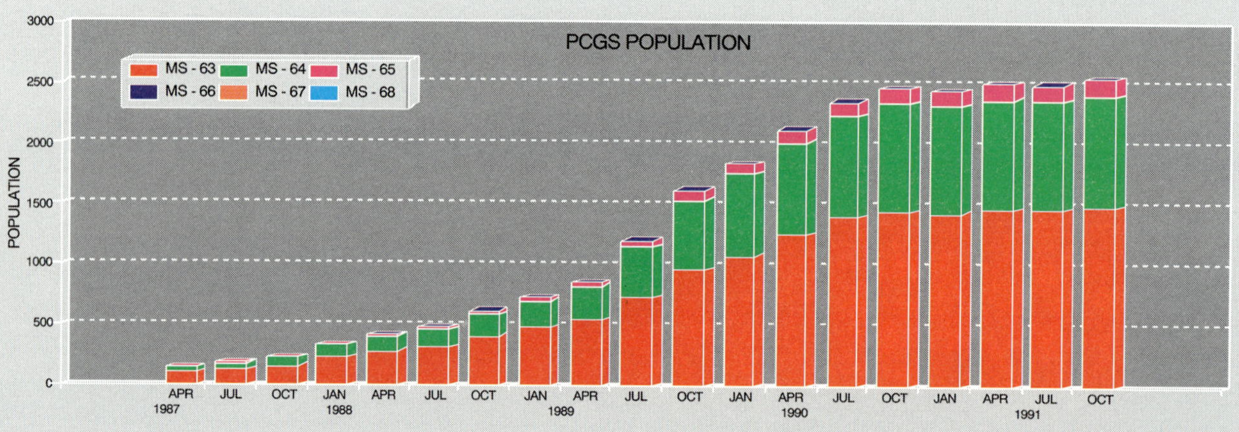

PCGS POPULATION

MS - 63 MS - 64 MS - 65 MS - 66 MS - 67 MS - 68

POPULATION: 0 500 1000 1500 2000 2500 3000

APR 1987, JUL, OCT, JAN 1988, APR, JUL, OCT, JAN 1989, APR, JUL, OCT, JAN, APR 1990, JUL, OCT, JAN, APR 1991, JUL, OCT

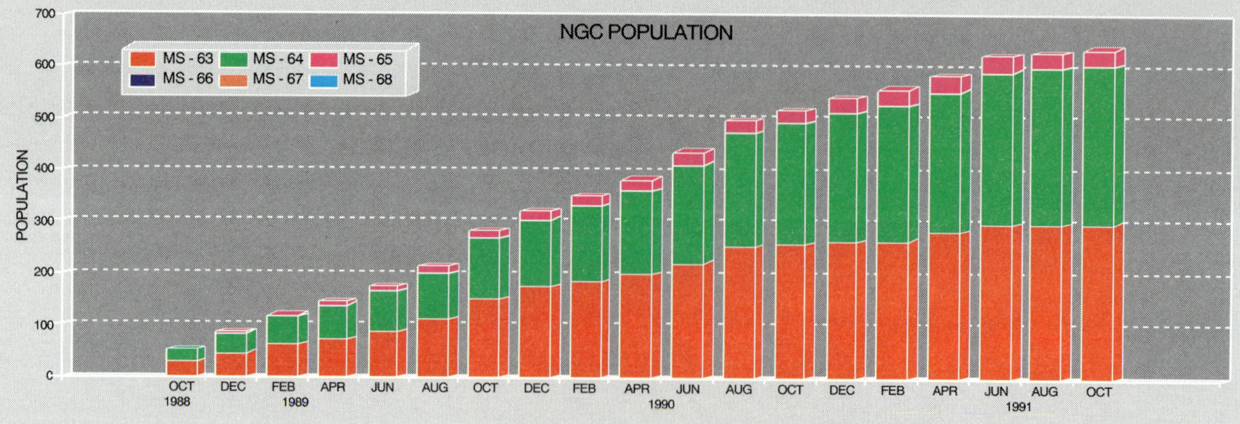

NGC POPULATION

MS - 63 MS - 64 MS - 65 MS - 66 MS - 67 MS - 68

POPULATION: 0 100 200 300 400 500 600 700

OCT 1988, DEC, FEB 1989, APR, JUN, AUG, OCT, DEC, FEB, APR 1990, JUN, AUG, OCT, DEC, FEB, APR, JUN 1991, AUG, OCT

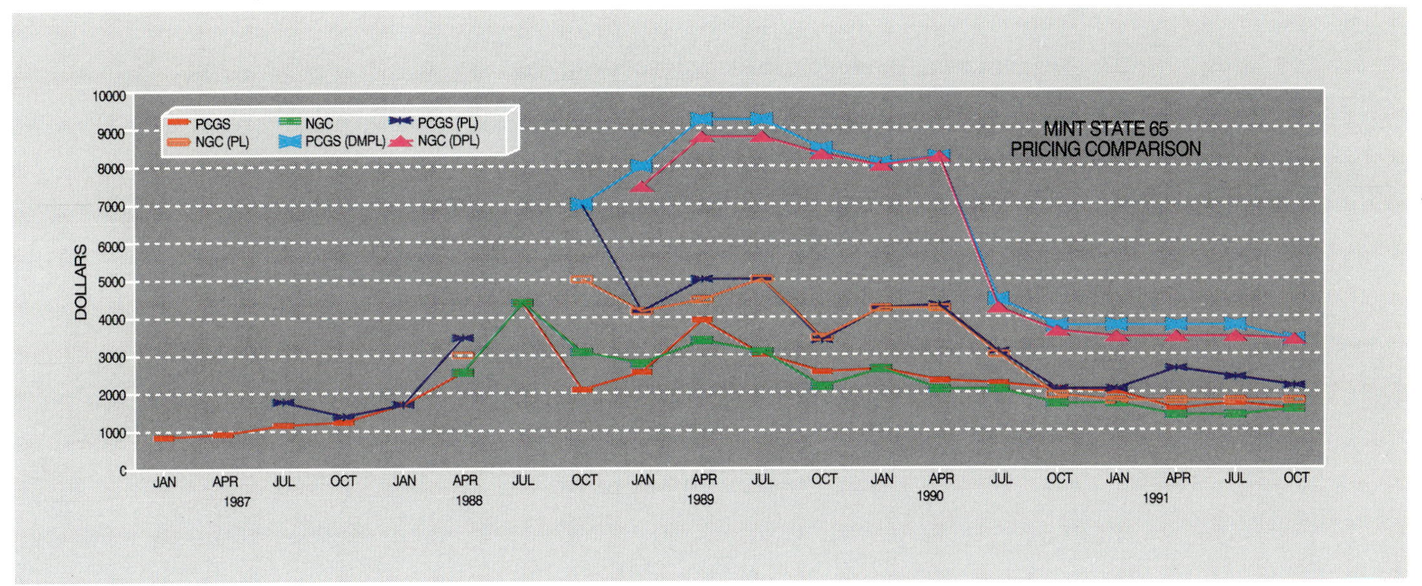
MINT STATE 65
PRICING COMPARISON
PCGS
NGC
PCGS (PL)
NGC (PL)
PCGS (DMPL)
NGC (DPL)
DOLLARS
10000
9000
8000
7000
6000
5000
4000
3000
2000
1000
0
JAN
APR
JUL
OCT
1987
1988
1989
1990
1991

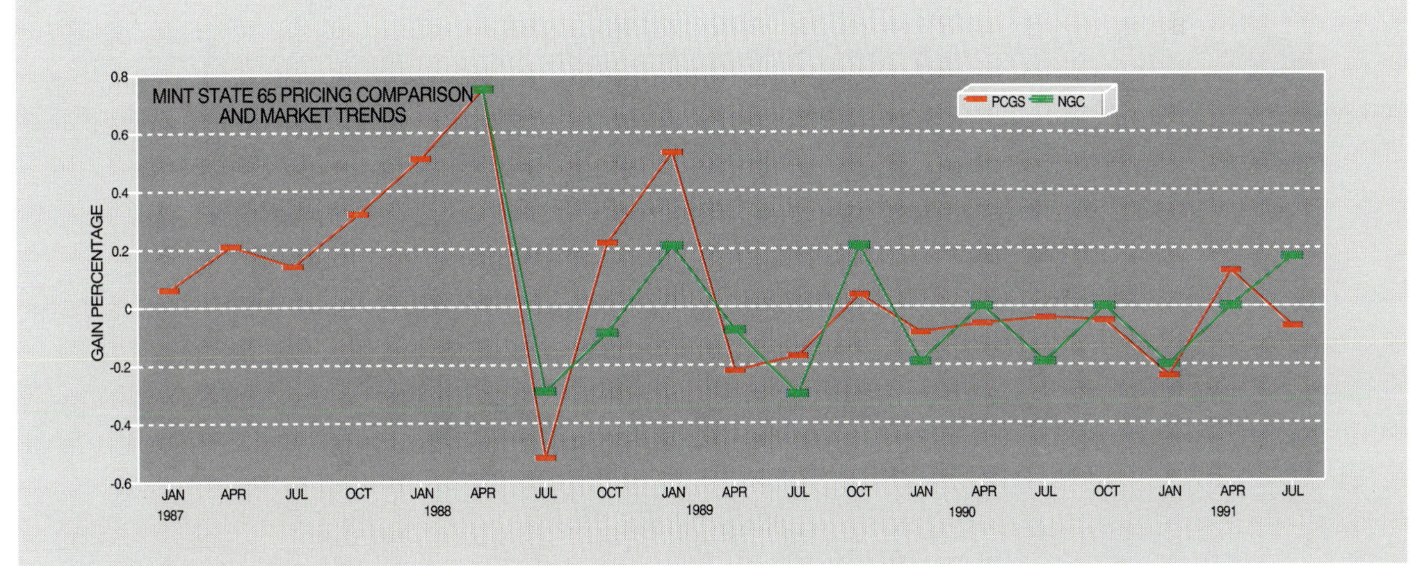
MINT STATE 65 PRICING COMPARISON
AND MARKET TRENDS
PCGS
NGC
GAIN PERCENTAGE
0.8
0.6
0.4
0.2
0
-0.2
-0.4
-0.6
JAN
APR
JUL
OCT
1987
1988
1989
1990
1991

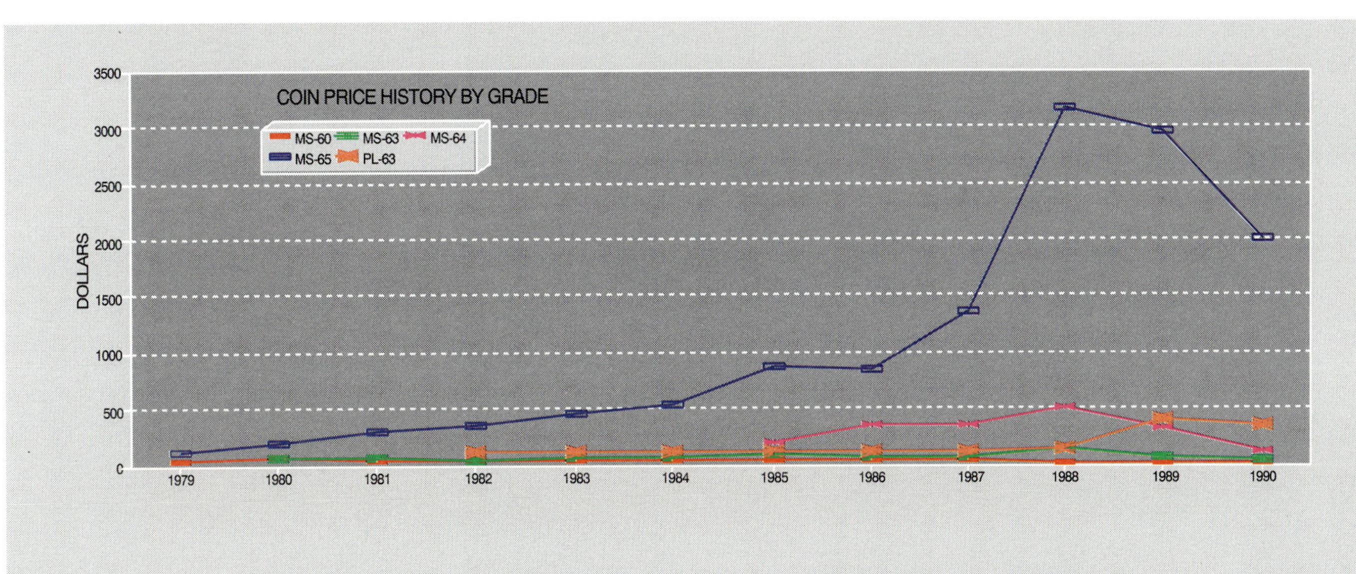
COIN PRICE HISTORY BY GRADE
MS-60
MS-63
MS-64
MS-65
PL-63
DOLLARS
3500
3000
2500
2000
1500
1000
500
0
1979
1980
1981
1982
1983
1984
1985
1986
1987
1988
1989
1990

1880-CC

All began as overdates, but many from worn dies no longer show more than microscopic traces. Seven vars. VAM 3 and 9 have large CC, the rest small.

Lower grade Uncs. form the majority of survivors, many from Treasury releases (1938).

Of the 131,529 in the GSA sales, all but 4,283 sold in the 1972-74 mail bid offerings (minimum bid $60 each); the rest in 1980. This was 22% of the total original mintage.

Recommended in MS 64 up. MS 60/63 rolls, also.

Prooflikes: Over twice as scarce as 1881-CC or 1885-CC in PL or DMPL. Scarce to rare above MS 65 PL, MS 64 DMPL. Many are cameos, but few are high grade.

MINTAGE	PROOF	STRIKE	LUSTER	BAG MARKS	REDFIELD
591,000*	0	Average To Bold	Good	Moderate To Heavy	No
DIES	**DIE VARIETIES**	**% OF PL**	**% OF DMPL**	**PIVOTAL GRADE**	**RARITY FACTOR**
25**	7	10.2	4.0	MS 65	R-4

*Includes estimated 500,000 1880-CC and estimated 100,000 1880-CC Rev 78 **Includes all dies used at the Carson City Mint -FY 1880

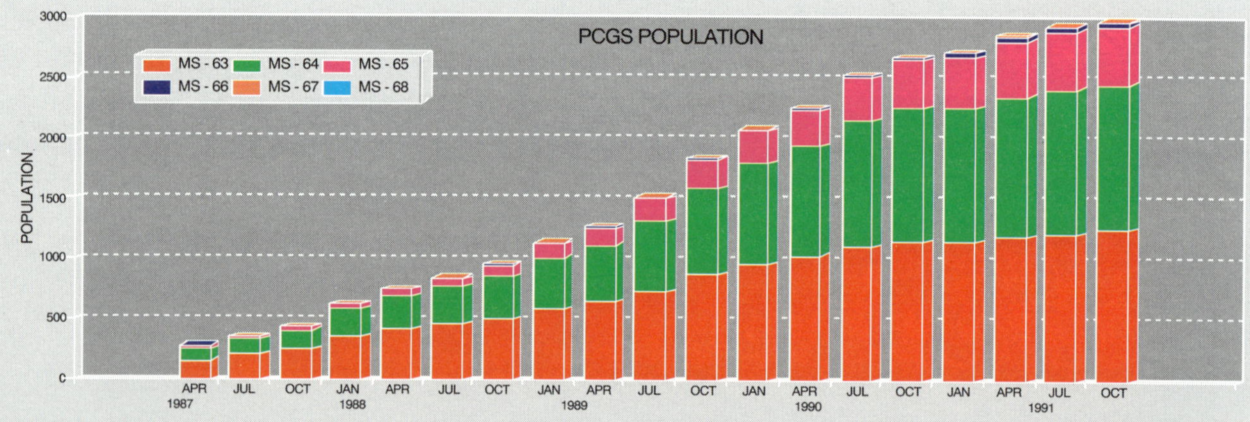

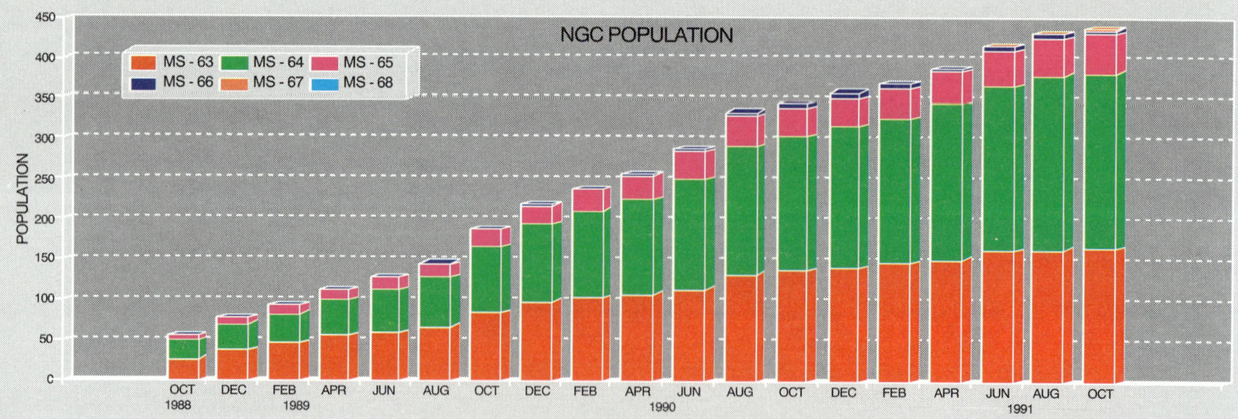

1880-CC

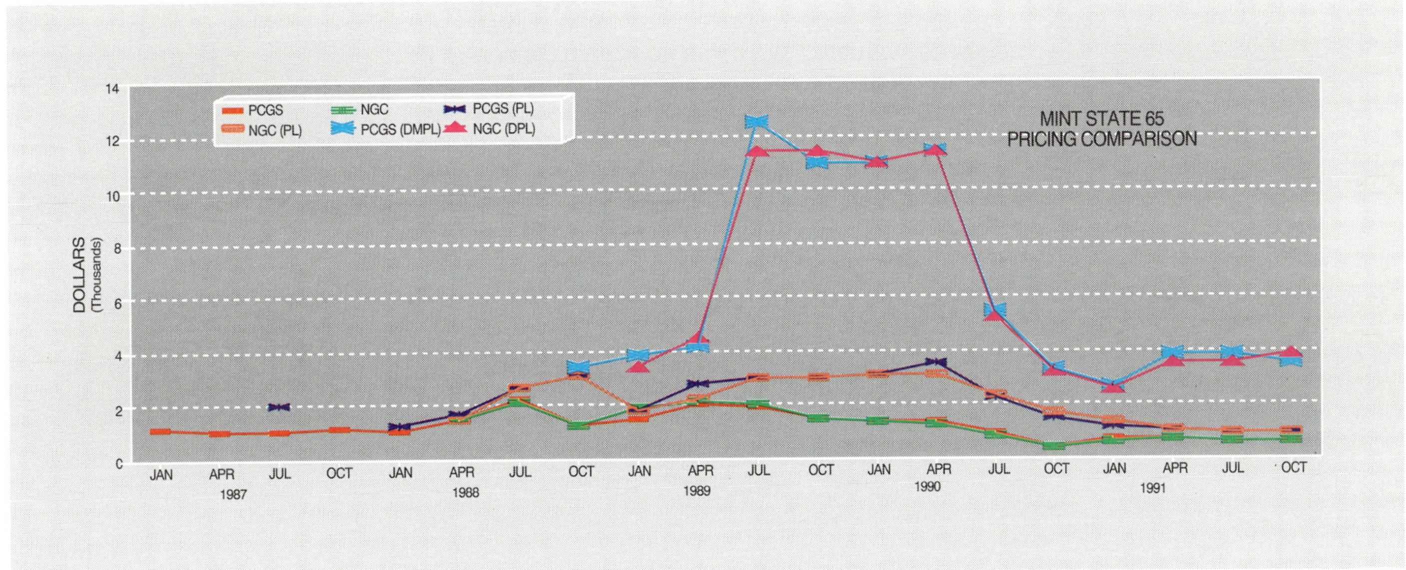

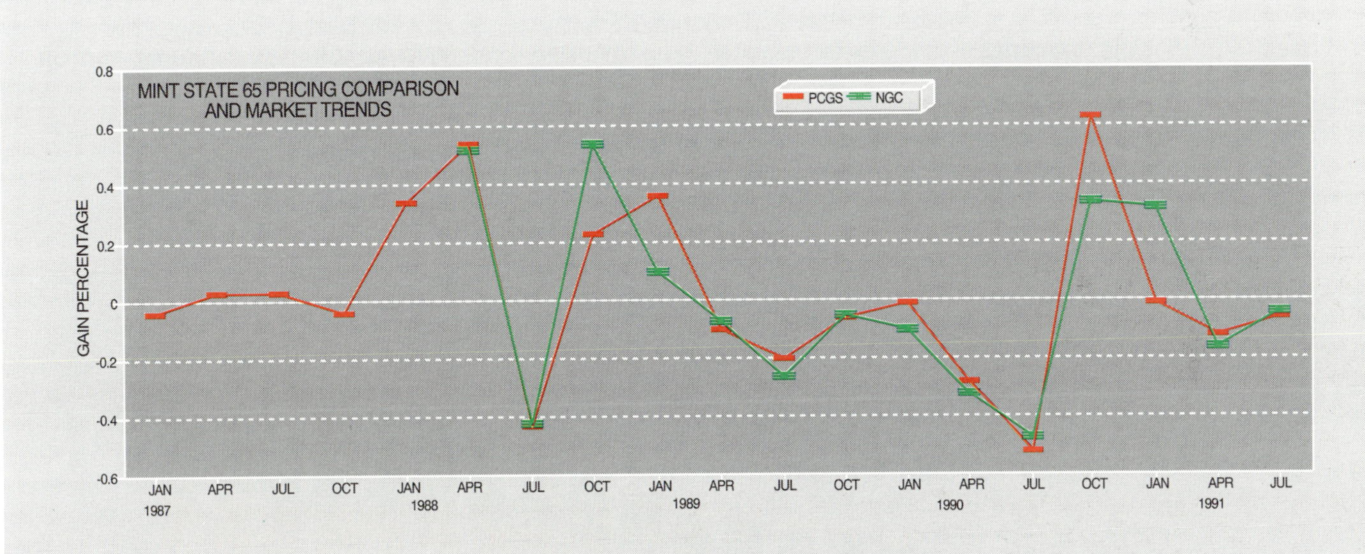

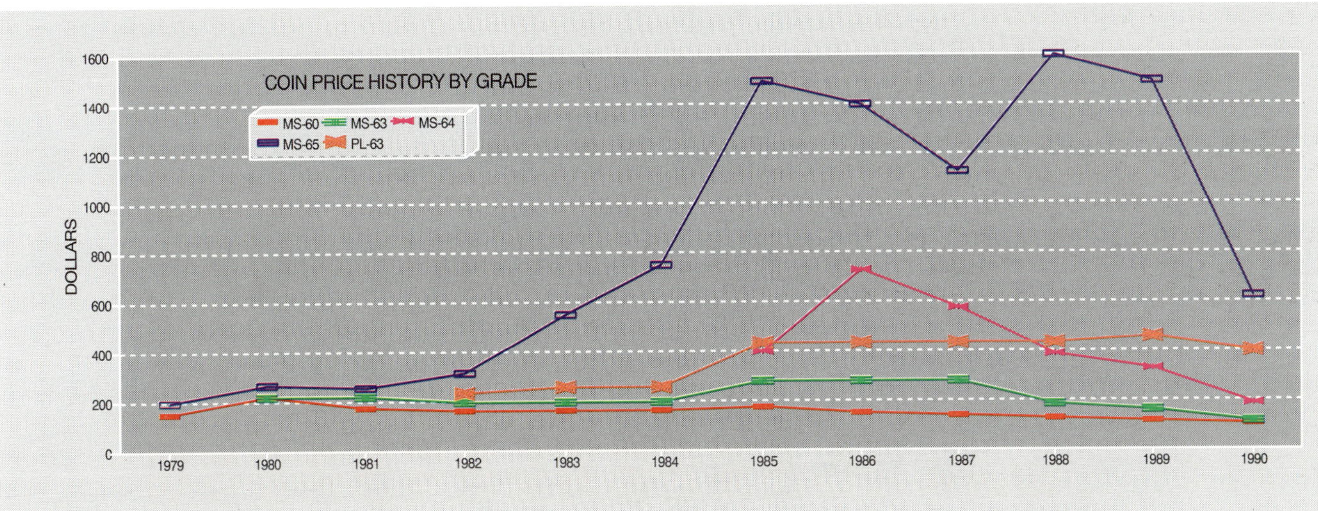

PCGS
1880-CC
S$1
MS66
REV 1878
7108.66/6271758

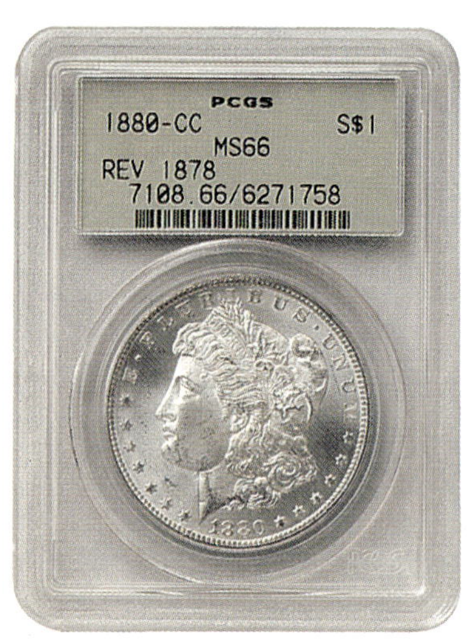

1880-CC (Reverse of '78)

Forms a small minority of 591,000 minted. All began as overdates, but some from worn dies (VAM 7) no longer show more than microscopic traces. Three varieties; the clearest, VAM 4, was discovered by Breen at the 1964 ANA Convention, among coins lately released by the Treasury. The 7 TF PAF coins were struck after August 1880, from improperly basined dies. When the Coiner complained about their appearance, Mint Engraver Barber ordered that all the 7 TF PAF reverses be returned to Philadelphia.

Popular type coins, recommended in MS 64 and above. MS 60/63 rolls, also.

Prooflikes: Very scarce to rare in all grades, PL and especially DMPL. Cameos occasionally turn up.

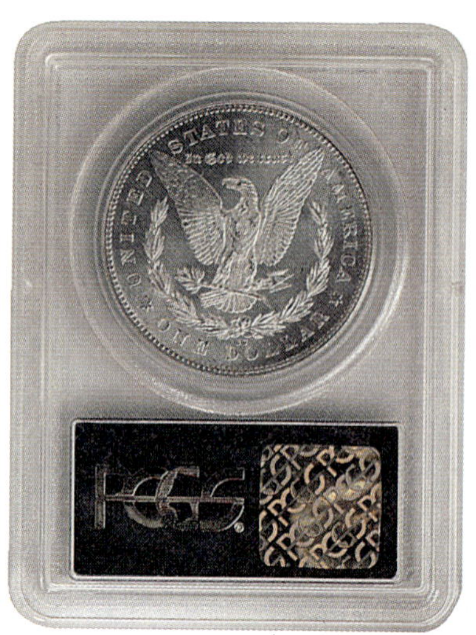

MINTAGE	PROOF	STRIKE	LUSTER	BAG MARKS	REDFIELD
100,000*	0	Average	Good	Moderate	No
DIES	**DIE VARIETIES**	**% OF PL**	**% OF DMPL**	**PIVOTAL GRADE**	**RARITY FACTOR**
25**	3	4.2	3.9	MS 65	R-2

*Includes estimated 500,000 1880-CC and estimated 100,000 1880-CC Rev 78 **Includes all dies used at the Carson City Mint - FY

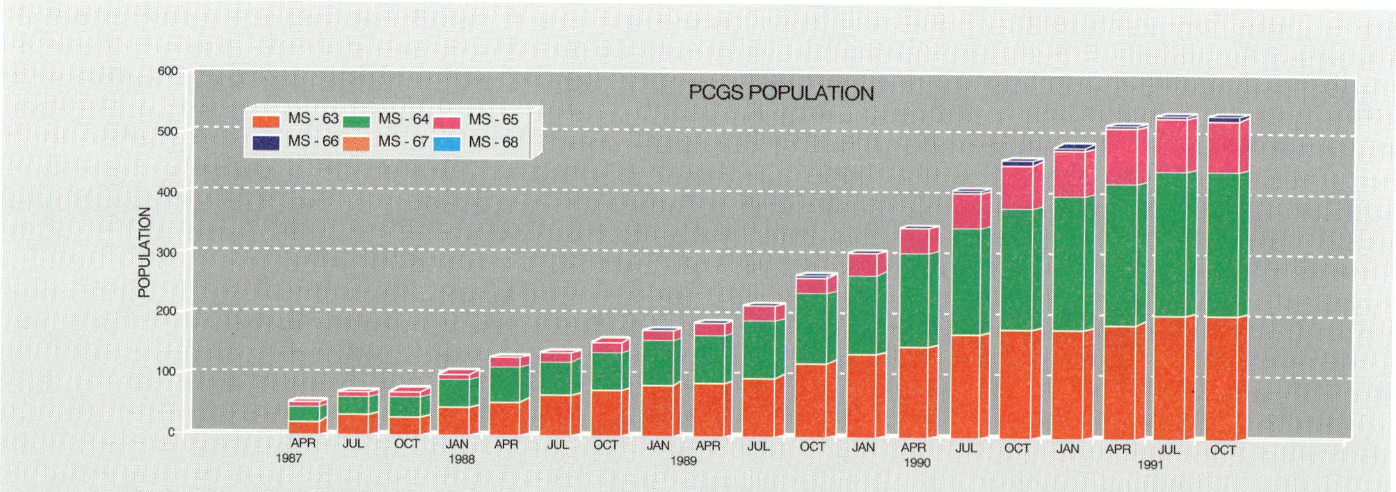
PCGS POPULATION
MS - 63
MS - 64
MS - 65
MS - 66
MS - 67
MS - 68
POPULATION
600
500
400
300
200
100
0
APR 1987
JUL
OCT
JAN 1988
APR
JUL
OCT
JAN 1989
APR
JUL
OCT
JAN
APR 1990
JUL
OCT
JAN
APR
JUL 1991
OCT

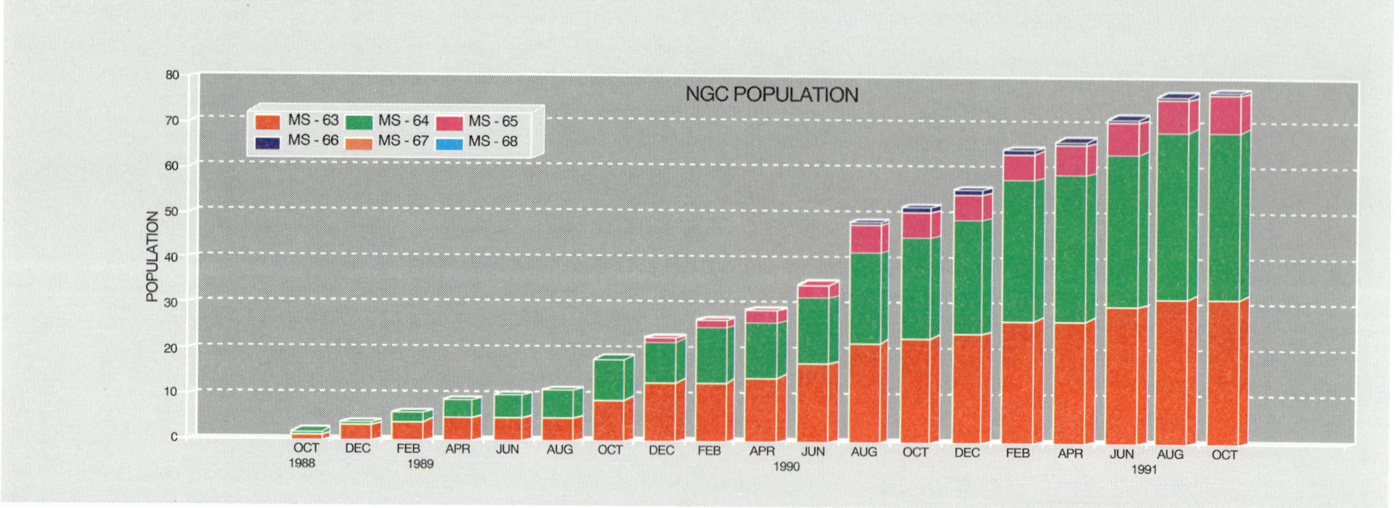
NGC POPULATION
MS - 63
MS - 64
MS - 65
MS - 66
MS - 67
MS - 68
POPULATION
80
70
60
50
40
30
20
10
0
OCT 1988
DEC
FEB 1989
APR
JUN
AUG
OCT
DEC
FEB
APR 1990
JUN
AUG
OCT
DEC
FEB
APR
JUN 1991
AUG
OCT

1880-CC (Reverse of '78)

NO PRICING DATA AVAILABLE FOR THIS DATE

NO PRICING DATA AVAILABLE FOR THIS DATE

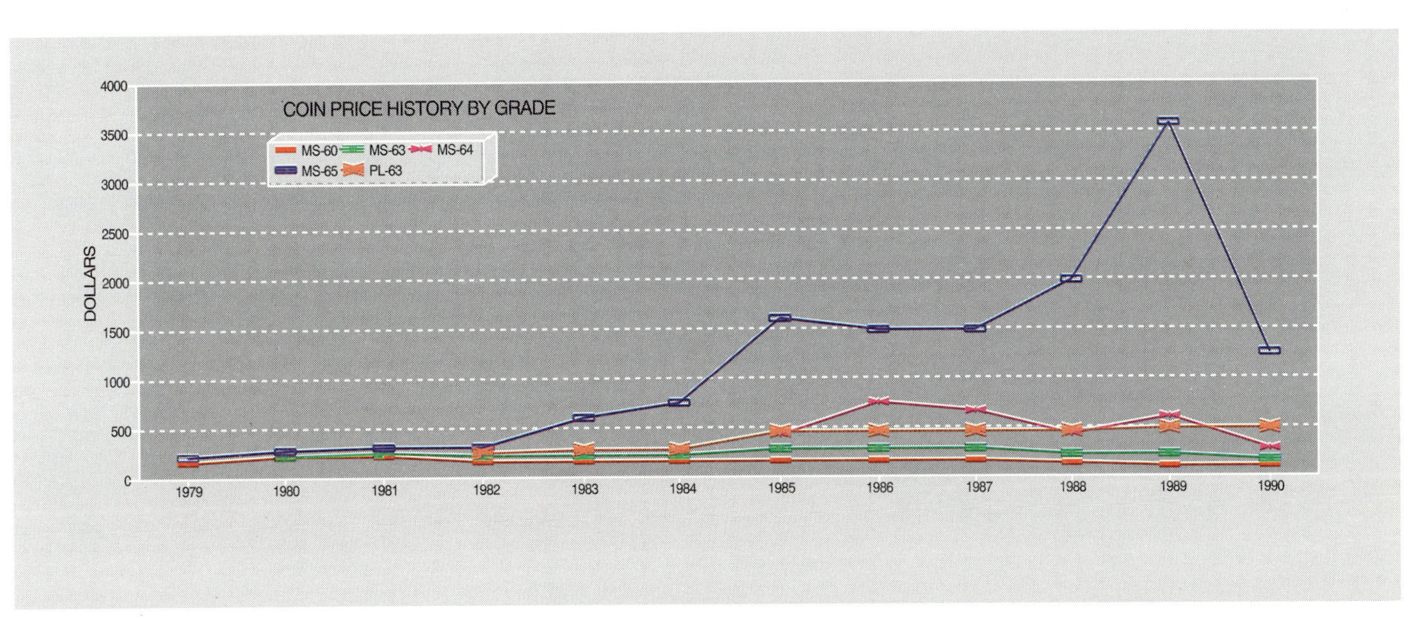

PCGS
1880-O
S$1
MS65PL
7115.65/3133951

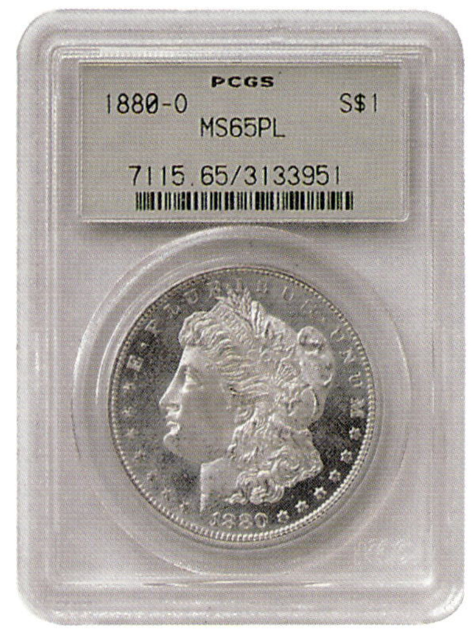

1880-O

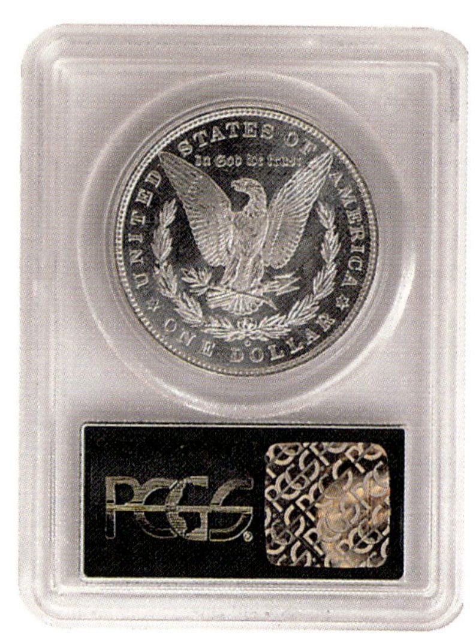

Many of the 5,305,000 minted were released, but quickly found their way back to banks, and were resealed into mint sacks; Dean Tavenner calls these "two-beer" coins. Hundreds of mint sewn bags turned up in the Continental Bank hoard; specimens are available from EF to MS 63. Beware of "original" bags; they are most likely to fall short of Unc.

But in MS 64 and above, this date tells another story. The first three graded PCGS MS 65 all sold for close to or above six digits! Professional guidance recommended for prospective buyers of MS 65's.

Overdates (80/79 and 8/7) are less spectacular than on Philadelphia or CC mints. Mintmark, on overdates and normal dates, comes small and round or large and oval (slit opening); not much difference in rarity.

Prooflikes: Because of a bag dispersed by Superior in 1977 (the R. D. Donovan hoard), PL cameos and even DMPL cameos are available, but most will be MS 63 and lower. To date, only one MS 65 PL has been certified; it also sold earlier in the six figure range.

MINTAGE	PROOF	STRIKE	LUSTER	BAG MARKS	REDFIELD
5,305,000	0	Average To Bold	Good	Moderate	No
DIES	**DIE VARIETIES**	**% OF PL**	**% OF DMPL**	**PIVOTAL GRADE**	**RARITY FACTOR**
80	39	5.0	5.2	MS 64	R-2

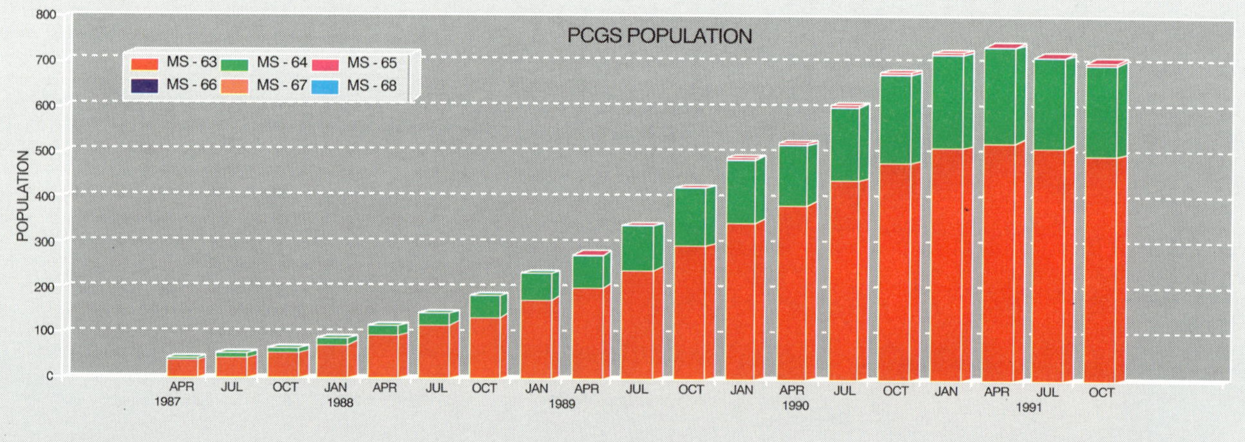
PCGS POPULATION
MS - 63
MS - 64
MS - 65
MS - 66
MS - 67
MS - 68
POPULATION
800
700
600
500
400
300
200
100
0
APR 1987
JUL
OCT
JAN 1988
APR
JUL
OCT
JAN 1989
APR
JUL
OCT
JAN
APR 1990
JUL
OCT
JAN
APR 1991
JUL
OCT

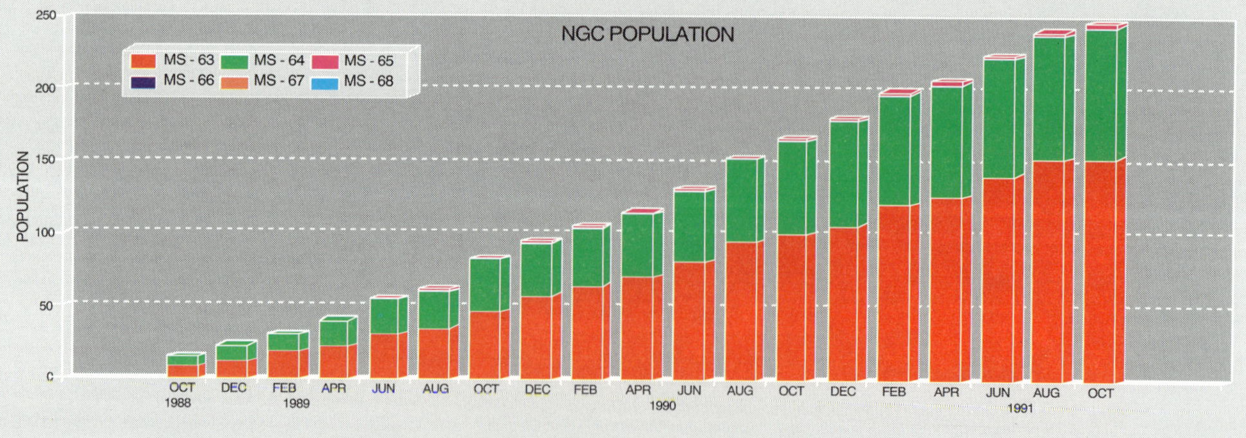
NGC POPULATION
MS - 63
MS - 64
MS - 65
MS - 66
MS - 67
MS - 68
POPULATION
250
200
150
100
50
0
OCT 1988
DEC
FEB 1989
APR
JUN
AUG
OCT
DEC
FEB
APR 1990
JUN
AUG
OCT
DEC
FEB
APR
JUN 1991
AUG
OCT

1880-O

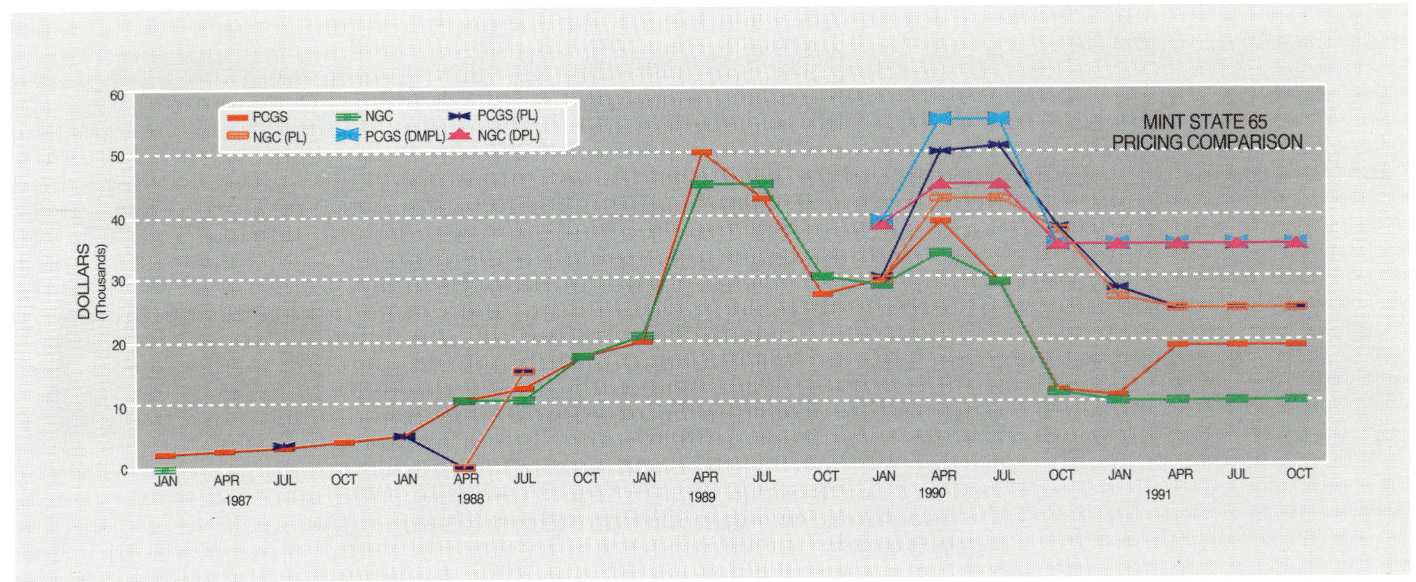

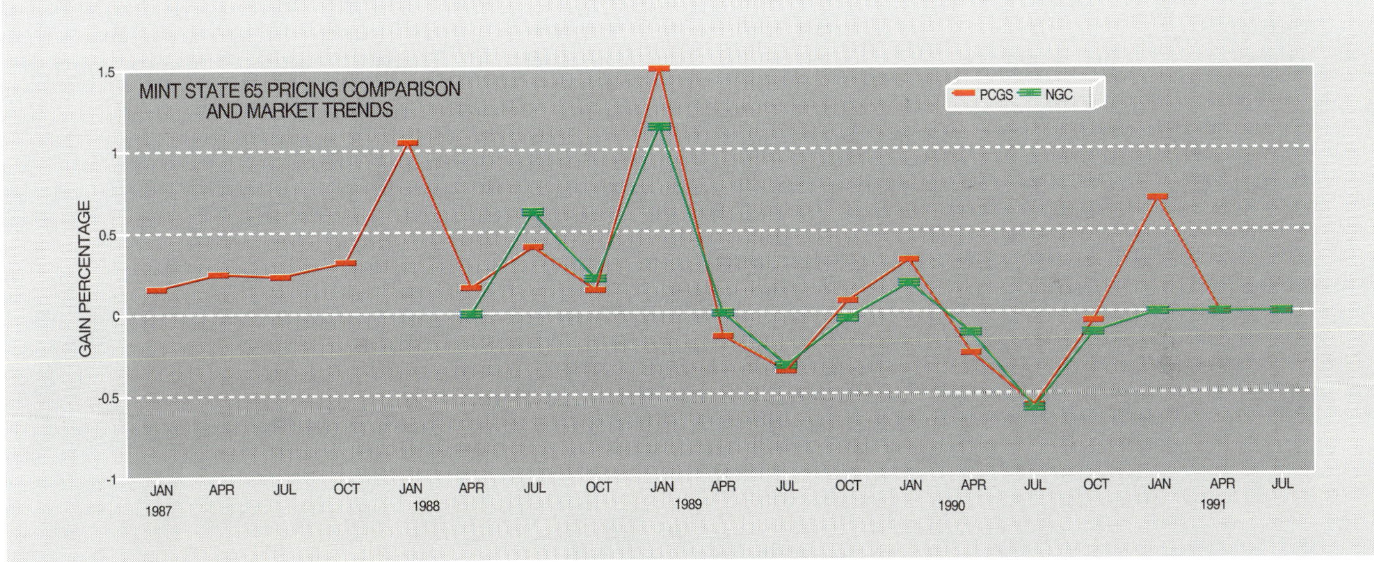

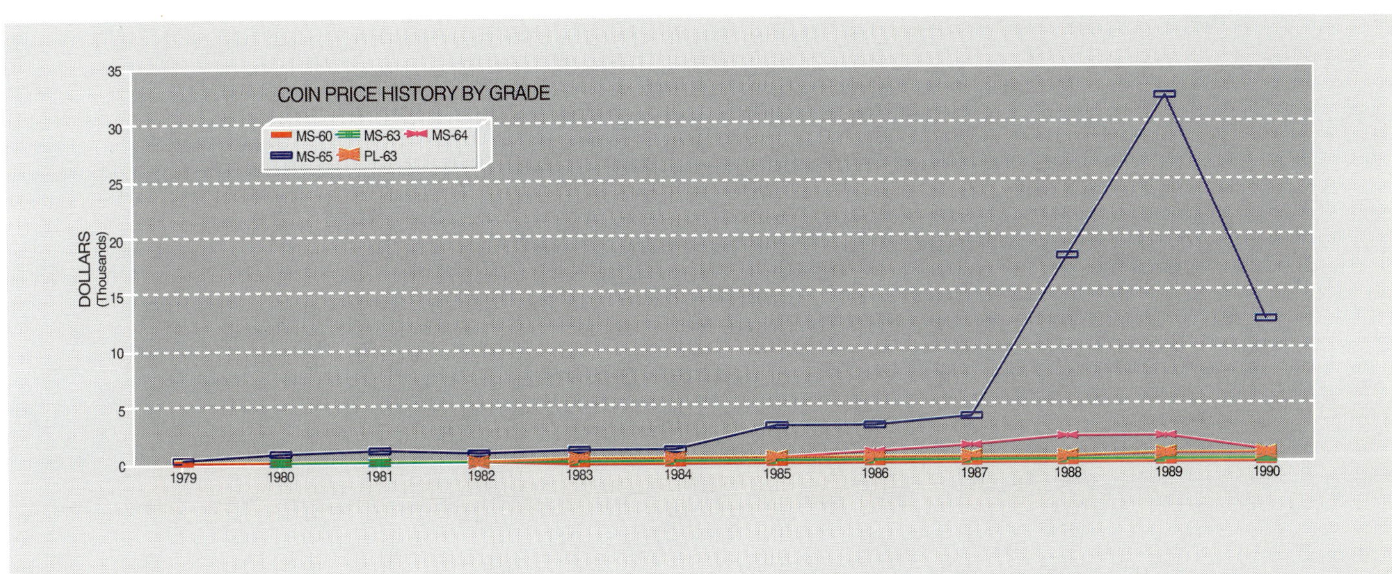

PCGS
1880-S S$1
MS69
7118.69/5096658

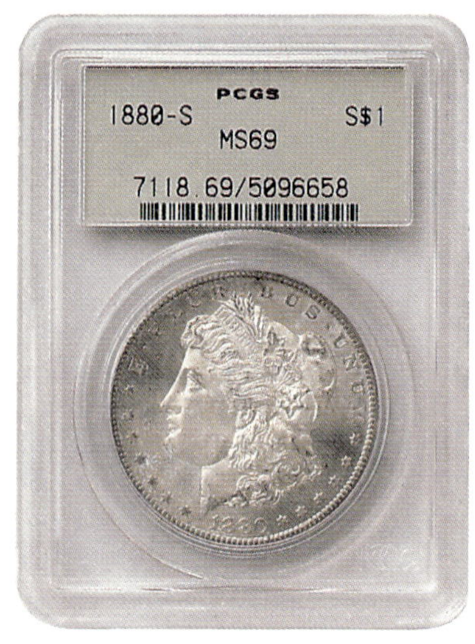

1880-S

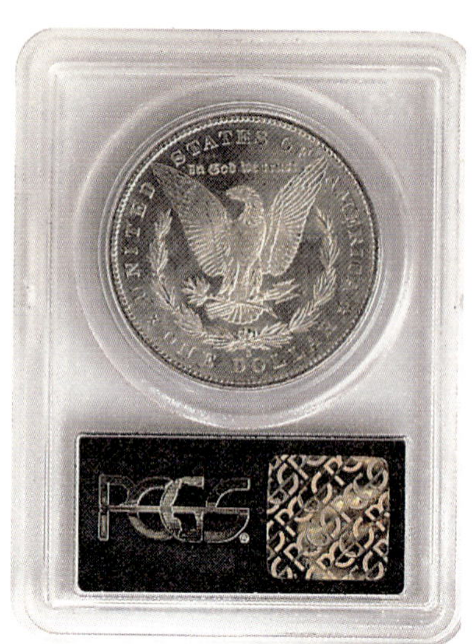

Despite its mintage of 8,900,000, this is the second commonest S Mint Morgan, from Treasury releases (1938 and 1963-4) augmented by Redfield and Continental Bank hoards. This date was second commonest in Redfield. Specimens are available in grades up to PCGS 69. They often have magnificent strikes, frosty luster, minimal bagmarks, and maximal eye appeal, more even than the 1881-S's of similar grade. Many from the Continental Bank hoard have rainbow tone. High grade examples are recommended, not as investments, just as things of beauty. They are the role model for all S mint Morgan dollars.

Overdates are plainer than on 1880-O but not as plain as on 1880-CC. Not much difference in rarity between medium and large mintmark varieties. See VAM, *Encyclopedia*, and Chapter 18 (Jeff Oxman).

Prooflikes: Abundant. DMPL's and cameos are readily available.

PCGS

MINTAGE	PROOF	STRIKE	LUSTER	BAG MARKS	REDFIELD
8,900,000	0	Sharp & Bold	Excellent	Light	Yes
DIES	**DIE VARIETIES**	**% OF PL**	**% OF DMPL**	**PIVOTAL GRADE**	**RARITY FACTOR**
110	69	12.9	2.8	MS 66	R-5

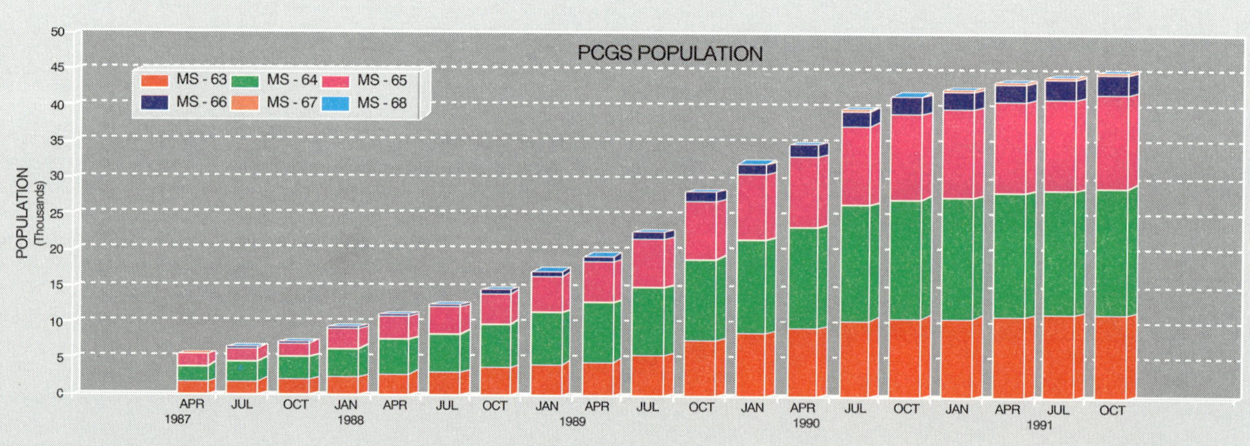
PCGS POPULATION
MS - 63
MS - 64
MS - 65
MS - 66
MS - 67
MS - 68
POPULATION (Thousands)
APR 1987
JUL
OCT
JAN 1988
APR
JUL
OCT
JAN 1989
APR
JUL
OCT
JAN 1990
APR
JUL
OCT
JAN
APR
JUL 1991
OCT

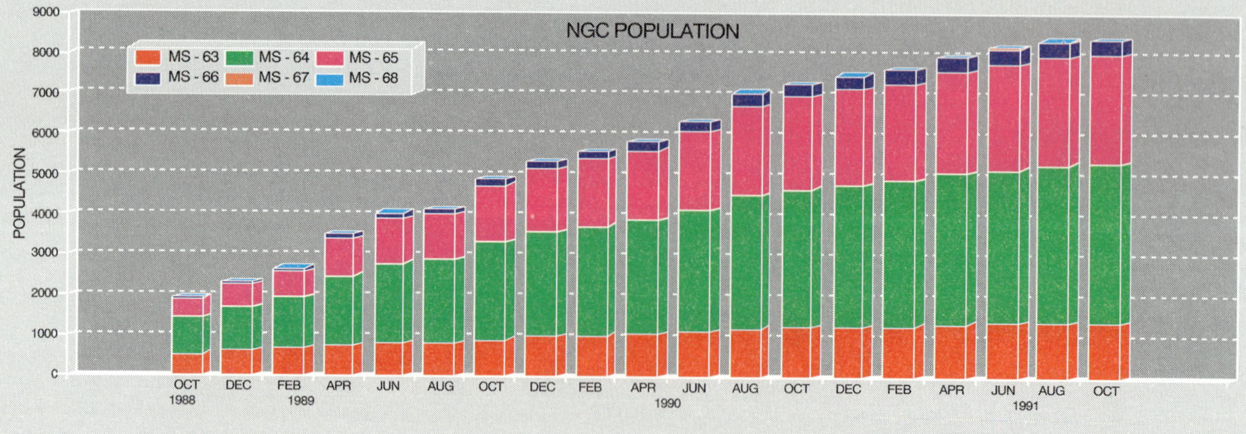
NGC POPULATION
MS - 63
MS - 64
MS - 65
MS - 66
MS - 67
MS - 68
POPULATION
OCT 1988
DEC
FEB 1989
APR
JUN
AUG
OCT
DEC
FEB
APR 1990
JUN
AUG
OCT
DEC
FEB
APR
JUN 1991
AUG
OCT

1880-S

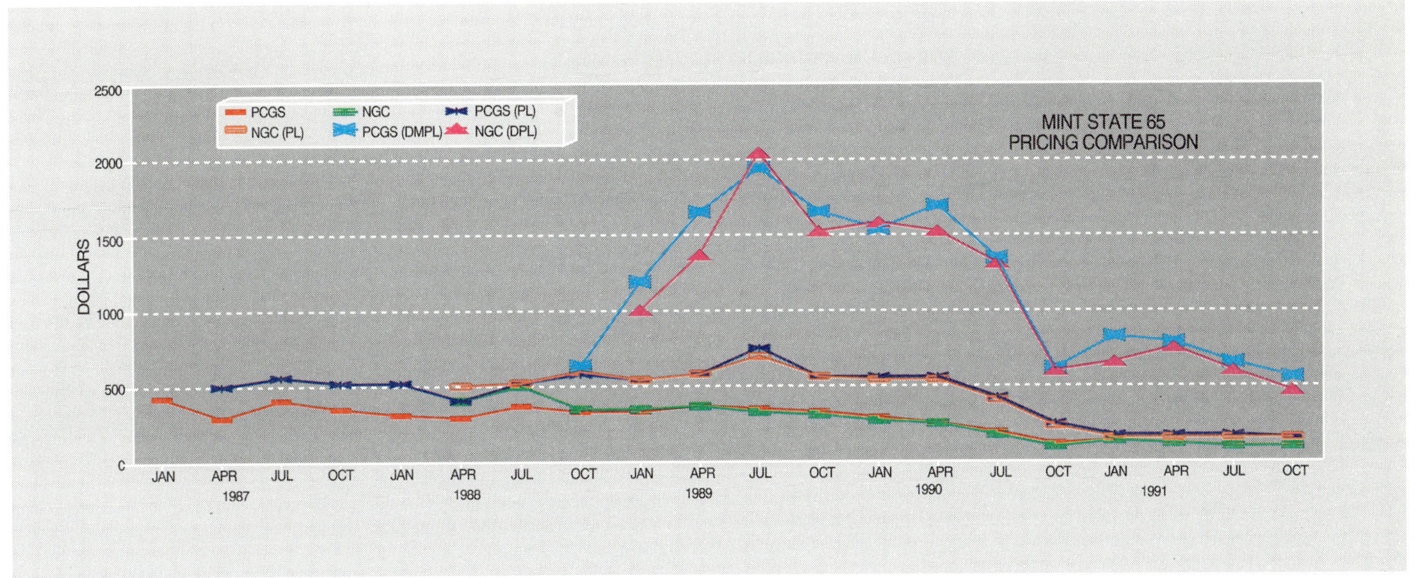

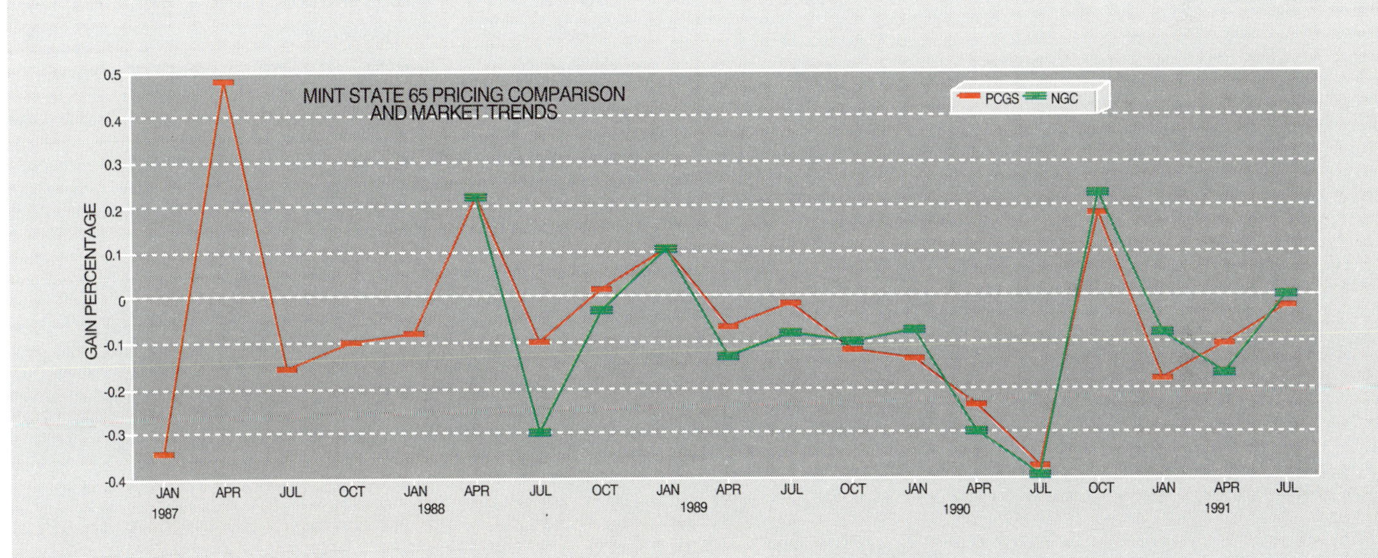

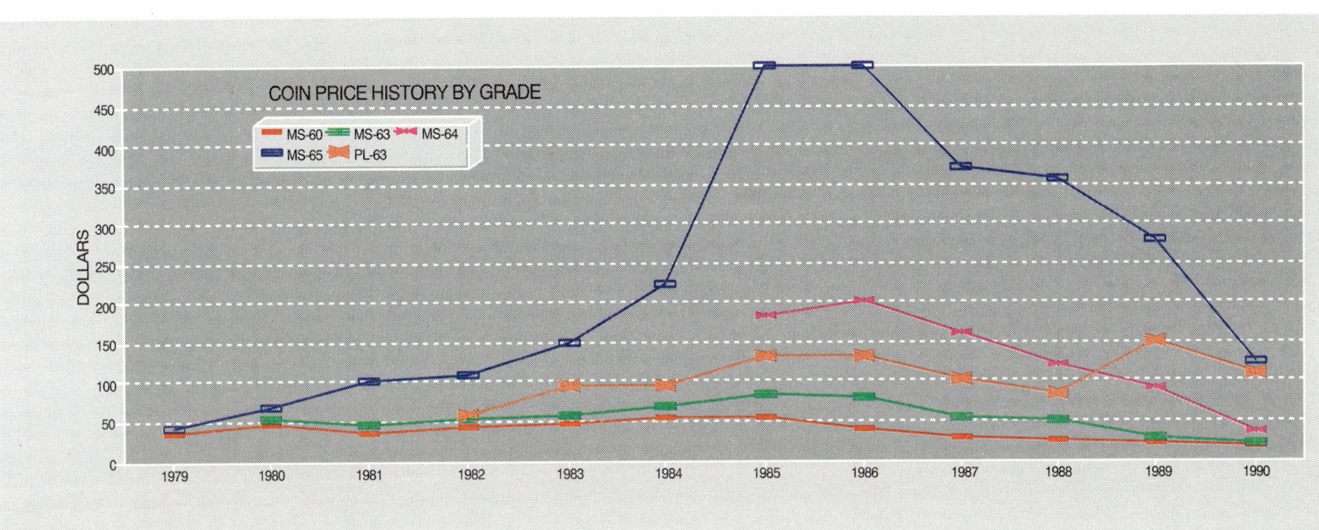

1881-P

PCGS
1881
S$1
MS65
7124.65/7142710

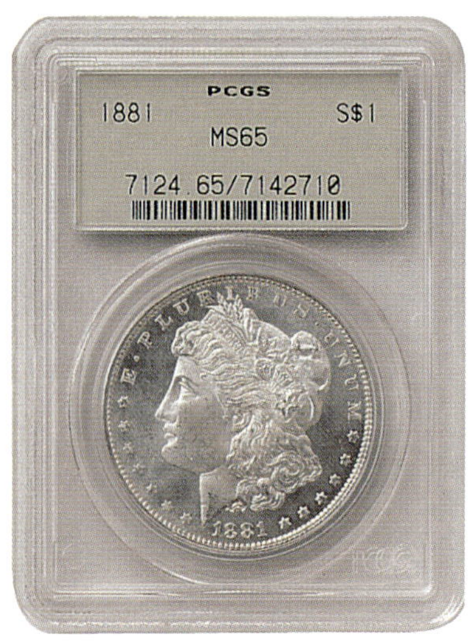

The 9,163,000 struck required 59 obvs., 47 revs. Flat strikes are common, from worn dies.

Available in roll and bag quantities in MS 60/62. Scarce above MS 64.

Proofs: Two pairs of dies for 984 struck. Only one obverse is identified (VAM 8); faintly repunched 18-1, die scratch crossing shaft of final 1; rev. wiggly die scratch (?) overlapping part of leg and wing at observer's right. The other rev. reappeared on 1882 proofs.

Recommended in MS 65 and up or by the roll in MS 63.

Prooflikes: Many one-sided. Very scarce two-sided in PL or DMPL in all grades; either is rare above MS 64.

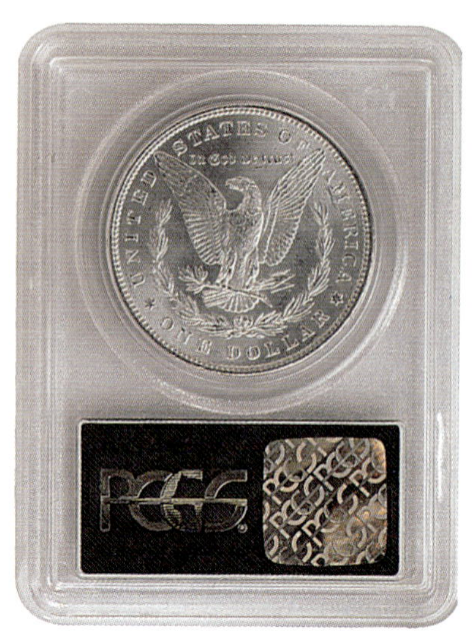

MINTAGE	PROOF	STRIKE	LUSTER	BAG MARKS	REDFIELD
9,163,000	975	Average To Bold	Good	Moderate	No
DIES	**DIE VARIETIES**	**% OF PL**	**% OF DMPL**	**PIVOTAL GRADE**	**RARITY FACTOR**
148	17	3.9	2.4	MS 65	R-4

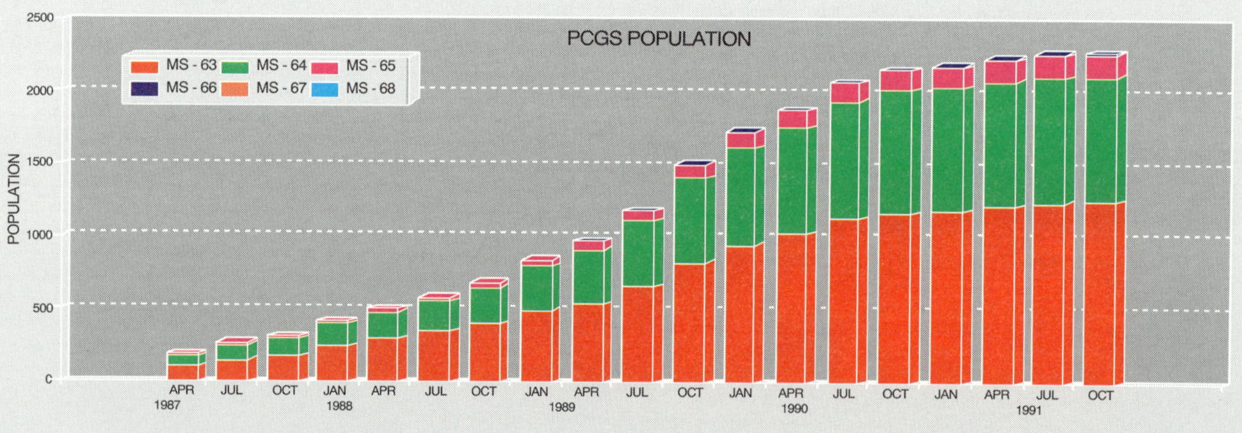
PCGS POPULATION
MS - 63
MS - 64
MS - 65
MS - 66
MS - 67
MS - 68
POPULATION
2500
2000
1500
1000
500
C
APR 1987
JUL
OCT
JAN 1988
APR
JUL
OCT
JAN 1989
APR
JUL
OCT
JAN
APR 1990
JUL
OCT
JAN
APR
JUL 1991
OCT

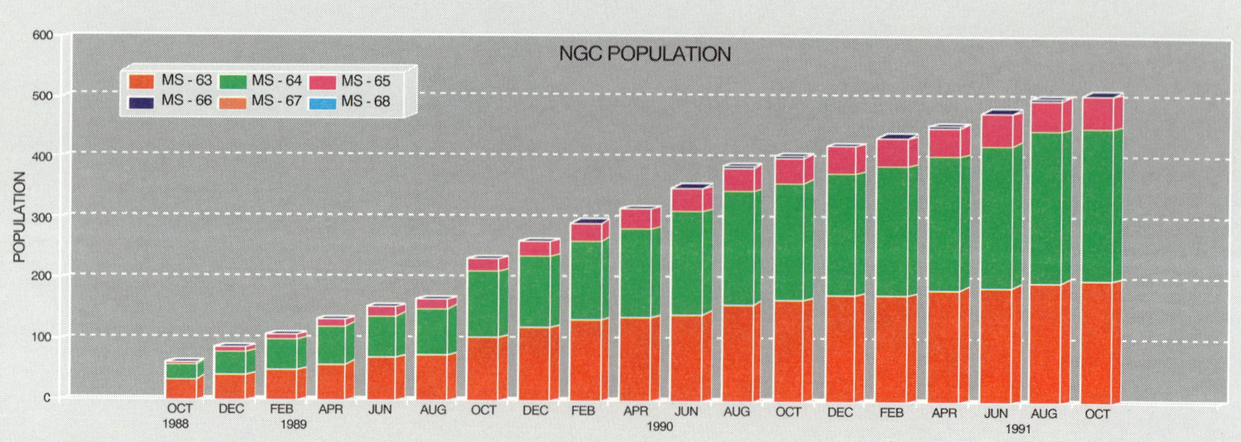
NGC POPULATION
MS - 63
MS - 64
MS - 65
MS - 66
MS - 67
MS - 68
POPULATION
600
500
400
300
200
100
C
OCT 1988
DEC
FEB 1989
APR
JUN
AUG
OCT
DEC
FEB
APR 1990
JUN
AUG
OCT
DEC
FEB
APR
JUN 1991
AUG
OCT

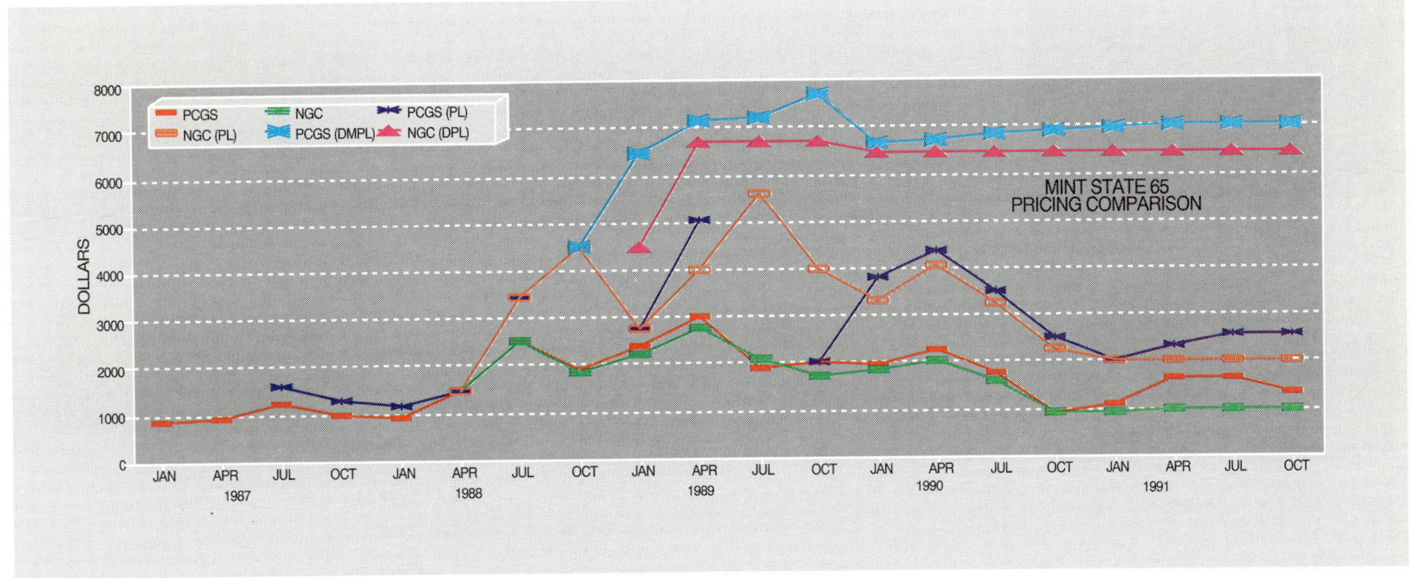
PCGS
NGC
PCGS (PL)
NGC (PL)
PCGS (DMPL)
NGC (DPL)
MINT STATE 65
PRICING COMPARISON
DOLLARS
8000
7000
6000
5000
4000
3000
2000
1000
0
JAN APR JUL OCT JAN APR JUL OCT JAN APR JUL OCT JAN APR JUL OCT JAN APR JUL OCT
1987 1988 1989 1990 1991

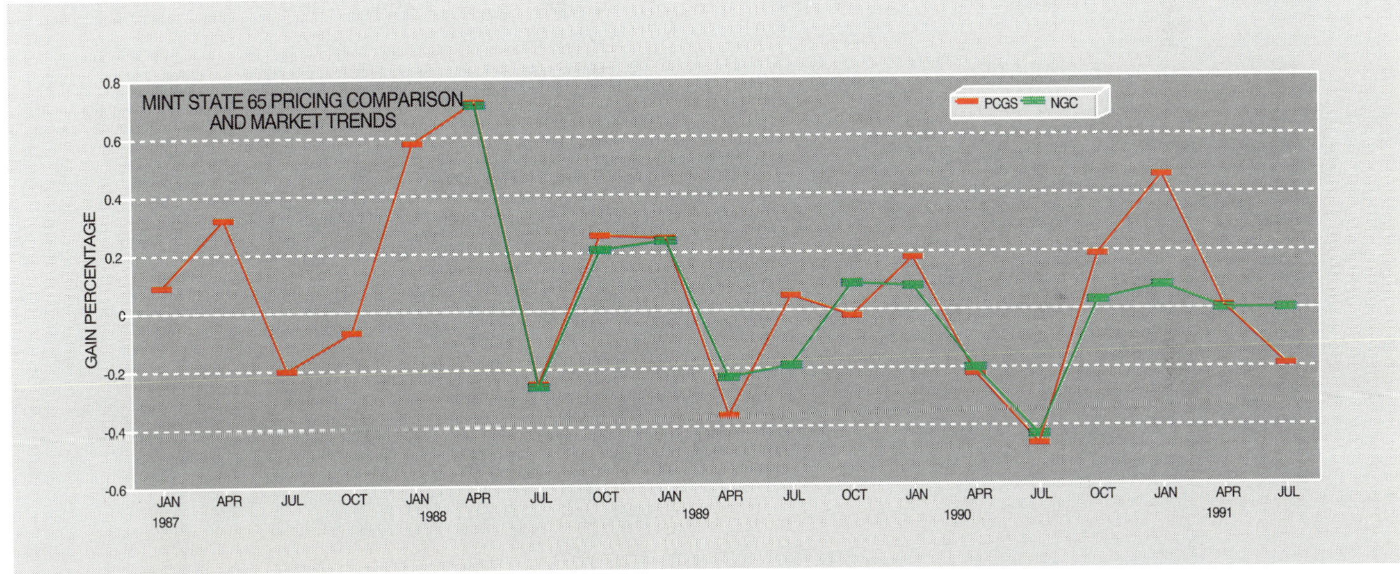
MINT STATE 65 PRICING COMPARISON
AND MARKET TRENDS
PCGS
NGC
GAIN PERCENTAGE
0.8
0.6
0.4
0.2
0
-0.2
-0.4
-0.6
JAN APR JUL OCT JAN APR JUL OCT JAN APR JUL OCT JAN APR JUL OCT JAN APR JUL
1987 1988 1989 1990 1991

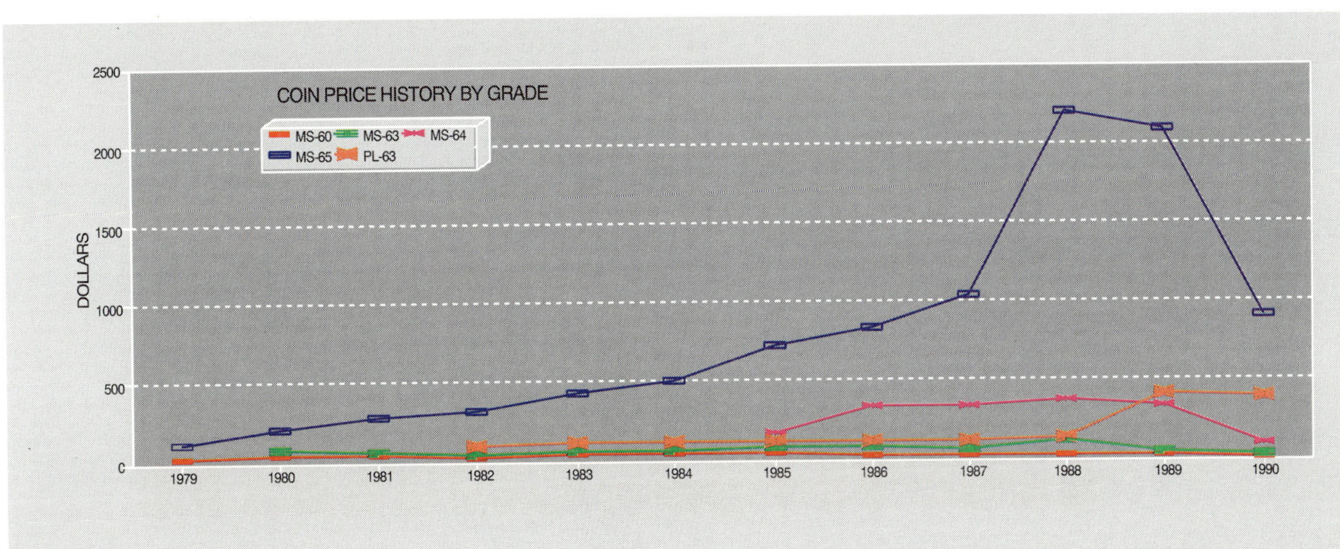
COIN PRICE HISTORY BY GRADE
MS-60
MS-63
MS-64
MS-65
PL-63
DOLLARS
2500
2000
1500
1000
500
0
1979 1980 1981 1982 1983 1984 1985 1986 1987 1988 1989 1990

1881-CC

Not all the 25 pairs of dies shipped to Carson City were used; the 296,000 coined could have been completed with two pairs but probably took 3 or 4. Available in well struck frosty MS 65. These are the role model for the entire CC dollar series. Many came from the 147,485 offered by GSA in mail bid sales 1972-74 (original bid $60). The last 19,020-odd were sold in spring 1980. The GSA holdings were 50% of the total original mintage!

Recommended in MS 65 or higher. By the roll in MS 60/63, also.

Struck only April 1— October 1, 1881. Seldom seen circulated.

Prooflikes: Sometimes hard to find, especially DMPL, particularly above MS 64. There are some awesome cameos.

MINTAGE	PROOF	STRIKE	LUSTER	BAG MARKS	REDFIELD
296,000	0	Sharp & Bold	Excellent	Light	No
DIES	**DIE VARIETIES**	**% OF PL**	**% OF DMPL**	**PIVOTAL GRADE**	**RARITY FACTOR**
50	6	7.0	6.4	MS 66	R-4

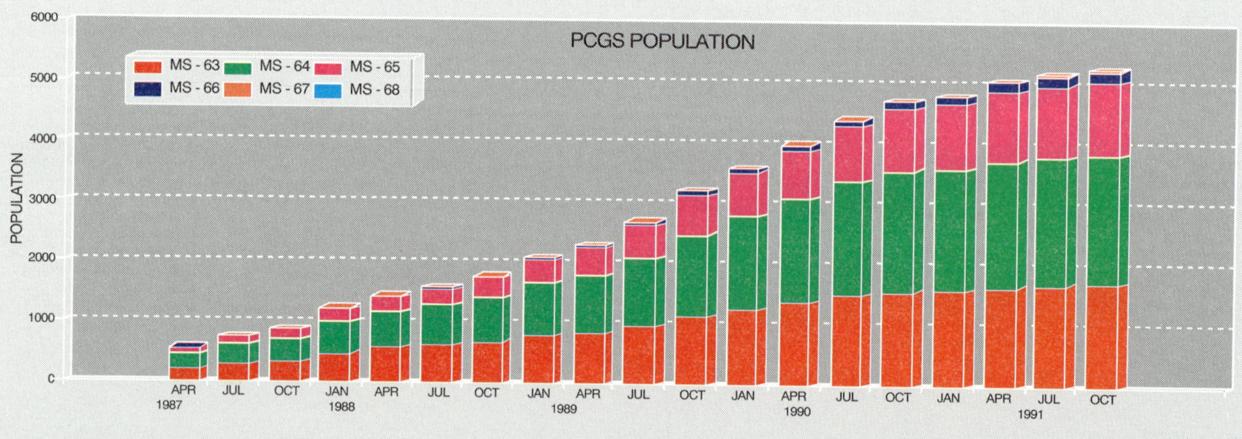

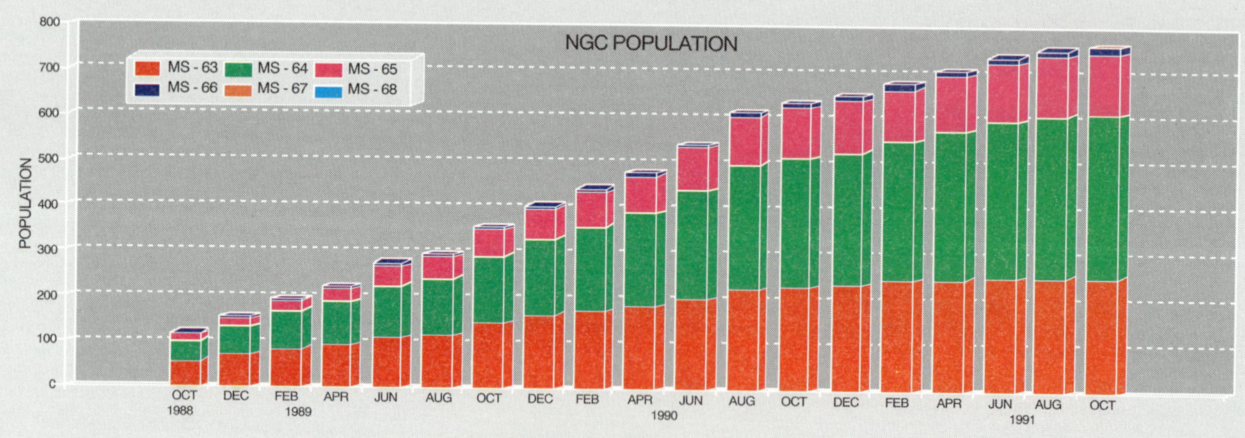

PCGS POPULATION

MS - 63 MS - 64 MS - 65 MS - 66 MS - 67 MS - 68

NGC POPULATION

MS - 63 MS - 64 MS - 65 MS - 66 MS - 67 MS - 68

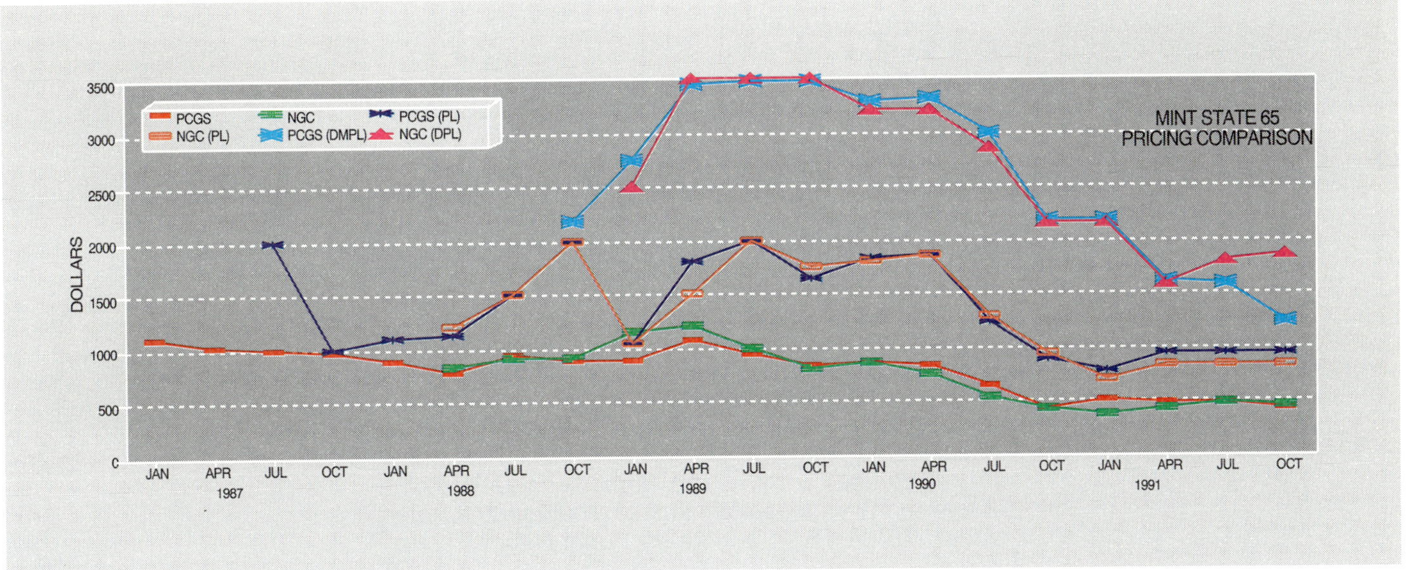
MINT STATE 65
PRICING COMPARISON
PCGS
NGC
PCGS (PL)
NGC (PL)
PCGS (DMPL)
NGC (DPL)
DOLLARS
3500
3000
2500
2000
1500
1000
500
0
JAN APR JUL OCT JAN APR JUL OCT JAN APR JUL OCT JAN APR JUL OCT JAN APR JUL OCT
1987
1988
1989
1990
1991

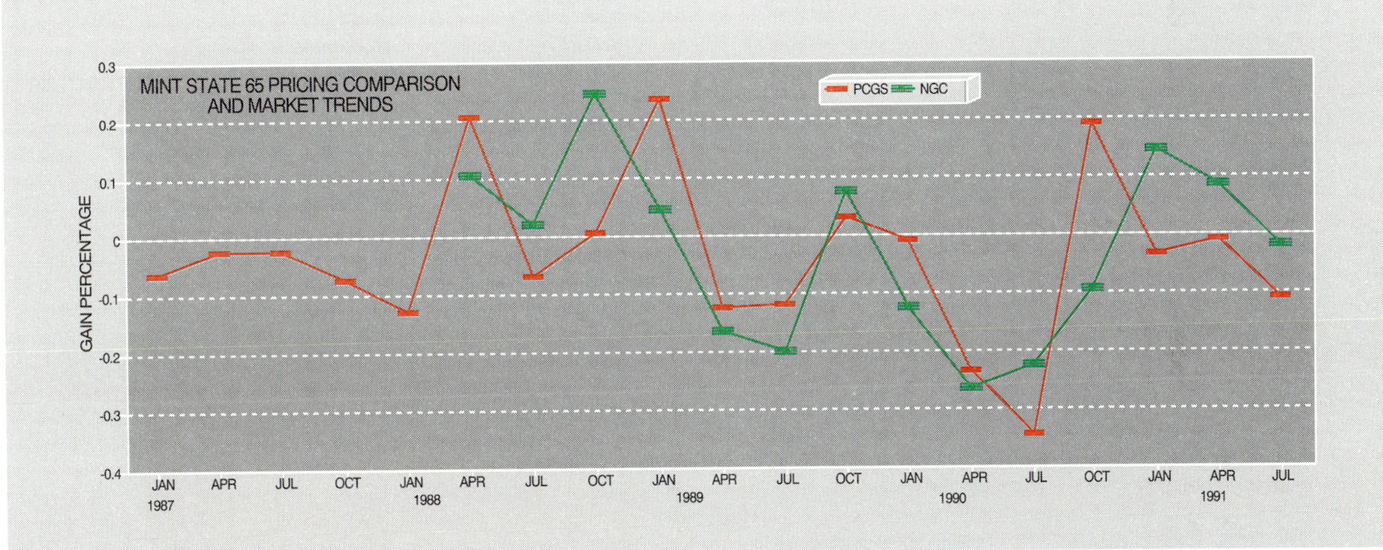
MINT STATE 65 PRICING COMPARISON
AND MARKET TRENDS
PCGS
NGC
GAIN PERCENTAGE
0.3
0.2
0.1
0
-0.1
-0.2
-0.3
-0.4
JAN APR JUL OCT JAN APR JUL OCT JAN APR JUL OCT JAN APR JUL OCT JAN APR JUL
1987
1988
1989
1990
1991

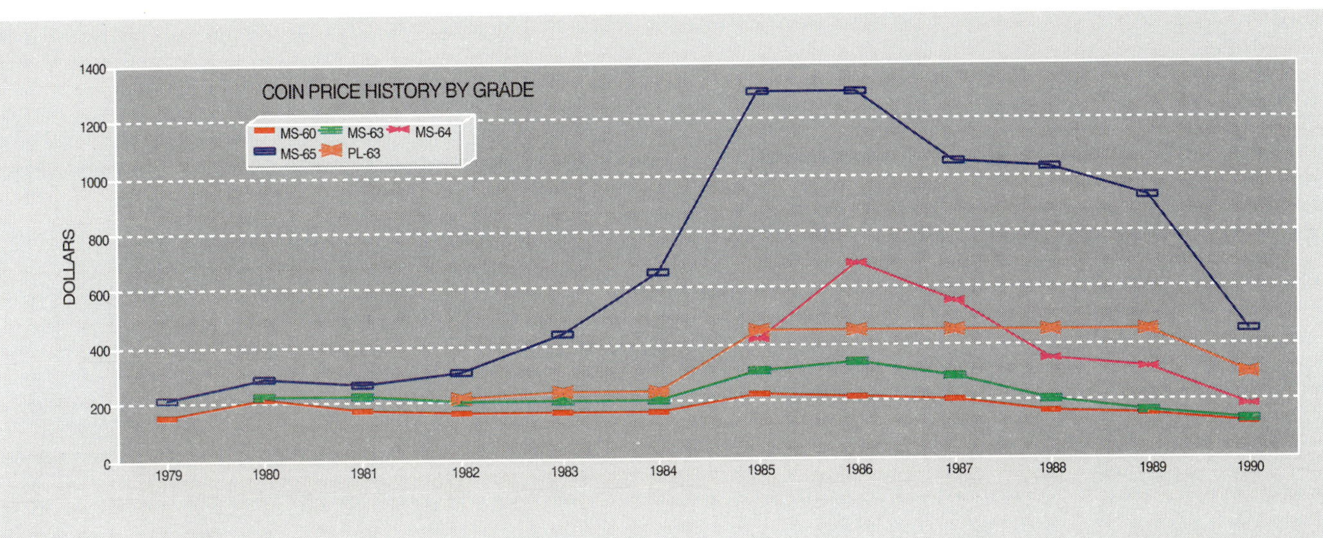
COIN PRICE HISTORY BY GRADE
MS-60
MS-63
MS-64
MS-65
PL-63
DOLLARS
1400
1200
1000
800
600
400
200
0
1979
1980
1981
1982
1983
1984
1985
1986
1987
1988
1989
1990

1881-O

Always with medium O. The 5,708,000 coined took 55 obvs., 40 revs. Some Uncs. are full bold strikes, many are flat, struck from worn dies. Luster is satiny rather than frosty. "Metal flow" is a constant problem.

AU's and sliders are common from resealed mint sacks found in the Continental Bank hoard (see 1879-S prior), and from bags released by the Federal Reserve branch bank at Missoula, MT, 1962-3. Roll lots are available in MS 60/62; those called "original" rolls may contain sliders.

Recommended in MS 65 and up or by the roll in MS 64.

Proofs: One reportedly turned up in 1982; discovered and reported by dealers in Beverly Hills and Dallas.

Prooflikes: Not too scarce one-sided. Two-sided are moderately scarce in all grades, rare above MS 64, DMPL's more so. Light cameos are a minority.

MINTAGE	PROOF	STRIKE	LUSTER	BAG MARKS	REDFIELD
5,708,000	0	Average	Average	Moderate	No
DIES	**DIE VARIETIES**	**% OF PL**	**% OF DMPL**	**PIVOTAL GRADE**	**RARITY FACTOR**
119	29	4.4	3.7	MS 64	R-4

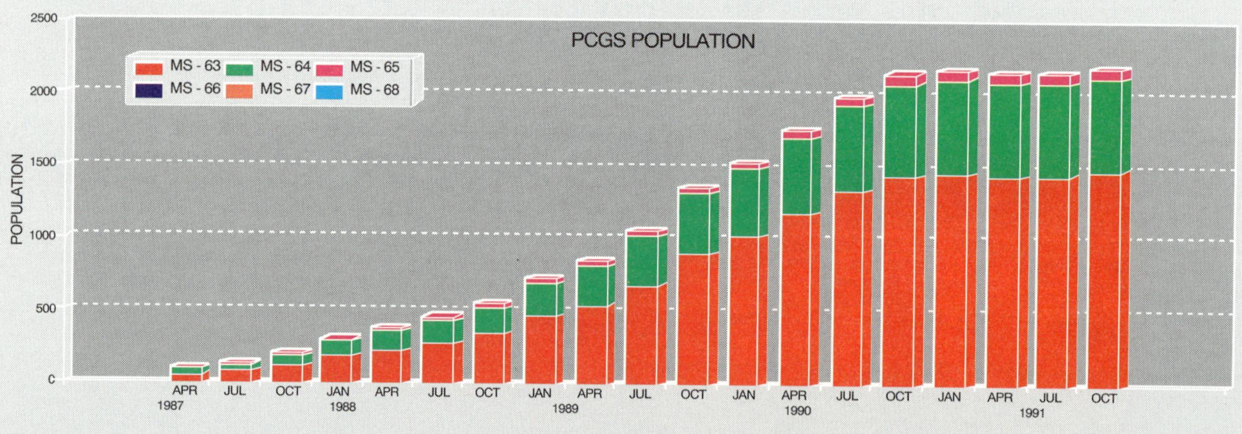

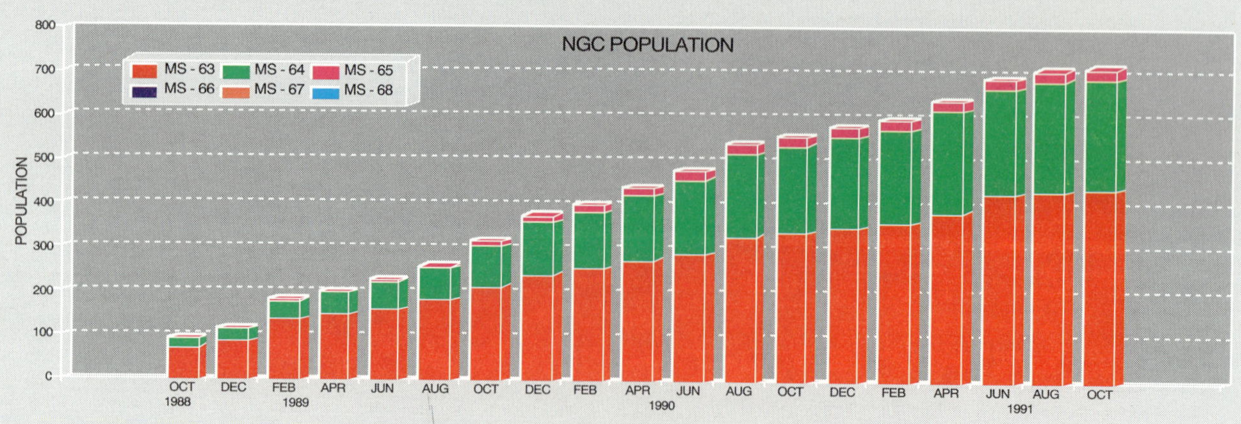

PCGS POPULATION

NGC POPULATION

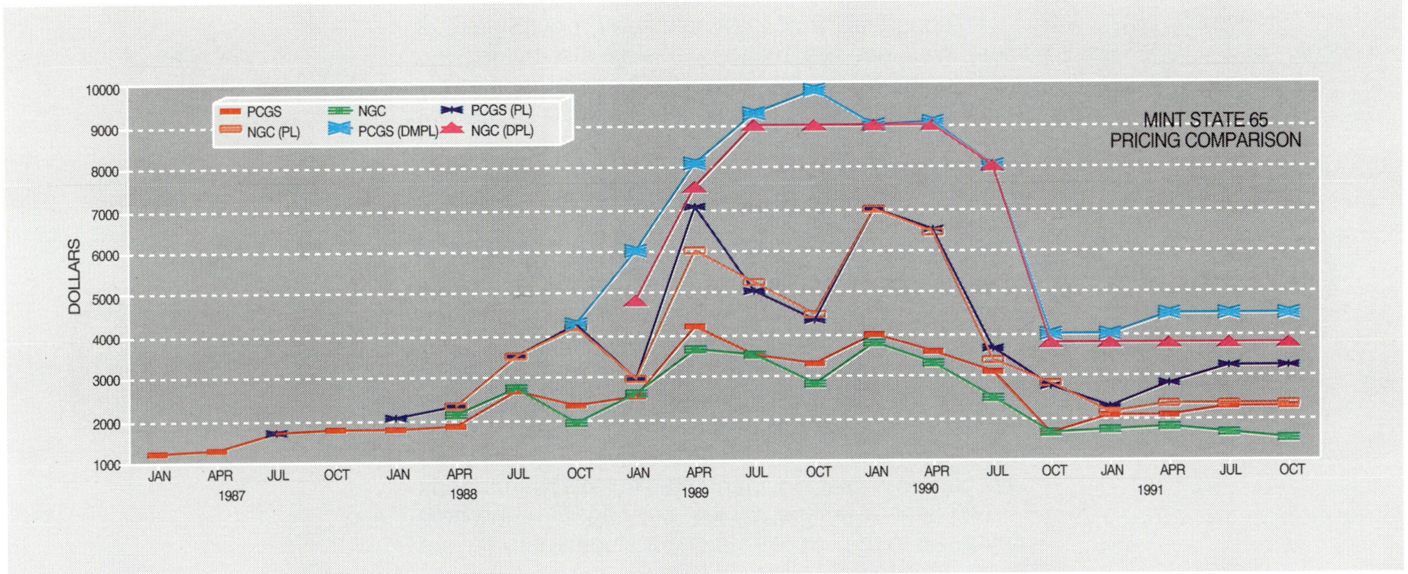

MINT STATE 65
PRICING COMPARISON
PCGS
NGC
PCGS (PL)
NGC (PL)
PCGS (DMPL)
NGC (DPL)
DOLLARS
10000
9000
8000
7000
6000
5000
4000
3000
2000
1000
JAN APR JUL OCT JAN APR JUL OCT JAN APR JUL OCT JAN APR JUL OCT JAN APR JUL OCT
1987
1988
1989
1990
1991

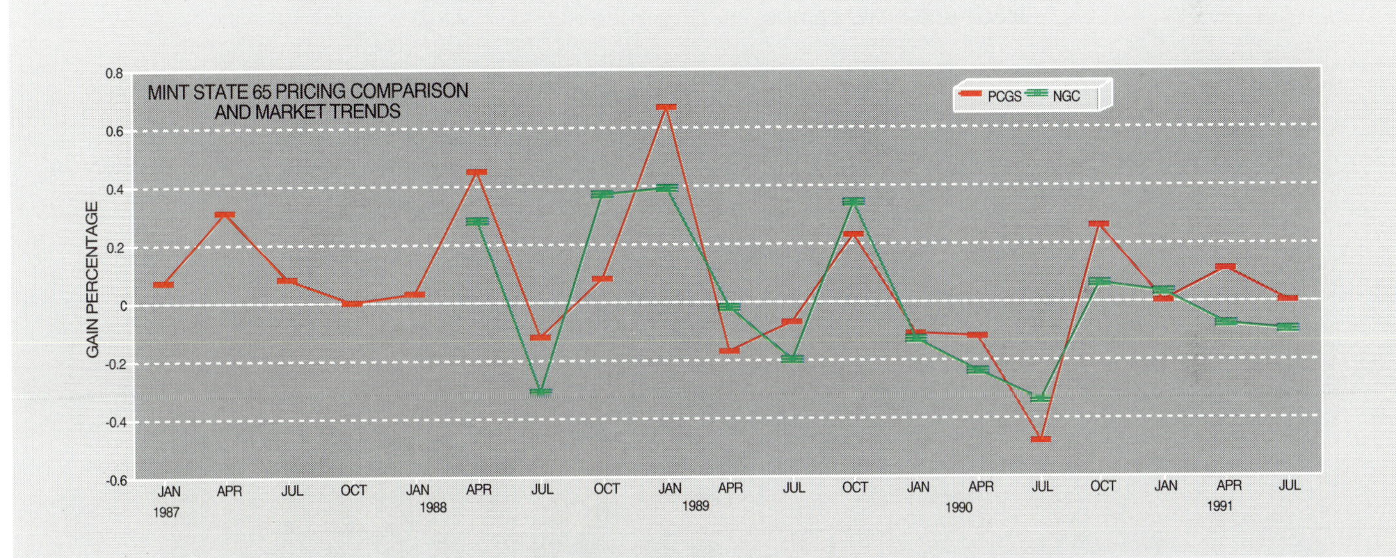

MINT STATE 65 PRICING COMPARISON
AND MARKET TRENDS
PCGS
NGC
GAIN PERCENTAGE
0.8
0.6
0.4
0.2
0
-0.2
-0.4
-0.6
JAN APR JUL OCT JAN APR JUL OCT JAN APR JUL OCT JAN APR JUL OCT JAN APR JUL
1987
1988
1989
1990
1991

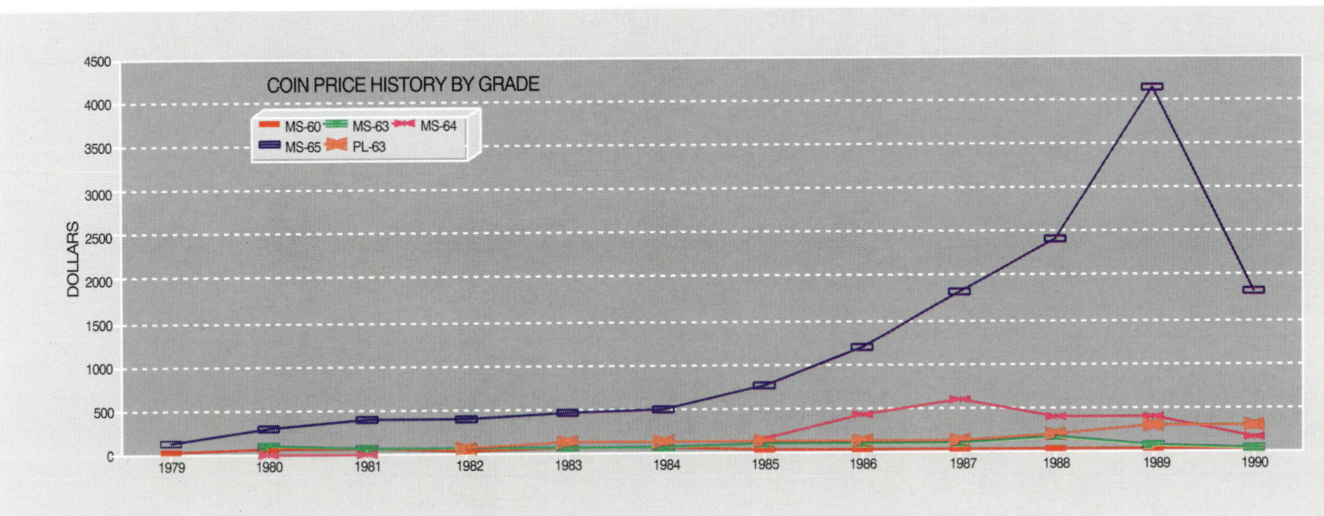

COIN PRICE HISTORY BY GRADE
MS-60
MS-63
MS-64
MS-65
PL-63
DOLLARS
4500
4000
3500
3000
2500
2000
1500
1000
500
0
1979 1980 1981 1982 1983 1984 1985 1986 1987 1988 1989 1990

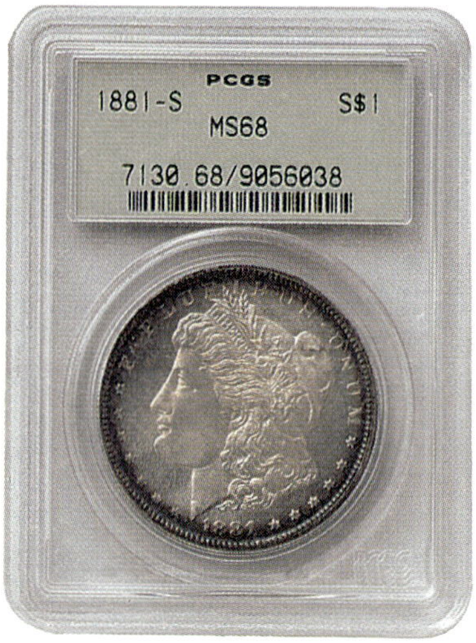

1881-S

Though its 12,760,000 mintage (from 85 pairs of dies) was not the highest, this is still by far the commonest S Mint Morgan, and the date most easily found in the highest quality. Available in all grades through PCGS MS 69. Recommended in the high end of MS not as investments but as things of beauty. This author (Highfill) has sold PCGS MS 65 1881-S dollars in bag quantity lots.

Plentiful from bags found in Treasury, Redfield (commonest of all Redfield coins), and Continental Bank hoards. Many of the Treasury bags contained PL's. John Ford told at an ANA Convention how New Netherlands bought 126 bags of this date alone (among thousands of others, 1962-64) from Harry Forman. Because, as junior partner, Ford had to carry the bags many blocks from wherever Forman's car was parked in midtown Manhattan to New Netherlands — two bags at a time, 60 lbs. per bag, then the next day down to the Express truck for shipment to buyers — he grew to hate silver dollars.

Prooflikes: Plentiful in all grades PL; more so one-sided. Notably scarcer in DMPL or complete black-and-white cameo.

MINTAGE	PROOF	STRIKE	LUSTER	BAG MARKS	REDFIELD
12,760,000	0	Very Sharp	Excellent	Light	Yes
DIES	**DIE VARIETIES**	**% OF PL**	**% OF DMPL**	**PIVOTAL GRADE**	**RARITY FACTOR**
200	53	6.5	1.0	MS 66	R-5

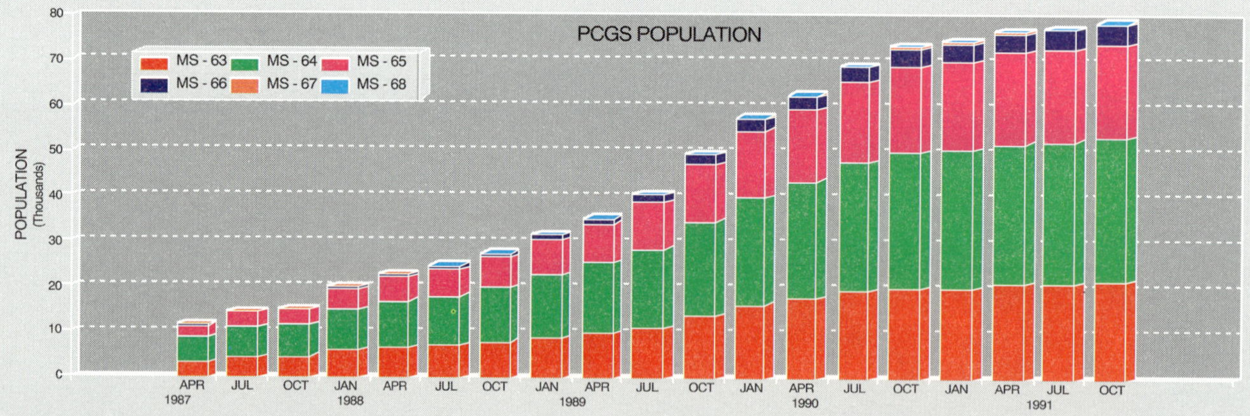

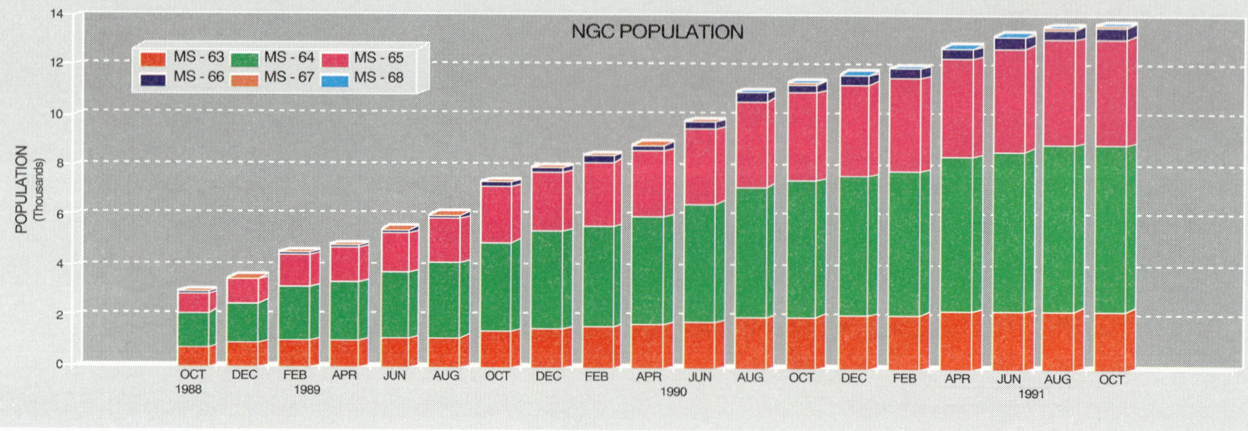

PCGS POPULATION

MS - 63, MS - 64, MS - 65, MS - 66, MS - 67, MS - 68

POPULATION (Thousands)

APR 1987, JUL, OCT, JAN 1988, APR, JUL, OCT, JAN 1989, APR, JUL, OCT, JAN, APR 1990, JUL, OCT, JAN, APR, JUL 1991, OCT

NGC POPULATION

MS - 63, MS - 64, MS - 65, MS - 66, MS - 67, MS - 68

POPULATION (Thousands)

OCT 1988, DEC, FEB 1989, APR, JUN, AUG, OCT, DEC, FEB, APR 1990, JUN, AUG, OCT, DEC, FEB, APR, JUN 1991, AUG, OCT

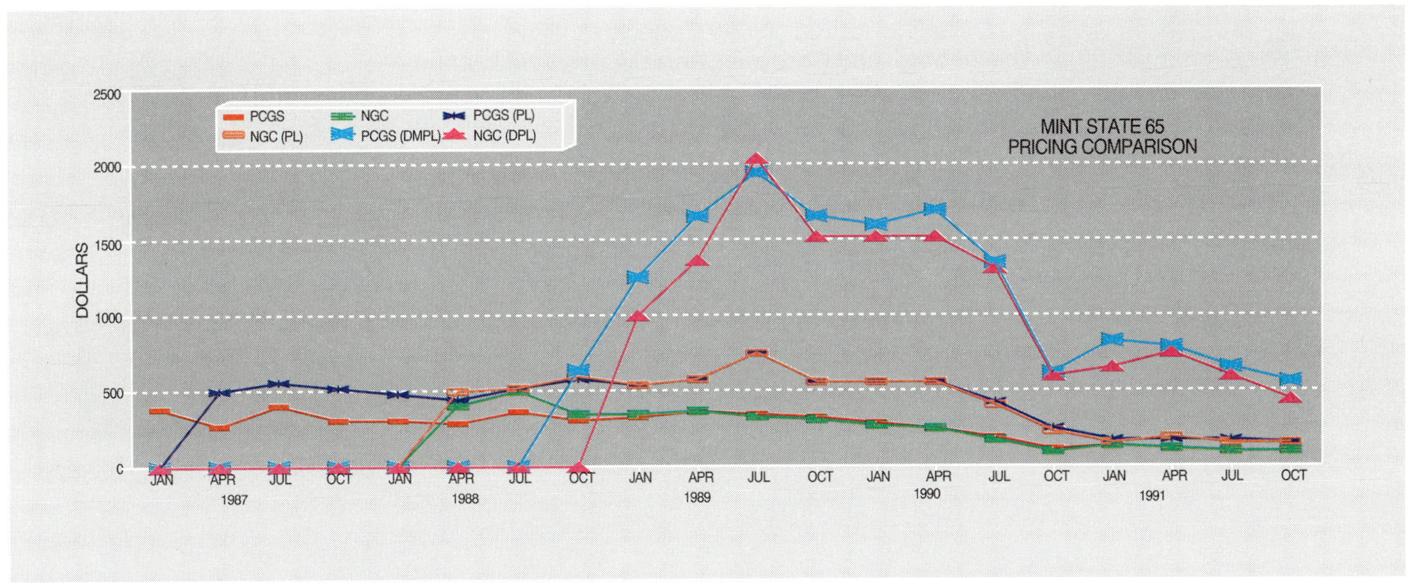
MINT STATE 65
PRICING COMPARISON
PCGS
NGC
PCGS (PL)
NGC (PL)
PCGS (DMPL)
NGC (DPL)
DOLLARS
2500
2000
1500
1000
500
0
JAN APR JUL OCT JAN APR JUL OCT JAN APR JUL OCT JAN APR JUL OCT JAN APR JUL OCT
1987 1988 1989 1990 1991

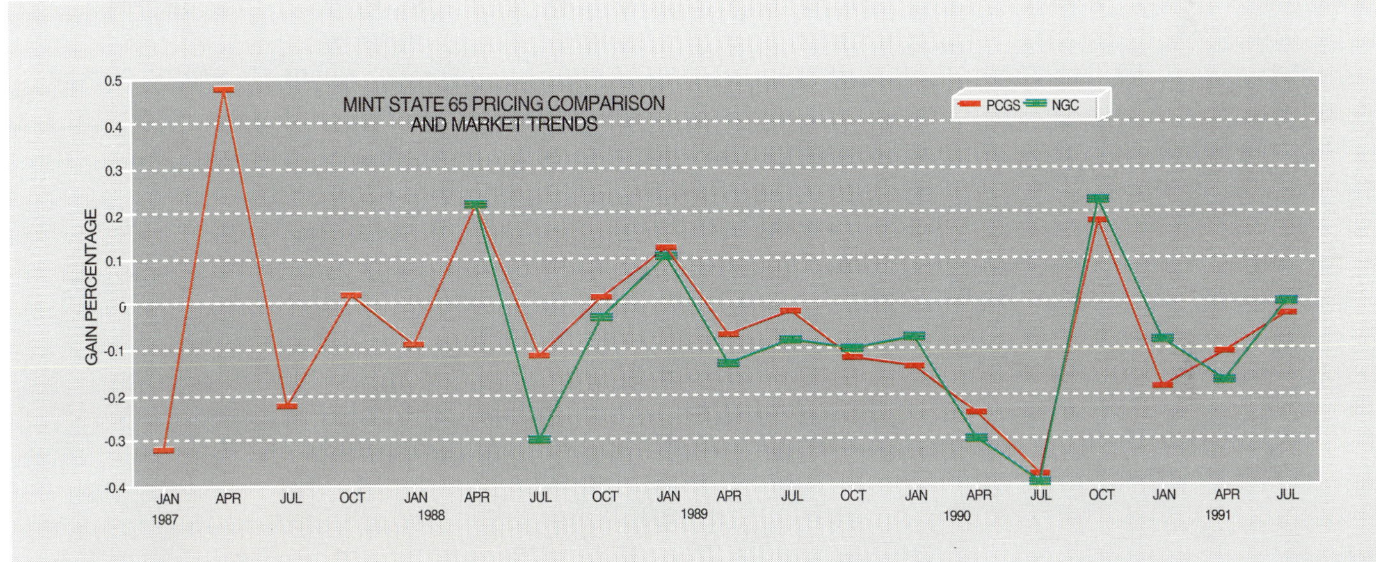
MINT STATE 65 PRICING COMPARISON
AND MARKET TRENDS
PCGS NGC
GAIN PERCENTAGE
0.5
0.4
0.3
0.2
0.1
0
-0.1
-0.2
-0.3
-0.4
JAN APR JUL OCT JAN APR JUL OCT JAN APR JUL OCT JAN APR JUL OCT JAN APR JUL
1987 1988 1989 1990 1991

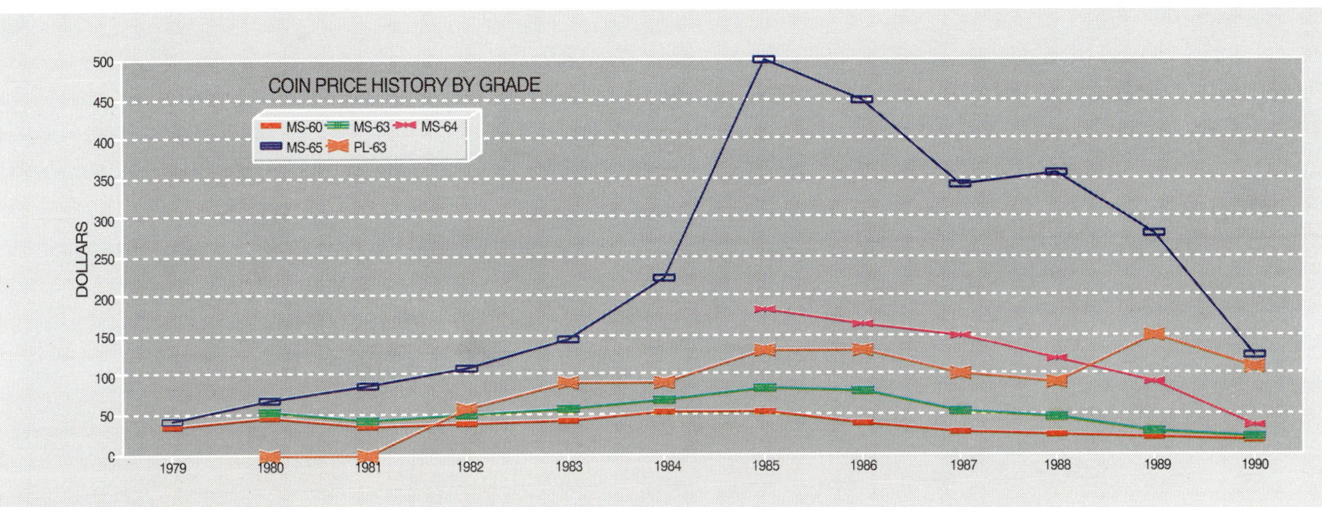
COIN PRICE HISTORY BY GRADE
MS-60
MS-63
MS-64
MS-65
PL-63
DOLLARS
500
450
400
350
300
250
200
150
100
50
0
1979 1980 1981 1982 1983 1984 1985 1986 1987 1988 1989 1990

PCGS
1882
S$1
MS65
7132.65/6165030

1882-P

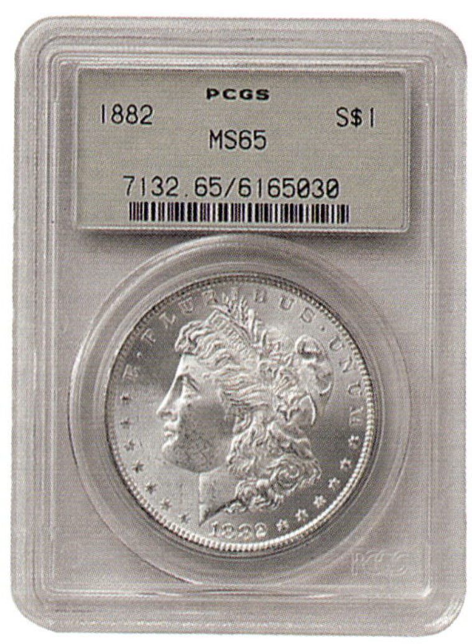

The 11,100,000 coined probably required most of the 58 obvs. and 60 revs. Generally well struck, often frosty. Many flat uncs. survive from worn dies. Die cracks are common for this issue. Bag quantities in MS 60/62 are available.

Recommended in MS 65 but may be hard to find at that level. Also by the roll in MS 64.

Proofs: At least 1,101 struck; two pairs of dies, the majority VAM 10, with repunching on 82, hollow in hair from die polish around Morgan's initial M.

Prooflikes: Cameos are rare, as are any PL's or DMPL's in MS 65 or better.

PCGS

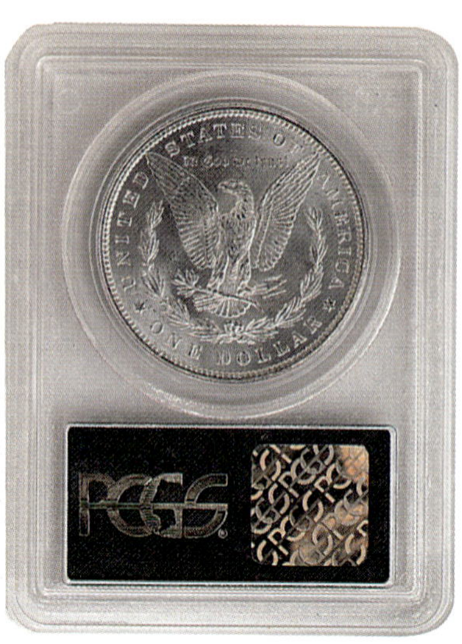

MINTAGE	PROOF	STRIKE	LUSTER	BAG MARKS	REDFIELD
11,100,000	1,100	Average	Good	Moderate	No
DIES	**DIE VARIETIES**	**% OF PL**	**% OF DMPL**	**PIVOTAL GRADE**	**RARITY FACTOR**
92	23	3.3	2.4	MS 65	R-3

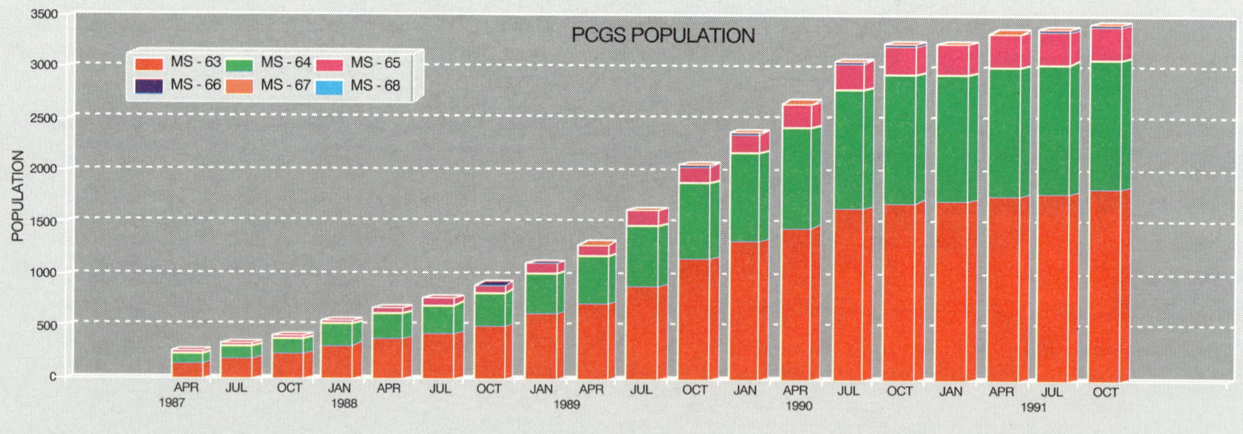
PCGS POPULATION
MS - 63
MS - 64
MS - 65
MS - 66
MS - 67
MS - 68
POPULATION
3500
3000
2500
2000
1500
1000
500
0
APR 1987
JUL
OCT
JAN 1988
APR
JUL
OCT
JAN 1989
APR
JUL
OCT
JAN
APR 1990
JUL
OCT
JAN
APR
JUL 1991
OCT

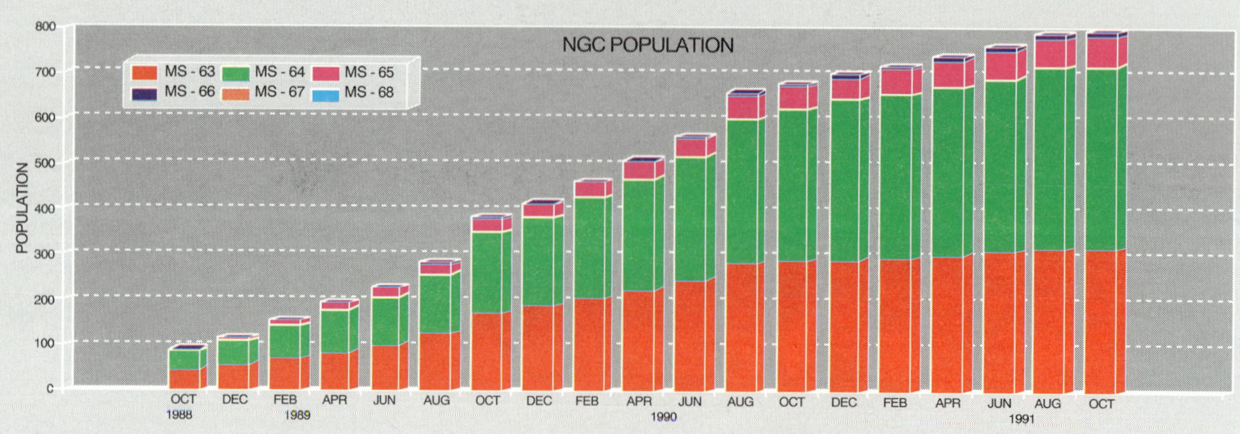
NGC POPULATION
MS - 63
MS - 64
MS - 65
MS - 66
MS - 67
MS - 68
POPULATION
800
700
600
500
400
300
200
100
0
OCT 1988
DEC
FEB 1989
APR
JUN
AUG
OCT
DEC
FEB
APR 1990
JUN
AUG
OCT
DEC
FEB
APR
JUN
AUG 1991
OCT

1882-P

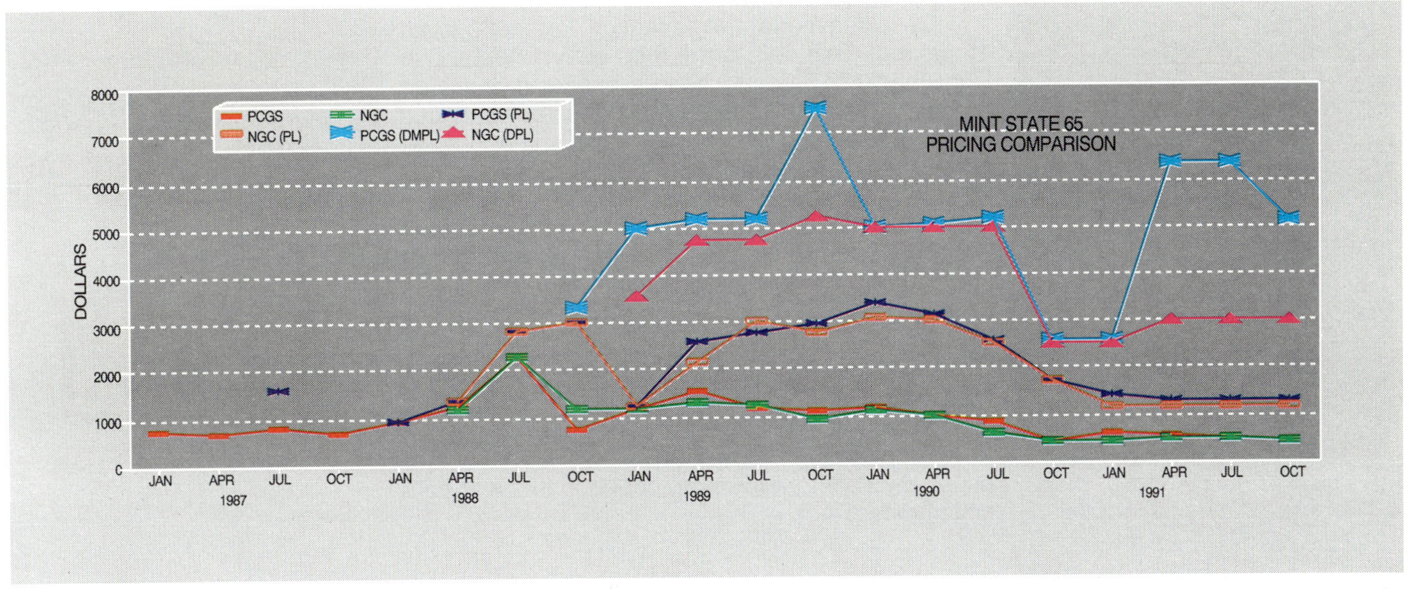

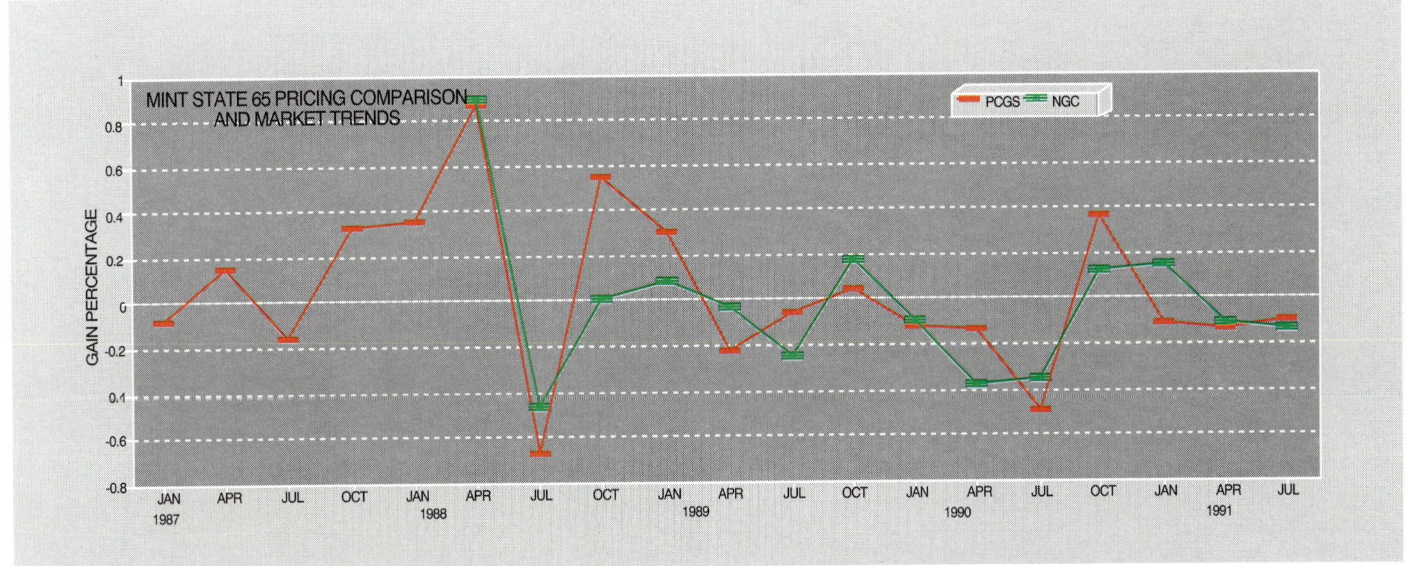

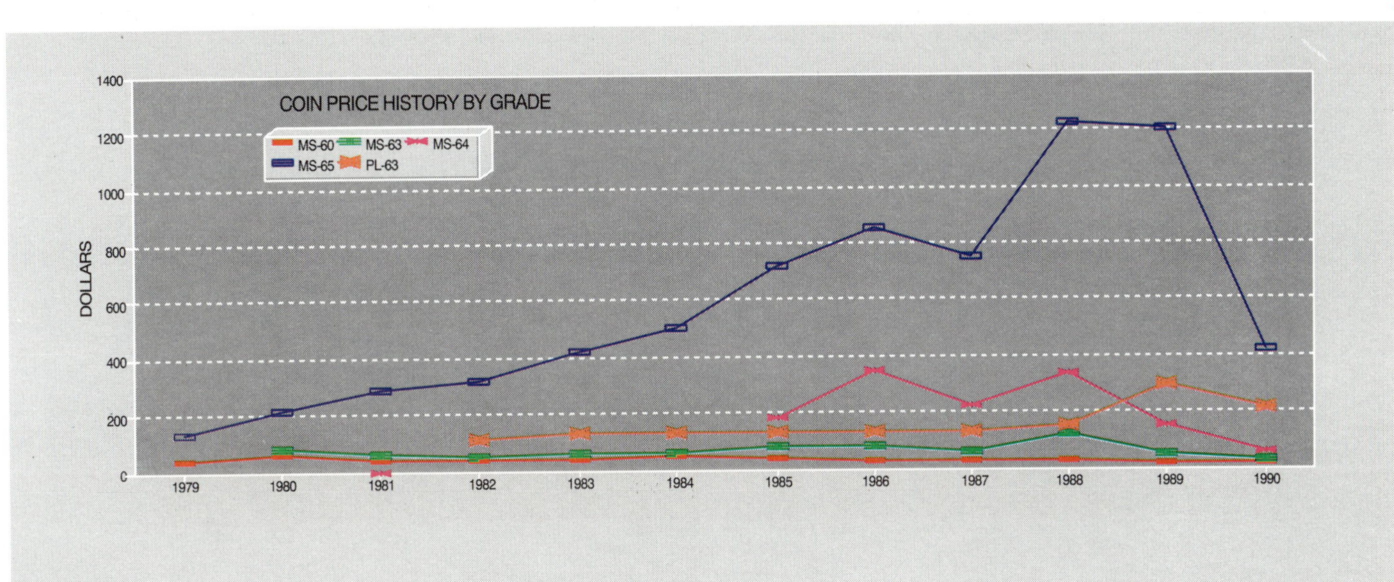

1882-CC

Despite a moderate mintage of 1,133,000 (from 15 pairs of dies), this is the third commonest CC in Unc., thanks to Treasury hoards; scarce in circulated grades. The 1972/74 GSA mail bid sales contained 605,029; minimum bid $30 per coin, limit of 5 coins per bidder. That's over "HALF" the original mintage! All were sold at $32 per coin, despite some higher bids. Most are well struck, lustrous, and bagmarked. Some circulated, 216,116 in all, at minimum bid of $15 each. The majority were in fact varying qualities of Mint State. Roll lots of MS 60/62 are still sometimes available.

Recommended in MS 65 up and by the roll in MS 60/63.

Proofs: One reported, not verified.

Prooflikes: Rare above MS 65, PL and especially DMPL. However, common in lower mint state grades.

MINTAGE	PROOF	STRIKE	LUSTER	BAG MARKS	REDFIELD
1,133,000	0	Bold	Good	Moderate To Heavy	No
DIES	**DIE VARIETIES**	**% OF PL**	**% OF DMPL**	**PIVOTAL GRADE**	**RARITY FACTOR**
30	6	9.8	8.0	MS 65	R-4

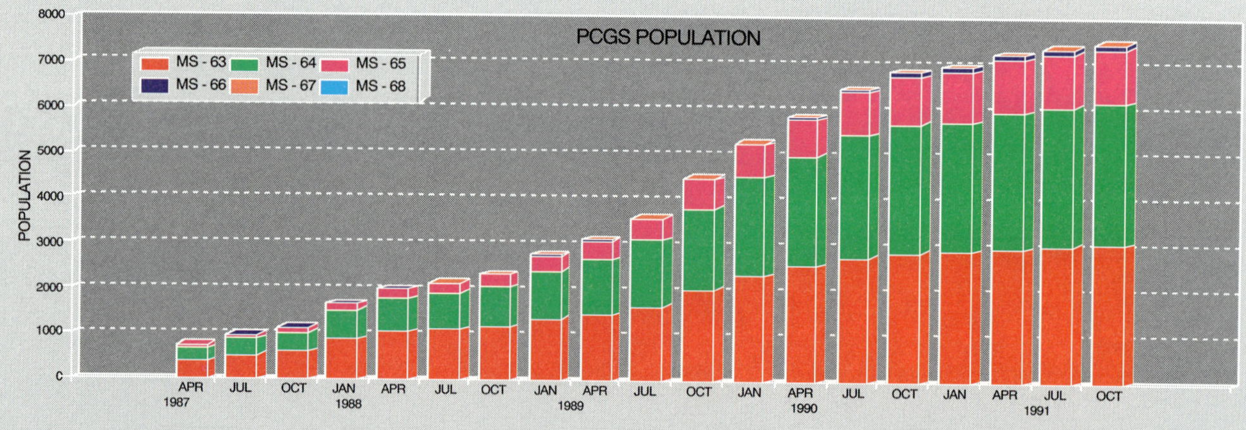

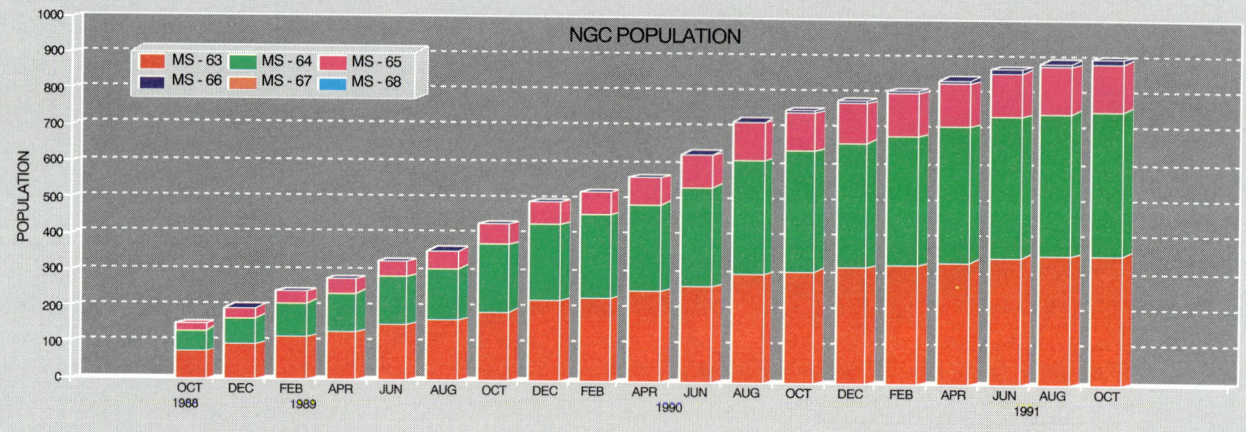

PCGS POPULATION

MS - 63 MS - 64 MS - 65 MS - 66 MS - 67 MS - 68

POPULATION: 0, 1000, 2000, 3000, 4000, 5000, 6000, 7000, 8000

APR 1987, JUL, OCT, JAN 1988, APR, JUL, OCT, JAN 1989, APR, JUL, OCT, JAN 1990, APR, JUL, OCT, JAN 1991, APR, JUL, OCT

NGC POPULATION

MS - 63 MS - 64 MS - 65 MS - 66 MS - 67 MS - 68

POPULATION: 0, 100, 200, 300, 400, 500, 600, 700, 800, 900, 1000

OCT 1988, DEC, FEB 1989, APR, JUN, AUG, OCT, DEC, FEB 1990, APR, JUN, AUG, OCT, DEC, FEB 1991, APR, JUN, AUG, OCT

1882-CC

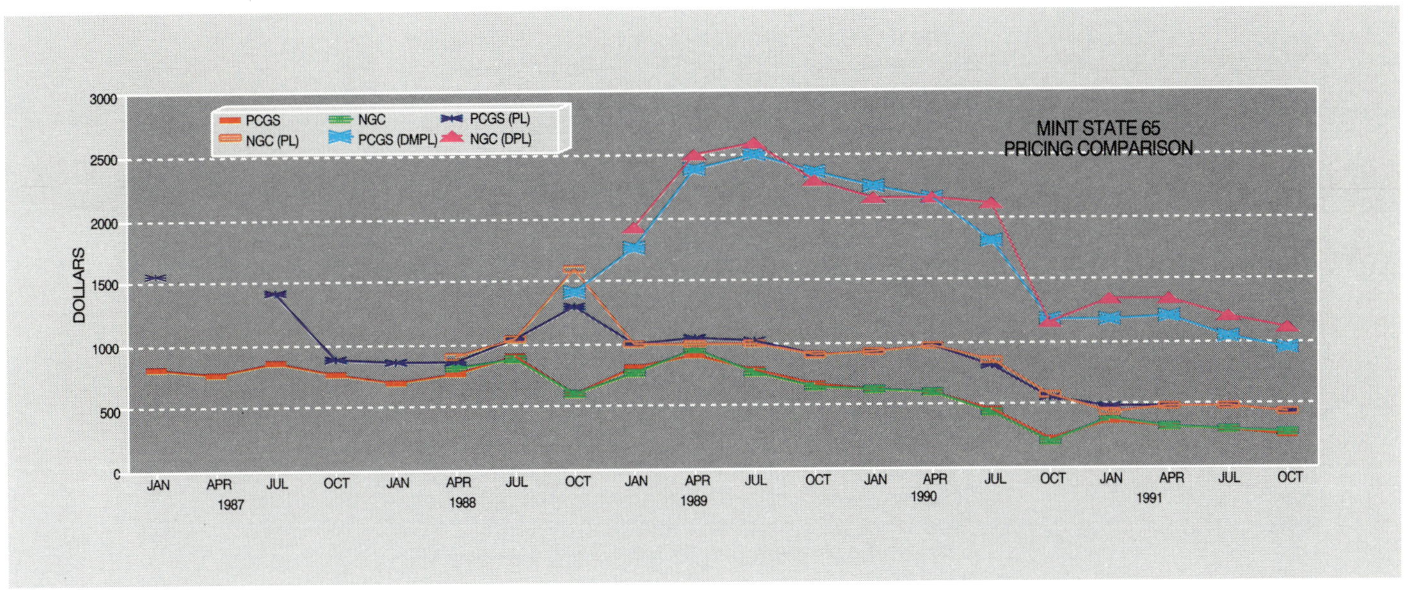

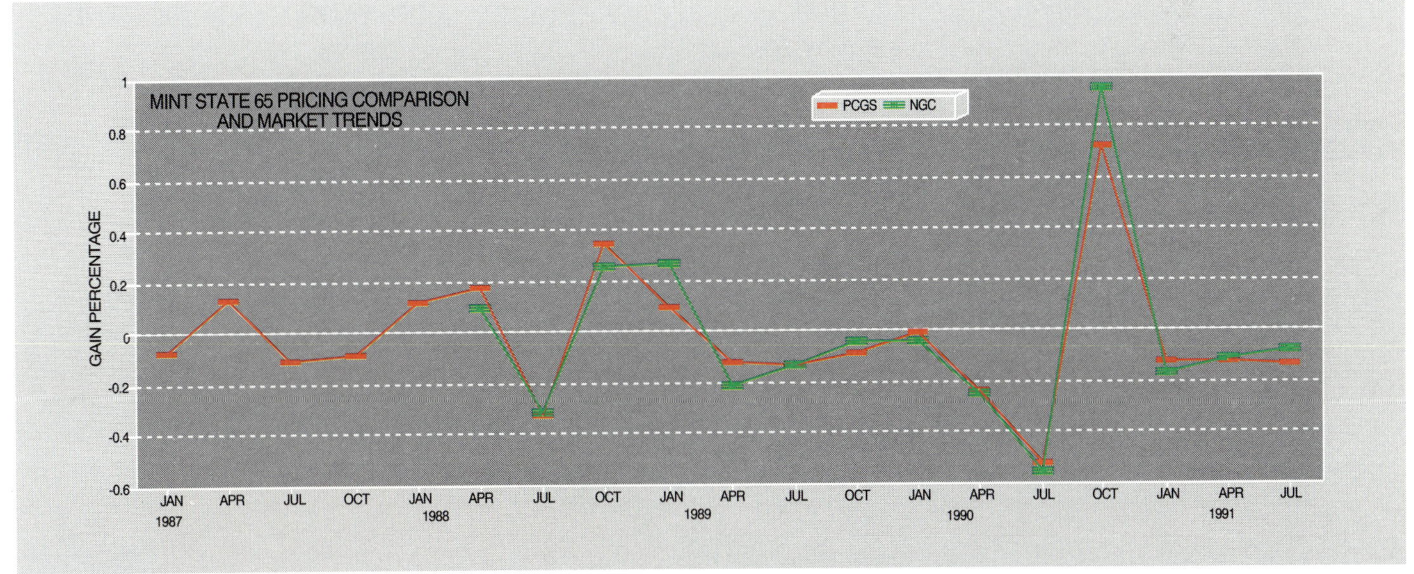

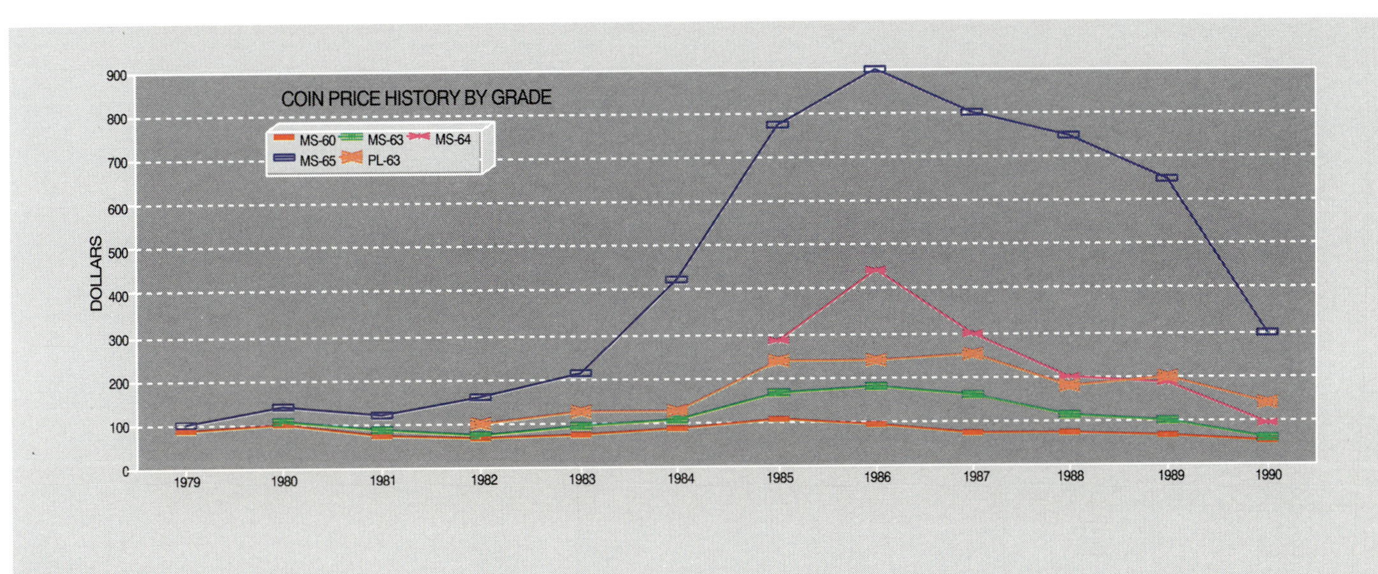

PCGS
1882-O
S$1
MS68
7136.68/4037153

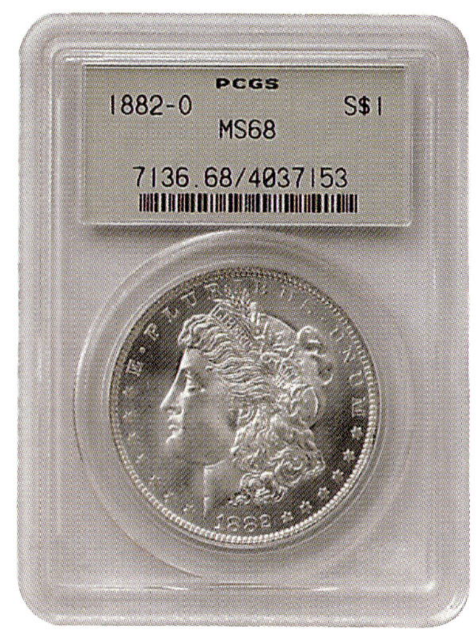

1882-O

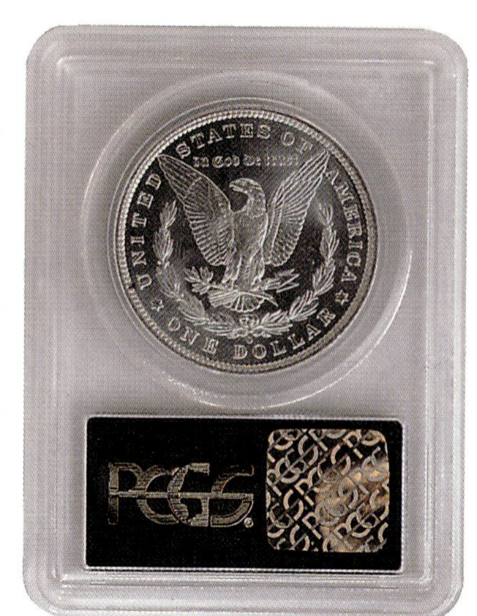

The 6,090,000 probably took most of the 33 pairs of dies made. Common in slider grade from resealed mint sacks (ca. 1882). Many such sliders were in the Continental Bank hoard. Leon Hendrickson, Ed Milas, Dr. George W. Vogt and Clark Samuelson will all attest to these findings. This practice recurred at New Orleans in 1887 and 1897, and in San Francisco in 1885.

Very scarce in MS 65 up, rare in MS 66 up. Fully struck, frosty and/or brilliant specimens may show light rubbing.

Beware of alleged original BU bags: look before buying. The same remark holds for rolls described as MS 60/62. All these may contain sliders.

Recommended in MS 64 or better.

Repunched mintmark ("O/O") is uncommon but has stimulated less collector interest than it deserves. But see 1882 O/S (next date analysis)

Prooflikes: Scarce in all grades, rare above MS 64, PL or DMPL.

MINTAGE	PROOF	STRIKE	LUSTER	BAG MARKS	REDFIELD
6,090,000*	0	Soft To Average	Dull	Moderate	No
DIES	**DIE VARIETIES**	**% OF PL**	**% OF DMPL**	**PIVOTAL GRADE**	**RARITY FACTOR**
50**	37	4.6	3.5	MS 64	R-4

*Includes estimated 6,080,000 1882-O and estimated 10,000 1882-O/S **Includes all dies used at the New Orleans Mint - FY 1882

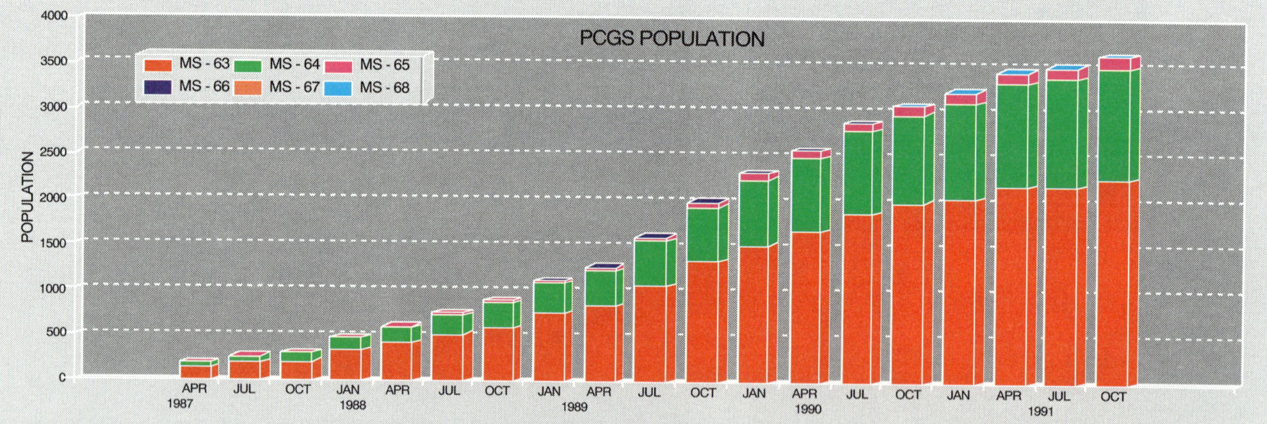
PCGS POPULATION
MS - 63
MS - 64
MS - 65
MS - 66
MS - 67
MS - 68
POPULATION
4000
3500
3000
2500
2000
1500
1000
500
0
APR 1987
JUL
OCT
JAN 1988
APR
JUL
OCT
JAN 1989
APR
JUL
OCT
JAN
APR 1990
JUL
OCT
JAN
APR
JUL 1991
OCT

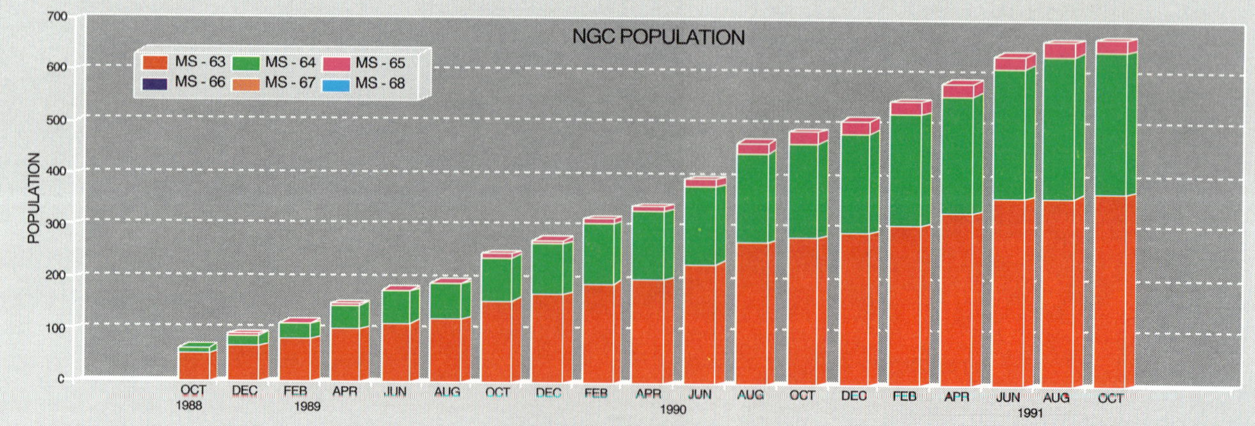
NGC POPULATION
MS - 63
MS - 64
MS - 65
MS - 66
MS - 67
MS - 68
POPULATION
700
600
500
400
300
200
100
0
OCT 1988
DEC
FEB 1989
APR
JUN
AUG
OCT
DEC
FEB
APR 1990
JUN
AUG
OCT
DEC
FEB
APR
JUN
AUG 1991
OCT

1882-O

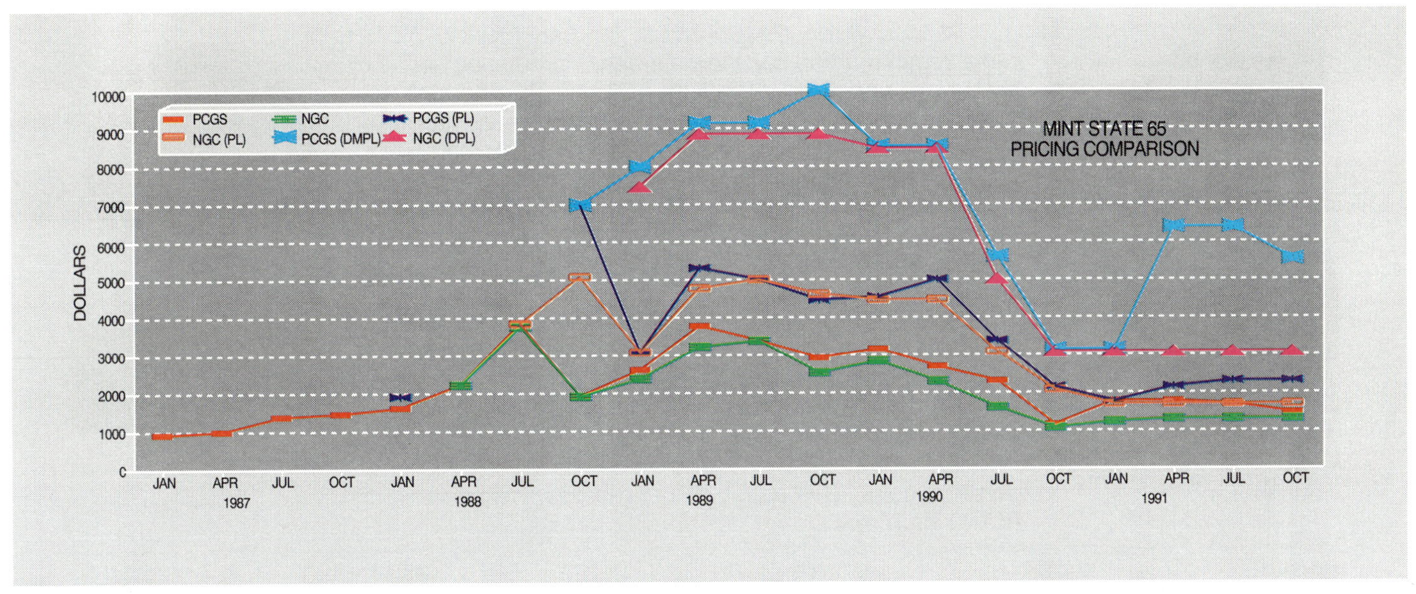

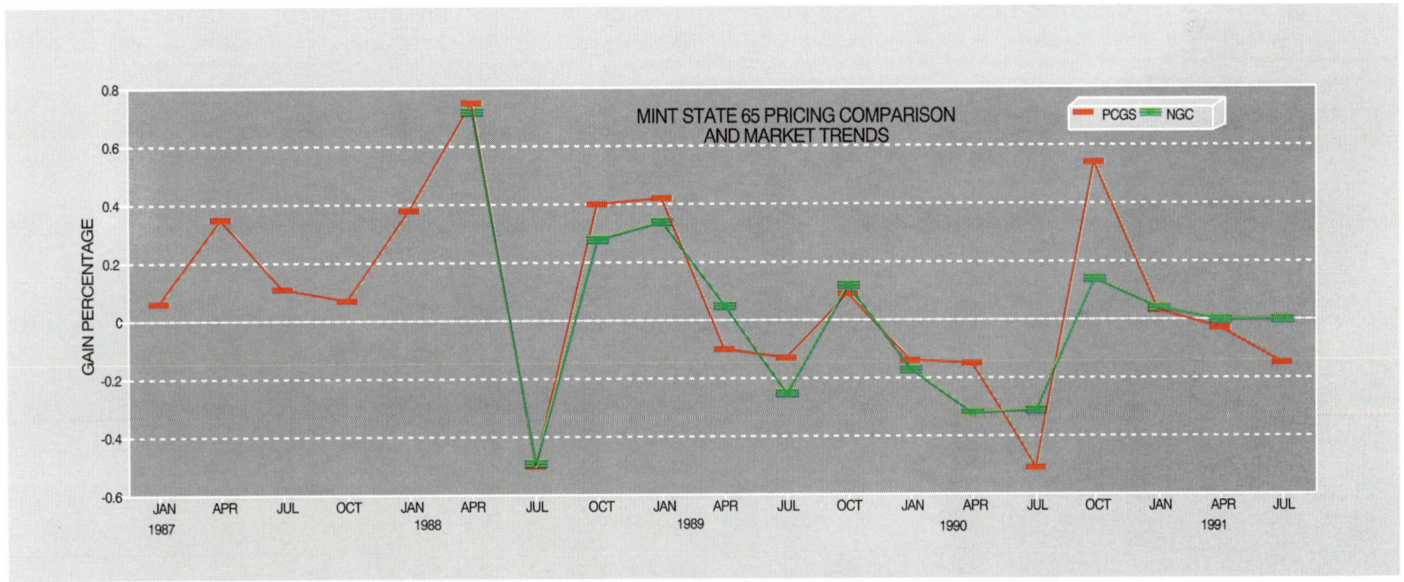

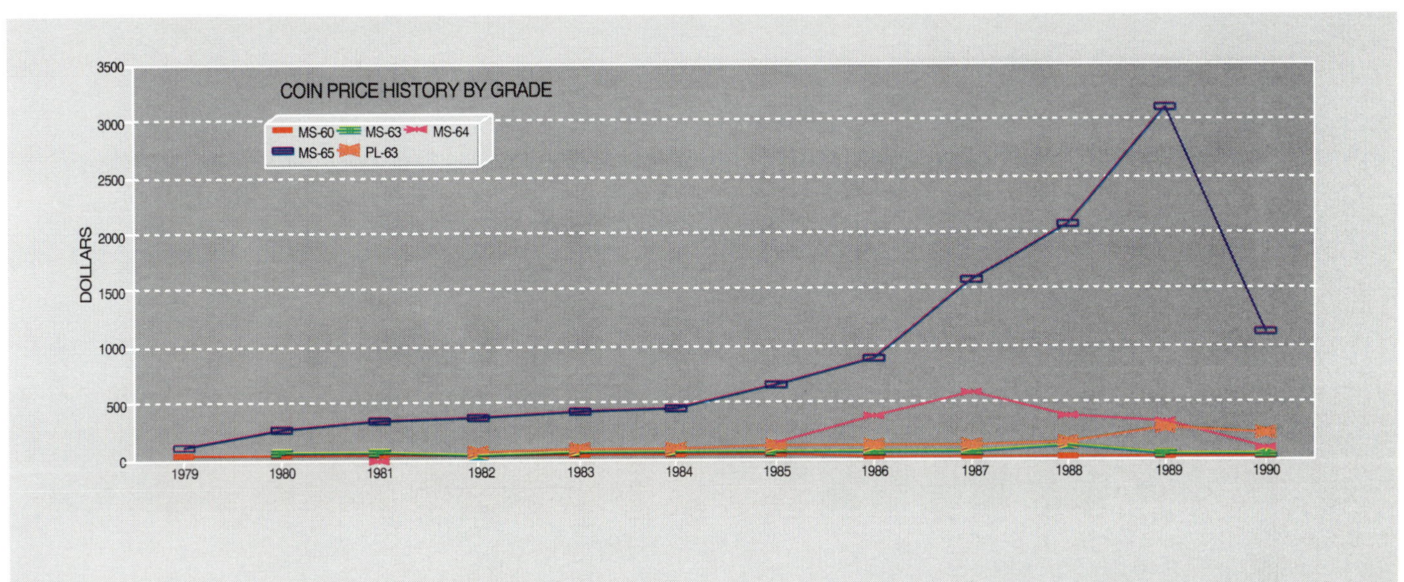

1882 O/S S$1
MS 64
203387-007

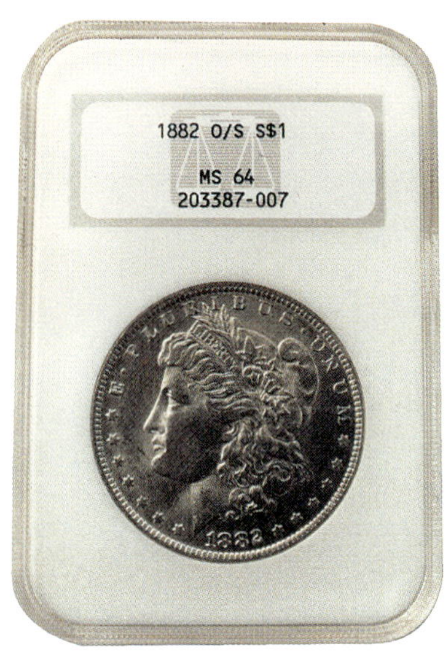

1882-O/S

At least three dies intended for San Francisco were remintmarked for New Orleans, producing six naked-eye varieties, VAM 2, 4, 5, 6, 17, 23 (the last three are actually earlier diestates of the first three: see the Jeff Oxman study in Chapter 18). All show rusted dies. This overmintmark is widely accepted as a key item, needed to complete a date and mintmark set. If this were a date, not a variety, it would be fifth rarest, behind 1884-S, 1889-CC, 1892-S, 1893-S, at least in mint state.

Scarce to rare in all circulated grades; not often available in any quality of Unc. Buy now in any BU grade, upgrade later, and happy hunting!

Prooflikes: Unknown in any grade or quality, though a few rumors have circulated.

***** The NGC 1882-O/S pictured here is Mr. Highfill's personal coin. This date was not represented on the PCGS Tour.

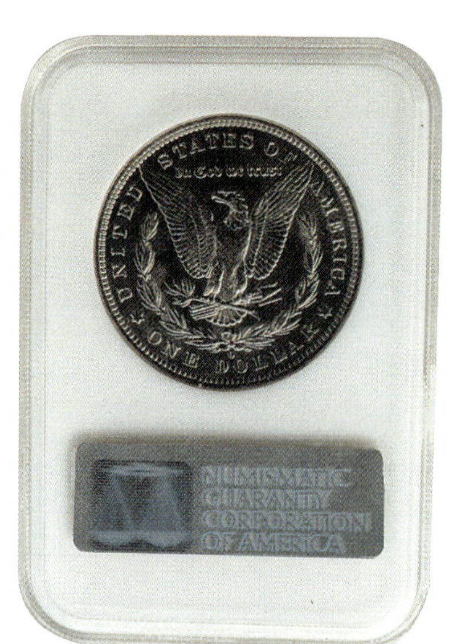

MINTAGE	PROOF	STRIKE	LUSTER	BAG MARKS	REDFIELD
10,000*	0	Weak	Good	Heavy	No
DIES	**DIE VARIETIES**	**% OF PL**	**% OF DMPL**	**PIVOTAL GRADE**	**RARITY FACTOR**
50**	6-7***	0.0	0.0	MS 64	R-1

*Includes estimated 6,080,000 1882-O and estimated 10,000 1882-O/S
**Includes all dies used at the New Orleans Mint - FY 1882
***Estimated (Van Allen-Mallis)

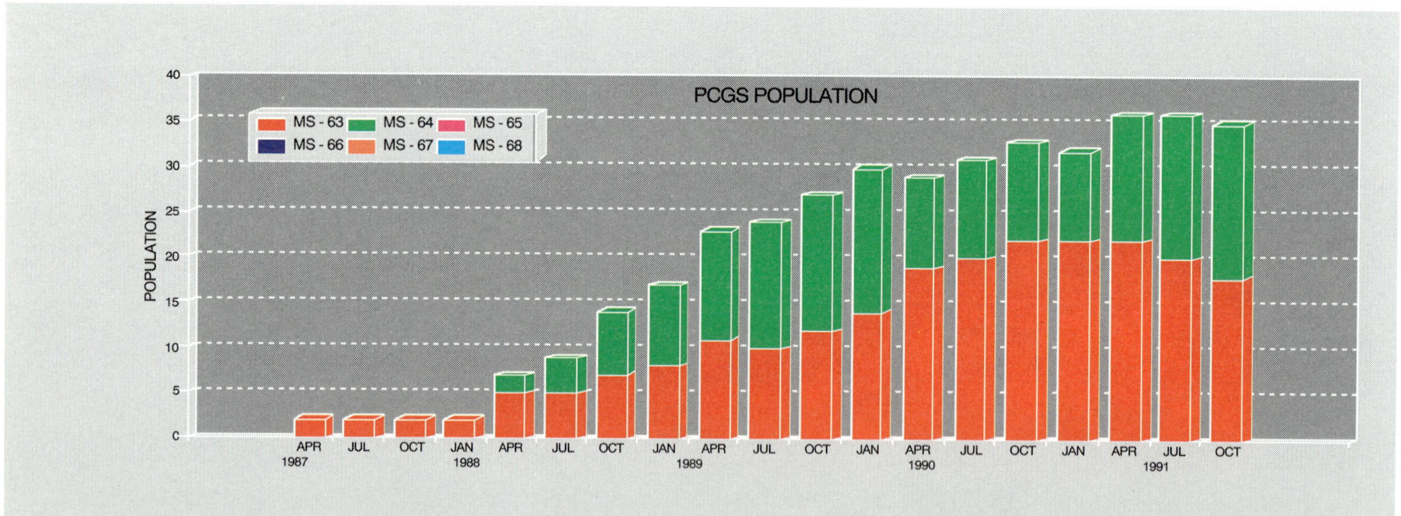
PCGS POPULATION
MS - 63
MS - 64
MS - 65
MS - 66
MS - 67
MS - 68
POPULATION
40
35
30
25
20
15
10
5
0
APR 1987
JUL
OCT
JAN 1988
APR
JUL
OCT
JAN 1989
APR
JUL
OCT
JAN
APR 1990
JUL
OCT
JAN
APR
JUL 1991
OCT

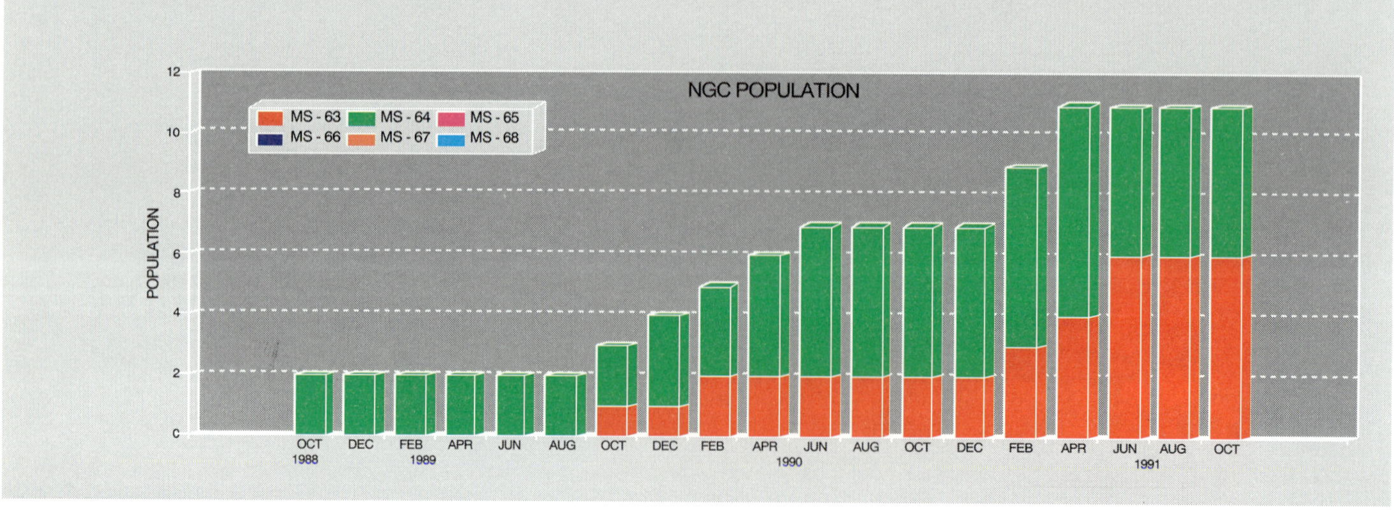
NGC POPULATION
MS - 63
MS - 64
MS - 65
MS - 66
MS - 67
MS - 68
POPULATION
12
10
8
6
4
2
0
OCT 1988
DEC
FEB 1989
APR
JUN
AUG
OCT
DEC
FEB
APR 1990
JUN
AUG
OCT
DEC
FEB
APR
JUN 1991
AUG
OCT

NO PRICING DATA AVAILABLE FOR THIS DATE

NO PRICING DATA AVAILABLE FOR THIS DATE

NO PRICING DATA AVAILABLE FOR THIS DATE

1882-S

The 9,250,000 struck may not have required all 55 pairs of dies. Fourth commonest S Mint Morgan; population probably about 1/4 that of 1881-S. Many came from Treasury, Redfield (Approximately 5 bags. 5th commonest Redfield date), and Continental Bank hoard bags. When this last group came to light, Clark Samuelson and Dr. George W. Vogt distributed many bags, including many high quality BU coins, some magnificently rainbow toned. They sold the 1882-S for a 30% premium over the 1879-S, 1880-S, and 1881-S.

Recommended in MS 65 up; MS 67's can be found with difficulty, but are worth the effort. Roll and bag lots of MS 60/63 are occasionally offered.

Prooflikes: PL's outnumber DMPL's about 20 to 1; cameos are scarce to rare, especially DMPL's. PL's are plentiful up to and including MS 66; DMPL's are hard to find above MS 64. The 1882-S comes in brilliant prooflike and cameos are actually scarce.

MINTAGE	PROOF	STRIKE	LUSTER	BAG MARKS	REDFIELD
9,250,000	0	Sharp & Bold	Excellent	Light	Yes
DIES	**DIE VARIETIES**	**% OF PL**	**% OF DMPL**	**PIVOTAL GRADE**	**RARITY FACTOR**
80	27	6.8	0.6	MS 65	R-5

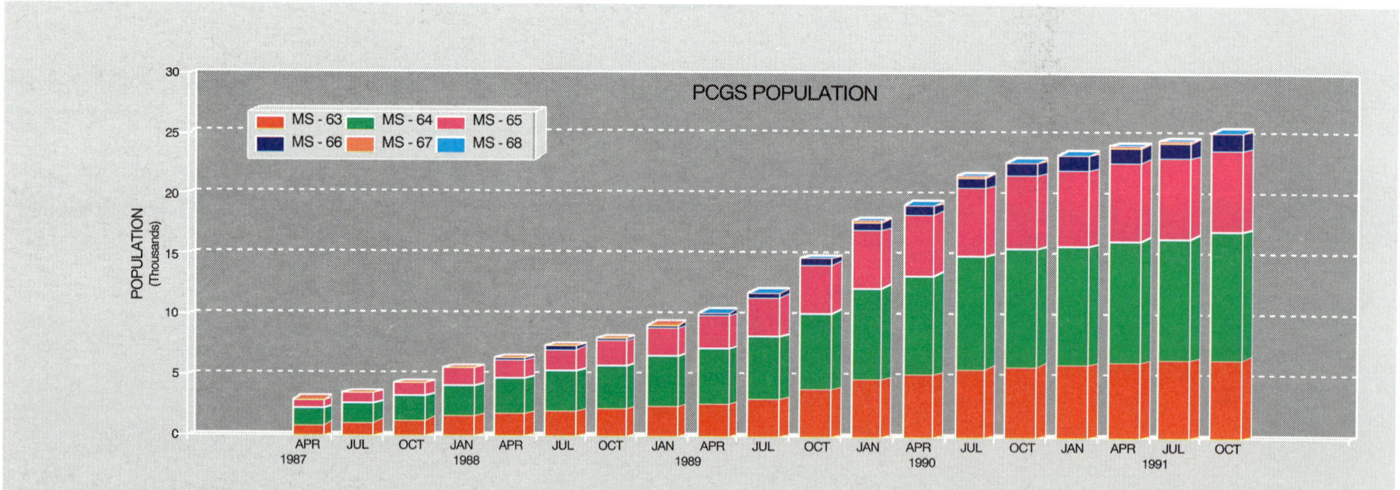

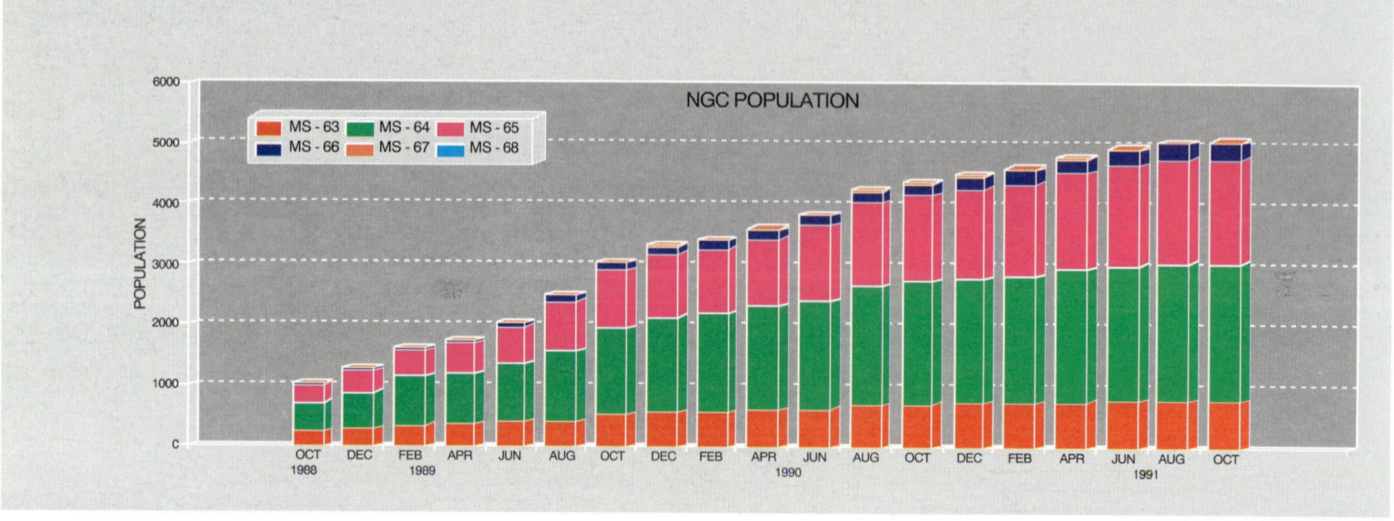

PCGS POPULATION

MS - 63 MS - 64 MS - 65 MS - 66 MS - 67 MS - 68

POPULATION (Thousands)

0 5 10 15 20 25 30

APR 1987 JUL OCT JAN 1988 APR JUL OCT JAN 1989 APR JUL OCT JAN 1990 APR JUL OCT JAN 1991 APR JUL OCT

NGC POPULATION

MS - 63 MS - 64 MS - 65 MS - 66 MS - 67 MS - 68

POPULATION

0 1000 2000 3000 4000 5000 6000

OCT 1988 DEC FEB 1989 APR JUN AUG OCT DEC FEB 1990 APR JUN AUG OCT DEC FEB 1991 APR JUN AUG OCT

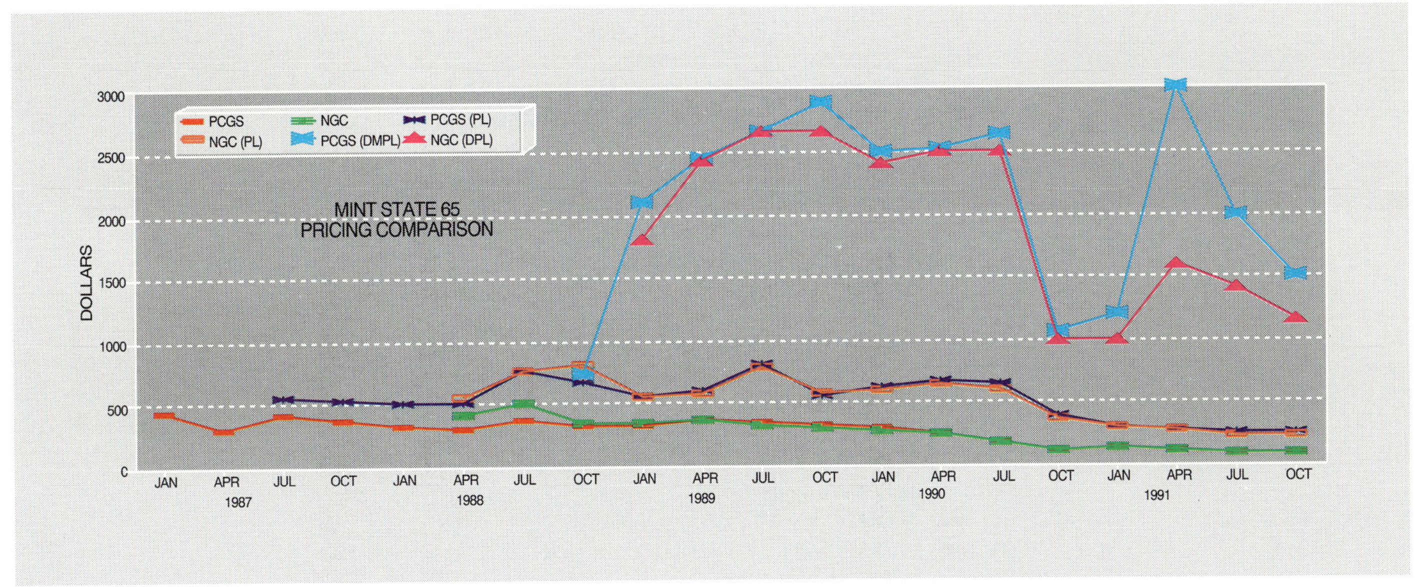

PCGS
NGC
PCGS (PL)
NGC (PL)
PCGS (DMPL)
NGC (DPL)
MINT STATE 65
PRICING COMPARISON
DOLLARS
3000
2500
2000
1500
1000
500
0
JAN
APR
JUL
OCT
1987
1988
1989
1990
1991

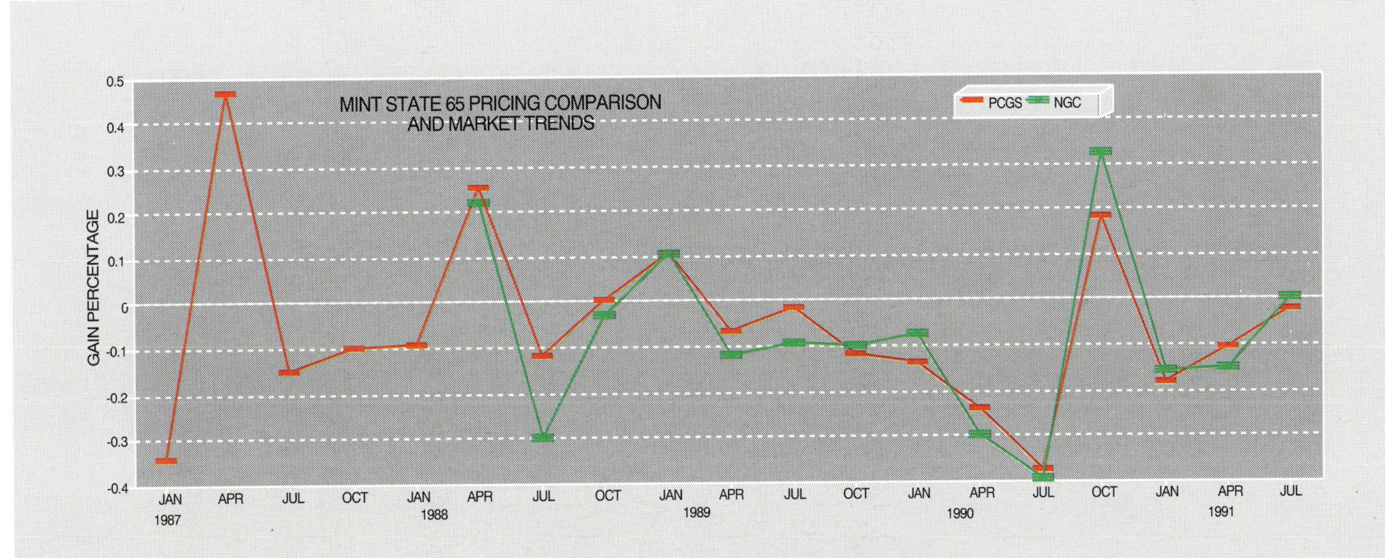

MINT STATE 65 PRICING COMPARISON
AND MARKET TRENDS
PCGS
NGC
GAIN PERCENTAGE
0.5
0.4
0.3
0.2
0.1
0
-0.1
-0.2
-0.3
-0.4
JAN
APR
JUL
OCT
1987
1988
1989
1990
1991

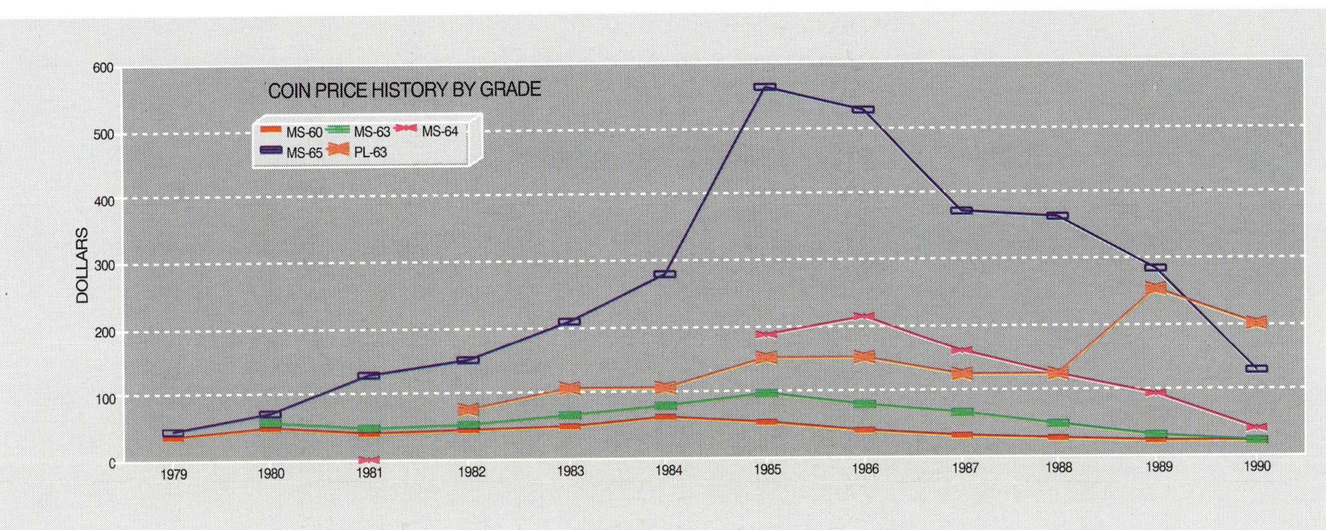

COIN PRICE HISTORY BY GRADE
MS-60
MS-63
MS-64
MS-65
PL-63
DOLLARS
600
500
400
300
200
100
0
1979
1980
1981
1982
1983
1984
1985
1986
1987
1988
1989
1990

1883-P

The 12,290,000 struck may have taken most of the 62 obs. and 59 revs. Common in lower qualities of Unc. from Treasury and Continental Bank Hoard bags. Roll and bag lots in MS 60/62 are still available. Clark A. Samuelson is quoted as handling 12 to 15 original mint sacks from the Continental Bank hoard, via Colonial Coins of Houston, Texas.

Many Unc. survivors, satiny or frosty, come with weak reverses; others show rusty dies.

Recommended in MS 65 up and by the roll in MS 64.

Proofs: 1,039 struck, from a single pair of dies (VAM 1); obv. has a wart on cheek (pit mark in die). A second variety may exist.

Prooflikes: One-sided pieces are common. Two-sided PL's are scarce to rare above MS 64; DMPL's and/or cameos rarer.

MINTAGE	PROOF	STRIKE	LUSTER	BAG MARKS	REDFIELD
12,290,000	1,039	Average To Sharp	Dull To Frosty	Moderate	No
DIES	**DIE VARIETIES**	**% OF PL**	**% OF DMPL**	**PIVOTAL GRADE**	**RARITY FACTOR**
127	15	3.1	2.8	MS 65	R-4

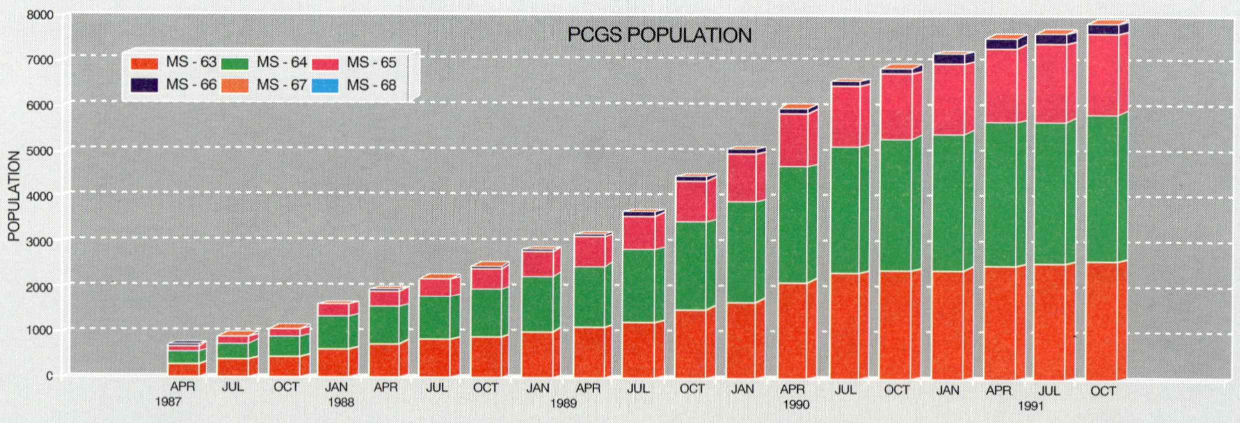

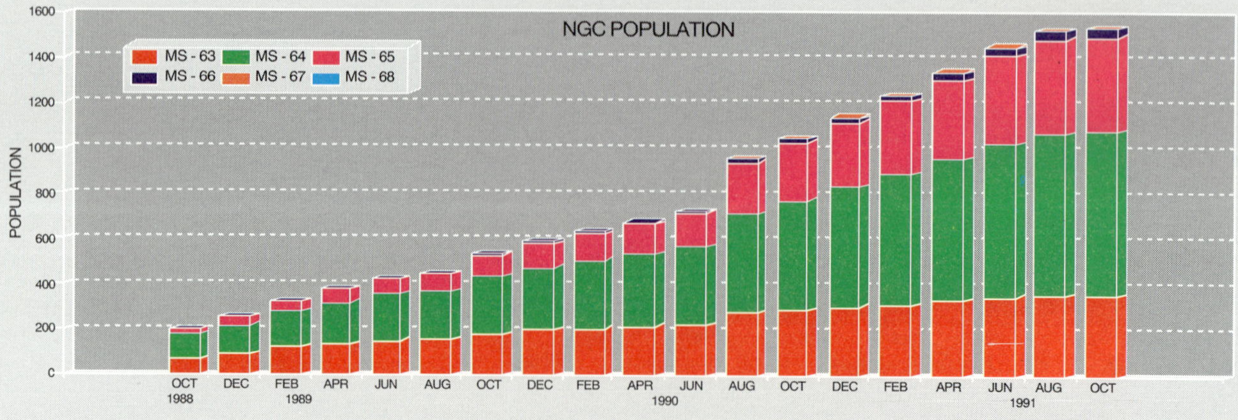

1883-P

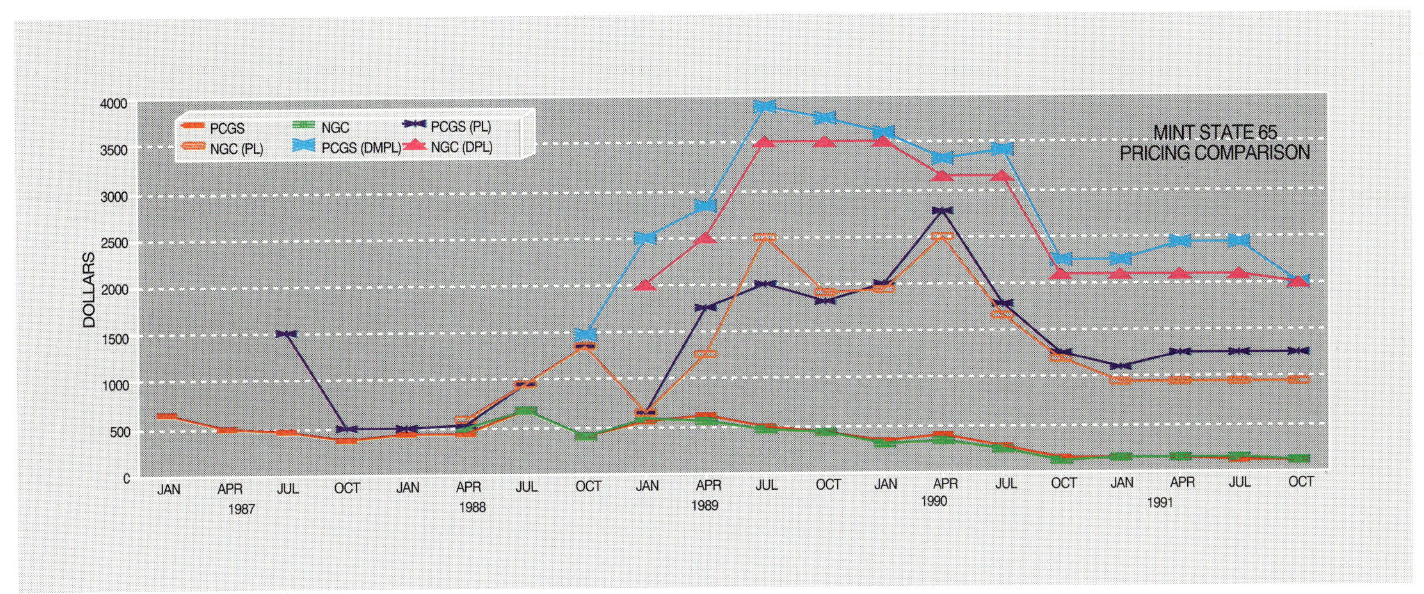

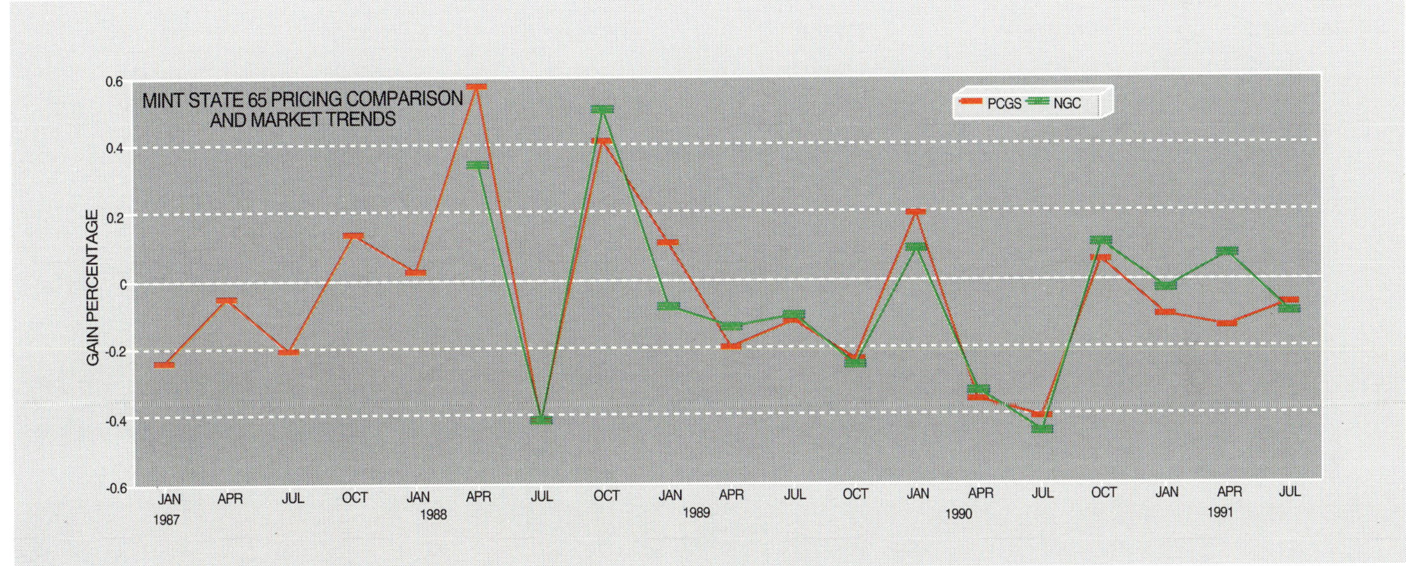

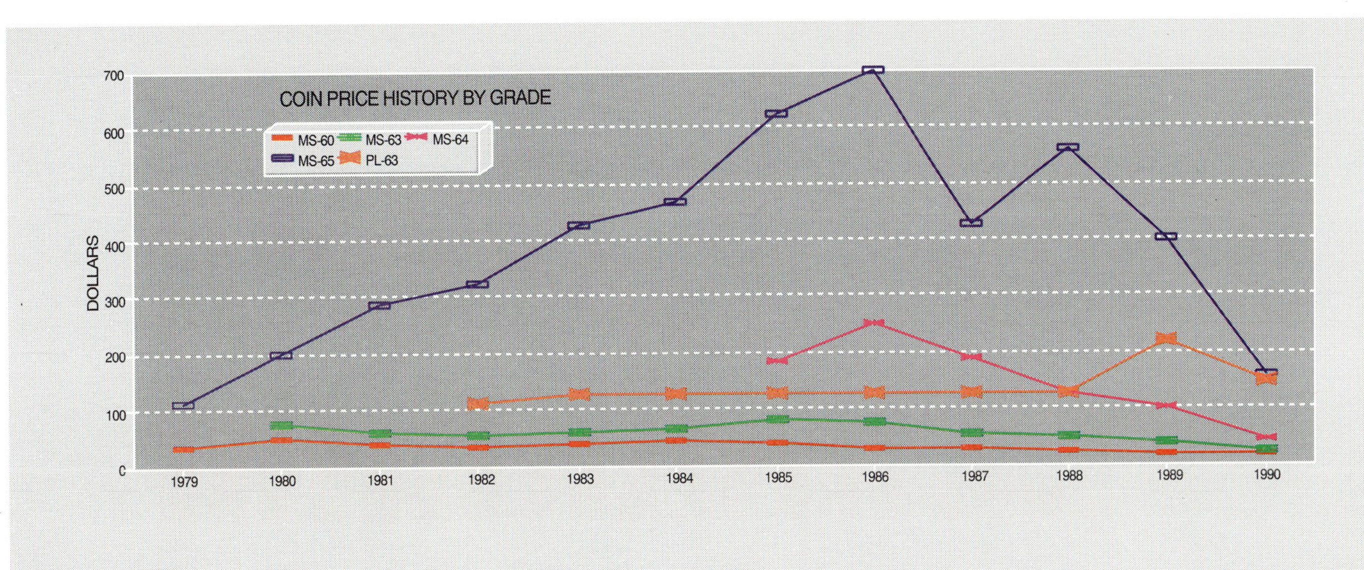

PCGS
1883-CC
S$1
MS67PL
7145.67/3082276

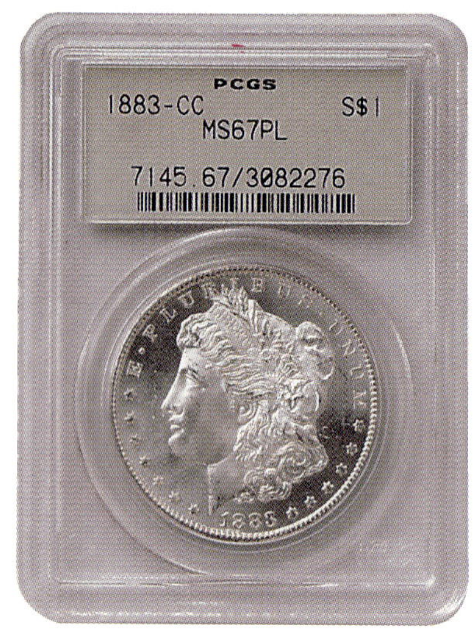

1883-CC

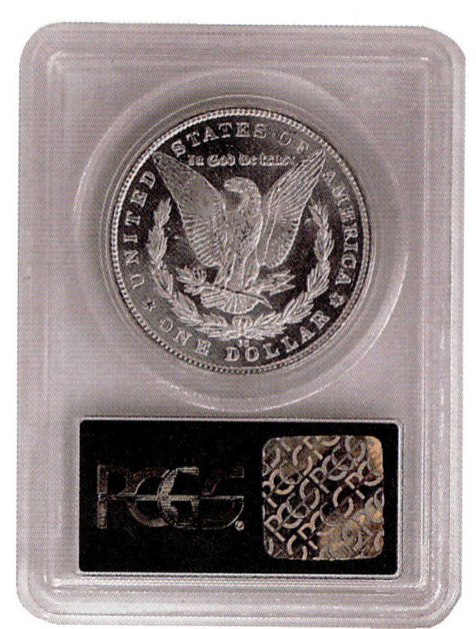

The 1,204,000 struck took 10 pairs of dies. One of two commonest CC's; the other is 1884-CC. Seldom seen circulated; plentiful in brilliant but bagmarked Unc., MS 60 through 65.

GSA offered 755,518 in the 1972-74 mail bid sales, minimum bid $30 per coin, limit of one per customer. About 62% of these were sold in their first offering. GSA offered 221,665 at a discount because of tarnish and surface scratches. The last Treasury 1883-CC's (195,748) were dispersed in 1980. The government had 63% of the entire original mintage in their vaults for over three-quarters of a century! BU rolls (MS 60/62) still show up from time to time.

Recommended above MS 65 and better or by the roll in MS 63/64.

Proofs: One from MARCA's 1986 San Diego Sale at $7,250 reappeared as Auction 87:1856 at $4,620. Unverified, but rumored to be the Amon Carter coin.

Prooflikes: Available in all grades, PL, DMPL, cameos. Rare above MS 65 PL or MS 64 DMPL.

MINTAGE	PROOF	STRIKE	LUSTER	BAG MARKS	REDFIELD
1,204,000	0	Average To Bold	Good	Moderate	No
DIES	**DIE VARIETIES**	**% OF PL**	**% OF DMPL**	**PIVOTAL GRADE**	**RARITY FACTOR**
20	4	10.8	8.3	MS 65	R-5

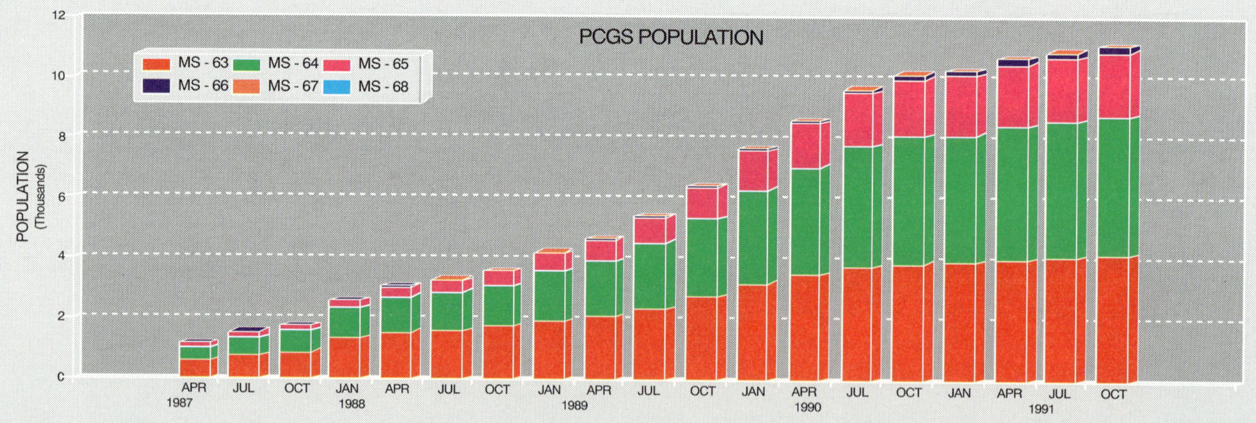
PCGS POPULATION
MS - 63
MS - 64
MS - 65
MS - 66
MS - 67
MS - 68
POPULATION (Thousands)
12
10
8
6
4
2
0
APR 1987
JUL
OCT
JAN 1988
APR
JUL
OCT
JAN 1989
APR
JUL
OCT
JAN
APR 1990
JUL
OCT
JAN
APR
JUL 1991
OCT

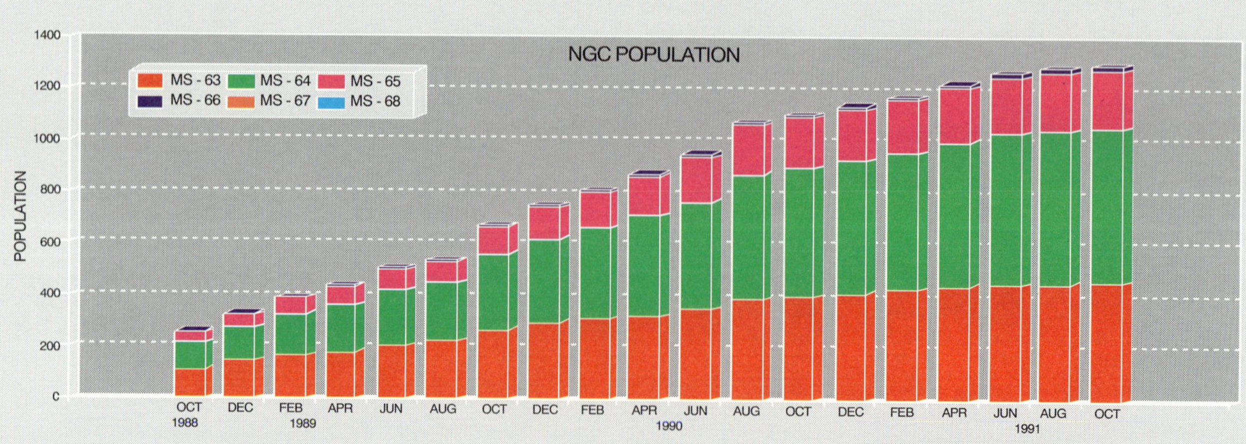
NGC POPULATION
MS - 63
MS - 64
MS - 65
MS - 66
MS - 67
MS - 68
POPULATION
1400
1200
1000
800
600
400
200
0
OCT 1988
DEC
FEB 1989
APR
JUN
AUG
OCT
DEC
FEB
APR 1990
JUN
AUG
OCT
DEC
FEB
APR
JUN 1991
AUG
OCT

1883-CC

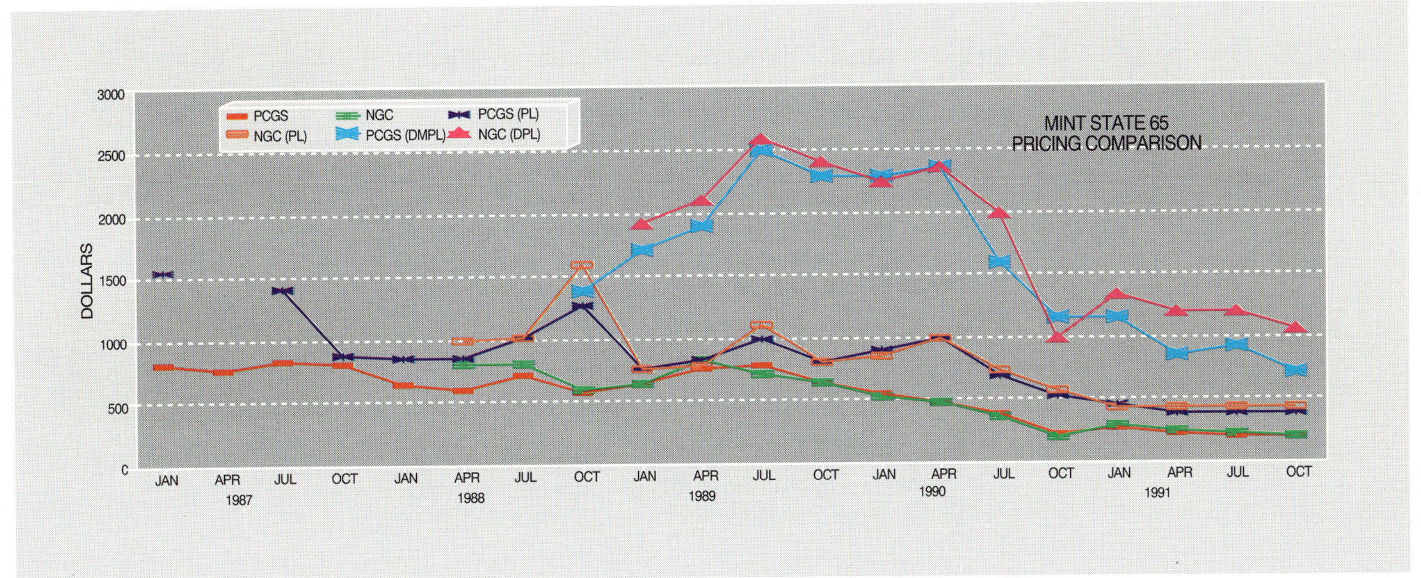

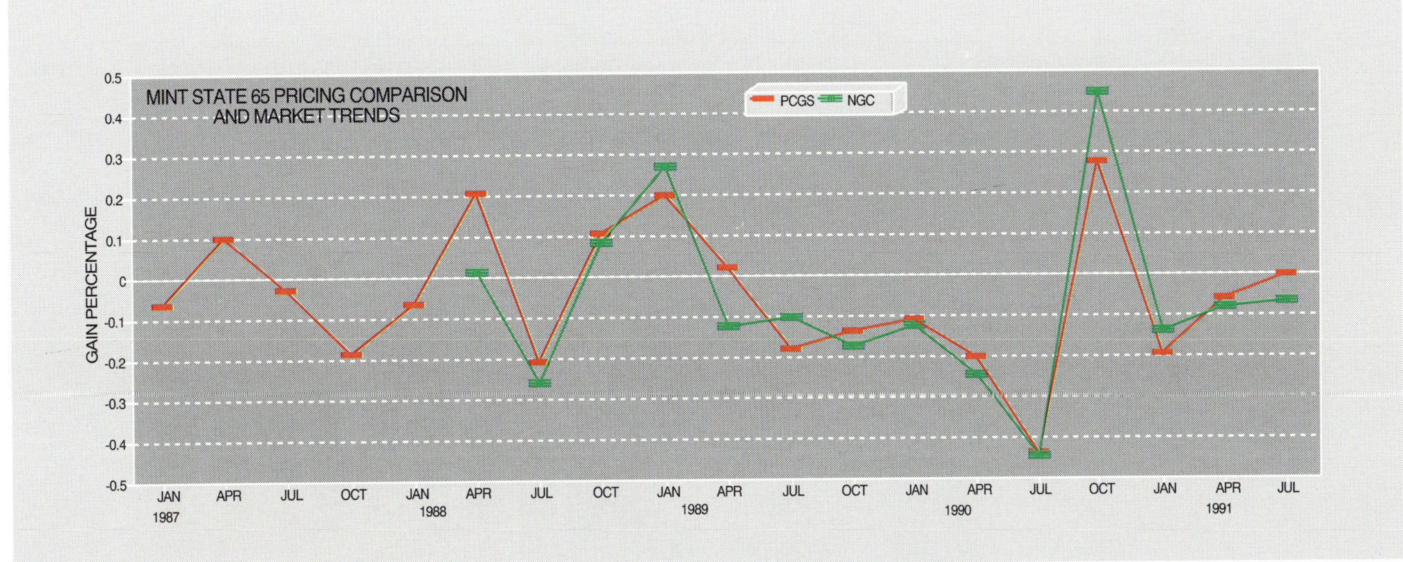

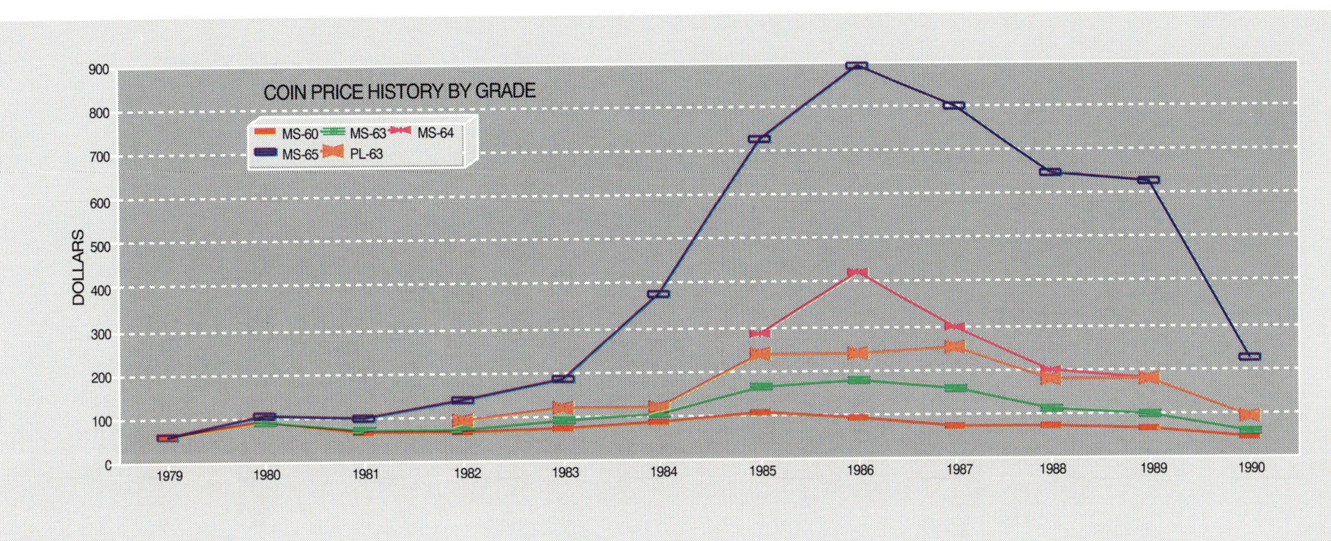

PCGS
1883-O
MS67
S$1
7146.67/8095043

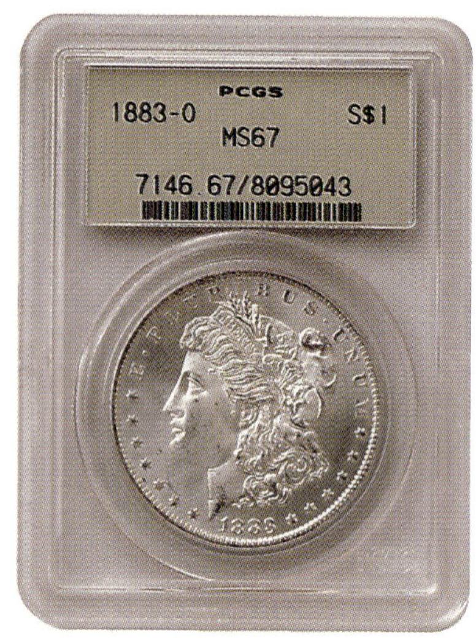

1883-O

The 8,725,000 struck took 40 obvs., 36 revs. Third commonest O Mint, partly from Treasury (1938) and Continental Bank hoard bags. Many of the latter were quietly distributed by Leon Hendrickson and Dr. G. W. Vogt. Often not well struck even when fully lustrous and free of rubbing; some of this is attributed to improper basining of the dies at New Orleans. Excessive metal flow (a "melted" wet look), thick rims and die breaks. Many show die cracks. VAM 4, with repunched O, is common. Bag quantities in MS 60/63 still survive.

Recommended as a single in MS 65 up, in rolls MS 64 up.

Proofs: Of the 12 minted, possibly three are traced.

Prooflikes: DMPL's are only half as common as PL's. Both are scarce above MS 65. Most cameos do not have as sharp contrast as on some other dates.

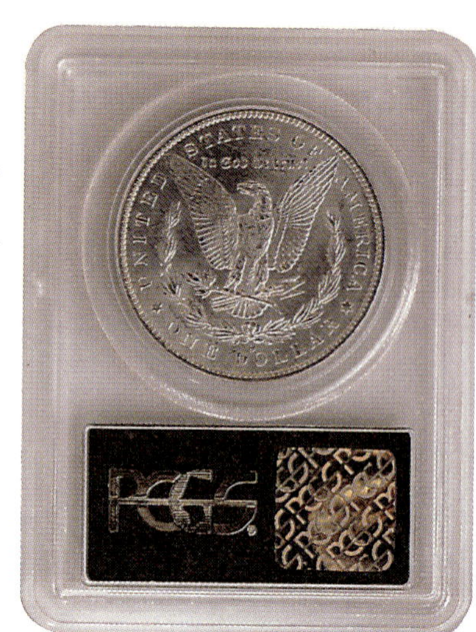

MINTAGE	PROOF	STRIKE	LUSTER	BAG MARKS	REDFIELD
8,725,000	0	Soft To Average	Good	Moderate	No
DIES	**DIE VARIETIES**	**% OF PL**	**% OF DMPL**	**PIVOTAL GRADE**	**RARITY FACTOR**
92	39	4.5	3.1	MS 65	R-5

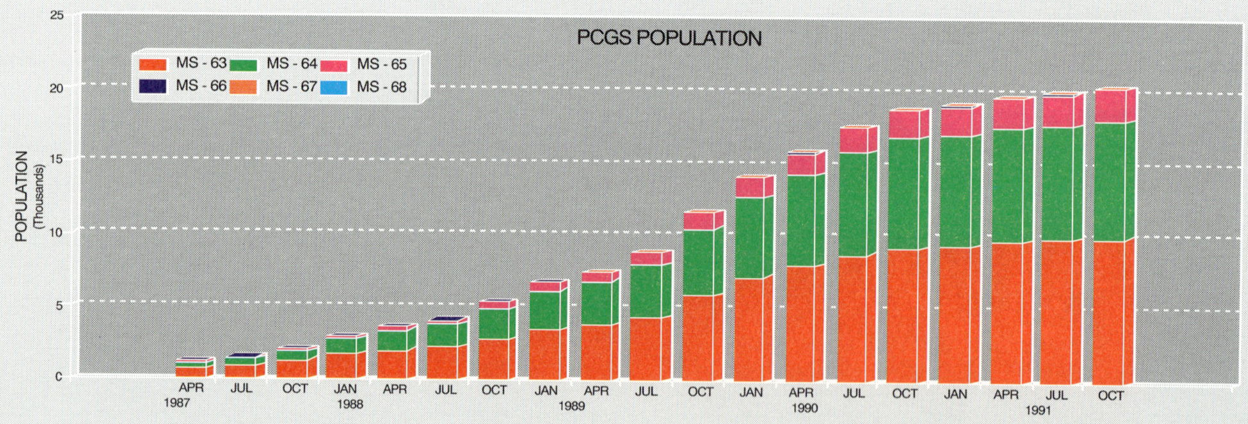
PCGS POPULATION
MS - 63
MS - 64
MS - 65
MS - 66
MS - 67
MS - 68
POPULATION
(Thousands)
25
20
15
10
5
0
APR
1987
JUL
OCT
JAN
1988
APR
JUL
OCT
JAN
1989
APR
JUL
OCT
JAN
APR
1990
JUL
OCT
JAN
APR
JUL
1991
OCT

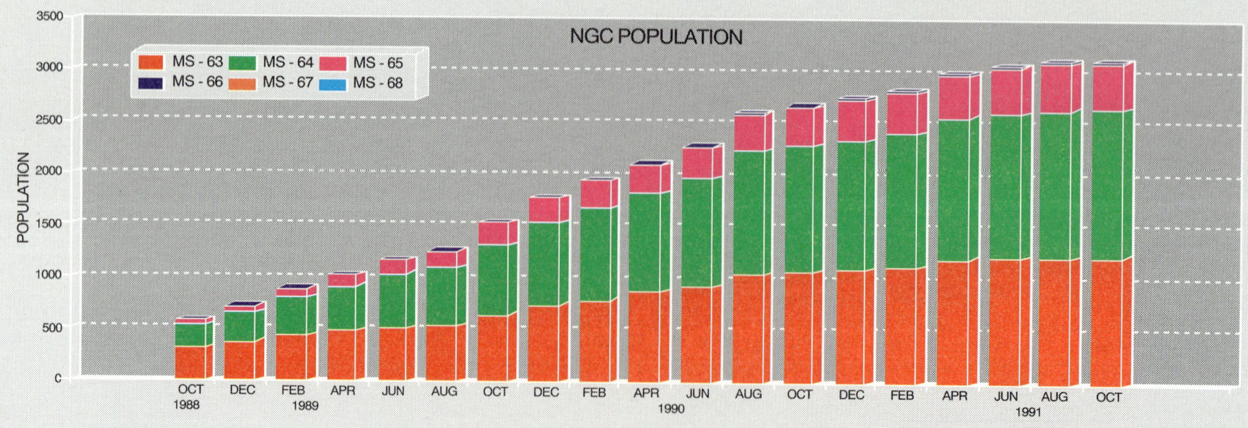
NGC POPULATION
MS - 63
MS - 64
MS - 65
MS - 66
MS - 67
MS - 68
POPULATION
3500
3000
2500
2000
1500
1000
500
0
OCT
1988
DEC
FEB
1989
APR
JUN
AUG
OCT
DEC
FEB
APR
1990
JUN
AUG
OCT
DEC
FEB
APR
JUN
1991
AUG
OCT

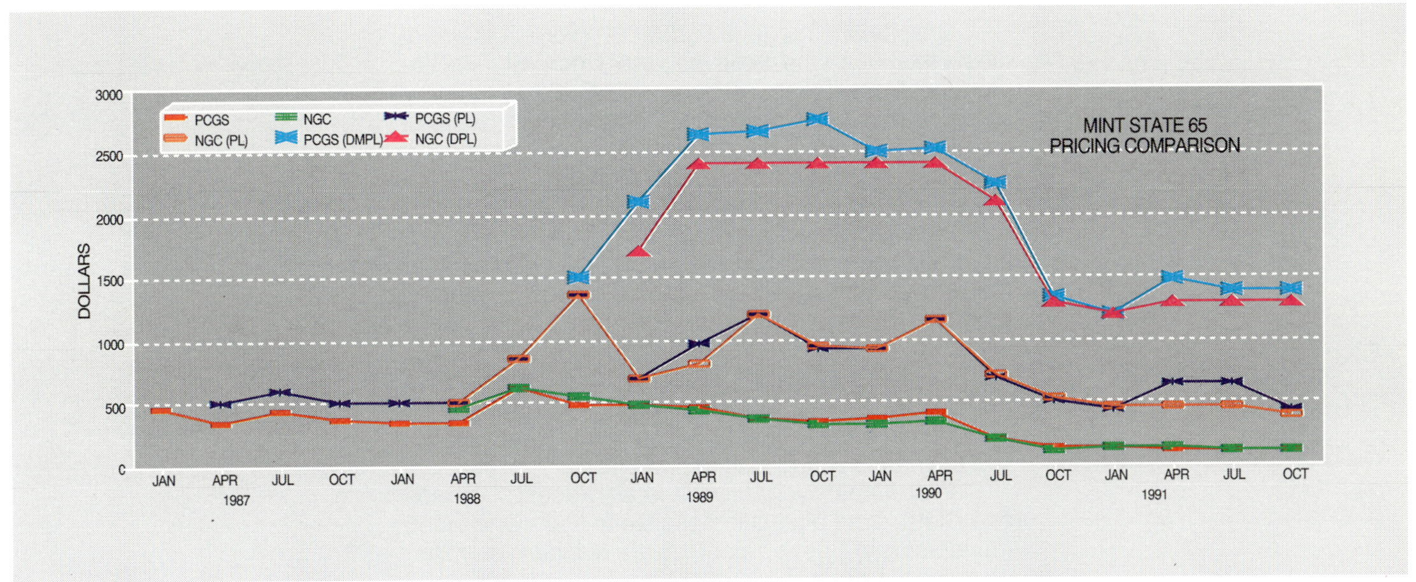
MINT STATE 65
PRICING COMPARISON
PCGS
NGC
PCGS (PL)
NGC (PL)
PCGS (DMPL)
NGC (DPL)
DOLLARS
3000
2500
2000
1500
1000
500
0
JAN
APR
JUL
OCT
1987
1988
1989
1990
1991

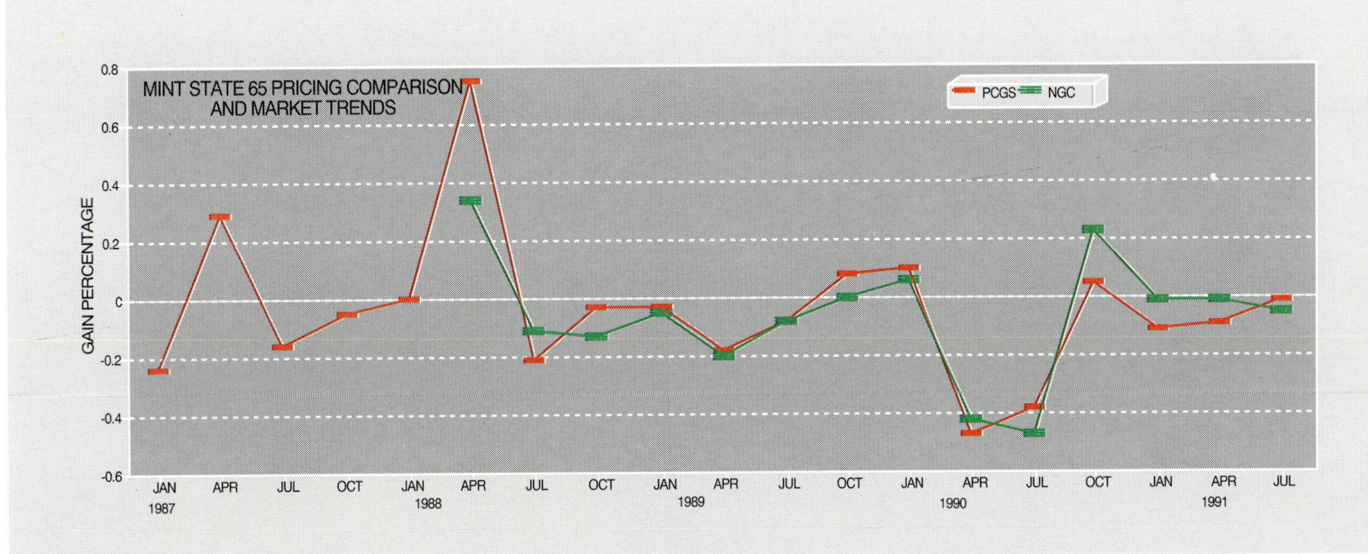
MINT STATE 65 PRICING COMPARISON
AND MARKET TRENDS
PCGS
NGC
GAIN PERCENTAGE
0.8
0.6
0.4
0.2
0
-0.2
-0.4
-0.6
JAN
APR
JUL
OCT
1987
1988
1989
1990
1991

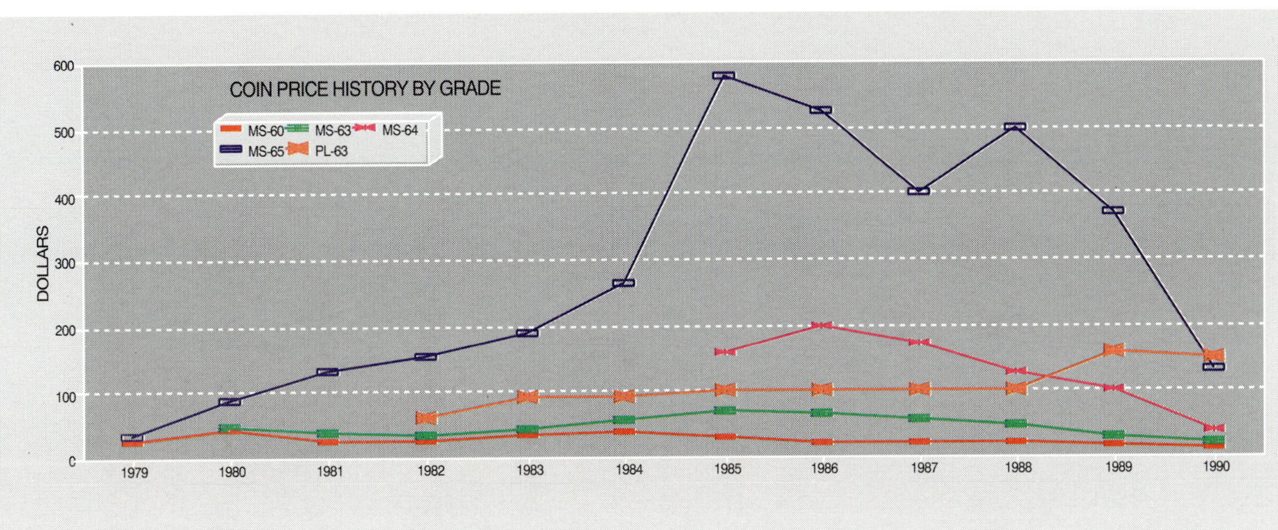
COIN PRICE HISTORY BY GRADE
MS-60
MS-63
MS-64
MS-65
PL-63
DOLLARS
600
500
400
300
200
100
0
1979
1980
1981
1982
1983
1984
1985
1986
1987
1988
1989
1990

PCGS
1883-S S$1
MS65
7148.65/2247242

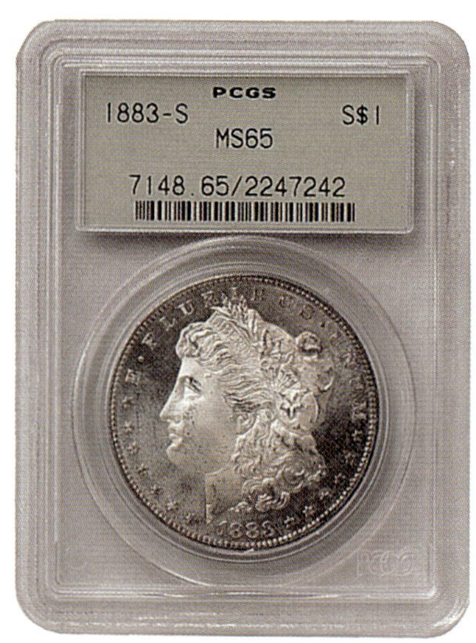

1883-S

Despite a mintage of 6,250,000 (from 40 pairs of dies), this was long believed rare Unc. Sliders are plentiful from Treasury bags (1963-4), apparently resealed "two beers" coins like the O Mints. Some of the slider bags were dispersed by Dean Tavenner and John B. Love, the Montana coin pioneers. (For more details see 1885-S analysis.)

Full Mint State specimens are not so easily found; most are sharp and lustrous but heavily bagmarked. Many are from the Redfield hoard; the 1883-S Redfield group Paramount distributed for A-Mark sold out at once. No bag lots are thought to survive, and roll lots will most likely be sliders. Beware of an added "S" to an 1883-P.

Recommended in MS 65 up when available, but you may have a long wait to find one.

Prooflikes: Very difficult in all grades. Cameos and DMPL's are almost impossible to find. One-sided (obverse only) PL's or semi-PL's are available in limited quantities.

PCGS

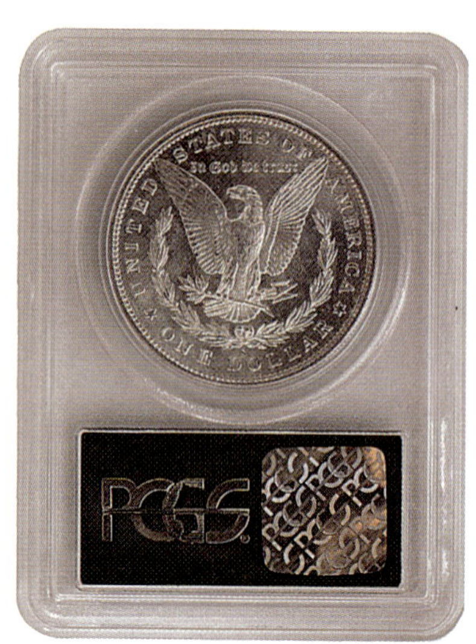

MINTAGE	PROOF	STRIKE	LUSTER	BAG MARKS	REDFIELD
6,250,000	0	Sharp & Bold	Very Good	Moderate To Heavy	Yes
DIES	**DIE VARIETIES**	**% OF PL**	**% OF DMPL**	**PIVOTAL GRADE**	**RARITY FACTOR**
105	8	2.9	0.1	MS 64	R-1

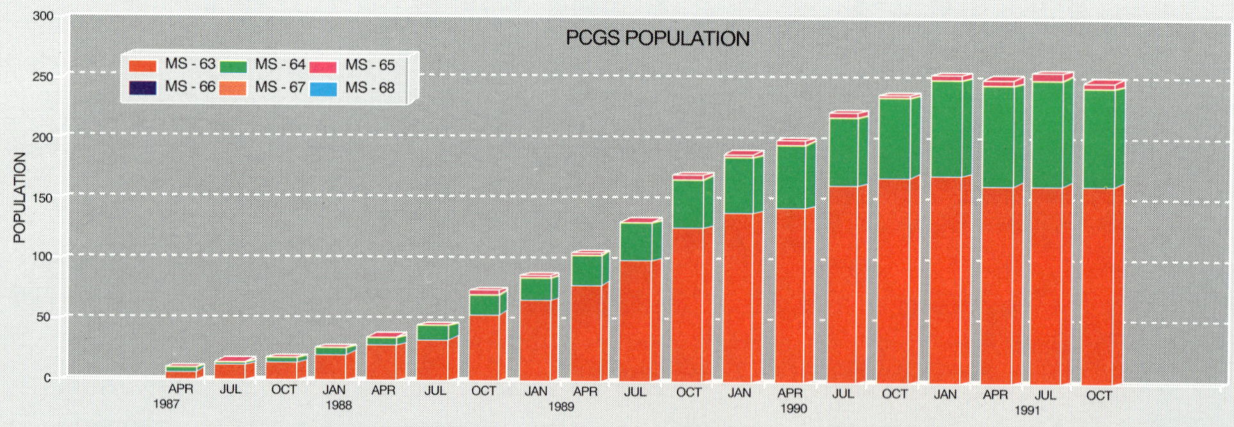

PCGS POPULATION
MS - 63
MS - 64
MS - 65
MS - 66
MS - 67
MS - 68
POPULATION
300
250
200
150
100
50
0
APR 1987
JUL
OCT
JAN 1988
APR
JUL
OCT
JAN 1989
APR
JUL
OCT
JAN
APR 1990
JUL
OCT
JAN
APR
JUL 1991
OCT

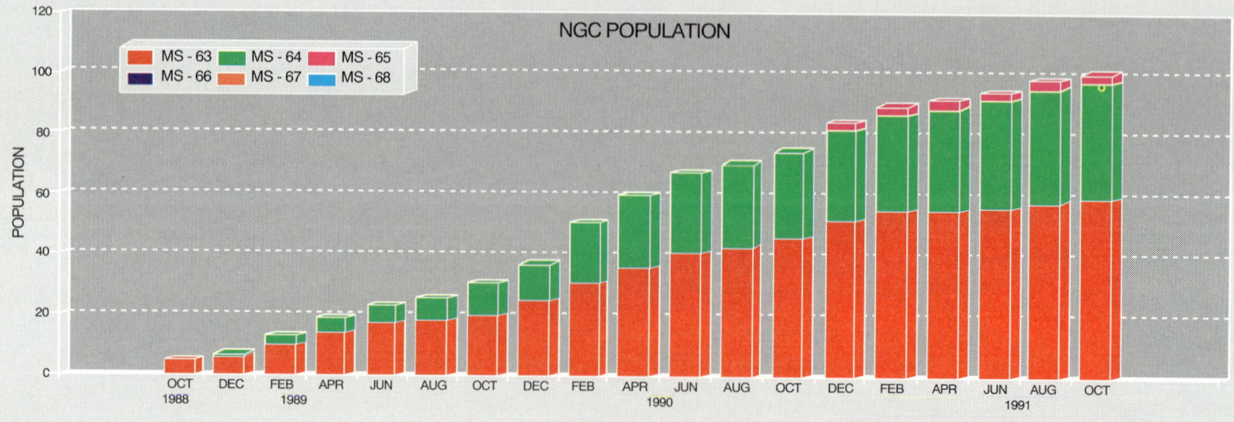

NGC POPULATION
MS - 63
MS - 64
MS - 65
MS - 66
MS - 67
MS - 68
POPULATION
120
100
80
60
40
20
0
OCT 1988
DEC
FEB 1989
APR
JUN
AUG
OCT
DEC
FEB
APR 1990
JUN
AUG
OCT
DEC
FEB
APR
JUN 1991
AUG
OCT

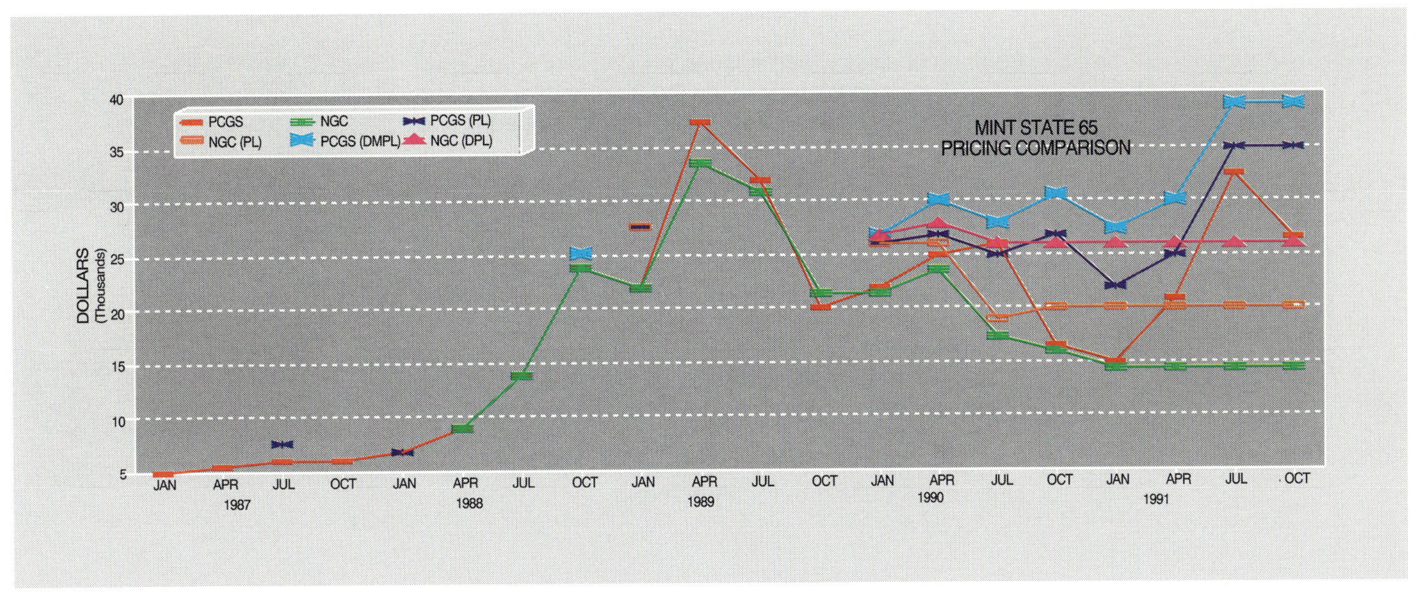
MINT STATE 65
PRICING COMPARISON
PCGS
NGC
PCGS (PL)
NGC (PL)
PCGS (DMPL)
NGC (DPL)
DOLLARS
(Thousands)
40
35
30
25
20
15
10
5
JAN
APR
JUL
OCT
1987
1988
1989
1990
1991

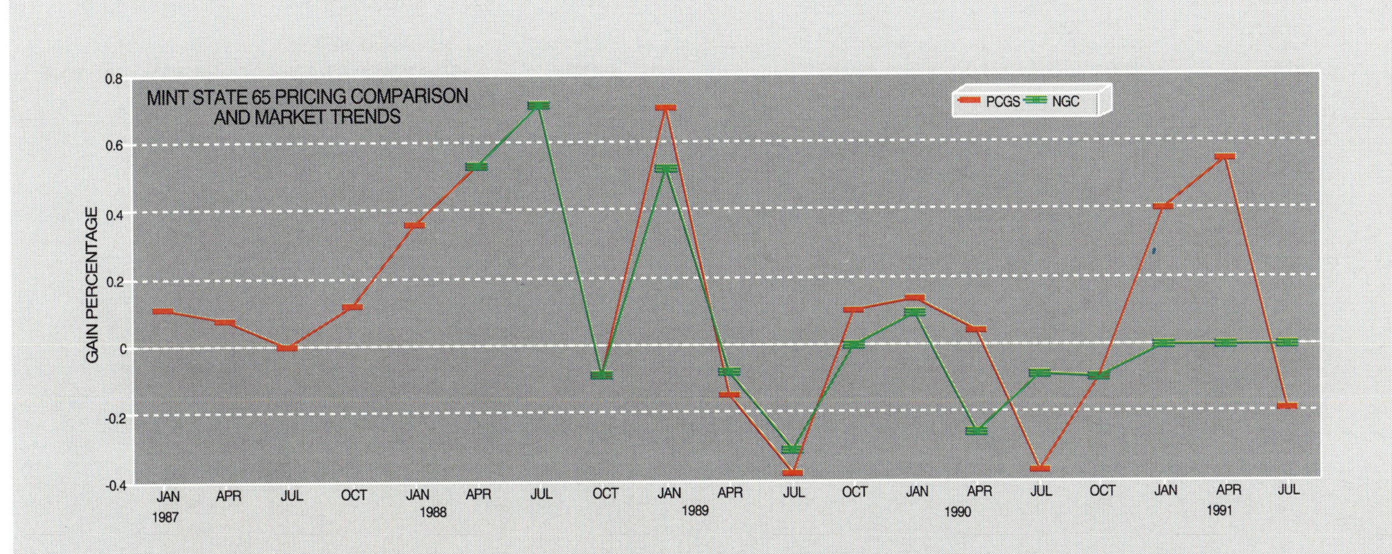
MINT STATE 65 PRICING COMPARISON
AND MARKET TRENDS
PCGS
NGC
GAIN PERCENTAGE
0.8
0.6
0.4
0.2
0
-0.2
-0.4
JAN
APR
JUL
OCT
1987
1988
1989
1990
1991

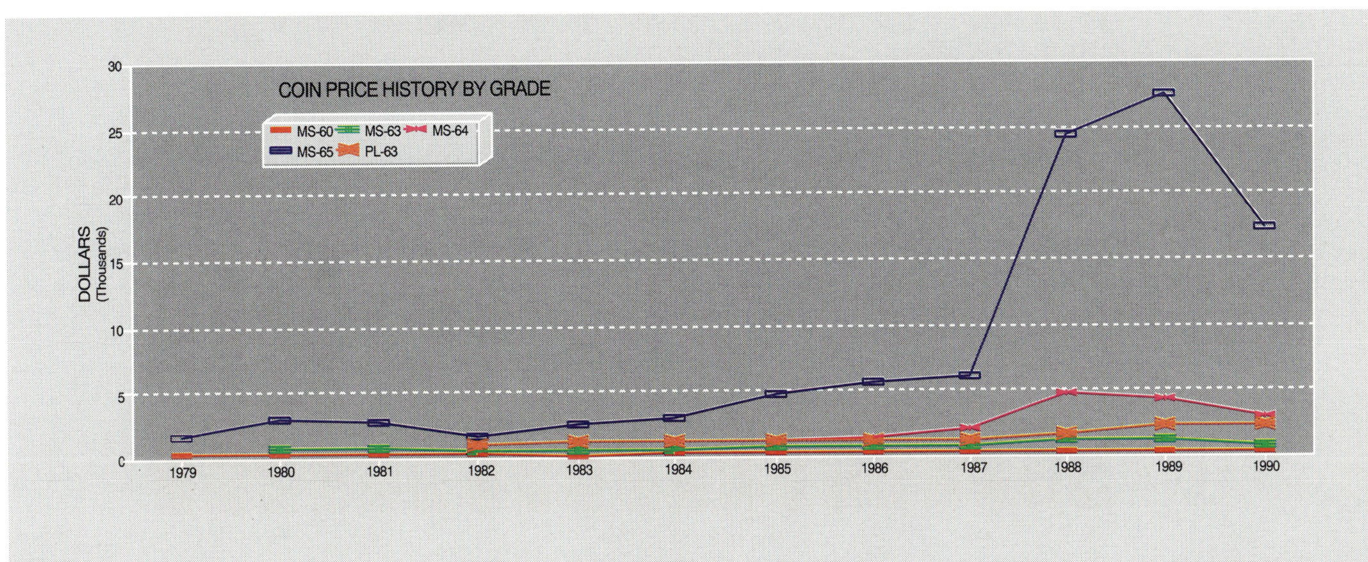
COIN PRICE HISTORY BY GRADE
MS-60
MS-63
MS-64
MS-65
PL-63
DOLLARS
(Thousands)
30
25
20
15
10
5
0
1979
1980
1981
1982
1983
1984
1985
1986
1987
1988
1989
1990

1884-P

Less common than its mintage (14,070,000, from 60 pairs of dies) would suggest. Many Uncs. are from 12 to 15 mint sewn bags in the Continental Bank hoard, dispersed by Dr. G. W. Vogt and Clark Samuelson. Roll and bag lots survive, mostly MS 60/62.

Recommended in MS 65 up or by the roll in MS 64. Check every specimen for the raised dot at Morgan's initial M on both sides; two obvs., one rev. die show it. See illustrations in VAM and Breen's *Encyclopedia* at 5576. These mysterious varieties are really scarce but have not been sought after.

Proofs: The 875 minted took only one pair of dies, VAM 1; rev. has much die polish within and around ribbon, an area not so efficiently polished on proofs of many other dates.

Prooflikes: Scarce to rare above MS 64, PL and DMPL. Cameos are not often found.

MINTAGE	PROOF	STRIKE	LUSTER	BAG MARKS	REDFIELD
14,070,000	875	Sharp & Bold	Good	Moderate To Heavy	No
DIES	**DIE VARIETIES**	**% OF PL**	**% OF DMPL**	**PIVOTAL GRADE**	**RARITY FACTOR**
128	12	3.2	2.5	MS 65	R-4

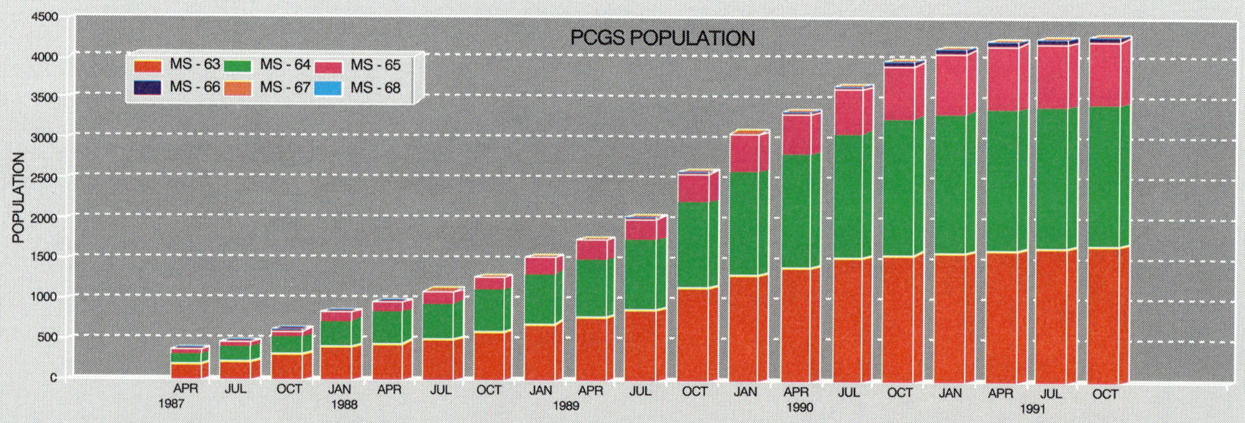

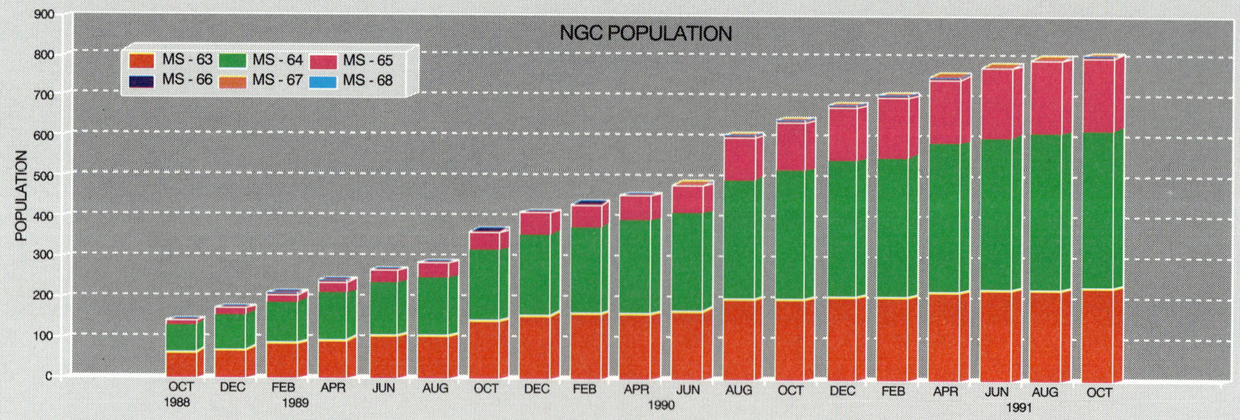

PCGS POPULATION

MS - 63 MS - 64 MS - 65 MS - 66 MS - 67 MS - 68

NGC POPULATION

MS - 63 MS - 64 MS - 65 MS - 66 MS - 67 MS - 68

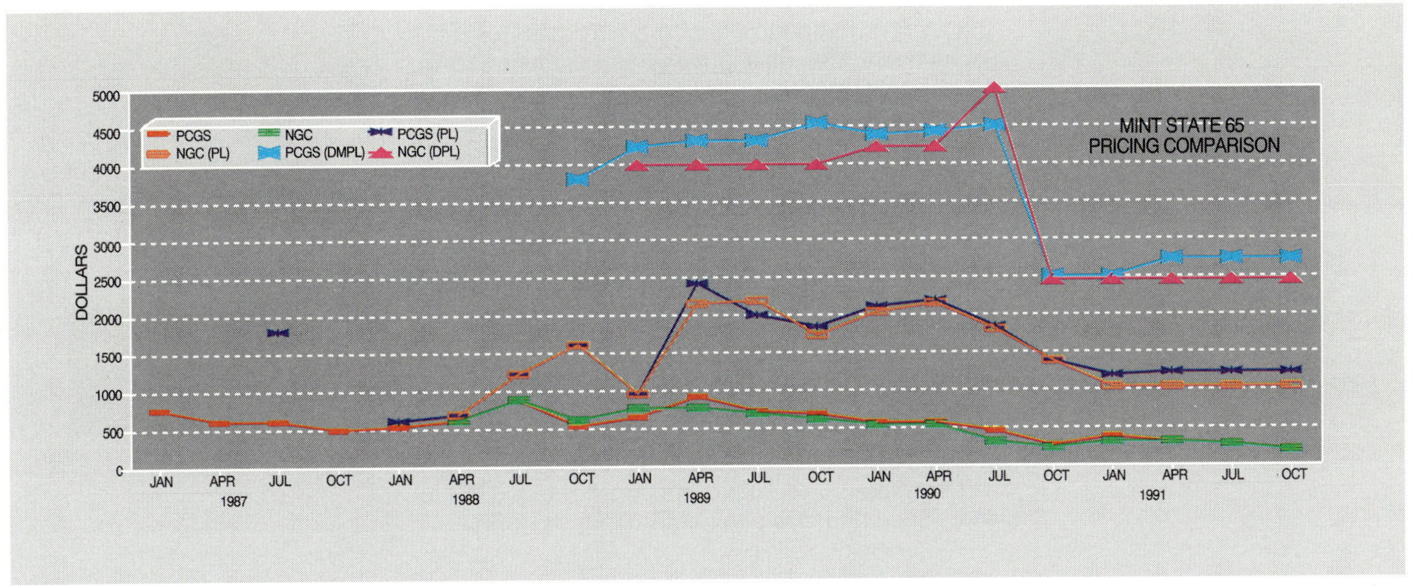
MINT STATE 65
PRICING COMPARISON
PCGS
NGC
PCGS (PL)
NGC (PL)
PCGS (DMPL)
NGC (DPL)
DOLLARS
JAN APR JUL OCT JAN APR JUL OCT JAN APR JUL OCT JAN APR JUL OCT JAN APR JUL OCT
1987 1988 1989 1990 1991

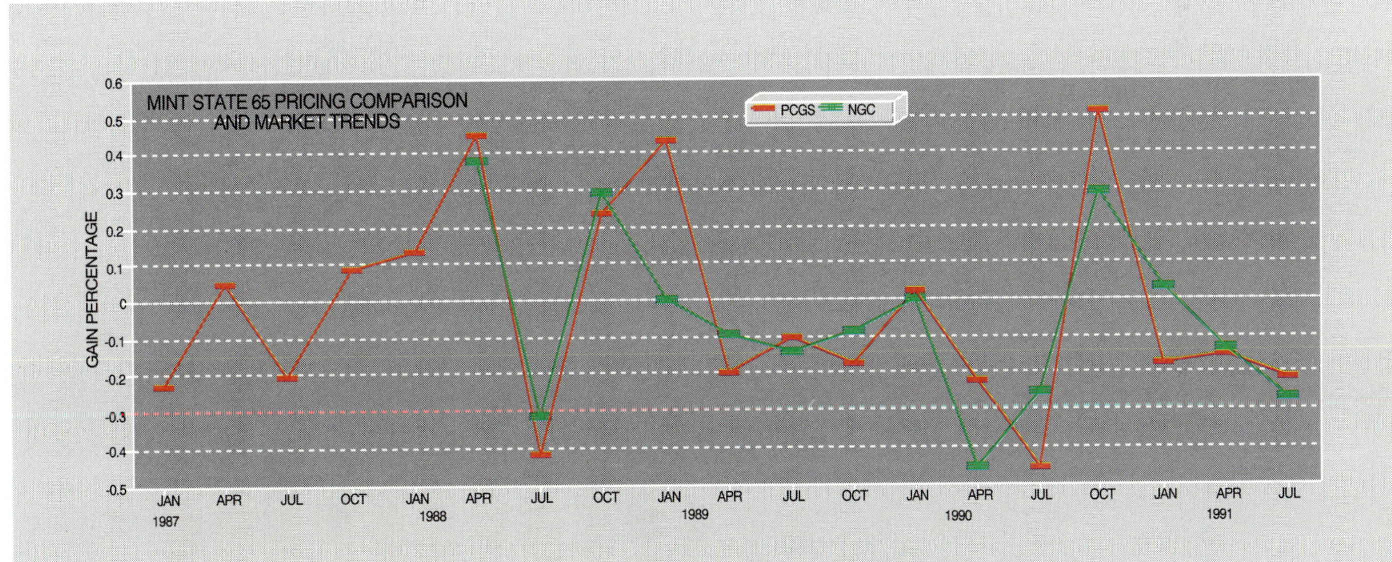
MINT STATE 65 PRICING COMPARISON
AND MARKET TRENDS
PCGS
NGC
GAIN PERCENTAGE
JAN APR JUL OCT JAN APR JUL OCT JAN APR JUL OCT JAN APR JUL OCT JAN APR JUL
1987 1988 1989 1990 1991

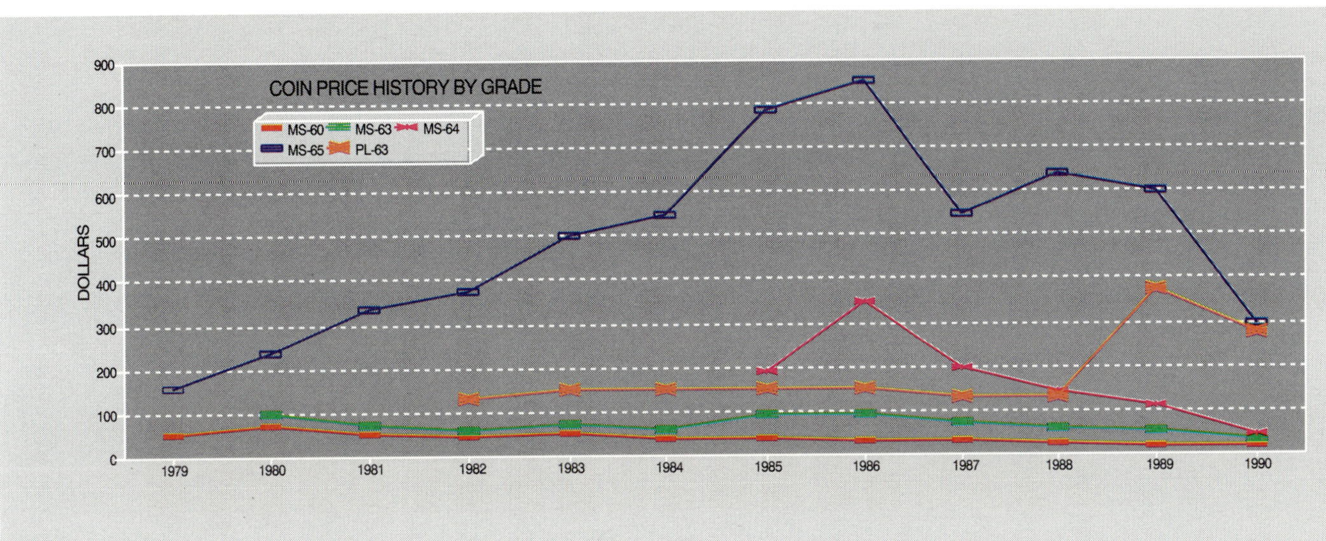
COIN PRICE HISTORY BY GRADE
MS-60
MS-63
MS-64
MS-65
PL-63
DOLLARS
1979 1980 1981 1982 1983 1984 1985 1986 1987 1988 1989 1990

1884-CC

Out of 1,136,000 minted (from 10 pairs of dies), GSA held 962,638, selling many at minimum $30 bid (one to a customer). In addition, they offered 159,008 as "undesirable" (scratched or circulated), at $15 minimum bid; many were actually Unc. In 1980 they disposed of the last 428,000. Others had been released by the Treasury in 1938 and 1961-63. That's a total of 85% from the original mintage! Unsurprisingly, rolls (MS 60/63) still survive. Seldom seen in circulated grades. One of two commonest CC's; the other is 1883-CC.

Recommended in MS 64 or better. Also by the roll in MS 63.

Proofs: At least two are reported with 4 believed to be known. One auctioned: Aug. 9-10, 1991, Racoa David W. Akers, Inc. Chicago ANA 100th Anniversary.

Prooflikes: Plentiful, but mostly in MS 64 or below. Scarce to rare above MS 65 PL or DMPL.

MINTAGE	PROOF	STRIKE	LUSTER	BAG MARKS	REDFIELD
1,136,000	0	Sharp & Bold	Good	Moderate	No
DIES	**DIE VARIETIES**	**% OF PL**	**% OF DMPL**	**PIVOTAL GRADE**	**RARITY FACTOR**
20	12	8.9	8.5	MS 65	R-5

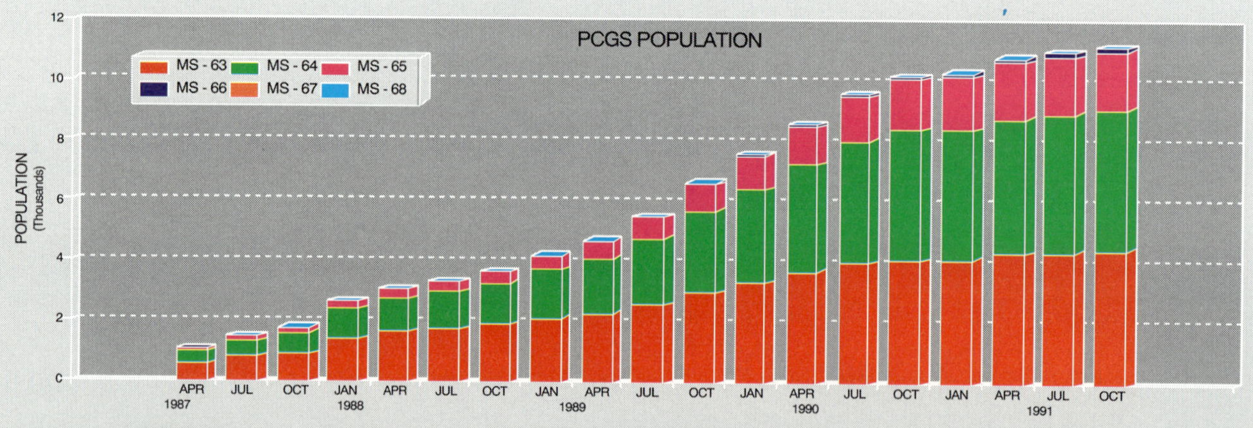

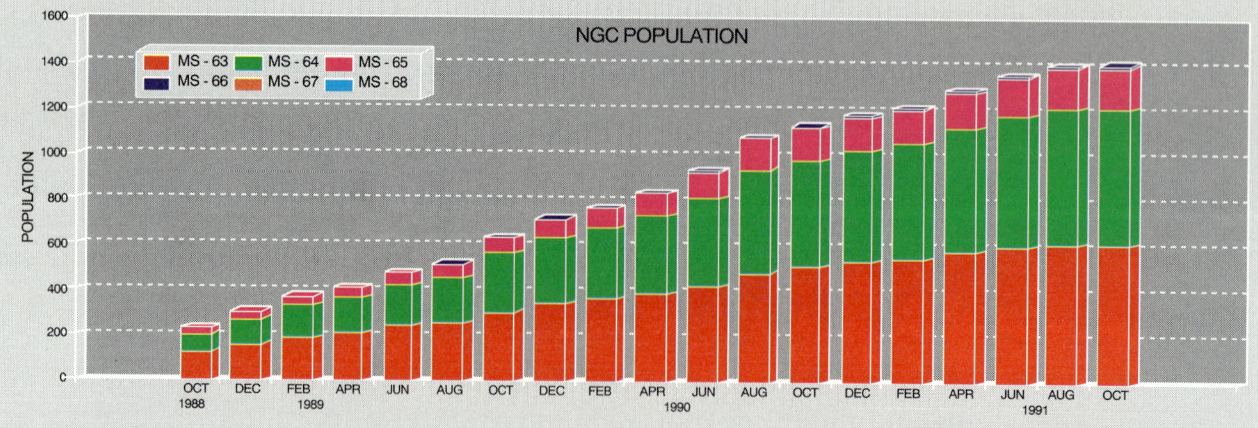

1884-CC

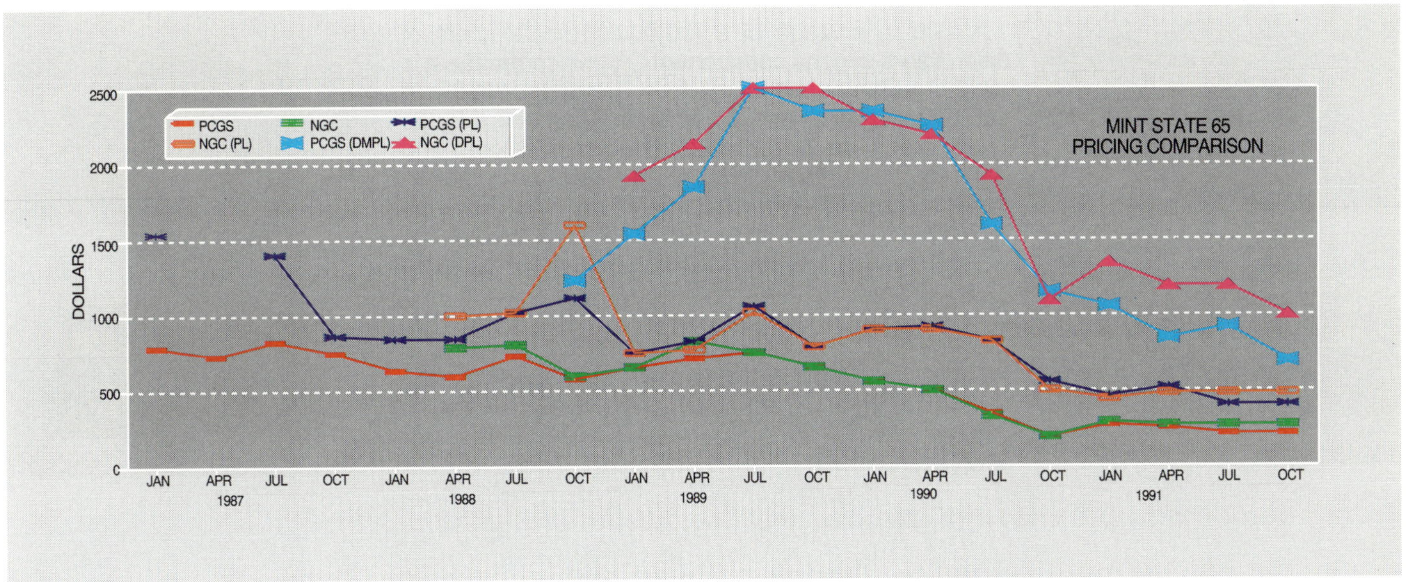

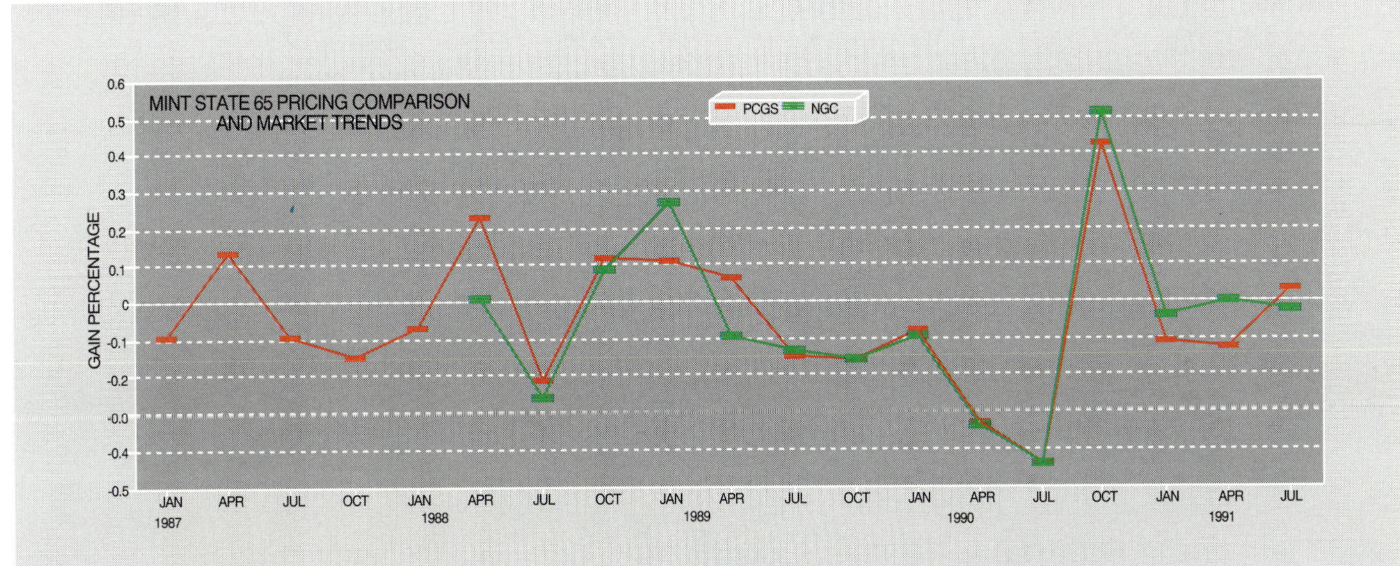

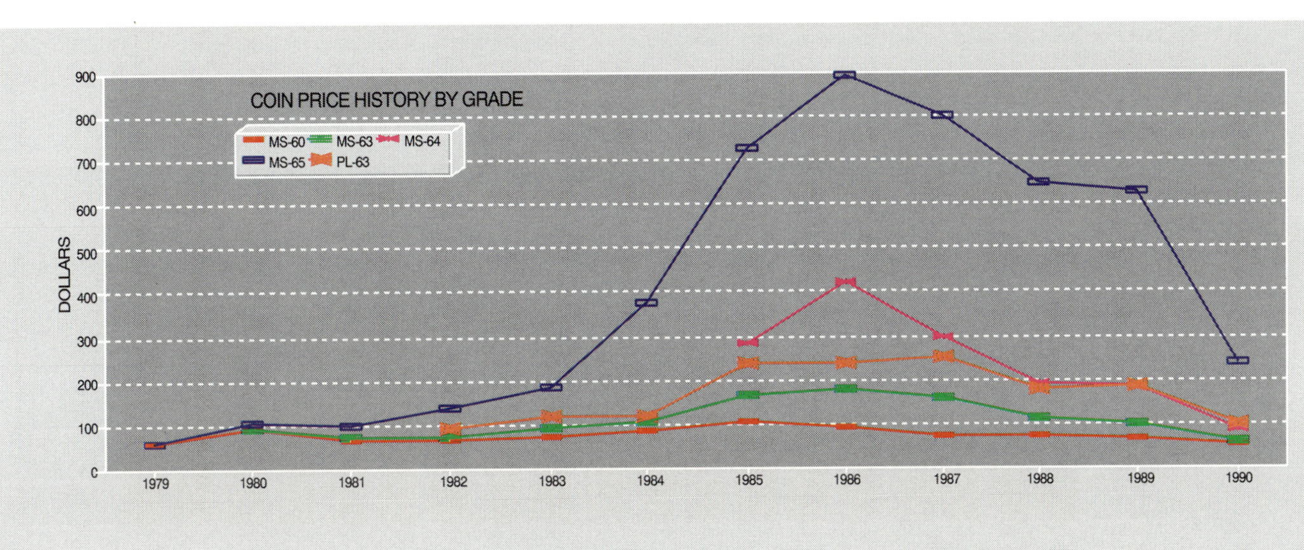

1884-O

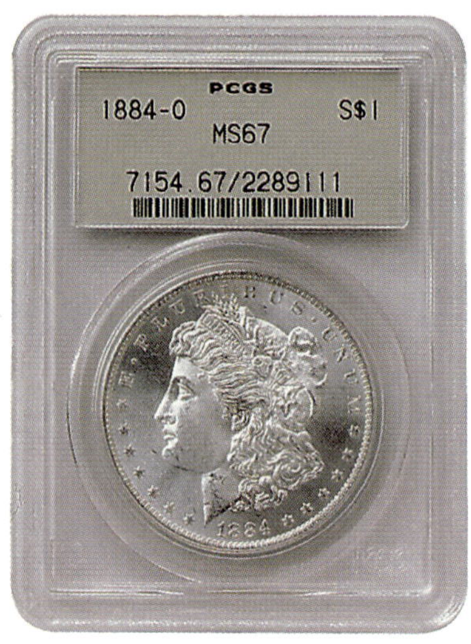

With a mintage of 9,730,000 (from 20 pairs of dies), this is second commonest O Mint; commonest is 1885-O. Many uncs. came from Treasury (1938 and 1960-62 releases) and Continental Bank hoard bags. These last were dispersed by Leon Hendrickson and Clark A. Samuelson. Uncs. are lustrous but often weak; improper basining and use of worn-out dies may be factors. Bag quantities (MS 60/63) still survive.

Most have oval O (slit opening); a small minority, round O (wide opening, VAM 2, 18).

Recommended in MS 65 up.

Proofs: One reported, ex Brock, University of Pennsylvania, Rovensky:99, Norweb:3858.

Prooflikes: Commonly one-sided. Two-sided one are scarce to rare above MS 65. Cameos are not often seen.

MINTAGE	PROOF	STRIKE	LUSTER	BAG MARKS	REDFIELD
9,730,000	0	Average To Bold	Good	Moderate	No
DIES	**DIE VARIETIES**	**% OF PL**	**% OF DMPL**	**PIVOTAL GRADE**	**RARITY FACTOR**
60	36	2.7	2.5	MS 65	R-5

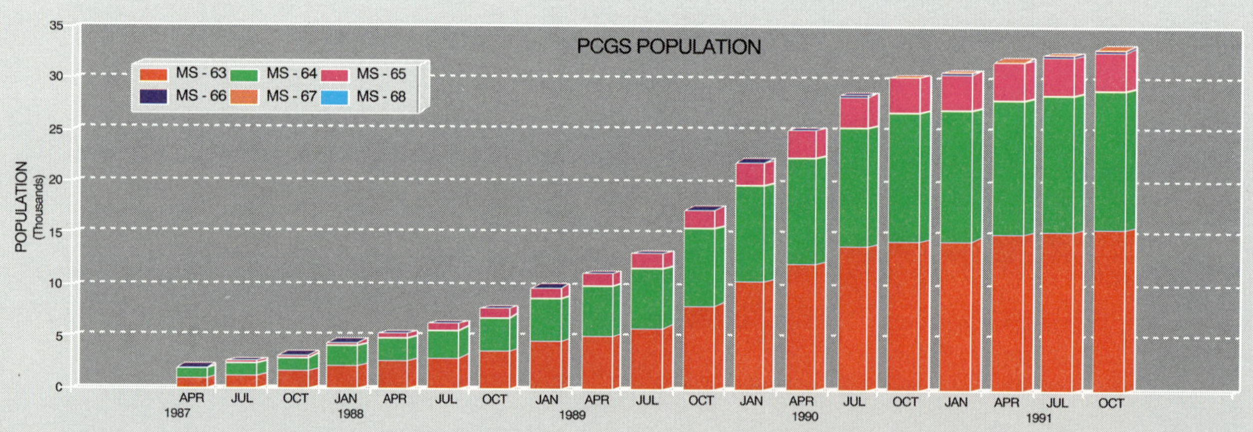

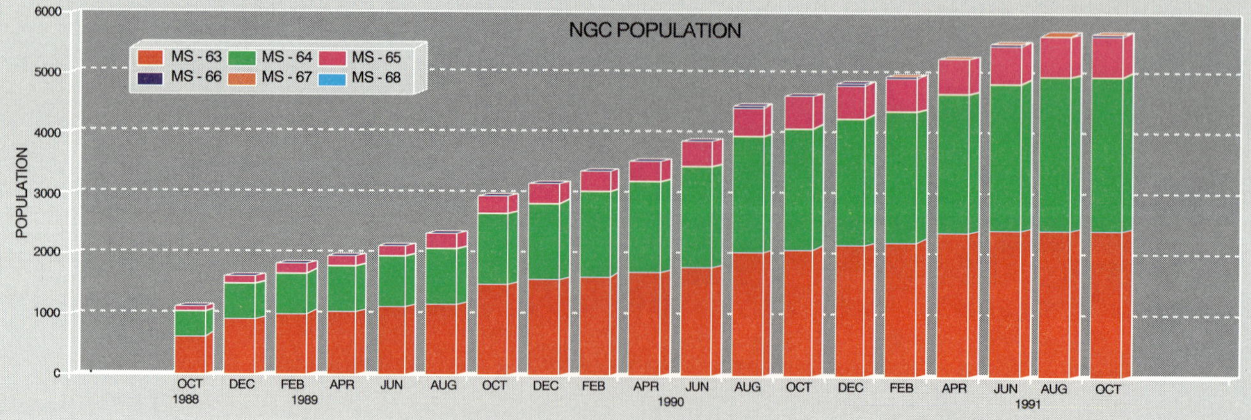

PCGS POPULATION

MS - 63 MS - 64 MS - 65 MS - 66 MS - 67 MS - 68

POPULATION (Thousands)

0 5 10 15 20 25 30 35

APR 1987 JUL OCT JAN 1988 APR JUL OCT JAN 1989 APR JUL OCT JAN APR 1990 JUL OCT JAN APR 1991 JUL OCT

NGC POPULATION

MS - 63 MS - 64 MS - 65 MS - 66 MS - 67 MS - 68

POPULATION

0 1000 2000 3000 4000 5000 6000

OCT 1988 DEC FEB 1989 APR JUN AUG OCT DEC FEB APR 1990 JUN AUG OCT DEC FEB APR JUN 1991 AUG OCT

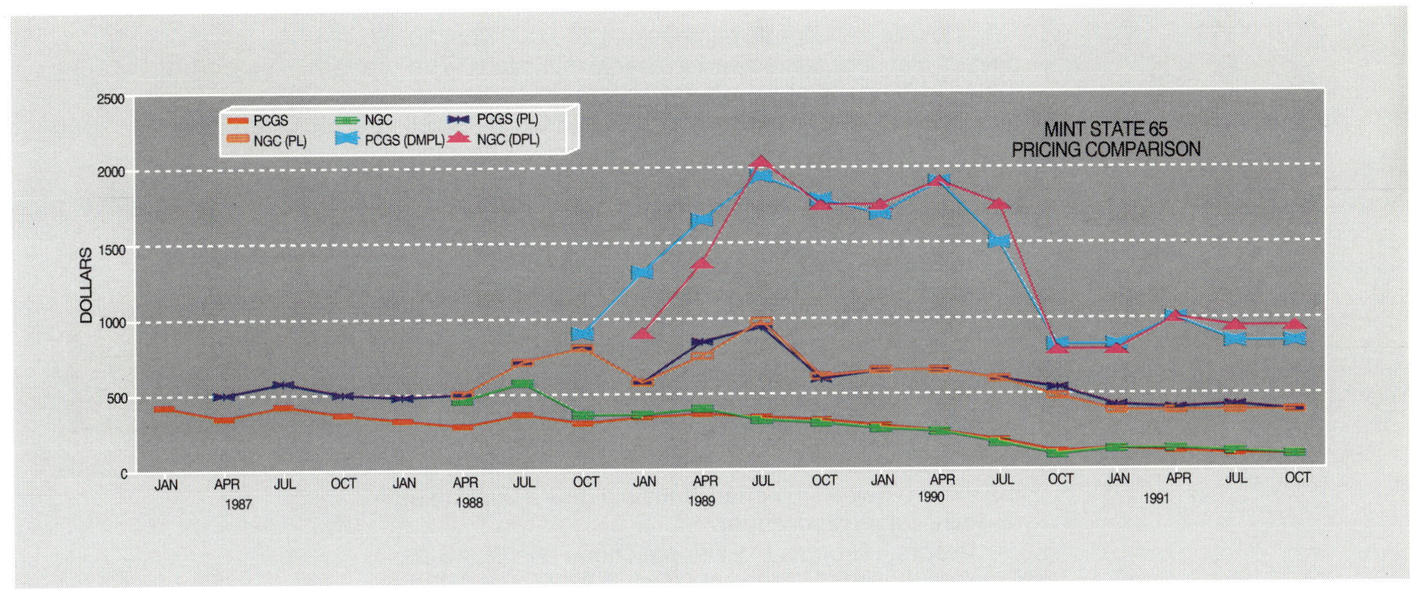
MINT STATE 65
PRICING COMPARISON
PCGS
NGC
PCGS (PL)
NGC (PL)
PCGS (DMPL)
NGC (DPL)
DOLLARS
2500
2000
1500
1000
500
0
JAN APR JUL OCT JAN APR JUL OCT JAN APR JUL OCT JAN APR JUL OCT JAN APR JUL OCT
1987
1988
1989
1990
1991

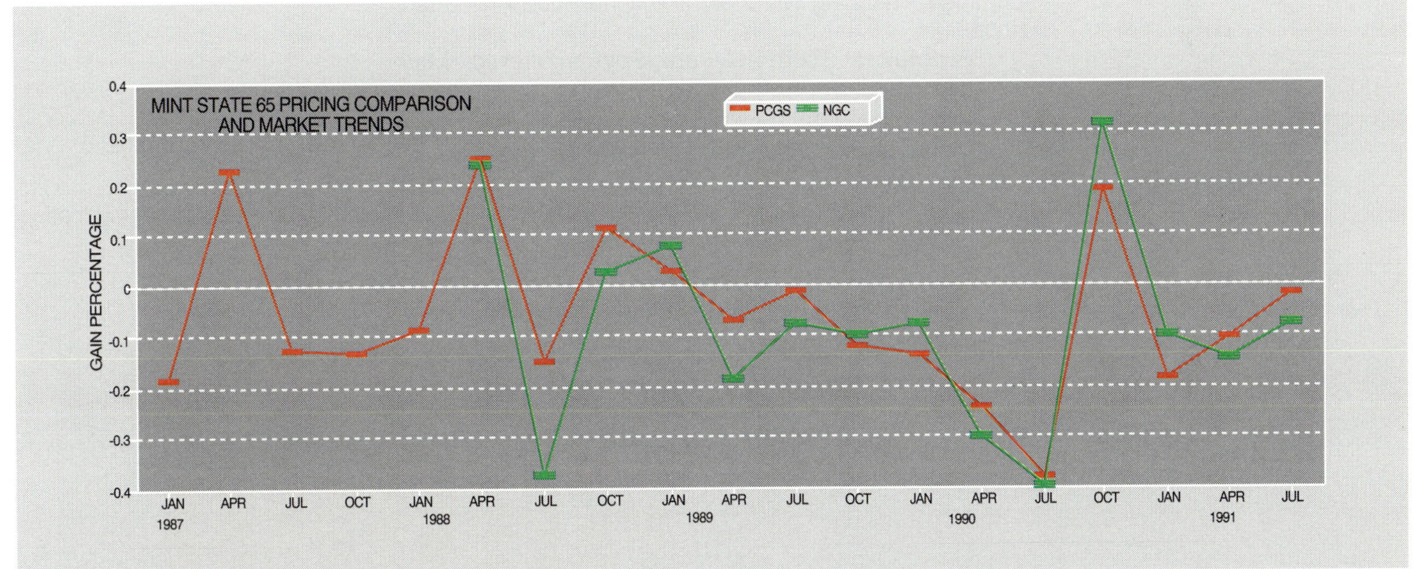
MINT STATE 65 PRICING COMPARISON
AND MARKET TRENDS
PCGS
NGC
GAIN PERCENTAGE
0.4
0.3
0.2
0.1
0
-0.1
-0.2
-0.3
-0.4
JAN APR JUL OCT JAN APR JUL OCT JAN APR JUL OCT JAN APR JUL OCT JAN APR JUL
1987
1988
1989
1990
1991

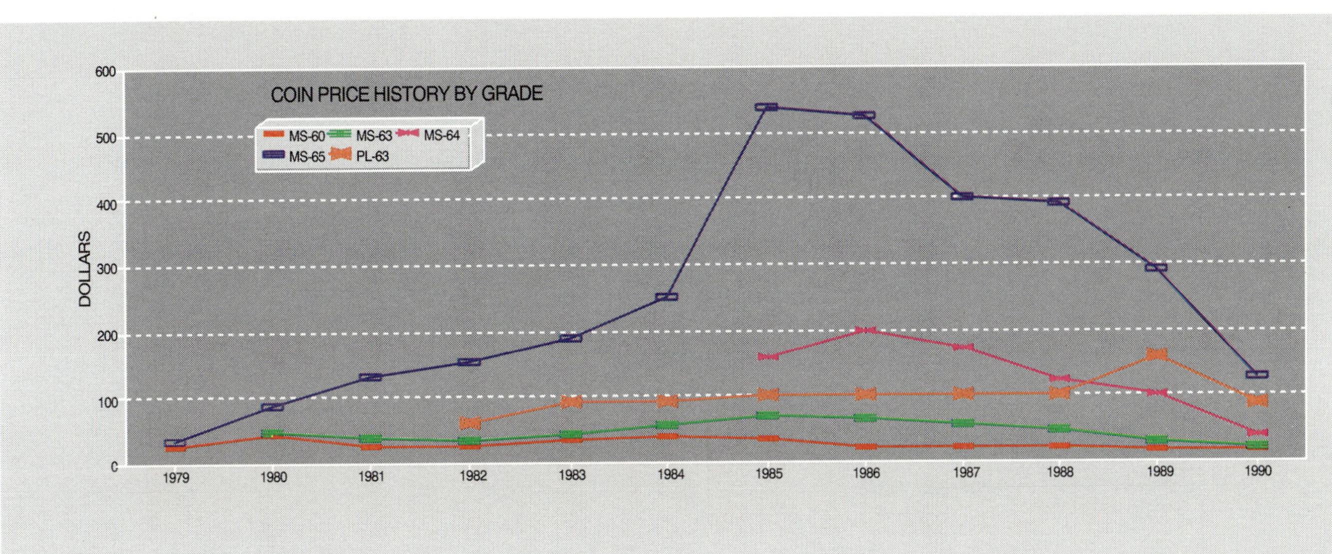
COIN PRICE HISTORY BY GRADE
MS-60
MS-63
MS-64
MS-65
PL-63
DOLLARS
600
500
400
300
200
100
0
1979
1980
1981
1982
1983
1984
1985
1986
1987
1988
1989
1990

PCGS
1884-S
S$1
MS67
7156.67/7005601

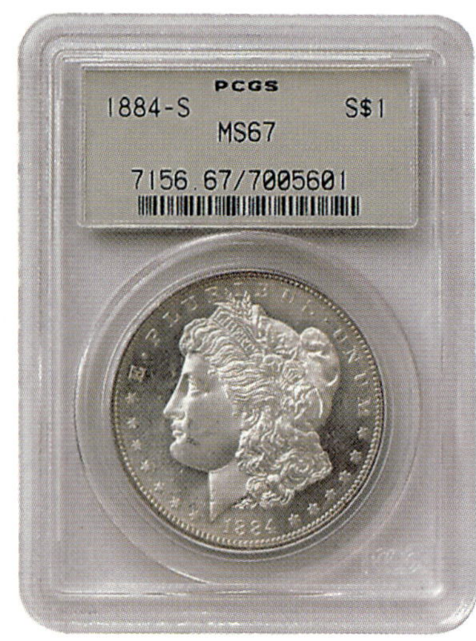

1884-S

Despite a moderate mintage of 3,200,000 from 20 pairs of dies, this has proved a rarity in mint state. The 1884-S has a soft strike. Many sliders from resealed mint sacks; for more details see 1885-S. On the other hand, real gems are almost unheard of. The only PCGS MS 64 traded for over $100,000; the PCGS MS 65 and MS 67 each sold around five times as high!

"There has never been documented an original BU roll for 1884-S Morgan silver dollars." — Dean Tavenner. Nor has the rumor of a bag in the western U.S. been confirmed.

Recommended in strict Mint State, the higher the grade the better. Professional advice may be necessary to avoid being taken in by sliders.

Fakes have been made by adding S to genuine 1884 Philadelphia dollars. These can be identified by the seam between mintmark and field (use a 20x glass or a binocular microscope).

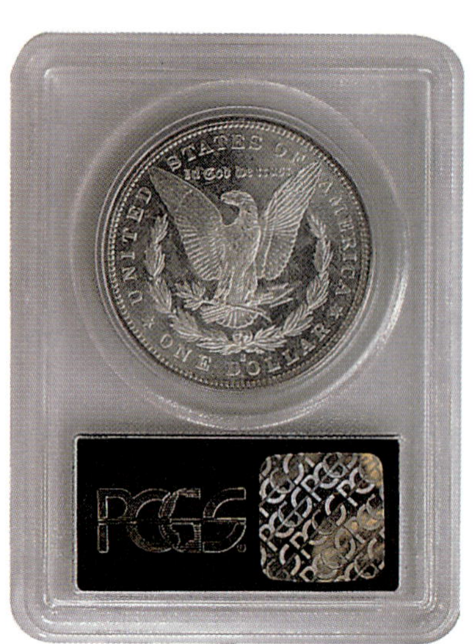

Proofs: Thomas L. Elder described an 1884-S as "Proof" in the J. B. Wilson sale (Oct. 5-7, 1908), lot 225. It went to a bidder designated as "Worth", not otherwise identified. Nothing remotely like it has been reported since.

Prooflikes: Extremely rare, Seldom offered. May not exist in DMPL.

MINTAGE	PROOF	STRIKE	LUSTER	BAG MARKS	REDFIELD
3,200,000	0	Soft	Good	Moderate	No
DIES	**DIE VARIETIES**	**% OF PL**	**% OF DMPL**	**PIVOTAL GRADE**	**RARITY FACTOR**
80	8	2.4	0.0	MS 63	R-1

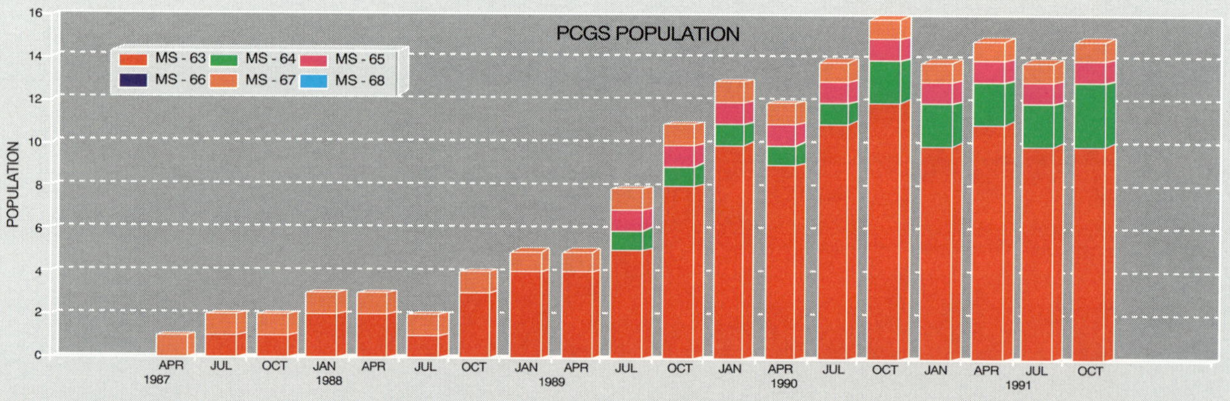

PCGS POPULATION
MS - 63
MS - 64
MS - 65
MS - 66
MS - 67
MS - 68
POPULATION
16
14
12
10
8
6
4
2
APR 1987
JUL
OCT
JAN 1988
APR
JUL
OCT
JAN 1989
APR
JUL
OCT
JAN
APR 1990
JUL
OCT
JAN
APR
JUL 1991
OCT

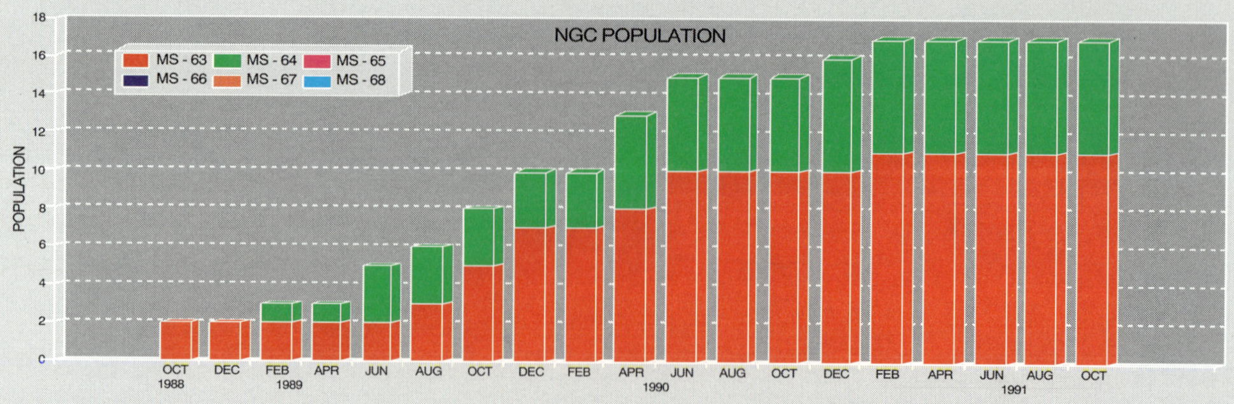

NGC POPULATION
MS - 63
MS - 64
MS - 65
MS - 66
MS - 67
MS - 68
POPULATION
18
16
14
12
10
8
6
4
2
OCT 1988
DEC
FEB 1989
APR
JUN
AUG
OCT
DEC
FEB
APR 1990
JUN
AUG
OCT
DEC
FEB
APR
JUN 1991
AUG
OCT

1884-S

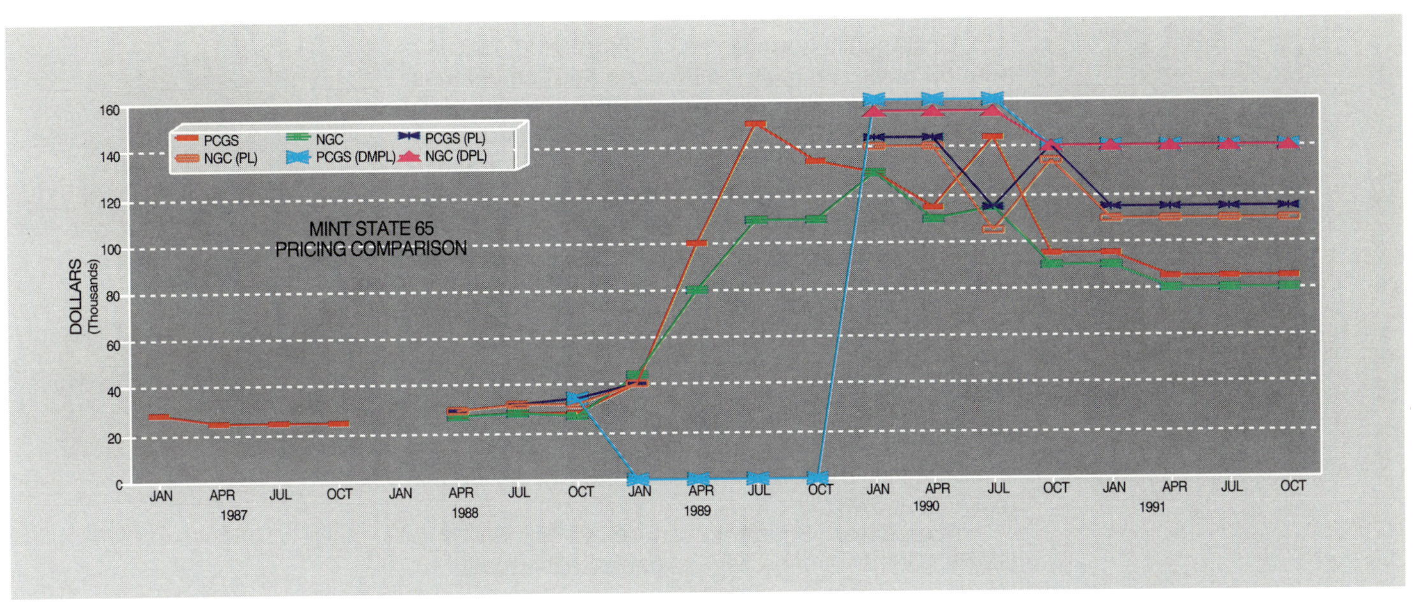

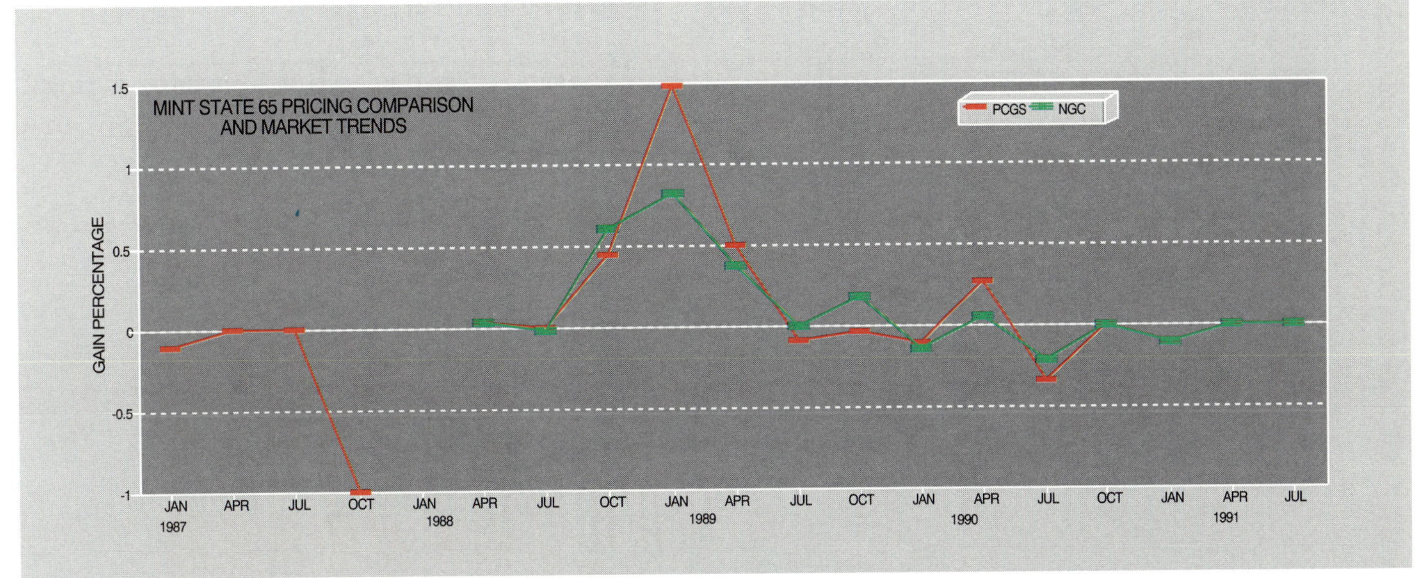

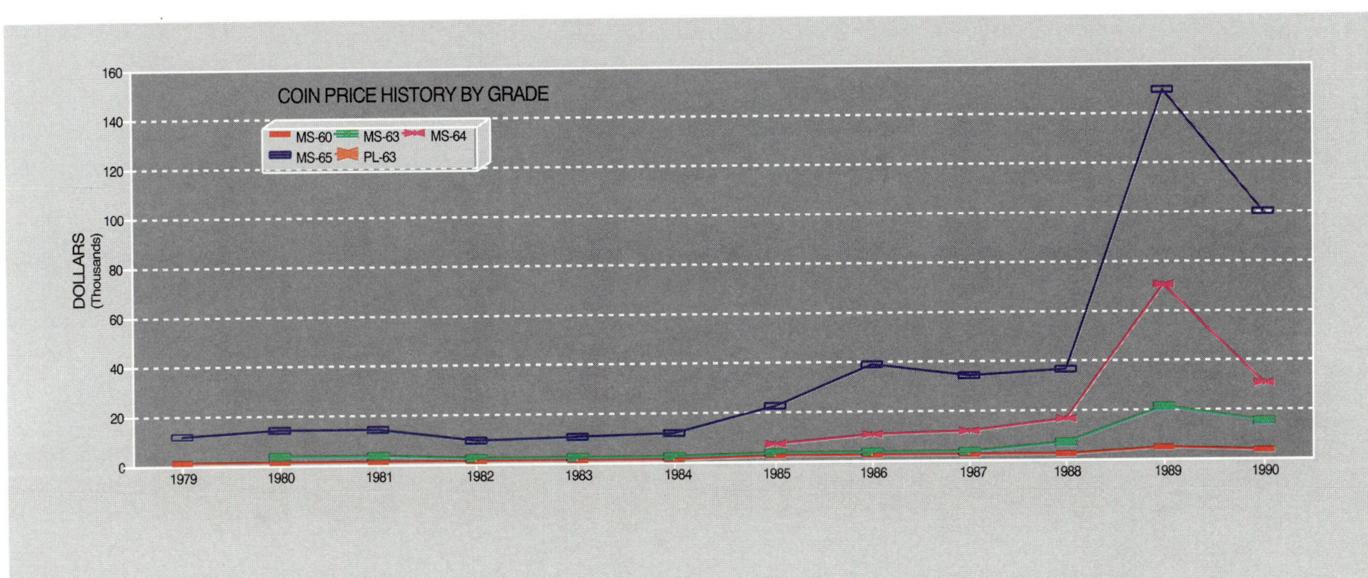

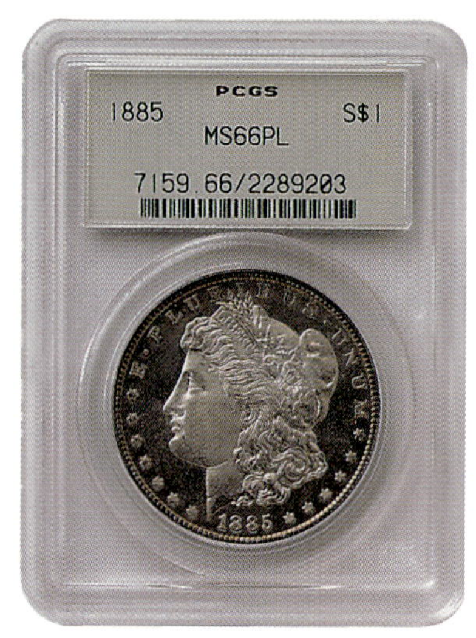

1885-P

PCGS
1885 S$1
MS66PL
7159.66/2289203

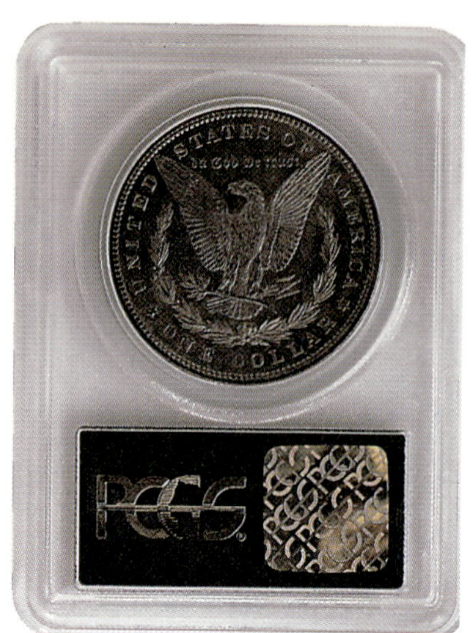

Unsurprisingly (given its mintage of 17,786,837, from 89 obvs., 88 revs.), this is the third commonest Philadelphia Morgan dollars prior to 1921, thanks partly to Treasury (1954) and Continental Bank hoard bags. The two commoner ones are 1886 and 1887. Plentiful in Unc. with bold strike and excellent luster; plentiful also with weak strikes and/or die cracks. This date has some of the best-struck Philadelphia Uncs. in the series.

Roll and bag lots (MS 60/63) survive. Both Silver Towne, Winchester, Indiana and Colonial Coins of Houston, Texas distributed many Continental Bank bags in 1984.

Recommended in MS 65 up by the roll only.

Proofs: The 930 struck took 2 obvs., 1 rev. VAM 2 has top of 5 double, VAM 2 bases of 85 double (plainest at 5).

Prooflikes: Scarce to rare above MS 65 PL or DMPL. Some cameos have exceptional contrast.

MINTAGE	PROOF	STRIKE	LUSTER	BAG MARKS	REDFIELD
17,786,837	930	Sharp & Bold	Very Good	Moderate	No
DIES	**DIE VARIETIES**	**% OF PL**	**% OF DMPL**	**PIVOTAL GRADE**	**RARITY FACTOR**
131	21	4.1	4.7	MS 65	R-5

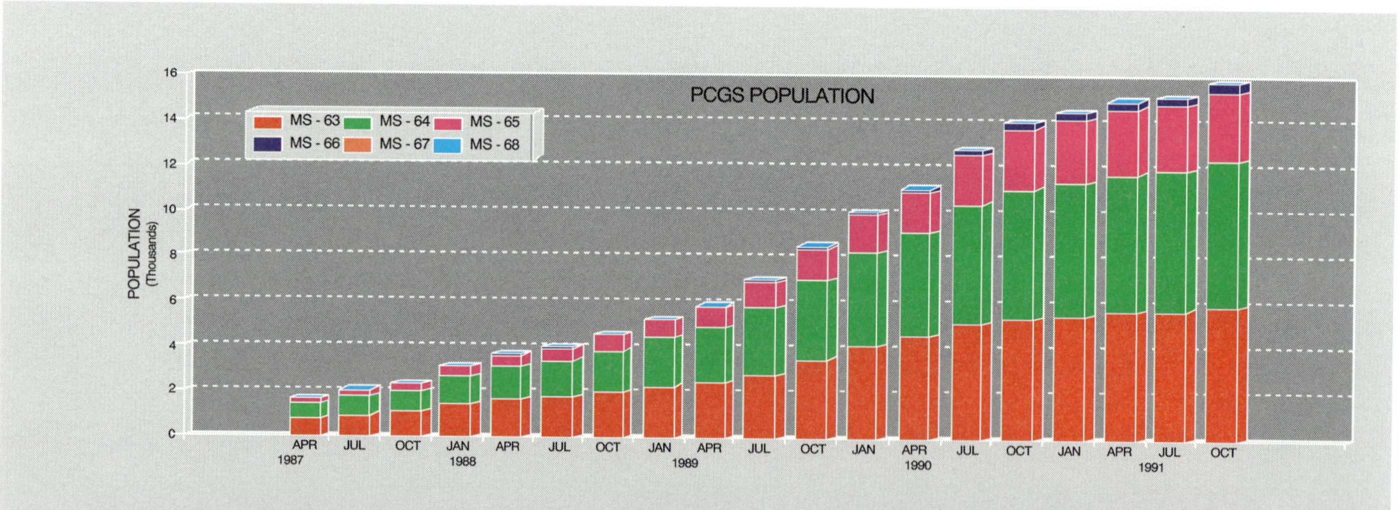
PCGS POPULATION
MS - 63 MS - 64 MS - 65
MS - 66 MS - 67 MS - 68
POPULATION (Thousands)
0 2 4 6 8 10 12 14 16
APR 1987 JUL OCT JAN 1988 APR JUL OCT JAN 1989 APR JUL OCT JAN APR 1990 JUL OCT JAN APR JUL 1991 OCT

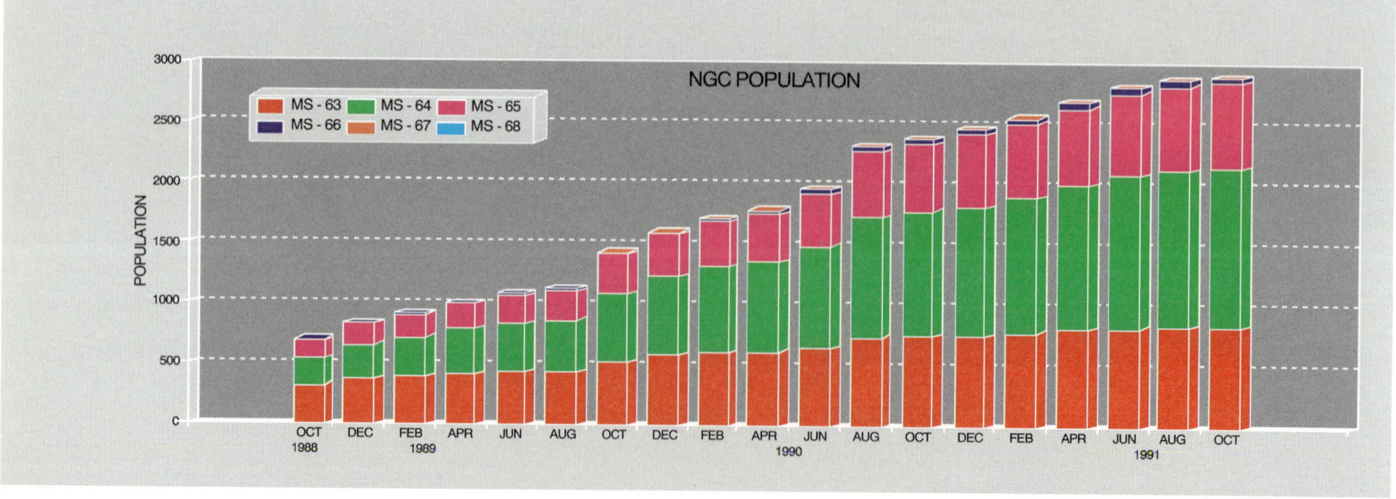
NGC POPULATION
MS - 63 MS - 64 MS - 65
MS - 66 MS - 67 MS - 68
POPULATION
0 500 1000 1500 2000 2500 3000
OCT 1988 DEC FEB 1989 APR JUN AUG OCT DEC FEB APR 1990 JUN AUG OCT DEC FEB APR JUN 1991 AUG OCT

1885-P

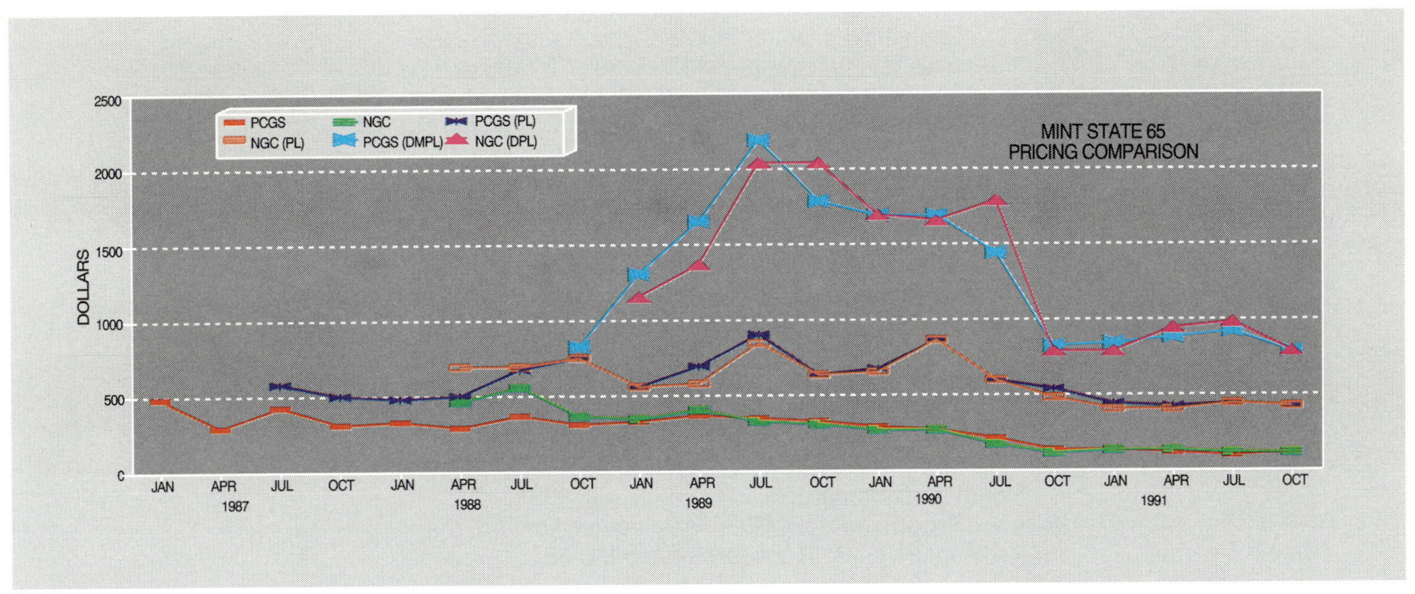

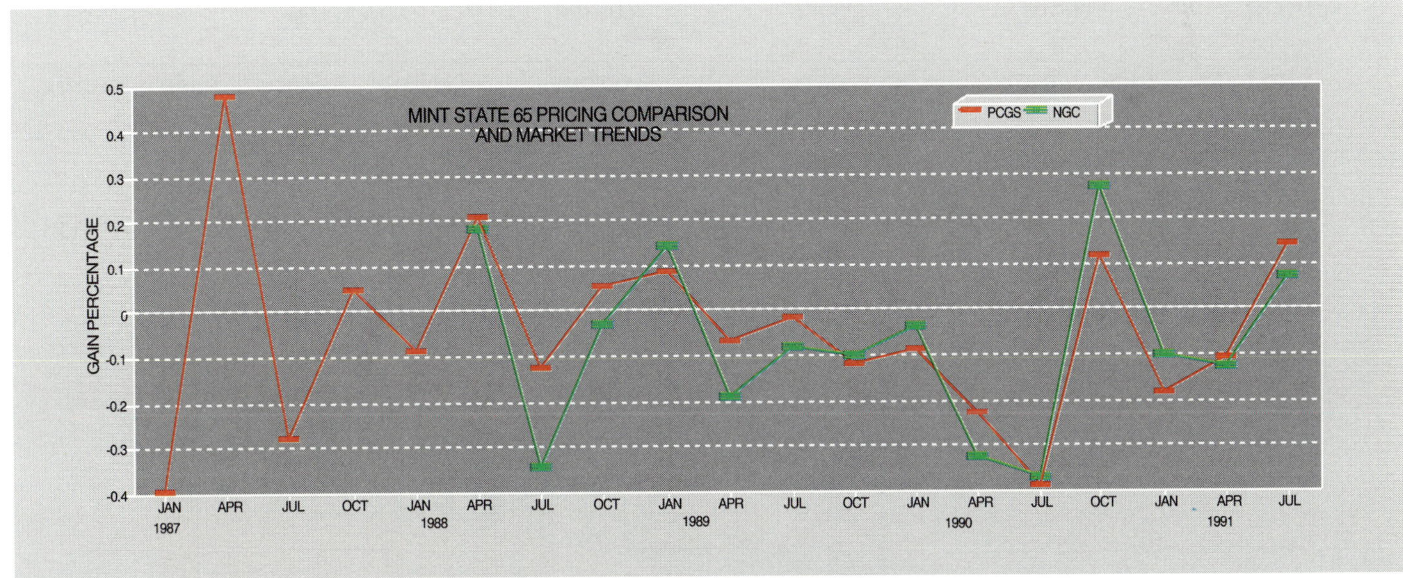

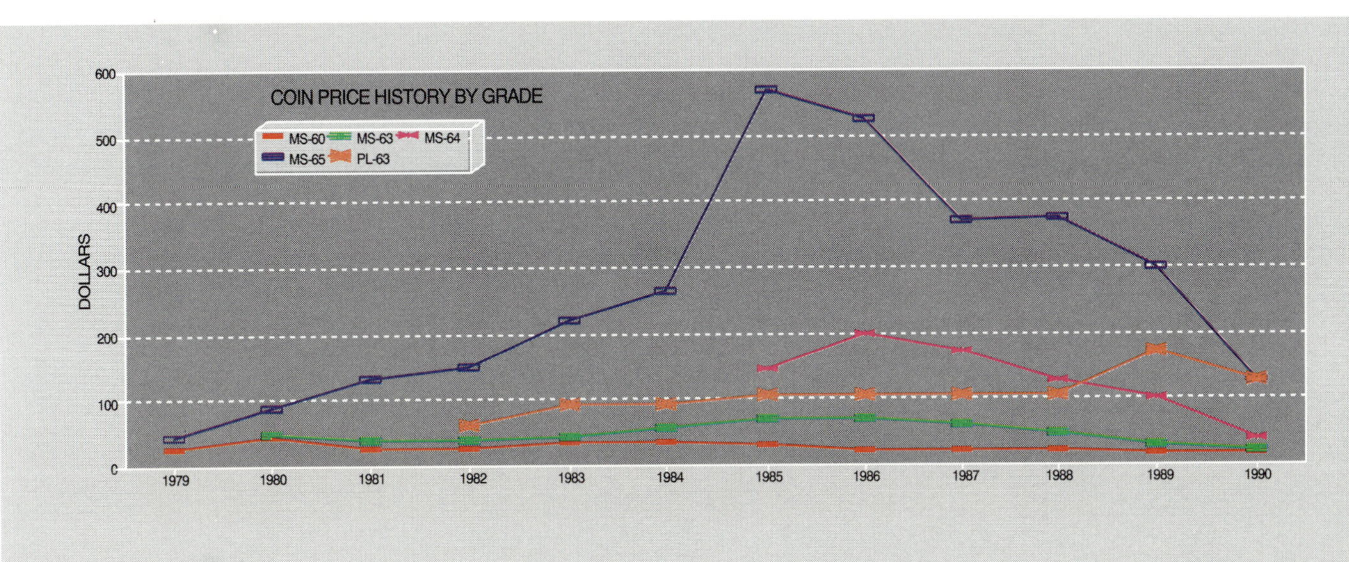

PCGS
1885-CC
S$1
MS68
7160 68/6271763

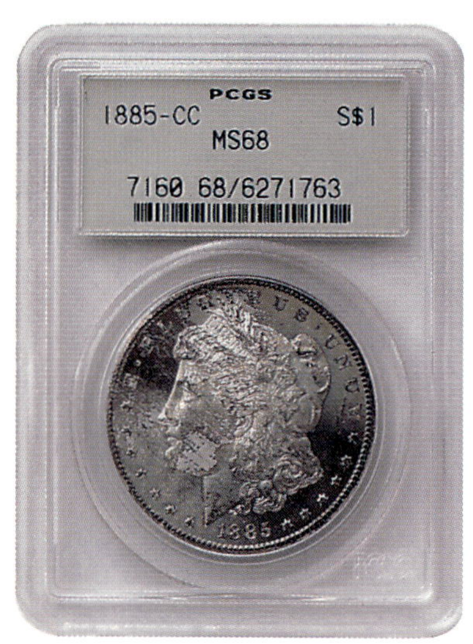

1885-CC

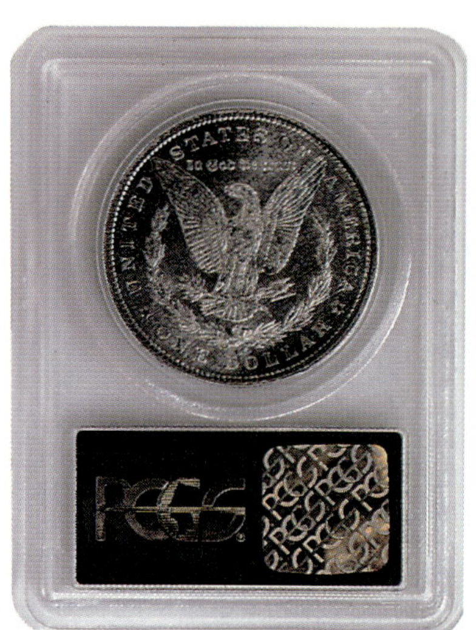

Though its mintage of 228,000 is fourth lowest in the series (the first three are 1895, 1893-S, 1894), it is far commoner than any of these. Many were released by the Treasury in Montana, 1958; GSA offered 148,285 Uncs. in the 1972-74 mail bid sales — minimum bid $60. The 31,569 unsold in those offerings were sold in 1980. This was nearly "two-thirds" of the entire mintage! There may have been as many as 1,000 in the Redfield hoard; it is listed as 6th scarcest Redfield date. Seldom seen circulated. Probably not all 10 pairs of dies were used.

Recommended above MS 64 or by the roll in any BU grade.

Fakes have been made by cementing CC mintmark to genuine Philadelphia coins.

The Carson City mint closed November 10, 1885, not to reopen until July 1, 1889.

Prooflikes: DMPL's are easier to find than ordinary PL's. Both are rare above MS 65.

MINTAGE	PROOF	STRIKE	LUSTER	BAG MARKS	REDFIELD
228,000	0	Sharp & Bold	Excellent	Moderate	Yes
DIES	**DIE VARIETIES**	**% OF PL**	**% OF DMPL**	**PIVOTAL GRADE**	**RARITY FACTOR**
20	4	7.4	7.7	MS 65	R-4

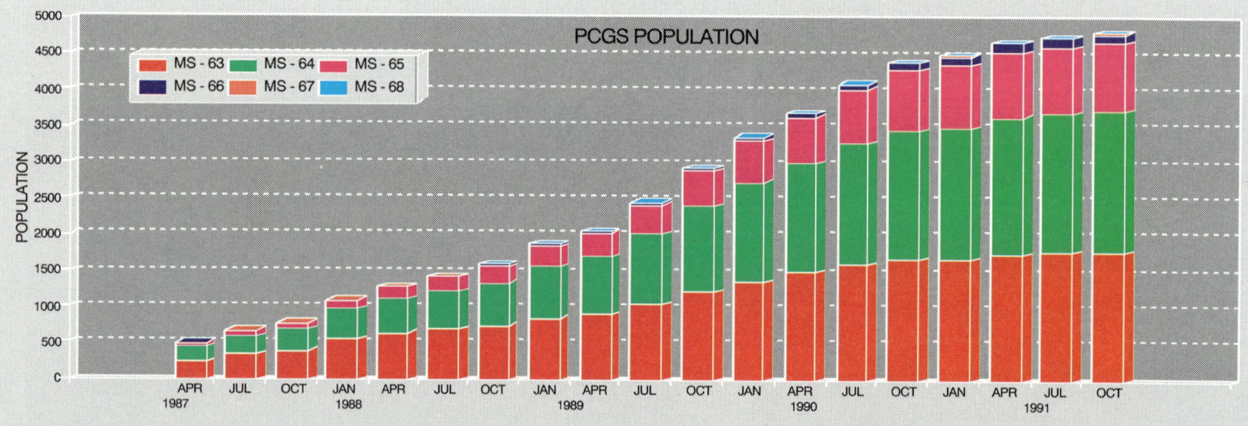
PCGS POPULATION
MS - 63
MS - 64
MS - 65
MS - 66
MS - 67
MS - 68
POPULATION
5000
4500
4000
3500
3000
2500
2000
1500
1000
500
0
APR 1987
JUL
OCT
JAN 1988
APR
JUL
OCT
JAN 1989
APR
JUL
OCT
JAN
APR 1990
JUL
OCT
JAN
APR
JUL 1991
OCT

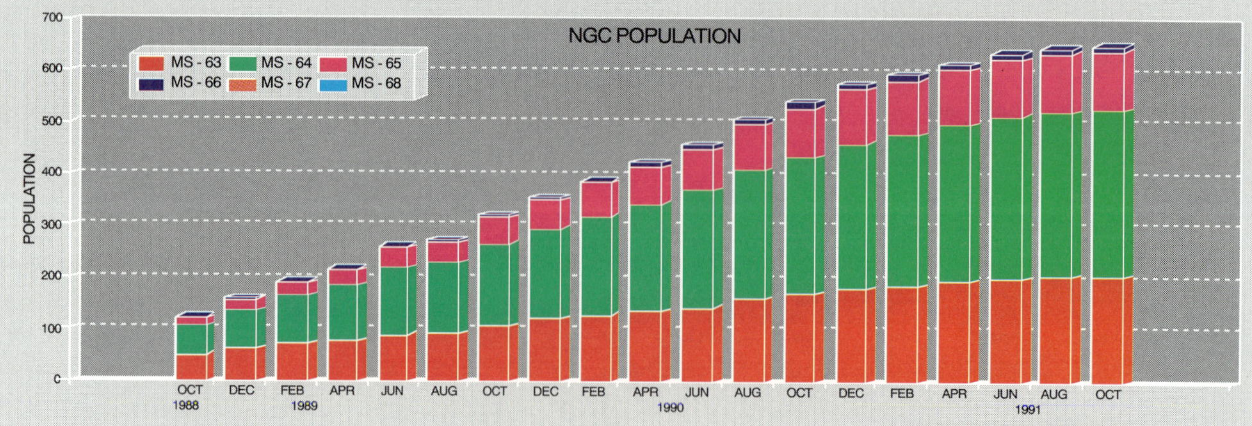
NGC POPULATION
MS - 63
MS - 64
MS - 65
MS - 66
MS - 67
MS - 68
POPULATION
700
600
500
400
300
200
100
0
OCT 1988
DEC
FEB 1989
APR
JUN
AUG
OCT
DEC
FEB
APR 1990
JUN
AUG
OCT
DEC
FEB
APR
JUN 1991
AUG
OCT

1885-CC

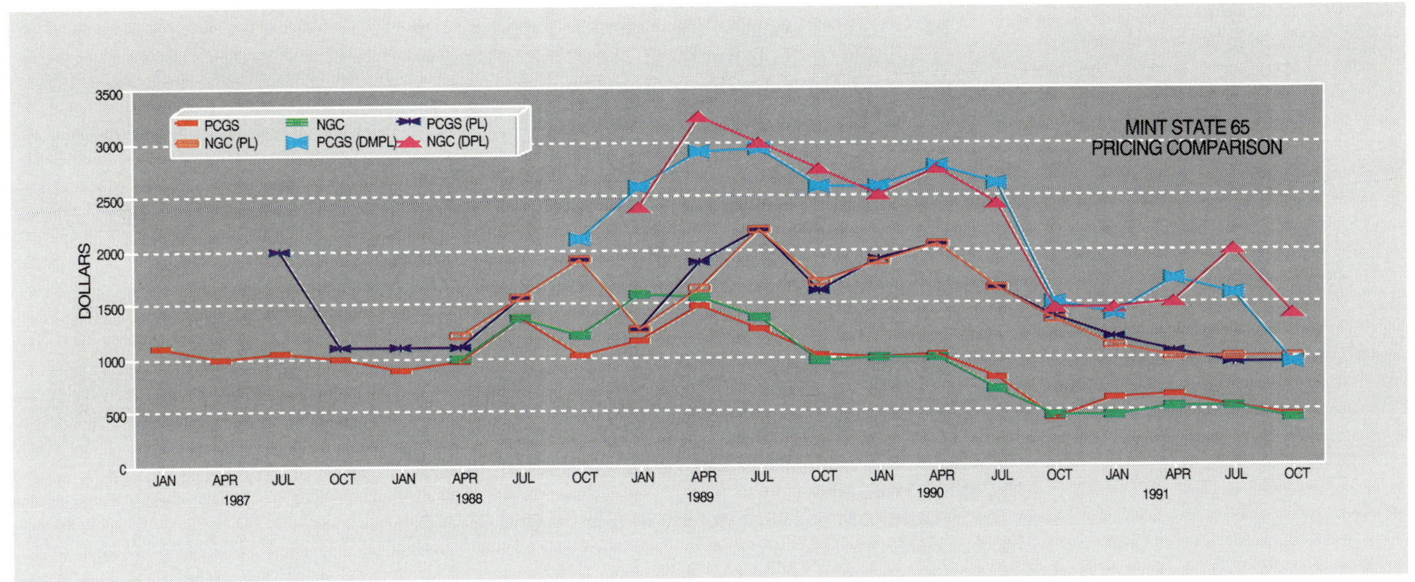

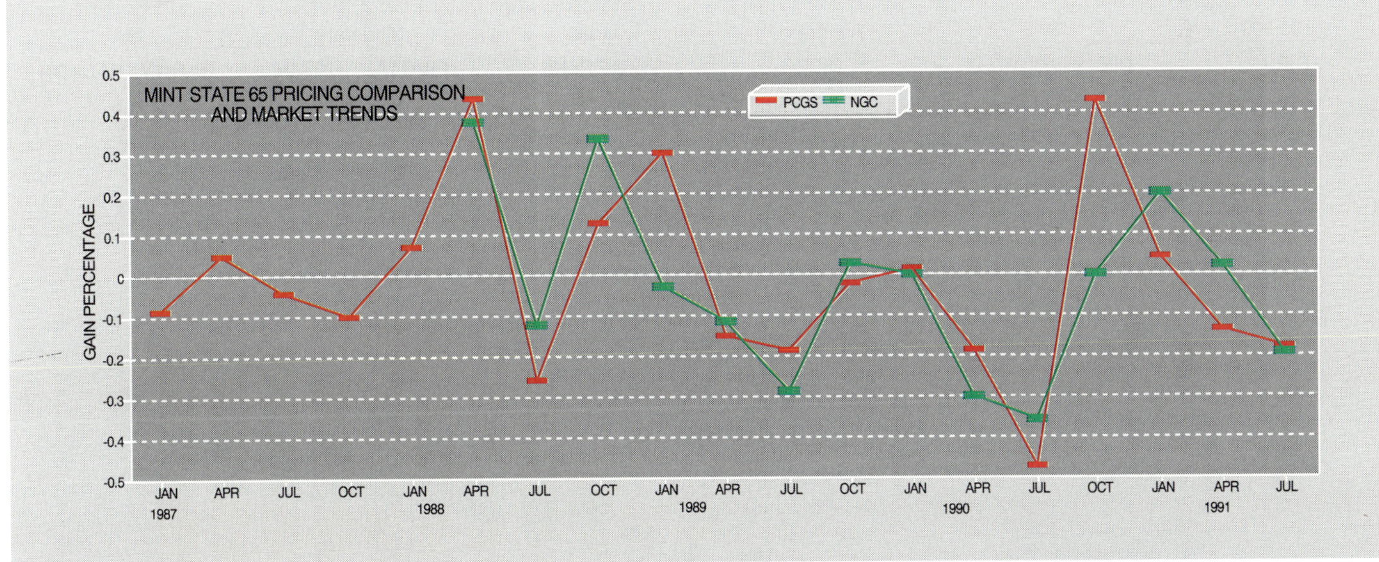

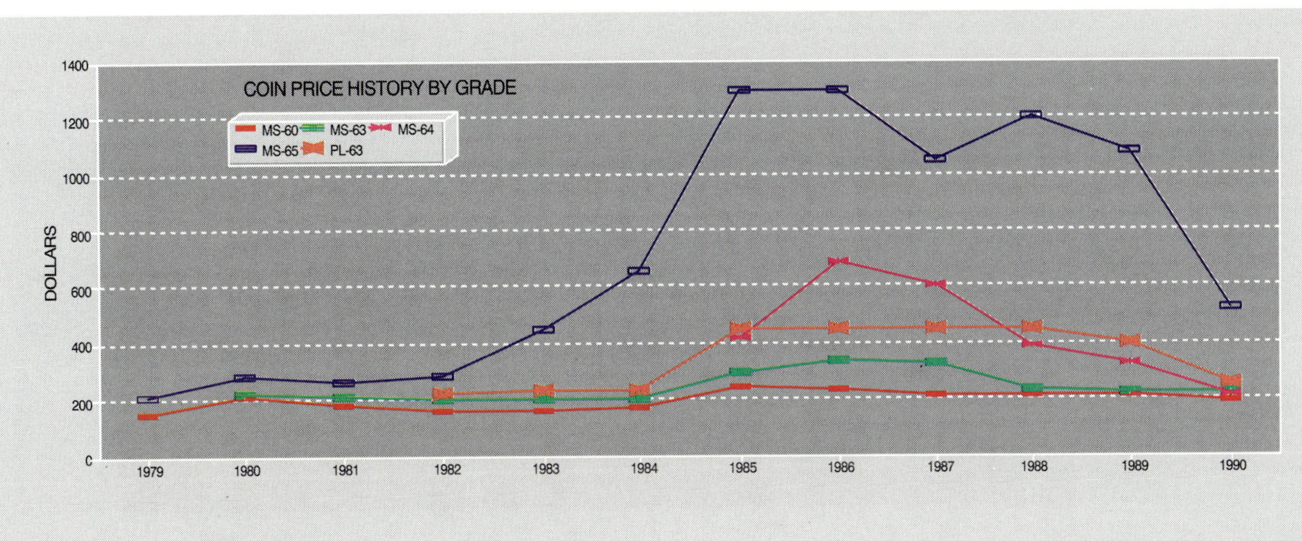

1885-O

The 9,185,000 coined took allegedly 10 pairs of dies: probably a typographical error for 40 pairs. Commonest O Mint; second commonest is 1884-O. That the higher mintages (1887-90-O, 1899-1901-O) did not survive in greater numbers than 1885-O may be blamed on the Pittman Act and World War II meltings. Striking quality of Uncs. ranges from flat to full; lustre is usually frosty.

Many BU bags were dispersed from the Continental Bank hoard. To nobody's surprise, rolls and bag lots are available, both original and assembled.

Recommended in MS 64/65 in roll lots only.

Proofs: One reported, from Brock, Univ. of Pennsylvania, Rovensky: 100, since unseen. This may have been similar to the 1884-O which ended up in the Norweb sale.

Prooflikes: Scarce to rare in MS 66 and above, PL or DMPL.

MINTAGE	PROOF	STRIKE	LUSTER	BAG MARKS	REDFIELD
9,185,000	0	Average	Good	Moderate	No
DIES	**DIE VARIETIES**	**% OF PL**	**% OF DMPL**	**PIVOTAL GRADE**	**RARITY FACTOR**
124	15	2.7	2.3	MS 65	R-5

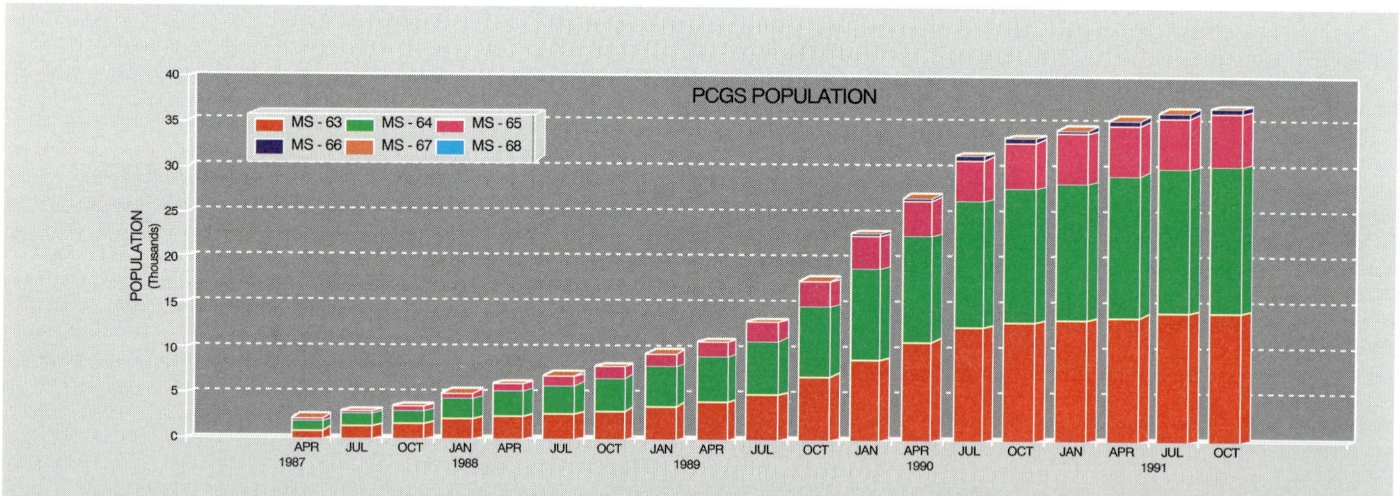

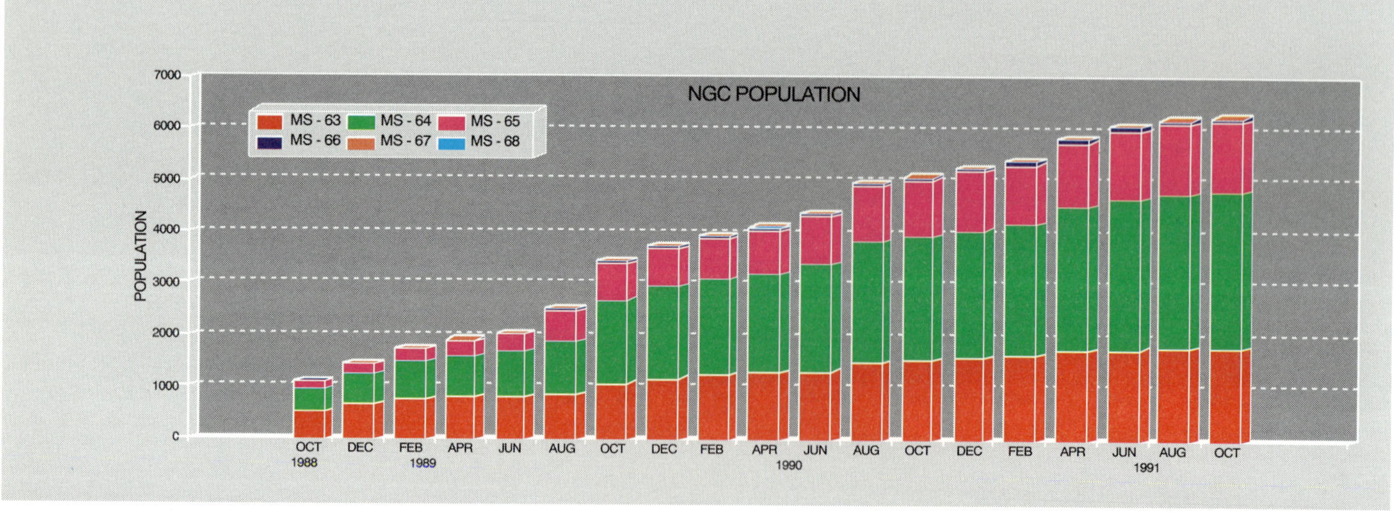

PCGS POPULATION

MS - 63 MS - 64 MS - 65 MS - 66 MS - 67 MS - 68

POPULATION (Thousands)

0 5 10 15 20 25 30 35 40

APR 1987 JUL OCT JAN 1988 APR JUL OCT JAN 1989 APR JUL OCT JAN 1990 APR JUL OCT JAN 1991 APR JUL OCT

NGC POPULATION

MS - 63 MS - 64 MS - 65 MS - 66 MS - 67 MS - 68

POPULATION

0 1000 2000 3000 4000 5000 6000 7000

OCT 1988 DEC FEB 1989 APR JUN AUG OCT DEC FEB 1990 APR JUN AUG OCT DEC FEB 1991 APR JUN AUG OCT

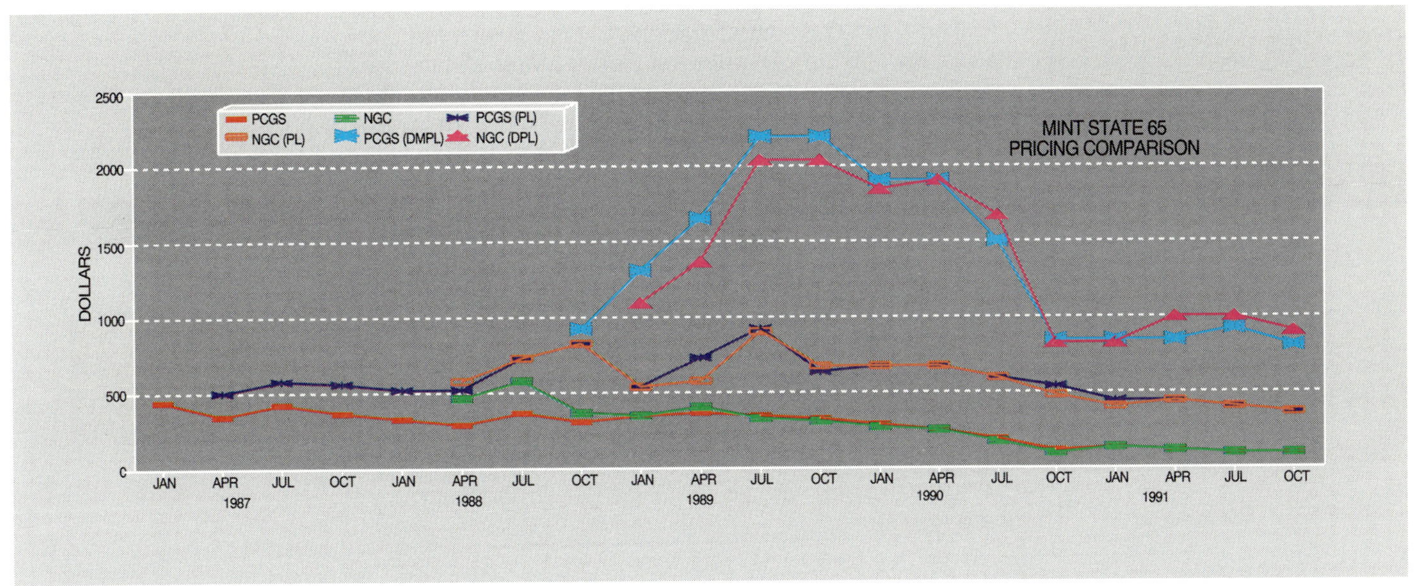

MINT STATE 65
PRICING COMPARISON
PCGS
NGC
PCGS (PL)
NGC (PL)
PCGS (DMPL)
NGC (DPL)
DOLLARS
2500
2000
1500
1000
500
0
JAN
APR
JUL
OCT
1987
1988
1989
1990
1991

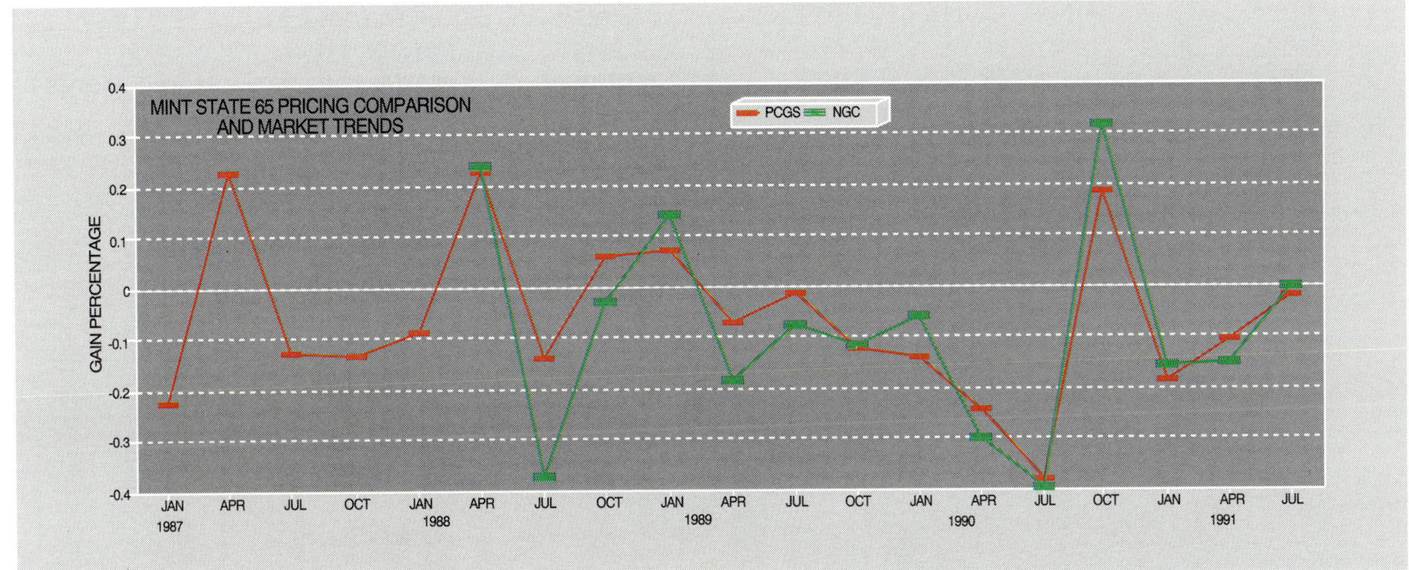

MINT STATE 65 PRICING COMPARISON
AND MARKET TRENDS
PCGS
NGC
GAIN PERCENTAGE
0.4
0.3
0.2
0.1
0
-0.1
-0.2
-0.3
-0.4
JAN
APR
JUL
OCT
1987
1988
1989
1990
1991

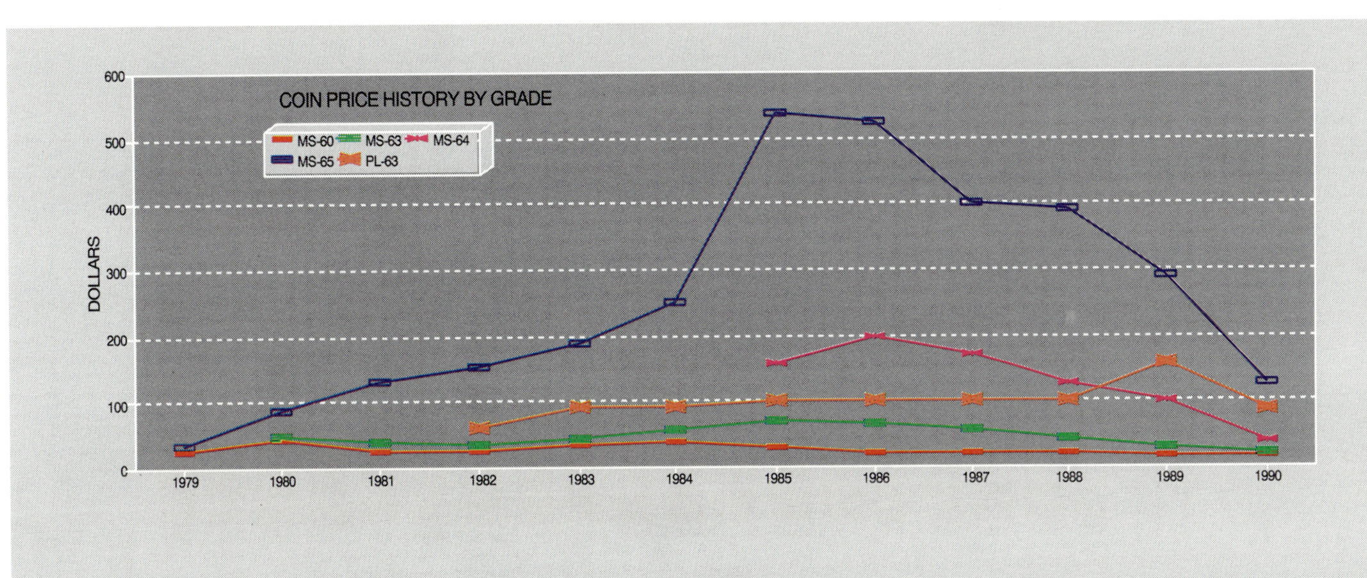

COIN PRICE HISTORY BY GRADE
MS-60
MS-63
MS-64
MS-65
PL-63
DOLLARS
600
500
400
300
200
100
0
1979
1980
1981
1982
1983
1984
1985
1986
1987
1988
1989
1990

PCGS
1885-S
S$1
MS67
7164.67/3079691

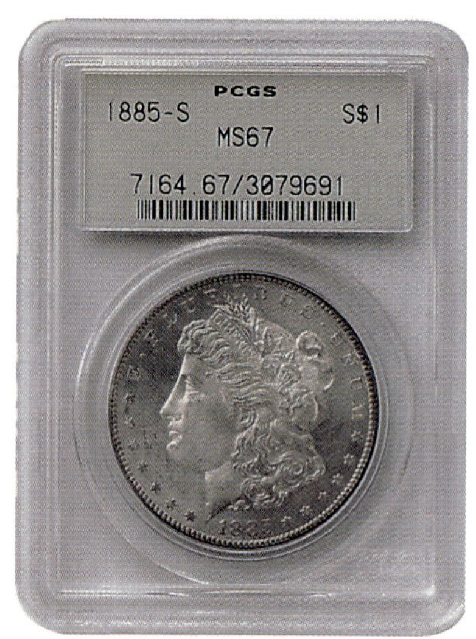

1885-S

The 1,497,000 coined probably did not need more than a few of the 20 pairs of dies. Many sliders ("two-beer" dollars) from resealed mint sacks. In the early 1960's, John Love handled a "mint-sewn" bag which proved to contain 1883-S, 1884-S and 1885-S, EF through slider grade. Other similar Treasury bags were reported later.

Claimed not to have appeared in the Redfield hoard; nevertheless, during the Redfield dispersal beginning in 1976, 30 to 40 roll offerings appeared. Some rolls survive, MS 60/62.

Real uncs. often have frosty lustre and weak striking in centers (hair above ear, breast feathers).

Recommended above MS 64.

Prooflikes: Often offered with striations on PL field, too often one-sided. PL's are scarce in all grades, DMPL's very rare, mostly from the R. D. Donovan hoard (1977).

PCGS

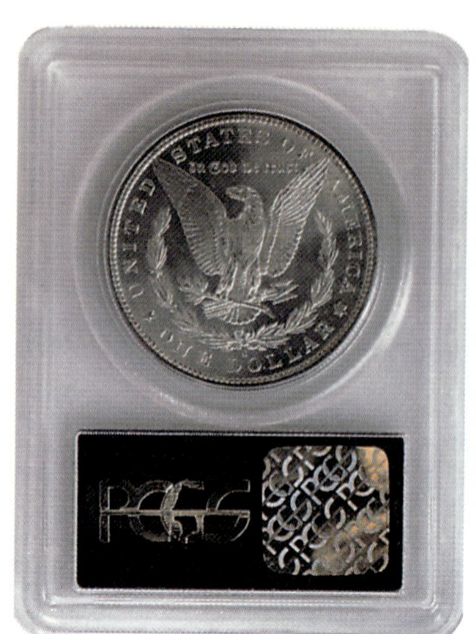

MINTAGE	PROOF	STRIKE	LUSTER	BAG MARKS	REDFIELD
1,497,000	0	Soft To Average	Good	Moderate To Heavy	No
DIES	**DIE VARIETIES**	**% OF PL**	**% OF DMPL**	**PIVOTAL GRADE**	**RARITY FACTOR**
40	8	4.0	0.1	MS 65	R-3

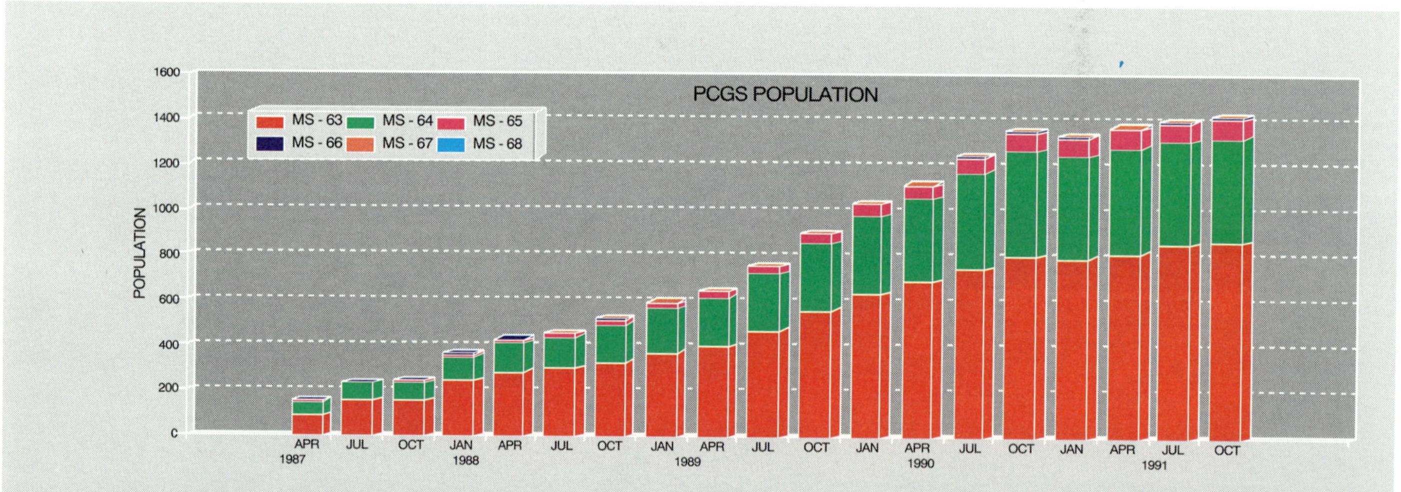
PCGS POPULATION
MS - 63
MS - 64
MS - 65
MS - 66
MS - 67
MS - 68
POPULATION
1600
1400
1200
1000
800
600
400
200
0
APR 1987
JUL
OCT
JAN 1988
APR
JUL
OCT
JAN 1989
APR
JUL
OCT
JAN 1990
APR
JUL
OCT
JAN 1991
APR
JUL
OCT

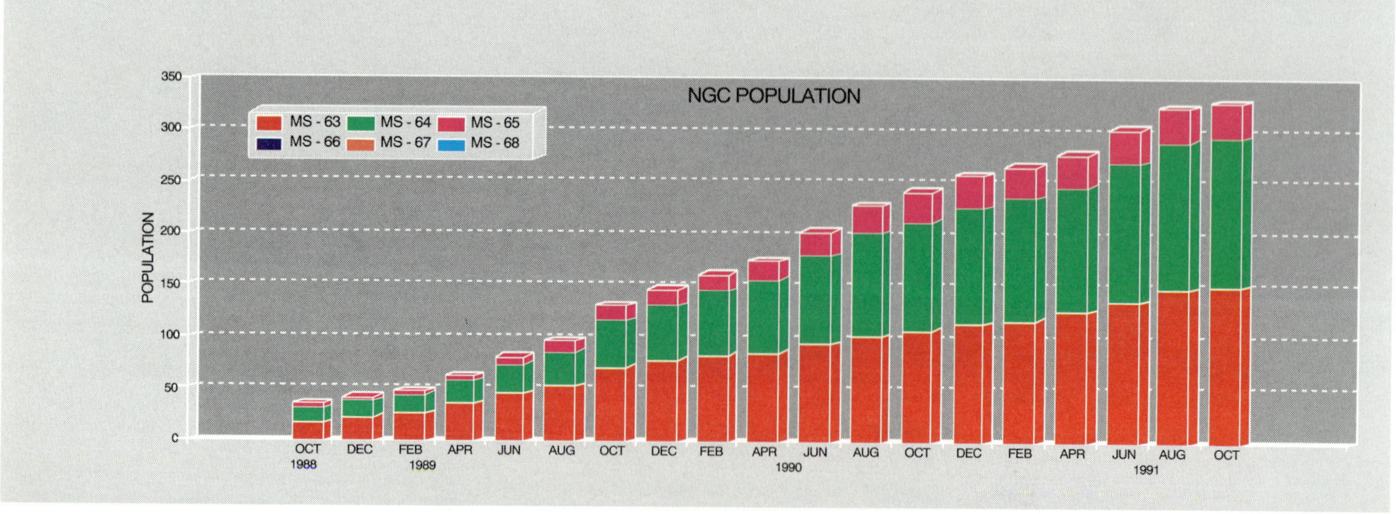
NGC POPULATION
MS - 63
MS - 64
MS - 65
MS - 66
MS - 67
MS - 68
POPULATION
350
300
250
200
150
100
50
0
OCT 1988
DEC
FEB 1989
APR
JUN
AUG
OCT
DEC
FEB
APR 1990
JUN
AUG
OCT
DEC
FEB
APR
JUN 1991
AUG
OCT

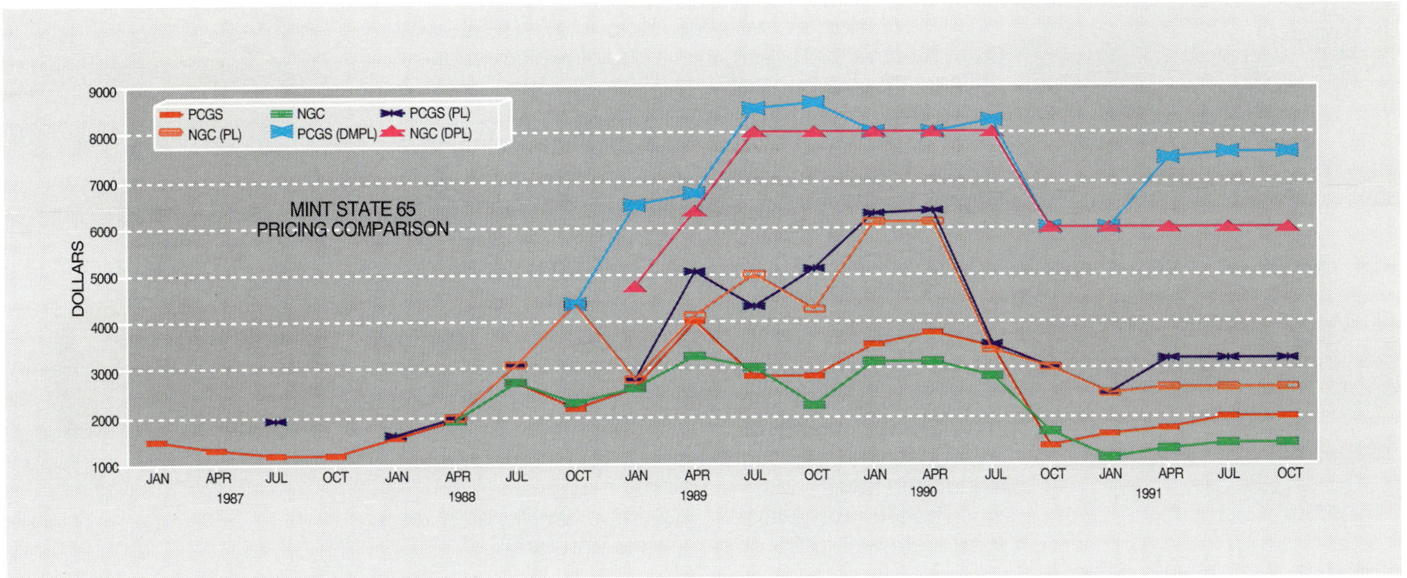

PCGS
NGC
PCGS (PL)
NGC (PL)
PCGS (DMPL)
NGC (DPL)
MINT STATE 65
PRICING COMPARISON
DOLLARS
9000
8000
7000
6000
5000
4000
3000
2000
1000
JAN APR JUL OCT JAN APR JUL OCT JAN APR JUL OCT JAN APR JUL OCT JAN APR JUL OCT
1987
1988
1989
1990
1991

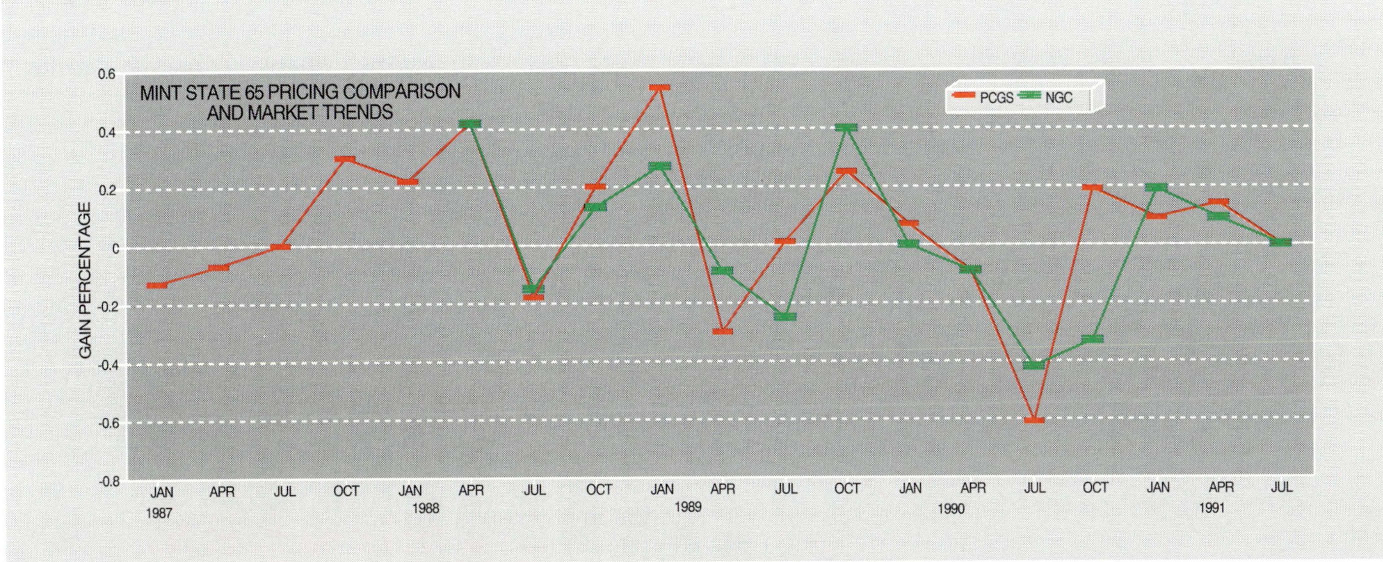

MINT STATE 65 PRICING COMPARISON
AND MARKET TRENDS
PCGS
NGC
GAIN PERCENTAGE
0.6
0.4
0.2
0
-0.2
-0.4
-0.6
-0.8
JAN APR JUL OCT JAN APR JUL OCT JAN APR JUL OCT JAN APR JUL OCT JAN APR JUL
1987
1988
1989
1990
1991

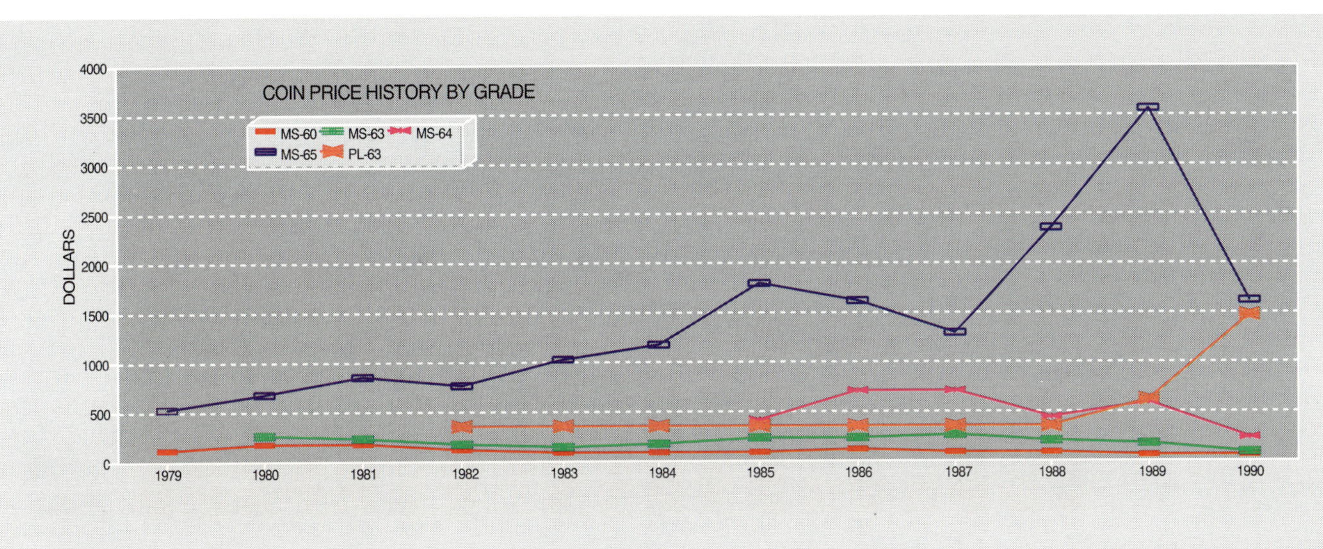

COIN PRICE HISTORY BY GRADE
MS-60
MS-63
MS-64
MS-65
PL-63
DOLLARS
4000
3500
3000
2500
2000
1500
1000
500
0
1979 1980 1981 1982 1983 1984 1985 1986 1987 1988 1989 1990

PCGS
1886
S$1
MS67
7166.67/2103492

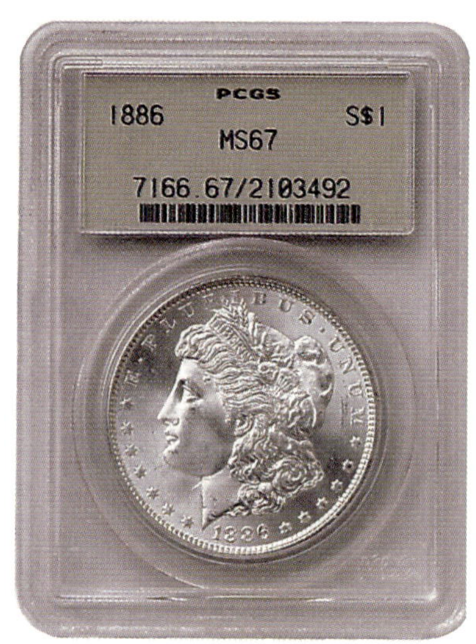

1886-P

Unsurprisingly with its mintage of 19,963,000 (from 63 obvs., 60 revs.), this is one of two commonest Philadelphia Morgans prior to 1921; the other is 1887. Many Unc. bags turned up in Treasury (1954) and Continental Bank hoards. Many of these coins have excellent lustre and good striking. Many others show metal flow, die cracks, from die wear (see Bill Fivaz's account in Chapter 17).

Both original and assembled bag lots survive.

Recommended above MS 65 or in MS 64/65 by the roll.

Proofs: The 886 minted took two pairs of dies, though only one was reported. The commoner, VAM 4, has repunched 1; the rarer (*Encyclopedia* 5587, not in VAM, discovered in 1974) has double date, first entered too low and slanting up to right, then corrected higher and level.

Prooflikes: Available in PL and DMPL; both are scarce above MS 65. Cameos are infrequent.

PCGS

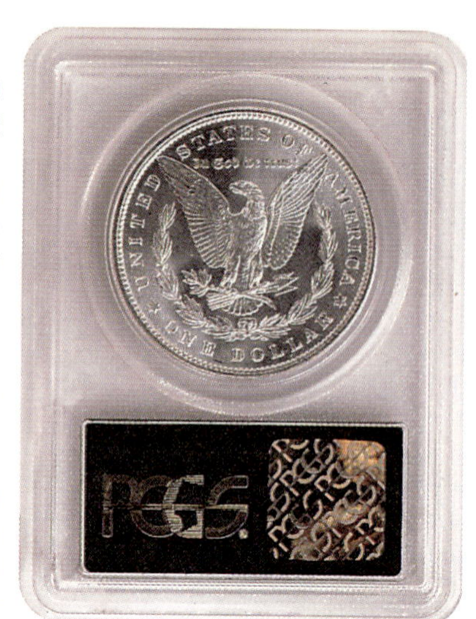

MINTAGE	PROOF	STRIKE	LUSTER	BAG MARKS	REDFIELD
19,963,000	886	Sharp	Excellent	Few	No
DIES	**DIE VARIETIES**	**% OF PL**	**% OF DMPL**	**PIVOTAL GRADE**	**RARITY FACTOR**
161	20	1.2	1.3	MS 65	R-5

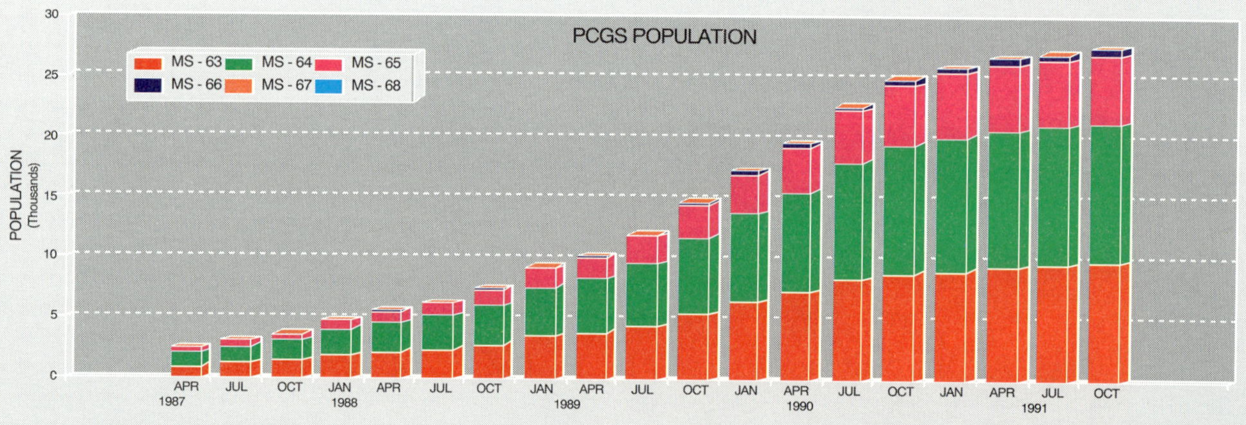
PCGS POPULATION
MS - 63
MS - 64
MS - 65
MS - 66
MS - 67
MS - 68
POPULATION (Thousands)
30
25
20
15
10
5
0
APR 1987
JUL
OCT
JAN 1988
APR
JUL
OCT
JAN 1989
APR
JUL
OCT
JAN
APR 1990
JUL
OCT
JAN
APR
JUL 1991
OCT

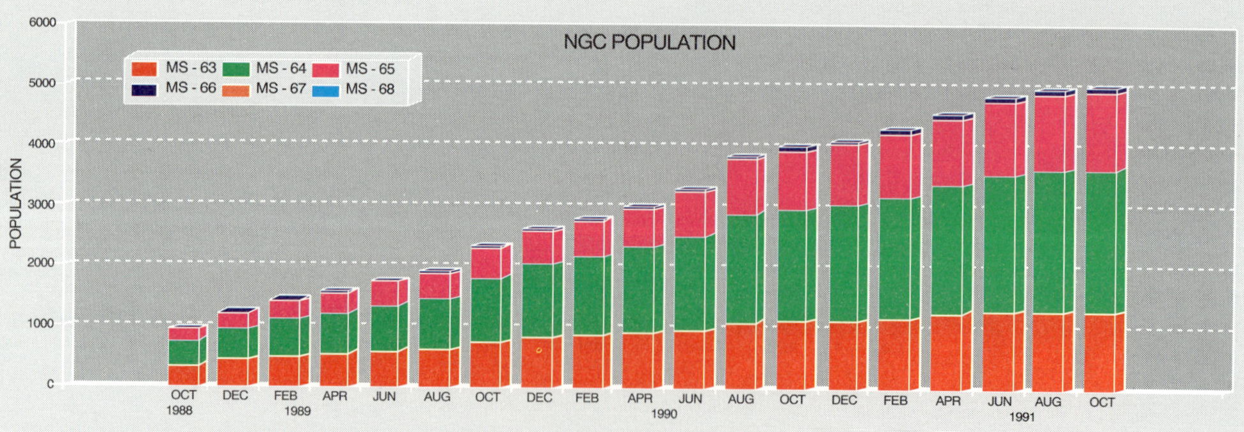
NGC POPULATION
MS - 63
MS - 64
MS - 65
MS - 66
MS - 67
MS - 68
POPULATION
6000
5000
4000
3000
2000
1000
0
OCT 1988
DEC
FEB 1989
APR
JUN
AUG
OCT
DEC
FEB
APR 1990
JUN
AUG
OCT
DEC
FEB
APR
JUN 1991
AUG
OCT

1886-P

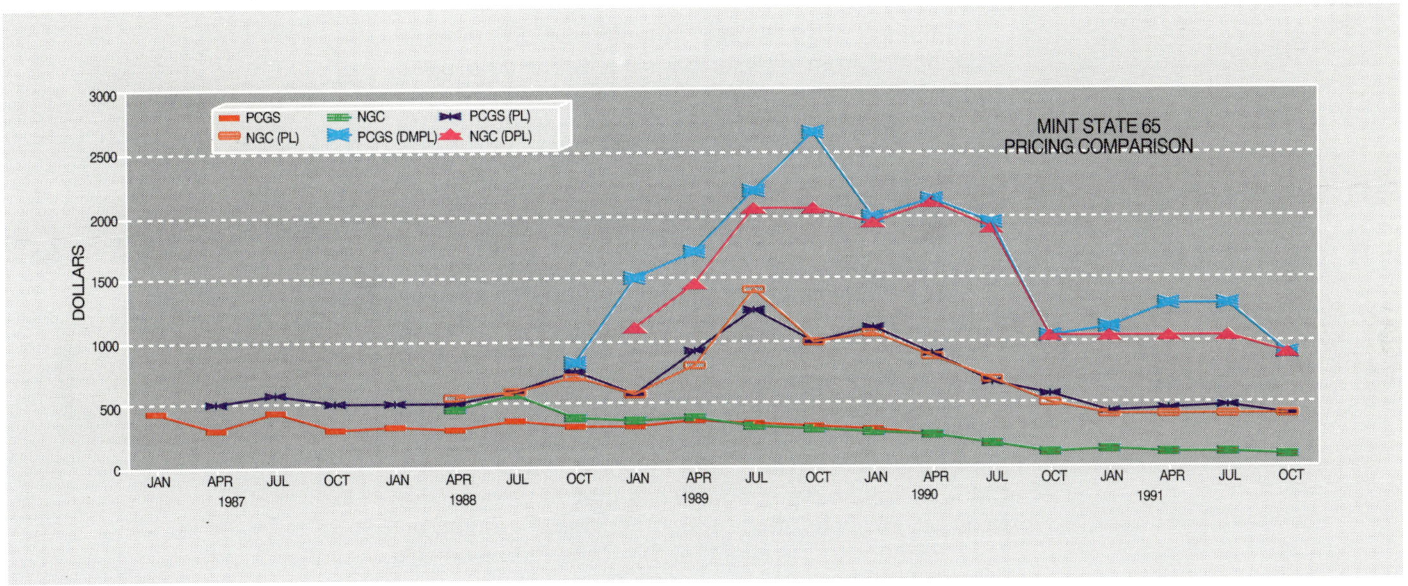

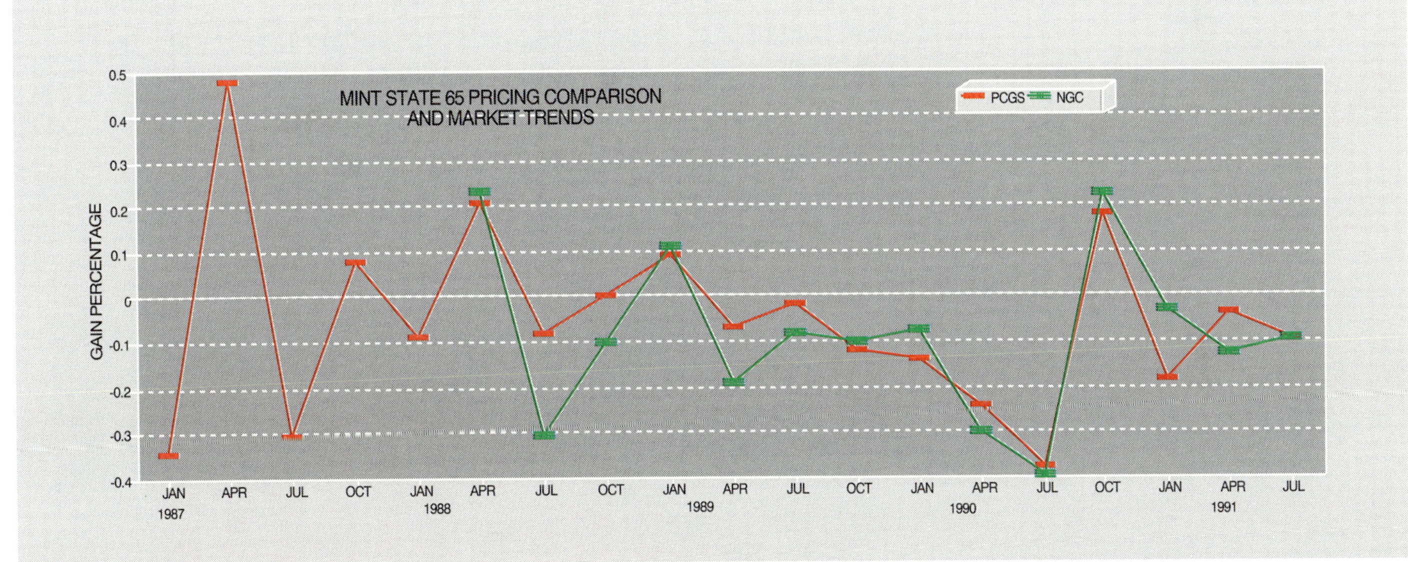

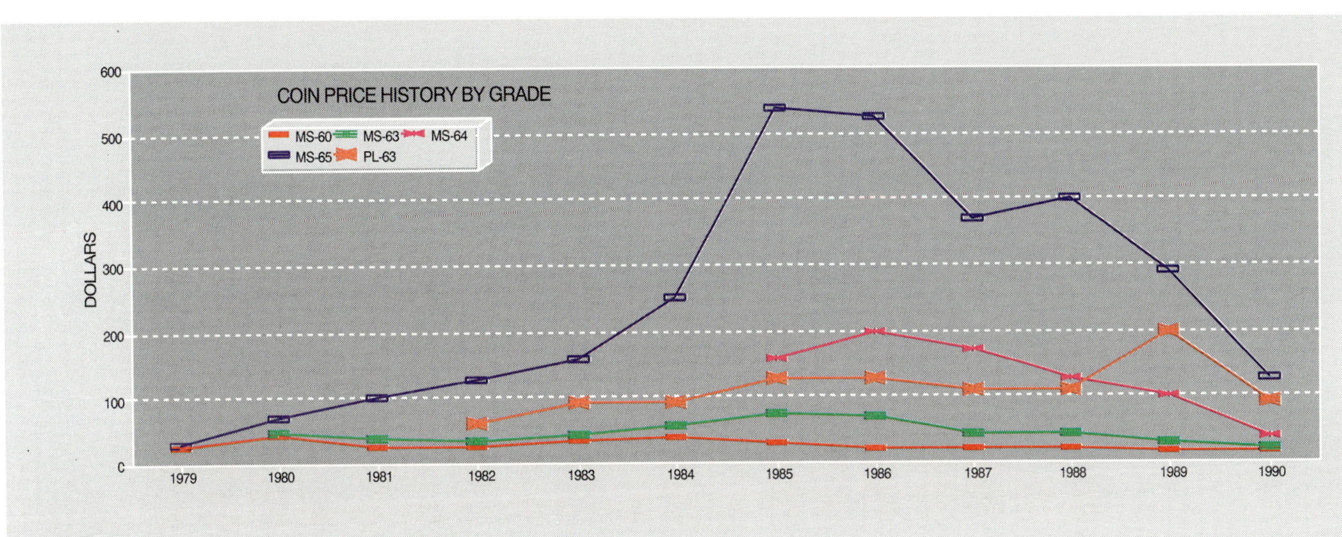

1886-O

Mintage, 10,710,000. Plentiful in EF through slider quality, from resealed bags (for further details see 1887-O). In mint state, this is beginning to be recognized as rare. A PCGS MS 64 sold at the 11th National Silver Dollar Convention (St. Louis, November 8-11, 1990) for $14,500. Only one better specimen has been slabbed: see DMPL's.

Recommended in MS 63 up, but be careful of sliders offered as "BU". There may also be fakes made by adding O mintmarks to genuine 1886 Philadelphia dollars. These can be detected (with 20x glass or binocular microscope) by the seam separating mintmark from adjacent field. Happy hunting!

Prooflikes: Extremely rare in all grades, PL and DMPL. Forget posted bid prices; you won't be able to get one at that level. The Tavenner, Wayne Miller DMPL is apparently unequalled; it may have been the NGC MS 67 DMPL that brought $231,000 (bought by Tony Terranova for a client) at the Chris Schenkel sale, Bowers & Merena, November 1990.

MINTAGE	PROOF	STRIKE	LUSTER	BAG MARKS	REDFIELD
10,710,000	0	Weak & Soft	Poor To Average	Moderate To Heavy	No
DIES	**DIE VARIETIES**	**% OF PL**	**% OF DMPL**	**PIVOTAL GRADE**	**RARITY FACTOR**
80	16	1.0	1.2	MS 64	R-1

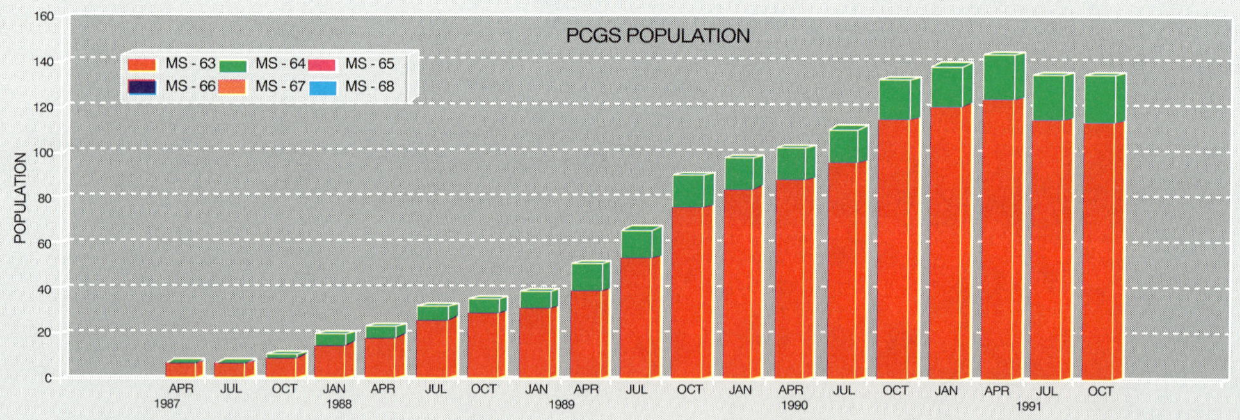

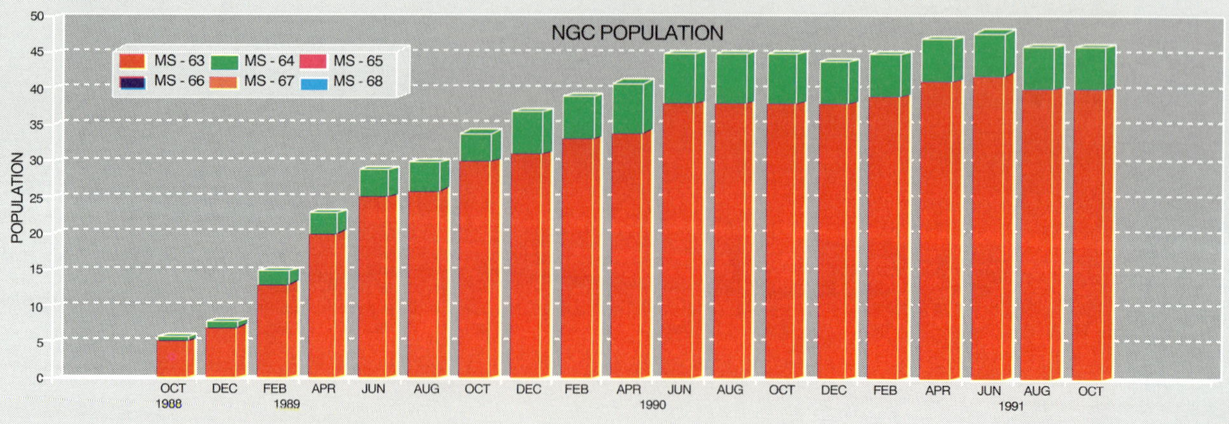

PCGS POPULATION

NGC POPULATION

1886-O

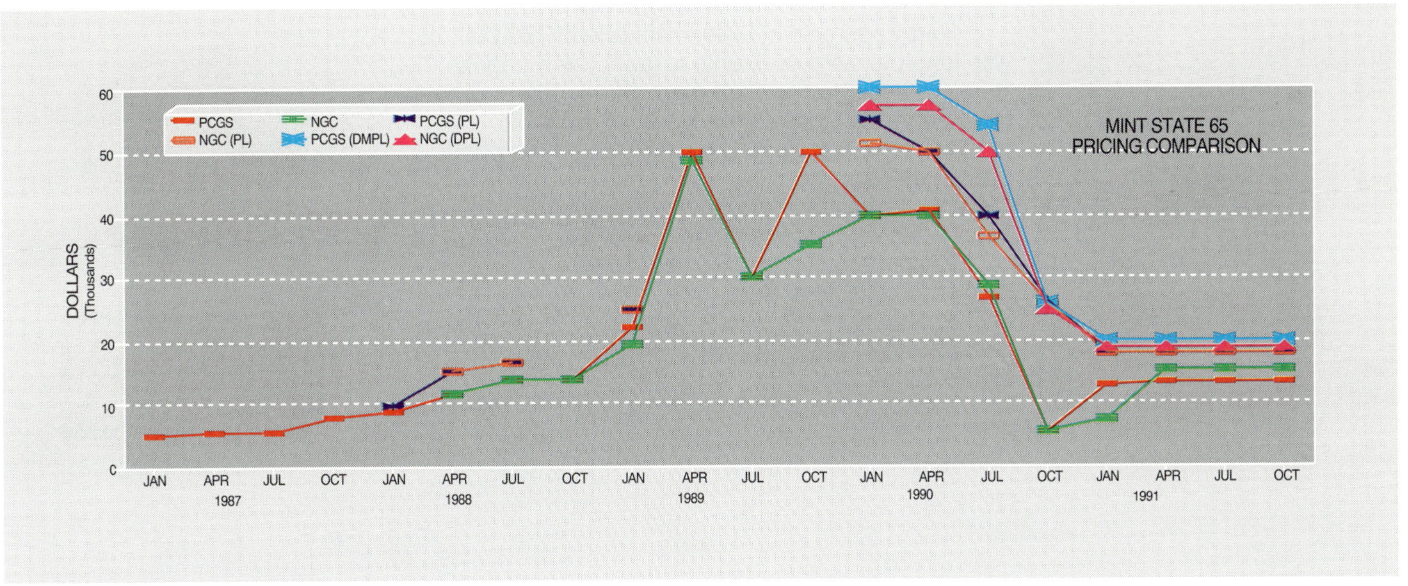

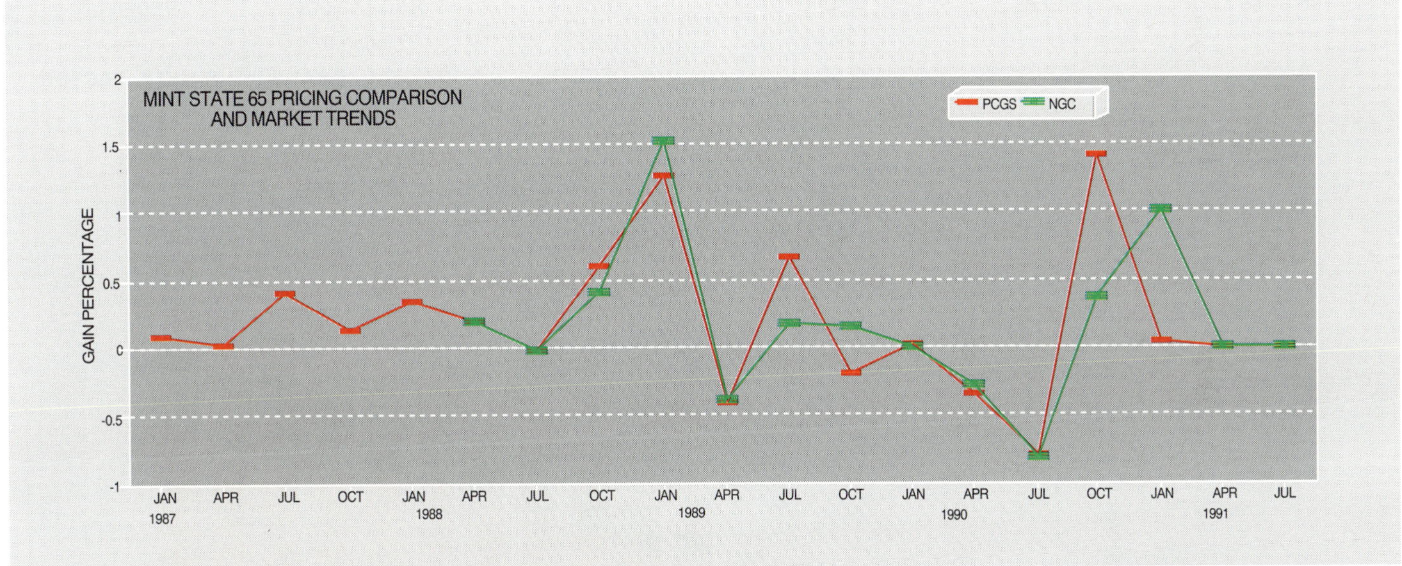

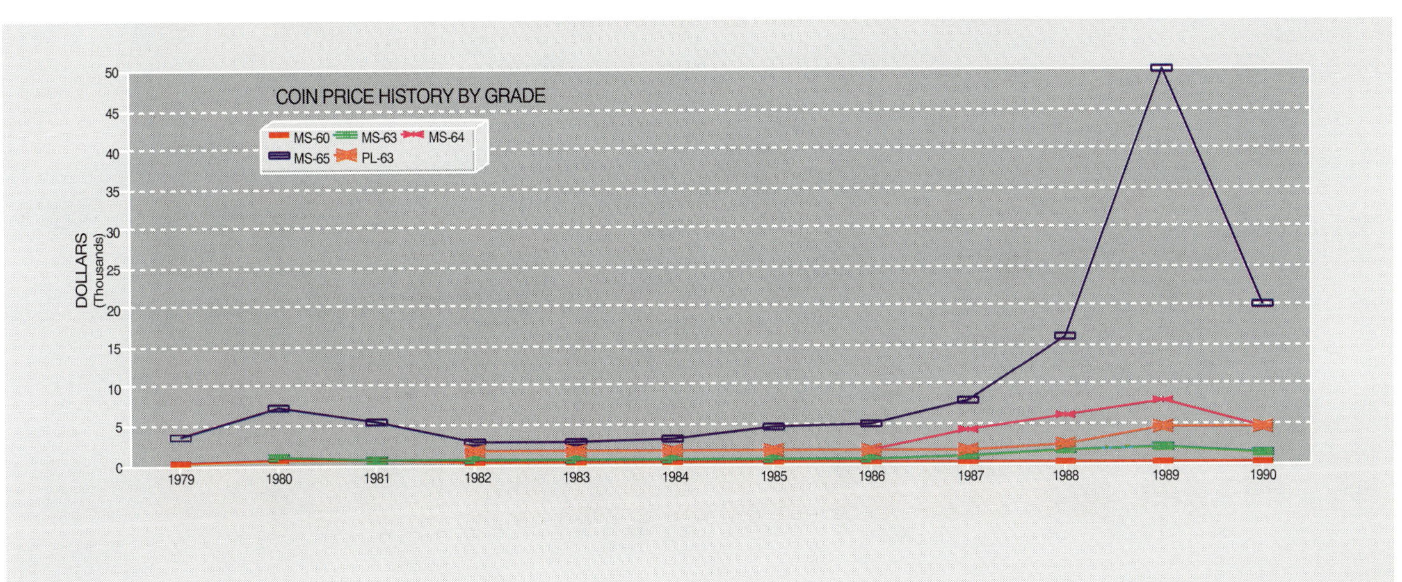

PCGS
1886-S
S$1
MS66
7170.66/3066175

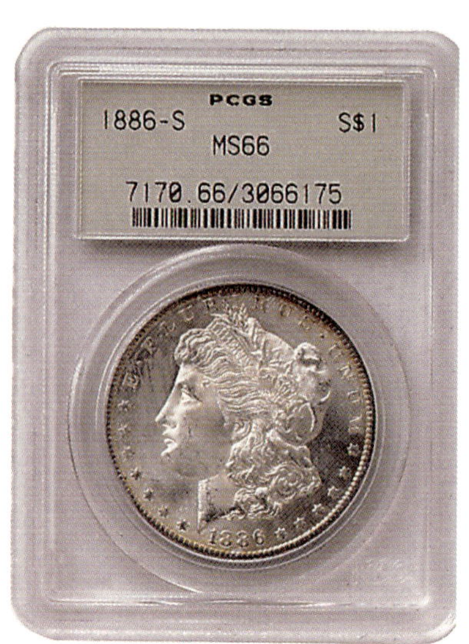

1886-S

Partly because of its low mintage of 750,000, this was long believed rare, until at least three bags in the Redfield hoard were dispersed; this is the source of most surviving Uncs. Most were MS 60/62.

Others were released by the Treasury in Montana, 1956. John Love (Cut Bank, MT) handled many of both groups. Circulated specimens are readily available, even in the EF to slider range.

Recommended in MS 64 up; 60/63 if you need the date for a collection.

Prooflikes: PL's are scarce in most grades; many are one-sided. DMPL's are rare above MS 64, as are cameos.

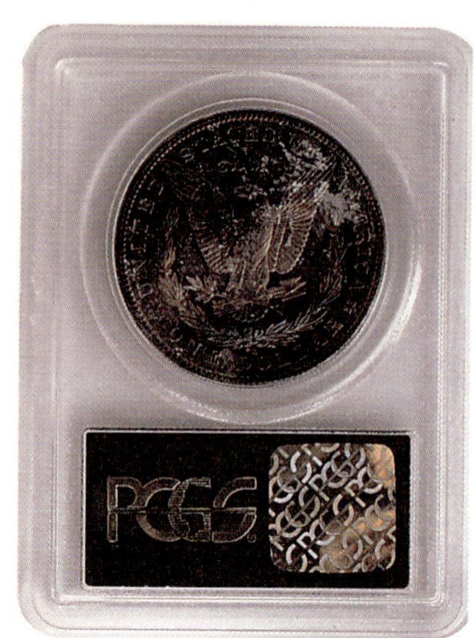

MINTAGE	PROOF	STRIKE	LUSTER	BAG MARKS	REDFIELD
750,000	0	Sharp	Good	Moderate	Yes
DIES	**DIE VARIETIES**	**% OF PL**	**% OF DMPL**	**PIVOTAL GRADE**	**RARITY FACTOR**
N/A	4	11.0	1.6	MS 65	R-2

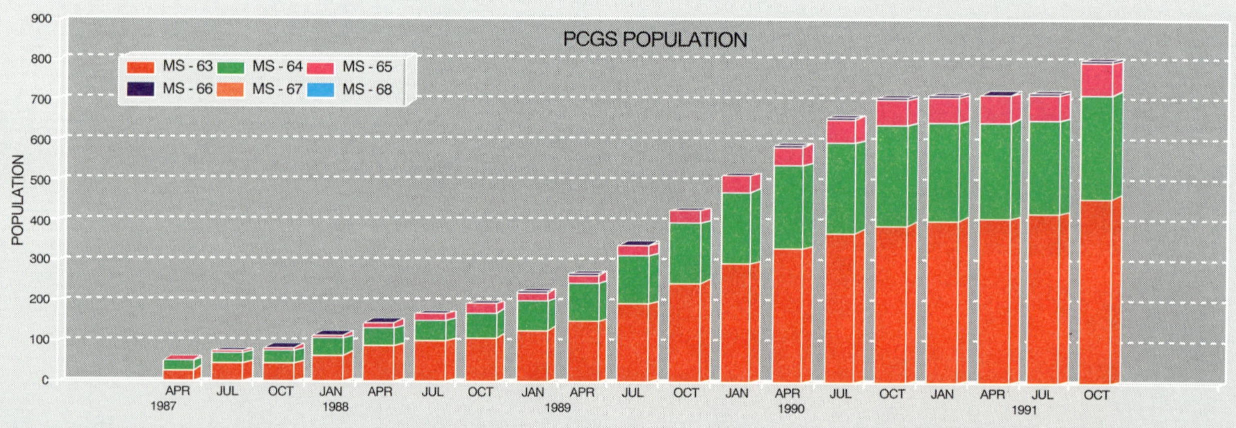

PCGS POPULATION
MS - 63
MS - 64
MS - 65
MS - 66
MS - 67
MS - 68
POPULATION
900
800
700
600
500
400
300
200
100
0
APR 1987
JUL
OCT
JAN 1988
APR
JUL
OCT
JAN 1989
APR
JUL
OCT
JAN
APR 1990
JUL
OCT
JAN
APR
JUL 1991
OCT

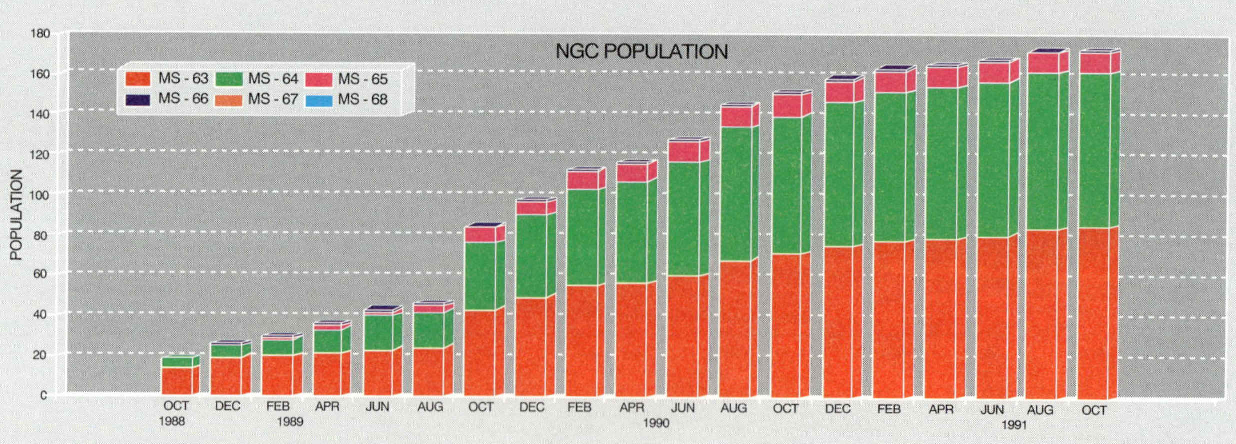

NGC POPULATION
MS - 63
MS - 64
MS - 65
MS - 66
MS - 67
MS - 68
POPULATION
180
160
140
120
100
80
60
40
20
0
OCT 1988
DEC
FEB 1989
APR
JUN
AUG
OCT
DEC
FEB
APR 1990
JUN
AUG
OCT
DEC
FEB
APR
JUN 1991
AUG
OCT

1886-S

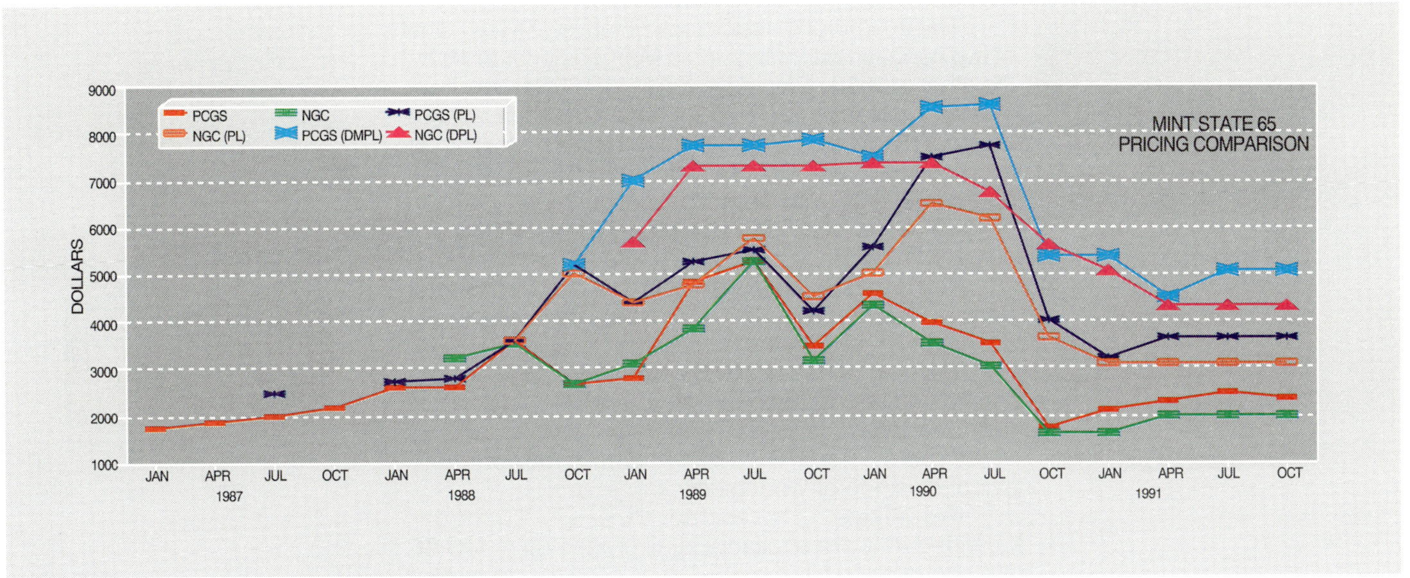

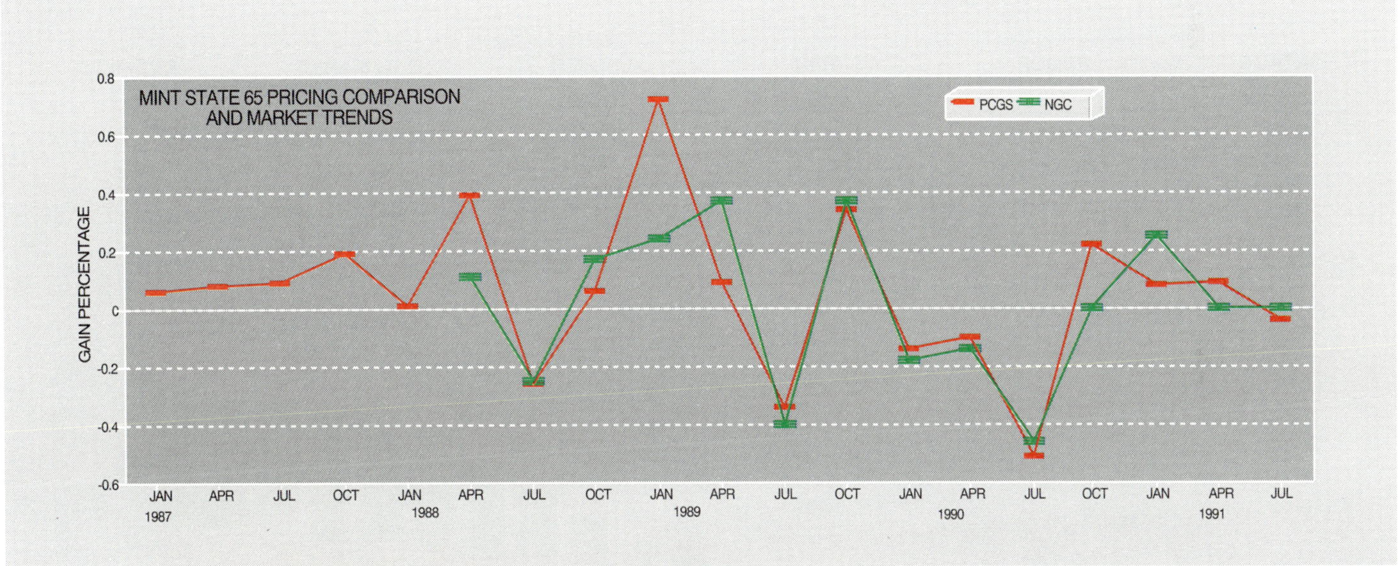

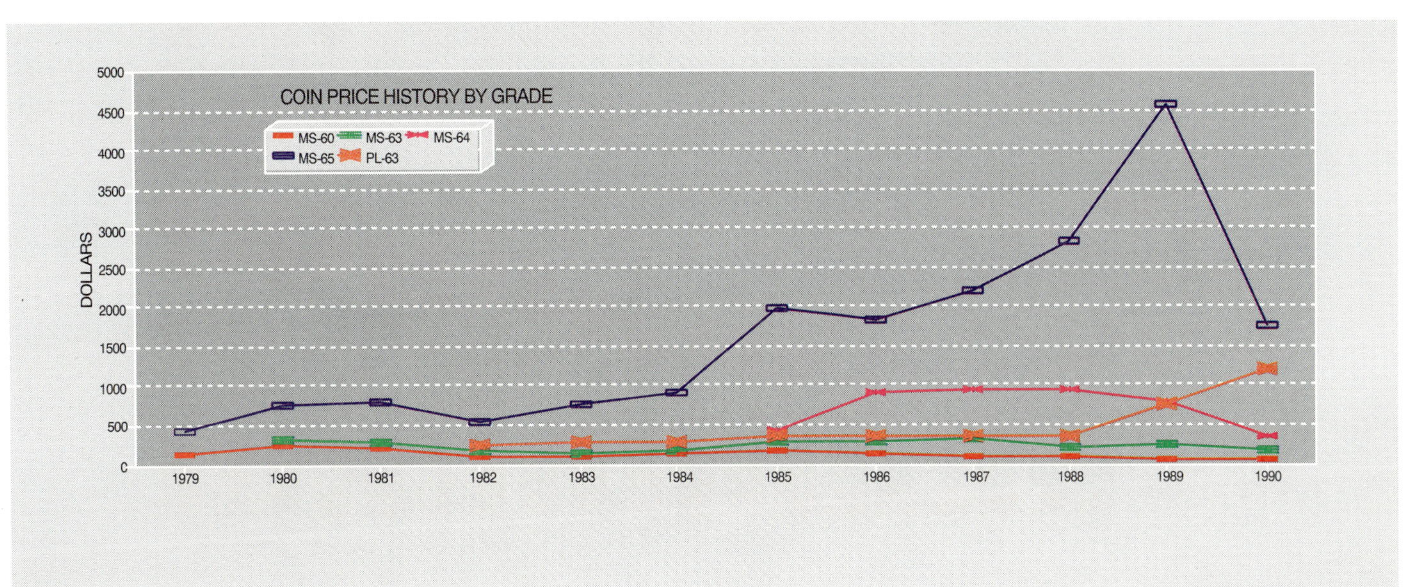

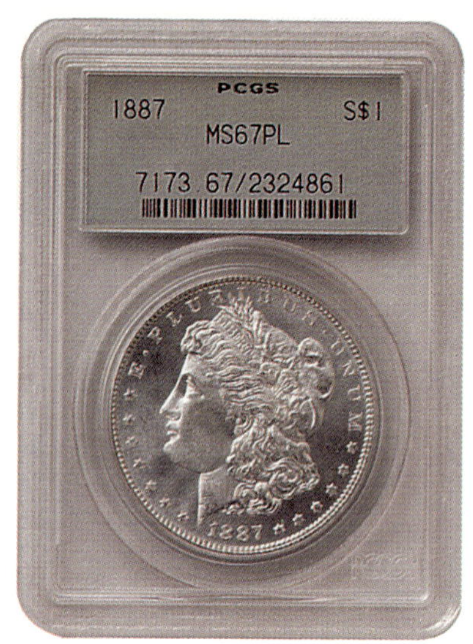

PCGS
1887 S$1
MS67PL
7173.67/2324861

1887-P

In God we trust
ONE DOLLAR
PCGS

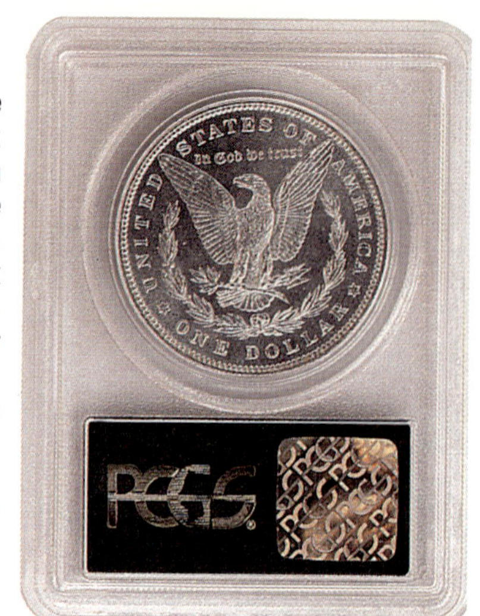

The 20,290,000 struck took 55 obvs., 54 rev. One of two commonest Philadelphia Morgans prior to 1921; the other is 1886. Plentiful even in MS 65, largely from Treasury released 1961-64, at least 100 bags. There are four qualities: 1) excellent strike and lustre; 2) average strike, dull; 3) poor strike, good lustre; 4) weak from worn dies with some of the brightest lustre in Morgan series. (These have plenty of metal flow; for details see Bill Fivaz's study, Chapter 17).

This was the latest date found in the Continental Bank hoard. Bags in MS 60/63 are still available; rolls are common, sliders more so.

Recommended in MS 65 or higher, but take your time to find one with plenty of eye appeal.

See 1887/6 in its own seperate anaylsis.

Proofs: The 710 struck apparently took only one pair of dies; top of 7 doubled.

Prooflikes: One-sided PL's are common; two-sided PL's are available in all grades up to MS 66, rare above it. DMPL's are twice as hard to find as PL's in any grade. Recommended above MS 65. Cameos are scarce to rare.

MINTAGE	PROOF	STRIKE	LUSTER	BAG MARKS	REDFIELD
20,290,000*	710	Average To Soft	Good	Moderate	No
DIES	**DIE VARIETIES**	**% OF PL**	**% OF DMPL**	**PIVOTAL GRADE**	**RARITY FACTOR**
107**	17	2.6	1.5	MS 65	R-5

*Includes estimated 20,290,000 1887-P and estimated 1,000,000 1887/6-P **Includes all dies used at the Philadelphia Mint - FY 1887

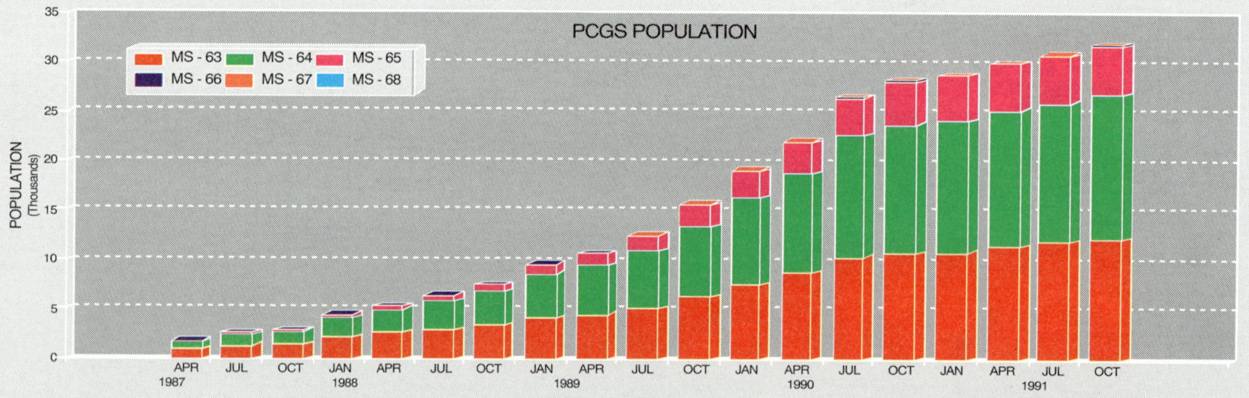

PCGS POPULATION
MS - 63
MS - 64
MS - 65
MS - 66
MS - 67
MS - 68
POPULATION (Thousands)
35
30
25
20
15
10
5
0
APR 1987
JUL
OCT
JAN 1988
APR
JUL
OCT
JAN 1989
APR
JUL
OCT
JAN
APR 1990
JUL
OCT
JAN
APR
JUL 1991
OCT

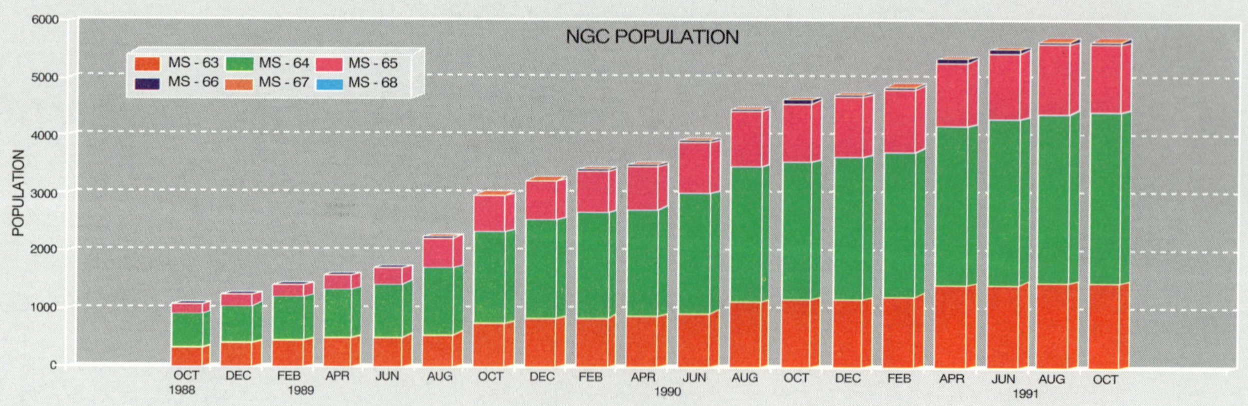

NGC POPULATION
MS - 63
MS - 64
MS - 65
MS - 66
MS - 67
MS - 68
POPULATION
6000
5000
4000
3000
2000
1000
0
OCT 1988
DEC
FEB 1989
APR
JUN
AUG
OCT
DEC
FEB
APR 1990
JUN
AUG
OCT
DEC
FEB
APR
JUN 1991
AUG
OCT

1887-P

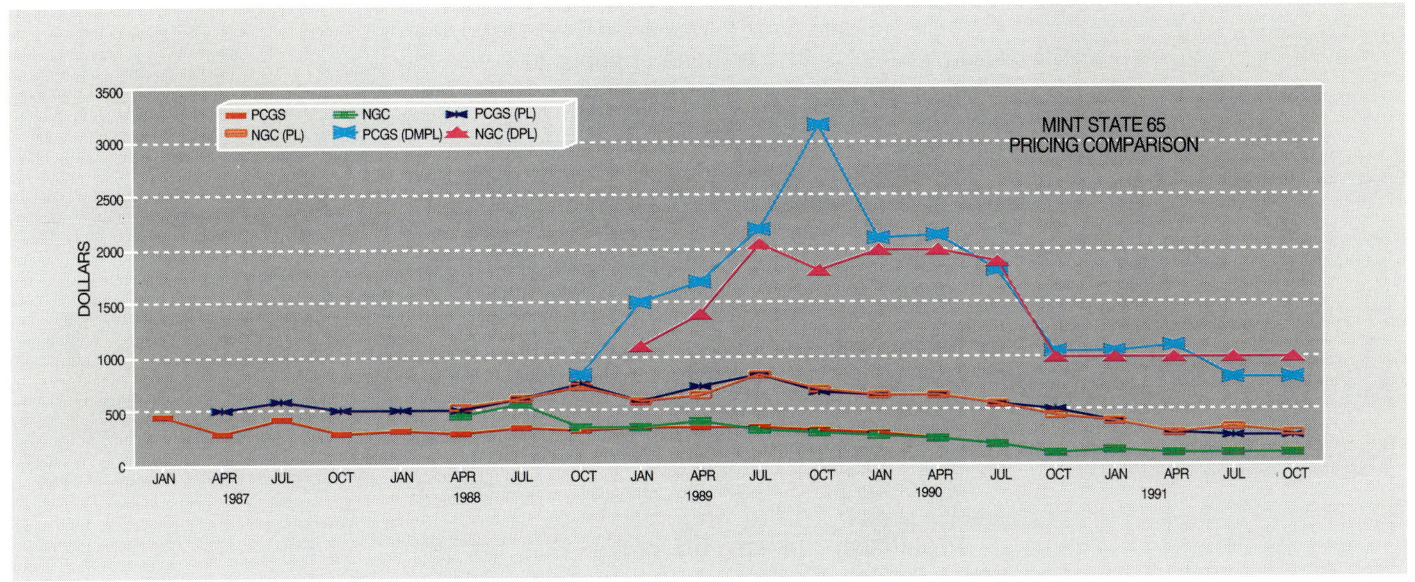

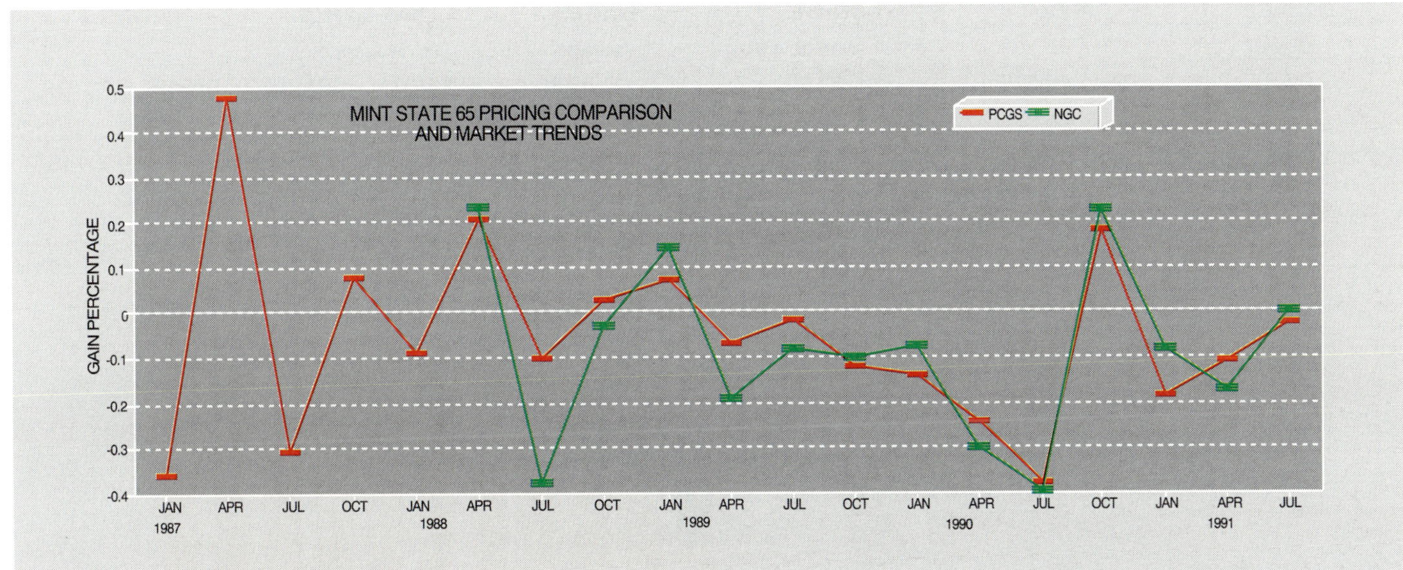

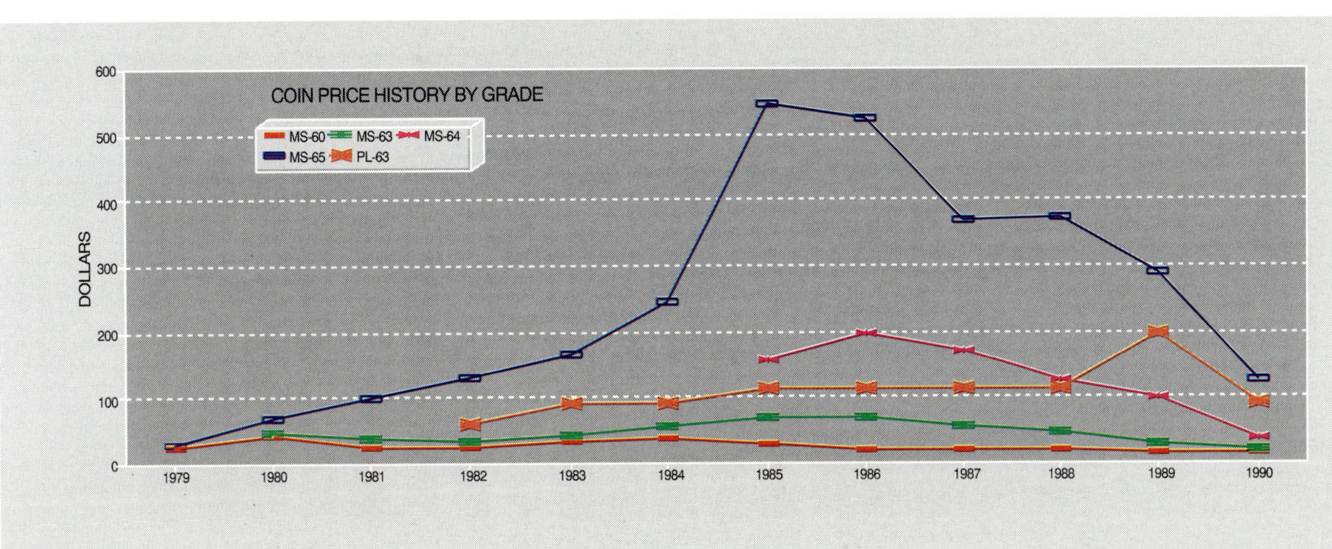

1887/6-P

PCGS
1887/6 S$1
MS65DMPL
97175.65/3151878

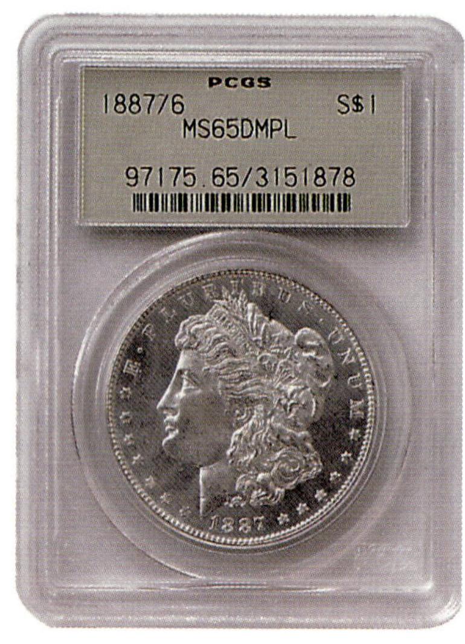

This overdate, VAM 2, was a Ted Clark Discovery, November 1971. The first one at public sale was lot 878 of Lester Merkin's sale, October 6-7, 1972, "brill, Unc. Prooflike." It realized a then high $550. Later ones, mostly in lower qualities of Unc., began showing up at lower prices. Nevertheless, in early 1990, in a single dealer-to-dealer wholesale transaction, a PCGS MS 65 brought over $10,000. To date fewer than 500 Uncs. have been slabbed; of these, under 20 have been graded MS 65, none higher. Unfortunately we have no statistics of how many were early states with both left and right arcs of 6 visible at base of 7. The 7 was repunched over the 6 of the original date. See ill., *Encyclopedia* 5593. As the die wore down, less and less of the 6 shows. In the latest states, the overdate may go unnoticed.

Recommended in all BU grades, especially in early die states.

Prooflikes: In any BU grade, PL's are rare, DMPL's very much rarer.

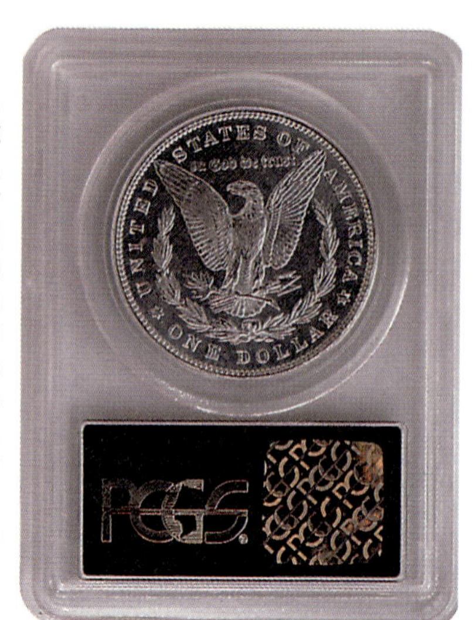

MINTAGE	PROOF	STRIKE	LUSTER	BAG MARKS	REDFIELD
1,000,000*	0	Average	Average	Moderate	No
DIES	**DIE VARIETIES**	**% OF PL**	**% OF DMPL**	**PIVOTAL GRADE**	**RARITY FACTOR**
107**	1	7.2	0.2	MS 65	R-1

*Includes estimated 20,290,000 1887-P and estimated 1,000,000 1887/6-P **Includes all dies used at the Philadelphia Mint - FY 1887

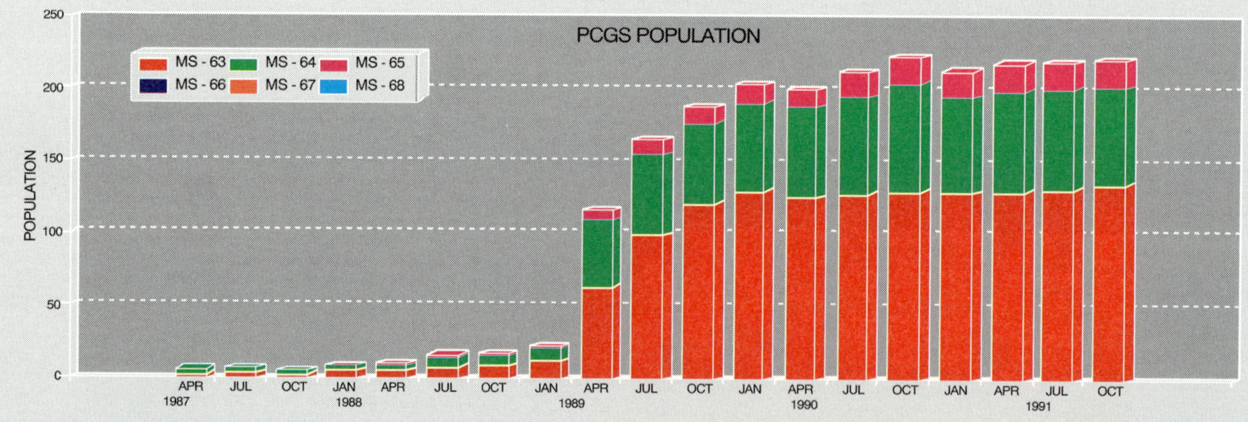
PCGS POPULATION
MS - 63
MS - 64
MS - 65
MS - 66
MS - 67
MS - 68
POPULATION
250
200
150
100
50
0
APR 1987
JUL
OCT
JAN 1988
APR
JUL
OCT
JAN 1989
APR
JUL
OCT
JAN
APR 1990
JUL
OCT
JAN
APR
JUL 1991
OCT

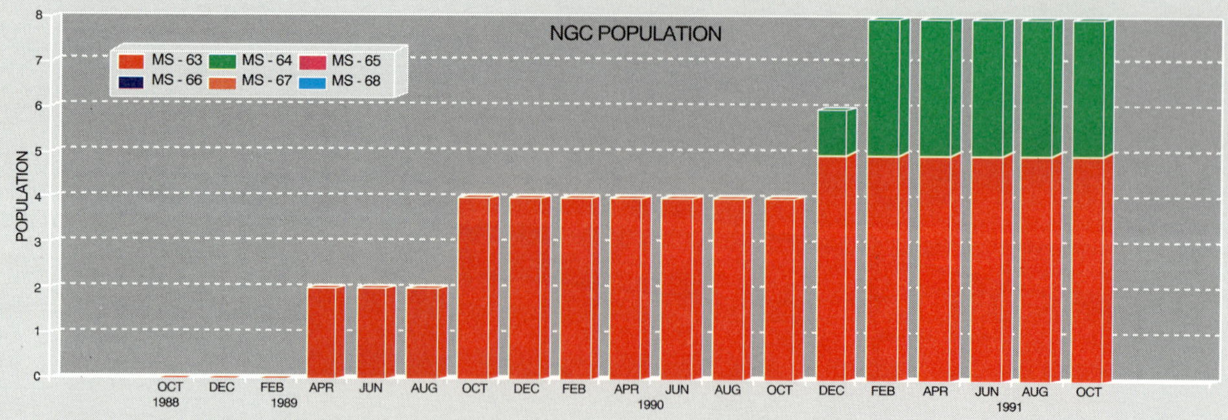
NGC POPULATION
MS - 63
MS - 64
MS - 65
MS - 66
MS - 67
MS - 68
POPULATION
8
7
6
5
4
3
2
1
0
OCT 1988
DEC
FEB 1989
APR
JUN
AUG
OCT
DEC
FEB
APR 1990
JUN
AUG
OCT
DEC
FEB
APR
JUN 1991
AUG
OCT

1887/6-P

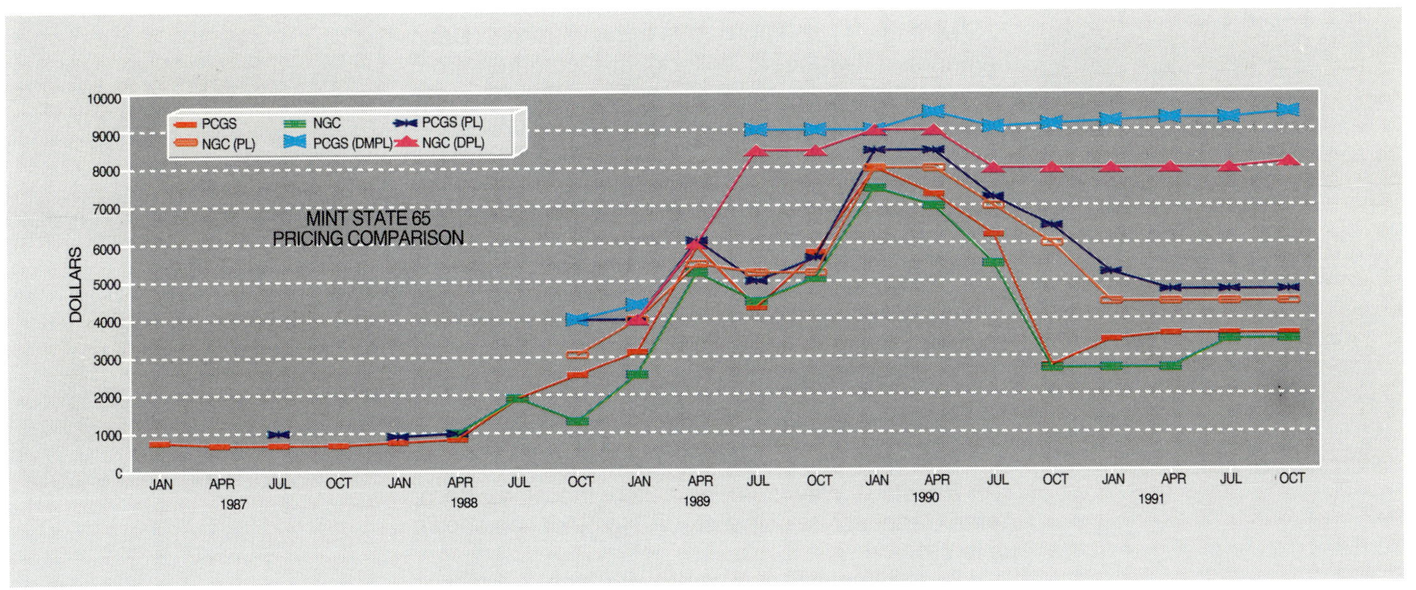

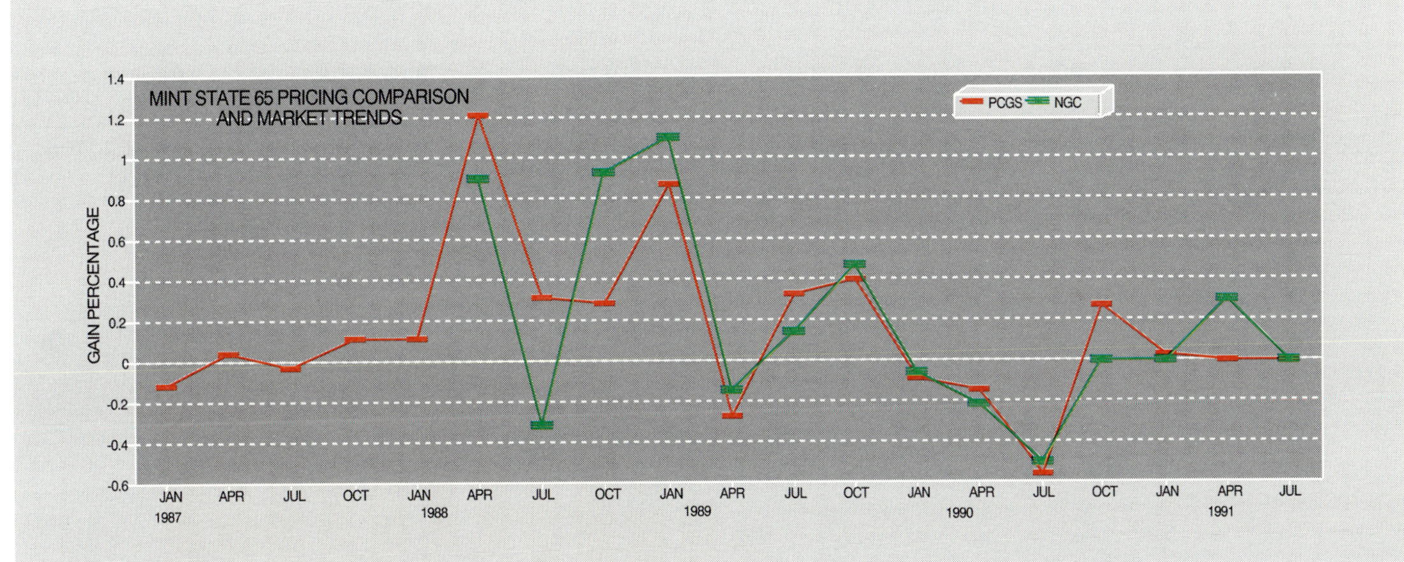

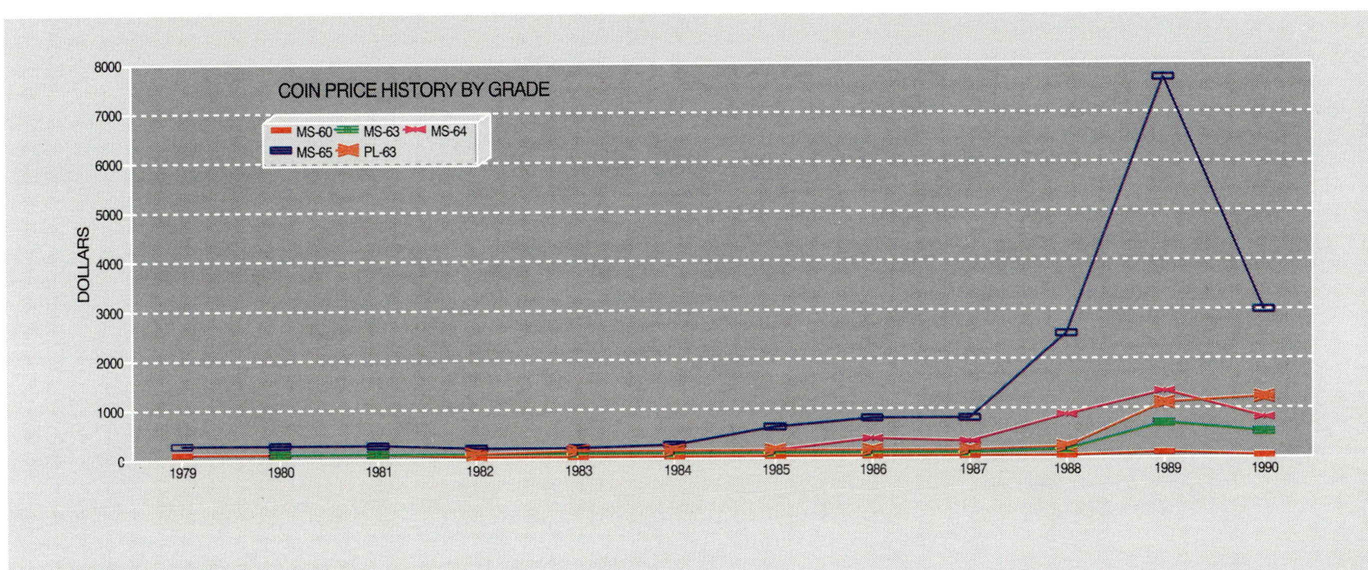

1887-O

Mintage, 11,550,000. EF's through sliders (Dean Tavenner's "two-beer" dollars) are common from resealed mint sacks (1887). These contained some 1886-O's in the same grade range. The next time this occurred: 1897-O. Full mint state specimens are not easily found; most (from Treasury bags, March 1964) are weak, dull, and bagmarked. Improper basining of dies, and use of some dies until they were worn out, causing thick rims and uneven metal flow explain some of the weakness. An original Unc. bag was bought and sold at the 1977 ANA convention, Atlanta, GA. MS 60 rolls are available.

Recommended in MS 64 up. You may have to buy an MS 63 and hope to upgrade sometime. In MS 65 and above this date is rare.

See 1887/6-O on seperate anaylsis.

Proofs: Wayne Miller called the Roe, Kern, Amon Carter estate coin a proof. No other has shown up to date.

Prooflikes: These come with highly reflective surfaces and good contrast but poor striking quality. This includes cameo MS 60 DMPL's. Rare in any grade above MS 64, PL or DMPL.

MINTAGE	PROOF	STRIKE	LUSTER	BAG MARKS	REDFIELD
11,550,000	0	Soft	Average	Moderate To Heavy	No
DIES	**DIE VARIETIES**	**% OF PL**	**% OF DMPL**	**PIVOTAL GRADE**	**RARITY FACTOR**
108*	21	6.1	4.8	MS 64	R-3

*Includes all dies used at the New Orleans Mint - FY 1887

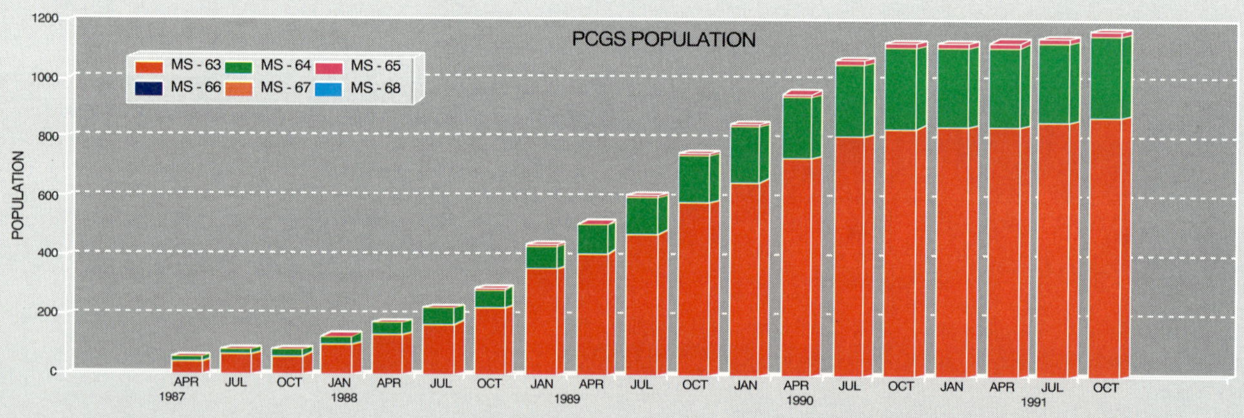

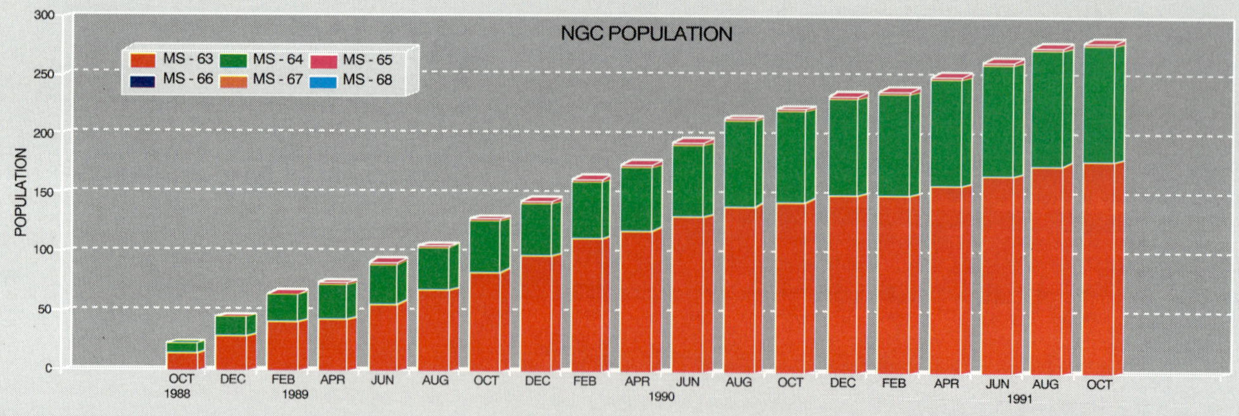

PCGS POPULATION

MS - 63, MS - 64, MS - 65, MS - 66, MS - 67, MS - 68

NGC POPULATION

MS - 63, MS - 64, MS - 65, MS - 66, MS - 67, MS - 68

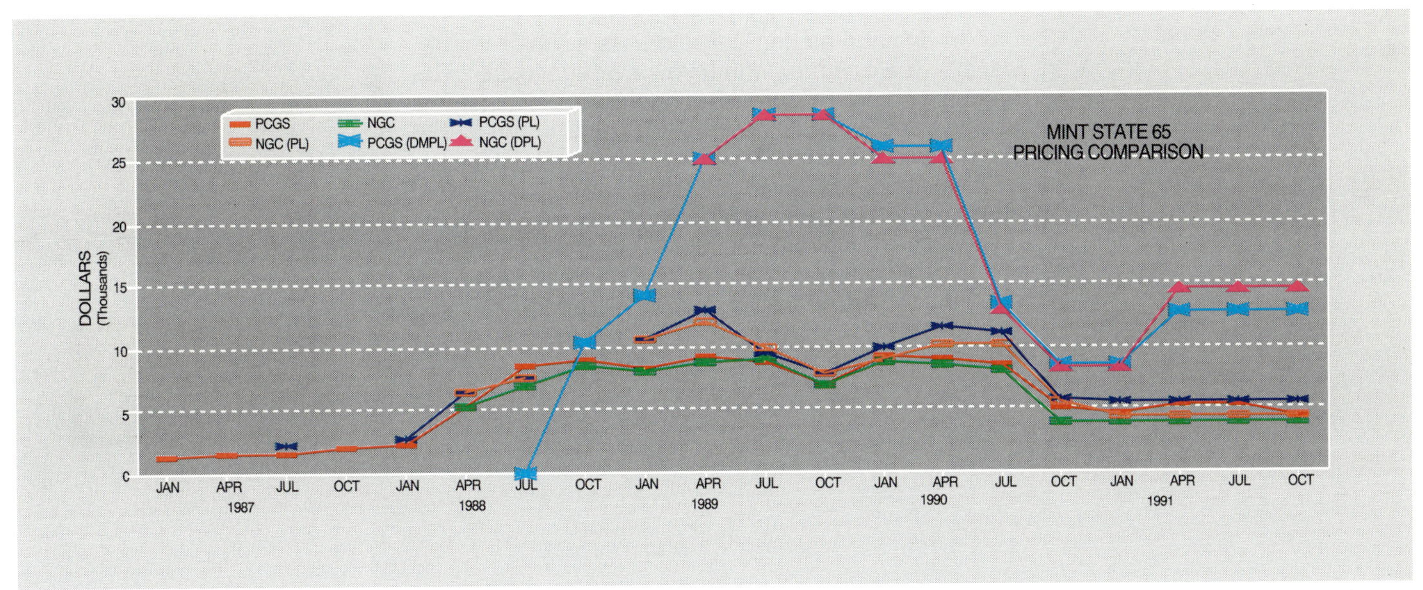
MINT STATE 65
PRICING COMPARISON
PCGS
NGC
PCGS (PL)
NGC (PL)
PCGS (DMPL)
NGC (DPL)
DOLLARS
(Thousands)
30
25
20
15
10
5
0
JAN
APR
JUL
OCT
1987
1988
1989
1990
1991

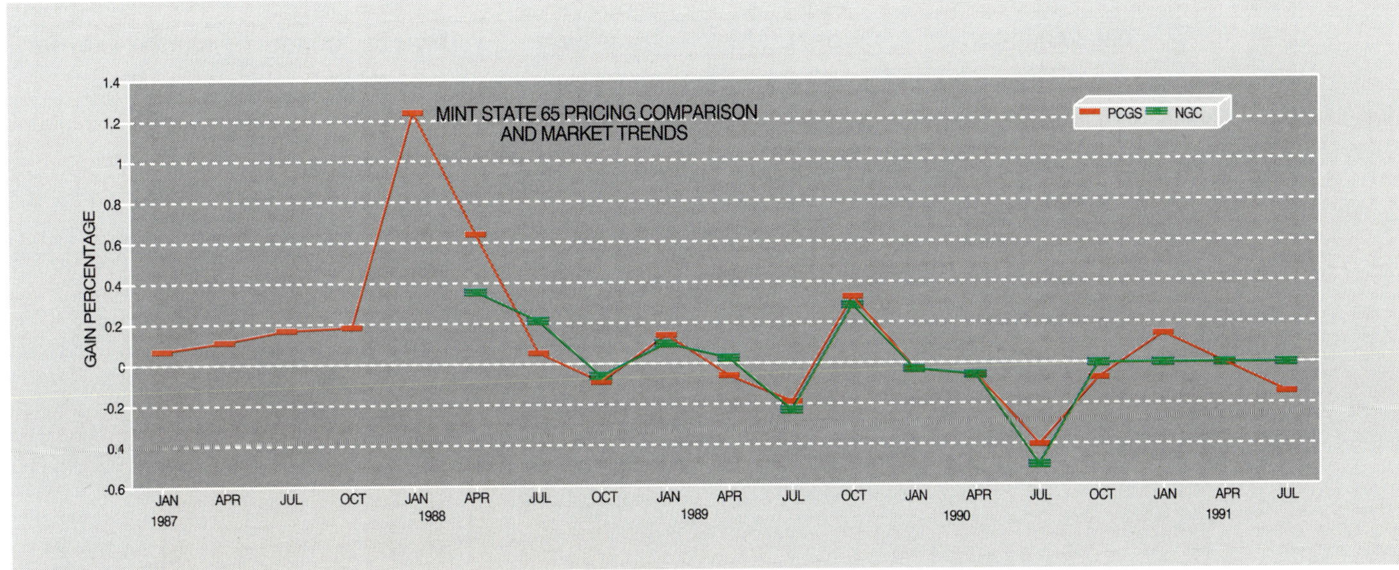
MINT STATE 65 PRICING COMPARISON
AND MARKET TRENDS
PCGS
NGC
GAIN PERCENTAGE
1.4
1.2
1
0.8
0.6
0.4
0.2
0
-0.2
0.4
-0.6
JAN
APR
JUL
OCT
1987
1988
1989
1990
1991

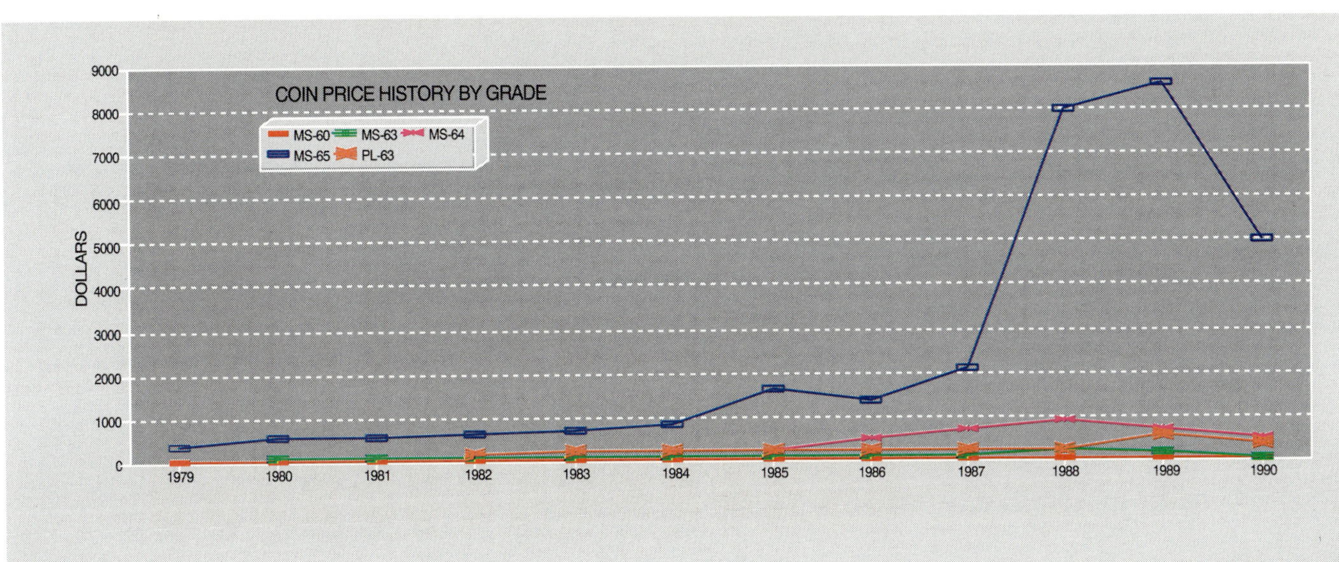
COIN PRICE HISTORY BY GRADE
MS-60
MS-63
MS-64
MS-65
PL-63
DOLLARS
9000
8000
7000
6000
5000
4000
3000
2000
1000
0
1979
1980
1981
1982
1983
1984
1985
1986
1987
1988
1989
1990

1887/6-O

In demand among collectors as a major variety. Usually weakly struck with below average lustre. The fragment of bottom loop of 6 at right base of 7 becomes fainter. See illustrations at VAM 3 and in the Breen *Encyclopedia*, no. 5597.

No quantities have turned up. Many survivors fall short of full mint state; those above MS 63 are rare.

Recommended in any or all grades of Mint State.

Prooflikes: No convincing ones seen. Cameos are virtually unknown in any BU prooflike grade.

MINTAGE	PROOF	STRIKE	LUSTER	BAG MARKS	REDFIELD
1,000,000*	0	Weak	Below Average	Moderate	No
DIES	**DIE VARIETIES**	**% OF PL**	**% OF DMPL**	**PIVOTAL GRADE**	**RARITY FACTOR**
108**	1	0.0	0.0	MS 64	R-1

*Estimated by this author (Highfill) **Includes all dies used at the New Orleans Mint - FY 1887

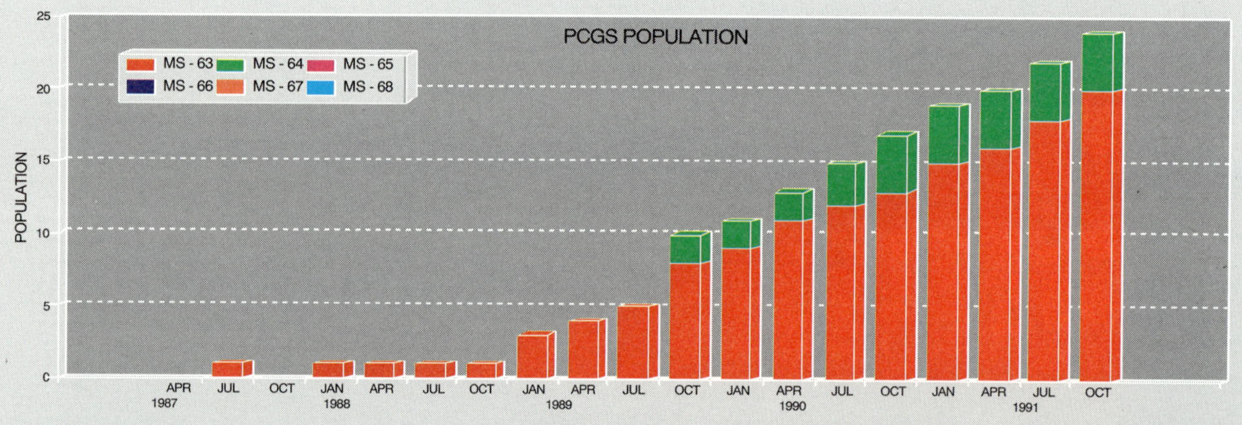

PCGS POPULATION

MS - 63 MS - 64 MS - 65
MS - 66 MS - 67 MS - 68

POPULATION

25 20 15 10 5 0

APR 1987 JUL OCT JAN 1988 APR JUL OCT JAN 1989 APR JUL OCT JAN APR 1990 JUL OCT JAN APR JUL 1991 OCT

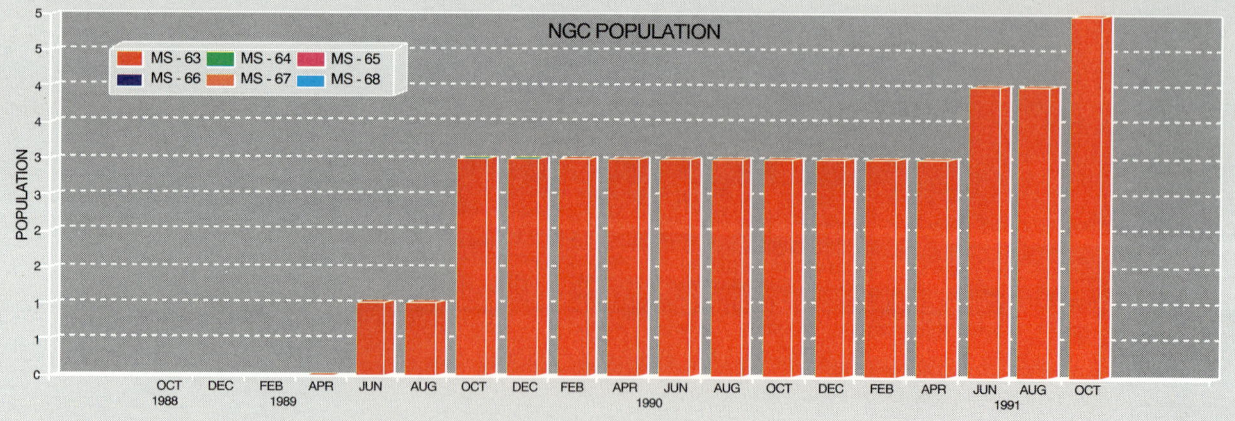

NGC POPULATION

MS - 63 MS - 64 MS - 65
MS - 66 MS - 67 MS - 68

POPULATION

5 5 4 4 3 3 2 2 1 1 0

OCT 1988 DEC FEB 1989 APR JUN AUG OCT DEC FEB APR 1990 JUN AUG OCT DEC FEB APR JUN AUG 1991 OCT

1887/6-O

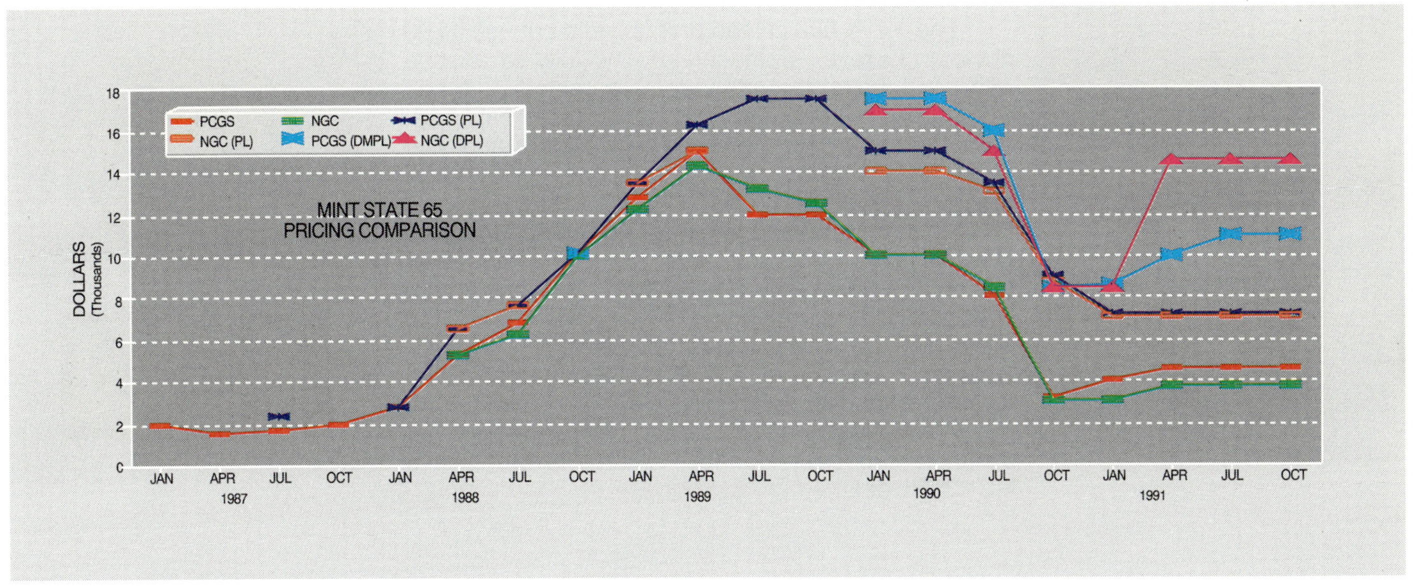

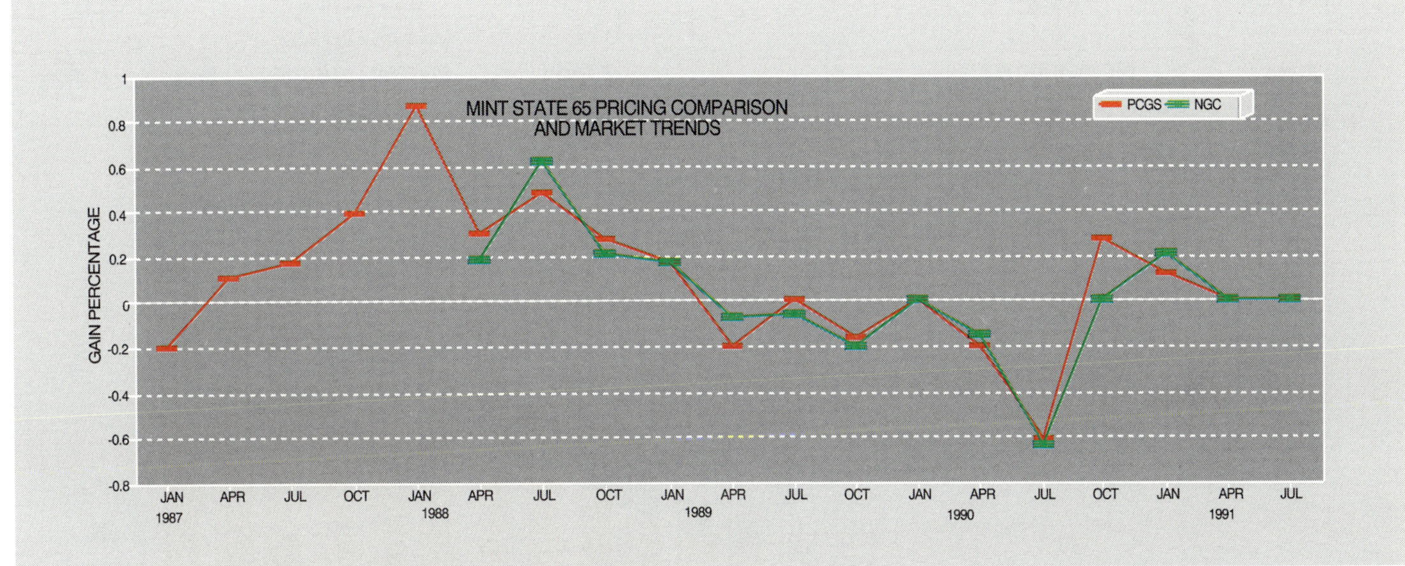

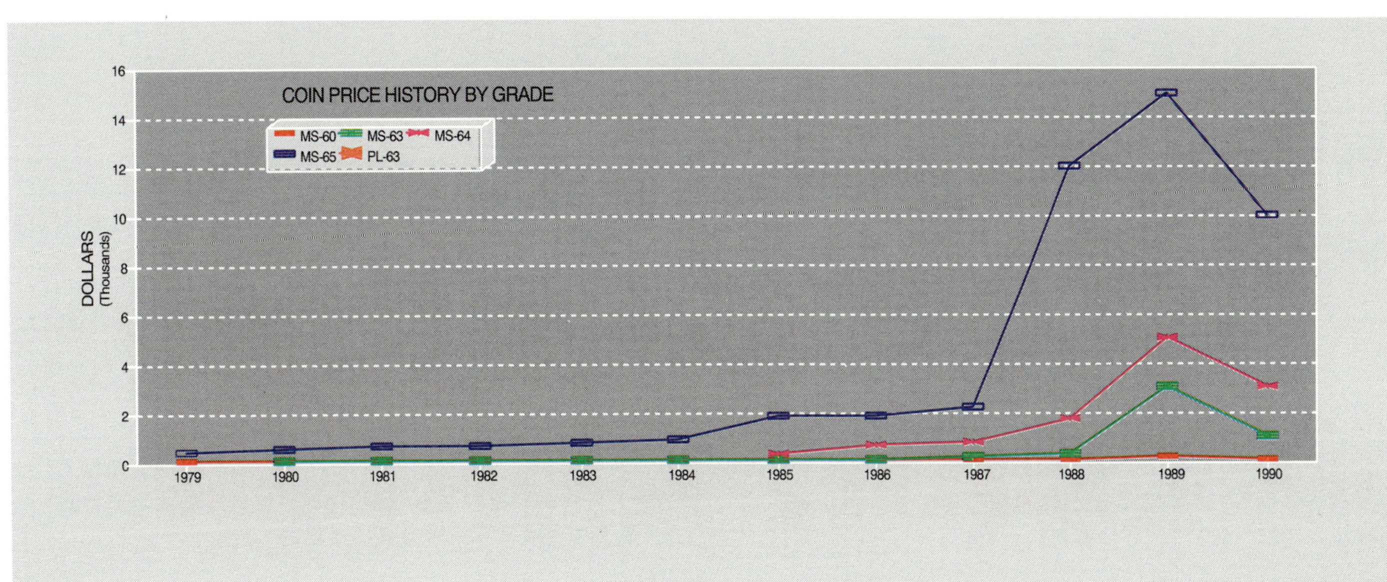

PCGS
1887-S S$1
MS65PL
7181.65/3174809

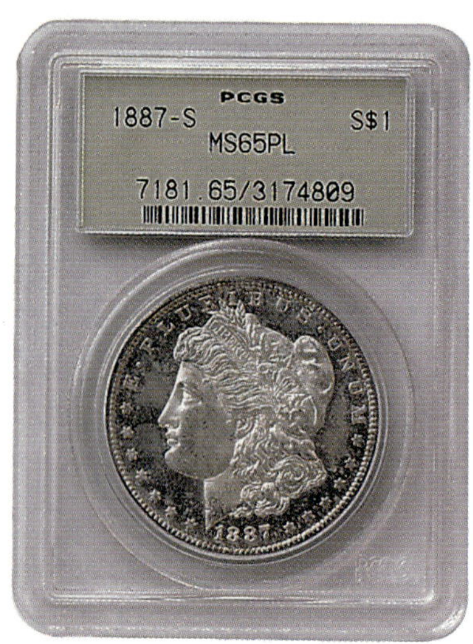

1887-S

The 1,771,000 coined probably did not use all 20 obvs. or 13 revs. Sometimes found fully struck and with good lustre; too often weak in center — in hair above ear and on breast feathers. Some real Uncs. have therefore been confused with sliders and vice versa. Many show obvious striations in field from repolishing of dies.

Reportedly 5 to 10 bags were dispersed from the Redfield hoard. Most coins seen from them have been MS 60/63 and heavily bagmarked. Roll lots in MS 60/62 are still available.

Recommended in MS 64 up. As with the 1887-O, you many have to buy a 60/63 as a space filler and upgrade when you get the chance.

Prooflikes: Many one-sided. Two-sided are not common, especially cameos. Scarce to rare above MS 63, PL or DMPL.

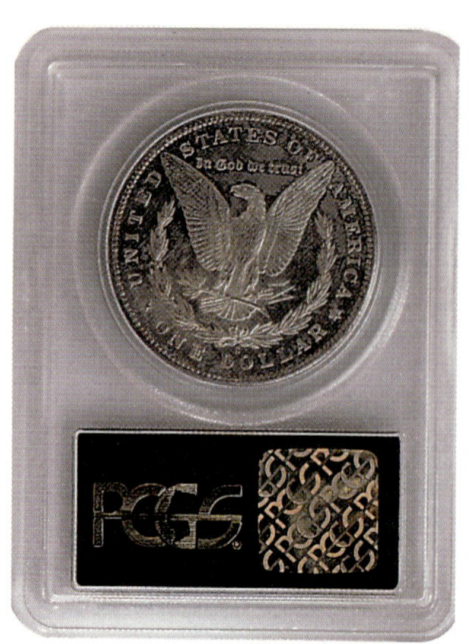

MINTAGE	PROOF	STRIKE	LUSTER	BAG MARKS	REDFIELD
1,771,000	0	Average	Good	Moderate To Heavy	Yes
DIES	**DIE VARIETIES**	**% OF PL**	**% OF DMPL**	**PIVOTAL GRADE**	**RARITY FACTOR**
8	8	3.4	1.9	MS 64	R-2

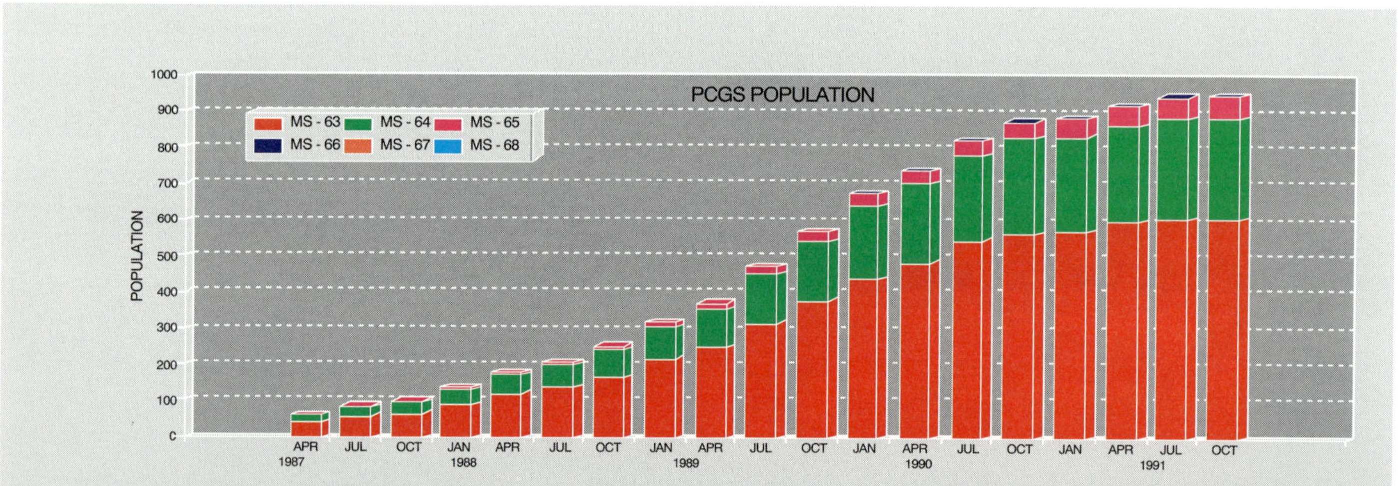

PCGS POPULATION
MS - 63
MS - 64
MS - 65
MS - 66
MS - 67
MS - 68
POPULATION
0
100
200
300
400
500
600
700
800
900
1000
APR 1987
JUL
OCT
JAN 1988
APR
JUL
OCT
JAN 1989
APR
JUL
OCT
JAN
APR 1990
JUL
OCT
JAN
APR
JUL 1991
OCT

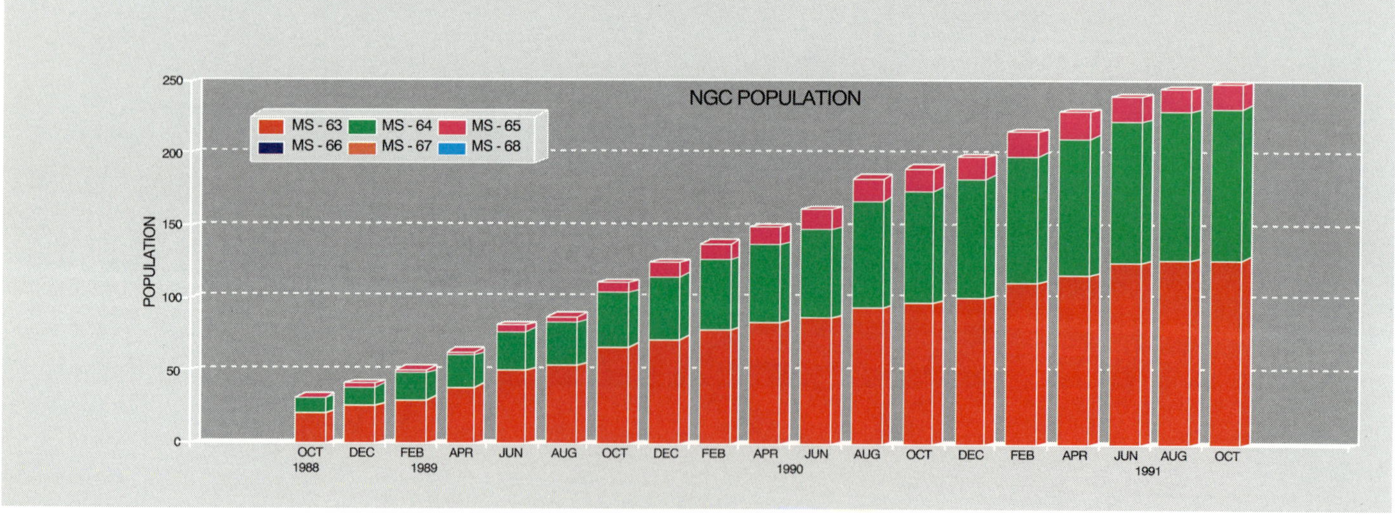

NGC POPULATION
MS - 63
MS - 64
MS - 65
MS - 66
MS - 67
MS - 68
POPULATION
0
50
100
150
200
250
OCT 1988
DEC
FEB 1989
APR
JUN
AUG
OCT
DEC
FEB
APR 1990
JUN
AUG
OCT
DEC
FEB
APR
JUN 1991
AUG
OCT

1887-S

PCGS
NGC
PCGS (PL)
NGC (PL)
PCGS (DMPL)
NGC (DPL)
MINT STATE 65
PRICING COMPARISON
DOLLARS
(Thousands)
12
11
10
9
8
7
6
5
4
3
2
1
JAN
APR
JUL
OCT
JAN
APR
JUL
OCT
JAN
APR
JUL
OCT
JAN
APR
JUL
OCT
JAN
APR
JUL
OCT
1987
1988
1989
1990
1991

PCGS
NGC
GAIN PERCENTAGE
0.5
0.4
0.3
0.2
0.1
0
-0.1
-0.2
-0.3
-0.4
-0.5
-0.6
MINT STATE 65 PRICING COMPARISON
AND MARKET TRENDS
JAN
APR
JUL
OCT
JAN
APR
JUL
OCT
JAN
APR
JUL
OCT
JAN
APR
JUL
OCT
JAN
APR
JUL
1987
1988
1989
1990
1991

COIN PRICE HISTORY BY GRADE
MS-60
MS-63
MS-64
MS-65
PL-63
DOLLARS
7000
6000
5000
4000
3000
2000
1000
0
1979
1980
1981
1982
1983
1984
1985
1986
1987
1988
1989
1990

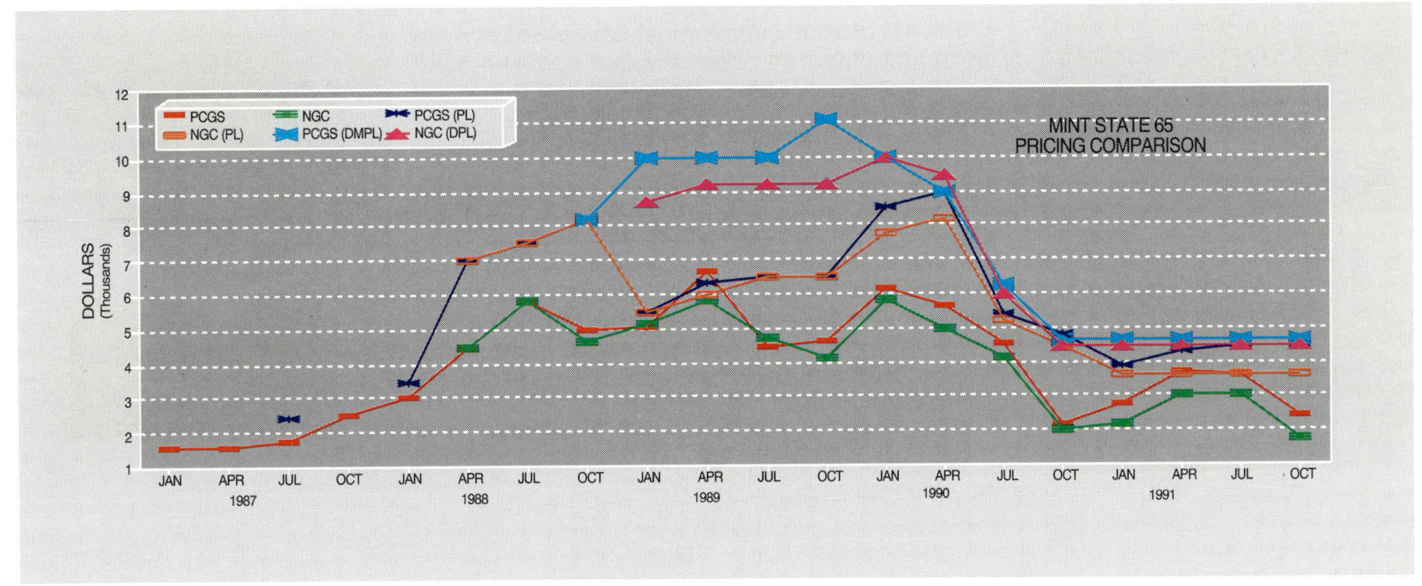

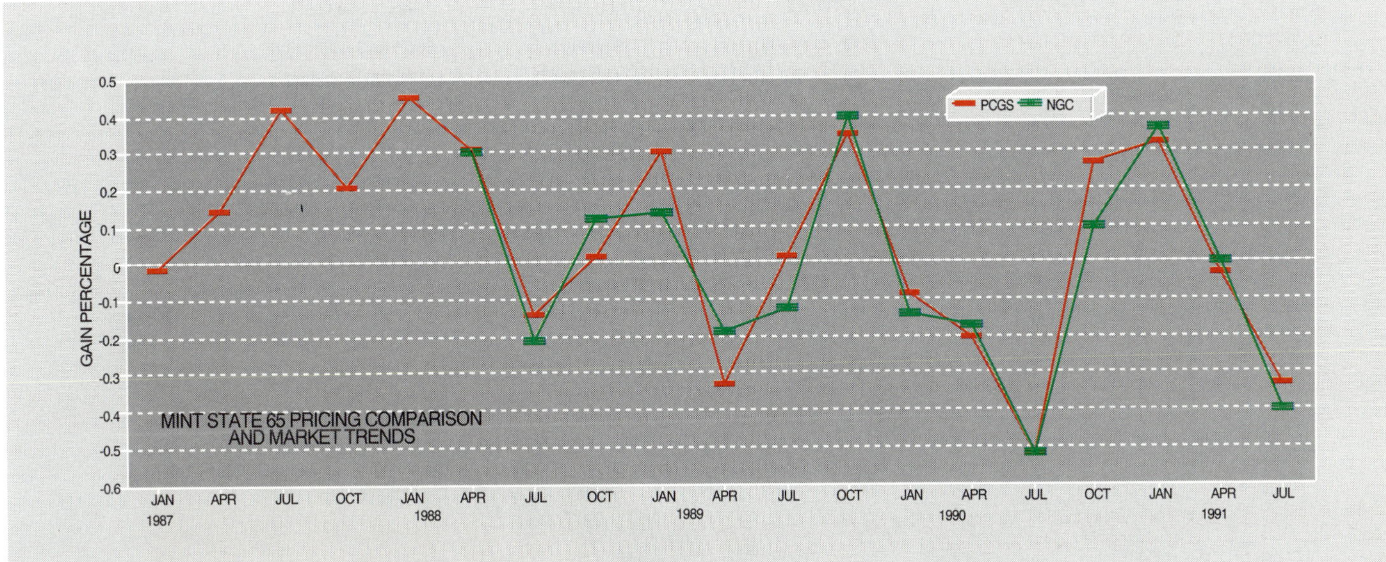

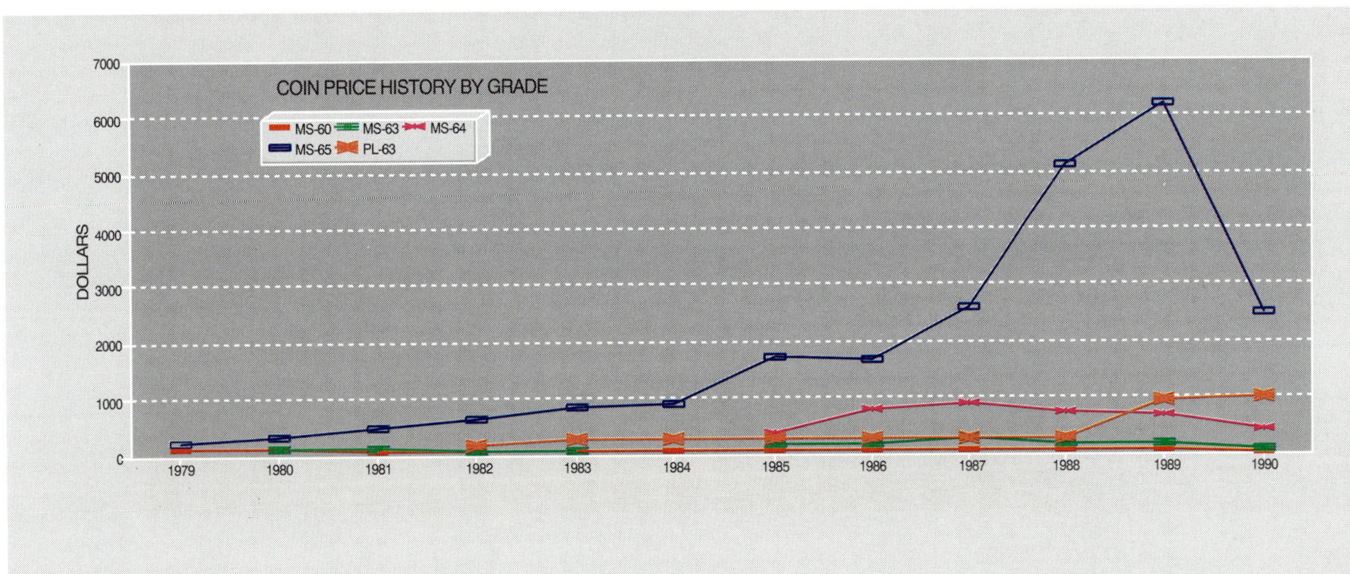

1888-P

The 19,183,000 coined must have needed most or all the 64 obvs., 54 revs. Another common date, though less so than 1885-87 Philadelphia. Found in all grades. BU roll and bag quantities still survive. Uncs. vary from flat to full strike, from dull to bright, though lustre is usually sub-par. Improper basining of the dies resulted in excessive "metal flow" and flat struck coins.

Recommended in MS 65 up; roll lots, MS 64 up.

Proofs: The 800 coined took two pairs of dies. Most have date slanting up to right (VAM 1). A few have obvious double date west (*Encyclopedia* 5800, first entered to left of final position); discovered 1954, discovery coin "Anderson Dupont":2586. Few others have been seen since.

Prooflikes: Surprisingly hard to find; scarce to rare in all grades above MS 64. Cameos are also scarce to rare.

MINTAGE	PROOF	STRIKE	LUSTER	BAG MARKS	REDFIELD
19,183,000	832	Soft & Weak	Average	Moderate To Heavy	No
DIES	**DIE VARIETIES**	**% OF PL**	**% OF DMPL**	**PIVOTAL GRADE**	**RARITY FACTOR**
116	19	1.6	1.5	MS 65	R-4

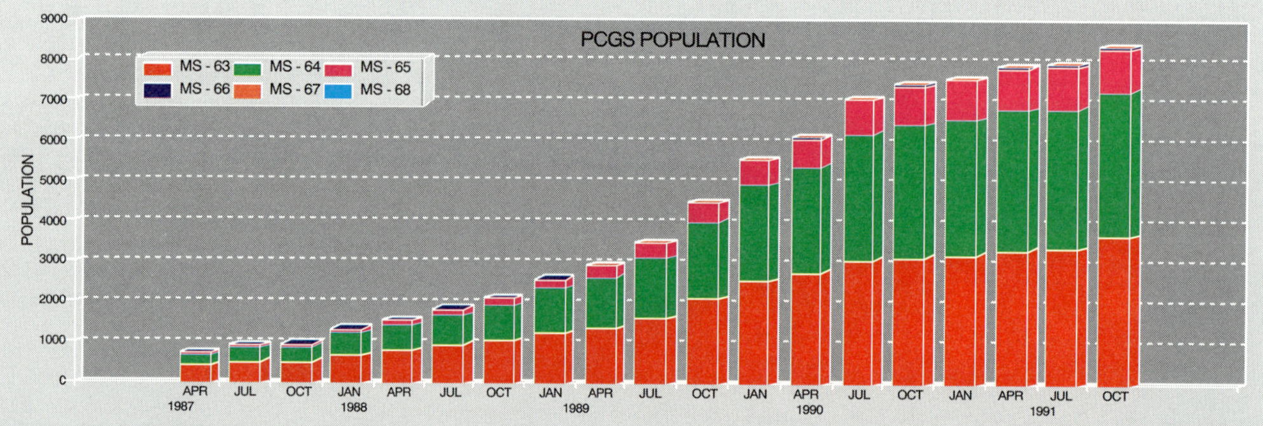

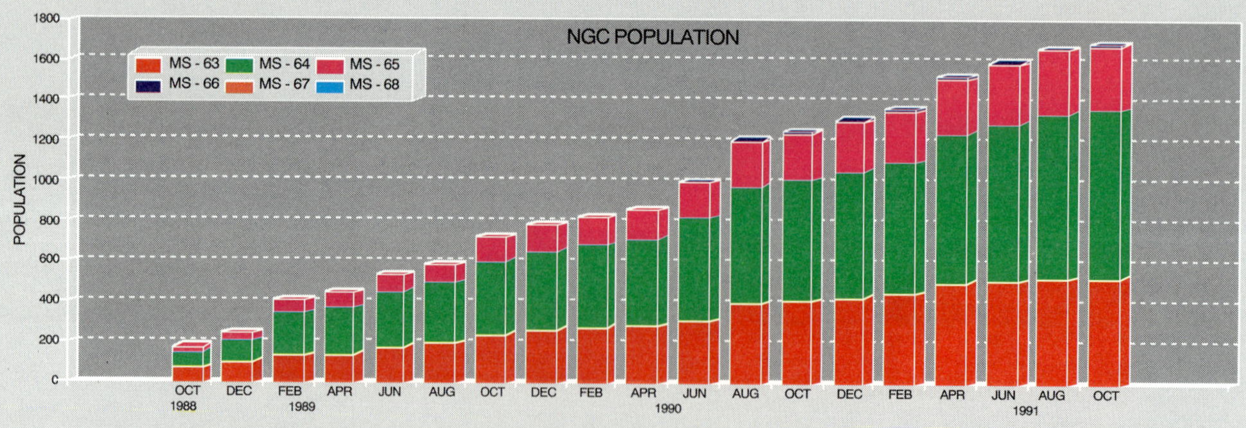

PCGS POPULATION

MS - 63 MS - 64 MS - 65 MS - 66 MS - 67 MS - 68

POPULATION

0 1000 2000 3000 4000 5000 6000 7000 8000 9000

APR 1987 JUL OCT JAN 1988 APR JUL OCT JAN 1989 APR JUL OCT JAN 1990 APR JUL OCT JAN 1991 APR JUL OCT

NGC POPULATION

MS - 63 MS - 64 MS - 65 MS - 66 MS - 67 MS - 68

POPULATION

0 200 400 600 800 1000 1200 1400 1600 1800

OCT 1988 DEC FEB 1989 APR JUN AUG OCT DEC FEB 1990 APR JUN AUG OCT DEC FEB 1991 APR JUN AUG OCT

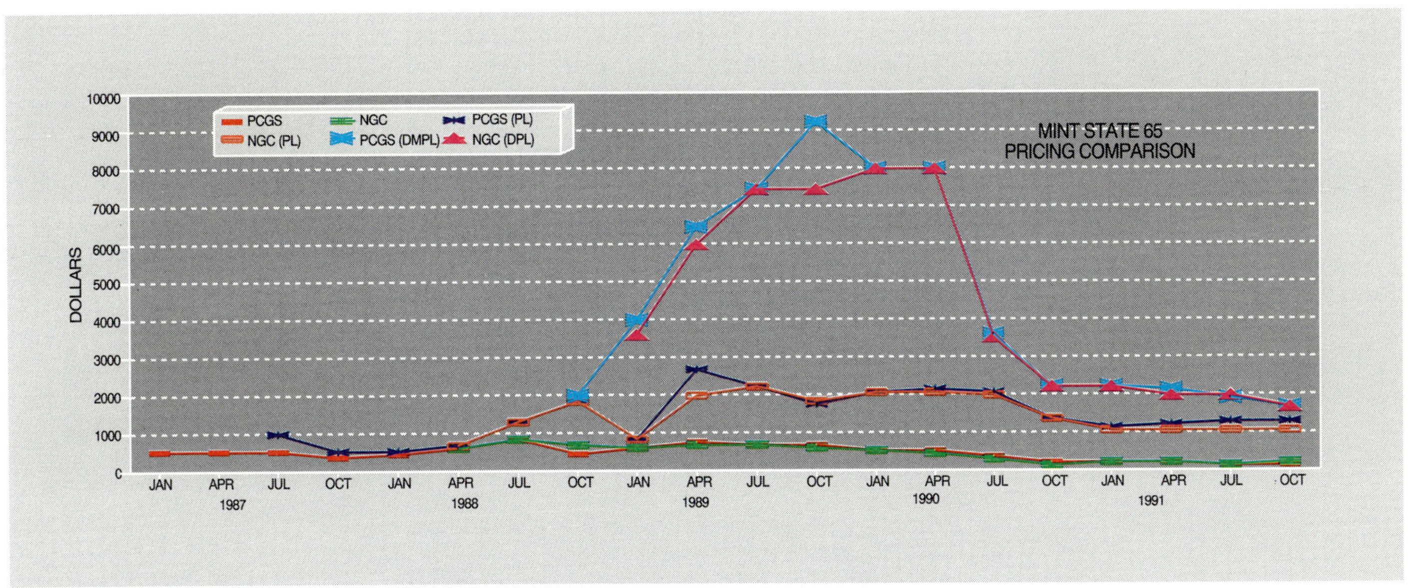

PCGS
NGC
PCGS (PL)
NGC (PL)
PCGS (DMPL)
NGC (DPL)
MINT STATE 65
PRICING COMPARISON
DOLLARS
10000
9000
8000
7000
6000
5000
4000
3000
2000
1000
0
JAN APR JUL OCT JAN APR JUL OCT JAN APR JUL OCT JAN APR JUL OCT JAN APR JUL OCT
1987
1988
1989
1990
1991

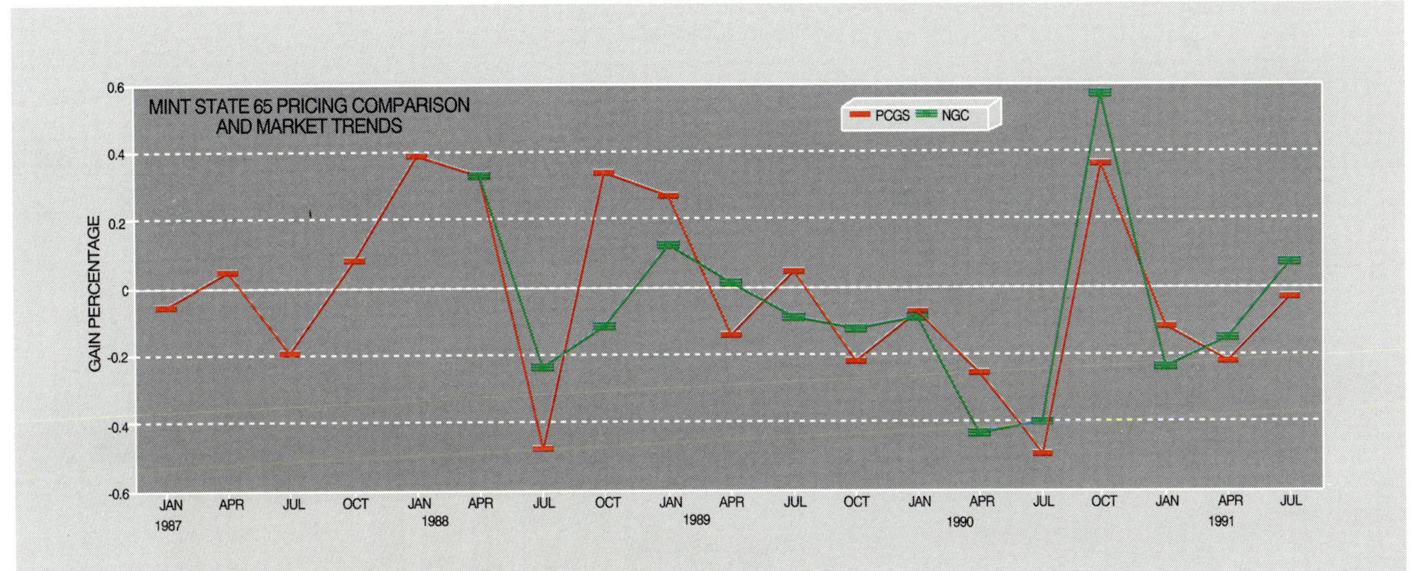

MINT STATE 65 PRICING COMPARISON
AND MARKET TRENDS
PCGS
NGC
GAIN PERCENTAGE
0.6
0.4
0.2
0
-0.2
-0.4
-0.6
JAN APR JUL OCT JAN APR JUL OCT JAN APR JUL OCT JAN APR JUL OCT JAN APR JUL
1987
1988
1989
1990
1991

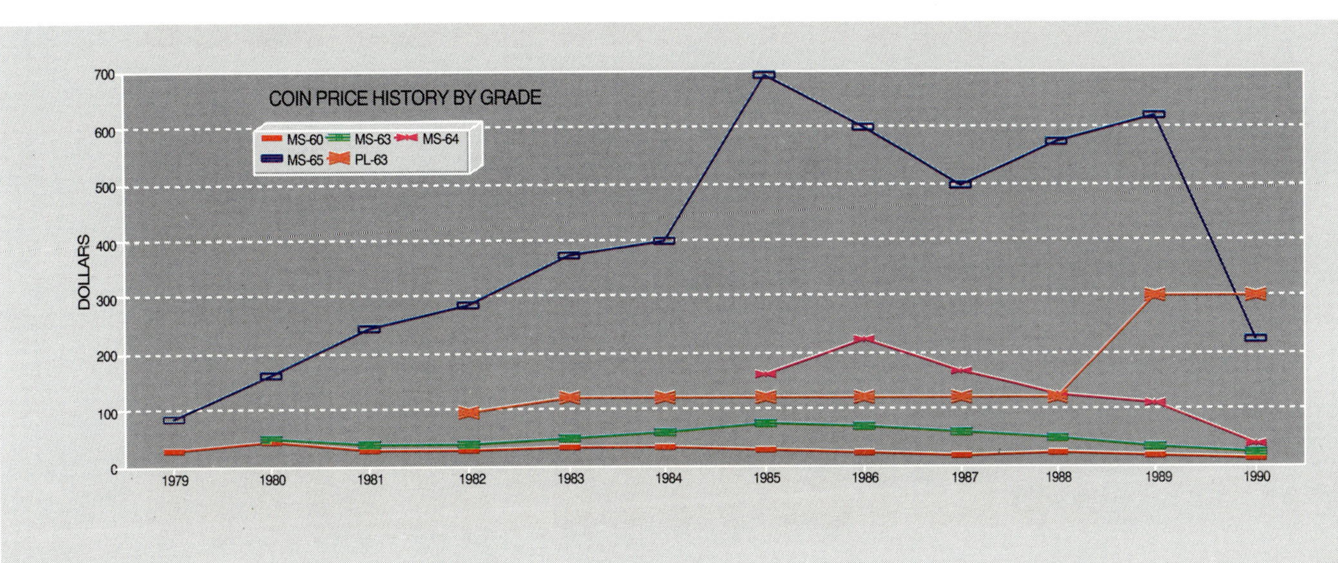

COIN PRICE HISTORY BY GRADE
MS-60
MS-63
MS-64
MS-65
PL-63
DOLLARS
700
600
500
400
300
200
100
0
1979 1980 1981 1982 1983 1984 1985 1986 1987 1988 1989 1990

PCGS
1888-O
S$1
MS66
7184.66/6264652

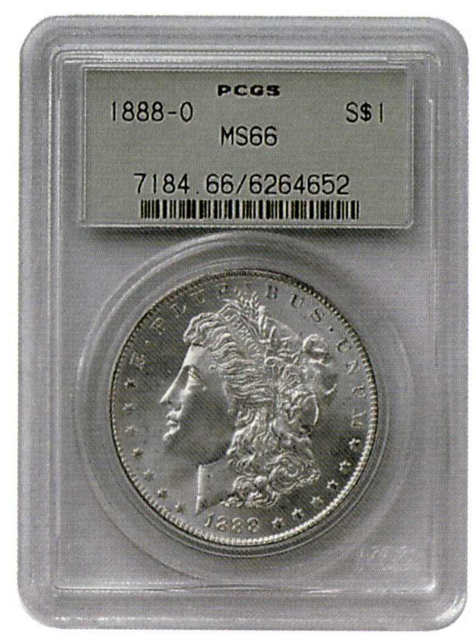

1888-O

Mintage 12,150,000. Often found with flat strikes, average lustre, and plenty of bag marks, much like 1887-O. Wayne Miller talked of examining 24 mint bags in eastern Montana, 1971-78. This author (Highfill) has also searched through bags of this date, only to find flat strikes in 80-90% of the coins. Roll and bag lots survive in MS 60/62.

Not much difference in populations between the oval O (slit opening) and the round O (wide opening).

Recommended in MS 65 up. You may have to buy a MS 64 for a space filler and upgrade at leisure.

The double obverse, VAM 4, more familiarly known as "Hot Lips," has become a favorite among collectors. It is very scarce in all grades (usually below AU), and unobtainable in full mint state; Bill Fivaz & J. T. Stanton report seeing only one. Discovered by Chester Bryk, 1962.

Proofs: One was described in the Woodin sale (1911). Not traced.

Prooflikes: Common one-sided. Two-sided are about equally often found PL and DMPL; both are scarce in MS 64 up. Many have good cameo effect. No "Hot Lips" coins are even rumored in PL.

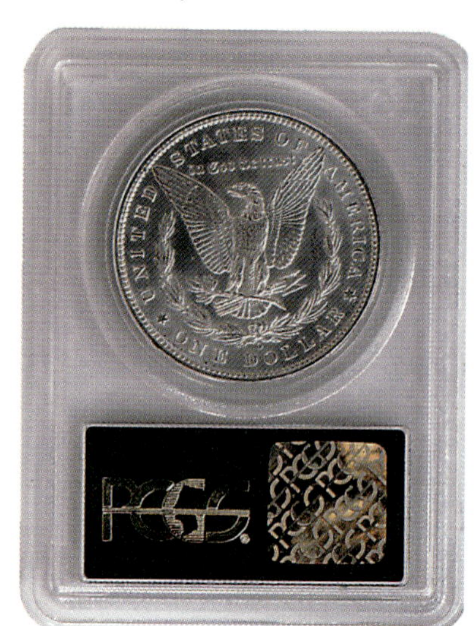

MINTAGE	PROOF	STRIKE	LUSTER	BAG MARKS	REDFIELD
12,150,000	0	Soft & Weak	Average	Moderate To Heavy	No
DIES	**DIE VARIETIES**	**% OF PL**	**% OF DMPL**	**PIVOTAL GRADE**	**RARITY FACTOR**
136	18	5.2	4.0	MS 65	R-4

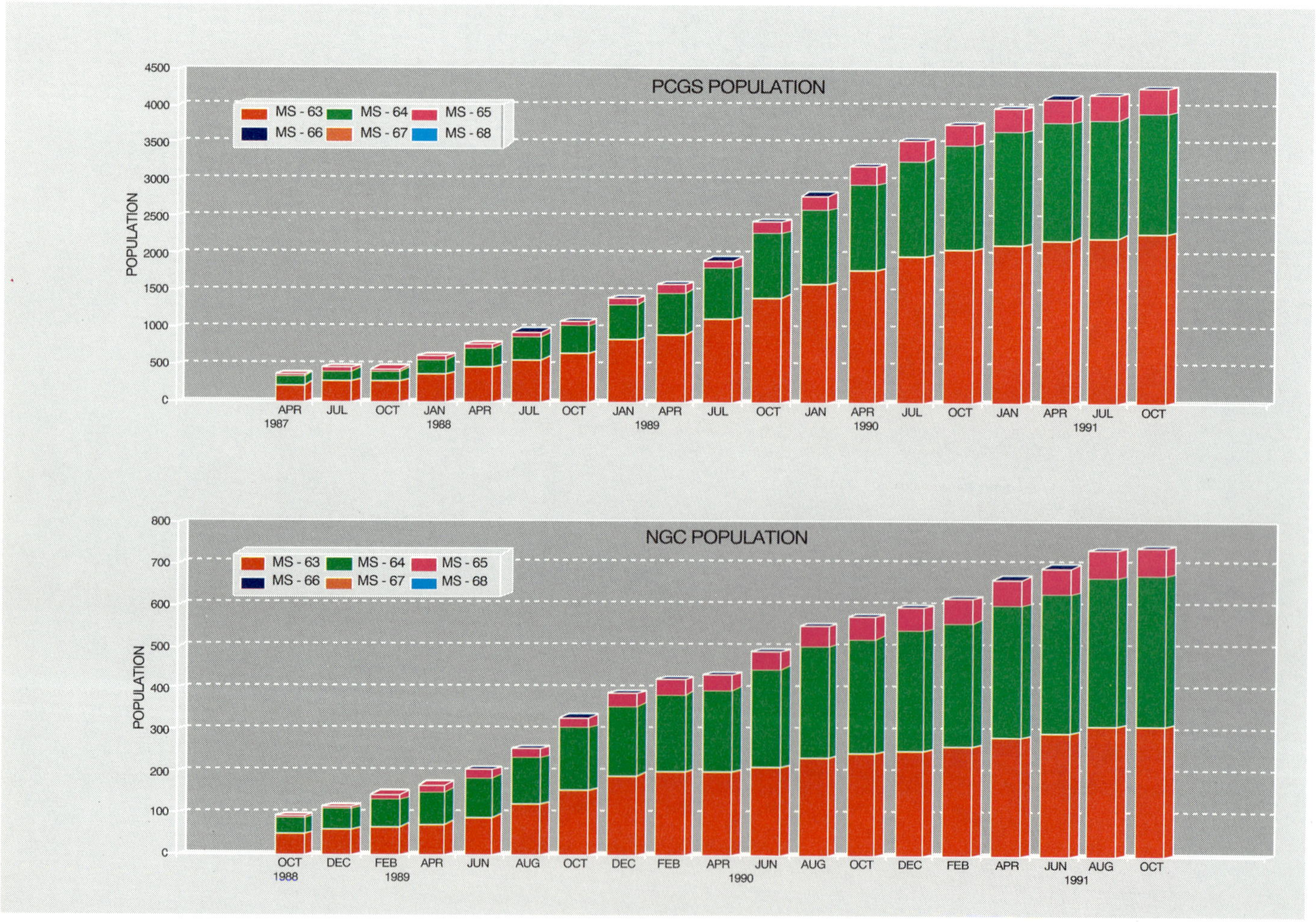
PCGS POPULATION
MS - 63
MS - 64
MS - 65
MS - 66
MS - 67
MS - 68
POPULATION
4500
4000
3500
3000
2500
2000
1500
1000
500
0
APR 1987
JUL
OCT
JAN 1988
APR
JUL
OCT
JAN 1989
APR
JUL
OCT
JAN
APR 1990
JUL
OCT
JAN
APR
JUL 1991
OCT
NGC POPULATION
MS - 63
MS - 64
MS - 65
MS - 66
MS - 67
MS - 68
POPULATION
800
700
600
500
400
300
200
100
0
OCT 1988
DEC
FEB 1989
APR
JUN
AUG
OCT
DEC
FEB
APR 1990
JUN
AUG
OCT
DEC
FEB
APR
JUN 1991
AUG
OCT

1888-O

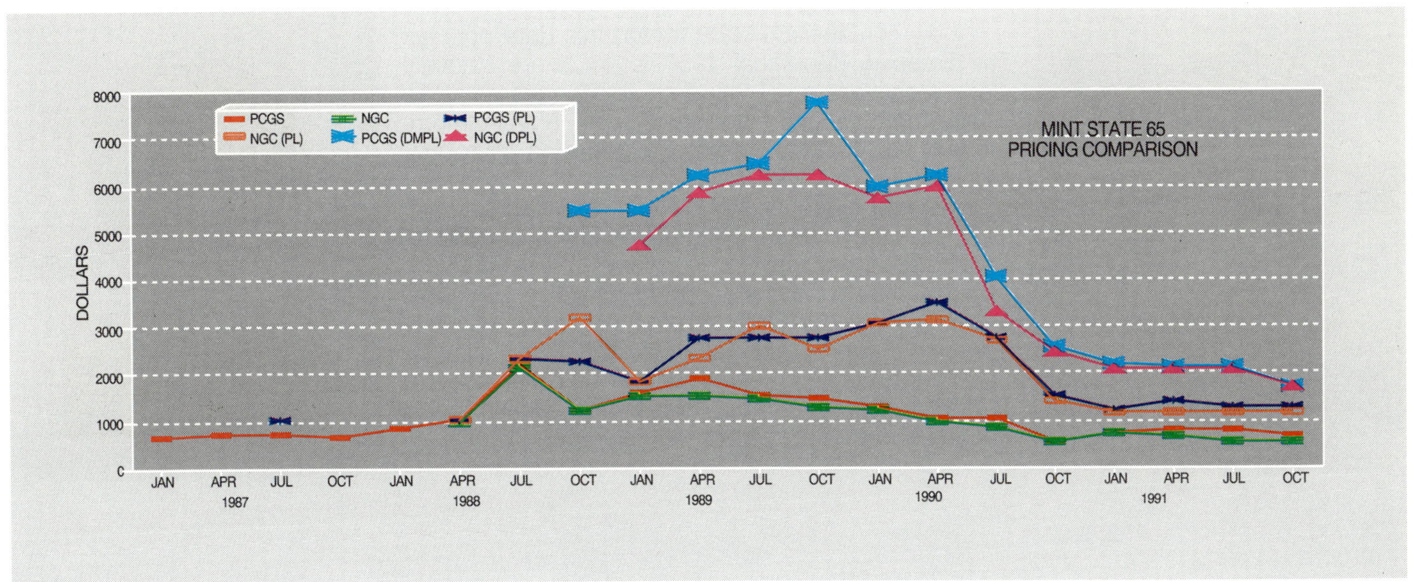

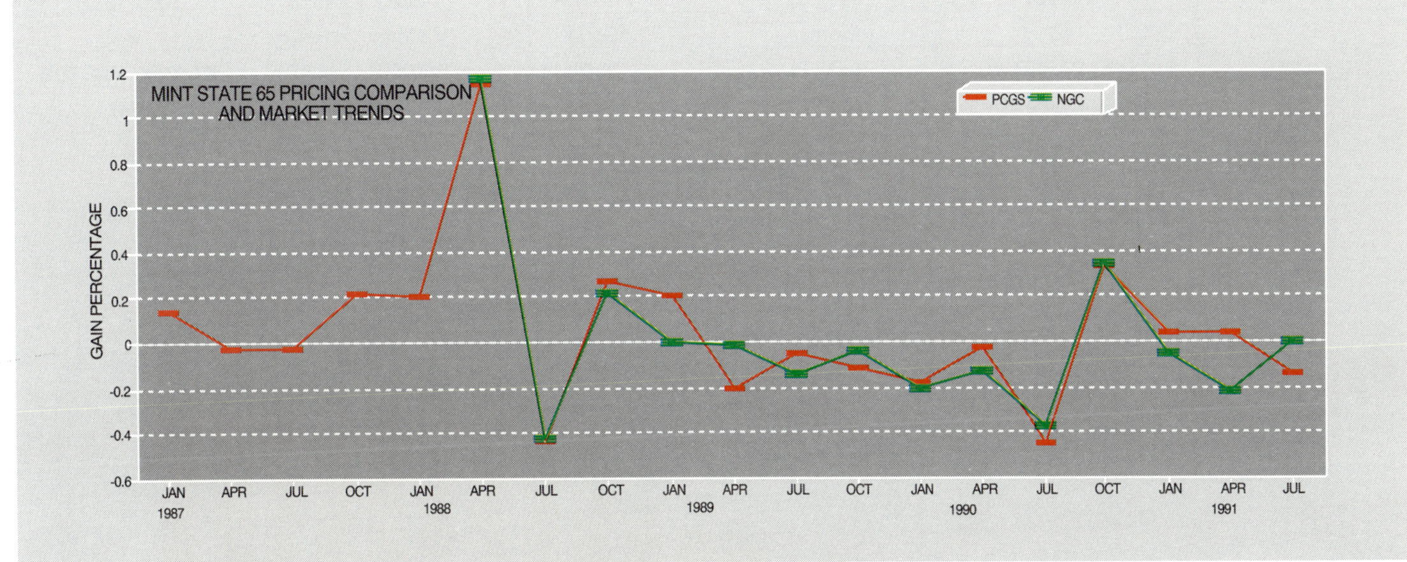

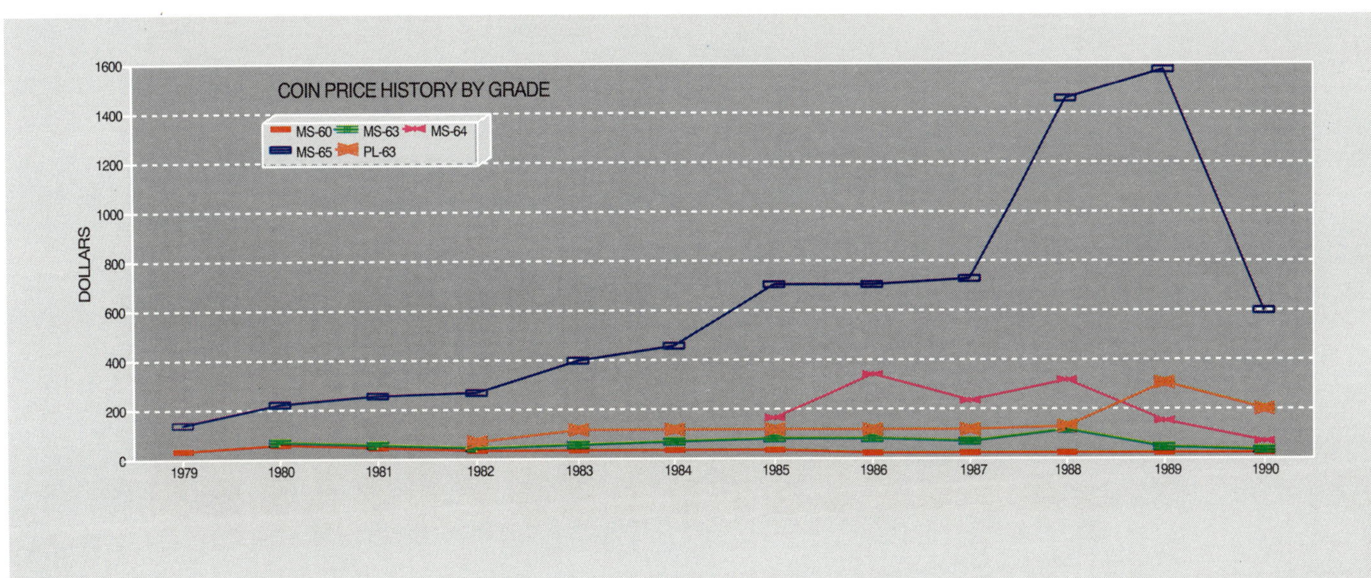

1888-S

Low mintage (657,000) made this date popular. The Treasury (Montana, 1956) and LaVere Redfield made it obtainable. Redfield's 5 to 10 bags were the source for many of the surviving Uncs. Many of them are soft strikes from heavily striated dies from over polished dies, but very lustrous.

Recommended in MS 65 up. Happy hunting!

Fakes have been reportedly made by cementing S mintmark to genuine 1888 dollars. To detect these, look at junction of mintmark and field with a 20x glass or, better, a binocular microscope. The fakes will show a seam separating mintmark from field.

Prooflikes: Usually coins so offered are semi-PL's, rarely cameo. This remark applies to the Redfield coins. Rare above MS 64, PL and DMPL.

MINTAGE	PROOF	STRIKE	LUSTER	BAG MARKS	REDFIELD
657,000	0	Average	Good	Moderate To Heavy	Yes
DIES	**DIE VARIETIES**	**% OF PL**	**% OF DMPL**	**PIVOTAL GRADE**	**RARITY FACTOR**
80	10	5.9	6.8	MS 65	R-2

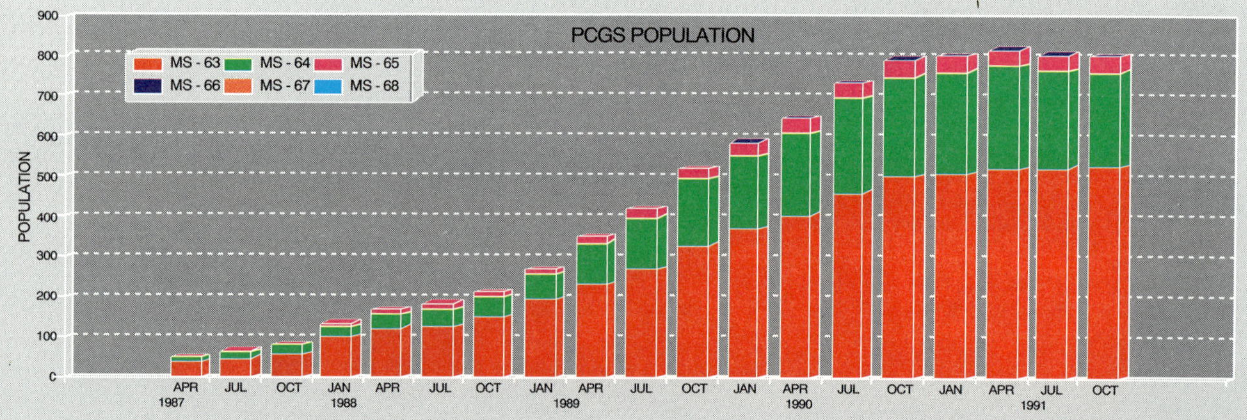

PCGS POPULATION

MS - 63 MS - 64 MS - 65
MS - 66 MS - 67 MS - 68

POPULATION

0 100 200 300 400 500 600 700 800 900

APR 1987, JUL, OCT, JAN 1988, APR, JUL, OCT, JAN 1989, APR, JUL, OCT, JAN, APR 1990, JUL, OCT, JAN, APR, JUL 1991, OCT

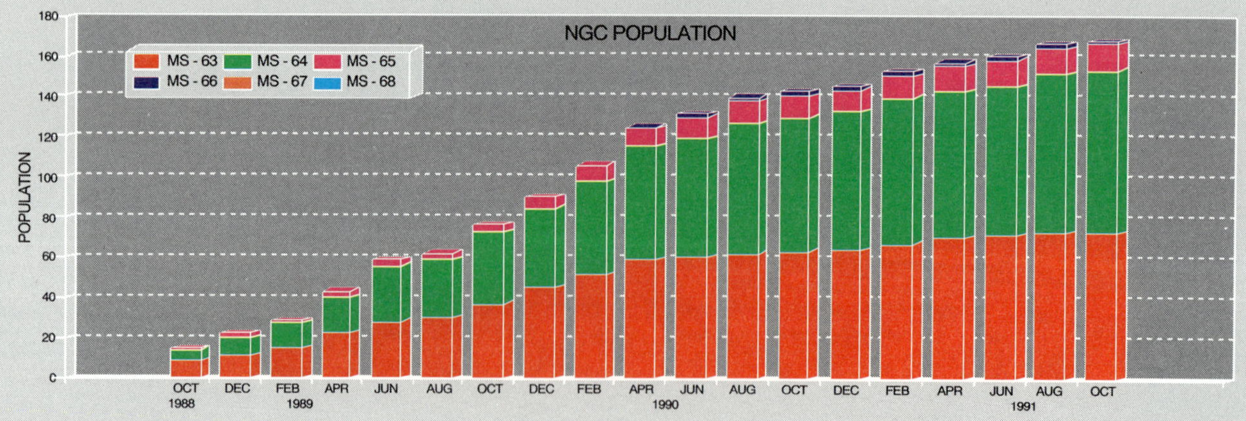

NGC POPULATION

MS - 63 MS - 64 MS - 65
MS - 66 MS - 67 MS - 68

POPULATION

0 20 40 60 80 100 120 140 160 180

OCT 1988, DEC, FEB 1989, APR, JUN, AUG, OCT, DEC, FEB, APR 1990, JUN, AUG, OCT, DEC, FEB, APR, JUN 1991, AUG, OCT

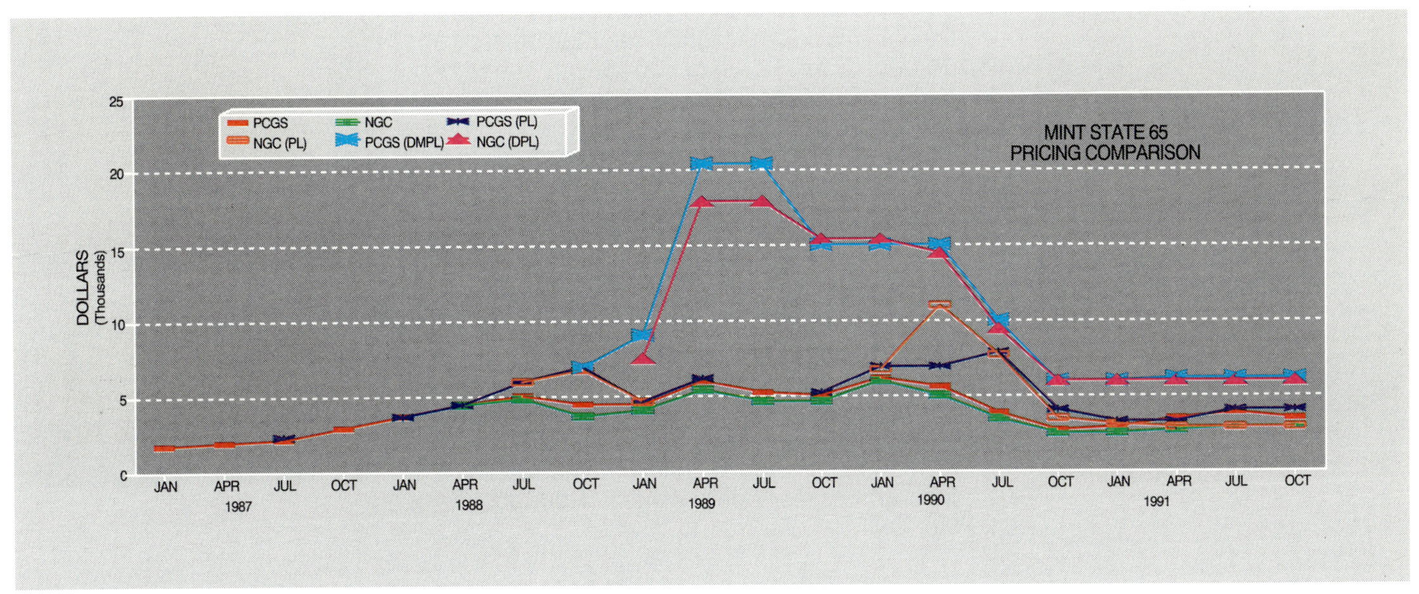
MINT STATE 65
PRICING COMPARISON
PCGS
NGC
PCGS (PL)
NGC (PL)
PCGS (DMPL)
NGC (DPL)
DOLLARS
(Thousands)
25
20
15
10
5
0
JAN APR JUL OCT JAN APR JUL OCT JAN APR JUL OCT JAN APR JUL OCT JAN APR JUL OCT
1987
1988
1989
1990
1991

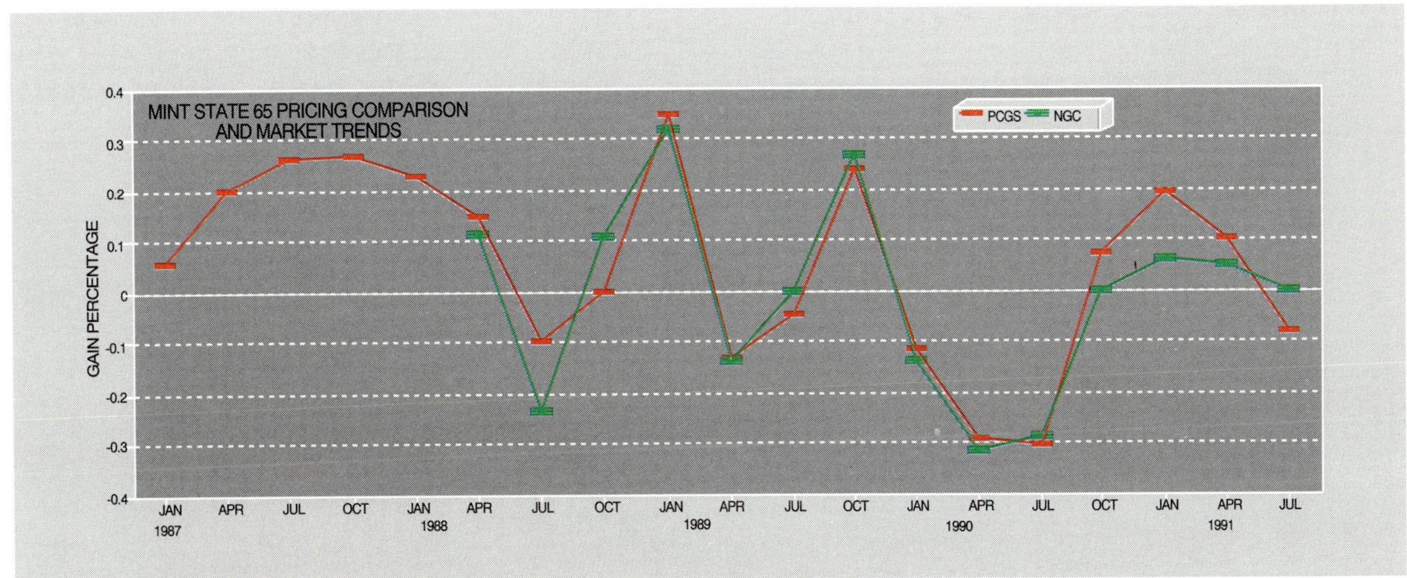
MINT STATE 65 PRICING COMPARISON
AND MARKET TRENDS
PCGS
NGC
GAIN PERCENTAGE
0.4
0.3
0.2
0.1
0
-0.1
-0.2
-0.3
-0.4
JAN APR JUL OCT JAN APR JUL OCT JAN APR JUL OCT JAN APR JUL OCT JAN APR JUL
1987
1988
1989
1990
1991

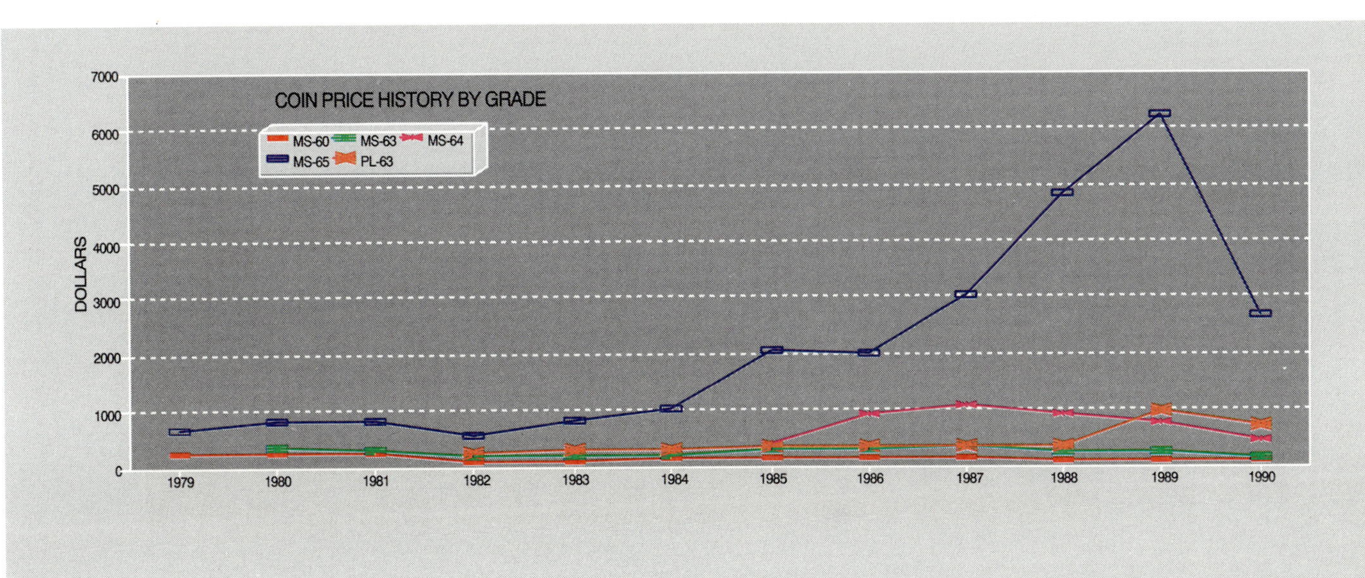
COIN PRICE HISTORY BY GRADE
MS-60
MS-63
MS-64
MS-65
PL-63
DOLLARS
7000
6000
5000
4000
3000
2000
1000
0
1979 1980 1981 1982 1983 1984 1985 1986 1987 1988 1989 1990

1889-P

PCGS
1889
S$1
MS67
7188.67/2241678

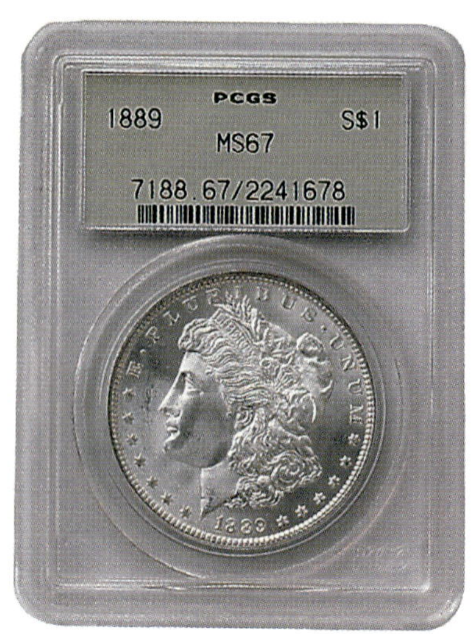

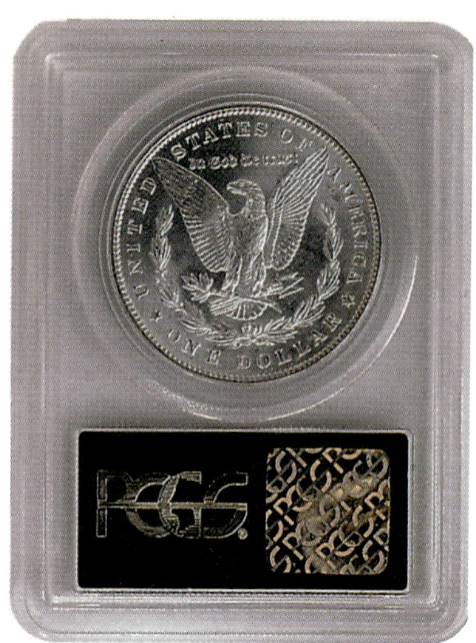

Though this has the highest mintage before 1921 (21,726,000, from 57 obvs. 50 revs.), most Unc. survivors — many from Treasury bags, 1954 — are low quality: subdued lustre, soft strike weak in centers. Many show evidence of badly worn, cracked, and/or rusted dies. "Metal flow" is very common for this date.

A Texas numismatic firm reportedly had several bags from the Redfield hoard. Though their holding is not documented, there are: an oversupply of sliders, rolls and bag lots in MS 60/62.

Recommended in MS 65. You may have to start with a MS 64 and hope to upgrade later.

Proofs: Only 811 made. Only one variety identified to date (VAM 1). Heavy date slants up to right; heavy die polish at eye and Morgans initial M.

Prooflikes: Scarce in semi-PL; the real thing is rarer in all grades, especially cameo. Rare above MS 64, PL or DMPL.

MINTAGE	PROOF	STRIKE	LUSTER	BAG MARKS	REDFIELD
21,726,000	811	Soft To Average	Average	Moderate To Heavy	No
DIES	**DIE VARIETIES**	**% OF PL**	**% OF DMPL**	**PIVOTAL GRADE**	**RARITY FACTOR**
104	22	1.6	1.2	MS 65	R-4

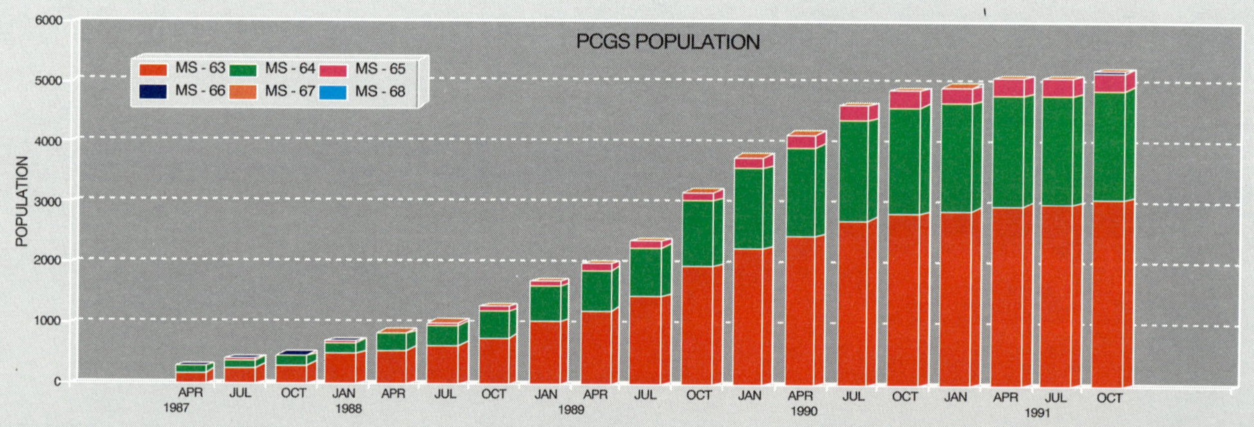
PCGS POPULATION
MS - 63
MS - 64
MS - 65
MS - 66
MS - 67
MS - 68
POPULATION
6000
5000
4000
3000
2000
1000
0
APR
1987
JUL
OCT
JAN
1988
APR
JUL
OCT
JAN
1989
APR
JUL
OCT
JAN
APR
1990
JUL
OCT
JAN
APR
JUL
1991
OCT

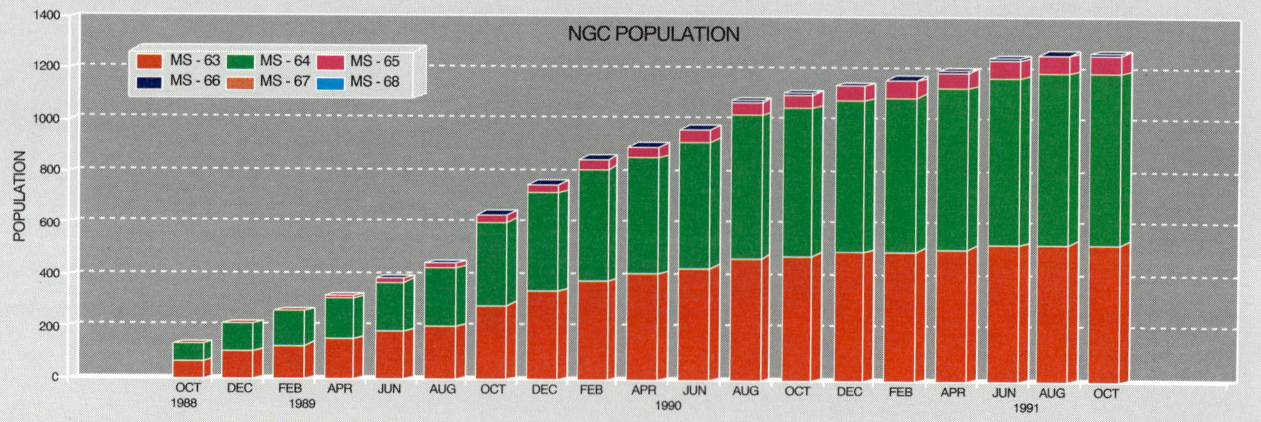
NGC POPULATION
MS - 63
MS - 64
MS - 65
MS - 66
MS - 67
MS - 68
POPULATION
1400
1200
1000
800
600
400
200
0
OCT
1988
DEC
FEB
1989
APR
JUN
AUG
OCT
DEC
FEB
APR
1990
JUN
AUG
OCT
DEC
FEB
APR
JUN
1991
AUG
OCT

1889-P

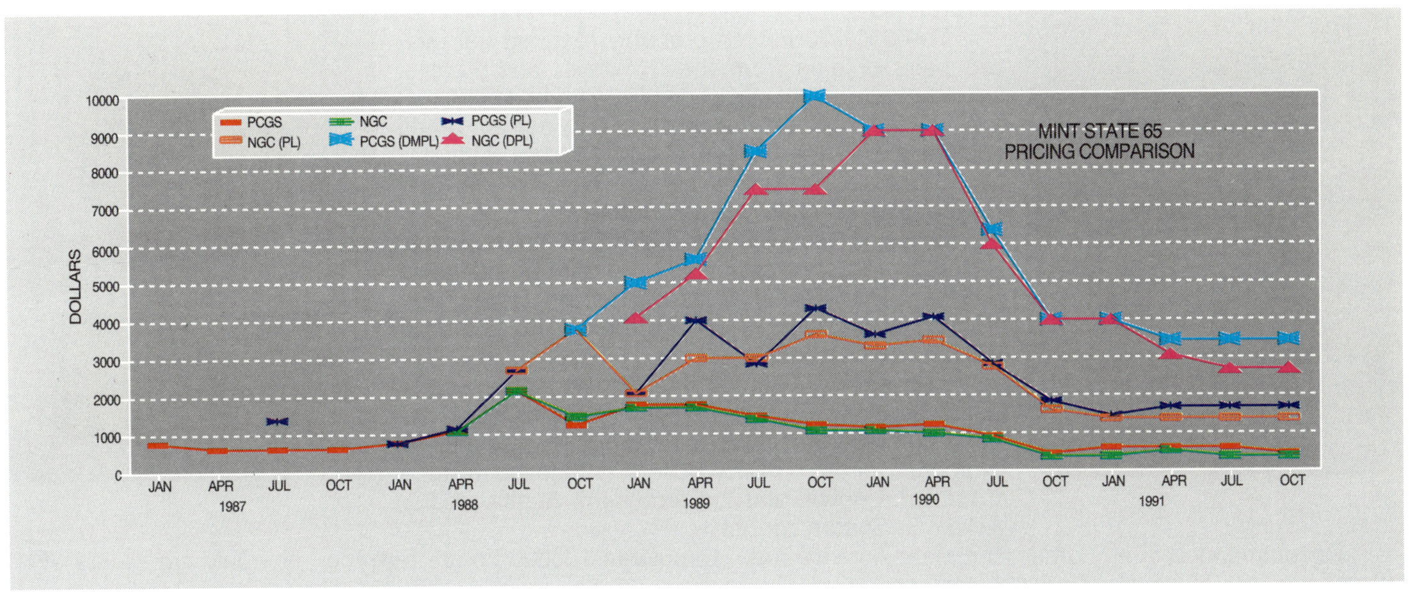

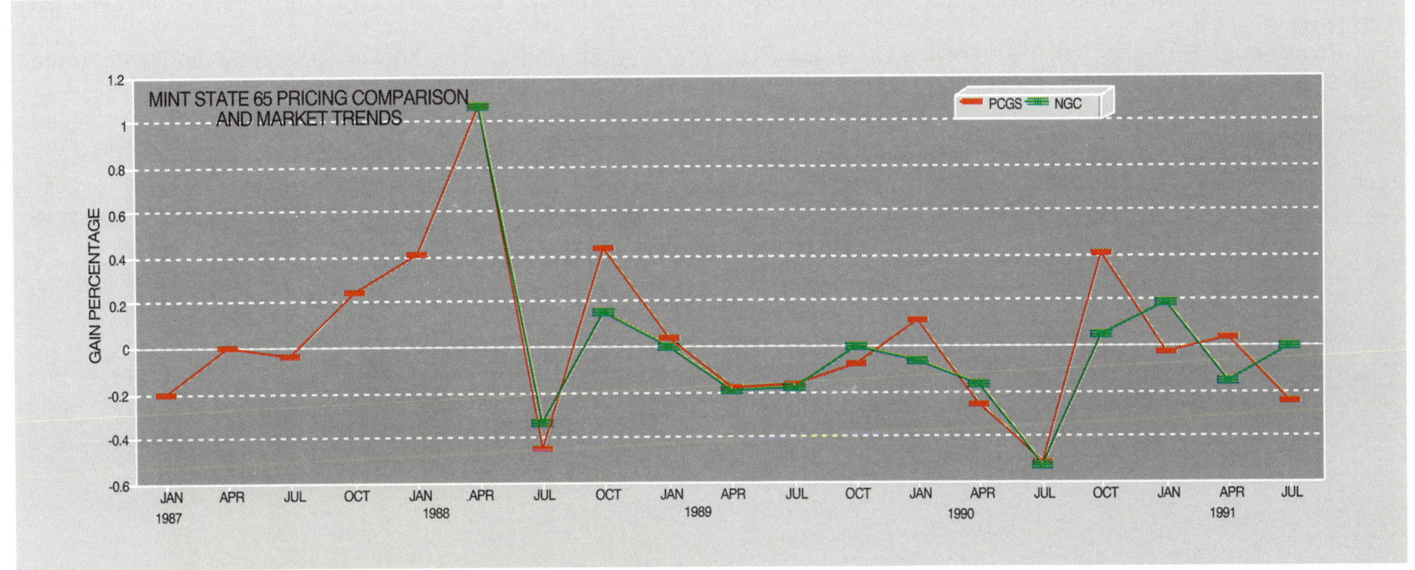

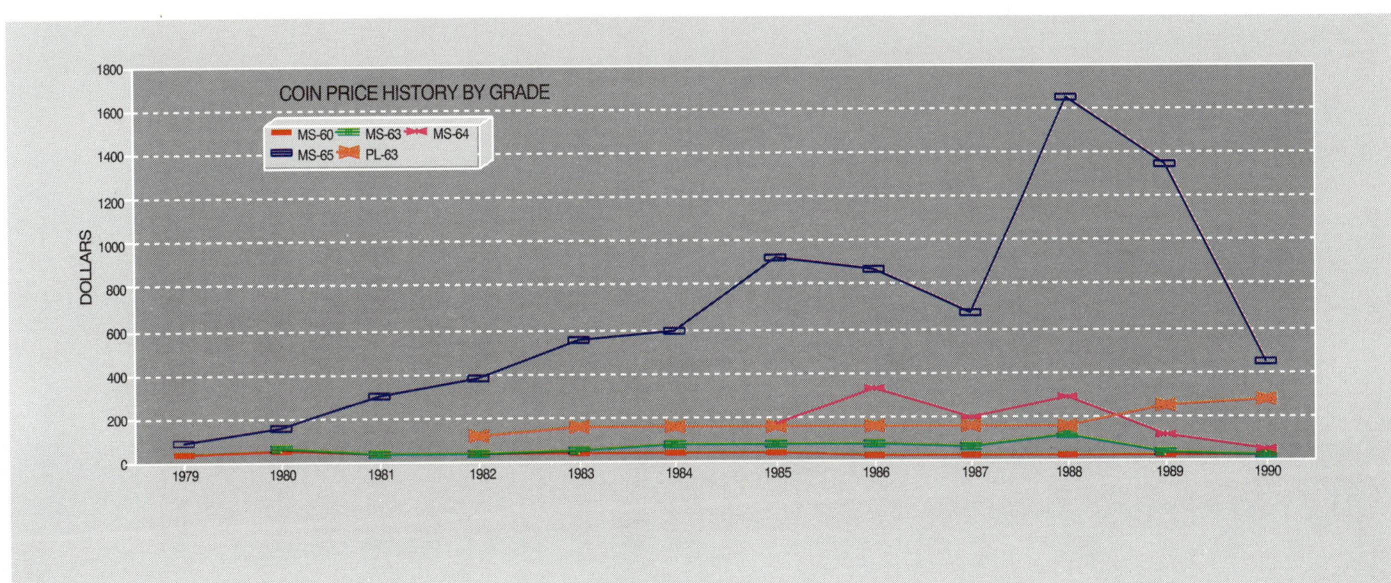

1889-CC

PCGS
1889-CC S$1
MS65
7190.65/6271764

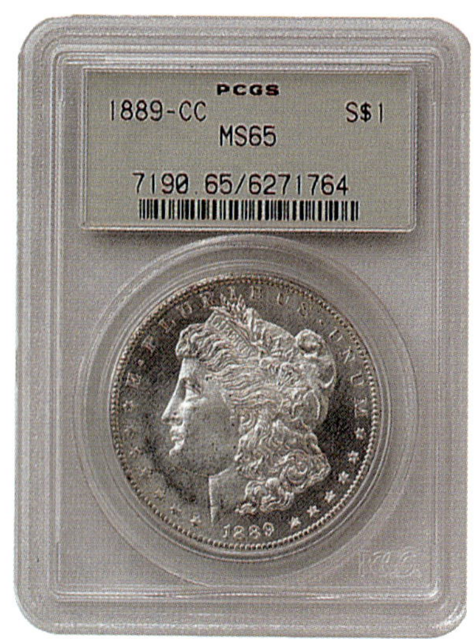

The 350,000 minted probably required not over two pairs of dies from the 10 obvs. and 7 revs. furnished. Rarest of all CC dollars, circulated or Unc.; the key to completeness of a CC set or a full date-mintmark set. Often strongly struck with dull luster (but see prooflikes below); rims are flat and broader than on 1889's of other mints.

Only one 1889-CC was in the GSA holdings; this was sold in the "mixed lot" CC group to an unknown winner. The Treasury bag reported from 1964 probably contained sliders, like the bag released on Montana in the 1950's.

This author (Highfill) has handled both of the PCGS MS 64 DMPL's for this date in the high 5 to the low 6 digit range. The only PCGS MS 65 was offered for about a third of a million dollars; I made the mistake of turning it down, and the prominent Seattle dealer William E. Spears bought it.

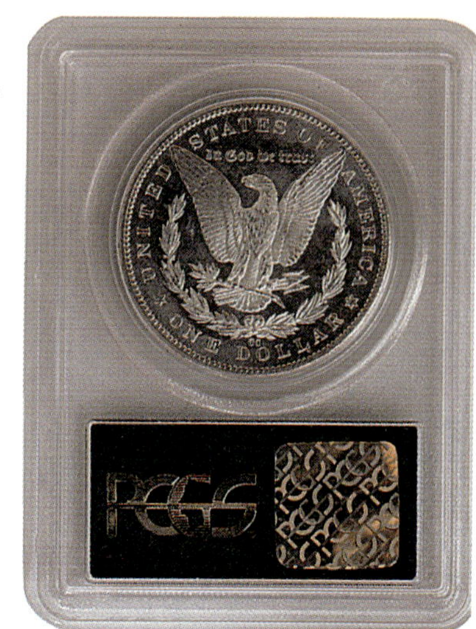

Recommended in any grade, but make sure it's real. Circulated 1889-CC's are rare too. Not only are sliders often offered as Unc., fakes are offered as genuine.

In fact, 1889-CC is probably more often counterfeited than any other Morgan dollar. Most often, fakes have CC cemented onto genuine 1889 dollars. Less often, 1883-CC coins have had the 3 changed to a 9. There are also fakes from false dies, said to be 90% silver.

Prooflikes: Probably half the surviving Uncs. are PL, many of them DMPL. The best is apparently the Tavenner coin (sold at $1,000, 1960, to John Hardenberg), which went in the late 1960's to Wayne Miller.

MINTAGE	PROOF	STRIKE	LUSTER	BAG MARKS	REDFIELD
350,000	0	Sharp & Bold	Good	Moderate	No
DIES	**DIE VARIETIES**	**% OF PL**	**% OF DMPL**	**PIVOTAL GRADE**	**RARITY FACTOR**
10	3	15.9	30.9	MS 63	R-1

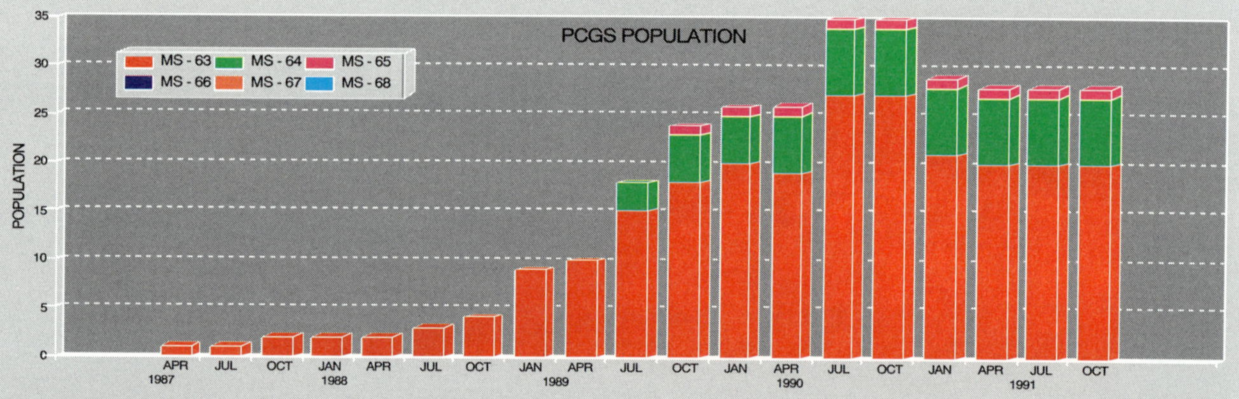

PCGS POPULATION
MS - 63
MS - 64
MS - 65
MS - 66
MS - 67
MS - 68
POPULATION
35
30
25
20
15
10
5
0
APR 1987
JUL
OCT
JAN 1988
APR
JUL
OCT
JAN 1989
APR
JUL
OCT
JAN
APR 1990
JUL
OCT
JAN
APR
JUL 1991
OCT

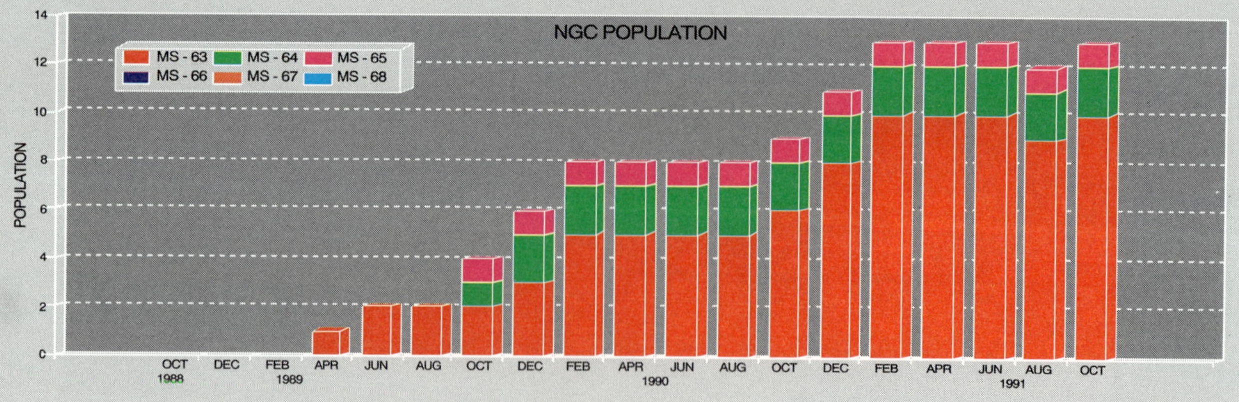

NGC POPULATION
MS - 63
MS - 64
MS - 65
MS - 66
MS - 67
MS - 68
POPULATION
14
12
10
8
6
4
2
0
OCT 1988
DEC
FEB 1989
APR
JUN
AUG
OCT
DEC
FEB
APR 1990
JUN
AUG
OCT
DEC
FEB
APR
JUN 1991
AUG
OCT

1889-CC

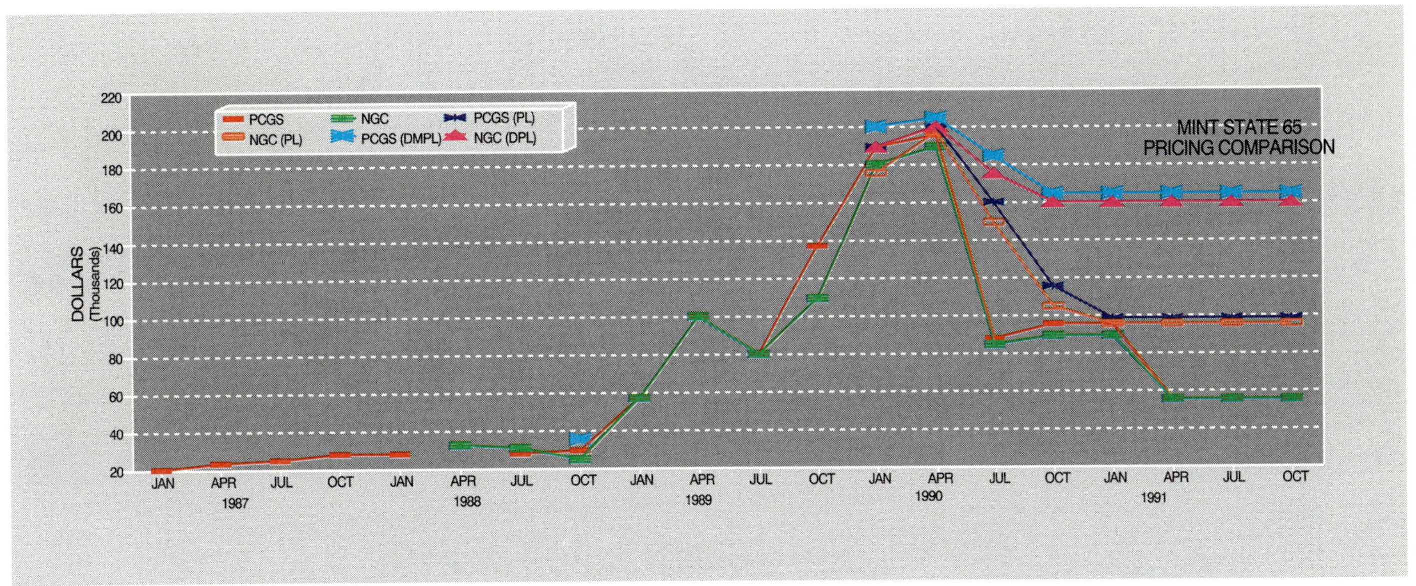

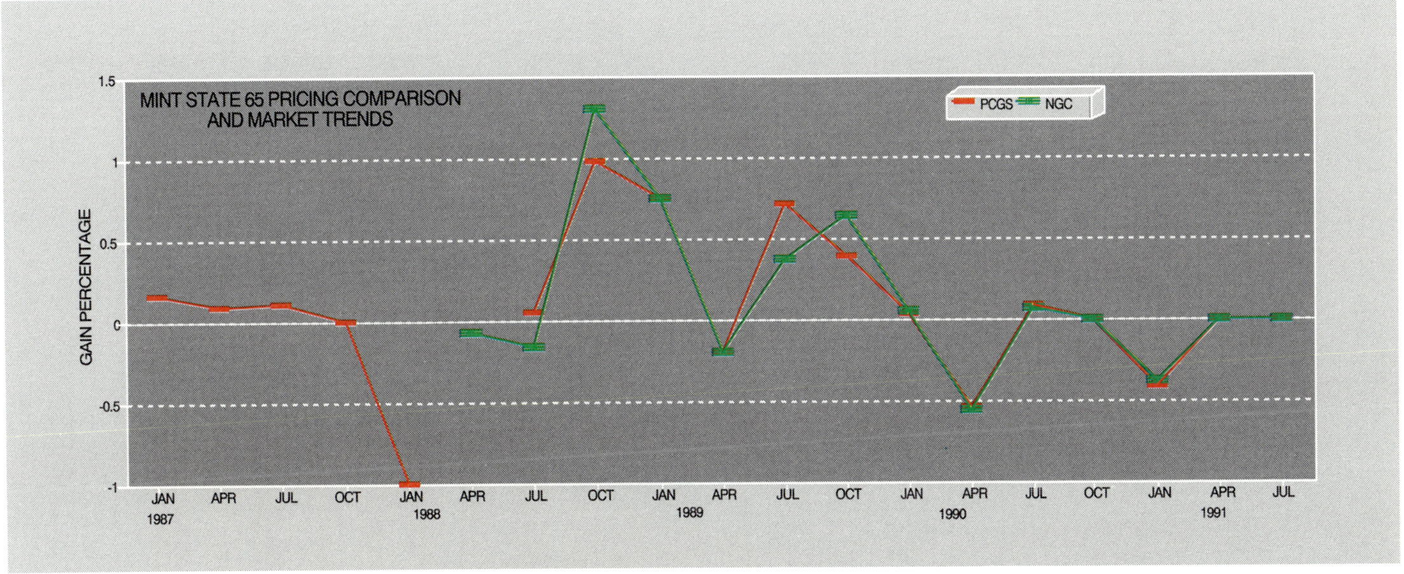

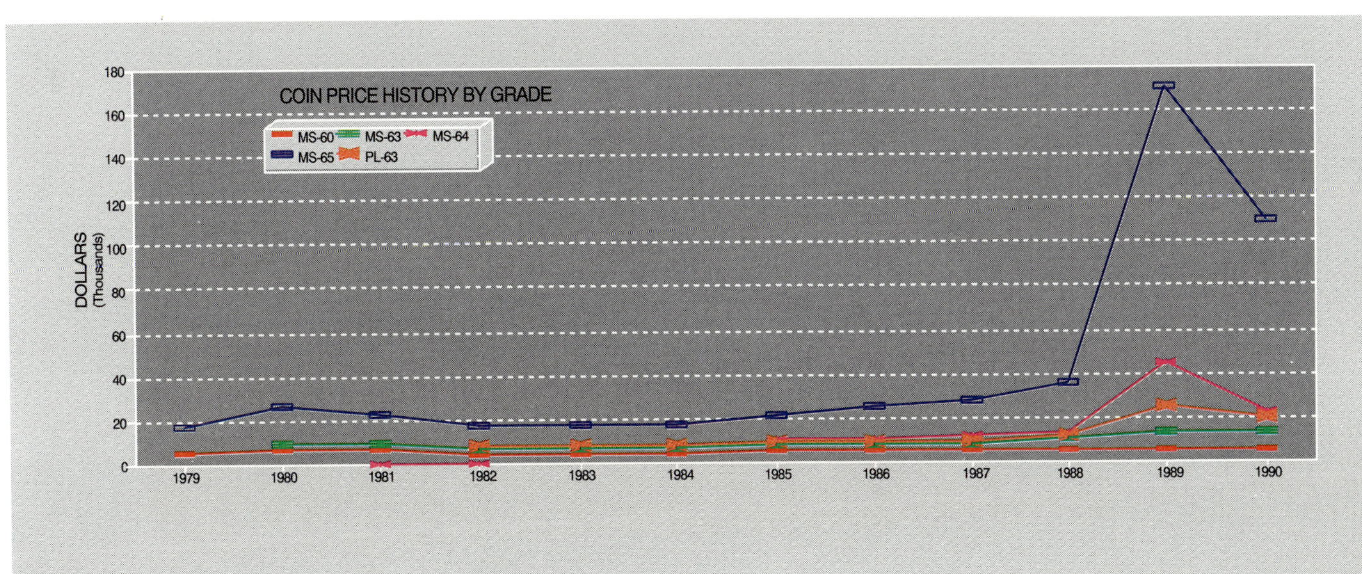

1889-O

Mintage 11,875,000. Uncs. often come flatly struck, with below average lustre; rarely brightly lustrous with minimal marks. Thick rims and "metal flow" probably have to do with improperly basined dies, as often from New Orleans. Uncs. are plentiful from Treasury releases, 1962-63.

Usually with round O (wide opening); VAM 2 has oval O (slit opening).

Recommended in MS 64 up. You may have to start with a 60/63.

Prooflikes: Scarce at all grade levels; rare above MS 64, PL or DMPL. Extreme cameo DMPL's occur, but they are really rare.

MINTAGE	PROOF	STRIKE	LUSTER	BAG MARKS	REDFIELD
11,875,000	0	Soft & Weak	Average	Moderate To Heavy	No
DIES	**DIE VARIETIES**	**% OF PL**	**% OF DMPL**	**PIVOTAL GRADE**	**RARITY FACTOR**
150	18	4.0	3.7	MS 65	R-2

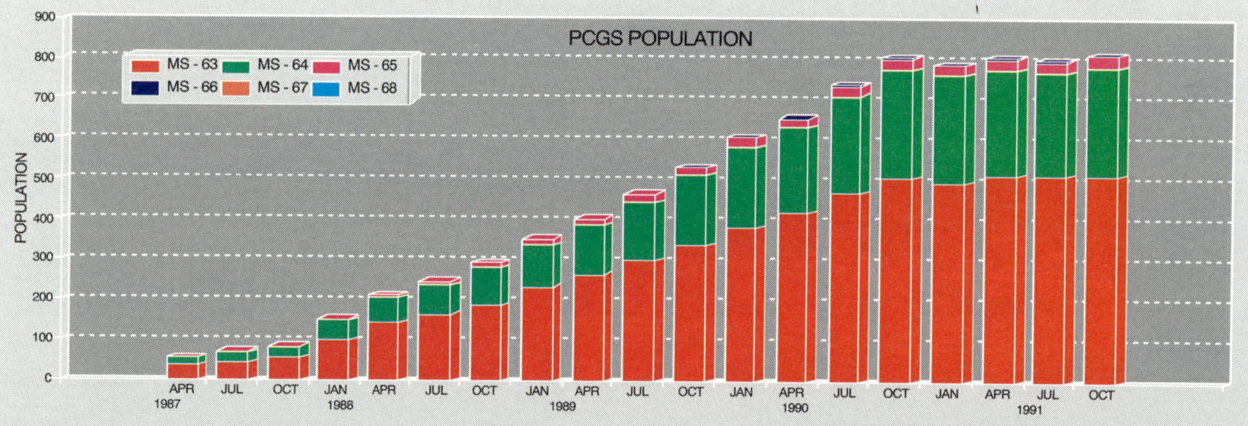

PCGS POPULATION

MS - 63 MS - 64 MS - 65
MS - 66 MS - 67 MS - 68

POPULATION

0 100 200 300 400 500 600 700 800 900

APR 1987 JUL OCT JAN 1988 APR JUL OCT JAN 1989 APR JUL OCT JAN APR 1990 JUL OCT JAN APR JUL 1991 OCT

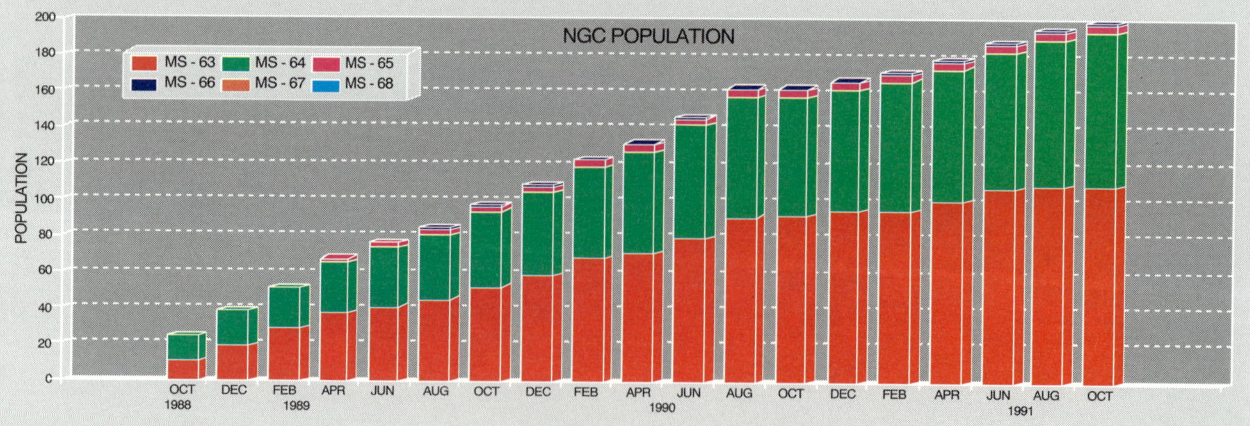

NGC POPULATION

MS - 63 MS - 64 MS - 65
MS - 66 MS - 67 MS - 68

POPULATION

0 20 40 60 80 100 120 140 160 180 200

OCT 1988 DEC FEB 1989 APR JUN AUG OCT DEC FEB APR JUN 1990 AUG OCT DEC FEB APR JUN AUG 1991 OCT

1889-O

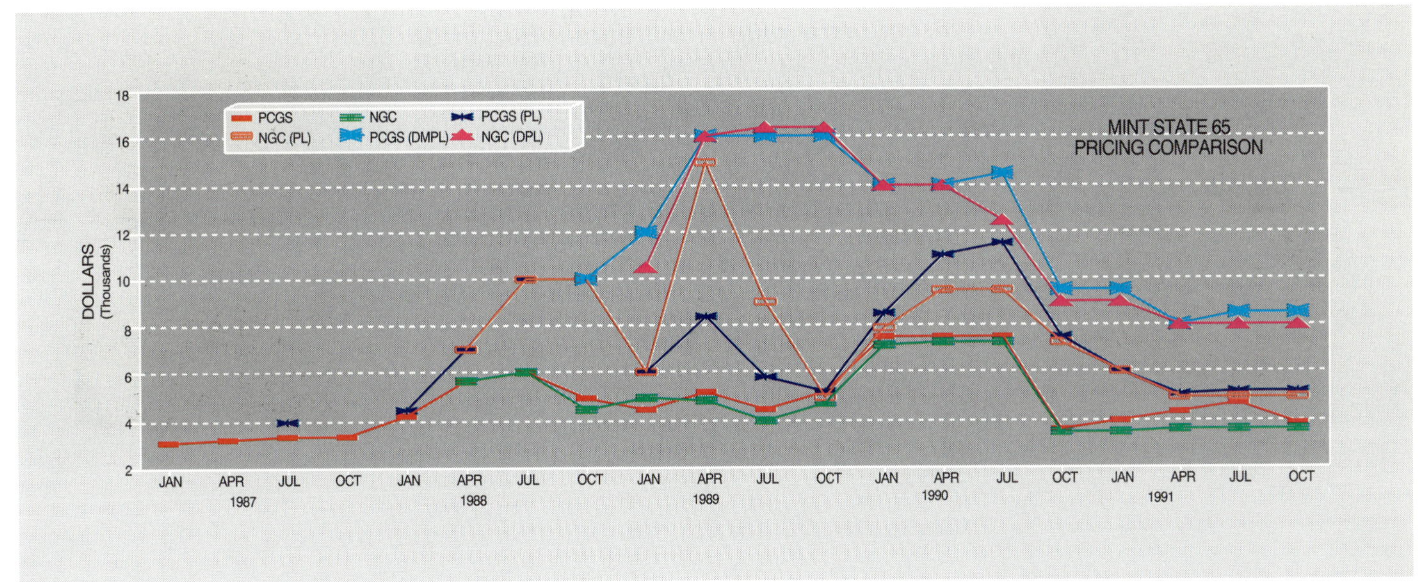

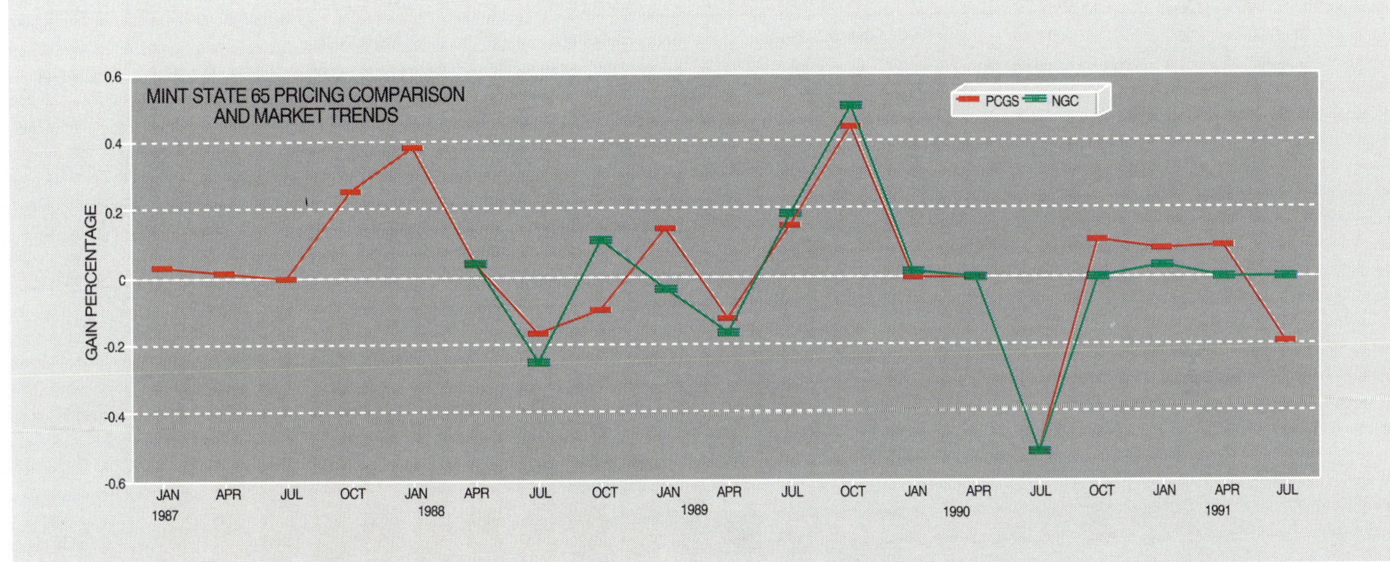

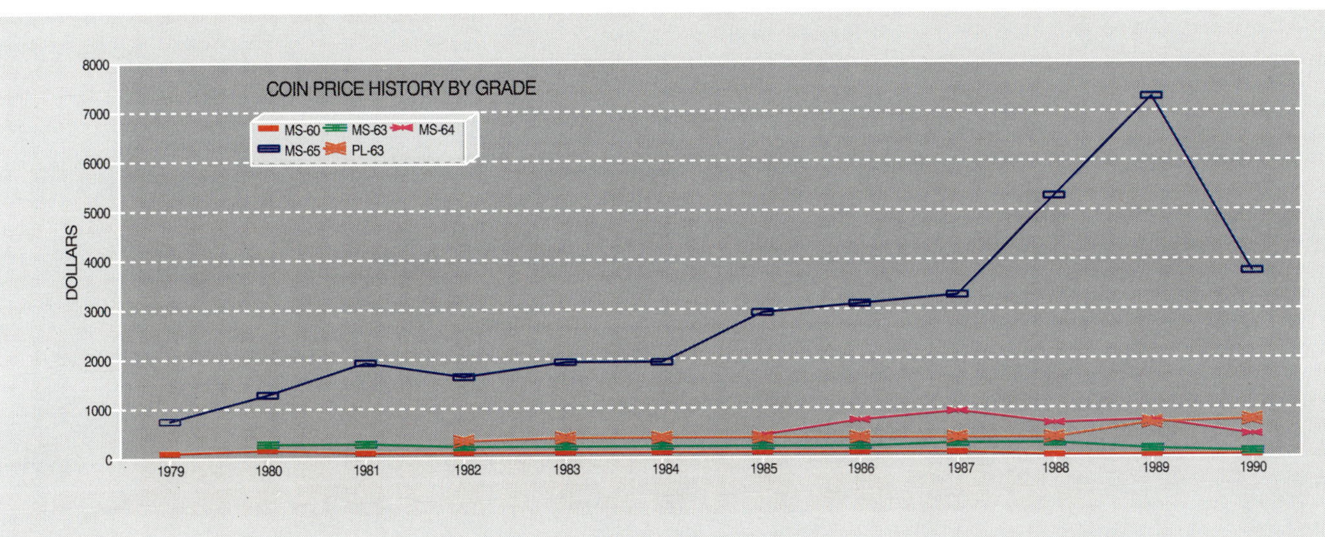

1889-S

The 700,000 mintage (from 5 pairs of dies) made this date popular; the Treasury (1937) and Redfield made it available. His hoard reportedly contained 3 to 5 bags; most were graded down to MS 60/63 from excessive bagmarks. A small minority will rival the 1881-S for high quality.

Recommended in MS 64 up, preferably 65.

Prooflikes: Most offered as such are one-sided (obverse only). Real ones are usually brilliant and without much depth; they are rare in MS 64 up. Real DMPL's are rare in any grade, especially cameo quality.

MINTAGE	PROOF	STRIKE	LUSTER	BAG MARKS	REDFIELD
700,000	0	Sharp & Bold	Excellent	Moderate	Yes
DIES	**DIE VARIETIES**	**% OF PL**	**% OF DMPL**	**PIVOTAL GRADE**	**RARITY FACTOR**
20	11	5.0	1.4	MS 65	R-3

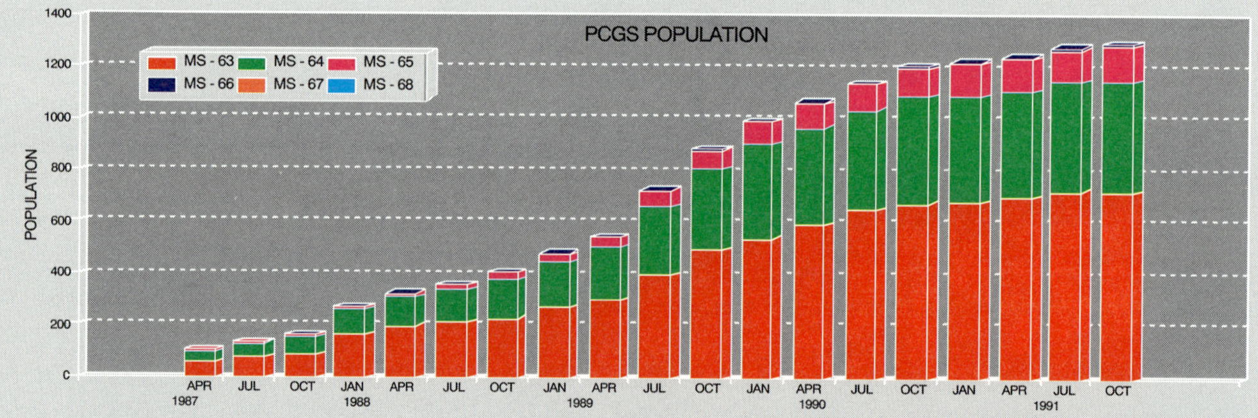

PCGS POPULATION

MS - 63, MS - 64, MS - 65, MS - 66, MS - 67, MS - 68

POPULATION: 0, 200, 400, 600, 800, 1000, 1200, 1400

APR 1987, JUL, OCT, JAN 1988, APR, JUL, OCT, JAN 1989, APR, JUL, OCT, JAN, APR 1990, JUL, OCT, JAN, APR, JUL 1991, OCT

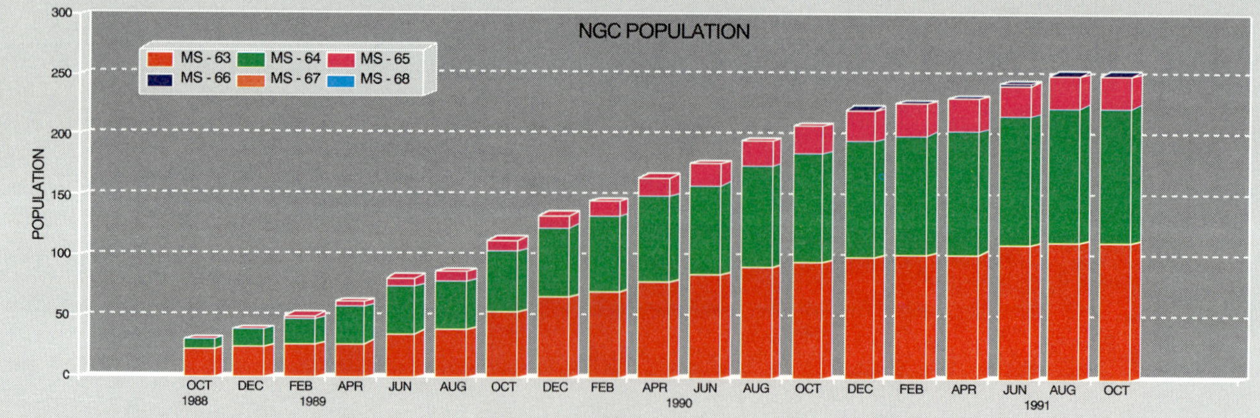

NGC POPULATION

MS - 63, MS - 64, MS - 65, MS - 66, MS - 67, MS - 68

POPULATION: 0, 50, 100, 150, 200, 250, 300

OCT 1988, DEC, FEB 1989, APR, JUN, AUG, OCT, DEC, FEB, APR 1990, JUN, AUG, OCT, DEC, FEB, APR, JUN 1991, AUG, OCT

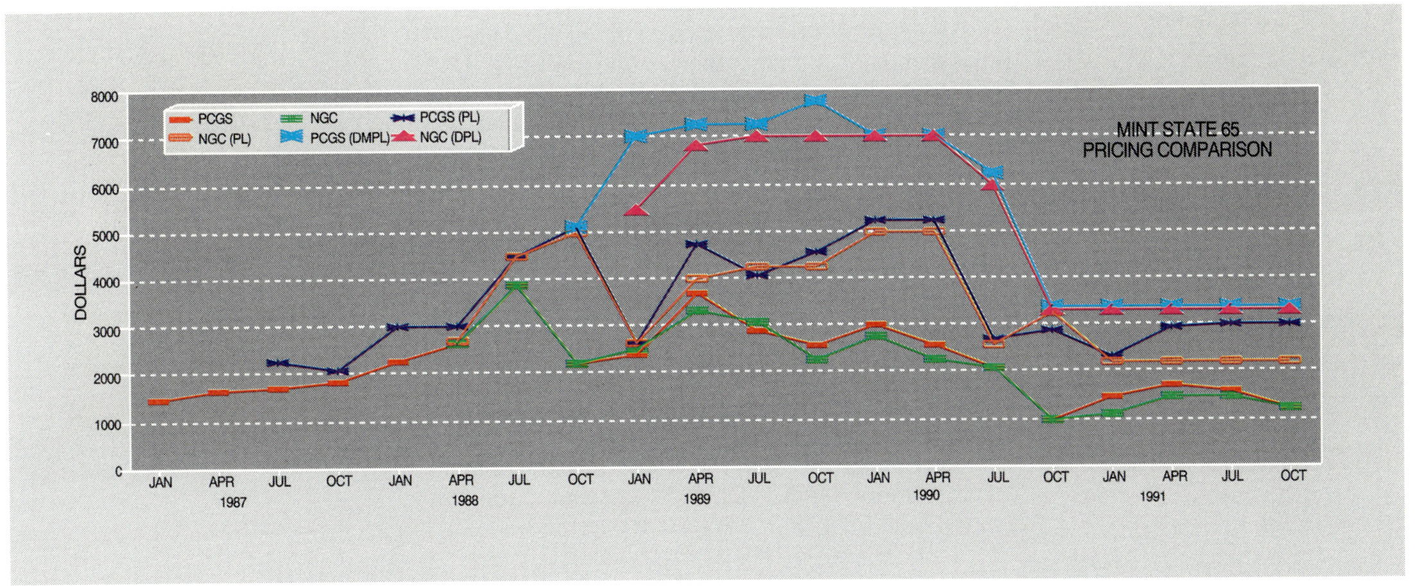
8000
7000
6000
5000
4000
3000
2000
1000
0
DOLLARS
PCGS
NGC (PL)
NGC
PCGS (DMPL)
PCGS (PL)
NGC (DPL)
MINT STATE 65
PRICING COMPARISON
JAN APR JUL OCT JAN APR JUL OCT JAN APR JUL OCT JAN APR JUL OCT JAN APR JUL OCT
1987
1988
1989
1990
1991

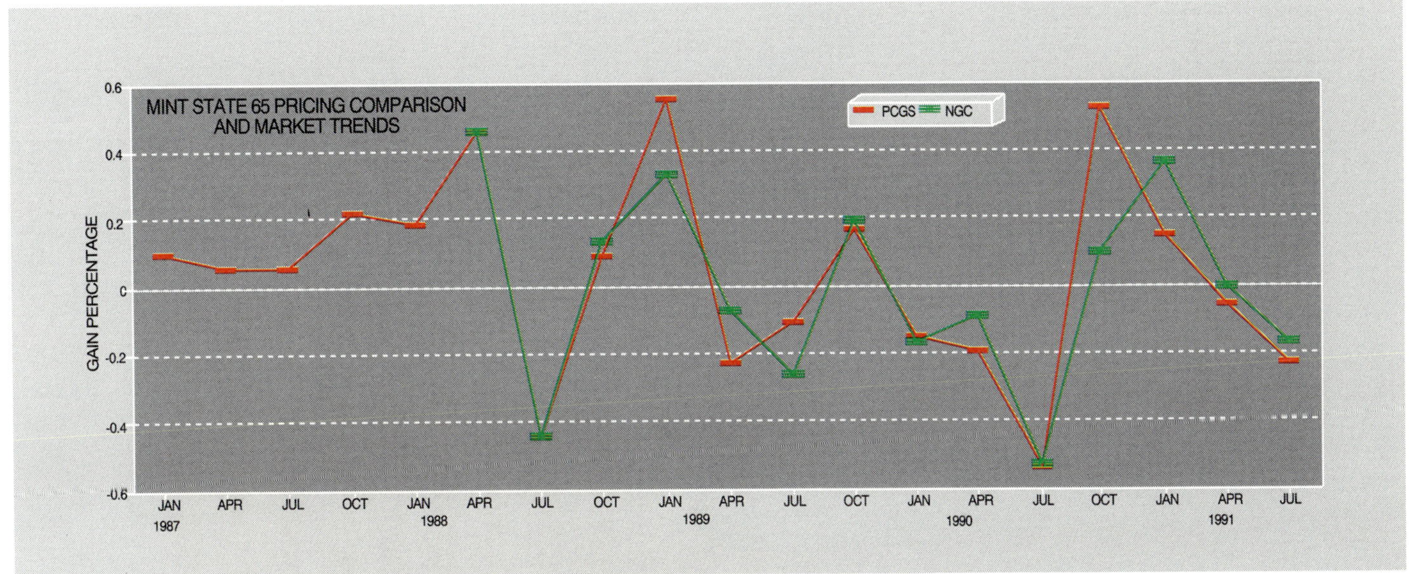
MINT STATE 65 PRICING COMPARISON
AND MARKET TRENDS
PCGS
NGC
0.6
0.4
0.2
0
-0.2
-0.4
-0.6
GAIN PERCENTAGE
JAN APR JUL OCT JAN APR JUL OCT JAN APR JUL OCT JAN APR JUL OCT JAN APR JUL
1987
1988
1989
1990
1991

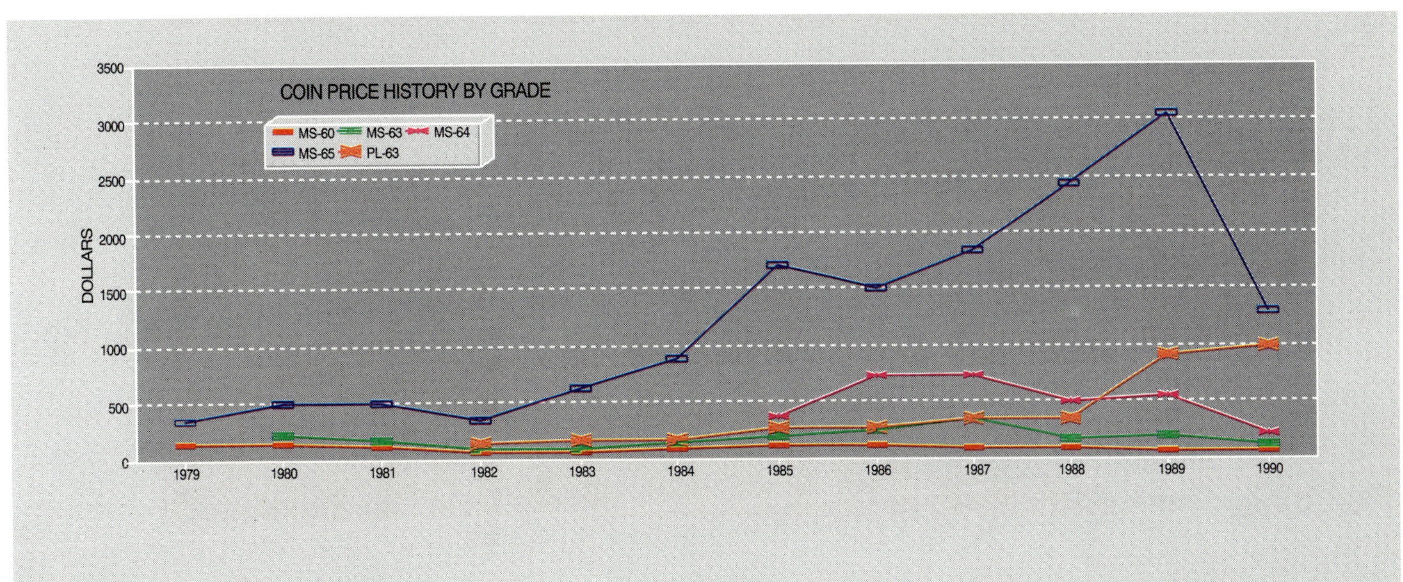
COIN PRICE HISTORY BY GRADE
MS-60
MS-63
MS-64
MS-65
PL-63
3500
3000
2500
2000
1500
1000
500
0
DOLLARS
1979 1980 1981 1982 1983 1984 1985 1986 1987 1988 1989 1990

PCGS
1890 S$1
MS65DMPL
97197 65/3088239

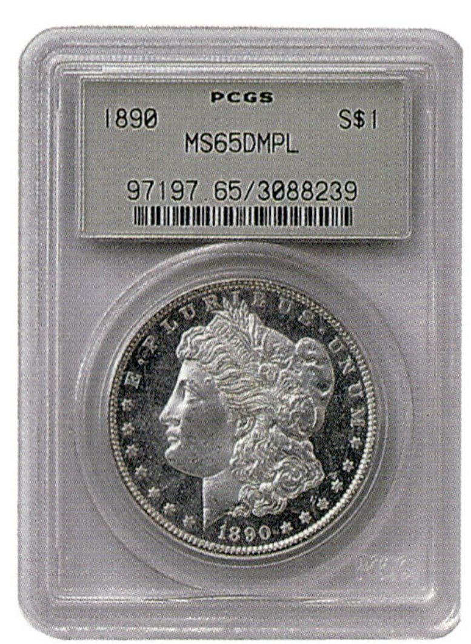

1890-P

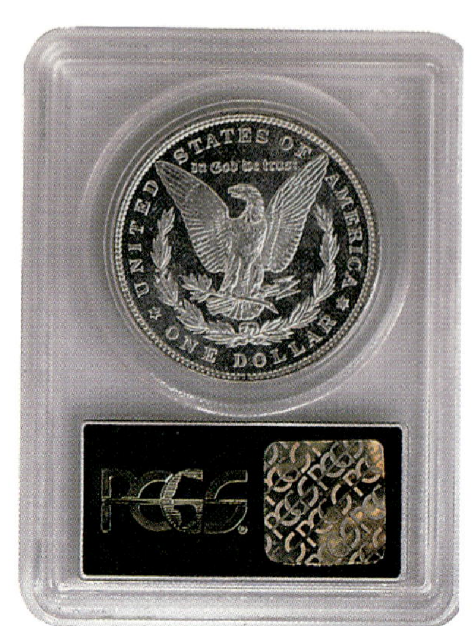

Mintage 16,802,000, from 48 obvs., 49 revs. One of the commonest dates. Sliders and low grade Uncs. are plentiful from Treasury & Redfield. Most are soft strikes, dull grayish lustre, plenty of bag marks, even grease. Many are from worn and/or cracked dies. In MS 65 and up the date is rare.

Rolls in MS 60/62 are available. Some original rolls have shown up in which the coins were stained with an unidentified dark greasy substance. This has yielded to a common liquid coin cleaner. Beware assembled rolls containing sliders.

Recommended in MS 65 up, but you may have to buy a 64 for a space filler.

Proofs: 590 minted; only one variety (VAM 1) The low mintage figure has created a demand.

Prooflikes: These only come brilliant, with little or no cameo effect. DMPL's are not particularly scarcer than PL's; both are rare above MS 64.

MINTAGE	PROOF	STRIKE	LUSTER	BAG MARKS	REDFIELD
16,802,000	590	Soft To Average	Poor	Heavy	Yes
DIES	**DIE VARIETIES**	**% OF PL**	**% OF DMPL**	**PIVOTAL GRADE**	**RARITY FACTOR**
95	14	2.7	2.5	MS 64	R-3

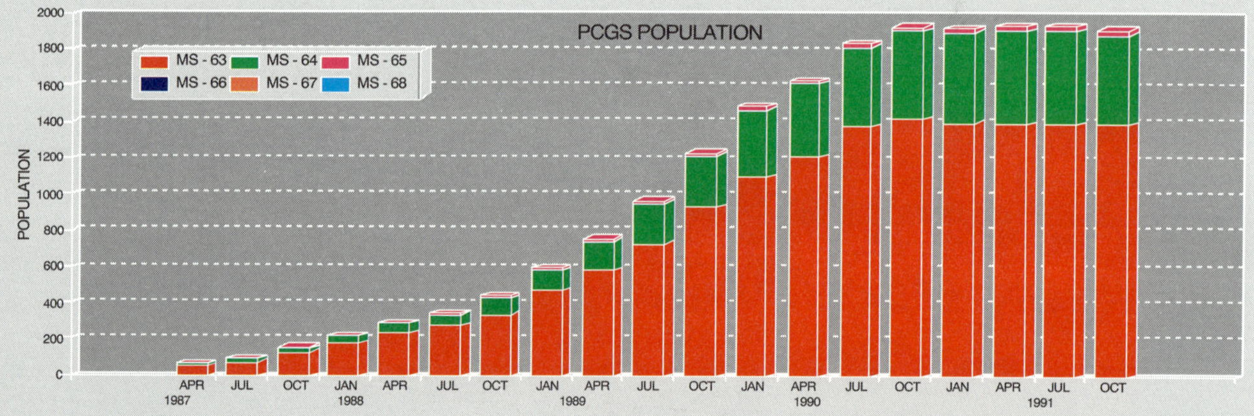
PCGS POPULATION
MS - 63
MS - 64
MS - 65
MS - 66
MS - 67
MS - 68
POPULATION
2000
1800
1600
1400
1200
1000
800
600
400
200
0
APR 1987
JUL
OCT
JAN 1988
APR
JUL
OCT
JAN 1989
APR
JUL
OCT
JAN 1990
APR
JUL
OCT
JAN 1991
APR
JUL
OCT

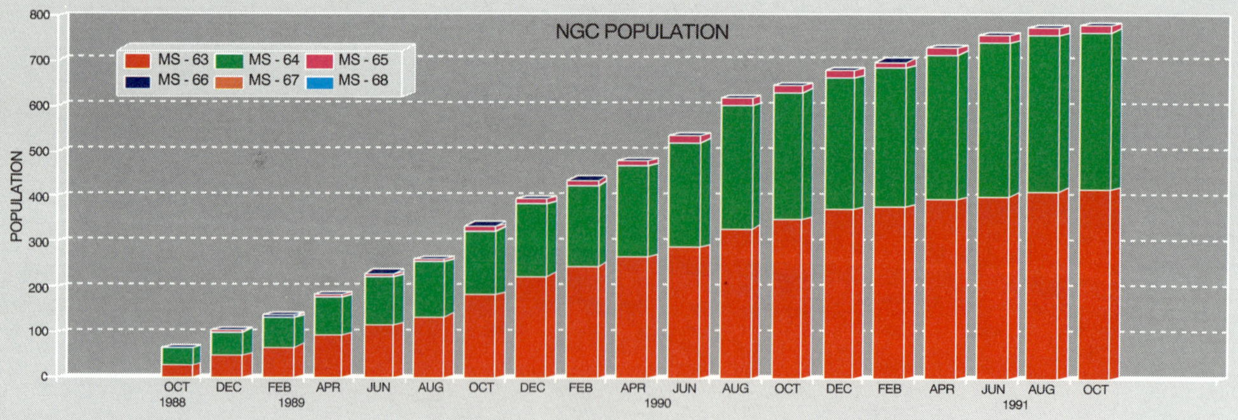
NGC POPULATION
MS - 63
MS - 64
MS - 65
MS - 66
MS - 67
MS - 68
POPULATION
800
700
600
500
400
300
200
100
0
OCT 1988
DEC
FEB 1989
APR
JUN
AUG
OCT
DEC
FEB 1990
APR
JUN
AUG
OCT
DEC
FEB 1991
APR
JUN
AUG
OCT

1890-P

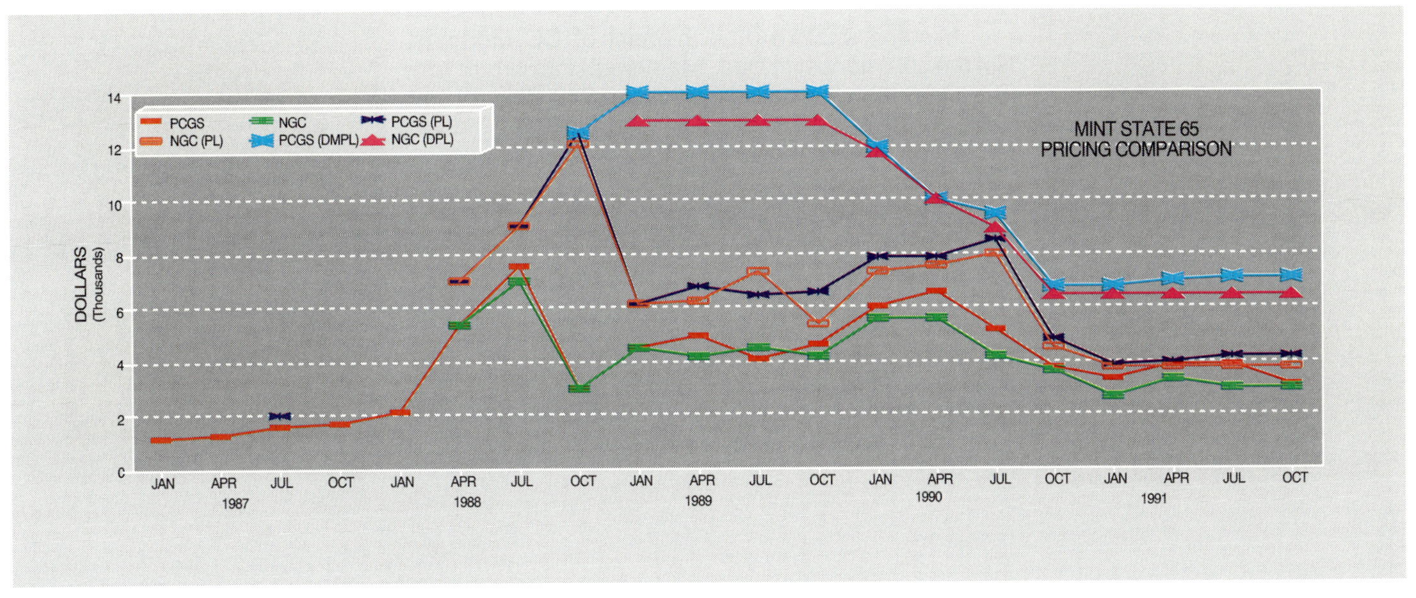

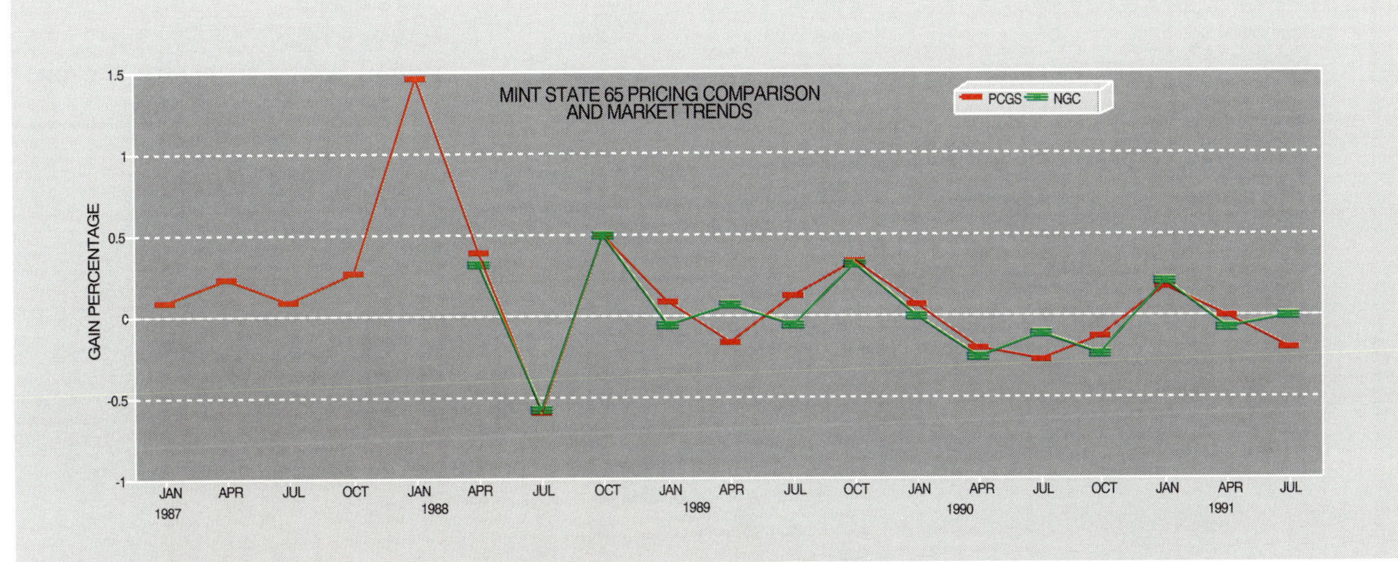

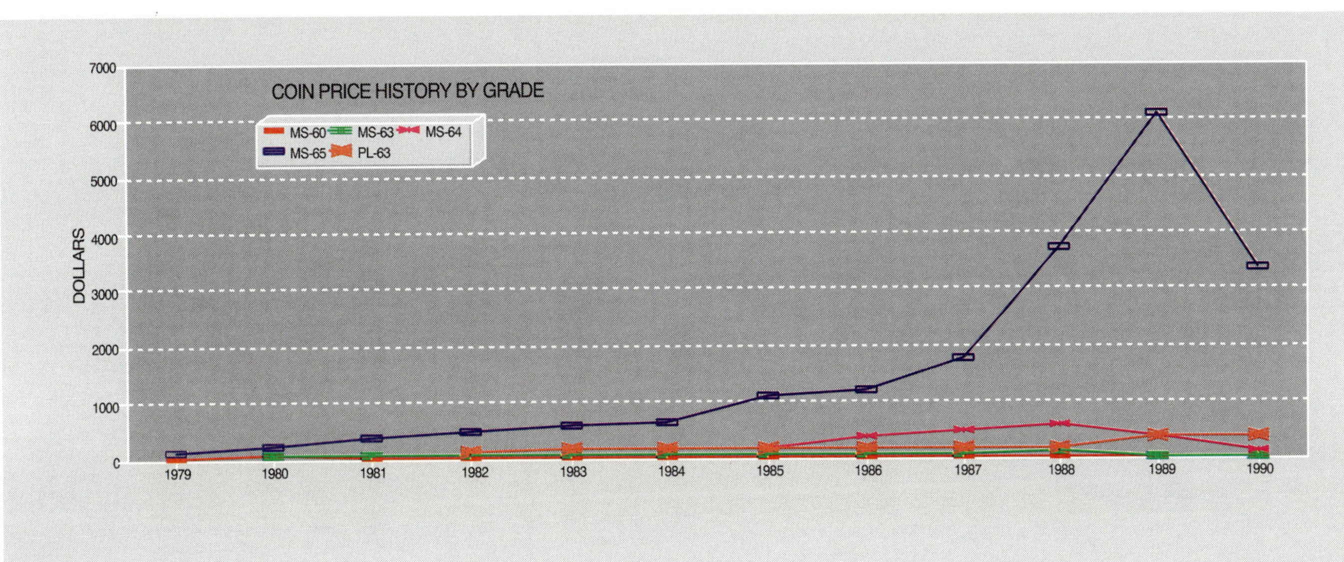

1890-CC

PCGS
1890-CC S$1
MS66
7198.66/6271765

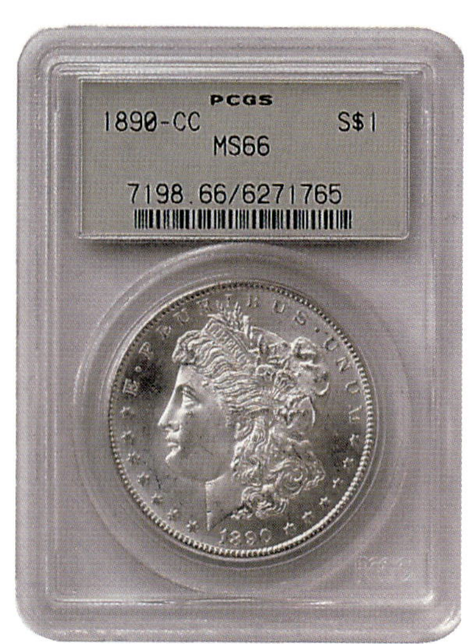

Mintage 2,309,041 — highest of CC Morgans. Not the commonest in Unc. Many went into circulation. The GSA mail bid sales included 3,949 BU's of this date, minimum bid $30 each, winning bid $46. Redfield hoard had at least 2 bags.

Recommended in MS 64 up.

The popular "Tail Bar" variety, VAM 4, is from a gouge in the die. It is very scarce. This author (Highfill) has only handled one PCGS MS 65 of this scarce variety.

Prooflikes: Plentiful in MS 60/63, even DMPL; some have estimated these at 20% of total Unc. survivors of this date. Wayne Miller said that Ivy sold nearly a full bag of DMPL's in 1978. These may have been from Redfield. Above MS 64, rare PL, scarce to rare DMPL.

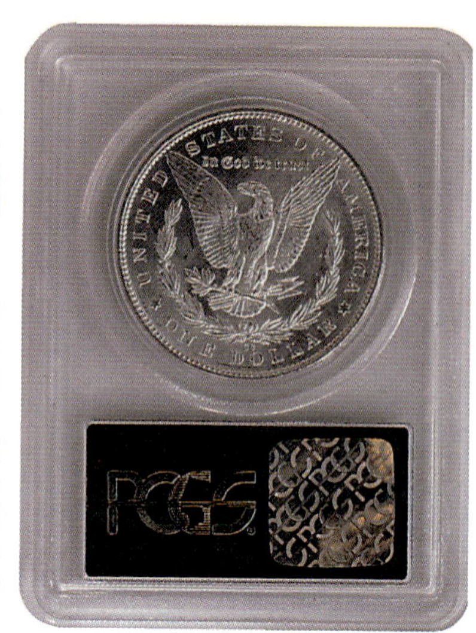

MINTAGE	PROOF	STRIKE	LUSTER	BAG MARKS	REDFIELD
2,309,041	0	Sharp & Bold	Good	Moderate To Heavy	Yes
DIES	**DIE VARIETIES**	**% OF PL**	**% OF DMPL**	**PIVOTAL GRADE**	**RARITY FACTOR**
50	13	5.2	14.3	MS 64	R-3

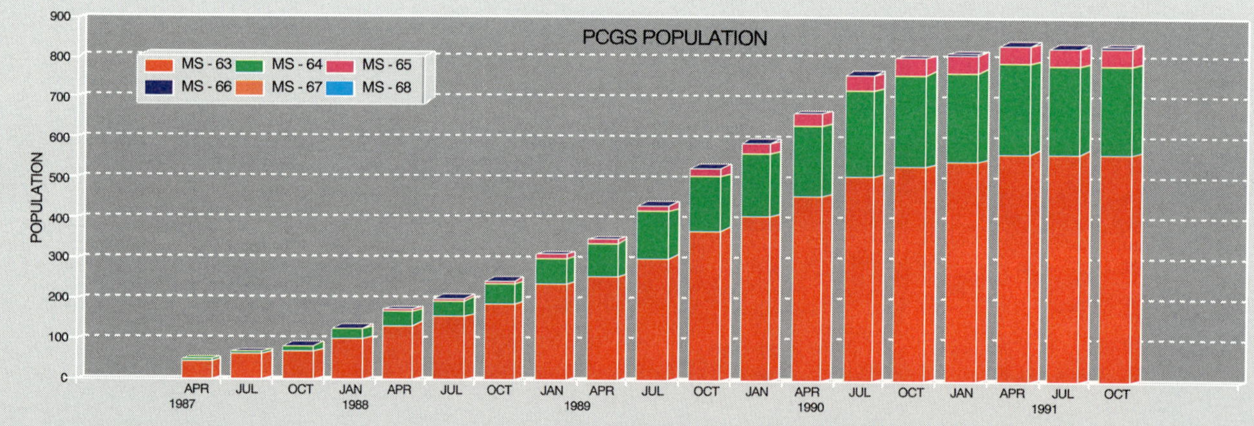
PCGS POPULATION
MS - 63
MS - 64
MS - 65
MS - 66
MS - 67
MS - 68
POPULATION
900
800
700
600
500
400
300
200
100
0
APR 1987
JUL
OCT
JAN 1988
APR
JUL
OCT
JAN 1989
APR
JUL
OCT
JAN
APR 1990
JUL
OCT
JAN
APR
JUL 1991
OCT

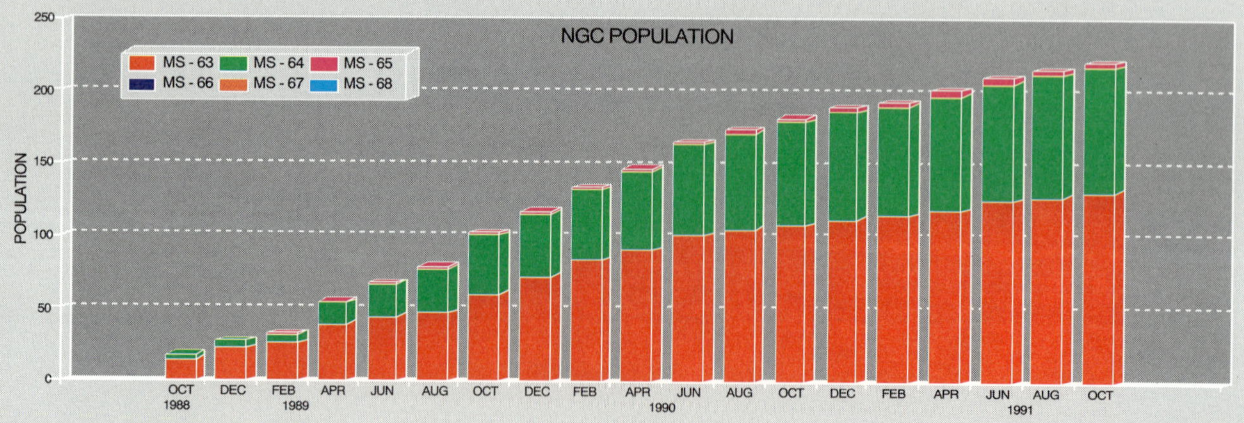
NGC POPULATION
MS - 63
MS - 64
MS - 65
MS - 66
MS - 67
MS - 68
POPULATION
250
200
150
100
50
0
OCT 1988
DEC
FEB 1989
APR
JUN
AUG
OCT
DEC
FEB
APR 1990
JUN
AUG
OCT
DEC
FEB
APR
JUN 1991
AUG
OCT

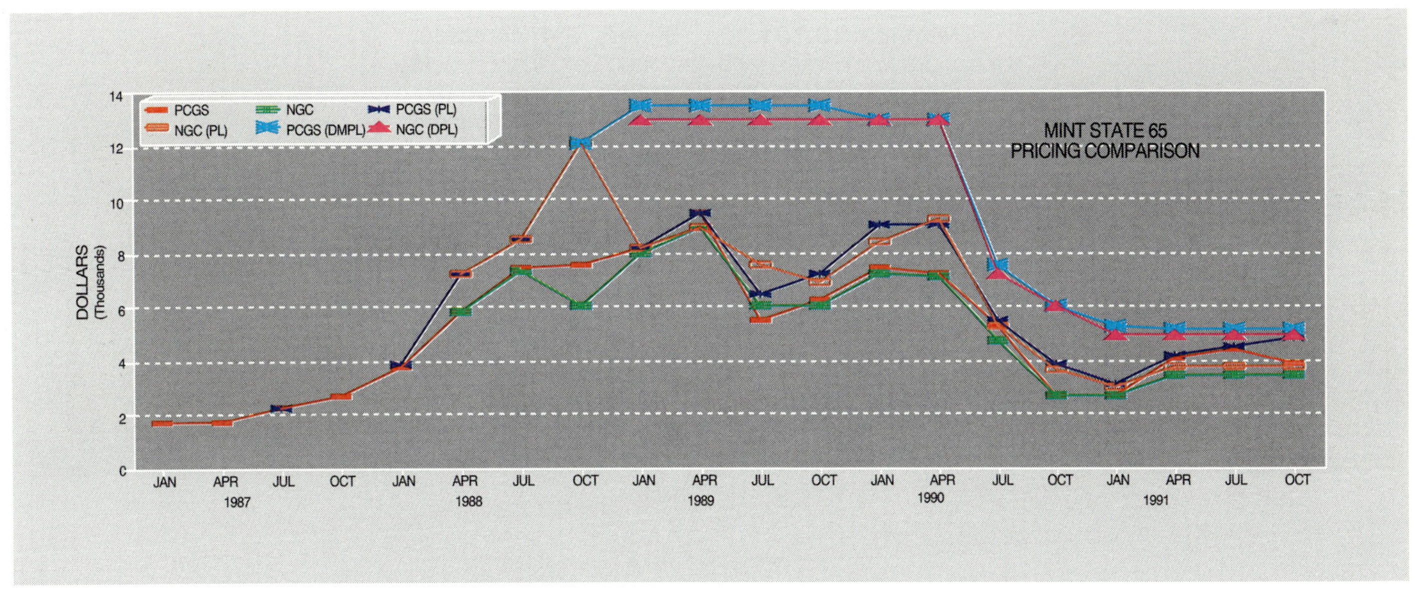
MINT STATE 65
PRICING COMPARISON
PCGS
NGC
PCGS (PL)
NGC (PL)
PCGS (DMPL)
NGC (DPL)
DOLLARS
(Thousands)
JAN APR JUL OCT JAN APR JUL OCT JAN APR JUL OCT JAN APR JUL OCT JAN APR JUL OCT
1987 1988 1989 1990 1991

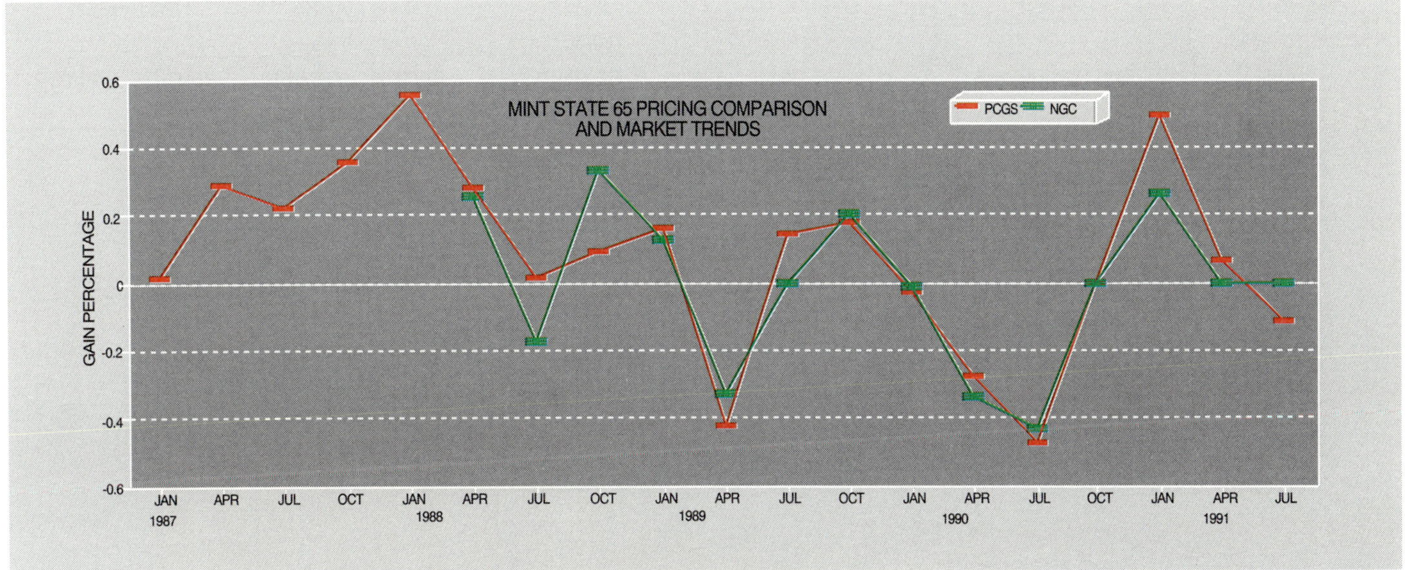
MINT STATE 65 PRICING COMPARISON
AND MARKET TRENDS
PCGS
NGC
GAIN PERCENTAGE
JAN APR JUL OCT JAN APR JUL OCT JAN APR JUL OCT JAN APR JUL OCT JAN APR JUL
1987 1988 1989 1990 1991

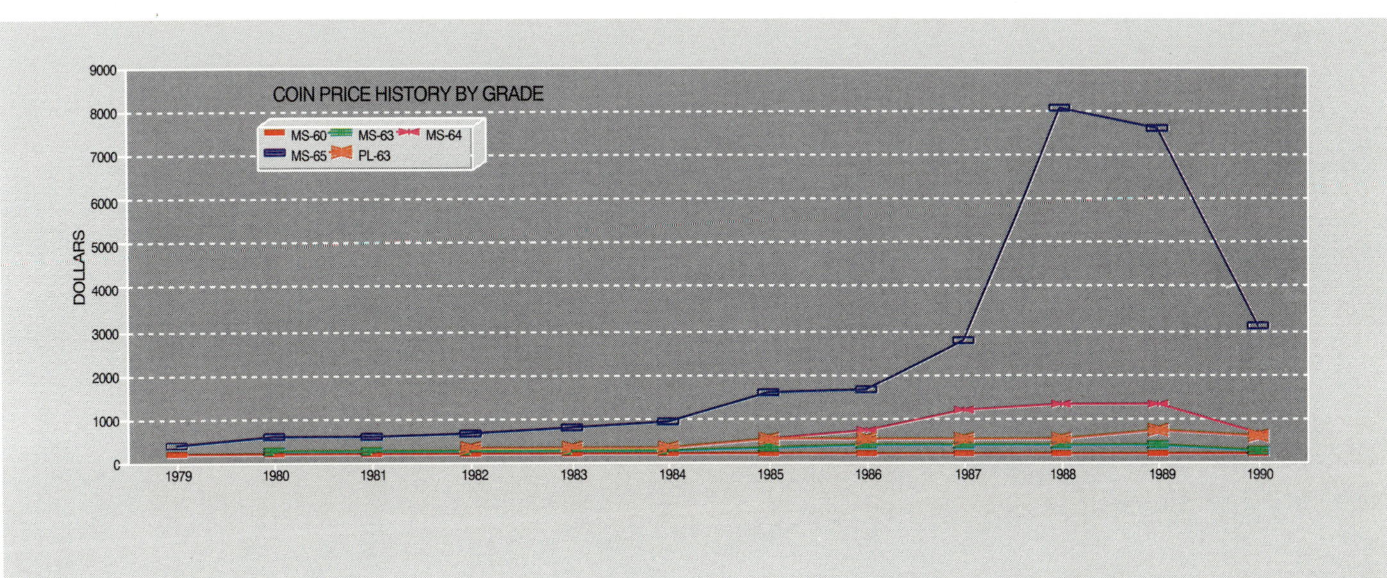
COIN PRICE HISTORY BY GRADE
MS-60
MS-63
MS-64
MS-65
PL-63
DOLLARS
1979 1980 1981 1982 1983 1984 1985 1986 1987 1988 1989 1990

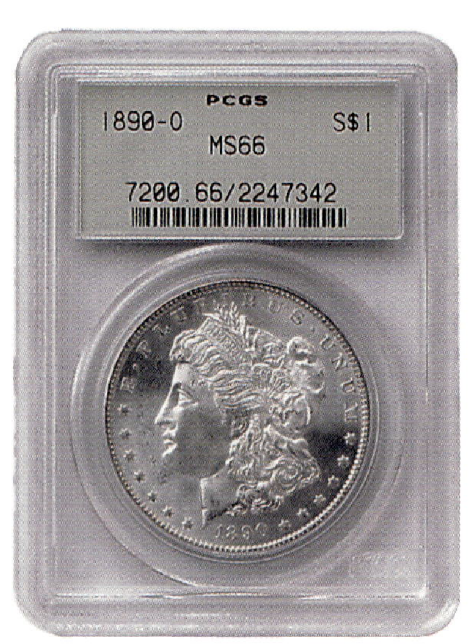

1890-O

Mintage 10,701,000. Sliders are common. Unc.'s are from Treasury bags; often very flatly struck. This date is a close runner-up to 1891-0 in the contest for the "Pancake of the Morgan Series" title. Rims are often thick, centers weak, lustre dull to frosty. Rolls are mostly MS 60/62. "Metal flow" is a constant problem.

Recommended in MS 65 up and by the roll in MS 60/63.

Prooflikes: Above MS 64, PL's are scarce, DMPL's rare, especially cameos.

MINTAGE	PROOF	STRIKE	LUSTER	BAG MARKS	REDFIELD
10,701,000	0	Weak & Soft	Good	Moderate	No
DIES	**DIE VARIETIES**	**% OF PL**	**% OF DMPL**	**PIVOTAL GRADE**	**RARITY FACTOR**
60	20	6.7	4.5	MS 65	R-3

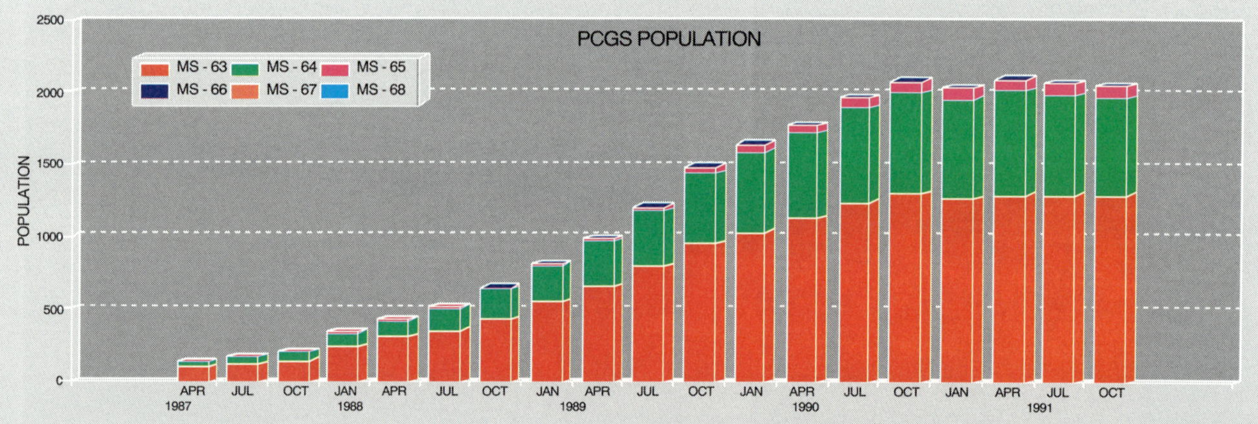

PCGS POPULATION

MS - 63 MS - 64 MS - 65
MS - 66 MS - 67 MS - 68

POPULATION

2500 2000 1500 1000 500 0

APR 1987 JUL OCT JAN 1988 APR JUL OCT JAN 1989 APR JUL OCT JAN 1990 APR JUL OCT JAN 1991 APR JUL OCT

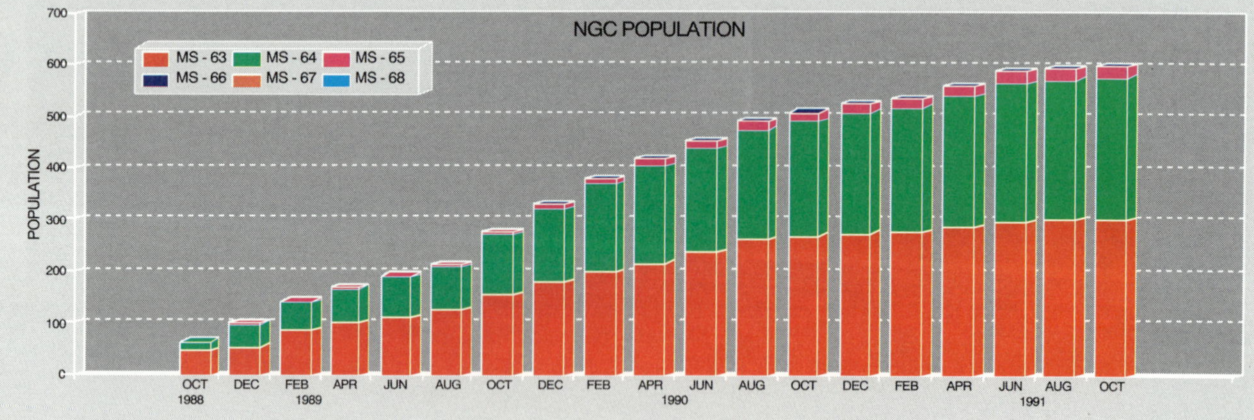

NGC POPULATION

MS - 63 MS - 64 MS - 65
MS - 66 MS - 67 MS - 68

POPULATION

700 600 500 400 300 200 100 0

OCT 1988 DEC FEB 1989 APR JUN AUG OCT DEC FEB 1990 APR JUN AUG OCT DEC FEB APR JUN 1991 AUG OCT

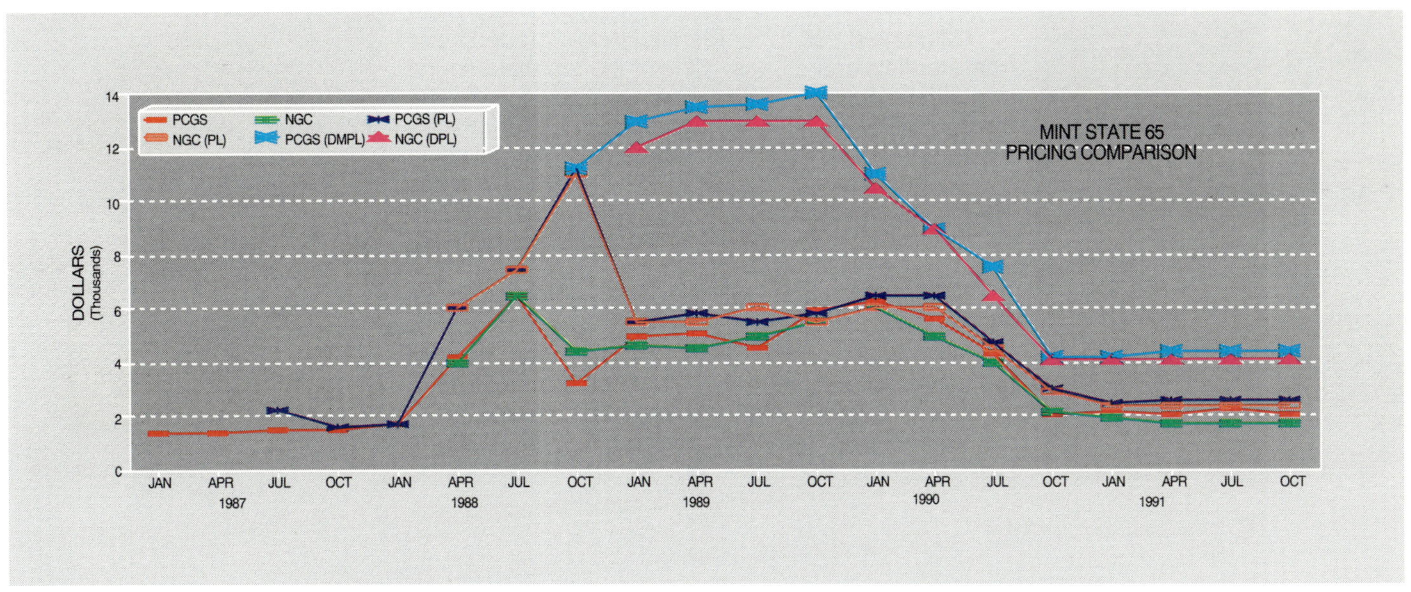
MINT STATE 65
PRICING COMPARISON
PCGS
NGC
PCGS (PL)
NGC (PL)
PCGS (DMPL)
NGC (DPL)
DOLLARS
(Thousands)
14
12
10
8
6
4
2
0
JAN APR JUL OCT JAN APR JUL OCT JAN APR JUL OCT JAN APR JUL OCT JAN APR JUL OCT
1987
1988
1989
1990
1991

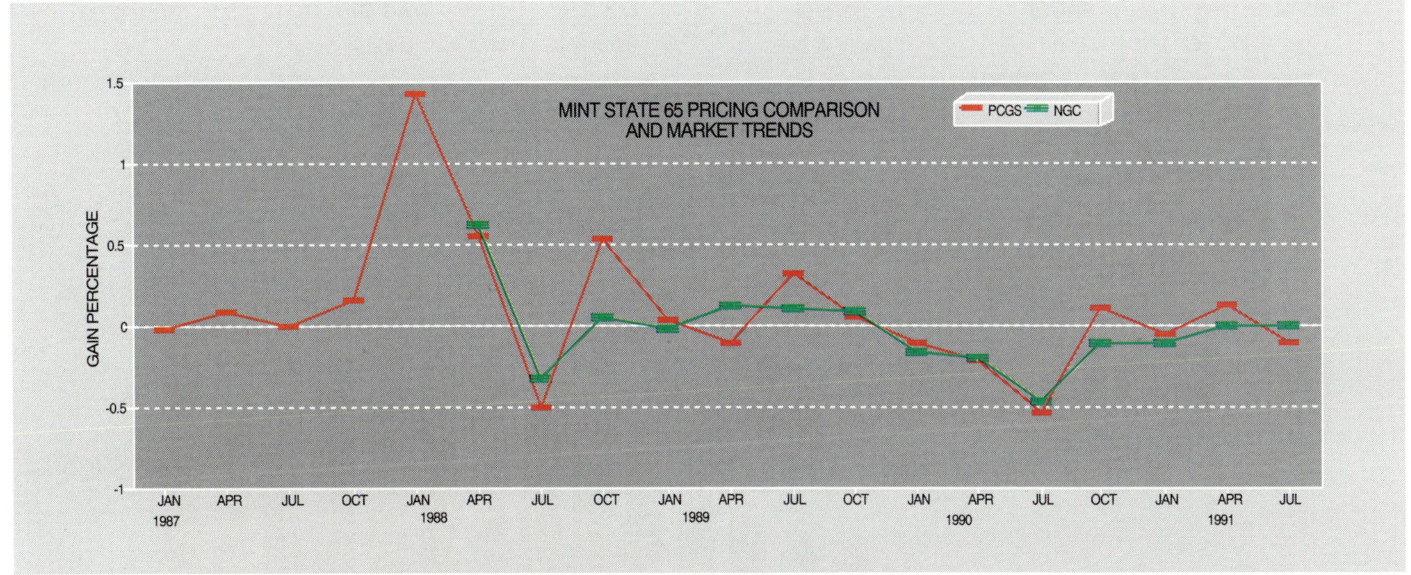
MINT STATE 65 PRICING COMPARISON
AND MARKET TRENDS
PCGS
NGC
GAIN PERCENTAGE
1.5
1
0.5
0
-0.5
-1
JAN APR JUL OCT JAN APR JUL OCT JAN APR JUL OCT JAN APR JUL OCT JAN APR JUL
1987
1988
1989
1990
1991

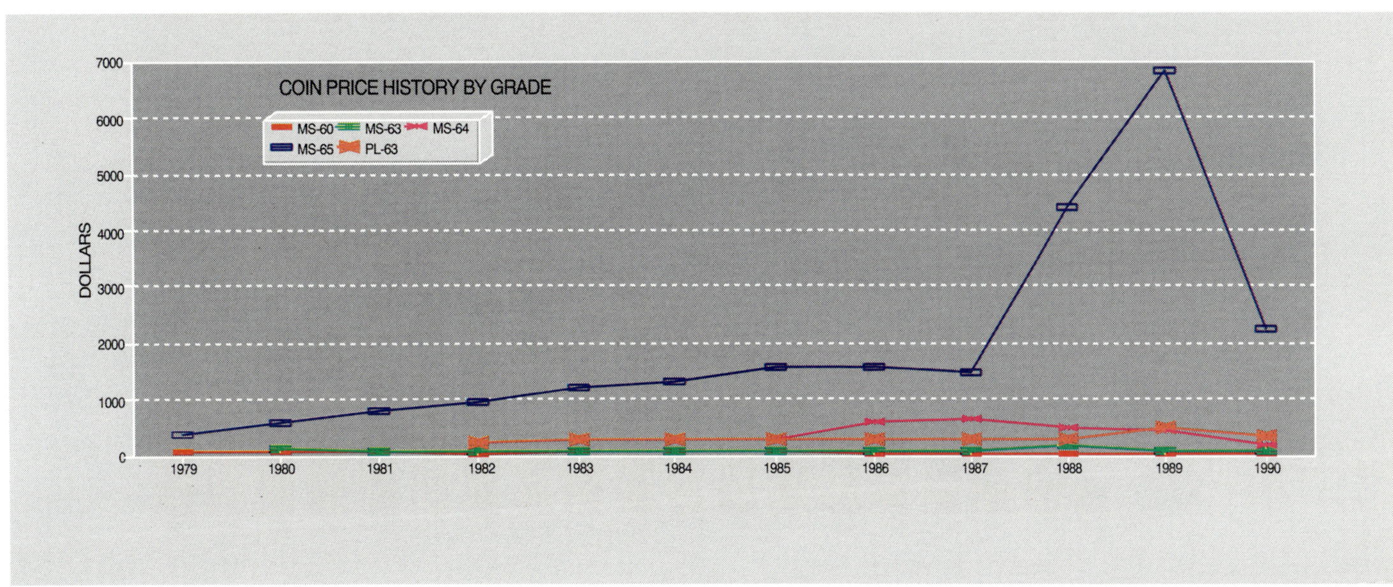
COIN PRICE HISTORY BY GRADE
MS-60
MS-63
MS-64
MS-65
PL-63
DOLLARS
7000
6000
5000
4000
3000
2000
1000
0
1979 1980 1981 1982 1983 1984 1985 1986 1987 1988 1989 1990

PCGS
1890-S
S$1
MS66
7202.66/2001265

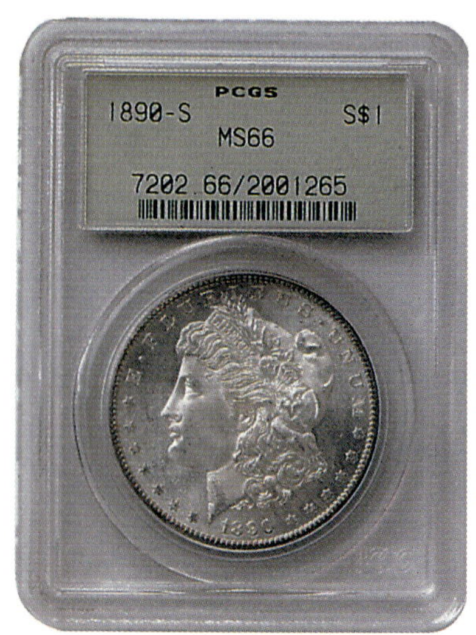

1890-S

Mintage 8,230,373. Plentiful in low grade Unc.'s from Redfield hoard bags. One of the ten dates found in greatest quantity in this hoard. They mostly run below MS 63 with plenty of bagmarks, though often well struck and brightly lustrous. Excessive die polishing has caused some examples to exhibit small striations leaving a semi-PL look. Some of the best 1890-S's rival the 1881-S's for overall quality. Rolls are available in MS 60/62.

Recommended in MS 64 up or by the roll in MS 63.

The double date, VAM 12 (illustration in VAM mislabeled 11) has date first slanting up to right, then corrected. It is very scarce but can be cherrypicked.

Prooflikes: Semi-PL's are plentiful; full PL's and DMPL's scarce, and above MS 64 rare.

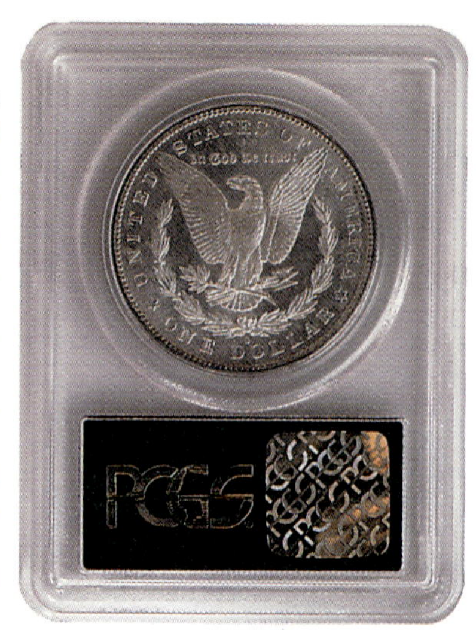

MINTAGE	PROOF	STRIKE	LUSTER	BAG MARKS	REDFIELD
8,230,373	0	Sharp & Bold	Excellent	Moderate	Yes
DIES	**DIE VARIETIES**	**% OF PL**	**% OF DMPL**	**PIVOTAL GRADE**	**RARITY FACTOR**
80	25	3.8	1.9	MS 65	R-3

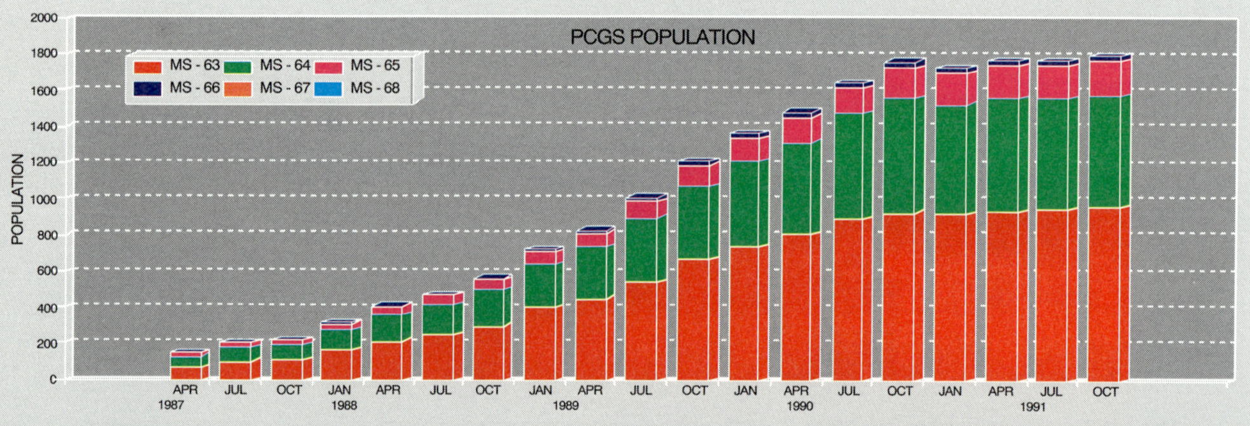
PCGS POPULATION
MS - 63
MS - 64
MS - 65
MS - 66
MS - 67
MS - 68
POPULATION
2000
1800
1600
1400
1200
1000
800
600
400
200
C
APR 1987
JUL
OCT
JAN 1988
APR
JUL
OCT
JAN 1989
APR
JUL
OCT
JAN
APR 1990
JUL
OCT
JAN
APR
JUL 1991
OCT

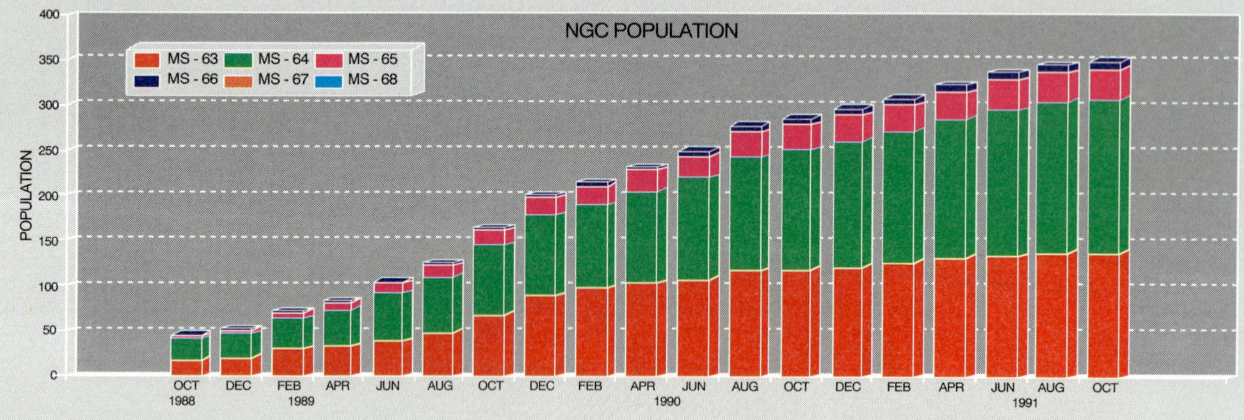
NGC POPULATION
MS - 63
MS - 64
MS - 65
MS - 66
MS - 67
MS - 68
POPULATION
400
350
300
250
200
150
100
50
C
OCT 1988
DEC
FEB 1989
APR
JUN
AUG
OCT
DEC
FEB
APR 1990
JUN
AUG
OCT
DEC
FEB
APR
JUN 1991
AUG
OCT

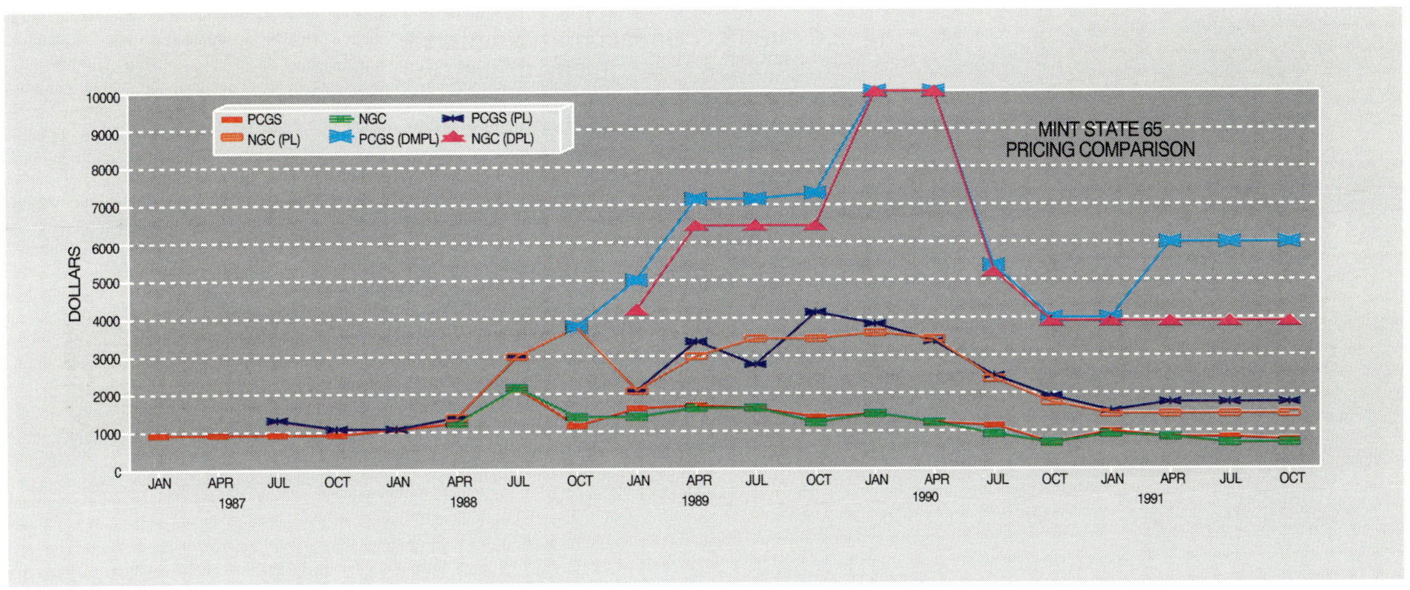
MINT STATE 65
PRICING COMPARISON
PCGS
NGC
PCGS (PL)
NGC (PL)
PCGS (DMPL)
NGC (DPL)
DOLLARS
10000
9000
8000
7000
6000
5000
4000
3000
2000
1000
0
JAN APR JUL OCT JAN APR JUL OCT JAN APR JUL OCT JAN APR JUL OCT JAN APR JUL OCT
1987
1988
1989
1990
1991

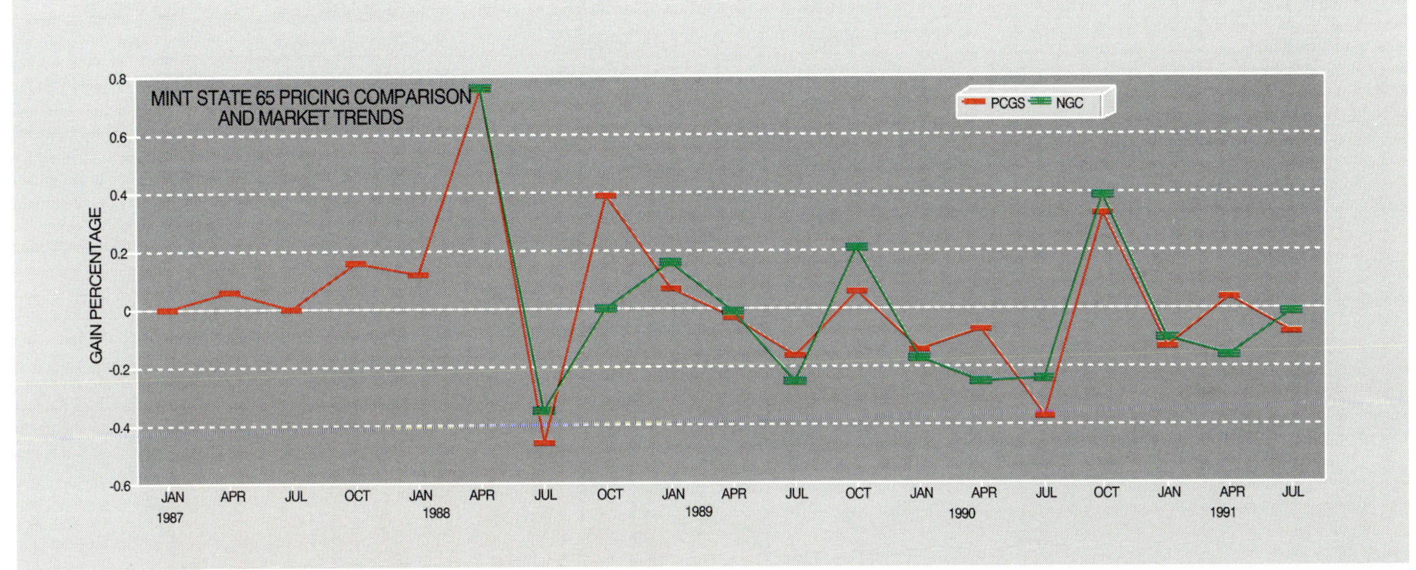
MINT STATE 65 PRICING COMPARISON
AND MARKET TRENDS
PCGS
NGC
GAIN PERCENTAGE
0.8
0.6
0.4
0.2
0
-0.2
-0.4
-0.6
JAN APR JUL OCT JAN APR JUL OCT JAN APR JUL OCT JAN APR JUL OCT JAN APR JUL
1987
1988
1989
1990
1991

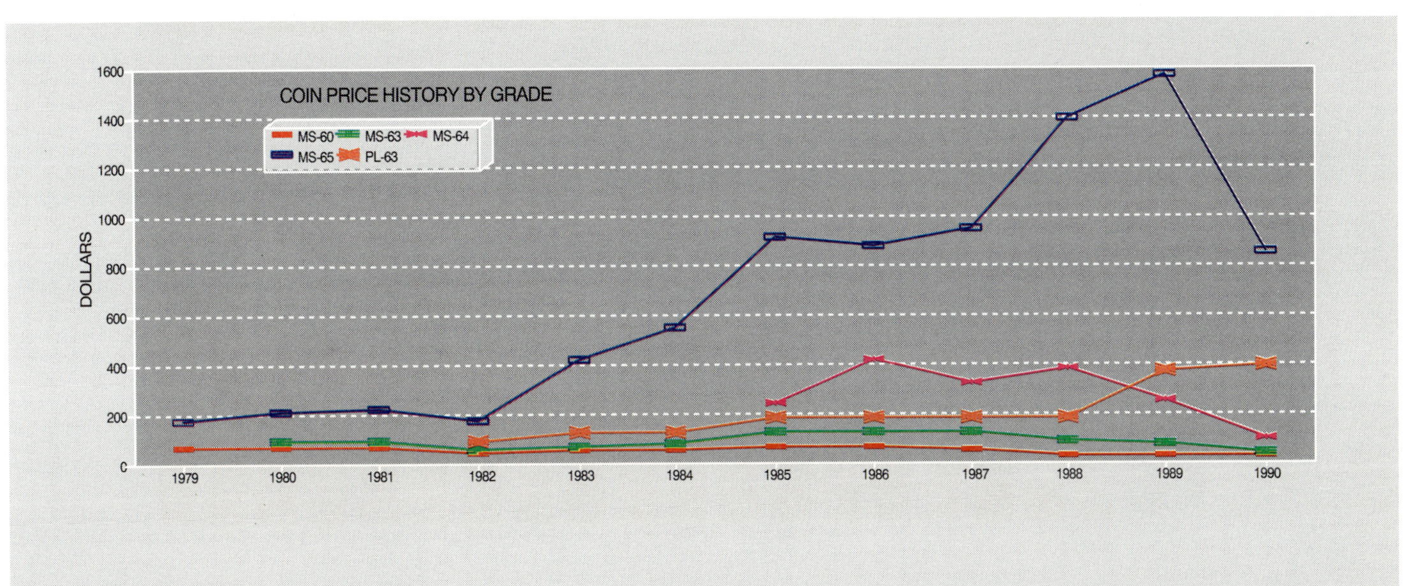
COIN PRICE HISTORY BY GRADE
MS-60
MS-63
MS-64
MS-65
PL-63
DOLLARS
1600
1400
1200
1000
800
600
400
200
0
1979 1980 1981 1982 1983 1984 1985 1986 1987 1988 1989 1990

1891-P

Mintage 8,693,556. Uncommon circulated (probably limited quantities spent, many of the rest melted). Plentiful in slider grades. Unc.'s often have reverses as flatly struck as some of the worst New Orleans dates; many are heavily bagmarked. Above MS 64, rare. One MS 60 bag reportedly in Redfield (not confirmed). Roll lots available in MS 60. Beware of sliders in MS 60 "put-together" rolls.

Recommended in MS 65, but you will probably have to make do with a MS 64 while you're hunting.

Proofs: Only 650 made. Only one variety seen to date (VAM 1). Date slants up to right.

Prooflikes: Rare in all grades, especially DMPL's.

MINTAGE	PROOF	STRIKE	LUSTER	BAG MARKS	REDFIELD
8,693,556	650	Weak	Poor	Moderate To Heavy	No
DIES	**DIE VARIETIES**	**% OF PL**	**% OF DMPL**	**PIVOTAL GRADE**	**RARITY FACTOR**
81	9	2.5	1.5	MS 64	R-2

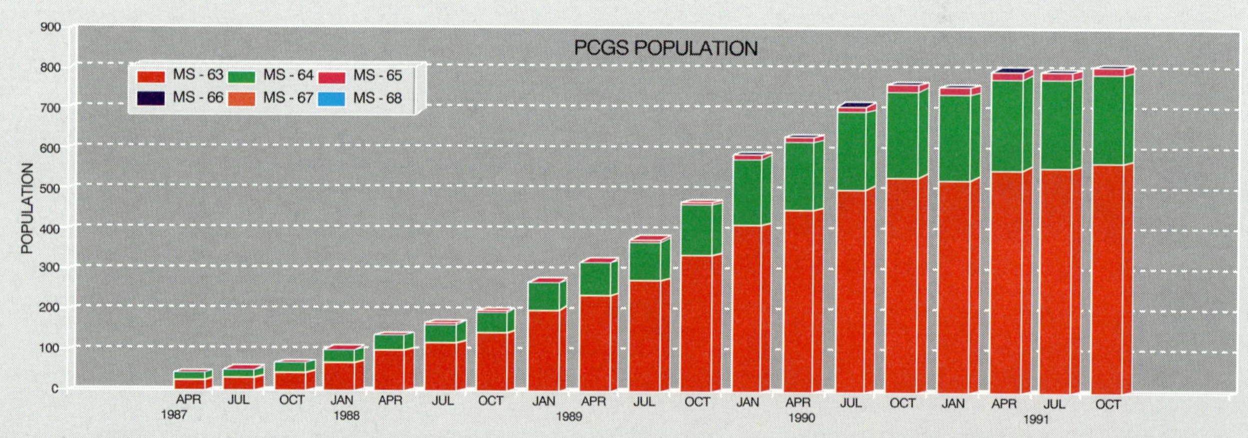

PCGS POPULATION

MS - 63 MS - 64 MS - 65
MS - 66 MS - 67 MS - 68

POPULATION

0 100 200 300 400 500 600 700 800 900

APR 1987 JUL OCT JAN 1988 APR JUL OCT JAN 1989 APR JUL OCT JAN APR 1990 JUL OCT JAN APR 1991 JUL OCT

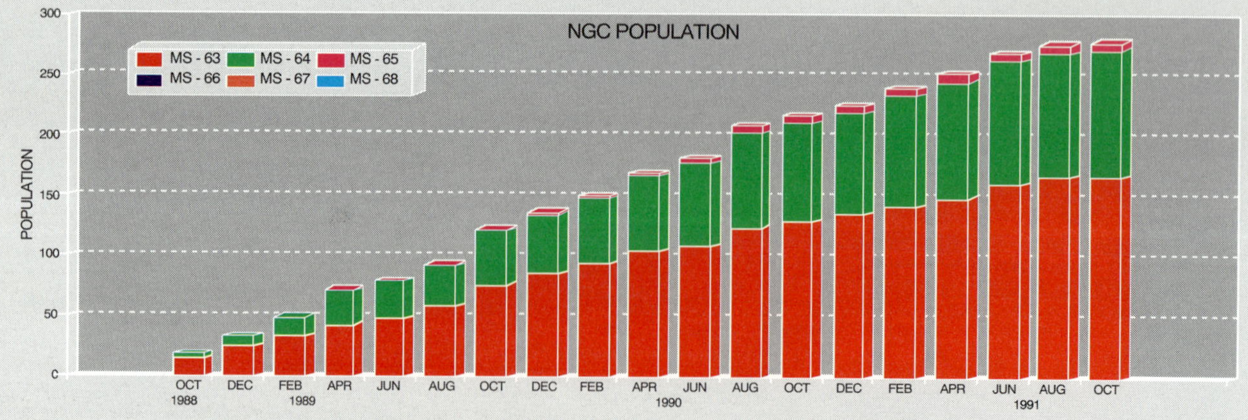

NGC POPULATION

MS - 63 MS - 64 MS - 65
MS - 66 MS - 67 MS - 68

POPULATION

0 50 100 150 200 250 300

OCT 1988 DEC FEB 1989 APR JUN AUG OCT DEC FEB APR 1990 JUN AUG OCT DEC FEB APR JUN 1991 AUG OCT

1891-P

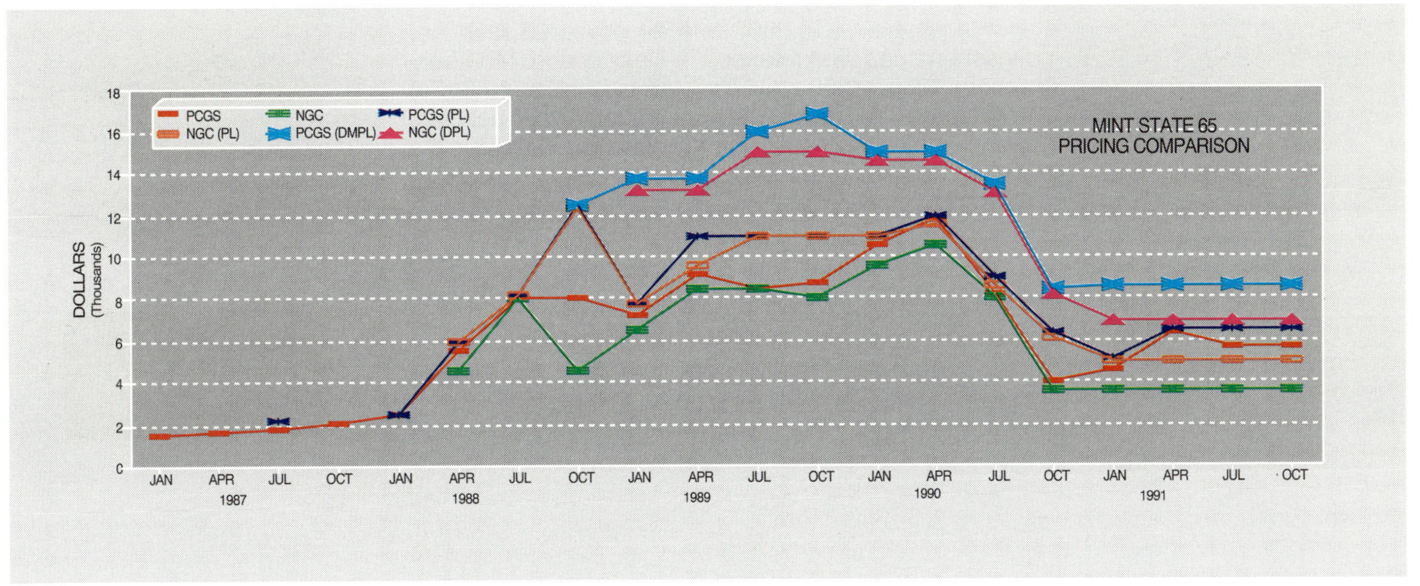

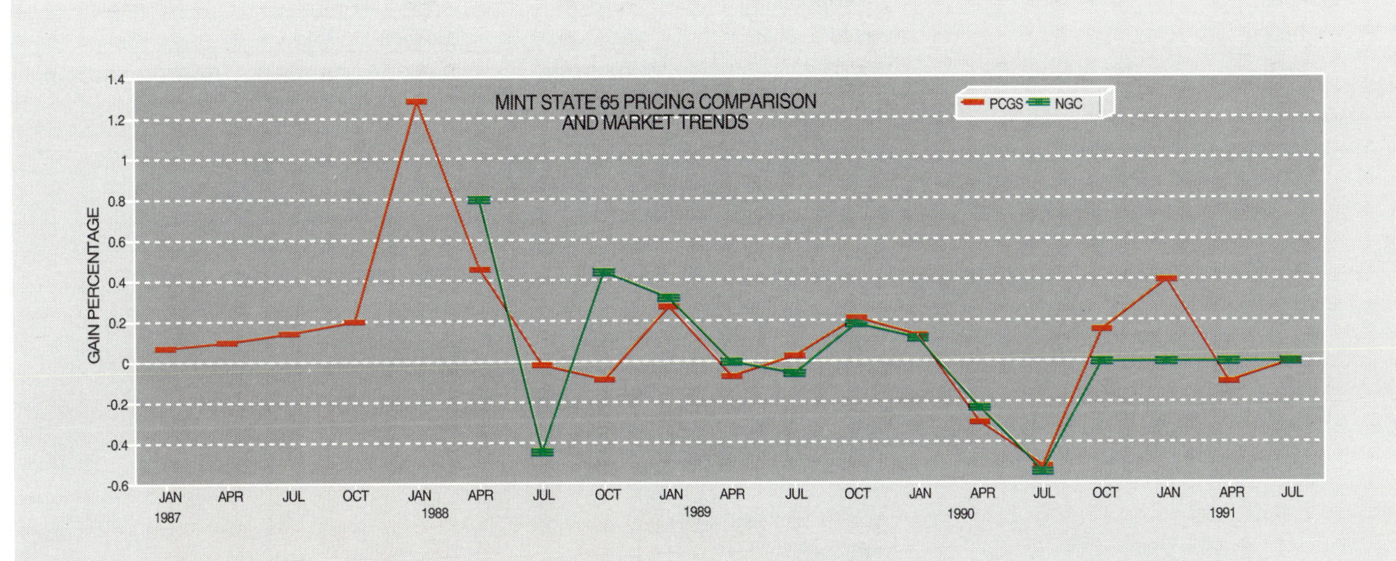

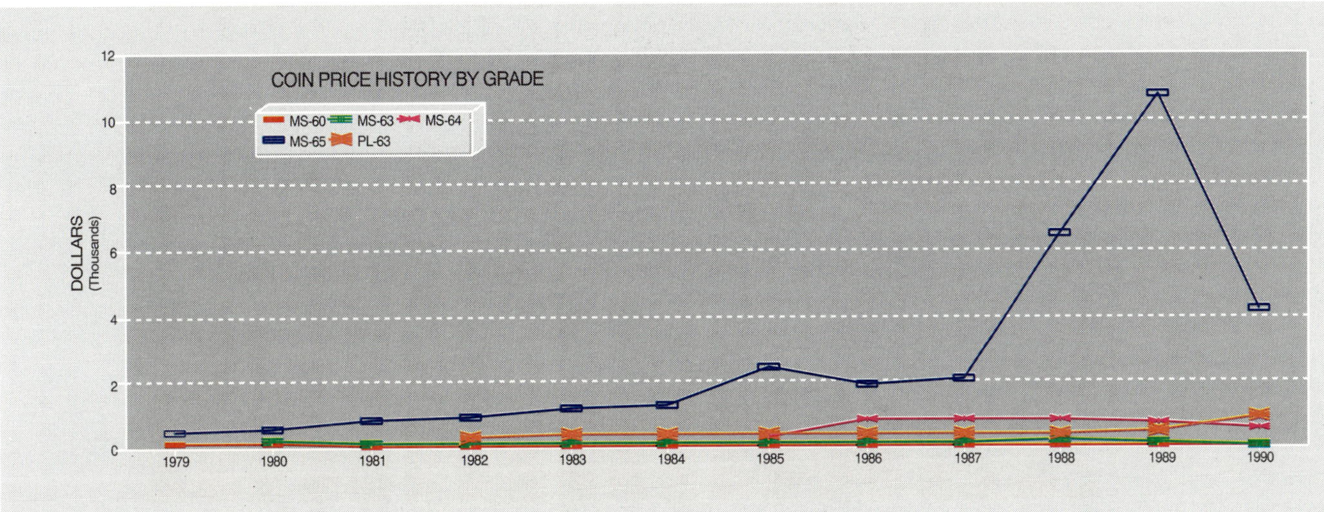

1891-CC

Mintage 1,618,000, from 24 obvs., 23 revs. At least one bag was released in Deer Lodge, Montana, about 1958 or '59. GSA's mail bid sales (1972-74) contained 5,687 of this date; minimum bid $30 per coin, winning bid $42. An additional 19 were later sold in the "mixed lot" offering. Many are well struck with excellent luster but plenty of bag marks. The Redfield hoard had possibly 3 to 5 bags of this date; these are probably the source of the MS 60/62 rolls. The 1889 through 1893 issues of CC dollars were widely opened to circulation.

Recommended in MS 64 up or MS 60/63 by the roll.

Prooflikes: Above MS 64, PL's are scarce, cameo specimens are rare, DMPL's rare.

MINTAGE	PROOF	STRIKE	LUSTER	BAG MARKS	REDFIELD
1,618,000	0	Average To Bold	Very Good	Moderate To Heavy	Yes
DIES	**DIE VARIETIES**	**% OF PL**	**% OF DMPL**	**PIVOTAL GRADE**	**RARITY FACTOR**
40	4	6.3	3.8	MS 64	R-3

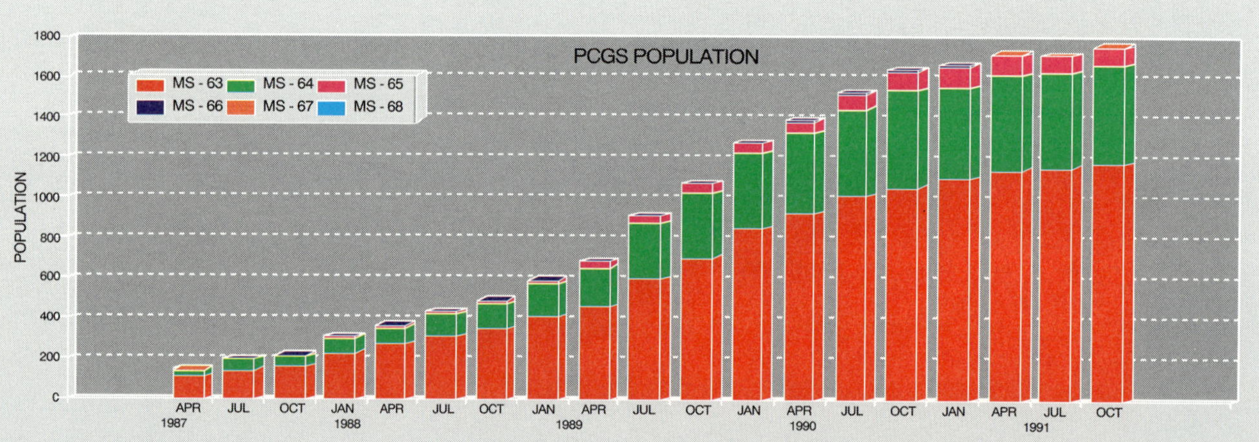

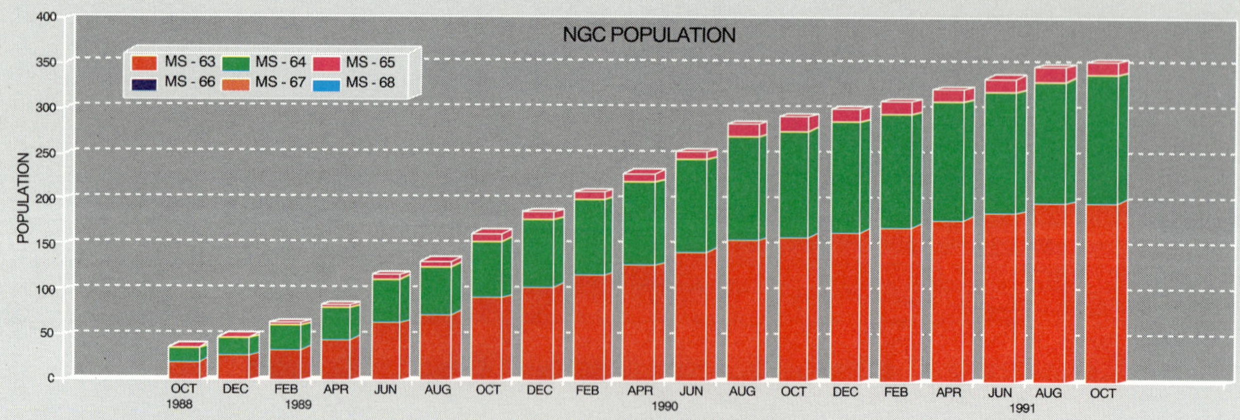

PCGS POPULATION

MS - 63 MS - 64 MS - 65
MS - 66 MS - 67 MS - 68

POPULATION

0 200 400 600 800 1000 1200 1400 1600 1800

APR 1987, JUL, OCT, JAN 1988, APR, JUL, OCT, JAN 1989, APR, JUL, OCT, JAN 1990, APR, JUL, OCT, JAN 1991, APR, JUL, OCT

NGC POPULATION

MS - 63 MS - 64 MS - 65
MS - 66 MS - 67 MS - 68

POPULATION

0 50 100 150 200 250 300 350 400

OCT 1988, DEC, FEB 1989, APR, JUN, AUG, OCT, DEC, FEB 1990, APR, JUN, AUG, OCT, DEC, FEB 1991, APR, JUN, AUG, OCT

1891-CC

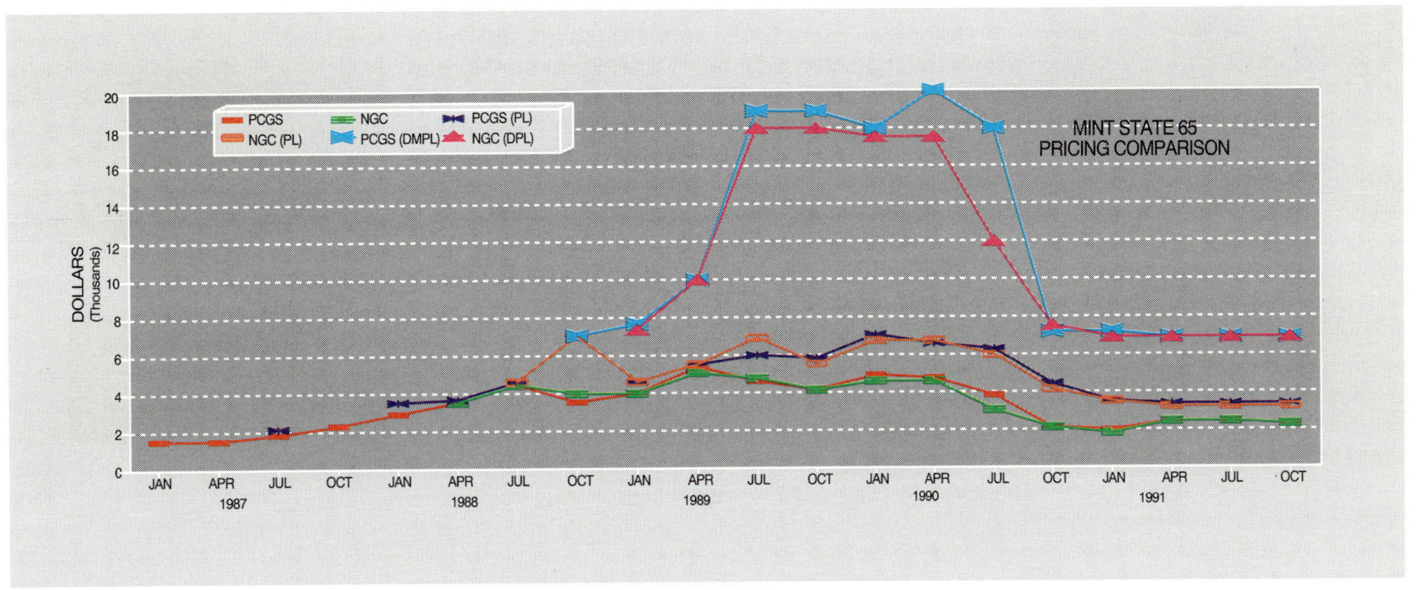

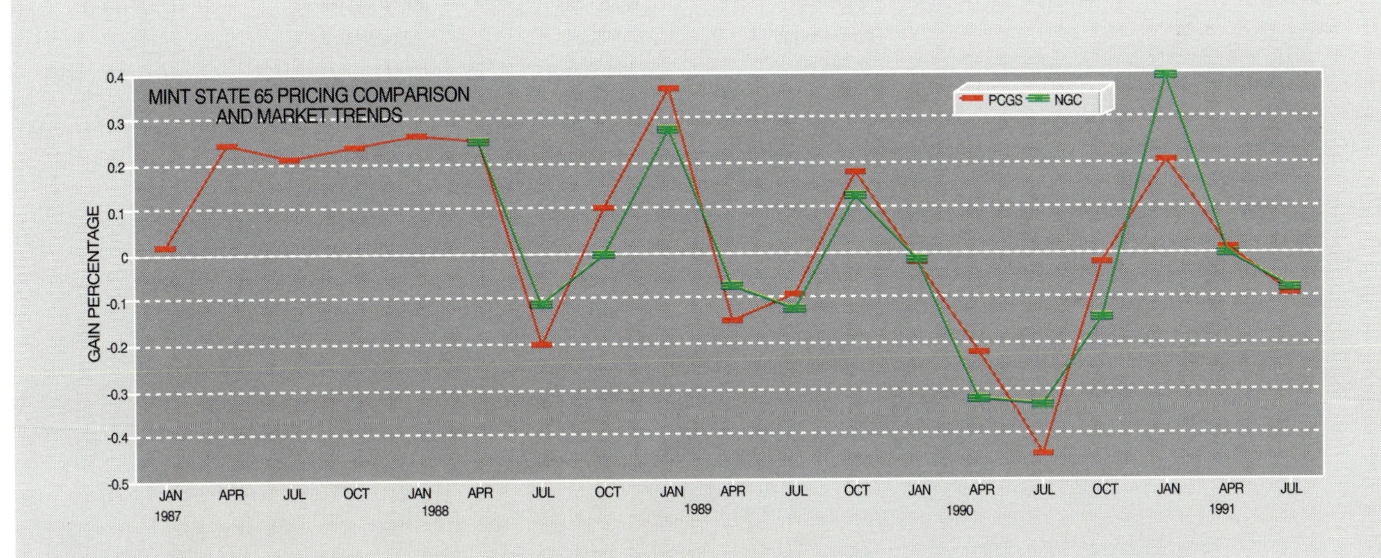

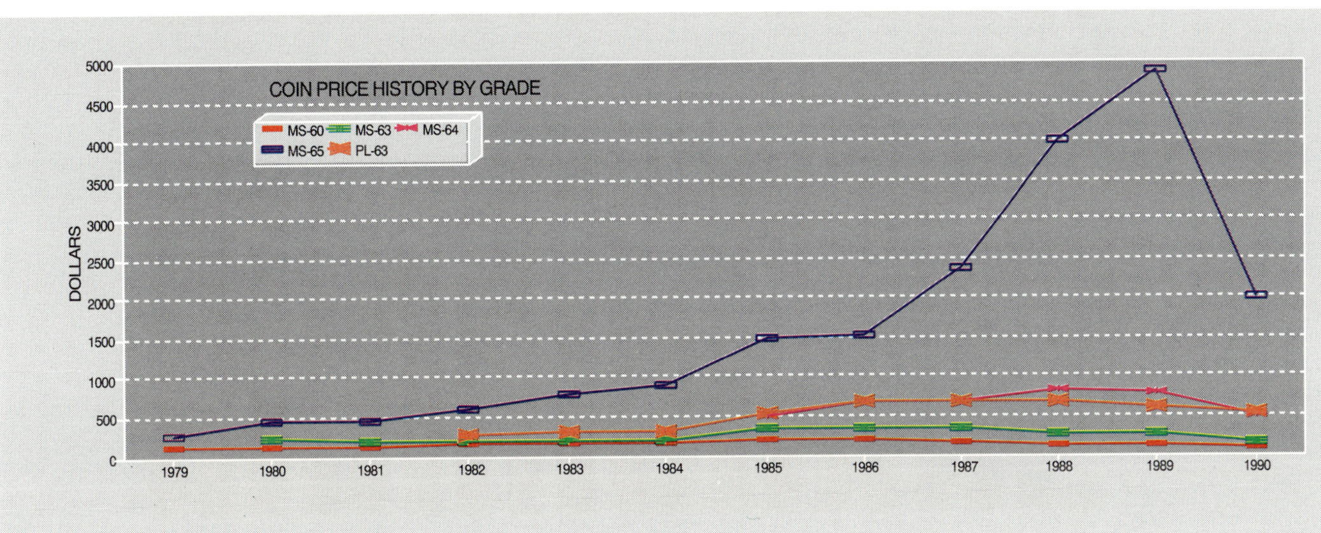

PCGS
1891-O S$1
MS65DMPL
97209.65/2241729

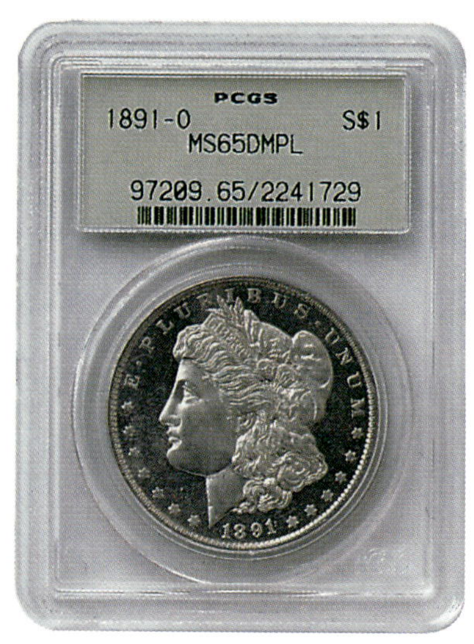

1891-O

Mintage 7,954,529, from 30 obvs., 29 revs. Winner of the contest for the "Pancake of the Morgan Series" title! Weak flat strikes, poor lustre, many bag marks. No one at the New Orleans Mint seemed to care about quality control (especially in the year of 1891).

Rolls occur, MS 60. The 1886-O, 1889-O, and 1891-O all experienced heavily clashed dies. The "E" and the bottom of the "R" of Liberty are visible without magnification under the reverse eagle's tail.

Recommended in MS 64 up, but you may have to settle for a 63 while you're hunting. Pivitol grade for this date is MS 64.

Proofs: Two reported, one from "Dupont", the other Amon Carter estate.

Prooflikes: Rare in all grades; not very impressive. Cameo's non-existive.

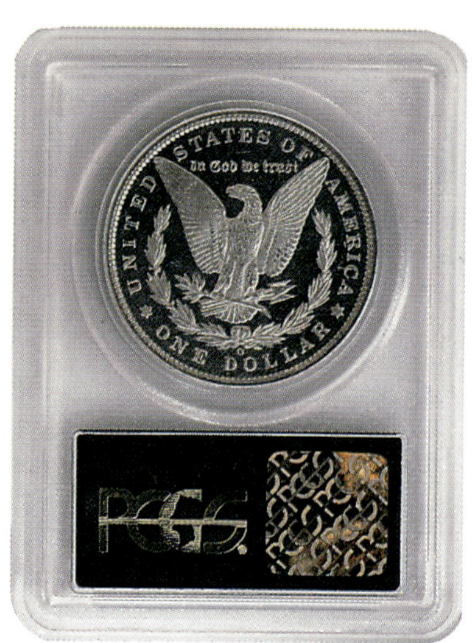

MINTAGE	PROOF	STRIKE	LUSTER	BAG MARKS	REDFIELD
7,954,529	0	Very Poor	Poor	Moderate	No
DIES	**DIE VARIETIES**	**% OF PL**	**% OF DMPL**	**PIVOTAL GRADE**	**RARITY FACTOR**
100	12	1.5	0.8	MS 64	R-2

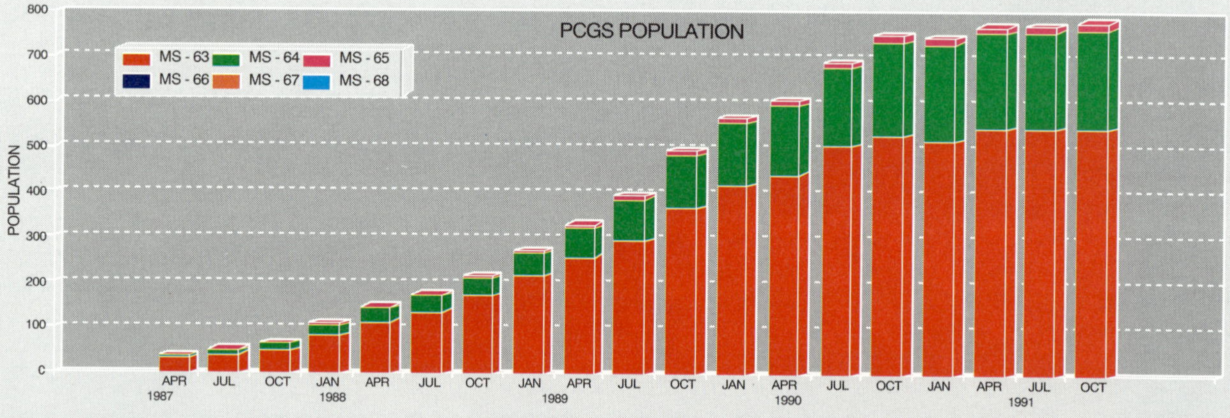
PCGS POPULATION
MS - 63
MS - 64
MS - 65
MS - 66
MS - 67
MS - 68
POPULATION
800
700
600
500
400
300
200
100
C
APR 1987
JUL
OCT
JAN 1988
APR
JUL
OCT
JAN 1989
APR
JUL
OCT
JAN
APR 1990
JUL
OCT
JAN
APR
JUL 1991
OCT

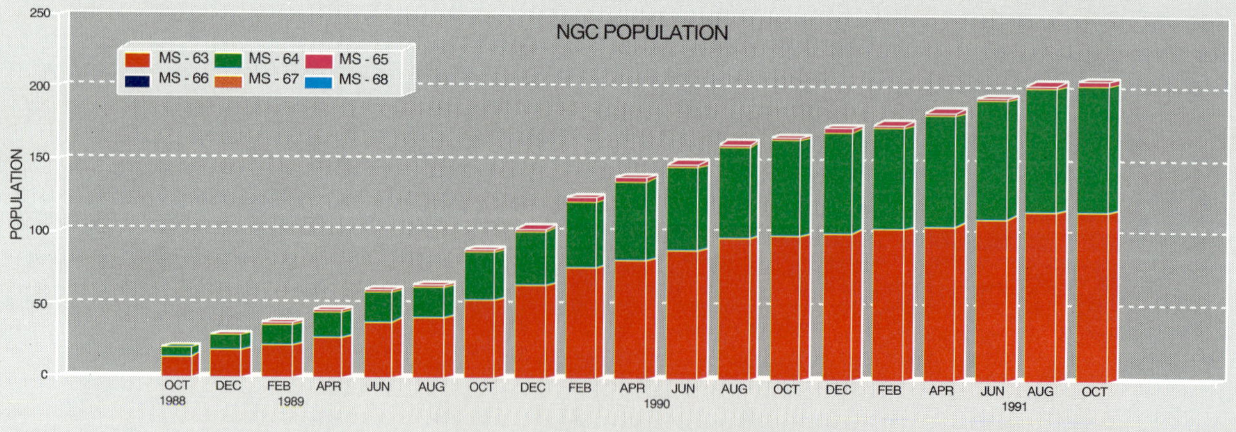
NGC POPULATION
MS - 63
MS - 64
MS - 65
MS - 66
MS - 67
MS - 68
POPULATION
250
200
150
100
50
C
OCT 1988
DEC
FEB 1989
APR
JUN
AUG
OCT
DEC
FEB
APR 1990
JUN
AUG
OCT
DEC
FEB
APR
JUN 1991
AUG
OCT

1891-O

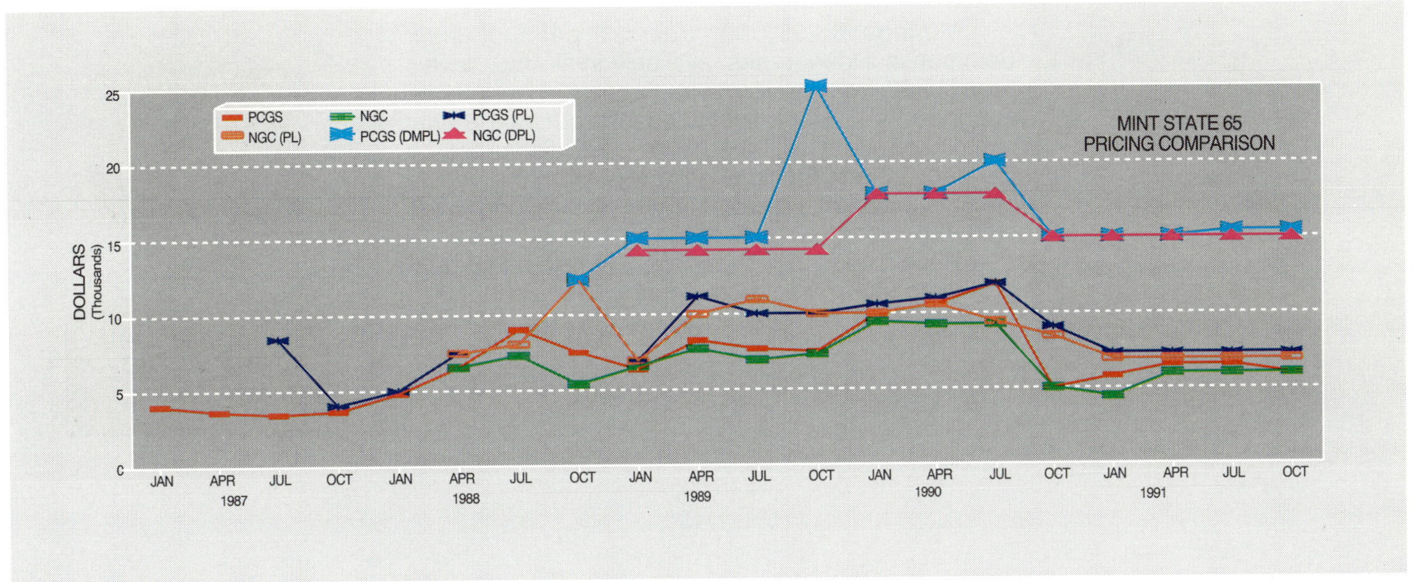

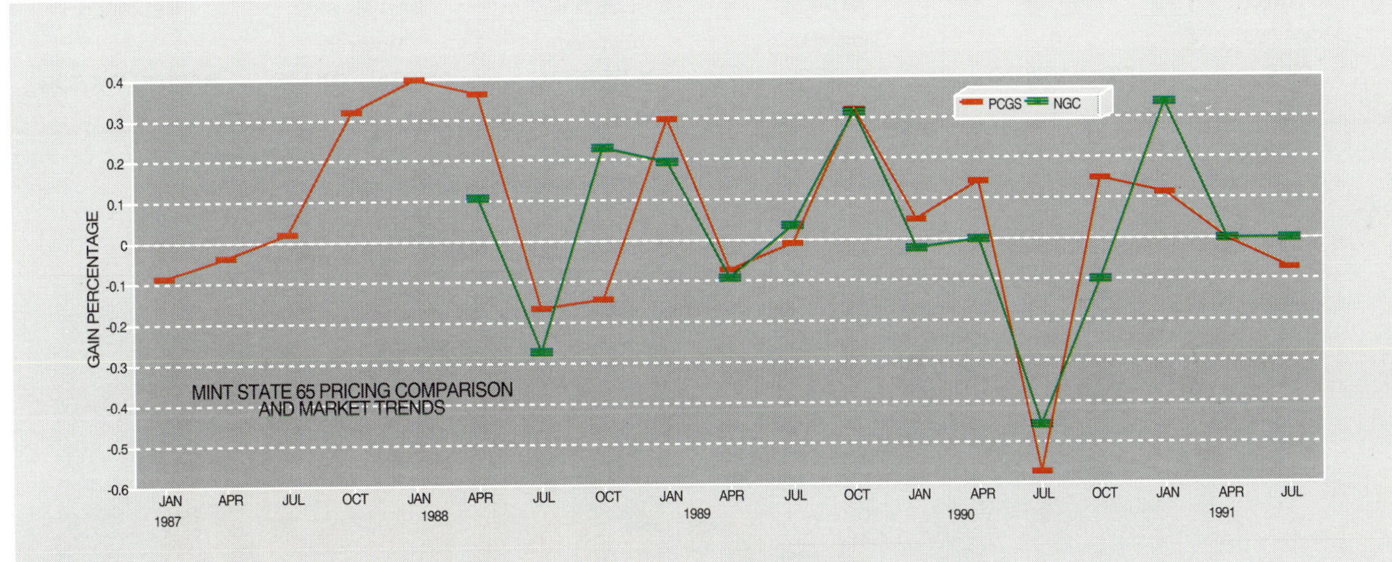

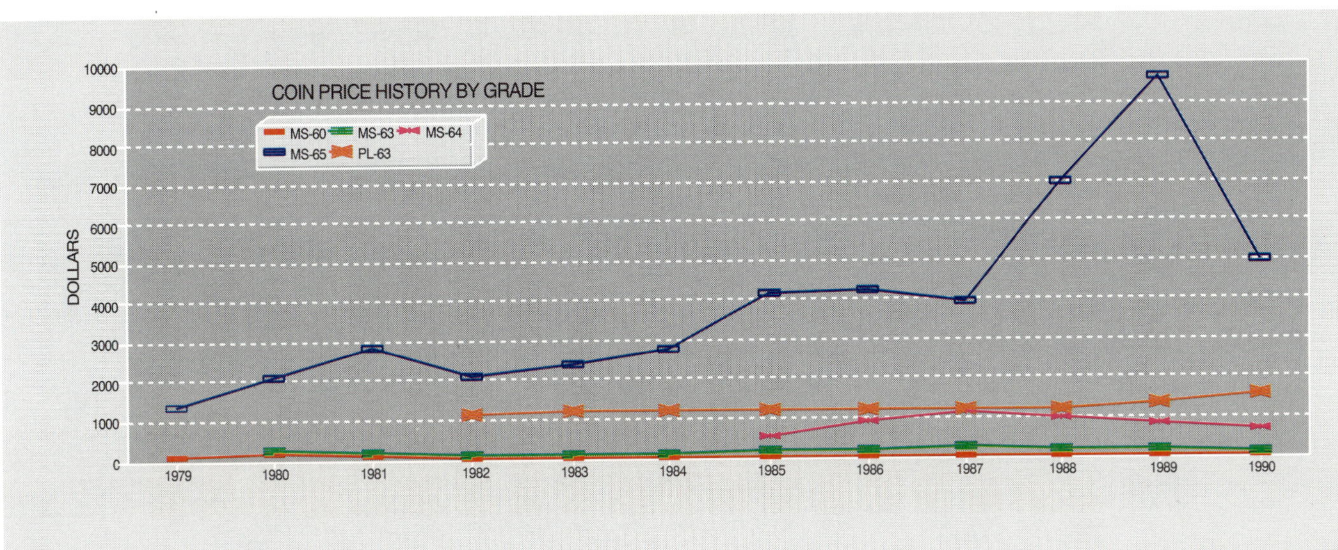

1891-S

Mintage 5,296,000, from 27 pairs of dies. Common in slider grades, available in all Unc. levels up to MS 67, from the Treasury. Redfield's hoard coins, supposedly 5 bags were described as heavily bagmarked, though some of the best (distributed by Paramount) were then graded MS 65; today they would be 63's. Quantities of MS 60/62 rolls and bags probably originate with Redfield.

Recommended in MS 64 up. Sliders are frequent.

Prooflikes: PL's outnumber DMPL's about 3 to 1. Cameos are very scarce. Above MS 64 all are rare.

MINTAGE	PROOF	STRIKE	LUSTER	BAG MARKS	REDFIELD
5,296,000	0	Sharp & Bold	Excellent	Moderate	Yes
DIES	**DIE VARIETIES**	**% OF PL**	**% OF DMPL**	**PIVOTAL GRADE**	**RARITY FACTOR**
73	13	8.7	3.0	MS 65	R-3

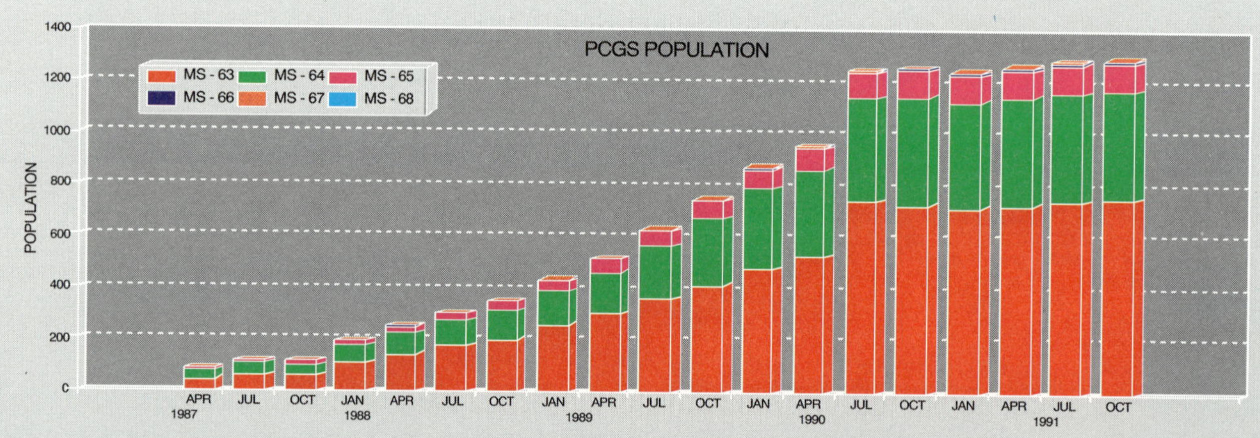

PCGS POPULATION

MS - 63 MS - 64 MS - 65
MS - 66 MS - 67 MS - 68

POPULATION

0 200 400 600 800 1000 1200 1400

APR 1987, JUL, OCT, JAN 1988, APR, JUL, OCT, JAN 1989, APR, JUL, OCT, JAN, APR 1990, JUL, OCT, JAN, APR, JUL 1991, OCT

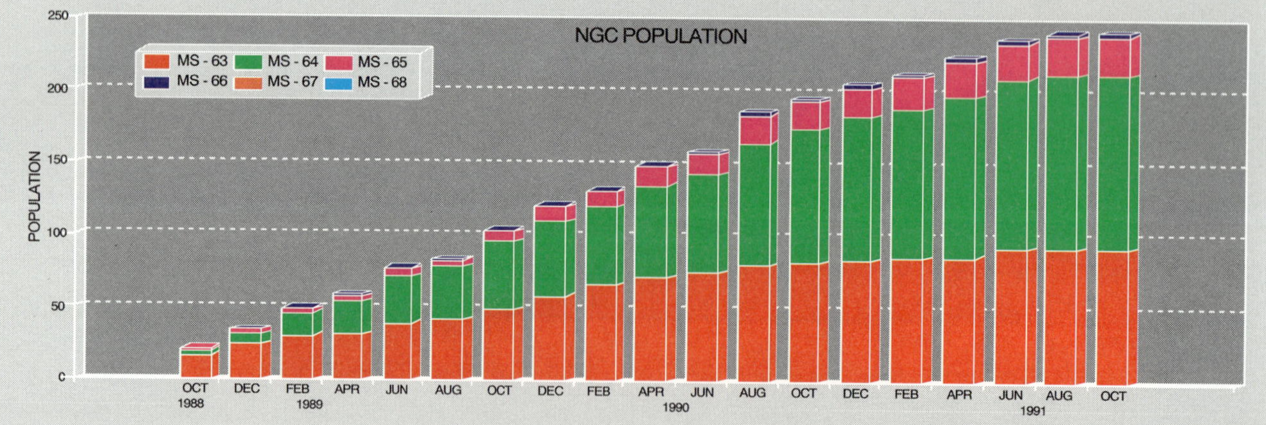

NGC POPULATION

MS - 63 MS - 64 MS - 65
MS - 66 MS - 67 MS - 68

POPULATION

0 50 100 150 200 250

OCT 1988, DEC, FEB 1989, APR, JUN, AUG, OCT, DEC, FEB, APR 1990, JUN, AUG, OCT, DEC, FEB, APR, JUN 1991, AUG, OCT

1891-S

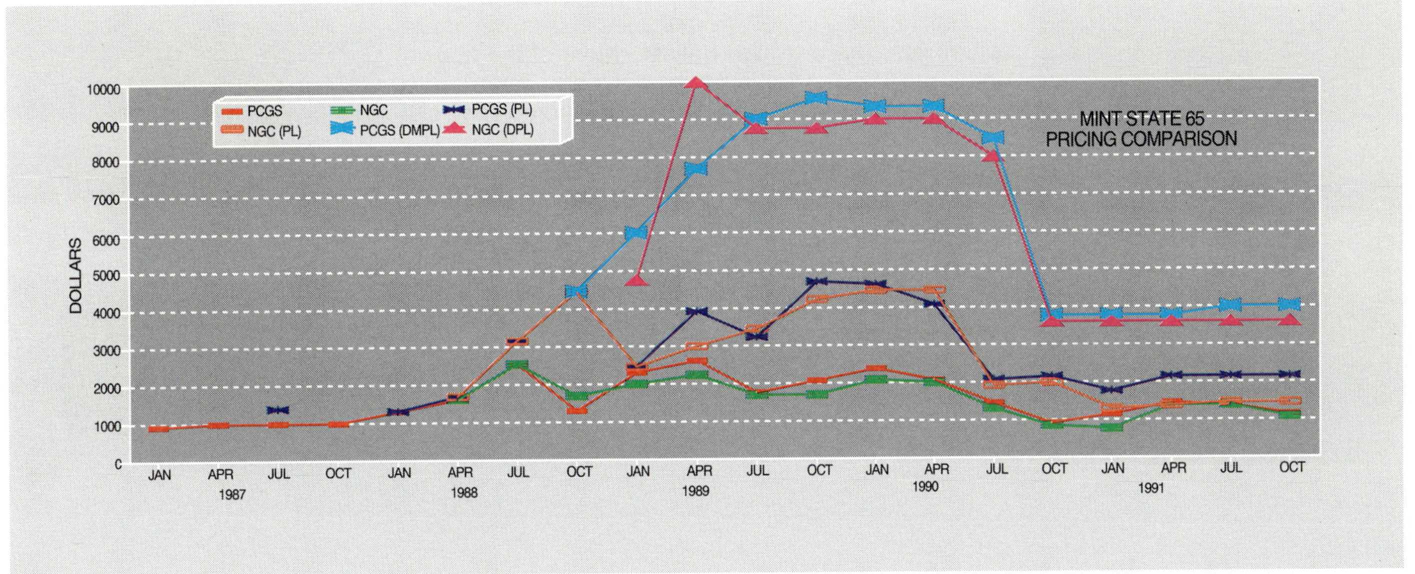

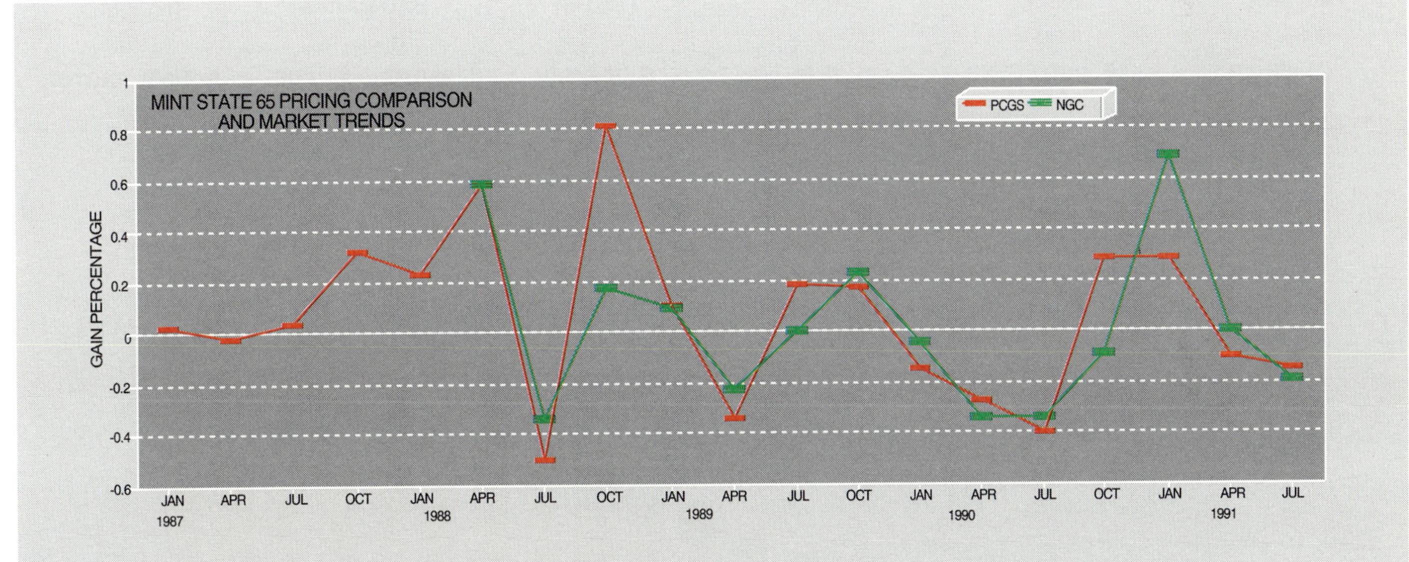

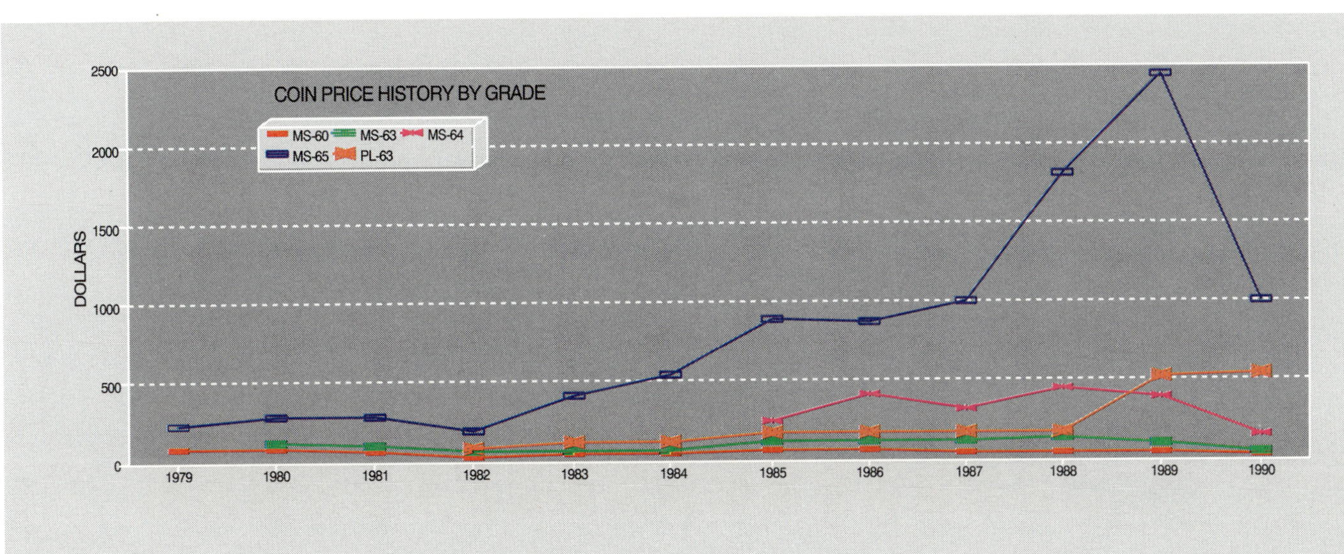

1892-P

Mintage 1,036,000, from 9 pairs of dies. Most are soft strikes, few are high quality. Most of the known Unc.'s are from Redfield's partial bag; these were primarily MS 60/62. Rolls from this source may still survive. Fourth scarcest Redfield date.

The 1892-P is a key coin. Recommended in MS 64 up, but you may have to make do with a MS 60/63 while hunting.

Proofs: 1,245 made, the larger number probably because of extra demand for proof sets of this first year with the new Barber silver coins. Closed 9, die polish in hair below Morgan's initial M.

Prooflikes: Scarce to rare in any grade. No intense cameos known.

MINTAGE	PROOF	STRIKE	LUSTER	BAG MARKS	REDFIELD
1,036,000	1,245	Average	Average	Moderate	Yes
DIES	**DIE VARIETIES**	**% OF PL**	**% OF DMPL**	**PIVOTAL GRADE**	**RARITY FACTOR**
15	7	2.8	3.5	MS 65	R-2

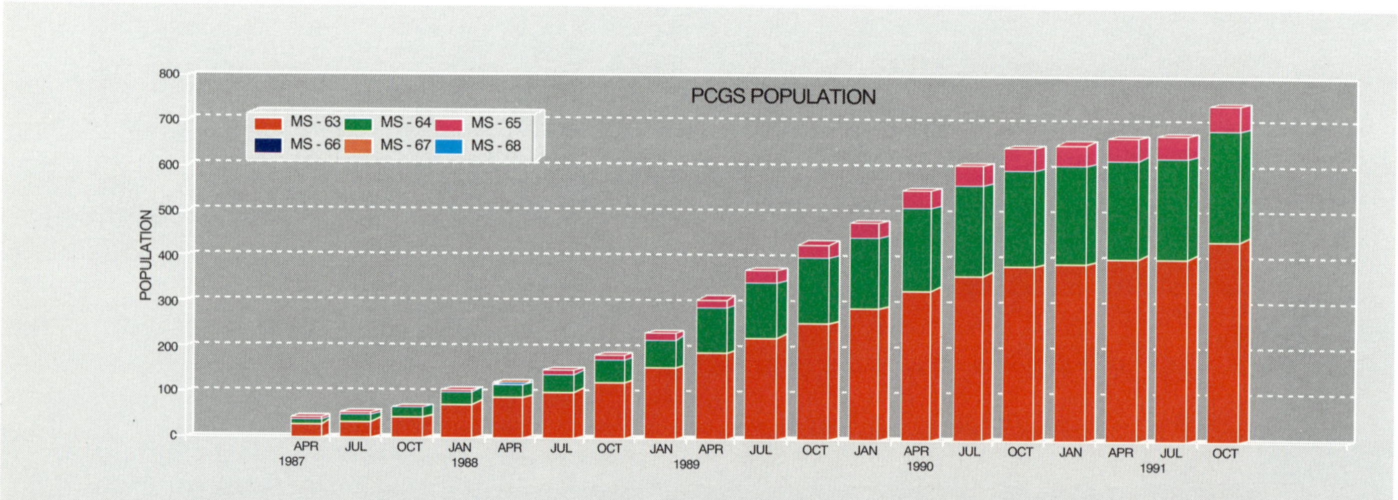

PCGS POPULATION

MS - 63 MS - 64 MS - 65 MS - 66 MS - 67 MS - 68

POPULATION

0 100 200 300 400 500 600 700 800

APR 1987 JUL OCT JAN 1988 APR JUL OCT JAN 1989 APR JUL OCT JAN APR 1990 JUL OCT JAN APR JUL 1991 OCT

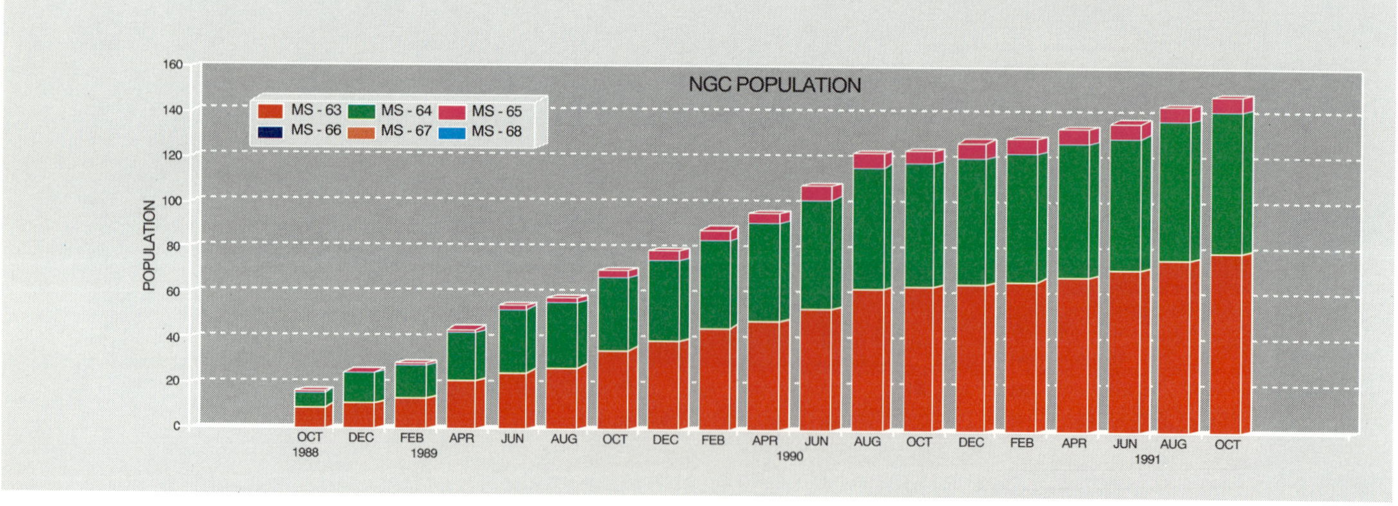

NGC POPULATION

MS - 63 MS - 64 MS - 65 MS - 66 MS - 67 MS - 68

POPULATION

0 20 40 60 80 100 120 140 160

OCT 1988 DEC FEB 1989 APR JUN AUG OCT DEC FEB APR 1990 JUN AUG OCT DEC FEB APR JUN 1991 AUG OCT

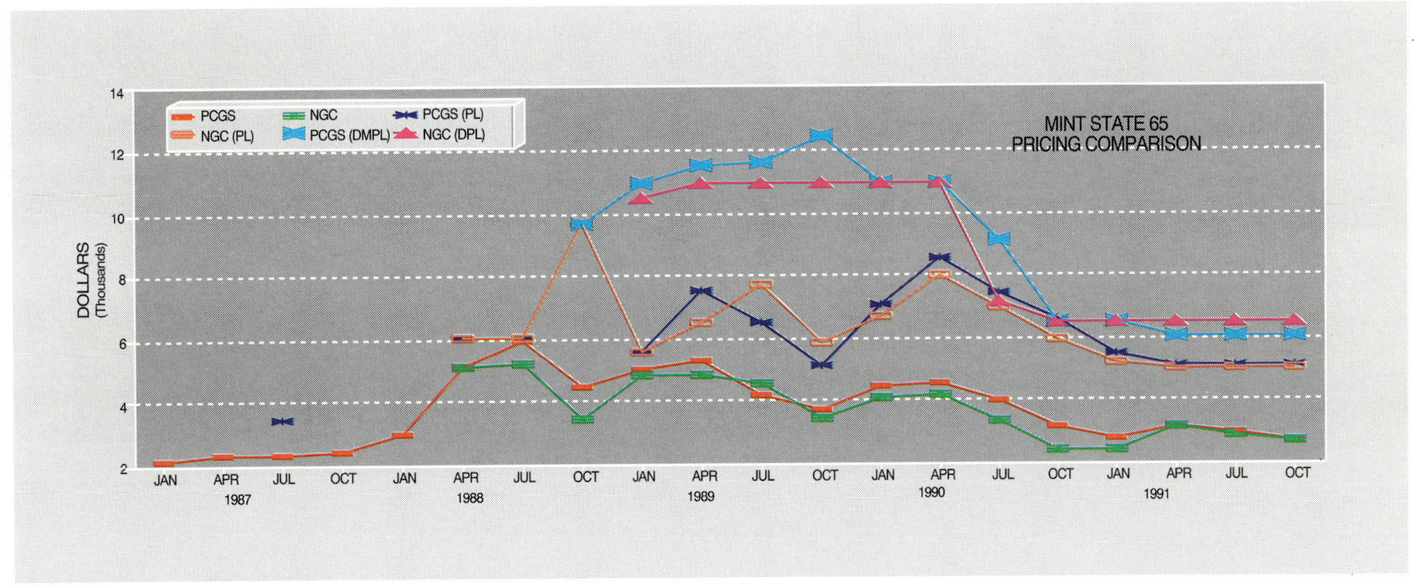
MINT STATE 65
PRICING COMPARISON
PCGS
NGC
PCGS (PL)
NGC (PL)
PCGS (DMPL)
NGC (DPL)
DOLLARS (Thousands)
14
12
10
8
6
4
2
JAN APR JUL OCT JAN APR JUL OCT JAN APR JUL OCT JAN APR JUL OCT JAN APR JUL OCT
1987
1988
1989
1990
1991

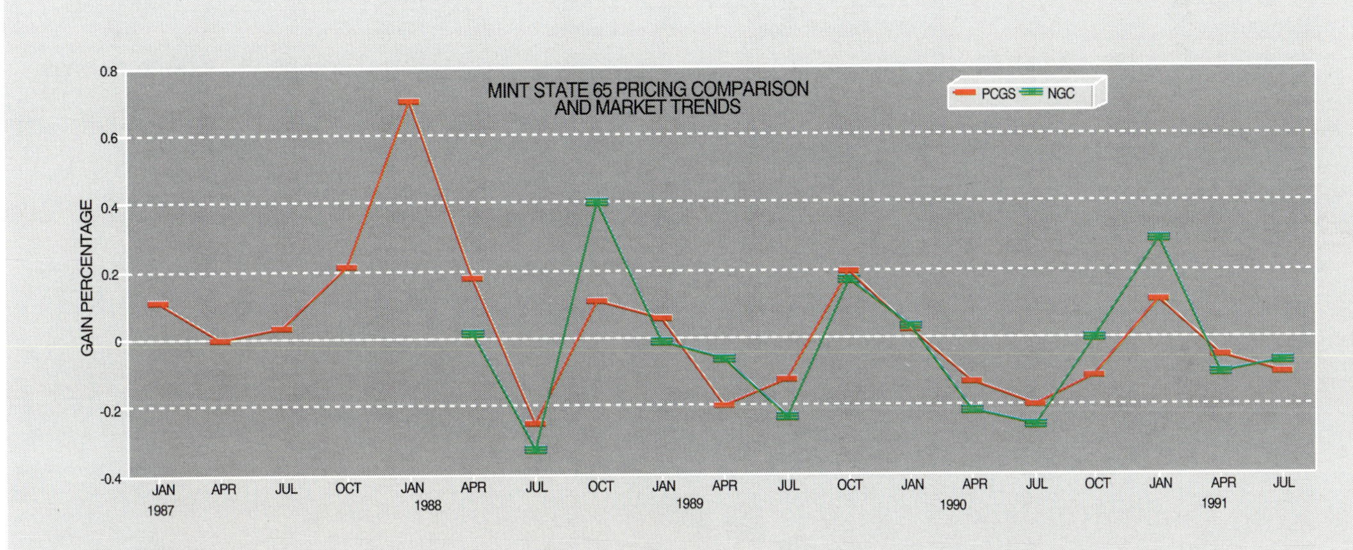
MINT STATE 65 PRICING COMPARISON
AND MARKET TRENDS
PCGS
NGC
GAIN PERCENTAGE
0.8
0.6
0.4
0.2
0
-0.2
-0.4
JAN APR JUL OCT JAN APR JUL OCT JAN APR JUL OCT JAN APR JUL OCT JAN APR JUL
1987
1988
1989
1990
1991

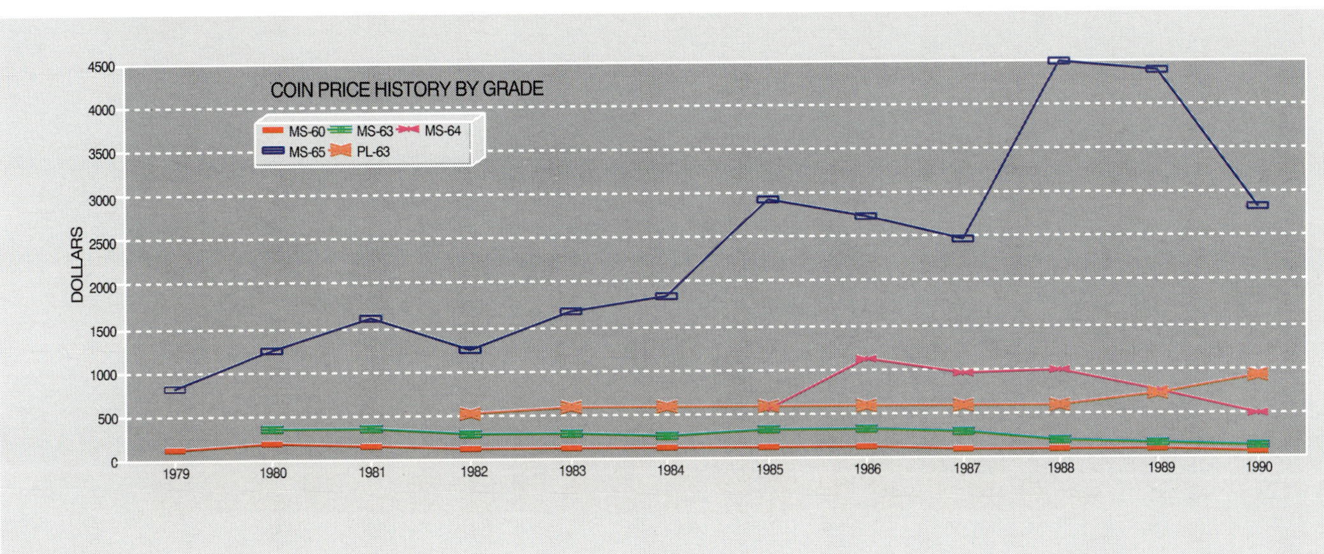
COIN PRICE HISTORY BY GRADE
MS-60
MS-63
MS-64
MS-65
PL-63
DOLLARS
4500
4000
3500
3000
2500
2000
1500
1000
500
0
1979 1980 1981 1982 1983 1984 1985 1986 1987 1988 1989 1990

PCGS
1892-CC S$1
MS67
7214.67/6271767

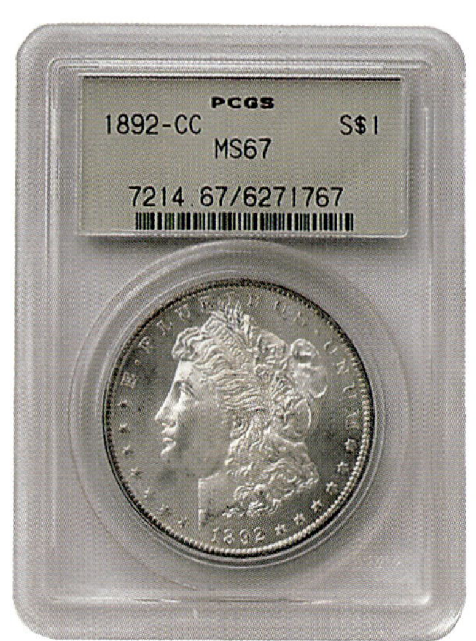

1892-CC

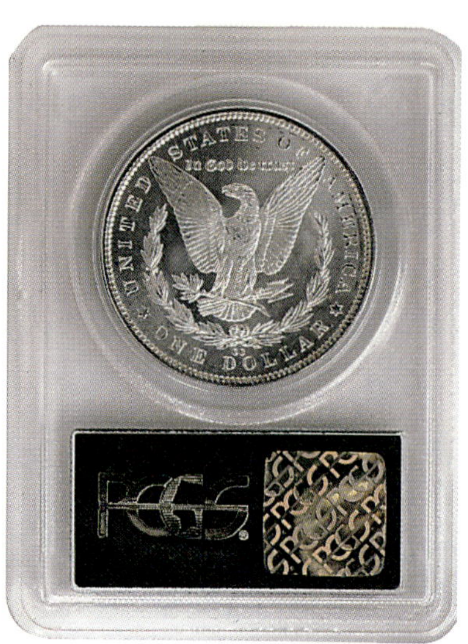

Probably most of the 1,352,000 mintage went to the melting pots. Ten pairs of dies. Unc. survivors are usually frosty with plenty of bag marks, in the MS 60/63 range, from a single Treasury bag. The GSA mail bid sales contained one 1892-CC in the "mixed lot" group (minimum bid $15); to date this has not surfaced in the original holder.

The Redfield hoard included an estimated 2 to 4 bags, many badly scratched on cheek by a counting machine. These may be the source of the occasional MS 60 rolls. Circulated pieces are scarce.

Recommended in MS 64 up.

Prooflikes: Low grade semi-PL's have been sold as PL's. Scarce to rare above MS 64 PL, MS 63 DMPL. The 1892-CC can come with a frosty cameo and deep mirror, but it is scarce.

MINTAGE	PROOF	STRIKE	LUSTER	BAG MARKS	REDFIELD
1,352,000	0	Average To Bold	Excellent	Moderate	Yes
DIES	**DIE VARIETIES**	**% OF PL**	**% OF DMPL**	**PIVOTAL GRADE**	**RARITY FACTOR**
30	9	9.4	5.0	MS 65	R-2

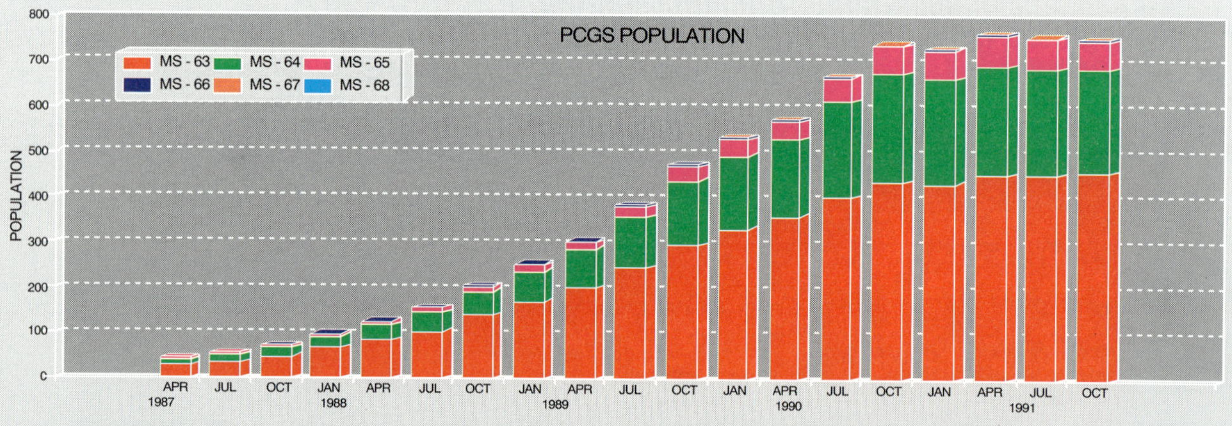

PCGS POPULATION
MS - 63 MS - 64 MS - 65
MS - 66 MS - 67 MS - 68
POPULATION
800 700 600 500 400 300 200 100 0
APR 1987 JUL OCT JAN 1988 APR JUL OCT JAN 1989 APR JUL OCT JAN APR 1990 JUL OCT JAN APR JUL 1991 OCT

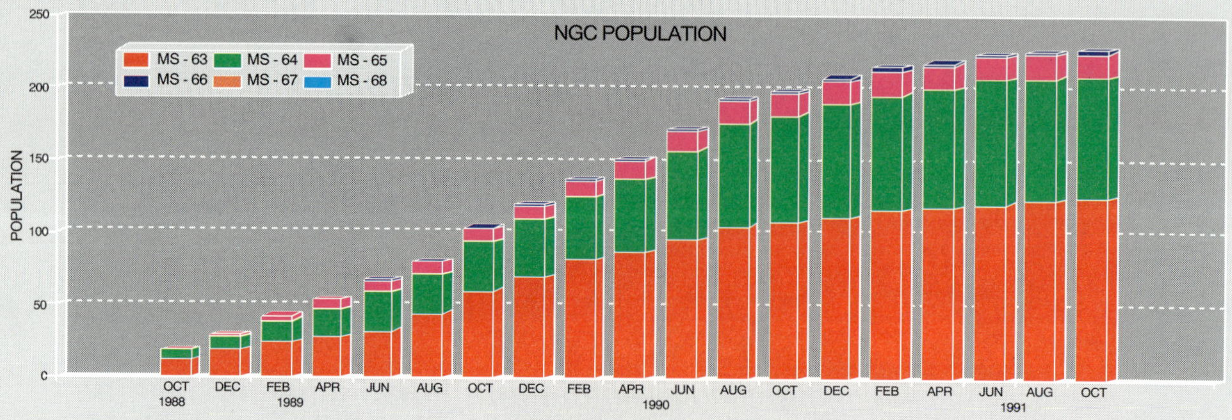

NGC POPULATION
MS - 63 MS - 64 MS - 65
MS - 66 MS - 67 MS - 68
POPULATION
250 200 150 100 50 0
OCT 1988 DEC FEB 1989 APR JUN AUG OCT DEC FEB APR 1990 JUN AUG OCT DEC FEB APR JUN 1991 AUG OCT

1892-CC

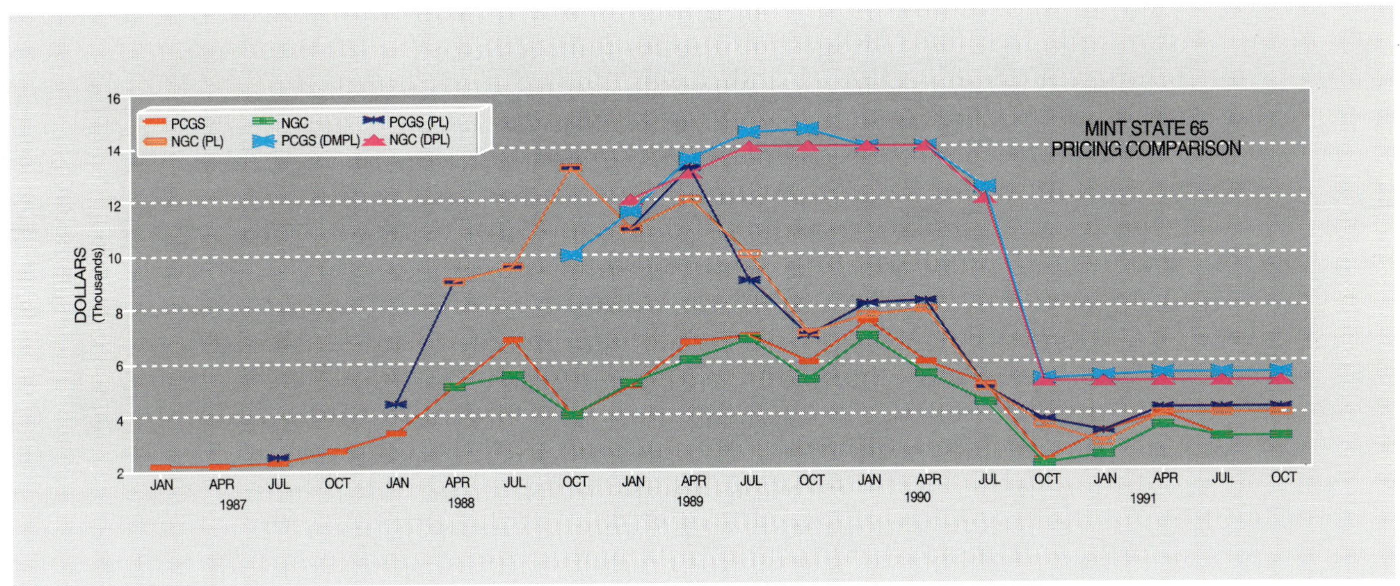

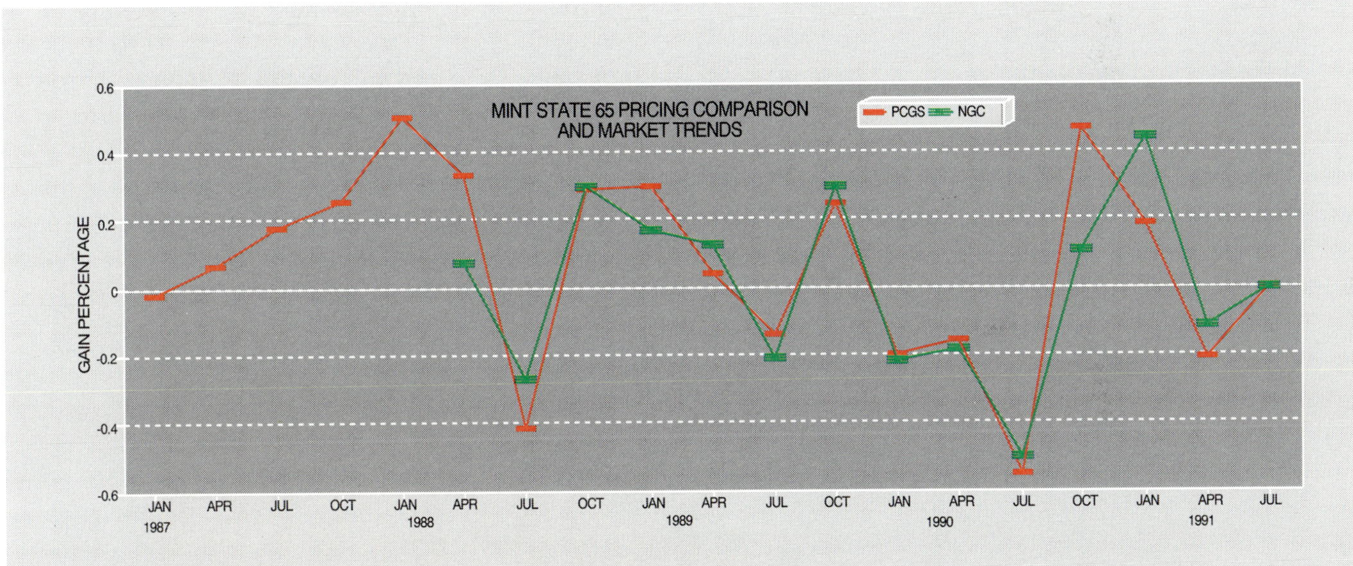

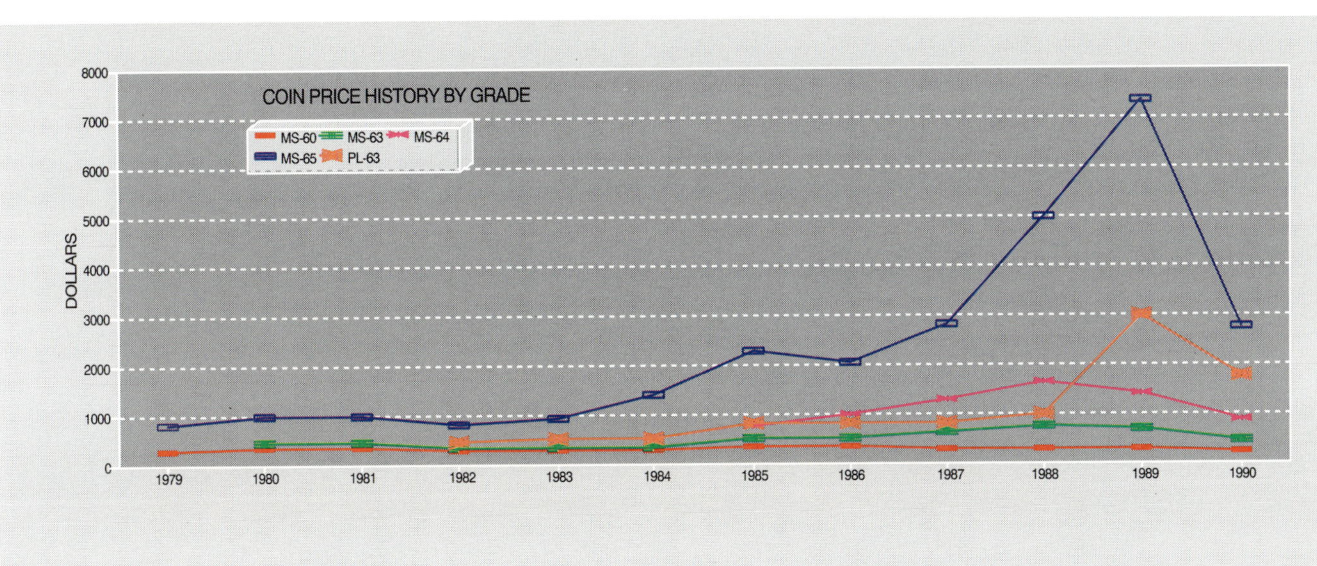

PCGS
1892-O S$1
MS65DMPL
97217.65/1156043
E PLURIBUS UNUM
1892

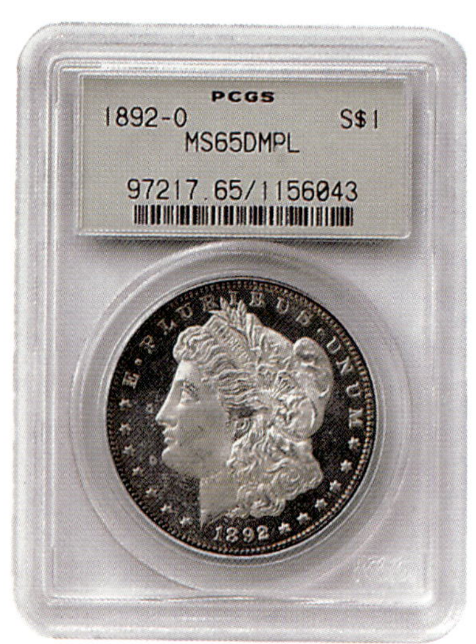

1892-O

Mintage 2,744,000. Third, or maybe tied for second, with 1890-O for "Pancake of the Morgan Series" title. Unc.'s have thick rims, weak centers, dull lustre, in the manner of 1887-O, 1889-O, 1891-O. Original rolls of MS 60/62 are known. High grade ones are from a bag found in 1977.

Recommended in MS 64 up. This coin should be a "keeper" in MS 65. Sell it only if needed.

Prooflikes: Rare in all grades. Cameos may not survive. The finest known DMPL is the Dean Tavenner, Wayne Miller coin.

UNITED STATES OF AMERICA
In God we trust
ONE DOLLAR
PCGS

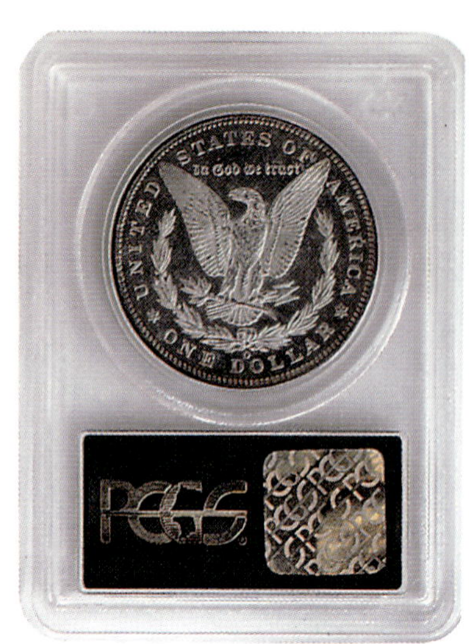

MINTAGE	PROOF	STRIKE	LUSTER	BAG MARKS	REDFIELD
2,744,000	0	Very Poor	Average	Moderate	No
DIES	**DIE VARIETIES**	**% OF PL**	**% OF DMPL**	**PIVOTAL GRADE**	**RARITY FACTOR**
30	11	0.4	0.3	MS 64	R-4

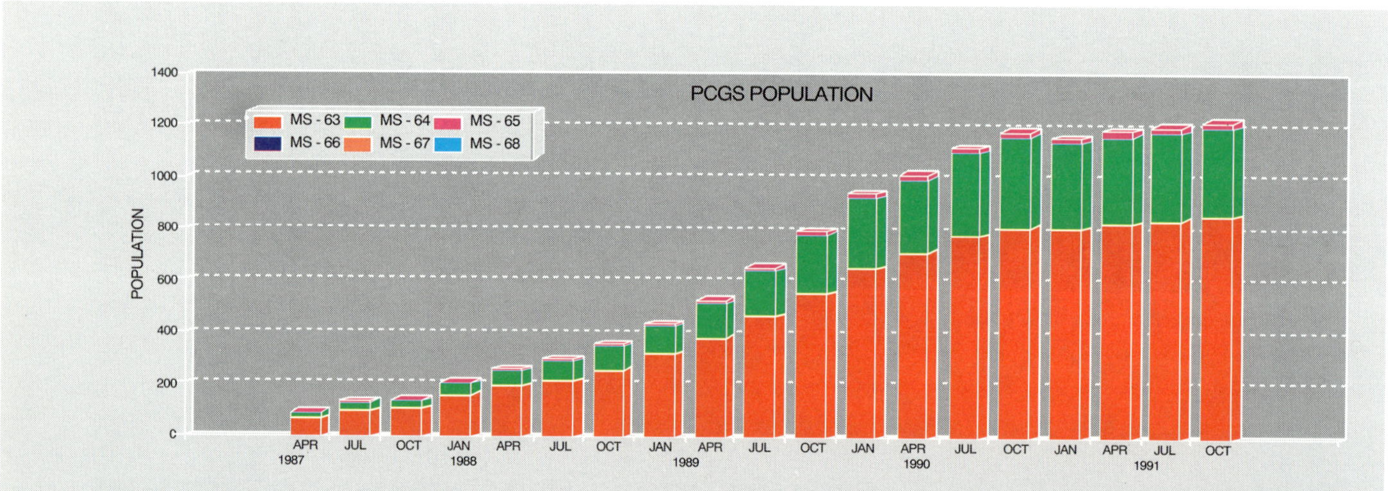
PCGS POPULATION
MS - 63
MS - 64
MS - 65
MS - 66
MS - 67
MS - 68
POPULATION
1400
1200
1000
800
600
400
200
0
APR 1987
JUL
OCT
JAN 1988
APR
JUL
OCT
JAN 1989
APR
JUL
OCT
JAN
APR 1990
JUL
OCT
JAN
APR
JUL 1991
OCT

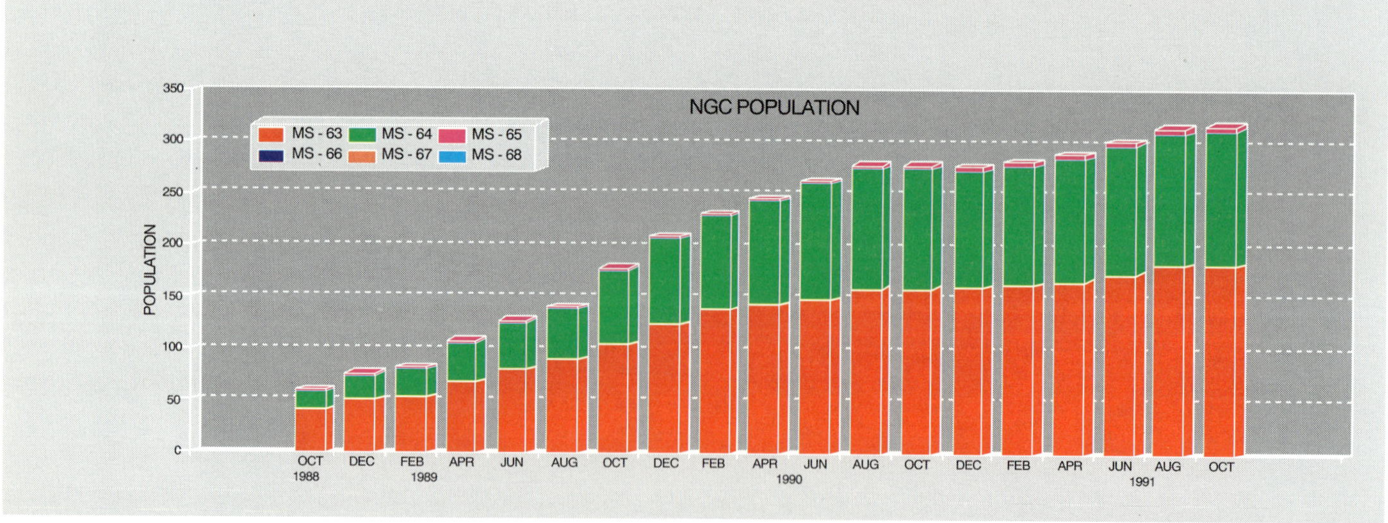
NGC POPULATION
MS - 63
MS - 64
MS - 65
MS - 66
MS - 67
MS - 68
POPULATION
350
300
250
200
150
100
50
0
OCT 1988
DEC
FEB 1989
APR
JUN
AUG
OCT
DEC
FEB
APR 1990
JUN
AUG
OCT
DEC
FEB
APR
JUN 1991
AUG
OCT

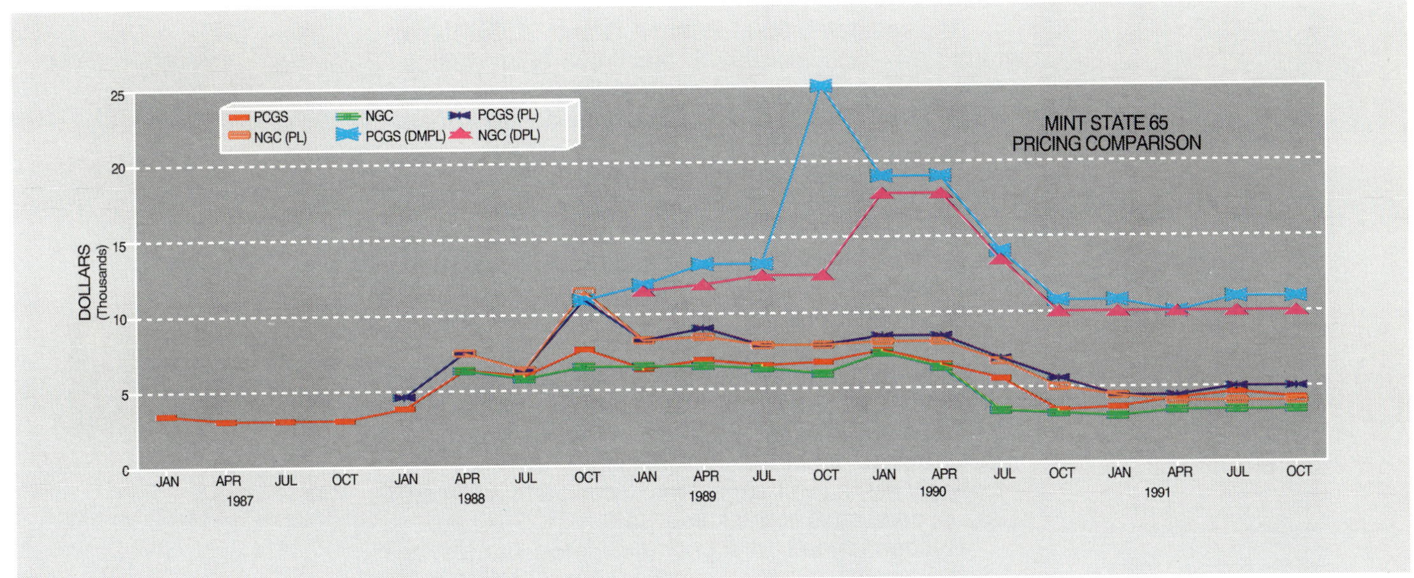
MINT STATE 65
PRICING COMPARISON
PCGS
NGC
PCGS (PL)
NGC (PL)
PCGS (DMPL)
NGC (DPL)
DOLLARS (Thousands)
25
20
15
10
5
0
JAN APR JUL OCT JAN APR JUL OCT JAN APR JUL OCT JAN APR JUL OCT JAN APR JUL OCT
1987 1988 1989 1990 1991

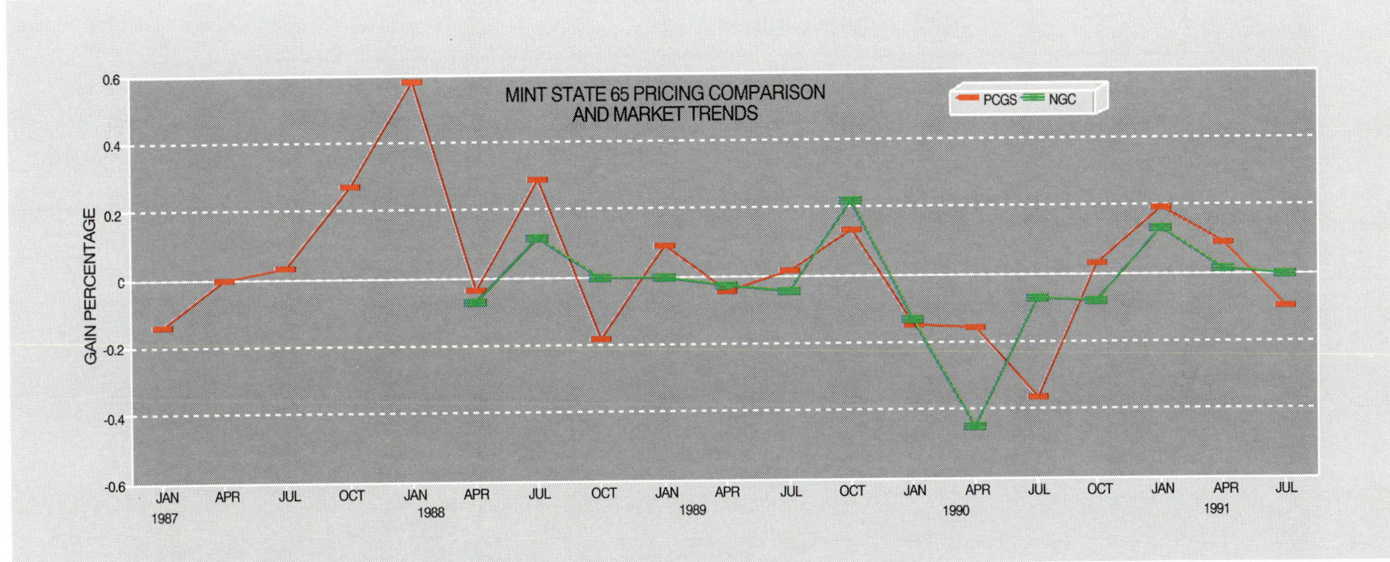
MINT STATE 65 PRICING COMPARISON
AND MARKET TRENDS
PCGS
NGC
GAIN PERCENTAGE
0.6
0.4
0.2
0
-0.2
-0.4
-0.6
JAN APR JUL OCT JAN APR JUL OCT JAN APR JUL OCT JAN APR JUL OCT JAN APR JUL
1987 1988 1989 1990 1991

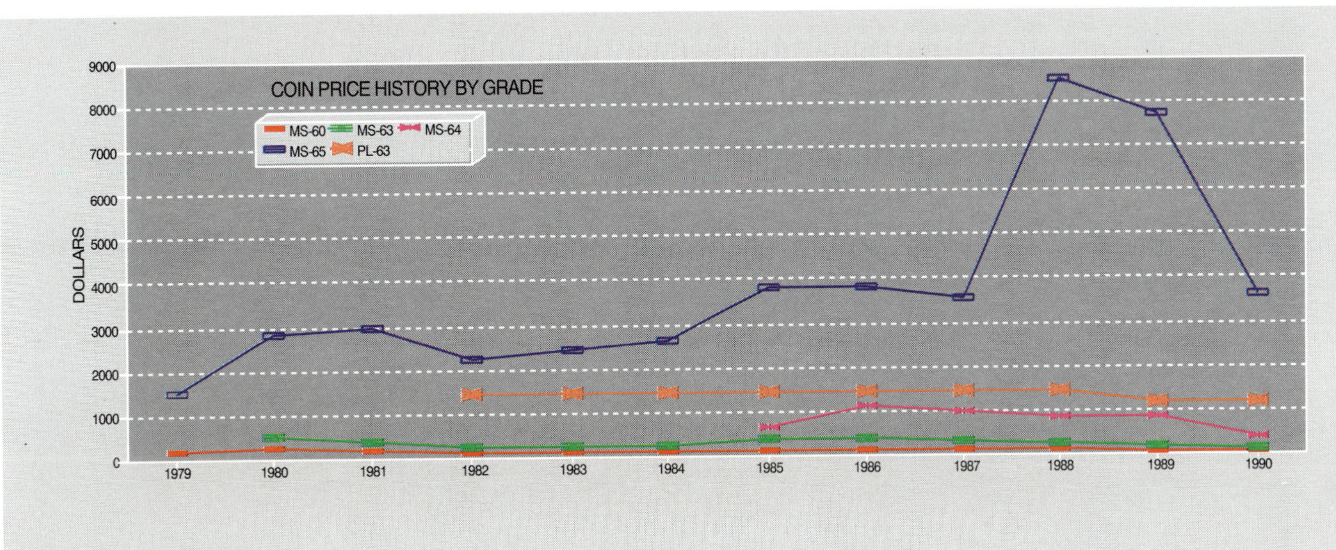
COIN PRICE HISTORY BY GRADE
MS-60
MS-63
MS-64
MS-65
PL-63
DOLLARS
9000
8000
7000
6000
5000
4000
3000
2000
1000
0
1979 1980 1981 1982 1983 1984 1985 1986 1987 1988 1989 1990

1892-S

Mintage 1,200,000. Both NCG and PCGS have graded 24 each of 1892-S and 1893-S in various grades of Unc., plus 5 PL's and one DMPL of 1892-S, vs. one MS 62 PL of 1893-S. Each of these has traded in six figures; the MS 65's around $500,000. But because the population reports say 30 1892-S's as against 25 1893-S's (but how many of each were resubmissions!), the 1892-S's, by comparison, have brought about half as much as the 1893-S's. Wayne Miller thinks that not over 200 Uncs. exist. Uncs. are usually well struck and very brilliant, most often semi-PL.

Most fakes have had mintmark cemented to genuine 1892 Philadelphia dollars; these are detectable by the seam separating mintmark from field (use 20x glass or binocular microscope). Others were reportedly made by changing the second 8 to a 9 in an 1882-S; detectable in the same way.

Recommended in higher circulated grades or sliders if properly graded and priced. Beware of sliders offered as MS 60 or above.

Prooflikes: Rare in all grades; only one DMPL reported. Cameos are unlikely.

MINTAGE	PROOF	STRIKE	LUSTER	BAG MARKS	REDFIELD
1,200,000	0	Sharp & Bold	Very Good	Light To Moderate	No
DIES	**DIE VARIETIES**	**% OF PL**	**% OF DMPL**	**PIVOTAL GRADE**	**RARITY FACTOR**
33	7	15.6	3.1	MS 60	R-1

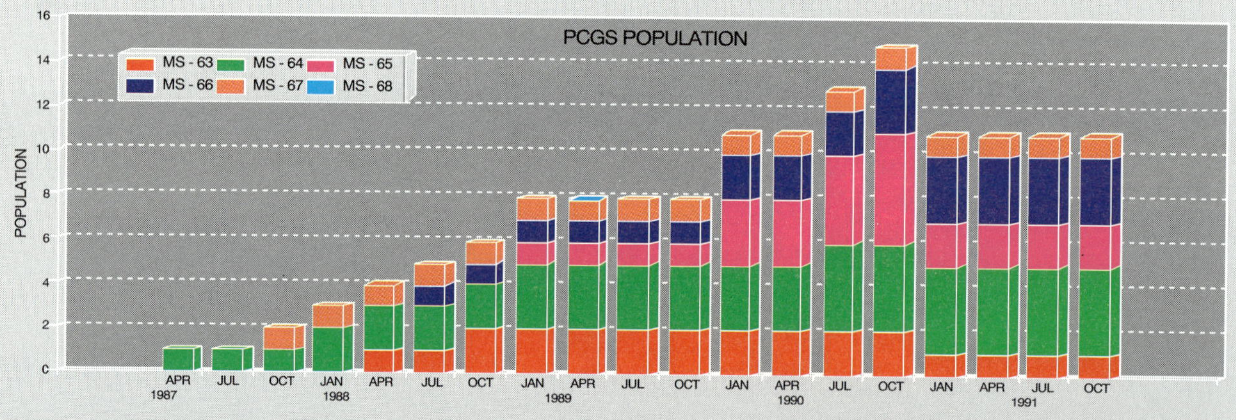

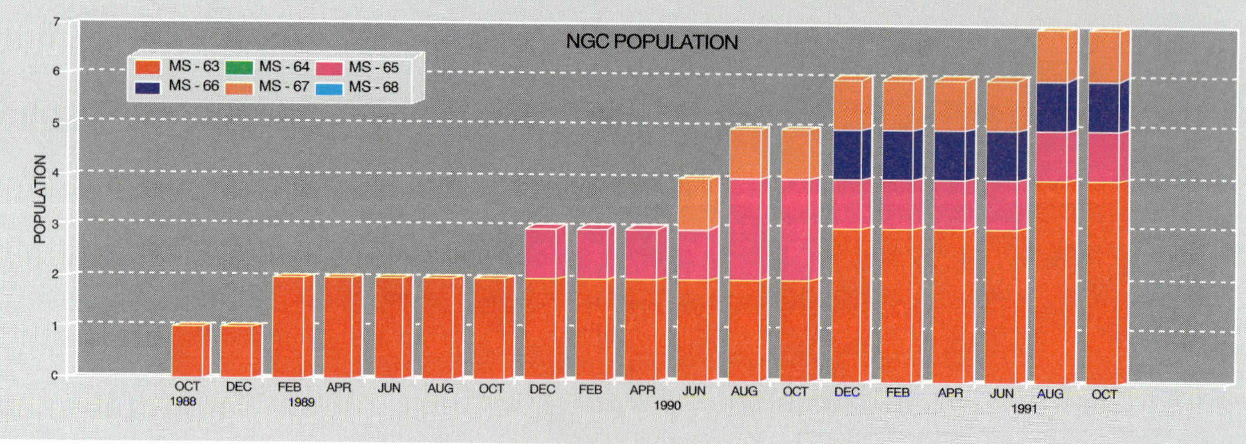

PCGS POPULATION

MS - 63 MS - 64 MS - 65 MS - 66 MS - 67 MS - 68

NGC POPULATION

MS - 63 MS - 64 MS - 65 MS - 66 MS - 67 MS - 68

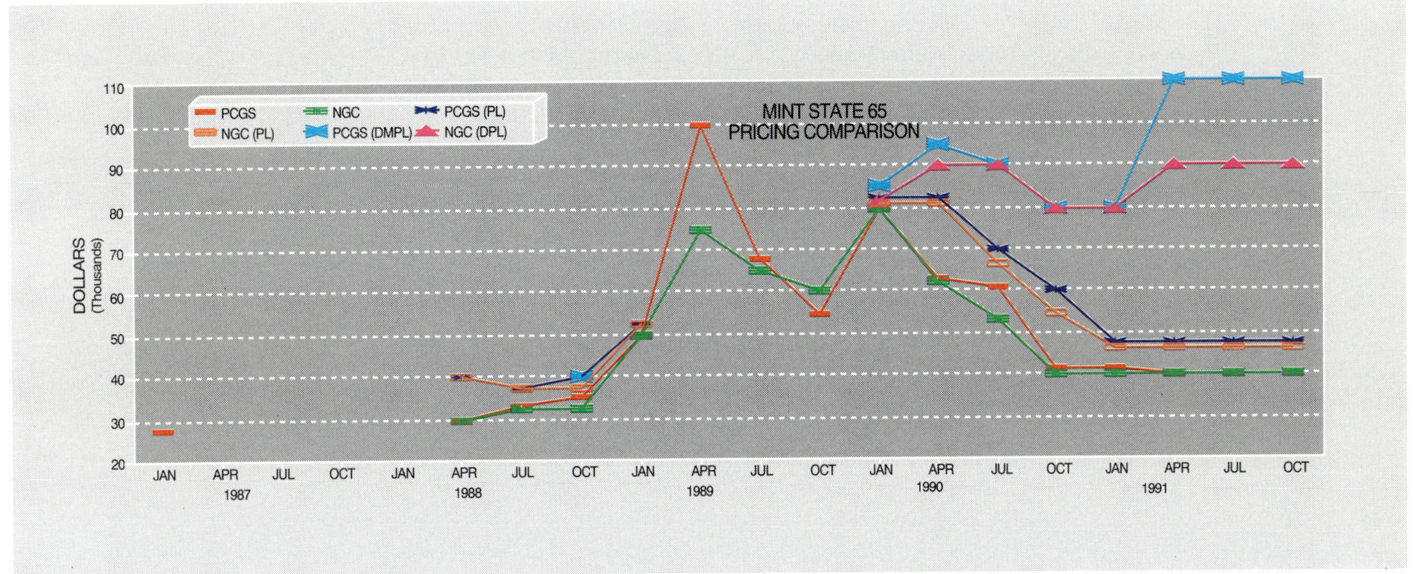
MINT STATE 65
PRICING COMPARISON
PCGS
NGC
PCGS (PL)
NGC (PL)
PCGS (DMPL)
NGC (DPL)
DOLLARS
(Thousands)
110
100
90
80
70
60
50
40
30
20
JAN
APR
JUL
OCT
1987
1988
1989
1990
1991

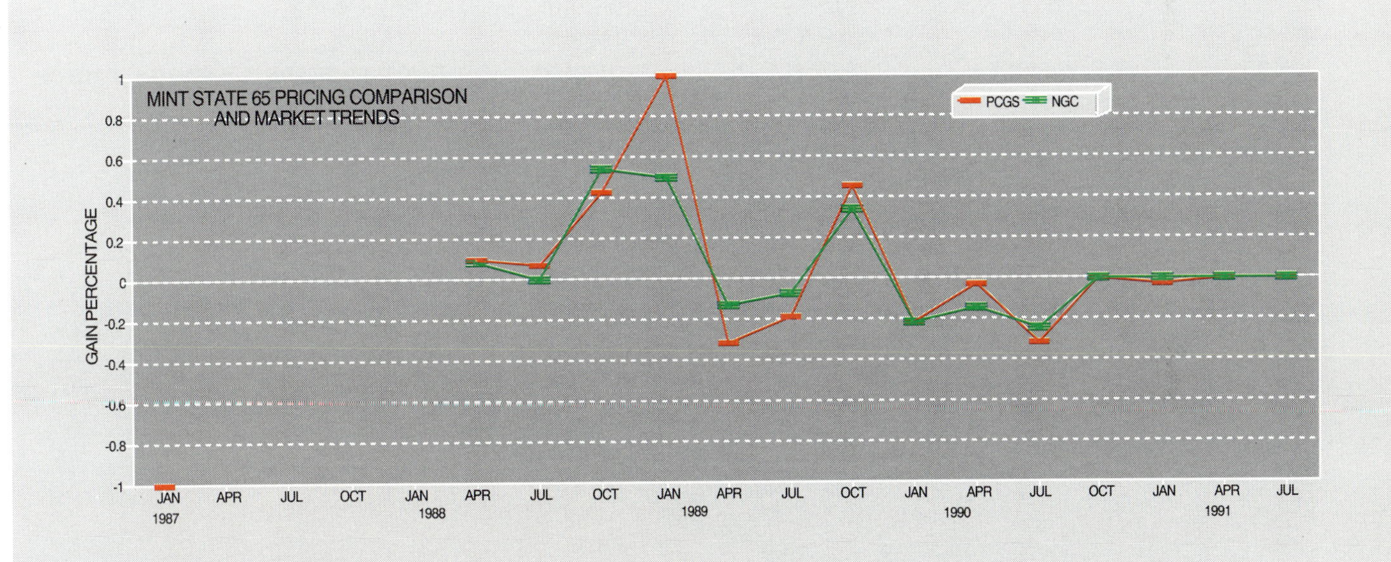
MINT STATE 65 PRICING COMPARISON
AND MARKET TRENDS
PCGS
NGC
GAIN PERCENTAGE
1
0.8
0.6
0.4
0.2
0
-0.2
-0.4
-0.6
-0.8
-1
JAN
APR
JUL
OCT
1987
1988
1989
1990
1991

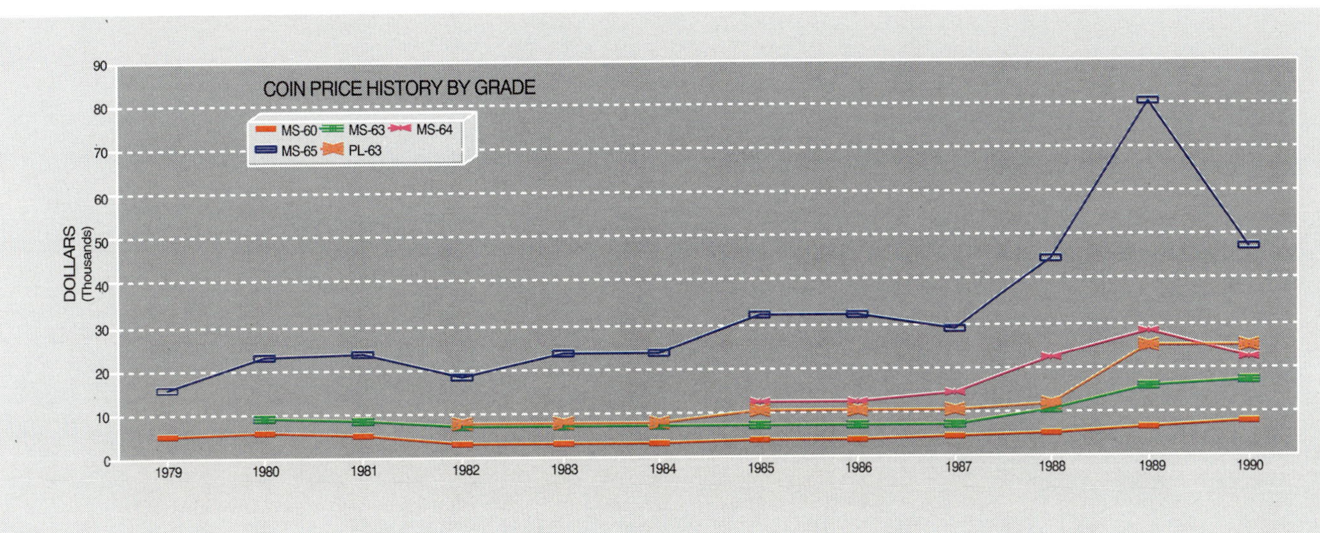
COIN PRICE HISTORY BY GRADE
MS-60
MS-63
MS-64
MS-65
PL-63
DOLLARS
(Thousands)
90
80
70
60
50
40
30
20
10
0
1979
1980
1981
1982
1983
1984
1985
1986
1987
1988
1989
1990

1893-P

Mintage 389,000, from 7 pairs of dies. Probably most were melted; circulated examples are seldom seen. Uncs. are mostly from Treasury bags about 1959, many dispersed by John J. Ford, Jr., another by John B. Love; bright, frosty, well struck. Third scarcest date in the Redfield hoard; this reportedly contained 2 to 3 bags, though LaVere Redfield supposedly sold another bag in the early 1970's. The only rarer Unc. Philadelphia Morgans are 1894 and 1901.

Recommended in any grade of Unc., preferably MS 63 up. BU rolls unlikely.

Proofs: Mintage 792. These have plain horizontal die file marks between back of neck and wing.

Prooflikes: Extremely rare; no DMPL's. Beware semi-PL's offered as full PL's.

MINTAGE	PROOF	STRIKE	LUSTER	BAG MARKS	REDFIELD
389,00	792	Average To Bold	Very Good	Light	Yes
DIES	**DIE VARIETIES**	**% OF PL**	**% OF DMPL**	**PIVOTAL GRADE**	**RARITY FACTOR**
16	5	0.1	0.1	MS 65	R-1

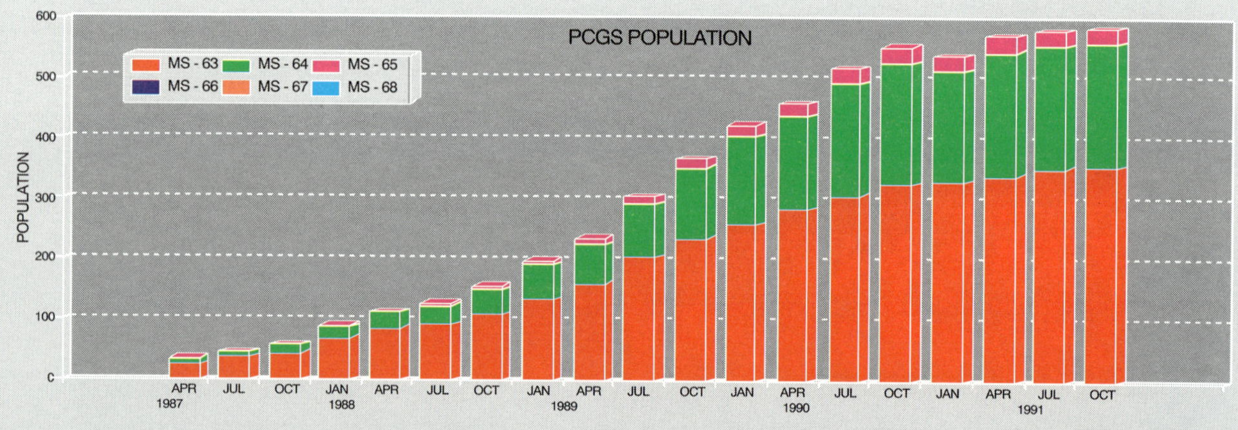

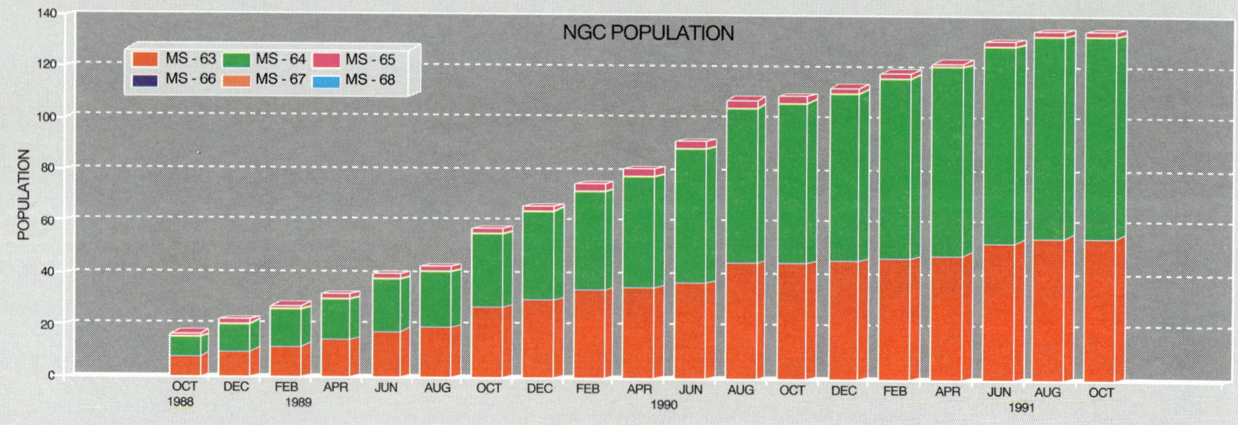

PCGS POPULATION

NGC POPULATION

1893-P

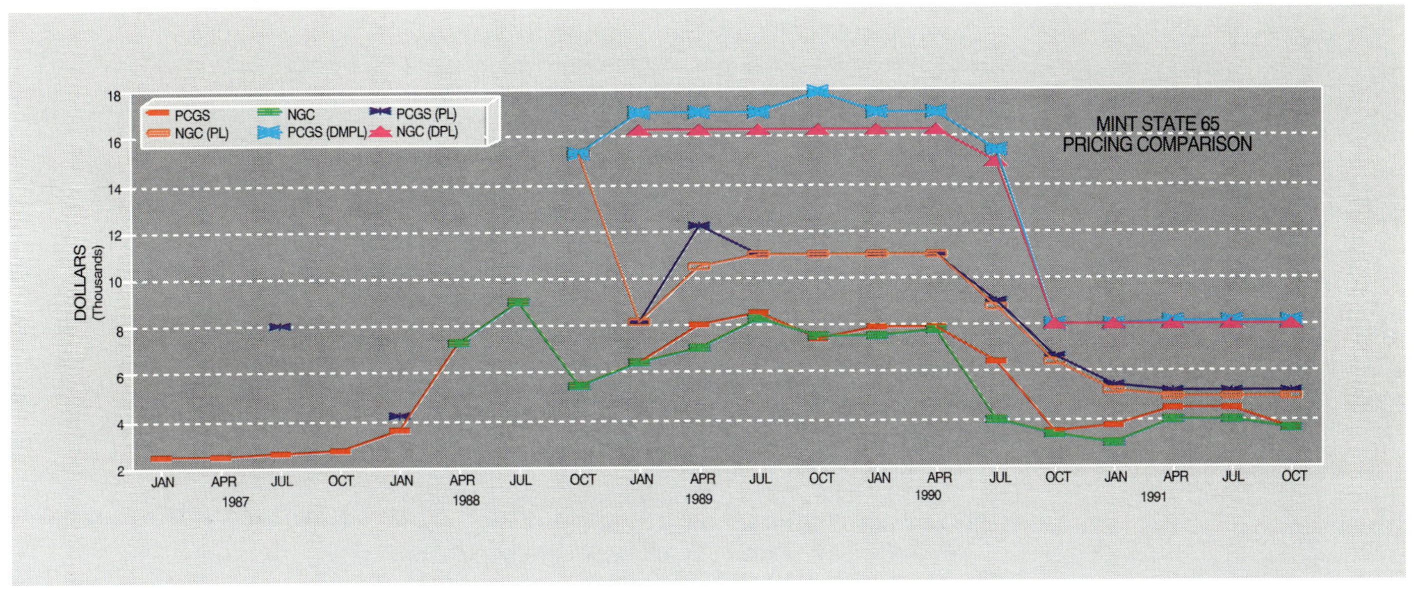

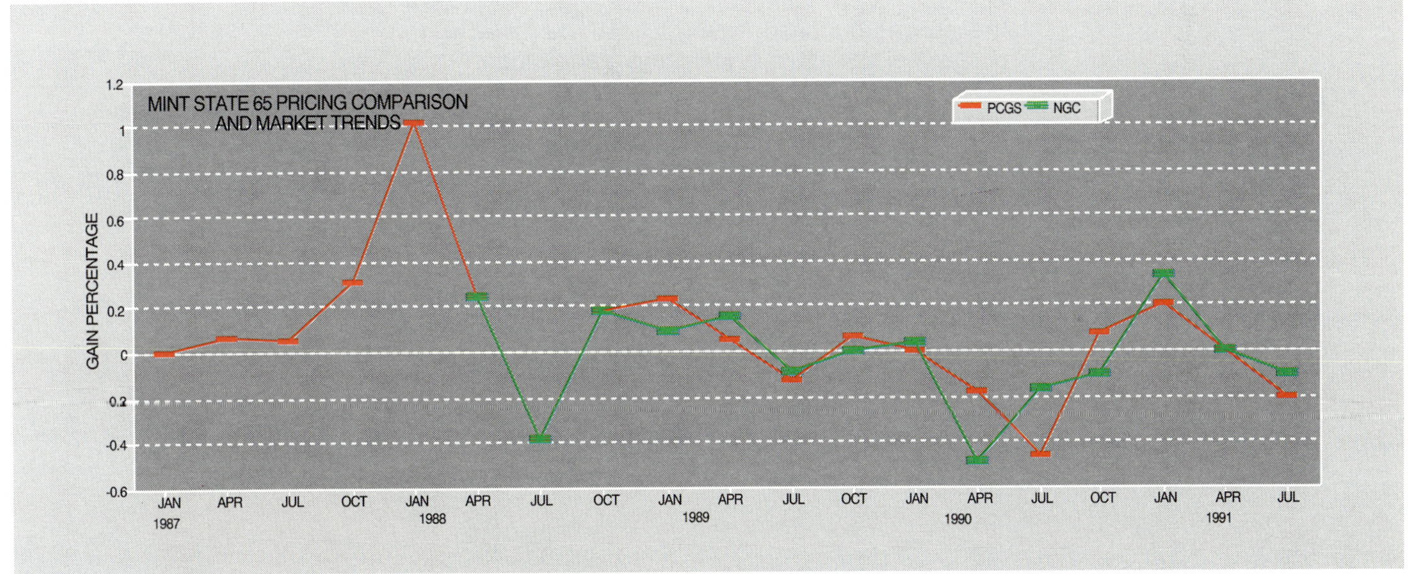

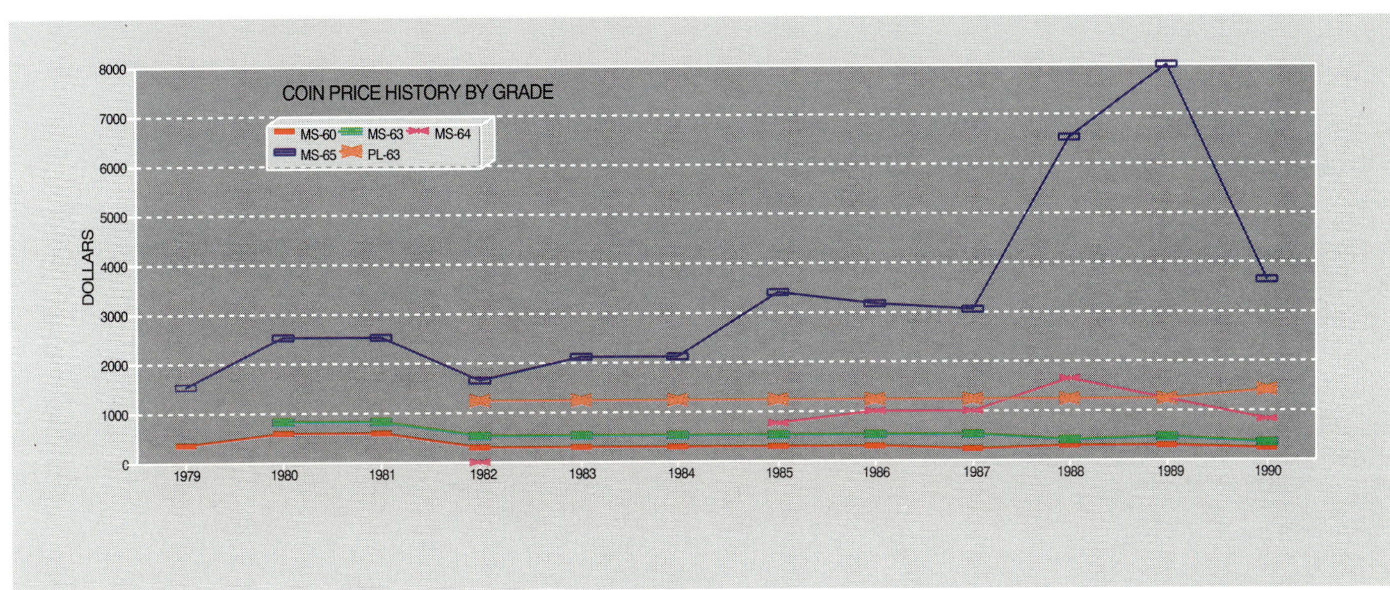

1893-CC

PCGS
1893-CC
S$1
MS65
7222.65/6271768

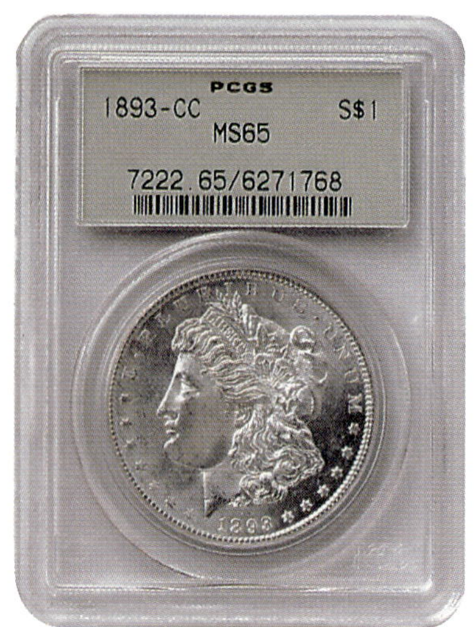

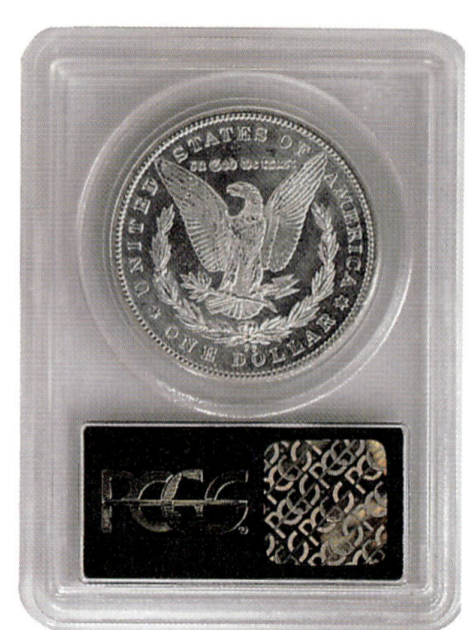

Mintage 677,000. Some of the Redfield hoard dollars were well struck and bagmarked; many were low quality PL's (below); others were flat strikes. Many Redfield pieces were scratched on cheek and eagle's breast, apparently from a coin counting machine. Paramount handled most of the Redfield 1893-CC's (reportedly less than 2 bags). Many Uncs. are flat strikes; some have no wing feather details, only mint lustre. Clashed dies also a problem for this date. The GSA mail bid sales contained only one 1893-CC, in the "mixed lot" group to date this has not surfaced in the original holder. Many worn examples are around. The Carson City Mint usually had the best dollars struck throughout its history, but in its final year put out one of the worst Morgans.

Recommended in MS 63 up.

Several fakes have turned up; these are genuine 1893 Philadelphia dollars with CC added.

Proofs: 12 struck for closing ceremonies in 1893. Norweb's brought $20,900.

Prooflikes: Rare above MS 63 or in any grade of DMPL. Many cameo PL's in MS 60/62 came from the Redfield hoard. Not to be confused with occasional semi-PL's in the same grade range.

MINTAGE	PROOF	STRIKE	LUSTER	BAG MARKS	REDFIELD
676,988	12*	Soft & Weak	Very Good	Moderate To Heavy	Yes
DIES	**DIE VARIETIES**	**% OF PL**	**% OF DMPL**	**PIVOTAL GRADE**	**RARITY FACTOR**
20	5	10.6	1.1	MS 64	R-1

*Estimate by the authors

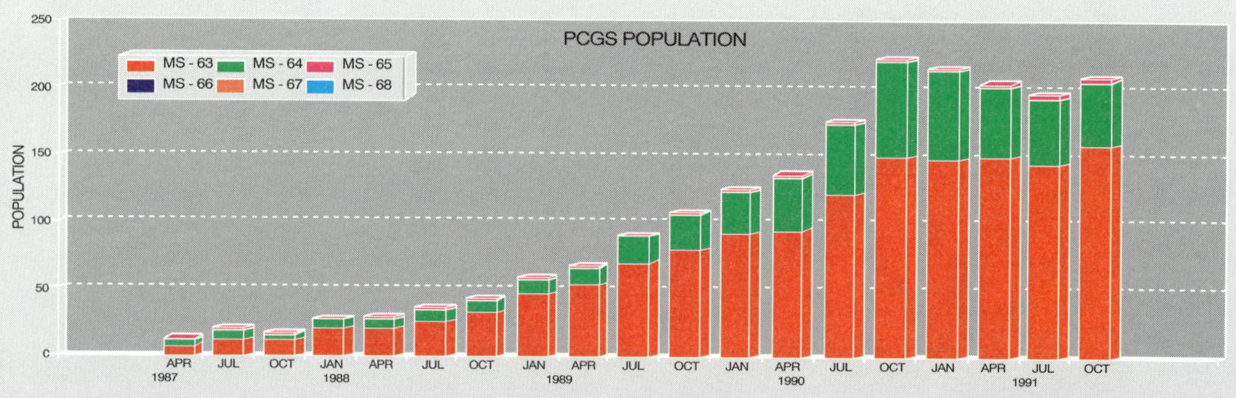
PCGS POPULATION
MS - 63
MS - 64
MS - 65
MS - 66
MS - 67
MS - 68
POPULATION
250
200
150
100
50
0
APR 1987
JUL
OCT
JAN 1988
APR
JUL
OCT
JAN 1989
APR
JUL
OCT
JAN
APR 1990
JUL
OCT
JAN
APR 1991
JUL
OCT

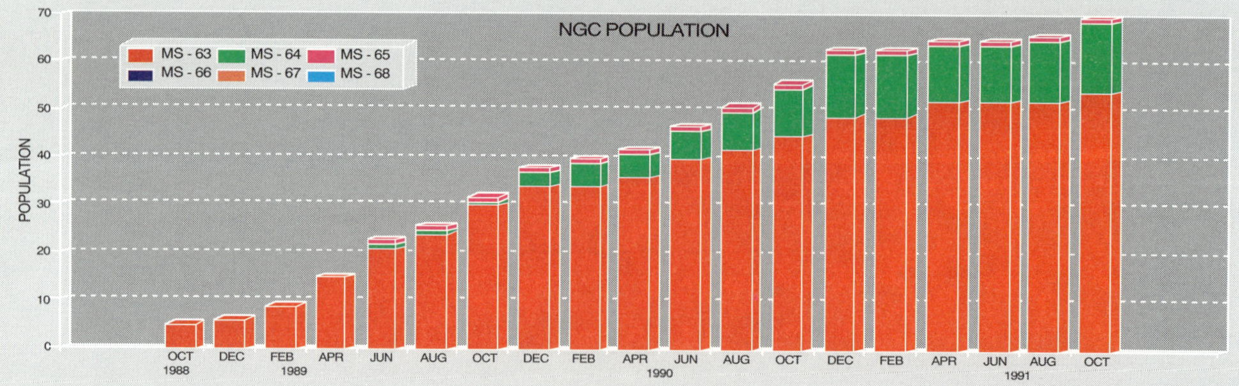
NGC POPULATION
MS - 63
MS - 64
MS - 65
MS - 66
MS - 67
MS - 68
POPULATION
70
60
50
40
30
20
10
0
OCT 1988
DEC
FEB 1989
APR
JUN
AUG
OCT
DEC
FEB
APR 1990
JUN
AUG
OCT
DEC
FEB
APR
JUN 1991
AUG
OCT

1893-CC

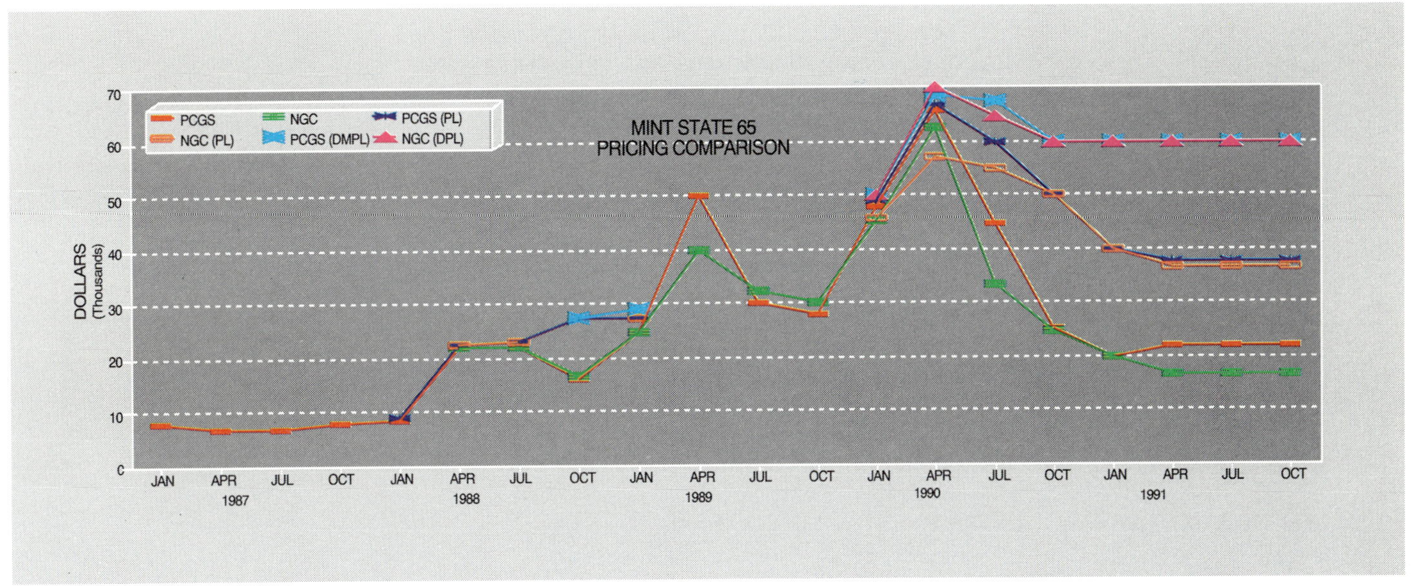

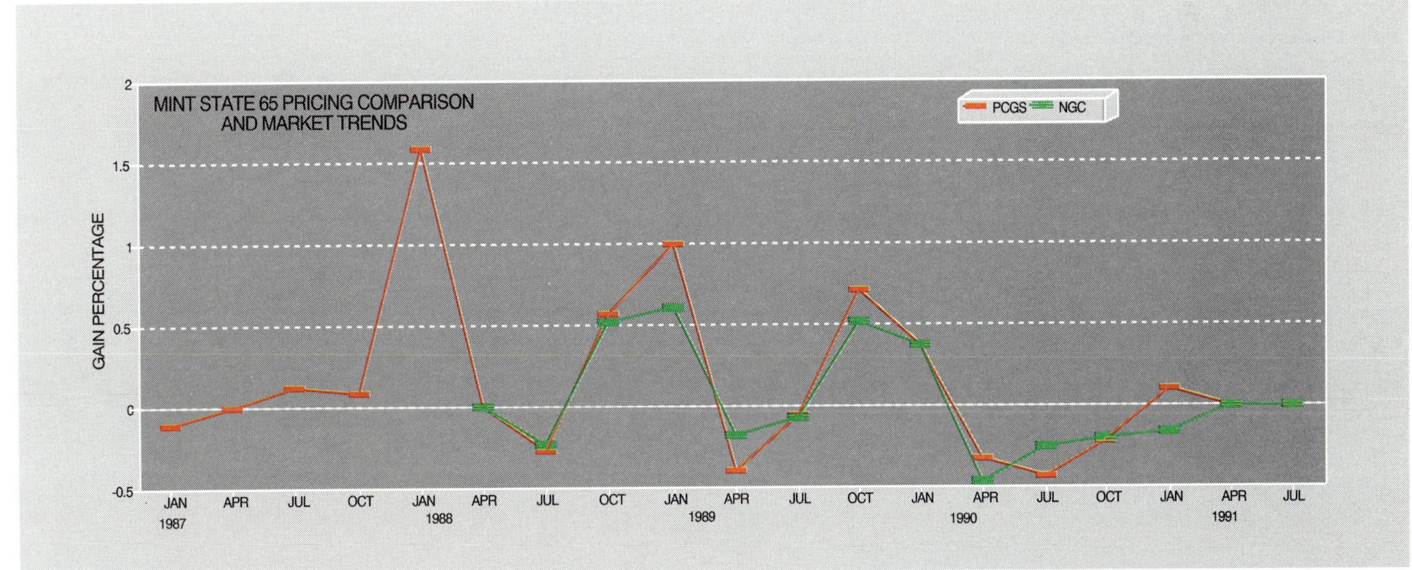

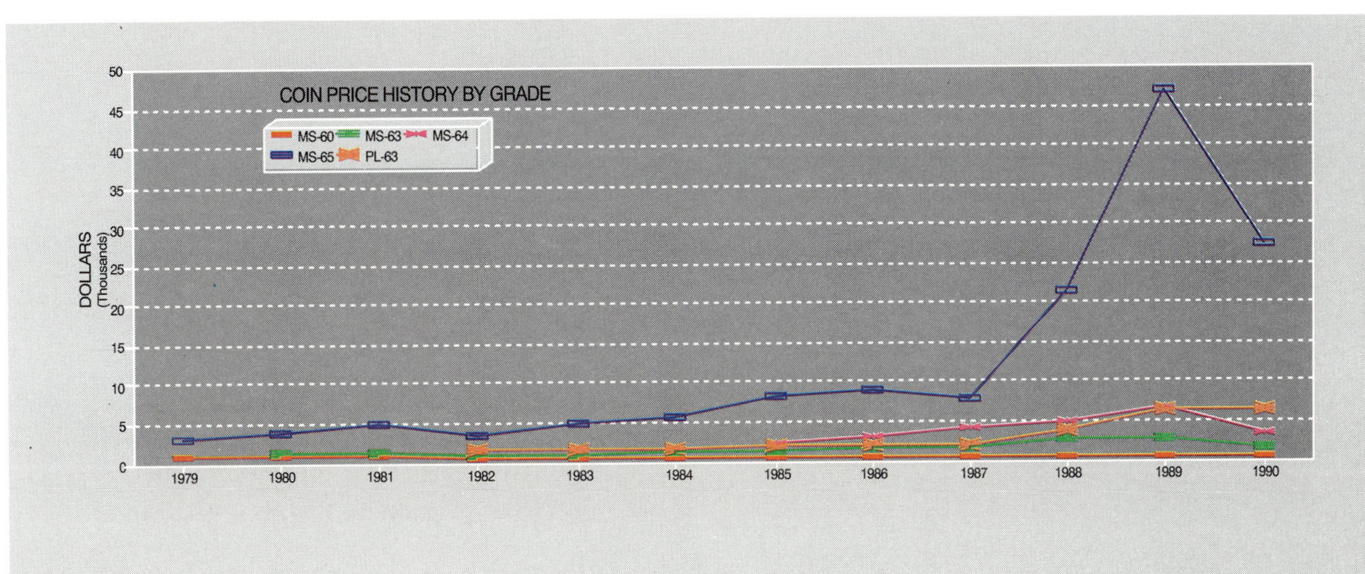

1893-O

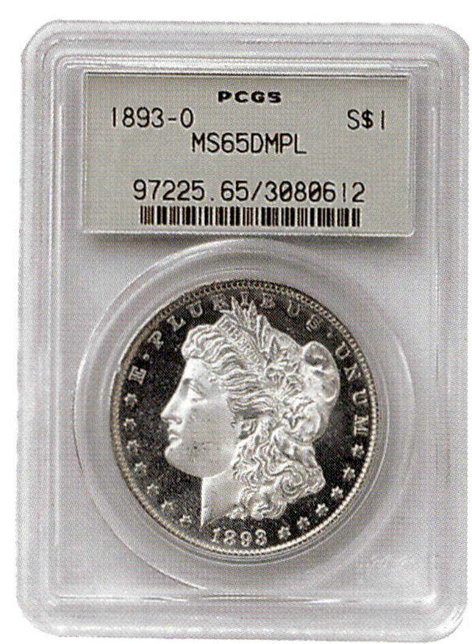

Mintage 300,000, the lowest Morgan issue from this mint. From 10 obv. dies and left over reverses. Uncs. are mostly low quality, weak in centers and bagmarked; except for a single DMPL (below). The finest one is probably the Amon Carter Jr. coin, which brought $14,300. This author (Highfill) sold the only PCGS MS 65 for $157,500 in the spring of 1991 to Elliot S. Goldman, Tucson, Arizona.

No BU rolls are reported.

Recommended in MS 60 up.

Prooflikes: Rare in all grades. The single PCGS MS 65 DMPL traded above $275,000 in a dealer-to-dealer wholesale transaction, 1990 San Diego Midwinter ANA. This was probably the Leo A. Young coin from Auction '80 at $57,500, Auction '87 at $71,500.

MINTAGE	PROOF	STRIKE	LUSTER	BAG MARKS	REDFIELD
300,000	0	Soft & Weak	Average	Moderate To Heavy	No
DIES	**DIE VARIETIES**	**% OF PL**	**% OF DMPL**	**PIVOTAL GRADE**	**RARITY FACTOR**
20	5	6.1	2.9	MS 64	R-1

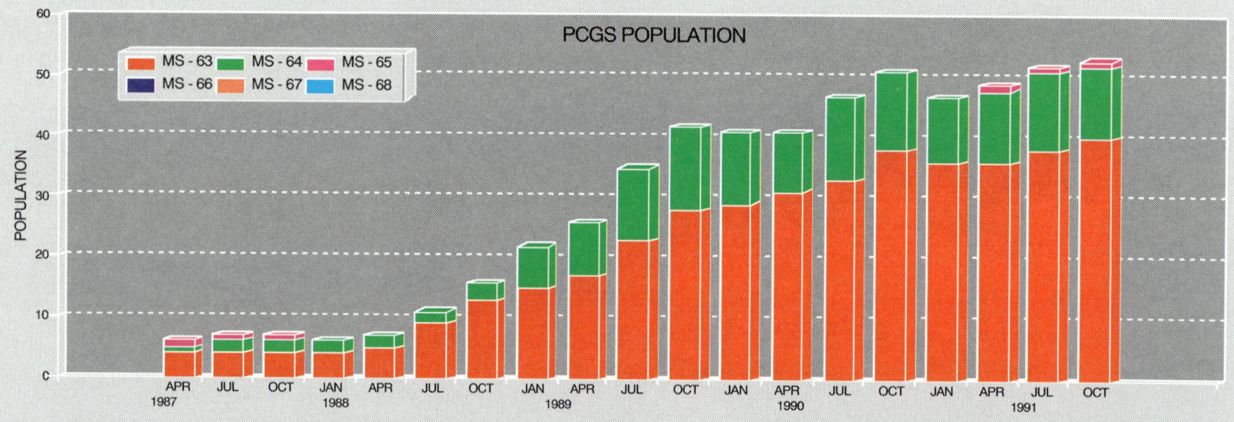

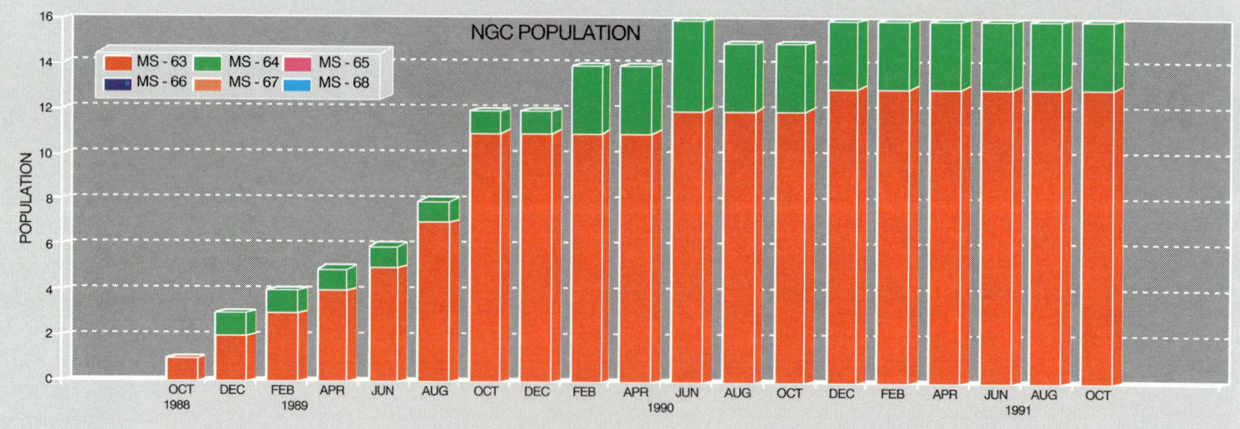

PCGS POPULATION

NGC POPULATION

1893-O

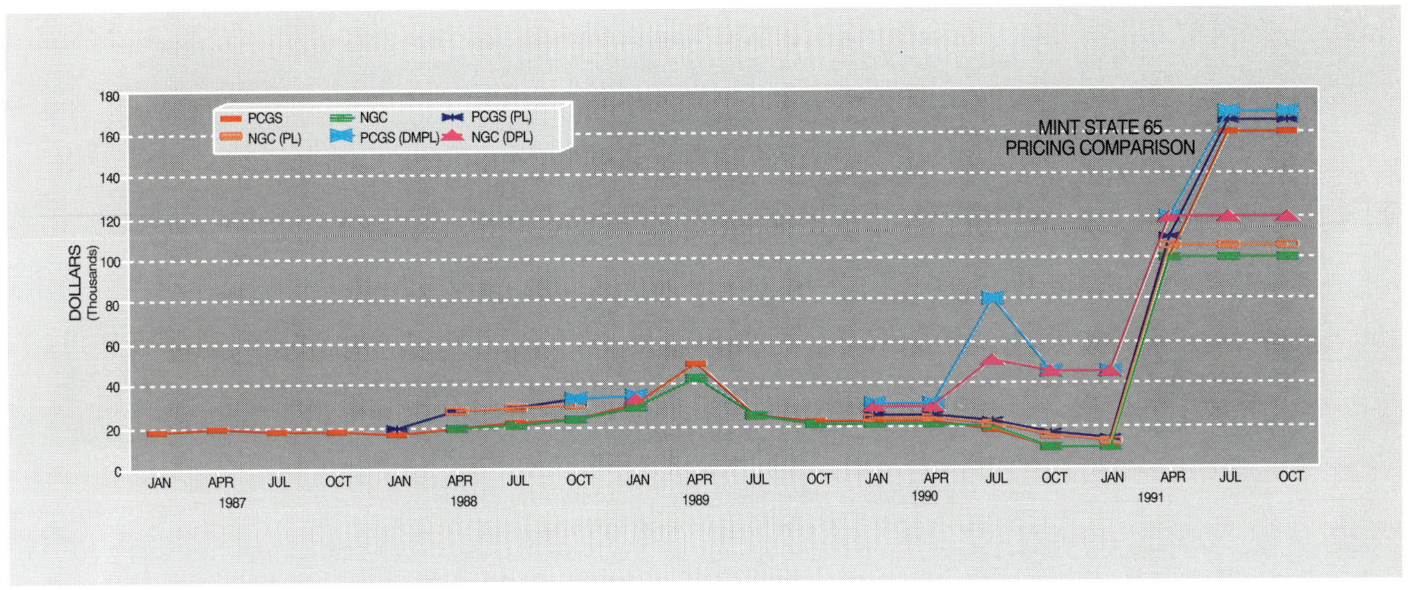

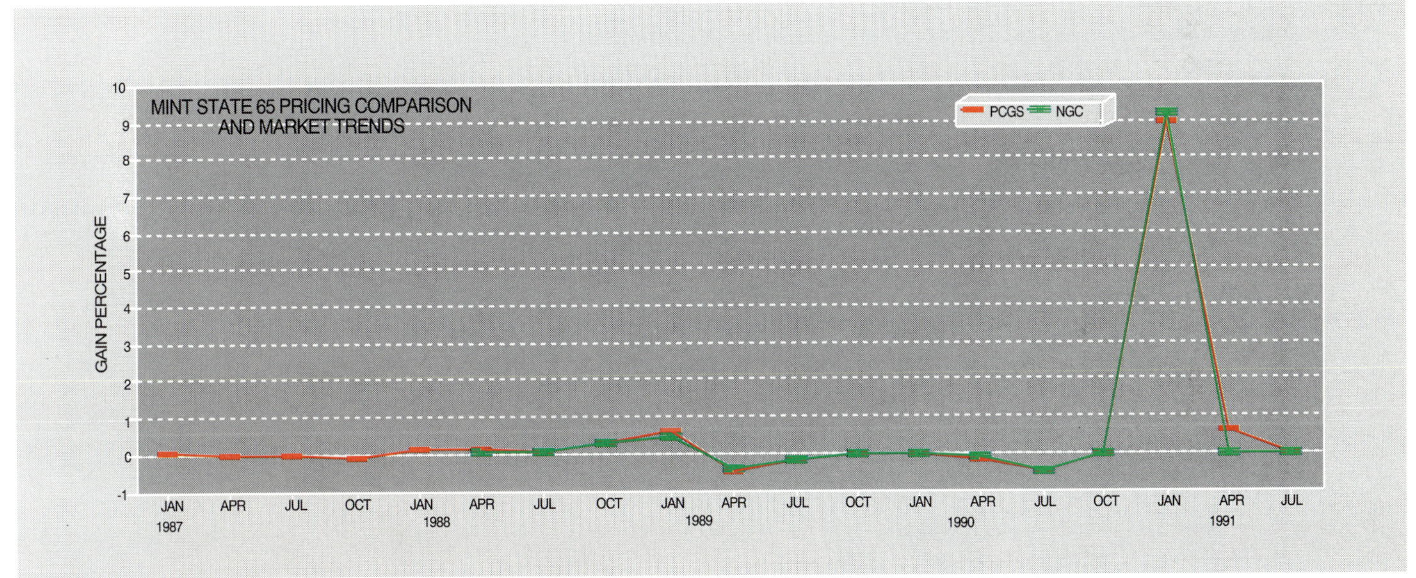

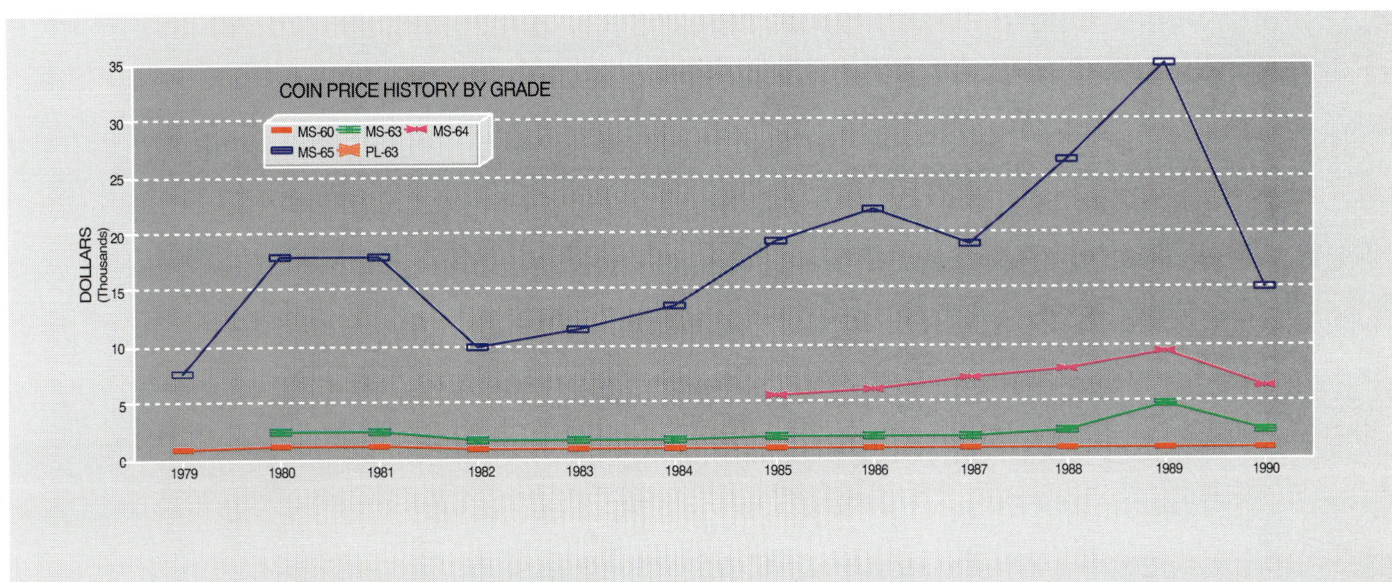

1893-S

The mintage of 100,000 apparently came from a single pair of dies. It was realeased into circulation early after production. Generally accepted as the rarest date-mintmark combination aside from the proof 1895; but see 1892-S prior. Uncs. are mostly boldly struck, with brilliant lustre and moderate bagmarks. Some are from the 20 found in a bag of 1894-S's in Great Falls, Montana, about 1952. The best one may be the Wayne Miller, Barbara Goldfreed, Auction '87 coin, which brought $41,250 in Auction '87. Its competitors include the Leo A. Young coin in Auction '80 at $48,000, and the Jerome Kern, Amon Carter coin at $57,750. Three PCGS MS 65 1893-S Morgans have all sold in the lower to mid 6 digit range.

Recommended in the highest grade you can find, but have the coin authenticated first.

Most fakes were made by attaching mintmark to genuine 1893 Philadelphia dollars—even in very worn grades. Others are genuine 1898-S dollars with final 8 altered to 3. (They may also exist altered from 1883-S) Look for seam (often with local discoloration) at junction of mintmark or 3 with field. None of these will show the raised line in T of LIBERTY found on all genuine specimens examined to date; this goes up from upper left edge of upright of T through crossbar. (See Counterfeit Chapter 20 by John W. Highfill)

Prooflikes: One PCGS MS 62 PL; no others available for comparison.

MINTAGE	PROOF	STRIKE	LUSTER	BAG MARKS	REDFIELD
100,000	0	Sharp & Bold	Excellent	Light	No
DIES	**DIE VARIETIES**	**% OF PL**	**% OF DMPL**	**PIVOTAL GRADE**	**RARITY FACTOR**
30	1	4.0	0.0	MS 60	R-1

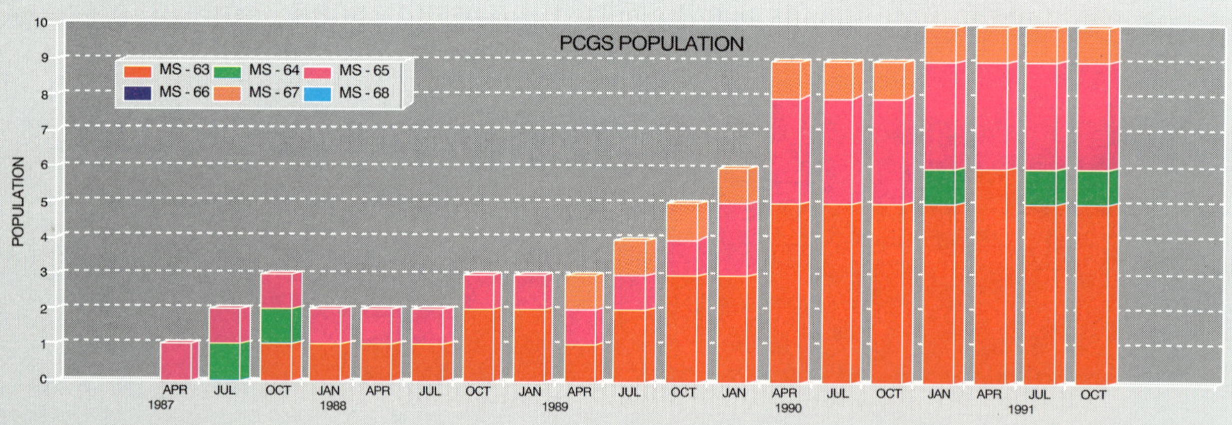

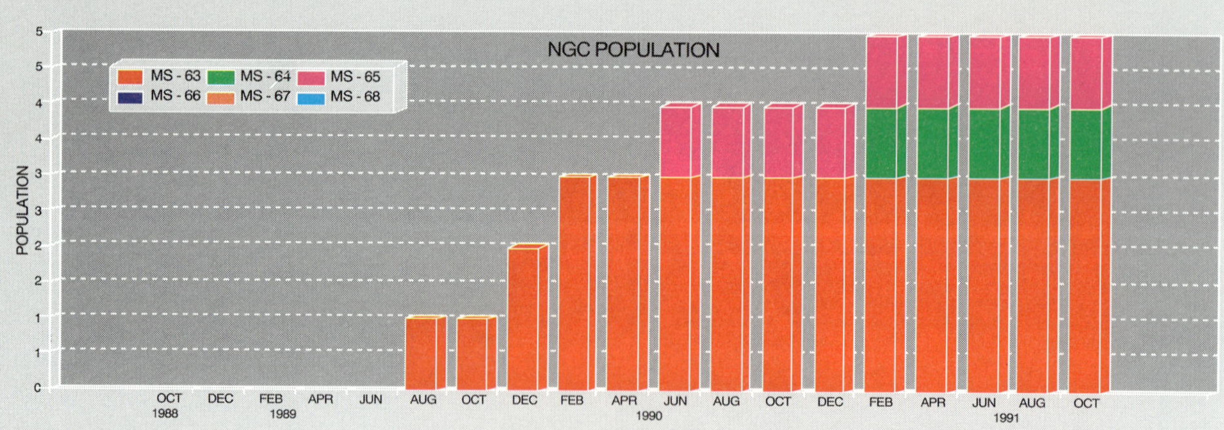

PCGS POPULATION

NGC POPULATION

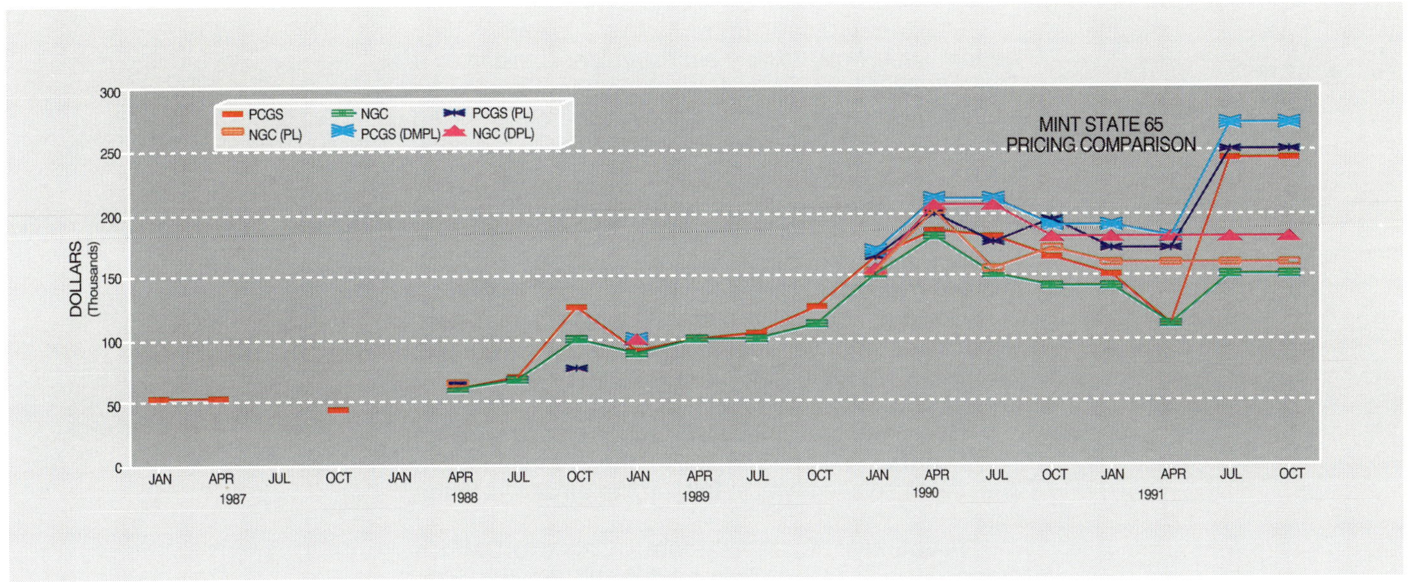
PCGS
NGC
PCGS (PL)
NGC (PL)
PCGS (DMPL)
NGC (DPL)
MINT STATE 65
PRICING COMPARISON
DOLLARS
(Thousands)
300
250
200
150
100
50
0
JAN
APR
JUL
OCT
1987
1988
1989
1990
1991

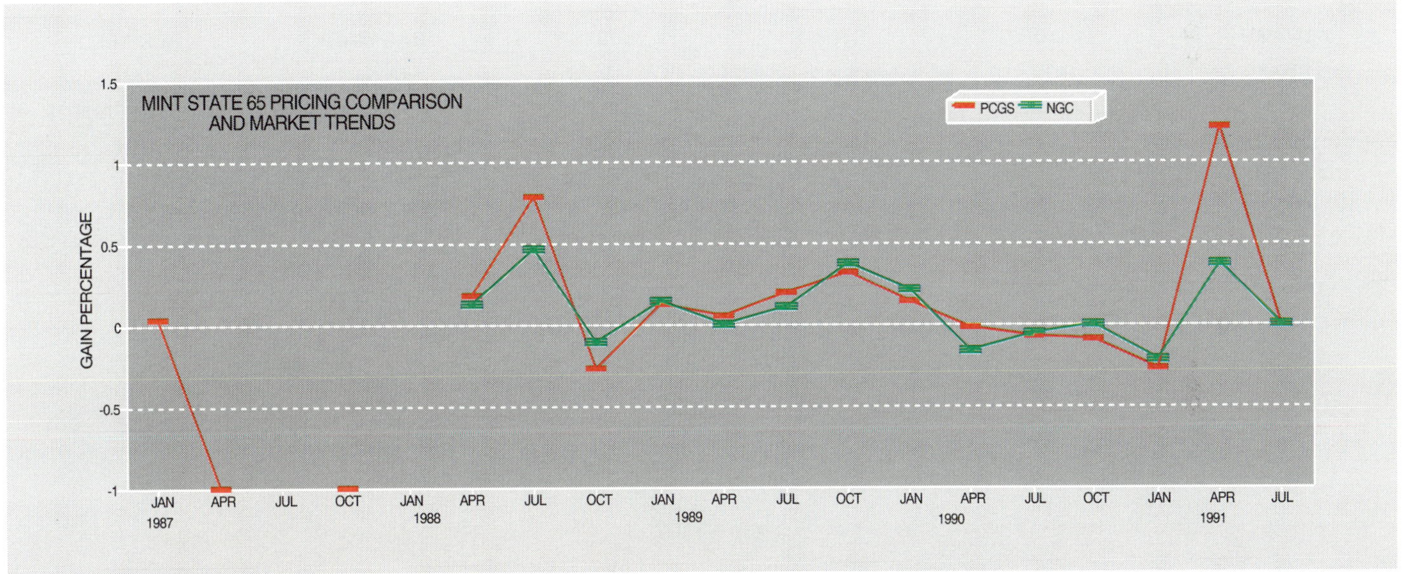
MINT STATE 65 PRICING COMPARISON
AND MARKET TRENDS
PCGS
NGC
GAIN PERCENTAGE
1.5
1
0.5
0
-0.5
-1
JAN
APR
JUL
OCT
1987
1988
1989
1990
1991

COIN PRICE HISTORY BY GRADE
MS-60
MS-63
MS-64
MS-65
PL-63
DOLLARS
(Thousands)
160
140
120
100
80
60
40
20
0
1979
1980
1981
1982
1983
1984
1985
1986
1987
1988
1989
1990

1894-P

PCGS
1894
S$1
MS65
7228.65/2241686

PCGS

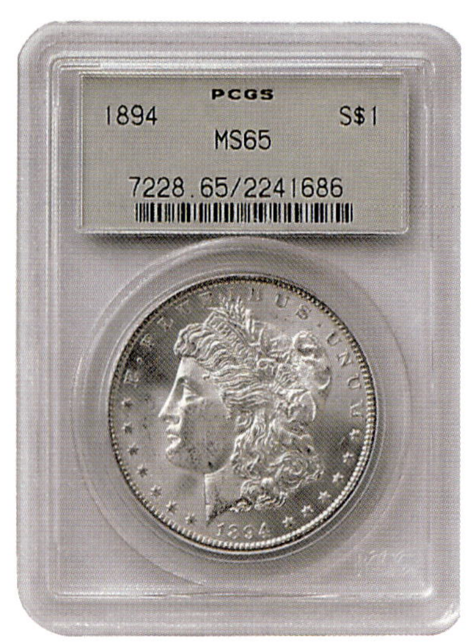

Mintage 110,000, from 7 obvs., 5 revs. Very seldom seen worn. Many surviving Uncs. are from a Treasury bag from Great Falls, Montana, handled by John B. Love about 1961. Others are from a mixed bag (1893, 1894) found in San Francisco in the early 1960's. Average to bold strikes, good lustre. Most likely the rest were melted long ago. The Bland-Allison Act was replaced by the Sherman Silver Purchase Act of 1890 (this resulted in very low mintages 1891-95).

Beware of 1894-O or 1894-S with mintmark removed, or with altered date (either 9 or 4). All these will show some abnormality of surface or color in the area.

Recommended in any BU grade. Happy hunting!

Proofs: Two pairs of dies for the 972 minted. On one, date is placed well to left, on the other it is to the right.

Prooflikes: Extremely rare. Only two DMPL's reported, one of them illustrated in the Wayne Miller Textbook.

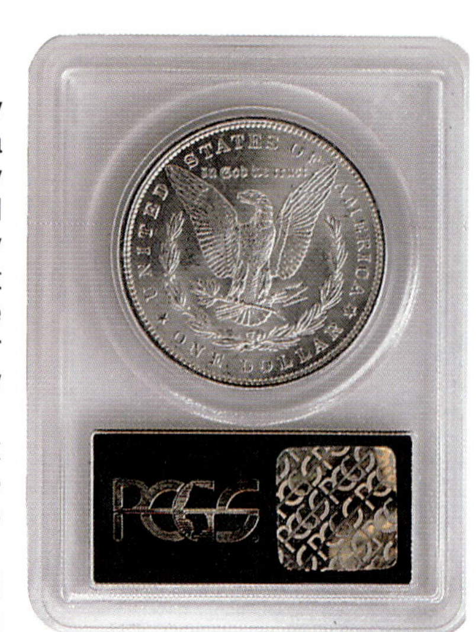

MINTAGE	PROOF	STRIKE	LUSTER	BAG MARKS	REDFIELD
110,000	972	Average to Bold	Good	Moderate	No
DIES	**DIE VARIETIES**	**% OF PL**	**% OF DMPL**	**PIVOTAL GRADE**	**RARITY FACTOR**
Not Available	2	0.6	0.3	MS 65	R-1

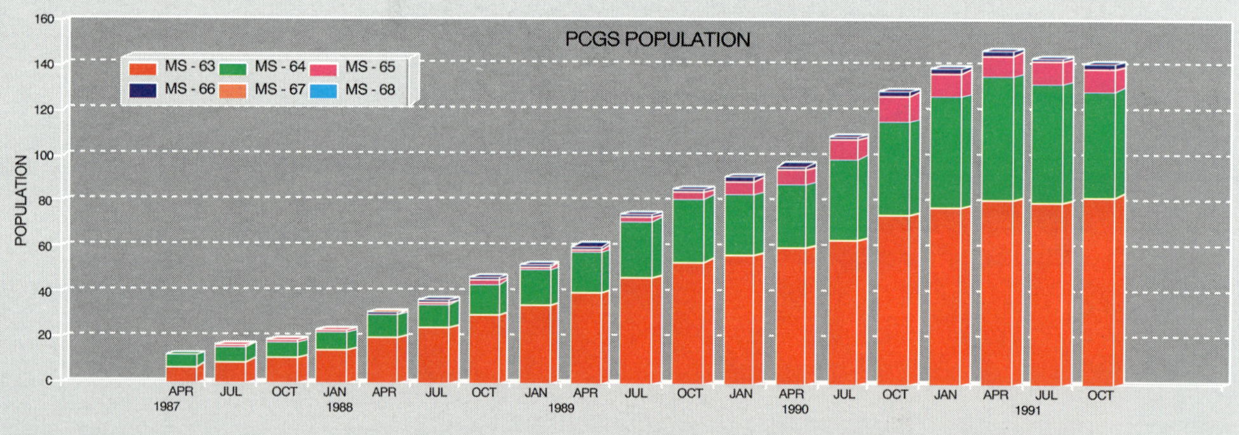

PCGS POPULATION
MS - 63
MS - 64
MS - 65
MS - 66
MS - 67
MS - 68
POPULATION
160
140
120
100
80
60
40
20
C
APR 1987
JUL
OCT
JAN 1988
APR
JUL
OCT
JAN 1989
APR
JUL
OCT
JAN
APR 1990
JUL
OCT
JAN
APR
JUL 1991
OCT

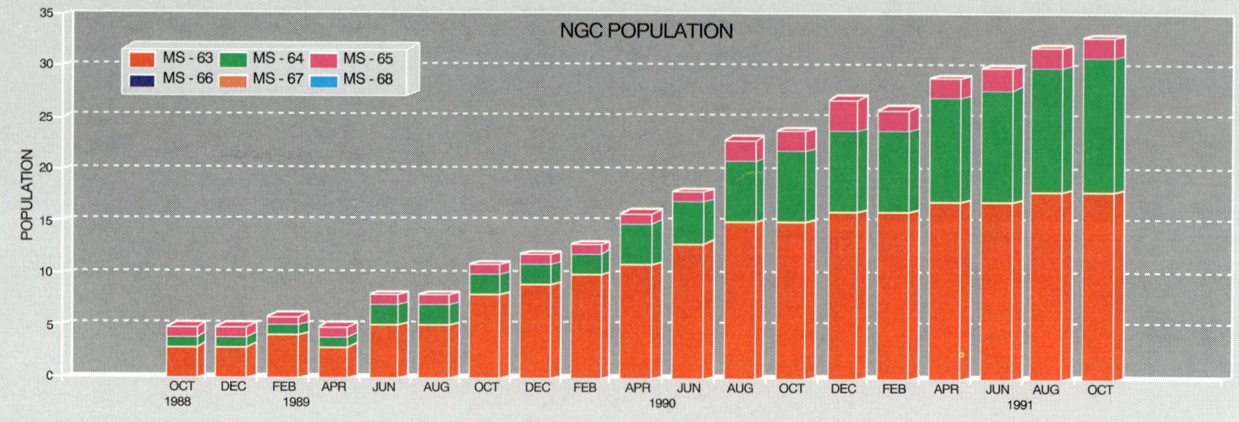

NGC POPULATION
MS - 63
MS - 64
MS - 65
MS - 66
MS - 67
MS - 68
POPULATION
35
30
25
20
15
10
5
C
OCT 1988
DEC
FEB 1989
APR
JUN
AUG
OCT
DEC
FEB
APR 1990
JUN
AUG
OCT
DEC
FEB
APR
JUN 1991
AUG
OCT

1894-P

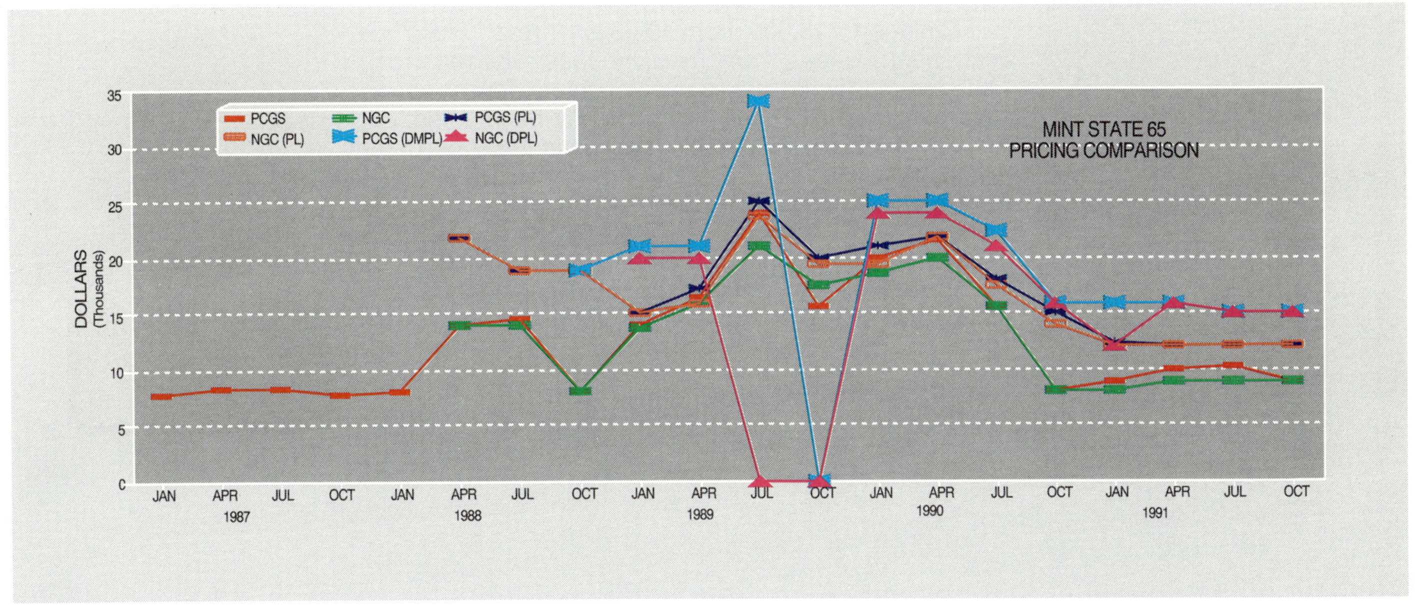

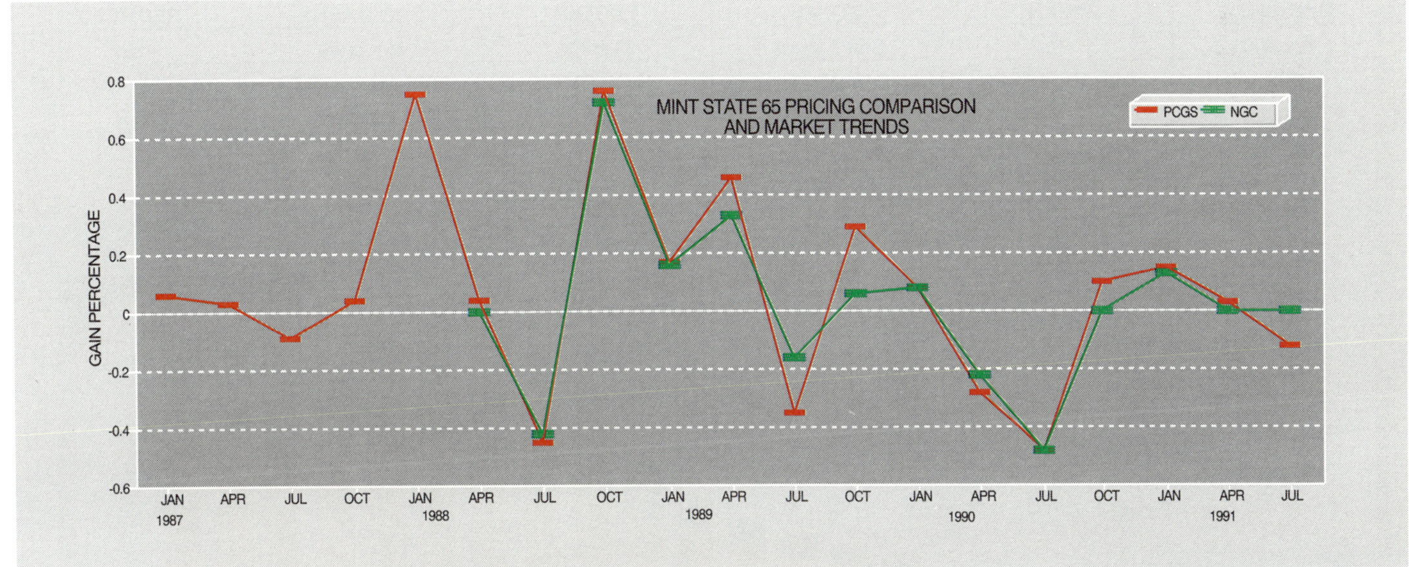

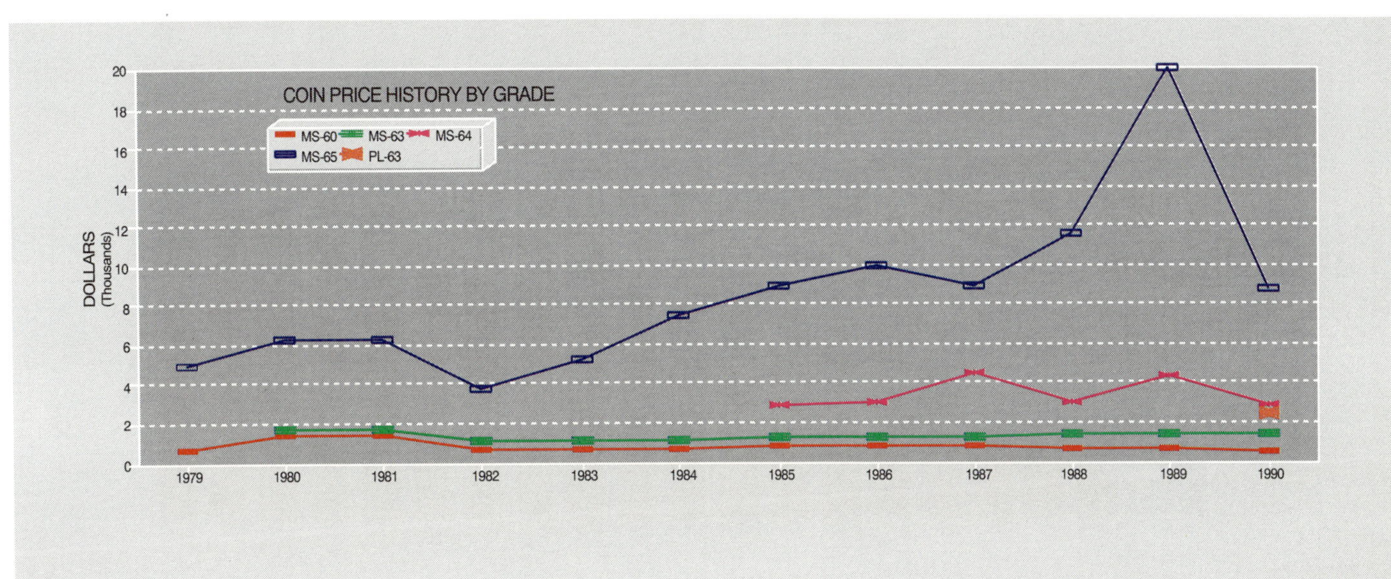

1894-O

Mintage 1,723,000, from 10 obvs., 7 revs. Many were spent. Uncs.., from Treasury bags released in 1963, are mostly flat strikes (weak centers, few or no wing feather details), dull lustre, heavily bagmarked; rare above MS 64. Honorable mention in the contest for the "Pancake" title. None in the Redfield hoard. Worn specimens occur in all grades. Counterfeits are unknown.

Recommended in all BU grades; beware sliders.

Prooflikes: So rare that specifics cannot be had about depth of field or frequency of DMPL's, if any.

MINTAGE	PROOF	STRIKE	LUSTER	BAG MARKS	REDFIELD
1,723,000	0	Soft & Weak	Average	Moderate	No
DIES	**DIE VARIETIES**	**% OF PL**	**% OF DMPL**	**PIVOTAL GRADE**	**RARITY FACTOR**
20	8	0.3	1.0	MS 64	R-1

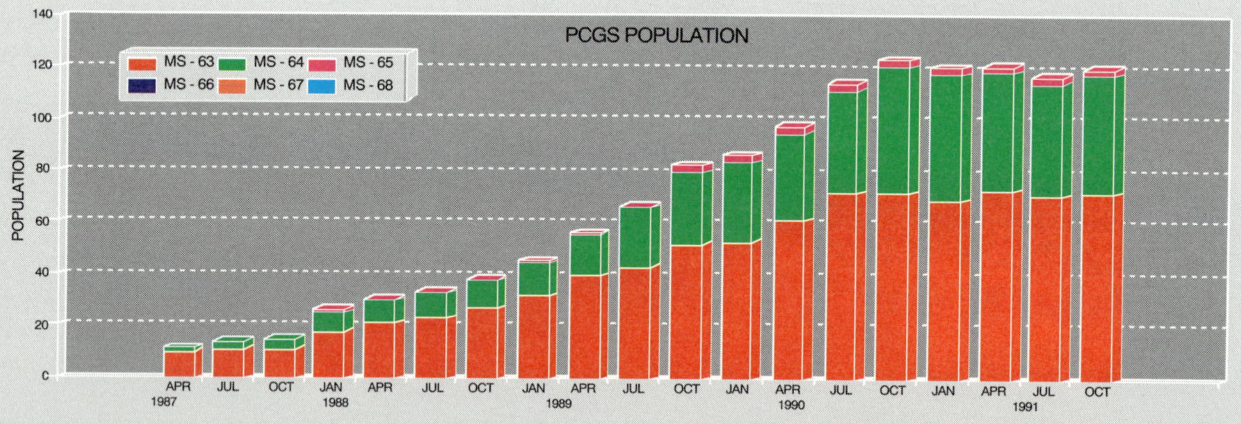

PCGS POPULATION

MS - 63 MS - 64 MS - 65 MS - 66 MS - 67 MS - 68

POPULATION

0 20 40 60 80 100 120 140

APR 1987 JUL OCT JAN 1988 APR JUL OCT JAN 1989 APR JUL OCT JAN APR 1990 JUL OCT JAN APR JUL 1991 OCT

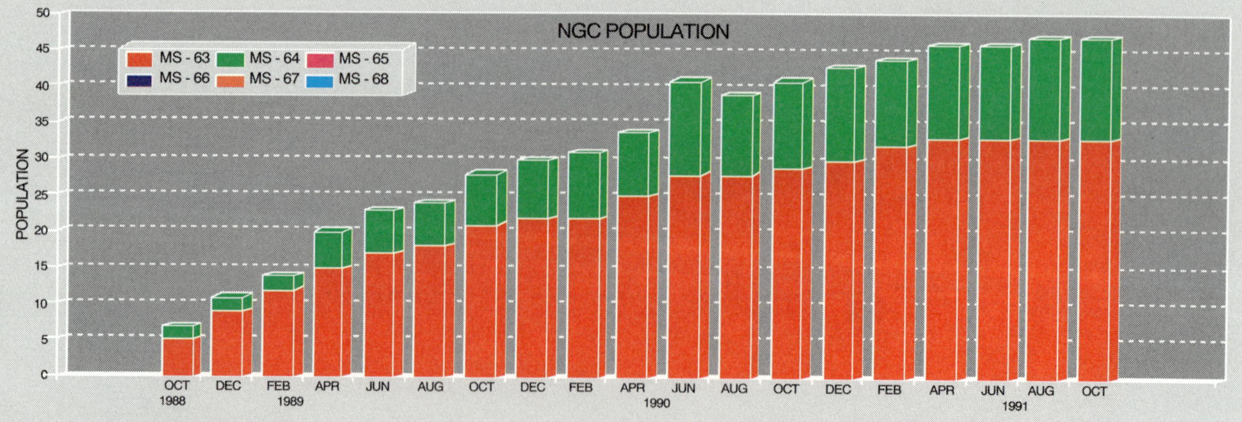

NGC POPULATION

MS - 63 MS - 64 MS - 65 MS - 66 MS - 67 MS - 68

POPULATION

0 5 10 15 20 25 30 35 40 45 50

OCT 1988 DEC FEB 1989 APR JUN AUG OCT DEC FEB APR 1990 JUN AUG OCT DEC FEB APR JUN 1991 AUG OCT

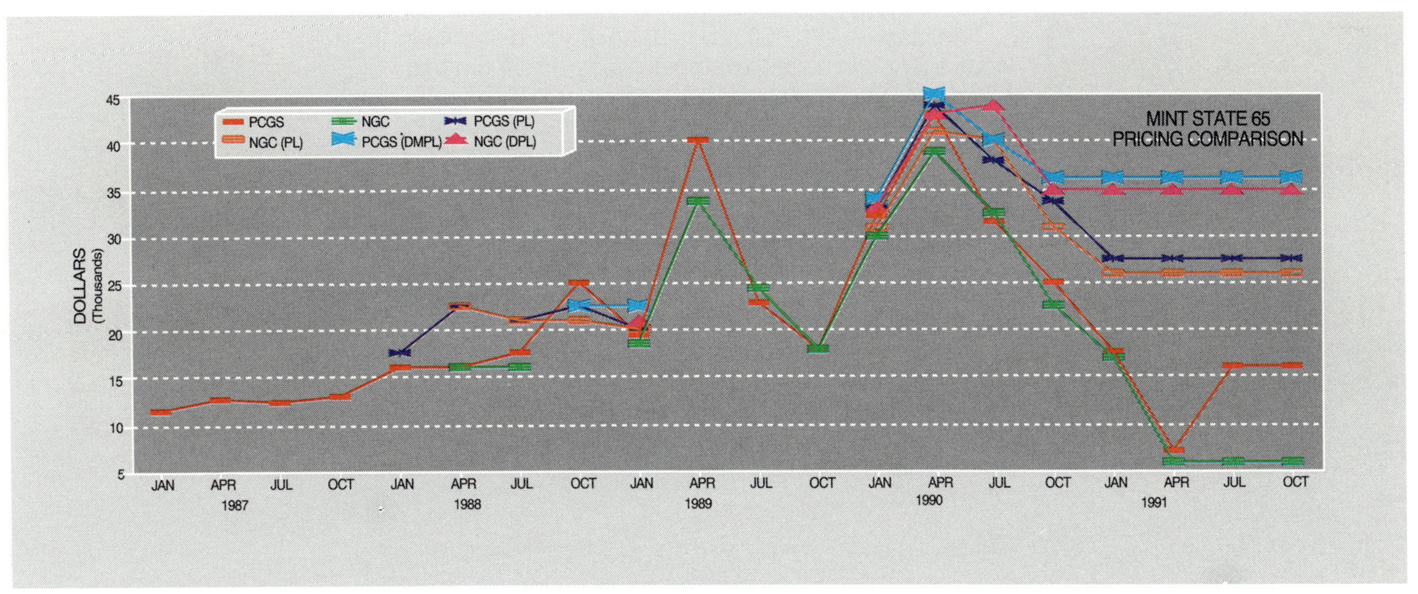
MINT STATE 65
PRICING COMPARISON
PCGS
NGC
PCGS (PL)
NGC (PL)
PCGS (DMPL)
NGC (DPL)
DOLLARS
(Thousands)
45
40
35
30
25
20
15
10
5
JAN
APR
JUL
OCT
1987
1988
1989
1990
1991

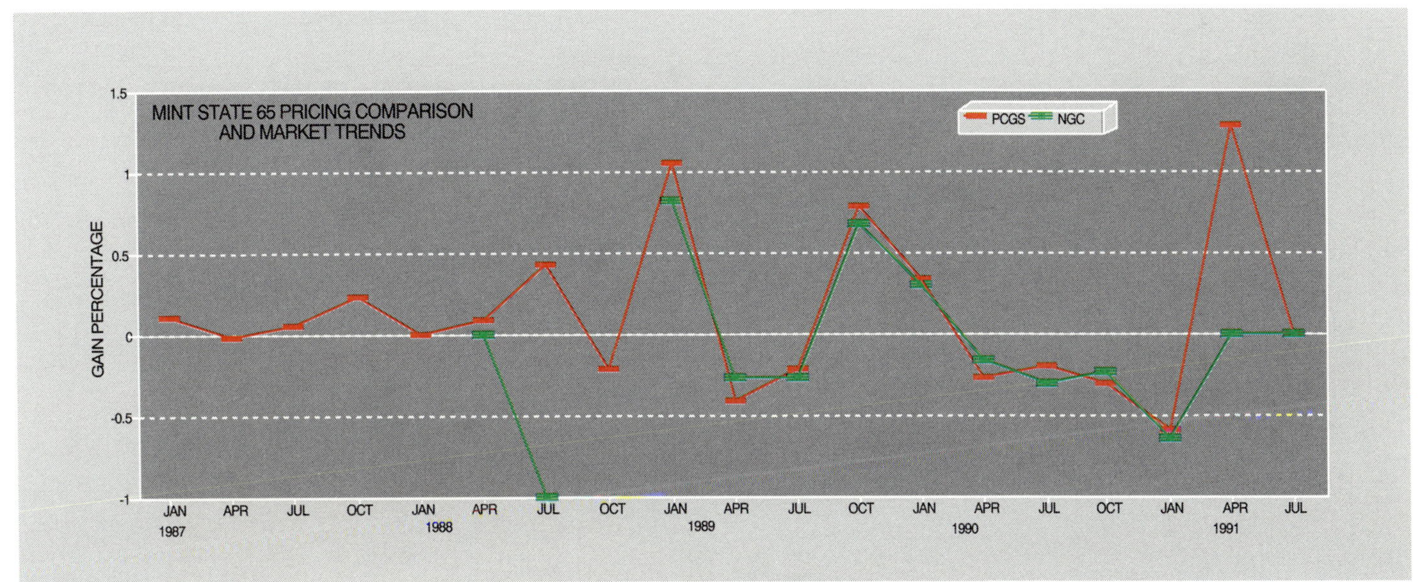
MINT STATE 65 PRICING COMPARISON
AND MARKET TRENDS
PCGS
NGC
GAIN PERCENTAGE
1.5
1
0.5
0
-0.5
-1
JAN
APR
JUL
OCT
1987
1988
1989
1990
1991

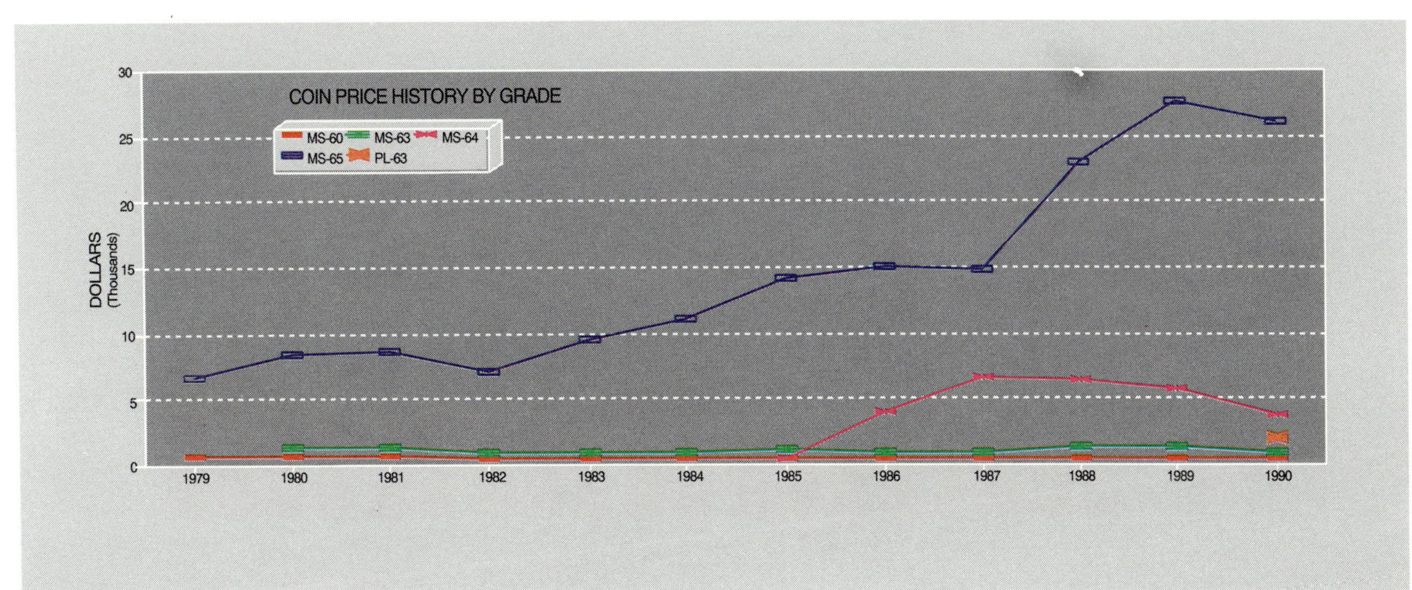
COIN PRICE HISTORY BY GRADE
MS-60
MS-63
MS-64
MS-65
PL-63
DOLLARS
(Thousands)
30
25
20
15
10
5
0
1979
1980
1981
1982
1983
1984
1985
1986
1987
1988
1989
1990

PCGS
1894-S
S$1
MS67
7232.67/3081798

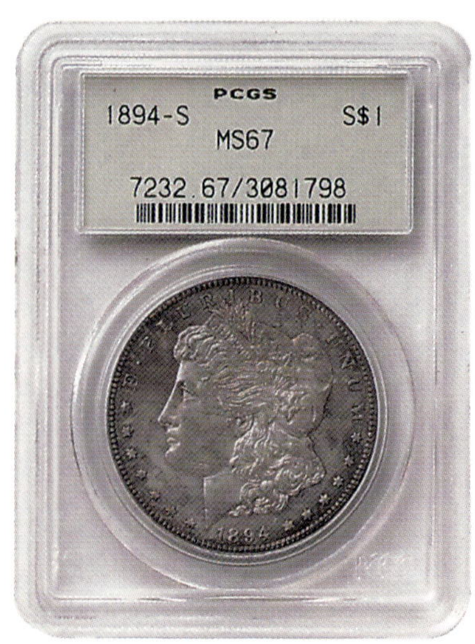

1894-S

Mintage 1,260,000, from 18 obvs., 13 revs. Most were spent; circulated examples occur in all grades. Sliders are uncommon, Uncs. are from a few Treasury bags, at least one before 1953, others in Deer Lodge, MT, about 1952 (the one with the twenty 1893-S's). The Redfield hoard had none. Surviving Uncs. are often bold with excellent lustre; some show die polishing marks in reverse field.

The millionth coin slabbed by PCGS is an 1894-S handled by this author (Highfill), PCGS had graded it MS 66. Serial #1,000,000 - What else!

Recommended in MS 63 up. Grades AU 50/58 difficult to locate.

Prooflikes: PL's outnumber DMPL's 10 to 1. Cameos are frequent in both. Rare above MS 63 PL, in any BU grade DMPL.

PCGS

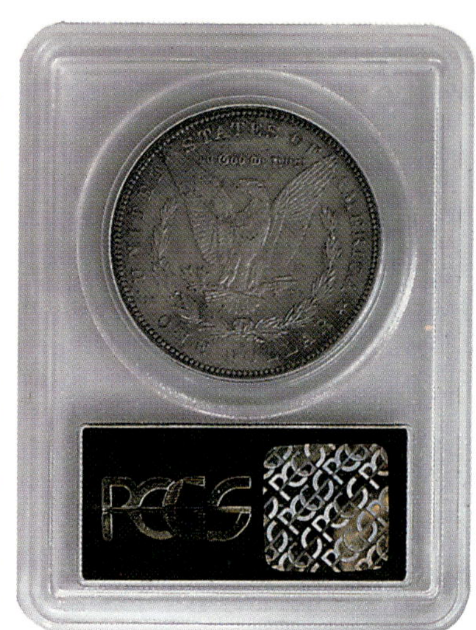

MINTAGE	PROOF	STRIKE	LUSTER	BAG MARKS	REDFIELD
1,260,000	0	Sharp & Bold	Excellent	Light	No
DIES	**DIE VARIETIES**	**% OF PL**	**% OF DMPL**	**PIVOTAL GRADE**	**RARITY FACTOR**
20	7	6.3	0.9	MS 65	R-1

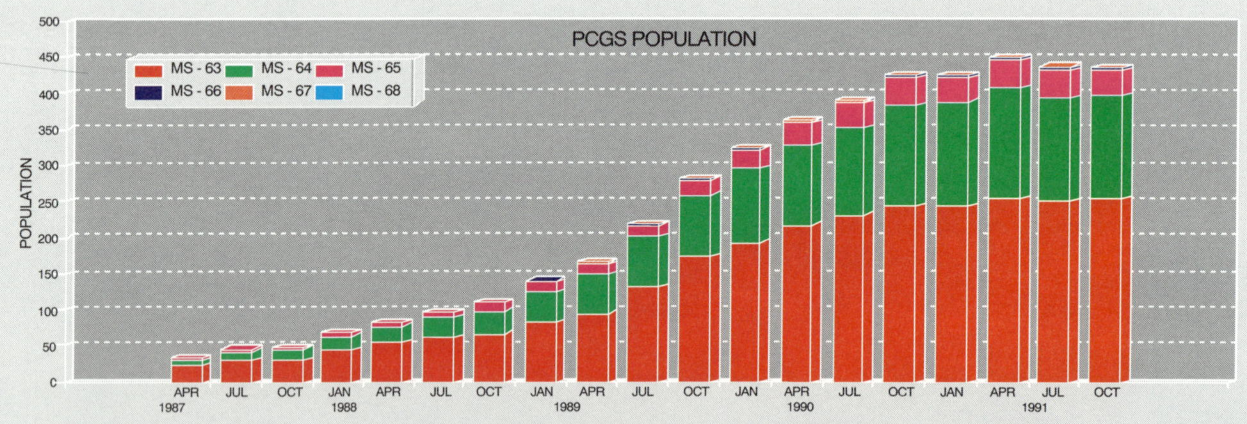
PCGS POPULATION
MS - 63
MS - 64
MS - 65
MS - 66
MS - 67
MS - 68
POPULATION
500
450
400
350
300
250
200
150
100
50
C
APR 1987
JUL
OCT
JAN 1988
APR
JUL
OCT
JAN 1989
APR
JUL
OCT
JAN 1990
APR
JUL
OCT
JAN 1991
APR
JUL
OCT

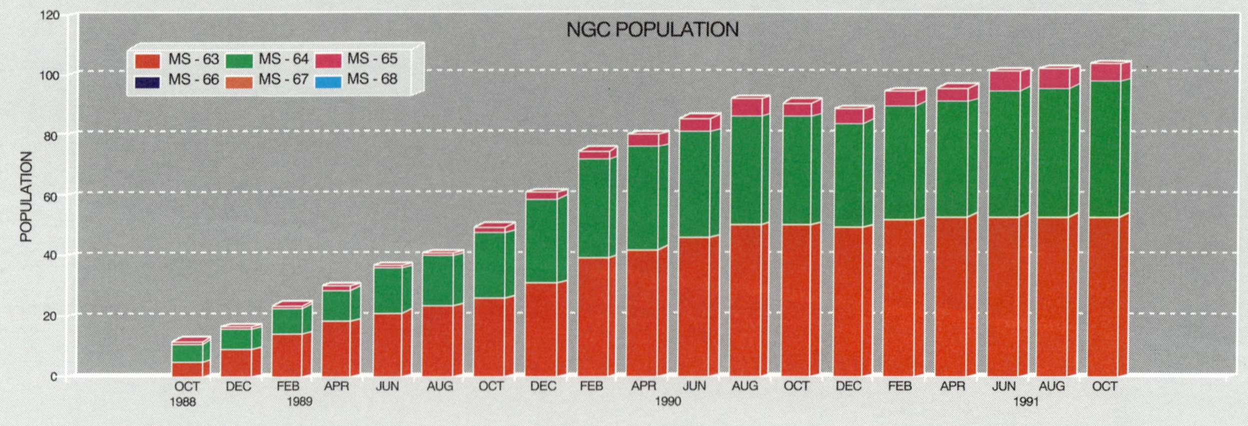
NGC POPULATION
MS - 63
MS - 64
MS - 65
MS - 66
MS - 67
MS - 68
POPULATION
120
100
80
60
40
20
C
OCT 1988
DEC
FEB 1989
APR
JUN
AUG
OCT
DEC
FEB 1990
APR
JUN
AUG
OCT
DEC
FEB 1991
APR
JUN
AUG
OCT

1894-S

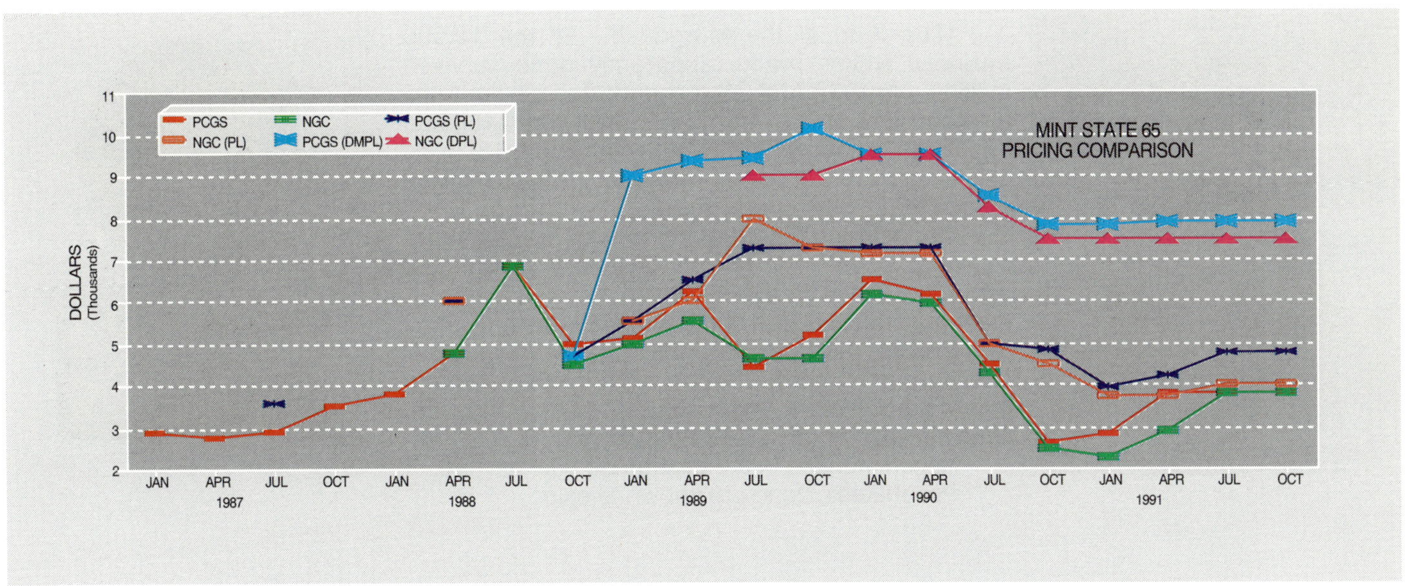

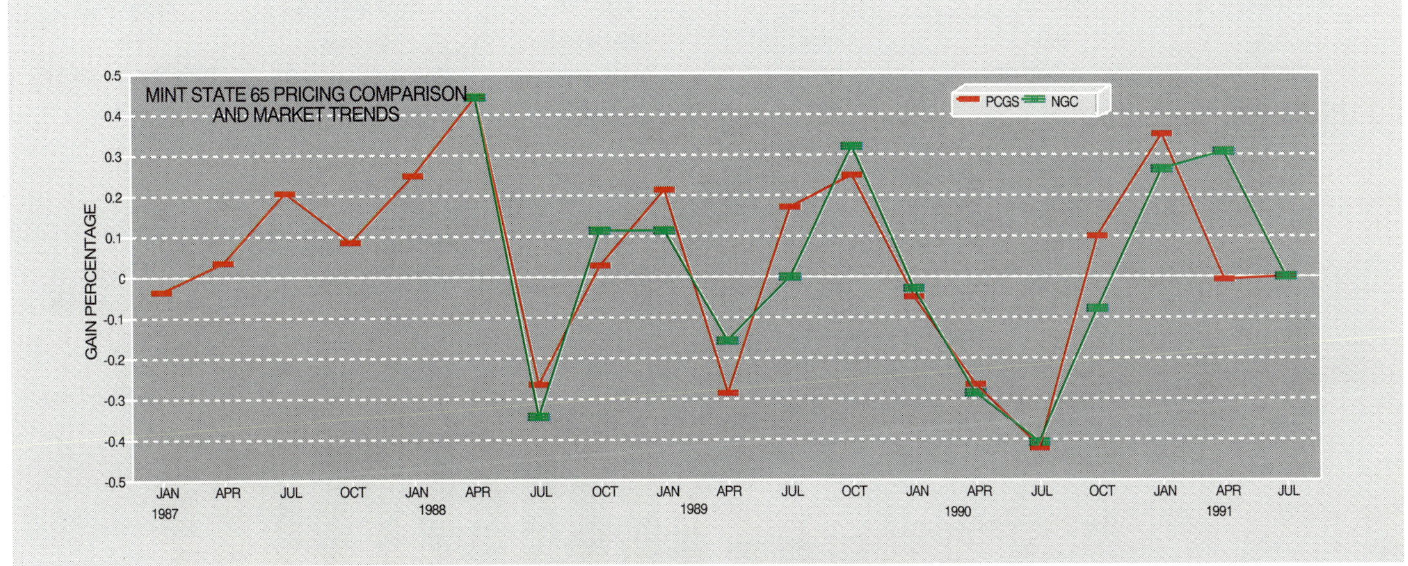

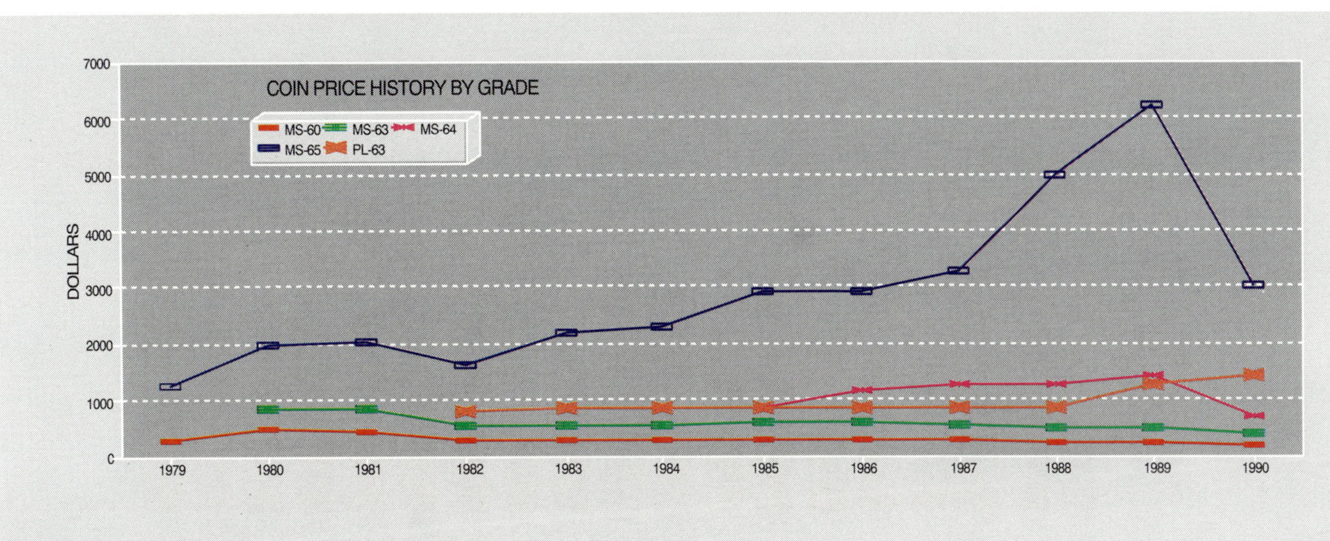

PCGS
1895
S$1
PR67
7330.67/1289217

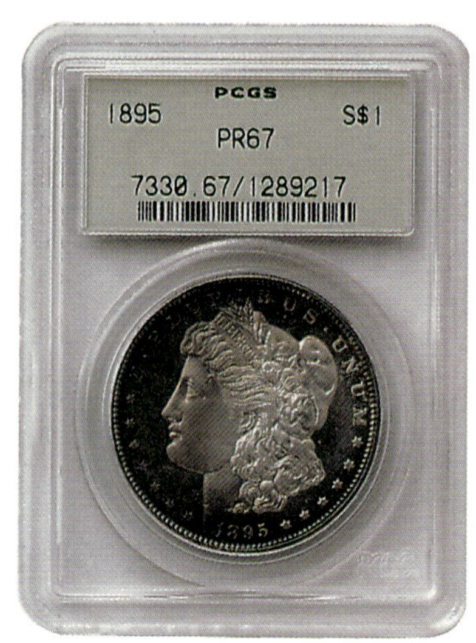

1895-P (Proof)

"The King of the Morgans!" Of the 12,000 business strikes made, apparently none survived melting. In 1974 ANACS authenticated a worn 1895 as a business strike. Many are convinced that it had begun as a proof. All 10-12 circulated 1895-P's examined by Walter Breen were from the same dies as proofs.

Occasional fakes have turned up: genuine circulated 1895-O or 1895-S dollars with mintmark removed. These always show tool marks, scrapes, or other abnormal surface in the mintmark area.

Proofs: Mintage 880. No more rare than other Morgan proofs, but under the most intense demand from date collectors. High cameo contrast, but most often hairlined or otherwise cleaned.

Recommended in the best grade you can find.

Prooflikes: None are known to exist.

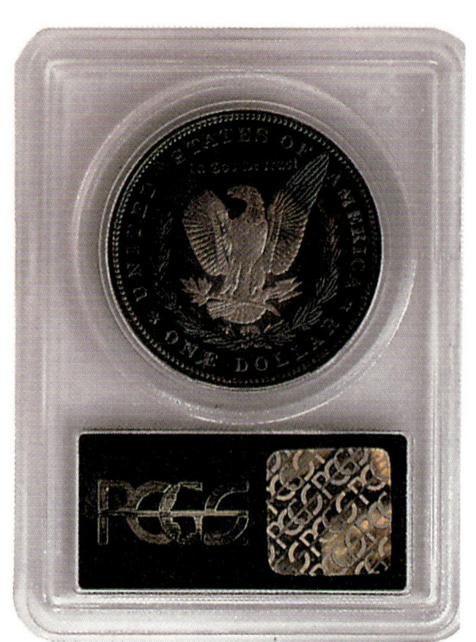

MINTAGE	PROOF	STRIKE	LUSTER	BAG MARKS	REDFIELD
12,000	880	Sharp	Excellent	Hairlines	No
DIES	**DIE VARIETIES**	**% OF PL**	**% OF DMPL**	**PIVOTAL GRADE**	**RARITY FACTOR**
Not Available	3	0.0	0.0	MS 65	R-1

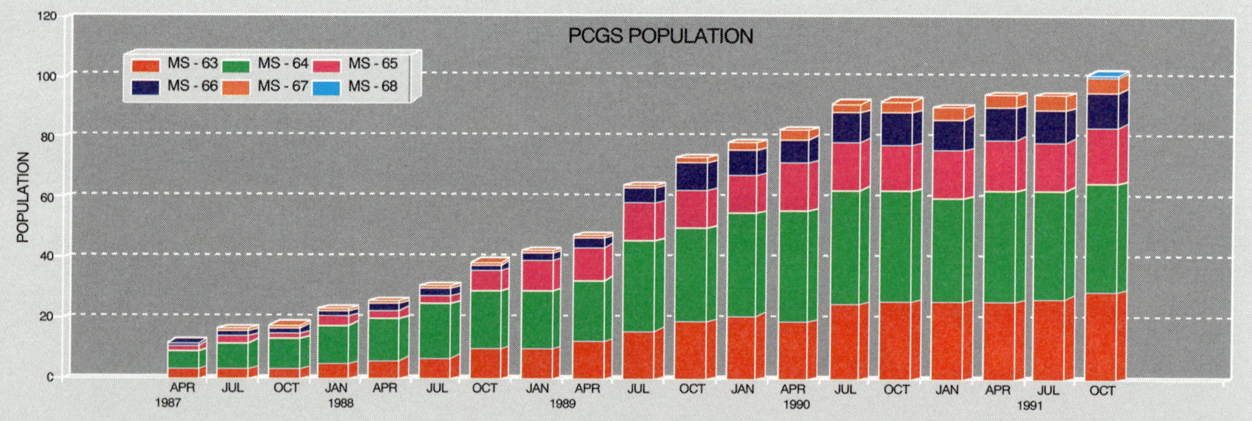
PCGS POPULATION
MS - 63
MS - 64
MS - 65
MS - 66
MS - 67
MS - 68
POPULATION
120
100
80
60
40
20
0
APR 1987
JUL
OCT
JAN 1988
APR
JUL
OCT
JAN 1989
APR
JUL
OCT
JAN
APR 1990
JUL
OCT
JAN
APR 1991
JUL
OCT

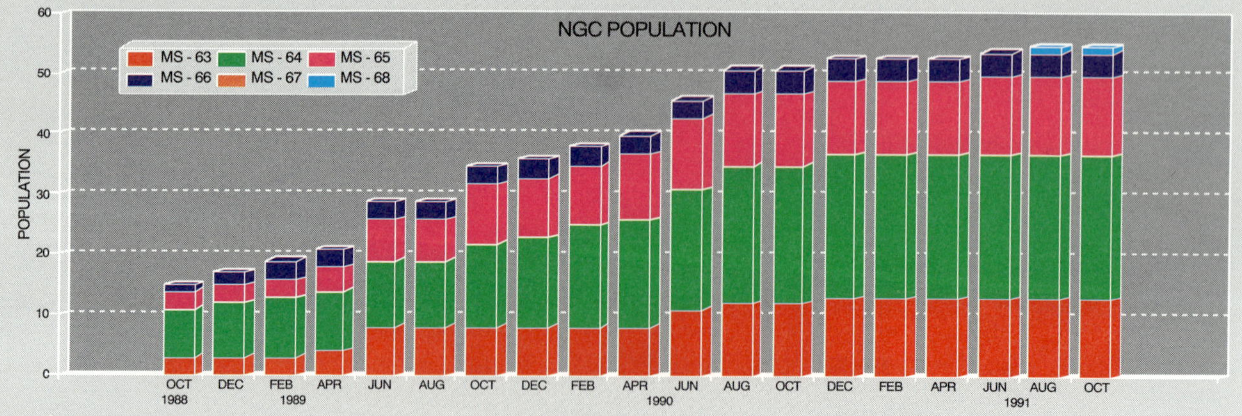
NGC POPULATION
MS - 63
MS - 64
MS - 65
MS - 66
MS - 67
MS - 68
POPULATION
60
50
40
30
20
10
0
OCT 1988
DEC
FEB 1989
APR
JUN
AUG
OCT
DEC
FEB
APR 1990
JUN
AUG
OCT
DEC
FEB
APR
JUN 1991
AUG
OCT

1895-P (Proof)

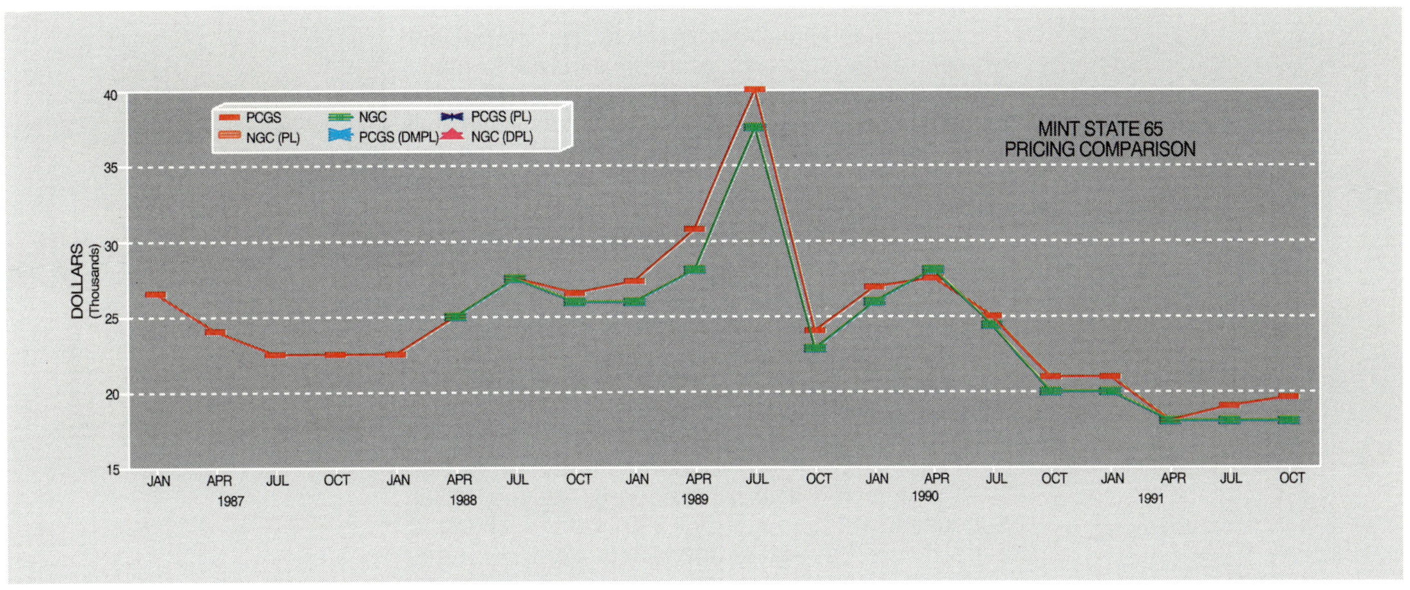

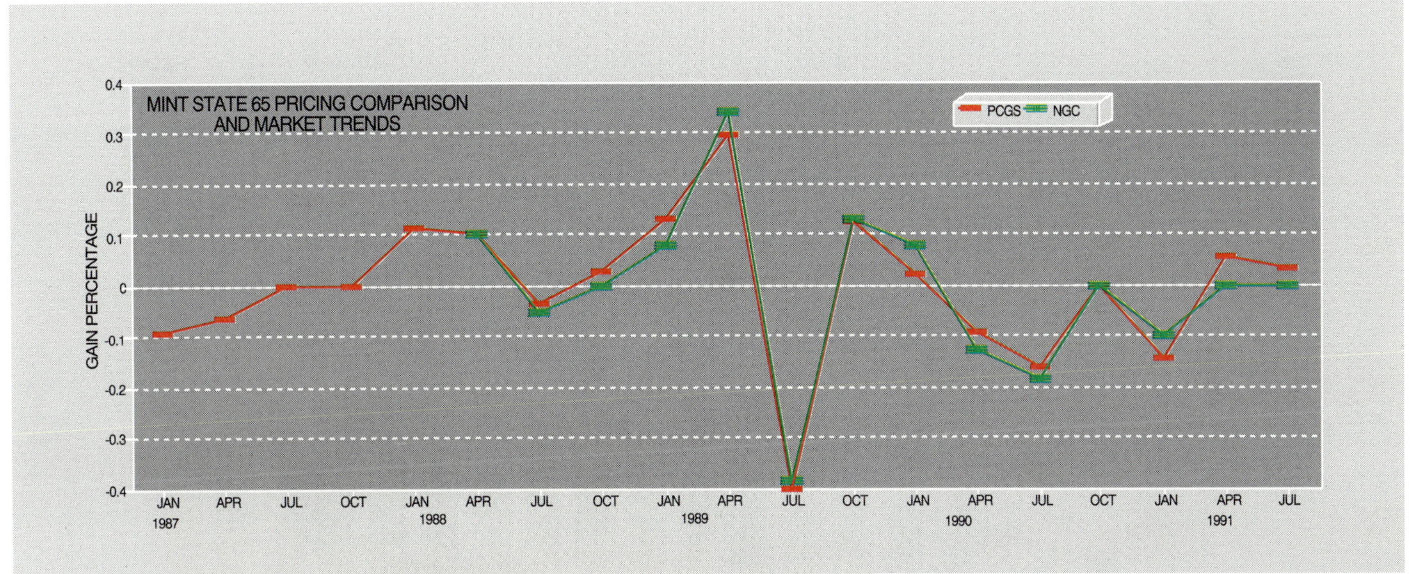

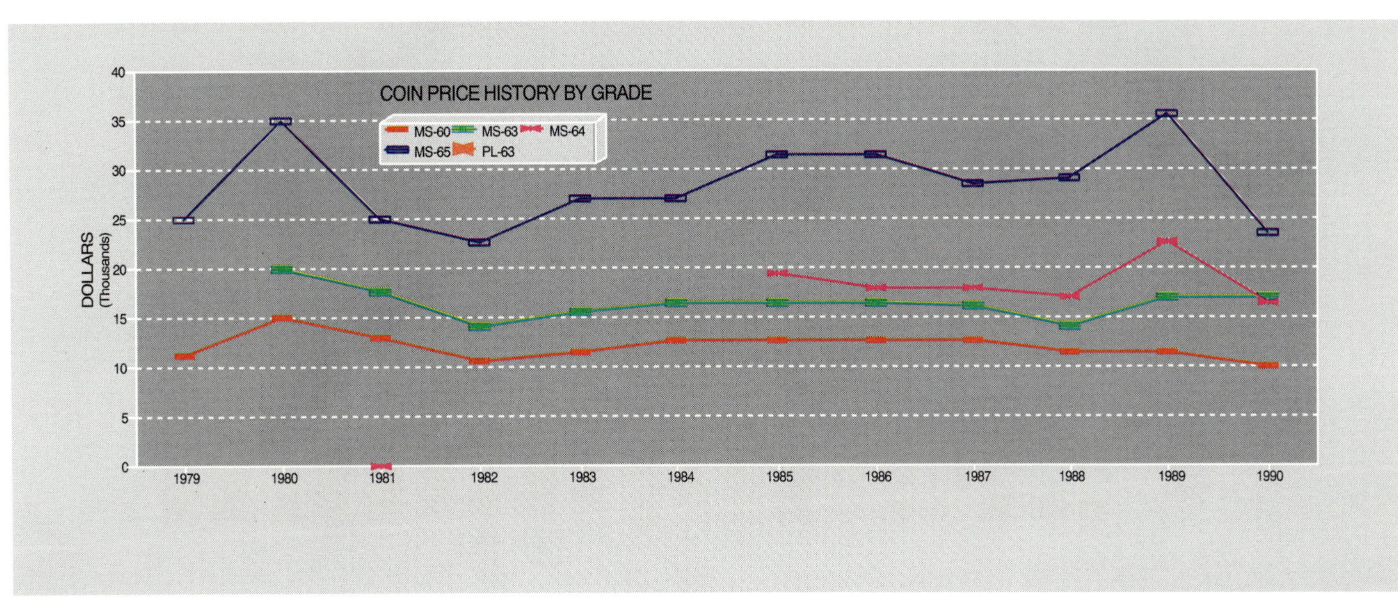

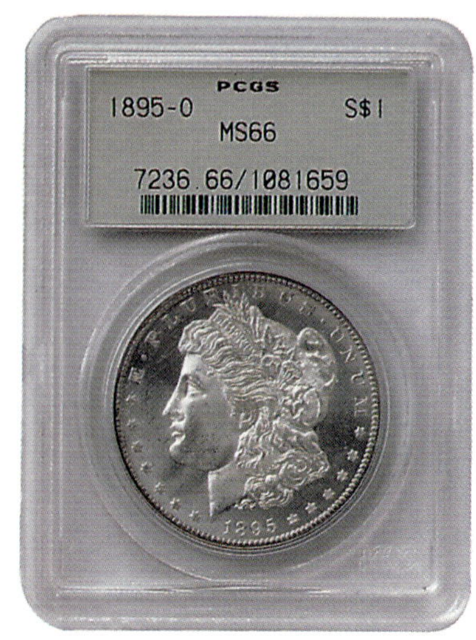

1895-O

PCGS
1895-O
S$1
MS66
7236.66/1081659

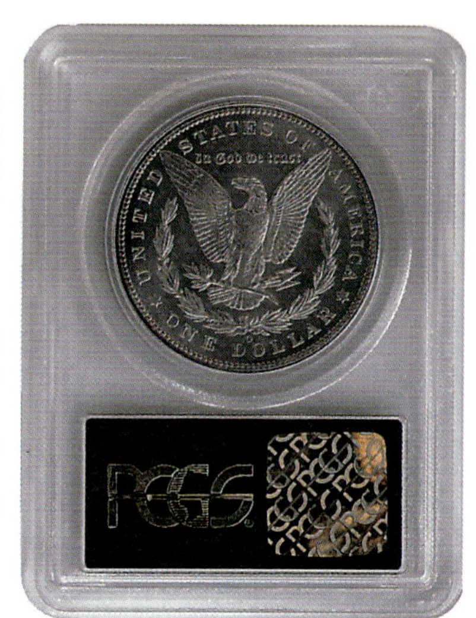

Mintage 450,000, from 5 pairs of dies. Many went into circulation; survivors occur in all grades, many AU's and sliders. Uncs. are rare, many weakly struck (though better than the "Pancakes") and with dull lustre; some sliders have sharper strikes than the Uncs. There are some very fully struck "sliders" around.

This author (Highfill) had a good lesson on grading changes and inconsistencies during the late 1970s and early 80s. I had purchased an 1895-O ANACS 63/65 in 1980 and later submitted it to PCGS and NGC in 1989. Both services graded it AU 55.

Recommended in any BU grade, but beware of sliders priced as Unc.

Proofs: None documented.

Prooflikes: Rare, seldom offered; very few DMPL's known. The Hardenberg, Wayne Miller "Subdued DMPL" brought $71,500. One PL changed hands in six figures at the 1986 Central States convention in Kansas City; in Auction '87 it only brought $50,600.

PCGS

MINTAGE	PROOF	STRIKE	LUSTER	BAG MARKS	REDFIELD
450,000	0	Soft & Weak	Poor	Moderate	No
DIES	**DIE VARIETIES**	**% OF PL**	**% OF DMPL**	**PIVOTAL GRADE**	**RARITY FACTOR**
10	4	12.5	2.1	MS 60	R-1

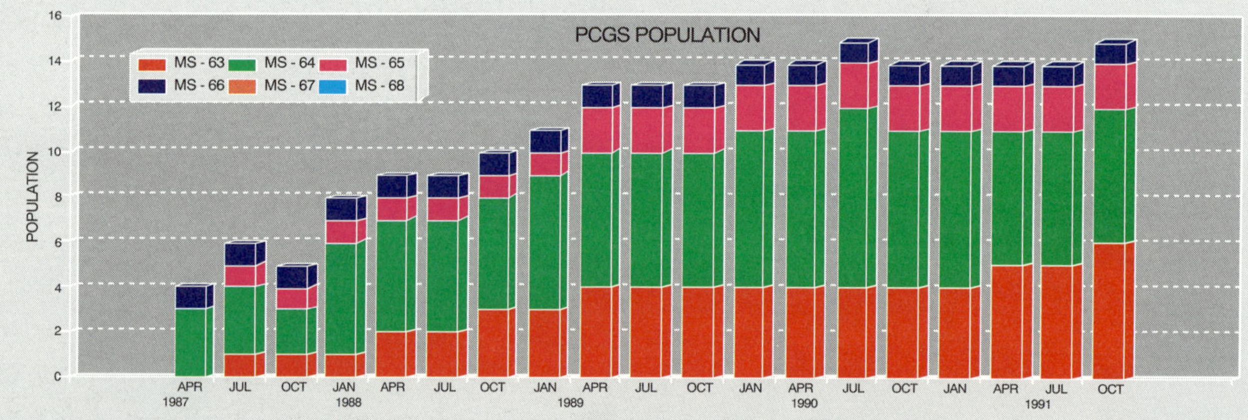
PCGS POPULATION
MS - 63
MS - 64
MS - 65
MS - 66
MS - 67
MS - 68
POPULATION
16
14
12
10
8
6
4
2
C
APR 1987
JUL
OCT
JAN 1988
APR
JUL
OCT
JAN 1989
APR
JUL
OCT
JAN
APR 1990
JUL
OCT
JAN
APR
JUL 1991
OCT

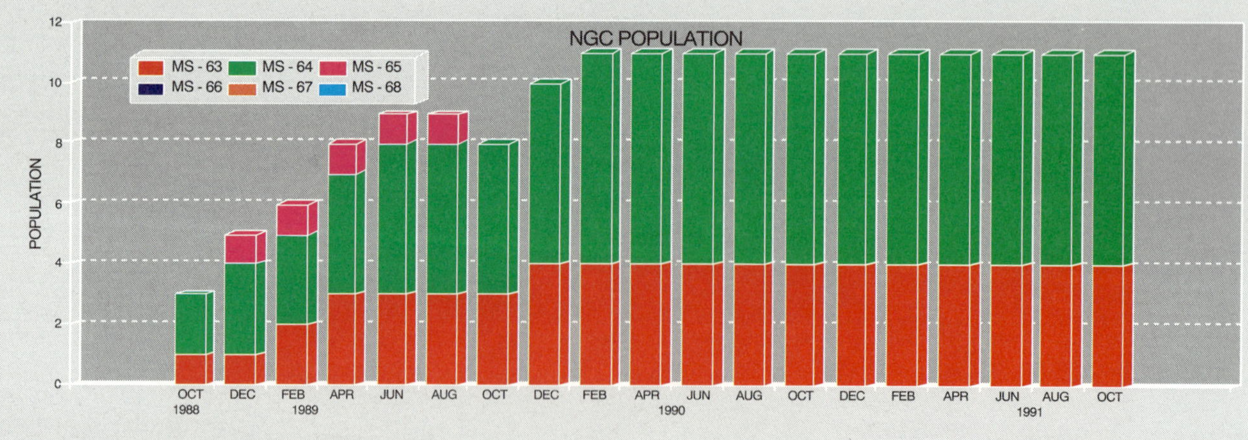
NGC POPULATION
MS - 63
MS - 64
MS - 65
MS - 66
MS - 67
MS - 68
POPULATION
12
10
8
6
4
2
C
OCT 1988
DEC
FEB 1989
APR
JUN
AUG
OCT
DEC
FEB
APR 1990
JUN
AUG
OCT
DEC
FEB
APR
JUN 1991
AUG
OCT

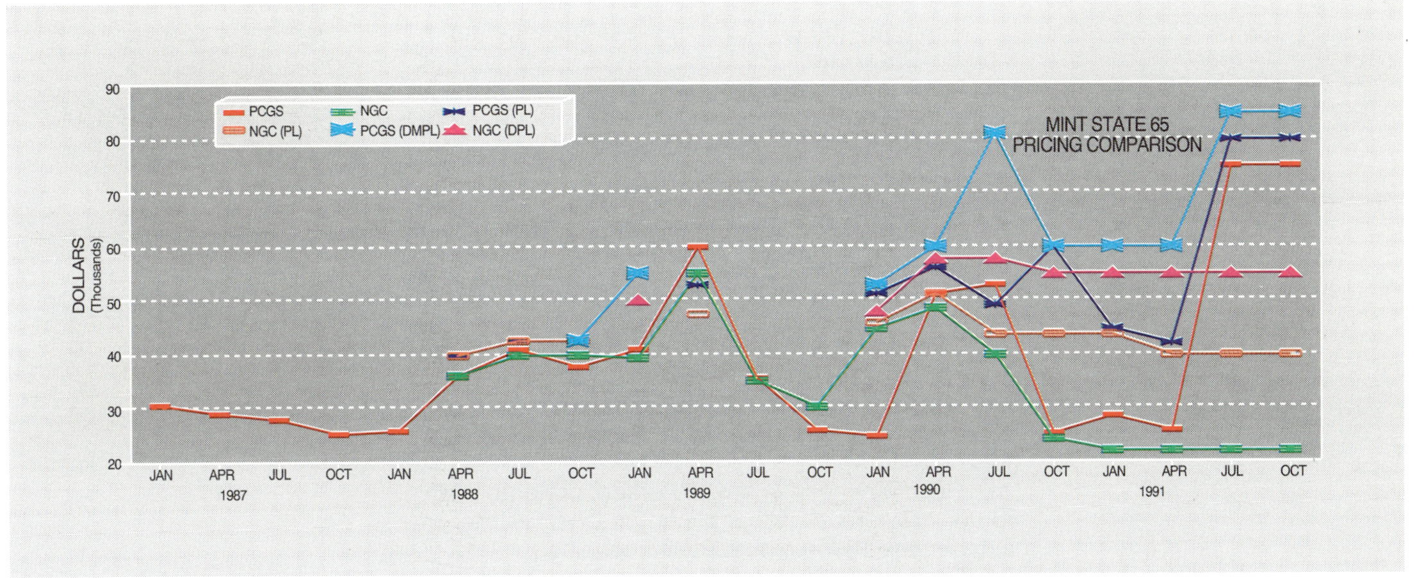
MINT STATE 65
PRICING COMPARISON
PCGS
NGC
PCGS (PL)
NGC (PL)
PCGS (DMPL)
NGC (DPL)
DOLLARS
(Thousands)
90
80
70
60
50
40
30
20
JAN
APR
JUL
OCT
1987
1988
1989
1990
1991

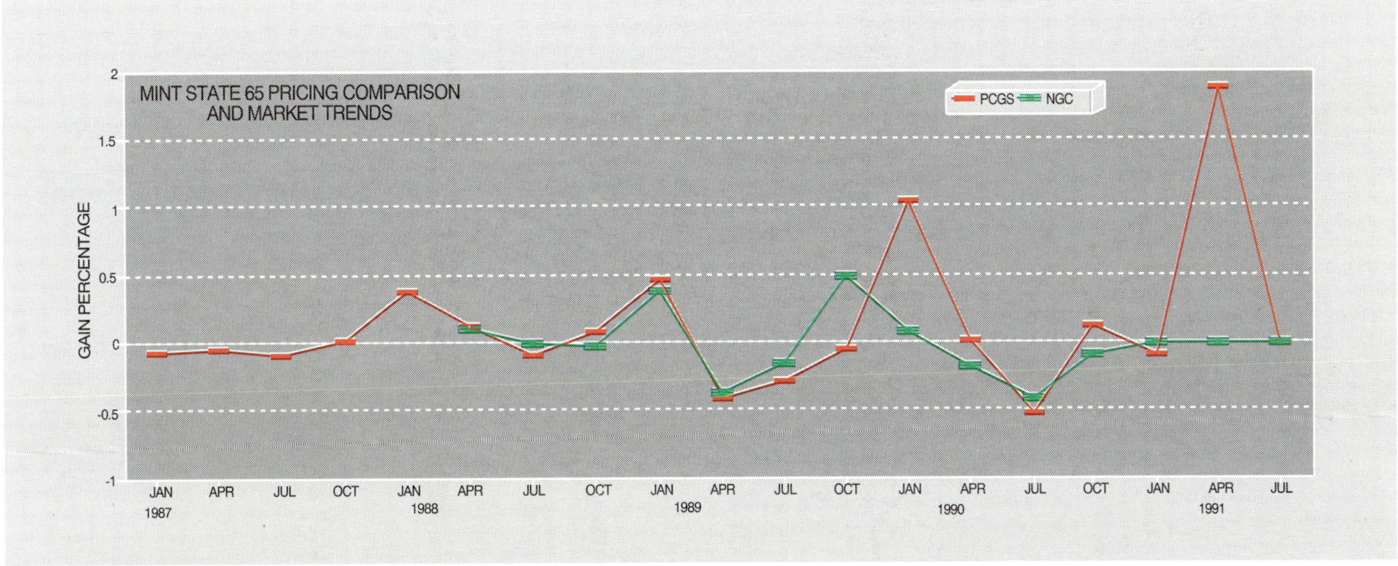
MINT STATE 65 PRICING COMPARISON
AND MARKET TRENDS
PCGS
NGC
GAIN PERCENTAGE
2
1.5
1
0.5
0
-0.5
-1
JAN
APR
JUL
OCT
1987
1988
1989
1990
1991

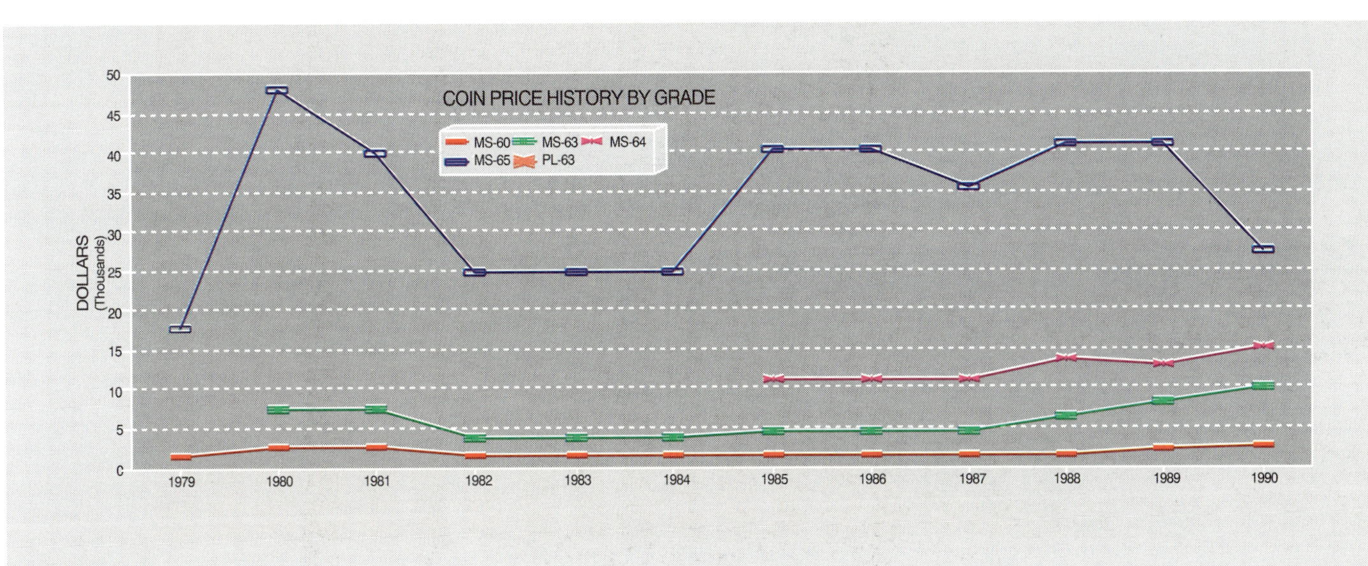
COIN PRICE HISTORY BY GRADE
MS-60
MS-63
MS-64
MS-65
PL-63
DOLLARS
(Thousands)
50
45
40
35
30
25
20
15
10
5
0
1979
1980
1981
1982
1983
1984
1985
1986
1987
1988
1989
1990

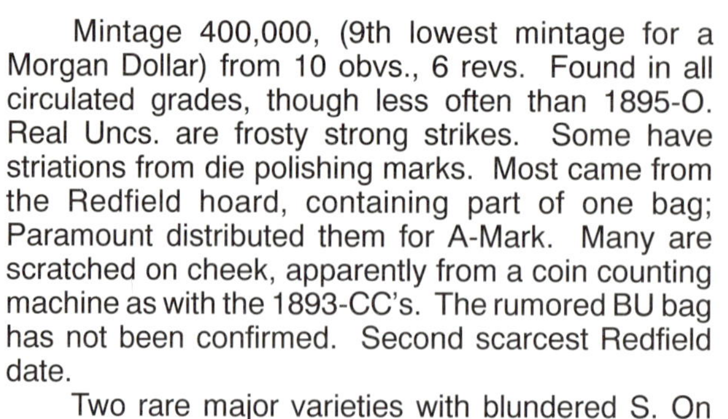

1895-S

Mintage 400,000, (9th lowest mintage for a Morgan Dollar) from 10 obvs., 6 revs. Found in all circulated grades, though less often than 1895-O. Real Uncs. are frosty strong strikes. Some have striations from die polishing marks. Most came from the Redfield hoard, containing part of one bag; Paramount distributed them for A-Mark. Many are scratched on cheek, apparently from a coin counting machine as with the 1893-CC's. The rumored BU bag has not been confirmed. Second scarcest Redfield date.

Two rare major varieties with blundered S. On *Ency* 5640 = VAM 3, mintmark was first entered too high and leaning far to left, then corrected lower and leaning to right. On *Ency* 5641, rarer still, S is over horizontal S.

Recommended in any BU grade, preferably MS 63 up. Beware of sliders priced as Unc. Harder to find than the 1895-O in circulated condition.

The S over horizontal S (*Ency* 5461 = VAM 4) is very rare but can probably be cherrypicked in circulated state.

Proofs: Three reported, occasion unknown.

Prooflikes: Scarce to rare in all grades. In the late 1980's, a PCGS MS 66 PL sold in six figures at the ANA convention, Cincinnati, August 1988.

MINTAGE	PROOF	STRIKE	LUSTER	BAG MARKS	REDFIELD
400,000	0	Average To Bold	Excellent	Moderate	Yes
DIE	**DIE VARIETIES**	**% OF PL**	**% OF DMPL**	**PIVOTAL GRADE**	**RARITY FACTOR**
38	4	6.2	4.8	MS 65	R-1

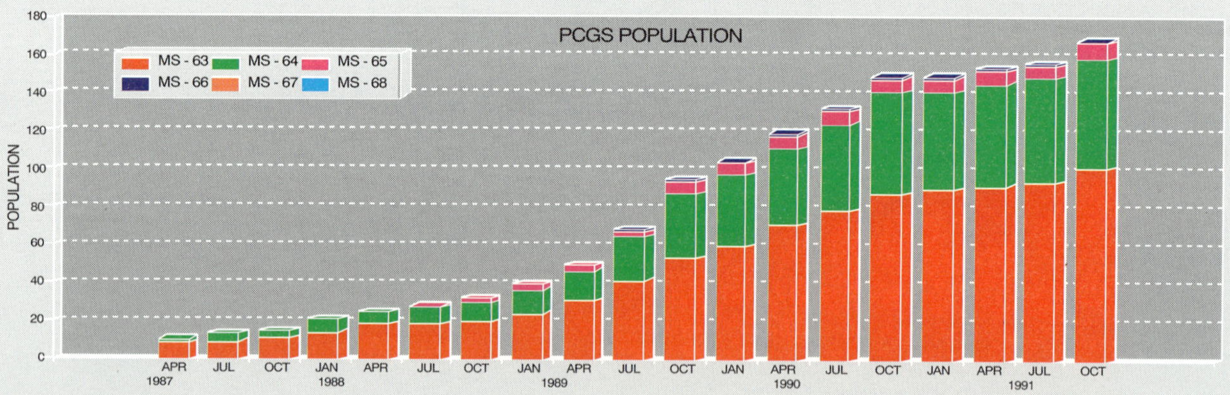

PCGS POPULATION

MS - 63 MS - 64 MS - 65 MS - 66 MS - 67 MS - 68

POPULATION

180 160 140 120 100 80 60 40 20 0

APR 1987 JUL OCT JAN 1988 APR JUL OCT JAN 1989 APR JUL OCT JAN APR 1990 JUL OCT JAN APR JUL 1991 OCT

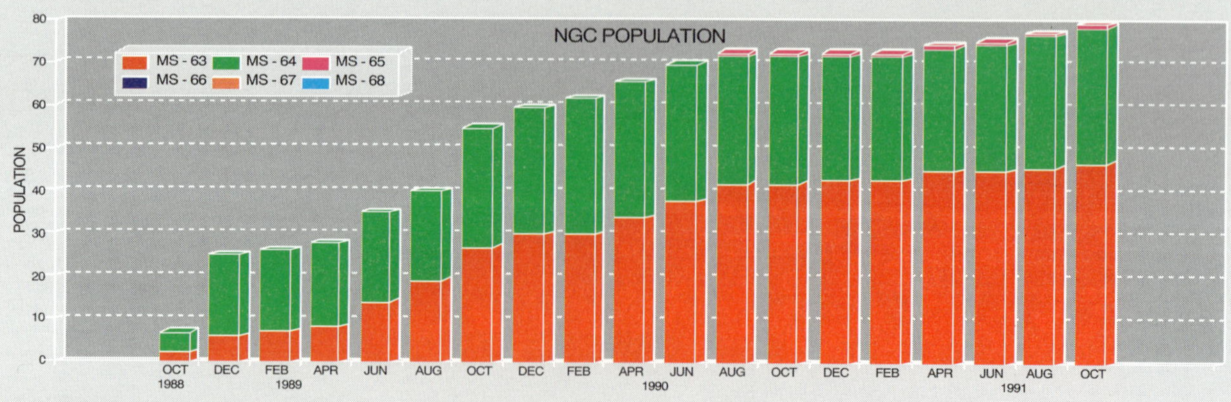

NGC POPULATION

MS - 63 MS - 64 MS - 65 MS - 66 MS - 67 MS - 68

POPULATION

80 70 60 50 40 30 20 10 0

OCT 1988 DEC FEB 1989 APR JUN AUG OCT DEC FEB APR 1990 JUN AUG OCT DEC FEB APR JUN 1991 AUG OCT

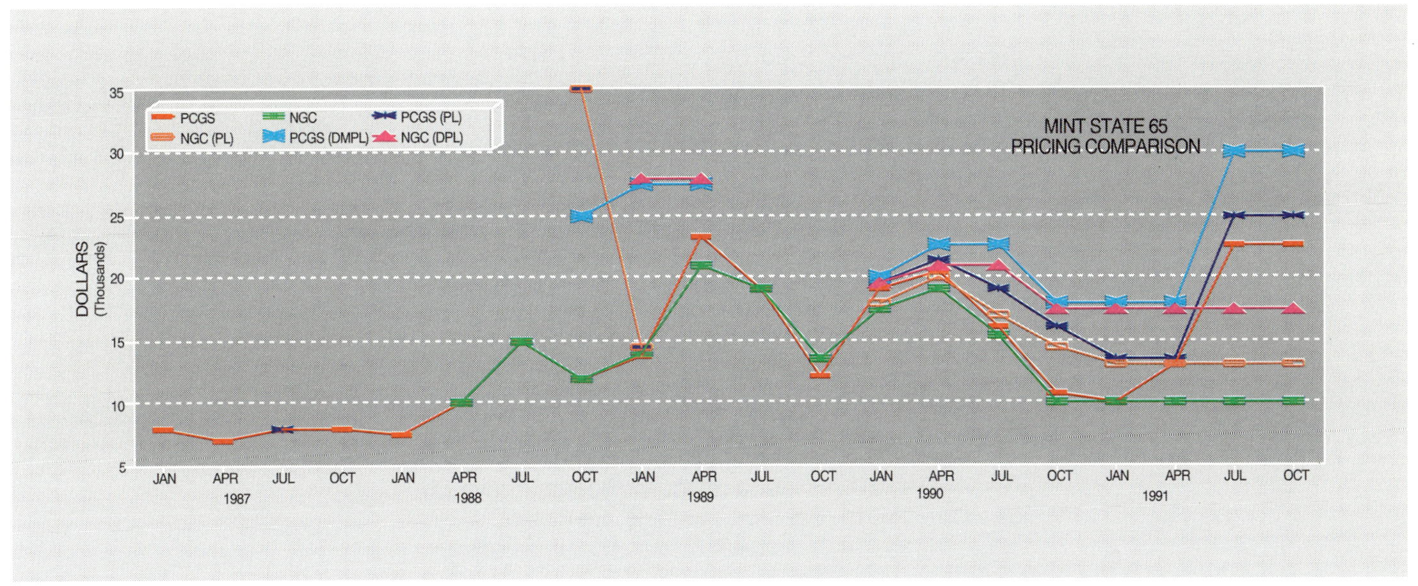
PCGS
NGC
PCGS (PL)
NGC (PL)
PCGS (DMPL)
NGC (DPL)
MINT STATE 65
PRICING COMPARISON
DOLLARS
(Thousands)
35
30
25
20
15
10
5
JAN APR JUL OCT JAN APR JUL OCT JAN APR JUL OCT JAN APR JUL OCT JAN APR JUL OCT
1987 1988 1989 1990 1991

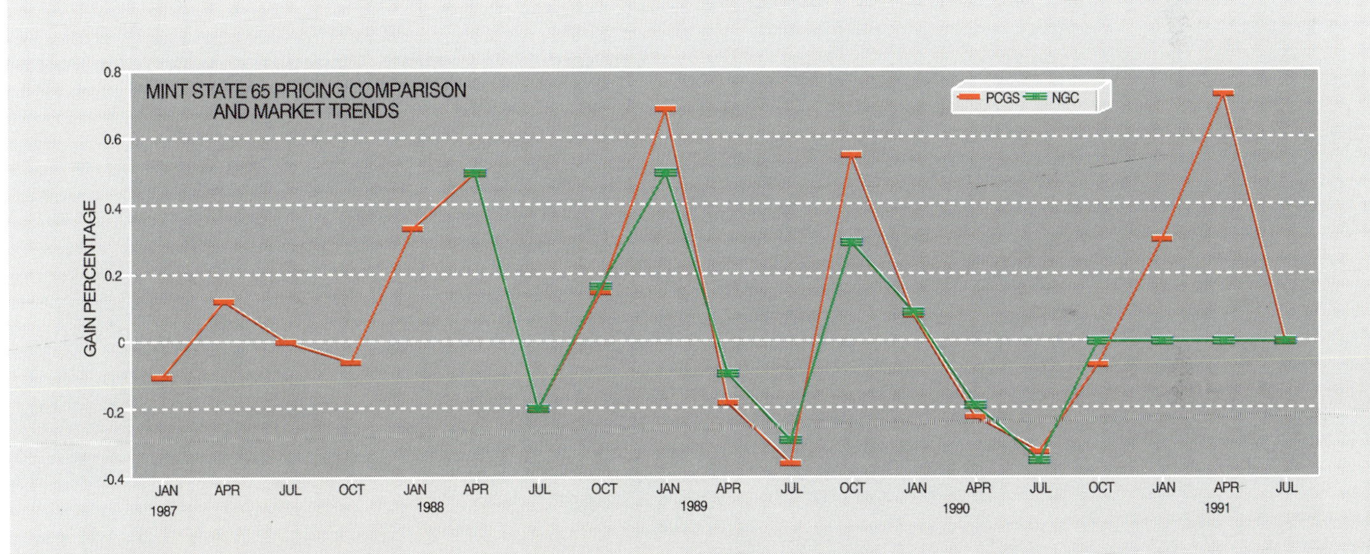
MINT STATE 65 PRICING COMPARISON
AND MARKET TRENDS
PCGS
NGC
GAIN PERCENTAGE
0.8
0.6
0.4
0.2
0
-0.2
-0.4
JAN APR JUL OCT JAN APR JUL OCT JAN APR JUL OCT JAN APR JUL OCT JAN APR JUL
1987 1988 1989 1990 1991

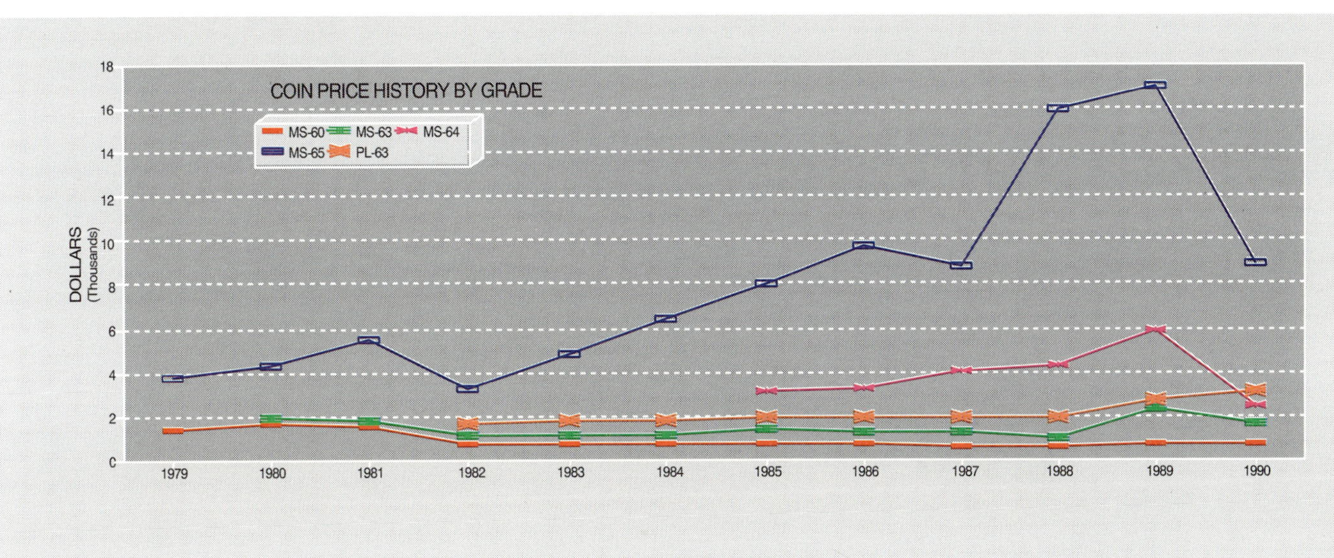
COIN PRICE HISTORY BY GRADE
MS-60
MS-63
MS-64
MS-65
PL-63
DOLLARS
(Thousands)
18
16
14
12
10
8
6
4
2
0
1979 1980 1981 1982 1983 1984 1985 1986 1987 1988 1989 1990

1896-P

Mintage 9,976,000. Uncs. are plentiful from Treasury and Redfield bags; many are high quality frosty sharp strikes, a large minority weaker strikes. John Love, Cut Bank, Montana, handled approximately 20 original mint sewn bags from the Redfield hoard, in a lot of about 100 bags of 1896-7-8 Philadelphia. Many of these went to John Kamin of the "Forecaster" newsletter. A few MS 60/63 bags still survive; rolls in that grade range are easier to find. Sliders are plentiful. Sixth commonest Redfield date.

Recommended in MS 65 up or in MS 64 by the roll.

Proofs: The low mintage of 762 took at least two obverse dies, both with date well to left of usual position.

Prooflikes: Most (several hundred) are from Redfield. DMPL's were a minority. Scarce above MS 64 PL or DMPL. Cameo Examples are scarce.

MINTAGE	PROOF	STRIKE	LUSTER	BAG MARKS	REDFIELD
9,976,000	762	Sharp & Bold	Average	Moderate	Yes
DIES	**DIE VARIETIES**	**% OF PL**	**% OF DMPL**	**PIVOTAL GRADE**	**RARITY FACTOR**
40*	21	3.5	3.0	MS 65	R-4

*Maybe an error in original mint records

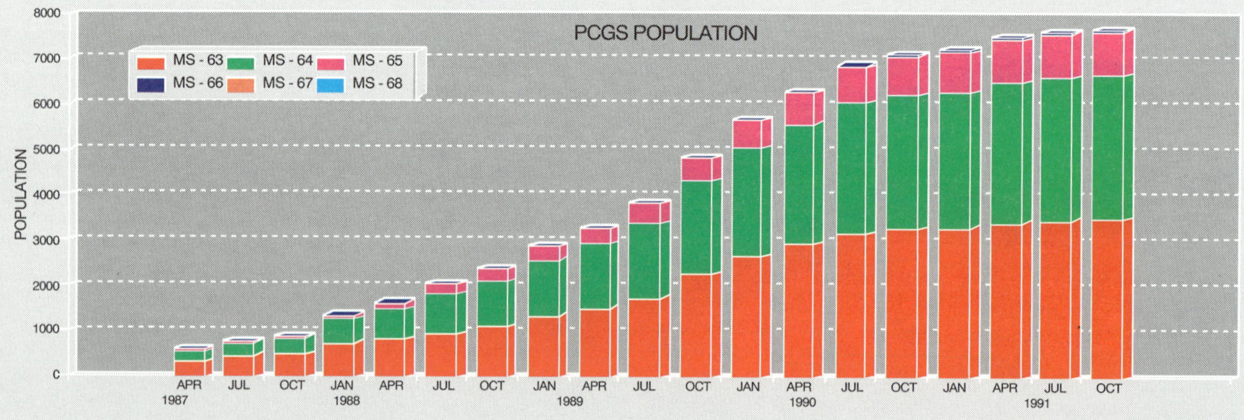

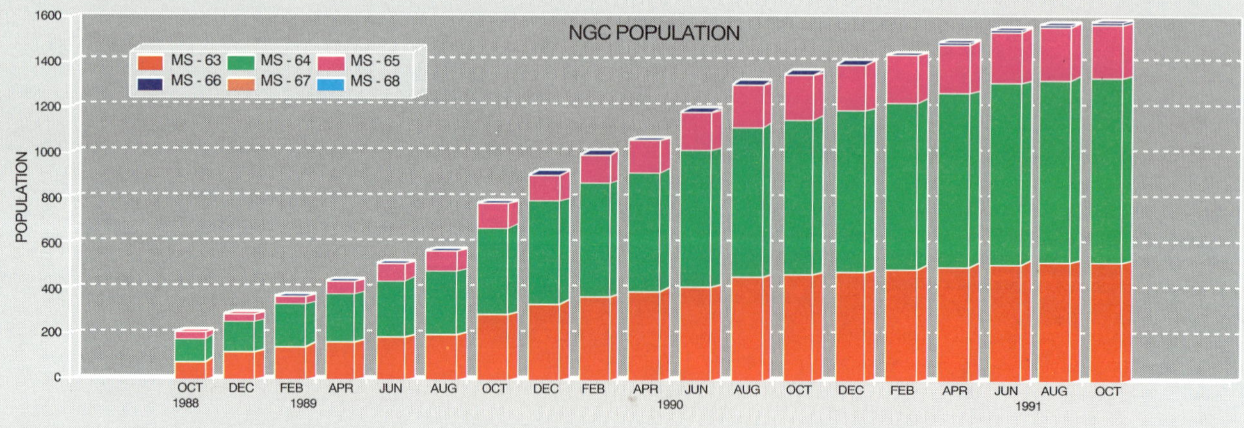

PCGS POPULATION

MS - 63, MS - 64, MS - 65, MS - 66, MS - 67, MS - 68

POPULATION: 0, 1000, 2000, 3000, 4000, 5000, 6000, 7000, 8000

APR 1987, JUL, OCT, JAN 1988, APR, JUL, OCT, JAN 1989, APR, JUL, OCT, JAN 1990, APR, JUL, OCT, JAN 1991, APR, JUL, OCT

NGC POPULATION

MS - 63, MS - 64, MS - 65, MS - 66, MS - 67, MS - 68

POPULATION: 0, 200, 400, 600, 800, 1000, 1200, 1400, 1600

OCT 1988, DEC, FEB 1989, APR, JUN, AUG, OCT, DEC, FEB 1990, APR, JUN, AUG, OCT, DEC, FEB 1991, APR, JUN, AUG, OCT

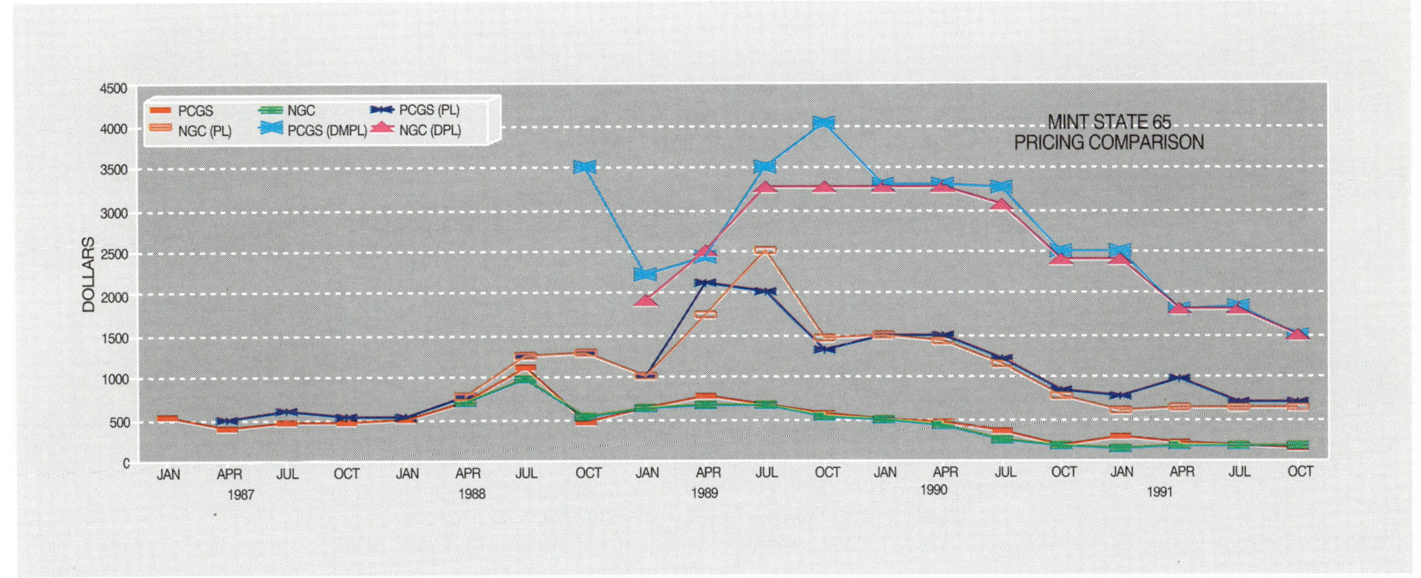
MINT STATE 65
PRICING COMPARISON
PCGS
NGC
PCGS (PL)
NGC (PL)
PCGS (DMPL)
NGC (DPL)
DOLLARS
4500
4000
3500
3000
2500
2000
1500
1000
500
0
JAN APR JUL OCT JAN APR JUL OCT JAN APR JUL OCT JAN APR JUL OCT JAN APR JUL OCT
1987 1988 1989 1990 1991

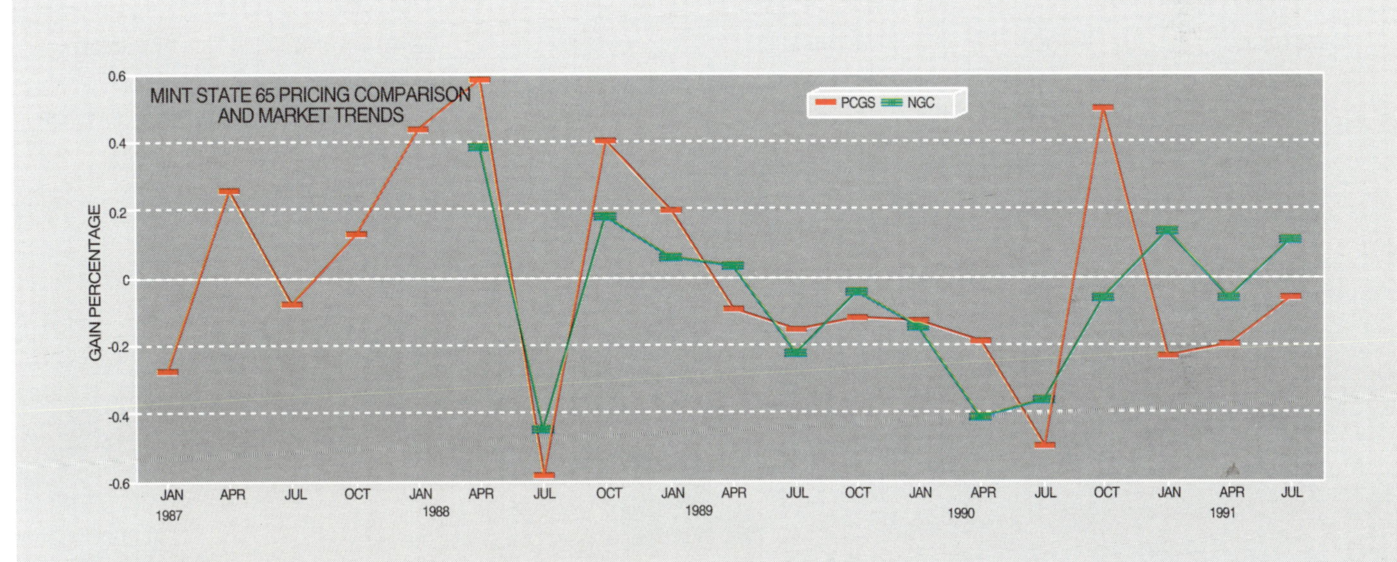
MINT STATE 65 PRICING COMPARISON
AND MARKET TRENDS
PCGS
NGC
GAIN PERCENTAGE
0.6
0.4
0.2
0
-0.2
-0.4
-0.6
JAN APR JUL OCT JAN APR JUL OCT JAN APR JUL OCT JAN APR JUL OCT JAN APR JUL
1987 1988 1989 1990 1991

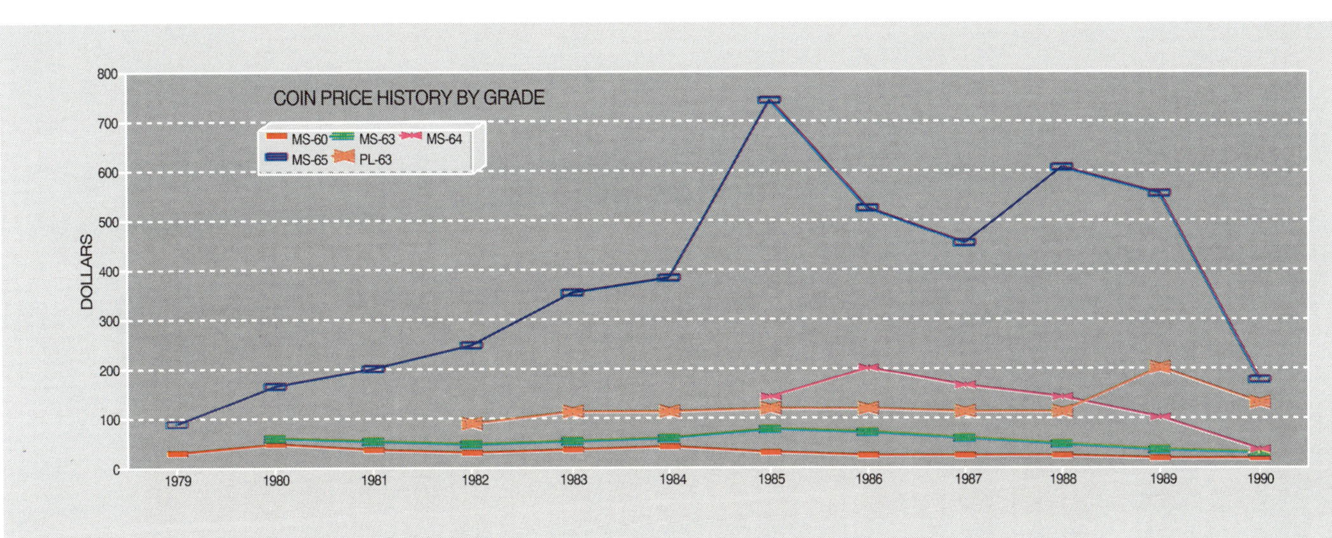
COIN PRICE HISTORY BY GRADE
MS-60
MS-63
MS-64
MS-65
PL-63
DOLLARS
800
700
600
500
400
300
200
100
0
1979 1980 1981 1982 1983 1984 1985 1986 1987 1988 1989 1990

1896-O

PCGS
1896-O
MS65
S$1
7242.65/3080611

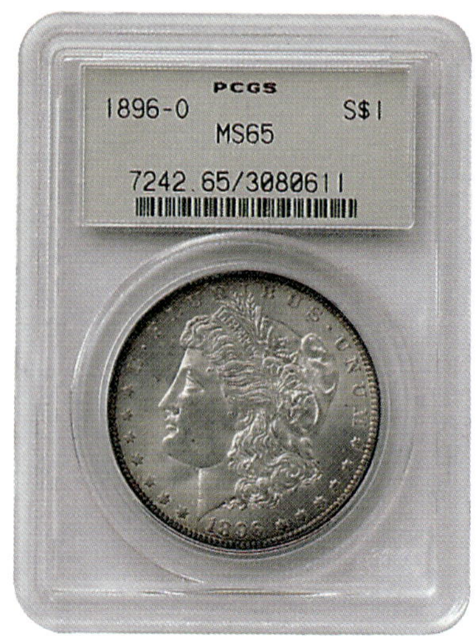

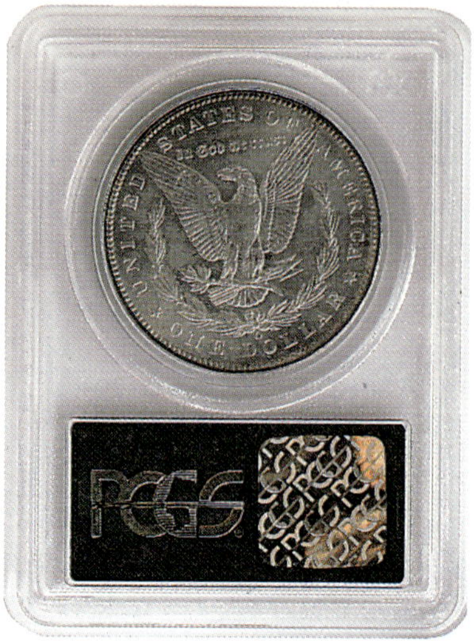

Mintage 4,900,000. Uncs. are usually dull weak strikes, rating honorable mention in the "Pancake" title competition. Many are from Treasury bags in the Billings, Montana, area, handled by John Love in the early 1960's. Many sliders show up. MS 65's are very seldom seen. They are RARE!

There was an "original" U.S. Mint sewn canvas bag of 1897-O morgans handled by Dean Tavenner of Deer Lodge, Montana in the early 1960s. This bag was not only "unoriginal" it was full of circulated "slider" Morgans. They were dated 1894-O, 1895-O, 1896-O and 1897-O. However, the majority of the coins were 1897-O, not 1896-O.

Recommended in all BU grades. Beware sliders priced as Unc. And beware fakes made by adding an O to genuine 1896 Philadelphia dollars. Circulated examples are available.

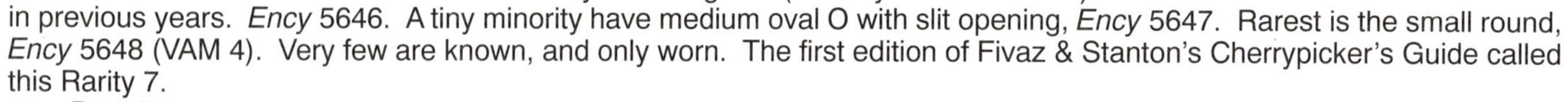

Usually with "large" O (actually medium round) as in previous years. *Ency* 5646. A tiny minority have medium oval O with slit opening, *Ency* 5647. Rarest is the small round, *Ency* 5648 (VAM 4). Very few are known, and only worn. The first edition of Fivaz & Stanton's Cherrypicker's Guide called this Rarity 7.

Prooflikes: Few, dull and nicked. A DMPL in Auction '87 brought $24,200. VERY RARE.

MINTAGE	PROOF	STRIKE	LUSTER	BAG MARKS	REDFIELD
4,900,000	0	Soft & Weak	Poor	Moderate to Heavy	No
DIES	**DIE VARIETIES**	**% OF PL**	**% OF DMPL**	**PIVOTAL GRADE**	**RARITY FACTOR**
40	19	1.5	1.8	MS 63	R-1

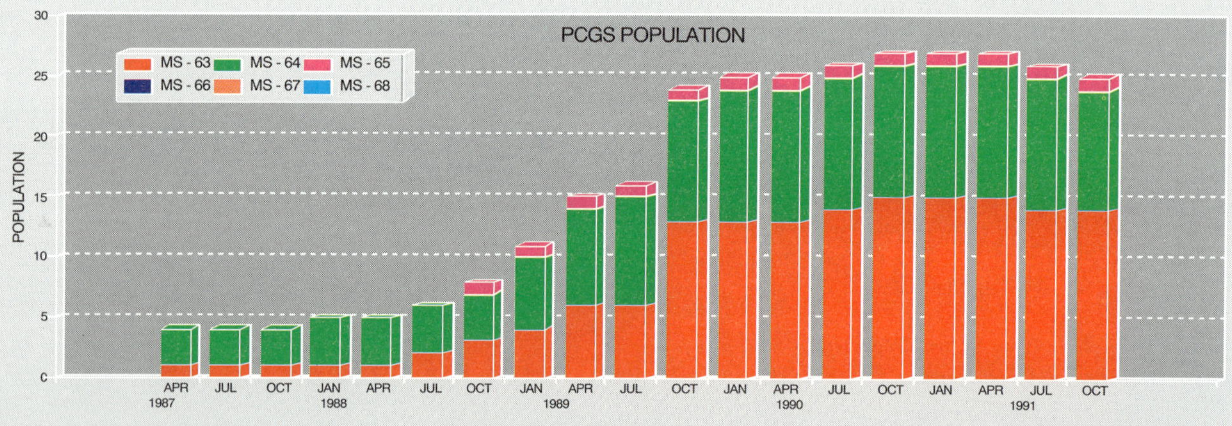

PCGS POPULATION
MS - 63
MS - 64
MS - 65
MS - 66
MS - 67
MS - 68
POPULATION
0
5
10
15
20
25
30
APR 1987
JUL
OCT
JAN 1988
APR
JUL
OCT
JAN 1989
APR
JUL
OCT
JAN 1990
APR
JUL
OCT
JAN 1991
APR
JUL
OCT

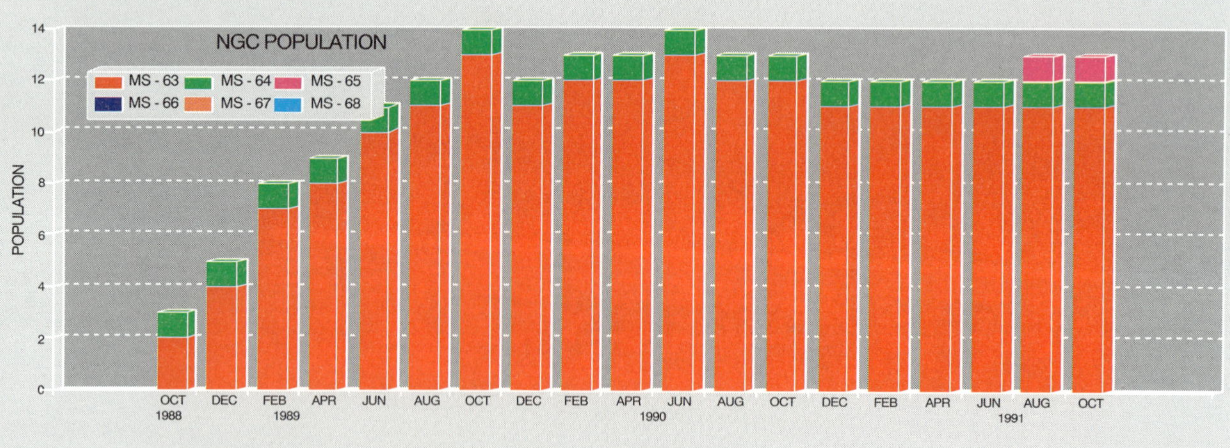

NGC POPULATION
MS - 63
MS - 64
MS - 65
MS - 66
MS - 67
MS - 68
POPULATION
0
2
4
6
8
10
12
14
OCT 1988
DEC
FEB 1989
APR
JUN
AUG
OCT
DEC
FEB 1990
APR
JUN
AUG
OCT
DEC
FEB 1991
APR
JUN
AUG
OCT

1896-O

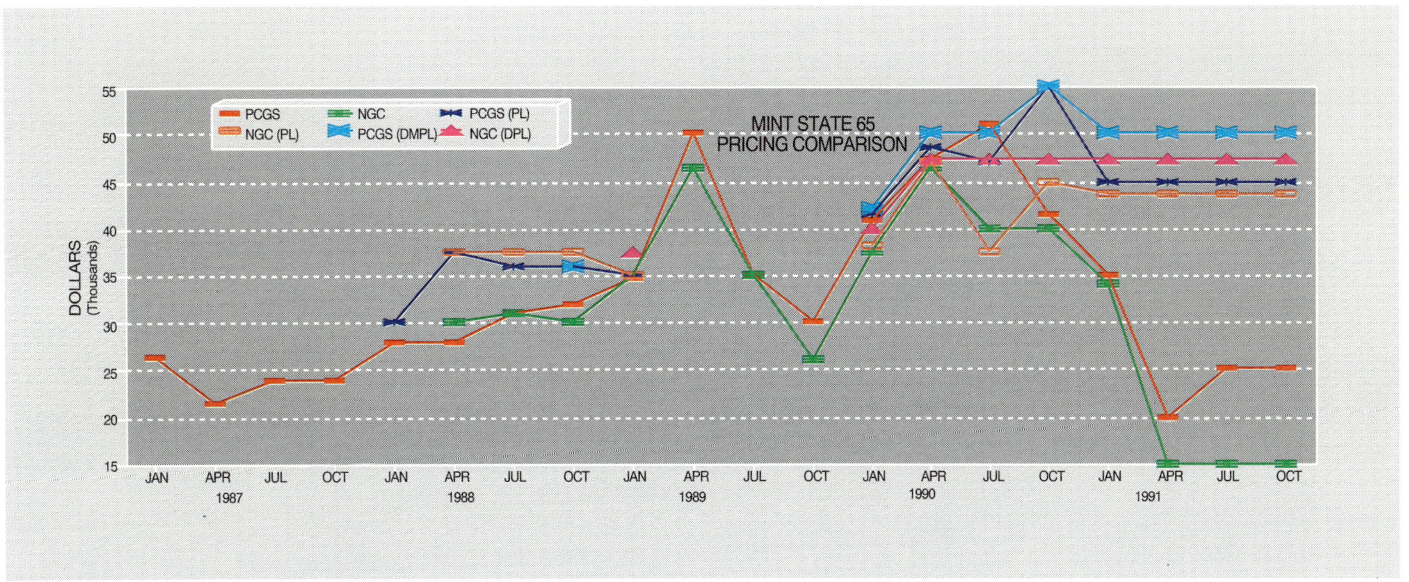

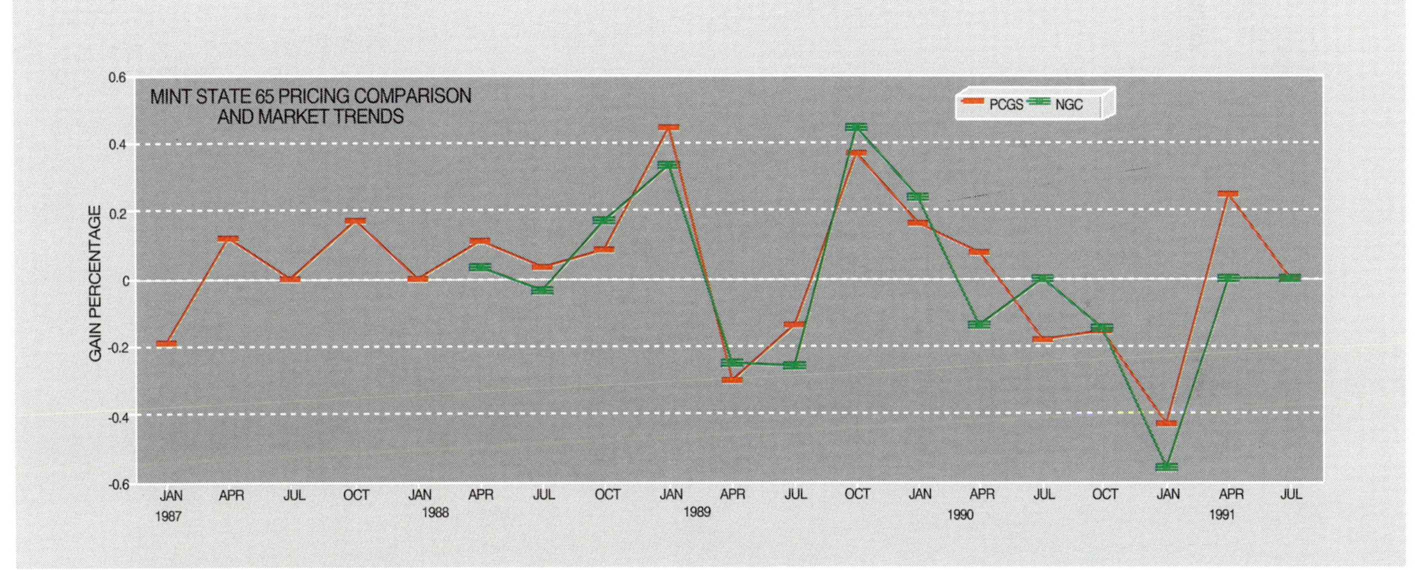

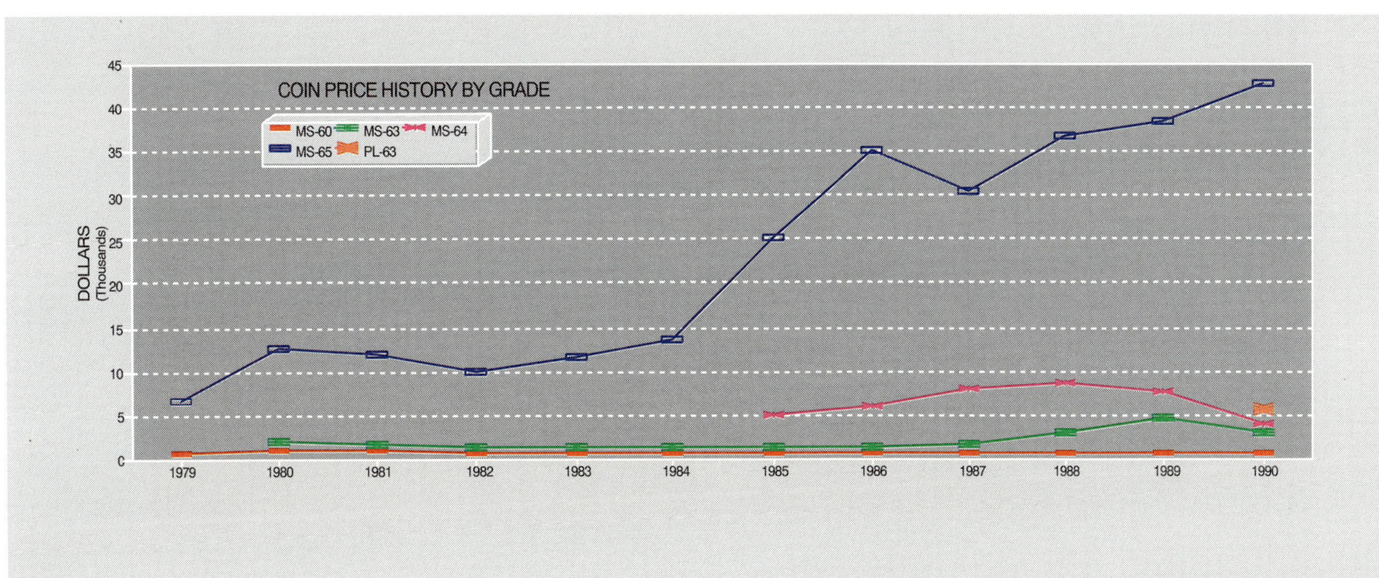

1896-S

Mintage 5,000,000. Uncs. are much harder to find than one would expect from that mintage. Worn examples (below VF) are obtainable, but higher grade circulated ones seldom show up. Hard to find in grades above Very Fine.

Uncs. are usually weak in centers and noticeably bagmarked. The Redfield coins (less than a full bag) mostly graded MS 63 and below. To date only 17 Uncs. have received PCGS grades of MS 65.

Recommended in all BU grades.

Beware fakes made by adding S mintmarks to genuine 1896 Philadelphia dollars. These altered date counterfeit methods are quite common and you should be very cautious.

Prooflikes: Very rare in all grades. Redfield had a few DMPL's. The 1896-S is the rarest Morgan in BU prooflike condition in direct proportion to its original mintage.

MINTAGE	PROOF	STRIKE	LUSTER	BAG MARKS	REDFIELD
5,000,000	0	Soft To Average	Average	Moderate To Heavy	Yes
DIES	**DIE VARIETIES**	**% OF PL**	**% OF DMPL**	**PIVOTAL GRADE**	**RARITY FACTOR**
40	8	0.4	0.0	MS 64	R-1

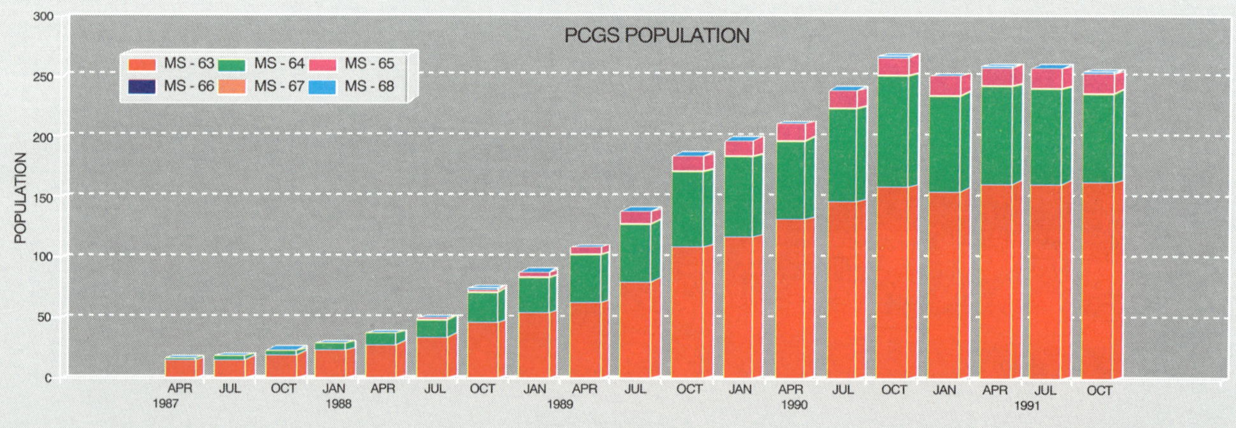

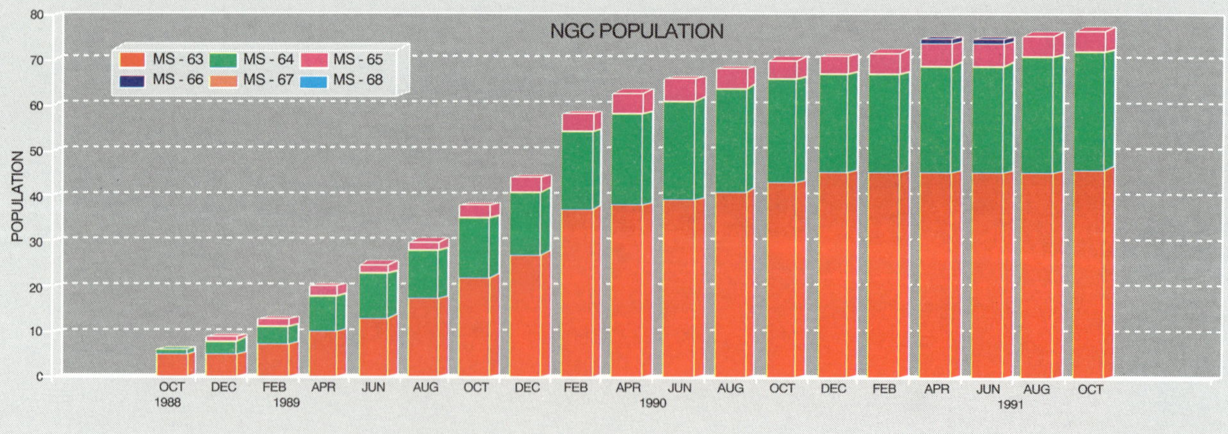

1896-S

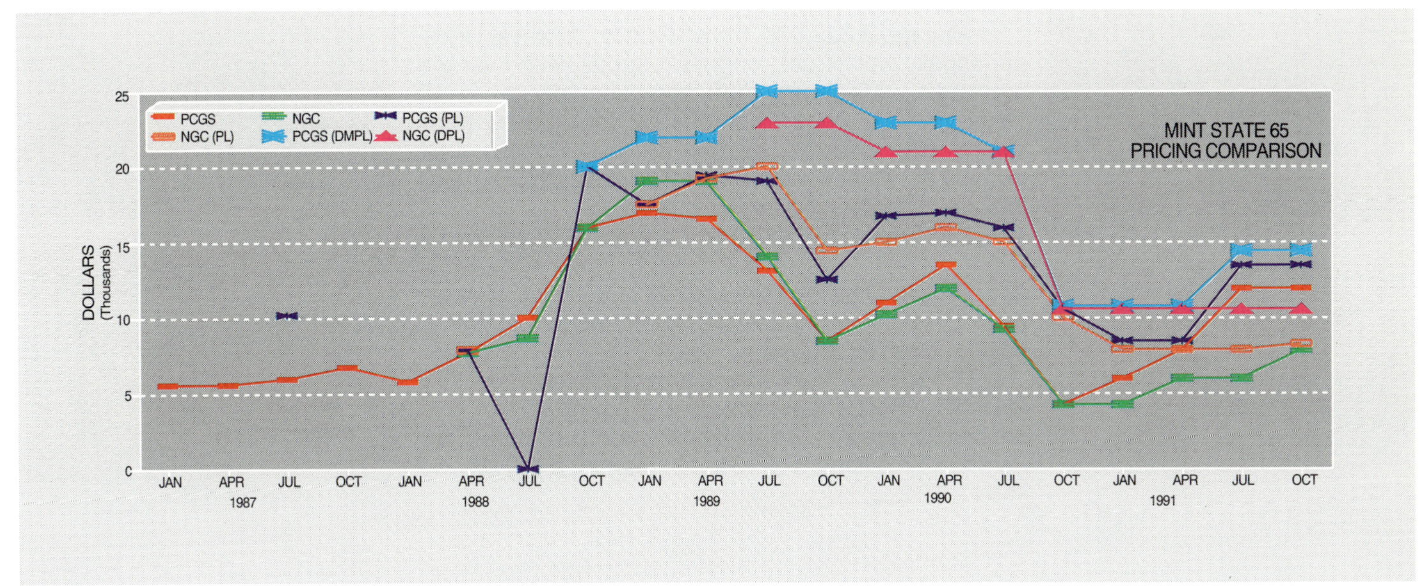

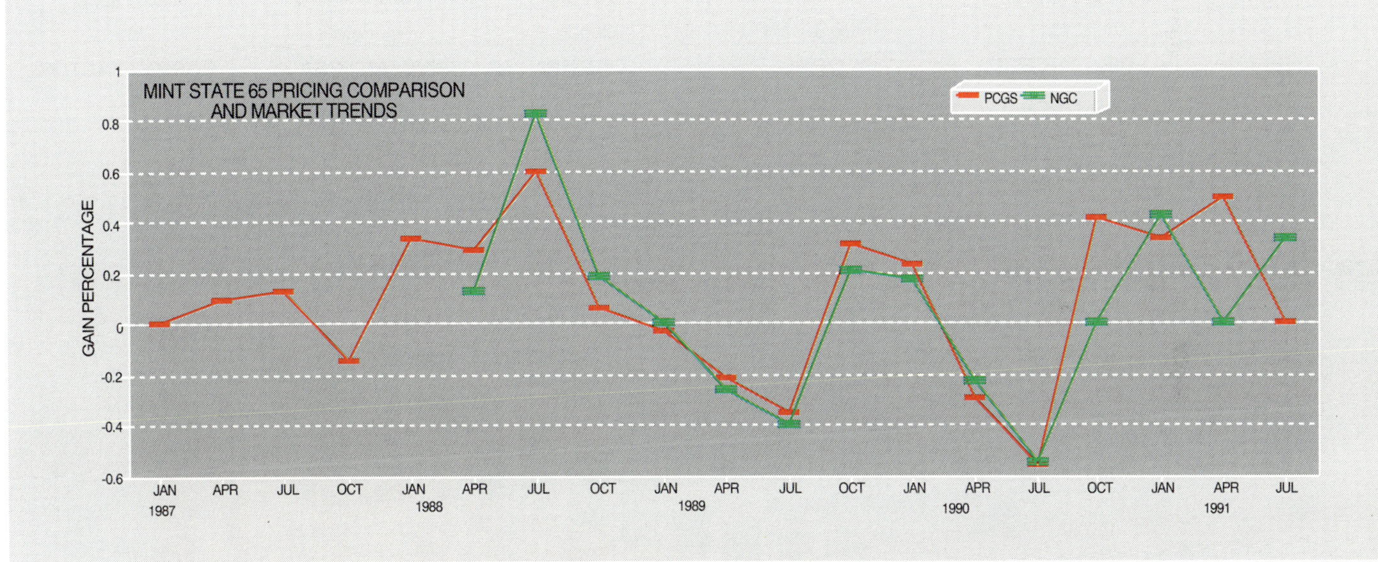

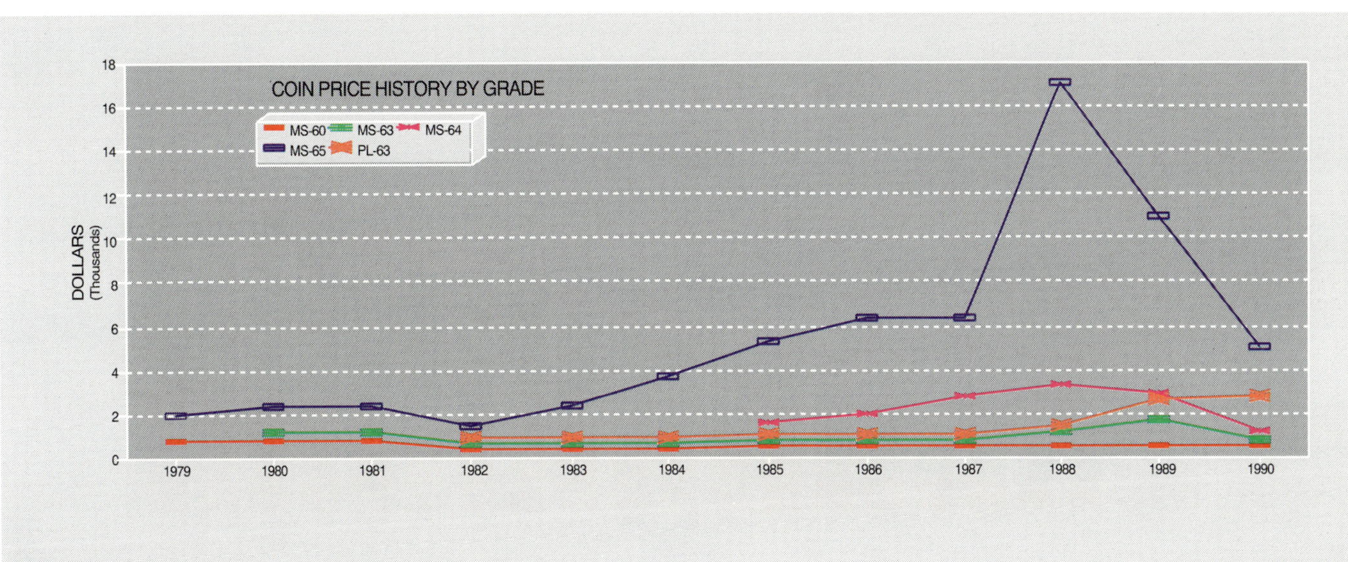

1897-P

Mintage 2,822,000, from 13 obvs., 12 revs. Uncs. are usually well struck, brightly lustrous, with average bagmarks. Many are from approximately 16 to 18 Redfield hoard bags dispersed by John Love, many reportedly to John Kamin of the "Forecaster" newsletter. Most were MS 60 to 63, fewer MS 64. Roll lots are available. Sliders are plentiful.

Recommended in MS 65 up or in MS 64 by the roll.

Proofs: The low mintage of 731 took two obverse dies. One of them has 18 lightly repunched; the other has not been described.

Prooflikes: Very scarce above MS 64, especially in DMPL. BU cameos are rare. Some DMPL's have amazingly deep mirrored fields. Some of these are from the "small hoard of 10 to 15" mentioned by Wayne Miller.

MINTAGE	PROOF	STRIKE	LUSTER	BAG MARKS	REDFIELD
2,822,000	731	Sharp & Bold	Good	Moderate	Yes
DIES	**DIE VARIETIES**	**% OF PL**	**% OF DMPL**	**PIVOTAL GRADE**	**RARITY FACTOR**
70	10	5.1	2.1	MS 65	R-4

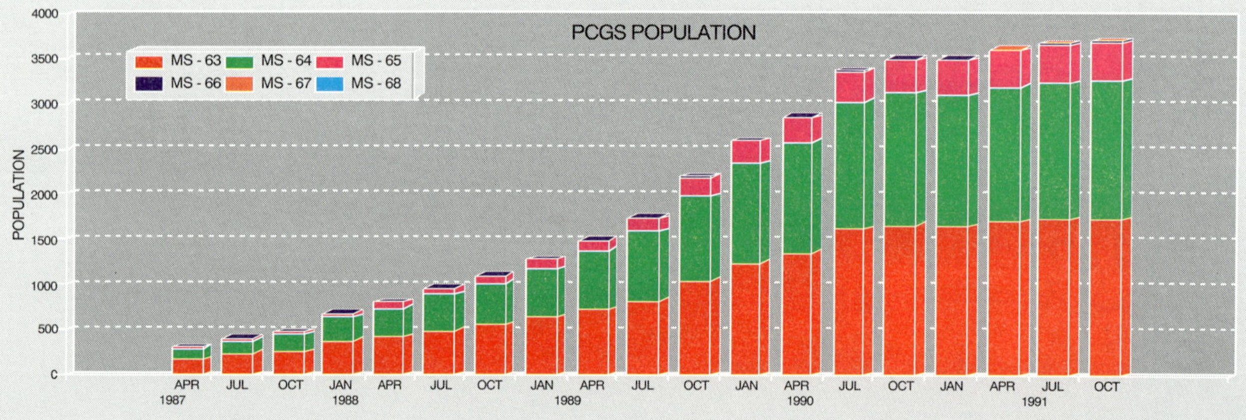

PCGS POPULATION

MS - 63, MS - 64, MS - 65, MS - 66, MS - 67, MS - 68

POPULATION

0, 500, 1000, 1500, 2000, 2500, 3000, 3500, 4000

APR 1987, JUL, OCT, JAN 1988, APR, JUL, OCT, JAN 1989, APR, JUL, OCT, JAN, APR 1990, JUL, OCT, JAN, APR, JUL 1991, OCT

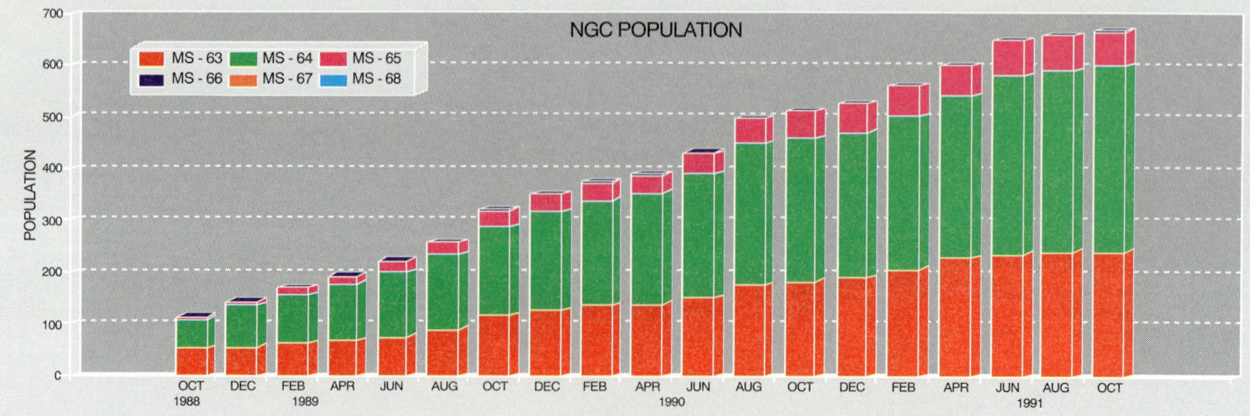

NGC POPULATION

MS - 63, MS - 64, MS - 65, MS - 66, MS - 67, MS - 68

POPULATION

0, 100, 200, 300, 400, 500, 600, 700

OCT 1988, DEC, FEB 1989, APR, JUN, AUG, OCT, DEC, FEB, APR 1990, JUN, AUG, OCT, DEC, FEB, APR, JUN 1991, AUG, OCT

1897-P

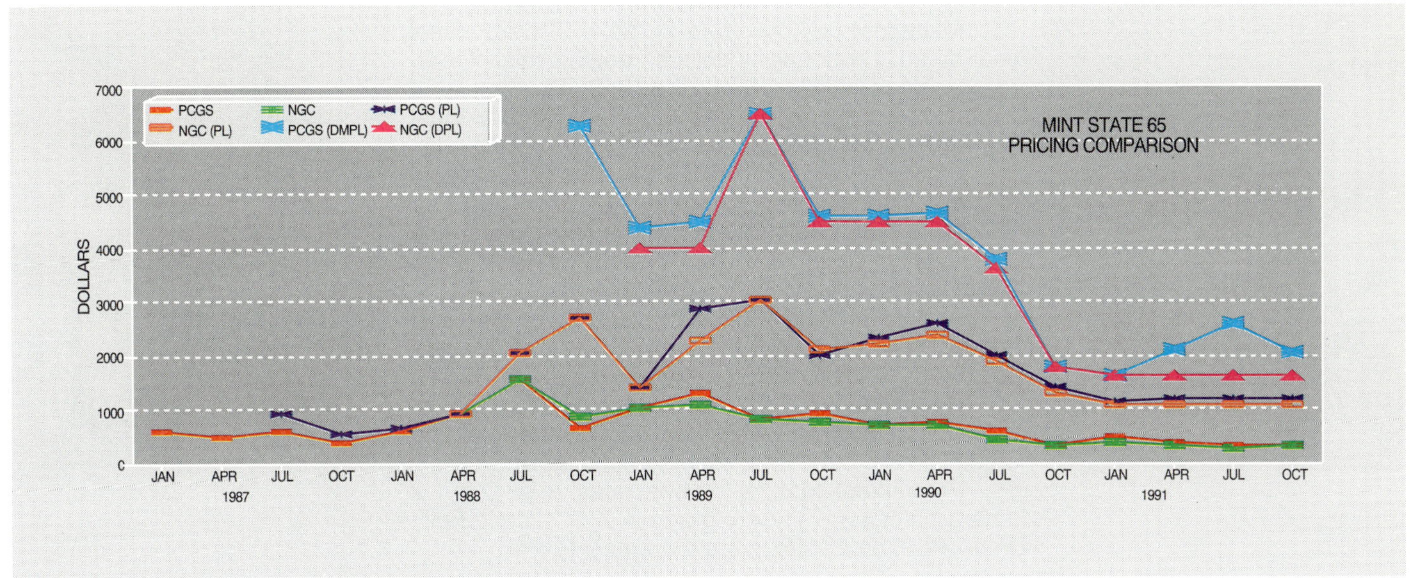

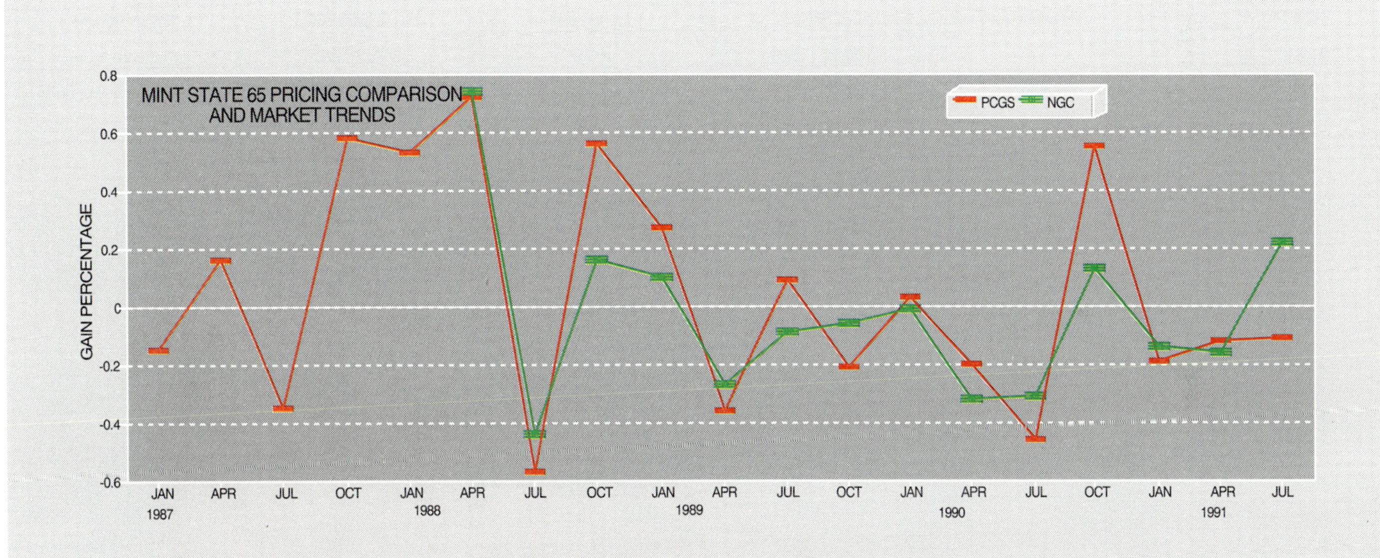

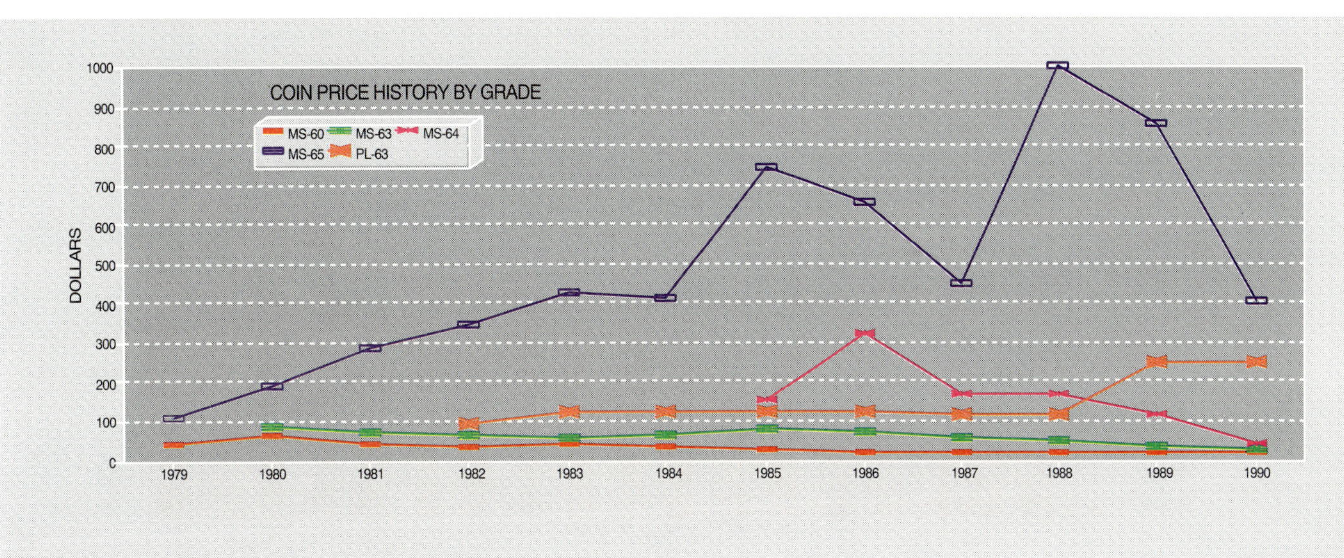

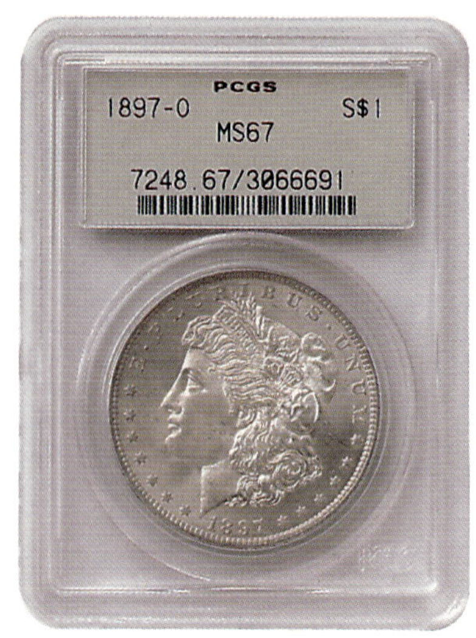

1897-O

PCGS
1897-O
S$1
MS67
7248.67/3066691

Mintage 4,004,000 from 22 pairs of dies. Final year of really poor quality dollars from this mint. Uncs. are weak and usually dull, like the 1896-O's. Circulated examples are scarce; no BU rolls are reported. Most likely the majority of this date went to the melting pots.

PCGS has graded two MS 67. One of these sold at the FUN convention (Orlando, FL), Jan. 1990, for $250,000. The other, not for sale, is currently touring the continents with the PCGS World's Finest Morgan Dollar Collection.

A mint sewn bag handled by Dean Tavenner (Deer Lodge, MT) in the early 1960's proved to contain sliders of 1894-O, 1895-O, 1896-O, and (the majority) 1897-O.

Recommended in MS 64 up, but you may have to settle for an MS 60/63 while hunting. Pivotal point and grade is MS 64. Beware sliders priced as Unc.

Prooflikes: Most of the best ones, even DMPL's (sharp cameos), will only grade AU or slider. Fully Uncs., PL's, and DMPL's are extremely RARE.

PCGS

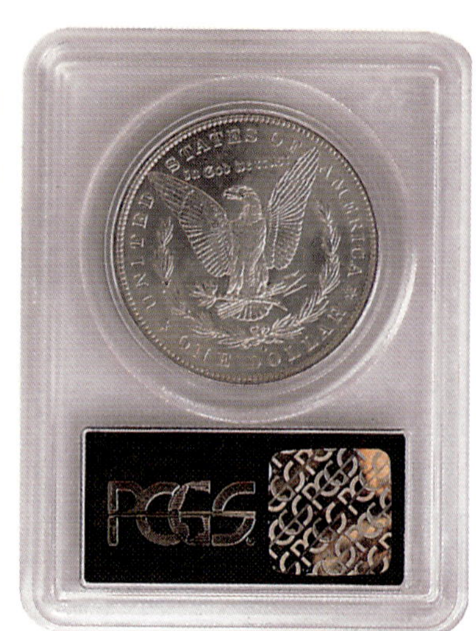

MINTAGE	PROOF	STRIKE	LUSTER	BAG MARKS	REDFIELD
4,004,000	0	Soft & Weak	Poor	Moderate	No
DIES	**DIE VARIETIES**	**% OF PL**	**% OF DMPL**	**PIVOTAL GRADE**	**RARITY FACTOR**
50	7	1.1	0.9	MS 64	R-1

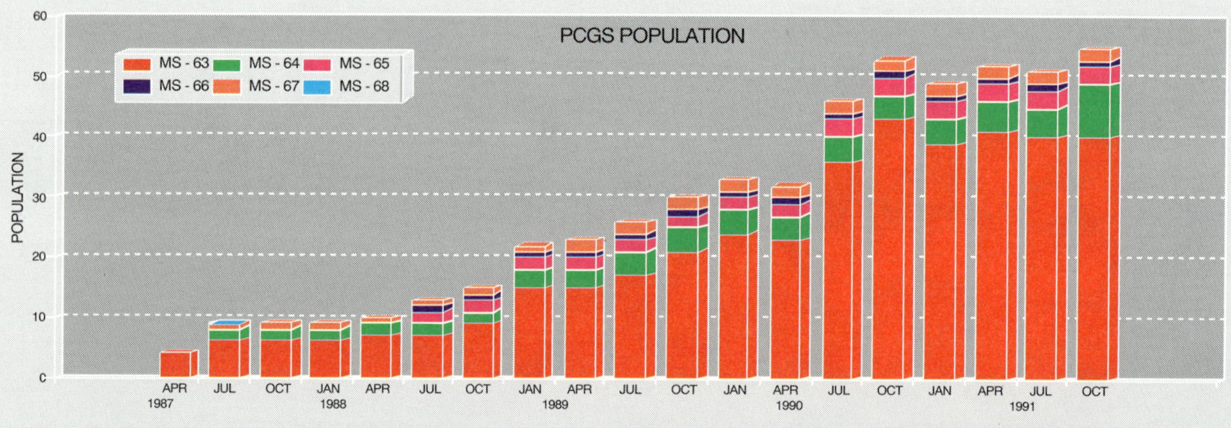
PCGS POPULATION
MS - 63
MS - 64
MS - 65
MS - 66
MS - 67
MS - 68
POPULATION
60
50
40
30
20
10
C
APR 1987
JUL
OCT
JAN 1988
APR
JUL
OCT
JAN 1989
APR
JUL
OCT
JAN
APR 1990
JUL
OCT
JAN
APR
JUL 1991
OCT

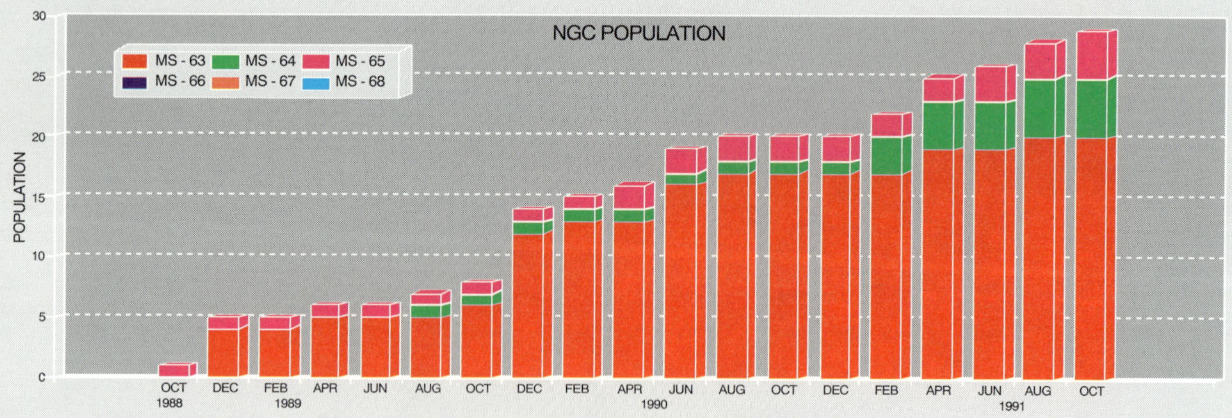
NGC POPULATION
MS - 63
MS - 64
MS - 65
MS - 66
MS - 67
MS - 68
POPULATION
30
25
20
15
10
5
C
OCT 1988
DEC
FEB 1989
APR
JUN
AUG
OCT
DEC
FEB
APR
JUN 1990
AUG
OCT
DEC
FEB
APR
JUN 1991
AUG
OCT

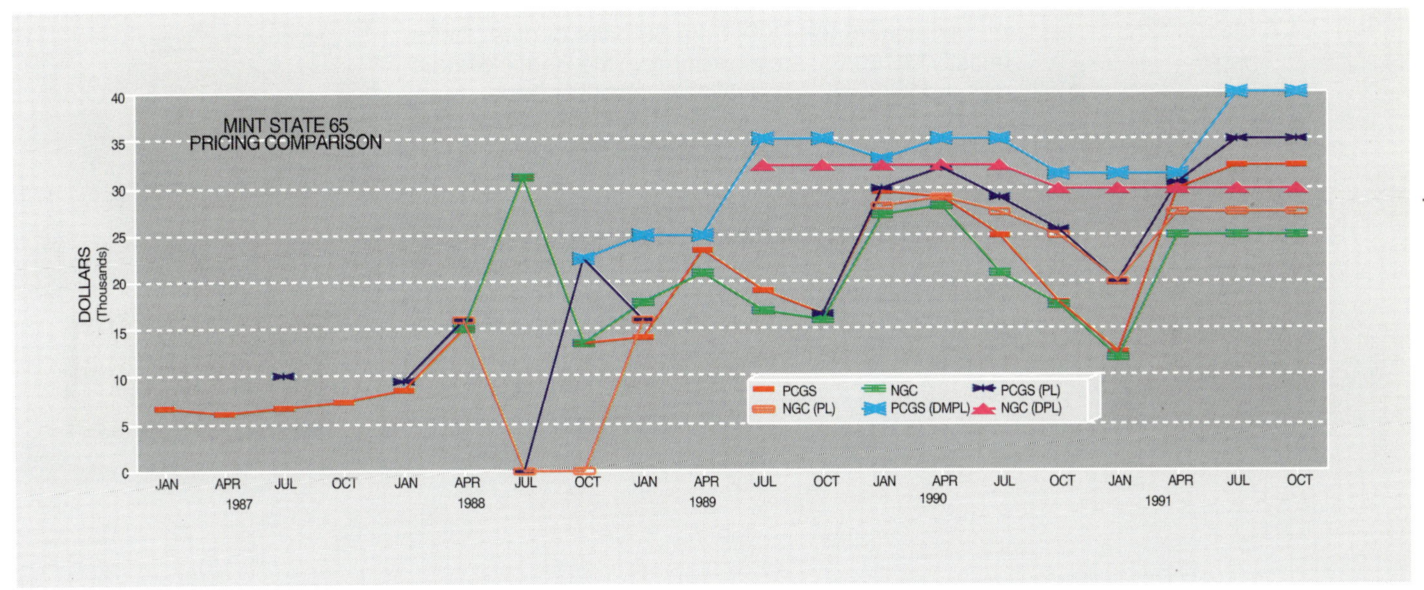
MINT STATE 65
PRICING COMPARISON
DOLLARS (Thousands)
40
35
30
25
20
15
10
5
0
PCGS
NGC
PCGS (PL)
NGC (PL)
PCGS (DMPL)
NGC (DPL)
JAN APR JUL OCT JAN APR JUL OCT JAN APR JUL OCT JAN APR JUL OCT JAN APR JUL OCT
1987
1988
1989
1990
1991

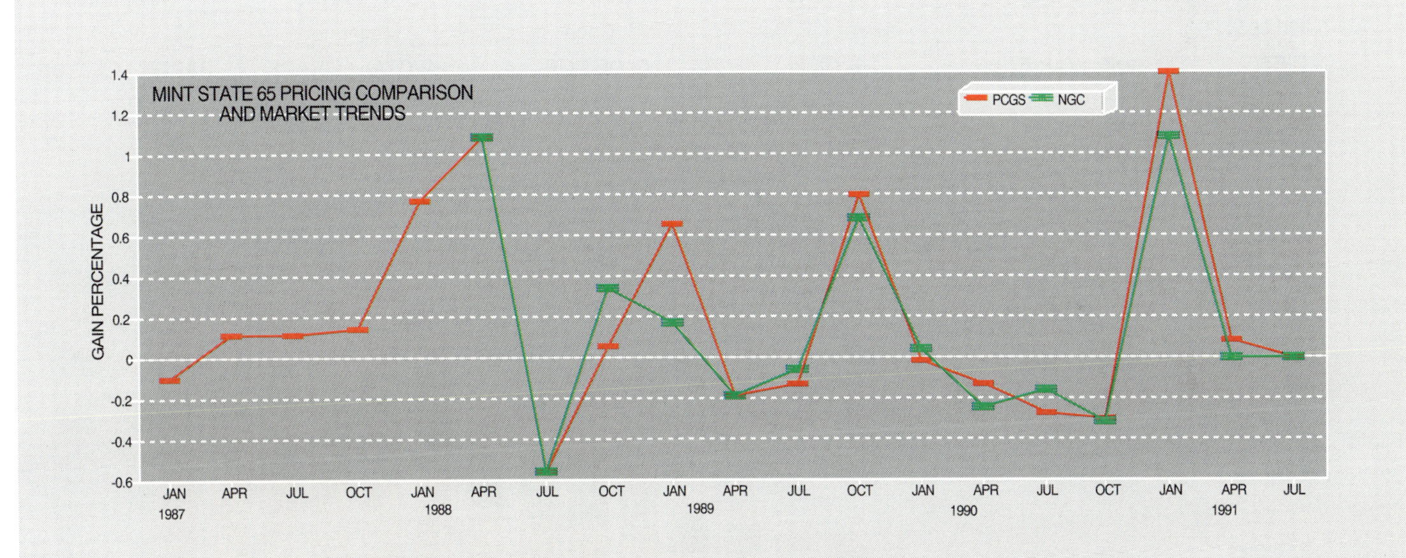
MINT STATE 65 PRICING COMPARISON
AND MARKET TRENDS
PCGS
NGC
GAIN PERCENTAGE
1.4
1.2
1
0.8
0.6
0.4
0.2
0
-0.2
-0.4
-0.6
JAN APR JUL OCT JAN APR JUL OCT JAN APR JUL OCT JAN APR JUL OCT JAN APR JUL
1987
1988
1989
1990
1991

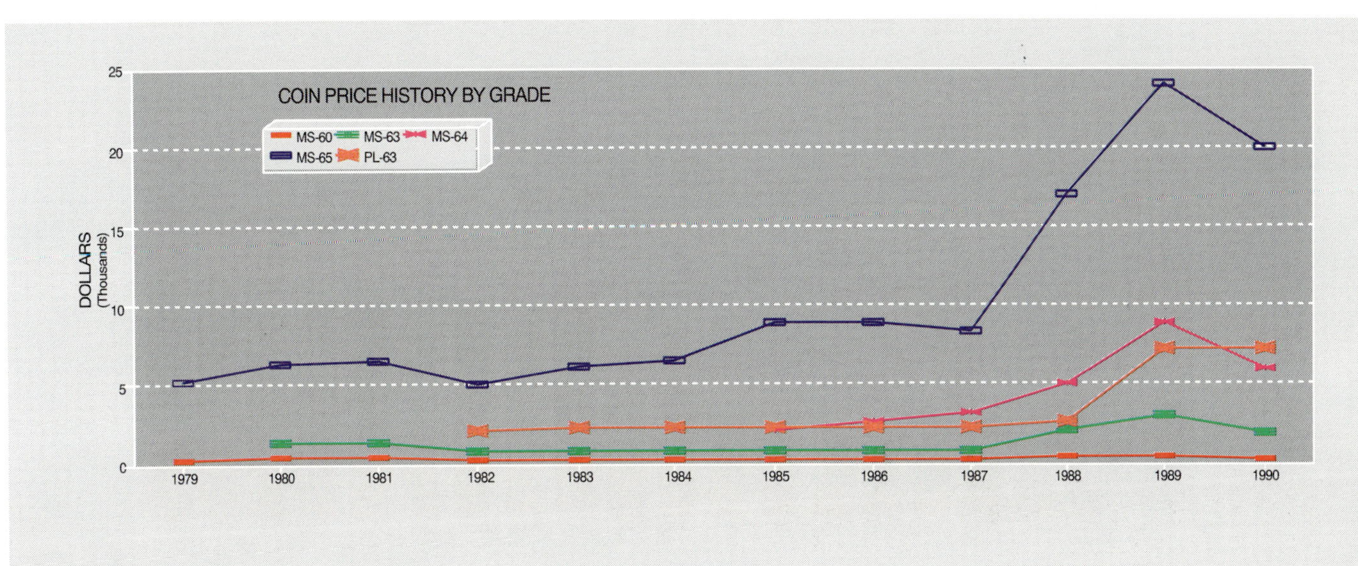
COIN PRICE HISTORY BY GRADE
MS-60
MS-63
MS-64
MS-65
PL-63
DOLLARS (Thousands)
25
20
15
10
5
0
1979 1980 1981 1982 1983 1984 1985 1986 1987 1988 1989 1990

PCGS
1897-S S$1
MS67
7250.67/9009349

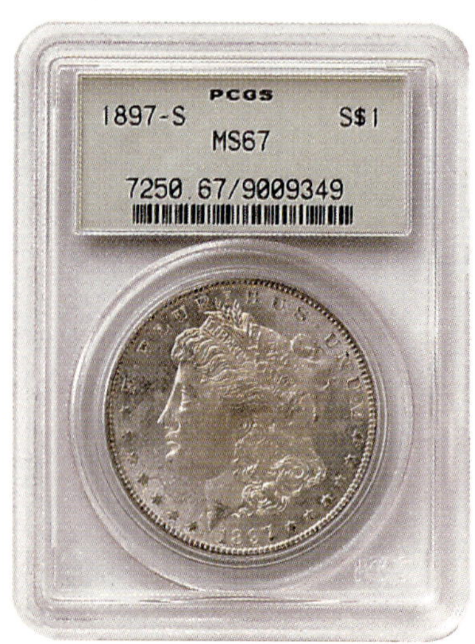

1897-S

Mintage 5,825,000, from 38 pairs of dies. Uncs. (mostly MS 60/63) are plentiful from the Redfield hoard; rolls in MS 60/62 are available, possibly bags. Many of these are well struck and brightly lustrous. A heavily melted date. Some have graded as high as PCGS MS 68.

Recommended in MS 64 up, preferably PL.

Prooflikes: Redfield had at least one full bag, mostly flat strikes with plenty of bagmarks. PL's comprise about 15-20% of all 1897-S Morgans. PL's outnumber DMPL's 5 to 1. PL's are very scarce above MS 64, DMPL's rare above MS 65.

PCGS

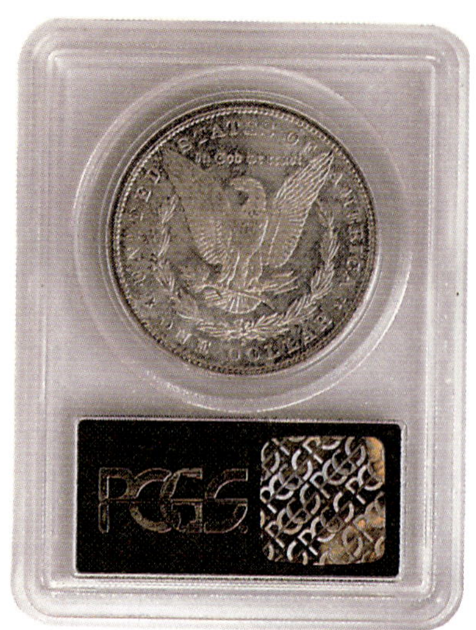

MINTAGE	PROOF	STRIKE	LUSTER	BAG MARKS	REDFIELD
5,825,000	0	Average To Bold	Good	Moderate	Yes
DIES	**DIE VARIETIES**	**% OF PL**	**% OF DMPL**	**PIVOTAL GRADE**	**RARITY FACTOR**
98	11	14.6	3.6	MS 65	R-4

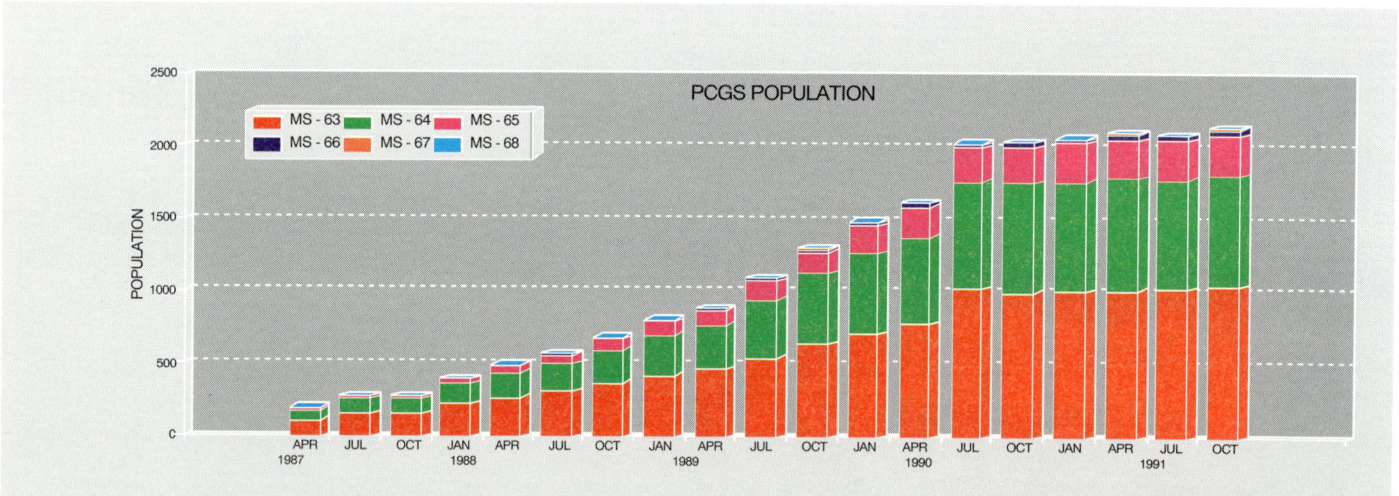
PCGS POPULATION
MS - 63
MS - 64
MS - 65
MS - 66
MS - 67
MS - 68
POPULATION
2500
2000
1500
1000
500
0
APR 1987
JUL
OCT
JAN 1988
APR
JUL
OCT
JAN 1989
APR
JUL
OCT
JAN
APR 1990
JUL
OCT
JAN
APR
JUL 1991
OCT

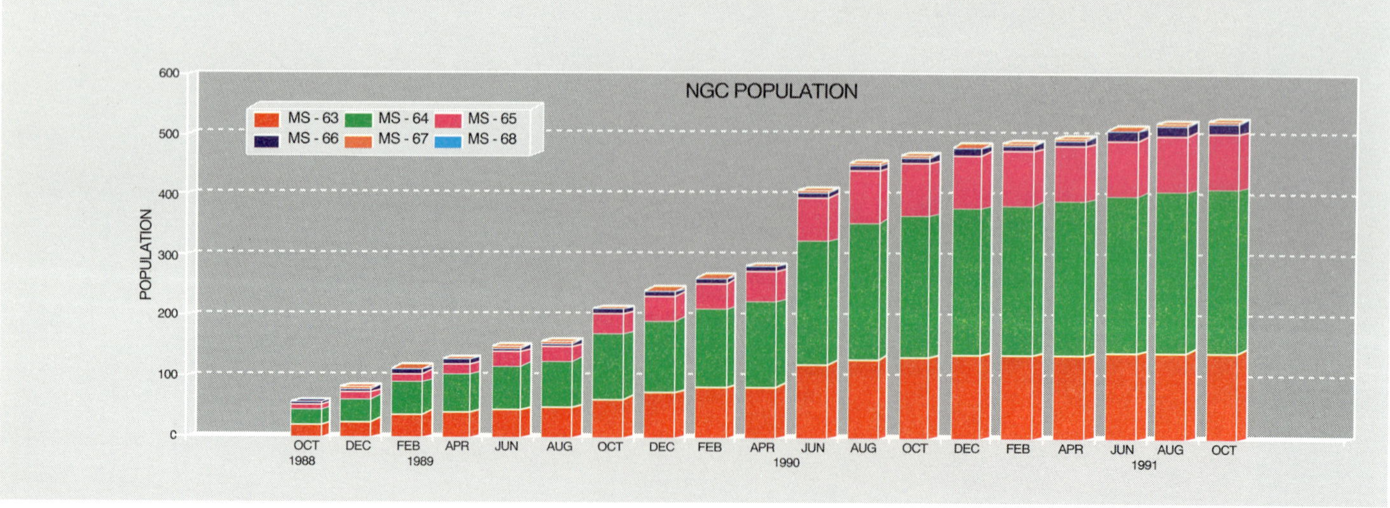
NGC POPULATION
MS - 63
MS - 64
MS - 65
MS - 66
MS - 67
MS - 68
POPULATION
600
500
400
300
200
100
0
OCT 1988
DEC
FEB 1989
APR
JUN
AUG
OCT
DEC
FEB
APR 1990
JUN
AUG
OCT
DEC
FEB
APR
JUN 1991
AUG
OCT

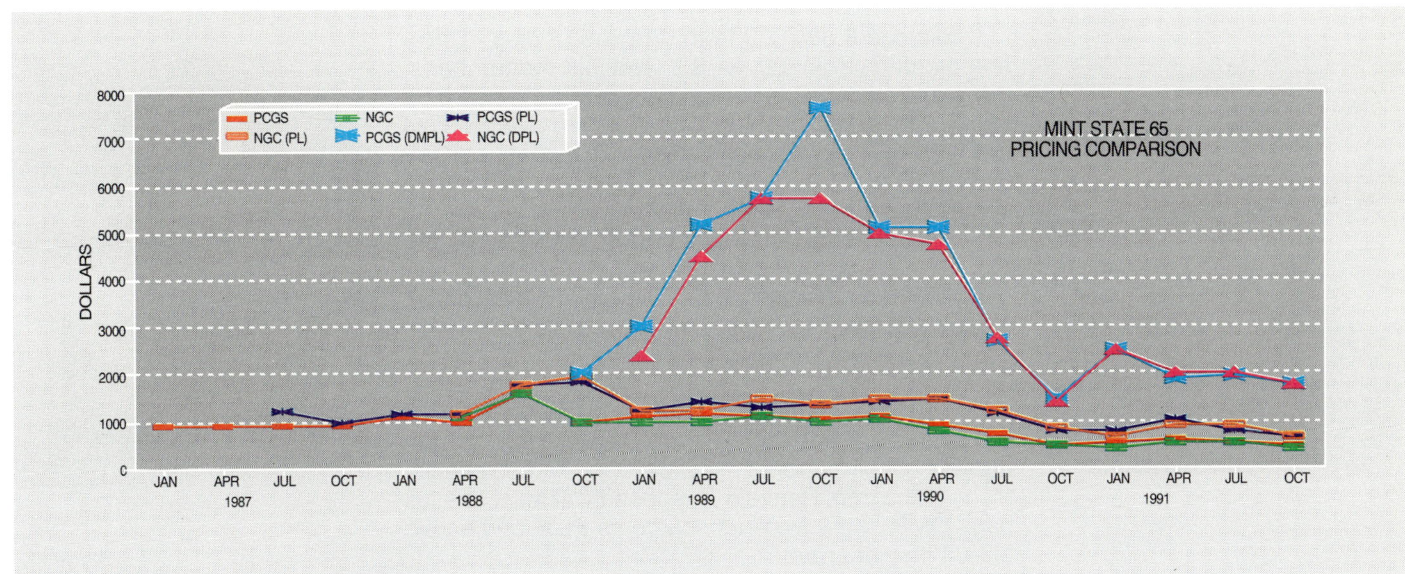
PCGS
NGC
PCGS (PL)
NGC (PL)
PCGS (DMPL)
NGC (DPL)
MINT STATE 65
PRICING COMPARISON
DOLLARS
8000
7000
6000
5000
4000
3000
2000
1000
0
JAN APR JUL OCT JAN APR JUL OCT JAN APR JUL OCT JAN APR JUL OCT JAN APR JUL OCT
1987 1988 1989 1990 1991

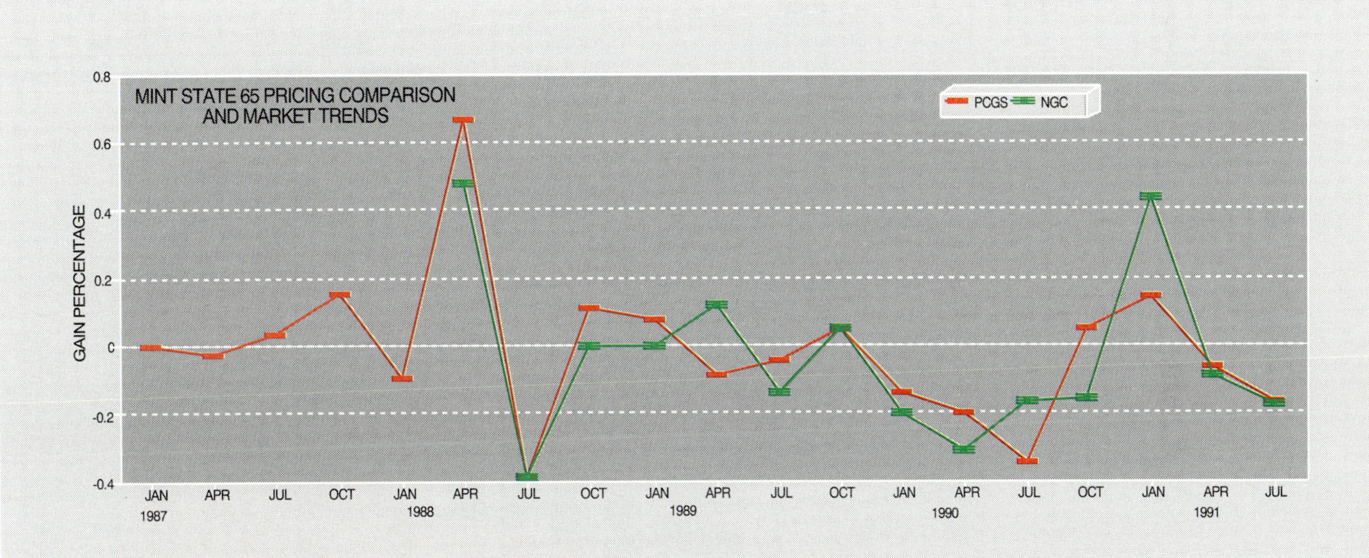
MINT STATE 65 PRICING COMPARISON
AND MARKET TRENDS
PCGS
NGC
GAIN PERCENTAGE
0.8
0.6
0.4
0.2
0
-0.2
-0.4
JAN APR JUL OCT JAN APR JUL OCT JAN APR JUL OCT JAN APR JUL OCT JAN APR JUL
1987 1988 1989 1990 1991

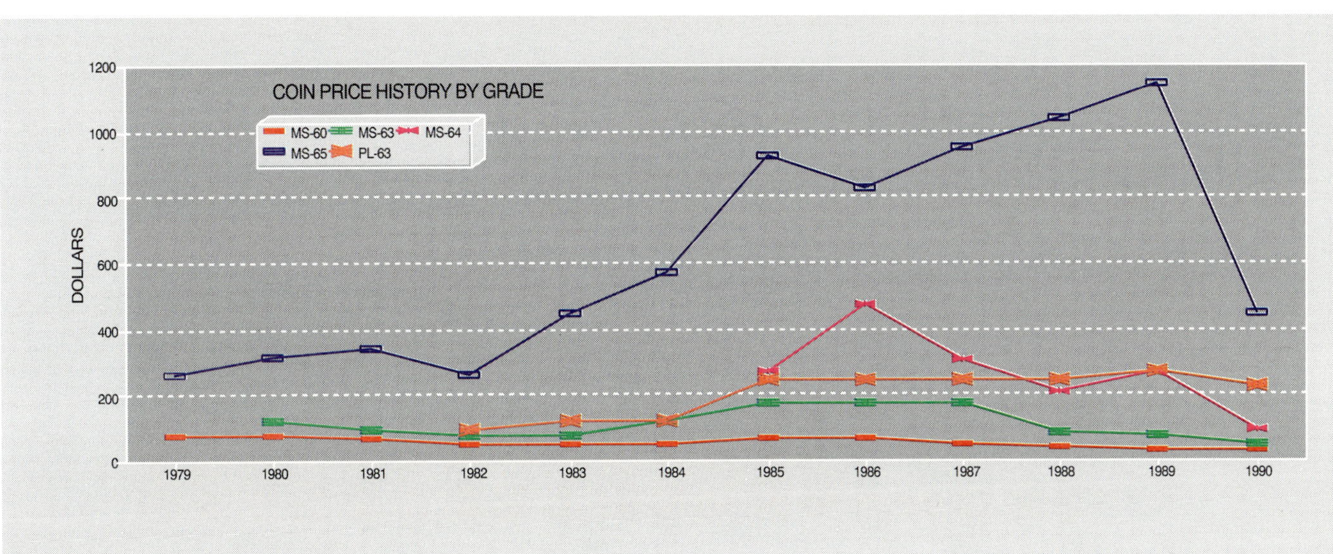
COIN PRICE HISTORY BY GRADE
MS-60
MS-63
MS-64
MS-65
PL-63
DOLLARS
1200
1000
800
600
400
200
0
1979 1980 1981 1982 1983 1984 1985 1986 1987 1988 1989 1990

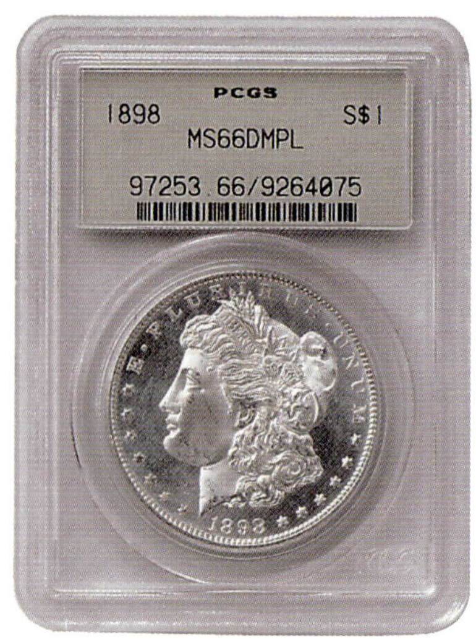

1898-P

Mintage 5,884,000 from 30 pairs of dies. Uncs. are plentiful from 20 to 30 Redfield hoard bags, dispersed by John Love, many going to John Kamin of the "Forecaster" newsletter. BU rolls are available, as are both original and assembled bags; most are MS 60/62. Many Uncs. are weak in centers: hair above ear, eagle's breast. Heavily melted.

Recommended in MS 65 up or in MS 64 by the roll.

Proofs: Mintage 735. Though 3 obvs. and 2 revs. were made for these, all seen to date are VAM 2's. Too many have been cleaned.

Prooflikes: One-sided (usually obverse) semi-PL's are common. Especially above MS 64, two-sided PL's are scarce in all Unc. grades, usually not very deeply mirrored nor with strong cameo effects. Many came from Redfield, supposedly at least one full bag. DMPL's are twice as scarce as PL's, and above MS 64 they are rare.

MINTAGE	PROOF	STRIKE	LUSTER	BAG MARKS	REDFIELD
5,884,000	735	Sharp & Bold	Good	Light	Yes
DIES	**DIE VARIETIES**	**% OF PL**	**% OF DMPL**	**PIVOTAL GRADE**	**RARITY FACTOR**
40	10	6.3	3.2	MS 65	R-4

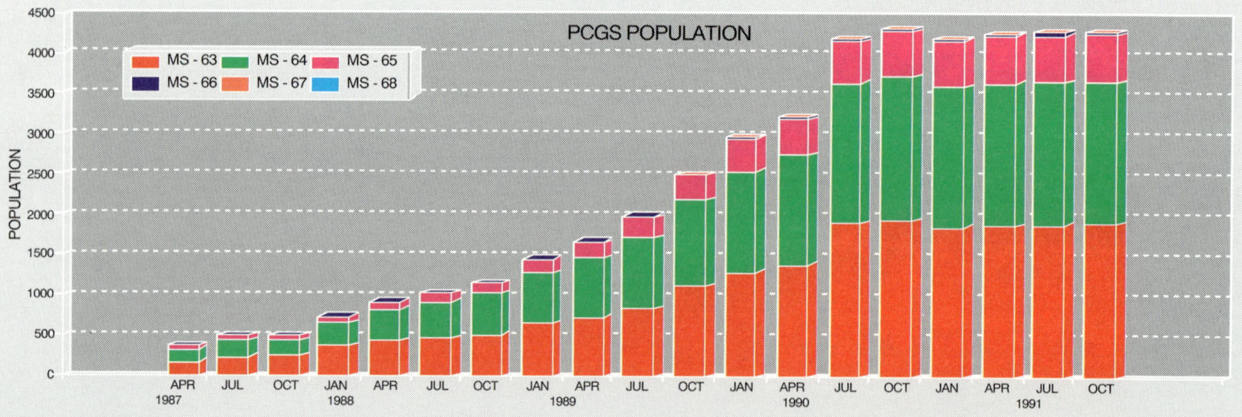

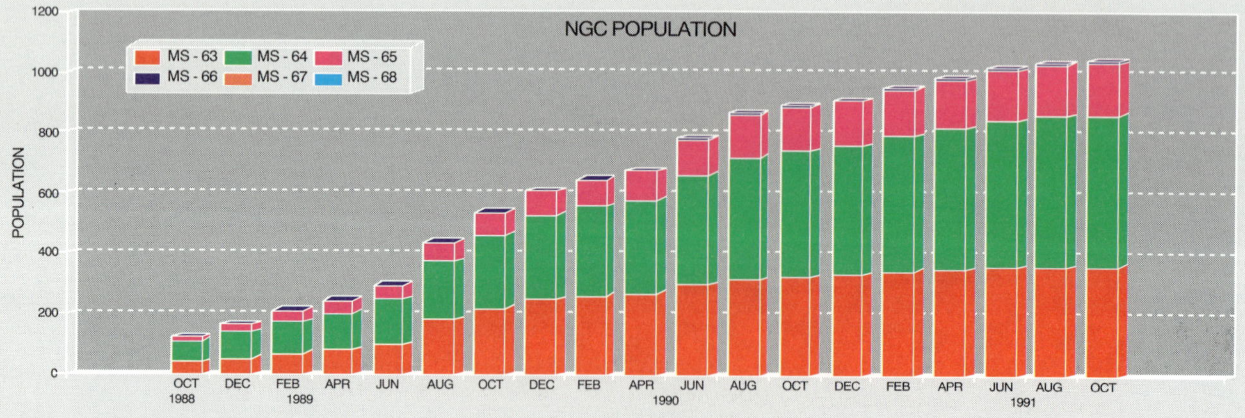

PCGS POPULATION

NGC POPULATION

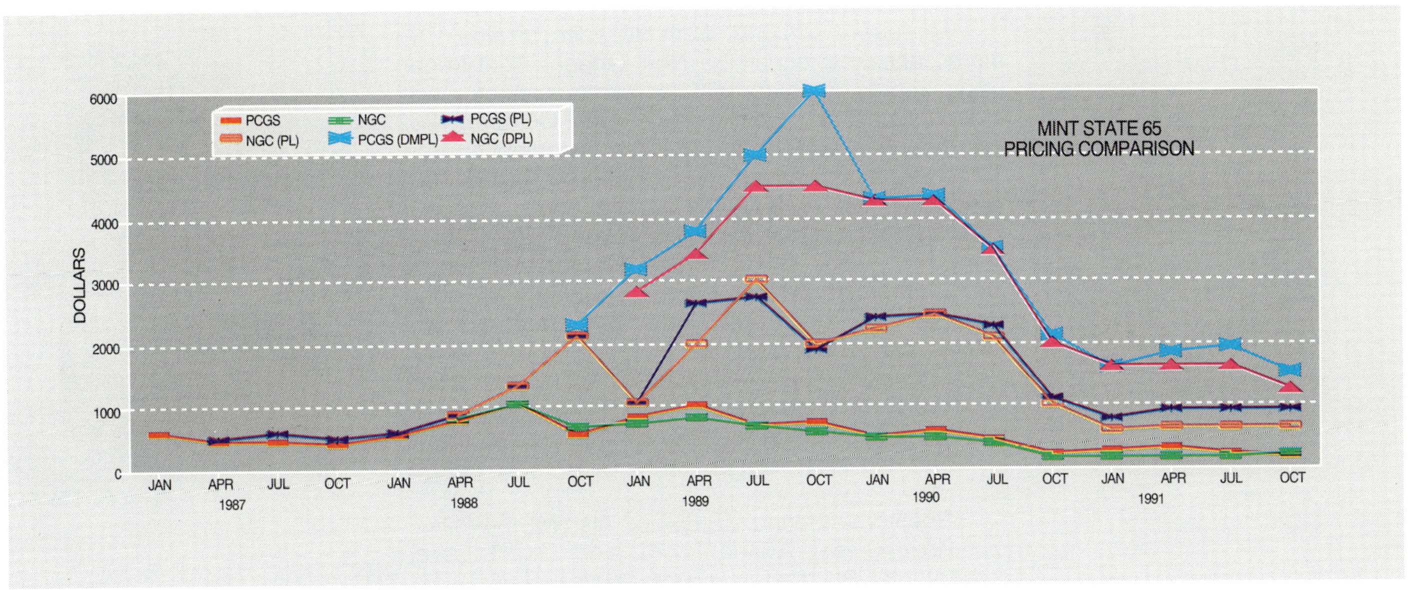

MINT STATE 65
PRICING COMPARISON
PCGS
NGC
PCGS (PL)
NGC (PL)
PCGS (DMPL)
NGC (DPL)
DOLLARS
6000
5000
4000
3000
2000
1000
0
JAN APR JUL OCT JAN APR JUL OCT JAN APR JUL OCT JAN APR JUL OCT JAN APR JUL OCT
1987 1988 1989 1990 1991

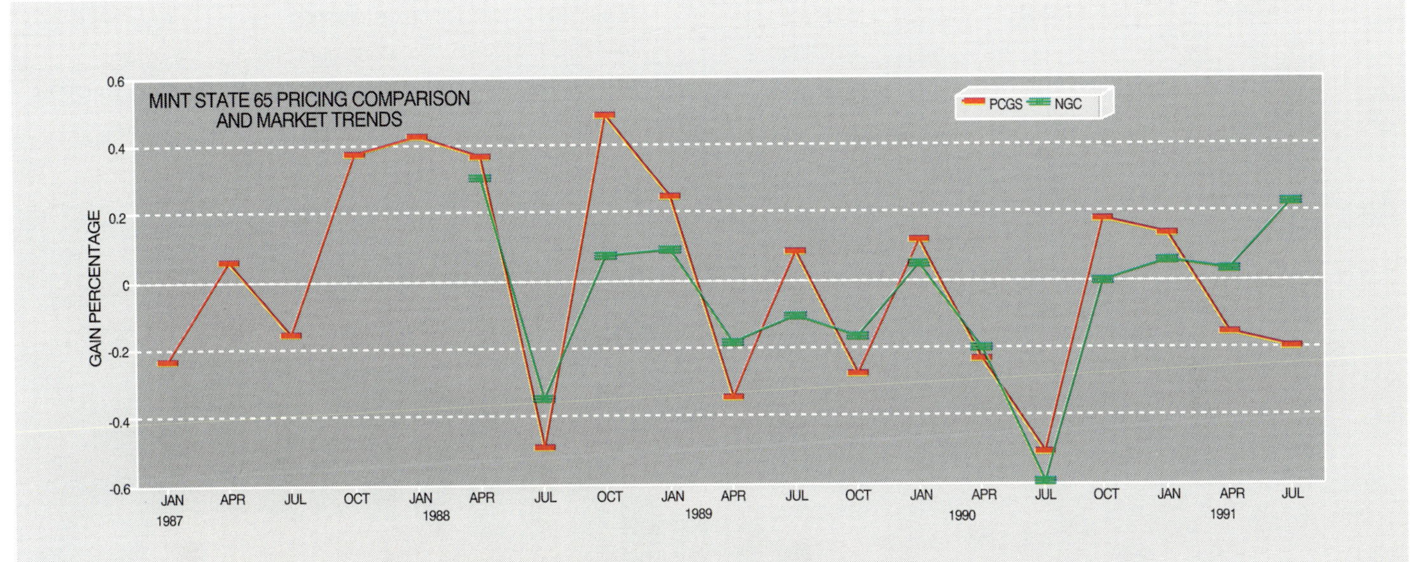

MINT STATE 65 PRICING COMPARISON
AND MARKET TRENDS
PCGS
NGC
GAIN PERCENTAGE
0.6
0.4
0.2
0
-0.2
-0.4
-0.6
JAN APR JUL OCT JAN APR JUL OCT JAN APR JUL OCT JAN APR JUL OCT JAN APR JUL
1987 1988 1989 1990 1991

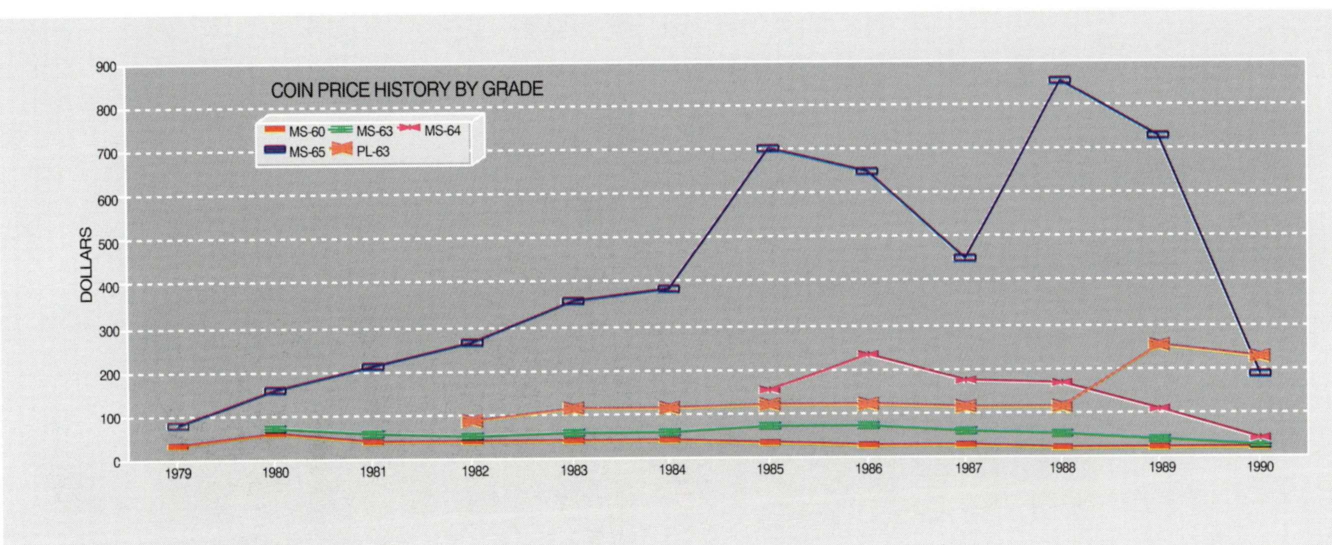

COIN PRICE HISTORY BY GRADE
MS-60
MS-63
MS-64
MS-65
PL-63
DOLLARS
900
800
700
600
500
400
300
200
100
0
1979 1980 1981 1982 1983 1984 1985 1986 1987 1988 1989 1990

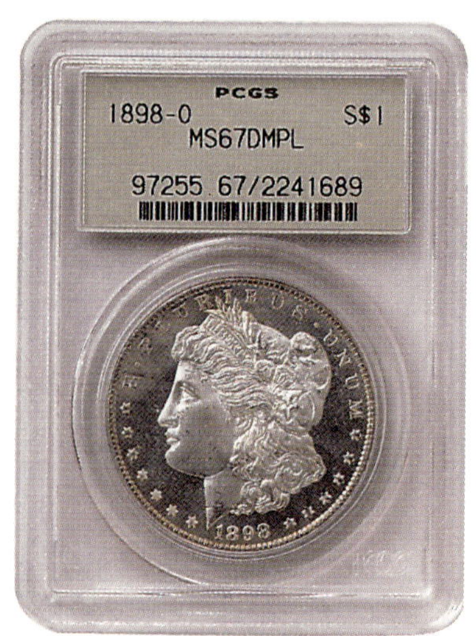

1898-O

PCGS
1898-O S$1
MS67DMPL
97255.67/2241689

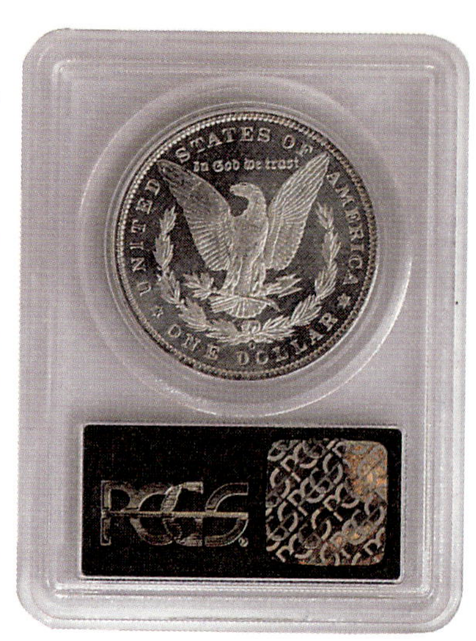

Mintage 4,440,000, from 30 pairs of dies. No more pancakes; either the New Orleans Mint began using improved equipment, or some inspector was more insistent on quality control. Until October, 1962 this date was a rarity; today Uncs. are plentiful from Treasury bags released 1958, 1962-64. In the 1963 "Redbook," the 1898-O was listed at $300. This was twice the price of the 1889-CC at the time! Though some have weak strikes, their frosty lustre is among the brightest from this mint. Redfield had none. Original and assembled rolls and bags are still available, mostly MS 60/62.

Circulated examples are seldom if ever seen. Thomas B. Phillips (Memphis, TN) was quoted as calling the 1898-O the rarest of all circulated Morgans: fewer around even than of 1889-CC, 1892-S, 1893-S, etc.

Recommended in MS 65 up. Also MS 64 rolls.

Prooflikes: Available PL and DMPL (even cameo) in all BU grades; scarce above MS 65.

MINTAGE	PROOF	STRIKE	LUSTER	BAG MARKS	REDFIELD
4,440,000	0	Average	Very Good	Moderate	No
DIES	**DIE VARIETIES**	**% OF PL**	**% OF DMPL**	**PIVOTAL GRADE**	**RARITY FACTOR**
34	19	3.1	1.8	MS 65	R-5

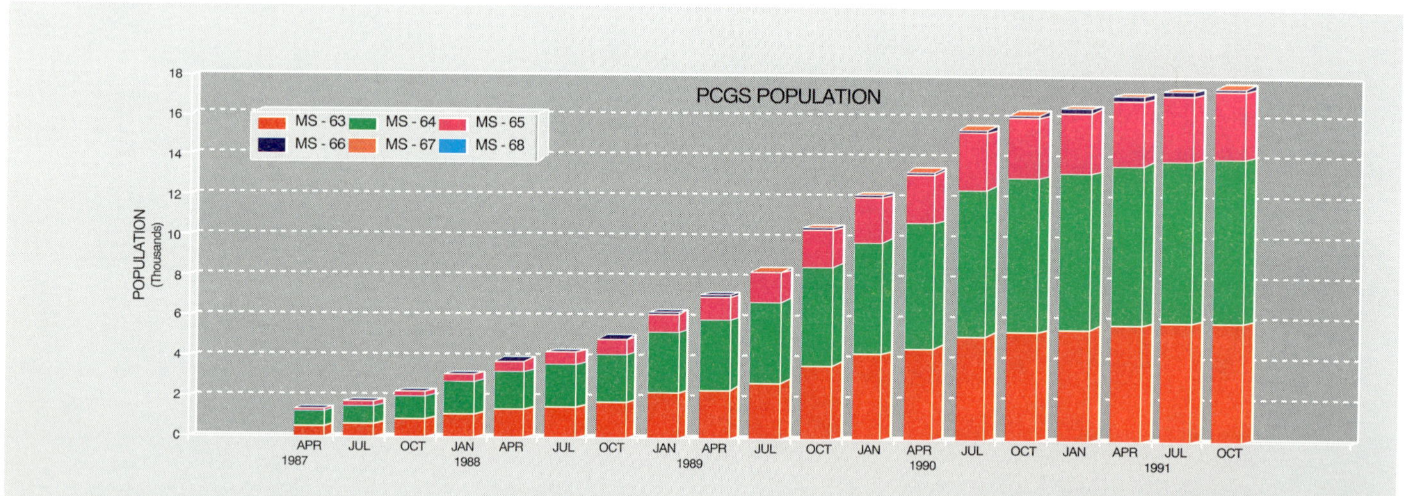
PCGS POPULATION
MS - 63
MS - 64
MS - 65
MS - 66
MS - 67
MS - 68
POPULATION (Thousands)
18
16
14
12
10
8
6
4
2
0
APR 1987
JUL
OCT
JAN 1988
APR
JUL
OCT
JAN 1989
APR
JUL
OCT
JAN
APR 1990
JUL
OCT
JAN
APR
JUL 1991
OCT

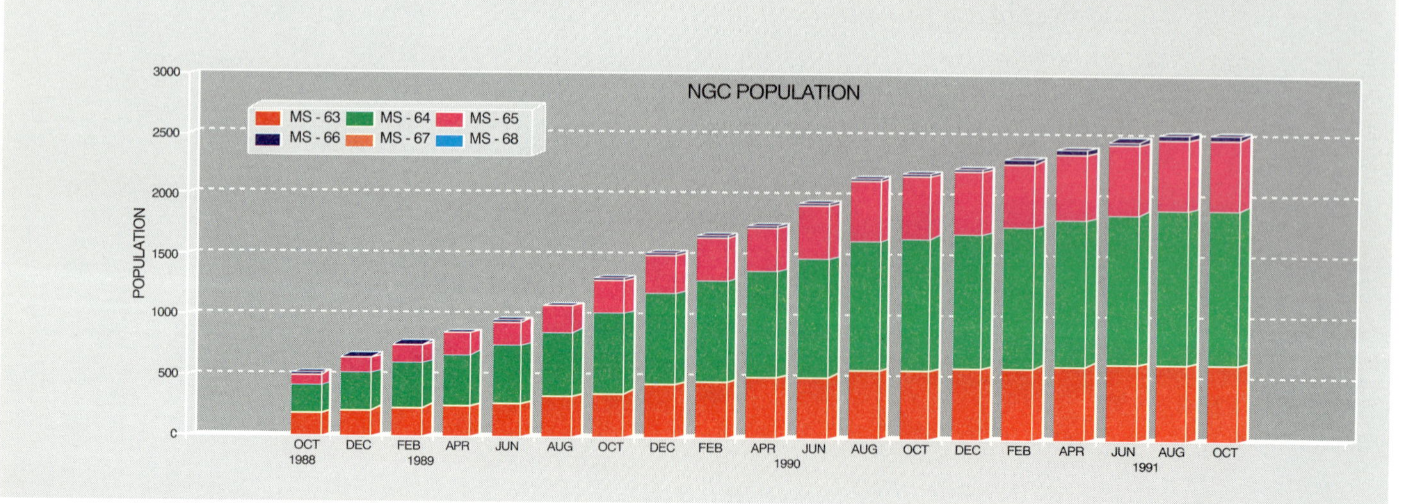
NGC POPULATION
MS - 63
MS - 64
MS - 65
MS - 66
MS - 67
MS - 68
POPULATION
3000
2500
2000
1500
1000
500
0
OCT 1988
DEC
FEB 1989
APR
JUN
AUG
OCT
DEC
FEB
APR 1990
JUN
AUG
OCT
DEC
FEB
APR
JUN 1991
AUG
OCT

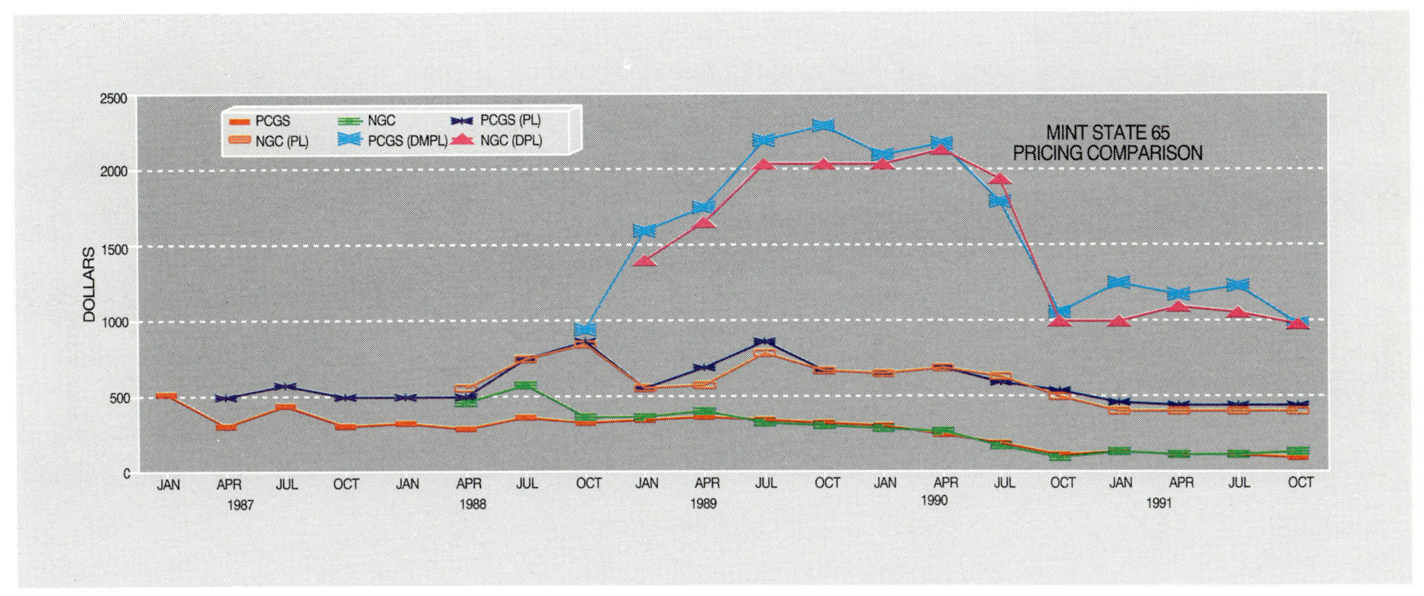
MINT STATE 65
PRICING COMPARISON
PCGS
NGC
PCGS (PL)
NGC (PL)
PCGS (DMPL)
NGC (DPL)
DOLLARS
2500
2000
1500
1000
500
0
JAN APR JUL OCT JAN APR JUL OCT JAN APR JUL OCT JAN APR JUL OCT JAN APR JUL OCT
1987
1988
1989
1990
1991

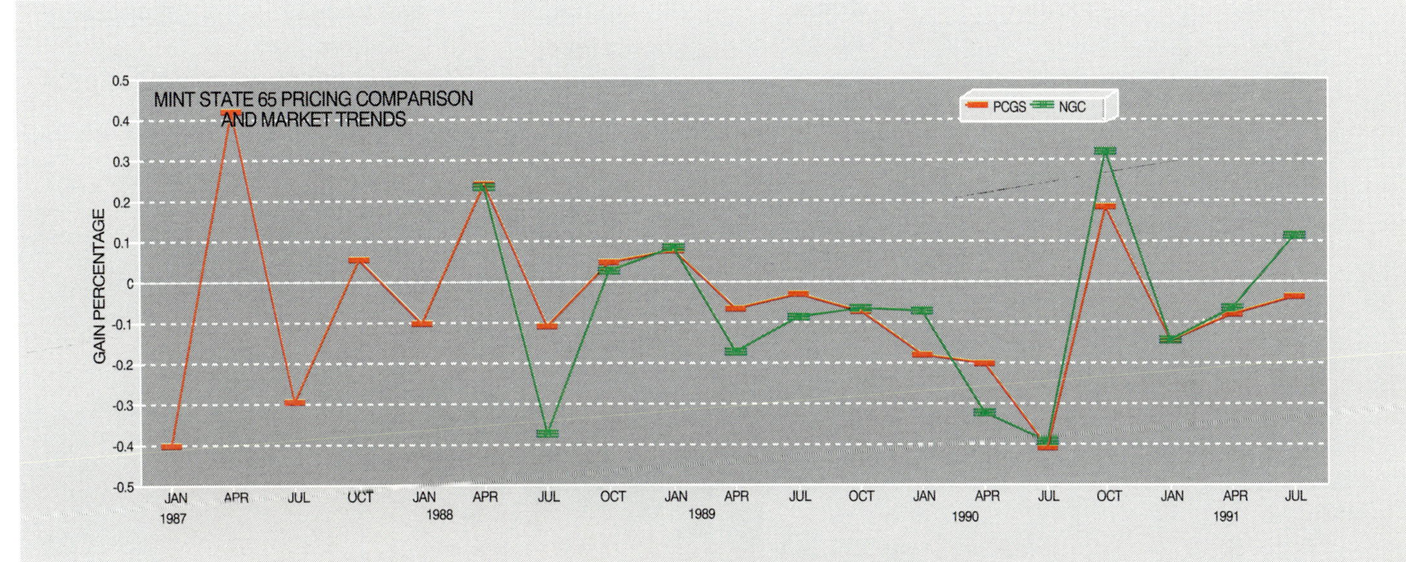
MINT STATE 65 PRICING COMPARISON
AND MARKET TRENDS
PCGS
NGC
GAIN PERCENTAGE
0.5
0.4
0.3
0.2
0.1
0
-0.1
-0.2
-0.3
-0.4
-0.5
JAN APR JUL OCT JAN APR JUL OCT JAN APR JUL OCT JAN APR JUL OCT JAN APR JUL
1987
1988
1989
1990
1991

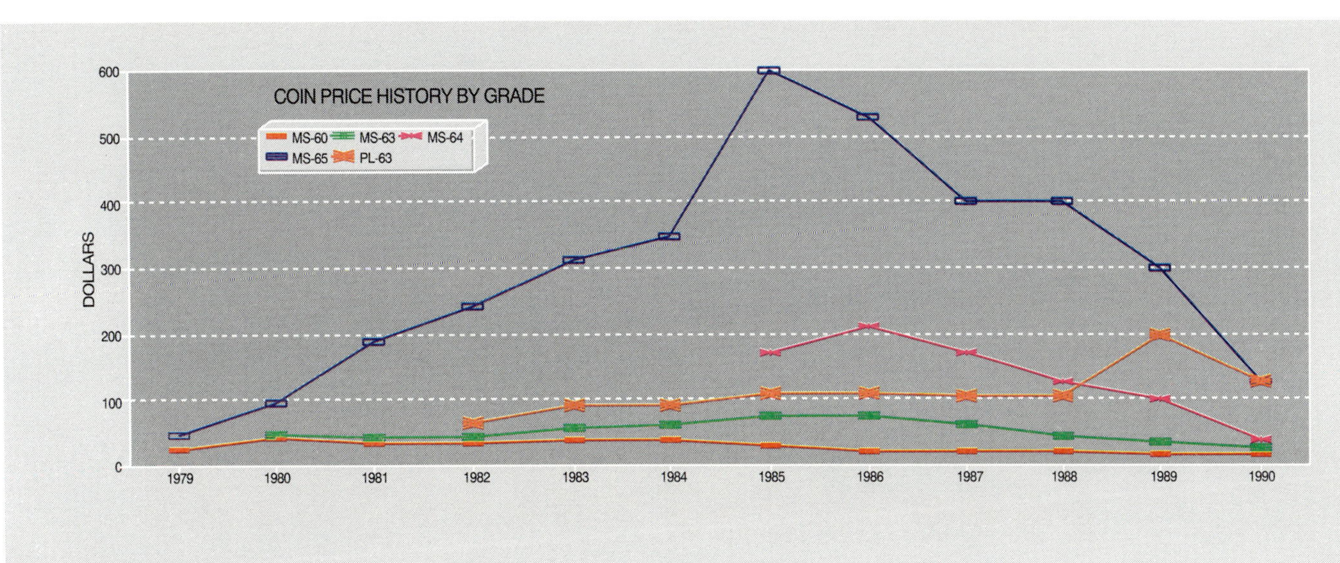
COIN PRICE HISTORY BY GRADE
MS-60
MS-63
MS-64
MS-65
PL-63
DOLLARS
600
500
400
300
200
100
0
1979 1980 1981 1982 1983 1984 1985 1986 1987 1988 1989 1990

1898-S

Mintage 4,102,000, from 20 obvs., 15 revs., Sliders are available, but real Uncs. remain in short supply; above MS 65 they are rare. The Redfield hoard yielded less than one full bag plus a lot of sliders; to date, PCGS has certified fewer than 1,000 as Unc. Many are soft strikes with full lustre.

Recommended in MS 63 up. Beware of sliders priced as Uncs.

"S" over "S" mint mark variety exists.

Prooflikes: Semi-Pl's are available, real ones scarce in all BU grades (especially above MS 63), DMPL's rarer in all BU grades. Redfield had several hundred nicked PL's.

MINTAGE	PROOF	STRIKE	LUSTER	BAG MARKS	REDFIELD
4,102,000	0	Average	Very Good	Moderate	Yes
DIES	**DIE VARIETIES**	**% OF PL**	**% OF DMPL**	**PIVOTAL GRADE**	**RARITY FACTOR**
58	13	6.6	3.6	MS 65	R-2

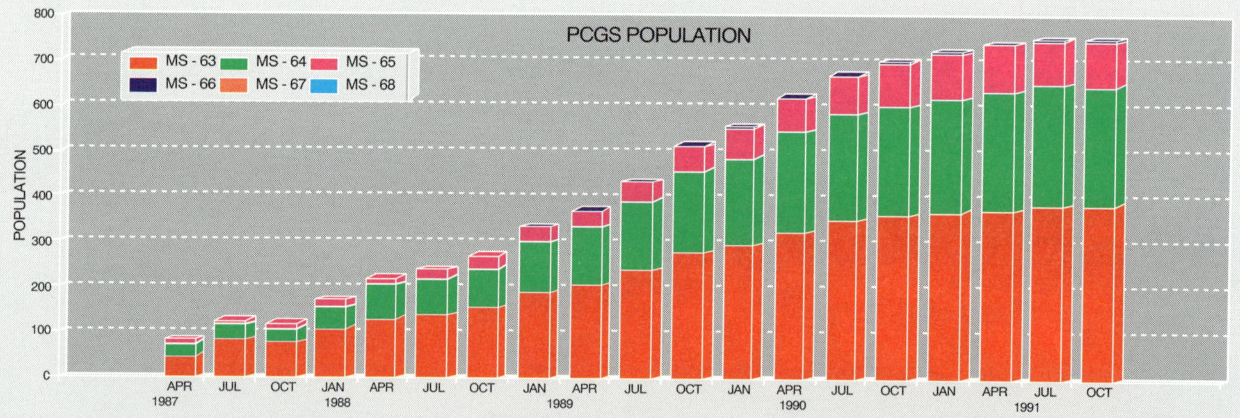

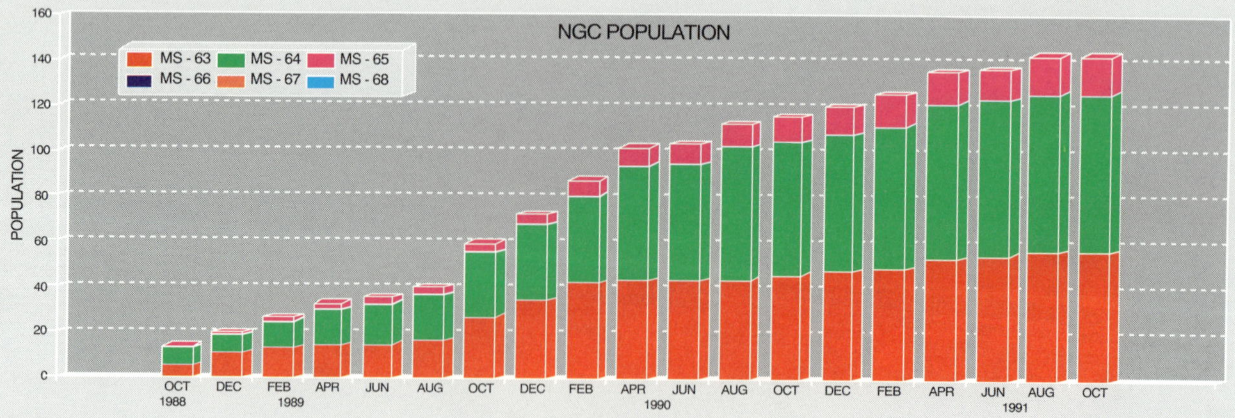

PCGS POPULATION

MS - 63 MS - 64 MS - 65 MS - 66 MS - 67 MS - 68

NGC POPULATION

MS - 63 MS - 64 MS - 65 MS - 66 MS - 67 MS - 68

1898-S

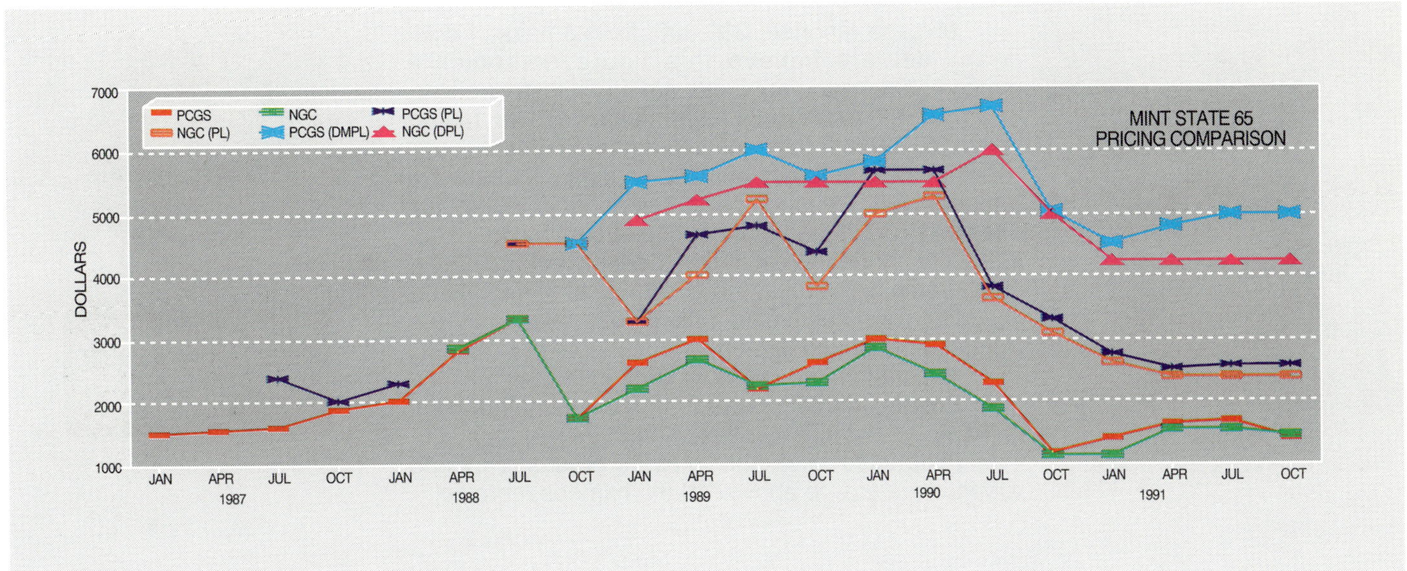

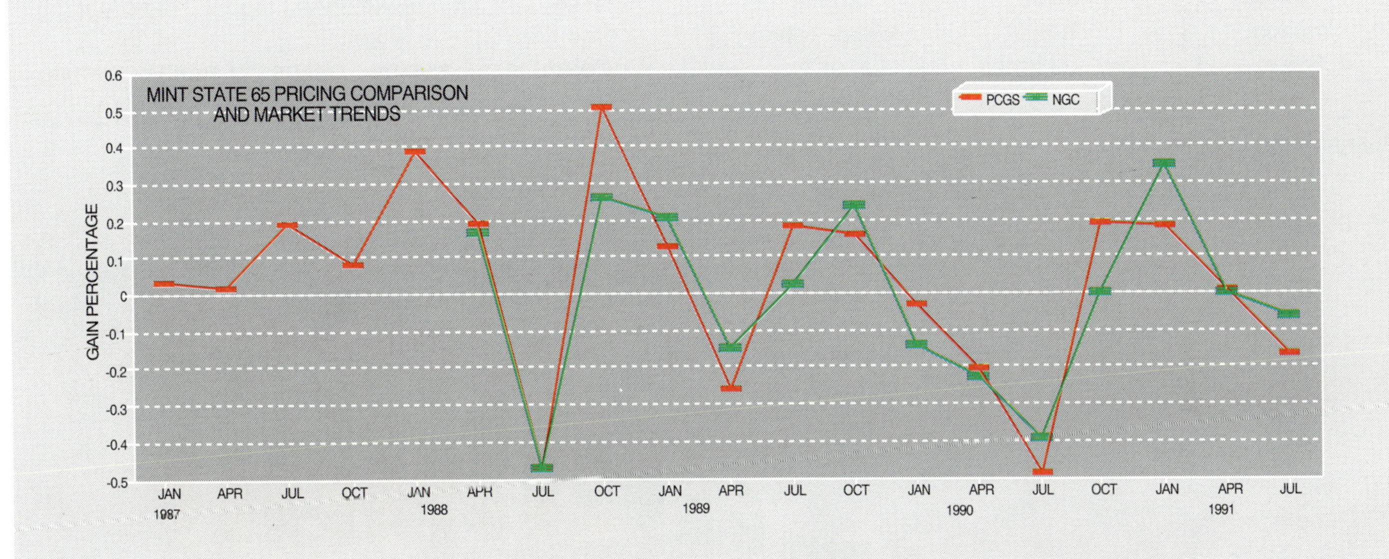

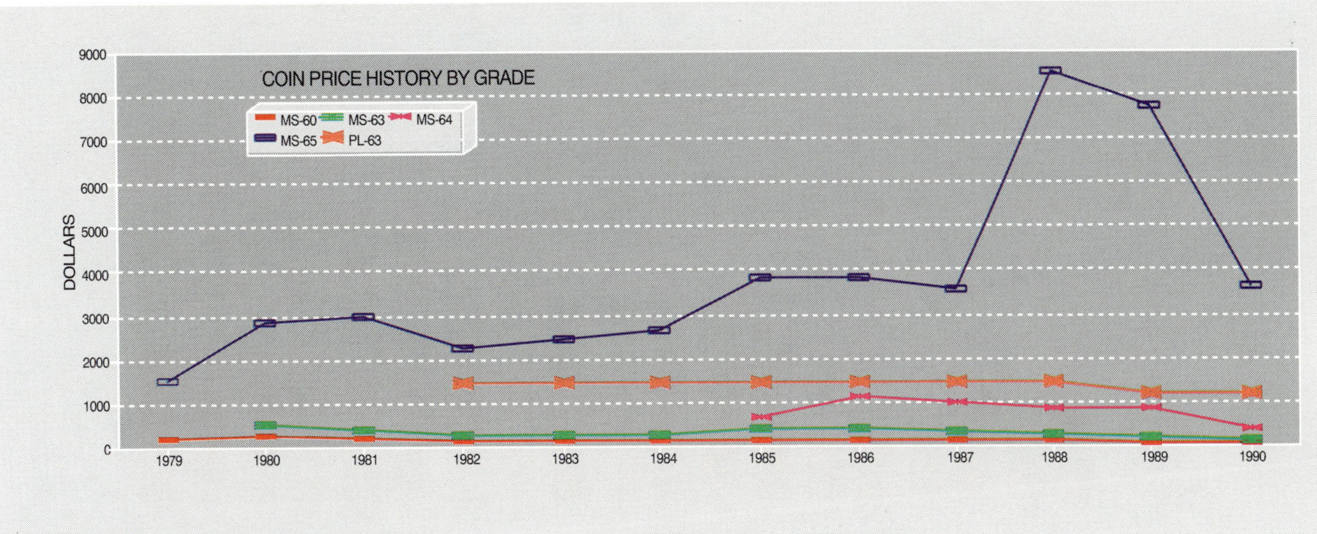

1899-P

Mintage reported, 330,000, from 3 pairs of dies. Many dealers believe this figure embodies a typographical error; survivors are much less rare Unc. than later Philadelphia Mint dollars of far higher mintage. (But if the real mintage were higher, one would expect a larger number of dies.) Uncs. are mostly from Treasury bags released in 1964; the Redfield hoard had none. Released by the U.S. Treasury in the "Great Silver Dollar Rush" of 1964. They come well struck with good lustre.

BU rolls survive in MS 60/62. Bag lots are rumored but not confirmed.

Recommended in MS 64 up.

Proofs: All 846 came from a single pair of dies, VAM 1.

Prooflikes: Available in all BU grades. PL's and DMPL's are scarce above MS 64, cameos more so.

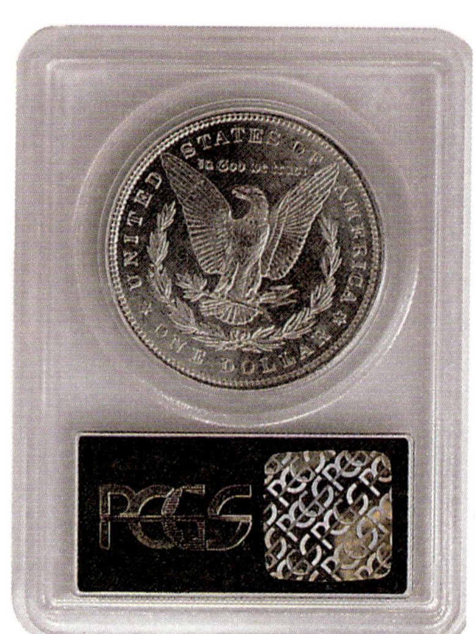

MINTAGE	PROOF	STRIKE	LUSTER	BAG MARKS	REDFIELD
330,000*	846	Average To Bold	Good	Moderate	No
DIES	**DIE VARIETIES**	**% OF PL**	**% OF DMPL**	**PIVOTAL GRADE**	**RARITY FACTOR**
37	6	6.1	4.2	MS 65	R-3

*Possible error in mintage report

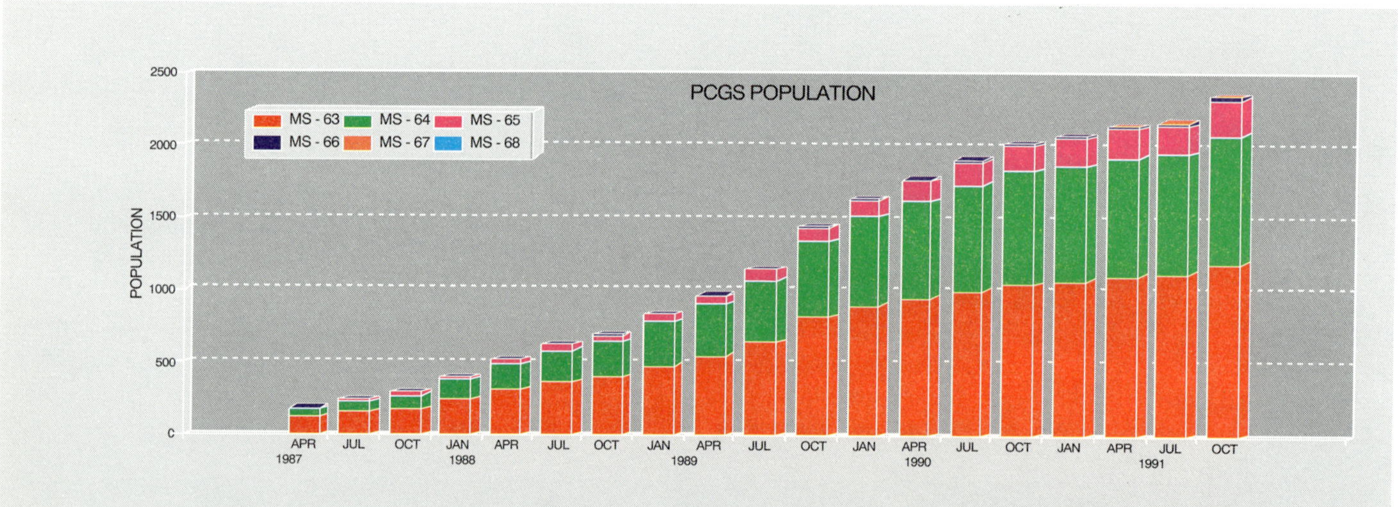

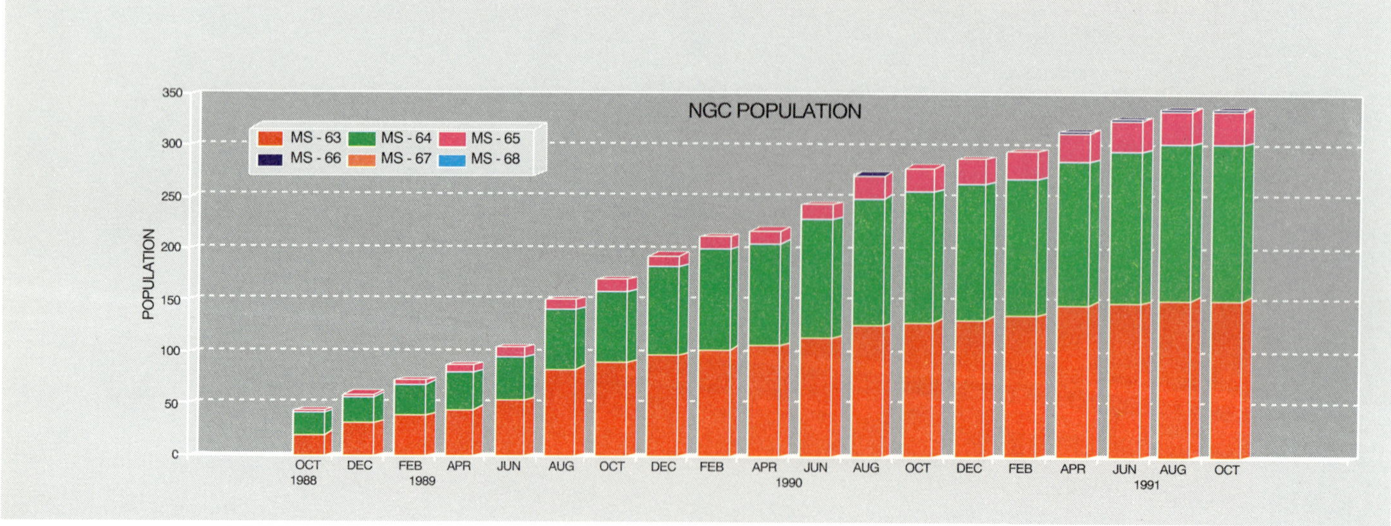

PCGS POPULATION

MS - 63 MS - 64 MS - 65 MS - 66 MS - 67 MS - 68

POPULATION: 0, 500, 1000, 1500, 2000, 2500

APR 1987, JUL, OCT, JAN 1988, APR, JUL, OCT, JAN 1989, APR, JUL, OCT, JAN 1990, APR, JUL, OCT, JAN 1991, APR, JUL, OCT

NGC POPULATION

MS - 63 MS - 64 MS - 65 MS - 66 MS - 67 MS - 68

POPULATION: 0, 50, 100, 150, 200, 250, 300, 350

OCT 1988, DEC, FEB 1989, APR, JUN, AUG, OCT, DEC, FEB 1990, APR, JUN, AUG, OCT, DEC, FEB 1991, APR, JUN, AUG, OCT

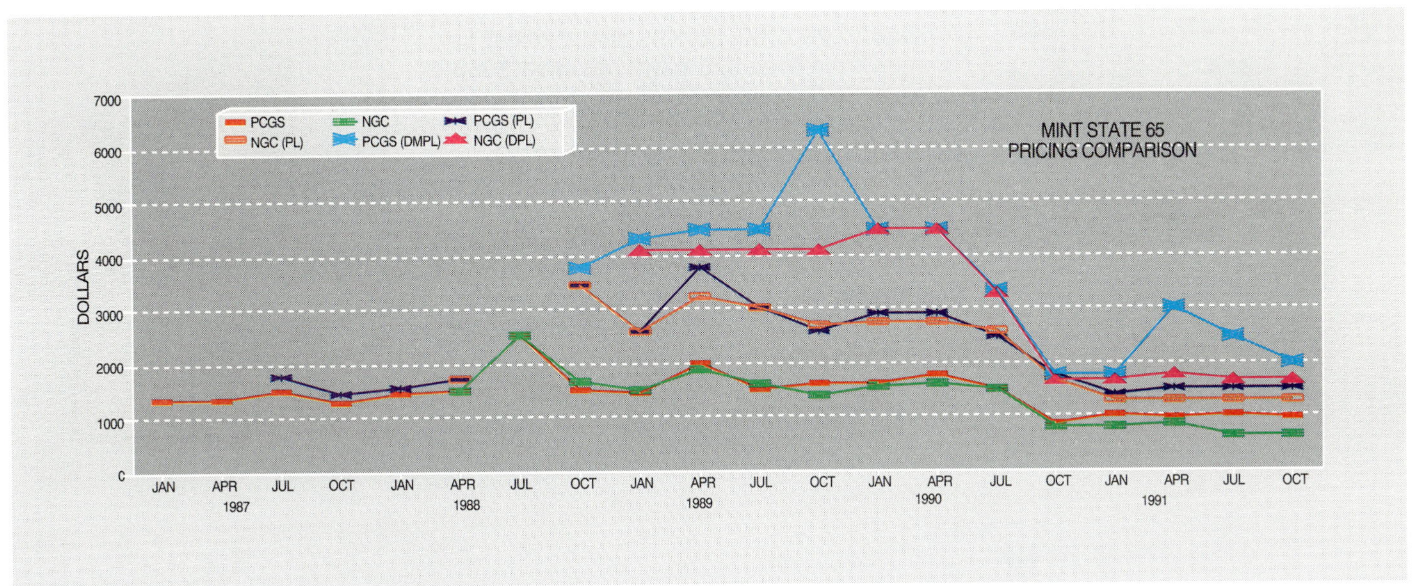
MINT STATE 65
PRICING COMPARISON
PCGS
NGC
PCGS (PL)
NGC (PL)
PCGS (DMPL)
NGC (DPL)
DOLLARS
7000
6000
5000
4000
3000
2000
1000
0
JAN APR JUL OCT JAN APR JUL OCT JAN APR JUL OCT JAN APR JUL OCT JAN APR JUL OCT
1987
1988
1989
1990
1991

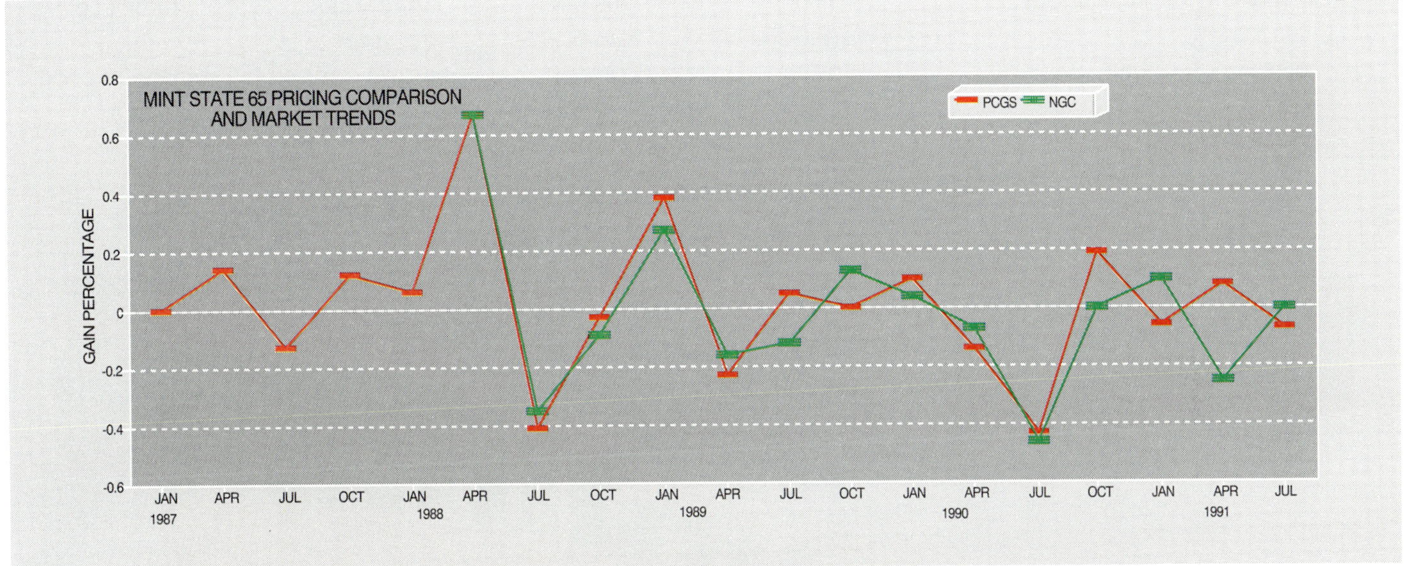
MINT STATE 65 PRICING COMPARISON
AND MARKET TRENDS
PCGS
NGC
GAIN PERCENTAGE
0.8
0.6
0.4
0.2
0
-0.2
-0.4
-0.6
JAN APR JUL OCT JAN APR JUL OCT JAN APR JUL OCT JAN APR JUL OCT JAN APR JUL
1987
1988
1989
1990
1991

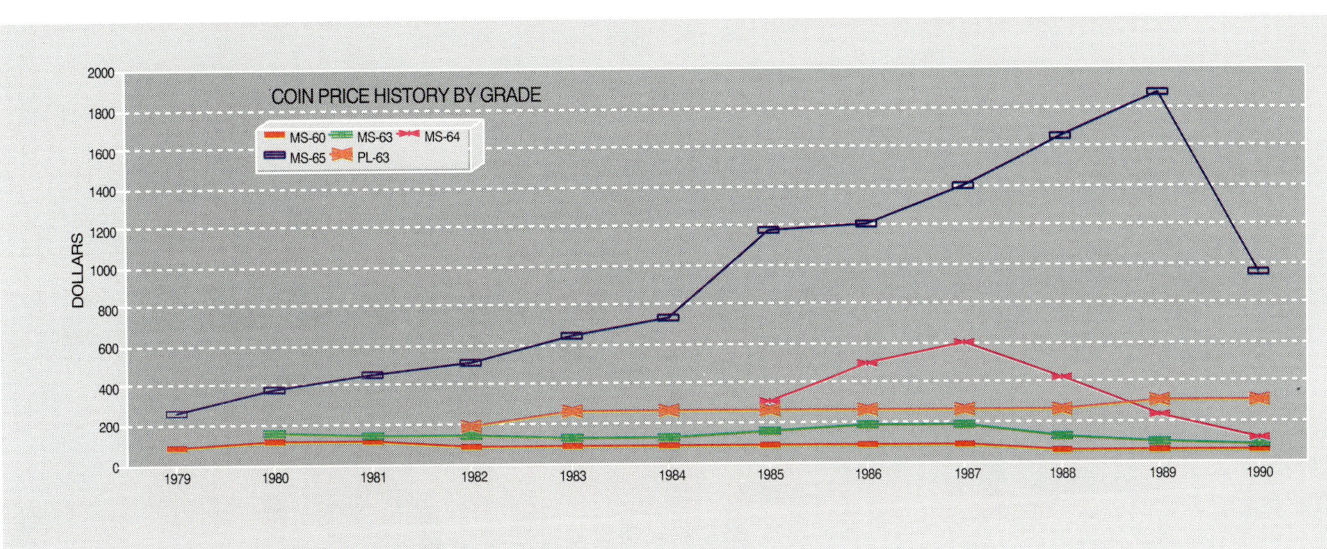
COIN PRICE HISTORY BY GRADE
MS-60
MS-63
MS-64
MS-65
PL-63
DOLLARS
2000
1800
1600
1400
1200
1000
800
600
400
200
0
1979 1980 1981 1982 1983 1984 1985 1986 1987 1988 1989 1990

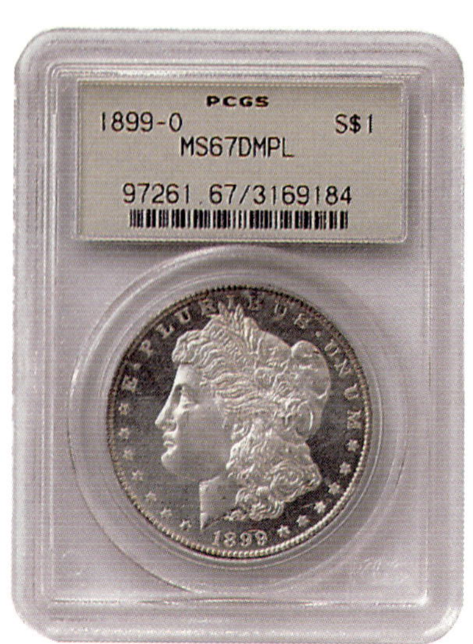

1899-O

PCGS
1899-O S$1
MS67DMPL
97261.67/3169184

Mintage 12,290,000, from 85 pairs of dies. Uncs. are common from Treasury bags released 1958-64, most of all in 1962; none in Redfield. Striking quality ranges from flat to full, with good lustre.

Rolls and bags are available in MS 60/62.

Recommended in MS 65 up. A "sleeper" common date. Advisable by the roll in MS 64.

Over 90% have large 0. The small round o variety (*Ency* 5660 = VAM 4, 5, 6) almost always comes worn.

Prooflikes: Scarce in all BU grades, rare in MS 65 up PL and DMPL. Light cameos are available. Many PL's are baggy.

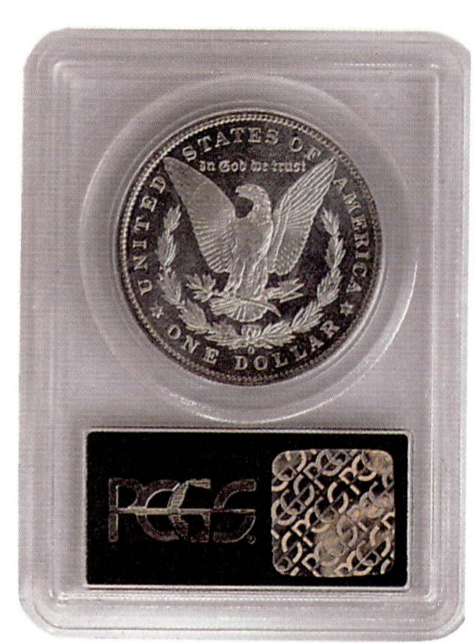

MINTAGE	PROOF	STRIKE	LUSTER	BAG MARKS	REDFIELD
12,290,000	0	Average To Bold	Excellent	Light	No
DIES	**DIE VARIETIES**	**% OF PL**	**% OF DMPL**	**PIVOTAL GRADE**	**RARITY FACTOR**
140	30	0.9	0.9	MS 65	R-5

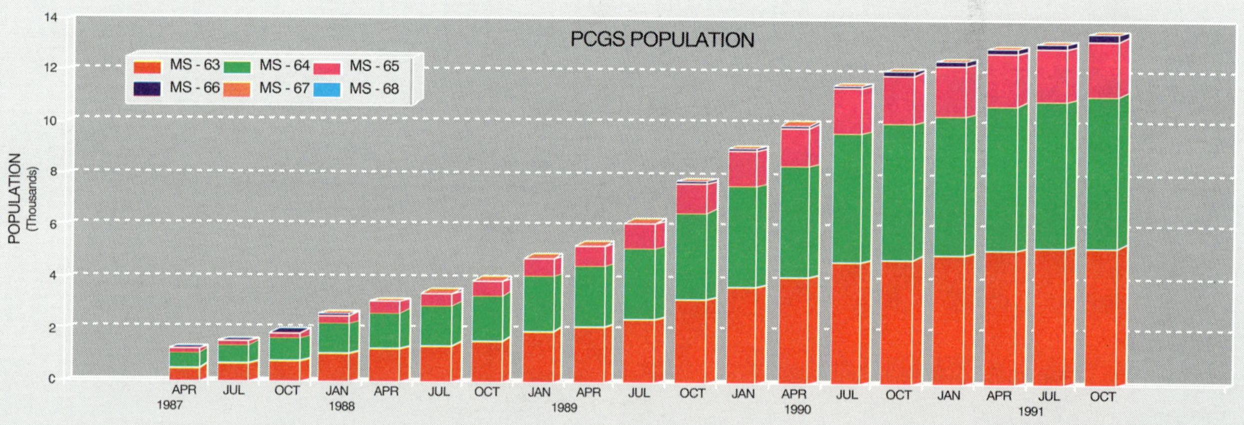
PCGS POPULATION
MS - 63
MS - 64
MS - 65
MS - 66
MS - 67
MS - 68
POPULATION (Thousands)
14
12
10
8
6
4
2
0
APR 1987
JUL
OCT
JAN 1988
APR
JUL
OCT
JAN 1989
APR
JUL
OCT
JAN
APR 1990
JUL
OCT
JAN
APR
JUL 1991
OCT

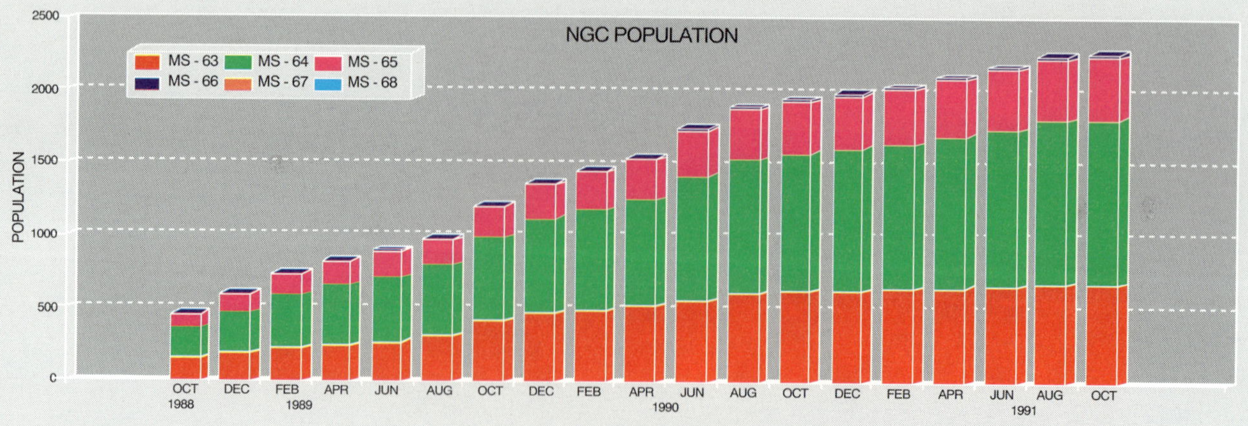
NGC POPULATION
MS - 63
MS - 64
MS - 65
MS - 66
MS - 67
MS - 68
POPULATION
2500
2000
1500
1000
500
0
OCT 1988
DEC
FEB 1989
APR
JUN
AUG
OCT
DEC
FEB
APR 1990
JUN
AUG
OCT
DEC
FEB
APR
JUN 1991
AUG
OCT

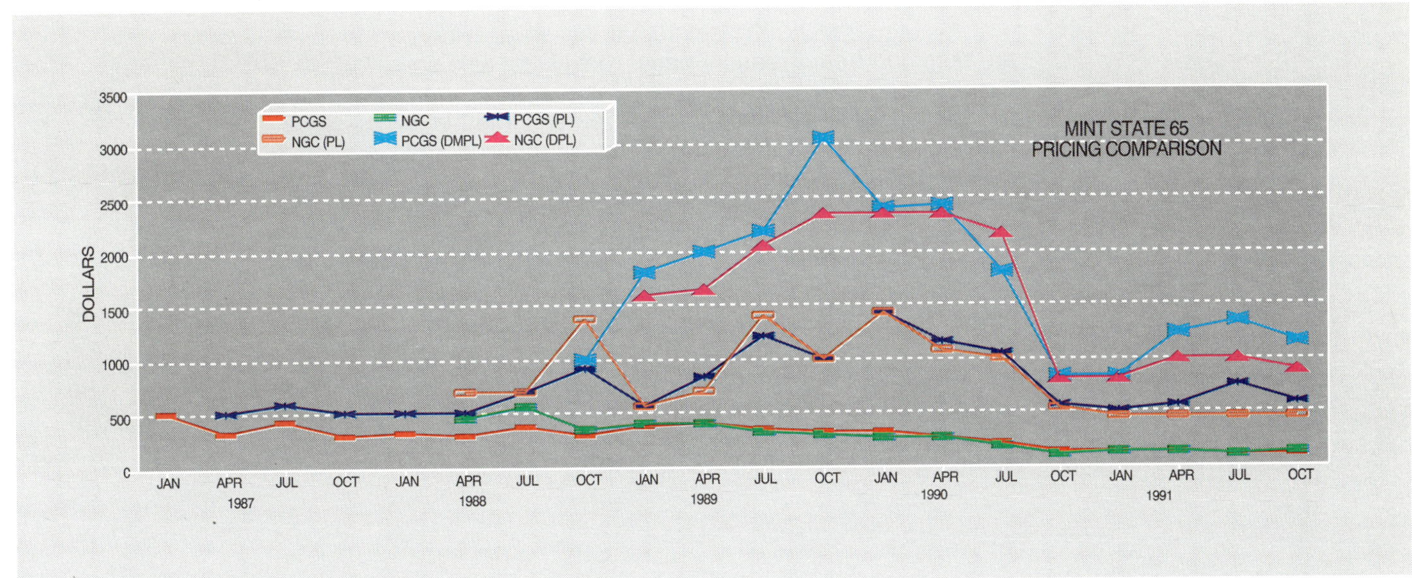
MINT STATE 65
PRICING COMPARISON
PCGS
NGC
PCGS (PL)
NGC (PL)
PCGS (DMPL)
NGC (DPL)
DOLLARS
3500
3000
2500
2000
1500
1000
500
0
JAN
APR
JUL
OCT
1987
1988
1989
1990
1991

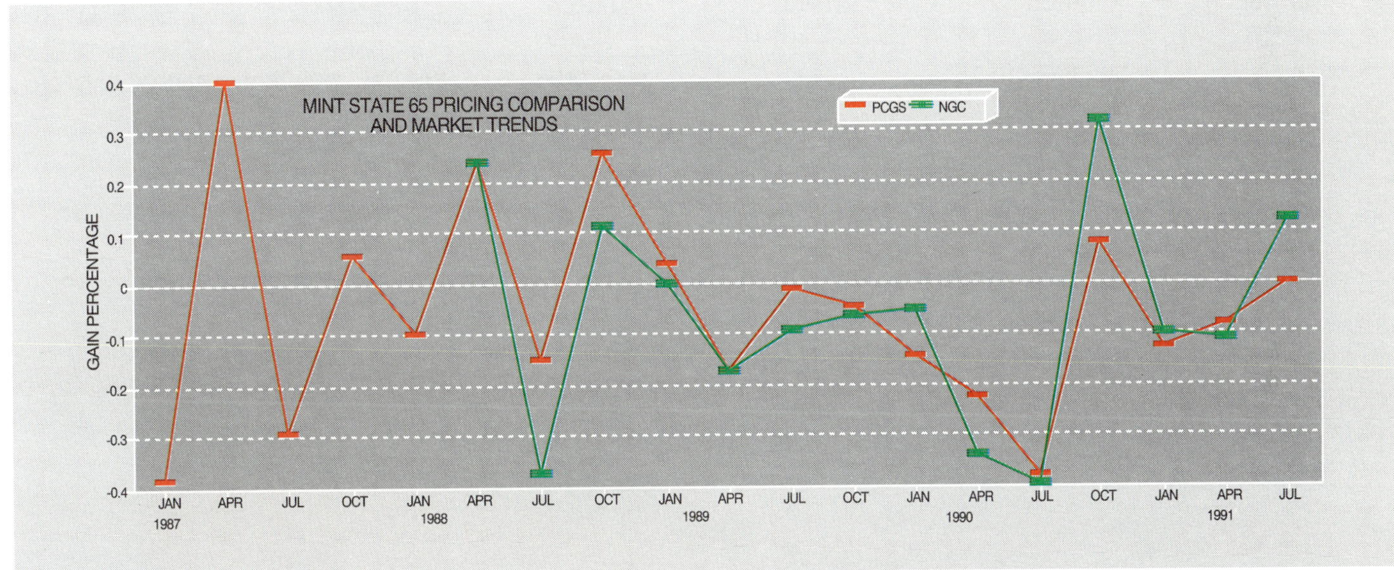
MINT STATE 65 PRICING COMPARISON
AND MARKET TRENDS
PCGS
NGC
GAIN PERCENTAGE
0.4
0.3
0.2
0.1
0
-0.1
-0.2
-0.3
-0.4
JAN
APR
JUL
OCT
1987
1988
1989
1990
1991

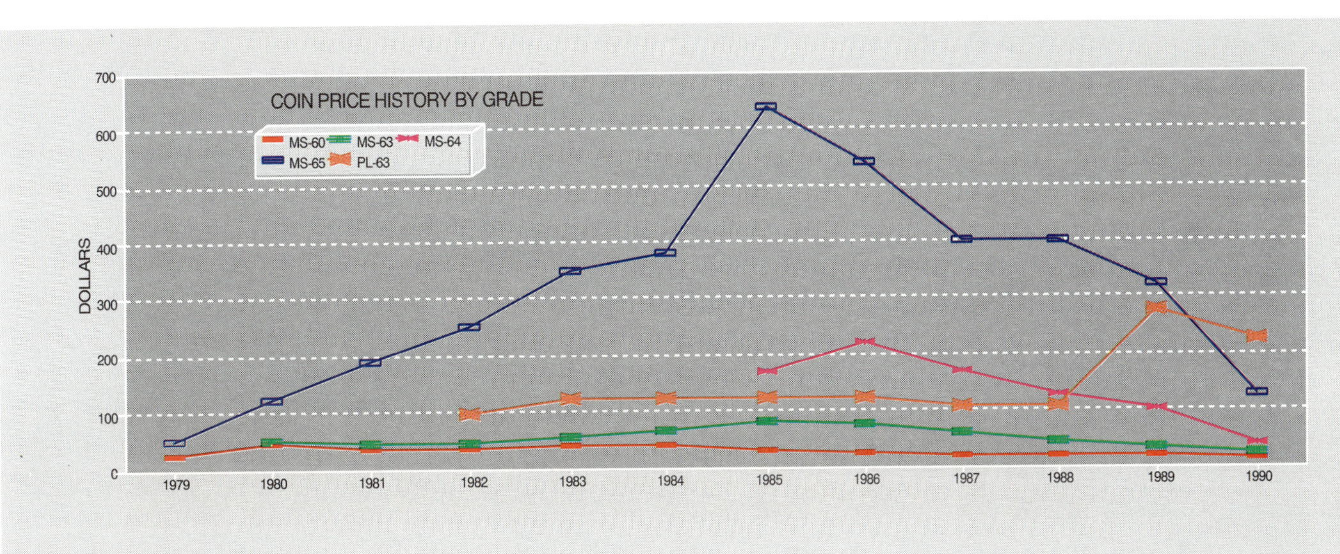
COIN PRICE HISTORY BY GRADE
MS-60
MS-63
MS-64
MS-65
PL-63
DOLLARS
700
600
500
400
300
200
100
0
1979
1980
1981
1982
1983
1984
1985
1986
1987
1988
1989
1990

PCGS
1899-S
S$1
MS67
7262.67/3000042

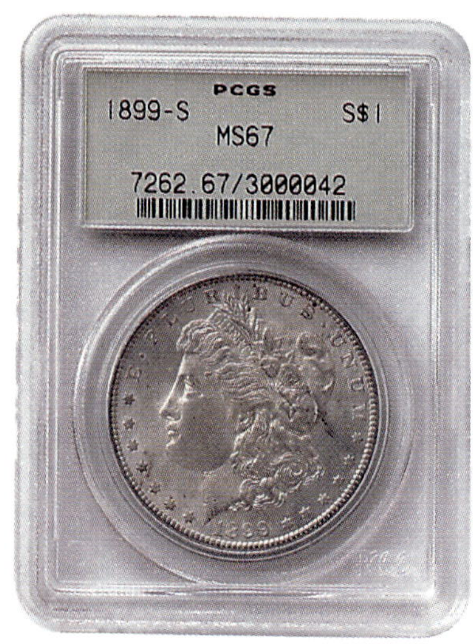

1899-S

Mintage 2,562,000 from 20 pairs of dies. Sliders are common from Treasury bags; real Uncs. less so. Circulated examples EF and above are very uncommon. The Redfield hoard apparently had less than one full bag of this date. Uncs. normally come bold and brightly lustrous.

More varieties have large wide S (serifs away from middle curve, as in 1900-04) than medium S. Neither can be called rare.

Recommended in MS 64 up, but you may have to buy a MS 63 as a space filler while hunting. Beware of sliders priced as Unc. This date would win the prize for "Most Often Encountered Slider".

Prooflikes: PL's are three times as often seen as DMPL's; cameos are seldom available. Rare in all grades above MS 64 PL, MS 65 DMPL.

PCGS

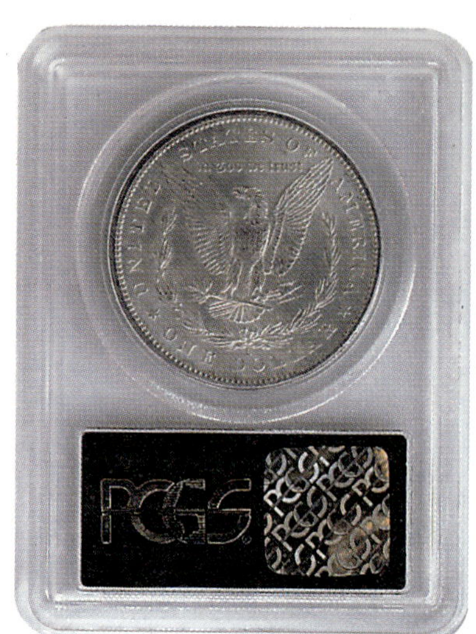

MINTAGE	PROOF	STRIKE	LUSTER	BAG MARKS	REDFIELD
2,562,000	0	Average To Bold	Good	Light	Yes
DIES	**DIE VARIETIES**	**% OF PL**	**% OF DMPL**	**PIVOTAL GRADE**	**RARITY FACTOR**
40	13	8.1	2.6	MS 65	R-2

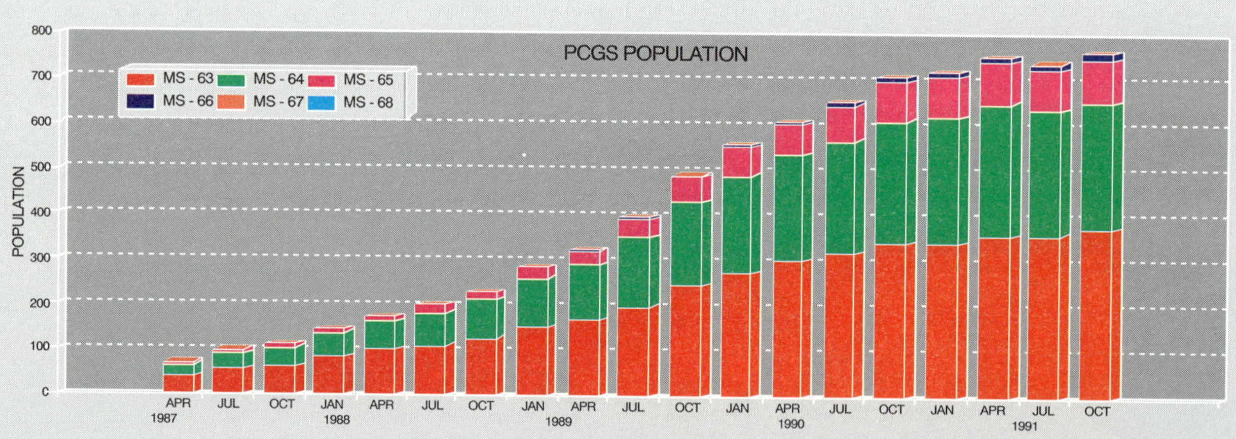

PCGS POPULATION
MS - 63
MS - 64
MS - 65
MS - 66
MS - 67
MS - 68
POPULATION
800
700
600
500
400
300
200
100
0
APR 1987
JUL
OCT
JAN 1988
APR
JUL
OCT
JAN 1989
APR
JUL
OCT
JAN
APR 1990
JUL
OCT
JAN
APR
JUL 1991
OCT

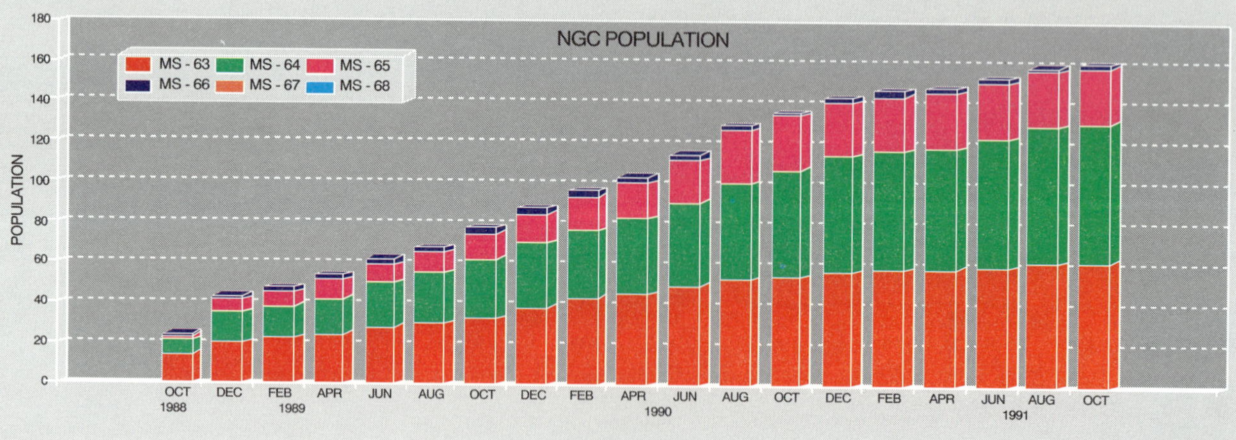

NGC POPULATION
MS - 63
MS - 64
MS - 65
MS - 66
MS - 67
MS - 68
POPULATION
180
160
140
120
100
80
60
40
20
0
OCT 1988
DEC
FEB 1989
APR
JUN
AUG
OCT
DEC
FEB
APR 1990
JUN
AUG
OCT
DEC
FEB
APR
JUN 1991
AUG
OCT

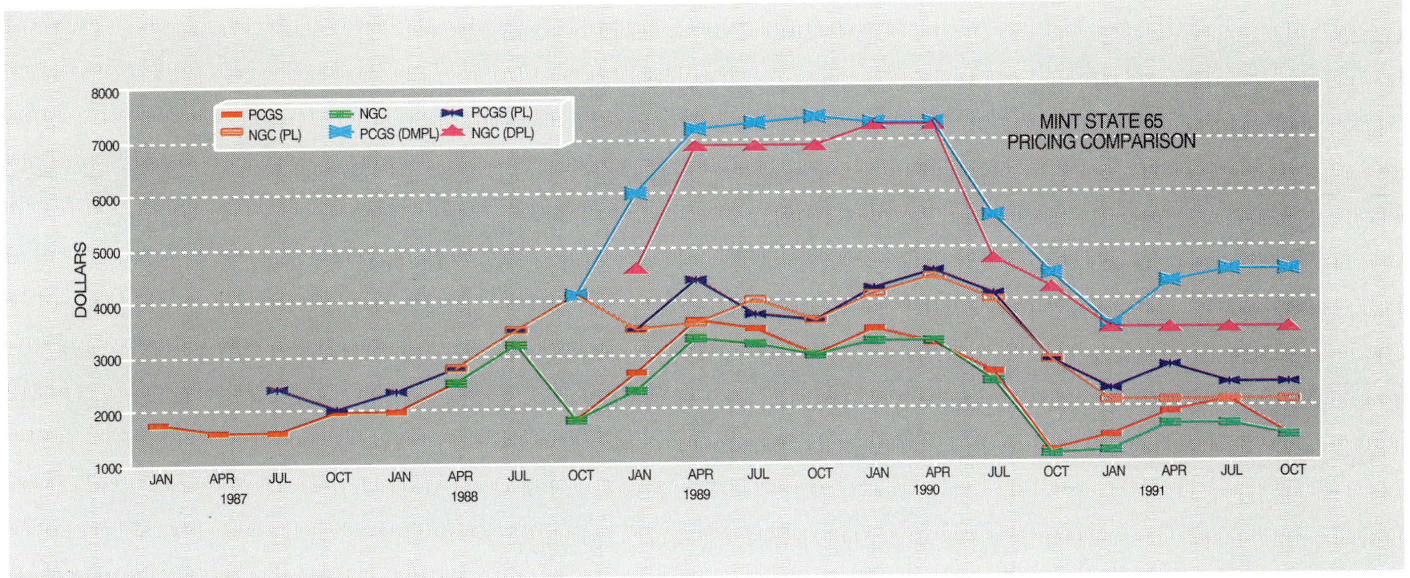
MINT STATE 65
PRICING COMPARISON
PCGS
NGC
PCGS (PL)
NGC (PL)
PCGS (DMPL)
NGC (DPL)
DOLLARS
8000
7000
6000
5000
4000
3000
2000
1000
JAN APR JUL OCT JAN APR JUL OCT JAN APR JUL OCT JAN APR JUL OCT JAN APR JUL OCT
1987
1988
1989
1990
1991

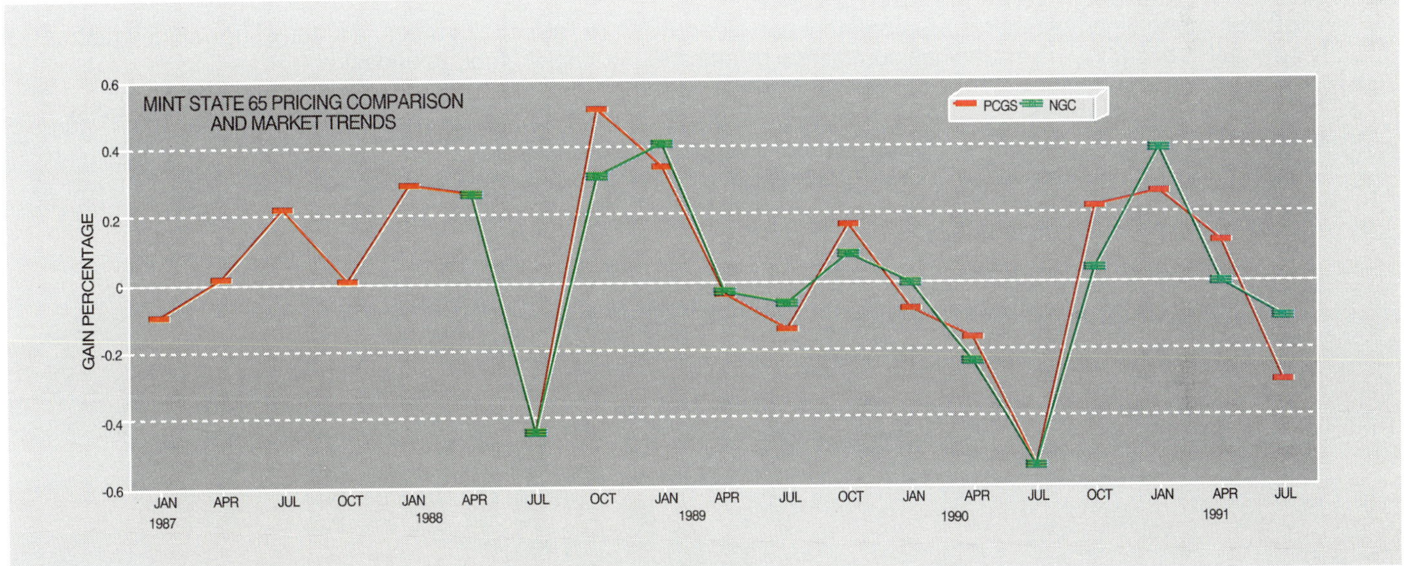
MINT STATE 65 PRICING COMPARISON
AND MARKET TRENDS
PCGS
NGC
GAIN PERCENTAGE
0.6
0.4
0.2
0
-0.2
-0.4
-0.6
JAN APR JUL OCT JAN APR JUL OCT JAN APR JUL OCT JAN APR JUL OCT JAN APR JUL
1987
1988
1989
1990
1991

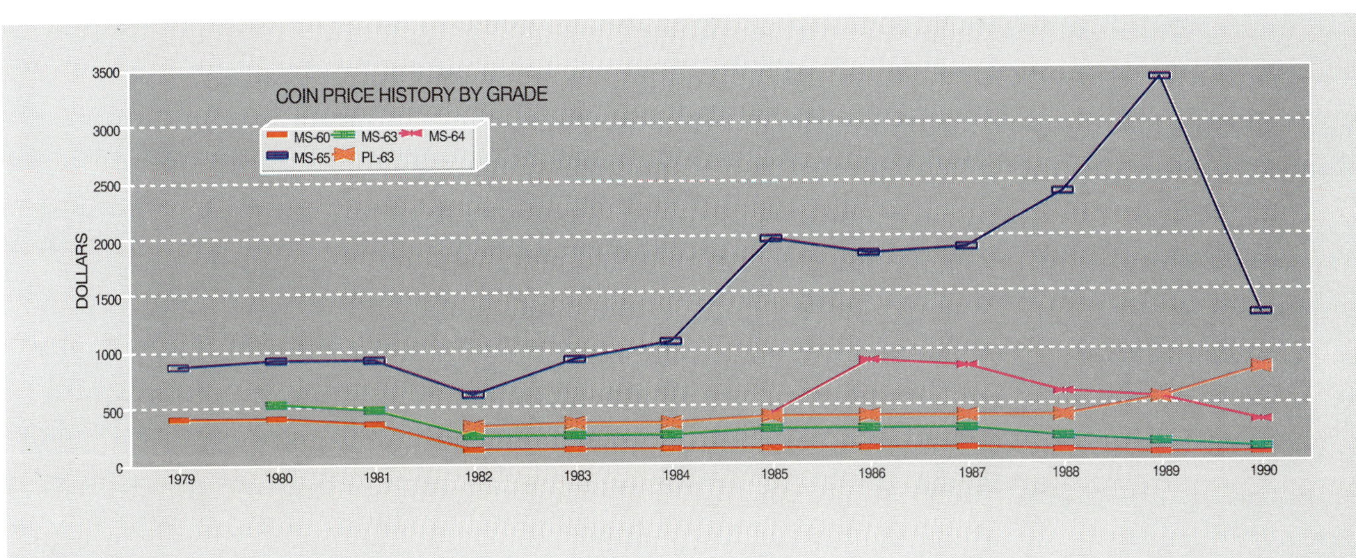
COIN PRICE HISTORY BY GRADE
MS-60
MS-63
MS-64
MS-65
PL-63
DOLLARS
3500
3000
2500
2000
1500
1000
500
0
1979 1980 1981 1982 1983 1984 1985 1986 1987 1988 1989 1990

1900-P

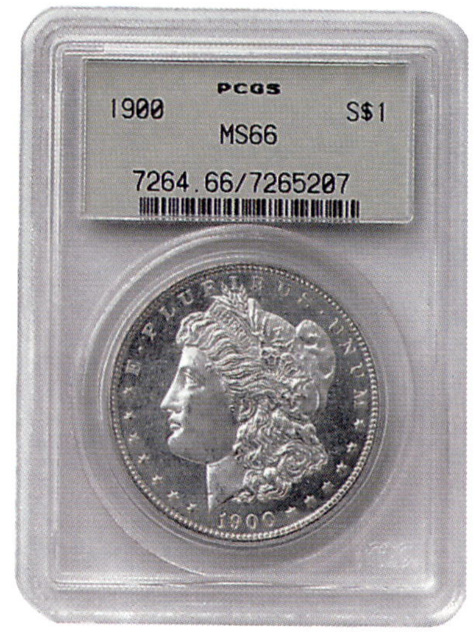

The first Morgan silver dollar of the 20th century from Philadelphia. Mintage 8,830,000, from 66 obvs., 61 revs. Less than four times as common as 1899 Philadelphia, though more than 25 times as many were minted, which is why many dealers think the 1899 mintage figure is in error (as before). Uncs. mostly come from Treasury bags; they range from flat to full strikes. with adequate lustre. Rolls and bags these days are mostly MS 60/62.

Two types for this date: old reverse, called C3 by VAM and "V" by some collectors, and new reverse, known as C4 or "U". On C3 dies (*Ency* 5664-5), junction of wing and neck forms a narrow V, stars are small; on C4 dies (*Ency* 5666-7), junction of wing and neck forms a wider U, stars are larger. Nobody knows which one is scarcer; both are available.

At least one double reverse die shows impressions from both hubs (see illustration at *Ency* 5668); notice the double olive. This is rare.

Recommended in MS 65 up or in MS 64 by the roll.

Proofs: Mintage 912, from two pairs of dies. One pair has C3 reverse (obv. similar to VAM 7 but with open 9), the other has C4 (obv. VAM 7). Nobody yet knows which is scarcer.

Prooflikes: One-sided semi-PL's are common; two sided PL's are rare in all grades. Nobody knows yet whether C3 or C4 is rarer in PL or DMPL. Die striations sometimes produce PL examples, though undesirable.

MINTAGE	PROOF	STRIKE	LUSTER	BAG MARKS	REDFIELD
8,830,000	912	Average	Good	Moderate	No
DIES	**DIE VARIETIES**	**% OF PL**	**% OF DMPL**	**PIVOTAL GRADE**	**RARITY FACTOR**
45	23	0.9	0.1	MS 65	R-4

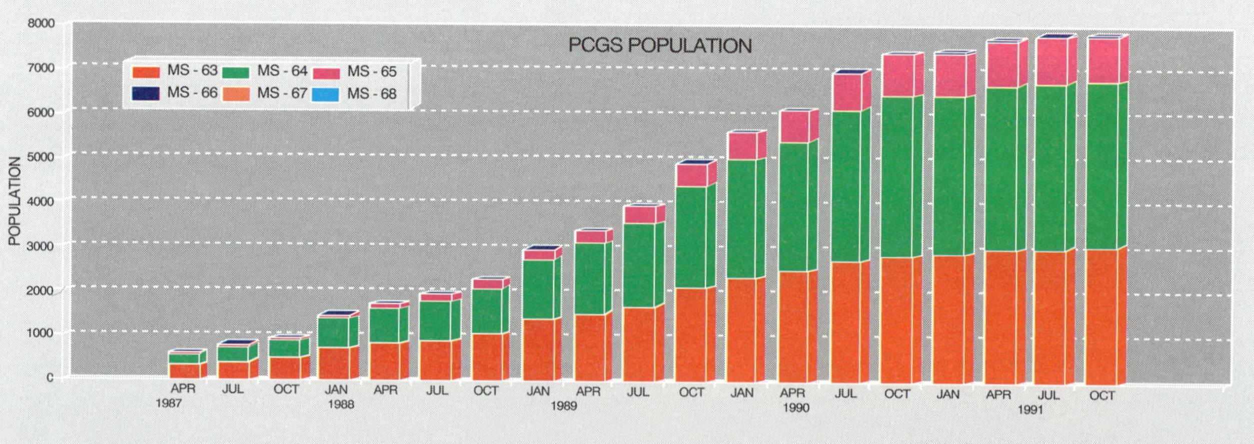

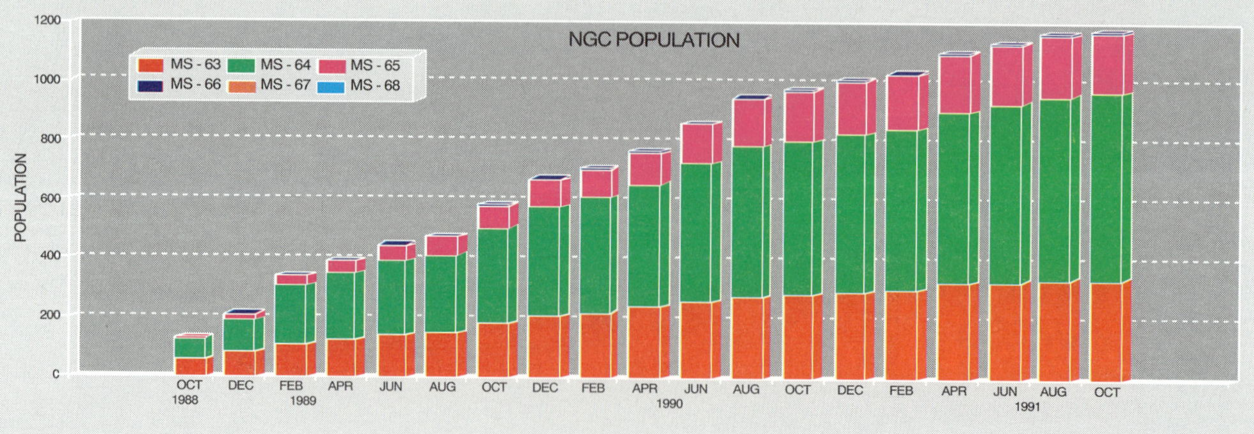

1900-P

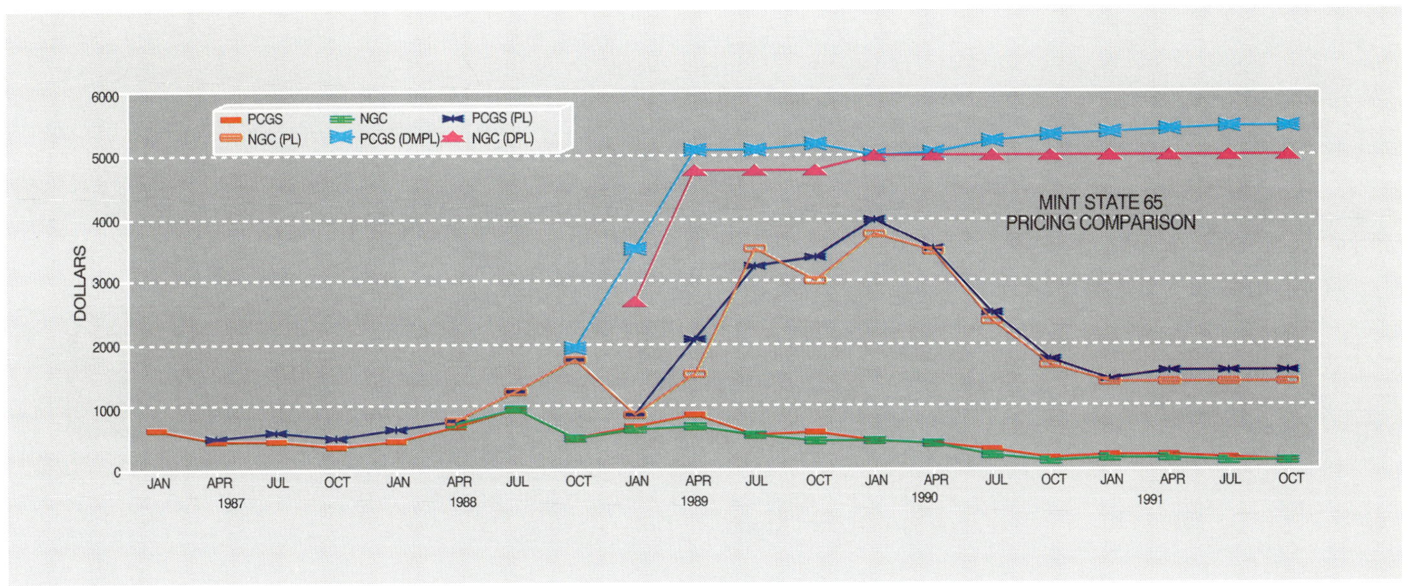

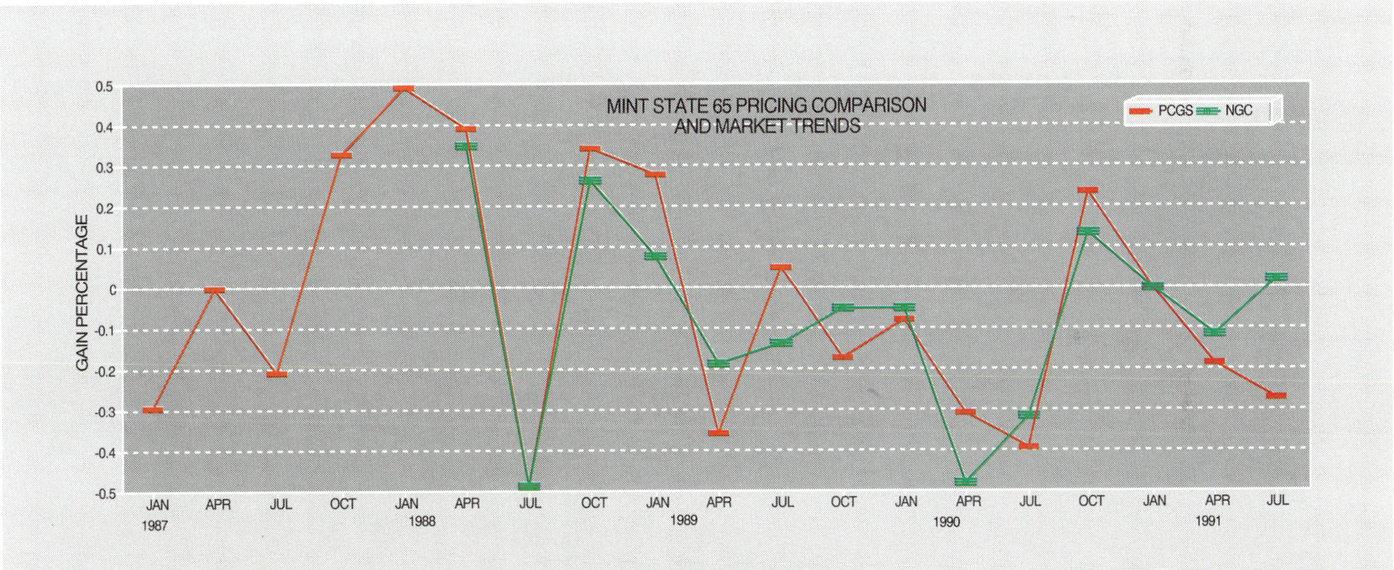

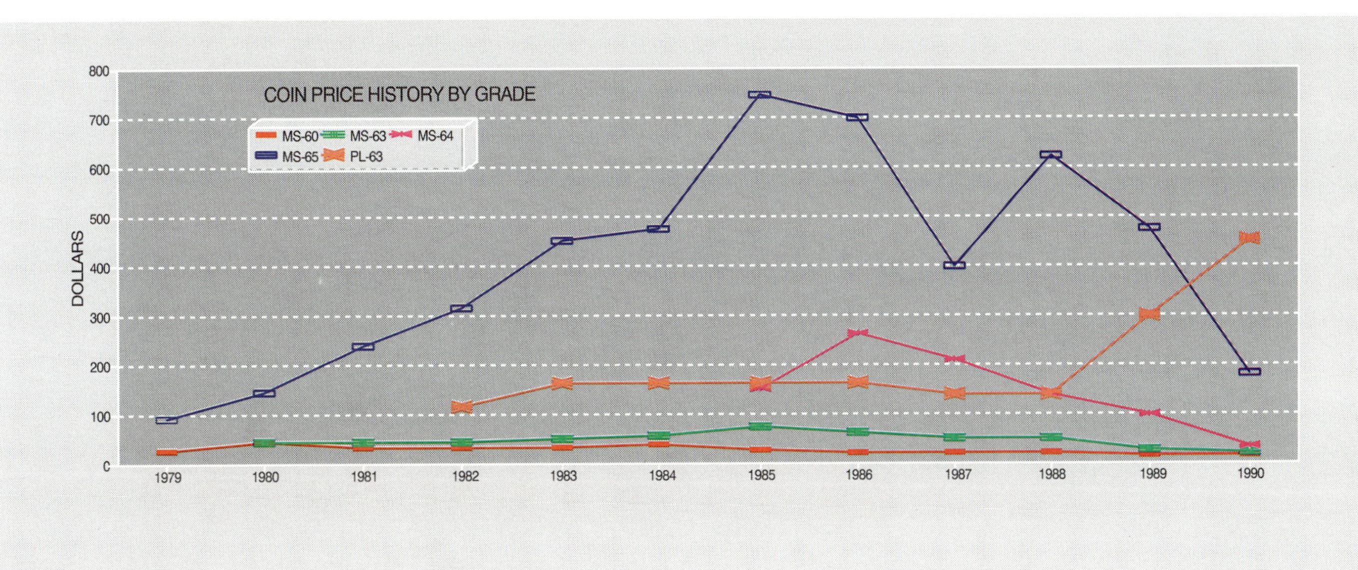

1900-O

Mintage 12,590,000, second largest among New Orleans Morgans. Usually weak in centers and sometimes elsewhere, but good frosty lustre. "Metal flow" was a nagging problem with this date. Uncs. are from Treasury bags; 1962-64, none in Redfield. BU rolls and bags of MS 60/62 are available.

Recommended in MS 65 up or by the roll in MS 64. Currently a "sleeper" common date.

See separate entry for 1900-O/CC

To date all reported are from old C3 reverses.

Most have large 0; a few have small round o as in 1880, 1896, and 1899. (*Ency* 5669 = VAM 5.) These are all worn. Fivaz & Stanton list the variety as Rarity 6.

Prooflikes: DMPL's are 8 to 10 times scarcer than regular PL's. Rare above MS 65 PL; scarce to rare in all Unc., grades of DMPL. High contrast cameos are seldom found.

MINTAGE	PROOF	STRIKE	LUSTER	BAG MARKS	REDFIELD
12,590,000*	0	Average	Very Good	Moderate	NO
DIES	**DIE VARIETIES**	**% OF PL**	**% OF DMPL**	**PIVOTAL GRADE**	**RARITY FACTOR**
230**	33	2.4	0.3	MS 65	R-4

*Includes estimated 11,590,000 1900-O and estimated 1,000,000 1900-O/CC ** Includes all dies used at the New Orleans Mint - FY1900

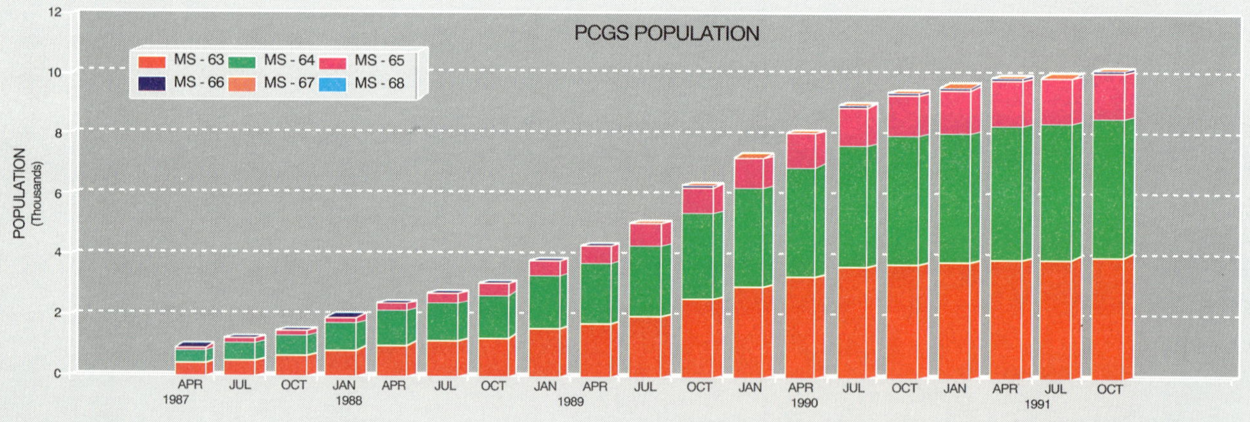

PCGS POPULATION

MS - 63 MS - 64 MS - 65
MS - 66 MS - 67 MS - 68

POPULATION (Thousands)

0 2 4 6 8 10 12

APR 1987, JUL, OCT, JAN 1988, APR, JUL, OCT, JAN 1989, APR, JUL, OCT, JAN, APR 1990, JUL, OCT, JAN, APR, JUL 1991, OCT

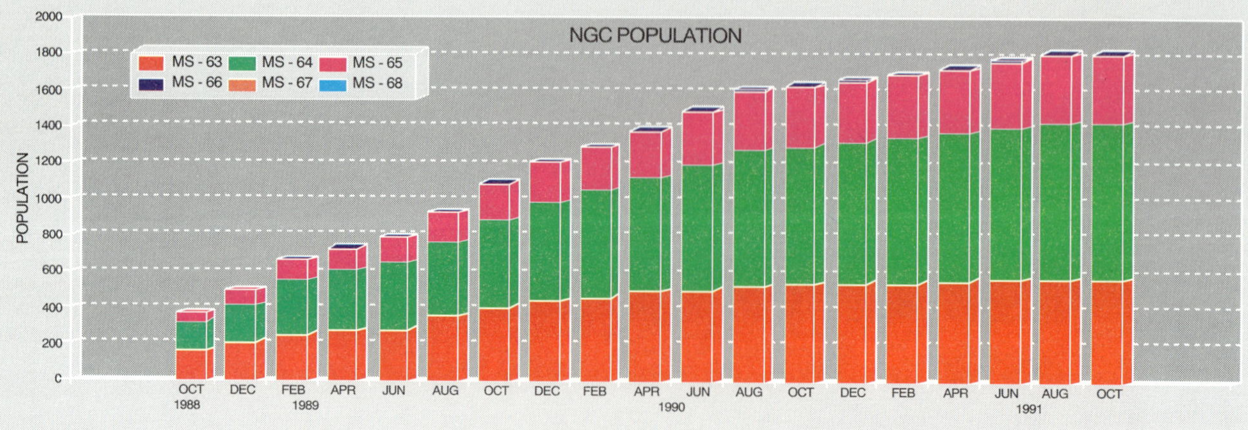

NGC POPULATION

MS - 63 MS - 64 MS - 65
MS - 66 MS - 67 MS - 68

POPULATION

0 200 400 600 800 1000 1200 1400 1600 1800 2000

OCT 1988, DEC, FEB 1989, APR, JUN, AUG, OCT, DEC, FEB, APR 1990, JUN, AUG, OCT, DEC, FEB, APR, JUN 1991, AUG, OCT

1900-O

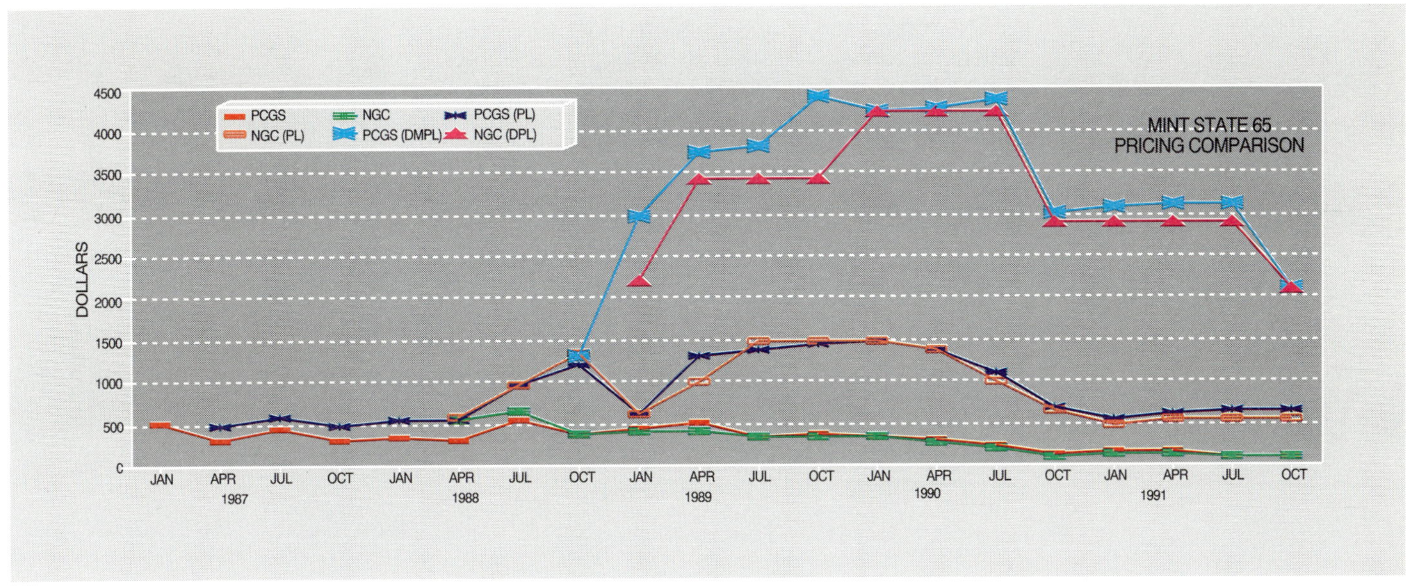

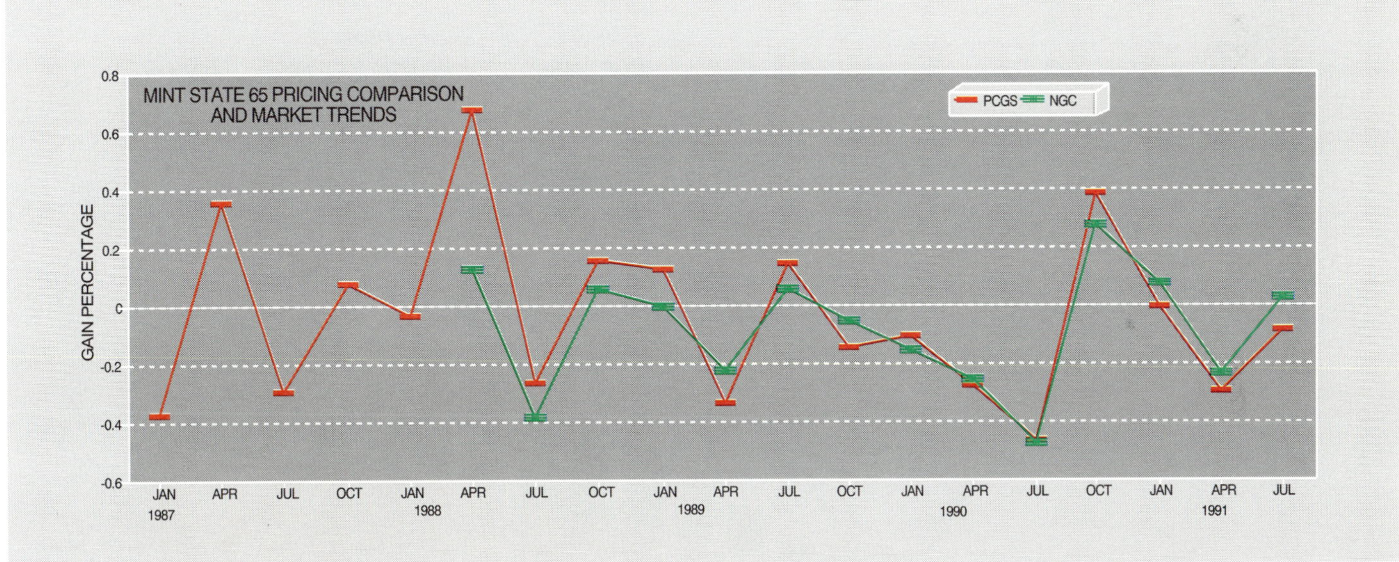

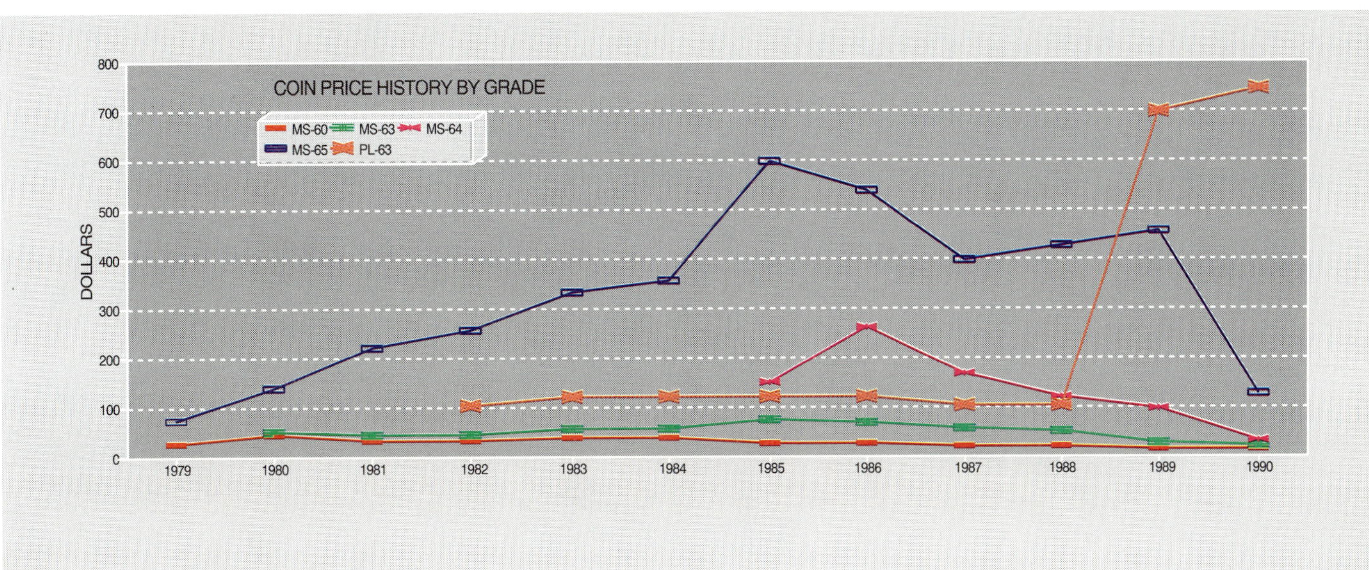

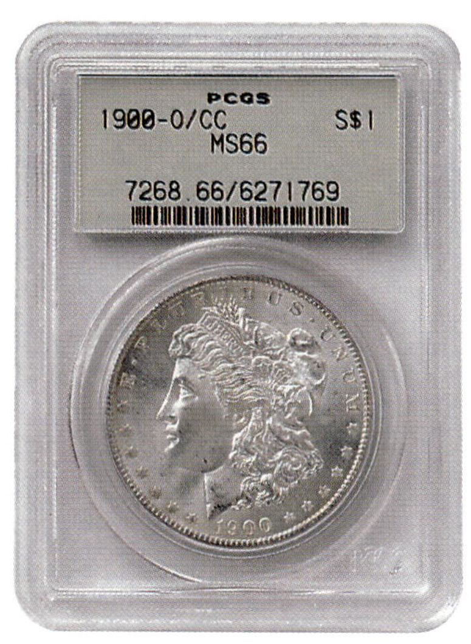

1900-O/CC

PCGS
1900-O/CC S$1
MS66
7268.66/6271769

Seldom seen very circulated; most survivors are sliders or Uncs., reported in and after the 1960's, suggesting that they turned up among Treasury bag coins before 1964. Redfield had none. A half dozen CC mint reverses, still fit for service, were discovered (1899) among the machinery of the closed Carson City Mint and sent back to the Philadelphia Mint, where Barber or assistants rebasined the dies, effacing much of the CC mintmarks, and re-mintmarked them for New Orleans service: VAM 7-12.

The variety has become popular enough to be defined and certified by both PCGS and NGC, to be listed on the CCE electronic exchange, and to be priced weekly in the greysheet. (CDN)

Recommended in MS 63 up. Circulated examples are quite scarce.

Prooflikes: None verified to exist.

PCGS

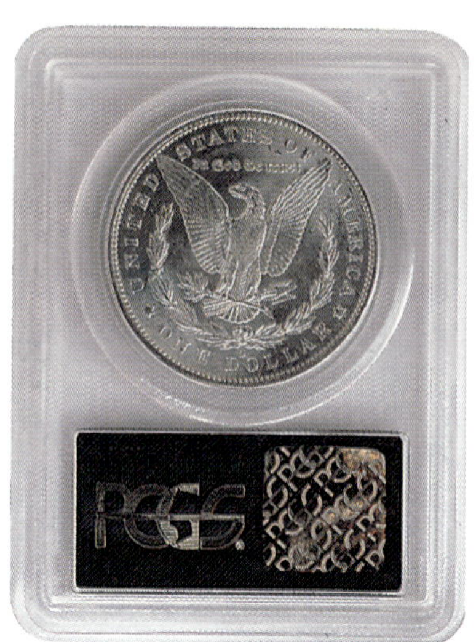

MINTAGE	PROOF	STRIKE	LUSTER	BAG MARKS	REDFIELD
1,000,000*	0	Soft	Good	Heavy	No
DIES	**DIE VARIETIES**	**% OF PL**	**% OF DMPL**	**PIVOTAL GRADE**	**RARITY FACTOR**
230**	7	0.0	0.0	MS 65	R-2

*Includes estimated 11,590,000 1900-O and estimated 1,000,000 1900-O/CC **Includes all dies used at the New Orleans Mint - FY 1900

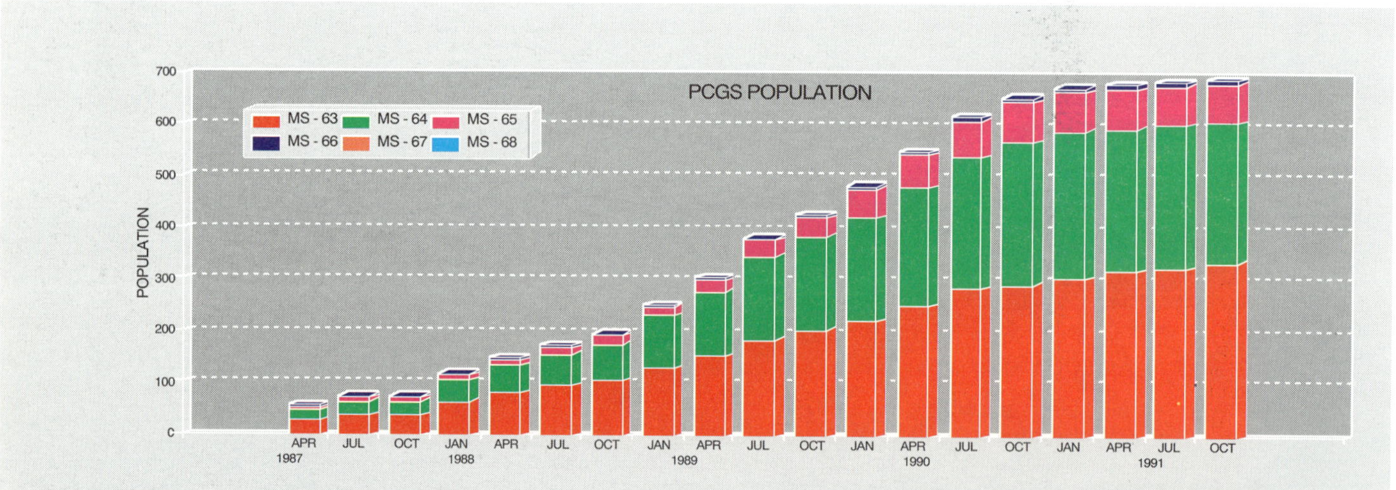
PCGS POPULATION
MS - 63
MS - 64
MS - 65
MS - 66
MS - 67
MS - 68
POPULATION
700
600
500
400
300
200
100
C
APR
1987
JUL
OCT
JAN
1988
APR
JUL
OCT
JAN
1989
APR
JUL
OCT
JAN
APR
1990
JUL
OCT
JAN
APR
JUL
1991
OCT

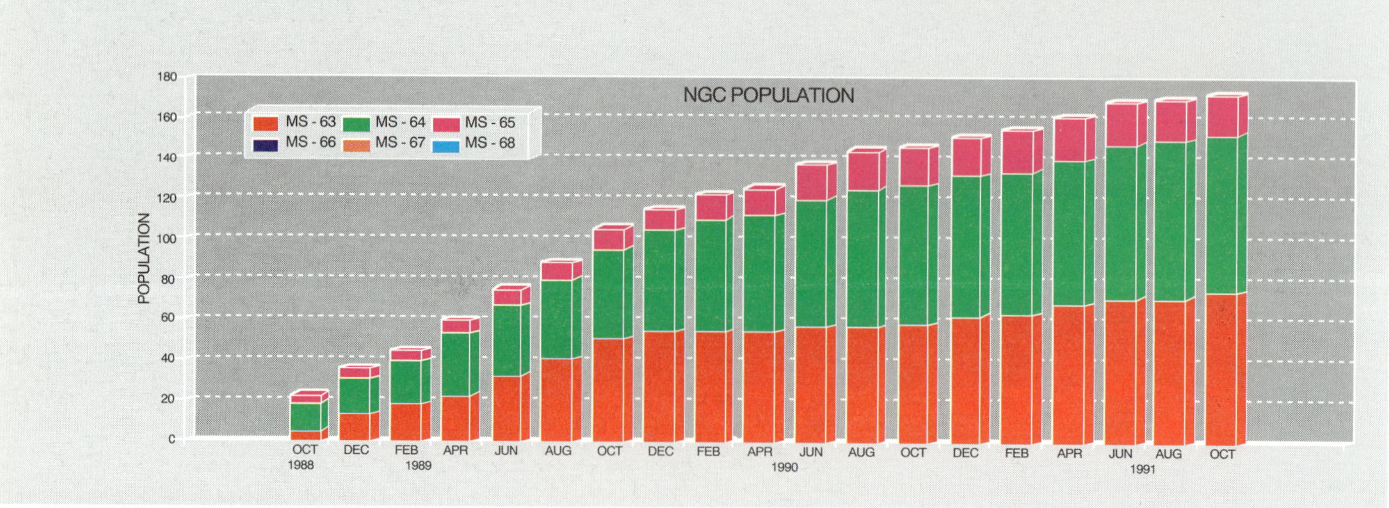
NGC POPULATION
MS - 63
MS - 64
MS - 65
MS - 66
MS - 67
MS - 68
POPULATION
180
160
140
120
100
80
60
40
20
C
OCT
1988
DEC
FEB
1989
APR
JUN
AUG
OCT
DEC
FEB
APR
1990
JUN
AUG
OCT
DEC
FEB
APR
JUN
1991
AUG
OCT

1900-O/CC

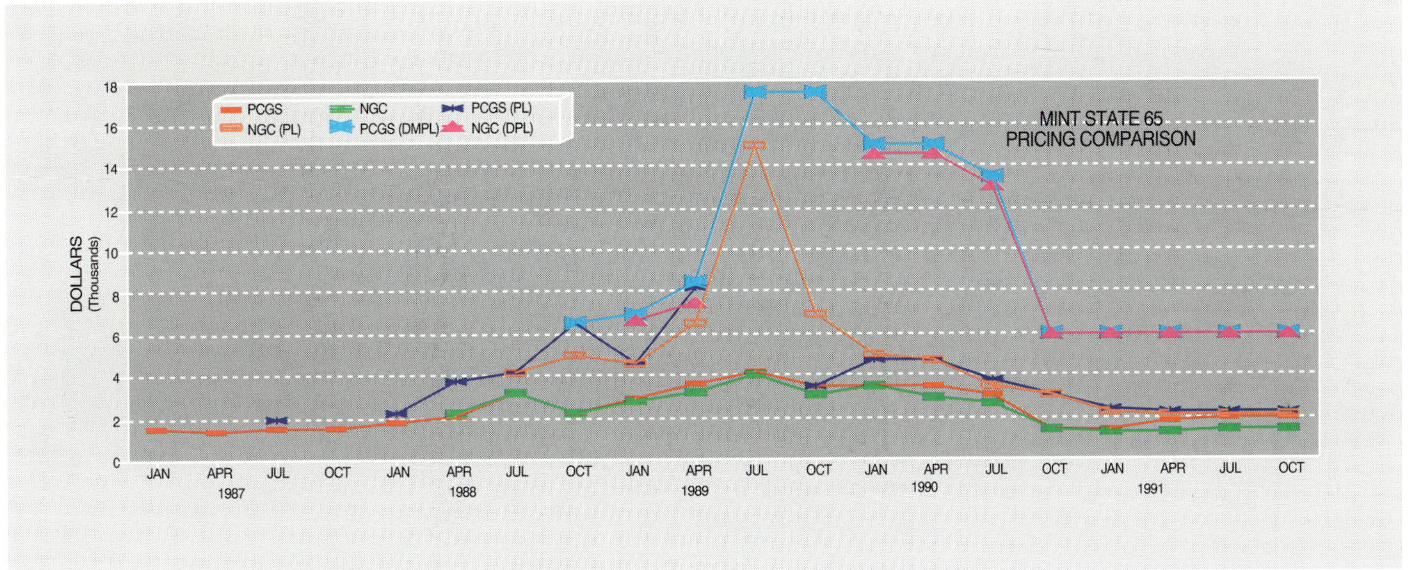

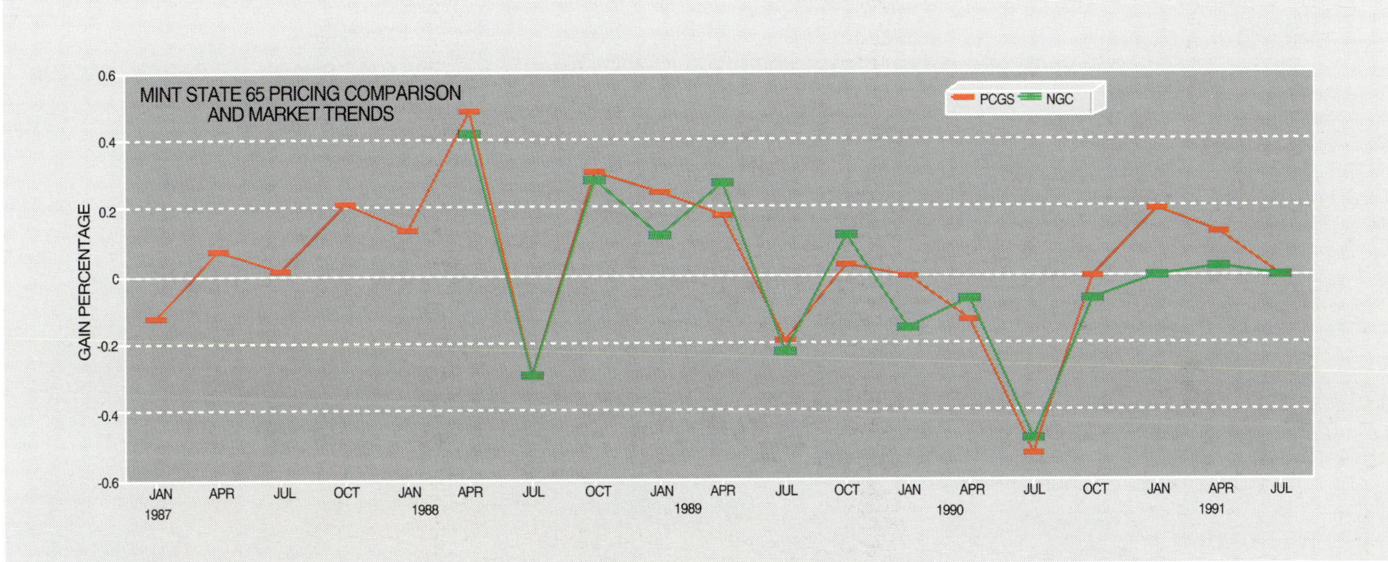

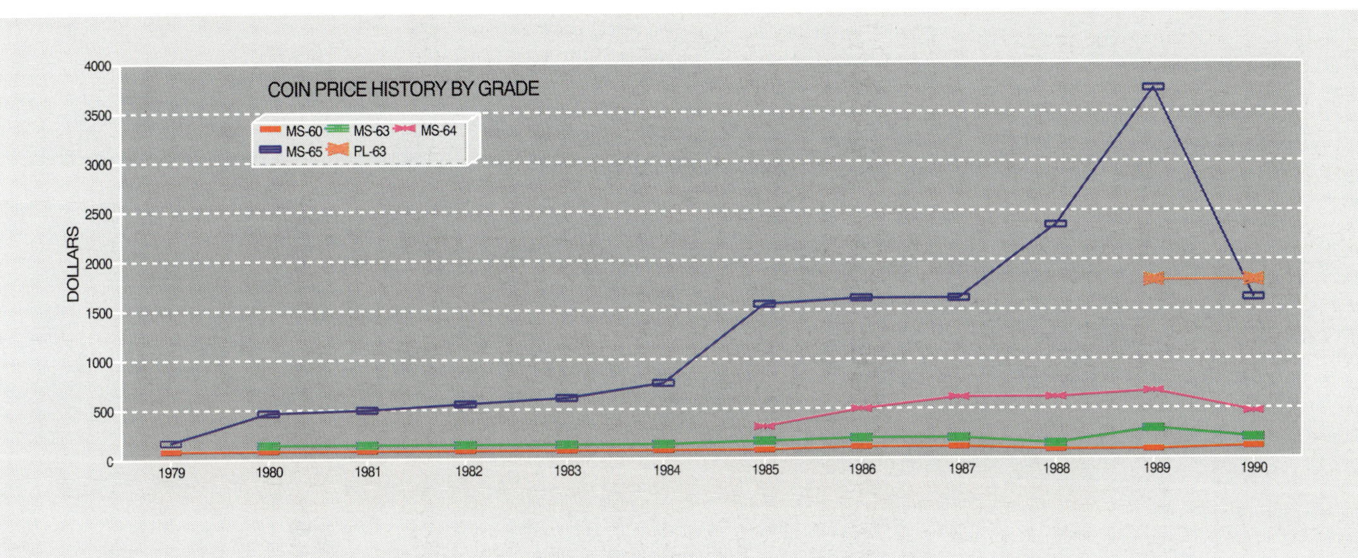

PCGS
1900-S
S$1
MS66
7270.66/7056748

1900-S

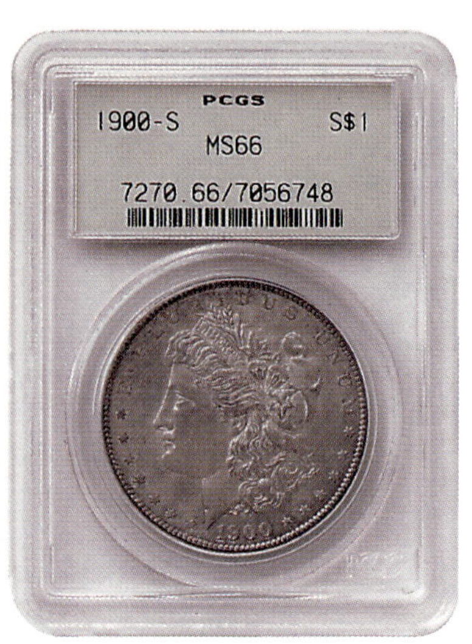

Mintage 3,540,000, from 35 pairs of dies. Treasury bags are the probable source of many Uncs. and sliders; Redfield hoard coins were mostly MS 60/63. Rolls in MS 60/62 survive; they may be Redfield coins. Striking quality on all these varies from weak to full; most are frosty.

C3 varieties come with narrow S (*Ency* 5674-5) or wide S (*Ency* 5676, VAM 2, 4).

C4 varieties to date come only with wide S (*Ency* 5677 = VAM 5); they are much scarcer. Don't mistake the C4 reverse variety as a weakly struck coin.

Recommended in MS 64 up. Beware of sliders priced as Uncs.. XF or higher grades command a premium.

Prooflikes: Rare above MS 64 PL, or in any BU grade DMPL. Many are from Redfield's few hundred, dull and spotty. Cameos are rare.

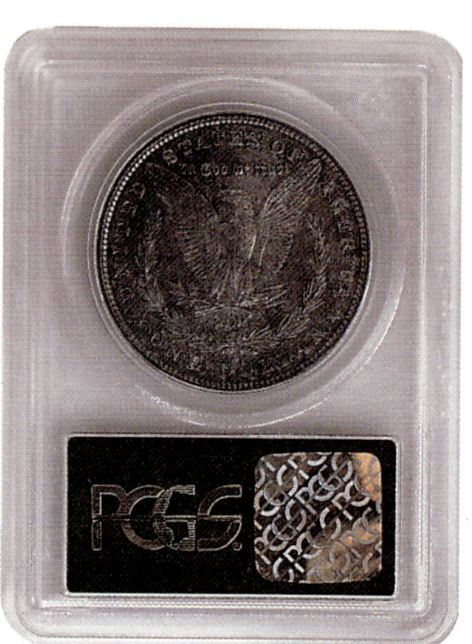

MINTAGE	PROOF	STRIKE	LUSTER	BAG MARKS	REDFIELD
3,540,000	0	Average	Good	Moderate	Yes
DIES	**DIE VARIETIES**	**% OF PL**	**% OF DMPL**	**PIVOTAL GRADE**	**RARITY FACTOR**
40	12	9.4	0.5	MS 65	R-2

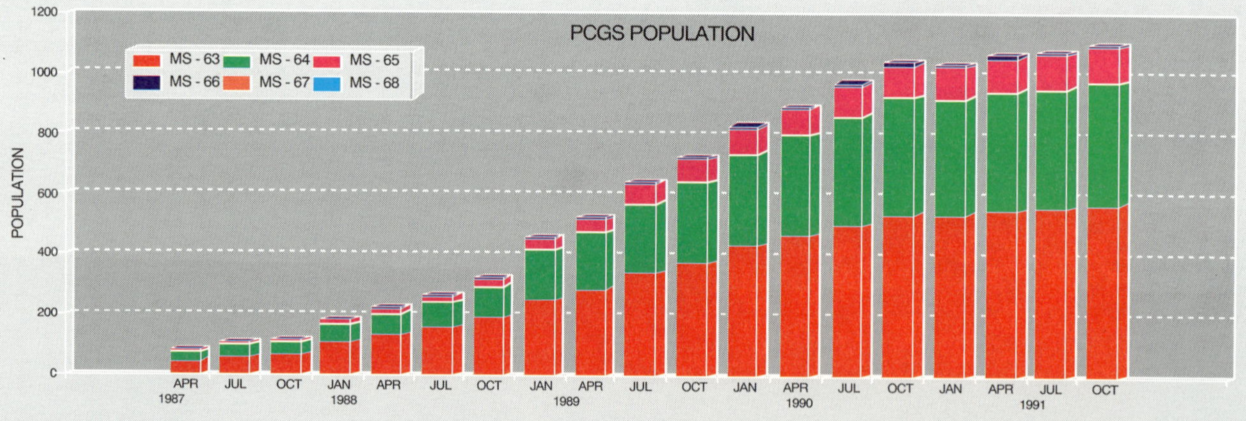
PCGS POPULATION
MS - 63
MS - 64
MS - 65
MS - 66
MS - 67
MS - 68
POPULATION
1200
1000
800
600
400
200
0
APR 1987
JUL
OCT
JAN 1988
APR
JUL
OCT
JAN 1989
APR
JUL
OCT
JAN
APR 1990
JUL
OCT
JAN
APR
JUL 1991
OCT

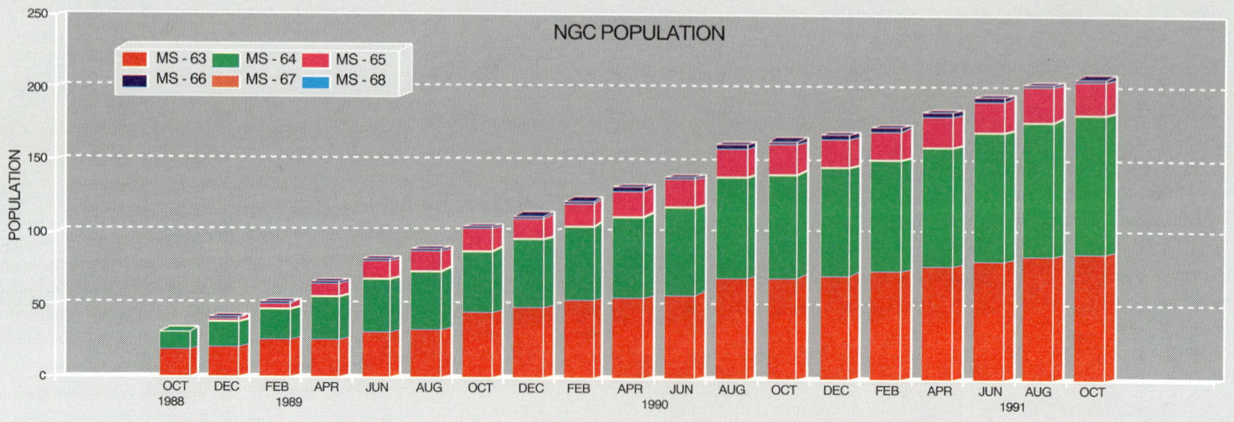
NGC POPULATION
MS - 63
MS - 64
MS - 65
MS - 66
MS - 67
MS - 68
POPULATION
250
200
150
100
50
0
OCT 1988
DEC
FEB 1989
APR
JUN
AUG
OCT
DEC
FEB
APR 1990
JUN
AUG
OCT
DEC
FEB
APR
JUN 1991
AUG
OCT

1900-S

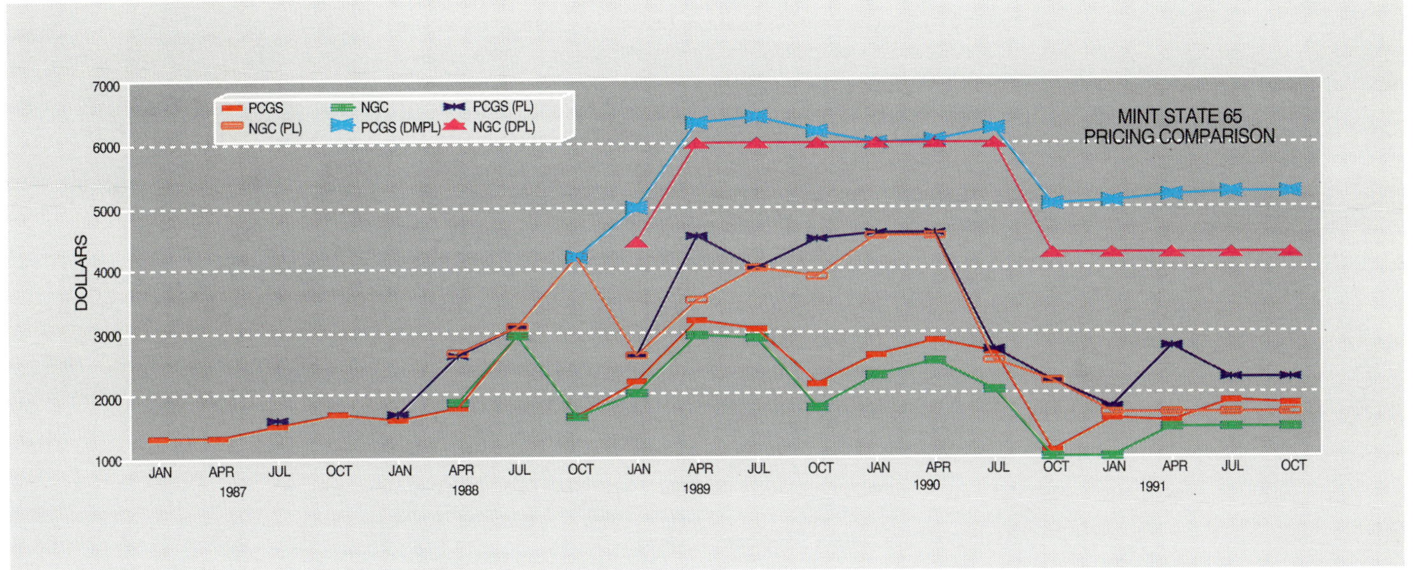

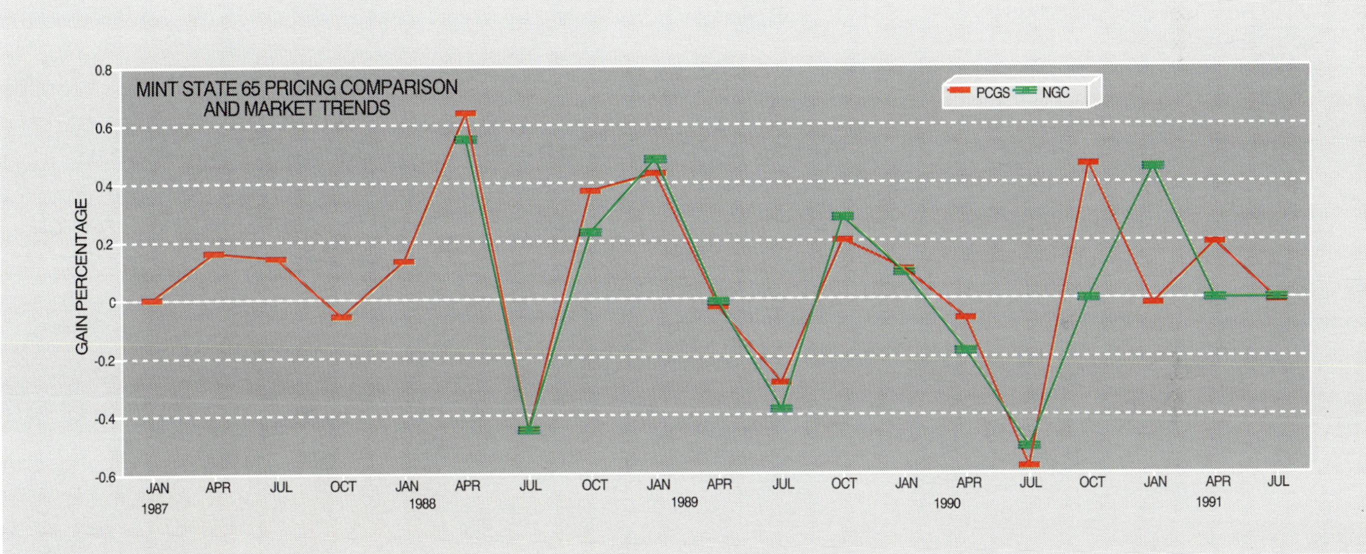

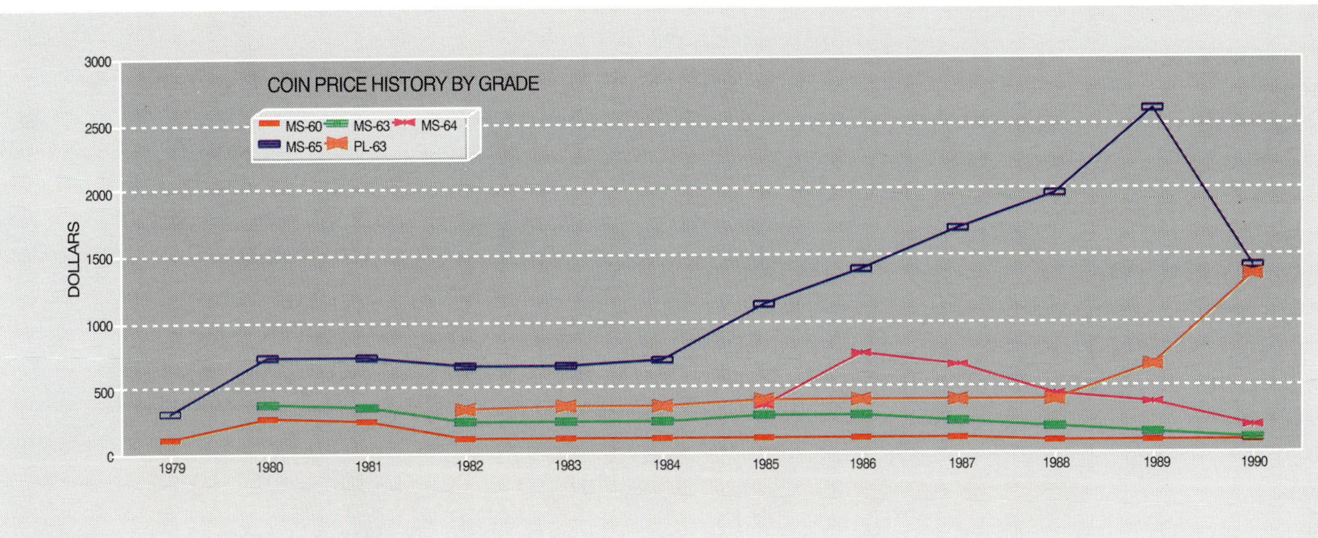

1901-P

KEY DATE! Mintage 6,962,000, from 43 obvs., 44 revs., mostly melted. Circulated survivors are not as often available as sliders. Uncs. are mostly low quality: flat strikes with dull gray lustre. Both of the PCGS MS 64's sold in 1989 for over $50,000 each. To date PCGS has graded only one MS 65, none higher. This 65 is in the PCGS traveling exhibit. Listed in the 1947 Redbook in BU condition for $3.25 and in the 1963 Redbook for $37.50. Times do change things!

This year (1901) the Philadelphia Mint replaced wood-burning annealing furnaces (for dies and planchets) by the gas-burning kind. From 1901 through 1904, the Mint released the same kind of low quality dollars.

Considered the 5th rarest Morgan for circulation, below 1895-O, 1884-S, 1892-S, 1893-S.

C3 reverses belong to Ency 5678 = VAM 1. These are a minority. Nobody yet knows how much scarcer this is than next.

C4 reverses belong to Ency 5679 = VAM 2. These are the majority.

The most famous of the doubled die reverses, also called "14 Feathers," is Ency 5680 = VAM 3 (new rev. hub). It is very scarce and to date always comes circulated. Much rarer but less well known is Ency 5681, with new over old hub; notice double olive left of claw, similar to illustration at Ency 5668.

Recommended in any BU grade you can find. Beware sliders prices as Unc. Beware fakes made by removing mintmark from 1901-O or 1901-S.

Proofs: All 813 were from one pair of dies (VAM 4); hollow places (overpolished die) in hair, especially around Morgan's initial M, reverse from the new C4 hub. Reverse is another doubled die; look at ONE DOLLAR, stars, and lower wreath. Under considerable pressure from date collectors because Uncs. are so unsatisfactory.

Prooflikes: PCGS certified one MS 61 DMPL. Possibly from the Spokane collection. Bruce Todd's coin had several sale records above $20,000. Dean Tavenner sold one to Barbara Goldfreed which reappeared in Auction '87. No others are reported, PL or DMPL.

MINTAGE	PROOF	STRIKE	LUSTER	BAG MARKS	REDFIELD
6,962,000	813	Very Weak	Very Poor	Moderate To Heavy	No
DIES	**DIE VARIETIES**	**% OF PL**	**% OF DMPL**	**PIVOTAL GRADE**	**RARITY FACTOR**
114	11	0.0	0.6	MS 63	R-1

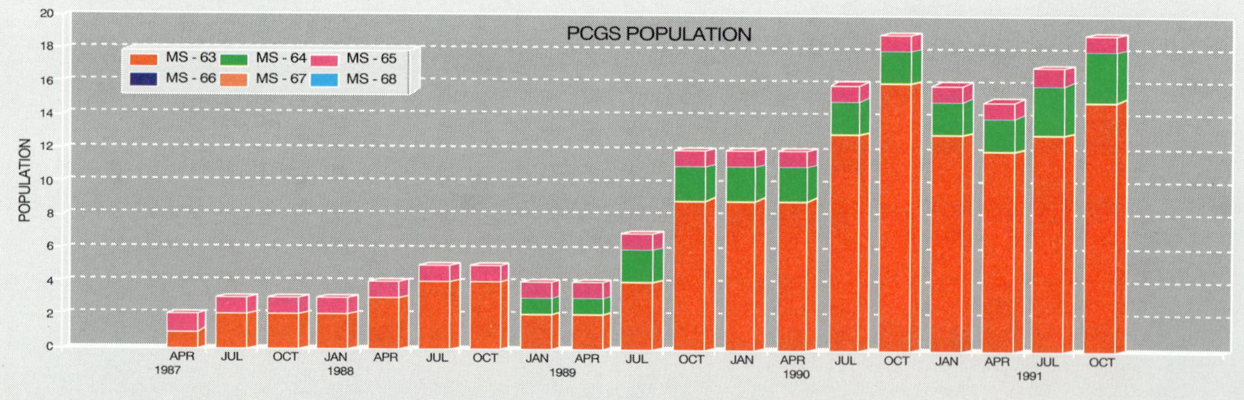

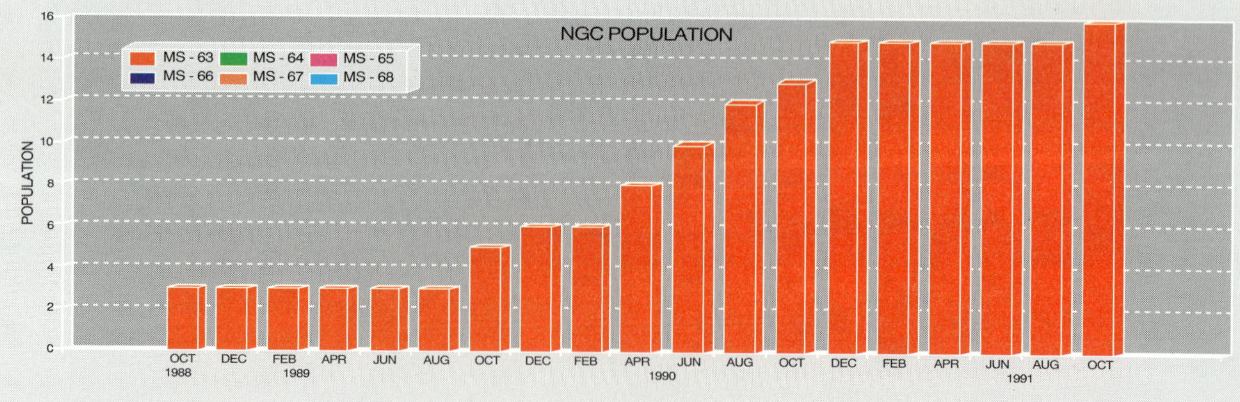

PCGS POPULATION

NGC POPULATION

1901-P

MINT STATE 65
PRICING COMPARISON
PCGS
NGC (PL)
NGC
PCGS (DMPL)
PCGS (PL)
NGC (DPL)
DOLLARS
(Thousands)
80
70
60
50
40
30
20
10
0
JAN
APR
JUL
OCT
1987
1988
1989
1990
1991

MINT STATE 65 PRICING COMPARISON
AND MARKET TRENDS
PCGS
NGC
GAIN PERCENTAGE
1
0.8
0.6
0.4
0.2
0
-0.2
-0.4
-0.6
-0.8
-1
JAN
APR
JUL
OCT
1987
1988
1989
1990
1991

COIN PRICE HISTORY BY GRADE
MS-60
MS-63
MS-64
MS-65
PL-63
DOLLARS
(Thousands)
60
50
40
30
20
10
0
1979
1980
1981
1982
1983
1984
1985
1986
1987
1988
1989
1990

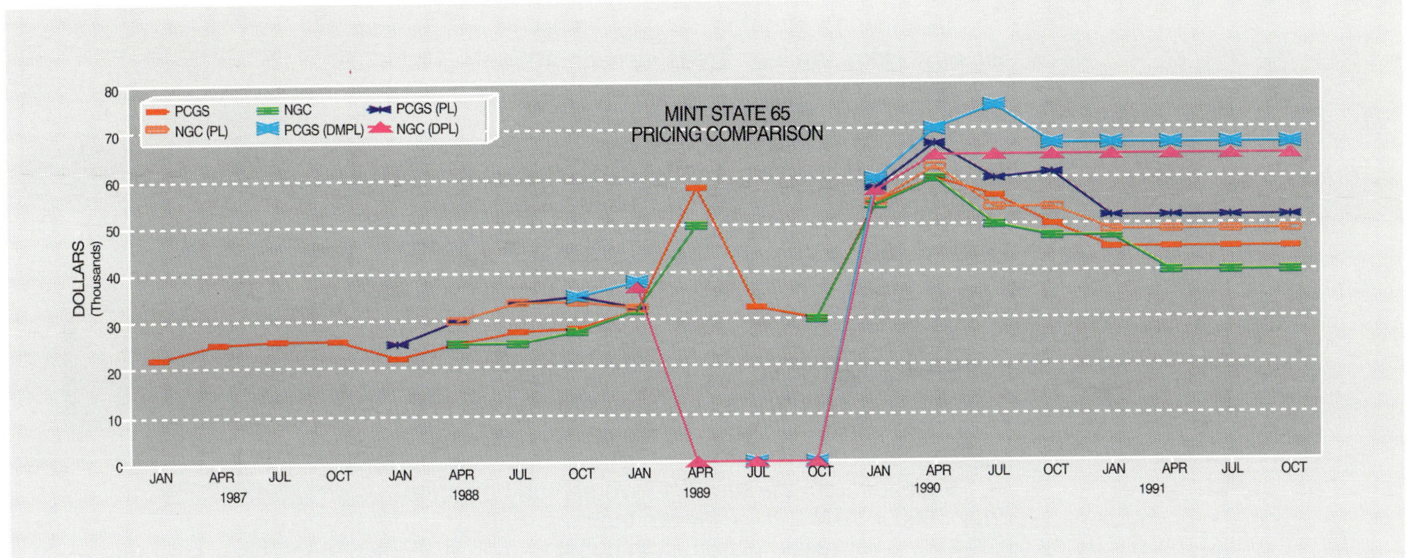

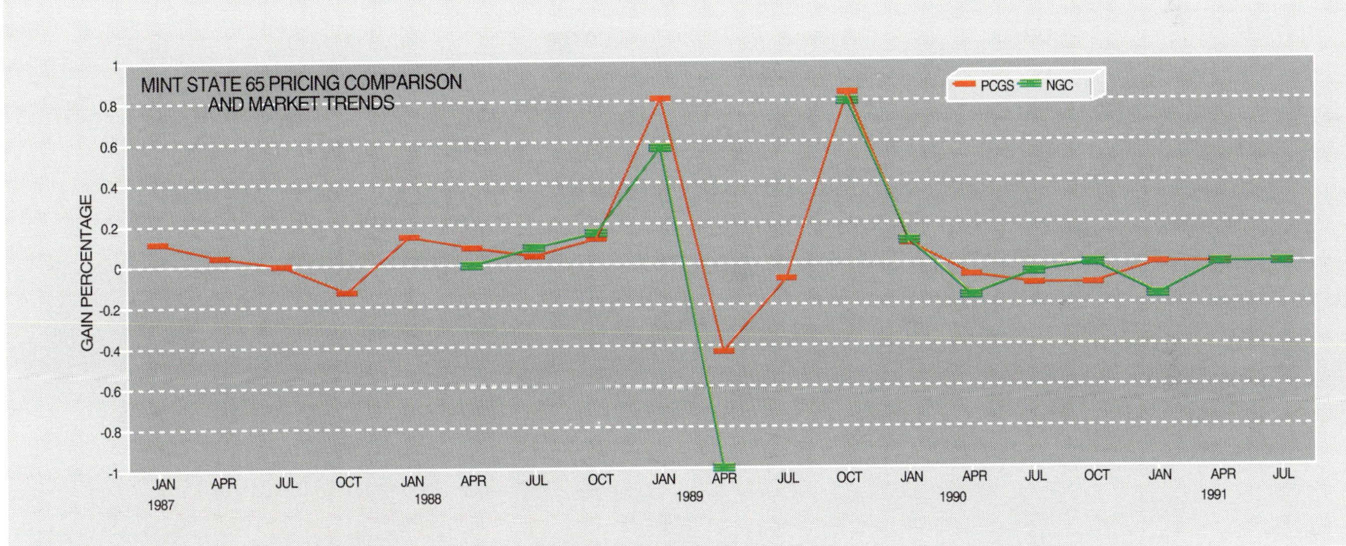

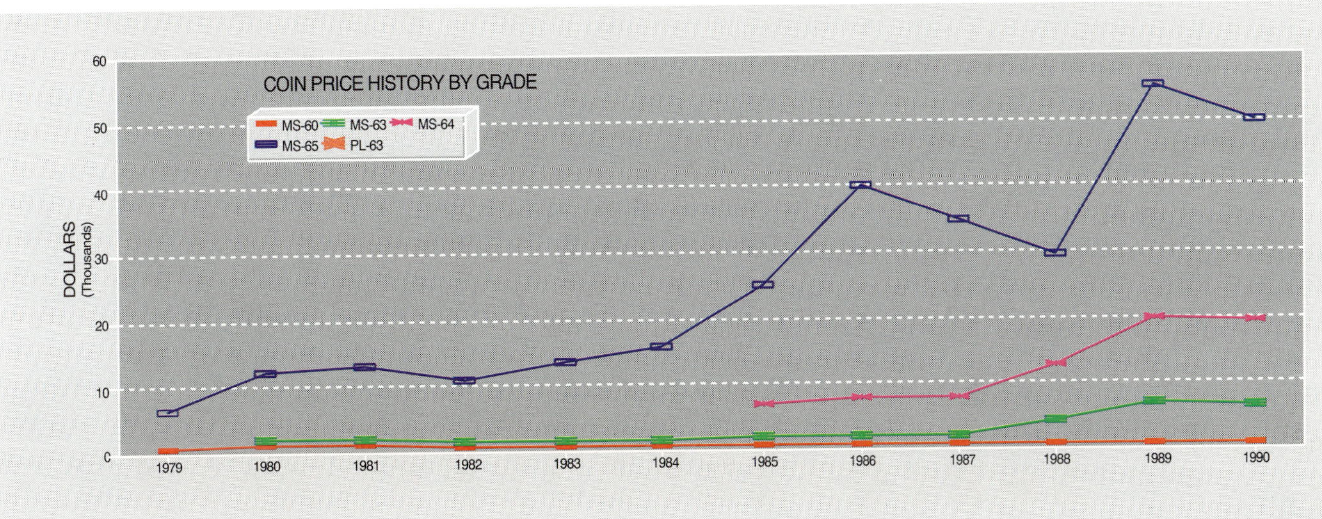

1901-O

Mintage 13,320,000, largest of all from New Orleans. Uncs. are from Treasury bags, 1958-64. Flat to full strikes, good lustre, sometimes very frosty. Rolls and bags survive in MS 60/62.

The 1901-O was priced $10 in the 1947 Redbook. It was valued higher than the 1883-S, 1886-S, 1887-O, 1888-S, 1889-CC, 1889-O, 1890-CC, 1890-O, 1891-CC, 1892-P, 1892-CC, 1892-O, 1893-P, 1894-P, 1894-O, 1895-P, 1896-O, 1897-O, 1898-S, 1899-S, 1900-S, 1901-P, 1901-S, 1902-S, 1904-P AND 1904-S. INCREDIBLE!

Multiple bag releases by the U.S. Treasury during the "Great Silver Dollar Rush" of 1958 - 1964.

Varieties from the old C3 reverse hub belong to *Ency* 5682 = VAM 1. They are a small minority of this date.

Varieties from the new C4 reverse hub belong to *Ency* 5683 = VAM 2-8. They are the majority.

One doubled rev. die (*Ency* 5681) shows impressions from both hubs, as in ill. at *Ency* 5668. This is still rare. Recommended in MS 65 up or in MS 64 by the roll.

Prooflikes: PL's outnumber DMPL's 10 to 1. PL's are rare above MS 65; DMPL's in all BU grades.

MINTAGE	PROOF	STRIKE	LUSTER	BAG MARKS	REDFIELD
13,320,000	0	Soft & Weak	Average	Moderate To Heavy	No
DIES	**DIE VARIETIES**	**% OF PL**	**% OF DMPL**	**PIVOTAL GRADE**	**RARITY FACTOR**
210	32	5.4	0.6	MS 65	R-4

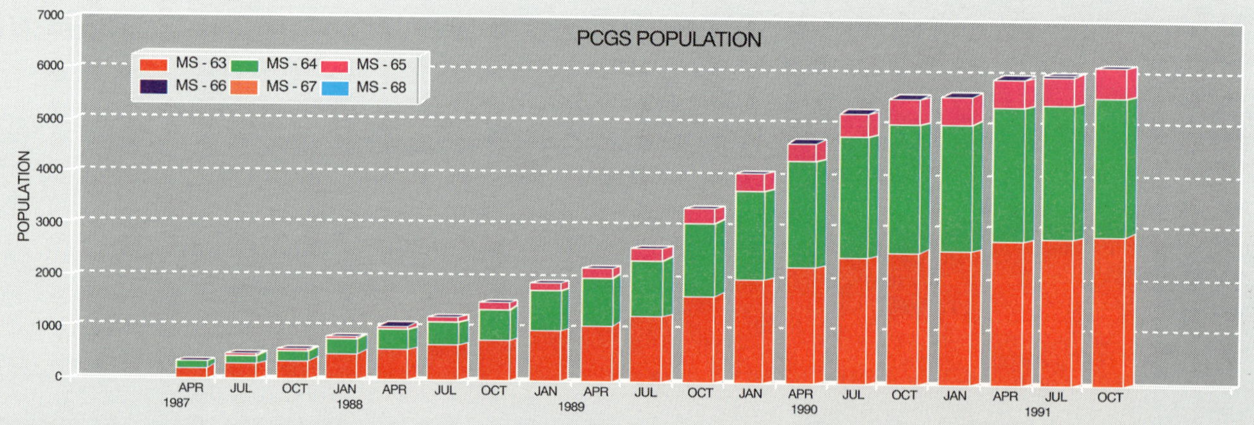

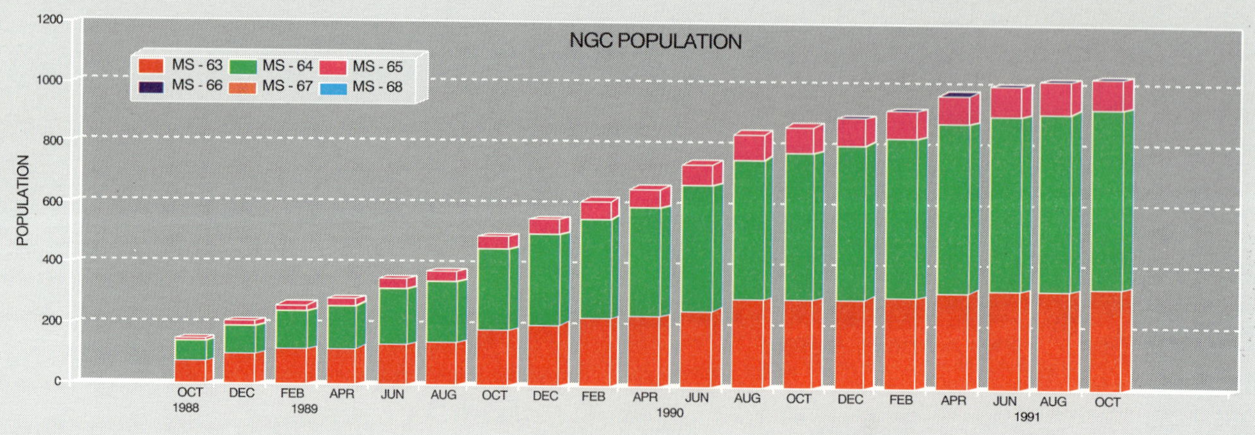

PCGS POPULATION

NGC POPULATION

1901-O

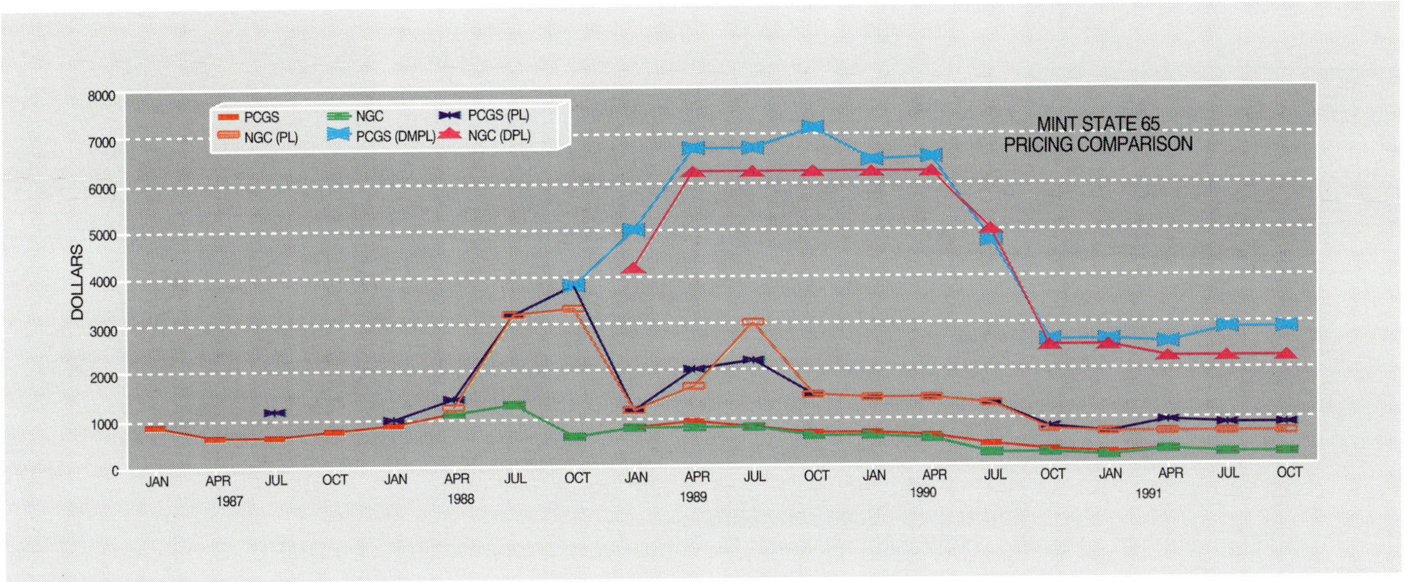

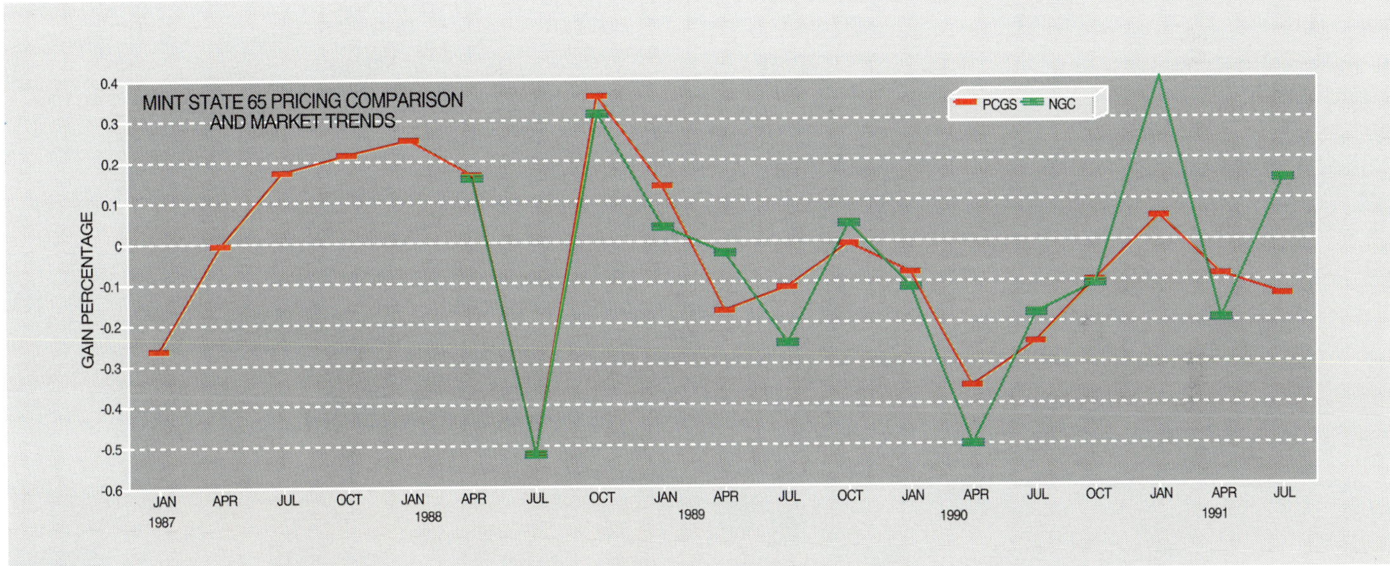

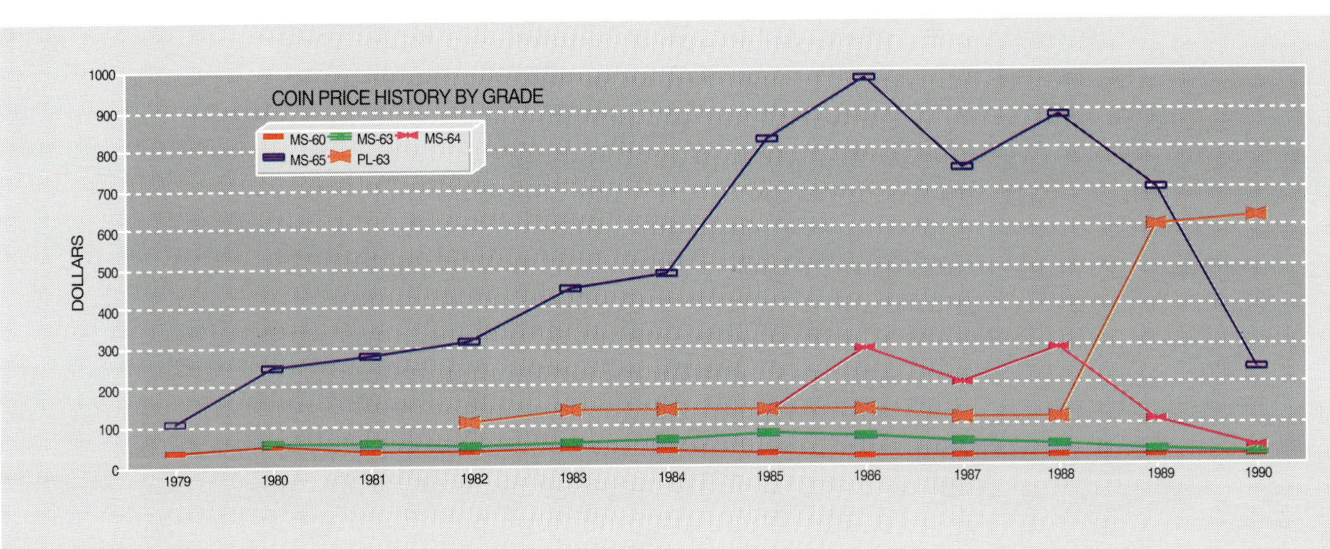

1901-S

Mintage 2,284,000, mostly melted. Uncs. are from Treasury bags (not many), notably two bags from Idaho handled by John B. Love in the early 1960's—for only 30% above face value! Quality is very variable; strike ranges from flat to full, lustre from dull to brilliant. Circulated pieces do not often show up.

The 1897-04-S are listed in rarity order of most rare to most common. They are 03-S, 04-S, 01-S, 99-S, 98-S, 02-S, 00-S, 97-S.

Recommended in MS 63 up.

Varieties with the old C3 reverse belong to *Ency* 5685 = VAN 1, 3.

Varieties with the new C4 reverse belong to *Ency* 5686 = VAM 2, 4. Uncs. are often of better quality than C3's. Nobody knows yet which is scarcer. Most of the C4 reverse are high quality strikes with good lustre.

A rare doubled reverse die shows impressions from both hubs (*Ency* 5687).

Prooflikes: Rare in all grades; contrast is minimal. Don't hold your breath waiting for a DMPL. Semi-prooflikes are scarce but available.

MINTAGE	PROOF	STRIKE	LUSTER	BAG MARKS	REDFIELD
2,284,000	0	Weak & Soft	Average	Moderate	No
DIES	**DIE VARIETIES**	**% OF PL**	**% OF DMPL**	**PIVOTAL GRADE**	**RARITY FACTOR**
80	9	1.5	0.1	MS 65	R-1

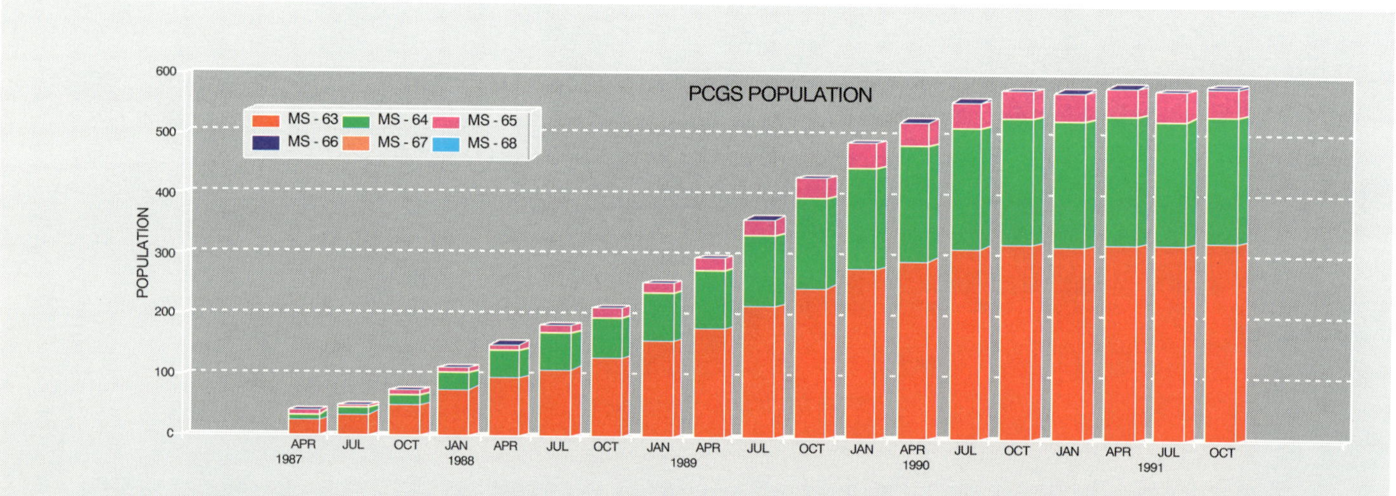

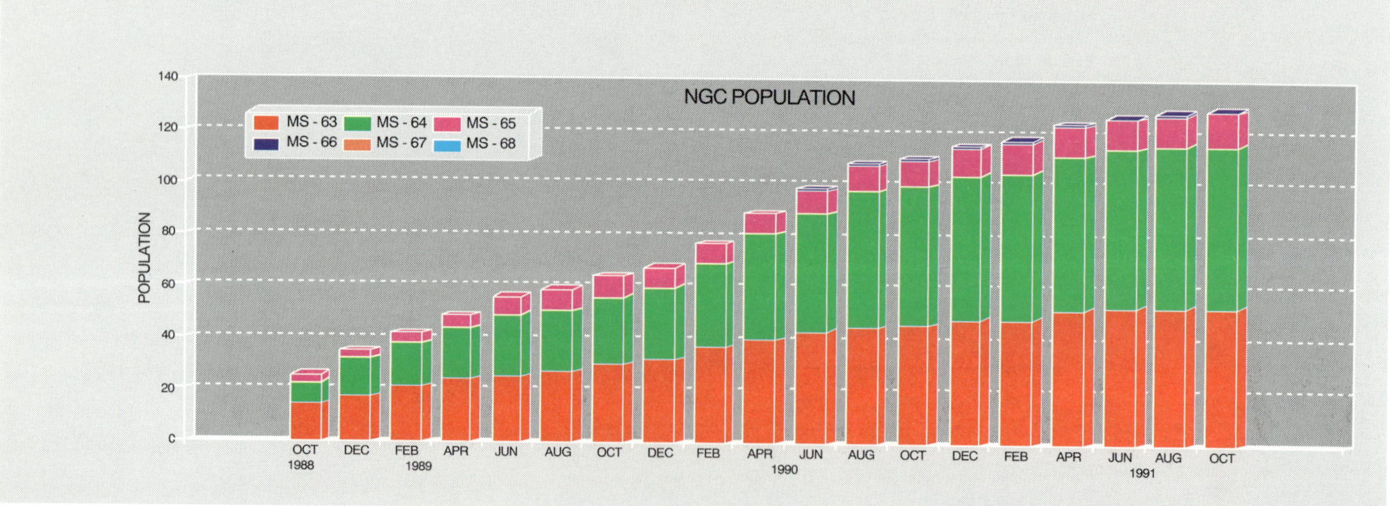

PCGS POPULATION

MS - 63 · MS - 64 · MS - 65 · MS - 66 · MS - 67 · MS - 68

POPULATION: 0, 100, 200, 300, 400, 500, 600

APR 1987, JUL, OCT, JAN 1988, APR, JUL, OCT, JAN 1989, APR, JUL, OCT, JAN, APR 1990, JUL, OCT, JAN, APR 1991, JUL, OCT

NGC POPULATION

MS - 63 · MS - 64 · MS - 65 · MS - 66 · MS - 67 · MS - 68

POPULATION: 0, 20, 40, 60, 80, 100, 120, 140

OCT 1988, DEC, FEB 1989, APR, JUN, AUG, OCT, DEC, FEB, APR 1990, JUN, AUG, OCT, DEC, FEB, APR, JUN 1991, AUG, OCT

1901-S

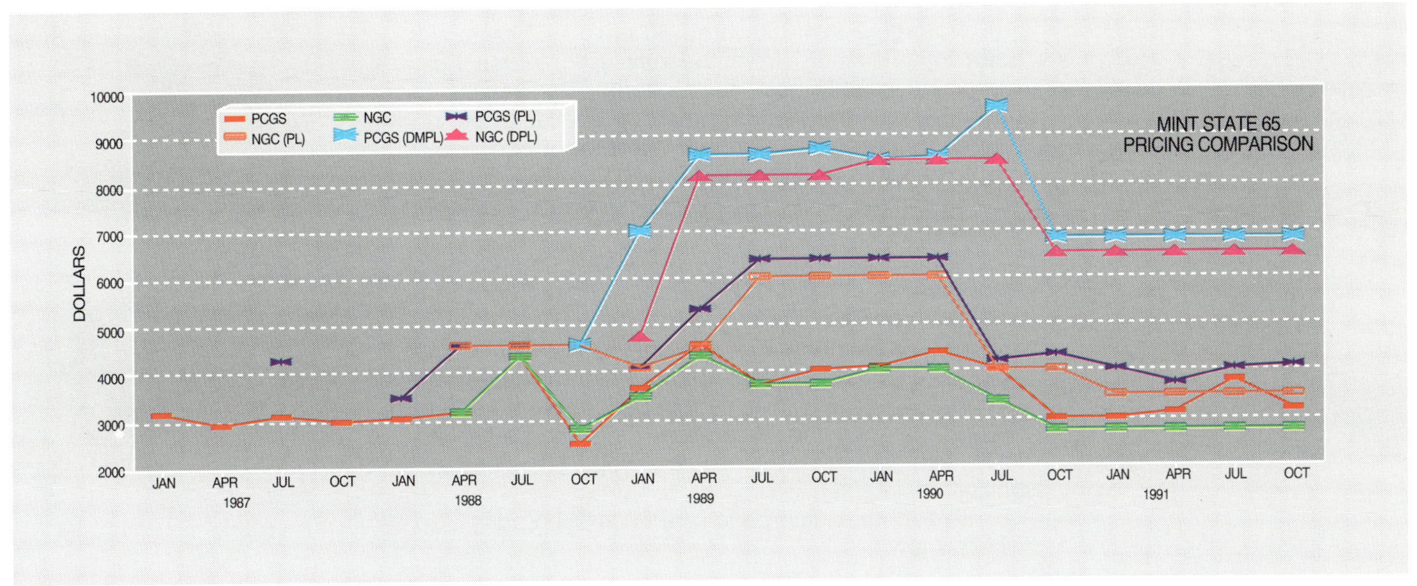

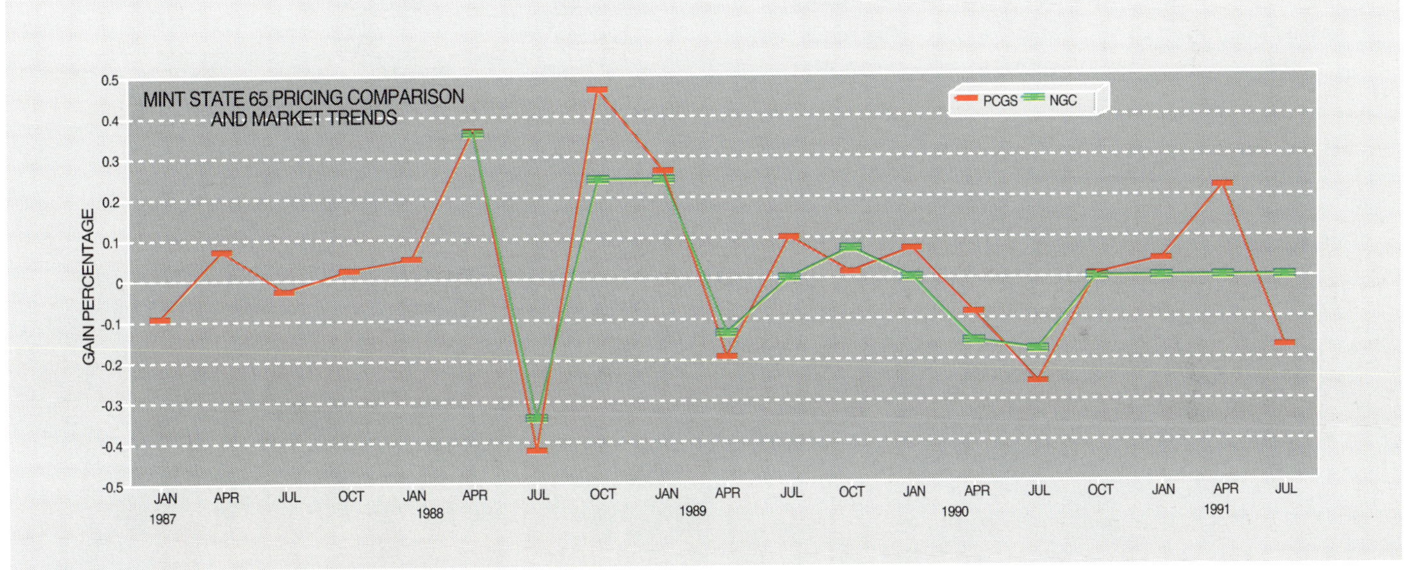

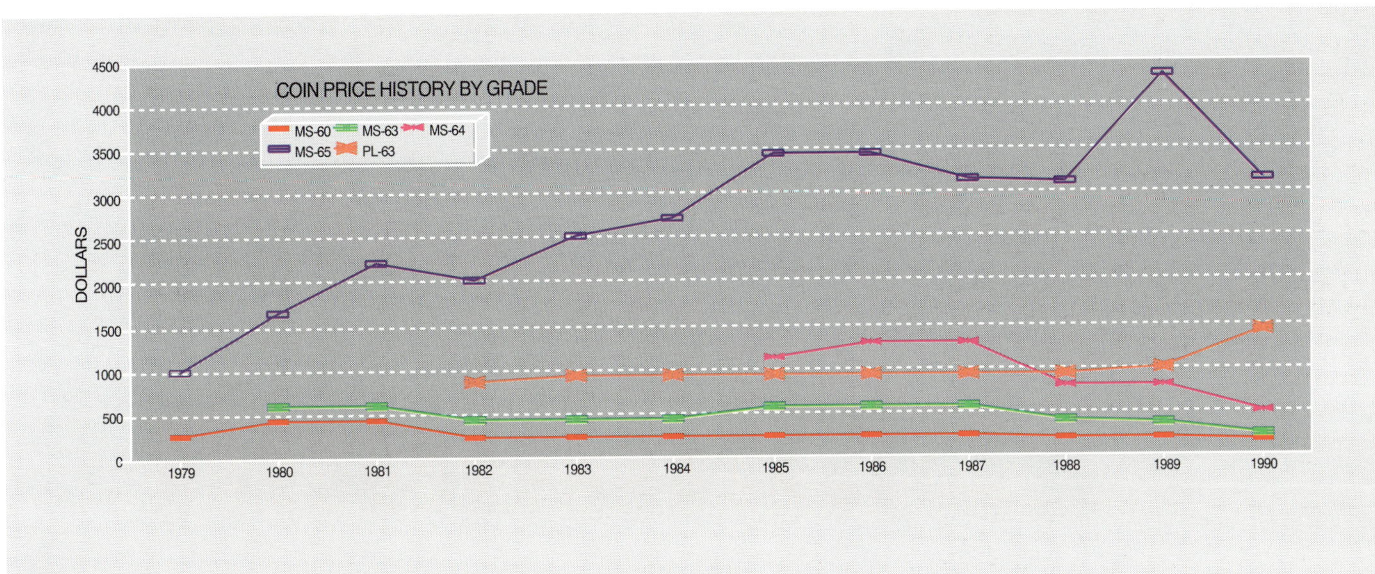

1902-P

Mintage 7,994,000, from 80 obvs., 67 revs. All seen to date come from the new C4 reverse hub. Uncs. are usually bold; lustre varies from satiny to brilliant. Rolls in MS 60/62 may be available, but no bags. Sliders are plentiful. Some of the same problems occur as described at 1901.

Recommended in MS 64 up. Beware of sliders priced as Unc.

A rare doubled reverse die shows impressions from both old C3 and new C4 hubs (*Ency* 5689), like illustration at *Ency* 5668.

Proofs: Mintage 777, all from the new C4 reverse hub; VAM 2, die file mark slants down to right at left ribbon bow. Proofs of all denominations from 1902 to 1904 no longer come as cameos. This apparently had to do with the way the dies were prepared. They are brilliant, not cameo.

Prooflikes: Scarce to rare in all BU grades. No DMPL known.

MINTAGE	PROOF	STRIKE	LUSTER	BAG MARKS	REDFIELD
7,994,000	777	Average To Bold	Average	Light	No
DIES	**DIE VARIETIES**	**% OF PL**	**% OF DMPL**	**PIVOTAL GRADE**	**RARITY FACTOR**
136	11	2.0	0.1	MS 65	R-3

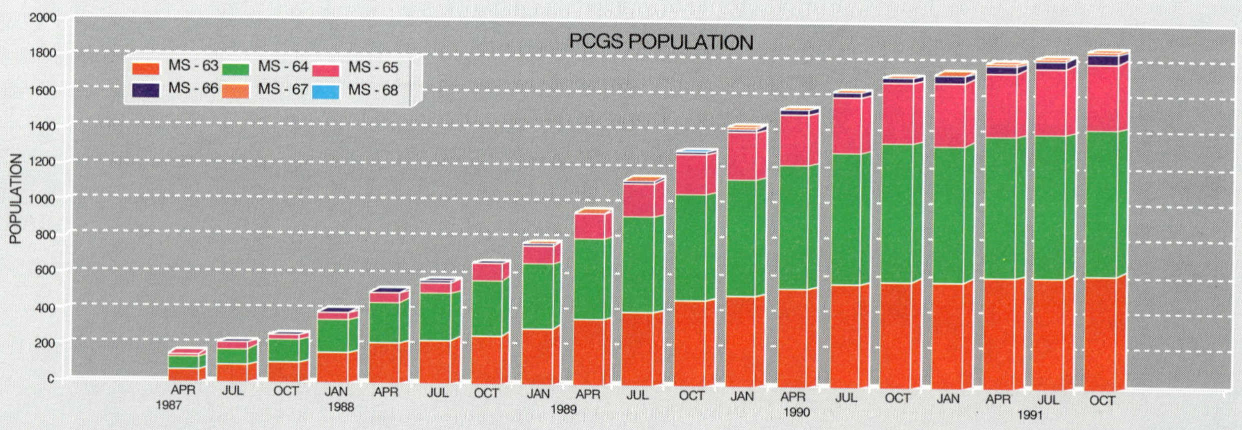

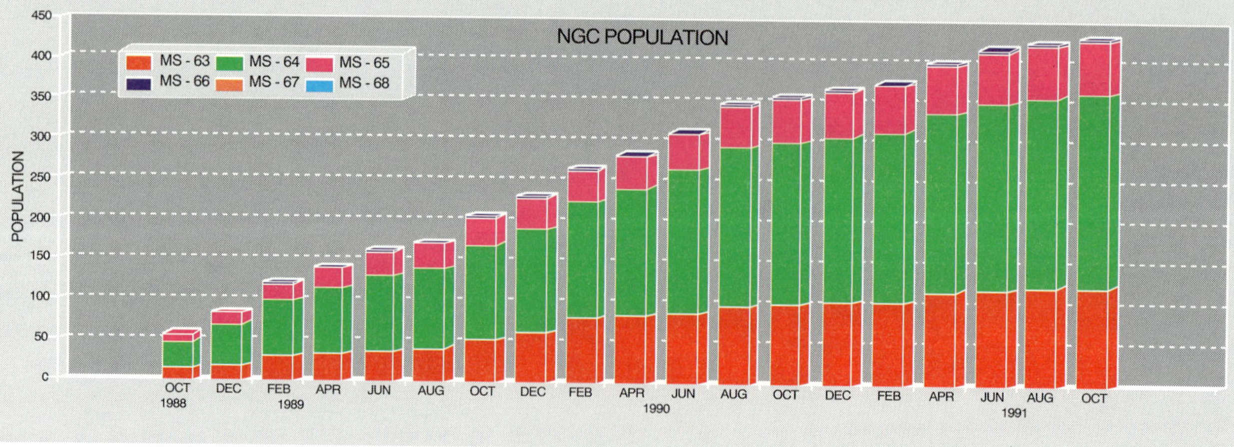

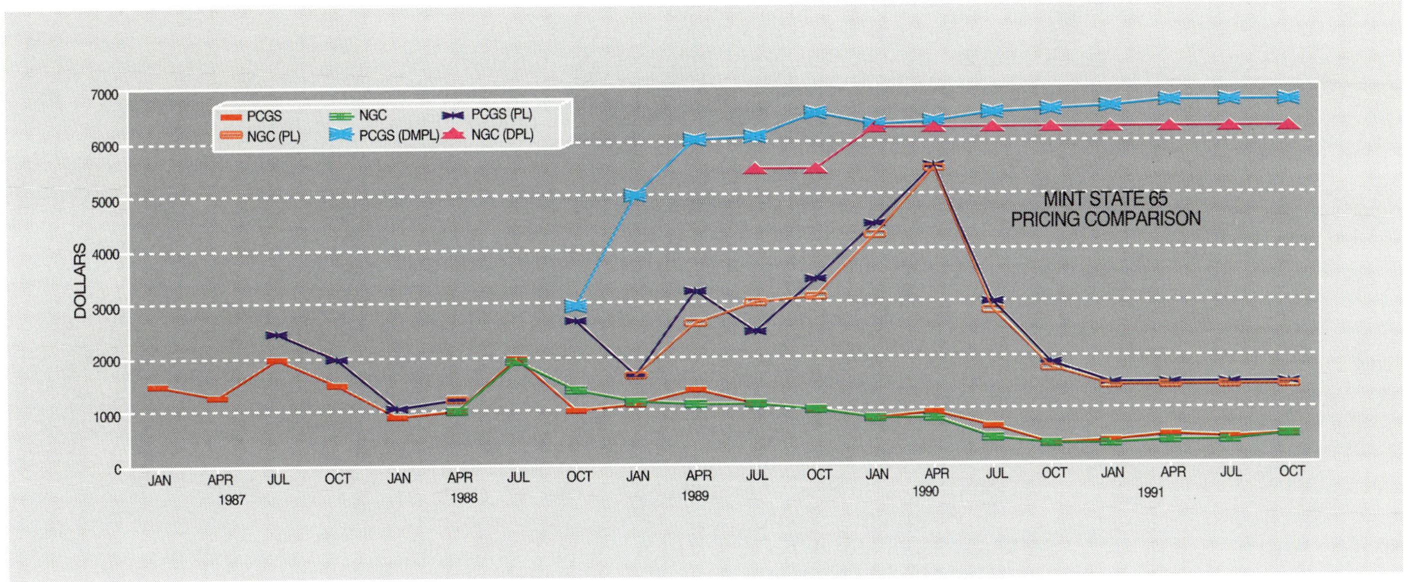
PCGS
NGC
PCGS (PL)
NGC (PL)
PCGS (DMPL)
NGC (DPL)
MINT STATE 65
PRICING COMPARISON
DOLLARS
7000
6000
5000
4000
3000
2000
1000
0
JAN APR JUL OCT JAN APR JUL OCT JAN APR JUL OCT JAN APR JUL OCT JAN APR JUL OCT
1987
1988
1989
1990
1991

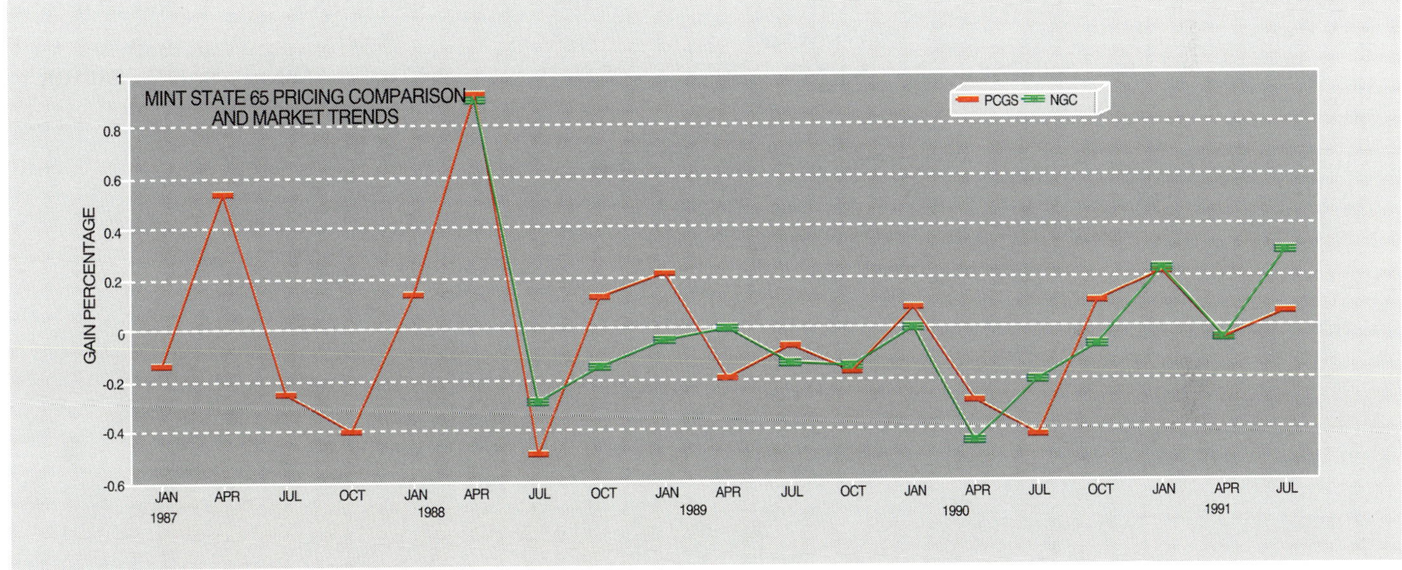
MINT STATE 65 PRICING COMPARISON
AND MARKET TRENDS
PCGS
NGC
GAIN PERCENTAGE
1
0.8
0.6
0.4
0.2
0
-0.2
-0.4
-0.6
JAN APR JUL OCT JAN APR JUL OCT JAN APR JUL OCT JAN APR JUL OCT JAN APR JUL
1987
1988
1989
1990
1991

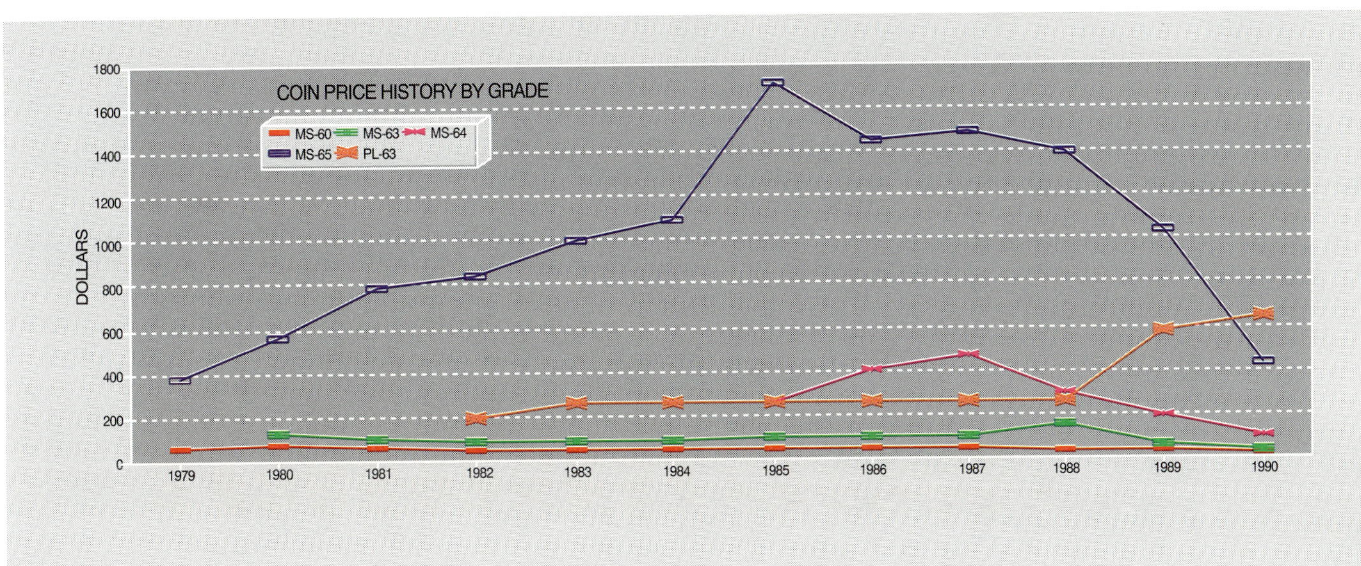
COIN PRICE HISTORY BY GRADE
MS-60
MS-63
MS-64
MS-65
PL-63
DOLLARS
1800
1600
1400
1200
1000
800
600
400
200
0
1979
1980
1981
1982
1983
1984
1985
1986
1987
1988
1989
1990

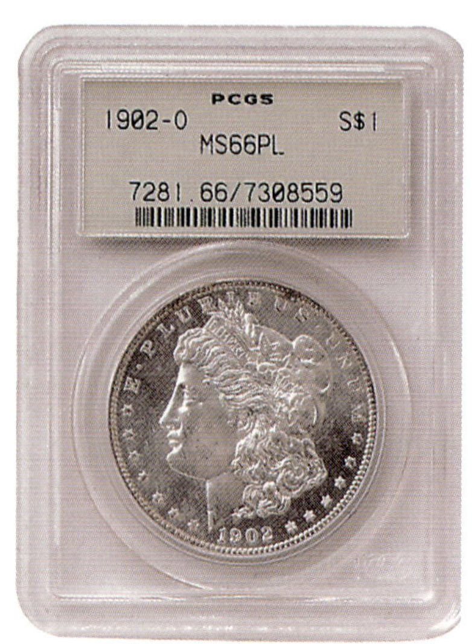

1902-O

Mintage 8,636,000, from 140 obvs., 107 revs. Uncs. are plentiful from dozens if not hundreds of Treasury bags released in October 1962; before then the 1902-O was very hard to find, priced higher than 1884-S. Rolls and bags in MS 60/62 are available. Sliders are common. In the summer of 1989, the 1902-O was over $1,400 wholesale in MS 65.

Recommended in MS 65 up or in MS 64 by the roll. Beware sliders priced as Unc. The rare small round o variety, *Ency* 5690 = VAM 3, is from the old C3 hub. Mintmark is as in 1880, 1896 and 1899. These only come worn. Fivaz & Stanton list this a Rarity 6.

The usual large O varieties, *Ency* 5691, are from the new C4 hub.

At least six doubled die reverses with large O (*Ency* 5692) show impressions from both hubs. Compare illustration at *Ency* 5668. These are rare.

Prooflikes: Scarce in all grades, mostly from two bags dispersed in 1968; DMPL's are rare especially above MS 64. None show much cameo contrast.

MINTAGE	PROOF	STRIKE	LUSTER	BAG MARKS	REDFIELD
8,636,000	0	Soft To Average	Dull To Average	Moderate	No
DIES	**DIE VARIETIES**	**% OF PL**	**% OF DMPL**	**PIVOTAL GRADE**	**RARITY FACTOR**
300	38	3.3	0.6	MS 65	R-5

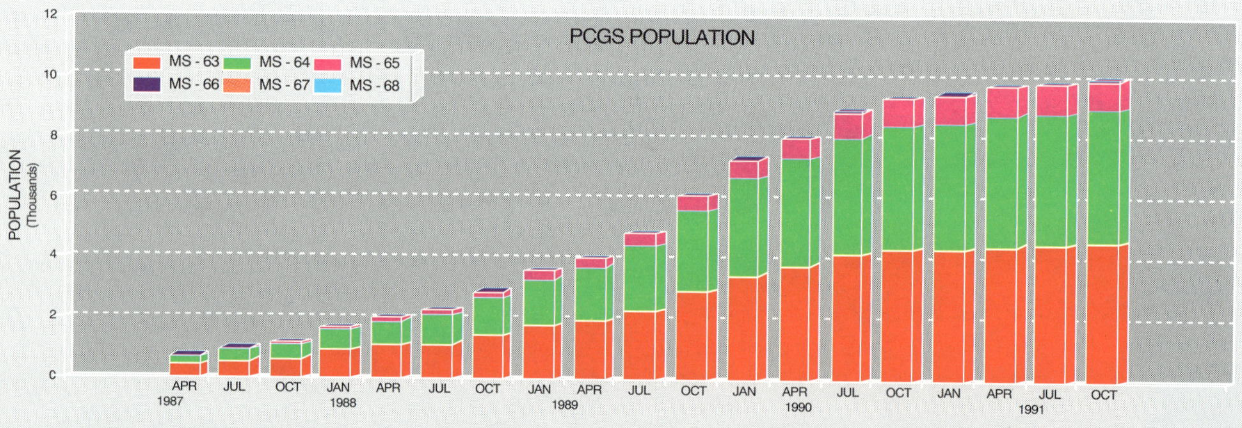

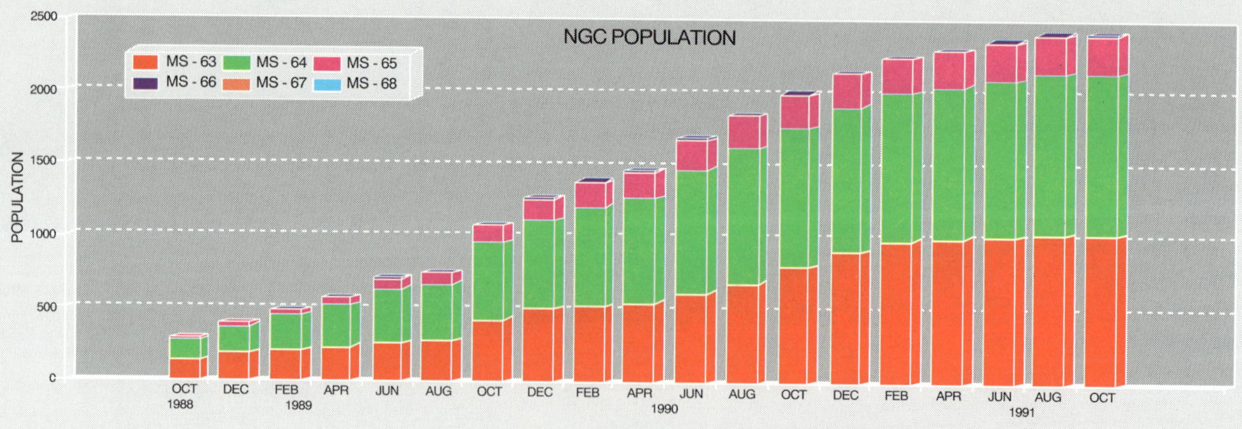

1902-O

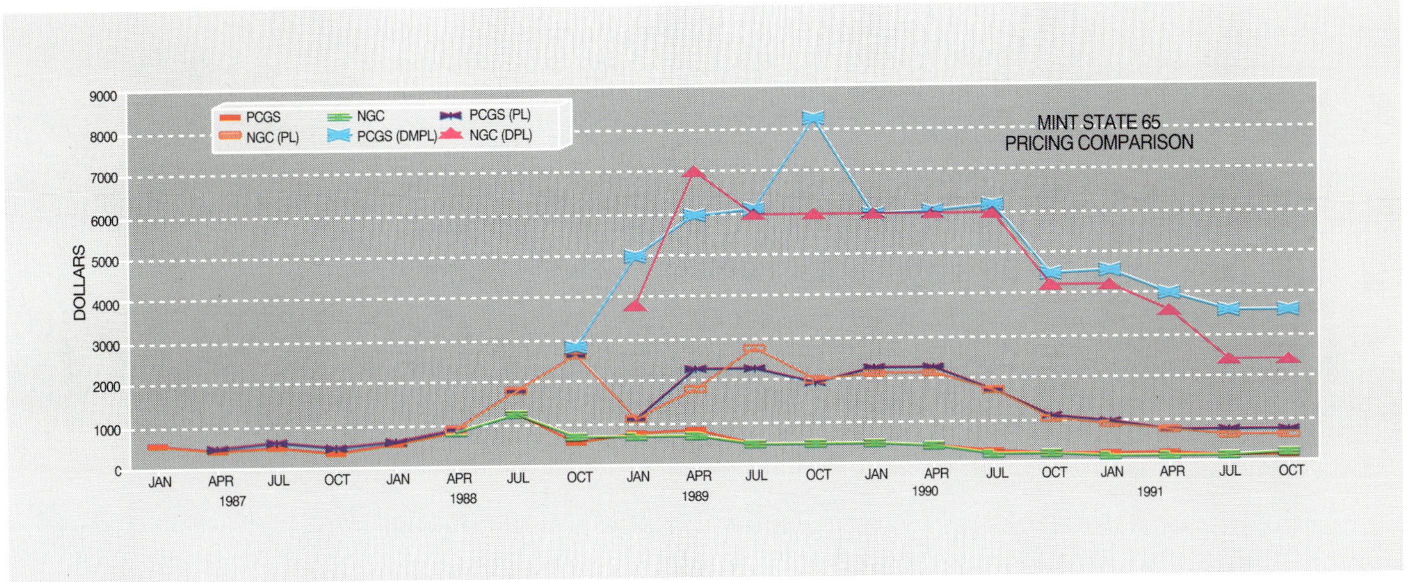

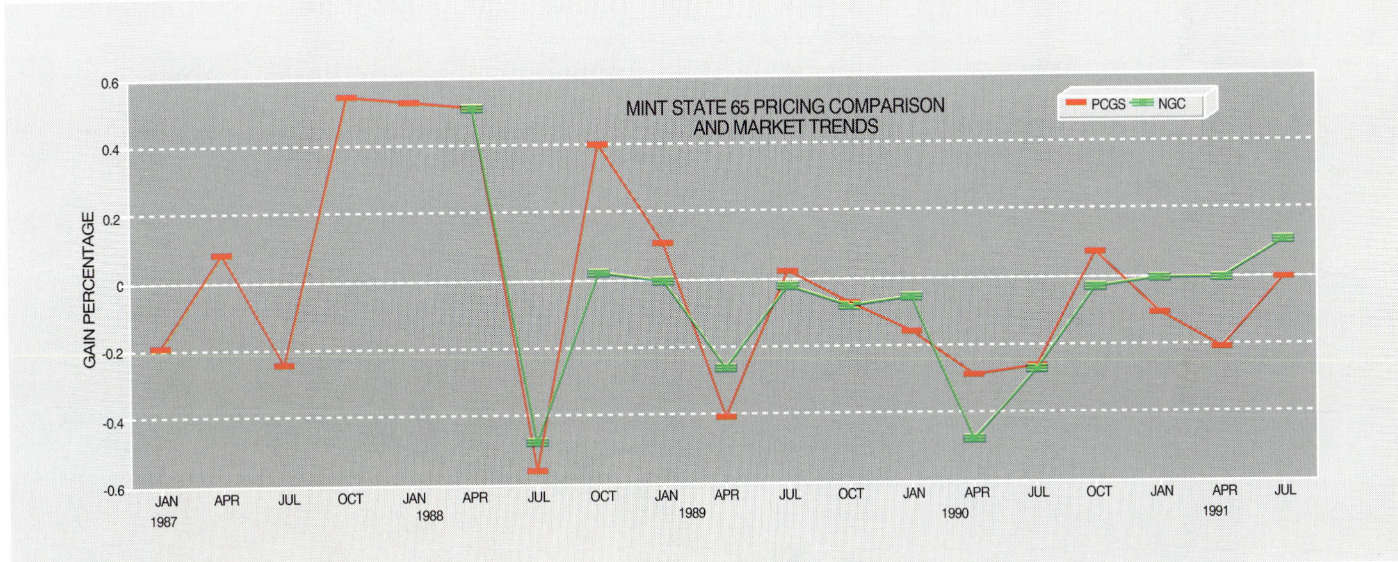

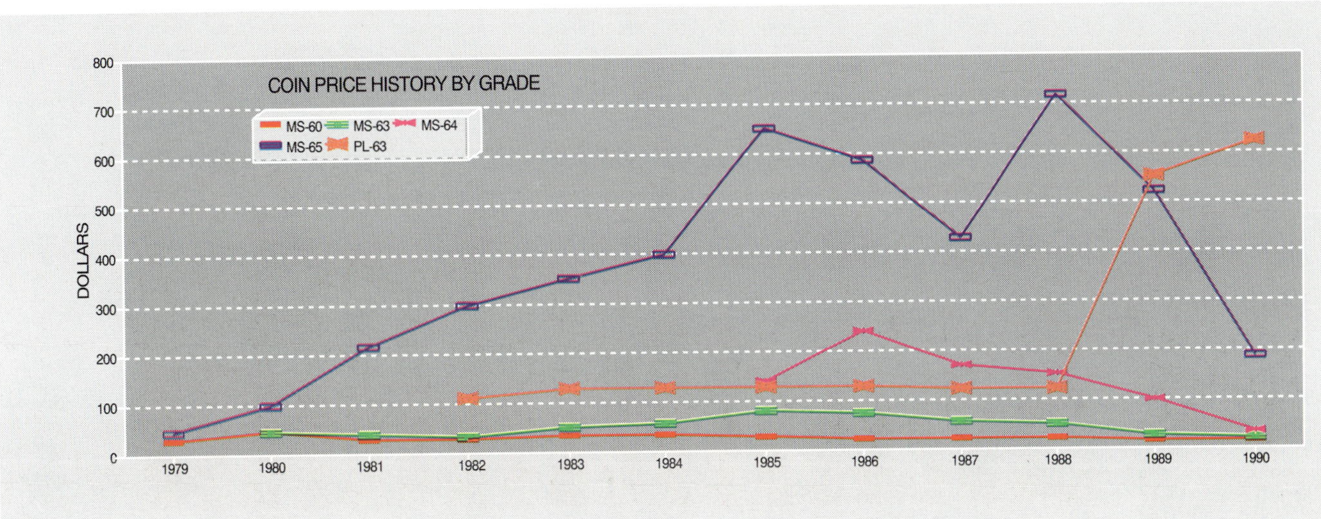

PCGS
1902-S
S$1
MS67
7282.67/2253895

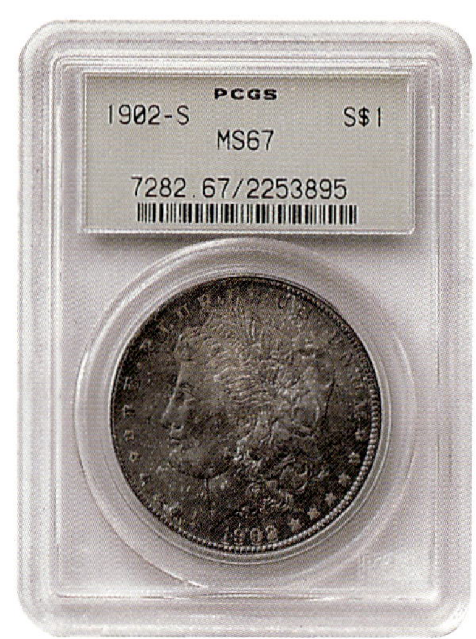

1902-S

Mintage 1,530,000, all from the new C4 hubs. Uncs. are among the least attractive San Francisco Mint Morgans: weak strikes from worn dies, heavily bagmarked, often showing striations (on the strip from which these blanks were cut). The Redfield hoard reportedly contained only one or possibly two bags of this date, mostly MS 60/63, many very baggy.

Recommended in MS 63 up. Circulated examples of this date are scarce. Beware of sliders priced as Unc.

At least two doubled die reverses show impressions from both old C3 and new C4 hubs (*Ency* 5694), like illustration at *Ency* 5668.

Prooflikes: Rare in all grades. Cameos very rare. A few semi-PLs exist.

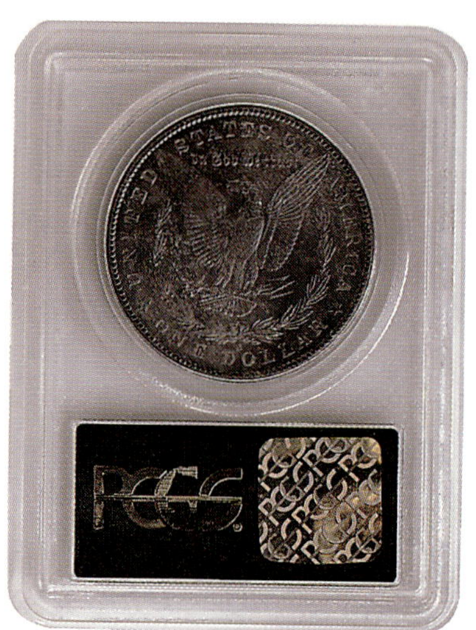

MINTAGE	PROOF	STRIKE	LUSTER	BAG MARKS	REDFIELD
1,530,000	0	Soft & Weak	Average	Moderate	Yes
DIES	**DIE VARIETIES**	**% OF PL**	**% OF DMPL**	**PIVOTAL GRADE**	**RARITY FACTOR**
40	8	0.8	0.1	MS 65	R-2

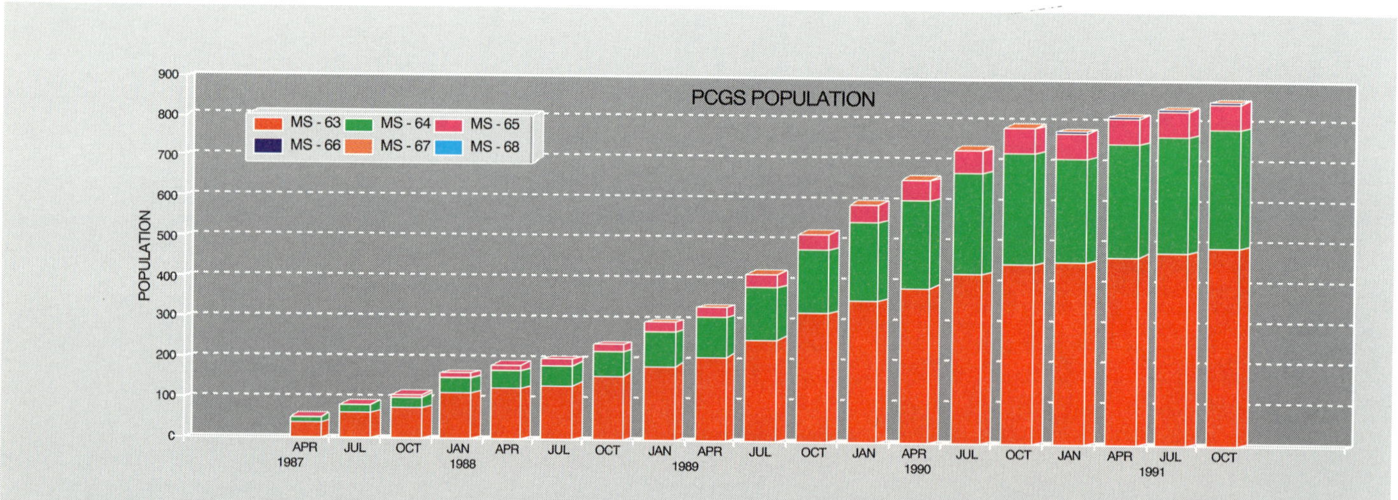
PCGS POPULATION
MS - 63
MS - 64
MS - 65
MS - 66
MS - 67
MS - 68
POPULATION
900
800
700
600
500
400
300
200
100
0
APR 1987
JUL
OCT
JAN 1988
APR
JUL
OCT
JAN 1989
APR
JUL
OCT
JAN
APR 1990
JUL
OCT
JAN
APR 1991
JUL
OCT

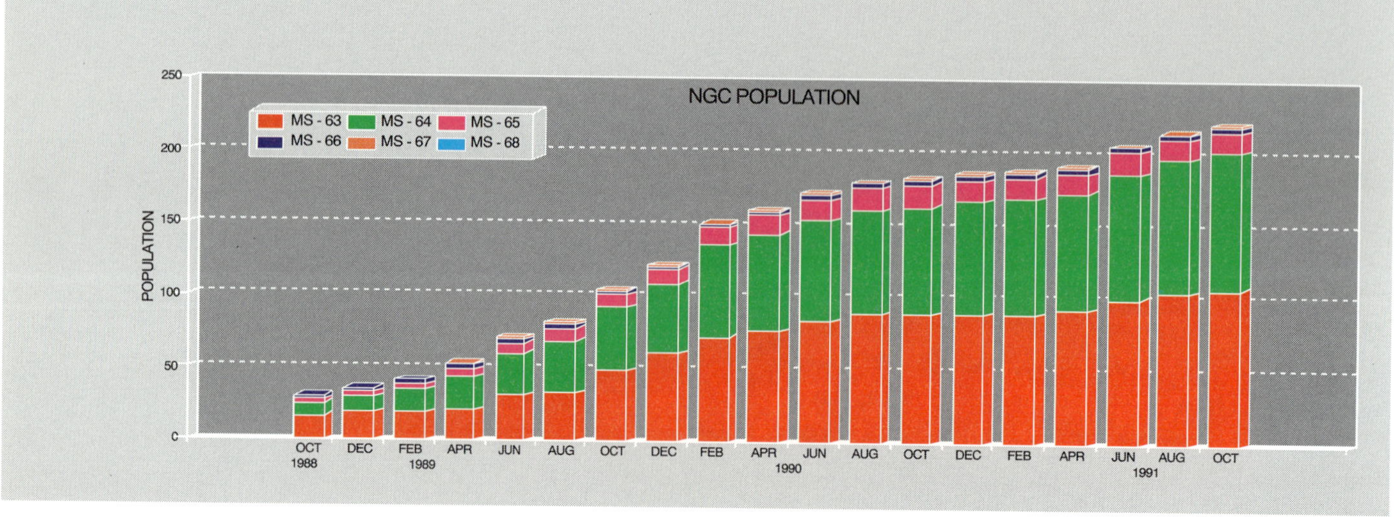
NGC POPULATION
MS - 63
MS - 64
MS - 65
MS - 66
MS - 67
MS - 68
POPULATION
250
200
150
100
50
0
OCT 1988
DEC
FEB 1989
APR
JUN
AUG
OCT
DEC
FEB
APR 1990
JUN
AUG
OCT
DEC
FEB
APR
JUN 1991
AUG
OCT

1902-S

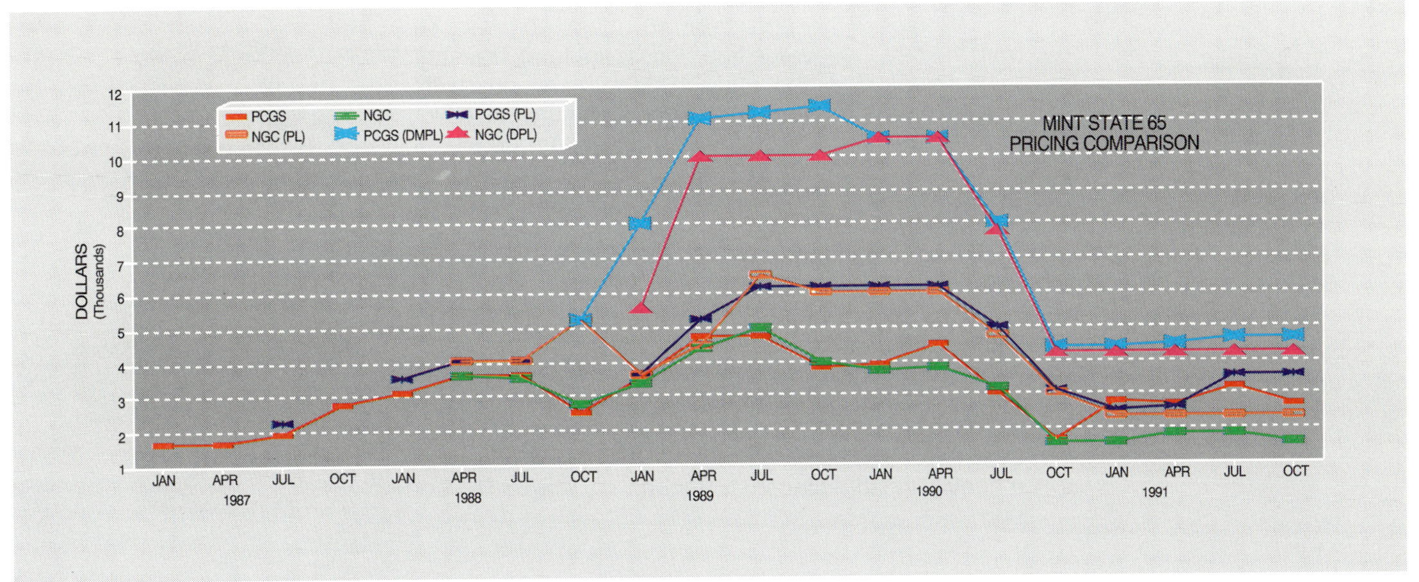

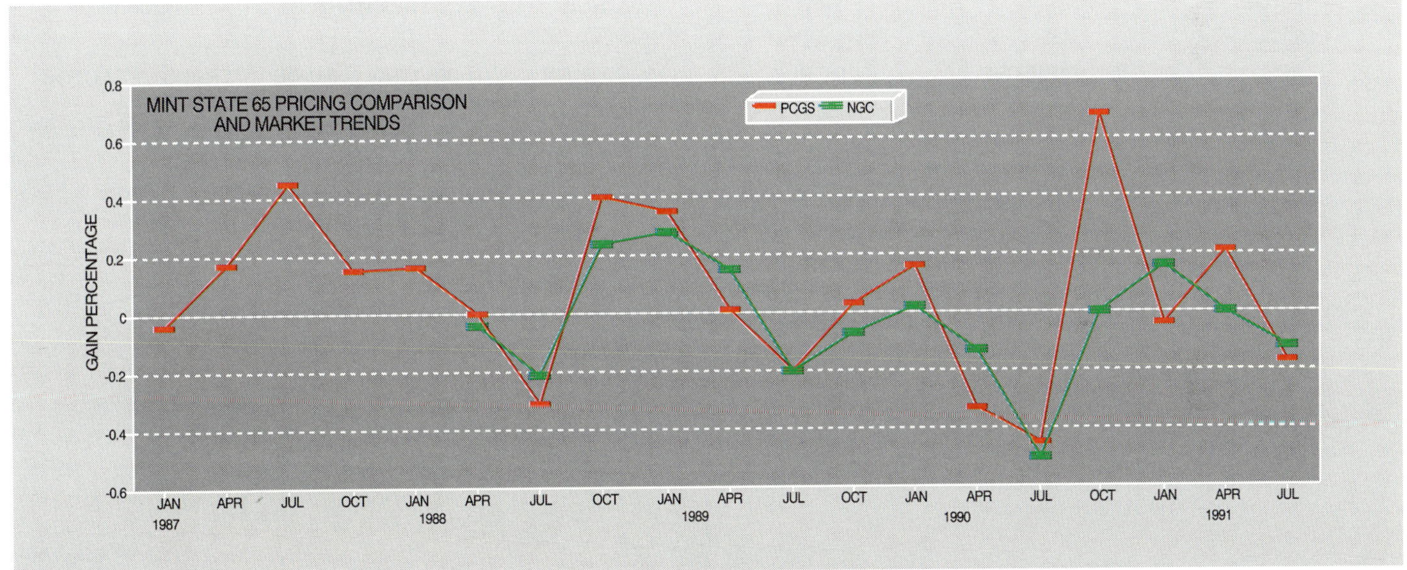

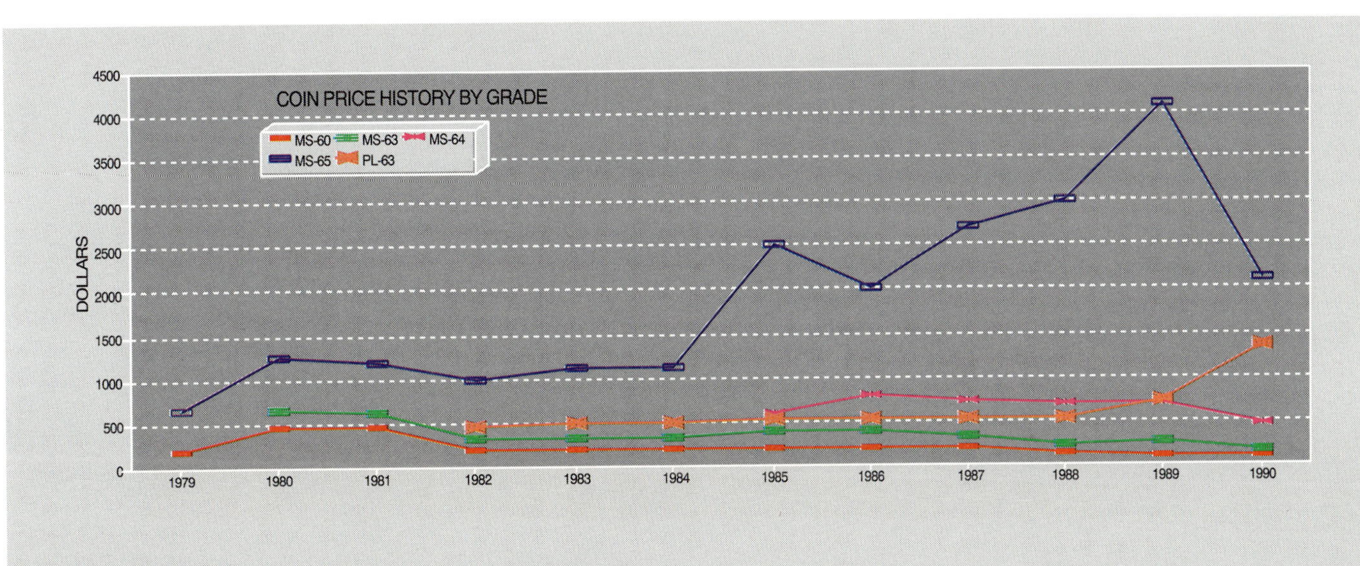

1903-P

PCGS
1903
S$1
MS66
7284 66/3149239

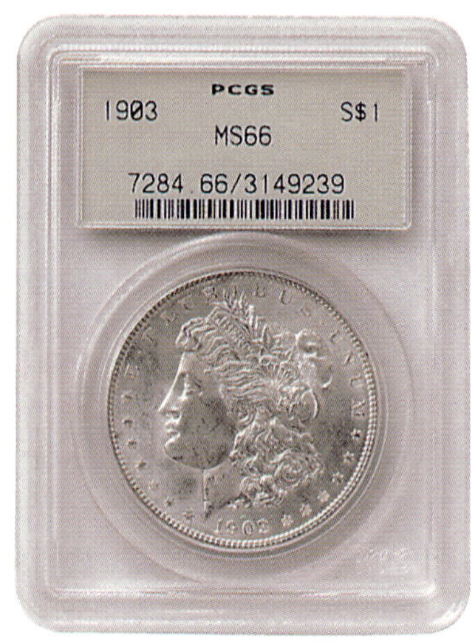

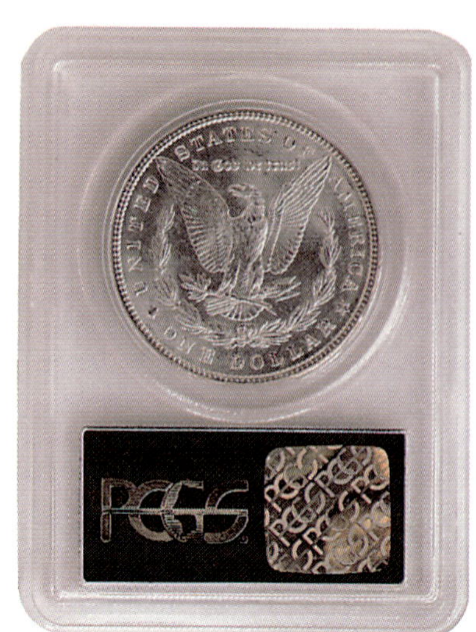

Mintage 4,652,000, from 46 obvs., 40 revs., all from the new C4 reverse hub. Uncs. are from Treasury bags released in the early 1960's, many on badly striated blanks. Lustre is excellent but satiny with a wet look rather than frosty. Some of the same problems persist as described at 1901. MS 60/62 rolls are available. Sliders are plentiful, be careful when purchasing.

Recommended in MS 65 up or in MS 64 by the roll.

Proofs: Mintage 755. Too many have been cleaned.

Prooflikes: Rare in all grades (many from a small group in the Redfield hoard); DMPL's may be impossible to find. Cameos are rare. Semi-PL's are available. One piece graded by NGC MS 65 PL is on a heavily striated planchet. Technically MS 65 PL, but ugly!

PCGS

MINTAGE	PROOF	STRIKE	LUSTER	BAG MARKS	REDFIELD
4,652,000	755	Sharp & Bold	Very Good	Light	Yes
DIES	**DIE VARIETIES**	**% OF PL**	**% OF DMPL**	**PIVOTAL GRADE**	**RARITY FACTOR**
142	5	1.3	0.2	MS 65	R-4

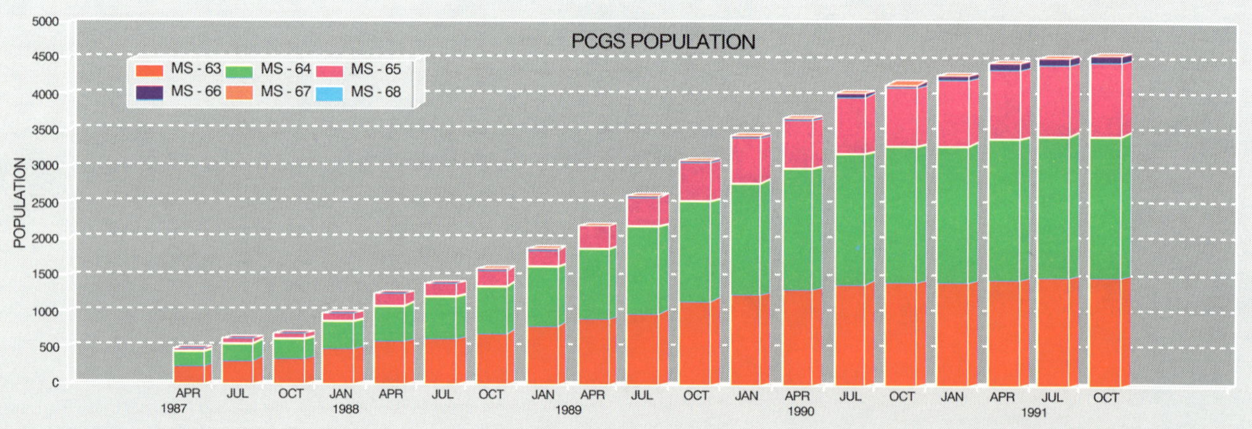

PCGS POPULATION
MS - 63
MS - 64
MS - 65
MS - 66
MS - 67
MS - 68
POPULATION
5000
4500
4000
3500
3000
2500
2000
1500
1000
500
C
APR 1987
JUL
OCT
JAN 1988
APR
JUL
OCT
JAN 1989
APR
JUL
OCT
JAN
APR 1990
JUL
OCT
JAN
APR
JUL 1991
OCT

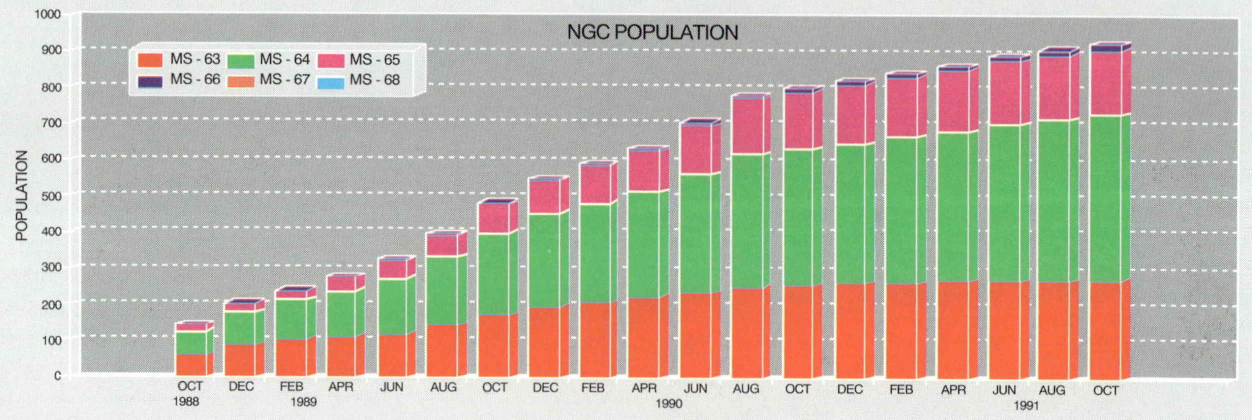

NGC POPULATION
MS - 63
MS - 64
MS - 65
MS - 66
MS - 67
MS - 68
POPULATION
1000
900
800
700
600
500
400
300
200
100
C
OCT 1988
DEC
FEB 1989
APR
JUN
AUG
OCT
DEC
FEB
APR 1990
JUN
AUG
OCT
DEC
FEB
APR
JUN 1991
AUG
OCT

1903-P

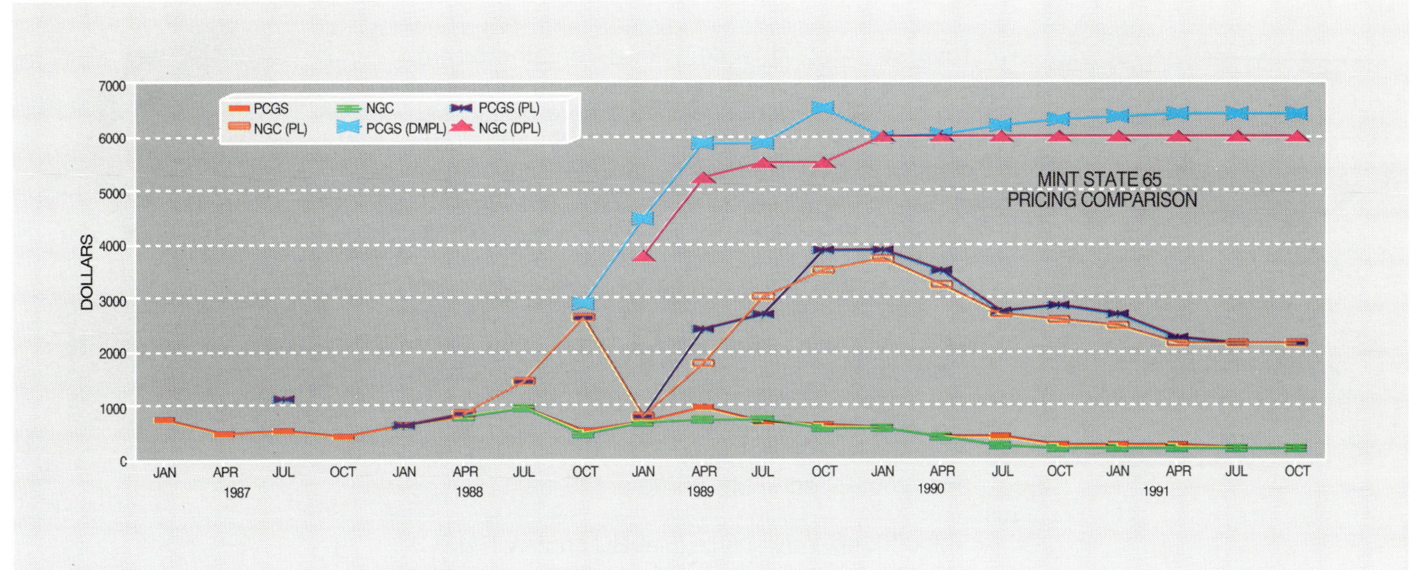

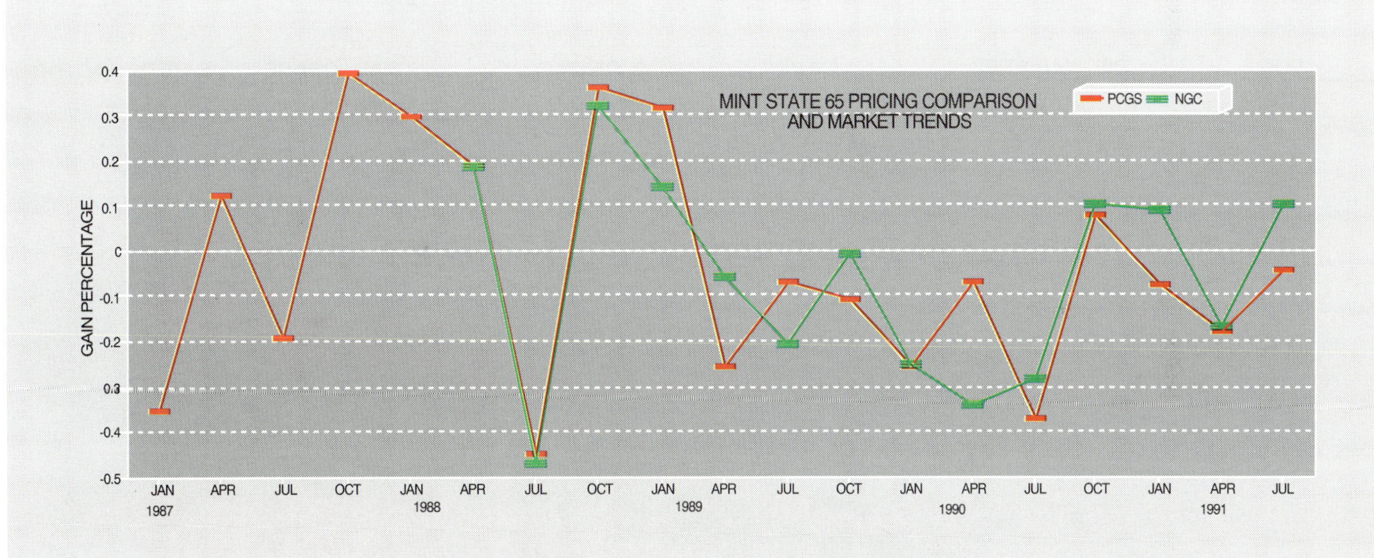

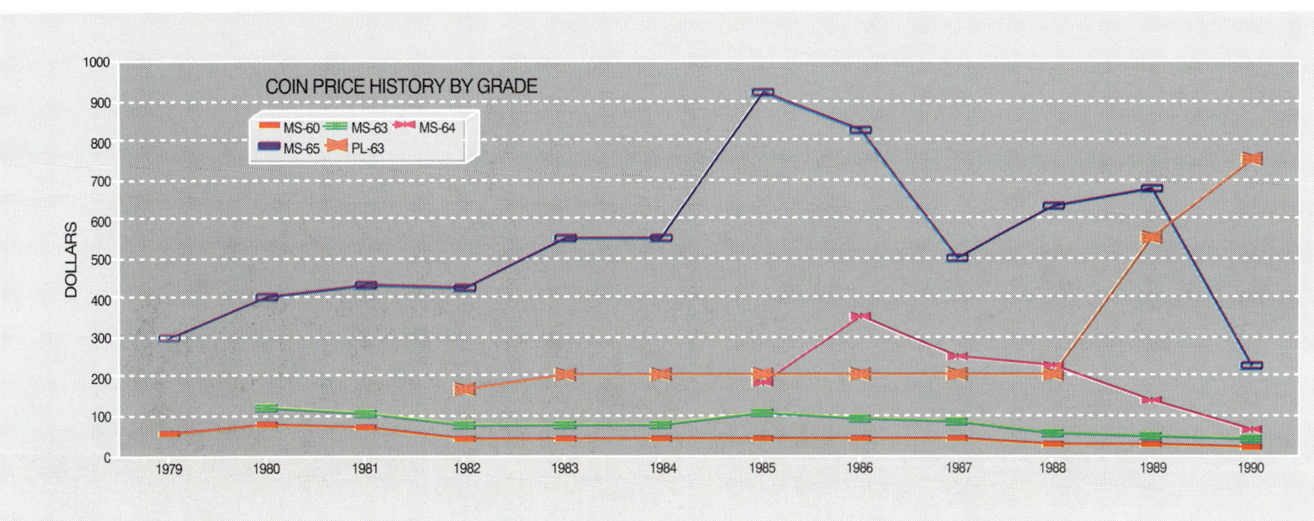

1903-O

Despite the mintage of 4,450,000 (all from the new C4 reverse hub), this coin long remained rare. Through early fall 1962 it was considered rarer than 1892-S or 1893-S; worn specimens were rarely seen (and still are), and Uncs. were quoted at $1,500. Then in October 1962 the Treasury began releasing bags — at least 60, possibly hundreds. Overnight the Unc. price dropped to $100 and even lower. How the mighty have fallen!

Uncs. sometimes come flat, sometimes strongly struck, with excellent lustre. MS 60/62 rolls are available. All are from the new C4 reverse hub.

This date is still one of the rarest circulated Morgan silver dollars. Since the 1962 Treasury release, over 95% of the existing 1903-O Morgans in the marketplace are BU coins.

Recommended in MS 65 up or MS 63/64 by the roll.

Prooflikes: Very scarce in all BU grades; DMPL's are rare especially above MS 64, far more so in cameo.

MINTAGE	PROOF	STRIKE	LUSTER	BAG MARKS	REDFIELD
4,450,000	0	Average	Excellent	Light	No
DIES	**DIE VARIETIES**	**% OF PL**	**% OF DMPL**	**PIVOTAL GRADE**	**RARITY FACTOR**
180	11	1.9	0.9	MS 65	R-4

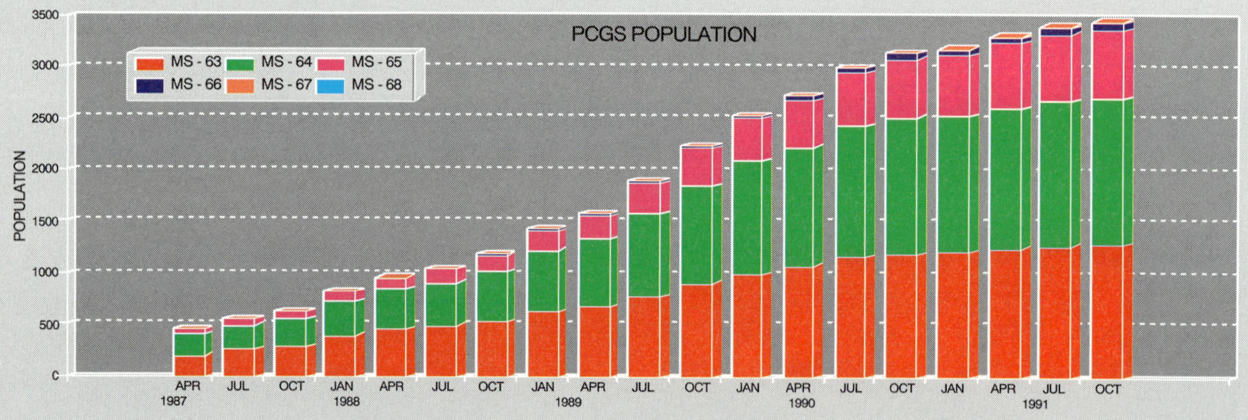

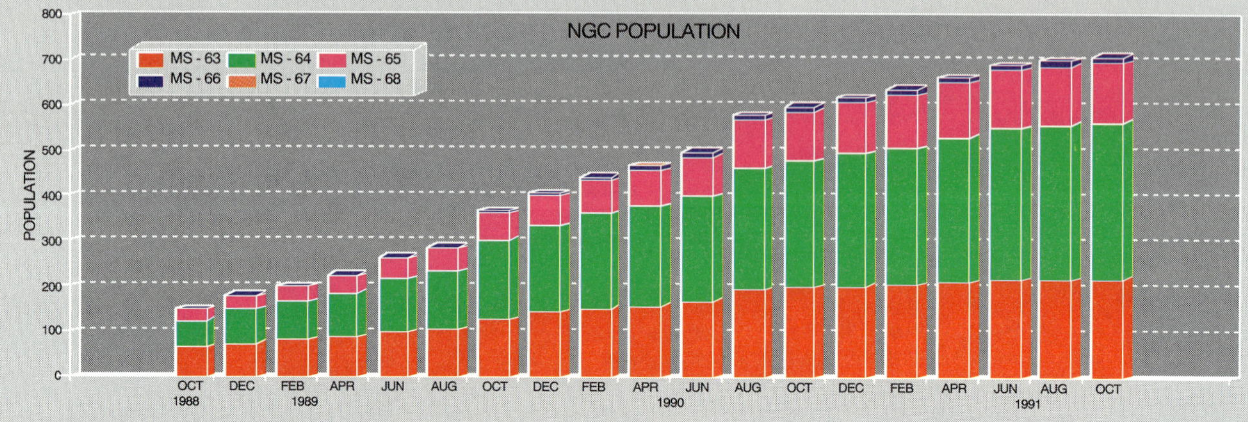

PCGS POPULATION

MS - 63 MS - 64 MS - 65 MS - 66 MS - 67 MS - 68

NGC POPULATION

MS - 63 MS - 64 MS - 65 MS - 66 MS - 67 MS - 68

1903-O

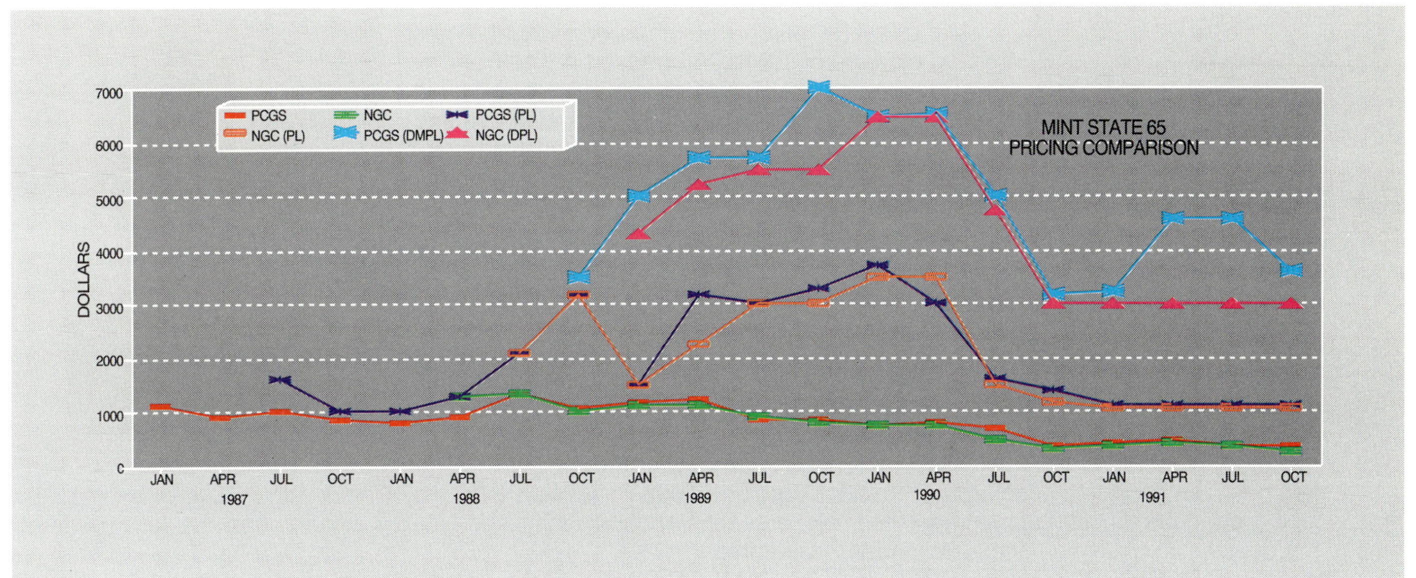

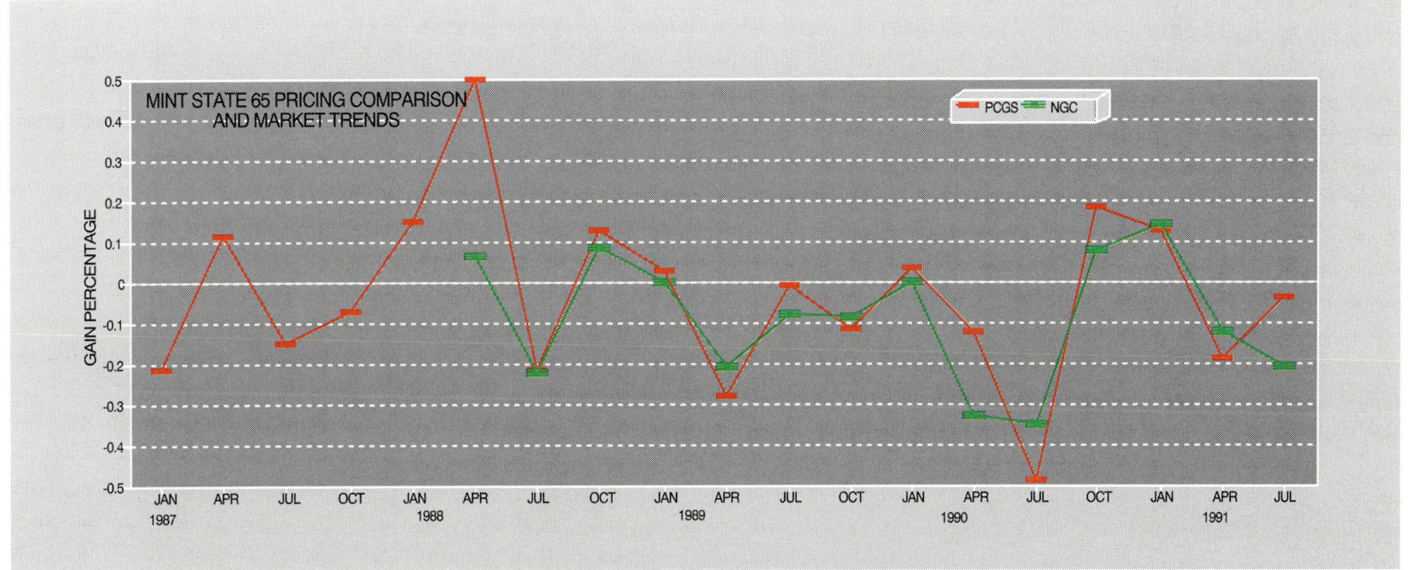

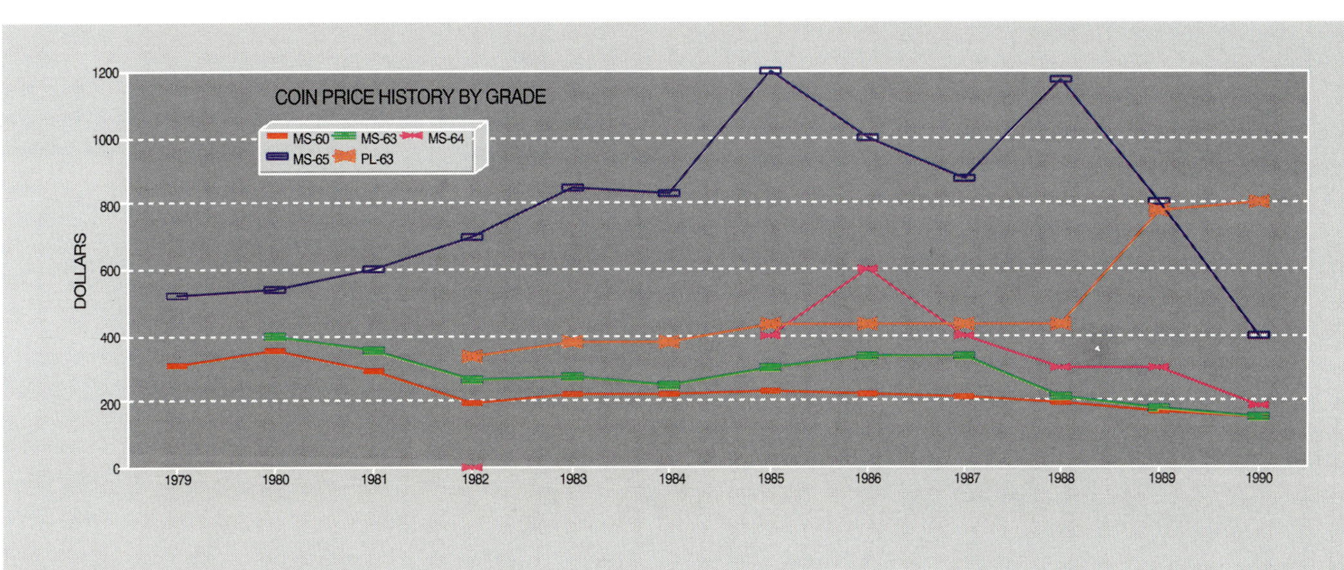

1903-S

KEY DATE! Much rarer than one would expect from its mintage of 1,241,000 (most if not all from the new C4 reverse hub). Worn specimens are available. Uncs. are few, and more often MS 64 and above than 63 or below (the only instance in the Morgan series); sharp strikes are usual. The Redfield hoard reportedly had some, evidently not many.

At least one doubled die reverse shows impressions from both old C3 and new C4 hubs (*Ency* 5699), like illustration of *Ency* 5668. This is rare.

Usually with large S (*Ency* 5698 = VAM 1, 3). The variety with small s (*Ency* 5697 = VAM 2, from the punch used for quarter dollars) is rare and almost always comes worn; Wayne Miller reports one PL as "marginally unc."

Recommended in any BU grade.

Fakes have been made by adding S mintmark to genuine 1903 Philadelphia dollars. Check with 20x glass or binocular microscope around the junction of mintmark with field; a seam identifies such fakes. Notice also the broader, less rounded, rims of the genuine S mint coin compared to the Philadelphia.

Prooflikes: RARE! PLs RARE! DMPL's RARE! CAMEOS RARE! EVERYTHING!

MINTAGE	PROOF	STRIKE	LUSTER	BAG MARKS	REDFIELD
1,241,000	0	Sharp & Bold	Excellent	Light	No
DIES	**DIE VARIETIES**	**% OF PL**	**% OF DMPL**	**PIVOTAL GRADE**	**RARITY FACTOR**
20*	9	0.4	0.0	MS 60	R-1

*Maybe an error in original mint records for dies produced

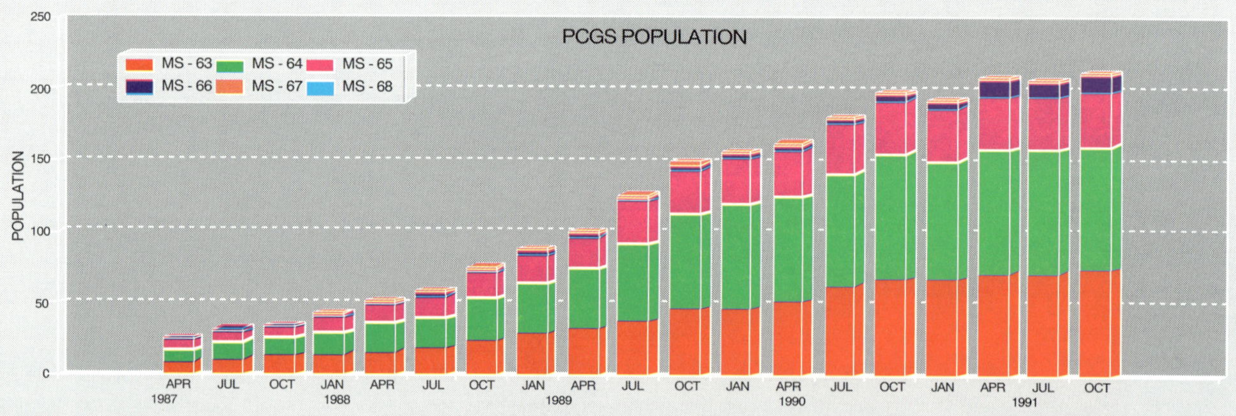

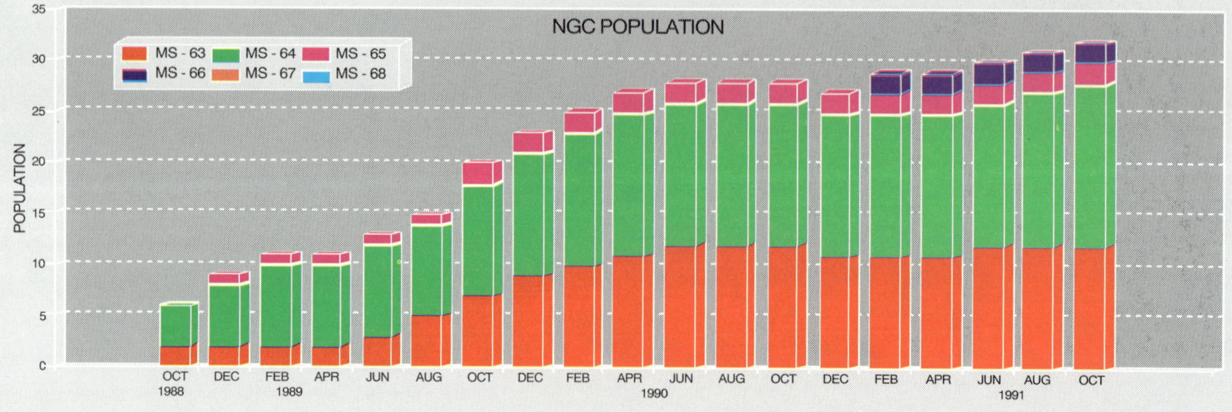

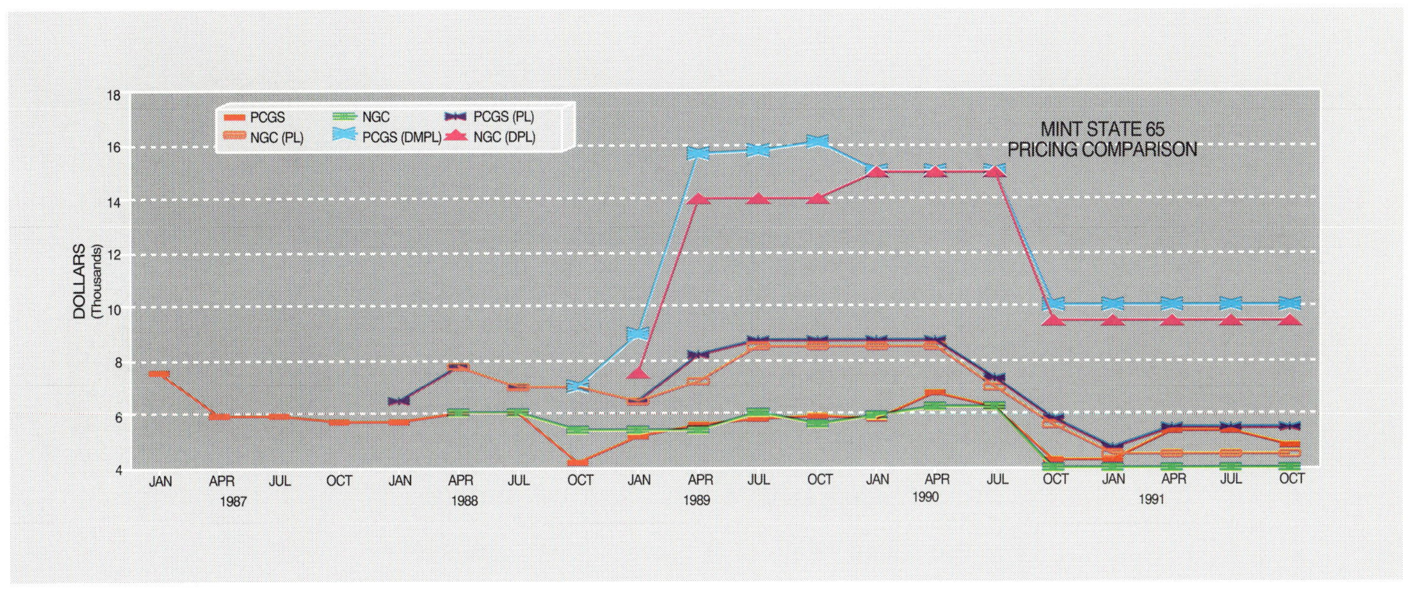
MINT STATE 65
PRICING COMPARISON
PCGS
NGC
PCGS (PL)
NGC (PL)
PCGS (DMPL)
NGC (DPL)
DOLLARS
(Thousands)
18
16
14
12
10
8
6
4
JAN
APR
JUL
OCT
1987
1988
1989
1990
1991

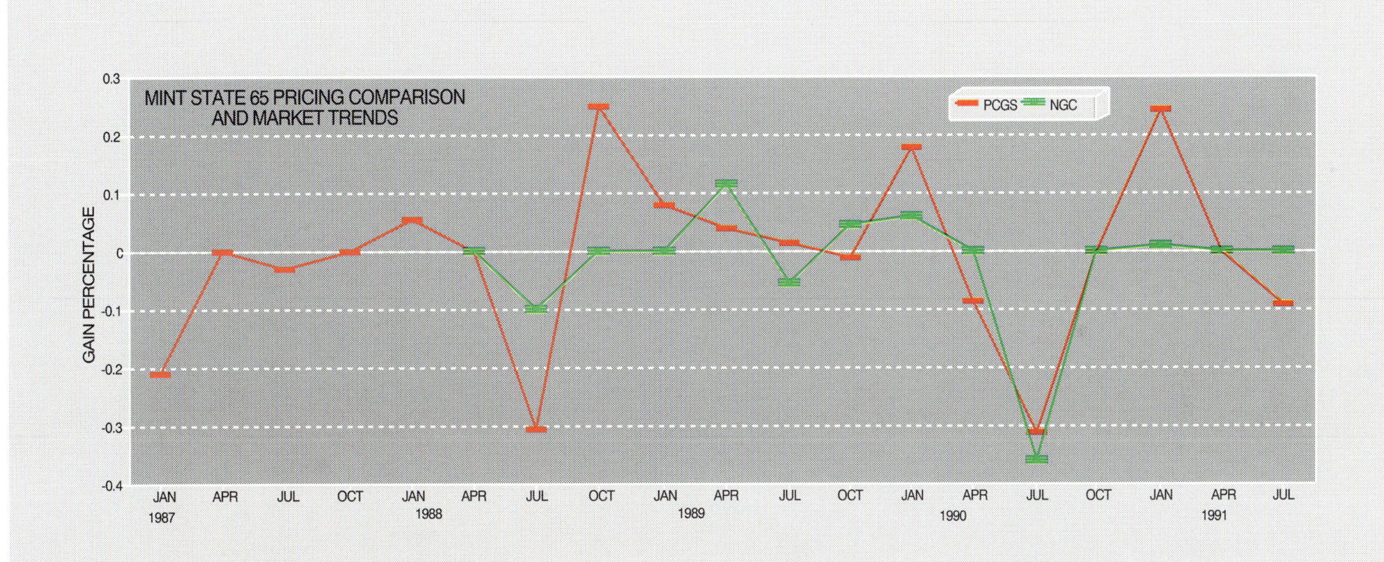
MINT STATE 65 PRICING COMPARISON
AND MARKET TRENDS
PCGS
NGC
GAIN PERCENTAGE
0.3
0.2
0.1
0
-0.1
-0.2
-0.3
-0.4
JAN
APR
JUL
OCT
1987
1988
1989
1990
1991

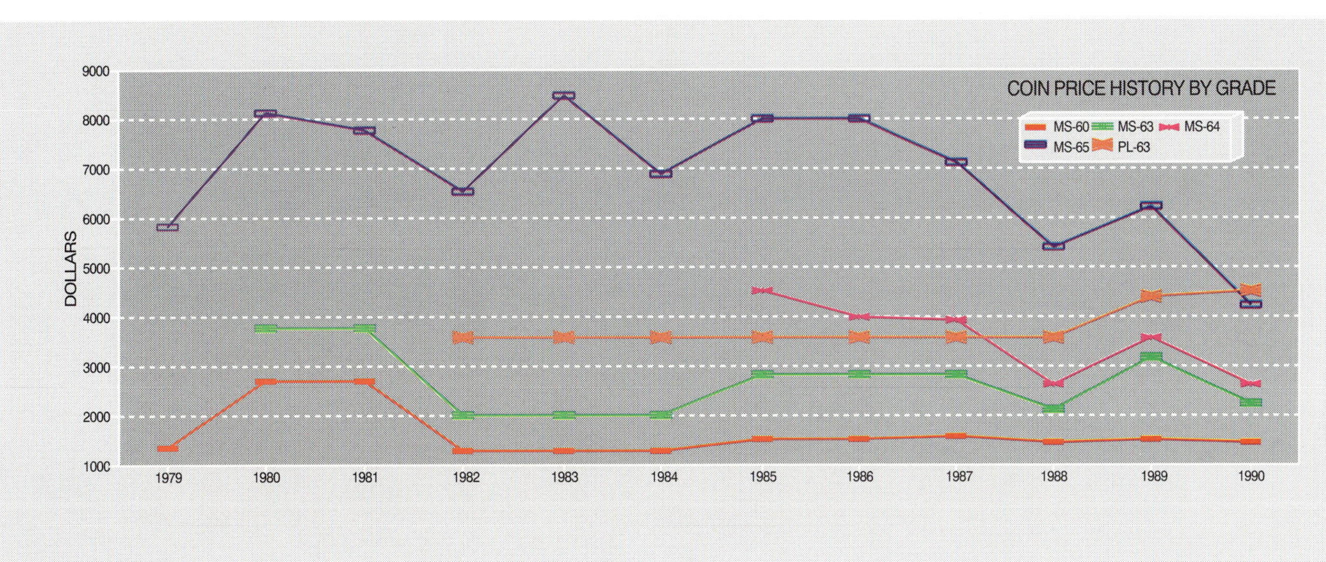
COIN PRICE HISTORY BY GRADE
MS-60
MS-63
MS-64
MS-65
PL-63
DOLLARS
9000
8000
7000
6000
5000
4000
3000
2000
1000
1979
1980
1981
1982
1983
1984
1985
1986
1987
1988
1989
1990

1904-P

Mintage 2,788,000, all from the new C4 reverse hub. Some of these were spent and come in low grades; many Uncs. were melted. Surviving Uncs. are usually low quality, from the problems described at 1901. The 1904-P Morgan usually has a dull metallic gray lustre. The vast majority are MS 60/61; sliders are common.

One "low end" Unc. bag was dispersed in 1979. Wayne Miller, Helena, Montana, who was one of the first to examine coins from it, said that there were "few if any gems". That was by 1979 grading standards also!

Recommended in MS 64 up, but you may have to settle for an MS 60/63 while hunting. Circulated examples can be found with small premiums.

Proofs: The low 650 mintage took two obverse dies, answering to VAM 1 but with different date positions.

Prooflikes: Rare in all grades. Don't expect to find cameos.

MINTAGE	PROOF	STRIKE	LUSTER	BAG MARKS	REDFIELD
2,788,000	650	Soft To Average	Poor	Moderate	No
DIES	**DIE VARIETIES**	**% OF PL**	**% OF DMPL**	**PIVOTAL GRADE**	**RARITY FACTOR**
142*	5	0.7	0.1	MS 65	R-2

*Fiscal year 1903 data

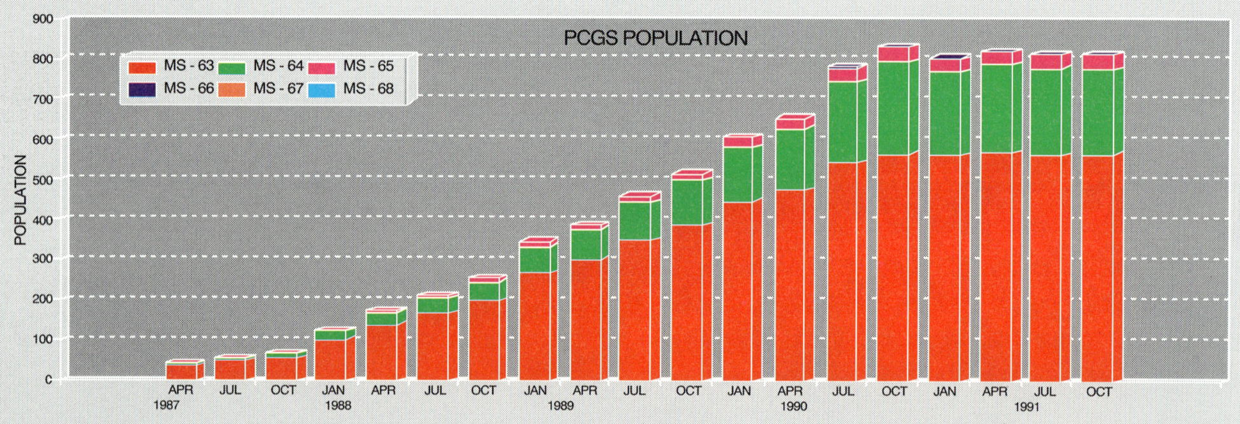

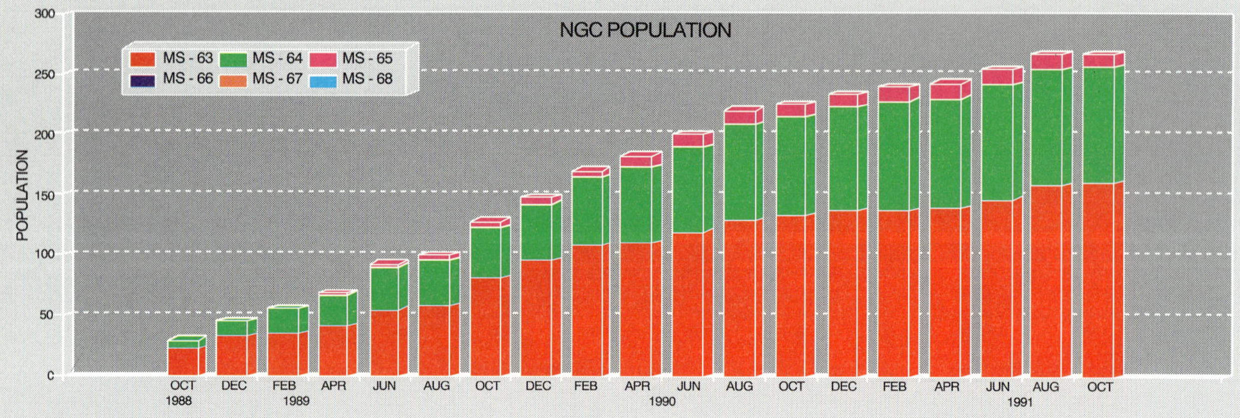

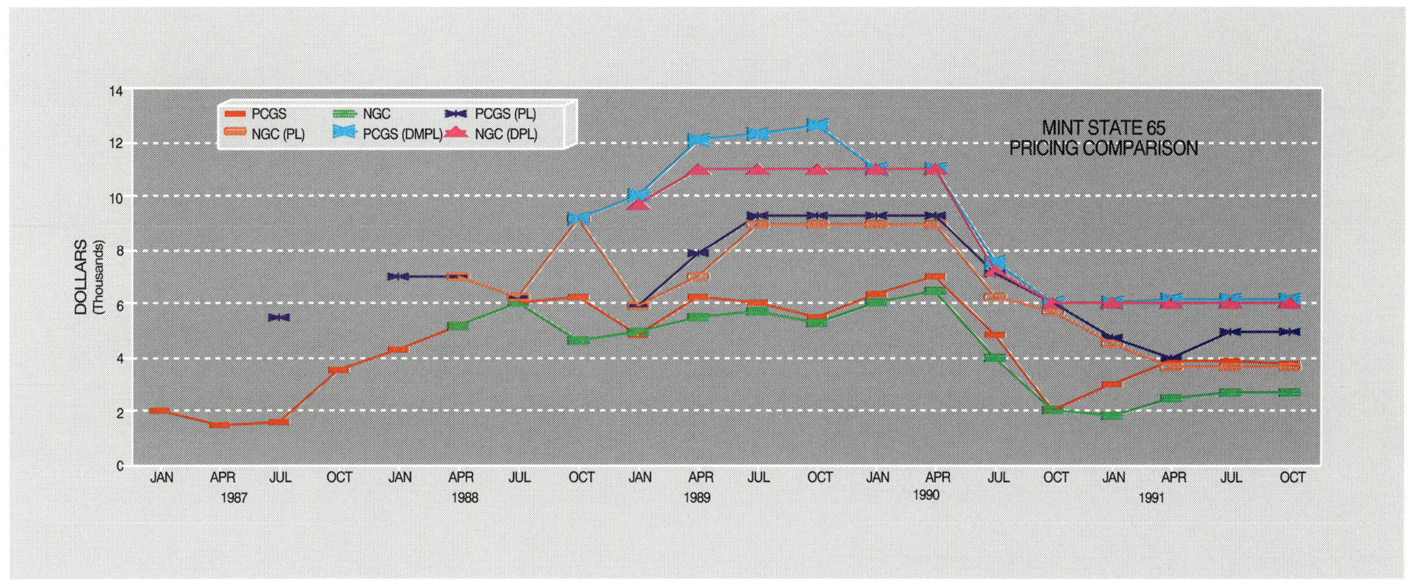
MINT STATE 65
PRICING COMPARISON
PCGS
NGC
PCGS (PL)
NGC (PL)
PCGS (DMPL)
NGC (DPL)
DOLLARS
(Thousands)
14
12
10
8
6
4
2
0
JAN
APR
JUL
OCT
1987
1988
1989
1990
1991

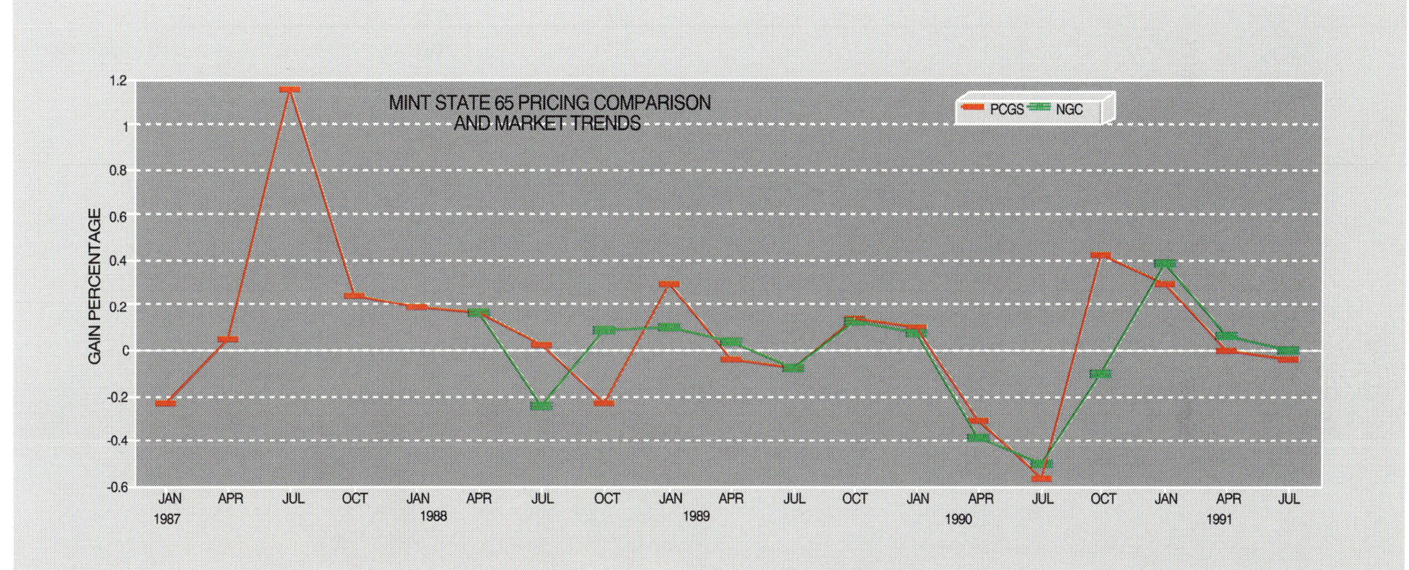
MINT STATE 65 PRICING COMPARISON
AND MARKET TRENDS
PCGS
NGC
GAIN PERCENTAGE
1.2
1
0.8
0.6
0.4
0.2
0
-0.2
-0.4
-0.6
JAN
APR
JUL
OCT
1987
1988
1989
1990
1991

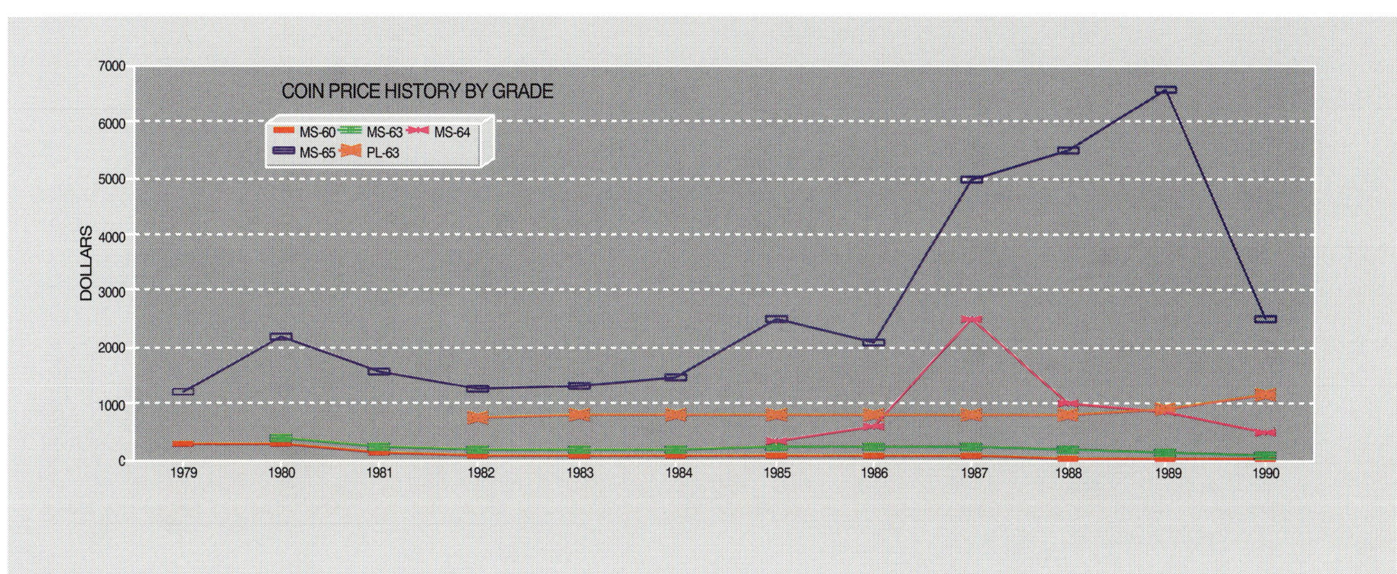
COIN PRICE HISTORY BY GRADE
MS-60
MS-63
MS-64
MS-65
PL-63
DOLLARS
7000
6000
5000
4000
3000
2000
1000
0
1979
1980
1981
1982
1983
1984
1985
1986
1987
1988
1989
1990

1904-O

The last New Orleans Morgan silver dollar. Mintage 3,720,000, all from the new C4 reverse hub. Like 1898-O and 1903-O, this was a rarity until October 1962, when the Treasury began releasing hundreds of bags. Unc. prices dropped from $350 to $3.50 literally overnight.

Worn examples are few; evidently most remained in Treasury vaults until the great meltings began. Uncs. vary in striking quality and lustre, though a great many are flat strikes. Rolls and bags are available in MS 60/63.

Recommended in MS 65 up. MS 64 rolls also.

Prooflikes: Available in quantity even in cameo DMPL, from a bag found in 1978, but they will be MS 60/62. Above MS 64 they are far less easy to find. Rare above MS 65.

MINTAGE	PROOF	STRIKE	LUSTER	BAG MARKS	REDFIELD
3,720,000	0	Weak To Average	Very Good	Moderate To Heavy	No
DIES	**DIE VARIETIES**	**% OF PL**	**% OF DMPL**	**PIVOTAL GRADE**	**RARITY FACTOR**
180*	31	4.9	1.1	MS 65	R-5

*Fiscal year 1903 data

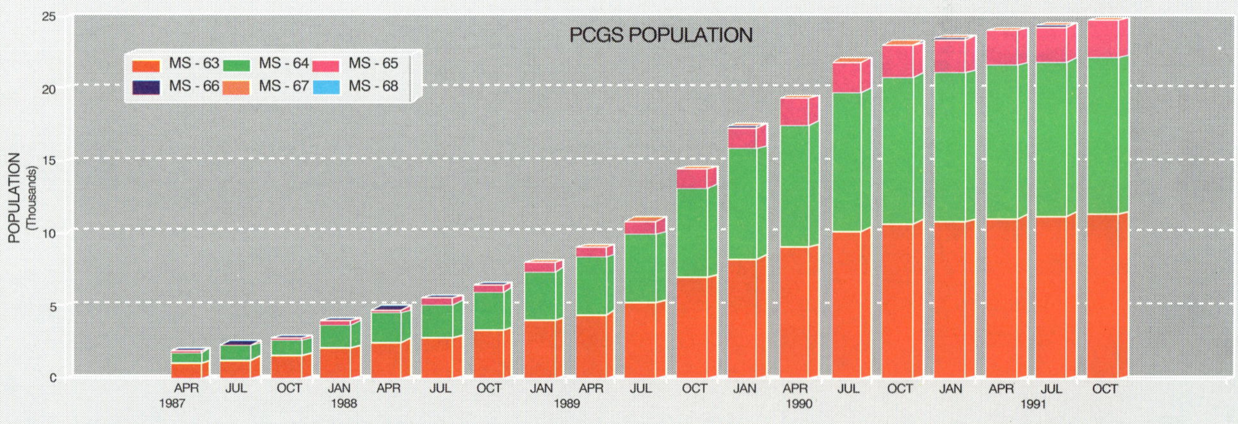

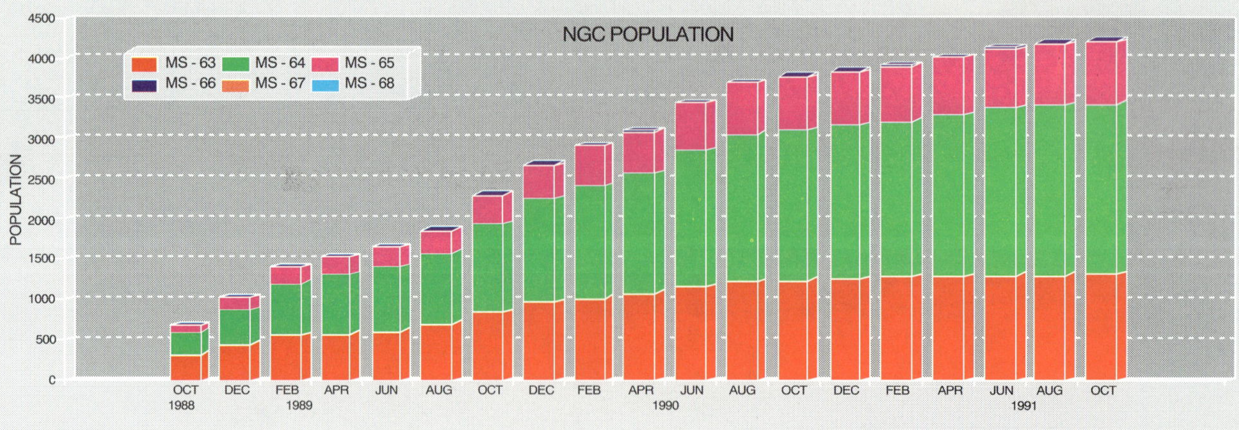

PCGS POPULATION

MS - 63 MS - 64 MS - 65 MS - 66 MS - 67 MS - 68

POPULATION (Thousands)

0 5 10 15 20 25

APR 1987 JUL OCT JAN 1988 APR JUL OCT JAN 1989 APR JUL OCT JAN 1990 APR JUL OCT JAN 1991 APR JUL OCT

NGC POPULATION

MS - 63 MS - 64 MS - 65 MS - 66 MS - 67 MS - 68

POPULATION

0 500 1000 1500 2000 2500 3000 3500 4000 4500

OCT 1988 DEC FEB 1989 APR JUN AUG OCT DEC FEB 1990 APR JUN AUG OCT DEC FEB 1991 APR JUN AUG OCT

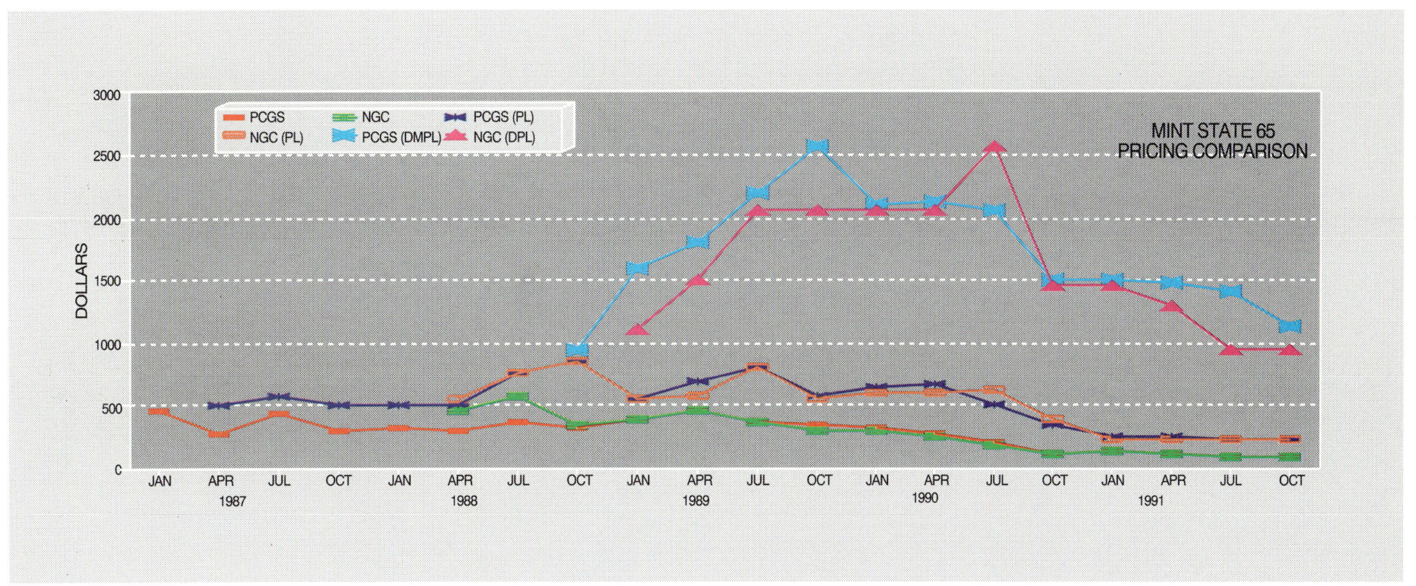
MINT STATE 65
PRICING COMPARISON
PCGS
NGC
PCGS (PL)
NGC (PL)
PCGS (DMPL)
NGC (DPL)
DOLLARS
3000
2500
2000
1500
1000
500
0
JAN
APR
JUL
OCT
1987
1988
1989
1990
1991

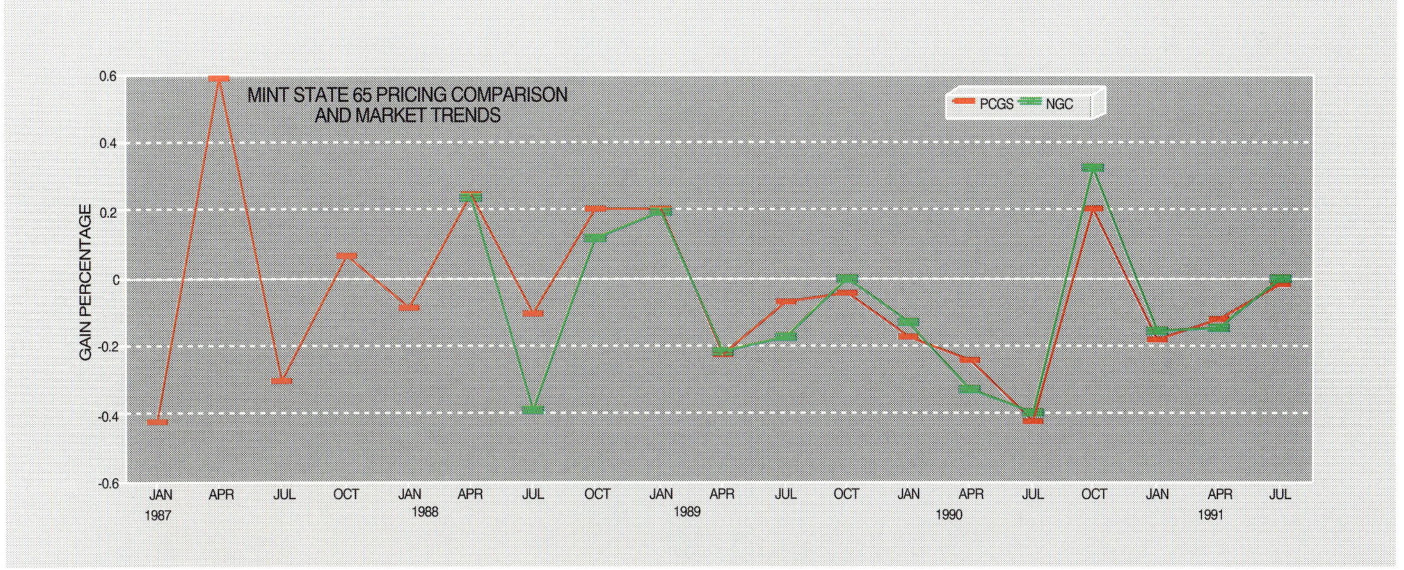
MINT STATE 65 PRICING COMPARISON
AND MARKET TRENDS
PCGS
NGC
GAIN PERCENTAGE
0.6
0.4
0.2
0
-0.2
-0.4
-0.6
JAN
APR
JUL
OCT
1987
1988
1989
1990
1991

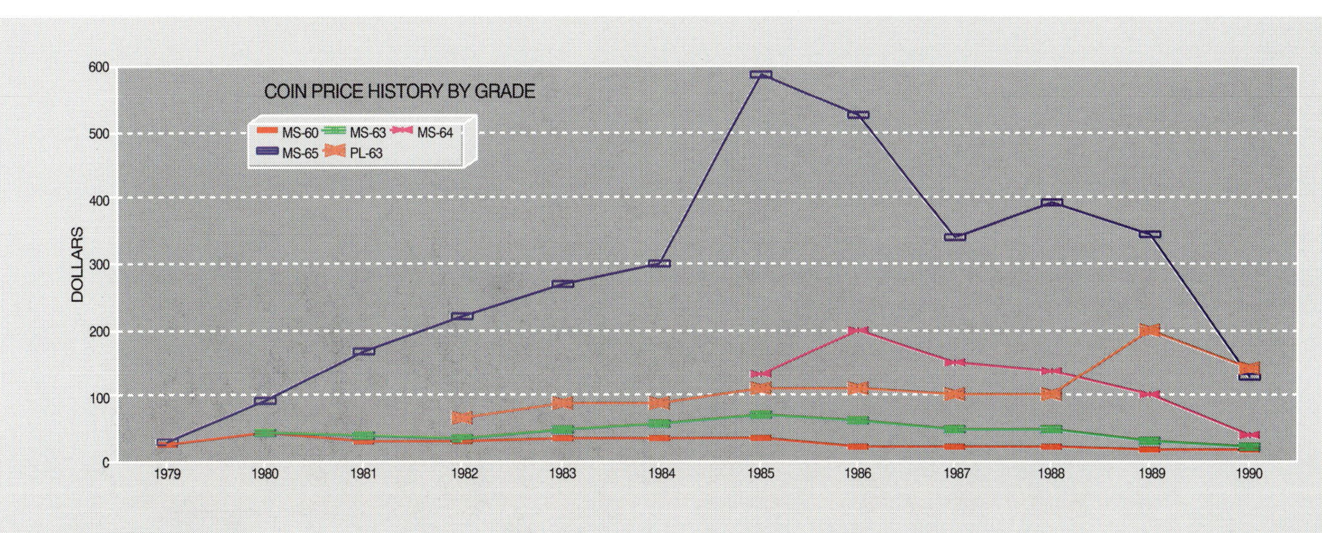
COIN PRICE HISTORY BY GRADE
MS-60
MS-63
MS-64
MS-65
PL-63
DOLLARS
600
500
400
300
200
100
0
1979
1980
1981
1982
1983
1984
1985
1986
1987
1988
1989
1990

1904-S

Mintage 2,304,000, all from the new C4 reverse hub. Worn examples are hard to find above VF. Uncs. are mostly from a bag that turned up in Los Angeles in the early 1950's. They are usually weakly struck, especially in centers; lustre is dull gray rather than brilliant or frosty. Rarer in MS 65 than 1903-S. None in Redfield hoard.

At least one doubled rev. die shows impressions from both old C3 (*Ency* 5703)and new C4 hubs; like of *Ency* 5668. There are examples with die cracks on the obverse.

Recommended in MS 63 up. You many have to settle for MS 60/62 while hunting.

Prooflikes: Rare in all grades; virtually unknown in cameo or DMPL.

MINTAGE	PROOF	STRIKE	LUSTER	BAG MARKS	REDFIELD
2,304,000	0	Weak To Average	Average	Moderate	No
DIES	**DIE VARIETIES**	**% OF PL**	**% OF DMPL**	**PIVOTAL GRADE**	**RARITY FACTOR**
20*	8	4.9	0.0	MS 65	R-1

*Maybe an error in original mint records (Fiscal year 1903 data)

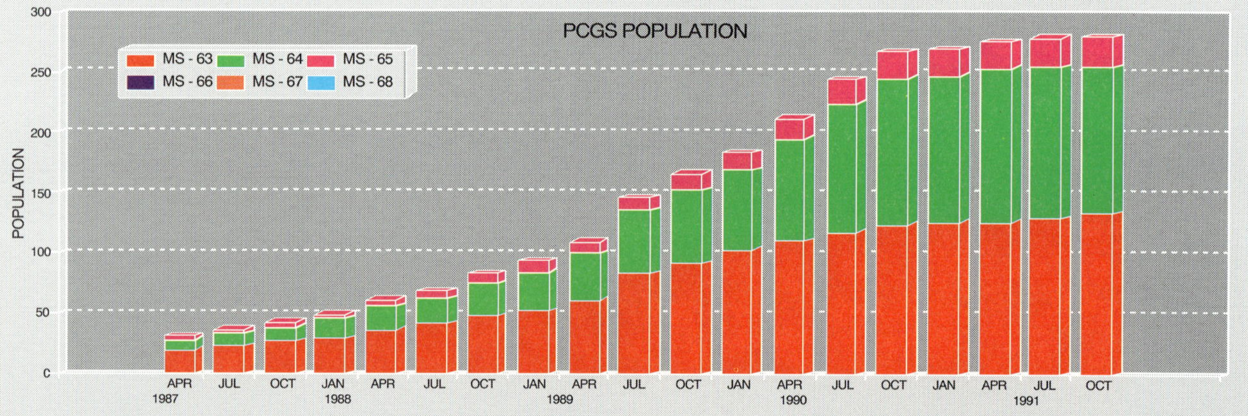

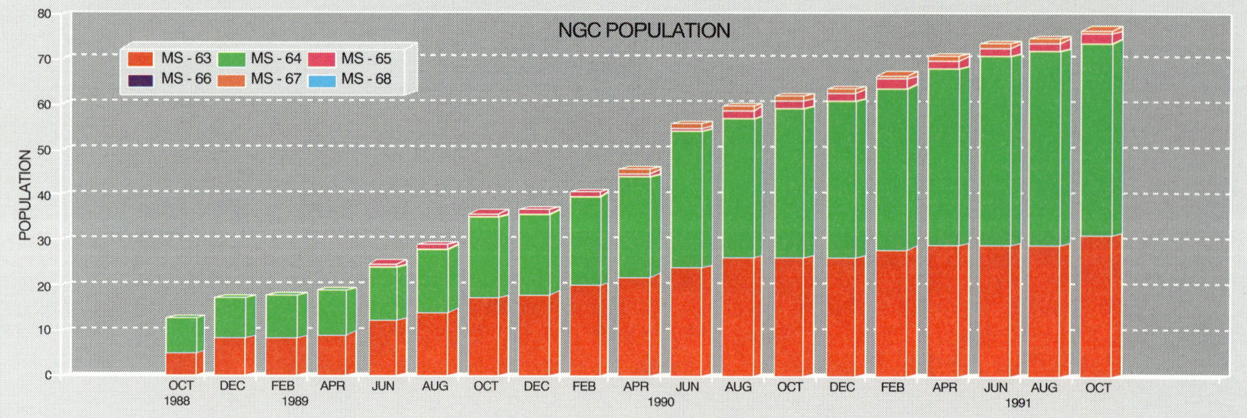

PCGS POPULATION

NGC POPULATION

1904-S

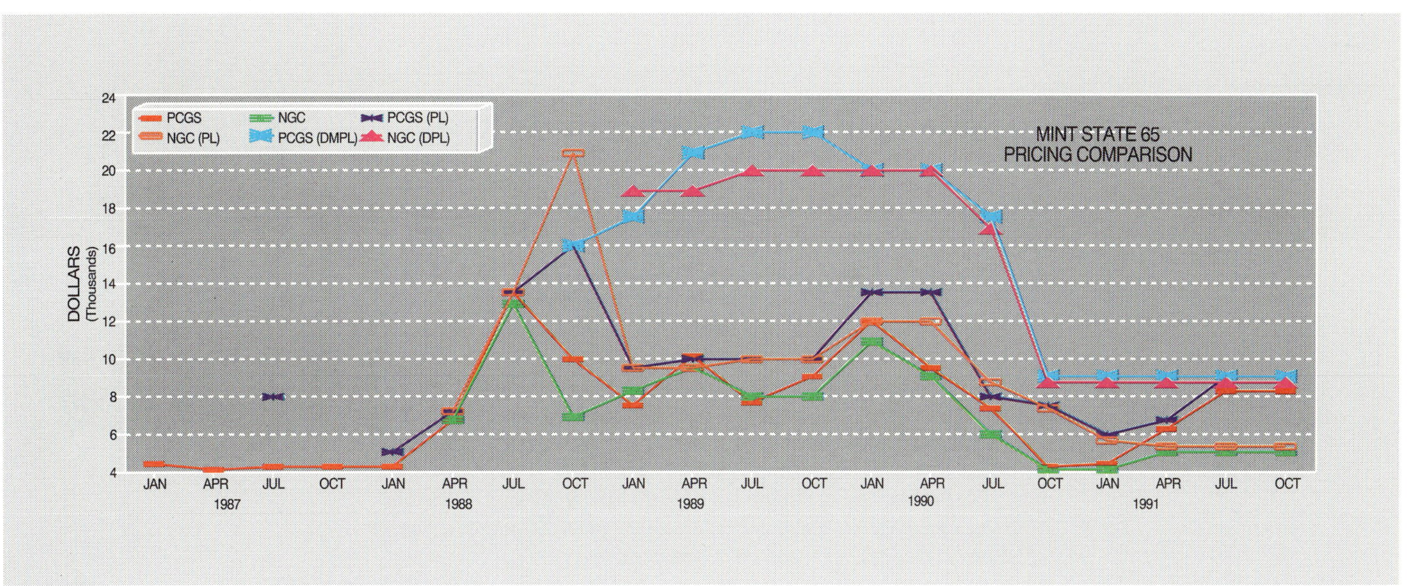

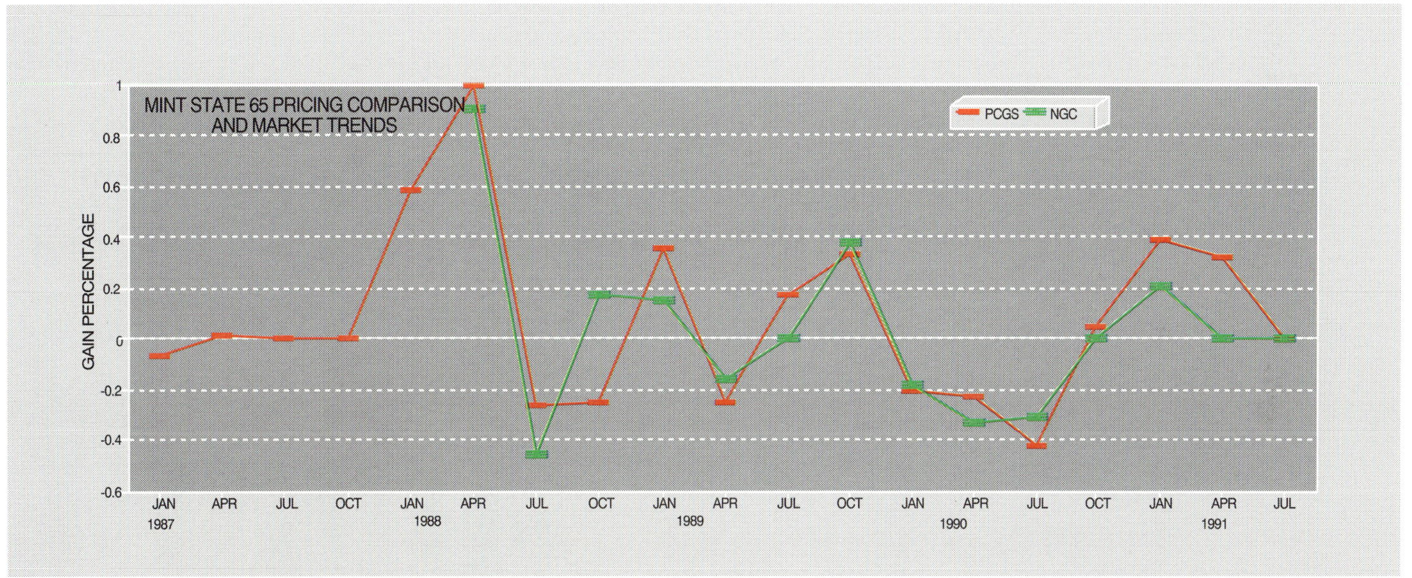

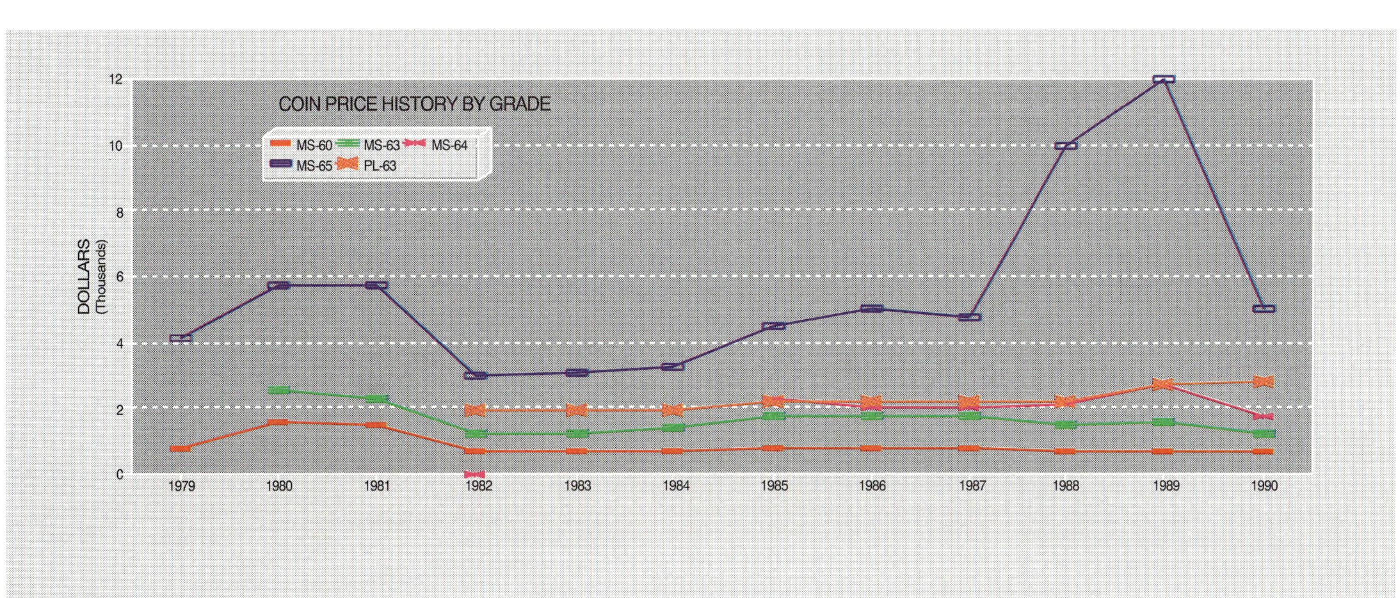

PCGS
1921 S$1
MS67
MORGAN
7296.67/3122440

1921-P

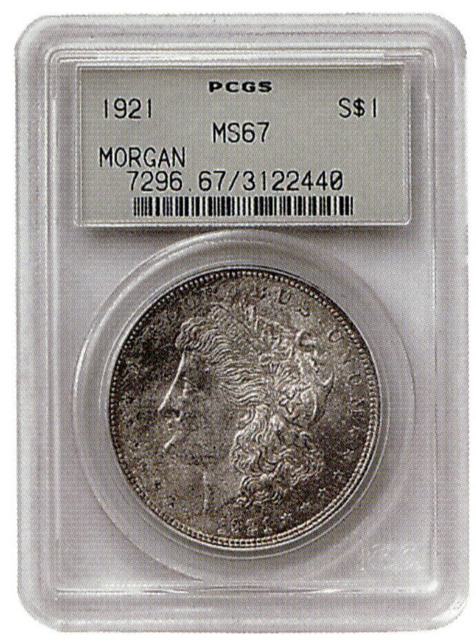

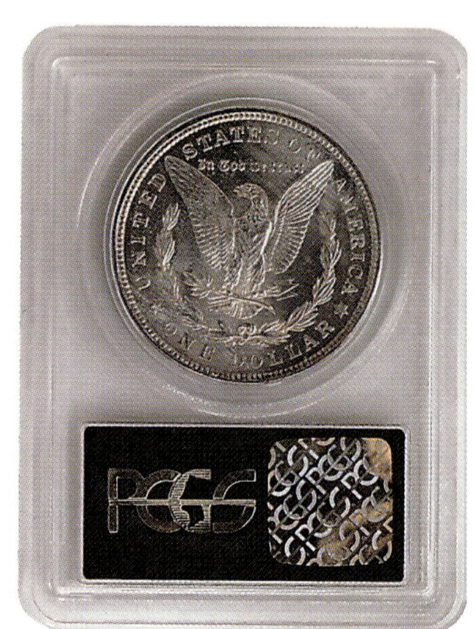

Last and commonest Philadelphia Morgan, despite extensive melting (1942) out of the 44,690,000 mintage. Circulated examples and sliders are abundant. Uncs. are common but usually flat strikes, noticeably bagmarked. They might not have graded MS 63 the moment they fell from the dies.

Because the Mint officials thought they were finished forever with Morgan dollars, the Engraving Dept. got rid of the original dies and hubs. When orders came through to make silver dollars in 1921, there was not time to make new designs, models, and original dies, let alone working hubs and dies. Morgan, probably with the help of John R. Sinnock, copied the old 1878 7 TF PAF design, keeping everything in low relief.

Not much difference in rarity between the 17 berry and 16 berry reverses. The 17th berry is within upper right wreath, opposite upright of R, and is often hard to see. Rolls and bags are available in MS 60/63.Recommended in MS 65 up or in MS 64 by the roll.

Proofs: Zerbe striking are from a 17 berry reverse. A few of these are really brilliant, but most are satiny with little contrast. The obverse die was later used on business striking.

Chapman striking (10, from a 16 berry reverse) are cameos. Hollow area (die polish) in hair around Morgan's initial M; faint scattered die striations around UN AM RICA. Leo A. Young's specimen brought $19,000 in Auction '80.

Morgan-Swasey striking (10, from 17 berry reverse, June 4, 1921): like the Chapman striking but from different dies. The description, from the three Norweb coins, was furnished by Andrew W. Pollock III: Short line from rim toward 3 star (ending about 1 mm from 2nd star); two die polish lines from rim to first 1; rev., dash between right star and wreath, touching neither; another (fainter) slanting up from left upright of I(C), still another between I(n) and first S of STATES.

Prooflikes: No real DMPL's. What passes for DMPL has little depth of field. What passes for PL is often satiny with little or no contrast.

MINTAGE	PROOF	STRIKE	LUSTER	BAG MARKS	REDFIELD
44,690,000	0	Soft & Weak	Average	Moderate To Heavy	No
DIES	**DIE VARIETIES**	**% OF PL**	**% OF DMPL**	**PIVOTAL GRADE**	**RARITY FACTOR**
Not Available	25	1.9	0.2	MS 65	R-5

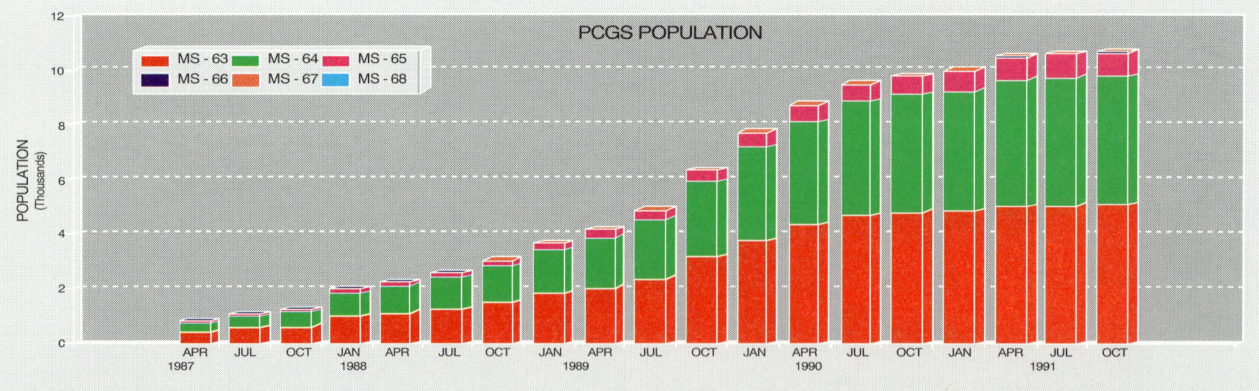
PCGS POPULATION
MS - 63
MS - 64
MS - 65
MS - 66
MS - 67
MS - 68
POPULATION
(Thousands)
12
10
8
6
4
2
0
APR 1987
JUL
OCT
JAN 1988
APR
JUL
OCT
JAN 1989
APR
JUL
OCT
JAN
APR 1990
JUL
OCT
JAN
APR
JUL 1991
OCT

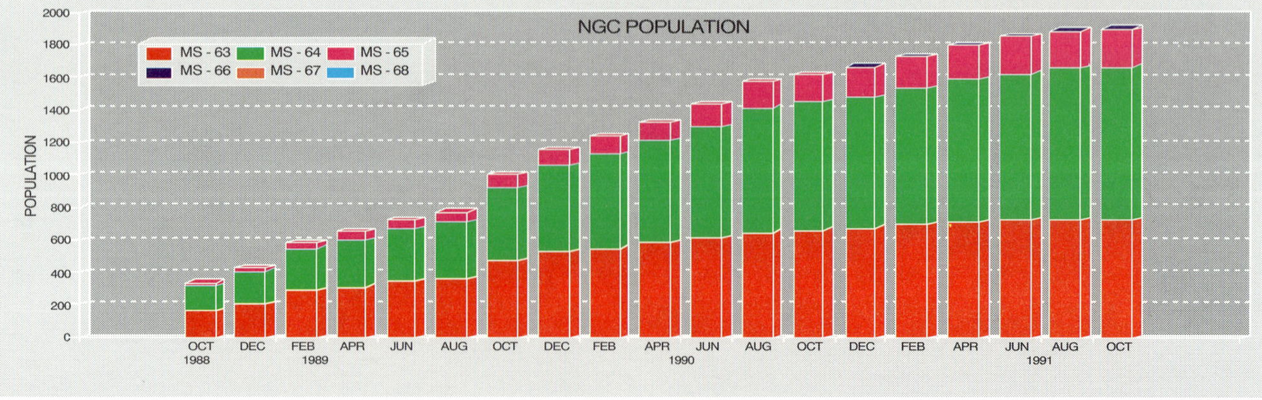
NGC POPULATION
MS - 63
MS - 64
MS - 65
MS - 66
MS - 67
MS - 68
POPULATION
2000
1800
1600
1400
1200
1000
800
600
400
200
0
OCT 1988
DEC
FEB 1989
APR
JUN
AUG
OCT
DEC
FEB
APR 1990
JUN
AUG
OCT
DEC
FEB
APR
JUN 1991
AUG
OCT

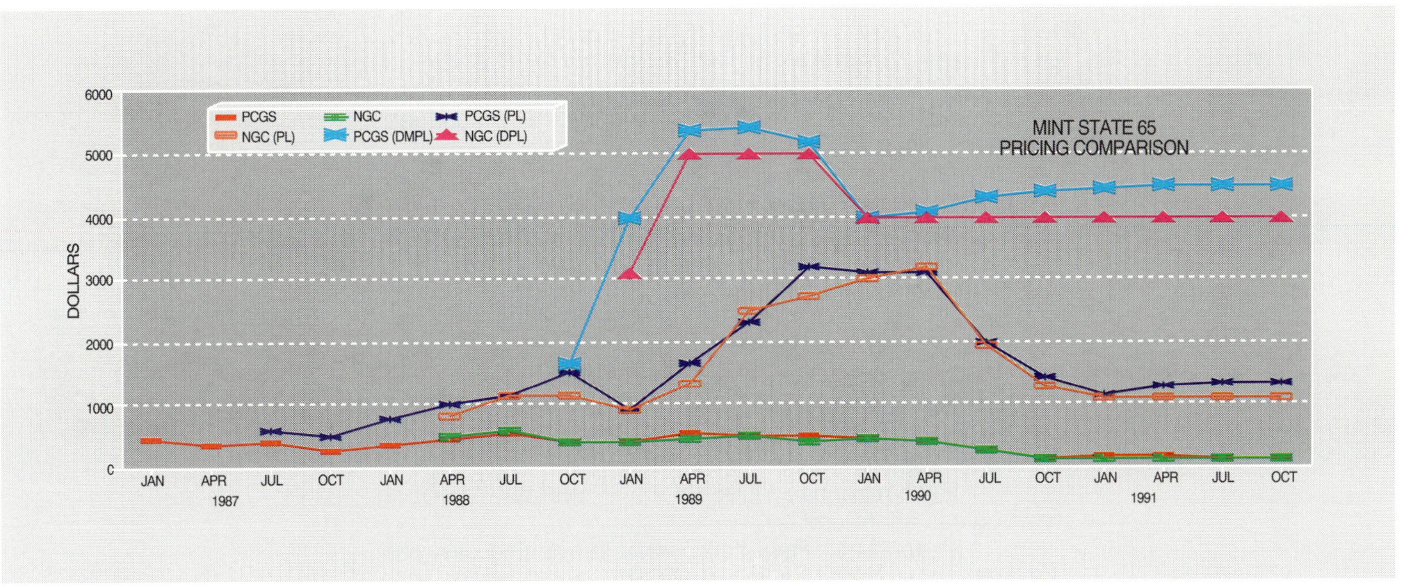
MINT STATE 65
PRICING COMPARISON
PCGS
NGC
PCGS (PL)
NGC (PL)
PCGS (DMPL)
NGC (DPL)
DOLLARS
6000
5000
4000
3000
2000
1000
0
JAN
APR
JUL
OCT
1987
1988
1989
1990
1991

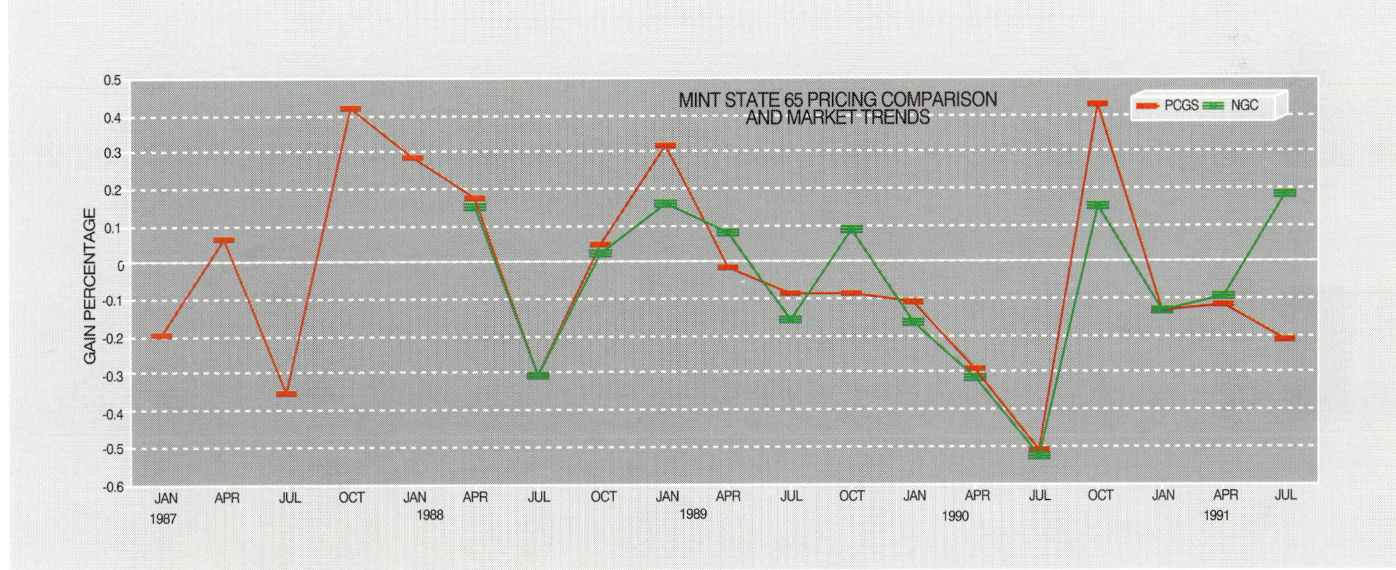
MINT STATE 65 PRICING COMPARISON
AND MARKET TRENDS
PCGS
NGC
GAIN PERCENTAGE
0.5
0.4
0.3
0.2
0.1
0
-0.1
-0.2
-0.3
-0.4
-0.5
-0.6
JAN
APR
JUL
OCT
1987
1988
1989
1990
1991

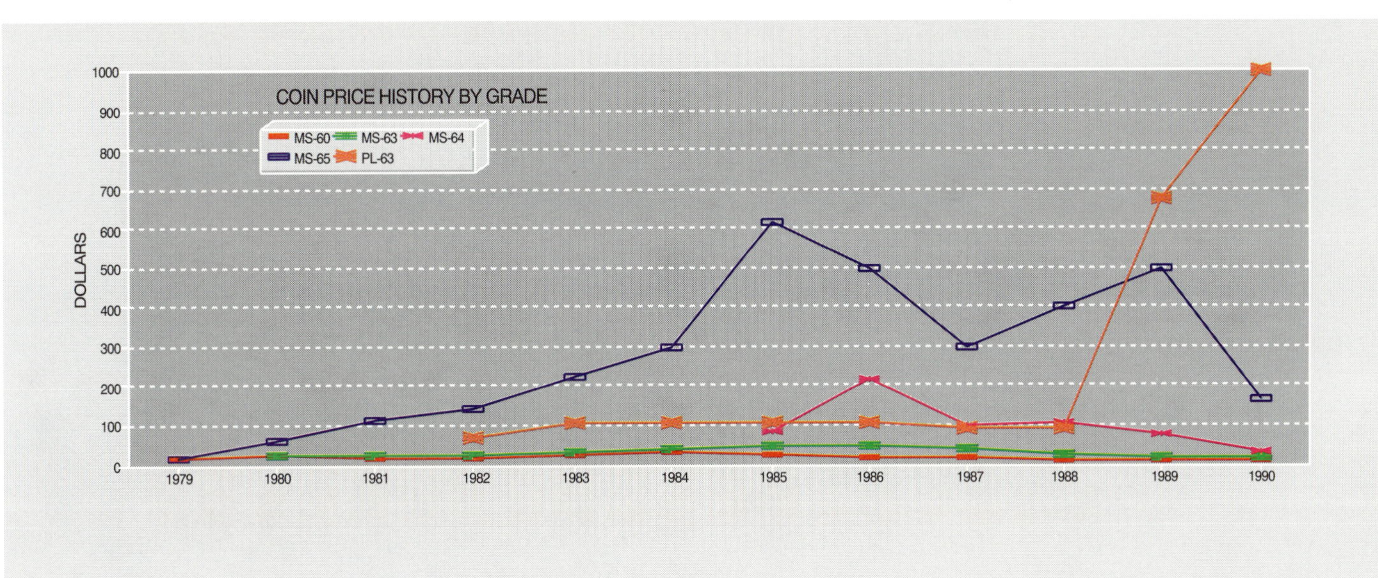
COIN PRICE HISTORY BY GRADE
MS-60
MS-63
MS-64
MS-65
PL-63
DOLLARS
1000
900
800
700
600
500
400
300
200
100
0
1979
1980
1981
1982
1983
1984
1985
1986
1987
1988
1989
1990

1921-D

THE FIRST, LAST AND ONLY DENVER MORGAN. Mintage 20,345,000, all with micro D most like that on $20's. Worn examples are not often seen. Sliders are common. Uncs. are often softly struck with subdued lustre. Rolls are mostly MS 60/62.

Of the first dozen struck, nos. 1 & 2 disappeared from Colorado School of Mines and Colorado Historical Society. Nos. 3 - 12 went from Denver Mint Superintendent Thomas Annear to C. W. Cowell, who had them engraved in left field 3RD (or other number through 12TH) DOLLAR RELEASED FROM 1ST 100 EVER COINED AT DENVER MINT THOMAS ANNEAR, SUPT. All ten of Cowell's appeared in a B. Max Mehl mail bid sale, December 18, 1923, lots 1040-49; eight are located. See Alan Herbert's write-up in Numismatic News Weekly, November 28, 1989, p. 58.

Recommended in MS 64 up. Preferably MS 65 if you can afford one.

Prooflikes: Few, none really convincing. Wayne Miller says those he has seen are usually weak, with foreign matter adhering to die in S of trust, sometimes also in E of STATES. A few semi-PL cameo examples exist. The only DMPL reported is in low grade.

MINTAGE	PROOF	STRIKE	LUSTER	BAG MARKS	REDFIELD
20,345,000	0	Soft & Weak	Average	Moderate To Heavy	No
DIES	**DIE VARIETIES**	**% OF PL**	**% OF DMPL**	**PIVOTAL GRADE**	**RARITY FACTOR**
Not Available	7	0.9	0.1	MS 65	R-4

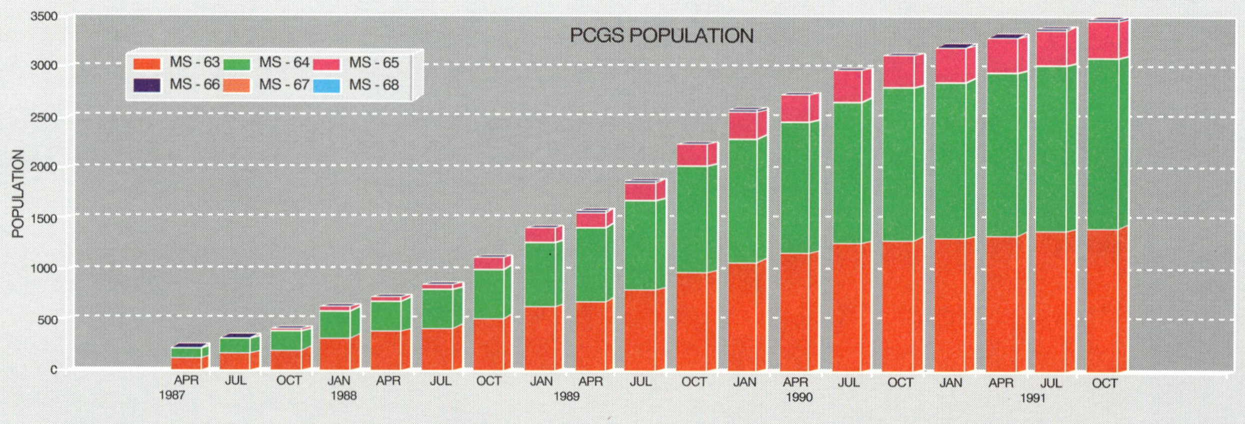

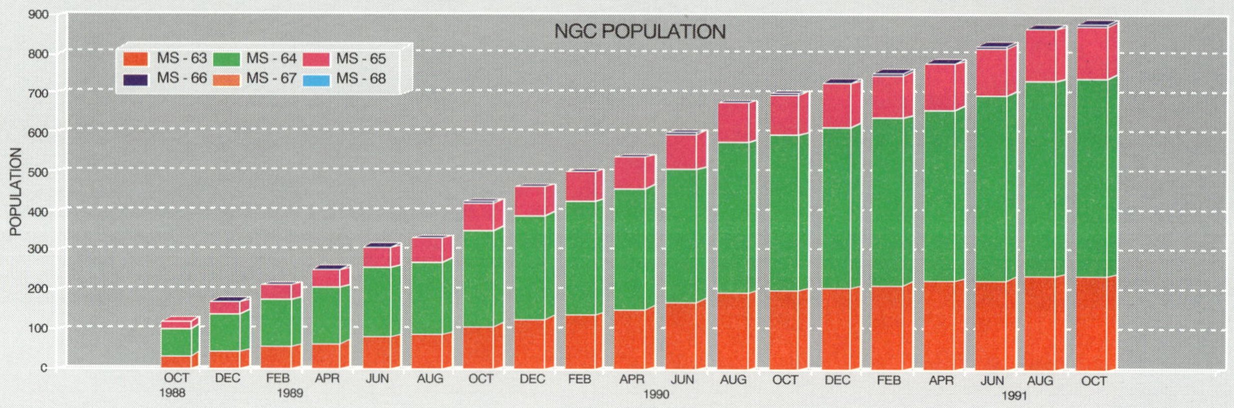

PCGS POPULATION

NGC POPULATION

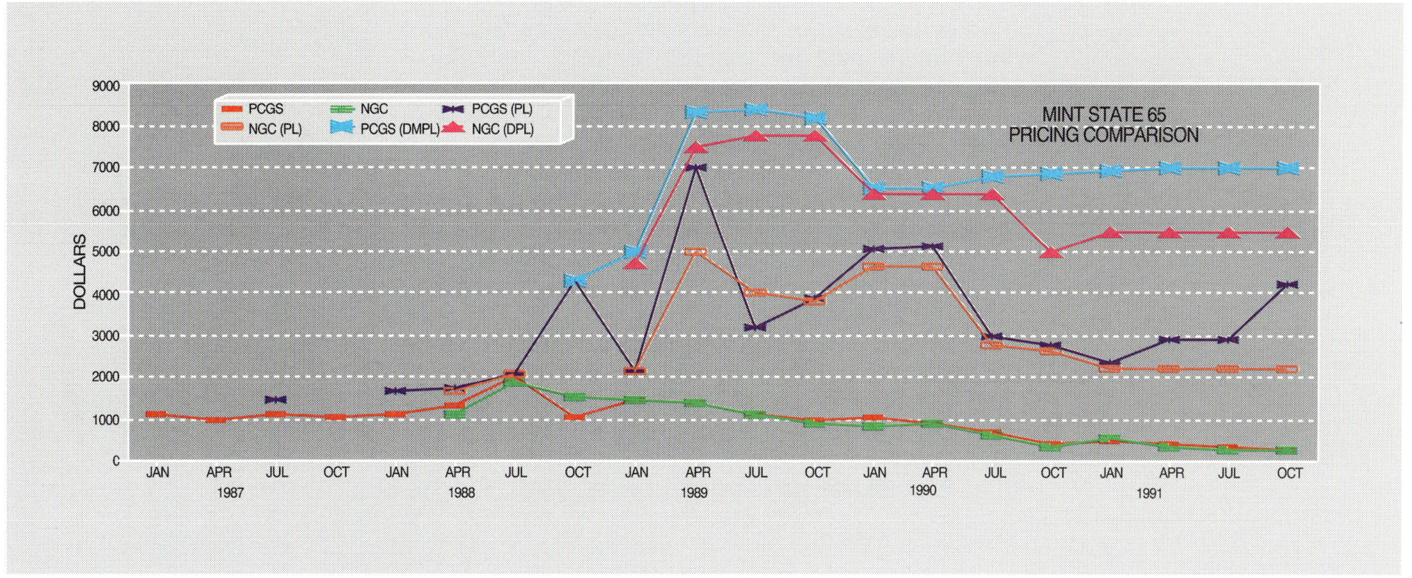
MINT STATE 65
PRICING COMPARISON
PCGS
NGC
PCGS (PL)
NGC (PL)
PCGS (DMPL)
NGC (DPL)
DOLLARS
9000
8000
7000
6000
5000
4000
3000
2000
1000
0
JAN APR JUL OCT JAN APR JUL OCT JAN APR JUL OCT JAN APR JUL OCT JAN APR JUL OCT
1987
1988
1989
1990
1991

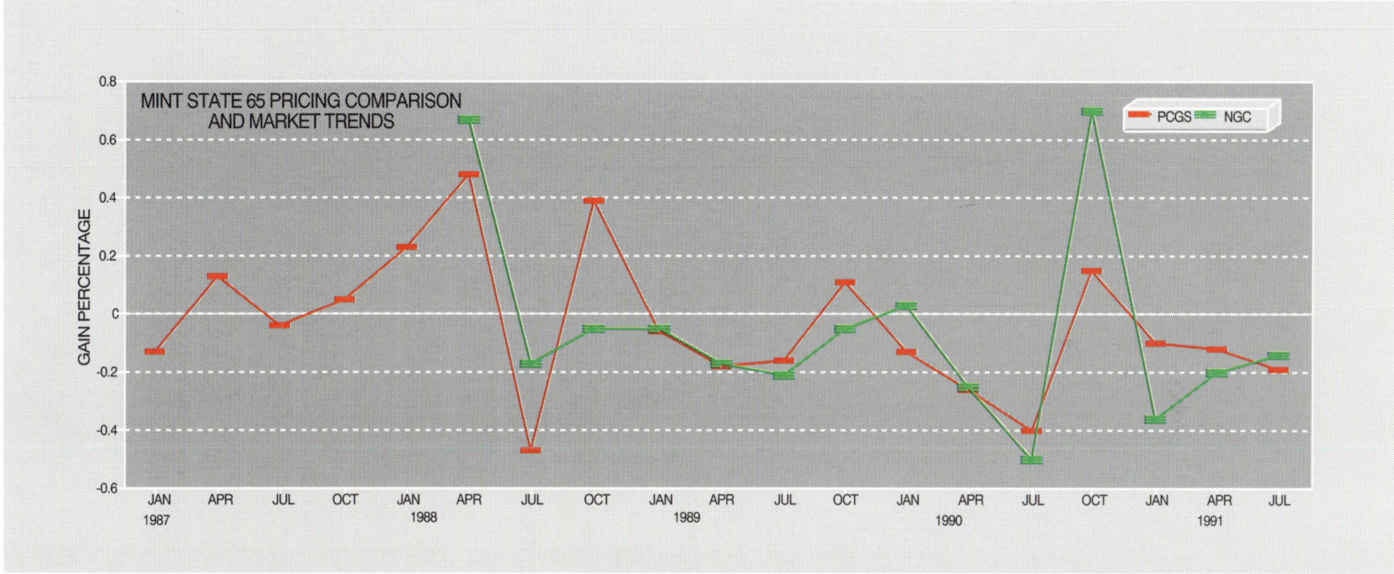
MINT STATE 65 PRICING COMPARISON
AND MARKET TRENDS
PCGS
NGC
GAIN PERCENTAGE
0.8
0.6
0.4
0.2
0
-0.2
-0.4
-0.6
JAN APR JUL OCT JAN APR JUL OCT JAN APR JUL OCT JAN APR JUL OCT JAN APR JUL
1987
1988
1989
1990
1991

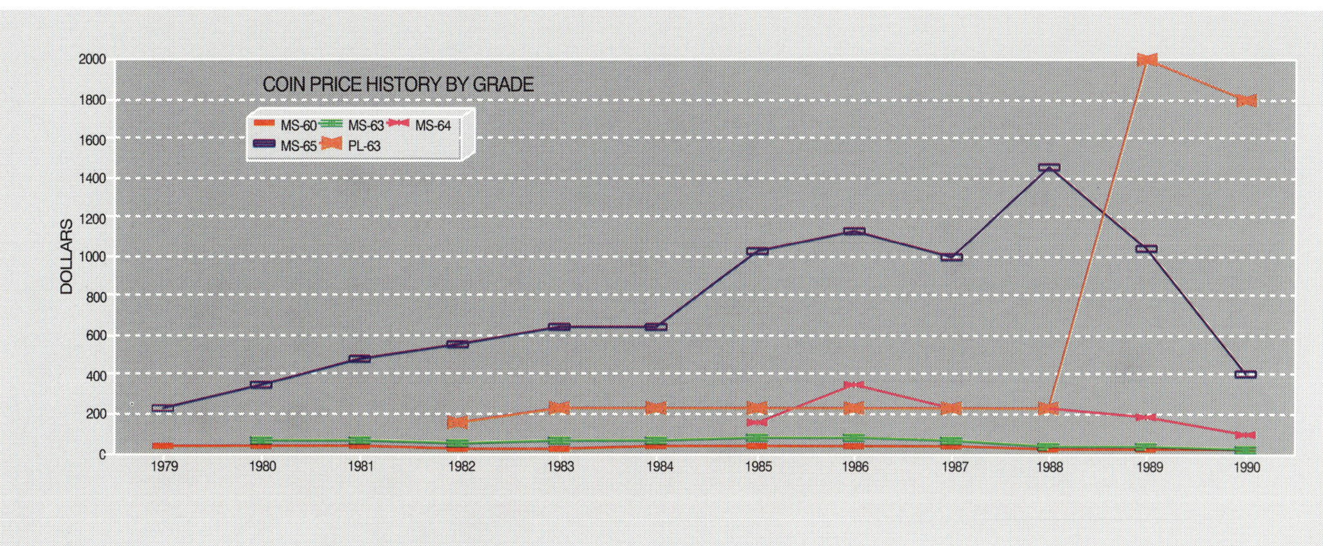
COIN PRICE HISTORY BY GRADE
MS-60
MS-63
MS-64
MS-65
PL-63
DOLLARS
2000
1800
1600
1400
1200
1000
800
600
400
200
0
1979 1980 1981 1982 1983 1984 1985 1986 1987 1988 1989 1990

1921-S
PCGS
S$1
MS65
7300.65/2241749

1921-S

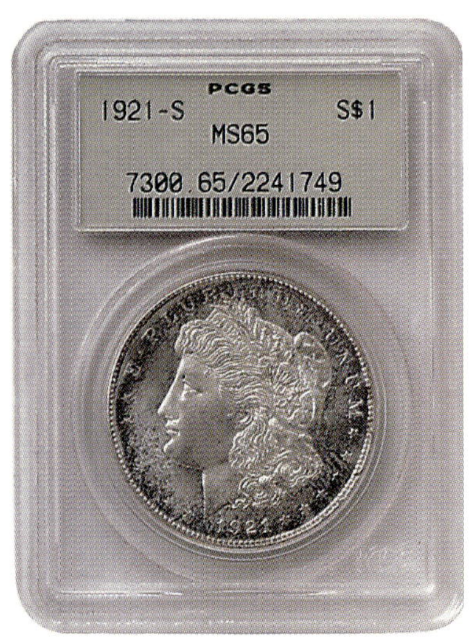

Mintage 21,695,000, all with 16 berries and micro s mintmark, after the style of 1878-S. The type IV obverse and reverse dies were used in all of the 1921-P, D and S Morgans. Coinage began May 9, 1921. Many were melted in 1942. Worn examples are not often seen. Uncs. are mostly flat strikes with plenty of bag marks. Sliders are common. The report of a small quantity in the Redfield hoard has not been confirmed. BU rolls in MS 60/62 are available.

Recommended in MS 65 up, but you may have to settle for a 64 while hunting.

Proofs: By Wayne Miller's accounts, 24 were struck at the urging of Farran Zerbe, however none have yet to be certified by PCGS nor NGC. Authencity is absolute from any accredited grading and certification service.

Prooflikes: No convincing ones. RARE!

PCGS

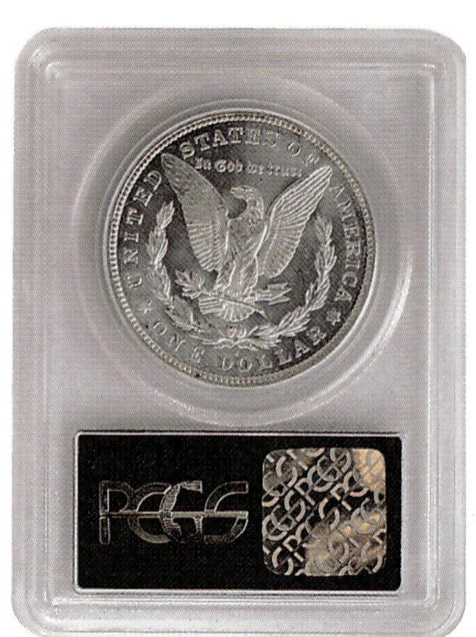

MINTAGE	PROOF	STRIKE	LUSTER	BAG MARKS	REDFIELD
21,695,000	0	Soft & Weak	Poor	Moderate To Heavy	No
DIES	**DIE VARIETIES**	**% OF PL**	**% OF DMPL**	**PIVOTAL GRADE**	**RARITY FACTOR**
Not Available	7	0.5	0.0	MS 65	R-3

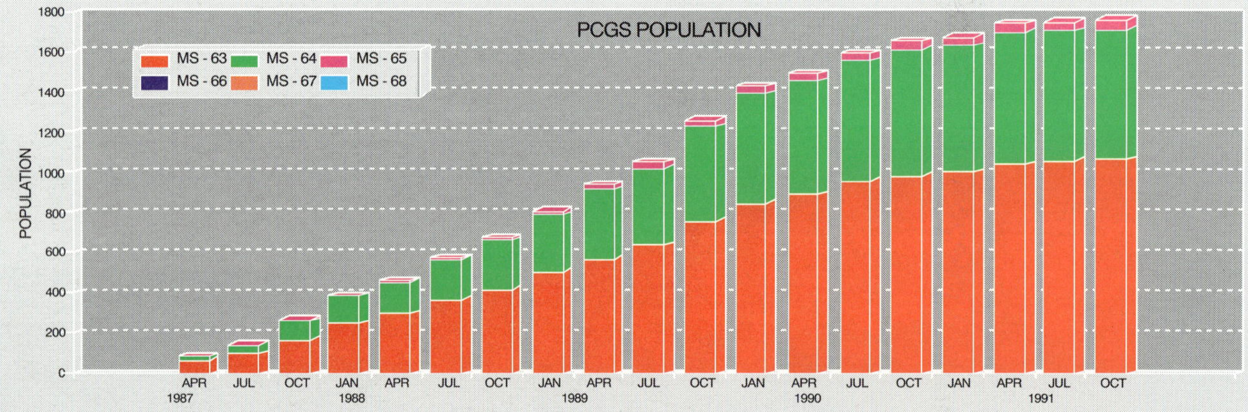
PCGS POPULATION
MS - 63
MS - 64
MS - 65
MS - 66
MS - 67
MS - 68
POPULATION
1800
1600
1400
1200
1000
800
600
400
200
C
APR 1987
JUL
OCT
JAN 1988
APR
JUL
OCT
JAN 1989
APR
JUL
OCT
JAN 1990
APR
JUL
OCT
JAN 1991
APR
JUL
OCT

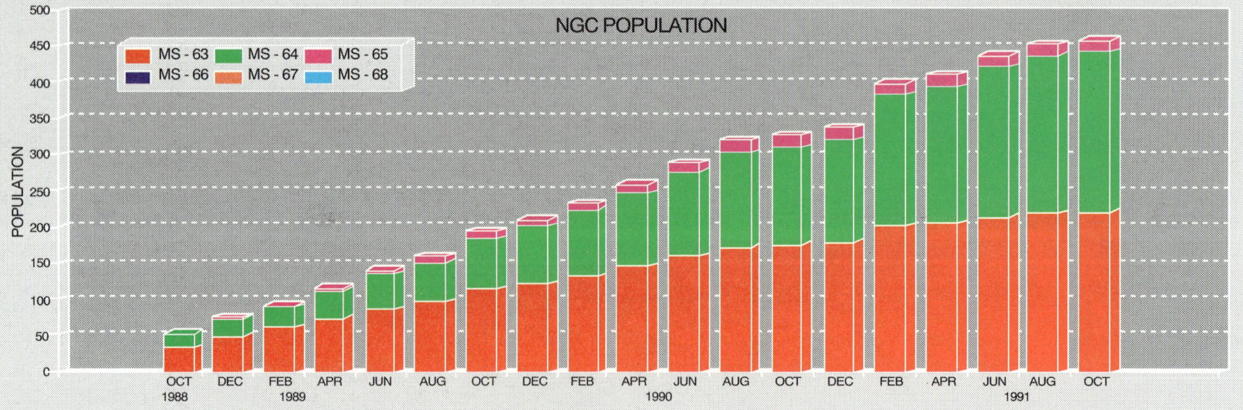
NGC POPULATION
MS - 63
MS - 64
MS - 65
MS - 66
MS - 67
MS - 68
POPULATION
500
450
400
350
300
250
200
150
100
50
C
OCT 1988
DEC
FEB 1989
APR
JUN
AUG
OCT
DEC
FEB 1990
APR
JUN
AUG
OCT
DEC
FEB 1991
APR
JUN
AUG
OCT

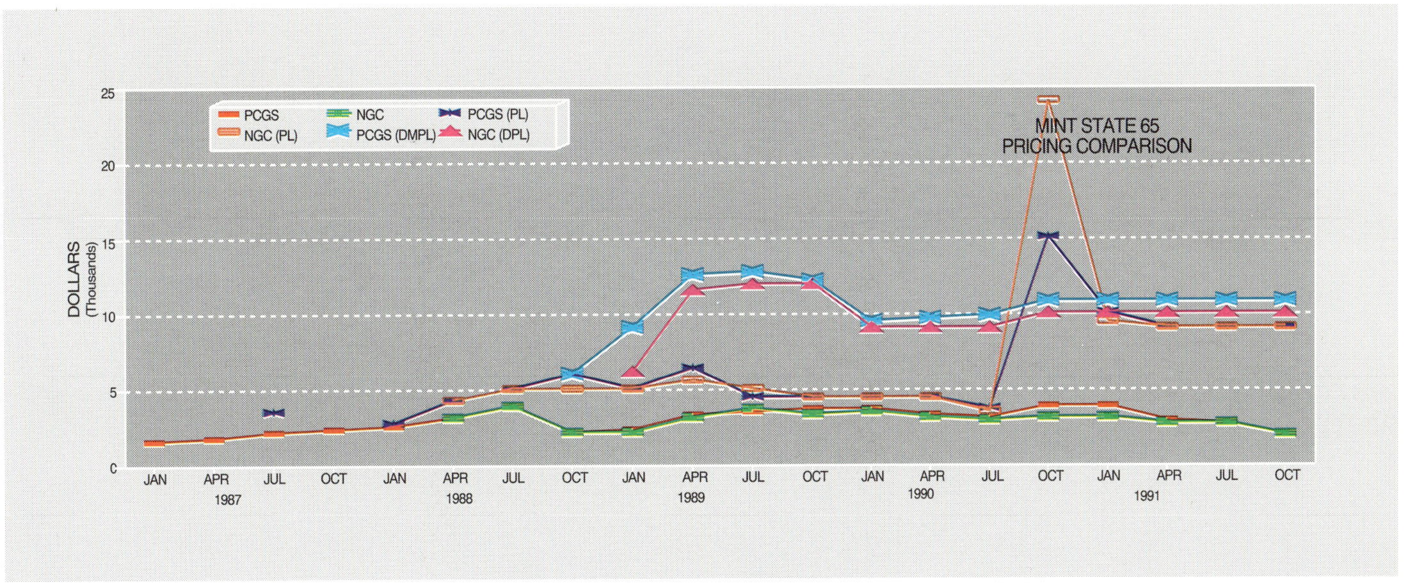
MINT STATE 65
PRICING COMPARISON
PCGS
NGC
PCGS (PL)
NGC (PL)
PCGS (DMPL)
NGC (DPL)
DOLLARS (Thousands)
25
20
15
10
5
0
JAN APR JUL OCT JAN APR JUL OCT JAN APR JUL OCT JAN APR JUL OCT JAN APR JUL OCT
1987
1988
1989
1990
1991

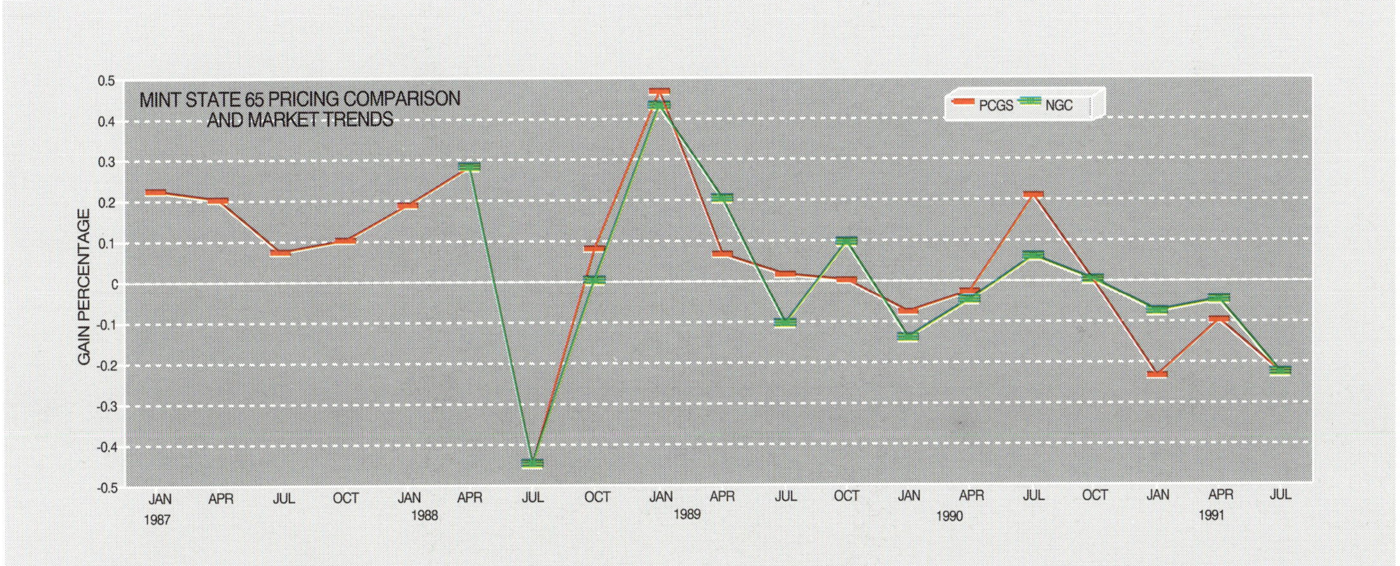
MINT STATE 65 PRICING COMPARISON
AND MARKET TRENDS
PCGS
NGC
GAIN PERCENTAGE
0.5
0.4
0.3
0.2
0.1
0
-0.1
-0.2
-0.3
-0.4
-0.5
JAN APR JUL OCT JAN APR JUL OCT JAN APR JUL OCT JAN APR JUL OCT JAN APR JUL
1987
1988
1989
1990
1991

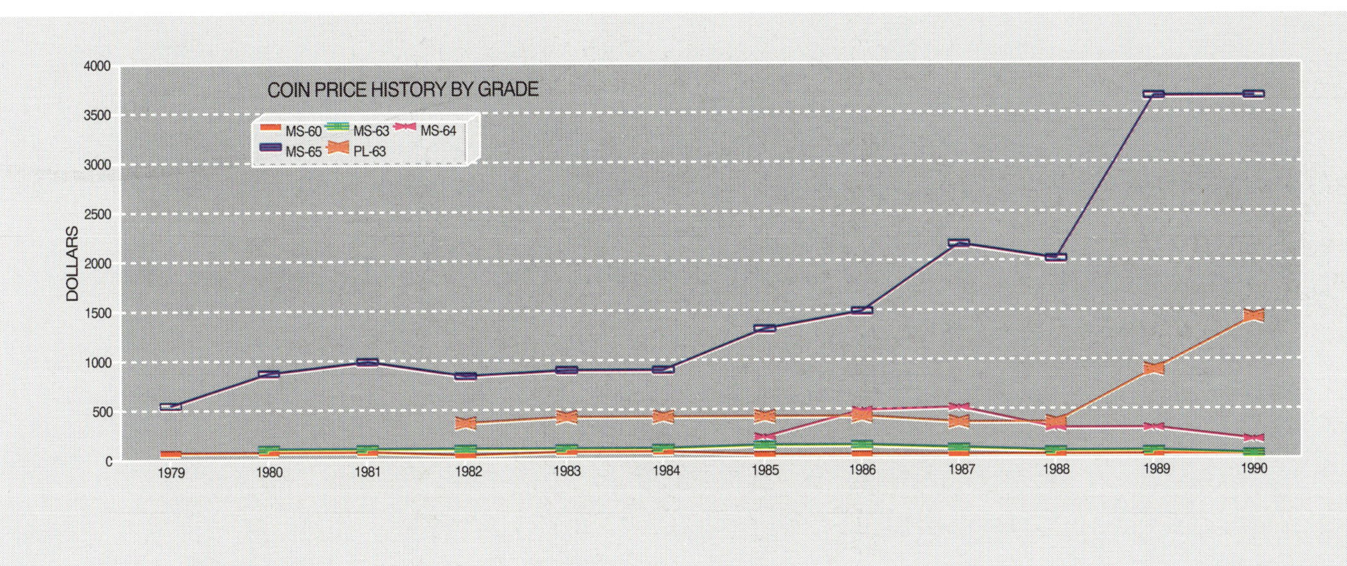
COIN PRICE HISTORY BY GRADE
MS-60
MS-63
MS-64
MS-65
PL-63
DOLLARS
4000
3500
3000
2500
2000
1500
1000
500
0
1979 1980 1981 1982 1983 1984 1985 1986 1987 1988 1989 1990

CHAPTER 81

Peace Dollars - Date By Date Analysis

by John W. Highfill, NLG

THE PEACE DOLLAR

(1921 - 1935)

IMPORTANT NOTE:

The color plate photos used for the Peace dollar date by date analysis were provided by Wayne H. Miller and are from his original *Morgan and Peace Dollar Textbook*, Adam Smith Publishing Co., Metairie, Louisiana.

PROPOSAL:

Farran Zerbe, San Francisco - historian for American Numismatic Association. Essay, "Commemorate the Peace with a Coin for Circulation," ANA convention on August 25, 1920. On May 9, 1921, Representative Albert Henry Vestal (chairman of the House Ways and Means Committee) introduced the Peace Dollar Coinage Bill as a joint resolution.

LEGISLATIVE COMMITTEE:

Judson Brenner - Chairman, with William A. Ashbrook, Dr. J.M. Henderson, Farren Zerbe, Albert Henry Vestal and Howland Wood.

INSPIRATION:

Treaty of Versailles marking the end of World War I.

AUTHORIZATION:

Coinage Act of 1890 and Pittman Act of April 23, 1918. Provisions for Secretary of the Treasury to approve change Morgan dollar design after 25 years.

COMPETITION:

Federal Commission of Fine Arts issued invitations to nine sculptors on November 23, 1921. Eight submitted sketches with Anthony de Francisci declared the winner.

DESIGNER:

Anthony de Francisci using his wife, Teresa, as the model, prepared the winning design of Miss Liberty accepted by the Commission of Fine Arts on December 19, 1921.

DESIGN:

Obverse: Liberty head with rays of light, LIBERTY around top, IN GOD WE TRUST on each side of Liberty's neck, and date at the bottom.

Reverse: Bald eagle perched on mountain top with sun-rays coming from lower right, olive branch in eagle's talons, UNITED STATES OF AMERICA around top with E PLURIBUS UNUM below, ONE DOLLAR on each side of eagle, and PEACE at the bottom. (modifications were later added by chief mint engraver George T. Morgan.)

SPECIFICATIONS:

Weight is 26.73 grams composed of .900 silver and .100 copper, giving a net weight of .77344 ounces of pure silver. Diameter is 38.1 millimeters with a reeded edge.

CONTRIBUTING MINTS:

Philadelphia, Denver, and San Francisco. There were no Peace dollars minted in New Orleans whose doors were permanently closed in 1909.

FIRST YEAR PRODUCTION:

From December 26 through December 31, 1921, 1,006,073 Peace dollars were struck at Philadelphia Mint. The first issue was given to President Harding on January 3, 1922.

PROOFS:

No official records were kept, but two different varieties were discovered for 1921 and 1922, respectively. These being a matte surface type and satin finish for each year.

***

1921-P

On December 19, 1921 (With no Congressional action on a May joint resolution) the federal Commission of Fine Arts approved a World War I commemorative silver dollar. Mintage 1,006,473, coined Dec. 26-31, 1921. Anthony de Francisco had completed his models in November 1921, portraying his wife, Teresa Cafarelli de Francisci, as Ms. Liberty.

Harry Forman said that he had never seen an unc. bag of this issue. Nobody else has reported any either.

Uncs. are moderately bagmarked; luster varies from dull or gray to brilliantly frosty. The key variable is striking quality; some are so weak in centers that hair details and feathers are blurred, others — a minority — sharper. The 1921-P can be found with "infrequent reeding" as a variety.

Recommended in MS 64 up, and the better it is struck, the better for both beauty and long-term potential. MS 67 or better unknown in certified grades.

Proofs: The first ones struck (at least the first 20) were satin finish; perhaps 10 are known today. They are sharply struck on central hair and wing and leg feathers and all other relief devices, far better than business strikes. The first three were delivered by messenger, to President Harding, Secretary of Treasury Andrew W. Mellon, and Mint Director Raymond T. Baker, January 3, 1922. Auction '87:1885, described as a "Satin Proof," came with a card reading "20th dollar coined in Philadelphia Mint 1921 New Peace Dollar." The same dies were used, individually and in combination, to make some of the earliest business strikes; but remember that all relief details are sharper on proofs than on the best uncs. These proofs first came to public attention at the 1975 ANA convention in Los Angeles.

Later proofs are matte or sandblast; they are also very sharply struck. Possibly 6 or 7 are known.

MINTAGE	PROOF	STRIKE	LUSTER	BAGMARKS
1,006,473	13-18*	Weak	Dull To Good	Moderate
REDFIELD	**CATEGORY**	**DIE VARIETIES**	**PIVOTAL GRADE**	**RARITY FACTOR**
No	Key	2	MS 65	R-2

*Estimated by the author (6-8 matte finish high relief) (7-10 satin finish high relief)

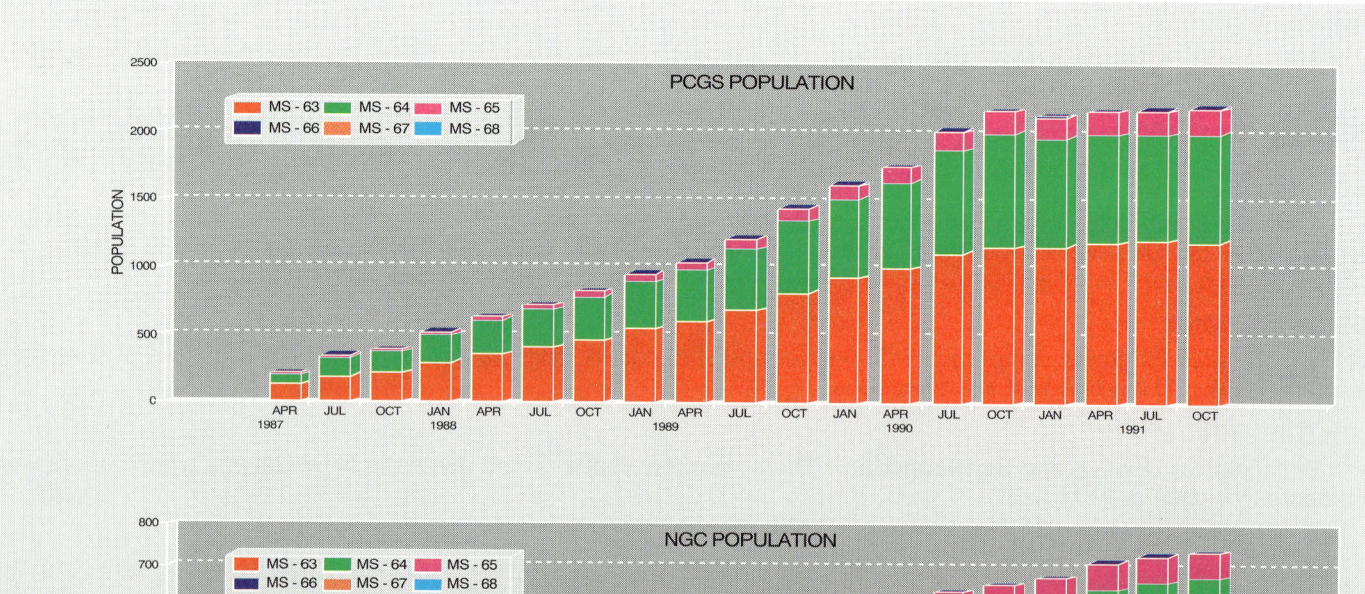

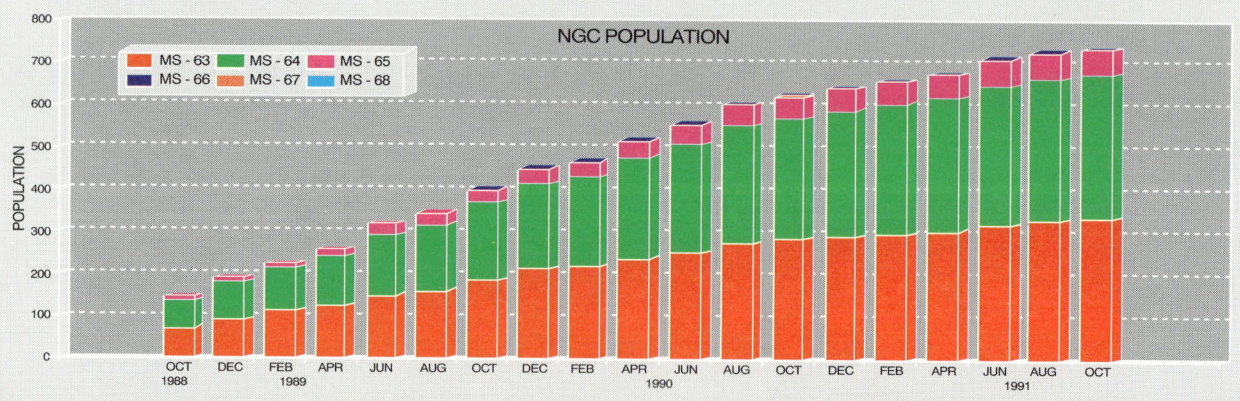

1921-P

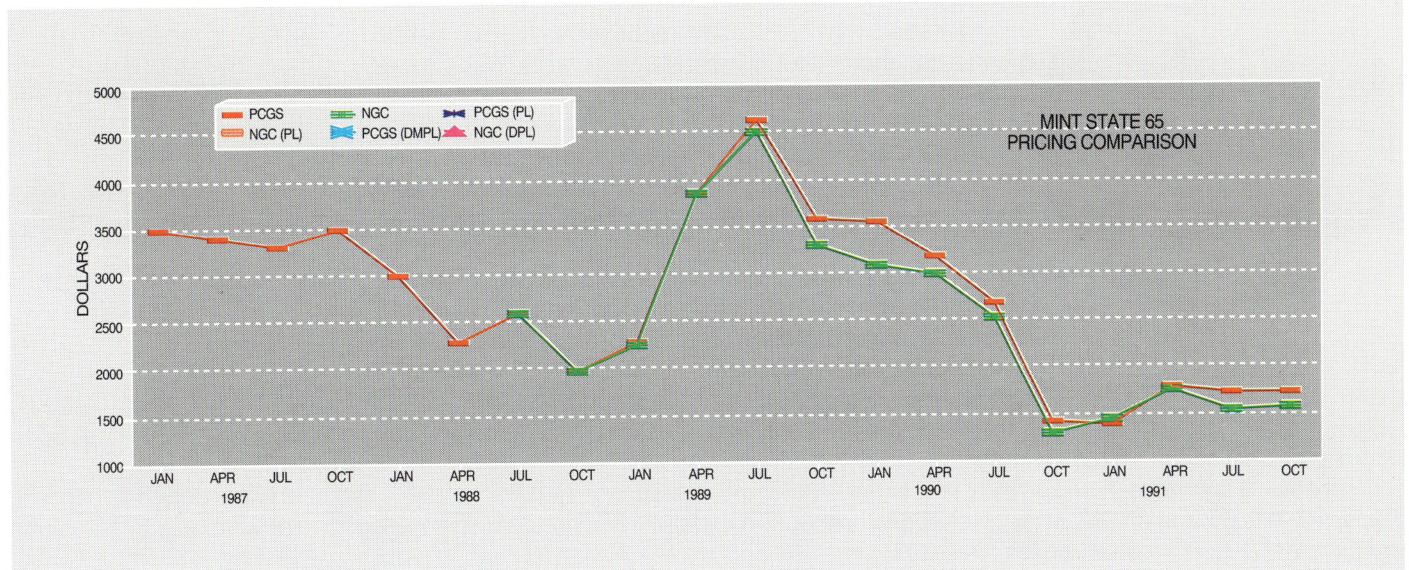

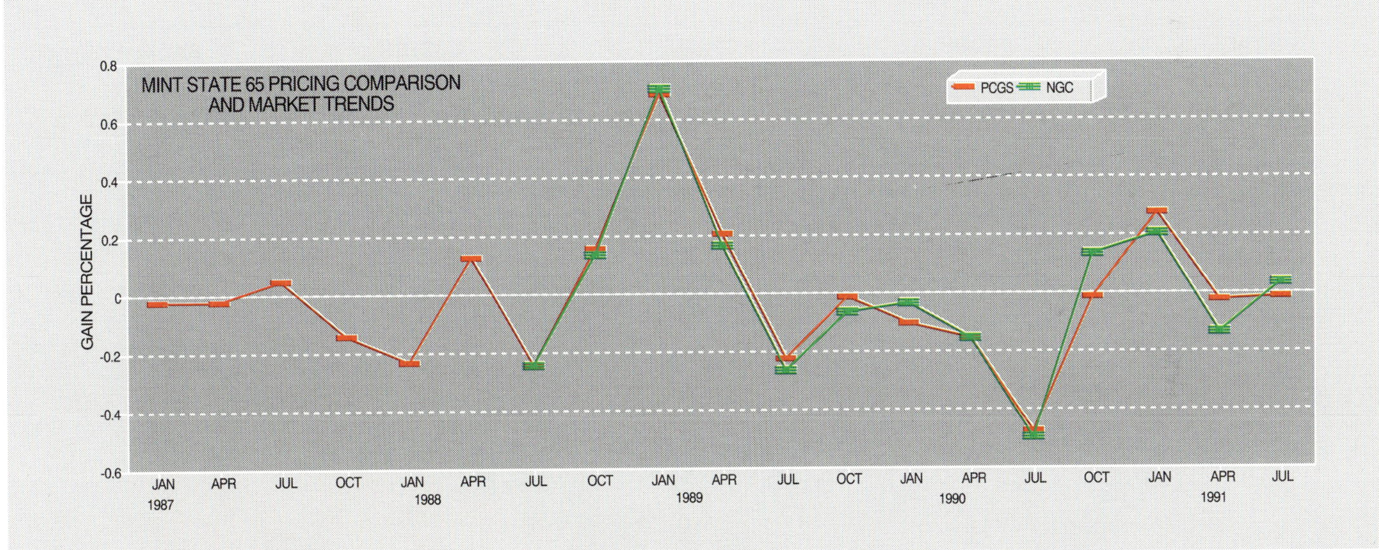

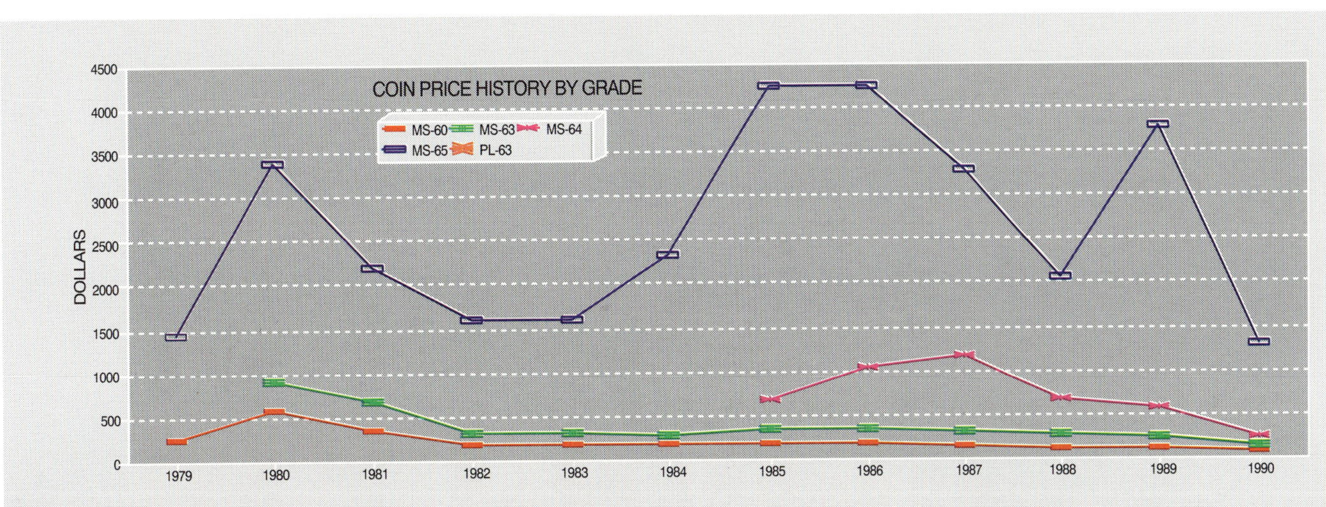

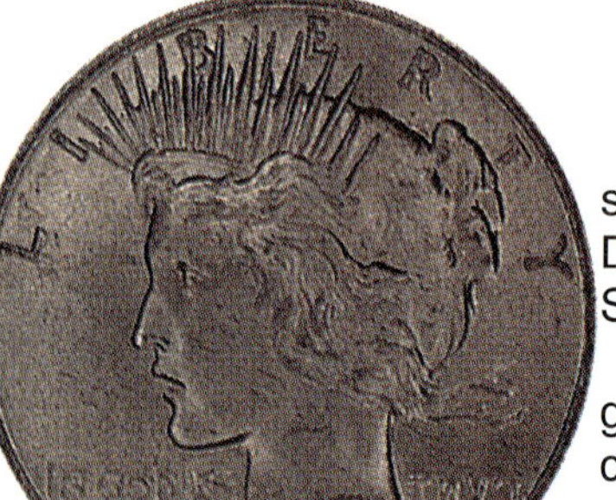

LIBERTY

1922-P

DOLLAR

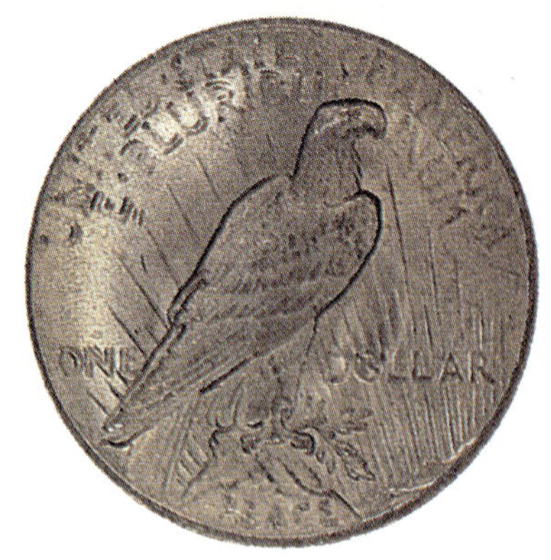

Mintage 51,737,000. Commonest U.S. dollar overall; second commonest Unc., exceeded only by 1923. See Drew Crowell's chapter on "Common Date Uncirculated Silver Dollars."

The Philadelphia Mint's chief engraver George T. Morgan made a lower relief copy of the Francisci design, with changes in rays and mountain; flat fields, thinner letters and numerals, long curved tail to R in TRVST. The object, as always, was to maximize die life and profits, to make the most coins from the fewest dies. Stacking of coins had become a major problem and die pressure led to daily adjustments. Often encountered with a flat milky unremovable stains.

Recommended only in the highest Unc. grade you can find. Only one 1922-P has been certified and graded in MS 67 or better.

Proofs: High relief, type of 1921, proofs only. Modified design, not identical to 1921; two short rays added to coronet, L and WE TRVST and mountain range changed in shape; hair details and feathers strengthened. *Encyclopedia* 5713. Matte or sandblast only. (+ roster from Norweb:3931)

Low relief, regular type, satin finish. At least 10 struck for Morgan, two given sandblast finish; Morgan sold these to Ambrose Swasey, March 1, 1922. (+ roster from Norweb: 3932-32)

MINTAGE	PROOF	STRIKE	LUSTER	BAGMARKS
51,737,000	9-11*	Average	Average	Heavy
REDFIELD	**CATEGORY**	**DIE VARIETIES**	**PIVOTAL GRADE**	**RARITY FACTOR**
No	Semi-common	3	MS 65	R-3

*Estimated by Walter H. Breen (6-8 Matte finish high relief) (3 satin finish lower relief)

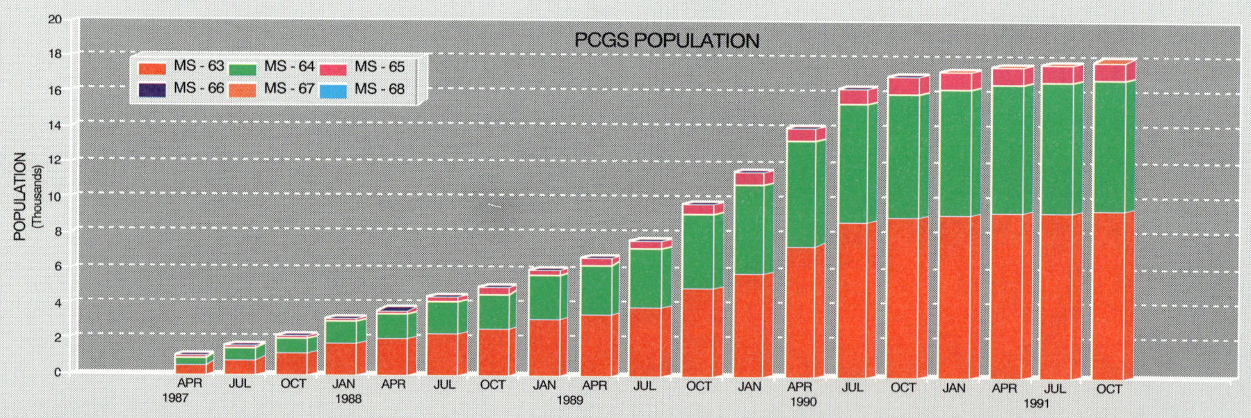
PCGS POPULATION
MS - 63
MS - 64
MS - 65
MS - 66
MS - 67
MS - 68
POPULATION (Thousands)
0 2 4 6 8 10 12 14 16 18 20
APR 1987
JUL
OCT
JAN 1988
APR
JUL
OCT
JAN 1989
APR
JUL
OCT
JAN
APR 1990
JUL
OCT
JAN
APR
JUL 1991
OCT

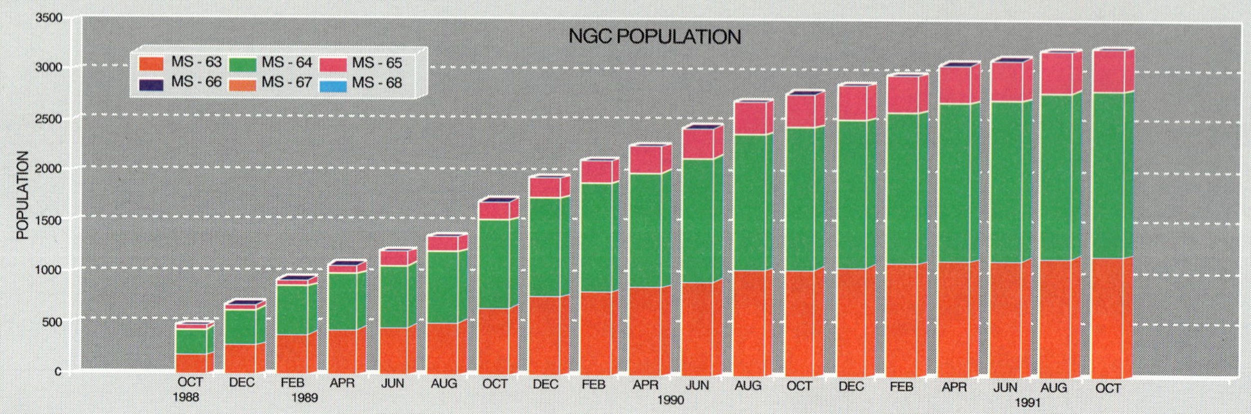
NGC POPULATION
MS - 63
MS - 64
MS - 65
MS - 66
MS - 67
MS - 68
POPULATION
0 500 1000 1500 2000 2500 3000 3500
OCT 1988
DEC
FEB 1989
APR
JUN
AUG
OCT
DEC
FEB
APR 1990
JUN
AUG
OCT
DEC
FEB
APR
JUN 1991
AUG
OCT

1922-P

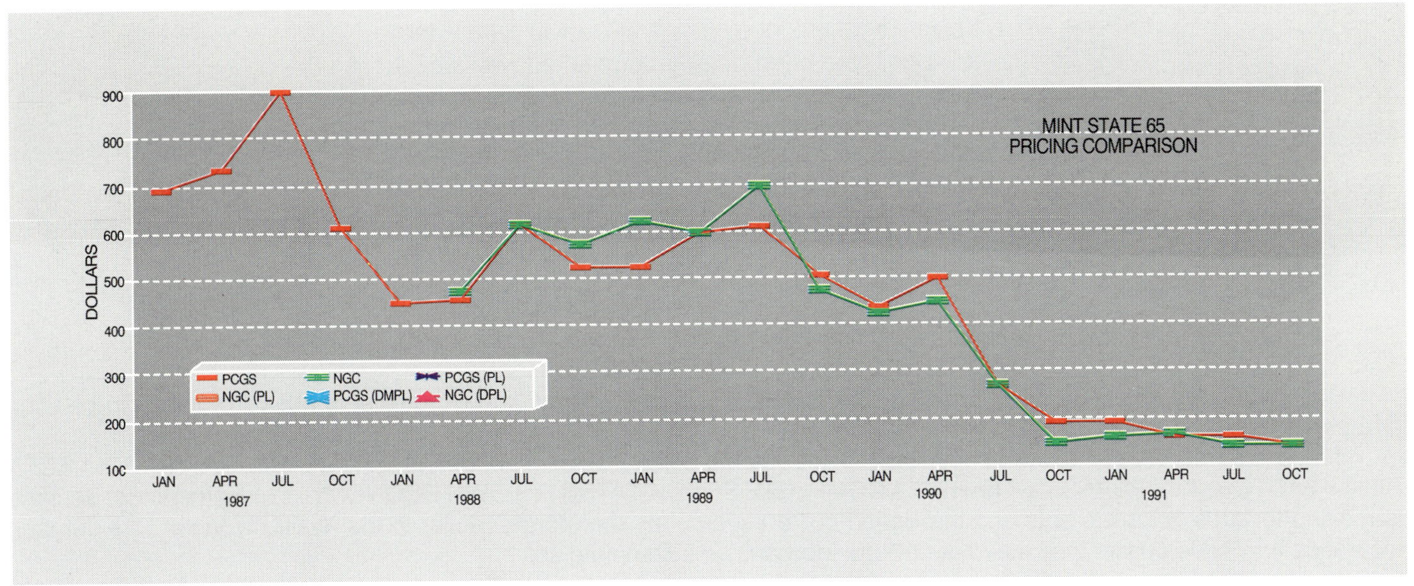

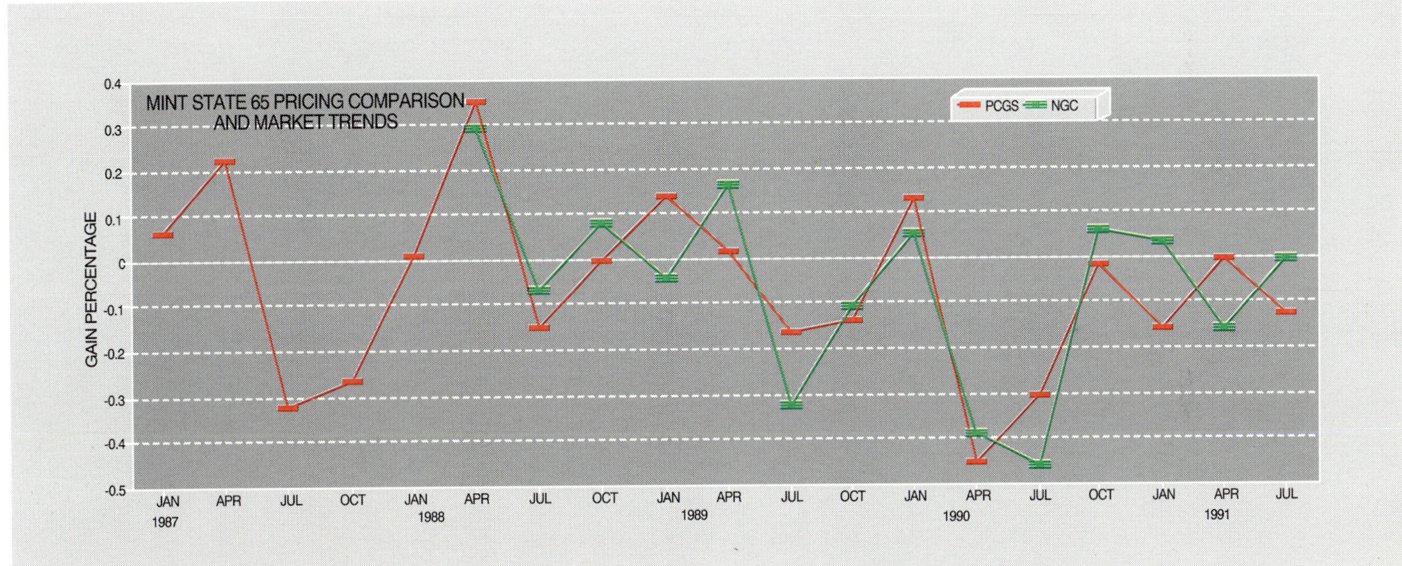

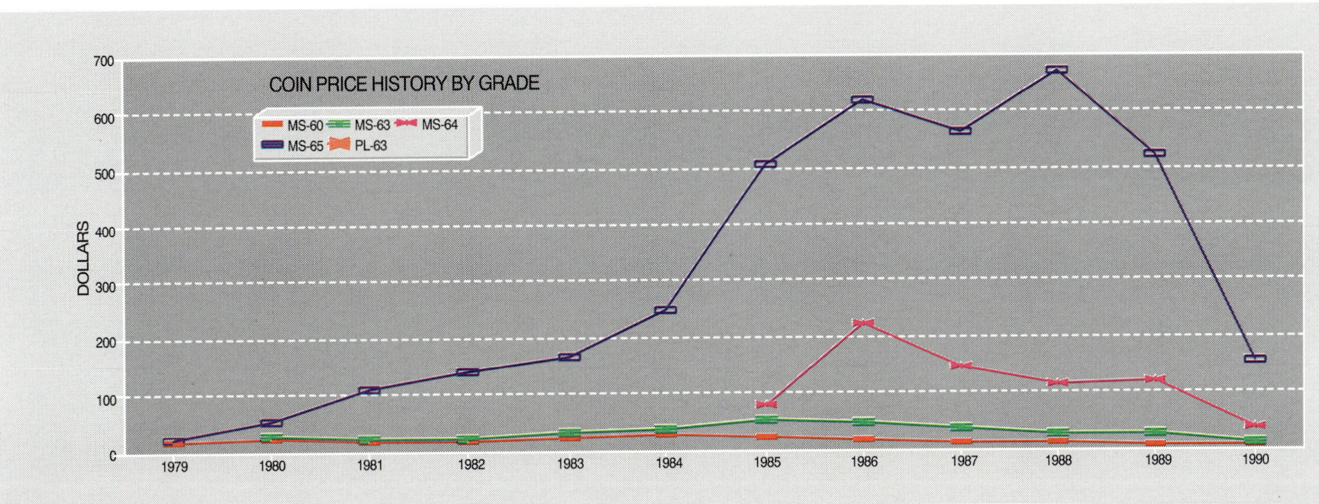

1922-D

Mintage 15,063,000. The first Denver Mint Peace dollar. Uncs. are often heavily bagmarked; well struck bags are available. Liberty's hairlines are distinct, however the reverse Eagle may come with softness on the feathers. Multiple obverse die breaks for this issue are common. Sliders are plentiful. An "orange-peel" surface roughness due to excessive die wear can also be a problem. Some examples exhibit a semi-prooflike appearence.

The Denver Mint struck Peace dollars for only five years. (excluding the 1964-D) These were 1922-D, 1923-D, 1926-D, 1927-D, and 1934-D.

Recommended in MS 64. Bag quantities of MS 60/63 still exist. None known to exist in MS 67 or better in certified grades.

The entire Peace dollar series is obtainable in grades MS 60/65. BECAUSE OF THIS AVAILABILITY AND COLLECTIBILITY FACTOR, THE PEACE DOLLAR AS A COMPLETE SET DICTATES ITS OWN ECONOMY. In simpler terms, demand is moving towards complete sets and the Peace dollar supercedes the Morgan dollar in the availibilty factor. As demand increases for Peace dollars they may out-perform Morgans as a complete set.

MINTAGE	PROOF	STRIKE	LUSTER	BAGMARKS
15,063,000	0	Average	Average	Heavy
REDFIELD	**CATEGORY**	**DIE VARIETIES**	**PIVOTAL GRADE**	**RARITY FACTOR**
No	Semi-common	3	MS 65	R-3

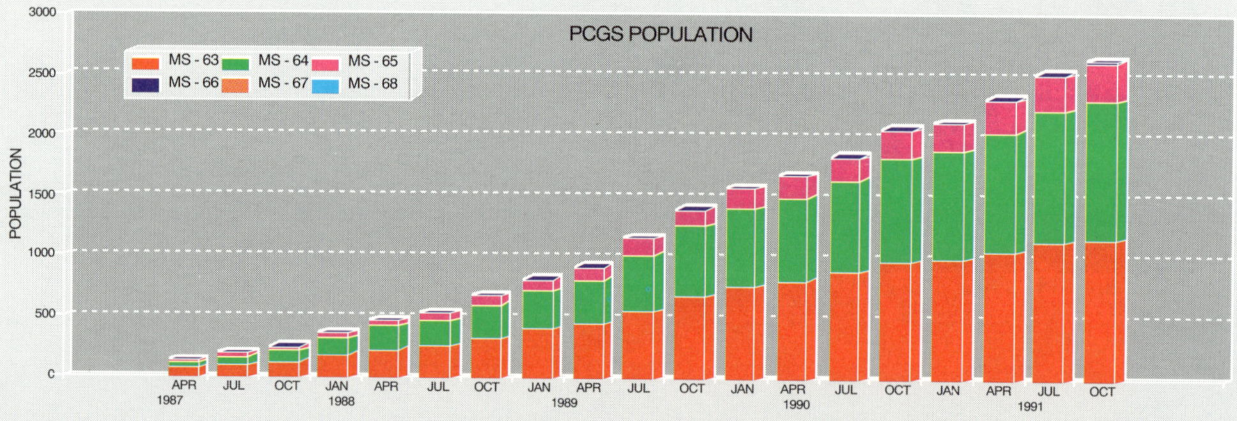

PCGS POPULATION

MS - 63 MS - 64 MS - 65 MS - 66 MS - 67 MS - 68

POPULATION: 0, 500, 1000, 1500, 2000, 2500, 3000

APR 1987, JUL, OCT, JAN 1988, APR, JUL, OCT, JAN 1989, APR, JUL, OCT, JAN, APR 1990, JUL, OCT, JAN, APR, JUL 1991, OCT

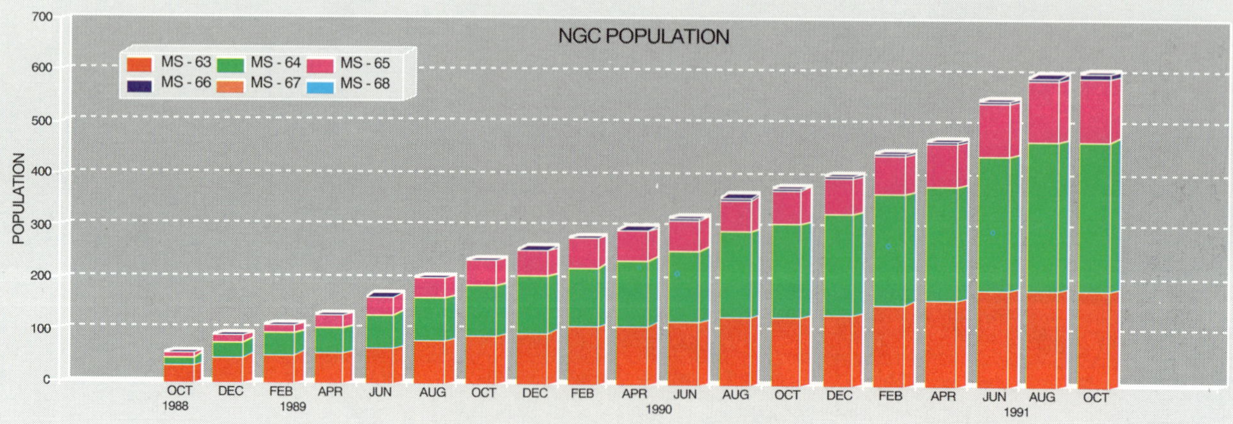

NGC POPULATION

MS - 63 MS - 64 MS - 65 MS - 66 MS - 67 MS - 68

POPULATION: 0, 100, 200, 300, 400, 500, 600, 700

OCT 1988, DEC, FEB 1989, APR, JUN, AUG, OCT, DEC, FEB, APR 1990, JUN, AUG, OCT, DEC, FEB, APR, JUN 1991, AUG, OCT

1922-D

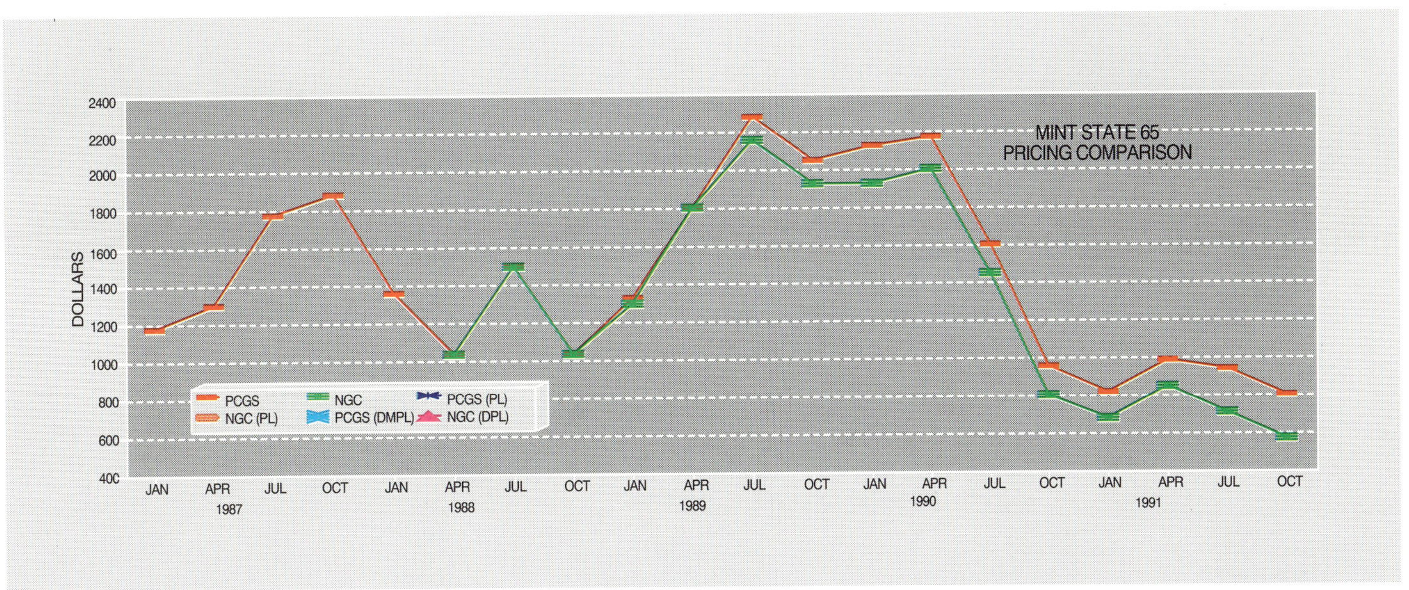

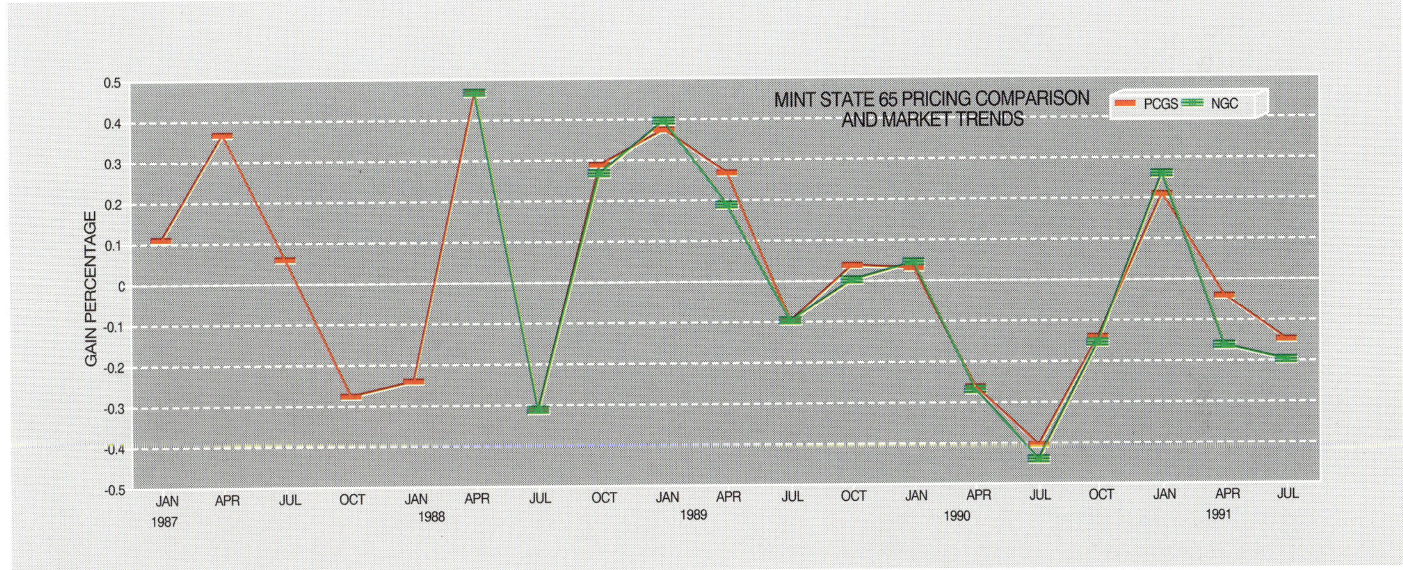

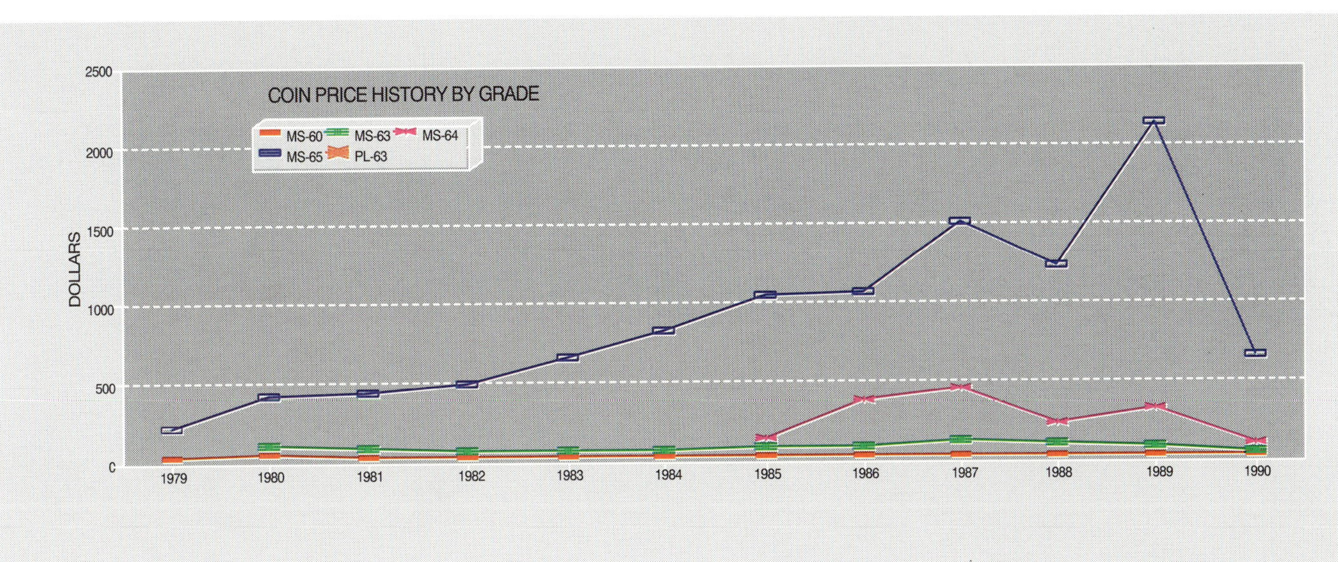

1922-S

Mintage 17,475,000. The first year of issue for the San Francisco Mint Peace Dollar. The great strikes that were so prevalent in the entire Morgan dollar series was "lost in the process" in the Peace dollar series. The 1922-S, 1923-S, 1924-S, 1925-S, 1926-S, 1927-S and the 1928-S are all weakly struck. "Fade Away" Rims, IN GOD WE, and centers often weak. Sometimes they appear to have no rim at all. This was the first of the Redfield Peace dates to be released. Paramount's promotion stimulated enough interest in dollars that the market went up rather than sagging under the huge quantities.

Roll quantities MS 60/63 coins exist. Recommended in MS 64 up if you can find it. An MS 65 example is 25 times more scarce than an MS 64. None known in MS 67 or better in certified grades.

MINTAGE	PROOF	STRIKE	LUSTER	BAGMARKS
17,475,000	0	Weak	Bold	Heavy
REDFIELD	**CATEGORY**	**DIE VARIETIES**	**PIVOTAL GRADE**	**RARITY FACTOR**
Yes	Semi-key	2	MS 65	R-2

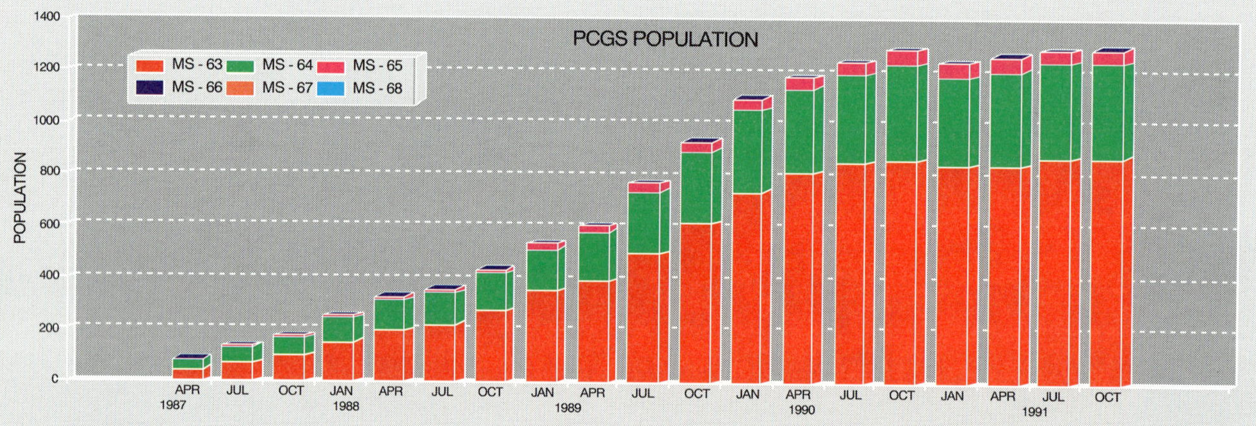

PCGS POPULATION

MS - 63 MS - 64 MS - 65
MS - 66 MS - 67 MS - 68

POPULATION

1400 1200 1000 800 600 400 200 0

APR 1987 JUL OCT JAN 1988 APR JUL OCT JAN 1989 APR JUL OCT JAN APR 1990 JUL OCT JAN APR JUL 1991 OCT

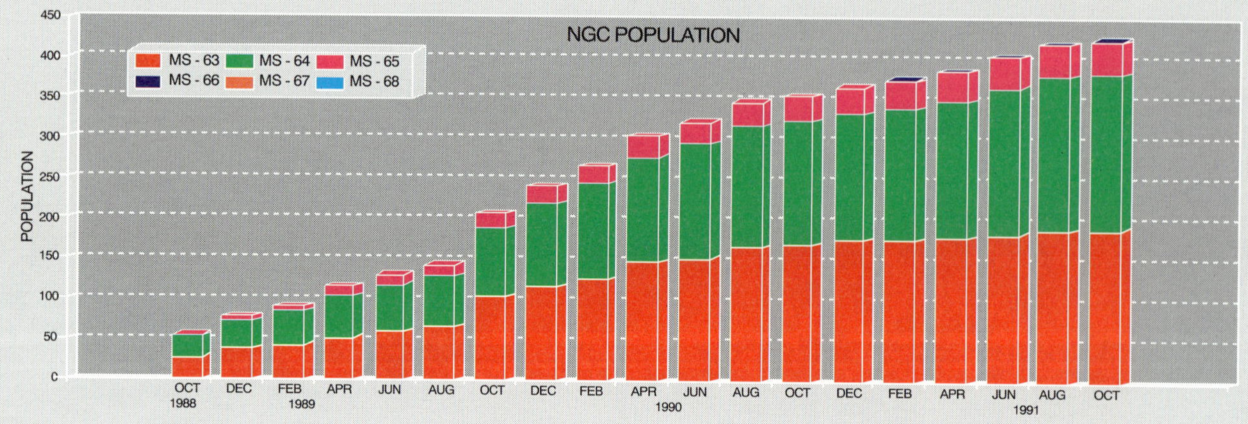

NGC POPULATION

MS - 63 MS - 64 MS - 65
MS - 66 MS - 67 MS - 68

POPULATION

450 400 350 300 250 200 150 100 50 0

OCT 1988 DEC FEB 1989 APR JUN AUG OCT DEC FEB APR 1990 JUN AUG OCT DEC FEB APR JUN 1991 AUG OCT

1922-S

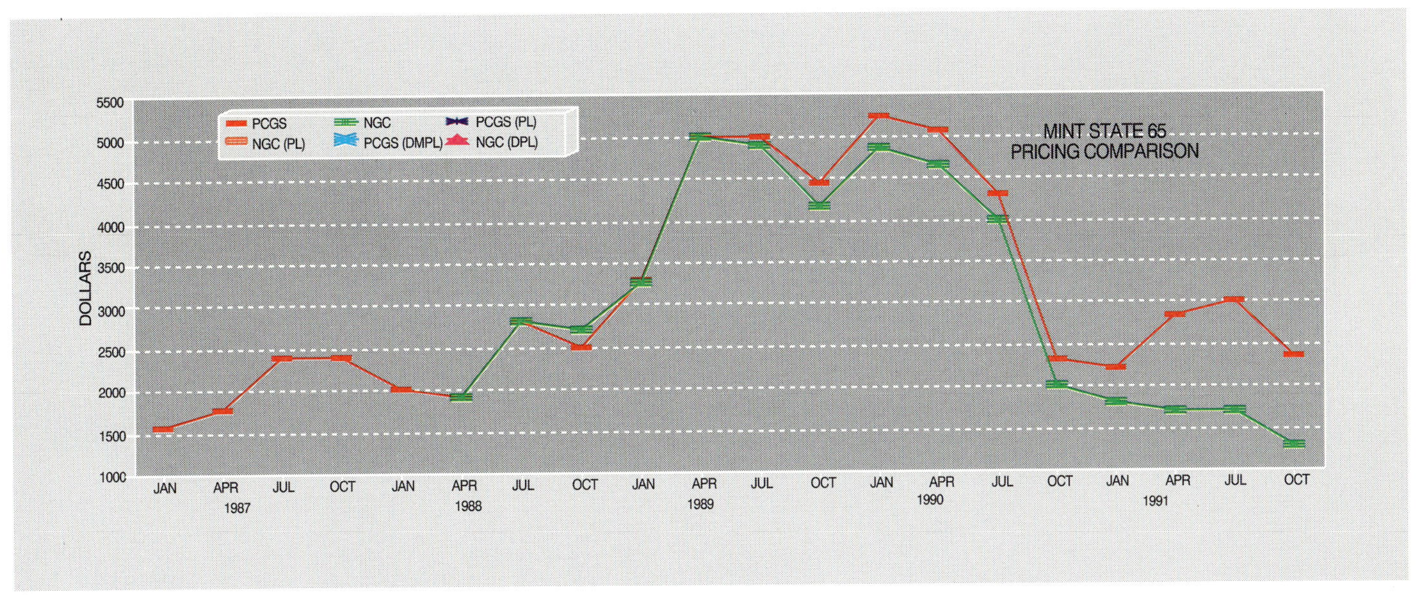

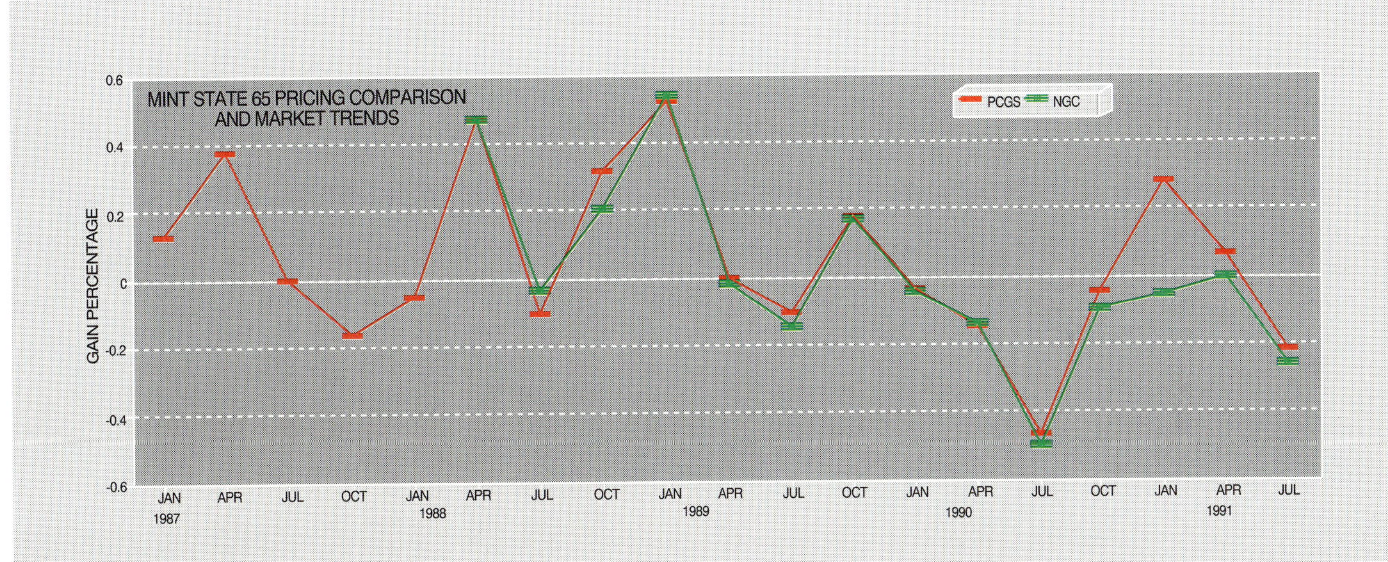

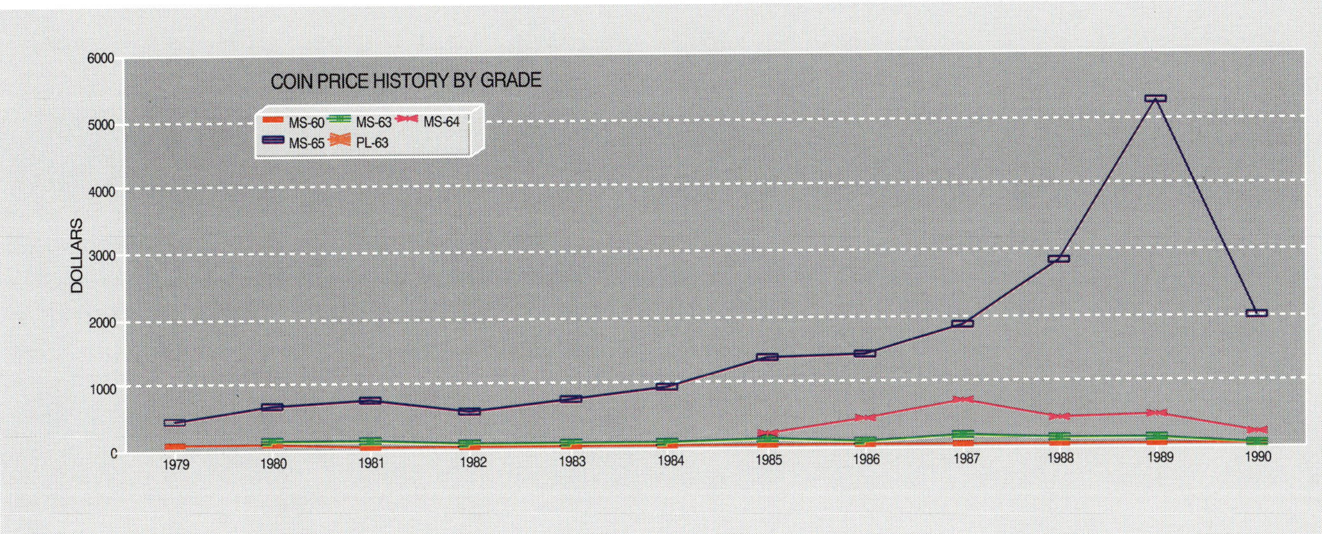

1923-P

Mintage 30,800,000. Commonest Unc. U.S. dollar, though not commonest in all grades. Good strike, and luster. Many Uncs. from Treasury bags released Nov. 1945; at least 40 in Chicago alone. Sliders common; so are gems. Circulated and MS 60/63 bags available. See Drew Crowell's chapter "Common Date Uncirculated Silver Dollars."

One variety has minor doubled reverse die. *Encyclopedia* 5717.

No explanation yet for the pieces with dull white stains. Unremoveable. The only PCGS MS 67 sold in lower to mid-five digits. None better known in certified grades. Recommended in MS 65 up. BU rolls in MS 64. Take your time and "cherry-pick" yourself good examples. They are plentiful.

MINTAGE	PROOF	STRIKE	LUSTER	BAGMARKS
30,800,000	0	Sharp	Good	Moderate
REDFIELD	**CATEGORY**	**DIE VARIETIES**	**PIVOTAL GRADE**	**RARITY FACTOR**
No	Common	8	MS 65	R-5

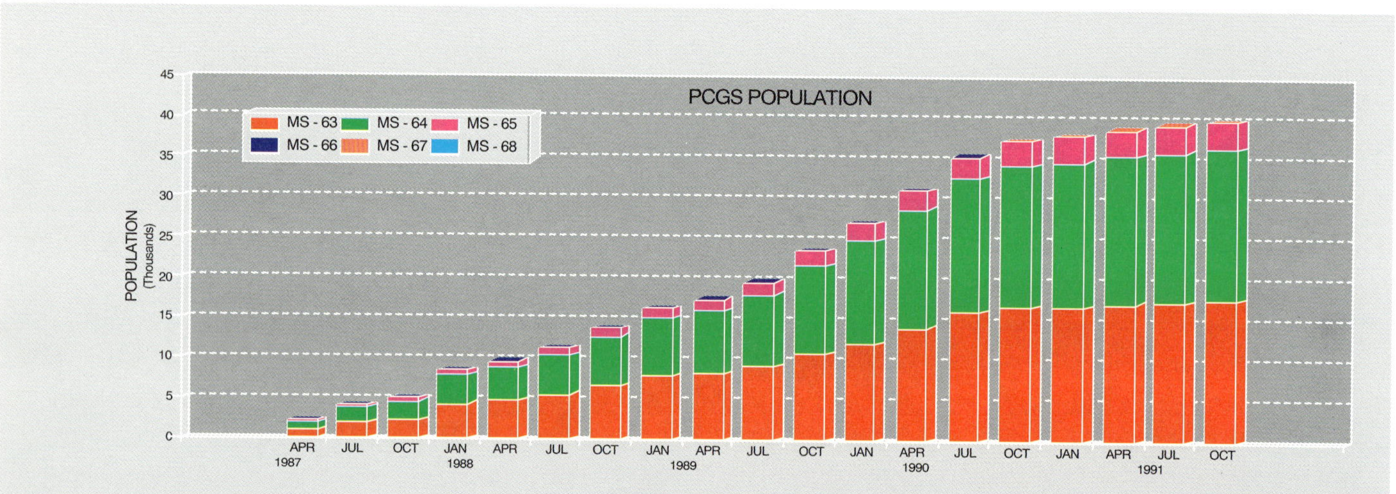

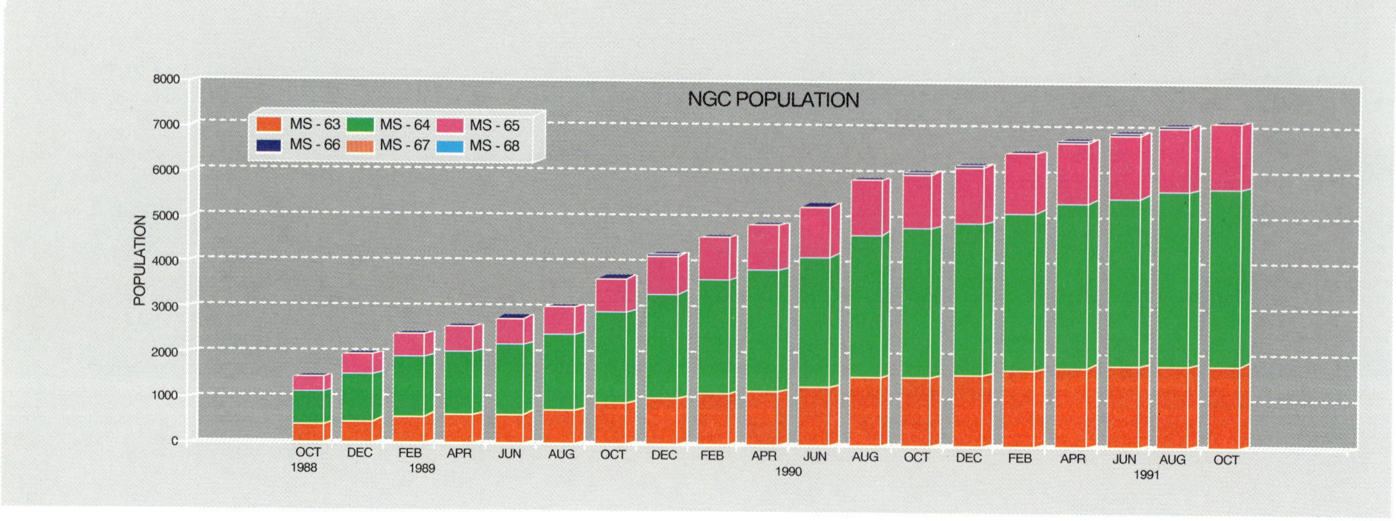

PCGS POPULATION

MS - 63 MS - 64 MS - 65
MS - 66 MS - 67 MS - 68

POPULATION (Thousands)

0 5 10 15 20 25 30 35 40 45

APR 1987, JUL, OCT, JAN 1988, APR, JUL, OCT, JAN 1989, APR, JUL, OCT, JAN, APR 1990, JUL, OCT, JAN, APR 1991, JUL, OCT

NGC POPULATION

MS - 63 MS - 64 MS - 65
MS - 66 MS - 67 MS - 68

POPULATION

0 1000 2000 3000 4000 5000 6000 7000 8000

OCT 1988, DEC, FEB 1989, APR, JUN, AUG, OCT, DEC, FEB, APR 1990, JUN, AUG, OCT, DEC, FEB, APR, JUN 1991, AUG, OCT

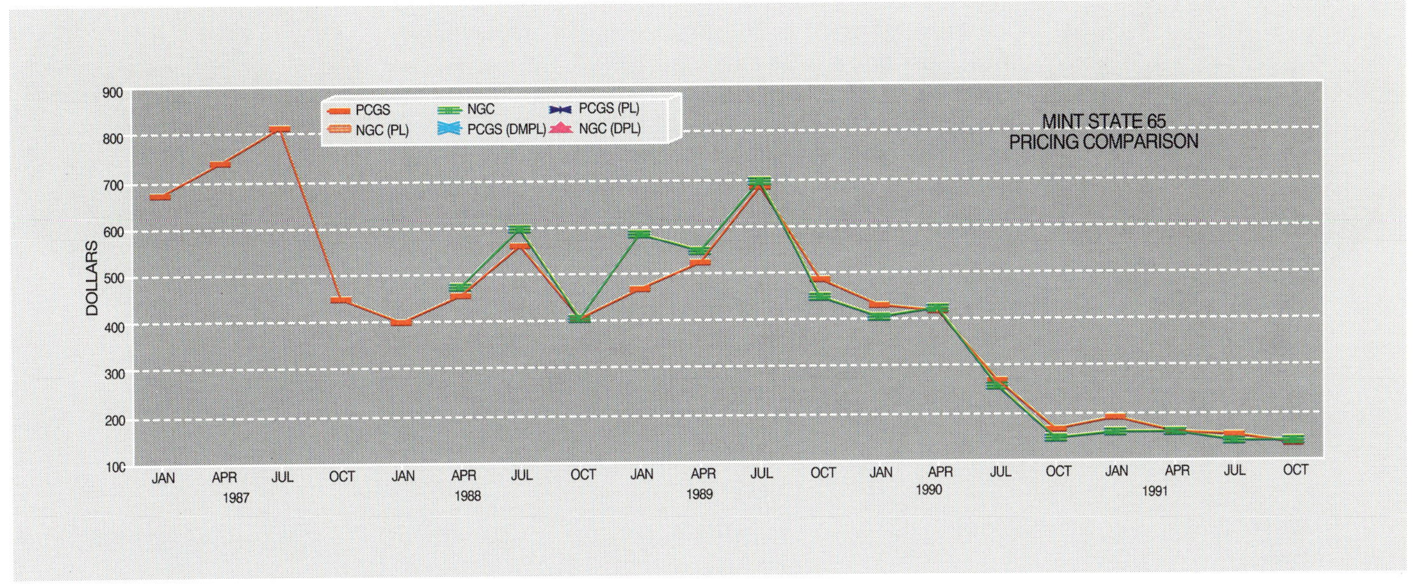
MINT STATE 65
PRICING COMPARISON
PCGS
NGC (PL)
NGC
PCGS (DMPL)
PCGS (PL)
NGC (DPL)
DOLLARS
900
800
700
600
500
400
300
200
100
JAN APR JUL OCT JAN APR JUL OCT JAN APR JUL OCT JAN APR JUL OCT JAN APR JUL OCT
1987
1988
1989
1990
1991

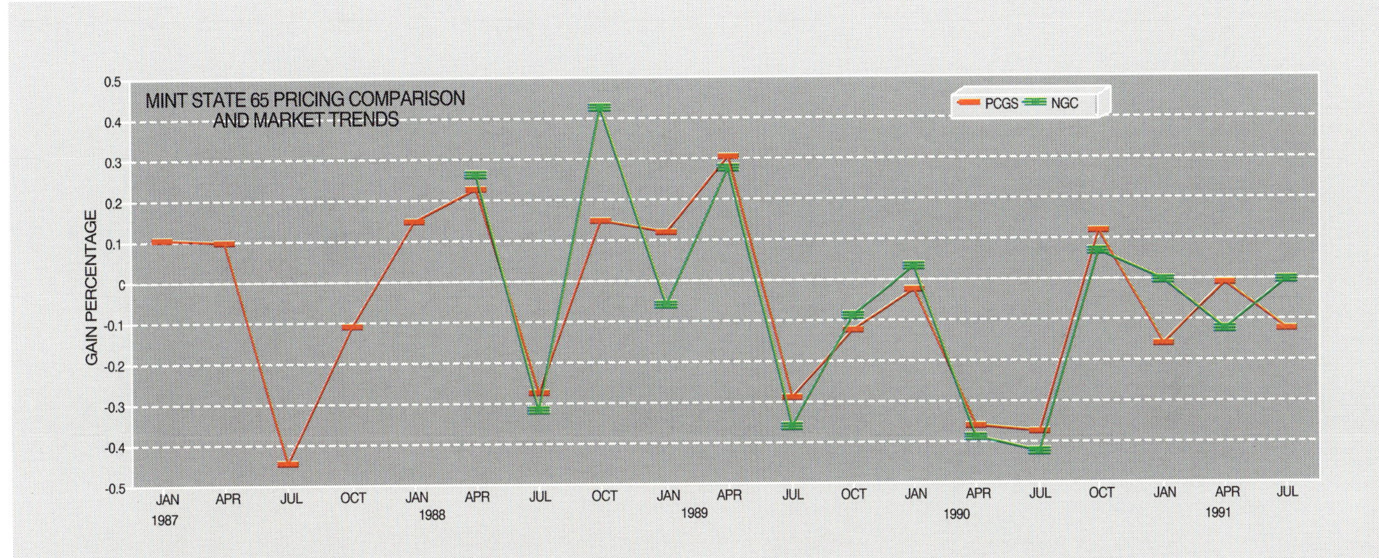
MINT STATE 65 PRICING COMPARISON
AND MARKET TRENDS
PCGS
NGC
GAIN PERCENTAGE
0.5
0.4
0.3
0.2
0.1
0
-0.1
-0.2
-0.3
-0.4
-0.5
JAN APR JUL OCT JAN APR JUL OCT JAN APR JUL OCT JAN APR JUL OCT JAN APR JUL
1987
1988
1989
1990
1991

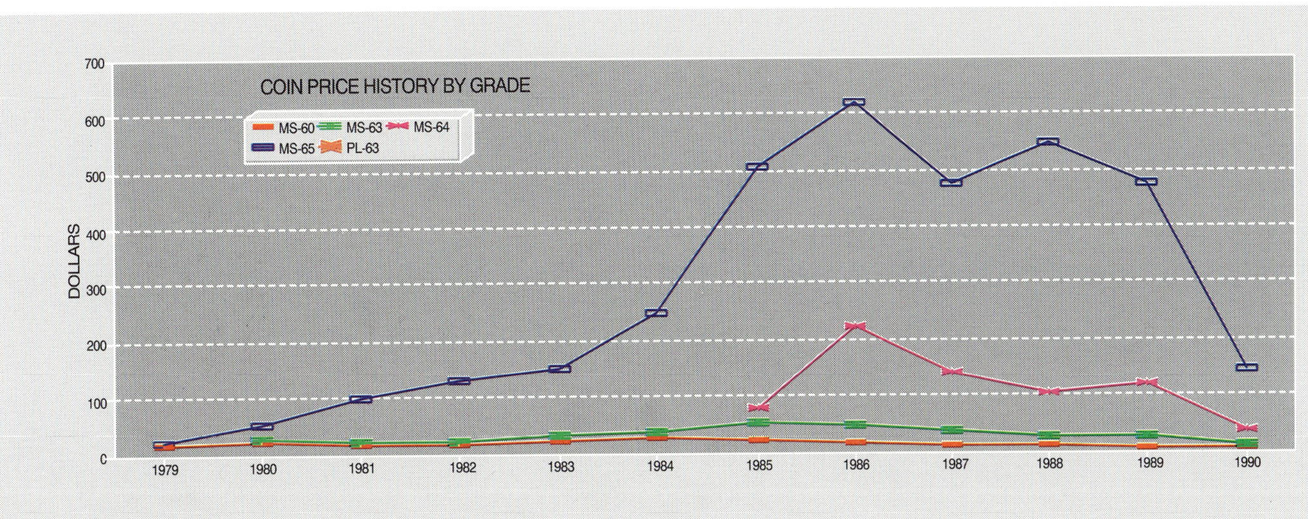
COIN PRICE HISTORY BY GRADE
MS-60
MS-63
MS-64
MS-65
PL-63
DOLLARS
700
600
500
400
300
200
100
0
1979 1980 1981 1982 1983 1984 1985 1986 1987 1988 1989 1990

1923-D

Mintage 6,811,000. Many sliders, many baggy uncs., few gems. Second best struck Denver Peace dollar; bettered only by 1926-D. Quantities of 1923-D Peace dollars have multiple obverse die cracks that appear as small hairlines running from the "Y" in LIBERTY to the bottom of Miss Liberty's neck. Sometimes, the die cracks can encircle the entire obverse. Bags of sliders and MS 60/63 are available. This date is very common as a slider.

Recommended in MS 65 up as a role model for what Peace dollars ought to look like. None certified and graded above MS 66 to date.

MINTAGE	PROOF	STRIKE	LUSTER	BAGMARKS
6,811,000	0	Average	Good	Moderate
REDFIELD	**CATEGORY**	**DIE VARIETIES**	**PIVOTAL GRADE**	**RARITY FACTOR**
No	Semi-key	1	MS 65	R-3

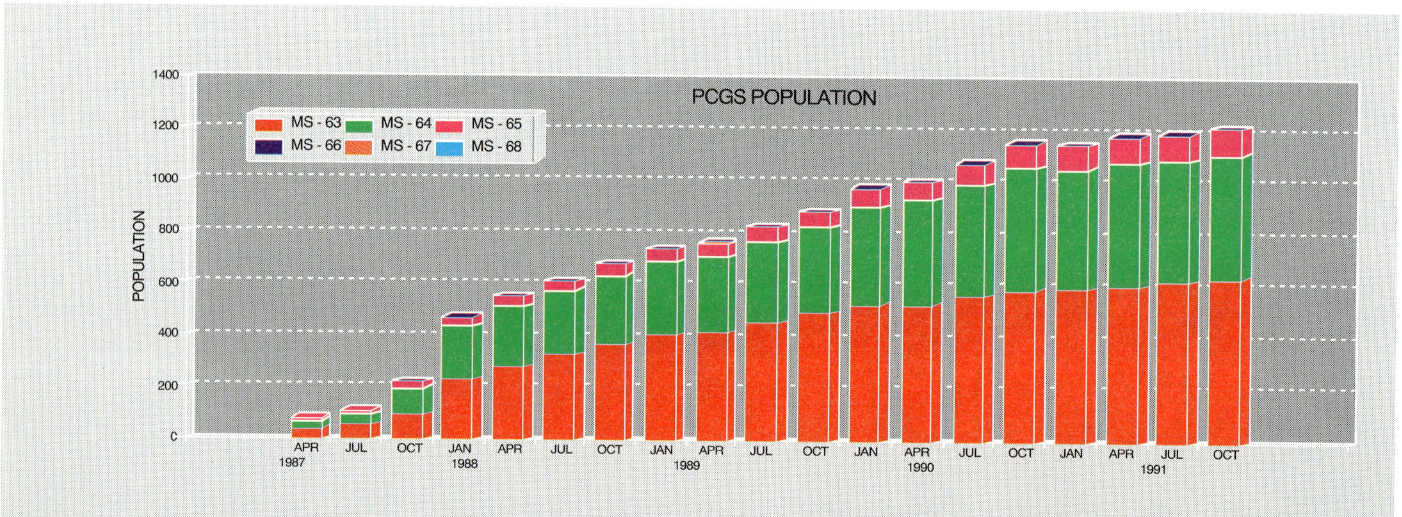

PCGS POPULATION

MS - 63 MS - 64 MS - 65
MS - 66 MS - 67 MS - 68

POPULATION

1400 1200 1000 800 600 400 200 0

APR 1987 JUL OCT JAN 1988 APR JUL OCT JAN 1989 APR JUL OCT JAN APR 1990 JUL OCT JAN APR JUL 1991 OCT

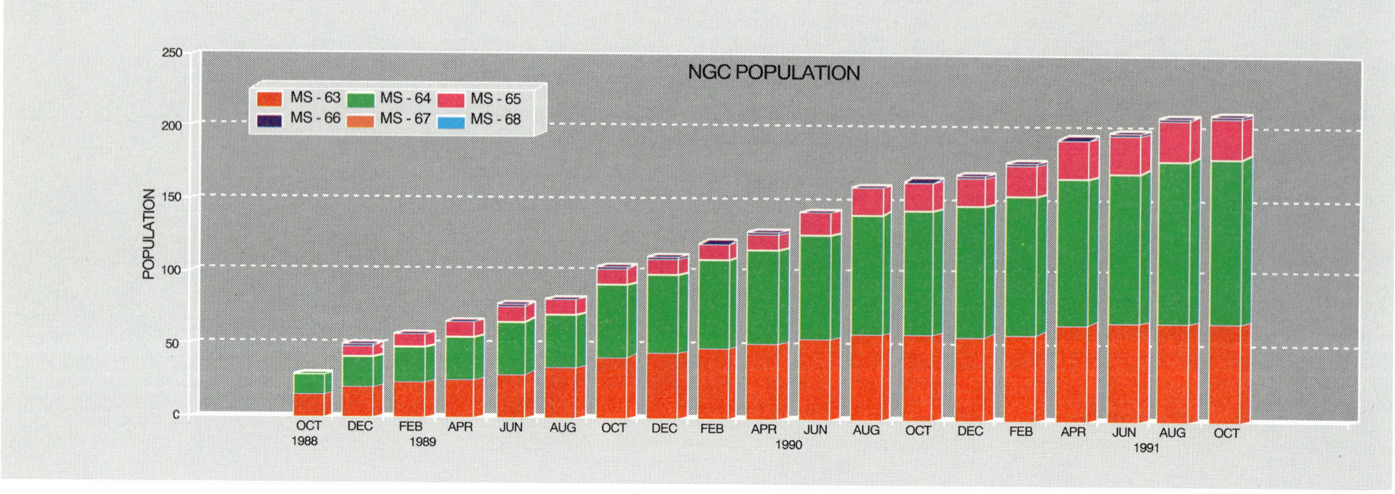

NGC POPULATION

MS - 63 MS - 64 MS - 65
MS - 66 MS - 67 MS - 68

POPULATION

250 200 150 100 50 0

OCT 1988 DEC FEB 1989 APR JUN AUG OCT DEC FEB APR 1990 JUN AUG OCT DEC FEB APR JUN 1991 AUG OCT

1923-D

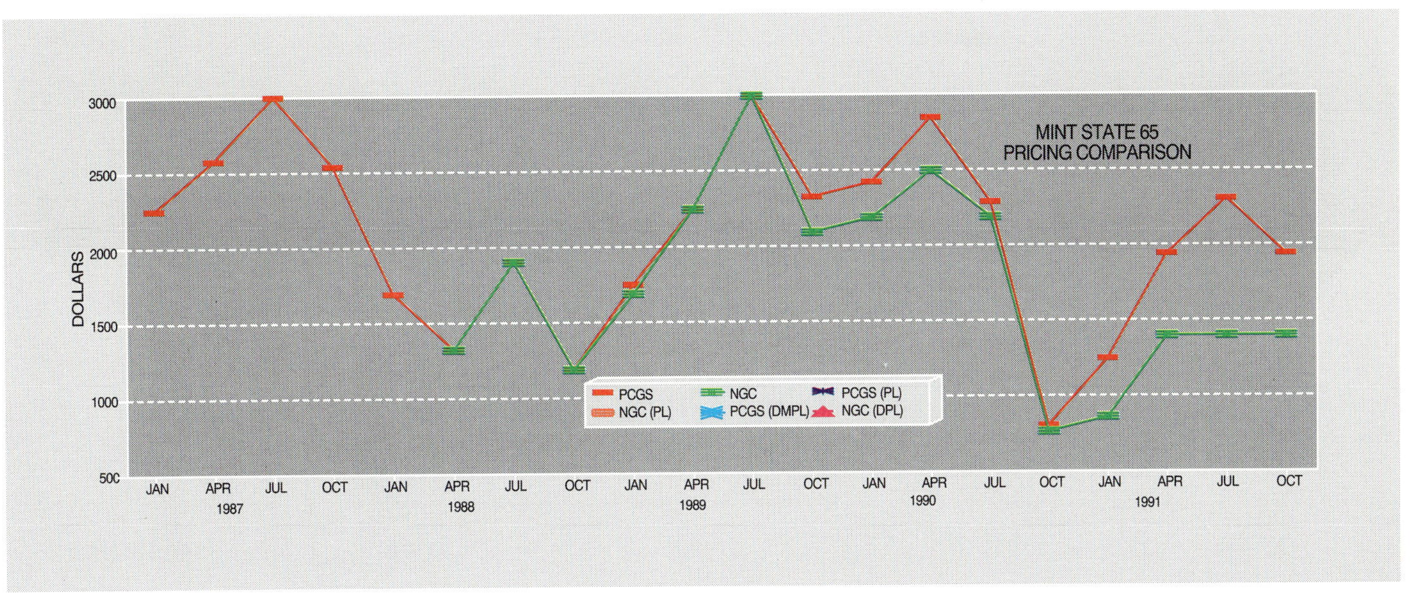

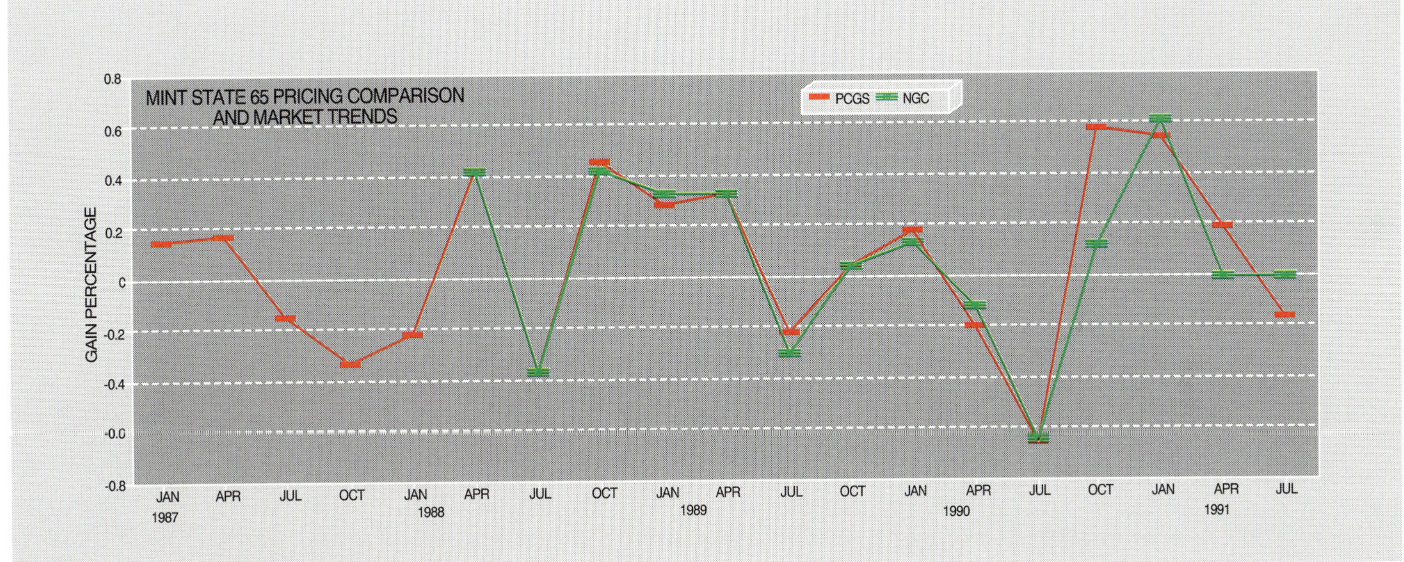

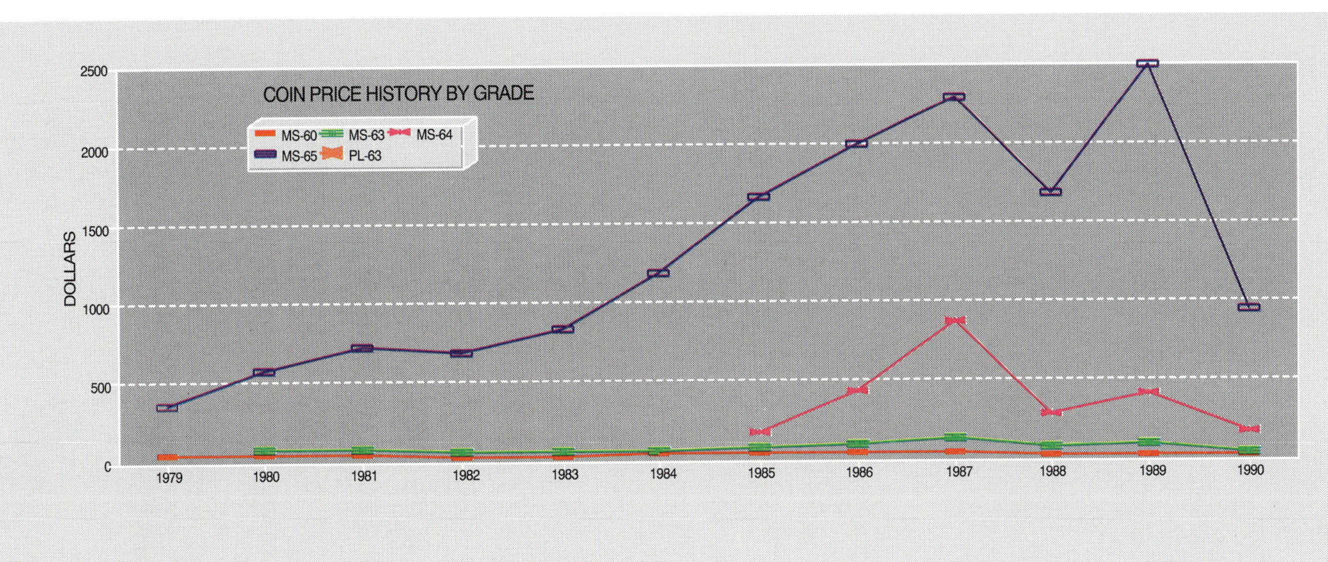

1923-S

Mintage 19,020,000. Terrible strike! Uncs. are the most poorly struck in the Peace design. This date is the worst strike of the entire Peace dollar series. Luster is often no better. Sliders are plentiful, gems few. Redfields' Uncs. are often very baggy.

Because of strike this date is exceptionally scarce in MS 65 and rare in all higher grades. Recommended in the highest Unc. grade you can find. You may have to settle for MS 64.

There are none graded in MS 66 by certification services. To date there is only one PCGS MS 67; this was successively owned by Steve Contursi, William E. Spears, and finally John W. Highfill. No higher grade known to exist.

MINTAGE	PROOF	STRIKE	LUSTER	BAGMARKS
19,020,000	0	Very Weak	Good	Moderate
REDFIELD	**CATEGORY**	**DIE VARIETIES**	**PIVOTAL GRADE**	**RARITY FACTOR**
Yes	Semi-key	2	MS 65	R-2

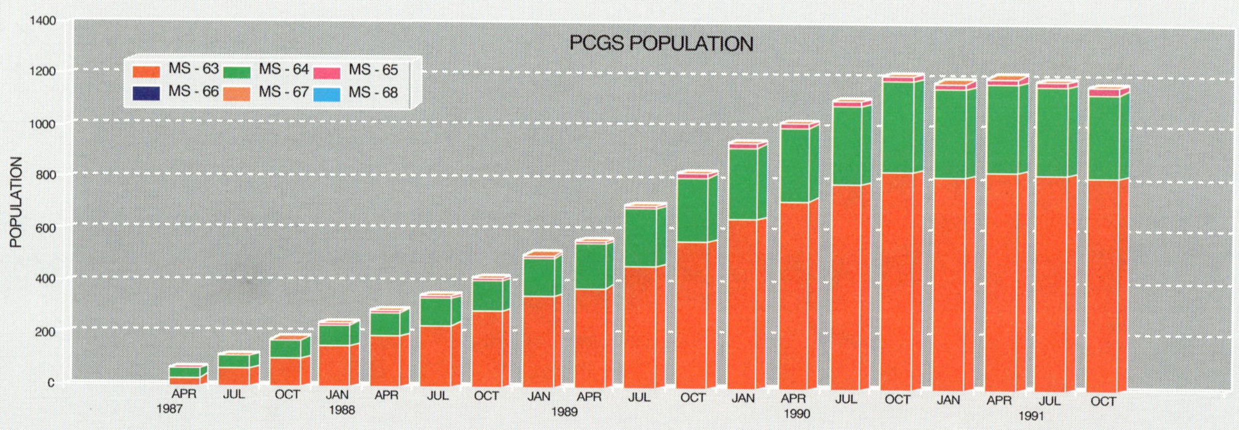

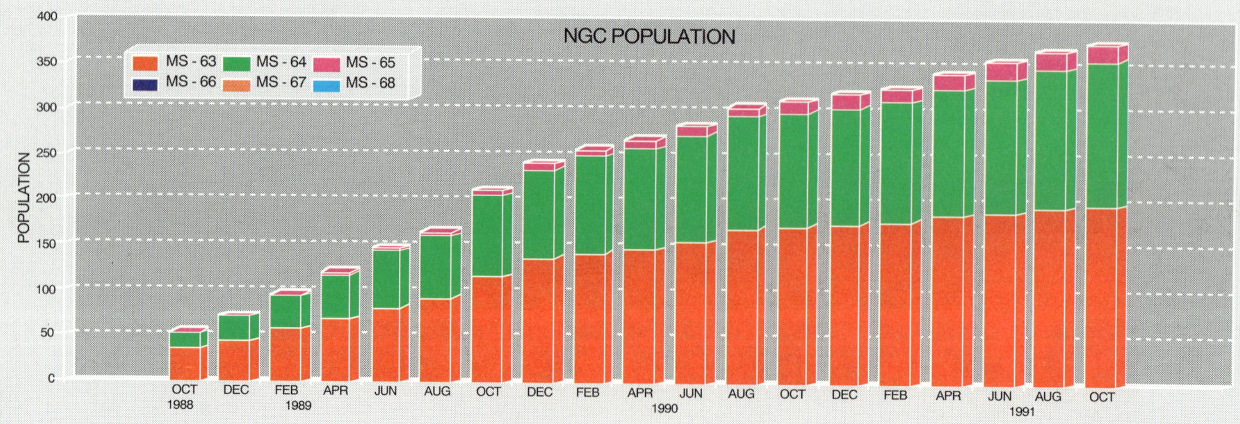

PCGS POPULATION

MS - 63 MS - 64 MS - 65
MS - 66 MS - 67 MS - 68

POPULATION

1400 1200 1000 800 600 400 200 0

APR 1987 JUL OCT JAN 1988 APR JUL OCT JAN 1989 APR JUL OCT JAN APR 1990 JUL OCT JAN APR JUL 1991 OCT

NGC POPULATION

MS - 63 MS - 64 MS - 65
MS - 66 MS - 67 MS - 68

POPULATION

400 350 300 250 200 150 100 50 0

OCT 1988 DEC FEB 1989 APR JUN AUG OCT DEC FEB APR 1990 JUN AUG OCT DEC FEB APR JUN 1991 AUG OCT

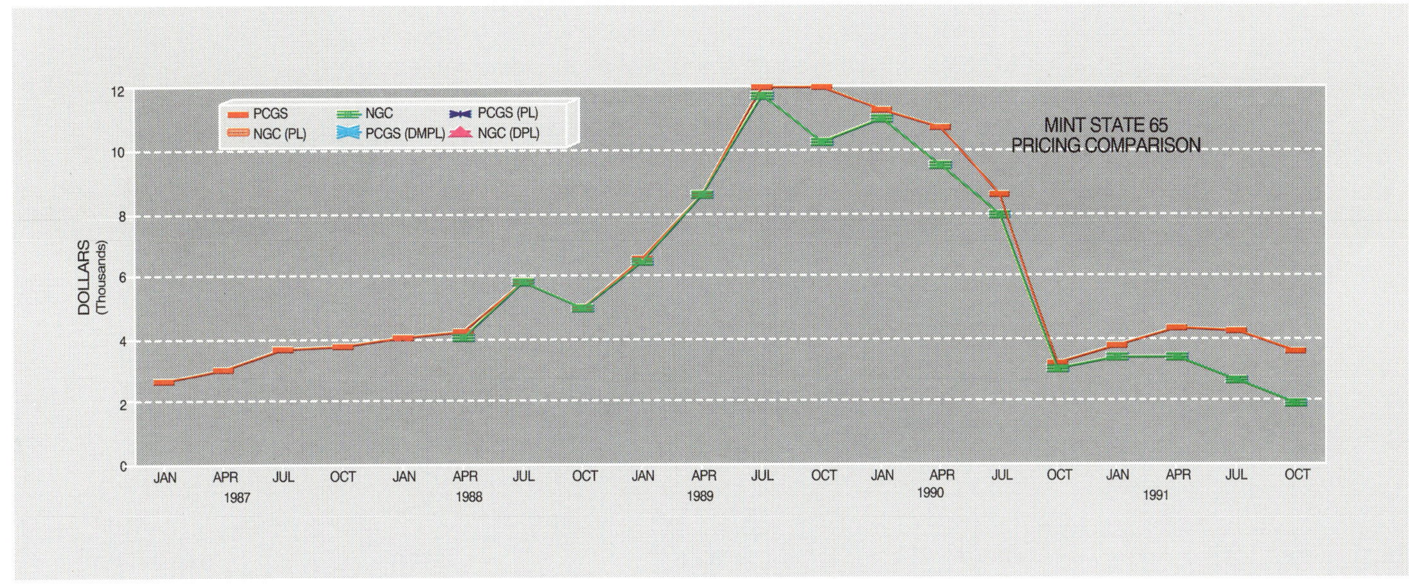
PCGS
NGC
PCGS (PL)
NGC (PL)
PCGS (DMPL)
NGC (DPL)
MINT STATE 65
PRICING COMPARISON
DOLLARS (Thousands)
12
10
8
6
4
2
C
JAN APR JUL OCT JAN APR JUL OCT JAN APR JUL OCT JAN APR JUL OCT JAN APR JUL OCT
1987
1988
1989
1990
1991

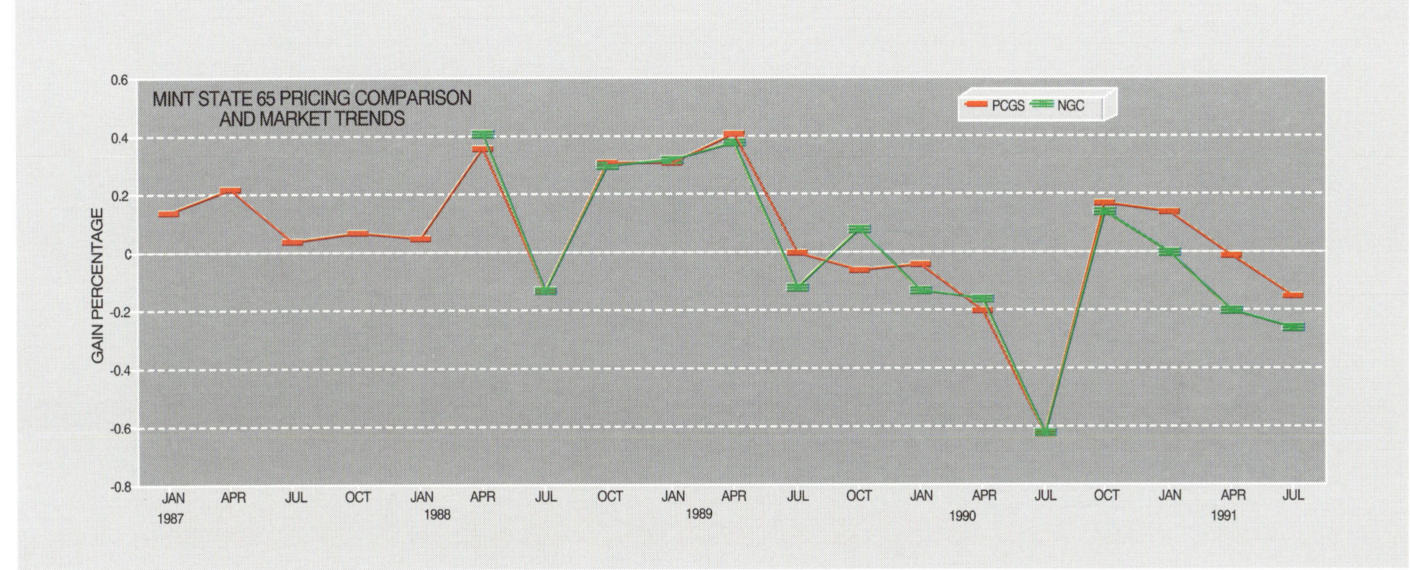
MINT STATE 65 PRICING COMPARISON
AND MARKET TRENDS
PCGS
NGC
GAIN PERCENTAGE
0.6
0.4
0.2
C
-0.2
-0.4
-0.6
-0.8
JAN APR JUL OCT JAN APR JUL OCT JAN APR JUL OCT JAN APR JUL OCT JAN APR JUL
1987
1988
1989
1990
1991

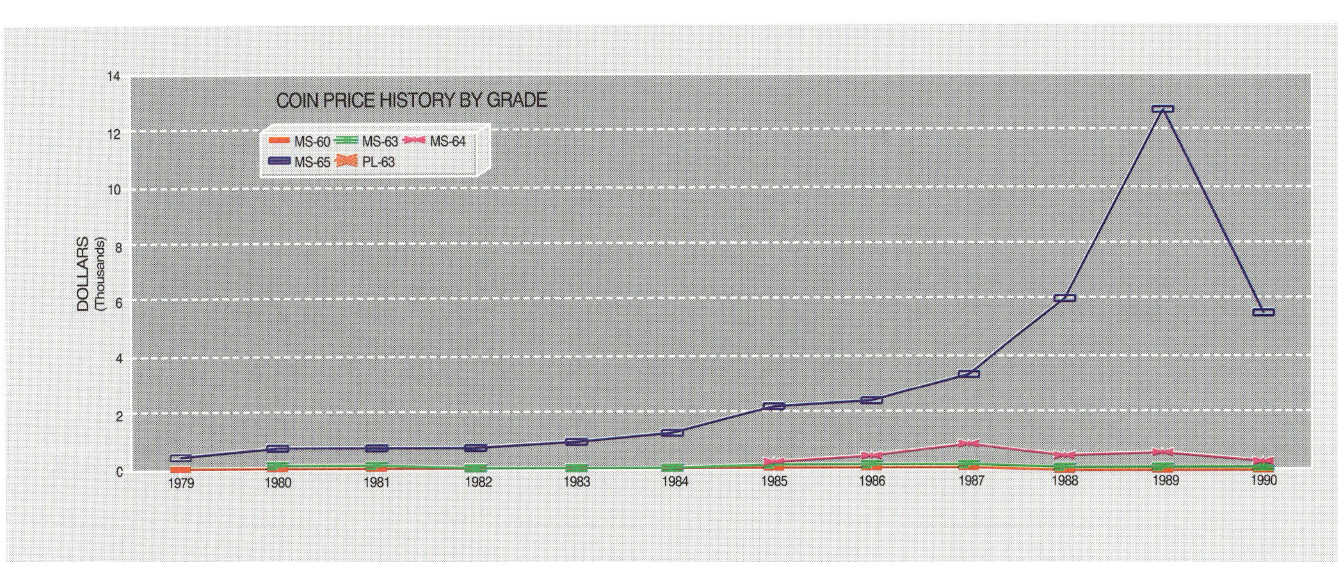
COIN PRICE HISTORY BY GRADE
MS-60
MS-63
MS-64
MS-65
PL-63
DOLLARS (Thousands)
14
12
10
8
6
4
2
C
1979
1980
1981
1982
1983
1984
1985
1986
1987
1988
1989
1990

1924-P

Mintage 11,811,000. Plentiful in all grades, sliders to gems, including some of the best struck coins of the design. Luster is brilliant, silky. Many have a golden hue toning. "Orange-peel" can be a problem.

Many bags have been assembled. Among the few original bags known are the twelve handled by John Love (Cut Bank, MT) in the late 1960's, and the two this author (Highfill) handled at the June 1980 Long Beach show. Beware. "Sliders" are everywhere! Original BU bags of MS 60/63 exist. The 1924-P is common but still 6 to 8 times scarcer than the 1923-P.

Recommended in MS 66 as another role model.

No MS 67 examples have been certified and graded to date.

MINTAGE	PROOF	STRIKE	LUSTER	BAGMARKS
11,811,000	0	Sharp & Bold	Good	Moderate
REDFIELD	**CATEGORY**	**DIE VARIETIES**	**PIVOTAL GRADE**	**RARITY FACTOR**
No	Common	5	MS 65	R-5

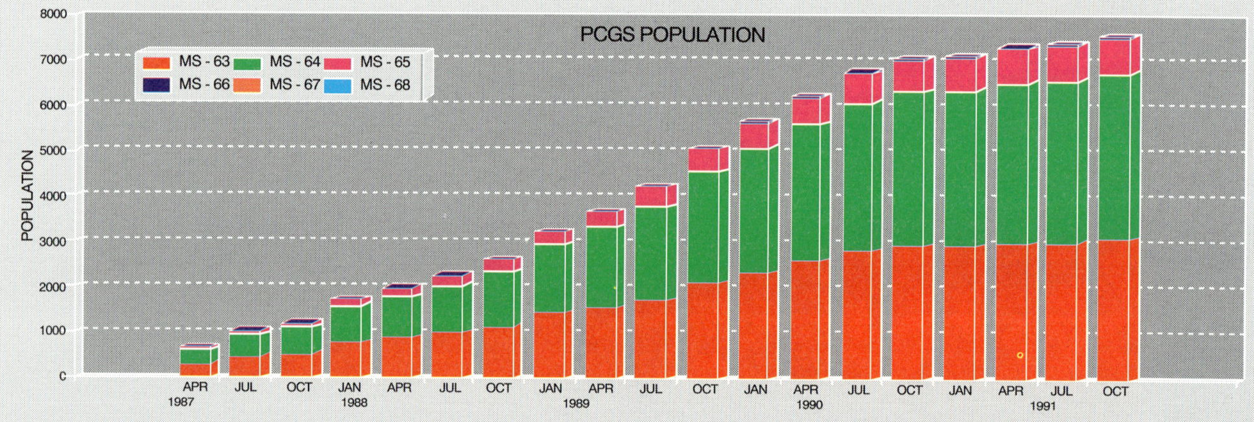

PCGS POPULATION

MS - 63 MS - 64 MS - 65
MS - 66 MS - 67 MS - 68

POPULATION

8000 7000 6000 5000 4000 3000 2000 1000 0

APR 1987 JUL OCT JAN 1988 APR JUL OCT JAN 1989 APR JUL OCT JAN APR 1990 JUL OCT JAN APR 1991 JUL OCT

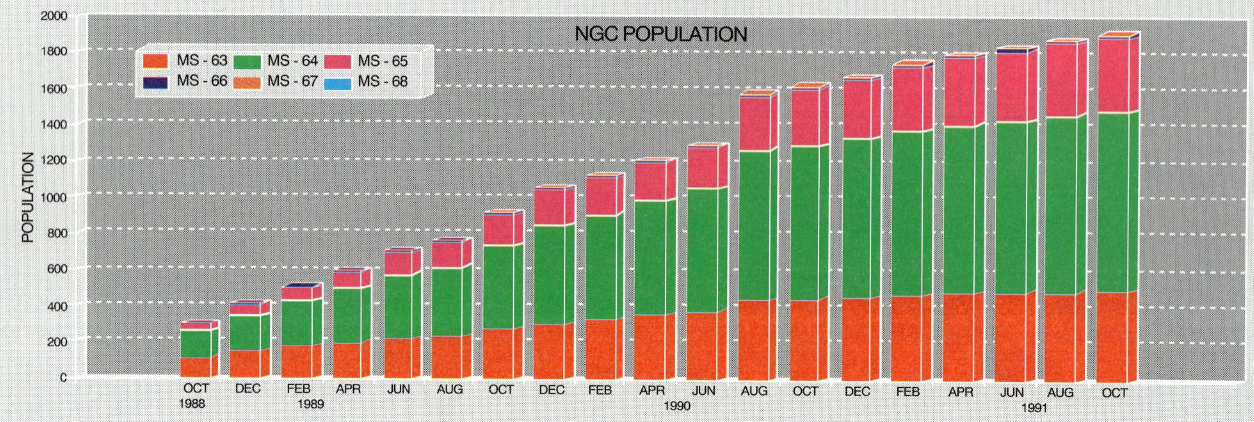

NGC POPULATION

MS - 63 MS - 64 MS - 65
MS - 66 MS - 67 MS - 68

POPULATION

2000 1800 1600 1400 1200 1000 800 600 400 200 0

OCT 1988 DEC FEB 1989 APR JUN AUG OCT DEC FEB APR 1990 JUN AUG OCT DEC FEB APR JUN 1991 AUG OCT

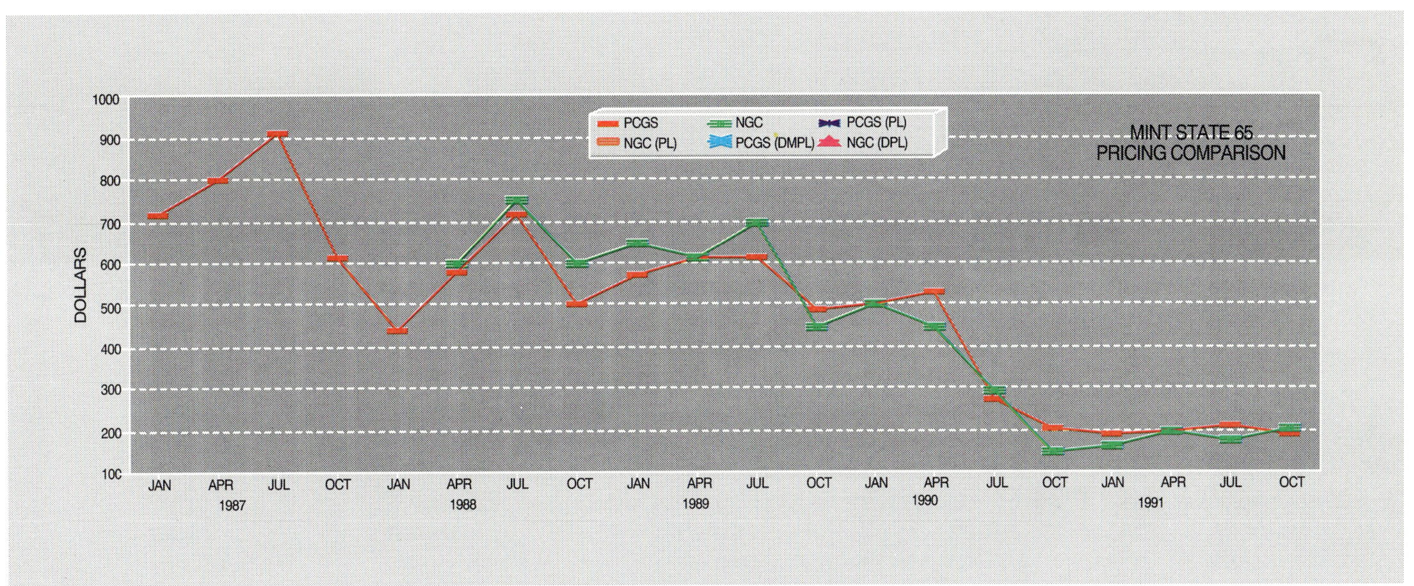
MINT STATE 65
PRICING COMPARISON
PCGS
NGC
PCGS (PL)
NGC (PL)
PCGS (DMPL)
NGC (DPL)
DOLLARS
1000
900
800
700
600
500
400
300
200
100
JAN
APR
JUL
OCT
1987
1988
1989
1990
1991

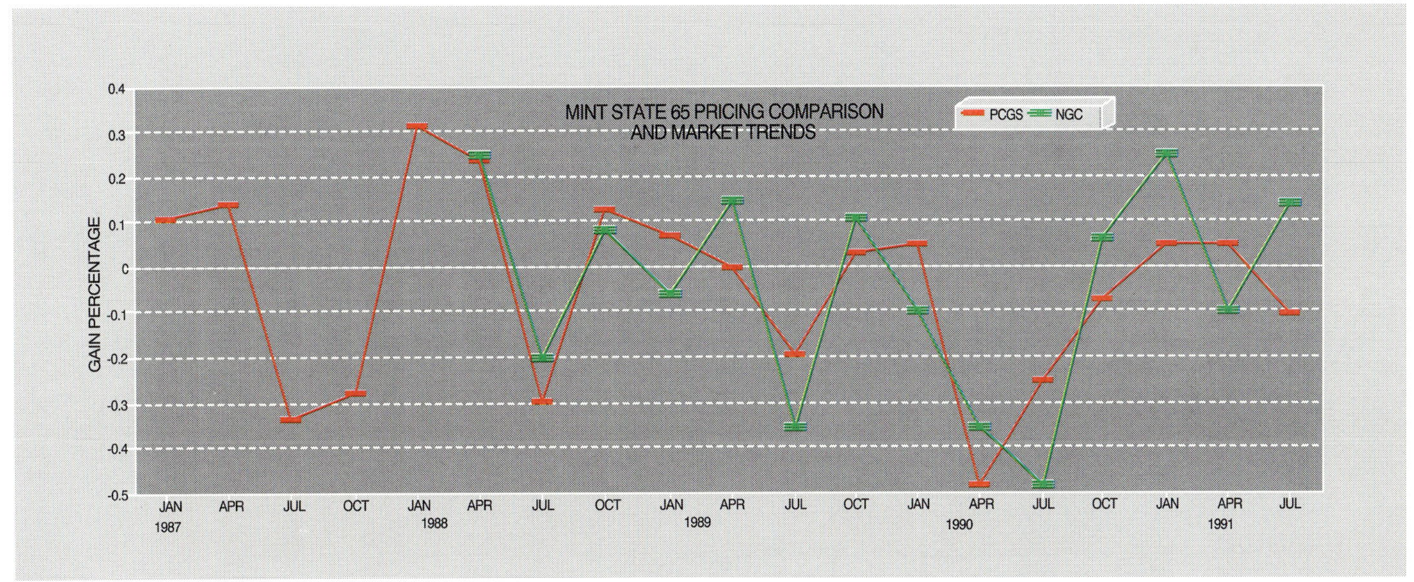
MINT STATE 65 PRICING COMPARISON
AND MARKET TRENDS
PCGS
NGC
GAIN PERCENTAGE
0.4
0.3
0.2
0.1
0
-0.1
-0.2
-0.3
-0.4
-0.5
JAN
APR
JUL
OCT
1987
1988
1989
1990
1991

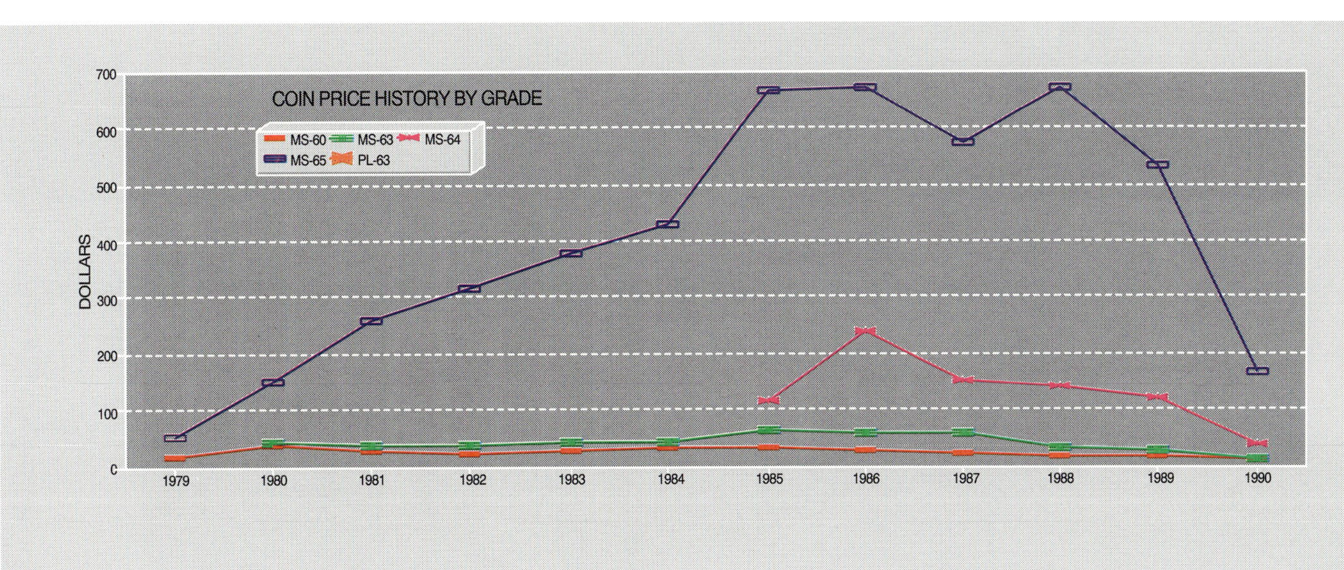
COIN PRICE HISTORY BY GRADE
MS-60
MS-63
MS-64
MS-65
PL-63
DOLLARS
700
600
500
400
300
200
100
0
1979
1980
1981
1982
1983
1984
1985
1986
1987
1988
1989
1990

1924-S

Mintage 1,728,000. Rims often weak. Strike weak, luster adequate. Beware of sliders being offered as BU. Many sliders, many baggy Uncs, ex Redfield (not as many as earlier S mints), few gems. The 1924-S is difficult to locate in circulated grades below AU 58. Coins with a matte-like finish can also be encountered.

Recommended in MS 64 up. MS 60/63 rolls are not readily available. None certified and graded above MS 65. A "keeper" date for collectors of MS 65 Peace dollars.

MINTAGE	PROOF	STRIKE	LUSTER	BAGMARKS
1,728,000	0	Soft & Weak	Good	Moderate To Heavy
REDFIELD	**CATEGORY**	**DIE VARIETIES**	**PIVOTAL GRADE**	**RARITY FACTOR**
Yes	Key	1	MS 65	R-1

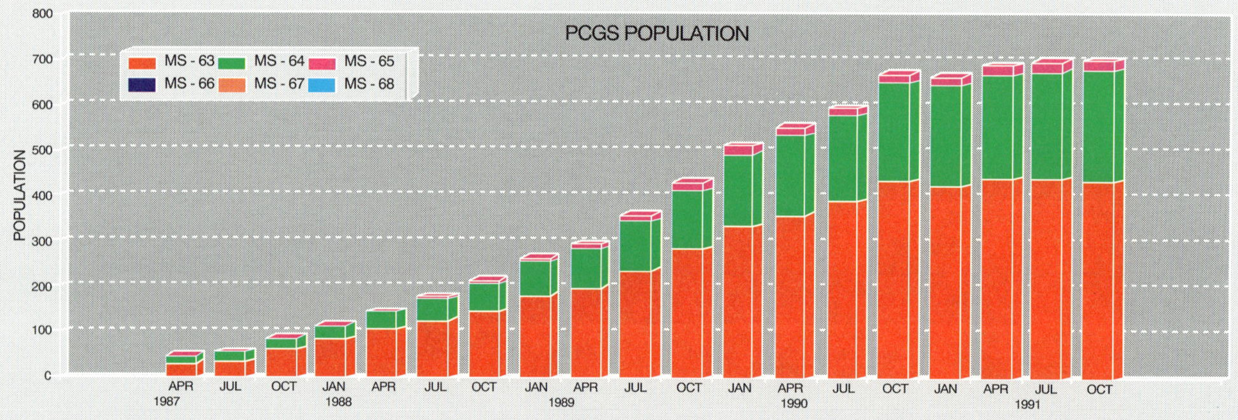

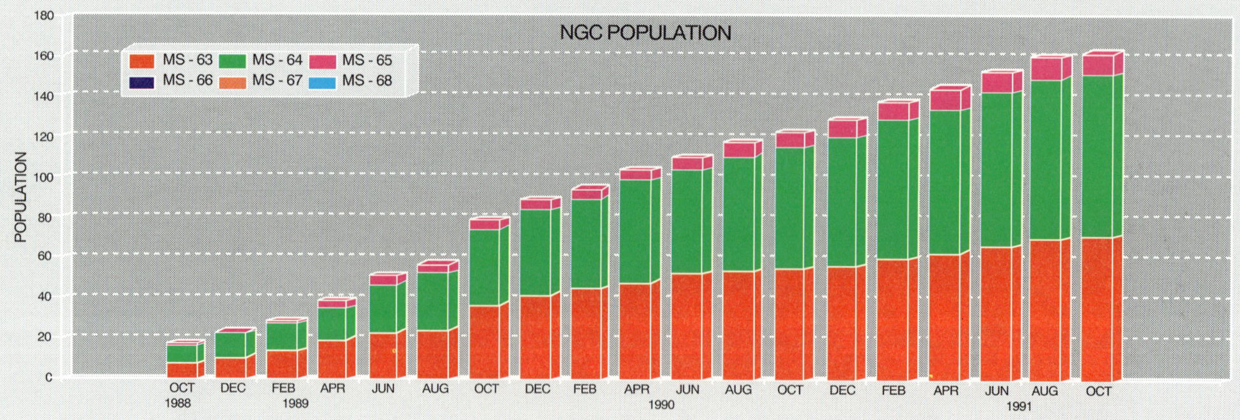

PCGS POPULATION

MS - 63 MS - 64 MS - 65 MS - 66 MS - 67 MS - 68

POPULATION

800 700 600 500 400 300 200 100 C

APR 1987 JUL OCT JAN 1988 APR JUL OCT JAN 1989 APR JUL OCT JAN 1990 APR JUL OCT JAN 1991 APR JUL OCT

NGC POPULATION

MS - 63 MS - 64 MS - 65 MS - 66 MS - 67 MS - 68

POPULATION

180 160 140 120 100 80 60 40 20 C

OCT 1988 DEC FEB 1989 APR JUN AUG OCT DEC FEB APR 1990 JUN AUG OCT DEC FEB APR JUN 1991 AUG OCT

1924-S

MINT STATE 65
PRICING COMPARISON
DOLLARS
(Thousands)
PCGS
NGC
PCGS (PL)
NGC (PL)
PCGS (DMPL)
NGC (DPL)
JAN APR JUL OCT JAN APR JUL OCT JAN APR JUL OCT JAN APR JUL OCT JAN APR JUL OCT
1987
1988
1989
1990
1991

MINT STATE 65 PRICING COMPARISON
AND MARKET TRENDS
GAIN PERCENTAGE
PCGS
NGC
JAN APR JUL OCT JAN APR JUL OCT JAN APR JUL OCT JAN APR JUL OCT JAN APR JUL
1987
1988
1989
1990
1991

COIN PRICE HISTORY BY GRADE
MS-60
MS-63
MS-64
MS-65
PL-63
DOLLARS
(Thousands)
1979 1980 1981 1982 1983 1984 1985 1986 1987 1988 1989 1990

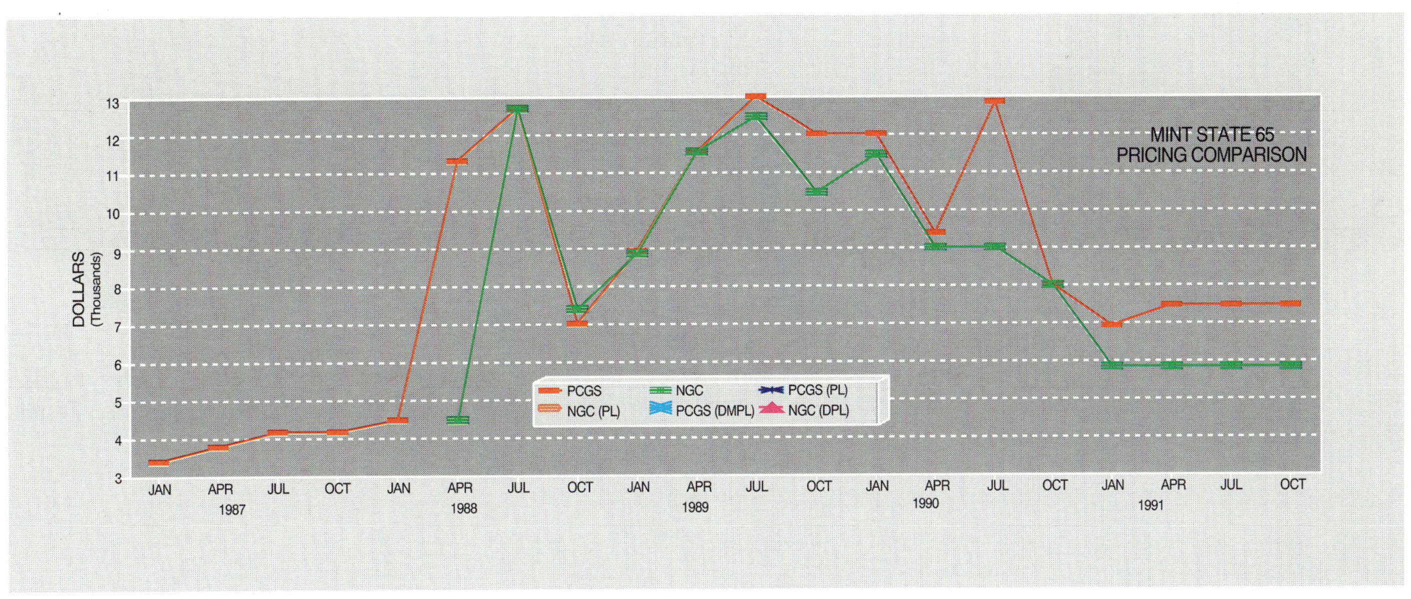

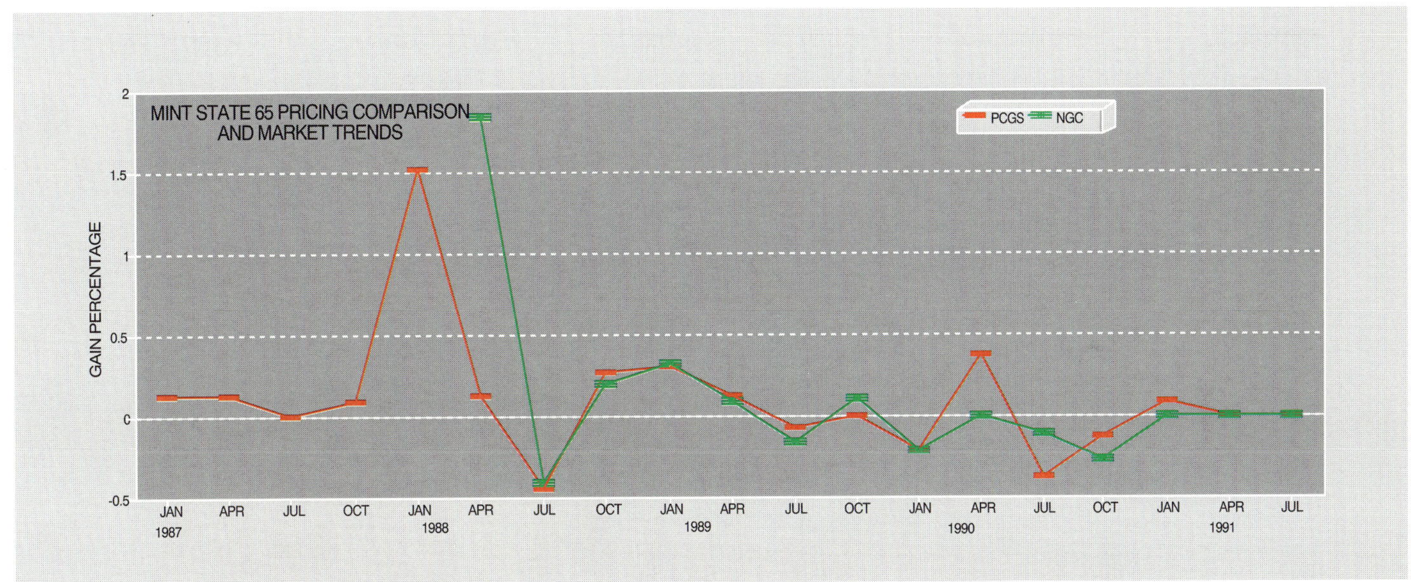

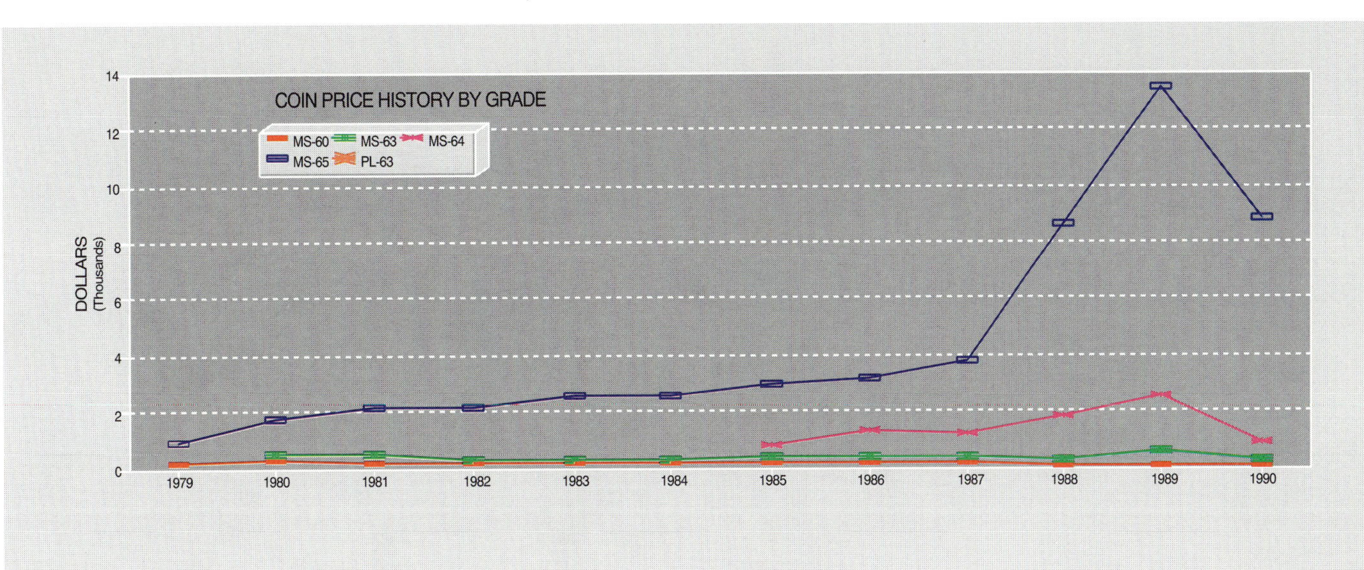

1925-P

Mintage 10,198,000. Good strike! Good luster! Many baggy Uncs. from Treasury releases, 1945. Often boldly struck with excellent luster. Sometimes satiny, even semi-PL.

The first original bag of peace dollars this author (Highfill) bought was from coin dealer and good personal friend, the late Ron Hyre, R. & M. Coins, Arkon, Ohio. He was one of the premier BU dollar roll dealers of all time.

Recommended in MS 65 up as a thing of beauty. Certified MS 64 rolls should be considered.

Both assembled and original bags are available, mostly MS 60/63. This Author (Highfill) handled several original bags in the early 1980's in which virtually every coin had a beautiful light gold tone. Toned Peace dollars are usually one gold tone. Very few other colors.

The only PCGS MS 67 so far graded sold a year or so back for well into five figures. There are currently nine Peace dollars graded MS 67 by PCGS and only two by NGC. None higher.

MINTAGE	PROOF	STRIKE	LUSTER	BAGMARKS
10,198,000	0	Sharp & Bold	Excellent	Light
REDFIELD	**CATEGORY**	**DIE VARIETIES**	**PIVOTAL GRADE**	**RARITY FACTOR**
No	Common	1	MS 65	R-5

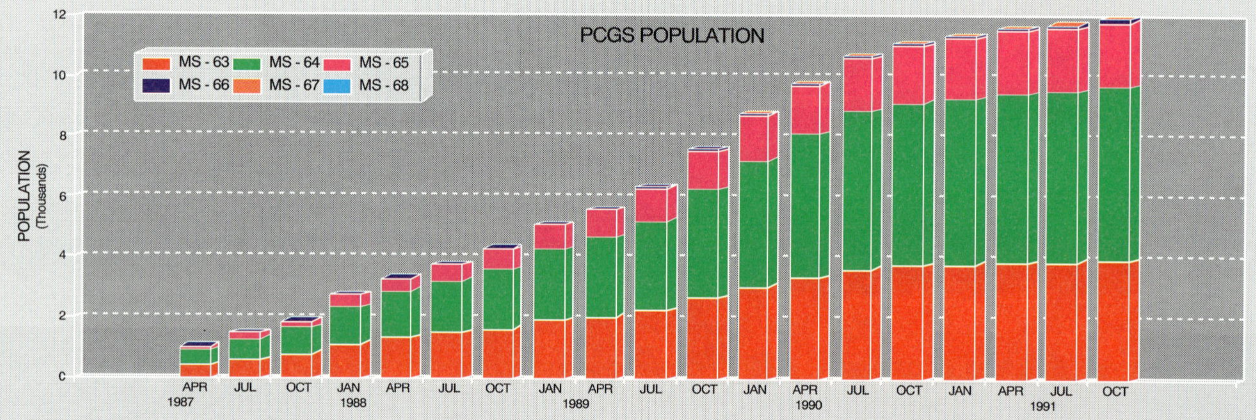

PCGS POPULATION

MS - 63 MS - 64 MS - 65
MS - 66 MS - 67 MS - 68

POPULATION (Thousands)

12 10 8 6 4 2 0

APR 1987 JUL OCT JAN 1988 APR JUL OCT JAN 1989 APR JUL OCT JAN APR 1990 JUL OCT JAN APR JUL 1991 OCT

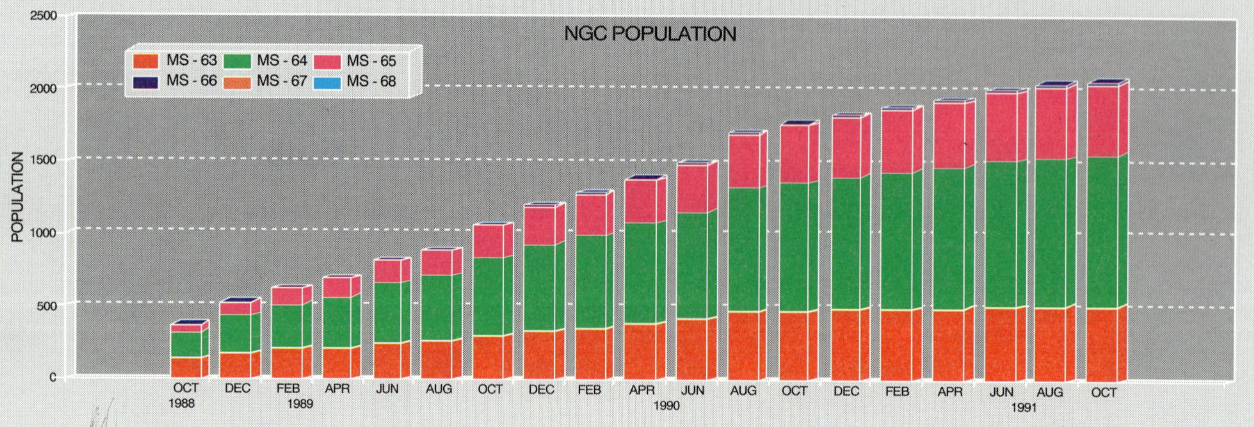

NGC POPULATION

MS - 63 MS - 64 MS - 65
MS - 66 MS - 67 MS - 68

POPULATION

2500 2000 1500 1000 500 0

OCT 1988 DEC FEB 1989 APR JUN AUG OCT DEC FEB APR JUN 1990 AUG OCT DEC FEB APR JUN 1991 AUG OCT

1925-P

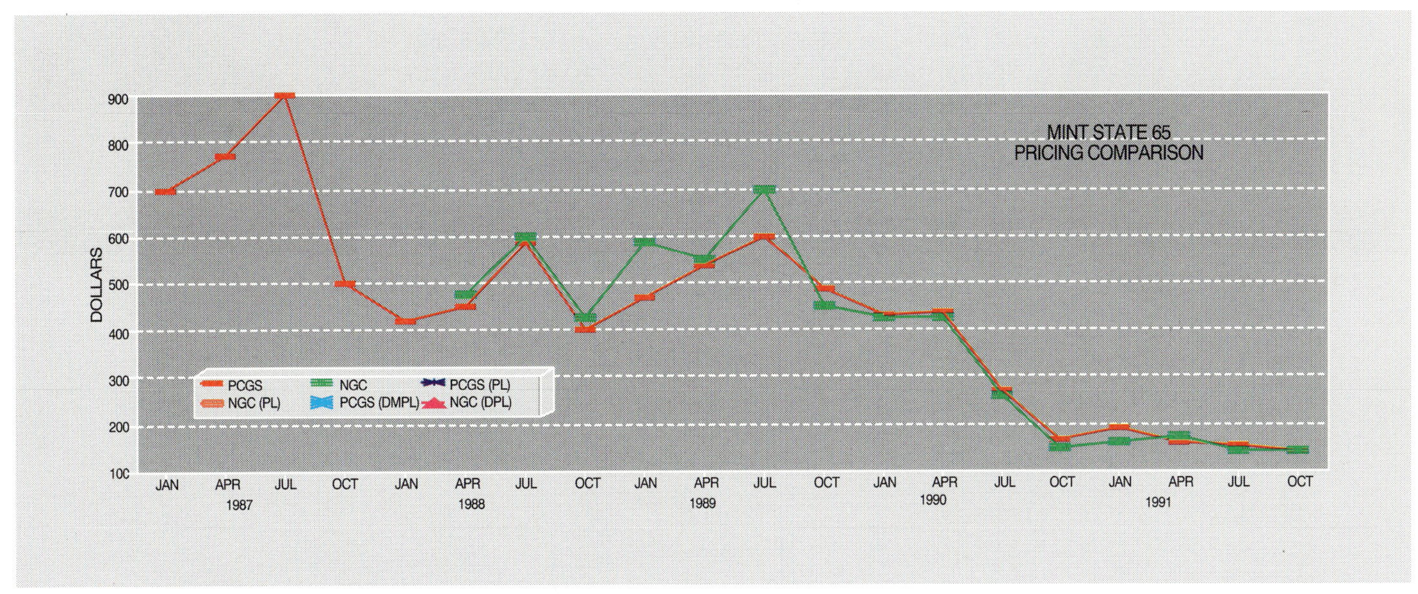

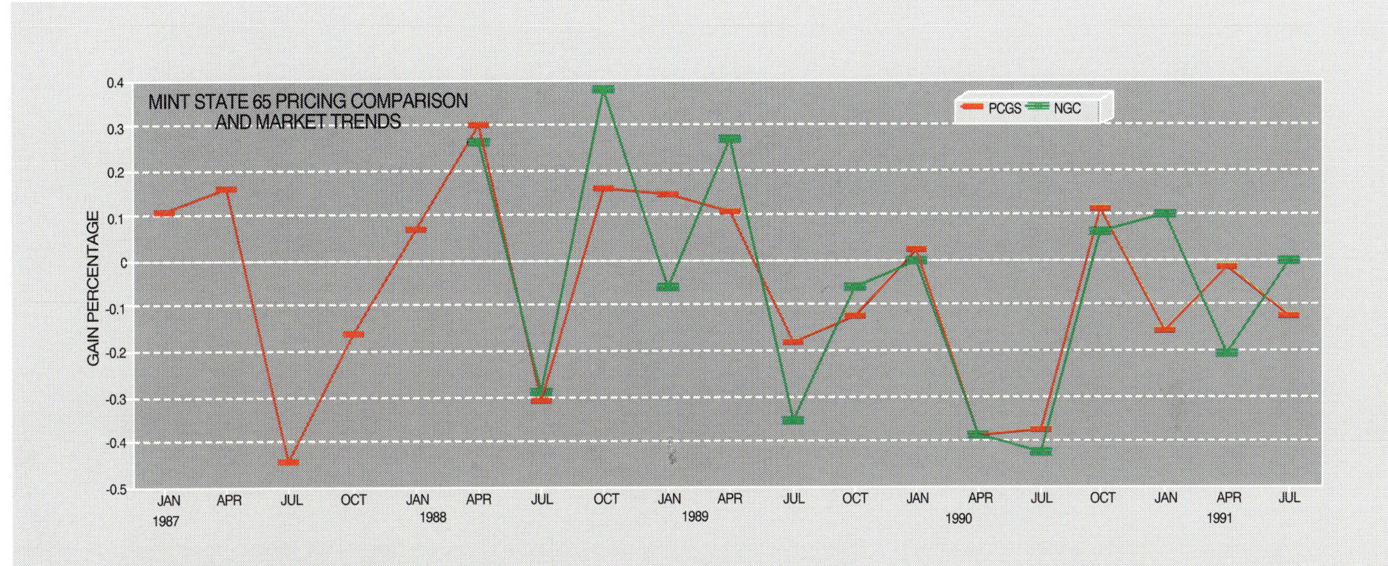

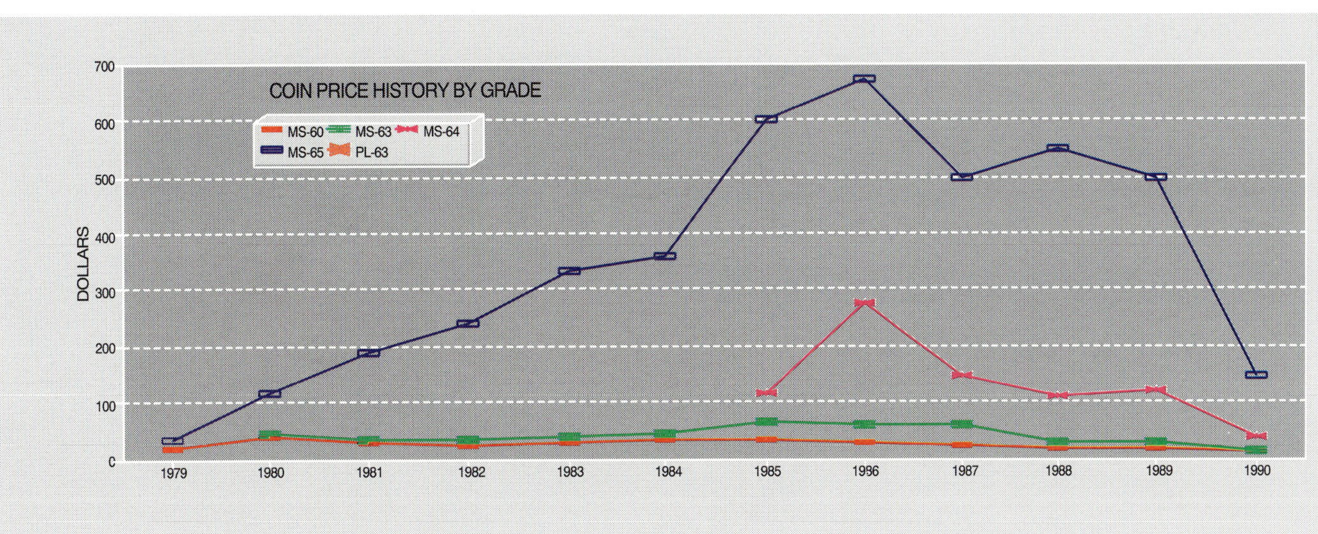

1925-S

Mintage 1,610,000. Rims often weak; deplorable striking quality, simular to the 1923-S, moderate to heavy bagmarks, average luster. No Treasury bags. Redfield reportedly had about 5 bags of weak Uncs., one of them sold in 1974. Even the few gems are weak. Pieces with matte surfaces should be avoided. The 1925-S is a key date.

Recommended in MS 64 up. MS 63 rolls should also be considered (if available). None graded above MS 65 by PCGS or NGC. This is definitely a keeper date in MS 65.

MINTAGE	PROOF	STRIKE	LUSTER	BAGMARKS
1,610,000	0	Soft & Weak	Average	Moderate To Heavy
REDFIELD	**CATEGORY**	**DIE VARIETIES**	**PIVOTAL GRADE**	**RARITY FACTOR**
Yes	Key	1	MS 65	R-1

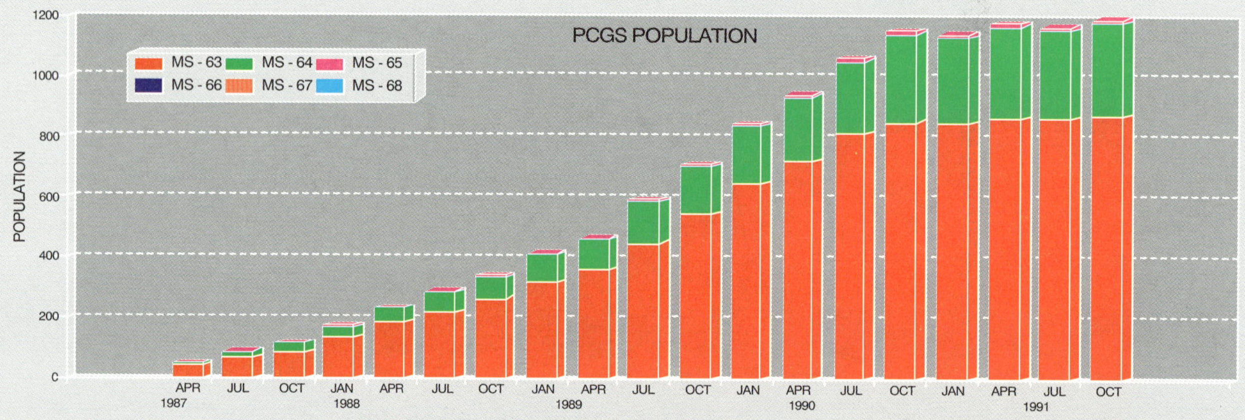

PCGS POPULATION

MS - 63 MS - 64 MS - 65
MS - 66 MS - 67 MS - 68

POPULATION

1200 1000 800 600 400 200 0

APR 1987 JUL OCT JAN 1988 APR JUL OCT JAN 1989 APR JUL OCT JAN APR 1990 JUL OCT JAN APR JUL 1991 OCT

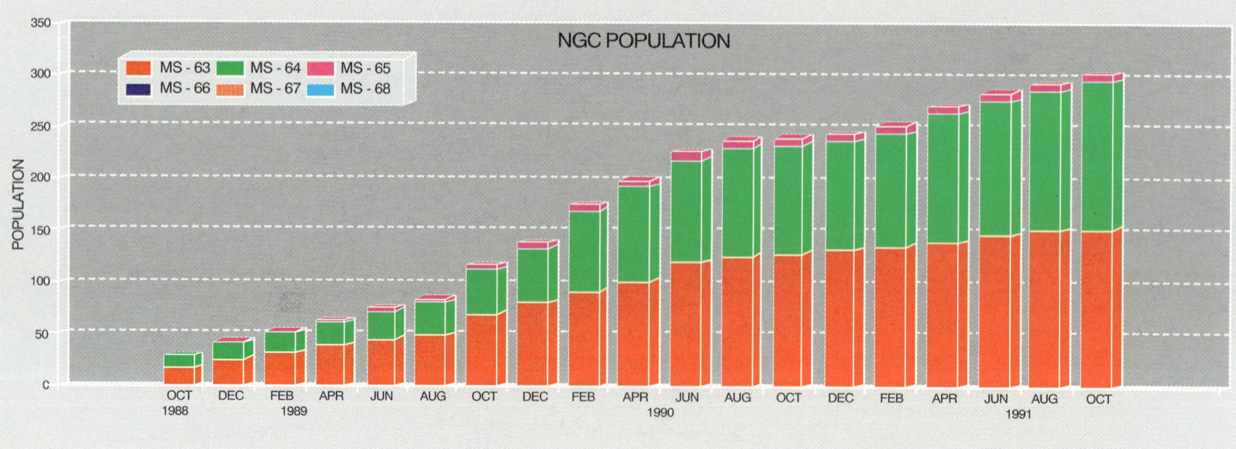

NGC POPULATION

MS - 63 MS - 64 MS - 65
MS - 66 MS - 67 MS - 68

POPULATION

350 300 250 200 150 100 50 0

OCT 1988 DEC FEB 1989 APR JUN AUG OCT DEC FEB APR 1990 JUN AUG OCT DEC FEB APR JUN 1991 AUG OCT

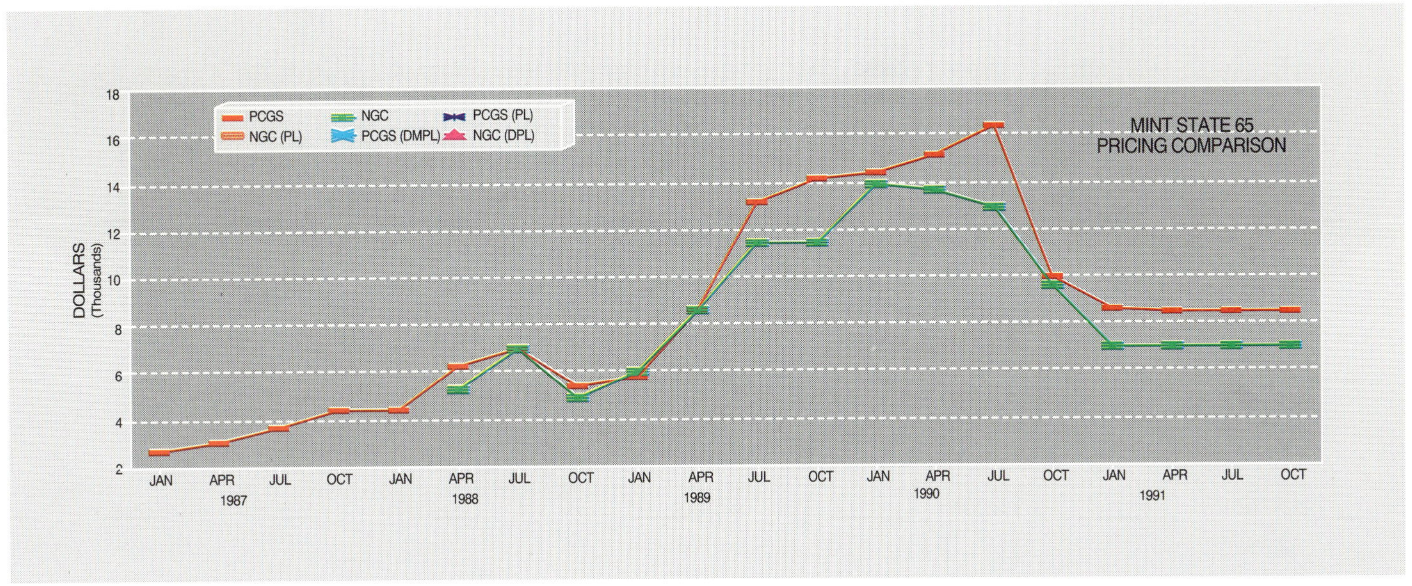
PCGS
NGC (PL)
NGC
PCGS (DMPL)
PCGS (PL)
NGC (DPL)
MINT STATE 65
PRICING COMPARISON
DOLLARS (Thousands)
18
16
14
12
10
8
6
4
2
JAN APR JUL OCT JAN APR JUL OCT JAN APR JUL OCT JAN APR JUL OCT JAN APR JUL OCT
1987
1988
1989
1990
1991

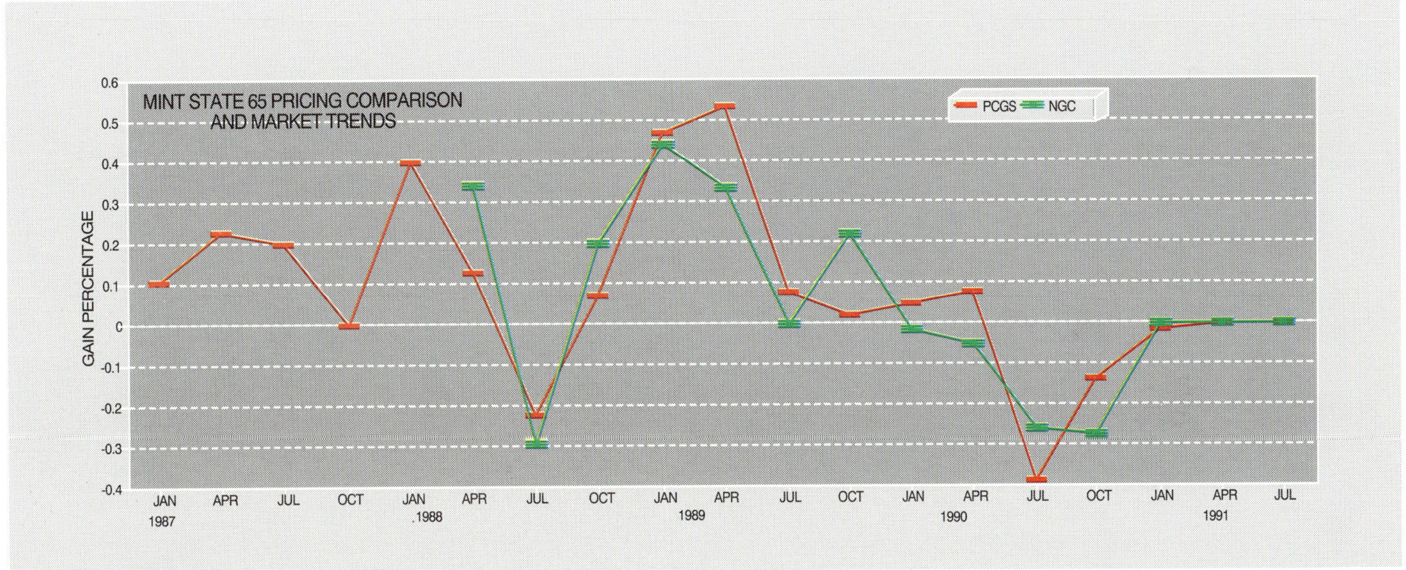
MINT STATE 65 PRICING COMPARISON
AND MARKET TRENDS
PCGS
NGC
GAIN PERCENTAGE
0.6
0.5
0.4
0.3
0.2
0.1
0
-0.1
-0.2
-0.3
-0.4
JAN APR JUL OCT JAN APR JUL OCT JAN APR JUL OCT JAN APR JUL OCT JAN APR JUL
1987
1988
1989
1990
1991

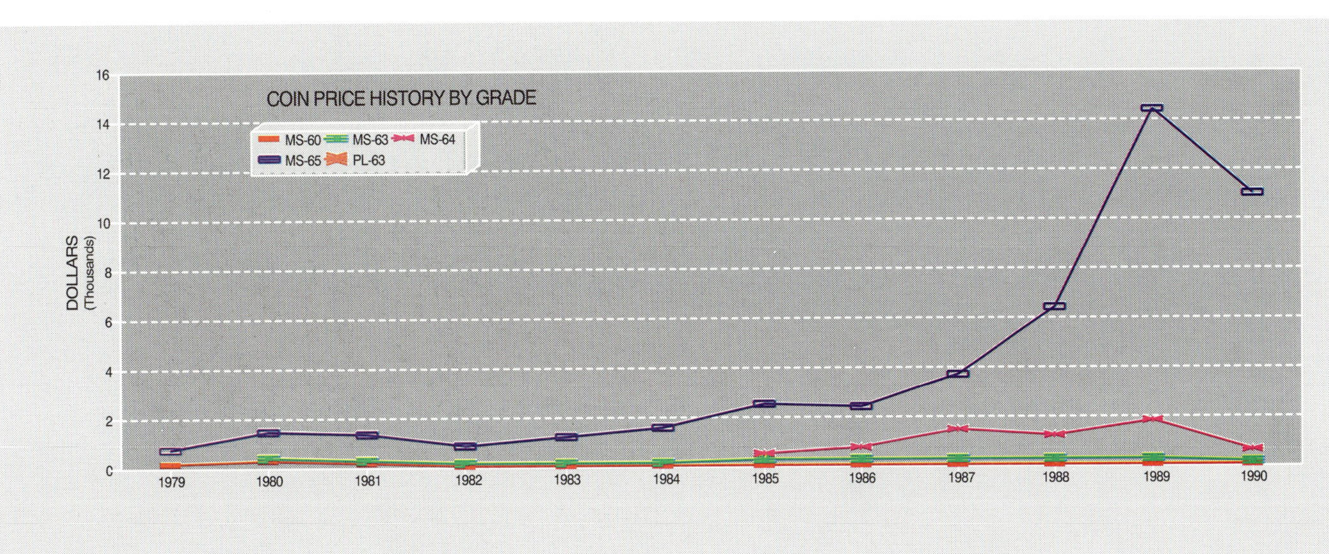
COIN PRICE HISTORY BY GRADE
MS-60
MS-63
MS-64
MS-65
PL-63
DOLLARS (Thousands)
16
14
12
10
8
6
4
2
0
1979 1980 1981 1982 1983 1984 1985 1986 1987 1988 1989 1990

1926-P

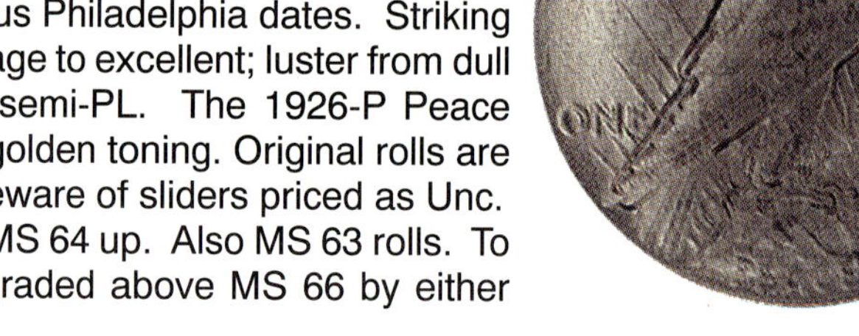

Mintage 1,939,000. Many baggy Uncs. from Treasury bags, 1944. There are unconfirmed rumors of small quantities in the Redfield hoard. Many sliders; fewer gems than previous Philadelphia dates. Striking quality from above average to excellent; luster from dull to a "wet look" almost semi-PL. The 1926-P Peace dollar can come with a golden toning. Original rolls are mostly MS 60/63, but beware of sliders priced as Unc.

Recommended in MS 64 up. Also MS 63 rolls. To date none have been graded above MS 66 by either PCGS or NGC.

MINTAGE	PROOF	STRIKE	LUSTER	BAGMARKS
1,939,000	0	Sharp & Bold	Good	Moderate
REDFIELD	**CATEGORY**	**DIE VARIETIES**	**PIVOTAL GRADE**	**RARITY FACTOR**
No	Semi-common	1	MS 65	R-4

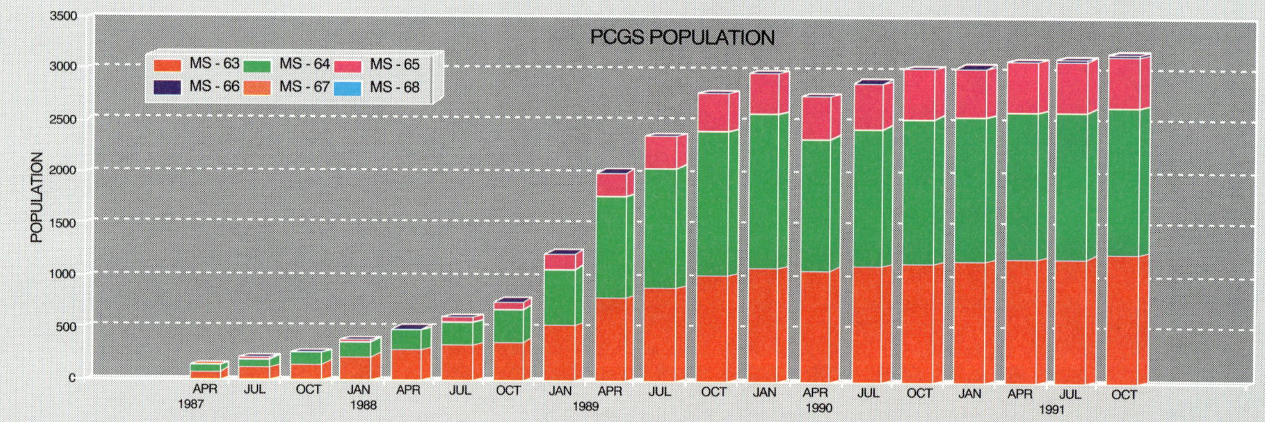

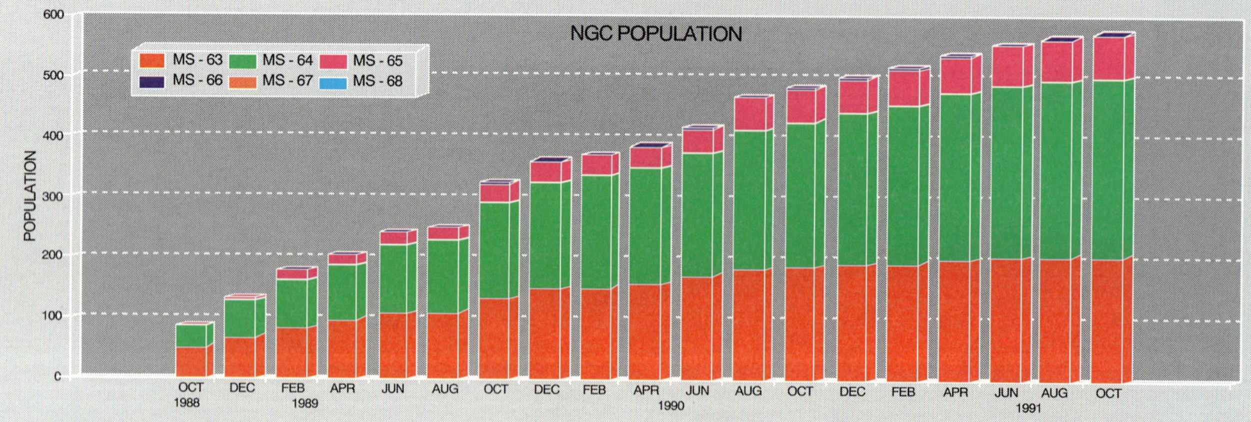

PCGS POPULATION

MS - 63 MS - 64 MS - 65
MS - 66 MS - 67 MS - 68

POPULATION

3500 3000 2500 2000 1500 1000 500 0

APR 1987 JUL OCT JAN 1988 APR JUL OCT JAN 1989 APR JUL OCT JAN APR 1990 JUL OCT JAN APR JUL 1991 OCT

NGC POPULATION

MS - 63 MS - 64 MS - 65
MS - 66 MS - 67 MS - 68

POPULATION

600 500 400 300 200 100 0

OCT 1988 DEC FEB 1989 APR JUN AUG OCT DEC FEB APR 1990 JUN AUG OCT DEC FEB APR JUN 1991 AUG OCT

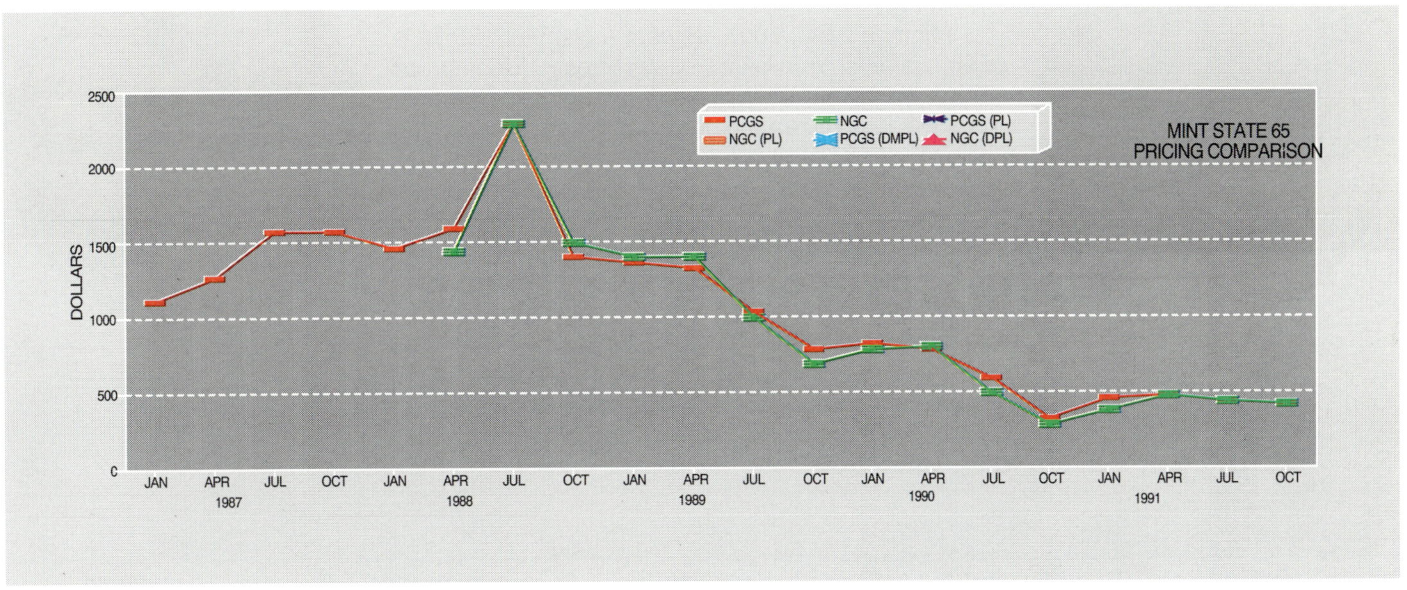
MINT STATE 65
PRICING COMPARISON
PCGS
NGC
PCGS (PL)
NGC (PL)
PCGS (DMPL)
NGC (DPL)
DOLLARS
2500
2000
1500
1000
500
0
JAN
APR
JUL
OCT
1987
1988
1989
1990
1991

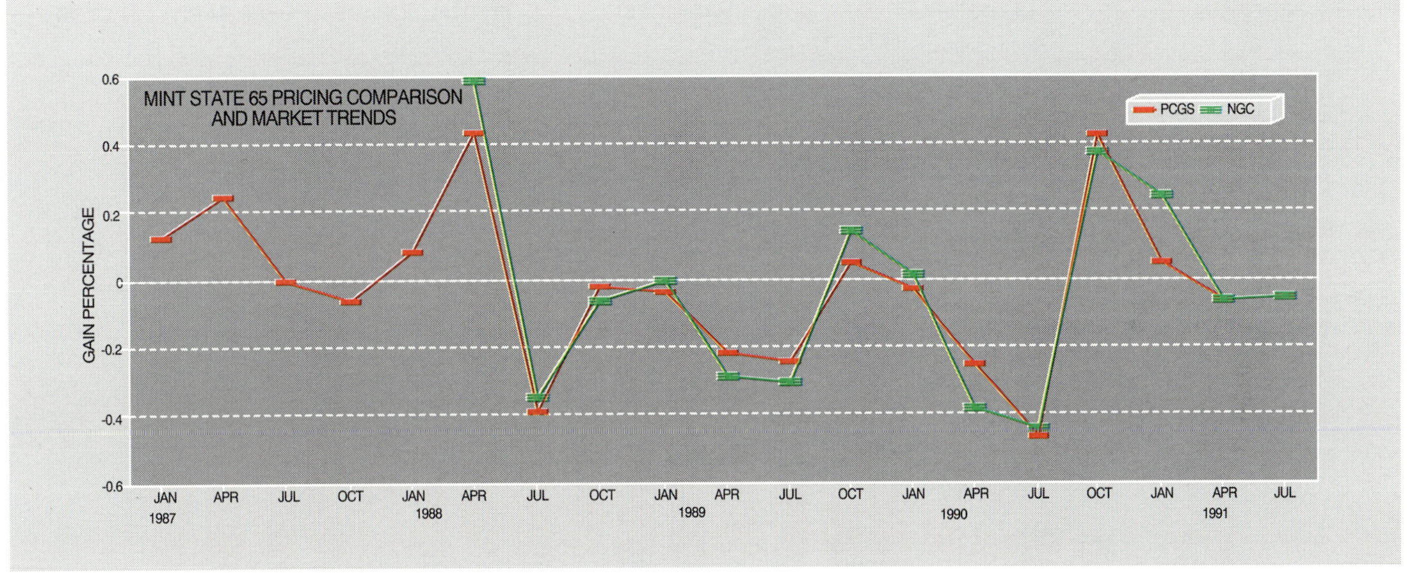
MINT STATE 65 PRICING COMPARISON
AND MARKET TRENDS
PCGS
NGC
GAIN PERCENTAGE
0.6
0.4
0.2
0
-0.2
-0.4
-0.6
JAN
APR
JUL
OCT
1987
1988
1989
1990
1991

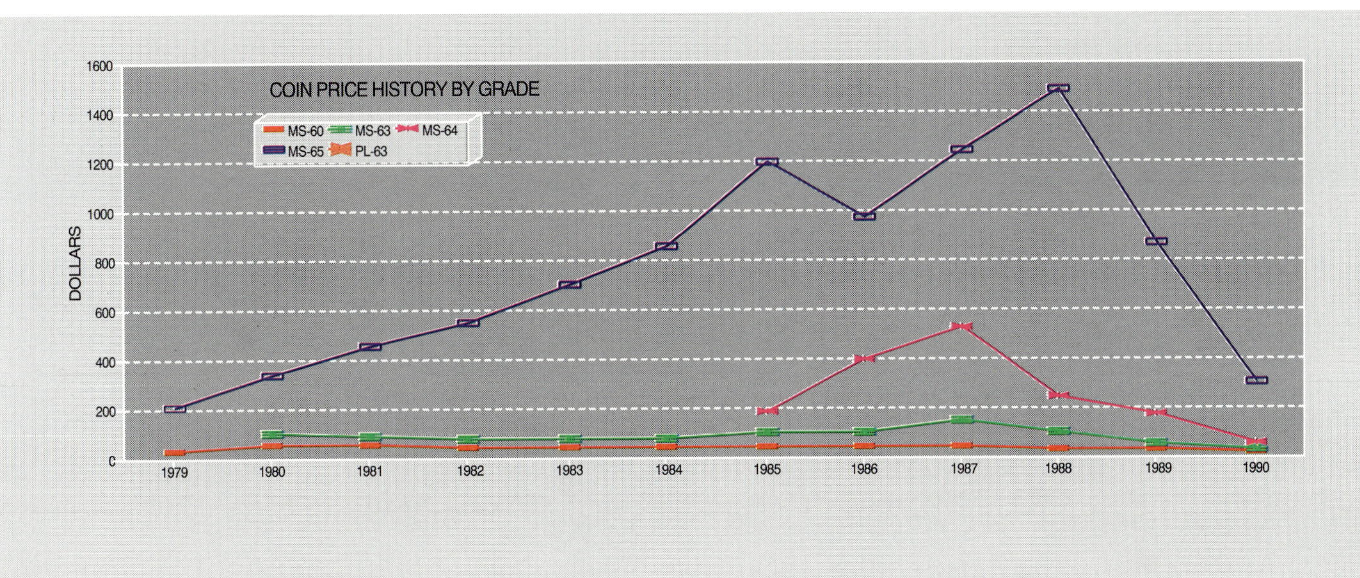
COIN PRICE HISTORY BY GRADE
MS-60
MS-63
MS-64
MS-65
PL-63
DOLLARS
1600
1400
1200
1000
800
600
400
200
0
1979
1980
1981
1982
1983
1984
1985
1986
1987
1988
1989
1990

1926-D

Mintage 2,348,700. Gems are plentiful. Strike is great, luster is often excellent and frosty. Best struck Denver Peace dollar. When strike is not full, the weakness will appear in the lower portions of both the obverse and reverse. Die cracks are a problem with this date. MS 60/63 rolls are available. Sliders are **NOT** frequent.

Out of 9 Peace dollars graded MS 67 by PCGS (and 2 NGC 67's), no less than 5 were 1926-D's. All of these traded wholesale within a few thousand of $30,000 each.

The "golden tone," from the sulphur content in the original mint sewn bags, is prevalent for this issue.

Recommended in MS 65 up as another role model. Otherwise MS 64.

MINTAGE	PROOF	STRIKE	LUSTER	BAGMARKS
2,348,700	0	Sharp & Bold	Excellent	Moderate
REDFIELD	**CATEGORY**	**DIE VARIETIES**	**PIVOTAL GRADE**	**RARITY FACTOR**
No	Semi-common	2	MS 65	R-3

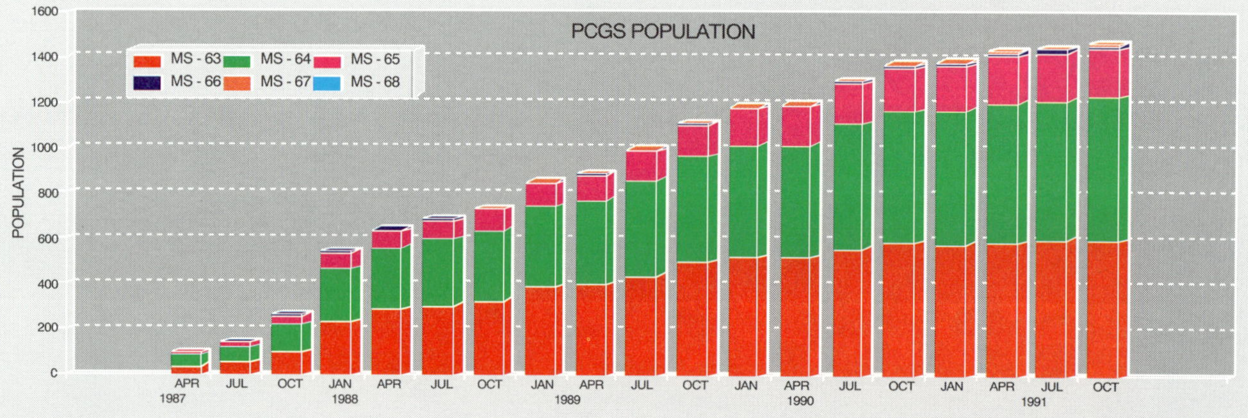

PCGS POPULATION

MS - 63 MS - 64 MS - 65
MS - 66 MS - 67 MS - 68

POPULATION

1600 1400 1200 1000 800 600 400 200 0

APR 1987 JUL OCT JAN 1988 APR JUL OCT JAN 1989 APR JUL OCT JAN APR 1990 JUL OCT JAN APR JUL 1991 OCT

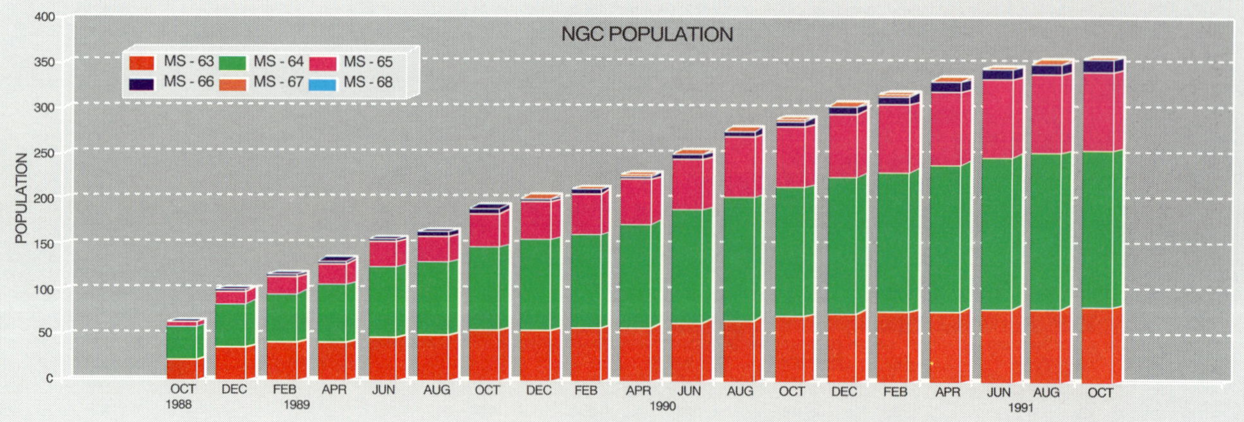

NGC POPULATION

MS - 63 MS - 64 MS - 65
MS - 66 MS - 67 MS - 68

POPULATION

400 350 300 250 200 150 100 50 0

OCT 1988 DEC FEB 1989 APR JUN AUG OCT DEC FEB APR 1990 JUN AUG OCT DEC FEB APR JUN AUG 1991 OCT

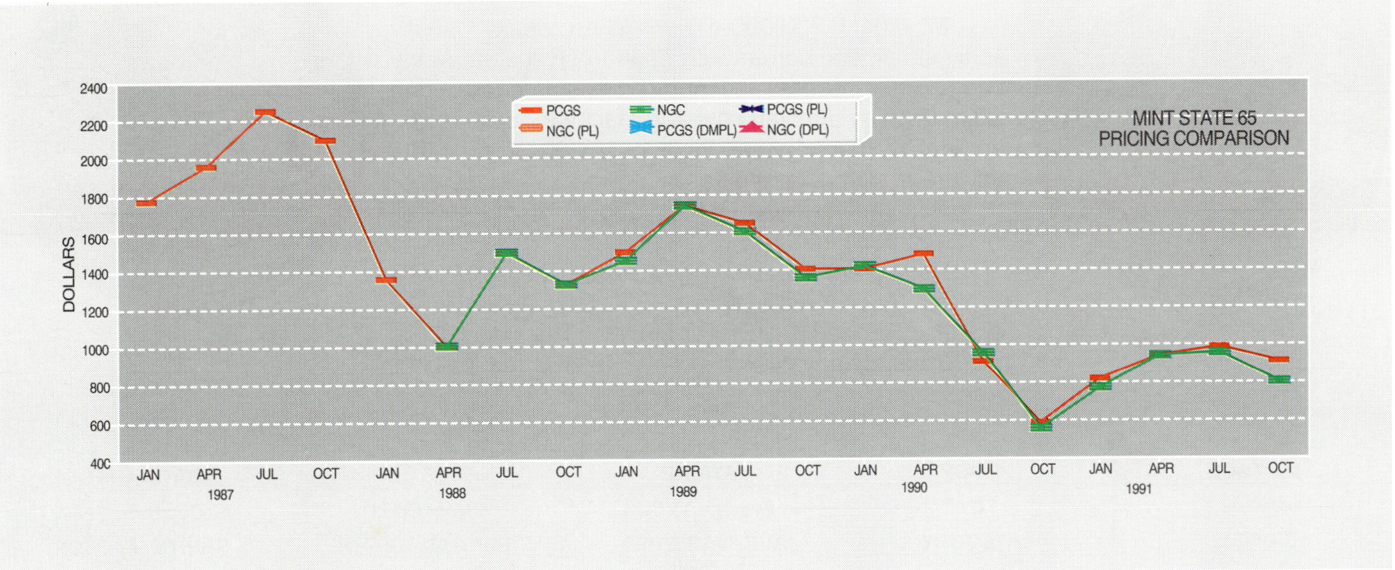
MINT STATE 65
PRICING COMPARISON
PCGS
NGC
PCGS (PL)
NGC (PL)
PCGS (DMPL)
NGC (DPL)
DOLLARS
2400
2200
2000
1800
1600
1400
1200
1000
800
600
400
JAN
APR
JUL
OCT
1987
1988
1989
1990
1991

MINT STATE 65 PRICING COMPARISON
AND MARKET TRENDS
PCGS
NGC
GAIN PERCENTAGE
0.5
0.4
0.3
0.2
0.1
0
-0.1
-0.2
-0.3
-0.4
-0.5
JAN
APR
JUL
OCT
1987
1988
1989
1990
1991

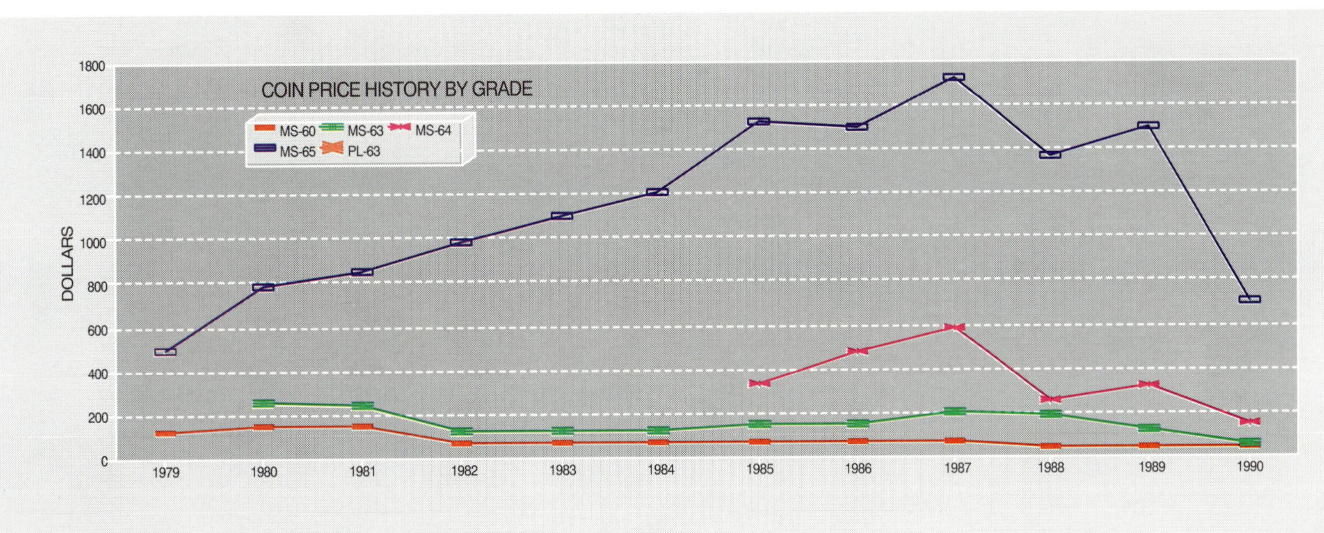
COIN PRICE HISTORY BY GRADE
MS-60
MS-63
MS-64
MS-65
PL-63
DOLLARS
1800
1600
1400
1200
1000
800
600
400
200
0
1979
1980
1981
1982
1983
1984
1985
1986
1987
1988
1989
1990

1926-S

Mintage 6,980,000. Rims often weak. Usually softly struck and comes with good frosty luster. Many baggy Redfield uncs., too many badly scratched during distribution by the coin counting machine. Lots of sliders, not so many gems. Rolls of MS 60/63 exist, but beware of sliders priced as Unc.

Recommended MS 64 and above. Also by the roll in MS 60/63.

None graded above MS 66 to date by either PCGS or NGC. ALL PEACE DOLLARS IN GRADES ABOVE MS 66 ARE CONSIDERED RARE. The only PCGS MS 67 example was sold in early 1991 in the $35,000 range.

MINTAGE	PROOF	STRIKE	LUSTER	BAGMARKS
6,980,000	0	Average To Bold	Very Good	Moderate To Heavy
REDFIELD	**CATEGORY**	**DIE VARIETIES**	**PIVOTAL GRADE**	**RARITY FACTOR**
Yes	Semi-common	3	MS 65	R-3

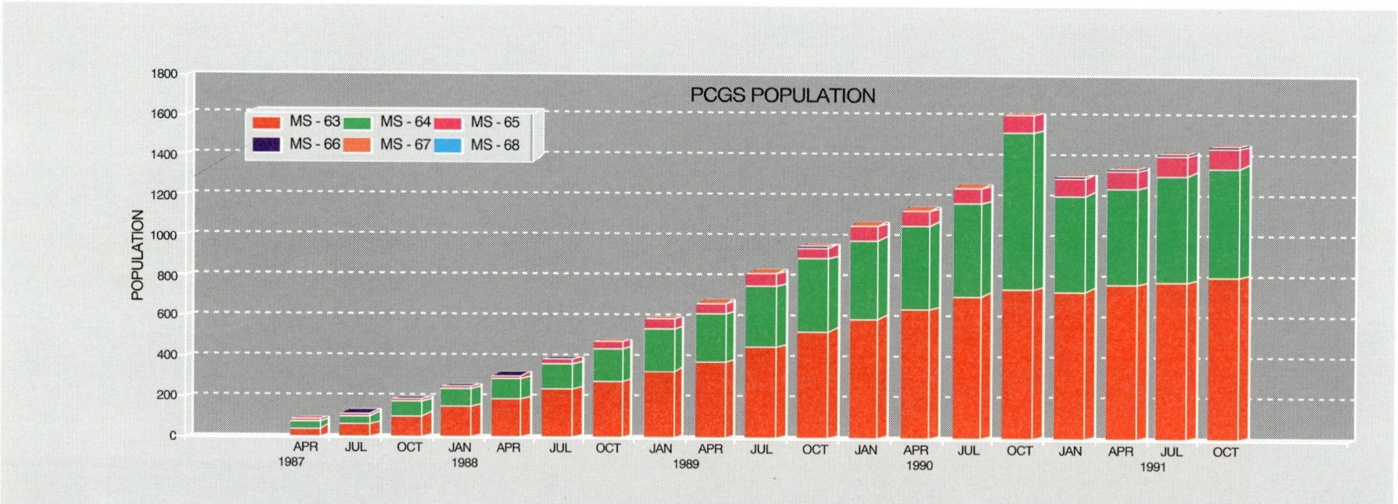

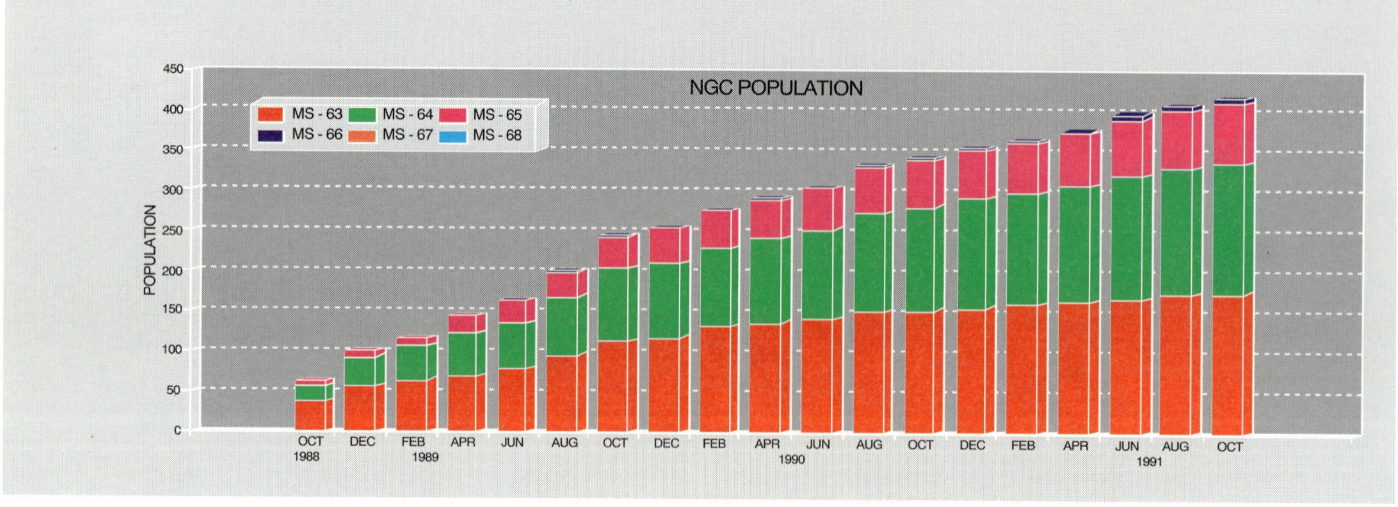

1926-S

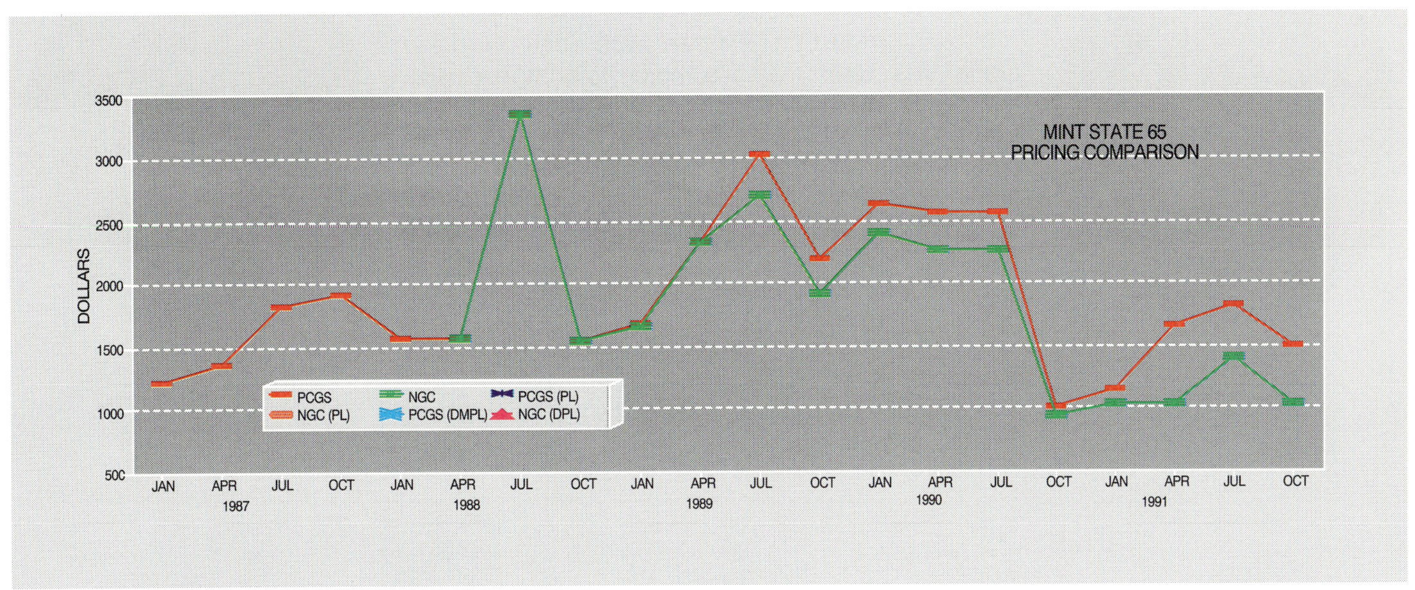

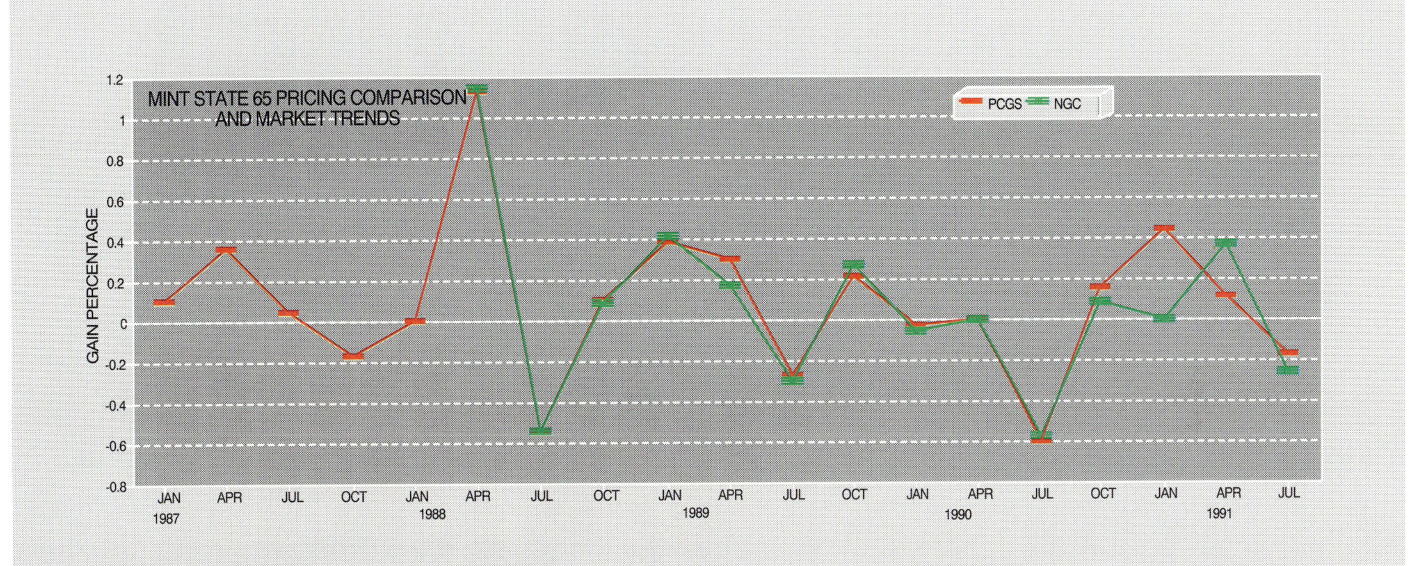

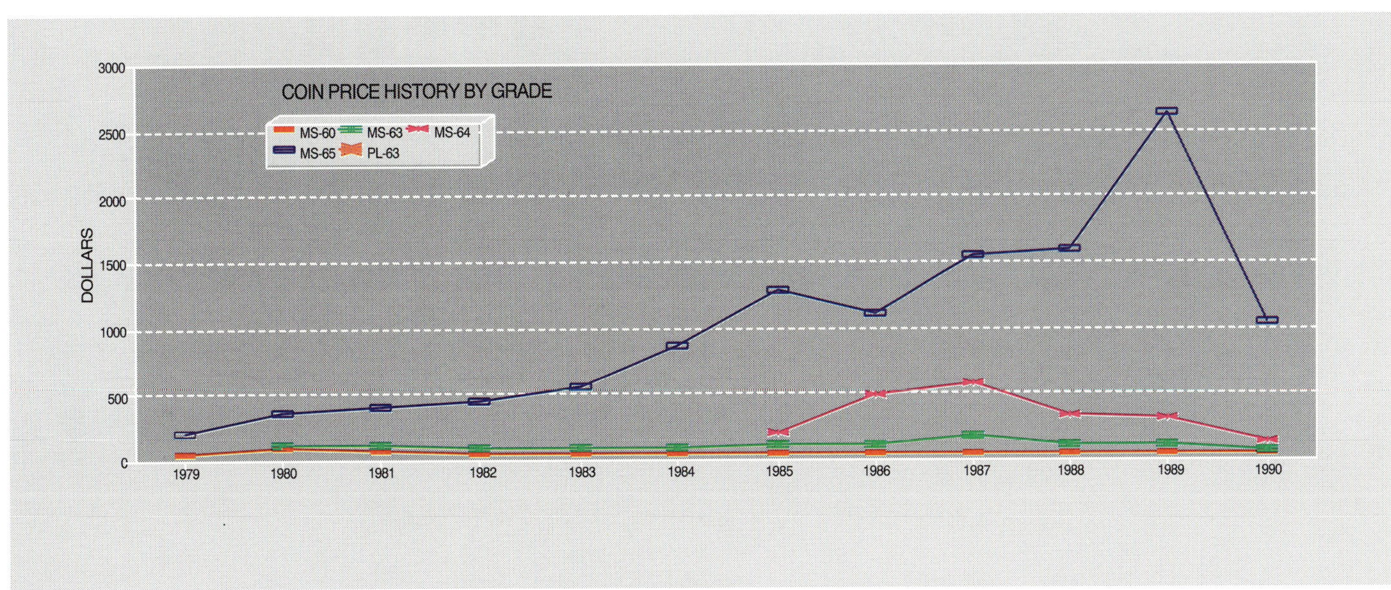

1927-P

Mintage 848,000. Plenty of sliders and low to mid grade Uncs. Gems are not common; this date is elusive above MS 64. Many have good strikes and excellent luster. As in most Peace dollars, bagmarks are a problem with this issue. The 1925-P, 1926-P and the 1927-P come with a beautiful golden hue toning. MS 60/63 rolls occasionally show up, but beware of sliders priced as Unc.

It is a semi-key issue. The low mintage assures collector interest.

Recommended in MS 63 and up. Another keeper date in MS 65.

Only one coin graded in MS 66 by PCGS and none by NGC. Higher grades unknown.

MINTAGE	PROOF	STRIKE	LUSTER	BAGMARKS
848,000	0	Good	Good	Light
REDFIELD	**CATEGORY**	**DIE VARIETIES**	**PIVOTAL GRADE**	**RARITY FACTOR**
No	Key	1	MS 65	R-1

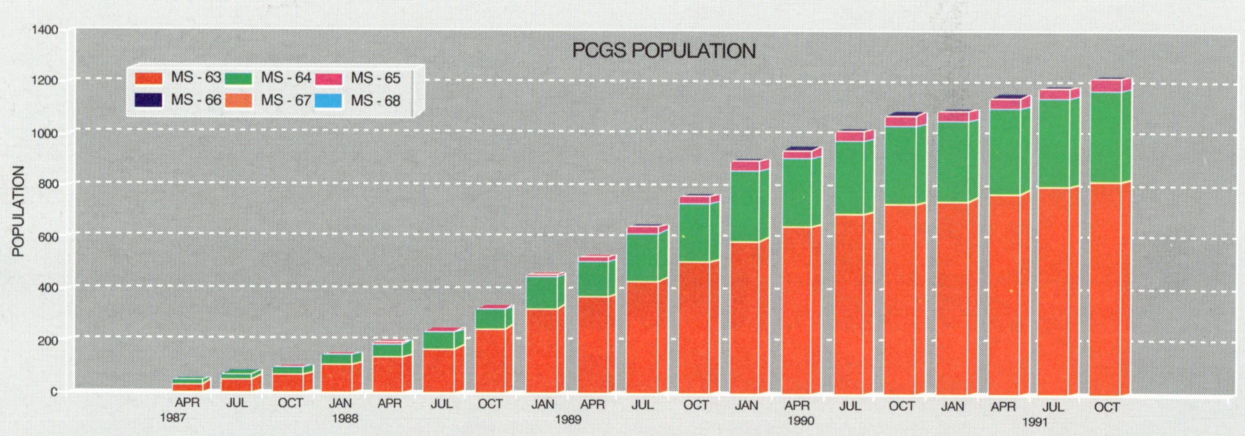

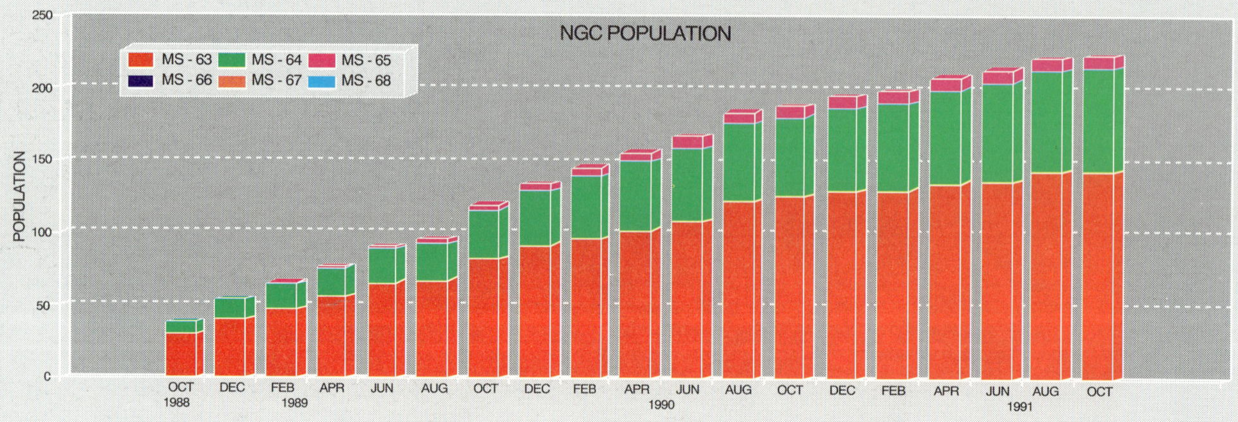

PCGS POPULATION

MS - 63 MS - 64 MS - 65
MS - 66 MS - 67 MS - 68

POPULATION

0 200 400 600 800 1000 1200 1400

APR 1987, JUL, OCT, JAN 1988, APR, JUL, OCT, JAN 1989, APR, JUL, OCT, JAN 1990, APR, JUL, OCT, JAN 1991, APR, JUL, OCT

NGC POPULATION

MS - 63 MS - 64 MS - 65
MS - 66 MS - 67 MS - 68

POPULATION

0 50 100 150 200 250

OCT 1988, DEC, FEB 1989, APR, JUN, AUG, OCT, DEC, FEB 1990, APR, JUN, AUG, OCT, DEC, FEB 1991, APR, JUN, AUG, OCT

1927-P

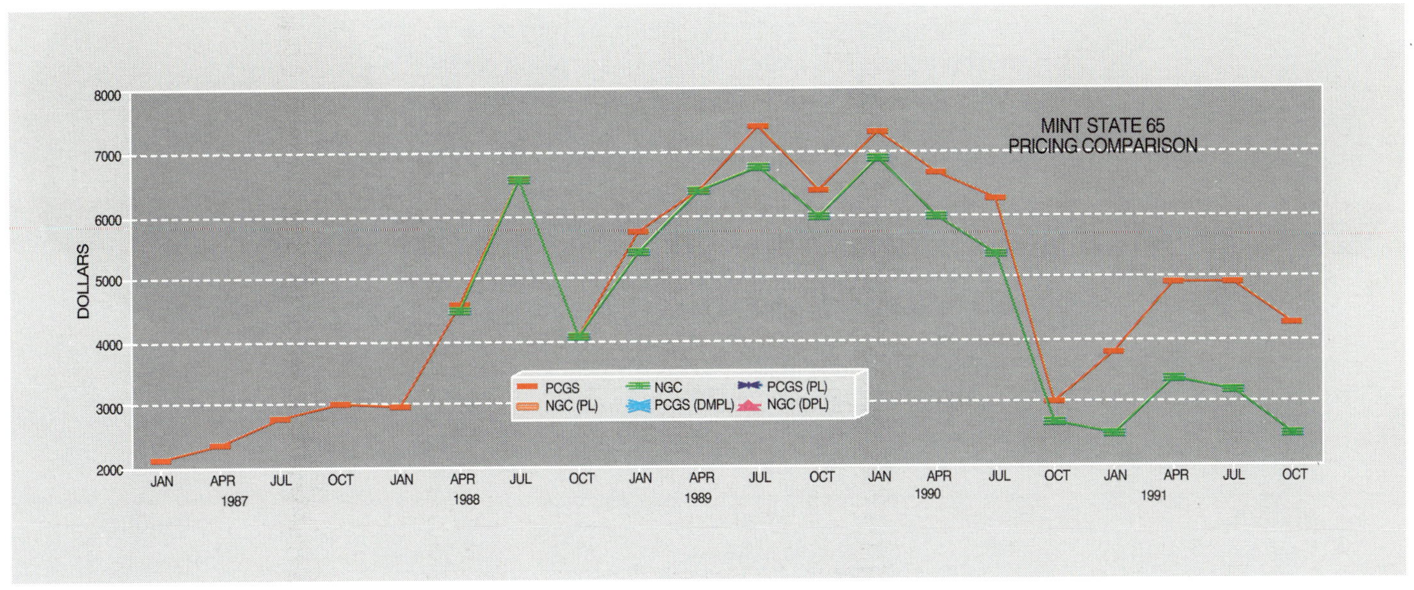

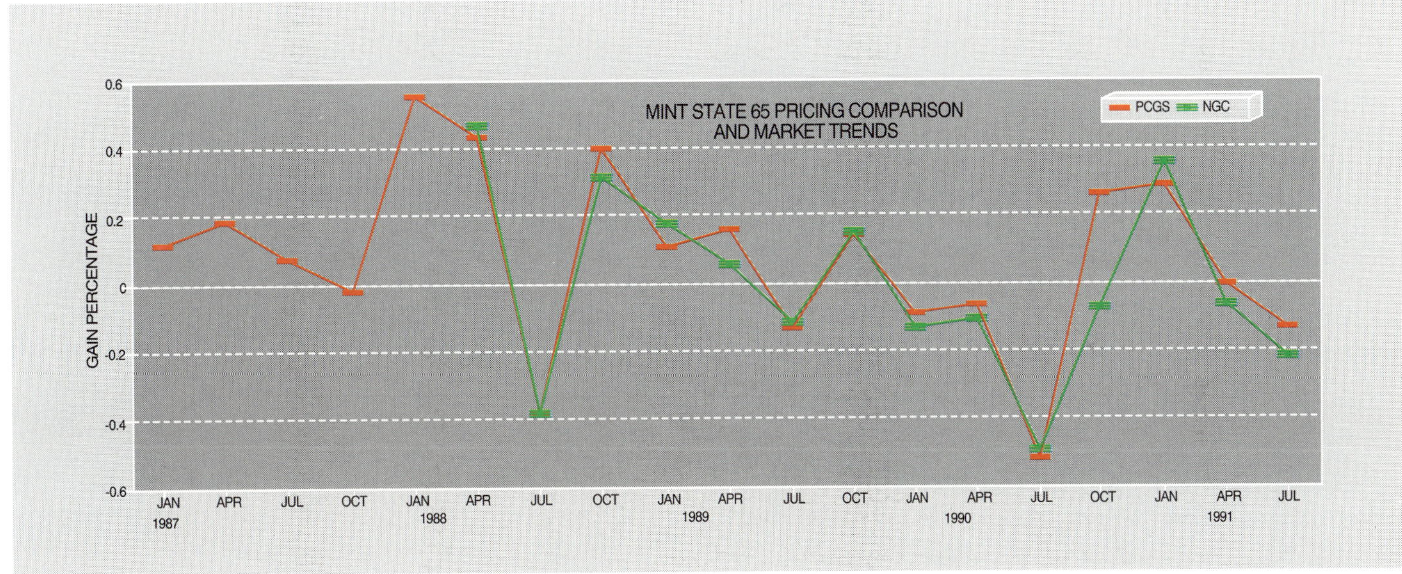

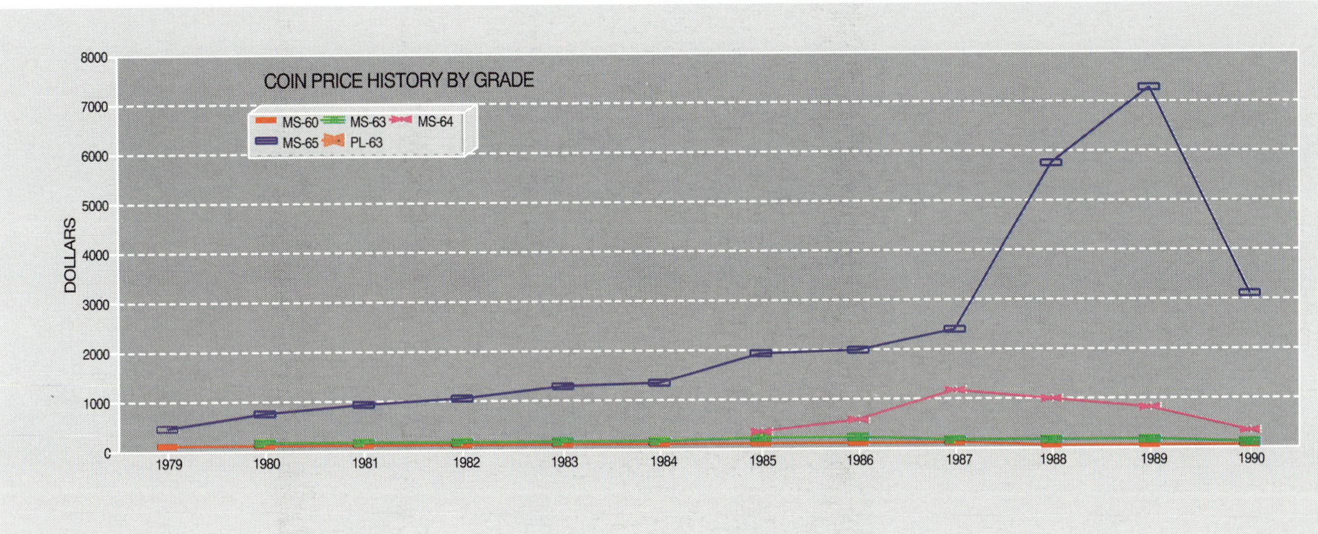

1927-D

Mintage 1,268,900. Tougher than 1927-P or S in most grades. The higher, the tougher. None certified and graded above MS 66 by either PCGS or NGC. Good strike, but not excellent. Luster is above average to frosty. Some of the better ones are well struck, though not in a class with 1926-D or 1923-D. No original rolls are known. Circulated specimens are in some demand by most collectors.

Due to it's low original mintage and current availability, the 1927-D is one of the key dates of the peace dollar series.

Recommended in MS 64 up. Another keeper in MS 65 or better. A "sleeper" in MS 64.

MINTAGE	PROOF	STRIKE	LUSTER	BAGMARKS
1,268,900	0	Average	Good	Moderate
REDFIELD	**CATEGORY**	**DIE VARIETIES**	**PIVOTAL GRADE**	**RARITY FACTOR**
No	Key	1	MS 65	R-1

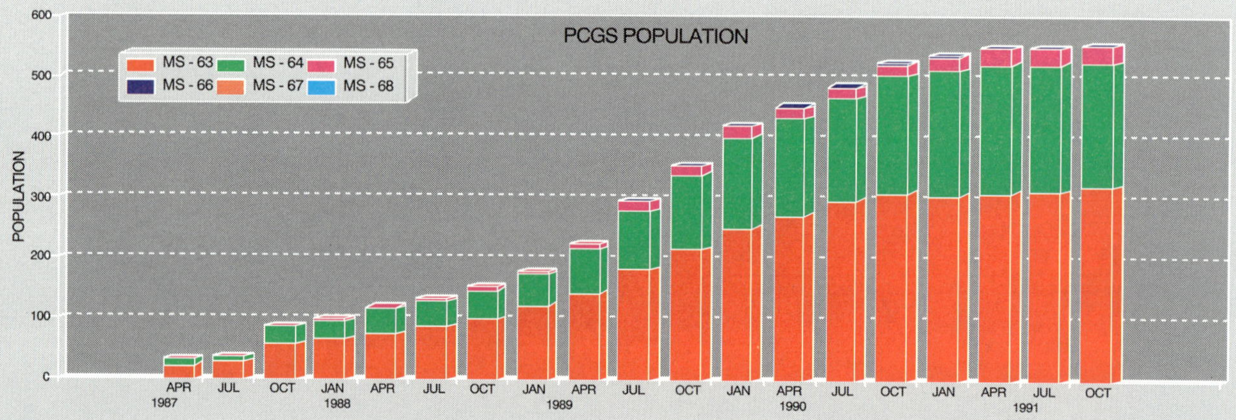

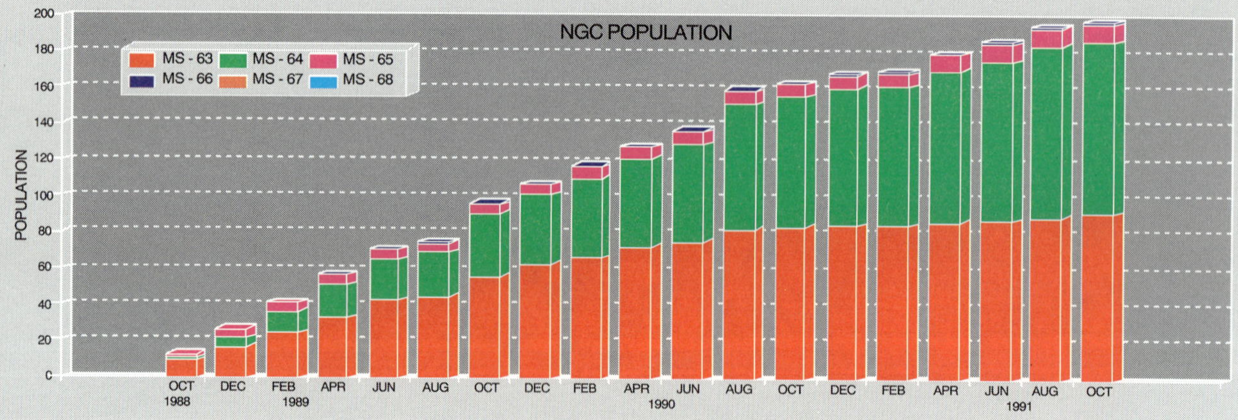

PCGS POPULATION

MS - 63 MS - 64 MS - 65 MS - 66 MS - 67 MS - 68

POPULATION

600 500 400 300 200 100 0

APR 1987, JUL, OCT, JAN 1988, APR, JUL, OCT, JAN 1989, APR, JUL, OCT, JAN 1990, APR, JUL, OCT, JAN 1991, APR, JUL, OCT

NGC POPULATION

MS - 63 MS - 64 MS - 65 MS - 66 MS - 67 MS - 68

POPULATION

200 180 160 140 120 100 80 60 40 20 0

OCT 1988, DEC, FEB 1989, APR, JUN, AUG, OCT, DEC, FEB 1990, APR, JUN, AUG, OCT, DEC, FEB 1991, APR, JUN, AUG, OCT

1927-D

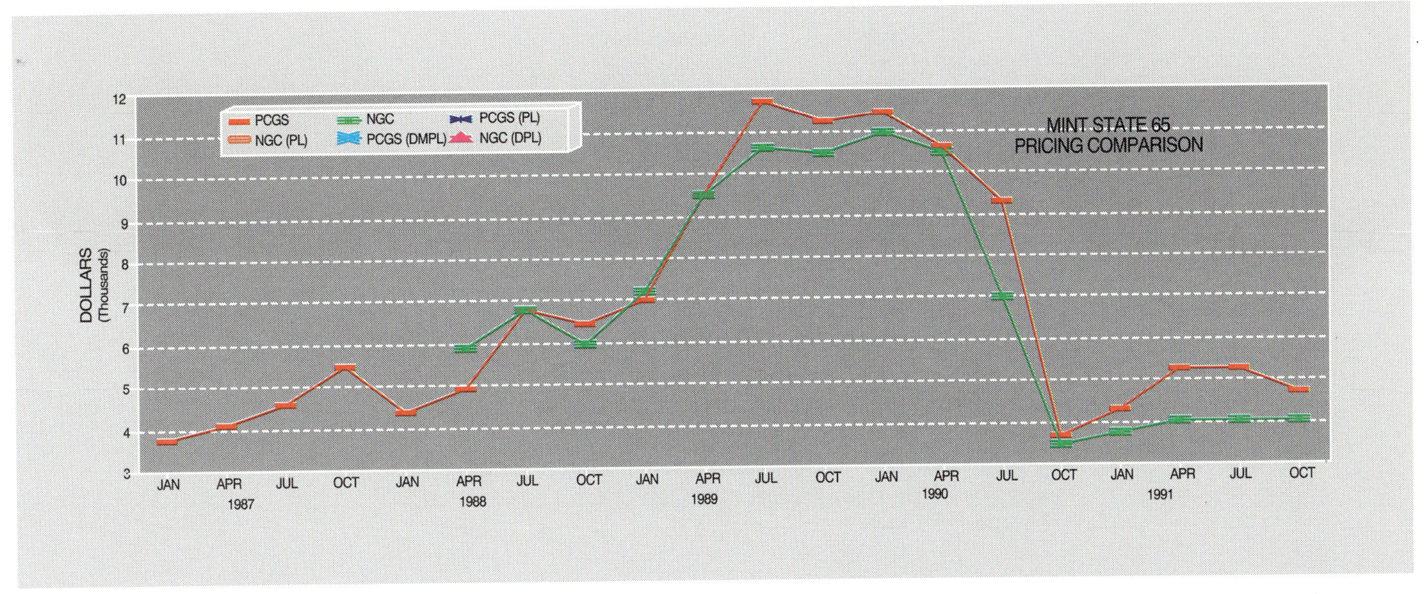

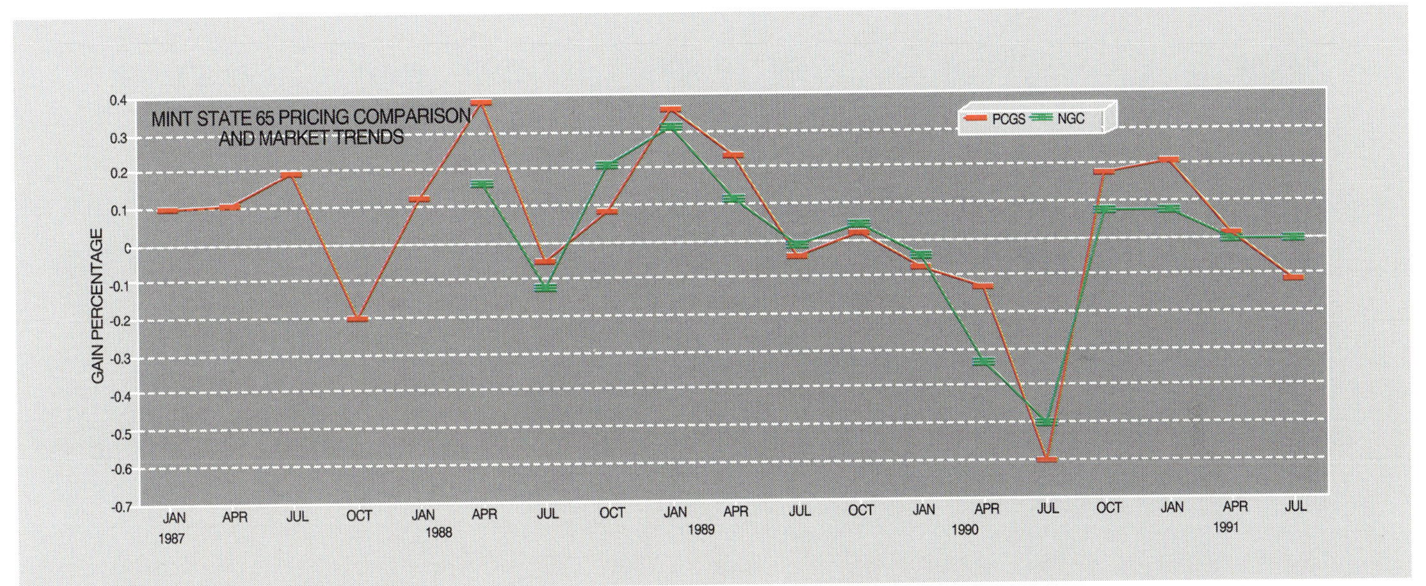

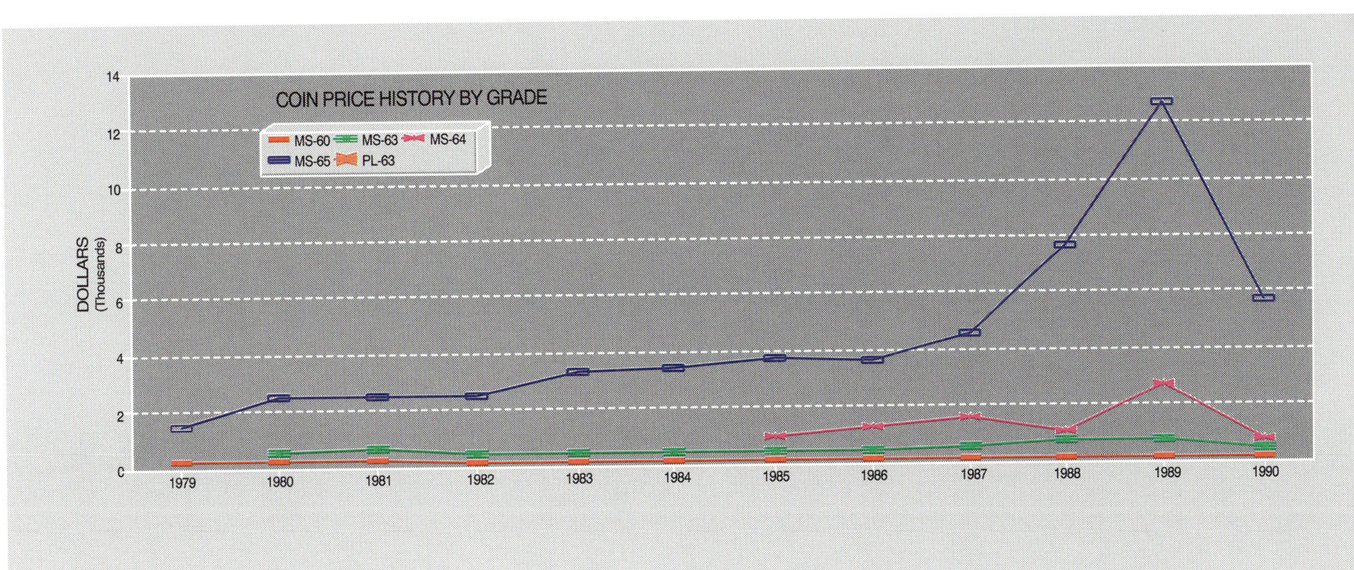

1927-S

Mintage 866,000. Rims and devices often weak; luster tends to be satiny. The Redfield hoard contained many baggy Uncs., mostly MS 60/63. Some of these were semi-PL with die striations on the obverse due to excess die polishing. Although some 1927-S Peace dollars exhibit a prooflike look, **TECHNICALLY SPEAKING, NO PROOFLIKES EXIST FOR THE ENTIRE PEACE DOLLAR SERIES**. Rolls in that grade range are available, but beware of sliders. Check for that slight "rub" that can turn an MS 63/65 coin quickly into a "slider" (AU 58). There is some collector demand even for circulated specimens.

Recommended in MS 64 up. Another key date and a keeper.

A total of two coins have been graded and certified in MS 66 by both PCGS and NGC. One each, none better.

MINTAGE	PROOF	STRIKE	LUSTER	BAGMARKS
866,000	0	Soft & Weak	Very Good	Moderate
REDFIELD	**CATEGORY**	**DIE VARIETIES**	**PIVOTAL GRADE**	**RARITY FACTOR**
Yes	Key	2	MS 65	R-1

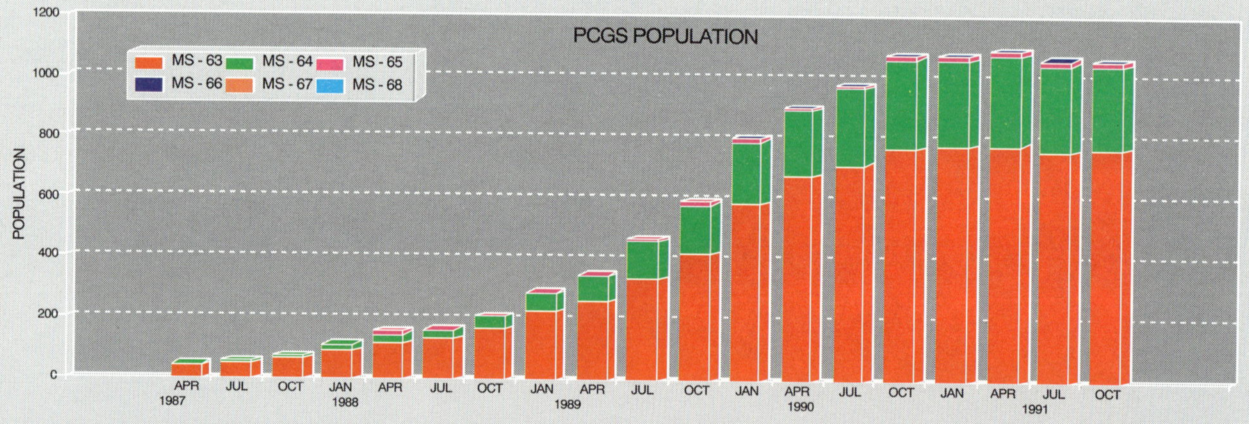

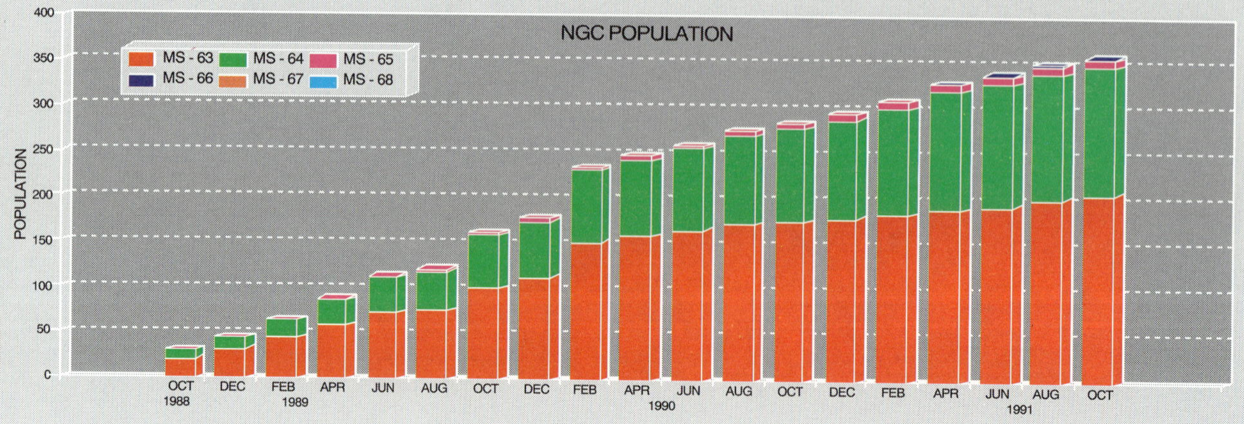

PCGS POPULATION

MS - 63 MS - 64 MS - 65 MS - 66 MS - 67 MS - 68

POPULATION: 0, 200, 400, 600, 800, 1000, 1200

APR 1987, JUL, OCT, JAN 1988, APR, JUL, OCT, JAN 1989, APR, JUL, OCT, JAN, APR 1990, JUL, OCT, JAN, APR 1991, JUL, OCT

NGC POPULATION

MS - 63 MS - 64 MS - 65 MS - 66 MS - 67 MS - 68

POPULATION: 0, 50, 100, 150, 200, 250, 300, 350, 400

OCT 1988, DEC, FEB 1989, APR, JUN, AUG, OCT, DEC, FEB, APR 1990, JUN, AUG, OCT, DEC, FEB, APR, JUN 1991, AUG, OCT

1927-S

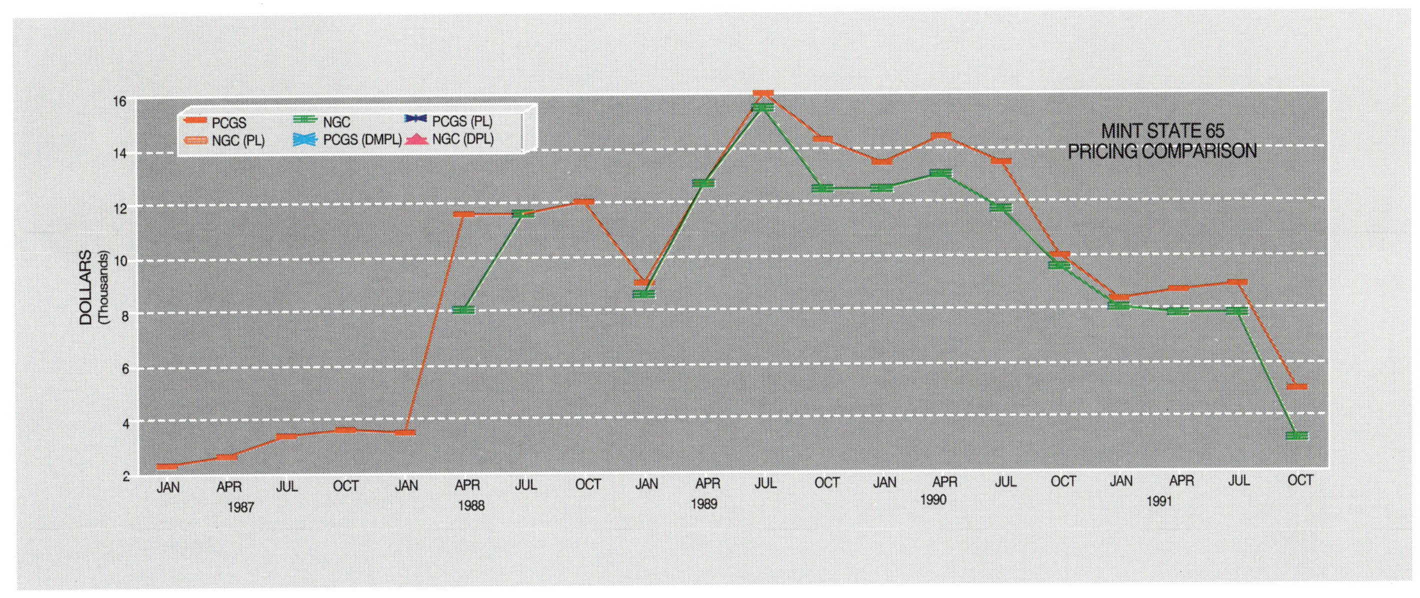

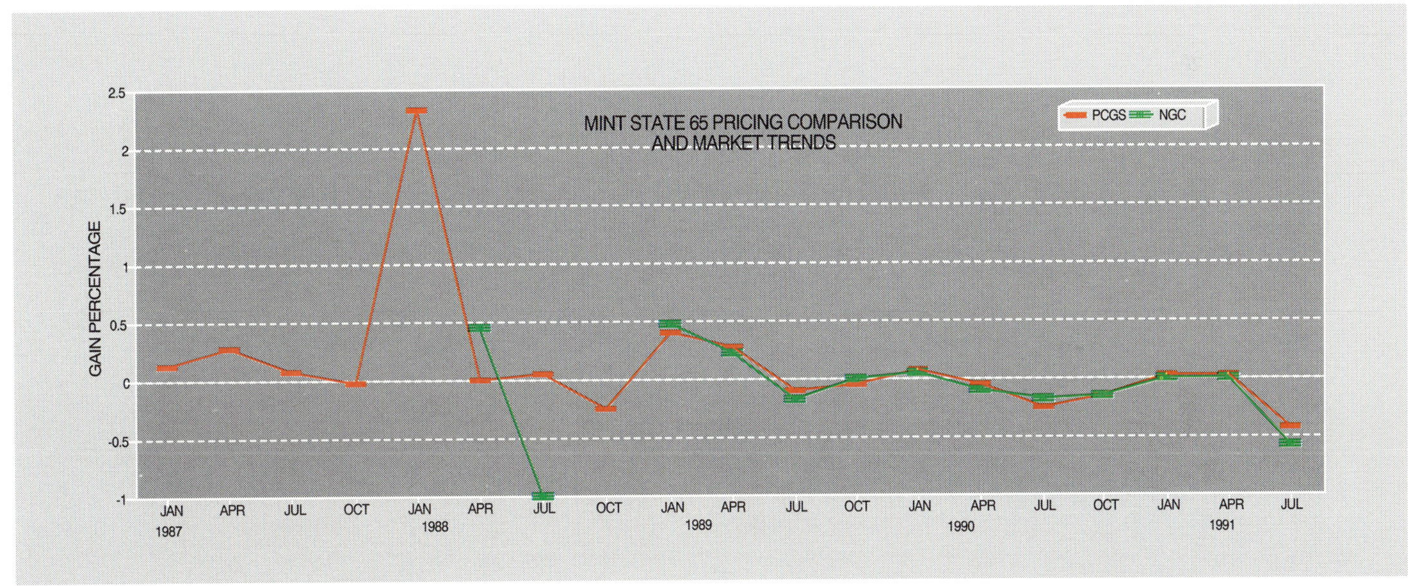

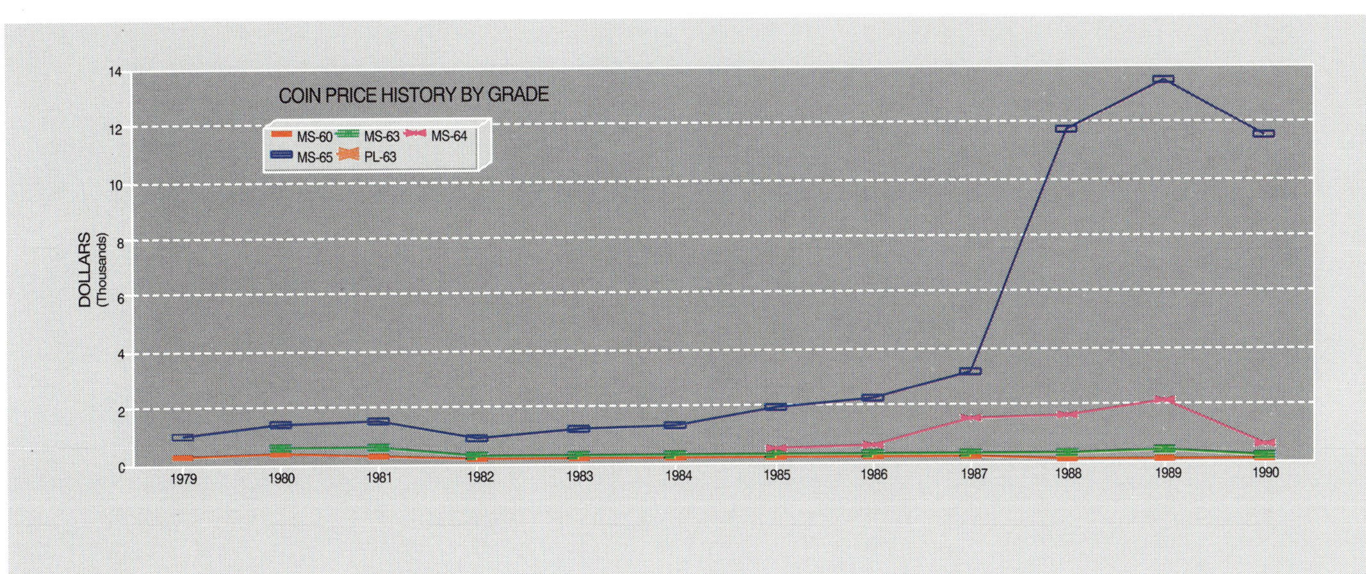

1928-P

Mintage 360,649; the key Peace date. These went into circulation in eastern Ohio and western Pennsylvania. Many survivors are worn. Bold strike, golden and/or satiny luster.

Only one coin graded MS 66 by PCGS and none by NGC. This key date issue is scarce to rare in all BU grades.

Recommended in any grade, the higher the better. Beware sliders priced as Unc. Circulated examples are scarce and highly sought after by collectors.

Some fakes were made by removing S mintmark from 1928-S, or altering the date of a 1923. Others are casts, many from Spain.

MINTAGE	PROOF	STRIKE	LUSTER	BAGMARKS
360,649	0	Average To Bold	Good	Light
REDFIELD	**CATEGORY**	**DIE VARIETIES**	**PIVOTAL GRADE**	**RARITY FACTOR**
No	Key	1	MS 65	R-1

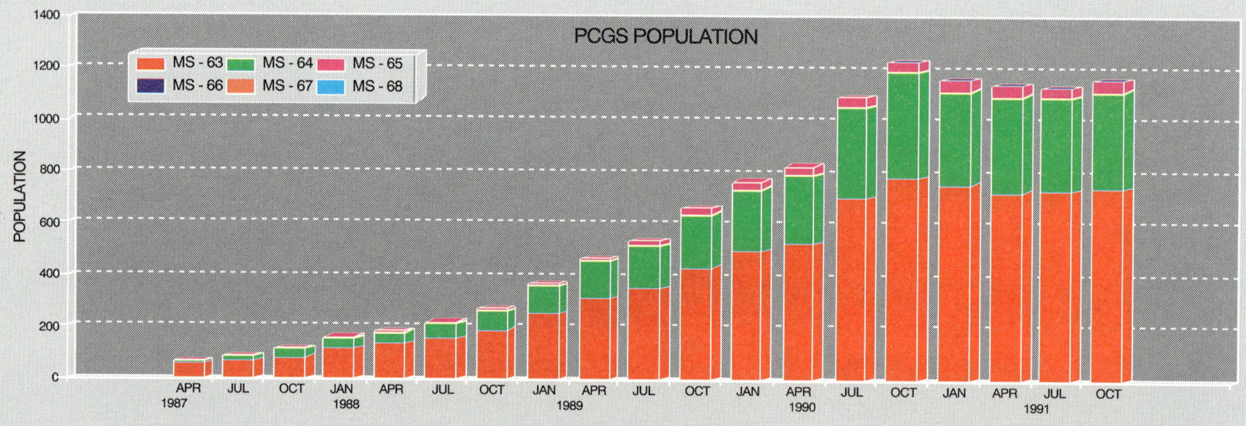

PCGS POPULATION

MS - 63 MS - 64 MS - 65 MS - 66 MS - 67 MS - 68

POPULATION

0 200 400 600 800 1000 1200 1400

APR 1987 JUL OCT JAN 1988 APR JUL OCT JAN 1989 APR JUL OCT JAN APR 1990 JUL OCT JAN APR JUL 1991 OCT

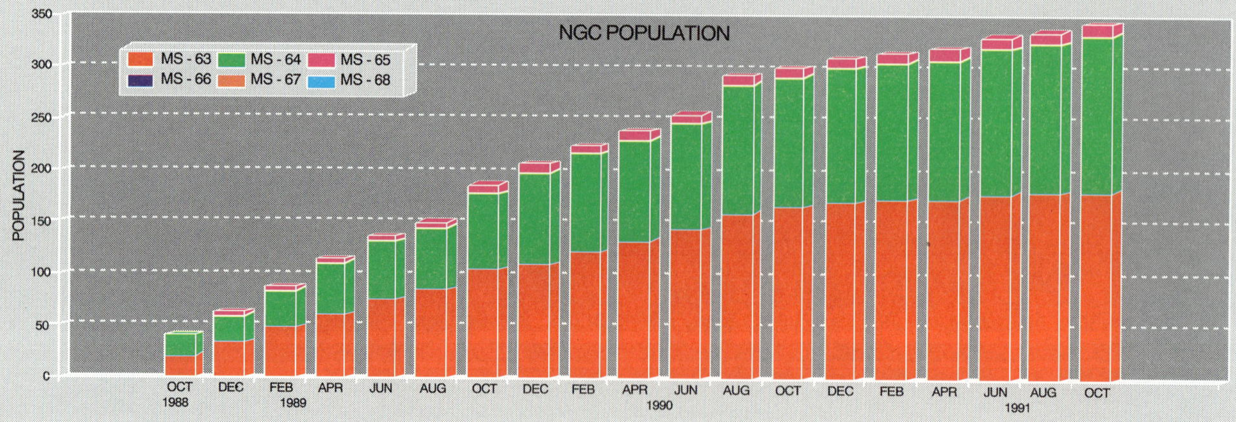

NGC POPULATION

MS - 63 MS - 64 MS - 65 MS - 66 MS - 67 MS - 68

POPULATION

0 50 100 150 200 250 300 350

OCT 1988 DEC FEB 1989 APR JUN AUG OCT DEC FEB APR 1990 JUN AUG OCT DEC FEB APR JUN 1991 AUG OCT

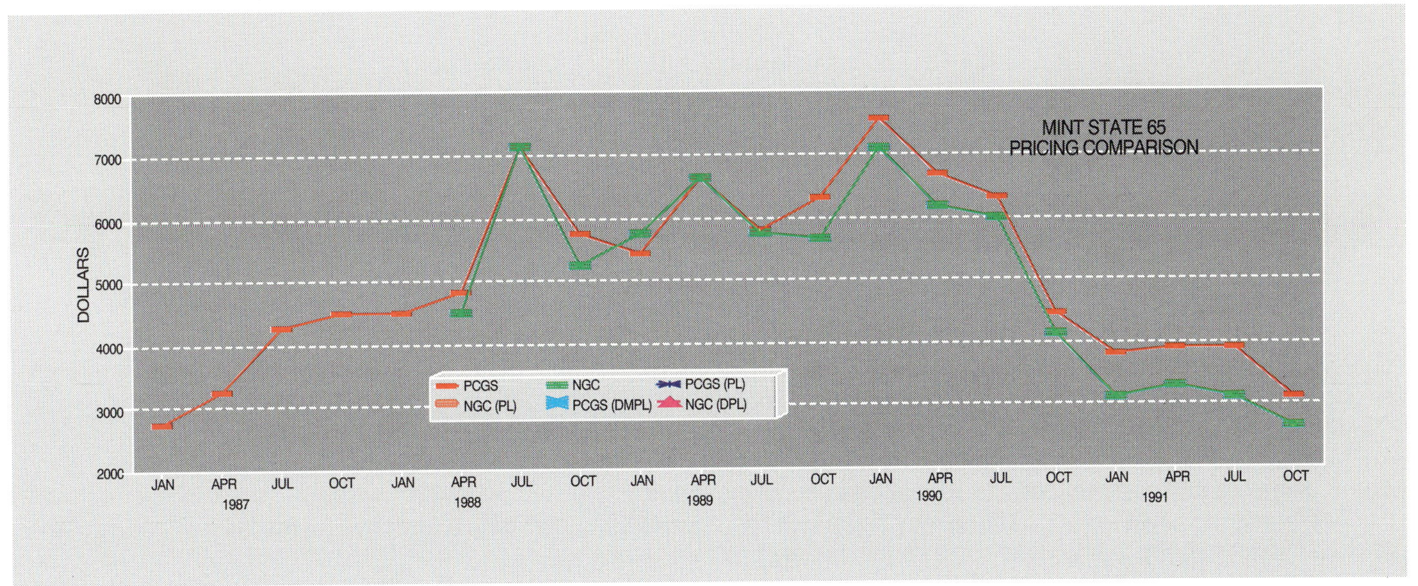

MINT STATE 65
PRICING COMPARISON
DOLLARS
8000
7000
6000
5000
4000
3000
2000
PCGS
NGC
PCGS (PL)
NGC (PL)
PCGS (DMPL)
NGC (DPL)
JAN
APR
JUL
OCT
1987
1988
1989
1990
1991

MINT STATE 65 PRICING COMPARISON
AND MARKET TRENDS
PCGS
NGC
GAIN PERCENTAGE
0.6
0.5
0.4
0.3
0.2
0.1
0
-0.1
-0.2
-0.3
-0.4
JAN
APR
JUL
OCT
1987
1988
1989
1990
1991

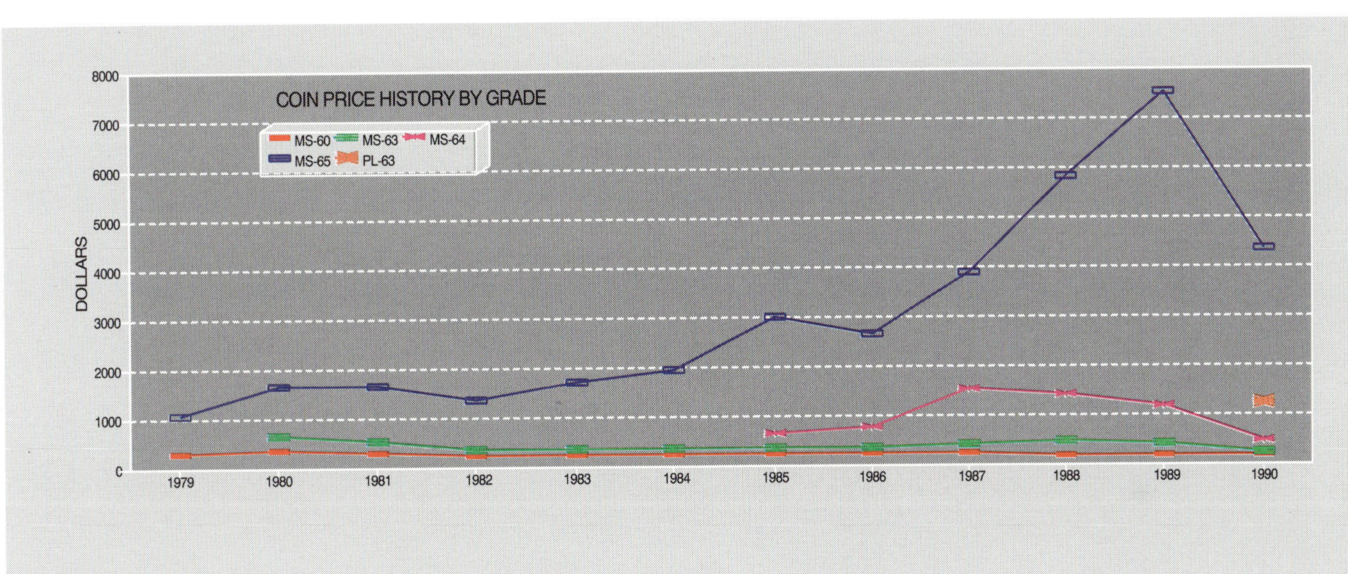

COIN PRICE HISTORY BY GRADE
MS-60
MS-63
MS-64
MS-65
PL-63
DOLLARS
8000
7000
6000
5000
4000
3000
2000
1000
0
1979
1980
1981
1982
1983
1984
1985
1986
1987
1988
1989
1990

1928-S

Mintage 1,632,000. Weak strikes, few gems. The 1928-S is a prime example of an extremely poorly struck Peace dollar. The counting machine which damaged Redfield's 1893-CC's did the same thing to his 1928-S's, notably on wings.

This author (Highfill) was lucky enough to "cherry-pick" (at a substantial premium) a roll of 1928-S from a multi-roll lot from Don Brown, (Tulsa, OK), 1975/6. They were simply gorgeous, with good strikes and blazing luster. PCGS later graded one of them MS 65. Many others had the same deep scratches from the counting machine as other Redfield coins, so this roll probably had the same original source. Circulated coins of this date are uncommon.

The vast majority in all grades belong to the small s variety. *Encyclopedia* (5731)

Mintmark as in some lower denominations: boldface (thick middle stroke), sharp vertical serifs. *Encyclopedia* (5732) large S coins are rare, but few collectors have been checking theirs.

Recommended in MS 64 up. MS 65 may be hard to find and will certainly sell in a few days for multiples of the published bid price. The 1928-S is a key date to the series, mainly due to its strike.

I would not be surprised to see fakes made by adding S mintmark to genuine unc. 1928 dollars. The real S mints price much higher than 1928-P in MS 65.

MINTAGE	PROOF	STRIKE	LUSTER	BAGMARKS
1,632,000	0	Very Weak	Good	Moderate To Heavy
REDFIELD	**CATEGORY**	**DIE VARIETIES**	**PIVOTAL GRADE**	**RARITY FACTOR**
Yes	Key	3	MS 65	R-1

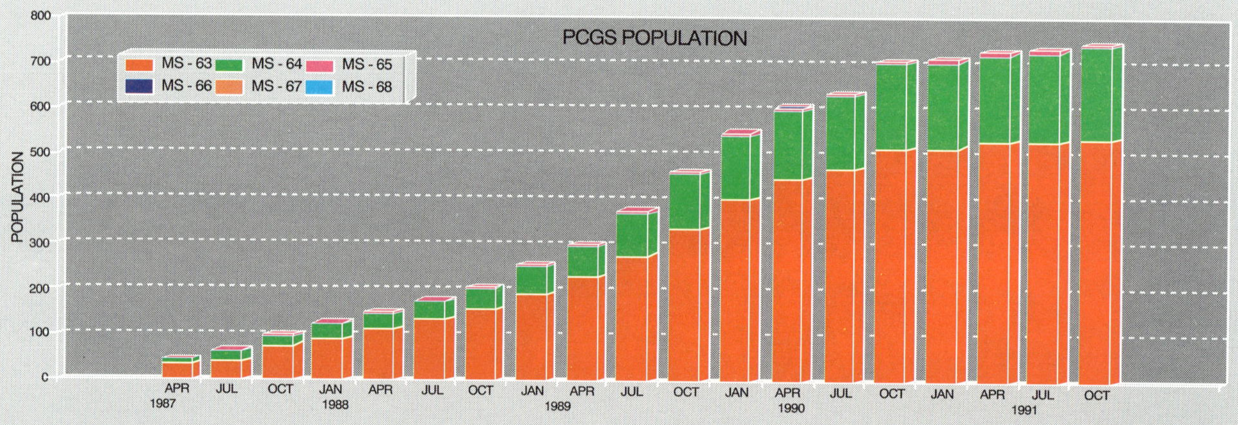

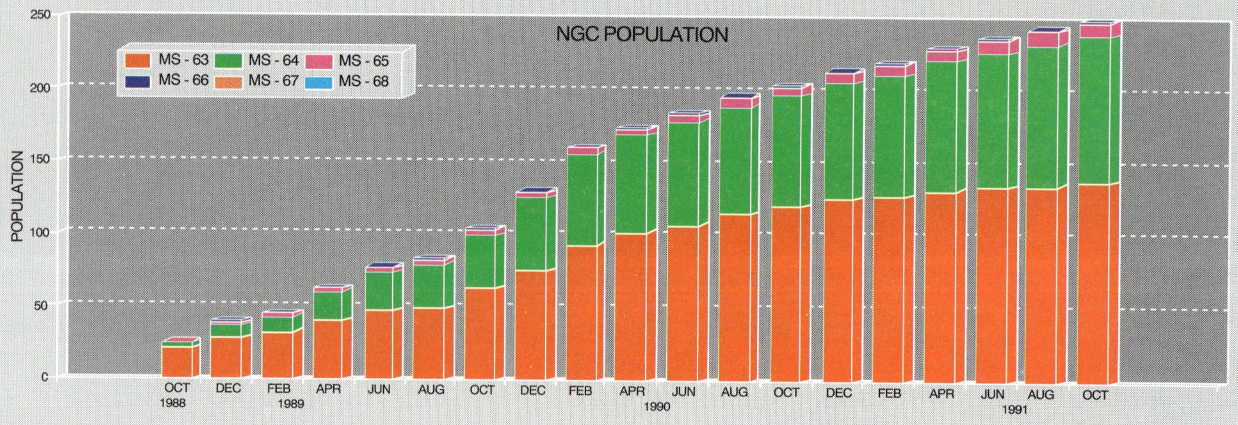

PCGS POPULATION

NGC POPULATION

1928-S

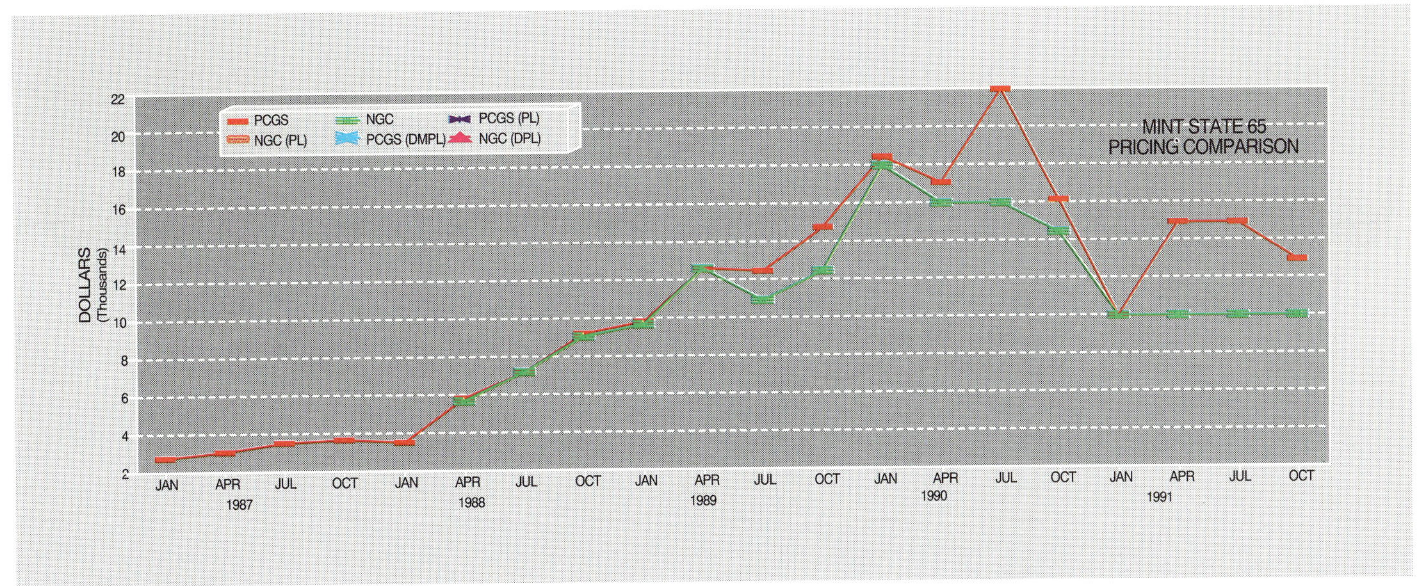

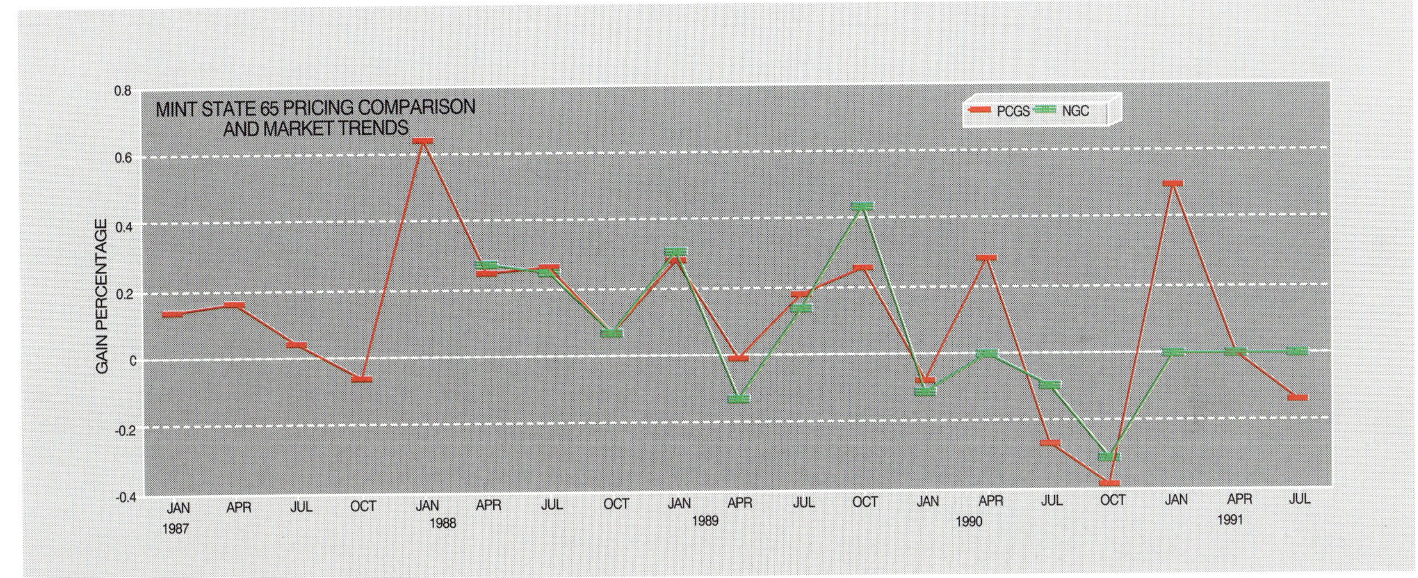

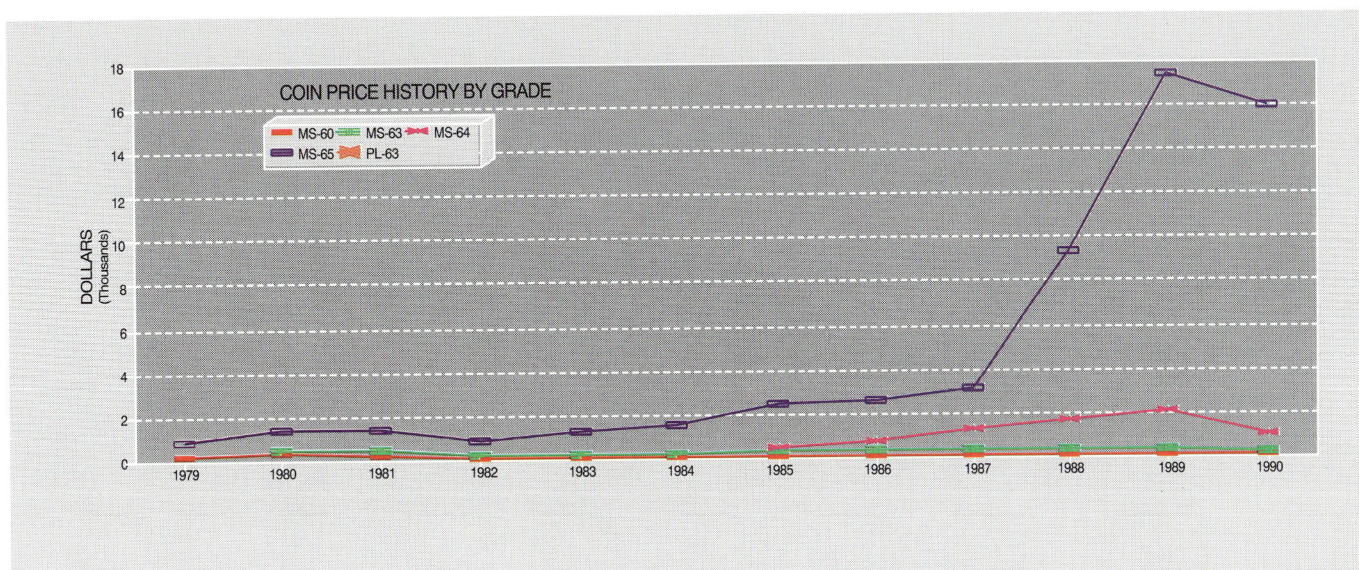

1934-P

Mintage 954,057, from new master dies and hubs. After a six year break, the Peace dollar series resumed production. Thinner letters, tail of R in TRVST almost straight. Plentiful as sliders and in all Unc. levels, gems less so. They include some of the best struck Philadelphia Peace dollars; weak strikes are unusual. Luster is brilliant and vibrant. Golden toning available on some pieces.

Recommended in MS 64 up. BU rolls of MS 60/63. Beware sliders priced as Unc. This date was released into circulation early, but circulated examples are still scarce.

MINTAGE	PROOF	STRIKE	LUSTER	BAGMARKS
954,057	0	Sharp & Bold	Dull To Good	Light
REDFIELD	**CATEGORY**	**DIE VARIETIES**	**PIVOTAL GRADE**	**RARITY FACTOR**
No	Semi-key	1	MS 65	R-3

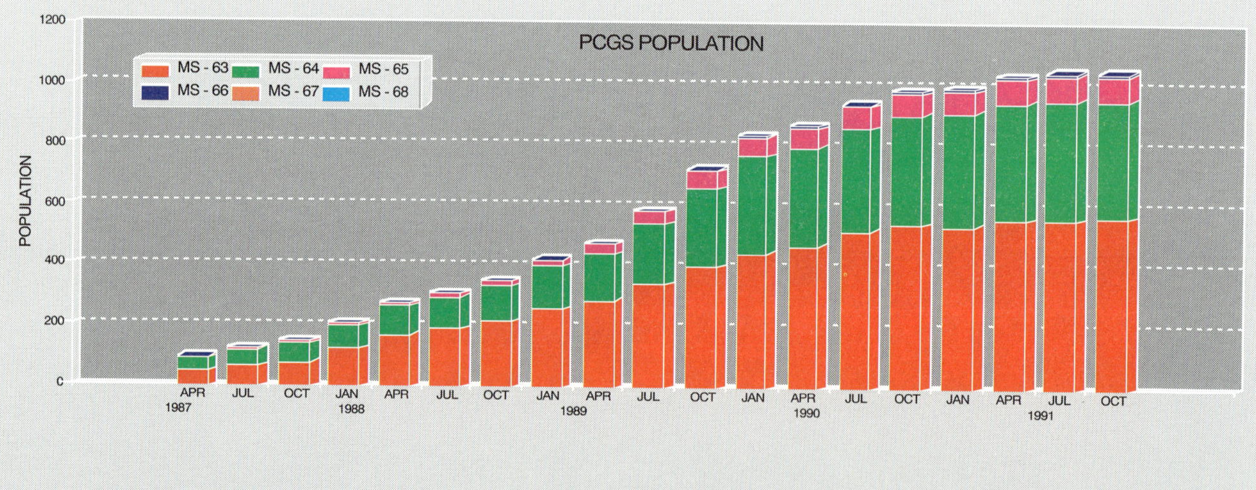

PCGS POPULATION

MS - 63 MS - 64 MS - 65
MS - 66 MS - 67 MS - 68

POPULATION

1200 1000 800 600 400 200 0

APR 1987 JUL OCT JAN 1988 APR JUL OCT JAN 1989 APR JUL OCT JAN APR 1990 JUL OCT JAN APR JUL 1991 OCT

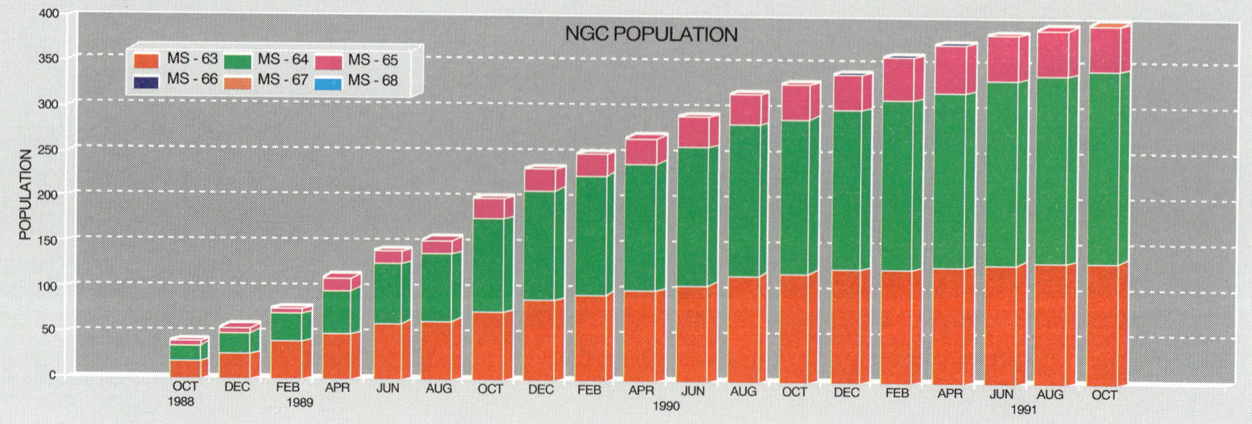

NGC POPULATION

MS - 63 MS - 64 MS - 65
MS - 66 MS - 67 MS - 68

POPULATION

400 350 300 250 200 150 100 50 0

OCT 1988 DEC FEB 1989 APR JUN AUG OCT DEC FEB APR 1990 JUN AUG OCT DEC FEB APR JUN 1991 AUG OCT

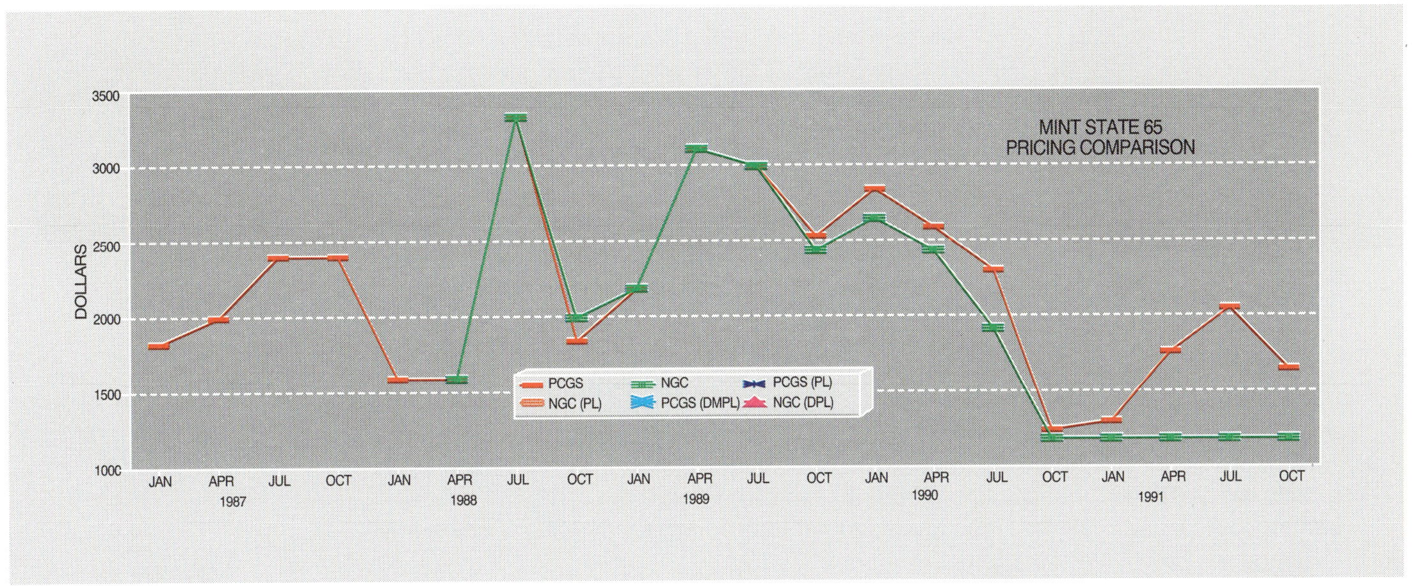
MINT STATE 65
PRICING COMPARISON
DOLLARS
3500
3000
2500
2000
1500
1000
PCGS
NGC
PCGS (PL)
NGC (PL)
PCGS (DMPL)
NGC (DPL)
JAN
APR
JUL
OCT
1987
1988
1989
1990
1991

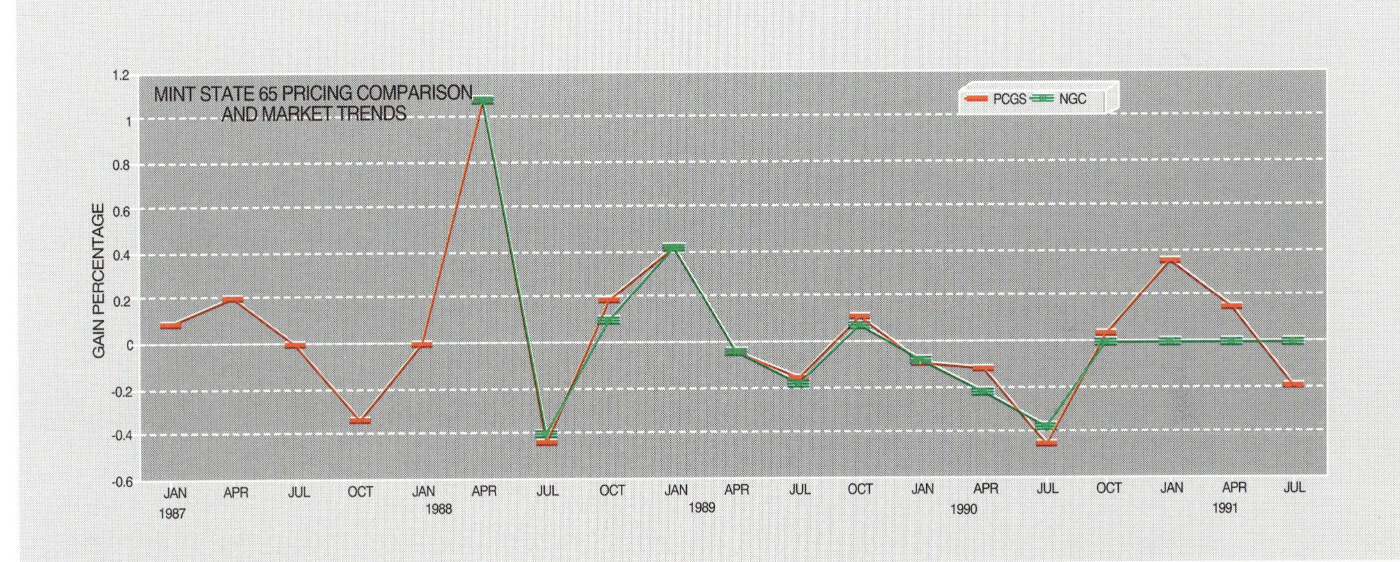
MINT STATE 65 PRICING COMPARISON
AND MARKET TRENDS
PCGS
NGC
GAIN PERCENTAGE
1.2
1
0.8
0.6
0.4
0.2
0
-0.2
-0.4
-0.6
JAN
APR
JUL
OCT
1987
1988
1989
1990
1991

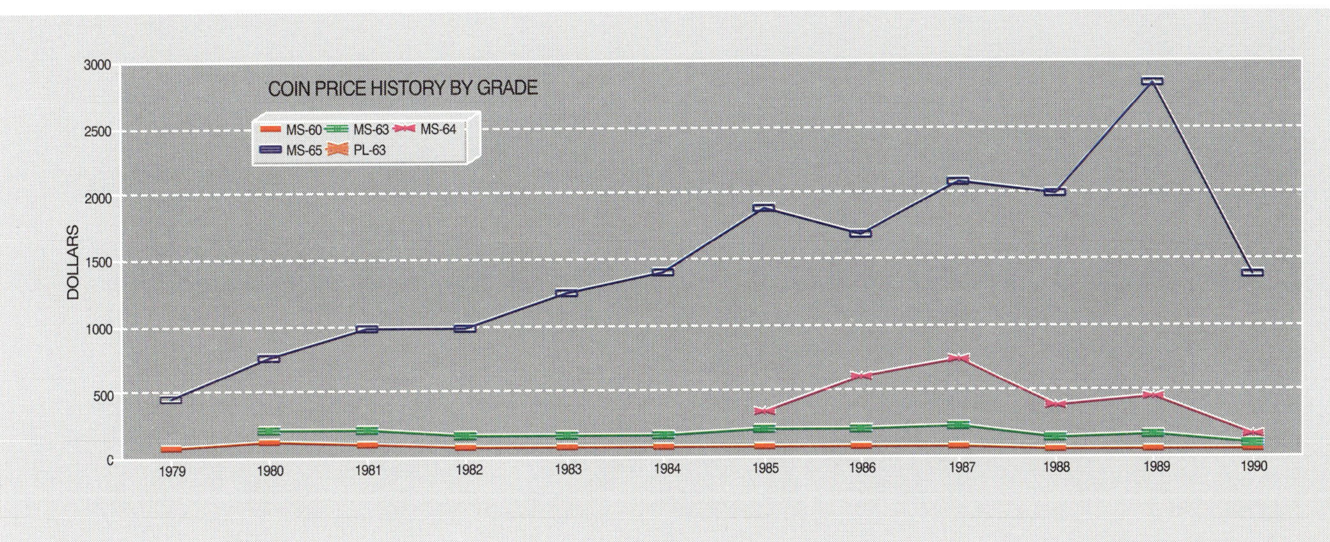
COIN PRICE HISTORY BY GRADE
MS-60
MS-63
MS-64
MS-65
PL-63
DOLLARS
3000
2500
2000
1500
1000
500
0
1979
1980
1981
1982
1983
1984
1985
1986
1987
1988
1989
1990

1934-D

Mintage 1,569,500. Last Denver Mint silver dollar. No Treasury bags. Lots of sliders, few gems. No original bag is confirmed to survive; Redfield had none. Uncs. are usually well struck; Luster varies from above average to frosty. Plenty of sliders around. Circulated examples scarce, but not rare.

This date has been bracketed in rarity side by side with the 1927-D; in fact, 1934-D is available in slightly larger quantities. Original MS-60/63 rolls exist.

Small D. *Ency* 5735 = VAM 1. D as in 1922-27. There is a doubled die obverse, *Ency* 5736 (look at rays below Ber); rare modified design.

Doubled ovberse die. *Ency* 5736.

Large D. *Ency* 5737 = VAM 2. heavy D as on the Washington Quarter. This also comes with doubled die obverse, *Ency* 5738 (look at profile, motto and rays); scarce. Fivaz & Stanton, Cherrypicker's Guide 1$-012.

Nobody has yet done a head count to tell if the small or large D is scarcer.

Recommended in MS 64 up. None graded to date above MS 66 by either PCGS or NGC.

MINTAGE	PROOF	STRIKE	LUSTER	BAGMARKS
1,569,500	0	Average To Bold	Good	Moderate
REDFIELD	**CATEGORY**	**DIE VARIETIES**	**PIVOTAL GRADE**	**RARITY FACTOR**
No	Key	5	MS 65	R-1

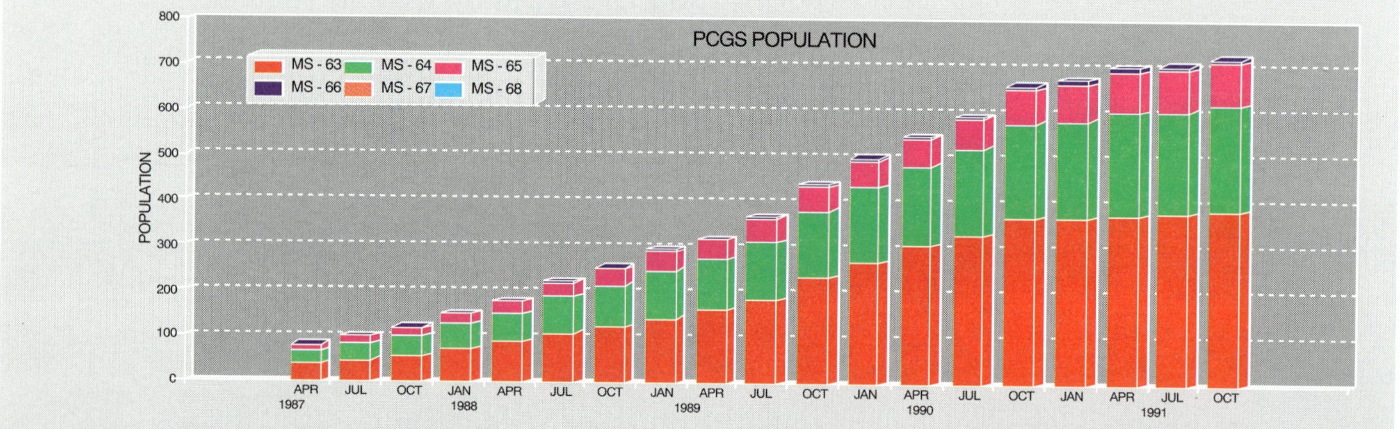

PCGS POPULATION

MS - 63 MS - 64 MS - 65 MS - 66 MS - 67 MS - 68

POPULATION: 0, 100, 200, 300, 400, 500, 600, 700, 800

APR 1987, JUL, OCT, JAN 1988, APR, JUL, OCT, JAN 1989, APR, JUL, OCT, JAN, APR 1990, JUL, OCT, JAN, APR, JUL 1991, OCT

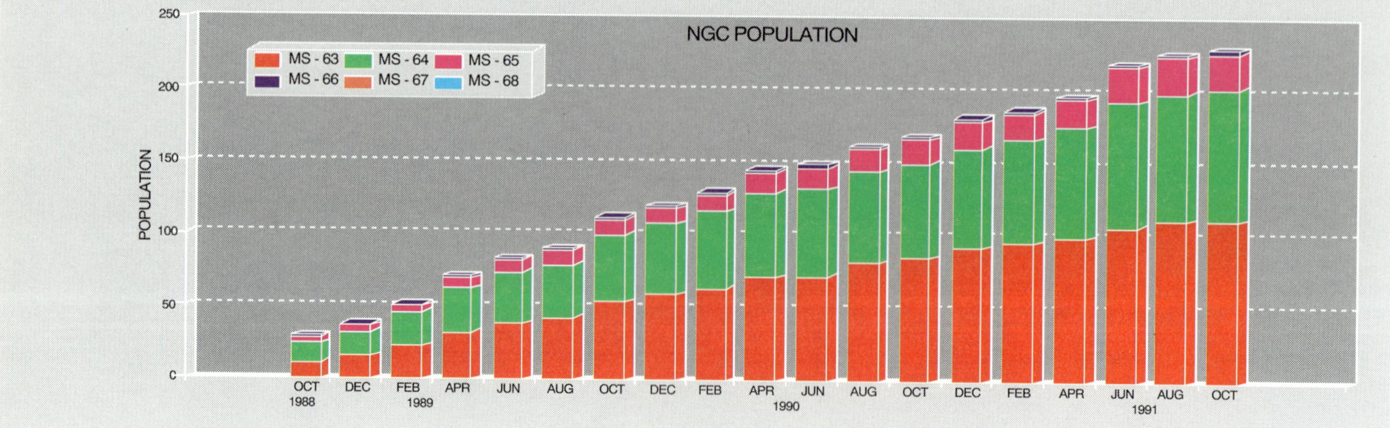

NGC POPULATION

MS - 63 MS - 64 MS - 65 MS - 66 MS - 67 MS - 68

POPULATION: 0, 50, 100, 150, 200, 250

OCT 1988, DEC, FEB 1989, APR, JUN, AUG, OCT, DEC, FEB, APR 1990, JUN, AUG, OCT, DEC, FEB, APR, JUN, AUG 1991, OCT

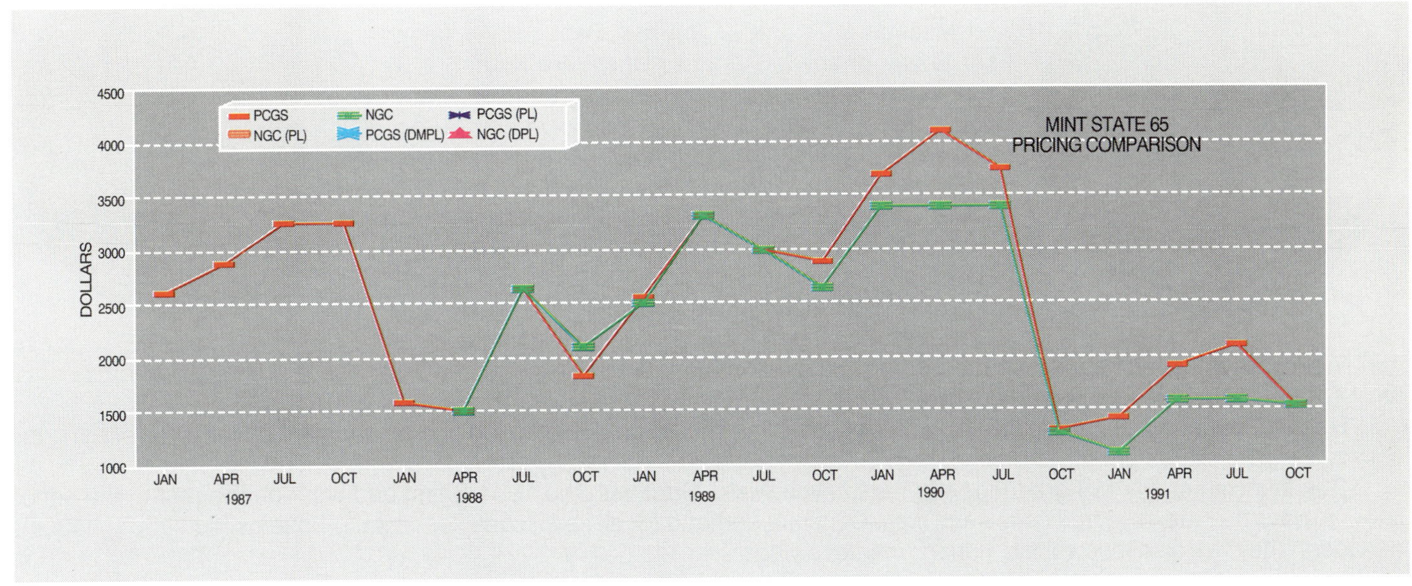
PCGS
NGC
PCGS (PL)
NGC (PL)
PCGS (DMPL)
NGC (DPL)
MINT STATE 65
PRICING COMPARISON
DOLLARS
4500
4000
3500
3000
2500
2000
1500
1000
JAN APR JUL OCT JAN APR JUL OCT JAN APR JUL OCT JAN APR JUL OCT JAN APR JUL OCT
1987
1988
1989
1990
1991

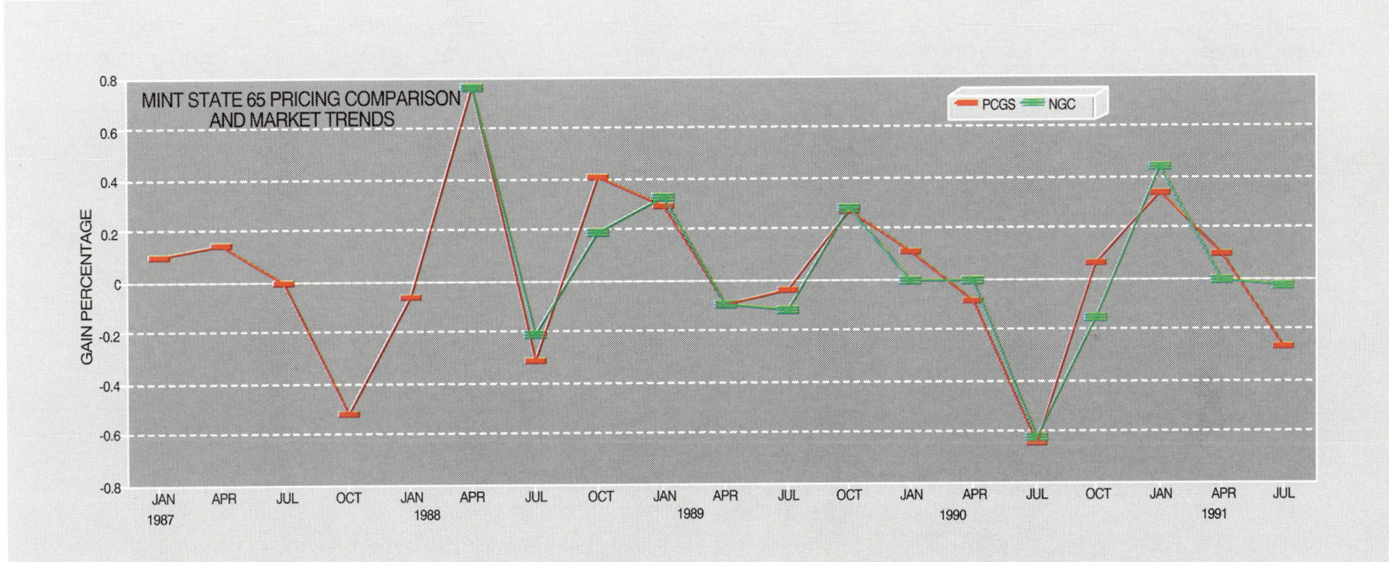
MINT STATE 65 PRICING COMPARISON
AND MARKET TRENDS
PCGS
NGC
GAIN PERCENTAGE
0.8
0.6
0.4
0.2
0
-0.2
-0.4
-0.6
-0.8
JAN APR JUL OCT JAN APR JUL OCT JAN APR JUL OCT JAN APR JUL OCT JAN APR JUL
1987
1988
1989
1990
1991

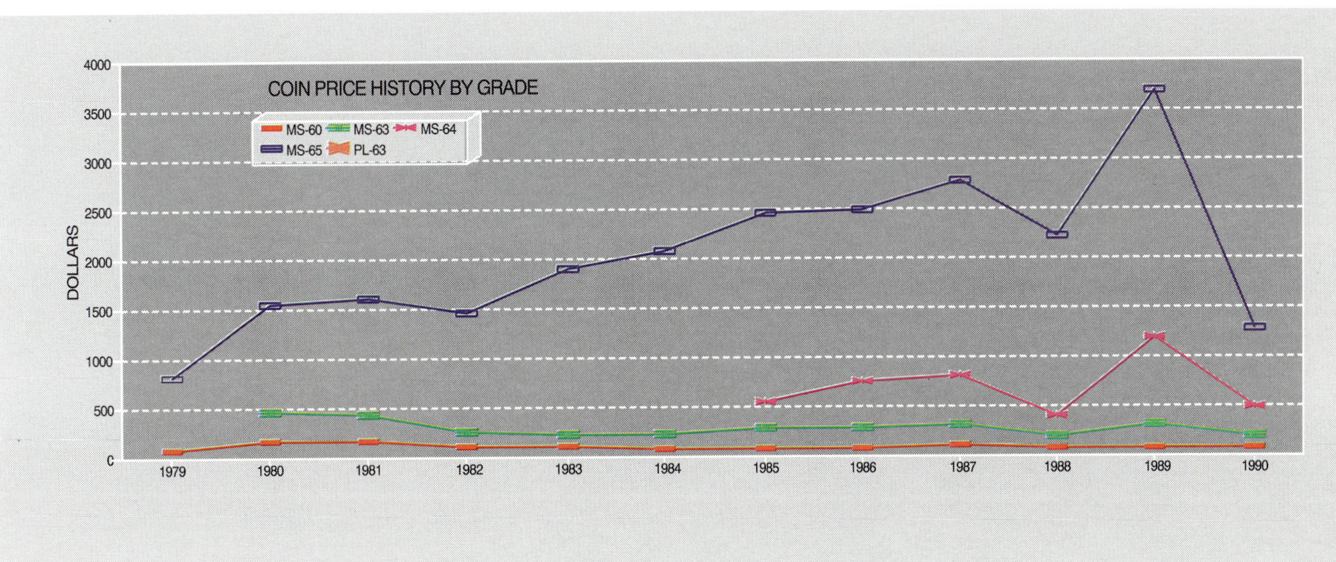
COIN PRICE HISTORY BY GRADE
MS-60
MS-63
MS-64
MS-65
PL-63
DOLLARS
4000
3500
3000
2500
2000
1500
1000
500
0
1979 1980 1981 1982 1983 1984 1985 1986 1987 1988 1989 1990

1934-S

Mintage 1,011,000. The key Peace date, fairly hard to find in any MS grade. Uncs. are from 2 or 3 small hoards, the biggest several hundred (San Francisco, 1962), 35 original BU pieces turned up at the 1978 F.U.N. Convention in Florida. Two original rolls changed hands in 1978; this author (Highfill) handled another at the 1982 National Silver Dollar Convention in Houston, Texas. Strike is average. Luster is blazing. Lots of sliders and circulated specimens abundant. Premiums required for those above EF 40.

Fakes have been made by adding S mintmarks to genuine Philadelphia dollars. Look for a seam around mintmark where it meets the field; use a 20x glass or a binocular microscope. Authentication recommended.

Recommended in any grade, the higher the better; this should probably be the first purchase of anyone just starting the series. Beware sliders prices as Unc.

Buy this coin in any MS grade for any reason you wish. Start with the 1934-S first and work on the rest of the series later. Always buy the keys and semi-keys first. Constant demand for all key issues keeps the premiums high throughout the decades. They are also less volatile during "market swings".

MINTAGE	PROOF	STRIKE	LUSTER	BAGMARKS
1,011,000	0	Average To Bold	Very Good	Light
REDFIELD	**CATEGORY**	**DIE VARIETIES**	**PIVOTAL GRADE**	**RARITY FACTOR**
No	Key	2	MS 65	R-1

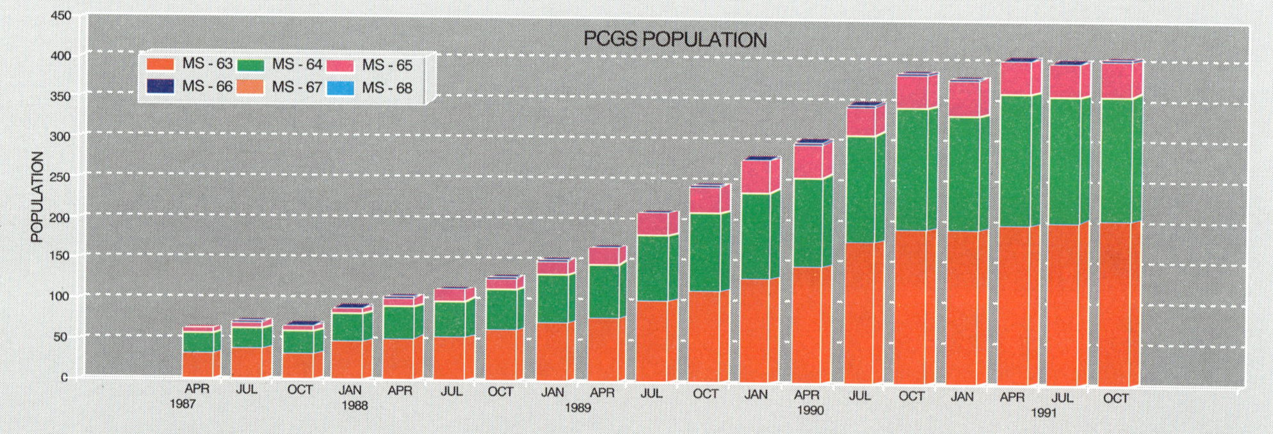

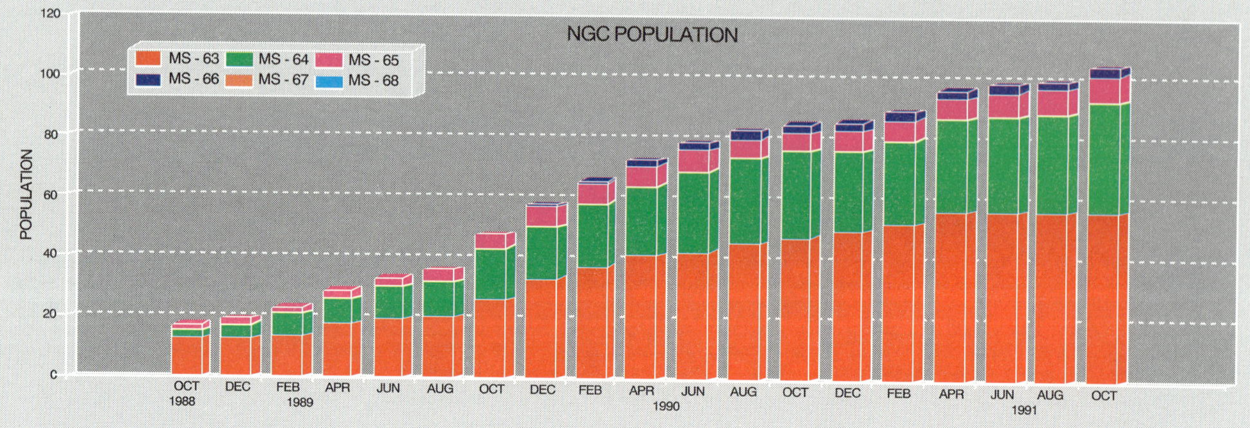

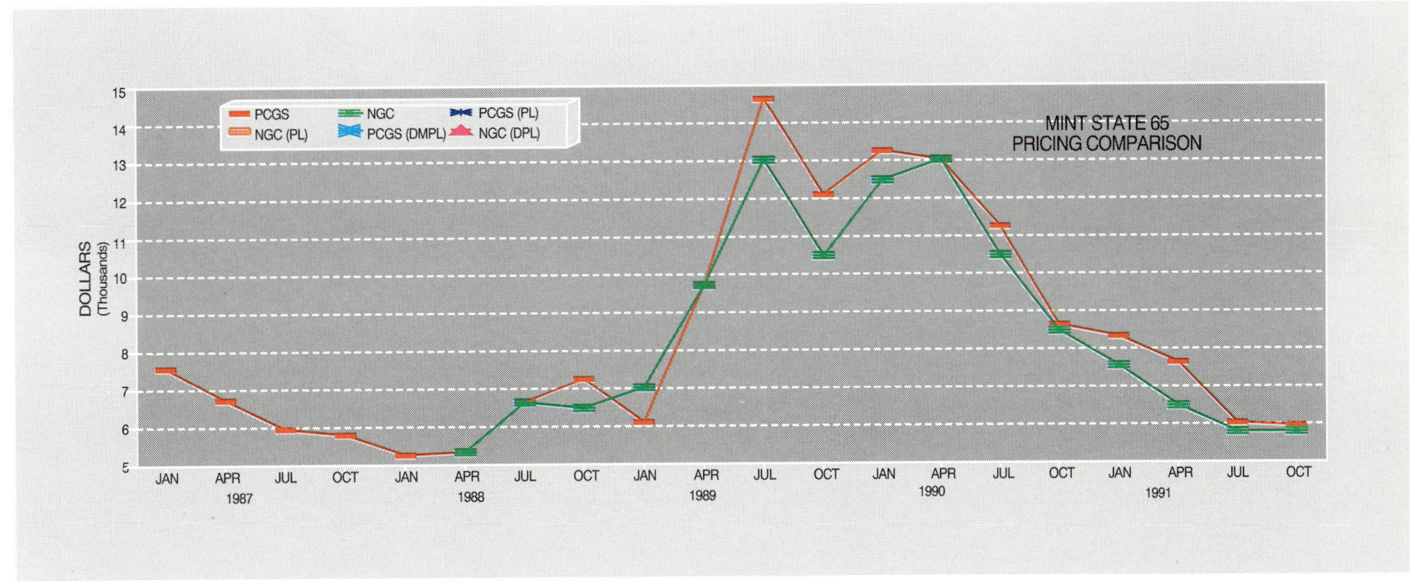
MINT STATE 65
PRICING COMPARISON
PCGS
NGC
PCGS (PL)
NGC (PL)
PCGS (DMPL)
NGC (DPL)
DOLLARS
(Thousands)
15
14
13
12
11
10
9
8
7
6
5
JAN APR JUL OCT JAN APR JUL OCT JAN APR JUL OCT JAN APR JUL OCT JAN APR JUL OCT
1987
1988
1989
1990
1991

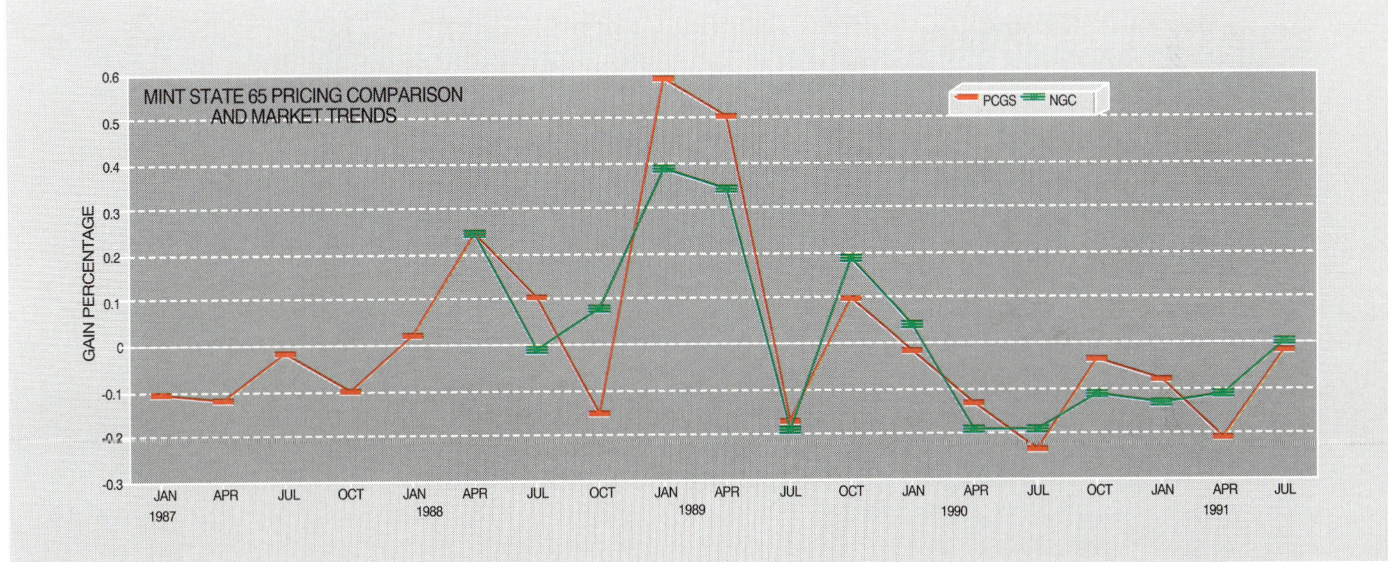
MINT STATE 65 PRICING COMPARISON
AND MARKET TRENDS
PCGS
NGC
GAIN PERCENTAGE
0.6
0.5
0.4
0.3
0.2
0.1
0
-0.1
-0.2
-0.3
JAN APR JUL OCT JAN APR JUL OCT JAN APR JUL OCT JAN APR JUL OCT JAN APR JUL
1987
1988
1989
1990
1991

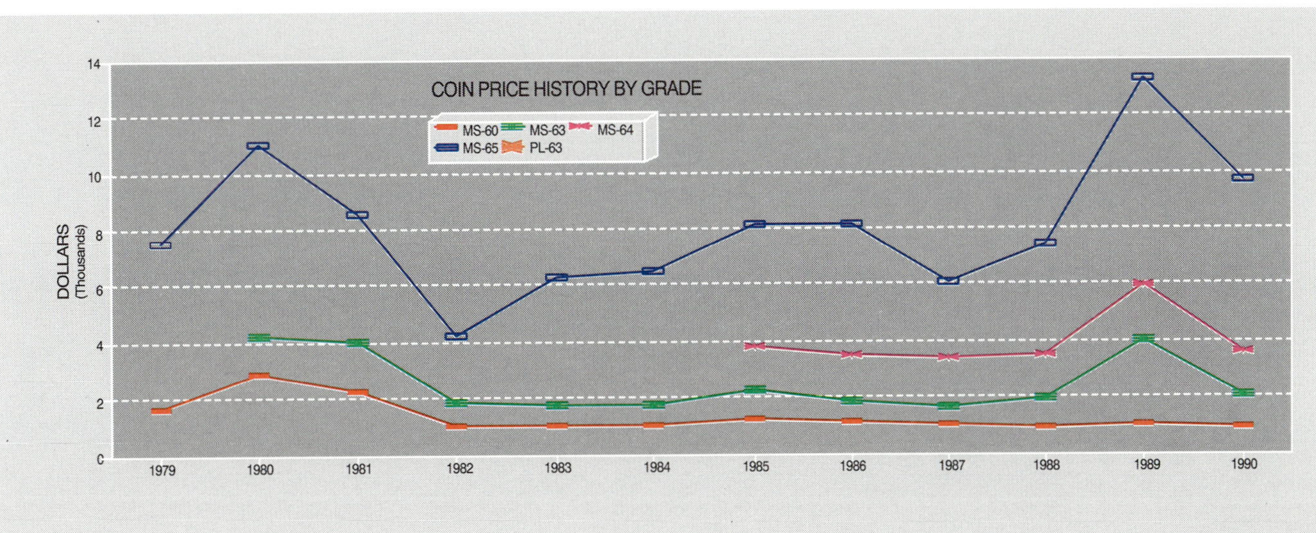
COIN PRICE HISTORY BY GRADE
MS-60
MS-63
MS-64
MS-65
PL-63
DOLLARS
(Thousands)
14
12
10
8
6
4
2
0
1979 1980 1981 1982 1983 1984 1985 1986 1987 1988 1989 1990

1935-P

Mintage 1,576,000. The last Philadelphia Peace dollar comes with great strike and good luster. Plentiful in all grades including gems. This date was released early into circulation. Sliders are abundant. The 1935-P is the most common issue that can be found with mint errors. This date is commonly available in circulated grades.

The 1935-P is twice as available in all grades above MS 63 than both the 1927-P or the 1934-P.

Recommended in MS 64 up. None graded above MS 66 by either service (PCGS or NGC).

MINTAGE	PROOF	STRIKE	LUSTER	BAGMARKS
1,576,000	0	Sharp & Bold	Very Good	Light
REDFIELD	**CATEGORY**	**DIE VARIETIES**	**PIVOTAL GRADE**	**RARITY FACTOR**
No	Semi-key	1	MS 65	R-3

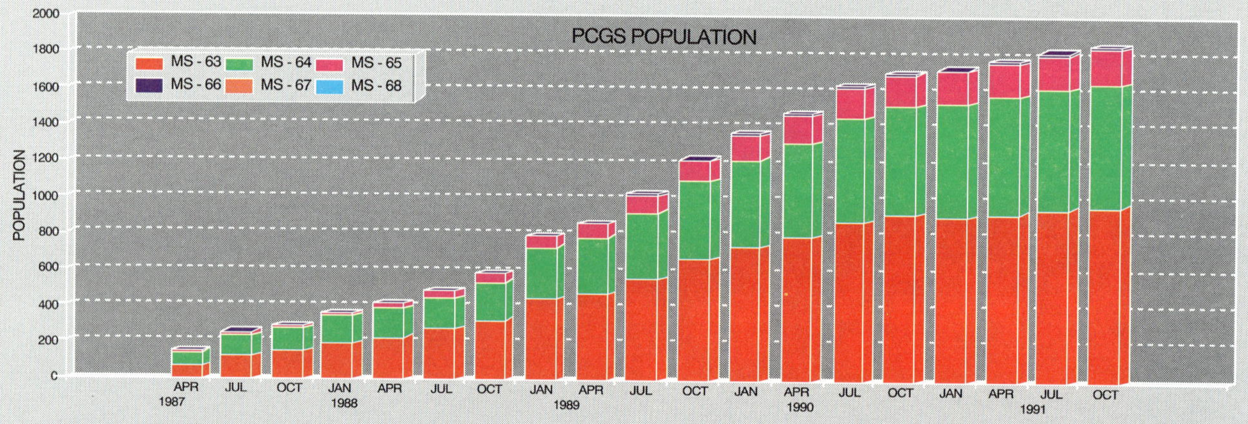

PCGS POPULATION

MS - 63 MS - 64 MS - 65 MS - 66 MS - 67 MS - 68

POPULATION

2000 1800 1600 1400 1200 1000 800 600 400 200 0

APR 1987 JUL OCT JAN 1988 APR JUL OCT JAN 1989 APR JUL OCT JAN APR 1990 JUL OCT JAN APR JUL 1991 OCT

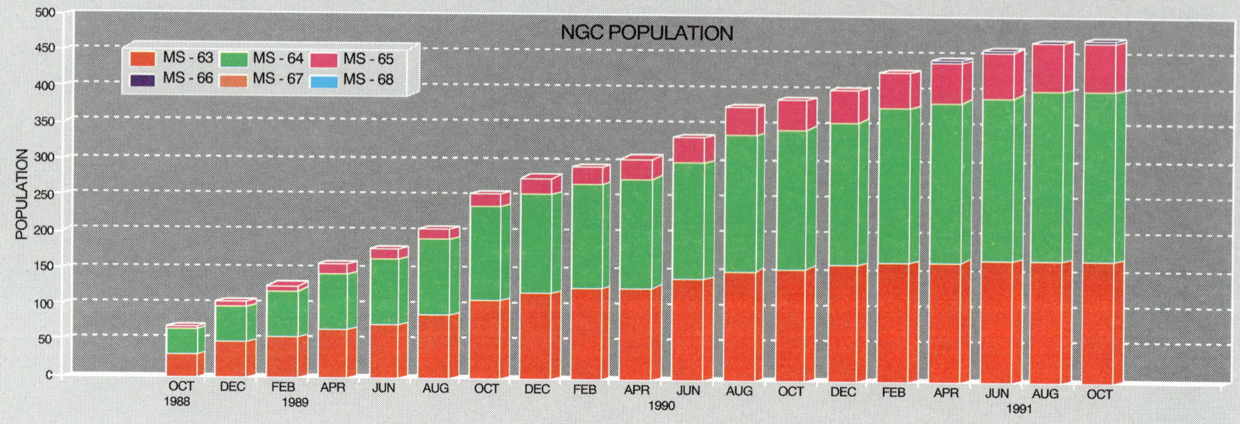

NGC POPULATION

MS - 63 MS - 64 MS - 65 MS - 66 MS - 67 MS - 68

POPULATION

500 450 400 350 300 250 200 150 100 50 0

OCT 1988 DEC FEB 1989 APR JUN AUG OCT DEC FEB APR 1990 JUN AUG OCT DEC FEB APR JUN 1991 AUG OCT

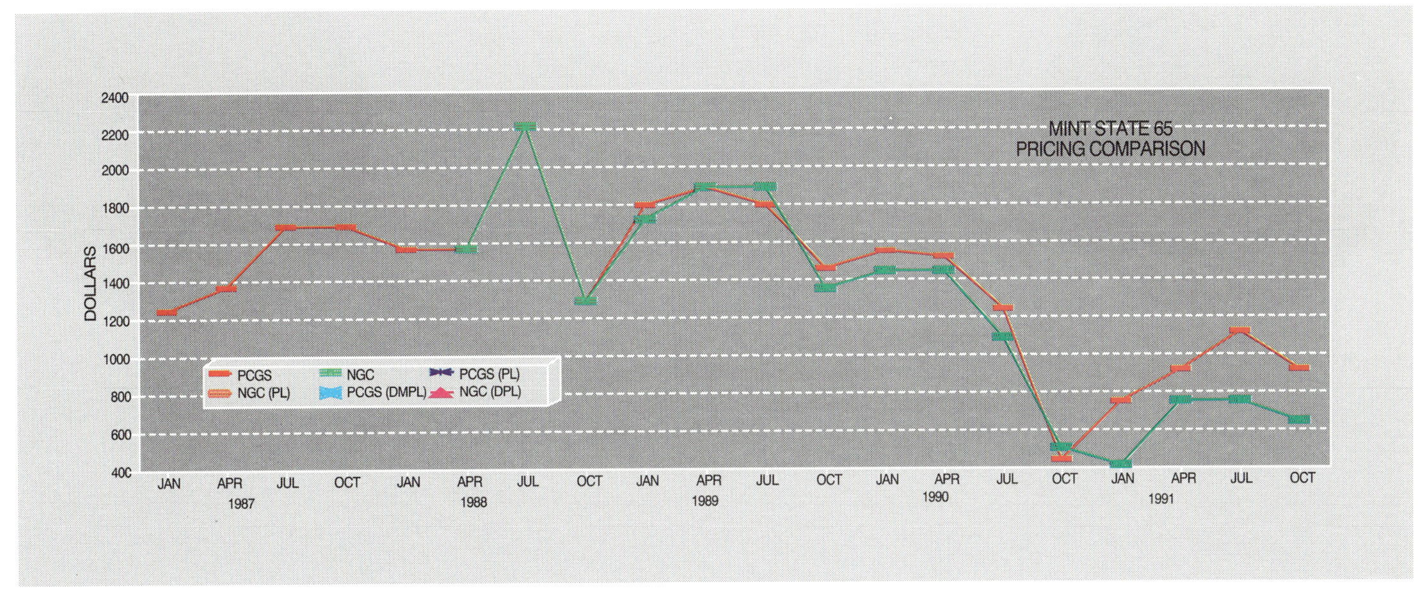
MINT STATE 65
PRICING COMPARISON
DOLLARS
2400
2200
2000
1800
1600
1400
1200
1000
800
600
400
PCGS
NGC
PCGS (PL)
NGC (PL)
PCGS (DMPL)
NGC (DPL)
JAN APR JUL OCT JAN APR JUL OCT JAN APR JUL OCT JAN APR JUL OCT JAN APR JUL OCT
1987
1988
1989
1990
1991

MINT STATE 65 PRICING COMPARISON
AND MARKET TRENDS
PCGS
NGC
GAIN PERCENTAGE
0.8
0.6
0.4
0.2
0
-0.2
-0.4
-0.6
-0.8
JAN APR JUL OCT JAN APR JUL OCT JAN APR JUL OCT JAN APR JUL OCT JAN APR JUL
1987
1988
1989
1990
1991

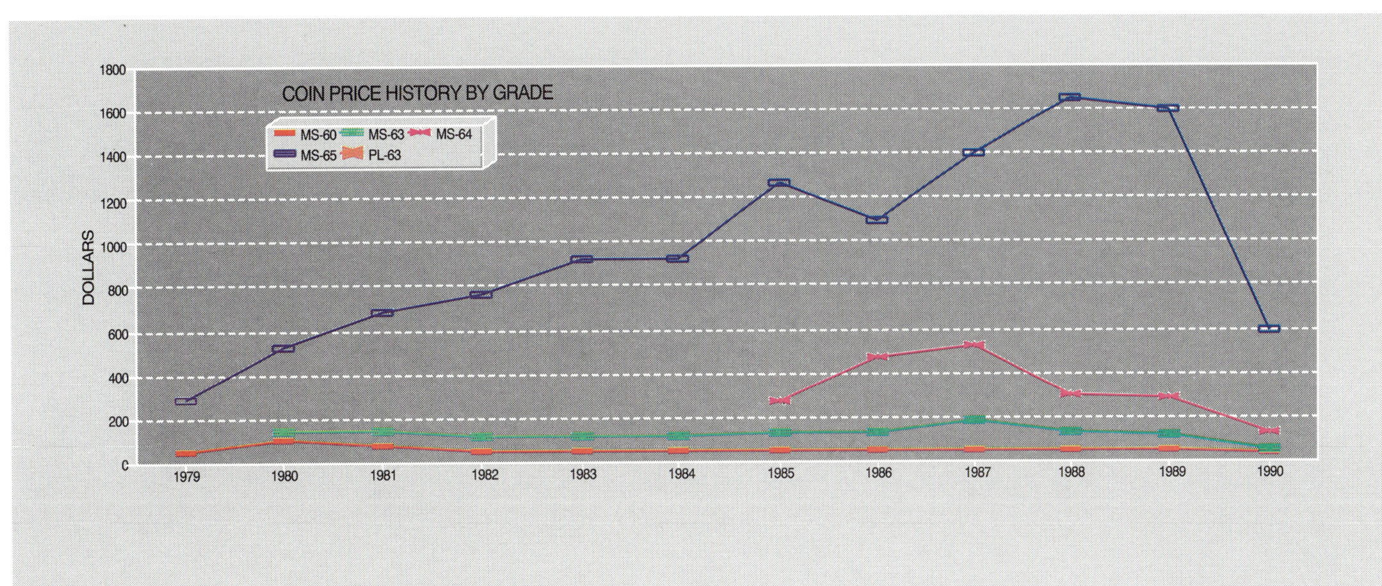
COIN PRICE HISTORY BY GRADE
MS-60
MS-63
MS-64
MS-65
PL-63
DOLLARS
1800
1600
1400
1200
1000
800
600
400
200
0
1979 1980 1981 1982 1983 1984 1985 1986 1987 1988 1989 1990

1935-S

Mintage 1,964,000. The last San Francisco Peace dollar. Gems are available, well struck, brilliant to frosty Luster. Redfield's (less that a full bag) were mostly weak MS 60/63.

The old design with 3 rays below ONE *Ency* 5740 and the modified version, (discovered by Thomas W. Voetter), with 4 rays below ONE *Encyclopedia* 5741 are both common. Nobody knows which is commoner. A variety collectors delight.

Recommended in MS 64 up. None certified in grades above MS 66.

A fully struck and frosty MS 65 or better can be the absolute best specimen for the entire Peace dollar series. WHAT A WAY TO END A TRADITION OF THE SILVER DOLLAR!

MINTAGE	PROOF	STRIKE	LUSTER	BAGMARKS
1,964,000	0	Average To Bold	Excellent	Moderate
REDFIELD	**CATEGORY**	**DIE VARIETIES**	**PIVOTAL GRADE**	**RARITY FACTOR**
Yes	Semi-key	3	MS 65	R-2

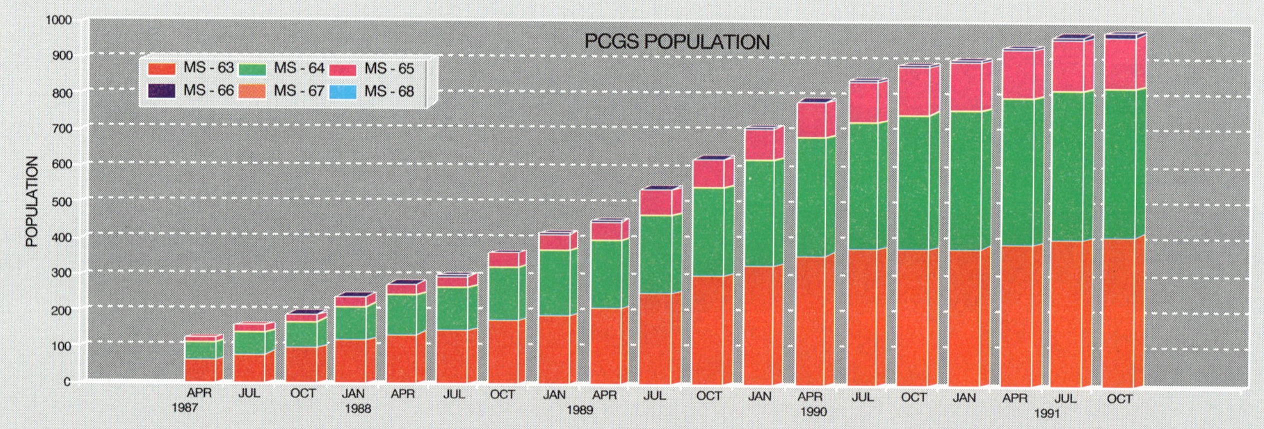

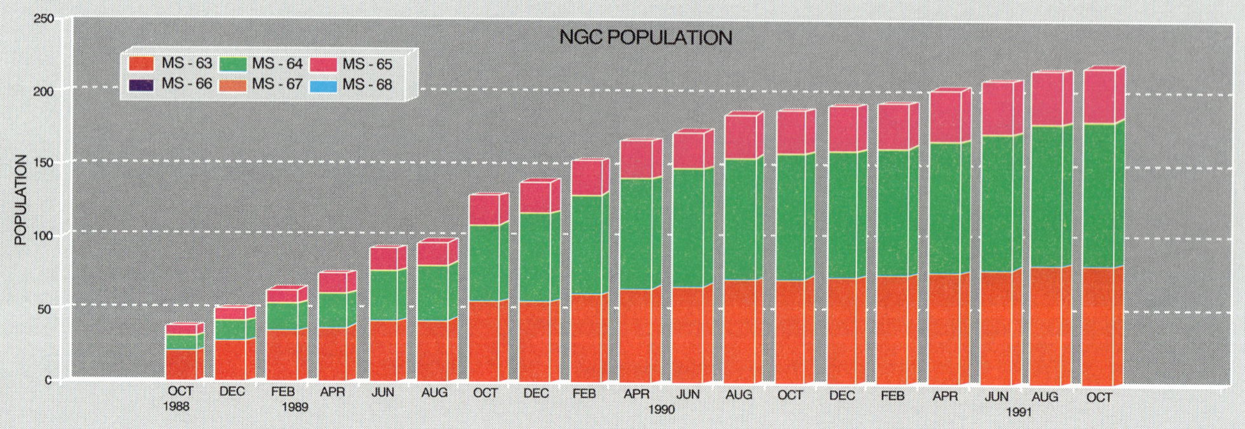

PCGS POPULATION

NGC POPULATION

1935-S

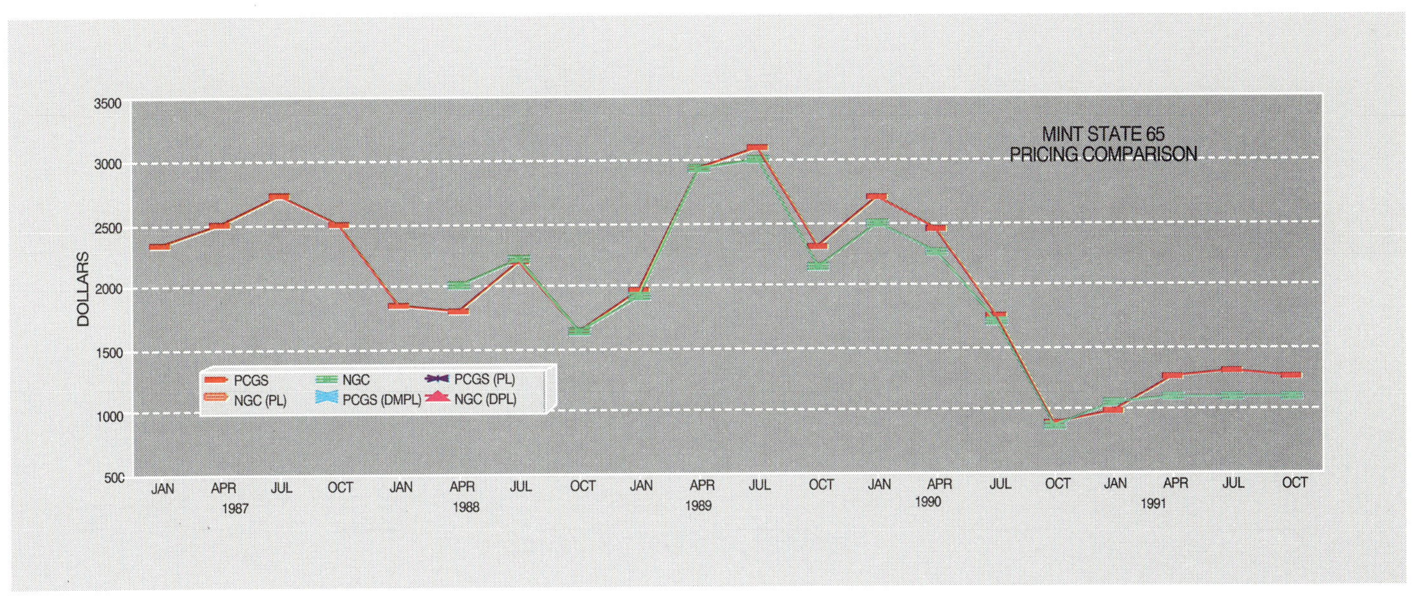

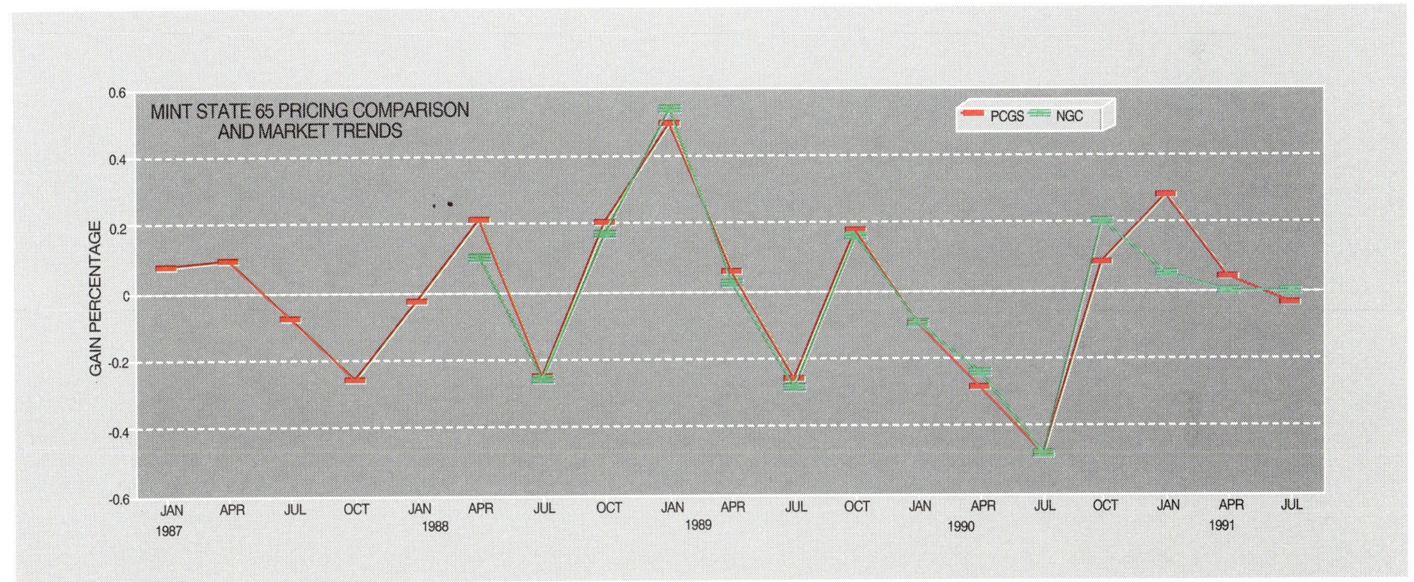

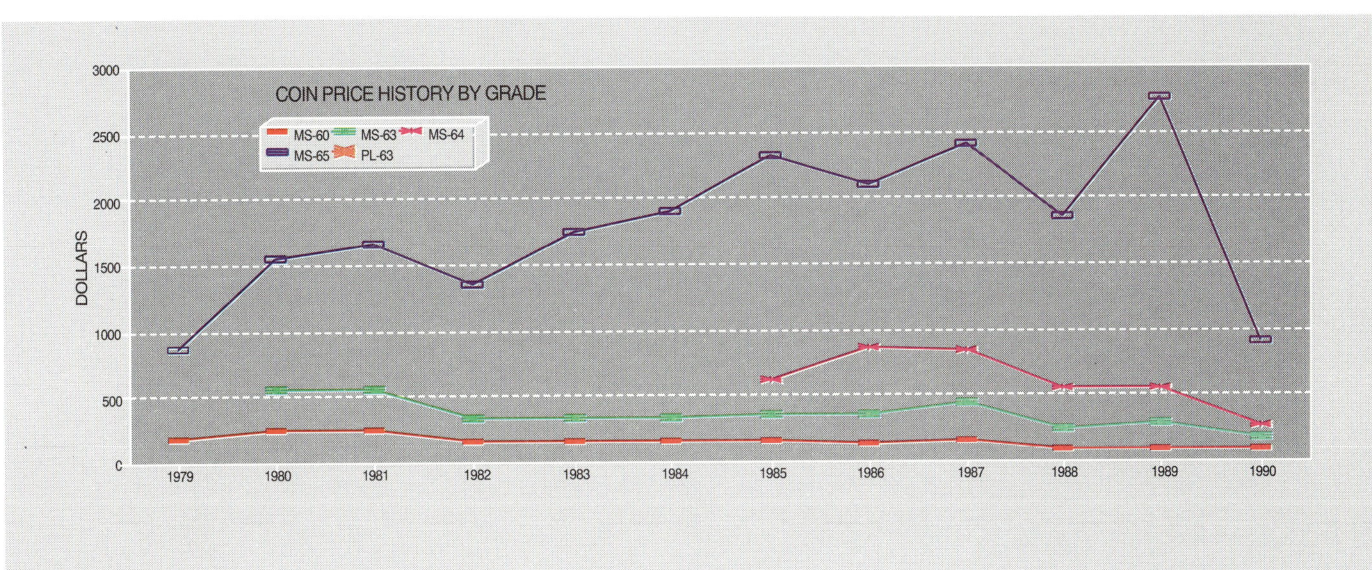

1964-D

Mintage 316,076. *Ency* 5742. THE 1934-D WAS THE LAST PEACE DOLLAR STRUCK AT THE DENVER MINT. HOWEVER, THE 1964-D TRIAL PIECES WERE STRUCK BUT NEVER RELEASED TO THE PUBLIC. NONE ARE KNOWN TO EXIST TODAY. Maybe someday one will turn up in the Smithsonian, and we'll know what it really looked like. I can dream, can't I? (Walter H. Breen)

No Analysis Data Available

Bibliography

Without the continuing knowledge, help, encouragement and assistance of the following friends, associates, inspirations, both alive and deceased, this book would not have been possible. Also, the listed organizations and their associates were indispensable in the creation of *The Comprehensive U.S. Silver Dollar Encyclopedia*™. Please accept my sincere apologies if I have left out your name by mistake. The fast approaching publisher's deadline made it physically impossible to thank everyone properly.

Organizations:

AccuGrade
American Airlines
Amos Press
American Coin Conventions Inc.
Broken Arrow, Oklahoma
ANA - American Numismatic Association
ANAAB - American Numismatic Association
Authentication Bureau
ANACS - American Numismatic Association
Certification Service
ANE - American Numismatic Exchange
American Numismatic Society
Astro Village Hotel - Houston, Texas
ATC/FACTS - American Teleprocessing Corporation
Bern's Steak House - Tampa, Florida
Blueberry Hill - Tampa, Florida
Brede Exposition Services - Orlando, Florida
British Royal Mint
Bureau of Engraving and Printing
Busch Gardens - Tampa, Florida
CABAP - Coin and Bullion Accreditation Program
Canadian Coin Dealer Newsletter
Capitol Plastics
CCDN - Certified Coin Dealer Newsletter
CCDN - Asksheet
CCE - Certified Coin Exchange
CDN - Coin Dealer Newsletter
Chester West Productions
China Mint
Clearwater Coin Club, Inc.
COINage Magazine
"CoinArt" Designer Series
Coin World
CompuGrade ™
CSNS - Central States Numismatics Society
Embassy Suites - St. Louis, Missouri
Entertainment Enterprises
Excel Decorators, Inc. - Tampa, Florida
FNN - Financial News Network
FUN - Florida United Numismatists
Gulfport and St. Petersburg Coin Clubs
Hallmark Grading Service
Harbour Island Hotel - Tampa, Florida
Hawaiian Mint
Heritage Numismatic Auctions
Highfill Press, Inc. - Broken Arrow, Oklahoma
Holiday Inn - St. Louis, Missouri
Hyatt Regency - Long Beach, California
Hyatt Regency - Tampa, Florida
ICTA - Industry Council for Tangible Assets
Johnson Matthey Metals
Joe Jones Agency
John Baumann Safe Company, St. Louis, Mo.
Krause Publications
Kurt Krueger Auctions
Long Beach Expositions
M & M World Travel Service, Inc.
Marriott - St. Louis, Missouri
McIntire Numismatic Auctions
Media Resources
Missouri Numismatic Society
NGC - Numismatic Grading Corporation
NGE - National Gold Exchange, Inc.
NSDR - National Silver Dollar Roundtable
National Gold Convention - Broken Arrow, Oklahoma
National Silver Dollar Conventions, Inc.
Broken Arrow, Oklahoma
North American Coin Conventions, Inc.
Broken Arrow, Oklahoma & Tampa, Florida
Numismatic News
NumisTech Publications
OFG&N - Oklahoma Federated Gold and
Numismatics, Inc., Broken Arrow, Oklahoma
PCGS - Professional Coin Grading Service
PCGS World's Finest Morgan Dollar Collection
Peoples Loan & Trust Co. - Winchester, Indiana
Photo Certified Coin Institute
PNG - Professional Numismatists Guild, Inc.
Pobjoy Mint
Positive Protection
Rarities Group
Riverside Hotel - Tampa, Florida
Riverfront "Becky Thatcher"
Ruth's Chris Steak House - St. Louis, Missouri
SafraBank - Encino, Ca.
Sheraton St. Louis Hotel
Sho-Mor Expositions, Inc. - Tampa, Florida
Spectrum Numismatics International
St. Louis Arch
St. Louis Cardinals Baseball Organization
St. Louis Cardinals Football Organization
St. Louis Coin Club
St. Louis Numismatic Expositions
St. Louis Police Department
Tampa Safe Company
Teletrade
T.I.S. - Tangible Information Services
T.W.A. - Trans World Airlines
U.S.R.C.E. - United States Rare Coin Exchange
U.S. Banknote Company
U.S. Bureau of Printing and Engraving
U.S. Coins - Houston, Texas
U.S. Mint
U.S. Postal Service - St. Louis, Missouri
U.S. Postal Service - Tampa, Florida
Unigold, Inc.
Unitrade
Valley National Bank - Tulsa, Oklahoma
Westex Expositions
Westside Forty-Four Security
Willard Scott "Today Show"

Individuals:

Steve Aaker
Cliff Aamoth
Bryan Abbott
Larry Abbott
Michael Abbott
John T. Abbott
Paul M. Abel
Wes Abel
Jay Abraham
Steven Abramovitz
Brian Abrams
Carl Abrams
Mike Abramson
Alan J. Ackerman
Manny Acosta
Laura Acree
Marc J. Achterhof
John Acton
Ronnie Adam
Al C. Adams, Jr.
Dalton Adams
David Adams
Dick Adams
Eva B. Adams
Gordon G. Adams
Jerry Adams
William T. Adams
Wayne Adcock
Massoud Adhoot
Bob Adisano
Charles M. Adkins
Gary Adkins
Jeff Adkins
Tony B. Adkins
Sheldon Adler
Edward W. Adomaitis
Carl E. Adrian
John Adrian
Thomas M. Affeldt
Phil Aftoora
Nader Agha
Carl Agostini
Robert Aguilar
Steve Ahajanian
Gary M. Ainsworth
Richard L. Ainsworth
George Akelis
David W. Akers
Wayne Akers
Rusty Akin
John Albanese
Mark Albarian
Ross Albergo
Tony Albergo
Audrey Alberto
Leonard Albrecht
John Albright
Stephen Album
Walt Alcott
Glen and Ruby Alderman
Ann Marie Aldrich
Edward J. Aleo
David T. Alexander
Gary Alexander
Meryl "Alex" Alexander
Jacquline E. Alford
Paul O. Alford
Patricia Alifraghis
Donald Allen
George Allen
John Allen
Johney Allen
Lyman Allen
Rod Allen
Stan Allen
Victoria Allen
Buddy Alleva
Phillip B. Alleva
William Allgeier, Sr.
Bill Allgood
Pat Allison
John Alman
Robert Alpigini
Michael Alster
Gary W. Alt
Martin L. Altbaum
Ted Althaus
Johnnie Alverson
Jake Amato
John Amos
Claude Amsellem
Bruce Amspacher
Charles O. Anastasio
Lisa Anastasio
Dave Anders
John M. Andersen
Wayne Andersen
Alan B. Anderson
Andy Anderson
Arthur A. Anderson
Burnett Anderson
Donna Anderson
Edna Anderson
James W. Anderson
Jim Anderson
Joel Anderson
John Anderson
Martin E. Anderson
Neil Anderson
Norbert Anderson
David Andrade
John F. Andres
Marie J. Andrian
Richard G. Andrian
Jeffrey Angello
Joseph M. Angello
Rob Anglemier
Walt Ankerman
Al Annibali
Michael C. Annis
Maney Anson
David Anthony
Ray Anthony
Frank Antino
John Antolino
William T. Anton
Don Antonio
Phil Antonio
Bill Apfelpaum
Dr. Richard S. Appel
Norman Applebaum
Duane Applegate
Jennifer Applegate
Donald Apte
Essy Arash
Miller B. Arbutine
Dan Archer
Robert Archer
Kerrilyn Ardeneaux
Gene Arensberg
Gus Argeris
Tony Argue
Sandra Armstron
Burl Armstrong
Dianne Armstrong
Dick Armstrong
Earl Armstrong
Evelyn Armstrong
Gabriele Armstrong
Glenn Armstrong
William R. Armstrong
Al Arndt
Elerie Arnett
Ed Arnold
Vince Arnold
Kelly Arnone
Thomas Arnone
Michael Aron
Irving Aronson
Gary Arrowood
Norm Ashby
Les Ashe
Charles Assetta
Eryck C. Aston
Robert L. Astrich
Mark Astroff
Gary Atkins
Irv Atkins
Tony Atkins
Thomas Atkinson
William Atkinson
R. J. Audet
Mark S. Auerbach
Richard August
Russell A. Augustin
Ed Auler
Richard Austin
Bobby Avena
Daniel J. Avena, Jr.
Daniel Avena, Sr.
Charles Avery
Thomas J. Avery
Jeffrey Ayers
Michael Ayres
John Babalis
Jerry Babcock
Richard Bacca
Francesca Bachtell
Michael Backus
Anne Badgett
Terry D. Baer
Richard A. Bagg, Ph.D.
Michael Bagley
Bill Bagwell
Don Bailey
L. M. Bailey
Luther Bain
Robert Bair
Judith Bajoris
Charles Baker
Dennis R. Baker
Don Baker
Keith Baker
Melissa Baker
Phyllis Baker
Wes Bakke
Peter Balanzategui
Charlotte C. Balbaton
Richard J. Balbaton
Clarence E. Baldwin
Clif Baldwin
Don Bale, Jr.
Robert Bales
Douglas Balik
Douglas Baliko
Robert M. Ball
Laymon Ballard
J. C. Ballentine
Lano Balulescu
Chuck Band
David G. Banner
Don Bannister
William Bannon
Dave Bara
Charles Barasch
Harry Barath
Paul Barattini
Michael Barber
Irv Bard
Joe Barger
Joanne Barham
Alex J. Barna
George D. Barnbaum
Loren Barnett
Ken Barr
Russell F. Barr
Wally Barr
Brian Barre
Gregg C. Barrett
Lisa Barrick
Teresa Barrick
Jordan Barrington
Gene Barron
John Barron
C. Bryon Barstow
Dr. Frederick Bart
Walt Bartee
David Barth
Robert Barth
Thomas E. Bartholomew
Charles R. Bartlett
Russell A. Bartlett
Bob Bartolo
Eugene Bascou
George Basehore
Ken Bashford
Stephen J. Bashinski
Sandy Bashover
R. W. Basket
R. Basler
Michael Bass
Emidio Bastianelli
John Bastolich
Robert F. Batchelder

Monte Batchelor
Dudley Batey
John W. Bates, III
Larry Bates
Joseph Battaglia
Joseph A. Battles
Eric Bauchner
Bill Bauer
John Bauer
Robert D. Bauer
Ruth W. Bauer
Timothy Bauer
Brian Bauman
Douglas Bauman
Gerald L. Bauman
John Baumnann
Jack M. Baxter
Mike Bay
James Bayer
George M. Beach
R. W. Beadle
Thomas M. Beahm
C. E. Bear
Jim Beard
John D. Bearden
Brian Beardsley
Hilda Bearinger
William A. Beasi
James T. Beasley
Dennis Beatty
Douglas S. Beatty
Richard Beaty
Jerry Beavers
Aubrey E. Bebee
Al Beck
Julie Beck
Paul Beck
Robert B. Becker
Tom Becker
Kevin Beckerman
Harry Becko
Lawrence J. Bedard
Bob Bednarski
Jeff Beem
Jim Beem
Jim Beer
Robert Behar
B. J. Behrends
Jack R. Behrends
Samuel J. Beil
Norman Belair
Tom Belcher
Joseph Belfer
Scott Belfer
Jim Belisle
Allyn Bell
Barbara Bell
Dianne Bell
Jeff Bell
K. C. Bell
Marvin Rex Bell
Lee J. Bellisario
Barry Bellefontaine
Steve Belman
Ralph Benavides
Larry Bence
Michael Bender
Joe Benedetti
Philip E. Benedetti
Nicholas Beneloque
Bernard Beneteau
Donald E. Benge
Charles H. Bengyak
C. H. Benjamin
Bob Bennett
Steve R. Bennett, III
Tom Bennington
Marcy Benouameur
Carl Benson
H. H. Benson
Lauren Benson
Mel Benson
Richard Benson
J.W. Bently
David A. Berg
Gordon W. Berg
Larry Berg
Jeffrey J. Bergelt
Neil Bergelt
Henry M. Bergen
Dwight W. Berger
Grace Berger
Guy Berger
Michael F. Bergin
Peter N. Berglund
John Bergman
Daniel Berk
Harlan J. Berk
Robert Berk
Louis Berkie
Larry Berkovits
Oliver Berliner
Allen G. Berman
Brad Berman
Christine Berman
Neil S. Berman
Jeffrey F. Bernberg
Mark Bernhardt
Robert Bernier
Norman Bernstein
Doug J. Berry
J. D. Berry
Mathis Berry
Van H. Berry, III
Yvonne "Vonnie"
A. Berry
Dave Berryman
Karlis Berzins
Erv Beskow
Jim Best
James W. Bethe
Mark Bettinger
John Bettinson
Diane Betts
C. L. Bewley
John S. Beyers
Michael Beyers
Jack H. Beymer
Sondra Beymer
Bob Bianchi
Michael Bianco
Diane Biard
Billy J. Biberstein
Bob Bible
Israel I. Bick
Jerry Bickers
Don Bickhart
Dorothy Bickmore
Glenn S. Biederman
John Bielasky
Andrew G. Bigos
Dr. Robert Bilinski
Daniel R. Bina
Don Bingaman
John Binna
Jerry Binsfield
Douglas F. Bird
George Birdsall
Paul Birkahn
Lucien Birkler
Hal Birt
Ed Bishop
Jerome Bishop
John Bishop
Sheri Bishop
Dale Bissett
Craig R. Bittner
Mike Bivins
Mitch Blachut
Chris J. Black
Ed Black
E. D. Black
Charles Hal Blackburn
David Blackburn
Peggy Blackburn
Teb Blackwell
Kenneth Bladsoe
Earl F. Blaisdell
Jan Blamberg
Larry Blamos
James U. Blanchard, III
David Bland, Jr.
Richard F. Bland
H. Clay Blaney, III
Bobbie Blankley
Robert Blaschke, Jr
Nora R. Blaser
Richard Blau
Michael Blauer
Gary D. Blevins
H.W. Blevins
J.D. Blight
Randy Block
Diane Blodgett
Michael W. Blodgett, Ph.D.
John Blois
David J. Bluestein
Steve Blum
Vincent Blume
Arthur Blumenthal
Burton S. Blumert
A. E. Blythe
James Blythe
H. H. Board
Michael M. Bobb
Jerry Bobbe
Sharon Bobbe
Emmett Bobbitt
Stephen Bobbitt
John Bobeng
Greg Bobitt
Tony Paul Bochicchio
Sheldon Bock
Rosemarie Bockhold
Bob Bodine
George E. Bodway, Ph.D.
Terry T. Bogert
R. A. Bohn
Brad Bohnert
Julie Boike
Ray Bolduc
M.H. Bolender
Robert C. Bollinger
Roger Boman
Albert Bonan
Jered Bonbrake
Craig Bond
Sue Bong
Anthony Bongiovanni
Don Bonser
Eldert A. Bontekoe
Martin Bookston
George T. Booth
Jack Borckardt
Mark R. Borckardt
Daniel J. Borda
R. O. Bordwine
Kathleen Borenitech
Fred Borgmann
Bo Borich
Jean Borkowski
Carl Borngasser
Lester Bortner
Ray Bos
William Bossert
Joseph M. Bossi
James M. Boswell
Remy Bourne
Larry R. Bovo
Ben Bowden
Brigitte M. Bowers
Norman L. Bowers
Q. David Bowers
Raymond Bowers
Dale Bowlin
Lynn Bowlin
Rosemary Bowlin
Wade Bowlin
Ray A. Bows
Charlie Boyd
Dan Boyd
Earl Boyer
Patrick Boyer
Peter A. Boyer
Suzanne Boyer
Gordon R. Boyle
R.W. Bradford
R. N. Bradley
Ronald Bradley
Will Bradley
Michael J. Brady
John Bragg
Richard A. Bragg, Ph.D.
Robert Brahms
Morris Bram
Virgil Brand
Gene Brandenburg
Joel Brander
William Brander
Robert J. Brandi
Ronald A. Brandow
Bob Brandt

Jeff Brant
Bob Brantley
David E. Brassfield
Frank Brazzell
Robert M. Breed
Walter H. Breen
Don L. Brennan
Mary Lee Brennan
Kent Brennen
John Brenner
Kenneth E. Bressett
Phil Bressett
Bruce Breton
Ruthann Brettell
Nelson Brewart
Dale R. Brewer
Pat Brewer
Gerald Breyer
Bill Brieske
Donald E. Brigandi
John E. Brigandi
Robert Brigandi
Ed Brigante
Christian R. Briggs
Gerald M. Briggs
Jerry Briggs
Jim Briggs
Larry Briggs
Bill Bright
Joe Bristol
Phillip Bristol
James Bristow
Nawana Britenriker
John Brndiar
Thomas Brody
Paul A. Brombal
Edward Brondback
Jan Bronson
Laurie Bronson
Barry Brooks
Mary Brooks
Harold R. Brosius
Irv Brotman
Al Brown
Alex Brown
Ann Brown
Bernie Brown
Bill Brown, Jr.
Bud Brown
Charlie Brown
Darrell Brown
Don Brown
Douglas Brown
Earl Brown
Gordon Brown
W. Herman Brown
Hy Brown
Jerry M. Brown
Kevin P. Brown
Mark Brown
Martin R. Brown
Norbert Brown
Paul Brown
Sandra Brown
Warren E. Brown
William K. Brown
Winford J. Brown, Jr.
Charles O. Browne
Chuck I. Browne
John Brownell
James H. Brownfield
Mike G. Brownlee
Charles A. Brownley, Jr.
Colin R. Bruce, II
Mike Bruce
Linda Brueggeman
Robert Brueggeman
Arnold R. Bruhn
Bill Brunner
F. L. Bruno
Larry Brush
Walter G. Brush
William J. Brutsche
Terry Bry
Ginger Bryan
John F. Bryan, III
Mary Megan Bryan
Mike "Wino" Bryan
Roger P. Bryan
Clayton Bryant
Dale Bryant
Jerry K. Bryant
Don Buchanan
R. J. Buchanan
Alvin M. Buckholtz
Charles T. Buckley
Charles Bukartis
Catherine Bullowa
Joseph Bumb
Douglas Bumgardner
Don Buntin
Gene Buonanno
William J. Burbridge
Chuck Burchfield
William Burd
Cecil Burden
Glen C. Burger
Craig Burgess
Calvin Burgin
Ronald Burhans
Gary L. Burhop
Patrick J. Burke
Paul R. Burke
Hall Burleson
James R. Burmeister
Charles A. Burnham
Frank Burns
Joseph D. Burns
June Burns
William A. Burns
Carl Burnstein
Jerry Burr
Gary Burton
Larry Busch
David L. Bush
Marcy Bush
Harry Busha
Lloyd E. Buss
Don J. Busselle
Gary Bustin
D. Butler
Eddie H. Butler
John Butler
John S. Buttles
Don Buttrey
Tye Buxton
Joe Buzanowski
Nick Buzolich, Sr.
Nick Buzolich, Jr.
C.B. Byers
Michael S. Byers
Mitchell Byers
Jordan Jill Byington
Walter Byler
William D. Byrd
David Caciola
Larry Cadle
Grover Lewis Cagle
Harry Cairns
Anthony Calcagno
Marc M. Calciano
Bruce Calder
Mark Caldwell
Thomas Caldwell
Bob Call
John Callahan
Anthony Calvacca
Joe Cameron
Jay A. Cammack
Willard Camp
Louis Campanara
John Campanella
Sterling F. Campaney
Bob Campbell
Randy Campbell
Richard Campbell
Randy Camper
Tony G. Campo
David L. Cannon
J. Lawrence Cannon
Thomas A. Capel
Victor Capo
Jim Capper
Louis E. Carabini
Dr. J. W. Carberry
Phil Carlino
Linda J. Carlo
Calvin Carlson
Eric Carlson
Gary J. Carlson
Carl W. A. Carlston
J. Carlton
William H. Carmack
Don Carmody
Helen Carmody
Jeff Carneal
Winthrop Carner
Tom Carney
Victor Caroddo
Robert Carolina
Chuck Carpenter
David Carpenter
Ken M. Carpenter
L.L. Carpenter
David Carr
Frank J. Carr
Jim Carr
Mildred Carr
Tim Carr
Janette Carrigan
Peter Carrigan
Andrew M. Carroll
Dennis Carroll
Tim Carroll
David Carruthers
Gerald Carsman
Amon Carter, Sr.
Amon G. Carter, Jr.
Barry Carter
Carl Carter
Daggert Carter
David A. Carter
Mike Carter
W. Scott Carter
Robert L. Caruthers
Robert A. Casabur
Rick Case
Roger Case
Ed Casey
Tim Casey
Leo N. Cashatte, Jr.
Eliot J. Cashdan
Cameron Cashwell
Harley Casper
Douglas S. Cass
Nick Cassarino
Craig Cassidy
Mark Castaneda
David E. Casteneda
David M. Casterline
David Castleman
John E. Castro
Roger Caswell
Charles E. Cataldo
John Catanzaro
Tom Catchings
Bob Cathcart
Victor R. Catts
Howland Caulkins
Bill Causey
Fred Causey
Bill Causseaux
Felix Cavaliere
David Cavanaugh
Wes Caves
John Cawley
Roger Cazin
Victor E. Cecil
Daniel T. Ceglia
Terry Celano
Chuck Ceraso
Glen E. Cerrato
Carl A. Cervellini
Chuck Cervellini
Peg Cervellini
Paul Chabot
David Chaffin
Larry Chambers
Michael Chambers
Armand Champa
Frank Chan
Jimmy Chan
Thomas Chan
John Chandler
Robert R. Chandler
Mark Chaplin
Richard K. Chapman
Robert G. Chapman
West Chappell
Cynthia Charatz
Larry Charbonneau
J.E. Charlton

Allan R. Charters
W. R. Chase
John L. Chass
Ed Chauncey
Larry D. Chauncey
Michael Checkan
Aurelia Chen
Lynn Chen
David Chermesino
Joel P. Cherry
Michael Cherry
Harvey Chew
Jack Chew
K. E. Chickering
Jeffrey Childs
Marty Childs
Sherry Childs
William H. Chisamore
Harold F. Chorney
Louis Chorney
Mark Chrans
John M. Christensen
William B. Christensen
Gene Christian
Rudy Christians
Gail Christopher
Corkey Christy
Frank Church
Herb Church
John Ciesielski
Richard Cincotta
Carol V. Cipot
John Cipriani
Alan Cirelli
Demetri Cirillo
Jim Clack
Bill Clark
D. J. Clark
Fred Clark
Greg Clark
Henry L. Clark
I. Nelson Clark
James R. Clark
Larry T. Clark
Lee Clark
Michael Clark
R. C. Clark
Tom Clark
William Clark
Chris Clarke
Neil Clasen
Robert Clausen
Dan Clay
Ritchie Clay
R. Claydon
Guy C. Clayton
Harry Clayton
Jim Clayton
Richard Cleland
Joe Clements
Samuel Clements
Dave Clenney
Steve Clenney
C.W. Clepper
Quentin Cler
Judson Cleveland
Jerry Cleworth
Terry Clift
Charles Cline
David C. Cline
Harold Cline
J.H. Cline
James Cline
Michael Cline
William F. Cloran
Karl Robt. Close
Thomas G. Cloud
Ken Clute
Dennis L. Cmunt
Jim Coad
Paul Cocheo
Bob Cochran
Jo Ann Cochran
Lee Cochran
Richard Cockwell
Joel D. Coen
R. B. Coen
J. M. Coffee
Ed Coffey
Edward Cogan
Edward M. Coggins
Alan R. Cohen
Bertram Cohen
Bob Cohen
Donald Cohen
James H. Cohen
Jeffrey Cohen
Jerry L. Cohen
Dr. Leonard Cohen
Stephen M. Cohen
Dennis Coit
Terri Coker
Nick Colaneri
Sam Colavita
E. A. Colby
John Colby
Mitchell Cole
Alfred S. Colella
James Coleman
Lou Coles
Carlie C.Coley
James M. Collier
Tracy Collier
Carl Collins
Charles Collins
Jerry Collins
Louis Collins
Robert Collins
John Collopy
Fred L. Colombo
Rosemary Colonna
Richard Coltrane
Edwin J. Colwell
Larry Comer
Patrick D. Comeskey, Sr.
Patrick D. Comeskey, Jr.
LeRoy Comnick
Larry M. Compton
Paul Compton
Henry Comstock
Emmett Concannon
William Condis
Dennis L. Conner
Larry W. Conner
John Connor
Michael J. Connor
John Conomos
William R. Conroy
S. Contursi
Steve Conway
Colonel B.G. Cook
Horace Cook
Hurley Cook
James O. Cook
John D. Cook
Larry Cook
Lee Cook
Nelda Cook
Peter H. Cook
Roy Cook
Tom Cook
David S. Cooke
Lester A. Coons
Andrew Cooper
Paul Cooper
Ronald L. Cooper
Fred Coops
Joseph Dean Cope, O.D.
Jack Copeland
R. Coquene
H. G. Corbin
Clarke Corby
Simon Cordova
Rich Corkran
James C. Corn
J. Cornelio
C. Cornelison
Dave Cornell
Robert H. Cornell
Robert Cornely
Joe Corrado
Ken Cortese
Burton Cosgrove
H. Coss
Brian Costakes
Lou Costanzo
Benny L. Costello
Rick L. Costello
David Coster
John Cotta
Michael A. Cotta
Larry W. Cotten
Marvin Couch
Howard J. Coulter
William Cousins
Don Cowen
Bobby Cox
Bruce K. Cox
David G. Cox
Samuel E. Cox
Charles R. Coyle
Edward Coyne
Mike Crabb
Jack Craddock
Warren Craden
Rickey Craft
Donald F. Craig
Freeman Craig
Louis M. Crain
Andrian Crandell
Dan Crandell
Lee Crane
Peter Crane
Allan Crawford
Bob Crawford
Eugene Crawley
Jack Crawley
Ron H. Crawley
Darrell Creekmur
Randy Crews
Vickie Crews
James Crim
D. A. Criss
Shirley Criss
Joe Cristman
Grover Criswell
Alan Crittenden
Richard Croci
Nick Crocker
Ray Crocker
William H. Crone
Leon C. Cronkright
James Crosby
Bill Cross
Jack Cross
James Cross
Richard E. Cross
W. K. Cross
Larry Crouch
Ron Crouch
Drew R. Crowell
LeRoy Crowell
Adam Crum
John Cubeddu
Paul Cuccia
Tom Culhane
C. H. Culpepper
Lawrence Culver
Rick D. Culver
Michael Cunio
Daniel Cunliffee
Melody Cunningham
Paul Cunningham
Verl Cunningham
Susanne Currie
Roger Currier
Wendell Curry
Jim Curtis
Larry Curtis
Delmer Cushing
David J. Cutitta
Barry J. Cutler
John B. Cychosz
Steven L. Cyrkin
Jim Czachowski
Edward F. Czajka
John Czapar
Michael J. Dady
William Dafcik, Jr.
Warren Dahl
Richard Dahlin
Connie Daigle
Ed J. Dalloz
Peter H. Daly
Stanley Dambrouckas
Henry G. Dammeyer
Jonathan Danch
Bobby Daniels, M.D.
Randy Daniels
Robert L. Daniels
Bela Danko
John W. Dannreuther

Paula Darais
Dennis A. Daray
Bill Darby
Jay R. Darby
Bud Dare
Tom Dariotis
Teresa Darling
Howard Darr, Jr.
Lester Davenport
Mike Davenport
Jean Davey
Tom Davey
Bob Davis
Dan Davis
Dennis Davis
Don Davis
Doug Davis
Gary W. Davis
Jack Davis
James W. Davis
John Davis
Ken Davis
Les Davis
Marion Davis
Michael S. Davis
Michael T. Davis
Ronald E. Davis
R. Coulton Davis
Sam Davis
Wayne L. Davis
Allan Davisson
Jeremy Day
Gary Dayton
Jack A. De Angelis
Dr. Ray De Biase
Gregory S. De Niro
Michael R. Del Greco
M. F. Deans
Henry Deatherage
Jim DeBerry
Ray DeBiase
Anthony DeChristopher
George Decker
Steve Deeds
Mike DeFalco
John DeFever
Gaston DeFilippo
Rick DeFrancis
Klaus J. Degler
Lou DeGregg
Neal Deibert
Beth Deisher
Dave Deitchman
John V. DeJohn
Phil DeJong
David Dekraker
Bill De Leonardis
Carl F. Dellmuth
Bob DeLong
Victor DeLong
Tom DeLorey
Larry Demangate
Larry Demerer
Robert Demers
Kenneth Demko
Jack Dempsey
Rob Dempsey
John C. Deniro
Jean L. Denis
Gary L. Denk
Thomas M. Denly
Jon Denney
Richard Denney
Anthony Denny
Vernon Denny
"Doc" Denton
Dana Derhammer
Matthew T. De Roma
David Derzon
Rick DeSanctis
James DeShong
Euclide Desruchers
Joseph Deter
Ernest DeTomaso
Chris Devine
Les DeVito
Dale DeVore
Don DeVore
Phillip DeVore
Gary Dew
Jack M. Dew
Raleigh Dew
Curtis E. Dexter
John M. Diacin
Tom DiBucci
Tami A. Dickason
Chuck Dickie
Gordon Dickie
Joe Diehl
John Diekhans
Rodney Diepersloat
Robert A. Dierking
Linda Dieter
H. F. DiFrancesco
Silvano DiGenova
James DiGeorgia
Lou DiGregorio
Jim Dillard
Nelson E. Dillehunt
Dan Dillman
Brenda G. Dillon
Thomas DiMaria
John DiMasi
Jerry DiMohner
Milton Dinkin
Doug DiPersio
Ken Dittmann
Kim M. Dixon
Richard Dixon
Tom Dixon
Susan Dodge
Lee Dodrill
Bill Dodson
Peter Doelger
John E. Doemel
David Doering
Larry Dolan
Patrick Dolan
John Dolhun
Greg C. Dollarhide
Richard Dollen
Michael N. Domingue
William Dominick
Tom Donahue
Al Donn
Barry Donnell
Lou Donnelly
Harry Donson
Willis B. Doolittle
Frank Dorcu
David Dorfman
William S. Dorman
John E. Dorn
Paul Dorney
Leonard Dorsett
Melba Dorsett
Ronald A. Dorval
Louis B. Doscher
James Dostalek
H. C. Dottery
Ed Douglas
Jennifer Douglass
Donald Downer
Gordon Downer
John Downey
Sheridan Downey
John Downing
Ron Downing
Shane Downing
Al Doyle
Donald Doyle
Fred E. Doyle
Augusto Dragoni
Douglas A. Drain
Greg V. Drajem
Victor Drajem
Mark Drake
Glen Drapeau
Frank Draskovic
Phil Dreis
Joe Dressel
Dick Driscoll
Jeff Drucker
John Drummey
Donn Drury
Elaine Ruth Dryer
Dan Drykerman
Ron Drzewucki, Jr.
Ron Drzewucki, Sr.
Joe Dubem
Judith Dubey
Bruce Dubin
Steve Dubinsky
Gordona Duca
Ron Ducharme
Joseph Ray Duclos
Marc Duclos
Jay Duda
Louis Dudderar
Gary D. Dudley
Thomas Dufour
Donald E. Dugas
Charles Dukto
Leroy Dull
Tim Dumm
Charles Duncan
Richard "Kenny" Duncan
Roger Dunham
Mike Dunigan
Richard Dunigan
Howard Dunklee
John W. Dunn
Burton P. Dupuy
Elliott P. Durann
M. J. Durben
James Durham
Mary Durham
Dennis L. Durigan
Tom Durkin
Gene E. Durrough
Ron Durs
Sanford J. Durst
Milton Dushane
Richard Duszynski
Richard Dutkin
Frank W. Duvall
Mickey Duzdevich, Jr.
Mike Dyer
Paul E. Dylewski
George Dysinger
Eric Dzin
Basil Dzwonchwk
Rick Eargle
F. A. Earle
Leon Eason
Bill Ebert
Buddy Ebsen
Denny Eckenrode
Joseph R. Eckman
Nicholas T. Economopoulos
Jon Edelman
Jay N. Edelson
Joel T. Edler
Jerry Edlin
Bob Edmiston
Paul Edmonds
Tom Edmondson
Dean Edwards
Gene Edwards
Arnoldo Efron
Mike Eggert
Tom Ehlers
T. Ehrlich
Jack A. Ehrmantraut, Jr.
Jeff Einbinder
Ira Einhorn
Jim Einhorn
Jerry and Mavis Eisenhower
William Eisenhower
Jim Elam
Leslie A. Elam
George Elbode, Jr.
Steve Eley
Herbert Elfvengren
Victor Elias
Louis Eliasberg
Jim Elicone
Jim Ellenburg
Bruce Elliott
Joe Elliott
Robert Elliott
Connie Ellis
Curtis L. Ellis
Donald E. Ellis
Joseph W. Ellis
Mike Ellis
Ray Ellis
Lawrence E. Elman
James F. Elmen
James G. "Jim" Elrod

Dr. K. B. Embler
Sid Emerson
Marc D. Emory
Bob Emmer
Marc Emory
Jim Endicott
Michael W. Endres
Jerry A. Enfield
Susanne Enfield
Fred England
Thomas England
Victor England
John R. Engle
Larry Engle
Clyde R. Englehardt
Jeffrey A. Englehardt
James P. English
John E. English, Jr.
Greg Engstrom
William Engvall
James Enright
Robert Enright
Bob Entlich
Robert E. Ephraim
Jim Epperson
Douglas Epstein
Peter M. Epstein
Ron Epstein
Gulay Erbil
Martin P. Erhardt
Patricia A. Erhardt
Leif Erickson
Jay Erlichman
David G. Ernest
Edward Esber
Jess H. Escalada
John Escove
Stephen Esterline
Daniel Estes
Steve Estes
Bob H. Estremera
Robert G. Euler
Larry Eulert
Steele Eunson
Emil N. Eusanio
John Evanoff
Jim Evans
John E. Evans, III
Warren Evans
Bob Everett
Steve Ewan
Steve Eyer
Becky Faber
Julio F. Fabregat
Alan Faden
Mary Fagan
Martin Fagin
Michael Fahey
Barry Faintich
Don Faircloth
Mark Faircloth
Patricia Faircloth
James Fairfield, Jr.
James W. Fairfield
Jennifer Fairfield
Joe Falater
Larry Falater
Salvatore Falcone
Frank Falgiani, Jr.
Frank Falgiani, Sr.
Michael Falk
Tina Falkner
Howard A. Faltz
Peter J. Falzone
Nick Fanale
William J. Fandison
Robert L. Fanger
Ken Fanning
Bill Fannon
Mike Faraone
Al Farber
Gary Farnsworth
Jessie Farnsworth
Rick Faro
William A. Farrer
Annette Fasano
Lawrence J. Fasano
Rita Fasano
Robert L. Fattore
R. K. Faulk
John Thomas Faulkenberry
Bob Faust
Carl H. Faust
Bryan Fazio
F. Fazzari
Skip Fazzari
Jim Fehr
David Feigenbaum
Norman Fein
Tony Fein
Joseph Feld
Mark Feld
Keith Feldbrugge
Carl R. Feldman
Mark R. Feldman
Steve Feldman
Frank Felice
Jesse Feliciani
Bruce A. Fenger
Harvey Fenton
Ned J. Fenton
Steve Fenyves
Daniel Fergot
Gary C. Ferguson
Kenneth R. Ferguson
Mark Ferguson
John Ferm
Ronn Fern
Albert W. Ferrante
Todd Ferrell
Michael H. Ferryman
John Fetto
Frank Fidnarick
Martin Field
Aaron Filbey
Robert Filbey
Ed Filipkowski
Gary B. Fillers
Vince A. Filpi
Paul Finck
Michael Findlay
David Finelli
Clarence Finger
Joseph Fink
Alan Finkelstein
James Finley, Sr.
Rita A. Finley
Leonard H. Finn
James Finney
Robert L. Finney
Wayne D. Finnicum
Martin Firman
David Fischer
Ed Fischer
Harry D. Fischer
Jeff Fischer
Joyce Fischer
L. V. Fischer
Max Fischer
Allen Fischler
Bill Fiscus
John Fish
Don Fisher
Jack H. Fisher
Ned L. Fishkin
Dr. Gerald Fishman
Arthur M. Fitts, III
Glynn Fitzgerald
Tom Fitzpatrick
Bill Fivaz
Fredric Flaig
Anthony Jaye Flagg
Wayne Flannigan
Harold Flartey
Horace P. Flatt
Larry G. Fleeman
Breck R. Fleeson
Samuel S. Fleisher
Edward Fleischmann
Gary Fleming
Jim Fleming
Marty Flesher
Bill Florentz
Sally Floto
William C. Floto
Joe Flynn
Stanley T. Fogle
Louis Fogleman
Kevin Foley
Mike Follett
Rebecca Fong
Robert Foppiano
Bob Ford
John Michael Ford
Bill Foreman
Bill Blue Foreman, Jr.
John M. Foreman, Sr.
Janie Foreman
Vineta Mae Foreman
Jerry Forewright, Sr.
Dennis Forgue
Harry J. Forman
Joel J. Forman
Phillip Forrester
Guy W. Forry
John T. Forsythe
Bill Foster
Coleman Foster
James D. Foster
John Foster
Ralph Foster
Steve Foster
Frank C. Fotti
David Fouke
Gene Fountain
Gloria Fouquet
Clarence Foust
Richard L. Fowlkes
Barry Fox
Bruce Fox
Donald Fox
Frank D. Fox
Les Fox
Randall W. Fox
Sue Chester Fox
Joseph M.Fragner
William J. Fragner
Jeffrey Franc
David Frances
Doyle Francis
Craig Franco
Benny Frank
John Frank
Stanley Frank
J. R. Frankenfield
A. P. Franz
John Fravel
Mike Frazier
Carmen Freda
Bart Frederick
Tom Fredericks
Jack Free
Lynn Dean Free
Cedric Freeman
Harvey Freeman
Wayne R. Freese
Tim Frein
Dennis French
Leo Frese
Arthur Friedberg
Goldye Friedberg
Robert Friedberg
Mike Friedman
Stephen P. Friedman
Edward E. Fritz, Jr.
H. D. Frizzell
Kent M. Froseth
Dwyaine Frost
Richard Frost
George Alexander Frudaki
Sam Frudakis
Howard Frydman
David Frye
Robert J. Frye
Barbara L. Fuente
Michael M. Fuertes
James D. Fugate
Dr. George Fuld
Michael Fuljenz
Larry Fuller
Joe Fulsom
Geoffrey E. Fults
Jack Fultz
Jeff Funderburke
Ronald Funk
Joe Furia
Carl J. Fusco
Joseph M. Fusco
Sal M. Fusco
Ray Futrell
John J. Gabarron
Caroline Gabel

Joel Gabrelow
Ron Gabriel
Tim Gabriel
Kenneth A. Gaida
Danny Gaines
James Gaines
Jan Gaines
Jimmy Gaines
Bruce Gainsley
Jessie Gainsley
Matt Gainsley
Aaron C. Gaizband
Harold Galary
Gary S. Galbo
Charlotte Gale
Evan Gale
Billy R. Gallier
Joe Gallo
Kenneth Galster
Jim Gambill
Sterling Gambino
G. W. Gamble
Don Gammel
Gary P. Ganguillet
Robert C. Ganter
David L. Ganz
J.P. Garbarini
Roger Gard
Chet Gardner
Paul Edmund Garner
Art Garnett
Frank L. Garofalo
Michael K. Garofalo
James Garraway
A. A. Garrett
Henry G. Garrett
Jeff Garrett
John Work Garrett
T. Harrison Garrett
Robert Gartenberg
M. J. Garvey
William Gase
Gary Gasperini
Laura Gasparrelli
Frank Gasparro
Don D. Gatrost
Andrew Gause
James R. Gautreaux
Jack Gauya
Michael Gauya
Bill Gavosto
William G. Gay
C. J. Gazier
James Geary
Roger L. Geary
Jerry Gebone
Ken Geer
Stephen J. Gehringer
M. Geiger
Jim Geise
Raymond P. Gelewski
R. G. Genis
Debra Gentile
Jerry George
John George
Michael Geppi
Lawrence F. Gerber
David B. Gere
Robert V. Gerenser
Sal Germano
Dorothy Gershenson
James Gerstel
Raymond Gesualdo
Richard J. Giacopelli
Anthony Giarla
Robert Gibbar
Alice Gibson
Roger Gibson
Richard Giedroyc
Jim Gilbert
Richard E. Gilbert
Elwood Gilboe
Kurt Gilge
Paul Gilkes
Ronald M. Gilkes
Debby Gillespie
Cory Gillilland
Dennis M. Gillio
Ronald J. Gillio
Johnnie B. Gilreath
Ed Ginn
Richard Giordano
Robert J. Giresi
Robert Gittis
Durwin L. Gjetley
Linda Glascock
R.A. Glascock
W.E. Glass
Jean Glazer
Len Glazer
Bob Glenn
Barry Glick
Diane Glover
W. B. Goble
Gerald Gochenour
Dennis Goddard
Brent Godlewski
Rusty Goe
Gary Goedken
Dr. Rayburne "Tex" Wyndham Goen, Sr.
Sally Goen
Tex Goen, Jr.
Jack Goetz
Daniel J. Goevert
Ira M. Goldberg
Joseph Goldberg
Lawrence S. Goldberg
Mark E. Goldberg
Steve Goldberg
Jim W. Golden
Steve Golden
B. Goldfinger
Barbara Goldfreed
Elliot S. Goldman
Irving Goldman
Kenneth M. Goldman
Max B. Goldman
Lloyd Goldsmith
Marc Goldsmith
Stephen Goldsmith
Jeffrey K. Goldstein
Lou Goldstein
Marc Goldstein
Michael Goldstein
Mike Golonka
Stewart Golub
Jerry Golz
Joseph G. Gomez
Keith Gomez
Lynn Gomillion
Robert Gomillion
Franklin Gonzales
Michael Gonzales
Victor Gonzalez
Jeffrey Goodman
Larry Goodman
Jaime Goodwin
Sam Goosay
Bruce Gordon
J. Gordon
Jonathan Gordon
Murray Gordon
Ron Gordon
Tom Gore
Ed Gorlick
David Gorlin
Gerald Gorman
Dieter Gorny
Ben F. Gorrell, Jr.
Bob Gothmann
David R. Gotkin
Craig Gottlieb
James H. Goudge
Steven D. Goulas
Maurice M. Gould
Roger R. Gower
Debbie Gowin
Don Gowman
Peter A. Goydos
Lawrence Grabarnick
Theodore Graepel
Robert Graf
Rita Graft
Bill Graham
Carolyn Graham
Harry Graham
Michael A. Graham
Robert Graham
Julius Graifman
Terry D. Gram
R. B. Grampp
David Grandinette
Clayton O. Grant
Raymond Grant
Mark Grasso
Rose Grasso
Joel Grauman
Laura A. Graves
Barry Gray
Keith Gray
L. G. Gray
Robert Gray
Edwin Grayson
Madge Grayson
Philip Greco
Ralph Greco
Al Green
Bob Green
Carol Green
Charles E. Green
Donald Green
Earl Green
Judy Green
Robert Green
James Greenbaum
Chaim Greenberg
Frank Greenberg
Gerald Greenberg
Paul J. Greene
Katharine Greenhouse
Phil Greenslet
Jimmy Greenspoon
Andy Greenstein
Robert Greenstein
Barbara J. Gregory
Glen Gregos
Howard Greiser
Gene C. Gress
Wayne Gretzky
Tony Gribi
Dan Griffin
Eugene A. Griffin
John I. Griffin
Kent Griffin
Robert R. Griffin
Mike Griffith
Barbara Griffiths
David Griffiths
Shelley Griffiths
Todd Griffiths
Sean E. Griggs
Rob Grill
Stanley L. Grissom
Michael S. Grodecki
Al Grodsky
Paul Groleau
John Groot
Charles Grosclaude
Steve A. Grosko
Larry Groskopf
Del Gross
Morris Gross
Richard Gross
Herman Grossfeld
Thomas Grossi
Gail Grossich
Paul Grosz
Donn Grouper
Maurice E. Grove
Becky Groves
Richard L. Groves
Nick Grovich
Robert K. Grubbs
Gary Gruenberg
Edward Grundy
Mark Gruner
Tony A. Gruppo
Walter J. Grzesczuk
August Guarniere
J. Guevrekian
Woodward Guidry
Richard J. Guignard
Jim Guinesso
R. D. Guiney
Marc Guitman
Clu Gulager
John Gulde
Richard Gulde
David Gulinello
Kent Gulley
Bruce Gumer

Mike Gumpel
Leeann Gunter
Howard L. Gurney
L. R. Gustafson
Ronald Guth
Jim Guthrie
Rich Gutman
Frank Gutschow
Hubert Guy
Patti Guynn
Adolfo E. Guzman
William Guzze, Sr.
Joe Guzzo
Herbert Haas
Ute Haas
Lee M. Haber
Martin E. Haber
Gene F. Haberstich
Sandra K. Haberstich
Kevin Hacker
R. D. Hacker
Charles Haddad
John Haddaway
Jim Hadley
John Hadley
Alan Hager
John Hager
Pat Hagerty
Sonja B. Hahl
Lloyd Hahn
W. A. Hahn
Dennis A. Haines
David A. Hakes
Mike Hakala
Kenneth A. Halagan
Arthur E. Hale, III, M.D.
James L. Halfon
Margaret Halfon
Bob Hall
Clayton Hall
Danny Hall
David Hall
Everett M. Hall
Frederick Hall
Jeff Hall
Jerry Hall
Kim Frances Hall
Nathan Hall
Roy Hall
Scott Hall
Terry Hall
Truman S. Hall
Kenneth L. Hallenbeck
Thomas G. Hallenbeck
George Hallock
Stephen J. Halloran
James L. Halperin
Natalie Halpern
Sam Halter
John Halvorson
Robert C. Hambleton
Leo Hammel
Bobby Hamilton
Harry Hamilton
John Hamilton
Peter F. Hamilton
Bob Hamling
Tom Hammel
Frank Hammelbacher
Robin G. Hammond
Thomas Hammond
Kenneth R. Hampshire
Bill Hampton
John B. Hamrick, Jr.
David Hancock
Jack Hancock
Russell G. Hancock
Virgil Hancock
Dorothy Hand
Joe Hand
Wayne Haney
Dennis Hankins
Robing Hankins
Larry Hanks
William Hanks
Kenneth J. Hanle
Terry Hanlon
James J. Hanna
Larry Hannick
Tom Hannick
Dusty Hanny
Herbert Hanrion
Dick Hanscom
Chris Hansen
Robert Hansen
Jon G. Hanson
Robert J. Hanson
Marc Harbour
John Hardenberg
Kevin Hardesty
Norman C. Hargaray
Tim Hargis
Raymond Harla
John E. Harland
William Harling
Robert S. Harlow
Bob Harmon
Don Harms
Jack H. Harper, Jr.
Janice Harper
James Harpet
Chris Harrell
Jim Harrell
Marv Harrenstein
Allen Harriman
Dale Harrington
Janet Harrington
Mary Harrington
Don Harris
Donna Harris
Neil Harris
David Harrison
Hillery Harrison
Jill Harrison
Richard Harrison
John M. Harrow
Bert Harsche
John Hart
Randy Hart
Steve Hart
L J. Hartley
David Hartman
John Hartman
Edward Hartmann
Quintin Hartt
Rich Hartzog
Greg Harvey
Craig Harwell
Robert L. Harwell, II
Winston Harwood
Steve P. Haslehurst
Raymond L. Hastey
Bill Hatchett
Bill Hatfield
George D. Hatie
William E. Haugen
Michael Haugh
Dottie Haun
Donald Hauser
Nicholas Hauser
James R. Hausknecht
James R. Hausman
G. E. Hawkins
Reed Hawn
Don Hawthorne
Stephen Hayden
William Hayes
Charles E. Hayes
Dennis Hayes
Jerry Hayes
George W. Haylings
Michael R. Haynes
Richard L. Hazel
Howard Hazelcorn
Jill Hazen
James R. Head
Carl Heartfield
June Heatley
David M. Hecht
Robert O. Heckmann
Dick Heisley
Karen Heitzman
Edward Helbig
C. L. Helderman
John Heleva
Norman Helfand
Leonard "Lenny" Helicher
Allan W. Heller
Dave Heller
Dennis Heller
H. Heller
Patrick A. Heller
Richard Heller
Cal Helmick
James A. Helzer
Brad Hemovich
Christian Hemphill
Brian Hendelson
Robert Hendershott
Alec Henderson
Bill Henderson
Glen S. Henderson
Oycie Henderson
Robert W. Henderson
Doris H. Hendrick
Ted H. Hendrick
David J. Hendrickson
Leon E. Hendrickson
Ruhama "Hamie" Hendrickson
Hank Hendrix
Joseph Hennessy
Gene L. Henry
Sonny Henry
Harry Hense
Alan Herbert
Frank Herbst
John Herlevic
David P. Herman
Roger Hermann
Clay Hermansky
Jerry Hermanson
Mark Hermanson
Henry Hermelin
Jack Herrera
Phillip Herres
C.B. Herron
Dan Herschberger
George Hersey
Tony Hershey
Jack C. Hertzberg
Todd Hertzberg
Harold W. Herz
Diana Herzog
John Herzog
Gene Hessler
Everett Hetzel
Jerry Heuer
Clifford Heverly
Lee F. Hewitt
Terri Lee Hewitt
Harold E. Hibler
Dana Lynn Hickman
John Hickman
Herbert Hicks
Ted Hicks
Howard Hickson
Levan F Hiemke
Lux Ann Higashida
Nathan Higashida
John Higgins
R.L. Higgins
Robert Higgins
Carol Highfill
Chelsea Marie Highfill
Frank Highfill
Howard Highfill
Jeffery James Highfill
John Wayne Highfill II
John William Highfill
Marlene Marie Highfill
Nicolette Lynn Highfill
Paul Highfill
Raymond Francis Highfill
Rebecca Ann Highfill
F.L. "Bud" Hildenbrand
Philip L. Hildenbrand
Bill Hill
David Hill
Edward L. Hill
Franky Hill
Gerard B. Hill
James Hill
John R. Hill
Lewis Hill
Martha Hill
Tony Hill
Don R. Hiltunen
Bill Himmelwright
Tommy Hindeliter
Wade Hinderling
Thomas Hines
James H. Hino

Martin A. Hinote
Wilbur Hinsen
Jim Hinton
Larry Hintz
Ed Hipps
John Hipps
Richard Hirsch
Steve Hirschhorn
David Hirschman
George J. Hirschman
Jim Hirtle
Dean Hitt
Craig Hively
Peter Hlinka
Roy P. Hoagland
Scott Hocevar
Robert A Hochman
Edmund Hock
Michael J. Hodder
Dempsey Hodges, Jr.
Robert R. Hodges
William R. Hodges
John Hodson
Kay Hoebake
Robert Hoebake
Arlyn Hoem
Daniel Hoem
Melissa Hoff
William Hoff
L.W. Hoffecker
Edward B. Hoffman
Lee Hoffman
Eugene J. Hogan
Robert W. Hoge
David Hogeland
Herbert R. Hogue
George R. Hohmann
Ken Holberg
Kevin Holcomb
Steve Holcomb
Calvin L. Holcombe
Randall P. Holder
Donald Holecek
Bob Holladay
Don Holladay
Tom Holland
Howard Hollenbeck
Joe Hollingsworth
Kenn Hollister
Greg Holloway
Erv Holly
Mark Holmes
Phyllis Holmes
Paul G. Holt
Don Holz
Ron Holzhauer
David C. Homer
Paul Honeywell
Jason Hong
Curt Honingford
Melanie Hoock
Walton Hood
Jess Hoogeveen
Gary J. Hoos
Robert P. Hoover
Dale Hopkins
Lew Hopkins
Kevin Hora
Eddie Horne
James E. Horne
Harry H. Horstman
Ronald L. Horstman
J. C. Horton
Lowell C Horwedel
Cammy Hosier
Don Hosier, Jr.
Donald W. Hosier
C. L. Hoskins
Charles Hoskins
Mark Hotz
Gwyn N. Houston
Cloyde Howard
Ed Howard
Judy A. Howard
Richard Howard
Ronald M. Howard
Dean F. Howe
Charles S. Howell
William Hoy
William Hub
Christian Hubscher
Marc Hudgeons
Doug Hudkins
C. E. Hudson
Jan Hudson
Louis Hudson
David Huff
John E. Huff
Richard Huff
J. W. Huffman
H. H. Hughes
Nancy Hughes
Robert L. Hughes
Brett Hull
Everett Hull
Linda J. Hull
Robert C. Hullar
Clinton Humbert
Leroy Huminsky
Wayne Hummel
Robert Humphrey
George B. Humphreys
Peter Humphreys
Seth Hunnington
Stan Hunsaker
David W. Hunt
Fred Hunt
J. P. Hunt
Jack Hunt
Ken Hunt
Jim Huntington
John D. Huntley
R. J. Huntzinger
Loy Hupp
Dave Hur
Al Hurry
Bill Hurst
Syed Hussain
James Hutchins
Jane Hutchins
Robert Hutchison
Danny Hutton
Joe Hylas
Gene E. Hynds
Ron Hyre
James S. Iacovo
John Imbriano
Wayne Imbrogno
Todd Imhof
Don Indendi
Dave Ingalls
Rosemarie Bockhold Ingenito
Howard Ingersoll
Fred Ingerson
Victor Ingraffia
Gregory Innace
Steve Innarelli
Charles Intriago
Joseph Iorio
Harry B. Ireland
James Irish
Joseph P. Irmen
Jim Irwin
Lou Irwin
Jeff Isaac
Paul Isbell
Jesse Iskowitz
Ron Iskowitz
Jeffrey Issler
Leona Ittelson
Robert Ittelson
Curtis Iversen
Phil Iverson
Steve Ivy
Anne Jackson
Larry Jackson
Richard R. Jackson
Jim Jacobs
Michael Jacobs
Robert H. Jacobs
Sandra Jacobs
Steve Jacobson
David Jadwin
Joe Jaffe
Alan Jaffre
Harold N. Jagger
Irma C. Jagger
Mark R. Jagger
Robert H. Jagger
Arlin James
Paul James
Wayne James
Gus Jammalo
Louis W. Jamme
Bob Jane'
Ed Jane'
Paul E. Janowsky
Alex Jaramillo
Tina Marie Jarnasino
Charles Jarrait
Graham E. Jarrett
Julian Jarvis
J. J. Jason
Mary Jeddoloh
Greg Jeffrey
Jay Jefferson
James J. Jelinski
Frederick L. Jenkins
Robert Jenkins
Rob Jenks
Brian Jenner
Steven Jennings
Don Jenright
James G. Jensen
R. S. Jensen
Roger Jensvold
Glenn Jeong
Gilbert L. Jesch
Jim Jessen
Mark S. Jewell
Timothy Jewison
Peter Johansen
Billie Johnivin
Alfred E. Johnbrier
JoAnn Johnbrier
Billie Johnivin
Bill Johns
Chris Johns
Douglas Johns
Alan Johnson
Bradley W. Johnson
Carl Johnson
Craig M. Johnson
Dean Johnson
Dennis Johnson
Edward R. Johnson
Gerald Johnson
James G. Johnson
Jerry K. Johnson
Lyndon B. Johnson
Pat Johnson
Richard G. Johnson
Robert R. Johnson
William Johnson
Johnny Johnston
A. I. Jones
Bob Jones
Chris Jones
Dale Jones
David C. Jones
Dennis Jones
H. Bruce Jones
H. Daniel Jones
Harold C. Jones, Jr.
Harry E. Jones
James A. Jones
James M. Jones
Jerry Jones
Jim Jones
Joe Jones
Paul Jones
Robert Jones
Thomas Jones
W. T. Jones
R. A. Jongsma
Peter Jordan
Glen Jorde
Tony Jordon
Art Jorgensen
Maurice Josefsen
Frank Joseph
David Josephine
Dan Josten
Jerry Jouben
Jerry Jouett
Michael Joyce
Terrell Joyner
Edward Judd
J. Hewitt Judd, M.D.
Evan L. Julber
Robert W. Julian
Laverne Junkins

Norman Junkins
Doug Juola
Kim Scott Jurnecka
Victor E. Jurusz
Stephen Juskewycz
J. Ross Justice
Antoninette Justus
Harry L. Kaatz
Steven M. Kaden
J. Kadish
Samuel H. Kaeppel
A.M. "Art" Kagin
Donald H. Kagin
Paul S. Kagin
Dante Kahn
Ronald Kahrimanian
K. Kaike
Joe Kalil
Richard Kalina
C. J. Kalnik
Jay H. Kamin
John V. Kamin
Bernie Kane
Greg Kankoskis
Kiran Kapadia
Winona Kapala
Kenneth A. Kapers
Gary Wayne (Highfill) Kaplan
Leonard Kaplan
Michael Wade (Highfill) Kaplan
Sol Kaplan
Terry Kaplan
Charles V. Kappen
John Kappy
Charles Karler
Ina Karler
Phillip Karler
Robert Karler
L. Karlin
Randy Karlin
Allen Karn
Edgar A. Karn, II
Eugene Karol
Brad Karoleff
Jules J. Karp
Ron Karp
Terry Karp
Peter S. Karpenski
Gerald Karschner
Len Karstadt
Steve Kary
Doug Kaselitz
Glen Kashuba
Frank Katen
Phillip Katrosh
Marvin Katz
Jim Kauffman
Karla Kauffman
Andrew J. Kaufman
Bonnie L. Kaufman
Mark Kaufman
Phil Kaufman
Richard Kaufman
Don Kaufold
Russell Kaye
Jack Keane
W. M. Kearley, Jr.
Daniel G. Keating
Robert Keck
Porter O. Keeble
David L. Keefe
Dennis Keefe
Douglas Keefe
Robert R. Keeler
Mike Keeley
Stu Keen
Thomas Keenan
Robert J. Keimig
Buddy Keller
Robert F. Keller
Phillip L. Kelley
Robert Kelley
James F. Kellison
Bob Kelly
Carole M. Kelly
David C. Kelly
Don C. Kelly
Eileen K. Kelly
Fredrick P. Kelly
James Kelly
Kirk Kelly
Robert D. Kelly
Rona Kelly
William M. Kelly
Keith N. Kelman
Don A. Kelso
Theodore Kemm
Ernest A. Kemmet
Bruce Kemp
James Kemp
W. A. Kemp
Michael Kempken
John Kendall
Edward M. Kennedy
Fred T. Kennedy
Michael Kennedy
Valda Kennedy
Chris Keogh
John Keogh
Harold R. Kercher
Arnold Kerkhof
Jonathan K. Kern
Don Kershner
Ervin Kery
Mike Kessel
Nelson W. Kessell
Rita Kettenhofes
Don Ketterling
Robert Kevorkian
Pat Kiddy
Jeff Kierstead
Dan Kihlstadius
Henry Killmeyer
Kevin J. Kilroy
Yeon-Sung Kim
Frank Kimball
Andrew Kimmel
Ralph W. Kimmel
Wes Kimmer
Michael A. Kincaid, D.D.S.
Benjamin King
Bill King
Don King
George D. King
Greg King
Harold King
Jay King
Jeffrey J. King
Johnny King
Mike King
Quinton S. King
Doug Kingsbury
Daryl Kinnard
James Kinoshita
Howard Kinsfather
Michael B. Kirke
Glen O. Kirsch
Murray Kirsh
Michael Kiscadden
Sheldon Kishner
Bill Kiszely
Denise Kitchen
William Kitts
Don Kittsmiller
Raymond Klabnik
Josef Klaus
William Klauser
Harlan Klave
Marcie Kleeman
David Klein
Gil Klein
Ken Klein
Mike Klein
Stan Klein
Bernard Kleinert
Jacob G. Kleinman
Jack K. Klemes
Harry Klepper
Mike Kliman
Myron M. Kliman
Ray Klinge
Jerry P. Klinger
Matthew Klovenkski
Jim Knapp
Kenneth Knapp
Bob Knauer
Tom Knebl
Barry L. Knechtle
Michael Knezivien
Alan M. Knieter
Arthur Knight
John Knight
Lyn F. Knight
Sandy Knight
John Knoblough
Paul Knox
Don Knutsen
Robert B. Kober
David Koble
Terry Koch
Richard Kodritsch
Colin Koeck
Donald L. Koehler
Steve Koelbe
Steve Koelbl
Elliot H. Koeppel
Robert Koga
Kazuo Koike
David Kokochak
George Frederick Kolbe
Tom Kolbrener
Kara Kolkman
Terry Kolkman
Valarie Kolkman
Richard Kollar
Michael Kolman
Den Komaromi
Ray Komka
Steve Kommor
Marion J. Konicki
Russell Konig
Susan M. Kono
John P. Konrad
Rita K. Konrad
Theodore Koopman
Brett Kopelman
Stan Kopkin
Robert S. Koppelman
Glenda Koppenhaver
Paul L. Koppenhaver
Bob Korosec
Robert Korver
Howard Kosanke
Michael J. Kosares
Abe Kosoff
Steve Kosoff
Richard A. Kosta
Edward Kostlery
Dale Kotalik
Mike Kotellos
William Kovach
Frank L. Kovacs
Timothy Kovel
John Kozicki
Bill Kraemer
Richard Kraft
W. L. Kraft
Kenny Kragen
Kenneth Krah
Arnold Kramer
James Kramer
Jerry Kramer
Michael Kramer
Scott Kransky
Elliott Krasnow
W. E. Krasowski
Chester L. Krause
Victor Kreatsoulas
Abner Kreisberg
Gene Kreitmayr
Marvin Krepps
Robert F. Kresge
Ron Kreske
Donald Kreus
Alan Kreuzer
Daniel Krick
Gregory Krill
Kris Kristofferson
Jay E. Kristofferson
Brian Kritt
Harold Kritzman
Jan P. Kritzman
K. Krivitsky
Edward A. krivoniak
Dennis J. Kroh
Gordon E. Krohn
Michael Krotz
John H. Krueger
Kurt R. Krueger
Robert E. Krueger

Karl R. Kruger
Jay Krugjohann
Barry Krumlauf
Betty Krummel
Gerald Krupa
Steve Kruth
George J. Kubal
Lieb Kudysch
Vanghn Kuehl
Joe Kuehnert
Michael Kulbacki
Craig Kumler
Debbie A. Kupfer
S. W. Kurek
Malcolm Kurin
Dennis Kurir
Donald Kurtz
S. Robin Kusinitz
Kenneth H. Kusumoto
Brian Kuszmar
Edward Kuszmar
Bruce Kutcher
Douglas Kuwano
Peter Kuzma
Ronald L. Kwaitkowski
Art Kyle
Colin Kyle
Natalie Kyle
Robert B. Kyts
Al LaBrec
Thomas W. Lacey
Peter LaConte
Daniel Ladd
Marilyn A. Ladd
John Ladoto
Dean Laffey
Craig LaGrone
Cloudy Lai
Harry Laibstain
Ian G. Laing
Lawrence S. Lajoie
Robert Lalas
James Lam
Ed Lamastus
James Lamb
Mike Lambert
Paul E. Lambert
Thomas Lambert
Marc Lamoureux
William A. Lamphere
Lamont Lee Lamport
Shirley J. Lancaster
James M. Land
Al Landis
John Landsberger
Al Lane
David Lane
J. Ron Laney
Bob Lang
Joseph E. Lang
Ralph C. Langham
Marc A. Langston
Wayne Lankford
David Lannom
William A. LaPietra
Barry LaPoint
Bruce LaPointe
Tim LaPointe
John LaPorte
L. D. Lappin
James Laravvso
A. L. Larkin
Maria LaRock
Dick Larsen
John Larsen
R. R. Larsen
Duane Larson
Larry D. Larson
Lew Larson
Ron Larson
Ronald E. Lasky
Jim Laszlo
John Latham
Kenneth Lau
Danial Laubler
Greg Lauderdale
D. F. Laufenburger
Brian Laufer
Michael R. Launi
Brian LaVane
Al Lavoie
Robert A. Lavoie
Mark A. Lavro
Douglas J. Law
Bobbi Lawrence
David Lawrence
Charles Lawver
Barry Lazaruis
Greg J. Lazeo
John Lazirko
Harold Leach
Anne Leady
Jim Leady
Jerry Leary
Elden Leasure
Jim Leauw
Mary Ann Leauw
Stanly H. Leavitt
Steve Leber
Ernest LeBlanc
Robert C. LeBlanc
Brian LeBoeuf
Robert B. Lecce
Alan D. Lederman
Jerome M. Lederman
David Leduersis
Becky Lee
Don Lee
Ed Lee
Jack R. Lee
Larry Lee
Robert D. Lee
Diane Lehman
Julian M. Leidman
Bret Leifer
Art Leister
Frank H. Leister, III
Darrell Lemieux
Dennis Lemke
Charlotte Lemons
Fred Lemons
Leroy Lenhart
Tracy Lenhart
James R. Lenig
Jim Lentz
Richard Leon
Robert Leonard
Jack Leonardo
Joe Leone, Jr.
Stuart Lerner
Jeffrey LeRose
Peggy Letson
Rocky Lerchitvikol
Keith LeSeure
Harry Leskauskas
Adrian P. Letendre
Robert J. Leuchten
Robert J. Leuver
Bill Levengood
David Leventhal
Ed Leventhal
Kevin Leventhal
J. C. Levesque
Richard Levesque
Thomas W. Levesque
Robert Levi
Benjamin Levin
Irwin Levin
Mike Levin
Charles Levine
Eli Levine
Howard Levine
Joe Levine
Stuart Levine
Ina E. Levinson
Ira Levinson
Mike Levinson
Allan R. Levy
Ken Levy
Martin Levy
Robert Levy
Tim Lewandowski
Chuck Lewensten
David Lewis
Dennis Lewis
Gil Lewis
Jean Lewis
Matthew Lewis
Michael O. Lewis
Russell Lewis
Warren A. Lewis
D. G. Liddell
Billie E. Lidikay
Carl Lieberman
Jeffery Alan Lieberman
David Liebert
Stephen S. Liebeskind
Larry Liebowitz
J. L. Lightcap
Michael Lightner
David L. Liljestrand
Peter Linden
H. S. Linder
Henry R. Linderman
Jim Lindsay
Ed Lindsey
Mark Lindsey
David E. Lindvall
Michelle Lineberger
Dana Linett
Donald R. Ling
Arthur J. Link
Steven W. Linthhicum
M.J. Lipford
J. B. Lipka
Jess Lipka
Kevin Lipton
Robert M. Liseno
Dean J. Liska
David Lisot
Dan Lisuk
Charles Litman
William Litt
George F. Little
John Little
John Livering
Alex J. Llorente
Dennis Loan
H. Haskell Lobb
Richard Lobel
Gina Lock
Janet R. Locke
Jerry Locke
Jon Locke
Norman Locke
Robert Lockhart
Rick L. Lockridge
Roger P. Loecher
Gerald Loegler
Millie Loeser
Roxane Loewenstein
Steven Loewenstein
Ed Lofton
Bill Lohmeyer
D. P. Lohoefener
Bob Long
Daniel R. Long
Darlene Long
David W. Long
James Long
Bruce Longyear
Gary D. L. Lonnon
Francis Loo
Orlando J. Lopez
Samuel L. Lopresto
Paul K. Lorenz
Bruce Lorich
William R. Lorman
Barry Louder
Stephen L. Louis
C. Louise
Carla Love
J.B. Love
John B. Love, Sr.
Keith Love
Fran Lovelette
Jeffrey Loven
James B. (Jim) Lovette
Stephen E. Lovick
Abbott A. Low
Fred Lowe
Ken Lowe
Vernon W. Lowe
Virgil Lowe
William Lower
Gordon Lowery
John D. Lowery
Fred Lowndes
Dick Lowrey
Edward Lowy
Tom Luba
Richard M. Lubbock

Fred Lucas
J. Lucas
Roger Lucas
James M. Luck
Michael Luck
Reginald Luck
James Ludowise
Walter Lukashevich
John Luke
Richard W. Luke
James E. Lukes
Stan Lukowicz
R. Lumsdon
Henrik O. Lunde
Ronald Lundy
Dick Lundsford
Marty Luster
Andrew P. Lustig
Ed Luszcz
Robert Lutz
Al Lutzi
Alan Luzzatto
G. Robert Lyles
Ray Lyles
Donald P. Lynch
James Lynes
Milton D. Lynn
John F. Maben, Jr.
Dorothy MacBurnett
Mark Machin
John W. Mackay
Ken Mackenzie
Thomas Macko
K. Macleane
Jeff Macpherson
"Katie" MacWilliams
William A. Maday
David S. Madis
Jim Madison
Tony S. Madren
H. E. Maeha
Irv Magaram
Denny Magden
Robert Magee
Lou Maggio
Nick Magnano
Walter Magnus
Ken Magreta
Rod Mahler
Michael A. Maino
Edward Majchrzak
Thomas A. Major
Clayton Makepeace
Jim Malanga
Michael Malicki
A. George Mallis
Alex G. Malloy
Glenn Malone
Al Maloof
Joel L. Malter
Charlie Mammoser
Joe Manchester
Donna Mancusi
Phillip Mancuso
Bob Mandel
Don Mandel
Morrie Mandell
Paul Manderscheid
Ronald Manganiello
Domenic J. Mangeno
Robert W. Mangels, Jr.
Robert W. Mangel, Sr.
Tom Manhard
Dwight N. Manley
John F. Manley
Shawn P. Manley
Joe Mann
Kathy Mann
Bill Manning
Paul Manseau
Martin Mansfield
Pat Maple
Thomas Maravelas
Anthony Marcello
Barbara J. Marcello
Joseph Marcinonis
Anthony Marcoaldi
Dick Marcus
Edward Marcus
Timothy I. Marcy
Mardy K. Mardegian
Alan Marek
Arnold Margolis
David Margulies
Richard Markley
Steve Markoff
Robert L. Markovits
Ben E. Marlenee
Jack Marling
George C. Maroskous
Keith I. Marsh
Sarge Marsh
Doug Marshall
Virg Marshall, III
Troy Marsing
Albert Martin
Chester Y. Martin
Chuck Martin
Dave Martin
Dick Martin
Greg Martin
J.P. Martin
J. W. Martin
Michael Martin
Patricia Martin
Phil Martin
Ray Martin
Reg Martin
Richard Martin
Richard A. Martin
Steve Martin
Tom Martin
Wilmer Martin
Fernando Martinez
Philip Martinez
Anthony Martini
Frank Martino
Ed Marusak
Richard Marusek
John P. Marvets
William Masi
James Mason
P. J. Mason
Sal Massa
David C. Massey
Billy Masters
D. E. Mastropolo
Tony Mat
Robin Mathias
Marlon Mathrey
Philip Mattcci, Jr.
Robert Matthews
Doug Mattox
Michell Mattrey
Robert N. Matylewicz
Mark Mauer
Edwin Maughan
Thomas Maus
Joseph Maushay
David Mave
Frances Lee Maxon
Bob Maxon
Julie Maxon
Gary L. Maxon
Mary Frances Maxon
Ritchie Maxon
R. E. Maxwell
Roy Maxwell
Bill Maybery
Steve Mayer
David Mayfield
Marsha Lynn Mayfield
James Mayoza
Bob Mays
Ron F. Mays
Richard H. Mazzei
Tom McAfee
Donald McAlvony
Ed McArtor
Art McBride
Jay McBride
Peggy McBride
Brian McCaffrey
Ed McCaffrey
Hank McCall
Robert L. McCammant
Joe McCarran
Tom McCarroll
A. A. McCarthy
Barry McCarthy
Ronald McCarthy
Tim McCarthy
Ann Marie McCartney
Clayton McClain
Daniel McCleary
John McCloskey
Larry McCloud
Steven McClure
Billy McCollom
Ed McConnell
Kay McConnell
Marie McConnell
Dennis McCormick
Matthew McCormick
C. McCoy
E. E. McCoy
Lonnie McCoy
Mike McCoy
Neil E. McCrabb
Craig McCulloch
R. McCurdy
Bernard McDaniel
James McDaniel
Michael T. McDevitt
David B. McDonald
Douglas B. McDonald
Edward McDonald
Hudson McDonald
Richard McDonald
"Sammy" McDonald
William E. McDonald
John McDonough
Ken McDowell
Chuck McElkiney
Scott McEvoy
Gary McFall
Edna M. McFarland
Ray McFarland
Michael McGivern
C. David McGlothin
Patrick L. McGohan
Lora McGovern
Larry McGowan
Dr. Terence McGrath
James R. McGuigan
M. J. McGuigan
Garry McGuire
Jaime McGuire
Raymond McGuire
Elton McGuyer
David McHenry
Peggy McIntire
Robert T. McIntire
John McIntosh
Tom McIntyre
Clarence A. McKee
Paul McKee
Thomas P. McKenna
Jim McKinley
Mal McKittrick
Milton McLain
William McLaughlin
Gary McMahon
Rick McNabb
Bruce P. McNall
Jay McNeal
F. Tom McNeelan
Louis R. McNeil
Tim McNeil
Richard McPheeters
Dennis McQuinn
Richard B. McTighe
Jack Meagher
Jeff Means
Don Medcalf
Gordon Medcalf
Virgil Medeiros
Richard Medina
Gene Medlar
Robert "Bob" Medlar
Stan Medlar
Chris Meeker
John Meeks
Kathi Meena
Jim Meenan
Daren Meenahan
M. Meghrig
Eugene G. Mehall
B. Max Mehl
Dennis Meierotto
John Meig
Steve Meinster

Joseph I. Mejia
Richard Melamed
Ralph Mellinger
Greg Mellon
Harry Melvin
Jim Melvin
Dave Memmer
Stanley Mena
Mark L. Mendelson
Thomas Mendonca
Ron Menichetti
Kip E. Meno
Arnie Mensch
James T. Merbs
John Mercanti
Daryl Mercer
Ray Mercer
Randy Merchant
John Meredith
Kirk Meredith
Raymond N. Merena
Lester Merkin
Bob Merrill
Bruce Merrill
Michael Merrill
Nels Merrill
Robert Mertens
Bill Mertes
Anthony Mesaros
Mark Messenger
Edwards Metcalf
William E. Metcalf
Nancy Metropoulos
Ed Metzger
Harvey P. Metzler
Blake Meyer
Gary William Meyer
Jack Meyer
Kurt Meyers
Morris Meyers
Ed Michaels
Steve Michaels
Mike Michalek
Joseph Michaud
Peter Michniewicz
Vic Michonski
Donald Mickelson
Ben L. Middleton
David Middleton
Jarod Middleton
Steve Middleton
James Miears
Tom Miels
David Miholer
Norman Mikat
Pauline Miladin
Ron Milan
V. Milano
Edward Milas
Ron Milcarek
Paul Milchak
Joe Mileham
Steven J. Mileham
Thomas R. Mileham
Jesse L. Miles
Mick Millard
Adam S. Miller
Billy Miller
Bob Miller
Bruce Miller
Cathy Miller
David C. Miller
Don Miller
Glenn Miller
Harold Miller
Howard Miller
J. A. Miller
Jack Miller
James Miller
Jan Miller
Jay C. Miller
Jim Miller
Lee Miller
Mary A. Miller
Michael P. Miller
Otis L. Miller
Randy Miller
Robert L. Miller
Robert W. Miller
Ronald L. Miller
Russell B. Miller
Samuel L. Miller
Thomas R. Miller
Warren Miller
Wayne H. Miller
Edward Millerd
Ernest Mills
Franklin L. Mills
Warren Mills
Russell Millsap
Patricia Minassian
Allen Mincho
Tom Mingolello
Robert Minichino
Tony Minicozzi
Stanley Minkinow
Jon Minor
Lee Minshull
A. R. Mintschler
Ron Mirr
Robert L. Mish
Cliff Mishler
Sally Mishler
Dennis P. Misiak
Don R. Mitchell
J. A. Mitchell
Newton Mitchell
Richard D. Mitchell
Robert Mitchell
Scott Mitchell
Joseph C. Mitchelson
William Mitkoff
Billy Mittlestadt
Donald A. Mituzas
E. J. Modesiti
Thomas Modzelesky, Jr.
Donald Moe
Tom Moehn
Robert W. Moffatt
Cindy Mohon
Colleen Mohrle
John Mokkosian
Michael C. Moline
Fred Mollenkramer
Michael Monachos
Jim Monday
Anthony Mongelli
Joseph Montalbano
Jerry Montana
Mary Anne Montana
Richard Montford
Paul Montgomery
Rick Montgomery
Renato Montorsi
Richard Moody
Al Moore
Amy Moore
Brent Moore
Brian Moore
Charles D. Moore
David W. Moore
Philip J. Moore
Randall Jack Moore
Sherry E. Moore
Steve Moore
Walter Moore, Jr.
Karen Mopsik
Alfred Morabito
Dan Moran
Thomas Moran
Anthony R. Morello
Louie Moreno, Sr.
Louie Moreno, Jr.
Patti A. Moreno
Robert Moreno
Scott Moreno
William Morford
Donald Morgan
Fred Morgan
George T. Morgan
Jack Morgan
James Morgan
Jeffrey Morgan
Jerry Morgan
Jim Morgan
John Morgan
William G. Morgan
John Morgan
W.C. Morgan
Eugene Morgulis
Steve Mormor
Stephen Moroney
A. M. Morris
Betty Morris
Cecil W. Morris
Michael Morris
Mike Morris
Thomas G. Morrison
Joseph Morrissey
Paul Morrow
Phoebe Morse
Shelby A. Morse
Robert Morton
Stanley Morycz
Edward J. Moschetti
Jerome Moskowitz
C. B. Mosley
James Moss
David Most
E. Mostrom
Jerry Moulton
Gina Mouret
Michael Mouret
Paul Mousseau
Jennifer Moussis
Steve Mower
Vance Mowery
Arthur Mueller
Howard Mueller
William Mueller
O. C. Muennink
John Muery
Carl Mujagic
Marsha Mullenax
Ed Mulhausen
James A. Mullaney, Jr.
Daniel Mullen
Andrew Muller, Sr.
Andy Muller, Jr.
John Muller
Ralph P. Muller
Ralph R. Muller
Cliff Mullinax
Thomas Mulrooney
Tom Mulvaney
Thomas Munson
Richard T. Munzner
Joseph Muraca
Joe Murat
Richard Muratori
John Murbach
Kenneth Murch
Claud Murphy, Jr.
Douglas Murphy
Fred A. Murphy
Jack Murphy
Loren Murphy
Lynn Murphy
Thomas Murphy
Tom Murphy
Col. Bill Murray
Donald M. Murray
James H. Murray
William Murray
Steven Musil
Louis E. Muzzillo
Bob Myers
Dale Myers
James A. Myhra
Alex G. Mykulowycz
Richard N. Nachbar
Emery Nadasdy
William J. Nagle
Steven Nardone
H. J. Naayer
Richard N. Nachbar
Steven Nagel
Bernard Nagengast
William J. Nagle
Dennis Nakano
Chris Napolitano
Steve Nardone
Neal Narmore
Ana Tams Nawee
Harold Naylor
David Nazzard
Melvin Neal
Anita Nebb
Edward H. Needham
Gene C. Neel
David Neff
Will W. Neil

David Nelkin
Douglas A. Nelson
Edmond Nelson
Gerry Nelson
Glen Nelson
Howard D. Nelson
Larry Nelson
Ralph Nelson
Richard A. Nelson
Rick Nelson
Webster Nesbitt
Mark Nestmann
Sanford Netburn
Peter Neubauer
Mike Neuman
Michael J. Nevin
Jay Newcomb
Del P. Newman
Eric P. Newman
Maggie Newman
Terry A. Newman
Ronna Newsom
Chris Newton
Danny L. Nicholson
Gary Nicholson
John Nicholson
John C. Nickell
Sue Nickrent
Doug Nicolary
Ron Nieburgs
Jim Niedzialkoski
William F. Niehaus
Edward C. Nielsen, Jr.
Armando Nieto
Dr. Pat Nilson
Richard A. Nixon
Eric L. Noah
Edgar F. Noble
Joe Noblin
Geoffrey Noe
Thomas W. Noe
Bob Nolan
Frank Norman
Mike Norman
Ron Norman
John Normyle
Dan Norris
Gary North
Howard Norton
Richard Norton
R. Henry Norweb
Doug Norwood
Wendell Norwood
Joseph Notini
Al Notowitz
David Notowitz
Jeff Notrica
Sylvia Novack
Wayne Nove
Paul A. Novitski
Art Novom
Frank A. Nowak
Robert P. Nowicki
Steve Nowlin
Casey Noxon
Joseph Nozinski
Robert J. Nuelle, Jr.
Paul B. Nugget

Larry Nunemaker
Sidney L. Nusbaum
Allen E. Nye
Daniel O'Brian
Art O'Brien
Mary O'Brien
Don O'Carmody
Helen O'Carmody
Joseph O'Connell
Edward L. O'Conner
Dean O'Connor
Joseph R. O'Connor
Pat T. O'Connor
Steve O'Day
Charles "Chuck" J. O'Donnell
Jim O'Donnell
Mitchell D. O'Donnell
Michael O'Higgins
Rick O'Neal
Gordon O'Rourke
Dean Oakes
James M. Oaks
Chris Odom
Dinah Oks
Valerie V. Olander
Robert Oldfield
Ron Olejniczak
Dennie Olevick
Bill Oliver
Fred Oliver
Mario Olivera
Mike Olle, Jr.
Larry D. Oller
David Olmstead
Bob Olmsted
Robert Olnhausen
Kenneth Olsen
Clay B. Olson
Greg Olson
Joel Olson
Margaret Olson
Sharon Olson
Thad Olson
Michael Omeluch
Ed Ondrick
Kent Oram
William M. Orendi
Duane Orfield
Sue Orlandi
Michael Orlando
Steven Ormond
Steven N. Orros
J. L. Orszulak
Maurice O. Ortiz, Jr.
Clayton Osborn
James B. Osborn
Donald Osborne
Neal Osborne
Neil Osina
John W. Osman
Francis Osmar
Mark Ostromecki
Vernon H. Oswald
Brian M. Ott
Fred Otto
John Ouellette
W. R. Overdorff

Lin Overholt
Arley C. Overstreet
Joel Overstreet
Gary A. Overton
Jeff G. Oxman
Billy Oyster
Michael Oyster
Paul Padget
Carmen A. Pagano
Joseph Pagano
David Page
Phillip Page
Henry C. Pahlas
Tom Paine
Ronald Paldino
Mike Palmadessa
Bob Palmatter
Allyn J. Palmer
Ed Palmer
Ernest E. Palms
Ted Pamperin
Richard M. Pandolfo
Greg Panik
John Panik
William S. Panitch
Joseph Pankratz
Bill Pannier
Nick Panos
Jurgen Pape
Andy Papertsian
James Pappas
Russ Pappas
Jim Pappy
John M. Paquette
Richard S. Parasiliti
Ben D. Parel
Gary W. Parent
Gary Parietti
Daniel Parisi Jr.
Ken H. Park
Bill Parker
Del Parker
Duane L. Parker
Harold E. Parker
John Parker
Leon B. Parker
Mickey Parker
Stephen F. Parker
Todd Parker
Alfred M. Parks
Thomas M. Parks
Gary R. Paro
David A. Parrella
Gene Parrella
Joseph Parrella
Jay Parrino
Charles C. Parrish
Barbara Parrotto
Glen R. Parshall
Richard Parsons
Louis Pascale
Christine Pasciuti
John Pasciuti, Jr.
John R. Pasciuti, Sr.
Sam Pashigian
Jay Passman
Bob Patchin
Preston H. Pate

Joseph A. Paterna
John Paton
Jesse Patrick
Bob Patterson
David T. Patterson
Elsie E. Patterson
G.M. "Pat" Patterson
James T. Patterson
Ray W. Pattillo
William Pattison
Bill Patton
Cheryl Paul
David Paul
Katherine M. Paul
Martin B. Paul
Robert M. Paul
William R. Paul
John Paulisin
Jerry Paulsen
Jerry Pauly
James Pavlakos
James Payette
Arnold "Arnie" Payne
Chris Payne
James M. Payne
Jasper D. Payne
Ronald W. Payne
Dan Pazsint
Elizabeth Peabody
Franklin Peale
Michael Pearce
Hal Pearl
Leonard Pearl
Donn Pearlman
Mark Pearlman
Larry Pearson
Robert L. Pearson
Ted Peck
John Peden
Jim Pedone
Ronald G. Peek
Oliver N. Peer
Gregg Pelnar
Earl Peltin
Dennis Peltonen
Stephen Pendergast
Bob H. Pendergrass
Michael A. Pendergrass
Trish L. Pendergrass
Bruce R. Penley
Arthur Penn
Ken Pennacchio
Brian C. Pennington
Ken Penter
O. Ernest Pepper
Alex G. Perakis
Edward M. Pereira
Lionel Pereira
Teresa Perez
Vince Pergino
Gary Pericual
Vincent A. Perillo
Dan Perlich
Darlene Perlich
Joel D. Perlin
Michael Perlin
M. Perlmutter
Robert A. Perrin

Robert A. Perrine
Ed Perry
Gerald Perry
Joseph J. Perry
Peter Perry
John R. Perschke
Walter Perschke
Joseph F. Person
Steve Person
Larry Pertcheck
Anthony Pesha
Michael A. Pesha
Vince Pesha
Gloria Peters
John Peters
Lloyd Peters
Michael A. Peters
Nancy Peters
Dean Petersen
Douglas Petersen
Earl N. Petersen
Amiel Peterson
Douglas Peterson
J. B. Peterson
Jerome Peterson
LaVern Peterson
Randy Peterson
Rex G. Peterson
Sanford W. Peterson
Scott A. Peterson
William J. Peterson
John Petrecca
Philip B. Petree
Jud Petrie
Jerry Petros
S. G. Petrucelli
Ron Pettit
E. Ralph Pfau
Paul J. Pfeil
Roy G. Phares
John Phillips
D. Harrison Phillips
John Phillips
Lewis K. Phillips
Rex Phillips
Thomas B. Phillips
Wayne C. Phillips
Randy Pias
William C. Pica
Robert J. Piccininni
Bruce Pichor
Albert Pick
David Pickens
Mary C. Pickering
Norman E. Pickering
Walter J. Pienciak
Peter R. Pienta
Jon W. Pierce
Tom Pierce
Warren L. Pierce
Wayne Pierce
Louis J. Pierini
Bob Pieroni
David Pike, Sr.
David Pike, Jr.
Gayle K. Pike
Si Pike
James V. Pilolli
Joe Pilolli
Bob Pimlott
Hollis Pincock
Kenneth D. Pines
Bruce Pinsof
Diane Augustyne Piret
Ron Pittenger
John Jay Pittman
Don Pitts
Angelo Pizzarella
Louis Pizzolatto
Byron L. Place
James G. Place
Jeff Place
Charles Platko
Gary Platteis
Phillip Plettner
Arthur M. Plitt
Ron Plunckett
Larry Plunkett
Bob Pockrandt
Kenneth Podrat
William J. Poland
Les Polansky
Neil Policow
Robert V. Polito
Bob Pollard
Andrew Pollock, III
Randall L. Pollock
Robert Pollum
Barry Polonsky
Thomas Polutanovich
Peter Pomeroy
R. V. Pomeroy
Donna Pope
William Popynick
Larry Porte
Marie Portell
Mitchell Porter
Thomas Ports
Kenneth R. Posing
David J. Posner
Ronald Posner
Alan Posnick
George F. Poth
Ken Potter
Russell L. Potter
Duane Powell
Gary Powell
Keith Powell
Neil Powell
Wayne Powell
Steve Powell
Susan E. Powell
John Powers
Mary Ellis Borglum Powers
Ken Prag
Wayne Pratali
Franklin Pratt
William A. Preston
Mike Prete
Marian E. Price
Robert Price
Tom Price
George I. Pritchett
Nancy L. Pritchett
Audrey Probert
Earl Proctor
W. L. Proctor
M. V. Proietti
Joni L. Propst
Ed Prout
Charles R. Provini
Jack Provost
Otis Pruitt
George Ptasnik
Jerry Puckett
Lee Puckett
Paul J. Puckett
Rodney Puckett
Ronald A. Pugh
Robert J. Pugliese
Gene Pullen
Norman W. Pullen
William C. Pullen
Jack Pulos
Jim Puma
Carl Pund
John A. Puro
James Pursell
J. D. Purvis
Pete Puskas
Gregory Putz
Larry Pyle
Toby Qualls
John Quist
Bob Raby
John Rackawack
John Raczkowski
Alex Radichevich
Charles Radler
Rick Radtke
Roger J. Radtke
Larry Rafert
Carl Ragan
Capt. Mitchell C. Ragland
Abe Raichek
Cosmos A. Raimondi
Jack W. Raines
Anthony Ramon
Robert Ramos
William Randel
Eddie Randell
Edward Randell
Elizabeth Rankin
William Rapanotti
Diane Rapanotti
Robert Rapoza
A. J. Rappaport
Art Rappaport
Howard Rappaport
Don Rapson
Lou Rasera
Jamie Raskansky
Larry Rasmussen
Jerry Rath
Earl Rathke
Walden Ratliff
Daniel Ratner
William Rattray
Roy Rauch
Clyde Ray
J. C. Ray
Henry Read
Jack Reames
Norman "Whimpy" Rau
Jim Reardon
Marcus Reaves
William Reaves
Louis J. Reback
Marilyn A. Reback
William Recksiek
Jerry Recob
Clifford Reed
Dick A. Reed
John Reed
Randall W. Reed
Richard Reed
Robert Reed, Sr.
Earl T. Reeder
Brian Reeds
Don C. Reeve
Bill Reeves
Jim Reeves
Warren J. Reeves
Greg Reff
R.J. Regan
E. T. Register
Sid Reichenberger
Victor I. Reichman
Mark E. Reid
Wayne Reinhardt
Ken Reinker
Paul Reiser
Darwin L. Reiswig
Scott Reiter
Paul Reitmeir
Dell Reitz
Pat Reitz
Wiley Reitzel
Jules Reiver
Eve Remmer
Roy Renderer
Lydia Resa
Joel Rettew
Joel Rettew, Jr.
Paul Revere
Charles Revier
Don Revis
Peter M. Rexford
Bill Reynolds
Gregory L. Reynolds
J. D. Reynolds
Jay M. Reynolds
Mervyn H. Reynolds
Michael P. Reynolds
Paul Reynolds
Tom Reynolds
Elbert Rhoads
E. H. Rhoden
Ray Rhodes
Robert Rhue
Craig Rhyne
Allan J. Richard
Frank G. Richards
Pete Richards
M. M Richardson
Rich Richardson
Teal Richardson
Vincent Steven Richardson
Edward Richins
Bob Richmond

Skip Richmond
Ed Richt
Tony Richter
Bob Rickard
Joe W. Rickman
Larry Rictert
Robert S. Riemer
Robert J. Riethe
Ronnie Rigsbee
Charles B. Riker
Mary Ellen Riker
Ron Riley
Robert Rimele
Robert E. Rimkus
William R. Rindome
Scott Rineer
Tony Rinella
Mike Ringo
Robert Rioux
Dale L. Rishel
Doug Rising
James C. Risk
James C. Ritchards
Dave Ritchey
Mike Ritchey
William Ritchie
Ron Rittenburg
Sonny Rivera
John Rizek
Sam Roakes
Frederick Robbins
Gerald "Skin" Robbins
Larry E. Robbins
Al Roberts
Earl Roberts
Greg Roberts
Fred Robertson
Beryl P. Robinson, Jr.
Bill Robinson
Danny R. Robinson
Doug Robinson
Edward Robinson
Emory M. Robinson
Frank S. Robinson
Jack Robinson
Johnny Robinson
Ray Robinson
Tom H. Robinson
Wiley H. Robinson
Steve Rocchi
Leo Roche
Edward C. Rochette
Brian Rock
Terry Rock
Floyd Rockholt
Charles C. Rockney
Ed Rockowitz
Brad Rodgers
Jay Roe
Gary Roessler
Geoffrey Roger
David D. Rogers
Jesse Gene Rogers
John F. Rogers
Kelly Rogers
Kenny Rogers
Paul D. Rogers
Rheta Rogers
Harold Rogg
Stanley Rogg
Gregory Rohan
Bob Rohl
Clark Rohmer
Joseph A. Rohner, III
W. L. Rohning
J.R. Rol
Danny Romano
Peter Romano
Tom Romano
Bernard Rome
Joseph Romeo
George Romeyn
Jerry Rominger
Tony Rood
Harmon Rooks
Len Roosmalen
Dave Roper
Don Ropiecki
Frank Rosa, III
Craig Rose
Donald Rose
Harvey Rose
Marshall Rose
Maurice Rose
Ray Rose
Robert C. Rose
Joseph H. Rose
Maurice H. Rosen
Michael J. Rosen
Ronald Rosen
R. Rosenbaum
Bob Rosenberg
Lee Rosenbloom
Daniel Rosenthal
Jon Ross
Larry G. Ross
Norm Ross
Ralph Ross
Robert L. Ross
Steven Ross
Joseph R. Rossi
Thereas R. Rossilli
Alfred H. Rossman
Gary D. Rossman
Will Rossman
Phil Rosso
William H. Roth
John Rothans
Edward M. Rothberg
Matthew H. Rothert, Sr.
Albert Rothstein
Joseph A. Rouillard, Jr.
Richard E. Rounds
Graves L. Rouse
Norman Rousseau
Tom Rowand
John N. Rowe
Stephen K. Rowley
Joseph Royack
Ronald R. Royce
O.E. "Dusty" Royer
Frank Roza, III
Bob Rozycki
Michael Ruben
Thomas L. Ruben
Frank Rubensohn
Martin H. Rubenstein
Marshall Rubin
Walter S. Rubin
Steven L. Rubinger
Art Rubino
Jerold Ruda
Steve Ruddel
Jack Ruditz
Dick Rudolf
John Rue
Howard J. Ruff
Larry Ruff
Russell Rulau
David A. Runfeldt
Lyn Runfeldt
Dorothy Runion
Paul Runze
Jefferey A. Rush
Robert D. Rush
Fred Rusher
Gregory Ruskin
Ray Russ
Vic Russ
Bill Russell
Jack Russell
Jim Russell
Kenny Russell
Margo Russell
Mike Russell
Teresa Russell
Robert Russow
Alvin Rust
Bryan Rust
Gaylen Rust
Albert D. Ruzzo
Chris Ryan
Kalla Ryan
Raymond Ryan
Steve Ryan
Thomas Ryan
James Ryder
Raymond D. Ryder
Steve Rye
J. J. Ryer
Bruce Ryndfleisz
Bojuka Rys
G. N. Sabath
John H. Sack
Brett Sadovnick
Albert Safdie
John Saffert
John J. Sage
Brian Sager
Henry M. Sager
Nicolas Salcedo
Bruce L. Salisbury
Mark Salzberg
Tom Sambola
Joe H. Samet
Ken Sampson
Paul D. Sampson
Russell Sampson
Larry D. Sams
Clark A. Samuelson
Dana Samuelson
Joe Sande
Robert A. Sandefur
Gene Sanders
Michael Sanders
Scott Sanders
Stephen L. Sanders
Gino Sanfilippo
Earl Sanford
Miguel Santalla
Vincent A. Santostefano
Carol Santy
Frederick Sarafino
Michael Sargent
George Sarkis
Fred Sarkowsky
Daniel T. Saros
Paul Saros
John Paul Sarosi
Gaylord Sartain
Dr. Arnold R. Saslow
John Saterfield
Charles Satlof
John Saunders
Leonard Saunders
Mary Sauvain
Kevin Savage
John Savarese
Kenneth D. Saville
Robin L. Savinelli
James Savoca
S. W. Sawyer
Iraj "Roger" Sayah
B. C. Sayers
Wayne G. Sayles
John M. Saylor
Byrd Saylor, III
Bob Scalze
David P. Scanlon
John Scanlon
James Scardino
William O. Schaffnit
M. Schander
Robert M. Scheckman
Henry F. Scheetz
Tom Schell
Steve Schenk
David Schenkman
Jerry Scherer
Cathy Schermer
Clement Schettino
Irving Schick
Ron Schieber
Robert L. Schillage
M. P. Schiller
Frank Schilling
Glenn Schinke
Joe Schlader
Dan Schlesener
Norman Schlesinger
David F. Schmidt
Dean Schmidt
Gerald A. Schmidt
Robert Schmidt
Don Schmitz
Norbert J. Schmitz
George Schneider
John D. Schneider, Jr.
Larry Schneider
Wayne Schneider
Kurt Schneider
Melaine Schnell

Bonnie Schoch
Vincent C. Schoemehl, Jr.
Allan Schoenberger
Frederick L. Scholl
Florence M. Schook
Steven M. Schooley
Steven Schor
Ina Schovcite
Jerry Schreiber
Rod Schriefer
Judy Schrock
Paul Schrock
Brad Schroeder
Bruce Schroeder
C. H. Schroeder
Don Schroeder
Joel Schroeder
Mark Schroeder
Donald J. Schroth
John L. Schuch
Don Schueler
Gary Schulte
E. Schultz
Sheldon Schultz
Steve Schultz
Paul Schuyler
Philip J. Schuyler
Fred Schwan
Ed Schwartz
Lyle J. Schwartz
Richard Schwartz
Stephen Schwartz
Richard J. Schwary
Ed Schwenk
Ed Schwinge
Anthony Sciabassi
Frederick M. Scicchitano
Anthony Scirpo
Joanne Scirpo
Tony Scirpo
Hugh J. Sconyers
Allen W. Scott
Cory G. Scott
Dewey Scott
Jim Scott
Linda K. Scott
Richard Scott
Robert Scott
Willard Scott
John D. Scritchfield
Don Seaberg
James Seamans
Rick Sear
William Searles
B.J. Searls
Ken Sears
Bob Sebenoler
Laurie Secard
Diana Sedgwick
Michael Sedgwick
Edward Sedo
Frank Sedwick
Harry Seebode
Stephen A. Seelig
Harry J. Seese
Jerry Sefranek
Neil Segal
Howard Segermark
James Sego
Alain Sehrapff
Dr. Joel Selbin
Jack Seldon
Everette Self
Malcolm Self
Bill Selfridge
Jim Selfridge
Tom Seligman
Jim Sellars
M. P. Sellers
Rich Sellers
Scott Semans
Andrew N. Seminerio
Dale Seppa
D. V. Seremetis
Carmen Serianni
Anthony J. Serlucca
Peter Setian
Stanley Setzer
Chris Seuntjens
Ronald Severa
Chris Severyn
Edward J. Seymour
Larry Seymour
Bill Shade
Leonard W. Shafer
Robert J. Shalowitz
Bill Shamhart
Monica Shamhart
George H. Shamlin
Mitchell Shands
Norman Shank
Edwin R. Shapiro
Margie Sharp
Mike Sharp
Douglas Sharpe
John D. Shattuck
L. J. Shatz
J. H. Shaw
Thomas R. Shaw
William Shaw
Charles F. Sheaks
Ray Shearer
D. W. Shebel
John Sheets, Sr.
Linda Sheldon
Richard J. Shelley
Fitzhugh L. Shelton
John Charles Shelton
Bill Shepard
Elba Shepard
Harry F. Shepherd
Larry Shepherd
Mike Sherman
Barry R. Sherwin
Howard Shields
Val J. Shilakes
Guy Shipler
Richard Shirk
Bob Shirley
James J. Shively
Ken Shoop
Fred B. Shore
Charles Shortt
Hugh Shull
Bonnie Shultz
Shelly Shultz
A. Shumshinen
George B. Shupp
Edward Shure
Janet Shure
Frank C. Shurteff
Vincent Sidebotham
Arlyn Sieber
Charles Siegel
Jimmie D. Siegelek
Alan Siegfried
Gerald Silbert
Nick Sileno
Steve Silliker
Gerald Silpoch
Gene Silvas
Fred Silver
Elvin Silverman
Peter A. Silverman
James A. Simek
Paul H. Simkin
Jim Simmons
Reubin A. Simmons
Stanley Simmons
Van Simmons
Peter A. Simon
Steve Simon
William E. Simon
Leslie Simone
Paul Simonetti
Valentino Simoni
Michael D. Simons
Robert Simonsen
David L. Sims
Paul Sims
Lloyd Singer, D.D.S.
Murray G. Singer
Ron Singer
Larry Siringer
Kevin Sisson
Robert E. Sisson
Alexius C.H. Sjoberg
Dwain Sjoberg
Ron Sjoberg
Robert Skaretka
Neil J. Skarzenski
James N. Skeen
W. J. Skelton
Craig Sklar
Keith M. Skole
Diana Skuratorwicz
John Skuratorwicz
Don Slabozcski
John Sladek
Robert D. Slamin
Stephen G. Slater
Russ Slaughter
Robert Slaven
John Slavic
A. Thomas Slemons
James E. Slemp
L. W. Slentz
Eric Slick
Ed Sliman
Lisa Sliman
Marty Sliman
Theodore Sliva
Jim Sloan
Robert Sloat
Sam Sloat
Frank Slomko
Jan Paul Slota
John Slota
John Slova
W. Pat Slusher
Leonard Slutsky
Dale Small
Gary Small
Jim Small
Ray L. Small
Grant Smallwood
Paula Smelly
David Smies
John J. Smies
Alan Smith
Albert Smith
Albert "Bo" Smith
Arthur J. Smith
Bill Smith
Bruce Smith
Charles Smith
Christina M. Smith
Craig R. Smith
Dan Smith
David L. Smith
Don Smith, Jr.
Grant H. Smith
Harry L. Smith
Hudson F. Smith
Ingrid Smith
Jim Smith
John Smith
Josef M. Smith
Katherine R. "Grandma" Smith
Kirk Smith
James V. Smith
Lew Smith
Lewis Smith
Maurice Smith
Michael D. Smith
Orville Smith
R. Clark Smith
Richard Smith
Rod Smith
Russell R. Smith
Samuel L. Smith
Tom Smith
William A. Smith
William H. Smith
R. W. Smithwick
Robert Smyth
R. P. Smythe
Lester D. Snell
A. L. Sneraglia
Ty C. Snider
Gary F. Snover
Charles F. Snow
Richard Snow
Betty Snyder
Bryon Snyder
Don Snyder
H. Jack Snyder
Rex Snyder
Sonny Snyder
John Sobiranski
Juan Socias
Stan Sokolowski

Marika Somogyi
Paul Song
Joe Sonner
Bryan Sonnier
George L. Sooter
Leslie Sorensen
Glenn Sorgenstein
Jim Sorn
Dave Sorrick
John South
Denny W. Southard, D.D.S.
Donald W. Southland, Sr.
Neal Sowards
Al. Spaeth
Larry Spanbauer
Kurt Spanier
Charles W. Sparboe
James A. Sparks
Scott D. Sparks
Stephen A. Sparks
Donald D. Spear
William E. Spears
Richard Speer
Don Speigel
Duane Spellman
Larry Spence
Rick Spence
Stuart Spence
Bill Spencer
Reid Spencer
Laurie Sperber
John Sperduti
Pat Spica
Paul Spiegel
Walter Spielman
Richard Spieskell
Don Spillane
Charles A. Spinella
Cheryl Spinner
Joel W. Spingarn
Dan Spiro
Tom Spittal
Maurice Spivak
Seth Spivak
R. W. Spivey
Joseph H. Sprague
Charles G. Springborn
Don Springer
Phillip C. Springman
John Sprinkle
Darwin Sprong
Mike Sprouse
Norman Spruce
Richard Stachurski
E. Stack
Harvey G. Stack
Lawrence R. Stack
Norman Stack
David C. Stagg, III
Mark Stallings
Carl D. Stamper
Scott Standafer
Burr Standish
Michael J. Standish
Leonard Standley
K. Bob Stanke
J. T. Stanton
John Stanziola
Mike Stapleton
Barbara Stark
Robert F. Stark
Frank Starkey
Neal Starr
Ken Starrett
Stanley Starsiak
Rick Statler
H. F. Statuti
Allan Stauber
Richard Stavrakis
Candie Stayton
Dave Steckling
Mario Stefani
Elvira Eliza
Clain Steffanelli
J. B. Steffens
Bryan Steger
George Steifle
Billy Steiger
Michael Stein
Norm Stein
Eric Steinberg
Mel Steinberg
Robert Steinberg
Stanley L. Steinberg
Michael B. Steinborn
Gene Steiner
Dennis E. Steinmetz
Tom Steinmetz
Richard Stelfox
Tom Stepanski
Kermit L. Stephen
Joseph H. Stephens, III
Karl Stephens
Sandra Stephenson
Jack Steppan
Lee Stern
Marcel Stern
Steven Stern
David Sternfeld
Butch Stevens
Chris Stevens
James Stevens
Millard J. Stevens, Jr.
Martha Stevenson
Scott Stevenson
Bobby Steverson
Fred Steward
Charles Stewart
Debbie Stewart
Dick Stewart
Gary Stewart
Robert Stiekle
Rick Stienecker
Bruce Stiles
Rich Stiles
Steve Stilgenbauer
James Stiller
Michael Stiller
Ray Stimac
Joachim Stimmel
James L. Stines
Richard A. Stinson
Jerry Stipp
Ray Stischok
Neil Stockbridge
Robert Stocking
R. Stockton
Paul Stohl
Nick Stolfi
Barbara Stone
Jack M. Stone
R. J. Stone
Daniel L. Stoner
Dean Stoner
Paul Stoner
Maurice A. Storck, Sr.
Michael R. Storeim
David D. Stouffer
Henry Stouffer
David Stout
W. W. Stout
James Stoutjesdyk
Ronald Stoutjesdyk
Ralph Strahan
J. Straus
Edwin B. Strauss
Larry Strauss
Edwin L. Strecher, Ph.D.
Eliot Streeper
Eric Streiner
A. E. Stricker
Paul R. Stricker
Mark H. Striley
Michelle Striley
Janelle Strombeck
Mark Strumpf
John Struzan
S. J. Stuart
Michael Stuckey
Barry Stuppler
Gary Sturtridge
Robin Sturtridge
Thomas A. Stutsman
Jon Subak
William Suky
Lenor K. Sullivan
Terrie Sullivan
Thomas J. Sullivan
Glenn W. Summers
Stan Sunde
James F. Sunderland
David Sundman
Rick Sundman
Brent Sunshine
Thomas J. Surina
Sam Susser
Barry Sutherland
Jeff Sutherland
Jack Sutton
Loren Sveen
Nico Swaap
Bob Swain
Elmer E. Swane
Dale L. Swanson
Glenn Swanson
Jerry Swanson
Robert Swanson
Sandra Swanson
Harry Swarthout
Fred Sweeney
Mike Sweeney
Terrance J. Sweeney
Gerald E. Swen
Betty Swenson
Robert Swenson
Jerry Swepston
Gordon L. Swetland
Anthony J. Swiatek
Tony Swicer
Gary Swieter
Gary Swieternt
Jerry Swindell
Gayl Swinehart
Ronald Swiney
Ronnie Swinney
Jim Syme
Michael Szapowah
Sharon Szapowah
Frank Szenay
Steven L. Szenay
George Szykier
Jeb Tabachnick
Scott Taber
Carl Tackett
Matthew F. Tackett
Nina Tafurt
Robert Tagliaferri
Richard P. Taglione
Carol Tailby
John M. Taitt
Dan Talbert
Norm Talbert
Thomas Tallarico
Peter Tam
Gary Alan Tanaka
Gary Tancer
Stephan Tanenbaum
Jerry Tannen
Dirk Tarman
Tom P. Taroski
Harry Tarr
Marie L. Tarrant
William Tarter
James Raye Tate
Dean Tavenner
Trish Tavenner
Don Taxay
Bill Taylor
Charles W. Taylor
Chet Taylor
David E. Taylor
Denise Taylor
James V. Taylor
Jerry Taylor
Dr. Lester Taylor
Mil Taylor
Peter Taylor
Rhonda Taylor
Richard Taylor
Robert J. Taylor
Sol Taylor, PH.D.
Steve Taylor
Wayne J. Taylor
William L. Taylor
Ken Teague
Steve Teal
Steve Tebo
Ira Teitelbaum
Steve Teitelbaum
Larry Tekamp
Teresa Teleshuk
Jay Tell

Louis M. Teller
C. E. Temple
Robert Tepper
Susan Teresco
Anthony Terranova
Lin Terry
Megan Terry
Michael Terry
David Terwillinger
Joe Tessier
John Tester
Ted Textor
Steven Theiner
Bill Theriault
Randy Thern
Kenneth M. Thimmel
David Thomas
John Thomas
Mark Thomas
Richard Thomas
Sara Thomas
Tom Thomas
William Thomas
John Thomasco
Doug Thomaston
R. Thomaston
Bruce Thompson
Danny E. Thompson
David Thompson
James Thompson
Joe Thompson
Michael Thompson
T. Thompson
Dean Thornberry
Michael Thorne, Ph.D.
Leon Thornton
Mark A. Thornton
Carl Thorpe
David Thorsheim
Debra L. Thorsheim
Denny Thostenson
Tom Throndsen
Mark Thurber
Greg Tibolt
Mike Tiesling
Norm Tietz
Aimee Tihonovich
Scott Tilson
Tom Tinney
Bruce Tippery
Ron Tipton
William E. Tipton, Jr.
Gustav R. Tiso
Kim Titley
Thomas S. Tkacz
Walter Tkacz
Roger C. Tobin
Bruce Todd
Elaine Todoroff
Michael Toledo
Claude Tolliver
Albert A. Tom
Thomas M. Toman
Rick J. Tomaska
Gwaine W. Ton
Lee Toner
Kenneth K. Tong
Monir Torabi
Jean R. Tordella
Al Toronto
Tim K. Torpin
David Torretta
Lance Touchette
Sonny Toupard
Scott Towe
Wayne Towe
Dennis Towne
Robert Towns
Don Townsend
Bill Townsley
Tim Toy
Christopher Tracey
Jerry Tralins
Alan Trammell
Frank R. Trask
Scott A. Travers
Robert L. Trayer
Barbara Traylor
Jerry Treglia
Kevin J. Trejo
E. S. Tremaine
David Trench
Frank Trenholme
Jeff Trestrail
Donald C. Tribit
Robert Tribow
Donald N. Trice
Tom Trice
Earl R. Trievel
Douglas Trinder
Henry Trippe
Harold F. Troglia
Bob Trosper
Ed Trout
Richard J. Trowbridge
Vincent Trypuc
John C. Tsagarakis
James Tsika
Gerald Tucker
Gregory E. Tucker
Hannes Tulving
Jim Tuma
Jerome Tupler
Charles A. Tuppen
Richard J. Turcotte
Robert L. Turcotte
Chester Turkiela
Steve Turnbo
M. C. Turnbow
Chip Turner
Clarence B. Turner
Ed Turner
Ester Turner
James H. Turner
John E. Turner
Mary S. Turner
Sandy Turner
Chuck Tutone
Kevin Twellman
Edmund J. Twohig
Mish Tworkowski
Danny Tyler
Ted Uhl
Walter Uhlhorn
John Uhlir
Mary Ulrich
Mel Ulrich
William J. Ulrich
Carl Ungar
Sam Ungar
Selby Ungar
Julie Uptegraff
Kenneth Urbach
Karl Urban
Jeffrey Ursin
Bob Usrey
Judy Usrey
Mitch Utz
Robert M. Uzelac
Charles S. Vaganis
Peter Vagelatos
David L. Vagi
Lee Vaillancourt
Joseph Valardi
Don Valenziano, Jr.
Harry a. Valk
Richard J. Valley
Dennis Valliere
Art Van
Leroy C. Van Allen
Marilyn Van Allen
Robert Van Bebber
Phillip Van Cleave
Jacob Jay Van Grover
Antonia J. Van Hanja
Richard Van Kerksen
Tom Van Kleeck
Robert R. Van Ryzin
Paul Van Sant
Desiree Van Seeters
Philip Van Slyke
Frank Van Valen
Alan Van Vliet
Stephanie Van Vliet
Mark Van Winkle
Bob Vanaman
Fred Vandergraff
Russ VanDerLinden
Jan Vandersande
Todd VanKleeck
Malcolm Varner
Al Varney
Fred F. Vasquez
Theodore Vassallo
Roberta Vaughan
Roy Vaughan
Eric Vaughn
Russell P. Vaughn
Tony Vecellio
George Vega
Bob N. Velis
Gale Venable
Roy Venable
Sharon Venne
Barbara Vento
Vincent M. Vento
Michael P. Ventrella
Rob Veres
S. R. Verges
Chris Verhaegh
Ernest Verina
Mary Vesely
Steven J. Vesely
Douglas Veshio
Al Vestal
Donald J. Vettel
R. P. Vick
Kyle Vick, III
Joanie Vicknair
Chris Victor-McCawley
Leo G. Viens
Dan Vierk
Jeffery Vierk
Joe Vignola
Paul Vining
Robert W. Vitt
Ron Vitro
Daniel J. Voccia
Fritz Voecks
Dave Vogel
Herb A. Vogel
Michael S. Vogel
Susan Vogel
George W. Vogt
W. W. Volkman
F.J. Vollmer
Gary L. Vollmer
Jim Vollmer
Marie Volpe
Ronald R. Volpe
Mike Volz
Yvonne Voorhees
James E. Vorus
Don Vosburgh
Leonard Vought
Sam Vuchkolch
Donald L. Waage
Mel Wacks
Edward J. Waddell
Joe Wade
Linda Wade
William W. Wages
Thomas E. Waggoner
Frank J. Wagner
J. Richard Wagner
Gary Wagnon, Sr.
Gary V. Wahl
Chuck Walanka
Karen "Kay" Waldner
Mose Waldner
Ernie Wale
Deborah Walker
Harry Walker
Jay A. Walker
Kevin Walker
Michael Walker
Thomas D. Walker
George Walko
Tom Wall
E. P. Wallaker
Gary Wallin
Edward Walter
Kimberly Walter
Robert B. Walter
Reed S. Walton
Sam Walton
Dr. Jiing T. Wang
Roger L. Wankel
John F. Ward
Larry Ward
Robert Ward
Roy E. Ward

Sue A. Ward
William Warden, Jr.
James Warmus
Harry Warner
James Warner
Dennis M. Warren
Harry Warren, Jr.
Fred Warsco
Philip M. Wartel
Ray Wasasky
Thaddeus Wasek
Tom Wass
Craig Watanabe
Don Waterhouse
Earl R. Waters
Bill Watkins
Aileen Watson
Gail Watson
Roger Watson
Susan A. Watters
Marc Watts
Hank Wavers
Jay Wayne
Leo Wazelle
Douglas Weaver
Jim Weaver
Richard Weaver
Bobbie J. Webb
Charles H. Webb
Marvin Webb
Val J. Webb
James Weber
Mike Weber
Calvin Webster
John J. Webster
Ron L. Webster
Allen Wechter
Ken Wecter
Sandra Wecter
Dennis E. Wegley
David K. Weigand
Eric B. Weigand
Dr. Bill Weikel
Fred J. Weiler
Ellen Weinberg
Fred Weinberg
Howard Weinberg
Jay Weinberg
Henry Weiner
George Weingart
David Weinstein
Michael Weinstein
Bill Weisbaun
Bernie Weisburgh
Arthur Weisel
David Weiss
Martin Weiss
Danny Weissman
Louis E. Weissman
Harold B. Weitz
C. E. Welcher
R. Wellman
Bill Wells
Bob Wells
Cory Wells
J. S. Wells
John Wells
Johnna Wells
Richard F. Wells
David C. Welsh
Walter Welsh
Jack Wene
Irv Wenger
Kenneth Wenger
Gordon L. Wenzel
Ed Werner
Thomas E. Werner
Walt Wescott, Jr.
Howard D. Wesely
Lester Wesner
Jon N. Wesson
Chester West
Danny West
Doug West
J. P. West
Terry West
Steward Westdal
Michael J. Westerman
Robert E. Westfall
Robert J. Westfall, Jr.
Kerry Wetterstrom
David C. Wetzel
Andrew Wetzler
William Wetzler
Sherwin Wexler
H. Weymouth
Scott Whary
Gene Wheeler
Hugh Wheeler
Guy Whidden
Zebedee Whindleton, Jr.
Bob White
C. Duane White
E. E. Sarge White
Forrest E. White
Greg White
Harlan White
Jack White
Lawrence E. White
Les White
Robert White
Shirley White
Thomas White
Weimer W. White
William H. White
Scott Whiteford
John C. Whitehead
Todd Whitehurst
Robert M. Whiteman
Harold Whiteneck
Rilla Whiteneck
Jan Whitinger
Larry Whitlow
Nelson Whitman
Paul R. Whitnah
Gregory Whitney
John Whitney
Raymond E. Whyborn
Robert W. Wiborg
John Wickham
Gary Wickwire
Gearld Wickwire
Rod Widok
Wayne Wiebe
Manfred Wieczorek
Ed Wielawski
Anthony Wiench
Henry Wiener
Morris Wiener
Seymour Wiener
Frank Wightman
Marlene Wilburn
Mike Wilcox
Rick Wilcoxon
Adna G. Wilde, Jr.
Galen E. Wilde
Robert E. Wilhite
Jim Wilhite
Arthur W. Wilkerson
Bill Wilkerson
John L. Wilkerson
Ron Wilkes
Fred Wilkins
Homer Wilkins
Robert Wilkins
Edward E. Wilkinson
John Wilkison
Kenneth Will
James Willard
Robert E. Willard
R. C. Willbanks
Bill Williams
Bob Williams
Bob W. Williams
Cheryl Williams
Crutch Williams
Curtis Williams
Dale L. Williams
Dennis R. Williams
Freda Williams
French Williams
G. R. Williams
Jack Williams
James Dudley Williams
Jerry Williams
Jerry A. Williams
Jim B. Williams
Kelly Williams
Leonard Williams
Michael D. Williams
Travis R. Williams
Victor L. Williams
Wendell C. Williams
Michael Williamson
Bill Williges
Bud Willis
Donald Willis
James A. Willms
Garry Willoughby
John Wills
Mike Wills
Bill Wilson
Dave Wilson
David Wilson
Floyd Wilson
George Wilson
George L. Wilson
John Wilson
Lori Wilson
Louis Wilson
Mitchell Wilson
Norman Wilson
Robert Wilson
John Wilson
Nancy Wilson
Ralph C. Windquist, Jr.
Sharon Wines
Augusto Wing
Phillip M. Wing
Russell Wingfield
Barbara D. Wingo
Brian Winquist
Henry R. Winsor, Jr.
Bill Winter
Douglas A. Winter
Ronald Winter
Christian Winterstein
Sheldon G. Wirt
Justin H. Wirtz
Bob Wise
Ron Wise
Dennis With
Wayne Witte
Marian Wittenberg
Dennis Witter
Phelps D. Witter
Augie Woicekoski
Geoffrey Wojcik
Clem Wojdak
Paul Wojdak
Stephen Wojdak
Wayne Wojdak
Douglas Wojtowicz
John H. Wold
Alan Wolf
Michael Wolf
Charles H. Wolfe
David Wolfe
Jim Wolfe
Keith Wolfe
Sandra Wolfe
Shawn Elaine Wolfe
Norman E. Wolfer
Stephen Wolff
Roger Wollam
Roger A. Wolver
Edmund Wong
Kam Ling Wong
G. Wake Wood
Howland Wood
Linda J. Wood
Michael Woodbury
Richard Woodbury
Robert E. Woodchek
David M. Woodland, Jr.
Charles W. Woodruff
J.J. Woodside
Jim Woods
Bruce Woodward
Jay E. Woodward
Eugene Wooldridge
John Wooten
Robert Woracher
Dick Wright
Jeff Wright
Kim Wright
Lynn Wright
Michael Wright
Stan Wright
Susan Wright
Tom Wright
William J. Wright

George W. Wrigley
A. R. Wrinkle
Michael Wrobleski
Gordon Wrubel
Jack Wunderman
Charles E. Wyatt
Gary Wycker
Bill Wynn
Myron Xenos
Alan Yaffe
Christel Yaffe
Mark S. Yaffe
Robert Yakavonis
C. Dennis Yandle
J. Yanesh
George Yanovitch
Steven Yant
Robert L. Yarbrough
Ron Yarbrough
J. Yasuk
Ron Yates
William M. Yates
Roberta Yeager
Ron J. Yeckrig
Ernest Yeckring
R.S. Yeoman
Curt P. Yemm
Michael L. Yergin
David Yesnick
Peter Yeung
Al York
Toshiyuki Yosehzawa
Grace I. Yost
Eugene T. Yotka
Gene Yotka
Larry J. Youness
David Young
Deborah Anne Young
Fred Young
Gary L. Young
Harold G. Young
Harry O. Young
James H. Young
Jim Young
Leo Young
Philip Young
Roland G.C. Young, Jr.
Shirley Young
Ted H. Young
Walter A. Young
William Youngerman
Eric J. Youngquist
Jack Yount
Brian D. Yutzy
Bennet Zager
Rick Zamarchi
Randolph Zander
Keith M. Zaner
Debbie Zappas
Jeffrey S. Zarit
Jan Zawadski
George Zawalonka
Calvin Zeboray
Suzanne Zeboray
Raymond A. Zekauskas, M.D.
Ingrida Zemzars
Bernard Zerof
John E. Ziegler
Chuck Zielinski
Darlene Ziemendorf
John Zillion
Kenneth Zimmerman
Chuck Zink
Walt Zitney
Evan Zlock
J. A. Zonca
Harry D. Zucker
Edward Zuckerberg
Doug Zuege
Paul M. Zuercher
John Zug
Stanley M. Zurawski, Sr.
Stanley M. Zurawski, Jr.
Robert Zurcher
Duke Zwahlen
Richard Zweifel

Entertainment:

J.W. Apperson
The Association *
Butch Wax and the Hollywoods
The Grass Roots *
Gregg Hosfeld
George Johnstone
Dale Jones
Royce Kelly
The Kings Manor
Phoenix
The Rascals featuring Felix Cavaliere *
Stephen A. Sparks
Jeff Sutherland
Three Dog Night *
Tinted Blue

* These are the original Rock n' Roll groups from the late 60s and the early 70s.

BIBLIOGRAPHY

Handbook of 20th-Century United States Gold Coins, by David Akers,

The Coin World Comprehensive Catalog & Encyclopedia of United States Coins, by David T. Alexander, project editor

Counterfeit Detection : A Reprint from *The Numismatist*, 1983, American Numismatic Association, Colorado Springs, Colorado

Counterfeit Detection: A Reprint from *The Numismatist*, Volume II, 1988, American Numismatic Association, Colorado Springs, Colorado

Library Catalogue of the American Numismatic Association, American Numismatic Association, Colorado Springs, Colorado

Official ANA Grading Standards For United States Coins, 1987, American Numismatic Association, Colorado Springs, Colorado

Annual Report of the American Numismatic Society, 1991, American Numismatic Society, New York, New York

American Teleprocessing Corporation (ATC), FACTS/Certified Quote System (CQS), Houston, Texas

Coin World Almanac, Sixth Edition 1990, Amos Press Inc., Sidney, Ohio

Coin World Comprehensive Catalog & Encyclopedia of United States Coins, 1990, Amos Press Inc., Sidney, Ohio

Coin World Guide to U.S. Coins, Prices & Value Trends, Third Edition 1991, Amos Press Inc., Sidney, Ohio

NumisTech Coin Price Activity Report, Edited by Russell A. Augustin, First Quarter 1991, NumisTech Publications, Osterville, Massachusetts

A Buyer's Guide to the Rare Coin Market, by Q. David Bowers

Abe Kosoff: Dean of Numismatics, by Q. David Bowers

Adventures With Rare Coins, by Q. David Bowers (Introduction by John J. Ford)

Buyer's Guide to United States Gold Coins, by Q. David Bowers

Coins and Collectors, by Q. David Bowers

The Coin Dealer Newsletter, A Study in Rare Coin Price Performance 1963-1988, Edited by Q. David Bowers, Bowers and Merena Galleries, Inc., Wolfeboro, New Hampshire

High Profits from Rare Coin Investment, by Q. David Bowers, 1980, Seventh Edition, Bowers & Ruddy Galleries, Inc., Los Angeles, California

The History of United States Coinage, by Q. David Bowers

How To Be A Successful Coin Dealer, by Q. David Bowers

The Numismatist's Bedside Companion, Edited by Q. David Bowers

The Numismatist's Fireside Companion, Edited by Q. David Bowers

United States Coins by Design Types, by Q. David Bowers

Virgil Brand: The Man and His Era, Profile of a Numismatist, by Q. David Bowers

Walter Breen's Complete Encyclopedia of U.S. and Colonial Coins, Walter H. Breen, Garden City: Doubleday, 1988

Walter Breen's Encyclopedia of United States and Colonial Proof Coins 1722-1989, by Walter H. Breen, 1989, Bowers and Merena Galleries, Inc., Wolfeboro, New Hampshire

Walter Breen's Encyclopedia of United States Half Cents, 1793-1857, by Walter H. Breen

Official ANA Grading Standards for U.S. Coins, by Kenneth Bressett and Abe Kosoff

Prices for Buying & Selling U.S. Coins, by Ken Bressett, 1983, Western Publishing Company, Inc., Racine, Wisconsin

A Guide to the Grading of United States Coins, by Martin R. Brown and John W. Dunn, Western Publishing Company, Inc., Racine, Wisconsin

American and Canadian Countermarked Coins, by Dr. Gregory Brunk

The Charlton Standard Catalogue of Canadian Coins, 44th Edition, 1991, The Charlton Press, Toronto

Comprehensive Guide to American Colonial Coinage, Its Origins, History and Value, by Sanford J. Durst, 1976, New York, New York

The Cherrypicker's Guide to Rare Die Varieties, by Bill Fivaz and J.T. Stanton

Fight Inflation With Silver Dollars, by Les and Sue Fox, 1981, Carson City Associates, West Palm Beach, Florida

Silver Dollar Fortune Telling, by Les and Sue Fox, 1977, 1978, 1980, 1983, 1987, Carson City Associates, Closter, New Jersey

A Comprehensive Guide To Eisenhower Dollars in Accugrade Uncirculated, Prooflikes and Proofs, by Alan Hager, 1986, Accugrade, Inc., Greenwich, Connecticut

A Comprehensive Guide To Morgan and Peace Dollars in Accugrade Prooflikes and Proofs, by Alan Hager, 1984, Silver Dollars Unlimited, Bedford, New York

A Comprehensive Guide To Morgan and Peace Dollars in Accugrade Uncirculated, by Alan Hager, 1984, Silver Dollars Unlimited, Bedford, New York

A Mercenary's Guide to the Rare Coin Market, by David Hall, 1987, American Bureau of Economic Research, Fort Worth, Texas

How to Grade U.S. Coins, by James L. Halperin, 1990, Ivy Press, Inc., Dallas, Texas

N.C.I. Grading Guide, by James L. Halperin, 1986, Ivy Press, Inc., Dallas, Texas

A Grading Guide For the Premium Uncirculated Coins, by George W. Haylings, 1981

Mint Marks, 1893. Reprint Edition, by Augustus G. Heaton

Official Investor's Guide, Buying, Selling Silver Dollars, by Alan Herbert, 1982, House of Collectibles, Orlando, Florida

The Comprehensive Catalog of U.S. Paper Money, by Gene Hessler, 1977, Henry Regnery Company, Chicago, Illinois

Mint Mark:CC The United States Mint at Carson City, Nevada, by Howard Hickson, Nevada State Museum, Carson City, Nevada

The Norweb Collection: An American Legacy, by Michael Hodder and Q. David Bowers

Official Investor's Guide, Buying, Selling Silver Dollars, by Marc Hudgeons, NLG, 1985 House of Collectibles, Orlando, Florida

Private Gold Coins and Patterns of the United States, by Donald H. Kagin

So-Called Dollars, by Harold E. Hibler and Charles V. Kappen, The Coin and Currency Institute, Inc., New York, New York

A Comprehensive Guide to United States Commemorative Coins, by James S. Iacovo, 1979, Ivy Press, Incorporated, Dallas, Texas

What Every Silver Dollar Buyer Should Know, by Steve Ivy and Ron Howard, 1984, The Ivy Press, Dallas, Texas

The Coin Collectors' Pricing Guide, JerNan Publishing, San Andreas, California

United States Pattern, Experimental, and Trial Pieces, Sixth Edition, by J. Hewitt Judd, M.D., 1977, Western Publishing Company, Inc., Racine, Wisconsin

Standard Catalog of World Coins, by Chester L. Krause and Clifford Mishler, 18TH Edition, Krause Publications, Inc., Iola, Wisconsin

Auction Prices Realized, Krause Publications, Inc., Iola, Wisconsin

Recollections of a Mint Director,by Frank A. Leach

Silver Dollar and Profits, by Richard C. Ludwig, 1979, Toledo, Ohio

Webster's Ninth New Collegiate Dictionary, 1988, Merriam-Webster Inc., Springfield, Massachusetts

An Analysis of Morgan and Peace Dollars, by Wayne Miller, 1976, Helena, Montana

The Morgan and Peace Dollar Textbook, by Wayne Miller, 1982, Adam Smith Publishing Co., Metairie, Louisiana

Jim Osbon's Silver Dollar Encyclopedia, by James B. Osbon, 1976, Headquarters Publishing Company, Richmond, Virginia

The Random House Encyclopedia, New Revised Third Edition, Random House, Inc., New York, NY 1990

The Complete Investor's Guide To Silver Dollar Investing, by Dick A. Reed, 1982, The English Factory, Phoenix, Arizona

The Other Side of the Coin, by Ed Rochette

The Comprehensive Catalogue and Encyclopedia of United States Coins, by Joseph H. Rose and Howard Hazelcorn, 1976, Scott Publishing Co., New York, New York

Photograde, by James F. Ruddy, 17th Edition, Bowers and Merena Galleries, Inc.

How To Prosper During the Coming Bad Years, by Howard J. Ruff, 1981, Warner Books, New York, New York

The History of the Comstock Lode 1850-1920, Grant H. Smith, 1943, Nevada Bureau of Mines and Geology, Reno, Nevada

The Coin Investor's Report, 1989, Southern Numismatic Publishing, Inc., Maitland, Florida

Investing in Morgan and Peace Dollars, by Richard Speer, 1981, Midway Coins, Louisburg, Kansas

The Encyclopedia of United States Silver & Gold Commemorative Coins 1892 to 1954, by Anthony Swiatek and Walter H. Breen, Arco Publishing, New York, 1981

An Illustrated History of Commemorative Coinage, by Don Taxay, 1967, Arco Publishing Company, Inc., New York, New York

U.S. Mint and Coinage, by Don Taxay

The Standard Guide to the Lincoln Cent, 2nd Edition, by Sol Taylor, Ph.D.

The Investor's Guide to Coin Trading, by Scott A. Travers

Coinage Act of 1965, Hearing Before the Committee on Banking and Currency, United States Senate, U.S. Government Printing Office, Washington, D.C. 1965

Treasury Staff Study of Silver and Coinage, United States Treasury Dept 1965

A Comprehensive Catalogue and Encyclopedia of U.S. Morgan and Peace Silver Dollars, by Leroy Van Allen and A. George Mallis, NY: FCI/Arco, 1976

The Liberty Seated Dollar 1840-1873, by Weimer W. White

A Catalog of Modern World Coins, by R.S. Yeoman, 1967, Whitman Publishing Company, Racine, Wisconsin

A Guide Book of United States Coins, by R.S. Yeoman, 44th Edition, 1991, Western Publishing Company, Inc., Racine, Wisconsin

1990 Handbook of United States Coins, Dealer Buying Prices, 47th Edition, by R.S. Yeoman, Western Publishing Company, Inc., Racine, Wisconsin

Periodicals

Certified Coin Dealer Newsletter (CCDN) and Coin Dealer Newsletter (CDN), Torrance, California

Coin World, Amos Press Inc., Sidney Ohio

COINage Magazine, Miller Magazines, Inc., Ventura, California

Coins Magazine, Iola, Wisconsin

NGC Census Reports, Numismatic Guaranty Corporation of America, Parsippany, New Jersey

Numismatic News, Krause Publications, Inc., Iola, Wisconsin

The Numismatist, American Numismatic Association, Colorado Springs, Colorado

The PCGS Population Reports, Professional Coin Grading Service, Newport Beach, California

Rome's Prices Realized, Rome Reports Inc., New York, New York

Auction Catalogs and Prices Realized Lists

David W. Akers, Inc., P.O. Box 530836, Miami Shores, Florida, 33153

Auctions By Bowers and Merena Galleries, Inc., P.O. Box 1224, Wolfeboro, New Hampshire, 03894

Butterfield & Butterfield, 220 San Bruno Avenue, San Francisco, California, 94103

Certified Coin Exchange (CCE), P.O. Box 19337, Houston, Texas, 77224

Christie's (New York), 502 Park Avenue at 59th Street, New York, New York, 10022

Harmer Rooke Numismatists, Ltd., 3 East 57th Street, New York, New York, 10022

Heritage Numismatic Auctions, Inc., The Heritage Plaza, Highland Park Village, Dallas, Texas, 75205

Kurt R. Krueger (Numismatic Auctions), 160 N. Washington Street, Iola, Wisconsin, 54945

Dana Linett (The San Diego Show & Auction, Inc.), P.O. Box 3341, LaJolla, California, 92038

McIntire Numismatic Auctions, Inc., P.O. Box 546, 27 Crestview Plaza, Jacksonville, Arkansas, 72076

Mid-America Rare Coin Auctions, Inc., 1707 Nicholasville Road, Lexington, Kentucky, 40503

Pacific Coast Auction Galleries, Inc., 1013 State Street, Santa Barbara, California, 93101

Paramount Numismatic Services, Inc., Doral Executive Office Park, 3785 N.W. 82nd Avenue, Suite 315, Miami, Florida, 33166

Rare Coin Company of America (Rarcoa), 6262 South Route 83, Willowbrook, Illinois, 60514

Sotheby's, 1334 York Avenue, New York, New York, 10021

Stack's, 123 West 57th Street, New York, New York, 10019

Superior Galleries, 9478 West Olympic Blvd., Beverly Hills, California, 90212

Teletrade, 885 Third Avenue, New York, New York, 10022

Authorized Distributors

Alco Distributors, Galena, Ohio

Allstate Coins, Tucson, Arizona

Arch City Supply, St. Louis, Missouri

Beymer, Jack H., Santa Rosa, California

Blanchard & Company, Jefferson, Louisiana

Brookman Coin Gallery, Brooklyn, New York

Bowers and Merena Galleries, Inc., Wolfeboro, New Hampshire

Centerville Coin & Jewelry, Centerville, Ohio

M.C. Clayton, South San Francisco, California

Harold Cohn & Co., Chicago, Illinois

Sanford J. Durst, Long Island City, New York

Harry Edelman Inc., S. Ozone Park, New York

Scott Edelman Supply Co., Fullerton, California

R.A. Glascock & Company, San Antonio, Texas

Gold Coast Coin & Stamp Supply, Ft. Lauderdale, Florida

Hamps Coin & Stamp Supplies, Houston, Texas

Charles R. Heisler, Inc., Lancaster, Pennsylvania

William J. Henderson Distributor, Puyallup, Washington

Virg Marshall, III, Inc., Wymore, Nebraska

National Gold Exchange, Inc., Tampa, Florida

Numismatic Arts of Sante Fe, Santa Fe, New Mexico

Pelco Coin Galleries, Columbus, Ohio

Pennies & Postage, Inc., Mercer Island, Washington

Pollard Coin & Stamp Supplies, Indianapolis, Indiana

R.M.F. Numismatics, Warrenton, Missouri

Rare Coin Investment, Inc., East Detroit, Michigan

Harold B. Rice, Buffalo, New York

Scott Western Distributing, Chino, California

Silver Towne, Winchester, Indiana

Spectrum Numismatics International, Santa Ana, California

Stone Mountain Coin & Stamp, Stone Mountain, Georgia

Lin Terry, Dumont, New Jersey

Tidewater Coin & Stamp, Chesapeake, Virginia

Trade Winds, Berlin, New Jersey

Unigold, Inc., Encino, California

U.S. Coins, Houston, Texas

West Texas Coin Supply, Lubbock, Texas

The Wholesale Company, New York, New York

Bud Willis, Greenfield, Indiana

Ralph Winquist, Rockford, Illinois

Sheldon Wirt Rare Coins, Menlow Park, California

Woodcock's Supplies, Sun City, California

***

Index

Numerical Entries

A

B

C

D

E

F

G

H

I

J

K

L

M

N

O

P

Q

R

S

T

U

V

W

X

Y

Z